Long-Term Debt an~~ROCKHURST COLLEGE LIBRARY~~ 4

Long-Term Sources 31

Management of Accounts Receivable and Payable 28

Mathematics of A

Mergers and A 33

Modern Portfol Theory and Management 17

Money and Capital Markets: Institutional Framework and Federal
   Reserve Control 1

"New" Financial Environment INTRODUCTION

Options Markets and Instruments 20

Overseas Money and Capital Markets 13

Pension and Profit-Sharing Plans 34

Performance Measurement 22

Planning and Control Techniques 25

Public Utility Finance 36

Real Estate Finance 23

Savings Institutions 7

Securities Industry: Securities Trading and Investment Banking 5

Security Analysis 16

Short-Term Money Markets and Instruments 10

Sources of Investment Information B

Specialized Fixed Income Security Strategies 19

State and Local Debt 3

FINANCIAL HANDBOOK

Fifth Edition

EDITORIAL CONSULTING BOARD

FINANCIAL HANDBOOK

Fifth Edition

Edited by

EDWARD I. ALTMAN

Professor of Finance
Chairman, MBA Program
Graduate School of Business Administration
New York University

ASSOCIATE EDITOR

MARY JANE McKINNEY

A Ronald Press Publication

JOHN WILEY & SONS   New York • Chichester • Brisbane • Toronto • Singapore

Library of Congress Cataloging in Publication Data:

Main entry under title:
Financial handbook.

  ''A Ronald Press Publication.''
  Includes index.
    1. Finance—Handbooks, manuals, etc. 2. Finance
—United States—Handbooks, manuals, etc.
3. Corporations—Finance—Handbooks, manuals, etc.
4. International finance—Handbooks, manuals, etc.
I. Altman, Edward I., 1941-   . II. McKinney,
Mary Jane.

HG173.F49   1981   658.1'5   81-10281
ISBN 0-471-07727-5   AACR2

Printed in the United States of America

10 9 8 7 6 5 4 3 2 1

To My Wife, Elaine, and Son, Gregory

Whose love and understanding
really do make a difference

PREFACE

In summer 1979 John Wiley & Sons asked if I would be interested in "taking on" the editing of the fifth edition of *Financial Handbook*. I soon realized that this assignment was more than simply supervising the compilation of another book of "readings." Ever since the appearance of the first edition in 1925, *Financial Handbook* has been widely accepted as a useful and authoritative reference by those who are active in business and finance, as well as their attorneys, accountants, and other professional advisers. Although many of my academic colleagues who were familiar with the book respected it as the finest reference book available in finance, the fourth edition was very much out of date. The field of finance had changed dramatically since 1967, when the last revision appeared. Hence there was a real need for a complete revision.

The final factor that prompted me to accept the assignment was the opportunity to follow in the footsteps of one of the most distinguished authorities in the world of finance, the late Dr. Jules I. Bogen. Indeed to follow the "Bogen book" is a distinct honor and privilege. Jules Bogen, who edited the third and fourth editions, following the work of Robert H. Montgomery, was a highly regarded scholar, economist, journalist, and financial consultant. My main objective is that the fifth edition be a worthy successor to the earlier versions.

Financial Handbook is unique in that it is an eclectic reference volume, covering the entire breadth of the world of finance. The sections are organized around four major subject areas: domestic (U.S.) financial markets and institutions (1–10), international financial markets and institutions (11–15), securities and portfolio management (16–23), and corporate financial management (24–38), with supporting appendices. A perusal of the *Contents* reveals several changes from earlier editions and, I hope, meaningful additions to the traditional contents of financial reference books. The emphasis on international finance is apparent, with all of Part Two devoted to that topic, as well as the section entitled "Financial Decisions for Multinational Enterprises" in Part Four. Several new sections also reflect current innovations and market relations, including "Specialized Fixed Income Security Strategies," "Options Markets and Instruments," "Futures and Commodities Markets," and "Performance Measurement" in Part Three, and "Financial Management in an Inflationary Environment" in Part Four. Finally, an expert on public utility finance was asked to provide a complete section to cover an area that usually is not presented in detail (see Part Four).

Recognized experts—including business executives, financial economists from the academic and business worlds, government authorities, and financial consultants—have synthesized the latest thinking and the most important literature contributions in their areas to present concise yet comprehensive studies of current principles and practice. My instructions to the authors were simple. Write about what you know best, present "modern finance" in a way that will be logical and understandable to an expected audience of practitioners and students of finance. The field of finance is constantly changing and new theories and innovations are being tested and implemented daily; it is my objective, however, that the bulk of the material presented here not soon be out of date.

I have been assisted by so many people that it is impossible to list them all. Two groups of experts have contributed their knowledge of the finance field in a direct way. First, of course, I am indebted to the section authors, who were given a most demanding task. I can truly appreciate their efforts because in preparing my own section I found that to write a reference-type chapter is far more difficult and challenging than to discuss a current research idea or market event. The second group, who both contributed ideas and recommended section authors, is our distinguished Editorial Consulting Board. Their guidance and counsel has been reassuring and appreciated.

The task of editing a compendium such as *Financial Handbook* is essentially a study of logistics combined with an understanding of the needs of the potential readership. In both areas I was most fortunate to have working with me, from the beginning, Mary Jane McKinney, a very talented editor. We have tried to integrate the many diverse topics and writing styles of the authors. In addition to working with the manuscripts, Mary Jane McKinney researched the field by interviewing librarians and other reference experts, to learn how they use handbooks of this type and to structurally improve upon previous editions.

Frankly, I had little idea of the logistical complexities of completing this project, and my small staff at New York University was absolutely indispensable. I would like to thank Diana Daniels, Donald Homolka, Janet Marks, and Tom O'Donnell, who assisted me. Several talented individuals from the publisher, John Wiley & Sons, were involved. Reflecting back on the process, I conclude that *Financial Handbook* was indeed a team effort.

Finally, I owe much to my wife, Elaine, and my son, Gregory for their enthusiastic support and tolerance over the long period required to put this work together.

EDWARD I. ALTMAN

New York, New York
July 1981

CONTENTS

INTRODUCTION   The "New" Financial Environment
ARNOLD W. SAMETZ

PART 1   U.S. FINANCIAL MARKETS AND INSTITUTIONS

1   **Money and Capital Markets: Institutional Framework and Federal Reserve Control**
JOSEPH BENCH

2   **Government Obligations: U.S. Treasury and Federal Agency Securities**
JOSEPH BENCH

3   **State and Local Debt**
RONALD W. FORBES

4   **Long-Term Debt and Equity Markets and Instruments**
ANDREW J. KALOTAY

5   **The Securities Industry: Securities Trading and Investment Banking**
MICHAEL KEENAN

6   **Commercial Banking**
NEIL B. MURPHY

7   **Savings Institutions**
DONALD M. KAPLAN
IRA D. MEASELL, III

8   **Insurance and Reinsurance**
OSCAR N. SERBEIN

9   **Consumer Finance**
A. CHARLENE SULLIVAN

10   Short-Term Money Markets and Instruments
TILDON W. SMITH

PART 2   INTERNATIONAL FINANCIAL MARKETS AND
INSTITUTIONS

11   The International Monetary System
JAMES L. BURTLE

12   Exchange Rates and Currency Exposure
RICHARD M. LEVICH

13   Overseas Money and Capital Markets
DENNIS E. LOGUE

14   International Commercial Banking
IAN N. GIDDY

15   International Portfolio Diversification and Foreign Capital
Markets
JAMES R. F. GUY
CLOSSON L. VAUGHAN

PART 3   SECURITIES AND PORTFOLIO MANAGEMENT

16   Security Analysis
JAMES L. FARRELL, JR.

17   Modern Portfolio Theory and Management
ROBERT L. HAGIN

18   Bond Management Issues
RAVI AKHOURY

19   Specialized Fixed Income Security Strategies
MARTIN L. LEIBOWITZ

20   Options Markets and Instruments
GARY L. GASTINEAU

21   Futures and Commodities Markets
RICHARD L. SANDOR
DALLAS JONES

22   **Performance Measurement**
     J. PETER WILLIAMSON

23   **Real Estate Finance**
     RICHARD T. PRATT
     R. BRUCE RICKS

PART 4   CORPORATE FINANCIAL MANAGEMENT

24   **Financial Statement Analysis**
     ROBERT L. HAGIN

25   **Planning and Control Techniques**
     NED C. HILL

26   **Financial Forecasting**
     GEORGE G. C. PARKER

27   **Cash Management**
     BERNELL K. STONE

28   **Management of Accounts Receivable and Payable**
     ROBERT W. JOHNSON

29   **Capital Budgeting**
     HAROLD BIERMAN, JR.

30   **Leasing**
     JOHN MARTIN

31   **Long-Term Sources of Funds and the Cost of Capital**
     THOMAS E. COPELAND

32   **Dividend Policy**
     JOHN T. HACKETT

33   **Mergers and Acquisitions**
     ALFRED RAPPAPORT

34   **Pension and Profit-Sharing Plans**
     ROGER F. MURRAY

35   **Bankruptcy and Reorganization**
     EDWARD I. ALTMAN

36　**Public Utility Finance**
EUGENE F. BRIGHAM

37　**Financial Management in an Inflationary Environment**
MOSHE BEN-HORIM and HAIM LEVY

38　**Financial Decisions for Multinational Enterprises**
ALAN C. SHAPIRO
RICHARD KARL GOELTZ

A　**Mathematics of Finance**
MARTI G. SUBRAHMANYAM

B　**Sources of Investment Information**

INDEX

CONTRIBUTORS

RAVI AKHOURY is vice-president, portfolio manager, and member of the Investment Policy Committee at Fischer, Francis, Trees and Watts, New York, a fixed income investment advisory firm. Previously he was vice-president and deputy head of the Bond Department at Equitable Life Assurance Society. Akhoury has broad-based experience in managing institutional portfolios of taxable fixed income securities. He is a graduate of the Indian Institute of Technology and received an MS degree from the State University of New York at Stonybrook.

EDWARD I. ALTMAN, professor of finance and chairman of the MBA program at the Graduate School of Business Administration, New York University, has been a visiting professor in France, Brazil, and Australia. Altman has an international reputation as an expert on corporate bankruptcy and credit analysis. Among his books are *Corporate Bankruptcy in America* (1971) and *The Analysis and Prediction of Corporate Bankruptcy* (1982). He was an adviser to the Commission on the Revision of the Bankruptcy Act, and he edits the international publication, *Journal of Banking and Finance* and the series *Contemporary Studies in Economics and Finance*. He also serves on the Editorial Board of *Journal of Business Strategy* and is a member of the Executive Committee of the European Finance Association. His primary areas of research include bankruptcy analysis and prediction, credit and lending policies, and capital markets. The editor of *Financial Handbook*, he has been a consultant to several government agencies, major financial and accounting institutions, and industrial companies. Altman received the MBA and PhD degrees from the University of California, Los Angeles.

JOSEPH BENCH is director of financial strategy, the Trading Company of the West, New York. He has also served as vice-president and economist of First Pennsylvania Corp. where he analyzed money market events and prospects; his other work experience includes director of financial analysis at Lionel D. Edie, an investment advisory subsidiary of Merrill Lynch, and economist at Chase Manhattan Bank. Bench has served as an adjunct professor of finance at numerous institutions, including Seton Hall University and Fairleigh Dickinson University. He received the BA, MA, and PhD degrees in economics from Case Western Reserve University, Cleveland.

HAROLD BIERMAN, JR. is Nicholas H. Noyes Professor of Business Administration, Graduate School of Business and Public Administration, Cornell University, Ithaca, New York. He formerly taught at Louisiana State University, the University of Michigan, and the University of Chicago. From 1964 to 1979 Bierman helped the University of the West Indies establish a management program. His industrial experience includes work with Arthur Young and Co., Shell Oil Co., Ford Motor Co., National Can Corp., and Boeing Corp. Bierman has been a consultant to a wide variety of firms including Owens-Corning Fiberglass and American Telephone & Telegraph, as well as the U.S. government. His teaching interests are in financial policy, investments, and accounting. He is the author or coauthor of more than ten books, including *The Capital Budgeting Decision, Financial Accounting, Managerial Accounting,* and *Decision Making and Planning for the Corporate Treasurer.* Bierman is a graduate of the U.S. Naval Academy, Annapolis, Maryland, and received the MBA and PhD degrees from the University of Michigan, Ann Arbor.

EUGENE F. BRIGHAM is graduate research professor of finance and director of the Public Utility Research Center at the University of Florida, Gainesville. Brigham has served as president of the Financial Management Association, and has written more than thirty journal articles dealing with the cost of capital, capital structure, and other aspects of financial management. The ten textbooks on managerial finance and managerial economics of which he is the author or coauthor are used at more than 1,000 universities in the United States and have been translated into six languages for worldwide use. Brigham has testified in numerous electric and telephone rate cases at both the federal and state levels, and has served as a consultant to many utility and industrial companies, and to the Federal Reserve Board, the Federal Home Loan Bank Board, the U.S. Office of Telecommunications Policy, and the Rand Corp. He received a BS degree from the University of North Carolina, Chapel Hill, and the MBA and PhD degrees from the University of California, Berkeley.

JAMES L. BURTLE, who is managing editor of *International Country Risk Guide*, New York, was an economist for the U.S. Economic Cooperation Administration of the European Recovery Program (Marshall Plan) in 1949 and later served as an economist for the International Labour Office in Geneva, Switzerland. In 1969 Burtle joined W. R. Grace & Co. and for more than ten years was responsible for advising on foreign exchange policy and forecasting foreign exchange rates. He has served as president of the New York Metropolitan Economic Association (1968–1969) and is the coauthor of *The Great Wheel* (1973), a book on the international monetary system. Burtle is an adjunct professor of finance at Montclair State University, Upper Montclair, New Jersey, and has taught at Long Island University. He received the BA and MBA degrees from the University of Chicago.

THOMAS E. COPELAND is an associate professor of financial economics at the Graduate School of Management of the University of California, Los Angeles. He is coauthor of *Financial Theory and Corporate Policy* (1979), a popular advanced-level text. Copeland has published articles in the numerous academic journals including *Journal of Finance, Journal of Financial and Quantitative Analysis, Journal of Economics and Business, Engineering Economist,* and *Journal of Accounting, Auditing, and Finance.* He is a member of the New York Stock Exchange Arbitration Board, does consulting in the area of corporate valuation, and is active in executive education. Copeland received a BA degree from Johns Hopkins University, Baltimore, and the MBA and PhD degrees from the University of Pennsylvania's Wharton School of Finance, Philadelphia.

JAMES L. FARRELL, JR. is chairman of MPT Associates, New York, a money management firm that emphasizes applied modern portfolio theory, and is affiliated with Manufacturers Hanover Trust. He is also chairman of the Institute for Quantitative Research in Finance, New York, and is a member of the finance faculty at the Graduate School of Business Administration, New York University. He has over fifteen years of experience in security analysis, portfolio management, and quantitative research at CNA Financial, College Retirement Equities and at Citibank, where he was most recently a vice-president of applied financial research. He has published several articles in professional investment journals. Farrell has a BS degree from the University of Notre Dame, Notre Dame, Indiana, an MBA degree from the Wharton School of Finance, Philadelphia, and a PhD degree from New York University.

RONALD W. FORBES is associate professor of finance and director of the Municipal Finance Study Group at the School of Business, State University of New York, Albany. Forbes also serves as a consultant to the Municipal Research Department of the First Boston Corp. and is a member of the board of directors of the Merrill Lynch Municipal Bond Fund, the Corporate Accumulation Fund, and the Municipal Accumulation Fund, all in New York. He has published extensively on the municipal bond market and served as coauthor of the Twentieth Century Fund Task Force on the Municipal Bond Market. Forbes received an AB degree from Dartmouth College, Hanover, New Hampshire, and a PhD degree from the State University of New York, Buffalo.

GARY L. GASTINEAU is manager of the Options Portfolio Service at Kidder, Peabody & Co., Inc., New York, where he manages individual and institutional accounts using options and their underlying securities. He is the author of *The Stock Options Manual* (2nd ed., 1979). Gastineau spent several years in the long-term planning department of a major oil company, came to Wall Street as a security analyst in 1966, and has been a portfolio manager since 1969. He is a frequent speaker before business and professional groups on the subjects of option evaluation and the use of options in portfolio management. Gastineau received an AB degree in economics from Harvard College and an MBA from the Harvard Business School, Boston, Massachusetts.

IAN N. GIDDY is an associate professor at the Graduate School of Business, Columbia University, New York. He has also been an assistant professor at the University of Michigan and a visiting assistant professor at the University of Chicago. Giddy has taught in a number of management development programs, including in-house programs at Price Waterhouse & Co., Citibank, and Manufacturers Hanover Trust Co., and has lectured in South Africa, Portugal, Mexico, and Brazil. He has been a consultant to several multinational corporations and to the U.S. Treasury Department. During 1978–1979 Giddy served as financial economist at the Office of the U.S. Comptroller of the Currency and in 1980–1981 at the International Monetary Fund and the Federal Reserve Board. He is coauthor of the recently published book, *The International Money Market* (1978). Giddy received the MBA and PhD degrees from the University of Michigan, Ann Arbor.

RICHARD KARL GOELTZ is vice-president of finance and a member of the board of directors at Joseph E. Seagram & Sons, Inc., New York. Goeltz received an AB degree from Brown University, Providence, Rhode Island, and an MBA degree from Columbia University, New York. He also studied at the London School of Economics and in the doctoral program at New York University. His papers on international finance have been published in magazines and newspapers, and he has given numerous speeches to professional societies, at university seminars, and to corporate and bank officers. Before joining Seagram in 1970, Goeltz was in the treasurer's department of Exxon Corp. He has appeared on panels at the Financial Executives Institute and the Financial Management Association.

JAMES R. F. GUY is a director of Lehman Management Co., New York, and an adjunct associate professor of finance and international business at the Graduate School of Business Administration, New York University. He was formerly an assistant professor of finance and international business, School of Business Administration, University of California, Berkeley, and did research at the International Institute of Management in Berlin. Guy's research on finance and international capital markets has appeared in *Financial Analysts Journal, Journal of Banking and Finance, Journal of Finance,* and other scholarly publications. Guy received his undergraduate degree from Oxford University, Oxford, England, an MBA degree from the Wharton School of Finance and a PhD degree from the University of Pennsylvania, Philadelphia.

JOHN T. HACKETT is executive vice-president and chief financial officer of Cummins Engine Co., Columbus, Indiana. He is a director of Cummins Engine Co., Cummins Engine Foundations, the Ransburg Corp., Irwin Union Corp., and the Camping and Education Foundation, and is a past director of the Federal Reserve Bank of Chicago. Hackett has served on the faculties of Ohio State, Case Western Reserve, and Kent State universities, and as assistant vice-president and economist of the Federal Reserve Bank of Cleveland. Hackett has contributed articles to *Financial Executives Handbook, Treasurer's Handbook, Harvard Business Review, Business Horizons,* and *Financial Executives Magazine,* and is a coauthor of a publication for the Conference Board on the impact of inflation. He has a BS and an MBA from Indiana University, Bloomington, and a PhD in finance and economics from The Ohio State University, Columbus.

ROBERT L. HAGIN is vice-president and director, quantitative research, at Kidder, Peabody & Co., Inc., New York. He is a distinguished researcher, educator, author, and investment professional. Hagin has been a leader in developing, testing, and applying elements of what is known today as "modern portfolio theory." He has had experience in both investment and management research, and has lectured in executive programs on financial analysis as well as on modern portfolio theory. In addition, Hagin has taught graduate level courses at the University of California, Los Angeles, and the Wharton School. He has written several books on investments including *The Dow Jones-Irwin Guide to Modern Portfolio Theory* (1980). Before joining Kidder, Peabody, Hagin worked at First Boston Corp. in New York. He received the PhD degree from the University of California, Los Angeles.

NED C. HILL is associate professor of finance at Indiana University, Bloomington. He is currently active in consulting in the cash management area and has also consulted in financial planning and forecasting. Hill developed a short-term financial management course at Indiana University and is a frequent participant in executive development programs. His paper "Determining the Cash Discount in the Firm's Credit Policy" won the competitive papers award at the Financial Management Association meeting in 1978. Hill is the author of numerous publications in such journals as *Financial Management, Journal of Financial and Quantitative Analysis,* and *Journal of Bank Research* and is on the editorial board of *Business Horizons.* He received his MBA and PhD from Cornell University.

MOSHE BEN-HORIM is a lecturer in finance at the Jerusalem School of Business at Hebrew University, Jerusalem, Israel. He has held financial research positions at institutions in the United States and Israel, including the (U.S.) National Bureau of Economic Research, the Israeli Institute of Financial Research, and the Hebrew University of Jerusalem. Teaching positions were at New York University, the University of Florida, and Montclair (New Jersey) State College. Ben-Horim has written several articles in professional journals and a book in business and economics statistics (1980). He received the BA and MA degrees in economics from the Hebrew University of Jerusalem, and a PhD degree in finance and economics from the Graduate School of Business Administration, New York University.

ROBERT W. JOHNSON is professor of management and director of the Credit Research Center, Krannert Graduate School of Management, Purdue University, Lafayette, Indiana. He was reporter-economist to the Special Committee on the Uniform Consumer Credit Code (1964–1974) and a presidential appointee to the National Commission on Consumer Finance (1969–1972). Johnson is a trustee of the National Foundation for Consumer Credit and is on the Policy Board of *Journal of Retail Banking.* During 1970 he was president of the newly formed Financial

Management Association. Johnson is the author of two books: *Financial Management* (4th ed., 1971) and *Capital Budgeting* (1977) and coauthor of *Self-Correction Problems in Finance* (3rd ed., 1975). He holds a PhD degree from Northwestern University, Evanston, Illinois, and was a fellow at the Institute of Basic Mathematics for Application to Business, Harvard University, Cambridge, Massachusetts.

DALLAS JONES is a financial futures trader for ContiFinancial Corp., Chicago. After a brief period as an equity research analyst for a regional dealer and a five-year tour as an Air Force and Air National Guard combat pilot, Jones returned to the financial arena as a bond manager for two New York bank trust departments. In 1979, after arbitraging financial futures for a major New York dealer, he joined ContiFinancial, where he has traded financial futures on both the Chicago Mercantile Exchange and the Chicago Board of Trade. Jones was a cofounder of the New York Bond Quant Group and received an MS degree in quantitative analysis from New York University.

ANDREW J. KALOTAY, Senior Analyst, Bond Portfolio Analysis Group, Salomon Brothers, New York, is a leading expert in financial theory and its application to the financial problems of regulated industries. He has worked extensively on financial and regulatory issues related to the management of corporate debt. Earlier he worked for Dillon, Read & Co., Inc., and the Bell Telephone System in a number of managerial and technical positions. Kalotay has published extensively in professional and academic finance journals, and his recent pragmatic work deals with long-term financing of corporations. He has taught at several institutions, including the Wharton School. Kalotay received a BS degree in mathematics from Queen's University, Ontario, Canada, and a PhD degree in mathematics from the University of Toronto, Ontario.

DONALD M. KAPLAN is managing associate with the financial consulting company of Kaplan, Smith & Associates, Inc., Washington, D.C. His prior experience includes several years as chief economist and director of the Office of Economic Research at the Federal Home Loan Bank Board, and membership on the finance faculty at the Harvard Business School, where he taught graduate and executive level corporate finance and financial institution management. Kaplan has also served as a consultant to savings and loan associations, commercial banks, and government agencies. He is a member of a number of economic, financial, and real estate professional associations and has written and spoken widely on the economy, the mortgage and housing markets, the savings and loan industry, and the Federal Home Loan Bank System. Kaplan received his undergraduate education at the University of California, Los Angeles, and an MBA and PhD degree from the Graduate School of Management, UCLA.

MICHAEL KEENAN is Associate Professor of Finance at the Graduate School of Business Administration, New York University. After teaching for three years at the University of California, Berkeley, he joined the faculty at NYU, where his primary teaching areas have been corporation finance and investments. Keenan's current research interests include mergers and acquisitions analysis, the economic structure of the securities industry, and the growth of the service sector type of economy. He has written several monographs on finance including *The New York-Based Securities Industry: 1979 Survey* (1980). Keenan received a BS degree from Case Western Reserve University, Cleveland, and a PhD degree from Carnegie-Mellon University, Pittsburgh.

MARTIN L. LEIBOWITZ is general partner and manager of the Bond Portfolio Analysis Group, Salomon Brothers, New York. He is coauthor (with Sidney Homer) of *Inside the Yield Book* (1972). Articles by Leibowitz have appeared in *Money Manager, Trusts and Estates, Euromoney, Financial Analysts Journal, Banker's Magazine, Financial Analysts Handbook,* and *Journal of Portfolio Management.* His recent work includes studies of mortgage-related securities, cash flow characteristics of mortgage securities, a series relating to bond immunization, and several studies developing a new approach to the analysis of financial futures. Leibowitz received his bachelor's and master's degrees from the University of Chicago, and his doctorate in mathematics from New York University.

RICHARD M. LEVICH is associate professor of finance and international business at the Graduate School of Business Administration, New York University. He is also a research associate with the National Bureau of Economic Research in Cambridge, Massachusetts. Levich was a visiting faculty member at the University of Chicago and at Yale University and visiting scholar at the Board of Governors of the Federal Reserve System. His research on international financial markets has appeared in *Journal of Political Economy, Columbia Journal of World Business,* and other scholarly publications; he is the author of *The International Money Market: An Assessment of Alternative Forecasting Techniques and Market Efficiency* and coeditor of *Exchange Risk and Exposure: Current Developments in International Financial Management* (1980). Levich received a PhD degree from the University of Chicago.

HAIM LEVY is professor of finance at Hebrew University in Jerusalem, Israel. He has taught extensively in the United States as a visiting professor at the University of Illinois, the University of California, Berkeley, the University of Florida, and the University of Pennsylvania. Levy has served as consultant to many firms as well as to the government of Israel, and has published almost 100 articles and books. He is an editor of *Research in Finance.* Levy received a BA degree in economics and statistics, an MA degree in statistics and finance, and a PhD degree in economics and finance, all from the Hebrew University of Jerusalem.

DENNIS E. LOGUE is professor of business administration at the Amos Tuck Graduate School of Business Administration, Dartmouth College, Hanover, New Hampshire, coeditor of the professional periodical *Financial Management,* and a consultant to a variety of organizations. He has served on the faculty of Indiana

University and as a visiting scholar at the U.S. Treasury, and has been a visiting faculty member at the University of California, Berkeley. Logue's professional research on international finance and capital markets has appeared in many journals, including *Quarterly Journal of Economics, Economica, Journal of Finance, Journal of Portfolio Management,* and *Financial Analysts Journal.* He is coeditor of two volumes on international financial topics: *Eurocurrencies and the International Monetary System* (1976) and *The Effects of Exchange Rate Adjustments* (1977). His most recent book is *Legislative Influences on Corporate Pension Plans* (1979). Logue received a PhD degree from Cornell University, Ithaca, New York.

JOHN MARTIN is visiting associate professor of finance at the University of Texas, Austin (on leave from Texas A & M University). He is coauthor of several texts including *Basic Financial Management* (1979) and *Guide to Financial Analysis* (1979), as well as numerous articles in finance, economics, and accounting. Martin presently serves on the editorial board for *Journal of Financial Research* and is finance editor for *Journal of Business Research.* Martin received the BA and MBA degrees from Louisiana Polytechnic Institute, Ruston, and a DBA degree from Texas Tech University, Lubbock.

MARY JANE McKINNEY is an editorial consultant specializing in business publications. A former journalist with Research Institute of America and Fortune Magazine, she develops newsletters for companies and conducts seminars in business writing for executives and at New York University Graduate School of Business Administration. Both her bachelor's and master's degrees are from the University of Texas, Austin.

IRA D. MEASELL III, vice-president and consulting associate for the firm of Kaplan, Smith and Associates, Inc., Washington, D.C., conducts economic and financial studies concerning financial institutions as well as the housing and mortgage markets. Previously he was vice-president of corporate planning for the Federal Home Loan Mortgage Corp., and he has served as a statistician with the Bureau of Economic Analysis, U.S. Department of Commerce. Measell holds a BA degree in economics from Washington College, Chestertown, Maryland, and a master of economics degree from North Carolina State University, Raleigh.

NEIL B. MURPHY is Oklahoma Bankers Professor of Finance in the College of Business Administration, University of Oklahoma, Norman, where he is responsible for teaching and curriculum development in areas related to banking. Previously he was senior vice-president at Payment Systems, Inc., a subsidiary of American Express Co. Murphy started his professional career on the research staff of the Federal Reserve Bank of Boston and has served on the research staff of the Federal Deposit Insurance Corp. Other positions include principal economist for Leasco Systems and Research Corp., and staff economist on the President's Commission on Financial Structure and Regulation (Hunt Commission). His academic experience includes an appointment as Professor of Finance, University of Maine, and visiting appointments with the Amos Tuck School, Dartmouth College, and Tel Aviv University. He has published extensively in books, scholarly journals, and trade publications and he writes in the *Comment* section of *American Banker*. Murphy received the BS and MS degrees in business administration from Bucknell University, Lewisburg, Pennsylvania, and a PhD degree in economics from the University of Illinois, Champaign-Urbana.

ROGER F. MURRAY is professor emeritus of finance, Graduate School of Business, Columbia University, New York, and currently serves as consultant to foundations and corporate pension funds. He is a member of the Pension Research Council, the Investment Advisory Panel of the Pension Benefit Guaranty Corp., the Investment Advisory Committee of the New York State Teachers' Retirement System, and the Board of Governors of the Investment Company Institute, and serves on the board of fifteen mutual funds and the Common Fund for Nonprofit Institutions. Murray previously served as a public director of the Chicago Board Options Exchange, an executive officer of College Retirement Equities Fund, director of the National Bureau of Economic Research pension study (1968), and member of the Securities and Exchange Commission Advisory Committee on Corporate Disclosures. He is past president of the American Finance Association and originator of the individual retirement account (IRA) concept. Murray received a BA degree from Yale University, New Haven, Connecticut, the MBA and PhD degrees from New York University, and an LLB degree from Hope College, Holland, Michigan.

GEORGE G. C. PARKER is senior lecturer in management and director of executive education at the Graduate School of Business, Stanford University, Stanford, California. He has also taught at the University of Valle, Cali, Colombia, and the Graduate School of Business, Columbia University. Parker is active in the management development programs of numerous companies including Morgan Guaranty Trust Co., Bank of America, Security Pacific National Bank, Citibank, and Fairchild Camera & Instrument Co. He is the author of a widely reprinted article "How to Get a Better Forecast" (*Harvard Business Review*, March/April, 1971) and has had articles published in many leading academic and professional journals. Parker received a BA degree from Haverford College, Haverford, Pennsylvania, and the MBA and PhD degrees from Stanford University.

RICHARD T. PRATT is a principal at Richard T. Pratt Associates, Salt Lake City, and is professor of finance at the College of Business, University of Utah, Salt Lake City. He is a member of the National Economic Advisory Council of the National Economic League, and public interest director at the Seattle Federal Home Loan Bank, where he served on the Board of Directors from 1970 to 1979. Pratt has extensive experience in government consulting and has served as liaison between the Presidential Commission on Financial Structure and Regulation (Hunt Commission) and the Federal Home Loan Bank Board. He has worked with the Agency for International Development, the Office of Housing, the Mortgage Guaranty

Insurance Corp., and the Federal Home Loan Mortgage Corp. Pratt received the BS and MBA degrees from the University of Utah and a DBA degree from Indiana University, Bloomington.

ALFRED RAPPAPORT is Leonard Spacek Professor of Accounting and Information Systems and director of the Accounting Research Center at the Kellogg Graduate School of Management, Northwestern University, Evanston, Illinois. He is an active consultant in strategic financial planning, mergers and acquisitions, and performance evaluation systems. His interactive time-sharing computer model has been used in many mergers, including several of the largest in U.S. history. Rappaport has written and edited numerous books and articles dealing with accounting and financial planning. He has served on Financial Accounting Standards Board task forces and as a consultant to the Securities and Exchange Commission. Rappaport received a BA degree from Case Western Reserve University, Cleveland, and the MS and PhD degrees from the University of Illinois, Champaign-Urbana.

R. BRUCE RICKS is a co-owner and manager of Becker & Ricks, Palo Alto, a shopping center management company, and senior lecturer in the Graduate School of Business at Stanford University, Stanford, California, where he teaches real property development. He has extensive and varied experience in real estate finance and investment. Ricks was a professor of finance at the University of California, Los Angeles, where he served as assistant dean, first of the Graduate School of Management, then of the School of Architecture and Urban Planning. He has held senior lecturer appointments at the Wharton School of the University of Pennsylvania and at American University. From 1969 to 1972 he was the chief economist and director of research for the Federal Home Loan Bank Board, Washington, D.C. He has written extensively on real estate finance and is the publisher of the *Ricks Report* on real estate investment. Ricks received the BS, MBA, and PhD degrees in finance and real estate from the University of California, Berkeley.

ARNOLD W. SAMETZ is professor of finance and director of the Salomon Brothers Center for the Study of Financial Institutions, New York, and the Institute of Finance, Graduate School of Business Administration, New York University. His professional and research interests include financial crises, financing the overseas subsidiaries of U.S. corporations, foreign investment in the United States, the National Securities Market System, and securities activities of commercial banks. Sametz has served as an expert witness on rate of return in utility rate cases for both companies and state commissions and also in stock valuation cases, including tenders, recapitalizations, and pension funds. He is an adviser to thrift institutions and associations, and trustee of the Empire Savings Bank. Sametz received an AB degree from Brooklyn College, Brooklyn, New York, and the PhD degree from Princeton University, Princeton, New Jersey.

RICHARD L. SANDOR is director, ContiFinancial Division, and vice-president, ContiCommodity Services, Inc., Chicago. Previously vice-president and chief economist of the Chicago Board of Trade, he earned the reputation as the "principal architect" of the interest rate futures markets. Sandor has been a faculty member of the School of Business Administration, University of California, Berkeley, and a visiting scholar and professor at Northwestern University. He is a member of the board of directors of the Chicago Board of Trade and Chairman of the Financial Instruments Committee. He was a member of the steering committee for the First International Commodities Conference, served as a moderator for all subsequent conferences, is a contributing editor to *Commodities Magazine* and is an honorary member of the Commodity Club of San Francisco. Sandor received a BA degree from City University of New York, Brooklyn College, Brooklyn, New York, and a PhD degree in economics from the University of Minnesota, Minneapolis.

OSCAR N. SERBEIN is professor of insurance at Stanford University, Stanford, California. He has taught at the University of California, Berkeley, Columbia University, and Escuela de Administracion de Negocios para Graduados (Peru). Serbein has a reputation as an authority on insurance issues and is the coauthor of *Property and Liability Insurance* (1967) and *Risk Management: Text and Cases* (1978). He is associate editor of *Journal of Insurance: Issues and Practices* and was the director of Stanford's doctoral program in business administration. Serbein received the BA and MS degrees from the University of Iowa, Iowa City, and a PhD degree from Columbia University, New York.

ALAN C. SHAPIRO is associate professor of finance at the Graduate School of Business Administration of the University of Southern California, Los Angeles. Previously, he was an assistant professor at the University of Pennsylvania's Wharton School of Finance. Shapiro has published extensively on problems in international financial management in a variety of journals, including *Journal of Finance, Journal of Financial and Quantitative Analysis, Financial Management*, and *Journal of Business*. His textbook *Multinational Financial Management* was published in 1980. Shapiro received a PhD degree in economics from Carnegie-Mellon University, Pittsburgh.

TILDON W. SMITH is a vice-president, Sales and Trading of Fixed Income Securities, Money Market Dept., First National Bank of Atlanta. Formerly with the Fixed Income Division of Goldman Sachs & Co., Philadelphia, Smith has held positions in data processing, cash management systems, and sales and trading of domestic and foreign money market instruments. He has been a guest speaker at the American Management Association, the Wharton Cash Management Seminar, Georgia Institute of Technology, Georgia State University, and the Georgia State University Financial Forum. Smith received a BBA in economics and an MBA degree in finance from Georgia State University, Atlanta.

BERNELL K. STONE is Mills Bee Lane Professor at Georgia Institute of Technology, Atlanta. He is editor of *Journal of Cash Management* and has served for a number of years as an associate editor for both *Financial Management* and *Journal* *of Financial and Quantitative Analysis*. Among his publications are nearly a dozen dealing with cash management and closely related areas. Stone's papers won awards in the Financial Management Association's annual competitions in 1974 and 1975. Stone received a BS degree from Duke University, Durham, North Carolina, an MS degree from the University of Wisconsin, Madison, and a PhD degree from Massachusetts Institute of Technology, Cambridge.

MARTI G. SUBRAHMANYAM is a professor of finance and chairman of the finance area at the Graduate School of Business Administration, New York University. He has taught finance and economics at the Massachusetts Institute of Technology, Cambridge, the Indian Institute of Management, Ahmedabad, and at École Supérieur de Sciènce Economics et Commerce (France). Subrahmanyam has published in several leading journals in finance and economics. His research interests are in the areas of capital market theory, corporation finance, and international finance. He is coauthor of the book *Capital Market Equilibrium and Corporate Financial Decisions* (1980). He serves as an associate editor of *Management Science* and *Journal of Banking and Finance*. Subrahmanyam received a bachelor's degree from the Indian Institute of Technology, an MBA degree from the Indian Institute of Management, Ahmedabad, and a PhD degree in finance and economics from the Massachusetts Institute of Technology.

A. CHARLENE SULLIVAN is assistant professor of management and research associate, Credit Research Center, Purdue University, Lafayette, Indiana, where she has been primarily engaged in research in consumer credit, studying the effects of restrictive rate ceilings and creditors' remedy laws on the supply of and demand for consumer credit. Sullivan is coauthor (with R. W. Johnson) of a handbook for the Small Business Administration on the management of consumer credit, *Credit and Collections for Small Stores*. She also coauthored a series entitled *Statistical Analysis of Bank Card Usage* for the American Bankers Association. Sullivan received a PhD degree in management from Purdue University.

CLOSSON L. VAUGHAN is a fixed income portfolio manager at Pacific Investment Management Co., Newport Beach, California. He was previously associated with the corporate and international bond rating departments of Standard & Poor's Corp., and was vice-president and fixed income portfolio manager at Lehman Management Co. Vaughan received an MBA degree in finance from New York University.

J. PETER WILLIAMSON is professor of business administration at the Amos Tuck Graduate School of Business Administration at Dartmouth College, Hanover, New Hampshire. He was formerly on the faculties of the Harvard Business School and the University of Toronto Law School, and was a visiting professor at the Colgate Darden Business School, University of Virginia, Charlottesville. Williamson is a consultant to a number of business and nonprofit organizations, provides expert testimony before public utility commissions, and is a trustee of the New

Hampshire Savings Bank and of the Common Fund. He has published several books on legal and financial subjects and is the author of a variety of articles on law, taxation, finance, and investments. Williamson has written several articles on performance evaluation, most recently for *Journal of Portfolio Management*. He received the MBA and DBA degrees from the Harvard Business School and the LLB from Harvard Law School, Cambridge, Massachusetts.

THE "NEW" FINANCIAL ENVIRONMENT

CONTENTS

MAJOR SHIFTS IN THE FINANCIAL ENVIRONMENT 3

Increased Rate and Unpredictability of Inflation 3
Increased Financial and Business Risk 5
Decreased Financial and Increased Economic Regulation 5
Increased Internationalization 6

ADJUSTMENTS AND INNOVATIONS IN FINANCIAL MARKETS AND

INSTITUTIONS: RESPONSES OF REAL AND FINANCIAL SECTORS TO CHANGING FINANCIAL ENVIRONMENT 6

The Real Sector 6
The Financial Sector 7
   Financial intermediation 7
   Financial markets 8
   Financial instruments 8
   Financial institutions 8

THE "NEW" FINANCIAL ENVIRONMENT

Arnold W. Sametz

Since 1968 when the fourth edition of the *Financial Handbook* was published, the **financial environment** of the United States—indeed of the world—has undergone radical change. Not since the 1930s, when depression and financial collapse led to radical restructure of **financial institutions** and instruments has there been such deep and widespread change in financial markets. By contrast to the 1930s, when deflation was the principal radicalizing factor (but like the 1890's when monetary expansion was the prime disturber) the initiating factor in the alteration of the financial environment was a quantum leap in the **underlying rate of inflation** and widened band of fluctuations around that higher average rate.

The rise of the underlying rate of inflation from the 2–3% of 1950–1965 to the 5% of 1965–1975 and the 9–10% of 1975–1980 (with an annual range of 6–12%) was accompanied or followed by at least three major shifts in the financial environment: **rises in both financial and business risks, increased internationalization** of **financial markets, and decreased regulation of financial markets.** It should also be noted that the 1970s were a decade during which the **real standard of living** of Americans ceased rising.

For our purposes, it is sufficient to assume that inflation was and is the prime instigator of the changed behavior by holders and issuers of financial assets and financial liabilities and thus of changes in financial institutions and instruments. This is not to say that **financial deregulation** may not have been a cause of inflation, but it surely was a reaction to inflation. Nor is it to deny that changes in **real economic growth and productivity** affect the rate of inflation; rather, we concentrate on how inflation and the accompanying changes in the financial environment affect the "real" economy, that is, the consumption and investment patterns in the United States. Inflation is discussed in detail in numerous sections of this *Handbook,* including "Money and Capital Markets: Institutional Framework and Federal Reserve Control," "Savings Institutions," and several of the sections in Part Two, on international finance, as well as "Performance Measurement," "Cash Management," "Capital Budgeting," "Long-Term Sources of Funds and the Cost of Capital," and "Financial Decisions for Multinational Enterprises." Finally, there is an entire section entitled "Financial Management in an Inflationary Environment."

The changes in the financial environment brought about a significant number of **innovations in financial instruments and institutions.** Financial markets today are quite different from what they were in 1965. We have a revolution to explain!

MAJOR SHIFTS IN THE FINANCIAL ENVIRONMENT

INCREASED RATE AND UNPREDICTABILITY OF INFLATION. The underlying rate of inflation doubled between 1965 and 1972, that is, **before** the oil crisis, rising from 2 to

4% yearly average with a peak of 6%. It doubled again between 1973 and 1980, rising from 4 to 8% on average, with a peak of 12% in 1974 and again in 1979. Moreover, the underlying rate of inflation not only doubled twice over the period, it became very erratic: as recently as 1975 through 1977 it averaged 6%, though in 1979 it broke 12%. In other words, not only did the **anticipated rate of inflation** rise, the shorter-run **unanticipated range** of inflation also increased to about 50% above and below the expected rate. Additional uncertainty about future price movements was injected because some major components of the price index (food, energy, and housing) also experienced wild fluctuations from year to year. Not only did consumers and businesses need to adjust patterns of spending to suit their changed purchasing power, they also had to adjust their **savings patterns.** This became necessary as relative prices and yields of **financial** "goods and services" changed radically along with the **consumer price index** or the **GNP deflator.**

For example, **interest rates** rose roughly to parallel price rises (though with leads and lags) as lenders required a stable "real" return on loans. This had four major financial impacts, two unfavorable, and two offsetting:

1. Holders of outstanding bonds experienced large capital losses, while issuers of such debt had to lock themselves into historically high long-term rates to raise fresh funds. **Both** borrowers and lenders at long term thus experienced increased risk and uncertainty in this financial market. Indeed there was talk of the impending demise of the **bond market.** The federal government as a debt issuer, however, was less affected by the inflation because federal taxes are heavily progressive, so that in effect government income is "indexed" to inflation, and thus its need to borrow is less pressing. Moreover, the bulk of federal debt is short term—both outstanding and new issues. Federal debt's relative stature improved during this turbulent period.

2. While it was no surprise that lenders were hurt by inflation, equities too turned out to be a poor **inflation hedge** from 1965 to 1980. New bonds could be issued as long as they carried the new higher interest rates; new stock was difficult to issue, and "real" stock prices fell even as consumer prices were rising. More than likely the cause of the decline in equity prices was the lower realized and expected **real return on investment** for U.S. companies.

It turns out that during an unanticipated, rapid, and erratic inflation, business is unable to adjust its prices to its costs fast enough to avoid profit erosion. Thus given price-earnings ratio (P/E) levels, stock prices lag, and the yield competition in capital markets that requires dividend yields to rise, requires that stock price **fall.** In addition, P/E ratios will actually fall as unpredictable inflation increases business risk. But as business learns to adjust to prices more rapidly, and as the inflation stabilizes even at higher rates, stock prices can revive. Indeed we saw a revival, of sorts, in equity prices in the first half of 1980. But for much of the period 1965–1980, total returns from stock included little or no capital gains; dividend yields rose to parallel bond interest rates, with capital losses to those who had to liquidate shares.

3. The only market that provided **inflation-offsetting yields** and no capital losses was the **short-term debt (deposit) market.** And those rates, as has been true for over 50 years, yielded a return that just matched the rate of inflation; that is, the real return was effectively zero. But that was a better return than the **negative** return on stocks and bonds over the past 15 years.

4. Positive real returns over this period were earned only on **nonfinancial assets.** The oldest law of how to live in inflationary times did indeed hold up in 1965–1980: flee to commodities or real assets like real estate, gold or diamonds, or fine art. This implies not only paucity of returns in financial markets, but increased **financial risk** to participants on both the supply and demand side. Our **traditional financial markets** failed to perform appropriately under inflationary conditions. The investing public will desert such markets unless inflation stabilizes or innovations in financial markets offset inflationary impacts.

INCREASED FINANCIAL AND BUSINESS RISK. In addition to the obvious increase in risk implied by the performance of the bond and stock markets as they adjusted to new higher average rates of inflation, there is the additional risk of fluctuations of returns, if average expected rates should become stable. Investors in the capital markets now require higher returns for term investment because **financial risk** of security price volatility has increased. Financial risks to issuers and users of funds have also risen. This is the result of the rise in **business risk** during inflationary periods (owing to increased swings in sales and costs) and the rise in **financial risk** implied in rising **debt-equity ratios,** rising ratios of short-term to long-term debt, and especially the fall in the **earnings coverage ratios** that are typical of inflationary eras. The average U.S. industrial ratio of debt to total assets rose from 34% in 1950 to over 52% in 1980, and these statistics fail, for the most part, to include the large increase in lease financing.

The impaired profitability of inflationary times threatens internal equity financing and raises the amount of required debt financing that is needed if investment plans are to be carried out. The impaired capital markets drive business away from stock and bond issues and toward short-term borrowing. The rise in debt plus the rise in interest rates results in sharp decreases in the "times (interest) charges earned," the cash flow indicator of financial risk.

DECREASED FINANCIAL AND INCREASED ECONOMIC REGULATION. The impact of the rise in business (real) and financial risk in the economy—primarily owing to the protracted but erratic inflationary trend—was made more precipitous by shifts in **regulatory policy. Deregulation of financial instruments and financial institutions** was stimulated partially by the inflation but in turn accelerated the spread or spiral of the inflationary effects. For example, lifting regulations prescribing interest ceilings on time deposits **(Regulation Q)** and on mortgages **(usury rates)** did allow small savers to keep up with inflation, but it also encouraged expanding **housing expenditures,** which fed the inflationary process. The restriction of housing expenditures used to inhibit inflation, as disintermediation and a credit crunch curtailed the financing of housing. As a result, this time, however, interest rates reached historic peaks (16% mortgage rates in 1980) and consumer credit controls had to be reimposed to break the inflationary spiral in early 1980. On the other hand, expanding regulatory controls in the business sector, such as environmental restrictions, safety requirements, and energy subsidies, resulted in increased **real costs of production.** Thus the regulatory sphere altered the financial environment substantially by raising the average base level of real economic and financial costs and prices.

It should be noted that the unleashing of aggregate **monetary policy**—which controls monetary reserves but leaves interest rates free to vary—leads to greater use of selective controls via **fiscal policy** depending on which taxes are cut and which expenditure streams are altered.

INCREASED INTERNATIONALIZATION.   Increased internationalization is the fruit of a variety of deregulatory and regulatory trends. Financial deregulation has been extensive, as exemplified by more **flexible exchange rates** and freer movement of portfolio investment (and even direct investment) and access to **overseas capital markets.** But the increased **economic** regulation in the form of oil cartels also has led to increased internationalization via overseas investment of Near East surpluses.

Increased and freer international financial flows, like domestic freer flows, results not only in more efficient financial markets—that is, lower **transactions costs** and greater information, and greater allocational efficiency—but also in more rapid and fuller **spread of inflation** and more volatile security price and interest rate fluctuations internationally. The **financial world** is more efficient but also more risky. And it is in response to these new conditions in the financial world that adjustments and innovations in financial instruments and activities have developed.

ADJUSTMENTS AND INNOVATIONS IN FINANCIAL MARKETS AND INSTITUTIONS: RESPONSES OF REAL AND FINANCIAL SECTORS TO CHANGING FINANCIAL ENVIRONMENT

THE REAL SECTOR.   **Households,** though of course remaining the prime surplus or saving sector in the economy, increased their borrowing, especially long-term **mortgage debt,** relative to their lending. The latter continued to be short term, though increasingly in **money market investments** rather than traditional savings accounts. Households fought against price inflation via short-term interest rate instruments and sheltered their income against **tax "inflation"** via tax-deductible mortgage interest and real estate taxes, even at the expense of curtailing net **personal savings.** The predominant "hedge" motivations of investors was also evidenced in the rise of **"options"** and **"futures"** and the revival of intermediation via **mutual funds of money market instruments, municipal bonds,** and **corporate bonds.** The business sector, like household investors, increased its debt ratio, though it is always a **net "deficit" sector.** While for much of the period business borrowed heavily in the short area, it is currently seeking to lengthen the debt and to devise painless ways to issue equity. Intermediate-term **convertible debentures** are a likely current means of adjustment. Business capital market requirements suggest that even **busier times are ahead for financial intermediaries serving the business sector.**

Compared to the household sector, the **business sector** has increased its **debt ratio** (to date) modestly. Business, suffering from restricted profits and thus lower retained earnings, was forced to finance itself externally, largely through debt, especially short-term debt. Business does not choose to sell new equity shares when profits and stock prices are relatively low; and when interest rates are at historic highs, borrowers are reluctant to lock themselves in to such rates via new issues of long-term corporate bonds. As a result, during the 1970s, nonfinancial business financial policy included new ways to economize on needs for short-term funds and means to raise such funds with new instruments.

Corporate finance departments developed new financial forecasting techniques to reduce liquidity needs and to minimize inventories, both of goods and receivables; long-term requirements or capital budgets were reduced by implementing strict **cost of capital hurdles** for fixed investments, based on high interest rates plus increased equity risk premiums. Furthermore, it was often found that outstanding fixed assets were available via merger or acquisition at bargain (stock) prices financed by private debt or through **leveraged leasing.**

And when business had to raise funds, it did so largely through the banks and short-term markets. While banks developed term loans, business developed extensive use of commercial paper, sold directly to other businesses and to financial institutions, including banks themselves. Business also developed new forms of intermediate-term (5–7 year) bonds and expanded its use of custom-made, longer term debt directly negotiated with insurance companies and pension funds. By 1980, while half of all bank term loans were **indexed,** over half of all corporate bonds were **privately placed.** As the 1980s begin, business is showing new interest in convertible bonds and is less reluctant in general to offer a share in equity to major lenders under certain conditions. Innovations in financing business over the long term are developing rapidly, with particular attention to attracting foreign sources of funding.

The government sectors have not been under borrowing pressure because their "incomes"—tax revenues—have been the best indexed streams in the economy. Consequently **government debt** has expanded less than **private debt.** Government finance in this sense has not been under pressure to innovate. Innovation in the governmental sector, however, has occurred in regulatory areas and in methods of executing **monetary and fiscal policies.**

THE FINANCIAL SECTOR.   The potential to provide detail in this area is so great that only typical examples of major classes of adjustments of the 1970s can be considered.

Financial Intermediation.   The decline of **term intermediation** by depository institutions—borrowing short and lending long—is a major adjustment to inflation, and was a serious step backward in the financial structure of the United States. The parallel rise of **money market certificates** and **variable rate mortgages** to displace **passbook savings accounts** and 30-year fixed rate mortgages is typical. Institutions like **savings and loan associations** were freed to issue savings shares indexed to open market Treasury bill rates and then were forced by competition to issue money market certificates. They then sought to **hedge** their high-cost, **variable interest obligations** by lending the funds out at high, variable rates rather than assuming the risk of high, fixed rate loan assets. The term risk in effect has been shifted from the intermediary to the household.

Term risk is the risk of persistently rising interest rates when fixed rate, long-term outstanding loans have been financed via short-term deposits or instruments; profits will be eroded as the short-term sources of funds have to be refinanced at higher and higher rates of interest, though the income from the mortgages, for example, is fixed. **Term intermediation** under alternately rising and **falling** interest rates rather than forever rising interest rates is another matter.

Default risk is pooled as always, but **term risk coverage** is not offered. Our financial services to households have been diminished. Similarly, commercial banks via **floating** (variable) **term loans** have diminished the "term" aspect of such loans with respect to interest cost if not to maturity. And even long maturity is not assured in the **"Canadian" 5-year rollover mortgage,** which is subject to periodic renegotiation of all terms. This marks a reversion to the financial practices of the 1920s, when term risk could not easily be intermediated.

The increase in **instrument intermediation,** or **hedging,** to cope with default risk further reduces the financial institutions' role in intermediation. As we will see, financial institutions are increasingly serving on a "service-for-a-fee" basis rather than serving a risk absorption function. Some financial institutions, for example, **insurance companies,** are curtailing their risks via **reinsurance contracts.** Sections in this *Handbook,* particularly those in Part One, discuss these issues in detail.

Financial Markets.   Across the board, financial markets have become more competitive. The listed stock brokers' fixed **commission schedules** were scrapped and negotiated rates mandated by the Securities and Exchange Commission in 1975; currently under discussion is the lifting of **price maintenance of new issues** while in distribution.

Increased competition among underwriters has also come about via commercial bank entry into the **private placement** of corporate securities, both stocks and bonds. Furthermore, **bank leasing financing** can substitute for new debt issues. In the wings is **automation of securities trading** to the point when execution of trades takes place via computer rather than exchange floors. The mechanization of price determination in standardized securities markets is not far off.

Not only have financial assets such as **certificates of deposit** (CDs) and **open market commercial paper** (CPs) become highly negotiable, instruments such as mortgages that are not directly negotiable owing to their uniqueness have in effect become so through **secondary market** and **pass-through** packaging of the nonnegotiable instruments. Many of these innovative markets and instruments were developed under government subsidy and protection; but most of them today are flourishing under private, nonsubsidized auspices.

Financial Instruments.   And of course **options and futures markets** are a substitute for buying the stocks or bonds themselves. So too the opening up of markets and expansion of information for foreign securities, especially equities and **Eurodollar deposits and loans,** provides competition for U.S. securities markets. Entire sections of the *Handbook* are devoted to these markets and instruments.

Innovations in the supply of **futures contracts** on financial instruments as well as commodities and other hedged contracts is directly responsive to the demand for instruments as shelters against the increased volatility of interest rates and the associated rise in both business and financial risk. Competition for ordinary savers' funds among **money market certificates, Treasury bills,** and **money market funds** is intense. Of these instruments only Treasury bills existed before 1975, and even they were not as well known or available as they are today.

A final example of adaptation to the new financial environment is the awakening of the **mutual fund industry,** not via stock funds but through **debt funds.** In addition to money market funds there are **municipal funds** and **corporate bond funds** and **government funds.** Each type is offered in funds of varying maturities and varying quality, in denominations of interest to even modest personal investors.

As the financial markets have expanded in new directions, they have replaced in part the intermediation of savers' funds through depositories and even insurance-pension contractual funds. We have come a long way since the early 1960s when CDs were first introduced. Today CDs are available to all savers, not just large depositors at large banks. A parallel development of the 1970s was the expansion of CPs as a substitute investment for large CDs. CPs rapidly became a substitute on the borrower side for commercial bank loans.

Financial Institutions.   Two polar developments in the structure and function of financial institutions are rapidly taking shape. First, we are on the upside of the long historical cycle toward large, multipurpose department stores of finance and away from specialized institutions. For example, **commercial banks** are entering the **investment banking** business. Second, and quite counter to the first trend, we are also developing highly **specialized financial boutiques,** which permit previously specialized financial businesses, such as securities firms, to restrict their activities to discount brokerage with little or no researching or advisory activities.

Both developments are common to American history, rising and falling depending on economic-financial events and governmental policy. For example, during the 1930s, the last period of radical change in the financial environment—a period of **deflation, depression,** then controls and planned recovery—financial institutions were segregated by law, and their specialized activities were subject to meticulous regulation. During the 1960s and 1970s, a period of inflation and competition and financial euphoria, financial institutions pushed out in all directions, and financial practices became highly flexible as measures of financial deregulation proliferated. Efficiency, competition, and flexibility typify this period, as contrasted with the concerns for safety, regulation, and measured change of the 1930s and 1950s. Currently the bias is toward allowing financial structure to evolve as financial entrepreneurs choose. Historically, such periods have ended when private financial overreaching, errors or misbehavior, and inadequate or misconceived public policy led to **financial crises** and then a period of restrictive financial regulation and supervision.

But since the early 1960s we have seen a remarkable **liberation of financial activity.** Consider the recent evolution of the large **commercial banks** toward continental style **department stores of finance.** In 1961 Citibank introduced the **certificate of deposit** the beginning of its effort to become a ''thrift'' institution, taking savings deposits and making long-term loans to all, as well as a traditional commercial bank, taking demand deposits and making short-term loans to business. By 1970 the larger banks, having grown far faster than the thrift institutions and having changed the practices in the industry, had shifted their attention to several other financial institution fields. For example, commercial banks, largely via the use of the **bank holding company** device, entered various financial service businesses such as leasing, data processing, and financial consulting. Commercial banks also began to enter the investment banking or securities business (which presumably had been proscribed by the **Glass-Steagall Banking Act of 1933**) such as **private placement** of corporate securities, **underwriting** of **municipal revenue bonds,** and offerings of **commingled trust funds** (mutual funds of securities) to the public.

On the other side, large securities firms like **Merrill Lynch** were opening ''deposit'' accounts for customers, entering the real estate and insurance businesses, and within the securities business proper, going into competition with the **New York Stock Exchange** for market making in listed securities. Some of the large thrift institutions are acquiring commercial bank functions: **negotiated order of withdrawal** (NOW) accounts, commercial savings deposits and loans, **real estate management,** and so on. **Insurance companies,** with their expanded term lending to business, annuity packages, real estate, equity positions and property management are also becoming all-purpose institutions.

This trend toward ''one big financial institution,'' with many functions falling between regulatory stools, is largely a reaction of the large institutions to rapidly changing financial needs and practices, and especially to increasing **financial and business risks.** The all-purpose business is one that is, by definition, widely diversified; thus it is cushioned against risk and well equipped to move in any direction the financial wind blows.

However, reaction to the very same events by less than giant financial institutions can and does result in quite different financial business developments. The **''boutique'' approach** (by contrast to the department store or, in this case, a variety store approach) is to specialize in particular financial functions that the business has unique capacity to deliver, for which a demand has been or can be developed, and for which profitable fee schedules can be arranged. For example, securities firms are specializing in **pure brokerage transactions at discount,** others are strictly research shops, selling expert opinions for a fee. Some thrift institutions are becoming mortgage **servicing** rather than mortgage holding businesses; that is, they pass through the loan to other lenders. Specialists in **options, reinsurance, second**

mortgages, and so on, are proliferating. Here the response to increased pace of change and risk is not to diversify but to strip down to lean, adaptable size and to specialize flexibly. In effect such activity involves unbundling the traditional packages of financial services, and leaving many of the money lending and capital functions to others, while offering profitable services at scheduled fees.

In addition to innovation in market procedures and in financial instruments, there have been **innovations in financial institutions.** To cope with inflation and increasing risk, the banks developed money market certificates; and then securities firms responded with **money market funds** and then short-term **municipal funds;** and the insurance-pension fund industries developed **variable annuities.** To cope with expanding volume of trade in less regulated financial security markets, the securities industries developed automated trading practices, competitive brokerage fees, and the beginning of a **national securities market;** then the banks moved into the securities business; brokerage firms shifted to option trading, and so on. Thus have the various financial institutions been responding to the changing environment by changing their structure and functions in free-form fashion.

BIBLIOGRAPHY

Altman, E. I., and Sametz, A. W., *Financial Crises*, Wiley, New York, 1977.

Federal Reserve Bulletin, various issues: "Recent Developments in Corporate Finance" and "Household Finance," Washington, D.C.

Federal Reserve Bulletin, *Commercial Paper Market*, Washington, D.C., June 1977, 525–536.

Friedman, B., "Postwar Changes in American Financial Markets," in M. Fieldstein, Ed., *American Economy in Transition*, University of Chicago Press, 1981.

Goldsmith, R. W., *The Flow of Capital Funds in the Postwar Economy*, Columbia University Press, New York, 1965.

Kaufman, Henry, et al., "Restoring Corporate Balance Sheets: An Urgent Challenge," Salomon Brothers, New York, July 21, 1980.

Polakoff, M. E., et al., *Financial Institutions and Markets*, Houghton-Mifflin, Boston, 1981.

Sametz, A. W., *Prospects for Capital Formation and Capital Markets*, Heath-Lexington Books, Lexington, MA, 1978.

———, et al., "Securities Activities of Commercial Banks," *Journal of Comparative Law and Securities Regulation*, No. 2, 1979, pp 155–193.

PART 1

U.S. FINANCIAL MARKETS AND INSTITUTIONS

MONEY AND CAPITAL MARKETS: INSTITUTIONAL FRAMEWORK AND FEDERAL RESERVE CONTROL

CONTENTS

THE INSTITUTIONAL FRAMEWORK: SAVINGS SURPLUS AND SAVINGS DEFICIT SECTORS   3

RISK AVERSION AND THE DEVELOPMENT OF THE FINANCIAL INTERMEDIARY   4

HOUSEHOLD DIRECT INVESTMENT AND DISINTERMEDIATION   4

FLOW OF FUNDS   4

Distribution of Assets Among Financial Intermediaries   6
   Savings institutions   6
   Life insurance companies   6
   Fire and casualty insurance companies   7
   State and local government retirement assets   8
   Private pension funds   12

INTEREST RATES: THE BALANCING MECHANISM   12

Capital Certainty Versus Income Certainty   12
The Equilibrating Process   13

THE FEDERAL RESERVE SYSTEM   13

The Fed in Operation   14
   The Board of Governors   14
   Federal Reserve Banks   16
   Collection of checks and other services   17

   Issuance of policy directives   17
Tools of the Fed   18

THE MONEY MARKET AND FEDERAL RESERVE CONTROL   19

Money Market Instruments   19
   Federal funds   19
   Repurchase agreements   19
   Treasury bills   19
   Bankers' acceptances   21
   Commercial paper   21
   Negotiable certificates of deposit   21

THE CORPORATION AND THE COST OF CAPITAL: SHORT-TERM FUNDING   24

Trade Credit   25
Bank Loans   25
Commercial Paper   26
Bankers' Acceptances   26
Finance Company Loans   26
Profit Tax Payable   26

THE CORPORATION'S LONG-TERM COST OF CAPITAL   27

THE CYCLICAL PATTERN OF INTEREST RATES   28

The Yield Curve: Relationships Between Yields and Term to Maturity   28
Quality Considerations   30
Inflation and Real Rates of Interest   32

MONEY AND CAPITAL MARKETS: INSTITUTIONAL FRAMEWORK AND FEDERAL RESERVE CONTROL

Joseph Bench

The financial officer of a corporation operates within a framework of institutions such as commercial banks, thrift institutions, life insurance companies, and pension funds. This section examines the roles these institutions play in determining interest rates. It also provides a brief introduction to the mechanics of monetary policy exercised by the Federal Reserve Bank. A better understanding of the Federal Reserve's operations—specifically its growth targets for monetary aggregates and its response when money and credit growth either falls short of or exceeds Fed objectives—will help the financial manager to cope with the constantly changing interest rate environment.

THE INSTITUTIONAL FRAMEWORK: SAVINGS SURPLUS AND SAVINGS DEFICIT SECTORS

In the traditional three-sector (households, businesses, and government) economy, there are **savings surplus** and **savings deficit** sectors. In the **savings surplus** sectors consumption is less than current income. In the **savings deficit** sectors current expenditures exceed current income and funds must be raised from external sources to make up the difference. Typically, the **household sector** is a net supplier of funds, since it is a savings surplus unit, whereas **businesses** are generally savings deficit units and therefore are seeking funds from the household sector. This does not mean to imply that every household has more income than it consumes. While there are many savings deficit units within the household sector, the sector collectively saves more than it borrows. In the business sector, there are both savings deficit units (the norm) and savings surplus units, firms that have extra money to invest. Collectively, however, businesses are viewed as savings deficit units attempting to make up the difference between spending on plant and equipment or inventories and income from operations.

Government has always been a deficit sector. The role of state and local governments and federal agencies as savings deficit units, however, is generally limited to periods of depressed economic activity when rising unemployment and welfare benefits, coupled with a slowdown in tax receipts, lead to a deterioration in municipal finances. As recently as

1978, state and local governments showed a net financial investment of $0.5 billion, acquiring $25.1 billion of financial assets and issuing $24.6 billion of financial liabilities.

RISK AVERSION AND THE DEVELOPMENT OF THE FINANCIAL INTERMEDIARY

The description of the savings surplus and savings deficit units suggests a natural flow of funds from saver to borrower. To smooth the flow of funds between surplus and deficit units, there has developed a variety of middlemen or **financial intermediaries.** These intermediaries, which include commercial banks, savings and loan companies, mutual savings, banks, and credit unions, provide a vehicle for diversifying the risks associated with investing in projects and at the same time provide investors with **liquidity,** should they need to use the funds (or wish to redeploy them in another investment offering a higher rate of return) before the project is complete.

The financial intermediary enables investors to **diversify** their portfolios by making them infinitesimally small shareholders of a wide variety of projects. The "law of large numbers" suggests only a small probability that any project will go bust, which allows investors to keep their capital intact. Moreover, the financial intermediary stands ready to redeem (refund) the capital plus accumulated interest on short notice, further assuring investors of the liquidity they desire. [Meanwhile, the financial intermediary recognizes the small likelihood that all investments of reasonably long maturities will go bad and therefore is willing to make long-term investments; even though its liabilities (deposits) are generally short-term.]

HOUSEHOLD DIRECT INVESTMENT AND DISINTERMEDIATION

The household sector does not always invest through financial intermediaries. Individuals do make direct purchases of corporate securities (including both equity and debt offerings), and in many cases will purchase tax-exempt securities to insulate themselves from the tax burden on the income derived from these investments. And when interest rates get high enough, individuals reverse the normal flow of savings through intermediaries, withdrawing funds to reinvest their capital in higher yielding, fixed income investments, such as U.S. Treasury obligations. This process is called **disintermediation.** Financial intermediaries generally react to this phenomenon by sharply cutting back their new investments in real and financial assets, which serves to dampen economic activity in areas deprived of new cash.

FLOW OF FUNDS

Exhibit 1 shows the supply and demand for funds in credit markets for 1978 and 1979. On the demand side, the chart is divided into five major groupings: government, corporate securities, mortgages, consumer credit, and short-term business demands. On the supply side are eight groupings: commercial banks, contractual savings institutions (insurance companies and pension funds), thrift institutions, foreign sources, monetary authorities (the Fed), non-bank finance companies, nonfinancial corporate business (corporations), and other (including individuals and mutual funds) investors. Exhibit 2 gives a more detailed breakdown of the flow of funds by sector.

EXHIBIT 1   FLOW OF FUNDS IN PRIVATE CREDIT MARKETS ($ BILLIONS)

Source of Funds	1978 Actual	1979 (Preliminary)	1980 (Forecast)
DEMAND FOR FUNDS			
Government	125	101	118
Federal	54	34	45
Agencies	30	22	30
State and local	23	19	20
Mortgage pool securities	18	26	23
Corporate Securities	29	39	45
Equity	2	5	4
Bonds and notes	20	25	30
Tax-exempt bonds	3	5	6
Foreign bonds	4	4	5
Mortgages	117	103	85
Residential			
Home	105	103	85
Multifamily	10	9	7
Commercial	23	23	20
Farm	10	14	8
(less agency holdings, mortgage pool securities, and state and local government sponsorship)	(31)	(46)	(35)
Consumer Credit	50	42	32
Policy loans	3	5	4
Short-Term Business	87	90	56
Bank loans N.E.C.	53	40	25
Open market paper	26	41	25
Finance company loans	8	9	6
	411	380	340
SUPPLY OF FUNDS			
Commercial Banks and Affiliates	122	112	105
Contractual Savings	87	97	105
Life insurance	36	34	36
Private pension funds	19	21	24
State and local retirement funds	16	21	23
Fire and casualty	16	21	22
Thrift Institutions	82	60	53
Savings and loans	64	48	43
Mutual savings banks	11	6	5
Credit unions	7	6	5
Foreign	38	11	2

EXHIBIT 1 CONTINUED

Source of Funds	1978 Actual	1979 (Preliminary)	1980 (Forecast)
Monetary Authorities	7	7	7
Nonbank Finance Companies	18	25	15
Nonfinancial Corporate Business	15	13	10
Net Trade Credit	6	19	9
Other [a]	36	36	34
	411	380	340

[a]Includes bond and money market funds, real estate investment trusts, individual investors, and other investors.
Source: Federal Reserve Board.

DISTRIBUTION OF ASSETS AMONG FINANCIAL INTERMEDIARIES. The largest asset in **commercial bank** balance sheets is bank loans. These constitute about one-third of the total, mortgages about one-fifth, consumer credit nearly one-sixth, U.S. Treasury and agency issues and state and local government obligations each about one-eighth of their investment portfolio. The remaining 10% is invested in a variety of financial assets including open market paper, security credit, and corporate bonds. A detailed breakdown of the size and proportion of each of these is presented in Exhibit 3.

Savings Institutions. Savings institutions include **savings and loan associations, mutual savings banks,** and **credit unions.** Their primary investment is in mortgages, which constitutes more than 75% of their assets. Home mortgages account for 60% of their investments; commercial mortgages and multifamily mortgages each account for 8% of their investment totals. Consumer credit and Treasury and Agency issues each account for 9% of the investments of savings institutions. The remaining 5% of their financial assets is invested in an assortment of long-term corporate paper and some state and local debt. A breakdown of these holdings is shown in Exhibit 4.

Life Insurance Companies. These institutions also invest a large share of their assets in mortgages. Mortgage investments account for 30% of total assets. The largest holding is corporate bonds, accounting for 45% of the total. Corporate equities are a distant third, accounting for about 10% of life insurance company assets. Policy loans also account for a considerable share (one-twelfth) of total holdings, with these totals gyrating over the interest rate cycle. Borrowing against cash values of policies becomes more attractive as interest rates rise and alternative sources of funds dry up. Exhibits 5 through 7 show that policy loan volume rises dramatically during high rate periods, making life insurance companies subject to disintermediation because of factors similar to those in the environment that triggers savings outflows at thrift institutions. Gyrations in policy loan volume at the 15 largest life insurance companies are shown in Exhibit 7, with Exhibits 5 and 6, respectively, giving gross policy loans made during various months, and the monthly holdings of policy loans

EXHIBIT 2   BREAKDOWN BY SECTOR OF FLOW OF FUNDS IN PRIVATE CREDIT MARKETS

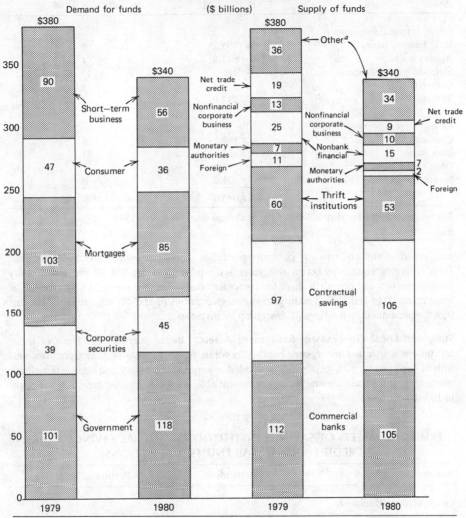

^aIncludes bond and money market funds, real estate investment trusts, individual investors, and other investors.

Source: Federal Reserve Board.

at the same institutions. Exhibit 8 gives a detailed breakdown of the distribution of life insurance company assets.

Fire and Casualty Insurance Companies.   Largely because of their higher marginal tax liability, which encourages them to invest in tax-exempt securities during profitable periods, these companies behave far differently from life insurance companies. However, when profits drop sharply (usually a consequence of high inflation rates forcing payouts of claims in excess of premium income), purchases of municipals drop off as well. Municipals constitute

EXHIBIT 3   COMMERCIAL BANK ASSETS AT YEAR-END 1978 ($ BILLIONS)

Assets	Outstanding	As Portion of Total (%)
Credit Market Instruments		
U.S. Treasury issues	$ 95.2	9
Agency issues	43.8	4
State and local obligations	126.2	13
Corporate bonds	7.4	1
Mortgages	214.0	21
Other Credit		
Consumer credit	167.2	16
Bank loans	358.2	34
Open market paper	13.0	1
Security credit	21.0	2
	$1,046.0	100

Source: Federal Reserve Board, *Flow of Funds Outstanding*, September 1979.

nearly half of fire and casualty company portfolios. Corporate bonds have taken the lead from corporate equities, whereas two years ago equities had one-fifth of fire and casualty company assets and one-sixth share for corporate bonds. The remaining 21% is invested in trade credit (9%) and U.S. Treasury and agency securities (8 and 4% respectively). Exhibit 9 outlines cumulative holdings of this group of investors.

State and Local Government Retirement Assets. Better than half the funds of these institutions is invested in corporate bonds. Corporate equities constitute little more than one-fifth of such assets, with the remainder divided among U.S. Treasury and agency securities, mortgages, and some state and local government obligations. A detailed breakdown appears in Exhibit 10.

EXHIBIT 4   ASSETS OF SAVINGS INSTITUTIONS: MUTUAL SAVINGS BANKS, CREDIT UNIONS, YEAR-END 1978 ($ BILLIONS)

Assets	Outstanding	As Portion of Total (%)
Credit Market Instruments		
U.S. Treasury issues	$ 18.6	3
Agency	40.8	6
State and local obligations	4.6	1
Corporate and foreign bonds	21.6	3
Corporate equities	4.8	1
Other Credit		
Home mortgages	421.7	61
Multi-family	52.6	8
Commercial	57.0	8
Consumer credit	62.0	9
Money market instruments	3.1	<1
	$686.8	100

Source: Federal Reserve Board, *Flow of Funds Outstanding*, September 1979.

EXHIBIT 5   GROSS POLICY LOANS MADE DURING EACH MONTH OF 3 YEARS BY 15 LIFE INSURANCE COMPANIES

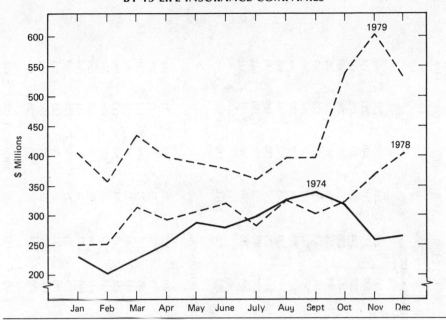

Source: American Council of Life Insurance.

EXHIBIT 6   MONTHLY CHANGES IN HOLDINGS OF POLICY LOANS FOR 15 LIFE INSURANCE COMPANIES

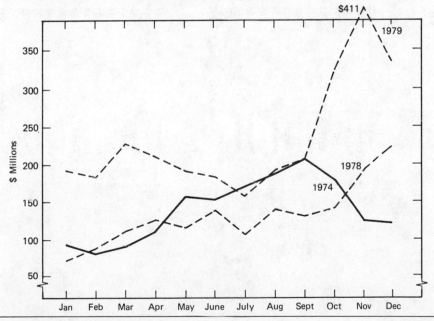

Source: American Council of Life Insurance.

EXHIBIT 7   POLICY LOANS OF 15 LIFE INSURANCE COMPANIES ($ MILLIONS)

	1971	1972	1973	1974	1975	1976	1977	1978	1979
GROSS LOANS MADE									
January	159	154	178	233	265	233	235	252	406
February	162	150	171	204	232	219	240	253	358
March	189	191	211	228	244	255	293	315	434
April	177	171	206	253	256	255	269	296	400
May	161	177	206	289	230	228	269	308	391
June	178	177	210	281	228	250	277	322	381
July	165	162	237	299	227	232	243	284	362
August	175	183	348	327	227	251	283	327	398
September	179	164	328	337	234	246	262	305	398
October	163	168	294	319	237	237	252	325	539
November	168	172	219	257	203	236	255	370	612ᵃ
December	186	177	214	265	235	269	262	403	531
Annual total	2,062	2,047	2,823	3,293	2,818	2,911	3,139	3,760	5,210
NET CHANGE IN HOLDINGS									
January	47	29	52	94	102	53	51	71	196
February	47	30	50	79	90	53	78	87	185
March	45	51	78	89	87	72	99	112	231
April	43	53	83	113	83	73	95	127	214
May	41	53	74	158	65	64	89	117	196
June	55	55	86	154	67	82	101	139	188
July	48	52	112	171	64	69	76	108	159
August	59	58	224	191	78	74	103	141	195
September	66	51	219	208	81	75	94	132	207
October	48	54	164	179	81	60	79	143	323
November	50	45	98	126	59	65	87	194	411
December	52	50	98	122	73	82	95	226	335
Annual net change	600	581	1,339	1,685	931	822	1,049	1,599	2,840

ᵃRevised figure.

Source: American Council of Life Insurance.

EXHIBIT 8 LIFE INSURANCE COMPANY ASSETS AT YEAR-END 1978 ($ BILLIONS)

Asset	Outstanding	As Portion of Total (%)
Credit Market Instruments		
U.S. Treasury issues	$ 4.8	1
Agency issues	6.5	2
State and local obligations	6.4	2
Corporate bonds	158.5	45
Mortgages	105.9	30
Open market paper	6.3	2
Policy loans	30.1	8
Corporate Equities	35.5	10
	$354.0	100

Source: Federal Reserve Board, *Flow of Funds Outstanding*, September 1979.

EXHIBIT 9 FIRE AND CASUALTY INSURANCE COMPANY ASSETS AT YEAR-END 1978 ($ BILLIONS)

Asset	Outstanding	As Portion of Total (%)
U.S. Treasury issues	$ 10.7	8
Agency issues	5.1	4
State and local obligations	62.5	48
Corporate bonds	21.4	16
Corporate equities	19.4	15
Trade credit	11.3	9
	$130.4	100

Source: Federal Reserve Bond, *Flow of Funds Outstanding*, September 1979.

EXHIBIT 10 STATE AND LOCAL GOVERNMENT EMPLOYEE RETIREMENT ASSETS AT YEAR-END 1978 ($ BILLIONS)

Asset	Outstanding	As Portion of Total (%)
U.S. Treasury issues	$ 10.5	7
Agency issues	12.4	8
State and local obligations	4.0	3
Corporate bonds	81.4	54
Equities	33.3	22
Mortgages	8.7	6
	$150.3	100

Source: Federal Reserve Board, *Flow of Funds Outstanding*, September 1979.

EXHIBIT 11   PRIVATE PENSION FUND ASSETS
AT YEAR-END 1978 ($ BILLIONS)

Asset	Outstanding	As Portion of Total (%)
U.S. Treasury issues	$ 17.5	10
Agency issues	4.7	3
Corporate bonds	48.0	26
Mortgages	3.1	2
Corporate equities	107.9	59
	$181.2	100

Source: Federal Reserve Board, *Flow of Funds Outstanding*, September 1979.

Private Pension Funds.   A greater preference for corporate equities over corporate bonds is seen in private pension funds. These assets constitute 60% of pension fund holdings. Corporate bonds equal about 25% of pension fund assets. Treasury and agency obligations account for another 10% and 3%, respectively, while mortgages account for only 2%. A breakdown of these holdings appears in Exhibit 11.

INTEREST RATES: THE BALANCING MECHANISM

Our analysis of the supply and demand for funds leads us to the determination of financial flows via some price mechanism. That price mechanism is the level of interest rates. If we assume that both issuers and investors are averse to risk, we can better understand the method by which equilibrium is determined.

CAPITAL CERTAINTY VERSUS INCOME CERTAINTY.   The investor faces two types of uncertainty in any investment.

> **Risk of Loss of Capital.** An investor who tries to liquidate a portfolio acquired at lower interest rate levels will incur some **loss of capital** in doing so.

> **Risk of Loss of Income.** In periods of high interest rates the investor has an opportunity to **"lock in"** high rates of return for long periods of time. Should the maturity of the asset be too short, the investor will find no vehicle available that offers the same high rate of return as that available on the original investment; thus he risks a loss of income.

A company that issues a security faces the same risks. Loss of income may result if in a period of rising interest rates, the company issues a security with a maturity that is too short. The firm will then have to pay too high a rate of return at the time when it wants to issue (roll–over) another debt obligation at maturity. Loss of capital is a risk in an environment of high interest rates, when a company sells an obligation whose maturity is too long, locking the firm into a high-cost obligation, and not permitting it to roll over its debt at lower rates some time down the road. In fact, the only way for the company to take advantage of the low interest rate environment after having issued high-cost debt is to refund that debt (buy back the outstanding obligations) at a considerable premium to the face value. A significant loss of capital would be incurred by a firm that took such action.

THE EQUILIBRATING PROCESS. Having demonstrated that investors and issuers (borrowers) are likely to be at odds, especially because maximizing returns to one group implies maximizing costs to the other, interest rates that will equilibrate these opposing forces will be a function of supply and demand and **interest rate expectations.** If interest rates are generally expected to rise, lenders will wish to keep their funds invested in reasonably short-term securities so that they may be able to reinvest at even higher rates later on. Issuers, by contrast, will want to issue longer-dated securities to insulate themselves from the rising cost of funds. On the other hand, if interest rates were widely expected to fall, the opposite would be true. Investors would seek to lock in high, long-term rates of return, while issuers (borrowers) would prefer to pay even higher rates for short-term funds in anticipation of being able to refund these obligations at lower interest rates when they mature.

There does not seem to be any mechanism that will bring about equilibrium and get the investor and issuer to agree on maturity and price (yield level). Flow of funds analysis suggests that disequilibrium results from either of the following:

1. A change in **portfolio preference** on the part of investors.
2. A change in **liability preference** on the part of issuers.
3. A change in **relative wealth.**

All these imply some imbalance between supply and demand. Equilibrium is achieved when the marginal investor (who has no particular preference) responds to exceptional values (purchases undervalued securities or sells overvalued securities) resulting from the imbalance. For this process to occur, **efficient markets** must exist that have (1) easy access to information about investor or issuer preferences, (2) well-functioning secondary markets, and (3) reasonably low transactions costs. The **broker and dealer** community meets these requirements, since both are only transient investors, buying securities with a view to trading them at a profit.

THE FEDERAL RESERVE SYSTEM

In 1908, following the Panic of 1907, Congress created a National Monetary Commission to investigate thoroughly the whole field of banking and currency and to recommend legislation. The fruit of its work was the Federal Reserve Act of 1913, a significant landmark in banking legislation.

The Federal Reserve is the central bank of the United States. It influences the availability of money through a complex system of operations that ultimately determine the level of interest rates.

A current interpretation of the **Federal Reserve Act,** including later amendments, would state the objectives broadly as (1) the establishment of an elastic currency and credit system, (2) the inauguration of a nationwide check collection system, (3) improved bank supervision, (4) aid in government financing, and (5) national credit management to achieve a high level of employment, avoidance of inflation, and economic stability with a sustainable rate of economic growth.

The Federal Reserve System consists of the Board of Governors, 12 Federal Reserve banks with 25 branches, the Federal Open Market Committee, the Federal Advisory Council, and member banks.

1. **The Board of Governors** is composed of seven members appointed by the President and confirmed by the Senate. It is the directing agency of the system. Members are appointed for 14 years, and a term expires every 2 years. One of the seven governors is appointed as chairman. The **Chairman of the Federal Reserve** testifies before the House and Senate Banking Committees at least once a quarter, alternating between the House and Senate each 3-month period. At these hearings, the Chairman identifies **Fed targets** for annual money and credit growth and gives a brief outline of the Fed's views on the economic outlook.

2. **The Federal Reserve banks,** one located in each of the 12 Federal Reserve Districts (Exhibit 12), supervise the member banks in each district. Each bank has its own board of directors and officers headed by a president, but its policies are largely determined by the Board of Governors.

3. **The Federal Open Market Committee:** Most of the Federal Reserve's policies regarding the availability of credit, money supply expansion, and interest rate targets are set by the Federal Reserve's **Open Market Committee** (FOMC), which meets on the third Tuesday of every month. This committee consists of eight permanent members, the Board of Governors and representative of the New York district, and four rotating members from the other districts, serving 2-year terms. **House Resolution 133,** passed in 1975, requires the Fed to publish up-to-date information on the discussions of its meetings. **Minutes** of the prior month's meeting are generally made available on the Friday following the FOMC meeting.

4. **The Federal Advisory Council** is composed of 12 members, usually commercial bankers, one elected by the directors of each of the Reserve banks. Its function is purely advisory.

5. **Member banks,** numbering over 5,000, include all national banks and those state banks that apply and are accepted for membership.

The Federal Reserve Act provided 12 regional banks rather than one central bank. This plan reflected the traditional American distrust of centralized financial control and was intended better to serve the diverse regional requirements of the nation. Such decentralization was, however, found to involve serious disadvantages, and the tendency since 1933 has been to increase greatly the authority of the Board of Governors in Washington.

A look at the currency in your pocket will indicate (1) that the currency is an obligation of the Federal Reserve and therefore is called a Federal Reserve note, and (2) the district bank that issued the money is denoted by the letters A through L appearing in the circle on the left of the bill, representing Boston, New York, Philadelphia, Cleveland, Richmond, Atlanta, Chicago, St. Louis, Minneapolis, Kansas City, Dallas, and San Francisco respectively.

THE FED IN OPERATION.

The Board of Governors.   The chief powers of the Board of Governors of the Federal Reserve System include (1) reviewing discount rates of the Federal Reserve banks, (2) reviewing the decisions of the Federal Open Market Committee, whose membership is numerically dominated by the board in any event: (3) raising or lowering reserve requirements for member banks within a specified range; (4) setting margin requirements on loans made for the purpose of buying or carrying listed securities; (5) defining the types of securities that member banks may purchase; and (6) fixing maximum interest rates payable by banks on

EXHIBIT 12   BOUNDARIES OF FEDERAL RESERVE DISTRICTS

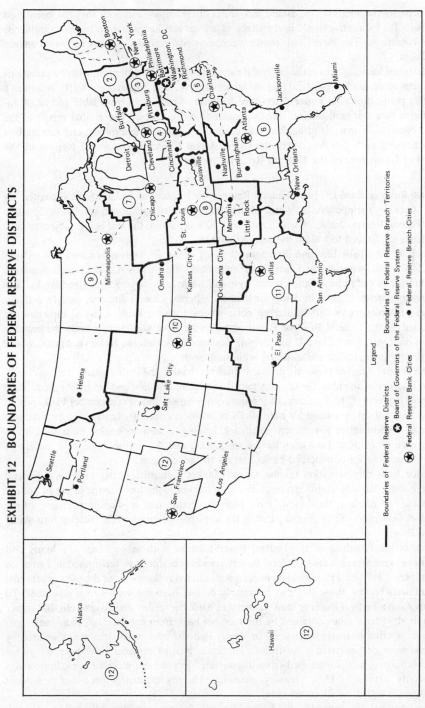

Legend

— Boundaries of Federal Reserve Districts
— Boundaries of Federal Reserve Branch Territories
— Boundaries of the Federal Reserve System
★ Board of Governors of the Federal Reserve System
● Federal Reserve Bank Cities
● Federal Reserve Branch Cities

Source: Board of Governors, Federal Reserve Systems, *The Federal Reserve System, Purposes and Functions.*

time deposits. In addition, the Board has broad discretionary authority that has been used as a basis for **"direct action"** in the shape of advice and instruction to banks to influence credit conditions. The Board also presents recommendations to Congress for new banking legislation.

The board has its offices at the Federal Reserve Building in Washington, where it maintains a permanent research, statistical, legal, administrative, and supervisory staff. It issues a monthly publication, the **Federal Reserve Bulletin,** which is an invaluable source of authoritative data and statistics on money, banking, and business. The annual report of the Board contains an analysis of banking and economic conditions and trends, and summarizes the actions of both the Board and the Open Market Committee (**Annual Report of the Board of Governors of the Federal Reserve System).**

Federal Reserve Banks.   Each Federal Reserve bank functions under a federal charter. Its stock is held by member banks, which must subscribe 6% of capital and surplus to the stock of its Federal Reserve bank, of which sum only 50% is paid in, the rest being subject to call. Dividends are limited to 6% on the amount paid in.

Each Reserve bank has nine **directors,** three of whom are known as Class A directors, three as Class B, and three as Class C. Member banks elect Class A and Class B directors, one director in each class being chosen by small banks, one by medium-sized banks, and one by large banks. Class A directors are bankers, whereas Class B directors must be actively engaged in business or agriculture but not connected with a bank. Class C directors are appointed by the Federal Reserve Board and may be from within or outside the banking profession. One of the Class C directors is designated as **Federal Reserve Agent,** whose special duty is to provide close liaison with the Board.

The Federal Reserve banks are primarily bankers' banks, and their deposits consist chiefly of the reserves of member banks, maintained as required by law and set by the Fed. They also hold deposits of the Treasury, of foreign central banks, and of nonmember banks whose checks they collect, but none for individuals or business concerns. Operations include note issuance, investment in government securities, lending to member banks, examination and supervision of member banks, collection of checks, and the performance of a variety of essential services for commercial banks and for the government.

Aside from representation on the **Open Market Committee,** the individual Federal Reserve banks have no major responsibility with respect to the formulation of credit policy. At times, nevertheless, their views have been very influential in shaping decisions of the Board of Governors. Their primary task is the implementation of credit policies formulated by the Board.

One of the functions of the Federal Reserve banks is to make temporary **loans and advances to members banks.** Federal Reserve credit is designed to accommodate banks for a short period only, that is, to help them cope with sudden withdrawals of deposits or seasonal requirements beyond those that can reasonably be met from the bank's own resources. To borrow from a Federal Reserve bank, a member bank may either **rediscount eligible paper** (such as short-term notes obtained by the member bank from commercial, industrial, agricultural, or other business borrowers) or it may issue its own promissory notes secured by eligible paper or government securities. The latter type of member bank borrowings are called advances, as distinguished from discounting. In practice, member bank borrowings are mainly secured by U.S. Treasury securities. The interest charge on either method of borrowing is called the **discount rate.**

The principal means used by the Federal Reserve System to influence the volume of bank reserves is the purchase and sale of U.S. government securities in the open market. By paying for purchases with a credit to member bank reserves, the Fed acts to expand the nation's credit base. Sales by the Federal Reserve, on the other hand, lead to a contraction in member bank reserve accounts as these are charged in payment for the securities sold. In addition, the System makes credit available on occasion to dealers in U.S. government securities through **repurchase agreements.** These agreements represent a pledge by the dealer to repurchase the securities within 15 days or less. To affect credit conditions, the Federal Reserve also buys bankers' acceptances.

During World War II, the Federal Reserve banks made large-scale purchases of U.S. government securities. This led to a tremendous **expansion** of member bank reserves and a vast wartime expansion of bank credit and currency in circulation. The banks' **principal liabilities** consist of Federal Reserve notes in circulation and the reserve balances of commercial banks.

Collection of Checks and Other Services.   A very important service performed for the entire commercial banking system by the Federal Reserve banks is the collection of checks drawn on banks throughout the country, deposited in banks located elsewhere than the towns in which the paying banks are located. The volume of checks handled by the Federal Reserve has grown rapidly over the years. All checks collected and cleared through the Federal Reserve must be paid at par—i.e., in full without deduction of any exchange charge by the paying bank. This check-clearing service is presently (1980) provided without charge not only for member banks but also for all banks that agree to remit at par. It is fairly certain that the FED will change its no-fee policy causing banks to incur greater costs, which will probably lead to bank strategies to limit their exposure.

Other services of the Federal Reserve banks include the collection of coupons and other items for member banks, transfers of funds between members, the safekeeping of securities for banks, supplying currency to banks, receiving and sorting currency returned from circulation, and the performance of certain tasks for foreign central bank correspondents.

A substantial part of the **personnel** of the Federal Reserve banks is engaged in providing fiscal agency, custodianship, and depositary services for the Treasury and other government departments and agencies. Most of this work is connected with the issuance, exchange, and redemption of government securities and the payment of government checks and coupons.

Issuance of Policy Directives.   The FOMC **policy directives** quoted below was approved unanimously at the Committee's meeting of January 8–9, 1980. It was issued to the Federal Reserve Bank of New York.

The information reviewed at this meeting suggests that real output of goods and services expanded somewhat further in the final quarter of 1979 and that prices on the average continued to rise rapidly. In November retail sales strengthened and nonfarm payroll employment rose considerably further, but industrial production declined somewhat and private house starts fell. The unemployment rate edged down from 6.0 to 5.8%. Producer prices of finished goods and consumer prices continued to rise rapidly, in part because of the spreading effects of earlier increases in energy costs. Over recent months the rise in the index of average hourly earnings has remained close to the rapid pace during 1978.

The trade-weighted value of the dollar against major foreign currencies has depreciated about 3% since mid-November, reflecting in large part the Middle East situation as well as a firming of monetary conditions in a number of foreign countries. The U.S. foreign trade deficit in October and November on the average was slightly below the rate for the third quarter.

Growth of the major monetary aggregates, which has slowed in October, remained at reduced rates in the final months of 1979. From the fourth quarter of 1978 to the fourth quarter of 1979 M-1 grew 5½%, M-2 about 8¼%, and M-3 about 8%. Most market interest rates have declined somewhat on balance since the Committee's meeting in late November.

Taking account of past and prospective developments in employment, unemployment, production, investment, real income, productivity, international trade and payments, and prices, the Federal Open Market Committee seeks to foster monetary and financial conditions that will resist inflationary pressures while encouraging moderate economic expansion and contributing to a sustainable pattern of international transactions. At its meeting on July 11, 1979, the Committee agreed that these objectives would be furthered by growth of M-1, M-2, and M-3 from the fourth quarter of 1978 to the fourth quarter of 1979 within ranges of 1½ to 4½%, 5 to 8%, and 6 to 9% respectively. It appeared that expansion of ATS and NOW accounts would dampen growth of M-1 by about 1½ percentage points over the year, half as much as assumed early in the year; thus after allowance for the deviation from the earlier estimate, the equivalent range for M-1 was 3 to 6%. The associated range for bank credit was 7½ to 10½%. The Committee anticipated that for the period from the fourth quarter of 1979 to the fourth quarter of 1980, growth may be within the same ranges, depending upon emerging economic conditions and appropriate adjustments that may be required by legislation or judicial developments affecting interest-bearing transactions accounts. Ranges for 1980 will be reconsidered at the meeting of the Committee scheduled for early February.

In the short run, the Committee seeks expansion of reserve aggregates consistent with growth over the first quarter of 1980 at an annual rate between 4 and 5% for M-1 and on the order of 7% for M-2, provided that in the period before the next regular meeting the weekly average federal funds rate remains within a range of 11½ to 15½%.

If it appears during the period before the next meeting that the constraint on the federal funds rate is inconsistent with the objective for the expansion of reserves, the Manager for Domestic Operations is promptly to notify the Chairman, who will then decide whether the situation calls for supplementary instructions from the Committee.

TOOLS OF THE FED.   The most frequently used Federal Reserve tool is the purchase and sale of government securities in the open market to affect the overnight cost of money to the banking system (**federal funds rate**) by expanding or contracting the availability of **bank reserves.** A **sale of securities** to the dealer community serves to absorb reserves and puts upward pressure on borrowing costs. A **purchase of securities** tends to expand the availability of reserves and puts downward pressure on interest rates. This almost daily procedure of buying and selling securities in the market to influence reserves and the cost of funds is called **open market operations.**

To influence reserve availability on a longer run basis, the Fed may decide to change the **reserve requirement** ratio, lifting the ratio of reserves that banks are required to hold against deposits to curb credit growth, and lowering reserve requirements to stimulate credit expansion. Since these are more permanent changes, the Fed is likely to make them much less frequently. On average, reserve requirement changes are made about once in 4 years.

Another tool available to the monetary authorities is a change in the **discount rate,** defined earlier as the rate at which banks may borrow reserves from the Fed. These changes are made as often as necessary to keep the rate in line with the banking system's overnight cost of funds. In the period 1976–1980, the Fed changed the discount rate about three or four times a year, on average.

It is important to remember that rates on government securities often determine prevailing **money market rates,** and as such, Federal Reserve actions materially affect the cost of short-term funds for corporations. Whether these funds are raised in the domestic commercial paper market, in the **bankers' acceptance market,** or even through bank loans, the government funds rate will usually set the floor on other domestic money costs to the corporation.

THE MONEY MARKET AND FEDERAL RESERVE CONTROL

The term **money market** refers to the marketplace where borrowers and lenders exchange short-term funds. Thus, "the" money market does not exist in one unique location. Instead, it is a complex of thousands of locations across the world where purchases and sales of short-term funds take place.

As the most important buyer and seller of short-term money the Federal Reserve influences daily money market conditions through the purchases and sales of securities defined earlier as **open market operations.**

The **New York Fed** is the dominant player of the 12-bank Fed system, conducting open market operations with some three dozen recognized **U.S. Government Securities Dealers.** Thus the New York Fed carries out the FOMC policy directive targeting reserve availability, money growth, and interest rates on Federal funds, which ultimately affect other interest rates.

While the New York Fed very significantly influences money market conditions via **open market operations,** other member banks also play a role in policing the use of member bank borrowings at their discount windows. Indeed, this is one of the few privileges allowed for Fed member banks. They can borrow funds temporarily from the Fed instead of selling money market securities to meet reserve deficiencies (see Exhibit 13).

MONEY MARKET INSTRUMENTS.

Federal Funds.   The monies that banks buy and sell among themselves to meet reserve requirements against deposits are called federal funds. Fed funds are usually bought and sold overnight, but **term funds** may be purchased for as long as a week. Fed funds are viewed as the most liquid, interest-bearing, near-cash asset.

Repurchase Agreements (RPs).   These are effectively collateralized deposits of corporations. Since corporations cannot buy and sell Fed funds, they have found a way to invest excess short-term funds in interest-bearing assets by temporarily purchasing Treasury securities from an owner (a bank) that agrees to buy these back (repurchase) at a higher price. The difference between the purchase and sale price effectively becomes the interest return earned on these securities. Since these short-term investments are collateralized, they represent the safest interest-bearing, near-cash asset. They often yield a little less than Fed funds. **Term RPs** can be arranged for as long as 3 months and sometimes even longer, though banks are often reluctant to show RPs on the books over quarterly statement periods.

Treasury Bills.   The next most liquid short-term investment is in Treasury bills, primarily because there is an active primary market for newly issued bills auctioned each week, as well as an active secondary market for older bill issues. Treasury bills are U.S. government obligations maturing within 12 months. Weekly bill maturities enable sophisticated corporate treasurers to synchronize their bill maturities with expected cash outflows. And in the event of an unexpected need for cash, bills can be liquidated readily with little or no loss of capital.

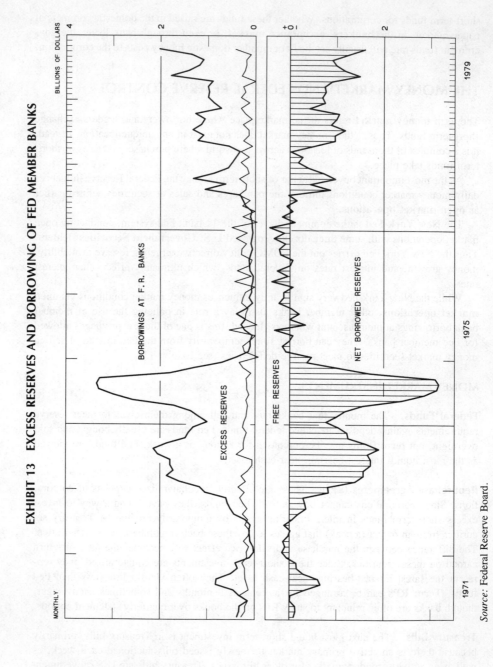

EXHIBIT 13   EXCESS RESERVES AND BORROWING OF FED MEMBER BANKS

Source: Federal Reserve Board.

Bankers' Acceptances (BAs).   Orders to pay special amounts at a given time are called bankers' acceptances. These orders are usually liabilities of a firm engaged in international trade, acknowledging an obligation to pay for goods in transit. Banks often finance these instruments, on behalf of their customers under a **letter of credit agreement,** making both the customer and the bank obligated to honor the liability. Thus there is a sense of double protection for the holder of the BA. If either the bank or the customer fails to pay, the paper is backed by the assets of the other.

The Federal Reserve Bank of Richmond (*Instruments of the Money Market,* 1977) provides an excellent description of the underlying BA transaction and acceptance financing:

> A domestic concern wishing to import goods from abroad may request its bank to issue a **letter of credit** on its behalf in favor of the foreign seller. If the bank finds the customer's credit standing satisfactory, it will issue such a letter, authorizing the foreign seller to draw a draft upon it in payment for the goods. Equipped with this authorization, the foreign exporter, on shipping the goods, can discount the draft with his bank, thereby receiving payment immediately. The foreign bank, in turn, forwards the draft together with appropriate shipping documents to its correspondent bank in this country with instructions respecting its disposition. Generally the U.S. correspondent bank will present the draft for acceptance at the drawee bank, which then forwards the shipping documents to the importer, who now may claim the shipment. The correspondent bank may be instructed to hold the acceptance until maturity as an investment for the foreign bank. Or it may be instructed to offer the acceptance for sale in the market and credit the deposit account of the foreign bank. In any event, the ultimate holder of the acceptance is the party actually financing the transaction.
>
> The **accepting bank** may, of course, buy the acceptance which it originated. In such a case, it earns the difference between the purchase price and the face amount which must be reimbursed by the customer on whose behalf the acceptance credit was opened. It also earns the commission charged for the letter of credit. When the bank follows such a course it is actually financing the transaction, and its position is much the same as when it extends a loan directly to the customer. On the other hand, if some other party buys and holds the acceptance, the originating bank has tied up no funds. It has merely lent the prestige of its name and assumed a contingent liability, for which it collects a small fee.

Commercial Paper.   This is another short-term investment vehicle, representing unsecured promissory notes of corporations whose credit rating is so high that their I.O.U.'s are immediately accepted for trading in the money market. Two major categories of commercial paper are available: those issued directly by a corporation (**directly placed**) and those issued through an underwriter, typically a private insurance company (**dealer placed**). These are further subdivided into **financial** and **nonfinancial** companies. Within the financial category the distinction is made between **bank-related** and **nonbank** paper. A sample Federal Reserve release shows these subdivisions and the consequent rate differentials paid by different issuers for different maturities (see Exhibits 14 and 15). Since the failure of Penn Central in 1970 left holders of commercial paper with illiquid assets, commercial paper issuers now follow an unwritten rule, namely, they maintain bank credit lines as a backup, in case the commercial paper issuer runs into difficulty.

Negotiable Certificates of Deposit (CDs).   Uncollateralized bank deposit liabilities of $100,000 or more are negotiable CDs. Banks started issuing CDs in 1961 but these were subject to **Regulation Q** interest rate ceilings imposed by the Securities and Exchange Commission until June 1970. At that time rate ceilings were lifted for shorter dated CDs (under 90 days), and 3 years later rate ceilings on CDs were lifted altogether. Domestic CD

EXHIBIT 14 COMMERCIAL PAPER OUTSTANDING, ($ MILLIONS—NOT SEASONALLY ADJUSTED)[b]

1980 Week Ended Wednesday	All Issuers Total	All Issuers Change	Financial Companies[c] Total	Financial Companies[c] Change	Dealer Placed Total	Dealer Placed Change	Directly Placed Total	Directly Placed Change	Nonfinancial Companies[d] Total	Nonfinancial Companies[d] Change
Mar. 26	119,561	−1,053	83,586	−1,611	18,669	+ 70	64,917	−1,681	35,975	+ 558
Apr. 2	119,425	− 136	82,931	− 655	18,465	− 204	64,466	− 451	36,494	+ 519
9	122,016	+ 2,591	85,722	+ 2,791	19,165	+ 700	66,557	+ 2,091	36,294	− 200
16	121,201	− 815	83,914	− 1,808	18,417	− 748	65,497	− 1,060	37,287	+ 993
23	122,993	+ 1,792	85,277	+ 1,363	18,433	+ 16	66,844	+ 1,347	37,716	+ 429

Memo Item: Bank-Related Paper Included in the Above[e]

1980 Week Ended Wednesday	All Issuers Total	All Issuers Change	Financial Companies[c] Total	Financial Companies[c] Change	Dealer Placed Total	Dealer Placed Change	Directly Placed Total	Directly Placed Change	Nonfinancial Companies[d] Total	Nonfinancial Companies[d] Change
Mar. 26	22,480	+ 28			3,142	+ 35	19,338	− + 7		
Apr. 2	21,820	− 660			3,180	+ 38	18,640	− 698		
9	22,104	+ 284			3,262	+ 82	18,842	+ 202		
16	21,737	− 367			3,301	+ 39	18,436	− 406		
23	22,345	+ 608			3,364	+ 63	18,981	+ 545		

[a]Short-term, negotiable, unsecured promissory notes sold by reporting companies with original maturities of 270 days or less, for which the reporting company has received but not yet repaid the proceeds of the sale. Amounts outstanding also include documented discount notes (i.e., paper accompanied by an irrevocable letter of credit issued by any bank or guaranteed by a private insurance company not related to the issuing company), borrowings under "type A" (payable on demand) master note agreements, and paper placed in the United States by foreign firms.

[b]These figures are preliminary and subject to revision. Since they are not adjusted for seasonal movements, caution should be exercised in interpreting intrayearly fluctuations.

[c]Financial companies are institutions engaged primarily in activities such as, but not limited to, commercial, savings, and mortgage banking; sales, personal, and mortgage financing; factoring, finance leasing, and other business lending; insurance underwriting; and other investment activities.

[d]Nonfinancial companies include public utilities and firms engaged primarily in activities such as communications, construction, manufacturing, mining, wholesale and retail trade, transportation, and services. Since only a few nonfinancial companies place commercial paper directly, a further breakdown of this category is precluded by an agreement to assure the confidentiality of individual company reports.

[e]Bank-related paper, as reported by banks, is commercial paper issued by bank holding companies, nonbank subsidiaries of the holding company, and nonbank affiliates of the bank.

Source: Domestic Reports Division, Federal Reserve Bank of New York.

EXHIBIT 15 COMMERCIAL PAPER OFFERING RATES[a]
(%/YEAR ON A DISCOUNT BASIS)

1980	Prime Paper Placed Through Dealers				Paper Placed Directly				
	30 days	60 days	90 days	120 days	30 days	60 days	90 days	120 days	180 days
Rates on Jan. 31	13.01	13.03	13.04	12.99	12.95	12.91	11.98	11.98	11.83
Changes									
Feb. 1	13.02	13.05	13.06			12.95	12.24	12.03	
4		13.07	13.07	13.03	13.04	13.04	12.70		
5			13.09		13.02	13.03			
6	13.03	13.08	13.10	13.01	13.00			12.05	11.85
7	13.01	13.07	13.09		12.95	13.01	12.68		
8	12.97	13.03	13.03	12.98			12.48	12.03	11.83
11	12.99	13.04	13.07	13.00	12.98		12.68		
13	13.02	13.08	13.10	13.07	13.02	13.02	12.73	12.13	11.95
14	13.03		13.11	13.09	13.09	13.01		12.25	12.08
15	13.37	13.41	13.38	13.34	13.55	13.06	12.74	12.20	12.03
19	13.74	13.83	13.88	13.88		13.55	12.78	12.45	12.20
20	14.02	14.11	14.18	14.18	13.88	13.85	12.65	12.68	12.48
21	14.04	14.13	14.32	14.35	14.03	14.03	13.15	12.93	12.73
22	14.25	14.38	14.46	14.43	14.26	14.29	13.25	13.00	12.78
25	14.31	14.49	14.60	14.68	14.30	14.33	13.58	13.10	12.88
26	14.38	14.61	14.79	14.70	14.44	14.46	13.76	13.28	13.18
27	14.52	14.69	14.81	14.77	14.48	14.43	14.00	13.33	13.23
28	14.51	14.68	14.83	14.86	14.51	14.47	14.15	13.55	13.45
29	14.55	14.67		14.90	14.52			13.70	13.60
Mar. 3	14.80	14.96	15.18	15.13	14.75	14.70	14.28	13.80	13.90
4	15.42	15.62	15.76	15.79	15.10	15.10	14.68	14.15	14.05
5	15.84	15.98	16.09	15.91	15.58	15.60	15.03	14.60	14.40

[a]Rates are the unweighted arithmetic average of rates reported by the five direct issuers, or six dealers, that report their rates. Before averaging, fractions are rounded to two decimal places.

Source: Domestic Reports Division, Federal Reserve Bank of New York.

EXHIBIT 16   NEGOTIABLE CDS, SEASONALLY ADJUSTED

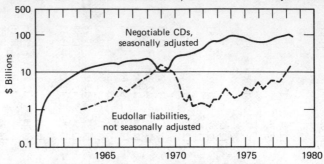

Source: U.S. Department of Commerce, *Business Conditions Digest.*

volume dropped sharply as market rates ran through the rate ceilings banks were allowed to pay in 1969–1970. Banks substituted **Eurodollar CD** borrowings during this period. Once rate ceilings were lifted, domestic CD volume expanded at the expense of Eurodollar borrowings (see Exhibit 16).

CDs are the least liquid of all the short-term assets, largely because there is no active secondary market in any but the top-name, large-bank CD liabilities. Also, during periods of intense interest rate pressure and robust loan growth, a **tiering** often develops in the marketplace such that smaller banks must pay a rate premium on CD liabilities over and above those paid by the largest, best known banks.

THE CORPORATION AND THE COST OF CAPITAL: SHORT-TERM FUNDING

Financial managers work within the institutional framework outlined above and, as such, have little influence on the cost of money. They generally look at two types of funding for their firm's assets: short-term and long-term. **Short-term funds** are available through one of the following sources: (*a*) **trade credit,** (*b*) **bank loans,** (*c*) **commercial paper,** (*d*)

EXHIBIT 17   SHORT-TERM LIABILITIES OF NONFINANCIAL CORPORATIONS OUTSTANDING YEAR-END 1978 ($ BILLIONS)

Type	Outstanding	As Portion of Total (%)
Bank loans	$224.0	54
Commercial paper	15.5	4
Bankers' acceptances	5.0	1
Finance company loans	54.1	13
Net trade credit	93.1	22
Profit tax payable	23.9	6
	$415.6	100

Source: Federal Reserve Board, *Flow of Funds Outstanding*, September 1979.

bankers' acceptances, and (*e*) **accounts receivable financing.** Exhibit 17 shows the relative importance of these sources of short-term credit.

TRADE CREDIT.   Trade credit is an asset of the vendor, who ships merchandise or provides services without immediate payment. Trade debt is a liability of the non-cash customer buying goods or services on credit. The **trade credit** figure in Exhibit 17 is a **net** figure, indicating the **difference between trade credit** and **trade debt.** The net figure indicates that trade credit is not as widely used as a short-term funding method compared to the much larger 54% share for bank loans. Companies that extend trade credit rarely use it as a source of funds. Many businesses, however, fund their short-term assets, especially inventories, through the use of trade debt. When the use of gross trade debt rather than net trade credit is compared to that of the other short-term methods, the proportions change markedly, as shown in Exhibit 18.

While trade debt is the largest source of short-term business credit under this second configuration, it is also the most expensive. Most finance books point out that the annual **cost of foregoing trade discounts** 2/10 net 30 is 36% + since the corporation really has the use of these funds for 20 days at a rate of 2% for that period.

Nevertheless, cash discounts are widely used first, because by paying later than net 30 days, a company is effectively reducing its annual borrowing cost. For example, if a firm pays in 60 days instead of 30, it has the use of money for 50 days and pays 2% interest for it. On an annualized basis, this is little more than 15%, probably less than the company can expect to pay for finance company loans and less than the bank prime rate, in the fall of 1979, and the spring of 1980. During tight money periods, small firms are likely to have little choice but to make extensive use of trade credit because money is not available elsewhere at any price. If a business is to continue to function, it must pay the high rates to get the merchandise it needs so that production may continue uninterrupted.

BANK LOANS.   Bank loans also play an important role in determining the availability of short-term financing for the corporation. Bank loans are generally tied to the prime lending rate, the rate banks charge their most favored borrowers. The amount in excess of the prime rate that is charged to less favored borrowers depends on the interest rate climate. When interest rates are generally low, banks allow almost all borrowers to borrow at the prime rate. Sometimes banks are so anxious to lend that they make loans below prime, that is, below the officially posted price for money. Another approach banks use to stimulate

EXHIBIT 18   SHORT-TERM LIABILITIES OF NONFINANCIAL CORPORATIONS ADJUSTED FOR TRADE DEBT OUTSTANDING AT YEAR-END 1978 ($ BILLIONS)

Bank Loans	Outstanding	As Portion of Total (%)
Bank loans	$224.0	38
Commercial paper	15.0	3
Bankers' acceptances	5.0	1
Finance company loans	54.1	9
Trade debt	262.5	45
Profit tax payable	23.9	4
	$585.0	100

Source: Federal Reserve Board, *Flow of Funds Outstanding*, September 1979.

demand for funds when interest rates are low is to make **fixed rate loans** lasting 5 to 7 years, at something over prime, allowing companies to protect themselves from an anticipated rise in interest rates before maturity. Another approach is to offer corporations **floating rate loans** with a ceiling on interest rates. These loans are often called **"cap loans,"** referring to the interest rate lid.

To qualify for bank credit, not only does a company have to pass certain credit checks, but it usually has to pay a fee for a **standby line of credit** the bank makes available to it. In addition, when the firm borrows the bank funds, it must keep some percentage of these borrowings on deposit with the bank as a **compensating balance.** Compensating balance arrangements require either a minimum level of funds kept in the account at all times, or some average balance of funds kept on hand over the period. The latter approach is certainly more lenient, allowing the corporate borrowers to let their bank balance go through much wider swings than would be permitted if an absolute minimum balance were required. The **prime rate** is usually set by adding on to the commercial paper rate. At Citibank, New York's largest commercial bank, the **prime formula** calls for $1\frac{1}{2}\%$ over the 3 week average of the bank's 90-day CD rate.

COMMERCIAL PAPER.   Commercial paper is an unsecured promissory note of a corporation, generally used to fund self-liquidating short-term assets, such as inventory. Most commercial paper is issued by financial corporations, such as finance companies, with the proceeds being used to fund short-term and intermediate-term assets such as consumer loans. In the second quarter of 1980 the volume of commercial paper outstanding was $111 billion, of which only $29 billion was issued by nonfinancial corporations.

Because it is unsecured, commercial paper is generally issued only by the largest corporations, such as General Motors, Ford Motor Co., General Electric, and Sears Roebuck. In addition, commercial paper issuers often have **bank lines** to **"back up"** these obligations, to be used to pay the holder of the commercial paper if for some reason the issuer cannot meet the outstanding obligations.

BANKERS' ACCEPTANCES.   Bankers' acceptances (BAs) are generally used to finance international trade. As such, they constitute little more than bank loans for international transactions, with the underlying merchandise serving as collateral. Many banks count BAs into their commercial and industrial loan totals, but others break out this category to show international lending explicitly.

FINANCE COMPANY LOANS.   This source of funds is important in the **funding of business equipment.** As the third largest source of corporate short-term funds, finance companies serve an important function. Most of the loans made by this group are usually to corporations that have limited ability to borrow at banks and no access at all to the commercial paper market. The same companies that rely on this source of financing are also likely to use trade credit heavily. As pointed out above, finance company loans and trade credit are the most expensive sources of short-term funds available to a corporation.

PROFIT TAX PAYABLE.   Although often overlooked, this can be an important source of funds to businesses, especially in periods of rising profits. Companies have the option of paying taxes on profits as they are earned or paying them at the same rate as last year, making up the shortfall the following March 15th or June 15th. Thus if a company experiences an improving profit situation, it can decide to pay taxes at quarterly estimates equal to those of its lower payment schedule a year earlier.

THE CORPORATION'S LONG-TERM COST OF CAPITAL

Financial managers often attempt to match the maturity of their company's liabilities with those of its assets. They are reluctant to fund long-term assets with short-term funds for more than a temporary period. Although it is not unusual for a new plant to be funded with a construction loan (a short-term bank loan), some form of long-term financing is usually sought.

Long-term financing generally falls into one of three categories. A popular source of long-term financing is corporate bonds. Three out of every five dollars of long-term corporate debt obligations are in corporate bonds, totaling $318.3 billion at the end of 1978.

Corporate bonds are classified according to **risk** categories primarily by two popular **rating services, Moody's** and **Standard & Poor's.** The ratings appear in Exhibit 19. The top four ratings are generally considered to be **"investment grade"** securities, those that are eligible for investment by institutional investors such as insurance companies, pension funds, and state and local government retirement funds. Securities rated below investment grade are deemed to be too risky for investment by institutional investors with a fiduciary responsibility to their clients.

Exhibit 20 shows the breakdown of long-term corporate debt financing as of December 1978. While corporate bond financing is the largest source of funds, mortgage financing is also an important source of long-term credit to the nonfinancial corporation. In fact, **commercial mortgages** provided 30% of corporate long-term debt requirements at year-end 1978. When multifamily and single-family mortgages are added to the totals, mortgage-related debt provides nearly 40% of the corporation's long-term source of borrowed funds.

With the passage of so much environmental legislation, a new source of funds was made available to the corporation, **pollution control revenue bonds.** These bonds are issued by state and local governments on behalf of a company to finance pollution control projects. Interest and principal are secured by the corporation, with the corporation getting a break on the cost of funds, since tax-exempt funds can generally be borrowed at a lower rate than taxable funds for similar risk and maturity.

EXHIBIT 19   BOND RATINGS FOR CORPORATE DEBT SECURITIES

Moody's	Standard & Poor's
Aaa	AAA
A	AA
A	A
Baa	BBB
Ba	BB
B	B
C	CCC
	CC
D	C

Source: Moody's Manual and Standard & Poor's Corp., both New York City.

EXHIBIT 20   LONG-TERM LIABILITIES OUTSTANDING FOR NONFINANCIAL CORPORATIONS AT YEAR-END 1978 ($ BILLIONS)

Type	Outstanding	As Portion of Total (%)
Corporate Bonds	$318.3	59
Mortgages		
Home mortgages	6.5	1
Multifamily	36.2	7
Commercial	164.7	30
Tax-Exempt Bonds	15.8	3
	$451.8	100

Source: Federal Reserve Board, *Flow of Funds Outstanding*, September 1979.

THE CYCLICAL PATTERN OF INTEREST RATES

Interest rates, or the price of money, are determined by the same factors that influence prices of other commodities, namely, the supply and demand for funds. In turn, supply and demand are a function of the borrowing and lending (investing) needs of money and capital market participants. These needs are volatile, fluctuating with the ups and downs of business activity. To some extent interest rates lag behind the economic cycle, peaking after the peak in business activity and bottoming out after the economy has turned upward (see Exhibits 21 and 22). Interest rates are therefore viewed as a **lagging economic indicator.** For example, note in Exhibit 22 that the **Federal funds rate,** the **Treasury bill rate,** the **corporate bond rate** and **municipal bond yields** all peaked several months after the business cycle turned into a recession in 1970–1971 and again in 1973–1974. It is not clear, as yet, whether the interest rate–economic cycle relationship continued in this fashion during the 1979–1980 recession, but it certainly appears that rates continued to climb while the economy turned down.

THE YIELD CURVE: RELATIONSHIPS BETWEEN YIELDS AND TERM TO MATU-RITY.   Over the interest rate cycle, the relationship between yield and **term to maturity** changes. Early in the interest rate cycle, short-term credit demands are generally sluggish, while long-term credit demands that had gone unsatisfied during the preceding interest rate period linger on. These relative pressures result from a desire on the part of borrowers to extend maturities of their liabilities, using the proceeds of long-term debt to repay short-term borrowings. One consequence of the corporation's repayment of bank loans is to put downward pressure on short-term interest rates, while the robust volume of long-term debt offerings keeps long-term interest rates from dropping. The resulting shape of the yield curve is an **upward sloping** line (March 15, 1977 in Exhibit 23).

As business activity picks up, accompanied by rising demands for short-term credit (as more money needs to be invested in working capital), short-term rates experience upward pressure. Long-term rates during this phase of the cycle also move higher but not nearly as

EXHIBIT 21   CYCLICAL INDICATORS BY ECONOMIC PROCESS

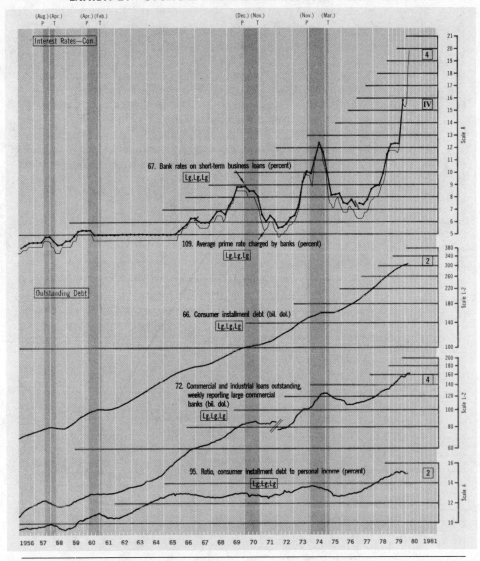

Source: U.S. Department of Commerce, *Business Conditions Digest,* April 1980.

much as short-term rates do. The resulting yield curve assumes a **flat** shape (November 15, 1977, Exhibit 23).

During the latter stages of the interest rate cycle, upward pressure on short-term rates increases. Both long- and short-term rates rise rapidly, with the upward movement short-term far outstripping the rise in long-term rates. This leaves the yield curve with a **downward sloping** shape, indicating borrowers' reluctance to lock in high-cost, long-term liabilities and their desire to fund long-term projects with short-term funds. Other borrowers may be locked

EXHIBIT 22   YIELDS ON VARIOUS OUTSTANDING DEBT OBLIGATIONS

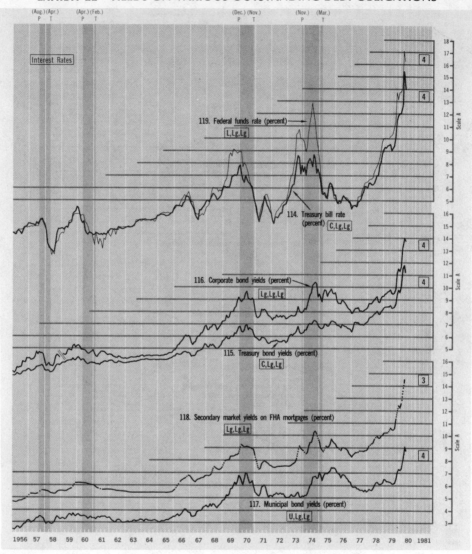

Source: U.S. Department of Commerce, *Business Conditions Digest,* April 1980.

out of the long-term market altogether, as the threat of economic slowdown or recession makes lenders increasingly **quality conscious.** Only after the economy has peaked, and inventories begin to be worked off do short-term interest rates begin to fall.

QUALITY CONSIDERATIONS.   Interest rate movement over the business cycle differs according to quality and maturity. Bond **yields on low quality** securities tend to increase more than **yields on high quality** securities, as the growing prospects of recession and

EXHIBIT 23 YIELDS ON U.S. GOVERNMENT SECURITIES

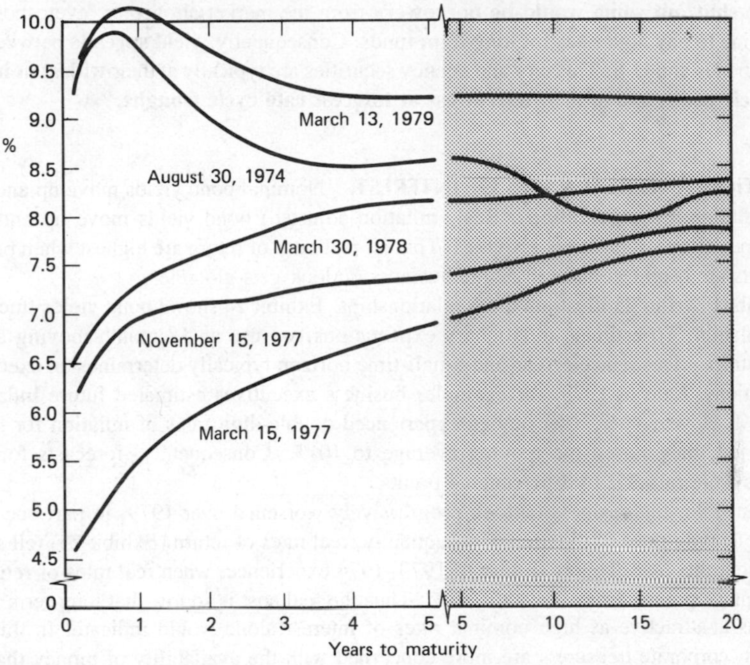

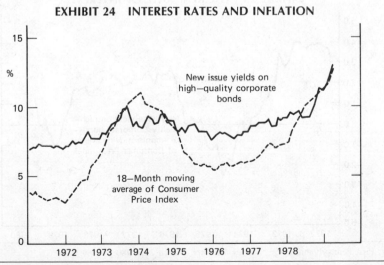

10.0
9.5
9.0
%
8.5
8.0
7.5
7.0
6.5
6.0
5.5
5.0
4.5
0
March 13, 1979
August 30, 1974
March 30, 1978
November 15, 1977
March 15, 1977
0 1 2 3 4 5 5 10 15 20
Years to maturity

Source: Federal Reserve Bank of St. Louis.

EXHIBIT 24 INTEREST RATES AND INFLATION

15
%
10
5
0
New issue yields on
high–quality corporate
bonds
18–Month moving
average of Consumer
Price Index
1972 1973 1974 1975 1976 1977 1978

Source: First Pennsylvania Corp., *Money Markets*, March 27, 1980.

business failure make investors increasingly quality conscious. The move to quality may work to **shut out some would-be borrowers** from the market altogether, even those who are willing to pay high rates for long-term funds. Consequently, **yield spreads** between low-quality bonds and U.S. Treasury and agency securities are typically at their **widest at interest rate cycle peaks** and at their **narrowest at interest rate cycle troughs.**

INFLATION AND REAL RATES OF INTEREST.   Nominal bond yields move up and down with **inflationary expectations.** Real (inflation adjusted) bond yields move up and down with expectations of business activities. That is, real rates of return are highest when business prospects are brightest and fall as the business outlook gets gloomier.

Exhibits 24 and 25 illustrate these relationships. Exhibit 24 shows bond yields fluctuating with inflation. To estimate inflationary expectations, we use an 18-month moving average of consumer prices, since a year-and-a-half time horizon typically determines an executive's expectations. Late in 1978, for example, business executives estimated future inflation at about 8%. A year later, after having experienced double-digit rates of inflation for most of that period, they raised the moving average to 10½%. Consequently, forecasts for future inflation were raised 2 to 3 percentage points.

Meanwhile, the business outlook progressively worsened over 1979, in part because of the accelerating rates of inflation. Consequently, real rates of return (Exhibit 25) fell sharply throughout the year. This is similar to 1973–1974 experience, when real rates of return fell 7 percentage points, from +4% to −3%. Thus the real cost is so low that long-term money is not as unattractive as high nominal rates of interest alone would indicate. In this environment, corporate treasurers are more concerned with the availability of money than with its price (yield).

EXHIBIT 25   THE REAL RATE OF INTEREST

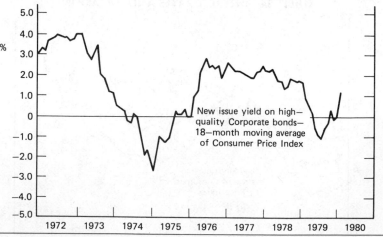

Source: First Pennsylvania Corp., *Money Markets,* March 27, 1980.

BIBLIOGRAPHY

Anderson, Carl G., Jr., "Farm Debt: A Problem for Some," *Federal Reserve Bank of Dallas Review,* June 1977, pp. 10–14.

Bowsher, Norman N., "Repurchase Agreements," *Federal Reserve Bank of St. Louis Review,* September 1979.

Budget of the U.S. Government, Fiscal Year 1980, 1981.

Burns, Arthur F., *Reflections of an Economic Policymaker: Speeches and Congressional Statements: 1969–1978,* American Enterprise Institute, Washington, D.C., 1978.

Business Conditions Digest, February 1980.

Controlling Monetary Aggregates, Federal Reserve Bank of Boston, June 1979.

Economic Report of the President, January 1979.

Economic Report of the President, January 1980.

Federal Reserve Chart Book, Board of Governors of the Federal Reserve System, February 1980.

Federal Reserve Readings on Inflation, Federal Reserve Bank of New York, February 1979.

Flow of Funds Accounts, Assets and Liabilities Outstanding, 1968–1978, Board of Governors of the Federal Reserve System, September 1979.

Instruments of the Money Market, Federal Reserve Bank of Richmond, 1977.

Lombra, Raymond E., "Reflections on Burns's Reflections," *Journal of Money Credit & Banking,* February 1980, pp. 94–105.

Policy Loan Developments of 15 Life Insurance Companies, American Council of Life Insurance, Washington, D.C., February 1980.

Survey of Current Business, selected issues 1979–1980.

Van Horne, James C., *Function and Analysis of Capital Market Rates,* Prentice-Hall, Englewood Cliffs, NJ, 1970.

GOVERNMENT OBLIGATIONS: U.S. TREASURY AND FEDERAL AGENCY SECURITIES

CONTENTS

THE NATIONAL DEBT   3

Evolution of the Debt   3
Interest on the Debt   3
Types of Obligations   3
Length of Debt Maturity   4
The Borrowing Cycle   6
Ownership of the Debt   6
Certainty of Payment   7
Debt in Foreign Currencies   8
Dealers in Government Securities   8

WHAT IS A REPO?   8

GOVERNMENT SECURITIES   9

Pricing Government Securities   9
Transactions in Government Securities   10
Delivery and Payment of Government Securities   10

GOVERNMENT OBLIGATIONS: AGENCY ISSUES   10

INTEREST RATE FUTURES: THEIR RELATIONSHIP TO CASH MARKETS   12

Government National Mortgage Association   12
Cash Pushes Futures   13
Futures Can Push Cash   13
Spread Trades   13
Trading the Yield Curve   16
Intermarket Trades   17
Hedging Against Rising MMC Costs   17
Financial Institutions Became Issuers of 6-Month Treasury Bills   17
Bill Futures: A Tool for Liability Management   17
When Bill Futures Rally, Insurance Premiums Go Up   17
    Scenario I: Interest rates rise   18
    Scenario II: Interest rates are unchanged   18
    Scenario III: Interest rates drop modestly   18
    Scenario IV: Interest rates drop sharply   18
Early 1980 Rally Provided Another Opportunity to Hedge Yield Backup   18

GOVERNMENT OBLIGATIONS: U.S. TREASURY AND FEDERAL AGENCY SECURITIES

Joseph Bench

THE NATIONAL DEBT

EVOLUTION OF THE DEBT.   Except for a few years during the early 1830s, the United States has never been out of debt. War and slumps in economic activity breed public debt. In 1791 the national debt was about $75 million. The War of 1812 raised the debt to $109 million, and the Civil War left a legacy of $2,776 million (including greenbacks) of indebtedness. By 1913 the debt had been reduced to less than $1 billion, but during World War I it soared above $26 billion. By 1929, the debt had been whittled down to $16 billion (Exhibit 1). During the ensuing decade the debt increased substantially for the first time without a war because of large Treasury expenditures for recovery and relief. Then came the tremendous debt expansion of World War II, from $48 billion at the time of the fall of France in 1940 to $279 billion early in 1946. By the end of 1948 the debt had been reduced to $253 billion, which was also the low point in the post-World War II period. The growth in the public national debt to $257 billion by the end of 1962 was largely due to the Korean War, Treasury deficits during several recessions, and large military and foreign aid commitments. Gross federal debt grew 20% from 1962 to the end of 1969. Of the $367 billion outstanding, $280 billion was publicly held. Gross federal debt expanded even more rapidly in the 1970s. The combination of the Vietnam War and the worst recession since the depression left the debt at $650 billion by the end of the decade. The total public debt, including national, state, and local, approached $1 trillion in 1979.

INTEREST ON THE DEBT.   A large government debt requires the levy of taxes to cover the interest payment on it, thus placing a burden on future generations. Interest on publicly held federal debt jumped sharply in 1979, approaching nearly four times 1969 outlays (see Exhibit 2). In part, this can be attributed to the rise in interest rates that accompanied the sharp uptrend in consumer prices during the decade.

TYPES OF OBLIGATIONS.   Roughly 23% of the public debt consists of **special obligations** held by trust account and state and local governments. **Foreigners** own 3%, while savings

EXHIBIT 1   PUBLIC AND PRIVATE DEBT

	1929	1945	1962	1979
National debt	$ 16	$253	$ 257	$ 650
State and local government debt	13	14	72	323
Long-term corporate debt	47	38	156	343
Short-term corporate debt	42	47	175	385
Urban real estate mortgages	31	27	211	1,163
Farm mortgages	12	7	29	99
All other private debt	29	20	101	569
Net debt, public and private	$190	$406	$1,001	$3,532

Source: Office of Management and Budget, Special Analysis of the Budget of the U.S. Government, Fiscal Year 1981.

bonds account for $8\frac{1}{2}\%$. Almost all the remainder, around 65% of the total, is represented by *marketable* securities. A tabulation of the debt by types of obligation is published in the **Monthly Statement** of the Public Debt of the United States, and in the **Treasury Bulletin** (Superintendent of Documents, Government Printing Office). Exhibit 3 gives the interest-bearing public debt (on April 30, 1980).

LENGTH OF DEBT MATURITY.   In recent years the Treasury has intensified its efforts to lengthen the maturity of the debt, which had declined substantially in the post-World War II period. In 1946 the average maturity of the marketable debt was 9 years and 1 month. It fell to as low as 2 years and 5 months in January 1976 (Exhibit 4).

EXHIBIT 2   COMPARISON OF TRENDS IN INTEREST ON FEDERAL DEBT
($ BILLIONS)

Fiscal Year	Total	Federal Government Accounts	The Public Total	The Public Federal Reserve System	The Public Other	Interest on Debt Held by Public as % of: GNP	Interest on Debt Held by Public as % of: Budget Outlays
1969	17.6	3.5	14.1	2.9	11.2	1.56	7.66
1970	20.0	4.4	15.6	3.5	12.2	1.63	7.95
1971	21.6	5.3	16.3	3.7	12.6	1.60	7.73
1972	22.5	5.8	16.6	3.7	12.9	1.50	7.16
1973	24.8	6.3	18.5	4.3	14.2	1.50	7.49
1974	30.0	7.7	22.4	5.5	16.9	1.64	8.29
1975	33.5	8.8	24.7	6.1	18.6	1.69	7.56
1976	37.7	9.0	28.7	6.3	22.5	1.77	7.84
TQ[a]	8.3	.6	7.6	NA	NA	1.78	8.07
1977	42.6	9.6	33.0	6.8	26.2	1.80	8.20
1978	49.3	10.2	39.2	7.3	31.8	1.92	8.68
1979[b]	60.3	11.6	48.7	NA	NA	2.13	9.87

[a]Transition quarter: budget year moved from July 1 to October 1.
[b]Estimated.
Source: Office of Management and Budget, Special Analysis of the Budget of the U.S. Government, Fiscal Year 1981.

EXHIBIT 3   INTEREST-BEARING PUBLIC DEBT, APRIL 30, 1980 ($ BILLIONS)

Interest-Bearing Debt: Public Issues:

Marketable Obligations

Treasury bills	$195
Treasury notes	292
Treasury bonds	78
Total marketable obligations	$565

Nonmarketable Obligations

U.S. savings bonds	$ 74
Government account series	179
State and local government series	24
Foreign:	
Dollar denominated	20
Foreign currency denominated	7
Total nonmarketable obligations	$304
Total interest-bearing public debt	$869

Source: Office of Management and Budget, Special Analysis of the Budget of the U.S. Government, Fiscal Year 1981.

EXHIBIT 4   AVERAGE LENGTH OF THE MARKETABLE DEBT, PRIVATELY HELD

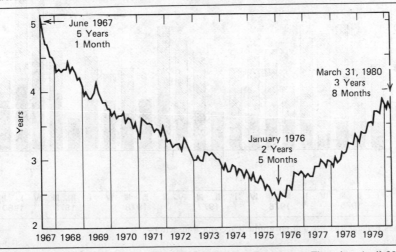

Source: Office of the Secretary of the Treasury and Office of Government Financing, April 29, 1980.

One reason for the sharp rise in interest expense is the Treasury's effort to **lengthen the average maturity** of its debt. This lengthening was accomplished by increasing the maximum maturity of Treasury notes not subject to **interest rate ceilings,** from 5 to 7 years (1967) and then from 7 to 10 years (1976). Another avenue of debt extension involved relaxing the $10 billion limit for bonds issued at rates above $4\frac{1}{2}\%$, which enabled the government to more easily float debt when interest rates grew so rapidly in the late 1970s. Exhibit 5 shows the rise in Treasury debt in recent years, particularly refunding operations.

THE BORROWING CYCLE.   Another by-product of the relaxation of restrictions on interest, volume, and maturity cited above is the **regularization** of Treasury debt offerings. The maturity, **frequency** of issuance, and size are illustrated in Exhibit 6.

OWNERSHIP OF THE DEBT.   A growing share of the **Treasury debt** is **held by commercial banks.** During the 1970s, increased reliance and emphasis on purchased funds' liabilities enabled banks to add both loans and investments near interest rate peaks. This is in sharp contrast with the earlier practice of liquidating investment assets to make room for loans. Despite bank additions to holdings of Treasury issues, their share of the total has declined progressively since 1976 (Exhibit 7). That year also marked the cyclical trough in interest rates.

Two sectors that have consistently added to their share of Treasury holdings are **state and local governments** and **nonbank financial institutions.** Municipalities that have benefited from revenue growth have increased their holdings of Treasury issues, especially in 1977 and 1978. State and local governments were heavy borrowers as rates fell in those years. Many took the opportunity to issue **advanced refunding bonds** at low interest rates,

EXHIBIT 5   TREASURY MARKET BORROWING,ᵃ CALENDAR YEAR QUARTERS

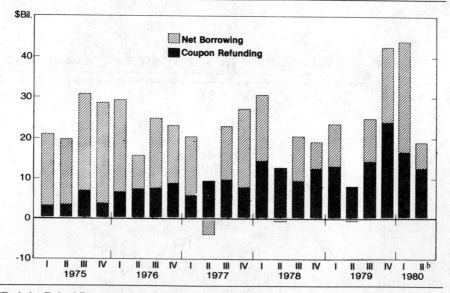

ᵃExcludes Federal Reserve and government account transactions.
ᵇEstimate.
Source: Office of the Secretary of the Treasury and Office of Government Financing, April 29, 1980.

EXHIBIT 6   TREASURY DEBT OFFERINGS

Type and Maturity	Approximate Size ($ Billions)	Approximate Frequency of Offering
3-Month bills	3.2	Weekly
6-Month bills	3.2	Weekly
1-Year bills	3.5	Monthly
2-Year notes	3.5	Monthly
3-Year notes	3.0	Quarterly—at midquarter refunding
4-Year notes	2.5	Quarterly—at end of quarter
5-Year notes	2.5	Quarterly—beginning last month of quarter
7-Year notes	2.5	Semiannually, alternate midquarter refunding
10-Year notes	2.0	Semiannually, alternate midquarter refunding
15-Year bonds	1.5	Quarterly—beginning first month of quarter
30-Year bonds	2.0	Quarterly—at midquarter refunding

Source: Department of Treasury, Monthly Statement of Debt Outstanding.

investing the proceeds in Treasury issues. They often earned more than they paid out, generating an interest arbitrage in the process. Congress eliminated this opportunity in September 1978.

Life insurance companies, pension funds, and other long-term investors have been aggressive buyers of Treasury debt since 1974, doubling their share of Treasury debt ownership in the process. This increased commitment to Treasury instruments can be traced to the **regularity of** Federal **long-term debt offerings** during these years, including 10-year, 15-year, and 30-year bonds offered at least once each quarter. It may also reflect the increased emphasis on **high-quality debt** securities that is an outgrowth of laws passed in 1974 and 1975 to protect citizens' retirement incomes (e.g., the **Employee Retirement Income Security Act (ERISA)** of 1974). Finally, it shows the growing reliance being placed by long-term investors on fixed income markets rather than equities.

CERTAINTY OF PAYMENT.   Despite the sharp rise in public and private debt since the 1930s, the obligations of the U.S. government continue to enjoy the highest confidence of investors. With the ownership of the public debt so widely distributed, throughout all segments of the population, **default** would be **inconceivable.** Ever since the credit of the United States was established on a solid foundation under the leadership of Alexander Hamilton, the determination of the American people to honor their obligations has hardly ever been questioned.

EXHIBIT 7   DISTRIBUTION (%) OF OWNERSHIP OF TREASURY ISSUES

Owner	1969	1970	1971	1972	1973	1974	1975	1976	1977	1978
Households	46	41	38	39	47	54	48	43	43	45
Nonfinancial business	3	3	5	3	1	1	4	4	2	0
State and local government	11	11	11	13	12	9	6	6	9	11
Commercial banks	27	30	33	33	29	27	30	32	29	26
Nonbank financial	14	14	12	12	11	9	12	15	17	18
	100%	100%	100%	100%	100%	100%	100%	100%	100%	100%

Source: Joseph Bench.

DEBT IN FOREIGN CURRENCIES.   The debt is almost entirely **internal** (i.e., payable in American dollars rather than in gold or foreign currencies). The government never lacks dollars with which to pay. At the end of 1977 **only $5½ billion of the Treasury debt was payable in foreign currencies.** The government can obtain funds through a virtually unlimited taxing power; it can borrow funds as needed by virtue of a control over the Federal Reserve System; or, should it so desire, it can print money in any denominations and amounts.

As part of dollar defense operations announced on November 1, 1978, the Treasury began a program of issuing deutschmark-, Swiss franc-, and yen-denominated intermediate notes. These have been nicknamed **"Carter bonds"** by the financial community. Only $6 billion worth of "Carter bonds" has been issued. Most of these were deutschmark-denominated and could be purchased only by foreign official institutions.

In actual practice, the Treasury meets most maturing obligations by **reborrowing.** The banking system provides a flexible mechanism for supplying the Treasury with any amount that cannot be borrowed on satisfactory terms from other investors. The lending power of the banks can be replenished almost indefinitely by means of reserves provided them through **open market operations** by the Federal Reserve banks. If commercial banks should fail to provide all funds required, the Federal Reserve banks would doubtless provide them. The **Treasury** is authorized at present to **borrow directly from the Reserve banks** but only to a limited extent. This has been done as a very temporary expedient, to prevent unsettlement of the money market. Direct borrowing of substantial amounts by a government from its **central bank** is regarded as a long step toward monetary inflation, and it is mentioned here to illustrate the ability of the Treasury under all circumstances to secure funds with which to meet its obligations.

There is no question that all obligations of the U.S. government will be paid promptly and in full as they fall due. This does not mean that the national debt will be paid off; the government can continue indefinitely to meet part of its maturing obligations by reborrowing. In fact, there are those who recommend that the Treasury refund some of its debt by issuing **perpetual obligations** bearing no maturity date, as the British Treasury has done with its "consols."

DEALERS IN GOVERNMENT SECURITIES.   The great bulk of transactions in government securities is affected by a few dozen dealers, most of whom have their headquarters in New York City. Larger firms maintain branch offices in principal cities throughout the country.

As the volume of trading in government securities increased after 1932, more and more dealers entered the field. Some represent old firms that formerly engaged in general investment banking or dealt in acceptances; others are new concerns organized primarily to deal in government securities. There are also **"dealer banks,"** commercial banks maintaining special departments to handle government securities business.

The dealer acts as middleman between those who wish to sell and those who wish to buy securities. The ultimate market for government securities is composed of the several classes of investors described above and dealers who provide the essential mechanism for buying and selling orders from these investors for their own account.

WHAT IS A REPO?

Securities dealers and banks often hold inventories of Treasury bills, notes, and bonds well in excess of their capital. This requires them to borrow to **finance securities inventories.**

By using their **securities as collateral,** they attract short-term (often overnight) funds from investors who have a temporary surplus of cash.

Such financing involves the temporary sale of securities by the bank or dealer, with the agreement to buy the securities back at some future date—often the next day, and settled in immediately available federal funds. This buy-back agreement is referred to as RP, or **repo,** referring to the repurchase transaction. The investor is usually willing to earn a return below the federal funds rate, since this overnight funds market is restricted to banks lending to one another. Thus the RP can be viewed as a collateralized deposit on which investors earn interest that otherwise would not be available to them.

Reverse repurchase agreements are the flip side of the RP transaction, or an RP viewed from the lender's perspective. The lender buys the security with the intent to resell it at maturity.

There are many advantages to RP transactions. Not only can corporations and other holders of excess cash earn a market rate of return on a secured basis, but banks have a source of nonreservable short-term deposits, flexible maturities, and no interest rate ceiling. That is in sharp contrast with bank Certificates of Deposit on which banks must maintain reserves, maturities must be at least 30 days, and interest rate ceilings exist for denominations of less than $100,000.

Exhibit 8 documents the **growth in the RP market** over the past decade. Two factors influencing growth in this market are **increased attention to cash management** on the part of corporate treasurers and the **growing volume of Treasury and agency securities** in bank portfolios that need to be **financed via purchased funds liabilities.**

GOVERNMENT SECURITIES

PRICING GOVERNMENT SECURITIES.   Government bonds and notes are quoted on a **percentage-of-parity basis.** Fractions are quoted usually in 32nds, sometimes in 64ths. A

EXHIBIT 8   OUTSTANDING RPs[a]

Year-End	Amount ($ Billions)
1969	4.9
1970	2.8
1971	4.9
1972	6.0
1973	13.3
1974	14.8
1975	15.5
1976	27.9
1977	36.3
1978	43.8
1979	45.0 (June)

[a]Estimates of RPs of all commercial banks with the nonbank public by staff of Federal Reserve Board of Governors.

Source: Federal Reserve Bank of St. Louis.

32nd is $312.50 per million par amount. Thus a quotation of 100.16 would mean a price of $1,015 for a bond with a par value of $1,000, or 1,015,000 per million of face value.

Treasury bills, by contrast, are quoted on a **discounted basis.** The size of the discount is directly proportional to **yield to maturity.** Thus, a one-year bill at 12% costs the investor $878,000 per $1,000,000 of maturity. The **coupon equivalent yield** is 13.44%, which is what the investor would earn if he were paid the $122,000 interest income on a semiannual basis. The actual return is even greater, namely, 13.9%.

TRANSACTIONS IN GOVERNMENT SECURITIES.   Almost always such transactions are at **net prices.** There is no tax involved and dealers rarely charge commissions as such. They obtain compensation for their services in the form of the **spread between bid and asked** quotations; that is, they buy at the bid price and sell at the asked price, the differential usually amounting to 2/32 of a point, sometimes less. Treasury bills are quoted in yield, with the higher yield bid (implying a greater discount and a lower price) and a lower yield offered. The **value of each 0.01** or **basis point** differs according to term to maturity. A 0.01 for a 3-month bill represents $25/million, on a 6-month bill $50/million, and on a 1-year bill $100/million.

Bonds and notes bear **semiannual interest coupons.** Quotations do not, of course, take into account the amount of interest accrued on the current coupons attached to the securities. This sum must be computed and added to the bill of the buyer. **Accrued interest** on government securities is computed on the basis of the actual number of days in the interest period, not on a uniform 30-day-month basis.

DELIVERY AND PAYMENT OF GOVERNMENT SECURITIES.   **Delivery** of securities and **payment** by check are normally made on the first business day following the transaction, Friday transactions being cleared on Monday. Arrangement can usually be made with the dealer for **delayed delivery** if the security cannot be delivered on the "regular delivery" date. Also, if the seller of securities wishes to be paid in "federal funds," by a check drawn on a Federal Reserve bank, on the regular delivery date or even on the day of the transaction, this can be arranged with the dealer at the time of the sale.

GOVERNMENT OBLIGATIONS: AGENCY ISSUES

Federal agency obligations generally fall into one of two major categories: borrowing by **government-sponsored** entities and **government-guaranteed** borrowing. Obligations of the first type are now entirely privately owned and are not subject to the federal budget review process, and their debt is not part of gross federal debt. Exhibits 9 and 10 summarize borrowing by government-sponsored agencies, and Exhibit 9 gives an estimate of debt outstanding at the end of 1981.

Fluctuations in government-sponsored agency borrowing are largely due to housing-related activity. The **Federal Home Loan Bank** increased **advances** by $12 billion in 1978 and by another $8 billion in 1979 to help savings and loan institutions cope with the slowdown in savings inflows due to high interest rates. The **Federal National Mortgage Association** ("**Fannie Mae**") and **Federal Home Loan Mortgage Corporation** ("**Freddy Mac**") increased their purchases of mortgages over that time as well.

Government-guaranteed borrowing consists of loans for which the federal government guarantees payment of principal and interest. Exhibit 11 illustrates the wide variety of purposes that guaranteed loans serve.

EXHIBIT 9 BORROWING BY GOVERNMENT-SPONSORED ENTERPRISES ($ MILLIONS)

Description	Borrowing or Repayment (−)				Debt Outstanding, End 1981, Estimate
	1978 Actual	1979 Actual	1980 Estimate	1981 Estimate	
Education Student Loan Marketing Association	235	530	670	−215	1,730
Housing and Urban Development: Federal National Mortgage Association	6,802	7,705	3,296	6,698	55,993
Farm Credit Administration[a]:					
Banks for cooperatives	775	1,089	523	777	8,143
Federal intermediate credit banks	444	2,725	2,310	2,603	20,738
Federal land banks	2,725	4,921	4,022	4,648	35,852
Federal Home Loan Bank Board:					
Federal home loan banks	7,792	5,194	2,197	−1,401	30,942
Federal Home Loan Mortgage Corporation	5,188	4,547	3,400	4,130	25,885
Total	23,961	26,712	16,418	17,240	179,283
Less increase in holdings of debt issued by government-sponsored enterprises	−98	962	244	578	4,355
Total, borrowing by government-sponsored enterprises	24,060	25,750	16,174	16,662	174,928

[a]The debt represented by consolidated bonds is attributed to the respective Farm Credit banks.

Source: Federal Reserve Board, July 1980.

EXHIBIT 10   NET NEW MONEY IN AGENCY FINANCE, QUARTERLY, PRIVATELY HELD

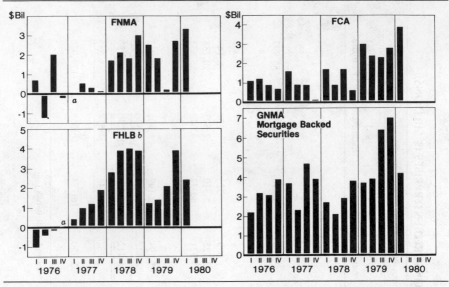

[a]Less than $50 million.

[b]Includes FHLB discount notes, bonds, and FHLMC certificates, mortgage-backed bonds, and mortgage participation certificates.

Source: Office of Secretary of the Treasury and Office of Government Finance, April 29, 1980.

In summary, federal and federally assisted borrowing has jumped sharply over the past decade (Exhibit 12). During that time, the proportion of government-related credit demands has grown relative to the total. In some periods, such as 1976, these public sector capital requirements have effectively **"crowded out"** some private sector borrowers. And while federal borrowing to finance budget gaps has declined sharply since 1976, federally assisted programs have proliferated, taking up much of the slack.

INTEREST RATE FUTURES: THEIR RELATIONSHIP TO CASH MARKETS

GOVERNMENT NATIONAL MORTGAGE ASSOCIATION.   In October 1975, **Government National Mortgage Association (GNMA)** interest rate **futures contracts** (also known as Ginnie Maes) were introduced on the **Chicago Board of Trade.** Since then, interest rate futures contracts have proliferated. Expanding markets for interest rate futures instruments now offer some of the best money management opportunities available to the investor or hedger. While some money managers, corporate treasurers and other cash market participants are reluctant to operate in the interest rate futures arena, much of this hesitancy will be overcome once cash market participants simply understand the relationship of the cash money market to the futures market.

Movements in the cash market tend to be less volatile than price changes for corresponding futures markets instruments. The direction of change in futures markets, however, is usually determined by factors directly influencing cash markets. Two of these factors are **financing costs** and the **available supply** of securities.

This is especially true for **Treasury bills**—relatively short-maturity instruments whose yields are influenced by their availability and the cost of financing them, namely, repurchase or RP rates. Bill yields rise and fall with RP rates, which, in turn, are influenced by the general availability of eligible collateral (Treasury bills, notes, and bonds) that needs to be financed.

CASH PUSHES FUTURES.   Treasury bill futures prices move inversely to yields. Cash prices usually determine futures prices. For example, the first contract month (December 1980) will influence the 3-month bill; the second contract (March 1981) will influence the 1-year bill and so on.

When financing costs or RP rates exceed yield levels in the cash Treasury bill market, holders of cash Treasury bills, who must finance them, incur a negative yield (carrying cost). One option they have is to avoid the cash market and buy the futures contract for delivery at a time when financing costs are expected to be lower than Treasury bill yields.

Normally, the futures market has already incorporated this **negative interest carrying** cost into its price by offering **futures contracts at a premium price to cash.** That premium disappears as the contract month nears. The opposite (futures will trade at a **discount to cash**) holds true when RP rates are below cash market yields.

Many arbitragers take advantage of these premium and discount anomalies by buying futures and selling cash, or vice versa, as the situation warrants.

Arbitrage strategies between cash and futures have merit only in a stable trend environment, that is, as long as interest rates are clearly moving in one direction. The danger arises when there is a changing perception of where interest rates are heading. Strategy must change as volatility increases.

FUTURES CAN PUSH CASH.   At interest rate **turning points,** the **futures market** tends to become the **dominant** market and influences the ultimate course of cash markets as well. The changing leadership role could prove to be a trap for the arbitrager who expects short-run aberrations to correct themselves when they may, in fact, go to even greater extremes. This is especially true for distant contracts that tend to overdramatize anticipated changes in future cash market interest rates.

Cash versus futures market relationships are not limited to Treasury bills. Treasury notes, bonds, and GNMAs are also repurchasable securities.

When RP rates are higher than current yields available on longer term fixed income securities, Treasury bond **futures** generally **trade at a premium** price to cash. When RP rates are below bond yields, **futures contracts trade at a discount** to cash, since the cash holder is earning income that the futures owner is not.

Thus the **size of the discount or premium** of futures to cash is **a function of the positive or negative interest carrying cost** incurred by the cash security holder. The greater the negative carrying cost, the bigger the premium of futures to cash. The greater the positive carrying cost, the bigger the discount.

SPREAD TRADES.   Since financing cost is known today but only anticipated for the future, the positive or negative carrying cost implied in the current array of interest rate futures prices may be well off the mark, since it is an extrapolation of current market conditions.

Opportunities exist for doing **intramarket spread trades** if it is assumed that financing costs will change. For example, say December 1980 **Treasury bonds** are trading at the same

EXHIBIT 11 DIRECT LOANS AND GUARANTEED LOANS BY FUNCTION ($ MILLIONS)

Function	New Direct Loans			New Guaranteed Loans		
	1978 Actual	1979 Estimate	1980 Estimate	1978 Actual	1979 Estimate	1980 Estimate
International Affairs						
Foreign economic and financial assistance	2,583	2,451	2,303	1,779	1,691	1,843
Export-Import Bank	1,260	1,578	2,199	4,213	4,845	5,572
Total	3,843	4,029	4,502	5,992	6,536	7,415
Natural Resources, Environment, and Energy						
National resources and environment	58	37	43	—a	—a	—a
Energy	881	1,100	1,150	2,095	3,297	4,800
Total	939	1,137	1,193	2,095	3,297	4,800
Agriculture farm income stabilization	13,670	11,016	8,990	4,219	3,883	3,021
Commerce and Housing Credit						
Mortgage credit and thrift insurance	7,042	7,942	9,619	33,482	35,471	40,883
Advancement of commerce	15,878	14,470	17,561	3,897	5,072	5,071

Transportation						
Ground transportation	863	1,096	578	160	266	15
Air transportation	—[a]	—[a]	—[a]	41	50	100
Water transportation	108	6	4	900	937	888
Total	37,561	34,530	36,752	42,699	45,679	49,978
Community and regional development	3,976	2,724	2,949	1,632	2,393	4,767
Total	3,976	2,724	2,949	1,632	2,393	4,767
Education, Training, Employment, and Social Services						
Higher education	564	638	496	4,284	4,857	5,300
Health	88	25	129	53	252	285
Total	652	763	625	4,337	5,109	5,585
Income security	191	204	205	9,448	11,310	14,193
Veterans benefits and services	174	35	139	—[a]	—[a]	—[a]
Veterans housing	430	527	542	14,849	16,259	18,264
Total	795	866	886	24,297	27,569	32,457
General government	6	6	3	128	74	45
General purpose fiscal assistance	839	149	159	729	500	250
Other programs	29	38	14	180	183	136
Grand total[b]	48,650	44,243	47,084	82,090	91,340	105,434

[a]Less than $0.5 million.
[b]Off-budget accounts are included (except sponsored agencies).
Source: Office of Management and Budget, Special Analysis of the Budget of the U.S. Government, Fiscal Year 1981.

EXHIBIT 12   FEDERAL AND FEDERALLY ASSISTED BORROWING

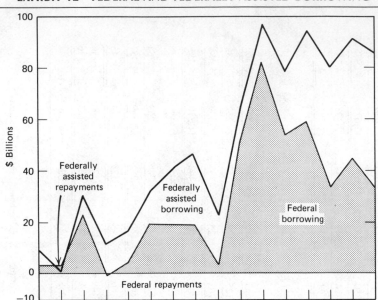

Source: Office of Management and Budget, Special Analysis of the U.S. Government Budget, Fiscal Year 1981.

price as those of June 1981. Current financing costs are higher than yields available on Treasury bonds and are not expected to fall any time soon. This credit situation suggests that the June 1981 contract ought to be purchased relative to the December 1980 contract because negative carrying cost resulting from high financing costs for cash market holders dictates the June 1981 contract will trade at a premium to cash. If financing costs remain high, the sale of the December 1980 contract and simultaneous purchase of the June 1981 contract will prove a moneymaker.

A similar strategy is applicable to **intramarket spreads for GNMA** futures contracts. Should financing costs rise even more, the spread trade strategy of purchasing the distant and selling the near-term futures contract will work out even better.

Of course, if financing costs drop sharply so that holders of cash market securities enjoy a positive carrying cost, the spread will not work.

TRADING THE YIELD CURVE.   One can also develop **strategies in anticipation** of the **changing shape of the Treasury yield curve** over the interest rate cycle. Historically, the Treasury yield curve begins the rate cycle with a significant upward sloping shape when short-term rates are well below long-term yields. Then the yield curve flattens and ultimately assumes a downward slope.

As the shape of the yield curve changes while interest rates move up, Treasury bill and note futures can be sold against Treasury bond futures on a ratio basis that provides maximum return and minimum risk. Conversely, one can implement strategies that incorporate the normal maturity extension that takes place as interest rates move down.

INTERMARKET TRADES.   Just as opportunities exist for anticipating changes in the Treasury futures market, opportunities also exist between markets. One example is the **changing relationship between GNMA futures and Treasury bond futures.**

As interest rates move up, GNMAs are a more desirable security than Treasuries. This is because the underlying mortgage-backed security pays principal and interest monthly, thus enabling its owner to reinvest the proceeds at higher yields.

Also, the supply of mortgage-backed securities shrinks as high interest rates make mortgage money scarce. Consequently, the price spread between Treasury bond futures and GNMA futures can be expected to narrow as rates rise. As rates fall, however, GNMAs become less desirable as the reinvestment rate drops and price spreads between GNMA futures and Treasury bond futures widen.

HEDGING AGAINST RISING MMC COSTS.   Since their introduction in June 1978, 6-month **money market certificates (MMCs)** have taken a growing share of savings deposits at banks and thrift institutions, including savings and loan associations and mutual savings banks. At the end of February 1980, MMCs outstanding equaled $307 billion. Nearly half of these were at savings and loans, 40% were at commercial banks, and 12% at mutual savings banks, representing 31, 28, and 26% of savings deposit totals at these institutions, respectively.

In late March 1980, institutions were paying as much as 16½% for these obligations. Yet, as recently as November 1979 they could have "locked in" considerably lower costs through the use of Treasury bill futures.

FINANCIAL INSTITUTIONS BECAME ISSUERS OF 6-MONTH TREASURY BILLS.   Indeed, few liability managers recognized that their institutions had effectively become issuers of 6-month bills through the MMC. The reason is that rates paid on these liabilities are a function of weekly auction yields for 6-month Treasury bills. And as bill yields rise and fall, so too does their MMC cost.

BILL FUTURES: A TOOL FOR LIABILITY MANAGEMENT.   Bill futures can be an effective tool for liability managers who would like to take advantage of interest rate swings that move the market to extremes in either direction. For example, in November 1979 and again in late April 1980, the market was overbought, enabling liability managers to "lock in" low-cost MMC yields by selling bill futures forward.

A hypothetical liability manager, thinking that the market was overbought, could have sold 3-month bill futures dated June 1980 and September 1980 against MMCs maturing in March and June, respectively. This would have been advantageous because the June 3-month bill future corresponds to the 6-month cash market for Treasury bills in March (i.e., it is a cash bill maturing on September 22 that is deliverable against the June bill futures contract). Similarly, it is the December 22 cash bill that is deliverable against the September 1980 3-month bill futures contract. Thus the September 1980 contract becomes the vehicle for hedging MMC costs in June, just as the June contract is the vehicle for hedging MMC costs in March.

WHEN BILL FUTURES RALLY, INSURANCE PREMIUMS GO UP.   Prices of the June 1980 and September 1980 bill contracts rallied so much in the fall of 1979 that yield levels dropped to lows in the neighborhood of 9 to 9½%. At these levels, the futures market was as much as 340 basis points rich (in price, but depressed in yield) to the cash market, and offered liability managers a tremendous incentive to lock in low-cost liabilities.

Let's examine four different scenarios that could have occurred subsequent to the taking of the short position, as the contract approaches its expiration date.

Scenario I: Interest Rates Rise.   For each percentage point that interest rates rise the hedger stands to make $2500/million (per contract). He can use the proceeds to effectively defray the higher borrowing costs in the cash market, which he must pay to MMC depositors.

Scenario II: Interest Rates Are Unchanged.   As the contract approached expiration, the price premium (yield discount) to the cash market disappears. The erosion of the 340 basis point premium to the cash market leaves the hedger with an $8500(340 × $25) profit per contract. That means the hedger, **instead of paying an insurance premium** for insulating the institution from rising interest rates, **was actually paid a premium** for hedging against rising money costs. The hedger will earn this bonus under both flat and rising interest rate trends (i.e., scenarios I and II).

Scenario III: Interest Rates Drop Modestly.   Because of the robust premium available to the hedger when the market is overbought, **the hedger can make money even when interest rates fall** (contrary to the hedger's expectations when the short position was taken). Indeed, if interest rates fall by less than the premium (340 basis points), the hedger will make money on his short position as the contract nears its expiration date and begins to approximate cash market prices.

Scenario IV: Interest Rates Drop Sharply.   The major risk to the hedger occurs when rates drop sharply. In our example, that drop would have to be more than 340 basis points before the contract expires. We have recently witnessed some fairly large swings in rates, indicating that such a development is indeed possible. But while our hedger is losing money on his short position in bill futures, the institution is benefiting greatly from the sharp drop in MMC costs and, in all likelihood, from the price appreciation of its fixed assets that are being funded at these lower costs. The drop in rates could also mean a much reduced negative yield spread between the yield paid on variable rate MMC liabilities and the yield earned on its fixed rate portfolio.

This relationship can be traced graphically through the use of a bond analysis system. Constant updating and tracking of these relationships are necessary to take advantage of what are historical abnormalities. The occurrence of such anomalies enables the hedger to get paid large premiums while insuring his institution against rising MMC liabilities. A graphical display of these yield spread relationships (Exhibit 13) shows the abnormally large (negative) insurance premiums that were available late in 1979 and returned again in Spring 1980, as indicated by a move above the average (mean) yield spread between cash bills and futures.

EARLY 1980 RALLY PROVIDED ANOTHER OPPORTUNITY TO HEDGE YIELD BACKUP.   For liability managers who do not believe that the recent fall-off in bill yields is sustainable, the bill futures market may once again be offering an opportunity to lock in low-cost MMC funds. The hedger would be protected against a "backing up" in bill yields or a flat market environment over the next several weeks. If rates are unchanged during this period, the yield on bill futures should move toward cash market yields, as the contract approached expiration. At this point, the June 1980 contract implies an 11.30% discounted yield on 3-month bills in June or 150 basis points protection against the outstanding 3-month bill, on a discounted basis, and over 200 basis points protection, on a coupon equivalent basis.

**EXHIBIT 13   NEGATIVE INSURANCE PREMIUMS: 6-MONTH BILL YIELDS LESS
JUNE 1980 BILL FUTURES**

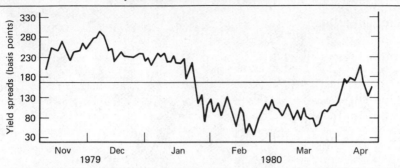

Source: American Council of Life Insurance.

BIBLIOGRAPHY

Bench, Joseph, "Ways to Trade an Interest Rate Outlook," *Commodities Magazine*, Fall 1979, pp. 14–16.

———, "Bond Market Still Vulnerable," *Bankers Monthly Magazine*, December 15, 1979, pp. 12–14.

———, "Credit Demands to Shrink Further in 1980," *Money Markets: A First Pennsylvania Report*, December 21, 1979.

———, "Stage Set for Credit Crunch," *Money Manager*, March 10, 1980.

Bowsher, Norman N., "Repurchase Agreements," *Federal Reserve Bank of St. Louis Review*, September 1979.

Budget of the U.S. Government, Fiscal Years 1980, 1981.

Burger, A. E., Lang, R. W., and Trasche, R. H., "The Treasury Bill Futures Market and Market Expectations of Interest Rates," *Federal Reserve Bank of St. Louis Review*, June 1977, pp. 2–9.

Jianakoplos, Nancy A., "The Growing Link Between the Federal Government and State and Local Government Financing," *Federal Reserve Bank of St. Louis Review*, May 1977, pp. 13–20.

Stevens, Neil A., "Government Debt Financing—Its Effect in View of Tax Discounting," *Federal Reserve Bank of St. Louis Review*, July 1979, pp. 11–19.

Treasury Bulletin, U.S. Treasury Department, selected issues 1979–1980.

STATE AND LOCAL DEBT

CONTENTS

RECENT TRENDS IN VOLUME 3

MARKETING TAX-EXEMPT SECURITIES 5

THE SECONDARY MARKET FOR TAX-EXEMPT SECURITIES 10

THE MUNICIPAL SECURITIES RULEMAKING BOARD 11

SECURITY FEATURES OF SHORT-TERM TAX-EXEMPT SECURITIES 11

Urban Renewal Project Notes 11
Local Housing Authority Notes 11
Tax Anticipation Notes (TANs) and Revenue Anticipation Notes (RANs) 12
Bond Anticipation Notes (BANs) 12

SECURITY FEATURES OF LONG-TERM BONDS 13

General Obligations 13
Special Assessment Bonds 13
Revenue Bonds 13

CHANGING TRENDS IN SECURITY FEATURES 14

CHANGING PURPOSES FOR PUBLIC DEBTS 16

TRENDS IN BOND SALES BY TYPE OF ISSUER 18

EVALUATING CREDIT RISK AND CREDIT QUALITY 18

GUARANTEED AND INSURED BONDS 22

PRIVATE BOND INSURANCE 23

THE DEMAND FOR TAX-EXEMPT SECURITIES 23

THE BEHAVIOR OF TAX-EXEMPT INTEREST RATES 25

THE MATURITY STRUCTURE OF TAX-EXEMPT YIELDS 27

TAX-EXEMPT YIELDS AND BOND RATINGS 28

YIELDS ON GENERAL OBLIGATION AND REVENUE BONDS 29

STATE AND LOCAL DEBT

Ronald W. Forbes

A distinctive characteristic of the debt securities issued by state and local governments and their agencies is the exemption of interest payments on such debt from federal income taxation. This tax exemption stems from the doctrine of **reciprocal tax exemption** outlined by Chief Justice Marshall in 1819 in the celebrated case of *McCulloch* v. *Maryland* (4 Wheaton 316). Under this doctrine, the interest income received by investors from the debt securities issued by states and their subdivisions is not subject to federal taxation. Most states also exempt from state taxation the interest income from securities issued by governmental units located within state boundaries. Because of the exemption from federal taxation, these state and local government securities and the markets they trade in have become widely referred to as the tax-exempt market. The tax-exempt feature permits states and local governments to borrow at interest rates lower than those available to other types of borrower such as the federal government and private corporations, whose interest payments on debt represent taxable income for investors. Moreover, tax exemption has its principal appeal to investors who are in high marginal income tax brackets. As discussed later in this section, this defines a special market of investors consisting primarily of commercial banks, property and casualty insurance companies, and high-income individuals.

RECENT TRENDS IN VOLUME

One of the outstanding features of the tax-exempt market has been the significant growth in volume of new debt issues. As noted in Exhibit 1, the dollar volume of new issues has expanded from $17.3 billion in 1966 to $69.6 billion in 1978, representing an annual compound growth rate of 12.3%.

Market convention generally distinguishes between **short-term tax-exempt securities,** which carry a final maturity of 13 months or less, and long-term debt issues with final maturities beyond 13 months. As noted in Exhibit 1, short-term tax-exempts (often called notes) increased rapidly between 1968 and 1971, from $6.3 billion to $26.3 billion. Since 1971, new note issues have generally increased during periods of high or rapidly rising interest rates and have declined during periods of low or falling interest rates.

Long-term issues, generally referred to as bonds, have recorded a consistent upward trend since 1966. In 1978, 5,695 new bond issues were marketed, raising $48.2 billion in funds. The $48.2 billion in bond sales is **more than double** the volume just 4 years earlier—in 1974—and more than **four times** the volume in 1969. The record of the past decade points out that new issues of tax-exempt bonds have doubled approximately every 5 years; between

EXHIBIT 1   NEW ISSUES OF TAX-EXEMPT SECURITIES, 1966–1978 ($ MILLIONS)

	Total New Issues		Long-Term Issues		Short-Term Issues	
	Number	Dollar Value	Number	Dollar Volume	Number	Dollar Volume
1978	8,031	$69,574	5,695	$48,190	2,336	$21,384
1977	8,333	71,457	5,358	46,706	2,975	24,751
1976	7.533	57,321	4,920	35,416	2,613	21,905
1975	8,072	59,632	4,689	30,659	3,383	28,973
1974	7,628	52,626	4,214	23,585	3,414	29,041
1973	8,061	48,488	4,655	23,821	3,406	24,667
1972	8,131	48,914	4,814	23,692	3,317	25,222
1971	8,493	51,210	5,143	24,929	3,350	26,281
1970	7,238	35,963	4,335	18,083	2,903	17,880
1969	6,167	23,485	3,824	11,702	2,343	11,783
1968	7,660	24,979	5,487	16,320	2,173	8,659
1967	7,552	22,430	5,417	14,405	2,135	8,025
1966	6,800	17,333	4,964	11,079	1,836	6,254

Source: Data files of the Public Securities Association.

1966 and 1978, the average annual compound growth rate in new bond volume was 13%.

Accompanying the growth in dollar volume has been an increase in the average size of each sale. In 1966, 4964 separate bond issues were marketed with a total dollar volume of $17.3 billion. In 1978, 5,695 issues were sold, raising $69.6 billion in funds. Thus, the **average size** of new bond issues increased from $2.2 million in 1966 to $8.5 million in 1978. Even more significant, the number of individual new issues over $25 million in par value has increased from 60 in 1966 to 408 issues in 1978. While these large issues accounted for only 7.2% of the **number** of new issues in 1978, they accounted for 63% of the total dollar volume of funds raised in the tax-exempt bond market (see Exhibit 2). Short-term note issues have also increased in size. In 1966, the average note issue amounted to $3.4 million; by 1978, the average note sale amounted to $9.2 million.

EXHIBIT 2   TRENDS IN SIZE OF TAX-EXEMPT BOND ISSUES, 1966 AND 1978

Range of Issue Size	1966		1978	
	% of Dollar Volume	Number of Issues	% of Dollar Volume	Number of Issues
< $1 million	10.5	3,331	2.1	2,229
1.0–5.0	25.4	1,271	10.4	2,015
5.0–25.0	29.9	302	24.4	1,043
25.0–100	21.7	52	35.1	338
> $100 million	12.4	8	28.0	70
	100.0	4,964	100.0	5,695

Source: Data files of the Public Securities Association.

**EXHIBIT 3   NEW OFFERINGS OF SECURITIES OF STATE AND LOCAL
GOVERNMENTS AND CORPORATIONS FOR SELECTED YEARS,
1966–1978 ($ MILLIONS)**

	State and Local Governments[a]		Corporations[b]	
	Total	Long-Term Bonds	Total[a]	Publicly Offered Bonds
1978	$69,574	$48,190	$47,230	$19,815
1974	52,626	23,585	37,837	25,337
1970	35,963	18,083	38,945	25,384
1966	17,333	11,079	18,074	8,018

[a]Data from Exhibit.
[b]Data from Board of Governors of the Federal Reserve System, *Federal Reserve Bulletin*, various issues.
[c]Includes public offerings and private placements of bonds and equity securities.

Some additional perspective on the tax-exempt new issue market is provided by the data in Exhibit 3, which compares tax-exempts with corporate security sales. Total public offerings of tax-exempts nearly matched total private and public corporate issues (equity and long-term debt) in 1966 and 1970. The volume of publicly offered tax-exempt **bonds** was approximately the same as corporate bond sales in 1974. By 1978, both total offerings and new bond sales in the tax-exempt market had eclipsed the total volume of new corporate debt and equity issues. As these comparisons demonstrate, the recent tax-exempt market is now larger than the market for corporate long-term securities. In the **bond** markets, new tax-exempt sales are more than twice the amount of corporate public issues.

MARKETING TAX-EXEMPT SECURITIES

Exhibit 4 provides some measures of the stock of outstanding state and local government debt over the 1966–1978 period. Long-term bond issues outstanding climbed from $99.9 billion in 1966 to $279 billion in 1978, which is equivalent to an annual compound growth

**EXHIBIT 4   TOTAL DEBT OUTSTANDING, STATE
AND LOCAL GOVERNMENTS FOR SELECTED
YEARS, 1966–1978 ($ BILLIONS)**

	Outstanding Debt		
	Total	Short-Term	Long-Term
1978	$291.4	$12.4	$279.0
1976	239.5	14.5	225.0
1974	207.7	18.8	188.9
1972	176.5	15.8	160.7
1970	144.4	13.3	131.1
1968	123.2	8.1	115.1
1966	106.0	6.2	99.9

Source: Board of Governors of the Federal Reserve System, Flow of Funds Statements, various dates.

rate of 8.9%. The fact that the stock of outstanding debt has increased at a much slower pace than the flow of new bond issues is largely attributable to the type of maturity structures commonly used on tax-exempt bonds. Short-term issues are usually retired during the fiscal year. Reflecting this, note issues outstanding at year-end have climbed less rapidly than new issues, from $6.2 billion in 1966 to $12.4 billion in 1978. Moreover, only a small proportion of new bonds is sold as term bonds, with a single long-term maturity and coupon rate. Instead, most tax-exempts are sold with **serial maturities;** that is, a portion of the total principal borrowed is scheduled to be repaid each year over the life of the issue. In effect, a bond issue with a final maturity of 25 years actually consists of a number of smaller issues each with its own yield, amount, and maturity. Exhibit 5 demonstrates a common form of serial bond maturity structure for a $300 million bond issue from the State of Oregon.

Municipal bonds are most often sold as **bearer bonds,** where ownership is presumed by possession. Holders of bearer bonds are not listed by name on the issuer's books. Payment of principal and interest is effected upon presentation of coupons or bonds to the issuer's paying agent. This practice differs from the corporate market, where ownership is typically registered with the issuer's agent and payment is effected by check from the agent. The bearer bond form permits tax-exempts to be exchanged among investors while owners remain anonymous to the issuer.

Most new issues of tax-exempt securities are sold to **underwriting syndicates.** In recent years, the Commonwealth of Massachusetts and a small number of municipalities have sold small amounts of bonds directly to investors. Private placements with institutional investors are somewhat rare in the tax-exempt market, and most of the privately placed issues in recent years have been related to New York City and New York State agencies.

Underwriters may be commercial banks or investment bankers, and syndicates may range in size from a single firm to as many as 100 firms. Under the Banking Act of 1933 (the **"Glass-Steagall Act"**), commercial banks are prohibited from underwriting most revenue bond issues. Underwriters serve as important intermediaries between the governmental units that issue securities and the investors who purchase them. The syndicate purchases the entire issue from the issuer and then attempts to resell the bonds to investors. Issuers can select underwriters in two ways: by **competitive bidding** or by **negotiated underwritings.** As noted in Exhibit 6, most general obligation issues are sold by competitive bidding, and most revenue bonds are sold by negotiation. As discussed later in this section, general obligations are secured by the full faith and credit and taxing power of the governmental unit, whereas revenue bonds are limited obligations secured by special user charges, not by general taxing power.

Under the competitive bidding method, issuers solicit bids from competing underwriting syndicates and award the bonds to the syndicate with the lowest interest cost bid. Under negotiation, an underwriting syndicate is selected well in advance of the sale date, and the terms of the bond issue are negotiated between the issuer and the syndicate.

While there are common services performed by underwriters regardless of which method of sale is used, there are important differences in the **level** of services provided by underwriters. These differences can be discussed under the three primary functions performed by underwriters: **origination services, risk bearing,** and **distribution.**

Origination services generally refer to the range of presale activities necessary to prepare a bond issue for the market. Under competitive bidding, the issuer carries out most of these activities, sometimes with the assistance of an outside financial advisor. Thus in a competitive offering, the issuing governmental unit determines the number of serial bond maturities and the final maturity for the bond issue, the par amounts of principal for each maturity, call features, and other components of the bonds. The issuer takes the responsibility of securing

EXHIBIT 5   DESCRIPTION OF $300 MILLION BOND OFFERING BY THE STATE OF OREGON

New issue   June 4, 1980

Interest on the bonds is exempt from present federal income taxes and tax exempt in the State of Oregon.[a]

These Veterans' Welfare Bonds, Series LXIII, in the opinion of counsel, are valid and legally binding general obligations of the State of Oregon.

Offering scale ($5,000 denominations)   Dated July 1, 1980

Noncallable prior to maturity.

Amount	Due	Rate (%)	Yield (%) or Price
$10,000,000	Jan. 1, 1994	20	7.40
20,000,000	Jan. 1, 1995	7.30	@100
20,000,000	Jan. 1, 1996	7.40	@100
20,000,000	Jan. 1, 1997	7.50	7.55
10,000,000	July 1, 1997	7.50	7.55
10,000,000	Jan. 1, 1998	7.70	@100
10,000,000	July 1, 1998	7.70	@100
10,000,000	Jan. 1, 1999	7.80	@100
10,000,000	July 1, 1999	7.80	@100
10,000,000	Jan. 1, 2000	8.00	@100
10,000,000	July 1, 2000	8.00	@100
10,000,000	Jan. 1, 2001	8.00	@100
10,000,000	July 1, 2001	8.00	@100
10,000,000	Jan. 1, 2002	8.00	@100
10,000,000	July 1, 2002	8.00	@100
10,000,000	Jan. 1, 2003	8.10	@100
10,000,000	July 1, 2003	8.10	@100
10,000,000	Jan. 1, 2004	8.20	@100
10,000,000	July 1, 2004	8.20	@100
10,000,000	Jan. 1, 2005	8.25	@100
10,000,000	July 1, 2005	8.25	@100
10,000,000	Jan. 1, 2006	8.25	8.30
10,000,000	July 1, 2006	8.25	8.30
10,000,000	Jan. 1, 2007	8.25	8.30
10,000,000	July 1, 2007	8.25	8.30
10,000,000	Jan. 1, 2008	8.00	8.30
10,000,000	July 1, 2008	8.00	8.30

[a]Accrued interest to be added.

a credit rating from one of the bond rating agencies; the issuer also prepares an official statement or prospectus of information necessary for underwriters and investors to gauge the investment merits of the bonds. In a competitive sale, the official notice of sale provides prospective underwriters with the necessary information on the date and time of bond sale and other terms on which the bids will be evaluated. The winning underwriter specifies the coupons and yields necessary to market the bonds and the total dollar amount to be paid to the issuer for the bond issue. In a negotiated sale, the underwriter works closely with the

EXHIBIT 6   NEW TAX-EXEMPT BOND SALES BY TYPE OF OFFERING, 1978 ($ MILLIONS)

Type of Offering	General Obligation		Revenue Bonds	
	Number	Amount	Number	Amount
Competitive bid	2,951	$13,686	743	$ 7,640
Negotiation	322	3,248	1,343	21,043
Private placement	11	819	186	1,576

Source: Public Securities Association, *Statistical Yearbook,* 1978.

issuer in carrying out many of these presale activities and the costs of these services are often incorporated in the compensation paid to underwriters.

Underwriters also provide risk-bearing services. Risk-bearing services are needed because once the issue has been purchased at a fixed price from the issuer, the underwriting syndicate faces uncertainty over the price at which these securities can be marketed to investors. This is basically an **inventory risk,** and underwriters expect compensation for incurring this risk. For negotiated issues, however, this risk should be lower than for competitive issues. The negotiated method of sale involves the underwriter in the early stages of a bond issue and enables the underwriter to engage in substantial **presale marketing** efforts. While presale marketing can and does take place in a competitive sale, there is much less incentive for underwriters to perform these services not knowing whether they will win or lose in the bidding.

Distribution services include the costs involved in selling and delivering bonds to investors and these transaction services are largely independent of the method of sale, be it competitive or negotiated.

The compensation received by underwriters is termed the **spread,** which is the difference between the price at which bonds are sold to investors and the price received by the issuer of the bonds. This underwriting spread typically ranges between 1 and 2% of the total par value of the issue, or $10–$20 per $1,000 bond. This total or gross spread is usually divided among four purposes. First, expenses incurred by underwriters for legal fees, advertising, travel expenses, and computer costs are deducted from the spread; Second, the managing underwriters receive a **management fee** as compensation for organizing and structuring the actual syndicate operations. The third and generally the largest component of the spread is the **concession,** which is paid to underwriters and dealers and their salespeople for actual selling effort. Finally, the **underwriting profit** is distributed among the syndicate members in proportion to the participation of each firm. Exhibit 7 provides an approximate breakdown of the components of an underwriting spread for a $20 million bond issue.

Underwriting spreads vary on different bond issues, reflecting differences in market conditions and in issue and issuer characteristics. Generally, spreads are higher (1) the more volatile the market conditions at the time of sale, (2) the greater the credit risk associated with the issue or issuer, and (3) the smaller the total bond size. Underwriting spreads are also generally higher on negotiated sales, reflecting in part the added services provided.

In negotiated bond sales, the underwriting spread is generally taken in the form of a discount from par value. That is, coupons are placed on each bond maturity such that given the yields required by investors, the bonds will be priced (or reoffered) at par. By convention,

EXHIBIT 7   COMPONENTS OF UNDERWRITING SPREAD FOR A $20 MILLION TAX-EXEMPT BOND ISSUE

Component	Amount per $1,000 Bonds	Total
Expenses	$2.00	$ 40,000
Management fee	4.00	80,000
Selling concession	7.50	150,000
Underwriting profit	1.50	30,000
	$15.00	$300,000

prices are typically quoted if bonds were issued in $100 units. Thus a price of par is quoted as $100. Bonds are typically issued in $5,000 denominations. After deducting the spread, the underwriter pays the issuer a total price below par.

In competitive sales, coupons on the bond issue are typically set to result in an aggregate reoffering price for the entire bond issue that is above par value, and after deduction of the underwriting spread, the issuer receives a total dollar value equal to or slightly above par value.

Most competitive sales are awarded to the underwriting syndicate that specifies the **lowest net interest cost** to the issuer. The **net interest cost** (NIC) method of awarding bonds:

is primarily a measure of the scheduled total dollar coupon interest payments over the life of the serial bond issue. It simply is the sum of the coupon payments that have to be made in each year, plus or minus the dollar amount by which the proposed purchase price (from the underwriter exceeds or falls short of, respectively, the aggregate par value of the issue. (Hopewell and Kaufman, *Improving Bidding Rules to Reduce Interest Costs in the Competitive Sale of Municipal Bonds: A Handbook for Municipal Finance Officers,* p. 13.)

Under the NIC method, the interest payments are equally weighted in calculating the interest rate of the bond issue; that is, a dollar of interest paid in 1 year is given the same weight as a dollar of interest paid in 40 years. In this sense, the NIC method ignores the time value (or present value) of interest payments. One result of this practice is that some bond issues carry high coupons in short maturities and lower coupons on longer maturities. Exhibit 8 provides an example of these **"coupon strategies"** for a $35 million bond issue by Albany County, New York, in 1978. For this issue, higher coupons (e.g., 7%) are placed on the short-term maturity, while lower coupon rates (5.5%) are placed on the long-term maturities. Yields to investors, on the other hand, increase with maturity, ranging from 4.90% on the 1979 maturity to 6.85% on the 2000 maturity. As a result of the coupon-yield relationship, short-term maturities are priced at premiums, while long-term maturities are priced as discounts below par. This practice is inefficient on several grounds. First, **discount bonds** generally carry **"penalty" yields** to compensate investors for the fact that the capital gain (the difference between par value and the purchase price) is taxable. Second, this practice "front loads" the total interest payments and raises the present value cost of borrowing. An analysis of these practices for bonds issued in 1973 estimated that the added borrowing costs may have exceeded $20 million.

EXHIBIT 8   MATURITIES, COUPON RATES, AND REOFFER YIELDS FOR $35 MILLION BOND ISSUE SOLD BY ALBANY COUNTY, NEW YORK, AUGUST 22, 1978

Principal Maturities ($ Millions)	Year	Coupon Rate (%)	Reoffer Yield to Investors (%)
$1,300	1979	7.80	4.90
1,300	1980	7.00	5.10
1,400	1981	7.00	5.25
1,400	1982	7.00	5.40
1,400	1983	7.00	5.50
1,400	1984	7.00	5.60
1,500	1985	7.00	5.70
1,500	1986	7.00	5.80
1,500	1987	7.00	5.90
1,500	1988	7.00	6.00
1,550	1989	7.00	6.10
1,550	1990	7.00	6.20
1,600	1991	6.30	6.25
1,650	1992	6.30	6.30
1,650	1993	6.30	6.35
1,650	1994	6.30	6.40
1,650	1995	6.50	6.45
1,900	1996	6.50	6.50
1,900	1997	6.50	6.55
1,900	1998	6.50	6.60
1,900	1999	5.50	6.85
1,900	2000	5.50	6.85

THE SECONDARY MARKET FOR TAX-EXEMPT SECURITIES

After new issues have been sold, trades are conducted in the secondary market, which is an "over-the-counter" market. While government units are most concerned with achieving the lowest borrowing costs possible at the date the bond issue is sold, efficient secondary markets are necessary to achieve low costs in the new issue market.

To investors, the ability to convert bonds into cash prior to final maturity is important from the standpoint of portfolio flexibility. To underwriters, the breadth of the secondary market for an issue is a determinant of the risk involved in distributing a new issue, and this risk is reflected in the underwriting spread and in the net interest cost to municipalities. For borrowers, a secondary market that provides investors with liquidity throughout the maturity range facilitates the sale of securities with longer final maturities than would otherwise be possible; this permits borrowers to hedge against future changes in interest rates, to some extent, by matching debt maturities to the useful life of capital assets.

The most comprehensive source of information on volume and activity in this market is the **Blue List of Current Municipal Offerings,** a daily financial publication that carries a listing of bonds offered for sale by dealers and banks. Approximately 700 securities dealers participate in the secondary market, ranging from large investment banking firms and commercial banks to small local or regional securities firms. In recent years, the average daily volume of bonds listed for sale in the Blue List has ranged between $700 million and $900 million in par value.

THE MUNICIPAL SECURITIES RULEMAKING BOARD

For the most part, the tax-exempt market has remained free from the widespread regulation that encompasses the corporate securities market. While transactions in tax-exempt securities have historically fallen under the umbrella of the general antifraud provisions of the federal securities laws, there never has been specific authority to regulate or otherwise control the reporting of information by the issuers of tax-exempt securities.

In 1975, however, the Securities Acts Amendments passed by Congress established an independent self-regulatory organization, the **Municipal Securities Rulemaking Board.** This agency was created as a response to the growing evidence of improper and unethical practices in the secondary market trading and selling of securities. Under the Securities Acts Amendments, the Board is required to adopt rules of conduct for market professionals, including standards for professional qualification, rules of fair practice, and record keeping, compliance examinations, quotations of municipal securities, and certain underwriting practices. Although the Board is an independent organization, its rules are subject to approval by the Securities and Exchange Commission and carry the force of law.

SECURITY FEATURES OF SHORT-TERM TAX-EXEMPT SECURITIES

Although market convention attempts to encapsulate the wide variety of tax-exempt securities into the broad categories of general obligations and revenue bonds, there are important distinctions recognized by credit analysts. Exhibit 9 provides a breakdown of short-term tax-exempt notes into five categories.

URBAN RENEWAL PROJECT NOTES.   These short-term issues are sold by local urban renewal agencies to provide funds for urban redevelopment projects. As described by one source:

> Although the Notes are obligations of Local Public Agencies, they are secured by a pledge of the proceeds of the loan which the United States Government has agreed to make pursuant to a loan and grant contract with a Local Public Agency. The Housing Act of 1961 amended Section 102(c) of the Housing Act of 1949 to authorize the execution of a Payment Agreement obligating the United States to pay or cause to be paid the principal of and interest on such obligations at maturity. The unqualified Payment Agreement setting forth the obligations of the United States is endorsed on each Project Note. Under the 1949 Act, as amended, the Payment Agreement is required to be construed by all officers of the United States separate and apart from the loan contract and is incontestable in the hands of the bearer. The funds which ultimately repay the temporary loans for urban renewal projects evidenced by Project Notes are derived from the proceeds of the sale of land in the urban renewal area and the provision of the Federal capital grant. (First Boston Corporation, *Handbook of Securities of the United States Government and Federal Agencies,* FBC, New York, 1978, p. 107.)

LOCAL HOUSING AUTHORITY NOTES.   These obligations of public housing agencies are centrally marketed through competitive sealed-bid auctions conducted by the U.S. Department of Housing and Urban Development (HUD). The security for these notes is an

EXHIBIT 9   SHORT-TERM TAX-EXEMPT NOTES, NEW ISSUES, 1978

Type	Volume ($ Millions)
Urban renewal	$ 1,062
Local housing authority	9,119
TANs and RANs	5,973
BANs	3,139
Other	2,091
	$21,384

Source: Data files of the Public Securities Association.

agreement between the local authority and HUD, whereby the government unconditionally agrees to make a loan to the local authority in an amount sufficient to pay the principal of and interest on the notes to maturity.

TAX ANTICIPATION NOTES (TANs) AND REVENUE ANTICIPATION NOTES (RANs).   Basically analogous to working capital loans, these obligations provide a cash flow bridge between nonsynchronous revenues and expenditures. In a number of governmental units, revenues tend to be realized during one or two concentrated periods of the fiscal year. Property taxes, for example, are often payable annually, semiannually, or quarterly as are such aid payments from other units of government as state aid to schools. Expenditures, on the other hand, tend to be more evenly spaced over the fiscal year. Thus notes payable from anticipated taxes (TANs) or other revenues including state aid (RANs) have become accepted means of financing periodic cash shortages over the fiscal year.

BOND ANTICIPATION NOTES (BANs).   Where legally permitted, these instruments are used to finance periodic construction work-in-progress payments. The use of BANs in this fashion can provide short-term funds for interim contract expenditures until projects are completed and final costs are estimated. Normally, BANs are retired through the issuance of long-term bonds. Thus, by contrast with TANs and RANs, BANs depend upon access to long-term bond markets for repayment. As summarized by one analyst:

> Market access is determined by two factors. One is the inherent quality of the loan in terms of ordinary debt structure criteria; this is a debtor characteristic controlled by the legal security, financial condition, and so on, of the borrower and is determinable by investor and analyst alike from data relating particularly to that borrower and instrument. The other determinant of market access is the condition of the market and its ability and willingness to meet the particular demand. (Smith, *The Appraisal of Municipal Credit Risk*, p. 102.)

It is noteworthy that the recent crises of municipal credit have been dramatized by failures associated with short-term debt issues. In February 1975, the New York State Urban Development Corporation, a state authority, defaulted on a BAN issue when it fell due. This default was occasioned by the unwillingness of the market to accept long-term bond issues backed by project revenues of dubious magnitude. **New York City** followed suit with a de facto default on notes maturing in late 1975. In the case of New York City, short-term borrowing had been used to fund years of operating deficits, as an alternative to increased taxes or reduced expenditures. The **City of Cleveland** defaulted on note issues in 1978 when investor concern about that city's credit quality and financial practices closed the door to further bond financing.

SECURITY FEATURES OF LONG-TERM BONDS

GENERAL OBLIGATIONS.   As defined by Wade Smith, dean of municipal bond analysts, the term "general obligation bond" should be reserved for bond issues with the following attributes:

> . . . First, it is the obligation of a governmental unit with the power to buy and collect taxes and is repayable, initially or ultimately, from the general revenues provided from such taxes as well as from other available revenues; and second, it is backed by a pledge of the full faith and credit of the issuer. (Smith, *The Appraisal of Municipal Credit Risk,* p. 140.)

In most instances, general obligations of local governmental units are backed by the ability of the city to levy **ad valorem** taxes on all taxable real property without limit. These bonds may be more completely described as **full faith and credit, unlimited-tax general obligations.**

Other tax-supported bonds can be described as limited-tax general obligation bonds. In some instances, the tax limit may be a general limit on the amount of tax levy for any governmental purpose; in other cases, the tax limit may apply specifically to levies for debt service payments. If, however, the debt also carries a pledge of the full faith and credit of the governmental issuer, revenues other than taxes may also be used to meet principal and interest payments, and these debts would be appropriately labeled full faith and credit, limited-tax general obligations.

SPECIAL ASSESSMENT BONDS.   In some jurisdictions, street paving and lighting, sewage lines, and other "neighborhood" improvements are constructed by the municipality but paid for by the residents in the form of special assessments. The improvements involve a substantial cost and carry useful benefits over future periods. Financing such improvements in a lump-sum outlay could create unexpected hardships on many residents. Therefore, the municipality may issue bonds to finance construction and pledge the special assessments as the source of funds for repayment. In effect, the municipality is issuing the debt on behalf of the residents who benefit. When such bonds are secured solely by the assessments levied against specific dwellings, the bonds are called **special assessment limited-liability bonds.** These bonds are not general obligations of the entire municipality, and the full faith and credit pledge is not applied.

REVENUE BONDS.   The distinguishing characteristic of the broad class of bonds commonly referred to as revenue bonds is that such debts are payable solely from revenue received from the users or beneficiaries of the projects financed. Here, the liability of the governmental issuer is limited, and neither the full faith and credit nor the general taxing power of the issuer is pledged as security.

Historically, one of the common uses of the revenue bond security has been to finance capital outlays of municipally owned utility systems. These utilities provide, for example, the generation, transmission, and distribution of electricity and water supply. These **utility revenue bonds** are repaid from charges to customers of the utility systems.

Also classified under the heading of revenue bonds are securities paid from the collection of special taxes. One relatively common application of the **limited-liability special tax bond** is used to finance state highway construction. State highway bonds are frequently designed to be repaid solely from the proceeds of motor fuel taxes or motor vehicle taxes levied by the states. Other examples of special taxes that have been pledged from time to time as revenues to secure bond issues include general sales taxes, excise taxes, including cigarette taxes, severance taxes, and utility taxes.

Revenue bonds are also used to finance other enterprise-type projects owned or operated by governmental units. Examples include regional sewage and solid waste disposal facilities, parking garages, bridges, tunnels, ports and airports, hospitals and other health-related facilities, and state university dormitories. Fees and user charges for services provided furnish the primary revenues available for meeting bond principal and interest payments.

Lease-rental and **mortgage-backed revenue bonds** represent a newer and rapidly growing form of tax-exempt bond financing. Under the lease-rental approach, public borrowing entities issue tax-exempt bonds and use the proceeds to construct facilities that are then leased to other governmental units, to nonprofit corporations, or to private enterprises. Under the lease agreement, lease-rental payments are pledged to fully cover the borrower's debt service requirements.

Mortgage revenue bonds are issued by state housing finance agencies, by local housing agencies, and by cities and counties. The bond proceeds are used to purchase pools of mortgages, and mortgage loan repayments are scheduled to meet the debt service requirements on the tax-exempt bond issues.

In a number of instances, the security features of both general obligations and revenue bonds are combined in one bond issue, creating what is sometimes referred to as a **double-barreled obligation.** In this type of financing, bond repayment is typically designed to be met first from specific user charges or fees levied on the direct beneficiaries of the facilities. However, to enhance the credit quality of the security, the bonds also carry a general obligation pledge of the governmental issuer. In this type of financing, the general revenues of the governmental unit serve as supplemental resources to be called upon in the event that shortfalls occur from the primary revenue stream.

A number of other public projects are financed by special purpose authorities organized solely for the delivery of a specific service or function to other governmental units. The authorities issue revenue bonds through which the revenues to retire debt are generated under long-term contracts for services provided to other governmental units. Although the issuing authority itself may not have general taxing power and may pledge only revenues derived from the service contracts, the contracts are often general obligations of the participating governmental units. These arrangements appropriately define an **indirect general obligation bond.**

CHANGING TRENDS IN SECURITY FEATURES

Parallel to the growth in volume and size of new issues have been equally significant changes in the forms and instruments used to raise funds from the tax-exempt market. Exhibit 10 records new bond sales by the type of pledge promised to bondholders and the sources of funds used to meet debt service (principal and interest) payments.

EXHIBIT 10   NEW BOND ISSUES BY TYPE OF SECURITY

	All	General Obligation	Revenue
1966	11,078,506	6,802,004	4,276,502
1967	14,405,352	8,944,606	5,460,746
1968	16,319,507	9,275,329	7,044,178
1969	11,702,028	7,735,674	3,966,354
1970	18,082,509	11,851,771	6,230,738
1971	24,929,063	15,218,492	9,710,571
1972	23,692,402	13,329,018	10,363,384
1973	23,821,477	12,169,799	11,651,678
1974	23,584,809	13,126,341	10,458,468
1975	30,659,442	15,974,335	14,685,087
1976	35,415,683	18,200,098	17,215,585
1977	46,705,886	18,118,339	28,587,547
1978	48,189,731	17,789,591	30,400,140

Source: Data files of the Public Securities Association.

A new tax-exempt bond issue most frequently used to be a **tax-supported** obligation of a general unit of government (state, city, school district, etc.). In the 1960s, over 60% of all new issues depended on tax support for repayment. By 1977 and 1978, however, tax-supported new issues had declined to less than 40 of all new bonds sold. As Exhibit 10 demonstrates, governmental units have turned increasingly to the revenue bond whereby debt repayments are linked to specific user charges, special taxes, or other nongeneral tax revenues. Revenue bonds now account for more than 60 of all new issues, amounting to $30.4 billion in 1978.

Many factors explain the decline of the tax-supported bond and the concomitant growth of the limited-liability revenue bond, including (*a*) the steady widening of public purpose to include special "enterprise-type projects," (*b*) the constraints imposed by statutory or constitutional limits on tax-supported debt, and (*c*) concern for equity, that is, the demand that the costs of projects or facilities be borne by the beneficiaries through user charges. One factor important in the shift to revenue bond financing is the reluctance by voters to approve new debt burdens.

Exhibit 11 traces the trend of bond election results over a 28-year period. Most general obligation bonds, but fewer revenue bonds, must pass the test of voter approval through referendum. This stamp of approval has often been cited as one source of strength behind the tax-supported bond. But, as the data in Exhibit 11 show, voter approval has become less certain. In the 1950s, more than 80% of new bond elections were routinely approved; by the early 1960s, this had declined to 75%. In the 1966–1970 period, only 62% of all proposed issues were agreed to by voters, and in the 1971–1976 period, the approval rate declined further, to slightly over 50% of bond elections.

One consequence of the taxpayer resistance evidenced through the bond election results is that a rapidly shrinking proportion of new bonds sold have first been ratified by the general public. Exhibit 11 points this out by relating approved issues to total new issues sold over this period. As noted, between 1966 and 1970, the ratio of approved issues to actual volume sold was 46%. Between 1971 and 1976, approvals amounted to 23% of new issues, and in 1977–1978, bonds passing election amounted to less than 15% of all issues sold.

EXHIBIT 11   BOND ELECTION RESULTS, 1951–1978

	Approved			
	Amount ($ Millions)	Amount of All Bond Elections (%)	Total Bond Sales ($ Millions)	Ratio of Bonds Approved to Bond Sales
1978	$8,413	63	$48,190	17.5
1977	5,437	61	46,706	11.6
1976	5,087	59	33,845	15.0
1975	3,392	29	29,326	11.6
1974	8,021	62	22,824	35.1
1973	6,036	52	22,953	27.5
1972	7,876	64	22,941	34.3
1971	3,143	35	24,370	12.9
1970	5,366	63	17,762	30.2
1969	4,287	40	11,460	37.4
1968	8,686	54	16,374	53.0
1967	7,365	74	14,288	51.5
1966	6,516	77	11,084	58.8
1965	5,612	73	10,544	50.6
1964	5,715	78	10,107	54.2
1963	3,627	63	8,558	35.9
1962	4,264	70	8,380	49.8
1961	2,544	67	7,230	30.4
1960	5,917	85	7,681	31.8
1959	2,753	72	7,449	35.8
1958	3,728	75	6,958	50.0
1957	2,733	77	5,446	39.3
1956	4,642	87	5,977	85.2
1955	2,886	65	6,969	48.3
1954	2,782	84	5,558	39.9
1953	1,852	83	4,401	33.3
1952	2,384	84	3,278	54.2
1951	2,250	88		68.6

Source: The Daily Bond Buyer, Municipal Finance Statistics, June 1978.

CHANGING PURPOSES FOR PUBLIC DEBTS

Additional perspectives on the dynamic uses of tax-exempt financing can be gained from a survey of the changing uses for public debt. Long-term financing through the bond market is a derived demand—it depends on the scope and purpose of the capital projects deemed necessary by governmental units and their constituents.

Capital expenditures and bonded debt sales reflect the interactions of several fundamental forces. Population growth carries with it the need for additional basic government services—education, public safety, transportation, and general administration. Rising standards of living also tend to raise expectations of the role of government in filling certain social welfare goals such as adequate housing, improved facilities and opportunities for health treatment and higher education, and other amenities such as parks and forest preserves. At some point, older capital facilities become obsolete and worn out and need to be replaced, so that an ever-increasing public capital base generates a continuing need for replacement capital. Finally, the trends in public capital spending mirror the changing forces at work in the overall economy: a notable example can be drawn from the current concern for environmental integrity and the growth of wastewater treatment and other pollution control facilities. The dynamics of these forces are reflected in the shifting purposes for which public debt is issued. Exhibit 12 records these trends. New debt issued for the "traditional" purposes of education, highways, and water and sewerage facilities has declined markedly, from 51% of the 1966–1970 market to 20.5% of the 1977–1978 market. The receding significance of these traditional uses for public debt is directly traceable to the abrupt slowdown in population growth and to the gradual completion of the interstate highway network.

But new areas for growth have more than taken up any slack created by the diminished need for traditional projects. Among these, bonds sold to meet social welfare goals have mushroomed. Social welfare projects, including housing, hospital and health facilities, and recreation facilities, accounted for over 21% of all new issues in 1977–1978, up from 7.2% of the 1966–1970 market.

Other uses of public credit, typically financed as revenue bonds, have increased in volume and proportion. Utility financing has more than doubled and accounted for over 10% of the market in 1977–1978. Many of these utility bond issues are among the most complex and specialized financings ever devised. Some, for example, involve joint undertakings between one public entity or a collection of municipalities and one or more private firms. Several projects involve the construction of entire new utility systems, including ancillary capital facilities such as railroad cars and other features of the vertically integrated system.

Exhibit 12 also points out that industrial aid bonds, including pollution control facilities, accounted for more than $9 billion in 1977–1978. These issues, which benefit private corporations, accounted for 9.5% of the market in 1977–1978, which is nearly double the 4.9% market share recorded in 1966–1970. Many of the new financings were formerly conducted in the taxable market from conventional lending sources. These trends demonstrate

EXHIBIT 12   TAX-EXEMPT NEW ISSUES CLASSIFIED BY USE OF PROCEEDS

Use of Proceeds	1966–1970		1971–1976		1977–1978	
	Volume	%	Volume	%	Volume	%
Education						
Elementary and secondary	19,533	21.7	25,799	12.2	6,584	6.9
Higher education and other	7,066	7.8	12,077	5.7	3,443	3.6
Highway transportation	10,033	11.1	12,447	5.9	2,896	3.1
Water and sewer	9,680	10.7	18,057	8.5	6,571	6.9
Electric, gas, other utility	3,909	4.3	25,714	12.2	9,695	10.2
Housing	1,639	1.8	13,794	6.5	9,391	9.9
Hospitals and health facilities	3,108	3.4	15,038	7.1	8,212	8.7
Parks, civic centers, etc.	1,763	2.0	5,372	2.5	2,401	2.5
Ports, airports, other transportation	6,958	7.7	9,500	4.5	3,532	3.7
Industrial aid (including pollution control)	4,387	4.9	13,600	6.4	9,036	9.5
Refunding, advance refunding	> N.A.	<	> N.A.	<	21,234	22.4
Multipurpose and all other	22,037	24.6	60,537	28.6	11,902	12.5
	90,113	100	211,395	100	94,896	100

Source: Data files maintained by the Public Securities Association.

that the concept of public purpose can be creatively defined to the point that such well-known corporations as U.S. Steel, and such diverse projects as shopping centers, branch banks, and catfish farms, have been included in the tax-exempt market.

Industrial aid bonds are tax-exempt bonds sold by state and local governmental units to finance facilities rented or leased by private businesses. The use of public credit to finance private purposes in this manner dates back to the 1930s and represents a type of subsidy that has often been rationalized as necessary to stimulate private economic development. In the present capital markets, the main incentive lies in the lower cost of tax-exempt financing when compared to taxable financing. Under the Internal Revenue Code (Section 103), tax-exempt bonds for these purposes are essentially limited to $12 million per project or facility; bonds sold to finance pollution control facilities are permitted without limit as to size.

TRENDS IN BOND SALES BY TYPE OF ISSUER

Exhibit 13 traces other changes in the tax-exempt market by classifying new bond sales by type of issuer. It is noteworthy that the proportion of bonds sold by general units of government—states, counties, municipalities, townships, and school districts—has declined, while the volume of debt raised by special districts and statutory authorities has increased. Nationally, the proportion of debt sold by general governmental units has fallen from 68% of all issues in 1966–1970 to 61% in 1971–1976 and 52% in 1977–1978. The increasing share of financing carried out by special purpose statutory authorities is one consequence of the broadened definition of public purpose. Statutory authorities also permit enterprise-type activities to be conducted with substantial autonomy and freedom from partisan politics.

EVALUATING CREDIT RISK AND CREDIT QUALITY

Although the value of tax-exempt income weighs most heavily in investors' decisions, other factors are important in determining which securities will be purchased or sold and what interest rate will be required. Important among these factors is an assessment of the relative risks on different securities. The risk arises because investors are purchasing claims on the future revenues of issuers of tax-exempt debts, and these future revenues cannot be known with certainty.

EXHIBIT 13   NEW BOND SALES CLASSIFIED BY ISSUER, 1966–1978

Type of Issuer	1966–1970		1971–1976		1977–1978	
	Amount ($ Millions)	% of Total	Amount ($ Millions)	% of Total	Amount ($ Millions)	% of Total
States	20,975	23.3	46,548	21.9	12,985	13.7
Counties	7,687	8.5	16,501	7.8	8,273	8.7
Municipalities	21,663	24.0	28,852	23.0	21,791	22.9
School districts	11,356	12.6	17,350	8.2	6,012	6.3
Special districts	4,772	5.3	9,673	4.6	5,082	5.5
Statutory authorities	23,645	26.2	72,987	34.4	40,755	42.9

Source: Based on data files of the Securities Industry Association.

The task for credit analysis is to collect and evaluate all relevant information in a timely fashion, so that the probable levels of future cash flows can be systematically evaluated and the likelihood of future payments difficulties can be estimated in advance.

Although the most serious risk faced by lenders is the possibility that a tax-exempt issuer will be declared in default on its obligations, investors are also concerned with any potential deterioration in credit quality. The marketability and the liquidity of bond portfolios are strongly conditioned by even small unanticipated changes in the credit standing of issues and issuers. In general, credit analysis measures the level and the variability of future cash flows of the borrower. Analysis focuses on the likelihood that the stream of cash flows actually available to the bondholder will be different in timing or in amount from the cash flows originally promised when the security was issued.

The multiplicity of issuers of tax-exempt debt and the remarkably varied security features and revenue sources have given rise to intermediaries that specialize in the collection and dissemination of credit information. Foremost among these intermediaries are the bond rating agencies, and two agencies—**Moody's Investors Service** and **Standard & Poor's Corporation**—have become the dominant information brokers in the tax-exempt market.

As stated by Moody's:

> A municipal bond rating is a judgment of the investment quality of a long-term obligation issued by a state or one of its subdivisions. It is based on an analysis that must ask, first, what has the debtor pledged to pay and, second, what is the likelihood that he will be able to keep his promises. (Moody's Investors Service, *Pitfalls in Issuing Municipal Bonds*, p. 13.)

Exhibit 14 summarizes the symbols used by Moody's in assigning ratings to bond issues and Exhibit 15 provides summary data on the volume of new bond issues by rating class in 1978. As these data indicate, virtually all new issues that carry ratings have investment grade ratings in the top four letter grades.

Bond rating agencies and other credit analysts generally follow similar approaches to the evaluation of credit risk. For tax-supported bonds, the principal factors that are evaluated are: (1) the economic base of the issuer, (2) the financial condition of the governmental units, (3) administrative factors, and (4) the debt burden.

Economic base analysis defines the basic indicators of the community's capability to support governmental functions (revenue capacity), and it indicates the main determinants of public expenditures. Important indicators include the level and growth of incomes, employment mix, unemployment rates, the level and growth of taxable property, and trends in population.

A cash flow shortage is the ultimate signal of a financial emergency that may lead to debt payment difficulties. Hence the aim of financial analysis is to study trends and conditions in the financial statements that may warn of potential cash flow crises.

The importance of financial analysis is reinforced by the findings of a major study of municipal financial emergencies, which noted that:

> The review of financial operations of the cities revealed certain common characteristics for those on the brink of financial trouble. Most important among these characteristics were:
>
> **a.** An operating fund revenue-expenditure imbalance in which current expenditures significantly exceeded current revenues in one fiscal period.
>
> **b.** A consistent pattern of current expenditures exceeding current revenues by small amounts for several years.
>
> **c.** An excess of current operating liabilities over current assets (a fund deficit).

   d.   Short-term operating loans outstanding at the conclusion of a fiscal year (or in some instances the borrowing of cash from restricted funds or an increase in unpaid bills in lieu of short-term operating loans).

   e.   A high and rising rate of property tax delinquency.

   f.   A sudden substantial decrease in assessed values for unexpected reasons.

Several other general conditions can cause financial problems. One is the existence of an underfunded locally administered retirement system. Secondly, poor budgeting, accounting, and reporting techniques may be indicators of impending financial problems. In some cases, inadequate financial management techniques may actually cause trouble because of the uncertainties they create. [Advisory Commission on Intergovernmental Relations, *City Financial Emergencies: The Intergovernmental Dimension,* ACIR, Washington, D.C., July 1973, p. 4.]

Administrative factors relate principally to the tax assessment and collection system, budgeting practices, and the contingent costs of possible litigation.

The most meaningful measures of debt for credit analysis are net debt and overall debt. **Net debt** refers to the total long- and short-term debt supported by the general revenues of the issuer. **Overall debt** includes the outstanding debt of all other governmental units that tap the same tax base as security for their debt. Typically, both debt figures are stated in ratio form relative to the full value of taxable property. These debt ratios measure the burden of debt in relation to a standard measure of community wealth.

Although many of the same factors are reviewed in developing revenue bond ratings, the growth of enterprise-type activities requires credit analysts to become informed about "industry" trends, with the associated analysis of the supply and demand conditions appropriate to the "product" or business that is financed with the tax-exempt debt. The risks here are familiar to the commercial loan analyst and include:

   1.   Competition from new or improved products or services.

   2.   Obsolescence or problems of maintenance and capital replacement.

   3.   Shifts in demand due to changing economic or social factors.

   4.   Risks of poor management.

   5.   The risks that the supply of essential "raw materials" may not be available.

Moreover, analyzing the bonds of public financial intermediaries, which hold asset portfolios of other debt instruments such as mortgage loans, requires information on the credit quality of each loan in the portfolio. Analysis also requires some measure of the "systematic risks" of the overall portfolio. These systematic risks—factors common to each of the loans in the portfolio—determine the likelihood that a decline in creditworthiness for one loan will be followed by similar deterioration in other components of the portfolio.

Computerized models for assessing the **default risk of municipalities** have met with mediocre success, at best. These models attempt to combine multivariate statistical analysis with measures of municipality "health" to forecast impending problems early enough to alert authorities and initiate rehabilitative programs. Multivariate analysis involves the simultaneous investigation of several default indicators, with each indicator objectively weighted and combined to arrive at a type of **credit score.** The reason for the relatively poor performance of those models compared to consumer and commercial credit scoring models is more than likely found in the quality of the data utilized. A related area of municipality, multivariate application is in the classification of those entities into relative risk rankings as portrayed by Moody's Municipal Bond Ratings (Exhibit 14). Here too, the results have not been impressive.

Aaa

Bonds which are rated Aaa are judged to be of the best quality. They carry the smallest degree of investment risk and are generally referred to as "gilt edge." Interest payments are protected by a large or by an exceptionally stable margin and principal is secure. While the various protective elements are likely to change, such changes as can be visualized are most unlikely to impair the fundamentally strong position of such issues.

Aa

Bonds which are rated Aa are judged to be of high quality by all standards. Together with the Aaa group they comprise what are generally known as high grade bonds. They are rated lower than the best bonds because margins of protection may not be as large as in Aaa securities or fluctuation of protective elements may be of greater amplitude or there may be other elements present which make the long-term risks appear somewhat larger than in Aaa securities.

A

Bonds which are rated A possess many favorable investment attributes and are to be considered as upper medium grade obligations. Factors giving security to principal and interest are considered adequate, but elements may be present which suggest a susceptibility to impairment sometime in the future.

Baa

Bonds which are rated Baa are considered as medium grade obligations; i.e., they are neither highly protected nor poorly secured. Interest payments and principal security appear adequate for the present but certain protective elements may be lacking or may be characteristically unreliable over any great length of time. Such bonds lack outstanding investment characteristics and in fact have speculative characteristics as well.

Ba

Bonds which are rated Ba are judged to have speculative elements; their future cannot be considered as well-assured. Often the protection of interest and principal payments may be very moderate, and thereby not well safeguarded during both good and bad times over the future. Uncertainty of position characterizes bonds in this class.

B

Bonds which are rated B generally lack characteristics of the desirable investment. Assurance of interest and principal payments or of maintenance of other terms of the contract over any long period of time may be small.

Caa

Bonds which are rated Caa are of poor standing. Such issues may be in default or there may be present elements of danger with respect to principal or interest.

EXHIBIT 14   CONTINUED

Ca

Bonds which are rated Ca represent obligations which are speculative in a high degree. Such issues are often in default or have other marked shortcomings.

C

Bonds which are rated C are the lowest rated class of bonds, and issues so rated can be regarded as having extremely poor prospects of ever attaining any real investment standing.

CON (. . .)

Bonds for which the security depends upon the completion of some act or the fulfillment of some condition are rated conditionally. These are bonds secured by (a) earnings of projects under construction, (b) earnings of projects unseasoned in operating experience, (c) rentals which begin when facilities are completed, or (d) payments to which some other limiting condition attaches. Parenthetical rating denotes probable credit stature upon completion of construction or elimination of basis of condition.

Those bonds in the A and Baa groups which Moody's believes possess the strongest investment attributes are designated by the symbols A 1 and Baa 1.

Source: Moody's Investors Service, *Moody's Bond Record,* January 1980.

EXHIBIT 15   NEW TAX-EXEMPT BOND ISSUES CLASSIFIED BY MOODY'S RATING, 1978 ($ MILLIONS)

Rating	General Obligation	Revenue
Aaa	$3,886	$ 1,832
Aa	3,599	5,980
A	6,119	14,491
Baa	1,155	2,015
Ba and lower	—	21
Unrated	2,195	4,465

Source: Data files of the Public Securities Association.

GUARANTEED AND INSURED BONDS

Borrowing costs for municipalities are strongly influenced by investors' perceptions of the creditworthiness of the issuer and its debt issues. The underlying risk factors that describe the ability of the issuer to meet its debt service payments tend to be long lasting and to require fundamental changes that are difficult to implement in the short run. Therefore, a number of credit assistance programs have been developed to improve the credit strengths of the bond issue, rather than the issuer. State governments have been active in implementing these programs, and there are three types of direct credit assistance used by states to help local governments: **guarantees, state financial intermediation,** and **debt subsidies.**

In its simplest form, a state guarantee is an explicit promise by the state to an investor in its local governments' bonds that any shortfall in local resources will be automatically replenished by the state. In its strongest form, a state guarantee places the full faith and credit of the state behind the contingent call on state funds.

State financial intermediaries issue tax-exempt bonds and use the proceeds to make loans to local governments. One major purpose of the intermediary device is to achieve economies in the sale of bonds by pooling numerous small local debt issues into a larger bond issue designed to reach a national market. The best known example is the bond bank concept, which has been implemented in several states. The bonds of the bond bank are secured in the first instance by the loan repayments from local governments. Most state financial intermediaries also pledge some form of added state assistance often in the form of a **"moral obligation."** under the moral obligation pledge, the state indicates its intent to appropriate funds in the future if the financial intermediary is unable to meet its debt service commitments. While the moral obligation serves as an indicator of intent, claims supported by it are legally unenforceable in the event that future state legislatures fail to appropriate the needed funds.

A third type of state credit assistance consists of debt service subsidy payments to local governments. Such subsidy payments are typically restricted to meeting bond principal and interest payments and usually are made directly to the local unit, although they may be sent to the paying agent or bondholder under certain circumstances.

PRIVATE BOND INSURANCE

Unique to the tax-exempt bond market in comparison with the public market for corporate securities is the availability of bond insurance from private insurance companies. This bond insurance, which may be purchased by investors or by issuers, is designed to protect bond-holders from losses occasioned by the default on debt payments by a governmental unit. If defaults do occur on insured bonds, the insurance company promises to purchase the bonds at par from the investor. Depending on the type of insurance, premiums are paid by either the borrower or the investor at the time the policy is issued.

THE DEMAND FOR TAX-EXEMPT SECURITIES

The exemption of interest income from federal income taxes is of greatest appeal to institutions or individuals in high marginal income tax brackets. Exhibit 16 points out that three sectors—commercial banks, households, and property and casualty insurance companies—account for over 90% of the holdings of outstanding tax-exempt securities.

Exhibit 17 reports data on the net change in holdings of these three investment sectors for the period 1964–1978. As the data indicate, there is a considerable degree of volatility in the participation rate by banks, households, and property and casualty insurance companies.

For most of the period from 1964 to 1971, commercial bank demand dominated the market for tax-exempts as banks regularly accounted for more than 60% of all new tax-exempts. In two years, 1968 and 1970, bank demand accounted for more than 90% of the

EXHIBIT 16   HOLDINGS OF TAX-EXEMPT SECURITIES BY INVESTMENT SECTOR, YEAR-END 1978

	Amount ($ Billions)	% of Total
Commercial banks	$126.2	43.3
Households	75.0	25.7
Property and casualty insurance companies	62.5	21.4
State and local governments	12.3	4.2
Other financial institutions	11.7	4.0
Nonfinancial corporations	3.7	1.4
		100.0

Source: Board of Governors of the Federal Reserve System, Flow of Funds Statement, September 15, 1979.

net change in outstanding, and in 1967 banks absorbed more than the net new supply offered by governmental units.

Recently bank demand has been generally lower, both in dollar amount and as a percentage of net new issues. On average, over the period 1972–1978, commercial banks have accounted for 32% of the net change in outstanding tax-exempts.

Participation by the household sector has been equally volatile. In 1966, for example, household sector demand accounted for $3.6 billion, or 64% of net new issues; one year

EXHIBIT 17   NET CHANGE IN HOLDINGS OF TAX-EXEMPT SECURITIES, 1965–1978

	Commercial Banks		Households		Property and Casualty Insurance Companies		Total Change in Outstanding Tax-Exempts ($ Billions)
	Amount ($ Billions)	% of Total	Amount ($ Billions)	% of Total	Amount ($ Billions)	% of Total	
1964	3.6	60	2.6	43	0.4	7	6.0
1965	5.2	71	1.7	23	0.4	5	7.3
1966	2.3	41	3.6	64	1.3	23	5.6
1967	9.1	117	−2.2	−28	1.4	18	7.8
1968	8.6	91	−0.5	− 5	0.9	9	9.5
1969	0.6	6	9.3	94	1.1	11	9.9
1970	10.7	96	−0.9	− 8	1.5	13	11.2
1971	12.6	72	0.1	1	3.5	20	17.4
1972	7.2	49	2.3	16	4.3	29	14.7
1973	5.7	39	5.3	36	3.6	24	14.7
1974	5.5	33	8.2	50	2.2	13	16.5
1975	1.8	11	6.2	39	2.6	16	16.1
1976	3.0	19	2.5	16	5.4	34	15.7
1977	9.2	39	2.6	11	10.7	45	23.7
1978	9.6	34	3.3	12	13.1	46	28.3

Source: Board of Governors of the Federal Reserve System, Flow of Funds Statement, September 5, 1979.

later, on 1967, households liquidated tax-exempt holdings of $2.2 billion. Again, substantial increases in holdings (of $9.3 billion) in 1969 were followed by net liquidations of $900 million in 1970. Since 1970, it is noteworthy that households have not recorded any further years of net liquidations in tax-exempt holdings.

Demand for tax-exempts by property and casualty companies remained exceedingly modest during the 1964–1970 period, averaging less than $1 billion per year. Since 1970, however, there has been a distinct upward trend in demand by these insurance companies, and in 1977 and 1978 demand exceeded $10 billion per year and absorbed over 45% of net new issues.

For the two institutional buyers of tax-exempts (commercial banks and property and casualty companies), demand is primarily determined by profitability and liquidity levels, and only secondarily by the relative attractiveness of tax-exempt interest rates. As summarized in one recent econometric study:

> When these investors have large profits to shield from taxes, they invest heavily in tax-exempts. When profits are small, these investors reduce their purchases of tax-exempts even if tax-exempt interest rates rise, because the exemption is valuable only if there exist profits to be shielded from taxation at the full corporate tax rate. (Hendershott and Koch, *An Empirical Analysis of the Market for Tax-Exempt Securities: Estimates and Forecasts,* p. 11.)

Thus these institutions will not generally respond to short-run movements in interest rates in their demands for tax-exempts; rather, most of their purchases will be determined by factors other than the relative yields.

Therefore, after the needs of these institutions are satisfied, the remaining volume of new securities must be absorbed by the household sector. Studies of the demand for tax-exempts from households conclude that investment behavior from this sector is especially sensitive to changes in interest rates. As noted by Hendershott and Koch:

> Households do substitute between tax-exempt and taxable bonds on the basis of relative after-tax yields. Whenever the longer-term tax-exempt yield rises (falls) in relation to the comparable taxable yield, households increase (decrease) their holdings of tax-exempt bonds. (*An Empirical Analysis of the Market for Tax-Exempt Securities: Estimates and Forecasts,* p. 33.)

Households also compare equity yields with tax-exempt rates, although the extent of portfolio switching based on relative yields is considerably less significant.

Over reasonably short periods of time, the amount of income in high marginal tax brackets is basically fixed. Thus increases in the supply of tax-exempt securities in the short run will need to attract new buyers from the household sector. These buyers will be in lower tax brackets and will require somewhat higher yields to substitute tax-exempts for taxable securities.

THE BEHAVIOR OF TAX-EXEMPT INTEREST RATES

Interest rates on tax-exempt securities serve as measures of the cost of borrowing to issuers and of the rate of return to investors. The most important determinants of tax-exempt interest rates are market conditions, issuer characteristics and issue characteristics.

Exhibit 18 traces the average annual interest rate on Aaa-rated long-term, tax-exempt bonds over the period 1965–1979. Also presented, for comparison, is the Aaa-rated corporate

EXHIBIT 18   YIELDS (%) ON LONG-TERM TAX-EXEMPT AND TAXABLE BONDS, 1965–1979

	Aaa-Rated Tax-Exempts, General Obligations	Aaa-Rated Corporate Bonds	Yield Spread, Corporate– General Obligations	Break-Even Marginal Tax Rate[a]
1979	5.92	9.63	3.71	38.5
1978	5.52	8.73	3.21	36.8
1977	5.20	8.02	2.82	35.2
1976	5.65	8.43	2.78	32.9
1975	6.42	8.83	2.41	27.3
1974	5.89	8.57	2.68	31.3
1973	4.99	7.44	2.45	32.9
1972	5.04	7.21	2.17	30.0
1971	5.22	7.39	2.17	29.4
1970	6.12	8.04	1.92	23.9
1969	5.45	7.03	1.58	22.5
1968	4.20	6.18	1.98	32.0
1967	3.74	5.51	1.77	32.1
1966	3.67	5.13	1.46	28.5
1965	3.16	4.49	1.33	29.6

[a]The break-even marginal tax rate is the tax rate on corporate bonds that reduce the aftertax return to the same yield as the tax-exempt security.

Source: Moody's Investors Service, Moody's Bond Record, January 1980.

bond yield. As these data indicate, yields in both markets move in general concert, reflecting the impact of macroeconomic forces such as the level of economic activity and expectations of inflation. Thus yields in general have moved considerably higher in both markets over the past decade and a half, because of the significantly higher rate of inflation recorded over this period. Rates also evidence cyclical volatility, reflecting the periodic episodes of tight money market conditions. For example, in 1966, 1969–1970, and 1974–1975, tax-exempt rates jumped to considerably higher levels because of the "credit crunches" in these years.

Exhibit 18 also reports the **yield spread** between taxable and tax-exempt interest rates. The data point out that the interest cost advantage of tax-exempt financing has widened considerably over the past 15 years, expanding from 1.33 percentage points in 1965 to 3.71 percentage points in 1979.

The break-even marginal tax rate at which after tax yields on taxable bonds equal the tax-exempt bond rate also appears in Exhibit 18. This break-even tax rate is the lowest marginal tax rate at which investors would be indifferent, on the basis of yield alone, in the choice between tax-exempt and taxable securities. Expressed another way, investors who pay taxes at a marginal rate **higher** than this break-even rate would earn higher yields from tax-exempt securities. The equation that relates tax-exempt yields to aftertax equivalent yields on taxable securities is: $R_{TE} = R_{TX}(1 - TR)$

$$\text{where: } R_{TE} = \text{tax-exempt yield}$$
$$R_{TX} = \text{taxable yield}$$
$$TR = \text{marginal tax rate on income}$$

To demonstrate, if the taxable rate R_{TX} is 9% and the tax-exempt rate R_{TE} is 5.4%, the break-even marginal tax rate TR is 40% (5.4 = 9 × .4). For investors in the 50% tax bracket, a 9% taxable bond yields only 4.5% after taxes, which is less than the tax-exempt yield (5.4%).

The concept of the break-even marginal tax rate has played an important role in national policy debates over the efficiency and equity of tax exemption. In its principal focus, this debate begins by adopting the views that tax exemption is a form of interest subsidy permitted state and local governments, and simultaneously, it is a form of tax shelter for wealthy investors. Accordingly, since the stock of outstanding tax-exempt debt is held by investors who, on average, pay taxes at a marginal rate in excess of the break-even rate, these investors are receiving windfall gains at the expense of the federal treasury. This debate became particularly heated in 1969–1970 and 1975, when the break-even marginal tax rate was extremely low—below 30%. Indeed, during these period several proposals were introduced in Congress that would have substantively altered the access of state and local governments to tax-exempt financing and would have substituted direct federal interest rate subsidies. (For a summary of these proposals, see Ronald Forbes and John Petersen, *Building a Broader Market: Report of the Twentieth Century Fund Task Force on the Municipal Bond Market*.)

The break-even marginal tax rate has steadily increased since 1975, thereby deflating any current attempts to radically alter this market. Nevertheless, the issues remain alive and can be expected to surface if at some future date the yield spread between tax-exempt and taxable securities again narrows.

THE MATURITY STRUCTURE OF TAX-EXEMPT YIELDS

Exhibit 19 reports yields on high-quality tax-exempt bonds by maturity for two recent cyclical peaks in interest rates, 1974 and 1980, and one recent cyclical low in interest rates. Also presented in this table, for comparison, are yields by maturity for U.S. Treasury bonds. The

EXHIBIT 19   TAX-EXEMPT AND TAXABLE BOND YIELD CURVES FOR SELECTED PERIODS

	Yields on Selected Maturities			
	1 Year	5 Year	10 Year	20 Year
June 1974 Peak in Rates				
U.S. Treasuries	8.92	7.98	7.42	8.06
Prime municipals	5.00	5.10	5.25	5.60
January 1977 Trough				
U.S. Treasuries	4.82	6.16	6.79	7.16
Prime municipals	2.40	3.50	4.20	5.10
April 1980 Peak in Rates				
U.S. Treasuries	15.80	13.25	12.63	12.40
Prime municipals	8.20	8.20	8.25	8.75

Source: Salomon Brothers, *Analytical Record of Yields and Yield Spreads.*

most interesting feature of these data is that the yield-maturity relationship is typically positive in the tax-exempt market, even at cyclical peaks when the U.S. Treasury yield-maturity relationship is negative (when short-term yields are higher than long-term yields). In April 1980, for example, the yield spread between 20-year and 1-year tax-exempts was a positive 0.44 percentage point (8.75% − 8.20%), while the 20-year–1-year Treasury yield spread was a negative 3.40 percentage points (12.40% − 15.80%). The striking contrast in the behavior of the yield-maturity relationships is generally believed to result from a weakness in the relative demand for long-term, tax-exempt bonds and a residual uncertainty in the market over the long-run value of tax-exempt income.

Somewhat consistent with these views is the observation that while yield-maturity spreads widen in both markets at cyclical lows in interest rates, the spread remains larger in the tax-exempt market. In 1977, for example, the 20-year–1-year yield spread on U.S. Treasury securities widened to 2.34 percentage points, while the spread on tax-exempts widened to 2.70 percentage points. Evidently, when interest rates in general are declining, long-term tax-exempt rates tend to decline somewhat less rapidly.

TAX-EXEMPT YIELDS AND BOND RATINGS

Exhibit 20 traces tax-exempt bond yields for Aaa-rated and Baa-rated bonds over the period 1965–1979. As expected, perceived credit risks are important determinants of interest rates. The yield on Baa-rated bonds has consistently been higher than the yield on Aaa-rated bonds. The record in Exhibit 20 also points out that risk spreads tended to rise over this period, with a notable and dramatic jump in 1975 and 1976. The markedly higher yields on lower rated securities in these years is a direct consequence of the 1974–1975 recession and the financial collapse of New York City. The more recent record for 1977–1979 indicates that the legacy of this earlier period remains, as risk spreads continued to be well above the average for the years before 1975.

EXHIBIT 20   YIELDS (%) ON TAX-EXEMPT SECURITIES BY RATING, 1965–1979

	Aaa-Rated General Obligations	Baa-Rated General Obligations	Spread (Baa–Aaa)
1979	5.92	6.73	0.81
1978	5.52	6.27	0.75
1977	5.20	6.12	0.92
1976	5.65	7.49	1.84
1975	6.42	7.62	1.20
1974	5.89	6.53	0.64
1973	4.99	5.49	0.50
1972	5.04	5.60	0.56
1971	5.22	5.89	0.67
1970	6.12	6.75	0.63
1969	5.45	6.07	0.62
1968	4.20	4.88	0.68
1967	3.74	4.30	0.56
1966	3.67	4.21	0.54
1965	3.16	3.57	0.41

Source: Moody's Investors Service, *Moody's Bond Record.*

**EXHIBIT 21   AVERAGE ANNUAL YIELDS (%) ON
10-YEAR MATURITIES OF Aa-RATED GENERAL
OBLIGATION AND REVENUE BOND NEW ISSUES,
1966–1979**

	General Obligation	Revenue	Spread, Revenue–General Obligations
1966	3.62	3.85	0.23
1967	3.61	3.79	0.18
1968	4.00	4.14	0.14
1969	5.18	5.26	0.08
1970	5.28	5.32	0.04
1971	4.26	4.38	0.02
1972	4.29	4.34	0.05
1973	4.52	4.59	0.07
1974	5.23	5.68	0.45
1975	5.63	6.23	0.60
1976	5.11	5.46	0.35
1977	4.56	4.72	0.16
1978	5.05	5.32	0.27
1979	5.54	6.04	0.50

Source: Data files maintained by the Public Securities Association.

YIELDS ON GENERAL OBLIGATION AND REVENUE BONDS

The interest rates on particular bond issues depend on other factors in addition to general market levels and maturities. One systematic factor that is important is the type of security feature. Exhibit 21 reports the average annual yield on Aa-rated general obligations and revenue bonds over the 1966–1979 period. As the data indicate, revenue bonds have consistently carried higher yields than general obligations. Yield spreads narrowed significantly from 1966 until 1971, when the differential was virtually nonexistent. Since 1971, the yield spread has widened considerably, reaching one-half a percentage point by 1979.

The recent trend toward widened yield spreads on revenue bonds has occurred in tandem with a marked shift in the type of financing from tax-supported debt to revenue bonds. In addition to the added relative supply of revenue bonds, many of these new financings are highly complex. Thus the higher costs to investors of understanding and evaluating the new types of risk in the tax-exempt market may be translated into added interest rate costs on these securities.

REFERENCES

Aronson, J. K., and Schwartz, E., *Management Policies in Local Government Finance*, International City Management Association, Washington, D.C., 1975.

Hendershott, P. H., and Koch, T., "An Empirical Analysis of the Market for Tax-Exempt Securities: Estimates and Forecasts," Monograph Series in Finance and Economics, New York University, Graduate School of Business Administration, New York, 1977.

Hopewell, M., and Kaufman, G., *Improving Bidding Rules to Reduce Interest Costs in the Competitive Sale of Municipal Bonds: A Handbook for Municipal Finance Officers,* Center for Capital Market Research, University of Oregon, Eugene, 1977.

Moak, L., *Administration of Local Government Debt,* Municipal Finance Officers Association, Chicago, 1970.

Petersen, John, "Changing Conditions in the Market for State and Local Government Debt," Joint Economic Committee, U.S. Congress, 94th Congr., 1976.

Smith, W., *The Appraisal of Municipal Credit Risk,* Moody's Investors Service, New York, 1979.

Twentieth Century Fund Task Force on Municipal Bond Credit Ratings, *The Rating Game,* Twentieth Century Fund, New York, 1974.

————, *Building a Broader Market,* McGraw-Hill, New York, 1976.

DEFAULT RISK CLASSIFICATION STUDIES

Carleton, W., and Lerner, E., "Statistical Credit Scoring of Municipal Bonds," *Journal of Money, Credit and Banking,* November 1969.

Hempel, G., *Measures of Municipal Bond Quality,* University of Michigan Press, Ann Arbor, 1967.

————, "Quantitative Borrower Characteristics Associated with Defaults on Municipal General Obligations," *Journal of Finance,* May 1973.

Horton, J., "A Statistical Rating Index for Municipal Bonds," *Financial Analysts Journal,* March–April 1969.

LONG-TERM DEBT AND EQUITY MARKETS AND INSTRUMENTS

CONTENTS

LONG-TERM DEBT
SECURITIES 3

Bond Types 3
  Mortgage bonds 3
  Collateral trust bonds 4
  Equipment trust certificates 4
  Debenture bonds 4
  Subordinated debentures 4
  Convertible bonds 4
    Exchange offers for convertible debt 4
    Advantages and disadvantages of
    exchange offers 5
  Income bonds 5
  Guaranteed bonds 5
  Participating bonds 5
  Joint bonds 5
  Voting bonds 5
  Serial bonds 5
  Adjustable rate bonds 5
Retirement of Bonds 6
  Callable bonds 6
  Tax treatment of debt discharge 7

SINKING FUNDS 7

Sinking Fund Purchases 7
Pricing Considerations on Sinking Fund
Bonds 7
  Price versus accumulation 8
  Advance purchase of a sinking fund 9
  Nominal versus realized cost 11

RATINGS AND RATING AGENCIES 15

Rating Agencies 15
The Rating Process 17

Rating Fees 21
Split Ratings 21

PRIVATE PLACEMENT MARKET 21

Advantages and Disadvantages 23
Market Participants 24
Dual Market 24
Resale of Private Placements 26
Outlook for the Private Market 26
Project Financing 27

PREFERRED STOCK 27

Sinking Fund Preferreds 27
Convertible Preferreds 28
Participating Preferreds 28
Preference Stocks 28
Par and Liquidation Values 29
Preferred Stock Ratings 29
Preferred Stock Issuers 29
Preferred Stock Purchasers 30

COMMON STOCK 30

Common Stockholders' Rights 30
Common Stock Characteristics 31
Common Stock Risk 32
Issuing Common Stock 32
  Advantages of issuing common stock 32
  Disadvantages of issuing common
  stock 32
  Registration with SEC 32
  Determining flotation costs 33
  Setting the offering price 33
Secondary Market 33

LONG-TERM DEBT AND EQUITY MARKETS AND INSTRUMENTS

Andrew J. Kalotay

The primary sources of permanent capital for U.S. corporations are long-term debt, preferred stock, and the common stock markets. The funds from these sources of capital are referred to as a firm's capital structure. One of the objectives of the firm is to combine these funds in such a way as to **minimize its overall cost of capital.** Although the issue of whether an optimal capital structure can be determined is still a question of debate among financial theorists, an understanding of the various sources of funds and the market in which they operate is important to the financial manager. For a discussion on the financial management issues and the cost of capital, see the section entitled "Long-Term Sources of Funds and the Cost of Capital."

This section describes and analyzes the various markets and instruments for corporate capital. It highlights the public markets for debt and preferred and common stock and also refers to the private or negotiated market for debt and preferred stock.

LONG-TERM DEBT SECURITIES

There are numerous types of long-term debt security, as well as various debt equivalents, that are alternative fixed income sources for corporations. The primary debt equivalent, leases, is discussed in depth in a separate section of this *Handbook*. Short-term debt instruments and sources are also discussed elsewhere.

BOND TYPES.

Mortgage Bonds. These are long-term obligations that are secured by specific property. In addition, mortgage bonds are unsecured claims on the general assets of the firm. In the event of default, holders of mortgage bonds receive ownership of the mortgaged property.

The author would like to express his appreciation to John T. Inglesby for his assistance in preparing this section.

Collateral Trust Bonds.   Backed by other securities, usually held by a trustee, collateral trust bonds are frequently used by a parent firm when it pledges the securities of a wholly owned subsidiary as collateral.

Equipment Trust Certificates.   Instruments backed by specific pieces of equipment or machinery frequently are used by airlines, railroads, and shipping companies. These certificates may be issued by a trustee who holds the equipment, issues obligations, and leases the equipment to the corporation that uses it. Cash received from the corporation is used to pay the interest and principal on the equipment trust certificates. Eventually the firm will take title to the equipment.

Debenture Bonds.   These general obligations of the issuing firm are unsecured credit. They are claims only on the general assets of the corporation and are protected by their indenture restrictions. The four most common types of indenture provision are (1) provisions against the issuance of more debt, (2) restrictions that limit dividend payments, (3) provisions restricting merger activity, and (4) restrictions on the disposition of the firm's assets.

Subordinated Debentures.   These debentures are junior debt. In the event of bankruptcy their claims against the firm will be met only after the claims of senior debtholders have been fully satisfied.

Convertible Bonds.   The trust indenture may give bondholders the privilege to convert their bonds into another security of the issuing company at a specified price, within a given time, and under stated terms and conditions. Bonds that carry this privilege are most often **debenture issues,** and the securities into which they are convertible are almost always **junior issues,** usually preferred or common stock, or units consisting of both. There have been instances among public utilities and railroads of short-term notes that were convertible into long-term mortgage bonds that were deposited as collateral to secure the notes. There are instances also in which bonds are made convertible into the securities of another company.

The typical convertible bond is one exchangeable for common stock of the same issuer at the option of the holder. The cost of capital in issuing such bonds is discussed in detail below.

Exchange Offers for Convertible Debt.   During 1980 three major airline companies (American Airlines, TWA, Eastern Airlines) undertook similar exchange offers for some of their outstanding convertible debt. Since at the time of the offer the conversion privilege on these issues had no value, having either already expired or being close to expiration, the bonds were selling at a deep discount.

In each case, in **exchange** for the outstanding bonds, the issuer offered **new convertible bonds** with somewhat higher market value and somewhat longer average life. In two of the exchanges the face amount of each new bond was significantly lower than that of the outstanding bond, while one exchange (American) was par for par. In each case, the total interest paid on a new bond exceeded the interest on the outstanding bond.

The exact structuring of these exchanges was influenced by the issuer's tax considerations. If an exchange is not **par for par,** the difference between the face amount of the outstanding security and the market value of the new security results in a gain that is taxable to the issuer. In the case of a **par-for-par exchange,** there is no such tax liability, although a gain is recognized for financial accounting purposes.

Advantages and Disadvantages of Exchange Offers.   The primary **advantages** to an issuer from such an exchange are threefold. First, the recognition of an extraordinary gain and the reduction in principal amount of debt outstanding allow him to **report improved earnings and an improved capital structure.** Second, by **delaying the sinking fund principal payments,** he alleviates possible cash flow problems in the near future. Third, the **likelihood of convertibility** for companies in need of common equity is enhanced.

There are two major **disadvantages** to the issuer: the cost of the transaction is substantial, and the restored conversion value to the debtholder is in fact at the expense of the equityholder. Moreover, the interest expenses increase, and the fixed charge coverage ratio drops.

As measured by their acceptance level of approximately 80%, these exchange offers were successful. The holders, of course, did receive an intrinsic increase in value. Moreover, in case bonds acquired in an exchange can be used by the issuer toward future sinking fund payments, the average life of bonds not exchanged is extended, and thus their market price at the expiration of the exchange offer may decline below the price prior to the offer.

Income Bonds.   Such bonds pay interest only when the corporation's net income is above a prespecified level. Occasionally they are called **adjustment bonds** because they may be issued to readjust fixed interest debt by corporations undergoing reorganization. Unfortunately, if the issue bears too many of the characteristics of equity, the Internal Revenue Service may view the interest payments as "essentially equivalent to a dividend" and taxable as such. In this event the interest payments are no longer deductible as an expense before taxes.

Guaranteed Bonds.   These instruments are guaranteed by the assets of a corporation other than the issuing firm. Usually the guaranteeing corporation is a parent firm.

Participating Bonds.   These provide fixed interest payments and, in addition, a portion of surplus earnings accruing over the life of the bond if earnings are above the fixed interest.

Joint Bonds.   Obligations jointly issued by two or more corporations (usually railroads) are sometimes called pooled or joint bonds because they provide joint collateral.

Voting Bonds.   Usually issued in connection with reorganizations, voting bonds give holders the right to vote for directors if interest payments are not paid for a certain length of time.

Serial Bonds.   These bonds have different portions of the issue maturing at different (sometimes random) dates. A default on any portion coming due constitutes default on the entire issue.

Adjustable Rate Bonds.   In 1980 several large insurance companies began experimenting with **variable or adjustable rate debt** to shield their extension loan portfolios against **unanticipated changes in inflation.** The interest rates on these securities are **tied (indexed) to the rates on Treasury securities** with maturities of 3–10 years, or longer. Investors usually charge a spread of 1–3% above the Treasury rates, although there is no single formula used by all. Rates can also be expressed as a percentage (e.g., 110%) above the Treasury rate to adjust for different levels of interest rates. Rates are adjusted periodically—a typical issue will have rate changes every year or perhaps every 2 years.

Prior to 1980 these adjustable rate securities were primarily restricted to **private placements** where the institutional lender could negotiate the type of **inflation hedge** or protection that suited its desires. The attractiveness of these securities spread to the public market in late 1980 (see "The Wave of Adjustable Rate Debt," *Business Week,* December 1, 1980, pp. 100–101) with issue size as high as the $250 million General Motors Acceptance Corp. (GMAC) 10-year adjustable rate debt, which is tied to the 10-year Treasury bond index. Although financial companies have floated these securities most frequently, the wave of new adjustable debt was beginning to spread to industrial and public utility companies as well.

Borrowers in the **adjustable rate market** are essentially making a choice between a **floating rate,** which may come down, and a high fixed rate, which firms could be forced to fund for up to 30 years. Adjustable rate debt is a more popular means of financing for firms when interest rate levels are historically high. The uncertainty about future rates, however, is what makes this market attractive to buyers and sellers.

RETIREMENT OF BONDS.   One of the important features of bonds is the method of principal repayment. The various types of refunding are discussed below with particular emphasis on sinking fund bonds.

Callable Bonds.   **Call provisions** give the firm the right to pay off a bond prior to maturity. This provides an increased degree of flexibility, since debt can be reduced, its maturity altered via refunding, and most important, expensive debt with high interest rates may be replaced with cheaper debt if rates decline. Frequently the **call price** is established above **par value.** Nevertheless, from the investor's point of view the call provision establishes an upper limit on the amount of capital gain that can be obtained if interest rates fall. For this reason, the investor will require a higher yield to maturity on callable bonds than on straight debt of equal risk and maturity.

In effect, a **callable bond** is equivalent to an ordinary bond with an **option contract.** On the date of issue the bondholder equates the market price of the callable bond B_0 with the present value of the cash payments from the bond (coupons plus face value) less the present value of the call option C_0, which gives the firm the right to call in the debt early at some predetermined price. Mathematically, this may be expressed as follows:

$$B_0 = \sum_{t=1}^{T} \frac{E(\text{coupon})}{(1 + K_c a)^t} + \frac{E(\text{face value})}{(1 + K_c a)^T} - C_0$$

where

$$B_0 = \text{present value of callable bond}$$
$$E(\text{coupon})_t = \text{expected coupon payment in year } t$$
$$E(\text{face value}) = \text{expected face value if bond is refunded at maturity}$$
$$K_c a = \text{true cost of issuing a callable bond}$$
$$C_0 = \text{present value of call feature (whose computation is}$$
$$\text{beyond the scope of this article)}$$

Investors are usually given some **call protection.** During the first few years an issue may not be callable. In addition, a premium may be paid when a bond is called. Often this amount becomes smaller, the closer the bond is to its scheduled maturity date. Sometimes an entire issue may be called and other times only specific bonds, drawn by lot by a trustee, will be called. In either case, a notice of redemption will appear in advance in the financial press.

Tax Treatment of Debt Discharge.   On December 13th, Congress passed the Bankruptcy Tax Act of 1980 (HR 5043). The Act, which became effective after December 31, 1980, provides tax rules applicable to debt discharge in the case of both bankrupt and solvent debtors. The Act affects the tax treatment of the **discharge of debt at a discount.** In particular, the rules permitting the reduction of the basis of assets in lieu of recognizing a gain on the extinguishment of discounted debt have been changed. It is no longer possible to reduce the basis in **nondepreciable assets.** Only **depreciable assets** can be utilized.

Prior to the passing of the Act, certain corporations, primarily holding companies, were able to avoid the payment of taxes on the gain (between par value and the repurchase price of the debt) by reducing the basis in nondepreciable assets, such as equity interest in a subsidiary. This is no longer the case.

SINKING FUNDS

SINKING FUND PURCHASES.   A **sinking fund** is almost always included with public industrial and pipeline issues, although it is notably absent from the issues of telephone and finance companies. Electrical utilities are commonly subject to a **"blanket" sinking fund requirement,** according to which the utility must spend a specified amount of cash annually, either for **retiring bonds** from any of several issues or possibly for improvements to existing plant. Moreover, most of the recent **preferred and preference equity issues** also carry sinking fund provisions.

The **standard sinking fund provision** requires the firm to retire a portion of an issue each year. In the case of a publicly held issue, this can be accomplished by one of two means. The issuer may make a **cash payment,** in the face amount of the bonds to be retired, **to the trustee,** who in turn **calls the bonds by lot.** The second option available to the issuer is the actual **delivery of the bonds to the trustee.** If the bonds are selling at a discount (below maturity value, $1,000) it is cheaper to make an **open market purchase** than to call at or close to par. In this case, the delivery of the bonds is the obvious option for the issuer. It is noteworthy that in certain instances the **bond indentures** do not allow for open market purchase; that is, they specify that the bonds be called by lot. Usually it is the **face amount** (par value) of the bonds that is specified in the indenture, and not the cash payment.

A variety of problems may arise in connection with bonds whose **coupon interest rate** is below the prevailing level of interest rates, that is, bonds that were issued when the prevailing rate was lower than the current rate. The prices of similar low-coupon bonds display a **high degree of variability.** If most of an issue has been accumulated by a single holder, the price may be close to par. As an extreme example, the asking price in fall 1980 for the Chase Manhattan 4.60s of 1990 was 100 (par), since virtually all the remaining approximately $100 million face amount bonds were held by a single institution. At the same time, there were several similar quality but widely held issues that sold at a substantial discount, **enabling their issuers** to make an attractive open market purchase. Thus, **accumulation** by one or a small number of purchasers constitutes a major threat to the issuer, while it provides holders with an opportunity to outperform the long-term bond market. Accumulators are large collectors of bonds for potential profit.

PRICING CONSIDERATIONS ON SINKING FUND BONDS.   To set the stage for the analysis below, the following facts are pertinent. The **institutional market for corporate bonds** consists primarily of **pension funds** (which are tax-exempt) and **life insurance companies** (whose marginal tax rate is normally much lower than that of the issuer). Consequently, the **role of taxes** is insignificant in the buying or selling decision of a holder. **Marginal tax rates** refer to the rate paid on the last dollar of income earned. Certain institutions, however, may be unable or unwilling to realize a book loss on a transaction, and therefore will not sell at a discount. Because of such institutional phenomena, several low-coupon preferred equity issues sell close to par. In the following analysis, the outstanding amount will be implicitly assumed to be lower due to the holdings of institutions unwilling to sell below par.

First, we examine the price of a **fully accumulated** (all securities are outstanding) **issue.** This situation bears a strong resemblance to a monopolist (i.e., the accumulator) who is faced with specified demands at various future time periods. At the sinking fund payment dates the demand is **price inelastic, up to par value.** What will be the minimum price demanded by the accumulator at time 0? The conventional valuation of a **private placement** with a sinking fund is directly applicable to this problem. First, the issue is segmented into various maturities; then the value of each segment is determined. Finally, the **value of the entire issue** is obtained **by summation.**

What will be the minimum price of a small block or a single bond? That can be determined by finding the **most valuable bond** (which in practice is always a **bond in the shortest maturity class in case of a low-coupon issue**). Of course, the minimum price demanded by the accumulator for the entire issue will be lower than that of a single bond. In general, the larger the size of the purchase, the lower the price per bond.

We now turn to the investigation of an arbitrary issue, and generalize the results obtained above for a **fully accumulated issue.** Subject to market efficiency, the price will normally be determined by the largest single holder, assuming that holders do not collude. If there is collusion, the colluding parties should be treated as a single entity.

In the general case the largest single holder will set the prices. We define the **guaranteed par value date (GPVD)** for a holder as the date at which he is assured of receiving par value for a single bond. The GPVD of the largest holder is the closest one to the present.

The price at which a holder is willing to buy or sell is dictated by his GPVD. Given the prevailing level of interest rates, the coupon rate, and the GPVD, the value of the bond to the holder can be determined. Presumably, he should be willing to buy below or sell above that value. It follows that the price of a widely distributed low-coupon issue, or one that is assumed to be widely distributed, will be determined by the **long-term interest rate.** Consequently, a widely held issue tends to be relatively cheap. In fact, such issues often sell at the same price as similar issues with the same maturity, but without a sinking fund.

Price versus Accumulation.   The opposition of these factors can be readily explained by the following example. Assume that an issue has a 7% coupon rate and a maturity of 15 years, with a sinking fund beginning at the end of the sixth year. The prevailing long-term rate is 10%. If an investor holds 100% of all the bonds outstanding, he will demand a price of $100 (par value) for each bond on the sinking fund date. The issuer having no other option must pay the $100 to the holder. However, if there are a large number of holders, each holding less than 10% of the bonds outstanding, the price to the issuer will be determined by the current long-term rate. In this case the price will be $81.31 per bond (see Exhibit 1 for the expected price for various percentages accumulated by the **largest holder**).

From the preceding discussion it follows that a widely held issue creates an opportunity for potential accumulation, since its price will be relatively low. However, once it becomes generally known that an issue has been partially accumulated, its price will rise appropriately, assuming no other market changes. At that point, the opportunity to realize further **profits from accumulation** should disappear.

How does the price of an accumulated issue behave over time, assuming a constant level

EXHIBIT 1   PRICES OF SINKING FUND BONDS UNDER VARIOUS ACCUMULATION ASSUMPTIONS

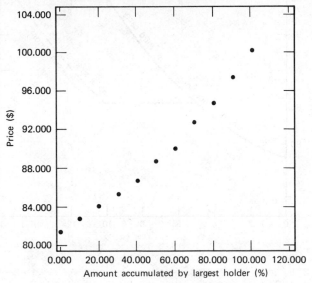

of interest rates? That depends on whether the **accumulator** sells before his GPVD. If he decides to hold, the price will rise from its current level to par at the accumulator's GPVD (the yield to the accumulator's GPVD will remain essentially constant). On the other hand, if the issuer's sinking fund purchases are satisfied by the accumulator, each sale will result in an extension of the accumulator's GPVD, and the price will remain constant, assuming a constant interest rate environment. Whenever possible, **the issuer should make his sinking fund purchase in a single block from the accumulator.**

As an illustration, consider an issue with 11 years left to maturity, 10 equal annual sinking fund payments, a 5% coupon rate, and a flat 10% interest rate environment (flat yield curve). The accumulator holds 50% of the issue, thus his initial GPVD is year 6. Exhibit 2 displays the price sequences corresponding to the two scenarios. As long as the issuer purchases the bonds from the **largest holder,** the accumulator's GPVD is pushed back; thus the price remains constant. This is displayed by the curve on the right. If, however, the issuer purchases from a different source, the accumulator's GPVD remains constant and the price increases (curve on the left).

Advance Purchase of a Sinking Fund.

We now turn to the problem facing the **corporate issuer.** His goal is to satisfy the sinking fund requirements at minimum cost. In contrast to the holder, for the issuer **taxes do play a significant role.** Taxes affect interest payments, the gain (face amount less purchase price), and the discount rate. Moreover, in considering an advance purchase, the **issuer's relevant horizon** is the next open **sinking fund date,** not the maturity date.

If the issue's maturity date is in the distant future and the prevailing long-term rate is much higher than the coupon rate, the bonds will normally sell substantially below par value. Superficial examination of the situation may suggest that the firm should retire the bonds in advance rather than wait until the sinking fund date and pay a significantly higher price.

In fact, the problem is quite complicated once the following considerations have been

EXHIBIT 2   PRICE SEQUENCES FOR ACCUMULATED ISSUE

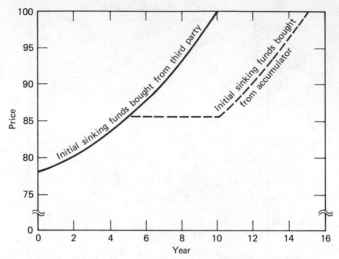

taken into account. First, interest rates manifest themselves not only in low bond prices, but also in **high borrowing or opportunity cost,** or equivalently, in a **high discount rate.** Second, the future price of the bonds is uncertain. It is entirely possible that even though the bonds are selling at a low price at the present, an even more advantageous situation will arise in the future.

As an illustration, assume that the bonds can be purchased either at the present or at the sinking fund date, but not at intermediate points in time. In this case, the problem can be approached in the following manner. For an assumed price at the sinking fund date, we determine the **present value of savings** due to a current purchase rather than purchase at the sinking fund date. We then compare the aftertax cost of current purchase with the present value of future liabilities in the manner described above. The only difference is that the **cost of retirement** at the sinking fund date is based on the assumed price rather than on par value. The procedure above can be repeated over a range of assumed prices at the sinking fund date. The higher the price, the more would be saved by making a purchase at the present time.

Consider the Series X debentures, with a coupon rate of 7% and 10 years left to maturity. The next **open sinking fund date** is 2 years from now and the current price is 71. The issuer's marginal tax rate is 50%, taxes on the gain are paid immediately, and the 2-year borrowing rate is 11%.

Exhibit 3 shows the savings to the issuer due to current purchase, rather than purchase at the sinking fund date at the indicated prices. Of particular interest is the break-even price 76, at which the issuer should be indifferent between buying at the present and buying at the sinking fund date. If he believes that the price will exceed 76, he should make his purchase at the present; otherwise he should wait.

The **maximum future price facing the issuer** is the sinking fund call price which is usually at par or slightly above. Purchase should never be made in advance if the break-even price exceeds the call price. A common mistake among financial analysts is to assume that the only alternative to current open market purchase is to retire the bonds at par at the sinking

EXHIBIT 3   SAVINGS DEPEND ON FUTURE PRICE

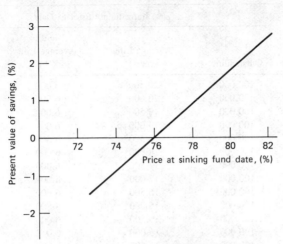

fund date. That assumption inevitably indicates that the issuer should make his purchase at the present. Having to pay par is the worst possible future outcome, not the expected outcome under reasonable assumptions.

The foregoing analysis can be presented in a different manner by considering the **bond's yield to maturity,** or possibly its **yield to average life,** instead of its dollar price. Returning to the example, we note that at the current price of 71, the corresponding yield to maturity is 12.07%. The yield at a price of 100 would be 7%. Thus the bond's yield to maturity would have to drop at least 5% within 2 years before the issuer would be forced to pay par.

Nominal Versus Realized Cost.   The conventional measure of the cost of a debt security to the issuer is the discount rate at which the resulting obligations equal the net proceeds, that is, the rate at which the net present value of the cash flows is zero or the **internal rate of return.** If the issue **does not have a sinking fund,** its cost can be computed at the time of issuance, since the interest payments are specified and the only principal payment to be made is at maturity date at par. Thus, the actual cost of an issue without a sinking fund is its nominal (i.e., coupon) rate, provided the net proceeds are equal to the fact amount.

In the case of publicly issued debt with a sinking fund, the **future principal payments are uncertain,** since the issuer has the option of satisfying the obligations by open market purchases, rather than by calling the securities at par. During periods of rising interest rates, the securities may be obtained at substantial discounts. (For the sake of simplicity, we assume that purchases are always made at the sinking fund date, not in advance.) The greater these discounts, the lower the realized cost of the debt to the issuer.

In typical studies concerning public sinking fund issues, the quoted cost is always the **"nominal" cost,** which is based on the assumption that the cost of all principal payments to the issuer is par. Moreover, the cost of a new issue, as quoted in the financial press, is also based on the same pessimistic assumption. But **having to pay par is clearly the worst case from the issuer's viewpoint.** In contrast to public issues, **sinking funds for private placements** must be retired by the issuer at par, and on a pro rata basis. Consequently, **the cost of a private placement** is known at the outset, and there is no opportunity to reduce the cost during periods of rising interest rates.

EXHIBIT 4   PUBLIC SINKING FUND

Date		% Outstanding	Average Life (years)	Yield to Average Life (%)	Market Price per Hundred
			Immediately Prior to Date		
Jun	1950	100.000	20.500	6.000	76.590
Dec	1950	100.000	20.000	6.000	76.838
Jun	1951	100.000	19.500	6.000	77.194
Dec	1951	100.000	19.000	6.000	77.510
Jun	1952	100.000	18.500	6.000	77.835
Dec	1952	100.000	18.000	6.000	78.170
Jun	1953	100.000	17.500	6.000	78.515
Dec	1953	100.000	17.000	6.000	78.870
Jun	1954	100.000	16.500	6.000	79.236
Dec	1954	100.000	16.000	6.000	79.613
Jun	1955	100.000	15.500	6.000	80.002
Dec	1955	100.000	15.000	6.000	80.402
Jun	1956	100.000	14.500	6.000	80.814
Dec	1956	100.000	14.000	6.000	81.238
Jun	1957	100.000	13.500	6.000	81.675
Dec	1957	100.000	13.000	6.000	82.125
Jun	1958	100.000	12.500	6.000	82.589
Dec	1958	100.000	12.000	6.000	83.066
Jun	1959	100.000	11.500	6.000	83.558
Dec	1959	100.000	11.000	6.000	84.065
Jun	1960	100.000	10.500	6.000	84.587
Dec	1960	100.000	10.000	6.000	85.124
Jun	1961	100.000	9.500	6.000	85.678
Dec	1961	95.000	9.500	6.000	85.678
Jun	1962	95.000	9.000	6.000	86.248
Dec	1962	90.000	9.000	6.000	86.248
Jun	1963	90.000	8.500	6.000	86.835
Dec	1963	85.000	8.500	6.000	86.835
Jun	1964	85.000	8.000	6.000	87.440
Dec	1964	80.000	8.000	6.000	87.440
Jun	1965	80.000	7.500	6.000	88.063
Dec	1965	75.000	7.500	6.000	88.063
Jun	1966	75.000	7.000	6.000	88.705
Dec	1966	70.000	7.000	6.000	88.705
Jun	1967	70.000	6.500	6.000	89.366
Dec	1967	65.000	6.500	6.000	89.366
Jun	1968	65.000	6.000	6.000	90.047
Dec	1968	60.000	6.000	6.000	90.047
Jun	1969	60.000	5.500	6.000	90.748
Dec	1969	55.000	5.500	6.000	90.748
Jun	1970	55.000	5.000	6.000	91.471
Dec	1970	50.000	5.000	6.000	91.471
Jun	1971	50.000	4.500	6.000	92.215
Dec	1971	45.000	4.500	6.000	92.215
Jun	1972	45.000	4.000	6.000	92.981
Dec	1972	40.000	4.000	6.000	92.981
Jun	1973	40.000	3.500	6.000	93.770
Dec	1973	35.000	3.500	6.000	93.770

EXHIBIT 4   CONTINUED

			Immediately Prior to Date		
Date		% Outstanding	Average Life (years)	Yield to Average Life (%)	Market Price per Hundred
Jun	1974	35.000	3.000	6.000	94.583
Dec	1974	30.000	3.000	6.000	94.583
Jun	1975	30.000	2.500	6.000	95.421
Dec	1975	25.000	2.500	6.000	95.421
Jun	1976	25.000	2.000	6.000	96.283
Dec	1976	20.000	2.000	6.000	96.283
Jun	1977	20.000	1.500	6.000	97.172
Dec	1977	15.000	1.500	6.000	97.172
Jun	1978	15.000	1.000	6.000	98.087
Dec	1978	10.000	1.000	6.000	98.087
Jun	1979	10.000	0.500	6.000	99.029
Dec	1979	5.000	0.500	6.000	99.029
Jun	1980	5.000	0.000	6.000	100.000

Source: Dillon, Read & Co., Inc., New York, 1980.

We shall compute the **"realized"** cost of a typical long-term, industrial sinking fund bond issue under a wide range of assumptions regarding the future interest rate environment. The maturity of the issue is 30 years, and its **level sinking fund** commences at the end of the eleventh year (thus the **average life** is 20.5 years).

We shall generate a **price sequence** for an issue over time by specifying a **constant yield to average life** (YTAL). For example, Exhibit 4 displays the price sequence for a 4% issue based on a constant 6% YTAL. According to our assumption, the issuer will purchase the bonds at the indicated prices near the sinking fund dates.

Exhibit 5 displays the issuer's realized cash flows in the absence of corporate income taxes. In particular, Exhibit 5 would be appropriate for a **preferred equity issue.** The **"realized"** cost is determined by finding the discount rate at which the net present value of the cash flows as of the time of issuance is 100. This assumes that net proceeds are equal to the face amount. In the example considered, the realized cost is 3.70%.

In the presence of corporate income taxes, the analysis must be modified. On the one hand, interest payments are tax deductible; on the other hand, the gain (face amount less purchase price) is taxable at the ordinary rate. Moreover, the timing of the tax on the gain also varies. In certain instances the tax is payable at the time of purchase; in other cases, the tax may be amortized over a period of several years.

Exhibit 6 displays the aftertax cash flows under the assumptions that tax on the gain is paid immediately and that the issuer's marginal rate is 46%. The discount rate yielding a present value of 100 is 1.98%, or equivalently, 3.66% on a pretax basis. If instead of being paid immediately, the tax on the gain is amortized over 10 years, the realized cost would be 3.64% on a pretax basis, whereas if the tax is never paid, the cost would drop to 3.37%.

As this example demonstrates, the realized cost may turn out to be considerably lower than the nominal cost, especially if tax on the gain is avoided. On a pretax equivalent basis (aftertax rate divided by 1 − tax rate) the realized cost to a **taxable issuer is always lower** than the cost to a **tax-exempt issuer.** The reason for this is that principal payments represent a larger percentage of the total cost to a taxable issuer than to one who is tax-exempt.

EXHIBIT 5 PUBLIC SINKING FUND CASH FLOW TO TAX-EXEMPT ISSUER (AMOUNTS AS % OF ORIGINAL PRINCIPAL)

Period Ended		4.000% Outstanding Issue		
		Interest	Principal Payment	Total Cash Flow
Dec	1950	2.000	0.000	2.000
Jun	1951	2.000	0.000	2.000
Dec	1951	2.000	0.000	2.000
Jun	1952	2.000	0.000	2.000
Dec	1952	2.000	0.000	2.000
Jun	1953	2.000	0.000	2.000
Dec	1953	2.000	0.000	2.000
Jun	1954	2.000	0.000	2.000
Dec	1954	2.000	0.000	2.000
Jun	1955	2.000	0.000	2.000
Dec	1955	2.000	0.000	2.000
Jun	1956	2.000	0.000	2.000
Dec	1956	2.000	0.000	2.000
Jun	1957	2.000	0.000	2.000
Dec	1957	2.000	0.000	2.000
Jun	1958	2.000	0.000	2.000
Dec	1958	2.000	0.000	2.000
Jun	1959	2.000	0.000	2.000
Dec	1959	2.000	0.000	2.000
Jun	1960	2.000	0.000	2.000
Dec	1960	2.000	0.000	2.000
Jun	1961	2.000	4.284	6.284
Dec	1961	1.900	0.000	1.900
Jun	1962	1.900	4.312	6.212
Dec	1962	1.800	0.000	1.800
Jun	1963	1.800	4.342	6.142
Dec	1963	1.700	0.000	1.700
Jun	1964	1.700	4.372	6.072
Dec	1964	1.600	0.000	1.600
Jun	1965	1.600	4.403	6.003
Dec	1965	1.500	0.000	1.500
Jun	1966	1.500	4.435	5.935
Dec	1966	1.400	0.000	1.400
Jun	1967	1.400	4.468	5.868
Dec	1967	1.300	0.000	1.300
Jun	1968	1.300	4.502	5.802
Dec	1968	1.200	0.000	1.200
Jun	1969	1.200	4.537	5.737
Dec	1969	1.100	0.000	1.100
Jun	1970	1.100	4.574	5.674
Dec	1970	1.000	0.000	1.000
Jun	1971	1.000	4.611	5.611
Dec	1971	0.900	0.000	0.900
Jun	1972	0.900	4.649	5.549
Dec	1972	0.800	0.000	0.800
Jun	1973	0.800	4.689	5.489

EXHIBIT 5   CONTINUED

Period Ended		4.000% Outstanding Issue		
		Interest	Principal Payment	Total Cash Flow
Dec	1973	0.700	0.000	0.700
Jun	1974	0.700	4.729	5.429
Dec	1974	0.600	0.000	0.600
Jun	1975	0.600	4.771	5.371
Dec	1975	0.500	0.000	0.500
Jun	1976	0.500	4.814	5.314
Dec	1976	0.400	0.000	0.400
Jun	1977	0.400	4.859	5.259
Dec	1977	0.300	0.000	0.300
Jun	1978	0.300	4.904	5.204
Dec	1978	0.200	0.000	0.200
Jun	1979	0.200	4.951	5.151
Dec	1979	0.100	0.000	0.100
Jun	1980	0.100	5.000	5.100
	Total	82.000	92.207	174.207

Source: Dillon, Read, & Co., Inc., New York, 1980.

As discussed earlier, **sinking funds of a private placement** must be purchased by the issuer at par. For this reason the realized cost of a private placement is the coupon rate, as long as the net proceeds equal the face amount.

In contrast to private placements, **sinking funds for publicly held debt** can be obtained by the issuer on the open market. During periods of rising interest rates, the issuer will normally purchase the bonds at a discount, rather than call them at par. Thus the **par "open market purchase"** is a valuable option to the issuer, and a detriment to the holders in aggregate.

RATINGS AND RATING AGENCIES

RATING AGENCIES.   Corporate debt securities, as well as other securities such as municipal bonds and preferred equity, often receive a rating from one or more rating agencies. In the case of debt securities, this rating represents that agency's judgment of the **credit-worthiness of the issuer** (and possibly third-party guarantors or insurers) with respect to the rated security issue. While differences exist in the policy and practices of the several rating agencies, there are enough similarities to warrant a general discussion of the rating process. Although rating systems vary from one agency to the next, securities are usually placed in one of two broad categories. Securities in the higher category are referred to as **investment grade securities** and possess a relatively low amount of default risk. The lower rated securities are referred to as **speculative grade.** For these securities, the opinion of the rater is that the **company's** outlook is sufficiently uncertain as to place significant **risk of default** on its fixed indebtedness.

The two most often quoted rating agencies are **Moody's Investors Service, Inc.** (Moody's) and **Standard & Poor's (S & P).** The rating categories used by these two

EXHIBIT 6   PUBLIC SINKING FUND CASH FLOW TO TAXABLE ISSUER (AMOUNTS AS % OF ORIGINAL PRINCIPAL)

Period Ended		4.000% Outstanding Issue		
		Aftertax Interest	Principal Payment	Total Cash Flow
Dec	1950	1.080	0.000	1.080
Jun	1951	1.080	0.000	1.080
Dec	1951	1.080	0.000	1.080
Jun	1952	1.080	0.000	1.080
Dec	1952	1.080	0.000	1.080
Jun	1953	1.080	0.000	1.080
Dec	1953	1.080	0.000	1.080
Jun	1954	1.080	0.000	1.080
Dec	1954	1.080	0.000	1.080
Jun	1955	1.080	0.000	1.080
Dec	1955	1.080	0.000	1.080
Jun	1956	1.080	0.000	1.080
Dec	1956	1.080	0.000	1.080
Jun	1957	1.080	0.000	1.080
Dec	1957	1.080	0.000	1.080
Jun	1958	1.080	0.000	1.080
Dec	1958	1.080	0.000	1.080
Jun	1959	1.080	0.000	1.080
Dec	1959	1.080	0.000	1.080
Jun	1960	1.080	0.000	1.080
Dec	1960	1.080	0.000	1.080
Jun	1961	1.080	4.613	5.693
Dec	1961	1.026	0.000	1.026
Jun	1962	1.026	4.629	5.655
Dec	1962	0.972	0.000	0.972
Jun	1963	0.972	4.645	5.617
Dec	1963	0.918	0.000	0.918
Jun	1964	0.918	4.661	5.579
Dec	1964	0.864	0.000	0.864
Jun	1965	0.864	4.678	5.542
Dec	1965	0.810	0.000	0.810
Jun	1966	0.810	4.695	5.505
Dec	1966	0.756	0.000	0.756
Jun	1967	0.756	4.713	5.469
Dec	1967	0.702	0.000	0.702
Jun	1968	0.702	4.731	5.433
Dec	1968	0.648	0.000	0.648
Jun	1969	0.648	4.750	5.398
Dec	1969	0.594	0.000	0.594
Jun	1970	0.594	4.770	5.364
Dec	1970	0.540	0.000	0.540
Jun	1971	0.540	4.790	5.330
Dec	1971	0.486	0.000	0.486
Jun	1972	0.486	4.810	5.296
Dec	1972	0.432	0.000	0.432
Jun	1973	0.432	4.832	5.264

EXHIBIT 6   CONTINUED

Period Ended		4.000% Outstanding Issue		
		Aftertax Interest	Principal Payment	Total Cash Flow
Dec	1973	0.378	0.000	0.378
Jun	1974	0.378	4.854	5.232
Dec	1974	0.324	0.000	0.324
Jun	1975	0.324	4.876	5.200
Dec	1975	0.270	0.000	0.270
Jun	1976	0.270	4.900	5.170
Dec	1976	0.216	0.000	0.216
Jun	1977	0.216	4.924	5.140
Dec	1977	0.162	0.000	0.162
Jun	1978	0.162	4.948	5.110
Dec	1978	0.108	0.000	0.108
Jun	1979	0.108	4.974	5.082
Dec	1979	0.054	0.000	0.054
Jun	1980	0.054	5.000	5.054
Total		44.280	95.792	140.071

Source: Dillon, Read & Co., Inc., New York, 1980.

organizations are listed in Exhibits 7 and 8. Securities rated in one of the **top four ratings** in each system are regarded as **investment grade.**

THE RATING PROCESS. The corporate issuer or an authorized representative usually requests that an agency rate a new security. **S & P** rates practically all corporate bonds and preferred stock issues of $5 million and over in principal amount with or without the request of the issuer. **Moody's** will rate securities only at the request of the issuer. Prior to a meeting with the management of the company, the rating agency requests information from the company. This information may include operating history, SEC registration statements, legal opinions, comparison of the issuer to similar companies, an analysis of capital spending, and other information that may affect the rating. The agency meets with management to discuss the **operating and financial plans** of the company. The basis of this discussion is the **security prospectus** and other information assembled by the company.

According to the rating agencies, the future outlook for the firm is important but ratings are not primarily based on **projections.** Instead, **projections** provide insight into **management's plans** for the future, how management assesses the **company's prospects** in light of past performance, and how it plans to deal with the **company's problems.** Projections

EXHIBIT 7   KEY TO MOODY'S CORPORATE RATINGS

Aaa

Bonds which are rated Aaa are judged to be of the best quality. They carry the smallest degree of investment risk and are generally referred to as "gilt edged." Interest payments are protected by a large or by an exceptionally stable margin and principal is secure. While the various protective elements are likely to change, such changes as can be visualized are most unlikely to impair the fundamentally strong position of such issues.

EXHIBIT 7 CONTINUED

Aa

Bonds which are rated Aa are judged to be of high quality by all standards. Together with the Aaa group they comprise what are generally known as high grade bonds. They are rated lower than the best bonds because margins of protection may not be as large as in the Aaa securities or fluctuation of protective elements may be of greater amplitude or there may be other elements present which make the long-term risks appear somewhat larger than in Aaa securities.

A

Bonds which are rated A possess many favorable investment attributes and are to be considered as upper medium grade obligations. Factors giving security to principal and interest are considered adequate, but elements may be present which suggest a susceptibility to impairment sometime in the future.

Baa

Bonds which are rated Baa are considered as medium grade obligations; i.e., they are neither highly protected nor poorly secured. Interest payments and principal security appear adequate for the present but certain protective elements may be lacking or may be characteristically unreliable over any great length of time. Such bonds lack outstanding investment characteristics and in fact have speculative characteristics as well.

Ba

Bonds which are rated Ba are judged to have speculative elements; their future cannot be considered as well-assured. Often the protection of interest and principal payments may be very moderate, and thereby not well safeguarded during both good and bad times over the future. Uncertainty of position characterizes bonds in this class.

B

Bonds which are rated B generally lack characteristics of the desirable investment. Assurance of interest and principal payments or of maintenance of other terms of the contract over any long period of time may be small.

Caa

Bonds which are rated Caa are of poor standing. Such issues may be in default or there may be present elements of danger with respect to principal or interest.

Ca

Bonds which are rated Ca represent obligations which are speculative in a high degree. Such issues are often in default or have other market shortcomings.

C

Bonds which are rated C are the lowest rated class of bonds, and issues so rated can be regarded as having extremely poor prospects of ever attaining any real investment standing.

Source: Moody's Investors Service, New York.

EXHIBIT 8   STANDARD & POOR'S CORPORATE AND MUNICIPAL BOND RATING DEFINITIONS

A Standard & Poor's corporate or municipal bond rating is a current assessment of the creditworthiness of an obligor with respect to a specific debt obligation. This assessment may take into consideration obligors such as guarantors, insurers, or lessees.

The bond rating is not a recommendation to purchase, sell, or hold a security, inasmuch as it does not comment as to market price or suitability for a particular investor.

The ratings are based on current information furnished by the issuer or obtained by Standard & Poor's from other sources it considers reliable. Standard & Poor's does not perform any audit in connection with any rating and may, on occasion, rely on unaudited financial information. The ratings may be changed, suspended or withdrawn as a result of changes in, or unavailability of, such information, or for other circumstances.

The ratings are based, in varying degrees, on the following consideration:

1. Likelihood of default-capacity and willingness of the obligor as to the timely payment of interest and repayment of principal in accordance with the terms of the obligation.
2. Nature of and provisions of the obligation.
3. Protection afforded by, and relative position of, the obligation in the event of bankruptcy, reorganization or other arrangement under the laws of bankruptcy and other laws affecting creditors' rights.

AAA

Bonds rated AAA have the highest rating assigned by Standard & Poor's to a debt obligation. Capacity to pay interest and repay principal is extremely strong.

AA

Bonds rated AA have a very strong capacity to pay interest and repay principal and differ from the highest rated issues only in small degree.

A

Bonds rate A have a strong capacity to pay interest and repay principal, although they are somewhat more susceptible to the adverse effects of changes in circumstances and economic conditions than bonds in higher rated categories.

BBB

Bonds rated BBB are regarded as having an adequate capacity to pay interest and repay principal. Whereas they normally exhibit adequate protection parameters, adverse economic conditions or changing circumstances are more likely to lead to a weakened capacity to pay interest and repay principal for bonds in this category than for bonds in higher rated categories.

BB, B, CCC, CC

Bonds rated BB, B, CCC, and CC are regarded, on balance, as predominantly speculative with respect to capacity to pay interest and repay principal in accordance with the terms of the obligation. BB indicates the lowest degree of speculation and CC the highest degree of speculation. While such bonds will likely have some quality and protective characteristics, these are outweighed by large uncertainties or major risk exposures to adverse conditions.

EXHIBIT 8   CONTINUED

C

The rating C is reserved for income bonds on which no interest is being paid.

D

Bonds rated D are in default, and payment of interest and/or repayment of principal is in arrears.

Plus (+) or Minus (−)

The ratings from "AA" to "BB" may be modified by the addition of a plus or minus sign to show relative standing within the major rating categories.

Provisional Ratings

The letter "p" indicates that the rating is provisional. A provisional rating assumes the successful completion of the project being financed by the bonds being rated and indicates that payment of debt service requirements is largely or entirely dependent on the successful and timely completion of the project. This rating, however, while addressing credit quality subsequent to completion of the project, makes no comment on the likelihood of, or the risk of default upon failure of, such completion. The investor should exercise his own judgment with respect to such likelihood and risk.

NR

"NR" indicates that no rating has been requested, that there is insufficient information on which to base a rating, or that S&P does not rate a particular type of obligation as a matter of policy.

Debt Obligations Of Issuers Outside The United states and Its Territories

These are rated on the same basis as domestic corporate and municipal issues. The ratings measure the creditworthiness of the obligor but do not take into account currency exchange and other uncertainties.

Bond Investment Quality Standards

Under present commercial bank regulations issued by the Comptroller of the Currency, bonds rated in the top four categories (AAA, AA, A, BBB, commonly known as "investment grade" ratings) are generally regarded as eligible for bank investment. In addition, the legal investment laws of various states impose certain rating or other standards for obligations eligible for investment by savings banks, trust companies, insurance companies, and fiduciaries generally.

Source: Standard & Poor's Bond Guide, New York.

also indicate the company's **financial strategy** in terms of its reliance on internal cash flows and outside funds. The information contained in the company presentation is often proprietary; therefore, it is kept **strictly confidential.**

Once all information has been gathered, the agency decides on a rating. The issuer is then notified of the rating and the major considerations behind the rating. The issuer is given the opportunity to respond to the rating by presenting new or additional data. Any such information is considered by the agency, and the final rating is published. In cases of particular types of security that the agency does not ordinarily rate, the right of publication rests with the issuer.

The rating agency **reserves the right to change or withdraw a rating,** once published. Such action may be the result of the issuance of new debt, failure on the part of the company to provide information needed for the periodic review of the rating, or change in the financial situation of the company. Most outstanding securities are reviewed at least once a year, although the **review process** is likely to be less comprehensive than that given to a **new issue.**

RATING FEES. For the rating, the issuer pays a fee to the rating agency. Moody's fee is based on the size of the issue and is in the neighborhood of 0.02% of the principal amount of the issue with minimum charge of approximately $1,000 and a maximum charge of about $20,000. S & P's fee is based on the amount of time and effort involved in rating the security. Typically, S & P's fee is between $500 and $15,000.

SPLIT RATINGS. The basic type of analysis used by the various rating agencies consists of traditional financial analysis, assessment of trends and future developments, and a good deal of subjective judgment. As a result, the process does not represent a scientific procedure and we can observe differences in ratings assigned to the same security. Such differences are referred to as **split ratings** or **mixed ratings.** It has been observed (Altman, "Computerized Bond Rating Replication: Worthwhile or Futile?," *Basis Point,* Equitable Life Assurance Society of America, Fall 1979, p. 11) that a comparison of all **electric utility bonds** rated by both Moody's and S & P in July 1979 showed that 17.6% of the bonds were rated differently by the two agencies. Morton ("A Comparative Analysis of Moody's and S & P's Municipal Bond Ratings," *Review of Business & Economic Research,* Winter 1975) found that as much as 30% of municipal bonds in 1972 possessed split ratings. Since ratings do affect bond yields, the split rating phenomenon is a matter of relevance for market participants and firms.

PRIVATE PLACEMENT MARKET

The private placement market is an important source of capital for U.S. corporations. During the 1970s **31% of the new corporate issues were sold privately.** Despite the size and importance of this segment of the capital markets, there is very little available information on individual financings sold or the private placement market as a whole. This is in contrast to the public market, where detailed descriptions of individual issues are available in prospectuses, and aggregate data on volume and interest rate levels are widely published.

The Securities Act of 1933, which was designed to secure full and fair disclosure on the part of companies proposing a public sale of securities, is the fountainhead of today's private placements. Section 4(2) of the law exempts offerings made to knowledgeable purchasers from the normal registration process that the Securities and Exchange Commission (SEC) enforces on public security offerings. Rule 146, issued by the SEC in 1974, provides detailed guidelines that issuers may elect to follow in arranging private placements. Basically the rule restricts qualified transactions to those marketed through contacts with purchasers who are directly solicited, well grounded in investment matters, informed about a financing (or at least able to become so), limited in number, and investment rather than resale oriented.

A private placement (also known as a **direct placement**) is a direct sale of securities to a limited number, at times only one, of sophisticated investors, usually life insurance companies. Like the public market for new issues, the private placement market is a system designed to permit the sale of securities. However, it differs from the primary public market in two important respects: **method of distribution** and **degree of liquidity.**

Customarily, when a company makes a public offering of securities, the issue is underwritten by an investment banking firm. For a fee, the underwriter assumes the risk of reselling them to the public. No such interim step occurs in a private placement; the issue is sold directly by the company to a limited group of investors.

When **purchasers of public issues** wish to dispose of their holdings, they normally encounter little difficulty because stock exchanges and brokerage houses facilitate such transactions. The **market in direct placement** is far less liquid, however: formal trading centers do not exist, and there is usually a paucity of holders in any given issue. Moreover, the investment qualifications (proscribing indiscriminate sale) imposed on purchasers of private placements inhibits turnover. Despite these obstacles, occasional trades of issues directly placed do occur.

During the 1970s the private placement market showed tremendous growth in both dollar volume and market share. The primary market in private placements demonstrated a 16% average annual growth rate in dollar volume between 1970 and 1979. During the same period, the average annual growth rate of new financings placed in the public sector was approximately 4.5%. The private sector increased its market share of new issues by 120% between 1970 and 1979 (see Exhibit 9).

Even though preferred stocks and equity instruments can be found in the private placement market, **debt offerings dominate.** For example, **bonds** made up approximately 87% of the newly issued private placements in 1979; **preferreds** accounted for 12%; and the remainder consisted of **common stock and equity in lease financings.** Private preferred issues are becoming more popular financial instruments. This sector of the private placement market increased its share of the private market from 1% in 1970 to 12% in 1979. This was partially due to the increased **use of preferred stocks in corporate mergers.** The growth can also be attributed to the increased participation of utility companies in the private sector. Traditionally, utility companies have used preferred stocks as an important source of capital.

EXHIBIT 9   NEW CORPORATE PUBLIC AND PRIVATE FINANCINGS ($ MILLIONS)

	Public	Private	Total New Financings	Percent Private (%)
1979	$36,584	$22,545	$59,129	38
1978	31,150	32,456	54,607	43
1977	36,693	25,748	62,441	41
1976	42,352	21,240	63,592	33
1975	46,828	13,515	60,343	22
1974	31,799	10,674	42,473	25
1973	22,701	12,183	34,884	35
1972	34,241	11,825	46,066	26
1971	39,148	9,067	48,215	19
1970	31,130	6,373	37,503	17

Source: Investment Dealers' Digest, New York, 1980.

The development of an intermediate preferred market in the last few years contributed to this expansion of the private preferred market. **Intermediate preferreds** usually have maturities of 12 years or less. The credit or finance divisions of U.S. firms are the major issuers of these intermediate preferreds.

The **creation of an intermediate preferred market** has coincided with the desires of investors to shorten the maturities of the investments they hold. This change in investment philosophy by investors was a direct result of the uncertain economic conditions and the rampant inflation seen in the late 1970s. Corporations also reacting to the adverse economic news have a tended to finance on a shorter term basis to maintain flexibility in a chaotic economic environment and in anticipation of declining long-term rates in the future. Thus, in response to the shifting needs of both borrowers and lenders, financings of debt with intermediate maturities (1–10 years) have become more prevalent.

ADVANTAGES AND DISADVANTAGES.   Raising capital in the private placement market frequently offers corporations many advantages not available in the public market. Among these advantages are **speed, ability to complete complex financings, reduced fees, and opportunity to sell issues in a variety of sizes.**

Funds can be raised more quickly in the private markets than in the public market place. Issuers of direct placements are not confronted with the delays encountered with the **SEC registration process** that most issuers of public issues must endure. This advantage can be particularly important during periods of volatility in the securities markets, when attractive financing opportunities can suddenly appear and just as suddenly disappear.

Since the investors who participate in the private placement market are highly sophisticated and a limited number of investors are contracted, it is often possible to complete financings that for many reasons may not be sold in public offerings. Complexity of financing, size, nature of credit, or a combination of all these factors may make it extremely difficult to sell unless a sophisticated investor is involved. However, even sophisticated investors can be confused by a multitude of complex terms. Therefore, it may be necessary for the issuer to fully explain the terms of the financing to the investor. This is almost inconceivable when issues are publicly offered.

Project financing, with many attendant complexities, e.g., large amounts of funds often required, and frequent need for a series of repayments over time, is a type of financing that is usually best suited to the private market. Project financing, as the name implies, involves capital raised for the completion of specific projects where the repayment scheme is often tied to the cash flow pattern of the project.

Fees and other **expenses** on direct placements tend **to be lower than those of publicly offered issues** of similar size. A simple and inexpensive **offering circular,** which is used to disseminate information about the new issue, is usually prepared by a corporation issuing a private placement. In contrast, a costly and elaborate prospectus must be prepared by the issuers (or investment banker) when they are going into the public sector for financing. When selling issues in the public markets, an **underwriter** is retained. The underwriter oftentimes assumes the ownership risks of the new offering. Therefore, this firm must be compensated for assuming such risks. However, corporations that issue private placements are not burdened with these **underwriting fees.** Advisers, usually investment bankers or corporate finance departments of commercial banks, are often retained by corporations to aid in **structuring the private placement agreement.** These advisers assume no ownership risks; therefore their fees tend to be much lower than the fees of underwriters.

The **public market** always used to be regarded as the appropriate medium for all issue sizes. However, this consensus no longer exists. In recent years, the direct placement market has demonstrated that it can handle large deals; 18 issues with sizes of at least $200 million were placed in 1978 and 1979. This market is now a viable competitor for major offerings. The private placement market has always been able to handle small issues. This, however, is not true for the public markets, since secondary markets in small issues tend to be illiquid and investors interested in reaping trading profits tend to shy away from small issues. Small issues are therefore not received well by investors in the primary public markets.

In light of all these advantages, it is no mystery why the direct placement is increasing its share of the primary, original issue, market. **The public market** does, however, have the advantage of flexibility. Private placement agreements are generally held to be more restrictive; they often include provisions that impose tighter controls—on additional debt issues, for example—than do covenants governing public security issues. This drawback, however, is offset to some degree by the comparative ease with which private agreement provisions can be amended or waived.

The use of a private placement also reduces the flexibility of issuers in meeting sinking fund requirements. Because of the repayment provisions that are attached to issues privately placed and because of the minor trading that takes place in them, **scheduled retirement payments are usually made pro rata to original owners** in cash in stipulated amounts. These conditions normally prevent private issuers from repurchasing their obligations at substantial discounts—a real possibility for public market issuers during periods when interest rates are sharply above those prevailing at the time of their "issues" origination.

MARKET PARTICIPANTS.   **Life insurance companies** have been the major source of capital in the private placement market. The tremendous growth in direct placements throughout the 1970s was in no small way related to the growth exhibited by life insurance companies in that decade. Recently, **pension funds** have shown some interest in the private placement market.

Participation in the private sector by pension funds is a direct result of the increasing presence of better rated companies issuing securities in the private market. In the past, most issuers found in the direct placement market had relatively poor **credit ratings.** These firms were forced to turn to the private placement market for funds because they were closed out of the public market. This situation was especially prevalent during periods of economic adversity. However, this is no longer true of the current markets. Recently, companies with ratings as low as B, or its equivalent, have been able to raise money in the public sector. Although the typical company in the private sector has a rating of BBB or Baa, companies with a rating of A or better have also been attracted to the direct placement market because of the advantages it offers.

Industrial companies have been the primary issuers in the direct placement market. However, utility companies have become extremely active issuers over the past couple of years. As previously noted, the growth in the private preferred stock was spurred by utility companies. **Credit and finance companies** have also increased the number of issues they have placed in the private sector. Again, the **private preferred stock sector** has received many of the new private issues placed by credit and finance companies. Issues of transportation companies, railroads, banks, and foreign and Canadian corporations are found in the private sector.

DUAL MARKET.   Traditionally, yields on issues placed directly have been approximately 35–50 basis points higher than public issues of similar maturity and credit rating. This yield differential is primarily a result of the **illiquidity of directly placed issues.** However, since mid-1974 this has not always been the case. The average spread between Baa/BBB quality paper publicly and privately placed since 1974 has ranged between -20 and -69 basis

EXHIBIT 10 SPREAD RELATIONSHIP FOR PRIVATE VERSUS PUBLIC MARKETS OF SIMILAR QUALITY

	A Quality		Baa/BBB Quality	
	Average Spread: Public vs. Private (b.p.)	Range (b.p.)	Average Spread: Public vs. Private (b.p.)	Range (b.p.)
1979	+28	+17 to -41	-20	+29 to -48
1978	+12	-3 to +43	-33	-5 to -48
1977	+6	-17 to +22	-36	-18 to -60
1976	+11	-9 to +42	-33	+14 to -89
1975	+16	-15 to +44	-69	-25 to -100
1974	+28	+21 to +59	-27	+25 to -68
3-Year average:	+14		-30	
6-Year average:	+16		-36	
Widest positive spread over 6 years:	+59, November 1974		+29, June 1979	
Widest negative spread over 6 years:	-17, March 1977		-100, November 1975	

Source: Investment Dealers' Digest, New York, 1980.

points. That is, issuers of Baa/BBB securities have had to pay **higher yields** if they decide to raise funds **in the public market** as opposed to the private market. The yield spreads between publicly and privately issued A-rated paper during the same period has tended to be "normal." Issuers of A-rated paper have found it more expensive to raise funds in the private market as opposed to the public market (see Exhibit 10).

Caution must be taken when analyzing **yield spreads.** In this situation, even though credit ratings were held constant, the average maturities of the various market segments were probably not similar. Publicly issued securities tend to have longer maturities than do similar securities issued in the private sector. Also it has been suggested that the private market lags the public market by a period of 4–6 weeks.

This **"lag" between the private and public markets** is a direct result of the time difference between the agreement to terms and the distribution of funds in the private sector. In the private market, borrowers and lenders usually agree to terms several weeks before the funds are actually transferred to the borrower. In the public market, on the other hand, the issuer generally takes possession of the funds once an agreement has been reached.

RESALE OF PRIVATE PLACEMENTS.   Sales of direct placements by investors tend to be inhibited by the illiquidity of the securities. However, a **secondary market in private placements** does exist. The resale of these securities can be completed only when certain legal requirements have been fulfilled. The issuer of the private placement **must register the securities with the SEC,** and a prospectus must be prepared for prospective investors. There are, however, certain exceptions to the rule. SEC Rule 144 describes requirements that, if met, exempt the directly placed issue from the registration process when it is sold in the secondary market. These requirements are:

1. The seller must have owned the securities for at least 2 years.

2. The amount sold in any 3-month period must not exceed 1% of the total number of securities outstanding or, if the securities are listed on an exchange, the greater of 1% or the average weekly volume of all the exchanges in which the security is listed during the 4 weeks prior to the sale. (However, holders of private placements not affiliated with the issuer for a period of 3 months prior to the sale can disregard this requirement if the securities are listed on an exchange and held for 3 years. If the securities are not listed on an exchange, the securities must be held for 4 years.)

3. The sale must occur as a normal broker's transactions.

4. Form 144 must be filed with the SEC at the time of the sale to provide the public with the necessary information about the issuer.

OUTLOOK FOR THE PRIVATE MARKET.   A number of trends are developing in the private placement market as we enter the 1980s. The market is beginning to take on an **international orientation.** In the late 1970s foreign investors, especially those from oil-exporting countries, became acquainted with the private sector. As their familiarity with the market increases, so will their participation. Foreign borrowers are also looking to the private market as an alternative source of financing.

The **merger** has long been a popular technique employed by corporations desiring to expand. In recent years mergers have been financed with capital raised in the direct placement market. As mentioned before, private preferred stocks have been increasingly used as a means to finance mergers.

The participation of better rated corporations in the private sector has forced firms with poorer ratings to add **equity "kickers"** to their issues. Without these sweeteners, the poorly rated corporations would be hard pressed to compete for funds with the better rated companies.

PROJECT FINANCING.   This type of financing is used primarily for large individual investment projects. Often a separate legal entity owns the project. Some of those projects are so large (e.g., oil and gas exploration, port facilities, aluminum plants) that a consortium of companies is formed to finance them through **equity participations, debt,** and **lease arrangements.** Often the financing is on a **nonrecourse basis** where the lender or lessor can look for repayment only to the earnings stream of the project. In other instances, the project's sponsor **guarantees the project's completion,** but after it is completed the return to investors is a function only of the project cash flows.

One type of project financing is a **take-or-pay arrangement** whereby each sponsor purchases a specific percentage of the project's output and pays a percentage of the operating costs and debt servicing charges. When pipelines are involved, this type of sharing arrangement is known as a **through put.** With the continuing energy needs of the 1980s and the large amounts of capital these needs require, **project financing** is likely to increase in importance. For a discussion of project financing, see Van Horne, *Financial Management & Policy*, 4th ed.

PREFERRED STOCK

Preferred stock represents a curious combination of various **features of debt and equity.** It is like common stock in that the instrument is called stock and is included in the equity section of the balance sheet; **payments** are considered dividends and are **not deductible for tax purposes;** the payment of dividends is not legally required; and the issue has **no fixed maturity.** Preferred stock is also similar to debt in that the **dividends have a fixed maximum rate;** investors in preferreds generally have **no vote** (unless a specified number—often four to six quarters—of dividends are not paid, in which case they may elect a minority of the board); holders are entitled to no more than the amount paid in to the firm in case of **liquidation;** and preferred stock may contain the same **call, sinking fund,** or **conversion feature as bonds.** In the event of liquidation, preferred stockholders are treated as creditors of the corporation. Their claims on assets are ahead of common stock but behind all bonds.

If a corporation has a poor year, it can forgo distributing dividends to holders of preferred stock without the danger of **bankruptcy.** Unlike bonds, failure to meet a stipulated dividend does not constitute default, and thus the legal ramifications resulting from such action are avoided. Preferred investors can protect themselves from this situation if their issue contains a provision for what are known as **cumulative dividends.** This provision specifies that all past preferred stock dividends must be paid in full before any dividends to common stock can be distributed. Companies that issue preferred stock with cumulative dividends can find themselves in the unenviable position of disbursing large amounts of money to preferred stockholders to pay off **dividend arrearages** before they can distribute dividends to their shareholders. Companies in such a position usually try to strike a compromise with the holders of the preferreds. Exchange of the preferred stock for debt or common stock has been the most popular solution to the problem at hand. Generally, no interest accrues on dividends in arrears. Therefore, preferred holders may be more inclined to an exchange offer than continuing to hold the preferred issue.

SINKING FUND PREFERREDS.   **Preferred stock with sinking funds** has become a popular financial instrument. The popularity has been stimulated by two factors: a ruling by the **National Association of Insurance Commissioners (NAIC)** and (2) the **inflationary and uncertain economic environment.**

As of December 31, 1978, the NAIC allowed insurance companies holding preferred stock with a sinking fund provision to carry these preferreds **at cost rather than market value** for statement purposes. Because of this ruling, changes in the market value no longer have an impact on the insurance companies' inventory of preferred issues with sinking funds. To take advantage of the ruling, the preferred stock must have a sinking fund that meets the following requirements: (1) 100% of the issue will be retired at a rate of not less than 2.5% per year, and (2) the sinking fund must begin within 10 years of the issuing date.

With the advent of the new NAIC ruling, preferred stocks with sinking fund have become an attractive investment alternative for insurance companies. Since the new ruling went into effect, the **yield spread** between preferreds with sinking funds and bonds has increased, with the preferred requiring a relatively lower yield.

Any provision that shortens the maturity of a financial instrument during periods of high inflation or economic uncertainty will be favorably received by all participants of the capital markets. Investors do not want to tie up their money for long periods of time. Borrowers also want to shorten the maturities of their obligations. Therefore, preferred issues with sinking funds are well received. The sinking fund gives the issue a final maturity date, in contrast to the perpetual nature of a preferred issue without a sinking fund. Also because of the sinking fund provision, preferreds with intermediate maturities (12 years or less) have been issued. As investors and issuers have become very attracted to intermediate preferreds, a large market for these intermediate issues, private as well as public, has developed.

CONVERTIBLE PREFERREDS.   Preferred stocks that are **convertible into common stock** have also become a popular security. Most companies use the convertible feature as a "sweetener." This provision is a technique used to make the preferred issue more attractive to investors and less costly for the issuer. Some investors are willing to accept a lower yield in exchange for a chance to participate in the potential appreciation of a firm's stock. Convertible preferred stock offers the investor such an opportunity.

Convertible preferred stocks have also become a popular means to **finance a merger.** Convertible preferreds offer the shareholders of the target company equity in potential higher earnings as well as in assets. If the combination proves to be successful, they can convert and reap the benefits of higher earnings. If, however, the potential increase in earnings does not materialize, they can keep their preferred stock and enjoy whatever protection and dividends it may produce. Preferreds with the convertible feature offer the stockholders of the target company a tax-free exchange. In contrast, a stockholder receiving bonds or cash in exchange for stock will have to pay **capital gains tax** on the amount received in excess of their cost. Mergers financed with convertible preferred stock are also beneficial to the shareholders of the acquiring firm. An exchange of convertible preferred for common will not immediately cause dilution of the earnings per share. With a convertible, preferred dilution will be gradual and could be absorbed by the growth in earnings.

PARTICIPATING PREFERREDS.   Some preferred stockholders participate with common stockholders in sharing the firm's earnings. This feature is rare, but in some cases this "sweetener" is used to sell preferred issues. **Participating preferred stock** generally works as follows: (1) the stated preferred dividend is paid, (2) dividends, up to an amount equal to the preferred dividends, are distributed to common stockholders, and (3) any remaining income is shared equally among common and preferred stockholders.

PREFERENCE STOCKS.   **Subordinated issues of preferred stock** are also found in the market. These are known as **preference stocks** and can have all the same features of preferred issues. However, the claims of holders of these preference stocks are subordinated to the claims of preferred stockholders. They tend to be more risky, and therefore will pay a higher dividend rate than a similar preferred issue.

PAR AND LIQUIDATION VALUES.   The preferred stock's par value serves two important functions. First of all, it establishes the amount due to the holder of the preferred issues in the event of the firm's liquidation. Second, the dividend of the preferred stock is frequently stated as a percentage of the par value. Dividend rates can also be stated in dollar values. Generally, the par value of a preferred stock is $100. Recently, preferreds with par values of $10, $25, and $50 have been issued to attract small investors.

PREFERRED STOCK RATINGS.   Preferred stock, like debt, is rated by **Moody's** and **Standard & Poor's.** Factors considered in arriving at a preferred stock rating are essentially the same as those reviewed in the case of a corporate bond. The most important are provisions of articles of incorporation, asset protection, financial resources, future earnings protection, and management.

Preferred stock will generally have a **lower rating than bonds** issued by the same corporation. This is true because preferred stockholders are ranked behind bondholders in the event of a firm's liquidation.

Preferred stock ratings represent a considered judgment of the relative security of dividends and the implied prospective yield stability of the stock. S & P ratings are as follows:

AAA	Prime
AA	High grade
A	Sound
BBB	Medium grade
BB	Lower grade
B	Speculative
C	Submarginal

Preferred stocks offer a number of advantages and opportunities for companies seeking to raise capital. First, a new source of funds is available to issuers of preferreds. Investors have various investment strategies and by offering a number of financial instruments (bond, preferreds, or equity) a company can tap a larger supply of capital. Second, a firm can increase its **equity base** by issuing preferred stock and therefore improve the **borrowing base** for future debt financing. Third, the control of existing shareholders is not diminished when nonconvertible preferred stock is issued. When convertible preferred stock is issued, the control of existing shareholders is threatened. However, as mentioned before, this process tends to be gradual and could be absorbed by future growth in earnings. Also since the conversion price is generally above the current market price, issuers of convertible preferreds are said to sell equity ahead of the market. Fourth, as previously noted, convertible preferreds can facilitate mergers or acquisitions.

PREFERRED STOCK ISSUERS.   The primary issuers of preferred stock are **utility companies.** This is because preferred stock dividends are treated as fixed costs and can be passed along to the customers. Corporations paying low or no taxes may find preferred stocks, rather than debt, a more attractive means of raising capital. Firms in this tax situation will not benefit by writing off their interest. Therefore, given the tax treatment of dividends on preferred stocks held by corporations, the yield on a preferred stock may be less than the yield on a bond. If a corporation's stock is depressed and it has a high debt-to-equity ratio, preferred stocks may be found to offer a viable source of capital. A company can effectively lower its debt-to-equity ratio by selling preferred stock instead of the more costly common stock.

PREFERRED STOCK PURCHASERS.   Corporations, especially **life insurance companies,** tend to be the primary holders of preferreds. This is due to the preferential tax treatment of preferred dividends paid to corporate holders of preferreds: 85% of the dividend received by corporations on their preferred investment is not taxable. Yields on preferred stock tend to follow yields on other fixed income securities rather closely. However, because of the 85% exclusion of preferred dividends, the **aftertax yield on preferreds** tends to be higher than a bond issued by the same corporation. Holders of preferred stocks receive other benefits from their investment. Preferreds provide reasonably steady income, and preferred stockholders have a preference over common stockholders in the event of liquidation.

COMMON STOCK

Common stock or, for unincorporated firms, the proprietors' or partners' interest constitutes the **ownership of the firm.** The laws of the state in which the company is chartered and the terms of the charter granted by the state define the rights of the holders of common stock. The rights and responsibilities attached to equity consist of positive considerations (income potential and control of the firm) and negative considerations (loss potential, legal responsibility, and personal liability).

COMMON STOCKHOLDERS' RIGHTS.   A number of common stockholders' rights are usually found in most **corporate charters.** Holders of common stock are usually given certain collective rights. Some of the more important rights allow stockholders (1) to amend the charter with the approval of the appropriate officials in the state of incorporation, (2) to adapt and amend bylaws, (3) to elect directors of the corporation, (4) to authorize the sale of fixed assets, (5) to enter into mergers, (6) to change the amount of authorized common stock, and (7) to issue preferred stock, debentures, bonds and other securities.

Stockholders also have specific rights as individual owners:

1. They have the right to vote in the manner prescribed by the corporate charter.
2. They may sell their stock certificates, their evidence of ownership, and in this way transfer their ownership interest to other persons.
3. They have the right to inspect the corporate books. This does not extend to an examination of the books of account or minutes of directors' meetings except under special circumstances.
4. They have the right to share residual assets of the corporation on dissolution; but the holders of common stock are last among the claimants to the assets of the corporation.

Stockholders, through their right to vote, have legal control of the corporation. However, in practice, holders of common stock do not run the corporation. Common stockholders **elect a board of directors** to oversee the running of the corporation.

It is the board of directors that names the management team that will direct the everyday business operations of the corporation. In effect, in a corporation, **ownership and control are separate,** but the goal of decisions made by management should always be to **maximize the wealth of the shareholders.** Also, it must be remembered that common stockholders have the right to vote on any matter that will have a large impact on the firm's operation. In most cases the shareholders temporarily transfer their voting rights. The instrument that transfers the voting rights is known as a **proxy.** The proxy is typically limited in duration, generally for a specific occasion such as the **annual meeting of stockholders.**

There are primarily two **methods of voting** employed in the **election of directors.** The first method which assigns one vote to one share of stock is the **majority voting system.** Thus a person who owns 100 shares has the right to cast 100 votes for each opening on the board of directors. The second method is known as **cumulative voting.** This method allows a shareholder to accumulate all his votes and cast them for one director. For example, if a person owns 100 shares of stock and there are three openings on the board of directors, the shareholder has 300 votes overall. When cumulative voting is permitted, the stockholder can cast 300 votes for one director. Cumulative voting is designed to enable a minority group of stockholders to obtain some voice in the control of the company by electing at least one director to the board.

Shareholders are usually given the first option to purchase additional issues of common stock. This is known as the **preemptive right.** This right protects the current position of the present stockholders in terms of **control** and **dilution.** The latter is usually more important since it provides for old shareholders to retain their respective proportion of outstanding shares. The former **prevents** management from issuing new shares to "friendly" persons to ensure management's continued control of the firm.

COMMON STOCK CHARACTERISTICS. Common stock is a **perpetual security** with no fixed payment schedule. Unlike debt securities, where failure to meet interest payments entails default and bankruptcy proceedings, a corporation is under no such pressure to pay out dividends to its stockholders. However, most large corporations pride themselves on their history of paying out dividends with no interruption regardless of economic conditions. **Dividends** on common equity **cannot be deducted for tax purposes;** therefore they are paid directly out of the aftertax profits of the firm.

Corporations can be classified by their dividend payment policies and the potential price appreciation of their stock. The shares of firms that do not generate large returns on their investment in assets but that pay out in such dividends most of what they do earn are called **income shares.** These stocks sell almost entirely on a pure **dividend yield basis,** because appreciation from retained earnings is limited. Income stocks may be above-average risk securities issued by declining firms that have exhausted their most profitable investment opportunities (e.g., railroad, fire and casualty, undiversified tobacco companies). On the other hand, income stocks may also be lower than average risk securities issued by firms that have their return on investment regulated by the government. These equities, which are usually stable and relatively safe even during periods of recession, may retain earnings and show capital appreciation. Nevertheless, their **growth rates** are constrained by the regulated rate of return that they are allowed to earn on plant and equipment. The best examples of low-risk income stocks are the shares of most American public utilities.

An equity whose average return is much better than the average increase in sales and earnings of all corporations for a consistent period of time is called a **growth stock.** These shares outperform the economy and most other equities in their respective industries. Growth companies typically pay negligible dividends because they can do better for their shareholders by retaining earnings and reinvesting in plant and equipment. They are aggressive in their search for new profitable opportunities, and they typically spend a great deal on research and development. The returns on their stocks are derived primarily from their price appreciation.

COMMON STOCK RISK.   In the event of a firm's liquidation, common stockholders are the last group to be compensated. The claims of creditors must be satisfied before assets can be distributed to equity holders. Because of its **low priority in liquidation** situations, common stock has the greatest risk of any security in the corporate structure. The **required rate of return on equity** (price appreciation plus dividends) must be high enough to compensate the holders of equity for the risk they are assuming. Therefore the rate of return on equity should be higher than the return on any other security in the same corporation or corporations with similar risk structures. If this were not the case, a corporation would be hard pressed to find any investors interested in holding its common stock.

ISSUING COMMON STOCK.   Usually a firm employs an **investment banker** when it decides to float a stock issue to raise capital. If the firm's stockholders have **preemptive rights,** the new stock must be offered to existing stockholders. Otherwise, the firm, in consultation with its bankers, must decide whether to offer the stock to existing stockholders. There are a number of issues that affect this decision. Among them are (1) **flotation costs,** (2) effects on **price of stock,** (3) **potential dilution** of earnings per share for current stockholders, and (4) **distribution of shares** held by the public.

Advantages of Issuing Common Stock.   From the viewpoint of the issuer, raising capital with common stock has a number of advantages. One major advantage is that common stock, unlike debt, entails **no fixed charges.** Second, common stock **increases the creditworthiness** of the corporation because it provides a cushion against losses for creditors. Usually, equity increases in value when the value of real assets rises during a period of inflation. Investors can benefit from holding common stock because the capital gain resulting from price appreciation is taxed at a lower rate than an investor's ordinary income.

Disadvantages of Issuing Common Stock.   Sale of new common stock, except in the case of a **preemptive rights offering,** reduces the control existing stockholders have over the company. As noted above, rights offerings provide for existing stockholders to purchase new shares so that their proportional ownership of the company is not diluted. Also, a sale of common stock may dilute earnings for existing stockholders. Dilution of earnings is a reduction in the earnings per share of stock. In this case, dilution may occur because the number of outstanding shares of common stock was increased. However, this can be prevented if the capital raised from the stock sale generates increased earnings. **Underwriting costs** tend to be higher for common stock than for debt or preferred issues. Also, if there is more equity than is called for in the optimum capital structure, the average cost of capital will be higher than necessary.

Registration with SEC.   Prior to the offering of any stock, a registration statement must be filed with the **Securities and Exchange Commission.** Upon filing, the investment banker must wait a specified period of time so that the SEC staff can analyze the accuracy of the registration statement. The SEC may file exceptions to the registration statement or may ask for additional information from the issuing company or the underwriters during the examination period. During this period investment bankers are not permitted to offer the securities for sale, although they may print preliminary prospectuses with all the customary information except the offering price.

Determining Flotation Costs. The firm and its investment banker must agree on the banker's compensation or the flotation cost involved in issuing the stock. **Flotation costs** to the firm consist of two elements—compensation to the **investment banker,** plus legal, accounting, printing, and other **out-of-pocket costs** borne by the issuer. The investment banker's compensation consists of the **spread** between the price the company is paid for the stock and the price at which the stock is sold to the public, called the offering price. Flotation costs historically have ranged from 23.7% of the size of the issue for small issues to 3.5% for issues involving stock with a value of over $50 million. Naturally the company wants to receive the highest possible price for its stock from the investment banker, so it bargains with the banker over both the offering price and the spread. The higher the offering price and the lower the spread, the more the company receives per share of the stock sold; and the more it receives per share, the fewer number of shares required to raise a given amount of money.

Setting the Offering Price. The offering price is not generally determined until the close of the registration period. There is no universally accepted practice, but a common arrangement calls for the **investment banker** to buy the securities at a prescribed number of points below the closing price on the last day of registration. Typically, such agreements have an **escape clause** that provides for the contract to be voided if the price of the securities ends below some predetermined figure.

The offering price may have to be set at a substantial discount from the preoffering market price. This will make it easier for the investment banker to market the new shares. However, this will have a detrimental effect on the position of existing shareholders. If the investors can be persuaded that the funds raised from the new stock can be used to enhance the future earnings potential of the company, the **offering price** of the stock need not be below the **preoffering market price.**

SECONDARY MARKET. The secondary market plays an important role in the issuance of new securities. The secondary market facilitates the buying and selling of seasoned securities. A security that is actively traded in the secondary market tends to be liquid. That is, a holder of a liquid security can sell his security with little difficulty. Also, a security that is actively traded tends not to fluctuate greatly in price. Therefore, the holder of an actively traded security does not face as great a risk of capital loss as does the holder of an illiquid issue.

It will be to the benefit of the holder, the issuer, and the investment banker if the banker is able to "make a market" for the issuer's securities. An investment banking firm will create an active secondary market for its clients if it expects to have referral business and keep its own brokerage customers happy.

REFERENCES AND BIBLIOGRAPHY

Altman, Edward I., "Computerized Bond Rating Replication: Worthwhile or Futile?" *Basis Point,* Equitable Life Assurance Society of America, Fall 1979, pp. 8–11.

Brigham, Eugene F., *Financial Management: Theory and Practice,* 2nd ed., Dryden Press, Hinsdale, IL, 1979.

Bowlin, O D., "The Refunding Decision: Another Special Case in Capital Budgeting," *Journal of Finance*, Vol. 20, No. 1, March 1966, pp. 55–68.

Boyce, W. M., and Kalotay, A. J., "Optimum Bond Calling and Refunding," *Interfaces*, November, 1979, pp. 36–49.

Callahan, J. R. and McCallum, J. S., "The Sinking Fund Decision: Buy Forward or Wait?" *Cost and Management*, January–February 1978, pp. 36–39.

Castle, G., "Project Financing–Guidelines for the Commercial Banker," *Journal of Commercial Bank Lending*, April 1975, pp. 14–30.

Crosby, John G. and Goodwin, J Barton, "Private Placements Market Review 1979," Kidder Peabody & Co. Inc. 1980.

Davey, Patrick J., "Private Placements: Practices and Prospects," *Conference Board*, No. 52, New York, January 1979.

Dyl, E. A., and Joehnk, M. D., "Sinking Funds and the Cost of Corporate Debt," *Journal of Finance*, Vol. 34, No. 4, September 1979, pp. 887–893.

Johnson, R., and Klein, R., "Corporate Motives in Repurchase of Discounted Bonds," *Financial Management*, Autumn 1974, pp. 44–49.

Kalotay, A. J., "On the Advance Refunding of Discounted Debt," *Financial Management*, Summer 1978, pp. 14–18.

———, "On the Management of Sinking Funds," *Financial Management*, Summer 1981.

Kintner, Earl, *Primer on the Law of Mergers*, Macmillan, New York, 1973.

Morton, T. Gregory, "A Comparative Analysis of Moody's and S & P's Municipal Bond Ratings," *Review of Business & Economic Research*, Winter 1975, pp. 74–81.

Van Horne, J. C., *Financial Management and Policy*, 4th ed. Prentice-Hall, Englewood Cliffs, NJ, 1977.

Weston, J. F., and Brigham, E. F., *Managerial Finance*, 6th ed., Dryden Press, Hinsdale, IL, 1978.

William, Edward E., and Findlay, M. Chapman, *Investment Analyses*, Prentice Hall, Englewood Cliffs, NJ, 1974.

Zwick, Burton, "Yields on Privately Placed Corporate Bonds," *Journal of Finance*, Vol. 35, No. 1, March, 1980, pp. 23–29.

THE SECURITIES INDUSTRY: SECURITIES TRADING AND INVESTMENT BANKING

CONTENTS

WHAT IS THE SECURITIES INDUSTRY? 3

A Small Industry 3
Scope of the Industry 3
Suppliers of Securities 3
Buyers of Securities 4
Supporting Services 4

FUNCTIONS OF THE SECURITIES INDUSTRY 5

Orderly Markets 5
Raising New Capital 6
Analyzing Financial and Economic Information 7
Managing Investment Capital 8

STRUCTURE OF THE INDUSTRY 8

A Little Bit of History 8
Legal Environment 10

Types of Brokerage Firm 12
Organized Exchange Marketplace 13
Government Regulatory Groups 15
Instability of Existing Structure 16

SECURITIES TRADING 16

Customer Classes 16
Types of Order 17
Exchange Execution: Old Processes and New 19
Impact of Computers 21
Internationalization of Securities Markets 24

INVESTMENT BANKING 25

Nature of Investment Banking 25
Types of Investment Banker 25
Sale of New Issues 26

SECURITIES INDUSTRY TRENDS: SOME SIGNIFICANT CHANGES 28

THE SECURITIES INDUSTRY: SECURITIES TRADING AND INVESTMENT BANKING

Michael Keenan

WHAT IS THE SECURITIES INDUSTRY?

A SMALL INDUSTRY. Most people have some idea of what constitutes the securities industry in this country. It is the brokerage firms with whom they do business and the securities exchanges on which the common stocks of larger firms are traded. And indeed, it is the securities brokerage firms and exchanges, plus related commodity broker groups, that constitute most of the industry as defined by the Standard Industrial Classification codes of the federal government. By this definition there are about 200,000 people employed in the securities industry throughout the United States. This is small compared to the more than 350,000 people employed by the Ford Motor Co. alone.

SCOPE OF THE INDUSTRY. This complex industry is broader than the narrow definition above suggests. The economic impact of the industry is far greater than the impact of any single firm of 200,000 employees. The securities industry includes: (1) the suppliers of securities—the industry's clients, (2) the buyers of securities—the industry's customers, (3) the inner industry—brokerage firms, exchanges, associations, (4) industry regulators—self-regulatory groups, the SEC, and others (5) direct supporting services—transfer of certificates, custodial services, special communications networks, and (6) other supporting services—legal, accounting, educational, outside computer support, office space, and indirect service requirements. Many of these groups are not counted as part of the securities industry, but they are essential to its operation.

SUPPLIERS OF SECURITIES. The suppliers can be divided into four categories: (1) the federal government and its agencies, (2) state and local governments, (3) private business firms, and (4) individuals. The problems in properly defining the scope of the securities industry are immediately apparent upon listing the suppliers of securities. For example, should trading and distribution of short-maturity securities be counted as part of the securities industry? In the case of short-term government debt and commercial paper, the primary intermediaries, banks and finance companies, are not counted as part of the securities industry. On the other hand, trading and promotion of some short-maturity, equity-type instruments such as options, commodity contracts, even commodity contracts in short-term government debt, are considered to be functions of the securities industry.

BUYERS OF SECURITIES.   The buyers are usually divided into two groups: individuals and institutions. It is sometimes said that the former are nonprofessionals or amateurs in the investment process, whereas the latter are "professionals" in securities transactions. There is no systematic difference between the two groups in investment returns earned over the long run but there are differences between the two groups. Pension fund managers, insurance companies, mutual funds, and other institutional buyers tend to transact larger amounts and with greater frequency than individuals. The typical institutional portfolio will be more diversified than the individual's portfolio, having a larger number of securities whose returns are not highly correlated than the typical individual's portfolio. And institutions are more likely to support their transactions decisions with formal research or background data for the issuer of the security being bought or sold. Institutions hold most of the debt instruments outstanding in the United States, including 80% of the corporate debt. Institutions are responsible for two-thirds of the public volume on the New York Stock Exchange, but individuals still own directly about 70% of the value of stock outstanding in this country.

SUPPORTING SERVICES.   These include direct supporting services—facilities necessary for the day-to-day conduct of the business, and other supporting services that are necessary more because this industry exists with people to be fed and housed than because of the particular nature of brokerage firm activities. Direct supporting services relate to the registration, transfer, custodial care, and physical transportation of securities. Providing such services has traditionally been a complex activity. Since more than one brokerage firm is involved, and since the valuable nature of the instruments requires considerable security, usually a third party participates. Commercial banks have long assumed major responsibility for registration and transfer activities and have been significant in providing custodial arrangements. Other firms have also specialized in such activities and in providing the bonded messenger services necessary to move securities. As long as physical delivery of securities was the customary mode of business, these services had to be in close proximity to the brokerage firms and major customer groups—and that meant the Wall Street area.

With the advent of computer balancing of securities transactions, with changes in the perceived legal requirements by major customer groups (particularly pension and mutual funds) so that direct physical possession of all securities is not always required, and with the increased volume of trading, the whole back office procedure is rapidly changing. Now regional consortiums associated with the various exchanges handle many of the clearing and custodial functions. Equity securities are increasingly immobilized (i.e., not subjected to actual physical transfer). This is the most significant technological change to occur in the securities industry this century. While the same sort of progress has not been made for debt securities, it is likely to develop over the next decade. By the end of the century, the "direct supporting services" as they existed at midcentury will be gone. Perhaps 50,000 jobs in close proximity to the financial community will be replaced by fewer than 5,000 jobs associated with a national clearing and depository service. That national center need not be located in close proximity to the financial community.

The other direct supporting service is the telecommunications network. The securities industry requires a higher level of rapid communication than do most industries. However, a significant portion of the hardware is not directly owned within the industry but is equipment rented or leased from outside suppliers.

Other supporting services may be divided into those that provide services to the firms in the securities industry and those that provide services to the employees in the industry. The following are included in first group: (1) real estate owners and brokers—most of the physical facilities in the securities industry are not owned by firms in the industry, (2) legal and accounting services, particularly for investment banking functions, (3) specialized printing firms—to produce securities, registration forms, industry reports, specialized newspapers, and so on, (4) external computer support groups, and (5) specialized educational units and libraries.

The second group includes: luncheon clubs, bars and sandwich shops, transportation services, small retail stores, and all the variety of indirect services supplied simply because a community of people exists—incremental police, fire, and hospital protection, grocery stores, and the rest.

FUNCTIONS OF THE SECURITIES INDUSTRY

There are at least four distinguishing functions performed by the securities industry. One is to make more orderly the buying and selling of existing securities. Another is to promote the raising of certain types of new capital for public and private groups. A third function is to analyze financial and economic information, to make the capital markets more efficient by relating such information to security value or to the proper utilization of new investment flows. A fourth function is to use such analysis and other tools in managing pools of investment capital.

ORDERLY MARKETS.   The primary function of a securities market is to provide a "meeting place" for buyers and sellers to effect transactions. Historically early security marketplaces (in France and England in the late seventeenth century, in this country at the end of the eighteenth century) were literally designated taverns or lanes where buyers and sellers could meet to transact. Eventually these places of convenience became organized into "exchanges." The markets were made orderly by promoting rules and standards for such matters as (1) the hours of operation, (2) the mode of payment for transactions, (3) the process for transferring securities, (4) the description of ethical behavior and the characterization of fraudulent practices, (5) the training required for those providing specialized services or acting as agents in the marketplace, and (6) the fees to be charged for various services provided.

Modern markets for the exchange of securities can be put together in numerous diverse ways. Exhibit 1 suggests three organizing elements: type of buyer representation, type of seller representation, and the market process for effecting transactions. There are 12 combinations of the buyer-seller-market process elements.

The buyer-seller representation can either be an **agency transaction** (acting on behalf of another) or a **principal transaction** (acting on behalf of oneself). The prices of the security may be posted, as is true for most retail goods markets. Or the pricing may be determined by direct negotiation between buyer and seller, as it usually is in a used car market. The

EXHIBIT 1   ORGANIZING ELEMENTS IN
A SECURITIES MARKETPLACE

Function	Element
Buyer representation	Agent or principal
Seller representation	Agent or principal
Market process	Posted pricing
	Negotiated pricing
	Auction pricing

price may be determined by some type of auction system, where buyers display their "bid" prices and sellers display their "offer" prices and there is a mechanism for insuring that transactions occur according to an agreed upon set of rules. There are many types of **auction market,** from the continuous auction market with specialist intervention of the New York Stock Exchange, to the periodic auction markets with round-robin calls once a day of some European exchanges.

Some examples may make the alternative structures clearer. Suppose that you want to buy a U.S. savings bond. This is likely to be a case of a buyer principal (you), buying from a selling agent (your bank), in a posted pricing market. If you ask your broker to buy an insurance stock not listed on any exchange, it could be buyer-agent–seller-principal–negotiated market pricing, meaning that your broker is buying for you a stock directly from the owner (who may be another broker holding it in inventory, or an individual or institution owning the stock), after at least a little negotiation. If you buy a stock on a major stock exchange it is most likely a buyer-agent (your brokerage firm)–seller-agent (seller's brokerage firm)–auction pricing transaction. Whatever the elements of a particular market structure, if that market is to successfully persist, there must be rules to give it order.

RAISING NEW CAPITAL.   An important part of the investment banking function of the securities industry is the raising of new capital. In the United States the securities industry is only one of the groups helping to raise new capital for public and private groups. Commercial banks, insurance companies, other financial institutions, and industrial corporations are all involved in this process. This competitive effort to provide funds for long-term investment has made the United States markets for new capital the largest and most efficient in the world.

The magnitude of capital raised is indicated by the benchmark figures in Exhibit 2, which show that less than 10% of the total credit market funds raised in a year consists of the long-term corporate capital usually associated with the investment banking function of the securities industry. But the securities industry also plays a role in helping to raise government debt

EXHIBIT 2   CREDIT MARKET FUNDS RAISED, 1979 ($ BILLIONS)[a]

Mortgages	$160
U.S. government securities	90
State and local obligations	20
Bank loans	50
Open market paper	40
Other loans	40
Consumer credit	40
Corporate bonds	30
Corporate stock	10
Total funds	$480

[a]Nonfinancial, nonfarm corporate business:

Net income	120
Dividends	− 50
Earnings retained	70
Depreciation	+ 120
Internal fund sources	190

capital (particularly state and local obligations), and increasingly has a role in making liquid the mortgage market.

It is important to note that for existing corporations most long-term funds are from internally generated sources—earnings retained in the business and noncash depreciation charges that provide funds if the firm is generating offsetting revenues. In 1979 these internal sources amounted to about $190 billion, while the new external capital sources from bonds and stocks amounted to $40 billion. The securities industry helped raise most of the $40 billion in new outside capital but did not play a direct role in the corporate decisions about inside sources—how much earnings to retain. Securities markets do play an important secondary role in this process, however. The earnings retained by the firms are generally "capitalized" by the marketplace over time. That is, stock prices increase in the expectation that these retained earnings will be reinvested by firms to generate even higher future earnings and dividends. If the capital markets were not reasonably efficient, this whole process could break down. Stockholders would not be as willing to invest in firms that retained earnings, more capital would have to be raised by directly selling new issues (at higher cost), and a smaller fraction of individuals' savings might be held directly in corporate securities.

ANALYZING FINANCIAL AND ECONOMIC INFORMATION.   To ascertain whether the earnings retained by firms are usefully invested (to generate even higher future earnings), someone must be prepared to analyze current financial information and future plans of these firms. To a degree, everyone who buys or sells a security must be a bit of a security analyst. But since it does take time and experience to perform this function, an area of professional expertise has developed. The securities industry supports several thousand professional security analysts, and additional thousands are found among the banks, insurance companies, pension fund advisors, and other groups responsible for the investment of significant pools of capital.

A security analyst has the task of analyzing all currently available information to evaluate and project the economic status of the firms, the industry, and the economy. These evaluations and projections are combined into an estimate of the true value of a security (or, more likely, a reasonable range for such value), hence a recommendation to buy or sell the security based on its current market price. Truly superior security analysis thus requires some combination of (1) better information than others have, (2) a superior way to screen out "noise" and get at the essential information, (3) a superior way to make future projections, and (4) more complete or better refined valuation frameworks than others are using. To the extent competitive conditions force professional security analysts to do the best possible job, and the information on how they do that job is quickly disseminated, there may be only a few relatively superior analysts at any one time. See the sections "Modern Portfolio Theory and Management" and "Performance Measurement" for a more extensive discussion of these issues.

The information professional security analysts utilize is supposed to be publicly available information. Though an analyst may talk to officers or managers of a firm, they are legally bound not to reveal any new information likely to have a significant impact on the firm's security prices that is not also made generally available.

For U.S. corporations with more than a few hundred shareholders, rather detailed financial income and balance sheet statements must be released at least yearly. These are distributed to shareholders, creditors, and other interested parties, and copies are filed with the Securities and Exchange Commission. For large, exchange-listed firms more abbreviated reports are distributed quarterly. A significant change in the structure or financial condition of any firm, is supposed to be quickly reported to the SEC and announced.

In addition to a firm's own reports, analysts can draw on a great deal of other data. Examples include: (1) government reports and studies, (2) industry trade association reports and magazines, (3) business news publications such as the *Wall Street Journal, Business Week, Forbes,* and *Fortune,* and (4) academic journals and special studies. This wealth of information is a development of the past 100 years in the United States. In some countries today corporations are still required to issue only very abbreviated financial statements. As an adjunct to security analysis, there is the industrial detective agency specializing in ferreting out private financial information. But it is clear that this approach makes value determination more uncertain, and the capital markets less efficient, than is the case when information is more readily available.

MANAGING INVESTMENT CAPITAL.   Different sectors of the industry are organized to provide investment capital management services for major capital pools such as mutual funds and pension funds, and for individual brokerage firm clients. Professional investment management is one of the most rapidly growing services offered by the securities industry. This growth results from a need by clients for greater expertise than has traditionally been required.

There are two factors contributing to the expanded specialization of investment capital management. One is the growth in the applications of modern portfolio theory to investment decisions. This requires specialists who have an understanding of the benefits and limitations of such theory, and who have access to the computers, data banks, and security analysts needed to implement the theory. (The theory is described in the section "Modern Portfolio Theory and Management.") A second factor is the broadened line of services many brokerage houses have begun to offer individual clients. In addition to advice on traditional stocks and bonds, clients are now being counseled about investment opportunities in real estate and tax shelters, and gold, silver, diamonds, and a variety of other collectibles that may be considered as investment vehicles. To provide such services the brokerage houses have created new subsidiaries, acquired existing firms, or hired special consultants. In addition, some of the larger brokerage firms have extended the scope of their services to include credit management and insurance agency activities, thus offering an almost complete package of financial services.

STRUCTURE OF THE INDUSTRY

A LITTLE BIT OF HISTORY.   To better understand the national structure of the securities industry and some currently evolving trends, it is useful to take a selective look at a little bit of history. Some securities trading began in this country with its first settlement. Many of the original colonies represented charter grants from the various crowns of Europe (primarily Spanish, English, and French) to groups that financed initial expeditions by issuing financial instruments to European capitalists. In the case of the land companies some of the deeds and other financial instruments, and some of the capitalists themselves, soon found their way to America. It was natural that some of these instruments would change hands— because of death or gifts, or because of a desire to move or a changed perception of the wealth potential of this new land. Most of these transactions either were private arrangements between the buyer and seller or were carried out in London or another European money center. There was hardly even an embryonic securities industry in what would become the United States.

The Revolutionary War provided the real impetus for the formation of the securities industry. During the war itself the Continental Congress, some states, and the Continental

Army, all issued various notes and forms of scrip. Washington's periodic pleas for more scrip for his army are well known, and the amount forthcoming and its subsequent market value (purchasing power) depended in part on perceptions of how the war was going. After the war the Congress of the newly formed United States funded part of the debt incurred by various states and the debt incurred by the Confederation. This funding of $80 million in federal debt provided the basis on which the securities industry was organized in this country.

As early as May 1792 a group of 24 brokers met in New York City to sign an agreement as to the minimum commission they would charge the public and the terms and conditions for trading among themselves. New York City was then the largest city in the nation (35,000), the state capital of New York, and a principal gateway to Europe. The rates and conditions for consummating trades within the group of brokers were of course more favorable than rates or conditions for brokers not a party to the agreement or for the public at large. This cartel of New York brokers was the precursor of today's **New York Stock Exchange.** In 1817 the brokers adopted a formal constitution and selected the name "New York Stock and Exchange Board." This name was shortened in 1863 to "New York Stock Exchange" (NYSE). Thus the original purpose of the 1792 group was to regulate prices for brokerage services to ensure minimum levels of profitability and to create a systematic procedure for transferring ownership of securities. These remained the principal objectives of the NYSE throughout the first 180 years of its history.

It should be noted that at the outset the Exchange was organized to deal in bonds—the $80 million in federal debt authorized by Congress in accepting most of Secretary of the Treasury Alexander Hamilton's report; other securities included small amounts of state paper and regionally backed transportation issues. Bonds remained the principal instrument of broker activity for a number of years. The federal government debt rapidly expanded for a period as a result of the War of 1812. After that war various types of transportation issue began to find their way to market. Initially demand for funds came from local turnpike authorities and canal charters, but by 1840 the age of railroads was beginning.

With the substantial reduction in federal government debt in the 1820s, the nature of the Exchange market began to change. Federal bonds became less important. Trading in the transportation bond–type securities became more important and stocks as an instrument of trading were gaining rapidly in popularity. Whereas most available domestic equities had been the stocks of banks or insurance companies, now some common stock of nonfinancial corporations began to appear. There were two other basic changes in the securities industry in the 1830s and 1840s. First, domestic investment banking houses largely replaced their European predecessors. While large amounts of capital continued to flow into the United States from European sources, it was now domestic investment bankers who arranged the terms of new securities issues and solicited domestic and foreign buyers.

A second change occurred about the time **gold was discovered in California.** The prospect of potential wealth from underground proved irresistible to many. Mines, mining claims, mining services—some real, some only imagined in the backroom of a bar—were all incorporated to sell shares of their stocks to an eager public. It did not seem to matter that many of the mines proved unproductive, or that many of the mining claims were fraudulent or nonexistent. People were willing to gamble on the rumor of a strike, or on the small probability that at the mine they had bought shares in, there would be a strike large enough to make all the owners rich. This sometimes happened, but for many investors the fact that gold was involved was incentive enough. The interesting points about this development from the securities industry viewpoint are that (1) this is probably the first instance of large-scale public participation in the equity markets in the United States, and (2) the securities were promoted and sold not in New York City or other eastern markets, but in the West. Exchanges were organized throughout the West, bringing brokers together to deal in mining stocks and local securities. In most cases these exchanges were short-lived, lasting only so long as the local mines were productive. In some cases not only did the mines peter out, the cities disappeared.

In cumulative numbers there seem to have been more than a hundred such exchanges in the United States. Only a few survived into the twentieth century, shifting focus from gold speculations to silver to oil or uranium as the type of prospecting activity shifted. Why did most of the mining exchanges die? They died because the brokers who organized them could not make enough money. It was not simply that the mines or the stocks listed failed or were worthless claims to begin with. Often the local exchanges were organized at a time of speculative excitement in each area. Much of the activity of the brokers consisted of issuing and promoting the sale of new stock. In the years before the creation of the Securities and Exchange Commission this could be done virtually at any time, in any amount, by anyone. The real money opportunities for brokers lay in this promotion of new stock. Although a few brokers might sustain themselves by acting purely as brokerage agents, these were exceptions. And only a few exchanges had enough activity to maintain any sort of existence once the initial new deals, the speculative phase, had passed. The exchanges that did survive were usually in already established cities such as San Francisco, Denver, and Salt Lake City.

The **modern structure of the securities industry** did not appear until 1934, with the enactment of the Securities Exchange Act. The legislation passed in 1933 and 1934 was a direct outgrowth of the collapse of the securities markets in the period 1929–1932. Stock volume and prices had advanced spectacularly in the late 1920s, financed by a very large amount of bank credit. As speculative fever rose and new issues all seemed to climb sharply after their initial distribution, the public crowded into the market. Throughout history, whenever the public—that is, those who were not part of the wealthiest classes in society—has entered a financial market in significant numbers, it has been a sign of excessive speculation. This was true of the tulipomania bubble of the 1630s, when Dutchmen paid fortunes for tulip bulbs. It was true of the Mississippi scheme of the early 1720s when the frenzied speculative excesses of Frenchmen in the shares of the Mississippi Company virtually bankrupted them and their entire country. We have already noted that in the U.S. one of the first great waves of public participation in the equity markets was in the short period of mining stock promotions. The game of chance being played toward the end of the 1920s ended in 1929 with the great market crash on Wall Street.

There are three points that can be made from this brief historical digression. First, New York City became the financial center of the nation because of its close proximity to the suppliers of securities (the Federal capital was in New York until 1790), because of the relative proximity to the suppliers of funds (primarily European investment banking groups in the beginning), and because the city had strong prospects of replacing Philadelphia as the commercial center of the nation. Second, for better or worse, the public at large has historically been active in security markets only when speculative instruments were available to be traded. Third, it is not economically feasible to maintain very many stock exchanges in a country. Like several other countries, at one time the United States had many local exchanges (more than 100). Now there are fewer than a dozen left. Most countries end up with one or two.

LEGAL ENVIRONMENT. With the collapse of the financial markets in the early 1930s a series of laws was passed to separate commercial banking from investment banking in the United States and to impose stricter federal regulatory oversight on the securities industry. Major laws include the Securities Act (1933); the Securities Exchange Act (1934); acts related to trustee responsibilities—the Trust Indenture Act (1939), the Investment Company

Act (1940), and the Investment Advisors Act (1940); and laws passed in the early 1970s—the Securities Investor Protection Corporation Act (1970), the Employmee Retirement Income Security Act (1974), and the "National Exchange Market System" (NEMS) Act (1975).

The primary thrusts of the 1930s acts were to inhibit fraud and deceit in the issuance and trading of securities, and to provide a regulatory framework for federal oversight of the securities industry. **The Securities Act (1933)** focused on new issues. New security issues must be registered with the Securities and Exchange Commission. Before the securities are offered for sale, audited financial statements, statements about the issuer's business, other securities outstanding, major contracts, salaries and other payments to officers and directors, and other matters must be filed. Much of this is summarized in a **prospectus,** a booklet that must be sent to every customer who purchases part of the new issues. Before the securities are issued, the SEC has a limited period to review the prospectus for completeness of disclosure. The SEC does not, however, pass judgment on the value of the security as an investment—that is the responsibility first of the selling investment banker and ultimately of the buying customer. Small issues, private offerings to a small group of knowledgeable investors, and secondary offerings of already outstanding securities were exempt from registration under the 1933 Act.

The **Securities Exchange Act (1934)** focused on providing information disclosure for already outstanding securities, and on the formal establishment of the Securities and Exchange Commission as the agency responsible for regulating nongovernmental securities markets. Under this law securities listed for trading must file registration statements and annual reports similar to those filed for new securities. Organized exchanges must register with the SEC, must abide by whatever rules the SEC promulgates, and must put forth bylaws or rules of their own to ensure the orderly operation of the exchanges and the ethical behavior of representatives of member firms. The 1934 Act also provides explicit rules for proxy solicitation (requests to shareholders for their votes), insider trading activities (e.g., officers, directors, and others inside the firm may not earn "speculative trading profits" by buying or selling stock before an important piece of information is made public), and price manipulation schemes. Finally, the Act and associated Federal Reserve regulations enabled a mechanism for controlling credit extended to brokerage firms and their customers in securities transactions.

The acts in the early 1940s primarily involved fiduciary responsibility and related institutional structures. **The Trust Indenture Act** (1939) promulgated rules to avoid some of the conflicts of interest between a firm and the bank or other institution that is trustee for some debt security of the firm. The **Investment Advisors Act** (1940) requires individuals who offer investment advice or analysis for money to register with the SEC, and permits rules to be specified placing limitations on the forms of compensation received and the forms of advertising for new clients. A third piece of legislation was the **Investment Company Act** (1940), which specified the structural form of operation for mutual funds and closed-end investment companies, as well as the responsibilities of officers, advisors, and others associated with such funds.

In a series of acts passed in the early 1970s, Congress significantly changed the protection accorded individual investors, and recommended procedural steps that will eventually change the structure of the exchange market in this country. The **Securities Investor Protection Act** (1970) **(SIPC)** provides insurance to small investors for their securities and cash left on deposit with a brokerage firm if that brokerage firm goes bankrupt. Currently the total claims limit is $100,000 per customer, but many firms have private insurance that increases this protection. The **Employee Retirement Income Security Act** (1974) **(ERISA)** and related pieces of legislation significantly changed the protection accorded individuals who participate in pension funds. For company-sponsored pension plans the law requires full vesting of an employee's share within a few years of work, and requires all underfunded plans to become fully funded within the next three decades. For all employees not covered by firm pension plans, and all individuals who are self-employed, there are tax-advantage opportunities to set up their own pension fund account plans. The securities industry has been one of the leaders in providing this service for millions of customers.

A third series of bills, including the **Securities Amendments Act** (1975) (the ''National Exchange Market System Act''), provided some structural direction for future developments in the securities industry. Congress set up a Commodity Futures Trading Commission (CFTC) to provide oversight regulation for the commodities markets and has encouraged some regulation of the markets for state and local government securities, an area outside the jurisdiction of the SEC. In the 1975 Act and during the associated hearings Congress made clear its preference for more competitive commission rates and related conditions, and encouraged the development of a technologically efficient National Exchange Market System within a reasonable period of time. Details were left to the industry, with the SEC having authority (and responsibility) to step in when necessary. Finally, a proposed new **''Federal Securities Code''** is being reviewed by the SEC and interested groups inside and outside the industry. Congress will hold hearings on this legislation in the early 1980s to determine whether the numerous rule changes in securities transaction codes should become law.

TYPES OF BROKERAGE FIRM.   In the mid-1970s there were more than 4,000 firms in the securities industry, almost 2,000 in the New York region alone. By the beginning of the 1980s the countrywide total had declined by 10% or so because of increased competitive conditions within the industry. As part of their reaction to new competitive conditions, many brokerage firms have been making fundamental changes in their organizational structure.

Traditionally brokerage firms were organized as small private partnerships. Even today, that is the primary form of legal organization. The ''typical'' firm has about 15 employees: 2 or 3 partners, perhaps 5 other professionals, and a small support staff. The firm operates out of one office and has its own equity capital of less than $100,000 invested in the business. Since 1953 the New York Stock Exchange has permitted its member brokerage firms to incorporate, but only as private corporations with restrictions. It was not until 1970 that public ownership of brokerage firm corporations was approved by the NYSE Board of Governors. Even in 1980 more than 200 of the member organizations of the NYSE remain partnerships. Of the more than 300 of these larger brokerage firms that have incorporated, about 15 have public shareholders.

These legal changes are not merely technical changes in the structure and report-filing formats for the firms. Often accompanying the legal change are possible fundamental changes (1) in the administrative structure of the firm (lines of responsibility are more clearly defined), (2) in firm goals (at least in public firms, profits and trends in profits become more important), and (3) in sources of capital for the firms (partnership-subordinated capital is replaced by debt and equity funds raised in the capital markets). Finally, many of the larger brokerage firms have not stopped at incorporation, but have gone on to set up holding company corporate structures. The traditional brokerage firm business thus becomes one subsidary of a parent company that may seek to diversify into other business opportunities.

Exhibit 3 indicates the variety of brokerage firms by reporting results of a 1979 study of the part of the securities industry that is based in New York. The ''principal product line'' designation is just a rough guess of the principal type of business, as revealed by directory listings. Only about 10 of the more than 1,300 firms represented are public firms that release standard financial reports. The rest of the firms do not. In this sense brokerage firms remain

EXHIBIT 3   NEW YORK DISTRICT FIRMS ENGAGED IN SECURITIES BUSINESS, 1979[a]

Principal Product Line	Number of Firms[b]		
	Small	Medium	Large
Multiple-line products	265	135	55
State and local bonds	90	40	0
Over-the-counter shares	125	15	0
Mutual funds	175	20	5
Floor traders	120	0	0
Specialists	30	30	0
Options	35	5	0
Others	55	15	0
Bank dealers	65	30	30
Foreign firms	10	10	5
Totals	970	300	95

REGIONAL BREAKDOWN

New Jersey	180
New York City	985
Other (New York State)	200
	1,365

[a]The number of NASD member firms in the district was approximately 900 in 1979.
[b]Firm size based on number of employees: small, 0–25; medium, 26–250; large, 250–up.
Source: Goldberg and Kelman, *The New York Based Securities Industry: 1979 Survey,* Occasional Papers in Metropolitan Business and Finance (1980, No. 2), New York University, New York.

more like partnerships of physicians than like banks or other regulated financial institutions.

Most firms in the New York area are, as expected, small firms operating either in some market-making role or specializing in a few lines of business. Omitted are probably hundreds of "investment counseling" organizations for which almost no information can be obtained. The district is headquarters for about two-thirds of the large brokerage firms in the country. Thus in the same area the firms competing for business range in size from fewer than 10 employees to more than 10,000 employees.

ORGANIZED EXCHANGE MARKETPLACE.   The existing stock exchanges plus the National Association of Securities Dealers (NASD) are the primary vehicles for regulation within the industry. Those groups are also the primary organizational structure for trading in already issued equity shares. That there is a potential conflict of interest in this setup is self-evident. Historically, much of the "self-regulation" was aimed at protecting the economic interest of current members by forming price-setting cartels, curtailing entry and exit from the groups, and controlling competition for business in a number of other ways. For a number of reasons this type of behavior began to break down rapidly in the 1970s. Now the focus is much more on providing brokerage exchange services and on auditing the behavior of member firms.

Exhibit 4 lists stock exchanges that were operating in the 1970s. In addition there are more than 10 active commodity exchanges in the United States. The most rapidly growing

EXHIBIT 4   SELF-REGULATING ORGANIZATIONS

	Employees
American Stock Exchange	600
Boston Stock Exchange	600
Chicago Board Options Exchange	300
Cincinnati Stock Exchange	100
Detroit Stock Exchange[a]	10
Intermountain Stock Exchange[a]	10
Midwest Stock Exchange	600
National Association of Securities Dealers (NASD)	600
New York Stock Exchange	1,500
Pacific Stock Exchange	400
Pittsburgh, Baltimore, Washington Stock Exchange (PBW)	200
Spokane Stock Exchange[a]	10

[a]Exchange virtually inactive.

segments of exchange business at the beginning of the 1980s are the options and financial futures lines of business. Most exchanges have set up subsidiaries to compete for some part of this business. The results are not always successful. The American Stock Exchange Commodities Exchange in effect went out of business in 1980, with the pieces absorbed by the New York Stock Exchange Futures Exchange.

The **New York Stock Exchange** is the largest stock exchange in the United States. Like many brokerage firms, the exchange was reorganized in the early 1970s to a structure that closely parallels that of a private holding company corporation. The Exchange is now governed by a Board of Directors, made up of about 10 public representatives, 10 representatives of exchange member groups, and a full-time paid chairman. He is assisted in operating management and policy planning by a number of executive officers. At present the Exchange has the following operating divisions: (1) market operations, to handle trading and facilities management; (2) member firm regulation and surveillance, to provide the regulatory oversight required of the exchange; (3) finance and office services management; (4) product development and planning; and (5) marketing services and customer relations. In addition there are specialized staff groups to handle legal problems and government relations, economic research, personnel relations, and similar activities. Some of the specialized functions in the operation of the Exchange have been transferred to subsidiary corporations, only partly controlled by the Exchange itself.

Important service-related corporations only partly controlled by the NYSE include the following three firms, each with its own officers and Board of Directors. The **National Securities Clearing Corp.** (NSCC), organized in 1977 and one-third owned by the Exchange, was formed by the merger of similar subsidiaries at the NYSE and American Stock Exchange with the National Clearing Corp. The NSCC is essentially a channel through which the books of brokerage firms, exchanges, and other clearing corporations are brought into balance. The **Depository Trust Co.**, organized in 1973 and about 40% owned by the Exchange, is a central certificate depository organized by the New York Stock Exchange, American Stock Exchange, banks, and other to immobilize the physical transfer of securities. The third organization, the **Securities Industry Automation Corp. (SIAC),** was organized in 1972 and is two-thirds owned by the NYSE and one-third owned by the American Stock Exchange.

SIAC provides much of the communications and computer facilities and systems now necessary to run the exchange.

At present the NYSE is limited to a total **voting membership** of 1,366. Only individuals may be members of the Exchange, though in most cases the individual is acting as a representative of a firm. There are about 550 brokerage firms represented on the Exchange. Almost 400 of these are firms dealing in some way with the public; the other 150 are specialists and others who do not deal directly with the public. One of the issues in the early 1970s was whether banks, insurance companies, or others who were major customers of Exchange member brokers, should be allowed to become Exchange members. In general the answer was no (though there were exceptions, particularly if the institution did no trading for its own account or was foreign based), and the issue died once negotiated commission rates became possible. At the beginning of the 1980s the issues are how to expand voting membership without decreasing the value of existing seats, and whether voting power should be shifted more toward the firms that provide much of the Exchange's revenues than is currently the case.

Typically the largest public corporations are listed for trading on the NYSE and they are handled by brokerage firms large enough to be members of the exchange. But there are thousands of traded securities not listed on any exchange, and thousands of individuals and firms in the brokerage industry that are not exchange members. Regulatory oversight for these usually smaller brokerage firms, and for the trading done in private securities away from an exchange floor, is provided by the National Association of Securities Dealers. The traditional role of NASD has been to help provide a structure for the training and registering of individuals and firms not part of an exchange, and to provide regulatory oversight for the trading and clearance of nonexchange-listed securities (called over-the-counter securities, hence OTC markets). In the past decade, however NASD and private computer firms have been developing a computerized communications network that permits member dealers to display price information and do some computer-linked trading for the more active OTC stocks. Moreover, recent SEC rule changes permit the trading of some exchange-listed securities on this system. Thus NASD is in the process of creating a new nationwide exchange with characteristics quite different from the other existing exchanges.

GOVERNMENT REGULATORY GROUPS. The principal government regulator for the securities industry since the 1930s has been the **Securities and Exchange Commission.** The commission is charged with regulating the issuance of securities, specifying the information to be provided periodically owners, and regulating the exchanges and brokerage firms that are at the core of the distribution-trading process. In addition to SEC regulations, the Federal Reserve Board has jurisdiction over the amount of credit that can be extended to customers and brokers for the securities they buy. The **Department of the Treasury** plays a minor role when international transactions are involved—particularly for foreign governments or agencies selling bonds in the United States, but also for private foreign purchases and sales.

Two new federal agencies were created in the 1970s to provide regulatory oversight. The **Securities Investor Protection Corp.** (1970) provides insurance to small investors for the cash and securities left on deposit with a broker. SIPC has authority to liquidate bankrupt brokerage firms and is seeking authority to merge or dissolve "troubled" firms before they become insolvent. The **Commodity Futures Trading Commission** (1975) was created to provide regulatory oversight for the rapidly developing commodities markets in the United States. Since both the exchanges and the products offered in this are relatively new or rapidly changing, there is considerable flux in the regulatory process. In addition to the federal agencies, a number of **offices of state attorneys general** became more active in securities regulation in the 1970s. In particular a number of states passed legislation to slow down tenders for the acquisition of firms with significant resources or employment in their state by a "foreign" corporation, whether that corporation was from another state or overseas. Since in many cases these laws directly conflict with SEC rules or practices, they are slowly being struck down in federal courts.

Despite this governmental regulation, the securites industry is still considered to be basically a **self-regulated industry.** The SEC establishes broad principles and some guidelines, but most of the day-to-day implementation of the regulations is left to industry groups—NASD or the exchanges. The SEC then audits the rules and performance of these groups. In most of the business report filings, the SEC has traditionally been most directly concerned about timeliness and format. Responsibility for content and accuracy falls mostly on the firm, its auditors, or the investment banking firms that help to prepare the document. Also a number of industry trade associations take part in the process. While the associations, as the **Securities Industry Association,** or the **Public Securities Association,** are not directly charged with regulation, they do promulgate standards of business ethics and professional practice. The associations also are active in representing member interests in any hearings on rule changes by the regulators.

INSTABILITY OF EXISTING STRUCTURE.   The structure of the securities industry as described in this section is much like the structure that might have been described one decade, or even three decades ago. Because of strong tradition, the complex interrelationships in the trading process, and an egalitarian approach to making changes in the industry, structural changes have come slowly.

There are two areas in which the structure of the securities industry may be unstable. First, there are few industries in this country where more than 4,000 firms, let alone 100 large firms, compete for the same type of business. Once the principle of competitive commission rates became established in 1975, economic pressure of "cost efficiency" began to be more important in traditional brokerage business. These cost pressures, and related competitive developments, have already forced a number of brokerage firms out of business (usually through merger with another firm, or through dissolution of the firm); more attrition is likely over the next two stock market cycles. While firms providing traditional brokerage services may decline, the ease of entry into this industry may lead to an increase in the number of small firms offering investment counseling or other specialty services.

The second area of obvious instability is in the number and relative sizes of the existing exchanges in this country. It is unlikely, for political reasons, that the number of exchange floors will drop much in the 1980s (though a severe market recession could well lead to the disappearance of the Boston Stock Exchange, the PBW Exchange, and a merger of the American Stock Exchange with another group). The economics of tied-together communications-computer systems for solving rapid transaction clearing and reporting problems is so overwhelmingly favorable that such a system will evolve. It is more likely to creep in as an expansion of "jointly owned" subsidiaries of exchanges to handle specific tasks than as an overt monopolization of trading by one exchange. But in fact, the subsidiaries will eventually dominate their respective parent exchanges in services provided.

SECURITIES TRADING

CUSTOMER CLASSES.   The traditional role of the securities industry is to facilitate and promote the trading of securities. The efficiencies of having a "marketplace" for doing this have led brokers to form associations to set common rules for transacting and stock exchanges to formalize marketplace administrative procedures. The customers attracted to this marketplace are sometimes divided into two different categories when discussing rationales for securities trading: individual versus institutional customers, and investors versus speculators. **Institutional** customers include such groups as private pension funds, mutual funds, life insurance companies, and property and liability insurance firms. Institutions hold about one-third the value of stock outstanding but account for more than half the trading on the NYSE. This is because institutions concentrate their stock holdings in the larger corporations listed on that exchange, and because they tend to turn over their portfolios more frequently than do individuals. **Individuals** (including personal trust accounts and other categories lumped into the "household" sector) still hold about two-thirds of the value of stock outstanding. Individuals own most of the stock, and do most of the trading, in the thousands of over-the-counter stock transactions and trades of the stocks listed on exchanges other than the NYSE.

Investors are generally regarded as customers who are buying or selling securities with the longer term in mind, and who undertake "fundamental analysis" of the economic performance of a firm whose shares they may be buying to try to estimate the true worth of the security. Most institutional buying is "professional," hence investor-oriented, transacting. **Speculators** are often defined as customers who are buying or selling securities with the expectation of short-term gain, who base buying decisions more on price fluctuations or other technical factors than on any fundamental analysis of underlying economic conditions. Speculation tends to be seen in pejorative terms as an activity that mostly benefits the speculator and may lead to unnecessary market excesses if speculators all decide to buy or sell a security at about the same time. Indeed, over the years the government and the NYSE have actively worked to reduce speculation. Actions taken include (1) closing down mining-type exchanges and inhibiting the trading of securities selling for less than $5 per share, (2) increasing the holding period for capital gains treatment from 6 months to a year, (3) increasing brokerage transactions cost to the point where "day trading" (buying and selling a stock the same day, or within a few business days) is no longer attractive to many investors, (4) inhibiting the activities of independent floor traders on the Exchange, and (5) slowing down the expansion of options and futures markets (e.g., postponing several proposals for futures instruments that are calls on stock price indexes such as the Dow Jones Industrial Average). Despite such attitudes, some speculative activity is regarded as beneficial because it (1) increases the liquidity of a market for a security, (2) attracts to the securities industry capital that would otherwise go elsewhere, and some of this capital seems to end up helping to finance new high-risk, enterprises, and (3) provides additional revenues for brokerage firms, thus helping to maintain the distribution network necessary to sell new securities to others. In **modern portfolio theory,** what constitutes investing and what is speculating becomes very blurred. It is no longer possible to designate as "probably speculative" the buying of a stock option or financial future, the buying and selling a bond within a week, or similar activities. Taken together with other decisions, such activities may lead to portfolios that are far less risky than if such "speculations" had not been undertaken (for a discussion of these issues, see the sections "Option Markets and Instruments" and "Futures and Commodities Markets").

TYPES OF ORDER.   Customers may specify a variety of terms relating to the execution of an order placed with a brokerage firm. **Market orders** are orders to buy or sell at the market price prevailing when the order reaches the specialist's post on the floor of the exchange. Under normal circumstances, this should take less than an hour for an order placed with a brokerage firm in the United States (but it may take longer for the confirmation of transaction to reach a given broker). **Limit orders** are orders by the customer to place limits on the price at which the order can be executed. For example, a limit order to buy IBM at

70 must be executed (if possible) at a price of 70 or less. Usually, some time limit is placed on limit orders. "Day orders" are automatically canceled at the end of the day given if not executed. "Good till canceled" orders remain on the books until executed or canceled by the customer.

Limit orders that cannot be executed as soon as they reach the exchange are left with the specialist in the stock, who notes the order in his book, showing amount, broker leaving the order, and time placed. Thus, 10 different brokers may place limit orders to buy IBM at 70. When this price is reached on a decline, the amount of stock available for sale at 70 may be only a fraction of the total of the buying orders. Then the rule of first come, first served applies. Brokerage firms do not encourage limit orders. Specialists' books for most securities are "thin," containing orders to buy or sell only a few hundred shares away from the current market.

Stop-loss orders are orders that can be used to help limit losses on existing positions. An order to sell "on stop" 100 shares of IBM at 65 is a type of limit order. When the market price of IBM reaches 65 or less, the customer's 100 shares are offered "at market." Thus if market conditions are unsettled, with many sell orders, the customer may get less than 65. Similarly, short sellers may seek to limit their losses by placing buy "on stop" orders. An order to buy IBM at 75 stop would trigger a market order to buy the required number of shares when the price reached 75 or more.

Short selling consists of selling securities that are not owned by the seller. Customers engaged in short selling do so in the expectation that they will be able to buy the stock later (or elsewhere) at a lower price, thus making a profit. Permitting short selling can have several advantages for a securities market: (1) the liquidity of the market will be increased; (2) to the extent that short sellers have contrary expectations, the sharpness of price fluctuations may be reduced as these customers sell as prices increase or buy back securities as prices drop; and (3) specialists and other market makers can better stabilize their markets without having large inventories, and can better arbitrage across markets selling the same security. The disadvantage of short selling is that under certain market conditions short selling focused on particular securities may temporarily accentuate price trends—for example, driving the prices too high as short sellers scramble to buy to cover their positions.

From the customer's viewpoint, short selling is simple. Suppose he tells his broker to sell 100 shares of IBM short as a market order, and the price turns out to be 70. The customer's broker arranges to "borrow" the stock from his own or another broker's inventory (or from the inventories of stock held in margin accounts at brokerage firms) for delivery to the buying customer's broker. To provide security for the loan of the stock, the borrowing broker deposits with the lender broker a sum of money equal to the market price of the borrowed shares ($7,000 here). Stock is usually loaned **flat,** that is, no interest is paid on the money put up as collateral, and a premium is not usually collected by the lender of the stock. The lender broker is compensated, however, for he can earn a return on the $7,000 as long as he has it. In addition, the short customer must turn over to the lender any dividends paid on the stock while it is loaned. The short customer's broker subtracts the amount from the short's account, transfers it to the lending broker, who adds it to the account of the customer from whom the stock was "borrowed." Short customers do not know from whom stock is borrowed, and lending customers do not know that "their" stock has been loaned. It is all a broker-to-broker arrangement. The Securities Exchange Act does require that customers of brokerage houses give permission to have their stock loaned; this permission is a standard part of the agreement signed by a customer opening a general account.

A general account is a customer account; the purchase of securities may be for cash or **on margin** (i.e., the customer pays down only a portion of the price of the security). Margin requirements are set by the Federal Reserve, with additional terms or conditions imposed by the stock exchanges and customer's brokerage firm. In a margin purchase, the customer is required to deposit with the broker, either in cash or in acceptable securities, a fraction of the purchase price (currently 50%). The balance is loaned to the customer by the brokerage house, which obtains the funds usually be pledging the purchased securities with a bank for a collateral loan.

Only listed securities, and the securities of certain larger over-the-counter firms may be carried in margin accounts. Stocks selling for less than $5 may not be purchased on margin. The New York Stock Exchange requires that customers maintain margin of at least 25% of the market value of all securities long or short in their accounts. Some brokerage firms set higher maintenance margins (usually 30%). When the margin in an account becomes inadequate, a "margin call" is sent to the customer requesting payment of any deficiency. If, payment is not forthcoming immediately, the broker may sell the margined stock at market and close out that transaction.

Suppose a customer bought 100 shares of IBM at 70 on margin. He would send a check to his broker for $3,500 (50% margin), and the broker would lend him $3,500. If the price of IBM suddenly dropped to 40, the customer's "equity" position would be only 500 (4,000, value of stock, minus 3,500 borrowed). The customer would receive a margin call to put up at least another 500 (for the maintenance margin requirement of 1,000). The interest that must be paid on the borrowed funds and the need to put up additional capital in declining markets are indications of the disadvantages of buying on margin. The advantages are those usually associated with financial leverage. If the price of the stock goes up enough (or dividends are higher than the customer's aftertax interest expenses), the customer will earn more money on his $3,500 equity investment than he would have if he had bought 50 shares for cash.

On exchanges in the United States, orders for fewer than 100 shares are generally regarded as **odd lots.** That is, the standard unit of trading is 100 shares or a multiple, and fractions of the standard unit are handled slightly differently from the regular order. Traditionally, odd-lot transactions were handled by a number of individuals and firms on the floor of, say, the NYSE who specialized in providing this service. The dealer stood ready to buy or sell the odd lot at the next price at which a round-lot (standard order) transaction took place plus a service charge of 12.5¢ (lower priced stocks) or 25¢ (higher priced stocks). Gradually, competition reduced the number of dealers to two, then to one. In the late 1970s, exchanges began experimenting with letting computers automatically process odd-lot orders and even small round-lot orders. The NYSE has not been entirely successful in this endeavor, so some major firms have begun processing odd-lot orders "in house" much as they might have been processed on the exchange. This competition, and the decision to let exchange specialists handle odd-lot business if they desired, forced the last major odd-lot firm out of business.

EXCHANGE EXECUTION: OLD PROCESSES AND NEW.   The large exchanges in the United States have, for a number of decades, operated under what is known as the "continuous auction" process. That is, specialists and others try to complete transactions any time orders arrive during the 6 hours the market may be open. Exchanges in other countries may follow other customs, such as having a round-robin call in a stock once a day at which time an attempt is made to match accumulated buy and sell orders.

In continuous auction markets the **specialists** and related market makers play an important role. At any given hour, orders arriving at the "trading post" for a particular stock may not be in balance. The specialist must decide, on the basis of his long training and experience, how much to adjust the quote on a stock to bring the market closer to balance. The quote is in terms of a **bid** price (offer to buy) and an **ask** price (offer to sell). For actively traded stocks, the bid-ask spread may be only one-eighth of a point (the standard price jump on U.S. exchanges) or sometimes a quarter-point. For small imbalances, the specialist may buy and sell from his own inventory, in the expectation of rebalancing his position by a transaction on the other side of the market later.

The trading post is likely to be a large circular counter (there are about 20 at the NYSE), with specialists standing around the edge and clerks inside. Each stock listed on an exchange is assigned to a specialist and post. Once two dealers, or a dealer and specialist, agree on a transaction, it is recorded on a machine-readable card. The card is fed into a computer system that quickly flashes the quotation on the ticker service and records the order for the exchange's back office clearing operation. Computer tapes with time-date records of every transaction are kept for a period in case of errors and to provide audit measures of the adequacy of specialist performance.

The **costs of transaction** from a customer's viewpoint are the brokerage charges for buying or selling a stock. Until the early 1970s these rates were fixed by mutual agreement of the members of the NYSE and were effectively the minimum rates charged throughout the industry. Exhibit 5 reports the last rate structure before competitive commission rates became effective in 1975. At that time the cost to buy or sell 100 shares of a $40 stock would have been almost $65 or 65¢ per share. Since then, despite rising inflation, those costs have remained stable or gone up slowly at major brokerage firms. For a small institutional-sized order of, say, 1,000 shares of a $40 stock, the 1975 basic cost might have been about $365 or 35¢ a share (even then, some firms were offering discounts). Since then, competition has forced rates down as low as 10¢ per share, though the current institutional rate is probably closer to 15¢ per share. For individuals, small "discount brokers" have gone into business to compete for individuals' orders by offering 30–50% discounts from the 1975 rates for no-frills brokerage service. In addition to these brokerage fees, there are small New York State and Securities and Exchange Commission transfer taxes, which aggregate to less than 3¢ per share.

EXHIBIT 5   BASIC COMMISSION RATES: FINAL COMMON SCHEDULE, 1975

	Money Involved	Basic Rate	Plus
On orders for 100 shares[a]	$2,000 and under	As mutually agreed	—
	Above $2,000 but under $2,500	1.3%	$ 12
	$2,500 and above	0.9%	$ 22
On multiple round-lot orders	$2,000 and under	As mutually agreed	—
	Above $2,000 but under $2,500	1.3%	$ 12
	$2,500 but under $20,000	0.9%	$ 22
	$20,000 but under $30,000	0.6%	$ 82
	$30,000 to and including $300,000	0.4%	$142

Plus, for Each Round Lot

First to tenth round lot	$6 per round lot
Eleventh round lot and above	$4 per round lot

[a]The minimum commission on any order for 100 shares could not exceed $65.

Once a transaction is completed, the information is routed through the exchange's computers and also messages go to the booths of the brokerage firms involved so that they may begin their own back office processing. On some of the smaller exchanges, for some of the smaller regional brokerage firms, this may be done automatically, for a fee, by the exchange's computer service corporation. If a broker is not too busy, he may call the customer the same day to tell him the results of the transaction. By late that night or early the following morning, the brokerage firm will have in the mail a **confirmation slip,** specifying the **transaction date** (when the order was executed on the exchange), the terms, the charges, and the **settlement date** (when the account of the customer will be debited or credited, as the case may be, for any cash or securities due). The settlement date was once as short as the end of the third working day after the transaction, but in recent years back office processing complications for some brokerage firms and delays in postal deliveries have increased the time before cash or securities are due in the broker's office to 5 working days.

As institutional trading on the NYSE has grown to the point where it constitutes the majority of public transactions on that exchange, special methods have had to be devised to handle **large block trades,** generally tabulated as trades of 10,000 shares or more. An indication of the vitality and liquidity of the American securities markets is that many such trades are handled every day on the floor of the Exchange in a regular way. For very large offers, or when there simply is no customer on the other side, the Exchange has a group of special methods to handle these trades away from the auction market at the specialist's post. Although these ''special method distributions'' may sometimes take place after regular trading hours, every attempt is made not to close out the public's opportunity to participate—particularly if there are limit orders on the specialist's book at the block distribution price.

Large block trades constitute more than 25% of the volume of trades listed on the NYSE. This has become one of the most competitive aspects of the brokerage industry. In addition to trades that occur on the NYSE, institutional block trades in NYSE-listed securities occur on some of the regional exchanges (where some institutions were permitted to buy membership in the early 1970s). Trades also occur in the ''third market'' (the over-the-counter market in exchange-listed securities), and in the ''fourth market'' (a market directly between institutions, perhaps facilitated by arrangements such as ''Instinet,'' which provides direct computer terminal links among institutions so they can display tentative volume interest and bid-ask quotes to others linked to Instinet). The third and fourth market arrangements have captured about 10% of the block trading business and the regional exchanges, smaller amounts.

IMPACT OF COMPUTERS.   Since the brokerage part of the securities industry is mostly a process of transferring orders from one point to another, then processing the paperwork that develops out of the transactions process, it ought to be the ideal industry for computerization. The cost savings and other benefits could be enormous. Such a changeover has not occurred, however, for at least three reasons.

1. With its thousands of small firms, many with partnerships passed down from father to son, tradition in the securities industry is very important—and is perceived as ''efficient,'' since new ways do not have to be learned.

2. There is no incentive for the firms and exchanges to set up a particular system. It does only limited good for one firm to set up a computer system if the exchange and broker on the opposite side of the transaction are utilizing normal systems or different computer systems.

3.   Hundreds of millions of dollars of capital would be required to develop a sophisticated
industrywide system. While the industry has been enormously successful in raising
capital for others, brokerage firms and exchanges have not always been able to raise
capital for their own needs.

Despite these factors slowing down industrywide computerization, the pressures to convert
are great. Pressures include rising volume that simply cannot be handled manually in the
short run because of the limited supply of trained industry personnel, rising labor costs,
and falling profit margins as commission rates became competitive. Recognizing these factors,
industry leaders began in the 1970s to establish a framework in which their own firms and
the exchanges could be modernized. The 1970s may be remembered as the decade that
computers came to Wall Street. The 1980s will be the decade when they began to be fully
utilized.

ITS, CLOB, BLOB, and CUSIP, to you DOTty NASDAQ. Which is to say, there are
a great many acronyms being bandied about today on Wall Street as names for the different
computer systems under development. Since new systems are evolving almost monthly, we
restrict this discussion to the thrust of these new systems. Primarily development focus seems
to be concentrated in three areas: electronic telecommunications, back office paper processing
after an order is completed, and the market transactions process. Systems cannot always be
placed in one of these areas, for the objective of the ultimate system is to integrate all parts
of the process.

Communications systems have been the most rapidly developing systems on Wall Street.
Ticker tape and the associated tickers that printed out each transaction are now mostly sold
as antiques. High-speed transmission facilities that can transmit thousands of characters a
minute send transactions data around the world, whereupon information may be displayed
on large electronic screens, fed to cable companies, or other vendors to send to home TV
screens or minicomputers, or sent directly to clients' computers for subsequent analysis and
use. To transmit this information, brokerage firms and exchanges are using land lines,
microwave, and even satellite facilities.

Most of the larger brokerage firms have direct lines to their exchange floor booths, and
at least in the bond areas, direct lines to other brokers and even major customers. A firm's
trader on the floor may carry an electronic beeper so that he can be called back to the booth;
in addition, all exchanges have message board systems to signal traders when they are
wanted. In 1980 the NYSE started an experiment to permit a few traders to carry around
miniature radio telephones, which could be used to call the booth without leaving the trading
floor. There have been some problems with this new technology. Specialists complained
about traders "standing in the crowd" all day and blocking opportunities for brokers who
came and went, to and from the post. More important, brokers could easily call "upstairs"
(headquarters management) or make direct long-distance calls to major customers. Since
those off the floor of the exchange are not supposed to have information on floor activity
until it is equally available to all via the transactions tape, the Exchange has had to rethink
this experiment.

Back office paper processing is in a sense the most difficult part of the securities
transaction process to fully automate, because it depends on the other systems being in place.
Still, cost pressures have forced virtually all firms to partially automate these activities. There
has been considerable success insofar as the number of employees in this area has remained
virtually constant in recent years (about 100,000 individuals), even though share volume
and number of transactions for most firms have more than doubled.

Three factors have contributed significantly to progress. First, after more than a decade of effort, most of the actively traded securities now have an identifying code (called CUSIP numbers), used in describing securities when certificates are exchanged. Not all firms use these codes in their internal inventory systems, however, and code identification has lagged for governmental-type securities and special instruments. Second, the physical transfer of certificates is slowly being curtailed as depository corporations become the resting places for the actual certificates. This has been a very slow process requiring changes in federal and state law, negotiated agreements with banks and others, and an educational program on the adequacy of a transactions slip and periodic statement of position as substitutes for the actual certificate. It will take at least another decade to get anything approaching full participation. The third factor contributing to back office computerization has been the ability of computer software companies to develop generic systems that can be installed in particular firms with only modest changes. Thus many smaller firms can afford to buy these systems, or to get their processing done by one of the computer service bureaus (both private ones and exchange-affiliated bureaus have developed) at reasonable fees.

Because customer identification has not been standardized, and because computer systems for larger firms tend to be self-designed with features unique to each firm, when brokerage firms merge there may be serious problems in putting the "books" of the two firms together. Indeed, in several cases in recent years the problems have been serious enough to impose a significant drain on the acquiring firm's capital base. The lack of standardization across firms has also caused external audit systems to lag the changes being made in back office processing. Thus, it remains a lengthy procedure to trace actual trading by source in a specific security, or to independently test a firm's net capital position.

Computer systems related to the **market transactions process** have been the most controversial in development. These systems have been the slowest to develop, and probably the most expensive to put in place. In the hearings for the 1975 Securities Act, Congress seemed to indicate an interest in a **"National Exchange Market System"** (NEMS) which would be, among other things, a truly national system that was highly automated, but preserved the regional exchanges, an exchange that maintained continuous auction markets but had competing **specialists** or market makers, and an exchange that had uniform standards for professionals' participation, though perhaps with different "levels" of standards participation. These goals are not precisely required by the Act. Development supervision was turned over to the SEC, which has delegated actual development to industry committees.

At the beginning of the 1980s a number of partial systems are under development. None are likely to evolve into a full-fledged NEMS, and some will eventually have to be abandoned. The reasons for this rather strange and collectively expensive type of evolution are both economic and political. It is reasonably clear that it is technically feasible to develop a highly automated transactions system, but at a cost of hundreds of millions of dollars. How will such development costs be funded? Once developed, the exchange would probably put out of business the regional exchanges **as they currently exist.** The new exchange would also change the nature of business for many on the "floor." Since many transactions would be semiautomated, there would be less revenues from floor brokerage and relatively more to be derived from the higher risk market-making activities where inventory positions must be taken.

There are three types of partial system under development. One type attempts to upgrade communications links between market makers to broaden the marketplace. An early version is found at the **Pacific Stock Exchange,** which was organized as a merger of the San Francisco and Los Angeles exchanges. Separate trading floors are maintained in each city, but the floors (and each specialist's post) are continuously linked, while the exchange is in operation. A second example of this type of linkage is the **NYSE's Intermarket Trading System** (ITS). This is a video-computer display system that links a specialist's post at the Exchange with specialists on the regional exchanges who are selling the same securities. The bid-ask quotes are displayed and are "firm" (good) for at least 100 shares, or more where indicated. By having a card marked, a broker standing in the crowd at the NYSE viewing the ITS screen may direct his order to another exchange if the quote there seems better. A third example of this type of system is the work the **National Association of Security Dealers** has done to develop its **NASDAQ** (automated quotation) system. Dealers, that is, brokerage firms taking positions in over-the-counter securities—but not required to be "specialists" making continuous markets— are linked in a nationwide computer system with video display units. Dealers interested in making a market in a particular security enter bid-ask quotes, good for at least 100 shares. Any dealer with a basic level screen may put on the screen the stock of interest, and if the price seems attractive, call the dealer to try to arrange a transaction at the desired volume. At higher levels, the system may be used to execute transactions for the volume displayed and to interface with other brokerage firms and exchange computer systems.

Another type of partial system automatically directs orders from a brokerage firm's computers to the specialist's post on an exchange. This step alone may save several minutes. The **specialist** presents the order to the crowd for execution at the best price available, and the completed order is routed back through the exchange and brokerage firm computers. The NYSE Designated Order Turnaround (DOT) system handles market orders for up to 299 shares and day limit orders up to 500 shares. Some regional exchanges, which developed such systems earlier, have even more sophisticated features permitting "automatic" execution at the current quote unless the specialist intervenes, or screening of ITS and other market makers for best quote.

A third type of system under development is known as the "Cincinnati experiment" because it is currently run under the nominal jurisdiction of the **Cincinnati Stock Exchange.** Actually, the computer systems involved and most of the participating brokers and their computers are based in New York and New Jersey. At the beginning of the 1980s the experiment is a small prototype with some of the features (but not all) that may be desirable in a NEMS. In the automated **"National Securities Trading System"** (NSTS) package being used in the Cincinnati experiment, brokerage firm computers enter orders in the NSTS computer, which matches orders there (or on limit books) and to the extent possible clears the orders back through the brokerage firms' computers. Small imbalances may be taken by the Cincinnati specialist or other market makers or laid off on one of the larger exchanges. The NSTS would like a direct link to ITS to do this automatically, but so strong is the opposition of the rest of the exchange community to this experiment that it has not been possible yet. As long as partial systems like this and the exchanges' computerized order execution systems continue, there is no national **"central limit order book"** (CLOB) to ensure that all limit orders left with the system receive the priority that time dating would suggest is due to them. Of course, there **never** has been such a system. Whether this desirable feature of a national market system is promoted or hindered by the currently evolving partial systems is a matter of much debate.

INTERNATIONALIZATION OF SECURITIES MARKETS.   Securities trading systems are not only becoming more national in scope, they are becoming more international. Already the trading desks of some major brokerage firms and banks are open 24 hours a day. Information passes back and forth from home-based computers to foreign branches at all hours. Activity is greater for credit and commodity instruments, but multinational equity trading is increasing.

The shares of several large American corporations are listed on foreign exchanges, and a number of foreign firms have shares or their equivalents listed on U.S. exchanges. Transactions by foreigners with Americans in both U.S. stocks and foreign stocks reached records by the beginning of this decade. The total, more than $50 billion, seems to increase yearly. Of the more than 1,500 corporations with stock listed on the NYSE, only about 40 are foreign firms, but the number is slowly increasing.

More than 100 foreign institutions have trading desks in the United States. The American subsidiary may be organized as a special bank or brokerage firm, but the foreign parent is likely to be a financial institution with a commercial bank as its main subsidiary. In the United States the law makes it very difficult for this country's commercial banks to have brokerage firm subsidiaries, so there may be some unevenness in regulatory burden applied. Of course, American financial institutions can usually operate in foreign countries according to the laws of the host country. With the rapidity with which funds are being switched from one country to another, and the increasing numbers of U.S. and foreign institutions doing nonhome-country trading, regulators are losing control over transaction audit trails and the real ownership–balance sheet position of some firms. In essence, the SEC itself and other regulatory groups have not kept pace with technology.

INVESTMENT BANKING

NATURE OF INVESTMENT BANKING.   Securities trading and investment is one major segment of a brokerage firm, and for most, the segment that generates the largest dollar volume of revenues. For some firms, however, the most profitable segment of business is investment banking and its related activities. The **"investment banker"** is the principal medium for bringing new securities to the market. His functions include the purchase of whole issues of securities from public bodies or corporate issuers and their distribution to institutional and individual investors.

In addition to the sale of new issues (**"primary distributions"**), investment banking divisions may offer a variety of other services related to financing issues. Such services include (1) using the distribution network for the sale by a few holders of large blocks of an outstanding security to the investing public (**secondary distribution**), (2) helping a firm design an appropriate **capital structure** and compute its **cost of capital,** (3) offering counsel and expertise on **mergers and acquisitions,** (4) advising on foreign transactions, **commodity contracts,** and other specialized financial instruments, (5) structuring and sometimes operating **dividend reinvestment plans** or employee stock saving plans for client firms. All these services can at times be very profitable in their own right to the brokerage firm offering them. But investment banking has become such a competitive business in recent years that the services are sometimes offered on a break-even basis to develop long-term client relationships.

TYPES OF INVESTMENT BANKER.   Within the securities industry investment banking is sometimes specialized by the type of role played in the distribution of new securities and by the type of securities being distributed. **Wholesalers** are investment banking firms engaged primarily in the origination and purchase of new issues of securities. The wholesaler purchases new issues (acts as the **"lead underwriter"**), usually in conjunction with other wholesalers, and markets them through **retail groups** (brokerage firms selling to client buyers) in which the wholesalers themselves may be participants.

Some idea of the relative role played in the distribution of a new issue may be gleaned by examing the **"tombstone advertisements"** often placed in financial papers or magazines for larger issues. A tombstone is a very plain advertisement; its contents are restricted by the SEC to the name of the firm selling securities, the amount, the date of offering, the names of the distributing investment bankers, and a couple of additional statements. The investment bankers' names are listed in a traditional format: at the top are the lead **underwriters,** and just under them are the participating wholesalers in an alphabetical group. Below them are the wholesaler-retailer and the smaller retailers in one or more alphabetical groups (for an issue of $200 million, there may be three or more of these groups).

The position of a brokerage firm depends basically on the amount of the issue it is underwriting for the client firm, and the amount of the issue it agrees to retail to the institutional or individual buyers. But there are exceptions. For example, a traditional wholesaler may not agree to participate in the issue unless his name can be a first bracket name, even though he is taking only a very small part of the issue. Since the lead underwriter may want to work with him on other issues (or wants the retailers the firm can "supply" on this issue), he may agree. At the beginning of the 1980s mergers had created new strong investment banking groups, and other firms were becoming more aggressive in the field; their dissatisfaction with old line traditional firms and the upgrading of the scope of operations caused some of the traditional groupings to begin to to break down.

Competition in investment banking is intensifying because of pressures generated both within the securities industry and, increasingly, from the outside. At the beginning of this century, much of the underwriting of corporate securities was done by investment banking subsidiaries of commercial banks. That is the way it is still done in most countries of the world. As part of the reorganization of the banking and securities industries in the early 1930s, Congress passed the **Glass-Steagall Act,** forbidding banks to underwrite corporate securities and many types of state and local bond issues; this role was given to the securities industry. In the past decade, banks (and other financial institutions) have steadily expanded the investment banking–related services offered and tried to get the Glass-Steagall laws modified. Of course, the competition is not all one-way. A few of the largest brokerage firms have begun to offer bank-type services of their own.

SALE OF NEW ISSUES.   The bread and butter business of the investment banking side of the securities industry remains the sale of new issues. New issuers may negotiate directly with an investment banker for financing an issue, or they may solicit competitive bids from various **syndicates (groups of investment banking firms** joined together by a lead underwriter to bid for and distribute an issue). For many **state and local government issues,** and the securities of regulated firms (railroads and utilities in particular) laws often require that competitive bids be solicited. There has been a trend to reduce this as an absolute requirement in recent years to give the issuer more flexibility in negotiating terms of the offering. Most corporate new issues are negotiated directly with lead investment bankers with whom the firm has had a long-standing relationship. Part of the increased competition within the investment banking industry is reflected in the attempts of investment bankers to encroach on these traditional relationships by offering the firm a better package of services.

There are several **steps in the sale of a new corporate issue.** First the firm's finance officers and advisors must decide that a new issue is needed—either to replace a maturing issue or to finance a planned captial expenditure. Firms with good planning systems will perceive these needs for additional outside capital at least a year before the issue goes to market. Next, there is usually some very preliminary discussion with an investment banking firm (or for smaller corporations that do not have a traditional relationship with one banker, several may be consulted) about the type of issue, size, and possible offering date. Once there is some tentative agreement, and the investment banker has made certain legal and accounting audits of the client firm, an underwriting contract between the lead underwriter and client firm is formulated.

The underwriter then proceeds to form the investment banking purchase group and to help the firm with a variety of procedural and legal requirements (printing certificates, notifying the firm's registrar, preparing the registration statement for the **SEC** and state authorities, etc.). The **registration statement** becomes effective about 3 weeks after it is filed with the SEC unless the SEC raises objections or amendments are filed. Once the statement has become effective, the underwriting syndicate may formally offer the issue, but each prospective customer must receive a prospectus detailing much of the information about the firm and proposed offering found in the registration statement. Note that SEC approval of new issues does not imply judgment on the appropriateness of price or use of funds. The intent of registration is to ensure that investment bankers and their customers have adequate disclosure about the issue and the risks involved in its intended uses. Finally, once the "cooling-off" period has passed and the registration is about to become effective, the final terms on issue pricing and investment banking fees can be filed (although these are "amendments" to the registration statement, the SEC usually accepts them the same day or overnight—conditions can change dramatically in the bond markets in 3 weeks). The **"preliminary prospectus"** circulated to customers during the waiting period can then be turned into a final prospectus, and the issue sold.

In recent years, the SEC has been experimenting with a number of ways to simplify the registration process. Very small firms (issues under $1 million) are mostly exempt from the federal requirements. **Issues** that are **privately placed** (about one-third of corporate debt is privately placed with an insurance company or other financial institution) have simplified registration requirements. Large firms that regularly file quarterly and annual reports and related documents may use them and only provide material information changes in certain cases. This makes it possible to create **"shelf registrations"**—new issues that are ready to be sold, for which the final administrative work can be completed in a day or two whenever the timing seems right. Simplified registration processes also permit more than 1,000 corporations to now sell new stock to shareholders directly—bypassing the investment bankers—if those shareholders participate in **dividend reinvestment plans,** shareholders agree to allow their dividends to be used to purchase new shares for them. While the individual purchases are usually small, more than $1 billion in new equity capital is now raised this way (see the section on "Dividend Policy").

When an investment banking syndicate agrees to distribute a new issue, it may make a **"firm commitment"** (an agreement to purchase all of the issue outright), a **"stand-by commitment"** (an agreement, with limits, to purchase part of an issue if the public or existing shareholders do not take all of it), or a **"best-efforts commitment"** (an agreement to use the syndicate's best efforts to sell the issue). The issues of most large firms in recent years have been on a firm commitment basis. This means that the investment banking syndicate must put up some of its own capital, and borrow the rest short-term (usually from commercial banks), to buy the issue from the originating corporation. The syndicate then tries to quickly distribute the issue to the buying public at a set price slightly higher than the price paid for the issue.

The **spread** between the investment banker's buying price and selling price determines his gross profits, from which expenses must be deducted. The magnitude of the spread decreases with the size of the issue, the size and financial well-being of the issuing firm, the status of the issue (from subordinate to senior secured debt issues), the type of investment banker's commitment, and other factors. The spread may range from a few basis points (fractions of 1%) for the debt issue of a large utility to a 25% or more differential for small equity issue (under $10 million) of a newly organized corporation. Obviously, the more competitive the investment banking process, the smaller these costs are likely to be.

SECURITIES INDUSTRY TRENDS: SOME SIGNIFICANT CHANGES

In the decade of the 1970s the securities industry was an industry in transition, subject to tremendous structural strains. These pressures included **deregulation of pricing** for its major product lines (brokerage commission rate deregulation), major **new product areas** and associated regulatory groups (options, commodities, financial futures mortage certificates), a **new technology** that is forcing changes in decades-old processing procedures, and a **new level of competition** within the industry and outside it. Most of these pressures were still present at the beginning of the 1980s.

Given these pressures and the difficulty some securities firms have in raising their own firm capital, it would not be surprising to see **further mergers within the industry**— particularly if there is a significant economic downturn in industry profitability. Over the past 5 years there have been at least 200 mergers involving securities firms with other securities firms or, less frequently, with firms outside the industry. But the industry still has a relatively low **concentration ratio,** so further consolidation can be expected if it follows a pattern similar to the development of most other industries. Such consolidations, and the increased competition from other financial institutions, will continue to make investment banking a particularly competitive activity.

The **operating leverage** of most securities firms is still very high. Thus periods of high brokerage transactions are associated with very good profits, and periods of relatively lower volume can result in substantial losses. The trend has been for the volume break-even point to steadily increase at most brokerage firms as "permanent employees," leased communications and computer facilities, and other fixed costs replace the traditional hiring and firing processes in the securities industry. While many brokerage firms are trying to diversify into other industries to offset part of this operating risk, their success has not been tested by a decline in market volume. The risk exposure of exchanges may be even greater; since their overhead is increasing even more rapidly and they cannot diversify away from their brokerage functions. It is likely that in a significant market volume decline one or more of the existing exchanges would be forced out of business.

Congress has not been entirely happy about the pace or evolving structure of the national market system. Because this is an area requiring considerable professional expertise not possessed by Congress, it is unlikely that anything will be done about the problem directly. But the SEC is likely to find it increasingly difficult to get support for budget increases unless NEMS begins to make more rapid progress. It now appears that 1985 is the earliest date for a functioning national market system, and it is more likely to be a decade before there is a fully integrated marketplace. Thus, the coming 5 years may subject the securities industry to at least as much stress as the past 5 years.

BIBLIOGRAPHY

Block, Ernest, and Schwartz, Robert A. (Eds.), *Impending Changes for Securities Markets: What Role for the Exchanges?* JAI Press, Greenwich, CT, 1979.

Bogen, Jules I. (Ed.), *Financial Handbook,* 4th ed., Ronald Press, New York; 1964, Sections 9 and 10 by David Saperstein, Loring C. Farwell, and Paul L. Howell.

Goldberg, Lawrence G., and White, Lawrence J. (eds.), *The Deregulation of the Banking and Securities Industries,* Lexington Books, Lexington, MA, 1979.

Hayes, Samuel L., III, "The Transformation of Investment Banking," *Harvard Business Review,* January–February 1979, pp. 153–170.

Keenan, Michael, *Profile of the New York Based Securities Industry,* New York University Monograph Series in Finance and Economics, NYU Graduate School of Business, New York, 1977.

New York Stock Exchange, *Fact Book,* NYSE, New York, 1980 and annually.

Securities and Exchange Commission, *Staff Report on the Securities Industry in 1978,* SEC Directorate of Economic and Policy Research, SEC, Washington, D.C., July 1979.

Securities Industry Association, *SIA Trends Report,* economic research staff of the SIA, New York, September 28, 1979, and previous reports.

Stoll, Hans R., *Regulation of Securities Markets: An Examination of the Effects of Increased Competition,* New York University Monograph Series in Finance and Economics; NYU Graduate School of Business, New York, 1979. This monograph also contains a more extensive bibliography of some of the academic research on the securities industry

Zarb, Frank G., and Kerekes, Gabriel T. *The Stock Market Handbook,* Dow Jones-Irwin, Homewood, IL, 1970.

COMMERCIAL BANKING

CONTENTS

**OVERVIEW OF CHANGES IN THE
COMMERCIAL BANKING INDUSTRY**   3

**WHAT IS COMMERCIAL BANKING
AND WHAT IS A COMMERCIAL
BANK?**   4

COMMERCIAL BANK REGULATORS   5

**BANKING PRODUCTS AND
SERVICES AS SHOWN IN ASSET
ACCOUNTS OF COMMERCIAL
BANKS**   6

Cash Account   **6**
  Check clearing   6
  Due-from accounts   7
  Currency and coin account   7
  Reserves with the Federal Reserve
  System   8
  Role of cash accounts   8
Investment Securities   **8**
  U.S. Treasury securities   8
  U.S. government agency securities   9
  State and local securities   9
  Federal funds and repurchase
  agreements   9
Commercial Loans   **10**
  Real estate loans   10
  Loans to financial institutions   10
  Agricultural loans   11
  Commercial and industrial loans   11
  Individual loans   12

**BANKING PRODUCTS AND
SERVICES AS SHOWN IN LIABILITY
AND CAPITAL ACCOUNTS OF
COMMERCIAL BANKS**   **12**

Demand Deposits   **12**
  Cash management systems   14
  NOW accounts   15

  Share drafts   15
  Automatic transfer service   15
  Current status of demand deposits   16
Time and Savings Deposits   **16**
  Certificates of deposit   16
  Commercial paper market   17
  Passbook savings accounts   17
Deposit Rate Ceilings   **18**
  Money market mutual fund
  competition   18
  Money market certificates   19
  NOW account legal and financial
  issues   19

**MAJOR CHANGES IN REGULATORY
ENVIRONMENT**   **20**

Bank Holding Company Act of 1970   **20**
International Banking Act of 1978   **22**
Depository Institutions Deregulation and
Monetary Control Act of 1980   **22**

**UNRESOLVED QUESTIONS AND
REGULATORY ISSUES**   **23**

Branch Banking   **23**
  Pros and cons of branching   23
  Economies of scale   24
  Concentration and competition   24
  Problem banks   25
  Recommendations on branching   25
Federal Reserve Credit Controls   **25**
  Bank credit cards   26
  Electronic funds transfer system   27
    Automated teller systems   27
    Point-of-sale funds movement   27
    Electronic reporting and movement
    of funds   28
    Automated clearing house   28
  Current status of EFT   29
Small Bank Outlook   **29**

SUMMARY AND CONCLUSION   **30**

COMMERCIAL BANKING

Neil B. Murphy

OVERVIEW OF CHANGES IN THE COMMERCIAL BANKING INDUSTRY

The **commercial banking industry** is in the process of adapting to an economic and technological environment that is both volatile and rapidly changing. This process has resulted in vast changes in services, delivery systems, organizational structure, and the type of regulation faced by banks. Indeed, the 1980 changes in federal legislation substantially removed distinctions among depository financial institutions (see subsection "Depository Institutions Deregulation and Monetary Control Act of 1980").

To comprehend the current banking industry situation and make reasonable judgments about its future directions, it is necessary to review the changes that have occurred in the past 15 years or so. This period may be characterized in the following manner:

- **Rapid innovation in liability products and management,** beginning with money market and wholesale products and culminating in retail products.
- Rapid changes in the organizational form of banking, with the **bank holding company** becoming the dominant organizational form.
- Substantial product and geographical **diversification,** largely through the bank holding company organization.
- A substantial **change in lending practices,** with a volatile interest rate environment moving lenders toward **floating rate pricing.**
- A **changing delivery system** resulting from increasingly automated internal operations and a growing number and dollar volume of electronic transactions.
- A growth in the number and type of **nonbank competitors,** including securities firms, thrift institutions, large retailers, and, recently, money market mutual funds.
- An **increase in the international activities** of U.S. banks.
- A **regulatory framework** that has responded, with a lag, to the external environment, in some cases creating opportunities for nonbank competitors.
- A continuing debate over the age-old question of **branching** within states and branching across state lines.

WHAT IS COMMERCIAL BANKING AND WHAT IS A COMMERCIAL BANK?

Before discussing the changes noted above, it would be helpful to define commercial banking and to indicate how one recognizes such a bank. These questions are neither easy nor trivial. The answers suggest the degree and amount of competition facing the banking industry.

The easiest, most precise, most accurate answer is probably also the least helpful. A commercial bank is one that is recognized as such and is called a "commercial bank" by governmental regulatory agencies. However, it is not clear that any set of products and services is so unique to commercial banking that one such institution would be instantly recognizable. For example, a major product of commercial banks is the **demand deposit,** or **checking account.** However, for the past 5 years, the **credit union industry** has offered its members (customers?) the **share draft.** Notwithstanding legal technicalities, the share draft account is an account on which the member may write drafts and transfer funds to a third party. In essence, it is a checking account. Similarly, mutual savings banks and certain savings and loan associations in New England have offered **negotiable order of withdrawal (NOW)** accounts since the early 1970s. These accounts are checking accounts that pay interest. Consider also the **Merrill Lynch Cash Management Account.** The nation's largest securities firm has tested in several markets an account in which credit balances are placed in a fund and may be transferred by check or credit card. The list could go on, but these examples show that through legislation, regulatory action, and technology, financial institutions other than banks have come to offer products traditionally thought to be the province of commercial banks.

An example or two in the lending area might also be instructive. For the past 15 or so years, banks have been active in issuing **bank credit cards** that may be used nationally even though issued by a local bank. That is, an international interchange system is operative permitting a customer with a bank card issued in Maine to use the same piece of plastic in California. However, several major retailers issue credit cards that are also valid in their stores nationwide. Indeed, **Sears Roebuck and Co.** has a consumer receivables portfolio exceeding that of any bank. Similarly the **American Express Co., Diners Club,** and **Carte Blanche** issue travel and entertainment cards that have many of the same features as bank cards. In the area of business lending, a highly developed market now competes with banks. In this market, which is known as the **commercial paper market,** large, well-known corporations issue unsecured, short-term debt directly to investors. Thus, corporate treasurers for large, creditworthy companies have the alternative of borrowing from a bank or placing debt directly in the commercial paper market. Commercial paper interest rates are competitively determined in the open market. Banks that lend to such corporations must consider commercial paper rates in setting loan terms.

Returning to our original question, the answer must be that **commercial banking is what commercial banks do,** and banks do what they are allowed to do by law and regulation. In addition, other firms, including but not limited to financial institutions, compete with banks in a variety of product and service markets.

Who gives any individual commercial bank the power to be in the commercial banking business, and who establishes the laws and regulations that determine what commercial banks may do? As above, the answer is less straightforward than it may seem. Basically, except for a small number of private banks, a commercial bank is given a **charter** by either the federal government or a state government. Under existing law, **such a bank may do business in only one state,** whether federally or state chartered. The process of granting a bank charter is by no means simple, but once a bank has successfully cleared the applicable regulatory hurdles, what can it do? In very basic terms, it gathers funds from customers by issuing liabilities on itself. The liabilities are generally known as **deposits** and have a wide variety of price and nonprice terms. The funds so acquired are then used to purchase the liabilities of other organizations and/or individuals. The types of liability issued by the other organizations are **loans and investments,** depending on their characteristics and terms. Both the issuing of liabilities to acquire funds and the use of funds by commercial banks are subject to a high degree of regulation.

COMMERCIAL BANK REGULATORS

Having indicated the arbitrariness in defining "commercial banking" and the regulated nature of the banking business in a general way, let us look at the asset/liability structure of the system and the particular regulators and major kinds of constraint on any commercial bank. The major regulators and their duties are summarized briefly as follows.

- Office of the **Comptroller of the Currency.** The Comptroller of the Currency is an official of the U.S. Department of the Treasury who has the primary responsibility for chartering and supervising **national banks.** All such banks **must** be members of the Federal Reserve System. The Comptroller of the Currency is bound by state laws in deciding on applications by national banks to establish branch offices. Only the Comptroller of the Currency may declare a national bank insolvent.

- The **Federal Reserve System.** This quasi-governmental agency has primary responsibility for the conduct of monetary policy. However, the implementation of the policy directly affects the use of funds by banks through the system's reserve requirements. In addition, the Federal Reserve handles **all** regulatory matters concerning bank holding companies as well as operating a substantial part of the check clearing system. Also, Congress gave the Federal Reserve the responsibility for writing regulations in the **consumer credit protection** area.

- **Federal Deposit Insurance Corporation (FDIC).** This agency insures deposits of insured banks up to $100,000 per account. The FDIC examines **state-chartered banks not members of the Federal Reserve System.** While it does not grant charters, the FDIC can refuse to grant deposit insurance; thus it is an effective partner to states in granting charters. The FDIC acts as receiver in all national bank insolvencies and must act in this capacity in state-chartered bank insolvencies if asked to do so by state authorities.

- **State Banking Departments.** Each state has an official and/or board (with various titles) that charters and examines banks under state law. It is important to note that state law determines the conditions and criteria (if any) under which banks may establish branch offices. State-chartered banks may join the Federal Reserve System voluntarily. Until the passage of the Depository Institutions Deregulation and Monetary Decontrol Act of 1980, a state-chartered bank would have generally had lower reserve requirements by not being a Federal Reserve member bank. However, this law puts **all** banks under the reserve requirements of the Federal Reserve. In addition, state banks may join the FDIC voluntarily. As a practical matter, the vast majority do so, since deposit insurance is a virtual necessity for being in the banking business.

BANKING PRODUCTS AND SERVICES AS SHOWN IN ASSET ACCOUNTS OF COMMERCIAL BANKS

The **asset and liability structure of banks** serves as an indication of their activities. Total assets represent the use of funds acquired by banks and indicate some of the types of products and services they provide. Assets for all U.S. banks are shown in Exhibit 1: it is important to know that this exhibit is for all banks and that the composition of assets for any one bank may vary greatly for many reasons including size, management preferences, and market conditions.

CASH ACCOUNT.   The first asset account to be examined is the cash account. It can be seen in Exhibit 1 that 18% of all bank assets are held in the form of cash. However it is perhaps more instructive to look at the breakdown of the cash account to learn the role of banks in the clearing and processing of the payments mechanism in this nation. For example, the largest component of the cash account is called **cash items in the process of collection.** This highlights the role of banks in managing the payments mechanism.

Check Clearing.   If a business, individual, or government agency receives payment by check, that check is deposited in the payee's checking account. Once the check is deposited,

EXHIBIT 1   ASSETS OF ALL COMMERCIAL BANKS IN THE UNITED STATES, DECEMBER 31, 1979 ($ THOUSANDS)

Cash and due from depositor institutions		$ 306,601,551
U.S. Treasury securities		88,426,476
Obligations of other U.S. government agencies		49,362,671
Obligations of state and local political subdivisions		132,807,784
Federal Reserves funds sold and securities held under repurchase agreements		61,276,639
All other securities		23,326,644
Net loans		923,859,842
Real estate loans	$249,291,258	
Loans to financial institutions	69,548,176	
Loans for purchase of securities	14,475,538	
Loans to finance agriculture production	31,441,881	
Commercial and industrial loans	351,126,743	
Loans to individuals	192,718,057	
All other loans	46,294,783	
Less: Unearned income and allowance for losses	(31,036,594)	
Direct lease financing		11,766,256
Bank premises, furniture, no fixtures		23,549,846
Real estate other than bank premises		2,131,620
All other assets		68,968,672
Total assets		$1,692,078,001

Source: Federal Deposit Insurance Corp., *Bank Operating Statistics, 1979,* FDIC, Washington, D.C., 1980.

the individual customer knows little of what goes on and frankly doesn't care. However, a number of steps are necessary to integrate the individual bank into the entire payments and clearing system. First, a simple internal transaction takes place if the account on which the check is drawn is in the depositor's bank. However, if the check is drawn on another bank, the receiving bank must collect that check. This can occur in various ways. To process local checks, for example, in many cases banks use a **local clearinghouse;** that is, all banks in the local area meet once a day and exchange checks drawn on each other. This makes it possible to record the net difference on clearinghouse books without a large number of accounting transactions between individual banks.

There are two major alternatives available to the bank that receives a nonlocal check. First, it can go to another bank. In this country many small banks have accounts with larger banks, called **correspondent banks.** The correspondent banks provide **clearing services** for small banks that are not members of the Federal Reserve System. The check is deposited, and the correspondent bank then collects it from the bank on which it is drawn. That correspondent bank may go to a local clearinghouse or, as is more likely, it will deposit the check in its own account at the local Federal Reserve office. The local Federal Reserve office will then clear the check itself or through another Federal Reserve bank. Thus the banking system is responsible, in conjunction with the Federal Reserve, for clearing checks, and that particular activity is shown on the books of the banking system as cash items in the process of collection. Banks have a tremendous incentive to collect those funds as quickly as possible, because while in the process of collection the funds cannot be used for loans or investments, which are the banks' primary source of revenue.

Due-From Accounts.   The next important category in the cash account is demand balance with banks in the United States, known as "due-from" accounts. This amounts to almost 26% of the total cash account. These accounts are held by **respondent banks** with their **correspondent banks.** This cash account also indicates the role of the banks in the process of collecting checks. When cash is collected, in the process of collection discussed above, it immediately turns into demand balances with U.S. banks. Now, in addition to the checks that are collected and increase the balance, respondent banks also have customers writing checks on their accounts for deposit in yet other banks. These other banks go through the same process of collecting the check, and in many cases collect through the correspondent bank. Thus, when a check comes in for collection, the respondent bank must have funds in its account against which the check may be drawn.

In addition to the role in the check collection process, there are other ordinary transactions for which the respondent banks use these balances. For example, bank transactions in the **federal funds market** (banks borrowing from other banks) are normally conducted through their correspondents, and those correspondent banks make the appropriate adjustment through the respondent bank's checking account. Until very recently, in many states, banks that were not members of the Federal Reserve System were allowed to count correspondent balances as reserves. However, the Monetary Control Act of 1980, discussed in detail later, makes all financial institutions that offer transactions accounts subject to Federal Reserve reserve requirements.

Currency and Coin Account.   The next interesting account indicating the activities of banks is the **currency and coin account.** This is an asset on which there is no return. Banks are involved in the process of supplying currency and coin as needed to the economy. The entire banking system is in partnership with the Federal Reserve Systsem in providing this service. Essentially anybody who has a checking account, or a savings account of most types, may withdraw currency and coin at any time. The needs of the public for currency and coin are served by the banking system, and its currency and coin account reflects this. All currency and coin comes initially from the Federal Reserve System and is shipped to individual banks, which then make distribution as needed. Banks maintain an inventory of currency and coin to meet the needs of the customers.

Reserves with the Federal Reserve System.   The next account of interest is the reserves held with the local Federal Reserve bank. Those balances, along with coin and currency, are counted as reserves to meet **reserve requirements** under Federal Reserve regulations. In addition those accounts serve as **clearing accounts** against which incoming checks are debited and outgoing checks are credited. In essence the Federal Reserve Bank acts not only as an institution establishing reserve requirements against deposit accounts, but it also serves as the ultimate correspondent bank for the entire system and handles much of the clearing of checks between different regions of the country. That is, even if a local bank never deposits its checks in the local Federal Reserve Bank, choosing instead to use its correspondent, eventually most checks clearing out of the area come through the local Federal Reserve bank. The level of reserve requirements and the extension of reserve requirements to banks not members of the Federal Reserve System had been a matter of substantial controversy in the banking industry for many years. However, that controversy has ended. It has ended in favor of the position long held by the Federal Reserve itself. That is, **all banks offering transaction accounts are subject to Federal Reserve requirements.**

Role of Cash Accounts.   The cash accounts of all banks in the United States serve to show their role in the process of clearing checks and in the process of assisting the monetary authorities in achieving their objectives. It is ironic to know that one usually views liquidity as the capability to realize cash from an asset and to be able to use that cash. Interestingly enough, many of the items in the cash account of the banking system are really not at all liquid. First, cash items in the process of collection have no value in terms of either earning a return or being used for any other purposes. Those balances with correspondent banks are used for clearing, meeting transactions needs, and also compensating those banks for services provided. Currency and coin also must be kept to meet the day-to-day needs of customers and the reserves with the Federal Reserve bank are established by regulation rather than by transactions needs, and hence cannot be utilized to meet any liquidity drains on the bank. Thus, we must look elsewhere on the balance sheet to determine how banks meet their liquidity needs.

INVESTMENT SECURITIES.   A major source of both liquidity and earnings in the banking system is investment securities. In December 1979 the banking system held about $355 billion worth of securities broken down into several different categories.

U.S. Treasury Securities.   The first category we might look at is the securities issued by the U.S. Treasury. These are **Treasury bills, Treasury bonds,** and **Treasury notes,** and in June 1978 banks held over $88 billion worth of such securities. Basically, those securities are sold by the Treasury on open market to all buyers. Banks have special interest in buying Treasury securities because the **risk of default is nonexistent** and because of the very high liquidity of many of the securities. However, there tends to be, most of the time, a relationship between yield and maturity that makes relatively short-term securities less attractive for earnings purposes or more attractive for liquidity purposes. Longer term securities tend to have higher yields, but greater risk of price fluctuations. Thus, in seeking liquidity, banks typically stay in the short end of the maturity structure.

U.S. Government Agency Securities.   Many other agencies in the federal government are permitted to issue securities, either directly by the agency or guaranteed by the U.S. Treasury. Over $49 billion worth of such securities was held by banks in December 1979. These securities are held mainly for earnings purposes because there is not an active **secondary market** for them. Hence the yields are somewhat higher and banks typically do not like to sell such securities before maturity.

State and Local Securities.   The obligations of state and local political subdivisions include those of state governments, local governments, and various other state and local governmental agencies such as school districts, water districts, and turnpike authorities. In December 1979 that category constituted the largest use of funds in the investments area, and almost $133 billion worth of such securities was held by banks. These securities are especially attractive for banks because they are **exempt from federal income tax.** Hence the market for such securities is generally known as the "tax-exempt market." Pension funds and mutual funds do not pay any taxes directly; hence state and local securities are of little interest to their managers; however those securities can provide very high aftertax yields to banks, which are subject to federal income tax. In addition to the yield characteristics, many banks have **deposit relationships** with their state and local governments; that is, local governments must maintain their checking accounts somewhere, and to compete for such business banks bid on the obligations of these agencies. This is an additional attractive feature of the obligations of many state and local political subdivisions. In addition to supporting the activities of various governmental organizations, the U.S. Treasury, federal agencies, and state and local political subdivisions, the banking system, by acting as a securities dealer, is actively involved in providing liquidity to the government securities market. Other organizations are securities dealers, but in 1980 banks held trading account securities worth approximately $6 billion, spread out among a relatively small number of banks that are actively involved in trading. By providing such services, banks add a substantial amount of liquidity to the government securities market, making these securities more valuable in the market place.

A bank involved in trading establishes prices at which it will buy and sell a list of government securities. Those securities are quoted on a bid-and-asked basis. The **spread** between the price to be paid for such a security and the price at which it is sold provides the income for trading account activity. This activity entails risk, however, because government security prices change from day to day. Hence the inventory of dollars is subject to change. Thus the spread is compensation to the bank for maintaining the activity and taking the risk. Because the banks provide this service, a substantially more liquid government securities market exists.

Federal Funds and Repurchase Agreements.   The final investment account to be examined consists of federal funds sold and securities purchased under **repurchase agreements,** or **"repos."** Banks held $61 billion worth of such securities in December 1979. Those securities, which represent a use of funds for extremely short periods of time, are perhaps among the more liquid assets held by any bank. When securities are purchased under repurchase agreements, the bank is essentially lending money for a day or two. Rather than actually making a loan, investigating the credit, and taking the risk, it simply takes title to securities for a few days; then, in accordance with the repo agreement, the securities are resold. The difference in the buying price and the selling price of the securities represents a return to the bank for that short period of time. If the securities are not repurchased, the bank of course holds the collateral.

"Federal funds" is shorthand for the **balances on the books of Federal Reserve banks.** Banks that have excess reserves lend those reserves, for a very short period, usually overnight, to other banks with deficiencies in their reserve positions. This market has developed quite recently, and it grew very rapidly in the 1960s and 1970s, reflecting the relatively high interest rates. This represents an alternative and more productive use of any funds that banks may have idle for a very short period of time.

Hence these two categories—federal funds sold and securities purchased under repurchase agreement—represent a very short term use of funds and may be viewed as a **highly liquid asset** turning into cash that may be used for other purposes very quickly.

COMMERCIAL LOANS.   By far the most important use of assets by banks is in the lending area. Almost 55% of all assets ($924 billion in 1979) were loans. Banks make a variety of loans to a large variety of customers. Data discussed here relate to the entire banking industry in the United States. However, individual banks in specific markets have very different patterns.

Real Estate Loans.   First, banks had over $249 billion worth of real estate loans outstanding in December 1979 (Exhibit 1). This was the second most important loan category, next to commercial and industrial loans. By far the most important categories are: loans for construction and land development, conventional single-family mortgage loans, and loans secured by nonfarm, nonresidential properties. Thus the banking industry contributes on several different levels to the construction and housing needs of both business and households. First, construction and land development loans support the very important domestic construction and building trade industries. This contributes both to the total stock of housing and building used by business, providing jobs and production for the entire economy. Most construction loans and land development loans are of relatively short duration and are maintained on the books while the project is under construction or development. At that time the builder usually seeks more permanent financing for the useful life of the project. In the case of housing, the individual buyers usually seek to have longer term mortgages that can be used to pay for the property and house. The builder then pays down the construction and land development loans. Most of the real estate loans made by commercial banks are in the conventional area. That is, they are not insured or guaranteed by either the **Federal Housing Authority (FHA)** or the **Veterans Administration (VA).** In addition, most of the loans to business for nonfarm, nonresidential properties are underwritten and funded by banks. Thus, banks play a major role in the financing of construction and real estate in the United States.

Loans to Financial Institutions.   In addition, banks make loans to other banks and other financial institutions, both domestically and in foreign countries. These institutions may be **real estate investment trusts** (REITS) and **mortgage companies,** which provide a further link between the banking industry and the real estate and construction business. They can be to **finance companies,** which essentially means that banks participate indirectly in the financing of the projects of individuals. Loans are often made to other depository financial institutions or to insurance companies.

In addition to making loans directly to financial institutions, banks make a number of loans to facilitate the functioning of securities markets. They make loans to **brokers and dealers** to purchase and hold securities and to individuals for purchasing securities. Thus, banks participate in the financing of the activities of securities markets that are essential to the allocation of resources and the raising of capital for the economy.

Agricultural Loans.   Banks are major lenders to farmers. In the aggregate, banks had over $31 billion worth of loans to farmers on their books in 1979. This represents 1.8% of total assets of the banking industry. At first glance this may appear to be a relatively low figure. However, these data represent all activities of all banks, and it is instructive to examine the commitment to farm lending of banks in the rural areas of an agricultural state. The results for Nebraska, which is primarily an agricultural state, are quite interesting. For all banks in the state 40% of all loans are made to finance agricultural production. For small banks located primarily in rural areas, having total assets less than $25 million, loans to finance agricultural production account for over 57% of all loans. This is clearly a different picture from that suggested by the national figures.

Commitment to agriculture is probably even greater than indicated above, since many of the commercial and industrial loans in rural regions are undoubtedly made to seed companies and suppliers and other providers of services to the agricultural industry. Hence, the commitment of the banking industry to any particular segment of the economy is related to the market in which it functions. Thus, while in the aggregate loans to farmers make up a small part of total bank loans, that proportion is much, much higher in agricultural regions. Similarly, small banks in suburban areas show a commitment to lending to households and individuals that probably is much higher than that of downtown metropolitan banks primarily engaged in business lending.

Commercial and Industrial Loans.   In the aggregate, the most important component of total loans consists of commercial and industrial loans. In December 1979 that figure exceeded $351 billion. Banks are the prime lenders to most business firms. A relatively small number of very large business firms have access to the **commercial paper market,** in which corporate treasurers can issue unsecured IOUs on the open market and have them purchased by institutional investors. These corporations have very high **credit ratings** and their securities are generally rated very high by agencies involved in evaluating the risk of lending to such institutions. However, most businesses are not in that fortunate situation and have a relatively small number of alternatives for seeking funds. Hence the term "commercial banking," which indicates the long-term substantial commitment of the industry to financing the needs of business.

The historic role of commercial banks looms very large in the development of individual firms. Indeed, commercial banks supply most of the funds and almost all the financial advice to most medium-sized and small business firms. Commercial lending is done on a variety of terms with a variety of contractual agreements between lender and borrower. Many years ago, banks provided primarily short-term loans that were liquidated according to the **seasonal cycles** of the particular business. In recent years, however, banks have provided a very large number of **"term loans,"** that is, loans that have maturity exceeding 1 year. These loans have many different characteristics; they vary greatly from business to business and are tailored to needs of the individual business. This flexibility is unique to the commercial banking industry. For example, the maturity may vary from relatively short seasonal loans to longer term loans, 10 years perhaps, to finance the purchase of equipment. The rate or price charged to the borrower may vary also: it may be fixed, or it may fluctuate with other interest rates in the economy. Indeed, in recent years the trend has been toward greater **floating of interest rates** that move as interest rates in the economy move. Other loans may be collateralized by business assets such as receivables or inventory, or by other assets such as government securities that are pledged as security. The collateral becomes the property of the bank if the loan results in a default. Most loans to business firms are made on the basis of an overall, long-term relationship between the bank and the firm. Typically, business firms make arrangements for needed funds, perhaps annually, under a **line of credit.** That is, at any time during the period of the agreement, the firm may **draw down** its line of credit and utilize those funds for business purposes. Typically the lines must be cleared up (i.e., have a zero balance) from time to time, and they are renegotiated, usually once a year. Thus, the firm can have continuous and flexible access to funds to meet its needs.

Individual Loans.   Loans made to individuals, or **consumer loans,** are another major use of funds in the banking industry. These loans may be made with collateral or they may be made unsecured, and they may have varying maturities. Loans to individuals are primarily a phenomenon of the past 50 years, with most of the growth coming in the post-World War II era. Before 1945, most banks did not make such loans, hence truly deserved the title "commercial banks." All banks in the economy in December 1979 had lent almost $193 billion to consumers, and this component was, in the aggregate, the next largest compared to commercial and industrial loans. These loans are made to purchase private automobiles and other types of consumer goods, to repair and modernize residential property, and in single payment loans; most recently there has been substantial growth in loans connected with **credit card** and **retail charge account plans.** Indeed, this was probably the fastest growing component of total consumer loans in the 1970s. Loans to individuals are an important component of the total bank balance sheet, and in some individual cases, depending on the market situation of the individual bank, are an even larger component of the earning assets of that bank.

BANKING PRODUCTS AND SERVICES AS SHOWN IN LIABILITY AND CAPITAL ACCOUNTS OF COMMERCIAL BANKS

The liability accounts of commercial banks are the major **sources of funds** necessary to make loan and investment services and products available. It is in this area that banks have seen the greatest changes in the past decade. These changes are due to a combination of volatile and relatively high interest rates, the persistent inflation of the decade, the inroads of nonbank competitors, and the movement and direction of technology. Exhibit 2 shows the **liability accounts of all commercial banks** in the United States as of December 31, 1979.

DEMAND DEPOSITS.   The first item of interest, namely demand deposits of individuals, partnerships, corporations (IPC), and the public sector, exceeded $430.7 billion. Over $330 billion represent the checking accounts of the private sector of the economy. The demand deposit is the most prevalent form of "third-party transaction service," although other products have been developed by banks and others to compete with demand deposits. The checking account has several important features:

- The owner may exchange his account balance for cash and currency on demand.
- The owner may use a highly efficient, well-developed system to transfer balances to another party.
- The owner may transfer funds by paper or electronically; the paper medium (checks) dominates such transactions, however.

EXHIBIT 2   LIABILITIES AND CAPITAL OF ALL COMMERCIAL BANKS IN THE UNITED STATES, DECEMBER 31, 1979 ($ THOUSANDS)

Total demand deposits	$ 430,775,791
Total savings deposits	206,668,739
Total time deposits	453,130,237
Deposits in foreign offices	171,493,380
Federal funds purchased and securities sold under repurchase agreements	112,346,888
Interest-bearing demand notes and other borrowing	39,526,304
Mortgage indebtedness	2,149,449
All other liabilities	71,493,618
Total liabilities	$1,588,584,406
Subordinated notes and debentures	6,252,770
Preferred stock, par value	125,890
Common stock, par value	20,273,743
Surplus	35,328,623
Undivided profits and capital reserves	41,512,569
Subordinated notes and debentures plus equity capital	$ 103,493,595
Total liabilities and capital	$1,692,078,001

Source: Federal Deposit Insurance Corp., *Bank Operating Statistics, 1979,* FDIC, Washington, D.C., 1980.

- Banks have not paid interest on balances in checking accounts since 1933, but inroads made by similar, competitive products have resulted in a change in the law effective December 31, 1980 (see below).

Although demand deposits are a major source of funds to banks and an essential component of any modern, diversified economy, they also are a major component of the **nation's money supply.** While the definition of the monetary aggregate has undergone substantial change, at least in part because of innovations designed to compete with demand deposits, the major component of the narrow definition of money (M1-A) is the demand deposits of banks. For a discussion of the various definitions of the money supply see the section on "Money and Capital Markets." Thus, the commercial banking industry is an important component of the process by which the **Federal Reserve** attempts to control monetary aggregates to accomplish its macroeconomic goals.

For the past 25 years, demand deposits have grown less rapidly than other forms of bank deposits. For example, at year-end 1954, demand deposits were almost 74% of the sum of demand and time deposits. By year-end 1979, demand deposits represented only 32% of total deposits. The primary reason for this was the tendency of business firms and individuals to economize on the balances held in checking accounts. Since banks could not then pay interest on such balances, there was an incentive for business firms and individuals to place those balances where they could earn money. With interest rates reaching record highs in the 1970s, these funds were viewed with great envy by other institutions, which devised new products to attract them out of demand accounts. Banks responded by offering services that may increase interest expense but nontheless keep the deposits in house.

A very large proportion of the dollar volume and number of transactions in the economic system moves through bank demand accounts. Some of the transactions move directly from one account to another, either inside a single bank or from one bank to another. However, as discussed above, even the vast number of cash transactions is facilitated by banks providing coin and currency to the public. It is estimated that in 1978 checks worth $30 billion were written in the United States, with an average value of $500 per check.

Another method of moving funds is through wire transfers. **Wire systems** for moving funds are offered both by the Federal Reserve and by a private company, Bank Wire Corp., owned by a group of banks. Interestingly enough, these wire systems handled only 20 million transactions, but the average value exceeded $1.7 million. Of course, these transfers are made from demand accounts to demand accounts. Often the transactions are between accounts of the same business firm to consolidate cash at one bank to invest in the money markets for periods as short as 1 day.

Further examination of demand deposit data reveals interesting patterns. Let us consider the distribution of accounts for a sample of banks participating in the Federal Reserve's Functional Cost Analysis program. For example, for 85 banks with deposits over $200 million, accounts with balances under $500 provide 59% of the accounts and approximately 3% of the funds. At the other end of the spectrum, accounts with balances exceeding $100,000 provide less than 0.5% of the accounts and 48% of the balances. The proportions are less extreme for smaller banks, but the direction is strongly confirmed. That is, a small proportion of the depositors provide the bulk of the funds available for lending and investing, while a large proportion of the depositors provide relatively small accounts that tend to be more costly to service (see *Functional Cost Analysis: 1978 Average Banks,* Federal Reserve Bank of Kansas City, 1979).

When the breakdown is altered to reflect commercial and personal accounts, a similar pattern emerges. For a sample of 100 banks providing such a breakdown, on average commercial accounts provided 65% of the funds (higher for larger banks) and approximately 14% of the accounts. Activity patterns for large banks show over 200 items processed per month, of which over 190 were checks written. Personal account activity averages approximately 25 items per account.

Major innovations in this area have occurred on three levels, all making the demand deposit account a more viable, but more costly product. Those three items are as follows:

- The use of technology to assist corporations in the aggressive **management of cash** to minimize idle funds (see section entitled "Cash Management").
- The development of substitutes for retail accounts by nonbank competitors.
- The adaptation of banks by accepting and competing effectively with new products, culminating in the authority to offer **NOW accounts** nationwide after December 31, 1980.

Any organization managing large amounts of cash has an incentive to move it into a form readily available for investment. This is especially true of organizations with customers, outlets, plants, and suppliers spread over the entire nation, indeed the world. The original movement toward aggressive cash management came from large corporations, but small corporations as well as governmental and nonprofit organizations have begun to follow suit.

Cash Management Systems.   These are varied in nature and degree of sophistication, but they work as follows. For incoming payments, a series of banks is selected based on location to minimize the time a check is in the mail from the customer to the corporation. Usually, the corporation instructs its customers to remit to it at a post office box. The chosen bank manages the box, known as a **"lockbox,"** and several times daily will remove all materials, send the checks for collection, and send all other materials plus a record of checks in process to the corporation. Those checks are available faster because of the strategic location of the bank. A corporation that has many retail outlets, for example, will have the local manager deposit funds daily. In both cases, the information may be relayed daily to a data center, which records the information from many sources and makes it available on a data terminal in the corporate treasurer's office. Armed with that information and knowing the cash needed to honor outstanding checks, the **corporate treasurer** will wire funds to a single, **lead bank** for disbursement and investment.

The number of wire transfers, undoubtedly reflecting the use of these techniques, has grown rapidly, as has the corporate use of **repurchase agreements,** a favorite way of investing funds for very short periods of time.

NOW Accounts.   The number of payment system innovations on the retail level has been substantial. In 1972 the NOW account was born in Massachusetts. **"NOW" means negotiable order of withdrawal,** and such an instrument is functionally equivalent to a check. The major innovation was the payment of interest on the balance in the NOW account. The NOW was pioneered by **mutual savings banks,** a thrift institution competitor, in Massachusetts and New Hampshire. After legislative, regulatory, and court skirmishes, Congress extended NOW account powers to all depository financial institutions in Massachusetts and New Hampshire in 1974. In March 1976, the NOW was extended to the rest of New England. In November 1978, NOW was extended to New York and in December 1979, to New Jersey. Thus, the entire Northeast, including two major financial centers, New York and Boston, was an experimental ground from 1974 to 1980. NOW accounts are a significant part of the money supply measure M1-B. Congress extended the NOW to all financial institutions beginning in 1981. For an extended discussion see Murphy and Mandell, *The NOW Account Decision: Profitability, Pricing and Strategies.*

Share Drafts.   While the NOW account was being introduced, a major new competitor appeared with a new product. In 1974 **credit unions** started to market their **"share draft"** account. This was again functionally equivalent to a check with two differences: interest was paid on the balance, and the draft (check) was "truncated," or not returned to the customer. Savings and loan associations, the dominant thrift institutions outside the Northeast, experimented with technology to transform their traditional product, the savings account, into a **transaction account.** This occurred in two basic ways. First, some savings and loan associations deployed point-of-sale terminals and automated teller machines to allow people easy access to their accounts at diverse locations. Second, some savings and loan associations pioneered the **telephone bill payment service** whereby a customer makes payments to selected vendors from his or her savings account by communicating with the financial institution through the telephone.

Automatic Transfer Service.   With all these products in the marketplace, the banking regulators authorized commercial banks to market a new service known as "automatic transfer service" (ATS) in November 1978. This may be thought of as a "clumsy" NOW account, because it works as follows. A customer agrees to maintain a savings account balance to cover any checks that may be written. The customer thus must have two accounts, a savings account and a zero-balance checking account. As checks are presented for payment, the bank automatically transfers the necessary funds to cover the checks. This was not a marketing success for reasons that are fairly obvious.

Current Status of Demand Deposits.   While IPC demand deposits are $333.5 billion, total demand deposits are $430.8 billion. Who has the rest? Other banks maintain correspondent balances and are referred to as **"due to" accounts.** Also, all levels of government maintain demand deposit accounts. These accounts have one unique feature. Securities must be pledged by banks to equal or exceed those balances of public funds. Thus, the securities portfolio is less liquid if pledgings are anywhere near the total investment portfolio.

In summary, demand deposits are an important source of funds to banks and a product over which the industry once had a virtual monopoly. As interest rates have risen, all sectors of the economy, especially the corporate sector, have economized on the holdings of non-interest-yielding assets. Nonbank competitors have innovated interest-yielding transactions accounts in various ways. Consequently, the trend noted above will continue until almost all balances pay some kind of return.

TIME AND SAVINGS DEPOSITS.   A major source of funds for commercial banking consists of time and savings deposits. These deposits have grown more rapidly than demand deposits and have substantially changed in offering terms in the past 20 years. The trend in economizing on cash balances had already begun in the decade of the 1950s, although it was limited to major corporate entities. The banking system had no deposit products to compete with **money market instruments** for the short-term use of idle corporate funds. During the 1946–1960 period, total commercial bank liabilities grew at an annual rate of only 3.7%, compared with a 10.5% growth rate for deposits at thrift institutions (savings and loan associations, mutual savings banks, and credit unions). As a result, commercial bank shares of total financial intermediation fell to a low of approximately 26% in 1960 (see Beebe, "A Perspective on Liability Management and Bank Risk").

Certificates of Deposit.   To counter the trend to economize on cash balances, commercial banks in New York City announced (in the early 1960's) that they would issue large-denomination negotiable **certificates of deposit (CDs)** and that a major securities dealer had agreed to "make a market" in them. The new instrument would be priced to compete with **U.S. Treasury bills.** Whereas previously the major deposit product at commercial banks had been the demand deposit, as a result of the introduction of CDs and other new market instruments, banks embraced a new management philosophy known as **"liabilities management."** Although banks used nonprice-competitive techniques such as opening conveniently located branches, staying open longer hours, mounting aggressive advertising campaigns, and other devices, the amount of funds available was not directly under their control. Hence, the asset portfolio was viewed as a major source of liquidity. With the advent of new markets and products, banks gained more control over deposit sources of funds, and the amount of money available to fund asset growth was a matter of bank discretion. The success of this strategy depended on the ability of banks to be able to price the CD's attractively; that is, Federal Reserve regulatory ceilings—in this case, the maximum interest rates payable to customers (Regulation Q)—had to respond to the movements in market rates. Such changes occurred in June 1970 and again in June 1973 when ceilings on CDs were lifted to enable banks to raise capital. (See below for a discussion of the stimulus prior to 1970).

The new financial instrument was an immediate success, growing rapidly to $18.6 billion in August 1966. At that time, money market rates rose rapidly and exceeded the ceilings set in place by **Regulation Q** of the Federal Reserve System. The result was a predictable "runoff" of CDs at commercial banks as corporate treasurers found better return-risk opportunities in other money market instruments. As rates fell in 1967, CDs renewed their growth and reached a high of $24.3 billion at year-end 1968. Shortly after this, interest rates rose once again, and the Regulation Q ceiling was not increased. A spectacular runoff ensued, and, at year-end 1969, only $10.9 billion worth of CDs was outstanding (see Nelson, "Negotiable Certificates of Deposit," in *Instruments of the Money Market*).

Commercial Paper Market. If banks could not offer competitive rates to attract funds through CDs, they would be hard pressed to meet loan requests. With corporate treasurers seeking funds but not finding them at banks, and placing funds but not purchasing bank CDs, some other market was needed to handle these requirements. A market that grew rapidly in this environment was the **commercial paper market. Corporate treasurers** issued these instruments that had no ceiling rates, and other corporate treasurers purchased them. Indeed, banks even began issuing commercial paper through holding company subsidiaries to avoid the effects of **Regulation Q.** Two major problems are associated with reliance on the commercial paper market to provide the services normally performed by financial intermediaries:

- Many business firms do not have the size or **credit rating** necessary to be able to issue commercial paper.
- No **loan loss reserves,** no **capital cushion,** and no **deposit insurance** exist to absorb losses in case of a default.

In June 1970 the **Penn Central Railroad** defaulted on its commercial paper obligations. As a result, the financial markets were severely disrupted, and the Federal Reserve moved quickly to suspend all ceilings on large CDs with maturities less than 90 days. This permitted the commercial banking system to provide a product with a competitive price to attract funds, and an alternative to commercial paper to meet corporate borrowing needs. In a series of moves over the next several years, all ceilings on all maturities of large CDs were removed, and the Federal Reserve System abandoned its attempt to regulate credit expansion through restrictive deposit interest ceilings.

As of 1980, it was the practice of banks to issue CDs in response to loan demand, and the aggregate amounts track the cyclical and secular changes in commercial and industrial loan demand. In August 1980, for banks with assets exceeding $750 million, large CDs averaged over $127 billion. The only remaining question is: Why do corporate treasurers receive an unregulated, market-determined rate on funds placed in large CDs while smaller deposits have a regulatory ceiling? That question is addressed below.

Passbook Savings Accounts. A traditional source of funds for commercial banks as well as thrift institutions is the "passbook savings account." While many banks no longer issue actual passbooks, the account itself is a very liquid asset with a yield (effective interest rate) that is bound by **Regulation Q.** Although Regulation Q was originally a Federal Reserve regulation, in 1966 Congress extended deposit interest ceilings to nonmember commercial banks, mutual savings banks, and savings and loan associations with regulations to be promulgated by the Federal Deposit Insurance Corp. for banks and Federal Home Loan Bank Board, for S & Ls, in addition to the Fed. The regulations were worked out in an interagency committee to assure uniformity. Then the entire set of deposit interest ceilings came to be known as "Regulation Q" or just "Reg Q." Another characteristic of the **traditional savings account** is **liquidity for the holder.** The account can be redeemed for cash at the option of the holder but does not have third-party transactions capability. Technically there is a (potential) 30-day waiting period for savings account funds, but as a practical matter it is rarely if ever invoked.

DEPOSIT RATE CEILINGS.   In the past decade, the ceiling rate permitted banks on savings accounts has been lifted several times. However, in most of the period, returns on money market alternatives were considerably higher than the ceiling on savings accounts. The inevitable result has been an erosion of this source of funds for commercial banks as savers looked for alternative instruments with higher yields, or, as has been the case in the past several years, simply saved less.

The reasons for maintaining a lower than market return for savers are related to the continuing battles between commercial banks and thrift institutions during the past two decades. As indicated above, commercial banks were not active in the savings deposit or time deposit areas until the post-World War II era and did not enter them aggressively until the 1960s. In 1966, interest rates rose rapidly and, among all depository financial institutions, commercial banks were best situated to reprice their assets and pay near-market rates to attract savers. Thrift institutions had a large proportion of their assets in longer term fixed rate mortgage loans with low rates locked in, while deposit costs were rising. The political solution to this was the passage of legislation in 1966 extending interest rate ceilings to all federally insured or regulated depository financial institutions. This legislation established a **"differential" for thrift institutions** allowing them to pay a slightly higher rate to savers. This legislation and all ensuing regulations and legislation served simultaneously to protect the institutions that were vulnerable to a rapid runup of deposits and to facilitate the flow of funds into the **housing sector.** The battle for reform of the financial system usually focused on the level of interest rate ceilings and the "differential" between commercial banks and other depository institutions.

While this set of constraints may have the appearance of accomplishing the objective, it neglected two major points:

- Savers could purchase instruments in the open market, bypassing financial institutions altogether.
- An unregulated competitor industry could design competing products with higher yields.

In practice, the decade of the 1970s included both phenomena. In June 1971 all savings deposits at commercial banks were $107,868 million, or 19.7% of all liabilities. In December 1979, savings deposits were $206,669 million, or 13% of total liabilities. Since we already know that demand deposit growth has been limited, it is clear that certificates of deposit, other time deposits, and purchased funds have accounted for most of the growth in bank liabilities.

Money Market Mutual Fund Competition.   Perhaps the most dramatic example of the behavior of an unregulated competitor has been the growth of the **money market mutual fund.** The product is a basic one; the investor (depositor) buys a share of a **portfolio of money market instruments** including Treasury bills, large certificates of deposit, bankers' acceptances, commercial paper, and other instruments, in varying proportions depending on individual's investment philosophy. After a management charge has been deducted, the interest income is passed through to the holder. While the size of a minimum investment and redemption policies vary, most money market funds (there were approximately 100 funds in 1980) have a low initial investment (several thousand dollars) and a liberal policy for redeeming the shares for cash. Indeed, some money market funds permit the holders to write checks on their shares, in effect creating an **interest-paying demand deposit.** In the high interest rate environment of the late 1970s, these funds reached approximately $80 billion in late 1980. This phenomenal growth explains in large part the final dismantling of the Regulation Q-type ceilings that was mandated by statute in March 1980. For a discussion of the growth in money market funds, see Dunham, "The Growth of Money Market Funds" (*New England Business Review*, September–October 1980).

Money Market Certificates.   In June 1978 federal bank regulatory agencies created a new deposit product known as the "money market certificate." Its primary purpose is to permit banks to compete with money market mutual funds. The maturity is 6 months, and minimum denomination is $10,000. The yield is tied to the yield on U.S. Treasury bills auctioned each week. Consumer response to this new product has been enthusiastic, and at year-end 1979, $103.2 billion in deposits had been issued by commercial banks, approximately 10% of all domestic deposits. In effect, the innovations in the **wholesale market** have "trickled down" to the **retail market** in response to competitive, technological, and financial developments of the decade.

NOW Account Legal and Financial Issues.   The final major development of the 1970s discussed here is the process of breaking down the prohibitions of interest payments on demand deposits. Since 1933, explicit interest payments on demand deposits had been forbidden for all federally insured banks. However, in July 1970, a mutual savings bank in Worcester, Massachusetts, filed a plan to offer "negotiable order of withdrawal" or NOW accounts to its customers. This deposit product allows a customer to transfer funds from a savings account to a third party with an instrument that is, for all practical purposes, a check. Thus, the product was a checking account that paid interest. The Commissioner of Banks in Massachusetts denied the request, but the Massachusetts Supreme Judicial Court found in favor of the savings bank, which along with several other savings banks began offering the service in the summer of 1972.

Now, if federal law prohibited the payment of interest on demand deposits, how could a Massachusetts savings bank offer it, and why is a state court rather than a federal court deciding the issue? The answer is that Massachusetts has a deposit insurance program for mutual savings banks, and the bulk of that industry, an important part of the financial institution market in that state, does **not** belong to the **Federal Deposit Insurance Corp.** Thus, there was no federal jurisdiction. However, the matter quickly became a federal issue as federally insured and regulated financial institutions, primarily commercial banks and savings and loan associations, perceived a competitive imbalance. After legislative deliberation, Congress chose a middle course between abolishing a product already in the market and inducing drastic changes in the entire nation: it allowed **all** depository financial institutions in Massachusetts and New Hampshire to offer NOWs. This was viewed as an experiment or an attempt to "quarantine" the matter to two states beginning on January 1, 1974. After several years, financial institutions in adjoining states felt competitive pressures, and the experiment was extended to the remainder of the New England states beginning March 1, 1976. The regional spread continued, adding New York in January 1979 and New Jersey in January 1980. NOWs became available nationally after December 31, 1980, eliminating a major part of the regulatory and statutory environment of the past 47 years.

Bankers and regulators were concerned about the impact of this development on their profitability and solvency. A substantial increase in interest expenses could have a devastating impact on earnings, depending on the pricing policies of financial institutions and the acceptance rate of the public. Thus, the experience in New England was monitored very closely. The evidence may be summarized as follows:

1. In the early days of the experiment in Massachusetts and New Hampshire, the worst of all possible worlds evolved. All financial institutions engaged in aggressive pricing, with the "free" NOW dominating the market. (A "free" NOW pays maximum allowable rates, has no minimum balance, and no service charges.)

2. The consumer response in the first two states, after an initial lukewarm response, was enthusiastic. The number of NOW accounts per 100 households exceeded 70 in 1978.

3. There was a substantial but not devastating impact on earnings in Massachusetts and New Hampshire in 1974 and 1975. However, some banks were particularly vulnerable.

4. In the the other New England states, the pricing patterns were considerably more conservative, with high balance requirements required to avoid service charges. Predictably, consumer response was slower, and the highest penetration rate in 1978 was approximately 20 NOW accounts per 100 households. Balances per account were considerably higher, and profitability impacts were much less.

All banks are presently faced with the problems of pricing and marketing NOWs, but they have 6 years of experience to review in establishing policy.

MAJOR CHANGES IN REGULATORY ENVIRONMENT

Despite the apparent or actual geographic limits placed on commercial banks by state laws, a number of changes in the regulatory environment have had the effect of removing the restriction on **where banks can operate.** In addition, there has been a major change in the kinds of regulation and restriction on bank product lines and prices. These developments portend a substantial and yet unknown change in the structure and operations of commercial banks. These developments are as follows:

- The Bank Holding Company Act of 1970 and subsequent interpretations and decisions.
- The International Banking Act of 1978.
- The Depository Institutions Deregulation and Monetary Control Act of 1980.

BANK HOLDING COMPANY ACT OF 1970.   This Act was an important milestone in the adaptation of the banking system to a changing financial environment. Prior to 1970, bank holding companies **owning or controlling more than one bank** were regulated by the Board of Governors of the Federal Reserve System. For our purposes, several important factors are noteworthy. First, bank holding companies were not permitted to own banks outside their state of incorporation unless both that state and the other state or states had enacted statutes permitting out-of-state entry. This prohibition is the subject of the **Douglas Amendment.** Second, for practical purposes, the bank holding company was confined to owning banks and firms with very narrowly restricted activities. Third, a holding company owning or controlling only one bank was exempt from regulation. For a complete discussion, see *The Bank Holding Company Movement of 1978: A Compendium* (Federal Reserve Board, Washington, D.C.) and Jesse and Seelig, *Bank Holding Companies and the Public Interest.*

The last exemption is crucial. In the late 1960s, the Federal Reserve was attempting to reduce the growth of bank credit by keeping the Regulation Q ceiling on large certificates of deposit beneath open market rates. The notion was that banks could not increase their lending if they could not pay market rates to attract funds. However, some major banks utilized the exemption to establish subsidiaries to issue commercial paper and avoid the interest rate ceilings. Thus a bank would form a holding company that initially owned nothing but that bank. Subsequently, the holding company would form a subsidiary to issue commercial paper at market rates. The subsidiary then used the funds **to purchase loans from the bank.** As a practical matter, there is little difference between a certificate of deposit of a large bank and **commercial paper issued by a subsidiary of the parent holding company** that owns the bank. Of course, the exemption existed for the purpose of eliminating the need to regulate thousands of holding companies owning small banks and other businesses in small towns across the United States. Notwithstanding the intent, the letter of the law was clear. Holding companies owning only one bank could own whatever else they wanted, anywhere in the United States. Most banks wished to assure themselves a stable source of funds when regulation threatened their traditional sources.

Using this scenario, however, what is to stop U.S. Steel, General Motors, or Texaco from **owning one bank,** perhaps one of the largest, through a holding company device? Recall that in 1968 there were some **conglomerate firms** growing very rapidly with high price-earnings multiples. One of these, Leasco Data Processing Equipment Co. (Leasco), determined that there were no statutory reasons to stop it from acquiring Chemical Bank and Trust Co. in New York, one of the top 10 banks in the nation. Leasco made a **tender offer** to Chemical stockholders. The transaction was never completed, and the subsequent stock market disenchantment with the conglomerates reduced their ability to make attractive offers to owners of bank stock. Nonetheless, no statutory nor regulatory barriers existed to prevent the takeover by Leasco.

Because of concern for the evasion of regulation, the potential blurring of distinctions between ownership and control of commerce and industry on the one hand and banking on the other (development of Japanese-style "zaibatsu"), and other reasons, Congress enacted legislation in late 1970 to **end all distinctions between one-bank and multibank holding companies and to regulate them.** A major facet of the law involved permission to own nonbank subsidiaries engaged in activities so closely related to banking or managing or controlling banks as to be a proper transaction. Congress conveniently left that determination to the **Board of Governors of the Federal Reserve System.** However, it is important to note here that while the **banks** are subject to geographic constraints inside the United States, this is **not** so for **nonbank subsidiaries.** Thus, a 36-month automobile loan made by a finance company subsidiary of a bank can be made from offices anywhere in the country, whereas a bank is limited to making such a loan from an office within a prescribed area. Is there much substantive difference between these loans? Ask a bank competing with **Citicorp's** *Person to Person Finance* or **Bankamerica's** *Finance America,* both finance company subsidiaries of major bank holding companies with nationwide offices.

The Federal Reserve Board has interpreted the recently liberalized legislation to include activities that essentially remove geographical restrictions from the asset products of commercial bank balance sheets. These include **finance companies** (consumer and commercial), **mortgage banking,** and **leasing.** These are credit activities that are similar to the lending done by banks themselves, and banks have penetrated, indeed dominated, those parts of the industry. For example, 6 of the top 10 mortgage banking firms are owned by banks. This is especially interesting because mortgage banks tend to be in the faster growing areas of the country and many of the purchasing banks are located in the Northeast metropolitan areas, with limited or no economic growth. Thus, the **holding company device** has permitted bank holding companies to circumvent the constraints placed on their bank subsidiaries in locating their lending activities. In addition, bank holding companies have major positions in finance company, factoring, and leasing industries. While there are no comprehensive data available for the geographical distribution of these lending offices of nonbank subsidiaries, it is generally accepted that the large holding companies have located them in most of the major growing areas of the nation.

INTERNATIONAL BANKING ACT OF 1978.   Another major step that is changing the regulatory environment was the passage of the International Banking Act (IBA) of 1978. In a strange anomaly of the laws regulating banks prior to 1978, branches of foreign banks were permitted to locate anywhere in the United States, but, of course, the branching capabilities of U.S. banks are constrained. The IBA solution was to allow previously established foreign branches to remain intact but to restrict all new foreign branches in the same way that American banks are.

For our purposes, a most interesting development was the relaxation of the restrictions on **Edge Act corporations** and their activities.

An Edge Act corporation is a subsidiary of a bank established to provide financial services to business firms engaged in foreign trade. A bank could establish such a subsidiary in a **location outside its home state.** However, each office was a separate corporation. In addition, the Edge Act corporation could finance only activities related to the **export of goods or services.** The IBA permitted the consolidation of all Edge Act corporations of a bank into a single, multibranch, interstate subsidiary. Also, under IBA, Edge Act corporations may finance activities related to the **production of goods for export.** Thus, IBA substantially increased the scope and flexibility of Edge Act corporations by giving them essentially interstate branching powers and broadening their lending powers. After all, almost all major U.S. corporations are engaged in some production for foreign trade, expanding the potential target market substantially.

DEPOSITORY INSTITUTIONS DEREGULATION AND MONETARY CONTROL ACT OF 1980.   A major change in the regulatory environment occurred on March 31, 1980, with the passage of the Depository Institutions Deregulation and Monetary Control Act (DIDMCA). This Act contains a number of major provisions that will **alter the nature of the banking industry** in the years to come. The various pressures and developments discussed above led to a consensus that the protection afforded by such regulatory props as Regulation Q was not appropriate, equitable, or effective. In 1971 the President's Commission on Financial Structure and Regulation (**Hunt Commission**) made a broad set of recommendations to alter the powers of and regulations applying to depository financial institutions. Those recommendations have been substantially incorporated into the DIDMCA. See the *Report of the President's Commission on Financial Structure and Regulation.*

There are a number of important changes in the DIDMCA:

1. Any depository financial institution offering transactions accounts is subject to **universal reserve requirements** set by the Board of Governors of the Federal Reserve System **regardless of the Federal Reserve membership status** of the financial institution.

2. Any financial institution with deposit-withdrawal transaction accounts or nonpersonal time accounts is entitled to the same discount and borrowing privileges as member banks.

3. The Federal Reserve must **charge for Federal Reserve bank services** such as check clearing, wire transfer, automated clearinghouse, and providing currency and coin. Services will be available to members and nonmembers on an equal basis.

4. **Interest ceilings on deposits** (Regulation Q) will be **eliminated** over a phaseout period of 6 years, with the Act containing suggested targets for raising the ceilings. The phaseout is to be administered by a Depository Institutions Deregulation Committee composed of the heads of the various federal regulatory agencies and the Secretary of the Treasury.

5. **All depository financial institutions** are **permitted** to offer **NOW accounts** effective December 31, 1980.

6. Thrift institution asset portfolio powers are broadened to lend up to 20% of assets in consumer loans, commercial paper, and corporate debt securities.

7. **State usury ceilings** are nonapplicable for 3 years.

In summary, the decade of the 1970s saw unprecedented changes in the commercial banking industry in response to volatile movements in prices, interest rates, and fund flows. Many new competitors entered the market with products that were close substitutes for traditional banking products. Through all this, banks have adapted fairly well, and the regulatory environment has changed, albeit with a lag, to meet the challenge.

UNRESOLVED QUESTIONS AND REGULATORY ISSUES

BRANCH BANKING.   "Perhaps the most important question of domestic banking policy before the country is that of branch banking." Charles Wallace Collins made that statement 55 years ago (*The Branch Banking Question,* Macmillan, 1926), but a casual perusal of the banking press indicates that it is far from a dead issue.

*   The Oklahoma legislature rejected proposed legislation to allow **multibank holding companies** in that state.
*   In November 1980 voters in Colorado resoundingly defeated a referendum to allow **branch banking**.
*   In Illinois banks are not an industry but are more like armed camps, with several trade associations representing different views on branching in that **unit bank state**.

The branching status of banking may change in two ways. First, individual states can change their laws. In recent years, there has been a trend in the direction of more permissive branching laws, with New York, New Jersey, Virginia, and Florida among states with large populations opting for wider branching powers. Second, the federal government could change its laws (primarily the **McFadden Act** and the **Douglas Amendment** to the Bank Holding Company Act of 1970) to permit wider branching. Indeed, the IBA contained an amendment directing the President to conduct a study that would review the federal statutes and recommend change if it is deemed appropriate. The study had not been released at the end of 1980, but its general outline has been sufficiently leaked to reveal the general thrust of the recommendations.

Pros and Cons of Branching.   Before discussing the possible recommendations and understanding the typical lag between recommendation and enactment, some of the issues that have been raised with regard to the branching issue are discussed. See the special issue (Summer 1980) of *Journal of Bank Research* for a detailed discussion. They are as follows:

1. Branching allows banks to grow sufficiently large to achieve scale economies necessary to produce financial services at low costs.
2. Branching results in an undue concentration of resources in a small number of financial institutions.
3. Branching protects local monopolies by not allowing banks outside a market to enter.
4. Branching achieves diversification of lending and investing necessary to promote the safety and soundness of the banking system.
5. Branching allows funds to flow from areas where supply is strong to areas where demand is strong.
6. Branching results in funds leaving rural areas for the financial centers.
7. Branching restrictions are an unwarranted government intrusion on the ability of private firms to decide where to conduct business.
8. Any change in federal laws will result in an unwarranted intrusion on the rights of the individual states.

Obviously, these issues are not mutually compatible. Branching cannot simultaneously increase and decrease competition. The issues are to a certain extent questions of fact, and there have been a number of studies to address them. The results are briefly summarized below. Unfortunately, they are not clear-cut.

Economies of Scale.   The existence of economies of scale has been studied by numerous researchers. Differences in approach, methodology, and data have characterized a wide variety of studies. Major questions have centered on the appropriate **definition of bank output**, recognizing several unique characteristics of banking activities. First, banks lend and acquire dollars, but costs are related to transactions. Second, the multiproduct nature of banking makes it difficult to disentangle joint costs and to determine the effect of changing any single output on costs. Keeping these difficulties in mind, a consensus of the results across studies may be summarized as follows:

1. While economies of scale exist in many bank activities, they are not sufficient to indicate that small and medium-sized banks are at a substantial cost disadvantage in competing.
2. The method of expansion affects the extent of scale economies. If expansion takes place by increasing the number of branches, the benefits of scale economies are largely offset.

The policy conclusion is that there appear to be no compelling **social reasons** to encourage large financial institutions; on the other hand, small and medium-sized banks do not have any inherent disadvantages that require special protection if they are to coexist with large banks.

Concentration and Competition.   The question of concentration and competition has been studied in two ways. First, the differences in concentration in different types of branching environments have been analyzed. Second, the effect of changing branching laws has been studied. That is, **concentration ratios** before the change in the law are compared to those following the change. The results suggest the following:

1. States with statewide branching tend to have fewer banks, higher concentration ratios, and more offices than limited or unit bank states.
2. States with statewide branching tend to have more competitors and more offices in individual retail banking markets. Concentration ratios in branch banking metropolitan areas were reduced between 1966 and 1975.

Problem Banks.   Studies regarding **availability of credit** consistently show higher ratios of loans to deposits over time for banks with branches. The results of analyses of the effect of branching on safety and soundness are inconclusive. That is, branching does not seem to affect the probability of a bank's being on the **problem list** or being closed. Unfortunately, there are few data available to use in assessing the geographic movement of funds under different branching regimes, and the question of the appropriate balance between state and federal regulation in banking is beyond the scope of this section.

Recommendations on Branching.   As indicated above, through several devices, banks have been able to achieve substantial geographical diversification under current statutes. While it is unlikely that interstate branching will be completely abolished in the near future, several changes might be politically acceptable and may occur in the next decade. First, a **removal of the restrictions of the Douglas Amendment in failing bank cases** might offer one kind of relaxation. Currently, when a relatively large bank approaches insolvency, the number of potential buyers is limited to banks in that state. One result is the purchase by foreign banks of banks facing financial difficulties. Foreign banks can sometimes gain a foothold in a large metropolitan area market more easily by purchasing a failing bank than in starting a de novo branch in that market. For example, in 1975 European American Bank purchased troubled Franklin National Bank. In any event, the regulators faced with closing a bank in the most efficient (least costly) manner now feel that their ability to do so would be enhanced if domestic out-of-state bank holding companies were permitted to bid along with in-state and foreign banks.

Another type of relaxation of interstate **presence** would be the permission of **electronic terminals across state lines** where metropolitan areas linked by economic and commuting patterns cross state lines. There is already a concept of an integrated metropolitan area (the Standard Metropolitan Statistical Area or SMSA) measured by the U.S. Bureau of the Census. For example, it would be both convenient and reasonable if banks in Kansas City, Missouri, could place electronic terminals in Kansas City, Kansas (and vice versa). Federal legislation would be required before any such arrangements could be implemented, however, because the U.S. Supreme Court has ruled that such terminals are branches for purposes of the law. Another possibility would be to permit bank holding companies to acquire banks in contiguous states. This selective, regional breakdown of state boundaries would bring the additional problem of establishing or acquiring a new bank, a somewhat more difficult proposition than establishing a branch office.

FEDERAL RESERVE CREDIT CONTROLS.   Another regulatory initiative occurred on March 14, 1980, and was withdrawn after several months. The Federal Reserve Board implemented a system of credit controls that placed a **"special deposit" of 15% on certain types of consumer credit**. This asset reserve requirement was viewed by many as a form of government credit allocation. The requirement was instituted for all lenders, including commercial banks, finance companies, credit unions, savings and loan associations, mutual savings banks, retail establishments, gasoline companies, and travel and entertainment card companies. Increases in credit beyond the amounts outstanding on March 14, 1980, were subject to the 15% special deposit requirement. This program and its demise were discussed in the *Federal Reserve Bulletin* (April and July 1980).

The effect of the requirement was to make certain types of consumer lending less desirable, thus reducing the amount of credit growth in the economy. But why select certain types of consumer credit and not others? Lending to business and government as well as certain types of consumer credit were exempt from the requirements. Under such a system, the decision to select or exempt a certain type of credit becomes a political one.

The special deposit was removed in phases, ending on July 3, 1980. The episode was a short-lived experiment in credit allocation in which certain types of credit were singled out for special treatment. The effects on the industry were minimal primarily because an environment was created in which banks could do patriotically and quickly what they would have done anyway. Several points, however, are unresolved.

1. Will the government be tempted to impose credit allocation measures in the future in response to unforeseen circumstances?

2. Can the commercial banking industry stay in the business of granting **fixed rate consumer loans** in an era of volatile and rising costs of funds, especially when their liabilities are becoming more closely tied to open market rates?

It is possible that **floating rate consumer loans** are the next pricing innovation, but it is not at all clear that such loans could be marketed as easily as **floating rate commercial loans**.

Bank Credit Cards.   Interest rates for funds acquired by banks were very high in the spring of 1980; hence consumer lending at fixed rates was not a profitable use of bank funds even before the special deposit was imposed. However, the requirement resulted in a substantial repositioning of the bank credit card. **Bank cards** had grown rapidly in the 1970s, and in 1977, 35% of all families used bank credit cards, with many families having more than one card. Usage of bank cards is much higher for families in upper income, higher education, and professional and managerial groups (see Durkin and Ellinghausen, *1977 Consumer Credit Survey*). Growth has been spurred by **"duality,"** a court-induced change in the rules of the credit card companies. That is, prior to duality, an issuing bank affiliated with one of the two major credit card companies, Visa or Interbank, could not issue the other's card. That rule was struck down in 1977, and, as a result, credit cards outstanding grew at rapid rates as banks issued Visa cards to their Mastercard customers, and vice versa.

An important result of the introduction of duality was the intense competition for merchant business. That is, before the change, merchants who accepted both Visa and Mastercard had to deposit their sales slips at two different banks, which was somewhat inconvenient. With duality, banks could compete for all of a merchant's business, and they did, reducing the rate of merchant discount as a source of revenue. Many customers use their cards, but avoid finance charges by paying their revolving charges every month. Thus, the bank credit card was not profitable prior to March 14, 1980, and expansion of business beyond levels outstanding that day would be even less profitable. For a discussion on bank credit card profitability, see Mandell and Murphy, *Bank Cards*.

The response of the industry was immediate. First, customer credit lines were not likely to be increased when requested. Second, new cards were issued very selectively. Third, minimum repayment schedules were increased. Fourth, many banks implemented an annual fee for the bank card. Finally, a number of banks sold their card receivables to other banks, preferring to get out of the business altogether.

Electronic Funds Transfer System.   The spread of **electronic banking**, generally referred to as the electronic funds transfer system (EFTS), is said by some to be the nonevent of the 1970s. In the late 1960s and early 1970s, it was fashionable to talk about the demise of the check and the emergence of a "checkless, cashless society." This did not happen, and the forecasts by electronic banking pioneers proved to be inaccurate. However, there has been slow growth in some areas and spectacular growth in others. In addition, the changes occurring because of the **Depository Institutions Deregulation and Monetary Control Act**, especially the removal of Regulation Q and the nationwide implementation of NOW accounts, should move the system a bit faster in the future. See *Management Perspectives on Payments Systems Change, 1980–1985*.

Automated Teller Systems.   A major development in the past 5 years is the explosion in the growth of **automated teller machines** (ATMs). In 1979 there were approximately 15,000 machines in place and several thousand on order. These machines permit customers to make deposits and withdrawals, move funds among accounts, and make balance inquiries. It was feared that these and other electronic machines would be installed and marketed by large banks only, the capital investment being too large for smaller banks. Many states passed mandatory sharing laws, forcing the banks that installed such systems to allow other banks to have access to them. The worst fears or hopes regarding the implementation of such systems have not been borne out, however. That is, a wide range of banks have installed ATMs both on and off their premises. Furthermore, banks have developed shared machines, shared systems, and individual proprietary systems depending on their strategic objectives in entering an ATM program. As time has passed, transactions volume on ATMs has increased substantially. Research on consumer demographics shows clearly that usage is related to age, income, and education levels. This is not surprising, since younger people are less likely to be reluctant to deal with electronic devices. This is also likely to be true for people with higher education levels. Families with higher income probably place a higher value on their time and appreciate the convenience and speed aspects of ATMs.

Point-of-Sale Funds Movement.   An EFT activity that has not grown as rapidly as was anticipated is the **point-of-sale (POS) electronic movement of funds**. As originally conceived, points of sale would be connected electronically with a number of financial institutions or a switch that would route the transactions. A debate over the appropriate management and control of any switch ensued, raising the following issues:

1. Private ownership and control of a switch could lead to a monopoly in the payments business.
2. Private ownership would tend to favor large banks that could afford the development and installation of large systems.
3. Public ownership would permit a public agency (the Federal Reserve?) to compete with the private sector on an unfair basis and would stifle innovation and competition in providing services.

The problem never really developed because POS experiments did not result in any consumer surge of enthusiasm for immediate, electronic movement of funds from an individual's account to a merchant's account. Several substantial systems were disbanded because the volume of activity was not sufficient to justify the cost of the system. Most point-of-sale terminals are used to authorize credit card transactions or to verify and/or guarantee checks. It is ironic that check guarantee systems are the most popular with consumers since such sytems enhance the attractiveness of paper compared to electronic transactions.

Electronic Reporting and Movement of Funds.   One area that has moved rapidly is the use of electronics in both the reporting and movement of funds by **corporations**. As interest rates have gone up in recent years, corporations have substantial incentives to economize on cash balances and to keep all excess funds fully invested. For a large corporation with receipts and expenditures throughout the nation, the information necessary to manage funds requires careful attention and an investment in services and systems. For example, companies maintain lockboxes (discussed in detail in the section entitled ''Cash Management'') to minimize the time that incoming checks spend in the postal system. The amounts of funds in a firm's lockbox accounts all over the nation are then communicated to the office of the corporate treasurer via a computer terminal. The **corporate treasurer** compares these funds with known disbursements and determines the amount available for investment. Funds are then sometimes moved via **wire transfer** to the corporation's major bank for investment, oftentimes for a single day. Existing variations on this type of system depend on the needs of the company, and systems are provided by banks and nonbank vendors. The volume of funds moved by corporations in this manner is substantial.

Automated Clearing House.   The final EFT activity that is discussed here is the Automated Clearing House (ACH). In principle, the function of the ACH is identical to that of the **bank clearinghouses** that have existed for many years. That is, instead of lugging huge sacks of checks to exchange on a net basis, banks bring to the ACH a **magnetic tape**, on which all necessary information is encoded. For example, if a corporation wishes to allow its employees to receive payroll amounts directly and automatically, it can use the ACH as follows. Each employee wishing to receive funds in this manner designates a bank and his or her account number at that institution. The corporation prepares a tape with all relevant information and delivers it to the bank that handles its payroll account. After making all internal transactions (i.e., crediting the accounts of its own customers), the bank prepares a tape for the ACH. Obviously, the tape could not move from bank to bank all around the nation. However, the local ACH (there were 37 ACHs in 1980 around the nation) shifts funds from the payroll bank to all other banks around the nation through the connection of all ACHs by the Federal Reserve's service, the ''Fed wire.'' The most successful promotion of the ACH system has come from the U.S. government, notably with **Social Security payments**. However, corporate payroll managers have not embraced the ACH system so enthusiastically because of the relative disadvantage of having instantaneous debit of funds versus being able to wait several days for payroll checks to clear. Corporate treasurers understand, measure, and use the **float** associated with payroll and other payments such as dividends. Indeed, they have devised remote disbursement schemes that have sent Federal Reserve float skyrocketing, much to the dismay of the Fed and the Congress. For this reason, and others, the Fed is taking steps to reduce float and to charge for its services, including check clearing. See the discussion in the section entitled ''Cash Mangement.''

The early EFT planners (dreamers?) viewed the preauthorized debit as a device for reducing the use of checks. In this procedure a consumer authorizes some institution to periodically and electronically debit his or her account. For example, the local utility could take all the electric bills, put them on tape, and periodically remove funds from the accounts of the customers who had signed an agreement to this procedure. However, most people would rather accept the inconvenience of writing checks than allow organizations to debit their accounts for unknown, variable amounts. The only successful preauthorization has been for known, invariable amounts, primarily insurance payments and installment payments on mortgage and automobile loans.

Current Status of EFT.   EFT has moved ahead in ways that make sense when reviewed after the fact. That is, corporate treasurers wishing to minimize nonearning assets have utilized electronic banking to accomplish that objective. Similarly, individuals have utilized electronic devices to conduct their traditional banking transactions faster and more conveniently.

The **outlook for electronic delivery systems** replacing people, brick and mortar, and paper depends on the perceived advantages of these new delivery systems. The consumer has two very good products in the check and the bank credit card. There are many advantages to the check, including convenience, reliability, control, float, and, importantly, pricing below costs as a result of competition for balances. Similarly, the bank credit card has, until recently, been issued free of charge and has permitted the user a substantial lag between purchase and payment. No wonder comsumers are not flocking to replace these payments devices. However, as banks must pay higher interest rates to attract funds, a trend of 20 years confirmed and accelerated by recent developments, it will not be possible to price services below cost. This is the opportunity to provide incentives for consumers by imaginative pricing schemes that charge more for services utilized by traditional delivery systems. In addition, while pricing is essential for both generating revenue and giving consumers incentives, it is reasonably clear that check volume will not be drastically affected. Thus **check truncation** is likely to be the only way to displace paper in the payment system. Experience with bank credit cards and credit union share drafts is encouraging, and perhaps the same kind of pricing incentive scheme could persuade consumers that they do not need their checks after all. For discussion of EFT, see Murphy, "Bank Credit Cards, NOW Accounts and Electronic Funds Transfer System: The Role of Explicit Pricing."

SMALL BANK OUTLOOK.   Given the economic, financial, technological, regulatory, and legislative developments of recent years, forecasts of the demise of the small bank have become familiar. For a number of reasons, however, it is not all clear that the small bank should be written off as a dinosaur at this point or in the foreseeable future. Before discussing those reasons, a few facts are in order.

First, it is true that the United States has many more banks than any other developed country. There were 14,738 commercial banks in the United States at year-end 1979. Only 33 of those banks had more than $5 billion is assets, and they were located in 10 states, with California and New York having 15 of them. Thus, there are a very small number of very large commercial banks in this country. If up to $50 million in assets for a bank is considered "small," then 11,374 banks are small banks. The demise of these small banks must be predicated on the basis of their inability to compete in a new environment. Ability to compete may be measured by a number of criteria, but the most important are related to earnings performance. As indicated below, the numbers do not seem to support the contention that smaller banks lack earnings capability.

One measure that is widely followed as a performance measure is the ratio of **net income to assets**, or return on assets (ROA). For all insured commercial banks operating in the United States throughout 1979, ROA followed the pattern shown in Exhibit 3. No size class has a lower ROA than the giant banks and, for the very small banks, ROA increases until

EXHIBIT 3   RETURN ON ASSETS AND EQUITY, EQUITY TO ASSETS FOR ALL INSURED COMMERCIAL BANKS OPERATING IN THE UNITED STATES THROUGHOUT 1979

Size Class, Assets ($ Millions)	ROA	ROE	Equity/Assets
Less than $5	0.98	8.03	11.5
5.0–9.9	1.04	10.90	9.5
10–24.9	1.13	13.14	8.6
25–49.9	1.14	14.10	8.1
50–99.9	1.10	14.30	7.7
100–299.9	1.05	14.52	7.2
300–499.9	0.93	13.49	6.8
500–999.9	0.88	13.49	6.5
1,000–4,999.9	0.75	12.72	6.2
5,000 and above	0.61	14.83	6.5

Source: Federal Deposit Insurance Corp., *Bank Operating Statistics, 1979,* FDIC, Washington, D.C., 1980.

the group having $50 million–$99.9 million in assets is reached, followed by a steady decline to banks with assets exceeding $5 billion. Another measure is the ratio of **net income to equity** (ROE), indicating the return to the stockholders and the potential for capital retention in the bank. Exhibit 3 shows a flatter pattern in ROE vs. ROA without as much consistent variation by size. However, this implies that large banks, with lower earnings per dollar of assets, must have fewer dollars of equity per dollar of assets to generate this type of return on equity pattern. As indicated, smaller banks have considerably more equity proportionally than large banks. Thus, the record shows that smaller banks have higher earnings and are more highly capitalized than large banks, hardly a scenario for doom.

Studies have shown that **entry by new banks into small towns** has not resulted in any systematic, substantial diminution of profitability of small banks already located in these towns. In addition, it is interesting to note that in California, where some of the largest banks in the nation are located, there were 177 banks out of 242 with assets less than $700 million in 1979. Thus, 73% of the banks are relatively small in the state most widely identified with statewide branching and giant financial institutions. While banks of all sizes must adapt to a new environment, the process has been continuous for at least a decade, and the banking system has remained a vigorous and essential part of the nation's economy.

SUMMARY AND CONCLUSION

This review of the structure, services, and functions of commercial banking has emphasized the rather dramatic recent changes in the industry's financial, legislative, regulatory, and technological environments. It was shown that an inflationary environment with attendant rising and volatile interest rates changes the attractiveness of product lines, encourages new product lines, and creates opportunity for nonbank competitors. In addition, the regulatory structure becomes unrealistic in the new total environment but, with a lag, it adapts to the altered situation.

However, it is important to note that these changes have been occurring for at least a decade. A brief list will suffice to demonstrate the point:

June 1970	Interest rate ceilings removed from large CDs with maturity less than 90 days.
June 1972	Mutual savings banks in Massachusetts begin issuing NOW accounts.
July 1973	All interest rate ceilings on large CDs removed.
Early 1974	Beginning of money market mutual fund growth.
August 1974	Credit unions permitted to offer share drafts.
March 1976	All financial institutions in New England permitted to issue NOW accounts.
June 1978	6-month money market certificate implemented.
November 1978	NOW accounts spread to New York; automatic transfer service (ATS) authorized nationally.
January 1979 to present	Explosive growth in money market mutual funds.

Thus, the industry has weathered a number of storms and changes. While banking has been viewed as a conservative, staid industry for many years, it is clear that increased competition and dramatic change have altered that situation for the foreseeable future.

REFERENCES

Annual Report of the Federal Deposit Insurance Corp., *1979*, FDIC, Washington, D.C., 1980.

Assets and Liabilities of Commercial and Mutual Savings Bank 1971–1979, Federal Deposit Insurance Corp., Washington D.C, 1980.

Board of Governors of the Federal Reserve System, *The Bank Holding Company Movement of 1978: A Compendium, 1978*, The Board, Washington D.C., 1979.

Beebe, John W., "A Perspective on Liability Management and Bank Risk," *Economic Review*, Federal Reserve Bank of San Francisco, Winter 1977.

Dunham, Constance, "The Growth of Money Market Funds," *New England Business Review*, September–October 1980.

Durkin, Thomas A., and Ellinghausen, Gregory E., *1977 Consumer Credit Survey*, Board of Governors of the Federal Reserve System, Washington, D.C., 1978.

Federal Deposit Insurance Corp. Banking Operating Statistics, 1979, FDIC, Washington, D.C., 1980.

Federal Reserve Bulletin, April and July 1980.

Functional Cost Analysis: 1978, Average Banks, Federal Reserve Bank of Kansas City, Kansas City, 1979.

Jesse, Michael A., and Seelig, Steven A., *Bank Holding Companies and the Public Interest*, Heath, Lexington, MA, 1977.

Journal of Bank Research, Summer 1980.

Kimball, Ralph C., "Wire Transfers and the Demand for Money," *New England Business Review*, March–April 1980.

Management Perspectives on Payments Systems Change 1980–1985, Payment Systems, Atlanta, GA, 1980.

Mandell, Lewis, and Murphy, Neil B., *Bank Cards,* American Bankers Assocation, Washington, D.C., 1976.

McNeill, Charles R., and Richter, Denise M., "The Depository Institutions Deregulation and Monetary Control Act of 1980," *Federal Reserve Bulletin,* June 1980.

Murphy, Neil B., "Bank Credit Cards, NOW Accounts, and Electronic Funds Transfer Systems: The Role of Explicit Pricing," *Magazine of Bank Administration,* August 1977.

——"The Impact of Payment Systems Innovation on Consumer Check Writing," *Journal of Retail Banking,* September 1979.

——, and Mandell, Lewis, *The NOW Account Decision: Profitability, Pricing, Strategies,* Bank Administration Institute, Park Ridge, IL, 1980.

Nelson, Jane F., "Negotiable Certificates of Deposit," in *Instruments of the Money Market,* 4th Ed., Federal Reserve Bank of Richmond, Richmond, VA, 1977.

Ogilvie, Nigel G., "Foreign Banks in the U.S. and Geographic Restrictions on Banking," *Journal of Bank Research,* Summer 1980.

Payments Systems Perspectives 1980, Payments Systems, Atlanta, GA, 1980.

Report of the President's Commission on Financial Structure and Regulation, The Commission, Government Printing Office, Washington, D.C., 1971.

Zimmer, Linda Fenner, "ATM Installations Surge: Customers Learning To Like Them," *Magazine of Bank Administration,* May 1980.

SAVINGS INSTITUTIONS

CONTENTS

ROLE OF SAVINGS INSTITUTIONS — 3

SAVINGS AND LOAN ASSOCIATIONS — 5

Overview — 5
Number of Associations — 6
Form of Organization — 6
Asset Size Distribution — 7
Asset and Liability Structure — 7
Savings Deposits — 10
Mortgage Lending — 12
Secondary Mortgage Market — 13
Composition of Revenues and Expenses — 13
Profitability Trends — 14
Sources of Variability in Profit Margins and New Loan Volume — 16
Federal Home Loan Bank Board — 17
Federal Home Loan Mortgage Corporation — 18
Federal Savings and Loan Insurance Corporation — 18
Legal and Regulatory Issues — 19
  Depository Institutions Deregulation and Monetary Control Act of 1980 — 19
    Regulation Q phaseout — 19
    New asset empowerments — 19
    Variable reserve requirements — 20
    Preemption of state usury laws — 20

    NOW accounts and overdraft privileges — 20
    Authorization of remote service units (RSUs) — 20
    Liquidity requirements — 20
    Mutual capital certificates (MCCs) — 20
    Increased insurance of accounts — 20
    Federal stock charters — 21
    Reserves on transactions accounts — 21
    Raising interest rates to market levels — 21

MUTUAL SAVINGS BANKS — 21

Nature of the Business — 22
Sources of Funds — 22
Uses of Funds — 23
Mortgage Lending — 23
Nonmortgage Assets — 25
Secondary Market — 25
Profitability — 26

CREDIT UNIONS — 27

Structure of the Credit Union Industry — 27
Asset Distribution — 28
Administration — 28
Regulation — 28
Sources and Uses of Funds — 29
Income and Expenses — 30
Credit Union Taxation — 31

SAVINGS INSTITUTIONS

Donald M. Kaplan
Ira D. Measell, III

ROLE OF SAVINGS INSTITUTIONS

The group of financial intermediaries known as savings institutions or thrift institutions includes savings and loan associations, mutual savings banks, and credit unions.

Savings and loan associations developed in the early 1800s as a means by which individuals could pool their savings for the purpose of building or purchasing houses, meeting halls, and so on. **Mutual savings banks** were also introduced in the early 1800s as a place where individuals and families could deposit their savings. The deposits were used to make loans and investments, and the income was used to pay the depositors a rate of return. **Credit unions** are a more recent phenomenon, having been created in the early twentieth century. These institutions were established as a place where people with a common bond (place of work, religious affiliation, etc.), could deposit their savings and obtain consumer loans.

Each of these institutions was started to meet the specific needs of its depositors, and each offered its own variety of savings accounts and types of loan. Over time these savings institutions have evolved into a more homogeneous grouping, with the different institutions moving toward offering much the same services to their depositors and borrowers. Today, these services include money market rate savings certificates, mortgage loans, consumer loans, and third-party payment mechanisms (allowed at savings and loans starting in 1981), and provide for increased competition not only among savings institutions, but among commercial banks as well.

The basic functions of each category of savings institution are virtually identical. Each obtains the majority of its funds in the form of savings accounts, is owned by the holders of the savings accounts (except for **stock savings and loan associations),** and places the largest portion of the funds received in mortgage loans or in some other form of consumer credit. Savings and loan associations and mutual savings banks invest predominantly in **residential mortgages,** while credit unions invest largely in **consumer loans** to their members. **Commercial banks** differ from savings institutions in that their primary purpose is to provide credit to businesses.

Savings institutions function as financial intermediaries. They provide a place where savers can deposit their funds and earn interest on their deposit balances. In turn, they provide a source of funds for borrowers who need funds to finance the purchase of housing or durable goods.

EXHIBIT 1   OVER-THE-COUNTER SAVINGS AT SAVINGS INSTITUTIONS AND COMMERCIAL BANKS: AMOUNT ($ BILLIONS) AND PERCENTAGE OF TOTAL

Year-End	Savings Associations[a]		Mutual Savings Banks[b]		Credit Unions[c]		Commercial Banks[d]		Total Amount	
1950	$ 14.0	20.1%	$ 20.0	28.7%	$ 0.9	1.3%	$ 34.9	50.0%	$	69.8
1955	32.1	29.5	28.2	25.0	2.4	2.2	46.0	42.3		108.7
1960	62.1	36.4	36.3	21.3	5.0	2.9	67.1	39.4		170.5
1965	110.4	36.5	52.4	17.3	9.2	3.0	130.8	43.2		302.8
1970	146.4	33.3	71.6	16.3	15.4	3.5	205.8	46.9		439.2
1975	285.7	34.8	109.9	13.4	33.0	4.0	393.4	47.9		822.0
1976	335.9	36.0	122.9	13.2	39.2	4.2	435.1	46.6		933.1
1977	386.8	36.9	134.0	12.8	46.8	4.4	482.0	45.9		1,049.6
1978	431.0	36.8	142.7	12.2	53.0	4.5	544.6	46.5		1,171.3
1979[e]	470.2	37.6	145.9	11.7	56.2	4.5	579.5	46.3		1,251.8
Compound annual growth rate (%)	12.9		7.1		15.3		10.2		10.5	

[a]All types of savings.
[b]Regular and special savings accounts.
[c]Shares and members' deposits.
[d]Time and savings deposits of individuals, partnerships, and corporations.
[e]Preliminary data.
Source: Federal Home Loan Bank Board; Federal Reserve Board.

Since the end of World War II, savings institutions have experienced rapid **growth in savings deposits.** Exhibit 1 shows that the three types of savings institution, plus the savings held by commercial banks, have grown at an annual rate of 10.5% from 1950 to 1979. The strongest savings growth has been in credit unions, which have experienced a 15.3% annual rate of growth since 1950, while the growth of mutual savings banks has been the slowest over this period, at only 7.1%.

Asset growth of these institutions since 1950 (Exhibit 2) has also been impressive. Total assets of savings institutions and commercial banks have grown at an annual rate of 8.6%. Again credit unions have been the fastest growing institution, with assets increasing at a 15.5% annual rate, compared to 13.0% for savings and loans and 7.1% for mutual savings banks.

Increased competition among institutions has produced significant changes in the services and operations each offers. Competition has resulted in new savings instruments offering higher rates of return, services such as third-party payment mechanisms, credit cards, broader lending powers, and electronic funds transfer. In effect, the forces of competition are moving savings institutions closer to operations that are similar to commercial banks, while still retaining their traditional role as depositories for savings and a source of funds for consumer borrowing.

The remainder of this section reviews savings and loans, mutual savings banks, and credit unions from the perspective of their operating nature and evolution.

EXHIBIT 2   TOTAL ASSETS OF SAVINGS INSTITUTIONS AND COMMERCIAL BANKS AT YEAR-END ($ BILLIONS)

Financial Intermediary	1950	1955	1960	1965	1970	1975	1979[a]	Average Annual Growth Rate, 1950–1979 (%)
Commercial banks	$168.9	$210.7	$257.6	$377.3	$576.2	$ 964.9	$1,480.3	7.8%
Savings associations	16.9	37.7	71.5	129.6	176.2	338.2	579.3	13.0
Mutual savings banks	22.4	31.3	40.6	58.2	79.0	121.1	163.4	7.1
Credit unions	1.0	2.7	5.7	10.6	18.0	38.0	65.9	15.5
Total	$209.2	$282.4	$375.4	$575.7	$849.4	$1,472.2	$2,288.9	8.6%

[a]Preliminary data.

Sources: CUNA International, Inc.; Federal Home Loan Bank Board; Federal Reserve Board; Institute of Life Insurance; National Association of Mutual Savings Banks; U.S. League of Savings Associations.

SAVINGS AND LOAN ASSOCIATIONS

OVERVIEW. The **modern savings and loan industry** evolved from building and loan associations that were established in the first half of the nineteenth century. These institutions were formed to encourage thrift by the general public and to foster the construction and purchasing of homes. In many respects, the early savings and loans were similar to modern credit unions in that they accepted deposits from members and made loans to members. Today's savings and loan is far more sophisticated than its early predecessor and operates as a true financial intermediary, with an ever broadening asset and liability structure and increasingly complex operating methods. Savings and loan associations are typically aggressive competitors for both deposits and mortgage loans. Their role in providing **mortgage credit** to the American public continues to be the dominant end product of savings and loan asset operations.

Savings and loan associations are private financial institutions established and operated under state and federal laws for the primary purpose of attracting funds in the form of savings deposits from the general public and making long-term loans on residential and other real estate. Savings and loans are the nation's **second largest financial intermediary,** with total assets of $579 billion at the end of 1979, compared to commercial banks, the largest, with asset holdings of $1,351 billion. At the close of 1979, savings and loans insured by the **Federal Savings and Loan Insurance Corporation (FSLIC)** held an estimated 88 million savings accounts with an average balance of about $5,210 and some 15.6 million mortgage loans with an average balance of approximately $30,500.

The industry is the dominant private mortgage lender, particularly for single-family (including two- to four-unit structures) residential dwellings in the country. Total mortgage holdings at the end of 1979 amounted to $476 billion, which represented approximately 44% of all residential mortgage credit outstanding (including federal agencies) and 47% of all single-family mortgage credit. Among major private financial institutions, savings and loans held about 63.5% of the total $621.4 billion in outstanding **single-family residential mortgage credit.**

NUMBER OF ASSOCIATIONS.   There were 4,709 savings and loan associations in the United States at the end of 1979, well below the peak of 6,320 in 1960 and somewhat down from the mid-1970s figure of 4,931 (Exhibit 3). The reduction in the number of associations is the result of a significant decline in the number of state-chartered associations through voluntary liquidations, mergers, and consolidations.

Associations chartered by the federal government and insured by the FSLIC totaled 1,989 at the end of 1979, or 42.2% of the total. State-chartered associations totaled 2,720, with 2,050 (75.4%) being insured by the **Federal Savings and Loan Insurance Corp.**, the instrumentality of the federal government that insures savings and loan savings deposits.

The **state-chartered associations** held 44.2% of total savings and loan assets as of December 31, 1979, with a total of $256.2 billion in assets (Exhibit 4). **Federally chartered associations** held 55.8% of industry assets, or $323.1 billion. State-chartered, nonfederally insured associations held only 1.9% of all association assets at the end of 1979, down from 2.4% in 1975 and 5.7% in 1960. Thus, with the exception of a few states (e.g., Maryland, Ohio, and Pennsylvania), the vast majority of associations are insured by the FSLIC.

FORM OF ORGANIZATION.   The majority (82.9%) of savings and loan associations have a mutual form of ownership. These associations are owned by their depositors and borrowers, who are entitled to vote on association affairs. **Mutual associations** cannot issue stock and must rely on aftertax income to raise additional permanent capital.

Approximately one-third of the FSLIC-insured, state-chartered associations are **capital stock associations.** The approximately 800 stock-chartered associations tend to be concentrated in a relatively few states—primarily California, Texas, Virginia, Ohio, Illinois, Kansas, and Washington. **Federal Home Loan Bank Board (FHLBB)** regulations, authorized in 1975, allow insured mutual associations to convert to capital stock form in states that allow stock chartering.

EXHIBIT 3   NUMBER OF SAVINGS ASSOCIATIONS, BY TYPE OF CHARTER

Year-End	Federally Chartered[a]	State-Chartered			Grand Total
		Total	FSLIC-insured	Noninsured[b]	
1950	1,526	4,466	1,334	3,132	5,992
1955	1,683	4,388	1,861	2,527	6,071
1960	1,873	4,447	2,225	2,222	6,320
1965	2,011	4,174	2,497	1,677	6,185
1970	2,067	3,602	2,298	1,304	5,669
1975	2,048	2,883	2,030	853	4,931
1976	2,019	2,802	2,025	777	4,821
1977	2,012	2,749	2,053	696	4,761
1978	2,000	2,725	2,053	672	4,725
1979[c]	1,989	2,720	2,050	670	4,709

[a]All federally chartered associations are insured by the Federal Savings and Loan Insurance Corp.
[b]Includes institutions insured by the Co-operative Central Bank of Massachusetts, the Maryland Savings-Share Insurance Corp., the North Carolina Savings Guaranty Corp., and the Ohio Deposit Guarantee Fund.
[c]Preliminary data.
Sources: Federal Home Loan Bank Board; U.S. League of Savings Associations.

EXHIBIT 4   ASSETS OF SAVINGS ASSOCIATION, BY TYPE OF CHARTER ($ MILLIONS)

| Year-End | Federally Chartered[a] | State-Chartered | | | Grand Total |
		Total	FSLIC-Insured	Noninsured[b]	
1950	$ 8,457	$ 8,436	$ 5,234	$ 3,202	$ 16,893
1955	20,035	17,621	14,163	3,458	37,656
1960	38,511	32,965	28,919	4,046	71,476
1965	66,715	62,865	57,861	5,004	129,580
1970	96,259	779,924	74,386	5,538	176,183
1975	195,410	142,823	134,849	7,974	338,233
1976	225,763	166,144	157,409	8,735	391,907
1977	261,920	197,321	188,078	9,243	459,241
1978	298,195	225,347	215,115	10,232	523,542
1979[c]	323,058	256,249	245,049	11,200	579,307

[a]All federally chartered associations are insured by the Federal Savings and Loan Insurance Corp.
[b]Includes the assets of institutions by the Co-operative Central Bank of Massachusetts, the Maryland Savings-Share Insurance Corporation, the North Carolina Savings Guaranty Corporation and the Ohio Deposit Guarantee Fund.
[c]Preliminary data.
Source: Federal Home Loan Bank Board; U. S. League of Savings Associations.

ASSET SIZE DISTRIBUTION.   The asset size distribution of the savings and loan industry is quite skewed, with a modest number of very large institutions at one end and a large number of very small institutions at the other. At the close of 1979, the average FSLIC-insured savings and loan held approximately $140 million in assets; however, just over 360 FSLIC-insured savings and loans had total assets in excess of $300 million, and only 84 institutions had assets in excess of $1 billion. At the top of the asset size distribution, the 100 largest associations each had over $884 million in assets and, as a group, held just over one-third of industry assets (Exhibit 5).

In contrast, the smallest associations hold a disproportionately small share of industry assets. As of December 31, 1979, the 831 smallest associations, those with assets of less than $10 million each, accounted as a group for assets of $3.3 billion, or only 0.6% of the $579.3 billion industry total.

ASSET AND LIABILITY STRUCTURE.   Savings and loan associations were established to encourage thrift and to finance home construction and purchases, and their statement of condition reflects this business focus (Exhibit 6). Mortgage loans outstanding accounted for 82.1% of all association assets at the end of 1979. This concentration in mortgage lending has not significantly changed over time because of regulatory requirements that limit the kinds of loan and investment that associations can make. However, over the past several years, new housing-related investments have entered association operations and are reflected on the balance sheet; for example, **mortgage-backed securities** and **insured mortgages** accounted for 3.5% of assets and together with mortgages outstanding accounted for 85.6% of industry assets.

Liquid assets in the form of cash and qualified short-term investments maturing in less than 1 year make up the second largest asset category at $39.8 billion, or 6.9% of assets. The level of liquid assets is regulated by the Federal Home Loan Bank Board, which sets

EXHIBIT 5   DISTRIBUTION OF SAVINGS ASSOCIATIONS, BY ASSET SIZE, DECEMBER 31, 1979[a]

Asset Size ($ Millions)		Number of Associations	% of Total	Assets ($ Millions)	% of Total
$1		234	5.0%	$ 108	—[b]
$1 and under	$5	279	5.9	790	0.1%
$5 and under	$10	318	6.8	2,447	0.4
$10 and under	$25	851	18.1	15,225	2.6
$25 and under	$50	957	20.3	36,466	6.3
$50 and under	$100	870	18.5	64,414	11.1
$100 and under	$150	406	8.6	51,814	8.9
$150 and under	$250	347	7.4	69,402	12.0
$250 and under	$500	250	5.3	85,525	14.8
$500 and under	$1,000	113	2.4	78,580	13.6
$1,000 and over		84	1.8	174,536	30.1
Total		4,709	100.0%	$579,307	100.0%

[a]Components may not add to totals because of rounding.
[b]Less than 0.05%.
Sources: Federal Home Loan Bank Board; U. S. League of Savings Associations. *Fact Book '80*.

the minimum percentage of liquid assets associations must have, based on deposits and borrowed funds.

The remaining assets of savings and loan associations are divided among a variety of other types of loan that account for only 2.8% of total assets and other items. Nonloan asset items include investments in securities that are not considered eligible for liquidity purposes, stock in Federal Home Loan Banks (FHLBs), investment in service corporations, buildings and equipment, real estate owned, and various other assets.

The **composition of savings and loan assets** over time has remained stable because of strict limits placed on the investment and lending activity by regulations. As a result, the historical concentration of savings and loans in the area of housing finance is maintained.

The liability portion of the balance sheet is dominated by savings deposits. As of December 31, 1979, 81.1% of all savings and loan liabilities plus net worth were in savings deposits. Three-fourths of these savings deposits were in some form of savings certificate, and one-fourth in passbook accounts.

Over time, the composition of savings deposits has shifted dramatically, with deposits being transferred from **passbook accounts** to higher yielding **certificate accounts.** This shifting in deposit composition is due largely to economic and investment conditions that have made the yield on passbook accounts comparatively unattractive to savers over the past 10 years. Such factors as a persistent high rate of inflation, high and rising yields on alternative investments, and the advent of new sources of investments such as **money market funds** have been the chief cause of the actions of savers who have placed their deposits in the higher yielding certificate accounts that better compete with alternative investments.

In addition to savings deposits, savings and loans can borrow funds from the FHL District Banks and other sources, such as commercial banks. These borrowed funds accounted for 9.6% of liabilities and net worth at the end of 1979. This source of funds has grown increasingly important to savings and loans as the competition for savings deposits has increased in recent years.

EXHIBIT 6   CONDENSED STATEMENT OF CONDITION OF ALL SAVINGS AND LOAN ASSOCIATIONS AS OF DECEMBER 31, 1979[a,b]

	Amount ($ Millions)	% of Total
Assets		
Mortgage loans outstanding	$475,797	82.1%
Insured mortgages and mortgage-backed securities	20,507	3.5
Mobile home loans	2,190	0.4
Home improvement loans	4,484	0.8
Loans on savings accounts	6,135	1.1
Education loans	898	0.2
Other consumer loans	1,576	0.3
Cash and investments eligible for liquidity	39,825	6.9
Other investments	6,716	1.2
Federal Home Loan Bank stock	4,900	0.8
Investment in service corporations	2,085	0.4
Building and equipment	7,583	1.3
Real estate owned	1,510	0.3
All other assets	5,101	0.9
Total assets	$579,307	100.0%
Liabilities and Net Worth		
Savings Deposits		
Earning regular rate or below	$118,906	20.5%
Earning in excess of regular rate	351,265	60.6
Federal Home Loan Bank advances	40,441	7.0
Other borrowed money	14,934	2.6
Loans in process	9,511	1.6
All other liabilities	11,684	2.0
Net worth	32,566	5.6
Total liabilities and net worth	$579,307	100.0%

[a]Components may not add to totals because of rounding.
[b]Preliminary data.
Sources: Federal Home Loan Bank Board; U. S. League of Savings Associations.

Loans in process, which represent the undisbursed portion of mortgage loans recorded as an asset on the balance sheet, amounted to $9.5 billion, or 1.6% of liabilities and net worth at the end of 1979. The loans in process category consists mostly of construction loans, which feature a series of cash advances to the builder as construction progresses. Therefore, the total amount of the construction loans is shown as an asset, while funds that have not been advanced to the builder are included in this liability category. All other liabilities accounted for 2.0% of the total. Included here are advance payments by borrowers of taxes and insurance premiums. Also included are such items as accrued federal taxes that have not been paid, accrued savings account interest that has not yet been paid, and other items.

Finally, **savings and loans net worth** amounted to $35.6 billion or 5.6% to total liabilities at the end of 1979. This category includes general reserves, paid-in surplus, and undivided profits.

SAVINGS DEPOSITS.   Maximum interest rates that savings and loans can offer savers on deposits were first set in 1966 under the **Interest Rate Adjustment Act.** Until that time the return paid by savings and loans had not been controlled. As a result of this law, savings and loans were prohibited from competing in the open market for deposits, and the rates of return that were offered were strictly controlled for all types of deposits. Exhibit 7 presents the **ceiling rates allowed on deposits of FHLB member associations** as of January 1, 1980. This exhibit shows that all categories of deposits, except those of $100,000 or more, have a fixed rate. Because savings and loans have had difficulty in recent years in competing for deposits against commercial banks, money market funds, and other investment alternatives, two **variable ceiling certificates** are now available through savings and loans with maturities of 26 weeks and $2\frac{1}{2}$ years. These certificates float according to market interest rates and are designed to better enable savings and loans to compete for deposits.

As noted above, almost three-fourths of savings and loan deposits are held in certificate accounts that yield greater than the 5.50% passbook rate. Exhibit 8 presents a more detailed breakdown of deposits by type of account as of September 30, 1979. The data show that 27.9% of deposits are in passbook accounts. **Money market certificates** (MMCs) represent 22.5% of deposits. The MMC was introduced in June 1978, and its interest rate ceiling floats with the 3-month Treasury bill rate. The MMC is the most popular type of deposit account at savings and loans at the present time. The 4-year floating interest rate ceiling certificate accounted for only 0.3% of deposits as of September 1979, and was discontinued as of December 31, 1979. The $2\frac{1}{2}$-year certificate introduced in January 1980 is not included in Exhibit 8. Certificates of less than $100,000 with fixed interest rate ceilings accounted for 43.1% of deposits, down from around 60% as of December 31, 1977, prior to the introduction of the market rate certificate.

In addition to these types of deposit, certificates in denominations of $100,000 or more accounted for 5.1% of total savings deposits. Recently **FSLIC insurance coverage** on savings deposits was raised to $100,000 from $40,000, bringing $100,000 denomination certificates under the coverage of the FSLIC.

Exhibit 8 also shows the changing composition of savings deposits at savings and loans. At the end of March 1973, passbook accounts represented nearly 50% of deposits, while at the end of September 1979 passbook accounts were down to 27.9% of deposits. This decline in passbook deposits has been due to the growth of certificate accounts, especially the money market certificate. These certificates rose from 5.0% of deposits at the end of September 1978, 3 months after they were authorized. One year later MMCs accounted for 22.5% of deposits, growing by over $80 billion. At the same time passbook savings fell by nearly $16 billion. Growth of the MMC has also come at the expense of other fixed ceiling certificate accounts which, until the advent of the MMC, had been increasing as a percentage of deposits.

Deposits in accounts of $100,000 or more, which have no regulated interest rate ceiling or maturity period, have grown from 3.3% of deposits at the end of September 1978 to 5.1% of deposits at the end of September 1979. As of April 1980 these certificates had risen to 6.9% of total deposits, indicating their popularity with savers who are increasingly sensitive to interest rates.

While savings and loans have become less dependent on passbook savings as a source of funds in favor of certificates, the liability structure has shifted toward increased borrowed

EXHIBIT 7   MAXIMUM RATES OF RETURN
PAYABLE ON SAVINGS ACCOUNTS BY SAVINGS AND LOAN ASSOCIATIONS
THAT ARE MEMBERS OF THE FEDERAL HOME LOAN BANK SYSTEM

Type of Account	Effective Dates and Percentage Rates, January 1, 1980
Regular	5.50
Transaction (NOW)	5.00[a]
90-day notice (for withdrawals)	6.00[b]

Certificate with Fixed or Minimum Term or Qualifying Period

Fixed Ceiling Accounts:

Balance less than $100,000

Owned by governmental units: All terms	8.00
Owned by others	
90 days to 6 months	6.00
6 months to 1 year	6.00
1 to 2 years	6.00
2 to 2½ years	6.50
2½ to 4 years	6.75
4 to 6 years	7.50
6 to 8 years	7.75
8 years or more	8.00
Individual retirement (IRA) or Keogh (H.R. 10) account with term of 3 or more years	8.00
Balance $100,000 or more: All owners, all terms	—[c]

Variable Ceiling Accounts

Money market certificate with 26-week term and minimum balance of $10,000	—[d]
4 years or longer	—[e]
2½ years or longer	—[f]

[a]Effective January 1, 1974, for associations with home offices in Massachusetts and New Hampshire, on February 26, 1976, for associations in other New England states, and on November 10, 1978, for associations in New York State.

[b]Beginning November 27, 1974, maximum rate for notice accounts owned by governmental units was the same as for certificate accounts owned by such units.

[c]No maximum rate.

[d]First authorized June 1, 1978. Maximum rate, as of each Thursday, was the average rate (discount basis) on 6-month U.S. Treasury bills (as determined at the immediately preceding auction) plus 25 basis points through March 14, 1979. Between March 15, 1979, and June 4, 1980, when the Treasury bill rate was less than 8.75%, the maximum continued as previously, but if the bill rate was between 8.75 and 9.00% the maximum was 9.00%; if the bill rate was 9.00% or higher the maximum was the bill rate. After June 5, 1980, the rates are as stipulated in the source, listed above.

[e]Authorized for July 1–December 31, 1979 only. Maximum rate for each month was equal to 1 percentage point less than the average yield on 4-year U.S. Treasury securities (as determined by the U.S. Treasury Department) for the 5 business days preceding the third business day before the end of the prior month.

[f]First authorized January 1, 1980. For the period January 1, 1980–May 1, 1980, the maximum rate for each month is equal to 0.5 percentage point less than the average yield on 2½-year U.S. Treasury securities (as determined by the U.S. Treasury Department) for the 5 business days preceding the third business day before the end of the prior month, but no higher than 12%.

Source: Federal Home Loan Bank Board Journal, October 1980, Vol. 13, No. 10, p. 51.

EXHIBIT 8   SAVINGS DEPOSITS AT INSURED SAVINGS AND LOAN ASSOCIATIONS, BY TYPE OF ACCOUNT ($ MILLIONS)[a]

Type of Account	March 31, 1973 Amount	%	September 30, 1978 Amount	%	September 30, 1979 Amount	%
Passbook	$103,814	49.5%	$142,061	34.5%	$126,324	27.9%
90-day notice	12,908	6.2	28,089	6.8	4,863	1.1
MMC	NA	—	20,750	5.0	101,911	22.5
4-year market rate certificate	NA	—	—[b]	—	1,292	0.3
Other certificates of less than $100,000	89,376	42.6	200,281	48.7	195,784	43.1
Subtotal	206,098	98.3	391,181	95.0	430,174	94.9
$100,000 minimum certificates	—[b]	—[b]	13,611	3.3	23,127	5.1
Other savings	3,500	1.7	6,957	1.7	—	—
Total savings	209,598	100.0%	453,297	100.0%	453,297	100.0%

[a]Data are based on reports from associations holding substantially all FSLIC-insured savings.
[b]Include in "Other certificates" data.
Source: Federal Home Loan Bank Board.

funds. Exhibit 9 shows total liabilities, including borrowings at three points in time. From December 31, 1973, to June 30, 1979, total borrowings as a percent of total liabilities rose from 6.9 to 9.1%. Both long-term (more than 1 year) and short-term **Federal Home Loan Bank advances** continue to be the major source of borrowings. The number of options available to savings and loans to borrow funds, however, has increased over time. As a result, FHLB advances as a percentage of all borrowed funds declined from over 87% in 1973 to around 72% in June 1979.

MORTGAGE LENDING.   Savings and loan associations are the largest originators and holders of **conventional mortgages** in the United States. At the end of 1979 savings and loans held 43.1% of the residential mortgage loans outstanding, compared to 15.8% for commercial banks, 8.2% for mutual savings banks, and 3.5% for life insurance companies. In 1979, according to data supplied by the Department of Housing and Urban Development, savings and loans originated $87.7 billion or 43.4% of the residential mortgage loans made. Of this total $84.8 billion, or 96.7%, were in conventional loans, with the remaining 3.3% in **FHA-insured or VA-guaranteed mortgage loans.**

Savings and loan mortgage lending has predominantly been in **single-family homes.** Exhibit 10 shows that in 1979, 78.5% of the savings and loan mortgage portfolio was in single-family homes. This percentage has risen in recent years as other lenders such as life insurance companies have reduced their single-family mortgage lending activity. The remaining 21.5% of savings and loan mortgage portfolios is made up of loans on two- to four-family structures (4.6%), multifamily structures for five or more families (7.2%), commercial properties (8.3%), and all other types of mortgage loan (1.3%).

In 1979, savings and loans made $98.7 billion in all types of mortgage loans (including residential), as shown in Exhibit 11. Loans to purchase real estate totaled $63.0 billion, or 63.8% of the total, while construction loans accounted for another 22.5% of savings and loan lending. In addition to these loans, savings and loans wrote $13.4 billion in refinancing agreements and other loans. The data demonstrate the commitment of these institutions to financing home purchases, along with their significant involvement in housing construction.

EXHIBIT 9   SAVINGS AND LOAN LIABILITIES, UNITED STATES ($ MILLIONS)

	December 1973		June 1978		June 1979	
	Amount	% of Total	Amount	% of Total	Amount	% of Total
Total liabilities	$247,899	100.0%	$452,996	100.0%	$512,734	100.0%
Total deposits	220,443	88.9	398,887	88.1	444,166	86.6
Total borrowings	17,019	6.9	33,485	7.4	46,764	9.1
Short-Term Borrowings						
FHLB advances	6,558	2.6	9,355	2.1	12,145	2.4
Commercial bank	—	—	1,032	0.2	1,011	0.2
Reverse repurchases	—	—	5,064	1.1	6,806	1.3
Other	1,719	0.7	443	0.1	1,892	0.4
Total	8,277	3.3	15,894	3.5	21,854	4.3
Long-Term Borrowings						
FHLB advances	8,285	3.3	15,043	3.3	21,691	4.2
Other borrowings	298	0.1	508	0.1	617	0.1
Subordinated debentures	98	—[a]	188	—[a]	190	—[a]
Mortgage-backed bonds	—	—	1,773	0.4	2,310	0.5
Association mortgages	60	—[a]	79	—[a]	102	—[a]
Total	8,741	3.5	17,591	3.9	24,910	4.9

[a]Less than 0.1%.

Source: Federal Home Loan Bank Board.

SECONDARY MORTGAGE MARKET.   In addition to originating mortgages, savings and loans are significant **participants in the secondary mortgage market.** Exhibit 12 shows savings and loan secondary market purchases and sales of mortgage loans and participations since 1970. Traditionally, savings and loans have purchased more loans and participations than they sold in the secondary market; however, savings and loan mortgage lending operations have been undergoing gradual changes in recent years as their historical role as holders of mortgage debt has become less financially feasible. As a result, many savings and loans are beginning to act as **mortgage banking** operations in that they originate mortgages and then sell them in the secondary market. The data in Exhibit 12 show that sales of loans and participations have risen steadily since 1970, while purchases reached a peak in 1977. As a result, in 1978 and 1979 the savings and loan industry sold more mortgages and participations than it purchased. This is a significant change in activity because associations, by selling more loans than they purchase, are now drawing funds from other sections of the capital markets into mortgage lending.

COMPOSITION OF REVENUES AND EXPENSES.   Savings and loans have relatively few major sources of revenues (Exhibit 13). The bulk (over 80% of gross operating income) comes from **interest earned on mortgage loans.** Mortgage loan fees, commissions and discounts, and premiums account for another 3–5%, bringing income from all aspects of mortgage lending activity to over 85% of total income. The bulk of these revenues is earned

EXHIBIT 10   MORTGAGE PORTFOLIO OF
INSURED SAVINGS AND LOAN ASSOCIATIONS, BY TYPE OF PROPERTY[a]

Type of Property	1974	1975	1976	1977	1978	1979[b]
AMOUNT ($ BILLIONS)						
Single family	$181.9	$202.9	$237.4	$283.2	$325.3	$367.0
Two to four family	13.0	13.9	15.6	18.6	21.1	21.7
Multifamily	23.0	24.6	27.5	31.4	34.9	33.7
Commercial	21.3	25.3	29.5	32.9	35.1	38.6
Other	4.0	4.6	5.3	6.3	7.1	6.3
Total	$243.1	$271.3	$315.3	$372.4	$423.5	$467.3
PERCENTAGE DISTRIBUTION						
Single family	74.8%	74.8%	75.3%	76.0%	76.8%	78.5%
Two to four family	5.3	5.1	4.9	5.0	5.0	4.6
Multifamily	9.5	9.1	8.7	8.4	8.2	7.2
Commercial	8.8	9.3	9.4	8.8	8.3	8.3
Other	1.6	1.7	1.7	1.7	1.7	1.3
Total	100.0%	100.0%	100.0%	100.0%	100.0%	100.0%

[a]Components may not add to totals because of rounding.
[b]Preliminary data.
Sources: Federal Home Loan Bank Board; U.S. League of Savings Associations.

on single-family residential loans, since the volume of lending on multifamily, commercial properties and interim construction lending is modest relative to total lending. Earnings on investments and other sources of revenue typically constitute 10–15% of total income.

The expense side of the savings and loan business is also relatively straightforward. In 1979 interest paid on all types of savings deposits equaled about 66% of total revenues. In addition, roughly 9% of operating income was paid out as interest on advances from the FHLB system and other borrowed money. General and administrative (G & A) expenses, which include compensation, occupancy, advertising, and miscellaneous items, accounted for just below 15% of total income, a figure that has shown some tendency to decline in recent years because of a steady rise in operating income and a smaller increase in operating expense, resulting in part from higher operating efficiencies. Personnel salaries and wages represent the principal operating cost of a savings and loan, typically accounting for nearly one-half of total G & A expenses.

Taxes constitute the remaining major expense category. Savings and loans pay federal income taxes and, where required, state income and other business taxes, as well. **The effective federal income tax rate** for most associations is about 30%, primarily as a result of their ability to shelter generally 40% of before-tax earnings as a bad debt loss reserve. The remaining 60% of earnings is taxes at the regular corporate rate of 46%.

PROFITABILITY TRENDS.   In analyzing **savings and loan profitability,** it is important to distinguish between long-run trends and short-run variations. As shown in Exhibit 14,

EXHIBIT 11   MORTGAGE LOANS MADE BY INSURED ASSOCIATIONS, BY PURPOSE OF LOAN[a]

	1979 ($ Millions)[b]	Percentage Distribution of Loans Acquired, 1979[b]
Construction Loans Closed		
Single-family homes	$17,301	17.5%
Two- to four-family homes	930	0.9
Apartments	1,979	2.0
Other structures	2,106	2.1
Purchase Loans Closed		
New single-family homes	17,576	17.8
Existing single-family homes	38,925	39.4
Two- to four-family homes	3,147	3.2
Apartments	1,962	2.0
Other improved real estate	1,430	1.4
Loans Refinanced	9,221	9.3
Loans for Other Purposes	4,156	4.2
Total loans closed	$98,730	100.0%

[a]Components may not add to totals because of rounding.
[b]Preliminary data.
Source: Federal Home Loan Bank Board.

EXHIBIT 12   SECONDARY MORTGAGE MARKET ACTIVITY FOR FSLIC-INSURED SAVINGS AND LOAN ASSOCIATIONS ($ MILLIONS)

Year-End	Loans and Participations Purchased	Loans and Participations Sold	Net Purchases: Purchase minus Sales
1970	$3,745	$1,108	$2,637
1971	7,529	2,165	5,364
1972	10,612	3,714	6,898
1973	7,229	3,457	3,772
1974	5,904	3,505	2,399
1975	8,544	5,206	3,338
1976	12,799	8,447	4,352
1977	14,497	13,846	651
1978	10,984	15,485	(4,501)[a]
1979	12,012	18,331	(6,319)[a]

[a]Sales exceeded purchases.
Source: Federal Home Loan Bank Board.

EXHIBIT 13   SELECTED INCOME AND EXPENSE ITEMS, ALL FSLIC-INSURED SAVINGS AND LOAN ASSOCIATIONS, 1965–1979 (% OF GROSS INCOME)

| | Interest Income | | Total | Expense Items | | Interest | Net | |
Year-End	Mortgage Loans	On Investments and Deposits	Operating Expense	Compen-sation	Adver-tising	on Savings Accounts	Operating Income	Net Income
1965	86.8	5.4	19.3	9.0	1.9	63.2	77.2	11.7
1970	84.3	7.7	17.8	8.1	1.8	64.6	75.0	8.7
1971	82.6	8.8	16.7	7.8	1.5	65.3	78.6	10.4
1972	82.9	7.9	16.3	7.6	1.6	65.5	80.5	11.1
1973	83.0	8.3	16.3	7.5	1.7	64.3	78.7	10.4
1974	82.0	9.0	16.4	7.6	1.7	65.0	75.6	7.1
1975	81.1	8.5	16.7	7.7	1.5	67.5	76.6	6.1
1976	79.9	7.5	16.2	7.6	1.2	67.7	78.8	7.9
1977	80.3	6.7	15.7	7.4	1.1	66.5	79.8	9.3
1978	80.2	7.4	15.2	7.2	1.2	64.1	80.2	9.6
1979	78.3	9.0	14.5	7.0	1.2	66.1	84.6	7.4

Source: Federal Home Loan Bank Board.

savings and loans earned high profits during the 1950s and early 1960s, when they faced relatively little savings competition from commercial banks and interest rates were generally low and stable, with upward sloping yield curves. Beginning in the mid-1960s, competitive pressures, the level of interest rates, and the federal tax burden on savings and loans increased, causing operating margins to narrow and to fluctuate substantially from year to year. Measured in terms of the ratio of **net income to average assets,** the industry's profitability hovered around 50 basis points during that period. Between 1975 and 1978, the industry's profitability increased to approximately 80 basis points. However, beginning in late 1979 and early 1980, industry profitability has fallen drastically from those levels, as a result of the performance of the economy and the cost pressures generated by the MMC and record **money market rates.**

SOURCES OF VARIABILITY IN PROFIT MARGINS AND NEW LOAN VOLUME.   The key to understanding the **operating economics of the savings and loan business** is to recognize that it is a classic example of a "margin" business. Savings and loans have rather limited control over their profit margins or yield spreads because of statutory and regulatory restrictions on deposit rates paid and competitive market limitations on mortgage rates charged. In contrast, savings and loan managers have more control over the volume of mortgage loans originated and purchased, except during periods of extremely tight money. Thus changes in savings and loan earnings are largely a function of changes in spreads and loan volume.

The impact of variations in loan volume and yield spreads on savings and loan earnings is shown in Exhibit 15. Loan volume affects net income immediately through income from origination fees, and more slowly through loan portfolio yields. **Portfolio yields** reflect long buildups over the years and tend to be relatively stable, moving substantially only in periods of rapid loan growth and high mortgage market rates. Thus, on a year-to-year basis, the average yield on the loan portfolio tends to increase steadily; 25–30 basis points per year is a representative figure for recent years. This is expected to change, since it is assumed

EXHIBIT 14   MEASURES OF INCOME AND PROFITABILITY, U.S. SAVINGS AND LOAN ASSOCIATIONS, 1950–1979[a]

Year-End	Total Net Worth ($ Millions)	Net Income After Tax ($ Millions)	Return on Average Net Worth (%)	Effective Tax Rate (%)	Profit[b] Margin (%)	Net Worth to Total Assets (%)
1950	$ 1,280	$ 179	15.1%	0.0%	24.9%	7.6%
1955	2,557	370	15.7	1.6	21.9	6.8
1960	4,983	577	12.4	0.7	15.5	7.0
1965	8,704	821	10.0	16.1	11.6	6.8
1970	12,401	904	6.7	21.5	8.2	7.0
1971	13,592	1,291	9.9	28.8	9.9	6.6
1972	15,240	1,729	12.1	27.3	11.1	6.3
1973	17,056	1,950	12.1	28.5	10.4	6.3
1974	18,436	1,532	8.6	30.8	7.1	6.2
1975	19,779	1,485	7.8	29.6	6.2	5.8
1976	21,998	2,300	11.0	30.8	7.9	5.6
1977[a]	24,365	3,198	13.8	30.6	9.3	5.5
1978[a]	28,126	3,920	14.9	31.6	9.6	5.5
1979[a]	31,624	3,620	12.1	30.4	7.4	5.6

[a]FSLIC-insured associations only.
[b]Net income after tax to total income.
Source: Federal Home Loan Bank Board.

that **variable rate mortgages** (VRMs) and **rollover or renegotiable rate mortgages** (RRMs) will begin to constitute significant proportions of savings and loans' mortgage portfolios.

Through 1978, savings and loans' cost of funds tended to increase slowly on a year-to-year basis, except when deposit interest rate ceilings were changed. Changes in deposit rate ceilings have caused rapid declines in savings and loan yield spreads and a corresponding decline in earnings after those changes were implemented.

This **"stair step" pattern** of behavior of savings and loan deposit costs was altered completely by the advent of the MMC in mid-1978; now savings and loan deposit costs move much more closely with short-term money market rates. Initially, about half of new MMC deposits constituted new money, the other half being transfers from existing accounts. However, as net new savings flows declined in the latter half of 1979, increasing amounts of new MMC accounts have come from existing deposits, including long-term certificates on which depositors have elected to incur a penalty to obtain the higher MMC rates. This "rollover" of lower cost deposits into MMCs has had increasingly severe effects on industry earnings, to the point that many savings and loans now have **negative yield spreads** (see Exhibit 15). However, the MMC undoubtedly has prevented, to date, what otherwise would have been the worst period of deposit losses in the industry's history, and the recent dramatic decline in rates will gradually, over a period of months, lower deposit costs. As of May 31, 1980, MMCs worth an estimated $171 billion were held by savings and loans nationally, representing 36% of total deposits.

FEDERAL HOME LOAN BANK BOARD.   The Federal Home Loan Bank Board (FHLBB) was created in 1932 to impart stability to the housing industry through support and regulation of the nation's housing finance institutions, namely, savings and loans. The FHLBB, through the FHLB System, provides a **central credit facility** to supply funds to member institutions

EXHIBIT 15   MORTGAGE LOAN VOLUME AND PROFITABILITY, FSLIC-INSURED SAVINGS AND LOAN ASSOCIATIONS, 1968–1979[a]

Year-End	Mortgage Originations		Effective Yields and Costs			Net Income After Taxes	
	Total ($ Millions)	Growth Rate (%)	Mortgage Portfolio (%)	Cost of Funds (%)	Yield Spread (%)	Total ($ Millions)	Growth Rate (%)
1968	$ 21,298	9.5%	6.13%	4.74%	1.39%	$ 863	39.7%
1969	21,169	(0.1)	6.32	4.89	1.43	1,036	20.1
1970	20,760	(1.9)	6.56	5.30	1.26	925	(10.7)
1971	38,341	84.6	6.81	5.38	1.43	1,314	42.0
1972	50,024	30.4	6.98	5.41	1.57	1,687	28.5
1973	48,193	(3.7)	7.17	5.60	1.57	1,897	12.4
1974	38,050	(21.0)	7.49	6.13	1.36	1,477	(21.8)
1975	53,799	41.4	7.69	6.30	1.39	1,443	(2.3)
1976	71,103	32.2	7.98	6.36	1.62	2,250	55.9
1977	105,287	48.1	8.22	6.41	1.81	3,198	42.1
1978	108,273	2.8	8.47	6.63	1.84	3,920	22.6
1979	98,730	(8.8)	8.83	7.45	1.36	3,620	(7.7)

[a]Parentheses indicate negative growth.
Source: Federal Home Loan Bank Board.

on a supplemental basis. Through its role as a supplier of additional funds, the FHLB System links the savings and loan industry to the capital markets. It also acts as a stabilizing influence, providing funds to associations during times of weak or negative savings flows.

The **FHLB System** is organized much like the **Federal Reserve System** and has 12 regional banks. Operations are controlled by the Federal Home Loan Bank Board, which has three members, all presidential appointees, who serve staggered terms of 4 years. The Bank Board is an independent agency of the federal government and is not tax supported. All expenses are paid through assessments on the regional banks and the Federal Savings and Loan Insurance Corporation, along with assessments from examination.

In addition to supplying the industry with supplemental funds, the FHLBB is the **regulator for the savings and loan industry.** In this role, the FHLBB sets standards for savings and loan operations. These standards range from the sources from which associations can borrow and the level of reserves that must be maintained, to the kinds of loan and investment that can be made.

FEDERAL HOME LOAN MORTGAGE CORPORATION.   The FHLBB also controls the operations of the Federal Home Loan Mortgage Corporation (FHLMC), which was established in 1970. FHLMC is designed to promote the flow of funds into the housing markets by purchasing mortgages in the secondary market and selling securities backed by those mortgages in the capital market. By doing this, FHLMC helps redistribute funds from areas of the country with a surplus of mortgage funds to mortgage deficient areas. It also brings additional funds into the mortgage market from the capital market. In 1979 FHLMC purchased $5.7 billion in mortgages, the vast majority of which were purchased from savings and loans.

FEDERAL SAVINGS AND LOAN INSURANCE CORPORATION.   One other major area under the control of the FHLBB is the Federal Savings and Loan Insurance Corporation

(FSLIC), which was established in 1934. FSLIC insures savings accounts, thus protecting savers from loss. As of December 31, 1979, FSLIC had assets of $5.9 billion. It has a line of credit with the U.S. Treasury and can assess its member institutions to cover its losses and expenses. FSLIC also requires insured associations to hold specified levels of reserves and net worth, which act as protection from loss. At the end of 1979 these reserves amounted to $31.7 billion, or 6.9% of total savings deposits.

Savings deposit insurance limits were raised to $100,000 in April 1980 from $40,000. To pay for this coverage, each insured association pays a premium of 0.0833% of its savings accounts. The FSLIC may levy additional premiums up to the full amount of its losses and expenses or up to a limit of 0.125% of the savings deposits of the member associations.

LEGAL AND REGULATORY ISSUES.   A number of **regulatory and legislative initiatives** that will have a profound influence on the savings and loan industry, and other thrift institutions in the 1980s and beyond, recently have been enacted, and others are currently under consideration by the Congress and by the banking regulatory agencies. These initiatives center around the two critical issues of raising the savings interest rates paid by commercial banks and thrift institutions to market levels and the granting of additional powers to thrift institutions to generate sufficient profits to enable them to pay market rates of interest.

Depository Institutions Deregulation and Monetary Control Act of 1980.   In the latter half of the 1970s, mounting pressures on financial institutions and consumers accentuated by continuing inflation and rising interest rates led to Congressional deliberation and action on financial reform. These concerns resulted in the passage of the **Proxmire-Reuss Depository Institutions Deregulation and Monetary Control Act of 1980,** which was signed into law by President Carter on March 31, 1980. As part of this legislation, a committee called the Depository Institutions Deregulation Committee (DIDC) was created to provide for the orderly implementation of certain sections of the statute. The full impact of the legislation will be spread over a period of up to 6 years.

A number of other legislative initiatives in this Act also affect the thrift industry directly. In fact, the legislation is felt by many observers to offer the most significant legislative reform since the 1930s. As the issues discussed below indicate, a major structural change is likely to result from the new authorities granted savings and loan associations and the lowering of competitive barriers between financial institutions. The major items that can be expected to have the greatest and most broadly based effects on the savings and loan industry are the following:

Regulation Q Phaseout.   A gradual elimination of **ceilings on interest rates** paid on savings deposits is to take place over a 6-year period with oversight provided by the DIDC. During this period, permissible rates are targeted for increases of 25 basis points in the passbook rates within 18 months after enactment. In addition, 50 basis point increases in maximum rates on passbook and all other accounts are provided for in the third, fourth, fifth, and sixth years after enactment until market rates of interest are reached.

At the end of the sixth year, all Federal Reserve Board **Regulation Q** authority expires. During the phaseout period, the maintenance of the differential between the rate payable on deposits by banks and that payable by thrift institutions will be examined and subject to change depending upon the effect on the viability of the thrift industry.

New Asset Empowerments.   In an effort to ameliorate the effects on the thrift industry of eliminating Regulation Q, broader asset powers have been given to savings and loan associations. Basically, the new authority allows a greater percentage of assets to be invested in instruments that are more sensitive to fluctuations in interest rates and, as such, bear shorter maturity than the predominant asset holdings of fixed rate mortgages.

The amendment allows federally chartered savings and loans to invest up to an aggregate limit of 20% of assets in secured or unsecured consumer loans, commercial paper, and corporate debt securities. Associations will also be allowed to invest in, redeem, or hold shares or certificates of open-end investment companies. Expanded authority to make acquisition, development, and construction loans will also be granted, and the maximum investment in service corporations will be raised to up to 3% of assets for certain types of investments.

Variable Reserve Requirements. The new legislation authorizes the FHLBB to determine the appropriate reserve requirements within a range of 3–6% of savings. This amendment removes the current statutory provision of a fixed 5% of savings and provides the Bank Board with a discretionary tool for implementing policy.

Preemption of State Usury Laws. State usury ceilings on mortgage loans made by savings and loan associations as well as other financial institutions and approved lenders were permanently preempted as of April 1, 1980, subject to a right of affected states to override the preemption within 3 years.

NOW Accounts and Overdraft Privileges. Authority to offer NOW (negotiable order of withdrawal) accounts for any federally insured financial institution is another major provision of the bill. Coupled with this authority is a provision granting overdraft authority on NOW accounts (i.e., preauthorized extensions of credit). These provisions became effective nationwide on December 31, 1980.

While the items above are considered to be major components of the act, a number of other items included in the legislation are also expected to significantly affect the thrift industry. Some of these are listed below.

Authorization of Remote Service Units (RSUs). RSUs will be authorized (by not being prohibited) for associations for the purpose of crediting and debiting savings accounts, crediting loan payments, and effecting related financial transactions under regulations set by the Bank Board. These provisions became effective on March 31, 1980.

Liquidity Requirements. Investments available to serve as eligible liquidity will be broadened to include shares or certificates of **open-end management investment companies** registered with the Securities and Exchange Commission.

Mutual Capital Certificates (MCCs). A new securities instrument will be authorized for federal mutual associations, allowing them to sell shares of MCCs that would qualify toward regulatory reserves. These MCCs will pay dividends (not interest) and, as such, will be **similar to preferred stock.** Basically, this authority will serve as a vehicle for a **mutual association** to acquire external forms of equity.

Increased Insurance of Accounts. Regular accounts insured by the FSLIC have had insurance coverage raised from $40,000 to $100,000 effective March 31, 1980, without any increase in the premium charged for insurance.

Federal Stock Charters.   Any **state-chartered stock association** will be allowed to transfer its charter to a **federal stock charter,** provided the association had never existed in mutual form.

Reserves on Transactions Accounts.   As part of the Federal Reserve Board's increased authority, it has been empowered to set (within prescribed ranges depending on the amount) reserve requirements on all transactions accounts including NOW accounts, effective March 31, 1980. This authority extends to all depository institutions. All depository institutions (including savings and loans) subject to those requirements will be eligible to borrow through the Federal Reserve discount window.

Raising Interest Rates to Market Levels.   The raising of interest rates on savings accounts to market levels has major and overriding consumer appeal. The high rates of inflation and short-term money market rates in 1979 and 1980 have made savers more interest rate conscious, particularly since the authorization of the popular MMC accounts and the pro-liferation of **money market funds,** both of which have been widely advertised.

On May 30 and again on December 31, 1979, financial institution regulatory agencies adopted regulations to raise interest rates for the small saver. The effect of these actions was to:

- Allow 0.25% increases in both the institutions' passbook and 90-day to 1-year certificate accounts, with the thrift institutions' differential being maintained.
- Reduce the minimum maturity of the 4-year certificate to $2\frac{1}{2}$ years with the rate based on similar maturity Treasury securities. (A maximum 12% rate was added late.)
- Eliminate minimum deposits on all accounts except MMCs and allow pooled funds by depositors, to take advantage of higher rates.
- Institute a less restrictive (severe) early **withdrawal penalty formula.**

Until recently these actions did not have a major impact on savings and loan earnings, since virtually all the industry's recent deposit growth was in 6-month MMCs and $100,000 certificates of deposit, both of which have had much higher interest rates than the accounts affected. However, when Treasury securities rates declined so dramatically (over 1,000 basis points on 6-month issues), the DIDC stepped in to make MMC rates more competitive with many market fund rates.

On May 29, 1980, the DIDC announced a number of interrelated actions for adjusting interest rate ceilings. Chief among these actions was the imposition of minimum ceilings of 7.75% on 6-month MMCs for all institutions and of 9.25 and 9.50% on 30-month MMCs for banks and thrift institutions, respectively. In doing so, the DIDC (1) effectively eliminated any meaningful differential on 6-month MMCs between commercial banks and savings and loans, but retained it on the 30-month accounts, and (2) effectively raised the minimum level to which overall savings and loan deposit costs can fall despite reductions in short-term interest rates.

MUTUAL SAVINGS BANKS

The **mutual savings banks,** which were first established in 1819, are similar to savings and loan associations. The purposes of this type of savings institution were to accept savings deposits and allow withdrawals of deposits, to invest funds safely, to use profits to cover expenses and add to reserves, and to make dividend payments to depositors. Like savings and loans, mutual savings banks are thrift institutions that encourage savings and act as financial intermediaries in making investments and extending loans to qualified borrowers. Mutual savings banks have not grown as rapidly as savings and loans, commercial banks, or credit unions since the end of World War II. They are, however, the fourth largest provider of residential mortgage funds in the country. At the end of 1979, mutual savings banks had assets of $163.4 billion of which 60.6% consisted of mortgage loans.

NATURE OF THE BUSINESS.   As thrift-oriented financial intermediaries, mutual savings banks encourage savings by offering interest-bearing savings accounts, through which individuals and institutions can invest their savings. With these savings deposits, mutual savings banks make investments and loans in a fairly wide variety of areas compared to savings and loans, including mortgages, U.S. government securities, state and local government securities, corporate securities, and other nonmortgage loan areas. Mutual savings banks are all private institutions owned by their depositors and individually controlled by a local board of trustees, who make the major decisions concerning operations. Unlike savings and loans, which are located in every state, mutual savings banks are located in only 17 states and are concentrated in the northeast. At the end of 1978 there were 465 mutual savings banks, with average assets of $340.2 million. Over 70% of these mutual savings banks were located in Massachusetts, New York, and Connecticut. There has been a net reduction in the number of savings banks in the country from 637 in 1910, to 540 in 1940, 494 in 1970, and 465 in 1980. There are no stock mutual savings banks. Therefore, these institutions are controlled by their members and board of trustees; the latter has a purely fiduciary role.

Each state within which mutual savings banks are domiciled provides the charter and regulates and supervises mutual banking activity. Because of this, allowable investments, permissible services, and operating practices vary somewhat from state to state. All mutual savings banks are members of either the **Federal Deposit Insurance Corporation (FDIC)** and/or the **Mutual Savings Central Fund, Inc.,** of Massachusetts. The FDIC and Central Fund insure savings accounts against loss as FSLIC insures savings accounts at savings and loans. At the end of 1978, 325 mutual savings banks were covered by FDIC insurance, while all 163 Massachusetts savings banks were insured by the Mutual Savings Central Fund, Inc., with 23 Massachusetts banks insured by FDIC as well. About 18% of the mutual savings banks are also members of the Federal Home Loan Bank System.

In addition to savings deposit insurance, mutual savings banks, like savings and loans, maintain a general reserve to protect against loss. In 1978 this figure amounted to 6.9% of total liabilities versus 7.6% for commercial banks and 5.9% for FSLIC-insured savings and loans. These reserves include **subordinated debentures.**

SOURCES OF FUNDS.   Over the years, the major source of funds for savings banks has been deposits of individuals and families. These deposits have been in accounts that are highly liquid and safe because of **deposit insurance** by the FDIC. As with savings and loans, significant new sources of funds have become available to savings banks in recent years. In addition to being able to offer **negotiable order of withdrawal (NOW) accounts,** mutual savings banks can offer market rate certificates such as the 6-month MMCs and other flexible ceiling savings instruments. Mutual savings banks are subject to the same rate limitations on savings accounts as are savings and loan associations.

Historically, passbook savings deposits have been the principal source of funds for mutual savings banks. This was a result of the savings banks' dependence on small savers. However, as economic conditions became more competitive in the 1970s with respect to achieving profitable rates of return on investments, savers became more sophisticated and investigated alternative investment opportunities. Thus mutual savings banks have had to compete for deposits, as have the savings and loans, with a growing number of alternative investments offering potential savers high yields. Because mutual savings banks are restricted by federal regulation as to the interest rates that they can offer on deposits, the composition of the deposits has shifted like that of savings and loans, but not to the same extreme. At the end of 1978, 43.8% of savings bank deposits were in time accounts (Exhibit 16) versus 68.1% for savings and loans. Passbook-type savings accounts amounted to 45.4% of mutual savings bank deposits, while all other deposits accounted for less than 1% at the end of 1978.

In addition to deposits, mutual savings banks had a modest amount of borrowings and other liabilities at the end of 1978. General reserve accounts at mutuals amounted to nearly $11 billion at the end of 1978 and were 6.9% of total liabilities plus reserves. Mutual savings bank reserves are similar to the "net worth" required for savings and loans.

USES OF FUNDS. Mutual savings banks have significantly greater diversity in their investment options than do savings and loans; however, mutuals are closely regulated in the loans and investments that they are allowed to make. Exhibit 16 shows that savings banks hold significant investment obligations of the federal government, federal agencies, and state and local governments, along with corporate bonds and stock and other similar securities. Despite their investment diversity, mutual savings banks are still large investors in mortgages, with 60.2% of their assets in this area.

Like savings and loans, mutual savings banks are allowed to originate loans in a number of other areas. These include education loans and home improvement loans, but these other lending areas only accounted for 4.6% of assets at the end of 1978.

The ability of mutual savings banks to make loans of different kinds varies from state to state. Not all states allow consumer installment lending or home improvement lending. Each state that charters savings banks has the sole authority to regulate the kinds of investments that are allowed.

MORTGAGE LENDING. In 1979 mutual savings banks held a total of $98.9 billion in **mortgage loans** (see Exhibit 17). This accounted for 60.6% of mutual savings banks assets, compared to 60.2% in 1978, and was down from 63.8% in 1975 and 73.4% in 1970. Because most mutual savings banks are located in the Northeast, the primary market demand for their supply of mortgage funds is weak compared to commercial banks and savings and loans, which have a great number of institutions located in the more growth-oriented states in the West and South. This has resulted in mutual savings banks having a lower percentage of their assets in mortgages than savings and loans.

Another factor affecting mortgage lending is that mutual savings banks experience fewer restrictions than do savings and loans in the number of alternative investments available to them. This allows mutuals greater freedom to invest in the safest, highest yielding instruments available.

Mutual savings bank holdings of mortgages historically have had a relatively high percentage of multifamily loans compared to savings and loans. In 1979 mutual savings banks held $17.2 billion (17.4% of their mortgage portfolio) in multifamily loans, compared to only 7.9% for savings and loans. The 17.4% of holdings in multifamily mortgages is about

EXHIBIT 16   ASSETS AND LIABILITIES OF MUTUAL SAVINGS BANKS, DECEMBER 31, 1978

	Total ($ Millions)	Distribution (%)
Assets		
Cash and due from banks	$ 3,665	2.3%
U.S. government obligations	4,959	3.1
Federal agency obligations	3,338	2.1
State and local obligations	3,333	2.1
Mortgage investments	105,179	66.5
Mortgage loans	95,157	60.2
GNMA mortgage-backed loans	10,021	6.2
Corporate and other bonds	21,566	13.6
Corporate stocks	4,870	3.0
Other loans	7,195	4.5
Guaranteed education loans	992	0.6
Consumer installment loans	1,333	0.8
Home improvement loans	722	0.5
Federal funds	2,140	1.4
Passbook loans	953	0.6
All other loans	1,055	0.7
Bank premises owned	1,396	0.9
Other real estate	413	0.3
Other assets	2,321	1.5
Total assets	$158,174	100.0%
Liabilities		
Regular deposits	$141,170	89.3%
Savings	71,816	45.4
Time	69,354	43.8
School and club	202	0.1
Other deposits	1,329	0.8
Total deposits	142,701	90.2
Borrowings and mortgage warehousing	1,594	1.0
Other liabilities	2,971	1.9
Total liabilities	147,267	93.1
Capital notes and debentures	356	0.2
Other general reserves	10,551	6.7
Total general reserve accounts	10,907	6.9
Total liabilities and general reserve accounts	$158,174	100.0%

Source: Federal Reserve Board.

the same as in the previous years, but it is up from 13.4% in 1970. Mutual savings banks held 13.1% of all multifamily loans outstanding at the end of 1979.

Holdings of one- to four-family mortgages at mutual savings banks amounted to $64.7 billion at the end of 1979, or 7.4% of the total outstanding. The growth rate in single-family holdings for mutual savings banks from 1970 to 1979 has been only 4.9%, compared to 12.6% for all holders combined. This is indicative of the lack of growth in the demand for

EXHIBIT 17   MORTGAGE LOANS HELD BY MUTUAL SAVINGS BANKS
($ MILLIONS, END-OF-YEAR TOTAL)

	1950	1960	1970	1975	1978	1979
Type of Property						
Total mortgages	8,262	26,935	57,948	77,249	95,157	98,924
One to four family	4,326	20,575	42,149	50,025	62,252	64,717
Multifamily	2,728	3,731	7,788	13,792	16,529	17,183
Nonresidential						
Type of Loan						
FHA	1,615	7,074	16,087	14,427	14,203	NA
VA	1,457	8,986	12,008	12,391	11,824	NA
Conventional	3,982	8,246	21,842	36,999	52,754	NA
GNMA, and other mortgage-backed securities	—	—	85	3,367	10,021	NA

Source: Federal Reserve Board.

mortgages in the mutual savings banks' general lending territory. To partially compensate for the weak local demand for mortgages in their own states, mutual savings banks have gone out of state to purchase mortgages in the secondary market. In 1978 (the latest year available), mortgage holdings out of state amounted to 31.8%. By comparison, savings and loans purchases from 1960 to 1978 were only 12.2% of closings. While this is not strictly comparable to holdings, it does show how savings banks have had to purchase loans in a higher proportion to holdings than savings and loans, which originate mainly for their own portfolios. Historically, mutual savings banks have had a relatively high proportion of their mortgage holdings in federally underwritten (FHA-insured and VA-guaranteed) mortgages. In 1979, 22.3% of mutual savings banks mortgage holdings were in FHA and VA loans, compared to 14.8% for all mortgage holders. In 1970, 48.5% of mutual savings bank holdings were in FHA-VA loans. This decline resulted from a resurgence in conventional mortgage lending precipitated in part by the **Emergency Home Finance Act of 1970,** which helped bolster the **secondary market for conventional loans.**

NONMORTGAGE ASSETS.   In addition to mortgages, mutual savings banks as of year-end 1978 held about 6.3% of their assets in mortgage-backed securities such as **GNMA pass-throughs** and other pass-through securities (see Exhibit 16). Mutual savings banks also held 23.9% of their assets in government and corporate securities. This was down from 25.5% in 1975, but up from 20.4% in 1970. Nonmortgage loans accounted for 4.5% of lending, while cash, real estate owned and other assets amounted to 5.0% of total assets. Unlike savings and loans, which had only 17.3% of their 1978 assets in nonmortgage loans, savings banks had 39.8%. This was because the states that charter and regulate savings banks have more broadly defined the kinds of investment in which the banks can participate. This has resulted in a much more diversified portfolio of assets.

SECONDARY MARKET.   Data from the Department of Housing and Urban Development (HUD) indicate that mutual savings banks are net purchasers of mortgages in the secondary market. This is not surprising, since these institutions are located predominantly in the

Northeast, where primary market loan demand is weak compared to supply. The HUD data show that in 1979, mutual savings banks acquired $16.0 billion in mortgages, of which $2.9 billion consisted of purchases. Mutual savings bank mortgage sales in 1979 amounted to only $577 million, or around 0.6% of the total amount of loans sold in the United States.

Mortgage purchases have historically been in single-family loans, accounting for 91.1% of the 1979 total. **FHA-VA mortgages** accounted for 43.7% of single-family purchases, which was less than the 51.1% national average.

PROFITABILITY.   **Mutual savings banks** pass on the majority of their earnings to depositors as interest, after deducting expenses and taxes and retaining a portion of income as reserves. In 1978 savings bank retained earnings as a percentage of total assets came to 0.58%, up from 0.55% in 1977 and 0.45% in 1976 (Exhibit 18). This resulted from a continued rise in total operating income relative to expenses and interest.

As with savings and loans, mutual savings banks hold the majority of their assets in long-term investments (mortgage loans), while their liability structure is dominated by short-term

EXHIBIT 18   INCOME AND EXPENSES OF MUTUAL SAVINGS BANKS, 1960–1978ᵃ

					Amounts ($ Millions)			
Year	Total Operating Income	Total Operating Expenses and Taxes	Net Operating Income After Expenses and Taxes	Interest	Net Operating Income After Expenses, Taxes, and Interest	Net Realized Losses on Asset Transactions	Retained Earnings	Retained Earnings (% of Total Assets)
1960	$ 1,687.2	$ 277.3	$1,409.9	$1,233.7	$176.2	$ 27.5	$148.7	0.37%
1961	1,835.1	297.8	1,537.3	1,326.3	211.0	0.4	210.6	0.51
1962	2,022.3	313.7	1,708.6	1,530.5	178.1	6.0ᵇ	184.0	0.41
1963	2,240.7	344.1	1,896.6	1,700.0	196.6	13.5ᵇ	210.1	0.44
1964	2,484.9	366.3	2,118.6	1,859.1	223.5	5.4ᵇ	228.9	0.44
1965	2,745.1	394.7	2,350.4	2,076.0	274.4	18.1	256.3	0.46
1966	2,990.0	429.3	2,561.6	2,383.0	178.6	16.0ᵇ	194.6	0.33
1967	3,301.5	454.1	2,867.4	2,712.8	134.6	6.2	128.4	0.20
1968	3,701.5	505.9	3,195.6	2,967.0	228.5	26.2ᵇ	254.7	0.37
1969	4,110.5	580.8	3,529.6	3,218.9	310.7	56.1	254.6	0.35
1970	4,487.3	685.1	3,802.3	3,451.8	350.5	142.8	207.7	0.27
1971	5,221.9	810.8	4,411.0	3,936.3	474.7	66.7	408.0	0.48
1972	6,081.1	979.5	5,101.6	4,516.7	584.9	25.3	569.6	0.60
1973	6,977.5	1,165.5	5,812.0	5,138.9	673.1	112.3	560.8	0.54
1974	7,471.4	1,275.2	6,916.3	5,620.4	575.8	198.5	377.4	0.35
1975	8,116.7	1,421.6	6,695.1	6,165.2	529.9	88.6	441.3	0.38
1976	9,275.6	1,714.8	7,560.8	6,970.4	590.4	13.7	576.6	0.45
1977	10,493.5	1,946.4	8,547.2	7,756.7	790.5	11.7	778.8	0.55
1978	11,842.2	2,355.1	9,487.1	8,524.4	962.8	69.0	893.8	0.58

ᵃData for 1971–1978 were compiled on a basis somewhat different from that used for earlier years. The differences are small in most cases, except for net realized losses on asset transactions.
ᵇNet realized gain.
Source: National Association of Mutual Savings Banks.

deposits. This has made them subject to the same problems with profitability that also have plagued savings and loans in recent years. Mutual savings banks generally have received lower rates of return on their assets than savings and loans, but their rates have been higher than those of commercial banks for most of the postwar period. In recent years, however, mutual savings bank earnings have lagged behind savings and loans and commercial banks, largely because of rising expenses and especially higher interest rates paid on deposits as depositors have shifted from lower cost to higher cost savings accounts (certificates).

Mutual savings banks are subject to the provisions of the **Tax Reform Act of 1969.** As a result, mutual savings banks pay ordinary corporate income tax rates on net income after interest is paid on savings deposits. Like savings and loans, however, a portion of net earnings may be sheltered through adding to bad debt reserves. In 1979 no more than 40% of otherwise taxable income could be used for tax-free additions to bad debt reserves, the same as for savings and loans.

CREDIT UNIONS

Credit unions in recent years have been the fastest growing group of financial intermediaries in the United States. The first credit union in the country was established in New Hampshire at St. Mary's Parish in the early 1900s. Like savings and loans and mutual savings banks, credit unions were formed to encourage thrift and to make loans to members. Unlike savings and loans and mutual savings banks, credit unions are nonprofit cooperative associations. They are formed by **people with a common bond** such as employment or affiliation with a religious or fraternal organization. Credit unions are the most numerous group of savings institutions, totaling more than 21,935 in 1978 compared to around 4,725 savings and loans and 465 mutual savings banks. Despite their large number, credit unions are, on average, very small, with estimated assets of only $62.3 billion at the end of 1978, or an average of $2.8 million per credit union. This compares to average assets of $110.8 million for savings and loans and $340.2 million for mutual savings banks. In 1979 credit unions held only 4.5% of total savings deposits at savings institutions, including commercial banks, up from only 2.9% in 1970 and 1.2 percent in 1950.

STRUCTURE OF THE CREDIT UNION INDUSTRY. Credit unions can be chartered under the laws of 46 states, or by the federal government under the Federal Credit Union Act of 1934. State-chartered credit unions made up 43% of the total number of credit unions in 1977 and like mutual savings banks and state-chartered savings and loans, are usually regulated by a state's department of financial regulation. Federally chartered credit unions are regulated by the **National Credit Union Administration (NCUA),** which also provides them, and some state-chartered credit unions, with share (savings) insurance of up to $40,000.

The number of state-chartered credit unions has declined in recent years, while the number of federally chartered institutions has remained relatively stable. The greatest growth in the number of credit union charters has been in California, New York, Pennsylvania, and Texas. Each of these states has a large population base, which is the key to the growth of credit unions.

Credit unions, being cooperative institutions, are organized around a common association of its members. In fact, credit union charters can be issued only if members have a common interest. This differentiates them from mutual savings banks and savings and loans, which are not membership based. In addition, unlike mutual savings and loans and mutual savings banks, whose primary obligation is to their depositors, or stock savings and loans, which are obligated to their stockholders, credit unions have obligations to both the shareholder-owners (savers) and their borrower-owners.

The granting of charters for credit unions usually requires a minimum of 100 potential members, although groups that may be too small to form their own credit union are able to become affiliates of an existing credit union. In 1978, 57% of all credit unions whose total membership was more than 40 million were organized around a **common occupational bond,** 16% by residence, 14% by association, and less than 10% by government. The trend in recent years has been for governmental agencies that issue charters to be increasingly liberal in defining the "common interest" necessary for a group to organize a credit union.

ASSET DISTRIBUTION.   Over time, there has been a significant shift in the concentration of assets between large and small credit unions. In 1969, nearly 38% of credit union assets were held in unions with assets of less than $100,000. Credit unions with assets of $1 million or more accounted for only 15% of assets. By 1978, credit unions with assets of less than $100,000 represented less than 12% of assets, while unions with $1 million or more in assets made up nearly 36% of total credit union assets. This distribution is highly skewed toward the large unions, with the largest credit union, Navy Federal Credit Union, having deposits of nearly $600 million in 1978.

ADMINISTRATION.   Each credit union is administered by a board of directors elected by the union's members. This board sets policies and procedures for operating the union and determines the specific services that will be provided. The officers of credit unions are the president, the vice-president, the secretary, and the treasurer. These officers are volunteers and are usually not paid, except for the treasurer, who is responsible for records and the operation of the organization.

REGULATION.   All federally chartered credit unions are regulated by the **National Credit Union Administration,** which was established in 1970. Before 1970, federal credit unions were supervised by the Bureau of Federal Credit Unions, which was a part of the Department of Health, Education and Welfare. NCUA is an independent agency, as is the **Federal Home Loan Bank Board (FHLBB).** As with the FHLBB, NCUA is completely financed by funds received from its own member organizations, that is, the credit unions, for services provided as well as for providing deposit insurance for the credit unions. Supervisory responsibilities of NCUA are exercised through the National Credit Union Board, which is made up of three persons appointed by the President of the United States.

The interest that credit unions can pay on shares is controlled by their regulatory agencies. The NCUA sets the rates for all federally chartered credit unions and many state-chartered credit unions. State-chartered credit unions are supervised by the regulatory agencies within the respective states that charter credit unions. The requirements for issuing a credit union charter vary from state to state, but state requirements tend to be somewhat consistent because NCUA and the **Credit Union National Association,** the main industry trade association, have had a standardizing impact on the industry.

Like savings and loans and mutual savings banks, credit unions can borrow funds from government agencies. The Federal Intermediate Credit Bank provides eligible customers with funds on an as-needed basis. Federal and state credit unions in most cases are also permitted to borrow funds from commercial banks, although the ability of state-chartered credit unions to borrow from this source varies from state to state.

SOURCES AND USES OF FUNDS.   Because credit unions have historically been thrift-oriented institutions, the vast majority of their liabilities are in the form of savings deposits, known as shares. Each share represents $5–$10 in deposits. Member shares made up more than 86.1% of credit union liabilities and reserves in 1977, while other borrowings and notes payable accounted for 8.1% of liabilities. Reserves and undivided earnings accounted for 5.7% of liabilities.

Credit union shares are insured through the **National Credit Union Share Insurance Fund (NCUSIF),** which was established in 1970. Since shares have been insured, the dollar volume of shares has risen by 244% (1970–1978). This represents more rapid growth in credit union savings than in either savings and loans savings, which grew by 194%, or in mutual savings bank savings, with growth of 99%. Like savings and loans and mutual savings banks, credit unions can offer savings certificates, including certificates whose interest rate ceiling varies according to money market conditions.

In recent years credit unions, like savings and loans and mutual savings banks, have turned increasingly to borrowing as a source of funds. Borrowed funds are largely in the form of certificates of indebtedness.

Credit union assets are highly concentrated in **consumer installment loans.** This is the result of historical limitations on the term and interest rate that credit unions were allowed to charge and the fact that they are small institutions aimed at meeting that portion of their shareholder's financing needs that has traditionally not been met by savings and loans, mutual savings banks, or commercial banks. Exhibit 19 shows credit union financial assets along with member share deposits (liabilities). In 1978 credit unions had total assets of $58.2 billion, up from $51.5 billion in 1977 and only $18.0 billion in 1970. Of the 1978 total, consumer credit amounted to $45.9 billion, or 78.9% of assets. Thus credit union lending and investing is dominated by consumer debt much the same way that savings and loan and mutual savings bank lending is dominated by mortgages. About 35% of credit union consumer credit is for the purchase of automobiles, while personal loans and loans to cover household expenses represented nearly 33% of loans made. Other consumer loans include those for furnishings, appliances, and so on.

EXHIBIT 19   CREDIT UNIONS STATEMENT OF FINANCIAL ASSETS AND LIABILITIES, 1970–1978 ($ BILLIONS)

	1970	1975	1976	1977	1978
Total Financial Assets	$18.0	$36.9	$43.2	$51.5	$58.2
Demand deposits plus currency	0.8	1.3	1.2	1.3	1.4
Time deposits	—	0.6	0.4	0.5	0.5
Savings plus loan shares	2.0	3.3	3.8	4.7	2.2
Credit Market Instruments	15.2	31.7	37.8	45.1	54.2
U.S. government securities	1.4	4.0	4.8	5.2	4.9
Home mortgages	0.8	2.0	2.5	2.9	3.4
Consumer credit	13.0	25.7	30.5	37.0	45.9
Credit Union Shares	15.5	33.0	39.0	46.8	53.0

Source: Board of Governors of the Federal Reserve System.

Federal credit unions received authorization in 1977 to issue **mortgage loans** with terms up to 30 years. Many state-chartered credit unions had been mortgage lenders before 1977; however credit unions have not been major suppliers of mortgage credit. Exhibit 19 shows that credit unions held $3.4 billion in mortgage debt at the end of 1978. This represented only 5.8% of assets. Since 1977 federal credit unions have become much more active in originating mortgages, but are still only a very small fraction of the market. In 1978 credit unions held less than 0.5% of this $761.8 billion in one- to four-family mortgage debt outstanding. Credit unions are only allowed to issue mortgages on one- to four-unit structures. A significant problem for credit unions trying to enter the mortgage field results from the relatively small size of most credit unions and their lack of experience in this kind of lending. Because credit unions are small, and given the price of housing and the corresponding dollar amount of mortgage loans, it is difficult for credit unions to originate a significant volume of mortgages. As the secondary mortgage market evolves to include credit unions, however, it is likely that they will become more active in originating and selling single-family mortgages.

In addition to loans of these kinds, credit unions are allowed to invest in U.S. government and federal agency securities. Because of the high demand for consumer loans and the increased interest in mortgage lending in recent years, increases in credit union investment in government securities has lagged behind the growth in total assets. Other asset areas include holdings of demand and time deposits from other financial institutions, which have been relatively stable since 1975, while deposits by credit unions in savings and loans have declined from 1975 to 1978.

INCOME AND EXPENSES.   The largest source of income for federal credit unions is interest paid on loans, which amounted to over 83% of total income in 1977 (Exhibit 20). Income from investments such as government securities and deposits at other financial institutions amounted to 16% of income, while income from other sources came to just over 1%. Total 1977 federal credit union income came to $2.6 billion.

On the expense side, employee compensation was by far the largest expense, at $309 million, or 32% of the $968 million in expenses. Other expense items are shown in Exhibit 20 and include office operation expenses, interest on borrowed money, borrowers' protection insurance, and professional and outside services.

The $1.6 billion in net income is the source for shareholder dividends, which in 1977 amounted to 85% of net income. The average dividend in 1977 for federally chartered credit unions was 6.33%, up from 6.15% in 1976. Like savings and loans and mutual savings banks, credit unions are subject periodically to savings withdrawals that exceed deposits because of high interest rates offered savers on alternative investments. The higher dividends in 1977 reflect credit union managers' attempt to hold their deposits by paying a more competitive rate of return. In addition to paying dividends, many credit unions refund a portion of the interest paid on borrowings as a means of competing with other lending institutions and as a direct benefit to credit union owners.

As the competition between savings institutions increases, each type of institution must develop new services that will attract and keep new customers. As noted earlier in this section, savings and loans and mutual savings banks are evolving rapidly into more complete financial institutions. Credit unions are also progressing. In addition to becoming more involved in mortgage lending, credit unions offer a variety of useful services. One of the major innovations is **share drafts.** These are similar to checking accounts in that they allow credit union members to write drafts against their account balance to pay bills. All federally chartered credit unions have authority to offer share draft accounts, as do many state-chartered

EXHIBIT 20   INCOME AND EXPENSES OF FEDERAL CREDIT UNIONS, 1977

	Amount ($ Millions)	Distribution (%)
Interest on loans	$2,143	83.1%
Income from investments	404	15.7
Other income	33	1.3
Total income	$2,580	100.0%
Employee compensation	309	31.9%
Borrower's protection insurance	79	8.2
Life savings insurance	46	4.8
Association dues	14	1.4
Examination and supervision fees	13	1.3
Interest on borrowed money	91	9.4
Office occupancy expense	30	3.2
Educational and promotional expense	20	2.1
Office operations expense	95	9.8
Professional and outside services	57	5.9
Conventions and conferences	17	1.8
Annual meeting expense	8	0.8
Share insurance premiums	18	1.9
Other expenses	172	17.8
Total expenses	$ 968	100.0%
Net income	1,612	—

Source: Adapted from the National Credit Union Administration, Annual Report, 1977.

credit unions. Share drafts pay interest on the average or minimum balance. In addition to share drafts, several large credit unions in 1977 began offering **credit cards** to their members. Credit unions are gaining access to automated clearinghouses, which provide **electronic funds transfer** among financial institutions. At the retail level, many credit unions have introduced automated teller machines and point-of-sale terminals at stores and shopping centers. Credit unions also can compete for deposits by offering market rate certificate accounts similar to those offered by savings and loans, mutual savings banks, and commercial banks.

CREDIT UNION TAXATION.   Credit unions, unlike savings and loans and mutual savings banks, are **exempt from paying income taxes** to the federal government and most state governments. This is because credit unions are considered to be nonprofit organizations that do business only with their owners. Member-owners receive earnings from the net income of their credit union in proportion to the amount of deposits (shares) they have in the union. The credit union must divide its net income among its members proportionately according to share balances. Following this division of earnings, no significant income remains in the credit union's name to be taxed. The privilege of tax exemption is a major benefit to credit unions and allows them to effectively compete for savings deposits by offering competitive market interest rates on deposits while still providing member-borrowers with loans at interest rates that do not have to cover the tax burden that is borne by savings and loans and mutual savings banks, or commercial banks.

BIBLIOGRAPHY

Benston, George J., "Savings Banks and the Public Interest," *Journal of Money, Credit, and Banking,* Pt. II, February 1972, pp. 133–226.

Board of Governors of the Federal Reserve System, *Federal Reserve Bulletin,* Washington, D.C., June 1980.

Bomar, Thomas A., "Conversion," *Federal Home Loan Bank Board Journal,* May 1974.

Credit Union National Association, Inc., *1978 Yearbook,* CUNA, Madison, WI.

———, *1979 Yearbook,* CUNA, Madison, WI.

Dougall, Herbert E., and Gaumnitz, Jack E., *Capital Markets and Institutions,* 3rd ed., Prentice-Hall, Englewood Cliffs, NJ, 1975.

Edmister, Robert O., *Financial Institutions: Markets and Management,* McGraw-Hill, New York, 1980.

Federal Home Loan Bank Board, *FHLBB Journal,* Washington, D.C., July 1980.

Friend, Irwin, *Study of the Savings and Loan Industry.* Vol. 1–4, Federal Home Loan Bank Board, Washington, D.C., 1969–1970.

Gerloff, Cecilia M., *The Federal Home Loan Bank System,* Federal Home Loan Bank Board, Washington, D.C., 1971.

Hempel, George H., and Yawitz, Jess B., *Financial Management of Financial Institutions,* Prentice-Hall, Englewood Cliffs, NJ, 1977, pp. 129–131, 148–152.

Jacobs, Donald, et al., *Financial Institutions,* Irwin, Homewood, IL, 1972.

Marvell, Thomas B., *The Federal Home Loan Bank Board,* Praeger, New York, 1969.

National Association of Mutual Savings Banks, *National Fact Book of Mutual Savings Banking,* NAMSB, Washington, D.C., 1979.

National Credit Union Administration, *Annual Report, 1977,* NCUA, Washington, D.C., June 1978.

Rose, Peter S., and Fraser, Donald R., *Financial Institutions.* Business Publications, Dallas, TX, 1980.

Smith, Paul F., *Economics of Financial Institutions,* Irwin, Homewood, IL, 1971.

U.S. League of Savings Associations, *Savings and Loan Fact Book,* USLSA, Washington, D.C., 1980.

INSURANCE AND REINSURANCE

CONTENTS

RISK IN BUSINESS	**3**	**INSURANCE CONTRACTS**	**16**
Definition of Risk	3	Types of Insurance Contract	16
Risk Identification and Analysis	3	Structure of Insurance Contracts	16
Classification of Risk	4	Property and liability insurance	17
Risk Measurement	4	Life insurance	17
Ways of Meeting Risk	5	Common Property and Liability	
Risk Management	5	Insurance Contract Provisions	**17**
		Basic Legal Doctrines Surrounding	
INSURANCE AS A WAY OF MEETING		Insurance Contracts	**19**
RISK	**6**	Indemnity	19
		Insurable interest	19
Characteristics of the Insurance		Representations and warranties	19
Mechanism	6	Concealment	20
Insurable Risks	6	Waiver and estoppel	20
Limitations on the Insurance Mechanism	7		
Basic Types of Insurance	7	**COMMERCIAL LIABILITY**	
Property insurance	7	**INSURANCE**	**20**
Liability insurance	9		
Life insurance	9	Liability and Negligence	**20**
Health insurance	9	Workers' Compensation and Employers'	
Commercial Insurance	10	Liability	**20**
Self-Insurance	10	Business Liability Other than Workers'	
		Compensation and Employers' Liability	**21**
STRUCTURAL CHARACTERISTICS OF		Liability of landlords and tenants	21
THE INSTITUTION OF INSURANCE	**11**	Product liability	22
		Liability for acts of agents	22
Number and Size of Insurers in the		Liability of owners and operators of	
United States	**11**	vehicles	22
Types of Insurer Based on Nature of		Liability of bailees	22
Ownership	**12**	Contractual liability	23
Types of Insurer by Domicile	**13**	Officers' and directors' liability	23
Types of Insurer by Line of Insurance		Insurance Contracts for Business Liability	
Sold	**14**	Risks	**23**
Internal Organization of Insurers	**14**	Professional Liability	**23**
REINSURANCE	**14**	**COMMERCIAL PROPERTY**	
		INSURANCE	**24**
Definition and Scope	**14**		
Reinsurance in Property and Liability		Insurance Against Physical Damage to	
Insurance	**15**	Property	**24**
Reinsurance in Life Insurance	**15**		

Fire and allied lines   24
Multiple-line insurance contracts for
the business firm   24
   Jewelers' block contract   24
   Mercantile block contract:
   Commercial property coverage   24
   Manufacturers' output contract   25
   Special multiperil contract   25
Ocean marine contracts   25
Inland marine contracts   26
   Transportation contracts   26
   Floater contracts   26
   Instrumentalities of transportation   26
Boiler and machinery contracts   26
Miscellaneous physical damage
contracts   27
Consequential Loss Contracts   **27**
Crime Insurance Contracts   **28**
Suretyship   **28**
   Fidelity bonds   28
   Surety bonds   29

**LIFE AND HEALTH INSURANCE
CONTRACTS AND THEIR BUSINESS
USES**   **29**

Key Man Insurance   **29**
Funding of Buy-and-Sell Agreements   **29**
Split-Dollar Life Insurance   **30**
Deferred Compensation   **30**
Group Life Insurance   **30**
Group Health Insurance   **30**
Retirement Income Plans   **30**

**INSURANCE MARKETS AND
MARKETING**   **31**

Definition   31
Capacity of Insurers   31
Market Availability   31
Methods of Distribution   31
   Agency systems   32
   Supervision of agents   32

UNDERWRITING AND RATING   **32**

Underwriting in Property and Liability
Insurance   32
Underwriting in Life Insurance   33
Basic Principles of Insurance Rate
Computations   33

SETTLEMENT OF LOSS   **33**

Functions of the Claims Department   33
Adjusters   33

INSURANCE FINANCE   **34**

Assets   34
Liabilities   34
Ratios   34
Underwriting Profit or Loss   35
Policyholders' Surplus   35
Accounting   35

SELECTION OF INSURERS   **36**

Solvency   36
Cost   36
Service   36

REGULATION OF INSURANCE   **36**

INSURANCE AND REINSURANCE

Oscar N. Serbein

RISK IN BUSINESS

Anyone who owns or manages a business is aware of the multitude of risks or uncertainties that are constantly present in day-to-day operations. These risks range from the usual uncertainties surrounding marketing, production, and financial activities that may result in a profit or loss, to the ever-present possibility of the destruction of real and personal property (including business personal property) through fire, windstorm, earthquake, flood, and other natural catastrophes. In addition, there is the possibility of loss of property of all types through criminal activities and lawsuits (particularly those alleging negligence), as well as losses of personnel through death, disability, resignation, and retirement. A principal objective of risk and insurance management is to lower the probability that loss will occur and to alleviate the financial consequences when it does.

DEFINITION OF RISK. In the field of risk management, **risk** is defined as **uncertainty** regarding the occurrence of gain or loss. The use of **insurance** as a way of meeting risk applies when a chance event brings about loss only. For the study of insurance, **risk** is uncertainty regarding the occurrence of an economic loss. The **degree** of risk may be quantified by attaching a **probability** to the happening of an event. Thus, if it is known that an event cannot occur, the probability that it will is zero and there is no uncertainty surrounding it. Likewise, if it is known that an **event** will occur, its probability of occurrence is 1, and there is no uncertainty. Maximum risk exists, and thus maximum uncertainty, when the probability that an event will occur is 0.5.

It is essential to distinguish between the word "risk" and the words "peril" and "hazard," which are sometimes used interchangeably with it. A **peril** is a cause of loss, such as fire, windstorm, fraud, infidelity of employees, or adverse legal decisions, whereas a **hazard** is a condition that makes occurrence of a peril more likely. It is possible to extend the definition of a hazard to include "conditions that make the loss more severe, once the peril has occurred and has caused a loss" (Greene and Trieschmann, *Risk and Insurance*), although this use of the word "hazard" is not common.

RISK IDENTIFICATION AND ANALYSIS.

One of the first steps in the management of risk is to **identify** all possible sources of accidental loss, and to analyze and estimate the **maximum** dollar amount of **potential loss** that could occur with each source. It is important to include in this measurement the aggregate of all losses that can result from a single event. A systematic procedure for identifying sources of loss is desirable. Greene and Serbein (*Risk*

Management: Text and Cases, p. 13) indicate that "three approaches to this problem are often recommended: (1) use of **questionnaires,** (2) **examination of balance sheets,** and (3) **flowcharts.**"

Questionnaires or **schedules** serve to list all possible sources of loss and go far toward reducing the likelihood that a serious source of loss will be overlooked. A rather extensive **Risk Analysis Questionnaire** is published by the American Management Association. Analysis of **balance sheets** and **income statements** can be helpful in identifying **loss exposures.** Balance sheets provide a starting point for the analyst in identifying the assets of the firm and the possible total dollar exposure to accidental loss. Since the balance sheet provides information in summary form only, it is necessary to investigate further to determine the location of the assets and the possible risks to which they are exposed. The income statement provides a considerable amount of help in suggesting areas for further investigation. An analysis of sales revenues might well lead to a determination, among other things, of the extent of **foreign sales, sales on credit,** and **product liability** exposures. The presence of miscellaneous income could suggest to the analyst the possibility of rental income and could raise questions about the protection of **real estate** from accidental loss. Expenses also serve to suggest various possibilities of loss, including use of employee automobiles, rented cars, continuing expenses in the event of **business interruption,** and exposures associated with leased property. **Flowcharts** may be of considerable use in identifying possible materials in manufacturing and the exposures associated with the manufactured product in its various stages, including sale of the finished product.

CLASSIFICATION OF RISK. Once risks have been identified and the extent and the magnitude of possible loss associated with them analyzed, it is useful to classify them as to type. A number of possible classifications have been suggested in the literature of risk and insurance. The most widely mentioned are **pure** versus **speculative, static** versus **dynamic,** and **particular** versus **fundamental.** A pure risk is one in which, if the event occurs, only loss can result. A speculative risk is one in which there can be either loss or gain. Static risks are ones that are not appreciably affected by changes in the economy, consumer tastes, technology, and similar factors; the probability of loss remains reasonably constant over time. Dynamic risks, on the other hand, are influenced by economic and societal changes that occur; they are typically less predictable than static risks and do not occur on a regular basis (Vaughan and Elliott, *Fundamentals of Risk and Insurance,* p. 10). Particular risks are associated with individual events such as the loss of a building by fire or windstorm. Fundamental risks affect large groups of people and may arise out of social as well as physical phenomena. Examples cited by Vaughan and Elliott are unemployment, floods, war, and inflation. One of the significant aspects of these classifications is that pure, static, and particular risks are typically transferable to private **insurers,** while speculative, dynamic, and fundamental risks are not. Some of the latter risks may be insurable, but usually only when the government is an insurer or reinsurer.

RISK MEASUREMENT. Decision making in **risk management** depends heavily on the ability to estimate the possible **severity** and **frequency** of future loss through the development of **loss distributions.** The assessment of the probabilities derived from these distributions that losses of given magnitudes will occur is useful in computing the expected monetary value of losses of various sizes. If this information is combined with an appropriate **utility distribution** (tolerance for risk) it can be decided, for example, whether to transfer risks to insurers and what deductible level is optimal (Greene and Serbein, *Risk Management: Text* *and Cases,* pp. 60–66). In some problems the arithmetic mean of a loss distribution is a useful way to assess the losses occurring to a group. For example, computing the average (arithmetic mean) loss for a given group is the first step in pricing some insurance contracts. Since this average has been computed from a sample, it will vary from the universe mean. The extent of this variation is measured by the **standard deviation** of the sample means and is a measure of the risk assumed by the insurer in basing its price on an estimated value. Since the standard deviation of means varies directly with the universe standard deviation and inversely with the square root of the sample size (i.e., less uncertainty as the sample increases), the insurer expects its risk to approach zero as the size of the sample increases.

WAYS OF MEETING RISK.   One of the ultimate objectives of the management of risk is to alleviate the financial consequences of chance losses. The four techniques that are typically used, either singly or in combination, are: (1) **avoidance,** (2) **control,** (3) **retention,** and (4) **transfer.** The avoidance of risk occurs when a company refuses to undertake a project. This is likely to occur when the costs of meeting risk would result in making the project unprofitable. Control of risk involves efforts to reduce the probability that loss will occur, and, after a loss, to limit the extent to which further damage will be done. The chief techniques are prevention and protection. Because the complete prevention of chance loss is difficult, many control activities are protective. "Retention of risk" means that a business (or individual) elects to bear the financial consequences of chance loss out of resources that may be available, such as accumulated assets or current income, or from formal arrangements including **self-insurance,** a **captive insurer,** or creation of loss reserves that do not involve segregation of assets for the specific purpose of meeting uninsured losses. Use of **deductibles** is one aspect of retention. Transfer of risk means the shifting of the financial consequences of loss to an individual or firm who is willing to accept the transfer. **Insurance** is the most widely known transfer technique, and **insurance companies** (insurers) constitute the principal **risk businesses** in the United States and throughout the world. Not all risks are transferable to insurers, but many of them, particularly pure risks, are. Insurance is not the only transfer technique. **Hedging, contracting out** (holding harmless agreements, bailment contracts), choice of **type of business ownership** (such as the corporation and the limited partnership), and use of **warranties** are examples of the transfer of risk that do not involve insurers.

RISK MANAGEMENT.   In the past 20 years risk management as a function of the firm has developed until today virtually all large businesses and many smaller ones have risk departments headed by a **risk manager.** There is a professional organization called the **Risk and Insurance Management Society (RIMS),** that publishes *Risk Management,* a journal that contains articles on topics of interest to professionals and scholars in the field.

Christy ("Selling Insurance to Risk Managers") has defined risk management as "the process for conserving the earning power and assets of the firm (or the individual) by minimizing the financial effect of accidental losses." Greene and Serbein (*Risk Management: Text and Cases,* p. 3) state that the responsibilities of the risk manager are "(1) risk identification and classification, (2) risk measurement, (3) methods of handling risk, (4) record keeping, (5) cooperation with other departments, (6) reports, (7) policy, (8) office management, (9) initiative, and (10) maintenance of professional skills." In addition, the risk manager should participate in top management decision making regarding risk policy, and in decisions relating to the level of authority of the risk manager and the place of risk management on the organizational chart.

INSURANCE AS A WAY OF MEETING RISK

Insurance as a way of meeting risk is a procedure under which members of a group agree to share the cost of insured losses that occur to the group. In commercial practice it is necessary to formalize the process and provide an **organization** to bring the **group** together and provide **capital,** to collect contributions, typically in advance, and to manage all the details associated with **selection of risks** and **adjustment of losses,** as well as to assume responsibility for financial and legal matters and record keeping.

CHARACTERISTICS OF THE INSURANCE MECHANISM. The **insurance mechanism** may be described by discussing its principal components. The **insured** in the process is either an individual or a firm seeking to **transfer specific risks** to an **insurer.** In the United States approximately 90% of insurers are stock or mutual corporations. Although individuals and unincorporated groups may serve as insurers, such arrangements are unusual. Ordinarily prospective insureds do not approach the insurer directly in the transfer process, but seek the assistance of **agents** or **brokers** who place the insurance with an insurer (see subsection "Methods of Distribution" for a definition of "agent" or "broker"). The details of the transfer and the promise of the insurer, as well as the responsibilities of the insured, are set forth in a **contract** between the parties. If loss occurs, the details of settlement often involve **adjusters,** individuals who represent the insurer or in some cases the insured (public adjusters). At times the insurer may wish to transfer a portion of the risks it has assumed to other insurers. When this occurs, the **primary insurer** is said to have **reinsured** some of its risks. The entire process of insuring is supervised by the government, and in the United States the detailed **regulation of insurance** is reserved to the various states, although the **federal government** may intervene in many ways.

INSURABLE RISKS. Not all risks are insurable. To be insurable a risk must meet four basic requirements:

1. *Large numbers and homogeneity.* The **law of large numbers** is a part of the theoretical foundation of insurance. The law of large numbers asserts that in respect to random events, the projected experience of an event (e.g., a loss) will tend to approach as a limit the actual experience, provided the forecast is based on a large enough number of exposure units. Typically, the larger the number of units involved, the more closely will the projected events approximate the actual events.

   The **homogeneity** requirement is essential to achieve equity in pricing among insureds. Insurers are interested in determining the average loss that will occur to the exposed units in a like class. Classification of insureds is a first step in computing the selling price of insurance contracts. The object is to charge those facing the same degree of risk the same price per unit of insurance. Complete homogeneity within particular classifications is usually difficult to achieve, and as a matter of practice, it is often necessary to balance the need for large numbers against the need for homogeneity.

2. *Loss must result from a chance event.* An underlying assumption in all insurance operations is that if loss occurs, it does so through the happenings of **chance.** It is necessary that neither the insured nor the insurer, apart from preventive activities, be in a position to control whether the event does or does not occur. Furthermore, the law of large numbers is based on the assumption of independent, random events.

3. *Loss must be determinable and measurable.* This requirement is essential because of the need for the accumulation of accurate historical data and also for the purpose of satisfactory loss settlement. All property and liability insurance contracts call for a **determination** of the value of the loss, which may be a value agreed upon at the time the contract was entered into, the actual cash value of the loss at time of loss, or replacement cost.

4. *Exposure units should not be subject to catastrophic loss.* **Catastrophe** is the occurrence of loss to a large group at the same time. This must be avoided if the independence assumption of the law of large numbers is to be met.

Other less crucial requirements that an insurable risk should meet are: (1) the probability of loss must be small enough to make the sale of insurance economically feasible, and (2) the insurer's cost of operation must be reasonably low. Perhaps the ideal situation for risk transfer is one in which the possible severity of a loss is substantial and the probability of its occurrence quite low. In other words, insurance tends to work best for low-frequency, high-severity losses.

The requirements of an insurable risk are not always met in practice, but sharp deviations from them may lead to difficulty in the insurance process.

LIMITATIONS ON THE INSURANCE MECHANISM. Although insurance works quite well as a way of meeting a large range of risks, it has its limitations: (1) only risks on which a **dollar value** can be placed are transferable to insurers; (2) most property and liability insurance contracts base the settlement of loss on the **actual cash value** (replacement new less depreciation) of the property at the time of loss; and (3) **controls** may be placed on the insured as a condition of the transfer (for example, physical examinations in life insurance, installation of fire extinguishers in fire insurance, and **coinsurance** clauses). Another limitation, in some ways the most important, is the existence of **moral hazard** or the deliberate bringing about of loss by the insured. Arrow (*Essays in the Theory of Risk Bearing*, pp. 134–143) has stated that one of the peculiarities of insurance is that the fact of a contract may "change incentives and therefore the probabilities on which the insurer relied."

BASIC TYPES OF INSURANCE. The four basic types of insurance are: property, liability, life, and health. In practice insurers sell either property and liability insurance or life and health insurance, although all lines may be sold by a group of companies under common ownership through the use of holding company arrangements. The parent company may be a property and liability insurer with a life and health insurance subsidiary, or vice versa. Historically, insurers tended to sell **property, casualty,** or **life insurance,** with **health insurance** being sold by both casualty and life insurers. With the advent of **multiple-line** underwriting powers in the 1950s, which gave nonlife insurers the right to sell virtually all types of insurance except life, the distinctions between casualty and property insurance tended to be blurred, and it was recognized that casualty insurance, with the exception of health insurance, tended to be either property or liability.

Property Insurance. This category includes **automobile physical damage insurance, fire** and **allied lines,** which encompass **sprinkler leakage, water damage, tenant's improvements and betterments, builder's risk, profits, rain insurance,** and **consequential loss,** for example, and **ocean marine, inland marine, burglary and theft, crop-hail, boiler and machinery, glass, credit,** and **aircraft physical damage.** The losses insured against are losses of property values and may include property in fixed single or multiple locations or in transit, or all these. A distinction is made between **real property** and **personal property.** The former includes (Magee and Serbein, *Property and Liability Insurance*) "buildings owned, rented or leased, and other real property or fixtures attached to real property which would embrace such things as alterations in progress, escalators, power machinery, signs, and pressure vessels." Personal property includes "inventory, cash and checks, furniture and fixtures, cars, trucks, boats, airplanes, and similar items."

Losses to property may be direct or indirect. If the cause of the loss has directly precipitated the loss, the loss is called a **direct loss.** Direct losses may be of two types: **on-premise** and **extended.**

> When the peril that causes the loss is actuated on the same premises where the damaged or destroyed property is located, the loss is an on-premise property loss. If the peril that causes the loss is actuated away from the premises where the damaged or destroyed property is located, the loss is an extended direct property loss. (Mehr and Hedges, *Risk Management in the Business Enterprise.*)

Two major sources of indirect or consequential property loss are **damage caused by a change in environmental conditions** and **damage to an integral part of a set.** For example, the flooding of an irrigation system might temporarily disrupt an on-premise power system. The damage to the power system might turn off all refrigeration units or shut down a production line, which might result not only in loss of production and related profits but also in partial or complete destruction of the inventory. Such damage to the power system would be a direct loss (loss due to flood), whereas the loss of the inventory would be an indirect loss, stemming from a common initial peril.

In addition to the loss to property itself, there may be expense associated with the damage, in particular the expenses incurred in **clearing the premises for rebuilding.** Local laws or regulations may require that when the damage exceeds a stipulated amount, the entire building must be torn down or completely modified to meet present building standards. A firm that sustains property damage may further find that even though the salvage value of the plant does not equal the cost of tearing it down, the expense will have to be incurred.

One of the **consequences** of direct loss of business property may be a **loss of profits** caused by the interruption of the business. Such interruption may also affect the profits and operations of other businesses. While the enterprise is unable to operate, it may well lose not only current business but also the future business of valuable customers who may have suffered losses because, for example, they lacked products to sell, or essential parts. The customer firm may be forced to purchase the goods elsewhere, perhaps at a higher price, with consequent decrease in profits brought about by increased costs of operation (Schultz and Bardwell, *Property Insurance*). This type of risk may be reduced by using several suppliers or by using a supplier that has spread its productive capacity geographically, to eliminate as much as possible the loss of its entire capacity. Some businesses, such as hospitals, cannot shut down, in which case it may be necessary to acquire substitute facilities at high cost, even though these facilities may be less satisfactory to the customer.

Other types of loss that may affect income are those associated with **rental or other agreements** and **losses due to destruction of records.** Losses associated with agreements may be caused by delay or other default of the party with whom the firm contracts, or a happening beyond the control of either party. Lease or rental agreements may contain a requirement that the tenant make rental payments even if a building is temporarily rendered uninhabitable. Destruction of records may result in losses associated with proving that payment was lost, in loss of income through the destruction of accounts receivable, or in the loss of particular customers.

Liability Insurance.   This type of insurance seeks to protect the insured from the financial consequences of damage suits that allege negligence on the part of the insured in causing property damage or personal injury to employees or members of the public. Since the **number and variety of claims and suits** seem to be limited only by the imagination of man, the cost of defending against them may be substantial. And when the injured are successful, the cost to the business may be much larger than that associated with most losses to physical property. The business may also be held liable for the **misconduct of any employee or agent** while acting within the scope of his employment. This type of exposure can be difficult to control.

The major types of **liability insurance** are those relating to (1) **business liability,** such as that of owners, landlords, and tenants; manufacturers and contractors; and elevators; products; as well as contractual; owners' protective; and employers'; (2) **professional liability,** including that of physicians, surgeons, dentists, pharmacists, and hospitals; (3) **personal liability** arising from activities such as ownership of a residence, participation in sports, and ownership of animals; (4) **contingent liability,** which includes owners' and contractors' protective and landlords' protective; and (5) **comprehensive liability,** including comprehensive general, comprehensive personal, and farmers' comprehensive personal. These comprehensive contracts cover off-premise as well as on-premise liability and combine in one contract a number of the separate coverages mentioned above.

Closely related to liability is **workers' compensation,** which is a legal remedy imposing liability for injuries to employees on the employer without regard to fault. Workers' compensation laws exist in every state and provide a procedure for compensating employee injuries that arise out of and in the course of employment. The statutes generally bar resort by the injured claimant to legal suit except, possibly, in cases of gross negligence. Schedules determining the amounts to be paid as compensation for different types of injury are established. The laws also provide that the employer demonstrate financial responsibility to provide benefits, typically through insurance or self-insurance. Insurance is available through private insurers, although six states have compulsory state funds and 11 additional states have funds that compete with private insurers.

Life Insurance.   This form of protection is designed to provide, on the death of the insured, cash **benefits** to third parties called **beneficiaries,** although the beneficiaries are not parties to the contract. The benefits provided are frequently intended as replacement of **income lost** on the death of the insured. The basic contracts are **term, whole life,** and **endowment,** although contracts combining these basic types are fairly commonplace. Contracts may be issued on an individual or group basis, with the latter type of contract forming the basis for a common **employee benefit.**

Health Insurance.   There are two kinds of health insurance: (1) **disability benefits** that provide partial replacement for income lost because of accident and sickness and (2) **medical expense benefits** that reimburse the insured for the costs of medical care, including surgical fees, charges for home and office calls, and hospital bills. Contracts may be written on an individual or a group basis. Health insurance is a valued **employee benefit,** and it is widely available among large firms. Contracts are sold by commercial insurers, but other groups such as Blue Cross and Blue Shield also participate in the area of medical expense benefits. Medical benefits are also offered by **independent practice plans, health maintenance organizations (HMOs),** and **group practice plans** that may not have qualified as HMOs.

COMMERCIAL INSURANCE. The activities of insurers may be classified by line of insurance, as above, or by **type of consumer** of the insurance product. In general, consumers are business firms or private citizens seeking to protect their estates. Insurance sold to business firms is called commercial insurance and that sold to individuals in their nonbusiness roles is called personal insurance. Commercial insurance is designed to provide protection against the risks that arise out of the ownership and operation of a business, and normally the firm buys insurance only after a careful review of alternative ways of handling risk. This section emphasizes commercial insurance.

SELF-INSURANCE. Although **self-insurance,** a program whereby the insured provides his own insurance, may be viewed as a **nontransfer** method of dealing with risk, it should be managed in a manner similar to that employed by insurers. In particular companies that self-insure should observe the requirements for an insurable risk. One of the chief advantages of self-insurance is possible **cost savings,** mainly from elimination of transfer costs. A company may also self-insure when commercial insurance is not available or is available only at a prohibitive cost.

Among the problems associated with self-insurance is the possibility that a serious loss will occur before adequate resources have been accumulated to meet it. The firm may also find that the alternative uses of the money committed to the fund offer a rate of return so attractive that the purchase of commercial insurance, although expensive in some respects, actually represents the optimal use of funds. Since pure risks are random not only in regard to **place of occurrence** but also in respect to **time,** it may be prudent to purchase commercial insurance until such time as self-insurance reserves are fully adequate.

One of the criteria in deciding on a method of dealing with risk is **comparative cost.** The following example, comparing the relative cost of funded risk assumptions and that of the purchase of commercial insurance, demonstrates a method used to evaluate the alternative means of providing for a risk.

Assume that a firm has a maximum loss exposure in respect to a particular asset of $100,000 and is studying the advisability of two alternatives: carrying commercial insurance to the full extent of the loss, or establishing a fund to cover potential loss. The following assumptions are made in evaluating costs:

Federal income tax rate applicable	48%
Municipal income tax rate applicable	8%
Total income taxes	56%
Internal, pretax rate of return on invested assets	22%
Rate of return on short-term investments	7%

Average loss exposure for this type of asset is such that losses paid for by the insurer have been running at 60% of premiums. The loss costs are related to the average loss rate. Average losses are $5,000 per year.

Risk Assumption Funded

Average loss		$5,000
Income on $100,000 funded at 7%	$7,000	
Potential income derived from internal investment of $100,000 at 22%	$22,000	
Opportunity cost		15,000
Gross cost of risk and loss before taxes		$20,000

Net cost if average loss materializes, after
allowance of 56% tax rate (net dollar amount
of loss, and potential income on the fund) $8,800

Commercial Insurance

Average losses of $5,000 assumed to be 60% of the premium
Premium $8,333
    Net cost of carrying insurance after
    allowance of applicable 56% tax rate $3,667

Given the assumptions of the illustration, the cost of commercial insurance is considerably less than that of risk assumption through a self-insurance fund. Not all the costs associated with self-insurance were taken into account in this illustration, but in practice, in comparing one alternative with another, all costs both direct and indirect must be considered. These may include the cost of defense in law suits arising out of the loss, costs of loss adjustments, and cost of records that must be maintained.

STRUCTURAL CHARACTERISTICS OF THE INSTITUTION OF INSURANCE

The organizations that have developed in the United States for the purpose of serving as insurers are varied as to their size, ownership, domicile, and the lines of insurance sold.

NUMBER AND SIZE OF INSURERS IN THE UNITED STATES.   In 1978 there were *4,762 insurers,* of which 2,938 were classified as property and liability insurance companies (*Insurance Facts,* 1979, p. 6), and 1,800 as life insurance companies (*1979 Life Insurance Factbook*). About 900 property and liability companies do business in all or most states and, in general, dominate the field from the standpoint of sales (*Insurance Facts,* 1979, p. 6). In 1978 approximately **1,776,000 persons** were employed in the insurance business, with approximately 40% of them serving in agency or brokerage operations. In terms of **premium volume** the United States leads the world, writing approximately 49% of the total premiums. **Premium receipts** of United States life insurance companies amounted to about $79 billion in 1978, separated by type of insurances as follows:

Type of Insurance	1978
Life insurance	$36,592,000,000
Annuities	16,339,000,000
Health insurance	25,829,000,000
Total	$78,760,000,000

Source: American Council of Life Insurance, *1979 Life Insurance Factbook,* ACLI, Washington, D.C., p. 7.

Net premiums written (premiums received less reinsurance) in the property and liability insurance industry by line of insurance amounted to approximately $82 billion in 1978. Net premiums by line of insurance are given in Exhibit 1.

EXHIBIT 1   NET PREMIUMS WRITTEN AND PRINCIPAL LINES IN 1978

Line of Insurance	Net Premiums Written (000 omitted)
Automobile liability, private passenger	$16,047,775
Automobile liability, commercial	4,335,232
Total automobile liability	$20,383,007
Automobile physical damage, private passenger	$10,540,718
Automobile physical damage, commercial	2,294,195
Total automobile physical damage	$12,834,913
Total, all automobile	$33,217,920
Medical malpractice	$ 1,215,789
Other liability	6,490,064
Total liability (other than auto)	$ 7,705,853
Fire insurance and allied lines	$ 4,675,368
Homeowners' multiple peril	7,792,293
Farmowners' multiple peril	434,478
Commercial multiple peril	5,829,795
Workers' compensation	11,300,144
Inland marine	1,867,189
Ocean marine	1,000,203
Surety and fidelity	1,076,183
Burglary and theft	132,855
Crop-hail	351,217
Boiler and machinery	255,873
Glass	34,951
Credit	42,572
Aircraft	156,482

Source: Insurance Information Institute, *Insurance Facts,* 1979 Edition, III, New York, p. 8.

Another measure of the **size of the insurance industry** in the United States is the **amount of assets** accumulated by the various insurers. The **total assets** for U.S. life insurance companies in 1978 was approximately $390 billion (*1979 Life Insurance Factbook,* p. 68) and for property and liability companies about $160 billion. These figures may be compared with the total assets of manufacturing companies in the United States, which in 1978 were approximately $1.085 trillion.

TYPES OF INSURER BASED ON NATURE OF OWNERSHIP.   From the standpoint of ownership organization, insurers may be classified as (1) **stock insurers,** (2) **mutuals,** (3) **Lloyd's,** (4) **reciprocals or interinsurers,** (5) and **governmental insurers** (Magee and Serbein, *Property and Liability Insurance,* pp. 691–692). Stock insurers are corporations owned by **stockholders** who seek to earn a profit on their investment. Mutuals are corporations owned by the **policyholders** and are **nonprofit** in that no need exists to earn a return on funds contributed by stockholders. Most large mutuals operate on an **advance-premium basis** and may write **assessable** or **nonassessable contracts,** although large insurers write on a nonassessable basis. A number of small mutuals do not collect premiums in advance but assess members at stated intervals to acquire money to pay losses and expenses. Over 90% of all insurers in the United States fall in one or the other of these two categories. The **stock form of ownership** is dominant in life insurance in the sense that the majority of all such insurers are stock corporations, although the largest firms in the field are mutuals and a large proportion of premiums is accounted for by these organizations. In the field of property and liability insurance the majority of the firms are organized as **mutuals,** although the largest insurers are mostly stock companies.

The use of individuals as insurers is rare in the United States, but one of the best known insurers in the world, **Lloyd's of London,** is organized on this basis. The **individuals** who accept risks at Lloyd's do so on their own responsibility and assume liability on the basis of "each for himself and not for one another." Financial responsibility extends to their nonbusiness assets. Within Lloyd's is a corporation that does not serve as an insurer, but performs various services including the keeping of a Lloyd's Shipping Register and maintenance of contingency funds.

Approximately 30 **American Lloyd's** associations operate in the United States. They are small and for the most part are domiciled in only one state. They are not affiliated with Lloyd's of London. Although they operate in a manner somewhat similar to the London institution, the insurers do not accept unlimited financial responsibility.

In 1979 New York State established the **New York Insurance Exchange,** to provide an international marketplace for the "insurance and reinsurance of large and unusual risks" (*Insurance Facts,* p. 5). Operations in many ways are similar to Lloyd's of London.

The **health insurance field** in the United States includes a variety of insurers. **Blue Cross** and **Blue Shield,** for example, in most states are established under special sections of the insurance laws. They are nonprofit, nontaxable associations governed by "boards of directors that represent the hospitals, doctors, and general public of a particular area" (Crane, *Insurance Principles and Practices,* p. 430).

Reciprocals or interinsurers are found in the property and liability insurance field and are unincorporated associations under the management of an attorney-in-fact. About 50 of these exchanges, some of which are very large, exist in the United States. The members of the reciprocal insure one another, and in the smaller ones separate accounts are kept with each member who is charged a share of all losses incurred by the group (Crane, *Insurance Principles and Practices,* p. 427).

Both **federal and state governments** serve as insurers for certain types of risk and now receive approximately 50% of the premiums collected in the United States. Examples of the involvement of the **federal government** are the **Old Age, Survivors, and Disability Insurance Program,** which is operated by the **Social Security Administration, Federal Deposit Insurance Programs,** and the **Federal Crop Insurance Program.** The various states are involved in insurance operations such as **unemployment insurance,** and six states operate **monopolistic state funds** that sell workers' compensation insurance. Twelve states operate competitive state funds. Another state-run undertaking is the **Maryland Automobile Insurance Fund.** The involvement of the government in insurance has increased considerably in recent years.

TYPES OF INSURER BY DOMICILE. Insurers operating in a particular state may be classified as **domestic, foreign,** or **alien,** depending on whether their home office is within the boundaries of the state, in another state, or in a foreign country. Insurers not domiciled in a particular state may nevertheless operate in that state if they seek admission to the state, gain approval of the commissioner, and agree to adhere to the insurance laws of the state in which they wish to operate. The number of domestic insurers in each state varies considerably throughout the United States. In the property-liability field, for example, the greatest number of insurers, 290, have their home offices in Illinois (*Insurance Facts*, p. 6). In Nevada, on the other hand, there is only one insurer with a home office in the state. Nine states have over 100 domestic insurers in the field of property and liability insurance: **California, Illinois, Iowa, Minnesota, New York, Ohio, Pennsylvania, Texas,** and **Wisconsin.**

TYPES OF INSURER BY LINE OF INSURANCE SOLD.   Historically insurers in the United States were organized on a monoline basis because of the requirements of the various state insurance laws. Thus insurers could be classified as **fire and allied lines, marine, casualty, title, surety, life,** and **health.** With the passage of multiple-line legislation many of the large property and liability insurers became **multiple-line insurers,** with the result that the distinction between property and casualty insurers became blurred.

INTERNAL ORGANIZATION OF INSURERS.   Whether insurers are stock corporations or mutuals, the **internal organizations** are similar. Each type has a *board of directors* that appoints a **chief executive officer.** Historically, the internal organization of property and liability insurers reflected the lines of insurance sold. For example, there would be a vice-president for fire insurance, marine insurance, and other lines, as well as a claims vice-president, and a vice-president of marketing and other functions, depending on the size of the insurer. In the past 10–15 years there has been a shift from this type of organization to one that reflects the type of customer. A number of insurers now have **vice-presidents of personal lines,** and **vice-presidents of commercial lines,** and perhaps an executive vice-president for underwriting.

Life insurers tend to organize internally in a way that reflects the type of business done by the insurer. Large insurers have **ordinary, group,** and **industrial divisions** and also have vice-presidents in charge of major functions, such as **actuarial, agency, legal, claims,** and other major aspects of life insurance activity.

Insurance associations are made up of cooperating insurers. Insurers, perhaps more than most businesses, have formed such groupings. There are more than 200 organizations in the field of property and liability insurance alone, some of which are rating bureaus (e.g., **Insurance Services Office).** Others are designed to assist in the education of employees, public relations, prevention, and underwriting. Some are national associations, others are regional or local in scope. Rating bureaus are unknown in life insurance. Associations in this field tend to promote life insurance education, the gathering of statistical data, or public relations.

REINSURANCE

DEFINITION AND SCOPE.   **Reinsurance** is the process of one insurer, called the **primary insurer** or **ceding insurer,** transferring a part or all of a risk it has accepted to another insurer, known as the **reinsurer.** Reinsurers may be engaged only in the reinsurance business or may sell insurance to the public as well. The transaction is called a **cession.** Reinsurers may also reinsure, in which case the procedure is called a **retrocession.** A paper that gives the details of each transaction used is a **bordereau.** One of the primary purposes of reinsurance is to enable a ceding insurer to transfer risk that may exceed its usual underwriting **retention** limits. Although reinsurance has been known for over 200 years, its widespread use has developed within the past 50 years.

REINSURANCE IN PROPERTY AND LIABILITY INSURANCE.   In property and liability insurance there are two reinsurance methods: (1) **facultative** (or specific or optional) and (2) **treaty** (or automatic). In facultative reinsurance, which was the first type offered, each risk is submitted separately by the ceding company to the reinsurer. Appropriate papers and description of the risk must accompany each offering. The **ceding insurer** may choose where it wishes to offer risks, and the reinsurer may accept or reject an offering. Although facultative reinsurance is still in use, it is declining in importance largely because of the time involved in placing the insurance.

   Treaty or automatic reinsurance is an arrangement whereby the ceding reinsurer agrees to cede and the reinsurer agrees to accept a portion of every risk involved (*Encyclopedia Britannica,* Vol. 19, p. 81). It is common to place treaties with more than one reinsurer with each one accepting a proportionate part of the business.

   Reinsurance treaties may be classified as (1) **quota-share,** (2) **surplus,** and (3) **excess of loss** and may be used with either the facultative or automatic type of agreement. In a **quota-share arrangement** the ceding insurer promises to cede a fixed share of every risk that it accepts from its customers (*Encyclopedia Britannica,* Vol. 19). A **surplus treaty** is based on the concept of a **retention** of the amount of each risk the ceding insurer is willing to keep in accordance with its underwriting practices. The excess above the retention is the surplus, and this part of the risk is distributed among the reinsurers in accordance with an agreed upon proportion. **Excess of loss** arrangements are not based on the concept of reinsuring a portion of each individual risk but rather on the concept of protecting against catastrophe by asking the reinsurer to cover the proportion of any one loss that goes beyond a specified, substantial dollar amount. There are a number of variations on the excess of loss concept, such as **excess of loss ratio** reinsurance, **catastrophe excess, spread-loss cover,** and **stop-loss cover.**

REINSURANCE IN LIFE INSURANCE.   As in property and liability insurance, the reinsurance of life insurance contracts may be on a facultative or a treaty basis. Either of two plans is used with facultative or automatic treaties to determine the reinsurer's liability in the case of loss: the **yearly renewable term plan** and the **coinsurance plan** (Heubner and Black, *Life Insurance,* p. 382).

   The **yearly renewable term plan** is based on the concept of transferring to the reinsurer all or part of the net amount of risk (face of the contract less the reserve) and the primary insurer "pays premiums on a yearly renewable term basis" (Huebner and Black, *Life Insurance,* p. 382). Since the net amount of risk decreases each year, retention of a flat amount results in a decreasing amount of reinsurance each year.

   In the **coinsurance plan** the ceding insurer transfers a part of each contract it writes to the reinsurer, which "assumes a share of the risk according to the terms that govern the original policy" (Huebner and Black, *Life Insurance,* p. 382). The reinsurer receives a proportionate share of the premium less certain deductions, including commissions and an agreed upon expense allowance. The reinsurer must also reimburse the ceding insurer for a proportionate amount of dividends paid. A **modified coinsurance plan** is available in which the ceding insurer retains the entire policy reserve. This plan may be preferred by small and medium-sized insurers for whom the retention of assets may be more crucial than for larger companies.

In recent years some of the **nonproportional reinsurance methods** of property and liability insurance have been introduced into life insurance. Examples are stop-loss reinsurance, spread-loss reinsurance, and catastrophe reinsurance. These forms have not yet been widely used.

INSURANCE CONTRACTS

Insurance **contracts** are **legal documents.** To be enforceable they must have certain characteristics. Required of all contracts are the following: (1) **offer and acceptance,** (2) **legal competence** to enter into the contract, (3) **consideration,** and (4) **legal purpose.** Although insurance contracts are similar to other contracts, differences exist because of their subject matter and use.

TYPES OF INSURANCE CONTRACT. There are no **standard** insurance contracts in the sense that all contracts read the same regardless of the insurer from which they are purchased. Nevertheless, there are a few forms such as the **1943 New York standard fire insurance policy** and the **standard workers' compensation and employers' liability policy** that are widely used by most, if not all, insurers and are approved by the majority of the states. In addition, every state has statutes requiring the inclusion of **standard provisions** in certain kinds of contract.

Apart from the specific subject matter of the contract (e.g., fire, inland marine, and crime), property and liability insurance contracts may be classified according to whether they cover property in fixed or variable locations and whether all or only a part of the property is covered in a single contract. A **specific contract** insures designated property for a stipulated amount. A **blanket contract** covers more than one class of property at a given location or property located at more than one location.

A **schedule contract** provides specific protection for more than one type of property or interest against several enumerated perils and hazards, or against several exposures to loss as enumerated in the schedule. A **package contract** is one that combines different lines of insurance (multiple-line type) such as fire, theft, personal liability, and often medical payments in one contract, and requires the purchase of fixed or minimum amounts of insurance under each coverage. This type of contract is to be distinguished from **multiple-peril contracts:** a number of perils may be included in one such contract, but not more than one line of insurance.

A **floater contract** insures property wherever it may be located, including **goods in transit,** but it usually excludes property on the premises of the insured's principal place of business. A **multiple-location contract** provides insurance for **fluctuating inventories at several locations.** Periodic reporting of the amounts of stock located at the various places is usually required. This contract is designed to meet the requirements of firms having many stores or warehouses, often in different states. Since it does not cover goods in transit, it is not a floater type of policy.

STRUCTURE OF INSURANCE CONTRACTS. The internal structure of all insurance contracts tends to follow a specific pattern, which is more obvious in some contracts than in others. Since the contract defines the conditions of the transfer, it must describe the risk being transferred, state what the insurer promises to do, and specify what conditions must be met for the promise to become a reality. Inasmuch as there are substantial differences between life and nonlife insurance contracts, it is useful to consider them separately.

Property and Liability Insurance.   In property and liability insurance the basic structure of the contract includes the **declarations, insuring agreement(s), exclusions,** and **conditions.** Endorsements and/or riders may also be added. The **declarations** contain a brief description of the insured and property that is the subject matter of the insurance. The **insuring agreement** describes the promise or promises of the contract. In a **named peril** contract perils that are not listed are not covered. The insuring agreement may be of the **"all-risk"** type, which means the contract insures against loss of property from any peril to which it might be exposed, subject to specific exceptions. "All-risk" contracts offer many advantages for the insurance buyer, but to the extent that they provide coverage of risks that the insured might prefer to bear in some other manner, they prevent rather than aid in the specialized treatment of risk.

The **exclusions** section serves to modify the insuring agreement by excluding property or perils or limiting the amount of recovery on certain types of property. Although there may be a specifically labeled exclusions section, exclusions and limitations can appear throughout the contract. The **conditions** section contains a variety of requirements that must be met by the insured before recovery can be obtained from the insurer. Among these requirements are **notice of loss, proof of loss, time limits on filing suit, assignment, cancellation,** and **assistance and cooperation of the insured.**

Life Insurance.   The **life insurance contract** closely resembles the internal plan found in property and liability insurance, although various parts of the contract are not labeled in the same way. There are few exclusions and limitations in the life contract, and in general, death from any cause is covered, so the insuring agreement is brief. Conditions are generally contained in the **general section** of the contract. Parts of the contract are peculiar to life insurance. If the contract is issued on a participating basis, a **dividends section** appears in the contract, and the insured is given at least four options, including receiving the dividends in cash, using them to help pay the premium, using them to purchase an additional face amount of insurance, or leaving them on deposit with the insurer. If a permanent form of life insurance is issued, such as whole life, paid for on a level premium basis, the contract will contain **nonforfeiture** and **loan sections.** The nonforfeiture options are payment of the cash value, extended term insurance, and paid-up insurance of a reduced face amount. Life insurers agree to pay the proceeds in a variety of ways, and **optional modes of settlement** sections are common in life insurance contracts. Thus proceeds may be paid in cash, as an annuity, or left on deposit with the insurer. Riders are often placed on life insurance contracts. Three that are typical are **double indemnity, waiver of premium in the event of disability,** and **guaranteed insurability.**

COMMON PROPERTY AND LIABILITY INSURANCE CONTRACT PROVISIONS.

Despite the nonstandard character of insurance contracts, a number of provisions are common to many of them. Among the most important of these provisions or clauses in property and liability insurance contracts are: (1) **coinsurance,** (2) **other insurance,** (3) **pro rata distribution,** (4) **replacement cost,** (5) **mortgage interests,** and (6) **subrogation.**

The **coinsurance clause** is fairly common in commercial property and liability insurance contracts. The requirements of the clause must be upheld if the insured is to collect in full on partial losses. Typically a coinsurance clause requires that the face of the contract equal 80% of the **actual cash value** of the property (replacement cost less depreciation) **at the time of loss.** Otherwise the insured becomes a "coinsurer" and, in effect, pays part of the loss. The operation of an 80% coinsurance clause may be illustrated as follows:

Value of the property	$250,000
Face amount of insurance	$150,000
Required face amount	$200,000
Loss	$5,000

Under the provisions of the coinsurance clause, the insurer pays the proportion of the loss that the face amount of the insurance bears to the amount of insurance required by the clause. In the example given above the insurer would pay

$$\frac{\$150,000}{200,000} \times \$5,000 = \frac{3}{4} \times 5,000 = \$3,750$$

The insured's share of the loss would be $1,250.

The coinsurance clause is introduced for the purpose of establishing **equity in rates.** In fire insurance, for example, rates are quoted per $100 of insurance and the rate does not vary with the amount of insurance carried. Since the majority of losses to property are only partial, the probability of a partial loss is greater than the probability of a total loss and the **rate** charged should be less for those insuring to value than for those who do not so insure. One way of avoiding use of the coinsurance clause is to establish a system of **graded rates,** although a graded system of rates would probably add substantially to insurance costs.

One of the problems that arises in property and liability insurance is that more than one contract may cover a particular loss. If a loss occurs under these circumstances, the contract provides for a method of settlement that will not permit the insured to recover more than the loss sustained. A typical provision is the **pro rata liability clause,** which limits the insurer's liability in a given loss to the proportion of the loss that the insurance bears to the total insurance covering the loss. The pro rata clause works best if all the contracts covering the loss are **concurrent,** that is, if they read alike. If the contracts are noncurrent, which may happen if different endorsements or clauses are attached, problems may arise in securing an adjustment of loss that would be fair to the insured as well as the insurer.

A provision that appears when a blanket contract covers several locations is the **pro rata distribution clause,** which distributes coverage among the different locations in the proportion that the values at the different locations bear to the total value of all locations at the time of loss. Without this clause, a small blanket contract might be adequate to give complete indemnity for losses to large property values at separate locations.

Although it is fairly typical for losses in property and liability insurance to be settled on the basis of **actual cash value** at time of loss, it is possible to obtain settlement on a **replacement cost new** basis, provided certain requirements are met—notably, the face of the contract must bear an appropriate relationship to the cost required to replace the building new at the time of loss, usually 80%. Replacement cost clauses are routine in homeowners' insurance and may be added to commercial contracts. For the insured to obtain a replacement cost settlement, he must actually replace the building lost, and a contract may require that replacement take place on the same premises and for the same occupancy and use.

Often real property is mortgaged and protection is needed for both the mortgagor's and mortgagee's interests. Such protection could be obtained by issuing separate contracts, but it is more usual to combine the interests in one contract through the use of the **mortgagee** clause. The clause fully protects the mortgagee's interest even to the extent that the right to receive payment is not invalidated by any action that the insurer may take against the mortgagor because of any act or neglect on his part. The mortgagee does assume certain responsibilities, among them notification of the insurer of "any change of ownership or occupancy or increase of hazard which shall come to the knowledge of said mortgagee (or trustee). . .and the mortgagee (or trustee) shall, on demand, pay the premium for such increased hazard for the term of use thereof.'' (*Study Kit for Students of Insurance*, p. 6.)

The **subrogation clause** is included in property insurance contracts in protection of the principle of indemnity (see below.) It may happen that the insured has a right to collect from the insurer under the terms of the contract, but also has a right to sue a third party because the loss was caused through the negligence of that party. There is a possibility that the insured could collect twice and thus receive considerably more than the value of the loss. The subrogation clause prevents this possibility by making clear the intention and right of the insurer, upon the payment of a claim to **take over the right of action** that an insured may possess against any party responsible or liable for the loss (Greene and Trieschmann, *Risk and Insurance*.)

BASIC LEGAL DOCTRINES SURROUNDING INSURANCE CONTRACTS.   In addition to the legal aspects of insurance contracts, already considered, there are a number of legal doctrines that govern the issuance, interpretation, and validity of insurance contracts, although the contract itself may not make specific reference to them. Chief among these doctrines are: (1) **indemnity,** (2) **insurable interest,** (3) **representation and warranty** (4) **concealment,** and (5) **waiver and estoppel.**

Indemnity.   In general, insurance contracts are regarded as contracts of indemnity, meaning that an insured should not recover more than he lost. There are some exceptions to this principle. Life insurance contracts are not contracts of indemnity in that the face of the contract is paid on death, and questions of value do not arise at the time the loss is settled. Marine insurance contracts in many instances also constitute an exception in that the settlement of a total loss is based on a value agreed upon at the inception of the contract.

Insurable Interest.   Typically insurance contracts may not be issued unless the person seeking the insurance has an **insurable interest** in the life or object being insured, which means that the insured must stand to suffer financially if loss occurs. In property and liability insurance the requirement prevents wagering, reduces the moral hazard, and serves as a measure of the loss. An insurable interest is required in life insurance to prevent wagering and to reduce the moral hazard. Whether an insurable interest exists in property and liability insurance depends on the type of legal grip the insured may have on the property. For example, ownership in fee simple absolute conveys an insurable interest. In life insurance insurable interests are conveyed by the nature of the relationships involved. A husband has an insurable interest in the life of his wife, for example, and the wife in the life of a husband. Presumably everyone has an insurable interest in his own life.

Representations and Warranties.   In negotiating an insurance contract, oral or written statements are made by the insured to the insurer often as a result of filling out an application. If any of the statements subsequently turn out to be false, grounds may exist for the voidance of the contract by the insurer. If the statements are regarded as **representations** (and except for the application in life insurance are not a part of the contract), materiality must be established before the contract can be declared void by the insurer. If the statements are regarded as **warranties,** and are thus a part of the contract, an incorrect statement, regardless of materiality, may serve as grounds for voidance. Today most statements made by insureds in connection with personal contracts are regarded as representations, although in some business contracts warranties are still in use (Crane, *Insurance Principles and Practices*, p. 50).

Concealment.   The failure to reveal a material fact or circumstance to the insurer, even if not asked, is called concealment. The usual rule is that a concealment must be a fraudulent or intentional withholding of a fact the applicant knows to be material. Furthermore, the fact must not be "readily apparent to the insurer" (Crane, *Insurance Principles and Practices*, p. 61). The effect of a concealment is to give the insurer grounds for voiding the contract.

Waiver and Estoppel.   After an insurance contract has been entered into, no changes in the contract are contemplated unless agreed to by the insurer. However, insurers are typically represented by people such as agents and adjusters, who may have the power to act for them and may through words or actions do something that constitutes a **waiver** or a relinquishment of a known right. Should it be legally held that a waiver has occurred, the insurer will be **estopped** from "denying liability on the basis of this violation at some time in the future" (Vaughan and Elliott, *Fundamentals of Risk and Insurance*, p. 162).

COMMERCIAL LIABILITY INSURANCE

Commercial liability insurance contracts are available to owners or operators of business firms to protect against the financial consequences of liability suits alleging bodily injury or property damage to employees or members of the public because of negligence by the owner or operator.

LIABILITY AND NEGLIGENCE.   Negligence may be defined as doing what a reasonable and prudent man would not do or failing to do what a reasonable and prudent man would do, acting in the same circumstances. Negligence may give rise to liability claims based not only on the actions of the owner and operator of the business but also on the acts of agents or employees. An injury to another person arising out of anything other than a breach of contract is a **tort.** An injury from a legal viewpoint arises when a person's rights are wrongfully invaded. Negligence is a tort, as are libel, assault, and slander. Although risk managers must be concerned about all torts that may bring about loss, major attention is given to torts arising from negligence, since these are chance events and are typically insurable.

For an act to be deemed negligent, it must be a **voluntary act.** The voluntary act may be intentional or unintentional; but even an unintentional negligent act is not excused under the law, and liability claims are not negated on this basis. Intentional negligence may give rise to both criminal and civil action, whereas unintentional negligence will give rise to civil action only.

For damages to be awarded as a result of a negligent act, the act must be the proximate (contributing) cause of the loss, and it must be possible to connect the injury with the act. Even when a party is guilty of a negligent act, **legal defenses** may be raised, including **contributory negligence** and **assumed risk.** Because of workers' compensation and employers' liability statutes, however, the latter defense, has been nearly eliminated in employee actions against employers.

WORKERS' COMPENSATION AND EMPLOYERS' LIABILITY.   Employers owe certain standards of care to their employees. Breach of these standards may give rise to damage suits or to the necessity for compensation under workers' liability statutes. The **standards of care** typically required are as follows:

The employer must provide a safe place to work, and when danger exists the employee must be warned.

The employer must employ reasonably competent individuals, and they must be provided with adequate tools.

The employer must have and enforce proper rules of conduct to minimize the possible hazards (Bickelhaupt, *General Insurance*).

The **workers' compensation and employers' liability** contract is designed to serve as a way for the employer to transfer his liability for payment to employees under **workers' compensation statutes** to an insurer. The contract is issued separately and typically does not appear as a part of package or multiple-line contracts. The insuring agreement of the contract provides that under coverage A the insurer will "pay promptly when due all compensation and other benefits required of the insured by the workers' compensation law" and under coverage B will pay "on behalf of the insured all sums which the insured shall become legally obligated to pay as damages because of bodily injury by accident or disease, including death at any time resulting therefrom, . . ." (*Study Kit for Students of Insurance*, p. 112).

In addition to the amounts payable under coverages A and B, the insurer also agrees to:

(1) defend any proceeding against the insured alleging such injury and seeking damages on account thereof, even if such suit is groundless, false, or faudulent . . ., (2) pay all premiums on bonds to release attachments for an amount not in excess of the applicable limit of liability of this policy, all premiums on appeal bonds required in any such defended proceeding or suit. . ., (3) pay all expenses incurred by the company, all costs taxed against the insured in any such proceeding or suit and all interest accruing after entry of judgment until the company (insurer) has paid or tendered or deposited in court such part of such judgment as does not exceed the limit of the company's (insurer's) liability thereon, and (4) reimburse the insured for all reasonable expenses, other than loss of earnings incurred at the company's (insurer's) request." (*Study Kit for Students of Insurance*, p. 112.)

BUSINESS LIABILITY OTHER THAN WORKERS' COMPENSATION AND EMPLOYERS' LIABILITY.

Business liability insurance includes primarily the **liability of landlords and tenants, product liability, liability for acts or agents, liability arising out of the ownership and operation of vehicles, bailment liability, liability imposed by contract,** and **officers' and directors' liability.** Knowledge of some of the basic characteristics of these forms of liability is essential to an understanding of the contracts issued by insurers to indemnify the insured in case of loss.

Liability of Landlords and Tenants.

The **owner** of real property and/or his **tenants** owe a certain degree of care to those who enter the premises. Three classes of individuals may be affected: **invitees, licensees,** and **trespassers.** The degree of care owed to these classes of persons varies widely.

The greatest degree of care is owed to an invitee, for example, a customer in a retail store. A **licensee,** such as a delivery man or messenger, might suffer injuries because of negligence by the owner or tenant, but the latter might be held innocent of negligence by the court if reasonable steps had been taken to warn the licensee of a particular danger. **Trespassers,** who are legally defined as all persons other than invitees or licensees, may also be injured while on the premises, but no positive standard of care is usually owed to such individuals. In most situations if a trespasser is injured by or through some hazard, even if hidden, the landlord or tenant will probably not be held liable. An exception may arise with respect to an attractive nuisance, such as, in some jurisdictions, a swimming pool.

It is generally accepted under the law that the operators, or **tenants,** of real property take on whatever legal duties the landlord normally owes to members of the public. In some cases courts have held that the landlord does not completely succeed in transferring his liability to the operator or tenant because, for example, the landlord may not have abandoned all of the premises to the occupant. There are some situations where responsibilities generally cannot be shifted. An example would be losses caused by violations of pertinent ordinances or failure to exercise reasonable care in making excavations.

Product Liability.   Product liability cases have increased considerably in recent years. From 1960 to the early 1970s, the number of product liability suits increased from approximately 50,000 to 500,000 (Greene, "The Changing Environment for American Liability Insurance *Kathleen Price Bryan Lectures,* University of North Carolina, Greensboro, N.C., November 18, 1977). Greene estimated that the number of liability suits were approaching 1 million in 1977. A firm may incur liability in connection with a product that it manufactures, processes, or distributes. If injury to a person or to property results from the use or consumption of a faulty product, there may be grounds for legal action in the courts. Such actions are generally based on **breach of warranty** or **negligence.** Negligence may arise with respect to particular products because of some impurity or foreign object or faulty construction.

Liability for Acts of Agents.   If an **agent** is acting within the scope of his authority or employment, the employer may be held liable for the agent's negligence. If through his voluntary act an agent brings injury to a third party, he may be held personally liable.

A distinction should be made between the actions of an agent and the actions of an **independent contractor.** Even though the independent contractor may be performing work for another, the latter is not usually held liable for the negligence of the contractor. On the other hand, if the employer controls or closely supervises the work of the contractor, he may be held liable for the contractor's work.

Liability of Owners and Operators of Vehicles.   In the event of an automobile accident caused by **negligence** or **misconduct,** three parties may be held legally liable: (1) the **driver,** whether owner or nonowner, (2) the **owner,** for the negligence of those operating his car, and (3) an **employer,** even though he may not be the owner, for the negligence of agents or employees using automobiles in the employer's business. Automobile insurance contracts are designed to provide financial protection in the event these parties become legally obligated to respond to damages. Responsibility for the operation of other vehicles, such as airplanes and boats, is similar to that for automobiles, and insurance contracts have been designed to take account of the nature and extent of the liability of those owning or operating them.

Liability of Bailees.   In the handling of property for another, a **bailee–bailor relationship** exists. The bailee, who has physical possession of the property, is required to exercise the care that a reasonably prudent man would exercise over his own property. Typical of the liability that is created by bailments is that which arises in respect to such businesses as automobile garages, dry cleaners and laundries, and various storage operations. The degree of care that may reasonably be expected is greater when the bailee accepts property for profit.

The liability of a bailee can be **altered by contract.** For such a contract to be binding, it must be consummated in accordance with the prescribed requirements of a particular jurisdiction. Some attempts to shift or avoid liability by invoking conditions stated on a parking lot ticket or bank deposit stub, for example, may not be recognized by a court as establishing an enforceable agreement.

Contractual Liability.   A business may agree to assume in whole or in part the common law or other liability of another party, provided the agreement is not in contravention of public policy or statute. A typical liability of this kind is found in permits from municipal authorities, in certain types of railroad agreement, and in contracts to supply goods or services.

Officers' and Directors' Liability.   In recent years officers and directors of businesses have been subject to an increasing number of liability suits alleging negligence in the performance of their duties. Charges of negligence may arise out of failure to attend board meetings, lack of care in decision making, or similar matters.

INSURANCE CONTRACTS FOR BUSINESS LIABILITY RISKS.   Insurance contracts for liability exposures may be purchased for particular types of liability, such as automobile, or they may be written on a **comprehensive** basis designed to cover in a single contract all or most of the exposure a business may have to various types of liability. Coverage for liability may also be a part of package contracts that include liability along with a variety of property risks.

Although each type of liability coverage has important provisions relating only to it, most liability contracts agree to the following types of payment: (1) the amount of judgments awarded by a court subject to the limits stated in the contract—these limits are typically stated separately in respect to bodily damage and property damage, with a maximum limit on behalf of any one person and a larger maximum stated as the amount that will be paid on behalf of all persons injured in an accident; (2) all costs in defense of a suit (see statements above in connection with workers' compensation and employers' liability); (3) expenses incurred in giving emergency medical and surgical aid at the time of an accident; and (4) expenses incurred in assisting in the defense against a suit at the request of an insurer, not including the loss of earnings.

There are a number of *exclusions* generally found in liability insurance contracts, including intentional injury; damage to property in the care, custody, or control of the insured; war risk; and liability assumed under contract. Other exclusions listed are usually designed to prevent duplication of coverage where the risk is expected to be covered by other insurance, such as automobile or workers' compensation.

PROFESSIONAL LIABILITY.   Providers of professional services are required to exercise reasonable care in the performance of their work, and if negligence can be shown, they may be required to respond to damages imposed by law. The financial liability may extend beyond that of the direct losses or costs to include **remuneration for psychic damages.** The professional persons who may be involved in liability suits include physicians, pharmacists, dentists, lawyers, accountants, fiduciaries, and insurance agents, as well as contractors. When brought against members of the medical profession, suits for negligence in the performance of professional duties are usually referred to as **malpractice suits,** and when brought against accountants, lawyers, and similar professionals as **errors and omissions suits.** Recent years have seen an upsurge in the number of suits against professionals as well as in the size of the awards. One of the results has been an increase in the amount of difficulty in obtaining such insurance, particularly at reasonable prices.

COMMERCIAL PROPERTY INSURANCE

INSURANCE AGAINST PHYSICAL DAMAGE TO PROPERTY.   As noted previously, many property insurance contracts are available to the owners and operators of businesses to protect against the financial consequences of fortuitous damage to property from various perils. Space does not permit a complete consideration of them all, and only some of the more widely known and utilized contracts are discussed here.

Fire and Allied Lines.   The basic standard fire insurance contract protects against the perils of **direct loss** by **fire and lightning,** and by **removal from the premises** of property endangered by the perils insured against. It covers only specific locations, and only the specific interests of the insured as described in the contract. It may cover both building and contents, or either separately, depending on the interest of the insured. The policy is subject to numerous stipulations, conditions, and exclusions.

The standard fire insurance contract is not issued by itself but must be completed by attaching an appropriate **form** or endorsement. The specific form attached will depend on whether a home or business building is being insured, on whether all-risk or named peril coverage is desired, and on the number of additional perils to be added. The form describes the property covered in more detail than the basic contract and extends the perils insured against. Thus the basic contract plus a form make the fire contract a multiple-peril coverage. The additional perils provided by the general property form include **windstorm, hail, smoke, explosion, riot, riot attending a strike, civil commotion, aircraft and vehicles,** and **vandalism or malicious mischief.** These added perils are subject to the same exact definition and to the same kind of conditions, exclusions, and limitations as the standard contract, but they are also subject to **special limitations** included on the form itself.

Multiple-Line Insurance Contracts for the Business Firm.   Although fire and allied lines insurance may be written on a monoline basis, increasingly they are included as a part of multiple-line contracts that cover, in addition to fire, many forms of casualty insurance.

Jewelers' Block Contract.   This contract was the first business multiple-line policy to be sold, and is used by jewelry retailers, wholesalers, or manufacturers. It is written as inland marine insurance (see below) and covers all risks of loss or damage to a jeweler's stock anywhere in the United States. It also protects property entrusted to the jeweler by others, and may be extended to include the theft of money.

Mercantile Block Contract: Commercial Property Coverage.   The mercantile block contract is prepared by attaching an appropriate form to the standard fire insurance contract. It insures against all risks of direct physical loss of or to property covered while anywhere in the continental United States or in transit in Canada. The property covered includes (1) stocks of merchandise, (2) fixtures, furniture, and equipment, and (3) the insured's interest in improvements and betterment of the premises.

This contract is written with a deductible and provides for the monthly reporting of values located at different places, as in the multiple-location fire insurance contract. As in all "all-risk" types of contract, the specific exclusions must be carefully analyzed by the insured.

Manufacturers' Output Contract.   The manufacturers' output contract provides manufacturers with all-risk protection of **personal property located off the insured's premises.** It is a separate multiple-line contract, not simply an extension of the standard fire contract. It is prepared on a reporting form basis and specifies three limits of liability: at each location, on any one conveyance, and while property is located at conventions or fairs. It does not cover real property except for improvements and betterments.

Special Multiperil Contract.   During the past 15–20 years numerous package contracts have been developed for business firms. Some of these are nonbureau, independent forms that vary among insurers. A bureau form that is frequently used is the **special multiperil contract,** which is now available to over 700 classifications of businesses (Vaughan and Elliott, *Fundamentals of Risk and Insurance,* p. 507). The coverages in the contract are divided into four sections: Section I, Property Coverage; Section II, Liability Coverage; Section III, Crime Coverage; and Section IV, Boiler and Machinery Coverage. The minimum coverage required consists of Section I and Section II.

Ocean Marine Contracts.   Ocean marine insurance is the oldest branch of the insurance business, and many of its features show the influence of the practices and customs developed among the individual underwriters in London.

Losses in marine insurance may be **partial** or **total,** falling on one interest alone, such as the owner of cargo, or shared by all interests involved in a voyage, including the owner of the ship and the owner of the cargo, as well as the owner of the freight interest.

The word **"average"** is used in ocean marine insurance to refer to a loss that is less than a total loss. Partial losses may be either a **particular average loss,** involving only one interest, or a **general average** loss, which is borne proportionally by all interests when it occurs because some or all cargo must be voluntarily sacrificed to save a ship. The settlement of general average losses is a highly technical matter, usually entrusted to specialized **general average adjusters.**

Ocean marine insurance contracts may be used to protect any one of four different interests. (1) that of the owners or charterers and of mortgagees in the **hull,** machinery, and equipment; (2) that of owners, consignees, commission merchants, and others in the **cargo;** and (3) that of owners or charterers of ships in **freight** charges that may be collectable only if the voyage is successfully completed (this interest is rarely insured in a separate policy, but is generally included in valuing the hull and cargo interests); (4) in addition, the owners of ships may be protected from the financial consequences of their negligence or that of their agents through **protection and indemnity coverage.**

The perils covered by a typical marine insurance contract are:

1. **Perils of the sea** such as sinking, stranding, overturning, collision, lightning, and action of wind and waves.

2. **Perils on the sea,** which include fire, jettisons, damage to the ship or the cargo due to barratry of the masters and mariners, and "all other perils," meaning the perils that are related to the ones already enumerated.

3. **Additional perils that may be added** by agreement. The contract may be extended to cover theft, leakage, spoilage of refrigerated foods, and pilferage.

A clause extending coverage to losses attributable to latent defects in machinery, hull, and appurtenances and known as the **Inchmaree clause** is frequently added. Liability for damage to another ship, its cargo, and other interests may be provided by an added endorsement or a **running-down clause.** A **warehouse-to-warehouse clause** may extend coverage to perils on the land, including fire, earthquake, flood, and collision.

Because of legislative modifications over the years, common carriers such as ships, railroads, trucks, and airplanes have a relatively low degree of liability for cargo for which they may be responsible. Therefore, the shipper or the receiving firm needs to consider carefully the risk he may be bearing in the sending or receiving of goods. Marine insurance can be very helpful in protecting against these risks.

Inland Marine Contracts. Inland marine insurance, like ocean marine is a form of **transportation insurance.** The distinction between the two is based on the fact that ocean marine is primarily concerned with transportation risks over water, whereas inland marine deals primarily with risks associated with transportation over land and in the air. Inland marine contracts fall into three major groups: transportation contracts, floater contracts, and contracts covering instrumentalities of transportation.

Transportation Contracts. The basic transportation contract is the **inland transit policy,** which is completed for each special class of transportation insurance by the attachment of special forms to fit the particular needs of the insured. Either the carrier or the owner of the cargo may obtain the coverage. The carrier is interested primarily in protecting itself against legal liability for loss and will typically not purchase insurance against direct physical loss. The principal contracts covering direct losses are: (1) **trip transit policies,** covering single shipments, and (2) **annual transit policies,** which may be written to cover incoming shipments as well as outgoing shipments and may be written on both an annual and an open form. The most widely used contract covering the liability of the carrier is the **motor carriers' cargo liability policy.**

Floater Contracts. A floater contract is one that covers property. Coverage under such contracts may be worldwide, although some of them are limited to the continental United States, and include all risks subject to listed exclusions. Some of the better known **commercial floaters** covering an owner's interest are: **contractor's equipment floater, installation risks floater, installment sales floater, mobile agricultural equipment floater, physicians' and surgeons' floater,** and **radium floater.**

Floaters may also be used to cover the liability of the bailee for goods entrusted to his care. The liability may be either legally imposed or voluntarily assumed. Aside from liability, a bailee may have an interest in the property of others because of the possible loss of payment for his services. Examples of floaters used for this purpose are **laundries' and dry cleaners' insurance, furriers' customers' insurance,** and **cold storage locker insurance.**

Instrumentalities of Transportation. Inland marine insurers are authorized to sell contracts that cover property that is not movable itself but is generally related to the transportation risk. Such property includes **bridges and tunnels, pipelines, wharves and piers, power transmission lines, telephone and telegraph lines,** and **neon signs.**

Boiler and Machinery Contracts. Boiler and machinery insurance is highly specialized, and losses covered by this insurance are often excluded from other property contracts. Insurers that sell insurance covering losses to steam boilers and machinery typically undertake periodic and extensive inspections as a way of minimizing losses. Thus the premium collected by these insurers is in many ways in the nature of a service charge.

The basic contract is completed by attaching a number of schedules that define the "object" to be insured and the "accident" with respect to that object. The contract covers the insured against loss to the object, as defined, caused by the accident in the schedules. The objects covered by the contract may be boilers and pressure vessels or machinery. Losses may be for damage to the property, and for property damage and bodily injury liability to others.

Miscellaneous Physical Damage Contracts.   A variety of other contracts are written to cover losses to property from a number of other perils. Some of these are necessary because of particular exclusions written into more comprehensive contracts. Among these contracts are those against flood, sprinkler leakage, and glass damage.

CONSEQUENTIAL LOSS CONTRACTS.   The fire insurance contract, even in its broadened and "all-risk" forms, provides indemnity only for **direct physical loss to property** resulting from the perils insured against. There are other losses that occur as a consequence of physical loss of property and the ensuing interruption of business that must be insured under separate contracts. The losses suffered may be related to the time period during which the business is not able to operate at full capacity, or they may be unrelated to the time taken to resume operations.

The **time element losses** include: (1) loss of income impossible to earn during the period of interruption, (2) inability to recover fixed expenses or any continuing expenses from operations during the period of interruption, and (3) extra expenses incurred if it is necessary to carry on operations in spite of loss to physical equipment. Among the consequential **losses that are unrelated to the time element are:** (1) losses to perishables on account of temperature changes, (2) loss of profit on goods already manufactured, and (3) loss of leasehold interests when a lease is cancelable following a fire.

The major types of insurance available for consequential loss are listed below:

1. Business interruption insurance, which provides indemnity for the insured or the loss of income that would have been realized had the business continued to operate; this insurance is available in several different forms adaptable to the special requirements of the type of business interrupted.

2. Contingent business interruption insurance designed to cover losses that are caused not by a loss to the insured's property but by a loss to the property of either suppliers of materials and parts or purchasers of the finished product of the insured business.

3. Extra expense insurance, which takes care of sizable additional expenses that might be required, for example, to carry on the business at a different location.

4. Rents and rental value insurance, which indemnifies for loss of use if the building is owner occupied, loss of rental income to the owner if occupied by a tenant, or loss to the tenant if he still must pay rent under a lease.

5. Leasehold interest insurance, designed to indemnify if a lease is canceled because of property damage.

6. Profits insurance for protection in case products ready for sale are destroyed by fire, say, before they can be marketed.

7. Temperature damage insurance, to provide protection when changes in temperature from a fire loss may bring about damage to refrigerating equipment.

CRIME INSURANCE CONTRACTS.   Crime insurance is written to protect the insured against losses by burglary, robbery, theft, forgery, embezzlement, and other dishonest acts. Crime contracts may be placed in three categories: (1) personal coverages providing for residence protection, (2) business coverage primarily for mercantile establishments, and (3) coverages for financial institutions.

Among the most important contracts for protecting businesses against the financial consequences of crime are: (1) the **mercantile open stock burglary policy,** which protects the insured against loss of merchandise that is not kept in a safe and is taken by a burglar or robber while the premises are not open for business; (2) the **mercantile open stock theft policy,** which adds the act of theft to the mercantile open stock burglary policy; (3) the **mercantile safe burglary policy,** designed to provide protection for money, securities, and other property usually kept in safes and vaults; (4) the **mercantile interior robbery, messenger robbery, and paymaster robbery policies,** all of which protect against losses resulting from robbery occurring under various conditions; and (5) the **money and securities broad-form policy,** designed to protect against dishonesty and for losses arising both inside and outside the premises, including destruction, disappearance, and wrongful abstraction.

Three comprehensive crime contracts provide the broadest form of crime insurance protection that mercantile, industrial, and commercial organizations can buy. These contracts are: (1) **blanket crime policy,** (2) **comprehensive dishonesty, disappearance, and destruction (3-D),** and (3) **broad-form storekeepers' policy.** The broad-form storekeepers' policy does for the owner of a small business what the 3-D does for the large organization. It does not provide, though, for the flexibility in coverages and amounts taken that the 3-D permits.

There are a number of crime insurance contracts written for **financial institutions.** Among them are several classes of **forgery bonds, bankers' blanket bonds,** the **bank burglary and robbery policy,** and the **combination safe depository policy.**

SURETYSHIP.   Suretyship is one of the oldest forms of providing financial protection against fortuitous loss. It protects against losses that may arise because a principal (e.g., an employee or contractor) does not perform as expected because of dishonesty or inability. In suretyship the contractual arrangement providing for indemnity against loss is called a bond, and there are three parties to the agreement: the **principal** whose actions may cause the loss, the **obligee** who is indemnified in case of loss, and the **surety** who serves a function similar to an insurer. Although multiple-line insurers often have surety departments, there are important differences between suretyship and insurance, and the two methods of meeting chance losses have different traditions. (For a discussion of the differences, see Crist, *Corporate Suretyship*).

The bonds sold by sureties are of two types: **fidelity bonds** and **surety bonds.** Fidelity bonds involve dishonesty and guilt, while surety bonds are more concerned with capacity or ability to perform. In practice some fidelity bonds are fairly close to insurance.

Fidelity Bonds.   Written to cover the possible dishonesty of employees, these bonds protect the employer against the loss of any kind of property and, within the scope of the contract, they cover against all losses. The bond applies only if there is dishonest intent on the employee's part. Examples of fidelity bonds are **individual bonds** covering a single employee; **name schedule bonds,** which cover several different employees named in the bond; **position schedule bonds,** which cover several different employees but identify them by position rather than by name; and **blanket bonds,** issued to cover a group of employees under a master contract. It is not necessary to identify a particular employee in a blanket bond, and two major blanket bonds are sold to commercial establishments: the **primary commercial blanket bond** and the **blanket position bond.**

Surety Bonds.   Typically surety bonds are contracts of indemnity paying to the extent an obligee has suffered loss. Some bonds, known as **forfeiture bonds,** provide that the amount of penalty will be paid under the conditions of the policy without need of proving loss. Some of the more important surety bonds are **court or judicial bonds,** such as probate bonds and litigation bonds (e.g., attachment bonds or appeal bonds), **contract bonds** (bid bonds and performance bonds), and **public official bonds.**

LIFE AND HEALTH INSURANCE CONTRACTS AND THEIR BUSINESS USES

Business uses of life insurance grow out of the need to provide for the financial problems that may arise because of uncertainties surrounding human health and survival. Death, disability, and sickness may disrupt a business as seriously as they do a family, and insurance offers a practical and effective way of meeting some of the uncertainties surrounding these events. Among the uses of life and health insurance in business are: (1) **key man insurance** (2) **funding of buy-and-sell agreements,** (3) **split-dollar insurance,** (4) **funding of deferred compensation plans,** (5) **group life insurance,** (6) **pension plans,** and (7) **group health insurance.**

KEY MAN INSURANCE.   The continued success of a business, particularly a small business, may depend on the life of one man or on the lives of a small group of men. These key men may be important because of special talents or knowledge, special skills in organization and management, or special creative drives and inspirations. The loss of key men can easily cripple a business. Life insurance on the lives of key men will provide cash for the company on the death of one or more of them, to help finance the replacement of such individuals or otherwise contribute to the financial needs of the firm. Furthermore, if a permanent form of life insurance is used, cash and loan values may provide funds in times of stringent credit conditions (Gregg and Lucas, *Life and Health Insurance Handbook,* p. 649).

FUNDING OF BUY-AND-SELL AGREEMENTS.   Small businesses, whether organized as **individual proprietorships, partnerships,** or **close corporations,** are often owned and managed by one or a few individuals whose death may be expected to lead to the cessation of the proprietorship or partnership. Often it is desirable for the business to continue, and one way to provide for this, while avoiding problems that may arise with other types of transfer, is to enter before death into a buy-and-sell agreement. This type of agreement provides for the transfer of the business or stock on the death of a proprietor, a partner, or stockholder to a party who has agreed to buy at a price set in the agreement or at a price determined by a specified valuation formula. This arrangement has a number of advantages, including the receipt by the estate of a fair price for the business, and, if the valuation is reasonable, at a price that is likely to be accepted by the government for tax purposes.

Since there has been an agreement to buy and sell, it is essential that funds to carry out the terms of the agreement be available immediately upon death of a proprietor, partner, or stockholder. Life insurance is one of the most practical ways of supplying these funds.

SPLIT-DOLLAR LIFE INSURANCE.   Split-dollar life insurance plans were originally developed for nonbusiness purposes, but today are often used as a type of employee benefit. They offer particular **advantages to younger executives** by providing large amounts of insurance during the early years when it is most needed. A **split-dollar plan** is an arrangement whereby an employer pays that part of the premium that represents the cash value of the policy in the first year and the increases in cash value in each subsequent year. The insured (the employee) pays only the part of the annual premium that exceeds the increase in the cash value on the policy, and the family of the employee receives the difference between the face amount of the policy and the cash surrender value. This arrangement results in substantial amounts of life insurance for the employee at very low cost to him.

DEFERRED COMPENSATION.   Current high income tax rates make attractive any legal and effective method of deferring compensation until a later age, when reduced income will usually place the individual in a lower income tax bracket. Employers may enter into agreements with highly paid employees to defer part of their income until after retirement. If the employee is to receive a **tax benefit,** the plan must be carefully drawn unless it is held by the IRS that he currently has vested rights in such compensation and should pay taxes on it. A possible difficulty with deferred compensation arrangements is that the employer may not have the funds to pay in accordance with the agreement. Thus consideration should be given to entering into suitable funding arrangements at the time the plan is drawn up. Life insurance may be used advantageously for this purpose, with the cash value of the policy being used to provide the promised payments.

GROUP LIFE INSURANCE.   Life insurance may be issued on an individual basis (i.e., the individual is the unit of selection) or on a group basis (i.e., the firm, labor union, or some other organization is recognized as a group for insurance purposes, and is the unit of selection). Groups may not be formed solely for the purpose of obtaining insurance. Group life insurance, issued typically on a renewable-term basis, is offered by many employers as a major employee benefit. A master contract is issued to the employer by the insurer in which life insurance benefits are made available to the employee for the ultimate benefit of their beneficiaries. Group life insurance has a number of advantages for the employee, including fairly low cash outlay because the employer contributes to the cost; substantial amounts of insurance often based on salary, position in the firm, and years of service; and absence of a physical examination requirement. **Group life insurance** in force in the United States has increased considerably over the years and now represents between 40 and 50 of the total face amount of life insurance on the books of insurers.

GROUP HEALTH INSURANCE.   The types of health insurance mentioned on page **8·9** may be written on a group or franchise basis, and these contracts find wide application in the area of employee benefits. Although insured benefits may form a large part of the health benefits offered employees, as a result of the **Health Maintenance Organization Act of 1973**, employers with an average of 25 or more employees must include in addition the option of membership in a qualified health maintenance organization, if such organizations exist in the area where the employees reside. The law recognizes that the HMO may operate on a group basis or as an **individual practice association** (IPA). If both types of organization exist in an area, the employees must be given a choice between these bases of operation.

RETIREMENT INCOME PLANS.   Plans designed to provide income during retirement have grown in importance especially from the standpoint of funding; they typically are either

trusteed or **insured.** In the United States in 1930, there were 100,000 persons covered by major pension and retirement programs that were insured with life insurance companies. By 1978 this figure had grown to well over 15 million. Retirement income plans may be classified as group annuities (including immediate participation guarantee and deposit administration plans), terminal funded group plans, individual policy pension trusts, tax sheltered annuities, individual retirement accounts (IRA), HR10 (Keogh) plans, and others (*1979 Life Insurance Fact Book*).

Pension plans, apart from their funding, are of two types: **defined contribution** and **defined benefit.** The former type of plan makes considerable use of **deferred annuities** as a way of providing benefits, although all types of plan may use some form of annuity. A trustee, for example, may be authorized, to purchase an **immediate annuity** at the time an employee retires as a way of fulfilling an obligation established by a pension plan. In the 1950s **variable annuities** were developed, based all or in part on common stock investments or on a cost of living index. By the end of 1976 some 2 million persons were covered by variable plans associated with life insurance companies.

In 1974 Congress passed the Employee Retirement Income Security Act (ERISA), which establishes standards for pension plans including reporting and disclosure, participation and vesting, fiduciary responsibility, and administration and enforcement.

INSURANCE MARKETS AND MARKETING

DEFINITION. In insurance terminology the word "market" is "used to indicate both the area of distribution and the available source of the different insurance coverages" (Magee and Serbein, *Property and Liability Insurance*, p. 31). The second use of the term is the one that is, perhaps, more often meant when one speaks of the availability of insurance markets, and **marketing of insurance** is the process of selling the product of insurers (insurance policies) to individuals and/or business firms.

CAPACITY OF INSURERS. Insurance markets are readily available for the traditional types of insurance coverage such as fire and extended coverage and workers' compensation, but may be unavailable, or available from only a few insurers, for more unusual coverages. Whether insurers are willing to provide a market depends on a number of factors, among the most important being the profit and policyholders' surplus position of the insurer, underwriting knowledge and skill, growth rate of insurers, reinsurance facilities, and the subjective attitudes of the underwriter toward risk (Greene and Serbein, *Risk Management: Text and Cases*, p. 366).

MARKET AVAILABILITY. As noted above, **market availability** may be a problem particularly for unusual coverages, and knowledge of where certain types of risk can be placed is important. Some possible sources of this type of information are: *The Insurance Market Place,* Rough Notes, Indianapolis, Indiana; *Agent's and Buyer's Guide* and *Who Writes What,* both National Underwriter Company, Cincinnati, Ohio. The first two references mainly cover the field of property and liability insurance; the last named is helpful in the field of life insurance.

METHODS OF DISTRIBUTION. Insurance contracts (policies) are generally sold through an intermediary who may be an **agent** of the insurer or a **broker** who represents the buyer.

Both are compensated by a commission paid by the insurer. In some cases one person may hold an agent's license as well as a broker's license.

Agency Systems.   In general, agents may be classified as **independent** or **exclusive.** Agents in both classifications are independent in that their relationship to the insurer is defined by an agency contract. They differ, however, in many ways, principally in that members of the first group retain ownership of their renewal lists and represent more than one insurer, while members of the second group are much closer to being employees. The independent agency system is widely used in the field of property and liability insurance, but the exclusive agency system is dominant in life insurance.

Another system of selling insurance is **direct writing,** in which the selling is done by employees of the insurer. The insurer, in effect, is contacting the public rather than acting through intermediaries.

Supervision of Agents.   Since many insurers operate over the entire United States, or at least over a wide area, supervision of agents becomes an important task. Three supervisory systems are used: (1) **general agency,** (2) **branch office,** and (3) **direct reporting** (Crane, *Insurance Principles and Practices,* p. 369). The first two systems are much more widely used than the last, with the first system being fairly typical in life insurance (although shifts in the direction of branch offices are occurring). The second system is widely used in property and liability insurance. Direct reporting is a system in which agents report directly to the insurer, especially if the latter does not have a general agency system or branch offices (Crane, *Insurance Principles and Practices,* p. 370).

A general agency system is one in which the insurer assigns a fairly large geographical area to a general agent and gives him the responsibility for developing business within that area, including the appointing of agents who work under his supervision. A **branch office** is an extension of the home office into the field. A manager, who is an employee of the insurer, is appointed to supervise the sales activities within the area the branch serves. The branch office performs a number of functions, and among its employees are claimsmen and underwriters as well as clerical staff.

UNDERWRITING AND RATING

Underwriting is the process by which an insurer selects the risks it wishes to accept from those risks being offered to it. One of the objectives of **underwriting** is to secure a risk portfolio that will produce experience at least as good as that assumed in rate making, and thus be profitable to the insurer. The underwriter must also aim for business that will produce "suitable volume and spread of risk" (Magee and Serbein, *Property and Liability Insurance,* p. 796).

UNDERWRITING IN PROPERTY AND LIABILITY INSURANCE.   Underwriting in property and liability insurance historically was done on a **monoline basis,** with underwriters specializing in particular lines. The introduction in the 1950s of **multiple-line** underwriting powers, hence multiple-line contracts, resulted in a gradual shifting of the underwriting process away from line specialization to a consideration of the multiple-line contract in its entirety.

Holton has described the **underwriting process** as consisting of five steps as follows: "(1) secure information, (2) develop alternative courses of action, (3) decide on the best course and take action, (4) evaluate the selected course of action, and (5) make corrections that are indicated." (Robert B. Holton, *Underwriting Principles and Practices,* National Underwriter Co., Cincinnati, 1973, p. 58).

UNDERWRITING IN LIFE INSURANCE.   In broad terms, the underwriting process in life insurance is not greatly different from that in property and liability insurance. Among the differences is that the property and liability agent has the power in most instances to bind the insurer, while the life insurance agent typically does not. Thus the property and liability agent, in effect, makes preliminary underwriting decisions, while the decision about acceptance or rejection in life insurance is not made until the insurer has had the opportunity to review the application.

BASIC PRINCIPLES OF INSURANCE RATE COMPUTATIONS.   Although underwriters are responsible for selecting the **rate** that is appropriate for a particular rate classification, the rates are computed, in the case of life insurance, by the actuarial departments of the various life insurers. In property and liability insurance, rates are prepared mainly by rating bureaus, which are associations of insurers, although a number of large nonlife insurers compute their own rates. All insurance rates are estimates for the future based largely on past experience and are intended to be sufficient to pay the losses that occur to the group to which they are applied, as well as the expenses of operation that may be attributed to the group. In addition, the rate should make some allowance for contingencies, and a reasonable profit, if the insurer is organized as a stock company. Except for nonfiled marine insurance rates, property and liability rates are subject to regulation. Rate regulatory laws vary, but the majority of states require prior approval of rates by the insurance commissioner before they may be used (Magee and Serbein, *Property and Liability Insurance,* p. 737).

SETTLEMENT OF LOSS

The settlement of losses is of vital concern to both the insurer and the insured. In many cases the impression the insured has of the insurer is obtained through the experience of reporting a loss and receiving reimbursement for it. This experience can be favorable or unfavorable depending on the skill and fairness with which the process is handled. The claims function has particular significance in property and liability insurance because of the complex problems that may arise in determining the value and cause of the many partial losses that occur.

FUNCTIONS OF THE CLAIMS DEPARTMENT.   The primary functions of the claims department are to determine whether the loss is covered by the contract and whether the contract is in force, and to establish the **amount of the claim** and the **time of payment.** Niggardly claims settlement or long delays in making the payment, or both, can cause much ill will and add to the insurer's expenses.

ADJUSTERS.   In establishing the amount of the claim, the insurer may use a **staff adjuster,** who is an employee of the insurer, or may seek the help of **independent adjusters** who are not staff members but may be retained as independent contractors to help with particular cases. Independent adjusters are often used in areas where insurers may not have regional or branch offices and may well expedite the settlement of claims. The insurer's claim department, of course, has the ultimate responsibility for determining the amount of the loss, applying the terms of the contract, and approving the payment of the claim.

A third type of adjuster is the **public adjuster,** who may be retained by the insured to represent him in loss settlements and to help with many of the details. An insured who has a large and complicated loss may find that such help is useful.

INSURANCE FINANCE

The financial safety of an insurer is of particular significance to the insured, and if doubt about the insurer's financial soundness exists, cost concessions should not persuade anyone to place business with that insurer. Financial soundness of an insurer may be judged by using many of the same principles followed in the analysis of any business firm. However, because of the nature of the insurance business and the requirements of statutory accounting, some special problems arise.

ASSETS.   Evaluation of the assets of an insurer involves not only a consideration of how the assets were valued, their quality, and distribution, but also recognition that in insurance there is a concept of **admitted** and **nonadmitted assets,** and only the admitted assets appear on the balance sheets in statutory accounting. Among nonadmitted assets are such items as agents' balances or uncollected premiums more than 3 months due; equipment, furniture, and supplies; loans on personal security, and the insurer's stock held as treasury stock (Strain, *Property-Liability Insurance Accounting,* p. 26). Furthermore, investments of insurers are regulated, although property and liability insurers have considerable freedom of choice in their investments for amounts over and above those that the regulatory authorities require to be held in the form of cash and high-grade bonds. In general, in property and liability insurance, funds equal to the minimum capital required must be invested in appropriate bonds and mortgages, and there must be investments in approved government or corporate bonds in an amount sufficient to meet the requirements of the various states regarding unearned premium and loss reserves. Investment regulation in life insurance is somewhat more stringent, and taking the New York law as an example, only a small percentage of the assets may be invested in common stocks and real estate.

LIABILITIES.   The principal liabilities of an insurer are represented by statutory reserves. In **property and liability insurance** the major reserves are the **unearned premium reserve** and the **loss reserve,** in **life insurance** the **policy reserve** is the major category. The manner in which these reserves are computed has an important bearing on the net worth of the insurer as reported on the balance sheet. For example, the unearned premium reserve in property and liability insurance is based on the premium paid by insureds and includes expenses as well as losses, even though the expenses are paid at the time they are incurred. Thus an equity in the unearned premium reserve arises in an amount roughly equal to the percentage of the premium represented by expenses.

RATIOS.   A number of **ratios** are used, particularly in property and liability insurance, to assess the financial performance of an insurer. Ratios are also used by insurance commissioners and form a part of an **early warning system** in regard to possible problems with solvency. Examples of ratios are (1) net worth to debt, (2) premiums written to net worth, (3) losses and expenses to premiums written, (4) total underwriting and investment profit to premiums written and (5) total gain (profit) to net worth (Greene and Serbein, *Risk Management: Text and Cases*, p. 367). A ratio that is often cited particularly for casualty insurers is premiums written to net worth (policyholders' surplus). If this ratio exceeds 2–1, there is an indication that the insured is less well protected from financial loss by the insurer than may be regarded as desirable. It is well in attempting to assess this ratio to consider other items, such as the product mix of the insurer and the experience of the insurer in regard to underwriting profit or loss.

UNDERWRITING PROFIT OR LOSS. In life insurance rate computations three **cost factors**—mortality, interest, and expense—are normally taken into account, while in property and liability insurance losses and expenses are the major factors considered. The result is that in property and liability insurance interest is not taken directly into account as one of the sources of funds for losses, and the premium charged is estimated to be sufficient to pay losses and expenses without the help of investment earnings. Investment gains and losses are, of course, considered in computing the overall profit of the insurer and may offset losses on the underwriting side. Major attention is given to underwriting profit or loss, which is the profit or loss obtained by deducting from earned premiums the incurred losses and loss adjustment expenses, and the expenses of the insurer other than those associated with losses. In addition, for summary purposes, a loss ratio is often computed (loss and loss adjustment expenses divided by earned premium) and an expense ratio (expenses other than loss adjustment expenses divided by earned premium). The combined ratio is the sum of these two ratios. If it is less than one, an underwriting profit has occurred; if it is greater than one, there has been an underwriting loss.

POLICYHOLDERS' SURPLUS. Policyholders' surplus is the net worth of the insurer. It is a measure of the protection the insured has against substantial losses of the insurer. Insurance regulatory laws require a minimum amount of capital and surplus, although the precise amount varies from state to state, and in the case of mutuals, the requirement is in terms of surplus. If the insurer does not maintain the requirement, insolvency ensues. Another reason for the importance of **policyholders' surplus** is that insufficiency of surplus can lead to curtailment of sales, which in turn has the effect of limiting the market. This phenomenon arises primarily out of the legal reserve requirements and the methods by which they are calculated. These methods can result in a drain on surplus, especially during times of rapidly increasing sales.

ACCOUNTING. In preparing the statements they submit to the insurance commissioners of the various states, insurers must use a statutory accounting basis, which differs in many ways from generally accepted accounting principles (GAAP). One of the distinguishing characteristics of **statutory accounting** is its conservatism, which results in a tendency to understate the financial position of the insurer. A person with little knowledge of insurance accounting could experience difficulty in arriving at a satisfactory evaluation of an insurer for investment purposes. This has led to the requirement that many insurers must submit statements based on generally accepted accounting principles in addition to the usual statutory statements. The requirement is, perhaps, most significant for insurers listed on stock exchanges who must meet Security and Exchange Commission requirements for GAAP statements in connection with the sale of securities.

SELECTION OF INSURERS

A significant decision in the purchasing of insurance is the selection of the insurer. A number of factors must be considered, three of which are primary: solvency, cost, and service (Greene and Serbein, *Risk Management: Text and Cases,* p. 351). A possible rule for making a choice is that, assuming solvency and service ratings (including benefits) are satisfactory, one should select the insurer with the lowest cost.

SOLVENCY.   An insurer's solvency may be judged by analyzing published statements and reviewing historical data. In addition, a great deal of published material bears on the solvency question. Alfred M. Best and Company publishes *Best's Insurance Reports, Property and Casualty; Best's Insurance Reports, Life and Health; Best's Fire and Casualty Aggregates and Averages;* and *Best's Key Rating Guide, Property and Liability,* all of which give a great deal of financial information for a large number of insurers. In addition, Best provides financial and policyholder ratings for each insurer.

COST.   In connection with buying insurance, **cost** means the net amount paid to the insurer for the product purchased. Thus cost may be the premiums paid less dividends, or in the case of the surrender of a participating whole life insurance contract after a period of years, the total premiums less total dividends less the cash surrender value; or cost may be premiums after adjustment for experience rating as in a retrospective rating plan. Although comparative cost data in property and liability insurance are not readily available, a fair amount of information is available in life insurance. Among the published sources are Best's *Flitcraft Compend* and *Interest Adjusted Index* (Gaines, Ed.).

SERVICE.   Insurers, in addition to the protection offered by their contracts, provide considerable **service** to the insured, sometimes directly and at other times through agents or other representatives. Service is not an easy factor to judge, especially on a comparative basis. Since published information of the type found for cost is not available, the insured must often rely on his own investigation of services offered and on the opinions of others.

REGULATION OF INSURANCE

In the *Southeastern Underwriters* case (*Southeastern Underwriters Association et al.,* 322 U.S. 533, 1944) it was established that insurance is interstate commerce and is therefore subject to federal regulation. Federal statutes apply in various situations, including in some instances those involving the federal antitrust acts. However, as a result of an act of Congress (Public Law 15), regulation has, for the most part, been left to the **individual states.** Insurers are regulated by the states in which they are incorporated and are also subject to extraterritorial regulation by other states in which they do business.

Each state may enact insurance legislation as it pleases, although there are a number of cases in which **uniform legislation** has been adopted by a majority of states. A major accomplishment of the **National Association of Insurance Commissioners,** composed of representatives from all the states, is the present trend toward uniformity in state insurance laws, which the association has encouraged.

The specific areas of regulation of insurance include licensing of insurers, solvency, examination of insurers, rates, reserves, policy forms, investments, unfair practices, and competence of agents (Vaughan and Elliott, *Fundamentals of Risk and Insurance* pp. 136–143).

REFERENCES

Agent's and Buyer's Guide, National Underwriters Co., Cincinnati, Ohio (Annual).

Arrow, Kenneth, *Essays in the Theory of Risk Bearing,* Markham, Chicago, 1971.

Best's Flitcraft Compend, Alfred M. Best Co., Morristown, NJ, 1979.

Best's Key Rating Guide, Property and Liability, Alfred M. Best Co., Morristown, NJ, 1979.

Best's Fire and Casualty Aggregates and Averages, Alfred M. Best Co., Morristown, NJ, 1979.

Best's Insurance Reports, Life and Health, Alfred M. Best Co., Morristown, NJ, 1979.

Best's Insurance Reports, Property and Casualty, Alfred M. Best Co., Morristown, NJ, 1979.

Bickelhaupt, D. L., *General Insurance,* 10th ed., Irwin, Homewood, IL, 1979.

Christy, James, "Selling Insurance to Risk Managers," *National Insurance Buyer,* Vol. 13, September 1966.

Crane, F. G., *Insurance Principles and Practices,* Wiley, New York, 1980.

Crist, G. H., *Corporate Suretyship,* 2nd ed., McGraw-Hill, New York, 1950.

Gaines, P., Jr., ed., *Interest Adjusted Index,* National Underwriter, Cincinnati, 1979.

Greene, M. R., and Trieschmann, X., *Risk and Insurance,* 5th ed. South-Western Publishing Co., Cincinnati, 1981.

————, and Serbein, O. N., *Risk Management: Text and Cases,* Reston Publishing Co., Reston, VA, 1978.

Gregg, D. W., and Lucas, V. B., eds., *Life and Health Insurance Handbook,* 3rd ed., Irwin, Homewood, IL, 1973.

Huebner, S. S., and Black, K., Jr., *Life Insurance,* 9th ed., Prentice-Hall, Englewood Cliffs, 1976.

Insurance Facts, Insurance Information Institute, New York, 1979.

Life Insurance Factbook, American Council on Life Insurance, Washington, D.C., 1979.

Magee, J. H., and Serbein, O. N., *Property and Liability Insurance,* 4th ed., Irwin, Homewood, IL, 1967.

Mehr, R. I., and Hedges, Bob A., *Risk Management: Concepts and Applications,* Irwin, Homewood, IL, 1974.

Schultz, R. E., and Bardwell, F. C., *Property Insurance,* Rinehart, New York, 1959.

Strain, R. W., ed., *Property-Liability Insurance Accounting,* Insurance and Statistical Association, Kansas City, MO, 1976.

Study Kit for Students of Insurance, American Mutual Alliance, Chicago, 1979.

The Insurance Market Place, Rough Notes, Indianapolis, 1980.

Vaughan, E. J., and Elliott, C. M., *Fundamentals of Risk and Insurance,* 2nd ed., Wiley, New York, 1978.

Who Writes What, National Underwriter Company, Cincinnati.

BIBLIOGRAPHY

Bachman, James E., *Capitalization Requirements for Multiple-Line Property-Liability Insurance Companies,* Irwin, Homewood, IL, 1978.

Bartleson, Edwin L., *Health Insurance,* 2nd ed., Society of Actuaries, Chicago, 1968.

Borch, Karl, *The Mathematical Theory of Insurance*, D. C. Heath, Lexington, MA, 1974.

Cooper, Robert W., *Investment Return and Property—Liability Insurance Ratemaking*, Irwin, Homewood, IL, 1974.

Fire, Casualty, and Surety Bulletins, National Underwriter Co., Cincinnati.

Jordan, C. W., Jr., *Life Contingencies*, 2nd ed., Society of Actuaries, Chicago, 1967.

Kenney, Roger, *Fundamentals of Fire and Casualty Insurance Strength*, Kenney Insurance Studies, Dedham, MA, 1967.

McGill, D. M., *Fundamentals of Private Pensions*, 4th ed., Irwin, Homewood, IL, 1979.

Rowe, W. D., *An Anatomy of Risk*, Wiley, New York, 1977.

Seal, Hilary L., *Survival Probabilities*, Wiley, New York, 1978.

———, *Stochastic Theory of a Risk Business*, Wiley, New York, 1969.

Strain, Robert W., *An Introduction to Reinsurance*, New York: College of Insurance, 1980.

Van House, C. L., and Hammond, W. R., *Accounting for Life Insurance Companies*, Irwin, Homewood, IL, 1969.

CONSUMER FINANCE

CONTENTS

**PRINCIPLES AND FORMS OF
CONSUMER CREDIT**   **3**

Definition of Consumer Credit   3
Growth of Consumer Credit Outstanding   3
Variability of Consumer Credit
Outstanding   5
Types of Installment Credit   5
Types of Noninstallment Credit   7
Holders of Consumer Credit   7
The Development of the Consumer
Credit Industry   8
   Consumer finance companies   10
   Commercial banks   10
   Credit unions   11
   Retailers   11
   Others   11
Changes in Market Share Over Time   **12**

**PRINCIPLES OF ADMINISTRATION
AND CONTROL**   **13**

Cost Factors in Determining Rate   **13**
   Risk-free rate   13
   Default risk premium   13
   Administrative expenses   13
Revenues from Consumer Credit   **13**
   Finance charges   13
   Origination fees   14
   Credit insurance fees   14
   Interchange fees and merchant discount   14
Methods of Specifying Finance Charges   **14**
   Annual percentage rate   15
   The add-on rate   15
   The discount rate   15
Nominal Rates Versus Yields on
Revolving Credit   **16**
   Previous balance   16
   Adjusted balance   16
   Ending balance   16

Risk Evaluation   **16**
   Judgmental system   17
   Credit scoring system   17
   Credit reporting agencies   17
Other Contract Terms   **17**
   Creditors' remedies   17
     Late payment charges   18
     Attorney's fee charges   18
     Repossession   18
     Deficiency judgment   18
     Blanket security   18
     Waiver of statutory exemption   18
     Garnishment   18
     Wage assignment   18
     Acceleration upon default   19
     Reaffirmation of debts after
     bankruptcy   19
     Cosignor agreement   19
     Contacting third parties   19
     Foreclosure   19
   Collection practices   19
   Prepayment provisions   19
     Rule of 78   20
     Actuarial method   20
   Credit insurance   21

**LAWS REGULATING CONSUMER
CREDIT**   **21**

Federal Laws   **21**
   Truth-in-Lending Act (1969)   22
   Fair Credit Reporting Act (1971)   22
   Fair Credit Billing Act (1969)   23
   Equal Credit Opportunity Act (1975)   23
   Fair Debt Collection Practices Act
   (1977)   23
State Laws   23
   Usury laws   23
   Small loan laws   23

CONSUMER USES OF CREDIT   23

Consumers Who Use Installment Credit   23
Trends in Consumer Debt Usage   24
   Installment debt and inflation   24

Installment debt and changes in
  demographic characteristics   25
Delinquency of Consumer Credit
Contracts   25
Personal Bankruptcies   25

CONSUMER FINANCE

A. Charlene Sullivan

PRINCIPLES AND FORMS OF CONSUMER CREDIT

DEFINITION OF CONSUMER CREDIT. Families and individuals use credit to provide for short- and intermediate-term financing and as a payment system to increase convenience of making transactions. As defined by the Federal Reserve Board, consumer credit includes short- and intermediate-term credit that is extended through regular business channels to finance the purchase of commodities and services for personal consumption, or to refinance debts incurred for such purposes. Thirty-day charge credit held by retailers, oil and gas companies, and travel and entertainment companies is not included in the consumer credit statistics published by the Federal Reserve Board. Loans against the cash value of insurance policies are not included. Home mortgage credit for financing the purchase of single-family or multifamily homes, which is long term and reported separately, is not included. However, personal loans secured by second mortgages are included in the statistics.

Consumer credit is subdivided for reporting purposes by the Federal Reserve Board into installment and noninstallment credit. **Installment credit** includes all consumer credit scheduled to be repaid in two or more payments; **noninstallment credit** includes credit scheduled to be repaid as a single, lump sum.

GROWTH OF CONSUMER CREDIT OUTSTANDING. Total consumer credit outstanding has grown rapidly in the past two decades, from a level of $44 billion outstanding in 1960 to $127 billion outstanding in 1970. By year-end 1979 there was $382.2 billion in short- and intermediate-term consumer credit outstanding. Exhibit 1 shows the amount of short- and intermediate-term consumer credit outstanding along with all net public and private debt outstanding. In 1970 consumer short- and intermediate-term credit made up 7.97% of total public and private debt. In 1975 it constituted 7.65% of total private and public debt, and in 1979 it grew to 9.0% of total debt outstanding. From these data, it is clear that the phenomenal growth in consumers' use of credit has been closely matched by the growth in total net public and private debt outstanding.

Total consumer borrowing including **mortgage credit,** as a percentage of total private and public debt outstanding, grew from 26.4% in 1970 to 29.2% in 1979. As Exhibit 2 indicates, the increase in home mortgages outstanding has accounted for the bulk of growth in household borrowing since 1972. Mortgages outstanding on one- to four-family homes rose by approximately $35 billion in 1972, compared to an increase of $108 billion in 1979. Consumer installment credit grew by approximately $20 billion outstanding in 1972 and

EXHIBIT 1 NET PUBLIC AND PRIVATE DEBT, SELECTED YEARS, 1970–1979 (BILLIONS)[a]

	1970	1975	1979
Public	487.4	781.3	1,229.4
U.S. government	343.0	558.1	916.7
State and local	144.4	223.2	312.7
Private Financial and Nonfinancial	686.2	1,154.2	1,775.4
Corporate and foreign bonds	201.6	317.3	455.7
Mortgages	178.5	315.9	474.9
Other debt	306.1	521.0	844.8
Consumer	421.7	686.2	1,241.1
Home mortgages	294.6	485.6	858.8
Consumer credit	127.1	200.6	382.3
Total	1,595.2	2,621.7	4,246.0

[a]Parts may not add to totals because of rounding.
Source: Federal Research Board, Flow of Funds series.

EXHIBIT 2   TOTAL HOUSEHOLD BORROWING

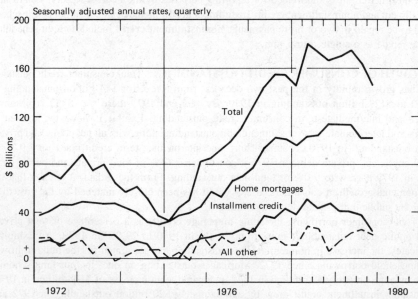

Source: Federal Reserve Board Chart Book, February 1980.

increased by approximately $42 billion in 1979. Exhibit 3 shows that until 1970 **installment credit** and noninstallment credit grew at about the same rate. However, since 1970, installment credit outstanding has grown rapidly relative to noninstallment credit outstanding. One of the major growth components of installment credit has been revolving credit.

VARIABILITY OF CONSUMER CREDIT OUTSTANDING. The volume of consumer credit outstanding has increased consistently during the past decade, although the rate of growth historically has slowed before periods of economic slowdowns. Exhibit 4, a chart of changes in consumer credit outstanding over time, reveals that consumer credit outstanding as well as mortgage credit outstanding fell sharply before and during the recessionary periods in 1969–1970 and again in 1973–1975. Data concerning the net change in consumer credit outstanding before the recessionary period in 1980 reveal that consumers sharply reduced their use of consumer credit several months before the recession started. This sharp reduction can be attributed to consumers' decreased demand for credit as well as to financial institutions' unwillingness to supply credit to that market. The effects of high money rates and restrictive usury ceilings in most states combined to limit creditors' ability to extend consumer credit profitably.

As Exhibit 4 shows, the growth rate of consumer installment credit outstanding has been considerably more variable than that of mortgage credit outstanding. Since 1974, there has been steady growth in home mortgages outstanding as a result of inflationary pressures on home prices and the switch of consumer savings from regulated savings vehicles at thrift institutions and banks into real estate and housing. As Kane stated in his discussion of the issue ("Accelerating Inflation and the Distribution of Household Savings Incentives," p. 29), real estate became the ordinary citizen's chief defense against accelerating inflation during the late 1960s.

TYPES OF INSTALLMENT CREDIT. The four types of installment credit are automobile paper, revolving credit, mobile home paper, and other loans. **Automobile paper** includes

EXHIBIT 3   CONSUMER INSTALLMENT AND NONINSTALLMENT CREDIT OUTSTANDING, 1950–1979

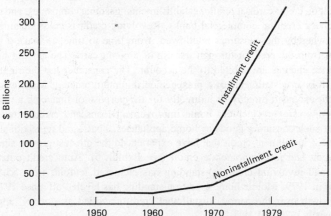

Source: Federal Reserve Board Chart Book, February 1980.

EXHIBIT 4   NET CHANGES IN CONSUMER AND MORTGAGE CREDIT OUTSTANDING

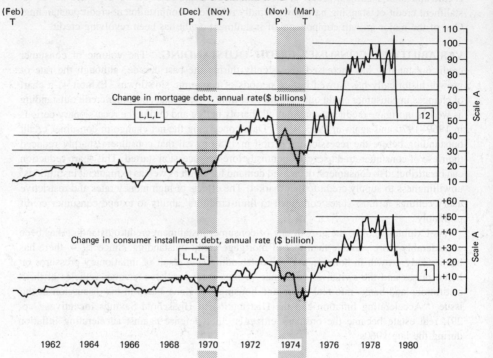

Source: U.S. Department of Commerce, *Business Conditions Digest,* March 1980, p. 32.

loans originated directly by the lending institution (direct paper) plus loans originated by a dealer and purchased by a creditor (indirect paper) for the purpose of financing a private automobile. The automobile generally serves as security for the loan. **Revolving credit** includes credit on credit cards at retailer establishments, gasoline companies, and commercial banks, and check credit at commercial banks. Revolving credit is credit obtained under an arrangement whereby the consumer is allowed, from time to time, to make a purchase or obtain a loan from the creditor through the use of a credit card. The amount financed and periodic finance charges are debited to the account. The consumer has the right to pay the account in full or in installments of a prespecified minimum amount. **Mobile home paper** includes credit extended directly or indirectly for the purpose of financing a mobile home. The **other loans** category includes home improvement loans and credit extended for the acquisition of such consumer goods as home appliances, boats, and recreational vehicles.

The types of installment credit that have experienced the greatest growth since 1970 are revolving credit and total automobile credit (see Exhibit 5). Auto credit outstanding has quadrupled, and revolving credit outstanding has increased tenfold, from $5.1 billion to $55.5 billion in 1979. Mobile home credit outstanding has leveled off since 1973, showing very little growth over the period. Installment credit classified as "other" approximately doubled between 1970 and 1980.

Installment credit contracts are also subclassified as open end or closed end. **Closed end**

EXHIBIT 5   INSTALLMENT CREDIT OUTSTANDING AT YEAR-END BY TYPE
OF CREDIT ($ BILLIONS)

	Total	Automobile	Revolving	Mobile Home	Other
1970	105.5	36.3	5.1	2.5	61.6
1971	118.3	40.5	8.5	7.2	62.0
1972	133.2	47.9	9.7	9.5	66.1
1973	155.1	53.8	11.7	13.6	76.0
1974	165.0	54.3	13.7	14.6	82.0
1975	172.4	57.2	15.0	14.4	85.7
1976	194.0	67.7	17.2	14.6	94.5
1977	230.8	82.9	39.3	15.1	93.5
1978	275.0	102.4	45.3	17.3	110.0
1979	311.3	115.0	55.5	17.4	123.4

Source: Federal Reserve Statistical Release G.19.

contracts are those under which the consumer borrows a specified amount and repays the loan through a prespecified number of periodic payments of a specific size over a specific period of time. **Open end** contracts or revolving credit allow the consumer to borrow up to a specified amount and repay principal plus interest over an unspecified period of time; however, the periodic payment must be at least as large as a specified minimum.

TYPES OF NONINSTALLMENT CREDIT.   The components of noninstallment credit are **single-payment loans, nonrevolving charge accounts,** and **service credit.** Most single-payment loans are extended by commercial banks. The nonrevolving segment includes traditional 30-day charge accounts of retailers, home heating oil accounts, and other credit card accounts. The most important component of service credit is debt to doctors and hospitals. A smaller portion is owed to public utilities and other service establishments. The Federal Reserve Board reports noninstallment credit outstanding as a single figure. Therefore, it is impossible to analyze the various classes of noninstallment consumer credit. Only about 20% of consumer debt is in the form of noninstallment debt.

HOLDERS OF CONSUMER CREDIT.   The Federal Reserve Board classifies amount of consumer credit by holder rather than by originator. A large portion of automobile paper is originated by an auto dealer and sold to a bank or finance company. Thus the bank or finance company, the ultimate supplier of the credit, is classified as the holder of the paper.

The holders of consumer credit include **banks, credit unions, retailers, gas and oil companies, savings and loan associations and mutual savings banks,** and all the corporations, partnerships, and proprietorships that comprise the **consumer finance business.** The primary purpose of the entities in the consumer finance business is to finance the consumer. The institutions specializing in financing the consumer are consumer finance companies (small loan), sales finance companies, industrial banks, and industrial loan companies.

Commercial banks provide the the largest proportion of consumer credit, followed by finance companies, credit unions, retailers, and others, including savings and loan associations, gasoline companies, and mutual savings banks (Exhibit 6).

A graph of consumer installment credit outstanding by holder shows that credit outstanding for commercial banks has grown most rapidly of all the financial institutions, from less than

EXHIBIT 6   INSTALLMENT CREDIT OUTSTANDING BY TYPE AND HOLDER AT YEAR-END 1975 AND 1979 ($ BILLIONS)

	1975	1979
Total Installment Credit	172.3	311.3
Commerical banks	82.9	149.8
Finance companies	36.0	68.3
Credit unions	25.7	48.2
Retailers	18.2	27.9
Others*a*	27.8	17.1
Automobile	57.2	115.0
Commercial banks	33.3	65.2
Indirect	19.3	37.2
Direct	14.0	28.0
Credit unions	12.7	23.0
Finance companies	11.2	26.8
Mobile Home	14.4	17.4
Commercial banks	8.7	10.0
Finance companies	3.4	3.4
Others	2.3	4.0
Revolving	15.0	55.5
Commercial banks	12.3	29.2
Retailers		22.1
Gasoline companies	2.7	4.3
Other	85.7	123.4
Commercial banks	28.7	45.4
Finance companies	21.3	38.2
Credit unions	12.7	24.6
Retailers	18.2	5.9
Others*a*	4.8	9.3

*a*Includes savings and loan, gasoline companies, and mutual savings banks.
Source: Federal Reserve Bulletin, "Consumer Installment Credit." Board of Governors of the Federal Reserve, Washington, D.C., January 1976 and 1980.

$60 billion in 1972 to almost $150 billion in 1979. Credit outstanding at finance companies and credit unions has shown a relatively slower rate of growth but has grown steadily since 1972.

THE DEVELOPMENT OF THE CONSUMER CREDIT INDUSTRY.   The consumer credit industry as it exists today developed from the first consumer credit law, conceived in 1916 to remedy the "loan shark" evil by creating a strictly regulated, legal consumer money-lending business. This remedial law was called the **Uniform Small Loan Law.** The small

EXHIBIT 7   CONSUMER INSTALLMENT CREDIT DISTRIBUTION BY TYPE AND HOLDER, MONTHLY

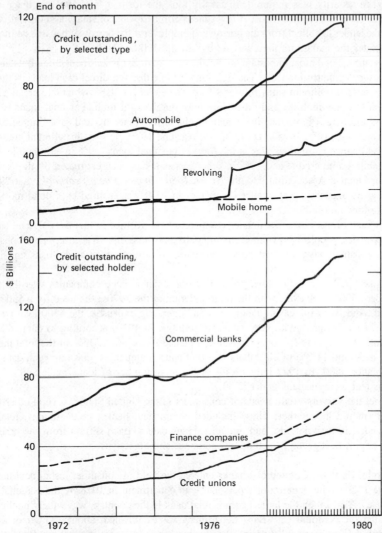

Source: Federal Reserve Board Chart Book, February 1980.

loan law contained only one permission, the right to charge an economically practicable rate, but it promulgated many stringent regulations designed to prevent abuse of borrowers and to deter people from borrowing except after careful consideration of their responsibilities. Consumer credit in the United States at the time the Uniform Small Loan Law was passed was limited to the charge accounts of wealthy customers, Morris Plan banks that made small loans secured by the borrowers' deposits, a few scattered credit unions, and few installment sales systems administered by manufacturers of durable goods, like the Singer Sewing Machine Co.

Consumer Finance Companies.   After the passage of the small loan law, consumer finance companies provided the bulk of small personal loans, often on an unsecured or signature basis. When security was required, it usually took the form of a chattel mortgage on an automobile or on household goods. A few states permitted wage or salary assignment, which enabled the lender to collect from the borrower's employer if the borrower became delinquent. In most states the maximum loan was set by law at $300 or $500.

Today, the second most important holder, in terms of dollar installment credit outstanding, is the consumer finance industry. The financing is done through direct cash loans or through the purchase of installment sales contracts from dealers or retailers, which are created when consumers buy automobiles and other consumer durables on time. Personal loans secured by second mortgages have become a major vehicle for financing and to a limited extent, finance companies offer revolving credit. At year-end 1979, 45% of installment credit outstanding at finance companies was in the form of personal loans, 39% in automobile credit, 5% in mobile home credit, and 11% in other loans. It has been estimated by the National Consumer Finance Association (Booth, *NCFA 1980 Finance Facts Yearbook*) that 29% of personal loans outstanding at finance companies in 1979 was secured by second mortgages on one- to four-family homes.

Traditionally most consumer finance companies have positioned themselves to be lenders of last resort for people who cannot obtain credit anywhere else. Recently many consumer finance companies have adopted polices designed to attract better credit risks and larger loans.

Until the 1970s the major loan product of consumer finance companies was the small loan (under $500). However, with the rapid inflation of the 1970s, the need for a $500 loan decreased. And, with increasing labor costs and operating expenses, the $500 loan was not profitable, even in states with very high rate ceilings. In 1970, according to data collected from its members by the National Consumer Finance Association, 33% of the total number of loans made and 11.3% of all dollars lent by finance companies reporting such data were in loans under $500. In 1977 only 19.4% of the total number of loans made and 4.2% of all dollars lent were in loans under $500.

To meet the varying credit needs of consumers in the United States, several other types of lender entered the market. These included commercial banks, credit unions, retailers, savings and loan associations, and mutual savings banks. Each differs from the others in terms of origin, background, method of operation, and objectives.

Commercial Banks.   Commercial banks entered the field of consumer installment lending in the late 1920s. The opening of a personal loan department in 1928 by the National City Bank of New York, then the largest commercial bank in the country, was widely publicized. A year after the National City Bank department was established, about 200 personal loan departments had been established in other banks, but many were discontinued during and shortly after the Depression. Bankers considered consumer installment lending to be outside their field of activity. However, after the Depression, the favorable experience of sales finance companies, consumer finance companies, and industrial banks showed commercial bankers that consumer installment lending could be safe and profitable.

While consumer installment lending is not the predominant type of lending for most commercial banks, it has steadily increased in importance both in proportion of total loans and in number of banks participating in the business. At year-end 1979, consumer loans accounted for about 17% of total loans and securities for all insured banks in the United States: 44% of installment credit outstanding at commercial banks was in the form of auto loans, 19% in the form of revolving credit, 7% in mobile homes, and 30% in other loans.

Automobile credit held by commercial banks is classified as either direct or indirect credit. About 57% of auto credit held by commercial banks is classified as indirect. Indirect auto credit arises when sales credit contracts are written by an auto dealer, with the vehicle as security, and the contract is sold to the bank. Direct auto credit arises when the consumer deals directly with an employee of the bank to acquire a personal loan to be used to purchase an automobile.

Revolving credit from commercial banks includes that which is extended through bank credit cards and bank check credit plans. Revolving credit extended by commercial banks more than doubled between year-ends 1975 and 1979, from $12.3 billion to $29.2 billion. There are two major bank credit cards, Master Card and Visa, which are singly or jointly issued by commercial banks extending revolving credit. The process of extending revolving bank credit involves the issuance of the card(s) to the customer, servicing the local merchants who accept the card, approving and processing transactions and billing to customer accounts, and financing the outstanding balances. Many banks only issue the cards and/or service the merchants. These are referred to as **agent banks.** Banks that carry the receivables are called **principal banks.** International information networks connecting institutions involved in the business of revolving bank card credit allow customers to use their cards at many thousands of locations all over the world.

Check credit plans account for a small percentage of revolving credit held by commercial banks. A check credit plan basically allows the customer to take out a loan by overdrafting the checking account. The customer has a preapproved overdraft line of credit from the bank and pays for the use of the line either on a charge per check basis or through a finance charge.

Credit Unions. Congress passed the Federal Credit Union Act in June 1934, enabling federally chartered credit unions to operate in every state with immunity from general usury laws. Credit unions developed rapidly after the passage of the Act. At year-end 1979, 48% of installment credit outstanding at credit unions was auto credit, 1% was mobile home credit, and 51% was classified as other credit.

Retailers. Retailers have historically originated much of the installment credit extended to consumers for the purchase of goods. Most retailers do not hold the contracts until they are paid off. Rather, they sell all or part of the contracts to a financial institution. Some of the large retailers like Sears and J.C. Penney do not sell their receivables but hold them through a captive finance company.

Retailers who sell on credit can choose from many different alternatives of open or closed end credit plans. Some retailers have their own credit plans, administered and financed in house. Frequently cited advantages to having an in-house credit plan are increased patronage, higher sales to customers who use the credit plan, ease of transaction and merchandise returns, and higher impulse buying. The disadvantage is the high cost of financing. Retailers can also choose to accept third-party revolving credit systems such as bank cards and travel and entertainment cards. The advantages are larger customer base, lower default losses, and lower financing needs. The disadvantages are high cost (merchants discounts) and the absence of a credit avenue for developing customer loyalty. A popular plan being provided by financial institutions to retailers is the private label financing plan, where retailers have revolving or closed end credit, but the credit operation is administered and supervised by a financial institution.

Others. The most notable other consumer lenders are the **industrial banks,** savings and loan associations, and mutual savings banks. The idea of industrial banking was developed by Arthur J. Morris, who maintained that he could profitably lend money on a comaker basis in sums as small as $50, to be repaid through monthly savings required for the purpose of liquidating the loan. The first industrial bank was established in 1910. After World War I, industrial banks performed many of the functions of commercial banks. In addition to making consumer loans, industrial banks, where permitted, were accepting time deposits and checking accounts.

Savings and loan associations and mutual savings banks have sought and won permission to provide consumer loans in an attempt to diversify their loan portfolios. At year-end 1979, about one-fifth of total assets of savings and loan associations and mutual savings banks was in the form of mobile home loans, home improvement loans, loans on savings accounts, education loans, and miscellaneous consumer loans.

CHANGES IN MARKET SHARE OVER TIME.   The relative positions of the principal lenders in the consumer installment loan market have changed dramatically since 1930 (Exhibit 8). The most significant change is the relative position occupied by commercial banks. In 1930 commercial banks held about 7% of all consumer installment credit outstanding. Since 1950 commercial banks have accounted for approximately 40% of all consumer installment credit outstanding. During the 1970s, commercial banks' share of total consumer installment credit outstanding grew to almost 50%.

Credit unions have grown rapidly since 1960. Their share of the consumer credit market grew from 9% in 1960 to 15% in 1979. Credit unions and banks have gained market share at the expense of finance companies and retail outlets. The market share of finance companies, which includes sales finance and consumer finance companies, has declined from a high of 50% in 1935 to 22% in 1979. Retail outlets' share has declined from a high of 48% in 1930 to 9% in 1979.

EXHIBIT 8   INSTALLMENT CREDIT OUTSTANDING, PERCENTAGE DISTRIBUTION BY HOLDER, 1930–1979

Year-End	Commercial Banks	Finance Companies[a]	Credit Unions	Retail Outlets	Others
1930	7	44	0	48	1
1935	15	50	1	34	0
1940	26	42	3	29	0
1945	30	38	4	28	0
1950	39	34	4	20	3
1955	37	38	6	16	4
1960	39	34	9	15	4
1965	41	33	10	14	1
1970	44	27	13	14	2
1975	48	21	15	11	6
1976	48	20	16	10	6
1977	49	19	16	10	5
1978	49	20	17	9	5
1979	48	22	15	9	5

[a]Finance companies include institutions classified as sales finance, consumer finance, and other finance companies.

Source: Federal Reserve Bulletin, Consumer Installment Credit, Board of Governors of the Federal Reserve. Washington, D.C., January, annually.

PRINCIPLES OF ADMINISTRATION AND CONTROL

COST FACTORS IN DETERMINING RATE.   In a perfect market setting with positive transactions costs, the equilibrium rate charged on any credit contract of given maturity is a function of three variables: the market-determined risk-free rate offered by securities with zero default risk with similar maturity; a risk premium to reward the lender for accepting the risk inherent in the contract; and the administrative costs of originating and enforcing the contract over the life of that contract.

Risk-Free Rate.   The risk-free rate considered in pricing consumer credit contracts is the rate of return attainable to the party investing in a security that has zero default risk and a maturity equivalent to that of the credit contract being priced, for example, yields to maturity on a Treasury security with equivalent maturity.

Default Risk Premium.   Consumer credit contracts normally have a short maturity (5 years or less). Therefore, the main source of risk incurred by the lender is default risk. Default risk of a contract is evaluated in terms of the borrower's creditworthiness. Methods commonly used to evaluate the creditworthiness of an individual are discussed later.

In an unrestricted market, the cost of credit or rate of charge will increase as the risk of default increases, holding everything else constant. However, the rates of charge allowed for various types of consumer loan are highly regulated. Given the creditworthiness of the individual, default risk of the credit contract can be reduced by adjustment of other terms of the contract. Holding all other things constant, default risk decreases as the size of the loan decreases, as maturity decreases, and as collateral requirements relative to the size of the loan increase. Types of collateral commonly used for security in consumer credit contracts are the durables being purchased with the proceeds of the loan, bank balances, household goods, wages, or the promise of a cosignor to pay the indebtedness.

Administrative Expenses.   Given the short maturity and small average size of consumer loans relative to other types of debt, the administrative costs of issuing consumer credit are high relative to the average amount outstanding. As a result, many sizes and maturities of consumer loans cannot be offered profitably unless rate ceilings allow explicit charges to be made to cover administrative expenses. Exhibit 9 shows the results of a simulation of the expected net rate of return (before default losses) for loans of various sizes and maturities as origination costs and monthly collection costs vary. These net returns are calculated for loans bearing a 12% annual finance charge (annual percentage rate).

From Exhibit 9 it is clear that variations in the administrative expenses have a sharp impact on the net rate of return for consumer loans and on the sizes and maturities of loans the credit grantor will be willing to offer. As administrative expenses increase, creditors are forced to increase the size and maturity of the loan, given fixed rate ceilings, to earn their economically justified rate of return.

REVENUES FROM CONSUMER CREDIT.   The main sources of revenue to an issuer of consumer credit are the **finance or interest charge, origination fees, credit insurance fees,** and **interchange fees** and **merchant discounts** in the case of revolving credit that are obtained by the use of internationally accepted credit cards.

Finance Charges.   Finance charges are usually limited by state law and vary considerably from state to state.

**EXHIBIT 9   NET RATES OF RETURN (BEFORE LOSSES) ON 12 PERCENT
CONSUMER LOANS, CONTRACT RATE = 12.00**

	Loan Size					
	$ 1,000			$ 2,500		
Contract Maturity (months):	12	24	36	12	24	36
Payment Collection Cost						
Origination Cost = $50.00						
$3.75	−5.574	−1.560	0.012	4.540	6.353	7.063
2.50	−3.006	1.181	2.790	5.660	7.505	8.206
1.00	0.131	4.499	6.121	7.013	8.892	9.578
0.50	1.190	5.612	7.232	7.467	9.355	10.036
Origination Cost = $25.00						
$3.75	−1.302	0.741	1.594	6.475	7.386	7.774
2.50	1.401	3.567	4.438	7.619	8.552	8.929
1.00	4.703	6.990	7.850	9.001	9.957	10.315
0.50	5.818	8.138	8.988	9.464	10.427	10.777
Origination Cost = $10.00						
$3.75	1.422	2.183	2.580	7.665	8.017	8.208
2.50	4.211	5.064	5.466	8.824	9.192	9.369
1.00	7.619	8.552	8.929	10.224	10.608	10.764
0.50	8.770	9.723	10.084	10.693	11.082	11.229

Origination Fees.   Origination fees are allowable charges to cover administrative costs of originating a loan. Origination fees are also limited by state law in terms of their size and the frequency with which they can be assessed.

Credit Insurance Fees.   Credit insurance fees are the insurance premiums on credit life, or accident and health insurance policies that are sometimes sold in conjunction with consumer credit. However, when insurance is required as a condition of obtaining credit, the premiums must be included in the quotation of the finance charge.

Interchange Fees and Merchant Discount.   Interchange fees are paid among credit card issuers to facilitate the ability of the cardholder to use the credit card universally at all merchant locations that accept the card. The merchant discount is a fee paid by the merchant who accepts a third-party revolving payment system to the financial institution for processing the resulting invoices. Both types of fee are expressed as a percentage of the face value of the invoice.

METHODS OF SPECIFYING FINANCE CHARGES.   The interest rate of charge for various types and sizes of consumer loan is limited by state law. The state statutes use a multitude of different methods to specify the permissible rates. This patchwork of rates, along with differences across institutions in terms of methods of quoting rates, motivated the passage of the **Federal Truth-in-Lending Act,** effective July 1, 1969, which says that rates on consumer loans must be expressed in a consistent format.

Annual Percentage Rate.   The truth-in-lending legislation established a common standard measure of rate, which is called an "annual percentage rate" (APR). Thus every consumer credit transaction carries an annual percentage rate and may be directly compared with every other such transaction. Financial institution managers are responsible for providing consumer borrowers with information on the total dollar finance charge and the APR of interest. The credit grantor may use loan terms of its choosing, but must compute and provide the individual borrower with the annual percentage rate equivalents.

Nonrevolving installment credit contracts specify that a series of equal payments at equal time intervals, usually a month apart, be made to retire the indebtedness. The APR charged on a consumer loan is the **internal rate of return** for the contract cash flows or the percentage discount rate that equates the scheduled periodic payments with the original principal amount of the loan extended. This concept is exemplified by the following equation:

$$P = \sum_{t=1}^{T} \frac{M_t}{(1 + r)^t}$$

where P = original principal balance
M = periodic monthly payment
r = periodic discount rate
T = number of regularly scheduled payments

The total dollar finance charge on an amount financed is equal to the difference between the sum of the scheduled periodic payments and the original principal balance of the loan.

Many of the relevant state laws specifying maximum rates predate the Truth-in-Lending Act. Thus maximum legal rates are not consistently stated as annual percentage rates but are sometimes specified as add-on or discount rates.

The Add-on Rate.   The maximum allowable rate of charge on consumer loans is stated in many states as an add-on rate, which must be converted to the annual percentage rate for disclosure purposes. The annual percentage rate is roughly double the "add-on" rate. To convert an "add-on" rate to an annual percentage rate the following procedure is used:

1. To determine the total amount to be repaid, multiply the stated add-on rate by the original principal balance of the loan. Multiply the product times the number of years the loan is outstanding. For example, a $1,000 loan with a 1 year to maturity at 10% add-on yields a total amount to be repaid of $1,100 ($1,000 × 0.10 × 1 year = $1,100).

2. To determine the size of monthly payments, divide the total amount to be repaid by the number of scheduled monthly payments. For example, $1,100 ÷ 12 = $91.67.

3. To calculate the equivalent monthly percentage rate, find the monthly internal rate of return for a $1,000 loan to be repaid in 12 monthly payments of $91.67 each (equation 1), $r = 1.49\%$.

4. Multiply the monthly rate by 12 to get the annual percentage rate: APR = 17.88%.

The Discount Rate.   A maximum discount per year rate is quoted in many state statutes. Under this method, the lender deducts the total interest charge from the principal amount of the loan and actually lends the borrower the difference. Thus for a $1,000 1-year loan at a 10% discount per year rate, the lender actually lends only $900.

The relationship between the discount rate and the annual percentage rate is a function of the number of payments specified in the contract and the maturity of the loan. For loans with long maturity, it is possible under a discount method for the amount of the discount to equal the total principal amount of the loan. Under these circumstances, the borrower gets nothing and the interest return to the lender approaches infinity. For this reason, most state statutes specify discount rates for loans with short maximum terms.

To convert a discount per year rate into an annual percentage rate, the amount actually lent to the borrower is set equal to the discounted value of the scheduled monthly payments as is shown in the equation above. The size of monthly payments is determined by the amount loaned plus the discount, divided by the number of scheduled periodic payments. The annual percentage rate is higher than the discount rate. The difference beteween the two rates increases as the term of the loan increases.

NOMINAL RATES VERSUS YIELDS ON REVOLVING CREDIT.   For revolving credit, the nominal monthly rate on the unpaid balance is frequently fixed by law, but the actual yield to the lender is a function of the methods used by lenders to assess finance charges. In their discussion of yields under various assessment methods, McAlister and DeSpain ("Bank and Retail Credit Card Yields Under Alternative Assessment Methods") stated that the yield is affected by the method of assessment as well as the timing of consumers' purchases and payments and the period of time over which the yield is calculated. The most common of the various methods of assessing finance charges on revolving credit accounts are **previous balance method, adjusted balance method,** and **ending balance method.**

Previous Balance.   In this approach, also known as the **"beginning balance" method,** the finance charges are calculated on any beginning unpaid balance shown on the current month's statement **before** deducting payments or credits received during the billing period and before adding purchases made during the billing period. If the previous balance is paid in full, no finance charge is assessed. If no payment is made, the unpaid finance charge may become part of the principal balance owed.

Adjusted Balance.   Finance charges are calculated on the basis of any beginning unpaid balance shown on the current month's billing statement **less** payments and credit received during the current billing period, but **before** adding the current month's purchases. The date of payment on an account is irrelevant to the calculation.

Ending Balance.   Finance charges are based on the balance owed at the end of each billing period, including purchases, payments, and credits occurring during the current month. Under this method, no "free period" is given to a customer who pays the account in full unless there is no outstanding balance at the end of the month.

In simulations of gross yields under the various billing methods, McAlister and DeSpain found that the adjusted ending balance, on average, provided 98.4% of the nominal annual rate followed by 86.6% of the nominal annual rate under the previous balance method. Finally, the adjusted balance method yielded 76.7% of the nominal annual yield.

RISK EVALUATION.   The rate that a creditor quotes on a loan is a function of the default risk assumed by the creditor when the loan is granted. The default risk for a particular individual is a function of the willingness and ability of the borrower to repay the loan according to the terms specified by the credit contract. Willingness and ability of an individual are evaluated on the basis of the credit applicant's type and duration of employment, stability of residence, income, past and current credit usage, financial assets, and personal characteristics. The **Equal Credit Opportunity Act** severely limits the personal characteristics of an individual that may be used in evaluating creditworthiness. The characteristics limited by the Equal Credit Opportunity Act are discussed below. To evaluate the default risk of an individual, given the necessary information, the credit grantor may use a judgmental system or a credit scoring system.

Judgmental System.   In a **judgmental risk evaluation system,** each credit application and the information contained therein are evaluated individually by an employee of the creditor. The success of a judgmental system depends on the experience and common sense of the credit evaluator.

Credit Scoring System.   Some creditors have used their historical experience with debtors to derive a quantitative model for the segregation of acceptable and unacceptable credit applications. With a credit scoring system, a credit application is processed mechanically and all credit decisions are made consistently. The scoring system is based on the addition or subtraction of a statistically derived number of points to the applicant credit score on the basis of responses given to a set of predictor variables, such as time on job or number of credit sources used. Given a statistically derived cutoff credit score, a creditor can thus segregate the acceptable from the unacceptable credit applicants.

Credit scoring has been criticized because statistical problems with the data used to derive the model frequently violate the assumptions of the statistical technique used to derive the points (multiple discriminant analysis). It is also pointed out that some of the variables used in a credit scoring system may have the effect of discrimination, although the variable may appear to be neutral. For example, using zip code in a scoring system may have the effect of discriminating against members of minority groups. Finally, the credit scoring model is derived by analysis of the characteristics of customers who were once granted credit by the creditor for whom the system is derived. The characteristics of the part of the population to which the credit grantor has not granted credit are not directly considered. Thus the scoring system may provide biased results when it is applied to new credit applicants. For a discussion of credit scoring systems, see Altman, Avery, Eisenbeis and Sinkey, *Application of Classification Techniques in Business, Banking, and Finance*.

Credit Reporting Agencies.   A credit reporting agency is a clearinghouse of credit information about consumers. To assist the creditor in the process of risk evaluation, the credit reporting agency or credit bureau assimilates information on the credit history of an individual. The credit report is coded in a common language that refers to the types of account a customer has with various creditors, the terms of the accounts, and the customer's usual method of payment.

The credit reporting agency does not assign a credit rating to an individual but rather provides the creditor, for a fee, with information about the applicant for purposes of evaluating creditworthiness. The type, condition, and distribution of information maintained by credit reporting agencies on consumers are restricted by the **Fair Credit Reporting Act.**

OTHER CONTRACT TERMS.

Creditors' Remedies.   Creditors' remedies are actions specified in the credit contract that the creditor may take in the event of delinquency or default to recover the accrued interest and outstanding balance of a loan or to reduce default losses. Creditors' remedies play the same role in consumer credit contracts that indenture provisions play in a commercial loan contract.

The methods that a creditor may use to collect past due accounts have become increasingly more restricted by state and federal law. Laws have been written and adopted that are meant to restrict or abolish creditors' remedies or collection practices that are likely to place undue hardship on the defaulting consumer. Feldman and Reiley ("A Compilation of Federal and State Laws Regulating Consumer Financial Services," pp. 540–573) have described the set of creditors' remedies available in most states.

The extent to which each of these remedies can be used is specified by state law and varies widely from state to state. These remedies are briefly summarized below.

Late Payment Charges. Legally allowed penalty charges to debtors for late payment—for example, $5 or 5% of the delinquent monthly payment.

Attorney's Fee Charges. Legal charges against a defaulting debtor for the creditor's costs of using attorneys to collect the debt. Such a charge is usually expressed as a percentage of the amount in default irrespective of the actual amount of attorney's fees incurred by the creditor.

Repossession. Legal seizure, initiated by a creditor, of property securing a debt. The role of the security in a debt contract is to secure payment or performance of an obligation. When the debtor defaults, the creditor has the right to take possession of the property specified as security without judicial process if this can be done without breach of the peace. In the event of repossession, the debtor must pay repossession costs, storing and selling costs, and attorney's fees.

Deficiency Judgment. A judgment or decree against a debtor for any part of a debt not recovered by sale of the collateral. Given depreciation and the obligation of the debtor to pay the cost of repossession, the total amount of the outstanding obligation may be significantly higher than the net resale value of the security.

Blanket Security. A lien taken by a creditor on all of the household goods of a debtor. This is also called cross-collateral.

Waiver of Statutory Exemption. A clause in a note waiving the laws shielding certain personal property from a creditor's claims. The effect of the waiver is that state laws are replaced by common law of absolute liability of the debtor, and any or all personal property can be seized to satisfy the obligation of the debtor to the creditor.

Garnishment. A legal procedure whereby some of the debtor's wages or other assets held by an employer or other third party may be assigned to the creditor. As it applies to wages and salaries, the process of garnishment requires an employer to withold part of an employee's compensation upon order of the court and pay it directly to, or for the account of, the employee's creditor. The maximum amount that may be withheld from a debtor's paycheck is specified by federal law as the lessor of a percentage of the check or some multiple of the federal minimum wage.

Wage Assignment. A voluntary assignment of wages made by the debtor to the creditor at the time a loan is made, which becomes effective in case of default. The function of the wage assignment is to provide the creditor with a speedy method of collection without the time and expense of a hearing on the underlying claim. It is usually an instruction to the employer to pay the creditor a portion of the debtor's wage.

Acceleration upon Default. A clause permitting the creditor to claim the entire balance due in the event of default on a credit agreement. In its most common form, the clause permits the creditor to accelerate when the debtor defaults. The credit contract specifies those actions that constitute default. In some cases, the acceleration clause allows the creditor to accelerate at will when he believes the loan to be insecure. Under common law the creditor has the burden of justifying the acceleration and proving his good faith.

Reaffirmation of Debts After Bankruptcy. An agreement made by a debtor who has declared bankruptcy, to repay a debt even though he is freed of the debt by the bankruptcy proceedings. Reaffirmation must be approved by the bankruptcy referee.

Cosignor Agreement. An agreement whereby parties other than the principal debtor agree to pay a debt if the debtor defaults.

Contacting Third Parties. A creditor's right to contact employers, relatives, or others in an effort to locate a delinquent debtor or to encourage payment of a delinquent balance.

Foreclosure. Legal seizure of property to liquidate a defaulted debt secured by a mortgage on the property.

Collection Practices. The collection practices of a credit grantor are the activities engaged in to obtain payment from a delinquent debtor, exclusive of creditor's remedies. Normal collection practices include letters, phone calls, and personal visits to the home or office of the debtor. Within the last several years, unfair collection practices have been defined and restricted by state law and the **Federal Fair Debt Collection Practices Act.**

The activities or practices that are considered to be harassment, hence unlawful, are:

1. The use of threats of violence, force, or criminal prosecution against the consumer in an attempt to enforce collection of a debt.
2. Communicating with the debtor or the debtor's family members frequently and at unusual hours to harass them concerning payment of the debt.
3. The use of communications, such as letters or telegrams, that simulate legal process or court suit papers.
4. Threatening or causing damages to a debtor's credit rating, knowing that the information is false or is being actively contested by the debtor.
5. Threatening legal action, directly or by implication, against a delinquent debtor unless such action can and will in fact be instituted as represented if the debtor fails to make payment or otherwise settle the account.
6. Communicating with the debtor's employer before securing a final judgment on the debt, challenging the debtor's creditworthiness except as permitted by statute for the purpose of determining the employment status of the debtor.

Prepayment Provisions. Most consumer credit contracts are written such that a schedule of periodic payments is specified over the life of the contract. The periodic payments are allocated between principal and the total interest that will be paid over the life of the contract. Because consumer loan contracts typically specify a fixed periodic payment, the interest is not paid at the same rate that it accrues. Therefore, in the event that a debtor prepays a loan, he may have paid a greater amount of interest than was justifiable, given the actual period over which the loan was outstanding. In the event of prepayment, the consumer is entitled to a rebate of the unearned finance charges that may have been paid. The amount of the rebate owed to the consumer is determined by one of two methods: the rule of 78 or the actuarial method.

Rule of 78.   As Johnson (testimony on S.2002 presented to the Consumer Affairs Sub-committee of the Senate Banking Committee at the invitation of the chairman of the Sub-committee, Senator Paul E. Tsongas, 1979) explained, when an installment debt was prepaid in full, the unearned portion of the finance charge was determined by the **Rule of 78.** This can be illustrated simply. Assume that you hire some workers to dig a hole that narrows as it becomes deeper. The first day you will use four workers, each at $1 per day. The next day you have three workers, the next two, and finally, one. Your total wage bill is $10 ($4 + $3 + $2 + $1). At the end of the second day, the workers quit. What do you owe them? Even though they have worked half the days, they have earned more than half the total wage bill. The unearned portion of the total wage bill is $3/10$; that is $3, the sum of the remaining days' wages, divided by $10, the total wage bill. This might be called the "rule of 10," since the sum of the digits—1, 2, 3, 4—is 10.

Since many installment contracts in the early 1900s were for 12 months, and since the sum of the digits 1 through 12 is 78, the refund rule became known as the "rule of 78," or the "sum-of-the-digits" method. To calculate the amount of unearned interest that should be refunded by the creditor, determine the proportion of the term of the contract that has expired before prepayment and multiply that by the total dollar finance charge. This determines the amount of the total finance charge that should be retained by the creditor. The difference between that amount and what the debtor actually paid is the amount to be refunded.

Actuarial Method.   An alternative method is to apply the annual percentage rate on a monthly basis to the declining balance on the loan. The monthly payment is thus allocated between principal and interest payments. Upon prepayment, the amount owed by the consumer is the sum of the remaining payment less the unearned finance charges by the actuarial method. For example, assume a 12-month loan for $1,200 at an 8% add-on, giving a finance charge of $96, total amount owed $1,296, and monthly payments of $108. Assume that the loan is prepaid at the end of the sixth month, with six payments to go. Those six payments total $648, but a portion is unearned finance charge that should be deducted. What portion? $(1 + 2 + \cdots = 60/78$, or $21/78 \times 96 = \$25.85$. Thus, the borrower must pay $648 − $25.85 = $622.15. If the refund were calculated under the actuarial method, the unearned finance charge would be $26.47, and the total payment owed would be $648 − $26.47 = $621.53—a difference of $0.62.

According to Johnson, the rule of 78 has been questioned for two main reasons. First, for longer contract maturities, the difference between the refund paid the consumer under the rule of 78 and under the actual method increases. As shown in Exhibit 10, when a loan is prepaid, the finance charges paid are always greater under the rule of 78 than under the actuarial method of determining the refund. And the maximum differential increases, the longer the term of the original installment contract.

Second, the rule of 78 has been challenged because computers are now available to calculate the unearned finance charge on the basis of the actuarial method. Presently, firms

EXHIBIT 10   INTEREST PAID TO MONTH OF PREPAYMENT: RULE OF 78 VERSUS ACTUARIAL METHOD

Interest paid under the Rule of 78 is always more than under the declining balance —

but how much more depends on:

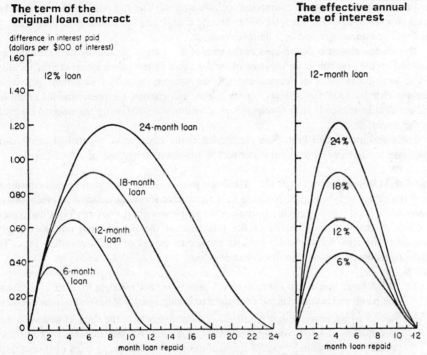

The term of the original loan contract

difference in interest paid (dollars per $100 of interest)

1.60
1.40
1.20
1.00
0.80
0.60
0.40
0.20
0

12% loan

24-month loan
18-month loan
12-month loan
6-month loan

0 2 4 6 8 10 12 14 16 18 20 22 24
month loan repaid

The effective annual rate of interest

12-month loan

24%
18%
12%
6%

0 2 4 6 8 10 12
month loan repaid

Source: Federal Reserve Bank of Chicago, *Business Conditions,* September 1973, p. 8.

having computers can compute the refund almost instantaneously under either the rule of 78 or the actuarial method, whichever is required by the applicable state law. Small credit grantors without computers will still find calculation of refunds under the actuarial method laborious.

Credit Insurance.   Credit insurance is usually life or accident and health insurance that is sold in conjunction with a credit contract. Credit life insurance insures the creditor against loss if the debtor dies. Accident and health insurance insures the creditor against loss if the debtor becomes sick or disabled. Rates on credit insurance are normally regulated by state law and stated as an amount per $100 of the original outstanding balance of the loan.

LAWS REGULATING CONSUMER CREDIT

FEDERAL LAWS.   The activities involved in the extension of consumer credit are highly regulated because of the extreme difference in the information and market power of the creditor compared to those of the individual consumer. There is a multitude of state and federal laws that apply to the extension of consumer credit although most are state laws. Below is a brief description of the major federal laws that apply to the activities of consumer credit issuers.

Truth-in-Lending Act (1969).   The Truth-in-Lending Act, part of the **Consumer Credit Protection Act,** is essentially designed to assure meaningful disclosure of credit terms to facilitate credit shopping and comparison of credit terms. The Act requires that the two key terms in a credit contract, the total dollar finance charge and the annual percentage rate, be disclosed conspicuously and in a uniform manner.

The finance charge is determined as the sum of all charges payable by the consumer and imposed by the creditor as an incident of or condition of the extension of credit. Included in the total dollar value of finance charges are interest, service, transaction, activity or carrying charges, loan fees, points, finder's fees, and charges for premiums for credit life and accident insurance if such is required as a condition for obtaining the amount advanced by the lender.

The Consumer Credit Protection Act prohibits the issuance of unsolicited credit cards and limits the liability of the cardholder to $50 for unauthorized use of a credit card.

Fair Credit Reporting Act (1971).   The basic purpose of this law is to protect consumers from inaccurate or obsolete information in a report that serves as a factor in evaluating an individual's eligibility for credit, insurance, or employment. It does not limit the type of information that can be gathered or the relevance of the information; nor does it give consumers the right to physically possess or receive copies of the information files. The major rights created by the law for consumers are:

1. *Disclosures by users to consumers.*   Consumers have the right to be told by the user the name and address of the consumer reporting agency if adverse action is taken.

2. *Access to information in a credit file.*   Consumers have the right of access to their information files to learn the contents of such files. All information in credit files is available to consumers except medical information and the sources of investigative information.

3. *Sources and recipients of information.*   Consumers have the right to be told the sources of information in their respective files and to have a list of recipients of the file for the previous 6 months.

4. *Confidentiality.*   Consumers have the right to have information in their files kept confidential and reported only for credit or business purposes.

5. *Reinvestigation of disputed entries.*   Consumer reporting agencies must reinvestigate disputed items and correct inaccuracies within a reasonable period of time.

6. *Care and accuracy.*   Consumer reporting agencies are required to provide reports only when these are requested for legitimate business purposes. They are also required to exercise care and accuracy in releasing the reports and in verifying that the reported information is not obsolete.

7. *Elimination of obsolete data.*   Credit reporting agencies must notify individual consumers when adverse information is being reported and must verify the current status of public information items.

8. *Obtaining information in a file by false pretenses.*   The law provides criminal penalties for obtaining information under false pretenses or for providing information to an unauthorized person.

Fair Credit Billing Act (1969).   This law specifies a billing dispute settlement procedure that allows customers to challenge perceived billing errors in their periodic statements. The act applies only to open end credit plans, which include credit cards and overdraft checking plans.

Equal Credit Opportunity Act (1975).   This act prohibits discrimination by creditors on the basis of sex, marital status, race, color, religion, national origin, age (provided the applicant has the capacity to enter into a contract), because all or part of the applicant's income comes from public assistance programs, or because the applicant has in good faith exercised any right under the Consumer Credit Protection Act.

Fair Debt Collection Practices Act (1977).   The purpose of this law is to protect debtors from harassment, deception, and other abuse in collection practices, while recognizing the legitimate need to collect consumer debts. The main thrust of the legislation is directed toward independent (third-party) professional debt collectors and collection agencies. The federal law regulates the following practices: (1) the acquisition of location information concerning the debtor, (2) communication to the debtor or third parties, (3) harassment or abuse, (4) false or misleading representations, and (5) unfair practices.

STATE LAWS.   The state laws relating to the extension of consumer credit are many and varied across states; they apply to all facets of the extension of consumer credit.

Usury Laws.   The usury or interest statutes set out the basic guidelines for permissible interest rates charged for the use of money. Some states have adopted the **Uniform Consumer Credit Code,** which specifies a uniform set of rules that apply to specified sales and loan transactions.

Small Loan Laws.   All states except Arkansas have adopted statutes specifically governing the extension of small loans. Small loans are defined by the individual statutes. These laws restrict the maximum term, maximum amount, and interest rate that can be charged by financial institutions making small loans, primarily consumer finance companies. Small loan laws frequently specify a graduated rate ceiling such that a higher rate may be charged on smaller loans and lower rates charged on larger loans.

CONSUMER USES OF CREDIT

CONSUMERS WHO USE INSTALLMENT CREDIT.   The demand for consumer credit is a derived demand, based on consumers' consumption decisions, given each individual's level of income and wealth. The results of a national survey of consumers cosponsored by the Federal Reserve Board of Governors, the Comptroller of the Currency, and the Federal Deposit Insurance Corporation and performed in 1977 by the Survey Research Center at the University of Michigan provide information about consumer installment credit and how it is used. Durkin and Elliehausen, discussing the use of installment credit in the population in general (1977 Consumer Credit Survey), analyzed the survey data and found that about half the families in the United States had installment credit outstanding during the summer of 1977 (excluding credit card and mortgage credit).

A comparison of the families that had installment debt outstanding and those that did not use installment debt revealed that the probability of installment debt usage and the amount of debt outstanding increased as income increased. Installment debt usage was also related to the age of the family head. Families with heads between the ages of 25 and 44 had the highest probability of having installment debt outstanding. Married couples with children with a family head younger than 45 had a 75% probability of using installment credit. An examination of other characteristics of credit users indicates that homeowners are more likely to use credit than renters, and that black families used more installment credit than white families.

TRENDS IN CONSUMER DEBT USAGE. Inflation, changing social attitudes toward the use of consumer debt, and alterations in the demographic characteristics of the general population can account for much of the growth and expected further growth in consumer installment credit outstanding.

Installment Debt and Inflation. Since 1970, the amount of total consumer installment debt outstanding has virtually exploded from a level of $102 billion to $308.7 billion at the end of February 1980, an increase of about 203%. Over the same period the Consumer Price Index increased from 115.0 to 236.5, an increase of about 105.6%. Much of the increase in debt outstanding can be attributed to the increase in prices of consumer durables purchased on credit. However, the relative percentage increases in consumer installment credit outstanding and in the Consumer Price Index suggest that individuals have become more willing or able to incur debt.

Inflation and expectations of higher inflation affects demand for credit in ways other than its effect on prices paid for consumer durables bought on credit. First, expectations of increased future rates of inflation may cause consumers to "buy now to avoid higher prices later." Much of the inflation experienced in 1978–1980 was attributed to this "buy now" psychology. Second, expectations of higher inflation make the increased use of credit a rational consumer choice, especially when the credit can be acquired at a fixed interest rate. The prospect of borrowing today and repaying with cheaper future dollars results in a transfer of real wealth from the creditor to the debtor.

Since the individual use of installment debt and the individual's level of debt outstanding is related to personal income, a valid analysis of trends in debt usage can only be made relative to the trend of personal income, which is highly correlated with inflation. A time series chart of consumer installment debt relative to disposable income (Exhibit 11) shows that in 1970 the ratio was about 13.0%, compared to a ratio of about 17% in 1977. These data also suggest that although much of the increase in installment credit outstanding is

EXHIBIT 11   RATIO OF CONSUMER INSTALLMENT DEBT TO PERSONAL INCOME

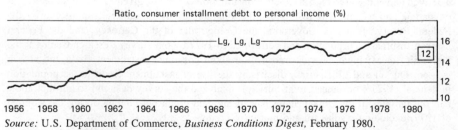

Source: U.S. Department of Commerce, *Business Conditions Digest,* February 1980.

attributable to the effects of inflation on prices and income, consumers have become more willing or able to incur consumer installment debt since 1970.

In a comparison of the debt burden by demographic characteristics of a national sample interviewed in 1970 and 1977, Durkin and Elliehausen found that middle- and upper-income consumers appeared more willing to be in debt in 1977 than in 1970.

Installment Debt and Changes in Demographic Characteristics. Changing demographic characteristics of the population in general may also account for some of the increase in outstanding consumer installment debt. As noted above, families in the family formation years, with family heads in the age bracket group of 25–44 years, are most likely to use debt. Statistics on the age structure of the population (Exhibit 12) indicate that there was a net increase of 8.3 million people in that age bracket between 1970 and 1977. Projections into 1985 suggest that there will be a further increase of 14.7 million in that age bracket. This phenomenon may result in the continued increase in demand for consumer installment credit between 1980 and 1985.

DELINQUENCY OF CONSUMER CREDIT CONTRACTS. Generally, the incidence of delinquency is low on consumer credit contracts but varies over the business cycle. Delinquency statistics for consumer finance companies that historically have extended loans to high-risk borrowers indicate that normally only about 2% of the dollar value of loans outstanding is classified as delinquent. During the recession period of 1974–1975 delinquencies reached as high as 4% for some firms in the industry. National statistics of installment credit delinquencies over time (Exhibit 13) suggest that during the 1974–1975 recession, delinquencies of 30 days and over rose to 3.0% from an average level of about 1.8%.

The main cause of delinquency, as indicated by a survey of creditors performed for the National Commission on Consumer Finance (*Consumer Credit in the United States*, p. 23) are unemployment, sickness, and overuse of debt. Most creditors did not believe that consumers who became delinquent were "deadbeats" who never intended to repay their debts.

PERSONAL BANKRUPTCIES. Most personal bankruptcies are voluntary: the assets of the bankrupt's estate are liquidated, exemptions are claimed, and the remaining fund is divided among the creditors according to the priority of their claims. When a creditor has a security interest in a debtor's property, he can enforce it even if a court has allowed an exemption for the property.

EXHIBIT 12   AGE STRUCTURE OF THE U.S. POPULATION (MILLIONS)

Age	1970	1977	1985
18–24	24.7	28.6	27.9
25–34	25.3	33.2	29.9
35–44	23.2	23.5	31.4
45–54	23.3	23.4	22.5
55–64	18.7	20.4	21.7
65+	20.0	23.5	27.3

Source: U.S. Department of Commerce, *Statistical Abstract of the United States,* Washington, D.C., 1979.

EXHIBIT 13   DELINQUENCY RATE, 30 DAYS AND OVER, CONSUMER INSTALLMENT CREDIT

Delinquency rate, 30 days and over, consumer installment loans
(% — inverted scale)

Source: U.S. Department of Commerce, *Business Conditions Digest*, March 1980, p. 33.

During the fiscal year ending June 30, 1979, there were 196,951 personal bankruptcy petitions filed, for an average of about 90 per 100,000 population. Because of the increased lenience under both Chapters 7 and 13 of the new Bankruptcy Code, the number of personal bankruptcies is expected and indeed has already begun to increase dramatically. The section "Bankruptcy and Reorganization" in this *Handbook* reviews the new Act in detail.

The personal bankruptcy rate varies considerably by state, with a high of 194 per 100,000 in Alabama compared to 14 per 100,000 in Texas in 1979. Personal exemption differences across states, as well as the legal ability to garnish wages, account for some of the variation in bankruptcy rates across states. However, it is difficult to account for the large variation in bankruptcy rates from state to state.

The new federal bankruptcy code increased the value of "bare necessities of life" that could be exempted in a personal bankruptcy case (see section "Bankruptcy and Reorganization" in this *Handbook*). The federal law overrides the various states' definition of "bare necessities" and generally results in an increase in the amount of personal property that can be exempted.

REFERENCES

Altman, Edward, Avery, Robert, Eisenbeis, Robert, and Sinkey, Joseph, *Application of Classification Techniques in Business, Banking, and Finance,* JAI Press, Greenwich, Conn., 1981.

Booth, S. Lees, *NCFA 1980 Finance Facts Yearbook,* National Consumer Finance Association, Washington, D.C., 1980.

Durkin, Thomas A., and Elliehausen, Gregory E., 1977 Consumer Credit Survey, Board of Governors of the Federal Reserve, 1978.

Feldman, Sheldon, and Reiley, Kimberly A., "A Compilation of Federal and State Laws Regulating Consumer Financial Services," Monograph No. 8, Vols. 1 and 2, Credit Research Center, Purdue University, Lafayette, IN, 1977.

Kane, Edward, "Accelerating Inflation and the Distribution of Household Savings Incentives," Working Paper No. 30, Credit Research Center, Purdue University, Lafayette, IN, 1979.

McAlister, Ray, and DeSpain, Edward, "Bank and Retail Credit Card Yields Under Alternative Assessment Methods," Working Paper No. 21, Credit Research Center, Purdue University, Lafayette, IN, 1978.

National Commission on Consumer Finance, *Consumer Credit in the United States,* NCCF, Washington, D.C., December 1972.

BIBLIOGRAPHY

Cole, R. H., *Consumer and Commercial Credit Management,* 5th ed., Irwin, Homewood, IL., 1977.

Eisenbeis, Robert A., "Problems on Applying Discriminant Analysis in Credit Scoring Models," *Journal of Banking and Finance,* Vol. 12, No. 3, October 1978.

Financial Publishing Co., *The Cost of Personal Borrowing in the United States,* Financial Publishing Co., Boston, 1979.

Hsia, David C., "Credit Scoring and the Equal Credit Opportunity Act," *Hastings Law Journal,* November 1978.

Redding, H. T., and Knight, G. H., *The Dun and Bradstreet Handbook of Credit and Collections,* Crowell, New York, 1974.

Sexton, Donald E., Jr., "Determining Good and Bad Credit Risks Among High- and Low-Income Families," *Journal of Business,* Vol. 50, No. 2, April 1977.

SHORT-TERM MONEY MARKETS AND INSTRUMENTS

CONTENTS

OVERVIEW OF SHORT-TERM MONEY
MARKETS   3

MONEY MARKET INSTRUMENTS:
STRUCTURE AND TRADING
CHARACTERISTICS   3

Bank Instruments   3
  Negotiable certificates of deposit (CDs)   3
    Domestic (U.S.) certificates of
    deposit   3
    Eurodollar certificates of deposit   5
    "Yankee" certificates of deposit   5
  Term deposits   5
    Eurodollar deposits   5
    Term Federal Funds   5
  Bankers' acceptances   5
Corporate Obligations   6
  Commercial paper   6
  Master notes   7
U.S. Treasury and Agency Obligations   7
  Treasury bills   7
  Securities of government-sponsored
  agencies   8

Federal Home Loan Bank discount
notes   8
Federal National Mortgage
Association discount notes   8
Federal Farm Credit System
discount notes   9
Money Market Instruments Denominated
in a Foreign Currency   9
Tax-Exempt Money Market Instruments   10
  Tax-free anticipation notes   10
  Project notes   10
  Tax-exempt commercial paper   10
Federal Funds Market   11
Repurchase Agreements and Reverse
Repurchase Agreements   11
  General description   11
  Yield determination on a repurchase
  transaction   12
    Type of security as collateral   12
    Maturity of collateral   12
    Delivery form of collateral   12
  Term repurchase transactions as an
  arbitrage instrument   12
  Dollar price repurchase agreement   13

SHORT-TERM MONEY MARKETS AND INSTRUMENTS

Tildon W. Smith

OVERVIEW OF SHORT-TERM MONEY MARKETS

The **money market** consists of the buying and selling of short-term instruments of debt. The major issuers of these instruments are **banks, corporations,** and **governmental** or **quasi-governmental** bodies. Initial maturities are 1 year or less, usually 6 months or less. The market is **unregulated** and has **no official central clearing agency;** rather, it consists of willing buyers coming to terms with willing sellers. As a practical matter, most transactions occur in New York through various securities firms and major banks, but London, Hong Kong, Tokyo, Chicago, and other financial centers all have functioning money markets. The market is highly liquid and is restricted by market custom to only the most creditworthy issuers. The various money market instruments and their characteristics are discussed below and summarized in Exhibit 1.

MONEY MARKET INSTRUMENTS: STRUCTURE AND TRADING CHARACTERISTICS

BANK INSTRUMENTS.

Negotiable Certificates of Deposit (CDs).

Domestic (U.S.) Certificates of Deposit. These CDs are obligations of banks chartered in the United States. They may be issued by a bank in minimum denominations of $100,000 with a minimum maturity of 14 days. The primary issue is typically directed to the bank's institutional and large individual customers; most initial maturities are 6 months or less. Large issues are often sold through major securities firms. Interest payments are on an **actual** (including nonwork days) 360-day basis with settlement in **Federal Funds,** usually in New York. Negotiable CDs differ in their size and marketability from those CDs available to smaller investors.

The **secondary market trades** are a round lot of $5 million, but trades of $1 million and less can be efffected at a concession to the market of 5–10 basis points (there are 100 basis points in a single percentage point of interest). The market is very liquid for maturities of

EXHIBIT 1 FACT SHEET ON MONEY MARKET INSTRUMENTS

	Treasury Bills	FHLB Discount Notes	FNMA Discount Notes	FFCB Discount Notes	FFCB Bonds	Domestic CDs	Eurodollar CDs	Bankers' Acceptances	Commercial Paper
Settlement[a]	Next business day, in federal funds	Next business day, in federal funds	Next business day, in federal funds	Next business day, in federal funds	Next business day, in federal funds	Next business day, in federal funds	Second business day, in clearing house funds	Next business day, in federal funds	Cash federal funds
Discounted or interest bearing	Discounted	Discounted	Either	Discounted	Interest bearing	Either	Interest bearing	Discounted	Either
Interest calculation	Actual 360	Actual 360	Actual 360	Actual 360	30-day month, 360 days	Actual 360	Actual 360	Actual 360	Actual 360
Form	Book entry	Physical	Physical	Physical	Book entry	Physical	Physical	Physical	Physical
Maturity range; new issue	91, 182, or 365 days	30–360 days	30–360 days	5–270 days	6 months, 9 months	14 days to 10 years	30 days to 10 years	30–270 days	1–270 days

[a]All money market instruments except Eurodollar can usually be settled for cash or same day until 11:00–11:30 A.M., but the investor must specify this requirement.

6 months and less and for the largest **money center banks** (usually top 10 deposit size). Smaller **regional bank CDs** trade at concessions of 5 to 30 basis points (and sometimes more) to money center banks.

Eurodollar Certificates of Deposit.   These are obligations of large U.S. or foreign commercial banks, payable usually in London in U.S. dollars. The minimum is $1 million with a maturity of 30 days. The primary issue is usually to large institutions and to major securities firms active in the secondary market. Interest payments are based on actual days on a 360-day basis. Normal settlement is in London in **clearinghouse funds. Federal funds** settlements and maturities can often be negotiated on secondary transactions.

Secondary market transactions in Eurodollar CDs are $5 million for a round lot; very few trades are for less. The market is very liquid for maturities of 6 months and less, however, not quite as liquid as the market for domestic U.S. CDs. Market convention restricts most activity to large **international banks.** Rates on domestic Eurodollar CDs are generally higher than for domestic U.S. CDs. **Foreign Eurodollar CDs** have slightly higher rates than U.S. Eurodollar CDs.

"Yankee" Certificates of Deposit.   These are obligations of non-U.S. banks issued in the United States by the foreign banks' U.S. branches. They are usually issued in minimums of $1 million for 30 to 180 days. Longer maturities of 180 to 360 days are issued with some frequency, usually through securities dealers. Interest is paid on an actual-day, 360-day basis. Settlement is in **Federal Funds,** usually in New York.

Secondary market transactions usually have a $1 million to $5 million minimum. There is a wide range in rates depending on availability and on the particular bank issuing the CD. Rates are higher than those for domestic CDs and usually are comparable to those for primary Eurodollar CDs.

Term Deposits.

Eurodollar Deposits.   These are obligations of major banks, both U.S. and foreign, placed with the London branch. Deposits are usually $1 million and larger for a **minimum of 1 day.** Deposits are placed for a **fixed time** at a **fixed rate.** No debt instrument is issued; therefore, there is **no secondary market** and **no liquidity.** Payment is made in clearinghouse funds by a transfer to the depository bank. Interest is on an actual-day, 360-day basis. Some deposits are placed directly, but a large portion are placed by **money brokers.** Most transactions are 6 months and less, but 1-year placements are not uncommon.

Term Federal Funds.   These are obligations of major U.S. banks. The normal transaction is $5 million, but some deposits can be made for as little as $500,000, at a concession to the market of 5 to 15 basis points. **Placements** can be made only by financial institutions and certain quasi-governmental bodies. Maturities are 2 days to 1 year, but most are 90 to 180 days. The placement is for a **fixed time** at a **fixed rate** and no instrument is issued; therefore, there is **no liquidity.** The effective interest rate is generally lower than that for term Eurodollar placements. Most institutions (primarily savings and loan associations) use this vehicle because of regulatory restrictions on use of the **Eurodollar placement market.**

Bankers' Acceptances.   A **banker's acceptance** (BA) is a **negotiable time draft** drawn on a bank, either U.S. or foreign, that is "accepted" by the bank on the **issue date.** That is, a bankers' acceptance is simply a "postdated check" insofar as the bank is willing to agree on the issue date that the draft will be accepted for payment on the postdated day.

BAs were devised to facilitate international trade but are now used domestically as well. To understand how a banker's acceptance is created, suppose that an exporter is selling goods that **will not be delivered for 6 months.** The exporter goes to his bank and draws a draft payable in 6 months, and the bank stamps the draft "accepted." The BA then can be sold as a money market instrument at a **discount from face.** The bank can provide this discounting service, or the customer may do it himself. The rate the BA trades at is a function of the bank on which it is drawn. As with CDs, the larger money center banks offer the lowest rates. Regional domestic banks and foreign banks will trade at higher rates.

The **secondary market for BAs** is similar to that for CDs. The larger the bank, generally, the **better the secondary liquidity.** Transactions are usually $1 million to $5 million. Settlement is in Federal Funds. BAs trade on a discount basis, and interest payments are on an actual-day, 360-day basis.

CORPORATE OBLIGATIONS.

Commercial Paper. Commercial paper consists of **unsecured promissory** notes issued by a corporation to meet short-term credit needs. These notes are **exempt from registration** under Section 3(a)3 of the Securities Act of 1933, which grants exception for any note "... which arises out of a current transaction or the proceeds of which have been or are to be used for current transactions, and which has a maturity at time of issuance of not exceeding nine months . . . or any renewal thereof . . . ."

Commercial paper has a usual minimum of $100,000 but some issuers will issue notes as small as $25,000. Commercial paper is **quoted on a discount actual 360-day basis** but can be purchased on an **interest-bearing equivalent.** Commercial paper can have a maturity from 1 to 270 days but the usual period is 15 to 45 days.

Commercial paper may be issued by two different methods.

"Direct." Commercial paper is issued **directly to the investor by the corporation.** The investor contacts the institution, usually a bank, that has been designated by the corporation as an approved intermediary. The bank acts strictly in an **agent capacity** and assumes no principal position.

"Dealer." Commercial paper is also issued by utilizing a securities firm to effect the placement. The securities firm, after consultation with the corporation, sells the paper and arranges all necessary money transfers.

There is **no secondary market for commercial paper.** Most direct issuers have some form of prepayment option. Liquidity for dealer paper is usually provided by the securities dealer's willingness to repurchase the paper at prevailing market rates. However, even though some liquidity is provided, it is usually assumed that all paper will be held to maturity.

Commercial paper, generally, is rated by **Moody's, Standard & Poor's,** and/or **Fitch Publishing Co.** It is the only short-term instrument with a **credit rating.** The ratings, in order of descending creditworthiness, are as follows:

Moody's	Standard & Poor's	Fitch
P-1	A-1	F-1
P-2	A-2	F-2
P-3	A-3	F-3

A rating of at least the second category is usually necessary to actively issue commercial paper.

Master Notes.   A master note is a variation of a commercial paper program negotiated between a direct commercial paper issuer and a large short-term investor. The arrangement usually calls for the investor to maintain some **minimum level of investment.** The investor can make adjustments in the amount of his investment up to some agreed-on maximum. The investor is usually paid an **interest rate based on a longer term investment**—say, 90 or 180 days, even though he has virtually a 1-day investment. The major advantage to the issuer is stability of funds. The major advantage to the investor is a higher interest rate and flexibility.

U.S. TREASURY AND AGENCY OBLIGATIONS.   The **U.S. Treasury** and various agencies of the government issue both long-term and short-term obligations. As long-term obligations move closer to maturity, they can be purchased in the secondary market as short-term investments. These obligations are interest bearing and are sold at the **market price plus the accrued interest** from the last interest payment date. Interest on government bonds and notes is calculated on an actual-day, 365-day basis, while agency obligations are calculated on the basis of a 30-day month and a 360-day year.

As a practical matter, most government and agency securities trading in the money market are those with **original maturities of 1 year or less.** These securities are **Treasury bills** and **discount notes.**

Treasury Bills.   Bills are direct obligations of the U.S. government; their minimum denomination is $10,000. They are sold on a discounted basis and calculated on actual days on a 360-day basis to pay par at maturity. Treasury bills are **auctioned** by the U.S. Treasury, and both **competitive** and **noncompetitive** bids are accepted. A person who submits a noncompetitive bid is paid the average rate of all the competitive bids.

Auctions are held **each Monday** for **settlement** on the next **Thursday** for a 91-day bill and for a 182-day bill. Every four weeks, an auction is held for a 1-year bill. The year bill is announced on **Tuesday,** auctioned on **Wednesday,** and settled the next **Tuesday.**

After issue, **a round lot trade** in the secondary market is $5 million, but trades can be executed for as little as $10,000 at some concession to the **round lot rate.** Most institutions charge an **"odd lot" fee** for transactions less than $100,000. Market terminology identifies the **most recently issued** 91-day, 182-day, and 1-year instruments as the "3-month bill," the "6-month bill," and the "year bill." Once a new bill has been issued, the old bill is identified by its maturity date.

The Treasury also occasionally issues shorter maturity bills on an as-needed basis. These are called **cash management bills** and usually have a minimum size of $1 million.

The **Treasury bill market** is the most liquid market place for money market instruments, since the market perceives no credit risk for this instrument; moreover, it trades as **a risk-free item.** Therefore, the yield on Treasury bills becomes the **base rate for all other instruments,** and all other instruments trade in relation to the "bill rate." As the market perceives **higher** credit risk or **less** liquidity for another money market instrument of comparable maturity, the yield will be correspondingly higher. For example, if a 6-month Treasury bill yields 16% and a 6-month domestic CD yields 18%, the 2% yield differential reflects the perceived higher credit risk and lower liquidity.

Treasury bills are not issued in a definitive form. U.S. government obligations are issued in book entry form and, therefore, **must be cleared through a commercial bank's account** at its respective Federal Reserve bank. Regular settlement is for the next business day, in Federal funds.

Securities of Government-Sponsored Agencies.   Various government agencies and/or government-sponsored institutions issue short-term securities. These securities are **not direct obligations of the U.S. government,** nor do they carry a guarantee from the U.S. government; however, the marketplace perceives these securities as being "moral" obligations of the government, and therefore, they command a premium rate, very close to the comparable maturity rate of a government security.

Federal Home Loan Bank Discount Notes.   The **Federal Home Loan Bank System (FHLB),** operating through 12 regional FHLBs, regulates and provides loans to the savings and loan industry. The system was established by the Federal Home Loan Bank Act in 1932. In 1974 the Federal Home Loan Bank Board implemented a program of issuing **consolidated discount notes,** which are joint and several obligations. These notes are issued in denominations of $100,000 and $200,000, and in increments of $50,000 above $200,000. Distribution is performed by a national syndicate of securities dealers comprised of the following:

Discount Corp.	First Boston Corp.
Bank of America	Aubrey G. Lanston Co., Inc.
William E. Pollock & Co.	Goldman, Sachs & Co.

The notes are sold at a discount to mature at par. Interest calculations are made on actual days on a 360-day basis. Maturities range from 30 to 360 days. The rates for each maturity reflect the FHLB's need for money in each period. Notes are issued in definitive form with New York delivery. Regular settlement is for the next business day in Federal Funds.

The **secondary market for FHLB discount notes** is good. Members of the underwriting group, as well as other securities dealers, make an active market. A **round lot transaction** is $1 million, with smaller amounts trading at a discount to the round lot rate.

Federal National Mortgage Association Discount Notes.   The Federal National Mortgage Association (FNMA; or **"Fannie Mae"**) was established in 1938 to provide support to the secondary market for federally guaranteed or insured mortgages. Although initially sponsored by the federal government, in 1968 the corporation became **privately owned.** In 1970 its scope was extended to include support for the secondary market for **conventional mortgages,** as well as **government mortgages.** In 1960 FNMA implemented a program of selling **discount notes** as a source of short-term financing. The minimum denomination is $50,000, and thereafter increments of $5,000 are allowed. These notes are sold through a national syndicate of securities dealers as follows:

Lehman Brothers Kuhn Loeb	Merrill Lynch, Pierce Fenner & Smith
Goldman, Sachs & Co.	Continental Bank
Salomon Brothers	Citibank
Bank of America	A. G. Becker

The rates are set by FNMA, are quoted on a discount basis, and are calculated on an actual-day, 360-day basis. Maturities range from 30 to 360 days. FNMA will, however, issue interest-bearing notes at the interest-bearing equivalent of the discount rate. Notes are issued in definitive form for New York delivery. Regular settlement is the next business day, in Federal funds.

A **secondary market for FNMA discount notes** is maintained by the dealers above, along with several others not in the syndicate. These notes have good liquidity, and $1 million is a round lot trade.

Federal Farm Credit System Discount Notes.   The Federal Farm Credit System provides credit services to farmers and farm-related enterprises through a network of 12 Farm Credit districts. Each district has a **Federal Land Bank,** a **Federal Intermediate Credit Bank,** and a **Bank for Cooperatives** (plus an additional Bank for Cooperatives in Denver, Colorado) to implement policies of the Federal Farm Credit System. The authority for the Farm Credit System is the **Farm Credit Act of 1971.**

In 1975 the Federal Farm Credit Bank System implemented a discount note program as a source of short-term financing. Notes have a minimum size of $50,000, purchasable thereafter in increments of $50,000. Distribution is through a national syndicate of securities dealers as follows:

Salomon Brothers

Merrill Lynch, Pierce Fenner & Smith

A. G. Becker

The rates are set by the Federal Farm Credit Bank and are sold only on a discounted basis. Interest calculations are made on an actual-day, 360-day basis. Maturities range from 5 to 270 days. Notes are issued in definitive form for New York delivery. Regular settlement is in 1 business day, in Federal Funds. An **active secondary market** for these discount notes is maintained by several securities dealers. A round lot is $1 million, with odd lots trading at some concession to the round lot rate.

The Federal Farm Credit System also sells **consolidated systemwide bonds** once a month. Each sale contains a 6-month bond and a 9-month bond. The bonds are sold in increments of $5,000 in book entry form. The rate is set by the Federal Farm Credit System. The consolidated bonds bear interest on a 30-day-month, 360-day-year basis. The **secondary market** for this bond is very good—in most cases **better** than the discount note market.

MONEY MARKET INSTRUMENTS DENOMINATED IN A FOREIGN CURRENCY.   In this highly specialized area of the money market, an investor with U.S. dollars purchases a security denominated in another currency. The investor first enters a **"spot" foreign exchange contract** to convert U.S. dollars to the foreign currency; simultaneously, he purchases the money market instrument with his newly acquired foreign currency and executes a contract to convert the foreign currency back to U.S. dollars at maturity.

The investor's ultimate yield has two components: first, the **stated yield on the purchased security,** and second, the **gain or loss on the forward foreign exchange contract.** An example would be as follows:

1. Investor has $10 million in U.S. dollars to invest.
2. Investor converts U.S. dollars to Canadian dollars in the spot market at $1.100, producing $11 million Canadian to invest.
3. Investor calculates that 11 million Canadian invested at 15% in a **Canadian bank certificate of deposit** for 180 days on a 365-day basis would yield proceeds at

maturity of $11,813,698 ($11,000,000 × 180/365). The investor, therefore, enters into a **forward** foreign exchange contract to convert the $11,813,698 in Canadian dollars to U.S. dollars at maturity (assume at cost, 1.080).

4. Therefore, on maturity, the $11,813,698 Canadian converts to $10,938,609 U.S. This converts to a U.S. yield, on a 365-day basis, of 19.03% ($938,609 ÷ $10,000,000 × 365/180).

This money market investment can be executed in amounts generally of $1 million and up. Liquidity is not very good insofar as liquidating the investment requires taking reverse positions in the foreign exchange contracts. Delivery is usually effected in the country in which the security is denominated. Some element of additional risk is injected as a result of the forward foreign exchange contract if the contract is executed in the name of a third party instead of the investor. It should also be noted that many foreign countries have a variety of duties to control capital movements (e.g., Canadian nonresident tax, Japanese duty stamps), and these can substantially reduce yields.

Interest rate calculations vary but are usually made on an actual-day, 360-day basis or an actual-day, 365-day basis, depending on the nature of the security. The most widely available securities are bank CDs, foreign commercial paper, and bonds under repurchase agreement.

TAX-EXEMPT MONEY MARKET INSTRUMENTS.   Securities that are **exempt from federal taxation** in the money market are somewhat less readily available than are other money market instruments. This limitation reflects to a large degree the long-term nature of the cash needs of most of the institutions that are authorized to issue tax-free debt. There are three major types of instrument: tax-free anticipation notes, obligations of local housing and urban renewal agencies (project notes), and tax-exempt commercial paper.

Tax-Free Anticipation Notes.   These obligations are a large part of the tax-exempt market. As the name suggests, they are issued ''in the anticipation'' of a more permanent source of money by states and other public agencies. The obligations fall into the categories of **tax or revenue anticipation notes** (TANs or RANs), which are redeemed by the collection of taxes and revenues, and bond anticipation notes (BANs), which are redeemed by the issuance of longer term bonds. These notes are usually sold on a **competitive bid basis.**

Anticipation notes range from $5,000 up. Some issues set minimums at $25,000. Notes are issued in interest-bearing form, and regular settlement is 5 business days, in Federal Funds; however, trades can usually be effected for cash or 1-day settlement. Interest is usually calculated on the basis of a 30-day month, 360-day year with interest at maturity. **Secondary market transactions** are usually $500,000 to $5 million.

Project Notes.   **Obligations issued by local housing and urban renewal agencies** are called **project notes** (PNs). They are administered under a U.S. Department of Housing and Urban Development program and are sold in **monthly auctions.** They carry the full faith and credit guarantee of the U.S. government. In price, form, settlement, calculation of interest, and secondary market transactions, PNs are like anticipation notes.

Tax-Exempt Commercial Paper.   Such instruments, which became more prevalent in the late 1970s, are issued by tax-exempt borrowers who have an ongoing need for short-term moneys. The minimum denomination usually is $100,000. The rate on tax-exempt commercial paper is established by the issuing institution for a range of maturities from 5 to 270 days. This offers a major advantage over anticipation notes and project notes because an **investor can select specific maturity dates.** Also, it is generally very difficult to obtain large blocks ($5 million or more) of anticipation notes and project notes in the secondary market—the commercial paper note will accommodate large orders, however. Rates are quoted on a discount basis and are figured on an actual-day, 360-day basis. Regular settlement is usually cash or next day, in Federal Funds.

FEDERAL FUNDS MARKET.   The Federal Funds market is an integral part of money market activities, even though **participation is limited to banking institutions, savings institutions,** and **certain government agencies.** Participants in the federal funds market buy and sell **excess reserves** for a period of 1 day (overnight). All transactions are **unsecured loans** and pay interest on an actual-day, 360-day basis. No security is created to evidence the transaction.

The market functions by two different methods. In the **"rollover" market** a seller/lender of money anticipates an ongoing sell position and places money with a regular purchaser/borrower. The seller then makes adjustments in his daily balance as necessary. The transaction is one of operational convenience that eliminates the movement of large amounts each day. The seller has the right to remove all his money on any day if he so desires. The rate paid is usually an average or composite rate of the individual day rates.

The second method involves the **"spot" market,** and each transaction is negotiated separately to establish the rate. The market is facilitated by **money brokers** who constantly query market participants via telephone to determine their market positions. The "spot" Federal Funds market is the most visible **money market indicator,** and this rate has significant implications for the monetary policies of the **Federal Reserve Open Market Committee.** Usually, the Open Market Committee has certian support levels at which it will enter the market as a participant in an attempt to effect its monetary policies. The support levels themselves, and any changes in them, exert a major influence on other money market rates. For more details on Federal Reserve activity, see the section entitled "Money and Capital Markets: Institutional Framework and Federal Reserve Control."

REPURCHASE AGREEMENTS AND REVERSE REPURCHASE AGREEMENTS.

General Description.   In a repurchase agreement **(repo),** securities are sold with the **simultaneous agreement to repurchase** the same securities at some point in the future at the **same price plus interest,** at an agreed on rate. Stated differently, a repurchase agreement is a form of **collateralized loan** wherein the investor is given a security as "collateral" for a loan of a fixed maturity at a fixed rate. A **reverse repurchase agreement** (sometimes called a **resell agreement**) is the mirror image of a repo. As a matter of convention, these transactions are identified from the vantage point of the securities dealer rather than that of the investor. Therefore, in market terminology, if an investor invests money in a repurchase agreement with a securities dealer of a commercial bank, the transaction is referred to by both parties as a "repo" even though it is in fact a reverse repurchase (resell) to the investor.

Repos as a practical matter are primarily very short-term vehicles with a **maturity of 1 to 5 days.** However, in recent years, the instrument has been used for terms as long as 1 year. Most repos use government bonds, agency bonds, or Government National Mortgage Association or Federal Home Loan Mortgage certificates as collateral. However, the trend in recent years has been to use many other items such as CDs, corporate bonds and gold as collateral.

The **1-day repurchase agreement** is the primary source of **financing by securities dealers** to finance trading positions and **commercial banks** to finance excess portfolio collateral. (Banks usually use this source of financing only when the 1-day repo rate is **below** the Federal Funds rate.) Therefore, this is one of the **key market rates** to track in analyzing money market rates because it is a significant ingredient in a securities dealer's profitability on a trading position. As the rate to finance a trading position rises, assuming that other market rates remain constant, the profitability of the position declines. This difference between the cost of financing and the yield on the security being financed is called the **"carry" spread.**

The repo, as a money market investment alternative, has experienced explosive growth in the past few years and is now one of the dominant money market instruments. Securities purchased under a repurchase agreement usually offer a substantial rate advantage over the outright purchase of the same instrument for the same maturity. Additionally, the maturity date and the size of investment can be tailored to meet the needs of the investor.

Yield Determination on a Repurchase Transaction.   The yield on a repo is negotiated between the two parties to the transaction. Some of the several factors that are considered in the negotiation are discussed next.

Type of Security as Collateral.   Since a repo is a form of collateralized borrowing, the creditworthiness and liquidity of the collateral is an integral part of the rate. The more creditworthy the collateral, the lower the rate. Therefore, for example, a repo using government bonds would receive a lower rate than the same transaction using bank CDs.

Maturity of Collateral.   Usually, given the higher volatility of securities with longer maturities, the shorter the maturity of the underlying collateral, the lower the rate. Large blocks of securities command a lower rate than do smaller blocks. For example, a $10 million repo transaction using one $10 million Treasury note as collateral would command a lower rate than the same transaction using 10 different $1 million notes. This difference reflects the higher operational and accounting costs associated with processing the larger number of transactions.

Delivery Form of Collateral.   **Collateral in book entry form** at the Federal Reserve will command a lower repo rate than collateral that is issued in definitive form. For example, Federal Home Loan Bank debentures issued in book entry, wireable form will command a lower rate than Federal Home Loan Bank discount notes issued in definitive form. This discrepancy, too, is related to the higher operational cost associated with physical delivery of securities.

Term Repurchase Transactions as an Arbitrage Instrument.   As discussed earlier, the creditworthiness and liquidity of the underlying collateral in a repurchase agreement determines the rate. Therefore, institutions that carry in their portfolios the most creditworthy and liquid instruments can often use these securities to borrow money and **arbitrage** into a less creditworthy and/or less liquid instrument.

As an example of such a transaction, consider a savings and loan association that owns in its portfolio $10 million government bonds. It has no plans to liquidate these during the next 6 months. The following steps might occur:

Step 1. The savings and loan enters into a reverse repurchase agreement with a security dealer wherein the bonds are sold at the prevailing market price of 98 and the S & L agrees to repurchase them at 98 plus interest at a rate of 10% in 180 days. Simultaneously, the savings and loan would use the proceeds of $9 million to purchase a $9 million CD, to mature on the same day as the reverse repurchase transaction, at a market rate of 10.5%.

Step 2. At the conclusion of 180 days, the proceeds of the maturing CD are calculated as $10,314, 500 (1 + $980,000 × 10.5 × 180/360), and this amount is applied to the repurchase of the government bonds at $10,290,000 (1 + $980,000 × 0.10 × 180/360). Thus the net profit on the transaction would be $24,500.

It should be noted that a **repo transaction** is treated for **accounting purposes as a borrowing.** Therefore, **no gain or loss is recognized** on the sale of the security, and the coupon payment on the underlying security continues to be accrued to the true owner during the term of the transaction.

Dollar Price Repurchase Agreement. A variation of a standard term repurchase agreement is a "dollar price repurchase agreement." This differs from a regular repo because the seller of the security does not continue to receive the coupon yield on the underlying security but realizes the coupon amount by selling and repurchasing the security at different prices. This transaction is primarily applied to Government National Mortgage Association (GNMA, or **Ginnie Mae) certificates.** A sample transaction would be as follows:

Step 1. A savings and loan that owns a $10 million GNMA 12.5% certificate agrees to sell the GNMA to a security dealer at a price of 94 and to repurchase at a price of $93\frac{1}{2}$ in 90 days. (Note that the repurchase price is different from the sell price.) The cost of borrowing under this method is calculated as follows:

$$\text{annualized lost interest income} =$$
$$\text{face amount} \times \text{coupon} =$$
$$\$10,000,000 \times 0.125 = \$1,250,000$$

$$\text{annualized price differential} =$$
$$(\text{sell price} - \text{repurchase price}) \times \text{yearly equivalent} =$$
$$(\$9,400,000 - \$9,350,000) \times 360/90 = \$200,000$$

$$\frac{\text{lost interest} - \text{price differential}}{\text{sell price}} = \text{interest cost}$$

$$\frac{\$1,250,000 - \$200,000}{\$9,400,000} = 11.17\%$$

Step 2. The savings and loan purchases a certificate of deposit to mature in 90 days at a yield of 11.67%, thereby earning a profit of $11,750 on a spread of 0.5% on $9,400,000 ($9,400,000 × 0.50 × 90/360 = $11,750).

For this transaction, a GNMA with the same coupon rate (in this case 12.5%) must be returned to the seller, but the certificate is not required to be from the same pool.

BIBLIOGRAPHY

An Introduction to the Interest Rate Futures Market, Chicago Board of Trade, Chicago, various dates.

Darst, David M., *The Complete Bond Book,* McGraw-Hill, New York, 1975.

Handbook of Securities of the United States Government and Federal Agencies, First Boston Corp., New York, 1978.

Handbook for the Money Market Investor, First National Bank of Atlanta, Atlanta, GA, 1973.

Hawk, William A., *The U.S. Government Securities Market,* Harris Trust and Savings Bank, Chicago, 1976.

Inside the Yield Book, Prentice-Hall, Englewood Cliffs, NJ, 1972.

Spence, Bruce M., Giaudenz, Jacob, Y., and Lynch, John, J., Jr., *Standard Securities Calculation Methods,* Securities Industry Association, New York, 1973.

ADDITIONAL SOURCES OF INFORMATION

Money Market Instruments, Federal Reserve Bank of Cleveland, Cleveland, Ohio, annually.

Lindow, Wesley, *Inside the Money Market,* Random House, New York, 1972.

Meiselman, David, *The Term Structure of Interest Rates,* Prentice-Hall, Englewood Cliffs, NJ, 1962.

Open Market Operations, Federal Reserve Bank of New York, New York, various dates.

PART 2

INTERNATIONAL FINANCIAL
MARKETS AND INSTITUTIONS

THE INTERNATIONAL MONETARY SYSTEM

CONTENTS

HISTORY OF THE GOLD STANDARD	**3**
Money Supplies and Price Levels	3
Payments Balances	3
Interest Rates: Role of the Bank of England	4
Technical Adjustments	4
THE GOLD EXCHANGE STANDARD	**4**
BRITAIN'S RETURN TO GOLD	**5**
THE GOLD BLOC	**5**
THE TRIPARTITE AGREEMENT	**5**
THE BRETTON WOODS SYSTEM	**6**
Plans of Keynes and White	6
Par Values	6
Foreign Exchange Intervention and the IMF	6
The Triffin Dilemma	7
THE SMITHSONIAN AGREEMENT	**7**
THE FLOATING RATE SYSTEM	**8**
Buying in Forward Markets	8
Selling in Forward Markets	8
EURODOLLARS AND EUROCURRENCIES	**8**
MANAGED FLOATING	**9**
Tied Exchange Rates	10
Basket currencies	10
SDR-tied currencies	10
Minidevaluation Systems	10
The European Monetary System	11
Parity grid system	11
Divergence indicator system	14
Financing the EMS	17
EXCHANGE CONTROLS	**17**
Tariffs, Subsidies, and Import Controls	17
Controls on Capital Movements	17
Multiple Exchange Rates	17
BALANCE OF PAYMENTS	**18**
Trade Account	18
Current Account	18
Capital Account	19
BALANCE OF PAYMENTS SETTLEMENTS	**19**
Foreign Exchange	19
Gold	24
Gold pool	24
Two-tier agreements	24
Jamaica agreement	24
Reserve Positions in the IMF	24
Conditionality	25
Special drawing rights (SDRs)	25
The Proposed Substitution Account	26

THE INTERNATIONAL MONETARY SYSTEM

James L. Burtle

Currency, bank deposits and other forms of money of one country that can be traded for the currency of another country, is the central element in an international monetary system. International monetary systems are distinguished from each other mainly in terms of policies that the leading governments apply to foreign exchange markets. The extremes of these policies range between rigid exchange rates fixed by governments and floating exchange rates determined by free market forces without government interference.

HISTORY OF THE GOLD STANDARD

Since ancient times there have been **foreign exchange markets,** sometimes operating freely and in other cases under strict government control. While much can be learned from earlier history, the gold standard, which applied from the latter part of the nineteenth centry until 1914, is a convenient starting point for a survey of the development of the monetary system as it exists today. Indeed, regardless of whether the apparent success of the gold standard was a historical accident, there has been a tendency to look back on the 1880–1914 era as a period of international monetary stability that helped to generate worldwide high productivity and employment.

MONEY SUPPLIES AND PRICE LEVELS. **The gold standard** operated without direct fixing of exchange rates between currencies but, in major countries, there was a fixing of units of each currency to its so-called **mint parity** in ounces of gold. In addition, the central bank of each country adjusted its money supply according to its holdings of gold. Thus, when gold moved into a country the money supply rose, and when gold moved out of a country the money supply fell.

Another requirement for a workable gold standard was flexibility in price levels such that they tended to move both up and down with money supplies. Thus a rise in the money supply in a country pushed up prices and a fall in the money supply lowered prices.

PAYMENTS BALANCES. When money supplies moved with gold supplies and prices moved with money supplies, the gold standard tended to be self-adjusting. If a country had acquired additional gold because of a balance of payments surplus, the rise in its money supply would push up prices. Because of its higher prices compared with the rest of the world, the country would sell less abroad. Moreover, since prices abroad were lower, it would import more. As a result, the trade surplus would be eliminated.

In a country with a trade deficit, the process would work in the opposite direction. The country would lose gold, and as its gold supply declined, the central bank would reduce the money supply. Prices would fall relative to those of other countries. As a result, exports would rise and imports would fall until the trade deficit was reduced.

INTEREST RATES: ROLE OF THE BANK OF ENGLAND. In actual practice the gold standard worked better with smaller gold movements and small relative price changes than might have been expected. Major reasons for the absence of disruptive gold movements and price changes were the dominance of London in the world money market and the policy of the **Bank of England** to adjust British interest rates to prevent excessive gold movements. When gold began to move out of London, the Bank of England usually raised interest rates, thus attracting money to London and improving the overall British balance of payments so that the gold outflow was reversed. Conversely, interest rates were usually lowered when gold moved into London.

TECHNICAL ADJUSTMENTS. It is also worth noting that under the **gold standard** the tie between gold supplies and money supplies was not as restrictive as might have been supposed. After 1890 new gold supplies were developed in South Africa and Alaska, and there were technological advances permitting the use of lower grade ores. Also the spread of checking accounts, not necessarily tied to gold holdings of central banks, increased world money supplies. Thus the gold standard did not lead to the stringency in world purchasing power that might have occurred without these favorable special circumstances.

THE GOLD EXCHANGE STANDARD

Major European countries abandoned the gold standard during World War I. Notes issued to pay for the war expanded more rapidly than gold supplies, and the convertibility of banknotes into gold was suspended because there was not enough gold for redemption. Nevertheless, most governments and central bankers looked back on the gold standard as a near-perfect system that they wanted restored. In the Genoa Conference of 1922 Britain proposed the so-called **gold exchange standard.** This system economized on gold by using as a reserve a **key currency** backed by gold. The key currency would have the same equilibrating function exercised by gold under the gold standard. Countries gaining the key currency would raise their money supplies and prices, and countries losing the key currency would lower their money supplies and prices. With higher prices, balance of payments surpluses would disappear, and with lower prices, balance of payments deficits would disappear. Britain wanted sterling to be the key currency because it was anxious to return sterling and the Bank of England to their central roles in the world monetary system.

Although the gold exchange standard was proposed in 1922, Europe remained on an essentially floating exchange rate system until 1925, when Britain went back on the gold standard. Britain, in effect, underwrote the gold exchange standard by promising that sterling would be redeemable in gold, though it was hoped that most countries would regard sterling as good as gold, as they had before 1914.

BRITAIN'S RETURN TO GOLD

Britain's **"return to gold"** was not a success. Instead of adopting a lower gold value for sterling, it was decided that confidence in **sterling** could be maintained only by using the prewar rate, which turned out to be too high for Britain to compete in world markets. Moreover, there had been a structural change in the world economy: relative wages and prices no longer moved downward easily, as had been the experience before 1914. The British coal strike and general strike in 1926 demonstrated these resistances to downward wage-price flexibility.

Under the gold exchange standard most of the British dominions and many of the smaller countries used sterling as a major part of their reserves. But the use of gold instead of sterling was the rule of major countries, notably the United States, France, and Germany (after the German mark was stabilized in 1924).

Already weakened and not fully supported by major financial centers, the gold exchange standard could not withstand the onslaught of the Great Depression. In September 1931, Britain was forced off the gold standard and sterling was allowed to float. There had been, of course, previous cases of countries abandoning gold convertibility, as in the United States from 1861 to 1879 and in France from 1971 to 1878, but these experiences were considered temporary and usually were related to recovery from wartime disturbances. The 1931 **sterling depreciation** was a shock: a leading financial power had dropped convertibility, and there was little hope that it would be restored.

THE GOLD BLOC

The reaction to the 1931 sterling depreciation—particularly from central banks that suffered losses from holding sterling reserves—was a total repudiation by major continental powers of the gold exchange standard. In the **World Economic Conference of 1933** the United States refused to stabilize the dollar, which had in effect gone off the gold standard when President Roosevelt took office in March 1933. Following the failure of the World Economic Conference, France, Belgium, the Netherlands, Switzerland, Italy, and Poland agreed to remain on the gold standard.

The gold bloc, as this group of countries was called, had basically the same problem as Britain. Their relative prices were too high and, in spite of trade restrictions, they suffered from chronic balance of payments deficits. The gold bloc came to an end when, after lengthy discussions with Britain and the United States on an appropriate exchange rate, France devalued its currency in September 1936.

THE TRIPARTITE AGREEMENT

In the period between 1936 and 1939 most currencies were floating or had fixed exchange rates subject to frequent change. Germany and a number of central European countries were maintaining balance of payments equilibria by means of complicated systems of **exchange controls.** There was, however, some recognition that there could be dangers in uncontrolled floating. **Stabilization accounts,** set up notably by the United States, France, and Britain, at least in principle were intended to smooth out erratic fluctuations in exchange rates. In the **Tripartite Agreement** issued in 1936 by the United States, Britain, and France simultaneously with the devaluation of the French franc, and in a subsequent statement in October

1936, it was agreed (*a*) not to use exchange rate changes to "obtain an unreasonable competitive advantage and thereby hamper the effort to restore more stable economic relations," (*b*) to maintain cooperation between exchange stabilization funds, and (*c*) to inform the other parties to the agreement of the exchange rate that would be maintained for the next 24 hours.

Prior to this agreement, the United States and the United Kingdom had indicated their opposition to a devaluation of the franc that would put France in an excessively competitive position. This fear of **competitive devaluation** was the major reason for the emphasis on exchange rate stability in the Bretton Woods Agreement of 1944.

THE BRETTON WOODS SYSTEM

The ideas advanced in negotiating the Tripartite Agreement might have been extended, since the world in the late 1930s seemed to be tiring of floating exchange rates. Before any action could be taken, however, World War II brought about exchange controls in most of the belligerent countries except the United States. Even before the end of the war, demands for monetary reconstruction were pervasive enough to lead to the **Bretton Woods Conference** of 1944.

PLANS OF KEYNES AND WHITE.   At Bretton Woods rival plans for world monetary reform were presented by John Maynard Keynes for Britain and by Henry Dexter White for the United States. The Keynes plan provided for a new international means of payment called the **bancor.** Member countries would agree to accept payments in bancors. A clearing process would be established among member countries with some limitations on the extent to which they could become debtors or creditors in bancors. The Keynes plan had the advantage that world trade would not be restrained by shortages of key currencies. White and the American delegation to the conference were, however, concerned that the expansion of bancor liabilities might become excessive. As an alternative to the Keynes plan, White proposed a plan that turned out to be a variant of the gold exchange standard in which dollars would be used as international reserves of central banks and dollars would be convertible into gold. The Bretton Woods Agreement emerged primarily as the White plan rather than the Keynes plan.

PAR VALUES.   In addition to the use of gold-convertible dollars as reserves, the agreement as it was actually implemented provided for essentially fixed exchange rates known as **par values.** Each member country was committed to maintain its exchange rate in the **1% band**—that is, not more than 1.0% above or below the par value. A country was permitted, however, to change its par value if there was a **"fundamental disequilibrium"** in its balance of payments. This term was not defined explicitly, but it appears that the Bretton Woods Agreement reflected the widespread viewpoint of the late 1930s that exchange rates should ordinarily remain stable. Thus a "fundamental disequilibrium" appears to refer to an extraordinary situation in which an exchange rate change could not be avoided by any realistic fiscal-monetary policy.

FOREIGN EXCHANGE INTERVENTION AND THE IMF.   Countries adhering to the Bretton Woods Agreement maintained their exchange rates within the 1% limit above or below par value by means of **foreign exchange intervention.** If a country's exchange rate went below the 1% lower limit, the central bank of that country would sell foreign exchange and thus buy back its own currency until the exchange rate was pushed above the lower 1% limit. On the other hand, if the currency went above the upper 1% limit, the central bank would sell its own currency, to bring its exchange rate to a point below the upper 1% limit. Under this system there was a possibility that countries might exhaust their gold and foreign exchange holdings while attempting to hold a currency above the 1.0% lower limit.

To make it easier for countries to maintain exchange rates during periods of temporary adversity, the Bretton Woods Agreement provided for the establishment of the **International Monetary Fund** (IMF). The IMF was set up to make loans (technically known as **drawings**) to countries experiencing balance of payments difficulties not severe enough to be considered "fundamental disequilibra." Thus as it was originally conceived, the IMF was intended to prop up exchange rates that were under temporary downward pressure. Loans from the IMF to member countries are provided from contributions by the members. Each country's **quota** in relation to other countries is determined on the basis of its gross national product, international trade data, international reserves, and other factors indicating the countrys' relative economic importance. Countries contribute 25% of their quota in gold or U.S. dollars and 75% in their own currency. Member countries are permitted to borrow 25% of their quota on a "no questions asked" basis. Larger borrowings from the fund require IMF approval and in many cases a **"letter of intent"** from the borrowing country indicating the measures that would be taken to improve its balance of payments.

THE TRIFFIN DILEMMA.   The Bretton Woods system in the earlier years of its operation appeared to be remarkably successful. World trade and output grew at record rates, fueled by the growth in dollar liquidity in a process roughly similar to the growth of gold supplies in the 1989–1914 period. In the 1960s, however, doubts began to arise about the basic soundness of the system. To increase world liquidity, a continuing U.S. dollar deficit was required; but as the cumulative deficit increased, it was not certain whether the value of the dollar could be maintained. This dilemma—sometimes called the **Triffin dilemma** after Professor Robert Triffin of Yale University—might have been the undoing of the Bretton Woods system.

Before there could be any test of the validity of the Triffin dilemma, however, for quite different reasons mainly related to military expenses and the overheating of the U.S. economy from the war in Vietnam, the dollar came under downward pressure in the late 1960s and early 1970s. In August 1971 President Nixon stopped conversions of the dollar into gold, thus ending the international monetary system that had been set up at Bretton Woods.

THE SMITHSONIAN AGREEMENT

Since the dollar was no longer supported by gold conversion, most exchange rates were allowed to float in world money markets from August to December 1971, when a new world monetary agreement, known as the **Smithsonian Agreement,** was adopted. In this agreement convertibility between gold and the dollar was not restored, but the theoretical gold value of the dollar was devalued 8.0%; that is, the price of gold was raised from $35 to $38 per ounce. Most other major currencies were valued up against the dollar by various amounts, including revaluations of the German mark and the British pound by 13.6 and 8.6%, respectively. To permit greater flexibility in exchange rates, fluctuations were permitted within 2.25% of parity instead of within 1% as under the Bretton Woods system.

In spite of high hopes for its success, the Smithsonian agreement lasted only about 14 months. By February 1973 it was evident that the revaluations against the dollar had been insufficient. The dollar was devalued an additional 10%, thus raising the official price of gold to $42.22 per ounce. But this devaluation was also insufficient to stabilize the dollar, and **since March 1973 most currencies of the world have been floating.**

THE FLOATING RATE SYSTEM

BUYING IN FORWARD MARKETS.   In the past many critics of floating exchange rates had questioned whether world money markets could adapt to the floating rate system. In particular, it was argued that for most major currencies there would be no forward markets. As a result, in the financing of international trade and investment, there would be inescapable risks of foreign exchange losses. It turned out, however, that for most major currencies there was a rapid development of **forward markets** that enabled the hedging of exchange risks. For example, an importer who was billed in deutsche marks (DM) could reduce the foreign exchange risk of higher costs from a rising mark by buying the currency forward. A **forward currency contract** is an agreement to buy or sell the stated currency at a fixed date ahead. Typically, foreign exchange contracts are available for periods of 1, 2, 3, 6, and 12 months. Thus the importer, by making forward contracts can guarantee the exchange rates at which payment will be settled.

Ordinarily, if an **exchange rate** is expected to appreciate, the seller of the foreign exchange forward contract will demand something more than the spot rate (today's price). He will want some compensation for his risk of having to supply marks at some date ahead, at which time he expects that the German currency will have revalued. The additional cost for delivery of a currency at a future date is called a **premium.** Premiums are often quoted on a percentage basis. For example, if the mark were selling at a spot exchange rate of 50¢ and the 6 months forward rate were 51¢, the nonannualized premium would be 2.0% = (0.51 − 0.50)/0.50. On an annualized basis the premium would be 4.0%. To annualize, multiply by 12/(duration of contract). For example, a nonannualized premium of 1.0% over 3 months would be multiplied by 12/3=4 to obtain an annualized premium of 4.0%.

SELLING IN FORWARD MARKETS.   Likewise, an exporter is concerned that there may be a devaluation of the currency in which he bills his sales abroad. He can **hedge** this risk by selling the currency forward—for example, by making an agreement that another party (usually a bank) will buy the proceeds from the export sale in lire at some period ahead. Ordinarily this kind of hedging takes place when a currency is likely to be devalued. Thus it can be expected that the buyer of the foreign exchange forward contract will be willing to trade dollars for the foreign currency only if the amount supplied is less than the spot rate. This negative difference between the spot rate and the forward rate is called a **discount.** For example, if the lira is 0.15¢ and it sells forward 6 months at 0.14¢, the discount on the lira would be 6.6% [(0.15 − 0.14)/0.15 = 6.6] nonannualized, or 13.2% annualized.

EURODOLLARS AND EUROCURRENCIES

External currency accounts have been another unique development in the post-World War II monetary system. These are bank deposits denominated in a currency different from the currency of the home country. Thus a bank deposit in London denominated in dollars rather than sterling is an external dollar account. External dollar accounts are commonly known as **Eurodollars,** though such deposits are not necessarily confined to Europe. They also exist in Asia and the Caribbean. External accounts in all currencies are commonly known as

Eurocurrency accounts or, for particular currencies, as Eurosterling, Euromarks, Euro-Swiss francs, and so on. For example, a deposit of British pounds in Luxembourg would be a Eurosterling deposit.

Eurocurrency deposits are believed to have begun when, after World War II, the Soviets deposited dollars in European banks to avoid danger of confiscation by the Americans. Growth of Eurodollar deposits received its strongest push with the imposing of various U.S. exchange controls in the 1960s. This created an incentive to keep dollar deposits out of the United States. Eurodollar deposits persisted after the lifting of U.S. exchange controls in early 1974, mainly because Eurodollar deposits were free of the Federal Reserve System's **Regulation Q** interest ceilings, bank deposit insurance, and various other costs that would be incurred in deposit banking in the United States. Eurocurrency deposits other than dollars also developed because of almost total freedom from regulation. The value of net Eurocurrency deposits at the end of 1979 was estimated at about $600 billion by the Morgan Guaranty Trust Co. This figure may involve some double counting, but it is nevertheless large compared with recorded outflows of dollars from the United States. It has been alleged that a **multiplier process** works in the Eurodollar market, with the proceeds of Eurodollar loans again becoming Eurodollar deposits. Although there are no formal **reserve requirements on Eurodollars,** there are "leakages" from this multiplier process because much Eurodollar borrowing is repatriated to the United States. Thus the extent of the Eurodollar multiplier is a matter of unsettled controversy.

Long-term lendings of Eurodollars are known as **Eurobonds.** This term is often used broadly to apply to offshore lending in any currency not of the host country of the bank making the loan.

MANAGED FLOATING

Although **forward foreign exchange markets** adapted readily in early 1973 to floating exchange rates, very few monetary authorities were willing to let their currencies float without intervention to influence exchange rates. Thus the financial world since 1973 has been compromising between floating rates and fixed rates. The wide differences in inflation between countries have made fixed rates almost impossible. On the other hand, freely floating rates are rejected by most central banks because of the possibility that speculative forces will produce a sharp decline in a weak currency or a sharp rise in a strong currency. As a general rule, neither of these extremes is desirable.

A strong currency depreciation will affect not only the price of imports but the price of all goods, imported or not, that compete with imports. To a greater extent than in the early postwar period, the proportion of a country's goods that is internationally traded—even in a somewhat self-sufficient country like the United States—is much larger than the percentage of imports. Today most U.S. consumer goods and vehicles compete with imports—a situation that certainly did not exist in the late 1940s and early 1950s.

Most monetary authorities are also afraid of sharp revaluations that raise the price of exports and thus damage export industries. Traditional economic theory states that this is a signal to move resources from export industries to domestic industries. For this shift to be politically acceptable, however, it must be gradual, and a strong currency appreciation is not likely to induce a gradual reaction.

Some countries—notably the United States, Canada, Japan, the United Kingdom, Switzerland, and Mexico—practice managed floating without any specific rule to guide the intervention process (where, as already discussed, a central bank sells foreign currencies to prevent its own rate from falling and sells its own currency to prevent its own rate from rising). In other countries, however, specific rules have been applied to guide the intervention process. Exhibit 1 classifies major currencies of the world in terms of how the currency is managed. Three systems of intervention are discussed in detail: tied exchange rates, mini-devaluation systems, and the **European Monetary System** (EMS).

TIED EXCHANGE RATES.   A currency that is **"tied"** moves parallel to some other currency or group of currencies. In spite of all its vicissitudes, the U.S. dollar remains the currency to which other currencies most frequently are tied. If the dollar rises 10%, the tied currency rises 10%; if the dollar falls 8%, the tied currency falls 8%. For example, the Trinidad and Tobago dollar was worth 41.7¢ as of February 29, 1980, an exchange rate that will hold as long as the tie lasts.

Most currencies in Central America, the Caribbean area, Bolivia, Paraguay, Ecuador, and a scattering of other countries are tied to the dollar. The second most important currency is the French franc, which is tied to most of the African countries (except Guinea) that were formerly French colonies. After World War II a number of British colonies were tied to the British pound, but as of August 31, 1979, the only currencies formally tied to sterling were those of Bangladesh, Gambia, and the Seychelles. Other intercurrency ties are the South African rand to the currencies of Lesotho and Swaziland and the Spanish peseta to the currency of Equatorial Guinea.

Basket Currencies.   Some tied currencies move in line with a group of more than one currency. Usually such a group of currencies is known as a **basket.** For example, a simple basket might consist of 50¢, American, one-half a British pound, and 3 French francs. For each trading day the value of the basket is calculated and the currency of the basket country adjusted in line with the overall percentage change in the value of the basket. In a simple case, suppose the pound is at $2 and the French franc at 25¢, and the pound gains 2% while the French franc loses 4%. The value of the basket is calculated as follows:

	First Period	Second Period	Change (%)
U.S. dollar	$0.50	$0.50	—
0.5 British pound	1.00	1.02	2.00
3 French francs	0.75	0.72	−4.00
Basket	$2.25	$2.24	−0.40%

Thus the basket currency in the second period would be lowered about 0.4 in value in relation to the U.S. dollar.

SDR-Tied Currencies.   In some cases, notably Sweden, the central bank of the "basket currency" country constructs its own basket, usually giving the most weight in the basket to the country's most important trading partners. (In some instances the actual weights in the basket are a central bank secret.) In other cases, exemplified by Kenya and Zambia, the currency is tied to the **Special Drawing Right (SDR),** which is a special basket used by the IMF for the valuation of a reserve asset.

MINIDEVALUATION SYSTEMS.   Among several Latin American countries, including Brazil and Colombia, it has become customary to make small monthly adjustments in exchange rates. These adjustments, known as **minidevaluations,** tend to reflect economic indicators, including price levels and reserve positions, but are usually less than 2% per month. In some cases, however, a series of minidevaluations may be insufficient to protect a country's reserve position; then it may become necessary to supplement the minidevaluations with a **"maxidevaluation."** This was done in the case of the 30% maxidevaluation of the Brazilian cruzeiro in December 1979. Ordinarily, after a maxidevaluation, a country will return to a new series of minidevaluations.

THE EUROPEAN MONETARY SYSTEM.   Of the schemes for coordinated intervention in currency markets, the **European Monetary System (EMS)** is the most important today. It now comprises the currencies of Germany, France, Belgium, Luxembourg, the Netherlands, Italy, Denmark, and Ireland. Up until March 1979 the EMS was known as the **joint float** or **"snake"** agreement and had been in operation since 1972. At various times the United Kingdom, Sweden, and Norway have belonged to the joint float, but they are not now participating.

In March 1979 the old joint float became the European Monetary System. The main provisions of the EMS agreement were:

1. The **parity grid system,** which places restrictions on the extent to which each EMS currency can rise or fall in relation to every other EMS currency. This system had been applied under the joint float.

2. A unit of account known as the **European currency unit** (ECU), which is a weighted average of EMS exchange rates.

3. A **"divergence indicator"** system that sets limits within which each currency is permitted to vary with respect to the ECU.

4. A fund for intervention in exchange markets, to maintain member currencies within their parity grids and divergence indicators.

The EMS is complicated because it involves two quite different limits on exchange rate movements. These limits—the parity grid and the divergence indicator—are discussed separately.

Parity Grid System.   One way to understand the parity grid system is to consider the dollar value of each currency for both its spot rate and its parity, as shown in Exhibit 2, for March 13, 1979.

For each currency the **"parity"** is an arbitrarily set exchange rate. On each working day a percentage change can be calculated between the spot rate and the initial parity. For example, on March 13 the spot rate on the Danish krone at 19.21¢ was 0.84% above parity at 19.05¢. Under the parity grid system the differences from parity are not permitted to vary more than the **2.25 percentage points band** (except for Italy, where by special agreement 6.0 percentage points are permitted). In Exhibit 2, the widest difference of percentages from parity is between Denmark and Belgium—from 0.84% above parity to 0.79% below parity. Since, however, this 1.63 percentage point difference is less than 2.25% the parity grid system is being followed.

But suppose that the Danish krone had been at 20.00¢. Then it would have been about 5.0% above parity (20.00 ÷ 19.05) with the range in differences from parity at 5.79 (5.00 percentage points above parity for Denmark plus 0.79 percentage point below parity for Belgium), which would have exceeded the 2.25% percentage point limit provided in the parity grid agreement. Under these conditions Denmark would sell kroner to bring down its

EXHIBIT 1 WORLD FOREIGN EXCHANGE INTERVENTION SYSTEMS (AUGUST 31, 1979)

Tied Exchange Rates					"Basket Currencies"	Minidevaluation Currencies	European Monetary System (EMS)	Other
U.S. Dollar	Pound Sterling	French Franc	Other Currency	SDR				
Bahamas	Bangladesh	Benin	Lesotho (South African rand)	Burma	Algeria	Brazil	Belgium	Afghanistan
Barbados	Gambia	Cameroon		Austria	Colombia	Denmark	Argentina
Bolivia	Seychelles	Central African Empire	Solomon Islands (Australian dollar)	Guinea	Cape Verda	Peru	France	Australia
Botswana		Chad		Guinea-Bissau	Cyprus		Germany	Bahrain
Burundi		Comoros	Swaziland (South African rand)	Jordan	Fiji		Ireland	Canada
Costa Rica		Congo		Kenya	Finland		Italy	Chile
Djibouti		Gabon	Equatorial Guinea (Spanish peseta)	Malawi	Kuwait		Luxembourg	China
Dominica		Ivory Coast		Mauritius	Malaysia		Netherlands	Ghana
Dominican Republic		Madagascar		São Tomé and Principe	Malta			Greece
Ecuador		Mali		Sierra Leone	Mauritania			Iceland
Egypt		Niger		Uganda	Morocco			India
El Salvador		Senegal			Norway			Indonesia
Ethiopia		Togo		Vietnam	Papua New Guinea			Iran
Grenada		Upper Volta		Zaire	Singapore			Israel
Guatemala				Zambia	Sweden			Japan
Guyana					Tanzania			Lebanon
Haiti					Thailand			Mexico
Honduras					Tunisia			New Zealand
Iraq								Nigeria
Jamaica								Philippines
Korea								Portugal
Laos Republic								Qatar
Liberia								Saudi Arabia
Libya								South Africa
Maldives								Spain

Nepal
Nicaragua
Oman
Pakistan
Panama

Paraguay
Romania
Rwanda
Somalia
Sudan

Surinam
Syria
Trinidad and
   Tobago
Venezuela

Yemen, North
Yemen, South

Sri Lanka
Switzerland
Turkey
United Arab
   Emirates
United
   Kingdom

United States
Uruguay
Western
   Samoa
Yugoslavia

Source: International Monetary Fund.

EXHIBIT 2   EUROPEAN JOINT FLOAT, DECEMBER 1978–MARCH 13, 1979

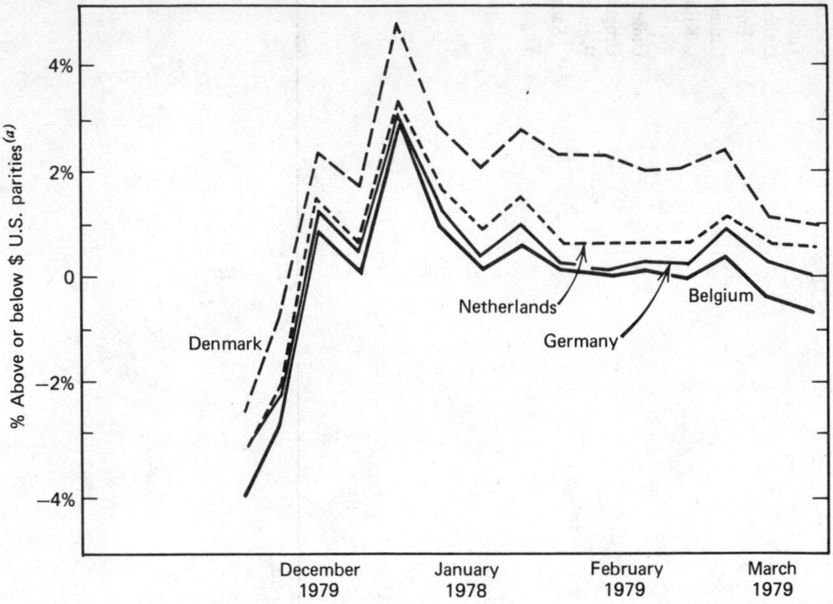

exchange rate, while Belgium would buy Belgian francs to push up its exchange rate until differences from parity were within the 2.25 percentage point limit.

The net result of the parity grid system (and the joint float that preceded it) is that the EMS currencies tend, with the 2.25% leeway allowed, to move together in relation to the dollar. In practice, however, the parity grid system is operated without reference to the dollar. Exhibit 3 shows how far each currency can move against each other currency under the 2.25% rule.

For example, the midpoint or parity of 100 German marks against 100 Dutch guilders is 110.537. Under the parity grid system, the German mark is permitted to move as high as 113.05 or as low as 108.0775. As another example, Exhibit 3 shows that 100 Danish kroner can move between the limits of 74.02 and 77.43 in relation to the French franc.

Divergence Indicator System.   In addition to the parity grid, a second limitation has been placed on exchange rate movements in the EMS. This is the **"divergence indicator"** system. Divergence indicators are variations in currency values from the European currency unit (ECU), which is a weighted average value.

Exhibit 4 shows the calculation of the value of the **ECU** at 135.21¢, as of March 13, 1979.

Each currency in the ECU has a market value in relation to every other EMS currency. Thus it is possible to calculate the value of the overall ECU in each EMS currency. As an example, Exhibit 5 shows how the market value of the ECU is calculated in Danish kroner.

Column 3 indicates the number of Danish kroner for each EMS currency. For example, on March 13 there were 2.7985 kroner per German mark (53.76 ÷ 19.21). Each other currency is likewise translated into kroner and multiplied by its weight in the basket (column 4). As a result, as shown in column 5, the value of the ECU is calculated in kroner. This market value of the ECUs can likewise be calculated daily for each other currency.

EXHIBIT 3   THE PARITY GRID IN THE EMS SYSTEM (NOVEMBER 30, 1979)

		(1)	(2)	(3)	(4)	(5)	(6)	(7)
		Belgium In Terms of Belgian Francs (BF)	Denmark In Terms of Danish Kroner (DKr)	France In Terms of French Francs (FF)	Ireland In Terms of Irish Pounds (Ir£)	Italy In Terms of Italian Lire (LIT)	Holland In Terms of Dutch Florins (HFL)	West Germany In Terms of Deutsche Marks (DM)
(1)	100 BF Belgium	—	18.9785 / 19.4105 / 19.8520	14.3680 / 14.6948 / 15.0290	1.64198 / 1.67934 / 1.71755	2,740.44 / 2,909.79 / 3,089.61	6.7420 / 6.89531 / 7.0520	6.0990 / 6.238 / 6.3800
(2)	100 DKr Denmark	503.75 / 515.5237 / 526.90	—	74.02 / 75.7054 / 77.43	8.45922 / 8.65169 / 8.84854	14,118.20 / 14,990.7 / 15,917.1	34.735 / 35.5237 / 36.33	31.42 / 32.1373 / 32.87
(3)	100 FFr France	665.375 / 680.512 / 696.00	129.15 / 132.091 / 135.095	—	11.1739 / 11.4281 / 11.6881	18,649. / 19,801.5 / 21,025.2	45.88 / 46.9235 / 47.99	41.505 / 42.4505 / 43.415
(4)	100 Ir£ Ireland	5,822.25 / 5,954.71 / 6,090.20	1,130.13 / 1,155.84 / 1,182.14	855.55 / 875.034 / 894.95	—	163,185. / 173,270. / 183,978.	401.45 / 410.597 / 419.95	363.20 / 371.457 / 379.90
(5)	100 LIt Italy	3.2365 / 3.43668 / 3.6490	0.62825 / 0.667078 / 0.70830	0.47560 / 0.505013 / 0.53620	0.0543545 / 0.0577136 / 0.0612801	—	0.223175 / 0.23697 / 0.25160	0.2019 / 0.21438 / 0.2276
(6)	100 HFl Holland	1,418.00 / 1,450.26 / 1,483.25	275.245 / 281.503 / 287.90	208.38 / 213.113 / 217.96	23.8130 / 24.3548 / 24.9089	39,743.4 / 42,199.5 / 44,807.4	—	88.455 / 90.4673 / 92.525
(7)	100 DM West Germany	1,567.40 / 1,603.07 / 1,639.55	304.23 / 311.165 / 318.26	230.330 / 235.568 / 240.930	26.323 / 26.921 / 27.553	43,931.20 / 46,646.0 / 49,528.70	108.0775 / 110.537 / 113.05	—

Source: Morgan Guaranty Trust Co., New York.

To calculate the divergence indicator, the market value of the ECU in a currency is compared to its arbitrary parity value. In the example above the **divergence indicator** is − 0.66%, since the market value of the Danish krone is 0.66% below the parity value. Because of their different proportional importance in the ECU, maximum permitted divergence indicators vary among currencies as follows:

Parities and Maximum Permitted Divergence Indicators in the EMS

	Parity (Units per ECU)	Maximum Divergence Indicator (%)
German mark	2.51064	1.13
French franc	5.79831	1.35
Netherlands guilder	2.72077	1.51
Belgian franc	39.4582	1.53
Italian lira	1148.15	4.07
Danish krone	7.08592	1.63
Irish pound	0.662638	1.67

EXHIBIT 4 VALUE OF THE EUROPEAN CURRENCY UNIT (ECU) IN U.S. CENTS (MARCH 13, 1979)

	(1)	(2)	(3) = (1) × (2)	(4)
	Value of ECU Currencies (U.S.¢)	Number of Currency Units in ECU Basket	Value of Currency Unit in ECU Basket	Each Currency as % of Total Basket
German mark	53.76	0.828	44.51¢	33.0
French franc	23.34	1.15	26.84¢	19.9
British pound[a]	204.7	0.0885	18.12¢	13.4
Netherlands guilder	49.80	0.286	14.24¢	10.5
Belgian franc	3.394	3.80	12.90¢	9.5
Italian lira	0.1182	109.0	12.88¢	9.5
Danish krone	19.21	0.217	4.17¢	3.1
Irish pound	204.7	0.00759	1.55¢	1.1
Total			135.21¢	100.0 %

[a]The United Kingdom as a member of the European Community has a weight in the ECU even though it is not a member of the EMS.

Source: From conversations with members of the European Economic Community, New York and Washington, D.C.

EXHIBIT 5 DIVERGENCE INDICATOR FOR THE DANISH KRONE (MARCH 13, 1979)

	(1)	(2)	(3)	(4)	(5) = (3) × (4)
	Dollar Market Rates				Calculation of
	Units per U.S. $	Cents per unit	Danish Kroner per unit	Units of Each Currency in ECU Total	Market Value of ECU in Danish Kroner
German mark	1.860	53.76	2.7985	0.828	2.3172
French franc	4.284	23.34	1.2150	1.15	1.3973
British pound	0.489	204.7	10.6559	0.0885	0.9430
Netherlands guilder	2.008	49.80	2.5924	0.286	0.7414
Belgian franc	29.46	3.394	0.1767	3.8	0.6715
Italian lira	846	0.1182	0.006153	109.0	0.6707
Danish krone	5.206	19.21	1.0000	0.217	0.2170
Irish pound	0.489	204.7	10.6559	0.00759	0.0809
		Market value of ECU (Danish kroner)			7.0390
		Parity value of ECU (Danish kroner)			7.08592
		Market value (below) parity value			(0.66)%
		Maximum divergence			±1.63%

Source: European Economic Community offices, New York and Washington, D.C.

Financing the EMS.   When the value of a currency in ECUs varies from its parity by more than its maximum permitted **divergence indicator** an EMS member country is required either to intervene in the foreign exchange market or to adopt monetary and other economic policies that result in an adjustment in the exchange rate. Another remedy, which applies to both the grid and the divergence indicator requirements, is to change the parity in the EMS. For example, when the Danish krone came under pressure in 1979, its parity was moved downward. This remedy is not expected to be used with great frequency, however, for this would vitiate the EMS goal of maintaining exchange rate stability among its members.

The EMS agreement also provides that member countries exchange 20% of their gold and foreign exchange reserves with the **European Monetary Cooperation Fund** for ECUs. ECUs may be used in settlements between EMS countries. Short- and medium-term credits available for currency intervention were raised from $13.5 billion under the joint float to $33.8 billion under the EMS system.

EXCHANGE CONTROLS

In addition to the various methods used by leading countries for intervention on foreign exchange markets, exchange rates are maintained or influenced by a wide variety of restrictions and controls on payments.

TARIFFS, SUBSIDIES, AND IMPORT CONTROLS.   Perhaps the best known method of protecting the value of a currency is the application of **tariffs** on imports and/or **subsidies** to exports. In many cases, when it is believed that tariffs are ineffective, **quantitative restrictions** are applied to imports. Quantitative restrictions limit amounts imported regardless of the import price. In developing countries where balance of payments equilibria are fragile, imports of nonessential consumer goods are often subject to quantitative restrictions. At the same time there are subsidies for exports, often in the form of tax relief. In some instances, notably in Latin American countries, a special **advance deposit** to the central bank may be required in addition to the payment for permitted imports. By tying up the importer's funds until the deposit is refunded—usually within 6 months or less—the advance import deposit tends to limit imports.

CONTROLS ON CAPITAL MOVEMENTS.   **Restrictions on capital movements outward and incentives on capital movements inward are also frequent.** In many cases capital outflows or inflows require approval from the central bank that the movement is in the country's interest. In some Latin American countries, for example, profit remittances are not permitted to exceed a specific return on capital. Another type of capital control—employed by countries attempting to avoid an unwanted appreciation of their currencies—is a reserve requirement on capital inflows. This type of control has been applied in West Germany.

MULTIPLE EXCHANGE RATES.   In some cases governments apply restrictions on both **current account** (trade and other noninvestment payments) and **capital account** by systems of **multiple exchange rates.** These have been used in Latin America and are currently used in Belgium. In Belgium there are two foreign exchange markets: the commercial market and the financial market. The first market includes most current account payments and receipts, while the second market includes most capital transactions and the collection of dividends and interest coming into Belgium. A separate foreign exchange market thus operates in each type of currency, and each day there are separate quotations for the Belgian "commercial franc" and "financial franc."

In the past, but not currently, **multiple exchange rates** were also applied in France and Italy. In Great Britain, up until 1979, a special exchange rate was required for the purchase of foreign securities by British residents. Earnings on the sale of British securities abroad were deposited in a "dollar pool." Foreign exchange in the dollar pool, minus certain taxes, was then auctioned off to British residents wishing to buy foreign securities. In effect, a **"dollar premium"** was required for the purchase of foreign securities. In South Africa a similar system is applied, with the result that the **"securities rand"** and the ordinary rand have different exchange rates.

In multiple exchange rate systems the two (or more, in a few cases, as in Chile in the 1960s) exchange rates cannot be widely different; otherwise **"false invoicing"** is likely to appear, in which funds are moved out of the country at a high rate and into the country at a low rate. However, there can be a wide disparity of rates when a special rate (usually lower than the principal exchange rate) is applied to a commodity, as in the case of Colombian coffee. Here, false invoicing can be easily detected when the price of the commodity is widely known. An excessively low exchange rate (or the equivalent in a tax on export proceeds) on an export commodity can lead to widespread smuggling.

BALANCE OF PAYMENTS

Thus far, this section has considered how the international monetary system determines exchange rates and the inflows and outflows of foreign exchange to and from a country. Since inflows and outflows are not necessarily equal, however, settlements are required to balance surpluses and deficits.

As discussed, under the pre-1914 gold standard a large part of international settlements was made with gold. Today, however, settlements are much more complicated; they are made with gold, foreign exchange, reserve positions in the **International Monetary Fund,** Special Drawing Rights, and changes in official liabilities of reserve currency countries. As background for considering these means of settlement, Exhibit 6 shows the U.S. balance of payments, 1970–1978.

TRADE ACCOUNT. Exhibit 6 shows the main "balances" in the overall **U.S. balance of payments** (lines 76–79) and also the main settlement items (lines 80 and 81). The first important balance is the trade balance, defined as exports minus imports (line 2 minus line 18). In addition to imports and exports, there are payments and receipts for services, including travel, transportation, military, fees and royalties, and earnings on investment abroad. These are totaled in lines 1 and 17, and the overall balance on goods and services is shown in line 77. Current transactions also include one-way or transfer payments such as foreign aid, pensions, and private remittances abroad (lines 34–36). The sum of the goods and services balance and transfer payments is the current account balance (line 79).

CURRENT ACCOUNT. Since the balance of payments is based on accounting principles, the current account deficit is financed by changes in assets and liabilities. If a country's current account is in deficit, it is financed by a decrease in its assets (or an increase in its liabilities) abroad.

In Exhibit 6 the 1978 **current account balance** at − $13,895 million is offset by changes in **U.S. assets abroad** at − $60,957 million (line 37) and changes in **foreign assets in the**

U.S. at $63,713 million (line 56). The net balance of these two capital account items is to $2,756 million, which is less than the current account balance at $13,895 million. This difference of $11,139 million consists of unreported items (including errors in trade accounts, delays in payment for imports and exports, unreported capital transactions, and illegal transactions) and is shown in line 75 as the **"statistical discrepancy."**

CAPITAL ACCOUNT.   Exhibit 6 indicates, many of the capital account items in the balance of payments represent government long-term lending and private investment, including direct investment, security transactions, and bank transactions. However, other changes in assets and liabilities are undertaken by central banks in a usually conscious effort to promote balance of payments adjustments. These official asset changes are listed in lines 39–42 for U.S. official assets and in line 57 less line 61 for foreign official assets in the United States. (Line 61 is excluded from foreign official assets used in official balance of payments settlements because these assets are short-term assets, while line 61 for "other U.S. liabilities" consists mainly of prepayments for military goods and services from the United States, an item that is considered a long-term asset.)

The items in the category represented by line 57 (excluding line 61) arise because the United States is a **reserve currency country.** This means that when foreign central banks acquire dollars, they do not necessarily sell them on foreign exchange markets as would ordinarily be done with nonreserve currencies. Instead the dollars acquired by foreign central banks are used to buy U.S. assets, mainly in the form of **government securities** (lines 59 and 60) and **bank deposits** (line 62).

BALANCE OF PAYMENTS SETTLEMENTS

Aside from the buildup of assets in reserve currency countries (which were only the United States and the United Kingdom before the 1967 devaluation of sterling, but currently include West Germany and Switzerland), international balances are settled by transfers of reserve assets, as shown under line 38 and also in line 80. Since an outflow of these assets contributes to the settlement of a deficit, outflows are shown with a plus sign and inflows with a minus sign. Thus there was in 1978 a $65 million gold inflow (line 39). Under the gold standard most international settlements in a country's own assets consisted of gold. Today, however, there are four assets used: foreign exchange, gold, reserve positions in the IMF; and Special Drawing Rights.

FOREIGN EXCHANGE.   Foreign exchange is defined to include short-term assets in a currency. It thus includes bank deposits and short-term government securities such as treasury bills. Under the IMF definition, foreign exchange included in reserves should be "readily available to support a currency" on foreign exchange markets. Thus long-term financial instruments (e.g., **long-term government bonds),** are excluded from the definition of **foreign exchange.**

Most official transactions in foreign exchange arise from **intervention.** As discussed, this takes place when a central bank buys its own currency to keep it from going too low or sells its own currency to keep it from going too high. Under the **Bretton Woods** system, intervention was required to maintain exchange rates within the 1.0% band above or below parity. Likewise, intervention is required in the EMS system to maintain currencies within the 2.25% band. In other cases there are no requirements for intervention, and in the amendment to Article 4 of the IMF agreement adopted at Jamaica in January 1976, freely floating exchange

EXHIBIT 6 U.S. INTERNATIONAL TRANSACTIONS ($ MILLIONS), 1970–1978

Line		1970	1971	1972	1973	1974	1975	1976	1977	1978
1	*Exports of Goods and Services*	65,666	68,830	77,491	110,214	146,604	155,721	171,761	184,592	220,849
2	Merchandise, adjusted, excluding military	42,469	43,319	49,381	71,410	98,306	107,088	114,745	120,816	141,884
3	Transfers under U.S. military agency sales contracts	1,501	1,926	1,364	2,559	3,379	4,049	5,574	7,441	7,744
4	Travel	2,331	2,534	2,817	3,412	4,032	4,697	5,742	6,150	7,284
5	Passenger fares	544	615	699	975	1,104	1,039	1,229	1,366	1,583
6	Other transportation	3,125	3,299	3,579	4,465	5,697	5,840	6,760	7,267	8,151
7	Fees and royalties from affiliated foreigners	1,758	1,927	2,115	2,513	3,070	3,543	3,531	3,793	4,806
8	Fees and royalties from unaffiliated foreigners	573	618	655	712	751	757	822	920	1,065
9	Other private services	1,287	1,539	1,764	1,960	2,259	2,920	3,584	3,769	4,284
10	U.S. government miscellaneous services	332	347	354	399	419	438	488	485	585
	Receipts of income on U.S. assets abroad:									
11	Direct investment	8,168	9,159	10,949	16,542	19,157	16,595	18,999	20,081	25,656
12	Interest, dividends and earnings of unincorporated affiliates	4,992	5,983	6,416	8,384	11,379	8,547	11,303	12,795	13,593
13	Reinvested earnings of incorporated affiliates	3,176	3,176	4,532	8,158	7,777	8,048	7,696	7,286	12,063
14	Other private receipts	2,671	2,641	2,949	4,330	7,356	7,644	8,955	10,881	15,964
15	U.S. government receipts	907	906	866	936	1,074	1,112	1,332	1,625	1,845
16	*Transfers of Goods and Services under U.S. Military Grant Programs, Net*	2,713	3,546	4,492	2,810	1,818	2,207	373	204	259
17	*Imports of Goods and Services*	−60,032	−66,548	−79,381	−99,191	−137,306	−132,769	−162,159	−194,015	−229,659
18	Merchandise, adjusted, excluding military	−39,866	−45,579	−55,797	−70,499	−103,649	−98,041	−124,051	−151,669	−176,071
19	Direct defense expenditures	−4,855	−4,819	−4,784	−4,629	−5,032	−4,795	−4,900	−5,762	−7,252
20	Travel	−3,980	−4,373	−5,042	−5,526	−5,980	−6,417	−6,856	−7,451	−8,475
21	Passenger fares	−1,215	−1,290	−1,596	−1,790	−2,095	−2,263	−2,568	−2,748	−2,922
22	Other transportation	−2,843	−3,130	−3,520	−4,694	−5,942	−5,621	−6,772	−7,784	−8,606
23	Fees and royalties to affiliated foreigners	−111	−118	−155	−209	−160	−287	−293	−243	−396
24	Fees and royalties to unaffiliated foreigners	−114	−123	−139	−176	−186	−186	−189	−191	−214
25	Private payments for other services	−810	−935	−1,017	−1,152	−1,211	−1,551	−1,991	−2,192	−2,359

#										
26	U.S. government payments for miscellaneous services	−725	−746	−788	−862	−967	−1,044	−1,227	−1,358	−1,545
	Payments of income on foreign assets in the United States:									
27	Direct investment	−875	−1,164	−1,256	−1,610	−1,331	−2,234	−3,110	−2,834	−3,958
28	Interest, dividends, and earnings of unincorporated affiliates	−441	−621	−687	−699	−266	−1,046	−1,451	−1,248	−1,628
29	Reinvested earnings of incorporated affiliates	−434	−542	−569	−910	−1,065	−1,189	−1,659	−1,586	−2,329
30	Other private payments	−3,617	−2,428	−2,604	−4,209	−6,491	−5,788	−5,681	−6,224	−9,188
31	U.S. government payments	−1,024	−1,844	−2,684	−3,836	−4,262	−4,542	−4,520	−5,540	−8,674
32	U.S. Military Grants of Goods and Services, Net	−2,713	−3,546	−4,492	−2,810	−1,818	−2,207	−373	−204	−259
33	Unilateral Transfers (excluding military grants of goods and services), Net	−3,294	−3,701	−3,854	−3,881	−7,186	−4,613	−4,998	−4,670	−5,086
34	U.S. government grants (excluding military grants of goods and services)	−1,736	−2,043	−2,173	−1,938	−5,475	−2,894	−3,146	−2,775	−3,152
35	U.S. government pensions and other transfers	−462	−542	−572	−693	−694	−813	−934	−971	−1,086
36	Private remittances and other transfers	−1,096	−1,117	−1,109	−1,250	−1,017	−906	−917	−924	−848
37	U.S. Assets Abroad, Net (increase/capital outflow (−))	−9,336	−12,474	−14,497	−22,874	−34,745	−39,703	−51,269	−35,793	−60,957
38	U.S. official reserve assets, net	2,481	2,349	−4	158	−1,467	−849	−2,558	−375	732
39	Gold	787	866	547	—	—	—	—	−118	−65
40	Special drawing rights	−851	−249	−703	9	−172	−66	−78	−121	1,249
41	Reserve position in the International Monetary Fund	389	1,350	153	−33	−1,265	−466	−2,212	−294	4,231
42	Foreign currencies	2,156	382	−1	182	−30	−317	−268	158	−4,683
43	U.S. government assets, other than official reserve assets, net	−1,589	−1884	−1,568	−2,644	366	−3,474	−4,214	−3,693	−4,656
44	U.S. loans and other long-term assets	−3,293	−4,181	−3,819	−4,638	−5,001	−5,941	−6,943	−6,445	−7,470
45	Repayments on U.S. loans	1,721	2,115	2,086	2,596	4,826	2,475	2,596	2,719	2,938

EXHIBIT 6 (CONTINUED)

Line		1970	1971	1972	1973	1974	1975	1976	1977	1978
46	U.S. foreign currency holdings and U.S. short-term assets, net	-16	182	165	-602	541	-9	133	33	-124
47	U.S. private assets, net	-10,228	-12,939	-12,925	-20,388	-33,643	-35,380	-44,498	-31,725	-57,033
48	Direct investment	-7,589	-7,617	-7,747	-11,353	-9,052	-14,244	-11,949	-12,898	-16,670
49	Equity and intercompany accounts	-4,413	-4,441	-3,214	-3,195	-1,275	-6,196	-4,253	-5,612	-4,606
50	Reinvested earnings of incorporated affiliates	-3,176	-3,176	-4,532	-8,158	-7,777	-8,048	-7,696	-7,286	-12,063
51	Foreign securities	-1,076	-1,113	-618	-671	-1,854	-6,247	-8,885	-5,460	-3,487
	U.S. claims on unaffiliated foreigners reported by U.S. nonbanking concerns:									
52	Long-term	-586	-168	-243	-396	-474	-366	-42	-99	-53
53	Short-term	-10	-1,061	-811	-1,987	-2,747	-991	-2,254	-1,841	-3,800
	U.S. claims reported by U.S. banks, not included elsewhere:									
54	Long-term	155	-612	-1,307	-933	-1,183	-2,357	-2,362	-751	-33,023
55	Short-term	-1,122	-2,368	-2,199	-5,047	-18,333	-11,175	-19,006	-10,675	
56	Foreign Assets in the United States, Net (increase capital inflow (+))	6,359	22,970	21,461	18,388	34,241	15,420	36,399	50,823	63,713
57	Foreign official assets in the United States, net	6,908	26,879	10,475	6,026	10,546	6,777	17,573	36,656	33,758
58	U.S. government securities	9,439	26,570	8,470	641	4,172	5,313	9,892	32,538	24,198
59	U.S. Treasury securities	9,411	26,578	8,213	59	3,270	4,408	9,319	30,230	23,542
60	Other	28	-8	257	582	902	905	573	2,308	656
61	Other U.S. government liabilities	-456	-510	182	936	301	1,517	4,507	1,240	2,754
62	U.S. liabilities reported by U.S. banks, not included elsewhere	-2,075	819	1,638	4,126	5,818	-2,158	969	773	5,411
63	Other foreign official assets	—	—	185	323	254	2,104	2,205	2,105	1,395
64	Other foreign assets in the United States, net	-550	-3,909	10,986	12,362	23,696	8,643	18,826	14,167	29,956
65	Direct investment	1,464	367	949	2,800	4,760	2,603	4,347	3,728	6,294
66	Equity and intercompany accounts	1,030	-175	380	1,890	3,695	1,414	2,687	2,142	3,964

Line	Item								
67	Reinvested earnings of incorporated affiliates	434	542	569	910	1,065	1,189	1,659	1,586	2,329
68	U.S. Treasury securities	81	−24	−39	−216	697	2,590	2,783	534	2,180
69	U.S. securities other than U.S. Treasury securities	2,189	2,289	4,507	4,041	378	2,503	1,284	2,713	2,867
	U.S. liabilities to unaffiliated foreigners reported by U.S. nonbanking concerns:									
70	Long-term	1,112	384	594	298	−90	406	−1,000	−520	−194
71	Short-term	902	−15	221	737	1,934	−87	422	993	1,834
	U.S. liabilities reported by U.S. banks, not included elsewhere:									
72	Long-term	23	−250	149	227	9	−280	231	373	
73	Short-term	−6,321	−6,661	4,605	4,475	16,008	908	10,759	6,346	16,975
74	Allocations of Special Drawing Rights	867	717	710	—	—	—	—	—	—
75	Statistical Discrepancy (sum of above items with sign reversed)	−230	−9,794	−1,930	−2,655	−1,609	5,944	10,265	−937	11,139
	Memoranda									
76	Balance on merchandise trade (lines 2 and 18)	2,603	−2,260	−6,416	911	−5,343	9,047	−9,306	−30,873	−34,187
77	Balance on goods and services (lines 1 and 17)	5,634	2,282	−1,889	11,022	9,298	22,952	9,603	−9,423	−8,809
78	Balance on goods, services, and remittances (lines 77, 35, and 36)	4,076	624	−3,571	9,079	7,587	21,234	7,752	−11,317	−10,743
79	Balance on current account (lines 77 and 33)	2,340	−1,419	−5,744	7,141	2,113	18,339	4,605	−14,093	−13,895
	Transactions in U.S. Official Reserve Assets and in Foreign Official Assets in the United States									
80	Increase (−) in U.S. official reserve assets, net (line 38)	2,481	2,349	−4	158	−1,467	−849	−2,558	−375	732
81	Increase (+) in foreign official assets in the United States (line 57 less line 61)	7,354	27,389	10,293	5,090	10,244	5,259	13,066	35,416	31,004

Source: Survey of Current Business, June 1979.

rates are permitted if countries do not manipulate them to their own advantage. Nevertheless most central banks intervene in foreign exchange markets to prevent wide swings in the exchange rates of their currencies.

GOLD.   As discussed, **gold** was the major medium of international settlement under the gold standard. With the breakdown of the gold standard, **reserve currencies**—particularly the pound and the dollar—were mainly used for international settlements. Reserve currencies under the Bretton Woods system were, however, expected to be convertible into gold.

Gold Pool.   Under the gold standard central banks had maintained the value of gold at $20.67 per ounce. This value was raised to $35 in 1934 when President Roosevelt devalued the dollar. There was little upward pressure on the price of gold until October 1960, when it was temporarily pushed up to $40 on the London market. The price of an ounce of gold was brought back down to $35 by central banks selling gold. This procedure was institutionalized in the so-called **gold pool** into which leading central banks contributed gold supplies. Gold from the gold pool was sold in sufficient amounts to hold the price of gold down to $35 until March 1968, when it was decided that gold sales by central banks could no longer stabilize the gold price. A "two-tier" system was adopted in which the gold price at $35 was maintained for transactions among central banks. In private markets, however, the price of gold moved freely. Central banks agreed not to sell gold on free markets.

Two-Tier Agreements.   The $35 gold price under the two-tier system lasted until August 1971 when the United States stopped free sales of gold to other central banks. In the **Smithsonian Agreement** the United States raised the theoretical gold price to $38, though this action did not have much meaning for U.S. gold because it remained inconvertible. In February 1973 the United States again raised the theoretical price of gold—this time to $42.22.

Jamaica Agreement.   It became evident, however, that $42.22 was not a realistic price for gold in view of market prices, which were much higher than the official price. By August 1975 gold on free markets had gone up to $160. In January 1976, in the **Jamaica Agreement** between major IMF member countries, it was decided to **demonetize gold.** Gold holdings of major countries were not to be increased for two years. One-sixth of gold holdings of the IMF would be returned to member countries that had contributed it, and another one-sixth would be sold on free markets, with the proceeds of the sale to be used for the benefit of less developed countries.

At the beginning of 1978 in accordance with the Jamaica Agreement, gold was officially demonetized. Central banks had the right to use their gold supplies in any way that they saw fit. By 1980 gold had reached a price exceeding $600 per ounce (it had exceeded $800 per ounce briefly in 1979), and most central banks continue to maintain their holdings intact. Very few international monetary transactions are currently in gold, but it is sometimes used as collateral for foreign exchange loans. One hint of **remonetization of gold** is found in the EMS agreement already discussed. Member countries in the EMS are required to exchange 20% of their gold and foreign exchange reserves into the European Monetary Cooperation Fund for ECUs. The gold in the fund is periodically revalued **at market prices.** This constitutes the first recognition by central banks of the actual price of gold on world markets.

RESERVE POSITIONS IN THE IMF.   As already discussed, the basic financing of the IMF arises from contributions in line with the member countries' **quotas.** Quotas are arbitrarily determined roughly in proportion to each country's economic importance in the world: the larger countries have the larger quotas and the smaller countries smaller quotas.

IMF quotas are three-quarters in the country's own currency and one-quarter in gold or dollars. The gold or dollar contribution of a country is also considered a reserve asset, along with dollars, gold, and SDRs. This is known as the **"reserve position in the IMF"** and is considered to be a reserve asset because a member country may borrow an equivalent amount from the IMF on a virtually "no questions asked" basis whenever it needs balance of payments financing. Additional conditions are required for further borrowing from the fund. (Actually in the formal IMF language there is no borrowing or repayment with the IMF. Countries "purchase" required currencies from the fund instead of "borrowing" and currencies are "repurchased" instead of being "repaid." But these actions have long since become identified with borrowing and repayment.)

Reserve positions in the fund, known also as the **gold tranche** or **reserve tranche,** are listed in a country's reserves unless there have been borrowings from the IMF, in which case the borrowed funds are deducted from the reserve position. In addition, a country's reserve position in the IMF is credited with the amounts of its own currency that have been lent out by the IMF. For example, a $100 million IMF lending of French francs would increase the French reserve position in the IMF by $100 million in addition to the unused part of the reserve tranche. (This statement oversimplifies how the reserve position is determined, but the actual calculation is not essentially different from the example presented here.)

CONDITIONALITY. In the 1940s and 1950s lending by the IMF was relatively simple, with the reserve tranche readily available and higher tranches, comprising the other 75% of the quota, available if a country could establish that it had balance of payments difficulties and was undertaking measures to overcome them. Currently, however, lending by the IMF has become much more complicated, exhibiting a wide range of types of lending, with different degrees of **"conditionality"** for granting loans. An extended discussion of types of fund lending (and also of the financing of IMF lending) is found in the *IMF Survey,* September 18, 1978.

In the Bretton Woods Agreement, **IMF quotas** were required to be adjusted every 5 years from 1951 forward. Quotas were unchanged in 1951 and 1956 but were raised by 50% in 1959, by 25% in 1965, and by 35.5% in 1970. A 32.5% increase was adopted for 1976. There have also been quota adjustments for particular countries. As quotas move upward, member countries raise their contributions to the IMF and thus increase their reserve positions in line with the rise in their quotas.

Special Drawing Rights (SDRs). SDRs are the most recent addition to **world reserve assets.** The SDR plan, adopted in 1969, authorized the IMF to create a special asset that would be accepted among IMF members in exchange for dollars and other currencies. Thus the SDR functions similarly to gold settlements and has been dubbed "paper gold." Each participating country received an amount of SDRs in porportion to its IMF quota. SDR issues have been 3.5 billion in 1970, 3 billion in 1971, and 3 billion in 1972. Originally each SDR was valued at the equivalent of one 1969 gold dollar. Thus given the devaluation of the dollar with respect to gold in 1971 and 1973, the value of the SDR was raised to $1.080 in 1971 and to $1.188 in 1973. In July 1974, however, the IMF decided to fix the value of the SDR for each business day in terms of a **basket of currencies,** a weighted average of exchange rates of the 16 major world currencies. Exhibit 7 shows how the value of the SDR was calculated for a particular day. As of September 18, 1979, the value of each SDR was

EXHIBIT 7   CALCULATION OF THE VALUE OF THE SDR ON SEPTEMBER 18, 1979

	(1)	(2)	(3) = (1) × (2)	(4)
	Exchange Rate (U.S. $ per Unit of Local Currency)	Number of Units of Local Currency per SDR	Value of Local Currency in One SDR (U.S. $)	% of Total Value of SDR
U.S. dollar[a]	$1.000	0.400	$0.40	30.77
German mark[a]	0.5525	0.320	0.18	13.85
British pound[a]	2.150	0.050	0.11	8.46
French franc[a]	0.2364	0.420	0.10	7.68
Japanese yen[a]	0.00446	21.000	0.09	6.92
Netherlands guilder	0.5028	0.140	0.07	5.37
Canadian dollar	0.859	0.070	0.06	4.62
Italian lira	0.00123	52.000	0.06	4.62
Belgian franc	0.03442	1.600	0.06	4.62
Saudia Arabian riyal	0.2984	0.130	0.04	3.08
Swedish krona	0.2322	0.111	0.03	2.31
Iranian rial	0.014	1.700	0.02	1.54
Australian dollar	1.120	0.017	0.02	1.54
Austrian schilling	0.0782	0.270	0.02	1.54
Norwegian krone	0.1999	0.100	0.02	1.54
Spanish peseta	0.01514	1.500	0.02	1.54
Total			$1.30	100.00%

[a]The parities for these currencies are as follows:

Currency U.S.¢
German mark 53.76
Netherlands guilder 49.61
Danish krone 19.05
Belgian franc 3.421

Source: International Monetary Fund, 1979.

$1.30. In the third quarter of 1980, the basket of currencies was again revised to include only the five major currencies (U.S. dollar, German mark, British pound, French franc, and Japanese yen).

SDRs, which are similar to **Keynes's bancors,** were authorized in 1969 because there was concern that with an improving U.S. balance of payments, the world monetary system would not have enough liquidity. Since the supply of gold was not increasing significantly, it was believed that if there was no U.S. balance of payments deficit supplying foreign exchange for central bank reserves, these reserves would not rise in line with world trade and investment. As it happened, however, the U.S. balance of payments after 1969 moved into a more severe deficit. Thus in more recent discussions the SDRs are viewed as a possible **substitute** for excess dollars in world reserves rather than as an addition to world reserves.

THE PROPOSED SUBSTITUTION ACCOUNT.   The participants at the IMF meeting in Belgrade in 1979 recommended further study of proposals for a substitution account, a plan to replace dollars by SDRs in international reserves. Though the plan was rejected in the IMF interim committee meeting in Hamburg in April 1980, its basic features would have been like that presented in Exhibit 8, which shows how the IMF would exchange SDRs with central banks for their reserves now held in short-term U.S. dollar securities. The short-term dollar securities received by the IMF would be exchanged with the U.S. Treasury for long-term U.S. government securities.

EXHIBIT 8   EXCHANGES OF ASSETS UNDER THE PROPOSED SUBSTITUTION ACCOUNT

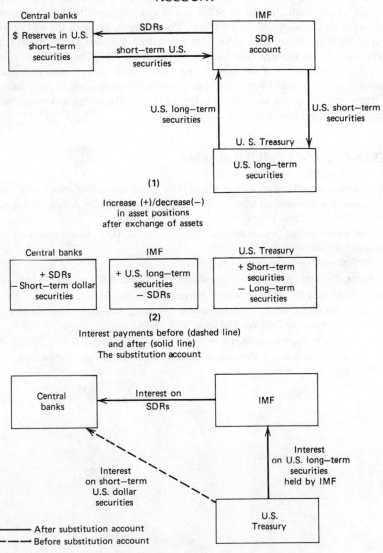

Thus as indicated in panel 2, central banks would end up holding fewer dollars and more SDRs, the IMF would hold fewer SDRs and more long-term U.S. bonds, and the **U.S. Treasury** would hold more short-term and fewer long-term U.S. government securities.

Interest payments would be made (1) by the United States to the IMF on the U.S. long-term bonds held by the IMF and (2) by the IMF to central banks on their SDR holdings. This would be a more indirect route of interest payments compared with the current situation in which payments (as shown by the dashed line in panel (3) are made by the United States to central banks on short-term U.S. dollar securities.

The exchange of dollars for SDRs would reduce the exchange risk of participating countries because the SDR is a weighted average of exchange rates. Thus the value of the SDR remains relatively steady because if some currencies go up, other currencies go down. If the dollar were to depreciate, holders of SDRs would lose on the dollar, but they would gain on currencies appreciating against the dollar. For example, between the end of May and October 4, 1979, the dollar value of the SDR increased 3.5% from $1.269 to $1.313, while the dollar value of the German mark increased 8.3% from 1.909 DM/52.38¢ to 1.762 DM/56.75¢. Because the value of the SDR is less volatile than that of most currencies, it is advocated as a reserve asset by proponents of the substitution account. In their view, central banks that would not accept any dollar funding of U.S. dollar obligations would be willing to accept the SDR because it has less exchange risk.

REFERENCES AND BIBLIOGRAPHY

Bank for International Settlements, *Annual Report,* BIS, Basel, Switzerland, issued each year.

Gilbert, Milton, *The International Monetary System: Growth, Breakdown, Reform,* Wiley, New York (for the Twentieth Century Fund), 1979.

International Monetary Fund, Annual Reports, IMF, Washington, D.C., Annual Reports on Exchange, Arrangements and Exchange *Restrictions.*

————, *IMF Survey,* published each month.

Mayer, Martin, *The Fate of the Dollar, Times Books,* New York, 1980.

Morgan Guaranty Trust Co., *World Financial Markets,* MGT, New York, monthly.

Rolfe, Sidney, and Burtle, James, *The Great Wheel, The World Monetary System,* Quadrangle, New York, 1973. (Paperback: McGraw-Hill, New York, 1975.)

Solomon, Robert, *The International Monetary System, 1945–1976,* Harper & Row, New York, 1977.

Yeager, Leland B., *International Monetary Relations: Theory, History and Policy,* 2nd ed., Harper & Row, New York, 1976.

EXCHANGE RATES AND CURRENCY EXPOSURE

CONTENTS

FUNDAMENTALS OF FOREIGN EXCHANGE   **3**

Basic Concepts, Terminology, and
Definitions   **3**
  Contracts   4
  Actors   7
  Activities   8
Foreign Exchange Trading   **9**
Dimensions of the Market   **10**
  Transaction costs   12
  Concepts of transaction costs   12
  Empirical measures   13
Managing Commercial Bank Traders   **13**

ECONOMICS OF EXCHANGE RATES   **14**

Describing Exchange Rate Movements   **14**
  Alternative measures of a currency's
  foreign exchange value   14
  Recent exchange rate behavior   16
Exchange Rate Determination   **19**
  Purchasing power parity theory   19
  Monetary theory and exchange rates   20
Exchange Rate Dynamics   **21**
  Causes of exchange rate volatility   21
  Exchange rate overshooting   23

Foreign Exchange Market Efficiency   **25**
  Definition   25
  Empirical evidence   26
Forecasting Exchange Rates   **27**
  Alternative forecasting techniques   29
  The forward rate as a forecaster   29
  Techniques for evaluating forecasting
  performance   30

CURRENCY EXPOSURE   **32**

Defining Foreign Exchange Exposure   **32**
  Sources of exposure to foreign
  exchange rate changes   32
  Accounting approaches to measuring
  foreign exchange exposure   33
  Economic approaches to measuring
  exposure   34
Management Strategies Toward Currency
Exposure   **35**
  Financial market hedging techniques   35
  Additional hedging techniques   36
  Impact of currency exposure   37
    Managerial behavior: Results from
    survey analysis   37
    Shareholder and stock market
    responses   38

EXCHANGE RATES AND CURRENCY EXPOSURE

Richard M. Levich

FUNDAMENTALS OF FOREIGN EXCHANGE

BASIC CONCEPTS, TERMINOLOGY, AND DEFINITIONS. The foreign exchange market establishes the link between financial activities in different currencies. As a simplifying assumption, it is convenient to associate each currency with a single country and to assume that only domestic currency is acceptable for domestic transactions. In an economy closed off to international trade, domestic residents need hold only domestic currency balances to carry out transactions. In the real world, which is highly open to international trade in goods and financial assets, we can sketch two separate arguments for the **development of foreign exchange markets.**

First, **international trade** in goods is an important, although not sufficient, explanation for the existence of foreign exchange markets. For example, if German residents would accept and hold U.S. dollars in exchange for Mercedes automobiles, and if U.S. residents would accept and hold German marks in exchange for Boeing aircraft, there would be no need to develop an elaborate foreign exchange market. The problem, of course, is that neither the dollar nor the deutschemark (DM) is particularly efficient as a **medium of exchange** in Germany and the United States, respectively. As a consequence, Mercedes is likely to demand payment in DM while Boeing is likely to demand payment in dollars. This forces foreign buyers to enter the foreign exchange market to trade their domestic currency for an acceptable means of payment. Then, unless the German buyer (who wants to exchange DM for dollars) meets a U.S. buyer (who wants to exchange dollars for DM), the German buyer must convince a satisfied holder of dollars (probably a U.S. resident) to hold DM instead. Why would a U.S. resident trade his dollars for DM—an unacceptable medium of exchange in the United States?

The answer constitutes our second major explanation for the rise of foreign exchange markets: residents of one country may desire to hold financial assets issued in a foreign country and/or denominated in a foreign currency. For example, the common solution to the international trade transaction described above is the presence of a **foreign exchange trader**—an agent who stands ready to buy and sell currencies out of inventory and plans to earn a fair profit for the costs and risks he incurs. The foreign exchange trader is an intermediary who smooths the transactions between German buyers of Boeing aircraft and American buyers of Mercedes automobiles, each of whom arrives at the market at irregular and unpredictable times.

But there are other important reasons for domestic residents to hold assets denominated in foreign currency. First, domestic currency may be subject to high and variable inflation and therefore domestic currency provides a poor **store of value.** As a consequence, domestic residents (of Brazil, Argentina, and Mexico, e.g.) desire foreign currency balances (very often U.S. dollars). Second, foreign currency balances may reduce risks. Also, foreign currency assets act to **hedge anticipated foreign currency liabilities.** In addition, a portfolio of international assets may diversify away some risks that are present in a portfolio containing only domestic currency securities. Finally, if domestic residents simply view foreign currency assets as undervalued, they may demand them for speculative or investment purposes. **Consols** (perpetuities) of the British government, common stock of a Japanese automobile company, or a **Eurobond issued** by a Swiss firm and denominated in Swiss francs may have particular characteristics (e.g., maturity, expected return and risk, or tax consequences) that are desired but unavailable in U.S. financial markets.

An excellent introduction to foreign exchange market terminology and operations has been prepared by Kubarych (*Foreign Exchange Markets in the United States,* Federal Reserve Bank of New York, New York, 1978). Much of the material that follows draws on this source.

Contracts.   The **spot foreign exchange market** involves an exchange of **bank drafts** denominated in different currencies. A **spot contract** implies an "immediate" exchange. In the New York foreign exchange market, immediate delivery is 1 business day for exchanges between North American currencies (i.e., U.S. dollar, Canadian dollar, and Mexican peso) and 2 business days otherwise. Same-day exchange and delivery of bank drafts is possible, but generally at a premium above standard quotations given by traders and reported in newspapers. A much smaller market, which we might call the **cash foreign exchange market,** exists for the immediate exchange of bank notes, traveler's checks, and paper currency. This market, located in international airports, hotels, and retail sections of commercial banks, incurs higher transaction costs and offers less favorable rates than those received by larger customers in the spot market.

The **forward exchange market** involves contracts for exchange of currency at some date in the future. The standard maturities for which contracts are available (and trading activity is greater) are 1, 2, 3, 6, and 12 months. A forward contract for any maturity can be negotiated, but **transaction costs** may be slightly higher than for the standard maturities. For the major industrial currencies, quotations on maturities less than 1 year are routinely available from commercial bank traders. Quotations on maturities from 1 to 5 years are available, but the markets here are much thinner.

Delivery conventions for forward contracts also require explanation. A 1-month forward contract will be delivered in 1 calendar month plus 2 business days (again, 1 business day for North American currencies). For example, a 1-month forward contract executed on July 28, 1980, matured on August 28 (a Thursday). In 1980 August 30 and 31 were a weekend, so no delivery was possible, and September 1 was Labor Day (a bank holiday). Therefore, delivery of clearinghouse funds would have been scheduled for September 2, **36 days** after the July 28 contract. The September 29, 1980, contract matured on October 29 (a Wednesday) for delivery of funds on October 31 (a Friday) or **32 days** after the original contract. The difference in actual horizons for seemingly similar 1-month contracts has strong implications for treasurers planning **exposure management strategies** or for analysts studying the forecasting and efficiency properties of forward rates.

Futures contracts, unlike forward contracts, are highly standardized. Futures contracts are always written against the **exchange clearinghouse** for a fixed number of foreign currency units and for delivery on a fixed date, say June 15. This high level of standardization makes a futures contract an asset that can be traded readily in a secondary market. The **International Monetary Market** (of the Chicago Mercantile Exchange) and the **New York Futures Exchange** are centralized auction markets where currency futures contracts are traded. This market organization is substantially different from the interbank market that specializes in forward contracts. Large corporations generally prefer to use forward contracts from the interbank market because forward contracts offer more flexibility (any amount of any currency on any delivery date) and also because banks supply many other services and information to corporations. (Corporations may have a bank line of credit that allows them to trade forward exchange contracts without explicit **margin requirements.** It may appear that forward trading is "free" once the corporation maintains, say, $1 million in bank balances. In contrast, futures contracts require an explicit margin. However, this margin can be in U.S. Treasury bills, which earn interest for the owner.) Smaller investors generally confine their activities to futures contracts. **Arbitrage** to ensure consistent pricing between forward and futures contracts is an important activity, discussed later.

The **swap contract** discussed by Kubarych, (*Foreign Exchange Markets in the United States,* Federal Reserve Bank of New York, 1978, pp. 10–11) represents "a simultaneous purchase and sale of foreign currency for two different value dates." The swap can be viewed as a simultaneous borrowing and lending operation, much like swap transactions in domestic money markets. An important point is that the swap represents a single transaction between two parties. Since the rates (for simultaneously buying and selling) are set in advance, the trader is not exposed to changes in the foreign exchange rate.

One purpose of a **swap transaction** is to allow a trader or corporate treasurer to invest (or protect) idle currency balances that will be needed at a later date. For example, a corporation with idle DM balances might use a "spot against forward" swap—a simultaneous sale of DM today for U.S. dollars and purchase of DM for delivery in, say, 1 month. As a strategy, this swap transaction will be profitable if the DM depreciates against the U.S. dollar and the extent of depreciation is not reflected in the price of the swap. (The price of a swap is the interest differential between the two currencies. If we expect DM to depreciate, the interest rate on DM should exceed the interest rate on U.S. dollars. In this case, the lender of DM receives more in interest than he pays in interest for the use of U.S. dollars for 1 month.) Another common swap is the **"rollover" or "tomorrow-next" swap.** Here, the first sell (or buy) transaction is for delivery tomorrow (i.e., the next business day) and the simultaneous buy (or sell) transaction is for delivery on the next day.

For our purposes, swap contracts help to illustrate two important points: (1) when quotations on outright forward contracts do not exist, swap transactions can be used to **construct a forward position,** and (2) because traders often use swap contracts to construct their outright forward quotations, the **interest rate parity theorem** (IRPT) will hold exactly within a trading room. Exhibit 1 is used to illustrate these points. A similar exhibit was used by Deardorff, in "One-Way Arbitrage and Its Implications for the Foreign Exchange Markets" (*Journal of Political Economy,* April 1979, pp. 351–364) to illustrate the interrelationships between transaction costs and deviations from interest parity.

Assume that on January 1 a U.S. firm orders a machine from Germany and on July 1, DM 100,000 will be required to pay for it. (In Exhibit 1 DM on July 1 are noted as cell D.) Assume further that the firm wishes to conclude all financial arrangements now rather than waiting until July 1 and buying DM in the spot market at the prevailing rate. There are two ways for the firm to proceed. If a forward market exists, the firm may obtain an outright forward quotation, say, $F = \$0.512195/\text{DM}$. This transaction represents a "direct" exchange of dollar balances for DM balances (between cells A and D in Exhibit 1). The T-accounts

EXHIBIT 1   DIRECT AND INDIRECT TECHNIQUES FOR EXCHANGE OF CURRENCIES AT A FUTURE DATE

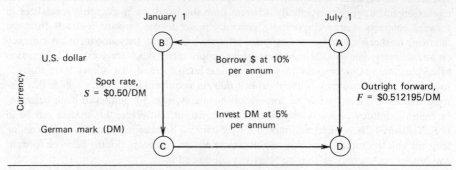

Source: Adapted from Deardorff, "One-Way Arbitrage and Its Implications for the Foreign Exchange Markets," *Journal of Political Economy, April 1979, pp. 351–364.*

show that using the forward market, the firm agrees to pay $51,219.51 for DM 100,000 (Exhibit 2).

What if a forward market does not exist and an outright forward quotation is unavailable? The firm can construct its own forward contract if domestic borrowing and lending are available. For example, if U.S. dollar and DM interest rates are 10 and 5%, respectively, the firm can complete the following transaction on January 1:

1.   Borrow $48,780.49 (= $51,219.51/1.05) for 6 months at 10% per annum.
2.   Use the loan proceeds to buy DM 97,560.98 in the spot market at $0.50/DM.
3.   Buy a DM security with 6 months maturity earning 5% per annum.

The T-accounts confirm that both the direct and indirect methods establish the same balance sheet positions. In this sense, and apart from transaction costs and any tax considerations,

EXHIBIT 2   T-ACCOUNTS FOR DM 100,000 BALANCES ON JULY 1

DIRECT METHOD (FORWARD CONTRACT)

January 1		July 1	
A/R July 1	A/P July 1	A/R July 1	A/P July 1
DM 100,000	$51,219.51	DM 100,000	$51,219.51

INDIRECT METHOD (SWAP CONTRACT PLUS SPOT TRANSACTION)

January 1		July 1	
DM security	Dollar loan	DM security plus interest	Dollar loan plus interest
DM 97,560.98	$48,780.49	DM 100,000	$51,219.51

the example demonstrates that **a forward transaction is fully equivalent to a spot market transaction combined with simultaneous borrowing and lending** (a swap contract). For currencies or maturities where active forward markets do not exist, firms may construct their own forward positions for any desired purpose (i.e., risk reducing or risk taking).

Naturally, the forward rate (F) we used in Exhibit 2 was not selected at random. We selected F so that

$$F = \$0.512195 = \$0.50(1.05/1.025) = \frac{S(1 + i)}{(1 + i^*)}$$

where S = spot rate, i = U.S. interest rate **per period** and i^* = DM (foreign) interest rate **per period.** When F is set according to the formula above, we see that both the direct and indirect methods for establishing forward positions lead to the same results. Traders must set an outright forward price very near the formula above for consistency; otherwise firms will choose the cheapest way to establish their desired forward position. In addition, the formula for F is the same as the equation for interest rate parity (discussed further in this section and elsewhere in the *Handbook*). **Risk-free arbitrage** profits are available if the trader does not quote a forward rate consistent with the prevailing spot rate and relative interest rates.

Actors. The primary actors in the New York foreign exchange market are brokers and traders. A **broker** is an individual who matches orders between people who want to buy foreign exchange and people who want to sell. Brokers do not hold an inventory of currencies and therefore they do not have any capital subject to foreign exchange risks. A **trader,** on the other hand, is an individual (generally employed by a bank or other large financial institution) who actively buys and sells currencies for his own account and for the purpose of making a profit. Traders, by definition, have capital invested in currency holdings (if only for a few minutes at a time) and therefore they are fully exposed to the risk of foreign exchange rate changes.

Transactions in the New York foreign exchange market can be arranged through brokers or **direct dealing.** Until September 1978, most U.S. banks, when trading among themselves, used brokers as intermediaries. Since 1978, practice has given way to greater direct dealing among banks. A few U.S. banks have always preferred to deal directly.

The **function of a broker** is to maintain a list of the best available prices offered by many foreign exchange traders. To accomplish this, the broker maintains direct telephone lines to as many as 150 bank traders. When a trader deals through the New York brokers market, he expects to trade at the best prices represented in the market. Since the cost of obtaining up-to-the-minute quotes can be very high, brokers can provide a very valuable service. In addition, the brokers' market provides anonymity, since the names of the trading parties are revealed to each other only after the transaction, for the purpose of completing delivery. In the brokers' market, size differences between banks will matter less. On the negative side, a broker may be unable to collect meaningful quotations in certain market conditions, or the quotations themselves may be very old. With direct dealing, the trader always receives a fresh quotation. In the interbank market, a trader (A) is obliged to make a **two-way quotation** (i.e., both bid and offer prices) without knowing whether the calling trader (B) wishes to buy or sell. And whether trader B hits A's bid price, offer price, or refuses to trade, trader A may interpret this as evidence that one or both of his prices are out of line.

Activities.   There are several activities in the foreign exchange market that are important for linking together the various prices and segments in the foreign exchange market. These trading activities are important because they contribute to the efficient operation of the market. An implication of efficiency is that at both the interbank (wholesale) and retail levels, individuals are assured of transacting at fair prices that full reflect available information.

Arbitrage is the simultaneous, or nearly simultaneous, purchase of securities in one market for sale in another market with the expectation of profit. **Spatial arbitrage** suggests arbitrage between segments of the foreign exchange market that are physically separated. Since foreign exchange traders are not housed in a centralized auction market (like the New York Stock Exchange), it is unlikely that all traders will quote exactly the same prices at exactly the same instant. This **price dispersion across traders** very likely represents the cost of searching for favorable prices and the uncertainty that comes from knowing that expected arbitrage profits may disappear before all transactions can be completed. Spatial arbitrage between a foreign exchange futures market and the interbank forward market is another important example. Finally spatial arbitrage to keep the DM/$ rate in Frankfurt equal to the reciprocal, that is, the $/DM rate in New York, represents another potential profit opportunity. However, since the 1978 agreement that standardizes interbank foreign exchange quotations in European terms (e.g., DM/$), this variety of spatial arbitrage may be very limited in the interbank market.

Triangular arbitrage suggests that ignoring transaction costs, the prices for any three currencies (e.g., U.S. dollars, DM, and Canadian dollars) must be consistant with the following relationship:

$$\frac{\$}{DM} = \frac{\$}{\$C} \times \frac{\$C}{DM}$$

This relationship applies to spot rates as well as to all forward rates. For example, if the U.S. dollar price of Canadian dollars is $0.85 and the Canadian dollar price of DM is $C0.64, the U.S. dollar price of DM must be $0.544/DM. Given the other two exchange rates, any price other than $0.544/DM establishes the opportunity for profits by triangular arbitrage.

In the above case, the $C/DM rate is called a **cross-rate,** a term used to describe exchange rates between non–U.S. dollar currencies. In a practical sense, a market for the **direct** exchange of $C for DM does not exist. The $C/DM cross-rate is most often calculated from the **direct rates** for $/$C and $/DM quoted in these active markets. A trader with Canadian dollars who instead wants to hold DM will most likely engage in two transactions: first, an exchange of $C for $, and second, an exchange of $ for DM. That these two transactions are preferred to a direct exchange between $C and DM suggests that the transaction costs must be lower. The time required to complete the two transactions may also be shorter than the time required to arrange a direct trade or DM for $C, suggesting that the **liquidity risk** is smaller by trading through the U.S. dollar. In fact, since both transactions involve the more active U.S. dollar market, the costs of two "indirect" transactions are less than the cost of one direct exchange between Canadian dollars and DM.

A more stark example would match a Brazilian exporter and a Swedish importer. Few Brazilians (Swedes) might willingly hold kroner (cruzeiros), but both would find it easier to trade their domestic currencies versus U.S. dollars. These examples illustrate that the volume of U.S. dollar transactions in the foreign exchange market may be very large relative to the U.S. share of world trade or the share of world trade denominated in U.S. dollars. In addition, the examples illustrate the role of the U.S. dollar as a **vehicle currency,** expediting the flow of transactions between smaller countries whose currencies have more limited circulation.

Our equation for **triangular arbitrage** illustrates another important relationship—with three currencies ($, $C, and DM) there are only two independent prices. Similarly, with four currencies there are only three independent prices and, in general, with N currencies only $N - 1$ prices are independent. This straightforward observation describes the role of the U.S. dollar during the **Bretton Woods** period (see section entitled "The International Monetary System"). As the Nth country, the United States passively absorbed exchange rate policies developed in the rest of the world. Under floating exchange rates, triangular arbitrage reminds us that exchange rate policies or targets must be consistent, or else periods of instability and profit opportunities will develop.

Covered interest arbitrage describes capital flows that seek risk-free profits based on differences between the forward premium and relative interest rates (see the discussion on forward contracts). Covered arbitrage transactions ensure consistent pricing of spot rates, forward rates, and interest rates on securities that are similar in all respects except currency of denomination.

All these examples reinforce the point that if exchange rate policies or targets and market prices are not internally consistent, there will be capital flows motivated by arbitrage profit opportunities.

Speculative transactions, in contrast to arbitrage, expose the individual to risk. However, speculation involves more than risk. For example, an investor who holds a widely diversified portfolio of stocks is exposed to risk, but he is not necessarily speculating. Holding risky stocks may simply reflect risk preferences rather than a desire to trade the portfolio actively and to exploit inside information or superior trading skills. **Speculation** implies financial transactions that develop when an individual's expectations differ from the market's expectations (Kohlhagen, "The Identification of Destabilizing Foreign Exchange Speculation," *Journal of International Economics,* August 1979, pp. 321–340). Speculators may transact in any international financial market. As a practical matter, because of low transaction costs, low margin requirements, and convenience, speculators prefer to use the forward market. It should be noted that some corporate transactions that, for accounting purposes or otherwise, might be called hedging, are actually speculation. For example, a firm may sell its product in Germany and hold DM accounts receivable. If the firm believes that the DM will appreciate (depreciate) relative to the current forward rate, the firm may maintain ("hedge") its DM receivables. Since the decision is selective (depending on expectations), the transactions are speculative.

FOREIGN EXCHANGE TRADING. The great majority of foreign exchange trading takes place in the **interbank market** between **traders or market makers** who represent large commercial banks or other financial institutions. The interbank market is worldwide with 24-hour trading. The foreign exchange market has the largest volume, the lowest cost of transacting, and the fastest pace of perhaps any financial market. However, there is no national or international agency (such as the Securities and Exchange Commission or the International Monetary Fund) that is charged with monitoring foreign exchange market practices and reporting fundamental market data. Market practices therefore depend on **self-regulation** (through the Foreign Exchange Brokers Association and the Forex Association of North America) and **competitive pressures.**

Unlike the New York Stock Exchange, there are no requirements for traders to divulge their **"inside information."** Accounting and reporting requirements for firms may be partially standardized, but macroeconomic data reported by countries are often difficult to compare, untimely, and inconsistent with meaningful accounting standards. If corporate operations require clarification to relieve market uncertainty, on the other hand, the SEC may halt trading and request clarifying statements from the firm. Great uncertainty and unstable market conditions may force a halt to foreign exchange trading (e.g., markets were essentially closed during the first few days of floating rates in February 1973), but it is market pressure and informal governmental pressures that eventually lead to clarifying statements and the resumption of trading. Finally, corporations intervene to repurchase their own stock and governments intervene to buy and sell foreign exchange. Presumably corporations are always guided by the profit motive, whereas the goals for government intervention are not so clearly identified.

The failure of **Bankhaus Herstatt** and **Franklin National Bank** in the mid-1970s, both closely associated with mismanaged or uncontrolled foreign exchange trading, has raised the awareness of both bank officials and government agencies of the lack of foreign exchange market regulation. Individual banks seem to have reduced their willingness to hold speculative positions (no formal statistics are available to support this). However, the number of banks trading foreign exchange has risen substantially since 1973. The U.S. government response has been to ask both banks and nonbanks to report their foreign exchange positions for various currencies and maturities on a regular basis (see *U.S. Treasury Bulletin,* monthly, Department of the Treasury, Washington, D.C.). But no formal regulations exist for interbank foreign exchange trading in the United States.

DIMENSIONS OF THE MARKET. A recent paper by Giddy, "Measuring the World Foreign Exchange Market" (*Columbia Journal of World Business,* Winter 1979, pp. 36–48), discussed several estimates of the size of the foreign exchange market. The author suggested that before the U.S. dollar devaluation of August 15, 1971, worldwide foreign exchange trading volume was less than $25 billion per day. During 1980 there is very good reason to believe that worldwide trading volume was $200 billion per day and perhaps much larger. This daily figure suggests annual volume more than $50 trillion!

These are enormous figures, many times larger than world GNP or the worldwide volume of foreign trade transactions. Thus, a great many foreign exchange transactions cannot be motivated directly by underlying real trade transactions. For another way to see this, consider Exhibit 3, which reports that 91.5% of transactions in the U.S. segment of the foreign exchange market are interbank transactions and only 8.5% are with final or retail customers.

Do these figures suggest that interbank trading is excessive and that many transactions are "unnecessary" or even "speculative"? Perhaps not. The retail market for foreign exchange has become highly competitive. Commercial bank traders must continuously interact with the market—to have fresh quotes, to have a sense of the market, and perhaps to have a small inventory of currencies to sell to retail customers. A retail customer who wants to purchase DM 10 million will calculate the difference between a $0.5321 and $0.5326 quote as $5,000. The treasurer for a large multinational corporation might trade these amounts weekly or even daily. Therefore, strong incentives exist for commercial bank traders to offer competitive quotes, and these pressures (along with a desire to exploit temporary informational advantages or trading expertise) may help explain the large percentage of interbank trading.

Exhibit 3 also illustrates the geographic breakdown of foreign exchange trading. London and the rest of Europe clearly hold a dominant position in the foreign exchange market. New York is a distant factor, with only $8 billion of an estimated $103 billion per day trading volume in 1977. The survey conducted by the Federal Reserve Bank of New York in March

EXHIBIT 3 DIMENSIONS OF THE FOREIGN EXCHANGE MARKET

Location	Volume ($ Billions)[a]	Currency	%[b]	Transaction	Volume ($ Billion/day)[c]	%	Volume ($ Billion/day)[c]	%
London	$ 29	U.S. dollar	99.0	Spot	315.5	64.2		
Germany	24	German mark	40.0	U.S. brokers	162.5	33.1		
Switzerland	18	British pound	15.0	Other interbank	137.9	28.1		
Amsterdam	9	Swiss franc	18.0	Customers	15.1	3.1		
New York	8	Canadian dollar	5.0	Outright forwards			29.4	6.0
Paris	5	French franc	6.0	Swaps			146.5	29.8
Brussels	2	Dutch guilder	5.0	Short-dated[d]			86.9	17.7
Far East	3	Belgian franc	2.0	Long-dated			59.6	12.1
Rest of world	5	Italian lira	1.0	Total	491.4	100.0		
	$103	Swedish krone	1.0	Total interbank	449.7	91.5		
		Other	6.0	Total customer	41.7	8.5		
			200.0					

[a]Daily volume, 1977 estimate.
[b]Estimated 1977 currency composition of worldwide foreign exchange trading. Total adds to 200% because two currencies are involved in every foreign exchange transaction. *Source:* Ian H. Giddy, "Measuring the World Foreign Exchange Market," *Columbia Journal of World Business,* Winter 1979, pp. 36–48.
[c]Monthly volume of transactions in the U.S. foreign exchange market, March 1980 estimate. *Source:* Federal Reserve Bank of New York, press release dated June 23, 1980.
[d]For 1 week or less.

1980 suggests that daily New York volume has risen sharply to $23.4 billion. Recent volume estimates for the rest of the world are not available.

Another important measure of the foreign exchange market is the currency composition of trading. Exhibit 3 indicates that the U.S. dollar is included in 99% of all transactions. (Note: a transaction involves **two** currencies.) This strongly confirms the **vehicle currency role** for the U.S. dollar. The second most actively traded currency (worldwide) is the German mark, followed by the Swiss franc and British pound.

Finally, Exhibit 3 also reports the **breakdown of U.S. foreign exchange market transactions.** Roughly two-thirds of all transactions are for spot delivery and about one-half of these transactions are arranged through brokers. Outright forward contracts comprise only 6% of daily volume. The remaining 29.8% of daily volume represents swap contracts.

Transaction Costs.   Professional interest in transaction costs has increased over the past 10 years. There are several reasons. First, **if markets are efficient,** transaction costs may be the only "true" cost of using the foreign exchange market. For example, foreign exchange risk management strategies sometimes use the forward premium as the **"cost of hedging"** or the differential between the forward rate and the expected future spot rate as an **"opportunity cost"** measure. In an efficient market, alternative hedging opportunities are priced fairly so transaction costs capture all of the real resource costs involved.

Second, by almost any measure, the cost of transacting has risen sharply over the floating rate period. On days when unexpected news reaches the market and uncertainty is high, transaction costs may increase dramatically and reduce, or even completely halt, the flow of trading. Therefore, transaction costs may be interpreted as a barometer for how well the **floating exchange rate system** is performing. Changes in transaction costs are one component of the real resource costs of operating a floating exchange rate system rather than a **pegged rate system.**

Concepts of Transaction Costs.   The **liquidity theory** argues that the **bid-ask spread** is only one component in the total cost of transacting. The spread represents the cost of making a quick exchange of a financial claim for money, that is, the cost of **liquidity services.** The theory suggests that the spread should decline as trading volume and the number of market makers increase. Notably, the spread ignores the costs of producing financial claims, the costs of being informed, and similar costs. More important, the liquidity theory assumes that prices are set at a fair or equilibrium level, and so the trader's major costs are associated with waiting for the arrival of buyers and sellers who want liquidity services. A transactor with inside information may be able to trade at a disequilibrium price and reduce his positioning cost below the quoted bid-ask spread.

The **adversary theory** explicitly considers the impact on transaction costs that results if there are two groups of investors with different information. Adversary theory suggests that there are indeed two groups of traders. One group is "informed," trading to earn unusual profits based on their information advantage. The second group is "uninformed," expecting to trade at fair prices for liquidity purposes only. In theory, the trader or market maker will respond differently to these two groups because he fears losing money to informed traders and he expects to earn a fair profit from uninformed traders. Adversary theory also helps us to refine the relationship between risk and transaction costs. **Price risk** suggests the price volatility of the underlying asset, while **liquidity risk** refers to the uncertainty from holding assets that trade a small volume per unit time. Transaction costs are positively related to both types of risk. According to this view, the percentage spread in spot gold prices should exceed the spread in U.S. Treasury bill prices. Furthermore, we expect that the (per unit) cost of trading DM 1 million is smaller than for a DM 1,000 transaction (because of economies of scale). However, the (per unit) cost of trading DM 100 million may **exceed** the cost for DM 1 million because of liquidity risks.

Empirical Measures.   The **bid-ask spread** measures the cost of buying and then immediately selling an asset. Therefore the cost of one transaction equals $\frac{1}{2}$(ask price − bid price)/ ask price. Estimates of transaction costs based on the bid-ask spread vary considerably across currencies and over time. During the early 1960s, spreads were extraordinarily small, roughly 0.01% for sterling, 0.02% for DM, and 0.03% for Canadian dollars. By the mid-1970s, these figures averaged 0.05% for spot contracts and 0.15% for forward contracts. But a substantial number of spreads in the 0.25–0.50% range were observed (Levich, *The International Money Markets: An Assessment of Forecasting Models and Market Efficiency*).

Triangular arbitrage offers another approach for measuring transaction costs. When transaction costs are stationary, the upper limits of the deviations from triangular parity (e.g., $/DM = $/$C − $C/DM) should equal the cost of one currency market transaction. Estimates using the triangular arbitrage approach should be larger than the bid-ask spread, since the costs required to monitor the deviations from triangular parity are included. Using the triangular approach for a 6-month period during 1976, McCormick, in "Covered Interest Arbitrage: Unexploited Profits? Comment" (*Journal of Political Economy*, April 1979, pp. 411–417), estimated spot transaction costs in the range 0.09–0.18%. It should be noted that these estimates of transaction costs are for major currencies during relatively tranquil periods. For less actively traded currencies or during turbulent periods, the cost of transacting can increase substantially. (See Frenkel and Levich, "Transaction Costs and Interest Arbitrage: Tranquil Versus Turbulent Periods," *Journal of Political Economy*, December 1977, pp. 1209–1226.)

MANAGING COMMERCIAL BANK TRADERS.   Some banks operate to break even on foreign exchange trading, treating it as an important service to provide for customers. Other banks see foreign exchange trading as another profit center, and traders are expected to earn profits. In either case foreign exchange trading activities are closely monitored.

Traders can be exposed to several types of risk. **Exchange rate risk** arises because of unexpected spot exchange rate volatility. Exchange rate risk is controlled by **limiting the open position** traders are allowed to hold. Often separate daytime and overnight limits are imposed. Position limits may vary further across currencies and individual traders. **Interest rate risk** pertains to unexpected shifts in the **structure of forward rates.** Restricting open positions at different maturities controls this variety of risk.

Credit risk is related to the fact that foreign exchange contracts, especially forward contracts, are an extension of bank credit. For example, Bank A may buy DM 10 days forward from Bank B. If Bank B fails in 7 days, Bank A will not receive its DM as originally planned. As a consequence, Bank A will have a shorter DM position than planned. The results would be identical if instead Bank B were a bankrupt firm (e.g., W. T. Grant or Penn Central). A bank's decision to trade with a particular bank or firm clearly involves credit risks. Consequently, bank lending officers rather than foreign exchange traders are responsible for setting trading limits for customers. **Country risk** is somewhat similar. It represents the possibility of unanticipated exchange controls or taxes that might alter the expected profitability of foreign exchange trades.

Foreign exchange trading income earned by major U.S. commercial banks is illustrated in Exhibit 4. The data suggest that for some banks (e.g., American Express, Chase, Citibank)

EXHIBIT 4   FOREIGN EXCHANGE TRADING INCOME ($ MILLIONS) OF MAJOR U.S. BANKS[a]

		1977		1978		1979	
		Income	%	Income	%	Income	%
1.	American Express International Bank	14.5	35.0	23.1	42.8	27.3	48.6
2.	Bank of America	54.1	8.4	63.7	7.5	90.2	9.5
3.	Bankers Trust	14.5	18.0	23.1	17.7	16.6	8.0
4.	Chase Manhattan Bank	48.5	24.8	74.7	20.5	77.0	14.0
5.	Chemical Bank	6.6	4.8	19.2	13.4	9.9	4.8
6.	Citibank	68.0	11.9	172.4	20.8	113.6	13.0
7.	First Chicago	8.4	5.6	13.1	7.7	11.2	7.7
8.	Irving Trust	2.9	4.3	1.9	2.6	10.0	10.0
9.	Manufacturers Hanover	8.5	3.1	13.4	4.4	16.1	4.7
10.	Morgan Guaranty Trust	40.3	11.2	56.4	13.4	35.9	8.2

[a]Foreign exchange income is exclusive of translation income; percentage of income is calculated before taxes and securities gains.
Source: Lynn Dominguez, "Management of Commercial Bank Foreign Exchange Trading Operations," MBA thesis, New York University, New York, 1980.

the contribution of foreign exchange trading to total profits is substantial. Furthermore, foreign exchange income varies considerably from year to year. It is not clear whether this variability reflects changing exposure to risk or changing volatility in foreign exchange markets.

ECONOMICS OF EXCHANGE RATES

DESCRIBING EXCHANGE RATE MOVEMENTS.   Tracing the value of a nation's currency is an important exercise. After we observe a time series graph of exchange rates, a number of questions demand attention. What factors determine the price of a currency? What causes currency prices to change? Are currency prices and price changes set fairly and in an orderly manner, or are foreign exchange markets inefficient and characterized by excessive price volatility? Before we explore these questions, we must define the notion of "currency value" more carefully.

Alternative Measures of a Currency's Foreign Exchange Value.   The most common notion of **currency value** is the **bilateral exchange rate** that is quoted by a foreign exchange trader or reported in a newspaper. This is a **nominal exchange rate** because it expresses the number of units of one currency that must be offered in exchange for a unit of another currency, such as, 220 yen/$, 0.50/DM, or $2.35/£. A nominal, bilateral exchange rate is essential, obviously, for translating cash flows in one unit of account, say DM, into the U.S. dollar equivalent.

The **real exchange rate,** however, expresses the value of a currency in terms of real purchasing power (i.e., the currency's value in purchasing real goods and services). Exhibit 5 illustrates the price of a hypothetical market basket of goods in the United States and in Germany. The market basket costs $500 in the United States and DM 1,200 in Germany. At the prevailing nominal exchange rate (we assume $0.50/DM), the real value of $500 (i.e.,

EXHIBIT 5   PRICE OF HYPOTHETICAL MARKET BASKET OF GOODS IN UNITED STATES AND GERMANY[a]

	United States	Germany
Television set	$325	DM 650
Two pair of blue jeans	50	125
Dinner for two at a nice restaurant	50	125
Hotel room for 1 night	75	300
	$500	DM 1,200

[a]If the exchange rate is $0.50/DM, the hypothetical market basket in Germany would cost 20% more than in the United States.

one market basket) exceeds the real value of DM 1,000 (i.e., five-sixths market basket). The real exchange rate is useful for measuring the price competitiveness of domestic goods in international markets. For example, Exhibit 5 suggests that blue jeans, dinners, and hotel rooms are less expensive in the United States than in Germany. Based on these price differences, we expect that German demand for U.S. blue jeans will be strong and that tourists will find vacations cheaper in the United States than in Germany. If we assume that economic agents make decisions based on real values, then we must utilize **real exchange rates** to calculate the real value of investment projects.

The difficulties of calculating and using real exchange rates are suggested by Exhibit 5. The price differences between U.S. and German hotel rooms and dinners may reflect quality differences and the fact that these goods cannot be traded. While blue jeans can be traded, some price difference may be the result of transportation costs and tariff barriers. The nominal exchange rate itself may reflect economywide factors (and as we argue shortly, expectations of these factors) that are not reflected in the posted prices for a particular market basket of goods. Notwithstanding these difficulties, the **real exchange rate** is an important concept, especially as it relates to future changes in trade patterns and evaluating long-term investment projects.

The **effective exchange rate** measures the overall nominal value of a currency in the foreign exchange market. It is calculated by forming a weighted average of bilateral exchange rates. For example, the effective U.S. dollar exchange rate combines many exchange rates (e.g., $/£, $/DM, $/yen, . . .) using a weighting scheme that reflects the importance of each country's trade with the United States. Several institutions (International Monetary Fund, Federal Reserve Bank, Morgan Guaranty Trust Co., and others) regularly calculate and report effective exchange rates. Each institution uses a slightly different weighting scheme. The effective exchange rate is a useful statistic for gauging the overall supply and demand for a currency on the foreign exchange market. By its nature, however, the effective exchange rate conceals the price behavior of individual bilateral markets.

The **real effective exchange rate** is calculated by dividing the home country's nominal effective exchange rate by an index of the ratio of average foreign prices to home prices. The real effective exchange rate attempts to measure the overall competitiveness of home country goods in international markets. While it is important to gauge international competitiveness, a summary statistic such as the real effective exchange rate should be interpreted with caution. A recent article on this subject by Hooper and Morton, "Summary Measures of the Dollar's Foreign Exchange Value" (*Federal Reserve Bulletin*, October 1978, pp. 783–789), has concluded that (p. 787):

Any such aggregate measure is subject to problems due to incorrect measurement of prices, incorrect weighting system, and an inability to measure sectoral shifts in productivity. In addition, real exchange-rate indexes are rough measures of price competitiveness only and do not measure important nonprice factors such as quality, dependability, and servicing, which have an important influence on trade patterns but may change relatively slowly.

Recent Exchange Rate Behavior.   Prior to the early 1970s, most exchange rates were pegged to the U.S. dollar, and their values were held within 1% of the central rate through official intervention. In response to a fundamental disequilibrium, the central bank would permit a discrete, step adjustment in the currency value and then resume its official support at a new central rate. Since March 1973, the values of major industrial currencies have been determined primarily by free-market forces in a **floating exchange rate system.** (The Canadian dollar began floating in June 1970 and the British pound in June 1972.) From time to time, central banks have intervened, ostensibly to smooth "disorderly" market conditions, making the term **managed floating** more appropriate. In either case, the volatility of exchange rates increased dramatically under the floating exchange rate system.

Exhibit 6 presents an index of selected bilateral exchange rates vis-à-vis the U.S. dollar. The graph clearly illustrates how the values of bilateral exchange rates, once pegged for long stretches of time, have strayed over a wide range since 1973. The Swiss franc, the German mark, and the Japanese yen demonstrated a strong tendency to appreciate over the

EXHIBIT 6   SELECTED NOMINAL EXCHANGE RATES

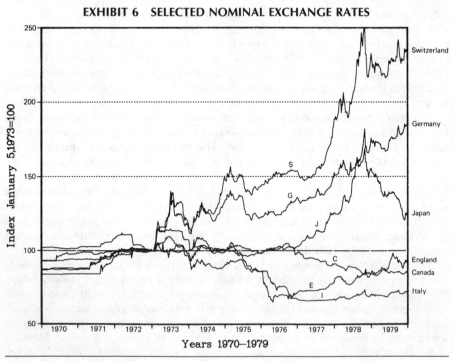

Source: Harris Bank Weekly Review.

period, while the Canadian dollar and the Italian lira generally weakened. The British pound depreciated sharply until late 1976, and has gradually appreciated since then. From 1973 through mid-1975, several currencies (noticeably the DM) demonstrated a cyclical pattern, leading observers to propose that exchange rates may overshoot their equilibrium value. During mid-1975 through mid-1977, exchange rate movements were relatively flat. The strong appreciation of the Swiss franc, the German mark, and the Japanese yen resumed in mid-1977, to be capped by the major U.S. intervention announced on November 1, 1978.

The **record** of **effective exchange rates** is illustrated in Exhibit 7. Since most countries will appreciate against some of their trading partners and depreciate against others, the pattern of effective exchange rates should be smoother than for bilateral exchange rates. The Swiss franc is an exception, since it appreciated vis-à-vis every currency, and it appreciated considerably more for some currencies (notably the Italian lira and British pound) than it did with respect to the U.S. dollar. The Italian lira depreciated against all other currencies. So the lira's effective depreciation (about 42% by 1980) exceeds its depreciation vis-à-vis the U.S. dollar (about 30%). Exhibit 7 also illustrates the effective value of the U.S. dollar. Even though the U.S. dollar depreciated substantially against the Swiss franc, the German mark, and the Japanese yen, the U.S. dollar appreciated against the Canadian dollar. And because the Canadian share of U.S. trade is large (roughly 50%), the effective value of the U.S. dollar has changed relatively little since 1973. At the end of 1979, the effective U.S. dollar exchange rate stood at 98.7. Thus, the average depreciation in the U.S. dollar of 1.3%

EXHIBIT 7   EFFECTIVE EXCHANGE RATES

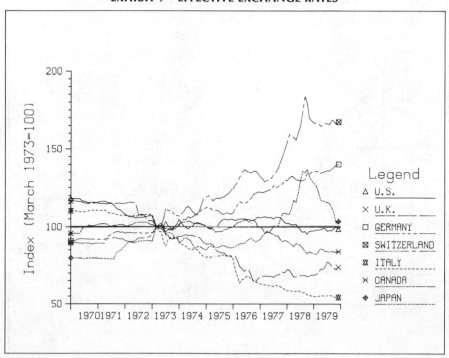

Source: Morgan Guaranty Trust.

since March 1973 thoroughly disguises the varied performance of the dollar against individual currencies.

A set of real effective exchange rates is illustrated in Exhibit 8. The pattern of real effective exchange rates is generally less volatile than other series because relative inflation rates often move to offset exchange rate changes. Several individual currencies are interesting to examine more closely. The effective exchange rates for Germany and Switzerland at the end of 1979 were 140.2 and 167.5, respectively, reflecting the substantial appreciation of these currencies vis à vis most others. However, the real effective exchange rates for Germany and Switzerland stood at 105.9 and 112.6, suggesting that most, but not all, of the exchange rate change was offset by differential inflation rates across countries. The figure for Switzerland suggests that the real purchasing power of the Swiss franc is up by 12.6% on average against its trading partners, compared to its purchasing power in March 1973. This is substantial **average** change.

On the other hand, the effective exchange rates for Canada and Italy at the end of 1979 were 84.0 and 54.4, respectively. With inflation adjustments, the real effective exchange rates stood at 92.9 and 95.2 for Canada and Italy, again suggesting that most, but not all, of the exchange rate change was offset by differential inflation rates. The United Kingdom presents an odd case. The end-of-1979 effective British pound exchange rate was 73.9 (a nominal devaluation), but the real effective exchange rate was 123.3, suggesting appreciation in real terms. By way of comparison, the real effective U.S. dollar exchange rate hit its low

EXHIBIT 8   REAL EFFECTIVE EXCHANGE RATES

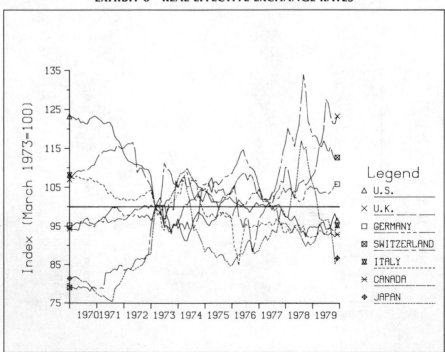

Source: Morgan Guaranty Trust.

value (88.6) in October 1978, just before the Federal Reserve Bank intervened to offset these rate movements. (In principle, the real value of a currency could be computed using one of several price indexes. The real value of the U.S. dollar adjusted with export price indexes, wholesale price indexes, consumer price indexes, and unit labor cost indexes is reported by Hooper and Morton in "Summary Measures of the Dollar's Foreign Exchange Value.")

EXCHANGE RATE DETERMINATION.   A central question facing economists and currency forecasters is the following: what data should be collected and how should the information be combined to explain past exchange rate behavior and to predict future exchange rates? To put it another way, **what is the model by which exchange rates are determined?** This is clearly a very complicated issue for which a huge literature exists. The interested reader should refer to the articles by Dornbusch ("Exchange Rate Economics: Where Do We Stand?" *Brookings Institution Papers on Economic Activity,* No. 1, 1980, pp. 145–185) and Isard ("Exchange Rate Determination: A Survey of Popular Views and Recent Models," *Princeton Studies in International Finance,* No. 42, May 1978), and the many studies cited therein. The goal of this subsection is to briefly outline the major themes of exchange rate models.

Purchasing Power Parity Theory.   Perhaps the most popular and intuitive model for exchange rate behavior is represented by the theory of **purchasing power parity (PPP).** The main thrust of purchasing power parity is that nominal exchange rates are set so that the real purchasing power of currencies tends to equalize. As a result, PPP suggests that in the long run, nominal bilateral exchange rate changes will tend to equal the differential in inflation rates between countries. The term "purchasing power parity" is associated with Gustav Cassel, who studied alternative approaches for selecting official exchange rates at the end of World War I and the resumption of international trade. As Frenkel has recently pointed out ("Purchasing Power Parity: Doctrinal Perspective and Evidence from the 1920s," *Journal of International Economics,* Vol. 8, No. 2, May 1978, pp. 169–191), the intellectual origins of purchasing power parity can be traced to the early nineteenth century and the writings of Wheatley and Ricardo. Economists have long debated whether the PPP doctrine applies to the short run or the long run and whether the relevant inflation rate is describing a narrow class of goods (e.g., traded goods) or a broad class of goods (e.g., all traded and nontraded goods in the consumer price index). Frenkel has argued that much of the controversy over the usefulness of the PPP doctrine results from the fact that PPP specifies a final, equilibrium relationship between exchange rates and prices without specifying the precise linkages and details of the process. If in the world economy, prices and exchange rates are determined by many other variables, then PPP represents an equilibrium relationship more than a precise theory of exchange rate determination.

The many writings on purchasing power parity have been surveyed by Officer in "The Purchasing-Power-Parity Theory of Exchange Rates: A Review Article" (*IMF Staff Papers,* Vol. 23, No. 1, March 1976, pp. 1–60). The following discussion of PPP is based on a recent book by McKinnon, *Money in International Exchange* (Oxford University Press, 1979, Chapter 6). The heart of PPP doctrine is the **law of one price,** that is, perfect **commodity market arbitrage.** For example, if the price of oil in New York is $40 per barrel, we expect the price in London to be £20 per barrel when the exchange rate is $2/£.

Absolute purchasing power parity requires that the exchange rate equalize the price of a market basket of goods in the two countries. Since the composition of market baskets and price indexes varies substantially across countries, and because many goods are nontraded or are subject to tariffs, it is unlikely that absolute PPP will hold in the real world. (McKinnon discusses the sufficient conditions in *Money in International Exchange,* p. 119.)

Relative purchasing power parity, however, requires that the **percentage change** in the exchange rate equal the differential **percentage change** in the price of a market basket of goods in the two countries. If the factors that cause absolute PPP to fail (e.g., tariffs, some goods being nontraded) are constant over time (i.e., zero percentage change), relative PPP might hold even when the absolute version does not. (See the subsection on **real** exchange rates. It should be clear that when relative PPP holds, the **real** exchange rate is constant, and the relative competitiveness of countries in foreign markets is unchanged.)

The empirical evidence on PPP is mixed. Moreover, the evidence may be sensitive to the countries, time periods, and price indexes that we select. Over long time periods and during periods of hyperinflation (when monetary factors swamp real changes), PPP offers a fairly good description of exchange rate behavior. However, over shorter time periods, say 3–12 months, it has not been uncommon to observe substantial exchange rate changes, say 10–20%, which are unrelated to commodity price changes. McKinnon, concluded that "Substantial and continually changing deviations from PPP are commonplace. For individual tradable commodities, violations in the 'law of one price' can be striking" (*Money in International Exchange,* p. 133).

The last statement refers to a study by Isard, "How Far Can We Push the Law of One Price?" (*American Economic Review,* Vol. 67, No. 6, December 1977, pp. 942–948), that compared the movement of the dollar prices of German goods relative to their American equivalents for specific goods selected at the 2- and 3-digit levels of the Standard Industrial Trade Classification (SITC). The results implied persistent violations of the law of one price. In part, Isard concluded that "In reality the law of one price is flagrantly and systematically violated by empirical data. . . . Moreover, these relative price effects seem to persist for at least several years and cannot be shrugged off as transitory" ("How Far Can We Push the Law of One Price?" p. 942).

Notwithstanding the arguments above, McKinnon concluded:

> Until a more robust theory replaces it, I shall assume that purchasing power parity among tradable goods tends to hold in the long run in the absence of overt impediments to trade among countries with convertible currencies. But . . . because commodity arbitrage is so imperfect in the short run, it cannot be relied on to contain nominal exchange rate movements within the predictable and narrow limits suggested by the law of one price. (*Money in International Exchange,* p. 136.)

As a consequence, economists have turned to monetary and portfolio balance models of exchange rate determination which are discussed below.

Monetary Theory and Exchange Rates. It is perhaps trivial to observe that whenever a voluntary foreign exchange transaction occurs, say between U.S. dollars and DM, it represents an excess demand for one currency (say DM) and an excess supply of the other currency (in this case, U.S. dollars). If we can identify the sources of this excess demand for DM (perhaps these sources include a transaction demand or a speculative demand for currency, or perhaps DM balances offer a more reliable store of real purchasing power), we have the basis for a **monetary theory of exchange rates.** The basic monetary approach to exchange rate determination is a direct outgrowth of purchasing power parity theory in combination with the quantity theory of money. While PPP concludes that the exchange rate is the relative price of goods in two countries, monetary theory suggests that the exchange rate is the relative price of two moneys. In this context, it follows that the exchange rate represents the **relative demand** for two moneys.

According to the monetary theory, factors that lead to an increase in the demand for domestic currency (i.e., the U.S. dollar) should lead to an increase in the price of domestic currency on the foreign exchange market. Two factors that would increase the demand for domestic currency balances are an increase in U.S. income (that increases the demand for transactions balances) and a fall in U.S. dollar interest rates (that lowers the opportunity cost of holding currency balances). Correspondingly, monetary theory predicts that these factors should cause the U.S. dollar to appreciate on the foreign exchange market. Notably, these predictions are contrary to more standard theories of trade and capital flows.

Trade models correctly argue that higher U.S. income will lead to greater demand for imports, and in turn an increased demand for foreign currency and a depreciation of the U.S. dollar. But capital flows would also respond to an increase in U.S. income, and monetary theory suggests that the net effect of higher U.S. income should be a U.S. dollar appreciation. Capital flow models correctly argue that high **real** U.S. interest rates should attract foreign capital that in turn, acts to appreciate the U.S. dollar. Monetary theory, however, emphasizes that high **nominal** U.S. interest rates that incorporate a large inflation premium actually imply low **real** interest rates. The data strongly confirm that currencies with high interest rates (e.g., Brazil and Argentina) generally have been characterized by depreciation, while currencies with low interest rates (e.g., Germany and Switzerland) generally have been characterized by appreciation.

The **portfolio balance theory** expands this framework, arguing that investors' excess demand is not for currency qua currency, rather investors desire to shift from one set of dollar financial assets into another set of DM financial assets. In the portfolio balance model, demand in the foreign exchange market for currencies is derived largely from demand for financial assets. As a consequence, if wealth accumulates (e.g., via current account surpluses) in a country that traditionally prefers DM assets, it is likely that the value of the DM will increase. To take another example, if the spending patterns of a country shift (e.g., the United States changes its taste toward German products) or if a country (e.g., Saudi Arabia) accumulates a substantial amount of financial wealth, prudent risk management principles suggest that investors in these countries will diversify their asset portfolios. And in our examples, diversification is away from dollar assets and toward DM assets.

Both the monetary and portfolio balance theories suggest that a relatively short list of factors determines the bulk of exchange rate movements. This list would include the **expected real interest rate** in each currency, the **expected productivity and income changes,** and other factors affecting **national wealth,** including the current account. Unfortunately, the numerical formula for combining these factors can only be estimated, and the results in terms of offering a complete explanation of exchange rate movements are far from satisfactory.

EXCHANGE RATE DYNAMICS.   Alternative models of exchange rate determination may agree that the equilibrium price of DM increased from $0.25/DM to $0.50/DM between 1973 and 1979, yet the models may disagree considerably concerning the **path of adjustment** between $0.25/DM and $0.50/DM. The topic of **exchange rate dynamics** examines the movement of exchange rates between two points in time, in addition to the beginning and end-of-period values of the exchange rate. Analyzing the movement of exchange rates over shorter time intervals is important for several reasons. We want to assess more closely the performance (i.e., efficiency) of foreign exchange markets. We also want to understand better the causes of these short-run movements and to gauge whether they are excessive and/ or predictable.

Causes of Exchange Rate Volatility.   The most fundamental change for exchange rate modeling in the 1970s was the realization that foreign exchange is a financial asset. And as

such, foreign exchange rates should exhibit characteristics common to other financial assets—namely, quick and sometimes large price changes in response to new information
(which is observable) or to changes in expectations (which cannot be observed). Therefore,
we expect to observe that foreign exchange rates move quickly and responsively relative to
commodity prices (e.g., automobiles and grocery items).

Exhibit 9 illustrates one measure of the daily volatility of exchange rate changes during
the current floating rate period. We see that it is not uncommon for exchange rates to change
by 0.5 to 1.0, or even 2.0% in a single day. We are interested in determining whether this
volatility is "excessive" relative to some standard.

Recent studies by Frenkel and Mussa ("The Efficiency of Foreign Exchange Markets
and Measures of Turbulence," *American Economic Review,* Vol. 70, No. 2, May 1980, pp.
374–381) and Levich ("An Examination of Overshooting Behavior in the Foreign Exchange
Market," Group of Thirty, *Occasional Studies,* No. 4, 1980) offer some insights on this
issue. Since exchange rates are determined by a list of variables (e.g., relative money supply
growth rates, income growth rates), we would expect the volatility of exchange rates to
reflect the volatility of underlying factors.

Exhibit 10 indicates that recent exchange rate volatility is considerably greater than the
volatility of relative **cost-of-living indexes.** This suggests that other factors (e.g., volatility
in relative income, government intervention, or unanticipated news events) have contributed
to exchange market volatility. Exhibit 10 also indicates that recent exchange rate behavior
has been less volatile than that of national stock markets. Most national stock markets are
felt to be fairly efficient in the sense that price swings in these markets represent a reasonably
accurate assessment of changing real economic events and changing expectations. By this

EXHIBIT 9   DAILY EXCHANGE RATE VOLATILITY

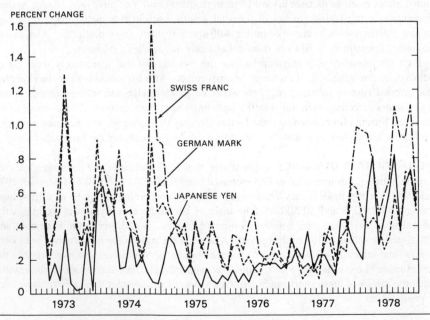

Source: Economic Report of the President, January 1979, p. 153.

EXHIBIT 10   MEAN ABSOLUTE PERCENTAGE CHANGES IN PRICES AND EXCHANGE RATES, (MONTHLY DATA: JUNE 1973–FEBRUARY 1979)

	Variable[a]				
Country	WPI	COL	Stock Market	Exchange Rate Against the Dollar	COL/COL$_{U.S.}$
United States	.009	.007	.038	—	—
United Kingdom	.014	.012	.066	.020	.007
France	.011	.008	.054	.020	.003
Germany	.004	.004	.031	.024	.004

[a]WPI = wholesale-price index: COL = cost of living.
Source: Frenkel and Mussa, "The Efficiency of Foreign Exchange Markets and Measures of Turbulence," *American Economic Review,* Vol. 70, No. 2, (May 1980), p. 375.

standard, recent exchange rate volatility does not appear to be "excessive" or "unprecedented." This does not contradict the viewpoint that world welfare and thè gains from international trade in commodities and capital would very likely increase if national economic policies were set to make exchange rate changes smoother and more predictable.

Exchange Rate Overshooting.   The recent period of floating exchange rates has caused some market observers to wonder whether exchange rate volatility, by some standard, is excessive. The term "overshooting" was coined to describe exchange rate changes in excess of this standard. Interest in overshooting arises from two general concerns. First, exchange rate overshooting may signal that the market is inefficient and profit opportunities exist, and/ or that some sort of corrective governmental action (**not** necessarily intervention) is required. Second, if the foreign exchange market is operating efficiently, overshooting may simply suggest that investing in foreign currency assets is somewhat riskier than is suggested by more simple models. The following discussion draws heavily on the study by Levich cited earlier ("An Examination of Overshooting Behavior in the Foreign Exchange Market").

Three **definitions of overshooting** can be stated briefly as follows:

1. The current spot exchange rate S_t does not equal some long-run equilibrium rate $\bar{S}$ that may be based on purchasing power parity or another long-run model.
2. The equilibrium exchange rate change that occurs in the short run ΔS_{sr} exceeds the equilibrium exchange rate change in the long run ΔS_{lr}.
3. The actual exchange rate change that occurs in the market place ΔS_t exceeds the equilibrium exchange rate change $\Delta S_t'$ that would be required if the market had full information about economic structure and disturbances.

The first definition reflects the conventional notion of overshooting as it is often reported in the press, such as "The Swiss franc is currently overvalued relative to any reasonable standard." If the exchange rate model $\bar{S}$ accounts for transportation costs, lags in price adjustment, and other factors, then profit opportunities exist when we can transact at S_t rather than $\bar{S}$. In this case when $S_t \neq \bar{S}$, the market is not efficient, and we should wonder why investors do not buy foreign exchange when $S_t < \bar{S}$ or sell it when $S_t > \bar{S}$.

Demonstrating empirically that the market does not establish a fair price $(S_t \neq \bar{S})$ is extremely difficult. Most empirical tests have been unable to reject market efficiency in favor of an alternative hypothesis. However, these tests of market efficiency are really tests of a joint hypothesis. That is, when we observe that $S_t \neq \bar{S}$, we cannot be sure whether it is because S_t is set too high (or low) and/or our estimate of $\bar{S}$ is too high (or low). Therefore this definition of overshooting is not likely to be an operational success. It is too easy to be led to the **efficient market tautology:** a price set by a freely competitive market must be a fair price, and so overshooting or undershooting is impossible.

If we maintain that $\bar{S}$ is the true, equilibrium exchange rate, then economic costs exist when the market fails to establish $S_t = \bar{S}$. However, if we can demonstrate valid reasons for the inequality of S_t and $\bar{S}$, this type of overshooting need not entail additional costs.

Interestingly, **overshooting** of this type could be explained by two very different stories: a **shortage** of **speculative capital,** so that transactions to stabilize S_t around $\bar{S}$ are not sufficient, or an **excess** of speculative capital, so that many speculative bandwagons push S_t far from $\bar{S}$. In either case unexploited profit opportunities exist for speculators who recognize the divergence between S_t and $\bar{S}$.

Both these explanations may reflect a confusion between ex ante and ex post results. Ex post, it may be clear that too little or too much speculative capital was committed to the foreign exchange market, but ex ante there would be no way to determine this. Similarly, the stock of speculative capital committed to the foreign exchange market may have been low in 1973, but if a slow and gradual building of capital was expected to be more efficient, then the resulting overshooting need not imply a resource misallocation once these capital adjustment costs have been considered.

The second definition of overshooting draws a distinction between short-run and long-run equilibria, while maintaining the notion that the exchange rate is priced fairly at all times, a perfect reflection of all information. Overshooting of this type might be viewed as the result of forcing a given amount of international adjustment through a limited number of channels, because it is assumed that other potential adjustment channels operate slowly or do not exist. Dornbush, in "Expectations and Exchange Rate Dynamics" (*Journal of Political Economy,* Vol. 84, No. 6, December 1976, pp. 1161–1176), elegantly formalized a monetary model of the exchange rate in which consumer prices adjust very slowly relative to the speed of adjustment in the foreign exchange market. Within this framework, an unanticipated change in the money supply leads to exchange rate overshooting (type 2) because domestic consumer prices cannot move immediately to reflect the money supply change. A similar overshooting result can be illustrated with a **portfolio balance model.** In this case, a desired accumulation of assets denominated in a foreign currency proceeds slowly through cumulative current account surpluses. As this slow process evolves, the foreign exchange rate overshoots to establish equilibrium in this market.

It seems intuitively clear that the greater the number of channels that exist and are free to operate, the less likely we are to observe overshooting behavior in exchange rates. A recent paper by Frenkel and Rodriguez, "Exchange Rate Dynamics and the Overshooting Hypothesis" (mimeographed, University of Chicago, 1980), formalizes this idea. Specifically, the authors show that if prices are free to adjust somewhat (in the Dornbusch model) or if investors elect to spend some of their wealth on nontradable domestic goods (in the portfolio balance model), overshooting behavior (of type 2) need not occur.

The third definition of overshooting rests on the idea that agents may have heterogeneous or incomplete information about the world, thus leading them to place "unfair" prices on financial assets (i.e., prices that do not reflect **all** available information). This framework posits that the actual exchange rate oscillates about the value that would be achieved if prices reflected **all** available information. If agents vary in terms of wealth, risk aversion, and confidence in their forecasts, or if they operate subject to constraints, it is easy to see how this type of overshooting might come about. Suppose that Widget Co. has a policy of using the forward exchange market to hedge real business transactions only. Widget Co. will transfer a DM 1 million dividend in 3 months; the 3-month forward rate is $0.55/DM, and Widget is very confident that the future spot rate will be less than $0.50/DM. Consequently, Widget sells its DM 1 million forward (causing the forward rate to decline slightly), but Widget does not continue selling DM until the forward market fully reflects Widget's expectation.

FOREIGN EXCHANGE MARKET EFFICIENCY.   Tests of the efficiency of asset markets as processors of information began in the 1950s and gained increasing popularity and significance during the 1960s. With the establishment of floating exchange rates in the early 1970s (presumably dominated by free-market behavior), it was natural to begin the investigation of foreign exchange market efficiency. The evidence on foreign exchange market efficiency is important for several reasons. First, macroeconomic models typically include price variables under the assumption that prices fairly aggregate bits of information that are dispersed throughout the economy. Economic agents who make decisions on the basis of observed prices will ensure an efficient allocation of resources. Second, if the foreign exchange market is judged inefficient, some corrective actions might be required. These might include increased profit-motivated private speculation, increased distribution of accurate market information, or central bank intervention. Finally, tests of market efficiency may influence financial management strategies. In an efficient market, managers would tend to favor **passive hedging strategies** to minimize **transaction costs** and maximize **diversification gains.** However, if the market is not efficient, **selective hedging strategies** to exploit available profit opportunities may be preferred.

Definition.   The classic definition of capital market efficiency was formalized by Fama in "Efficient Capital Markets: A Review of Theory and Empirical Work" (*Journal of Finance,* Vol. 25, No. 2, May 1970, pp. 383–417). We can compress a definition into one sentence: **a market is efficient** if market prices "fully reflect available information." The key words are in quotation marks. The expression "fully reflect" implies the existence of an equilibrium model. But your model, which concludes that $2.25 is the fair spot price of sterling, may not agree with my model, which draws a different conclusion. Similarly, one forecaster who uses only public information may conclude that $2.30 is the fair spot price of sterling, while another forecaster with "inside" information may disagree strongly, even though both forecasters use the same framework for predicting exchange rates.

These arguments have been refined in two important directions. First, when information itself is costly to collect, market participants, in their self-interest, will never choose to be completely informed. As a result, market prices will never reflect all information, although they still may reflect available information. Furthermore, if investors are heterogeneous in terms of their wealth, expectations, forecasting accuracy, and risk aversion, actual market prices will reflect a "mixture" of diverse opinions. However this "mixture" will correspond to investors' "dollar votes" rather than a set of optimal weights.

In economic jargon, the remarks above imply that **tests of market efficiency** are testing a "joint hypothesis." Any investigation that rejects market efficiency might be explained in two ways: (1) profit-seeking private investors had information they could have used to earn unusual profits, but they failed to do so (i.e., in reality, the market is inefficient), or (2) our empirical tests are in error—we have used a false measure of "fair value" insofar as we assumed that the investor used information that, in fact, was not available to him, or we forgot to include the costs of learning about or exploiting these profit opportunities.

Naturally, in a market populated with thousands of sophisticated, profit-seeking investors who can transact at low cost, the second explanation seems more reasonable. This takes us dangerously close to the efficient market tautology, namely, that any free market must be efficient. But since there is little agreement on what constitutes the "true" or "fair" value of foreign exchange, tests of market efficiency are difficult both to formulate and to interpret.

Empirical Evidence.   The literature on foreign exchange market efficiency increased greatly during the 1970s. Surveys of this literature have been prepared by Kohlhagen (*The Behavior of Foreign Exchange Markets—A Critical Survey of the Empirical Literature,* New York University Monograph Series in Finance and Economics, Salomon Brothers Center, No. 1978–3) and by Levich ("Further Results on the Efficiency of Markets for Foreign Exchanges," in *Managed Exchange-Rate Flexibility: The Recent Experience,* Federal Reserve Bank of Boston, Conference Series No. 20, 1978). We briefly discuss three aspects of this evidence.

Tests of **covered interest arbitrage** have clearly established that the market efficiently polices risk-free profit opportunities in the Eurocurrency markets. Studies of arbitrage between traditional or onshore securities (e.g., U.S. and U.K. Treasury bills) suggest that covered differentials do appear in the market. However, it is not clear whether these differentials are the result of known costs (e.g., transaction costs, exchange controls, taxes, and other barriers), perceived risks (e.g., future controls and taxes), or an actual market failure to exploit **risk-free arbitrage** profits.

Tests of **spot market efficiency** began by analyzing the time series properties of spot rates. Several studies examined the **random walk hypothesis,** that is, that changes in spot exchange rates are serially uncorrelated. For a number of reasons, including the fact that exchange rates are driven by economic factors, which themselves may be serially correlated, **random walk exchange rate behavior** (1) is not necessary for spot exchange market efficiency and (2) is not sufficient to prove spot exchange market efficiency.

Other studies of the spot foreign exchange market have analyzed the performance of investment strategies that use a filter rule as a guide for picking speculative positions. A **filter rule** is a mathematical rule that can be applied mechanically to produce buy signals and sell signals. For example, if the $/DM rate rises 1% above a previous low, this could be interpreted as a buy signal, under the assumption that momentum will carry the $/DM rate still higher. However, if international financial markets are efficient, **Eurodeposit traders** should also recognize the expected momentum in the exchange market. As a result, Eurodeposit traders would set relatively low DM interest rates and high rates that tend to offset the anticipated exchange rate change. This summarizes the efficient market process—Eurodeposit interest rate differentials should exactly offset the expected exchange rate change, so there are no expected profits from the filter rule strategy.

The results of empirical studies of filter rules are mixed. Some academic studies have concluded that simple filter rule strategies could have been profitable, especially during periods of exchange rate volatility. Studies of commercial technical or momentum advisory services have also suggested that their predictions could have led to profitable results. However, none of these studies has suggested that their trading profits are risk free. On the contrary, we know that investors who seek to profit from "market timing" lose the "time diversification" associated with maintaining a steady portfolio over time. It is therefore unclear whether filter rule profits are unusually large relative to the risk involved.

Tests of **forward market efficiency** have focused on the relationship between the **current** n-period forward rate $F_{t,n}$, the **expected** future spot rate $E(\bar{S}_{t+n})$, and the **actual** future spot rate S_{t+n}. Market efficiency requires that market agents be able to process available information and form reasonable expectations; that is, $E(\bar{S}_{t+n}) = S_{t+n}$. However, market efficiency allows for the possibility that investors may demand a risk premium on forward contracts, much the same as long-term interest rates may reflect liquidity premiums rather than simply pure interest rate expectations. Therefore, market efficiency does not require that $F_{t,n} = E(\bar{S}_{t+n})$. As a result, the relationship between the current forward rate $F_{t,n}$ and the actual future spot rate S_{t+n} is ambiguous, **even in an efficient market.**

Numerous empirical tests of the relationship between today's forward rate $F_{t,1}$ and the future spot rate S_{t+1} have been published over the past 5 years. Some of the econometric tests are too technical for our purposes and some of the details of the analyses might be disputed, but the general thrust of this literature is as follows:

1. The forward rate is an unbiased predictor of the future spot rate. The average forecast error is approximately zero, and in most cases the serial correlation of forecast errors is also zero. In a linear regression, variation in F_t generally explains more than 90% of the variation in S_{t+1}.

2. The forward premium $(F - S)/S$ is an unbiased predictor of the future exchange rate change $(S_{t+1} - S_t)/S_t$; however, it is a poor predictor in the following sense: in a linear regression, variation in $(F - S)/S$ generally explains less than 10% of the variation in $(S_{t+1} - S_t)/S_t$. This suggests that the bulk of the short-run exchange rate changes are dominated by unanticipated events (i.e., **news**) and that the forward premium sits roughly in the middle of a wide distribution of exchange rate expectations. Exhibit 11 illustrates the wide variation in exchange rate changes relative to the forward premium for the DM.

3. Empirical studies do not support the existence of a positive risk premium in forward contracts. This may be because the premium actually is zero, the premium is too small to measure in the limited history of floating, or the premium changes signs and averages near zero.

4. Adding variables beyond the current forward rate may improve our ability to **fit** a regression equation explaining S_{t+1}. But in postsample comparisons, the forward rate by itself generally has better **predictive** ability.

These results suggest that the foreign exchange market is fairly efficient and that the forward rate may offer stiff competition to other forecasters.

FORECASTING EXCHANGE RATES. As we have discussed already, the **character of international financial markets** has changed dramatically in recent years. In particular, we have noted that the **volatility of foreign exchange rates** has increased significantly. Correspondingly, professional and academic interest in currency forecasting has increased, and a large number of commercial foreign exchange advisory services have developed. In the current environment, firms that maintain exposure to foreign exchange risks are likely to find exchange market volatility reflected in volatility of the firm's financial statements and in changes in the firm's competitive position. The discussion in this subsection is based on recent studies by Levich that address these issues in more detail: "The Use and Analysis of Foreign Exchange Forecasts" (in Antl, Ed., *Foreign Exchange Risk*, Euromoney Publications, 1980, pp. 98–104) and "Analyzing the Accuracy of Foreign Exchange Advisory Services: Theory and Evidence" (in Levich and Wihlborg, Eds., *Exchange Risk and Exposure*, Heath, 1980, pp. 99–128).

EXHIBIT 11 MONTHLY PERCENTAGE CHANGES OF THE U.S. AND GERMAN CONSUMER PRICE INDEXES (COL U.S. AND COL G, RESPECTIVELY), OF THE $/DM EXCHANGE RATE, AND THE MONTHLY FORWARD PREMIUM

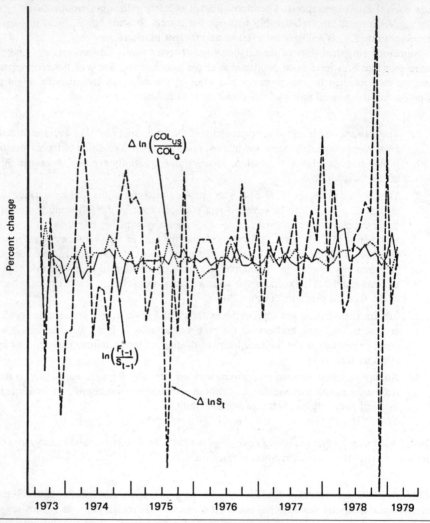

Source: Frenkel and Mussa, "The Efficiency of Foreign Exchange Markets and Measures of Turbulence," *American Economic Review,* May 1980, p. 376.

For the **multinational firm,** exchange rate forecasts play a role in a wide variety of decisions. Obviously, any foreign borrowing or investment decision requires a forecast of future exchange rates, to permit the conversion of future foreign cash flows into units of domestic currency and the competition of a comparable domestic cost of funds or return on investment. A currency forecast is generally required for the firm to manage its currency exposure that results from current and planned holdings of foreign currency. Currency forecasts can play a role in marketing, specifically with respect to pricing decisions. Suppose a Japanese automobile that sells for 1.2 million yen in Japan is priced at $6,000 in the United States when the exchange rate stands at 200 yen/$. If the yen appreciates to 180 yen/$, each U.S. auto sale will earn only $6,000 × 180 yen/$ = 1,080,000 yen. The Japanese firm is now in a worse position, and it is clear that the decision to raise U.S. prices will depend on many factors, including the future yen/$ exchange rate. From this example we can see that assessing subsidiary performance will also require exchange rate projections. Finally, exchange rate forecasts may be valuable for long-range or strategic planning. If the real **exchange rate** is expected to change, the U.S. firm can maximize its dollar profits (revenues − costs) by incurring costs in countries where the currency has depreciated below its PPP level (so that the real value of production costs is lower) and by earning revenues in countries where the currency has appreciated above its PPP level (so that the real value of revenues is higher).

Alternative Forecasting Techniques.   Among the commercially available **forecasting services,** it is convenient to classify companies as using either an **econometric** or a **judgmental approach.** This distinction is somewhat artificial, since the decision to accept one forecasting equation and reject all the others clearly involves judgment. The econometric forecasts are very often based on a **single-equation model,** and most of these appear to be inspired by purchasing power parity or monetary models, with other variables added. For example, the money supply, inflation rate, national income, industrial production, and interest rates are typical explanatory variables. The advantage of this approach is simplicity, and the ability of the user to easily simulate other scenarios. In fact, several companies offer this simulation facility on an **interactive computer basis.** The disadvantage of the single equation approach is that the simple equation may not adequately represent the real world. Forecast errors may result even when the right-hand-side variables are known with some confidence.

Other econometric advisory services prepare their forecasts using models based on 50–900 equations, sometimes allowing for interaction and feedback between economic regions. These complex models attempt to be a better reflection of the real world. But more regression coefficients and variables have to be estimated, so forecasting performance need not improve beyond the simple models. In fact, some large econometric services add judgment factors to the pure econometric forecast. It is important for a user to be able to isolate these judgment factors to evaluate the pure econometric model.

Other forecasting companies follow a more **judgmental approach.** Some may consider econometric estimates of important (and **quantifiable**) variables (e.g., money supply, trade balance, inflation rate). However, economic factors that are difficult to quantify (e.g., currency expectations, changes in capital controls or tax policy), along with other factors (e.g., political elections and appointments) are also considered. All these factors are combined in some unspecified way to determine a forecast.

Some forecasting companies specialize in very short-run forecasts. These so-called **technical or momentum services** advise their customers primarily on the direction of exchange rate movements in the very short run and correspondingly whether customers should hold long or short positions in particular currencies. These directional forecasts are typically based on a statistical analysis of recent exchange rate behavior, although judgment may play an equally large role.

The Forward Rate as a Forecaster.   Our interest in the forward rate as a forecaster of the future spot exchange rate is linked closely with the efficient market hypothesis, which states that market prices reflect available information. Since investors' expectations of the future spot rate are part of the available information set, and these expectations should be reflected in market prices under certain strict assumptions (which were outlined in connection with forward market efficiency), it is correct to argue that today's forward exchange rate is (1) the single market price that represents all investor expectations of the future spot rate and (2) an unbiased forecast of the future spot rate. If these assumptions were met, many multinational firms would view the forward rate as a very attractive forecast to use—first, because it represented the collective wisdom of many well-informed, profit-seeking traders; second, because the forward rate would be revised quickly as new information became available; and third, because the forward rate would be a very inexpensive forecast to use.

However, there are three **counterarguments against the forward rate** as an unbiased predictor—first, the forward rate may be influenced by official intervention; second, the forward rate may reflect a risk premium as well as exchange rate expectations (much the same as an interest rate can include a liquidity or risk premium); and third, expectations themselves may be weakly held or very imprecise. This final point suggests that the forward rate prediction may be very inaccurate, even though it is unlikely that investor expectations will be wrong consistently. The forecasting accuracy of the forward rate is an extremely important question, but one that remains unsettled, given the empirical research to date.

Techniques for Evaluating Forecasting Performance.   How can we evaluate and choose among alternative currency forecasts? As in other similar problems (e.g., evaluating the performance of mutual fund managers or of individual subsidiaries or profit centers within a firm), evaluating foreign exchange forecasting performance is a tricky procedure. Basically, we need to establish a **standard of performance** and to calculate how a forecast compares to the standard.

There are two general approaches for analyzing the performance of an individual forecaster. The first general approach concentrates on the **forecast error** (forecast error = predicted exchange rate − actual exchange rate) and its various statistical properties. One desirable property of a forecast is small forecast errors. However, even this simple criterion needs qualification. For example, assume that today's forward rate is $2 and two alternative forecasts of the future spot rate are $S_1 = \$1.99$ and $S_2 = 2.08$. If the actual spot rate turns out to be $2.02, the forecast error associated with S_1 (− \$0.03) is smaller than the forecast error associated with S_2 ($0.06). However, forecast S_2 is superior because it leads investors to take long and profitable forward positions in sterling; that is, forecast S_2 leads to a "correct" decision.

As a further qualification, suppose that a third forecast, $S_3 = \$2.14$, also exists. Even though its forecast error is + $0.12, it does not follow that this forecast is "twice as bad" as forecast S_2. If, for example, the firm is remitting a dividend from its U.S. parent and the firm is considering an "all-or-nothing" hedging decision, it will make the same decision using either S_2 or S_3 as a guide, thus there is no additional cost associated with S_3's larger forecast error. On the other hand, forecast S_3 may be "more than twice as bad" as forecast S_2. If the firm is considering investing a variable amount in U.K. bonds, based on the substantial appreciation predicted by S_3, the firm may invest 10 times as much in the United Kingdom as it would have, based on forecast S_2. As a consequence, the firm forgoes other profitable investments; these opportunity costs of using S_2 may exceed twice the costs of using S_3.

Therefore we conclude that there is no simple and unique relationship between the magnitude of forecast errors and the cost of forecast errors for investors. The implication of this statement is that there is no unique statistic for evaluating or ranking forecasters that will be correct for all investors. An "all-or-nothing" hedger will be concerned only that the forecast tell the correct direction, regardless of the magnitude of the forecast error. Investors who feel that exchange gains and losses are proportional to the forecast error will rank forecasters on the basis of mean absolute errors. Investors who feel that exchange gains and losses are proportional to the forecast error squared will rank forecasters on the basis of mean squared errors. It is an empirical question whether these criteria will rank forecasters in similar order.

If we ignore the magnitude of forecast errors, we can evaluate a forecast by calculating the fraction of periods where the forecast correctly predicts only the **direction** of exchange rate movement. We can define direction relative to the current forward rate or some other decision variable (e.g., the forward rate plus a risk premium). For example, in our earlier example S_2 and S_3 were "correct" forecasts (relative to the forward rate), while S_1 was incorrect. If the fraction of correct forecasts is unusually high, we can conclude that the forecast advisory service has expertise.

A numerical example will help to illustrate the procedure above. In a sample of 100 observations (n), suppose there are 60 correct forecasts (r), or a 60% track record. Is this an unusually good track record that demonstrates expertise, or is it simply the result of a sequence of lucky guesses? The question is analogous to another basic statistics problem: if a fair coin is tossed 100 times, what is the probability that it will land on "heads" 60 or more times? The answer is, this event would occur with roughly 2.3% probability. There are two ways to interpret this track record.

1. The forecaster does not have any special expertise in picking the direction of currency movements. A fairly rare event happened—the forecaster guessed correctly on 60 of 100 trials.

2. The forecaster does have special expertise. His track record for picking the direction of currency movements correctly is close to 60%, significantly greater than 50%, which would result from simply guessing.

In this case, we would probably pick interpretation 2. The track record appears too high to be the likely result of guessing alone.

The second general approach for evaluating forecasting performance is to calculate the stream of returns that an investor could earn by following the forecast. We would conclude that the advisory service has expertise and that the forecasts are useful if the stream of investment returns (adjusting for risk) is high relative to alternative investments. Again, this straightforward evaluation procedure raises two difficult questions.

First, how does an investor translate a set of currency forecasts into a set of investment decisions? The investor recognizes that forecasts are seldom perfect. If the forward rate stands at $2, the investor may not be willing to buy forward contracts unless the forecast is $2.02, $2.06, or perhaps higher. Furthermore, the investor is free to increase the number of forward contracts he purchases as his expected profits, and the confidence in those profits, increases. These issues are often handled by assuming that the investor uses the forecast to determine a "lump-sum" investment rather than an investment that increases with the expected returns predicted by the forecast or decreases with the expected variance of returns.

The second difficult question involves how the **risk associated with currency investment** should be measured. This calculation is necessary so that we can determine whether the return on currency investment is high relative to the risk incurred. Since the measurement of this risk factor is somewhat controversial, many analyses will simply compare the returns from selective currency investments based on a forecast with returns from (1) always holding U.S. dollar assets or (2) always holding foreign currency assets. These latter alternatives correspond to the statements (1) always hedge foreign exchange risk strategy and (2) never hedge foreign exchange risk strategy, which are simple rules of thumb for comparison.

To summarize, we have drawn a distinction between "correct" forecasts (those that correctly predict the direction of change relative to the forward rate) and "accurate" forecasts (those with low mean squared forecast errors). We noted earlier that many exchange rate changes are very large, and most are unanticipated by the market. Therefore, including these as large forecast errors may bias (upward) our estimate of forecasting inaccuracy and our estimate of the potential for profits. In this sense, calculating the "percentage correct forecast" may offer a more meaningful measure of forecasting expertise.

CURRENCY EXPOSURE

DEFINING FOREIGN EXCHANGE EXPOSURE.   Business operations by their nature are exposed to many kinds of uncertainties. International business operations and foreign exchange transactions have often been treated as a separate, and perhaps different, source of uncertainty when compared to domestic operations. However, it has recently been argued by Wihlborg ("Currency Exposure: Taxonomy and Theory," in R. Levich and C. Wihlborg, Eds., *Exchange Risk and Exposure*) that the **distinction between exposure in foreign and domestic operations** is exaggerated. For example, a Minnesota firm that heats its plant with oil might be concerned about (i.e., exposed to uncertainty because of) competition from a Texas firm that requires smaller expenditures on heating. Similarly, a Pennsylvania chocolate maker might be concerned about (i.e., exposed to uncertainty because of) a change in consumer tastes for Washington apples or a change in the relative price of apples to chocolate.

Notably, the uncertainties above might arise because domestic inflation need not proceed at the same pace in different states, or in different factor and goods markets. Clearly, the domestic firm is concerned about (i.e., exposed to uncertainty because of) the unpredictability of domestic inflation. When the value of domestic currency is uncertain, the firm can only estimate the **real value** of its expenses and the **real value** of its revenues and profits. These conditions are analogous for the domestic firm with international operations. In this case the domestic firm is concerned about the **real value** of transactions denominated in foreign currency and the potential competitive impact from foreign firms that face lower real costs. Therefore, the exposure of domestic and foreign operations appears to be similar in many respects.

Sources of Exposure to Foreign Exchange Rate Changes.   Firms that maintain long-term assets (receivables) or liabilities (payables) denominated in foreign currencies may be subject to **translation exposure**—namely, the possibility that an exchange rate change will alter the U.S. dollar value of foreign currency items when they are translated and consolidated for accounting purposes. **Translation gains and losses** represent a stock amount that has not been realized, but it may be realized in future transactions. For example, the cost of repaying a loan of 1 million Swiss francs increases by $100,000 when the exchange rate moves from $0.40/Swfr to $0.50/Swfr. This additional cost must be borne by the firm if the $0.50 exchange rate is sustained.

Current payables and receivables denominated in foreign currencies give rise to **transaction exposure.** These transactions that are settled during the current accounting period represent a **flow** amount of **realized** gains and losses.

Economic exposure is a broader concept that suggests how currency realignments affect future cash flows, and therefore, the present value of the firm. For example, a U.S. dollar devaluation may assist the domestic firm to increase its export sales; however it also would increase the costs for firms that rely on foreign inputs. The full impact of the exchange rate change on the firm's cash flows would depend, of course, on the price elasticity of demand for U.S. products, the ability of U.S. firms to substitute away from higher priced foreign inputs, and other factors.

The discussion of economic exposure suggests that in a world economy open to trade and capital flows, even "fully domestic" firms might be concerned about currency realignments. Clearly U.S. automobile makers or steel producers with no foreign currency balances or contracts might benefit (or lose) because of unanticipated changes in the $/DM or $/yen rates. To the extent that economic exposure reflects real economic changes, this further suggests that financial transactions may be insufficient to completely eliminate the risks of currency realignments.

Accounting Approaches to Measuring Foreign Exchange Exposure.   Quantifying exposure to foreign exchange movements is important because of two sets of factors. First, managers require an estimate of the firm's exposure to formulate their hedging (i.e., exposure management) decisions. Second, investors and financial analysts require similar information to reassess a firm's value in response to exchange rate changes.

Accounting approaches measure translation exposure and apply the reported results on balance sheets. The firm's net exposure is defined as the difference between exposed assets and exposed liabilities. These categories are determined following a particular accounting rule.

Throughout the 1960s and early 1970s, U.S. firms could choose between two alternative accounting rules for translation. The **current-noncurrent approach** classified current assets and liabilities as exposed (while noncurrent items were not exposed). The **monetary-non-monetary approach** classified all monetary assets and liabilities as exposed (while non-monetary items were not exposed). Long-term debt was the major item treated differently under these two accounting rules. For example, a 5-year loan of 1 million Swiss francs would be exposed under the monetary-nonmonetary approach but not exposed under the current-noncurrent approach.

A study by Aliber and Stickney, "Accounting Measures of Foreign Exchange Exposure: The Long and Short of It" (*Accounting Review,* Vol. 50, No. 1, January 1975, pp. 44–57), argued that accounting conventions implicitly make a statement concerning macroeconomic relationships. For example, the monetary-nonmonetary approach is consistent with the view that purchasing power parity holds, while the Fisher open effect (described below) does not. Recall that if PPP holds, the U.S. dollar value of a foreign asset would be maintained (i.e., not exposed) because exchange rate changes offset foreign currency inflation. The **Fisher open effect** implies that the real cost of funds (or real return on funds) is the same in any currency because exchange rate changes reflect different (and offsetting) interest rates on the two currencies. The evidence presented by Aliber and Stickney suggested that among industrial countries, the data offered stronger support for the **Fisher open effect** than for PPP. If departures from PPP are small enough to maintain that nonmonetary items are not exposed, logic would lead us to conclude that monetary items are not exposed either, because the departures from the Fisher open effect are still smaller.

While the precise calculations and interpretation of the results of this study may be subject to varying interpretations, the underlying thrust of the analysis should be clear. If there are no changes in real exchange rates (i.e., if PPP holds) and the expected real interest rate is the same in every currency (i.e. if the Fisher open effect holds), the firm with international operations bears no exposure to currency realignments. This view of international financial markets may represent an extreme, or polar, case, but it is useful as a reference point for measuring a firm's actual exposure.

The **current-noncurrent approach** might also be cast in economic terms. This accounting approach would be consistent with a world in which PPP and the Fisher open effect held in the long run but not in the short run. In this case we would expect the U.S. dollar value of noncurrent items to be maintained, while in the short run, substantial changes in U.S. dollar value would be possible.

The **temporal approach** became the required standard for all U.S. firms in 1976 with the adoption of **Financial Accounting Standards Board Statement No. 8** (FASB-8). The temporal approach required that items valued in terms of foreign currency at a particular date must be translated to U.S. dollars using an exchange rate from the same date. Therefore, if a firm purchased a plant site in London on April 23, 1980, for £1 million when the exchange rate was $2.30/£, the closing December 31, 1980, balance sheet would show a £1 million or $2.3 million asset. However, if the firm purchased a £1 million 10-year U.K Treasury bill on April 23, 1980, the closing December 31, 1980, balance sheet would restate this to reflect current market values (say, £925,000) and (to maintain temporal consistency) current exchange rates, $2.45/£, or $2,266,250 translation value. Since monetary items are usually reassessed at current market values, the temporal approach and the monetary-non-monetary approach lead to similar results. The primary difference is for nonmonetary items (e.g., inventories) that may be restated to reflect the lower of cost or market value. These items are exposed under the temporal approach but not exposed under the monetary-non-monetary approach.

On August 28, 1980, the Financial Accounting Standards Board proposed a major change for measuring exposure. The FASB recommended the **current rate approach.** Under this guideline, **all** foreign currency assets and liabilities of U.S. firms would be translated to U.S. dollars at the current exchange rate; that is, for accounting purposes, all foreign currency assets and liabilities are exposed. The reasoning that the FASB puts forward (see their Exposure Draft dated August 28, 1980, especially paragraphs 43–45) is that long-term debt should be translated at current rates (because the amount to be paid is a more relevant attribute of the debt than the amount that was borrowed) and for consistency, fixed assets should be translated at current rates (because the fixed assets will be used to generate foreign currency revenues and may have been financed by long-term debt). This framework suggests a "net investment view" of foreign currency exposure rather than an individual asset and liability view.

Another major aspect of FASB-8 was to include all translation gains and losses in the income statement. Given recent exchange rate volatility, this rule had the effect of **raising the volatility of reported earnings.** The proposal of August 28, 1980, calls for all translation gains and losses to be consolidated into retained earnings, rather than the income statement (effective after December 15, 1981). This may have the effect of smoothing reported earnings, although it may not keep the information content of exchange rate changes away from investors and financial analysts.

Economic Approaches to Measuring Exposure.   Assessing the impact of exchange rate changes on the market value of a firm raises many difficult challenges. When exchange rate changes are nominal rather than real (i.e., when PPP holds), there is strong agreement that no currency exposure exists, so market values should be unaffected. Furthermore, when financial markets are efficient, Logue and Oldfield have argued, in "Managing Foreign

Assets When Foreign Exchange Markets Are Efficient'' (*Financial Management*, Vol. 6, No. 2, Summer 1977, pp. 16–22), that any hedging strategy will not affect the total market value of the firm (except for transaction costs). However, deviations from PPP can be sizable and persistent. And continuous, strong-form market efficiency can also be questioned. Therefore, it seems likely that currency realignments have an impact on the market value of firms, although the magnitude and the time lag of the response are variable and are not measured with certainty. Several hypothetical, but illustrative, examples are analyzed in Eiteman and Stonehill (*Multinational Business Finance*, pp. 80–90).

MANAGEMENT STRATEGIES TOWARD CURRENCY EXPOSURE. It is correctly argued that shareholder welfare and resource allocation are best served when firm managers select projects with positive expected value and ignore risk. Shareholders then engage in other financial transactions to reach their desired risk levels. This scenario, however, ignores transaction costs, the manager's risk preferences, and other factors. The burgeoning literature on these issues suggests that managers are not leaving foreign exchange risk management to shareholders. This may be because managers are protecting their own short-run interests rather than maximizing expected profits for the firm. It may also be the case that debt capacity is increased and the cost of debt is decreased if the perceived riskiness of company profits is reduced through hedging.

It is important to note that this subsection considers only financial strategies to currency exposure rather than **operating strategies.** The latter group of strategies would include diversification into more factor markets, goods markets, and production locations. Operating strategies reduce the risk of real cash flow changes that might result from real exchange rate changes.

Financial Market Hedging Techniques. Consider a U.S. firm with a DM 1,000 net asset exposure that represents a royalty to be received in 1 year. To offset or hedge this asset exposure, the firm must establish a corresponding DM liability. The most direct way to accomplish this is to sell a DM 1,000 forward contract for delivery in 1 year. This forward contract obligates the U.S. firm to delivery DM 1,000 in 1 year (an account payable, or liabiliy) and to receive a fixed amount of U.S. dollars.

Let the current spot rate be $0.50/DM and the current 1-year forward rate be $0.55/DM. One traditional measure of the cost of hedging is the percentage forward premium, $(F - S)/S$, which equals 10% in this case. It thus appears as if the U.S. firm locks in a 10% profit (i.e., it incurs **negative** costs) by hedging. This calculation basically represents a **sunk cost,** the amount by which the market has already realigned the value of DM. A second measure of the cost of hedging is the percentage difference between the forward rate and the expected future spot rate, $(F - ES_{t+1})/F$. If we expect that the spot rate will be $0.60/DM in 1 year, the cost of hedging is $(0.55 - 0.60)/0.55 = -9.1\%$. This calculation represents an **opportunity cost,** the amount we stand to lose if we hedge today at the forward rate rather than maintaining an open position and selling at the expected future spot rate. The second, opportunity cost measure corresponds more closely to the notion of economic cost. However, it may be difficult for a firm to assess its expected spot rate and measure the opportunity cost. Also, the realized spot rate may differ greatly from the firm's expectation, so that in advance, the realized hedging cost can only be estimated.

Other financial transactions besides the forward contract can be used to establish an offsetting DM liability. Using a **money market hedge,** the U.S. firm borrows DM 1,000 for 1 year, buys $500 in the spot market, and invests the $500 for 1 year. Using these three transactions, the U.S. firm "constructs its own" forward contract. If the interest differential between the U.S. dollar investment and the DM loan equals the percentage forward premium, the costs of a forward market hedge and a money market hedge are identical. (See Exhibits 1 and 2 and the earlier discussion of forward contracts.)

If well-functioning forward markets are unavailable, firms may carry the "do it yourself" strategy further to "construct their own" offsetting DM liability positions. Consequently, these strategies might be more applicable for developing countries in which forward markets do not exist or strict controls on local borrowing are present. The basic alternative strategy is for the U.S. firm to arrange a **swap** between two private parties. A **swap** is an agreement to exchange a given amount of one currency for another and, at a prearranged time, to return the original amounts swapped. A broker or investment banker may be involved to match the two parties and to negotiate the terms (i.e., cost) of the swap.

A **basic swap arrangement** is illustrated in Exhibit 12. Suppose a U.S. firm in Brazil has accumulated 1 million cruzeiros in retained earnings, but these funds are blocked (i.e., cannot be repatriated to the United States) and a forward market for cruzeiros does not exist. The brazilian affiliate of the U.S. firm must locate in Brazil another foreign firm (e.g., from France) that wants to borrow cruzeiros. The U.S. affiliate lends cruzeiros to the French affiliate, while the French parent lends dollars to the U.S. parent. The terms of the swap would be negotiated, to some extent reflecting the gains to the U.S. affiliate from lending its blocked funds and the gains to the French affiliate of acquiring spot cruzeiros and working capital through a private arrangement.

The variations on this basic swap (e.g., the back-to-back loan, the parallel loan, the currency swap, and the credit swap) are similar in many ways but may differ in terms of costs, parent guarantees, and tax aspects. Some of these variations are described in more detail by Eiteman and Stonehill, (*Multinational Business Finance*, pp. 138–145).

Additional Hedging Techniques.   In our earlier example, we considered a U.S. firm with a DM 1,000 net asset exposure. Suppose this same firm also held a liability position of 2,000 French francs (= 1,000 DM × \$0.50/DM × 4 Fr fr /\$). If we believe that movements in the \$/DM and \$/Fr fr rates are very highly correlated, the combination of these two positions may be very nearly offsetting, so that the net exposure approaches zero. This example illustrates two points. First, using **third currencies** may offer a useful alternative to normal hedging procedures. An asset exposure in DM can be hedged by establishing a **liability** position in a currency that is closely (and **positively**) correlated with DM, or by establishing an **asset** position in a currency that is strongly **negatively** correlated with DM.

Second, this example suggests that the risk of a currency position should not be considered in isolation, but rather in the context of a portfolio. Just as a portfolio of two securities is likely to produce a more favorable risk-return tradeoff than either security individually, one can make a similar argument for currency exposure. The merits of a portfolio approach to currency management have been argued in the literature for some time (see, e.g., Lietaer, *Financial Management of Foreign Exchange*, MIT Press, 1971, and Makin, "Portfolio Theory and the Problem of Foreign Exchange Risk," *Journal of Finance*, Vol. 33, No. 2, May 1978, pp. 517–534), but managers have been slow to adopt these principles.

A further extension of the many currencies case is the U.S. firm with many foreign subsidiaries. In this case, the firm must weigh the tradeoffs between centralized versus decentralized management strategies. Centralization allows the firm to implement a netting model (that will reduce aggregate foreign exchange trading and transaction costs worldwide) and a worldwide portfolio approach (based on consolidated foreign exchange positions). Furthermore, **centralization** may allow the firm to direct hedging operations to those affiliates

EXHIBIT 12   ILLUSTRATION OF A SWAP TRANSACTION[a]

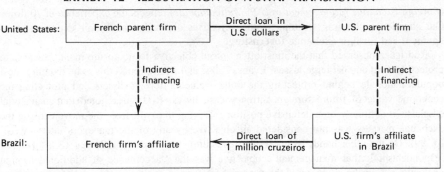

[a]The terms of the swap, including the amount of the direct U.S. dollar loan, must be negotiated.
Source: Adapted from Eiteman and Stonehill, *Multinational Business Finance,* Addison-Wesley, Reading, MA, 1979, p. 139.

that enjoy certain tax advantages. **Centralized financial information collection and management** may also represent an advantage. On the other hand, decentralized management maintains performance incentives for foreign affiliates and avoids the problem of ordering individual affiliates to retain foreign exchange exposures that are contrary to their own interests. Foreign exchange information may be more accurate and timely when used by the foreign manager. Finally, **decentralization itself leads to portfolio diversification** because it is unlikely that all foreign managers will follow the same hedging strategies based on the same exchange rate expectations.

One additional method for dealing with exposure is through the selection of a contract or **invoice currency.** In the context of our earlier examples, the U.S. firm might have contracted for its royalty payments to be paid in U.S. dollars rather than DM, and it might have chosen to invoice its exports to Brazil in U.S. dollars rather than in cruzeiros. This strategy eliminates foreign exchange exposure at its source by transferring the exposure to the other party in the transaction. This pricing strategy therefore may reduce sales, but it may be a more effective way to lay off foreign exchange risks in some situations. Technical details of invoice currency selection are discussed by Rao and Magee ("The Currency of Denomination of International Trade Contracts," in R. Levich and C. Wihlborg, Eds., *Exchange Risk and Exposure*) and by McKinnon (*Money in International Exchange*).

Impact of Currency Exposure. The preceding subsections are testimony to the great current interest in how one measures exchange rate variability, how one forecasts exchange rates, and how one sets up accounting rules to measure exposure and provide useful information for managers and shareholders. These are obviously complicated and interrelated issues. Now, we focus on two points: the managerial response to currency exposure and the shareholder response to managerial decisions and exchange rate changes.

Managerial Behavior: Results from Survey Analysis.   In the past few years, two surveys have been published on managerial attitudes and practices toward foreign exchange risk management. The survey by Evans, Folks, and Jilling (*The Impact of Statement of Financial Accounting Standards No. 8 on the Foreign Exchange Risk Management Practices of Amer-*

ican Multinationals) represents 156 U.S. multinationals, and the survey by Rodriguez (*Foreign-Exchange Management in U.S. Multinationals*) reflects the experience of 70 firms. Our attention centers on two topics—the **objectives of foreign exchange exposure management** and **foreign exchange forecasting.**

Rodriguez observed that the most often voiced objective for exposure management is to protect the firm against large losses. Evans, Folks, and Jilling found this to be the third most popular rationale behind protecting the dollar value of foreign assets and protecting the economic value of future foreign currency cash flows. Rodriguez noted that managerial emphasis is definitely on a defensive position: "Trying to **profit** from the movements in the exchange markets was not considered an objective by any of the managers interviewed" (p. 99). On the other hand, Evans, Folks, and Jilling reported (p. 132) that 13.5% of their respondents felt that management's objective was the "acceptance of additional foreign exchange risk in the short run if the potential for foreign exchange gains exists."

The latter result is more consistent with the other evidence in Rodriguez and Evans, Folks, and Jilling, as well as our casual empiricism. If a firm has a "natural" long (short) position in a currency that is appreciating (depreciating), the firm is likely to maintain its open position, especially if the forward premium is less than the expected currency change. Management may rationalize this situation as a potential windfall gain rather than speculation. The firm may try to hedge or close out only the natural positons that are going against it. In this regard, Rodriguez has suggested the possibility of risk asymmetry within a firm. That is, the firm may be unwilling to maintain open positions that are presently valued at losses or for which large losses are possible. However, if uncertainty is skewed toward gains, the firm will not bother to hedge.

Rodriguez correctly pointed out that problems of exposure management often are generated in the treasury area as a result of insufficient planning in operations and marketing areas. Long-range business plans are often executed assuming that financial exposure problems will be small.

The most extensive **information on exchange rate forecasting practices** is presented in the survey by Evans, Folks, and Jilling. It suggests that nearly all major U.S. firms collect and attempt to utilize foreign exchange forecasts. These authors reported that 55% of the firms in their sample purchased forecasts from outside consultants. Of this group, about 50% began purchasing their forecasts after FASB-8 became effective. The average number of currencies forecasted was 16; the modal value was 10, and the maximum was 70. Over 55% of the managers agreed that their firms had greatly increased their resources devoted to exchange rate forecasting since 1976. However, only 31% felt that they had become more skillful in forecasting. Along these lines, Evans, Folks, and Jilling reported that 58% agreed that foreign exchange rate forecasting was the "weakest link" in their **exposure management program.** This figure is nearly twice as large as that reported in a 1975 survey by the same authors. They observed that despite corporate efforts, forecasting appears to be an "increasingly weaker link" in firms' exposure management programs. Perhaps, however, firms are coming to understand that forecasting is at the center of any exposure management program and because of this awareness, they are devoting greater efforts to forecasting.

Shareholder and Stock Market Responses.   Evidence on the stock market's reaction to exchange rate changes and currency exposure management strategies is sketchy and understandably difficult to interpret. Standard trade theory suggests that if the U.S. dollar is devalued, U.S. exports should appear less expensive while imported foreign goods appear more expensive. If these predictions are true (in real terms), we expect the market value of firms that export their products (or produce import-competing goods) to rise, while the market value of firms that sell imported goods (or use imports in the production process) will fall. Any number of factors may alter this chain of reasoning. For example, if exporters face tough overseas competition and buyers are sensitive to small price change, U.S. exporters will not gain much by devaluation. If U.S. importers are able to easily substitute domestic goods for more expensive foreign sources, however, U.S. importers would not necessarily lose much by devaluation. In either case, the stock market may have predicted the exchange rate change in advance, and the share prices of U.S. firms would have been adjusted by the time the change actually occurred.

Accounting research on the other hand, has focused on the definition of exposure and the impact of reporting practices. For example, if managers changed their behavior (again in real dimensions) in response to a new accounting rule (e.g., FASB-8) the market value of shares should change. Market values might also change if the new accounting rule brought new information to public awareness. However, an accounting change that shifts reported foreign exchange gains from a footnote to the income statements, or to retained earnings, should not affect market values because such a rule change does not affect the information available to investors.

An early study by Giddy, *Devaluations, Revaluations and Stock Market Price* (unpublished Ph.D dissertation, University of Michigan, 1974) examined the stock market response to several discrete exchange rate changes during the 1960s and the early 1970s. Giddy's analysis suggests that domestic stock prices respond favorably to domestic currency devaluations. The favorable effect appeared to be stronger for export-oriented firms. A more recent study by Dukes, *An Empirical Investigation of the Effects of Statement of Financial Accounting Standards Number 8 on Security Return Behavior*, attempted to measure the impact of FASB-8 on stock prices during a period of floating exchange rates. Dukes's analysis could not reject the hypothesis of zero impact on stock prices. However, as we have suggested, the studies cited are not conclusive because of the complexity of the problem. The net impact of hedging strategies and currency volatility on stock prices remains an important question that has not been resolved.

REFERENCES

Aliber, Robert Z., and Stickney, Clyde P., "Accounting Measures of Foreign Exchange Exposure: The Long and Short of It," *Accounting Review,* Vol. 50, No. 1, January 1975, pp. 44–57.

Deardorff, Alan V., "One-Way Arbitrage and Its Implications for the Foreign Exchange Markets," *Journal of Political Economy,* Vol. 87, No. 2, April 1979, pp. 351–364.

Dominguez, Lyn, "Foreign Exchange Trading In Banks," unpublished MBA thesis, New York University, New York, 1980.

Dornbusch, Rudiger, "Expectations and Exchange Rate Dynamics," *Journal of Political Economy,* Vol. 84, No. 6, December 1976, pp. 1161–1176.

———, "Exchange Rate Economics: Where Do We Stand?" *Brookings Institution Papers on Economic Activity,* No. 1, 1980, pp. 145–185.

Dukes, Roland E., *An Empirical Investigation of the Effects of Statement of Financial Accounting Standards No. 8 on Security Return Behavior,* Financial Accounting Standards Board, Stamford, CT, December 1978.

Eiteman, David K., and Stonehill, Arthur I., *Multinational Business Finance,* 2nd ed., Addison-Wesley, Reading, MA, 1978.

Evans, Thomas G., Folks, William R., Jr., and Jilling, Michael, *The Impact of Statement of Financial Accounting Standards No. 8 on the Foreign Exchange Risk Management Practices of American Multi-nationals,* Financial Accounting Standards Board, Stamford, CT, November 1978.

Fama, Eugene F., "Efficient Capital Markets: A Review of Theory and Empirical Work" *Journal of Finance,* Vol. 25, No. 2 May 1970, pp. 383–417.

Frenkel, Jacob A., "Purchasing Power Parity: Doctrinal Perspectives and Evidence from 1920s," *Journal of International Economics,* Vol. 8, No. 2, May 1978, pp. 161–191.

———, and Levich, Richard M. "Transaction Costs and Interest Arbitrage: Tranquil Versus Turbulent Periods," *Journal of Political Economy,* Vol. 87, No. 6, December 1977, pp. 1209–26.

———, and Mussa, Michael L., "The Efficiency of Foreign Exchange Markets and Measures of Turbulence," *American Economic Review,* Vol. 70, No. 2, May 1980, pp. 374–381.

———, and Rodriguez, Carlos, "Exchange Rate Dynamics and the Overshooting Hypothesis," mimeographed, University of Chicago, August 1980.

Giddy, Ian H., "Devaluations, Revaluations, and Stock Market Prices," unpublished Ph.D. dissertation, University of Michigan, Ann Arbor, 1974.

———, "Measuring the World Foreign Exchange Market," *Columbia Journal of World Business,* Vol. 14, No. 4, Winter 1979, pp. 36–48.

Hooper, Peter, and Morton, John, "Summary Measures of the Dollar's Foreign Exchange Value," *Federal Reserve Bulletin,* Vol. 64, No. 10, October 1978, pp. 783–789.

Isard, Peter, "How Far Can We Push the Law of One Price?" *American Economic Review,* Vol. 67, No. 6, December 1979, pp. 942–948.

Kohlhagen, Steven W., *The Behavior of Foreign Exchange Markets—A Critical Survey of the Empirical Literature,* New York University Monograph Series in Finance and Economics, Salomon Brothers Center, No. 1978–3, New York, 1978.

———, "The Identification of Destabilizing Foreign Exchange Speculation," *Journal of International Economics,* Vol. 9, No. 3, August 1979, pp. 321–340.

Kubarych, Roger M., *Foreign Exchange Markets in the United States,* Federal Reserve Bank of New York, New York, 1978.

Levich, Richard M., "Further Results on the Efficiency of Markets for Foreign Exchange," in *Managed Exchange-Rate Flexibility: The Recent Experience,* Conference Series No. 20, Federal Reserve Bank of Boston, Boston, 1978.

———, *The International Money Market: An Assessment of Forecasting Techniques and Market Efficiency,* JAI Press, Greenwich, CT, 1979.

———, "An Examination of Overshooting Behavior in the Foreign Exchange Market," Group of Thirty *Occasional Studies,* No. 4, New York, 1980.

———, "Analyzing the Accuracy of Foreign Exchange Advisory Services: Theory and Evidence," in *Exchange Risk and Exposure* (R. Levich and C. Wihlborg, Eds.), Heath, Lexington, MA, 1980.

———, "The Use and Analysis of Foreign Exchange Forecasts," in *Foreign Exchange Risk* (Boris Antl, Ed.), Euromoney Publications, London, 1980.

Lietaer, Bernard A., *Financial Management of Foreign Exchange,* MIT Press, Cambridge, MA, 1971.

Logue, Dennis E., and Oldfield, George S., "Managing Foreign Assets When Foreign Exchange Markets Are Efficient," *Financial Management,* Vol. 6, No. 2, Summer 1977, pp. 16–22.

Makin, John H., "Portfolio Theory and the Problem of Foreign Exchange Risk," *Journal of Finance,* Vol. 33, No. 2, May 1978, pp. 517–539.

McCormick, Frank, "Covered Interest Arbitrage: Unexploited Profits?: Comment," *Journal of Political Economy,* Vol. 87, No. 2, April 1979, pp. 411–417.

McKinnon, Ronald I., *Money in International Exchange,* Oxford University Press, New York, 1979.

Morgan Guaranty Trust Co., *World Financial Markets,* various issues, MGTC; New York.

Officer, Lawrence H., "The Purchasing-Power-Parity Theory of Exchange Rates: A Review Article," *International Monetary Fund Staff Papers*, Vol. 23, No. 1, March 1976, pp. 1–60.

Rao, Ramesh K. S., and Magee, Stephen P., "The Currency of Denomination of International Trade Contracts," in *Exchange Risk and Exposure* (R. Levich and C. Wihlborg, Eds.), Heath, Lexington, MA, 1980.

Rodriguez, Rita M., *Foreign-Exchange Management in U.S. Multinationals*, Heath, Lexington, MA, 1980.

U.S. Office of the President, *Economic Report of the President*, Government Printing Office, Washington, D.C., 1979.

Wihlborg, Clas G., "Currency Exposure: Taxonomy and Theory," in *Exchange Risk and Exposure*, (R. Levich and C. Wihlborg, Eds.), Heath, Lexington, MA, 1980.

OVERSEAS MONEY AND CAPITAL MARKETS

CONTENTS

ROLE OF INTERNATIONAL FINANCIAL MARKETS 3

Function of International Markets 3
  The current account 3
  Size of financing 4
  Other roles for international financial markets 4
Sources of Financing for Current Account Deficits 4
International Investing and Borrowing 6
Petrodollar Recycling 6
Centers for International Investing and Financing 6
Currencies for Investment and Borrowing 7
Multicurrency Financing 9

THE EUROCURRENCY SYSTEM AND FOREIGN BOND MARKETS 10

Eurocurrencies 10
  Origin 11
  Size 11
Interest Rates 12
Deposits 14
Eurocredits 14
  Size 16
  Interest rates 16
  Banking concentration 16
Eurobonds 16
  Instruments 17
  Size 17
  Sale of Eurobonds 18
Foreign Bonds 19
  Size 19
  Sale of foreign bonds 20

THE INTERNATIONAL STRUCTURE OF INTEREST RATES 20

Interest Rate Levels 20

Financial Market Integration 20
  Measurement of market integration 21
  Interest rate parity theory 21
  Asset pairs, sovereign risk, and transaction costs 22
  Forward exchange rates 23
Term Structure of International Interest Rates 24
  Expectations theory 24
  Liquidity preference 25
  Preferred habitat 25
  Variability 25

RISK IN INTERNATIONAL FINANCIAL MARKETS 25

Interest Rate and Currency Risk 25
Default Risk 26
Effects of Risk 26
Sovereign Risk 28
  Capital controls 28
  Currency controls 28
  Taxes 28
  Confiscation 29

WORLD FINANCIAL CENTERS 29

Leading Securities Exchanges 29
Controls 29
Major International Capital Markets 30
  New York 30
  London 31
  Luxembourg 31
  Germany 31
  Switzerland 31
  Japan 32
  Emerging centers 32
Official International Financial Institutions 33

OVERSEAS MONEY AND CAPITAL MARKETS

Dennis E. Logue

ROLE OF INTERNATIONAL FINANCIAL MARKETS

FUNCTION OF INTERNATIONAL MARKETS. Since the end of World War II, there has been explosive growth in international trade and investment. To accommodate this growth and the imbalances in countries' balance of payments accounts that result, international financial markets have flourished.

If all countries in the world experienced the same trade and investment cycles, and the magnitudes of these cycles relative to the sizes of their economies were identical or nearly so, only minimum sized international financial markets would be needed. However, business cycles among economies are not synchronized; hence funds must be transferred from savings surplus countries to savings deficit countries. As one economy enters an upswing in economic activity and aggregate demand for goods and services, including imports, rises, that economy may not be able to finance itself internally. The expansion must be at least partially financed internationally. Similarly, in a contracting economy, there may be a surplus of financial resources. The owners of these resources will search abroad for risk-adjusted investment returns that exceed those available domestically. **International financial markets** serve to bring together the economies that have demands for financing that exceed their capacity to supply funds internally and those that have supplies of funds in excess of domestic needs.

The Current Account. **The current account** is a balance of payments account that indicates the magnitude of international financing that a country, its corporations, or its citizens must do to remain in equilibrium with the rest of the world. It represents a minimum estimate of the magnitude of international financial transactions that must take place. The current account shows the difference between imports and exports, services sold to or bought from foreigners, dividend and interest income paid to foreigners or derived from abroad, and transfer payments. The current account surplus roughly indicates the amount of international financing that a country, its corporations, or its citizens can supply to the rest of the world. The amount of international financing a country needs is revealed by its current account deficit. To these estimates of available or required financing, one ought to add the amount by which a country wishes to increase its official reserve holdings or its holdings of foreign currencies.

If **the current account surpluses and deficits** for the world as a whole were added up, the result would approximate zero. It would differ from zero only to the extent that new international reserves were created by the **International Monetary Fund** or the mining of gold, and to the extent that reporting of international transactions was incomplete. The incomplete reporting category is represented in the "errors and omissions" section of the balance of payments statement.

To get a rough estimate of the minimum of international financing that must take place every year, one must add up the amounts by which current account deficit countries are in deficit. This equals, again adjusting for changes in **international reserves** that are independent of any single country's monetary policies, the sum of surplus countries' current account surpluses.

If the world were in **general economic equilibrium** or if every country imposed sufficient limitations on its imports and other international transactions, the size of any country's current account surplus or deficit would be small, and the international financial market, which facilitates the financing of current account deficits and the investment of surpluses, would necessarily be small. Since the end of World War II, there has been nearly consistent reduction in the number and type of restrictions that most countries impose on foreign transactions. Countries' economic cycles have tended not to become more synchronized, however, and accordingly, the need for international financing has increased.

Apart from helping countries balance their current accounts, international financial markets enable domestic investors to diversify their liquid asset holdings among many countries. When properly done, such **diversification** reduces **portfolio risk** for investors without impairing expected returns. Financial markets develop to accommodate this desire for diversification. Furthermore, given the attractions of international portfolio diversification, international financial markets would exist even in the absence of large current account surpluses or deficits.

Size of Financing.   Exhibit 1 offers some perspective on the growth in the size of current account surpluses and deficits. It shows what happened with respect to current account balances in 1970 and in 1977 for industrialized countries. Note the major change in the magnitude of the range between the largest surplus and the largest deficit between 1970 and 1977. In 1970 the largest surplus was $2.357 billion and the largest deficit was $0.832 billion. In 1977, the largest surplus was $10.911 billion and the largest deficit was $15.276 billion. Even though Exhibit 1 does not show results for less developed countries, it does reveal that in the volume of money and capital market transfers between current account surplus and deficit countries grew enormously, as did the volume of transactions in international markets over the same period.

Other Roles for International Financial Markets.   It is important to recognize that while countries are either in net current account surplus or deficit, all international financial market transactions for any category of country in any one period are not unidirectional. For instance, even though the United States had a huge current account deficit in 1977, many U.S. corporations and individuals were investing rather than borrowing abroad. The current account data show only the magnitude of the net financing need. They do not say anything about the gross amount of international financial market transactions that private parties enter into irrespective of their nation's economic position.

SOURCES OF FINANCING FOR CURRENT ACCOUNT DEFICITS.   Large current account deficits do not necessarily imply that a country is living beyond its means. They may

EXHIBIT 1   CURRENT ACCOUNT BALANCES FOR INDUSTRIALIZED COUNTRIES ($ U.S. MILLIONS)

	1970	1977
Ireland	−189	−261
Italy	902	2,285
New Zealand	−29	−630
United Kingdom	1,755	596
Japan	1970	10,911
Austria	−18	−3,003
Finland	−240	−151
Netherlands	−381	363
France	67	−3,296
Australia	−832	−2,512
Belgium	715	−373
Denmark	−544	−1,681
West Germany	842	3,799
Canada	1,078	−3,930
United States	2,357	−15,276
Norway	−242	4,937
Sweden	−265	−2,815
Switzerland	70	3,333

Source: World Bank, World Development Report, 1979, p. 151.

be a consequence of the fact that the country is experiencing **real economic growth** at a more rapid pace than other countries. In this case, the financing necessary to sustain a large current account deficit typically is provided autonomously. That is, it can occur without any official government involvement in the financing process. On the other hand, when a country is living beyond its means, there may be official government financing of the deficit to protect the exchange rate, the price of that country's currency in terms of other countries' currencies. In either case, the methods and sources of international financing are much the same, the only exception being that the government can borrow from the **International Monetary Fund (IMF)**, an international agency that supplies liquidity to countries whose balances of payments are not in equilibrium.

Corporate, individual, and governmental investment and borrowing activities play a role in financing current account deficits. The minimum amount of international financial transactions has to equal the size of the collective deficit or surplus, but there are many more transactions that take place because, for example, the investor believes the risk-adjusted rate of return to be better abroad than at home. These transactions may run counter to the direction of the current account in the home country of the investor. That is, the transactions may add to rather than reduce the amount that must be transferred internationally to accommodate the current account position without affecting the exchange rate.

There are a number of sources for financing a current account deficit. Borrowing from foreign banks will help finance a deficit, as will accepting foreign deposits in a domestic bank. In addition, corporations, individuals, or governments can borrow in the Eurocurrency markets. The public sale of debt or equity securities abroad will help finance a deficit in the current account. Finally, the sale to foreigners of domestic assets, such as equity or debt securities or real assets, will help finance a current account deficit. Conversely, the same activities in reverse will dispose of a current account surplus.

INTERNATIONAL INVESTING AND BORROWING.   Most transactions in international financial markets take place without regard to current account balances. This is particularly true during periods when exchange rates are not heavily managed. Such autonomous transactions arise when an investor believes that a better deal is available if money is invested abroad. At the same time, economic actors who believe that funds they find necessary for the conduct of their activities are available on more favorable terms abroad than domestically will seek those funds abroad. Other reasons for investing or borrowing internationally include the **portfolio diversification opportunities** that foreign financial markets provide, opportunities to hold or owe foreign currencies that appear to be overvalued, opportunities to evade domestic taxes, and opportunities to hold investments in countries that are politically stable, avoiding investments in countries that are not.

PETRODOLLAR RECYCLING.   In the early 1970s the **Organization of Petroleum Exporting Countries (OPEC)** began raising the price charged for oil at a precipitous rate. Accordingly, these nations' oil-related revenues rose rapidly. For many of these countries, international revenues ran far ahead of international expenditures on goods and services. A few of these **OPEC nations,** particularly Saudi Arabia, Kuwait, and Libya, experienced large and persistent current account surpluses. These surpluses along with other OPEC members' surplus funds collectively became known as **petrodollars.**

At the time when the OPEC began to build massive international reserves, there was great concern that the nations that were running corresponding current account deficits (owing to their high bills for imported oil) would not be able to finance their deficits. The problem underscored by policymakers was "recycling," that is, encouraging OPEC wealthholders to invest their surpluses in such a way as to finance the deficit nations' oil purchases.

The efficiency of the international financial markets, the ability of these markets to channel investment flows from surplus to creditworthy deficit nations with minimum cost and disruption, was put to the test. Financial markets responded well. Indeed, while OPEC investment tended to be concentrated in a small number of world financial centers, principally London and New York, these centers redistributed the funds to borrowers in countries that may not have attracted OPEC investment directly. At the same time, the OPEC members provided direct development assistance to some less developed countries that were hard hit by the oil price rise and were unable to obtain private financing on acceptable terms. Over the period 1975–1978, OPEC made loans and grants to less developed countries totaling roughly $22 billion.

The international financial markets in combination with voluntary OPEC contributions to less developed countries have to date successfully recycled petrodollars in rough proportion to various nations' current account deficits, which, in the case of developed countries, approximates the size of their own internal money and capital markets.

CENTERS FOR INTERNATIONAL INVESTING AND FINANCING.   Virtually every non-Communist bloc country in the world has some resources owned by foreign countries. Some bank deposits and equity and bond investments in nearly every country are owned by foreigners. At the same time, every country has corporations or citizens who own foreign financial assets. But this does not mean that every country is a world financial center. Some countries serve not only as domiciles for foreign financial investment, but also as conduits for international investment. These countries' banking systems will accept deposits from nearly anywhere in the world and put those funds to work nearly anywhere in the world. They serve as places of accommodation for borrowers and lenders from different nations. Moreover, they are places where the choice of currency is comparatively free. There is no need to deal in any specific currency, least of all the currency of the country where the transaction is taking place. No matter what the currency to be invested or borrowed, simultaneous transactions in the financial and foreign exchange markets can deliver to the investor or borrower whatever is required.

World financial centers that play the role of bringing foreign lenders and foreign borrowers together are known as **entrepôt** financial centers. The countries in which these centers are located may or may not be capital exporters or importers, but they are channels through which international funds pass. **London** is an example of an entrepôt center. Money moves through London, but little in the way of financing comes out of the United Kingdom, and little of what is invested through London remains there. **Luxembourg** plays a similar role. **New York** is an example of a world financial center that is not really an entrepôt center. Money deposited in New York by international investors is typically reloaned in U.S. markets, and money raised in New York often represents investment by U.S. investors.

There is a relatively high concentration of resources among world financial centers. Not every major country has a particular city that serves as a world financial center. Indeed, why they sprang up where they did is somewhat of a mystery. Most probably they resulted from the absence of disadvantageous domestic controls on the local banking system, the political stability of the countries in which they are located, the size and customer base of the domestic banking system before the area became an international financial center, the wealth of the country and the demands by its inhabitants for international investment outlets, and the ability to exploit economies of scale in the investment business.

There is no generally accepted method for determining what a world financial center is, nor is there a neat way of ranking world financial centers. Nevertheless, one crude approach to identifying world financial centers entails measuring the size of external liabilities of the banks operating within a country's borders and counting the number of foreign banks in that country. Exhibit 2 shows such an approximation. By the definitions employed, the places represented in Exhibit 2 are the major world financial centers.

CURRENCIES FOR INVESTMENT AND BORROWING.   Investing or borrowing that takes place in a country that is not a world financial center is typically done in the currency of that country. For instance, if a U.S. investor wishes to purchase Brazilian equities, the dealing must be done in cruzeiros; if a Mexican subsidiary of a U.S. multinational corporation borrows in Mexico, it will borrow in pesos.

Dealing in the international markets, however, does not limit currency choice to the currency of the financial center. A borrower may borrow U.S. dollars, German marks, or French francs in Luxembourg or London. Similarly, an investor may place any of a variety of currencies in these markets. The banking system will then convert the deposit to whatever currency it needs for investment.

Risk plays an important role in currency choice. Borrowers, of course, would prefer to borrow in weak currencies, which will tend to depreciate relative to other currencies. In this way, they will face interest payments and principal repayment that decline in real terms. Lenders would prefer to lend in strong currencies. The interest rate for loans in particular currencies when juxtaposed against possible devaluations and revaluations of that currency will move investors and borrowers together. Generally, the parties will coalesce around a comparatively stable currency, which brings only limited risk of depreciation or appreciation to both.

According to one authority (Mendelsohn, *Money on the Move*) in 1977 nearly 60% of all international bond issues, **Eurobonds plus foreign bonds,** were denominated in U.S. dollars. This percentage varies depending on the strength (rise) or weakness (fall) of the

EXHIBIT 2   WORLD FINANCIAL CENTERS, 1978

	External Assets ($ Billion)	Number of Foreign Banks
London	173	308
New York	78	274
Bahamas	83	285
Frankfurt	61	172
Luxembourg	53	67
Zurich	73	111
Paris	58	194
Amsterdam	35	73
Brussels	31	68
Toronto	20	90
Milan	18	40
Tokyo	17	137
Panama	10	111

Source: IMF International Financial Statistics, March 1979; taken from M. S. Mendelsohn, *Money on the Move,* McGraw-Hill, New York, 1979, p. 259. Mendelsohn's compilation yields cities, not countries, and groups the Bahamas with New York and Luxembourg with Frankfurt.

dollar versus other currencies. Moreover, roughly 80% of all Eurocurrency transactions are denominated in U.S dollars.

The preeminence of the U.S. dollar as the currency of denomination for most international financial transactions is due principally to the U.S. financial authorities and Congressional willingness to let the U.S. dollar serve as an **international reserve currency** and the U.S. monetary authorities' meritorious failure to develop the kinds of restrictive controls on foreign borrowing by U.S. corporations and individuals that many foreign governments have imposed and continue to impose.

Other important international currencies include the German mark, the Swiss franc, the Dutch florin, the Canadian dollar, and the Japanese yen. The removal of withholding taxes on interest payments to foreigners from Canadian securities with maturities of more than 5 years led to the expansion in the use of that country's currency. The other currencies noted above are all soundly managed and because of their stable values are generally highly desirable currencies for international financial transactions. The countries noted, however, tightly regulate the issue of international bonds in their currencies, and Germany and Japan impose withholding taxes on interest income received by nonresident investors in domestic securities. Moreover, **none** of these countries seems to want its currency to serve as **official international reserve assets;** this suggests that this group will continue to adapt measures to hinder the free flow of capital into (as well as out of) their countries. Until this attitude changes, these countries' currencies are unlikely to replace the U.S. dollar as the premier international investment currency.

The British pound is another currency sometimes used in international financial transactions. Its use is limited, however, since the U.K. monetary authorities, while attempting to attract foreign financial investment, have for many years been quite active in trying to inhibit capital outflow. Only recently (October 1979) have the British authorities begun to dismantle the controls placed on outflows of British capital. In addition, over the past two decades, the pound sterling has been viewed as a weak currency, that is, one likely to depreciate in value, hence one not particularly attractive to foreign investors.

MULTICURRENCY FINANCING. From time to time, debt that is offered internationally is denominated in a "basket" of currencies, to diversify currency risk for both borrower and lender. The mechanics of such arrangements are quite complex, but multicurrency units can be used as a prototype, and they work as follows. A borrower offers an instrument denominated in the **portfolio of currencies.** The purchasers of the security buy the security with a specific currency allowed by the borrower; the amount necessary for any given purchase will be a function of that currency's value relative to the other currencies in the portfolio and current exchange rates. For instance, suppose that a multicurrency bond were initially offered to the public on July 1, 1980, and the market basket was comprised of 1 DM, $1 and £1, that is, equal amounts of the three currencies. Furthermore, suppose that on the issue date 1 DM = $1 U.S. = £1. To purchase the bond at issue price, an investor would have to pay either $1,000 U.S., £1,000, or 1,000 DM. Suppose that on January 1, 1981, the U.S. dollar has declined to $2 U.S. = 1 DM = £1. The trading price of the bond will have risen in U.S. dollars, provided no general changes in interest rates have occurred. To purchase a bond, an investor would have to pay the dollar equivalent of $333.33 plus 333.33DM, plus £333.33 (these reflect initial weights), and since $2 must now be spent to acquire each unit of foreign currency, the investor must pay $1,666.65 to buy the bond on the secondary market. Equivalent price changes would occur if the investor wished to pay for a bond in some other currency.

Interest payment and repayment of such bonds work in much the same way. If interest is set at 12% on par value of $1,000 equivalent, the investor will get $120 per year, provided there are no currency changes. If the dollar depreciates relative to other currencies, the dollar amount of interest will rise. So if the dollar declines as above, the dollar amount of interest will be $40 plus the dollar equivalent of 40 DM, plus the dollar equivalent of £40, or $200.

At the time of purchase of such an instrument, the investor could specify the currency in which interest is to be paid, but with some instruments the borrower specifies the currency that is to be used for repayment. Since the values of the **composite currency basket** are frequently adjusted, this choice of currency for payment is a matter of convenience, there being no currency that will be disadvantageous relative to any other. The values of various composite currency units are published daily in the financial press.

There are several such multicurrency units in existence. Each has some special features that might cause it to differ somewhat from the prototypical composite. The most famous is the **Special Drawing Right** (SDR), issued by the IMF. The currencies included are those countries belonging to the IMF that account for 1% or more of world exports. The weightings of the currencies in the basket and the listing of currencies in the basket are changed periodically. Values of SDR are published frequently in the financial press. Issues of SDR-denominated bonds can be of any type. They need not be connected with the IMF. They only use the SDR as a measure of value.

Another composite currency unit or currency portfolio is the **European composite unit,** or **Eurco.** This includes the sum of each of the European Community's currencies, with weights attached to each that are in rough proportion to the "importance" of the currency. This is a private unit of account, meaning that private banks rather than official government agencies developed it. The Eurco's original formula was 1 Eurco = 0.9 DM + 1.2 French francs + (0.075 U.K. + 0.005 Irish £) + 80 Italian lire + 4.50 Belgian francs + 0.20 Danish krone + 0.5 Luxembourg franc.

Two other multicurrency units exist. The first is the **European unit of account (EUA).** The second is the **European currency unit** (ECU). Both are based on European currencies.

The intent of all these is the reduction of the variation in the real value of the currency in which debt is denominated. Use of a composite reduces fluctuations in the real value of interest payments and principal repayment for both the borrower and lender.

However, according to Mundelsohn (*Money on the Move*) between 1962 and 1977 less than 2% of Eurobond issues were denominated in composite currency units. This is largely due to the complexity of multicurrency bonds. They are not popular because they are hard to understand and extremely complex to evaluate.

THE EUROCURRENCY SYSTEM AND FOREIGN BOND MARKETS

EUROCURRENCIES.   A Eurocurrency is a bank deposit in a currency other than the currency of the country in which the bank is located. A deutsche mark (DM) deposited in Frankfurt is simply a DM, but if the same DM were deposited in London or Luxembourg, it becomes a Euro-DM. Similarly, a U.S. dollar deposited in London or Frankfurt is a Eurodollar.

The term "Eurocurrencies" is used to describe virtually any currency on deposit in a land where the currency is different. Hence, there are, in essence, Eurodollars, Panama dollars, Hong Kong dollars, and so forth. These geographical distinctions have long since broken down, however. Currently any U.S. dollar on deposit outside the United States is termed a Eurodollar, irrespective of location. Eurodollars comprise approximately 70% of Eurocurrencies.

Principal Eurocurrencies include U.S. dollars, German marks, British pounds, French francs, Swiss francs, and Japanese yen. There is no official restriction on the development of Eurocurrency markets in other currencies. These are the important ones owing to the size of the relevant economies, the importance of their currencies in world trade, and the relative stability of these currencies.

A Eurocurrency deposit comes into being with the deposit of a currency in a bank outside that currency area. The receiving bank in turn makes a deposit of equal size in a bank in the country where the currency is legal tender. So a dollar deposit in a major New York bank's London branch would soon be reflected as a liability on the books of the New York parent, but not as a liability to any party other than the bank's branch. Similarly, any foreign bank that accepts a dollar deposit must make a corresponding deposit at a U.S. bank. This can be done directly or indirectly (through a deposit at some other bank, which in turn makes a deposit in a U.S. bank). In fact, this is generally true of any Eurocurrency deposit. The receiving bank must deposit a corresponding amount in the banking system of the country whose money it accepts as a deposit.

If the process stopped here, there would be no real Eurocurrency system. Indeed, before 1957 the process generally did stop here, with Eurobanks investing foreign currency deposits in financial assets of the countries where currencies were deposited. But in 1957 banks in Europe, particularly London, began to loan on an international scale the external currency funds that were deposited in them. It thus became possible for someone seeking a dollar loan to deal in London, rather than in the United States. Now, one can seek a loan in any of the major currencies in a world financial center of one's choice. Today, if a Eurobank cannot lend the funds it has at its disposal to a final borrower, it may lend them to another bank through the interbank market.

Origin.   One expert (Paul Einzig, *The Eurodollar System*, 5th ed., St. Martin's Press, 1970, p. 30) attributes the **birth of the Eurocurrency system** to the practices of the Moscow Narodny Bank in the late 1940s and early 1950s of camouflaging their dollar holdings by depositing them not in the United States, but in a foreign bank, which in turn held them in the United States. While this may have given birth to the system, it does not account for the growth of the system. This practice could not account for the growing importance of the Eurocurrency system in world financial affairs.

George McKenzie (*The Economics of the Euro-Currency System*) points out that in 1957 a significant stimulating event occurred. **The Bank of England** restricted the granting of sterling credits to limit speculative activity against the pound. In response, U.K. banks began to lend dollars to the borrowers who originally sought pounds. The borrowers, of course, could convert to pounds what they wished, but they still would owe dollars. Since the U.S. dollar was a respected currency, convertible into other currencies or into gold (when presented to the U.S. Treasury by foreign governments), and an international reserve currency, it was ideally suited to this purpose.

Since that time, the **Eurocurrency system** has grown substantially. Other impetuses to its growth were: (*a*) the expansion of large U.S. multinational businesses in Europe, and U.S. banks' following them there to maintain these firms as clients; (*b*) foreign banks trying to obtain business from U.S.-based multinationals as well as foreign-based multinationals; (*c*) controls on the outward flow of capital imposed by the U.S. government and other governments, which made it difficult for firms to borrow domestically for investment abroad; and (*d*) government-imposed limitations on interest rates that could be paid by U.S. banks on deposits, which made investment in the Eurodollar market very attractive compared to investment in U.S. banks.

Size.   All the published estimates of the size of the Eurocurrency markets differ somewhat. These discrepancies are in part due to differences in the concepts employed to measure the size of the system and, in part, due to differences in coverage, survey techniques, and data sources.

The two most widely respected and most often used sources for estimates of the **size of the Eurocurrency market** are those published by the Bank for International Settlements (BIS) in its annual report and those published by Morgan Guaranty Trust Co. in its publication *World Financial Markets*.

Both organizations publish estimates of the gross size of the Eurocurrency market and estimates of net size. The details are complex, but in rough terms they are as follows. Gross size estimates add Eurobanks' liabilities to all other banks and to all other depositors. Net size estimates distinguish among the liabilities banks have to other banks. In particular, the net size estimates typically exclude Eurobanks' liabilities to banks outside the country of the currency in which the liability is denominated.

By way of illustration of the gross–net size concept, suppose there were only two Eurocurrency banks, one a French subsidiary of a U.S. bank, the other a British bank. A depositor places $100 into the U.S. subsidiary. The subsidiary, in turn, places a $100 deposit into its parent. The subsidiary then loans $50 to a regular borrower and deposits $50 in the British bank. The British bank then owns a $50 deposit in the United States (the U.S. parent may or may not hold the deposit), and the U.S. Eurobank owns a $50 U.S. deposit. The gross size measure would indicate that the Eurocurrency market's size is $150; the $100 liability of the U.S. bank's subsidiary plus the $50 liability of the British bank. The net size would be $100, the interbank deposit of the U.S. subsidiary. The British bank would not be counted. The gross size can vary greatly in the very short run.

The example above represents the concept, but intervening influences make actual measurement more difficult. One of the most troublesome problems arises as a result of **Eurobank** activities in the foreign exchange market, where currency denominations may be obscured. That is, a Eurobank can convert a dollar asset into any other type of asset it wishes.

The BIS estimate of gross size represents external liabilities in foreign currencies of banks in Belgium, Luxembourg, France, Germany, Italy, the Netherlands, Sweden, Switzerland, and the United Kingdom. In its estimates of net size, the BIS subtracts inter-Eurobank deposits channeled through Eurobanks in the reporting area. At the end of 1977, the BIS estimated the gross size of the Eurocurrency system as $310 billion and the net size as $262 billion.

Morgan Guaranty's estimates of gross and net size are conceptually similar to BIS estimates. However, Morgan Guaranty has more extensive banking center coverage. Its estimates include not only Eurobanks surveyed by the BIS, but also those in Canada, Japan, Singapore, Hong Kong, the Bahamas, the Cayman Islands, and Panama. The more complete coverage results in Morgan's estimates being substantially larger than those of the BIS. For 1979 Morgan Guaranty estimates the gross size as $860 billion and the net size as $480 billion; these amounts exceed BIS estimates by approximately 20%.

By any measure, the Eurocurrency system is a very large financial market. Two authorities (Dufey and Giddy, *The International Money Market*) present data suggesting that Euromarkets are larger than every country's domestic financial markets except for those of the United States.

Knowledge of the size of the Euromarkets may be interesting, but by itself it is not terribly important. What is important is that the **liquidity of any financial market is directly related to its size.** Accordingly, given the size of the Euromarkets, they are likely to be extraordinarily liquid. This means that large amounts of funds can be invested or borrowed in a short period of time without much effect on the price of funds; that is, much money can be moved without disturbing prevailing interest rates.

INTEREST RATES.   The **Eurodollar** is the principal currency in the Eurocurrency market, and for it the key interest rate is seemingly the **London Interbank Offer Rate (LIBOR).** This is the rate at which a Eurobank proposes to lend (or offers) Eurodollars to another Eurobank of the highest creditworthiness. Neither bank need be in London, but by convention, LIBOR is the term used. Eurobanks that are riskier than the most creditworthy banks sometimes are able to borrow from other banks, but during periods of financial turbulence they must pay a premium over the rate for top quality banks. Such premiums range from 0.25 to 3%.

Corresponding to LIBOR and other interbank offer rates is the **interbank bid rate.** This is the rate that is proposed by banks to purchase funds. It is typically 0.125% less than the offer rate. But the spread between bid and offer prices can fluctuate with market conditions. The more volatile the market, the higher the spread.

The Eurocurrency interbank offer rates typically will track short-term, low-risk interest rates in the relevant domestic markets. Exhibit 3 shows rates on U.S. Treasury bills, rates on large **negotiated certificates of deposits** in the United States, and Eurodollar deposit rates for several recent periods. Corresponding data are also presented for Euro-Sterling. Although the Eurobank deposit rates tend to be higher than domestic money market rates, the two sets vary quite closely. The same appears to be true for other Eurocurrencies. The higher rates are attributed to higher risks in the Eurocurrency markets than in domestic markets. These risks include the fact that Eurobanks, unlike most domestic banks, cannot rely on domestic central bank support during turbulent times, nor are Eurobanks required to hold a given

EXHIBIT 3   COMPARISON OF EUROMARKET INTEREST RATES AND DOMESTIC RATES

Date	Treasury Bill Rate	Representative 3–4 Month Money Market Rates (excluding Treasury Bills)	3-Month Euro Deposit Rate
		UNITED STATES	
December 1975	5.27	5.91	5.81
December 1976	4.41	4.75	5.00
December 1977	6.33	6.84	7.19
December 1978	9.42	10.57	11.69
November 1979	11.68	12.90	14.00
		UNITED KINGDOM[a]	
December 1975	10.78	10.69	11.00
December 1976	13.98	14.38	16.12
December 1977	6.42	6.50	6.62
December 1978	12.01	12.50	12.62
November 1979	16.75	16.81	16.50

[a]Three-month deposit not given for Eurosterling
Source: Morgan Guaranty Trust Co., *World Financial Markets,* various issues.

portion of their deposits as reserves. Eurobanks are riskier than those in their respective countries, hence must pay higher rates to attract deposits.

For the Eurodollar, LIBOR and LIBOR's counterparts in other Eurocurrencies, are the **key rates.** Deposit rates are generally a function of these rates, and regular borrowing rates are normally set at, say, LIBOR plus some premium or margin. Moreover, the interest rate on the loan will generally vary over the life of the loan as LIBOR varies. For most borrowers, the **base rate** will be adjusted every 6 months or so. Adjustments to the size of the premium are negotiable. While in earlier years premiums were set for the life of the loan, in recent years an increasing number of loan agreements call for changes in the premium over the base rate during the credit's life. Typically, the longer the term of the loan, the larger the premium over LIBOR.

The overall level of rates in the Eurocurrency markets for loans in any one currency is dependent on the level of domestic interest rates in that currency, the amount of competition between domestic and European financial markets for that lending business, and the amount of competition for that business among Euromarkets in different currency denominations.

Whenever a country imposes controls on the foreign lending activities of its domestic banks, the gap between the external (Euro) rate for loans in that currency and the internal rate can be expected to broaden to the point at which borrowers find it attractive to borrow in a different currency denomination.

As in domestic financial markets, there is a **term structure of interest rates in Eurocurrency markets.** Sometimes longer term credits carry lower interest rates than short-term credits, sometimes there is no difference, and sometimes short-term credits carry lower interest rates than longer term credits. The term structure in any Eurocurrency will typically resemble the term structure of interest rates that prevails in domestic financial markets. This may not be true, however, if there are domestic programs to control external lending that affect some maturities more than others. (For more detail on this issue see Dufey and Giddy, *The International Money Market.*)

DEPOSITS. Eurocurrency banks derive deposits from two principal sources. The first is time deposits. These account for the bulk of the funds deposited in the Eurobanking system. They typically range in maturity from 7 days to 6 months, but some are for as short a period as 1 day or as long as several years. Deposits generally come from the interbank brokering system. Sometimes, direct deposits are made, then rates are negotiated between the depositor and the bank. Because there is intense competition among banks for funds, the deposit rate will often be quite close to **LIBOR** or its equivalents.

The second way in which Eurobanks attract money is through the sale of certificates of deposit (CDs). As Dufey and Giddy point out (*International Money Markets*), there are two common types of certificates of deposit. The first is a **"tap" CD.** The issuing bank sets an interest rate, a particular amount, and a maturity. It searches for an investor seeking this sort of instrument. Normally, banks do this with the idea of financing a particular loan. It is analogous to a private placement of securities.

The second type of CD is a **"tranche" CD.** The Eurobank offers the total amount of funds it wishes to raise in small portions. These are sold through brokers or agents in small denominations to final investors who generally are outside the banking system. This is analogous to a public sale of bonds or notes.

Both types of CD are negotiable; however, because of the wider distribution of tranche CDs and their smaller denominations, their secondary market is substantially more liquid than that for tap CDs. The price of any of these negotiable instruments will be a function of the prevailing level of interest rates, the promised interest payments on the instruments, and the degree of risk involved in dealing with the issuing bank.

The interest on Euromarket deposits and CDs typically exceeds that which could be obtained in domestic markets on instruments with similar characteristics. This is likely due to the higher risk of Eurocurrency deposits. Unlike domestic banks in the United States and most domestic banks in European countries, Eurobanks have no required reserve requirements. In addition, if a Eurobank develops financial problems, there is no central bank, acting as lender of last resort, that has an obligation to help the troubled bank out of its difficulties. As a practical matter, if a major Eurobank were to face failure, the bank's parent bank or the central bank of its domestic parent, or perhaps even the central bank of the country in which the bank was doing business, might come to its aid. But there is no legal obligation to help, so a deposit in a Eurobank is at somewhat greater risk than it would be in a domestic financial institution.

EUROCREDITS. "Eurocredit" is the term often used to describe the short-, medium-, and sometimes long-term loans in the Eurocurrency markets that are made directly by banks. They differ from **Eurobonds** because with **Eurocredits,** the banks provide the funds directly. Eurobonds, on the other hand, are marketable and are sold to outside investors by merchant and investment bankers, and the investors generally would not be other bank-like entities.

Sometimes single Eurobanks provide an international corporation or national government with a loan. However, much of the lending in this market is done through syndicates. A **lead bank** will develop the lending business and then arrange with other banks to take a portion of the loan. For arranging the financing, the lead bank receives a management fee, which may range from 0.5 to 2.5% of the size of the loan. This is an up-front cost to the borrower, and must be paid no matter what portion of the credit is drawn. Typically, the lead bank will pass along a portion of this management fee to other banks participating in the loan; this is termed a **participation fee.** In syndicated lending, an agent bank must ultimately be appointed to oversee the loan. This entails collecting interest, paying interest to syndicate banks, and checking on whatever indenture agreements exist; for this the bank is paid depending on its negotiating position vis-à-vis the other banks.

Two types of credit are common in the Euromarkets. The first is a regular **term loan.** The second, more widely used type of credit arrangement is a **rollover credit.** This may be set up for a period similar to that for a term loan, but periodically it is rolled over or reestablished, perhaps at different interest rates but rarely with different conditions. So this is much like a succession of very short term loans for a medium term, but conditions will not change.

In contrast with the fairly standard practice in the Eurobond markets, where interest rates are fixed, rollover credits carry variable interest rates. Typically, a Eurocredit's interest rate is set at some specified premium above LIBOR, or its equivalent. Every time the credit is rolled over, the base borrowing rate—generally not the premium over that rate—is adjusted to reflect changes in the lenders' own cost of funding the loan. The borrower, in this case, bears the risk of rising interest rates but also reaps any benefits from falling interest rates. The Eurobank lender is assured that the value of the commitment will not rise or fall with the general level of interest rates beyond a 6-month period. Of course, the value could rise or fall as a result of changes in the riskiness of the underlying credit. Recently some loans have been written that call for a floating premium. For example, a 7-year credit may be set at LIBOR plus 0.5% for the first 3 years, and LIBOR plus 1% for the remainder of the loan. This presumably will compensate the lenders for any change in the credit worthiness of the borrower. The borrower in this market also pays a **commitment fee** on the unused portion of the loan to compensate lenders for setting the funds aside.

Borrowers in this market face somewhat higher interest rates than they would if an equal amount with an identical maturity were borrowed in a domestic market. One reason for this is that in the Eurocredit market, banks normally would not require compensating balances (i.e., funds that the borrower must keep on deposit in the lending institutions); also, lending is typically done on an unsecured basis. The financing is not secured for an asset in place. In addition, in the Eurocredit markets, the sort of restrictive covenants that domestic banks impose, such as working capital requirements, are generally not used. There are some covenants, the most prominent being the **negative pledge,** which prevents borrowers from subordinating the loan to others. Furthermore, a great deal of attention in loan contract clauses is focused on neutralizing the effect of any changes in tax laws or restrictions on foreign payments. For example, all the following must be included and administered: (a) special clauses in the loan agreement relating to the borrower's responsibility for general increases in lenders' costs, such as those resulting from a domestic central bank's imposition of a reserve requirement on a Eurobank's deposits in the relevant domestic market, (b) clauses relating to currency options, and (c) clauses relating to the appropriate jurisdiction in the event of default. Finally, the cost of administering a Eurocredit may be higher than a domestic credit.

In turn, borrowers are willing both to pay higher interest rates than they might face domestically, and to bear the risk of **floating interest rates** because of the greater flexibility of Eurocredits. Possible restrictions on operating activities are minimal. Large pools of capital can be mobilized with very little formality, and there are typically no restrictions as to how or where these funds can be used. Finally, for very strong borrowers, the loans can be repaid prematurely without penalty. They may choose to pay off credits when interest rates in the Eurobond or foreign bond markets appear more favorable. Thus, they are encouraged to seek long-term financing.

Size.   Exhibit 4 gives some perspective on the size and structure of the Eurocredit market. It shows the volume of publicized Eurocredits for the period 1974–1979 by borrower and by currency. These represent commitments to lend, not actual amounts raised. Of course, there are many unpublicized Eurocredits, such as private single-lender deals, that are not recorded. But one may safely assume that the volume and mixture of these corresponds closely to those of the publicized deals.

With this magnitude of financing provided annually by the Eurocredit market, there is no significant liquidity problem. Indeed, in 1978 the government of Canada secured a Eurocredit of $3 billion without any substantial impact on prevailing market rates.

Interest Rates.   Interest rates in the Eurocurrency markets tend to be slightly higher than comparable domestic rates (see Exhibit 3). This implies that risks are higher in the Eurocurrency markets. (See the section on "International Structure of Interest Rates" for more detail on interest rates.)

Banking Concentration.   Though there are approximately 500 Eurobanks, a small portion of these play an active role in the Eurocredit market. The most active participating banks are the world's leading commercial banks; the others all accept deposits and join in Eurocredit syndications, but they do not do much loan origination, nor do they play a major role in managing syndicates. According to data published in *Euromoney,* an important periodical on international financial markets, the leading 10 managers typically manage approximately 50% of publicized Eurocredits. Through the late 1970s, the leading managers were Citicorp, Chase Manhattan, Morgan Guaranty, and Bank of America, with other American and European banks playing lesser roles.

EUROBONDS.   The principal distinction between Eurobonds and Eurocredits is that the former are sold to outside investors and are marketable. In the case of Eurocredits, syndicate members themselves provide the funds. With Eurobonds, the funds are obtained by members of the syndicate's selling group by sale of the bonds to nongroup members. Chief participants in **syndicates** include merchant banks, commercial banks' merchant bank subsidiaries, and investment banks.

Eurobonds are bonds sold internationally. A simultaneous offering of Eurobonds is made by an international syndicate to an international clientele. In this, they may be distinguished from foreign bonds, which are bonds offered by one borrower in another country. They may be issued by governments, government-sponsored organizations, or corporations.

EXHIBIT 4   PUBLICIZED EUROCREDITS ($ MILLIONS)

Domicile of Borrower	1975	1976	1977	1978	1979 (Prelim.)
Industrial countries	7,231	11,254	17,205	28,952	24,639
Developing countries	11,098	15,017	20,976	37,300	44,832
Communist countries	2,597	2,503	3,394	3,767	7,244
International organizations	65	74	190	160	275
Total	20,992	28,850	41,765	70,179	76,990

Source: Morgan Guaranty Trust Co., *World Financial Markets,* various issues.

Although the World Bank estimated that between 1957 and 1962, $500 million in Eurobonds was publicly offered or privately placed, the chief impetus to the development of the Eurobond market appears to have been the imposition of the **interest equalization tax** in the United States in 1963. This tax imposed a penalty against foreign borrowers in U.S. financial markets. In effect, it made foreign borrowing in the United States more costly by an amount equal to 15% of the interest rate by imposing a 15% tax on foreign interest payments in this country. Accordingly, to compete effectively, foreign borrowers were compelled to offer interest rates on securities to be sold here that were approximately 18% greater [i.e., 1/(1 − tax rate)] − 1 than those prevailing on domestic securities of comparable risk and maturity. This tax was removed in 1974.

The Eurobond market fills an important gap in the international capital markets. It provides long-term capital with none of the regulation that usually accompanies foreign bond issues, that is, bonds of one country sold in another country. The Eurobond market deals only with the most creditworthy borrowers, so the need for national securities supervision such as **U.S. Securities and Exchange Commission** is minimized.

There is some dispute concerning what actually constitutes a Eurobond (see Mendelsohn, *Money on the Move*). The market itself prefers to view Eurobonds as any bonds that are issued internationally. Some, however, prefer a narrow definition that excludes bonds that require the prior authorization of the government of the currency of issue. Using this narrow definition, only the U.S. dollar, the Canadian dollar, and the unit of account issues qualify as true Eurobonds.

Instruments.   According to Mendelsohn (*Money on the Move*), there are four major types of Eurobond instrument: (*a*) straight debt issues; (*b*) debt issues convertible into the common stock of the issuing company; (*c*) currency option bonds, which offer investors the option of buying in one currency while taking payment in another, and (*d*) floating rate notes, wherein the interest rate is periodically adjusted to reflect short-term interest rates.

Approximately 85% of Eurobonds are conventional debt issues, and 10% are convertibles. The remainder are more or less evenly divided between currency options bonds and floating rate notes.

Currency option bonds are among the more innovative creations of Eurobond market. The rate of exchange on these bonds has typically been set at the time of offering. The lender can specify the currency in which interest payments are to be made. Suppose that such a bond were offered by a British company when $1.50 = £1.0, and this was the set rate. Suppose further that the interest rate was 10%. Initially the borrower would pay, on a $1,000 bond, $100 or £66.67 in interest. However, if the actual rate of exchange became $2 = £1, the same $100 interest payment would cost only £50. So an investor who opted for payment in pounds sterling would suffer. The sword cuts both ways, though, and if the exchange rate were to move against the pound sterling, the issuer would have to pay more pounds. In addition, if the principal were to be repaid in dollars, more pounds would be needed by the issuer to repay. The alternative to a fixed exchange rate option is a floating exchange rate option. In this arrangement, the exchange rate of the bond contract floats with actual exchange rates. Accordingly, issuers and lenders are protected against adverse exchange rate fluctuations.

Size.   Exhibit 5 shows the volume of Eurobonds sold over the past several years. It is broken down by borrower and by currency. It shows liquidity for primary offerings. Furthermore, the secondary market is not as large as the Eurocredit market, but it is quite liquid, with more than 25 major market-makers, mostly major commercial and investment banks.

EXHIBIT 5   EUROBOND FINANCING ($ MILLIONS)

Bonds Financed	1975	1976	1977	1978	1979 (Prelim.)
By Category of Borrower					
U.S. companies	268	435	1,130	1,122	2,872
Foreign companies	2,903	5,323	7,347	4,540	6,988
State enterprises	3,123	4,138	4,667	3,291	4,508
Governments	1,658	2,239	2,936	3,643	2,346
International corporations	615	2,193	1,691	1,529	1,664
By Currency of Denomination					
U.S. dollar	3,738	9,125	11,627	7,290	12,320
German mark	2,278	2,713	4,131	5,251	3,529
Netherlands guilder	719	503	452	394	531
Canadian dollar	558	1,407	655	—	425
European unit of account	371	99	28	165	253
Other	903	482	878	1,025	1,310
Total	8,567	14,328	17,771	14,125	18,378

Source: Morgan Guaranty Trust Co., *World Financial Markets,* various issues.

In addition to secondary trading through market makers, most Eurobonds are traded on major European stock exchanges. Dollar Eurobonds are traded in London and Luxembourg; French franc Eurobonds are traded in Luxembourg; and external deutsche mark bonds are traded in Luxembourg and in German stock exchanges.

Sale of Eurobonds.   Eurobonds are sold through **underwriting syndicates,** much as domestic U.S. bonds are sold. The investment banking fee is typically in the vicinity of 2.5%, though for short maturity bonds (i.e., less than 6 years) it will be lower, and for longer maturity bonds (8 years or more) it may be 2.5% or more. This spread also tends to vary inversely with the size of the offering and will widen during turbulent periods and narrow during tranquil times.

The distribution of the **investment banking spread** normally approximates the following breakdown. The lead underwriter, the originator of the business, will take 0.5%. Another 0.5% will be divided among the underwriters, the risk-bearing group, to compensate for their costs and the risk they bear during the distribution period. The remainder is a selling concession, divided among those underwriters and others who are brought into the syndicate for the purpose of selling bonds only, in rough proportion to the number of bonds actually sold by each.

The spread plus any other issuing costs are borne by the issuer. These are netted against the gross proceeds of the issue to determine how much the issuer receives.

In contrast to spreads such as those noted above, the typical **spread of a high-quality U.S. bond** in the United States is 0.875%. In further contrast, U.S. investment bankers agree among themselves to sell the new bond issue to all investors while the syndicate is in force at the same price. This is called the **fixed price offering system.** In the Eurobond market (and in the part of the foreign bond market that is external to the United States), the investment bankers can discriminate among customers, effectively reducing the size of their spread in favor of an investor. In turn this means that some investors pay full price for the new bond while others purchase new bonds at discount.

Sales to residents of various countries is controlled by national authorities. For instance, the U.S. Securities and Exchange Commission prohibits the purchase of a Eurobond by a U.S. resident unless the bond has been registered with the SEC or has been "seasoned," that is, traded, for at least 90 days. The Canadian authorities impose similar restrictions. However, Switzerland, France, Belgium, Germany, and the Netherlands have for a long time now allowed their residents to purchase Eurobonds, and the United Kingdom recently allowed domestic investors to purchase such bonds.

FOREIGN BONDS.   These are bonds issued by a government or juridical resident of one country in another country. The distinction between these and Eurobonds is blurry, though bonds are put in one or another category by various data collecting agencies depending on the composition of the investment banking group. If it is comprised of banks from only one country, it is generally classified as a foreign bond; if the syndicate's composition is international, it is categorized as a Eurobond. An ideal characterization would depend on who the ultimate investors were, but such data are, for all practical purposes, impossible to gather.

Size.   Exhibit 6 shows the volume of foreign bond issues over the past several years. It is broken down by borrower and currency. The market is quite large, and capable of absorbing large bond offerings.

EXHIBIT 6   FOREIGN BOND SALES ($ MILLIONS)

Foreign Bonds	1975	1976	1977	1978	1979 (Prelim.)
Outside United States					
By Category of Borrower					
U.S. companies	61	28	40	245	217
Foreign companies	1,386	1,654	1,421	2,110	3,437
State enterprises	1,314	2,439	2,427	3,163	3,206
Governments	765	1,307	2,043	5,771	7,600
International organizations	1,358	2,158	2,846	3,070	2,682
By Currency of Denomination					
German mark	1,089	1,288	2,181	3,789	5,234
Swiss franc	3,297	5,359	4,970	5,698	9,564
Netherlands guilder	182	597	211	385	75
Japanese yen	67	226	1,271	3,826	1,707
Other	248	116	144	671	562
Total	4,884	7,586	8,777	14,359	17,142
In United States					
By Category of Borrower					
Canadian entities	3,074	6,138	3,022	3,142	2,193
International organizations	1,900	2,275	1,917	5,795	1,100
Other	1,488	2,191	2,489	2,194	1,222
Total	6,462	10,604	7,428	5,795	4,515

Source: Morgan Guaranty Trust Co., *World Financial Markets,* various issues.

Sale of Foreign Bonds.   Foreign bonds are sold like Eurobonds. One very important feature is worth noting, however. The investment banking spreads differ substantially among foreign bonds. For instance, spreads on foreign bonds sold in the United States (so-called Yankee bonds) are in the order of 1% of par. However, typical spreads on foreign bonds denominated in yen ("Samurai" bonds), deutsche marks, and Swiss francs approximate 2, 1.75–2.25, and 4%, respectively. In addition, in the market external to the United States and as in the Eurobond market, some investors may be able to negotiate discounts from the offering price. The size of the investment banking spreads in foreign bonds in non-U.S. markets suggests some inefficiencies in the new security distribution systems of many foreign countries.

THE INTERNATIONAL STRUCTURE OF INTEREST RATES

INTEREST RATE LEVELS.   Nominal interest rates in any one country are typically a function of (*a*) the demand for and supply of loans, (*b*) the expected inflation rate, (*c*) the rate of growth in the money supply, and (*d*) government credit controls and interest rate regulations, which tend to vary among countries as each of the underlying factors varies among countries. While there is no general agreement, there is much support for the notion that anticipated inflation plays the most important role in setting nominal interest rates.

Most authorities argue that over the past several years the principal course of interest rate changes internationally has been from the U.S. market through the Eurodollar markets through the other Eurocurrency markets and finally to the domestic financial markets of Eurocurrency countries. This might be termed the direction of causality. Of course, interest rate disturbances can originate in the other countries and be transmitted backward through the network mentioned above, but because of the overwhelming size of the U.S. markets relative to others, disturbances initiated elsewhere are very diffused by the time they are experienced in the U.S. market.

FINANCIAL MARKET INTEGRATION.   International financial markets are said to be integrated when the risk ratios across all markets are similar. This means that an investor from one market cannot expect rewards that are unjustified by risk when investing in another. In an integrated financial market, there are no opportunities for systematic investment returns that exceed those attributable to the risks associated with investment in those markets. The process of **international financial market arbitrage**—the simultaneous purchase and sale of like financial assets—keeps the various expected returns in line. From the view of the investor or borrower, the more integrated the markets, the more like a single market they appear. Like assets promise like returns; like loans carry similar costs.

Financial market integration is an **ex ante** or expectational concept. Before the fact, one should not anticipate reaping rewards that exceed those justified by the amount of risk borne. This is to be distinguished from the **ex post** reality. Sometimes actual received returns in some markets are excessive when compared to risk. In an ex post sense, the markets may not appear to have been integrated if the return-risk relationship was substantially more favorable in one country or if the financial assets were denominated in a particular currency more than in others. The fact that such anomalies occur does not mean that international financial markets are not integrated ex ante; it may simply mean that some wholly unanticipated events occurred during the period in which the assets were held, which led to this result.

Measurement of Market Integration.   One set of experts (Dennis E. Logue, Michael A. Salant, and Richard James Sweeney, "International Integration of Financial Markets: Survey, Synthesis, and Results," in Stem, Makin, and Logue, Eds., *Eurocurrencies and the International Monetary System,* pp. 91–138) suggests that there are three ways to **measure international financial market integration.**

The first approach to measuring international financial market integration focuses on the degree to which **international interest rates move jointly,** after adjusting for anticipated exchange rate changes and other systematic types of risk. If there is joint movement—that is, if interest rates among countries are highly correlated—it may be assumed that the rates are affected by common factors. To the extent that they are all influenced by the same set of international economic determinants, such as the growth of world money supplies and industrial production, the financial markets are internationally integrated. Available evidence shows that when integration is defined in this way, international financial markets seem to be highly integrated. What this means in a practical sense is that before taking tax differences and other special factors into account, an international borrower or lender is not likely to do substantially better by borrowing or lending in one country rather than another.

The second approach is generally termed the **portfolio or capital flow approach** to financial market integration. It examines the behavior of international capital flows in response to enhanced expected return opportunities (risk constant) in other countries. Enhanced return opportunities are presumed to arise from changes in interest rate differentials among countries, adjusted for expected exchange rate changes. If a pair of countries initially have identical sets of interest rates and no change is expected in their exchange rates, one would assume that if the interest rate rose in one country, other things constant, funds would flow to that country out of the low-interest country until interest rates were again equalized. Under this approach the degree of international financial market integration is assessed by estimating the sensitivity of international capital flows to interest rate differentials, adjusted for anticipated exchange rate changes. The more sensitive the flows, the speedier the return to interest rate equilibrium, hence the more highly integrated the financial markets.

The final and most common approach to the measurement of international financial market integration derives from the **interest rate parity theory.** The theory holds that there should be no difference in the expected return on any pair of otherwise identical financial assets after adjusting for the expected change in the exchange rate between the currencies of denomination. This is one of the most durable and indispensable concepts to anyone involved in international finance.

Interest Rate Parity Theory.   The interest rate parity theory assumes that two financial assets issued in two different currencies can be made comparable by adjusting for exchange rate risk through the use of **forward currency markets.** An investor can purchase a foreign security instead of an otherwise identical domestic security and make them comparable by also purchasing a contract to convert the foreign currency received when the foreign instrument matures back to domestic currency at a price that is known at the time the investment is undertaken. (Contracts to purchase domestic currency for foreign currency at specified prices can also be made to cover interest payments in foreign currency over the life of the asset.) Because forward exchange contracts can be purchased, a domestic investor is able to neutralize foreign exchange risk. Moreover, because foreign exchange risk can be neutralized, a domestic investor can effectively compare the returns and rewards of domestic investment with foreign investment. If after guarding against foreign exchange risks, a foreign yield exceeds the yield on a comparable domestic asset, funds will be placed abroad. If the converse is true, funds will be withdrawn abroad and placed domestically. This process is known as covered interest arbitrage. To the extent that international capital flows are unimpeded by the policies of governments, interest rate parity should generally prevail.

The relationship between foreign and domestic interest rates and the **price of forward currency** (the forward rate) is as follows:

$$\frac{F - S}{S} = \frac{i - i^*}{1 + i^*}$$

where F is the forward exchange rate, S is the current spot rate, i is the domestic interest rate, and i^* is the foreign interest rate. If the theory is to hold, the pair of securities must be identical with respect to business and default risk, maturity, and tax status.

Suppose the current interest rate on 1 year commercial paper in the United States is 10% and on a comparable security in Germany, the rate is 5%. The entire difference in interest rates, if the theory is correct, will then be attributable to the difference between the spot and forward exchange rates between the U.S. dollar and the German mark. The premium or discount on the DM. relative to the current spot rate will be $(0.10 - 0.05)/1.05$, or approximately 4.8%. This means that between the present time and the time of maturity of these two financial assets, the DM is expected to rise by 4.8% versus the dollar. The forward premium on DM is thus 4.8%.

Of course, if an international investor observes that the premium on forward DM exceeds 4.8%, funds will be invested in the U.S. and flow out of Germany. Conversely, if it is less, funds will be placed in Germany by foreign investors.

Because of the astuteness of **covered interest arbitrageurs** (economic actors who will invest or borrow anywhere and simultaneously cover foreign exchange risks by covering in forward currency markets where foreign exchange can be bought or sold for future delivery at specified prices), interest parity generally ought to prevail. Interest differentials ought to be fully offset by expected exchange rate changes. As it turns out, straightforward tests of the theory have not been conclusive; however, they do show that the theory tends to hold.

Asset Pairs, Sovereign Risk, and Transaction Costs.   Three problems have hindered interest rate parity theory testing. The first is associated with the **choice of asset pairs.** It is very difficult to identify securities in two countries that are identical except for currency of denomination. Business and default risk must be constant, maturity must be identical, and taxes that must be paid by investors ought to be similar. Generally, short-term treasury securities from pairs of countries, commercial paper in pairs of countries, and certain bank liabilities are about the only securities that approach comparability.

The second problem has to do with **sovereign or political risk.** Any country can at any time impose controls designed to prevent funds from flowing out of or into that country. A country can impose capital controls, exchange market restrictions, or tax impediments to deter the flow of capital to or from it. This effectively means that the identification of comparable securities between two countries has to take account of the risk that one or both countries may prevent the international investor from repatriating funds. To surmount this problem, researchers have used rates from the Eurocurrency markets. Here financial flows into and out of different currency financial assets are generally beyond the reach of domestic policies. To obtain comparable securities, one might compare 90-day rates on dollar-denominated certificates of deposit issued in London with rates on similar instruments denominated in pounds sterling issued in Paris. Using Eurocurrency rates effectively neutralizes the influence of political risk.

Finally, in covered interest arbitrage, there are **transaction costs.** To invest in a DM-denominated security, U.S. investors must buy DM in the spot exchange market, sell DM in the forward exchange market, and buy the asset. Some U.S. investors will even have to sell dollar-denominated assets to generate the cash to begin the series of transactions. All these transactions cost something.

In each market that must be dealt with, there is a market maker who will buy at a low price and sell at a higher price. This difference is known as the bid-ask spread. In recent years, an investor may pay anywhere from 0.5 to 1% to transact in the foreign exchange markets, both spot and forward, and 0.03 to 0.1% to transact in the relevant securities markets. The higher costs tend to be associated with periods of turbulence and uncertainty in international currency and financial markets. These transaction costs could cause deviations from interest rate parity, thus prompting one to conclude that international financial markets are not highly integrated when in fact they are.

Available evidence (see e.g., Jacob A. Frankel and Richard M. Levich, "Transaction Costs and Interest Arbitrage: Tranquil versus Turbulent Periods," *Journal of Political Economy,* November–December 1977, pp. 1209–1226) shows that when sovereign risks and transaction costs are incorporated in the analysis, interest parity generally holds. What this means for practicing international financial managers is that in the absence of special considerations, interest rate differences in most international financial markets are the result of the anticipated exchange rate changes that will occur over the lives of the financial instruments. The premium or discount on forward exchange accounts for the differences.

Exhibit 7 illustrates the range of interest rates that prevailed in the short-term Euromarkets in November 1979. It also shows the 3-month forward premium (or discount) on the U.S. dollar that prevailed at that time. The 3-month premium and 3-month deposit rates are compared in a set of interest parity computations. For this randomly chosen sample, the deviations seem to be sufficiently small to be attributed to transaction costs.

Forward Exchange Rates.   Interest rate parity between financial assets will occur when the forward exchange rate is precisely related to interest rate differentials. However, if the forward exchange rate is not a good estimate of what the spot exchange rate will be when

EXHIBIT 7   COMPARISON OF EUROCURRENCY DEPOSIT RATES AND THE FOREIGN EXCHANGE RATE ON THE U.S. DOLLAR

Eurocurrency	3-Month Deposit Rates at Prime Banks' Bid Rate, December 29, 1978	Forward Premium (+) or Discount (−) of Currency against U.S. Dollar (annual percentage rate, on December 29, 1978)	Deviation from Interest Parity[a] (%)
Eurodollar	11.69	—	
Euromark	3.31	8.31 +	0.20
Eurosterling	12.62	1.12 −	−0.29
Euro-French franc	9.87	1.63 +	−0.02
Euroyen	0.62	11.44 +	−0.16

[a]Calculated as the difference between the actual forward premium or discount and the premium or discount that is obtained from the formula $(i - i^*)/(1 + i^*)$, where i is the dollar rate and i^* are foreign rates.

Source: Morgan Guaranty Trust Co., *World Financial Markets,* December 1979, p. 15, and *Euromoney,* October 1979, p. 261.

the financial assets mature, that is if the forward exchange rate consistently exceeds or lies below the spot exchange rate that prevails when the forward contract is settled, then although interest rate parity may hold in an arithmetic sense, it does not work in a conceptual sense. This is because a higher or lower return could have been realized on a financial asset than was justified by risk, including exchange risk. For instance, if interest rate parity exists in computations and if the forward premium on currency X versus currency Y is almost always positive, but the spot rates that prevail when the forward contracts mature always equal the spot rates that exist at the time the contracts are entered, an international investor has the opportunity to earn excess returns by buying currency Y securities and by avoiding the forward market. In this case, the forward premium on currency X would be unjustified; furthermore, the forward rate would be a biased predictor of the expected future spot rate. So even if interest parity prevails computationally, it still does not signal international financial market integration.

Available evidence (see Bradford Cornell, "Spot Rates, Forward Rates, and Market Efficiency," *Journal of Financial Economics,* May 1977, pp. 55–65) shows that at least for the U.S. dollar relative to other currencies, the forward exchange rate is an unbiased predictor of future spot exchange rates. While it has not been a terribly good predictor, it is useful nonetheless because systematically it is neither too high nor too low.

TERM STRUCTURE OF INTERNATIONAL INTEREST RATES. "Term structure of interest rates" is the expression used to describe the relationship between yields to maturity on debt instruments and the maturity of those instruments. If the term structure slopes upward, short-term yields are lower than long-term yields. If it slopes downward, long-term yields are lower than short.

International borrowers and lenders use the term structure of interest rates to help guide financial decisions, much as domestic financial managers use the term structure to guide their decisions. In the Euromarkets, when Eurobond rates in various currencies seem low relative to short-term Eurocredit rates in those currencies, borrowers try to obtain long-term financing. Conversely, when rates seem high, borrowers use the Eurocredit markets. Note that Eurocredit lenders will release many prime quality borrowers from revolving credit and intermediate credit arrangements if they suddenly chose to seek longer term financing in the Eurobond markets.

As short-term and long-term interest rates in the United States bear some relationship to each other, so do Euromarket interest rates for various maturity instruments. There are three important theories of the term structure of interest rates. For the United States, none of the theories has proved to be perfectly accurate; nor have they shown themselves to be precisely accurate in the Euromarkets or in other foreign financial markets. However, each theory deserves some explanation insofar as they do attempt to explain the relationship between promised yields and the maturity of internationally traded financial assets in robust fashion.

Expectations Theory.   The expectations theory holds that long-term rates reflect the current short-term rate and expectations about future short-term rates. The long-term rate is nothing more than the geometric average of the present and expected future short-term rates. Suppose the yield on a 1-year asset is 5% and the yield on a 2-year asset is 5%. Under this theory, the expected rate on a 1-year asset 1 year from now would be 5%. Similarly, suppose a 1- and a 2-year asset have yields of 5 and 10%, respectively. The rate expected on a 1-year asset available in one year would be $(1.10^2/1.05) - 1$ or approximately 15.2%. The general formula used to find a 1-period rate that will prevail in the future at time t is

$$\frac{(1 + i_t)^t}{(1 + i_{t-1})^{t-1}} - 1$$

where i_t is the current yield on a financial asset of t-period maturity.

If this theory is correct, a borrower or lender should be indifferent to the choice between a short-term or long-term loan or investment.

Liquidity Preference.   The liquidity preference theory is nearly identical to the expectations theory except that it maintains that investors insist on a slight premium for purchasing assets with long maturity. Borrowers are willing to pay this premium because they avoid the cost of reentering the market frequently, as they would have to do if they borrowed for only short periods when long-term financing was what they needed. Liquidity premiums are anticipated to be larger, the longer the maturity of the instrument. Much evidence suggests this is a reasonable approximation to reality.

Preferred Habitat.   The preferred habitat theory of the term structure is sometimes referred to as the "segmentation" theory. It holds that there is little relationship between promised yields on short- and long-term instruments. The reason for the absence of a strong relationship concerns the preferences of investors and borrowers. Some investors and borrowers strongly prefer the long end of the maturity spectrum; others prefer the short end. To overcome these preferences, significant departures from the expectations theory or the liquidity premium theory are necessary. Major deviations must occur before investors will switch from their preferred maturity range to consider opportunities in the other area. As a consequence, there is no strong relationship between short and long-term yields owing to an absence of investor–borrower arbitrage of the maturity spectrum. This theory has not been as substantially verified empirically as the prior two.

Variability.   The term structure of interest rates shifts quite frequently and unpredictably. It may be downward sloping at one time and shortly thereafter it may slope upward. This is true in the U.S. financial markets, the Euromarkets, and in most other foreign money and capital markets. Typically, short-term rates are more volatile than long-term rates, so much of the variation in the shape of the yield curve is due to variation in short-term rates.

Exhibit 8 depicts some short- and long-term rates in the Eurodollar market for particular points in time. It offers insight into the volatility of the relationship between long and short rates, showing, among other things, that the slope of the yield curve can rise or fall rather dramatically in comparatively short periods of time.

While it would prove fruitful to know more about the relationships among yield curves in various currencies, very little is presently known about their correspondence. If the U.S. dollar curve shifts, economists do not really know how quickly the yield curves in foreign countries or in the nondollar Euromarkets will shift, or indeed, whether they will shift at all.

RISK IN INTERNATIONAL FINANCIAL MARKETS

INTEREST RATE AND CURRENCY RISK.   International borrowers and investors must cope with **interest rate risk** in their activities. Conceptually, this is no different from the sort of interest rate risk that domestic economic agents confront. If interest rates, in general,

EXHIBIT 8   TERM STRUCTURE OF THE EURODOLLAR MARKET

Deposit	Eurodollar Rates (%)		
	December 1976	December 1978	November 1979
Overnight	4.63	10.62	12.87
7-day fixed	4.75	10.62	13.00
1 Month	5.13	11.00	13.56
3 Months	5.00	11.69	14.00
6 Months	5.38	12.31	13.94
12 Months	5.56	12.00	12.87
Bond yields	7.39	8.55	10.07

Source: Morgan Guaranty Trust Co., *World Financial Markets,* November 1979, p. 15.

rise unexpectedly, borrowers gain at the expense of investors who have put up funds at low rates. If rates unexpectedly fall, investors win and borrowers lose, unless the borrowers are able to refinance expensive loans with lower cost loans.

To help control interest rate risk in Eurocredit markets, most loans are written at **floating rates.** The interest rate is set equal to the **London Interbank Offer Rate** LIBOR) (or its equivalent in other currency markets) plus a premium that reflects, among other things, the creditworthiness of the borrower. As general economic conditions vary, LIBOR moves up and down; with a floating rate loan, the interest rates that borrowers and lenders face move up and down as well. In this way the risk of interest rate changes is distributed between borrowers and lenders.

Currency risk exists because the currency of denomination of the loan or investment will vary in value. It has much the same effect as interest rate risk. If the currency in which borrowing takes place is devalued relative to other currencies, the borrower wins; if it is revalued, the lender wins.

Because **interest rate parity** (after adjustment for sovereign or political risk and transaction costs) generally prevails, the expected effect of currency risk is normally reflected in relative interest rates. Interest rates in currencies that are likely to be devalued relative to another currency tend to be higher by the amount that the financial market can best guess to be the possible magnitude of the devaluation.

DEFAULT RISK.   Default risk refers to the borrower's ability to meet interest and principal payments on schedule. Because the nature of a borrower's activity may change over time, default risk varies over the life of an investment. Through poor management a borrower who originally borrowed under favorable terms may increase the likelihood of default over the term of the loan; correspondingly, good management of an entity may reduce the likelihood of default over the life of the loan.

Interest rates are likely to vary directly with risk. Similarly, the maturity of a loan is likely to be negatively related to default risk. The less certain lenders are about an entity's prospects, the more likely are they to try to control the period of exposure by limiting the maturity of a loan.

EFFECTS OF RISK.   Exhibit 9 shows for a selected group of borrowers from various countries the weighted average spread over LIBOR and weighted average maturity of published Eurocredits during the first 9 months of 1979. It also shows the number of loans to each

EXHIBIT 9   RISKS ASSOCIATED WITH SELECTED COUNTRIES IN 1979

	Weighted Average Spread Above LIBOR	Average Maturity	Number of Loans in First 9 Months of 1979
France	0.480	10.7	3
China	0.500	5.0	3
United Kingdom	0.500	10.0	1
Denmark	0.596	9.3	4
Australia	0.612	11.5	2
Venezuela	0.777	5.1	14
Argentina	0.801	10.6	7
Mexico	0.811	7.6	25
U.S.S.R.	0.625	8.0	2
Hungary	0.651	8.5	2
Bulgaria	0.652	8.5	2
Iceland	0.670	10.0	3
Italy	0.673	7.2	12
Hong Kong	0.796	8.7	3
Spain	0.807	8.9	38
Yugoslavia	0.910	10.6	9
Brazil	0.997	11.1	20
Algeria	1.181	7.8	14
Pakistan	2.151	4.2	3

Source: Excerpted from *Euromoney*, October 1979, pp. 130–138.

country. The borrowers include privately and publicly owned corporations, government-owned organizations, and governments. There is not a great deal of comparability across countries, since the mixes of borrowers vary. Nonetheless, the exhibit does reveal the range of possible spreads on Eurocredits and the range of maturities that might prevail in loans to differentially risky borrowers. In the period evaluated, Pakistan was determined by the market to be the riskiest borrower, paying on average fully 215 basis points above LIBOR on loans with an average maturity of only 4.2 years. France appears to be one of the least risky, bearing spreads of less than 50 basis points and enjoying maturities of nearly 11 years.

Though lenders can insist on higher promised returns from lending to risky borrowers, just as they do in domestic financial markets, the recourse of lender in international markets is much more limited. With regard to nongovernment organizations, principally corporations, that default on loans, the legal processes necessary to recoup even partially through the takeover of assets is cumbersome and expensive. Concerning governments that default on loans, there is virtually nothing that private investors can do. In both instances, the investor (lender) must generally be satisfied with the knowledge that these entities will find borrowing difficult in the future.

Incidentally, international investors and lenders often press the **International Monetary Fund** (IMF) to invest in a country's government if the country goes into default or approaches default. The proceeds are not used to repay privately advanced loans; but since the IMF is the international lender of last resort, it is often able to impose conditions and economic restraints on the borrowing country that may enhance its ability to repay all its outstanding loans. This feature of IMF loans is known as **conditionality.** Furthermore, to avoid write-offs of bad loans to countries, banks often renegotiate the maturity of the loans in the hope that the longer term will enable borrowers to repay.

SOVEREIGN RISK. The most difficult sort of risk to analyze in international financial arrangements is **sovereign risk.** This is the risk that the government of the borrowing country will inhibit the flow of capital out of the country to repay loans. It also often entails the government's willful neglect in paying its own loans. Finally, it sometimes entails governmental prevention of investment in a country. In short, sovereign or political risk is a consequence of government power to hinder the free flow of capital among nations. It may or may not be correlated with economic conditions.

Sovereign risk takes four main forms: (*a*) outright limitations on the flow of capital among nations, (*b*) limitations on the conversion of domestic currencies into other currencies, (*c*) taxes that tend to separate or segment foreign from domestic money and capital markets, and (*d*) outright confiscation of domestic investment owned by foreigners.

Most often governments pursue these sorts of actions to prevent capital from flowing out of their countries, thus reducing downward pressure on their foreign exchange rate and upward pressure on domestic interest rates. Sometimes, however, governments impose such controls to inhibit capital inflows that would tend to raise the exchange rate, reduce domestic interest rates, and possibly increase internal inflationary pressures. Finally, from time to time governments simply act selectively for overt political reasons.

Capital Controls. Capital controls are typically designed to inhibit the flow of domestic capital abroad. Most analyses suggest that they do not work terribly well, but governments nonetheless continue to use them. The United States had a capital control program during the latter half of the 1960s and the early 1970s. It was aimed at reducing bank lending abroad and the movement of investment funds out of the country by **U.S. multinational corporations.** These measures were eliminated in 1974.

Some countries, surprisingly, impose controls on the inflow of capital. Certain financial instruments in West Germany cannot be purchased by foreigners. Germany also does not allow its companies to offer Euro-DM issues without approval of the Bundesbank. Switzerland also currently (1980) impedes foreign investment in that country in Swiss domestic securities.

Currency Controls. **Controls on foreign exchange** are quite common in major countries (the United Kingdom did not eliminate its most hindering controls until October 1979), and they are pervasive in most developing countries. The conversion of domestic currency into foreign currencies by private citizens is sometimes completely prohibited. Sometimes the rate of exchange is determined by the use to which the funds will be put; if the foreign currency is to be used to purchase industrial machinery for domestic use, the exchange rate will often be substantially more favorable than if the funds are to be used, say, to purchase equity securities in New York.

The present incidence and continuing prospect of currency controls makes international investing risky. Borrowers in a particular country may be able and willing to pay interest and principal, but they may be unable to obtain the currency with which to do it. Indeed, international investors face the risk that the returns earned from investments may not be readily converted to a desirable currency.

Taxes. Governments often attempt to drive wedges between international investment returns and domestic investment returns by imposing **differential taxes.** Countries that are trying to prevent the outflow of capital will tax foreign investment returns more heavily than domestic returns. For example, the United States imposed the **interest equalization tax** in the early 1960s. This was a special tax of 15% on the interest from foreign investments. (Canada and less developed countries, and international organizations such as the World Bank were exempt.) The interest was to stem the outflow of U.S. capital. This tax succeeded in allowing London to replace New York as the world's leading financial center and also succeeded in establishing the Bahamas as an important financial center. In the latter case, funds from the United States were permitted to flow to the Bahamas, where they could be invested at the discretion of the receiving banks. The tax was removed in 1974.

Countries that want to limit capital inflows will often impose withholding taxes on interest and dividend payments to foreign investors. This sort of tax makes investment in those countries comparatively less attractive.

There is an almost infinite variety of taxes and fees that governments can impose to hinder international financial market integration.

Confiscation.   Governments now and again confiscate or expropriate foreign investments in their countries. This is more often done for political than for economic reasons. For instance, in 1979 the U.S. government blocked all the official investments of the Iranian government in the United States. Thus Iran lost control over the use of the funds. Confiscation is the highest form of sovereign risk because when a government begins to confiscate, the investor is likely to wind up with absolutely nothing.

WORLD FINANCIAL CENTERS

LEADING SECURITIES EXCHANGES.   The **size of a domestic capital market** is an important statistic. The larger the size, the more liquid a capital market is likely to be. And the more liquid, the slighter will be the price impact on disruption in the market when a large transaction takes place. In large markets, large amounts can be raised or invested without noticeable impact.

Using this general criterion to define leading exchanges, Exhibit 10 lists the world's most important securities exchanges. It reports the total value of outstanding listed bonds and the total value of new issues of bonds in 1978 for the largest securities exchanges. It also shows the market value of listed equities on these exchanges. Finally, it shows the total value of listed foreign bonds and debentures and the issue volume for 1978. Of course, many of the securities sold within a country are not subsequently listed on exchanges; rather they are traded in over-the-counter markets. Nonetheless, the over-the-counter volume is likely to be highly correlated with the volume of listed securities.

The **relationship between foreign securities and domestic securities** is important as an indicator of the "openness" of various capital markets to foreign issues. The absolute **quantity of foreign securities** is also a telling piece of information. While such data reveal the receptiveness of countries to foreign securities, they tell very little about the receptiveness of the respective countries to **inflows** of foreign capital or investment of foreign funds in their securities.

A number of countries do not allow foreign issuers to sell securities to the public, but they do allow their banks and financial institutions to lend to foreigners or purchase foreign securities privately. These countries are typically most prone to official controls over foreign capital inflows and, particularly, to controls on outflows of domestic capital to foreign borrowers.

CONTROLS.   The openness of a country's capital markets generally depends on the country's current account balance and exchange rate policies. Some countries that have positive

EXHIBIT 10   VALUE OF LEADING WORLD SECURITY EXCHANGES
($ MILLIONS OF LISTED SECURITIES AS OF DECEMBER 31, 1978)

| | Outstanding Bonds and Debentures | | Par Value Newly Listed Bonds and Debentures in 1978 | | Market Value of Listed |
	Total	Foreign	Total	Foreign	Equities
American (AMEX)	4,850	327	441	70	39,200
Amsterdam	31,635	0	3,772	292	26,600
Basle	51,319	13,624	7,526	2,525	33,700
Brussels	46,408	0	10,067	0	12,500
German (all)	289,100	34,850	30,252	5,666	83,700
Geneva	43,171	13,424	6,767	2,509	33,800
Hong Kong	789	381	145	20	12,900
London	162,256	15,447	22,572	2,887	129,400
Luxembourg	39,876	39,021	5,026	4,944	1,000
Milan	93,190	7	54,859	0	9,800
New York (NYSE)	508,800	17,900	N.A.	N.A.	822,700
Osaka	173,723	1,670	52,550	722	293,800
Paris	83,105	0	14,015	0	45,400
Rome	87,008	2,251	21,857	0	8,200
Tokyo	177,935	5,454	54,127	3,779	342,000
Zurich	59,494	16,587	7,718	2,537	38,100

Source: Fédération Internationale des Bourses de Valeurs, *Statistical Data.*

current accounts do not want to experience the exchange rate appreciation that could result if they allowed free foreign investment in their countries. These countries may in fact encourage capital outflows investment by citizens abroad, while discouraging domestic investment by foreigners. Other countries that experience current account deficits but do not want their exchange rates to depreciate try to discourage the outflow of capital while encouraging inflows. All the encouragement and discouragement is accomplished through special taxes, formal and informal quantitative restrictions on capital flows, controls over foreign exchange, and interest rate policy.

MAJOR INTERNATIONAL CAPITAL MARKETS.   The leading international financial centers are New York, London, and Luxembourg. Switzerland, Germany, and Japan are important, but not of the same stature; this is by design, given the types of controls they use. France, Italy, and the Netherlands are reasonably active, but strong controls on international capital flows limit the significance of these international capital centers. Finally, Hong Kong, Singapore, Panama, and the Bahamas are emerging as important international centers.

New York.   At present, the United States has no restrictions on the international flow of capital. A large volume of funds for international use flows through New York commercial banks and investment banks. Most of the capital flowing abroad comes from the United States, and most flowing into the United States is invested in this country.

New York has not established itself as an **entrepôt** financial center, where deals with two foreign parties—investor and capital raiser—are consummated. Recent legislation in the State of New York, if allowed by the Federal Reserve Board, will create an **international banking tax haven** in New York, which would attract substantially more entrepôt activities.

Presently foreign issuers are free to sell stocks and bonds (these are called "Yankee bonds") in the United States and can borrow from the banking sector with no more difficulty than domestic firms have. Sellers of Yankee bonds face a somewhat higher investment banking spread than domestic firms face, namely 1.0% versus 0.875%. The **Securities and Exchange Commission** has equally stringent requirements for foreign issuers and domestic issuers. This is considered by many foreign borrowers as detrimental, given the costs of such registration and the disclosure of information on business activities that the SEC requires.

London.   Prior to October 1979, London was principally an **entrepôt financial center.** Exchange controls essentially put into effect by the British government in 1947 had stifled the flow of British capital abroad. But in October 1979 the government lifted them, retaining, of course, authority to impose controls during critical periods in the future.

Foreign borrowers wishing to obtain funds in London typically look to Euromarket capital, which is principally centered there. Before exchange controls were lifted there were no restrictions on the borrowers of foreign deposits, and presumably there will be no restrictions of any sort on foreign security offerings in the United Kingdom to domestic investors.

London was always, and will surely continue to be, receptive to foreign capital inflows. Foreigners can own stocks, bonds, or bank deposits.

Luxembourg.   The tiny country of Luxembourg is an international financial center of major proportions. It principally deals with Euro–DM, Euro–guilder, and Euro–Swiss franc securities. Few restrictions are currently placed on borrowing and investing in this market.

Many German banks have subsidiaries there. They were established primarily to circumvent restrictions imposed by the German banking authority. Recently, however, arrangements between German banking authorities and the banks have been made that give the Bundesbank, the German central bank, some measure of control over the activities of these banks.

Germany.   Germany has over the past decade enjoyed a chronic current account surplus. At the same time, it has tried to prevent capital inflows to limit the amount of appreciation in the DM relative to other currencies.

Germany has strict restrictions on the inflow of investment capital. Principally, these take the form of withholding taxes on interest income of nonresident investors in domestic securities. Other restrictions include the periodic declaring of **negative interest rates** on foreign DM deposits in German banks and prohibitions against the purchase of certain types of security.

The German authorities do allow foreigners to raise capital in the German market, but the amount is controlled. In addition, they authorize the sale of Euro-DM securities. Nonresident investors who purchase these DM-denominated securities issued by foreign borrowers are exempt from withholding taxes.

Switzerland.   Switzerland has over many years earned a well-deserved reputation as a country that understands how to manage its economy, with particular emphasis on the stability of its currency. As a consequence, during turbulent economic times Switzerland is viewed as a haven for capital. In response, Switzerland tightly controls capital inflows and outflows to limit the amount of appreciation in its currency and, not inconsequentially, to keep domestic inflation in check.

Switzerland allows foreign capital raising activities through the domestic sale of foreign bonds, private placements of foreign securities, and bank borrowing. The raising of capital, however, requires official approval. Foreign investment is very restricted. Foreigners can buy only foreign securities. Currently (1980) Swiss franc deposits by foreigners are subject to negative interest rates. These negative interest rates are imposed or lifted depending on the Swiss banking authority's interpretation of current domestic economic conditions.

Japan. Japan has been struggling with the idea of becoming an international financial center. Through various policy choices it has indicated ambivalence toward the notion. The country has not discouraged foreign investment, though there is a withholding tax on interest income that varies from 10 to 20% depending on the status of foreign investors. In recent years Japan has been more accommodating toward foreign borrowers, although it remains ambivalent toward foreign capital-raising activities. Foreign bonds sold in Japan are known as "samurai bonds."

Foreign-owned, but juridical Japanese corporations can qualify for subsidized government loans, though other foreign firms may experience credit rationing in the tightly organized Japanese market.

Emerging Centers. Singapore, Hong Kong, the Bahamas, and Panama have made the conscious decision to become international entrepôt centers. Within the past several years all have removed restrictions on international capital flows and altered tax codes, and have generally been receptive to foreign commercial and investment banking locations within their borders. These centers are principally entrepôt centers channeling money from developed countries to developing countries in their regions.

EXHIBIT 11   REPRESENTATIVE DEVELOPMENT BANKS

	Resources in 1978	Purpose
European Investment Bank	$4.82 billion (approx.)	Loans in the European Economic Committee
European Coal and Steel Community	N.A.	Coal and steel sectors
European Development Fund	$7.3 billion (approx.)	Sales financing to less developed countries
Andean Development Corporation	$400 million	Projects in Bolivia, Colombia, Ecuador, Peru, Venezuela
Caribbean Development Bank	$259.1 million	Projects in Caribbean
Inter-American Development Bank	$9.65 billion	Long-term loans in Latin America
Adela Investment Company	$544.9 million	Private firm that invests in Latin America
Central American Bank for Economic Integration	N.A.	Medium- and long-term credits
Asian Development Bank	$8.71 billion	Loans and equity investment
African Development Bank	$888 million (approx.)	Development in Africa
Arab Bank for Economic Development in Africa	$631 million (approx.)	Development in Africa (government loans)

Source: Business International Corporation, *Regional Development Banks,* May 1979, New York.

OFFICIAL INTERNATIONAL FINANCIAL INSTITUTIONS.   In addition to private markets for international capital, there are a variety of official institutions whose goal it is to supplement private capital markets, to invest in worthwhile development projects that cannot otherwise obtain funds.

The most important of these agencies is the **World Bank.** It consists of three separate financial institutions. The **International Bank for Reconstruction and Development** (IBRD) makes loans to developing countries for high-priority projects, offering interest rates and maturities at conventional terms. The **International Development Agency** (IDA) lends at concessionary terms to countries that might not be able to obtain funds otherwise. The **International Finance Corporation (IFC)** finances private sector investments with both debt and equity.

The IBRD lends only to governments, official institutions, and to the private sector, but only with the guarantee of the government. The IFC lends to private sector firms. At the end of June 1978, IBRD had loans outstanding equal to $6.1 billion, IDA had loans outstanding of $2.3 billion, and at the end of 1977, IFC had loans and equity investments of $980 million outstanding.

In addition to the giant World Bank, there are many other regional development banks and official (and semiofficial) financial institutions. Exhibit 11 lists some of the more important of these and shows estimates of the resources they control or have access to.

REFERENCES

Dufey, Gunter, and Giddy, Ian, *The International Money Market*, Prentice-Hall, Englewood Cliffs, NJ, 1977.

Lessard, Donald R., Ed., *International Financial Management: Theory and Applications*, Warren, Gorham, and Lamont, New York, 1979. (A book of readings.)

McKenzie, George W., *The Economics of the Euro-Currency System*, MacMillan, New York, 1976.

Mendelsohn, M. S., *Money on the Move*, McGraw-Hill, New York, 1979.

Stem, Carl H., Makin, John H., and Logue, Dennis E., Eds., *Eurocurrencies and the International Monetary System*, American Enterprise Institute, Washington, D.C., 1976.

These periodicals offer helpful current analysis and are excellent sources of data:

The Banker.   An excellent periodical analyzing international economic events, with a focus on the United Kingdom (London).

Business International Corporation, *Financing Foreign Operations* (New York). Periodically issued pamphlets on foreign money and capital markets, rich in detail and data.

Euromoney (London).   A monthly that is indispensable reading for the international financial executive.

International Currency Review (London).   An extremely analytical periodical that not only covers important international economic and political events, but also provides lengthy evaluations of the economic conditions in a wide variety of countries.

Morgan Guaranty Trust Co., New York, *World Financial Markets*.   A superb source for Euromarket data; also contains short articles on issues of interest.

INTERNATIONAL COMMERCIAL BANKING

CONTENTS

**INTERNATIONAL BANKING
ACTIVITIES** 3

Changes in the International Banking
Environment 5
Strategies for International Bank
Expansion 5

**ORGANIZING FOR INTERNATIONAL
BANKING** 9

Legal Versus Managerial Organization 9
Export Financing Department 9
International and Regional Departments 9
Service or Functional Organization 10
Global Customer Organization 11
Legal Entities for International Banking 12
Correspondent Banking 12
Foreign Branches 12
Representative Offices 12
Foreign Affiliates 13
Joint Banking Ventures and Consortia 13
Majority-Owned Banking Subsidiaries 14
Edge Act Subsidiaries 14

**THE FINANCING OF
INTERNATIONAL TRADE** 14

Problems and Risks of Export Financing 15
Financing by the Exporter 16
  Shipment on open book account 16
  Consignment 16
  Collection drafts 16
Financing by the Importer 17
  Payment with order 17
  Partial payment in advance 17
  Payment on documents 19
Financing by the Exporter's Bank 19
  Advance on drafts 19

Discount of drafts 19
Refinancing bill 19
Financing by the Importer's Bank **19**
  Commercial letter of credit 20
  Import and export letters of credit 22
  Revocable and irrevocable letters of
  credit 22
  Confirmed and unconfirmed letters of
  credit 23
  Revolving letter of credit 23
  Assignable letter of credit 24
  Authority to purchase 24
  Documents attached to draft 24
Public Sources of Export Financing **25**
U.S. Export-Import Bank **25**

**FOREIGN EXCHANGE AND
INTERNATIONAL PAYMENTS** **26**

The Foreign Exchange Market **26**
Types of Foreign Exchange Transactions:
Spot, Forward, and Swap **27**
Quotation of Rates **28**
Forward Exchange Rates **29**
Covered Interest Arbitrage **30**
Mechanics of International Payments **31**

INTERNATIONAL LENDING **32**

Borrowers from International Banks **33**
Eurocurrency Lending Practices **33**
  Unbundling of services **34**
  Loan syndication **35**
Eurocurrency Loan Pricing: Rollover
Credits **37**
Loan Agreement Provisions **38**
Swaps, Credit Swaps, and Parallel Loans **39**
Eurobanking Risk Protection **40**

FUNDING IN INTERNATIONAL
BANKING   **40**

Funding in the Eurocurrency Market   **40**
Eurobank Liability Management   **41**
Interbank Lines of Credit   **41**
Euromarket Funding Instruments   **42**
Onshore Versus Offshore Funding   **43**

INTERNATIONAL BANKING
REGULATIONS   **44**

U.S. Regulation of American Banks
Abroad   **45**
U.S. Regulation of Foreign Banks   **45**
Other Countries' Regulation of Foreign
Banks   **51**

INTERNATIONAL COMMERCIAL BANKING

Ian N. Giddy

INTERNATIONAL BANKING ACTIVITIES

The present **international banking system** is without precedent both in size and in character. The system has its origins in the global expansion of corporations during the 1960s. Today's international banking system constitutes a wide-ranging network of deposit and ownership linkages around the world, and as a result, banks can easily move money from one country to another, and from one currency to another. The **growth and spread of international banking** is shown most clearly in:

1. The number of countries that admit foreign bank offices.
2. The greatly increased number of foreign banks in traditional financial centers such as London and New York, and newer centers such as Singapore.
3. The growth of the Eurodollar banking market.
4. The growth in foreign exchange trading.

Almost all the banks that dominate the world of international commercial banking come from the large industrial countries with well-developed monetary systems. In these countries, multinational corporate expansion has been accompanied by the expansion of **multinational banks.** Their success depends not only on their size, skills, and aggressiveness, but also on the degree of support extended by the parent bank's monetary authorities. Exhibit 1 lists the world's 30 biggest banks, at the start of 1980, based on a compilation from *The Banker,* annually. The reader should be aware that some of these banks, despite their size, do not have extensive international activities; Crédit Agricole, for example, is almost entirely a domestic French bank.

The primary activities of international banks are the same as those for domestic banks: receiving deposits and making loans. The difference is that the deposit and loan business is often done with foreign depositors and borrowers, usually booked in a foreign location, and sometimes denominated in a foreign currency. In addition to these three differences, multinational banks engage in certain unique functions, such as export-import financing and documentation, foreign exchange trading, Eurocurrency borrowing and lending, and international payments clearing. Moreover, the difference between commercial and investment banking is blurred in the international context; hence U.S. commercial banks engage in

EXHIBIT 1   THE WORLD'S 30 BIGGEST BANKS, 1979

Rank by Assets	Bank	Location
1	Crédit Agricole	Avignon
2	Bank of America	San Francisco
3	Citibank	New York
4	Banque Nationale de Paris	Paris
5	Deutsche Bank	Frankfurt
6	Crédit Lyonnais	Paris
7	Société Générale	Paris
8	Dresdner Bank	Frankfurt
9	Barclays Bank	London
10	Dai-Ichi Kangyo Bank	Tokyo
11	National Westminster Bank	London
12	Chase Manhattan Bank	New York
13	Westdeutsche Landesbank Girozentrale	Düsseldorf
14	Fuji Bank	Tokyo
15	Commerzbank	Frankfurt
16	Sumitomo Bank	Osaka
17	Mitsubishi Bank	Tokyo
18	Sanwa Bank	Osaka
19	Norinchukin Bank	Tokyo
20	Banco do Brasil	Brasilia
21	Bayerische Vereinsbank	Munich
22	Industrial Bank of Japan	Tokyo
23	Banca Nazionale del Lavoro	Rome
24	Manufacturers Hanover Trust Co.	New York
25	Cooperatieve Centrale	Utrecht
26	Midland Bank	London
27	Amsterdam-Rotterdam Bank	Amsterdam
28	Swiss Bank Corp.	Basel
29	J. P. Morgan Bank	New York
30	Bayerische Landesbank Girozentrale	Munich

Source: The Banker, "The Top 500 in World Banking," June 1980.

activities such as bond underwriting abroad that they are not able to do at home. For example, Chemical Bank described its **international activities** in its 1979 Annual Report as follows:

> International services include bank, business and government loans and deposits, correspondent banking arrangements, letters of credit, acceptances, collections, leasing, foreign exchange and Eurocurrency activities, cash management and merchant banking.

The same bank's **merchant banking activities** are described more specifically as follows:

> Syndicated lending, international bond financing, private placement, distribution and trading of international securities, government-sponsored export financing, project financing, corporate financing, and merger and aquisition advisory services.

This section surveys commercial rather than merchant banking activities as well as the legal and regulatory environment faced by international banks.

CHANGES IN THE INTERNATIONAL BANKING ENVIRONMENT. The character of international banking underwent rapid changes during the 1960s and 1970s. Many banks entered international activities for the first time during these decades, and those that were already international expanded the range and size of their international activities. These banks encountered an environment that was altering several ways, including:

1. The move from fixed to **floating exchange rates.**
2. The removal of many **controls** on the flow of funds between countries.
3. The development of the **Eurocurrency market.**
4. The need for foreign exchange trading, hedging, and advisory services by **multinational corporations** faced with the possibility of exchange losses.

These elements gave rise to new opportunities, but may also have encouraged an excessively rapid expansion abroad by many American and non-American banks. By the end of 1974 a number of banks had failed, and several major rescues were engineered by the central banks of the United States, Germany, and the United Kingdom. Exhibit 2 lists a number of banks that faced problems during this period. Subsequently, bank managers have engaged in international expansion in a more cautious fashion, seeking the proper match between customer needs, regulatory opportunities and constraints, and the banks' own strengths before choosing the degree and form of international involvement.

Apart from foreign exchange-related losses, international banks have recently experienced problems such as inept and fraudulent management, inadequate controls and guidelines from headquarters, the difficulties associated with lending to sovereign borrowers, overconcentration of lending, maturity mismatching during periods of volatile interest rates, and the unavoidable exposure of the international banker to global political and economic events. In many respects today's environment is more conducive to international banking: capital controls have been reduced, central banks provide more support and exercise more well-informed control, and communications and management information have improved. The same factors, however, make it easier for inexperienced management to enter international banking more rapidly. This was the source of the relatively high incidence of international banking problems during the 1970s.

STRATEGIES FOR INTERNATIONAL BANK EXPANSION. Banks can engage in international banking activities in two ways: from their home countries, or abroad. Much of traditional international banking could be carried out without ever establishing a foreign office, since the principal activities of international banking have long been the **financing of exports and imports** and the effecting and clearing of international payments. Both of these require no more international presence than the establishment of **correspondent balance** relationships with foreign banks.

More recently, many banks with little or no international involvement have found it advantageous to create offshore branches in low-tax and low-regulation jurisdiction such as the Bahamas, the Cayman Islands, or Singapore, to take advantage of the absence of reserve requirements and certain other regulatory constraints.

In a 1978 survey of senior international bank managers, Steven Davis sought to identify the most important facets of **long-term international banking strategy.** By far the most frequently mentioned competitive strategy was **speed and flexibility of decision making.** Other strategies accorded top priority included specialist expertise, the existence of a large customer base, and the ability to commit relatively large amounts of funds. Canadian and

EXHIBIT 2 INTERNATIONAL BANKING PROBLEMS IN 1974

Bank	Total Assets[a]	Losses[a,b]	Cause
I. D. Herstatt (Germany)	DM2,075m ($807m)	DM1,200m + ($467m +) (P)	Foreign exchange losses
Hessische Landesbank Girozentrale (Germany)	DM34,396m	DM800m ($311m) (K)	Losses incurred by subsidiary on industrial loans
Banca Privata Italiana (Italy)		L170,000m ($254m) (E)	Withdrawal of deposits following collapse of Franklin National Bank, whose chief shareholder, Michele Sindona, also owns Banca Privata
Bau-Kredit Bank (Germany)	DM600m ($233m)	DM456m ($177m) (K)	Losses incurred on loan to bankrupt building firm
Union Bank of Switzerland (Switzerland)	SF40,479m ($14,007m)	$150m (E)	Foreign exchange losses
U.S. National Bank of San Diego (United States)	$1,200m	$45m (K) $98m (P)	Allegedly fraudulent loans to associated companies
Westdeutsche Landesbank Girozentrale (Germany)	DM54,000m ($21,012m)	DM270m ($105m) (K)	Foreign exchange losses
Lloyds Bank International (United Kingdom)	£7,586m ($17,675m) (Group Figure)	£33m ($77m) (K)	Foreign exchange losses
Franklin National Bank (United States)	$5,007m (Group figure)	$59m (K)	Foreign exchange losses
J. H. Vavasseur & Co (United Kingdom)	£51m ($119m) (Group figure)	£17·9m ($42m) (K)	Domestic liquidity squeeze; fall in value of share and property investments
Scottish Co-operative Wholesale Society Ltd, Bankers (United Kingdom)		£3·6m ($8m) (K) £12·9m ($30m) (P)	Losses on forward dealings in sterling CD market
London & County Securities Group (United Kingdom)	£129m ($301m) (Group figure)	£16m ($37m) (P)	Fall in share and property values prompted withdrawal of interbank deposits
Chase Manhattan Bank (United States)	$36,791m	$34m (K)	Overvaluation of bond trading portfolio

Triumph Investment Trust (United Kingdom)	£153m ($356m) (Group figure)	£9·7m ($23m) (K)	Domestic liquidity squeeze
Cedar Holdings (United Kingdom)	£147m ($343m) (Group figure)	£0·19 ($0·44m) (K)	Domestic liquidity squeeze
Banque de Bruxelles (Belgium)	BF302,000m ($7,865m) (Group figure)	£8·8m ($21m) (P) BF600m–1,500m ($16m–39m) (E)	Foreign exchange losses
Banco Halles (Brazil)	Cr3,860m ($560m)	Unknown	Domestic liquidity squeeze
International Credit Bank (Switzerland)	SF651m ($225m)	Unknown	Withdrawal of deposits and bank credits following uncertainty about bank's future
Cannon Street Acceptances (United Kingdom)	£62m ($144m)	Unknown	Domestic liquidity squeeze; falling investment values
Israel-British Bank, London (United Kingdom)	£59m ($137m)	Unknown	Collapse of parent company, Israel-British Bank
Israel-British Bank (Israel)	IL524m ($125m)	Unknown	Post–Herstatt international liquidity squeeze
Cosmos Bank (Switzerland)	SF185m ($64m)	Unknown	Post–Herstatt international liquidity squeeze
Interbank House Group (including International Bank of Grand Cayman and Sterling Bank & Trust) (Cayman Islands)	$45m (Group figure)	Unknown	Post–Herstatt international liquidity squeeze
Bass und Herz Bank (Germany)	DM70m ($27m)	Unknown	Domestic liquidity squeeze
Bankhaus Wolff (Germany)	DM55m ($21m)	Unknown	Domestic liquidity squeeze
Frankfurter Handelsbank (Germany)	DM14m ($5m)	Unknown	Large stake held by Michele Sindona (chief shareholder of Franklin National Bank) aggravated liquidity pressures

[a]Figures in local currency converted into dollars at exchange rates prevailing mid-October, 1975.
[b]Key: P = possible losses, K = known losses, E = estimated losses.
Source: The Banker, 1975.

other foreign banks differed from U.S. banks in their strong emphasis on a large existing customer base. As Davis pointed out, this reflects the historical relatively defensive objectives of many European and other banks in protecting their customer base from the assault of U.S. banks and the latters' relative lack of such a base. (See Steven I. Davis, *The Management* Function in *International Banking*.)

International involvement permits a commercial bank to take advantage abroad of skills and resources developed at home. These include **existing customers, geographic location, industry expertise, existing services,** and **loyal depositors.** Such resources must be sufficient to enable the bank to compete against the foreign competition it may encounter, and to overcome the special risks and costs arising from crossing national boundaries and entering unfamiliar banking environments. It follows that the bank's management should choose a strategy for international expansion that concentrates on the activities in which the bank possesses a special advantage, and employs the form of involvement that minimizes the costs of banking abroad.

A domestic bank entering international banking has the advantage of familiarity with the needs of existing customers. To capitalize on this familiarity with only moderate international involvement, a bank will normally begin its international involvement in one of two ways:

1. By extending **letters of credit** and **export or import financing** for existing customers' international trade financing needs.
2. By establishing a **nominal** or **"shell" branch** in an offshore banking center.

Once a bank develops familiarity with trade credit or offshore (Eurocurrency) deposit taking, it can extend its scope into the foreign exchange area. Customers will frequently require foreign exchange for overseas purchases, and a hedge or cover for their foreign exchange risk. The bank should therefore develop a facility in buying or selling foreign exchange in the spot and forward foreign exchange market. At some point the bank will have sufficient international business and experience to be ready to establish a full-fledged overseas branch. The most common locations for such branches are London, New York (for non-U.S. banks), Singapore, and Hong Kong. Typically such branches engage in trade financing participation in **loan syndications, interbank trading of dollar** and **foreign currency deposits, foreign exchange trading,** and **corporate advisory services.** They may also serve as a useful source of funds or as a repository of funds for the parent bank.

Many American banks have followed their initial establishment of a foreign presence by setting up other branches and/or **Edge Act subsidiaries.** Edges, as they are called, enable U.S. banks to have offices in other states for international banking activities, and in other countries to engage in activities not permitted at home.

At this point the bank can be said to have a limited international banking network, and such a network is sufficient for most banks' purposes. Some banks, however, have developed a degree of business with foreign firms or governments that warrants their presence, in the form of **representative offices, agencies,** or **branches,** in certain host country banking markets. Later they have sought further penetration by buying partial or whole **equity participation in a local financial institution.** Indeed the latter activity has proved to be the most effective way of penetrating the local currency banking market.

Few banks have a truly **global network of branches and affiliates** in a large number of countries. Such a network brings many benefits in the form of on-the-spot knowledge and the ability to service the worldwide needs of multinational corporations, but it is costly and gradual and subjects banks to the vagaries of capital controls, economic nationalism, and other forms of business and political risk. Only three American banks (Bank of America, Citibank, and Chase Manhattan Bank) have such a multinational network, and only a few foreign banks do—primarily those from countries with colonial histories.

ORGANIZING FOR INTERNATIONAL BANKING

LEGAL VERSUS MANAGERIAL ORGANIZATION.   The back pages of any large U.S. bank's annual report will provide the reader with an idea of the complex and diverse forms of legal organization employed by multinational banks. One should not be deceived, however, into thinking that the legal entities reflect the true organization of the bank. The **legal organization** is designed to minimize taxes, reserve requirements, and constraints on activities and to conform with government requirements. The **managerial organization** is concerned with who makes decisions and how they are communicated and implemented, how controls are exercised, and how line and staff functions relate to each other. It is concerned with the **translation of strategy into revenues,** with the allocation of responsibility, accountability and rewards.

The **managerial organization** of international banking can be **geographical,** the prototype being a division between domestic and international banking. On the other hand, many banks have found more logic in **structuring responsibility by service** or **function;** and a few have geared their organizations to **groups of customers,** worldwide.

EXPORT FINANCING DEPARTMENT.   The early entry of many American banks into international business was in the form of a rather passive response to the financing needs of their customers entering international markets. The **export financing group** was regarded as an eccentric, specialist bunch playing, at best, a supporting role. Services included collections, letters of credit, and the provision of foreign exchange; the only international expansion was the establishment of correspondent relationships with individual banks abroad. Being a passive service organization dealing primarily with foreign banks, the group and its head tended to be removed from the mainstream of corporate deposit and lending activities and from the bank's management team.

INTERNATIONAL AND REGIONAL DEPARTMENTS.   Later, many banks found that the establishment of specific entities or representative offices abroad was necessary to service customers' growing international facilities and to draw on the foreign exchange and deposit resources of the international money market. Foreign exchange trading and directly solicited loan business warranted the establishment of a specific organization to handle the increasingly varied international business. It is now acknowledged that the nature of financing international transactions is unique enough to justify creation of a separate international banking department: procedures, terminology, and legal regulations differ markedly from those of domestic banking. In addition, the profits realized through international banking activity have grown to such an extent that for internal accounting purposes a separate international department is warranted.

The activities of such a department encompass the following: issuing letters of credit and bank acceptances, offering forward exchange contracts, serving as collecting agents for drafts drawn by exporters and others, buying and selling foreign exchange, and lending to exporters, overseas subsidiaries, local foreign firms, governments and government agencies, and financial institutions. In addition, international departments act in more informal ways. They provide customers with information on exchange rates, foreign credit, and trade; advise them

**EXHIBIT 3   INTERNATIONAL DIVISION AND REGIONAL STRUCTURE FOR A
TYPICAL AMERICAN BANK**

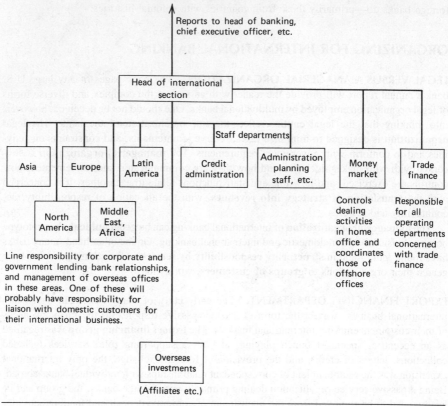

Source: Steven I. Davis, *The Managerial Function in International Banking*, Halsted, New York,
1977, p. 49.

on accounting and related problems stemming from foreign exchange, and assist them in the
development of foreign trade.

The **geographically divided organizational form** evolved from the international division
for banks that declined to undertake a radical shift in organizational form. This traditional
form of organization implicitly assumes that particular regions, such as the Far East or
Latin America, have more in common for bank management than do services offered or
global customer relationships. A typical American bank's regional structure is depicted in
Exhibit 3.

SERVICE OR FUNCTIONAL ORGANIZATION.   Because of the openness of their economies and the relative thinness of their capital markets, many Japanese and continental
European banks supplement a limited international department with other functionally oriented departments that have global rather than domestic responsibilities. During the 1970s
a number of American banks placed their domestic and international **treasury functions**
under a single department, and integrated bond, money market, and foreign exchange trading

in a single room. A service or functional organization is geared to particular functions of the banks, such as money dealing, bond underwriting, or data processing. Functions that are staff related, such as planning, or functions that possess other indivisible features, such as transfers, must serve the global bank. In European banks, such functions as customer lending and treasury dealing are centralized on a bankwide basis, rather than falling under the international department. The latter may be charged chiefly with trade financing and international correspondent relationships. Exhibit 4 illustrates a typical functionally oriented managerial structure.

GLOBAL CUSTOMER ORGANIZATION.   Recognizing the integration of domestic and foreign markets and the global nature of many of their multinational customers, several U.S. banks have abandoned the traditional distinction between domestic and international banking and sought to gear their respective organizations to **customer types.** Thus a single industry group or specialist might service a particular multinational firm's worldwide financing needs. Other groups might be oriented to purely domestic entities, or to foreign governments. On the other hand, since geographical or functional expertise often is required to supplement the customer-oriented group, a geographic and/or service-oriented group of specialists interacts with the customer specialists to provide needed support. This approach is particularly suited to **multinational corporations** whose own treasury management function has become globally centralized.

EXHIBIT 4   TYPICAL FUNCTIONAL STRUCTURE FOR INTERNATIONAL BANKING

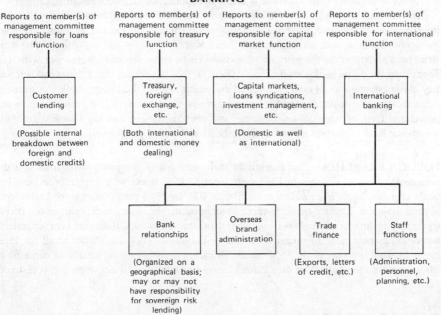

Source: Steven I. Davis, *The Managerial Function in International Banking,* Halsted, New York, 1977, p. 50.

LEGAL ENTITIES FOR INTERNATIONAL BANKING. There are various legal forms by which U.S. commercial banks can participate in international activities. The legal entities chosen will depend on the degree to which the bank seeks to become involved in such activities. If a minimal presence is desired, a bank may simply maintain a correspondent relationship with a local foreign bank. Total presence would necessitate the establishment of a branch or subsidiary office. The following lists the full range of options:

1. Correspondent banking relationships.
2. Representative office.
3. Minority foreign affiliate.
4. Joint banking ventures and consortia.
5. Branch office.
6. Majority foreign subsidiary.
7. Edge Act subsidiary.

CORRESPONDENT BANKING. Most of the major domestic and foreign banks maintain a two-way channel of "correspondence" through cable and mail, specifying activities to be undertaken and fees to be charged. **Correspondent banks** typically maintain deposit balances with one another. The services provided via this channel concentrate on the collection or payment of foreign funds stemming from import-export transactions. They include accepting drafts, providing credit information, and honoring letters of credit. In addition, the correspondent banking network is used to invest funds in short-term foreign government securities and money market instruments. While neither of the correspondent banks maintains its own personnel in the other country, there is direct but limited contact between managements.

The **advantage** provided by the correspondent bank network of an international bank is the provision of services in whatever country the correspondent is located, by knowledgeable, indigenous bankers, well acquainted with their country's customs and regulations. The main **drawback**, however, is the inability of a customer to make deposits, borrow, or withdraw funds from the home bank's own offices. There is, too, the chance that a correspondent will pay closer attention to its own established customers than to the foreign bank's customers. Nevertheless, the maintenence of overseas correspondent balances is a prerequisite to any substantial form of international banking, and even the largest and most sophisticated international banks maintain numerous correspondent banking relationships.

FOREIGN BRANCHES. The **foreign branch network of international banks** is a development of recent vintage. In 1965 there were 13 U.S. banks with foreign branches. Ten years later that figure had swelled to more than 100; by 1980 such offices abroad numbered several thousand. Legally speaking these branches function as an integral part of the parent bank: they are an extension of the bank rather than separate entities. Books are kept separately, but branches hold none of their own assets or liabilities. They are subject to all the legal encumbrances applying to the U.S. banks. Branches do enjoy the advantage of name identification with the parent, but they cannot engage in nonfinancial activities and investment banking.

REPRESENTATIVE OFFICES. This form of presence involves the posting of one or more individuals in a foreign host country to represent the parent bank's interests, to serve a very limited range of clients' needs, and to seek out new business opportunities. **No banking**

business is transacted by representative offices, and under U.S. law they have no formal authority to bind the head office to any contractual obligation.

Such offices provide certain **advantages.** First, their existence does not pose a threat to correspondent relationships previously established. Indeed, by directing clients to local banks for needed services, representatives could enhance and solidify existing correspondent relationships. Second, under host country law, the head office is not deemed to be "present" for the purpose of being sued, or taxed in the host country on global earnings. Third, because of its familiarity with foreign and domestic operations, a representative office is in a better position than say, a correspondent, to determine rapidly and precisely the type of information the head office or a client may need. Fourth, a representative may leave the host country, if necessary, to arrange transactions in a third country where the head office maintains no presence. Should a head office decide that a branch office is needed in the host country, the representative is available to oversee its establishment.

The **drawbacks** to this form of representation are largely attributable to the limited nature of its activities. The need to rely on local institutions can lead to unwieldy transactions. Also, because many decisions must be referred back to headquarters, delays are inevitable. Representative offices are small, thus staff members are physically limited in the amount of work they can assume. Accordingly, the research produced may lack the precision and scope that a large staffed organization might provide.

Nonetheless, as a "listening post," or as an "ambassador of goodwill," the representative office well suits the objectives of certain U.S. commercial banks that seek a presence abroad, but not a deep commitment.

FOREIGN AFFILIATES.   A number of U.S. commercial banks have found it advantageous to acquire an **equity interest in a foreign bank.** This is accomplished by outright purchase of voting shares in an existing bank or by setting up a new bank and retaining a minority voting stock interest. With the former method, controlling interest remains in the hands of the person(s) who controlled the bank prior to the stock purchase. The latter method places controlling interest in local hands, with the U.S. bank, or with a third party.

The activities undertaken by affiliated banks are the same as those undertaken by indigenous banks. Often an affiliated bank will also perform all or most correspondent services needed by the U.S. parent. The advantages to this form of banking stem from the fact that the institution is not "foreign" in the host country—it is staffed with nationals, and all its contacts with the local population are through them. If the institution existed prior to the affiliation, it will also benefit from its former reputation. There are of course, disadvantages. Frequently the U.S. presence, however discrete, is construed by local banking interests as an intrusion. Because the U.S. bank does not exercise controlling interest, its recommendations may be ignored or vetoed by local shareholders.

JOINT BANKING VENTURES AND CONSORTIA.   **Joint ventures** are associations, often for a finite period of time, of two or more banks seeking to pool efforts toward a particular task. This might be a risky project or one beyond their normal scope of activity. The banks bound together in joint ventures provide technical or financial services for each other or explore uncharted areas of development. Typical projects include construction of motorways and hydroelectric facilities; or the result of a joint venture would be an affiliated bank with distinguishing nonlocal characteristics.

Prominent U.S. banks have been invited to join **consortium banks,** which are joint ventures separately owned and incorporated by two or more parent banks of different nationality. The consortium banks service the clients of the parents and also actively develop new business. Activities include the arrangement of global syndicates for very large or very long-term loans; underwriting and distribution of corporate securities; and involvement in mergers and acquisitions. Located in **major banking capitals,** these consortia are more permanent than joint ventures and, as multinational organizations, are unfettered by central bank controls.

MAJORITY-OWNED BANKING SUBSIDIARIES.   While similar to the affiliated bank by virtue of its local charter in the host country, the subsidiary is distinguished by its nonlocal ownership. The key legal difference between the two is that the U.S. parent bank exerts controlling interest in its subsidiary. As a separate corporation, however, the banking subsidiary must adhere to all local laws. Because it is often perceived as a local bank by the host population, it is more likely than a branch office to participate in both domestic and international business. Subsidiaries are often established where host country laws prohibit branch banking.

One disadvantage of the subsidiary form is that, being a separately incorporated legal entity, its obligations are not automatically the liability of the parent bank. This may make it more difficult or costly to raise funds, even though the parent would ordinarily stand behind the credit of all subsidiaries. On the other hand, the parent bank may have good reason for wishing to limit its direct liabilities.

EDGE ACT SUBSIDIARIES.   Passed in 1919, the **Edge Act** permitted U.S. banks to transact international business from U.S. offices, and to engage in certain banking and investment activities not otherwise permissible in the United States. Subsidiaries are restricted to dealings with overseas or multinational clients exclusively.

Edge Act subsidiaries are particularly useful in **serving large multinational companies.** When established in several different U.S. cities, they can increase competitive pressures on other U.S. banks. For example, a California state-chartered bank can set up an Edge Act bank in New York City. Although restricted to international operations, Edge Act subsidiaries can accept deposits related to such operations, refer new customers to the parent, and obtain new international business in unchartered states.

Overseas Edge Act subsidiaries are permitted by the **Federal Reserve Board** to engage in activities common in foreign countries but not possible for U.S. banks. This factor, plus the Edge Act bank's separate corporate structure, and its ability to be located outside the parent's state of incorporation, make such subsidiaries valuable to many U.S. banks.

Under the **International Bank Act of 1978,** the restrictions on the capitalization and geographical expansion of Edge Act subsidiaries was eased by the Federal Reserve Board. In addition, foreign banks with U.S. branches were permitted to establish **out-of-state Edge Act subsidiaries.**

THE FINANCING OF INTERNATIONAL TRADE

International trade financing, one of the oldest functions of commercial banks, is also one of the least glamorous. Nevertheless, for the majority of firms engaged in international business, export financing forms the core of international finance. While the techniques are standardized, the range of applications is as varied as the content and destinations of a nation's exports, and things can easily go wrong. If managed properly, therefore, export-import financing can be one of the most profitable of a bank's international activities. Exhibit 5 provides a list of typical export-related services provided by commercial banks.

EXHIBIT 5   BANK SERVICES TO EXPORTERS

Collecting drafts (outgoing and incoming)
Granting advances to exporters
Discounting drafts
Opening credit lines
Opening letters of credit (for importers)
Confirming letters of credit (acting for foreign banks)
Negotiating letters of credit
Creating bankers' acceptances
Collecting payments for creditors from foreign debtors
Opening accounts for customers in foreign branches or banks abroad in which export proceeds may be
   collected (e.g., Eurodollar accounts)
Buying and selling foreign currencies and making foreign remittances
Extending loans against merchandise in warehouses or in transit
Providing credit information on foreign buyers
Providing services incidental to export transactions, such as on customs, interest rates, and collection
   experience

PROBLEMS AND RISKS OF EXPORT FINANCING.   The first basic problem of export
financing is that payment must involve conversion from one currency to another, and between
one jurisdiction and another. The second basic problem is that payment must be made at a
distance, and across time, so that the exporter, the importer, or both, need credit during part
or all of the period from the initial manufacture of the goods by the exporting firm, through
to the time of final sale and collection by the importer.

The first task for the export financier is to establish a means for making **international
payments.** This is done through the foreign exchange market, addressed later. The second
is to provide the requisite financing in an appropriate form. The third is to identify and
manage the several risks that may or may not accompany a particular trade financing deal.
Among these risks are:

1. Credit risk.
2. Convertibility risk.
3. Currency risk.
4. Interest rate risk.
5. Collateral risk.

In **international trade financing,** a bank may issue a letter of credit to an importer, or
confirm a letter of credit issued by a foreign bank, or provide a loan directly to the exporter.
Credit risk arises from the provision of loans or guarantees to the importer or exporter to
a foreign bank.

When a domestic bank confirms a letter of credit issued by a foreign bank, the foreign
government might impose exchange controls that prevent the foreign bank from meeting its
obligations in foreign currencies. The domestic bank thus faces a risk termed **"convertibility
risk."**

Currency risk arises when a bank holds an acceptance (an asset) denominated in a foreign
currency, or when the bank issues a letter of credit (a liability) in favor of a customer making
payment in a foreign currency. Normally, a bank may offset the curency risk of an asset

(future cash inflow) in a foreign currency by selling the foreign currency in the forward market, (i.e., contracting for a future cash outflow). The same **"hedging" effect** may be achieved by borrowing in the same currency as the bank's asset (again, contracting for a future cash outflow to match the future cash inflow in the foreign currency).

Interest rate risk arises when the bank holds in its portfolio an asset, such as a **discounted acceptance,** without having a corresponding fixed interest liability of the same maturity. This is the normal risk of **maturity mismatching** in a bank's portfolio.

Since export financing is normally collateralized by the goods being shipped, **collateral risk** arises from the possibility that the bank financing itself will incur expense and difficulty trying to sell the goods in a market with which it has little familiarity. The collateral risk can be shifted back to the exporter by discounting an acceptance with recourse.

The reader new to this field will no doubt find many of the terms used above somewhat unfamiliar. Not to worry: descriptions of most standard trade financing techniques are provided.

FINANCING BY THE EXPORTER. There are various methods by which the exporter may finance his transactions.

Shipment on Open Book Account. If an exporter has maintained business relations with an importer over a number of years and the credit standing and good faith of the importer are unquestionable, the exporter may agree to sell on an open account basis, as in domestic trade. Such an arrangement is extremely advantageous to the importer because it permits him to receive the goods and even sell them before making payment. The exporter runs the risk that in time of stress the importer may give preference to pressing domestic obligations, and efforts to collect by legal proceedings may prove difficult and expensive. Banks may be willing to grant exporters loans on the evidence of the sales contract and shipment of the goods.

Consignment. An exporter may ship goods to his branch, agency, or resident salesman abroad and order sale of the goods while in transit or upon arrival at a fixed or the best obtainable price. Proceeds from the sale are remitted to the exporter in his currency. The exporter then not only ties up his funds until the goods are sold and paid for, but also assumes the exchange risk.

Collection Drafts. An exporter draws a draft on the importer at the time of shipment. Depending on the credit terms specified in the sales contract, the draft, drawn either in the exporter's or importer's currency as agreed, may be either sight or time, clean, or documentary. A **sight draft** is payable on presentation, whereas a **time draft** is payable either at a specified future date or at a certain period after sight. A **clean draft** is drawn by an exporter to collect an amount due from an importer for a shipment of goods. Such a draft is not accompanied by documents and is used when the exporter has complete confidence in the integrity of the importer. Banks generally do not discount clean drafts unless the credit rating of the exporter warrants it.

A **documentary draft** is accompanied by documents conveying title to the goods and may be either a **D/P draft** (documents against payment) or a **D/A draft** (documents against acceptance). In a D/P draft the exporter turns over the draft, together with the documents, to his bank for collection, with instructions not to release the documents to the importer until the draft is paid; in a D/A draft the bank is ordered to withhold documents until the importer has accepted the draft. The accepted draft—called **trade acceptance**—becomes a ''clean'' bill.

The exporter retains control of the goods when he employs a documentary draft, because the importer cannot obtain shipping documents from the collecting bank until he pays or accepts the draft. If a clean draft is used, the importer can secure the merchandise upon arrival of the documents by mail, even though the draft still has a period to run.

If the distance between the exporter and importer is great, and the draft and annexed documents sent by mail steamer or air mail will reach their destination long before the goods arrive, it is customary to allow the importer to postpone payment or acceptance of the draft until the goods have arrived.

A bank that undertakes the service of collection must receive detailed **instructions from the exporter** (drawer) so that it may protect his interests in accordance with the sales contract. The instructions are given on a printed form supplied by the bank (see Exhibit 6). The instructions given in each instance are determined by the sales contract, the policy of the exporter, and any special requirements of the moment. Since the bank must follow instructions explicitly, it is advisable that the exporter designate a representative located near the importer (drawee), with instructions ''in case of need, refer to.'' This **local representative** knows the exporter's policies, and reference to him implies that he may be trusted by the bank to modify original instructions to meet emergencies.

The exporter's bank forwards the draft and documents with the exporter's instructions to its branch or correspondent bank in the country of the importer. Upon receipt of payment from the importer the foreign bank remits the funds to the exporter's bank, which in turn makes them available to the exporter. In case of a D/A draft, the **correspondent bank** will hand over the documents to the importer upon his acceptance of the draft. On the due date, the correspondent bank presents the acceptance to the importer, and when it is paid remits the amount to the exporter's bank. Although the exporter's bank selects the correspondent abroad, the latter acts as the agent of the exporter and not of the bank. Should the correspondent bank become insolvent or bankrupt before it has remitted the collected funds to the exporter's bank, the loss will be borne by the exporter.

FINANCING BY THE IMPORTER.   The importer has three principal means for financing his operations.

Payment with Order.   This term means that the importer must pay for the goods at the time he places the order with the exporter. He would probably purchase from his bank a draft on a bank located in the city of the exporter, or in the financial center of the exporter's country. In normal times sales on such terms are rarely encountered in foreign trade, except when the credit standing of the importer is unsatisfactory or not known. The exporter receives payment before he ships the goods, often even before he has manufactured them. The importer thus not only finances the entire transaction and assumes the foreign exchange risk involved, but pays over cash without security, except for the credit standing of the exporter. Should the order not be filled, should the goods be unduly delayed or prove to be of inferior quality, the importer's only redress is to bring legal action on the basis of the sales contract unless the exporter makes an adjustment voluntarily.

Partial Payment in Advance.   To protect himself against the contingency that goods ordered by importers might be rejected on delivery, an exporter may stipulate in the sales contract that importers must remit in advance a partial payment on the order as evidence of good

EXHIBIT 6   CUSTOMER'S INSTRUCTIONS TO A BANK FOR COLLECTION OF A DRAFT

MORGAN GUARANTY TRUST COMPANY
OF NEW YORK
Direct Collection Form

ATTACH THIS COPY TO
SHIPPING DOCUMENTS

Via Airmail To —

NIPISHI BANK LTD
OSAKA
JAPAN

DATE July 3, 19*

REFER TO
COLLECTION 1-111000

We enclose the following draft and documents for collection in accordance with the instructions shown below. Please accept this collection FOR ACCOUNT OF MORGAN GUARANTY TRUST COMPANY OF NEW YORK as if received directly from them and SEND PAYMENT, ALL REPORTS AND YOUR ACKNOWLEDGEMENT TO MORGAN GUARANTY TRUST COMPANY OF NEW YORK, ATTN. COLLECTION SECTION, 23 WALL STREET, NEW YORK, N. Y. 10015 MENTIONING THE COLLECTION NO. SHOWN ABOVE, SUBJECT TO UNIFORM RULES FOR COLLECTIONS (1978 REVISION) INTERNATIONAL CHAMBER OF COMMERCE, BROCHURE NO. 322.

DRAWERS REFERENCE NUMBER	DATE OF DRAFT	TENOR	AMOUNT
INV 1234-201	July 3, 19*	120 D/S	$5,321.68

DRAWER Coast Textile Machine Supply Inc.
AND
ADDRESS Portland, Oregon

DRAWEE Shoji Merchandise Ltd.
AND
ADDRESS Osaka, Japan

BILLS OF LADING ORIG DUP	PARCEL POST RECEIPTS	INSUR. CERT'S.	INVOICES	CONSULAR INVOICES	PACKING LISTS	WEIGHT CERT'S.	CERT'S. OF ORIGIN	OTHER DOCUMENTS
1/3 Neg 1			2	2				

X DELIVER DOCUMENTS AGAINST	X ACCEPTANCE PAYMENT	ALL CHARGES INCLUDING STAMPS, EXCHANGE, TAXES, ETC. FOR DRAWEE'S ACCOUNT PLUS MORGAN GUARANTY TRUST COMPANY CHARGE OF $25.00.
X ADVISE BY CABLE	X NON-ACCEPTANCE X NON-PAYMENT	
REMIT PROCEEDS BY CABLE	DRAWEE'S EXPENSE OUR EXPENSE	
X REMIT PROCEEDS BY AIRMAIL		X WAIVE CHARGES IF REFUSED
PROTEST	NON-ACCEPTANCE NON-PAYMENT	DO NOT WAIVE CHARGES
X DO NOT PROTEST		X HOLD FOR ARRIVAL OF MERCHANDISE

X IF DOLLAR EXCHANGE IS NOT IMMEDIATELY AVAILABLE AT MATURITY (OR ON PRESENTATION IF DRAWN AT SIGHT) AND IT IS NECESSARY TO PROVISIONALLY ACCEPT LOCAL CURRENCY PENDING AVAILABILITY OF DOLLAR EXCHANGE, IT MUST BE DISTINCTLY UNDERSTOOD THAT THE DRAWEE SHALL REMAIN LIABLE FOR ALL EXCHANGE DIFFERENCES. AT TIME OF DEPOSIT OF LOCAL CURRENCY OBTAIN FROM DRAWEES THEIR WRITTEN UNDERTAKING TO BE RESPONSIBLE FOR ANY EXCHANGE DIFFERENCES. THE DRAFT MUST NOT BE SURRENDERED TO DRAWEES UNTIL FINAL PAYMENT FOR FACE AMOUNT IN U.S. DOLLAR EXCHANGE.

ALLOW A DISCOUNT OF   IF PAID

COLLECT INTEREST AT THE RATE OF   % FROM

IN CASE OF NEED REFER TO

WHO IS EMPOWERED BY US: TO ACT FULLY ON OUR BEHALF I.E. AUTHORIZE REDUCTIONS, EXTENSIONS, FREE DELIVERY, WAIVING OF PROTESTS ETC.

WHO MAY ASSIST IN OBTAINING ACCEPTANCE OR PAYMENT OF DRAFT, AS DRAWN, BUT IS NOT TO ALTER ITS TERMS IN ANY WAY.

OTHER INSTRUCTIONS

This letter of instructions and attached draft (below) are prepared by the exporter and sent directly to the collecting bank, with a copy to Morgan Guaranty.

FROM_____
(DRAWER'S NAME)

AUTHORIZED SIGNATURE

SOLE BILL OF EXCHANGE

$ 5,321.68   DATE July 3, 19*   NO. 201

120 DAYS AFTER SIGHT   of this SOLE BILL OF EXCHANGE

pay to the order of MORGAN GUARANTY TRUST COMPANY OF NEW YORK

FIVE THOUSAND THREE HUNDRED TWENTY ONE DOLLARS SIXTY EIGHT CENTS*************************

Payable for face amount by prime Banker's sight draft on New York, New York
Value received and charge to account of

To Shoji Merchandise Ltd.

Osaka, Japan

Coast Textile Machine Supply Inc.

Source: The Financing of Exports and Imports, Morgan Guaranty Trust Co., New York, 1980.

faith and intention to pay the balance as agreed. Such provision is usually made when the order is for specialized equipment, or when the goods involved cannot be satisfactorily disposed of in the country of destination if the importer fails to take them as agreed. The partial payment by the importer should suffice to cover the cost of freight out and back, insurance, and other expenses incidental to the shipment of goods abroad.

Payment on Documents.   When the contract stipulates payment on documents, the importer must provide funds in the exporter's country to pay for the shipment on the day the exporter turns over to a designated bank documents evidencing shipment of the goods ordered. The importer thus raises the funds, converts them into the currency of the country of the exporter, and carries the financing burden while the commodities are in transit.

FINANCING BY THE EXPORTER'S BANK.   The exporter's bank may finance his transactions by the following means.

Advance on Drafts.   Under this arrangement, the financing is done jointly by the exporter and his bank. An exporter who is unwilling to have his funds tied up while the goods are en route to the importer may borrow from his bank a percentage of the amount of the draft. The draft on the importer and pertinent shipping documents, turned over by the exporter to his bank for collection, constitute **collateral** for the advance. In case the drawee (importer) fails to pay the draft when due, the bank has recourse against the drawer, whether the draft is made out to the order of the drawer (exporter) and endorsed by him to the bank, or to the order of the bank. Thus the credit risk rests on the exporter just as when he hands the draft to the bank for collection only. After the draft has been paid by the drawee, the bank retains the amount of the advance plus interest and collection fees, crediting the balance to the exporter.

The amount that an exporter can borrow on foreign drafts depends on the financial responsibility of exporter and importer, and the collateral behind the draft. The **character of the merchandise** shipped determines its value as collateral. Staple commodities not subject to rapid deterioration (cotton, wheat, wool) and traded on organized markets are obviously better collateral than perishable goods or manufactured articles requiring expert selling to be disposed of without loss.

Discount of Drafts.   The bank may discount the draft drawn by the exporter on the importer when the credit standing of the exporter is high, and particularly if he already has a line of credit. The exporter then receives the face amount of the draft, less interest and collection charges, unless custom requires the drawee to absorb all charges.

Refinancing Bill.   Under this arrangement, an exporter hands over to the bank the draft and documents for collection, and the bank allows the exporter to draw on itself a time draft of a maturity identical with that of the draft upon the importer. The bank accepts the draft on itself, and this refinancing bill becomes a banker's acceptance that the exporter can sell in the open market at a very low rate of discount. When the original draft has been paid by the importer abroad, the bank uses the funds to pay off its own acceptance at maturity.

FINANCING BY THE IMPORTER'S BANK.   The importer may finance transactions through his bank in several ways.

Commercial Letter of Credit.   This is a device that substitutes a bank's credit for that of the importer by giving the exporter the right to draw drafts on a designated bank, instead of on the importer. Such drafts, upon acceptance, become **bankers' acceptances** that command a low rate of discount. A commercial letter of credit may be defined briefly as a notification issued by a bank to an individual or firm authorizing the latter to draw on the bank, its branch, or a correspondent bank for amounts up to a specified sum, and guaranteeing acceptance and payment of the drafts if drawn in accordance with the terms stipulated in the letter.

A letter-of-credit transaction may be illustrated by the following example. An importer in London purchases from an exporter in New York a quantity of goods, agreeing to make payment by a letter of credit. The importer applies to his bank in London for a letter of credit in favor of the exporter. If his credit standing at the bank is satisfactory, the importer is requested by the bank to fill out and sign an "application and agreement for commercial letter of credit" (see Exhibit 7; the agreement appears on the reverse side of the application). In the application the importer asks the bank to open, by cable or mail, a credit for a stipulated amount to be made available to the beneficiary (exporter) by drafts drawn on the bank or its correspondent, upon delivery by the exporter to the drawee bank of specified documents evidencing shipment of goods ordered by the importer.

The agreement usually provides that the importer must put up the funds to meet acceptances in advance of their maturity. It stipulates that the bank is the owner of the merchandise and documents until the importer has met all his obligations to the bank. It provides that neither the bank nor its correspondents shall be responsible for the existence, character, quality, quantity, condition, packing, value, or delivery of the property purporting to be represented by the documents.

The **importer's bank** will then instruct its branch or correspondent bank in New York to open a letter of credit in favor of the exporter under the conditions stipulated by the importer in his application. The New York bank, in turn, notifies the exporter that it will accept his drafts if drawn in compliance with the terms of the credit. This notification to the exporter, specifying conditions stipulated by the importer, constitutes the letter of credit (see Exhibit 8).

If the importer's bank has substantial resources and is well known abroad, such as one of the large London banks, it may send a letter of credit directly to the exporter in New York. The exporter then draws on the importer's bank in London and sells the draft to a New York bank, surrendering to it the letter of credit and the shipping documents specified therein. The New York bank will buy (negotiate) the draft only when the exporter is its customer or known to it, and the documents conform exactly to the stipulations. The New York bank then forwards the draft, letter of credit, and shipping documents to its correspondent in London for collection. The importer's bank must pay or accept the draft, unless the documents do not conform to the provisions of the letter of credit.

A letter of credit not only shifts the burden of financing to a bank or the money market, but also gives the exporter a **bank guaranty** that he will receive cash or a bank acceptance once he has turned over the goods ordered to a common carrier for shipment to the importer in accordance with the letter of credit. An importer supplying a letter of credit is usually able to buy at somewhat lower prices than those quoted to open book account customers, since the exporter neither carries the burden of financing nor assumes the credit risk.

Once a time draft has been "accepted" by a well-known bank, it becomes a readily negotiable instrument (see Exhibit 9). In recent years the acceptance market has witnessed substantial growth; New York and San Francisco are the main market centers. Acceptances enjoy a good market among foreign institutions and foreign investors, since these holders are exempt from U.S. federal income taxes.

EXHIBIT 7 APPLICATION AND AGREEMENT FOR COMMERCIAL LETTER OF CREDIT

Morgan Guaranty Trust Company of New York
Commercial Credits Department
23 Wall Street, New York, N.Y. 10015

April 2nd 19*
(Date)

Gentlemen:
Please issue an irrevocable letter of credit for our account and transmit it through your correspondent via
☒ Airmail   ☐ Cable   ☐ Brief Cable   ☐ Return to us for transmission

BENEFICIARY	AMOUNT (Not to Exceed a Total of)
Guarani Mendoza & Co. Santos, Brazil	ABOUT U.S.$50,000.00

APPLICANT (If other than ourselves)	EXPIRY DATE
	May 10th 19*

Available by drafts (Check One) ☐ Sight   ☐ 30 Days Sight   ☐ 60 Days Sight   ☒ 90 Days Sight
Drawn at your Option on you or any of your correspondents
For. . .100%. . . . . invoice value (Full invoice value unless otherwise stated)
DRAFTS TO BE ACCOMPANIED BY: (AS CHECKED)
☒ Commercial invoice describing the merchandise as indicated below   ☒ Special customs invoice
☐ Marine-War insurance policy or certificate   OR   ☒ Insurance covered by us

OTHER DOCUMENTS

☒ Full Set On Board ocean steamer Bills of Lading drawn to the order of Morgan Guaranty Trust Company of New York.
☐ Airway Bill of Lading consigned to_____
☒ Indicating Notify Party as __James Williams & Co., New York__
   Indicate Merchandise here (Omitting details as to grade, quality, price, etc., if possible)

   1,000 (one thousand) bags of COFFEE during April, 19*

Check One ☐ F.O.B. Steamer   ☐ F.A.S. Steamer   ☒ C. & F.   ☐ C.I.F.

SHIPMENT LATEST (If Applicable)...........................	PARTIAL SHIPMENTS	TRANSSHIPMENTS
FROM: Santos, Brazil	☒ Permitted	☒ Permitted
TO: United States Atlantic Port	☐ Prohibited	☐ Prohibited

Unless otherwise stated herein, you may authorize the negotiating/paying bank to send all documents to you in one airmail.

SPECIAL INSTRUCTIONS

U.S. importer uses this form to request issue of irrevocable letter of credit by Morgan Guaranty in favor of exporter. See overleaf for letter of credit issued in response.

Unless otherwise expressly stated, the letter of credit is to be issued subject to the uniform customs and practice for documentary credits (1974 Revision) International Chamber of Commerce Publication No. 290, as well as subject to your letter of credit agreement, which agreement has been or will be duly executed by us. In case of any conflict, your rights under your letter of credit agreement shall prevail.

James Williams & Co.......................

....
Authorized Official(s)

Form 11-4-671B 7-1-74

Source: The Financing of Exports and Imports, Morgan Guaranty Trust Co., New York, 1980.

EXHIBIT 8   IRREVOCABLE DOCUMENTARY LETTER OF CREDIT

IRREVOCABLE DOCUMENTARY LETTER OF CREDIT   7

issued by
Morgan Guaranty Trust Company of New York
Commercial Credits Department, 23 Wall Street, New York, N.Y. 10015; *Cable* Morganbank

Advising bank	☐ This credit is a confirmation of the credit opened by cable under today's date and is available only for the amount not already availed under the cable advice, and is not available at all unless attached to and as part of the advising bank's notification of such cable advice, the two jointly constituting evidence of the outstanding amount of this credit.
Bank of South America Santos Brazil	
Beneficiary	☐ This refers to our cable of today through the advising bank. ☒ This credit is forwarded to the advising bank by airmail.
Guarani Mendoza & Co Santos Brazil	**Date** April 2nd 19* **Issuing bank's Credit No.** 89054 **Advising bank's Credit No.**
Applicant	**Amount** ABOUT U.S.$50,000.00 (ABOUT FIFTY THOUSAND U.S. DOLLARS)
James Williams & Co. New York New York	
	Expiry date May 10, 19*

Dear Sirs:
We hereby issue this letter of credit in your favor available by your draft drawn on us at 90 days sight

bearing the clause: "Drawn under Morgan Guaranty Trust Company of New York Letter of Credit No. 89054 "
accompanied by the following documents:
    Commercial invoice, describing the merchandise as indicated below
    Special Customs Invoice
    On board ocean steamer bills of lading drawn to the order of Morgan Guaranty
    Trust Company of New York, marked "Notify James Williams & Co., New York."

Import letter of credit. Morgan Guaranty as issuer sends this copy to advising bank, which fills in block at lower right and forwards to beneficiary (the foreign exporter).

covering: 1,000 (one thousand) bags of COFFEE during April 19*   Cost and Freight

Shipment from: Santos, Brazil	**Partial shipments**	**Transhipments**
to: United States Atlantic Port	permitted	permitted

Special conditions
    We are informed marine and war risk insurance to be effected by James Williams & Co.

    The negotiating bank may, at their discretion, forward the draft and documents in
    one airmail.

| The amount of each draft negotiated, with date of negotiation, must be endorsed hereon by the negotiating bank.

We hereby agree with you and with negotiating banks and bankers that drafts drawn under and in compliance with the terms of this credit shall be duly honored upon presentation to us at 15 Broad Street, New York, N.Y. 10015 if negotiated, or presented at this office together with this letter of credit, on or before the expiry date.

Yours very truly,

Morgan Guaranty Trust Company of New York

Issuing bank (authorized signature) | **Advising bank's notification**

Place, date, name and signature of advising bank |

This credit is subject to the Uniform Customs and Practice for Documentary Credits (1974 revision), International Chamber of Commerce Publication No. 290.

Source: The Financing of Exports and Imports, Morgan Guaranty Trust Co., New York, 1980.

Import and Export Letters of Credit.   American banks usually distinguish between and handle separately import and export letters of credit. When an American bank, on the application of an American importer, issues a commercial letter of credit in favor of an exporter located abroad, it is termed an import letter of credit. An export letter of credit is one issued by a foreign bank in favor of an American exporter for the account of an importer abroad buying goods in the United States.

Revocable and Irrevocable Letters of Credit.   A revocable letter of credit may be canceled by the importer's bank before drafts drawn by the exporter under the letter of credit have

EXHIBIT 9   BANKER'S ACCEPTANCE (TIME DRAFT STAMPED "ACCEPTED" BY A BANK)

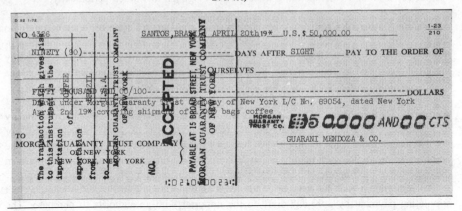

Source: The Financing of Exports and Imports, Morgan Guaranty Trust Co., New York, 1980.

been negotiated by the correspondent bank. Banks do not favor revocable letters of credit, some banks refusing to issue them, because they may become involved in resulting litigation. The correspondent bank acting as agent for the importer's bank (credit-issuing bank) assumes no obligation. An irrevocable letter of credit cannot be canceled by the importer's bank for the period specified without the consent of the beneficiary. Exporters generally insist upon irrevocable letters of credit.

Confirmed and Unconfirmed Letters of Credit.   When a **correspondent bank** located in the country of the exporter confirms a letter of credit to the exporter by obligating itself to pay or accept his drafts, the instrument is called a confirmed letter of credit. The confirmation binds the correspondent bank to honor drafts drawn under the credit even if the importer's (issuing) bank should refuse or be unable to meet its obligation. An unconfirmed letter of credit does not give the exporter this additional security. Exporters insist on confirmed letters of credit when the foreign issuing bank is not well known. It is obvious that the correspondent bank will confirm only irrevocable letters of credit, since a bank would not guarantee an agreement that might be canceled at will by the issuing bank.

Revolving Letter of Credit.   If an importer maintains continuous business relations with an exporter and receives repeated shipments of goods, a revolving credit in favor of the exporter is often used. A revolving letter of credit assures automatic renewal of the amount of the credit when it becomes exhausted. Revolving letters of credit are issued in various forms, of which three types are most frequently employed. (1) The letter of credit provides that when drafts drawn under the letter of credit are paid by the importer, new drafts in equal amounts may again be drawn, so that the stipulated maximum amount may be continually outstanding. Thus, if the letter of credit is for $100,000 and the bank has honored the exporter's draft for $20,000, the credit is reduced to $80,000. But after the importer has paid this draft, the full amount of the credit, or $100,000, again becomes available to the exporter. (2) The exporter draws drafts for the full amount of the credit, and when these drafts have been paid by the importer the original amount again becomes available to the exporter. (3) The exporter is permitted to draw drafts up to a stated amount for a specified period, say a month, corresponding to deliveries of goods forwarded periodically.

Assignable Letter of Credit.   A beneficiary may transfer this type of letter of credit to another party. An assignable letter of credit is employed by importers who maintain representatives abroad. It is issued in favor of the foreign representative, who is ordered to buy the goods specified by the importer. When the representative has contracted for the goods on the stipulated terms, he assigns the letter of credit to the seller (exporter).

Authority To Purchase.   The "authority to purchase" (abbreviated **A/P**), or "authority to negotiate," is a letter or cable sent by the importer's bank to its branch, agent, or correspondent aborad, instructing him to buy an exporter's draft drawn on an importer. The authority to purchase, used mainly in Far Eastern trade, shifts the burden of financing from the exporter to the importer's bank. Its operation is illustrated by the following example.

An importer in Asia has bought goods from an exporter in San Francisco, the contract stipulating payment by a 90-day draft on the importer with an authority to purchase. The importer applies to his bank for an authority to purchase, specifying the amount, expiration date, shipping documents, and other conditions. When the bank approves the application, the importer signs **"a letter of guaranty"** in which he obligates himself to accept and pay the draft, pledging the documents conveying title to the goods as collateral security. The bank then instructs its agent in San Francisco to buy the exporter's draft drawn in compliance with the stated conditions. The San Francisco agent sends a notice (advice of authority to purchase) to the exporter, informing him of the terms on which the draft on the importer will be purchased. After the exporter has delivered the goods to the shipping company, he presents the draft with the required documents to the agent and receives payment. The authority to purchase thus enables the exporter to sell the draft immediately without using up any of his line of credit with his bank.

In contrast to the letter of credit, which gives rise to bankers' acceptances, the authority to purchase gives rise to a trade acceptance, with the importer as acceptor. Although under both methods the exporter is only secondarily liable, that is, only if the acceptor should fail to pay, it is obvious that an exporter is less likely to be called on to pay a dishonored bank acceptance than a trade acceptance. The exporter may, however, be relieved from his liability by being authorized to endorse his draft on the importer with the words "without recourse." Thus, if the importer (drawee) refuses to accept or pay the draft, the exporter (drawer) cannot be called on to refund the money he received from its sale. But authorities to purchase authorizing the exporter to endorse "without recourse" are rarely issued.

The authority to purchase may be revocable or irrevocable. In a revocable authority to purchase, the issuing bank has the right to cancel the authorization given to its agent to buy the exporter's draft. In such circumstance the agent's advice of authority to purchase contains a clause stipulating that the authority may be canceled by giving notice to the exporter.

Documents Attached to Draft.   A full set of documents accompanying an exporter's draft under a letter of credit or authority to purchase consists usually of a negotiable bill of lading (two or more copies), an insurance certificate or policy, commercial invoice, consular invoice, certificate of origin, and other documents that may be needed to bring the goods into the foreign country, such as an antidumping certificate, inspection certificate, or health certificate. The latter is often required for shipments of agricultural and livestock products. These shipping documents are ordinarily endorsed in blank or to the bank negotiating the exporter's draft. To establish the indisputable legal right of the negotiating bank to the goods represented by the documents, the bank usually requests the exporter to execute a **letter of hypothecation and general assurance.** This instrument contains a number of provisions, of which the most important are those in which the exporter obligates himself to deliver to the bank all the necessary documents, to indemnify the bank against losses and costs arising in connection with the draft, including loss from exchange fluctuations, and to pay the amount of the draft upon notice of protest. It grants the bank discretionary power to dispose at public or private sale, for its own and the exporter's protection and for account and sole risk of the exporter, all its own and the exporter's protection and for account and sole risk of the exporter, all or part of the merchandise represented by the title-conveying documents, and to apply the net proceeds toward payment of the draft secured by these documents.

PUBLIC SOURCES OF EXPORT FINANCING.   To promote employment and thereby to better balance of payments, governments frequently provide export credit, guarantees, and other services for various types of trade financing, with an emphasis on long-term, capital equipment financing. The **U.S. Export-Import Bank (Eximbank)** is the largest and most diversified export credit institution in the world. In addition, export credit is provided by government-backed financing agencies in Austria, Belgium, Canada, Denmark, Finland, Germany, Italy, Japan, the Netherlands, Norway, Sweden, Switzerland, and the United Kingdom.

U.S. EXPORT-IMPORT BANK.   In 1934 the U.S. government entered the field of foreign banking by organizing the **Export-Import Bank,** which in 1945 was made an independent agency of the federal government. The bank is empowered to do a general banking business and to make any type of loan for the purpose of aiding in the financing and facilitating of exports and imports and the exchange of commodities between the United States or any of its territories or insular possessions and any foreign country or the agencies or nationals thereof.

The bank makes long-term loans to finance purchases of U.S. equipment, goods, and services for projects undertaken by private enterprises or governments abroad and guarantees direct loans extended by financial institutions to overseas buyers. It also finances or guarantees payment of medium-term commercial export credits granted by exporters and, in partnership with private insurance companies, offers short- and medium-term export credit insurance.

One unique feature of Eximbank is that it will **guarantee political risks,** which include inconvertibility of foreign currency into dollars, cancellation of export and import licenses, or other governmental actions preventing importation of goods, war, civil strife, and expropriation of confiscation by government action.

The Foreign Credit Insurance Association is a joint enterprise of a number of private insurance firms. It works with Eximbank to provide coverage of the following kinds: short-term comprehensive risk, medium-term comprehensive risk, all-term comprehensive master policy, catastrophe policy, small business policy, and political risk policy.

The Private Export Funding Corp. (PEFCO), established in 1970, provides private funding, guaranteed by Eximbank, to finance U.S. exports. Typically, PEFCO provides middle-maturity financing (5–12 years) in a financial package of substantial size where one or more commercial banks take the shortest maturities and Eximbank the longest.

Many additional sources provide information on export financing techniques. The reader may refer to a booklet published in various updated editions by the Morgan Guaranty Trust Co., New York, *The Financing of Exports and Imports: A Guide to Procedures*. Other major banks provide similar guides.

FOREIGN EXCHANGE AND INTERNATIONAL PAYMENTS

THE FOREIGN EXCHANGE MARKET.   Foreign exchange trading involves the exchange of one national currency for another. Foreign exchange is traded by banks around the world in a **24-hour market.** Somewhere in the world, banks are buying and selling dollars for, say, German marks, regardless of whether the banks in the United States and Germany are open for business. Banks in the Far East, including branches of major U.S. and European institutions, begin trading in Hong Kong, Singapore, and Tokyo at about the time most traders in San Francisco are going home for supper. As the Far East closes, trading in Middle Eastern financial centers has been going on for a couple of hours, and the trading day in Europe is just beginning. Some of the large New York banks have an early shift to minimize the time differential of 5–6 hours with Europe. By the time New York trading gets going in full force around 8 A.M., it is lunch time in London and Frankfurt. To complete the circle, West Coast banks also extend "normal banking hours" so they can trade with New York or Europe, on one side, and with Hong Kong, Singapore, or Tokyo, on the other. While foreign exchange deals frequently take place between residents of different countries, the money being traded never actually leaves the country of the currency. Thus when German marks are exchanged for U.S. dollars in London, the marks and the dollars stay in Germany and the United States, respectively. The act of trading only effects a **change in ownership** of the money. The money itself, being in the form of bank deposits, merely gets shifted from one deposit to another in the home country of the currency.

This characteristic of foreign exchange trading has two implications. One is that for a currency to be actively traded, it must be **freely convertible**—that is, ownership must be transferable between residents and nonresidents, and among nonresidents of the country. The second is that the "market" can be anywhere and everywhere, since there is no need to be near the money to trade it.

Thus the **foreign exchange market has no central location.** It is, instead, a network of telephone and cable communications between banks, foreign exchange brokers, and ultimate buyers and sellers of foreign exchange such as corporations, commodity trading firms, governments, and central banks.

Although much foreign exchange trading (or **dealing,** as it is called outside the United States) arises from international trade, the great majority of transactions are deals between banks. When banks purchase currencies, they do not leave them idle in noninterest-bearing clearing accounts, but rather place them on deposit for some period with other banks. Thus the foreign exchange market is closely linked to the **deposit market.** The deposit market, or more generally the **money market,** involves the interbank **buying** (borrowing) and **placing** (depositing) of funds in given currencies in given centers. When the funds are deposited outside of the country of the currency, the money market is the **Eurocurrency market.** As is shown in Exhibit 10, banks organize their foreign exchange and money market activities in such a way as to recognize the linkage between the two.

The foreign exchange and **international money market** is made up of banks and others that exchange currencies and place funds throughout the world. They are linked by telephone and cable and by information transfer services that provide instantaneous summaries of events and rates in other parts of the world. Although it is an over-the-counter market with no central trading floor, banks and their dealing departments do find it advantageous to be in the same location, or at least in the same time zone, as other banks dealing in the same currencies. Moreover, because foreign exchange trading results in payments being made through each currency's payments mechanism, local banks may benefit from closer access to domestic money markets. They usually have an advantage in trading their local currency.

EXHIBIT 10   ORGANIZATION OF FOREIGN EXCHANGE AND MONEY MARKET ACTIVITIES

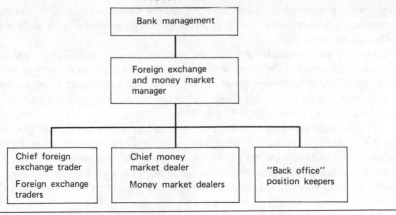

Source: Nigel R. L. Hudson, *Money and Exchange Dealing in International Banking,* Halsted, New York, 1979, p. 34.

For instance, buying and selling sterling for dollars is most active among the banks in London. Similarly the major market for Swiss francs is in Zurich; for Japanese yen, in Tokyo. But the local advantage is by no means absolute. Thus dollar–Swiss franc trading is active in London and dollar–sterling trading is active in Zurich. Moreover, New York banks trade just as frequently with London, German, or Swiss banks in all major currencies as they do with other New York banks.

Within most individual centers, and even between centers, banks deal with one another to a large extent through **foreign exchange brokers.** Brokers do not deal themselves, but serve as a go-between among banks, preserving anonymity and passing quotes on rapidly to their numerous clients.

The remainder of this subsection provides some details on the mechanisms of foreign exchange trading and the corresponding international payments system. It draws heavily on *Foreign Exchange Markets in the United States,* by Roger M. Kubarych.

TYPES OF FOREIGN EXCHANGE TRANSACTIONS: SPOT, FORWARD, AND SWAP. Whenever two currencies are exchanged, each party promises to pay a certain amount of currency to the other on an agreed-upon date. The most common transaction, a **spot transaction,** involves the purchase of and payment for foreign exchange with delivery and payment to be completed at once or within 1 or 2 business days. A typical spot transaction might involve a U.S. company arranging for the immediate transfer of £1 million to the account of a client in London. The company and a U.S. bank would agree on an exchange rate for the transaction: say, $2 per pound sterling. The U.S. company would pay its bank $2 million and the bank would cable instructions to London that the equivalent amount of pounds (£1 million) be credited immediately to the account of the London client.

A **forward exchange contract** calls for delivery at a fixed future date of a specified amount of one currency for a specified amount of another currency. The exchange rate is established at the time the contract is agreed on, but payment and delivery are not required until maturity. Forward exchange rates are normally quoted for fixed periods of 1, 3, or 6 months; but actual contracts in major currencies can usually be arranged for delivery at any specified date up to 1 year, and on occasion for longer periods up to 3 years. Forward contracts in less commonly used currencies are not readily available. Forward contracts on particularly unstable currencies can be expensive, since someone has to pay for the risk of exchange rate changes.

Although most contracts have specific maturity dates, it is possible to arrange, usually at slightly greater cost, for **forward option contracts** that permit delivery at the beginning of a month (first to tenth days of the month), at the middle (eleventh to twentieth), or at the end (twenty-first to thirty-first). Such contracts are desirable when the customer does not know the exact day of receipt of foreign funds.

If the forward exchange rate for a currency is higher than the current spot rate, dealers say the currency is trading at a **premium** for that forward maturity. If the forward rate is below the spot rate, the currency is said to be trading at a **discount.** In the exceptional case when the spot and forward quotations are the same, traders say the forwards are **"flat."** For instance, sterling for value 3 months from now is at a discount if the spot rate is $2 and the 3-month forward rate is $1.97.

Banks active in the foreign exchange market find that **interbank currency trading** for any specific value date in the future is inefficient, and they do it infrequently. Instead, for future maturities banks trade among themselves, as well as with some corporate customers, on the basis of a transaction known as a **swap.** A swap transaction is a simultaneous purchase and sale of a certain amount of foreign currency for two different value dates. The key aspect is that the bank arranges the swap as a single transaction with a single counterparty, either another bank or a nonbank customer. This means that unlike outright spot or forward transactions, a trader does not incur any **foreign exchange rate risk,** since the bank contracts both to pay and to receive the same amount of currency at specified rates.

A swap allows each party to use a currency for a period in exchange for another currency that is not needed during that time. If the objective is to get a better return in the other currency without incurring exchange risk, the swap is being used to undertake covered interest arbitrage; more on this below. Swaps also provide a mechanism for a bank to accommodate the outright forward transactions executed with customers or to bridge gaps in the maturity structure of its outstanding spot and forward contracts.

The two value dates in a swap transaction can be any pair of future dates. But, in practice, markets exist only for a limited number of standard maturities. One of these standard types is called a "spot against forward" swap. In a spot against forward swap transaction, a trader buys or sells a currency for the ordinary spot value date and simultaneously sells or buys it back for a value date a week, a month, or 3 months later.

Another type of particular interest to professional market-making banks is called a **"to-morrow-next" swap** or a "rollover." These are transactions in which the dealer buys or sells a currency for value the next business day and simultaneously sells or buys it back for value the day after. A more sophisticated type of swap is called a **"forward-forward,"** in which the dealer buys or sells a currency for one future date (say, a month later) and sells or buys it back for another future date (say, 3 months later). Only a handful of banks specialize in such transactions.

QUOTATION OF RATES.   When a **corporate treasurer** asks a foreign exchange trader to quote a rate for spot sterling or German marks, the trader will quote not one rate but two. The first price is the one at which he will buy a currency and the second is the price at which he will sell. For example:

$/£   1.9320−1.9325

Using the rates above, in the first case either £1,000 = $1,932.00 or £1,000 = $1,932.50. Therefore, if a trader is being asked to purchase £1,000 and to sell the equivalent amount of currency, the deal will be done at 1.9320, since the trader has to part with $1,932, not $1,932.50. If, however, the trader is being asked to sell sterling, then in exchange the trader would wish to obtain as many dollars as possible. Therefore, the deal is done at $1.9325.

In theory, any two currencies can be traded in an exchange transaction. Swiss francs can be bought for French francs, German marks for sterling. In practice, such transactions are common only between banks and nonbank customers. Virtually all interbank transactions, by market participants here and abroad, involve a purchase or sale of dollars for a foreign currency. This is true even if a bank's aim is to buy German marks for sterling.

The reason is that since the dollar is the main currency for international trade and investment, the dollar market for each currency is much more active than the bilateral market between any pair of foreign currencies. By going through the dollar, large amounts can be traded more easily. Of course, a German mark rate in sterling terms can be readily calculated from the respective dollar rates. The calculation produces what is called a **crossrate.** If the dollar–mark rate is 2.2250–60 (marks per dollar) and the sterling–dollar rate is $1.8200–10 (per pound), then the sterling–mark crossrate is 4.0495–4.0535 (marks per pound). Analogously, if the dollar–Swiss franc rate is 1.9000–10, the Swiss franc–German mark crossrate is 1.1704–16 (marks per Swiss franc).

FORWARD EXCHANGE RATES.   Forward exchange rates can be expressed in three ways. Like spot rates, outright forward prices are expressed in dollars and cents per currency unit, or vice versa. Traders normally quote forward prices to corporate customers or correspondent banks seeking to buy or sell a currency for a particular future date. For instance, a trader may quote an outright 6-month rate to buy sterling of $1.8450, while by comparison a quotation to buy spot sterling might be less (say $1.8200) or more (say $1.8625).

In **swap transactions,** the trader is interested only in the difference between spot and forward rates, the premium or discount, rather than the outright spot and forward rates themselves. Premiums and discounts expressed in points ($0.0001 per pound sterling or DM 0.0001 per dollar) are called swap rates. For the first spot rate above, the premium is 250 points ($0.0250). For the second, the discount is 175 points ($0.0175).

Since in a swap a trader is effectively borrowing one currency and lending the other currency for the period between the two value dates, the premium or discount is often evaluated in terms of percent per annum. For the examples above, the premium of 250 points is equivalent to 2.75% per annum, while the discount of 175 points is equivalent to 1.88% per annum.

The premium or discount is calculated by taking the difference between the forward and spot rate as a percent of the spot rate and multiplying this by $12/n$, where n is the number of months in the forward contract. The formula is as follows:

$$\frac{\text{forward rate} - \text{spot rate}}{\text{spot rate}} \times \frac{12}{\text{number of months forward}} \times 100 = \begin{array}{l}\text{forward premium}\\ \text{or discount as a}\\ \text{per annum percent}\end{array}$$

Applying the formula to the British pound (spot rate, 1.8200; 6-month forward rate, 1.8450):

$$\frac{1.8450 - 1.8200}{1.8200} \times \frac{12}{6} \times 100 = +2.75\%, \quad \text{or} \quad \text{a premium of 2.75\% per annum}$$

COVERED INTEREST ARBITRAGE.   Spot exchange rates, forward exchange rates, and interest rates on deposits are not all determined independently but are linked to one another through **covered interest arbitrage.** Such arbitrage ensures that in the absence of legal obstacles, the forward premium or discount on a currency relative to the dollar, expressed as a percentage of the spot rate, will tend to (about) equal the differential between interest rates available in that currency and dollar interest rates. Otherwise, traders would have opportunities to make profits by moving funds from one currency to the other. This relationship is called **interest rate parity.** The precise relationship is shown in Exhibit 11.

A tendency toward interest rate parity is achieved through the movement of funds into or out of a currency when the forward discount or premium is out of line with the relative interest rate differential. Suppose the relevant sterling interest rate was 8%, the corresponding dollar interest rate was 4%, and the discount on forward sterling was only 2%. A trader could earn 6% on dollars by selling dollars spot for sterling and investing the sterling at 8%, while selling the sterling forward at a discount of 2%. Obviously, the trader would rather earn 6% than 4% on dollars.

EXHIBIT 11   INTEREST RATE PARITY

F is the 1-year sterling rate. To buy £1 a year forward costs $F \times £1$.

S is the spot rate. The 1-year sterling interest rate is $R_£$. The dollar interest rate is $R_\$$.

Buying $£1/(1 + R_£)$ spot and investing it for a year at $R_£$ would yield £1 a year from now. In dollars, it would cost $S \times £1/(1 + R_£)$.

The foregone dollar interest is:

$$S \times £1 \times R_\$/(1 + R_£)$$

Adding the two costs together—actual and foregone—gives the total dollar cost of the second option:

$$\frac{S \times £1}{(1 + R_£)} + \frac{S \times £1 \times R_\$}{(1 + R_£)}$$

Or collecting terms:

$$S \times £1 \times (1 + R_\$)/(1 + R_£)$$

If that equals $F \times £1$, then the two options cost the same.

Divide both expressions by $S \times £1$, and the result is the interest parity condition:

$$\frac{F}{S} = \frac{1 + R_\$}{1 + R_£}$$

$(F/S) - 1$ is the percentage forward premium or discount. So, when the interest rate parity condition holds:

$$\frac{F}{S} - 1 = \frac{1 + R_\$}{1 + R_£} - 1 = \frac{R_\$ - R_£}{1 + R_£}$$

In other words, the percentage premium or discount on forward sterling is just about equal to the difference between dollar and sterling interest rates when the interest rate parity condition holds. (To be perfectly equal $R_£$ would have to be zero!)

As that trader and other traders sought to take advantage of such a lucrative opportunity, the net selling of forward sterling would put downward pressure on the forward rate and the net buying of spot sterling would put upward pressure on the spot rate. Both would tend to widen the forward discount on sterling. At the same time, the investment in sterling assets would tend to lower sterling interest rates and therefore narrow the interest rate differential. In principle, the process would continue until the percentage forward discount just about equaled the sterling–dollar interest rate differential, thereby eliminating the profitable arbitrage opportunity.

MECHANICS OF INTERNATIONAL PAYMENTS. All U.S. dollar receipts and payments outside the United States, whether they involve trade, investment, Eurodollar, or foreign exchange transactions, are ultimately effected through the transfer of funds between bank accounts in the United States. Similarly, German mark and French franc transactions are effected in Germany and France, respectively. Thus every foreign exchange transaction involves at least two shifts of bank deposits in national currencies. If Barclays Bank buys German marks from Crédit Lyonnais, Barclays will arrange for funds to be transferred from its correspondent account in New York to that of Crédit Lyonnais. At the same time, in Frankfurt, funds will be transferred from a correspondent account of Crédit Lyonnais to one of Barclays.

Since practically all major interbank foreign exchange transactions involve the U.S. dollar, every foreign exchange dealer must maintain at least one bank account in the United States to make and receive payments in dollars.

An account at a foreign correspondent or branch through which a bank pays or receives foreign currency is called a **nostro** or **clearing account.** On the value date of a foreign exchange transaction, the correspondent debits or credits the clearing account in response to instructions received in a cable message. For many years, virtually all foreign exchange transactions of any size were settled through cable transfers, that is, debits and credits of bank accounts in response to cable messages. In September 1977 an automated system known as SWIFT began sending payment instructions written in a standardized format among European and North American banks. **SWIFT** is short for "Society for Worldwide Interbank Financial Transactions." It is based in Brussels. A foreign bank or U.S. regional bank pays or receives dollars in foreign exchange transactions through a clearing account at a New York correspondent. The correspondent debits or credits the clearing account on the value date in response to cable or computer messages.

The method of settlement on the dollar side of a foreign exchange transaction differs from the settlement on the foreign currency side. Abroad, settlement in foreign currency is made in **immediately available funds.** That is, the recipient can always use the funds as if they were cash and make another payment on the same day as the value date of the foreign exchange transaction. In New York, dollar settlement is made in what are called **clearinghouse funds.** The term derives from the name of the institution through which interbank settlements among major New York banks are made: the **New York Clearing House Association.** Clearinghouse funds are not available for the recipient to make further payments—until the first business day after the value date of the foreign exchange transaction. At that point, clearinghouse debits and credits are settled in "immediately available" or Federal funds, which are balances on deposit at a Federal Reserve bank. The steps in a typical foreign exchange settlement (illustrated in Exhibit 12) are as follows:

1. Barclays Bank buys German marks from Crédit Lyonnais; to consummate this it must transfer funds in the U.S. to Crédit Lyonnais' account in Chemical Bank, New York.

EXHIBIT 12   THE INTERNATIONAL DOLLAR PAYMENTS SYSTEM

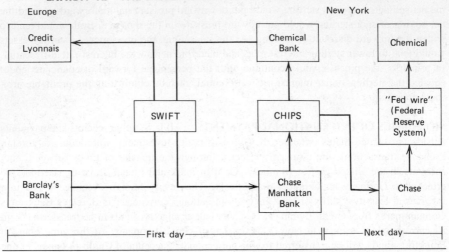

Source: Ian H. Giddy, "Measuring the World Foreign Exchange Market," *Columbia Journal of World Business,* Winter 1980, p. 40.

2. Barclays uses SWIFT, a worldwide financial communications network, to instruct Chase to transfer funds out of the Barclays account.

3. Chase debits the Barclays account and transfers the funds through the clearinghouse of international payments (CHIPS), the payments clearing system for international transactions; in effect it sends an electronic check to CHIPS; those "clearinghouse funds" get credited to Chemical on the same day. Night falls.

4. Next day, the net amount is settled between Federal Reserve member banks by transfers in "Fed funds"—deposits held at the various Federal Reserve banks. This is done through the domestic interbank clearing system, the "Fed wire."

5. Chemical credits Crédit Lyonnais' account and notifies Crédit Lyonnais, again through the SWIFT network.

INTERNATIONAL LENDING

Much of international banking evolved in response to the growing international financing needs of corporate customers that were "going multinational." So too with **international lending**—loans initially were to well-established domestic clients. Because of this, credit analysis and loan terms for international loans did not necessarily differ importantly from domestic loans.

As the international money market grew during the 1960s and 1970s, however, these Eurocurrency markets took on a life and character of their own. The Eurocurrency market is explained in greater depth in the section, "Overseas Money and Capital Markets." For the present purpose, it is worth recalling that **Eurobanking** consists of the taking of deposits denominated in currencies other than that of the host country and either redepositing the funds in other banks at home or abroad, or lending them to governments or corporations.

The **Eurocurrency market** is dominated by Eurodollars, which consist of dollar-denominated deposits in banks outside the United States, including Canadian banks and overseas branches of U.S. banks. The primary reason for the existence of the Eurocurrency market is the absence of reserve requirements and certain other regulatory constraints imposed on domestic deposits or loans. See Dufey and Giddy, *The International Money Market*.

While international lending is by no means limited to Eurocurrency loans—many foreign loans are still made out of the home offices of large banks, in their own currency—the unique features of such loans are of particular relevance to the international banker. This is because a special set of techniques has arisen in the market, techniques that have come to dominate all forms of international lending, and which, most recently, have been increasingly adopted in purely domestic lending.

BORROWERS FROM INTERNATIONAL BANKS.   At one time, corporations borrowing from international banks were primarily those whose name, size, and good standing enabled banks to make loans to them with little more than a cursory analysis of creditworthiness. In recent years, however, the range of corporate (and government) borrowers has spread to a wide variety of virtually unknown firms, as a result of (1) the volume of funds available for lending, (2) guarantees provided by foreign banks on loans made to foreign corporations, and (3) the vastly superior knowledge of foreign business systems that international banks have developed through their overseas branches. Even domestic firms with no international activities are learning to rely on Eurodollar loans when local credit conditions become tight and interest rates are high.

While the participation of corporations in the international money market continued to expand, the 1970s saw an even greater expansion of governments and government-related borrowers. This applies particularly to the **medium-term Eurocredit market,** which public authorities around the world have increasingly tapped for industrial and infrastructure projects and even to finance balance of payments deficits. In addition, international institutions, such as the **World Bank** and its affiliates, various regional development banks, and the **European Economic Community** have been regular borrowers.

Corporations in particular are attracted by the size of the market—of all the sources of funds in the world, only the U.S. market is larger, and only if one takes into account all segments of the U.S. money market. Whereas in national markets there is invariably **credit rationing** during periods of tight credit, often mandated by government, in the Euromarkets the funds are always available for those willing and able to pay the price.

A second advantage to international firms is that the funds raised in the international money market are not restricted to where they can be deployed once lenders have been satisfied that the intended purpose will not jeopardize the prospects for servicing the loan(s).

Similarly, as borrowers, governments find loans granted without conditions except those that affect the collective assessment of credit risk by a competitive system of profit-seeking financial institutions. And this freedom has apparently been sufficient for many countries to pay market rates of interest instead of the subsidized rates that are usually available in intergovernmental borrowing and similar traditional ways of financing balance of payments deficits.

EUROCURRENCY LENDING PRACTICES.   Domestic banking markets around the world traditionally have been protected from change by government regulation and barriers to entry. In contrast, the very rationale for the existence of the Euromarkets has always been their freedom from certain regulations, taxes, and other costs. This freedom has allowed an unprecedented influx of international banks and their customers to Eurocurrency centers such as London, and these institutions have brought a variety of novel techniques and instruments to the market. Exhibit 13 lists some **Euromarket innovations.** As may be seen, some innovations did not succeed.

Techniques that have survived generally represent efficient responses to the high degree of competition and volatility of interest rates and funds flows in the Eurocurrency market. Three practices in the Euromarket are of particular interest:

- The unbundling of financial services and the decline of "relationship" banking.
- Formal multibank syndication of large loans.
- Rollover credits and floating rate notes.

Unbundling of Services.   The **bundling of financial services,** such as tying deposit taking to loan making, is a product of a protected market and tends to disappear when competition

EXHIBIT 13   INTERNATIONAL FINANCIAL INNOVATIONS IN THE POSTWAR ERA

Instrument or Technique and Date of Introduction	Supply Factors	Primary Functions or Demand Factors	Degree of Success
Swaps (late 1950s)	Currency flexibility in loans, deposits in a single money market	Potentially higher cost than alternative	High
Eurobonds (1958)	Severe secondary market difficulties at first	Domestic taxes and issue regulations	High
Eurodollars (1959)	Easy to issue	Domestic bank regulation	High
Currency basket bond (1961)	Minimal secondary market	Ready-made diversification	Minor
Rollover credits (early 1960s)	Lenders match assets' maturity to liabilities'	Transfer of interest rate risk to borrower	High
Parallel loans (early 1960s)	High cost of matching participants' needs	Credit and exchange controls	Modest
Currency option bond (1965)	Highly risky for borrower	Assurance of gains but not losses from exchange rate changes	Minor
Dual-currency convertible bonds (mid-1960s)	Thin secondary market	Issue and exchange controls	Minor
London dollar CDs (1967)	Secondary market slow to grow at first	Liquidity	Modest
Forward-forward CDs (late 1960s)	No secondary market; available in different form	Transfer of interest rate risk	Minor
Forfaiting (late 1960s)	Transfer of country risk to special institution	Adaptation of traditional technique	Modest

EXHIBIT 13 CONTINUED

Instrument or Technique and Date of Introduction	Supply Factors	Primary Functions or Demand Factors	Degree of Success
Floating rate notes (1970)	Small secondary market	Transfer of interest rate risk	Modest
Eurocommercial paper (1971)	Secondary market difficulties	None under existing regulatory system	Minor
Multicurrency option loan	Increases risk for banks	Provides borrower flexibility	Modest
Eurocurrency loan participation certificates (early 1970s)	No secondary market	Standardization, potential liquidity	Minor
Currency futures (1973)	Institutional framework in place	Standardization, negotiability; transfers default risk	High
Floating rate CDs (1977)	Small secondary market	Transfer of commitment period risk	Minor so far
Foreign exchange options (1970s)	Hedge currency risk of uncertain cash flows	Regulatory obstacles	Minor
Eurodollar interest rate futures (introduction under discussion)	Institutional framework exists	Standardization, negotiability; transfers default risk	—
Euroequity (rare)	Secondary market assured	None at present	None
Commodity-linked bonds (rare)	Hedge price fluctuation of reference commodity	Unrelated to cash flow of issues or investor	Minor
Index-linked bonds (rare)	Avoid risk of unexpected inflation	No objective index available, secondary market difficulties	Minor

Source: Gunter Dufey and Ian H. Giddy, "Innovation in International Financial Markets," *Journal of International Business Studies*, 1980.

sets in, at least in commercial loan markets. Because the bank that offers the most competitive loan terms is frequently not the bank that gives the most attractive rates on deposits, or on foreign exchange, Eurobanks have had an incentive to provide these services separately. The declining use of **compensating balances** is the most advanced manifestation of the unbundling trend in the United States.

Loan Syndication. The formal **Eurocurrency syndication** technique arose primarily because of the large size of term credits required by governments and multinational firms and the wide variety of banks providing the funds. The syndication procedure is also a means for banks to diversify some of the unique sovereign risks that arise in international lending. Syndicated Euroloans involve formal arrangements in which competitively selected **lead banks** assemble a management group of other banks to underwrite the loan and to market shares in it to still other participating banks.

As described in "The Pricing of Syndicated Eurocurrency Credits" by Goodman (*Federal Reserve Bank of New York Quarterly Review*, Summer 1980), there are generally three levels of banks in a syndicate: the **lead banks,** the **managing banks,** and the **participating banks.** Most loans are led by one or two major banks who negotiate to obtain a mandate to raise funds from the borrower. Often a potential borrower will set a competitive bidding procedure to determine which lead bank or banks will receive the mandate to organize the loan.

After the preliminary stages of negotiation with a borrower, the lead bank will begin to assemble a management group to underwrite the loan. The management group may be in place before the mandate is received, or may be assembled immediately afterward, depending on the loan. The lead bank is normally expected to underwrite a share at least as large as that of any other lender. If the loan cannot be underwritten on the initial terms, it must be renegotiated or the lead bank must be willing to take a larger share into its own portfolio than originally planned.

Once the management group is firmly in place and the lead bank has received a mandate from the borrower, a **placement memorandum** will be prepared by the lead bank and the loan will be marketed to other banks who may be interested in taking up shares (the participating banks). This placement memorandum describes the transaction and provides information about the borrower. The statistical information regarding the financial health of the borrower given in the memorandum is generally provided by the borrower. The placement memorandum emphasizes that reading it is not a substitute for an independent credit review by the participating banks. Bank supervisory authorities normally require sufficient lending information to be lodged in the bank to allow bank management to make a reasonable appraisal of the credit.

In a successful syndication, once the marketing to interested participants is completed, the lead and managing banks will keep 50–70% of their initial underwriting share. Not all credits are sold to participants. In smaller credits to frequent borrowers, **club loans** are often arranged. In a club loan, the lead bank and managers fund the entire loan and no placement memorandum is required. This type of credit is most common in periods of market uncertainty when all but the largest multinational banks are reluctant to do business.

It takes anywhere from 15 days to 3 months to arrange a syndication, with 6 weeks considered the norm. Generally speaking, the more familiar the borrower, the more quickly the terms can be set and the placement memorandum prepared; the smaller the credit, the shorter is the time needed for negotiating and marketing.

After the loan is arranged, one of the banks serves as agent to compute the appropriate interest rate charges, to receive service payments, to disburse these to individual participants, and to inform them if there are any problems with the loan. The lead bank usually serves as agent, but another member of the management group may do so.

The most common type of syndicated loan is a **term loan** in which the funds can be drawn down by the borrower within a specified period of time after the loan agreement has been signed (the drawdown period). The loan is usually repaid according to an amortization schedule, which varies from loan to loan. For some loans it may begin as soon as the loan is drawn down. For other loans, amortization may not begin until as long as 5 years after the loan agreement has been signed. The period before repayment of principal begins is known as the **grace period.** This is one of the most important points of negotiation between a borrower and a lead bank, and borrowers are normally willing to pay a wider spread to obtain a longer grace period.

The vast majority of **syndicated credits** are **denominated** in dollars, but loans in German marks, Swiss francs, Japanese yen, and other currencies are also available.

In contrast to Euroloans, U.S. domestic large loans or facilities are generally less formal arrangements even when provided by a group of banks. Although one bank may act as agent for the group, normally the corporate treasurer will himself organize a multibank facility and draw on each line of credit as he sees fit. This is possible because the borrower is more familiar to the various lending banks and facilities tend to be smaller and for more limited periods. In the future, as a wider range of both borrowers and banks participate in the prime loan market, it seems probable that U.S. and Euromarket syndication techniques will merge. But the sovereign risk of Euroloans is nonexistent for U.S. domestic loans and size is not yet the problem it is in Eurolending. Thus, there seems to be no immediate pressure for formal syndication of prime U.S. loans on a widespread basis.

EUROCURRENCY LOAN PRICING: ROLLOVER CREDITS. Euroloan pricing practices reflect the nature of the market as a pure financial intermediary, in which funds are "bought" and "sold" on a highly competitive basis. The primary manifestation of this is the rollover credit pricing technique.

Rollover credits, which enable banks to separate a loan's maturity from its interest contract period, were a direct result of the absence of a "deposit base" in the Euromarket. Eurobanks are specialized wholesale banks that rely on a sole funding source—large time and call deposits, mostly from banks and other highly interest-sensitive depositors. The Eurobanks' cost of funds therefore varies directly with the level of short-term rates. To protect themselves from substantial **interest rate risk** when they arrange to commit funds to the borrower for medium-term periods, such as 3 years, they establish that the interest rate will be altered every 3 or 6 months, bearing a fixed relationship to the **London Interbank Offered Rate (LIBOR),** the average rate paid by large banks in the Eurodollar interbank market. Whereas rollover Eurodollars bear a rate tied directly to money market and interbank cost of funds and the rate is changed only at fixed intervals, in the United States changes in a bank's **prime rate** are policy decisions that affect the rates on existing as well as new loans. Eurolending **spreads** are normally negotiated with the borrower prior to the initiation of the loan and either remain constant over the life of the loan or change after a set number of years. Customers have found these arrangements acceptable because it permits them to avoid the risk of unavailability of funds.

In addition to the interest costs on a Eurocurrency loan, there are also **commitment fees,** front-end fees, and occasionally an annual agent's fee. **Commitment fees** are charged to the borrower as a percentage of the undrawn portion of the credit and are typically 0.5% annually, imposed on both term loans and revolving credits. **Front-end management fees** are one-time charges negotiated in advance and imposed when the loan agreement is signed. Fees are usually in the range of 0.5–1% of the value of the loan. These front-end fees include participation fees and management fees. The participation fees are divided among all banks in relation to their share of the loan. The management fees are divided between the underwriting banks and the lead bank. The **agent's fee,** if applicable, is usually a yearly charge but may occasionally be paid at the outset. These fees are relatively small; the agent's fee on a large credit may run $10,000 per annum.

The charges on syndicated loans may be summarized as follows:

$$\text{annual payments} = (\text{LIBOR} + \text{spread}) \times \text{amount of loan drawn} + (\text{commitment fee})$$
$$\times \text{amount of loan undrawn} + \text{annual agent's fee (if any)}$$

$$\text{front-end charges} = \text{participation fee} \times \text{face amount of loan} + \text{management fee} \times \text{face}$$
$$\text{amount of loan} + \text{initial agent's fee (if any)}$$

Front-end changes are an important component of the banks' total return on a credit. Consider a $100 million, 7-year credit with no grace period. If the loan is priced at 100 basis points over a LIBOR of 10%, annual payments of interest and principal repayment total slightly over $21 million. A 1% fee requires that $1 million be paid to the banks in the syndicate at the outset. This raises the effective interest to the borrower from 11 to 11.31% per annum. If banks paid, on average, 9.75% for their funds, the front-end fees increase their margin on the loan from 125 to 156 basis points. This represents a 25% increment to their return on a credit.

LOAN AGREEMENT PROVISIONS. As a rule, Eurocurrency loan agreements are simple, containing fewer restrictive covenants than do many domestic (U.S.) loan agreements. This is in part because loans to multinational corporations' affiliates are regarded as the obligation of the parent company, and loans to governments cannot impose many conditions for obvious reasons. Another reason is that such agreements typically contain a **cross-default clause,** which stipulates that the loan is in default if and when the parent is in default on its own loans: for example, by not complying with restrictive covenants contained in its own loan agreements.

In addition to the usual clauses referring to pricing, interest payment dates, and amortization dates, Euroloan agreements contain a number of provisions that reflect their international character.

First, special clauses are required to specify the **jurisdiction** as well as the **judgment currency** for loans. A loan may be funded in the Bahamas, booked in London, and made by a diverse group of international banks to a borrower in Japan. The determination of jurisdiction requires careful consideration. Not only must the applicable law and legal practice be sophisticated, but courts must be willing to accept jurisdiction, and it helps when the country is one that has the power to enforce judgments. New York is often chosen because of the extensive case law on banking matters that has been built up, even in cases involving lenders and borrowers not residents of that country. Judgment currency clauses are necessary because the courts in many countries, notably the United Kingdom, will render a judgment in domestic money only.

Similarly, the **place and method of payment** must be stipulated. Payment is normally effected by means of the transfer of funds from one bank account to another in the country of the currency in which the loan is denominated, although the well-developed U.S. dollar payments system in New York is often used for payment of interest and principal on loans denominated in other currencies. Some banks have sought to insert a clause that states that banks can **deliver** the funds from any financial center they choose. Borrowers sometimes succeed in including the right to **receive** the funds in the place of their choice.

Several clauses are designed specifically to protect banks. A **guarantee clause** will be required if the borrower's own credit standing does not suffice. A frequently used clause is the **reserve requirement** clause stipulating that the borrower has to absorb any additional cost the lender incurs when interest-free reserve requirements are imposed on the lending bank, effectively increasing the cost of money. Banks also ask that all payments of principal and interest be made **free and clear of taxes** and similar charges. Some go further and insist on a clause protecting them against general increases in cost. Many agreements also contain a **Eurocurrency availability clause,** permitting the bank to call for prepayment if sufficient dollar funds are not available.

In contrast, several typical clauses favor the borrower. A **prepayment clause** gives the borrower the right to repay a loan before maturity. A **multicurrency option clause** permits the borrower to switch currencies and draw down funds in currencies other than the one specified in the loan agreement. A different **currency option clause** allows the borrower to alter the currency of denomination of the loan entirely. This choice can be valuable at times of anticipated currency revaluation. Recent agreements have also provided borrowers with the option of two or more different financial markets (e.g., Eurodollar and U.S. dollar) in which to take down a commitment.

SWAPS, CREDIT SWAPS, AND PARALLEL LOANS.   While international loans are normally funded and denominated in a single currency, there exists a set of techniques for making loans across currencies and across national boundaries. These normally involve an explicit or implicit purchase of a foreign currency and simultaneous sale of that currency for a future date. This coupling of a spot and forward foreign exchange deal is called a **swap.** A **currency swap** is simply an agreement to exchange certain amounts of two currencies on a spot basis (today) and to reverse the transaction at an agreed-upon exchange rate at a specified time in the future. The term "swap" is also used frequently to refer to a credit swap, which matches the currency swap to a pair of loans.

A typical **credit swap** might involve a firm in country A providing (hard) currency funds for its affiliate in a weak-currency country. The parent company will lend, for example, dollar funds to an intermediary, a commercial bank, or even the central bank of the weak-currency country, which, in turn, lends local currency funds to the foreign affiliate. At a predetermined date in the future, the transaction will be reversed. The cost of the transaction contains the following elements: the interest rate on the funds less the interest rate on the local currency funds, adjusted for any difference between the prevailing spot rate, and the implicit rate used to reconvert the local currency funds on repayment date. Because of these contractual relationships, it is the intermediary (local bank or foreign central bank) that bears the burden of the exchange risk on the (dollar) principal. The interest on the local currency loan, however, is subject to **exchange risk** in dollar terms.

Why would firms and intermediaries undertake such complex deals instead of simpler alternatives such as direct loans in dollars, borrowing in the local money market, or lending dollar funds covered with a forward contract? From the viewpoint of the firm, it is primarily market imperfections that provide the compelling reason. Neither forward cover nor access to local credit markets may be available at reasonable rates. For the intermediaries, such credit swaps are a means of bolstering their foreign exchange reserves, using the financial needs of captive foreign affiliates to obtain these reserves at a lower cost than might be available through outright borrowing. And since they are close to the political powers that determine extent and timing of devaluations, they may be convinced of their ability to assess the foreign exchange risk better than private companies. Indeed the intermediary bank is frequently the central bank itself.

A **parallel loan** is an arrangement under which two corporations (or other institutions) in different countries make loans to each other in their own countries and currencies. The classic example is that of an American firm making a dollar loan to the U.S. subsidiary of a British company, while the British firm simultaneously makes a sterling loan to the U.S. subsidiary of the American firm. Such dollar–sterling parallel loans have been concluded at interest rate differentials reflecting the difference between long-term interbank rates, avoiding the respective borrowing-investing spreads.

Each loan serves as collateral for the other, and bears an interest rate related to local credit conditions plus the putative cost of a long term forward exchange contract. Unlike some of the earlier examples, this technique is purely a product of regulation; it enables firms to avoid capital (and perhaps also credit) controls. In concept, it is a costly and clumsy arrangement; two parties with matching needs have to be brought together, and the agreement is a combination of three financial contracts: two loans plus one implicit forward transaction.

EXHIBIT 14   RISK PROTECTION TECHNIQUES OF EUROBANKS

Lending Risk	Source of Risk	Risk Reduction Strategy
Interest risk	Mismatched maturities coupled with unpredictable movements in interest rates	Matching assets to liabilities by pricing credits on rollover basis
Funding risk	Possibility that funds will not be available to particular banks on normal terms	Floating rate notes and floating rate CDs
Currency risk	Exchange loss when currency of loan depreciates or currency of liability appreciates	Fund in same currency as loan or cover mismatched currencies with swaps
Credit risk	Ability of an entity to repay its debts	Syndication of credit and diversification of bank's loan portfolio; corporate and government guarantees
Country risk	Ability and willingness of borrowers within a country to meet their obligations	Syndication of credit and diversification of bank's loan portfolio
Regulatory risk	Imposition of reserve requirements or taxes on banks	Clause in contract that forces borrowers to bear this risk

Source: Adapted from Laurie Goodman, "The Pricing of Syndicated Eurocurrency Credits," *Federal Reserve Bank of New York Quarterly Review,* Summer 1980.

Only regulations that constrain credit allocation or prevent free capital flows justify its existence.

A variant of the parallel loan **across** currencies is a similar construct that involves two offsetting transactions in the domestic and the external (Euro-) sector of the credit market in a **single** currency. This technique requires the same constellation of actors and regulations, but has the advantage that the security of each party (i.e., the right of offset) is not affected by changes in the exchange rate.

EUROBANKING RISK PROTECTION.   As should be evident, international banks have accumulated a fair degree of experience in Eurocurrency lending and funding techniques. Because the market is so competitive, there remains little margin for loss. Therefore, most of the risks are explicitly managed through diversification, pricing, hedging or insurance of some sort or another. Some of the principal risks and banks' responses to them are contained in Exhibit 14.

FUNDING IN INTERNATIONAL BANKING

FUNDING IN THE EUROCURRENCY MARKET.   Prior to the development of the Euromarkets, the primary source of funding for international lending was the deposit base of the parent bank plus funds bought in the domestic money market. The Eurodollar market changed this feature dramatically, providing a huge pool of primary and interbank deposits that new entrants to the international banking scene could draw on. The Eurocurrency market is the market for bank deposits and loans denominated in currencies other than that of the country in which the bank or bank branch is located. The **Eurocurrency interbank market**

now has a depth comparable to any of the world's money markets, including that of the United States.

For their international loans, therefore, banks have come to rely very heavily on the Eurocurrency or "offshore" markets. This changes when a bank enters a country intent on doing local currency business with domestic companies. Here, it is usually desirable to fund local currency loans with local currency deposits—otherwise the bank might expose itself to serious exchange losses should the local currency devalue. In some countries the local money market is so poorly developed or so restricted that banks are forced to obtain funds from abroad—for example, American banks relied on funds borrowed abroad for yen-denominated loans extended in Japan during the 1970s. In such cases the borrowed funds are typically hedged by means of a **swap,** usually arranged with the central bank. Dollars could be exchanged into yen for lending purposes, with an agreement to reverse the exchange at some later date at a prearranged exchange rate. In some cases banks have chosen to fund local loans abroad because they are cheaper—for example, Canadian banks' U.S. offices fund much of their U.S. lending by drawing on the large pool of Eurodollar deposits placed with their parent banks in Canada.

EUROBANK LIABILITY MANAGEMENT. As pointed out in *The International Money Market* (Dufey and Giddy), liability management in a Eurobank aims to (1) assure the continued availability of funds at a reasonable cost (i.e., at close to prevailing market rates), (2) maintain a stable deposit base, (3) minimize the cost of funds, and (4) minimize the "mismatch" between maturities of assets and those of liabilities. In addition, some banks seek to profit from such money market techniques as arbitrage (taking advantage of differences in yields between similar money market instruments) and "riding the yield curve" (borrowing at short maturities and depositing at longer maturities, or vice versa, to profit from differences between the bank's forecast of future interest rate and those implied by the prevailing yield curve).

While in most respects the **international bank liability management** task is similar to domestic funding, there are certainly differences of emphasis, arising partly from the fact that the Eurodollar market is largely a wholesale banking system. A substantial proportion of day-to-day Eurobanking activities consists of the active "trading" of Eurocurrency deposits—that is, borrowing short-term funds from other banks and redepositing these funds in the interbank market. This means that the **liability management** of a Eurobank is closely tied in with the management of cash and liquid assets. In this respect, a Eurobank is most closely comparable with the money market departments of large money market center banks in the United States.

Exhibit 15 illustrates a hypothetical balance sheet of an offshore branch of an international bank. The major sources of funds are short-term borrowings from other international banks, nonbank time deposits, and (for London branches), **Eurodollar certificates of deposit.** Other funding sources are **floating rate loan notes** and **floating rate CDs, Eurobonds,** loans from other branches, and loans or equity from the parent bank.

Eurobanks are not subject to reserve requirements imposed by monetary authorities —indeed the absence of noninterest-bearing reserve requirements and other costs such as taxes and fees of the **Federal Deposit Insurance Corp.** (FDIC) enable them to compete with domestic deposits and offer more attractive rates. Therefore if they hold noninterest-bearing deposits, they do so purely for precautionary and transactions purposes.

INTERBANK LINES OF CREDIT. Because Eurobanks are not subject to reserve requirements, they do all they can to minimize amounts held in demand deposits. Interbank lines

EXHIBIT 15   SIMPLIFIED BALANCE SHEET OF A EUROBANK

Assets	Liabilities
1. Reserve balances	1. Interbank deposits
2. Liquid assets	2. Nonbank time deposits
3. Loans	3. London dollar CDs
	4. Notes and bonds
	5. Loans from other branches
	6. Loans from parent bank
	7. Share capital held by parent bank

of credit enable them to hold negligible clearing balances. All active international banks retain and extend a network of credit lines, based on the relative creditworthiness of banks with which they place funds. These lines are drawn on whenever the bank's daily cash outflows exceed its cash inflows. Since Eurobanks maintain almost no immediately payable checking accounts, and since almost all international payments are effected 1 or 2 business days after completion of a transaction, these inflows and outflows can be managed rather tightly. Since **interbank deposits** form the prime Eurocurrency funding source for the bulk of international banks as well as enabling them to manage cash flows, the establishment of credit lines, formal or informal, is paramount to the banker entering the Euromarket.

In addition, many Eurobanks doing business in a particular currency seek to maintain lines of credit with banks from the country of that currency. Thus a bank in London taking Euromark deposits will establish German mark lines with, say, Deutsche Bank, Dresdner Bank, and DG bank. The concern is that, should Euromarket funding sources for some reason "dry up," the Eurobank will nevertheless have access to the domestic market to meet its obligations.

Because the Euromarket does not create new funds, but only attracts business away from domestic markets, the disappearance of the market is not a serious concern—the funds could only return to their domestic money markets, and the interbank market would reshuffle them to those banks willing to pay competitive interest rates. On the other hand, banks do face a funding risk from time to time, as a result of the phenomenon of **tiering.** Tiering refers to the grouping of banks according to some characteristic, such as size or nationality, that serves as a proxy for creditworthiness assessments during periods of great uncertainty. The number of tiers and the differences between them have tended to increase when events focus attention on the possibility of **bank default.** Such an event was the suspension of Bankhaus Herstatt in 1974: for some time after that, interbank deposit rates indicated the existence of six or more tiers of Eurobanks. Some banks effectively found themselves cut off from the market, at least temporarily.

For a more detailed discussion of the granting of interbank lines, see Davis, *The Eurobank* (Wiley, 1976, Chapter 4).

EUROMARKET FUNDING INSTRUMENTS.   The bulk of deposits in the Eurocurrency market is time deposits at fixed interest rates, usually of short maturity. According to figures published by the Bank of England in the *Quarterly Bulletin,* approximately 70% of deposits in London Eurobanks have a maturity of less than 3 months. Many of these deposits are on **call,** meaning that they can be withdrawn without notice; but since payment is normally effected by means of transfers in the currency's home country, these are not really checking accounts. While checking account facilities are offered by some Eurobanks, these are chiefly for small transactions and do not form an important part of the funding portfolio.

Most of the time deposit placements are made by other banks, but many are also made by governments and their central banks and by multinational corporations. A few are made by wealthy individuals, often by proxy—for example, through a Swiss bank.

Negotiable Eurodollar certificates of deposit, sometimes called **London dollar CDs,** appeared in London in 1970. These provide greater liquidity and so often bear a slightly lower interest rate than Eurodollar time deposits of the same maturity. While the original intention was to attract a greater proportion of corporate and individual deposits to the market, the bulk are probably held by banks. There is an active secondary market in London dollar CDs, although its depth does not match that of the U.S. CD market. A number of institutions, such as affiliates of U.S. investment banks as well as U.K. merchant banks and discount houses, assure the continuation of the secondary market by acting as market makers.

The usual form of issuance of Eurodollar certificates of deposit is as **tap CDs.** Tap CDs are issued in round amounts (say $5 million) whenever a bank requires funds for a particular maturity—say 3 months. The usual purpose would be to fund a Eurodollar loan made on a 3-month rollover basis. The issuing bank "taps" the market at very short notice by setting a rate and informing brokers of the terms of the issue.

The distinctive feature of the alternative form of London dollar CD, **tranche CDs,** is that they are "sliced" into several portions with greater appeal to those investors who prefer an instrument with smaller denominations than those of conventional CDs. Unlike tap CDs, tranche CDs are "managed" issues, offered to the public for sale through brokerage houses in a fashion similar to a securities issue.

To obtain funds at longer maturities without locking themselves into a fixed interest cost, some banks have issued **floating rate notes** (FRNs) and, more recently, **floating rate CDs.** These two differ only in terms of subordination. Floating rate liabilities enable banks to assure themselves of the longer term availability of funds, while allowing the interest rates on their liabilities to vary periodically with market rates. Thus they can match the interest period of their liabilities with those of their assets (rollover loans), and avoid a funding risk.

Finally, a **forward forward,** or more correctly, a **forward Eurodollar CD,** is a contract to issue a Eurodollar CD at a fixed interest rate at a given date in the future. Such contracts, in conjunction with the issue of ordinary (spot) CDs, effectively constituted CDs of longer term than was at one time legally permitted in the United Kingdom. However, since the same effect can now be achieved as easily by simultaneously buying and selling CDs of different maturities, participants in the Eurodollar market have not employed this technique to any great extent. A more promising development is the introduction of standardized futures contracts in Eurodollar CDs.

ONSHORE VERSUS OFFSHORE FUNDING.   The banker familiar with sources of funds in the Euromarket is able to use the market not only to fund Eurocurrency loans, but also for domestic purposes. Indeed U.S. banks have made extensive use of their Bahamian and London branches to obtain funds when tight credit in the United States impelled depositors to place their funds in a market free of interest rate ceilings—**Regulation Q** of the **Federal Reserve Board.**

To compare the cost of funding onshore with the cost of borrowing Eurodollars, however, it is not sufficient to know the interest rates on the two types of deposit. Domestic deposits, unlike Eurodeposits, are subject to reserve requirements and FDIC premiums. While offshore deposits themselves face no such costs, the Federal Reserve Board has from time to time imposed a reserve requirement on Eurodollars used in the United States; this is called **Regulation M.** Hence to compare costs, one must adjust the interest rates as follows:

cost of domestic deposit in United States = domestic bank deposit rate
+ cost of reserve requirement
+ FDIC premiums
cost of Eurodeposit used in United States = Eurodollar deposit rate + cost of Regulation M reserve requirement

If banks have substantial domestic funding needs and are otherwise indifferent between onshore and offshore deposits, **arbitrage** between the **U.S. and Eurodollar money markets** will occur until the two adjusted rates are equal. Indeed, because of the cost of reserve requirements and FDIC fees, banks can and usually do offer higher interest rates on Eurodeposits than on domestic deposits.

INTERNATIONAL BANKING REGULATIONS

No treatment of international banking would be complete without a discussion of the **legal and regulatory constraints** facing the international banker. Because banks have the means to garner and allocate a nation's savings, governments around the world seek to influence the behavior of banks. Banks are constrained, secured, protected, discriminated against, and sometimes even owned by governments. International banks face multiple and often overlapping jurisdictions and almost universally must confront restrictions on entry into foreign markets. On the other hand, their flexibility has, to some extent, given them a choice of jurisdiction for certain activities, thus reducing the burden of regulation. Banking authorities viewing international banking are thus faced with the choice of constraining banks and thus isolating their country from the free world market's interchange of financial resources, or easing regulations in such a way as to reduce the relative attractiveness of doing banking in offshore jurisdictions. Among the issues faced by the U.S. banking authorities are:

- The problem of **gaps in regulatory coverage.**
- The **problem of regulating foreign portfolios** and activities of U.S. banks that receive Federal Reserve and FDIC support.
- The problem of maintaining U.S. banks' international **competitiveness** without sacrificing their soundness.
- The problem of **national versus reciprocal treatment of foreign banks** in the United States.
- The problems of **appropriate jurisdiction** for U.S. banks abroad.
- The problem of maintaining an effective **monetary policy** despite international capital mobility and continual innovations.
- The problem of maintaining the appropriate **allocation of credit** in the domestic economy.

The regulation of U.S. banks abroad and foreign banks in the United States is made more difficult by the fragmentation of banking jurisdiction between federal and state agencies and between the **Federal Reserve Board,** the **Comptroller of the Currency,** and the **Federal**

Deposit Insurance Corp. at the federal level. The tendency has been toward a concentration of jurisdiction at the federal level, especially under the Federal Reserve Board and the Comptroller of the Currency.

The framework of U.S. and foreign regulation of international banking is outlined next. For more detail, the reader is referred to the references and bibliography.

U.S. REGULATION OF AMERICAN BANKS ABROAD.   Since most international banking is done through foreign branches, and because branches are legally an integral part of the bank, U.S. banking abroad is in principle subject to all the regulations (e.g., reserve requirements) and legal limitations (e.g., on the concentration of loans to a single borrower) to which domestic branches are subject. In practice, some regulations, such as reserve requirements and strict limits on the nature of commercial banks' activities, are eased. Others, such as limits on loan concentration and provisions for adequate capital to meet deposit outflows, are enforced in the interest of bank soundness.

For all banks, granting permission to **open a branch abroad** is the preserve of the **Federal Reserve Board.** The Board also regulates direct equity participations in foreign banks (or nonbanks) by U.S. banks or by bank holding companies, and branches, agencies, and subsidiaries of Edge Act banks.

The U.S. Comptroller of the Currency has responsibility for examination and supervision of overseas branches of national banks. Jurisdiction over activities of state-chartered banks that are not Federal Reserve System members is held by state banking authorities but in practice is shared with the FDIC. The state authorities also share jurisdiction over activities of state-chartered member banks with the Federal Reserve Board.

U.S. REGULATION OF FOREIGN BANKS.   The 1970s saw a proliferation of non-American banks in the United States. While these banks at first entered to service their multinational clients' U.S. banking needs, a later acceleration of entry was motivated by the desire to establish access to the U.S. money markets to support international dollar-based banking, and simply to compete profitably with U.S. banks for the loan and deposit business of large domestic customers.

Some foreign banks establish **representative offices,** which can drum up business but may not carry on any borrowing or lending. Banks wishing to make loans but not requiring deposits can establish **agencies.** To both take deposits and make loans, they must set up either a **branch** or a **subsidiary.** Subsidiaries are merely domestic banks owned by foreigners, and so are subject to the normal range of state and federal regulations.

While in the past the regulation of foreign banking in the United States rested primarily with state governments, the **International Banking Act (IBA)** of 1978 placed foreign banks under explicit federal jurisdiction, prohibiting cross-state branching and investment-banking subsidiaries, imposing reserve requirements and, for small deposits, requiring FDIC insurance.

Until the present the United States has adhered rather strictly in its regulation of foreign banks to the **national treatment principle,** whereby insofar as is possible, foreign banks are accorded the same privileges and subjected to the same constraints as are domestic banks. The rationale is that this provides the greatest competitive equality and best serves the public. Some state regulators and some officials at the national level, however, have argued for consideration of the principle of **reciprocity,** whereby a foreign bank from country A would be permitted only the activities allowed U.S. banks doing business in A. Prior to the implementation of the IBA, New York State's treatment of foreign banks adhered to this principle.

EXHIBIT 16 CLASSIFICATION OF RESTRICTIONS ON BANK ENTRY INTO HOST COUNTRIES AS OF 1979[a]

Country	No Foreign Presence	No New Foreign Commercial Bank Entry	No Foreign Commercial Banking Except Representative Offices	No Foreign Commercial Bank Branches	No Equity Interest in Indigenous Commercial Banks	No Controlling Interest in Indigenous Commercial Banks	No Restrictions Found	Restrictions Indeterminate
1. Afghanistan	X	X		X	X	X		
2. Algeria			X	X	X	X		
3. Argentina							X	
4. Australia			X	X		X		
5. Austria							X	
6. Bahamas							X	
7. Bahrain				X		X		
8. Bangladesh					X	X		
9. Barbados							X	
10. Belgium							X	
11. Belize		X			X	X		
12. Benin			X	X		X		
13. Bermuda			X	X		X		
14. Botswana				X				
15. Bolivia							X	
16. Brazil		X			X	X		
17. Bulgaria	X			X	X	X		
18. Burma				X	X	X		
19. Burundi								X
20. Cameroon								
21. Canada				X		X		
22. Republic of Cape Verde							X	
23. Cayman Islands							X	
24. Central African Empire						X		
25. Chad							b	
26. Chile								X

#	Country								
27.	China, Peoples Republic			X	X	X	X		
28.	Colombia			X	X	X	X		
29.	Congo, Peoples Republic			X		X			
30.	Costa Rica			X					
31.	Cuba			X	X	X		X	X
32.	Cyprus			X	X				
33.	Czechoslovakia			X^c		X		X	X
34.	Denmark								
35.	Republic of Djibouti		X	X		X			
36.	Dominican Republic			X		X			
37.	Ecuador			X		X			
38.	Egypt								
39.	El Salvador			X	X	X	X	X	
40.	Ethiopia			X	X	X			X
41.	Federal Republic of Germany		X						
42.	Fiji		X	X		X			
43.	Finland			X		X			
44.	France		X						
45.	Gabon		X						
46.	The Gambia			X		X			
47.	German Democratic Republic			X	X	X	X		
48.	Ghana					X			
49.	Greece			X	X	X			
50.	Guatemala			X	X	X	X	X	
51.	Guinea								X
52.	Guinea-Bissau	X							
53.	Guyana			X	X^d	X	X	X	X
54.	Haiti					X	X		
55.	Honduras				X	X			
56.	Hong Kong			X		X			
57.	Hungary			X	X	X			
58.	Iceland			X	X	X			
59.	India				X	X	X		
60.	Indonesia				X		X		
61.	Iran			X	X	X		X	X
62.	Iraq	X							

EXHIBIT 16 CONTINUED

Country	No Foreign Presence	No New Foreign Commercial Bank Entry	No Foreign Commercial Banking Except Representative Offices	No Foreign Commercial Bank Branches	No Equity Interest in Indigenous Commercial Banks	No Controlling Interest in Indigenous Commercial Banks	No Restrictions Found	Restrictions Indeterminate
			Current Restrictions on Foreign Commercial Bank Entry					
63. Republic of Ireland				X	X			
64. Israel							X	
65. Italy							X	
66. Ivory Coast							X	
67. Jamaica								
68. Japan						X		
69. Jordan				X			X	
70. Kenya								
71. Republic of Korea				X	X	X		
72. Kuwait		X		X	X	X		
73. Laos	X	X		X	X	X		
74. Lebanon							X	
75. Lesotho								X
76. Liberia						(X)		
77. Libya	X	X		X	X	X		
78. Luxembourg							X	
79. Madagascar	X	X		X	X	(X)		
80. Malawi				X		X		
81. Malaysia							X	
82. Mali				X		X		
83. Malta				X	X			
84. Mauritania							X	
85. Mauritius							X	
86. Mexico			X	X		X		
87. Morocco				X		X		
88. Mozambique							X	

#	Country	1	2	3	4	5	6	7	8
89.	Nepal			X	X	X			X
90.	Netherlands-Antilles			X	X	X		X	
91.	Netherlands			(X)					
92.	New Zealand	X		X	X	X	X		
93.	Nicaragua								
94.	Niger								
95.	Nigeria			X	X	X			
96.	Norway			X	X	X			
97.	Oman			X					
98.	Pakistan								
99.	Panama		X	X					
100.	Papua New Guinea		X		X				
101.	Paraguay		X						
102.	Peru			X	X	X			
103.	Philippines			X	X	X			
104.	Poland			X	X	X			
105.	Portugal			X	X	X			
106.	Qatar								
107.	Romania			X	X	X			
108.	Rwanda		X	X	X	X			
109.	Saudi Arabia			X	X	X			
110.	Senegal		X	X					
111.	Seychelles		X	X					
112.	Sierra Leone		X	X	X	X			
113.	Singapore			X	X	X			
114.	Somalia		X	X	X	X	X	X	X
115.	Solomon Islands		X	X	X	X			
116.	South Africa		X	X	X	X			
117.	Spain								
118.	Sri Lanka		X	X		X			
119.	Sudan			(X)		(X)			
120.	Surinam		X	X	X	X		X	
121.	Swaziland		X	(X)	X	X	X		
122.	Sweden			X	X	X			
123.	Switzerland			X					
124.	Syria		X	X	X	X			

EXHIBIT 16 CONTINUED

Country	Current Restrictions on Foreign Commercial Bank Entry							
	No Foreign Presence	No New Foreign Commercial Bank Entry	No Foreign Commercial Banking Except Representative Offices	No Foreign Commercial Bank Branches	No Equity Interest in Indigenous Commercial Banks	No Controlling Interest in Indigenous Commercial Banks	No Restrictions Found	Restrictions Indeterminate
125. Taiwan								f
126. Tanzania		X		X	X	X		
127. Thailand				X				
128. Togo							X	
129. Trinidad and Tobago		X	X	X	X			
130. Tunisia			X	X	X	X		
131. Turkey			X	X	X	X		
132. USSR		X	X	X	X	X		
133. United Arab Emirates		X		X	X	X		
134. United Kingdom								
135. Upper Volta						X		
136. Uruguay				X	X	X		
137. Venezuela			X	X	(X)	(X)		
138. Yemen Arab Republic					X	X		
139. Yugoslavia			X	X				
140. Zaire				X				
141. Zambia							X	

[a]Parentheses.

[b]Either a representative office or a branch is permitted, but not both.

[c]De novo subsidiaries are permitted.

(X) indicates that the situation is unclear but entry might be possible. This exhibit is an overview of restrictions on foreign bank entry in countries recognized by the U.S. plus Taiwan and the Cayman Islands. The classifications are based on current practices (August 1979), not status. In most cases where restrictions were found to be indeterminate, foreign banks have not attempted those specific forms of entry, so that clear conclusions about current practices cannot be drawn. Other instances represent cases where government practices are unclear or not defined.

[d]Equity participation is unclear.

[e]No representative offices are permitted.

[f]Branch and representative offices are permitted.

Source: U. S. Treasury Department, Office of the Comptroller of the Currency, *Report to Congress on Foreign Government Treatment of U. S. Commercial Banking Organizations,* 1979.

OTHER COUNTRIES' REGULATION OF FOREIGN BANKS.   As noted above, banks are often a major instrument for the implementation of social goals. Hence the banking systems of many countries are relatively restricted. The free entry of foreign banks would undermine the influence exercised by the host government to allocate credit, set interest rates, and so forth. Nevertheless U.S., British, French, Japanese, and other banks have established substantial presences in the domestic markets of many countries.

Official constraints on foreign banks take the form of (1) **entry restrictions,** and (2) **restraints on the operations** of banks already established in the host country's market.

Restrictions on entry may be by law or, more often, by administrative policy or practice. They range from prohibition of foreign bank presence to various limitations on the legal form allowed. Particular forms of entry, such as establishment of branches, or subsidiaries, or acquisition of equity interest in an existing bank, may be specifically restricted. Or foreign bank presence may be limited to representative offices, which may not engage in any direct banking transactions.

In 1979 the **U.S. Treasury Department** undertook a major survey of foreign countries' treatment of U.S. banks. One result of this was a table listing the entry restrictions of 141 countries (Exhibit 16). The reader should be aware that many of these classifications were judgmental, and in any case many regulations are in a state of flux.

Even when established in a country, foreign banks are frequently subjected to treatment that differs from that accorded domestic banks. Most **restrictions on bank operations** increase the cost of doing business and thus have effects that are equivalent to the imposition of a tax. An example of a **"taxlike"** restriction is special reserve requirements. A second category of regulation is **"quotalike"** restrictions that set absolute limits on the amount of credit or services that banks may offer. Examples of both types of restraints may be found in Exhibit 17.

EXHIBIT 17   EXAMPLES OF "TAX-LIKE AND QUOTALIKE" RESTRICTIONS ON FOREIGN BANKS

"Taxlike" Restrictions[a]

Differential reserve requirements
Prohibitions against accepting retail deposits
Prohibitions against foreign exchange transactions
No access to rediscount facilities
No access to subsidized funds for export financing

"Quotalike" Restrictions

Credit and lending ceilings
Specified loan portfolio structure
Swap limits
Required capital-to-asset ratios combined with capitalization limits
Ceilings on loans in domestic currency
Ceilings on loans in foreign currencies
Prohibition or limitation on branching

---

[a]Most of these restrictions effectively increase funding or other costs.
Source: U. S. Treasury Department, Office of the Comptroller of the Currency, *Report to Congress on Foreign Government Treatment of U. S. Commercial Banking Organizations*, 1979.

REFERENCES AND BIBLIOGRAPHY

Angelini, Anthony, Eng, Maximo, and Lees, Francis A., *International Lending, Risk and Euromarkets*, Macmillan, New York, 1979.

Baker, James C., *International Bank Regulation*, Praeger, New York, 1978.

———, and Bradford, Gerald M., *American Banks Abroad: Edge Act Companies and Multinational Banking*, Praeger, New York, 1974.

Coninx, Raymond G. F., *Foreign Exchange Today*, Wiley, New York, 1978.

Davis, Steven I., *The Management Function in International Banking*, Halsted, New York, 1979.

———, *The Eurobank: Its Origins, Management and Outlook*, Macmillan, New York, 1976.

Donaldson, T. H., *Lending in International Commercial Banking*, Halsted, New York, 1979.

Dufey, Gunter, and Giddy, Ian H., *The International Money Market*, Prentice-Hall, Englewood Cliffs, NJ, 1978.

Einzig, Paul, *Roll-Over Credits*, Macmillan, New York, 1973.

Eiteman, David K., and Stonehill, Arthur I., *Multinational Business Finance*, 2nd ed., Addison-Wesley, Reading, MA, 1979.

Harfield, Henry, *Bank Credits and Acceptances*, 5th ed., Ronald Press, New York, 1974.

Hayes, Douglas A., *Bank Lending Policies: Domestic and International*, 2nd ed., University of Michigan Press, Ann Arbor, 1977.

Henning, Charles N., Pigott, William, and Scott, Robert Haney, *International Financial Management*, McGraw-Hill, New York, 1978.

Hudson, Nigel R. L., *Money and Exchange Dealing in International Banking*, Halsted, New York, 1979.

Kubarych, Roger M., *Foreign Exchange Markets in the United States*, Federal Reserve Bank of New York, New York, 1978.

Lees, Francis A., *International Banking and Finance*, Wiley, New York, 1974.

Mandich, Donald R., Ed., *Foreign Exchange Trading Techniques and Controls*, American Bankers Association, New York, 1976.

Mathis, John, Ed., *Offshore Lending by U.S. Commercial Banks*, Robert Morris Associates, Philadelphia, 1975.

Quinn, Brian Scott, *The New Euromarkets*, Macmillan, New York, 1975.

Riehl, Heinz, and Rodriguez, Rita M., *Foreign Exchange Markets*, McGraw-Hill, New York, 1977.

Shaw, Ernest D., *Practical Aspects of Letters of Credit*, Irving Trust Co., New York, 1963.

Steuber, Ursel, *International Banking: The Foreign Activities of Principal Industrial Countries*, Sijthoff, Amsterdam, 1976.

Stigum, Marcia, *The Money Market: Myth, Reality and Practice*, Dow-Jones Irwin, Homewood, IL, 1978.

SECTION **15**

INTERNATIONAL PORTFOLIO DIVERSIFICATION AND FOREIGN CAPITAL MARKETS

CONTENTS

INCREASED INVESTMENT EFFICIENCY	3
EMPIRICAL STUDIES ON INTERNATIONAL PORTFOLIOS	5
Analysis of the Structure of Returns	7
Models of the International Capital Market	8
Performance of Some International Funds	8
Costs of International Investment	8
INVESTING IN MULTINATIONAL CORPORATIONS	9
INVESTING IN MAJOR CAPITAL MARKETS	9
The Euromarket	10

Foreign Markets	**14**
Japan	14
Stock exchanges	15
Bond market	17
Securities trading	18
United Kingdom	19
Securities trading	19
Gilt market	20
Investors in the U.K. market	21
Regulation of the U.K. market	21
West Germany	22
Securities trading	22
Fixed income securities market	23
Investors	24
Tax laws	24
France	24
Securities trading	25
Restrictions and taxes	25
Investors	26

INTERNATIONAL PORTFOLIO DIVERSIFICATION AND FOREIGN CAPITAL MARKETS

James R. F. Guy and Closson L. Vaughan

Studies on the effects of diversifying an investment portfolio internationally started to appear in the academic literature in the late 1960s. It is only recently, however, that individual U.S. investors and the popular press have shown significant interest in the field. This has been due in large part to the divergence of economic growth rates and inflation rates among the major industrialized nations since 1974, which have had an impact on **relative market performance, interest rates,** and **currency exchange rates** in the various countries.

Although these dramatic economic gyrations have highlighted the benefits of international diversification, previously published research on the subject had already made a strong case for creating **international portfolios.** Tackling the subject from many different directions, this research created the empirical and theoretical rationale for forming internationally diversified portfolios. These scientific foundations are reviewed first; then we consider the mechanics of developing an international portfolio.

INCREASED INVESTMENT EFFICIENCY

In 1968 H. Grubel ("Internationally Diversified Portfolios: Welfare Gains and Capital Flows," *American Economic Review)* extended the risk-return ideas of Markowitz to the international area to illustrate the benefits of **international diversification.** Markowitz had developed some basic and increasingly familiar ideas on portfolio selection in a book published in 1959 *(Portfolio Selection: Efficient Diversification of Investments,* Wiley). He argued that an investor, by using forecasts of the future over some anticipated holding period, could at any point in time calculate the return he expected on any security. This expected return, however, might not be realized because any one of the investor's forecasts could materialize. The resulting range of possible returns would provide the investor with a measure of an investment's riskiness, which was conveniently summarized by the statistical measure, **standard deviation.** Extending this analysis to the universe of securities facing the investor, for any set of forecasts, one can estimate the expected return and risk for each security considered. When combining securities into a portfolio, the investor's perception changes insofar as he is now interested in the **risk-return characteristics** of the overall portfolio rather than the individual securities comprising the portfolio. In estimating the volatility of anticipated portfolio returns, the investor is interested not only in the anticipated volatility of the individual securities, but also the manner in which the securities are likely to covary with each other, that is, their **covariance.** Other things being equal, if securities are chosen that have a high covariance with each other, the resulting portfolio will be riskier than one composed of securities that have low covariances with each other. When securities have a low covariance or a low correlation with each other, their selection in a portfolio enables the portfolio manager to reduce portfolio risk or diversify away some risk unique to a particular security.

Markowitz was able to take the diversification philosophy advocated by portfolio managers and **represent it mathematically.** He showed that if a portfolio manager could estimate the expected return, the standard deviation of returns for each security, and the covariance of returns between all securities in the investment universe, a computer program could derive a list of optimal or **efficient portfolios.** He defined an efficient portfolio as one that had a maximum expected return for any level of risk or a minimum level of risk for any expected return. The locus of efficient portfolios became known as an **efficient frontier.** Exhibit 1 depicts the general form of an efficient frontier for domestic portfolios.

Some important characteristics of this frontier are first, it is **positively sloping.** Generally, a portfolio manager is able to increase his expected rate of return only by accepting a high level of risk. Second, the curve is **concave to the risk axis** because securities are less than perfectly correlated with each other. Third, any portfolio in the area *A* is inferior to a portfolio lying on the efficient frontier, because for the same level of risk, an efficient portfolio could be derived that has a higher level of expected return. If we are confining our attention to domestic securities, no portfolios exist in the areas labeled *B* and *C*.

One of the key arguments behind **international diversification** is that if the portfolio manager included foreign investments in his universe of potential investments, they would provide **additional diversification benefits,** because these foreign securities would have a

EXHIBIT 1   EFFICIENT FRONTIERS FOR DOMESTIC AND INTERNATIONAL PORTFOLIOS

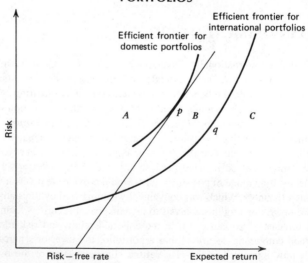

low correlation with domestic securities, and the efficient frontier would move to the right as indicated in Exhibit 1. Now for each level of risk, a higher level of return is earned on the portfolio by the inclusion of foreign securities; that is, the availability of foreign securities enables the portfolio manager to obtain the same level of return at a lower risk. In this case, no portfolios could be constructed that would lie in C.

The benefits of international diversification can be illustrated graphically by the extent to which the efficient frontier moves to the right. The exact combination of securities on each efficient frontier is shown by points p and q. This analysis leads to an important question: whereas in theory the benefits of international diversification can be explained, what are their magnitudes? In other words, how much does the efficient frontier move to the right? This **empirical question** is hard to answer.

The preceding analysis was based on future anticipations by an investor of the level, variability and covariability of returns. The empirical scientist did not have access to a data base of these forecasts, and instead, has concentrated on examining historical return data over different time periods. This methodology assumes that the time periods selected are sufficiently representative of economic cycles, that they represent a good approximation of what an investor could have anticipated. Several independent empirical analyses have followed this approach. For an in-depth discussion on risk-return analysis, see the section "Modern Portfolio Theory and Management."

EMPIRICAL STUDIES ON INTERNATIONAL PORTFOLIOS

Grubel (1968) calculated the monthly rates of return from the U.S. point of view on common stock market averages from 11 countries (the United States, Canada, the United Kingdom, West Germany, France, Italy, Belgium, the Netherlands, Japan, Australia, and South Africa) for the period 1959–1966. By constructing the **efficient set of portfolios** based on these data, he concluded that "recent experience with foreign investment returns would have given rise to substantial gains in welfare to wealthholders. If past experience is considered to be indicative of future developments, then these data suggest that future international diversification of portfolios is profitable, and that more of it will take place." The six most important countries for the U.S. investor were Japan, Australia, South Africa, the United States, Canada, and the United Kingdom. During this period, **Moody's Industrial Average** had an average annual return of 7.54%, with an annual standard deviation of 47.26%. The exact portfolio chosen by an investor would depend on his risk and return preferences, but Grubel concluded:

It can be said, unambiguously, however, that if an investor had wanted to maintain the same variability in return found in the New York investment, international diversification would have permitted him to earn 12.6 percent as against 7.5 percent, a gain of 68.0 percent in the annual rate of return.

Levy and Sarnat (1970) calculated rates of return from the U.S. viewpoint on market indices from 28 countries for the period 1951–1967 and similarly concluded there were substantial gains from diversification. They summarized their results in an interesting way by allowing the portfolio manager to invest in a combination of a **domestic risk-free asset** and one of the efficient portfolios. The best efficient portfolio for the investor to choose is one defined by the point of tangency of a straight line from the risk-free rate to the efficient frontier. In Exhibit 1, this corresponds to point p for the efficient frontier for domestic portfolios. Using this approach, Levy and Sarnat quantified the gains from diversification by listing the mean rates of return and standard deviations of the optimal portfolios for various subsets assuming a 5% interest rate. This is given in Exhibit 2. The systematic nature of risk reduction through **international diversification** is clearly seen as the opportunity set broadens.

Grubel and Fadner ("The Interdependence of International Equity Markets," *Journal of Finance,* March 1971) calculated weekly rates of returns from the U.S. viewpoint on 108 industry indices from the United States, the United Kingdom, and West Germany from the start of 1965 to the middle of 1967 and showed that the gains from diversifying among these 108 industries were greater than those from diversifying solely among the 51 U.S. industries.

All these studies were based on **index data.** In 1974, Solnik ("An International Market Model of Security Price Behavior," *Journal of Financial and Quantitative Analysis,* September 1974) extended it to data on individual companies. Using weekly price movements from 1966 to 1971 on over 300 European stocks selected from the United Kingdom, Germany, France, Switzerland, Italy, Belgium, and the Netherlands, he considered how a portfolio's risk declined as the number and type of securities contained in it increased, and he concluded that an internationally well-diversified portfolio would be significantly less risky than a well-diversified portfolio of U.S. stocks with the same number of holdings.

To overcome the limitations of small national samples and the exclusion of dividends, Guy ("The Performance of the U.K. Investment Trust Industry," *Journal of Finance,* May 1978) analyzed total returns on 99 U.K. and 99 U.S. companies, for the period February 1960–January 1971, from the U.K. viewpoint. Assuming that U.S. securities could be bought and sold each month using spot currency, the study showed that the risk of the portfolio was reduced through international diversification. Over the complete period, the average monthly percentage investment return in pounds sterling for an equal weighted portfolio of 99 U.S. companies was 0.896%, with a standard deviation of 4.29%, and that for U.K. companies was 1.07% (4.05%). For the combined portfolio of 198 U.S. and U.K. companies, however, while the mean return was the average of the two preceding national means, 0.983%, the standard deviation of the portfolio at 3.302% was much less than that for the two national portfolios. Of course, during this period the U.K. investor had to buy foreign securities through the investment currency market and suffer the cost of U.K. exchange controls; this impediment is discussed later in the subsection "Costs of International Investment."

EXHIBIT 2   MEAN RATES OF RETURN AND STANDARD DEVIATIONS OF OPTIMAL PORTFOLIOS FOR A 5% INTEREST RATE

	Mean Rate of Return (%)	Standard Deviation (%)
Developing countries	5.0	26.5
Common market	15.5	25.0
Western Europe	15.5	23.5
High-income countries	13.0	12.5
All countries	12.0	8.0

Source: H. Levy and M. Sarnat, "International Diversification of Investment Portfolios," *American Economic Review,* September 1970, p. 673.

This general approach has been extended to the **debt markets** by Barnett (*Euromoney,* April 1979). Using bond data from the International Monetary Fund (IMF), the Organization for Economic Cooperation and Development (OECD), and the U.S. Department of Commerce, monthly rates of return were calculated from 1970–1977 on 5- to 10-year government bonds in nine countries. Because the **U.S. bond market** had the second lowest average monthly return in dollars (7.3% annualized), the returns on an internationally diversified bond portfolio with a varying U.S. content and the eight other markets equally weighted provided returns better than those of the U.S. market. The standard deviation of monthly returns on the U.S. market was the lowest, 1.5%; but when an international portfolio was constructed, the volatility of the portfolio declined to a minimum of 1.32% with a 70% U.S. content before rising again. These results are given in Exhibit 3. Recently, this study was updated and extended by J. Hanna ("Why Americans Should Have Diversified," *Euromoney,* March 1980). This study again showed the benefits of international investing.

ANALYSIS OF THE STRUCTURE OF RETURNS. So far we have observed that when the returns on individual securities move together, there is less opportunity for **risk reduction through diversification.** Generally, it is very likely that **international diversification** will result in significantly larger gains than diversification within single countries, if (1) returns within each country share a strong common element of variance, and (2) the common elements for each country are largely independent of those of the other countries. This assumes there are no restrictions on capital flows. The existence of these two conditions can be determined by examining the covariances of returns on individual stocks. This approach is unlikely to reveal the complex patterns of association among securities.

Lessard ("International Portfolio Diversification: A Multivariate Analysis," *Journal of Finance,* June 1973) chose instead to use the methods of **factor** and **principal component analysis.** This approach assumes that each single-period return on a common stock is a function of several underlying factors and a unique element. Lessard examined the returns on equity markets from four Latin American countries (Colombia, Chile, Argentina, and Brazil) from 1958 to 1968. His results demonstrated the existence of conditions for substantial gains, but the magnitude of the gains could not be shown. This methodology has been applied with similar results to a series of **national and international indices.** In these studies, the low covariance between the country factors indicates the potential advantages from international diversification, but the precise magnitude of these gains would depend on whether

EXHIBIT 3   RISK-RETURN CHARACTERISTICS OF INTERNATIONALLY DIVERSIFIED BOND PORTFOLIO

Percentage of Portfolio Invested in		Average Monthly Return From the U.S. Viewpoint	Standard Deviation
U.S. Bonds	Foreign Bonds		
100	0	7.32%	1.50%
90	10	7.76	1.41
80	20	8.14	1.34
70	30	8.52	1.32
60	40	8.90	1.33
50	50	9.28	1.38

Source: G. A. Barnett, "The Best Portfolios are International," *Euromoney,* April 1979.

the **markets were segmented or integrated.** These concepts introduced by Agmon ("The Relations Among Equity Markets," *Journal of Finance,* September 1972) state that in a **segmented market,** expected returns are determined by the **undiversifiable risk** of each security in the context of an appropriate national portfolio, while in an **integrated market,** expected returns are determined by the undiversifiable risk of each security in the context of a world portfolio. Consequently, with fully integrated markets the advantage of international diversification is a **pure diversification effect,** while with fully segmented markets, gains might be greater as prices adjusted to reflect the emerging diversifiability of some heretofore undiversifiable risk.

MODELS OF THE INTERNATIONAL CAPITAL MARKET.   In the 1960s, financial theorists developed an equilibrium model for the **pricing of domestic capital assets.** One of the conclusions of this model was that an investor need consider only two portfolios in his investment decision, the **market portfolio of securities** and the **riskless asset.** Solnik ("An Equilibrium Model of the International Capital Market," *Journal of Economic Theory,* August 1974) extended this model and developed an **equilibrium model** of the international capital market, in which an investor need only consider three portfolios, the **world market portfolio,** a portfolio of bonds, and the risk-free asset in the investor's country of residence. Although these models rest on strong simplifying assumptions—for example, no **transactions costs, taxes,** or **capital controls**—and have not been and possibly cannot be verified empirically, they represent a strong theoretical argument in favor of international diversification.

PERFORMANCE OF SOME INTERNATIONAL FUNDS.   Another approach to examining the effects of international diversification has been through the historical performance of internationally diversified portfolios. McDonald ("French Mutual Fund Performance," *Journal of Finance,* December 1973) examined monthly returns on eight French mutual funds from April 1964 to November 1969 and found that generally they produced risk-adjusted returns that were superior to the domestic French market, and that during the rising French market, from 1967 to 1969, the **risk to variability performance** measure paralleled the degree of international diversification.

Guy ("An Examination of the Effects of International Diversification from the British Viewpoint on Both Hypothetical and Real Portfolios," *Journal of Finance,* December 1978) extended the analysis and considered the risk-adjusted performance of 47 internationally diversified British investment trusts from February 1961 to January 1971; he found that the trusts' performance increased with international diversification. This effect, however, was marginal, reflecting the onerous **exchange controls** affecting British residents trading in foreign securities during this period. However, even if a British investment trust had restricted the extent of its trading during this period, it could probably have realized significant gains from international investing.

COSTS OF INTERNATIONAL INVESTMENT.   Most of the work on international diversification stressed the benefits of international diversification but ignored the costs of international investing. Black ("International Capital Market Investing," *Journal of Financial Economics,* January 1974) theoretically examined the effects of these costs on international investing, but it remained an empirical question whether the effect of institutional restrictions on the cost of foreign investment significantly reduced the benefits.

An investor resident in the United Kingdom for exchange control purposes used to purchase securities outside the sterling area only by paying the **dollar premium** in the **investment currency market.** If the current rate of exchange in the spot market was x

dollars for every pound sterling, and the dollar premium was y percent, for every pound sterling the U.K. investor could purchase $1/(1 + 0.01y)$ investment dollars. From 1960 to 1970, the **British investor** on the New York Stock Exchange was affected by exchange controls in three major ways: first, the capital cost of the foreign investment included the dollar premium, while the dividend or interest payment had to be converted into sterling at the **official spot rate.** This reduced the yield on foreign investments and effectively ruled out the possibility of investing in foreign fixed income securities. Second, the value of the dollar premium fluctuated with the demand for and supply of investment dollars, and a British investor in American stocks had to account for this additional uncertainty in his investment decision. Third, the **"quarter surrender rule,"** introduced in April 1965, acted as a tax on switching investments.

Until 1965, if a British investor had sold a security denominated in a foreign currency, that is, a **"foreign currency security,"** he could have converted the proceeds of the sale into pounds sterling by selling them in the investment currency market and using the dollar premium existing at that time. In 1965 a new rule was introduced, whereby, when foreign currency securities were sold, one-quarter of the proceeds had to be sold at the official rate, and three-quarters could be sold with the benefit of the dollar premium. This rule applied even when the proceeds of the sale were used to invest in other foreign currency securities. When the dollar premium was 30%, for example, the effective tax on switching investments was 5.77%.

INVESTING IN MULTINATIONAL CORPORATIONS

It has been suggested that investors could obtain all their desired international exposure by buying equity securities of **multinational corporations** quoted on the New York Stock Exchange, particularly when they considered the costs of international investment, which could be lower for corporations than for individuals. Agmon and Lessard ("Investors' Recognition of International Diversification," *Journal of Finance,* September 1977) and Jacquillat and Solnik ("Multinationals Are Poor Tools for Diversification," *Journal of Portfolio Management,* Winter 1978) have among others investigated this problem. Jacquillat and Solnik concluded that the issue was whether investing in U.S. multinational firms could be regarded as a direct substitute to international portfolio diversification. The answer seems to be mostly negative. Others have found that diversification over all multinational firms reporting foreign sales proved less beneficial than did diversification over internationally selected securities.

INVESTING IN MAJOR CAPITAL MARKETS

The practical application of international portfolio diversification requires investors to be familiar with the major capital markets of North America, Europe, and the Far East. This must include the **Euromarket,** which lacks specific nationality but operates on a worldwide basis and represents one of the largest capital markets. Factors to be considered include:

1. **Structural and operational characteristics,** including the location and operating hours of exchanges, procedures for execution of trades, clearing procedures, market liquidity and turnover, volatility, the availability of current market information, and

familiarity with the principal market participants. Where over-the-counter markets are active, similar information on such markets will be required.

2. **Regulation and taxation** can easily make a market unattractive to foreign investors. Regulation may limit market entry or exit by investors, and it often specifies required operating procedures and legal liabilities of all market participants. Taxation has a more direct cost. Investors must be aware of the tax codes in foreign markets as they pertain to domestic and foreign investors, application to each different type of security, and reporting requirements.

3. **Investment opportunities** vary from market to market. Securities are often unqiue to specific markets either because the issuing entity participates only in one market, or because the security is unique in its own characteristics. An investor must be able to determine the important characteristics of the issuing entity, the rights and claims of both investor and issuer arising from the existence of the security, and the trading **liquidity and volatility of the security** in the market.

4. **Currency risks** affect foreign investments in a variety of ways. The value of the asset will change as exchange rates vary, dividend and interest payments will be **repatriated** based on the exchange rate at the time of the disbursement, and restrictions on capital flows may be imposed as a result of volatile **exchange rate fluctuations.** Furthermore, the earning power and asset value of an issuing entity will change to the extent that earnings and assets are located outside the investors' domestic environment.

Currency risk and exchange rate fluctuations are topics requiring an examination of sizable magnitude in their own right. This section does not provide information on the subject. Investors, however, should note that the preceding empirical research included adjustments for exchange rate movements and should always remember the major impact that such movements can have on the risk and return of international diversification.

This section provides a practical description of factors noted above as they relate to the Euromarket and to the largest national markets outside of North America. The following description of national markets includes Japan, the United Kingdom, West Germany, and France. Exhibit 4 indicates that these represent the largest national capital markets outside North America. Although **Canada** also qualifies as a major non-U.S. market, it is not covered here. Previous empirical work has shown that Canada has a **high level of correlation with the U.S. market,** and many of the major issuers in that market also participate directly or through related organizations in the U.S. market.

THE EUROMARKET. This is a truly international market that operates worldwide. Although operations are largely based in London for reasons of convenience and efficient communications, the Euromarket has no real geographic base. This market is unique for a number of reasons:

1. Since the market has no legal domicile, it is **not subject to the regulatory controls** of any government.

2. The absence of a regulatory body, such as the SEC, allows new issues to reach the market very quickly and with a **minimum of disclosure.**

3. Most securities are in **bearer form,** and the identity of investors is not easily discernible.

EXHIBIT 4   MARKET CAPITALIZATION AND TURNOVER

| | 1978 | | | | | 1977 | | | | |
| | Total Market Capitalization | | Annual Turnover[a,b] | | | Total Market Capitalization | | Annual Turnover[a,b] | | |
	$ Billion	% Total	$ Billion	% Total Turnover	In % of Each Market	$ Billion	% Total	$ Billion	% Total Turnover	In % of Each Market
United States	$ 815.2	54.8%	$199.9	47.8%	24.5%	$ 800.7	60.9%	$154.8	54.7%	19.3%
Canada	60.6	4.1	10.9	2.6	18.0	52.9	4.0	6.9	2.4	13.0
Europe										
United Kingdom	110.1	7.4	18.6	4.4	16.9	86.4	6.6	17.6	6.2	20.4
Germany	73.3	4.9	17.3	4.1	23.6	57.3	4.4	12.0	4.2	20.9
France	37.6	2.5	10.6	2.5	28.1	25.7	2.0	4.5	1.6	17.5
Spain	14.6	1.0	1.5	0.4	10.3	17.9	1.4	1.5	0.5	8.5
Netherlands	21.0	1.4	4.5	1.1	21.4	18.1	1.4	3.6	1.3	19.8
Italy	9.1	0.6	2.3	0.6	25.7	7.4	0.6	1.0	0.4	14.2
Sweden	9.3	0.6	0.4	0.1	4.3	9.1	0.7	0.4	0.1	4.4
Belgium and Luxembourg	11.4	0.8	1.2	0.3	10.9	9.5	0.7	1.1	0.4	11.5
Japan	278.7	18.7	142.4	34.1	51.1	189.7	14.4	77.4	27.3	40.8
Hong Kong	14.8	1.0	5.8	1.4	39.4	11.5	0.9	1.3	0.5	11.4
Singapore	9.2	0.6	1.5	0.4	16.3	6.3	0.5	0.5	0.2	7.5
Australia	23.1	1.6	0.9	0.2	3.9	21.8	1.7	0.7	0.2	3.2
"World"	$1,488.0	100.0%	$417.8	100.0%	28.1%	$1,314.3	100.0%	$283.3	100.0%	21.6%

[a]The annual figures for turnover values in U.S. dollars are calculated by converting monthly values at month-end exchange rates.
[b]Turnover data refer to common stocks only. It includes foreign shares listed, except in Germany and the Netherlands.
Source: Walter P. Stern, *Size and Liquidity of Foreign Stock Markets*, Capital Research Corp., New York, February 1979, p. 7.

4. There is **no withholding tax** associated with investments in this market. Investors, however, still must report income and gains on Euromarket securities as required by applicable domestic laws.

5. The market has historically been a **new issue market,** with limited secondary market liquidity in all but the largest issues outstanding. The growth of the market has expanded the secondary market to such a degree that **secondary market liquidity** is now improving substantially.

6. The market is dominated by **fixed income securities.** Although there are a number of equity issues and convertible issues outstanding, they were generally issued in the early years of the market, and the lack of liquidity in these issues reduces their acceptability as investment opportunities.

7. The market includes **securities denominated in a number of currencies,** including U.S. dollars, pounds sterling, German marks, and Dutch guilders. There are also several issues denominated in yen, French francs, and currencies with smaller international float. Quite unique to this market are securities denominated in Special Drawing Rights **(SDR's),** and other **basket currencies.**

A brief history of the Euromarket will provide a background for understanding its current structure and help to explain why the market is predominantly a new issue market. From the end of World War II until the early 1960s, most of the capital used in the reconstruction of Europe and the Far East was generated within the United States. Although the government provided most of the capital, large amounts were provided also by the U.S. capital markets and foreign direct investment by U.S. corporations.

The speed and strength of the recovery in Europe and Japan, together with the massive inflow of capital from the United States, resulted in continuing **U.S. balance of payments deficits** and a growing accumulation of dollar balances held outside the country. The dollar came to be used as an **international unit of account,** and it provided liquidity to financial markets in a number of European countries.

By the early 1960s the continuing payments deficits and capital outflows were causing substantial concern in the U.S. government. This prompted the imposition of the **interest equalization tax** (IET) in July 1963. This was a levy, initially up to 15%, on all subsequent purchases by Americans of foreign debt or equity securities of developed countries. The measures effectively closed the U.S. capital markets to foreign borrowers. In 1965 the Johnson administration issued a set of voluntary guidelines asking for a **limit on the transfer of capital from U.S. parent companies** to their foreign subsidiaries. Simultaneously, the Federal Reserve released a program of **voluntary foreign credit restraints** (VFCR) to restrict foreign lending by U.S. banks and other financial institutions. In 1968 these voluntary measures were replaced by the mandatory **foreign direct investment program** (FDIP), and capital flows from the United States to Europe virtually disappeared. The IET subsequently was removed in 1974.

The **first example** of a **true Eurobond issue** came to market in July 1963, only weeks after the imposition of the IET. According to data presented in *Euromoney's Inter-Bond Annual,* the volume of new issues totaled $90 million in 1963 (U.S. dollar equivalent). From this base, the volume expanded at a fantastic rate, reaching a peak of $18,087 million in 1977. Volume dipped somewhat in 1978 and 1979 as rising interest rates restricted the market.

The absence of regulatory control has played an important role in the growth of the market. Nearly any borrower of recognizable quality can use the Euromarket as a source of funds. New issues can be modified in structure, size, or price right up to the time of the offering, thus allowing maximum flexibility in adapting to market conditions.

Underwriting syndicates in the Euromarket are quite different from those in the United States. As many as 200–300 underwriters may participate in a syndicate. There is no **Glass-Steagall Act** in the Euromarket, so commercial banks join investment banks and other financial institutions in these syndicates. As a practical matter, only 25–35 of these underwriters are major factors in the market. Major multinational banks and the largest investment banking houses represent the greatest part of this group, and their strength is based on their **financial expertise, existing relationships with many issuers,** and **strong placing power.**

Until very recently, the liquidity of the secondary Eurobond market was limited. New issues would trade readily for a period of 6–9 months; then the trading volume would trail off as securities found their way to long-term holders. This pattern can be explained by the nature of the investors in the Euromarket. Mendelson and Sanderman reported in their "Eurobond Survey" (*The Banker,* September 1977 pp. 75–98) that **individuals** made up 60–65% of the investing group and banks with the discretionary authority to buy securities for their individual clients made up another 15%. These investors were more concerned with current yield and security of principal than with the maximization of portfolio total return. This often resulted in a buy-and-hold posture. Furthermore, most of these individuals, with support from their banks, demanded **protection of their identity.** This made it particularly difficult for traders to locate securities when they received orders in the secondary market.

Institutional investors, with the objective of professional investment management, historically accounted for only 20–25% of the Euromarket investor group. This compared to approximately a 60% representation by institutional investors in the U.S. bond market. The combination of a more easily identified investor, and the willingness of that investor to trade securities, accounts for the better liquidity of the U.S. market.

The presence of institutional investors in the Euromarket has grown since the mid-1970s, reflecting a trend toward greater international diversification and expanded reliance on **professional money managers** during a period of greater market volatility. As expected, this growing representation by institutional investors is improving the liquidity of the secondary Eurobond market. Note that high interest rates and market volatility periodically disrupt the trend toward improved liquidity.

Trading and clearing procedures are largely **separate functions on the Euromarket. Trading** is conducted through a **negotiated over-the-counter market** centered in London. The London market is linked to all other major financial markets around the world by telephone, telex, and mail. Most major U.S. brokerage firms, a few of the largest U.S.-based multinational banks, and most of the major European and Japanese banks are active participants in the Euromarket. International investors operate through one or more of these participants much as they would through brokers in the U.S. over-the-counter market. Orders can be placed to buy into new issue offerings, or to buy or sell outstanding securities. These orders can be placed at the market or with limits. An **order will remain open for one day;** however, there is no firm rule in this regard, and investors are advised to specify the period for which an order can remain open.

Euromarket trades are not conducted on any exchanges; however, many of the more popular issues are listed on the **Luxembourg Stock Exchange.** These listings provide representative prices and are the source of most price information reported in financial newspapers. For trading purposes it is necessary to get actual bid and offer prices from dealers. When comparing Eurobonds to U.S. securities, it is important to note that **yields on Eurobonds** are calculated using a single annual interest payment.

Following the execution of a trade, emphasis shifts to the **clearing procedures** to be used in settling that trade. **Two clearing systems** are normally used in the Euromarket: **Cedel and Euroclear.** These organizations are made up of dealer members that use the system to make book entry settlements through affiliated custodian banks around the world. The physical movement of securities is kept to a minimum by reassigning security holdings among investor accounts as indicated by trading operations. Physical delivery of securities can be made on request, and only against payment in a predetermined currency. Transaction settlements are on the basis of the settlement date stipulated by the participant delivering the securities; in normal practice this is usually 7 calendar days. Cedel and Euroclear also provide for the primary distribution of new issues, including the collection of **subscription payments,** remittance of funds to the **underwriting syndicate,** and distribution of the securities in the form of definitive certificates or **temporary global certificates.**

Each system has an approved list of securities that can be cleared through its operations. The most commonly traded issues are settled through both systems, and for these issues the two systems are linked through an intersystem working agreement. In the case of less liquid issues, investors may be restricted to whichever system carries the corresponding listing. In addition to clearing, the systems are prepared to maintain **custody arrangements** for their clients at affiliated banks. Included in this service is the presentation of coupons for payment and the allocation of bond redemptions using a lottery system.

FOREIGN MARKETS. **Foreign markets** operate within the boundary of foreign national or regional governments and under their regulatory control. These markets may encompass both formal exchanges and over-the-counter markets. Unlike the Euromarket, these financial markets are normally **subject to governmental regulation and taxation.** Foreign investors may be subject to limitations on capital movements or on the types of investments that are permitted. There are usually withholding taxes on income, but foreign investors can recapture all or part of these taxes when double taxation agreements exist between governments.

As a representative sample of foreign markets, this section covers the four largest financial markets outside of the United States and Canada as measured by market capitalization. These are the markets of Japan, the United Kingdom, West Germany, and France.

Japan.* The Japanese capital markets were established in the late nineteenth century; however, they were almost exclusively the domain of the major domestic banks and large **trading companies** until after World War II. Following the war, the financial markets of Japan were restructured under American supervision along lines similar to the U.S. markets. The power of the banks and trading companies was also broken down, though they remain significant factors in today's markets.

Japanese equity and debt markets grew quickly during the last half of the 1960s and throughout the 1970s (Exhibit 5). The **equity market growth** was spurred by the increasing efficiency and technological innovation of Japanese industry and the ability of industry to adapt quickly to changing domestic and export market conditions. The debt markets were expanding as a result of sharply higher levels of government borrowing. Banks also increased the frequency with which they tapped the debt markets.

Although the **Japanese capital markets** were structured along the lines of the U.S. markets, numerous differences between the Japanese and U.S. economies have a material impact on the actual operation of these markets. The **savings rate** in Japan is substantially higher than in the United States. This provides a large source of funds for new investment

---

*The authors acknowledge the assistance of personnel from Daiwa Securities and N. Reitenbach & Co.

EXHIBIT 5   JAPANESE SECURITIES MARKETS

	1974	1975	1976	1977	1978	1979
MARKET VALUE (YEN BILLIONS)						
Stocks	36,042	43,245	52,994	51,574	66,341	67,734[a]
Bonds	46,227	58,999	73,814	91,652	120,000(E)	150,000 (E)[a]
AVERAGE DAILY STOCK TRADING VOLUME, TOKYO STOCK EXCHANGE						
Shares (millions)	179	183	245	249	346	343[b]
Yen volume (billions)	43.5	54.8	82.7	75.2	114.2	122.2[b]
AVERAGE DAILY BOND TRADING VOLUME, OVER-THE-COUNTER (YEN BILLIONS)						
	132.9	196.1	249.6	467.4	687.6	716.0[b]

[a]November.
[b]January–November.
Source: Tokyo Stock Exchange (market value and daily stock trading data) and Japanese Securities Dealers' Association (Tokyo) (bond trading data). Assistance of personnel from Daiwa Securities, New York and Tokyo, is acknowledged.

capital. This capital reaches the economy either through direct individual investment or through the banks as they reinvest funds placed on deposit.

A sizable part of the outstanding equity capital is frozen in cross-ownership between companies. It is common practice for a company's shares to be held by its banks, suppliers, customers, and related firms. These shares are not traded under most circumstances, resulting in a substantial reduction in the amount of equity capital actually traded in the market. It is estimated that individuals control about 25% of the outstanding equity capital but account for nearly 70% of the market turnover. **Mutual funds** account for approximately 5% additional turnover. The high turnover of the Japanese equity market appears even more astounding in light of the relatively small proportion of total capital available for trading. Accordingly, **liquidity** is very good.

The **bond market,** which is principally an over-the-counter market, is a much more concentrated market. That is, the bulk of new and outstanding issues is found in the government and financial sectors (Exhibit 6). Many smaller industrial and commercial firms obtain funds from the strong banking system rather than through entering the public market.

Banks and mutual funds are major investors in the fixed income market. Although individuals hold a significant amount of the outstanding bonds (comparable to their ownerships of outstanding equities), trading is limited and their presence is not as significant as it is in the equity market.

Stock Exchanges.   There are eight **Japanese stock exchanges,** but Tokyo accounts for approximately 85% of total turnover, and Osaka contributes another 12% of the total. At

EXHIBIT 6   AMOUNTS ISSUED[a] AND OUTSTANDING BALANCES[b] OF PUBLIC AND CORPORATE BONDS[c], JAPANESE MARKETS (YEN BILLIONS)

Fiscal Year	Government Bonds[d]	Local Government Bonds	Government-Guaranteed Bonds	Industrial Bonds	Convertible Debentures	Financial Debentures	Yen-Based Foreign Bonds	Total
1974	2,200.1	176.5	471.9	986.7	283.5	6,516.3	0.0	10,635.0
	8,403.6	756.9	2,456.6	4,518.2	903.0	13,318.7	163.3	30,520.3
1975	5,362.7	311.1	549.9	1,504.2	331.0	8,079.6	35.0	16,173.5
	13,295.4	990.9	2,703.2	5,537.5	1,079.2	15,919.7	197.3	39,723.2
1976	7,148.0	441.4	964.0	1,166.4	55.5	9,436.7	62.0	19,274.0
	20,023.1	1,349.0	3,368.2	6,199.9	1,012.4	18,397.9	256.3	50,606.8
1977	9,866.3	556.9	1,219.6	1,240.8	162.5	10,492.7	454.0	23,992.8
	29,534.4	1,811.5	4,303.4	6,820.7	1,098.0	20,692.1	702.9	64,963.0
1978	10,792.1	696.9	1,552.4	1,313.3	277.0	11,394.0	657.0	26,682.7
	39,612.0	2,398.0	5,451.2	7,300.2	1,237.0	22,856.3	1,343.0	80,197.7
1979 (April–June)	3,730.5	174.0	412.8	285.5	198.0	2,683.8	83.0	7,484.6
	43,342.5	2,542.3	5,800.9	7,462.5	1,371.6	23,207.0	1,422.8	85,149.6

[a]First line, for each year.
[b]Second line, for each year.
[c]Includes bonds underwritten by the Trust Fund Bureau of the Ministry of Finance and the Postal Life Insurance.
[d]Includes both interest-bearing and discount bonds.
Source: Securities Public Information Center of Japan, *Japanese Securities Markets, 1979*, SPICJ, 1980, p. 12.

the end of 1978 there were 1,709 companies listed on the Japanese exchanges, of which 1,404 were listed on the Tokyo exchange. Exhibit 7 presents some characteristics of the stock market in Japan.

On the Tokyo exchange, trading is conducted two ways. At 12 of the 13 trading posts, **specialists** receive buy and sell orders for shares assigned to their respective posts. A price is then established at which a maximum turnover of shares can be accomplished. The specialists are not permitted to take positions in shares on their own behalf, and they are primarily responsible for matching orders. The thirteenth trading post is restricted to shares of larger companies, which have a sizable investor following and exhibit a high rate of turnover. At this post there is no specialist, and trading is conducted between **brokers** in a continuous **auction system.**

Investors place buy or sell orders with their brokers, specifying a **limit** at which orders are to be executed or the timing of the order (i.e., at the opening or close). This practice is common among international investors, since when the Japanese markets operate, it is the middle of the night in Europe and the United States. The exchanges are open from 9:00 A.M. to 11:00 A.M. and again from 1:00 P.M. to 3:00 P.M., Tokyo time; the over-the-counter bond market is not restricted to specific trading hours.

Bond Market.   The **bond market** is substantially larger than the equity market in capitalization and turnover, however there is a much smaller diversity of issues available to investors. As noted in Exhibit 6, the government bond and financial debenture sectors are the most active areas, while the yen-based foreign bond sector (known as **samurai bonds**) is one of the fastest growing segments.

Since the rise in world oil prices in 1974, the Japanese government has greatly increased the volume of new bond offerings to the extent that government bonds accounted for 50% of all the bonds outstanding at the end of 1978. The growth of the government bond sector has made it the most liquid area of the market and the sector attracting the greatest investor interest. The government sector is broken down into markets for long-term bonds (those with maturities exceeding 5 years), medium-term bonds (3- or 5-year original maturity) and short-

EXHIBIT 7   JAPANESE STOCK MARKET CHARACTERISTICS

	1974	1975	1976	1977	1978	Jan.–June 1979
Number of listed companies	1,709	1,713	1,716	1,724	1,709	1,708
Aggregate stated capital of listed companies (billions)	9,154.6	10,145.7	10,631.6	11,236.6	11,779.2	12,070.3
Number of shares listed (billion shares)	158.6	173.0	181.8	192.8	199.5	203.1
Aggregate market value (billion)	37,469.0	44,779.8	54,922.5	53,638.1	69,064.7	69,321.7
Sales volume (million shares)[a]	65,081 (228)	62,855 (221)	82,597 (289)	85,111 (297)	118,494 (416)	60,475 (429)
Sales value (billion)[a]	15,933.3 (55.9)	18,976.2 (66.8)	27,929.8 (97.7)	25,527.0 (89.2)	38,880.0 (136.4)	20,552.5 (145.8)

Numbers in parentheses are daily averages (excluding foreign–listed companies).
Source: Securities Public Information Center of Japan, *Japanese Securities Markets, 1979,* SPICJ, 1980.

term bills (maturities of approximately 60 days). The long-term bonds are **coupon bonds,** while the medium-term bonds are issued at a discount or in coupon form. Bills are always discount instruments.

Local government bonds of prefectures and cities are coupon securities of various maturities; however, a large portion of the bonds are **privately placed issues.** This limits the public trading in local government bonds. There are also bonds of government-related organizations, which carry a full government guarantee on the payment of interest and principal. These are growing in importance as a percentage of total bonds outstanding.

The largest segment of the bond market after the government sector is the financial debenture market. The issuers consist of the six long-term credit banks of Japan, specifically, the Industrial Bank of Japan, the Long-Term Credit Bank of Japan, Nippon Credit Bank, Bank of Tokyo, Central Cooperative Bank for Agriculture and Forestry, and Central Bank for Commercial and Industrial Cooperative Associations. **Bank debentures** may be issued as coupon bonds or in discount form.

Industrial bonds, including convertible issues, are also major components of the market; however, the volume of new issues is more sensitive to market conditions. A large number of industrial and electric utility issues of various quality make up the market. Nearly all straight bonds are secured by mortgage instruments. **Convertible issues,** unlike most bonds, are traded almost exclusively on the established exchanges because they are predominantly viewed as equity securities.

The last sector of the market, the **Samurai bond market** is particularly important to international investors. Although the sector is still small, the issuers consist of major international organizations (World Bank, Asian Development Bank, European Investment Bank, and others), foreign governments, and government-related organizations. These are generally high-quality organizations with worldwide financial borrowing capability. More important, the interest from these issues is exempt from Japanese withholding taxes. More information is provided on tax considerations later in this section.

Most publicly traded bonds are in **registered form,** and are listed on the exchange. Although listed bonds are normally traded on the over-the-counter market, their prices are restricted to a narrow bargaining range centering on the exchange prices. Unlisted securities are based solely on dealer quotes without being directly influenced by exchange prices.

Investors should be aware that the Japanese method of calculating yield to maturity and accrued interest differs from the U.S. system. Whereas in the United States the yield-to-maturity calculation is a variation of an internal rate of return, in Japan the following procedure is used for coupon bonds. The difference between the purchase price and the redemption price is divided by the number of years to maturity and added to the annual coupon. This amount is then divided by the purchase price and multiplied by 100 to obtain the **"yield to maturity"** as a percentage.

Securities Trading.   Settlement procedures for stocks and bonds can be for cash or normal settlement. **Cash settlement** takes place the day after the trade date. When special trading problems require variations in settlement procedures, the date can be extended; however, the investor must assume any related carrying costs.

Although there are no official restrictions on the purchase of Japanese equities or bonds, **trading restrictions** are usually imposed when the foreign ownership of any Japanese company exceeds 20%. Both domestic equity and fixed income securities are subject to withholding tax on the payment of interest and principal. **Double taxation agreements** reduce but do not eliminate this withholding tax. For example, U.S. citizens are subject to a 15% withholding tax on dividends and 10% on interest income. For fixed income securities, there is also a 0.03% transfer tax levied on the proceeds of the seller. International investors can avoid all withholding taxes through the purchase of samurai bonds because taxes are not levied on these securities. Note that regulations and tax laws are subject to change. Investors should verify tax considerations applicable to their specific investment decision before taking action.

United Kingdom.*   The capital markets of the United Kingdom began as early as the seventeenth century with the creation of the joint stock trading companies such as the East India Company and the Hudson Bay Company. The British government entered the market in the mid-1700s with its first debt offering, thereby giving birth to the **gilt-edged securities** market (gilts). The U.K. markets expanded rapidly with the industrialization of that nation in the early twentieth century. Private industry used the public market to obtain equity and debt capital to fund expansion, and the government used the gilt market to finance the heavy costs of World Wars I and II. Historically, there were numerous stock exchanges throughout the United Kingdom, but in 1973 all these exchanges were unified into a **single exchange system** with the main trading floor in London, and regional exchanges in Birmingham, Glasgow, Liverpool, and Manchester in the U.K., and Dublin, Ireland.

The U.K. economy and its business community share a common heritage with those of the United States. Business practices, accounting standards, and regulatory control are similar in the two countries. The capital markets, however, were created differently, so the international investor should become familiar with the operating procedures of the U.K. market.

Virtually all securities trading in the United Kingdom is conducted on the exchanges, with only a limited over-the-counter market. Furthermore, the over-the-counter market is closely tied to the exchange operations and is subject to many of the same regulatory controls. There were approximately 8,200 securities listed on the exchange in 1978, including both debt and equity issues. About 2,600 of these securities were ordinary capital shares of British and Irish companies, many of which were small in capitalization. There were also about 450 securities of non-U.K. companies, with U.S. firms representing a substantial part of that total. Since large firms dominate this group, the combined capitalization of these foreign firms made up 74% of the total market capitalization at year-end 1977. British government and government-guaranteed fixed income securities made up another large segment of the market, accounting for approximately 41% of the capitalization of U.K. securities and 15% of all securities on the U.K. exchange. More important, the gilt market provided about 80% of the total market turnover.

Securities Trading.   The operational structure of the exchange is built on two principal groups, brokers and jobbers. There are more than 3,000 individuals registered as brokers who serve solely as agents for their clients, and more than 400 registered as jobbers, acting only as principals and dealing exclusively with dealers or other jobbers. The **jobbers** make markets in all listed securities and many unlisted securities. At least two jobbers deal in any of the more important securities to ensure competitive pricing.

The jobbers' risk in making a market in securities is reduced by the existence of an **account system.** Under this system all trades completed within a 10-day period are combined for a single settlement date, which occurs on the **seventh business day** after the end of the dealing period. This allows jobbers flexibility in matching buy and sell orders during the

*The authors acknowledge the assistance of Vickers da Costa, Ltd., N.Y. and London, and Mr. O. John Olcay, General Partner, W. Greenwell Associates.

trading period, thereby reducing their exposure. The account system applies to all securities except gilts and new offerings. **Gilt trades** and allotment letters take place for cash, requiring next-day settlement.

When an investor wishes to buy or sell a security, his broker will contact one or more jobbers for a quotation, without disclosing whether the investor is a buyer or seller. The jobber in turn will provide both a bid and offered price. This spread will vary based on the size of the trade and on the market liquidity of the security involved. **Spreads** are considerably narrower on gilt trades than on corporate debt or equity security transactions. On each business day, the Stock Exchange produces an official record of transactions called the **Daily Official List,** which provides officially quoted bid and offered prices, **markings** (prices at which blocks are traded), and dividend information. Daily prices and other market information can also be obtained from independent financial publications such as the *Financial Times*. The Stock Exchange is officially open Monday through Friday from 9:30 A.M. to 3:30 P.M.; however, brokers may conduct business outside these official hours. Brokerage operations with international clients may remain open 24 hours a day. Investors may place orders by mail, telex, or telephone, and care should be taken in describing the security, any price limit, requirements for foreign exchange conversion, and settlement procedures.

Gilt Market.   Since the gilt market accounts for much of the total market turnover, and since these securities are held to be of the highest quality, they are of substantial interest to many international investors. For these reasons more details concerning this market are provided.

At the shortest end of the gilt market maturity spectrum are **Treasury bills.** The principal type of bill is the **discount bill,** which has a 91-day maturity and is issued weekly by tender in denominations of £5,000, £10,000, £50,000, £100,000, £250,000, £500,000, and £1,000,000. The **secondary bill market** is very active, and liquidity is excellent. **Trading spreads** are quite narrow, and transaction costs are low.

Gilts with longer maturities are divided into four groups:

1. *Shorts*. Issues with maturities of less than 5 years.
2. *Mediums*. Issues with maturities from 5 to 15 years.
3. *Longs*. Issues with maturities over 15 years.
4. *Undateds*. Issues redeemable only at the option of the government.

Prices on shorts are usually quoted in multiples of 1/64, while longer issues are quoted in multiples of 1/16. **Redemption characteristics** can affect the value of gilt securities. There are issues that have single- and double-dated maturity dates. Double-dated issues may be redeemed on or after the first date at the option of the government (upon 3 months notice) but must be redeemed at par by the final date. If a double-dated issue is trading at a premium, the yield to maturity is calculated using the initial date, otherwise the later date is used.

Accrued interest also affects quoted prices. When dealing in short dated bonds, the quoted price does not include the interest accrued since the last interest payment date. The purchaser, therefore, will have to pay accrued interest in addition to the purchase price of the bond (similar to U.S. bond market procedures). When dealing in mediums and longs, the quoted price includes adjustments for interest accruals. When the basis of the quotations changes from **cum-dividend to ex-dividend,** the price is automatically reduced by the amount of the pending interest payment (similar to U.S. preferred stock market procedures). In most cases securities are quoted ex-dividend 5 weeks and 2 days before the interest payment date.

Different gilt issues are subject to different tax liabilities, as discussed later. Because of the difference in tax characteristics, yields on gilt issues are quoted in different forms. The term **"yield"** usually refers to **yield to redemption** except in the case of undateds, where it implies a current yield. It also commonly means **gross yield**, which refers to the yield to maturity before any deduction for tax liabilities. By contrast, **net redemption yields** are calculated after the deduction for the appropriate tax on interest payments. Net yields account for the deduction of both income and capital gains tax.

As previously noted, settlement on gilt trades is normally done for cash with the transaction completed on the next day. Extension of this settlement period can be arranged; however, the purchaser is usually required to assume any **carrying costs** incurred beyond the normal cash settlement date. This additional charge is commonly included in an adjustment to the quoted price, so it is important to specify any unusual settlement requirement when asking for quotes. The practice of extending settlement dates in the gilt market is referred to as **forward dealing** and it is covered by Stock Exchange Rule 97.

Nearly all U.K. securities are in registered form, and this can present a problem for domestic investors who trade frequently, or foreign investors who require ownership certificates at the time of settlement. There may be a delay of 2–4 months between the purchase date and the date the certificates are delivered. Foreign investors can alleviate this problem somewhat by having securities registered in the name of a **nominee company** (such as a custodian bank) located in London. Lending and borrowing of securities is available only to those securities possessing a **"Z" account** with the **Bank of England,** but under most circumstances, these "Z" accounts are not available to foreign investors.

It is possible for investors to have gilt issues in either **registered or in bearer form** with coupons attached. There is a small fee for the conversion from one form to another. Note that bearer bonds cannot be traded ex-dividend, since bonds with coupons removed will not be accepted for delivery in London.

Investors in the U.K. Market.   Investors in the U.K. market include individuals, banks, insurance companies, pension funds, mutual funds, and foreign investors. A study conducted by a committee under the direction of Harold Wilson reported the growing **concentration of institutional investors** in the U.K. markets. The report noted that between 1963 and 1975, the proportion of ordinary shares in listed U.K. companies held by individuals fell from 54 to 37.5%, while the proportion held by institutional investors climbed from 30.5 to 48%. The trend has continued since 1975, and some research reports have suggested that institutions may hold 70–85% of the value of U.K. equities by the year 2000. Factors contributing to this concentration include high personal tax rates, the advantages of professional management in volatile market environments, and the ability to offset insurance premiums and pension fund contributions against taxes.

Regulation of the U.K. Market.   Regulation of the U.K. financial market rests with the Stock Exchange and its related agencies. In addition to the rules and regulations of the Exchange, there is a controlling council elected by the members. The government is not directly involved beyond the creation of a general legal framework and the execution of central bank monetary policy through the **Bank of England's** day-to-day activities (much like the U.S. Federal Reserve System open market operations). In July 1978 the Parliament released a white paper on proposed changes in the regulation of the markets. Of major importance was a substantial tightening of the regulations against **insider trading,** with the right to impose civil or criminal sanctions.

The tax laws in the U.K., as they apply to the financial markets, can have a material impact on the suitability of investments to domestic and foreign investors alike. Two types of tax levy exist: taxes on transactions and taxes on income or gains. Securities registered in the United Kingdom (excluding foreign issues) are subject to a **government stamp duty** on purchases equal to 2% of the consideration paid. Charitable institutions and foreign investors are charged the stamp duty at 1%. No stamp duty is payable on gilt-edged bonds, debentures, loans, or bearer bonds. There is a contract stamp tax payable on both purchases and sales, which varies from 10 to 60 p, depending on the amount of the consideration paid. U.K. residents and individual investors (not institutions) within the Common Market are also subject to a **value-added tax** (VAT) equal to 8% of any commission charges. Other foreign investors are exempt from the VAT.

Under present **U.K.** tax law all **dividend payments** and most **interest payments** are made **net of withholding taxes.** U.K. residents are able to offset these taxes against their regular income tax liability; however, foreign investors are able to recapture this withholding tax only where double taxation agreements exist between the United Kingdom and the investor's domestic government. Before consideration of **double taxation agreements,** dividends are currently subject to a 30% withholding tax; however, certain **gilt issues** are subject to special withholding tax considerations. Certain issues are designated tax-free to residents abroad, and an investor can receive interest payments free of withholding tax by filing the appropriate forms with the Inspector of Foreign Dividends.

For investors in countries having double taxation agreements with the United Kingdom, the withholding tax on nonexempt dividends and interest is reduced to 15%. Until February 1980 the double taxation agreement between the United States and the United Kingdom had been suspended. With the approval of the new tax treaty, U.S. residents will have their U.K. withholding tax reduced to 15%. For residents of the United Kingdom, capital gains are subject to tax, but foreign investors incur no capital gains liability as long as they do not have a residence or conduct a business in the United Kingdom.

West Germany.   Germany's political and economic history before the twentieth century was strongly influenced by the independence and segregation of the various states. **Local capital markets** developed, but they were so small that little activity was generated. The German banking system dominated the economic system even in these early days. Although the latter part of the nineteenth century saw the consolidation of the German states, the ravages of war and depression limited investment opportunities in that country until the end of World War II. Even during the decade following the war, most capital transfers were conducted by government-to-government exchanges or from governments to the German banking system.

The late 1950s was a period of substantial change in the German financial system. The domestic economy was staging a strong recovery, and there was a growing international interest in the German markets. The German government gradually removed most foreign exchange restrictions, culminating in the full convertibility of the deutsche mark in 1958.

Note in Exhibit 4 that **West German market capitalization** and turnover are significantly below those of Japan and the United Kingdom. Furthermore, market capitalization is a smaller percentage of gross national product than in either of the other countries.

Securities Trading.   In the German system, the **brokerage function** in securities transactions is handled exclusively by the banks. Trading on the exchanges is not compulsory; however, banks are bound by general agreement to channel all trades through the exchanges unless expressly instructed by clients to do otherwise. There is often the need for trading off the exchanges, since they are only open on weekdays from 11:30 A.M. to 1:30 P.M. Trading on **official exchanges** requires that securities meet listing requirements much as they would on the New York Stock Exchange. Approximately 465 stocks and 10 times that many bonds are listed on the German exchanges; the capitalization of these securities is heavily concentrated among a few very large firms, however, and many of the listed securities are not actively traded.

The shares of companies that are actively traded receive **consecutive market quotations** during trading hours, allowing for continuous trading. Shares that are traded less actively are quoted only **once a day.** In the case of consecutive quotations, **specialists** post a new quotation each time a buyer and seller can be matched. By contrast, the shares that are quoted only once a day are priced by the specialists to maximize share turnover in those securities. Specifically, specialists receive orders between 11:30 A.M. and 12:00 P.M. each day, and then determine the price at which the most buyers and sellers can be satisfied. Fixed income securities are almost exclusively quoted on the basis of a **single price fixing per day.** Share prices are quoted in deutsche marks per share, while bonds are quoted as a percentage of par value. For fixed income securities, accrued interest is not included in the quoted price but must be included in the amount paid or received.

Unofficial trading takes several forms. The regulated over-the-counter market is for trading on the stock exchanges in securities that meet weaker listing requirements. The pricing method follows the single daily pricing system, but no official prices are posted. Securities traded on the **unregulated over-the-counter** market, also referred to as telephone dealings, are commonly the smallest German companies, or companies that do not wish to meet listing requirements. Also, foreign securities that are actively traded outside Germany but are not closely followed within the country may be traded on the unregulated over-the-counter market.

Investors may place orders through any bank that is a member of the stock exchange. These orders may be placed in person at the bank, or by letter, telegram, telex, or telephone. Orders are considered valid until further notice but at the latest, the last business day of the current month. Orders should clearly specify the desire to buy or sell, the customer's name and account number, and the number of shares or nominal value of fixed income securities to be traded. Orders should give an exact description of the security involved and its reference number from the official quotation list. Finally, the investor should specify execution at the market (at best), or at a specific price (limited).

Settlement on security transactions takes place 2 business days following the trade date, and delivery against payment may be made either in the form of actual certificates or shares in a central deposit account for securities. Most German equity shares and fixed income securities are in bearer form, and the latter method is used most frequently.

Fixed Income Securities Market. The **market for fixed income securities** in Germany is substantially larger than the equity market based on capitalization. The supply of debt securities is provided by deficit financing on the part of the German federal and local governments and by federal agencies. A substantial part of the capitalization of German banks and industrial companies is also provided by fixed income debt financing. Furthermore, foreign entities seeking capital in Germany usually do so through debt offerings.

The Federal Republic may issue bonds or treasury bills; however, foreign investors are effectively precluded from buying bills. Bond issues of the federal government may be in **serial form** (partial maturity in each year) or in **term form** (single maturity), but the single maturity bond has been more common in recent years. By contrast, industrial issues commonly use sinking fund provisions to retire principal debt before maturity.

In trading practices, a distinction is commonly made between maturity classifications. Short bonds usually mature within 5 years. In recent years new issues have been offered with maturities in the 5–10 year range. Therefore, bonds maturing past 10 years are often referred to as long-term issues.

Investors.   In the German stock market the major investor group consists of the **banks,** which act for their own account and as trustees for individual and corporate investors. **Individual investors** make up the largest single group of shareholders, but they are not active market participants as a group. **Mutual funds** are also becoming increasingly important to the German equity markets, because of the liquidity they provide the market and as a vehicle for individuals to obtain professional money management. **Insurance companies** and nonfinancial companies also own German equities; their representation is not large, however, and they are not active market participants.

By contrast, the German fixed income markets are more heavily dominated by **institutional investors.** Banks and insurance companies are particularly dominant in these markets, though the insurance companies weight their activity toward the private placement market just as they do in the United States.

Foreign investors were attracted to the German financial markets in the latter part of the 1970s by the strength of the currency. The comparatively low coupon yield of bonds denominated in deutsche marks has been more than compensated for by the strength of the currency. In particular, foreign investors have concentrated on **foreign DM bonds,** that is, the fixed income securities on **non-German government and industrial entities.** Such issues are exempt from withholding taxes on the interest income paid.

Tax Laws.   **German tax laws** applying to security transactions and the yield on investments are complex. Foreign investors must be aware of the **stock exchange turnover tax,** which applies to all purchases of securities if transacted within Germany and is applied as a small percentage of the purchase value. German domestic securities that are held by foreign investors are subject to a withholding tax of 25% on dividends and interest income. **Double taxation agreements** between West Germany and other countries allow residents of those countries to obtain partial or complete refund of the withholding tax.

Foreign investors escape the withholding tax liability with the purchase of foreign DM bonds, since these securities are not subject to German tax liabilities. Issuers of foreign DM bonds include non-German governmental and quasi-governmental entities, including the U.S. government. Other **issuers** include **supranational organizations** and **multinational corporations.**

France.   The French financial markets are materially different from those previously reviewed. In large part this is due to the high degree of regulation and intervention by the French government in nearly all areas of the domestic economy. Following World War II, nearly 25% of the business capital in France was brought under direct government control through the **nationalization** of 125 companies. Price controls, market allocations, and other forms of governmental control were imposed on nearly all economic sectors. This type of environment was not conducive to equity investment by French citizens and was even less favorable for foreign investors. A limited amount of French equity investment was directed to Geneva, Switzerland, but the more common practice was to divert capital to fixed interest savings. The **savings rate** in France during 1979 was approximately 17% of disposable income, compared to 3–4% in the United States. The French capital markets reflect this orientation toward fixed income securities, with market capitalization being two-thirds fixed income securities and one-third equities. Market turnover in both sectors is small: the 1979 trading volume in equities equaled 20% of outstanding market value, and fixed income securities experienced an even lower turnover (11.5%). Furthermore, the most actively traded equities accounted for 27% of the total turnover.

Securities Trading. Fixed income and equity securities are traded in France on seven exchanges, and no security is listed on more than one exchange. The Bourse, the **Paris exchange,** accounts for nearly all actively traded issues, and it is the exchange on which all companies of national or international importance seek listings. All transactions on French exchanges are carried out between brokers, with **no specialists** or jobbers as intermediaries. There are only about 74 brokers on the Paris exchange, and 28 brokers on the six other exchanges. The Paris exchange operates 5 days a week from 11:30 A.M. to 2:30 P.M. The exchanges are regulated by the Ministry of Economy and Finance, and by the **Commission des Operations de Bourse** (the French equivalent to the SEC). These organizations establish operating procedures, ensure that listed companies report required information on a timely basis, police insider trading, and investigate complaints.

There are three types of trading on the exchanges. In the **cash market,** trades require immediate payment and delivery. All listed securities can be traded on a cash basis. Trading in the **forward market** is limited to the more actively traded securities (162 French stocks, 20 French bonds, and 58 foreign stocks in 1978). In forward market trades, transactions are effective immediately, but **settlement takes place only at the end of the month** in which the trade is completed. A 20% **margin** in cash is required for trades in the forward market, otherwise brokers will execute trades in the cash market.

The third type of exchange trading is called the **conditional market or the marché à primes.** On this market, buyers have the right to cancel their trade the day before settlement date. If trades are canceled, the buyer pays a premium to the seller. Premiums are fixed in advance by the Board of Governors for each security according to its price. Buyers may also choose between three **forward settlement dates.** This conditional market bears a resemblance to the U.S. options market. Most securities traded on the forward market can also be traded on the conditional market.

On these exchanges, quotations are established by designated brokers for each security. Brokers do not maintain positions in securities, rather they consolidate and match orders. Price quotes are set at levels at which the maximum number of trades can be executed, and the brokers enforce such prices for all clients who have agreed to deal within specified price limits.

There is also an **over-the-counter market** in France, where unlisted securities are traded exclusively between brokers on a cash basis. In this market, brokers may either match orders as they do on the exchange (called *procédure normale*), or they may act as principals and set prices at which they are willing to execute transactions (called *procédure spéciale*).

Currently (1980), the **Paris Bourse** is considering a proposal to transform its trading operation to a **continuous auction market** similar to the major U.S. stock exchanges.

Restrictions and Taxes. Since the removal of restrictive regulations in 1971, foreign investors are permitted to buy or sell all French and foreign securities on the exchanges or the over-the-counter market. However, no more than 20% of the capital of any French company can be purchased without prior government approval. Brokers must open a foreign account for their international clients, but securities deposited in these accounts can be exported from France at any time. Securities may be in bearer or registered form.

A recent ABD Securities Corp. (New York, 1979) report indicates that foreign investors are subject to **operational taxes and income taxes.** Operational taxes include a **stamp duty** imposed on trades for all securities except bonds maturing in less than 7 years. The stamp duty ranges from 0.15 to 0.30% of the transaction amount, depending on the amount of the trade. There is also a **tax on financial activities** (TAF) amounting to 17.6% of commissions paid on transactions.

Income taxes imposed on foreigners take the form of a 25% withholding tax on dividends and interest paid on French securities. Interest and dividends on securities of non-French entities, as well as capital gains on all securities, are exempt from withholding taxes for foreign investors. Tax treaties between France and other countries provide for the recapture by investors of part, but not all of the withholding taxes.

Investors. Investment in the French domestic market is dominated by the major French banks, mutual funds, and insurance companies. While individuals hold about 50% of the outstanding bonds, they hold only about 25% of the outstanding equities. This is due in part to the individuals' orientation toward saving, but it also reflects the lack of high-quality investment research available on most French companies. Accounting practices are quite different from those used in the United States, and provisions for various reserves disguise the true financial condition of the reporting entities.

An international investor is likely to confront lower **liquidity in the French market.** Withholding taxes further reduce the attractiveness of domestic securities, but do not detract from foreign issues traded on the Paris exchange. Despite the disadvantages of investment in the French market, there are some unique securities that may attract certain investors. In the equity market there are companies that are unlike any others, including champagne vineyards, Perrier, BIC, the Club Meditéranée, and the nationally protected oil and defense companies. In the fixed income markets, there are securities backed by gold or natural resources, lottery bonds through which a chance at lottery winnings is obtained in addition to interest payments, and certain utility bonds on which the amount of interest paid is related to the total revenues earned by the utility.

REFERENCES

Agmon, T., ''Country Risk—The Significance of the Country Factor to Share Price Movements in the United Kingdom, Germany, and Japan,'' *Journal of Business,* January 1973, pp. 24–32.

———, ''The Relations Among Equity Markets: A Study of Share Price Comovements in the United States, United Kingdom, Germany and Japan,'' *Journal of Finance,* September 1972.

———, and Lessard, D., ''Investor's Recognition of Corporate International Diversification,'' *Journal of Finance,* September 1977, pp. 1049–1056.

Arenson, K. W., ''Ways to Invest Funds Abroad,'' *New York Times,* June 12, 1979.

Barnett, G. A., ''The Best Portfolios Are International,'' *Euromoney,* April 1979, p. 165.

Black, F. ''International Capital Market Equilibrium with Investment Barriers,'' *Journal of Financial Economics,* January 1974, pp. 337–352.

———, ''The Ins and Outs of Foreign Investment,'' *Financial Analysts Journal,* May–June 1978, pp. 1–7.

Fountain, J., ''Premium Dollars,'' *Financial Analysts Journal,* March–April 1975.

Grauer, F. L. A., Litzenberger, R. H., and Stehle, R. E., "Sharing Rules and Equilibrium in an International Capital Market Under Uncertainty: An Abridgment," *Journal of Financial Economics*, 1976, pp. 233–256.

Grubel, H. G., "Internationally Diversified Portfolios: Welfare Gains and Capital Flows," *American Economic Review*, December 1968, pp. 1299–1314.

———, and Fadner, K., "The Interdependence of International Equity Markets," *Journal of Finance*, March 1971, pp. 89–94.

Guy, J., "An Examination of the Forward Exchange Market During Pegged and Floating Systems: United States, Canada, Germany, and United Kingdom," *Journal of Financial and Quantitative Analysis*, November 1977, p. 631.

———, "The Behavior of Equity Securities on the German Stock Exchange," *Journal of Banking and Finance*, 1977, No. 1, pp. 71–93.

———, "An Examination of the Effects of International Diversification from the British Viewpoint on Both Hypothetical and Real Portfolios," *Journal of Finance*, December 1978, pp. 1425–1438.

———, "The International Capital Asset Pricing Model in Discrete Time," University of California, Berkeley, Working Paper, International Bureau of Economic Research, March 1976.

———, "The Performance of the British Investment Trust Industry," *Journal of Finance*, May 1978, pp. 443–455.

———, "The Stock Exchange, London: An Empirical Analysis of Monthly Data from 1960 to 1970," in *European Finance Association, 1975 Proceedings*, R. Brealey and G. Rankine, Eds., North Holland, Amsterdam, 1976.

Hanna, J. "Why Americans Should Have Diversified." *Euromoney*, March 1980.

Jacquillat, B., and Solnik, B. H., "Multinationals Are Poor Tools for Diversification," *Journal of Portfolio Management*, Winter 1978, pp. 8–12.

Lessard, D. R., "International Portfolio Diversification: A Multivariate Analysis for a Group of Latin American Countries," *Journal of Finance*, June 1973, pp. 619–633.

———, "World, Country and Industry Relationships in Equity Returns," *Financial Analysts Journal*, January–February 1976, pp. 2–8.

———, "World, National, and Industry Factors in Equity Returns," *Journal of Finance*, May 1974, pp. 379–391.

Levy, H., and Sarnat, M., "International Diversification of Investment Portfolios," *American Economic Review*, September 1970, pp. 668–675.

McDonald, J. G., "French Mutual Fund Performance: Evaluation of Internationally Diversified Portfolios," *Journal of Finance*, December 1973, pp. 1161–1180.

Mossin, J., "Equilibrium in a Capital Asset Market," *Econometrica*, October 1966, pp. 768–783.

Pogue, G. A., and Solnik, B. H., "The Market Model Applied to European Common Stocks: Some Empirical Results," *Journal of Financial and Quantitative Analysis*, December 1974.

Shohet, R., "Investing in Foreign Securities," *Financial Analysts Journal*, September–October 1974.

Solnik, B. H., "An Equilibrium Model of the International Capital Market," *Journal of Economic Theory*, August 1974.

———, "An International Market Model of Security Price Behavior," *Journal of Financial and Quantitative Analysis*, September 1974, pp. 537–554.

———, "The International Pricing of Risk: An Empirical Investigation of the World Capital Market Structure," *Journal of Finance*, May 1974, pp. 365–378.

———, "Why Not Diversify Internationally Rather than Domestically?" *Financial Analysts Journal*, July–August 1974, pp. 48–54.

Stevens, G. V. G., "Two Problems in Portfolio Analysis: Conditional and Multiplicative Random Variables," *Journal of Financial and Quantitative Analysis*, December 1971, pp. 1235–1250.

PART 3

SECURITIES AND PORTFOLIO MANAGEMENT

SECURITY ANALYSIS

CONTENTS

INVESTMENT PRINCIPLES	**3**
Investment Defined	3
Classes of Investments	3
Risk and Return	3
Return on investment	3
Sources of risk	4
Diversification	4
Risk-return tradeoff	4
Marketability	4
Tax Status	5
Security Analysis in an Efficient Market	5
Role of the analyst	5
Efficient markets	6
SOURCES OF INVESTMENT INFORMATION	**7**
Traditional Published Sources	7
Information on economic conditions and the business outlook	7
Information on industries and companies	8
The press	8
Trade journals	8
Investment services	8
Information on companies and securities	9
Computer-Based Information	10
Standard & Poor's Compustat Services, Inc.	10
Interactive Data Corporation	10
Value Line Data Services	11
FIXED INCOME SECURITIES ANALYSIS	**11**
Bonds: Terms, Yield Concepts, and Yield Tradeoffs	**11**
Contractual provisions	11
Typical discretionary contractual clauses	11
Bond yield concepts	12
Yield tradeoffs	12
Corporate Bond Analysis	**13**
The credit of the issuer	13
Earnings coverage of interest charges	13
Earnings coverage of junior bonds interest	13
Asset coverage	14
Liquidity	14
The size factor	14
Protective provisions of bond issue	14
Bond ratings	15
Municipal Bond Analysis	**16**
Analytical concepts	16
General obligations	16
Revenue bonds	16
Technical aspects	17
Legality	17
Maturities	17
Redemption provisions	17
Contractual position and remedies	17
Credit analysis of municipals	17
Credit quality factors	17
Preferred Stock Analysis	**18**
Nature of contract	18
Major weakness of preferred stock contracts	18
Yields and taxes	18
COMMON STOCK ANALYSIS	**19**
Characteristics of Common Stock	**19**
Common Stock Valuation Concepts	**19**
Risk-Return Tradeoff	**20**
Financial Statement Analysis	**20**
The income statement	20
The balance sheet	21
Sources and uses of funds statements	22
Deficiencies of financial statements	23
Projecting Earnings	**24**
Historical growth rate	24
Aggregate approach using regression analysis	24

Return on investment approach	25
The industrial life cycle	25
Variations in the Analytical Technique	**26**
Industrial securities	26
Nature of the industry	26
Industry analysis	26
Financial securities	27
Distinctive features	27

Bank stocks	27
Insurance stocks	28
Other financial stocks	28
Public utility securities	29
Franchises	29
Utility rates	29
Utility valuation	30
Commission regulation	30
Challenges for the future	31

SECURITY ANALYSIS

James L. Farrell, Jr.

INVESTMENT PRINCIPLES

INVESTMENT DEFINED.   The term "investment" has three different meanings in common usage. In the broadest sense, investment refers to the placement of funds in protective assets to earn a return, regardless of whether such investment is accompanied by management. In this sense, investment refers to the acquisition by a business of assets for its own use, as well as the purchase of securities in businesses managed by others. A second definition of investment is the acquisition of assets to secure a return in the form of interest, dividends, rents, or capital appreciation, but without assumption of responsibility for management. The third and most narrow definition of investment is the acquisition of assets to secure income, but limiting the degree of risk so far as is practicable. In this third sense, investment is distinguished from **speculation,** which involves the deliberate assumption of substantial risks to secure capital appreciation or a high rate of return, and **gambling,** which involves the making of wagers rather than the acquisition of interests in property. Ownership of **cash** does not constitute investment. Only when cash is used to acquire income-producing assets, whether as creditor or owner, does investment occur.

In this section, the term "investment" is used in the second sense stated above, that is, the placement of capital, without assuming responsibility for management, to obtain a return in the form of interest, dividends, rents, or capital appreciation.

CLASSES OF INVESTMENTS.   Investments fall into two main classes: **fixed income** and **equity.** Fixed income investments include bonds and preferred stocks. Equity investments include common stocks and real estate ownership. In addition, it is sometimes possible to find combinations of the two basic types in a single issue and, for purposes of classification, such securities may be designated "**hybrids.**"

Each asset possesses a number of characteristics that determine its suitability and desirability for individual or institutional investors. The two most important characteristics are **risk** and the **rate of return.** Other significant characteristics are **marketability** and **tax status.**

RISK AND RETURN.

Return on Investment.   Investors seek to obtain the highest return available on investments that provide the kind and degree of safety they desire. The return on fixed income investments like bonds, mortgages, and preferred stocks is limited to the contractual interest or preferred dividend rate. Common stocks, by contrast, constituting the ownership element in businesses, provide not only a current dividend yield, but also the prospect of future increases in **cash dividends** and price appreciation that may result from reinvestment of retained earnings and the cash flow from depreciation allowances, research and development outlays, and other management efforts to increase profits. At the same time, however, common stocks are subject to the risk of declines in earnings, dividends, and market price that unfavorable developments affecting the economy or the company may cause.

Sources of Risk.   Each security has its own degree of risk that reflects the following major uncertainties: (1) interest rate risk, (2) purchasing power risk, (3) business risk, and (4) financial risk. There is the chance that other securities may offer larger returns and lower the worth of the presently owned security. This is commonly called the **interest rate risk.** There is also the chance that inflation will erode purchasing power and reduce the amount of goods and services that the dollars of accrued return are worth. This is called the **purchasing power risk.** There is the risk that business competition and conditions may impair the ability to provide the return. This is called the **business risk.** There is also the risk that the methods used to finance the corporation may impair the ability to provide the return. This is called the **financial risk.** Fixed income securities are primarily subject to interest rate, purchasing power, and usually financial risk, while common stocks are subject to one degree or another of all four risks.

Diversification.   When considering the risk of a security in a portfolio context, it is useful to divide the total risk or total variability of return of an asset into two parts: systematic and unsystematic. **Systematic risk** is the portion of total variability in return caused by factors that simultaneously affect the prices of all securities. Systematic variability of return is found in nearly all securities in varying degrees because most securities move together in a systematic manner. **Unsystematic risk** is the portion of total risk that is unique to a firm. Unsystematic variations are thus independent of factors affecting other securities.

Since unsystematic variations are unique to each firm, they can be diversified away to nearly zero by spreading the funds to be invested across the securities of several unrelated firms. Systematic risk, on the other hand, is more difficult to diversify because it is common to all assets in the market to some extent. Within a given market, assets with high degrees of systematic risk must be priced to yield high rates of return to induce investors to purchase them.

Risk-Return Tradeoff.   Studies of the probability distributions of returns indicate that securities with high total and high systematic risk tend also to have high average rates of return. For example, short-term fixed income instruments, like Treasury bills, have displayed the least variability and provided the lowest return over time. Common stocks have shown the largest variability and provided the highest return, while bonds have provided intermediate variability and return, as would be expected. It should be noted that these are longer term tendencies, with the data also showing that over shorter periods of time there is frequently an inverse relationship, with less risky investments actually earning more than high-risk ones.

MARKETABILITY.   The ability to readily sell or buy a security is called marketability. When a security can be bought and sold in large amounts without disrupting its price, it is said to possess a **broad market;** if only small amounts can be bought or sold at the prevailing price, it has a **narrow** or **thin market.** When the bid and asked prices are not far apart, a security is said to enjoy a **close market.** When prices for a security do not fluctuate widely between sales or over a period of time, the security has a **stable market;** when a security's prices move over a wide range, its market behavior is **volatile.** (See also discussions of marketability in the section "Short-Term Money Markets and Instruments" and risk-return tradeoff in "Modern Portfolio Theory and Management.")

Liquidity refers to the ability to convert investments into cash at any time without material loss. **Short-term U.S. government obligations** are a prime source of liquidity, as are **commercial paper** and deposits in banks. The short maturity and the high quality of these instruments assure their liquidity. In addition, short-term U.S. government securities and commercial paper possess very broad, close, and stable markets, which enhance their liquidity characteristics.

TAX STATUS. High rates of income taxation make the tax status of investments a matter of major significance to individual investors in the middle and upper income brackets, and to taxed institutional investors. In their appraisals, such investors should be concerned primarily with the return from an investment after taxes, rather than with the gross return before taxes. Among fixed income investments, tax-exempt obligations hold a particularly favorable position for higher bracket individual investors and taxed institutional investors like commercial banks. Dividend income enjoys an 85% credit when received by corporate investors. Appreciation is taxed only when realized, and long-term capital gains are currently taxed at only half or less of the rate applicable to ordinary income of individuals.

SECURITY ANALYSIS IN AN EFFICIENT MARKET. The relevance of security analysis has been controversial for several decades. Originally the debate centered on the relative merits of "fundamental" security analysis as opposed to a set of charting techniques referred to as **"technical analysis."** More recently, evidence of efficiency in the capital market pricing mechanism has been interpreted by some to imply the uselessness of both fundamental security analysis and technical analysis. Since this section is a description of security analysis, it is important to consider the question at this point.

Role of the Analyst. Curley and Bear *(Security Analysis and Portfolio Management)* describe the role of the analyst as follows. Fundamental **security analysis** involves the processing of available information concerning a firm to arrive at a subjective estimate of the expected return and risk to an investor who purchases the firm's stocks or bonds. Fundamental analysis can also be defined more narrowly as the process of calculating a firm's **intrinsic value;** this is an equilibrium price that can be compared to the current market price to identify undervalued and overvalued securities. The term "fundamentalist" is more closely associated with the narrower definition.

Relevant information is both quantitative and qualitative. Quantitative information includes the firm's stock price history, financial data, reaction of the firm to changes in macroeconomic variables, and other data that may be used to forecast return on investment. Qualitative information includes such items as the assessment of competence of a firm's management. Information can also be classified as publicly available or as inside; the former is generally available at little or no cost, while the latter is known only to a limited number of persons. Notwithstanding its usual definition as data available to corporate insiders (e.g., employees), **inside information** may be generated externally from publicly available information through private techniques developed by an analyst.

Security analysis is not a unique and codified set of techniques. There is basic agreement about the general analytical formulation, but forecasting techniques and qualitative adjustments vary from one analyst to another. Research has provided increasingly better **forecasting methods,** but the search for superior techniques continues. A large part of security analysis consists of routine forecasts using a model that is considered to be most reliable by the analyst; risk and return elements are estimated on the basis of anticipations formed from existing information. As new information is received, it is compared with anticipated values, and the forecasting process is repeated. On occasions, new information may concern an unexpected and major event. In this case, windfall gain or loss accrues to shareholders as market price adjusts to reflect that information; equilibrium risk-return dimensions may also be altered significantly. The quality of the analytical process depends on the ability to anticipate events.

Efficient Markets.   The most recent challenge to security analysis arose because of the statement and testing of the **efficient market hypothesis.** An efficient market is defined as one in which security prices fully reflect all available information. New information is discounted as it arrives, meaning that its value is assessed by investors. Price quickly adjusts to a new and correct level. Under the circumstances, detailed analysis of existing information would appear to be fruitless. In fact it is not. As Lorie and Hamilton (*The Stock Market*) have pointed out, it is the interaction of investors in analyzing new information and in adjusting portfolios that causes price to respond in an efficient market; paradoxically, if investors accepted the efficiency hypothesis, and abandoned security analysis, market efficiency would decrease.

Curley and Bear (*Security Analysis and Portfolio Management,* p.7) indicate three reasons why security analysis remains relevant in a generally efficient market:

1. In an efficient but less than perfect market, there is a time lag between the arrival of information and its subsequent reflection in price. During that interval, security analysis provides an opportunity to adjust portfolios profitably. Market efficiency in this respect has not been fully established but evidence which is available suggests that price response is fairly rapid; this may imply that rewards arising from security analysis are captured by institutional investors and others with the capacity to process large amounts of data quickly and efficiently.

2. Superior analytical techniques may allow the analyst to transform publicly available information into inside information. This possibility is difficult to document because there is little motivation for making superior techniques public. But some evidence is available which supports the proposition.

3. Security analysis is critical to the investment process even in the case of instantaneous price response because securities must be evaluated in a portfolio context. Correct pricing of individual assets in an efficient but less than perfect market does not imply investor indifference to the choice of assets which are held in a portfolio. As the price of an individual security responds to new information, reflecting change in risk and expected return, the security in question may no longer be desirable as part of the portfolio for some investors. Other investors, in contrast, may wish to acquire the asset because of the change in risk and return. Portfolio management is clearly a continuing process with portfolio revision dependent upon evaluation and reevaluation of asset risk-return elements. Security analysis and portfolio selection are therefore complementary; they are both compatible with, and necessary to, an efficient capital market.

SOURCES OF INVESTMENT INFORMATION

If the conceptual framework that investors use to assess their position in the market is to be valuable, it must have information inputs. Information can be gathered from published sources, and these can be grouped into the following categories: (1) information on economic conditions and the business outlook, (2) industry and company data sources, and (3) information on companies and securities. Much of this information is also available in computer-based format, and these sources are described following a review of the sources of published information. An appendix on sources of investment information is provided at the end of this *Handbook*.

TRADITIONAL PUBLISHED SOURCES.

Information on Economic Conditions and the Business Outlook.   The reference citations listed below are good sources of background information on economic developments, statistical data on the economy as a whole, and some industry statistics. The data offered in these publications are quite useful for measuring the performance of a given company or industry against that of the entire economy. These volumes do not, however, give any of the specific data on individual companies that are the direct tools of security analysis.

A number of banks publish reports or surveys dealing with the business outlook and other topics. **Citibank** publishes a *Monthly Economic Letter.* The leading article is always "General Business Conditions." *The Morgan Guaranty Survey* is published monthly by the Morgan Guaranty Trust Co. of New York. The Bank of New York issues **General Business Indicators,** which is a statistical tabulation of selected economic indicators. Manufacturers Hanover publishes the "Financial Digest," a weekly economic commentary along with selected financial data and business indicators. The Chase Manhattan Bank publishes *Business in Brief,* issued bimonthly by its Economic Research Division. The first article usually presents an analysis of the business outlook.

The 12 Federal Reserve banks publish monthly bulletins devoted to banking, economic, and financial topics. The Federal Reserve Bank of New York, for example, publishes a *Monthly Review.* The Federal Reserve Bank of Philadelphia publishes the *Business Review* monthly. The Federal Reserve banks of Chicago and St. Louis also issue monthly reviews. The Board of Governors of the Federal Reserve System in Washington, D.C., publishes the *Federal Reserve Bulletin* monthly. It contains the "National Summary of Business Conditions." The Federal Reserve also publishes a *Chart Book on Business, Economic, and Financial Statistics* monthly, as well as an annual *Historical Chart Book.*

The federal government provides a number of useful sources of information on developing business trends. The *Survey of Current Business* is published monthly by the U.S. Department of Commerce. It has two principal parts. The first deals with basic business trends. The second section is an elaborate compilation of basic statistical series on all phases of the economy. The President's Council of Economic Advisors publishes the monthly *Economic Indicators* and the *Annual Economic Review,* which deal with the state of the economy and the outlook.

For economic forecasting purposes, a useful government publication is *Business Conditions Digest,* issued monthly by the U.S. Department of Commerce. This report brings together many of the available economic indicators in convenient form for analysis and interpretation. *Business Week,* in its "Business Outlook" section, reviews the indicators from time to time and regularly provides an analytic review of changing business and economic developments. It provides coverage of major developments in many areas of business and finance. *Fortune* magazine has a section in each issue entitled "Business Roundup," a bi-monthly report on the economic outlook.

On corporate profits, overall trends can be seen in the *Quarterly Financial Report for Manufacturing Corporations,* published jointly by the Federal Trade Commission and the Securities and Exchange Commission. Each year, in its Monthly Economic Letter, Citibank publishes the results of its survey of the profits performance of U.S. corporations. Both report profits on two bases, as percent return on net worth and as percent margin on sales, and permit an investor or a securities analyst to compare a given company with the reported industry average, or with a larger universe of companies.

Information on Industries and Companies.

The Press. General news offers information that may be of consequence in the evaluation of a firm or industry. Dow Jones and Co. and Reuters operate a news ticker that disseminates items in a matter of moments. Several magazines, such as *Time, Newsweek, Business Week,* and *U.S. News and World Report,* carry substantial business and financial news in addition to political and social news. The daily newspapers *(N.Y. Times, Washington Post)* are a major source of general information. The more financially oriented papers, such as the *Wall Street Journal,* provide a wealth of financial news with an emphasis on news of significance to individual industries, companies, or markets.

Several journals are also specifically devoted to finance. *Barron's* and the *Commercial and Financial Chronicle* are both financial publications that discuss specific corporate, industry, and economic events in addition to providing stock price and market statistics. Other journals provide specific investment suggestions. Among these are *Forbes, Financial World,* and publications like the *Economist* and *Financial Times* that cover overseas events.

Trade Journals. Every major industry grouping has at least one trade journal that covers the events of the industry and the companies in it. *Advertising Age* and *Chemical Week* are two such publications. Because of their narrower interest, these journals are among the first to gather news on product development, management change, pertinent general economic considerations, and other corporate developments. These journals are probably closer to the heart of an industry than any other published source of information. The **Business Periodicals Index** lists articles in all major trade journals.

Investment Services. **Standard & Poor's** issues a series of **Industry Surveys,** covering 45 industries. In each case a **Basic Analysis** is issued, usually annually, followed by supplementary sections. The "Current Analysis and Outlook" updates the figures in the basic survey, provides a short-run forecast, gives brief analyses of representative companies in the industry, and provides updated data on the comparative statistical position of leading common stocks in the industry.

Forbes publishes an "Annual Report on American Industry" at the beginning of each calendar year. It covers each of the major industries and within the industry makes comparisons of companies based on yardsticks of performance. Examples are: growth (5-year compounded rate for both sales and earnings) and profitability (5-year average for return on equity, and on total capital). Each industry reviewed is analyzed for both past and prospective performance.

Information on Companies and Securities.   **Moody's** publishes six bound manuals annually, with weekly or semiweekly loose-leaf supplements: Bank and Finance, Industrial, Municipal and Government, OTC Industrial, Public Utility, and Transportation. This service provides information on a considerable number of corporations or issuers, usually including a brief history of the company and its operations, products, and officers, as well as income statements, balance sheets, selected financial ratios, a description of outstanding securities, and market price data.

Another established source of financial information is **Standard & Poor's Standard Corporation Records.** This loose-leaf service in six volumes, kept current with bimonthly supplements, provides information similar to that found in Moody's manuals. It also includes a well-indexed "Daily News Section" and a "Daily Dividend Section," with weekly and annual cumulations. Another particularly useful feature of this service is its "List of Subsidiary Companies," which enables the user to obtain company information in greater detail.

The **Standard & Poor's Stock Guide** is a condensed handbook, issued monthly, containing a brief sketch of essential facts about some 5,000 common and preferred stocks, listed and unlisted. Most of the 5,000 stocks are rated for earnings and dividend stability and growth. At the back of the guide each month are to be found "quality ratings of utility preferred stocks" and a section on the performance of 400 mutual funds.

Both Moody's and Standard & Poor's publish compendia of individual companies. *Moody's Handbook of Common Stocks* is issued quarterly and covers over 500 companies. For each company there is a chart, showing the industry group stock price trend and the company's stock price performance. Basic financial statistics for the past decade are given. The written analysis covers the company's financial background, recent financial developments, and prospects. The Standard & Poor's compendium is called **Standard N.Y.S.E. Stock Reports.** It covers about 2000 stocks. Financial facts are given for each company. A chart shows the market performance of the stock, the average performance of stocks in its industry, and the performance of the stock market as a whole, in addition to the trading volume of the stock. Each report usually carries a Standard & Poor's opinion of the investment merits of each stock.

Two other Standard & Poor's publications of interest are the *Analysts Handbook* and the *Earnings Forecaster.* The *Analysts Handbook* provides composite corporate per share data on a comparative basis. It provides continuity since 1946 for 95 industries and the **Standard & Poor's 400 Industrial Index,** making possible a great variety of significant per share comparisons. It is available annually with monthly updatings. The *Earnings Forecaster* provides weekly new and revised earnings estimates on the companies prepared by Standard & Poor's and other leading investment organizations and brokerage firms, and offers a check of the various estimates against one another.

The **Value Line Investment Survey** covers 1,800 stocks in 91 industries. It is essentially a reference and current valuation service. Each stock in the list is reviewed in detail once every 13 weeks. Interim reports are provided in weekly supplements on any new developments between the time of the regular quarterly reports. Each week the new edition of the Value Line Investment Survey covers four to six industries on a rotating basis. Each industry report contains full-page reports on individual stocks.

Corporate annual and quarterly reports with financial statements are usually available from companies on written request. Some companies will also place interested persons on a permanent mailing list to receive future reports and other information published by the company. Current stockholders receive such reports automatically. These reports represent the direct source of most financial data on particular companies.

10K reports sometimes provide valuable information, in addition to that contained in annual reports, that is helpful in the security analysis of a company. These reports are available in major business libraries, from the companies themselves, and from the Securities and Exchange Commission.

COMPUTER-BASED INFORMATION.   **Machine-readable financial data** can now be utilized by investors who have access to computer facilities. Companies specializing in computer-based information supply either data bases or computer-based services, or both. **Data bases,** sometimes called data banks, are magnetic tape storehouses of financial information about companies and markets, taken from the published sources described earlier. Clients can receive magnetic tapes directly, to be used on their own computers, or they can receive data remotely by sharing computer time with other clients. The major firms in the data base field are Compustat Services, Inc. (a Standard & Poor's subsidiary), Interactive Data Corporation, and Value Line. Other organizations supply related computer-based data which can be used in conjunction with financial data; for example, Data Resources Inc. (DRI) and the Center for Research in Securities Prices (CRSP).

Computer-based services are processing systems, programs, and software packages, which enable the client to gain access to the data bases. The client's place of business may contain an input-output device connected to a remote computer, which enables the client to "access" stored information. All three previously mentioned data base organizations offer these services.

These services and the use of data bases make possible the high-speed retrieval and analysis of data. Analysts can use these new research tools to gain greater insights into company, industry, and market characteristics. Among other advantages, the preliminary statistical analysis of data can be done quickly. Furthermore, computers and processing systems can be used to classify industry characteristics, such as growth rates, yields, and price-earnings ratios. These can be compared with statistics of other companies, other industries, or with various indexes. Screening for desired characteristics of individual companies can be performed rapidly. Finally, computers can be used to test characteristics of stocks that have done well or poorly in the market, to determine what characteristics should be examined as possible indicators of performance in future periods.

Standard & Poor's Compustat Services, Inc.   S&P uses the name **Compustat** for its data base. Compustat offers basic annual data files covering over 5,000 stocks. The basic Compustat service contains 120 items of annual data on each of the companies covered. This includes income statement data, balance sheet data, and other miscellaneous information of value to the analyst, such as information on stock prices. Many adjustments are made to the data to achieve comparability between time periods and companies.

Interactive Data Corporation (IDC).   IDC provides four major data bases and several smaller ones. The **Securities Price Data Base** contains daily closing price and volume data for all New York and American Stock Exchanges stocks and for 1,800 over-the-counter stocks. Daily information is also available for about 130 NYSE, Amex, Dow Jones, NASDAQ (the National Association of Securities Dealers' automated quotations system), and Standard & Poor's daily and **weekly market indexes.** IDC's Corporate Financial Data base consists of Compustat balance sheet, income statement, and company ratio data. Its economic data base contains weekly, monthly, quarterly, and annual time series describing more than 6,000 economic variables and are grouped into 14 categories, among them GNP and Components by Industry, Consumer and Wholesale Price Indexes, and Monetary Statistics. The fourth major data base is the Value Line Data Base, which provides annual and quarterly financial information and ratios for about 1,800 major companies.

Value Line Data Services.   Value Line produces a number of data services that are available from IDC and other vendors, as well as its own Value Line Data Services. The basic data file is their Value Line Data Base. This base consists of over 150 income statements, balance sheets, sources and applications of funds, and financial ratio variables on 1650 companies beginning in 1955. In addition, the base consists of a file of calendarized per share earnings forecasts covering 1650 corporations for the 12-month period ending a half-year hence. Finally, the base provides a systematic evaluation of the probable reliability of earnings per share forecasts of the 1650 companies.

FIXED INCOME SECURITIES ANALYSIS

BONDS: TERMS, YIELD CONCEPTS, AND YIELD TRADEOFFS.

Contractual Provisions.   The essential features of a bond contract (*indenture*) are relatively simple. First, the issuer promises to pay a specific amount of dollars per bond unit (*par value*) on specified dates each year known as the coupon payments. Because it is an unconditional promise, failure to meet the required coupon payments means default and possible insolvency. Second, the issuer promises to repay the principal amount of the debt at a specified future date. This date is known as the **maturity date** of the bond.

These two provisions are the heart of the bond *indenture*, and offer two major advantages to investors: (1) a known amount of income in dollar terms and (2) considerable pressure on the corporation to pay. It may be assumed that the debtor will meet these obligations if at all possible because the penalties for default are drastic. As a result, relative to other types of investment, the bond provides a greater certainty of a given income. But the contract alone does not guarantee payment of the return. Actual payment still depends on the continued financial ability of the borrower to fulfill the promise; it is thus necessary to appraise the quality and prospects of the company. The main disadvantage of the bond is that income return is restricted. The bondholder continues to receive only the indicated contractual income even if the profits of the company grow dramatically.

Typical Discretionary Contractual Clauses.   Although a specified amount of income and a fixed maturity are the essential components of a bond contract, two other provisions may also be of considerable significance to the investor. First is the **call provision,** which gives the corporation the right to redeem the outstanding bonds at a specified price either immediately or after some future date (*deferred call*). The price is usually a few dollars more than par.

The call provision is always disadvantageous to the investor. A company will exercise its option to redeem its bonds at the call price if doing so is to its advantage. In most cases, the company advantage arises from a decline in interest rates or an improvement in the credit position of the company, if not both. Such developments enable the company to redeem a high-cost issue with the proceeds from the sale of a new issue at a lower interest cost. On the other hand, if interest rates rise or the company's financial position deteriorates, the company will not exercise its option to call the issue, and the full impact of any market or credit losses will be borne by the investor holding the issue.

A second provision that is common to many bonds and some preferred stocks is one that requires an annual **sinking fund payment** by the corporation, to retire the issue gradually. The specific bonds or preferred stock to be retired at any given time may be selected at random and ''called'' at a specific price, or they may be bought in the open market if a sufficient supply is available at less than the call price.

Sinking funds are disadvantageous to investors in one respect. After investors have gone to all the trouble of evaluating and purchasing a security at what they consider to be an attractive rate of return, they may find the security taken away from them by a sinking fund call. And at that time interest rates may be considerably lower than when the issue was purchased; thus reinvestment in an equally attractive issue may not be possible.

Bond Yield Concepts.   The **value** of a bond can be defined as the present value of the future stream of the income payments (coupon rate) plus the present value of the principal payment at maturity, both discounted at the appropriate rate of interest for bonds of that maturity and quality. This rate is known as the **yield to maturity** or **effective yield.** The formula is expressed as follows:

$$V = \frac{rp}{(1 + i)} + \frac{rp}{(1 + i)^2} + \cdots + \frac{rp}{(1 + i)^n} + \frac{p}{(1 + i)^n}$$

where V = value of bond
  r = coupon rate on bond
  i = discount rate
  p = principal of bond
  n = years to maturity

In actual practice, this precise formula is not used because the principal p, the market price V, the coupon rate r, and the years to maturity n are the known data. The unknown quantity is the discount rate i that would be obtained if the bond were purchased at its existing price and held to maturity. The formula demonstrates two important features of bonds as an investment medium. First, their prices vary inversely with changes in interest rates; if market interest rates i go up, price V declines. Second, the amount of price variation necessary to adjust to a given change in interest rate is a function of the number of years to maturity.

If the discount rate based on prevailing interest rates i is above the coupon rate r, the price V of the bond will be less than 100 ($1,000); that is, the bond will be selling at a **discount.** If the opposite relationship prevails (the coupon rate is above the level of interest rates), the bond will sell at a **premium** above par. At a given price, therefore, the effective yield on a bond has two components: the annual coupon rate and the appropriate annual amount of the total discount added to (or premium subtracted from) the coupon rate.

A book of bond yield values or financial calculators can be used to compute both the **effective yield to maturity** and the appropriate annual discount or premium that should be added to or subtracted from the coupon for the bond to yield the indicated rate of return.

Yield Tradeoffs.   The bond market consists of three components:

1. U.S. government obligations.
2. Municipal obligations of state and local government units.
3. Corporate obligations.

Government bonds represent obligations of highest credit quality and are available in a wide spectrum of maturities; they are the benchmark against which yields on all other bonds are evaluated. The coupon payments on **municipal bonds** are exempt from federal income taxes. As a result their nominal pretax yields are usually lower than others. **Corporate bonds** as a class provide higher yields than government and municipal bonds. They carry credit risk that the government obligations do not, and at the same time do not provide the tax advantage of municipals. The rest of this section evaluates corporate bonds as well as municipals, since these are the two types that require credit analysis.

CORPORATE BOND ANALYSIS. As noted before, investors in bonds sacrifice most of the benefits that may ensue from a company's future growth. Since bond investors forego the benefits of growth, they must try to assure themselves that the issuers will be able to fulfill their obligations. In this regard investors in corporate bonds should be primarily concerned with the capacity of the issuer to pay interest and principal as they fall due. The chief indices of such capacity are:

1. The credit of the issuer.
2. Protective provisions of the bond issue being analyzed.
3. Bond ratings.

The Credit of the Issuer. The credit of the issuer, that is, his ability to meet all debts as they mature, is the most important factor in bond analysis. The credit of the obligor is measured by: (1) earnings or cash flow coverage of interest charges; (2) level of debt in relation to equity; (3) the debtor's liquidity position; and (4) the size and economic significance of the company and its industry.

Earnings Coverage of Interest Charges. In the past the most widely used yardstick for bond quality was the ratio of earnings available to pay interest (profits before income taxes) to fixed charges. In stable industries, earnings coverage of two or more times interest charges may be regarded as adequate, whereas in industries subject to wide fluctuations in earnings coverage of three, four, or more times may be required for a good credit rating. In industries sensitive to the business cycle, coverage of fixed charges under recession conditions is the significant ratio.

The factor of safety in **fixed charge coverage** is the percentage by which earnings before taxes may decline before they fail to cover fixed charges. If earnings before taxes are $2.4 million and fixed charges are $960,000, then such earnings can decline by as much as 60% or $1.44 million and still cover fixed charges. Investors also consider the number of times that a firm's cash flow (earnings after taxes plus noncash expenses, e.g., depreciation) cover fixed charges.

If substantial **lease rental obligations** have been incurred, they should be taken into account in computing earnings coverage of fixed charges. However, rentals under long-term leases may include not only a return on the investment of the lessor, but also the principal return of such investment. In that event, the rentals are equivalent to both the interest and the sinking fund payments on a bond issue. See the section entitled "Leasing" for a more detailed discussion.

As long-term creditors, bondholders are concerned with future far more than with past or present earnings coverage of fixed charges. Hence the probable trend of earnings over a period of years and their vulnerability to cyclical declines in business activity and other unfavorable influences are major factors affecting the credit of the issuer.

Earnings Coverage of Junior Bonds Interest. If a corporation has both senior and junior (subordinated to the senior) debt outstanding, the significant measure of earnings coverage of interest on junior debt is the ratio to total fixed charges. Thus a corporation with a $20 million issue of 4.5% debentures and $10 million of 5% subordinated debentures has total interest charges of $1.4 million. If it earns $2.8 million before income taxes, the coverage of interest on the subordinated debentures would be two times, since prior charges of $900,000 must be paid along with $500,000 on the subordinated issue. To say that earnings after deducting $900,000 of interest on the debentures, or $1.9 million, cover interest requirements on the 5% subordinated debentures 3.8 times is misleading. But it is accurate to say that interest of $900,000 on the 4.5% senior issue is being covered 3.1 times.

Asset Coverage.   Another quality measure is the proportion of total capitalization represented by debt versus equity. The individual bond or preferred stock owner would be best off if that issue were the only senior security outstanding, because earnings coverage then would be at a maximum. Thus to the bondholder or preferred stockholder, the greater the equity capital as a percentage of total capitalization, the better. An analysis of the corporation's capital structure is, therefore, a sort of asset coverage measure that supplements the earnings coverage measure.

Liquidity.   Some companies that appear to have satisfactory earnings and asset coverage may however not have enough cash on hand to pay their claims as they come due. The following ratios are the principal ones in use for measuring liquidity:

1. *Receivables collection period.*   This ratio measures the number of days it takes, on average, to collect accounts and notes receivable. A firm's day's sales (annual sales ÷ 360) are divided into accounts receivable to solve for the collection period.

2. *Number of days to sell inventory.*   Analogous to the ratio just described, this **inventory turnover** ratio is derived by dividing average daily cost of goods sold into the average of beginning and ending inventory.

3. *Number of days' bills outstanding.*   Here, the average daily cost of goods sold is divided into average accounts payable.

4. *Working capital ratios.*   Whereas ratios 1–3 dissect working capital (current assets minus current liabilities) into its major components—accounts receivable, inventory, and accounts payable—it is also useful to take an overall view of a company's ability to meet current liabilities. The most common measures are:

    a. Current ratio.   Current assets divided by current liabilities.
    b. Quick asset, or acid-test, ratio.   Current assets exclusive of inventory, divided by current liabilities.
    c. Cash ratio.   Bank deposits plus liquid securities owned, divided by current liabilities.

The Size Factor.   Although the basic economics of the company's product line and cost structure are of great importance, the competitive position of the company is perhaps of equal significance. By and large there is good reason to have much greater confidence in the long-term continuity of big companies that are competitive leaders in their industry. Although size alone does not guarantee a profitable level of operations, seasoned firms that are dominant in their industry area naturally tend to be better able to withstand adversity. It is true, however, that we do occasionally observe large firms with great difficulties requiring drastic rehabilitative action. See the section "Bankruptcy and Reorganization."

Protective Provisions of Bond Issue.   A bond issue may be given specific protection, over and above that provided by the credit of the obligor, by a **mortgage** on physical property, a pledge of securities under a **collateral trust agreement,** or a preference over other creditors of the issuer through a **covenant of prior or equal coverage** or the **subordination** of other indebtedness. The chief protection such provisions give is priority in the event of a future reorganization, should the corporation become unable to meet its interest charges on debt maturities. Because of the specific added protection they have been given, such bond issues sell at lower yields than other obligations of the corporation. In some instances, the protection provided by a mortgage or by a pledge of collateral may be so great that the bond issue is considered strong and sells at a relatively low yield even if the credit of the obligor is weak. Perhaps the best example of this is **equipment trust certificates** issued by railroads. The collateral in this case is considered so marketable that the credit of the certificate is appraised separately from the railroad.

The collateral provisions of bonds, which used to be very heavily stressed by investors, are much less emphasized today. This is because property value is a function of the earnings the property can produce. Most property that serves as bond collateral is in the form of specialized plant and equipment. When the economics of the issuing company deteriorate to the point of bankruptcy, the likelihood is that its property is incapable of earning an adequate rate of return and is therefore not worth very much.

Bond Ratings.   Widespread use is made of ratings accorded publicly owned bond issues by investment services. These ratings are based on a few broad investment tests, and on the subjective evaluation of the future by the raters. This should not take the place, however, of a thorough analysis of a bond issue unless the investor cannot perform this evaluation. However, because many investors are guided by ratings in buying and selling bonds, they influence bond yields to a large extent. Institutional investors are particularly influenced by ratings if, as in the case of commercial banks, supervisory authorities use them to determine the suitability of bonds for bank investment. Changes in the rating given to a bond, therefore, can considerably affect its price and yield.

The two primary systems of rating are those of **Moody's Investors Service** and **Standard & Poor's.** The rating or rank assigned to a security under each of these systems has the following stratifications:

Moody's	Standard & Poor's	Quality Designation
Aaa	AAA	Highest quality
Aa	AA	High quality
A	A	Upper medium grade
Baa	BBB	Medium grade
Ba	BB	Speculative elements
B	B	Speculative
Caa	CCC-CC	Default possible
Ca	C	Default, some recovery possible
C	DDD-D	Little recovery possible

Bond ratings are designed essentially to rank issues in order of the probability of default. Thus, triple-A bonds are those judged to be of highest quality because they have a negligible risk of default. Double-A bonds are of high quality also but are judged not to be quite as free of default risk as triple-A. Bonds rated A and BBB by Standard & Poor's are generally referred to as medium-quality obligations, with the BBB possessing a higher risk of default than the A. Bonds not falling within the first four rating categories are believed to contain a considerable "speculative" element, and are sometimes referred to as **"junk bonds"** or **high yield bonds.**

Hickman (*Corporate Bond Quality and Investor Experience,*) found that "the agency ratings serve as rough indexes to price and yield stability. On the average, realized yields on low grades were somewhat above those on high grades, but investors seeking price stability should have avoided the low-grade issues." He also found that the incidence of failure among firms with lower rated securities was greater than that of higher rated ones.

MUNICIPAL BOND ANALYSIS.   Because of the excellent empirical credit record of most municipal obligations, the need to engage in a penetrating analysis of their quality has sometimes been doubted. After 1975, however, the fiscal difficulties of some cities, notably New York City and Cleveland, led to the view that careful appraisal of the relevant credit factors should precede investment in municipal bonds. Therefore, it would seem highly desirable for investors in municipals to become reasonably competent in the techniques of municipal credit analysis. For an in-depth discussion of municipal bonds, see the section "State and Local Debt."

Analytical Concepts.   Hayes and Bauman (*Investments: Analysis and Management*) note that the **appraisal of municipal obligations** is a highly specialized area of investment analysis. In fact, the techniques for evaluating the quality of these issues are quite different from those used in corporate bond analysis. The major reason for the singular nature of municipal bonds rests in their status as obligations or governmental units. These units are not established to derive earnings from economic activities; their purpose is to supply services to the general public. Taxation is the typical means of financing these services. Under ordinary circumstances tax levies are designed to cover only the operating costs of municipal services plus any requirements for debt service, including interest charges and annual maturities.

As a consequence, a substantial **"coverage" of interest payments** is not expected on municipal obligations, and there is no residual equity to backstop the bondholders' claim. Indeed, in most cases there are no assets to which the bondholders can look in case of default. There is, of course, the estimated value of the real and personal properties subject to tax levies within the geographic area. But these properties are not available for foreclosure in case of default; moreover, estimates of taxable property values are not subject to conventional rules of determination as are corporate asset values.

General Obligations.   These may be described as bonds issued by state governments or municipal corporations chartered by the states under which all taxing powers are pledged for payment. Most general obligations arise from the financing of capital improvements undertaken by states, cities, counties, and special districts. The latter are merely municipal corporations chartered for a particular governmental function, the most important and widespread example being school districts. These bonds are generally regarded as the basic type of municipals, and, unless otherwise qualified in the bond description, it is usually presumed that a bond of a municipal corporation is a general obligation.

Revenue Bonds.   There are three major categories of revenue obligations classified according to the source of funds for debt servicing:

1. Those issued to finance physical facilities that provide economic services sold directly to users, with the service revenues pledged to debt servicing. Water and sewer, toll roads, and airport services are examples of this type of obligation.

2. Those issued to finance special purpose facilities, which are then leased to a user,

with the lease rentals pledged to debt servicing. If the user is a municipal corporation, general tax revenues may indirectly support the issue as they become the effective source of the lease payments.

3. Those issued to provide services that benefit certain products with special taxes levied on these products and pledged to service the bonds. A large volume of state highway bonds fall into this group, since fuel taxes and auto license fees are specifically pledged to service the bond interest and principal payments.

The quality of revenue bonds tends to vary over a considerable range. Those that receive support from a high-quality corporate credit or a highly assured usage fee, may carry quality ratings equal or superior to the general obligations of the related municipal unit. Others have gone into partial or total default as revenues fell short of bond service requirements.

Technical Aspects.

Legality.   In most states municipal borrowings are subject to restrictions under statutory law, and in some jurisdictions the power to borrow funds is not assumed to result from the general powers of municipal corporations.

Maturities.   Except for revenue bonds, it is customary for municipal bonds to carry **serial maturities.** Such maturities are often required by law, and their purpose is to encourage **prudent debt management** by automatically retiring debt out of taxes or other sources of revenue on a periodic, regular basis.

Redemption Provisions.   Most general obligations issued in serial form are not subject to a call price. Revenue bonds are more likely to be subject to redemption before maturity. The redemption provision is similar to that on corporates; they may be callable as a whole or in part at certain specific dates, and the premium above par at which the bonds are callable may decrease as they approach maturity.

Contractual Position and Remedies.   In the case of corporate bonds, the willingness to pay the required interest and principal is always assumed to be strong, because the very life of the corporation is in jeopardy if there is a default. The situation is not quite so clear-cut in the case of municipal obligations. A municipality cannot be liquidated to satisfy a bond-holder's claim. As a result, the analyst needs to make a special inquiry of the willingness to pay, or the indicated desire of the municipality to manage the debt in a prudent way.

Credit Analysis of Municipals.

Credit Quality Factors.   As in corporate analysis, the factors bearing on credit quality have two dimensions: (1) the broad economic factors and their trends, and (2) the financial data and trends.

The most significant general economic factors pertinent to the appraisal of any municipal credit are population trends and the nature and diversity of the economic base.

A number of financial ratios and data trends have been suggested for inputs to credit quality decisions on a municipal credit, including tax-dependent debt as a percentage of true valuation of taxable real estate, per capital net overall bonded debt, debt trend, property valuation trend, tax collection record, and budget record.

Revenue bonds are very much like the bonds of business corporations. Therefore, the key ratio in revenue bond analysis is **earnings coverage.** Since civic facilities are not profit-making operations in the business sense—fees are usually designed to meet operating expenses and debt service only, with a small addition for contingencies—coverage ratios are not expected to be as substantial as for corporate bonds. Ratios of 1.5–2 times charges are common for good-quality obligations.

PREFERRED STOCK ANALYSIS.

Nature of Contract.   The investment implications of the preferred stock contract are for the most part analogous to those of a bond. First, both provide a limited fixed income. Second, both often include the redemption provision. Because of the resemblance between the two types of securities, the techniques for analyzing them are almost identical. The grouping of preferred stocks and bonds for purposes of analysis is in distinct contrast to legal and accounting concepts, which view the preferred shares as a part of the equity along with the common stock and establish the creditors in a separate category. In one major respect only the preferred contract resembles common stock more closely than bonds: like common stock, there is no maturity. But this is of much less significance than the fact that **both bonds and preferreds** are **fixed income securities.**

Major Weakness of Preferred Stock Contracts.   The corporation is under much less compulsion to pay preferred dividends than it is to pay bond interest, because preferred stock is merely given the right to receive its specified dividend before any dividends are paid on the common shares. When a corporation fails to meet interest charges on bonds, the result is default. But the penalty for failure to declare preferred dividends is not as onerous. Such an omission merely means that the company does not pay dividends on the common stock until the preferred dividends have been paid in full; that is, preferred dividends are **cumulative.** Still, most analysts view the omission of preferred dividends as a serious sign of firm deterioration.

Yields and Taxes.   Because of the fixed rate of return and prior claim on assets and earnings, the market action of high-grade preferred stock tends to be governed by interest rates. As in the case of other types of security, preferred stocks range in quality from sound investments to highly speculative issues. The price action of the more speculative issues may more frequently be affected by the business risk of the issuer than by interest rates.

Except for **public utilities** and other companies with a similar need to maintain a certain equity-debt relationship, corporations have not generally desired to issue preferred stock as a source of new capital because of the tax burden. In particular, present income tax laws allow corporations to deduct interest payments on debt before computing taxable income, but dividends on preferred stock are not similarly treated. They are paid from income after taxes. This has not only reduced significantly the issuance of new preferreds, but has caused corporations to eliminate preferreds from their capitalizations when possible. The exception to this trend, however, is the practice of issuing preferred stock, usually **convertible,** to effect **mergers and acquisitions.**

Even though new preferred issues are not frequent and even though their appeal to the individual investor is questionable when their return and risk are considered, preferreds have a special attraction for any organization that **pays taxes** as a corporation. Dividends on preferred stock owned by a corporation or by certain institutions are taxable as income only to the extent of 15%. After-tax yields on good-quality preferreds have thus been very attractive relative to bond yields for these investors.

COMMON STOCK ANALYSIS

CHARACTERISTICS OF COMMON STOCK. Common stock represents a share in the ownership of the firm. It has the last claim on earnings and assets of all other securities issued, but it also has an unlimited potential for dividend payment and capital gain through rising prices. Other corporate securities (i.e., corporate bonds and preferred stock) have a contract for interest or dividend payout that common stock does not have. If the firm should fail and be forced to liquidate, common stockholders get what is left after everyone else has been repaid. Risk is highest with common stock and so must be its expected return.

COMMON STOCK VALUATION CONCEPTS.   It was noted earlier that value of a bond at a given time can be defined as the present value of the stream of coupon payments plus the present value of the principal payment to be received at maturity, both discounted at the prevailing rate of interest for that maturity. Following analogous reasoning, the value of a common stock can be defined as the present value of the future dividend stream in perpetuity. This concept is consistent with the assumption that the corporation will indeed have a perpetual life in accordance with its charter. In mathematical terms, the formula is that of a value for a **perpetual annuity** with a constant level of payments:

$$V = \frac{D}{r}$$

where V = value
$\quad D$ = dividends per share
$\quad r$ = percentage discount rate

If the **dividends are assumed to grow** at a certain **constant rate,** the formula becomes

$$V = \frac{D}{r - g}$$

where g = annual constant percentage growth in dividends per share

Since this model assumes that the growth rate for the corporation to be analyzed is constant, it is most suitable for use in estimating value for stable mature companies, with public utilities perhaps best illustrating this type. Companies with a more erratic or cyclical earnings pattern or companies showing quite rapid growth rates require a more complex dividend capitalization model framework to accommodate those differing dividend growth patterns. These models are described in the investment literature and have most recently found practical implementation at various investment organizations.

While more elaborate variations of the dividend capitalization model are needed for practical applications, the simplified form provides a convenient means of analyzing the determinants of stock value. To begin with, the value of the stock should be greater, the greater the earning power and capacity of the corporation to payout current dividends D. Correspondingly, the higher the growth rate g of the dividend, the greater the value of the corporation's stock. Finally, the greater the risk of the corporation and thus presumably the higher the discount rate (r), the lower the value of the stock.

The prime role of the analyst is to evaluate the basic earning power of the firm and to project the potential growth of earnings and dividends into the future and that is the focus of this section on common stock analysis. The discount rate r is considered to be a function of the corporation's **systematic risk** and is thought of as being determined in a broader economic framework. After briefly discussing the determinants of the discount rate, we describe the role of financial statement analysis in evaluating corporate earning power and discuss the methods of projecting dividend growth rates.

RISK-RETURN TRADEOFF.   As noted before, **systematic risk** is that component of total risk that cannot be diversified away because it is common to all stocks, hence should be the relevant risk in a portfolio context. In the stock market, stocks with high degrees of systematic risk must be priced to yield high rates of return to induce investors to accept high degrees of risk that are essentially undiversifiable within that market. Stocks with high systematic risk should have higher discount rates r than stocks with lower systematic risk.

Correspondingly, we should expect to observe stocks with higher systematic risk earning higher returns over longer periods of time than stocks with lower systematic risk. Several empirical studies have in fact addressed this question of the risk-return tradeoff in the stock market, with one by Sharpe and Cooper ("Risk-Return Classes of NYSE Common Stocks," *Financial Analysts Journal,* March–April 1972) providing perhaps the best example. This study analyzed the price behavior of all listed stocks over the 1926–1967 period, and used the **beta coefficient as the measure of systematic risk of stocks.**

Essentially, the study showed that stocks with high observed betas tended on average to earn higher returns than stocks with medium betas, which in turn tended to earn higher returns than stocks with low betas. The results supported the theory that high systematic risk should be associated with higher return and low systematic risk with lower return. The level of systematic risk might well be used as a means of establishing the appropriate discount rate for a stock. Using this approach in practice, however, requires adequate estimates of systematic risk, and investors should be aware of the deficiencies of standard beta measures for this purpose. For a discussion of the properties of beta, see W. Sharpe, *Investments,* Chapter 11.

FINANCIAL STATEMENT ANALYSIS.   The financial statements of a company consist of an **income statement, a balance sheet,** a **sources and uses of funds statement,** and the footnotes to each. From the analysis of these statements it may be possible to gather certain information and indications about basic corporate earning power. Certain pertinent ratios, trends, and figures may provide clues to the company's future. Financial statement analysis should, however, proceed with the caution that these statements suffer from certain deficiencies. An entire, separate section in this *Handbook* is devoted to financial statement analysis.

The Income Statement.   The **annual income statement** issued by a company is an accounting picture of the past year's income, expenses, and profits. The **common size income statement** is an income statement in which all figures are expressed as a percentage of sales. The major advantage of a common size income statement is the standardized presentation, which eliminates the bias of size and makes all companies directly comparable. The following tabulation illustrates the income statement of a hypothetical company presented in common size form.

Model of Income Statement

Sales	$200,000,000	100%
Less: Cost of goods sold	100,000,000	50
Gross operating margin	100,000,000	50
Less: Selling, administrative expenses and depreciation	50,000,000	25
Net operating income	50,000,000	25
Less: Interest expense	10,000,000	5
Taxable income	40,000,000	20
Less: Taxes	20,000,000	10
Net income	20,000,000	10
Less: Dividends to common equity	10,000,000	5
Retained earnings	10,000,000	5

Ratios can be calculated from income statement figures and used for common comparison among various companies and among years for the same company. Ratio analysis is generally used only in comparison with certain accepted ratio standards. Particular ratios and trends may be especially helpful in evaluating the earning capacity of the firm. Among the more useful ratios are the following:

1. Pretax profit margin: Income before taxes/Sales
2. Operating margin: Operating income/Sales
3. Earnings per share: Net profit/Outstanding shares
4. Tax ratio: Taxes paid/Earnings before taxes

The **payout ratio** is the common dividend earnings available to common stock and reveals the percentage of net profits paid to stockholders. The amount and percentage of retained earnings (1 minus the payout ratio) may give some indication of the funds available for investment that will generate future earnings. A higher retention rate may indicate increased future earnings.

The Balance Sheet. The **balance sheet** represents the company's financial position at a point in time. Income statements deal with flows, whereas balance sheets present data that reflect the amount of assets and liabilities at a point in time. The **common size balance sheet** is a balance sheet in which all the figures are expressed as a percentage of total assets or total liabilities. As in the case of the common size income statement, it offers a standardized presentation that eliminates the bias of size and makes all companies directly comparable. The illustrative balance sheet that follows shows the liability side as representing sources of funds and the asset side as uses of funds.

The balance sheet reveals information on the company's liquidity, utilization of assets, and financing, all of which may aid in appraising the company's earning power. A company's liquidity position is an indication of its ability to meet the more immediate cash needs of normal, as well as unusual, operating conditions. **Current assets** are the most quickly converted to cash, and **current liabilities** present the most immediate need for cash. Therefore, the analysis of liquidity concentrates on these areas. The **working capital position,**

Balance Sheet Model

Uses of Funds	Sources of Funds
Current assets	Current liabilities
Long-term assets	Long-term liabilities
Other assets	Net worth
Total assets	Total liabilities and equity

which is current assets minus current liabilities, is a frequently used indication of liquidity. Certain working capital ratios are indicative of the quality and adequacy of the working capital position. Among the ratios that indicate the quality of the working capital position are (1) the **current ratio** (current assets to current liabilities), and (2) the **quick ratio** (cash, marketable securities, and accounts receivable to current liabilities).

An important indication of **basic earning power** may be found in the efficiency with which management is utilizing its assets to produce sales and profits. Indications of efficient asset management are:

1. Return on investment: Net profit/Total assets

2. Net profit to common equity.

3. Fixed asset turnover: Sales/Assets

The balance sheet also reveals how a company has financed itself among the various sources of funds available. The **capital structure** is the proportion of long-term debt, preferred stock, and stockholders' equity in a firm's financing. The more debt in a capital structure (the higher the debt-equity ratio), the more cash expense obligations the company has. A large cash obligation in relation to the company's cash generation is indicative of great financial risk.

In addition to affecting the risk associated with future earnings, the use of debt also affects earnings. **Leverage** is the use of debt in an attempt to increase return on equity. The difference between the return on an investment and the cost of financing the investment is the residual to the common stockholders. If the difference is positive, the stockholders benefit but if it is negative, the stockholders must make up the difference. This causes a decrease in the return on equity and **magnifies** the decrease in earnings per share. The key aspect of the use of financial leverage is its **magnification effect.**

Sources and Uses of Funds Statements.   The **sources and uses of funds statement** for a corporation tells where the cash came from and where it went. It indicates what assets were acquired and how they were financed. It is, in many respects, wider in scope than either the income statement or the balance sheet and, indeed, integrates the two statements.

Uses of funds are increases in assets and decreases in liabilities. For example, increases in cash, accounts receivable, inventory, and plant, property, and equipment; and decreases in accounts payable, long-term debt, and stockholders' equity are uses of funds. Sources of funds are the reverse; that is, decreases in assets and increases in liabilities.

The sources and uses of funds statement may be constructed by comparing the company's balance sheets from one period with another and recording the increases and decreases in assets and liabilities. One format for portraying these flows might be referred to as the

reconciliation of working capital. The focus here is on changes in total working capital (current assets minus current liabilities) and is illustrated as follows:

Reported net income			$20,000,000
Plus:	Noncash charges (depreciation, deferred tax reserve, etc.)		4,000,000
Equals:	Working capital provided by operations		$24,000,000
Less:	Capital expenditures	$10,000,000	
	Common stock dividends	10,000,000	(20,000,000)
Equals:	Increase in working capital		$ 4,000,000

Deficiencies of Financial Statements.   A company's financial statements provide valuable information about the level and trend of its earning power. However, investors cannot accept at face value the figures designated by a company as net income or net worth. This is because in preparing financial statements accountants have latitude in the way that business trans- actions are reported. This generally leads to less than uniform statements of income and balance sheets of companies even within the same industry. The rest of this section reviews the areas where the divergences may be greatest.

To begin with, there can be problems in determining when revenues or sales are to be recognized for certain types of company. These can be illustrated by the case of producers of expensive equipment, who often lease their products to customers rather than sell them outright. Accounting guidelines have been issued on minimally acceptable answers to this and other questions, but some companies choose an accounting policy more conservative than that suggested by the guidelines, while others follow only the minimally acceptable standards.

For example, companies may use first in, first out or last in, first out (**FIFO** or **LIFO**) **methods for valuing inventories.** During periods of falling prices, LIFO usually produces higher earnings than FIFO, because the less costly inventory is "sold" first. During periods of rising prices, the earnings effect is reversed. In recent years, LIFO has produced lower earnings but higher cash flows, since taxes have been reduced. In analyzing earnings, it is important to be aware of any earnings increase or decrease that may have arisen because of a shift from LIFO to FIFO, or vice versa. It is also important to be aware of the LIFO versus FIFO effects on earnings when comparing different companies.

Companies may use **straight-line** or **accelerated methods of depreciation.** Accelerated depreciation increases depreciation costs in the early years of a new asset's life; it thereby decreases profit, income tax, and net accounting profit when the asset is new. The total depreciation expense is unchanged; only the timing is altered. Differing methods, however, can affect any particular year's reported accounting income significantly.

Intangible **investment in research and development** (R & D) activity is expensed periodically under conventional accounting procedures. This is correct only when R & D expenditures contribute nothing to the generation of future cash flows; in that case there is little rationale for pursuing research. The analyst should consider this in making comparisons among research-intensive and nonresearch-oriented companies.

A company's financial obligations under its **pension plans** can be divided into two major segments: the **past service liability** and the **current service liability.** There are various legal, tax, and personnel relations reasons for putting money aside in advance to provide for these liabilities. This is known as funding. But the rate at which pension liabilities are funded, and reflected in current net income, is a matter of managerial discretion within rather broad guidelines. Given this range of discretion, some companies have manipulated their pension charges in a way that artifically smoothes reported earnings.

Finally, one of the most difficult tasks of balance sheet analysis is to determine the nature and extent of liabilities that are not shown on the balance sheet. In the past, probably the most significant of these obligations was the **long-term lease.** The method of determining the debt equivalent amount of a lease is fairly simple in concept, but in practice a number of rather subjective judgments are involved. Even after these judgments have been made, it has been difficult for the accounting profession to decide whether these amounts should be shown in footnotes or directly on the liability side of the balance sheet, together with an offsetting fixed asset representing the value of property acquired through the lease. As of January 1980, most long-term leases must be shown directly on the balance sheet on a capitalized basis (i.e., the present value of future lease obligations).

PROJECTING EARNINGS.   Once an evaluation of the earning power of the corporation and its capacity to pay dividends has been obtained, the analyst needs to evaluate the growth rate potential of the corporation and its dividends. With a stable rate of growth and environment, the company's past performance may be a reasonable indication of the future. This stability allows forecasting future earnings and dividends with statistical methods, such as historical growth rate extrapolation, aggregate economic forecasting using regression analysis, and the rate of return approach. Evaluating growth potential under more dynamic conditions requires more subjective analysis, but the life cycle framework may be one that is a useful aid for this analysis.

Historical Growth Rate.   Assuming that the circumstances under which the firm operated in the past will continue unchanged in the future, the investor may use the **historical growth rate** in forecasting future earnings. Various methods of computing the historical growth rate can be used such as the compound growth rate, the moving average, and a fitted trend line.

The investor must be careful in interpreting **compound and trend growth rates,** especially as indicators of future earnings patterns. Among the most important considerations are the selection of the base and terminal years and hidden patterns of intervening years. By selecting different base and terminal years, the growth rate will also be made to differ.

The **moving average approach** lessens the problem of base and terminal year distortion and gives weight to the intervening years. The effects of an abnormal base or terminal year are tempered by the inclusion of other years. The major disadvantage of the moving average is its sluggish response to a significant change.

When using any of these methods for forecasting, it must be assumed that the conditions that prevailed during the selected time span will continue in the future. Stable conditions imply that such important considerations as industry technology, competition, and political environment are constant. If the conditions are unstable, forecasts may be more misleading than helpful.

Aggregate Approach Using Regression Analysis.   The application of historical growth rates in forecasting earnings relies solely on earnings information and assumes a continuation of the previous earnings pattern. The **aggregate approach** broadens the investigation for indicators of future earnings beyond the earnings themselves into the general economic, industry, and company operating environments.

The procedure is first to isolate and estimate the major economic influences on the firm's profits. The analyst must then relate the appropriate economic indicator to the industry sales, through **regression analysis.** After the regression analysis has established this relationship, the analyst must obtain an estimate of the future value of this indicator. Applying this relationship to the projected economic indicator value, the analyst arrives at an estimate of projected industry sales.

The firm's share of the market is the third step in estimating future earnings under an aggregate approach. It is easier to determine the firm's historical market share if the industry is well defined and there are only a few major companies than when there are a large number of small companies. If the conditions are stable, the firm's historical market share can be applied to the projected industry sales to determine the projected company sales. When the firm's sales projection has been made, the investor's final step is to apply the historical profit margin ratio to sales to derive the total profits of the company.

The major **advantage of the aggregate approach** is its consideration of more than earnings alone. This approach recognizes the influence of the economy on a firm's earnings. Furthermore, it allows for more flexibility than the mechanical projections of the historical earnings growth rate approach.

The aggregate approach assumes that conditions identical to those in the past will prevail in the future. If the relationship between economic variables and industry sales, the firm's market share, or the firm's profit margins changed, the stable conditions assumption would be violated. The problem of the base and terminal years selection also remains in the aggregate approach. The choice of an abnormal base or terminal year may distort the regression results.

Return On Investment Approach.   A third method for forecasting earnings is the **return on investment** approach, which applies the historical rate of return on investment to a projected total investment base. The rationale for using this approach is that the necessary information is readily obtainable, and firms have target rate of return objectives that they attempt to maintain. It is argued that investment plans are made in advance and can be readily estimated by a scrutiny of the company's reports and its capital sources. The target rate of return is the return on investment that the firm attempts to earn from each investment. Under stable conditions, it may be reasonable to assume that future investments will return the historical rate of return.

The advantage of the return on investment approach is the relative ease with which it can be computed. The information is relatively easy to obtain, and the computational procedures are quick. This approach continues to assume, however, that stable conditions will prevail and that investment plans are unlikely to change rapidly. The accuracy of this method may be reduced in industries of low capital investment. If earnings increases arise with no additional investment expenditures, it is difficult to correlate future earnings with investment. Accuracy may also be impaired if unforeseen startup costs or delays are encountered in the development of the investment's profit potential.

The Industrial Life Cycle.   The **industry life cycle theory** is a framework for analyzing companies under more dynamic conditions. According to this theory, an industry evolves over time through several different growth patterns or stages of development. The first stage is the pioneering stage, during which the infant industry develops a new product. Sales and profits grow rapidly, and other companies enter the young industry because of the high profit opportunity. This leads to overcapacity, severe competition, merger of weaker companies, and withdrawal of others from the industry. After the turbulence of the **pioneering stage,** the industry enters the **expansion stage.** Growth during this stage is above the national economic average but is more stable than in the earlier stage. As the rate of technological improvements within the industry decreases, and as the product market becomes fully penetrated, the industry enters the **maturity stage.** The industry then grows at or below the rate of the economy, depending on whether it is able to maintain its position or is being gradually displaced by other expanding industries. The final period is the **decline stage,** when the firm experiences negative growth.

The investor who tries to forecast industry performance within the life cycle framework faces several serious analytical problems. There is no guarantee that a specific industry will systematically pass through the four stages described above. Another difficulty associated with this theory is in determining in advance, when an industry will change from one stage to another. Because changes in stock prices tend to lead changes in industry growth rates, it is desirable to anticipate each shift in stage. Perhaps the greatest value of the life cycle framework is that it conditions the analyst to look for certain clues that may help him detect a shifting tide in the industries he analyzes. At the same time, it prevents him from blithely extrapolating abnormally high or low industry growth rates into the distance future.

VARIATIONS IN THE ANALYTICAL TECHNIQUE.   The foregoing discussion provides a broad outline that should be of use generally in analyzing individual companies. Differing companies will require variations of the general process of analysis. The discussion below outlines some of the major differences that should be considered when evaluating companies in the following categories: industrial securities, financial securities, and public utilities.

Industrial Securities.

Nature of the Industry.   Since the category of industrial securities embraces every type of corporate enterprise except financial corporations, public utilities, and railroads, it comprises a very wide variety of businesses. Although basic principles of investment analysis are the same in each case, their application varies with the character of the business.

The major classes of industrial concerns are:

1.   Mining, petroleum, and other extractive enterprises that depend on natural resources, the supply of which is usually limited.
2.   Manufacturers of industrial materials like metals and chemicals.
3.   Manufacturers of producer durable goods and military equipment.
4.   Manufacturers of consumer nondurable goods, including textiles, foods, and tobacco.
5.   Manufacturers of consumer durable goods and building materials.
6.   Wholesale and retail distributors.
7.   Service industries like air transport and bus lines that may have public utility characteristics.

Numerous concerns diversify their activities, so that they manufacture and sell products falling in two or more of the classifications given above. Thus, a petroleum company produces chemicals and the General Electric Co. manufactures equipment for industry and consumer durable goods.

Industry Analysis.   In the analysis of industrial securities, an essential step is to identify and study dominant influences that affect earnings and other elements of value of companies in each industry. These influences not only vary from industry to industry, but also from time to time within the same industry. Examples of such key analytical factors are given in the following summary:

Oil stock values are largely affected by the location of crude reserves and other properties, the proportion of its crude requirements produced by the company, and the relation of product to crude prices. **International petroleum companies,** with a large part of their operations outside the United States, are subject to political risks that do not apply to companies operating mainly within this country. For domestic companies, close regulation of crude production and imports will result in relatively high crude oil costs if a large part of the company's crude requirements must be purchased from others. Recent events in the OPEC countries and the tremendous increase in crude oil prices have made the oil industry a very high risk and return industry. Investors have, through 1980, been handsomely compensated for the increased risks.

Automobile stocks are very much influenced by cyclical fluctuations in demand, as well as by the ability of car manufacturers to adapt their products to changing public tastes. The latter factor has accounted for wide variations in the percentage of the market captured by individual companies in particular years. For the most part, U.S. companies have suffered from foreign competition in recent years. The imports have been able to meet the demand for smaller, more fuel-efficient cars providing a real challenge for the U.S. car companies in the 1980s.

Chemical and drug stock values may be very much influenced by development of new products. Staple chemicals and drugs are subject to intense price competition, but new products and those sold under brand names to consumers and having a wide acceptance often give quite satisfactory profit margins. The record of each company's research program is thus a major analytical consideration.

Retail stocks are greatly influenced by a company's adaptability to shifting population patterns and buying habits. In the mail order field, the success of a company in establishing stores and in competing with discount house operations has been of great importance. In grocery chains, the shift from small stores to supermarkets has played a similar role. Widespread automobile ownership and suburbanization were the underlying forces that made such adaptation important. In recent years there has been a great increase in **firm failures** in the retail industry due to shrinking profit margins, overexpansion and heightened competition.

Tobacco stock values have been affected by the success of managements in adapting their product to consumer concern with health considerations. Shifts in demand to filter cigarettes and consumer response to advertising stressing health factors have favored some companies at the expense of others.

After analyzing financial statements and other pertinent data, the security analyst will want to identify and appraise such key industry influences, and the management's ability to cope with them, to arrive at a realistic appraisal of future earning power and of the value of an industrial stock.

Financial Securities.

Distinctive Features.   Securities of financial enterprises are peculiar in that assets of these institutions consist mainly of loans and securities. The methods of analysis differ, therefore, from those applicable to industrial companies. Quality of assets and effective cost of funds, for example, may be quite significant analytical factors.

Bank Stocks.   The most important group of financial securities are bank stocks. Analysis is made more difficult because of the limited information provided by annual and other reports in many cases. When assets are understated or left out of the balance sheet entirely, the regulatory authorities interpose no objections. They do not regard it as their function to require accurate accounting for investors—they are concerned primarily with the safety of the funds of depositors.

Because of the highly liquid character of bank assets, book value is of more importance than for industrial companies. **Reported book value** is readily determined from the condition statement, as the bank's balance sheet is called. However, **asset value** may vary considerably from the figure shown on the books. Securities are usually carried at cost less a reserve built up through sales of investments at a profit. Loans are shown net of reserves for possible losses. Real estate may be carried at figures varying widely above or below current market values. Many bank managements like to accumulate **hidden reserves,** usually by carrying assets taken over when loans go into default far below their true worth.

Banks derive their **earnings** mainly from interest on loans and investments. Fees and charges for services are a relatively small part of income for most banks. Banks customarily report operating earnings from these two sources and deduct expenses and taxes attributable to such operating income to show **net operating income.** Gains and losses on securities and additions to reserves are then listed, to arrive at net income.

Analysis ratios commonly used in studying bank stocks are net operating earnings after applicable taxes per share, market price as a percent of book value, earning assets per share, and the ratio of time to total deposits. When relatively high rates of interest are paid on time deposits, the time deposit ratio may be significant. The rate of growth of deposits and earning assets and the average return on assets, allowing for the tax advantage of tax-exempt securities, are also important indicators of investment value.

Insurance Stocks.   Analysis of insurance stocks involves an appraisal of both underwriting and investment results. The investment funds of most insurance companies are derived chiefly from reserves that belong to policyholders. In **fire and casualty insurance companies,** these are the unearned premium reserves and the loss reserves. In life insurance companies, they are the reserves against policies outstanding.

Fire and Casualty Insurance Companies.   These companies report underwriting and investment results separately. Some companies rely mainly on underwriting for their earnings, and others chiefly on investment income, including appreciation of the stock portfolio that accounts for a large percentage of the assets of most of these companies. The analyst must recognize this and stress the underwriting or investment outlook accordingly in appraising such stocks.

Life Insurance Companies.   Life insurance stock analysis stresses the rate of growth of the company and the types of policy outstanding, as well as such general factors as the trend of interest rates, life expectancy, and taxation of life insurance companies. Although life insurance companies invest mainly in fixed income securities, some have put a material percentage of their funds in common stocks. Because of the high degree of leverage in life insurance stocks, this can substantially affect investment values.

Other Financial Stocks.   Analysis of stocks of **finance companies,** including installment finance, business finance, and personal loan companies, stresses profitability and quality of assets, cost of funds, and rate of growth. Similar considerations affect stocks of **savings and loan holding companies,** as well as the impact of special tax law provisions to which they are subject.

Public Utility Securities.   Securities of electric, gas, telephone and telegraph, water, and transit companies are classified as public utilities. Railroads are public utilities in the legal sense, but their securities are classified separately because of economic, regulatory, and other peculiarities.

From an investment viewpoint, public utility companies are distinguished from other corporations in the following respects:

1. Public utilities must generally obtain from a regulatory authority a franchise to provide the specified service.
2. The franchise is, as a rule, exclusive, giving them a **"legal monopoly"** to serve the area specified.
3. Rates charged, financing, and other aspects of operation are subject to regulation in the public interest.

Franchises.   The chief provisions of a public utility franchise, affecting directly or indirectly the investment standing of the utility securities, are:

1. The kind of service to be performed.
2. The duration of the franchise.
3. The exclusiveness of the right to perform the service permitted.
4. Territorial limitations in the performance of the service.
5. Restrictions and regulations regarding rates and charges.

A franchise may limit a utility company to a single service, such as supplying electricity, operating a telephone system, or running a transit company. As a rule, however, the utility is permitted to furnish the services that its equipment renders economically possible, even though the franchise does not specify some services. Thus a telephone company may make its wires available for the transmission of messages by telegraph.

A franchise may be limited as to **duration,** it may be perpetual, or it may be of indeterminate duration. Under a limited franchise a renewal by the political authority is required at the time the franchise expires. A perpetual franchise cannot be revoked, except for some breach of the franchise agreement. Under the "indeterminate permit," the political authority reserves the right to revoke the franchise under specified conditions. It is frequently provided that in the event of revocation, the utility company is to receive compensation for its property, either from the municipality or from a successor corporation.

When a franchise is **exclusive,** the utility company receives a monopoly to perform the specified service within a prescribed territory. This eliminates direct competition and duplication of equipment, but it does not exclude indirect competition such as exists between a gas and an electric company. The present-day tendency of public authorities is to avoid duplication of services and wasteful competition by granting exclusive franchises or by refusing to grant additional franchises for the performance of a service that is or can be adequately supplied by existing public utility facilities.

A franchise is usually limited to a **specified area,** although in some cases the area is not definitely outlined. Thus, it may be limited to a single municipality or to a county. Gas and electric companies often operate under a number of different franchises acquired by merger or acquisition, each confined to a limited area.

Utility Rates.   Utility rates reflect the value of the service and the cost of the service. The value of the service is what consumers can afford to pay for it; the cost of service is the cost of furnishing it, including a fair return on invested capital. Neither principle can be applied independently of the other. The cost basis of rate making is impracticable if, under it, rates would be higher than the consumers could afford to pay. On the other hand, rates based on the "value of service" may be so high as to yield unreasonable profits at the public's expense. Utility rates, under judicial precedents, are generally set at levels that give a reasonable return on the capital invested and provide service at rates consumers can readily afford to pay.

Utility Valuation.   Adjustment of public utility rates is closely linked to the valuation of property used in performing the service. Courts have sought to define a **"fair value"** for utility property as a base on which a fair rate of return could be computed. In a number of decisions in the 1920s, fair value was held to be chiefly present-day cost of reproduction, less depreciation, irrespective of original cost. This formula linked earning power of utility enterprises to the fluctuating purchasing power of the dollar, rather than to a return on the dollars invested.

Subsequently the **original cost basis of utility valuation** has come into the ascendency. This valuation basis would limit the rate base of public utilities to the dollars "prudently" invested in their property. This view has prevailed in rulings of the Federal Power Commission in rate cases affecting companies subject to its jurisdiction, decisions of the Securities and Exchange Commission on issues of securities under the Public Utility Holding Company Act, and rulings by a number of state regulatory commissions that have been influenced by these federal agencies and the Uniform Classification of Accounts issued by the National Association of Railway and Public Utility Commissioners.

In 1944 the U.S. Supreme Court, in the **Hope Natural Gas case** (320 U.S. 591), virtually discarded the "fair value" rule for rate making. Instead of any rigid rate formula, the highest court ruled that "rates which enable the company to operate successfully, to maintain its financial integrity, to attract capital, and to compensate its investors for the risk assumed certainly cannot be condemned as invalid, even though they might produce only a meagre return on the so-called fair value rate base." Thus the Supreme Court greatly widened the discretion given regulatory commissions in setting rates. This epoch-making decision said further:

> From the investor or company point of view, it is important that there be enough revenue not only for operating expenses but also for the capital costs of the business. These include services on the debt and dividends on the stock. . . . By that standard the return to the equity owner should be commensurate with returns on investments in other enterprises having corresponding risks. The return, moreover, should be sufficient to assure confidence in the financial integrity of the enterprise, so as to maintain its credit and to attract capital.

Commission Regulation.   State commissions set up in most states have the widest power of regulation. The commission's authority differs from state to state. It usually embraces (1) franchises, (2) rates and services, (3) security issues, and (4) accounts and reports.

The attitude of the state commission is particularly important in the investment analysis of utility securities, now that the courts are disinclined to overrule such rate decisions, as we have seen above.

Analysis of a Utility Company.   In the investment analysis of public utility stocks, prospective earning power and cash flow are primary considerations, as with other securities. Some items to be taken into account are discussed next.

Demand for Service.   The rate of growth in the demand for service in the area served is the major point for analysts. Competition from other services and other fuels must be taken into account in appraising potential demands for utility service.

Throughout their history, with very few exceptions, public utilities other than transit companies have enjoyed an expanding demand for their services. But growth rates vary greatly with population, employment, industrial, and living standard trends.

Load Factor.   This may affect earning power substantially. A utility is required to have capacity adequate to meet the maximum demand for its service at any time. This maximum is the **peak load.** Actual output in a given period, such as a month or year, divided by what would have been produced at continuous peak load operation, is the load factor. The higher the load factor, other things being equal, the more profitable the operation, for plant capacity is idle a lesser percentage of the time.

Capitalization.   Regulatory authorities, both federal and state, have sought to maintain a reasonable balance between bond and stock capitalization of public utilities, to avoid the excessive fixed charges that have plagued railroads. The SEC has favored a capital structure for an operating company that comprises 50% debt, 20–25% preferred stock, and the balance common stock, though the commonly accepted ratio for an electric utility is 50% debt, 15% preferred stock, and 35% common stock.

Reported Earnings.   A utility's reported earnings are affected by the accounting treatment of the tax credit from the use of more rapid depreciation methods for tax purposes. A number of jurisdictions require that only taxes actually paid be deducted from earnings, so that tax reductions **flow through** to net income, thereby increasing the reported amount, and could become an argument for lower rates. Elsewhere, the tax reductions go into a "reserve for deferred federal income tax" and so are kept out of net income, which is then said to be **normalized.** The cash flow is the same in each case, but the investment quality of reported profits is affected by the accounting procedure employed. Utilities are permitted to add a percentage of construction in progress to earnings.

An in-depth discussion of the major microeconomic issues related to public utility companies can be found in the section "Public Utility Finance."

Challenges for the Future.   The public utility industry has witnessed, in recent years, dramatic shifts in public and investment community acceptance of its operating and financial performance. Although the industry is still a regulated monopoly with little or no **failure risk** potential among the more than 100 publicly owned companies, clearly the environment within which they operate is far from secure and certain. The remainder of this section discusses some of the major challenges and uncertainties facing the industry as it moves into the 1980s.

Fuel Sources and Costs.   The primary operating expense of a public utility is its fuel costs. A utility's balance between the main available sources is a critical ingredient in assessing the potential risks and returns. The recent increases in oil prices along with the environmental and investment problems of nuclear fuel have caused analysts to rethink optimal fuel-mix strategies for operating an electric or gas public utility.

Environmental Conditions.   The trend in the industry during the 1970s was to move toward a greater reliance on nuclear fuel. With the near disaster of the Three Mile Island nuclear plant in Pennsylvania and heightened environmental pressure group activities, government agencies have been very cautious about granting permit proposals for building new plants of this type. The threat to the industry, and the country, from additional nuclear problems is real and must be considered.

Regulatory Climate.   The ability of a public utility to pass along cost increases to customers in the form of rate changes is a function of the **regulatory climate** that it operates in. A permissive, "understanding" public service rate commission that acts promptly and favorably on rate increase petitions is a great advantage to a utility. A critical, more deliberate commission is less favorable. An analyst must be aware of the recent history and trends in the regulatory environments around the country.

Sources of Capital.   As public utility "risks" increase and regulators scrutinize requests for rate increases more stringently, the ability of utilities to attract investment capital at competitive rates can become a problem for individual electric and gas companies. There are currently relatively few "top"-rated (Aaa) senior debt securities and far more lower-rated (Baa and Ba) bonds outstanding in 1980 than there were in 1970. This reflects lower interest coverage ratios and increased uncertainties. Operating performance of utilities must be monitored and, in many cases, improved in order to attract debt, preferred, and common equity capital. To the extent this is not done effectively, capital will either move elsewhere, despite the monopolistic nature of the industry, or be provided at extremely high costs of capital.

REFERENCES

Babcock, Guilford C., "The Concept of Sustainable Growth," *Financial Analysts Journal*, May–June 1970, pp. 108–44.

Bolten, Steven, *Security Analysis and Portfolio Management*, Holt, Rinehart & Winston, New York, 1972.

Brealey, Richard A., *An Introduction to Risk and Return from Common Stocks*, MIT Press, Cambridge, MA, 1969.

Cohen, Jerome B., Zinbarg, Edward P., and Zeikel, Arthur, *Investment Analysis and Portfolio Management*, Irwin, Homewood, IL, 1973.

Curley, Anthony J., and Bear, Robert M., *Security Analysis and Portfolio Management*, Harper & Row, New York, 1979.

Francis, Jack Clark, *Investments: Analysis and Management*, McGraw-Hill, New York, 1979.

Graham, Benjamin, Dodd, David L., and Cottle, Sidney, *Security Analysis*, 4th ed., McGraw-Hill, New York, 1962.

Hagin, Robert, *Modern Portfolio Theory*, Dow Jones-Irwin, Homewood, IL, 1979.

Hayes, Douglas A., and Bauman, Scott W., *Investments: Analysis and Management*, Macmillan, New York, 1976.

Hickman, W. B., *Corporate Bond Quality and Investor Experience*, Princeton University Press, Princeton, NJ, 1958.

Ibbotson, Roger G., and Sinquefeld, Rex A., *Stocks, Bonds, Bills and Inflation: The Past (1926–1976) and the Future (1977–2000)*, Financial Analysts Research Foundation, Charlottesville, VA, 1977.

Latané, Henry A., Tuttle, Donald L., and James, Charles P., *Security Analysis and Portfolio Management*, 2nd ed., Ronald Press, New York, 1977.

Lorie, James H., and Hamilton, Mary T., *The Stock Market: Theories and Evidence*, Irwin, Homewood, IL, 1974.

Sharpe, William F., *Portfolio Theory and Capital Markets*, McGraw-Hill, New York, 1970.

———, *Investments*, Prentice-Hall, Englewood Cliffs, NJ, 1978.

Williamson, J. Peter, *Investments: New Analytic Techniques*, Praeger, New York, 1970.

MODERN PORTFOLIO THEORY AND MANAGEMENT

CONTENTS

DEFINITION	3	RISK: CLASSIFICATION AND MEASUREMENT	15
CLASSICAL SECURITY ANALYSIS	3		
MPT DECISION PROCESS	5	Capital Asset Pricing Model	15
		Market Model	16
ROLE OF JUDGMENT IN MPT	6	Security Characteristic Lines	17
		R-Squared	18
THEORETICAL FOUNDATION FOR MPT	7	VALUATION THEORY	18
RELATIONSHIPS AMONG SECURITIES	8	USE OF VALUATION THEORY	19
Concept of Utility	8	DIVIDEND DISCOUNT MODELS	22
Indifference Curves	9	IS MPT-BASED VALUATION A	
Inefficient Sets	10	"LONG-TERM" FORECASTING	
Efficient Sets	11	TOOL?	23
RISK AND RETURN	13	MPT-BASED RESEARCH RESULTS	23
Markowitz Model	14		
Portfolio Theory	15	WHAT WILL HAPPEN IF MORE	
Capital Market Theory	15	PEOPLE USE MPT?	25

MODERN PORTFOLIO THEORY AND MANAGEMENT

Robert L. Hagin

DEFINITION

Broadly speaking, **modern portfolio theory** (MPT) is an **investment decision process.** As the term is used today, MPT encompasses far more than the individual words—"portfolio" or "theory"—suggest. Today, MPT embraces all modern investment and portfolio theories, including the applications and decision processes based on these theories. As a result, terms such as "new investment technology," "modern investment theory," "applied investment theory," and "quantitative investment theory" are all synonymous with MPT.

The essence of MPT, and the characteristic that distinguishes it from other investment approaches, is its quantification of the relationship between **risk and return.** Furthermore, what has evolved from once-theoretical constructs is a **practical decision-oriented process** that allows an investor to classify, estimate, and then control both the type and the amount of expected risk and return.

CLASSICAL SECURITY ANALYSIS

Classical security analysis and **portfolio construction** focuses on expected return without quantifying risk. A close look at classical security analysis and portfolio construction illustrates the significance of omitting risk from the analysis and highlights the problems that arise from using any approach that is not based on the capital market theory. (Capital market theory, which is discussed in a subsequent section, holds that investors must be compensated for assuming risk).

Classical security analysis begins with estimates of near-term earnings. Typically, such forecasting involves much time and effort. Moreover, some people are very good at it. The problem with purely earnings-based analysis is that—assuming that the earnings estimates are accurate—it is then necessary to estimate, with almost equal accuracy, the **price-earnings ratio (P/E)** that will prevail during the same period. The product of the estimated earnings and the estimated price-earnings ratio results in the estimated stock price. Then a comparison of the estimated and actual prices reveals both the direction and the magnitude of any implied mispricing.

**EXHIBIT 1   PRICE-EARNINGS RATIOS FOR THE DOW JONES INDUSTRIAL
AVERAGE, 1961–1980.**

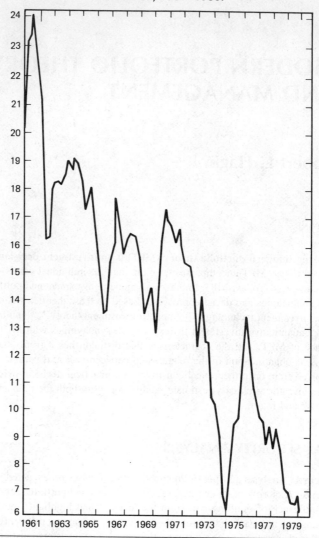

Source: Kidder, Peabody & Co., Inc., *Modern Portfolio Theory: Topics and Applications,* No. 2,
June 1980.

    Two factors complicate the apparent simplicity of classical security valuation. First, this
type of analysis does not incorporate any explicit estimate of risk—stocks can only be said
to appear to be over- or undervalued. Second, since accurate earnings estimates need to be
combined with accurate estimates of subsequent price-earnings ratios, the absence of the
decision-making framework provided by capital market theory can present insurmountable
forecasting problems.

To illustrate some of the problems associated with price-earnings estimates, suppose that, over the past 20 years, one could have forecast the earnings on the **Dow Jones Industrial Average (DJIA)** for each coming year with perfect accuracy. (In MPT jargon, this means that there would have been a "perfect" information coefficient, or IC, for 1 year earnings estimates.) The point to emphasize is that for an analyst to have had perfect foresight in forecasting earnings of the DJIA over the past 20 years, this forecasting ability would have to have been combined with a "reasonably accurate" estimate of the price-earnings ratio in order to forcast the price of the DJIA in each succeeding time period. Thus, unless there is an accurate estimate of both the absolute and the market-relative price-earnings ratios, the accuracy of the earnings forecast is "lost."

Unfortunately, classical security analysis does not provide the tools with which to estimate future price-earnings ratios. This deficiency is compounded by the fact that P/E's are highly volatile. This volatility is illustrated in Exhibit 1, which depicts the P/E ratios for the DJIA between 1961 and 1980. (Since the DJIA is representative of 30 stocks, it is much less volatile than any of the component stocks.) Over the past 20 years the P/E on the DJIA has fluctuated from a high of over 24 to below 7.

The application of MPT implies significant departures from the "old school" investment selection processes. The most significant of these changes is the shift in emphasis from examining the characteristics of individual investments toward the analysis of investments within the context of a complete, appropriately designed portfolio.

In this regard, MPT has demonstrated that the investment selection process requires far more than just assembling a portfolio of what is believed to be the "best" available securities. MPT has shown us that portfolio construction should go far beyond simply determining, and then summing, the characteristics of the individual component securities. MPT has demonstrated that either the construction or the analysis of portfolios must address the **statistical relationships** between the individual securities that comprise the aggregate portfolio.

MPT DECISION PROCESS

The MPT-based investment decision process is composed of four distinct steps—**security valuation, asset allocation, portfolio optimization,** and **performance measurement.** These four steps are depicted in Exhibit 2 as the legs on a table.

The first, and cornerstone, step of the MPT decision process is **security valuation.** Basically, security valuation is the description of a universe of stocks in terms of two dimensions: expected return and expected risk.

Next, the descriptive information from the security valuation step is used for the **asset allocation decision.** One first arrays information on the expected risk and expected return for various classes of assets (stocks, bonds, etc.). Then the decision maker compares the relative attractiveness of the various investment instruments (e.g., stocks vs. bonds) and determines the proportion of assets to be allocated to each category.

The next step (also using information from the security valuation step) is **portfolio optimization.** In terms of equity optimization, this step involves determining which portfolio of stocks offers the highest expected return for a given level of expected risk or, conversely, which portfolio of stocks offers the lowest expected risk for a given level of expected return.

It is important to recognize that the asset allocation and portfolio optimization decisions use different kinds of information derived from the security valuation process. **Asset allocation** decisions use information on the **absolute** aggregate expected return and expected risk, for each category of assets. This means that for the asset allocation decision, each

EXHIBIT 2   THE FOUR STEPS IN THE MPT DECISION PROCESS

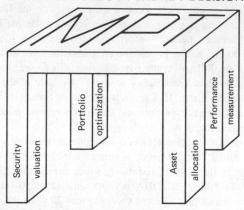

Source: Kidder, Peabody & Co., Inc., *Modern Portfolio Theory: Topics and Applications,* No. 1, May 1980.

analyst's assessment of an individual company's expected return is important only to the degree that it contributes to the overall average expected return for all equities.

Portfolio optimization decisions, on the other hand, use information on **relative** expected returns and risks for each stock within the valuation universe. Here, the objective is to select the "best" portfolio of stocks from the valuation universe. When selecting a portfolio, the individuality of separate company-by-company forecasts is not lost through aggregation (as in the case of the asset allocation decision). In this case, the companies are compared one against another.

Because of the inherent differences between the asset allocation decision and the portfolio selection decision, many organizations separate the responsibility for these decisions. Frequently, the responsibility for how a firm allocates its assets among different categories of investments rests with an **investment strategy or investment policy group.** The responsibility for portfolio selection (how assets are allocated within a category such as "stocks") rests with an **investment selection group.**

The dichotomy between asset allocation and portfolio optimization is reflected in the fourth, and final, **performance measurement** "leg" of the MPT-based decision process. This step divides the sources of each stock's performance into two parts: market related (systematic) and industry and/or security related (residual).

ROLE OF JUDGMENT IN MPT

Some people mistakenly assume that judgment has no role in MPT. In truth, each step in the MPT decision process involves judgment. Valuation estimates are based on analysts' judgments about expected risk and expected return. Asset allocation also is based on judgments. After valuing a universe of securities on the basis of expected risk and return, a judgment is made as to how much money should be allocated to stocks as opposed to alternative forms of investments. Next, an investor selects the "optimum" portfolio from the valued universe. That is, the investor selects the portfolio that (given the investor's preferences for yield, etc.) will provide the maximum level of return for a given level of risk, or alternatively, provide the minimum level of risk for a given level of return. Judgments, such as the desired level of risk, which are made as part of the asset allocation process, "drive" the portfolio optimization process.

Finally, the performance measurement process involves looking back at the judgments that were made in the security valuation, asset allocation, and portfolio optimization processes to determine the sources of the performance and, the accuracy of the decisions.

THEORETICAL FOUNDATION FOR MPT

Modern portfolio theory is based on a series of theoretical constructs dealing with how the market processes information, how investors behave, how investors' behavior drives a price-setting mechanism, and how the constructs can be quantified.

The essence of MPT is the quantification of the relationship between risk and return. To do this, modern portfolio theory draws from, and combines, elements of the efficient market hypothesis, portfolio theory, capital market theory, and capital asset pricing theories.

By drawing on the **efficient market hypothesis,** MPT assumes that the market is "reasonably" efficient. In this context, "efficient" means that through the combined actions of the market's myriad participants, all information that influences stock prices is quickly, thoroughly, and accurately impounded into the price of each stock. In economic terms, this means that at any given moment, the market is in equilibrium.

Another premise underlying MPT, which is drawn from **portfolio theory,** is that all investors have the same preferences for risk and return. That is, according to portfolio theory, all **rational investors** prefer more return to less return and less risk to more risk. The significance of portfolio theory is that it describes the way investors normally behave. According to this theory (also known as **Markowitz's theory**) all investors, other things being equal, prefer higher returns. Thus portfolio theory provides a normative description of every investor's preferences.

The combination of the high level of market efficiency with the universal aversion to risk and preference for high return results in a predictable equilibrium relationship between expected risk and expected return. Significantly, however, portfolio theory says nothing about the way prices adjust to the way investors behave—saying only that since all investors have the same preferences, investors will act in a consistent and predetermined manner. It is **capital market theory** that describes (hence allows us to predict) the relationship between expected risk and expected return whereby investors demand higher returns for higher risks.

In an almost mechanical sense, capital market theory can be thought of as the price-setting mechanism that is driven by the "normal" behavior of investors. That is, if investors act as portfolio theory suggests they do, and the price-setting mechanism spelled out by capital market theory operates consistently, the relationship between expected risk and expected return can be predicted.

The **capital asset pricing model (CAPM)** is a simplified statement of the capital market theory. By making certain simplifying assumptions, the CAPM provides a usable and explicit statement of the **equilibrium relationship between expected risk and expected return** whereby, as indicated above, investors demand higher returns for higher risks. Other theories, such as the **arbitrage pricing theory** and the **options pricing theory** have been proposed as alternative descriptions of how assests are priced.

Over the years these theoretical constructs have been tested and, when appropriate, have been applied to the investment decision process. Today, with the increased understanding of these theories, the applications have spread to virtually all facets of the investment decision-making process. As a result, instead of connoting "theories," or even certain "applications" based on these theories, the term **"modern portfolio theory"** now represents an integrated **investment decision process** that addresses the relationships among securities.

RELATIONSHIPS AMONG SECURITIES

The relationships among securities that make up a portfolio are easy to understand but difficult to measure. It is obvious to most people, for example, that holding two substantially different securities is less risky than holding a single security. If two quite different securities are held and one suddenly turns "sour," there is a chance that the second security, possibly in a different industry, will turn in an offsetting "good" performance.

But what is the chance? The answer to this question depends on the degree to which the two securities can be expected to move together. One would not expect, for example, the same degree of offsetting performance from a two-stock portfolio drawn from the airline industry and from a two-stock portfolio representing two widely different sectors of the economy.

Most portfolio managers are intuitively aware of the various kinds of **market comovement**—the tendency for certain stocks, or groups of stocks, to move in the same, or opposite, direction. It is a giant step, however, to move from this intuitive awareness of interrelationships among securities to the development of techniques to measure and forecast these interrelationships.

The length of the MPT evolution is best illustrated by the fact that Harry Markowitz (accurately referred to as the father of MPT) published the theoretical foundation for MPT in 1952 (Markowitz, "Portfolio Selection," *Journal of Finance*, March 1952). Before Markowitz's article, it was more or less taken for granted that the proper way to construct an investment portfolio was just to select the "best securities."

Markowitz correctly pointed out that the **goal of modern portfolio management is not solely to maximize the expected rate of return.** (If this were the only aim, and diversification were not important, investors should concentrate all their assets in the securities with the highest expected returns—regardless of risk.) Markowitz demonstrated instead that the objective of modern portfolio management is to **maximize "expected utility."**

CONCEPT OF UTILITY.   The concept of utility is based on the fact that different consumers have different desires, and individuals derive personal satisfaction in varying ways. Consumers purchase goods that satisfy their needs or desires. To avoid the complex task of attempting to measure the relative importance of these needs and desires, economists have devised the concept of utility. Thus, from the perspective of an economist, purchases are said to provide the consumer with some measure of "utility."

In the context of MPT, the concept of "utility" is used in much the same way. Basically, **utility** embraces all that an investor wants to get and all that an investor wants to avoid. If we set the complexities aside, "utility" can be viewed as synonymous with "satisfaction"—as the consumer sees it. If satisfaction is translated into investment terms, each investor's preferred combination of investments depends on the individual's preference for positive returns relative to personal distaste for risk. In turn, then, the goal of all rational investing can be thought of as that of maximizing each investor's utility.

Although utility cannot be gauged on an absolute scale, it is possible to evaluate it on a relative scale, much as temperature can be gauged without a thermometer. That is, various states of hot and cold can be distinguished even if the absolute differences cannot be determined. Similarly, a consumer, without an explicit scale of measurement, can still express judgments about **relative levels of satisfaction and dissatisfaction.** For any individual, these relative judgements can be put in the form of **indifference curves.**

INDIFFERENCE CURVES.   A typical **investor's indifference curve** or utility function is shown in Exhibit 3. The horizontal axis shows risk and the vertical axis plots expected return. To provide a point of reference, the investor's indifference curve in Exhibit 3 has been divided into four quadrants—*A, B, C,* and *D*. Imagine that an investor's risk is currently *M*—designating the market's level of risk. For this degree of risk, the investor is assumed to receive a "normal" rate of return, *N*. Moving from the intersection of this level of risk and expected return, *Q*, the investor would prefer any point in quadrant *A*—with a higher expected return and less risk. Conversely, the investor would be less satisfied with any point in quadrant *D*—with a lower expected return and more risk.

The choice of the points in the other quadrants depends on the individual's personal preferences; in this case, the preference for return and the distaste for risk. Thus, moving along the curve in quadrant *B*, this "typical" investor will be willing to accept more risk, since the proportionate increases in expected return would offset the increases in risk. Conversely, moving along the curve in quadrant *C*, this "typical" investor will be willing to accept a lower expected return as long as the proportionate decline in risk progressively exceeds the reduction in expected return.

Note, however, that by moving to **different points along the curve,** the investor neither increases nor decreases the total level of satisfaction derived from the various combinations

EXHIBIT 3   TYPICAL INVESTOR'S INDIFFERENCE CURVE

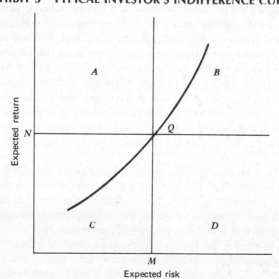

Source: Hagin, *The Dow Jones-Irwin Guide to Modern Portfolio Theory,* Dow Jones-Irwin, Homewood, IL, 1979, p. 149.

EXHIBIT 4   TYPICAL INVESTOR'S INDIFFERENCE MAP

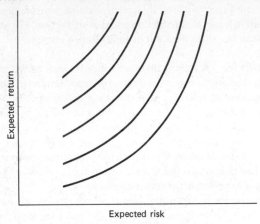

Source: Hagin, *The Dow Jones-Irwin Guide to Modern Portfolio Theory,* Dow Jones-Irwin, Home-wood, IL, 1979, p. 150.

of risk and expected return. Hence, investors are indifferent to being at any point along their own indifference curves.

Exhibit 4 shows a typical investor's **indifference map**—a set of indifference curves that profile an investor's willingness to trade off changes in risk against changes in expected return. The important characteristic of an investor's indifference map is that each successive curve moving upward to the left represents a **higher level of investor satisfaction.**

Thus, depending on the available alternatives, a rational investor would always prefer a higher curve—one with less risk and a greater expected return. However, given the highest available curve, the investor's personal preferences are such that the individual will be indifferent to any combination of risk or expected return along that particular curve.

Different investors have varying indifference curves. Exhibit 5 shows two cases in which the indifference curves labeled 1 through 3 provide different types of investors—"adventuresome" and "conservative"—with increasing levels of satisfaction. Exhibit 5 illustrates that while both investors are averse to risk, the "adventuresome" investor is willing to trade relatively smaller increases in incremental expected return for a given increment of risk than the "conservative" investor is willing to trade.

INEFFICIENT SETS.   Modern portfolio theory is based on the premise that investors want either the highest available rate of return for a given level of risk, or the lowest level of available risk for a given rate of return. The relationship between what investors want and what is expected is best illustrated by asking the question: Which investment in Exhibit 6 best meets the **objective of maximum return with minimum risk?**

Investment alternatives A and B each have the same expected return, but B carries more risk. Thus, since investment A would be preferred by any rational, risk-averse investor, B can be eliminated from consideration. Of alternatives A and C, both have the same risk, but A has a higher expected return. Accordingly, alternative C can be eliminated from consideration. A comparison of the two remaining alternatives, A and D, reveals that A has both a higher expected return and a lower risk than D. Thus investment A—with the highest expected return and the lowest risk—is the preferred alternative.

EXHIBIT 5   RISK-RETURN TRADEOFFS FOR TWO INVESTORS

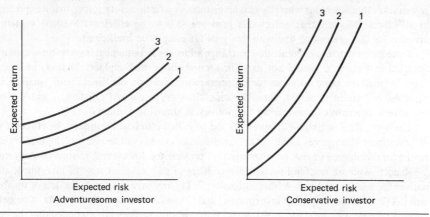

Source: Hagin, *The Dow Jones-Irwin Guide to Modern Portfolio Theory,* Dow Jones-Irwin, Homewood, IL, 1979, p. 151.

EFFICIENT SETS.   What would happen, however, if the four hypothetical investment alternatives in Exhibit 6 existed in a freely competitive real-world marketplace (while maintaining the assumption that everyone has the same estimates of expected return and risk)? In a competitive marketplace, since all investors would prefer investment A to the other alternatives, their demand for investment A would drive up its price. As the price of investment A increased, the expected return per unit of investment would decrease. Simultaneously, the lack of demand for investment C would drive its price down, in turn increasing its expected return.

Thus, while investors have different risk-return preferences, rational investors will always attempt to find portfolios that provide the maximum rate of return for every level of risk, or conversely, the minimum level of risk for every possible rate of return. This normal

EXHIBIT 6   INEFFICIENT SET OF INVESTMENT ALTERNATIVES

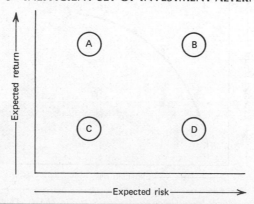

Source: Hagin, *The Dow Jones-Irwin Guide to Modern Portfolio Theory,* Dow Jones-Irwin, Homewood, IL, 1979, p. 154.

behavior of investors—and a distaste for risk—will cause adjustments in prices that eliminate any **market inefficiencies** whereby one investment is so attractively priced that it is preferred to all others. Markets that reflect this goal are said to be **efficient.** Markets containing investments that are out of line with this goal are said to be **inefficient.**

Since inefficiencies are eliminated by competition, the hypothetical investment alternatives depicted in Exhibit 6 would not exist in a competitive marketplace. Instead, as long as everyone used the same estimates for expected return and risk, the "inefficient" marketplace depicted in Exhibit 6 would, through price changes, become "efficient," and the **new** investment alternatives would array themselves as shown in Exhibit 7.

The curve *XYZ* in Exhibit 7 represents the so-called **efficient boundary, or efficient set,** of investment alternatives. That is, the investments on this curve offer the highest level of return for this degree of risk or, alternatively, provide the lowest risk for this rate of return.

Readers who are not familiar with the concept of an "efficient set" of investment alternatives are encouraged to note that in Exhibit 7: (1) any investments to the left of or above curve *XYZ* would be **superior** investments, and (2) any investments to the right of or below curve *XYZ* would be **inferior** investments. Furthermore, readers are reminded that the competitive forces of the marketplace will eliminate—through price changes—any agreed-upon superior or inferior alternatives.

Working from the three investment alternatives depicted in Exhibit 7, suppose it was necessary to select an investment for someone whose investment preferences closely reflect those of the classical "widow or orphan." Presumably, this individual would want to attain the **highest available return that is consistent with a minimum level of risk.** Of the three alternatives shown in Exhibit 7, the investment with the lowest risk—the overriding consideration for this person—is investment X.

At the other extreme, suppose that an investment must be selected for a classic **"speculator."** Here, the objective would be to select the alternative with the **lowest available risk that is consistent with the highest expected return.** Of the three hypothetical investments shown in Exhibit 7, the one with the highest expected return—the overriding preference for this person—is investment Z. The middle ground between the two ex-

EXHIBIT 7   EFFICIENT SET OF INVESTMENT ALTERNATIVES

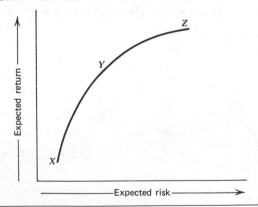

Source: Hagin, *The Dow Jones-Irwin Guide to Modern Portfolio Theory,* Dow Jones-Irwin, Homewood, IL, 1979, p. 155.

tremes—essentially a balance between risk and expected return—is represented by investment Y.

RISK AND RETURN

At this point, the terms **"expected return"** and **"risk"** require more explicit definitions. One's best estimate of the future return of any investment is the expected value, or mean, of all the likely returns. It is this mean, or "expected return," that an investor attempts to maximize at each level of acceptable risk. The distributions of the likely returns and the mean, or expected, returns for two hypothetical investments are shown in Exhibit 8.

A comparison of investments A and B reveals that both have the same average, or expected, return. The distributions of the likely, or expected, returns are quite different, however. Specifically, investment A has more dispersion, or **variance,** around the mean than the distribution of likely returns for investment B. Thus, based either on a comparison of the graphic representations in Exhibit 8, or on the explicit numerical measures for the variance of the distributions of the expected returns for the two investments, investment B emerges

EXHIBIT 8   DISTRIBUTIONS OF EXPECTED RETURNS

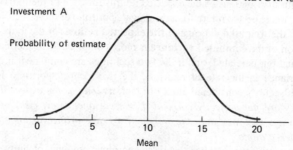

Investment A

Probability of estimate

Mean

Estimates of expected annual return (%)

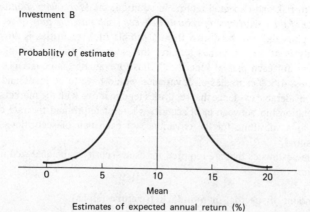

Investment B

Probability of estimate

Mean

Estimates of expected annual return (%)

Source: Hagin, *The Dow Jones-Irwin Guide to Modern Portfolio Theory,* Dow Jones-Irwin, Homewood, IL, 1979, p. 157.

as superior because it offers the same expected return but with less variance of estimated returns.

Exhibit 8 dramatizes the importance of variance. The higher an investment's variance (i.e., variability around the expected value), the more its actual return is likely to deviate from the expected return. From an investor's point of view, the more assurance that the actual results will parallel the expected results, the better the investment. Since we operate under the maxim that rational, risk-averse investors will always seek investments with a minimum level of risk for a given level of expected return, the use of the statistical variance (or its square root, the **standard deviation**) of the distribution of possible expected returns emerges as a measure of risk.

MARKOWITZ MODEL. According to **Markowitz's formulation,** the selection of an efficient portfolio begins with an analysis of three estimates:

1. The **expected return** for each security.
2. The **variance of the expected return** for each security.
3. The possibly offsetting, or possibly complementary, interaction, or **covariance,** of return with every other security under consideration.

Beginning with distributions of the expected returns for each of the individual securities, the calculation of the expected return for an aggregate portfolio of these securities is relatively easy. It is merely the **weighted average of the expected returns** of the individual securities.

The calculation of the **combined variance** is more complicated. If the returns on the two securities are equal but unrelated, and if the two securities are combined into a two-security portfolio the variance in the rate of return of the two-security portfolio is only half the variance for each security considered alone. In fact, *as long as the expected rates of return of the two stocks are not perfectly correlated, the variance (i.e., risk) of a two-security portfolio will always be lower than the weighted average of the variance of either of the securities considered alone.*

Unfortunately, covariance analysis requires enormous amounts of human and computational resources. For example, to evaluate 100 securities, an analyst must prepare 100 timely estimates of both risk and expected return. In addition, the *Markowitz solution requires an explicit estimate of the covariance of returns between each possible pair of securities.* Since the number of pairs that can be drawn from a sample of N securities is $N(N - 1)/2$, the Markowitz analysis of 100 securities requires the estimation and processing of $100(99)/2$ covariances—one for each pair of securities. Thus to evaluate the covariance between 100 pairs of securities, 4,550 estimates of covariance would have to be made and processed.

Given the considerable evidence that securities tend to move with the market, a "shortcut" is to use the relationship between each security's rate of return and the rate of return on a **market index** as a substitute for the covariance of each pair of securities—the so-called **single-index model.**

Thus the three estimates that are required for each security to be analyzed using a single-index model are:

1. The amount of **specific, or nonmarket, return** (alpha).
2. A measure of **responsiveness to market movements** (beta).
3. The **variance of the nonmarket return.**

PORTFOLIO THEORY.   Portfolio theory is a **normative theory.** Normative means "normal" or "standard." In economics, a normative theory refers to the "normal" way consumers behave. Portfolio theory delineates the decisions that will be made by a population of normal investors—each exercising his or her personal preferences.

CAPITAL MARKET THEORY.   Capital market theory is a **positive theory.** The distinction between a normative and a positive theory is best explained by an analogy to a machine. In a mechanical sense, a "positive" mechanism is "definite, unyielding, constant or certain"; its outcomes are "determined by unyielding parts, or controlled movements." In this sense, capital market theory can be thought of as the unyielding and **constant price-setting mechanism** that is driven by the "normal" behavior of investors.

   Portfolio theory holds that all investors are risk averse and that in satisfying their individual preferences they will act in a consistent, predetermined way. Portfolio theory says nothing about the way prices of individual assets adjust to investor behavior. It follows, however, that if investors are rational and risk averse, and act as portfolio theory suggests (all logical assumptions), the price-setting mechanism relating risk and expected return will be consistent and can be predicted. This is the **function of capital market theory**—to describe (hence, to allow us to predict) the relationship between expected risk and expected return.

RISK: CLASSIFICATION AND MEASUREMENT

To better understand the classification of risk, it may be useful to imagine a **market portfolio**—one consisting of all outstanding assets. The total return for accepting the level of risk associated with the market portfolio is the aggregate rate of return society pays to suppliers to risk capital. This return and its associated risk are tied to the overall capital market system. Accordingly, such returns are called **systematic or market-related returns.** Similarly, the risk that is linked to the overall capital market system is referred to as systematic or market-related risk.

   Any risk beyond market-related or systematic risk is known by a variety of names, including **residual risk, nonmarket risk, unsystematic risk,** and **selection risk.** "Residual" merely defines what is left over. The nonmarket and unsystematic nomenclature parallels the "market" and "systematic" terminology. So-called selection risk pinpoints the source of the risk as the selection of investments that are different from the total market. In turn, **residual risk** can be broken down into **specific risk** (arising from factors that are specific to the company) and **extramarket risk** (arising from components of homogeneous groups whose movements are independent of the market as a whole).

   From the perspective of the overall market, each investor's selection risk is always offset by some aggregation of other investors' selection risk. For the **market as a whole, there is no selection risk.** Looked at another way, the capital market system cannot, and does not, reward investment selection. The capital market system only rewards **capital market risk.** Any gains derived solely from astute investment selection are at the expense of the investors who have the offsetting selection losses.

CAPITAL ASSET PRICING MODEL.   Two concepts—efficient capital markets and risk premiums—are brought together in the **capital asset pricing model (CAPM).** The concept of an efficient capital market leads to the conclusion that prices cannot be expected to diverge "by much" or "for long" from the consensus view of an equitable rate of return for a given level of risk. The concept of a **risk premium** is basically that investors must be paid to take any risk above that of a "riskless" investment.

The classic example of a **riskless investment** is a short-term obligation of the U.S. government. Since the government can always print money, there is no default risk with such an instrument. According to the CAPM, investors who select a risk-free investment (such as short-term government securities) can expect to be compensated for the use of their money, but not for market-, extramarket- or company-related risk.

Other investors, however, opt for risky investments, including common stocks. Such investors logically expect a higher rate of return than the riskless rate as compensation for the risk that they assume. The difference between the risk-free rate of return and the total return from a risky investment is called a **risk premium.**

Given the assumption of an efficient capital market, the pricing of the market portfolio, at any point in time, accurately reflects an equilibrium relationship between the market's consensus expectation for risk and return. Thus the **CAPM** is the facet of capital market theory that provides an explicit statement of the equilibrium expected return for all securities. Specifically, the CAPM states that the prices of assets in a capital market will be in equilibrium where the expected return on a security is equal to a riskless rate of return plus a premium that is proportional to the amount of **market-related risk—beta. Beta** is a measure of the relative volatility of a security compared to that of the market.

Stated another way, the CAPM holds that any expected **excess return** for a security, or portfolio, will come entirely from the **market component of return.** This is because in equilibrium a security with zero systematic risk (beta) will have the expected return that is available for a riskless asset. Furthermore, in equilibrium, the expected excess return from the nonmarket component is always zero.

MARKET MODEL.   The **market model** provides the conceptual foundation for the **single-index model,** also known as the **diagonal model,** or the **one-factor model.** The market model **describes the relationship between returns on individual securities (or portfolios) and the returns on the market portfolio.** Specifically, the market model holds that the returns on an individual security (or portfolio) are linearly related to an index of market returns.

The **capital asset pricing model** (CAPM) is a very distinct model. Neither the market model nor the CAPM depends in any way on the other. The **CAPM provides an explicit expression of the expected returns for all assets.** Basically, the CAPM holds that if investors are risk averse, high-risk stocks must have higher expected returns than low-risk stocks. In equilibrium, a security with zero risk will have an expected return equal to that of a riskless asset. Increases in risk beyond that of a riskless asset will be accompanied by proportional increases in expected return.

Thus the CAPM is indeed a pricing model—it indicates the price of **immediate consumption and the price of risk.** That is, when consumers choose to direct their funds to immediate **consumption,** they do so in preference over the alternative of **investing** these funds in riskless securities. The "price" of immediate consumption is consequently the "reward" that could have been earned from waiting. Similarly, when investors choose **risky investments,** they also do so in preference over the alternative of holding **riskless investments.**

However, to attract capital to the risky alternatives, the marketplace must reward investors in proportion to the amount of risk they undertake. Since "price" to the buyer is the "reward" to a seller, these returns can also be thought of as rewards—the reward for waiting and the reward for taking market risk. From the opposite point of view, these returns can be thought of as the "price of immediate consumption" and the "price of assuming risk."

While the CAPM is an abstraction and simplification of capital market theory, the market model is not explicitly linked to a particular theory. The market model merely describes the relationship that exists between security and market returns. As such, the market model tells us nothing about what **determines** returns.

SECURITY CHARACTERISTIC LINES. The market model describes the relationship between the excess return on a security and the overall market (represented by a single market index). **Excess return** is defined as the return **expected** from the security (during a specified holding period) less the estimated return from holding a riskless security (such as a short-term government obligation) during the same period. According to the market model, a security's "excess return" is either: market related (systematic), or nonmarket related (residual).

The estimation of a security's expected excess return may be best understood from the following representation of the underlying equation:

Since a security's

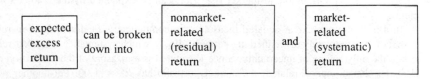

it follows that a security's

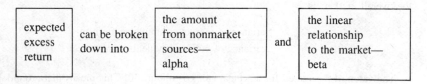

therefore,

and since the equation for a straight line is:

$$Y \quad = \quad a \quad + \quad bX$$

the values of a security's **alpha** and **beta** represent the vertical intercept and the slope, respectively, of the **security's characteristic line.**

The **security characteristic line** contains a subtlety that needs to be emphasized. Although

beta is an estimate of a **relationship** to another variable, **alpha** is an estimate of an **amount**—a specific rate or return. In practice, therefore, **alpha is the average, or expected value,** of the nonmarket component of expected excess return. Accordingly, estimates of alpha are presumed to fluctuate around the expected, or "best guess," value.

R-SQUARED.   It is useful to be able to show symbolically a measure of the proportion of the total risk that is market related. Therefore,

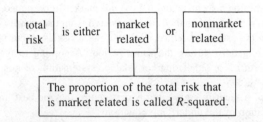

Thus, much as alpha and beta have taken on very narrow and explicit meanings within the context of MPT, **R-squared** defines the proportion of the total risk of either a security or a portfolio that is attributable to market risk (i.e., can be explained by the market's movement).

In a portfolio context, R-squared measures the completeness of **diversification** relative to that of the completely diversified market portfolio, in which systematic, or market-related, risk is the only source of uncertainty. Since R-squared is a measure of the proportion of the total risk that is market related, the market portfolio has $R^2 = 1.00$. Put another way, a portfolio with an R-squared of 1.0 has **zero selection risk.**

Technically, R-squared is the **coefficient of determination (R^2).** The formula for computing R-squared, the proportion of total risk (measured by variance) that is attributable to the overall market, is

$$R^2 = \frac{\text{variance of market component of return}}{\text{variance of both components of return}}$$

The value of R-squared for a typical stock is about .30. This means that around 30% of a typical stock's behavior (hence, risk) is explained by the behavior of the market. On the other hand, the R-squared for a well-diversified portfolio will typically exceed .90. This means that more than 90% of a well-diversified portfolio's total price movements can typically be explained by the market's behavior.

VALUATION THEORY

The feature that distinguishes the modern portfolio theory decision process from other approaches is that MPT begins with—and is based on—explicit estimates of both risk and return. For the return dimension, MPT adopts an aspect of **classical valuation theory** to the effect that the present value of an asset can be derived from the income stream and the discount rate, which is commensurate with the risk. One problem with this approach is the difficulty in determining the appropriate discount rate.

MPT-based valuation approaches the problem of determining the discount rate by analyzing equities much as we analyze bonds. This involves using the analyst's estimate of the dividend stream and the present market value of the stock to derive the implied discount rate.

The expected return number can be thought of as the equity equivalent of a bond's **yield to maturity.** However, since stocks do not mature, the term "yield to maturity" does not apply. When working with stocks, therefore, terms such as **"implied discount rate,"** **"implied rate of return,"** **"internal rate of return,"** and **"expected return"** are used instead. (The most widely used term is "expected return.")

Thus if we combine analysts' estimates of the dividend stream with the market price of the security, we can derive the expected rate of return. This is the annual rate of return that one expects if one pays the current market price for the projected dividend stream. This measure of expected return, along with each stock's expected risk, represent the two cornerstones of MPT valuation.

USE OF VALUATION THEORY

Basically, valuation theory can be used in either of two ways:

1. **Expected return** can be derived from (*a*) the "next" dividend, (*b*) the projected dividend growth rate, and (*c*) the current price.
2. **Theoretical price** can be derived from (*a*) the "next" dividend, (*b*) the projected dividend growth rate, and (*c*) an estimate of the expected rate of return commensurate with the expected risk.

Assuming that we would like to calculate the annual expected return inherent in the pricing of the **Standard & Poor's 500** on June 27, 1980, we would start with:

1. The "next" annual dividend—an estimate of the current year's dividend times an estimate of the dividend growth rate.
2. An estimate of the long-term average dividend growth rate of the **S&P 500 index.**
3. The closing price of the **S&P 500.**

Because this example assumes constant dividend growth (the equation is much more complex without this assumption), the equation for **expected return** is:

$$ER = \frac{d_1}{P_0} + \bar{g}$$

where ER = expected average long-term rate of return
 d_1 = next year's dividend (i.e., \$6.715)
 P_0 = the June 27, 1980 closing price (\$116)
 $\bar{g}$ = constant annual rate of growth in dividends (0.1191)

Assuming the estimates and the price for the **S&P 500** index shown in parentheses above:

$$ER = \frac{\$6.715}{\$116} + 0.1191$$
$$= 0.1770$$

Similarly, to calculate the **theoretical price** of the **S&P 500,** we could start with:

1. The "next" annual dividend.
2. The long-term average dividend growth rate.
3. The average expected long-term annual rate of return (i.e., the discount rate).

Because this illustration assumes constant dividend growth, the total value of the discounted present value of all dividends, to infinity, can be determined from another rather simple equation (without the assumption of constant dividend growth, this equation also becomes much more complex):

$$P_0 = \frac{d_1}{ER - \bar{g}}$$

where P_0 = today's price
$\quad d_1$ = next year's dividend ($6.715)
$\quad ER$ = expected average long-term rate of return (0.1770)
$\quad \bar{g}$ = constant annual rate of growth in dividends (0.1191)

Assuming the estimates shown in parentheses above:

$$P_0 = \frac{\$6.715}{0.1770 - 0.1191}$$
$$= \$116 \text{ (rounded)}$$

The illustration of the statement that the value of stock is the sum of the present values of the dividends that will be received—to infinity—is illustrated in Exhibit 9. The present value column shows that if the discount rate is 17.70%, an investor would be willing to pay 84.96¢ for $1.00 to be received 1 year from today. Or, alternatively 84.96¢ invested for 1 year at 17.70% would be $1.00. In 10 years, however, the present value of $1.00 to be received in that year is only 19.60¢. Thus $4.34 (84.96 ÷ 19.60) in the tenth year will make approximately the same contribution to present value as $1.00 received next year. By the twentieth year, the present value of a dollar is only 3.8¢.

This means that $22.13 of dividends in the twentieth year contributes as much to the present value of the stock as a $1.00 dividend that is received next year (84.96 ÷ 3.84). If we go to the thirtieth year, the present value of $1.00 is approximately 0.7¢. Thus it would take approximately $113.28 in dividends in the thirtieth year to have the same contribution to present value as a $1.00 dividend next year (84.96 ÷ 0.75).

The third column in Exhibit 9 shows the projected dividend stream. Here the simplifying assumption is that this year's dividend for the **S&P 500** of $6 will grow at a constant compound annual rate of 11.91%. Using another simplifying assumption that dividends are received only once a year, the dividend will grow by the tenth year to $18.49; by the twentieth, to $56.97; by the fiftieth, to $1,666.80; and, by the one-hundredth, to $463,034.06.

What is important, however, is that while the dividend grows to an astronomical size (in comparison to today), the present value of each dollar's worth of dividends falls at an even faster rate. Column 2 shows, for example, that the (approximate) present value of a $1 dividend in 10 years is 19.6¢; in 20 years, 3.8¢; in 50 years, roughly 0.03¢; and in 100 years, it is so small that it does not appear when the calculation is carried to six decimal places.

EXHIBIT 9 SAMPLE CALCULATION OF THE PRESENT VALUE OF AN ASSET[a]

(1) Year	(2) Present Value of $1.[b]	(3) Projected Dividend	(4) Present Value of Dividend	(5) Sum of Dividend	(6) % of Total Present Value of Dividend
1	$0.849618	$6.715	$5.705	$5.70	4.9
2	0.721850	7.515	5.424	11.13	9.6
3	0.613297	8.410	5.158	16.29	14.0
4	0.521068	9.411	4.904	21.19	18.3
5	0.442708	10.532	4.663	25.85	22.3
6	0.376133	11.787	4.433	30.29	26.1
7	0.319569	13.191	4.215	34.50	29.7
8	0.271511	14.762	4.008	38.51	33.2
9	0.230681	16.520	3.811	42.32	36.5
10	0.195991	18.488	3.624	45.94	39.6
11	0.166517	20.691	3.445	49.39	42.6
12	0.141476	23.155	3.276	52.67	45.4
13	0.120200	25.913	3.115	55.78	48.1
14	0.102124	29.000	2.962	58.74	50.6
15	0.086767	32.454	2.816	61.56	53.1
16	0.073718	36.320	2.677	64.24	55.4
17	0.062633	40.646	2.546	66.78	57.6
18	0.053214	45.488	2.421	69.20	59.7
19	0.045211	50.906	2.302	71.50	61.6
20	0.038412	56.970	2.188	73.69	63.5
21	0.032636	63.756	2.081	75.77	65.3
22	0.027728	71.350	1.978	77.75	67.0
23	0.023558	79.849	1.881	79.63	68.6
24	0.020015	89.360	1.789	81.42	70.2
25	0.017005	100.004	1.701	83.12	71.7
26	0.014448	111.916	1.617	84.74	73.1
27	0.012275	125.247	1.537	86.28	74.4
28	0.010429	140.165	1.462	87.74	75.6
29	0.008861	156.861	1.390	89.13	76.8
30	0.007528	175.546	1.322	90.45	78.0
40	0.001476	540.924	0.798	100.57	86.7
50	0.000289	1666.795	0.482	106.68	92.0
60	0.000057	5136.039	0.291	110.37	95.1
70	0.000011	15826.119	0.176	112.60	97.1
80	0.000002	48766.391	0.106	113.95	98.2
90	Nominal	150268.109	0.064	114.76	98.9
100	Nominal	463034.062	0.039	115.25	99.4
Infinity				116.00[c]	100.0

[a]Calculated as being equal to the sum of the present values of the dividend income to be received, using the following assumptions:

Current dividend = $6.00
Constant dividend growth rate = 11.91% per year
Expected return = 17.70% per year

[b]Based on discount rate equal to expected return.
[c]In this sample calculation, the total present value of dividends to infinity is $116.

Source: Kidder, Peabody & Co., Inc., *Modern Portfolio Theory: Topics and Applications*, No. 2, June 1980.

Column 4 shows the present value of the dividend that appears in column 3. This column is merely the product of the present value in column 2 and the dividend in column 3. One year from today the present value of a $1 dividend is approximately 85¢ (as shown in column 2). Thus the present worth of a contract to receive a $6.715 dividend 1 year from today (if the discount rate is 17.70%) is $5.705. By the one-hundredth year, the present value of the dividend of $463,034.06 is 3.9¢! Looked at another way, this means that 3.9¢ invested for 100 years at an annual return of 17.70% would compound to $463,034.

Since valuation theory holds that the value of an asset is the sum of the present values of each of the dividends that will be received if the asset is held until infinity, the present worth of the asset can be determined by merely summing the present values in column 4 to infinity. This year-by-year summation is shown in column 5.

Column 6 shows the progressive summation of present values (in column 5) as a percentage of the theoretical price (calculated earlier as $116). Thus by the end of the tenth year, the summation represents 39.6% of the total value (if summed to infinity). Similarly, by the end of the twentieth year, the summation represents 63.5% of the total value. Looking down column 6 it is easy to see that although theoretically the summation goes on to infinity, the contributions that successive dividends make to present value are heavily weighted toward the earlier years.

Notice, for example, that by the fourteenth year the dividend summation exceeds 50% of the total value. This means that the dividends from the fourteenth year to infinity contribute as much to the present value as the dividends in the first 14 years. Since it is in the early years that an analyst has forecasting expertise (and after which valuation models make the assumption that the dividends of different companies grow at similar rates), it is precisely this information that is captured by the dividend discounting process.

Some skeptics respond to the idea of dividend discounting by asking, "How can anyone forecast an 'infinite' stream of dividends?" Fortunately, forecasting an infinite stream of dividends is not the problem that it might appear to be for two reasons: (1) the present value of distant dividends becomes progressively smaller—hence distant dividends become less important, and (2) distant forecasts of dividend growth rates for different companies tend to be very similar. Thus, even though valuation is based on a theoretically infinite stream of dividends, the differences between the resultant expected returns are derived largely from differences in analyst's estimates of the near-term dividend growth rates.

DIVIDEND DISCOUNT MODELS

Dividend discount models translate an analyst's forecasts of near-term dividend growth and assumptions about plateau, transition, and steady-state growth rates into an explicit year-by-year forecast of the dividend stream. One can then calculate the annual expected rate of return that equilibrates the projected dividend stream with the current price of the stock.

Dividend discount models typically break the future into several time periods. For example, in a three-period model, the **near-term period** is one in which there is reason to believe that dividends can be forecast with a reasonable degree of accuracy. In the **final period,** it is assumed that the dividend growth rate for all industries—and companies—will approximate the steady-state growth rate of the economy. For the **middle period,** dividend discount models typically use some kind of mathematical smoothing function to bridge the specific near-term forecasts in the first period to the steady-state growth rates in the final period.

Two things happen with progressively more distant dividend forecasts: differences between forecasted growth rates becomes smaller, and the importance of the differences is minimized through the discounting process. Thus, in a properly designed dividend discount model, the differences in relative valuation of securities result primarily from differences in the analysts' estimates of near-term dividend growth rates.

IS MPT-BASED VALUATION A "LONG-TERM" FORECASTING TOOL?

MPT-based valuation is definitely not a "long-term" forecasting tool! Many people wrongly assume that because the expected-return dimension of MPT-based valuation is based on an "infinite" forecast of a company's dividend stream, the results of such valuation must therefore also be measured over long periods of time. The reason this is not true is best understood by the analogy between the use of **yield to maturity** in bond valuation and **expected return** in stock valuation.

When working with long-term bonds, the yield to maturity figure is derived from the price and income stream—the periodic coupon payments and eventual repayment of face value. The yield to maturity figure gives bond investors a common descriptor that can be used to compare different bonds on the basis of long-term expected annual rates of return. If two bonds that are similar in terms of risk and other features have different yields to maturity, the market will adjust to these expectations.

Modern portfolio theory assumes that stock prices are set by the marketplace in much the same way as bond prices—on the basis of expected risk and return. Thus the expected return in MPT-based valuation is—as yield to maturity is for bonds—a relative measure of expected return. When analysis reveals that a disproportionate amount of return is available for a given level of risk, it is assumed that the market will react—by adjusting the price of the underlying stock—over a relatively short time horizon. In practical terms, this means positive correlations between expectation and performance 3, 6, and 12 months later.

MPT-BASED RESEARCH RESULTS

Modern portfolio theory-based research, like fundamental research, actually combines two elements—a methodology that spells out which variables are important, and analysts' estimates of those variables. Forgetting that this is a two-part process can lead to erroneous conclusions. Some people assume, for example, that because some users of **dividend discount models** have had below-average performance, dividend discount models are no good. Such reasoning overlooks the fact that a dividend discount model is "driven" by analysts' estimates of dividend growth. Poor results could be attributable to the model, the inputs, or both.

Equally fallacious is the reasoning of researchers who start with analysts' estimates that have been shown to have predictive value and, then, by coupling these estimates to a dividend discount model, point to the model's predictive ability. All that can really be said from such research is that the model accurately translated accurate predictions into another format. The objective of MPT-based research is to capture analysts' forecasts of specific variables, which in and of themselves cannot be used to estimate either risk or return accurately but, when combined in the framework of MPT, can produce significant value added.

Recognizing that it can be misleading to draw conclusions from limited experience, it is unfortunate that only limited historical data are available on the MPT-based valuation systems. Nonetheless, with this caveat in mind, it is useful to examine the record of one valuation system with which this author is familiar, namely, the **Kidder, Peabody Security Valuation System,** called SALUS, for 1979 (the first full year that the system was in use).

Exhibit 10 compares expected and actual returns for each quintile in the valuation universe during 1979. That is, on December 31, 1978, the stocks in the valuation universe were divided into five quintiles on the basis of expected returns. The stocks with the highest expected returns were placed in quintile 5 and those with the lowest, in quintile 1. One month later, the actual return was calculated for the stocks in each quintile. This process was then repeated for each of the 12 months and the total return (dividends plus price changes) tallied for the entire year. This performance (before transaction costs) summary is shown in Exhibit 10.

The data in Exhibit 10 indicate that during 1979 the combination of Kidder, Peabody's valuation system and analysts' estimates was for the most part able to discriminate between over- and undervalued stocks. The exception is in the second quintile, which had the lowest actual return.

Exhibit 11 compares the expected and actual alphas for the same 12 months. **Alpha** is the "return above, or below, that required to offset the risk inherent in the investment." The data in Exhibit 11 indicate that except for the first, second, and third quintiles, during 1979 the valuation system was able to discern significantly the better performing stocks when forecast and measured on a risk-adjusted basis.

While the foregoing results are encouraging, it should be emphasized that the performance figures reported here are historical. It should not be assumed that future results will either be profitable or equal to past performance.

EXHIBIT 10   KIDDER, PEABODY'S SECURITY VALUATION SYSTEM PERFORMANCE SUMMARY: RETURN FROM DECEMBER 31, 1978 TO DECEMBER 31, 1979

	Total Return (%)
Dow Jones 30	10.14
Standard & Poor's 500	18.50
Expected Return Quintile	
5	34.71
4	28.28
3	19.86
2	11.87
1	16.90

Source: Kidder, Peabody & Co., Inc., *Modern Portfolio Theory: Topics and Applications,* No. 1, May 1980.

**EXHIBIT 11   KIDDER,
PEABODY'S SECURITY
VALUATION SYSTEM
PERFORMANCE SUMMARY:
ALPHA FROM DECEMBER
31, 1978 TO DECEMBER 31,
1979**

Expected Alpha Quintile	Actual Alpha (%)
5	10.89
4	2.81
3	0.12
2	0.75
1	−0.16

Source: Kidder, Peabody & Co.,
Inc., *Modern Portfolio Theory: Topics and Applications*, No. 1, May
1980.

WHAT WILL HAPPEN IF MORE PEOPLE USE MPT?

Nothing. Again, it is important to separate the methodology from the estimates that go into
the methodology. If everyone used fundamental analysis, would everyone get the same
results, want to own the same stocks, and so on? Certainly not. Even though everyone uses
fundamental analysis, everyone does not have the same expectations. MPT-based research
is not different; it says that certain variables are important and that these variables are related
to other variables in certain ways. But we must also consider the users' estimates of the
values of the variables. Hence, when using MPT, or any other methodology, it is the user's
expectations that cause the results to be different.

REFERENCES

Black, Fischer, Jensen, Michael C., and Scholes, Myron, "The Capital Asset Pricing Model: Some
Empirical Tests," in *Studies in the Theory of Capital Markets* (Michael C. Jensen, Ed.), Praeger,
New York, 1972.

Blume, Marshall E., "Portfolio Theory: A Step Towards Its Practical Application," *Journal of Business*,
Vol. 43, No. 2, April 1970, pp. 152–73.

———, "On the Assessment of Risk," *Journal of Finance*, Vol. 26, No. 1, March 1972, pp. 1–10.
Reprinted in James Lorie and Richard Brealey, Eds., *Modern Developments in Investment Management: A Book of Readings*, 2nd ed. Dryden Press, Hinsdale, IL, 1978, pp. 432–441.

———, "Betas and Their Regression Tendencies," *Journal of Finance*, Vol. 30, No. 3, June 1975,
pp. 785–796.

Brealey, Richard A., *An Introduction to Risk and Return from Common Stock Prices*, MIT Press,
Cambridge, MA, 1969.

Brealey, Richard A., *Security Prices in a Competitive Market,* MIT Press, Cambridge, MA, 1971.

Evans, John L., and Archer, Stephen H., "Diversification and the Reduction of Dispersion: An Empirical Analysis," *Journal of Finance,* Vol. 23, No. 12, December 1968, pp. 761–767.

Fama, Eugene F., "Efficient Capital Markets: A Review of Theory and Empirical Work," *Journal of Finance,* Vol. 25, No. 2, May 1970, pp. 383–417. Reprinted in James Lorie and Richard Brealey, Eds., *Modern Developments in Investment Management: A Book of Readings,* 2nd ed., Dryden Press, Hinsdale, IL, 1978, pp. 109–153.

———, "Components of Investment Performance," *Journal of Finance,* Vol. 27, No. 5, June 1972, pp. 551–567. Reprinted in James Lorie and Richard Brealey, Eds., *Modern Developments in Investment Management: A Book of Readings,* 2nd ed., Dryden Press, Hinsdale, IL, 1978, pp. 448–465.

Fouse, William, "Risk and Liquidity: The Keys to Stock Price Behavior," *Financial Analysts Journal,* Vol. 32, No. 3, May–June 1976, pp. 35–45.

———, "Risk and Liquidity Revisited," *Financial Analysts Journal,* Vol. 33, No. 1, January–February 1977, pp. 40–45.

Hagin, Robert L., *The Dow Jones-Irwin Guide to Modern Portfolio Theory,* Dow Jones-Irwin, Homewood, IL, 1979.

——— (with Chris Mader), *The New Science of Investing,* Dow Jones-Irwin, Homewood, IL, 1973.

Jensen, Michael C., "Tests of Capital Market Theory and Implications of the Evidence," Research Paper No. 1, Financial Analysts Research Foundation, 1975.

Lintner, John, and Glauber, Robert, "Higgledy Piggledy Growth in America," paper prepared for the Seminar on the Analysis of Security Prices, University of Chicago, May 1967. Reprinted in James Lorie and Richard Brealey, Eds., *Modern Developments in Investment Management: A Book of Readings,* 2nd ed., Dryden Press, Hinsdale, IL, 1978, pp. 594–611.

Markowitz, Harry M., "Portfolio Selection," *Journal of Finance,* Vol. 7, No. 1, March 1952, pp. 77–91. Reprinted in E. Bruce Fredrikson, Ed., *Frontiers of Investment Analysis.* International Textbook Co., Scranton, PA, 1965, pp. 353–366, and in James Lorie and Richard Brealey, Eds., *Modern Developments in Investment Management: A Book of Readings,* 2nd ed., Dryden Press, Hinsdale, IL, 1978, pp. 310–324.

———, *Portfolio Selection: Efficient Diversification of Investments,* Wiley, New York, 1959.

Molodovsky, Nicholas, *Investment Values in a Dynamic World: Collected Papers of Nicholas Molodovsky,* Irwin, Homewood, IL, 1974.

Roberts, Harry V., "Stock Market 'Patterns' and Financial Analysis," *Journal of Finance,* Vol. 14, No. 1, March 1959, pp. 1–10. Reprinted in Paul H. Cootner, Ed., *The Random Character of Stock Market Prices.* MIT Press, Cambridge, MA, 1964, pp. 7–16, in Richard E. Ball, Ed., *Readings in Investments,* Allyn and Bacon, Boston, 1965, pp. 369–379, and in James Lorie and Richard Brealey, Eds., *Modern Developments in Investment Management: A Book of Readings,* 2nd ed., Dryden Press, Hinsdale, IL, 1978, pp. 154–163.

Rosenberg, Barr, and Marathe, Vinay, "The Prediction of Investment Risk: Systematic and Residual Risk," *Proceedings of the Seminar on the Analysis of Security Prices,* University of Chicago, Vol. 20, No. 1, November 1975, pp. 85–225.

Rosenberg, Barr, and McKibben, Walt, "The Prediction of Systematic Risk in Common Stocks," *Journal of Financial and Quantitative Analysis,* Vol. 8, No. 3, March 1973, pp. 317–333.

Sharpe, William F., "A Simplified Model for Portfolio Analysis," *Management Science,* Vol. 9, No. 2, January 1963, pp. 277–293. Reprinted in James Lorie and Richard Brealey, Eds., *Modern Developments in Investment Management: A Book of Readings,* 2nd ed., Dryden Press, Hinsdale, IL, 1978, pp. 325–341.

———, "Capital Asset Prices: A Theory of Market Equilibrium Under Conditions of Risk," *Journal of Finance,* Vol. 19, No. 3, September 1964, pp. 425–442. Reprinted in James Lorie and Richard Brealey, Eds., *Modern Developments in Investment Management: A Book of Readings,* 2nd ed., Dryden Press, Hinsdale, IL, 1978, pp. 366–383.

Sharpe, William F., "Risk, Market Sensitivity and Diversification," *Financial Analysts Journal,* Vol. 28, No. 1, January–February, 1972, pp. 74–79. Reprinted in James Lorie and Richard Brealey, Eds., *Modern Developments in Investment Management: A Book of Readings,* 2nd ed., Dryden Press, Hinsdale, IL, 1978, pp. 342–347.

———, "Adjusting for Risk in Portfolio Performance Measurement," *Journal of Portfolio Management,* Vol. 1, No. 2, Winter 1975, pp. 29–34. Reprinted in James Lorie and Richard Brealey, Eds., *Modern Developments in Investment Management: A Book of Readings,* 2nd ed., Dryden Press, Hinsdale, IL, 1978, pp. 442–447.

BOND MANAGEMENT ISSUES

CONTENTS

**HISTORICAL PERSPECTIVE ON
BOND RETURNS** 3

BOND CHARACTERISTICS 4

Mortgage Bonds 4
Debenture Bonds 4
Subordinate Debenture Bonds 4
Equipment Trust Certificates 4
Convertible Bonds 5
Bond Definitions 5
 Principal amount 5
 Coupon rate 5
 Maturity date 5
 Quality 5
Call and Refunding Features 5
Sinking Fund Provisions 5
Maintenance and Replacement Fund 6

BOND MATHEMATICS 6

Yield to Maturity 6
Horizon and Realized Compound Yield 7
Price Amortization 8
Analysis of Yield Curves 10
Term Structure of Interest Rates 11

RISK MEASUREMENT 12

Risk of Call and Sinking Funds 12
Quality Risk 14
Reinvestment Risk 15
Price Volatility Risk 15
Term to Maturity 15
Duration 15

Horizon Volatility 16
Mean Absolute Change 16

**MANAGEMENT OF BOND
PORTFOLIOS** 17

Active Management Strategies 18
Passive Fixed Income Management 21
 Index funds 21
 Passive strategies emphasizing constant
 maturity 24
 Immunization 24
Private Placements 24
Guaranteed Investment Contracts 25

QUANTITATIVE TECHNIQUES 25

Portfolio Simulations 25
Performance Measurement 26
 Yield-to-maturity effect 27
 Interest rate effect 27
 Sector-quality effect 27
 Residual effect 27
 Frank Russell Index 27
Valuation Models 27

FUTURE DEVELOPMENTS 28

Floating Rate Securities 28
Mortgage-Related Securities 29
 Government National Mortgage
 Association 29
 Federal Home Loan Mortgage Corp. 29
 Conventional mortgage pass-through
 certificates 29
 Cash flow patterns of GNMAs 30

BOND MANAGEMENT ISSUES

Ravi Akhoury

Management of bond portfolios has evolved dramatically in the past decade primarily because of the increasingly attractive yields available in bond investments. Daniel Ahearn ("Strategic Role of Fixed Income Securities," in *The Theory and Practice of Bond Portfolio Management*, P. L. Bernstein, Ed.) notes that **fixed income yields** are at levels that are truly competitive with average earning yields on common stock and other types of investments.

HISTORICAL PERSPECTIVE ON BOND RETURNS

To truly evaluate fixed income securities, it is essential to look at the historical performance of bonds. In a study completed in 1979 for the Financial Analysts Research Foundation entitled *Stocks, Bonds, Bills and Inflation: Historical Returns (1926–1978)*, Ibbotson and Sinquefield show that over the period studied, annual return and **standard deviation of return** for common stock were 8.9 and 22.2%, respectively; for long-term corporate bonds these returns were 4.0 and 5.6%, while **inflation** grew at an annual rate of 2.5% with a standard deviation of 5%. Incremental return from common stocks was achieved at the cost of a substantially higher standard deviation of 22.2% versus 5.6% for long-term corporate bonds. It is also interesting to note that during the same period **bond returns** were positive 42 out of 53 years as compared to 35 out of 53 years for common stock.

In their study, the common stock return was measured by the return on **Standard & Poor's Composite Index.** Long-term bond performance was measured by the **Salomon Brothers High-Grade, Long-Term Corporate Bond Index** from 1969 to 1978; from 1946 to 1969 the index was backdated using Salomon Brothers monthly yield data and similar methodology. For the period 1926–1945, the investigators employed S & P monthly high-grade corporate bond composite data using 4% coupon and 20 year maturity. During the last 10 years covered in the study, 1969–1978, a period of rising inflation, the record for long-term bond performance was even more impressive. During that period long-term bonds on an annual basis achieved a rate of return of 5.8% as compared to 3.2% for common stocks.

More fundamental than these historical comparisons, however, is that **bond yields** are presently higher than the **historical returns from common stocks,** namely, 8.9%. Even in an absolute sense, the yield levels are attractive, since these contracts for future returns are presently higher than most actuarial assumptions used in **pension plans.**

In an inflationary environment, there are no clear choices, but it is interesting to note that even though **principal values** of bond portfolios are negatively affected by rising inflation and interest rates, the reinvestment of interest income provides a valuable **inflation hedge.** Andrew Carter ("Value Judgements in Bond Management," *Seminar on Bond Portfolio Management,* Financial Analysts Federation, 1977) points out that over two-thirds of return from an 8% bond comes from the reinvestment of interest income; that is, two-thirds of the return from the bond would be affected by future interest rates and inflation.

In the same example, it is demonstrated that $1 million invested in an 8% bond with coupon reinvested at 8% would grow to $10,519,627 in 30 years. However, should rates rise to 10%, the $1 million invested in bonds would drop in market value by approximately $190,000, but at maturity the loss would be recovered. At the same time reinvestment of the coupon at 10% would cause the final value to grow to $15,143,349, an increment of $4.63 million. The yield to maturity grows to 9.3% from the promised 8% at purchase. As can be seen, bond compounding offers a built-in inflation hedge that requires no special management techniques. Interestingly enough, the higher the **coupon,** the larger the impact of **reinvestment returns** on bond returns. During late 1979 and 1980 for the current coupon bonds, over 90% of the returns for long-term bonds came from reinvestment.

Investing in an **inflationary environment** is a challenging asset allocation decision. In an increasingly risky and uncertain environment, **fixed income securities** offer **lower levels of risk and volatility** relative to equity portfolios, provide a competitive rate of return that in most instances exceeds the actuarial requirements of many plans, and offer an attractive inflation hedge in their reinvestment mechanism. The role of fixed income securities can thus be viewed as adding **diversification** to the overall portfolio.

BOND CHARACTERISTICS

In reviewing the characteristics of corporate bonds, it is useful to summarize a few types that dominate the corporate bond market.

MORTGAGE BONDS.   Most utility companies issue mortgage bonds. These bonds are secured by the pledge of specific property. There are usually a number of conditions in the **indenture** that provide protection for bondholders' interest, specifically limiting the corporation from using that property in a manner that would be detrimental to the bondholder. In addition to the property, the holders of mortgage bonds have an unsecured claim on the corporation.

DEBENTURE BONDS.   Debentures usually refer to the general obligation of the corporation and therefore are not secured specifically. The indentures of debentures usually prevent the corporation from ignoring the rights of the holders of debenture bonds. It is important to thoroughly understand the provisions in the indentures of debentures.

SUBORDINATE DEBENTURE BONDS.   Subordinate debentures are generally considered one step lower than debentures in the hierarchy of corporate bonds. In case of insolvency, these instruments represent claims **junior to debentures** and **in theory** are considered only if senior claims are fully compensated.

EQUIPMENT TRUST CERTIFICATES.   These are usually secured by title to a specific piece of equipment and by the pledge of the lease under which the corporation is using the equipment. Because of the ease with which the specific property pledged is transferred and used by other corporations, the investment record of equipment trust certificates has been quite good.

CONVERTIBLE BONDS.   A convertible bond is generally a bond of junior status with an option to exchange a specific number of shares of common stock of the company for each bond. The ratio of the number of shares per bond varies from bond to bond and is specified in the indenture. The characteristics of a convertible bond are similar to a fixed income security in that they pay semiannual coupons and have a final value. However, because of the conversion features, investment in a convertible security in some circumstances also provides for participation in the underlying common stock.

BOND DEFINITIONS.   Before proceeding with an analysis of the management of bond portfolios, it may be constructive to define some characteristics of a specific issue.

Principal Amount.   The term usually refers to the redemption value of the bond if held to maturity. Corporate bonds are generally issued in units that have a **face value of $1,000.**

Coupon Rate.   This is the annual interest rate, expressed as a percentage of the principal amount, which the company **pays semiannually.**

Maturity Date.   This is the date on which the issuer must redeem all outstanding holdings of the given issue. It is generally regarded as the remaining life of the bond and in many instances also serves as a measure of **interest rate risk.** This point is elaborated on later when dealing with risk. The last coupon payment coincides with the maturity date.

Quality.   Quality of a corporate bond usually refers to the rating assigned by any or all of the three standard rating services, **Moody's, Standard & Poor's,** and **Fitch.**

   Standard & Poor's in many instances affixes a plus or minus to indicate a better or worse than average bond in a rating category. Elsewhere in the *Handbook*, definitions of various rating categories are provided.

CALL AND REFUNDING FEATURES.   Most corporations include in their indentures **call provisions,** which give them flexibility to call some or all of the issue from the bondholders before maturity. However, since investors wish to be compensated for this additional risk, the provisions specify some premium at which the bonds may be called. The premium is usually a function of the coupon rate. Furthermore, to reduce the uncertainty for the investor, many corporate bonds are noncallable for a specified period. When the issue is called, specifically with the intention of reissuing debt at lower interest rates, the process is referred to as a **refunding** and is most relevant to bond investors. **Refunding protection** is sought most dearly by bond investors. Most long-term bonds provide periods of refunding protection. Refunding protection is a form of call protection; however, it is not as complete. A bond that is nonrefundable may yet be called as long as funds are not derived from the refunding operation.

SINKING FUND PROVISIONS.   Sinking fund provisions require the issuer to make annual deposits of cash or bonds of the same issue to the trustee on behalf of the bondholders. The indenture also allows the corporation to call bonds at par, to satisfy sinking fund requirements.

   This feature makes it advantageous for corporations to deposit bonds rather than cash because if at the time the sinking fund requirement is to be satisfied, the market price of bonds is above the sinking fund call price, the corporation can call the bonds. If, however, the price is lower than the sinking fund call price, the corporation can buy the bonds in the marketplace. In either case, retired bonds can be used to satisfy sinking fund requirements.

MAINTENANCE AND REPLACEMENT FUND.   Bond investors have traditionally ignored provisions in the indentures of many utility bonds giving the issuer the option of retiring bonds at special redemption prices to satisfy **maintenance and replacement fund requirements.** However, the issue became significant in March 1977, when Florida Power & Light decided to call $63 million of its 10.125% bonds due in 2005 under this provision at a redemption price of $101.65. The regular redemption price at that time was $111.39.

The only way to clearly understand this provision is to study the **indenture** carefully; the general "mechanics" are as follows. Utilities are required by indenture to contribute annually a certain defined percentage of their operating revenues to a replacement fund. Usually, the indenture allows this to be done in a number of different ways: by pledging additional property, by purchasing bonds in the open market, and by depositing cash and then retiring bonds at special redemption prices. This final provision transforms into another source of risk to bondholders and is covered later.

In some cases the provisions of the fund state that bonds cannot be called during the refunding protection period. However, **refunding protection** does not apply in most cases. The best way to understand the provision is to study the indenture carefully, since provisions differ from issue to issue. See the Section on "Long Term Debt and Equity Markets and Instruments" in this *Handbook* for an in-depth discussion of the bond market.

BOND MATHEMATICS

YIELD TO MATURITY.   Since bond investments are contractual, with predetermined cash flows, they lend themselves more to analysis than do most forms of investment. Despite conceptual drawbacks of the simple **yield-to-maturity** calculation for bonds, in reality, it continues to be the most widely used measure of bond value. It remains one of the important measures utilized by traders for short-term trading tactics, as well as by **portfolio managers** for the construction of longer term strategic portfolios.

A frequently used method for determining yields involves **yield tables.** Yield tables are published by Financial Publishing Co., in Boston. A page of the yield book is organized by coupon sections, with each column representing time remaining to maturity in years and months and each row signifying the yield level (Exhibit 1). An entry in the table then represents the dollar price of a bond with a specified coupon, time to maturity, and yield to maturity levels.

Recently, however, yield tables have more or less been replaced by **programmable calculators** with special features to perform all bond mathematics calculations. These calculators are presently being used on the trading desks by portfolio managers and traders. The appendix "Mathematics of Finance" discusses and utilizes programmable calculators.

Fundamental to yield-to-maturity calculations is the concept of the **time value of money.** Bonds can be viewed as a contract whereby the investor receives from the issuer semiannual coupon payments and the par amount principal payment at maturity, ignoring for the moment other call, refunding, or sinking fund features. On that basis, the most common and practical way of viewing yield to maturity is to consider it as that **discount rate** which would equate the present value of all future payments to the present price of the bond. On that basis, yield to maturity can quite correctly be viewed as the **internal rate of return** over the bond's remaining life. Mathematically, one can derive the formula for yield to maturity by considering the following.

Combining the present value of final principal (PRINC) after N semiannual periods, discounted at Y interest rate per period plus the present value of a stream of N semiannual coupon payments (COUP), discounted at the same rate Y, we get the price of bond (PRICE):

$$\text{PRICE} = \sum_{t=1}^{n}\frac{\text{COUP}}{(1 + Y/2)^t} + \frac{\text{PRINC}}{(1 + Y/2)^n}$$

The formula above relates in a simplistic way the price and yield to maturity of the bond. PRICE represents the market price and Y represents the **yield to maturity of the bond.**

The formula, for the sake of simplicity, assumes that a bond has a remaining life of equal multiple, semiannual interest periods. If, however, a bond transaction does **not** take place on a **coupon payment date,** the buyer of the bond receives the full semiannual coupon at the first coupon payment date. Since he held the bond for only a fraction of that period, he is entitled to only a fraction of the payment. The balance belongs to the seller of the bond. The settlement between the buyer and seller takes place at the time of the transaction in the form of **accrued interest.** In addition to the price of the bond, the buyer of the bond pays to the seller accrued interest, which is the seller's portion of the first semiannual coupon payment. "Total proceeds" in a transaction usually refers to the sum of market value and accrued interest. The calculation of accrued interest is performed by way of a fairly simple linear interpolation technique. For a detailed derivation of formulas, the reader is referred to *Standard Securities Calculation Methods* (Spence, Graudenz, and Lynch) and also to *Inside the Yield Book* (Leibowitz and Homer).

Here we develop the concept of yield to maturity and discuss the implications of various assumptions implicit in the calculation. As should be clear from the formula, one of the most powerful implicit assumptions in the yield-to-maturity calculation is the **reinvestment of all future cash flows** at the yield-to-maturity rate. Specifying reinvestment rates for future cash flows is an uncomfortable burden for most practitioners. It should be recognized, however, that by not specifying and utilizing yield to maturity as a measure of return, bond managers are assuming future reinvestment at yield to maturity rates. There is no easy way to avoid this very important component of bond returns.

HORIZON AND REALIZED COMPOUND YIELD. Utilizing bond yields to maturity as a measure of bond returns and then comparing returns ignores the issue of **horizon.** The comparison can be misleading because for each bond the computation could be made to **different time horizons and reinvestment assumptions.** A concept called **realized compound yield,** developed by Leibowitz and Homer in *Inside the Yield Book*, overcomes to a large extent these drawbacks. Realized compound yield is the interest rate required to produce the future value per dollar invested in the bond compounded at a specified interest rate.

$$\text{\textbf{future value of a bond at maturity (FV)}} = \text{PRINC} + \text{COUP}\left[\frac{(1 + R)^n - 1}{R}\right]$$

where R is the reinvestment rate.

$$\text{\textbf{realized compound yield to maturity}} = \left[\left(\frac{\text{FV}}{\text{PRICE}}\right)^{1/n} - 1\right]$$

EXHIBIT 1   YIELD TABLES FOR 7%

Yield	Time to Maturity (Years, Months)							
	26, 6	27, 0	27, 6	28, 0	28, 6	29, 0	29, 6	30, 0
4.00	148.74	149.26	149.76	150.26	150.74	151.22	151.68	152.14
4.20	144.51	144.96	145.41	145.85	146.28	146.69	147.11	147.51
4.40	140.44	140.84	141.24	141.62	142.00	142.37	142.73	143.08
4.60	136.54	136.89	137.24	137.57	137.90	138.22	138.53	138.84
4.80	132.79	133.10	133.40	133.69	133.97	134.25	134.52	134.79
5.00	129.19	129.46	129.71	129.96	130.21	130.45	130.68	130.91
5.20	125.73	125.96	126.18	126.39	126.60	126.80	127.00	127.19
5.40	122.41	122.60	122.78	122.96	123.14	123.31	123.48	123.64
5.60	119.21	119.37	119.53	119.67	119.82	119.96	120.10	120.23
5.80	116.14	116.27	116.40	116.52	116.63	116.75	116.86	116.97
6.00	113.19	113.29	113.39	113.48	113.58	113.67	113.75	113.84
6.10	111.75	111.84	111.93	112.01	112.09	112.17	112.25	112.32
6.20	110.34	110.42	110.50	110.57	110.64	110.71	110.77	110.84
6.30	108.96	109.03	109.09	109.15	109.21	109.27	109.33	109.38
6.40	107.61	107.66	107.72	107.77	107.82	107.87	107.91	107.96
6.50	106.28	106.32	106.37	106.41	106.45	106.49	106.53	106.56
6.60	104.98	105.01	105.04	105.08	105.11	105.14	105.17	105.20
6.70	103.70	103.72	103.75	103.77	103.79	103.82	103.84	103.86
6.80	102.44	102.46	102.47	102.49	102.50	102.52	102.53	102.55
6.90	101.21	101.22	101.22	101.23	101.24	101.25	101.25	101.26
7.00	100.00	100.00	100.00	100.00	100.00	100.00	100.00	100.00
7.10	98.81	98.81	98.80	98.79	98.78	98.78	98.77	98.77
7.20	97.65	97.63	97.62	97.61	97.59	97.58	97.57	97.55
7.30	96.51	96.48	96.46	96.44	96.42	96.40	96.39	96.37
7.40	95.38	95.35	95.33	95.30	95.28	95.25	95.23	95.21
7.50	94.28	94.25	94.21	94.18	94.15	94.12	94.09	94.07
7.60	93.20	93.16	93.12	93.08	93.05	93.01	92.98	92.95
7.70	92.14	92.09	92.05	92.01	91.96	91.93	91.89	91.85
7.80	91.09	91.04	90.99	90.95	90.90	90.86	90.82	90.78
7.90	90.07	90.01	89.96	89.91	89.86	89.81	89.77	89.72

When the reinvestment rate is equal to the yield to maturity, the **realized compound yield** is the same as **yield to maturity.** Realized compound yields can also be computed to a time horizon other than maturity. If in the computation, the principal value is replaced by price of the bond at some other time period and N is replaced by the number for semiannual periods to the desired time horizon, the realized compound yield to the derived time horizon can be computed. This is indeed the most commonly used measure for **total return in bonds.** It allows two bonds to be compared on a total return basis using the same reinvestment rate for intermediate cash flows and the same time horizons. If the manager is more comfortable with using a set of variable reinvestment rates for intermediate cash flows, the formula can be quite easily adapted.

PRICE AMORTIZATION.   Another aspect of **total return calculation** to horizons other than maturity that makes the bond practitioner uncomfortable is the determination of bond

EXHIBIT 1 CONTINUED

| | \multicolumn{8}{c}{Time to Maturity (Years, Months)} | | | | | | | |
Yield	26, 6	27, 0	27, 6	28, 0	28, 6	29, 0	29, 6	30, 0
8.00	89.06	89.00	88.95	88.89	88.84	88.79	88.74	88.69
8.10	88.08	88.01	87.95	87.89	87.83	87.78	87.72	87.67
8.20	87.11	87.04	86.97	86.91	86.85	86.79	86.73	86.68
8.30	86.15	86.08	86.01	85.94	85.88	85.82	85.76	85.70
8.40	85.22	85.14	85.07	85.00	84.93	84.87	84.80	84.75
8.50	84.30	84.22	84.14	84.07	84.00	83.93	83.87	83.81
8.60	83.39	83.31	83.23	83.16	83.08	83.01	82.95	82.88
8.70	82.51	82.42	82.34	82.26	82.19	82.11	82.04	81.98
8.80	81.63	81.55	81.46	81.38	81.30	81.23	81.16	81.09
8.90	80.78	80.69	80.60	80.52	80.44	80.36	80.29	80.22
9.00	79.93	79.84	79.75	79.67	79.59	79.51	79.43	79.36
9.10	79.11	79.01	78.92	78.83	78.75	78.67	78.59	78.52
9.20	78.29	78.20	78.10	78.01	77.93	77.85	77.77	77.70
9.30	77.49	77.39	77.30	77.21	77.12	77.04	76.96	76.89
9.40	76.71	76.61	76.51	76.42	76.33	76.25	76.17	76.09
9.50	75.93	75.83	75.73	75.64	75.55	75.47	75.39	75.31
9.60	75.17	75.07	74.97	74.88	74.79	74.70	74.62	74.54
9.70	74.43	74.32	74.22	74.13	74.04	73.95	73.87	73.79
9.80	73.69	73.59	73.49	73.39	73.30	73.21	73.13	73.05
9.90	72.97	72.86	72.76	72.66	72.57	72.48	72.40	72.32
10.00	72.26	72.15	72.05	71.95	71.86	71.77	71.69	71.61
10.20	70.87	70.77	70.66	70.56	70.47	70.38	70.29	70.21
10.40	69.53	69.42	69.32	69.22	69.13	69.04	68.95	68.87
10.60	68.24	68.13	68.02	67.92	67.83	67.74	67.65	67.57
10.80	66.98	66.87	66.77	66.67	66.57	66.48	66.40	66.31
11.00	65.77	65.65	65.55	65.45	65.36	65.27	65.18	65.10
11.20	64.59	64.48	64.37	64.27	64.18	64.09	64.01	63.93
11.40	63.45	63.34	63.23	63.13	63.04	62.95	62.87	62.79
11.60	62.34	62.23	62.13	62.03	61.94	61.85	61.77	61.69
11.80	61.27	61.16	61.06	60.96	60.87	60.79	60.70	60.63
12.00	60.23	60.13	60.02	59.93	59.84	59.75	59.67	59.60

Source: Financial Publishing Co., Boston.

prices at time horizons other than maturity. In most instances when a bond manager purchases a bond or consummates a trade, he has some expectation of market behavior. This expectation is transformed into the price of the bond at the desired time horizon. If the manager is reluctant to make market judgments, an acceptable price for horizon other than maturity is a price computation based on **scientific amortization.** Price is computed assuming that the yield to maturity remains the same as the yield to maturity of the bond at the time of purchase. This can be a very acceptable procedure if the manager intends to hold the bond to maturity and is interested in computing returns at intermediate time horizons.

Even though the **total return** is probably the most complete measure to compute and use to compare bond returns, in practice, bonds are quoted and traded on a yield-to-maturity basis. There are two primary reasons for this: first, the time horizons of the participants vary; therefore total return computations are necessarily different. Second, even though many trades are consummated at certain **yield spreads,** they are made with certain reversals or changes in spread relationships in mind. Implicit in those assumptions is a certain total rate of return expectation from the two securities. These aspects are covered in more detail under "Active Management Strategies." Suffice it to say that the yield-to-maturity concept is important, flexible, and ingrained in the thinking of most practitioners.

ANALYSIS OF YIELD CURVES. The yield curve usually refers to a **plot of yield to maturity** and **time to maturity.** When plotted across the same type of bond (e.g., public utilities), and quality (e.g., Aa bonds), it usually signifies the tradeoff between yield and maturity within the given sector and quality. Market participants have different interpretations and applications of the yield curve. Perhaps the most widely followed use of the yield curve is the analysis of the **Treasury yield curve** or the pure **"default-free" yield curve.** Most often the shape of the yield curve changes dramatically over the course of a business and interest rate cycle. Many participants have studied historically the shape of yield curves at different stages of the business and interest rate cycle and so use the shape of the yield curve to gauge the stage of a business cycle. In many cases this analysis leads to some conclusions regarding the relative values of certain groups of securities. The changing shape of the yield curve then can be used to position the portfolio.

Exhibit 2 is a three-dimensional representation of the corporate bond yield curve from 1900 to 1975 as presented in the analytical record of yields and yield spreads prepared by Salomon Brothers. The shape of the yield curve changes dramatically over the course of an **interest rate cycle.** Early in the cycle, where yields are generally lower, the shape of the yield curve is generally positive sloping, with higher yields for longer maturity bonds. As the cycle matures and yields rise, the curve tends to flatten until eventually toward the end of the cycle the yield curve actually inverts, with longer maturity bonds yielding less than shorter maturity bonds.

Some view the yield curve as a consensus of market participants and therefore try to extract mathematically implicit market forecasts. This practice is covered in some detail later.

It is important to recognize that the shape of the yield curve is affected quite dramatically by the **supply and demand of securities.** It is not uncommon to have a certain shape of yield curve in one sector of the market and a different shape in another sector. For example, in October 1979 the market expectation of supply of intermediate Treasury securities was quite high and the Treasury yield curve was inverted. However in January and February 1980, the strong demand for intermediate corporate securities caused a dramatic flattening of the yield curve, with long rates rising more than intermediate rates. At the same time the market expectations of a large supply of intermediate Treasury obligations relative to corporate bonds caused the yield curve to remain inverted in the Treasury sector but not in the corporate sector.

One word of caution: the yield curve should not be viewed as a **risk-return tradeoff curve.** As discussed later, risk in bonds is multidimensional, and maturity is probably not a good proxy for risk in bonds. Furthermore, equating yield to maturity with return is probably an equally serious error, as noted earlier. The analysis of yield curves using a measure of **horizon return** rather than yield to maturity has been addressed by Leibowitz in *Total Return Management*. See the section in this *Handbook* by Leibowitz, "Specialized Fixed Income Security Strategies."

EXHIBIT 2   BASIC YIELDS OF CORPORATE BONDS BY MATURITY, 1900–1975

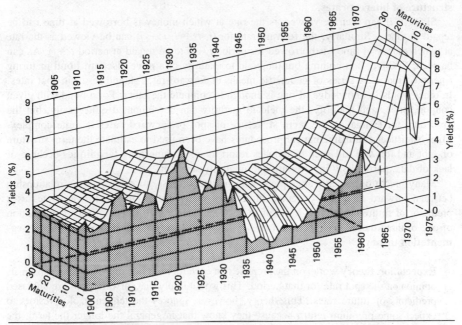

Source: Salomon Brothers, ''An Analytical Record of Yields and Yield Spreads,'' May 1976.

TERM STRUCTURE OF INTEREST RATES.   Despite its many conceptual problems, yield to maturity in practice continues to be the most widely quoted concept in bond management. Conceptually a much sounder formulation and explanation of the structure of interest rates for a default-free bond with no tax consequences can be made by a series of one-year **forward rates.** As Malkiel (*The Term Structure of Interest Rates*) states, ''the most intriguing structural relationship among market interest rates is the functional relationship among yields of the securities which differ only in their term to maturity. This relationship is called the term structure of interest rates.'' The concept of term structure using forward rates and a discount function has been extensively covered by many academicians and is gaining some popularity in the investment community.

All **bond pricing models** essentially discount future payments at a discount rate that is relevant to the time of payment. In yield-to-maturity calculations some simplistic assumptions are made regarding future discount rates. In the case of **forward** and **spot rate** estimation, a much more precise methodology is used.

$$\text{PRICE}(t) = \frac{\text{COUP}_1}{1 + \text{SPOT}(t, 1)} + \frac{\text{COUP}_2}{[1 + \text{SPOT}(t, 2)]^2} + \cdots \frac{\text{COUP}_n + \text{PRINC}}{[1 + \text{SPOT}(t, i)]^n}$$

where PRICE(*t*) = price of bond at time *t*

COUP = semiannual coupon payment

n = number of semiannual coupon payments

SPOT(*t*, *i*) = discount rate implied by market for payment received *i* periods after time *t*

PRINC = par amount principal payment at maturity

A series of spot rates SPOT(t, i) where ($i = 1,. . ., n$) is referred to as **spot rate term structure of interest rates.**

SPOT(t, i) can then be viewed as the rate at which money is borrowed at time t to be repaid in time i. Similarly, the forward rate for (t, $t + i$, $t + j$) can be viewed as the rate at which money at time t is borrowed for period $t + i$ to be repaid at period $t + j$. As can be seen, SPOT(t, i) is nothing but the yield to maturity of a **pure discount bond** maturing i periods from t. A series of geometric means of forward rates should result in spot rates. In other words, a knowledge of one is enough to compute the other. For a bond with given coupon, price, and maturity, the yield to maturity can be computed quite easily, but the procedure for estimating the **term structure of spot** or **forward rates** is quite complex. Many statistical and mathematical procedures have been used to estimate the term structure of spot and forward, all such techniques resort to some **smoothing techniques** because of lack of data, particularly in certain longer maturity segments.

Many practitioners have attempted, with limited success, to determine the relationship between forward rates and expected future spot rates, that is, to use forward rates as a predictor of future spot rates. Most of these techniques utilize some form or combination of one of three theories: **expectation theory, liquidity preference theory,** or **market segmentation theory.**

Expectation theory works on the premise that each forward rate represents the consensus opinion on the spot rate for that period. This would imply that forward rates are unbiased predictors of future rates. This theory, however, ignores the tendency of investors to expect some premium return because they know that in general the longer the term, the greater the risk associated with the investment.

Liquidity preference theory compensates for this expectation by adjusting the forward rate structure by a liquidity premium that increases with time.

Market segmentation theory suggests that there are many institutional constraints that result in the preference of certain maturity instruments and that only a major adjustment in rates of different maturity instruments can change that preferred pattern for both buyers and sellers of bonds.

There is some empirical validation for the market segmentation theory, but the liquidity preference hypothesis is supported by more evidence.

RISK MEASUREMENT

Measurement of risk in bonds is perhaps the most elusive and complex process in bond portfolio management. As an asset class, bonds are unique in that the cash flow aspects and the features that affect cash flow are contractual. This feature of bonds makes their future return dependent on the present and past returns. Therefore, the definition of **horizon,** or the time period over which risk and return is to be measured, is of utmost importance. To manage bond portfolios, the portfolio manager must be aware of the role the bond portfolio is playing in the overall investment plan. If the role of the bond portfolio is clearly defined, the contractual nature of bonds renders the portfolio manager better equipped to manage each element of the risk and return to the appropriate time horizon.

RISK OF CALL AND SINKING FUNDS.   As was described earlier, an **issuer** maintains the option to retire the bonds at a **premium call price** from the bondholder. If the proceeds used to retire bonds are not from internally generated cash but are obtained by raising funds at lower interest rates in the open market, the process is called **refunding.** The risk to bondholders is generally from the latter scenario. Corporations seldom use cash to retire bonds except in the case of telephone bonds. A very simplistic approach to incorporate the impact of call is to compute **yield to call** and **yield to maturity** and use the lower of the two (minimum yield) as a measure of return. This is a conventional and simplistic measure because it assumes that since the option is in the hands of the issuer, investors will necessarily receive the minimum yield.

Yield to call is computed by replacing **principal value** at maturity by the first refunding price or first call price and by replacing **maturity date** by first refunding date or first call date. A slightly more realistic approach is to consider the process of calling as an investment decision on the part of the issuer, who in effect pays the call price to buy back the bonds. The yield to maturity of this bond can then be compared to the estimate of the **cost of issuing new bonds** by the issuer at the call date. It is safe to assume that unless the cost of new bonds is less than the computed yield to maturity, the bonds will not be called.

In an interesting paper by Einhorn, ''Breaking Tradition in Bond Portfolio Investment'' (in *The Theory and Practice of Bond Portfolio Management,* P. L. Bernstein, Ed.), the author points out that a **price to call price ratio** greater than 1 had a significant impact on price movements of callable bonds in response to interest rate changes, but that **time to call** had little or no effect.

This would indicate that bond investors pay more attention to the market price, and as the price of the bond approaches and exceeds the call price, investors become more concerned about bonds being called, irrespective of any call protection the bonds may have. This added concern results in further price movements in the bond less dependent on interest rate changes. Finally, more attention has recently been given to the optionlike features of call and procedures to value options are being developed for **callable bonds**.

The **sinking fund risk** presents a more interesting situation because in most cases the requirements are mandatory. If the bonds are trading above par, the corporation will retire the bonds at par; but if the bonds are trading below par, it would attempt to buy the bonds at market price. This feature creates a built-in demand for bonds with sinking funds, and in many instances investors have tried to take advantage of the situation by controlling a large portion of a discount bond with a sinking fund provision forcing the corporation to buy bonds from the investors to satisfy the sinking fund requirements. Also, because of this built-in demand, the bonds have tended to be less volatile. Because of the contractual retirement, in many instances these bonds trade on a **yield-to-average-life basis**.

The indenture of an issue often gives the option to the issuer to **double the sinking fund provision**. This is a powerful option, and the risks to the investor are quite significant. The issuing corporation clearly will exercise this option only if the environment is in its favor. In effect, it is a way of retiring bonds at no premium with low supplementary costs. Furthermore, nonredemption clauses have no effect on sinking fund calls, so in effect the corporation does not need cash. It could easily raise cash if the environment were to become more attractive, and use the proceeds to double the mandatory sinking fund requirement. From the bondholders' point of view, this is a threat to call protection that would be applicable only if the environment were advantageous to the issuer, therefore disadvantageous to bondholders.

In summary, the risk of call refunding is real but manageable. The risk clearly is applicable only if interest rates drop fairly dramatically. More than the **act of call**, the **threat of call** produces interesting cyclical price behavior in securities and, if understood, can be managed effectively. The only **way to eliminate call and refunding risk** is to buy lower coupon bonds, for which calling would not be economically justified, or to buy U.S. Treasury bonds, which either are noncallable or are protected from call for a longer period than applicable to most corporate bonds.

QUALITY RISK.   The most widely used **quality risk measures** in the bond market are the ratings assigned by rating services as mentioned earlier. Even though the classifications appear to be very distinct, in reality, within those classifications securities trade differently. For example, all AAA securities would not trade at the same yield. Securities considered to be weak AAA would trade at higher yields than those considered to be strong AAA. The risk a portfolio manager takes in buying an AAA security is not necessarily a default risk because it is extremely unlikely that such a security would default. The risk, rather, is the risk that the quality of the company may deteriorate such that the security might start trading in the lower end of the quality spectrum or, even worse, it might be **downgraded** by the rating agencies. Bond markets are very sensitive to such changes and in most instances react before the rating agencies change the ratings. For example, in late 1979 when **Ford Motor Co.** announced serious problems in its North American operations, both Ford Motor Co. and Ford Motor Credit Co. bonds, which were rated AAA by rating agencies, started trading at higher yields than many AA rated bonds within their industry classification. Subsequently Ford Motor Co. bonds were downgraded. Such a situation results in opportunity losses in the portfolio. To avoid such risks, many institutions have credit analysts who monitor working lists of securities, hoping to identify changing situations before the market. Like any risk, these situations can also present opportunity if the analyst can properly identify any potential change in ratings.

Besides the financial characteristics of the issue, probably the most important element affecting **quality risk** is maturity, because over an extended period the risk of unforeseen developments increases. The **yield spreads** between securities of various quality classifications also change dramatically with the business and interest rate cycle. Management of that aspect of quality risk is a very important ingredient of **active bond management**.

It should be understood that even though the hierarchy of risk classes is established by rating services, there is no specific measurement of the **risk differential** among credit ratings. In addition, the existence of split ratings among agencies further complicates the issue. It has been estimated that between 15 and 20% of outstanding bond securities receive differential ratings from Moody's and Standard & Poor's; see Altman, "Computerized Bond Ratings" (*Basis Point*, Equitable Life Assurance, Fall 1979).

In managing lower grade securities, the **risk of default** is much more important than the risk of securities being downgraded. More in-depth analysis is required, and the estimate of default premium becomes a critical issue. Default premium estimation is extensively defined in the book *Investments*, by Sharpe (Prentice-Hall, 1978). Many practitioners have also resorted to computer models utilizing multiple discriminant analysis to predict bankruptcies. One such model that has been used fairly extensively was developed by Altman, Haldeman, and Narayauan ("Zeta Analysis," *Journal of Banking and Finance*, Vol. 1, June 1977). Similar statistical analysis techniques have also been used to predict rating reclassifications by the various rating agencies. See the references in this section and in the Section entitled "Bankruptcy and Reorganization."

The risk inherent in low-rated securities is clearly quite high, but a number of studies have shown that returns in many instances adequately compensate for the risk. This writer believes that the low-rated **market is inefficient**. Many institutions do not participate in the market. In many instances, the stigma attached to defaulted bonds is so severe that securities can trade at a discounted value more extreme than the fundamentals may warrant. The market recently, however, has been dominated by institutions as more and more funds establish high-yield, low-quality funds. This change will tend to make the market **more efficient**.

REINVESTMENT RISK.   **Reinvestment risk** is a more obvious element, but perhaps it is the most overlooked **quantifiable risk** in fixed income securities. Return from the reinvestment of semiannual coupon payments in many instances could account for as much as 90% of the total return to maturity in a long-term fixed income security. Implicit in **yield-to-maturity calculation** is a reinvestment rate equal to yield to maturity. If interest rates rise, reinvestment will be at higher rates and the realized return will be higher than promised returns. If, on the other hand, interest rates decline, the reinvestment will be at lower rates and the realized returns will be lower. This aspect of risk, along with the **price volatility risk**, plays an important and sometimes overlooked role in judging risk from **bond portfolios**.

PRICE VOLATILITY RISK.   Price volatility risk is probably the most widely analyzed and applied form of risk in fixed income securities. Measurement of this risk has evolved considerably, and perhaps is still quite incomplete. Here we identify various measures and conclude with a thought on measurement of the **combined price and reinvestment risk**.

One of the crudest and earliest measures of price volatility was **yield value 1/32**. This measure is the change of basis points (1 basis point equals 0.01 percentage point) necessary to cause a change in price of the security by 1/32. By comparing yield value 1/32 for different securities, it was possible to get an estimate of their price volatility.

TERM TO MATURITY.   The next stage in the evolution of price risk measurement is **term to maturity**. Even though utilizing the time dimension as a measure of price risk has merit, term to maturity puts major emphasis on the last principal payment, ignoring all other interim cash flow. As Leibowitz and Homer discuss in *Inside the Yield Book*, the price volatility of bonds is a function of **years to maturity, coupon payment**, and **yield levels**. The dramatic changes in the shape of the yield curve during most of the 1970s have clearly demonstrated the fallacy of equating maturity with risk. On numerous occasions intermediate-term securities have outperformed long-term bonds in rallies, and vice versa. Despite this, term to maturity continues to be the most important measure used by many practitioners.

Average maturity of portfolios is used by many to compare risk of portfolios. Average maturity is also a means of communicating strategy changes to clients by investment managers. Even if maturity were a complete measure of price risk in bonds, **weighted average maturity** of a portfolio would not be a good risk measure for the portfolio. There are a number of combinations available with bonds of different maturities that would result in the same average maturity of the portfolio. However, since the relationship between price change and maturity is not linear, the different combinations of bonds with the same average maturity would have different risk levels. Yawitz, Hempel, and Marshall, in "Is Average Maturity a Proxy for Risk?" (in *The Theory and Practice of Bond Portfolio Management*, P.L. Bernstein, Ed.) point out not only that the price volatility-maturity relationship is nonlinear, but that from May, 1953 to November, 1972 **yield volatility** also **decreased with maturity** in a **nonlinear fashion**. These drawbacks of using average maturity as a price risk measure led to the revival of the **duration concept**.

DURATION.   The **concept of duration** was introduced by **F.R. Macaulay** in 1938. Duration is a more complete measure of bond life that takes into account the timing of all cash flows. **Duration** is the number of years in the future when cash is received, **weighted** by the proportion the present value of the cash flow contributed to the total present value of all cash flows. The formula for duration is:

$$D = \sum_{t=1,n} t \left\{ \frac{\dfrac{\text{cash}(t)}{(1 + YTM)^t}}{\displaystyle\sum_{t=1,N} \frac{\text{cash}(t)}{(1 + YTM)^t}} \right\}$$

where t = time in (years)

N = years to maturity

cash (t) = total cash flow at time t

YTM = yield to maturity

If duration did nothing but measure the average term for bonds, the concept would not be used extensively. What made duration an acceptable and popular tool was the property that duration adjusted by a factor that could relate **yield change in bond to its price change:**

$$\frac{\Delta P}{P} = - \frac{D}{1 + R} \Delta R$$

where ΔP = change in price of the bond

P = price of bond

D = duration

R = yield level

ΔR = change in yield rate level

Duration takes into account all the factors that affect **price volatility**. The problem arises in using **average duration** of a portfolio as a measure of price risk for the portfolio. The principal serious objection to the concept is its implication of a parallel **shift in yield curves**, which is not realistic. Practitioners have seen the shape of the yield curve change so dramatically that their faith in duration as a measure of price risk of the overall portfolio is limited. Another technical problem associated with using duration as a measure of price risk is that the relationship that equates yield changes to price changes using duration is true only for small changes in yield. Nevertheless, average duration is a better measure of price volatility than **average maturity**.

HORIZON VOLATILITY. Another measure developed by Leibowitz is the concept of **horizon volatility** ("Horizon Analysis for Managed Bond Portfolios," in *The Theory and Practice of Bond Portfolio Management,* P.L. Bernstein, Ed.). Horizon volatility is a precise mathematical term, which is expressed as basis point of price move. This measure has the same drawback when applied to the **total portfolio** in that a parallel shift in yield curve is implicit in its applicability as a risk measure for the total portfolio. Similar to duration, this measure is more informative than average maturity.

MEAN ABSOLUTE CHANGE. Finally, a measure developed by Yawitz, Hempel, and Marshall ("Risk Return Approach to the Selection of Optimal Government Bond Portfolios,"

Financial Management, Autumn 1976), has intuitive appeal. This measure is an empirical determination of the **mean absolute change in price** (MACP) over a 1-month time horizon. Because the relationship between price volatility and maturity is nonlinear, and because empirically it can be shown that yield volatility also decreases with increasing maturity, these authors suggested that the best measure of risk is an empirical determination of relationships between price and maturity.

To define risk characteristics of the portfolio, it is important to determine the role that bonds are expected to play and to establish a horizon or planning period. If we focus only on the risk that is market related, that is, **reinvestment risk** and **price volatility risk**, it becomes apparent that the holding period is a key item. If the holding period is very short, price risk is probably the only risk the manager needs to focus on. If, however, the holding period is very long, clearly reinvestment risk will dominate. To define risk characteristics of the portfolio, it is important to determine the role of bonds in the portfolio. It is equally risky to buy long-term bonds for the portfolio having an extremely short planning period than to buy short-maturity bonds for a portfolio with a long planning period as a horizon. Each portfolio is subject to an inordinate amount of risk; in the first case it is price risk and in the second case it is reinvestment risk.

Risk could also be defined as the probability of not realizing the promised contractual yield. If this were truly the definition of risk, a good measure would be the difference between the duration of the portfolio and the planning period horizon. This is principally the concept behind **immunization** and is discussed at length in the section by Leibowitz entitled "Specialized Fixed Income Security Strategies."

In the discussion above, we have identified various elements of risk without any attempt either to combine them or to make judgments as to preference of risk measure. In measuring risk in bonds, first define the objective and then determine the horizon. When the objective is known, and therefore the horizon, the definition and also the measurement of risk become more manageable tasks.

MANAGEMENT OF BOND PORTFOLIOS

To manage bond portfolios, it is imperative that the long-term objectives of the portfolio be clearly defined, to permit the setting of appropriate techniques for the measurement of risk and return by the client and the portfolio manager. With objectives and horizon well defined, it should be possible to construct a **baseline portfolio** appropriate to the long-term objectives. The **value added by divergence** from the baseline portfolio then can be interpreted as the manager's ability to use his judgment to add value to the baseline portfolio's risk and return objectives. The value added could also be measured in terms of incremental risk and return incurred on the portfolio. The concept of baseline portfolio has been developed more fully by Leibowitz in "*Total Return Management*." At this point it is sufficient to say that a client-manager dialogue is critical in determining the usefulness of any particular management style and that no portfolio management style should lose sight of the ultimate long-term objective.

This subsection covers a number of portfolio management strategies, both active and passive. There is no single strategy that is dominant. Each strategy has certain risk-return characteristics and satisfies certain objectives. It is critical to recognize this basic premise and then select a strategy that best suits the needs of the plan. It is not necessary that any one strategy meet the needs. In fact, in many instances it may be desirable to select more than one strategy, perhaps even a combination of active and passive strategies, such that the combination has the **optimum risk-return characteristics** for the plan.

ACTIVE MANAGEMENT STRATEGIES.   Proponents of active bond management strategies cite two principal reasons for pursuing them.

1. **Volatile interest rates** in the bond markets, in terms of both levels of interest rates and changes in the shape of the yield curve, have dramatically increased risks in the bond markets in the past 10 years. Along with increased risks, the market presents increased opportunities to participants willing to exercise calculated judgments.

2. Historic evidence suggests that in the **inflationary environment** of the past decade, the real rates of return generated by most fixed income **buy and hold strategies** have been less than satisfactory.

Perhaps the most widely implemented and followed active management strategy is the **market timing strategy** or strategy emphasizing the cyclical nature of interest rates. The key element of this strategy is **forecasting interest rates**. The investment process and style of management under such an active strategy is covered precisely by Meyer in "Forecasting Interest Rates: Key to Active Bond Management" (*Financial Analysts Journal*, November–December 1978). Practitioners of this style have historically analyzed the cyclical nature of interest rates and have carefully identified various economic and monetary statistics that assist in their determination of the stage of the **interest rate cycle**. This style of management generally requires a thorough understanding of the business cycle and economic and monetary events that affect interest rates. Once a judgment regarding the stage of interest rate cycle has been made, the **maturity structure of the portfolio** is adjusted to reflect that judgment.

Since interest rate forecasting is not an exact science (clearly the events of 1979 and 1980 have made the best of forecasters very humble), most practitioners lengthen maturities close to their estimate of interest rate peaks and shorten maturities close to troughs of interest rate cycles. This activity usually does not require a precise determination of interest rate peaks but rather a judgment on the state of the interest rate cycle and the general direction in which the interest rate is moving. The extreme to which the maturity of the portfolio is lengthened or shortened is determined between the client and manager and should be a function of the client's long-term objective.

Besides maturity, quality coupon and sector selection should also be consistent with the interest rate cycle. These features have coincided enough with the interest rate cycle to permit the development of a consistent, disciplined process of averaging in and out of these categories. It is risky to attempt to time these developments precisely, since most bond investors have a less hearty appetite for increased risk. Bond managers, by active management, should attempt to add modest value to general market returns and not necessarily attempt to time the markets perfectly. The risk of such a **market timing strategy** is twofold:

1. Since interest rate forecasting is not an exact science, any strategy for which acceptance is so dependent on the accuracy of the forecast has to add an extra element of risk that must be consciously offset by the implementation process of the strategy.

2. The strategy is by definition very dependent on the business and **interest rate cycle.** It would appear that the horizon on any such strategy would be the duration of a cycle and could be inconsistent with the horizon for most **pension funds.**

The rewards of timing the interest rates perfectly are high as Meyer has demonstrated. He indicates that in the cycle covering the period April 1971 to December 1976 the annual compound rate of return for an investor making perfect timing decisions was 11.6%, as compared to the **Salomon Brothers Index,** which had a return of 7.6%. Over the same period, an investor making wrong decisions in attempting to time the market would have realized a rate of return of just 2.9%.

These additional risks in a **market timing strategy** can be controlled in two ways:

1. By controlling the extent of portfolio restructuring in the implementation process.
2. By utilizing a **number of bond managers** with different styles, to compensate for the added market timing risks. Multiple managers diversify a number of different types of risks.

The second form of **active management** is based on **determination of value.** Adherents to this style of management believe that interest rate forecasting is not the optimal way of managing bonds. To a large extent, they believe that timing risks is not justified in most bond portfolios. In their view, bonds must be managed with a longer term fundamental view. Carter, in "Value Judgments in Bond Management" *(Proceedings of the Seminar on Bond Portfolio Management,* 1977) points out that bond managers should make two judgments.

Do bonds offer good value?

Which bonds offer the best value?

In our opinion, Carter's views would suggest that owning or not owning bonds is a much more basic asset allocation question. It has to be determined in the context of the overall portfolio consisting of all permissible asset classes. Since the characteristics of bonds are contractual, these obligations lend themselves to analysis, and ownership should therefore depend on the ability of a given bond to meet the long-term objectives of the plan. Once the role of bonds in the overall portfolio has been determined, the portfolio manager's primary responsibility is to seek out bonds that offer the most value.

Bond markets have become increasingly volatile and segmented. Supply and demand of securities, level of interest rates, and the cyclical nature of interest rates have varying impacts on different sectors of the bond market. An astute bond manager can take advantage of these changing characteristics. Such a strategy certainly reduces the risks of market timing. However, in my opinion, it introduces another element of risk. A clear definition of long-term objectives is essential to the formulation of this strategy, and the risk is in the proper construction of the **baseline portfolio** to meet those objectives.

A third style of management is a unique blend of the two styles above, that captures the advantages of both such that the risks offset each other and minimize the risk of the total portfolio. To achieve these objectives, the portfolio is structured along two distinct tiers.

Tier I of Active Bond Portfolio Management.   An actively managed strategic tier is one in which maturities, sectors, and quality are altered according to the interest rate expectations. Maturity shifts are made in small increments. The emphasis is on averaging into interest rate peaks or troughs, not trying to time them exactly. This tier is managed to achieve returns that are comparable to a long-term bond market index during **bull market phases,** and to prevent excessive loss of capital during **bear market phases.**

Tier II of Active Bond Portfolio Management.   This involves a core of fixed income securities, carefully selected after simulations of historical cycles such that the return over full market cycles should be better than the long-term bond indexes, with volatility of these securities considerably less. The purpose of the core is to anchor the risk-return characteristics of the accounts in a range acceptable to most pension clients and to minimize the negative effects of errors in interest rate forecasts.

In tailoring an account to the specific risk-return parameters of an individual client, the mix of tier I and tier II can be altered. This style attempts to capture the benefits from market timing but recognizes the risks involved by subjecting only tier I of the portfolio to those risks. In addition, tier II, or the "**core portfolio,**" is constructed to anchor the risk-return characteristics of the total portfolio. The core portfolio is so selected that the characteristics are not adjusted with the interest rate cycle; rather it must be adjusted only if there is a secular change in the trend of interest rates. The core portfolio is primarily a portfolio that is active, where within certain predetermined characteristics, value is sought. Core portfolio offsets some of the risks of market timing without sacrificing return.

The three **active management strategies** discussed above are utilized by most active bond managers. Another style that gained some popularity has been a strategy emphasizing securities with **active sinking funds.** This strategy attempts to "collect" a high percentage of the amount outstanding of low-coupon securities with active sinking funds. The strategy takes advantage of the contractual nature of sinking funds, which creates a demand for securities with active sinking funds. The thrust of this strategy is that the investors controlling a very large percentage of the amount outstanding can demand a price close to par, since the issuer has to retire bonds. The strategy tends to reduce the volatility of the return and, in a secularly rising interest rate environment, has also provided very competitive rates of return.

Risks involved with this strategy are:

1. To control the issue, the portfolio is largely concentrated in **smaller size issues,** and the average **quality** of the portfolio is generally low.

2. The **liquidity of the portfolio** is poor because the expected demand is from the issuer who only retires certain specified bonds each year.

3. Since the success of the portfolio depends on the extent of **control over the amount outstanding,** the strategy can be followed by only a limited number of managers. This is normally not a serious problem unless the portfolio is illiquid, as was discussed earlier.

4. If the **secular trend in interest rates** changes, the attractiveness of such a strategy is further diminished.

All the active management styles discussed have one thing in common. Generally, their **turnover rates** are higher than those of managed equity portfolios. The nature of turnover in actively managed bond portfolios needs explanation. **Turnover in bond portfolios** can be classified in two broad categories.

Strategic Turnover.   This usually refers to **trading activity** resulting from the **strategy** representing the **style of management.** For example, in the market timing strategy, it would represent maturity, sector, and quality shifts in the portfolio resulting from interest rate expectations. Since bond market strategies are not generally **issue oriented** but rather are **sector oriented,** strategic turnover could at times be large (this is an important distinction, which makes turnover in bond portfolios larger than in equity portfolios) simply because large sector moves are not uncommon.

Tactical Trading.   This generally refers to the **"arbitrages"** or the **"substitution swaps."** Bond markets are not efficient because they are **dealer-quoted markets** and because of the simultaneous existence of participants with different time horizons and different tax rates. This inefficiency presents opportunities to alert bond managers. The extent to which this form of trading is utilized is a matter of investment philosophy and should be discussed between the bond manager and the plan sponsor. Tactical swapping done in a manner consistent with the overall strategy can generally add value.

Finally, turnover rate in bond portfolio is so misunderstood that it is computed in many different ways, and care should be exercised in interpreting the statistics.

PASSIVE FIXED INCOME MANAGEMENT.   Before we proceed with a discussion of **passive fixed income management,** it may be useful to define passive strategy for fixed income portfolios. For equity portfolios, passive strategy is generally synonymous with **index funds.** Passive strategy requires no special knowledge of the market and is generally a **buy and hold strategy.** Characteristics of fixed income securities are nonstationary, that is, they change with the mere passage of time. Thus no passive strategy in fixed income securities can be strictly a buy and hold strategy and still maintain its characteristics over time. The basic premise of most passive strategies remains the same (i.e., the manager claims to have no special knowledge of the market). The transactions are made in a very calculated, systematic manner without regard to market levels. Passive strategy in bonds \is more stable than active management strategies.

Index Funds.   The first and most obvious form of passive strategy is one of indexing. **Bond index funds** are commonly created to mirror any of the three bond indexes, namely, the Salomon Brothers Index, the Lehman Brothers Kuhn Loeb Index, and the customized type.

The **Salomon Brothers Index** is the oldest and most widely used index for measuring rates of return from the **corporate bond market.** Exhibit 3 is a summary of the characteristics of these indexes as prepared by Salomon Brothers personnel. It should be recognized that all indexes are long-term indexes.

The **Lehman Brothers Kuhn Loeb Index** is a series designed by the research staffs at Lehman Brothers Kuhn Loeb. A definition of each component of this index appears in Exhibit 4.

With the exception of the long-term, quality bond index and the GNMA Pass-Through index (described later), all other indices have an intermediate-term section of 1–10 years and a long-term section of 10 or more years. When a **rating change** on a security takes place, the issue remains for the month in its prior rating class and the following month moves to its new rating class. Also, if bonds are called, they leave the index at the call price at the end of the month.

The **GNMA Pass-Through Index** measures the total returns of pools backed by 30 year, single-family mortgages. The index, in addition to price and income changes, includes the principal repayments both scheduled and unscheduled.

The inability of the major bond market indexes to truly represent desired risk-return characteristics of funds has led many managers to attempt to create **customized indexes.** Such an index is usually created with bond market sectors that accurately represent the long-term needs of the plan. In a sense, **the index is the baseline portfolio for the fund.**

After the index has been decided on, there are a number of ways to create an **index fund.** Generally, creation of any index fund suggests transactions to maintain the portfolio such

EXHIBIT 3 SUMMARY OF SALOMON BROTHERS BOND INDEXES AS OF JANUARY 1, 1980

	High-Grade Corporate Index	Single-A Corporate Index	Composite High-Grade and Single-A Corporate Index
Minimum maturity	1992	1992	1992
Average maturity	December 15, 2004	August 7, 2002	January 21, 2004
Average Coupon (%)	8.042	8.415	8.185
Weightings (%)			
Utilities	60.73	62.54	61.42
Industrials	27.78	32.68	29.65
Financials (including banks)	11.49	4.78	8.93
Total par amount outstanding (billions)	$83.45	$50.73	$134.18
Quality groups	AAA/AA	A	AAA/AA/A
Minimum size outstanding (millions)	$25	$25	$25
Range of coupons monitored	3¼–11¾	4¼–12¾	3¼–12¾
Total market sectors monitored	62	31	93
Total utility market sectors monitored	39	20	59
AAA utility sectors	19	—	19
AA utility sectors	20	—	20
A utility sectors	—	20	20
Total industrial market sectors monitored	14	8	22
AAA industrial sectors	7	—	7
AA industrial sectors	7	—	7
A industrial sectors	—	8	8
Total financial market sectors monitored	9	3	12
AAA financial sectors	4	—	4
AA financial sectors	5	—	5
A financial sectors	—	3	3

Source: Salomon Brothers, New York.

EXHIBIT 4   THE LEHMAN BROTHERS KUHN LOEB BOND INDEXES

DEFINITIONS

The Lehman Brothers Kuhn Loeb Bond Index is comprised of all publicly issued, fixed-rate, non-convertible, domestic debt of the three major corporate classifications: industrial, utility and financial. Bonds included have a rating of at least Baa by Moody's Investors Service, BBB by Standard & Poor's Corporation or, in the case of bank bonds not rated by either Moody's or Standard & Poor's, BBB by Fitch Investors Service. Only bonds with a minimum outstanding principal amount of $1,000,000 and a minimum maturity of one year are included. All pass-through issues are excluded.

The Lehman Brothers Kuhn Loeb Government/Agency Bond Index is comprised of all publicly issued, non-convertible, domestic debt of the U.S. Government or any agency thereof, quasi-Federal corporation, or corporate debt guaranteed by the U.S. Government. Only bonds with a minimum outstanding principal amount of $1,000,000 and a minimum maturity of one year are included. All pass-through issues are excluded.

The Lehman Brothers Kuhn Loeb Government/Corporate Bond Index is comprised of all the issues in both the Government/Agency Bond Index and the Lehman Brothers Kuhn Loeb Bond Index.

The Lehman Brothers Kuhn Loeb Long-Term, High-Quality Bond Index is comprised of all Aaa- or Aa-rated issues contained in the Lehman Brothers Kuhn Loeb Long-Term Bond Index plus the Long-Term Government/Agency Bond Index.

The Lehman Brothers Kuhn Loeb GNMA Pass-Through Index is comprised of all GNMA single family, 30 year pools with 6½, 7¼, 7½, 8, 8¼, 8½, 9, 9½, and 10 percent coupons.

The Lehman Brothers Kuhn Loeb Yankee Bond Index is comprised of all SEC-registered, publicly issued, non-convertible, debt of foreign Sovereign Governments, Municipalities, Government Agencies with Sovereign guarantee and International Agencies, which were previously subject to Interest Equalization Tax, issued since its elimination in January 1974. Bonds or notes included are all rated Aaa by Moody's Investors Service and/or AAA by Standard & Poor's Corporation.   Not included are Canadian issues, issues of International Agencies such as the International Bank for Reconstruction and Development, The Inter-American Development Bank, and Asian Development Bank and issues of Developing Countries; all these issues were granted specific exemption from Interest Equalization Tax.

All of the indices have an intermediate-term section of one to ten years and a long-term section of ten or more years with the following exception. The Long-Term, High Quality Bond Index and the GNMA Pass-Through Index are not subdivided.

Source: Lehman Brothers Kuhn Loeb, New York.

that it includes the market proportion of all outstanding issues in the index. In the case of bond portfolios this presents problems. Two main problems are:

1. The number of issues in most indexes is very large, suggesting excessive transactions and applicability only to very large portfolios.

2. The large number of new issues coming to the market presents unique problems for the **index fund manager in fixed income securities.** Such a manager cannot risk waiting until **after the pricing** for fear of not being able to participate in the deal or having to bid up the prices in the attempt to acquire bonds after pricing, if the

deal is successful and attractive. However, in case there is interest in all new issues, the market will reflect this enthusiasm, resulting in an unattractive pricing for the deal. In either case, the prospects are not good.

To circumvent both problems, a second approach suggests **breaking the index into cells** consisting of bonds with similar characteristics, then appropriately selecting a set of bonds to represent each cell. Perhaps the most obvious way of doing this would be to compute the average characteristics of each cell and find a set of bonds with similar average characteristics.

This strategy, however, would be grossly inaccurate, because, as has been discussed earlier, it is easy to demonstrate that two groups of bonds with the same **average maturity** could have a different set of bonds in each group, and so the response of each group to interest rates would be different. Furthermore, the relationship between average maturity and return is not linear. The only solution to the problem is to divide the index into the largest **number of cells that is practical,** depending on the size of the portfolio. An attempt should be made to select subjectively securities that best represent each cell. Care should be exercised to ensure that all characteristics, including risk of the securities, are consistent with each cell.

Passive Strategies Emphasizing Constant Maturity.   Strategies in this category include **barbell, laddered,** and **buy long and hold.** Academicians have done much research in this area, and readers are referred to "Bond Portfolio Strategies, Returns and Skewness" (Fogler, Groves, and Richardson, *Journal of Financial Quantitative Analysis,* March 1977) for details. The **barbell strategy** emphasizes only bonds with long maturities and short maturities, excluding all intermediate terms. A **laddered maturity** strategy, however, favors investment of a proportion in all maturity instruments. Both strategies rebalance automatically to ensure their composition. The authors report that when using the holding period returns criterion, the laddered strategy dominated (outperformed) the barbell strategy on a **risk-adjusted basis.** They conclude that perhaps the earlier results conflicted because many earlier studies ignored capital gains and losses when these were unrealized, ignored transactions costs, or assumed certain cash flows that favored barbell strategies.

Most empirical results in this area are not conclusive. There is only one rationale for any of these strategies. If it is determined that the objectives of the portfolio are best met by any of these strategies over the investment horizon and the manager further determines that the risk of adding value by deviating from the strategy is not consistent with the objective, then perhaps the strategy could be employed. All such strategies have different characteristics, and it would be impossible to make a fair comparison.

Immunization.   In this investment strategy a portfolio is structured to achieve a **targeted rate of return** for a given holding period regardless of interest rate fluctuations. Immunization relies on the principle of **matching the average duration of the portfolio assets** to the **average duration of liabilities.** It can be demonstrated that by so structuring the portfolio, reinvestment risk is eliminated and therefore the rate of return over the horizon is assured.

PRIVATE PLACEMENTS.   The **private placement market** has emerged as a powerful force in the realm of corporate financing. The key to the emergence of this market is the ability of issuers to issue debt that is exempt from the **SEC Disclosure Act of 1933** as long as debt is sold to a limited group of sophisticated investment professionals, knowledgeable in corporate financing.

An excellent detailed description of the market is presented by Davey (*Private Placements, Practice and Prospects*, Conference Board Information Bulletin No. 32, January 1979), who shows that the choice of private or public offering ultimately is made after careful consideration of several issues, summarized below.

The **market characteristics of the private placement issue** reflect the tendency of the issuers to consider the size of the offering and the supply demand factors affecting the public versus the private markets at the time of issuance. It was generally believed that for large offerings the public market was more desirable, whereas private placement market was to be preferred for small offerings. This perception, however, is changing as the growth of the private placement market has accommodated fairly large offerings of up to $250 million. It is still true, however, that the public bond market is more receptive to larger size ($50 million or more) offerings because of its liquidity in the **secondary market.**

Since only a few **sophisticated investors** participate in the market, the issuer can find them more receptive to an innovative financing scheme. For similar reasons, even though covenant provisions are restrictive, it is easier to modify a covenant than to make changes in an indenture for a public offering. Furthermore, the small number of investors also allows for raising funds rather quickly compared to public markets. Finally, despite the **interest rate premium,** some issuers may find the process less expensive than a public offering.

From an investor's point of view, the added covenants provide an extra level of comfort and protection. They also provide for periodic review of the company. **Private placement buyers** claim that the lack of liquidity is compensated by the incremental yield. Most investors in the private placement market are yield buyers and prefer to deal in lower quality, where the structure of the covenants becomes a key element and the incremental yield justifies the lack of liquidity. It should be recognized, however, that loan agreements can become extremely complex. An experienced legal staff generally is needed to review and structure the agreements.

GUARANTEED INVESTMENT CONTRACTS.   During the period 1976–1980, guaranteed investment contracts (GICs) became a major force in fixed income markets. As the yield levels rose in the marketplace, investors were attracted to GICs because of the certainty they offered. It should be pointed out that the GIC is not an investment or **portfolio management strategy** but rather a **marketing strategy.** It is a marketing strategy employed generally by **insurance companies** to attract **pension assets,** when fund managers are seeking a guaranteed rate in an increasingly volatile and uncertain investment environment. The portfolio management strategy behind GICs varies among institutions that bear the investment risk of having a rate of return from the portfolio different from the guaranteed rate of return. Generally, behind GICs is either a **private placement portfolio** or an **immunized portfolio.**

From an investor's point of view, the guarantee is backed by the assets of the insurer's general account and has equal claim on the assets. The plans are offered by life insurance companies to qualified pension and profit-sharing plans. The contracts vary in their complexity, and each contract is generally structured to the needs of the investor. The safety of interest guarantee contracts is regulated by the various **state insurance departments.** In analyzing the risk of a contract, an investor must investigate the credit-worthiness of the insurance company.

QUANTITATIVE TECHNIQUES

PORTFOLIO SIMULATIONS.   Of all the quantitative tools employed for bond portfolio management, simulation is perhaps the procedure most widely used among investment managers. The procedure allows the manager to identify the sources of return from his portfolio based on the **interest rate forecast.** There are a number of commercially available models, and many brokerage houses offer some intricate and sophisticated models that cover this aspect.

The more sophisticated models allow the investor to enter the interest rate forecast. Since forecasting is not yet an exact science, the better models allow the investor to enter a range of possible interest rate forecasts, with a range of probabilities associated with each scenario. Also associated with each scenario is an estimate of change in yield spreads for **quality, coupon, and sector.** Change in interest rates has the major impact on most portfolio returns. The incremental return, however, for change in **quality spread, coupon spread, and sector** can also be significant. Many of the more sophisticated models provide an analysis of the returns broken down by the contribution of various components. Also, in some models that maintain a historical data base, the user has the option of entering historical spreads that may have existed at the forecasted levels. This added capability provides the user with some reference at which point the spreads can be adjusted to reflect personal biases.

A few models have added capabilities to **optimize portfolios.** This feature allows the investor to determine how close the structure of the portfolio is to the long-term objectives of the portfolio. Also, by allowing for some sensitivity analysis, most of these models permit the investor to determine the more sensitive **constraints of the objective function.** Furthermore, given a universe of bonds, the investor can optimize the portfolio such that the model will suggest the transactions that would lead to a portfolio that best provides for the needs of the plan.

As should be intuitively obvious, a model is critically dependent on the **interest rate forecast.** The "optimum" portfolio is also a function of the interest rate forecast. The most useful function the model serves is quantification of the impact of various strategies on the interest rate forecast and allowing for an explicit determination of the effect of different interest rate forecasts on the strategy. The **sensitivity analysis** function of the model is perhaps the most useful one because it allows the investors to test the effects of all their assumptions on portfolio returns and risk.

PERFORMANCE MEASUREMENT.   Existing performance measurement techniques for fixed income portfolios are inadequate. Perhaps the most important reason, as discussed earlier, is our inability to define an **adequate risk measure for bond portfolios.** Williamson explores those issues in depth in his section "Performance Measurement" in this *Handbook.*

Perhaps the most publicized fixed income performance measurement technique is one designed by **Frank Russell and Co.** The objective of the technique is to decompose the return from bond portfolios into the following four components:

Yield-to-maturity effect.
Interest rate effect.
Sector-quality effect.
Residual effect.

Before defining the four effects, it is useful to define the index, which consists of all issues in the **Telestate Pricing Tapes** with a minimum quality of Baa or BBB and a minimum of $50 million par value outstanding. The purpose of the index is to allow for a framework to compare returns from the portfolio. Also, it is used to determine the **sector-quality effect.**

In computing a return from the portfolio for a specified period, the portfolio is assumed to be static as of the beginning of the period. Next, for each security the four effects are computed for the portfolio.

Yield-to-Maturity Effect.   This is the component of return if **no market change occurs.** It is the result of accrued **coupon payments, price change** due to amortization of the difference from par value, the "**roll-effect,**" which affects the yield to maturity by way of the slope of the yield curve with the passage of time.

Interest Rate Effect.   For each security, this is computed by assuming that the yield on a security over the measuring period moves precisely the same amount as a **Treasury security with the same maturity.** The return from this component assumes no change in the sector quality spread.

Sector-Quality Effect.   This is computed by determining the sector-quality matrix for the index. For each security in the index, the yield to maturity and the interest rate effect are calculated. The difference between the **total return for the security** and the **yield-to-maturity effect** and the **interest rate effect** is the basis for determining the **sector quality effect.** Next, a matrix with each row representing the seven major sectors (corporate, utilities, financial, telephone, foreign, GNMA, agencies) and four columns representing quality (AAA, AA, A, Baa) is constructed. Each cell of the matrix is the average of the sector-quality effect of each security belonging to the particular cell. The entry in each cell then becomes the sector-quality return for each issue of that classification held in the portfolio being measured.

Residual Effect.   The difference between the total return from the security and the three factors just discussed is the **residual.**

Frank Russell Index.   The **performance of a portfolio** can be analyzed in terms of its four components and can be further compared against the **component returns of the Frank Russell Index.** Perhaps the best use of the model is to analyze the components of return over an extended period. This may allow the plan sponsor to identify the strengths of the manager and perhaps conclude whether the manager is capable of delivering the style of management promised by him.

There are two primary drawbacks of the system, which could introduce errors in the process and make the validity of results questionable. First, pricing of bond holdings is a serious problem in the industry; this model is critically dependent on the pricing tapes produced by **Telestat.** Second, sector-quality breakdown should be further classified by maturity. The assumption that sector-quality effect does not change with maturity is not valid. In all fairness, however, the concept is a useful one and perhaps would benefit from some refinements.

VALUATION MODELS.   There has been some recent interest by academicians in precisely **computing the value of bonds** and all their features. This has been an evolutionary process resulting in the application of some **option valuation techniques** to various features of bonds. One such model has been developed by **Barr Rosenberg and Associates.** Briefly, the model arrives at a **fitted bond price** by investigating two distinct characteristics of bonds. The first characteristic is the stream of payments, both **future coupons** and **principal payments**, including redemption value and any sinking fund purchase. The second involves call, sinking fund, conversion, liquidity, default risk, and current yield characteristics.

To properly discount the stream of payments, the model determines the **term structure of interest rates** of the **government bond market.** This provides for a consistent set of **spot and forward rates** used to discount all streams of future payments for all securities. For the second set of characteristics, a precise present value of these features called "**indexes** of value" is determined. The model next recognizes that since the market may not be valuing these features in the same precise manner, the way the market is valuing these indexes must be determined. The combination of the **indexes of value** and the **market assessment of value** determines the value of the feature in the model.

The innovation in the model is the determination of indexes of value. Most of the features described can be viewed as options. For example, **default risk** of a bondholder can be viewed as a stockholder's **put option.** If the firm encounters problems, the stockholders have the option to **put the company** to the bondholders and walk away. Similarly, **convertibles** are clearly the option of bondholders to convert to equity. Both these options depend on the value of the firm. A model using **option theory** for determining the future of the firm allows it to arrive at an estimate of the two characteristics.

Call and sinking fund features are similarly viewed as the option of the issuer to either call or sink the bonds. In this instance, however, the value of the option is more a function of uncertainty in interest rates. A stochastic model for interest rates is then used to determine the index of value for these options. Once an index of value for each bond is determined, the market assessment factor across all bonds is determined. The two values together provide a value for the feature, which together with the present value of all payments constitute the **fitted price of a bond.** The valuation model provides the basis for the bond model. The valuation model is then extended to compute **future holding period returns** (similar to other models discussed earlier by specifying both the future term structure and if necessary any changes in future value of the features).

The model forces the investor to investigate thoroughly each option in a bond indenture and analyze precisely its value. Furthermore, by using forward and spot rates, the model mathematically discounts the future streams with fewer assumptions. Since the model is new, its accuracy and usefulness are yet to be determined.

FUTURE DEVELOPMENTS

Looking ahead, it is reasonable to assume that the fixed income markets will witness more innovative methods of financing. It will be a challenge to bond portfolio managers to analyze new features of more traditional offerings and in some instances new financings. Types of financing developed within the past few years that have been received with enthusiasm and are expected to continue in the decade ahead are (1) floating rate securities and (2) mortgage-related securities.

FLOATING RATE SECURITIES.   In response to **rising inflation and interest rates** and reluctance by investors to accept long-term, fixed coupon securities, an array of floating rate, or **adjustable rate,** securities with varying optional features emerged in the U.S. markets during the late 1970s. The trend had originally developed in the European markets for similar reasons. The issuer attempts to reduce his reliance on money markets by **locking in financing** for a long term. In doing so, he reduces financing costs but does assume interest rate risk. The lenders, on the other hand, find the scheme attractive because of its **inflation-adjusting features.**

The arrangements for some of these publicly traded **floating rate securities** are very complex and have to be reviewed individually. However, most are issued at a **spread** of either 3- or 6-month Treasury bills, adjusted periodically, with the spread changing over time. Other features include options on the part of the holder to sell the bonds back to the issuer at par. The issuer may be able to call the bond, or there may be options on the part of the holder to **convert to a long-term debenture.**

Depending on the issuer and the features attached to a particular security, the spread against 3- or 6-month Treasury bills is determined. At the time of issuance of this type of security it was believed by some that all "floaters" at the time of change in coupon should trade near par. There is no reason to expect securities with different features to all **trade at par** around the coupon change date. Furthermore, after initially trading quite well in early 1979, floating rate securities lost their defensive appeal later in the year as they began to trade at **substantial discounts.** It became critical to evaluate the characteristics of all features of these securities. There are a number of ways to do it. Perhaps the simplest is to project interest rates and discount all expected cash flows from the security in the projected interest rate environment. The **Fixed Income Portfolio Service,** offered by Harris Trust Bank in Chicago in the paper "Valuation of Floating Rate Securities," covers this topic well, noting that three factors should be considered:

1. Transaction cost.
2. Credit risk.
3. Formula for adjusting spread against Treasury bills with time.

This area is relatively new, and valuation procedures are quite subjective. However dramatic growth can be expected, just as in Europe. As new innovative schemes are developed, valuation procedures will have to improve. The majority of **floating rate issues,** so far, have been issued by financial institutions that can **hedge** against uncertain interest costs by putting proceeds into **floating rate earning assets.**

MORTGAGE-RELATED SECURITIES. To reduce reliance solely on the **thrift industry** to provide for the capital needs of the **single-family housing market,** the government and the private sector have taken steps to strengthen the single-family **secondary mortgage market** by introducing the **mortgage-backed pass-through security.** The market for pass-through securities has increased dramatically to over $80 billion dollars. There are essentially three types of pass-through security, each representing an undivided fractional interest in a pool of single-family mortgages that provide for monthly payments of interest and principal. The principal payment includes the scheduled portions as determined by the amortization schedule as well as unscheduled prepayments.

Government National Mortgage Association (GNMA). GNMA pass-through securities represent fractional undivided interest in pools representing Federal Housing Administration and Veterans Administration mortgages. Furthermore, the certificate is also backed by the full faith and credit of the U.S. government. The guarantee by the federal government has made GNMAs the most widely accepted pass-through security.

Federal Home Loan Mortgage Corp. (FHLMC). This corporation, created by the **Emergency Home Finance Act of 1970** issued "Freddie Mac" **pass-through securities** representing undivided interests in pools of primarily **single-family conventional mortgages.** These securities do not carry the guarantee of the federal government; rather, payment of principal and interest is guaranteed by the Federal Home Loan Mortgage Corp., which is in turn owned by regional **Federal Home Loan Banks.**

Conventional Mortgage Pass-Through Certificates. These instruments, issued by commercial banks and savings and loan associations, were introduced in 1977. The securities are backed neither by government nor by the sponsoring financial institution. The credit of the securities is a direct function of the quality of mortgages.

The Bank of America and First Federal Savings and Loan of Chicago were able to pool mortgages from their own portfolios and generate funds for reinvestment in new housing.

Cash Flow Patterns of GNMAs. The complex cash flow patterns are important to the understanding of the GNMA markets. The cash flow of GNMAs has three components.

> Coupon income.
> Scheduled amortization principal payments.
> Unscheduled principal prepayments.

Since the third component is unknown, the measures of computing **risk and return for GNMA** are necessarily **an approximation.** Most approximations attempt to estimate the speed and timing of the unscheduled principal prepayments. The speed and timing in the industry is measured in terms of FHA experience, specifically, the results of a study conducted by FHA to examine prepayment as a function of age. An **average GNMA pool** is then assumed to be prepaying at 100% FHA experience rate, which refers to a schedule determined by the study. The speed of prepayment for most mortgages can then be defined relative to the average FHA experience.

There are two commonly used methods for computing returns of GNMAs.

1. Most tables are constructed using **"GNMA yield"** or "yield to 12-year average life." This technique first assumes normal interest and scheduled principal payments for 12 years with no prepayments; then all remaining principal is assumed to be paid back at the end of the twelfth year. The use of this yield is justified because 100% FHA experience corresponds to roughly a 12-year average life. Although this is the most commonly quoted yield in the trading environment, the errors in this methodology are numerous. First, most GNMAs do not prepay at 100% FHA. Second, pools with different ages and different speeds are all computed to give the same result.

2. A more popular method is called **cash flow yield.** This is a calculation based on some specified speed and using a constant FHA experience for prepayments over the life of the mortgage. The cash flow patterns are more realistic, however, the computation is extremely dependent on the specified speed, which is also at best an approximation based on historical evidence. This methodology is clearly the better of the two, but it ignores the fact that prepayment experience is not necessarily constant.

Perhaps the best risk measure for GNMAs is computing **duration** using some constant prepayment experience (consistent with the "cash flow" yield computation). The supply and demand characteristics of **mortgage-related securities** also tend to be cyclical and are important considerations in making value judgments on these securities.

REFERENCES

Altman, E. I., "Computerized Bond Ratings," *Basis Point* (Equitable Life Assurance), New York, Fall 1979.

Altman, E. I., Haldeman, R., and Narayanan, P., "Zeta Analysis," *Journal of Banking and Finance,* Vol. 1, June 1977.

Bernstein, P. L., Ed., *The Theory and Practice of Bond Portfolio Management*, Institutional Investor Books, New York, 1977.

Davey, P. J., *Private Placements: Practice and Prospects*, Conference Board Information Bulletin No. 32, New York, 1979.

Fogler, H. R., Groves, W. A., and Richardson, J., "Bond Portfolio Strategies, Returns and Skewness: A Note," *Journal of Financial and Quantitative Analysis*, March 1977.

Financial Analysts Federation, *Proceedings of Seminors on Bond Portfolio Management*, New York, 1977.

Harris Trust Bank, "Valuation of Floating Rate Securities," Chicago, 1977.

Ibbotson, R., and Sinquefield, R., *Stocks, Bonds, Bills and Inflation: Historical Returns (1926–1978)*, Financial Analysts Research Foundation, Charlottesville, VA, 1979.

Leibowitz, M., *Total Return Management*, Salomon Brothers, New York, 1979.

———, "An Analytic Approach to the Bond Market," *Financial Analysts Handbook* (Summer M. Levince, Ed.), Dow Jones-Irwin, Homewood, IL, 1975.

Leibowitz, M., and Homer S., *Inside the Yield Book*, Prentice-Hall, Englewood Cliffs, NJ, Institute of Finance Publication, 1972.

Macaulay, F. R., *Some Theoretical Problems Suggested by the Movements of Interest Rates, Bonds Yields, and Stock Prices in the United States Since 1865*, National Bureau of Economic Research, New York, 1938.

Malkiel, B. G., *The Term Structure of Interest Rates*, Princeton University Press, Princeton, NJ, 1966.

Meyer, K., "Forecasting Interest Rates: Key to Active Bond Management," *Financial Analysts Journal*, November–December 1978.

Sharpe, W., *Investments*, Prentice-Hall, Englewood Cliffs, NJ, 1978.

Spence, B., Graudberg, J. Y., and Lynch, J. J., Jr., *Standard Securities Calculation Methods*, Securities Industry Association Publications, New York, 1973.

SPECIALIZED FIXED INCOME SECURITY STRATEGIES

CONTENTS

THE CONCEPT OF IMMUNIZATION	3
Immunization and Reinvestment Risk	4
The Macaulay Duration	6
Duration Equivalents of Zero-Coupon Bonds	8
A View of Immunization Over Time	9
DURATION AND CONTROL OF VOLATILITY RISK	11
OTHER RISK CONTROL STRATEGIES	14
Immunization Under Multiple Rate Changes	17
Rebalancing Using Duration	18
Rebalancing as a Proxy for a Zero-Coupon Bond Over Time	20
An example with declining rates	20
An example with rising rates	23
General sequences of parallel shifts	25

Improved Rebalancing Using Horizon Volatility	25
THE YIELD CURVE CASE	26
Portfolio Rebalancing Along the Yield Curve	26
The Rolling Yield	27
Parallel shifts of the yield curve	30
Parallel movements of actual yield curves	30
Simulation tests of the YTM target	32
Simulation test of the rolling yield target	33
Changing yield curve shapes	33
Simulation of actual yield curve sequences	34
THE INTRICACIES OF REBALANCING	36
VULNERABILITY OF ANY IMMUNIZATION PLAN	37

SPECIALIZED FIXED INCOME SECURITY STRATEGIES

Martin L. Leibowitz

In recent years, the marketplace has developed a series of approaches to specialized fixed income portfolio management that represent fairly major departures from tradition in both technique and motivation. Fundamentally, most of the techniques involve an effort to obtain better control of the "risk" associated with a particular fixed income portfolio posture. Several different definitions of "the risk to be avoided" are implied in these new techniques. In some cases, the risk is the simple **volatility risk** that has been associated with the **modern portfolio theory (MPT)** approach to equity portfolios. In other cases, the risk is the uncertainty associated with realizing a specific target return over a defined period of time, usually 3–10 years. In the latter category, the most highly articulated and studied technique is **bond immunization.** To understand these and other specialized risk control approaches, this section focuses on the concept of immunization and the technical underpinnings that make it applicable in the bond market. An effort is made to show how the concept of **duration** and related techniques can be applied in risk control strategies that are more general than the narrow immunization framework.

THE CONCEPT OF IMMUNIZATION

Immunization is a specialized technique for **constructing and rebalancing** a **bond portfolio** to achieve a specified return target. The idea is to closely approach or exceed this return target in the face of **changes** in **interest rates,** even radical changes in interest rates. In other words, one is trying to "immunize" the portfolio against the "disease" of changing rates. This is not a new concept. It was introduced in 1952 by F. M. Redington in a paper in the (British) *Journal of the Institute of Actuaries*. In the three decades since its introduction, the theory of immunization has been the subject of a wide range of research studies that have advanced and refined the theoretical foundation underlying bond immunization. (See References and Bibliography for a sampling of the large body of research papers in this area, e.g., Bierwag, Bierwag and Kaufman, Leibowitz, Shedden, and Marshall and Yawitz.)

Much of the material in this section is taken from articles and volumes published by Salomon Brothers, New York, as listed under "References and Bibliography."

Immunization techniques are relevant for many fixed income investment funds that must achieve a well-defined level of realized return over a specified investment period. This need may arise from a variety of motivations. For example, one fund might have a lump-sum liability payment coming due at the end of the period. Another fund may need a relatively well-assured return for actuarial or accounting purposes. Another may have a simple desire to lock up what is thought to be a sufficiently high level of returns. In yet another instance, the fund sponsor may wish to reduce the uncertainty in his overall portfolio by devoting a portion of assets to achieving a specified return over a given period.

It should be noted that immunization in the narrow sense is only one way of achieving the objective of immunization in a broader "risk reduction" sense. There are other routes to this broader goal—**guaranteed investment contracts** (GICs), "matchings" of cash flows against liabilities, and the so-called **R-cubed techniques.**

IMMUNIZATION AND REINVESTMENT RISK.   Since bonds do mature eventually, they tend to provide a certain natural immunity to changing rates, at least over planning periods ending with their maturity. However, there still remains the uncertainty associated with the future rates at which bond coupon payments can be reinvested. It is this **reinvestment risk** that the **portfolio manager** is trying to reduce to even closer tolerances.

For example, when asked to secure a target return over a given period such as 5 years, a portfolio manager might at first respond by selecting a portfolio of bonds having a maturity of 5 years. If these bonds were of sufficiently high grade, the portfolio would essentially be assured of receiving all the **coupon income** due during the 5 years, then the redemption payment in the fifth year. However, coupon income and principal payments are only two of the three sources of return from a bond portfolio. The third source of return is the **interest-on-interest** derived from the reinvestment of coupon income (and/or the rollover of the maturing principal). Since this reinvestment will take place in the interest rate environments that exist at the time of the coupon receipts, there is no way to ensure that one will obtain the amount of interest-on-interest required to achieve the target return.

Exhibit 1 illustrates this point. A 5-year 9% bond will provide $450 of coupon income and $1,000 of maturing principal over its 5-year life. This would amount to an added return of $450 beyond the original $1,000 investment. However, to achieve a 9% compound growth rate in asset value over the 5-year period, the original $1,000 would have to reach a cumulative value of $1,553, which is an incremental dollar return of $553. This $103 gap in return has to be overcome through the accumulation of interest-on-interest. As Exhibit 1 shows, this amount of interest-on-interest will be achieved when coupon reinvestment occurs at the same

EXHIBIT 1   REALIZED RETURN FROM 5-YEAR 9% PAR BOND OVER A 5-YEAR HORIZON

Reinvestment Rate (%)	Coupon Income	Capital Gain	Interest-on-Interest	Total Dollar Return	Realized Compound Yield (%)
0	$450	$0	$ 0	$450	7.57
7	450	0	78	528	8.66
8	450	0	90	540	8.83
9	450	0	103	553	9.00
10	450	0	116	566	9.17
11	450	0	129	579	9.35

9% rate as the bond's original **yield to maturity.** At lower reinvestment rates, the interest-on-interest will be less than the amount required and the growth in asset value will fall somewhat short of the required target value of $1,553.

This reinvestment problem becomes even more severe over longer investment periods. Exhibit 2 shows the total dollar amount and the percentage of the target return that must be achieved through interest-on-interest for various investment periods ranging from 1 to 30 years. This "reinvestment risk" is a major problem in achieving any assured level of target return. However, there are ways of limiting this reinvestment risk. For example, Exhibit 3 shows the total return and cumulative asset value for a 5-year bond over investment horizons ranging from 1 to 5 years. For the periods shorter than 5 years, the bond's price in Exhibit 3 has been determined by the simplistic assumption that the yield to maturity coincides with the indicated reinvestment rate. This set of assumptions corresponds to a scenario where interest rates immediately move to a flat **yield curve** at the level of the indicated reinvestment rate, and remain there throughout the entire investment period.

Exhibit 3 illustrates the well-known facts that over the short term, lower interest rates lead to increased returns through price appreciation, while over the longer term, lower interest rates lead to reduced returns through reduced interest-on-interest. For periods lying between the short term and the longer term, it is not surprising to find these two effects somewhat compensating for each other.

This leads to the question of whether there might be some intermediate point during a bond's life when these **compensating effects** precisely offset each other. Again, from Exhibit 3, we can see that for a 7% reinvestment rate this offset does exist and occurs at 4.13 years. That such an offset point should exist is not, of course, surprising in a situation characterized by two conflicting forces—**reinvestment and capital gains**—with one force growing stronger and the other force growing weaker with time. What may be somewhat more surprising is that with reinvestment rates of 7, 9, and 11%, this offset point occurs at the same 4.13 years. (This is not perhaps intuitively obvious, although it can be readily demonstrated through mathematical analysis.)

In the context of the fund seeking an assured level of return, this finding has great significance. To achieve the guaranteed 9% return over 4.13 years, Exhibit 3 shows that there would be no problem in doing so with the 5-year bond, no matter what reinvestment

EXHIBIT 2 MAGNITUDE OF INTEREST-ON-INTEREST TO ACHIEVE 9% REALIZED COMPOUND YIELD FROM 9% PAR BONDS OF VARIOUS MATURITIES

Maturity (years)	Total Dollar Return	Interest-on-Interest at 9% Reinvestment Rate	Interest-on-Interest (%) of Total Return
1	$ 92	$ 2	2.2%
2	193	13	6.5
3	302	32	10.7
4	422	62	14.7
5	553	103	18.6
7	852	222	26.1
10	1,412	512	36.2
20	4,816	3,016	62.6
30	13,027	10,327	79.3

EXHIBIT 3   REALIZED RETURN FROM A 5-YEAR 9% PAR BOND OVER VARIOUS HORIZON PERIODS

| | Horizon Period (years) | | | |
	1	3	4.13	5
Coupon Income:	$ 90	$270	$372	$450
7% Reinvestment Rate and YTM at Horizon				
Capital gain	$ 68	$ 37	$ 16	$ 0
Interest-on-interest	$ 2	$ 25	$ 51	$ 78
Total dollar return	$160	$331	$439	$528
Realized compound yield	15.43%	9.77%	9.00%	8.66%
9% Reinvestment Rate and YTM at Horizon				
Capital gain	$ 0	$ 0	$ 0	$ 0
Interest-on-interest	$ 2	$ 32	$ 67	$103
Total dollar return	$ 92	$302	$439	$553
Realized compound yield	9.00%	9.00%	9.00%	9.00%
11% Reinvestment Rate and YTM at Horizon				
Capital gain	−$ 63	−$ 35	−$ 16	$ 0
Interest-on-interest	$ 2	$ 40	$ 83	$129
Total dollar return	$ 29	$275	$439	$579
Realized compound yield	2.89%	8.26%	9.00%	9.36%

rates existed (as long as they followed the simplistic "flat yield curve pattern" assumed in the construction of Exhibit 3).

THE MACAULAY DURATION.   This offset effect occurs because the **"duration"** of a 5-year 9% par bond is 4.13 years. This same offset can be achieved over the original 5-year horizon by buying a somewhat longer bond having a maturity of between 6 and 7 years. The precise maturity that gives this "magical" immunization over the 5-year period is determined by seeking a bond whose duration is 5 years.

Duration is a concept that was first proposed by Frederick R. Macaulay (1938). He was searching for a way to characterize the average life of a bond in a way that would reflect the present value of its total cash flow. Exhibit 4 illustrates the dollar value of a level payment stream. The average life of this stream would fall at the simple fulcrum point indicated in the diagram. Exhibit 5 shows a similar level stream, but also illustrates the present value of each of the payments. Macaulay argued that a more appropriate measure of the life of any cash flow would be the average time point of the flow of **present values,** as opposed to simply the flow of raw dollar amounts. Since earlier payments have a higher present value than later ones, this would lead to a fulcrum point that is shorter than the conventionally calculated average life (Exhibit 6). Macaulay used the term ''duration'' to represent this measure of the time to each payment, weighted by the present value of that payment.

Thus a 1-year bill has a duration of 1. A 2-year bill, if you could buy one, would have a duration of 2. **Coupon securities,** however, have durations that are always less than their maturity. As discussed earlier, a 5-year 9% par bond has a duration of 4.13 years. Exhibits 7 and 8 show how the durations of 9% par bonds grow with increasing maturity. Because of the way this curve bends at the longer maturities, it turns out that durations of 10 or 11 are about the longest values that can be obtained in the market. At higher rate levels such as the 12% rate level shown in Exhibit 8, there is an even further **shrinkage** in the maximum duration values. Macaulay defined duration in this way because he felt that it represented a more logical measure of a bond's life. At the time, he failed to recognize that the duration

EXHIBIT 4   AVERAGE LIFE OF PAYMENT STREAM

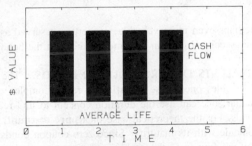

EXHIBIT 5   PRESENT VALUE OF PAYMENT STREAM

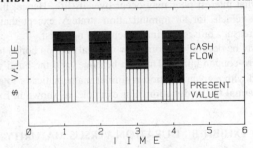

EXHIBIT 6   DURATION OF PAYMENT STREAM

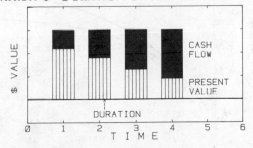

EXHIBIT 7   DURATION OF VARIOUS BONDS, ALL
PRICED TO YIELD 9%

Maturity (years)	Coupon (%)			
	0	7.5	9.0	10.50
1	1.00	0.98	0.98	0.98
2	2.00	1.89	1.87	1.86
3	3.00	2.74	2.70	2.66
4	4.00	3.51	3.45	3.38
5	5.00	4.23	4.13	4.05
7	7.00	5.50	5.34	5.20
10	10.00	7.04	6.80	6.59
20	20.00	9.96	9.61	9.35
30	30.00	11.05	10.78	10.59
100	100.00	11.61	11.61	11.61

also had another, perhaps even more valuable, property—it served as a gauge of the percentage price change associated with an incremental move in the bond's yield.

DURATION EQUIVALENTS OF ZERO-COUPON BONDS.   The combination of the foregoing properties enables one to use **duration** to relate complex cash flows to simple cash flows. In particular, one can use the duration concept to find real bonds that behave like zero-coupon bonds. For the theoretical case of a **pure discount, zero-coupon bond,** the duration will coincide with its maturity. Since zero-coupon bonds have no cash flows before maturity, they are free from the problem of coupon reinvestment. A 5-year zero-coupon bond priced to yield 9% would always provide the targeted 9% return over its maturity period, no matter what interest rates may occur over its life. Hence, the zero-coupon bond would be the ideal vehicle for an immunization strategy except that beyond the 1-year maturity range of Treasury bills, such instruments do not exist.

It would obviously be desirable to somehow use real coupon bonds to obtain some of the characteristics of zero-coupon bonds. This can be done, and the bond's duration is the key link. A coupon bond with a given duration is similar mathematically to a **zero-coupon bond having a maturity equal to the duration.** For example, as shown in Exhibit 7, a 9% target

EXHIBIT 8   DURATION VERSUS MATURITY

EXHIBIT 9   REALIZED RETURN OVER A 5-YEAR HORIZON FROM A 9% PAR BOND HAVING A 5-YEAR DURATION[a]

Reinvestment Rate and Yield-to-maturity at Horizon (%)	Coupon Income	Capital Gain	Interest-on-Interest	Total Dollar Return	Realized Compound Yield (%)
7	$450	$25	$ 78	$553	9.00
8	450	13	90	553	9.00
9	450	0	103	553	9.00
10	450	− 13	116	553	9.00
11	450	− 26	129	553	9.00

[a]For illustrative purposes, this table is based on the somewhat artificial case of a bond that can be purchased free of accrued interest.

return over a 5-year period could be achieved by either a 5-year maturity zero-coupon discount bond at a 9% yield rate or a 6.7-year 9% par bond. Both these bonds have the same duration—5 years. Thus the first step in a simple immunization procedure is to construct a portfolio having a duration corresponding to the length of the planning horizon.

Returning to the original objective of providing an assured 9% target return over a 5-year period, one should choose a 6.7-year bond having a **duration** of 5 years, as opposed to a maturity of 5 years. Exhibit 9 shows how such a bond will indeed achieve the growth in overall asset value required to provide the 9% return compounded semiannually. In the face of interest rate changes, this 9% growth is maintained through the compensating increases (or declines) in the **interest-on-interest** and the **capital gain** components of return.

A VIEW OF IMMUNIZATION OVER TIME.   Immunization can be viewed as a dynamic process over time through the illustration shown in Exhibits 10, 11, and 12. Exhibit 10 shows the growth in value from a 9% par bond (of any maturity) under the assumption that

EXHIBIT 10   ASSET GROWTH FROM 9% PAR BOND WITH ALL RATES CONSTANT AT 9%

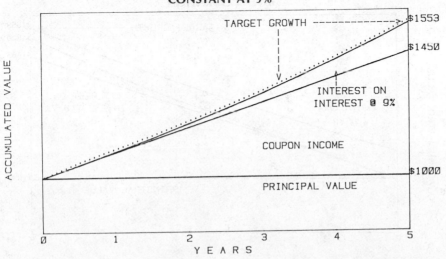

EXHIBIT 11   SHORTFALL FROM 7% REINVESTMENT

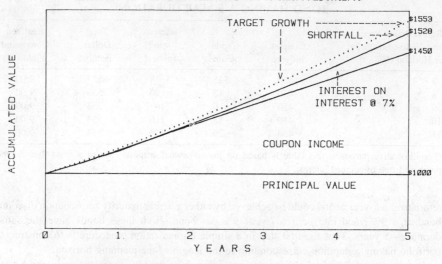

rates remain constant at 9%. Now suppose rates dropped to 7%. Without any consideration of capital gains, Exhibit 11 shows how the reduced reinvestment income would result in a shortfall in interest-on-interest and a consequent failure to meet the 9% target return. Exhibit 12 shows the capital gain associated with a 6.7-year 9% par bond (i.e., a bond having a duration of 5 years). The assumption here is that all rates move immediately to the 7% level. Hence there is a sudden capital gain at the outset, which declines as the bond ages over the 5-year investment horizon. Exhibit 12 shows how the remaining capital gain at the 5-year horizon is just sufficient to compensate for the reduced reinvestment income, and thereby maintain the original 9% target. This compensation process is the key to the basic idea of

EXHIBIT 12   COMPENSATING CAPITAL GAIN FROM 9% PAR BOND WITH 5-YEAR DURATION

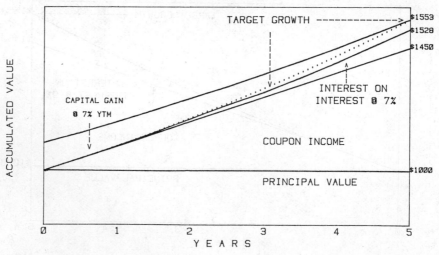

immunization. In turn, the fundamental concept underlying the compensation process is Macaulay's duration—the present-value-weighted average life of the bond's cash flow.

DURATION AND CONTROL OF VOLATILITY RISK

In addition to its role as a measure of the average time to repayment of a bond's cash flow (or indeed of **any** specified cash flow over time), duration has an important interpretation with respect to **price volatility of a bond.**

It is, of course, well known that maturity functions as a rough guide to the volatility of bonds as interest rates change. Longer term bonds tend to be more volatile than shorter term bonds. However, this crude gauge has a number of problems associated with it, especially when one seeks to achieve a more refined volatility analysis. For example, while a 2-year bond is almost twice as volatile as a 1-year bond, it is **not** true that a 30-year bond is twice as volatile as a 15-year bond. This effect is illustrated in Exhibit 13, which shows the price movement of 9% par bonds of various maturities under a ±100 basis point change in **yield to maturity.** It is clear from this figure that the incremental increase in volatility tends to diminish with each additional year of maturity. Thus a **perpetual bond** is not a great deal more volatile than a 30-year bond. In fact, under some circumstances, there are bonds with maturities in the 30–50 year range that may be more volatile than the perpetual.

The general shape of Exhibit 13 is reminiscent of the curves in Exhibit 8 tracing the relationship of duration to a bond's maturity. This immediately raises the possibility that duration might function as a useful gauge of bond price volatility. In Exhibit 14, the duration of a 9% par bond is overlayed on the price movements shown in Exhibit 13. This demonstrates that there is indeed a close relationship between duration and volatility. A slight adjustment in the basic duration number has been made to achieve the fit as shown in Exhibit 14, the adjusted duration is derived by simply multiplying the original duration value by a scale factor consisting of $1/(1 + \text{yield rate})$. This relationship can be developed mathematically.

All this suggests that the duration (on adjustment) can serve as adequate first approximation for the basic price volatility of a bond. This remains true even when dealing with discount and premium bonds. Indeed, as noted earlier, this general result applies beyond the realm of simple bond-type cash flows to **any** prescribed cash flow over time: the price sensitivity can be approximated by the adjusted duration value.

At first glance, the earlier definition of duration as a measure of present-value-weighted average life seems to clash curiously with its interpretation as a price volatility measure. While these two interpretations are immediate consequences of the mathematical specifications of duration, the connection remains somewhat difficult to grasp at an intuitive level. Macaulay introduced duration in an effort to find an appropriate measure of the time that a given loan remains outstanding. He did not realize the role that duration could play as a volatility measure. In fact, it was not until many years later that this fundamentally simple connection was finally uncovered.

To understand why duration functions so well as a volatility measure, it may be useful to think in terms of how volatility would be assessed in a "simple interest" environment. For example, consider a 10-year 9% par bond. Now further suppose that interest rates rise suddenly, so that the bond's price falls 5 points to a level of 95. Over the bond's 10-year life, these 5 points of discount will be translated into 5 points of capital gain. In turn, this capital gain provides a certain increment to the bond's yield. To estimate this yield increment using a very crude simple-interest-like calculation, the 5-point capital gain could be amortized over the 10-year life of the bond. This would provide, roughly speaking, an additional 50

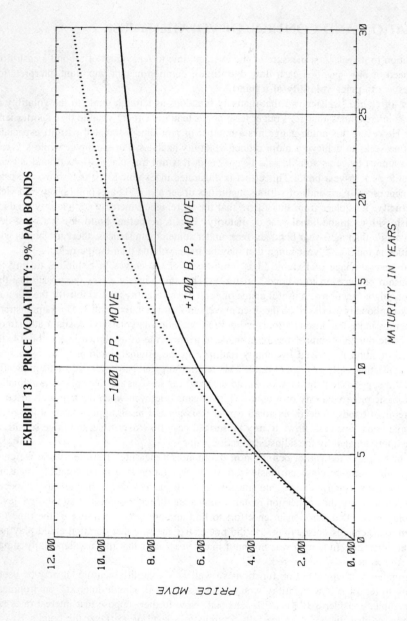

EXHIBIT 13 PRICE VOLATILITY: 9% PAR BONDS

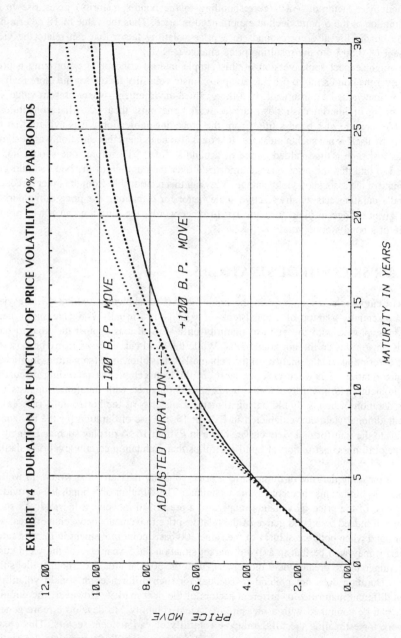

EXHIBIT 14   DURATION AS FUNCTION OF PRICE VOLATILITY: 9% PAR BONDS

basis points per year of yield. In other words, the $+50$ basis point yield move, when multiplied by a factor of -10 (corresponding to the bond's maturity) gives rise to an approximation of the 5-point decline experienced in price. Thus the value of 10 determined from the bond's life also corresponds to a price volatility factor that can relate the yield movement ($+0.50\%$) to the resulting price change (-5%).

One might expect some version of this simple interest concept of amortizing a price change over the bond's life to provide an approximate **volatility factor** for the more realistic case of a time-valued environment. In a time-valued environment, where present value and compounding of interim cash flows are at work, one must then ask what constitutes a reasonable measure of a bond's life. From the preceding subsections, it is evident that the **maturity** by itself is not such a measure. It should also be evident that duration was designed to act as just such a time-valued gauge of a bond's "life." Therefore, one should not be surprised to find that the price change amortized over the duration of the bond should give an estimate of the associated yield change. Viewing this relationship from the other direction, the bond's duration acts as an effective scale factor for estimating the price move derived from a given change in yield to maturity. In other words, the duration can act as a good measure of a bond's price volatility.

OTHER RISK CONTROL STRATEGIES

The yield curve is a key concept in the bond market. As shown in Exhibit 15, the yield curve is essentially a graph of a consistent series of issues, usually U.S. Treasury "near-par" bonds, plotted with the yield to maturity on a vertical axis against the time to their respective maturities on the horizontal axis. While the yield curve serves many purposes in both the description and the analysis of the debt market, it is often used (sometimes implicitly) as a representation of **reward-risk tradeoff.** In this connection, the preceding discussion of the problems with maturity and the better results obtained with duration, suggests that perhaps duration of bonds should be substituted for maturity as the horizontal "risk" axis. For the traditional yield curve depicted in Exhibit 15, the use of duration for the horizontal axis leads to the transformed yield curve shown in Exhibit 16. A display such as Exhibit 16 can be helpful in a construction of bond portfolios that maintain a certain level of volatility risk.

Before pursuing the role of duration as a price volatility measure, one would do well to recognize the limitations inherent in this technique. The duration of a bond does provide a useful gauge of the price movements relative to a prescribed movement in yield. As such, duration will indeed be a good gauge of the relative price movements between a 30-year and a 5-year bond when both are subject to the same 100 basis point movement in interest rates. However, it may well be that in a given market situation the 5-year area of the yield curve may be vulnerable to greater yield movements than the 30-year area (i.e., nonparallel shifts in rates). Duration does not pretend to account for such differences in "yield volatility" between different maturities or different sectors of the debt market. However, the duration measure can be combined with a measure of "yield volatility" to develop a more general framework for estimating the **total market volatility** of various debt sectors. This entails a more involved procedure than can be described in this section. For a complete description see Leibowitz, *The Risk Dimension* (1977) and Bierwag, Kaufman, and Khang (1978). Such measures of total market volatility should theoretically be the next step in constructing a comprehensive horizontal "volatility risk axis" for evaluating reward-risk tradeoffs.

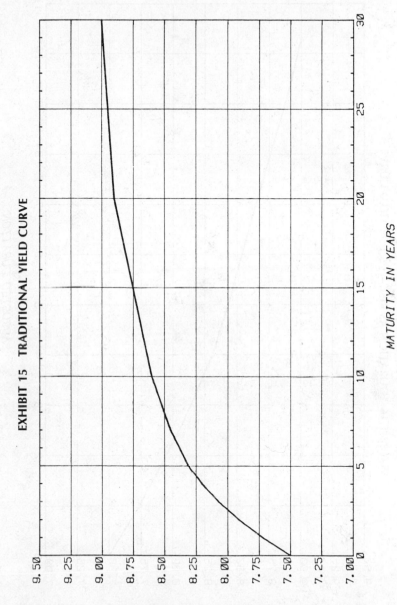

EXHIBIT 15 TRADITIONAL YIELD CURVE

YIELD TO MATURITY

MATURITY IN YEARS

EXHIBIT 16   DURATION AS RISK AXIS FOR YIELD CURVE

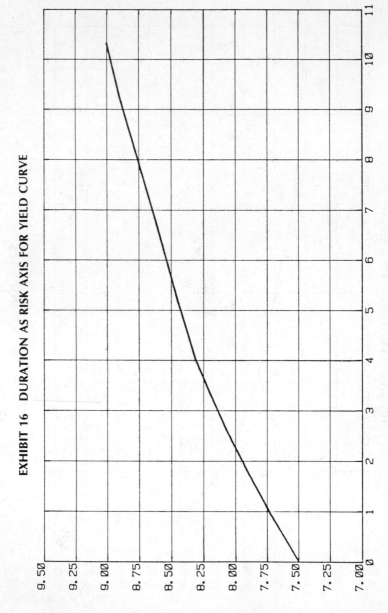

YIELD TO MATURITY

ADJUSTED DURATION

To obtain a more generalized framework, the vertical reward axis should also be extended beyond the simple concept of yield to maturity. Again, there are various ways for trying to achieve this, and they are also described in Leibowitz, *The Rolling Yield* (1977).

The key to these approaches, as well as to other methods for achieving various forms of risk control over specified horizons, lies in a deeper understanding of the time value and volatility characteristics of fixed cash flows. Although the concept of immunization is a relatively narrow version of these many possible approaches, it provides a clear insight into the volatility-reinvestment factors that form the foundation for any risk control strategy. While it is impossible within the confines of this section to dwell at great length on these broader techniques, the following discussion represents an attempt to clarify the main issues that arise from efforts to develop practical immunization strategies.

IMMUNIZATION UNDER MULTIPLE RATE CHANGES.   As seen earlier, by setting the portfolio's duration equal to the planning period, **immunization** can be achieved for the case of a single, immediate jump in interest rates. The key assumption is that interest rates immediately move from their current level to some given level and remain there for the entire planning period. Under this assumption of "a single move to a flat yield curve," the new level determines the reinvestment rate for coupon income as well as the final price of the portfolio. For an initial bond investment whose **Macaulay duration** corresponds to the length of the planning period, these conditions would result in a realized compound yield that closely matches the promised yield to maturity. However, this finding would have only theoretical interest unless one could find ways to deal with more general and more believable assumptions. In particular, before the immunization procedure can really be put into practice, one must come to grips with the assured fact that there will be **multiple changes in rates** during the course of the planning period. Here we explore how rebalancing procedures can be used to accommodate such multiple changes in rates.

It is easy to demonstrate the problems that arise when one drops the "single-move" assumption and allows for "multiple movements." If rates remained at 9% throughout the 5-year period, a $1,000 investment in this bond would compound to $1,552.97, thereby providing the 9% return that one would expect in the "no move" case (Exhibit 17A). To illustrate the effects of a "single move" in rates, suppose that rates immediately jumped to 12% and then stayed there for the remaining 5-year period (Exhibit 17B). This bond would then generate a coupon income of $436.67, interest-on-interest of $162.49, and a capital loss of $42.91, which is slightly better than the 9% target level of return.

There is another way of viewing the events in Exhibit 17B. The sudden rate move generates an immediate capital loss of $131. For the remaining asset value of $869 to grow to the target level, a compound growth rate of 12% must be achieved throughout the next 5 years, for example,

$$\$869 \times (1.06)^{10} = \$1,556.25.$$

In this sense, the 5-year return of 12% is needed to compensate for the immediate price loss incurred as rates jumped from 9 to 12%. In any case, the example in Exhibit 17B illustrates that under the "single move" assumption, even when the move is as large as 300 basis points, we still manage to realize the required target return.

However, let us see what happens under a simple case involving a "multiple move" in rates. Suppose, as before, that the first move in rates happens immediately after purchase and changes the yield curve to 12%. This rate persists for the next 5 years. But then, just before the bond is sold at the fifth year, there is a second jump in interest rates to 13% (Exhibit 17C). All numbers are then the same as in the earlier example, with the exception

EXHIBIT 17   PORTFOLIO VALUES DEVELOPED UNDER VARIOUS INTEREST RATE PATTERNS: INITIAL PORTFOLIO, $1,000 INVESTMENT IN 6.7-YEAR 9% PAR BOND; INITIAL DURATION, 5 YEARS

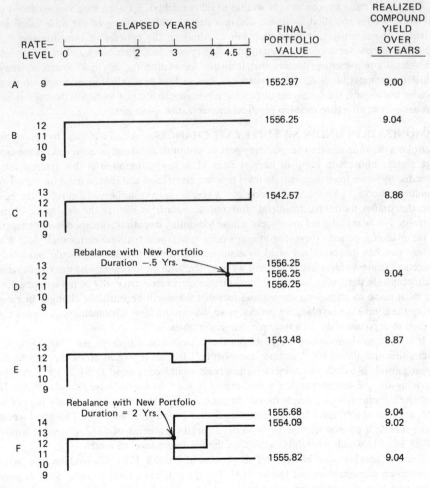

of the capital loss, which now amounts to $56.58. This greater capital loss brings the total **future value** down to $1,542.57, for a total realized compound yield of 8.86%. Thus, under this two-move assumption, the portfolio falls short of its target by more than 14 basis points.

If immunization procedures could not deal with such simple "multiple movements" in rates, there would clearly be a problem in achieving any sort of application in real life. Fortunately, techniques exist involving **portfolio rebalancing** that can overcome this difficulty.

REBALANCING USING DURATION.   The problem arising from multiple rate movements can be traced to the way a bond ages over time. Exhibit 18 illustrates how our theoretical bond, having a starting **duration** of 5 years, ages on a year-by-year basis. With each passing year, the maturity obviously gets shorter by 1 year, but the duration becomes shorter by less than a year. For example, over the first year, the bond's duration "ages" from 5.0 to 4.4, a drop of only 0.6 for the year. At the end of the fifth year, when we would clearly like to have a duration of zero, the original bond has a duration of 1.5 years, even when combined with the cash flow generated by coupon reinvestment, the blended duration of the portfolio becomes seriously mismatched with the passage of time.

This **"duration drift"** can be overcome by periodic rebalancing of the portfolio. For example, suppose that at the end of 4.5 years, the portfolio had been "rebalanced" in the following fashion. The bond was sold at a yield to maturity of 12%, leading to a capital loss of $54.22 and a total future value of $1,468.16 (Exhibit 17D). The entire proceeds were then invested in a 12% par bond, having a **duration** of precisely 0.5. Clearly, this instrument would assure us of achieving a 12% rate of return over the final 0.5-year period. In turn, this would provide a 12% return over the entire 5 years, bringing the total value of the portfolio up to $1,556.25. In other words, by rebalancing before the second movement in interest rates, we would have immunized ourselves to the effects of that movement.

As a further example, suppose that a second move to 11% had occurred at the end of the third year, and had been followed by a third move to 13%. Coupons from the original 9% bond would have been reinvested for 3 years at 12%, for 1 year at 11%, and for the remaining year at 13%. At the end of the fifth year, the bond would have been sold at 13% yield to maturity, engendering a sizable capital loss. This would lead to a total future value of $1,543.48, well below our target level (Exhibit 17E). However, suppose that the portfolio had been rebalanced at the end of the third year, just before the interest rate jump, to give a duration of exactly 2.0 years. This reset in duration will help ensure that the final 2 years realize a 12% return. This lockup of the 12% rate over the final 2 years is just what is needed, together with the return achieved over the first 3 years, to ensure realizing the original target return of 9% (Exhibit 17F).

The preceding example illustrates the **key idea underlying the immunization process.** By rebalancing to continually maintain a duration matching the remaining life of the planning period, the bond portfolio is kept in an immunized state throughout the period. This guarantees that the portfolio will achieve the target return promised at the outset of every subperiod. By working backward, this implies that the original target return of 9% can be met in the face of multiple movements in interest rates. (The actual proof of this statement entails somewhat involved mathematics, which are treated at great length in the references, e.g., Bierwag, 1977.)

Even when carried out only once a year, this rebalancing procedure can have a dramatic immunizing power in the face of radical changes in interest rates. This is illustrated in Exhibit

EXHIBIT 18   CHANGES IN DURATION OF A 9% 6.7-YEAR PAR BOND WITH PASSAGE OF TIME (YEARS)

Elapsed Time	Maturity	Bond's Duration	Target Duration	Mismatch
0	6.66	5.00	5.00	0.00
1	5.66	4.42	4.00	0.42
2	4.66	3.79	3.00	0.79
3	3.66	3.11	2.00	1.11
4	2.66	2.35	1.00	1.35
5	1.66	1.53	0.00	1.53

19 where interest rates increase by 100 basis points at the end of each year. Through annual rebalancing based on duration, the total portfolio value grows to within 4 basis points of the original 9% target. With more frequent rebalancing one could have an even closer tracking of the original target return.

REBALANCING AS A PROXY FOR A ZERO-COUPON BOND OVER TIME.   At first glance, the success of this rebalancing procedure in keeping the portfolio on target may seem to be somewhat magical. An insight into the rebalancing principle can be provided by thinking in terms of our old friend, the **zero-coupon bond.** For any change in yield level, the zero-coupon bond automatically retains sufficient asset value to provide the original return over its life. For example, in Exhibit 17B, when interest rates jump from 9 to 12%, a $1,000 investment in a 5-year zero-coupon bond would decline from $1,000 to $867.17. Suppose one were to sell the "zero-coupon" bond immediately after this jump in rates, realize the $867.17 proceeds, and hypothetically invest these funds into another 5-year zero-coupon bond at its market yield of 12%. Over the remaining 5 years, the assured 12% compounding would enable the original $867.17 to grow to $1,552.97, thereby satisfying the original 9% return goal.

The **rebalancing process** just described is, of course, equivalent to **continued holding of the zero-coupon bond.** The 5-year zero-coupon bond purchased at 9% has truly locked in the targeted 9% return over the 5-year planning period. Regardless of the magnitude or frequency of subsequent rate movements, the zero-coupon bond stays "on target." Moreover, the zero-coupon bond obviously remains continually "on target" even with the passage of time. In other words, it always retains the precise amount of asset value needed to realize the original target when compounded at the **then** yield rate for the remainder of the period.

The key idea here is that the price of the zero-coupon bond moves in lock step with the change in the required dollar investment at the new interest rate level. Another way of saying this is that, with respect to interest rate movements, the volatility of the zero-coupon bond coincides with the volatility of the assets required to provide the promised payment in the fifth year. Thus, for a bond portfolio to retain the assets needed to stay "on target," it must have the same volatility as the 5-year zero-coupon bond. Moreover, it must maintain this volatility equivalence as time passes. As shown in the preceding discussion, a bond's volatility is related to its **duration.** In particular, the duration of a zero-coupon bond coincides with its remaining life. Thus, to stay "on target" over time—as the zero-coupon bond does automatically—an "immunizing bond portfolio" must maintain the same duration over time as the zero-coupon bond. An "immunizing" bond portfolio can maintain this equivalence through **duration-based rebalancing.** Thus, duration-based rebalancing can provide a bond portfolio that mimics the automatic "immunizing" behavior of the zero-coupon bond in the face of multiple interest rate movements over time.

An Example with Declining Rates.   Assume that this rebalancing can be accomplished on an essentially continuous basis. The initial portfolio consists of a 6.7-year 9% par bond appropriate to the 5-year planning period. Suppose that interest rates move down 100 basis points a year in each of those 5 years. After the first year, the portfolio will show a nice capital gain, providing a total return over that 1-year period of 13.07% (Exhibit 20). The portfolio will have a greater dollar value than would have been expected at a constant rate of 9%. That is the good news. The bad news is that this greater asset value can be invested only at the lower rate of 8%. For an immunized portfolio, the good news and the bad news offset each other—they combine into "no news." The increased asset value is just sufficient, when invested at the new lower 8% rate, to keep the portfolio "on target" toward its original

EXHIBIT 19 PORTFOLIO GROWTH WITH DURATION-BASED REBALANCING: INITIAL INVESTMENT, $1,000

| Period Ending Date (years) | Rebalanced Portfolio at Start of Period | | Results Over Year | | | Realized Coupon Yield (%) | | |
	New Rate Level (%)	Duration (years)	Maturity	Coupon Flow and Interest-on-Interest	Capital Gain	Total Proceeds	Over Year	Cumulative	Blended[a]
1	9	5.00	6.66	$ 92.02	$41.18	$1,050.84	5.02	5.02	8.99
2	10	4.00	5.14	107.72	−33.03	1,125.52	6.98	6.00	8.99
3	11	3.00	3.66	127.22	−24.12	1,228.61	8.96	6.98	8.97
4	12	2.00	2.27	151.86	−13.61	1,366.87	10.95	7.97	8.97
5	13	1.00	1.00	183.47	0	1,550.34	13.00	8.96	8.96

[a]The 5-year return that would result if the portfolio value at that date were to be compounded at the existing new rate level for all remaining periods.

EXHIBIT 20   IMMUNIZATION THROUGH MATCHING OF REALIZED AND FORWARD RETURNS: 9% TARGET RATE, FLAT YIELD CURVE WITH ANNUAL SHIFTS OF −100 BASIS POINTS

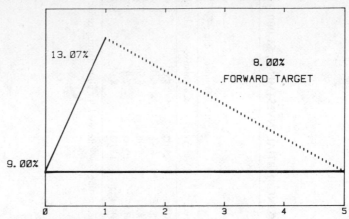

goal of 9% over the full 5-year period. As depicted schematically in Exhibit 20, the portfolio's return is like a string pinned down at the 0-year and 5-year points. The change in rates at year end acts to pluck the string away from the horizontal, but it still provides the same 9% cumulative return over the full 5-year period.

At the end of the first year, the portfolio is reinvested into a new 8% par bond having the required duration value of 4. Over the second year, interest rates decline by another 100 basis points to the 7% level. This results in a further capital gain, and a total cumulative return of 12.05% (Exhibit 21). The portfolio is now rolled into a 7% par bond having a duration of 3. This process continues year by year, with 100 basis point declines followed by a total reinvestment into par bonds (Exhibit 22). At the end of the fourth year (Exhibit 23), the cumulative return of 10.02% is just sufficient so that, when blended with the 5% rate available over the last year, the 5-year target of 9% will be realized.

EXHIBIT 21   IMMUNIZATION EXAMPLE: SECOND YEAR

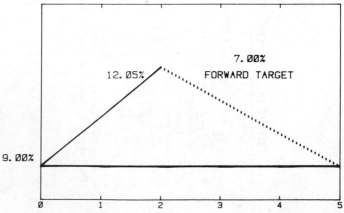

EXHIBIT 22 IMMUNIZATION EXAMPLE: THIRD YEAR

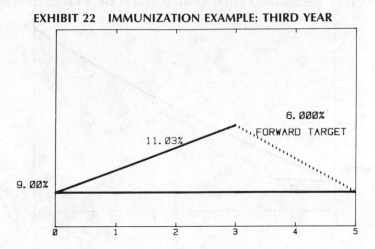

An Example with Rising Rates. The preceding scenario moved in the happy direction of lower interest rates and nice capital gains. Suppose the market moves in the opposite direction: higher interest rates and big capital losses. Assume that interest rates increase 100 basis points a year. The proper duration is again assumed to be maintained continuously. To gain a somewhat different viewpoint, a new schematic will be used to represent the **growth** of the portfolio's asset value over time (Exhibit 24). At the outset, let the asset value be $1,000. It would have to grow to $1,552.97 over the 5-year period to achieve the 9% target rate. The scenario now is that, after the first year, interest rates increase to 10%. This results in a capital loss, for a total return of 5%. This reduced asset value is still sufficient, given the higher 10% rate at which it can now be invested, to achieve the original 9% target. After rebalancing, this process continues with +100 basis point increases in the second year (Exhibit 25), the third year (Exhibit 26), and the fourth year (Exhibit 27). Finally, in the fifth year (Exhibit 28), there is just enough dollar value in the portfolio to reach the original $1,552.97 target after investment for the last year at the 13% rate. In this sequence of rate

EXHIBIT 23 IMMUNIZATION EXAMPLE: FOURTH YEAR

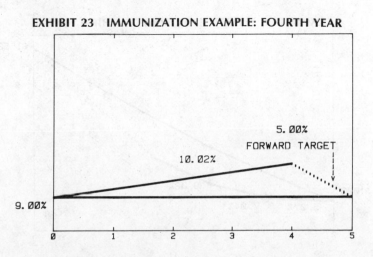

EXHIBIT 24   PORTFOLIO GROWTH THROUGH IMMUNIZATION: 9% TARGET RATE, FLAT YIELD CURVE WITH ANNUAL SHIFTS OF +100 BASIS POINTS

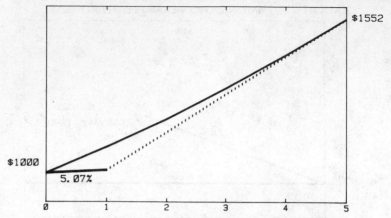

EXHIBIT 25   PORTFOLIO GROWTH: SECOND YEAR

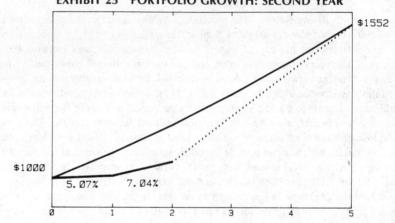

EXHIBIT 26   PORTFOLIO GROWTH: THIRD YEAR

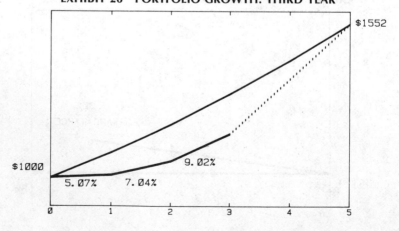

EXHIBIT 27   PORTFOLIO GROWTH: FOURTH YEAR

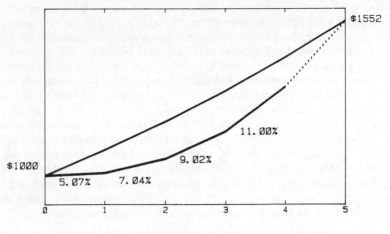

EXHIBIT 28   PORTFOLIO GROWTH: FIFTH YEAR

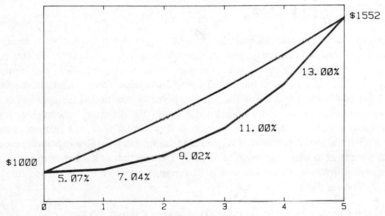

moves, the portfolio realized a capital loss every single year, but was able to exactly compensate for this loss through its increased earning power at the higher rates.

General Sequences of Parallel Shifts.   In the two extreme interest rate scenarios just described, rates moved either consistently up or consistently down in successive years. The same results with varying interest rate moves could be achieved as long as the correct rebalancing procedure is followed. For example, rates could move up 100 basis points the first year, down 100 basis points the next year, and so on. Any such sequence of steps, as long as the duration is continuously maintained, should theoretically lead to the original target return.

IMPROVED REBALANCING USING HORIZON VOLATILITY.   The preceding theoretical results would require rebalancing continuously so as to maintain a duration equal to the remaining life of the planning period. In practice, rebalancings are more likely to be scheduled for specific points in time (e.g., annually). In departing from the concept of a continuous rebalancing, we can assume a well-defined rebalancing horizon, with the impact of yield movements concentrated at the horizon. Under these assumptions, the volatility of the portfolio is affected by a certain **horizon effect.** The classical definition of duration, while serving well in the case of continuous rebalancing, fails to readily accommodate this "horizon effect." For **annual rebalancings,** such as those used in Exhibit 19, this "horizon effect" accounts for a good portion of the portfolio's 4 basis point shortfall below the target return.

The concept of **horizon volatility** was specifically developed to accommodate this "horizon effect." This term was introduced in 1975 in a chapter by Leibowitz in the *Financial Analyst's Handbook,* and then refined in subsequent articles. The horizon volatility does provide a better surrogate for the volatility of the **ending portfolio** than the duration, even over 1-year horizons. This raises the prospect of using **horizon volatility** as the rebalancing yardstick in an immunization procedure. Exhibit 29 shows the results of rebalancing based on horizon volatility as applied to 16 different interest rate scenarios involving ±100 basis point annual jumps in interest rates. These results provide an empirical illustration of the improvement that can be obtained through the use of **horizon volatility** (rather than the classical duration) as the **basis for rebalancing** in an immunization procedure.

THE YIELD CURVE CASE

All the preceding discussion took place in the context of a rather restrictive set of assumptions. In particular, the model focused on parallel movements of a flat yield curve. We now consider **yield curves** that are truly curves (i.e., not flat). With this modification, one immediately runs into a rather surprising problem: finding an appropriate return target. In the flat yield curve case, it was clear that the initial yield to maturity constituted the appropriate target. However, with a more generally shaped yield curve, the necessary rebalancings force the portfolio into a sequence of yields and returns that may bear very little relation to the yield to maturity of the initial portfolio. This situation complicates the immunization process and reduces the extent to which the yield to maturity can function as a satisfactory return target. The following discussion shows how this "targeting" problem can be solved through the use of the **rolling yield.**

PORTFOLIO REBALANCING ALONG THE YIELD CURVE.   Most of the academic literature on immunization focuses on yield curves consisting of hypothetical forward rates or zero-coupon bonds. Under such circumstances, the return target is readily defined. However, when market participants speak of the "yield curve," they are generally referring to a maturity plot of the yields to maturity of Treasury par bonds. We shall adopt this market view of a **par bond yield curve** for the following discussion.

Exhibit 30 illustrates a particularly simple par bond yield curve. This yield "curve" is a straight line with a positive slope of 50 basis points per year. In the preceding discussion, it was stated that a rebalancing procedure based on the **horizon volatility** provides the required portfolio volatility for the flat yield curve. This technique works equally well for the general yield curve case.

Exhibit 31 shows the horizon volatility associated with each maturity point along our simple yield curve. At the outset, a horizon volatility of 4 is needed, and this can be achieved by a 6.41-year 9% par bond. At the end of the first year, however, a horizon volatility of 3 is required and this is achieved with a maturity of 4.8 years.

Using the sequence of **annual rebalancing maturities** derived in this fashion, we can proceed to determine the total returns achieved under the scenario of "no change in the market"; that is, the yield curve remains constant. This sequence of calculations is shown

EXHIBIT 29   PORTFOLIO GROWTH ACROSS 16 DIFFERENT INTEREST RATE SCENARIOS: REBALANCING BASED ON HORIZON VOLATILITY[a]

FINAL VALUES

	ASSET VALUE PER $1000	REALIZED COMPOUND YIELD
8.02 / 9.01	1553.46	9.01
11.00 / 13.00		
8.51 / 9.01	1553.49	9.01
13.01 / 11.00		
8.51 / 9.01	1553.46	9.01
9.01 / 11.00		
9.01 / 9.01	1553.45	9.01
11.01 / 9.00		
8.51 / 9.01	1553.49	9.01
9.01 / 11.00		
9.01 / 9.01	1553.48	9.01
11.01 / 9.00		
9.01 / 9.01	1553.43	9.01
7.01 / 9.00		
9.51 / 9.01	1553.45	9.01
9.01 / 7.00		
8.51 / 9.01	1553.44	9.01
9.01 / 11.00		
9.01 / 9.01	1553.43	9.01
11.01 / 9.00		
9.01 / 9.01	1553.38	9.01
7.01 / 9.00		
9.51 / 9.01	1553.40	9.01
9.01 / 7.00		
9.01 / 9.01	1553.43	9.01
7.01 / 9.00		
9.51 / 9.01	1553.45	9.01
9.01 / 7.00		
9.51 / 9.01	1553.44	9.01
5.00 / 7.00		
10.02 / 9.01	1553.39	9.01
7.00 / 5.00		

[a]Legend: $12 \lfloor \frac{7.03}{9.02}$

where interest rate at end of year = 12%
cumulative realized compound yield = 7.03
realized compound yield over prior year = 9.02

in Exhibit 32. The resulting total return is 8.56%, well below the initial yield to maturity of 9%. Clearly, the yield to maturity of an initial portfolio cannot function as an immunization target, even for this simple yield curve case. It remains for us to show that the 8.56% figure can constitute a target return that is indeed realized by the immunization procedure, and to then try to understand the nature of this new "targeting process."

THE ROLLING YIELD.   In a series of articles published beginning in 1977, we tried to formalize the total return associated with the age-old investment concept of "rolling down the yield curve." The term **"rolling yield"** was defined as the total return associated with

EXHIBIT 30   SIMPLE PAR BOND YIELD CURVE

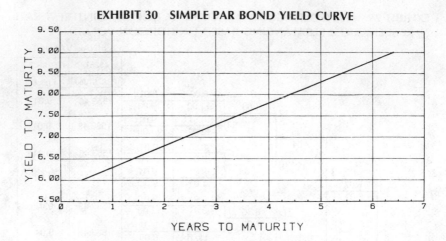

an investment at a maturity point along the yield curve under the assumption that the yield curve remained constant. From this assumption, it follows that the investment could be priced at the end of the horizon on the basis of its "aged" position on the curve. For example, for the curve shown in Exhibit 30, the 1-year rolling yield associated with an investment into the 6.41-year 9% par bond would correspond to the results of subsequently pricing that investment 1 year later at the 5.41-year point on the yield curve (i.e., at a yield of 8.50%). For any common horizon, one can compute rolling yields for investments at every maturity point. The resulting curve is referred to as the **rolling yield curve.**

Exhibit 33 superimposes the rolling yield curve on the par bond yield curve from Exhibit 30. For positively sloped yield curves such as this one, the rolling yield characteristically will lie above the yield curve itself. This results from the incremental return associated with the implied ability to sell out the investment at a "rolldown" yield that is lower than the initial purchase yield.

Exhibit 33 highlights the specific rolling yield values associated with the sequence of maturities required by the annual rebalancing procedure. As one compares the rolling yield values with the immunization procedure followed in Exhibit 32, it becomes apparent that

EXHIBIT 31   HORIZON VOLATILITY

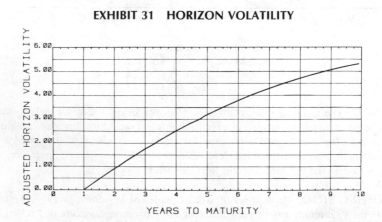

EXHIBIT 32   IMMUNIZATION PROCEDURE APPLIED TO A YIELD CURVE SITUATION: INITIAL INVESTMENT, $1,000; STATIC SCENARIO

Period Ending (years)	Rebalanced Portfolio at Start of Period			Results Over Year			Realized Compound Yield (%)			
	Parallel Shift (b.p.)	Initial Yield Level (%)	Maturity (years)	Coupon Flow and Interest-on-Interest	Capital Gain	Total Proceeds	Over Year	Cumulative	Forward Target[a]	Blended[b]
1	+ 0	9.00	6.41	$92.03	$21.18	$1,113.21	11.02	11.02	7.94	8.56
2	+ 0	8.17	4.76	92.81	17.56	1,223.58	9.69	10.35	7.37	8.56
3	+ 0	7.46	3.33	92.98	12.81	1,329.37	8.46	9.72	6.82	8.56
4	+ 0	6.85	2.12	92.62	6.91	1,423.90	7.35	9.12	6.29	8.56
5	+ 0	6.29	1.00	91.29	0	1,520.23	6.29	8.56	0	8.56

NO CHANGE IN CURVE OVER TIME

[a] The return realized from the immunization procedure for the remainder of the planning period, assuming that the then-existing yield curve remains unchanged.
[b] The 5-year return that would result if the portfolio value at that date could be compounded at the "forward target rate" for all the remaining periods.

EXHIBIT 33   THE ROLLING YIELD CURVE

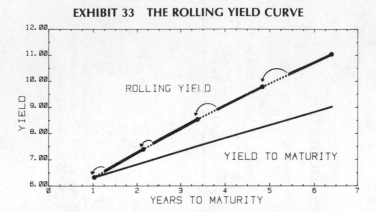

the year-by-year realized compound yields achieved by immunization are nothing more than the sequence of rolling yields indicated in Exhibit 33. This result suggests that return targets for the yield curve case may be found by stringing together the appropriate **sequence of rolling yield values.**

Parallel Shifts of the Yield Curve.   We have yet to demonstrate that this procedure maintains the target level of return in the face of changing yield curves. We retain the assumption that the yield curve changes through parallel movements. A + 100 basis point parallel move in the yield curve simply means that the yields associated with every maturity are increased by + 100 basis points. As before, we allow for multiple movements concentrated at the end of each year. Exhibit 34 illustrates a scenario consisting of annual jumps of − 100 basis points each. Rebalancing is carried out in accordance with the **horizon volatility** technique. The year-by-year returns are obviously different from those achieved under the static case of Exhibit 32. However, the total return comes in at 8.54%, only 2 basis points under the target level determined by the sequence of rolling yields. These results provide encouraging support for the rolling yield as a "targeting" process.

Parallel Movements of Actual Yield Curves.   The foregoing example is based on one extremely simple positively sloped yield curve. But does this technique apply to more general yield curve shapes? To study this question within a more realistic framework, a series of computer-based simulations was developed. In the initial studies, the basic research tool was a simulation of 5-year immunization plans using simple point portfolios. These portfolios consisted of a single maturity point along the yield curve. The simulations utilized a data base consisting of U.S. Treasury yield curves for the beginning of each month starting with January 1958 and ending in December 1979.

Exhibit 35 illustrates the procedure followed in the first series of studies. The analysis began with the actual yield curve shape on a given date. Then, at the end of each year, the curve was moved in a parallel fashion by a specified yield increment. Exhibit 35 illustrates the case of an annual 50 basis point downward move. Rebalancing takes place on an annual basis. By evaluating the immunization strategy in this context, one can determine the effect of the historical starting yield curve shape. In other words, this will expose and isolate problems arising from the flat yield curve assumption.

EXHIBIT 34 IMMUNIZATION PROCEDURE APPLIED TO A YIELD CURVE SITUATION: INITIAL INVESTMENT, $1,000; ANNUAL RATE MOVEMENTS

Period Ending (years)	Rebalanced Portfolio at Start of Period: Parallel Shift (b.p.)	Rebalanced Portfolio at Start of Period: Initial Yield Level (%)	Rebalanced Portfolio at Start of Period: Maturity (years)	Results Over Year: Coupon Flow and Interest-on-Interest	Results Over Year: Capital Gain	Results Over Year: Total Proceeds	Realized Compound Yield (%): Over Year	Realized Compound Yield (%): Cumulative	Realized Compound Yield (%): Forward Target[a]	Realized Compound Yield (%): Blended[b]
−100 B.P. PARALLEL SHIFT PER YEAR										
1	−100	9.00	6.41	$92.03	$65.24	$1,157.27	15.16	15.16	6.93	8.55
2	−100	7.13	4.67	83.98	55.55	1,296.80	11.71	13.43	5.35	8.54
3	−100	5.41	3.24	71.10	40.78	1,408.69	8.45	11.75	3.81	8.54
4	−100	3.83	2.07	54.44	21.84	1,485.00	5.34	10.13	2.30	8.54
5	−100	2.29	1.00	34.20	0	1,519.20	2.30	8.54	0	8.54

[a] The return realized from the immunization procedure for the remainder of the planning period, assuming that the then-existing yield curve remains unchanged.
[b] The 5-year return that would result if the portfolio value at that date could be compounded at the "forward target rate" for all the remaining periods.

EXHIBIT 35   IMMUNIZED POINT PORTFOLIO OVER TIME

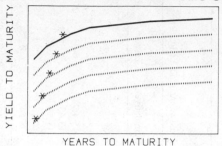

Simulation Tests of the YTM Target. The first series of simulations used to test the immunization procedure employed the traditional yield to maturity as the return target. The results are shown in Exhibit 36. Each point along the horizontal axis represents a different starting yield curve. For example, the first immunization plan began in January 1958. An initial point portfolio was constructed that had a duration of 5 years in the context of that yield curve. This initial portfolio had a yield to maturity (YTM) of 2.78%. In accordance with the usual procedure, this value of 2.78% was then taken as the return target for the 5-year immunization plan. At the end of each year, the market was assumed to have undergone a 50 basis point downward move across all maturities. The simulation was then carried out with the portfolio being rebalanced every year.

The cumulative return realized by this immunization process turned out to be 2.76%. This represented an error of −2 basis points relative to the original YTM-based target of 2.78%. The vertical axis in Exhibit 36 indicates the magnitude of the "tracking error." This "miss" of −2 basis points for the January 1958 curve is the leftmost point in Exhibit 36. The next point corresponds to the miss relative to the initial YTM target for the 5-year immunization plan beginning with the yield curve for February 1958. The plot thus depicts the tracking errors for different immunization plans starting on successive months from January 1958 through December 1974.

The worst variation occurred on March, 1971, a tracking error of −21 basis points. At first, that does not sound so bad. In fact, Exhibit 36 would seem to provide evidence that

EXHIBIT 36   SIMULATED IMMUNIZATION RETURNS OVER YTM TARGET: ANNUAL PARALLEL SHIFTS OF −50 BASIS POINTS

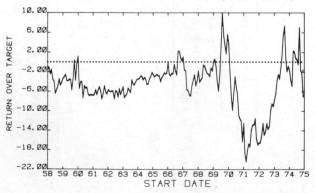

immunization strategies have done very well. The problem is that these results are based on **parallel moves.** These are the idealized conditions under which immunization is supposed to function **perfectly.** Under such idealized circumstances, it is rather disappointing to see the sequence of misses shown in Exhibit 36.

Simulation Test of the Rolling Yield Target.   We next tested the concept of a rolling yield-based target using the simulation procedure described earlier. The worst miss is − 5 basis points, compared with a − 21 basis point miss for the YTM target. To facilitate comparison of the targeting techniques, Exhibit 37 shows both sets of simulation results on a single graph. The rolling yield target is clearly superior. The result can be proved mathematically: the rolling yield provides the correct return target for the case of parallel movements of par bond yield curves.

However, much as the portfolio manager interested in immunization might wish to see parallel movements, the real world often deals out a sequence of rate movements that are anything but parallel. For example, consider just one segment of the yield curve—the spread of 5-year maturities over 1-year bills. Under parallel shifts, this spread would remain constant over time. As Exhibit 38 indicates, there have actually been wide, and often wild, variations in this spread.

This brings us to the second subject of our simulation studies—the problem of nonparallel shifts.

Changing Yield Curve Shapes.   To appreciate the problems caused by nonparallel shifts, consider the situation of an initially inverted yield curve that snaps down to a positive shape in subsequent years. Exhibit 38 shows that this situation was not uncommon—it happened in 1969, 1973, and 1974. Exhibit 39 provides a more detailed view of the snapdown that occurred over the year following September 1974.

When faced with a yield curve shape such as that of September 1974, the rolling yield targeting process will count on rolling "up" the curve and capturing the higher yields.

EXHIBIT 37   COMPARISON OF YTM AND ROLLING YIELDS AS TARGETS: ANNUAL PARALLEL SHIFTS OF − 50 BASIS POINTS

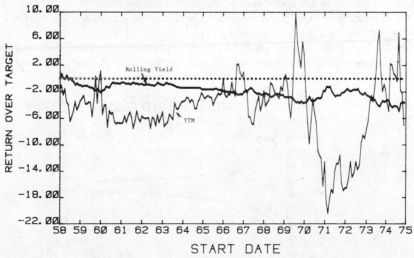

EXHIBIT 38   5-YEAR–1-YEAR TREASURY CURVE SPREAD

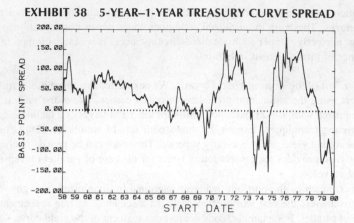

Parallel downward shifts would, of course, reduce these yields but would also generate sufficient capital gains for an immunized portfolio to remain "on target." However, when the yield curve snaps down as shown in Exhibit 39, the yield loss in the short-term maturities may far exceed the yield move in the intermediate-term maturities. In the early years of an immunization plan, the portfolio will probably be concentrated in this intermediate range. Consequently, the smaller yield move in these intermediate maturities may not generate sufficient capital gains to provide the needed offset to the much lower yields that will be encountered in the plan's later years.

Thus one should anticipate problems for the immunization-oriented portfolio manager in the face of snapdowns like those that followed the inverted yield curves that occurred in 1969, 1973, and 1974.

Simulation of Actual Yield Curve Sequences.   The next set of computer simulations utilized the same data base of monthly U.S. Treasury yield curves stretching from January 1958 to December 1979. However, the immunization plan now had to deal with market movements defined by the **actual** sequence of historical curves.

The first case to be examined at this detailed level is a 5-year immunization strategy using a point portfolio with annual rebalancing. This sequence of tracking errors is shown in Exhibit 40. The results are quite satisfactory for plans begun in 1958–1966. Over this period, the immunization plans usually did better than the target. Then, in 1967, 1968, and 1969,

EXHIBIT 39   HISTORICAL YIELD CURVES

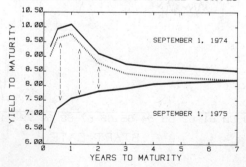

EXHIBIT 40   HISTORICAL IMMUNIZATION RETURNS OVER ROLLING YIELD TARGET: ACTUAL SEQUENCE OF YIELD CURVES

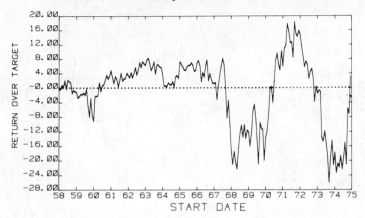

there developed a series of instances of the immunization strategy underperforming the target by 20–24 basis points. Over the next 3 years, from mid-1970 through the end of 1972, the immunization plans always met their target and, in some cases, outperformed by as much as 18 basis points. The results turn sour once again in 1973, reaching the worst miss of −26 basis points in September 1973. By the end of 1975, the results had begun to improve.

In comparing Exhibit 40 with the 5- to 1-year spread graph shown in Exhibit 38, one can roughly identify the most difficult times for immunization plans. An inverted yield curve followed by a snapdown to a positive curve causes trouble in the standard immunization strategy. If this situation occurs within the first 2–3 years of the plan's life, it can create distortions that may lead to underperformance. It is not surprising that this situation would place a particular strain on targets based on the rolling yield.

To assess the role of the targeting procedure in these underperformance situations, this series of simulations was repeated using return targets based on the yield to maturity of the original portfolio. As pointed out earlier, this YTM target is theoretically incorrect for the hypothetical situation of parallel yield moves. However, one might expect the YTM to provide a more conservative, hence somewhat better target estimate, in just the inverted yield curve situations that spell trouble for the rolling yield. From the simulation results presented in Exhibit 41, it is evident that the YTM target actually does perform somewhat better in those troublesome times. In contrast with the early results shown in Exhibit 40, there are fewer starting months shown in Exhibit 41 where the immunization plan underperformed by more than 16 basis points.

Another approach to dealing with this problem of yield curve reshaping is to find portfolio structures that may prove more resilient to actual market movements. In the preceding discussion, all analyses and all simulation results have been based on a point portfolio. This is a hypothetical portfolio consisting of a single par bond having the needed maturity. There are actually many other portfolio structures that can generate the needed sequence of duration (or horizon volatility) values. It is reasonable to expect that some of these portfolio structures can perform much better than others over time.

As one delves into this question of characterizing the various dynamic structures, one finds a virtually limitless variety of potential portfolio forms and rebalancing procedures. Our research has encompassed a large number of different portfolio structures, many more than can be described in the context of this section. However, the basic thrust of our research

EXHIBIT 41   HISTORICAL IMMUNIZATION RETURNS OVER YTM TARGET: ACTUAL SEQUENCE OF YIELD CURVES

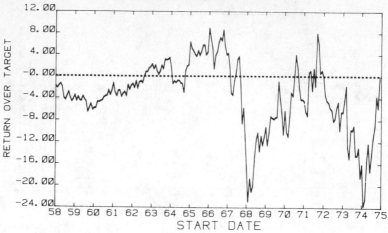

findings confirm that considerable improvement in tracking accuracy can be attained through selection of the right portfolio structure.

THE INTRICACIES OF REBALANCING

It turns out that there is much more flexibility and many more questions in the area of rebalancing than is generally realized. Research into many of these variables has shown that there are numerous surprises that can have a fairly substantial impact on tracking accuracy. For example, while most of the work presented here is based on **annual rebalancing,** other studies have been performed on the effects of using different rebalancing frequencies. The theory suggests that apart from the practical considerations involved, more frequent rebalancing should prove to be superior. Curiously, the historical simulations tend to suggest that too frequent rebalancing may introduce more problems than it solves. In fact, these results raise the question of whether rebalancing should be specified in terms of the time dimension alone. For example, it appears that improved duration matching may be obtained by having more adaptive scheduling of the rebalancing action, such as those triggered by certain thresholds of rate moves, cash inflows, and so on.

Another important facet of this problem is the rebalancing criterion itself. This presentation has been cast in the context of the traditional **Macaulay duration** and the **horizon volatility.** In actuality, both these specifications probably should be viewed as special cases of a class of volatility measures. Each volatility measure turns out to be appropriate for a particular set of assumptions regarding the rebalancing horizon, the nature of the market movement, and the procedure for reinvesting interperiod cash flows. In fact, for most of the situations analyzed, the Macaulay duration has turned out **not** to be the best choice from within this class of volatility measures. A full discussion of this subject would lead too far astray for the purposes of this section.

Another aspect of the rebalancing question involves the range of choices involved when using specific securities. There are a host of such questions, ranging from the most efficient application of coupon flows, to the selection of the optimal security for liquidation, to the broader issue of constructing initial portfolios using a combination of highly liquid and relatively illiquid securities. Once again, a full discussion of this subject is beyond the scope of this presentation. However, it is important to note that the choice of the best rebalancing procedure is a weighty problem in its own right.

Simulation results indicate that when effective rebalancing procedures are combined with carefully chosen portfolio structures, one can achieve tracking accuracy that is far better than that illustrated in Exhibits 40 and 41 for the point portfolio. If immunization could reliably and consistently provide such tracking accuracy, this technique would indeed have to be taken seriously as a route to reducing uncertainty in an uncertain world.

VULNERABILITY OF ANY IMMUNIZATION PLAN

However, it should immediately be pointed out that any such results clearly run the danger of being specific to the historical sample that was used for these simulations. Even with portfolio structures that seem to have a reasonable conceptual justification, one must always be skeptical of such extraordinary tracking accuracy. Moreover, any portfolio structuring and/or targeting procedure will have its own particular set of vulnerabilities. These vulnerablilities may not have fully surfaced even under the range of yield movements and yield curve reshapings that have occurred during the 22-year period used in this simulation.

Indeed, with a little insight, a pathological sequence of yield curve movements can **always** be found that will defeat **any** immunization strategy. Thus if one develops a rebalancing procedure for defending against snapdowns and/or snapups, the portfolios created will be vulnerable to other types of yield curve movement. This is a very important point. The theoretical models of immunization all place some limits on the nature of yield curve movements. Without such limits, or some statistical approach specifying the probability of various pathologies, it is impossible to define an immunization scheme that will always work, one that will **always** provide tracking within some specified (reasonable) tolerance of the target.

In summary, in the course of exploring practical applications of an immunization strategy using actual securities from U.S. Treasury, agency, and/or corporate markets, we have found that it is better to develop initial and rebalanced portfolios based on criteria involving the rolling yield–horizon volatility approaches. These procedures can be readily combined with active management techniques to enable portfolio managers to integrate their market judgments with immunization strategies. This combined approach could even be used to attune the portfolio risk to levels deemed appropriate for different funds. For example, on the one hand, with stringently specified targets, a manager would follow a rather basic immunization strategy using market insights primarily to provide additional insurance that the return target will indeed be met. On the other hand, a fund with a greater risk tolerance might establish a more relaxed target for minimum return, thereby allowing the manager to aggressively seek incremental return in the short term while still maintaining a risk-controlled portfolio posture relative to the longer term.

REFERENCES AND BIBLIOGRAPHY

Bierwag, G., "Measures of Duration," Preprint, University of Oregon, August 1976.

——, "Immunization, Duration, and the Term Structure of Interest Rates," *Journal of Financial and Quantitative Analysis,* December 1977, pp. 725–742.

——, "Dynamic Portfolio Immunization Policies," *Journal of Banking and Finance,* Fall 1977.

Bierwag, G., and Grove, M., "A Model of the Term Structure of Interest Rates," *Review of Economics and Statistics,* February 1967, pp. 50–62.

Bierwag, G., and Kaufman, G., "Bond Portfolio Strategy Simulations: A Critique," *Journal of Financial and Quantitative Analysis,* September 1978, pp. 519–525.

———, "Coping with the Risk of Interest-Rate Fluctuations: A Note," *Journal of Business,* July 1977.

Bierwag, G., and Khang, C., "An Immunization Strategy is a Minimax Strategy," *Journal of Finance,* May 1979, pp. 389–399.

Bierwag, G., Kaufman, G., and Khang, C., "Duration and Bond Portfolio Analysis: An Overview," *Journal of Financial and Quantitative Analysis,* November 1978, pp. 671–681.

Bierwag, G., Kaufman, G., Schweitzer, R., and Toevs, A., "Risk and Return for Active and Passive Bond Portfolio Management: Theory and Evidence," paper presented at Institute for Quantitative Research in Finance, October 1979, New York, Columbia University.

Bildersee, J. S., "Duration as a Determinant of Price Spreads in Bond Markets," University of Pennsylvania, March 1978.

Blocker, E., and Stickney, C., "Duration and Risk Assessments in Capital Budgeting," *Accounting Review,* January 1979, pp. 180–188.

Blume, M. E., "Bond Betas," Wharton School, University of Pennsylvania, December 1973.

Boquist, J. A., Racette, G. A., and Schlarbaum, G. C., "Duration and Risk Assessment for Bonds and Common Stocks," *Journal of Finance,* December 1975, pp. 1360–1365.

Boyle, P., "Immunization Under Stochastic Models of the Term Structure," *Journal of the Institute of Actuaries* (U.K.), Vol. 105, 1978, p. 177.

Buse, A., "Expectations, Prices, Coupons and Yields," *Journal of Finance,* September 1970, pp. 809–818.

Caks, J., "A Refutation of Duration," paper presented at the Annual Meeting of the Midwest Finance Association, April 1976.

Carr, J. L., Halpern, P. J., and McCallum, J. S., "Correcting the Yield Curve: A Reinterpretation of the Duration Problem," *Journal of Finance,* September 1974, pp. 1287–1294.

Cooper, I. A., "Asset Values, Interest-Rate Changes, and Duration," *Journal of Financial and Quantitative Analysis,* December 1977.

Cox, J. C., Ingersoll, J. E., and Ross, S. A., "Duration and the Measurement of Basis Risk," *Journal of Business,* Vol. 52, January 1979.

———, "A Theory of the Term Structure of Interest Rates," Working Paper, University of Chicago, 1978.

Diller, S., "The Impact of Changing Interest Rates in a Bond Portfolio," *Money Manager,* February 13, 1979.

Durand, D., "Growth Stocks and the Petersburg Paradox," *Journal of Finance,* September 1957, pp. 348–363.

Einhorn, M., "Breaking Tradition in Bond Portfolio Management," *Journal of Portfolio Management,* Spring 1975.

Ezra, D., "Immunization: A New Look for Actuarial Liabilities," *Journal of Portfolio Management,* Winter 1976.

Fisher, L., "An Algorithm for Finding Exact Rates of Return," *Journal of Business,* January 1966, pp. 111–118.

———, and Weil, R., "Coping with the Risk of Interest-Rate Fluctuations: Returns to Bondholders from Naive and Optimal Strategies," *Journal of Business,* October 1971, pp. 408–431.

———, "Returns to Bondholders from Naive and Optimal Strategies," University of Chicago, August 1970.

Grove, M. A., "On Duration and the Optimal Maturity Structure of the Balance Sheet," *Bell Journal of Economics and Management Science,* Autumn 1974.

Grove, M.A., "A Model of the Maturity Profile of the Balance Sheet," *Metroeconomica,* Vol. 18, 1977, pp. 40–55.

Haugen, R. A., and Wichern, D. W, "The Elasticity of Financial Assets," *Journal of Finance,* September 1974, pp. 1229–1240.

Hainer, M. M., McLeod, C. C., and Strowger, G. G., "The Practical Application of Immunization to the Financial Management of New Money Business," paper presented at the November 1978 meeting of the Canadian Institute of Actuaries.

Hicks, J. R., *Value and Capital,* 2nd ed., Clarendon Press, Oxford, 1946.

Hopewell, M. H. and Kaufman, G. C., "Bond Price Volatility and Term to Maturity: A Generalized Respecification," *American Economic Review,* September 1973, pp. 749–752.

Ingersoll, J. E., Skelton, J., and Weil, R. L., "Duration Forty Years Later," *Journal of Financial and Quantitative Analysis,* November 1978, pp. 627–650.

Kaufman, G., "Measuring Risk & Return for Bonds: A New Approach," *Journal of Bank Research,* Summer 1978.

Khang, C., "Bond Immunization When Short-Term Rates Fluctuate More than Long-Term Rates," revised preprint, University of Oregon, November 1978.

Leibowitz, M. L., *The Rolling Yield,* Salomon Brothers, New York, 1977.

———, *The Risk Dimension,* Salomon Brothers, New York, 1977.

———, "Bond Immunization: A Procedure for Realizing Target Levels of Return," Salomon Brothers, New York, 1979.

———, "Bond Immunization, Part II: Portfolio Rebalancing," Salomon Brothers, New York, 1979.

———, "Bond Immunization, Part III: The Yield Curve Case," Salomon Brothers, New York, 1979.

———, *Pros & Cons of Immunization,* Salomon Brothers, New York, 1980.

Livingston, M., and Caks, J., "A Duration Fallacy," *Journal of Finance,* March 1977.

———, "Duration and Risk Assessment for Common Stocks: A Note," *Journal of Finance,* March 1978.

McEnally, R. W., "Duration as a Practical Tool for Bond Management," *Journal of Portfolio Management,* Summer 1977, pp. 53–57.

Macaulay, F. R., *Some Theoretical Problems Suggested by the Movements of Interest Rates, Bond Yields, and Stock Prices in the United States Since 1865,* National Bureau of Economic Research, New York, 1938.

Marshall, W., and Yawitz, J., "Lower Bounds on Portfolio Performance: A Generalized Immunization Strategy," prepublication draft, revised January 1979.

Redington, F. M., "Review of the Principles of Life-Office Valuations," *Journal of Institute of Actuaries,* Vol. 78, 1952.

Samuelson, P. A., "The Effect of Interest Rate Increases in the Banking System," *American Economic Review,* Vol. 55, 1945.

Shedden, A. D., "A Practical Approach to Applying Immunization Theory," *Transactions of the Faculty of Actuaries,* Vol. 35, 1977, p. 313.

Springbett, T. M., "Valuation for Surplus," *Transactions of the Faculty of Actuaries,* Vol. 28, 1977.

———, and Cavage, C. M., "Actuarial Note on the Calculation of Premium Rates Using a Decreasing Rate of Interest and Allowing for the Benefit of Immunization," *Transactions of the Faculty of Actuaries,* Vol. 28, 1977.

Tilley, J. A., "The Matching of Assets and Liabilities," *Transactions of the Society of Actuaries,* Vol. 32, 1977.

Trainer, F. H., Yawitz, J. B., and Marshall, W. J., "Holding Period Is the Key to Risk Thresholds," *Journal of Portfolio Management,* Winter 1979.

Vanderhoof, I. T., "The Interest Rate Assumption and the Maturity Structure of the Assets of a Life Insurance Company," *Transactions of the Society of Actuaries,* Vol. 24, October 1972.

Vanderhoof, I. T., "Interest Rate Assumptions and the Relationship Between Asset and Liability Structure," Education and Examination Committee of the Society of Actuaries, Part 7 study notes; 79–12–76.

Wallas, G. E., "Immunization," *Journal of Institute of Actuaries, Student's Society,* Vol. 15, 1959.

Weil, R. L., "Macaulay's Duration: An Appreciation," *Journal of Business,* Vol. 46, October 1973, pp. 589–592.

Whittaker, J., "The Relevance of Duration,"*Journal of Business and Finance,* Spring 1970.

Wissner, L., "Bond Immunization: How Today's High Bond Yields Can Be Locked In," Smith Barney, Harris Upham & Co., Inc., New York, December 1978.

———, "The Neutral Bond Portfolio," Smith Barney, Harris Upham & Co. Inc., New York, September 1978.

———, "The Unmanaged Bond Portfolio," Smith Barney, Harris Upham & Co. Inc., New York, September 1978.

Yawitz, J. B., "Is Average Maturity a Proxy for Risk?" *Journal of Portfolio Management,* Spring 1976.

———, "The Relative Importance of Duration and Yield Volatility on Bond Price Volatility," *Journal of Money, Credit and Banking,* February 1977, pp. 97–102.

———, Hempel, G., and Marshall, W. J., "A Risk-Return Approach to the Selection of Optimal Government Bond Portfolios," *Financial Management,* Vol. 5, No. 3, Autumn 1976.

———, "The Use of Average Maturity as a Risk Proxy in Investment Portfolios," *Journal of Finance,* May 1975.

OPTIONS MARKETS AND INSTRUMENTS

CONTENTS

INVESTMENT CHARACTERISTICS OF BASIC OPTION CONTRACTS 3

Definitions 3
  Option 3
  Call option 3
  Put option 3
  Combination option 3
  Straddle 3
  Striking price or exercise price 3
  Option premium 4
  Expiration date 4
  Option buyer 4
  Option writer 4
  Spread 4
Risk Modification 4
Risk-Reward Characteristics of Put and Call Contracts 4

SIGNIFICANCE OF EXCHANGE-LISTED OPTIONS 6

Important Changes Initiated by CBOE 6
  Standardization of terms 6
  Fungibility 7
  Lower transaction costs 7
  Organized secondary market 7
  Published transaction prices 7
  Certificateless clearing 9
Comparison of Conventional and Listed Options and Markets 9
Comparison of Transaction Costs 9

ROLE OF OPTIONS IN INTELLIGENT PORTFOLIO MANAGEMENT 10

Background 10
Risk-Reward Characteristics of Options 10
Covered Call Writing 12
Risk-Return Tradeoff 13

Covered Calls and Modern Portfolio Theory 14
Improving Risk-Adjusted Returns 15
Variations in Option Premium Levels 15
Option Evaluation and Portfolio Management 16
Analysis of Risk 17

INVESTMENT SIGNIFICANCE OF LISTED PUT OPTIONS 18

Background 18
Basic Risk-Reward Characteristics of Put Contracts 18
Conversion: Key to Analyzing Puts 19
Conversion, and Calculation of Risk Equivalents 20
Early Exercise of Puts 21

TAX TREATMENT OF OPTION TRANSACTIONS 22

Tax Treatment from Viewpoint of Option Buyer 22
Tax Treatment from Viewpoint of Option Writer 22
Special Tax Problems and Opportunities 22
  Using capital loss carry-forwards 28
  Nonresident aliens 28
  High tax bracket individuals 28

EVALUATION OF AN OPTION CONTRACT 28

Significance of Option Evaluation 28
Probability Models 28
  Sprenkle and Samuelson-Merton 31
  Black-Scholes model 31
  Recent attempts to deal with probability distribution problem 34

Cox, Ross, and Rubinstein   35
Gastineau–Madansky model   35
Using an Option Evaluation Model   35

**PROFITABILITY OF OPTION
TRADING**   37

Studies of Option Profitability   37
  Kassouf   37
  Merton, Scholes, and Gladstein   37
  Common flaws in simulations   37
Historic Profitability Record   38

**OPTIONS AND THE CORPORATE
TREASURER**   40

Evaluating Corporate Securities   40
Put and Call Provisions on Corporate
Securities   40
Pension and Profit-Sharing Investments   40
Management of Corporate Funds   40
Options on Fixed Income Securities   41
Merits of Option Listing   41

OPTION ADVISORY SERVICES   44

OPTIONS MARKETS AND INSTRUMENTS

Gary L. Gastineau

INVESTMENT CHARACTERISTICS OF BASIC OPTION CONTRACTS

DEFINITIONS. Before we examine the investment characteristics of puts and calls, it will be helpful to define a few terms:

Option. A negotiable contract in which the writer, for a certain sum of money called the option premium, gives the buyer the right to demand, within a specified time, the purchase or sale by the writer of a specified number of shares of stock at a fixed price called the striking price. Unless otherwise stated, options are written for units of 100 shares. They are ordinarily issued for periods of less than 1 year.

Call Option. An option to buy stock from the writer.

Put Option. An option to sell stock to the writer.

Combination Option. An option consisting of at least one put and one call. The individual option contracts that make up the combination are originally sold as a unit, but they may be exercised or resold separately.

Straddle. A combination option consisting of one put and one call with a common striking price and a common expiration date.

Striking Price or Exercise Price. The price at which an option is exercisable, that is, the price per share that the buyer of a call option must pay the writer for the stock or the price that the writer must pay the holder of a put option.

Option Premium.   The price of an option contract. In this section the convention of stating the option premium in terms of dollars per share under option is adopted. If the total premium for a 100-share option is $1,000, the option premium is given as $10.

Expiration Date.   The date after which an option is void.

Option Buyer.   The individual or, less frequently, the institutional investor who buys options.

Option Writer.   The individual or institutional investor who sells or writes options.

Spread.   (1) For listed options: the purchase of one option and the sale of another option on the same stock; the investor setting up the spread hopes to profit from a change in the difference between the prices of the two options. (2) In the conventional option market: a straddle in which the put side and the call side are written at different striking prices; typically, the put striking price is below, and the the call striking price is above, the market price of the stock at the time the spread is established. In the listed option market this position is usually called a **spraddle.** (3) The put and call dealer's margin between the option premium paid by the buyer and the premium paid to the writer is also called a **spread.**

The reader will find these basic definitions and opening pages of Section 17 useful in understanding this material.

RISK MODIFICATION.   No matter how intricate an option investment strategy the investor may adopt, **the principal result of any option purchase or sale is to modify the risk characteristics of an investor's position.** This feature of options can have an important impact on portfolio structure and on the investor's overall risk exposure.

Stock options provide the investor with a unique way to modify exposure to market risk. In particular, listed options traded on securities exchanges around the world are extremely versatile instruments for the modification of risk. This statement appears to be at odds with the popular view of call options as speculative tools that permit the small investor to obtain superior leverage on a small amount of capital. Options can fulfill much more important functions in an investment portfolio than this popular view suggests. Options can be of substantial aid to investors, large or small, who wish to modify the exposure of their portfolios to market fluctuations and improve their risk-adjusted return on investment.

RISK-REWARD CHARACTERISTICS OF PUT AND CALL CONTRACTS.   Exhibit 1 illustrates the basic investment characteristics of a call option from the respective viewpoints of the buyer and the writer. As most investors who have any familiarity with options are aware, an option buyer can never lose more than the premium paid for the option contract. On the other hand, if the price of the stock rises substantially over the life of the call option, the buyer's potential reward is theoretically unlimited. This position is illustrated by the line that begins in the lower left-hand corner of Exhibit 1.

The uncovered or "naked" call writer's position is, in many respects, the exact opposite of the call buyer's position. As the line that begins in the upper left-hand corner of Exhibit 1 illustrates, the call writer keeps the entire premium unless the stock price rises above the exercise price at the time the option expires or is exercised. In return for the option premium received, the writer of the call agrees to sell the stock at the striking price, no matter how high the stock may go. If the writer does not own the shares covered by the option, the writer's position deteriorates by $1 per share for every point by which the price of the stock exceeds the exercise price.

EXHIBIT 1   PROFIT AND LOSS POSITIONS OF THE BUYER AND WRITER OF A CALL

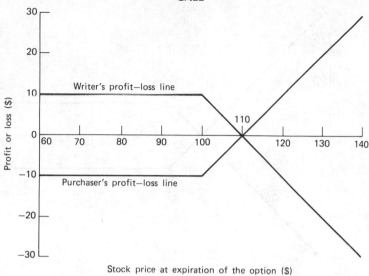

Stock price at expiration of the option ($)

The essence of the uncovered call writer's position is that he or she can earn no more than the amount of the option premium and can lose a large amount if the price of the underlying stock runs up. In contrast to the call buyer who is fixing the risk at the amount of the premium and accepting the possibility of a widely varying reward, the uncovered writer is fixing the reward at the amount of the premium and accepting a highly variable risk. Exhibit 2 illustrates the profit and loss positions of the buyer and writer of an uncovered put. In return for a fixed premium, the buyer of a put obtains the right to receive a reward that increases as the price of the underlying stock declines. As in the case of the call, both the buyer and the writer of a put option fix one side of the risk-reward equation and permit the other side to vary.

The offsetting risk-reward features of the buying and writing positions are clarified by Exhibits 1 and 2. Any profit to the option buyer is exactly offset by a loss to the writer, and vice versa. Neglecting transaction costs, **the net effect of an option transaction is simply a reallocation of risk and reward between buyer and writer.**

It is no accident that the word **"premium"** is used in both the insurance business and the option business. Option contracts, like insurance policies, are used to protect the investor, whether writer or buyer, from unacceptable risk. In Exhibits 1 and 2, the option buyer appears to be in a position analogous to that of the owner of an insurance policy. The option writer is like the insurance underwriter who accepts risk in return for premium income. When options are incorporated in an overall portfolio plan, however, the risks and rewards can change remarkably. For example, the call writer who has a position in the underlying stock will actually be **reducing** the overall volatility or market risk of his portfolio by writing the option because the premium he receives protects his assets in the event of a price decline, while his writer's obligation limits his gain on the up side. Although options do not increase or decrease the total level of risk in the financial system, **both parties to a particular option transaction can reduce their portfolio risk simultaneously through a combination of stock, option, and short-term debt positions.**

EXHIBIT 2   PROFIT AND LOSS POSITIONS OF THE BUYER AND WRITER OF A PUT

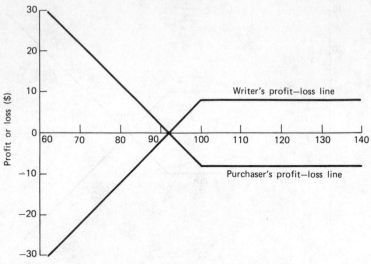

Stock price at expiration of the option ($)

SIGNIFICANCE OF EXCHANGE-LISTED OPTIONS

Although options in one form or another have been around since the days of ancient Greece (some would argue since the days of the Old Testament), both modern theory and the widespread use of option contracts awaited development of the **listed option,** initiated by the **Chicago Board Options Exchange (CBOE)** in 1973.

IMPORTANT CHANGES INITIATED BY CBOE.   Before 1973 the market in options on securities was one of the less significant segments of the securities business. In that year the Chicago Board Options Exchange, a division of the Chicago Board of Trade, introduced standardized listed option contracts. Neither the stock market nor the option market will ever be the same. Innovations introduced by the CBOE have been adopted by virtually every other securities options market in the world.

Standardization of Terms.   The importance of standardized option terms in the development of a secondary market in option contracts cannot be overemphasized. Standardization facilitates secondary trading because the number of distinct contracts a buyer or seller must evaluate is reduced. In contrast to the conventional option market, where it is possible to buy or write an option with practically any striking price or expiration date, the terms of contracts available on the exchanges are more limited. The striking price of a listed option always ends in $5, $2.50, or $0 unless a stock dividend or other capital change occurs after trading in the option begins. If American Telephone and Telegraph is selling at $51 a share at the time options for a new expiration month are being listed for trading, the new AT&T option will have a striking price of $50 per share. If the stock price closes above $52.50, the exchange will add $55 contracts for each expiration date beyond 60 days. Barring stock dividends, splits, or other capital changes, it will be impossible to buy or write an AT&T option on the exchange with a striking price between $50 and $55 per share.

In addition to standardization of striking prices, the exchanges have standardized **expiration dates.** The expiration date is the Saturday after the third Friday in the month. While most options expire in January, April, July, and October, some underlying stocks have options expiring in February, May, August, and November cycles, and a few use March, June, September, and December cycles.

Fungibility.   Fungibility, or interchangeability, is a second important characteristic of listed options necessary for the development of an active secondary market. Fungibility means substitutability or equivalence. Each listed option with a common expiration date and striking price is interchangeable with any similar listed option.

Either party to a listed option can usually, without undue sacrifice, close out a position that no longer meets his needs. The buyer and writer in a listed option transaction have no direct connection. Each has a contract only with the **Options Clearing Corp.,** which is the issuer of listed options. The option buyer relies on the Clearing Corporation to make good on the contract. The writer's obligation is an obligation to the Clearing Corporation, not to the buyer his broker happens to meet on the exchange floor. Either the option buyer or the writer can close out his position by simply reversing the initial transaction. For a more complete explanation of the relationship between the Clearing Corporation and the other parties to an option contract, the reader should examine the relevant sections of the **Options Clearing Corp. Prospectus.**

Lower Transaction Costs.   A third important characteristic of listed options is their relatively low transaction cost. The total transaction cost of any listed option trade is substantially lower than the transaction cost of a similar conventional option trade. Lower transaction costs have an important effect on trading volume and market liquidity. As the spread between the premium paid by the buyer and the premium received by the writer grows smaller, the number of transactions will tend to grow larger. If the option premium paid by the buyer is $500 and the amount received by the writer, net of transaction costs, is only $400, a writer who was willing to accept a net premium of $425 and a buyer who was willing to pay a premium of $475 would be excluded from the market. On the other hand, if the spread were narrower, both the buyer and the writer could be accommodated and the total volume of option transactions would increase. Relatively low transaction costs have been an important factor in the high trading volume of listed options.

Organized Secondary Market.   In contrast to the conventional options market, where both buyer and writer are literally locked into a transaction until the expiration date unless they can reach agreement for an earlier liquidation of their positions, depth of the market in listed options often exceeds the depth and liquidity of the market in the underlying stock.

Because both writer and buyer can close out positions relatively quickly, trading and investment strategies that require the use of options for only a short period of time are feasible. Strategies that depend on an investor's ability to buy or sell additional options as time passes are facilitated by a secondary market.

Published Transaction Prices.   The prices at which listed option transactions actually take place are published daily. Published prices and known commission rates assure both buyer and writer of a fair market. In spite of the apparent absence of any widespread abuse of the relative obscurity of conventional option dealer spreads, the mere fact that daily trading

EXHIBIT 3 COMPARISON OF CONVENTIONAL AND LISTED OPTIONS AND MARKETS

	Conventional	Listed
Type of options traded	Calls, puts, combination options	Calls, puts, combination orders permitted
Striking price	Any price buyer and writer negotiate	Standardized price ending in $5, $2.50, or $0
Expiration date	Any date buyer and writer negotiate	Saturday after the third Friday in the designated expiration month
Expiration time	3:15 P.M. eastern time	5 P.M. eastern time
Last date and time option can be sold	Same as expiration date and time	2 P.M. central time 3 P.M. eastern time on the business day immediately prior to the expiration date
Adjustment for cash dividend	Striking price reduced on ex-dividend date	No change in striking price
Adjustment for stock dividends, stock splits, and reverse splits	Both striking price and number of shares covered by options are adjusted to reflect the capital change	
Adjustment for rights or warrants issued to common shareholders	Striking price reduced by the value of the rights or warrants	
Limitation on purchase or sale of options on one stock	None, but limits have been proposed	2,000 contracts on the same side of the market (e.g., long calls **and** short puts); limit applies to all expiration dates
Unit of trading	One contract is an option on 100 shares of the underlying stock before any adjustments	
Method of option price determination	Buyer and writer negotiate through put and call broker	Central auction market
Secondary market	Limited; special options advertised in newspaper	Very active secondary market
Buyer's recourse to obtain performance on option contract	Primary responsibility for performance belongs to the endorsing broker who may be any member of the NYSE	The Options Clearing Corp. is the primary obligor guaranteeing the writer's performance
Evidence of ownership	Bearer certificate	Broker's confirmation slip
Method of closing out transaction when stock sells above striking price	Option may be exercised by buyer or sold to put and call broker who exercises the option and sells the stock	Exercise is rare; contract is usually closed out in a closing purchase-sale transaction
Transaction costs	High	Moderate
Commission structure	Basic charge is negotiated by put and call broker as a spread between premium paid by buyer and premium paid to writer	Negotiated commission rates since May 1, 1975
Stocks on which options are available	Almost any stock	Over 200 selected stocks in the United States and a growing list of stocks elsewhere in the world

EXHIBIT 3 CONTINUED

	Conventional	Listed
Pricing information	Brokers publish indicated premiums to buyers or writers	Actual transaction prices published daily
Procedure for exercise	Buyer exercises by notifying endorsing broker	Buyer's broker notifies the Options Clearing Corp. which selects writers essentially at random
Extensions	Available if writer agrees	Not available
Tax treatment	Identical	

Margin Requirement

Call buyer	100% of the option premium
Covered writer	No margin required beyond that needed to carry stock position
Uncovered writer	Minimum requirement is related to price of stock with adjustment for amount of premium received and amount by which option is in or out of the money. Margin requirements should be checked in detail with each brokerage firm.

summaries are published in the newspapers removes some of the mystery and, quite frankly, some of the suspicion from the option market.

Certificateless Clearing.   In some respects, one of the most important innovations pioneered by the CBOE is the introduction of certificateless clearing. Except in unusual cases when an option trader insists on evidence of the transaction in addition to a brokerage firm confirmation slip, the Options Clearing Corp. does not issue an actual option contract or certificate. This feature of listed option trading reduces the amount of paperwork and eliminates the physical movement of securities, in this case option contracts, between brokerage firms. The Options Clearing Corp. has sharply reduced the time required to clear a transaction and, as the brokerage community gains additional experience with certificateless trading, the cost of clearing a transaction should decline. The CBOE was a pilot project not only for organized trading of option contracts but also for the introduction of certificateless trading to the securities markets. On the basis of results to date, both features of the pilot project can be called unqualified successes.

COMPARISON OF CONVENTIONAL AND LISTED OPTIONS AND MARKETS.
Exhibit 3 compares conventional and listed options and markets.

COMPARISON OF TRANSACTION COSTS.   Probably the single most significant contribution of **listed option trading** to the expansion of the option market is that it sharply reduces the cost of a transaction. Both the writer and the buyer of a call can fare better on an exchange than with a conventional call. If commission and other transaction costs are too large, they act as a deterrent to trading. Commissions on the exchange are low enough to permit the buyer to consider purchasing options for a relatively small expected move in the stock. The writer has reasonable assurance that the commission cost to close out the transaction will not consume most of the premium. The lower transaction cost leads to more active trading and, consequently, to more liquid markets. The example chosen for Exhibit

4 illustrates a typical difference between transaction costs for a listed option and those for a conventional option. The actual difference in a particular case always depends on what happens to the price of the stock and what the parties do to close out their respective sides of the contract.

Nonetheless, examination of Exhibit 4 reveals that the costs of the conventional option transaction are, in this case, more than 2.5 times as high as for the comparable listed option transaction. In fact, commissions and other charges paid by the two parties to the conventional option trade are equal to about two-thirds of the total option premium paid by the buyer. If one assumed that the transaction involved **one** call rather than 10, the costs would consume an amount nearly equal to the entire premium. With transaction costs of this magnitude, neither buyer nor writer can realistically expect superior performance unless premiums are grossly out of line with any measure of fair value.

ROLE OF OPTIONS IN INTELLIGENT PORTFOLIO MANAGEMENT

BACKGROUND. One reason options are avoided by many investors is that the successful use of options requires more attention and analysis than most people devote to their portfolios. Much of the aura of complexity that surrounds options is due to a tendency to view them as unique or unusual investments. It is far more useful to relate the **risk-reward characteristics** of **options** to those of stocks and bonds than to emphasize the differences between options and other investment vehicles. The idea that "highly leveraged" options fit into the same risk-reward hierarchy as corporate bonds or common stocks can be difficult for many investors, including some experienced option traders, to accept at first. Nonetheless, most investors find options easier to understand when they examine them in terms of their impact on total portfolio risk.

This subsection demonstrates that the intelligent use of options requires evaluation of option contracts combined with measurement and control of portfolio risk. This discussion is directed at the investor who attempts to analyze investment positions in terms of **risk** and **reward.** Such an investor is sensitive to the tradeoff between opportunities to obtain high rates of return and the increased risk of loss which usually comes with such opportunities. Those who view investments in this framework can improve their decision-making process, and perhaps their results, by understanding the **risk-reward characteristics** of stock **options.**

To test their understanding of these principles, readers should compare the ideas presented here with the principles of **modern portfolio theory** outlined in the section entitled "Modern Portfolio Theory and Management."

RISK-REWARD CHARACTERISTICS OF OPTIONS. To illustrate the risk-reward characteristics of options, let us analyze the covered writing of a call option. In Exhibit 5 the ownership of shares of common stock is designated by the solid line $(A-A')$. The ownership of common stock, combined with the sale of a call option on that underlying stock, is designated by the broken line $(B-B')$. The vertical axis represents the profit or loss from each of these positions at a particular stock price on the day the option expires. The horizontal axis represents the price of the stock on that day. In this example the stock is purchased at $95 per share. The shareholder who does not sell the call option participates point for point in every increase or decrease in the price of the stock. His profit is theoretically unlimited on the upside, and his loss is limited only by a stock price of zero on the downside.

The alternative strategy of **covered call writing,** illustrated by the broken line, is based on the sale of a call option against the stock position. The hypothetical call option used in

EXHIBIT 4   COMPARISON OF TRANSACTION COSTS: CONVENTIONAL VERSUS LISTED OPTION MARKETS[a]

Assumptions

Buyer buys 10 calls at $500 each with a $50 striking price. Stock rises to $60 where buyer sells or exercises calls, receiving $1,000 per contract before costs. Writer initially buys 500 shares of stock or enough to cover one-half of his obligation. All figures are expressed on a per contract basis with commissions calculated on the assumption that the transaction consists of 10 contracts.

	Conventional	Listed
Buyer's Position		
Premium paid by buyer	$ 500.00	$ 500.00
Commission to buyer's broker	12.50	12.70
Cost to buyer to establish position	$ 512.50	$ 512.70
Gross proceeds from selling call		
($60–$50) × 100 shares	$1,000.00	$1,000.00
Listed option commission		(17.20)
Round-trip stock commission on sale of options	(107.06)	
Transfer taxes	(5.00)	
Subtract: Cost to establish position	(512.50)	(512.70)
Net profit to buyer	$ 375.44	$ 470.10
Writer's Position		
Premium paid by buyer	$ 500.00	$ 500.00
Option commission paid by writer to his broker	(12.50)	(12.70)
Put and call broker's spread (est.)	(75.00)	
Net premium to writer	$ 412.50	$ 487.30
Cost of repurchasing call from buyer	$1,000.00	$1,000.00
Add: Listed option commission		17.20
Purchase commissions initial stock position	30.13	30.13
Sale commission initial stock position		33.58
Purchase commission additional stock called	33.58	
Sale commission on stock called	50.83	
Transfer taxes	5.00	2.50
Subtract: Net premium received	(412.50)	(487.30)
Profit on stock owned	(500.00)	(500.00)
Net loss to writer	$ 207.04	$ 96.11
Net profit to buyer	$ 375.44	$ 470.10
Subtract: Net loss to writer	(207.04)	(96.11)
Net profit to investors	$ 168.40	$ 373.99
Total transaction costs	$ 331.60	$ 126.01
Less:	(126.01)	
Difference in transaction costs: Conventional vs. listed calls	$ 205.59 per contract	

[a]Note the following: (1) If the writer had written conventional straddles instead of two calls against each round lot owned, he would have fared better but the **total** transaction cost would have been even higher. (2) If the stock declines, total transaction costs may drop slightly faster for the conventional option but they are always substantially higher than listed option costs. (3) Transfer taxes are based on New York residence. (4) Commissions are calculated on the basis of an initial position of 10 calls and a stock position of 500 shares bought by the writer. Stock and option commission rates are those in effect prior to May 1, 1975, on the NYSE and CBOE, respectively. These commission charges are then stated on a per call basis. The total charges are 10 times the figures listed.

EXHIBIT 5   COMPARISON OF PROFIT AND LOSS: LONG STOCK POSITION VERSUS COVERED WRITER POSITION

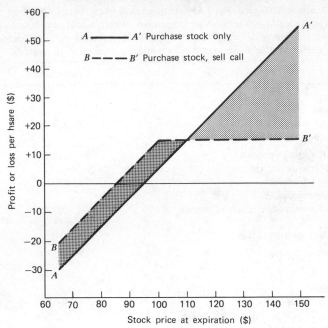

Exhibit 5 has a $100 striking price and a life of about 6 months from the time it is sold. The writer obtains a $10 per share premium. Any loss on the long stock position will be reduced by the $10 per share obtained from the option.

The covered call writer's position does have some disadvantages. If the price of the stock rises above $110 per share (the striking price plus the call premium), the investor would have been better off not selling the call. In return for a degree of downside protection, he has given up the opportunity to participate in any rise in the price of the underlying stock above $110 per share.

The downside protection provided by the option premium received is designated by the cross-hatched trapezoidal area to the left of the intersection of the two profit-loss lines in Exhibit 5. The upside opportunity given up by the covered call writer is represented by the shaded triangular area to the right of the intersection of the two lines.

COVERED CALL WRITING.   Exhibit 5 highlights several features of covered call writing. Note that the seller of the covered call option **reduces the variability of his return on investment.** If the stock rises sharply, the return on the stock position will be reduced by the amount of any loss on repurchase of the option. If the stock is called away at a price of $100 per share when the market price at the time of exercise is much higher, the investor may experience a sizable opportunity loss. If the stock declines, the loss will be reduced by the amount of the premium collected. Regardless of the direction in which the stock price moves or how far it moves, **covered call option writing reduces the variability of the return from a portfolio of equity securities.** The importance of this point is hard to overemphasize.

If the value of the premium received is too small relative to the value of the opportunity for appreciation given up, the covered writer will obtain a substandard return on investment over a period of time. When the value of the premium received equals the value of the opportunity forgone, after adjustment for risk, the option is said to be **fairly priced.** When the value of the protection is inadequate, the option is **underpriced.** When the premium is more than adequate to compensate for the capital appreciation opportunity given up, the option is **overpriced.**

To appreciate the importance of the size of the **option premiums** in determining investment results, compare Exhibits 5 and 6. In Exhibit 6 the option premium received by the covered call writer is only $1, not the $10 assumed in Exhibit 5. With this very low premium for a 6-month option, the cross-hatched area representing the downside protection afforded by the premium is much smaller, and the shaded area depicting the upside opportunity loss is considerably larger. A change in the size of the option premium affects the size of **both** areas, with obvious implications for investment results. Exhibit 6 provides an excellent demonstration that covered call writing is not a simple technique that almost magically adds to the income of a portfolio. Actually, as we will see momentarily, **covered call writing is more likely to reduce portfolio returns than it is to increase them.**

RISK-RETURN TRADEOFF.   Perhaps the significance of overpriced and underpriced options and their effect on investment results can be brought into perspective best by an examination of Exhibit 7, which represents the expected risk-return tradeoff characteristics of a variety of investment opportunities. The vertical axis (Y) measures the investor's expected

EXHIBIT 6   COMPARISON OF PROFIT AND LOSS: LONG STOCK POSITION VERSUS COVERED WRITER POSITION WITH LOW OPTION PREMIUM

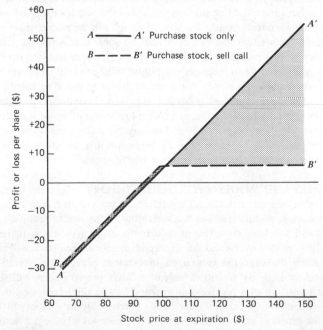

EXHIBIT 7   THE RISK-RETURN TRADEOFF

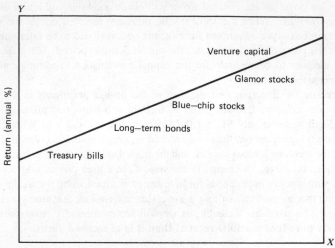

Risk (standard deviation of return)

annual return on investment for different investment opportunities. The horizontal axis (*X*) measures the degree of risk associated with a particular investment. Risk is expressed as the **standard deviation** (or variability) of the rate of return.

Treasury bills show essentially no variability of return relative to the yield anticipated at the time the bills are purchased. Though the interest rate structure as a whole can move up or down, the Treasury bill rate is fixed for the life of each bill at the level the investor accepts when he buys the bill. If an investor wishes to increase his expected return, he can purchase long-term **corporate bonds.** Because of changes in the market value of bonds due to interest rate fluctuations and the risk of default by some borrowers, the return from an investment in bonds for a particular time period may be greater or less than the risk-free rate of return on Treasury bills. Most investors will not be willing to hold long-term bonds unless they have the **expectation** of a higher rate of return than they would be able to obtain from Treasury bills. The same argument holds for any other investment. Investors who buy **common stocks** generally require a higher expected total rate of return than they would be willing to accept from long-term bonds or Treasury bills. To compensate for the risk to principal and the consequent variability in the return on investment, investors in **venture capital** projects require an even higher expected rate of return.

COVERED CALLS AND MODERN PORTFOLIO THEORY.   Like any other investment vehicle, options fit into this risk-reward structure. As we saw in Exhibit 5, selling a call option against a stock position reduces the variability of the rate of return on investment. Thus selling a call will have the effect of reducing portfolio risk levels. If the call option an investor sells is neither overpriced nor underpriced, sale of the option will also have the effect of **reducing the expected return on investment** because the overall risk of the portfolio will be reduced. By definition, **sale of a fairly priced option will simply move the risk-return position of a portfolio downward and to the left along the risk-return tradeoff line** of Exhibit 7. On the other hand, purchase of an option will increase the variability of the expected return from a portfolio. An investor who buys a fairly priced call option demonstrates willingness to accept greater variability of return in exchange for the expectation of a higher average rate of return.

The prospective option investor should keep in mind that selling call options will tend to move the expected risk-reward position of a portfolio down and to the left along the risk-reward tradeoff line of Exhibit 7, whereas the purchase of call options will tend to move the expected return up and to the right. Theoretically, it is possible to reduce the risk level of a portfolio of glamour stocks to the risk level of a portfolio of Treasury bills through the sale of an appropriate number of call options. In practice, commissions and other trading costs make it difficult to maintain such a low risk level with options. Within reasonable limits, however, it is possible to use options to adjust the risk posture of a portfolio rather closely to an individual's risk preferences.

IMPROVING RISK-ADJUSTED RETURNS.   The opportunities for risk modification that options provide are extremely important, but they are not the principal reason for using options. It is possible, if option premiums are too high or too low relative to their fair value, to structure a portfolio that provides a **higher expected return per unit of risk** than any portfolio of conventional securities lying along the risk-return tradeoff line. If a call option is **overpriced** and an investor sells that option, the risk-reward structure of the portfolio will move not only to the left along the risk-return line but also **above** the line. If the investor starts with Treasury bills or other short-term debt instruments and **buys underpriced** call options with a portion of his assets, it is possible to achieve an expected rate of return **above** the line while obtaining a degree of risk equivalent to the risk associated with owning a portfolio of long-term bonds or common stocks.

In contrast to the seller of overpriced call options, the investor selling underpriced calls will be reducing his return **more than proportionately to the reduction in risk.** This investor would generally be better off reducing the risk exposure of a portfolio by selling a portion of the stock and investing the proceeds in bonds or some other lower risk investment rather than accepting inadequate option premiums. The risk-return position of a portfolio will fall below the risk-reward tradeoff line in Exhibit 7, if underpriced options are sold against stock positions or if overpriced options are bought.

Selling a call option in a diversified equity portfolio will **always** reduce risk, as measured by the variability of the expected total return on the portfolio. Selling the option will **not** always (or even usually) enhance the overall rate of return. **By consistently selling overpriced options and/or buying underpriced options as part of a program of risk management, an investor can break away from the risk-reward tradeoff line.** Few serious investors will use options for any reason other than to enhance the rate of return per unit of risk.

VARIATIONS IN OPTION PREMIUM LEVELS.   Exhibit 8 shows a monthly **index of listed option premium levels** since shortly after the beginning of listed option trading on the Chicago Board Options Exchange. The index roughly approximates the degree of price variation in a "typical" option contract with the striking price and market price equal. The index indicates that a typical premium was just under 1.0 on the index, or the approximate equivalent of $4 for a 6-month option on an "average" $40 stock at the end of April 1974. The index rose to about 1.75, or the rough equivalent of about a $7 premium for the same option in November 1974. In early 1978 the index was consistently below 0.70 or the equivalent of less than $3 for the "typical" 6-month option on a $40 stock.

The index is based on premium levels of options on 14 of the first stocks listed on the CBOE. The fluctuations in option premium levels for individual stocks or the fluctuations for the most overpriced or most underpriced options on a specific stock show even more

EXHIBIT 8   AN INDEX OF LISTED OPTION LEVELS: BASE PERIOD STOCK PRICE VOLATILITY, OCTOBER 1968–SEPTEMBER 1972 = 1.0

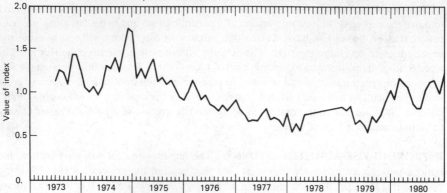

Source: Gastineau, *The Stock Options Manual*, 2nd ed., McGraw Hill, New York, 1979. Recent data courtesy of Kidder, Peabody & Co. Inc.

dramatic changes. It is not at all unusual for premium levels on some stocks to vary by a factor of 2 or 3 over the course of a year. Given the magnitude of these premium fluctuations, opportunities for **portfolio risk adjustment and return enhancement** through the purchase and sale of options are obviously extensive.

OPTION EVALUATION AND PORTFOLIO MANAGEMENT.   Most individuals and portfolio managers who use options take one of two approaches to the use of options. Some investors focus strictly on the fundamental or technical outlook for the underlying common stock and, on the basis of their fundamental or technical analysis, construct either a bullish or a bearish investment position using options or stock and options. Investors accustomed to conventional analytical and portfolio management approaches frequently pay little heed to computerized evaluation of option contracts.

In marked contrast to those who focus strictly on their investment attitude toward the underlying common stock, there is a sizable group of investors who focus strictly on **computerized option evaluation.** This group believes that no analytical technique can forecast stock price direction but that an investor can consistently make money selling overpriced and buying underpriced options. Overpricing and underpricing will be consistently determined by complicated computer programs.

Who is correct? Both. And neither. I agree with the conventional investor who says it is ridiculous to sell an overpriced naked call option on IBM if there are sound reasons for believing that IBM's stock will rise in price over the life of the option. I also agree with the computer evaluation advocate who argues that one should not buy that option. Fortunately, the approaches are not as contradictory as they may seem.

A **portfolio manager** or an individual investor can integrate conventional stock selection techniques with computerized option evaluation. The resulting portfolio would be carefully designed to reflect a desired degree of risk exposure. Each position in the portfolio would reflect the best analysis of the outlook for the particular stock in question and would integrate that analysis with evaluation of the option contract. For example, a covered writing position in IBM would be appropriate if the option was overpriced and the investor felt the stock was going up. Because selling the option reduces the risk associated with a long position in IBM, the investor should **buy more IBM stock** as a covered writer than as an owner who was not using options.

Fundamental analysis should also have an impact on the computerized evaluation of the option contract. Nearly all the more sophisticated option evaluation models base their calculation of the fair **value of an option** on five factors:

1. Time remaining until expiration.
2. Money market interest rates.
3. The size and pattern of dividend payments on the underlying stock.
4. The relationship between the current stock price and the striking price of the option (sometimes divided to make six factors).
5. The expected volatility (range of price movement) of the underlying stock.

All these factors except future stock price volatility can be easily observed and appropriate values supplied to the computer. Most users of computerized option evaluation models derive a stock price volatility estimate from the past volatility pattern of the underlying stock. While historic stock price volatility data are important, intelligent portfolio managers and individual investors temper their use of historic data with judgments based on fundamental analysis of the stock.

No option strategy is inherently superior to any other. At times option premiums on particular stocks are so high that it makes no sense to purchase these options. At other times premiums are so low that it is impossible to justify a covered writing position on any rational basis. If an investor is flexible in his choice of option strategies, there will almost always be attractive investment opportunities based on the use of options.

ANALYSIS OF RISK.   While evaluation of the expected profit from buying or selling a particular option can be complex, analysis of the risk impact of an option position on a portfolio is straightforward. To appraise the risk position quantitatively, the investor must translate each option into a risk-equivalent position in the underlying stock. If the option contract used in the example in Exhibit 5 moves up or down in price by one-half point for each one-point change in the price of the underlying stock, that option contract is the risk equivalent of 50 shares of the stock. The dollar gain or loss from a long or short position in that option will be approximately one-half the gain or loss from movement in a corresponding long or short position in a round lot of the underlying stock. If an investor wants to establish a position that is the risk equivalent of owning 100 shares of this stock, he can do so in any one of three ways:

1. Buy 100 shares of stock.
2. Buy 2 options (50 shares equivalent × 2 contracts = 100 shares).
3. Buy 200 shares of stock and sell 2 options [200 shares − (50 shares equivalent × 2 contracts) = 100 shares].

The fraction of a point by which an option price is expected to change when the underlying stock price changes by a full point is called the **neutral hedge ratio.** The concept of the neutral hedge ratio and the notion of options as stock equivalents are basic to the informed use of options.

Any option or option and stock position, no matter how complicated, can be readily translated into the risk equivalent of a specific number of shares or a dollar investment

in the underlying stock. If this analysis is undertaken for the entire portfolio, it is a surprisingly simple matter to convert all positions into stock equivalents. Once this has been done, the portfolio can be analyzed using the techniques of conventional portfolio management to appraise diversification and market risk exposure. Obviously, the fraction of a point that an option price will change for each one-point move in the stock will vary as the option nears expiration and as the relationship between the option striking price and the stock price changes. Consequently, the investor must analyze the risk structure of a portfolio frequently to be certain that the risk exposure to a particular underlying stock has not changed beyond acceptable limits. In turbulent markets the risk exposure to a particular stock may change significantly in a short period of time. The alert and flexible investor can usually maintain adequate diversification and appropriate overall market risk exposure, even when the market is unsettled.

INVESTMENT SIGNIFICANCE OF LISTED PUT OPTIONS

BACKGROUND.   Most of the previous examples have been based on **call option strategies.** This focus on calls reflects the interest of most option users and the fact that an option to buy seems to be easier to comprehend than an option to sell. While many investors will never use puts, an investor will never fully understand calls without some knowledge of the relationship between calls and puts.

BASIC RISK-REWARD CHARACTERISTICS OF PUT CONTRACTS.   Examining a possible transaction with the aid of a pair of diagrams should help clarify the risk-reward features of the put contract. Someone who **buys** an option to **sell** (a put) will not exercise that option unless the actual market price falls below the striking price. Consequently, the buyer of a put who holds the option until the expiration date will lose the entire premium paid for the put option unless the stock falls below the striking price. As the stock drops further below the striking price, the put buyer will begin to recover the premium paid and eventually earn a profit. The **writer** of a put will not be required to buy stock unless the market price of the stock falls below the striking price. The writer retains the entire premium if the stock price remains above the striking price.

Exhibit 9 shows the risk-reward positions for investors on both sides of a put contract with a $40 striking price and a $4 option premium. In Exhibit 9a the put buyer's profit-loss position is shown as of the date of exercise or expiration. The buyer loses the entire $4 premium if the stock price stays above $40 per share because the right to sell at $40 is worthless if a higher price is available on the stock exchange. The put buyer begins to recover premium as the stock drops below $40 and fully recovers the premium at the break-even price of $36 per share.

If the put buyer can buy stock on the market at $36 and deliver it to the writer of the put contract at a price of $40, the difference of $4 exactly equals the put premium before commissions. Below $36, the put buyer profits point for point as the stock continues to decline because the stock can be purchased at the lower price and sold to the writer of the put at $40. The put buyer's profit per share is equal to the $40 striking price less the sum of the $4 premium and the price at which the stock is ultimately purchased.

Exhibit 9b, the put writer's profit-loss line, contrasts with Exhibit 9a. The put writer's profit is the put buyer's loss, and vice versa. If the stock sells above $40, the put writer keeps the entire premium. As the stock drops, the put writer will still be required to buy stock at $40. The put writer's loss per share, like the put buyer's profit, is equal to the $40

EXHIBIT 9   COMPARISON OF PROFIT AND LOSS: BUYER OF PUT (*A*) VERSUS WRITER OF PUT (*B*)

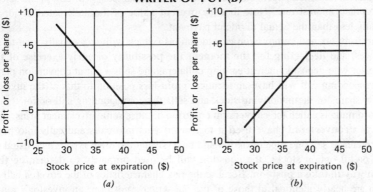

(a)   (b)

striking price less the sum of the $4 premium and the price at which the stock can be sold after the put is exercised.

Comparison of Exhibits 5 and 9*b* reveals in both cases the same general shape that characterizes the covered call option writer's profit-loss position. The covered call writer, like the put writer, has a fixed profit if the stock is above the striking price on the date the option expires. The covered call writer also has a measure of downside protection, represented by the option premium. The profit-loss diagrams for the put writer and the covered call writer look the same because, **in most important respects, they are the same.**

CONVERSION: KEY TO ANALYZING PUTS.   A thorough understanding of puts requires an understanding of the **conversion** process. Through conversion, calls can be transformed into puts, and puts transformed into calls. Most of the confusion surrounding puts will be eliminated if the investor keeps in mind that the sale of a put option, margined by a Treasury bill or similar short-term debt instrument, should be the approximate risk-reward equivalent of a covered call writing position using the corresponding listed call option (i.e., the call with the same striking price and expiration date as the put).

The **conversion formula** expressed in terms of the present value of a put is:

$$P_p = P_c - P_s + D + \frac{S}{1 + nr}$$

where P_p = price of a put

P_c = price of a corresponding call with identical striking price and expiration date

S = striking price of options

P_s = price of underlying stock

n = life of options expressed as fraction of a year

r = intermediate-term interest rate on Treasury bills or high-grade commercial paper

D = present value of all dividends expected to be paid before expiration of options

For some investors the appropriate rate r may be the interest rate a broker charges on debit balances. Learned papers can be written (and undoubtedly will be) on the selection of an appropriate interest rate. Note that the **present value** of the anticipated dividends will be slightly less than the actual dividend payment.

Apart from tax and commission considerations (which will occasionally lead to material differences) and **neglecting for the moment the possibility of early exercise of the put,** the investor who deposits interest-earning collateral and sells a put at conversion parity with the corresponding call will have an identical profit-loss position to that of the investor who buys 100 shares of the underlying stock and sells the corresponding call option.

This formula is called the **conversion equation** because some investment firms, popularly known as **"converters,"** have used it to convert puts into calls and calls into puts when writers prefer to sell one type of option and buyers want the other type. Once listed puts are trading on all option stocks, the equation will be used primarily **to determine the most efficient way to take a position.** Because the risk characteristics of the covered call writer's position are nearly identical to those of the put writer's position, an investor's return may be improved by taking one of these positions in preference to the other and earning a small arbitrage profit if the prices of the two options differ from the appropriate relationship. **Arbitrage** opportunities based on conversion relationships between puts and calls may be consistently available to certain investors, but understanding these possible arbitrage opportunities will be easier if the reader is able to calculate **stock risk equivalents** for simple stock and option positions.

CONVERSION, AND CALCULATION OF RISK EQUIVALENTS. Earlier I introduced the idea that it is possible to translate any listed call option position into a risk equivalent position in the underlying stock by calculating the fraction of a point by which the price of the option will change if a one-point move occurs in the underlying stock (the **neutral hedge ratio**). **Specifically, if the price of an option changes by one-half point when the price of the underlying stock changes by a full point, then that option, over a reasonable period of time and a range of stock prices, will behave in essentially the same manner as 50 shares of the underlying stock.** If a call changes in price by one-quarter point for each one-point move in the stock, the option will behave like 25 shares of stock.

The same concept holds for translating put options into stock equivalents. Because the put writer's position is the risk equivalent of covered call writing, **the number of equivalent shares represented by a put is equal to 100 minus the number of equivalent shares represented by the corresponding call.** If a call behaves like the equivalent of 25 shares of the stock, by moving one-quarter point for each one-point move in the stock, then a position in the analogous put contract will be the equivalent of 75 shares (100 shares minus 25 shares). The buyer of the put is "buying" the risk equivalent of a 75-share short position in the stock because, through the conversion mechanism, buying a put is the risk equivalent of buying the analogous call (plus 25 shares) and selling the underlying stock short (minus 100 shares).

Complex option positions are usually less attractive than relatively simple ones because transaction costs rise as the complexity of the position increases. The **risk-reward characteristics** of complex positions can also be difficult to evaluate. An investor may find that a position he meant to be bearish was, in fact, bullish. A position that is bullish at current stock prices may **become** bearish if the stock advances sharply. **The best way to keep track of a complex position is to translate each component into its common stock equivalent and total these equivalents to get the stock equivalent risk exposure of the entire position.**

Exhibit 10 shows the **risk equivalents** of a number of simple and complex stock and option positions. The security or combination described in the left-hand column is usually the most common way to establish a position. The other securities or combinations in the same row are risk equivalents of the left-hand column. **Unusual combinations may be the most efficient way to establish a position if they can provide the expectation of an arbitrage-type profit. The opportunity for arbitrage will arise if the market mechanism does not force put and call prices into conversion parity adjusted for the possibility of early exercise of the put.**

EARLY EXERCISE OF PUTS.   Sellers of calls are familiar, sometimes distressingly so, with the phenomenon of early exercise. Though other factors occasionally lead to early exercise of calls, the most common cause is the call buyer's desire to obtain a dividend paid on the underlying stock. Consequently, early exercise is most common when the call is in the money and there is a relatively short time period between an ex-dividend date and expiration of the option.

Sellers of puts must be prepared for early exercise under a different set of circumstances. Specifically, the seller of a put that is in the money (i.e., the stock is selling significantly

EXHIBIT 10   RISK COMPARABILITY OF INVESTMENT POSITIONS[a]

1. Buy 100 shares	Buy a call Sell a put	Buy 100 shares
2. Buy a call	Buy 100 shares Buy a put	
3. Buy 200 shares Sell two calls	Sell two puts	Buy 100 shares Sell a put Sell a call
4. Sell a call	Sell 100 shares short* Sell a put	
5. Buy a put	Sell 100 shares short* Buy a call	
6. Sell a put Sell a call	Buy 100 shares Sell two calls	Sell 100 shares short* Sell two puts
7. Buy a put Sell a call	Sell 100 shares short*	
8. Buy a put Buy a call	Sell 100 shares short* Buy two calls	

[a]The security or combination in the left-hand column is usually the most common of several possible ways of establishing an investment position. If all puts and calls are assumed to have the same striking price and expiration date, the positions in each row have equivalent risk characteristics. Positions marked with an asterisk involve a short sale of the underlying common stock and are unattractive for most investors.

below the striking price) will frequently experience early exercise **after** the stock goes ex-dividend if the option has a relatively short remaining life. Whereas sellers of calls find early exercise a problem when the dividend is sizable and the call is in the money, sellers of puts will find early exercise a problem when future dividends will be small or nonexistent and the put is in the money. Early exercise of in-the-money puts will be a particular problem in less volatile stocks. A moment's reflection will suggest that early exercise of puts may become quite common in bear markets and during any period when interest rates are high.

The reasons behind the early exercise of a put are related to the economics of short selling. The total investment return to the holder of **any** security consists of the algebraic sum of any periodic dividend or interest payment and any capital gain or loss. Frequently, there will be no dividend due on the underlying stock during the remaining life of a put. Consequently, the holder of a deep-in-the-money put will not benefit from a stock price reduction on an ex-dividend date. The holder of this put will be carrying the equivalent of a short position in the stock. Only if the put is bought **below** intrinsic value will the buyer of the put get credit for the proceeds of the implicit short sale. On the other hand, if the put is selling below its intrinsic value, an **arbitrageur** can profit by exercising it and reinvesting the cash received in a security with a higher expected total return. A deep-in-the-money put is an unstable position.

Call writers have learned that the buyer of a call has absolute control over who will receive a particular dividend on the underlying stock. The call buyer may exercise this control to deprive a call writer of the dividend. The owner of a put exercises similar control over who will receive a dividend. Ordinarily, the holder of a put will choose to "receive" dividends or get "credit" for them in the form of a probable decline in the stock price on the ex-dividend date. If there will be no dividends during the remaining life of an in-the-money put option, it can sell at or slightly below intrinsic value. There will probably be a greater tendency to exercise in-the-money puts than in-the-money calls because, in effect, **the carrying cost of a long position can be eliminated by exercising the put.** The effect of early exercise on the value of a put can be significant. Because of the potential for early exercise, the value of a put will always be greater than the value given by the conversion equation.

TAX TREATMENT OF OPTION TRANSACTIONS

TAX TREATMENT FROM VIEWPOINT OF OPTION BUYER. Exhibit 11 summarizes the tax treatment of the options buyer if the buyer is an **individual** or some other entity that treats options as capital assets. Tax treatment for broker-dealers and certain other options holders will be different.

TAX TREATMENT FROM VIEWPOINT OF OPTION WRITER. Exhibit 12 shows tax treatment from the viewpoint of an **individual** who is writing put and call options. As in the case of the option buyer, the tax treatment may be somewhat different for other entities.

SPECIAL TAX PROBLEMS AND OPPORTUNITIES. Before the passage of the **Tax Reform Act of 1976,** the focus of this subsection would have been on tax problems for pension and profit-sharing plans, mutual funds, and other tax-exempt organizations. Today there are virtually no tax problems except for a degree of uncertainty on the tax treatment to be accorded **foundations** on the purchase of options and certain problems that **Section 1244** and **Subchapter S corporations** might have. The focus is on tax opportunities. A more

EXHIBIT 11   TAX TREATMENT FROM OPTION BUYER'S VIEWPOINT

Description of Transaction	Tax Treatment of Option Premiums			Effect on Common Stock Holding, if any	Comments (Also See Text)
	Holding Period of Option	Nature of Gain or Loss	Timing of Recognition of Gain or Loss		
Buy put					
Having owned underlying stock less than 12 months and 1 day					
Sell put	Short-term	Short term capital gain or loss	Date of sale of option	Holding period of stock is eliminated for purposes of long-term gains by purchase of put. Any gain on stock is long-term 12 months and 1 day after put is sold. Any loss on stock is long-term 12 month and 1 day after stock was purchased.	This is a change from an earlier IRS position that if a put was sold (as opposed to being exercised or expiring), the short sale rule did not apply.
	Long-term	Long-term capital gain or loss			
Exercise put	Immaterial	Cost of put is deducted from proceeds of sale of stock	Date of exercise	Any gain on common stock is short-term. Any loss will be long-term if the date of exercise is more than 12 months and 1 day after purchase of the stock.	
Let put expire	Short-term	Short-term capital loss	Date of expiration	Holding period of stock for purposes of determining long-term gain begins on date of expiration of put. For purposes of determining loss, holding period begins on day stock was purchased.	
	Long-term	Long-term capital loss			

20 · 23

EXHIBIT 11 CONTINUED

Tax Treatment of Option Premiums

Description of Transaction	Holding Period of Option	Nature of Gain or Loss	Timing of Recognition of Gain or Loss	Effect on Common Stock Holding, if any	Comments (Also See Text)
Then buy underlying stock one or more days later					
Sell put	Short-term	Short-term capital gain or loss	Date of sale of option	If stock is sold for a gain holding period starts on day option is sold. If stock sold at loss, holding period starts on day stock was puchased.	
	Long-term	Long-term capital gain or loss			
Exercise put	Immaterial	Cost of put is deducted from proceeds of sale of stock	Date of exercise	Gain on common stock is short-term after deducting cost of put from proceeds. Loss will be long-term if stock held more than 12 months and 1 day.	
Let put expire	Short-term	Short-term capital loss	Date of expiration	For purposes of determining taxation of gain, holding period of stock begins on day put expires. If a loss, holding period begins on a day stock was purchased.	
	Long-term	Long-term capital loss			
Buy underlying stock on same day and identify put as intended to be used with this stock position					
Sell put	Short-term	Short-term capital gain or loss	Date of sale of option	If stock is sold for a gain, holding period starts on day option is sold. If stock sold at loss, holding period starts on day stock was purchased.	
	Long-term	Long-term capital gain or loss			

Exercise put	Same as stock	Cost of put is deducted from proceeds of sale of stock	Date of exercise	Loss is short- or long-term depending on holding period from date of purchase.
Let put expire	Same as stock	Add cost of put to basis of stock	Date of sale of stock	Gain or loss on sale of stock is short- or long-term depending on holding period. Holding period of stock starts on day stock and put are purchased. Note recognition of put loss is deferred until stock is sold.
Do not own related stock during life of put				
Sell put	Short-term	Short-term capital gain or loss	Date of sale of option	
	Long-term	Long-term capital gain or loss		
Let put expire	Short term	Short-term capital gain or loss	Date of expiration	
	Long-term	Long-term capital gain or loss		
Buy Call				
Sell call	Short-term	Short-term capital gain or loss	Date of sale of option	Purchase of call can cause wash sale.
Exercise call	Immaterial	Cost of call added to purchase cost to determine basis of stock	Date of sale of stock	Purchase of call can cause wash sale. Holding period of stock starts on day call is exercised. Short sale of stock does not affect holding period of call. Long-term loss on call can be avoided by exercising call and selling stock even if call has been owned more than 12 months and 1 day. Note that recognition of gain or loss on call is deferred until stock is sold.
Let call expire	Short-term	Short-term capital loss	Date of expiration	Purchase of call can cause wash sale.
	Long-term	Long-term capital loss		

EXHIBIT 11 CONTINUED

Tax Treatment of Option Premiums

Description of Transaction	Holding Period of Option	Nature of Gain or Loss	Timing of Recognition of Gain or Loss	Effect on Common Stock Holding, if any	Comments (Also See Text)
Buy Straddle or Other Combination Option		Same as separate put and call		Same as separate put and call.	On conventional options cost of straddle is allocated 55% to call and 45% to put unless there is a substantial reason to allocate in another way. No effect on income, gain or loss, or tax basis.
Adjustment of Striking Price or Number of Shares for Dividends or Other Capital Changes					

EXHIBIT 12   TAX TREATMENT FROM OPTION WRITER'S VIEWPOINT

Description of Transaction	Holding Period of Option	Nature of Gain or Loss	Timing of Recognition of Gain or Loss	Effect on Common Stock Holding if any	Comments (Also See Text)
Write Put					
Put expires	Immaterial	Short-term capital gain	Date of expiration	No effect.	Holding period of stock starts on day put is exercised. Note that recognition of tax effect of premium is deferred until stock is sold.
Put exercised	Immaterial	Proceeds from sale of put reduce basis of stock purchased	Date stock acquired through exercise is sold	Reduces basis.	
Put repurchased	Immaterial	Short-term capital gain or loss	Date of repurchase	No effect.	
Write Call					
Call expires	Immaterial	Short-term capital gain	Date of expiration	No effect if shareholder is an individual.	
Call exercised	Immaterial	Call premiums added to proceeds of sale of stock, character of gain or loss on stock determines nature of total gain	Date of exercise if stock delivered long; date of covering purchase if stock delivered short	No effect except on lot of stock delivered against exercise.	Holding period of stock extends from purchase date to exercise date if stock is delivering long.
Call repurchased	Immaterial	Short-term capital gain or loss	Date or repurchase	Might create wash sale in rare instances.	
Write Straddle or Other Combination	Immaterial	Same as separate put and call	Date or repurchase	Same as separate put and call.	Special treatment of straddles was eliminated by the **Tax Reform Act of 1976.**
Adjustment of Striking Price or Numbers of Shares for Dividends, Splits, or Other Capital Changes					No effect on income, gain or loss, or tax basis.

comprehensive discussion of tax considerations can be found elsewhere (Gastineau, *The Stock Options Manual*, pp. 127–171). Special tax opportunities are available to selected groups of investors such as investors with **capital loss carry-forwards, nonresident aliens** and even **high tax bracket individuals.**

Using Capital Loss Carry-Forwards. Investors with capital loss carry-forwards can obviously benefit by structuring a portfolio with the same risk characteristics as a conventional common stock portfolio but with a strong orientation toward realizing as much return as possible in the form of short-term capital gains that are not taxable until the loss carry-forward is used up. The notion of options as stock equivalents spelled out in Exhibit 10 should be useful in such an endeavor.

Nonresident Aliens. Nonresident alien shareholders are generally subject to a 30% **withholding tax** on interest and dividends from sources in the United States. While the tax is sometimes reduced by a tax treaty between the United States and the individual's country of residence, this withholding tax and the reporting requirements associated with it can be a substantial drawback to investment in U.S. securities.

It is easy to understand how options can help a foreign investor avoid the 30% tax if we assume that the investor's ideal portfolio consists of dividend-paying common stocks with listed options. The obvious way to construct such a portfolio would be to buy the stocks. Unfortunately, the dividends on the stocks would be subject to the withholding tax. In addition, the nonresident would find it difficult to obtain a tax deduction for any margin interest charges if a leveraged position were desired.

Using options, an investor can establish a portfolio with equivalent risk and with a similar or superior pretax return to that available on the common stock portfolio. Because the withholding tax is avoided, the aftertax results will probably be significantly improved. Funds not used in taking options positions would be invested in Treasury bills or Eurodollar certificates or deposited in banks. Income from these sources, if handled carefully, is not subject to the withholding tax.

High Tax Bracket Individuals. Options, even though they give rise only to short-term capital gains and losses, can be extremely useful to the high bracket tax payer in deferring gains or losses and in helping this investor to accumulate as much return as possible in the form of **long-term capital gains.**

Though this may seem contradictory at first, it will become clear if the reader will visualize the opportunity for timing the realization of short- and long-term capital gains that an active option trading strategy will provide. Basically, the higher tax bracket investor attempts to offset short-term gains against short- or long-term losses rather than offsetting these losses with hard-earned long-term capital gains.

EVALUATION OF AN OPTION CONTRACT

Evaluation of an option relative to the **risk-reward characteristics** of the underlying stock is the single most important step an investor must take to achieve superior investment performance using options.

SIGNIFICANCE OF OPTION EVALUATION. Many option services and option users stress calculations based on (1) the leverage inherent in a particular option contract, (2) the option premium as a percentage of the stock price or the striking price, or (3) the stock price parameters within which an option writing strategy is profitable. While it is helpful to know the leverage potential of an option relative to a possible price change in the underlying stock, the option premium as a percentage of the stock price, or the range of prices over which a given strategy will be profitable, a far more useful approach is to try to arrive at a single figure for the **fair value of an option.** Not only will that figure tell the investor whether, other things being equal, he should buy or write that option, but on the basis of that single figure, he also can make any other appropriate calculations easily.

Whether the fair value of an option is expressed in dollars and cents or the desirability of the option to a buyer or writer is appraised by calculating the ratio of the market price of the option to the fair value of the contract, the important thing is to arrive at a single figure that provides meaningful guidance to the use of that option in a possible investment strategy.

Exhibit 13 illustrates the process of determining the value of an option from the viewpoint of the buyer. Evaluation of the writer's position is essentially similar. This discussion deliberately omits several points that have an important bearing on any practical application of this approach or on any advanced discussion of the theoretical value of an option. The most important of these points is the notion of risk adjustment illustrated by Exhibit 7 and described in the accompanying discussion. Any option evaluation must be adjusted to reflect the effect of the purchase or sale of that option on the **risk-reward characteristics** of the portfolio. While this simplified discussion omits this risk adjustment, any working option evaluation model must take it into account.

The buyer's profit-loss line begins in the lower left-hand corner of Exhibit 13, runs parallel to the horizontal axis until it reaches the striking price (in this case, $100 per share), and rises toward the upper right-hand corner. The approximately bell-shaped curve superimposed on the graph is a hypothetical probability distribution of the stock price on the day the option expires. The shape and the location of the stock price distribution curve are a

EXHIBIT 13   CALL BUYER'S PROFIT-LOSS LINE AND STOCK PRICE PROBABILITY DISTRIBUTION

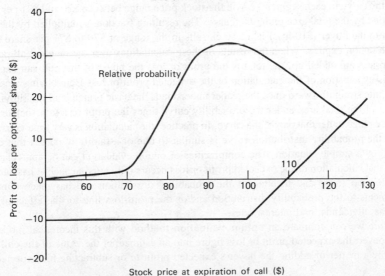

Stock price at expiration of call ($)

function of the price of the stock at the time the option is purchased, interest rates, the volatility of stock price changes, and the time remaining before the option expires. In the present instance, the price of the stock is assumed to be $95 on the day the buyer purchases the 6-month call at an option price of $10. The interest rate is the intermediate-term, low-risk interest rate. For simplicity, the volatility of the stock is assumed to be the average volatility over some past period.

While it is not possible to determine the exact price of the stock on the date 6 months in the future when the option will expire, it is possible to estimate the **probability** that it will sell at any particular price. This probability estimate is based largely on the way common stock prices have behaved in the past. The probability estimate should not be confused with technical analysis of stock price behavior. Derivation of the probability curve neither requires nor provides a forecast of the **direction** of any change in the stock price. It is concerned only with the likely **magnitude** of stock price changes.

Certain characteristics of this probability distribution are intuitively obvious. For example, most observers, whether they are avid chart readers or exponents of the random walk hypothesis, would agree that the price of a typical stock is more likely to be close to the present price 6 months from today than it is to be selling for either twice or half the present price. As the time period is extended from 6 months to, say, 2 years, the probability distribution will tend to spread out. Over the longer period, doubling or halving the stock price will become more likely events.

Some stocks are more likely to double or collapse than others. Both **Asarco** and **American Telephone and Telegraph** were selling near $45 per share in early 1980. Regardless of their opinions on the merits of the two issues, most market participants would expect Asarco stock to trade over a broader price range than AT&T over the next several years. Beyond these areas of agreement, there is considerable controversy over the exact shape of the probability distribution of future stock prices. The curve shown in Exhibit 13 is for illustrative purposes only, though it does approximate the shape of observed probability distributions.

Once the difficult task of estimating the characteristics of the probability distribution has been completed and both shape and location of the probability curve have been determined, it is a relatively simple matter to calculate the expected profitability of a call option. Using the example in Exhibit 13, we divide the probability curve into small segments. The area under the curve in each segment, say in the stock price range between $70 and $71 per share, is divided by the total area under the curve. The resulting fraction is multiplied by the profit or loss to the buyer ($10 loss) if the stock sells in the range of $70 to $71 per share on the day the option expires. When the results of these calculations over the range of all possible stock prices are added up, the total is the profit or loss the buyer of that call can expect.

This explanation of the calculation of the expected profit or loss from buying a call will seem quite straightforward once the reader understands the basic principle of multiplying the fraction of the total area under the probability curve times the profit or loss associated with the price range under that part of the curve. In practice, the calculation is very time-consuming unless the probability distribution curve is similar to one of a family of curves that can be defined by a simple equation. The complexities of option evaluation can be appreciated by noting that calculation of the expected profit or loss occurs only after an analyst has carefully estimated the shape and location of the probability distribution and has made numerous adjustments to the probability distribution and/or the profit-loss line for the effect of commissions, dividends, and interest rates.

Before we can compare an **option evaluation method** with this theoretical model, we must convert the expected profit or loss figure into an estimate of the **value of the call.** This is simply a matter of adding the buyer's expected profit *to* or subtracting his expected loss from the market price of the call and subtracting an additional amount as an adjustment for risk.

The importance of the **fair value or an option contract** is hard to overestimate. Once this value has been determined, it can serve as the foundation for any further work the investor might wish to do. It can also serve as part of a simple decision rule such as:

A call option is never written unless the premium received by the writer exceeds the fair value of the call, and a call option is never purchased unless the premium falls below the fair value of the option.

The fair value of a call or the ratio of the call price to fair value can serve as the basis of a whole series of calculations that permit the investor to structure the risk and return parameters of his investment position in virtually any desired way.

If we use an expected value calculation, such as the fair value of a call, as the sole criterion for a decision, we implicitly assume that the investor is neutral toward risk. Stated another way, relying solely on the expected value of an option implies that an individual is indifferent to the choice between, say, a 100% chance of gaining $1 and a 10% chance of gaining $10, combined with a 90% chance of no gain. While there is considerable evidence that this assumption is not valid when the amounts of money involved are quite large, the calculation of expected value provides a useful starting point. An individual's risk preferences can be reflected in the development of an investment strategy once the expected value has been calculated.

PROBABILITY MODELS. At one time or another a number of leading economists have written articles on option or **warrant pricing.** Most of this work has used options or warrants as a tool to study some other phenomenon that interested the author. To the reader who appreciates the nuances of academic literature, few of the option value models developed by these economists are exactly identical. To the reader less concerned with nuances, the similarities among these models are either comforting or boring, depending on one's mood.

Sprenkle and Samuelson-Merton. One of the more important probability models was derived by **Case M. Sprenkle** in his doctoral dissertation at Yale University in 1960. Sprenkle's work was published in *Yale Economic Essays,* and reprinted in *The Random Character of Stock Market Prices,* edited by **Paul Cootner.** The Sprenkle model is similar in most respects to other classical option and warrant models based on the probability approach. Apart from a few practical considerations that limit its usefulness, Sprenkle's model describes fairly well the relationship between the probability distribution of stock price changes and option or warrant values. The Sprenkle model approximates the description of the probability approach already given and soon to be developed further.

A second important model was developed by **Paul Samuelson** and **Robert Merton** of MIT and described in an article in the Winter 1969 issue of *Industrial Management Review*. The unique feature of this model is that it is based on what the authors call a "util-prob" or combined utility and probability distribution. Though most observers would argue that some of the complexities of the Samuelson-Merton model are rendered obsolete by the work of **Fischer Black** and **Myron Scholes,** this model in its most general form is one of the most flexible approaches to warrant and option evaluation.

Black-Scholes Model. Almost as if it were timed to coincide with the opening of the **Chicago Board Options Exchange,** a theoretical valuation formula for options, derived by

Fischer Black and **Myron Scholes,** was published in *The Journal of Political Economy* for May–June 1973. The principal difference between the Black-Scholes formulation and the techniques proposed by other economists over the years is that Black and Scholes focus on the **neutral option hedge** as the key to the determination of option value. The Black-Scholes formula and its major assumptions are outlined in Exhibit 14.

While the mathematical derivation of the formula is an important feature of the Black-Scholes article, the focus here is on the principle behind the Black-Scholes approach and its usefulness as a practical method of evaluating options.

The Black-Scholes model is based on the fact that it is possible, subject to a number of assumptions, to set up a **perfectly hedged position** consisting of a long position in an underlying stock and a short position in options on that stock, or a long position in the

EXHIBIT 14   THE BLACK-SCHOLES MODEL[a]

$$V_c = P_s N (d_1) - Se^{(t - t)} N(d_2)$$

$$d_1 = \frac{\ln (P_s/S) + (r + \frac{1}{2}v^2)(t^* - t)}{v\sqrt{(t^* - t)}}$$

$$d_2 = \frac{\ln (P_s S) + (r - \frac{1}{2}v^2)(t^* - t)}{v\sqrt{(t^* - t)}}$$

V_c = fair value of option

P_s = stock price

S = striking or exercise price

$N(d)$ = cumulative normal density function

r = "risk-free" interest rate

t = current date

t^* = maturity date of option or warrant

v^2 = variance rate of return on stock

e = base of natural logarithms = 2.71828

$\ln$ = natural logarithm

Key assumptions of the Black-Scholes Model:

1. The short-term interest rate is known and is constant through time.

2. The stock price follows a random walk in continuous time with a variance rate proportional to the square of the stock price.

3. The distribution of possible stock prices at the end of any finite interval is lognormal.

4. The variance rate of return on the stock is constant.

5. The stock pays no dividends and makes no other distributions.

6. The option can only be exercised at maturity.

7. There are no commissions or other transaction costs in buying or selling the stock or the option.

8. It is possible to borrow any fraction of the price of a security to buy it or to hold it, at the short-term interest rate.

9. A seller who does not own a security (a short seller) will simply accept the price of the security from the buyer and will agree to settle with the buyer on some future date by paying him an amount equal to the price of the security on that date. While this short sale is outstanding, the short seller will have the use of, or interest on, the proceeds of the sale.

10. The tax rate, if any, is identical for all transactions and all market participants.

Source: Fischer Black and Myron Scholes, "The Pricing of Options and Corporate Liabilities," *Journal of Political Economy,* May–June 1973, pp. 637–654.

options and a short position in the stock. "Perfectly hedged" means that over a stock price interval close to the current price, any profit resulting from an instantaneous increase in the price of the stock would be exactly offset by a loss on the option position, or vice versa. The Black-Scholes formula, then, is developed from the principle that **options can completely eliminate market risk from a stock portfolio.** Black and Scholes postulate that the ratio of options to stock in this hedged position is constantly modified at no commission cost to offset gains or losses on the stock by losses or gains on the options. Because the position is theoretically riskless, the option premium at which the hedge yields a pretax return equal to the risk-free short-term interest rate is the fair value of the option. If the price of the option is greater or less than fair value, the return from a risk-free hedged position could be different from the risk-free interest rate.

Readers familiar with **modern capital market theory** should recognize that the Black-Scholes evaluation of options with a **neutral hedge** and the risk-reward analysis that accompanied the discussion of options in portfolio management is an extension of modern capital market theory. Establishing the relationship of options to other securities was one of the more important contributions of the Black-Scholes papers (Black and Scholes, "The Valuation of Option Contracts and a Test of Market Efficiency," *Journal of Finance,* May 1972, pp. 399–417, and "The Pricing of Options and Corporate Liabilities," *Journal of Political Economy,* May–June 1973, pp. 637–654). The Black-Scholes articles are an appropriate starting point for anyone wishing to explore option theory in greater depth.

Probably the most important **shortcoming of the Black-Scholes model** is that it relies heavily on the assumption that the probability distribution of future stock prices is a **log normal distribution.** Unfortunately for the usefulness of the Black-Scholes model, virtually every significant empirical study ever made of the distribution of stock price changes indicates that the actual probability distribution of stock prices deviates materially from the log normal curve.

While economists are satisfied that the log normal distribution provides a better approximation to the actual probability distribution of stock prices than the standard normal distribution, the log normal distribution does not fit observed data on stock prices well enough to permit its use for all purposes. Empirical studies have shown that the probability distribution of stock prices differs from the log normal approximation in several ways. First, there is a slight tendency for future stock prices to cluster more around the current stock price than might be expected on the basis of the log normal distribution. Second, and even more significant when options are involved, there is a pronounced tendency for stock prices to be more concentrated in the tails of the distribution than predicted by the log normal curve.

Exhibit 15 illustrates for comparative purposes the difference between the log normal distribution (dashed line) and the observed distribution with its higher peak and fatter tails.

Option evaluation techniques based on the log normal distribution give reasonably satisfactory results as long as the market price and the exercise price are identical. When these prices differ materially, however, an option evaluation based on a log normal distribution of expected stock prices is subject to substantial error. For example, a call option selling well out of the money might appear, from the log normal distribution, to have little value. The "skinny" tails of the log normal distribution suggest a low probability of a large price advance. Using the **empirical distribution,** with its fatter tails, the value of the out-of-the-money call would be much higher.

Although very little has been said about the problems of estimating the precise characteristics of the probability distribution applicable to a particular stock at a particular time, practical use of a probability model for option evaluation is difficult and time-consuming, even with the help of a computer.

**EXHIBIT 15   COMPARISON OF EMPIRICAL DISTRIBUTION OF STOCK PRICES
WITH LOG NORMAL DISTRIBUTION**

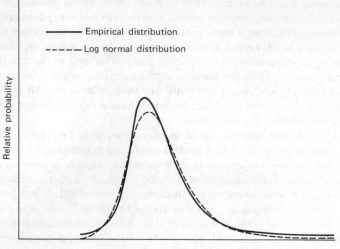

Stock price at end of selected period ($)

Recent Attempts to Deal with Probability Distribution Problem.   Even before the Black-Scholes articles were published, a number of writers focused on the analytical complexities caused by the fact that the actual distribution of stock price changes is not log normal. The work of **Mandelbrot, Fama,** and **Press** preceded the Black-Scholes articles and focused primarily on finding a standard function that fit the observed data better than the log normal curve. More recent articles have explored the **whys** of non-log normality with the analytical tools provided by Black and Scholes. Although the authors referred to in subsequent paragraphs have much more to say, we focus on their analysis of why the distribution of stock price changes is not log normal.

Robert Merton has probably done as much to extend and improve the realism of the theoretical framework developed by Black and Scholes as any one. Though their work differs in some respects from Merton's, John Cox and Stephen Ross have also attempted to reconcile the Black-Scholes model with empirical data. A major contribution of Merton, Cox, and Ross has been to develop models that combine the log normal Black-Scholes equations with a **"jump" process.** Their explanation for non-log-normality is that the log normal movement of stock prices in the absence of new developments is combined with jumps caused by major events that significantly change the mean value around which log normally distributed fluctuations take place. In essence, they argue that the observed stock price distribution is really a combination of several interacting distributions. Merton points out that this **dual distribution** approach helps explain not only the observed stock price distribution but also the tendency for certain options to sell for relatively more or less than the Black-Scholes model predicts.

Robert Geske has proposed another explanation for the observed distribution of stock price changes that is consistent with the work of Merton and of Cox and Ross. His approach also helps tie option theory more closely to capital market theory, a process initiated by Black and Scholes. Geske argues that a call option is really an option on an option if the firm's capitalization consists of debt as well as common stock. Because common shareholders cannot be assessed if a firm is bankrupt and because they have an "option" to purchase the balance of a firm's assets and cash flows from bondholders by redeeming the bonds, **common stock can be evaluated as an option to purchase the entire firm.** A call option on common stock is therefore best analyzed as an option on an option. Like the Merton-Cox-Ross dual distribution analysis, Geske's **compound option approach** improves on some of the empirical weaknesses of the simple Black-Scholes model. In addition to explaining the Black-Scholes undervaluation of deep-out-of-the-money options, Geske's model explains the tendency of stock price volatility to increase as the stock price declines.

The problem with these extensions of the Black-Scholes model is that the user of these complex models is called on to deal with more unknowns than the average human mind can handle. It is almost certain that several probability distributions do interact to determine the observed pattern of stock price changes. Likewise, the leverage characteristics of the firm do affect the volatility of the stock and the shape of the stock price distribution. These models may be intuitively more satisfying, but they require a user to deal with too many variables. Whereas the Black-Scholes model has five variables, four of which are known, Geske's model has seven variables, and four of them require complex estimation techniques. The practitioner needs a model that is as easy to use as the Black-Scholes formulations but gives results closer to the more sophisticated extensions that attempt to deal with the non-log-normality of the distribution of stock prices.

Cox, Ross, and Rubinstein.   Most of the alternative derivations of the Black-Scholes evaluation model have been of value primarily in explaining the mechanism behind the model from different perspectives. One of these derivations, by Cox, Ross, and Mark Rubinstein was published as Working Paper 79 of the Institute of Business and Economic Research at the University of California at Berkeley and has appreciably extended the usefulness of the Black-Scholes model. Specifically, the use of the **binomial approximation** to the log normal distribution permits a more accurate adjustment for dividends. Good dividend adjustments had been a major problem with the traditional Black-Scholes formulation. The binomial approach is also of value in dealing with the early exercise problem in put evaluation. Although a binomial model requires more computer memory and operating time than the traditional Black-Scholes model, the improvement in accuracy may be worth the cost.

Gastineau-Madansky Model.   The development of the **Gastineau-Madansky model,** described in Gastineau (*The Stock Options Manual*), has drawn heavily on the work of the authors whose formulations were discussed above. In general form, the Gastineau-Madansky model is a probability model. By modifying an assumption here and dropping an equation there, it is possible to reduce the Gastineau-Madansky formulation to the format of any of the probability models, including the Black-Scholes model.

The fair value of an option determined by the Gastineau-Madansky model can be adjusted for dividends, interest rates, and option commission charges. The model can also be adjusted for tax rates. One feature, but by no means the only unique feature, of the Gastineau-Madansky model is that it does not use a simple mathematical function to represent the stock price probability distribution. The complex **empirical probability distribution** gives more useful results than the commonly used log normal distribution.

USING AN OPTION EVALUATION MODEL.   Exhibit 16 lists some of the data generated by the Gastineau-Madansky computerized option model for listed options on **McDonald's Corp.** and **Polaroid.** Even a casual examination of these data suggests, under the assumptions incorporated in the model, that the McDonald's option was slightly underpriced and that the

EXHIBIT 16   PARTIAL LISTING OF THE OUTPUT OF THE GASTINEAU-MADANSKY COMPUTERIZED OPTION MODEL: DATE OF ANALYSIS, AUGUST 12, 1974[a]

	Stock	
	McDonald's	Polaroid
Symbol	MCD	PRD
Expiration month	January	January
Striking price	$50.00	$30.00
Stock price	$41.125	$26.375
Call price	$ 2.75	$ 3.75
Stock price variance assumption	0.8	1.0
Gastineau-Madansky fair value	$ 3.00	$ 2.79
Call price–fair value	0.92	1.34
Black-Scholes fair value full adjusted	$ 2.82	$ 2.72
Neutral hedge ratio (pretax)	0.37	0.47
Net margin required for uncover writer (30% rate) per share	$ 0.71	$ 0.53
Probability option will be exercised	31%	39%
Probability uncovered writer will lose money or buyer will make money	25%	26%
Probability writer of pretax neutral hedge will lose money	36%	24%
Profit parameters pretax neutral hedge	$33.72–$59.62	$18.47–$40.40
Expected annualized return on equity from a neutral hedge	5.8%	34.9%
Implied stock price variance	0.7	1.6

[a]Note the following:

1. Stock and option prices are closing prices for the previous Friday.

2. Margin requirements are based on an assumed 30% margin rate for uncovered writers and expressed net of any credit for the premium received by the writer.

3. The profit parameters are simply the prices that bracket the stock price range over which a neutral hedge is profitable.

4. The expected annualized return on equity from a neutral hedge is annualized probability weighted profit or loss from a neutral hedge divided by the net equity of the investor in the hedge after option premiums received are credited.

5. Implied stock price variance is the level of stock price volatility that is consistent with the market price of the option.

Polaroid option was substantially overpriced. At the risk of repeating a point, it should be emphasized that the terms "overpriced" and "underpriced" do not imply **anything** about the likely direction of stock price movement; they suggest **only** how an option should be used.

If an investor is bearish on McDonald's, he might not be interested in buying a call just because it is cheap. Instead, an underpriced call might be reversed to create a put, or the call might be purchased to hedge a short sale. Likewise, a bull on Polaroid might want to write uncovered puts, write straddles against a long position, or set up a bullish spread. The option evaluation model is a tool to help the investor choose a strategy that is appropriate to his attitude on the stock, the value of the option contract, and his personal risk preferences.

A careful examination of Exhibit 16 will indicate that some of the calculations are based on the fair value of a call option. Others, such as the probability that an option will be exercised or the probability that an uncovered writer will lose money, require direct reference to the probability curve of the stock price distribution. Still others, such as the required margin calculation, are easy enough to obtain without reference to a particular model and are included on the computer run for convenience.

While the amount of data that a computerized model generates can be truly staggering (most of the computations that can be furnished by the computer are not listed in Exhibit 16), very few data need be understood or evaluated to reach an intelligent decision on a **particular** option strategy. In fact, the most important lessons that a **portfolio manager** who uses options must learn are to analyze assumptions about the underlying stock carefully and to organize the computer output in a format that is relevant to a decision. Usually, organizing the output means disregarding all but a few pertinent numbers.

PROFITABILITY OF OPTION TRADING

Many people believe that determining the "inherent" profitability of an option strategy should be easy. It is not. In many respects the issue of option profitability is the most controversial of all option topics.

STUDIES OF OPTION PROFITABILITY.   The academic community was fascinated with the issue of option profitability even when the high transaction costs of conventional options made it difficult to believe that either option buyers or option writers could enjoy consistently superior results in the absence of brilliant investment decisions to overcome the cost disadvantage of dealing in options. Most of the **early studies of option profitability** reached the conclusion that the option writer enjoyed a modest advantage over the option buyer. However, none of these early surveys of option profitability covered a long enough period to assure representative market behavior.

Kassouf.   The leading apologist of the "covered writing is best" school is probably **Sheen Kassouf.** His documented simulation of option profitability appeared in an article entitled "Options Pricing: Theory and Practice" (*Institute for Quantitative Research and Finance,* Columbia University Spring Seminar, Palm Springs, CA, 1977). The principal weakness of this simulation is that it systematically used option premiums that were too high.

Merton, Scholes, and Gladstein.   Perhaps, in spite of themselves, Merton, Scholes, and Mathew Gladstein are usually considered to be advocates of option buying. Their study "A Simulation of the Returns and Risks of Alternative Option Portfolio Investment Strategies" appeared in the *Journal of Business* (April 1978, pp. 183–242). This simulation combined option premiums that were systematically too low with failure to maintain a consistent degree of stock equivalent risk exposure within and between simulation periods. Exhibit 17 compares the Merton, Scholes and Gladstein results with those of Kassouf.

Common Flaws in Simulations.   Gastineau and Madansky, in their article "Why Simulations Are an Unreliable Test of Option Strategies" (*Financial Analysts Journal,* September–October 1979, pp. 61–76), carefully analyzed the weaknesses of the Kassouf and

EXHIBIT 17   OPTION STRATEGY SIMULATIONS: KASSOUF VS. MERTON, SCHOLES, AND GLADSTEIN

Period Covered by Study	Kassouf	Merton, Scholes, and Gladstein
	(Quarterly Returns): February 1, 1950– January 31, 1975	(Semiannual Returns): July 1, 1963– December 31, 1975
Return from Dow Jones unoptioned stock portfolio	2.74%	4.1%
Standard deviation	6.74	13.7
Return from at-the-money covered call writing	4.20	2.9
Standard deviation	3.63	6.2
Return from 90% money market instruments, 10% at-the-money call purchase strategy	−1.60	5.1
Standard deviation	5.71	10.1

Merton-Scholes-Gladstein simulations and developed a list of common flaws inherent in the use of simulation techniques to evaluate option strategies. By far the most important criticism of **all** option simulations is that they fail to maintain a consistent degree of stock equivalent risk exposure between the simulated option portfolio and the market indexes with which the option portfolio is compared. In other words, a portfolio that starts out with approximately the same risk exposure as the **Standard & Poor's 500 stock index** will have a great deal more or a great deal less risk exposure by the end of the simulation period.

Although inconsistent changes in stock equivalent risk exposure are the primary cause of misleading results in option strategy simulations, other factors can lead to misleading results as well. Factors mentioned in the Gastineau-Madansky article include various techniques by which option premiums are systematically over- or underestimated. Among the reasons for misestimation are failure to adjust properly for risk, use of an inappropriate risk-free interest rate, and use of an inappropriate option evaluation model. Option premiums can be incorrectly estimated as a result of secular changes in the volatility of the underlying stocks. In addition, decision rules for constructing simulation portfolios may overweight or underweight various sectors of the market.

HISTORIC PROFITABILITY RECORD.   The only meaningful study of **historic profitability** in the **listed options market** is provided in the Gastineau-Madansky article. Exhibit 18 compares option premium levels with fair values as measured by subsequent stock price volatility: when the solid line was above the dashed line, options were overpriced and the risk-adjusted advantage lay with the seller of options; when the solid line was below the dashed line, the advantage lay with the buyer of options because options were underpriced. Over the entire period covered by the graph there was a modest advantage accruing to option sellers. In the subsequent period there are indications that this advantage has reversed. Since the inauguration of listed option trading in 1973, there has been no material net advantage to the option buyer versus the option seller, or vice versa.

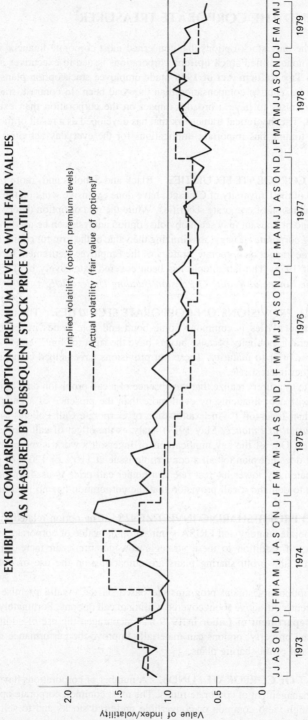

EXHIBIT 18 COMPARISON OF OPTION PREMIUM LEVELS WITH FAIR VALUES AS MEASURED BY SUBSEQUENT STOCK PRICE VOLATILITY

Implied volatility (option premium levels)

Actual volatility (fair value of options)[a]

*a*The actual volatility is shown one quarter early, to permit calculation of the degree of option overpricing or underpricing.

OPTIONS AND THE CORPORATE TREASURER

Until recently, the only stock options that concerned most corporate financial officers were the **qualified** or nonqualified **stock options** corporations issued to executives and other key employees. The **Tax Reform Act of 1976** made employee stock option plans a much less attractive form of executive compensation than they had been. In contrast, trading in listed stock options promises to have a broader impact on the corporation than executive stock options ever had. The theoretical framework that has developed as a result of the introduction of listed option trading has important implications for the everyday activities of corporate treasurers.

EVALUATING CORPORATE SECURITIES.   Black and Scholes and, more recently, **Jonathan Ingersoll** of the University of Chicago, have done extensive work on the use of option theory in the evaluation of corporate securities. While the role of option theory in evaluating a convertible bond or warrant may seem obvious, option analysis can be used in such diverse areas as planning corporate strategy, maximizing the value of the firm for equity shareholders, and evaluating the impact on corporate strategy of the Employee Retirement Income Security Act **(ERISA)** of 1974. The latter topic has been covered extensively by Treynor, Regan, and Priest in *The Financial Reality of Pension Funding Under ERISA*.

PUT AND CALL PROVISIONS ON CORPORATE SECURITIES.   The use of **call provisions on debt securities** is common. Some bond and note issues in recent years have received considerable publicity because buyers have the right to ''put'' bonds to the issuing corporation at par prior to maturity. These put provisions have helped companies sell their debt at a lower net interest rate.

Few corporate treasurers realize that the absence of a call provision on a bond can reduce the interest cost of debt financing by even more than the presence of a put provision. An article by Jonathan Ingersoll (''An Examination of Corporate Call Policies on Convertible Securities,'' *Journal of Finance*, May 1977) analyzes the effect of call provisions on convertible securities. One of the key implications of Ingersoll's work is the probability that a corporation that does not plan to call a convertible issue at 110% or 120% of parity will be able to pay a materially lower interest rate if a higher call price is used. In other words, it makes no sense to demand a call provision that the corporation has no intention of using.

PENSION AND PROFIT-SHARING INVESTMENTS.   The option-related implications of **ERISA** for corporate strategy and ERISA's impact on the value of corporate securities were described above. In addition to these strategic considerations, an increasing number of corporate pension and profit sharing plans are embarking on the use of options in their portfolios.

Most such option investment programs are based on the invalid premise that there is something inherently attractive about covered writing of call options. Fortunately, a regulation issued by the **Department of Labor** in 1979 has encouraged the use of additional options strategies. If used properly, options can materially improve the performance results of corporate pension and profit-sharing plans.

MANAGEMENT OF CORPORATE FUNDS.   A number of corporations have begun using options in the management of corporate funds. The most common corporate options strategy is to purchase high-yield common or convertible preferred stocks and to sell call options.

This strategy can limit exposure to stock price fluctuations while the corporation takes advantage of the 85% intercorporate dividend deduction. This option strategy can work very well if two basic rules are observed. First, the option sold should be overpriced. Any investor, corporate or individual, who consistently sells underpriced call options will probably experience a substandard return on investment in the long run.

A second basic rule may be of even greater significance to the corporate seller of call options. Section 246(c) of the Internal Revenue Code requires a corporate taxpayer to hold shares on which the 85% dividend deduction is claimed for a period of more than 15 days. The holding period will be reduced by any period in which the taxpayer has an option to sell, is under a contractual obligation to sell, or has made (and not closed) a short sale of substantially identical stock or securities. The key provision for the covered call option writer is whether the corporation is under an obligation to sell the underlying stock. The IRS has issued a private ruling that selling a covered call does not create a contractual obligation to sell within the meaning of this statute. If this private ruling is used as a basis for aggressive conversion of short-term capital gains into qualified dividends, it may be modified.

A more sophisticated corporate option strategy uses put and call options on interest-sensitive common stocks to hedge the interest rate risk of a preferred stock or municipal bond portfolio. Because most preferred stock dividends qualify for the 85% intercorporate dividend deduction and because municipal bond interest is totally tax exempt, a hedged portfolio of this nature should provide an **aftertax** yield advantage over commercial paper or certificates of deposit. The basis of this technique is the use of options to remove a substantial element of risk from an investment vehicle that has unique tax advantages for the corporate investor. A similar effect can be achieved through the use of interest rate futures contracts that hedge a preferred or utility common stock portfolio.

OPTIONS ON FIXED INCOME SECURITIES.   Several of the existing options exchanges have announced plans to introduce put and call options on fixed income securities, typically long-term government bonds. While it is too early to tell when and if such plans will be implemented, there is a distinct probability that the volume of option trading on fixed income securities eventually will exceed volume in the interest rate futures markets.

MERITS OF OPTION LISTING.   A few corporations have taken steps to discourage the listing of their stocks for option trading. A far greater number of corporate managements have launched campaigns to interest the listing committees of the options exchanges in their stocks. Although the evidence is not definitive, an active option market appears to reduce the tendency for the underlying stock price to fluctuate. This stock price volatility reduction results from the **risk transfer characteristics of options.** A brokerage firm asked to bid on a block of stock or an institutional investor offered part of the block can offset some of the risk of the stock position in the option market. Because volume in the option market is a proxy for volume in the underlying stock, each option trade increases the depth and the liquidity of the market in the stock, with a consequent reduction in stock price fluctuations.

The significance of lower stock price volatility to the financial officer is that lower volatility helps reduce the corporation's cost of capital. Other things being equal, a less volatile stock is a more desirable investment. Lower volatility means lower risk. Investors will accept a lower return on a lower risk investment. A lower future return expectation means a higher current stock price and a lower cost of equity capital. Even a slight reduction in stock price volatility should tend to improve the average price-earnings multiple or reduce the dividend yield that investors will demand from a common stock.

EXHIBIT 19 INFORMATION PROVIDED BY OPTION ADVISORY SERVICES

Name and Address	Evaluation of Premiums								Stock Information			
	Values Provided		Hedge Ratio	Type Model	Volatility Estimates or Data	Return Data	All Option Stocks Covered	Statistical	Recommendations	Technical or Fundamental	Data on Nonoption Securities	Market Opinions
	Calls	Puts										
Advanced Investment Strategies Thomas C. Nodding & Associates, Inc. 135 S. LaSalle St. Chicago, IL 60603	No	No	No	None	None	None	Selected strategies	Ltd	Convertibles	Tech	Convertibles, dual funds	No
Fisher Black 50 Memorial Dr. Cambridge, MA 02139	Yes	Yes	Yes	Prob	Calc	None	Yes	D	No		No	No
CMI's Option Trader CMI Business Services, Inc. 1133 N. North Camano Dr. Camano Island, WA 98292	No	No	No	None	Hist	ORC	56	No	Yes	Tech	No	Yes
Chartcraft Weekly Option Service Investor's Intelligence, Inc. 2 East Ave. Larchmont, NY 10538	No	No	No	None	None	RE, RU	Yes	P&F charts	Yes	Tech	No	Yes
Dunn and Hargitt's Option Guide 22 N. Second St. Lafayette, IN 47902	No	No	No	None	Hist	No	209 stocks	Ltd	Yes	Tech Fund	Some	Yes
EVM Stock Option Letter EVM Analysts, Inc. 1001 Gayley Ave. Suite 208, Westwood Village Los Angeles, CA 90024	Yes	Yes	Yes	Econ	Calc	RE, RU	Yes	Ltd	Yes	Tech	No	Yes

The Holt Trading Advisory T.J. Holt & Company, Inc. 277 Park Ave. New York, NY 10017	Limited	No	Tech Fund	Yes	Ex	156 stocks	No	Hist	Econ	No	Planned	Yes, graphs
The Option Trader 119 W. 57th St. New York, NY 10019	Yes	No	Fund, Tech	Yes	Ltd	No	ORC	Hist	None	No	No	No
Option Weekly 4838 Randolph Dr. Annandale, VA 22003	No	No	No	No	No	102	ORC	Calc	Econ	No	Some	Some
Stock Option Guide Daily Graphs P.O. Box 24933 Los Angeles, CA 90024	No	No	No	No	Ex	Yes	Yes	Calc	Prob	Occasional	Yes	Yes
Systems and Forecast P.O. Box 1227 Old Village Station Great Neck, NY 11023		Yes	Tech Fund	Yes	Ltd	No	No	Hist	Prob	Occasional	Occasional	Occasional
Trade Levels Option Report Trade Levels Inc. Suite 400 Mutual Savings Building 301 E. Colorado Blvd. Pasadena, CA 91101	Yes	Yes	Tech	Yes	No	Yes	RE, RU	Calc, beta	None	No	No	No
Value Line Options and Convertibles Arnold Bernhard & Co., Inc. 5 E. 44th St. New York NY 10017	No	Convertibles, warrants	Fund	Yes	D	Yes	None	Hist	Econ	Yes	Yes	Yes

Source: G. Gastineau, *The Stock Options Manual,* 2nd ed., McGraw-Hill, New York, 1979, pp. 363–364.

In addition to the generally favorable effect of an option listing on liquidity and stock price volatility, an option listing can reduce the **corporation's cost of capital** in another way. A growing number of individual investors and institutional portfolio managers work extensively or even exclusively with options and their related stocks. For these investors it is frequently a case of "no options, no interest." A growing number of advisory services and brokerage firm research departments are influenced by the combined trading volume in stocks and options when they select stocks for statistical and analytical coverage. Obviously, if a corporation has problems, more attention is not always desirable. After weighing positive and negative factors, however, managements of most large corporations have concluded that they want increased interest from the investment community.

A corporation can do relatively little to encourage one or more of the option exchanges to list its stock. While an investment banker can help with a presentation to the exchange's listing committee, these committees are usually controlled by floor members. Consequently, listing decisions are based on the floor members' expectations for option trading volume. With few exceptions (e.g., Bally Manufacturing) most companies listed for option trading after 1975 have experienced only modest option trading volume. If a company has not already been selected for option trading, management should not expect too much from an option listing.

It is a relatively simple matter for a corporation to **discourage** an option listing if the preceding paragraphs have not been persuasive. Because option terms must be modified in the event of a noncash dividend or a stock split, any corporation that declares small quarterly stock dividends will soon have an unmanageable number of option series with irregular striking prices and unusual numbers of shares underlying each option. Traders will shy away from the issue, volume will dry up, and the option exchange will rue the day the stock was admitted to trading.

OPTION ADVISORY SERVICES

Exhibit 19 summarizes the information provided by some advisory services with respect to options.

Following is a list of abbreviations used in the exhibit, with their definitions:

Prob	Probability type, usually a variant of Black and Scholes
Econ	Econometric type, usually a variant of Kassouf
Hist	Historical volatility, weighted or unweighted
Calc	Calculated volatility, including historic and implied volatilities
RE	Return if exercised
RU	Return if stock price unchanged
ORC	Other return calculations
D	Dividend information
Ltd	Limited but more than, or different from, earnings and dividend data
EX	Extensive data on underlying stocks
Tech	Technical ratings of stocks
Fund	Fundamental ratings of stock

BIBLIOGRAPHY

Black, Fischer, "Fact and Fantasy in the Use of Options," *Financial Analysts Journal,* July–August 1975, pp. 36–72.

————, and Cox, John C., "Valuing Corporate Securities: Some Effects of Bond Indenture Provisions," *Journal of Finance,* May 1976, pp. 351–367.

————, and Scholes, Myron, "The Valuation of Option Contracts and a Test of Market Efficiency," *Journal of Finance,* May 1972, pp. 399–417.

————, and ————, "The Pricing of Options and Corporate Liabilities," *Journal of Political Economy,* May–June 1973, pp. 637–654.

Brennan, Michael J., and Schwartz, Eduardo S., "Convertible Bonds: Valuation and Optimal Strategies for Call and Conversion," Working Paper No. 336, University of British Columbia, Vancouver, July 1976.

Cootner, Paul, Ed., *The Random Character of Stock Market Prices,* MIT Press, Cambridge, MA, 1964.

Cox, John C., and Ross, Stephen A., "The Valuation of Options for Alternative Stochastic Processes," *Journal of Financial Economics,* January–March 1976, pp. 145–166.

————, ————, and Rubinstein, Mark, "Option Pricing: A Simplified Approach," Working Paper No. 79, Institute of Business and Economic Research, University of California, Berkeley, September 1979.

Gastineau, Gary L., *The Stock Options Manual,* 2nd ed., McGraw-Hill, New York, 1979.

————, and Madansky, Albert, "Why Simulations Are an Unreliable Test of Option Strategies," *Financial Analysts Journal,* September–October 1979, pp. 61–76.

Geske, Robert, "The Valuation of Compound Options," unpublished working paper, University of California, Berkeley, December 1976.

Ingersoll, Jonathan E., Jr., "A Contingent Claim Valuation of Convertible Securities," *Journal of Financial Economics,* May 1977.

————, "An Examination of Corporate Call Policies on Convertible Securities," *Journal of Finance,* May 1977, pp. 463–478.

Kassouf, Sheen T., "Option Pricing: Theory and Practice," Columbia University Graduate School of Business, Institute for Quantitative Research and Finance, Spring 1977 Seminar.

Merton, Robert C., "Theory of Rational Option Pricing," *Bell Journal of Economics and Management Science,* Spring 1973, pp. 141–183.

————, "Option Pricing When Underlying Stock Returns Are Discontinuous," *Journal of Financial Economics,* January–March 1976, pp. 125–144.

————, Scholes, Myron S., and Gladstein, Mathew L., "A Simulation of the Returns and Risk of Alternative Option Portfolio Investment Strategies," *Journal of Business,* April 1978, pp. 183–242.

Parkinson, Michael, "Option Pricing: The American Put," *Journal of Business,* January 1977, pp. 21–36.

Ross, Stephen, "Options and Efficiency," *Quarterly Journal of Economics,* February 1976, pp. 75–89.

Rubinstein, Mark (assisted by John C. Cox), *Option Markets,* Prentice-Hall, Englewood Cliffs, NJ, 1981.

Samuelson, Paul, and Merton, Robert C., "A Complete Model of Warrant Pricing that Maximizes Utility," *Industrial Management Review,* Winter 1969, pp. 17–46.

Treynor, J. L., Regan, P. J., and Priest, W. W., Jr., *The Financial Reality of Pension Funding Under ERISA,* Dow Jones-Irwin, Homewood, IL, 1976.

SECTION **21**

FUTURES AND COMMODITIES MARKETS

CONTENTS

**DEVELOPMENT OF FUTURES
TRADING**   3

Growth in Futures Trading   3
Origins of Futures Markets   3
Contract Attributes   3
Contract Features   4
Securities Portfolio Contracts   5
Hedging Strategies Using Portfolio
Futures   5
Location, Volume, and Other Data on
Futures Markets   5
Necessary Conditions for a Viable
Contract   8

**PARTICIPANTS IN FUTURES
CONTRACT TRADING**   10

Hedging   11
Speculation   12
Futures Market Functions   12
Functions of the Futures Exchange   13
Function of the Clearinghouse   13
Exchange Operations   13

MECHANICS OF FUTURES TRADING   15

Margin Mechanics   15
Contract Liquidation   15

Futures Accounting   15
Types of Order   18
Flow of Orders   18
Types of Trading   18
The Basis   19
Carrying Charge Market   20
Inverted Market   20
Other Markets   21

HEDGING   21

Types of Hedge   21
   Short hedge 1: Price change hedge   23
   Short hedge 2: Interest rate change
   hedge   24
   Long hedge   25
      Buy hedge 1: Exchange rate
      change hedge   25
      Buy hedge 2: Interest rate change
      hedge   26
   Spreading and rolling positions   26

FEDERAL REGULATION   27

Early Regulation   27
The Commodity Futures Trading
Commission   27
Required Reporting   29

FUTURES AND COMMODITIES MARKETS

Richard L. Sandor
Dallas Jones

DEVELOPMENT OF FUTURES TRADING

GROWTH IN FUTURES TRADING. In a period of just less than two decades, **futures trading** in the United States has grown from a level of 3.7 million contracts in 1960, to 12.4 million in 1970 and to 74.3 million in 1979. Annual volume increases amounted to 13% during the 1960s and 21% during the 1970s as shown in Exhibit 1. Before 1960, trading was confined to **primary agricultural commodities.** Although trading volume has expanded in the latter area, the success of a wide variety of new contracts such as lumber, precious metals, currencies, and financial futures has been a significant factor in the growth of futures trading.

ORIGINS OF FUTURES MARKETS. The origins of futures markets can be traced to the needs of individuals and commercial enterprises that produced, merchandised, and processed commodities. An examination of the history of exchanges reveals that commercial participants entered into **forward contracts** (the actual purchase or sale of a specific quantity and quality of a commodity for delivery at some specific time in the future) to prevent losses that might arise from price changes. These forward contracts were eventually traded by individuals who wanted either to hedge themselves against price changes or to attempt to make profits from fluctuations in market values.

Organized futures markets evolved from these **spot** or **cash markets** (markets for immediate and possible deferred delivery) where forward contracting became prevalent. The oldest and largest of these exchanges, the **Chicago Board of Trade,** came into existence in 1848, offering opportunities for trading for immediate and deferred delivery. During the decade of the 1860s, **trading in futures contracts** for **grain** evolved. The **futures contracts** differed from **forward contracts** in several important ways. For example, futures contracts were not tailored to the needs of a specific buyer and seller but were (more) standardized with terms set by the exchange, and prices were determined in a **competitive auction market.**

CONTRACT ATTRIBUTES. **Futures contracts** are defined as contracts for future delivery of a specific quantity and quality of a commodity at prices determined today. The exchanges establish contract specifications for the various commodities which are traded under their

EXHIBIT 1   TOTAL FUTURES CONTRACTS TRADED

Fiscal Year	Contracts ($ Millions)	Annual Increase (%)
1960	3.7	
1970	12.4	13.0
1974	25.0	19.2
1975	26.3	5.1
1976	34.0	29.3
1977	39.7	16.9
1978	52.1	31.0
1979	74.3	42.6

Source: Commodity Futures Trading Commission, 1980.

auspices. For example, the Chicago Board of Trade corn contract specifies 5,000 bushels of USDA No. 2 Yellow Corn as the **contract grade.** Prices are quoted for this particular grade, although other grades can be delivered at premiums or discounts to the quoted prices. **Contract months** are May, July, September, December, and March. Trading takes place as much as one year and more into the future. Delivery can occur at any time during these months, at the option of the seller, in warehouses in Chicago, St. Louis, or Toledo, cities that have been approved by the exchange.

It is important to emphasize that although futures contracts are firm and binding, there are usually **sellers' options** regarding both the specific day of the month when delivery occurs and the contract grade. There is also a seller's option regarding the location of the delivery when more than location is specified by the exchange. For example, as indicated previously, the corn contract provides for delivery at Chicago, St. Louis, or Toledo.

CONTRACT FEATURES.   Additional salient features include maximum and minimum daily price fluctuations. For example, corn is traded in units of quarter-cents per bushel and ranges during the day from 10¢ higher to 10¢ lower than the previous day's close. Other features include method of delivery, hours of trading, and method of payment. **Delivery** of corn is accomplished by exchanging a **warehouse receipt** issued by an approved grain elevator and registered by the exchange for a check drawn on an approved bank or a cashier's check. Grains in general, and corn in particular, are traded from 9:30 A.M. to 1:15 P.M., central time.

Despite common fiction of unwanted commodities, such as corn, being delivered to homes of individuals participating in the market, this is not possible under the rules and regulations of the exchanges. Contract specifications and contract grade vary enormously among commodities. In the case of currencies, contract specifications simply state the amount of the currency that can be delivered in satisfaction of the contract. For example, if the amount of currency required to satisfy a contract is 25,000 British pounds, only this amount can be submitted, and there is no tolerance for different grades of currency. This is also true for the other currencies traded on the International Monetary Market of the **Chicago Mercantile Exchange.**

In other **financial futures** the contract specifications allow for the delivery of certain types of **government security** with certain terms to maturity. For example, the **U.S. bond futures market** on the Chicago Board of Trade allows for the delivery of any government bond having a maturity with at least 15 years to call. The contract grade is $100,000 par amount of a hypothetical 8% 20-year bond. For delivery, the price of this contract is then adjusted by a predetermined factor to determine the price of any other bond that might be tendered.

SECURITIES PORTFOLIO CONTRACTS.   The development of **new futures contracts** has widely altered terms, such as contract grade, from the straightforward definitions in primary agricultural commodities to hypothetical standards such as the bond contract. Furthermore, the proposal of the Chicago Board of Trade for **futures on stock indices** creates totally new definitions of a commodity. The concept of a futures market in stock indices is not new. The Chicago Board Options Exchange was an outgrowth of this idea. One proposed new approach, invented by Richard Sandor, calls for the creation of a **portfolio futures contract for different industries.** For example, in the oil industry, delivery could be satisfied by a portfolio of 300 common shares of Atlantic Richfield, Exxon, Gulf, Mobil Oil, and Standard Oil of Indiana. The particular stocks and number of shares to be delivered for other industries were chosen using both **modern portfolio theory** and the art of contract design prevailing in futures markets. In general, portfolios were designed to be representative of price movements for the particular industry.

HEDGING STRATEGIES USING PORTFOLIO FUTURES.   Numerous types of **hedges** (see detailed discussion below) may be used with a **portfolio futures complex.** For example, in the simplest case a **portfolio manager** could hedge against a fall in prices for the oil stock complex. Furthermore, if a portfolio manager chose stocks that outperformed the industry, it would be possible to produce income irrespective of whether the prices of the oil stocks in the portfolio rose or fell. A particular strategy exemplifying the latter might be to buy Exxon and Standard Oil of Indiana and simultaneously sell or go short the oil complex. If prices for all oil stocks rose, and the assumption was correct, then Exxon and Standard Oil of Indiana prices would rise by more than the prices of the other stocks in the oil complex. The price appreciation associated with the purchase of the two stocks would more than offset the loss associated with the sale or short position in the oil complex. If the price of the two stocks fell, and these stocks outperformed the other stocks in the complex, net income would be produced for the portfolio manager. A similar strategy could be used by a portfolio manager who was capable of choosing the industries that would outperform the general stock market. In this particular case, if the manager felt that the oil industry would outperform an index of the overall market, the appropriate strategy would be to purchase a select group of oil stocks and sell or go short the **overall market index.**

This **portfolio complex** could also be used to **hedge anticipated cash flow** into a portfolio. If there were a forecast that a particular industry would be prospering at the time of the inflow of cash to the institution that employs the manager, he could simply buy a portfolio futures contract in that industry complex for that particular time in the future, thereby assuring the price of the portfolio. Numerous other strategies can be contemplated that might be of enormous value to any portfolio manager. It is interesting to note that this complex would not only provide a market forecast of stock prices in the future but would imply some forecast of projected dividends as well.

LOCATION, VOLUME, AND OTHER DATA ON FUTURES MARKETS.   Exhibits 2–4 summarize data on location and trading volume for the largest futures contracts traded in the world. Exhibit 2 provides a current **list of all commodities** that are traded on U.S. futures markets and the exchanges that trade them. Exhibit 3 gives **primary foreign futures exchanges** and their contracts. Exhibit 4 shows the **10 largest contracts** in terms of **trading**

EXHIBIT 2a COMMODITIES TRADED ON U.S. FUTURES MARKETS

SYMBOLS

MA	Mid America
CBT	Chicago Board of Trade
CME	Chicago Mercantile Exchange
KC	Kansas City
MPLS	Minneapolis
CEX	Coffee Sugar & Cocoa Exchange
CMX	New York Commodity Exchange
CTN	New York Cotton Exchange
NYFE	New York Futures Exchange
NYM	New York Mercantile Exchange
NO	New Orleans (in formation)

Commodity	Exchange

GRAINS AND FEEDS

Corn	CBT, MA
Oats	CBT, MPLS, MA
Sorghum	CME
Soybeans	CBT, MA
Soybean meal	CBT
Soybean oil	CBT
Sunflower seeds	MPLS
Wheat	CBT, KC, MPLS, MA

FOODS

Butter	CME
Cocoa	CEX
Coffee	CEX
Eggs	CTN
Orange juice	CTN
Potatoes	CME, NYM
Sugar	CEX

LIVESTOCK AND MEAT

Boneless beef	CME
Imported beef	NYM
Iced broilers	CBT
Feeder cattle	CME
Live cattle	CME, MA
Skinned hams	CME
Live hogs	CME, MA
Pork bellies	CME
Turkeys	CME

Commodity	Exchange

OTHER RAW MATERIALS

Cotton	CTN
Rubber	CEX
Wood lumber	CME
Plywood	CBT
Stud lumber	CME

CURRENCIES

British pound	CME, NYM
Canadian dollar	CME, NYM
German mark	CME
French franc	CME
Japanese yen	CME, NYM
Mexican peso	CME
Swiss franc	CME, NYM

ENERGY

Crude oil	CTN
Heating oil	NYM
Industrial fuel oil	NYM
Liquid propane	CTN

METALS

Copper	CMX
Gold	CBT, CME, CMX, NYM
Palladium	NYM
Platinum	NYM
Silver	CBT, CMX
Zinc	CMX

FINANCIAL INSTRUMENTS

Commercial paper	CBT
Government National Mortgage Association paper	CBT, CMX
Treasury bills	CME, CMX
Treasury bonds	CBT
Treasury notes	CBT, CME

EXHIBIT 2b CONTRACTS PROPOSED AND PENDING BEFORE THE CFTC

Contract	Exchange
Agricultural	
Sunflower	CBT
Soybeans	NO
Rice	NO
Cotton	NO
Wood	
Southern yellow pine	CBT
Energy	
Heating oil	CBT
Currencies	
Italian lira	CME
British pound	NYFE
Canadian dollar	NYFE
German mark	NYFE
Japanese yen	NYFE
Swiss franc	NYFE
Financial Instruments	
Treasury bills	NYFE, CET
Treasury bonds	NYFE
Treasury notes: long and short term	CBT, CMX
Domestic CDs	CBT, CME
Eurodollar CDs	CBT, CME
Value Line Stock Index	KC
Standard & Poor's Stock Index	CME
Portfolio Stock Index Complex	CBT

volume and estimated trading volume. Exhibit 5 describes what are generally termed the **salient features** of futures contracts, as illustrated by three widely differing examples: corn, U.S. Treasury bonds, and British pounds.

NECESSARY CONDITIONS FOR A VIABLE CONTRACT.   A brief discussion of some of the factors that are necessary for a successful futures contract is appropriate here. All the previously discussed commodities tend to have a number of significant elements in common. All are subject to great **price volatility** and exist in an environment where **prices are competitively determined.** The commodities are **homogeneous** in that there are close price

EXHIBIT 3 FOREIGN EXCHANGES AND COMMODITIES

Winnipeg Commodity Exchange (WPG)

Barley
Flaxseed
Gold
Oats
Rapeseed
Rye
Wheat

Coffee Terminal Market Association of London, Ltd.

Coffee

Grain & Feed Trade Association, Ltd.

European Economic Community Grains
(wheat, barley)

Hong Kong Commodity Exchange, Ltd.

Cotton
Sugar
Soybeans

London Bullion Market

Gold
Silver

London Cocoa Terminal Market Association, Ltd.

Cocoa

London Metal Exchange

Aluminum
Copper
Lead
Silver
Tin
Zinc

London Rubber Terminal Association, Ltd.

Rubber

EXHIBIT 3   CONTINUED

London Vegetable Oil Terminal Market Association, Ltd.

Palm oil
Soybean oil

London Wool Terminal Market Association, Ltd.

Wool

São Paulo Exchange

Coffee
Cotton
Maize
Soybeans

Sydney Futures Exchange Ltd.

Boneless beef
Live cattle
Gold
Greasy wool

Currencies
Australian dollar
British pound
Swiss franc
Japanese yen

United Terminal Sugar Market Association, Ltd.

Sugar

movements among different grades. There is also an **active cash or spot market** for the commodities. These conditions are necessary but certainly not exhaustive. There must be appropriate **contract design** and **professional speculators** on the floor of the exchange, as well as other fulfilled conditions, for the contract to be viable.

PARTICIPANTS IN FUTURES CONTRACT TRADING

Futures markets attract two broad classes of users: **hedgers** and **speculators. Hedging,** is defined as a temporary substitute for a transaction in the spot market to protect against adverse price movement. A multinational grain company that receives an order from a foreign government for corn may not be able to find a sufficient number of farmers or grain elevator

EXHIBIT 4   LARGEST CONTRACT DATA, 1978

	Exchange	Trading Volume (000 Omitted)

10 LARGEST CONTRACTS, TRADING VOLUME

Soybeans	CBT	8,477
Corn	CBT	6,127
Live cattle	CME	5,592
Silver	CMX	3,822
Gold	CMX	3,742
Soybean oil	CBT	2,909
Gold	CME	2,812
Silver	CBT	2,658
Wheat	CBT	2,556
Soybean meal	CBT	2,493

	Estimated Trading Value ($ Billions)

10 LARGEST CONTRACTS, ESTIMATED TRADING VALUE

Treasury bills	704
Soybeans	284
Silver	192
Gold	139
Cattle	138
Currencies	105
GNMA mortgages	90
Corn	77
Wheat	57
Treasury bonds	53

Source: Futures Industry Association.

operators willing to sell the spot commodity for deferred delivery. The company will use the futures market as an interim substitute to fix the price of the commodity.

HEDGING.   Commercial enterprises use the futures market to hedge for three principal reasons:

1. Price or cost effectiveness.
2. Flexibility.
3. Financial integrity of the contract.

The grain company that entered into a contract with a foreign government might not be able to buy a sufficient quantity of the corn that is needed within a short time or without

EXHIBIT 5   SALIENT FEATURES OF THREE FUTURES CONTRACTS

CORN

Grade	5,000 bushels USDA #2 yellow
Delivery points	Chicago, Toledo, and St. Louis
Price increments	$\frac{1}{4}$ cent per bushel or $12.50 per contract
Delivery instrument	Registered warehouse receipts issued by warehouses approved by the Exchange
Delivery months	March, May, July, September, December
Daily price limits	10¢ per bushel ($500 per contract) above or below the previous day's settlement price
Trading hours	9:30 A.M.–1:15 P.M., central standard time

U.S. TREASURY BONDS

Grade	$100,000 face value 8% bonds maturing at least 15 years from delivery day if not callable: and if callable are not so for at least 15 years from delivery day
Price increments	$\frac{1}{32}$ of a point or $31.25 per contract
Delivery instrument	Federal Reserve book entry wire transfer system; invoice is adjusted for coupon rates and maturity or call dates
Delivery months	March, June, September, December
Daily price limits	$\frac{64}{32}$ ($2,000 per contract) above or below the previous day's settlement price
Trading hours	8:00 A.M.–2:00 P.M., central standard time

BRITISH POUNDS

Contract size	25,000£
Price increments	$0.0005 or $12.50 per contract
Delivery instrument	Foreign currency delivered to a designated bank
Delivery months	March, June, September, December
Daily price limits	$0.0500 ($12.50 per contract) above or below the previous day's settlement price
Trading hours	7:30 A.M.–1:24 P.M., central standard time

forcing prices significantly higher. Similarly, a pension fund that would like to sell bonds from a portfolio might have to do this quickly, possibly depressing prices for the particular bond that is being sold. In these cases, the purchase or sale of a futures contract could act as a hedge against pricing problems.

SPECULATION.   **Speculation** is the use of a futures market to profit from a movement in prices and **is unrelated to any business activity** of the participant. It is important to distinguish between speculation and gambling. In the former, uncertainty exists in the system and the only question is, Who can bear its costs more efficiently? Gambling risk, on the other hand, is created, and generally is assumed for the purpose of leisure.

FUTURES MARKET FUNCTIONS.   Futures markets provide for the **redistribution of risk** by allowing hedgers the ability to fix the price of commodities that are used in commercial enterprises at an earlier time in the process. This **price insurance** function is the critical

element in these markets. In addition, futures markets perform a function of **price discovery.**
The open dissemination of price data signals farmers, millers, bakers, and so on, the prices
that crops not yet planted may have. In addition, in some circumstances these markets may
be used as an alternate market for producers, merchants, and other users.

FUNCTIONS OF THE FUTURES EXCHANGE.   It is appropriate to begin a discussion of
the **functions of Exchanges** by quoting directly from the Rules and Regulations of the
Chicago Board of Trade:

> The objects of the Association are: to maintain a Commercial Exchange; to promote uniformity
> in the customs and usages of merchants; to inculcate principles of justice and equity in trade;
> to facilitate the speedy adjustment of business disputes; to acquire and to disseminate valuable
> commercial and economic information; and, generally to secure to its members the benefits of
> co-operation in the furtherance of their legitimate pursuits.

In promotion of "uniformity in the customs and usages of merchants," the exchange
standardizes the contracts as discussed previously. The exchange establishes the physical
environment where transactions occur. In addition, the highest bid and lowest offer must
prevail, and buyers may not bid below another bid to insure a competitive market environment. The exchange also provides that if delivery occurs, the grade and quality delivered
must be consistent with the contract specifications. The exchanges specify the conditions
under which different commodities can be delivered and the physical instrument of delivery.
In the case of grains, **warehouse receipts** are utilized. Delivery of other commodities occurs
through a **shipping certificate** (a promissory note that a processor or shipper will deliver
a certain commodity within a certain period of time). Only exchange-approved warehouses
and shippers can issue instruments that can be used for delivery. The approval of warehouses
and shippers is accomplished through inspection procedures outlined by the exchange. The
process is greatly simplified in commodities such as Treasury Bills and Bonds because no
intermediate instrument is necessary—the financial instruments are delivered directly.

FUNCTION OF THE CLEARINGHOUSE.   Financial integrity is established by the existence of the **clearinghouse.** Trading can be done only by members of the exchange, and
only those designated as **clearing members** can assume the financial responsibilities associated with initiating a position in the market. The clearinghouse (or clearing corporation,
when it is a separate firm) mediates between buyers and sellers. When a buyer meets a seller,
the clearinghouse serves on the opposite side of the contract for both parties. In this triad,
the clearinghouse interposes itself as buyer from the seller and as seller to the buyer.

EXCHANGE OPERATIONS.   The management of the exchange is executed jointly by a
professional staff and committees of members. Most exchanges are operated as if they were
nonprofit membership associations. Membership in the exchange implies privileges in addition to equity. These include permission to act as **futures commission merchants** (brokers),
clearing members, and **floor brokers** (individuals executing orders on the exchange floor),
as well as to trade from the floor. It should be noted that **floor traders (professional
speculators** located on the exchange floor, sometimes referred to as **locals**) often speculate
in more than one commodity and may behave as market makers or specialists. Officially,
they are not charged with this function. Some evolution has occurred in recent times in
exchanges that have issued conditional memberships requiring owners of this type of membership to execute a certain proportion of their trades in a commodity designated by the
exchange. Exhibit 6 lists 10 futures exchanges, indicating size and other characteristics.

EXHIBIT 6   CHARACTERISTICS OF 10 FUTURES EXCHANGES

Exchange	Number of Members	Cost of Full Membership, December 1979 ($ Thousands)	Trading Volume, 1978 ($ Thousands)	Estimated Value of Commodities Traded, 1978 ($ Billions)
Chicago Board of Trade	1,402 regular 150 restricted	$225	$27,363	$ 730
Chicago Mercantile	500 regular 950 restricted	258	15,154	1,078
Mid-America (Chicago)	1,205	14	2,121	12
Kansas City Board of Trade	214	58	756	12
Minneapolis Grain	420	9	284	4
New York Commodity Exchange	386	125	8,964	205
New York Cocoa	183	24	223	11
New York Coffee & Sugar	344	24	1,203	19
New York Cotton	450	34	1,441	41
New York Mercantile	408	27	927	8

Source: Futures Industry Association.

MECHANICS OF FUTURES TRADING

Initiating a position in the futures market is accomplished by placing an order with a firm that is known as a **futures commission merchant.** The purchase of a futures contract is referred to as taking a **long** position in the market, while the sale of a contract is referred to taking as a **short** position. When buying or selling a contract, an **initial margin** deposit is required. These deposits differ from margins in the stock market. **Commodity margins** are actually **performance bonds.** They generally vary between 2 and 10% of the full value of the contract. Individual exchanges set the levels of margins for their respective commodities. Once a position is established, each position is marked to market daily. If the equity in a participant's account falls below a predetermined level termed **maintenance margin,** additional monies known as **variation margin** must be posted.

MARGIN MECHANICS. For example, a speculator may choose to buy a contract for $100,000 of 20-year, 8% Treasury bonds for December delivery priced as 80-00 to yield 10.394%. Once the position has been established, an initial margin of $2,000 is posted with the futures commission merchant and maintenance margins are set at $1,500. Since a 1-point move on the contract is worth $1,000, when prices fall to 79-00 and yields rise to 10.539% the equity in the account is reduced to $1,000. This is below the **maintenance level** of $1,500, so the participant must post an additional $1,000 with the futures commission merchant to restore the $2,000 margin. Conversely, if prices rose to 81-00 to yield 10.253%, the participant would be credited with $1,000. It is important to emphasize that although the $1,000 is an unrealized profit, the participant may withdraw it from the account or use it as margin for the purchase of additional contracts.

CONTRACT LIQUIDATION. Positions in the futures market can be liquidated by either making or taking delivery or by **offset.** In the former case, buyer and seller exchange the specific commodity for cash at the **settlement price,** or the last price at which trading occurred when the buyer received notice from the seller that delivery will be made. To continue our example, if the settlement price of the December contract were 90-00 on the last day of trading and delivery of the 20-year bond had been made, the buyer would pay the seller $90,000. It is important to recall that since the buyer has been credited with $10,000 as a result of the **mark to market** (i.e., valuation using current market prices) of his position, his purchase price of 80 has been achieved; that is, $90,000 settlement price less $10,000 in profits equals $80,000 purchase price.

Either long or short positions may be liquidated before delivery by establishing an equal and opposite position in the market. This is known as the **offset provision** of a futures contract. Thus the buyer of a contract would sell an equal amount of the same contract and the seller of a contract would buy a contract. In our example, the purchaser of $100,000 of a 20-year 8% U.S. Treasury bond for December delivery at a price of 80-00 on April 1 might sell the contract one week later at a price of 81-00. At that particular time, the initial margin of $2,000 would be returned, plus the $1,000 in profit, less commissions. **Commissions on futures contracts** are generally quoted as **round turn** (including both the purchase and sale) and are charged at the time the contract is liquidated. As a practical matter, **less than 1% of all futures contracts are settled by delivery.** The **offset provision accounts for 99%** of positions being liquidated prior to the delivery month.

FUTURES ACCOUNTING. The mechanics of establishing and liquidating positions is quite simple. The clearing corporation establishes accounts for the positions of its clearing members. For purposes of exposition, a simplification of the delivery example is presented in the form of ledgers maintained at the clearing corporation (Exhibit 7). In the example,

EXHIBIT 7 FUTURE CONTRACT DELIVERY EXAMPLE

	Purchase	Sale
ESTABLISHMENT		
Clearing Member A		
April 1	1 December U.S. Treasury bond @ 80	
December 31		
Credit	$10,000	
Full purchase price	90,000	
Initial margin	2,000	
Profit	+ 10,000	
Clearing Member B		
April 1		1 December U.S. Treasury bond @ 80
December 31		
Debit		$10,000
Full sale price		90,000
Initial margin		2,000
Loss		10,000

LIQUIDATION

Clearing Member A

April 1	1 December U.S. Treasury bond @ 80
April 8	1 December U.S. Treasury bond @ 81

Initial margin ... 2,000
Profit ... 1,000

Clearing Member B

April 1	1 December U.S. Treasury bond @ 80
April 8	1 December U.S. Treasury bond @ 81

Initial margin ... 2,000
Debit ... 1,000

Clearing Member C

April 8	1 December U.S. Treasury bond @ 81

Initial margin ... 2,000

the seller (A) liquidated his position by purchasing a December contract from a third participant (C), and the clearing corporation substituted the new seller (C) for the original seller (B). (The seller could have liquidated his position with the original buyer, but this is very improbable.) The number of transactions in the market that take place during any given day is termed the **volume.** The number of positions remaining outstanding at the end of a day that have not been offset is termed the **open interest** (the outstanding purchases or sales).

TYPES OF ORDER.   Futures markets allow a wide variety of orders to be entered. Orders fall into three broad classes: market orders, limit orders, and contingent orders. A **market order** is an order to buy or sell at the best possible price available in the market. A **limit order** is an order to buy or sell at a predetermined price. In our example the purchaser of the December U.S. Treasury bond might have entered his order with a limit of 81-00 or better. (A limit order can always be satisfied at a lower price if it is a purchase or a higher price if it is a sale.) **Contingent orders** may refer to actions that must be taken if certain prior conditions are satisfied. The most widely used contingent orders are stop limits and orders that have time contingencies. A **stop limit order** specifies that a contract should be bought or sold only if a particular price is reached. For example, if an individual had sold one contract of December U.S. Treasury bonds at 80-00, he might place an order to buy one December contract at 83-00 stop. If the market price increases to 83-00, this order will be transformed into an order to buy one December U.S. Treasury bond at market. This mechanism is frequently used by participants to limit the losses they might incur. Another type of contingent order refers to the time of day an order is to be executed. The purchaser of one December U.S. Treasury bond might enter an order to buy at the close as **market on close** (MOC). Limit or contingent orders may be entered for a single day or perhaps for a longer period of time such as a month. The latter case is referred to as an **open order.**

FLOW OF ORDERS.   Orders to buy or sell may reach the trading floor in several distinct ways. An order may be entered through an **account executive** or a **Registered Commodity Representative** (RCR) at the branch office of a **futures commission merchant.** The order might then be telexed to a central order deck, which wires the order to the floor. The order is transmitted by a runner, who carries the order to the trading pit or ring, where it is executed by a **floor broker,** who is licensed by the exchange and by the **Commodity Futures Trading Commission** (CFTC) to perform this function. All orders are made by open outcry, often supplemented by hand signals. The **trading pit** is divided in such a manner that different delivery months are executed in different portions of the pit or ring. Once the order has been executed, the process takes place in reverse, and the market participant is notified of his action by the RCR. A confirmation of the action is then sent by mail on the following day. Orders might reach the exchange floor by telephone from the RCR directly or from an order desk. To facilitate the quickest possible execution, large market participants often call the trading floor directly and place an order with a member of the exchange. In many instances, large participants have direct lines to the trading floor.

TYPES OF TRADING.   The trading pit or ring contains not only floor brokers but speculators, as well. There are a wide variety of speculators in the pit or ring who fill different functions. They include **market makers,** who are referred to as **scalpers.** These individuals may simply agree to make a market or buy or sell in a particular delivery month. **Day traders** buy and sell throughout the day but normally do not hold positions overnight. Both types of participant provide liquidity and bridge the gap between orders from buyers to sellers who trade from outside the exchange floor.

Another type of pit or ring trader is the **spreader.** This individual buys and sells different contract months of the same commodity. The spreader's function is to maintain equilibrium between the prices in different delivery months. Subsequent examples discuss this technique in greater detail.

Floor traders may also be professional speculators, who establish positions in the marketplace for longer periods of time. They provide great liquidity for hedgers and perform the same function that public speculators do.

THE BASIS.   The **basis** is the **difference between the cash commodity and the corresponding futures contract** at a particular point in time. Factors that influence the basis include:

1. Specific futures contract month.
2. Carrying costs including storage, financing, and insurance.
3. Price relationships between deliverable grades of the cash commodity.
4. Seasonal supply and demand factors.
5. Transportation costs.
6. Costs of making or taking delivery.
7. Changing supply and demand conditions or variations in quality over time and/or location.
8. Yield curve.
9. Interest rate differentials.

Exhibit 8 shows how cash and futures prices, as well as the basis for four commodities with widely varying delivery characteristics, are tracked daily. Exhibit 8a depicts the last month of trading for the June 1980 British pound contract, which has no variation with respect to quality, quantity, and delivery date. Note not only convergence at maturity for the cash and futures but also the much smaller range in the **basis** than either cash or futures prices alone.

Exhibits 8b and 8c illustrate two sellers' option contracts with apparent nonconvergence in basis. Since making delivery costs roughly 10–15¢, the corn example actually confirms convergence and illustrates several of the factors underlying the basis. The bond data in Exhibit 8c illustrate a different type of basis adjustment peculiar to **financial instrument futures** as previously mentioned. When the futures price is adjusted by the factor, the basis converges to within $\frac{4}{32}$ of the cash price.

Finally, Exhibit 8d illustrates the important concept of **cross-hedging,** whereby the cash commodity differs from that underlying the future one; the latter is used as a **hedging proxy** because of basic characteristics that generate similar price movements. Although price correlation is not as high between the IBM corporate issue and the 8% 20-year Treasury future as it was for the $9\frac{1}{8}$% Treasury issue, it may still be acceptable for one wishing to hedge a position in the corporate security.

In addition to deciding on the specific futures contract to use for hedging, the extent of the hedge as determined by the number of contracts employed, and probable movement in the basis, one must choose a **contract month** to employ. Since a future structure of prices from nearby to distant contracts is rarely flat, one must often make judgments regarding

EXHIBIT 8a   BRITISH POUND BASIS[a]

	Cash, Interbank, Spot	Future June 1980, IMM (b.p.)	Basis
May 12	2.2875	2.2725	150 (H)
13	2.2870	2.2745	125
14	2.2985	2.2885	100
15	2.2885	2.2735	150
16	2.2850 (L)	2.2715 (L)	135
19	2.2850	2.2745	105
20	2.2945	2.2835	110
21	2.3295	2.3190	105
22	2.3290	2.3205	85
23	2.3540	2.3425	115
27	2.3750 (H)	2.3650 (H)	100
28	2.3610	2.3515	95
29	2.3300	2.3285	15
30	2.3480	2.3430	50
June 2	2.3220	2.3245	75
3	2.2920	2.2860	60
4	2.3220	2.3135	85
5	2.3350	2.3255	95
6	2.3355	2.3300	55
9	2.3415	2.3375	40
10	2.3285	2.3220	65
11	2.3475	2.3400	75
12	2.3372	2.3300	72
13	2.3460	2.3475	−15(L)
16	Expired		

[a]H = high; L = low.

changes in the shape of the curve through time. It is helpful to distinguish between normal market conditions and temporary aberrations and to recognize implications of certain basic market structures.

CARRYING CHARGE MARKET. When futures prices increase with maturity, it is considered a **normal** or **carrying charge** market. The **spreads,** or differences between successive contracts, are negative. For example, during the course of a crop year beginning with the harvest when supplies are usually most plentiful, futures prices generally follow an increasing pattern. Month-to-month differences often reflect and are generally only limited on the upside by **carrying costs,** including storage, financing, and insurance. Part A of Exhibit 9 depicts a typical market structure for corn.

INVERTED MARKET. The opposite condition, an **inverted** market, occurs when succeeding prices decrease with contract maturity, resulting in positive spreads. A nearby shortage, strong expectations for lower prices, or interest rate differentials may lead to such a condition. Unlike a normal market, there is generally no limit to the magnitude of the spreads. Part B of Exhibit 9 illustrates an **inverted market** brought on by a combination of the foregoing factors in the British pound market.

OTHER MARKETS. Hybrid markets such as V or inverted-V shapes are less common and sometimes result from a combination of the two basic types of market. Bond future prices and corn prices shown in Parts C and D of Exhibit 9 illustrate an inverted V and a V, respectively.

HEDGING

The concept of **hedging** is based on the assumption of both high **correlation and convergence between cash and futures prices** through time. Both prices should move in the same direction, since they are affected by the same factors. On average, differences between the two should narrow through time as the futures contract becomes nearly interchangeable with the cash commodity while approaching its expiration date. As long as certain basic relationships between futures and cash do not change, price movement in the cash commodity can be offset by an equal and opposite futures position.

TYPES OF HEDGE. A **short hedge** is appropriate when one owns or expects to own the cash commodity and accordingly sells the future to protect against downward price moves. If the positions are equal, it is considered a **total hedge;** if the futures sale is less than the

EXHIBIT 8b   CORN BASIS

November	Cash, No. 2 Yellow Corn (Boxcar)	Future, December 1979, CBT Corn	Basis
1	236	258¼	−22¼
2	239	260¾	−21¾
5	243½	263¼	−19¾
6	241¼	261	−19¾
7	242½	262¼	−19¾
8	241¼	261¼	−20
9	242¼	262	−19¾
12	245¾	265½	−19¾
13	249	268¾	−19¾
14	254¼	274	−19¾
15	251¾	271½	−19¾
16	250¾	271	−20¼
19	250¼	270½	−20¼
20	257¾	273	−15¼
21	262	277¼	−15¼
23	261¼	276¼	−15¼
26	257½	272¾	−15¼
27	256¾	271½	−14¾
28	258½	271¼	−12¾
29	257½	269¼	−11¾
30	261½	273½	−12

EXHIBIT 8c   TREASURY BOND BASIS

January	Cash 9⅛% 5/15/09	Future, March 1980 CBT, Treasury Bond	Basis
2	90-16	80-28	9-20
3	89-26	80-16	9-10
4	89-12	80-04	9-08
7	89-13	80-09	9-04
8	89-29	80-25	9-04
9	89-28	80-20	9-08
10	90-07	81-01	9-06
11	89-08	79-29	9-11
14	88-30	79-20	9-10
15	88-26	79-26	9-00
16	89-00	79-25	9-07
17	88-08	79-01	9-07
18	87-05	78-05	9-00
21	85-20	76-22	8-30
22	86-22	77-18	9-04
23	86-20	77-16	9-04
24	85-02	75-29	9-05
25	84-04	75-02	9-02
28	83-23	74-25	8-30
29	83-04	74-01	9-03
30	83-02	74-08	8-26
31	83-16	74-16	9-00

EXHIBIT 8d   CORPORATE BOND BASIS

May	Cash, IBM, 9⅜% 10/1/04	Future, June 1980, CBT Treasury Bond	Basis
1	89-09	78-12	10-29
2	88-18	80-06	8-12
5	90-31	80-18	10-13
6	91-25	81-27	9-30
7	92-20	81-17	11-03
8	92-20	80-20	12-00
9	92-20	80-10	12-10
12	92-20	79-25	12-27
13	90-18	80-12	10-06
14	90-18	80-24	9-26
15	89-25	78-24	11-01
16	88-07	78-08	9-31
19	88-07	77-03	11-04
20	88-31	79-03	9-28
21	89-25	80-06	9-19
22	89-25	79-30	9-27
23	90-18	81-29	8-21
27	91-13	81-12	10-01
28	91-13	80-22	10-23
29	90-18	79-25	10-25
30	90-06	79-14	10-24

EXHIBIT 9   FUTURES MARKETS PRICE STRUCTURES

October 1, 1979, CBT Corn Futures Prices		May 1, 1980, CBT British Pounds Prices	
A. NORMAL MARKET		**B. INVERTED MARKET**	
Dec	79	290¾	June	80	2.2515
Mar	80	305½	Sep	80	2.2430
May	80	313¼	Dec	80	2.2280
Jul	80	317			
Sep	80	319			
Dec	80	320			

August 1, 1979, CBT Treasury Bond Prices		June 1, 1976, CBT Corn Futures Prices	
C. INVERTED V		**D. V**	
Sep	79	90-23	Jul	76	292
Dec	79	90-24	Sep	76	283¼
Mar	80	90-26	Dec	76	274¼
Jun	80	90-24	Mar	77	282¼
Sep	80	90-22	May	77	287½
Dec	80	90-19			
Mar	81	90-16			
Jun	81	90-13			
Sep	81	90-10			
Dec	81	90-08			

cash, it is a **partial hedge.** The hedge is usually **lifted;** that is, the future is bought to offset when the cash is sold.

The success of a hedge is gauged not only by the downside risk protection it affords but also on fluctuations in the basis. On net, the short hedger benefits by a **narrowing of the basis** if the future is sold over the cash and a **widening of the basis** if the future is sold under the cash. The examples of hedges that follow reflect a favorable change in the basis as well as a favorable movement in the futures prices in relation to the position the hedger wishes to protect. This may not always be the case, however, and the alternative possibility should be considered by a hedger. A hedged position can protect against unfavorable market movements but **can also limit potential profits.**

Short Hedge 1: Price Change Hedge.   On November 1 an elevator operator with excess storage capacity buys 100,000 bushels of #2 corn for $2.36 (plus a $0.10 loading fee), which he expects to sell to a baker by the end of the month. December CBT corn is quoted at $2.58¼. Feeling that the basis of 12¼¢ is wide, he decides on a **total hedge** and accordingly sells 20 December corn contracts MOC. The following reflects a breakdown of his short hedge.

Cash	Basis	Futures
	NOVEMBER 1	
Buys 100,000 bushels of #2 corn at 236 + 10 = 246	$-12\frac{1}{4}$	Sells 20 contracts (100,000 bushels) December CBT corn at $258\frac{1}{4}$
	NOVEMBER 30	
Sells 100,000 bushels of #2 corn at $261\frac{1}{2}$ + 10 = $271\frac{1}{2}$	-2	Covers 20 December CBT corn at $273\frac{1}{2}$
	RESULTS	
$25\frac{1}{2}$ cent gain	$10\frac{1}{4}$ narrowing	$15\frac{1}{4}$ cent loss

While securing protection from downside price movement in the corn that was bought, the operation was able to profit by a $10\frac{1}{4}$ narrowing of the basis. It is important to emphasize that the basis might have moved in the opposite direction, thereby generating a basis loss.

Short Hedge 2: Interest Rate Change Hedge.   A corporate treasurer plans to issue $50 million in 30-year debt in February to finance a certain project that depends rather sensitively on financing costs, but on January 2 he becomes apprehensive about the bond market. Since his filing for financing is tied up in **SEC registration** for 3 weeks and therefore cannot be priced, he decides to **cross-hedge,** using CBT bond futures. He assumes that his issue will require 1% or 100 basis points (b.p.) concession to a Treasury issue of comparable maturity, such as the $9\frac{1}{8}$% of 5/15/09 selling at 90-16 to yield 10.15%. If he could sell his bonds today at par with a coupon of 11.15%, the project would be successful. Since his authorization to cross-hedge is restricted by the corporate charter, it is understood that by selling 500 bond futures at 80 ($40 million) he will not be completely hedged. The partial cross-hedge analysis is as follows:

Cash	Basis	Futures
	JANUARY 2	
Proxy: Treasury $9\frac{1}{8}$ of 5/15/09 90-06 = 10.15% Firm's estimated coupon = 11.15%	9-10	Sells 500 March bond contracts @ 80-28

Cash	Basis	Futures

JANUARY 23

Cash	Basis	Futures
Proxy: $9\frac{1}{8}$ of 5/15/09 86 - 20 = 10.60% Sells $50 million bonds at par coupon = 11.65%	9-04	Buys 500 March bond contracts @ 77-16

RESULT

Cash	Futures
Opportunity loss (based on 50 b.p. higher coupon) $2,250,000	$1,687,500 gain

While unable to obtain complete protection with the partial cross-hedge because of internal constraints, the corporation was able to mitigate against 75% of a 50 basis point (or $2.25 million) rise in borrowing costs. Not only was the firm **underhedged** 20% in a falling market, but the basis versus the futures market widened with the drop in bond levels costing $225,000 alone. Nonetheless, the $1.7 million profit on the **short sale** offset most of the increased financing costs sustained during the 3-week period.

Long Hedge. A **buy hedge** utilizes a long position in the futures market to protect against a rise in the cost of honoring a future commitment. In this case, the hedger benefits from a narrowing of the basis if the future is bought under the cash and a widening if it is bought over the cash.

Buy Hedge 1: Exchange Rate Change Hedge. An importer contracts to buy 100,000£ of wool payable in 30 days. His cash flow and credit are such that he is unable to buy pounds at present, but wishes to lock in his profit margin figured at current exchange rates. Accordingly, he buys 4 CME British pound contracts totaling 100,000£.

Cash	Basis	Futures

MAY 12

Cash	Basis	Futures
Future commitment to deliver 100,000 pound sterling @ 2.2875	150	Buys 4 IMM June BP @ 2.2725

JUNE 12

Cash	Basis	Futures
Delivery commitment 100,000 pound sterling @ 2.3372	72	Sells 4 IMM June BP @ 2.3300

RESULT

Cash	Futures
Opportunity $4,970 loss	$5,750 profit

Since the basis narrowed during this period, the importer actually improved his situation by this change of $780.

Buy Hedge 2: Interest Rate Change Hedge. A performance-oriented bond manager learns that a contribution expected to be in the neighborhood of $25 million will be made into a fund in a couple of weeks. Management forecasts that rates are peaking and wishes to lock in current yields. It is unable to obtain a **forward delivery commitment** from bond dealers because of the uncertainty in quantity and settlement date. While the intention is to immediately invest the entire amount in corporate bonds when the contribution is received, it is decided to hedge only $20 million by going long or buying 250 contracts trading at 78-12.

Cash	Basis	Futures
	MAY 1	
IBM 9⅜ of 04 @ 89-09 to yield 10.61%	10-29	Buys 250 June 1980 bond contracts @ 78-12
	MAY 22	
Buys $22 million IBM 9⅜ of 04 @ 89-25 to yield 10.55%	9-27	Sells 250 June 1980 bond contracts @ 79-30
	RESULT	
Opportunity cost 6 b.p. in yield or $5,600 per $1 million of contribution	1-02 narrowing	$390,625 profit

As a result of a favorable change in the basis, the portfolio manager was able to more than compensate for the lower yields prevailing in the market when the contribution was finally available for investment.

Spreading and Rolling Positions. A **spread** or **straddle** is a simultaneous long and short position in two different contract months of the same commodity so that the net position is zero. While often used to take advantage of forecasted changes in intermonth relationships, spreading can also be used by hedgers to maintain a futures position in an expiring contract. For example, an elevator operator sells 250 December corn contracts to protect his inventory. In November the operator is still long cash corn and wishes to retain his hedge. This is done by purchasing 250 December contracts and simultaneously selling (250) March. He is now long the cash corn and short March corn futures.

EXHIBIT 10   PROFESSIONAL FUTURES PERSONNEL

	Fiscal Year	
Registration or Reregistration	1978	1979
Futures commission merchants	372	357
Associated persons (2-year registrations)	12,266	22,058
Floor brokers	2,901	3,076
Commodity pool operators	670	717
Commodity trading advisers	971	1,216
	17,180	27,424

Source: Commodity Futures Trading Commission.

FEDERAL REGULATION

EARLY REGULATION.   Congressional interest in commodity futures dates back to the 1830s. Since 1900 an average of more than two regulatory bills have been introduced per year. In 1922 Congress enacted the **Grain Futures Act,** replacing the Futures Trading Act, which had been found to be unconstitutional. Revamped in 1936 as the **Commodities Exchange Act,** this legislation established a ruling agency under the U.S. Department of Agriculture, namely, the Commodities Exchange Authority (CEA).

THE COMMODITY FUTURES TRADING COMMISSION.   The 1936 Act was amended intermittently until Congress established the **Commodity Futures Trading Commission (CFTC)** in a complete legislative overhaul in 1974. The scope of the CFTC Act includes two broad mandates: (1) to protect and strengthen the functional aspects of the futures markets, and (2) to protect the participants themselves. Specifically, the following areas and practices are regulated or prohibited:

1. Market manipulation.
2. Dissemination of false information.
3. Unfair trading practices.
4. Market emergencies.

EXHIBIT 11   POSITION LIMITS SET BY CFTC

Commodity	Minimum Reporting Level
Wheat, corn, soybeans	500,000 bushels
Oats, rye, barley, flaxseed	2,000,000 bushels
Cotton	5,000 bales
Silver	250 contracts
Copper, gold, cattle, soybean oil and meal	100 contracts
Hogs, silver coins, sugar	50 contracts
All others	25 contracts

EXHIBIT 12   TRADING VOLUME FOR FISCAL 1978

	Volume	Deliveries	%
Corn	6,264,936	25,352	0.4
U.S. Treasury bonds	291,555	3,313	1.1
British pounds	230,461	1,576	0.7

Source: Commodity Futures Trading Commission.

EXHIBIT 13   MONTH-END TRANSFER COMMITMENT, CFTC: AN EXAMPLE

	Bushels (Thousands)	% Held by Each Group	Number of Traders
CBT CORN, OCTOBER 1977			
Open interest	677,390	10.0	202
Speculative			
Long	48,515	7.2	45
Short	13,270	2.0	21
Spreaders			
Long	66,115	9.8	59
Short	66,760	9.9	59
REPORTING (LARGE) TRADERS			
Hedging			
Long	422,130	62.3	
Short	405,675	59.9	
Total			
Long	536,760	79.2	
Short	485,705	71.7	
NONREPORTING (SMALL) TRADERS			
Long	140,630	20.8	—
Short	191,685	28.3	—

Source: Commodity Futures Trading Commission, Month-End Trader Commitment, October 1977.

5. Customer moneys.
6. Registration of appropriate firms and individuals.
7. Record keeping.
8. Mandatory reporting requirements.

While jurisdiction as specified by the CFTC Act includes all commodities traded in organized contract markets, various agencies and governmental units provide input to the commission.

In civil regulatory matters, the CFTC retains jurisdiction over the exchanges and registered participants, while allowing the individual states enforcement capability against those dealing with the public. In addition to overseeing the exchanges to ensure that they perform their self-regulation function as well as enforcing stringent standards among futures professionals, the CFTC is charged with establishing a **National Futures Association** (NFA) similar to the National Association of Securities Dealers. When operational, the NFA will assume certain CFTC responsibilities such as customer arbitration.

Professional futures personnel, under the auspices of the CFTC as indicated in Exhibit 10, include futures commission merchants, floor brokers, and associates or others actively involved with the futures industry.

REQUIRED REPORTING.   Besides requiring certain filing information for individuals, the **CFTC** requires financial statements, certain minimum financial standards, thorough record keeping, and reporting by the futures commission merchants. The agency also acts as a watchdog and sets guidelines for commodity trading advisors, pool operators, and floor brokers to protect customers. To curb excessive speculation, the CFTC sets **position limits** on certain commodities and establishes minimum reporting levels as outlined in Exhibit 11. Volume and delivery figures are also available monthly or on an annual basis, as shown in Exhibit 12.

In addition to its regulatory capacity, the CFTC regularly publishes pertinent information regarding participant composition and deliverable supply status. Excerpts from the agency's month-end trader commitment appear in Exhibit 13.

It is important to stress that both organized exchanges through their extensive self-regulatory efforts as well as the Commodity Futures Trading Commission provide the framework in which the economic and social benefits of futures markets can be realized. Increased volatility in current markets as well as innovation in new areas should provide an environment for futures markets to prosper and serve the hedging needs of a wide variety of users.

REFERENCES

Rules and Regulations, various exchanges.

Statistical Annuals and Yearbooks, various exchanges.

Commodities Futures Correspondence Course, Futures Industry Association, Inc., One World Trade Center, New York, NY, 10048.

Commodity Futures Correspondence Course, New York Institute of Finance, Two New York Plaza, New York, NY 10004.

Annual Databook, Commodity Futures Trading Commission.

Commodity Futures Trading Commission, Annual Report, Government Printing Office, Washington, D.C., 1974.

The Dow Jones Commodities Handbook, A Guide to Major Futures Markets, Dow Jones Books, Princeton, NJ (annual).

Emery, Walter L., (Ed.), *Commodity Year Book,* Commodity Research Bureau, New York (annual).

BIBLIOGRAPHY

Commodity Futures Trading: Bibliography, Chicago Board of Trade, Chicago, 1978.

Sources of Financial Futures Information, Chicago Board of Trade, Chicago, 1980.

Bibliography of Finance and Investment, Brealy and Pyle, MIT Press, Cambridge, MA, 1973.

General

Arthur Andersen & Company, *Interest Rate Futures Contracts: Accounting and Control Techniques for Banks,* Andersen, Chicago, 1978.

————, *Federal Income Tax Implications,* Andersen, Chicago, 1979.

Burns, Joseph, *A Treatise on Markets,* American Enterprise Institute, Washington, D.C., 1979.

Chicago Board of Trade, *Futures Trading Seminar IV, Chicago, 1976, A Research Symposium: Proceedings,* CBT, Chicago, 1978.

————, Working, Holbrook, Ed., *Readings in Futures Markets,* Vol. 1, CBT, Chicago, 1977.

————, *Views from the Trade,* Vol. 3, J. Peck, Ed., CBT, Chicago, 1978.

————, *Commodity Trading Manual,* CBT, Chicago, 1980.

Commodity Futures Trading Commission Act of 1974 and amendments, Publication No. 5720-02640 Government Printing Office, Washington, D.C., 20036.

Gold, Gerald, *Modern Commodity Futures Trading,* Commodity Research Bureau, New York, 1975.

Hieronymous, Thomas, *Economics of Futures Trading for Commercial and Personal Profit,* Commodity Research Bureau, New York, 1977.

Kaufman, Perry J., *Commodity Trading Systems and Methods,* Wiley, New York, 1978.

Kroll, Stanley, and Shishki, Irwin, Ed., *The Commodity Futures Market Guide,* Harper & Row, New York, 1973.

Labys, W. C., and Granger, C. W. J., *Speculation, Hedging and Commodity Price Forecasts,* Heath, Lexington, MA, 1970.

Loosigian, Allan, *Interest Rate Futures,* Dow Jones, Princeton, NJ, 1980.

Schwartz, Edward, *How to Use Interest Rate Futures,* Dow Jones-Irwin, Homewood, IL, 1979.

Teweles, R. J., Harlow, C. V., and Stone, H. L., *The Commodity Futures Trading Guide,* McGraw-Hill, New York, 1969.

Research

Black, Fischer, "The Pricing of Commodity Contracts," *Journal of Financial Economics,* January 1976.

Dusak, K., "Futures Trading and Investor Returns: An Investigation of Commodity Market Risk Premiums," *Journal of Political Economy,* Vol. 81, November–December 1973, pp. 1387–1406.

Gray, Roger W., "Risk Management in Commodities and Financial Markets," with discussion by Clifford Heldreth, Konrad Biedermann, and Richard L. Sandor, *American Journal of Agricultural Economics,* Vol. 58, No. 2, May 1976, pp. 280–285, 296–304.

Houthakker, H. S., "Can Speculators Forecast Prices?," *Review of Economics and Statistics,* 39, May 1957, pp. 143–151.

Long, Richard W., and Raasche, Robert H., "A Comparison of Yields on Futures Contracts and Implied Forward Rates," *Federal Reserve Bank of St. Louis Review,* Vol. 60, No. 12, December 1978, pp. 12–30.

Martin, Robert B., Jr., "How T-Bill Spreads Can Be Used for Hedging and Tax Deferral Opportunities," *Journal of Taxation,* Vol. 48, No. 2, February 1978, pp. 102–105.

McCall, James W., "Taxation: Commodity Straddles as an Income Sheltering Device," *Oklahoma Law Review,* Vol. 31, No. 1, Winter 1978, pp. 233–246.

Poole, William, "Using T-Bill Futures to Gauge Interest Rate Expectations," *Federal Reserve Bank of San Francisco Economic Review,* Spring 1978, pp. 7–19.

Samuelson, P. A., "A Random Theory of Futures Prices," *International Management Review,* Vol. 6, June 1965.

Sandor, Richard L., "Trading Mortgage Interest Rate Features," *New York Times,* November 9, 1979, p.D 5–6.

Selig, Stephen F., and Schmittberger, Wayne, "Tax Aspects of Commodity Futures Trading," *Hofstra Law Review,* Vol. 6, No. 1, Fall 1977, pp. 93–114.

Stoll, Hans R., "Commodity Futures and Spot Price Determination and Hedging in Capital Market Equilibrium," *Journal of Financial and Quantitative Analysis,* Proceedings Issue, Vol. 14, No. 4, November 1979.

Working, Holbrook, "New Concepts Concerning Futures Markets and Prices," *American Economic Review,* Vol. 52, June, 1962, pp. 431–459.

PERFORMANCE MEASUREMENT

CONTENTS

EVOLUTION OF PERFORMANCE	
MEASUREMENT	**3**
Demand for Measurement	**3**
Competition in the 1960s and 1970s	**3**
Pension Fund Emphasis on Performance	**4**
State of the Art	**4**
RATE OF RETURN FOR A SINGLE	
PERIOD	**4**
Simplest Performance Measurement	**4**
Valuation	**5**
Market value versus cost or book value	**5**
Obtaining market values	**5**
Bond valuation	**6**
Nonmarketable assets	**6**
Income Measurement	**7**
Total Return	**7**
Income Yield	**7**
Appreciation	**8**
Calculation	**8**
AVERAGE RATE OF RETURN OVER	
SEVERAL TIME PERIODS	**9**
Method of Averaging	**9**
Dealing with Cash Flows	**10**
Internal or dollar-weighted rate of	
return	**10**
Time-weighted rate of return	**11**
Use of unit values	**11**
Approximations	**13**
MEASUREMENT OF RISK	**14**
Quantitative Measures	**14**
Measures of uncertainty	**14**

Standard deviation	15
Measures of market risk	16
Calculation of beta coefficients	16
Published sources of betas	17
Importance of investor time horizon	**18**
COMBINING RISK AND RETURN	
MEASURES	**18**
Purposes	**18**
Risk-Adjusted Rate of Return	**18**
Adjusting for beta	19
Sources of error and bias	20
EVALUATING PERFORMANCE	**20**
Purpose	**20**
Meeting Objectives and Expectations	**20**
Analyzing Sources of Performance	**21**
COMPARING PERFORMANCES	**21**
Purpose	**21**
Rate of Return Comparisons	**22**
Indexes	**22**
Choosing an index	**22**
Risk-Adjusted Comparisons	**23**
Special Services	**24**
Usefulness of Comparisons	**24**
NONCOMMON STOCK PORTFOLIOS	**25**
Bond Portfolio Performance Evaluation	**25**
Components of performance	**25**
Isolating components of performance	**25**
Portfolios of Short-Term Securities	**26**
Real Estate Portfolio Evaluation	**26**

PERFORMANCE MEASUREMENT

J. Peter Williamson

EVOLUTION OF PERFORMANCE MEASUREMENT

DEMAND FOR MEASUREMENT. The 1960s saw the beginning of careful and systematic **investment performance** evaluation. Prior to that time investors, including most institutional investors, were generally content to monitor their portfolios without numerical measures. The change was brought about by a number of forces, including competition among money managers in a rapidly rising market and the preoccupation of pension fund managers with pension cost reduction. For the most part these forces are still at work, and while there is somewhat less faith in the profitability of the securities market in 1980 than there was in the 1960s, interest in performance measurement appears to be undiminished.

The basic methodology for measuring rate of return has been pretty well worked out, although there is still disagreement over risk measurement and over the choice of benchmarks for performance evaluation. Some of this disagreement rests on matters of judgment and probably will never be resolved. To some extent, performance measurement still suffers from the lack of information available and from the infrequency and questionable reliability of security valuations.

COMPETITION IN THE 1960s AND 1970s. Competition among money managers was the principal force in bringing about systematic and frequent investment performance measurement. This was particularly evident in the mutual fund industry. Investors in mutual funds, who had never before paid close attention to the performances of these funds, were confronted in the 1960s with evidence of some spectacular rates of return. Magazines and newspapers began to feature the most successful fund managers, and the funds themselves began to sell numerical performance results rather than relying on the traditional description of investment philosophy.

It was during the 1960s that publication of **comparative performance statistics** began. For a few years the Lipper Reports gave managers and institutional investors weekly rates of return for several hundred mutual funds. A. G. Becker began to publish comparative rates of return on a quarterly basis for pension funds. The investment committee of the National Association of College and University Business Officers began to circulate annual comparative performance statistics for college and university endowment funds.

Throughout the investment world, money managers were discovering that performance evaluations had become an important element in competition. And those responsible for selecting managers discovered a new, if sometimes treacherous, device for making their selections.

PENSION FUND EMPHASIS ON PERFORMANCE. A second factor at work during the 1960s was the increasing emphasis among **pension plan sponsors** on investment performance. For the first time, many corporations with large **trusteed pension plans** began to relate investment performance to the level of contributions and even to the level of benefits payable. The performance of the stock market during the 1960s suggested that substantial reductions in pension fund contributions might be achieved through superior investment management. Pension plan sponsors began to call for more frequent and more accurate measures of fund performance, and indeed much of the development of measurement techniques was brought about to satisfy these demands.

Investment manager selection for trusteed pension plans became a much more important activity in the 1960s than it ever had been. The realization that investment performances of individual managers could show spectacular differences and that these differences could have a major impact on pension fund contributions led to an almost frenzied search for the high performing managers.

STATE OF THE ART. It appeared for a while during the 1960s that a single reliable performance statistic might be agreed on, one that would provide a complete measure of the investment ability of a manager and could therefore be used for purposes of hiring, firing, and monitoring performance. It is generally accepted now that no such single statistic exists. Evaluation of an investment manager's performance requires a variety of statistics. There are still differences of opinion as to the accuracy of valuation data and the best way to obtain accurate data. And there are differences of opinion as to the use of approximations when numerical data are inaccurate or missing. But these disagreements are minor and should become less significant in the future as data processing and record keeping improve.

The important issues in calculation methodology have been resolved. The issues that remain are not concerned with methodology but with the usefulness of performance calculations.

Probably the most discouraging discovery in the evolution of performance measurement, and the discovery that led to the realization that no single performance statistic will ever tell the whole story, was that most historic performance records simply do not furnish a reliable basis for **predicting future performance.** This discovery then raises the question of whether performance measurement has any value at all. The answer must be that it has less value than many at one time hoped. It is hardly surprising that there should not exist a single reliable statistic on which to confidently base predictions of the relative success of fund managers. A variety of performance measurements will give insights into the strengths and weaknesses of various managers, styles of management, and strategies. What still remains is the task of sorting out the measurements that are most useful and combining them effectively to gain those insights. Despite all the past work on computational techniques, it is this task that largely remains to be completed.

RATE OF RETURN FOR A SINGLE PERIOD

SIMPLEST PERFORMANCE MEASUREMENT. The simplest performance measurement for an investment, or for a portfolio, is the **total return rate** and its two components: income yield and growth rate. Income yield is income (interest and dividends for a securities portfolio) expressed as a percentage of the portfolio value. If a $1 million portfolio produces $50,000 in interest and dividends, the yield is $50,000/$1 million or 5%. The growth rate measures appreciation as a percentage of value. If the $1 million portfolio appreciates to a value of

$1,060,000, the growth rate is $60,000/$1 million or 6%. The total return, measuring the total investment performance of the portfolio, is 11% (5% + 6%).

Total return is the measure most useful in evaluating the quality of investment management, but yield and growth have their own uses. The determination of the rate of return requires first a set of valuations—for income and principal—and second a method of calculation.

VALUATION.   Valuation requires a clear understanding of the difference between market value and book value or cost. Market value is the appropriate choice for performance evaluation and raises some practical problems.

Market Value Versus Cost or Book Value.   A number of financial institutions normally report their investment portfolios at **market value,** while others report at cost, or **book value.** Mutual funds always use market value. Life insurance companies, banks, and savings institutions generally use cost. Pension funds traditionally report investments at cost, but are increasingly reporting market values as well. Charities and college and university endowment funds once reported only cost figures and many continue this practice. Others report individual portfolio holdings at cost but disclose the market value of their total portfolios. Still others report all holdings at market.

Book value is quite useless for the usual purposes of performance measurement. It records the original cost of a portfolio (e.g., the original amount of gifts to an endowment) plus realized gains, less realized losses. It does not reflect **unrealized gain or loss.** A portfolio with a high turnover is likely to have a book value close to market value, because gains and losses are constantly being realized. But if the turnover is low, the book value may be far below market value. Some institutions, particularly colleges and universities, calculate performance figures based on book value and use these figures for comparison. Sometimes the error is easy to spot. When an institution boasts of an income yield of 10% on a growth stock portfolio, there is obviously something wrong. The explanation is likely to be that an income of $1,000 is being expressed as a percentage of a $10,000 original cost instead of a $25,000 market value. The point is that when growth stocks can be purchased to produce a yield of about 4% (dividends of $4 for every $100 invested in the stock), a portfolio of such stocks yielding 10% would indeed be remarkable. But when it turns out that the portfolio is a very ordinary one, producing 4% on its market value, the 10% figure can be seen to derive from the original cost, something that has nothing to do with how well the portfolio is currently invested.

Correct performance measurements demand market values for a portfolio. Precise performance measurements may require market valuations at frequent intervals. Mutual funds, for example, value their portfolios at least daily. Other institutions generally make less frequent valuations and are satisfied with less precise measurements. The subject of frequency of valuation is discussed later.

Obtaining Market Values.   It is not difficult to obtain usable valuations for common stocks traded daily on a stock exchange, but even for these investments the valuation process is not absolutely certain. For example, if a portfolio is being valued as of December 31 and one security held is common stock of a company listed on the New York Stock Exchange, there are at least three numbers that might go into the value used for the stock: the "close" (the price at which the last trade took place on December 31), the "bid," or the "ask" at the close of trading. Generally the "close" is the number used. If there was no trading in the stock on December 31, the average of the **bid and ask quotes** is usually used. For

over-the-counter stocks only the bid and ask quotes are generally available: sometimes the average of the two is used and sometimes the bid is used alone.

The procedure just described is satisfactory for most valuation purposes, but it can be questioned on a number of grounds. First, the closing price for a particular stock on a particular day may well reflect an aberration in the price performance of the stock. The price may have bounced up briefly as the result of a large purchase order placed late in the day. Or it may have dropped briefly as the result of a large sell order. One generally expects that aberrations of this sort will cancel out over all the portfolio holdings. A more serious question is raised if the portfolio includes a large holding of a single stock, and it is quite clear that the entire holding could not have been disposed of on the valuation day at the closing price for that day. Selling a large block would have required a price concession. So the procedure described above will overstate what could have been realized in cash if the entire portfolio of securities had been liquidated on the valuation date. The second objection is generally answered by pointing out that at least for purposes of evaluating investment performance, the **liquidation value of the portfolio,** under conditions of almost instant liquidation, is not relevant.

Bond Valuation.   For bonds, the valuation process is not as simple. It is quite likely that on the valuation date there were no trades in many of the bond issues held in a portfolio. **Bid and ask quotes** may have been available from bond dealers on that day, but these are not systematically collected and tabulated as they are for listed or even unlisted common stocks. Generally, one must rely on a bond firm to use its trading expertise to place values on bond issues in the portfolio. Some firms have developed matrices for pricing thousands of issues of untraded bonds, using as guidelines the prices at which the traded issues changed hands. But there is no generally accepted matrix calculation, so in using the valuations one is essentially relying on the judgment of the firm. There are bound to be some errors in the valuations of individual issues; but just as in the case of common stocks, one hopes that the errors will cancel out across the entire portfolio.

Nonmarketable Assets.   Some investments must be classified as essentially nonmarketable, and for these there is no market value. Examples are real estate and mortgages. The best way to treat these investments is to separate them for reporting purposes from marketable investments. The investment performance of the latter can then be calculated, and indeed it is useful to examine the marketable bond portfolio and the marketable stock portfolio separately. If nonmarketable investments make up a small proportion of the total portfolio, it may not be necessary to calculate an investment performance for them. To find out how well the nonmarketable investments are doing, it is possible to arrive at an approximate market value. Real estate holdings, for example, can be appraised. But it is important to bear in mind when reviewing such performance measurements that appraisals are only an approximation of market value, and the investment performance figures cannot be compared to figures based on true market values. This is particularly true when the performance of a real estate portfolio is being reviewed. Whether or not the real estate portfolio appears to have been more profitably invested, almost always the investment performance will appear to have been much smoother than the performance of a stock or bond portfolio. That is, the values will seem to have risen steadily over time without the wide fluctuations that can be found in the value of a stock or bond portfolio. This smoothness is essentially the result of using appraisals rather than true market values; it does not reflect any inherent superiority of real estate as an investment. This is especially important to understand because the **variation of returns** is a standard measure of portfolio riskiness.

INCOME MEASUREMENT.   For many portfolios the measurement of income suffers from inadequate record keeping. For bond portfolios it is important to calculate accrued income at the beginning and end of a measurement period and to include an increase in accruals as income for the period, and vice versa for a decrease in accruals.

For stocks, the dividend should be attributed to the period in which the stock goes **"ex-dividend."** (The New York Stock Exchange advances the date when stocks shall be quoted and sold on an ex-dividend basis to the third full business day before date of record.) So if the measurement period ends on December 31 and a dividend is payable in January but the stock goes ex-dividend in December, the dividend should be included in income for the measurement period. This is because the stock price at the end of December will have declined to correspond to a buyer's ineligibility to receive the dividend. This procedure will lead to a small upward bias in the performance measure, since the investor does not actually have the use of the dividend at the end of the measurement period. The amount of the bias, probably a few one-hundredths of a percent a year, could be estimated and an adjustment made.

TOTAL RETURN.   Total return is the best single measurement of investment performance. Any single measurement must fall short of a complete description of performance, as will be seen, but total return is a widely used and generally accepted indicator that comes closest to the ideal statistic for comparison purposes.

Anyone responsible for the supervision or safeguarding of investment assets—a pension fund trustee, a foundation or college or university trustee, a mutual fund director, or a member of an investment committee—must know the rate of total return for the portfolio of assets. This is the starting point for evaluating management of the assets.

INCOME YIELD.   For many portfolios there is no particular advantage to breaking down the rate of total return into income yield and appreciation. For a pension fund, income is added to the principal of the fund, both income and appreciation are free of tax, and all that matters is the total performance of the fund. For a **taxable entity,** however, if the tax rate on realized appreciation differs from the rate on income, income and appreciation are not equivalent and there is good reason to examine each.

Consider a **bank-administered trust fund,** with the beneficiary taxed at 70% on dividend and interest income and at 28% on long-term capital gains (the maximum personal rates in 1980). A total return of 12%, consisting of 5% income and 7% growth, may be more attractive than a total return of 14%, consisting of 9% income and 5% growth. If the growth were all in the form of realized long-term capital gain, the aftertax total returns would be respectively, $[(5\% \times 30\%) + (7\% \times 72\%)]$ and $[(9\% \times 30\%) + (5\% \times 72\%)]$ or 6.54% and 6.30%. If the growth is all or even partly in the form of unrealized appreciation, a comparison becomes more difficult because appreciation is not taxed at all until it is realized. There is no standard accepted method of calculating comparable rates of total return in this case, but probably the most used comparison would treat the appreciation as if it were all realized and would show pretax total return rates of 12 and 14% and aftertax rates of 6.54 and 6.30%.

Regardless of whether an aftertax rate of total return is actually calculated, the importance of the income and growth components is obvious. In other cases taxes may not be an important factor, but legal distinctions between income and appreciation may be.

A trust with one **income beneficiary** and another **remainderman,** or principal beneficiary, is an example. To the income beneficiary the income yield is what matters; to the remainderman growth is what counts. Endowment funds are generally subject to a rule that income may be spent but appreciation may not be (although in the 20 or more states that have adopted the **Uniform Management of Institutional Funds Act** a portion of appreciation is expendable). So income yield has an importance of its own.

APPRECIATION.   While there are cases in which income yield, as opposed to or in addition to total return, may be of considerable interest, it is only rarely that appreciation alone is a matter of concern. This is why reports often show total return and income yield separately, but without any figure for growth.

CALCULATION.   The calculation of total return or income yield is fairly simple in principle, but it can become complicated in practice. Consider a straightforward example: the market value (or net asset value, at market) of a unit in a fund rises from $10 to $10.7368 in the course of a year, and the fund produces income of $0.4211 per unit. On the assumption that all the income was received at year-end, the yield can be calculated as 0.4211/10 or 4.21%, and the appreciation as 0.7368/10 or 7.37%, for a total return of 11.58%.

But the income was almost certainly not all received at year-end. A better assumption may be that on average it was received at midyear. Since income received early (midyear) is generally more valuable than income received late (year-end), the performance of the fund has probably been a little better than 11.58%. There is no standard "correct" way to make the adjustment. For college and university endowment funds the usual convention is to assume that income is received at midyear and could have been invested in the fund at that time, and that the value of the unit at midyear was the average of the beginning and end of year unit values.

In the example above, the average of the beginning and end of year unit values was $10.3684. The year-end value of $10.7368 represents growth of 0.3684/10.3684 or 3.55% during the second half-year. If the income of $0.4211 per share had grown at this rate over the second half-year, it would have amounted to $0.4361 at year end. The sum of $0.4361 and $0.7368 is $1.1729, or 11.73% total return on a $10 initial value.

The conventional formula is:

$$\text{total return} = \left(\frac{\text{income}}{(\text{beginning} + \text{ending unit values})/2} + 1 \right) \frac{\text{ending value}}{\text{beginning value}} - 1$$

Obviously the assumptions used in the formula are not entirely valid. As long as educational endowment funds only are being compared, this should not matter much. If funds using this formula were compared to other funds for which the rate of return is calculated differently, the errors could become serious.

If the time period for the measurements were so short that all the income was actually received at the end of the period, there would be no need for an approximation; an exact total return rate could be calculated. The more frequent the valuation and calculation, the more valid the assumptions and the more reliable the rate of total return.

Exhibit 1 shows, for a large common stock portfolio (in excess of $1 billion), total return rates over 5 years based on monthly, quarterly, and annual valuations, using the formula described above. The figures suggest that monthly valuations do not add much accuracy to quarterly valuations, but that quarterly valuations give much more reliable return figures than do annual valuations.

EXHIBIT 1   COMPARISON OF CALCULATED RATES OF TOTAL
RETURN (%) USING MONTHLY, QUARTERLY, AND ANNUAL
VALUATIONS

Year	Computed from Monthly Data	Computed from Quarterly Data	Computed from Annual Data
1	11.86	11.70	11.39
2	13.62	13.27	12.65
3	2.51	2.43	1.96
4	− 22.97	− 22.83	− 22.30
5	46.67	46.40	41.46

AVERAGE RATE OF RETURN OVER SEVERAL TIME PERIODS

METHOD OF AVERAGING.   Having computed the rate of total return on a portfolio for
a series of periods, months or quarters or years, one would like to be able to compute an
average rate of return over several such periods. During the early 1960s a number of
institutions showed a certain amount of confusion in this averaging process. By 1980 the
confusion had largely vanished, but it may still be worth pointing out the difference between
the **arithmetic average** and the **compound average,** and the reasons for preferring the latter.

Suppose that the total return on a portfolio is measured for four quarters and the results
are 10, − 2, − 9, and 1 for the quarters. The simplest average that can be deduced from
these four numbers is the arithmetic average, which is the sum of the numbers divided by
4:

$$\text{arithmetic average} = \frac{10 - 2 - 9 + 1}{4} = \frac{0}{4} \neq 0\%$$

A second average figure that can be deduced is the compound or geometric average rate of
return. The compound average answers the question; What rate of return earned for four
quarters in a row is equivalent to earning 10% the first quarter, losing 2% the second quarter,
losing 9% the third quarter, and earning 1% the fourth quarter? The following equation
shows how the compound average rate R is calculated:

$$(1 + R)^4 = (1 + 0.10)(1 - 0.02)(1 - 0.09)(1 + 0.01)$$
$$= 0.9908$$
$$1 + R = 0.9977$$
$$R = -0.0023$$
$$= -0.23\%$$

The compound average rate of total return is slightly negative. In general, the compound
average will always be smaller than the arithmetic average (unless by some chance the
individual period returns are identical, in which case the compound average will be the same
as the arithmetic average). This is because the positive rates of return are applied to a smaller
base than are the negative rates of return. The greater the fluctuation in rate of return over
the periods being averaged, the greater the difference will be between the compound and
arithmetic averages. To take an extreme case, consider a rate of return of 50% in one quarter

and -50% in the second quarter. The arithmetic average rate of return is 0%. The compound average rate of return is -13.5%. A \$100 investment would increase to \$150 during the first quarter and then decline to \$75 during the second quarter, leaving a net loss of \$25.

For purposes of performance evaluation, the compound average is the one to use. In the example above, the compound average rate of -13.5% per quarter faithfully reports the conversion of \$100 into \$75 in two quarters.

DEALING WITH CASH FLOWS.   Another source of considerable confusion in the early 1960s was the flow of money into or out of an investment portfolio. A pension fund receives investment income that is normally added to the capital of the fund. Investment income does not produce any special problems. It constitutes part of the investment return and was dealt with in various examples above. But a pension fund also receives contributions from the plan sponsor, contributions that are not a part of investment performance. And the fund makes benefit payments, that again are not part of investment performance. It is necessary in calculating the rate of return on the fund to allow for the effects of the receipts and disbursements that are not a part of the investment performance.

There are two computational methods for calculating the rate of return in the context of these cash flows. The methods serve different purposes, and only one of them is appropriate for evaluating the quality of investment management. The confusion surrounding the two methods was cleared up in 1968 when the Bank Administration Institute published *Measuring the Investment Performance of Pension Funds*. The following discussion identifies the two methods, explains the calculations, and describes the purpose each method serves.

Internal or Dollar-Weighted Rate of Return.   Exhibit 2 gives the set of cash flows for a pension fund over four calendar quarters. The fund begins with a value of \$1 million. At the end of the first quarter the plan sponsor contributes \$60,000 to the fund and the fund pays out \$12,000 in benefits to participants. At the end of the second quarter there is no contribution, but \$12,000 in benefits are paid out. At the end of the third quarter contributions are \$80,000 and \$12,000 benefits are paid out. And at the end of the fourth quarter benefits of \$12,000 are paid out and the resulting value of the fund is \$1,240,000. It is assumed that all investment income received by the fund is held in the fund and shows up at the end of the year in the \$1,240,000 value.

The net cash flows for the fund are arrived at as follows: at the beginning of the first quarter, the fund sponsor gives the fund \$1 million. At the end of the first quarter the fund takes in \$60,000 and pays out \$12,000, so the net flow is an inflow of \$48,000. At the end of the second quarter there is an outflow of \$12,000. At the end of the third quarter there is a net inflow of \$68,000. At the end of the fourth quarter there is an outflow of \$12,000, and the fund value is \$1,240,000, for a net of \$1,252,000. (A negative cash flow is one from the sponsor to the fund; a positive flow is one from the fund.) To calculate the so-called dollar-weighted or internal rate of return, we form the following equation:

$$1,000,000 = \frac{-48,000}{1 + R} + \frac{12,000}{(1 + R)^2} - \frac{68,000}{(1 + R)^3} + \frac{1,252,000}{(1 + R)^4}$$

where R is the dollar-weighted or internal rate of return. The expression essentially says that the \$1 million initial value is the discounted present value of a \$48,000 flow into the fund one period hence, a \$12,000 flow out of the fund two periods hence, a \$68,000 flow into the fund three periods hence, and a \$1,252,000 flow from the fund four periods hence. Solving for the rate R is a trial-and-error process, and it turns out in this case that R is 3.36% per quarter. This corresponds to an annual rate of 13.4% compounded quarterly.

The correct interpretation of the internal rate of return is that the combination of contributions, benefit payments, and investment performance of this fund led to an average rate of return of 3.36% per quarter over the four-quarter period. It is not correct to say that the investment performance alone accounted for a return of 3.36% per quarter. Indeed it is impossible to extract from the internal rate of return the contribution made by investment management. The internal rate of return is, however, useful for describing the total experience of the fund, in light of investment performance and cash flows.

Time-Weighted Rate of Return.   Exhibit 3 adds some further numbers to the data of Exhibit 1. Specifically, what is now supplied is the value of the fund at each quarter-end. It can be seen that investment performance carried the \$1 million value to \$1,100,000. The net cash flow brought the value up to \$1,148,000 and investment performance in the second quarter carried this value down to \$1,040,000. The \$12,000 net cash flow further reduced the fund's value to \$1,028,000, but during the third quarter investment performance carried this value up to \$1,158,000. The end of the third quarter net cash flow brought the fund value up to \$1,226,000, and the investment performance for the fourth quarter carried the value up further to \$1,264,000. It is now possible to identify the role of investment performance alone, and to calculate the contribution this performance made in terms of a rate of return. For each quarter the total return, reflecting the investment performance, has been calculated. The compound or geometric average of these four quarterly returns is 3.71% or 14.8% per year compounded quarterly. It is this figure that is the so-called **time-weighted rate of return.**

This time-weighted rate of return, or **compound average total return,** provides a measure of investment performance unaffected by the cash flows. In the particular example, the time-weighted rate of return is a little higher than the **dollar-weighted rate of return,** about 0.35% higher per quarter. The explanation can be seen from the set of figures above. The fund did very well during the first quarter. At the end of this quarter a substantial amount of money was added, and during the second quarter the performance was poor. At the end of the second quarter money was withdrawn, and during the third quarter the performance was very good. At the end of the third quarter another substantial sum was added, and the fourth quarter performance was mediocre. In other words, money was consistently put into the fund just before a bad performance and taken out just before a good performance. The timing of the cash flows tended to offset the quality of investment management, and pulled down the overall performance of the fund. Sometimes the timing of cash flows will worsen the overall performance; sometimes it will improve the overall performance. The time-weighted rate of return is unaffected by the timing of cash flows and therefore gives the truer picture of the quality of investment management.

Use of Unit Values.   The calculation of the time-weighted rate of return as described above may seem to be an awkward and cumbersome process. It is made a good deal easier if the record keeping for the fund includes the calculation and tabulation of **unit values.** Then all that is necessary to arrive at the investment performance over any particular period of time is to examine the beginning and end of period unit values, and to take account of income per unit if this is not already incorporated in the unit values. Mutual funds calculate unit values, or per share values, at least once a day. The investor in a mutual fund need not be

EXHIBIT 2   CASH FLOWS FOR A PENSION FUND

	First Quarter		Second Quarter		Third Quarter		Fourth Quarter	
	Beginning	End	Beginning	End	Beginning	End	Beginning	End
Contributions to fund	—	$60,000		—		80,000	—	—
Benefits paid out	—	12,000		12,000		12,000		12,000
Value of fund	$1,000,000						1,240,000	1,252,000
Net cash flows	−1,000,000	−48,000		12,000		−68,000		12,000

EXHIBIT 3   EXPANSION OF NET CASH FLOW EXAMPLE

	Value of Fund				
	Before Contributions Received and Benefits Paid: $1,000,000	End First Quarter: $1,100,000	End Second Quarter: $1,040,000	End Third Quarter: $1,158,000	End Fourth Quarter: $1,264,000
Net cash flow		−48,000	12,000	−68,000	12,000
Value after net cash flow		1,148,000	1,028,000	1,226,000	1,252,000
Total return		$\dfrac{1,100,000}{1,000,000} - 1$ $= 10\%$	$\dfrac{1,040,000}{1,148,000} - 1$ $= -9.4\%$	$\dfrac{1,158,000}{1,028,000} - 1$ $= 12.6\%$	$\dfrac{1,264,000}{1,226,000} - 1$ $= 3.1\%$

Compound average $(1 + R)^4 = (1 + 0.10)(1 - 0.094)(1 + 0.126)(1 + 0.031)$
$R = 3.71\%$ per quarter

concerned about the cash flow of the fund as shares are redeemed. The investment performance of the mutual fund is entirely reflected in the per share value and the income distributions
per share.

The calculation and use of unit values is described in some detail in a publication of the
Ford Foundation included in the References and Bibliography. Briefly, for the example
above, one could arbitrarily establish the number of units in the fund at 100,000 at the
beginning of the first quarter. The initial unit value would then be $10. At the end of the
first quarter the unit value is the fund value, $1,100,000, divided by the number of units,
or $11 per unit. At a value of $11.00 per unit, the net cash flow of $48,000 into the fund
represents the addition of 4,364 units (48,000/11). The total number of units then grows to
104,364. At the end of the second quarter, the unit value has declined to $9.965. The net
cash flow of $12,000 represents a withdrawal of 1,204 units (12,000/9.965), leaving 103,160
units. At the end of the third quarter these units are worth $1,158,000, or $11.225 each. The
net inflow of $68,000 adds 6,058 units (68,000/11.225) for a total of 109,218 units. These
units are worth $1,264,000 at the end of the fourth quarter, or $11.573 each. The unit values
at the five points in time are then $10, $11, $9.965, $11.225, and $11.573. From these five
numbers it is easy to calculate the quarterly total returns, or to go directly to a calculation
of the rate of return over the entire year. For the entire year, the $10 value grew to $11.573,
so the rate of return is [(11.573/$10) − 1)] or 15.7%. This is the annually compounded rate;
the corresponding rate with quarterly compounding is 14.8%.

Unit values have other uses besides the calculation of investment performance. But for
the performance calculations alone they offer great convenience. From a permanent tabulation
of the unit values calculated above, one can quickly calculate the investment performance
over any particular sequence of time periods.

APPROXIMATIONS.   The correct calculation of the time-weighted rate of return, and of
the unit values, requires valuation of the total fund on each date on which contributions were
made or benefits paid out. For some funds, where cash flows are not frequent, these valuations
present no difficulty. But if the cash flows are frequent, corresponding valuations of the
entire fund may be difficult and costly. As time goes on the cost and the difficulty should
decline. Data processing routines and sources of stock and bond valuations are common
enough that most institutional managers of funds and almost all bank custodians should be
able to deliver valuations as often as daily without great difficulty. Nevertheless, valuations
are not being made available to all pension funds and other institutional investors on a daily
basis.

If a portfolio valuation is not available at the time of each cash flow, it is necessary to
make some approximations in estimating the time-weighted rate of return. The Bank Administration Institute study referred to above described some method of approximation. A simple
and widely used approximation for the total return on pension funds was proposed in 1966
by Peter Dietz. It begins with this expression:

$$M_2 = M_1 + C + R\left(M_1 + \frac{C}{2}\right)$$

where M_2 is the market value of the pension fund at the end of the period of time, M_1 is the
market value at the beginning of the period, C is the net contribution to the fund during the
period (the contribution made by the plan sponsor less benefit payments made by the fund),
and R is the rate of total return for the period. In essence the equation says the ending market

value is made up of the beginning market value, net contributions, and investment performance over the period. Investment performance is represented by the return on the beginning of period assets plus half the contributions, based on the assumption that the net contribution is received at the middle of the period, or half at the beginning and half at the end.

Rearranging the expression gives:

$$R = \frac{M_2 - M_1 - C}{M_1 + C/2}$$

So if M_1 = \$1,000,000, M_2 = \$1,060,000, contributions are \$40,000, and benefits are \$30,000, so that C = \$10,000, we have

$$R = \frac{1,060 - 1,000 - 10}{1,000 + 0.10/2} = 5.0\%$$

This formula can be used for charitable endowment funds too, but care must be taken in calculating C, which is gifts or other capital additions less all withdrawals (including income spent) for spending. So if \$5,000 is received as a gift addition, \$12,000 is withdrawn from principal to be spent, and \$40,000 of income is all spent as received, C = \$5,000 − \$12,000 − \$40,000 or − \$47,000. If M_1 = \$1,000,000 and M_2 = \$1,060,000,

$$R = \frac{1,060 - 1,000 + 47}{1,000 - 0.47/2} = 11.0\%$$

MEASUREMENT OF RISK

QUANTITATIVE MEASURES.   Probably the major accomplishment of performance measurement over the past two decades has been the development of quantitative measures of risk. None of these measures is entirely satisfactory, since to some extent risk in the mind of the investor remains subjective and difficult to quantify. It seems clear that any quantitative approach to risk involves limitations that will never be eliminated. But the measures that have been proposed have a high degree of plausibility, and they are steadily winning acceptance from investment practitioners.

Until the 1960s, few efforts were made to quantify risk, but it was generally accepted that rate of return comparisons between two portfolios were legitimate only if the portfolios reflected approximately equal investment risk. This meant that there was simply no way to compare portfolios with extremely different risks. Given quantitative risk measures, however, the rates of return on two portfolios can be adjusted for the different risks of the portfolios and the so-called **risk-adjusted rates of return** can be compared. This offers the possibility of comparing the performance of any portfolio with the performance of any other portfolio or the performance of any index.

Measures of Uncertainty.   Risk in an investment portfolio has to do with uncertainty about the future performance of that portfolio. The performance over the next 6 months of a portfolio of 6-month Treasury bills is very certain. The rate of return over the next 6 months on a portfolio of long-term U.S. government bonds is much less certain. While the coupon interest on the portfolio may be easily predictable, the market value of the portfolio at the end of 6 months is uncertain, and so, therefore, is the rate of total return. The investment performance over the next 6 months for a portfolio of common stocks is still more uncertain. And there are some common stocks for which the next 6 months' performance is more uncertain than for others. If one pictures uncertainty about the future performance of a portfolio as a range of possible outcomes, with very high returns and very low returns highly unlikely, with moderately high and moderately low returns more likely, and average returns the most likely, one has some basis for quantifying the uncertainty. If the outcome of an investment is very uncertain, the range of possible outcomes is very broad. If the outcome is fairly certain, the range is quite narrow.

Standard Deviation.   A useful statistical measure of the range of outcomes is the so-called standard deviation. It is this measure that has become widely accepted as the most appropriate measure of **total risk in an investment.** In principle, one arrives at the standard deviation for a particular portfolio by establishing the range of possible future investment performances and attaching a probability to each of those performances. In practice, one usually relies heavily on the past performance of a portfolio or of the securities within that portfolio as a guide to the future uncertainty. An investment for which the future is very uncertain is generally an investment for which the past performance has shown wide fluctuations, whereas for an investment having a highly certain future performance, the past performance is likely to have shown very little fluctuation. For this reason, it is customary to calculate the **standard deviation of performance** for a portfolio or a security from a series of past performances, and to use this standard deviation as the measure of future uncertainty.

Exhibit 4 shows 16 quarterly rates of return for the several billion dollar, all common stock portfolio of College Retirement Equities Fund (CREF) and for the Standard & Poor's

EXHIBIT 4   QUARTERLY TOTAL RETURN RATES

			CREF Unit (%)	S&P 500 Index (%)
1976	Q	1	12.89	15.01
	Q	2	2.91	2.42
	Q	3	0.79	1.86
	Q	4	3.51	3.12
1977	Q	1	−8.34	−7.45
	Q	2	4.19	3.26
	Q	3	−2.12	−2.80
	Q	4	0.09	−0.25
1978	Q	1	−4.15	−4.90
	Q	2	9.03	8.51
	Q	3	8.77	8.70
	Q	4	−4.39	−5.00
1979	Q	1	6.89	7.03
	Q	2	2.62	2.79
	Q	3	7.43	7.65
	Q	4	−1.71	0.13
Arithmetic average, quarterly rate			2.40	2.51
Compound average, quarterly rate			2.25	2.34
Compound average, annual rate			9.31	9.69
Standard deviation of quarterly rate			5.74	5.95

500 Index. The standard deviation of the 16 quarterly rates has been calculated and is shown at the bottom of the tabulation for both the CREF unit and the S&P Index. The two values are very close; the risk in the CREF portfolio is just a little below the risk in the S&P 500 Index, which is probably about the same as the risk in the stock market as a whole.

Measures of Market Risk.   Standard deviation is the commonly accepted statistic for representing the total uncertainty or risk in a portfolio or a security. For some evaluation purposes, however, it may be appropriate to break down total risk into two or more components. Since all securities tend to move somewhat with the market as a whole, some of the uncertainty over the future performance of a portfolio or a security reflects uncertainty about the future of the market. To put the matter another way, if one could predict the stock market with perfect accuracy, one could substantially reduce the uncertainty about the future performance of any common stock portfolio. One component of total risk then is the sensitivity of the performance of a portfolio to the performance of the market. This is the so-called **beta coefficient** of the portfolio. A portfolio with a beta coefficient of 1 moves with the market. When the market is up 10%, the portfolio is up approximately 10%. And when the market drops 10%, the portfolio value drops about 10%. A portfolio with a beta greater than 1 moves more than the market, and one with a beta less than 1 moves less than the market. Most reasonably diversified portfolios of common stocks have beta coefficients between 0.5 and 1.5.

Almost no investment portfolio tracks the market perfectly. Thus even a perfect forecast of the market's performance will not enable an investor to make a perfect forecast of the performance of a portfolio. There is therefore a second component of total risk in the portfolio, the **residual** or **nonmarket-related risk.** An investor can reduce this residual risk to just about any desired level, simply by increasing the **diversification** of the portfolio. It is **not** possible to reduce market-related risk through diversification.

In a world of reasonable investors one would expect the taking of risk to be accompanied by the expectation of returns commensurate with that risk. That is, one would expect investors to take large risks only in the expectation of large returns. Modern portfolio theory goes one step beyond this and proposes that in this tradeoff of risk and expected return, only **market-related risk** is to be taken into account. This is because investors can reduce nonmarket-related risk by way of diversification. They can justify taking market-related risk only by the expectation of an appropriately higher rate of return.

Calculation of Beta Coefficients.   The beta coefficient is usually calculated from a series of historic rates of return. Exhibit 5 plots the 16 quarterly rates of return on the CREF unit and the S & P 500 Index. As can be seen, the performance of CREF tracked the Index very closely. A straight line has been fitted to the points representing the quarterly rates of return, and the slope of this line, 0.95, is the beta coefficient for CREF over the 16 quarters. In this particular case, the straight line can be adequately fitted by eye, but there is a mathematical procedure—least squares regression—that does a more precise job. It is from a regression that the 0.95 slope coefficient was calculated.

While the method shown in Exhibit 5 for estimating a beta coefficient is simple to apply, it does have some weaknesses. Over time, there may be changes in the beta coefficient for a portfolio. The changes may be the result of conscious decisions by the portfolio managers or the result of chance, but in either case the historic beta coefficient may not be a satisfactory measure of the risk in the portfolio at a particular time. In the case of CREF there have been deliberate shifts in the volatility of the fund, although these have taken place within a narrow range. It might be noted at this point that if the manager of a portfolio is free to change the beta coefficient over time and indeed can be expected to do so, a further element of uncertainty

EXHIBIT 5   RELATIONSHIP BETWEEN QUARTERLY PERFORMANCE OF CREF UNIT VALUE AND S&P 500 INDEX, 1976–1979

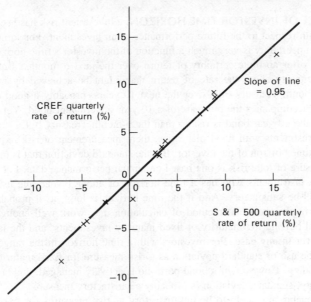

with respect to future performance is introduced. There seems to be as yet no clear methodology for measuring this risk.

A second way to calculate the beta coefficient for a portfolio is to calculate the coefficient for each security in the portfolio, as described above using a regression, and then compute a weighted average of the betas for the securities. The average is the **beta for the portfolio.** This procedure corrects for the fact that the portfolio was not the same in all 16 quarters because over 4 years some securities were added and others dropped. The second method would lead to a beta coefficient of close to 1.00 for CREF at the end of 1979. For planning purposes, predicting the future reaction of a portfolio to a market movement, this method of calculating a beta coefficient is preferable. For purposes of estimating the risk in the portfolio over a historic period however, in evaluating past performance, the first method is preferable because it records what actually happened.

A third method of estimating portfolio beta coefficients goes somewhat further than the second, and makes use of **"fundamental" beta coefficients** for the securities making up the portfolio. The historic coefficient for a particular stock suffers from a weakness similar to that noted above for the historic coefficient for a portfolio. The company may have changed its business or financial structure over the years, and its risk may have changed. The calculation of fundamental betas attempts to incorporate both historic response to the market and current characteristics of the company. Once again, this method of estimating beta coefficients is appropriate for prediction purposes, rather than for historic performance evaluation.

Published Sources of Betas.   Beta coefficients for individual common stocks are available from a number of sources. Merrill Lynch, Pierce, Fenner & Smith publishes monthly tables. Value Line Investment Survey provides beta coefficient estimates for the stocks it reviews.

Fundamental betas are not generally available in published form but must be obtained from consulting firms.

IMPORTANCE OF INVESTOR TIME HORIZON.   Investment risk has been presented as uncertainty with respect to the future performance of an investment. For some investments, however, this uncertainty is very much a function of the investor's time horizon. Six-month Treasury bills offer absolute certainty of return over the next 6 months. But there is considerable uncertainty about the rate of return that might be achieved by investing in 20 successive 6-month Treasury bills over the next 10 years, probably a good deal more uncertainty than accompanies the purchase of a 10-year government bond. Yet for a 6-month time horizon, the 10-year bond is riskier than the 6-month Treasury bill.

Among investments with fixed maturities, then, measurement of risk requires some attention to the time horizon of the investor. But the standard deviation that is most commonly used as a measure of total risk is one based on annual performance data. For an investor in fixed maturity instruments who has a time horizon of about 1 year, the usual method of calculation will be satisfactory. And if the time horizon is long, as it probably will be for most pension funds, the usual method of calculation may work well enough because the horizon is well beyond the maturity of fixed maturity investments, and the latter will have to be rolled over in any case. For investors with a time horizon in the range of one to 10 or 15 years, the use of standard deviation as a risk measure for fixed maturity investments may be misleading. However, if a bond portfolio is actively managed, and bonds are rarely held to maturity, standard deviation is probably a satisfactory measure.

Beta coefficients are likely to be unsatisfactory as risk measures for fixed maturity securities regardless of investor time horizons. The point is discussed toward the end of the section.

COMBINING RISK AND RETURN MEASURES

PURPOSES.   The measurement of investment risk in a portfolio has some value for its own sake. Communication between the owner of a portfolio and the portfolio manager on the subject of risk objectives is made more effective if there is an acceptable way of quantifying and measuring risk. But for purposes of performance evaluation, the real benefit in risk measurement lies in ability to combine risk and return measures to produce risk-adjusted rates of return and so make possible performance comparisons among investments of different risks.

As noted above, the hope that performance measurement might lead to agreement on a single performance statistic by which all managers and portfolios might be evaluated has largely disappeared. Nevertheless, risk-adjusted rates of return do have a use in the evaluation process.

RISK-ADJUSTED RATE OF RETURN.   Risk adjustment to rates of return rests on some propositions of portfolio theory. The first of these is that the rate of total return one can anticipate on an investment, above the return available on a risk-free investment, is proportional to the risk in the investment. So if the chosen measure of risk is the standard deviation of return, a successful performance is one that delivers a high total return, above the risk-free rate, per unit of standard deviation. The **risk-adjusted return** is given by:

$$\text{risk-adjusted return } R = \frac{\text{average return on portfolio } - \text{ risk-free rate of return}}{\text{standard deviation of returns}}$$

The average return and standard deviation for the CREF unit for a 16-quarter period were given in Exhibit 4. For comparison purposes, the arithmetic average quarterly return and standard deviation for the same 16 quarters for the Common Fund were 3.73 and 5.89%, respectively. The Common Fund equity portfolio is an all common stock portfolio of under $100 million, representing endowment investments of colleges and universities.

Calculation of the risk-adjusted return above requires a figure for the risk-free rate of return. Over the 16 quarters 1976–1979, the **average quarterly rate** of return on 30-day Treasury bills was 1.67%. Using this as the risk-free rate of return leads to the following calculation for the risk-adjusted rates of return over the 16 quarters for CREF, the Common Fund, and the S&P 500 Index:

$$\text{For CREF} \qquad R = \frac{2.40 - 1.67}{5.74} = 0.13\%$$

$$\text{For Common Fund} \qquad R = \frac{3.73 - 1.67}{5.89} = 0.35\%$$

$$\text{For S\&P 500 Index} \qquad R = \frac{2.51 - 1.67}{5.95} = 0.14\%$$

In other words, the S&P 500 Index achieved a rate of return of 0.14 percentage point per quarter above a Treasury bill rate, for each percentage point of standard deviation in return. CREF performed almost as well, achieving 0.13 percentage point above the Treasury bill rate for each percentage point of standard deviation. The Common Fund performed much better over these 16 quarters, delivering 0.35 percentage point of quarterly return above the Treasury bill rate for each percentage point of standard deviation.

Adjusting for Beta.   The process of adjusting the rate of return for the beta coefficient is somewhat more complicated; it rests on portfolio theory relating expected return to market risk. It is common practice to substitute the beta coefficient for the standard deviation in the equations above, but while this generally leads to the proper ranking of performances, it is not strictly correct. The correct adjustment was described some years ago by Jack Treynor in an article in the *Harvard Business Review*. The explanation is not repeated here, but the calculation of an index by which performances can be ranked is given by:

$$\frac{\text{index for ranking}}{\text{performance}} = \frac{(\text{regression line intercept}) + (\text{beta} - 1)(\text{risk-free rate of return})}{\text{beta}}$$

The regression line is the line drawn in Exhibit 5. The intercept is the rate of return on the portfolio, where the regression line intercepts the vertical axis, which is at 0.0122% in Exhibit 5, for CREF. Using this equation gives the following ranking index values (the beta and the intercept for the Common Fund for the 16 quarters were 0.927 and 1.41, respectively):

$$\text{ranking index for CREF} = \frac{0.0122 + (0.954 - 1) \times 1.67}{0.954} = -0.068$$

$$\text{ranking index for Common Fund} = \frac{1.41 + (0.927 - 1) \times 1.67}{0.927} = 1.39$$

$$\text{ranking index for S\&P 500 Index} = \frac{0 + (1 - 1) \times 1.67}{1} = 0$$

The ranking index for the S&P 500, the reference for the calculation of the beta and the intercept, will always be 0. The ranking for a portfolio that underperforms the S&P 500 on a risk-adjusted basis will be negative, as is the case for CREF. The ranking index for a portfolio that outperforms the S&P 500 will be positive, as is the case for the Common Fund.

Sources of Error and Bias.   The calculation of a beta coefficient requires selection of a reference index. Common stock betas are generally based on the S&P 500 Index, but other indexes could be used. Portfolio theory demands that the index incorporate all risky assets—stocks, bonds, real estate, commodities, and everything else one can invest in. No such index has been tabulated, although indexes more broadly based than those now available could certainly be devised. In the absence of this ideal index, any choice of index is somewhat arbitrary, therefore beta coefficients themselves have a degree of arbitrariness. As a practical matter, use of the S&P 500 Index as the reference appears to work well. Some sources of bias have been discovered. Over the 20 years 1959–1978, portfolios of stocks of smaller companies appear to have performed better, on the basis of a beta-adjusted return, than they really did. The same is true of portfolios made up of high-yield common stocks.

EVALUATING PERFORMANCE

PURPOSE.   The preceding discussion centered on measurement of performance in terms of both rate of return and risk. The usual purpose of performance measurement is performance evaluation. This may involve comparing a performance with an expectation, analyzing sources of good and bad performance, comparing a performance with a benchmark like a market index, or comparing a performance with performances of other managed portfolios. Comparisons among managers, portfolios, and indexes are discussed later. We deal next with evaluation in terms of objectives and expectations, and the analysis of strengths and weaknesses.

MEETING OBJECTIVES AND EXPECTATIONS.   In general there is not much point in expecting managers to achieve **short-run objectives** set in terms of total return. One may hope that in the long run a common stock portfolio will average, say, 15% a year total return. But to anticipate a 15% return in any particular year flies in the face of the known volatility and unpredictability of the stock market and the major influence of market action on any stock portfolio.

It does, however, make sense to establish risk objectives and expect them to be achieved over the short term. If the portfolio owner and manager agree on a beta coefficient between 0.95 and 1.05, for example, only a few quarters of performance data will indicate whether this objective is being achieved. There are, of course, bound to be random deviations from a target beta coefficient, but one measure of manager quality is the manager's ability to control risk within a narrow range.

Risk-adjusted rates of return may suggest a basis for short-term evaluation in terms of expectations, but here random fluctuations present a serious problem. In principle, the risk-adjusted measures discussed above for CREF and the Common Fund are applicable to short periods of time, but in practice these measures vary so much from period to period for any one manager or portfolio that in the short run they are a poor guide to management ability to meet objectives.

Dissatisfaction with total return and risk-adjusted total return as measures by which to judge performance against expectations has led to a search for more useful criteria, and one factor that shows some promise is **income growth.** For a charitable or educational endowment, from which only income will be spent, the rate of income growth is obviously important. Even for a pension fund, if in the long run the income yield will fluctuate around some average, the capital appreciation will in the long run equal income growth. Income growth has other features to recommend it. It is generally more consistent and more predictable than total return. It does lend itself to abuse, however. A manager can produce a high rate of income growth in a short time simply by shifting from low to high yielding securities. This device will not work for long, and in the short run its effects can be identified and allowed for in a performance evaluation.

As an example, the average growth in dividends on the S&P 500 Index over the 10 years 1970–1979, calculated by a least squares regression, was 7.3% a year. The rate of inflation over the same 10 years, as measured by the Consumer Price Index, was 7.4% per year. So the dividend income from the S&P Index almost kept up with inflation. This may be a more important result than the total return on the investment, especially if one objective for a portfolio is an income stream that maintains its purchasing power.

ANALYZING SOURCES OF PERFORMANCE.   The two obvious sources of performance are security selection and market timing. The latter involves either successful switching of funds among stocks and bonds and short-term investments to take advantage of relative ups and downs in the three markets or successful changes in the volatility of a stock portfolio, becoming aggressive in rising markets and defensive in falling markets. The former involves selection of the best performing stocks, bonds and other instruments.

The effects of switching are determined by calculating the results of investing in stock, bond, and short-term indexes in the proportions indicated by the manager's decisions. Use of indexes eliminates any effects due to security selection. If the manager begins with a portfolio equally divided between stocks and bonds, and after a month changes the proportions to 70% stocks and 30% bonds, and after another month changes back to half and half, one calculates the result of holding a stock and a bond index in equal proportions for a month, then switching to 70% stock index and 30% bond index for a month, then switching back to equal proportions. Comparing this result to the result of simply maintaining constant proportions will indicate whether the switching was successful. The effects of shifting the volatility of a stock portfolio can be determined in a similar way, by tracking the performance of a mix of a stock index and a short-term index, or by correlating the volatility shifts with subsequent stock market performance.

Once the timing contribution to a portfolio's performance has been estimated, it is subtracted from the total return and the balance of the performance is attributed to selection ability.

COMPARING PERFORMANCES

PURPOSE.   An obvious purpose of performance measurement is to compare managers with one another, to hire and keep only the best. A closely related purpose is to determine whether there is any value to management, whether an actively managed portfolio has outperformed a simple and less expensive passive strategy. This is a difficult area and obviously an important one. There is no single all-revealing method of comparison. Nor is there much general agreement even on the best comparisons. The following discussion suggests a number of considerations that should enter into the choice of a comparison method.

RATE OF RETURN COMPARISONS.   The most common comparisons between the performance of a portfolio and the performance of an index, or among the performances of managed portfolios, are based on rates of total return. This approach is not inappropriate if the risk levels of the portfolios or indexes in the comparison are roughly the same. A quick inspection of beta coefficients or standard deviations of return may confirm that they are about the same. Even a qualitative description, giving the kind of stocks or bonds held in the portfolio or represented by the index, may be enough to support a comparison of total returns. But one frequently finds performances being compared on a total return basis when risk levels are not at all the same. Total return comparisons among a common stock portfolio, a bond portfolio, and a mixed stock and bond portfolio are not uncommon. Often the results are presented without drawing attention to the fact that the portfolios are not comparable on a risk basis.

It is also not uncommon to find that the return figures themselves used in a comparison are not really comparable. Because it is often difficult to obtain accurate data on the income generated by a portfolio and on the income corresponding to an index, comparisons are sometimes based strictly on capital appreciation, ignoring income. The comparisons will be fair only if the incomes generated by the portfolios or index being compared are equal. But making a comparison strictly on the basis of appreciation between a growth stock portfolio, with a low level of income, and an income stock portfolio obviously biases the result in favor of the growth stocks. A more subtle lack of comparability may arise from the treatment of management fees. Sometimes rates of return are calculated net of (less) management fees and sometimes they are calculated before deduction for fees. Mutual fund results are always reported net of management fees. Rates of return reported for educational endowment and charitable funds are often before deduction of management fees. With fees running in the range of a few tenths of a percent up to 1 or 2% of asset value, a substantial bias can be introduced by an inconsistency here.

If rates of return alone are to be compared, the time period chosen for the comparison may be significant. Even small differences in volatility among portfolios will lead to substantial differences in reported rates of return during periods of extreme market movement. Comparisons that extend over a full market cycle will generally avoid the biases of shorter periods.

Indexes.   Rate of return comparisons between portfolios and indexes are fairly common. At one time it was argued that no investor could actually buy an index, and therefore the comparisons meant nothing. It is clear today that investors **can** buy an index, or at least a portfolio as close to an index as they care to come. A number of investment managers offer "index funds," investing in a portfolio that matches the composition of an index—the Standard & Poor's 500 Index, for example. So the comparisons do have a real meaning. They show the difference between the actual performance of a portfolio and what the performance would have been if an index fund had been chosen. The record of an index, of course, does not reflect any transaction costs. To the extent that the manager of the portfolio was required to buy and sell securities to account for cash flows into and out of the portfolio, an adjustment should be made. Otherwise the index comparison is biased against the manager. No adjustment for other transaction costs is appropriate, since the index fund alternative avoids such costs.

Choosing an Index.   It is important that an appropriate index be chosen, and many are available. Exhibit 6 shows 10 years of annual total returns for the most commonly used stock and bond reference indexes—the **S&P 500 Stock Index** and the **Salomon Brothers Long-**

Term, High Grade Corporate Bond Index. The S&P 500 includes 500 common stocks and represents a broad cross section of the U.S. stock market. It is a "value-weighted" index, with each of the 500 stocks represented in proportion to the market value of the company's common stock. This means that the index reflects the experience of investors in general. IBM, for example, plays a major role in the S&P 500 Index, just as it does in the experience of the investment community. The S&P 500 can easily be found in newspapers, and dividend figures corresponding to the index are available, allowing anyone to calculate yield, appreciation, and total return. The Salomon Brothers bond index is also a broad index, covering industrial and utility bonds, and is one of the few bond indexes for which income is tabulated. It is restricted to high-quality bonds (AA and AAA) with long maturities, however, and it includes no U.S. government issues.

For most performance evaluations the S&P 500 provides a suitable stock index benchmark. It may be desirable to compare performance of a portfolio to a more specialized set of stocks, however. Managers of growth stock portfolios should use a growth stock index for comparisons.

The usefulness of the Salomon Brothers bond index is more limited. Because it is an index of high-grade corporate bonds, it is not entirely suitable for judging a portfolio that includes lower grade bonds or U.S. government bonds. And because it includes only bonds with long maturities, it is not always suitable for judging portfolios with short or shifting maturities. It is valuable, of course, for identifying the performance contribution of a maturity strategy that differs from simply holding long bonds.

Evaluating the performance of a portfolio containing both stocks and bonds may require an index reflecting both stocks and bonds, and one can easily combine the index results in Exhibit 6 in any desired proportions to provide a benchmark.

RISK-ADJUSTED COMPARISONS. The chief weakness of simple rate of return performance comparisons lies in the requirement that the portfolios and indexes being compared have approximately the same investment risk characteristics. In theory, comparisons of risk-

EXHIBIT 6   ANNUAL RATES OF TOTAL RETURN

	Standard & Poor's Composite (500) Stock Index (%)	Salomon Brothers Long-Term, High-Grade Corporate Bond Index (%)
1970	4.0	18.4
1971	14.3	11.0
1972	19.0	7.3
1973	− 14.8	1.1
1974	− 26.5	− 3.1
1975	37.3	14.6
1976	23.7	18.7
1977	− 7.3	1.7
1978	6.6	− 0.1
1979	18.6	4.1
Arithmetic average	7.5	6.6
Compound average	5.8	6.2
Standard deviation	19.3	8.7

adjusted rates of return overcome this weakness. But the risk-adjusted comparisons bring with them some problems of their own.

The mechanics of calculating risk-adjusted returns have already been described. The two methods, one involving the standard deviation, a measure of total portfolio risk, and the other involving the beta coefficient, a measure of market-related risk, suggest at least one dilemma. Although portfolio theory would indicate that it is the return adjusted by the beta coefficient that is the more appropriate, in reality this is not so clear. As long as the comparison is limited to common stock portfolios and indexes, the beta coefficient is generally a satisfactory risk measure for adjusting return. The calculation of the beta coefficients is based on a broad stock market index, like the S&P 500 Index. But if the portfolios include fixed income securities or other noncommon stock investments, there is no general agreement on the reference index against which beta coefficients are to be measured. And in general, beta coefficients for fixed income securities are much less satisfactory than beta coefficients for common stocks.

For most comparisons of common stock portfolio performances, rankings using returns adjusted by standard deviation will be almost identical to rankings obtained from rates of return adjusted by beta coefficients. Where the portfolios to be compared involve more than common stocks, returns adjusted for standard deviation are preferred.

SPECIAL SERVICES. A number of firms offer performance comparisons. A. G. Becker was one of the first and may still have the largest set of pension fund performance figures available for comparison purposes. Merrill Lynch offers a widely used service. Peat, Marwick, Mitchell & Co., through its Investment Supervision Consulting Group, publishes statistics on performances of U.S. and Canadian institutional funds. Computer Directions Advisers maintains large sets of computerized performance data. Wilshire Associates offers performance measurement coupled with a large data base. Lowry Associates, a manager selection consultant, also maintains a large set of data on manager performance, as does dé Marche Associates. These are among the better known sources of comparisons, but many consulting firms and brokerages can supply data, calculations, and interpretation.

Reference has already been made to improvements in data processing and the capability of bank custodians in delivering accurate and frequent portfolio valuations. Some banks and trust companies have made a specialty of this. The master trust arrangement, which puts the record keeping and overall control of a plan sponsor's total pension assets in the hands of a single bank, usually offers detailed performance statistics on the entire fund and each of its separately managed components.

USEFULNESS OF COMPARISONS. The most important question with respect to performance comparisons is whether they can be relied on to indicate true relationships. One would hope that superior management ability would lead to consistently superior performance, and therefore be readily identifiable. But there will always be some chance element in the performance of a portfolio, whether that performance is expressed in terms of a rate of return, or in terms of a risk-adjusted rate of return. The important question is whether the role played by management ability in determining investment performance is strong enough to permit this quality to be identified by the methods described above, or whether the element of chance is strong enough to obscure the effects of ability.

The evidence seems to be that it is extraordinarily difficult to identify consistently superior management through performance rankings. Over any particular time period it is of course possible to rank the performances of any set of portfolios or portfolio managers. But generally the rankings over one time period show little correlation with rankings over another time period. This suggests rather strongly that performance rankings do not provide reliable evidence of differences in management ability.

This discovery may be disappointing, but it should not come as a surprise. If it is true, as seems likely, that the majority of investment managers have about the same ability and that even very good managers do not produce performances far above average, one should not expect to be able to find in performance rankings a reliable ranking by ability. This does not mean that rankings are useless. A ranking that is very high or very low over a long period of time suggests superior or inferior ability. Now the evaluation task is to see whether that suggestion is confirmed by other characteristics of the manager. A careful examination of risk level and control, consistency of style, disciplined analysis, and other managerial qualities, coupled with a review of the sources of performance, discussed briefly above, will help to establish whether the extreme ranking position is the result of ability or chance.

NONCOMMON STOCK PORTFOLIOS

BOND PORTFOLIO PERFORMANCE EVALUATION.

Components of Performance.   The measurement of income yield, appreciation, and total return for a bond or bond portfolio presents no special problems. As noted above, accrued interest at the beginning and end of the measurement period must be allowed for, as well as accrued interest paid (negative income) when bonds are purchased. But **risk measurement** for a **bond portfolio,** and the measurement of risk-adjusted returns, presents some special difficulties.

Standard deviation of total return as a risk measure is probably appropriate for bonds as well as stocks. For many investors, however, particularly regulated financial institutions that carry bond portfolios on their books at cost, market value fluctuations are not regarded as important. This means that total return, and standard deviation of total return, may not be important. But for the investor who is equally concerned about bond value fluctuation and stock value fluctuation, standard deviation is a good risk measure.

In principle, a measure of market risk should be appropriate for bonds. But the beta coefficient used for stocks and stock portfolios does not work well for bonds. Bonds have a fixed maturity, and as a result their rates of total return will follow a pattern over time.

So total return adjusted for standard deviation, as described above for stock portfolios, will serve many investors as a risk-adjusted performance measure for bond portfolios. But what is of much more interest is the **dissection of bond performance into its components.** The analysis of sources of performance for stock portfolios was discussed briefly above, and consists generally of separating the contributions of timing and stock selection. For bond portfolios the process has been carried somewhat further.

Isolating Components of Performance.   A number of methods of analysis have been proposed to isolate components of bond portfolio performance. In general, they distinguish between how performance is affected by changes in interest rates, which depends on the maturity structure of the portfolio, and how it is affected by the selection of individual bonds. The contribution of bond selection can be divided further into the results of quality choice, sector choice (e.g., industrial or utility or government bonds), and choice of individual issues within a sector and quality range. This process was described by Dietz, Fogler, and Hardy

("The Challenge of Analyzing Bond Portfolio Returns"). Other proposed methods go into further detail, identifying the contribution of a manager's choices with respect to size of issue, sinking fund provisions, conversion features, coupon level, and other characteristics.

As a practical matter, the major source of uncertainty about the future performance of a bond portfolio, and therefore the major factor accounting for a superior or inferior performance record is change in interest rates and in the term structure of interest rates. So identification of the contribution of this factor alone tells a good deal about the quality of performance.

PORTFOLIOS OF SHORT-TERM SECURITIES.   In principle, short-term portfolios should be measured as stock and bond portfolios are. Reporting practices, however, frequently fail to provide correct figures.

Corporations and other institutions maintaining short-term portfolios for temporary investment of surplus cash often rely on cost or book value in reporting portfolio returns. In times of stable interest rates, the failure to use market value may not lead to significant errors. But when rates are rising or falling, the true performance may be very different from what is reported.

Money market mutual funds generally follow a practice of maintaining the share or unit value constant, most often at $1 per unit. As interest rates change, of course, the value of the portfolio changes, but what is reported as "income" (and income is normally credited daily to each unit holder's account) is adjusted to keep the unit value at $1. Comparisons of reported income, or yield, among these funds may not mean much because of the relationship between unit value and income. Only a total return comparison can be relied on. The calculation of total return, however, requires the maintenance of an account with no contributions or withdrawals, since income is being added daily and the funds generally do not disclose their total return performance record.

REAL ESTATE PORTFOLIO EVALUATION.   In principle, the measurement of performance of real estate investments is no different from measurement of security portfolio performance. In practice, there are significant differences. First, **the value of a real estate portfolio** is always based on appraisals. Appraisals represent the subjective judgment of the appraiser and can never achieve the status of market quotations for stocks and bonds. As noted above, the use of appraisals tends to create the appearance of steadily moving values and a stable rate of return. This is not necessarily misleading for an investor with a long time horizon and little interest in the results of quick liquidation of a portfolio. But it is not appropriate to contrast the apparently stable appreciation of a real estate portfolio to the highly variable price record of a stock or bond portfolio and conclude that the former is much safer.

Income from a real estate portfolio is often not as precisely measurable as interest and dividends from a securities portfolio. For the participant in a pooled fund, income is what the fund distributes as income. For the sole owner of a portfolio, the determination of income may involve a number of accounting conventions and assumptions. For performance reporting purposes, income before depreciation and before income tax is the figure used. Essentially, this figure is the cash flow before-income tax. Ignoring depreciation is appropriate, assuming that expenditures on repairs and maintenance are adequate, because the property value is being recorded along with income. Repairs and maintenance of course present an opportunity for more or less arbitrary manipulation of income. Income measurement is somewhat more objective than property valuation, but it is subjective enough to render comparisons to security portfolios inappropriate.

REFERENCES AND BIBLIOGRAPHY

Bank Administration Institute, *Measuring the Investment Performance of Pension Funds,* BAI, Park Ridge, IL, 1968.

Dietz, P. O., *Pension Funds: Measuring Investment Performance,* Free Press, New York, 1966.

——, Fogler, H. R., and Hardy, D. J., "The Challenge of Analyzing Bond Portfolio Returns," *Journal of Portfolio Management,* Vol. 6, Spring 1980, pp. 53–58.

Ford Foundation, *Measuring Investment Results by the Unit Method,* Ford, New York, 1975.

Leibowitz, M. L., "Sources of Return in Corporate Bond Portfolios," Salomon Brothers, New York, August 3, 1978. (Reprinted as Chapter 6 in *Total Return Management,* Salomon Brothers, New York, 1979.)

——, *Total After-Tax Bond Performance and Yield Measures,* Salomon Brothers, New York, 1974.

Murphy, J. M., "Why No One Can Tell Who's Winning," *Financial Analysts Journal,* Vol. 36, May–June 1980, pp. 49–57.

Rosenberg, B., "A Critique of Performance Measurement," unpublished paper, University of California, Berkeley, 1980.

Sharpe, W. F., "Adjusting for Risk in Portfolio Performance Measurement," in *Portfolio Management and Efficient Markets,* Peter L. Bernstein, Ed., Institutional Investor Books, New York, 1977, pp. 113–127.

——, "Mutual Fund Performance," *Journal of Business,* Vol. 39, January 1966, pp. 119–138.

Treynor, J. L., "How to Rate Management of Investment Funds," *Harvard Business Review,* Vol. 43, January–February 1965, pp. 63–75.

Williamson, J. P., *Performance Measurement and Investment Objectives for Educational Endowment Funds,* Common Fund, New York, 1972.

REAL ESTATE FINANCE

CONTENTS

SOURCES OF REAL ESTATE LENDING	3
Financial Institutions	3
Savings and loan associations	3
Commercial banks	7
Life insurance companies	7
Mutual savings banks	8
Mortgage Companies	8
Federal and Quasi-Federal Mortgage Credit Agencies	9
Real Estate Investment Trusts (REITs)	10
FINANCIAL ASPECTS OF THE MORTGAGE INSTRUMENT	10
Interest Rates on Mortgages	10
Frequency Compounding	11
Maturity	11
Amortization and Repayment Plans	12
New Mortgage Instruments	14
Charges and Fees	15
Prepayment charges	15
Closing costs and origination fees	15
Late charges	17
Mortgage Liens	17
Mortgage Insurance	18
SPECIAL TYPES OF MORTGAGE	18
Construction Loans	18
Land Development Financing	18
Wraparound Mortgages	19
Leasehold Mortgages	19
Open-End Mortgages	20
Package Mortgages	20
Deposit Collateral Mortgages	20
ALTERNATIVE FORMS OF REAL ESTATE FINANCING	20
Long-Term Leases	20
Net leases	21
Gross leases	22
Typical Provisions of Leases	22

Variable Rent Leases	22
Sale-Leaseback Financing	22
OPTIONS, ESCROWS, AND LAND TRUSTS	23
Real Estate Options	23
Real Estate Escrows	23
Land Trusts	24
EFFECTS OF MARKET INTEREST RATES ON MORTGAGE CREDIT MARKETS	24
Money Market Certificates	24
Behavior of MMCs and Its Relationship to Mortgage Interest Rates	25
MORTGAGE FUTURES AND FORWARD MARKETS	25
INVESTMENT FEATURES OF REAL ESTATE	26
Risk Characteristics	26
Environmental and physical characteristics	26
Type of property	26
Market trends and lease terms	26
Financing arrangements for investor	28
Governmental influence	28
Taxes	29
Real Estate Valuation	31
Market comparison approach	31
Income capitalization analysis	31
Cost of replacement approach	31
Investment Characteristics by Property Type	32
Office buildings	32
Shopping centers	32
Apartments	32
Single-family houses	33

REAL ESTATE FINANCE

Richard T. Pratt
R. Bruce Ricks

This section looks at the changes over time in financial institutions' emphasis on real estate lending, the terms of mortgage loans, especially in times of high interest rates and inflation, and valuation and investment analysis, with particular focus on aftertax returns.

SOURCES OF REAL ESTATE LENDING

FINANCIAL INSTITUTIONS. At the end of 1979 **mortgage debt** outstanding was in excess of $1.3 **trillion.** Of this, the major financial institutions held over $940 billion, with federal and related mortgage credit agencies issuing $97 billion directly and guaranteeing $111 billion of **mortgage pools** and **trusts.** Individuals and others held approximately $177 billion or 13%. Exhibit 1 shows these totals and subtotals by type of property. One- to four-family (mostly single-family) housing dominates total mortgage debt with $840 billion of the total.

Savings and Loan Associations. The largest single type of financial institution providing home mortgage loans is **savings and loan associations** (S & Ls) with $394 billion of the $822 billion one- to four-family debt in 1979. The portfolio concentration of S & Ls is also shown in Exhibit 1. Of their $476 billion mortgage holding, 83% are one- to four-family loans, 8% are multifamily loans, and 9% are commercial loans. This specialized lender may be a federal institution chartered under the Homeowners Loan Act of 1933 or a state-chartered institution. All "federals" are regulated directly by the three-member **Federal Home Loan Bank Board** in Washington, D.C. This Board also has certain regulatory powers over state-chartered institutions, since the same individuals constitute the Board of the **Federal Savings and Loan Insurance Corp.,** the entity that insures to $100,000 each deposit in almost all S & Ls. Since most state regulation gives state-chartered institutions at least as much lending and operating power as is granted to "federals," the operations of federally chartered and state-chartered S & Ls are quite similar. Most of the S & L's portfolio must be in home mortgages, with limited but increasing percentages permitted in other real estate loans and still less in ownership of real estate. The investment powers of S & Ls are slowly being broadened, but with a continuing emphasis on residential real estate lending.

EXHIBIT 1   MORTGAGE DEBT OUTSTANDING ($ MILLIONS END OF PERIOD)[a]

Type of Holder, and Type of Property	1977	1978	1979	1978	1979			
				Q4	Q1	Q2	Q3	Q4[b]
All Holders	1,023,505	1,172,754	1,334,373ʳ	1,172,754	1,206,213	1,252,426	1,295,644	1,334,373ʳ
One- to four-family	656,566	761,843	872,191ʳ	761,843ʳ	784,546	816,940	846,115	872,191ʳ
Multifamily	111,841	121,972	130,758ʳ	121,972	123,965	125,916	128,256	130,758ʳ
Commercial	189,274	212,746	239,093ʳ	212,746	217,495	224,499	232,120	239,093ʳ
Farm	65,824	76,193	92,331ʳ	76,193	80,207	85,071	89,153	92,331ʳ
Major Financial Institutions	745,011	848,095	940,268ʳ	848,095	865,974	894,385	919,967	940,268
Commercial banks[c]	178,979	213,963	246,763	213,963	220,063	229,564	239,363	246,763
One- to four-family	105,115	126,966	146,077	126,966	130,585	136,223	142,038	146,077
Multifamily	9,215	10,912	12,585	10,912	11,223	11,708	12,208	12,585
Commercial	56,898	67,056	77,737	67,056	68,968	71,945	75,016	77,737
Farm	7,751	9,029	10,364	9,029	9,287	9,688	10,101	10,364
Mutual savings banks	88,104	95,157	98,924	95,157	96,136	97,155	97,929	98,924
One- to four-family	57,637	62,252	64,717	62,252	62,892	63,559	64,065	64,717
Multifamily	15,304	16,529	17,183	16,529	16,699	16,876	17,010	17,183
Commercial	15,110	16,319	16,695	16,319	16,488	16,662	16,795	16,695
Farm	53	57	59	57	57	58	59	59
Savings and loan associations	381,163	432,808	475,797	432,808	441,358	456,543	468,307	475,797
One- to four-family	310,686	356,114	394,436	356,114	363,723	377,516	387,992	394,436
Multifamily	32,513	36,053	37,588	36,053	36,677	37,071	37,277	37,588
Commercial	37,964	40,641	43,773	40,641	40,958	41,956	43,038	43,773
Life insurance companies	96,765	106,167	118,784ʳ	106,167	108,417	111,213	114,368	118,784ʳ
One- to four-family	14,727	14,436	16,193ʳ	14,436	14,507	14,489	14,884	16,193ʳ
Multifamily	18,807	19,000	19,274ʳ	19,000	19,080	19,102	19,107	19,274ʳ
Commercial	54,388	62,232	71,137ʳ	62,232	63,908	66,055	68,513	71,137ʳ
Farm	8,843	10,499	12,180ʳ	10,499	10,922	11,477	11,864	12,180ʳ

Federal and Related Agency	70,006	81,853	97,293	81,853	86,689	90,095	93,143	97,293
Government National Mortgage Association	3,660	3,509	3,852	3,509	3,448	3,425	3,382	3,852
One- to four-family	1,548	877	763	877	821	800	780	763
Multifamily	2,112	2,632	3,089	2,632	2,627	2,625	2,602	3,089
Farmers Home Administration	1,353	926	1,274	926	956	1,200	1,383	1,274
One- to four-family	626	288	417	288	302	363	163	417
Multifamily	275	320	71	320	180	75	299	71
Commercial	149	101	174	101	283	278	262	174
Farm	303	217	612	217	191	484	659	612
Federal Housing and Veterans Administration	5,212	5,419	5,764	5,419	5,522	5,597	5,672	5,764
One- to four-family	1,627	1,641	1,863	1,641	1,693	1,744	1,795	1,863
Multifamily	3,585	3,778	3,901	3,778	3,829	3,853	3,877	3,901
Federal National Mortgage Association	34,369	43,311	51,091	43,311	46,410	48,206	49,173	51,091
One- to four-family	28,504	37,579	45,488	37,579	40,702	42,543	43,534	45,488
Multifamily	5,865	5,732	5,603	5,732	5,708	5,663	5,639	5,603
Federal Land Banks	22,136	25,624	31,277	25,624	26,893	28,459	29,804	31,277
One- to four-family	670	927	1,552	927	1,042	1,198	1,374	1,552
Farm	21,466	24,697	29,725	24,697	25,851	27,261	28,430	29,725
Federal Home Loan Mortgage Corporation	3,276	3,064	4,035	3,064	3,460	3,208	3,729	4,035
One- to four-family	2,738	2,407	3,059	2,407	2,685	2,489	2,850	3,059
Multifamily	538	657	976	657	775	719	879	976
Mortgage pools or trusts[d]	70,289	88,633	119,278	88,633	94,551	102,259	110,648	119,278
Government National Mortgage Association	44,896	54,347	76,401	54,347	57,955	63,000	69,357	76,401
One- to four-family	43,555	52,732	74,546	52,732	56,269	61,246	67,535	74,546
Multifamily	1,341	1,615	1,855	1,615	1,686	1,754	1,822	1,855
Federal Home Loan Mortgage Corporation	6,610	11,892	15,180	11,892	12,467	13,708	14,421	15,180
One- to four-family	5,621	9,657	12,149	9,657	10,088	11,096	11,568	12,149
Multifamily	989	2,235	3,031	2,235	2,379	2,612	2,853	3,031
Farmers Home Administration	18,783	22,394	27,697	22,394	24,129	25,551	26,870	27,697
One- to four-family	11,397	13,400	14,884	13,400	13,883	14,329	14,972	14,884
Multifamily	759	1,116	2,163	1,116	1,465	1,764	1,763	2,163
Commercial	2,945	3,560	4,328	3,560	3,660	3,833	4,054	4,328
Farm	3,682	4,318	6,322	4,318	5,121	5,625	6,081	6,322

EXHIBIT 1 CONTINUED

Type of Holder, and Type of Property	1977	1978	1979	1978 Q4	1979 Q1	Q2	Q3	Q4^b
Individual and Others^e	138,199	154,173	177,534	154,173	158,999	165,687	171,886	177,534^r
One- to four-family	72,115	82,567	96,047^r	82,567	85,354	89,345	92,565	96,047^r
Multifamily	20,538	21,393	23,439	21,393	21,637	22,094	22,920	23,439
Commercial	21,820	22,837	24,979^r	22,837	23,230	23,770	24,442	24,979^r
Farm	23,726	23,376	33,069^r	27,376	28,778	30,478	31,959	33,069^r

^{a}Based on data from various institutional and governmental sources, with some quarters estimated in part by the Federal Reserve in conjunction with the Federal Home Loan Bank Board and the Department of Commerce. Separation of nonfarm mortgage debt by type of property, if not reported directly, and interpolations and extrapolations when required, are estimated mainly by the Federal Reserve. "Multifamily debt" refers to loans on structures of five or more units.

^b_r = Revised (Notation appears on column heading when more than half of the figures in that column are changed).

^{c}Includes loans held by nondeposit trust companies but not bank trust departments.

^{d}Outstanding principal balances of mortgages backing securities insured or guaranteed by the agency indicated.

^{e}Other holders include mortgage companies, real estate investment trusts, state and local credit agencies, state and local retirement funds, noninsured pension funds, credit unions, and U.S. agencies for which amounts are small or separate data are not readily available.

Source: Federal Reserve Bulletin, May 1980, Table A41.

EXHIBIT 2   AVERAGE SPREADS, FSLIC-INSURED SAVINGS AND LOAN
ASSOCIATIONS

	1974	1975	1976	1977	1978	1979
Interest return on mortgages held (%)	7.43	7.66	7.95	8.21	8.47	8.83
Average cost of funds	6.14	6.32	6.38	6.44	6.67	7.47
Spread (%)	1.29	1.34	1.57	1.77	1.80	1.36

Source: Federal Home Loan Bank Board Journal, November 1979, and May 1980, Tables S4.10 and
S4.8.

The liberalized lending and deposit powers from the Federal Home Loan Bank Board
and from Congress, (e.g., the Depository Institutions Deregulation and Monetary Control
Act of 1980) is usually expressed in terms of allowing S & Ls to earn a sufficient spread
between the interest returns on mortgages held and the average cost of fund sources (i.e.,
deposits, advances from the Federal Home Loan Banks, and other commercial and open
market borrowings). Exhibit 2 illustrates this spread. As market interest rates rise during
periods of high interest levels, S & Ls suffer reduced savings inflows, known as **disintermediation,** as savers are attracted to open market debt instruments issued by government
entities and corporations. The drop in spread of 44 basis points during the 1979 credit crunch
is illustrative of this problem. See "New Mortgage Instruments" in this section for a
discussion of alternate mortgage terms instituted to help alleviate this squeeze.

Commercial Banks.   **Commercial banks** have a somewhat greater concentration of their
real estate loan portfolio in commercial loans and construction loans than do S & Ls. Exhibit
1 showed that of the $247 billion of mortgage debt outstanding at commercial banks, 59%
is in one- to four-family loans, 5% in multifamily loans, 32% in commercial loans, and 4%
in farm real estate loans. It is common for another institutional investor such as a **life
insurance company** to issue a commitment to make the long-term loan on property with
a local commercial bank making, servicing, and supervising the **construction loan** to a
builder and the drawing down of funds by the borrower as construction progresses. In addition
to direct mortgage lending, commercial banks loan to real estate-related institutions and
many have mortgage companies that originate, sell, and service loans for others. Exhibit 3
shows such loan portfolio composition for insured commercial banks.

Commercial bank participation in mortgage investments has been sensitive to economic
and interest rate cycles. Banks tend to shy away from long-term, fixed rate loans during
periods of high rates and tight money. When excess bank funds are available, banks have
shown renewed interest in the long-term mortgage sector.

Life Insurance Companies.   Exhibit 1 shows that life insurance companies as an industry
hold approximately one-half as much mortgage debt as commercial banks and one-fourth
as much as S & Ls. Of $119 billion outstanding as of December 31, 1979, 14% was in one-
to four-family debt, 16% in multifamily loans, 60% in commercial loans, and 10% in farm
real estate loans. In the late 1940s and 1950s when money market interest rates were low,
insurance companies were heavy buyers of home loans, mostly FHA and VA insured,
originated and serviced by **mortgage bankers.** As market rates rose and as commercial loans
and equity investments became more attractive to life insurance companies, they reduced
their emphasis on direct investment in home mortgages. This trend has continued. Exhibit

EXHIBIT 3   INSURED COMMERCIAL BANKS: LOANS OUTSTANDING, SEPTEMBER 30, 1979

	Loans ($ Millions)
Real Estate Loans	$203,386
Construction and land development	25,621
Secured by farmland	8,418
Secured by residential properties	117,176
One- to Four-Family Residences	111,674
FHA-insured or VA-guaranteed	7,503
Conventional	104,171
Multifamily Residences	5,502
FHA-insured	399
Conventional	5,103
Secured by other properties	52,171
Loans to Financial Institutions	37,072
REITs and mortgage companies	8,574
Domestic commercial banks	3,362
Banks in foreign countries	7,359
Other depositary institutions	1,579
Other financial institutions	16,198

Source: Federal Reserve Board Bulletin, Table A18, December 1979.

1 shows that just since 1976, insurance company holdings of one- to four-family mortgages decreased by approximately $1 billion, while commercial loans held increased by $20 billion—a dramatic shift. In recent years, however, insurance companies have become substantial buyers of **mortgage-backed securities,** which offer more bondlike characteristics.

Mutual Savings Banks.   Chartered in only a few states, notably Washington, New York, and the New England states, **mutual savings banks** had $98 billion in mortgages as of December 31, 1979–only $20 billion less than the much larger life insurance industry. Of this, 66% was in one- to four-family loans, with 17% each in multifamily and commercial loans. This industry, being more concentrated in financial centers, is more susceptible to **disintermediation** when money market interest rates rise.

MORTGAGE COMPANIES.   A **mortgage company,** sometimes called a **mortgage banker** or **mortgage bank,** is not actually a bank but a company whose principal activity is originating mortgage loans, selling them to others, and retaining the servicing of the monthly payments. They also cure defaults and process foreclosure for the investor when necessary. Mortgage companies earn **origination** and **servicing fees,** profits on resale of loans, and a profit or loss from the spread between mortgage yields and the cost of their borrowings (usually from commercial banks under credit lines), during the short time that a given mortgage is held or "warehoused" before sale. To protect against negative spreads and to assure the presence of a subsequent buyer for mortgages originated, mortgage companies secure commitments from institutional lenders or purchase them from the **Federal National Mortgage Association** (see Federal Mortgage Credit Agencies) or the **Government National Mortgage Association.** Thus, mortgage companies play an important part in maintaining the flow of mortgage funds but not in holding outstanding mortgages.

FEDERAL AND QUASI-FEDERAL MORTGAGE CREDIT AGENCIES. The most rapid percentage growth in mortgage holdings comes from federally sponsored agencies—an alphabet soup of acronymic entities that have become of pivotal importance to the growing **secondary market** for **mortgages.** The **Federal Housing Administration** (FHA), the grandfather of such agencies, was a response to the depression of 1929–1933 and was founded to insure lenders against loss on home mortgages. It also standardized construction and housing tract layouts with its underwriting standards for insurance eligibility. The Veterans Administration (VA) loan guarantee program was established in 1944. Together the VA and FHA programs encouraged lenders to increase the **loan-to-home price ratio** on owner occupied homes.

The Federal National Mortgage Association (FNMA), nicknamed **"Fannie-Mae,"** was created in 1938 to purchase FHA and VA mortgages. Mortgage companies, the most active users of FNMA, can purchase commitments and subsequently deliver mortgages to FNMA if they cannot find a private institution to purchase them on better terms. Thus, FNMA makes its profit both on commitments sold but not exercised and by the spread between mortgages subsequently delivered to it and the cost of selling FNMA debt securities in the money markets. While sellers to FNMA were required to buy its stock, the federal government was the controlling stockholder. This changed when the **Housing and Urban Development Act of 1968** made FNMA a government-sponsored corporation owned solely by private investors. This law took the subsidized mortgage purchase programs part of FNMA and put it into a new government corporation within the Department of Housing and Urban Development titled the **Government National Mortgage Association** (GNMA), nicknamed **"Ginnie Mae."**

In the Emergency Home Finance Act of 1970, FNMA was permitted to deal in conventional mortgages (those not FHA insured or VA guaranteed) and the **Federal Home Loan Mortgage Corporation** (FHLMC) was created. FHLMC (referred to as the Mortgage Corporation or **"Freddie Mac"**) is owned by the 12 District Federal Home Loan Banks and is governed by the Federal Home Loan Bank Board. While empowered to deal in FHA and VA mortgages, FHLMC concentrates on conventional mortgages sold to it by S & Ls. **GNMA's principal activity** is to insure securities issued by FNMA and FHLMC and by private institutional issuers where the collateral for these securities is FHA and VA mortgages. The Farmers Home Administration provides a similar insurance for loans in rural areas and smaller communities.

The decade of the 1970s showed a dramatic rise in **mortgage-backed bonds, pass-through securities,** and **mortgage participation interests** issued by FNMA, FHLMC, savings and loan associations, commercial banks, and mortgage companies, and purchased by other thrift institutions in areas of capital surplus. More importantly, these mortgage-backed securities have become attractive to diversified financial institutions such as life insurance companies, pension funds, and even foreign buyers who want to avoid the bother of dealing with individual mortgage payments and **risks** but want a safe, negotiable security with bondlike terms and more nearly mortgagelike yields.

REAL ESTATE INVESTMENT TRUSTS (REITs). The **Real Estate Investment Trust Act** of 1960 sanctioned firms known as REITs, which distribute to their shareowners 90% of ordinary income and meet other qualifications to be nontaxable. This awarded the same tax status to REITs as that long enjoyed by mutual funds. REITs became popular in the 1960s and early 1970s. Some REITs chose to specialize in equity investment, while others made mortgage loans. The **mortgage REITs** concentrated on riskier lending for land acquisition, development, and construction, and on short-term first and second mortgages on completed projects that were not yet eligible for long-term financing. Unfortunately, growth was rapid and little attention was paid to real estate project quality. Also, much of the heavy debt structure was borrowed from commercial banks and insurance companies at rates tied to the prime rate. As the **prime rate** moved to 12%, and as tight money and recession caused projects to slow down and fail, a large portion of the **mortgage REIT industry** was forced to default on loans. This segment of the REIT industry is still working out **"asset swaps"** and other debt compromises to its creditors. It remains to be seen whether REITs will again be a major factor in mortgage lending.

FINANCIAL ASPECTS OF THE MORTGAGE INSTRUMENT

The prominence of the mortgage as a credit instrument in real estate finance markets prompts a closer inspection of the financial aspects of the mortgage and their implications for investment purposes. Following is a discussion of several financial components that determine the nature of the mortgage as a credit and investment instrument.

INTEREST RATES ON MORTGAGES. The **rate of interest and the maturity** combine to determine the monthly payments necessary to amortize a mortgage loan. Exhibit 4 shows the relationship between these two components. An important characteristic of interest rates is that an increase in **higher level mortgage interest rates** results in a greater increase in the monthly payment amount than an equal increase at a lower rate. For example, an increase in rate from 9 to 10% on a 30-year loan increases the monthly payment 73¢ per $1,000 borrowed, while an increase from 13 to 14% on a loan with the same maturity causes a 79¢ increase in payment. Similarly, changing the maturity of a loan affects monthly payment

EXHIBIT 4   EFFECT OF INTEREST RATE AND MATURITY ON MONTHLY PAYMENT (ASSUMES A $1,000 LOAN)

Interest Rate (%)	Maturities					
	5 Years	10 Years	15 Years	20 Years	25 Years	30 Years
6	$19.33	$11.10	$ 8.44	$ 7.16	$ 6.44	$ 6.00
7	19.80	11.61	8.99	7.75	7.07	6.65
8	20.29	12.13	9.56	8.36	7.72	7.34
9	20.76	12.67	10.14	9.00	8.39	8.05
10	21.25	13.22	10.75	9.65	9.09	8.78
11	21.74	13.79	11.37	10.32	9.80	9.52
12	22.24	14.35	12.00	11.01	10.53	10.29
13	22.75	14.93	12.65	11.72	11.28	11.06
14	23.27	15.53	13.32	12.44	12.04	11.85
15	23.79	16.13	14.00	13.17	12.81	12.64

EXHIBIT 5   KEY INTEREST RATES, 1975–1980

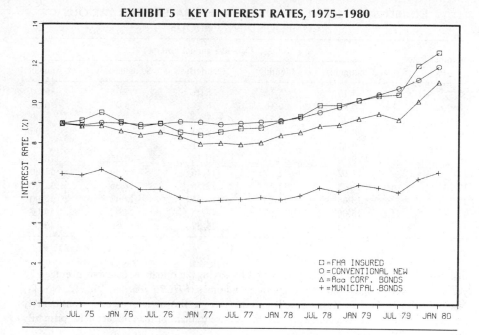

Source: Richard T. Pratt Associates, Salt Lake City, UT, 1980.

amounts unequally at different interest rates. Extending a loan maturity from 20 to 25 years at an interest rate of 14%, decreases monthly payments 40¢: at 10%, the same extension decreases payments by 56¢.

Long-term interest rates for mortgages and bonds are shown in Exhibit 5. From 1975 through 1979, Federal Housing Administration (FHA) mortgage rates have fluctuated between 7 and 12%. During the same period the corporate bond rate has tended to correspond with the mortgage rate, while the rates for tax-free bonds have moved from about 5 to 7%.

FREQUENCY COMPOUNDING.   The period of interest compounding on a loan usually corresponds to the timing of cash payments. Long-term mortgage loans involving monthly payments are normally compounded on a monthly basis. Construction loans and other loans with nonmonthly payments may be compounded on a variety of other bases. Frequency of compounding affects return in that a standard mortgage loan with monthly payments and compounding at a stated nominal rate carries a higher **effective yield** than another financial instrument at the same stated interest rate having less frequent compounding periods. Exhibit 6 illustrates the effect of various compounding periods on the actual yield of a financial investment, showing that a mortgage with a nominal interest rate of 9% compounded monthly has an actual annual effective rate of 9.38%, whereas a bond of 9% nominal interest (compounded semiannually) returns a yield of only 9.2% on an annual basis. This difference would allow a 9% mortgage with monthly payments invested at 9% to support the interest payments necessary on a bond of 9.17%.

MATURITY.   The maturity of a mortgage is the contract life and is the maximum time for which the mortgage can remain outstanding without being renegotiated. In 1979 the contract

EXHIBIT 6   EFFECTIVE ANNUAL INTEREST RATE UNDER VARIOUS COMPOUNDING PERIODS

Nominal Rate (%)	Effective annual rate (%)				
	Continuous	Monthly	Quarterly	Semiannually	Annually
5	5.13	5.11	5.09	5.06	5.00
6	6.19	6.16	6.14	6.09	6.00
7	7.25	7.23	7.19	7.12	7.00
8	8.33	8.30	8.24	8.16	8.00
9	9.41	9.38	9.31	9.20	9.00
10	10.50	10.47	10.38	10.25	10.00
11	11.62	11.57	11.46	11.30	11.00
12	12.75	12.68	12.55	12.36	12.00
13	13.68	13.80	13.65	13.42	13.00
14	15.02	14.93	14.75	14.49	14.00
15	16.18	16.07	15.87	15.56	15.00

maturity for home mortgage loans originated by savings and loan associations averaged 27 years for existing homes and 28.6 years for new homes (*FHLBB Journal*, Vol. 12, No. 11, November 1979, p. 52). However, the actual average life of mortgages is considerably shorter than the contract maturity because of early retirement of the contract debt, primarily due to resale of property and refinancing.

For commercial and industrial property, loan maturities vary considerably depending on the purposes of the financing, relative positions of the lender and the borrower, and the degree of participation of the seller in the lending arrangements. Frequently, amortization periods are relatively long, incorporating a large **"balloon payment"** after a short time (e.g., 5 or 10 years).

AMORTIZATION AND REPAYMENT PLANS.   The amortization process provides for the gradual extinction of a mortgage debt through periodic payments on the principal balance. Although other types of mortgage are still used (notably the straight-term and partially amortized mortgages) the **fully amortized loan** has become the most popular form of financing for residential real estate. A typical loan of this sort requires equal monthly payments on principal and interest, with an increasing portion of each payment available for reduction of the principal balance. By maturity, the principal payments have completely discharged the original debt.

An example of the amortization of a **level payment mortgage loan** is provided in Exhibit 7: while the payment for principal and interest is a level amount throughout the life of the loan, the early payments in the amortization of the loan are almost entirely interest payments. In this example of a 30-year, $60,000 loan at an interest rate of 12%, only $17.17 of the first month's $617.17 payment is used to amortize the principal of the loan. The principal component of the level payment will increase each period by $1 + r$ times the previous principal payment, where r is the interest rate. Thus, if a real estate contract is payable on a yearly basis with level payments and bears an interest rate of 10%, each subsequent principal payment will be 10% larger than the previous principal payment. Later in the amortization life, the portion of the payment going to principal is greatly increased, while the portion for interest continues to decline.

Straight-term loans require no payments on the principal during the mortgage term. They usually involve periodic payments on the interest of the total debt outstanding with the

EXHIBIT 7   PAYMENTS ON A $60,000, 30-YEAR LOAN AT 12% INTEREST; TWO TYPES OF ANNUITY

Monthly Payment Number	Total Payment	Interest Portion	Principal Portion	Loan Balance
		LEVEL PAYMENT ANNUITY		
1	$617.17	$600.00	$ 17.17	$59,982.83
13	617.17	597.82	19.35	59,762.89
25	617.17	595.37	21.80	59,515.06
37	617.17	592.60	24.57	59,235.88
49	617.17	589.49	27.68	58,921.13
109	617.17	566.88	50.29	56,637.74
169	617.17	525.81	91.36	52,489.53
229	617.17	451.19	165.98	44,953.49
289	617.17	315.64	301.33	31,262.79
360	617.17	6.03	611.14	−8.53
		VARIABLE PAYMENT ANNUITY		
1	$766.67	$600.00	$166.67	$59,833.33
13	746.67	580.00	166.67	57,833.29
25	726.67	560.00	166.67	55,833.29
37	706.67	540.00	166.67	53,833.25
49	686.67	520.00	166.67	51,833.17
109	586.67	420.00	166.67	41,832.97
169	486.67	320.00	166.67	31,832.77
229	386.67	220.00	166.67	21,832.57
289	286.67	120.00	166.67	11,832.37
360	168.32	1.65	166.67	−1.20

full amount of the debt due at the end of the loan term. Generally only 50–60% of the pledged property is covered by a straight-term mortgage, and the maturity is relatively short, seldom exceeding 5 years. Such loans are used principally for interim financing situations.

When refinancing of the unamortized portion of the mortgage is expected, a **"partially amortized"** or **"balloon payment"** loan may be created. Equal monthly payments on interest and principal are required (as in a fully amortized mortgage) until a specified portion of the original debt is repaid. At that time, a lump sum or "balloon" payment covering the outstanding principal balance on the loan discharges the debt. Instead of making a cash payment, the borrower can then refinance the balance with a new loan.

In nonresidential mortgages and real estate contracts, numerous payment programs exist for the purchase of real estate. One alternative to the level payment mortgage is a real estate contract which calls for equal principal payments per period with interest payments on the unpaid balance. The second half of Exhibit 7 provides an example of this type: the principal payment is constant for each payment during the life of the loan, while the interest payment declines by a constant amount per period; as a result, the total payment amount declines as interest payments decrease. The implication of this characteristic for the purchaser of real estate is that amortizing a specified amount over a given period using the **equal principal**

payment approach will ordinarily place greater financial burden on the purchaser than amortizing under a different plan, inasmuch as the early payments will be larger than the later payments. This approach to the financing of real estate is also substantially more burdensome on an aftertax basis, since interest is deductible, a greater proportion of the early payments must be made with aftertax funds.

NEW MORTGAGE INSTRUMENTS.   In response to conditions of substantial economic instability and chronically high levels of inflation in which mortgage markets have been forced to operate in recent years, new forms of mortgages have been developed and long-forgotten approaches have been resurrected and are being discussed and utilized as answers to the problems of mortgage finance. In the residential mortgage lending arena, two primary mortgage types have received considerable attention recently.

The first of these is the **graduated payment mortgage** (GPM). The GPM is an instrument that incorporates increasing payments over a limited period of time. For example, the FHA-245 program presently allows for payment growth rates of 2.5, 5, or 7.5% per year during the early years of the mortgage term. The FHA-245 mortgage is a government-sponsored graduated payment mortgage that is insured by the Federal Housing Administration.

The **conventional GPM** has been unavailable to S & Ls in the past because of a regulation of the Federal Home Loan Bank Board prohibiting loans from having "any subsequent payment larger than a previous payment." The FHLBB has recently approved the GPM, but the regulation cited is still in force.

Before FHLBB regulations approved the GPM, variations of that instrument were created that were designed to comply with regulations, while duplicating GPM payment patterns. These mortgages incorporate a **pledged savings account** in connection with the loan. An individual having a 20% down payment may opt for a mortgage loan program where perhaps half the amount available for the down payment is placed in a savings account, and the balance goes as an actual down payment on the property. During the early years of the loan, while the nominal loan payment is at a level amount, a portion of the savings account is withdrawn to pay a portion of the mortgage payment with a smaller amount being withdrawn each subsequent year so that the net out-of-pocket cash requirement from the borrower for his monthly mortgage payments appears to be the same as for a GPM.

The second major alternative form of mortgage instrument commonly available at present is the **variable rate mortgage** popularized in California by state-chartered savings and loan associations. The variable rate mortgage is **indexed** to market interest rates and may be changed periodically as interest rates change. Under current regulations in California, if interest rates increase, lenders may increase mortgage interest rates at their option with a minimum and a maximum specified increase allowed over a given time period. The total amount of escalation that the institution may impose on the mortgage is limited. In the event that interest rates decrease sufficiently to trigger the minimum adjustment mechanism, lenders must comply with a mandatory decrease in interest rates in accordance with the indicated decrease in market rates.

Several other mortgage instruments are being introduced and experimented with, including the **reverse annuity** and the **Canadian rollover mortgage** (CRM), an instrument that provides periodic renegotiating of a loan with the same lender at current interest levels. The CRM approach to mortgage lending combines a long-term amortizing mortgage and a balloon payment at the end of a relatively short period. For example, a mortgage may be made at an interest rate of 13% based on a 30-year amortization, including a 3- or 5-year balloon payment clause or, more realistically, an adjustment period. At the end of the specified period, the mortgage is examined in the context of existing economic conditions in mortgage markets and is adjusted to carry a comparable interest rate. In a common approach to this adjustment program, if the borrower does not agree with the adjustment suggested by the lending institution, he may prepay the mortgage and refinance his property without penalty.

The **reverse annuity mortgage,** still in its formative period, allows a homeowner to purchase an annuity using the equity built up in his home while retaining the right to live there. It is a real estate loan, the principal of which is not repayable until the death of the borrower or upon sale of the real estate, and the proceeds of which are used to supply an annuity to the borrower until his death or until he sells the home. This type of mortgage is particularly attractive to older homeowners on fixed incomes who have considerable equity in their homes, since it provides an income supplement without the need to incur any cash repayment obligation. Lending institutions have been less than enthusiastic about this product, however, because of the risk exposure associated with an unknown mortgage term and cash disbursements based on a fixed rate in the context of changing market interest rates.

CHARGES AND FEES.

Prepayment Charges.   The main justification for a lending institution's incorporating a **prepayment charge** in the mortgage contract is to **protect itself againt a decrease in interest rates,** which would allow borrowers to refinance their loans at lower rates and thus reduce the yield on the portfolio of the lending institution. Such charges frequently follow the pattern enumerated in Federal Home Loan Bank Board regulations. A federally chartered association may impose a prepayment charge equal to 6 months' interest on the amount of principal prepaid less 20% of the original mortgage balance.

From the point of view of the refinancing-oriented borrower, this alternative would not be attractive unless interest rates were to drop to a lower level than the one he would have considered refinancing at in the absence of such a prepayment charge. The impact of the prepayment charge is shown in Exhibit 8.

Variable rate mortgages usually do not carry prepayment charge provisions, inasmuch as it is presumed that the lender is constantly adjusting his portfolio to market rates and therefore has no legitimate reason to impose fees for the early retirement of a mortgage loan.

Despite federal and state regulations on home mortgages, no regulations exist on the nature or extent of prepayment charges for commercial and industrial loans. Quite often, the financing of industrial or commercial properties will incorporate a prohibition against pre-payment for a certain period, a balloon payment requiring prepayment at a later date, and a floating charge for prepayment between those two dates. For example, a loan on an office building may have a 30-year amortization schedule with a balloon payment required at the end of 15 years. Prepayment may be prohibited for the first 5 years of the loan, and then a sliding scale may exist for prepayment charges from the fifth through the tenth or fifteenth years. For example, a prepayment at the end of the fifth year might require the payment of a charge equal to 5% of the then outstanding balance at the end of the sixth year; it would be 4.5% at the end of the seventh year, and so on, until the end of the fifteenth year when the balloon payment is required.

Closing Costs and Origination Fees.   The mortgage borrower is generally charged certain fees at the time of the loan's origination. The fees on residential loans normally amount to 1–2% of the loan amount and may be either deducted from the face amount of the loan or added as a cash cost. A $20,000 loan with origination and closing costs of 1.5 points would

EXHIBIT 8   EFFECT OF ORIGINATION FEES AND LOAN PREPAYMENT ON EFFECTIVE MORTGAGE LOAN INTEREST RATE (ORIGINATION FEE OF 1%)

Contract Rate on Loan (%)	Loan of 25 Years' Maturity Prepaid in				Loan of 30 Years' Maturity Prepaid in			
	5 Years	10 Years	15 Years	No Prepayment	5 Years	10 Years	15 Years	No Prepayment
7.00%	7.25%	7.16%	7.13%	7.12%	7.25%	7.15%	7.12%	7.10%
8.00	8.26	8.16	8.13	8.12	8.25	8.16	8.13	8.11
9.00	9.26	9.17	9.14	9.13	9.26	9.16	9.13	9.12
10.00	10.27	10.17	10.15	10.13	10.26	10.17	10.14	10.12
11.00	11.27	11.18	11.15	11.14	11.27	11.17	11.15	11.13
12.00	12.28	12.18	12.16	12.15	12.27	12.18	12.15	12.14
13.00	13.27	13.19	13.16	13.15	13.28	13.18	13.16	13.14
14.00	14.28	14.19	14.17	14.15	14.28	14.19	14.16	14.15
15.00	15.29	15.20	15.17	15.16	15.29	15.19	15.17	15.16

result in a disbursement of funds in the amount of $19,700 to the borrower. The combined effects of fees, interest rates, maturities, and periods to prepayment are shown in Exhibit 8.

Closing costs and origination fees can be conceptually viewed as (1) charges for out-of-pocket expenses incurred by the lending institution in the actual origination of the mortgage, and (2) payments to the lender for the purpose of increasing the mortgage yield above the nominal contract rate. The hard expenses include application processing, appraisals, and other functions necessary to consummate the transaction.

It is evident that (1) origination fees have a greater effect on realized interest rates at higher contract interest rates, (2) the effect of origination fees is greater on loans of shorter maturity, and (3) the effect of origination fees is increased on a loan that is prepaid relatively early.

The consumer is protected from the use of these fees to hide the true cost of the mortgage loan by the **Federal Reserve Board's Regulation Z,** "Truth-in-Lending." This regulation requires disclosure of the percentage rate, including all charges and fees, on noncommercial loans. Mortgage lenders are generally free to charge various mixes of rates and fees that seem to best serve their market.

Late Charges. Monthly installments that become overdue incur late charges. Generally, the mortgage lender provides a grace period before the late charge is imposed. The imposition of a late charge is justified by pointing out that (1) the handling of delinquent accounts forces additional costs on the lending institution, (2) the existence of the charge encourages the borrower to maintain his loan on a current basis, thus mitigating the probability of foreclosure, and (3) the late charges help to maintain the cash flow into the lending institution, providing for additional mortgage funds. Late charges are generally some proportion of the late payment. Recent legislative and regulatory changes in some states have prohibited basing late payment charges on the loan balance outstanding or adding unpaid late charges to the unpaid balance of the loan, or "pyramiding."

MORTGAGE LIENS. Institutional mortgages usually carry a first claim against the real estate pledged as security. There are many situations in real estate finance in which second and third mortgages are also used.

Under a **second mortgage** the mortgagee's claim to the property is subordinated to a previously existing pledge. The second mortgage is common in commercial financing, but appears most often in the sale of houses by individuals when the price exceeds the combined amount of an available first mortgage and the buyer's cash resources. In such instances, if the seller is willing to extend credit to the buyer, he frequently takes a second mortgage. Maturities of the notes are usually shorter than those of the first mortgage loan, commonly running 3 to 5 years. Second mortgages or contracts are especially popular when a low interest rate, assumable first mortgage exists.

The **purchase money mortgage** is used when a purchaser buying property partly on credit from the seller pledges as security the property being purchased. The purchaser takes the property subject to the claim of the seller, which has priority over any other mortgage loan the buyer may subsequently obtain. Since no note or bond exists in this arrangement making the purchaser personally liable, the seller is secured only by the value of the pledged property. As a result, sellers will generally accept purchase money mortgages only if the amount of cash down is sufficient to compensate the seller in the event of default, or if the pledged property is valuable enough to secure the loan without the buyer's personal liability. The purchase money mortgage is used often in land acquisition and subdivision development projects. It is common for the seller to agree that his lien will be subordinated to a claim of an institutional lender supplying either land development or construction funds.

MORTGAGE INSURANCE.   The bulk of all mortgages are conventional, or uninsured, loans. Lending institutions making conventional loans bear all risks of loss associated with the loans.

To decrease the risks borne by lending institutions, the Federal Housing Administration and the Veterans Administration developed government-insured loan programs that provide standards for loan terms and properties eligible for security, and insure lending institutions producing qualifying loans against loss. The FHA program calls for 100% insurance on each eligible loan, whereas the VA guarantee is for 60% of the loan, but not in excess of $25,000. (See "Federal and Quasi-Federal Mortgage Credit Agencies" in this section.)

Loan eligibility requirements for **private mortgage insurance companies** are generally less strict than those for loans underwritten by government. These companies set no maximum on qualifying loans, and will insure loans for which the borrower has as little as 5% equity or a combination of equity and pledged collateral totaling 5%. However, they ordinarily insure only the top 20–25% of the mortgage balance. Fees for private mortgage insurance are paid by the borrower and typically are composed of an initial premium of 0.5% of the loan amount with annual renewal premiums of 0.25% of the then outstanding loan balance.

SPECIAL TYPES OF MORTGAGE

CONSTRUCTION LOANS.   The construction loan, involving irregular disbursement schedules adapted to the particular situation, is the most common type of construction financing. The loan is evidenced by a note or a series of short-term notes drawn at intervals during the construction period. This interim financing is repaid from the proceeds of the regular mortgage loan once the project is completed.

Disbursement schedules may be determined in any of several ways. In some loans, disbursements occur after completion of certain phases of the construction project. For example, 25% may be paid out when the foundation is completed, 25% when the structure is under roof and rough plumbing and wiring are installed, 35% when the structure is completed and ready for occupancy, and 15% after the period for filing mechanics' liens has elapsed. Other plans require the builder to submit bills to the lender for payment as the building progresses, and another payout system permits the borrower to draw loan funds in amounts equal to a certain percentage of the cost of the work completed for which payment has not already been made. Construction loans, then, are highly adaptable to the situation for which financing is required.

Construction loans are usually issued at rates 1–2% over the prime lending rate. They typically carry **origination fees** of 1–2.5% of the loan amount. The resulting effective yields on construction loans are relatively high because of the effects of short maturity periods, partial disbursement of funds, and high closing costs. The effects of these factors and a typical disbursement pattern are illustrated in Exhibit 9. Carrying a nominal interest rate of 14% (assume the prime rate is 12%), and with a 5-month disbursement period with 2% closing costs, the effective yield to the lender at the end of the 9-month loan is 17.44%.

LAND DEVELOPMENT FINANCING.   Subdivision developers typically are responsible for the installation of the necessary capital facilities, which are generally costly and consequently require credit arrangements. The cost of converting a farm into residential sub-

EXHIBIT 9   EFFECTS OF DISBURSEMENT SCHEDULE: $45,000 LOAN, 9-MONTH MATURITY, 14% INTEREST, 2 POINTS

Disbursement Schedule Time Period	Amount	
0	$14,850	37% less fees
1	8,816	20% less interest
2	6,461	15% less interest
3	6,382	15% less interest
4	6,304	15% less interest

Amount due at maturity $47,687

Yield to lender without points   14.00%
Yield to lender with points   47.44%

division lots, for example, usually runs from three to six times the investment in the raw land. Most of the institutional lenders are permitted to grant loans for land development, federally chartered savings and loan associations and some state associations having specific authority to make such loans.

The form of mortgage note most often used in land development financing of subdivisions is the **blanket mortgage,** which attaches to each lot in the subdivision. As the project is completed and the lots are ready for sale, an individual lot may be removed as security for the loan upon the payment of a stipulated sum. The release payments typically are set at such levels that the entire loan will be repaid before all the pledged lots have been presented for release.

WRAPAROUND MORTGAGES.   A **wraparound mortgage** is all-inclusive and involves an existing mortgage. If a property is subject to an existing mortgage at less than current mortgage interest rates and if the borrower wishes additional funds, a new mortgage can be issued to include (1) the existing mortgage and (2) the additional amount lent under the wraparound mortgage. The wraparound mortgage is amortized as if it were the first mortgage.

Typically, the **wraparound mortgage** is at an interest rate higher than the existing mortgage rate, has a longer term, and requires payments in excess of those required for the existing loan. The lender of the wraparound mortgage receives payments on the new loan, makes payments on the old mortgage, and retains the difference between the two payments. The resulting yield may provide an attractive return to lenders producing wraparounds.

Suppose, for instance, that A owns a house on which an 8% assumable mortgage with a $50,000 balance is outstanding. A sells the house to B for $90,000. B approaches the Acme Savings and Loan Association seeking financing. Acme agrees to assume the 8% mortgage and creates a wraparound mortgage of $80,000 at 12% interest, to be amortized by B. Acme, in turn, makes payments on the $50,000 loan at 8% and earns the difference between the payments as a return on the investment of $30,000 ($80,000 − $50,000).

LEASEHOLD MORTGAGES.   Leasehold mortgages are common in the financing of large-scale properties such as office buildings, shopping centers, and some industrial properties. They are often used in combination with other types of financing in the subdividing of property interests in a single unit of real estate. In a leasehold mortgage one party leases a piece of property from another with the intent to develop the property so it can be leased to other tenants. A mortgage is obtained for the development of the property secured by the mortgagor's rights as a lessee in the land and the future rents due under lease contracts with the tenants. In effect, the security for the mortgage is the credit standing of future tenants.

OPEN-END MORTGAGES. An open-end mortgage includes provisions for future advances to the borrower by the lender. If the future advances are an **obligation** of the lender, the lender need only acquire a note, since the advance is secured by the original mortgage, which stipulates that the mortgage is to secure the original debt plus additional advances that may be made. This note is generally repayable over the unexpired term of the original mortgage. If additional advances are **optional,** the mortgagee uses his discretion to decide whether to lend additional funds.

Open-end mortgages are used most frequently in residential financing to cover improvements, expansion, or remodeling of the property financed by the original mortgage.

PACKAGE MORTGAGES. A package mortgage is a standard first mortgage created when all personal property and fixtures attached permanently to a piece of real estate are included with the real estate as the security in a mortgage transaction. The package mortgage is frequently used in residential financing. The items to be covered are listed in the mortgage and are included in the value of the real estate, thus eliminating the need for the borrower to negotiate separate installment loans on each item.

DEPOSIT COLLATERAL MORTGAGES. The deposit collateral mortgage allows savings and loan institutions to lend not only on the security of real estate but also on their own deposits. Such loans are used only when a qualified borrower requires a loan in excess of 80% of the appraised value of the property. Because of the extra protection available to the lending institution through lending on security it controls, associations unwilling to make 90% government-underwritten loans may be willing to make deposit collateral loans for the same amount.

For example, assume that the DEF Savings and Loan Association makes conventional home loans with no more than an 80% loan-to-value ratio. A potential home buyer comes to DEF seeking a loan for a $60,000 home, on which the buyer can make only a $2,000 down payment. DEF is willing to provide no more than a $48,000 mortgage on the home. However, a third party agrees to put $10,000 in pledged account at DEF as collateral for the loan. Based on 80% of the home's value ($48,000) and 100% of the pledged account ($10,000), DEF Savings and Loan Association makes a loan of $58,000 to the buyer. By agreement, the pledged account will gradually be released to the third party so that the amount in the account will not exceed the difference between the outstanding balance on the loan and $48,000, as the mortgage is paid off. The third party will collect all interest on the unreleased balance in the pledged account.

ALTERNATIVE FORMS OF REAL ESTATE FINANCING

LONG-TERM LEASES. A **long-term lease** is often used instead of mortgage financing by firms wishing to conserve working capital or even to free working capital invested in real estate. In some instances the deductibility of interest as an expense for income tax purposes makes leasing more economical for business firms than buying real property on a mortgage, since interest is deductible as a business expense whereas principal repayments are not. Long-term real estate leases are of two types: net leases, under which the tenant pays all charges of every description, and gross leases, under which the tenant pays a given rental to the owner, who assumes the entire burden of management.

Net Leases.   There are three standard forms of the net lease: the long-term, often 99-year lease to a developer, the 21-year lease, and the lease to a user-tenant of improved space. The 99-year lease is likely to appear to the owner of the real estate as a sale on an annuity basis. This type of lease is usually made on large pieces of valuable land and is typically regarded as a well-secured, long-term investment on a net basis. Frequently it results from inability to sell the property because of complications with an estate, or a desire to avoid reinvestment of proceeds of the sale or to defer payment of a capital gains tax.

Ninety-nine-year leases are often used on prime commercial or office building sites. The lessee may agree to purchase for cash any buildings on the site and then replace them with a new building or buildings. The lessor receives a net rental—that is, in addition to the rent the tenant pays the taxes, water rates, insurance, and operating expenses of the building. Typically, 99-year leases made after 1945 include provisions for rental adjustments to combat inflation.

The **21-year** lease, characteristic of New York real estate, is basically a ground lease. It differs from the 99-year lease mainly in that under the ground lease, if there are improvements the tenant purchases the improvements, but is not obliged to erect a new building. If there are no improvements, or if the improvements are obsolete, the tenant may, at his option, erect a new structure. The 21 year lease usually gives the tenant one to three options to renew for additional terms of 21 years each. The rent paid is also net; the tenant paying all other charges. There may or may not be step-up provisions for the rentals. The renewal options provide that 1 or 2 years prior to the expiration of the original term the tenant must signify his intention to exercise his renewal privilege. The renewal options may specify that the rent be set at a percentage of the market value at the time of renewal or at a predetermined figure, but, in any event, the rental in the renewal period is hardly ever set at a figure below the amount paid in the preceding term.

In the early days of **sale-leaseback transactions,** in the 1940s and 1950s, particularly when insurance companies were involved, the initial rental was set at a figure sufficient to completely amortize the initial investment with interest on the outstanding balances during the first term lease. The renewal options then called for sharply reduced rentals for the succeeding term. But **sale-leaseback transactions** are more like financial arrangements between insurance companies and substantial tenants than they are like real estate transactions. In these cases, the credit rating of the tenants, the former owners, is at least as important as the value of the property as security for the lease. These leases were found to be too generous to the tenant and to give up the opportunity for value appreciation for the owner.

In the **long-term net lease,** the lessee is typically the property user, who will occupy all or the greater portion of the building. The term of the lease is usually 20 years or shorter and is written on a net rental basis. Ordinarily it is on improved property, and the lessee is not expected to erect a structure or provide improvements to it.

Long-term net leases usually have the following provisions:

1. The landlord has no problems of management, the tenant relieving him of this burden and paying all operating charges. The landlord receives his monthly or quarterly rental and pays interest and amortization on the mortgage, if there is one.

2. The landlord is not obligated to make any repairs. In the event of fire or other casualty causing damage or destruction of the building, the tenant is obligated to repair or rebuild; and if the insurance proceeds are insufficient, the tenant makes up the deficiency. Rent does not cease for any reason.

Gross Leases.   Gross leases represent the most common type of lease contract and are typical of rental situations involving short-term tenancy. Normally they contain no provision for periodic rent adjustments, and there are no standard arrangements regarding renewals.

The tenant pays a given rental to the owner, who has the burden of management. The leases sometimes require the lessee to pay the real estate taxes in excess of a certain stipulated amount. Tenants may also be assessed for operating expenses of certain types, such as snow removal, and institutional advertising and grounds care in the case of shopping centers. The more operating costs rise, the less landlords are willing to write gross leases.

On commercial properties the rent is frequently based on gross revenues of the tenant, with a stipulated minimum below which rents may not fall. A summary of percentage lease rates on selected types of properties is given in *Percentage Leases* (National Institute of Real Estate Brokers).

TYPICAL PROVISIONS OF LEASES.   The essential parts of the real estate lease are the names of the parties, the extent and boundaries of the properties, the term of the lease, the amount of the rent, and the time of payment and execution by the parties.

VARIABLE RENT LEASES.   The longer the term of the lease, the greater the possibility that the real flow of rent to the lessor will be diminished by inflation, rising taxes, or changes in the productive capacity of the property. Several devices have been used to alter lease payments to meet changed conditions. Among such variable leases are the expense-participating lease, the step-up or step-down lease, the reappraisal lease, the percentage lease, and leases based on a cost-of-living index. Leases calling for reappraisals are likely to be burdensome to one or the other of the parties and difficult to administer because the rent to be paid during certain periods of the term of the lease will be determined by strangers to the contract. The uncertainty about rent level is a mental hazard to both the landlord and the tenant and a hindrance to the sale of the building as well as to the sale of the tenant's business.

In addition to objecting to the uncertainty attending appraisals, the parties often object to the inconvenience and expense incident to the process. It appears that if the appraisal accomplishes its purpose, the inconvenience and expense are amply justified by the result.

Leases adjusted according to changes in some price index, such as the Consumer Price Index (CPI) may frustrate as well as protect the parties to a lease. To guard against too frequent readjustment, the leases usually prohibit an adjustment more frequently than once a year, and then only if the CPI has changed by not less than a stipulated percentage.

The **percentage lease** is the most common of all the variable leases. Inasmuch as the rent payment is expressed as a percentage of gross sales, such a lease automatically takes into account inflation, changes in the productivity of the site, and variable performances by the tenant. Current operating data provide the basis for rent determination without the necessity for special calculations or reviews. The disadvantages are (1) underreporting of sales by tenants and (2) failure of weak tenants to produce enough sales.

SALE-LEASEBACK FINANCING.   A sale and leaseback arrangement is created when the owner of real estate, usually a well-established business corporation, sells property to an institution with funds to invest and then leases the property from the purchaser for a stipulated period. Office buildings, retail outlets, and industrial properties are types of real estate commonly covered by this type of financing, which may also be referred to as a **"purchase and leaseback"** or a **"liquidating lease."**

Terms of sales and leasebacks typically range from 20 to 40 years. Provisions for renewal or repurchase may be included in the contract. The lessor receives a net rental; that is, the lessee pays maintenance and repair costs, taxes and assessments, utility charges, insurance, and so on. The net rent is fixed so that the lessor's original investment will be repaid by the end of the first term of the lease and a return comparable to rates currently available on government bonds will be yielded by the rent payments. The rate of return may be graduated, rather than level, over the life of the lease, with higher rates during the early years of the lease. This enables the lessor to recover his investment more rapidly.

The price at which the property is sold to an institutional investor is not necessarily the same as the current market price. The purchaser might be willing to pay a premium price that would be reflected in the higher rents received under the lease. The selling corporation, in turn, would have a gain taxable at capital gains rates while the higher rents would be tax-deductible as operating expenses.

The **main advantages** to the seller initiating a **sale-leaseback** are: (1) the seller retains possession of real estate with no capital investment, (2) the seller may deduct rent as an operating expense, and (3) the proceeds of the sale provide capital for business purposes. Advantages to the purchaser-lessor include the following points: (1) a relatively high rate of return is obtained after amortization of the principal of the investment, (2) the lessor maintains more control over real estate it leases than over that on which it holds a mortgage, (3) the sale and leaseback arrangement is a long-term investment involving no early pre-payments, with the burden of taxes, maintenance, repairs, and insurance expenses borne by the lessee, (4) the sum of money invested is usually quite large, thus involving relatively low investment management costs, and (5) the purchaser is in a position to realize any capital gains from appreciation after the lease term.

The disadvantage to the purchaser-lessor is the long-term, relatively fixed nature of the lease.

OPTIONS, ESCROWS, AND LAND TRUSTS

REAL ESTATE OPTIONS.   An option is a contract that gives the buyer the right to complete a real estate transaction in accordance with predetermined terms within a given time period in return for a consideration. If the option is exercised in compliance with all terms of the agreement, the consideration (i.e., option price) ordinarily becomes part of the purchase price of the real estate. If, however, the holder of the option fails to act before the expiration of the option, his consideration is forfeited and he loses any further rights in the property.

An option contract may prove extremely valuable to its holder in that the option holder, with no commitment to buy, has secured property at a known price and on known sale terms. This enables the buyer to negotiate for other property, obtain zoning amendments, secure financing, process a subdivision plot, or abandon his original plan and let the option expire if other factors make completion of the project infeasible.

REAL ESTATE ESCROWS.   An escrow is an arrangement wherein a **disinterested third party** serves to protect the interests of two or more contracting parties while a **title transfer** is being effected or **after a default** has occurred. An escrow agent performs many functions that the parties to the contract would normally undertake themselves in completing the transaction. According to the instructions of the escrow agreement, the escrow agent may collect all the papers, releases, and money necessary to the transaction and effect the exchanges with full protection to all parties. The escrow holder coordinates the activities of the interested parties, making certain that all legal and contractual obligations have been fulfilled before a title is transferred. For example, it is not unusual in real estate transactions for the seller to be unable to satisfy his mortgage until he receives the proceeds from the buyer. The buyer, in turn, or his mortgagee, will be unwilling to pay the full purchase price to the seller until the mortgage claim against the seller's property has been satisfied. The escrow arrangement allows this impasse to be overcome.

The escrow period may be a relatively short time, to allow for the completion of a **title search** or the arrangement of financing. It may, however, extend for months or years, during which a long-term contract for the purchase of land is fulfilled.

LAND TRUSTS.   A land trust is created by a deed in trust under which the grantor conveys to a trustee, usually a corporate trustee, a title to property to be held for a specified beneficiary. The warranty deed conveying the title of property must be recorded in the public records, but the trust agreement need not be recorded and, accordingly, the identity of the beneficiary need not become public information. The beneficiary may be the creator of the trust.

The land trust is used both for the holding of single properties and for the assembling of parcels of land. It permits privacy of ownership, limited liability for beneficiaries, and multiple ownership without the legal complexities of joint tenancies or tenancies in common. Interests in trusts may be conveyed simply by assignment of the beneficial interest.

EFFECTS OF MARKET INTEREST RATES ON MORTGAGE CREDIT MARKETS

The economics of real estate finance markets have necessitated the creation of new financial mechanisms to supply mortgage credit. During the latter half of the 1960s and the 1970s, mortgage credit markets, especially those dominated by savings and loan associations, suffered several periods of disintermediation. **Disintermediation** (withdrawal of savings from thrift institutions) typically occurs when market interest rates rise relative to the controlled interest rates paid by banks and thrift institutions operating under regulations of the Federal Reserve System and the Federal Home Loan Bank Board. These periods of disintermediation created a serious lack of loanable funds for mortgage lending institutions, substantially affecting the housing and construction industries. To counteract the ill effects of disintermediation on these industries, and to reduce the volatility of real estate markets in the long run, the financial regulatory authorities in 1978 instituted the **money market certificate for banks and thrift institutions.**

MONEY MARKET CERTIFICATES.   Money market certificates (MMCs) allow these institutions to pay the same interest rate on 6-month certificates as can be obtained on U.S. Treasury obligations. The instrument demonstrated its value immediately. During 1978 and 1979 the Federal Reserve Bank of New York raised its discount rate from 6 to 12% while 3-month Treasury bill rates increased from an average of 7.22% in 1978 to a level of 12.22% at the end of 1979. This caused massive withdrawals of funds from mortgage lending and thrift institutions. However, institutions issuing MMCs, particularly savings and loan associations, were able to maintain their supply of loanable funds, although at a substantially higher cost. As a result, the credit rationing process for real estate funds during that period was one controlled by price, rather than by availability. The institution of the money market certificate seems to bode well for stability and availability of funds in real estate finance markets, but it is an indisputable indication that the cost of funds in these markets will no longer be sheltered by subsidy and regulation to rates below general interest rates in the United States. Instead, the cost of such funds will be closely tied to market rates in the future.

BEHAVIOR OF MMCs AND ITS RELATIONSHIP TO MORTGAGE INTEREST RATES. The initial favorable reaction to money market certificates indicated their potential impact on the cost of loanable funds. Money market certificates did not exist at the beginning of 1978; by the end of 1979 FSLIC-insured savings and loan associations had issued over $114 billion in money market certificates, over 25% of all savings at these institutions. During late 1979, the cost of these certificates rose as high as 12.65% and by early 1980 the rate exceeded 15%, substantially increasing the weighted cost of funds at mortgage lending institutions and applying significant upward pressure on required mortgage interest rates. It appears, then, that the practitioner in real estate finance can no longer expect special institutional regulations to provide real estate funds at lower cost than those available in other sectors of the economy, but must look to the basic economic conditions of the country and the returns available on alternative investments in the market to determine the cost of loanable funds.

MORTGAGE FUTURES AND FORWARD MARKETS

In addition to the primary real estate lending market that is apparent to the parties on either side of a real estate finance transaction, substantial **secondary markets** exist that deal both in spot loans and in future and forward contracts. In secondary markets dealing in spot loans, mortgages can be bought or sold for immediate delivery. A typical selling institution for the secondary market would be a **mortgage banker** in the business of **originating mortgage loans,** selling them to investors, and servicing the loans for the investors.

Secondary mortgage markets range from highly organized to very informal organizations. The **major formal secondary markets** in the United States consist of the **Federal National Mortgage Association** (FNMA), which has historically been the primary purchaser of FHA and VA loans; the **Government National Mortgage Association** (GNMA), which serves as a guarantor for modified mortgage pass-through securities issued by lenders in conjunction with traditional underwriting houses; and the **Federal Home Loan Mortgage Corp.** (FHLMC), which serves as the primary formal secondary mortgage market for savings and loan institutions in the United States. The ultimate borrower needs little knowledge of the existence or function of secondary markets. However, they are important to real estate finance transactions inasmuch as they serve to move real estate funds from areas of capital surplus to areas of deficit. They have further served the function of standardizing many real estate finance instruments so that a mortgage originated in one part of the country will tend to closely resemble a similar mortgage originated in another part of the country. Both the Federal National Mortgage Association and the Federal Home Loan Mortgage Corp. require that mortgages be originated on approved forms before these loans can be purchased.

In addition to the spot secondary markets, formal markets exist for both **forward and future trading.** Forward trading is maintained by FHLMC, FNMA, and GNMA **underwriters.** Primary lending institutions may sell for forward delivery a package of mortgages using a number of possible vehicles. This sale for forward delivery allows the mortgage lender to quote a certain and specified rate to large builders, developers, and individual customers who may be seeking real estate loans. Normally such a commitment on the part of the lender will be associated with a commitment fee. Organized futures trading is carried on by the Chicago Board of Trade and the American Commodities Exchange in **GNMA modified pass-through securities.** The mortgage futures market operates similarly to the futures market in grain or other commodities. It allows mortgage lending institutions to hedge portfolio positions and remove interest rate risk, and serves functions similar to those served by the forward delivery market, except that mortgages are generally not actually traded in the futures market, since futures positions are normally closed out prior to the delivery date.

INVESTMENT FEATURES OF REAL ESTATE

Real estate features of major interest to both lenders and equity investors are **value stability, investment safety, investment yield** (in terms of certainty and stability), **marketability** or investment liquidity, **capital appreciation,** protection from **inflation,** and **tax minimization** opportunities. Real estate, however, cannot be rated as a homogeneous investment asset. Different types of real estate have different investment attributes. Exhibit 10 classifies the principal types of real estate according to their investment qualities.

RISK CHARACTERISTICS.   The risks inherent in any real estate investment may arise from the following factors: (1) environmental and physical characteristics of the real estate, (2) type of property, (3) market trends, (4) financing arrangements of the investor, (5) governmental influence, and (6) taxes.

Environmental and Physical Characteristics.   The physical characteristics of real estate obviously determine its capacity to produce useful services. One of the most significant criteria is the **functional character of the design,** which may influence the profitability of operations of a business using the structure, maintenance costs, and, of course, the rents that can be obtained from the property. Other important physical attributes are quality of construction, convertibility, architectural style, and adaptation of the structure to the site.

The **quality of construction** should be measured in terms of whether the building will be capable of performing its functions satisfactorily during the entire economic life of the structure. Another test is whether the physical qualities will require unusually heavy maintenance expense.

The **architectural style** and the **adaptation of the structure to the site** each may influence the uses to which the building may be put as well as the efficiency with which the property can be used. To a great extent, the value characteristics of real estate are determined by the attributes of the neighborhood, the district, or the immediate environment of the property.

Type of Property.   Exhibit 10 showed generalizations about different types of property for investment. Some properties such as **shopping centers** provide cubes of space for various retail and office tenants. If the tenant does poorly or sells a fad item that drops from favor, the tenant ordinarily asks to terminate the lease and the request is granted because the first tenant can be replaced with another who is more popular. However, if the property type is a racketball club, for instance, and the sport decreases in popularity or the market area becomes oversaturated with facilities, then the next best use for the property, such as warehousing, may produce much less rent and incur high conversion costs. In contemplating a specific use for improving land, one must consider carefully the current and future market demand for the property type and its alternative future uses.

Market Trends and Lease Terms.   Since real estate improvements are long-lived assets whose present value is based primarily on long-term net operating income streams, analyzing present market conditions at the time of conception of the development is not sufficient. It is important to make projections into the future for population, employment, incomes, space

EXHIBIT 10 RATING OF REALTY INVESTMENTS[a]

Type of Investment	Safety of Initial Investment	Safety of Annual Earnings	Capital Appreciation	Liquidity	Income Tax Shelter	Inflationary Protection
Apartment houses (middle income)	E	E	E	E	G	E[b]
Apartment houses (luxury)	F	F	F	F	G	E[b]
Office buildings (multitenant, in city)	G	G	G	E	F	E[b]
Office buildings (one national tenant, suburb)	F	G[c]	P[c]	E[c]	E	N
Office buildings (multitenant, suburb)	P	F	P	P	E	G
Retail property (average tenant, in city)	F	P	N	F	P	F
Retail property (one national tenant, in city)	F	G[c]	P	E	P	N[d]
Retail property (shopping centers)	F	G	G	G	E	P[d]
Retail property (one national tenant, suburb)	G	G[c]	P[c]	E[c]	E	N[c]
Loft buildings (multitenant)	G	G	F	F	G	G[b]
Industrial buildings (one national tenant)	G	G[c]	P[c]	E[c]	E	N
Gas stations (one national tenant, highway)	F	F[c]	P[c]	E[c]	E	P
Gas stations (one national tenant, in city)	E	G[c]	G	E[c]	F	P

[a]Code: E = excellent; G = good; F = fair; P = poor; N = negative.

[b]Under free market conditions, otherwise poor.

[c]Assume rental is at market, lease has many years to run, and purchase price is fair.

[d]Unless percentage lease, then excellent.

Source: S. Kahn, F. Case, and A. Schimmel, Real Estate Appraisal and Investment, Ronald Press, New York, 1963.

needs, buying power, consumer preferences, inflation rates, and so on. The investor can insulate himself, to some degree, against divergent trends by preleasing and agreeing to long-term net leases. However, in doing so, he often sacrifices the opportunity for future value appreciation. In the last 40 years or so, we believe that more real estate value has been lost or postponed by charging too little rent for too long than has been lost by overcharging or by ill-considered projects.

Financing Arrangements for Investor.   The investment character of a fee interest in improved property is directly related to the financial obligations involved. A leaseholder's interest may have risk characteristics comparable to those of a **fee holder,** depending on the position of the leasehold and whether the leaseholder is an investor in improvements. The greater the number of mortgage commitments and subleases a leaseholder has, the greater the risks of the leasehold position tend to be.

The amount of leverage involved in either a fee or a leasehold situation is a factor in determining whether a particular program represents an investment or a speculation. The **loan-to-value ratio** was for many years the principal measure of leverage and financing risk. A 75% first mortgage, at a fixed interest rate lower than the ratio of net operating income to cost, would give the 25% equity holder positive leverage. The simplified arithmetic is that if the property produced a 10% return on cost and 75% of cost could be borrowed at 8% interest, then the investor was left with 4% for his 25% of cost or a 16% rate of return; that is,

	% of cost
Operating income	10
Interest 75% × cost × 8%	6
Residual to owner	4
÷ Owner's investment	25
Owner's rate of return	16

This simplification ignores, however, both required amortization of the mortgage and changes in operating income over time. Increasingly, as interest rates have risen to double digits, the **income-to–debt service ratio** test is being utilized to compare the adequacy of fluctuating operating income to cover required mortgage payments for interest and amortization, yet still leave the owner a cushion for repairs, vacancies, dips in rent, unexpected costs, and so on. This ratio looks more to the property's income performance to service the debt and less at how much the lender thought the borrower had invested in the property as the principal financial risk factor. This shift in emphasis is part of the trend for lenders (1) to be more interested in future profitability of projects, (2) to accept shorter leases with more frequent opportunities to increase rents and to pass on increases in operating costs, (3) to require equity participations in loans, (4) to be more willing to finance all the cost if the income justifies it, and (5) to become direct equity investors.

Governmental Influence.   It is increasingly necessary to carefully consider the role of local, state, and federal government in assessing the risks of real estate investment. Local planning and zoning processes can (1) delay projects, (2) change the design, access, density and pricing, and (3) impose large percentage costs for fees, site work, payment for schools, inclusion of low-income housing units, and so on. State laws can impose energy regulations and air and water quality requirements. Federal laws can change the expensing versus capitalizing tax status of development costs and alter other tax aspects such as depreciation and interest. All levels of government can condemn the property or change its environment for better or worse from an investment standpoint.

Taxes.   Two forms of tax are important to real estate: property tax and income tax. Property tax, the principal revenue source for most municipalities, is based on value, but tends to lag changes in value over time—depending on the astuteness and aggressiveness of the assessor. Movements to limit property taxes in many municipalities in the country increase the present and future value of real estate. Leases on commercial property, and increasingly on offices and residential property, pass through to the occupant increases in property taxes from initial levels at the time of the beginning of the leases.

   Income tax assumes a major importance in real estate because of the tendency to finance a high portion of cost through long-term debt, and because of the depreciation deduction for structures, fixtures, and personal property. **Tax "shelter"** has become emphasized, often overemphasized. Shelter is the ability of real estate investments to show a negative taxable income, which not only frees the owner's property income from tax but reduces the tax he would otherwise have to pay on other income. It is wisely said that tax shelter cannot make a bad real estate investment good, but it can certainly make a good one better. Consider the following example:

Investment Returns

Operating income, first year		$10.00
Less:	Interest, 75% loan at 12%	9.00
	Amortization	0.30
Residual to owner		$ 0.70
÷ Owner's investment		25.00
Owner's rate of return, pretax		2.8%

The owner's return of 2.8% looks inadequate. However he is allowed to deduct depreciation. Let us assume that 75% of cost is depreciable and that the owner uses **component depreciation.** (The structure, carpets, roof, paving, etc., are depreciated over their separate useful lives.) Assume that this averages 30 years. The resulting straight-line rate would be 2.5% of cost per year (75% × cost × 3.33%). The taxable income for the first year would be:

Operating income		$ 10.00
Less:	Interest	9.00
	Depreciation	2.50
Taxable income		$(−)1.5%
× Tax rate of 50%		$(−)0.75
÷ Owner's investment		$ 25.00
Owner's return from tax loss		3%

This simple illustration shows that the investor has **tax-free cash flow** in the first year equal to 2.8% of his cash investment. The tax saving from otherwise taxable income equals 3% of his cash investment. The total is 5.8%. This is the equivalent of a fully taxable investment of 10.6% at the 50% tax bracket. Additionally, if operating income goes up over time 20% from 10% of cost to 12% of cost, and all other factors remained constant (and ignoring the slight increase in amortization), the results would be as follows:

Operating income	$12.00
Less: Interest	$ 9.00
Depreciation	2.50
Taxable income	$ 0.50
× Tax rate of 50%	$ 0.25

Cash Flow to Investor

Operating income	$12.00
Less: Interest	9.00
Amortization	0.30
Income tax	0.25
Cash flow after tax	$ 2.45
÷ Owner's investment	$25.00
Owner's rate of return after tax	9.80%

This return equals 19.6% pretax to an investor in the 50% bracket. Thus, a 20% increase in operating income has caused the owner's single-year return percentage to go up 69%, from 5.8 to 9.8% after tax. The increase in operating income could come from percentage rents, cost-of-living clauses in leases, or from replacing the initial tenants with others at higher rents. Note, however, that a decrease in operating income of only 7% (from 10% of cost to 9.3% of cost) would eliminate the investor's pretax cash flow from the property, since 9.3% operating income less 9% of cost for interest and 0.3% for amortization uses all the property cash flow. The decrease in operating income increases the tax shelter. In fact, it would take a 39% decrease in operating income, from 10% of cost to 7.1% of cost, to make the 50% tax bracket investor have zero total return as follows:

Operating income	$7.10
Less: Interest	9.00
Depreciation	2.50
Taxable income	(−)4.40
× Tax rate of 50%	(−)2.20

Aftertax Cash Flow to Investor

Operating income	$7.10
Less: Interest	9.00
Amortization	0.30
Plus: Tax saving	2.20
	0.00

This shows the combined effects of leverage and income tax. The last example shows that tax benefits cushion the return impact of a decrease in operating results. However, a property that has turned bad and shows a trend to substantially lower operating income cannot be "made good" simply by its tax benefits. The reader should be aware that the computations in this section are partial, single-period analyses used for simplicity and are no substitute for multiperiod analysis of internal rate of return and net present value. (See the discussion on those techniques in a later section in this *Handbook* entitled "Capital Budgeting.")

REAL ESTATE VALUATION. Appraisals made for mortgage lenders differ little from analyses made for equity investors. The mortgage lender seeks to determine the probability that the debt will be satisfied according to schedule and that in the event of default, the property value will be large enough to cover the outstanding loan balance. The equity investor seeks essentially the same information, since the probable rate of return on his equity is closely related to the value of the property and the mortgage terms. He is also interested in depreciation allowances, in the property's value stability, and especially in the prospects for capital gains.

Three standard approaches to **value analysis** are in use: (1) market comparison, (2) income capitalization, and (3) cost of replacement. It is rare that data are available that permit the satisfactory use of all three methods in a single value analysis.

Market Comparison Approach. Whenever a property is of a type actually traded in the real estate markets, the appraiser or analyst will endeavor to ascertain the consensus of the market as to the present worth of the property, as determined by what has been paid for similar properties. The basic technique of the market comparison method is to find evidence of sales of properties that took place under market conditions comparable to those at the given time. The **comparison units** should be properties with physical, legal, environmental, and financing characteristics similar to those of the property being evaluated. To find truly comparable situations is the most difficult part of market comparison appraising. This method is used in the valuation of all kinds of property and is employed whenever possible, even though other appraisal methods may also be used in the analysis.

Income Capitalization Analysis. The capitalization of income approach is used whenever it is possible to estimate the net operating income stream of the property. The value analysis of investment property almost always involves income capitalization appraising. The basic objective is to estimate a **reasonable net operating income stream** for the economic life of the property and to translate this into a present worth estimate, frequently through the use of annuity factors. This requires estimating the remaining economic life of the property, gross income potentials, and probable operating expenses.

Market comparison techniques also come into play in the income capitalization analysis, since the process involves the application of appropriate capitalization rates to the projected income. The rates selected must be close to those being earned by investors in properties of comparable risks.

Cost of Replacement Approach. Certain kinds of real property are not readily traded in the market and produce no measurable money income. Ordinarily, special purpose amenity producing properties are valued or analyzed on a cost of replacement basis. In an effort to determine the value of a nonmarket, nonincome-producing property, the question is posed: What would it cost to replace the present property with a newly created unit of real estate that would offer a totality of future services similar to those of the property under consideration?

Since a new structure would embody technological advances in the given field, the analysis technique is divided essentially into two parts: (1) estimation of the cost to replace the subject structure with new facilities that would render comparable services, and (2) measurement of the differences in productivity between the subject property and the hypothetical replacement. The differential is called depreciation or penalty, so that the method of valuation is called either the **"replacement cost less depreciation"** method or the **"penalized cost of replacement"** approach.

The market comparison and replacement cost methods can be combined to compare a proposed new development with the price of existing properties of the same type in the area. If a new shopping center costs $100 per square foot of leasable space while existing centers are available for $70, the investor **and** his lender must be able to show why the new center can produce sufficiently higher operating income to justify the development.

INVESTMENT CHARACTERISTICS BY PROPERTY TYPE.   While there are often major differences among properties of the same type in different geographic markets, some general statements can be made.

Office Buildings.   Many of the major office buildings in urban centers are built for a specific corporate user who may own the building or **net lease** the entire space. This type user may hire a management and leasing firm to rent out space not currently needed. Some corporations are selling their buildings to institutional investors and leasing them back so that the using corporation can keep its operating capital in its own business. Rising utility and other operating costs and increased emphasis on rising operating income and value have caused office building landlords to seek shorter leases and to pass on cost increases to tenants. With the movement of the population to suburbia and more people ''doing their own business thing,'' there is a rise in **suburban office parks.** Within and near these parks are ''incubator'' offices, with small spaces available on very short leases—even month to month. Sometimes, central secretarial and computer services, exercise rooms, and luncheon facilities are provided.

Shopping Centers.   The downtown retail hubs of the cities are normally in very fractionated ownerships. It is not unusual for a family that bought property and started a business downtown to retire and become landlords to the successor occupants. Then, from the late 1940s through the 1970s, a boom took place in **major suburban regional shopping centers.** These centers with major department stores as ''anchors'' and perhaps 50–150 other stores in malls succeeded so well that they sometimes became almost the new downtowns, at least from a retail and weekend social standpoint. Some feel that the high cost of suburban housing and costs of commuting to work and to shop will slow this rapid growth. Indeed, there are retail revitalization projects in many downtowns, with intown shopping centers and mixed use projects—retail, office, and housing all in one complex. Neighborhood shopping centers continue as strong as the communities they serve, provided owners and managers perform good maintenance, refurbish the appearance regularly, and pay attention to securing a strong tenant mix. In shopping centers, it is typical for the tenants to pay for all increases in operating costs. They pay their own utilities and pay common area charges for the mall, parking area, and open space maintenance.

Apartments.   The **ownership of an apartment building** has long been a popular type of investment for individuals. Smaller buildings have the owners living there as managers. This frequently makes it difficult for the owners to raise rents, evict tenants, and enforce rules, however. Many foreigners coming to the United States have purchased apartment buildings as an inflation hedge and to have their money in relatively safe U.S. real estate, denominated in dollars. In some markets these buyers have pushed prices to the point where there is little or no cash flow for the equity investor. Concern about the ability to raise rents high enough and frequently enough to keep ahead of rising operating costs, as well as concern about rent control, are causing some investors to more carefully evaluate this investment type. Similarly, lenders are questioning the **income-to–debt service ratios,** particularly for new properties.

Yet, vacancies are low. This is certainly not an equilibrium situation, and it makes for higher risk; but there also exists the possibility for higher capital appreciation returns. Some investors are buying apartments and selling houses by converting rental apartments to **condominium** ownership units.

Single-Family Houses.   An area of increasing importance, about which there is little published information, is investment in single-family homes. Most of us are aware of the large share of personal wealth that is represented by the ownership of one's own home for personal residence. It is the best investment that most people make in their lifetime. Increasing equities in homes help to finance education for children and to provide the capital for small family businesses and many other transactions useful to society. Some individual investors have carried this one step further by buying homes to rent to others. With annual rents in the range of 7–10% of cost and mortgage rates in the 12–14% range, the **cash flow to the investor is negative.** However, the mortgage terms are liberal in the sense that the loan-to-price ratio is high, say 80%, the maturity of the loan is long, usually 30 years, and the interest rate is fixed or varies slowly.

In areas of the country where demographic growth is high, the economy strong, and utility costs not too high, houses are appreciating rapidly. If a home goes up 10% in price in a year and the investor's down payment is 20% of cost, then the appreciation on his equity is 50%. This can more than offset the negative cash flow.

Some lenders are beginning to look at **equity returns on houses** and other investment real estate compared to the cost of long-term fixed rates on mortgages and are structuring **equity participations** to increase yield and to hedge against inflation. In summary, real estate is usually a long-term investment, and its liquidity is limited compared to stocks and bonds. It requires careful analysis of the economic, physical, financial, and tax aspects of each transaction.

BIBLIOGRAPHY

Denz, R. E., "Lease Provisions Designed to Meet Changing Economic Conditions," *University of Illinois Law Forum,* Fall 1952.

Kahn, Sanders A., *Real Estate Appraisal and Investment,* Ronald Press, New York, 1977.

Leider, Arnold, "How to Wrap Around a Mortgage," *Real Estate Review,* Winter 1975, pp. 29–34.

Levinson, D., "Basic Principles of Real Estate Leases," *University of Illinois Law Forum,* Fall 1952.

Plant, Kenneth M., "Playing the Futures Market Game," *Federal Home Loan Bank Board Journal,* November 1975, pp. 15–21.

Smith, David L., "Reforming the Mortgage Instrument," *Federal Home Loan Bank Board Journal,* May 1976, pp. 2–9.

PART 4

CORPORATE FINANCIAL MANAGEMENT

FINANCIAL STATEMENT ANALYSIS

CONTENTS

DEFINITION AND USES	3	Earnings per share	18
		Dividend payout ratio	19
BALANCE SHEET	3	Dividends per share	19
		Income retention rate after preferred	
Terms and Structure	3	dividends	19
Shortcomings of Balance Sheets	4	Sustainable Dividend Growth	21
Comparative Analysis	4	Income reinvestment rate	22
Trend Analysis	6	Sustainable growth rate	22
		Equity Valuation Index	23
INCOME STATEMENT	7		
		TRADITIONAL RATIO ANALYSIS	25
Terms and Structure	7		
Comparative Analysis	7	Liquidity Ratios	25
Trend Analysis	7	Current ratio	25
Percentage income statement	10	Quick ratio or acid test	26
Base 100 income statement	10	Financial Leverage Ratios	26
		Balance sheet ratios	26
FINANCIAL ANALYSIS	12	Income statement ratios	27
		Profitability Ratios	27
Objective of Financial Analysis	12	Profit margin on sales	27
Key Financial Ratios	12	Return on total assets	27
Analysis of Return on Equity	13	Return on common equity	27
Asset turnover	13	Turnover or Asset Management Ratios	28
Return on sales	13	Inventory utilization	28
Return on assets	13	Average collection period	28
Financial leverage	15	Asset utilization	29
Return on equity	15	Fixed assets utilization	29
Components of Return on Sales	15	Total assets utilization	29
Return on sales before interest and		Market Value Ratios	29
taxes	16	Price-earnings	29
Income retention rate after net interest		Price-book	29
expenses	16		
Income retention rate after taxes	16	DISCRIMINANT ANALYSIS AND	
		FINANCIAL RATIOS	29
THREE AVENUES BEYOND RETURN			
ON EQUITY	16	Credit Scoring	30
		Applications	31
Earnings and Dividends per Share	18		
Book value per share	18		

FINANCIAL STATEMENT ANALYSIS

Robert L. Hagin

DEFINITION AND USES

Financial statements report how capital that has been entrusted to a corporation by its creditors and stockholders has been used. Broadly speaking, financial statements are analyzed by people who wish to evaluate the potential risks and rewards of loaning money to corporations as creditors or owning shares of corporations as stockholders; in addition, financial statements permit internal assessment of strengths and weaknesses.

The complexity of financial analysis stems from the fact that no two companies are identical. Clearly, Ford is different from General Motors; IBM is different from Digital Equipment, and so on. But how do these companies differ? To answer this question one must analyze the accounting-related data that appear on a company's financial statements. Techniques that facilitate this kind of comparative analysis are presented in this section.

Specifically, the goals of this section are to clarify frequently used accounting terms, to suggest a convenient technique for comparing balance sheets and income statements, to illustrate a system of ratios that links data on the balance sheet and on the income statement, and to analyze and interpret these ratios to enhance the information content of numbers found on financial statements.

BALANCE SHEET

TERMS AND STRUCTURE. Within the accounting profession, different terms are used to describe the same thing. Each of the following terms, for example, refers to the same document: balance sheet, statement of financial condition, position statement, statement of assets, liabilities, and owners' equity. The **balance sheet** (as it is most commonly known) is the basic financial statement for a firm. It shows, on the left-hand side, what the company owns (valued at acquisition cost plus installation minus accumulated depreciation) and, on the right-hand side, the sources of the funds that were used to acquire those assets.

By definition, the total amounts represented on each side of a balance sheet are numerically equal—they balance. Specifically, the equation for a balance sheet is:

(Left Side)	(Right Side)
Assets	Liabilities + owners' equity
(What is owned)	(How it was funded)

SHORTCOMINGS OF BALANCE SHEETS.   An **asset** is something of sustained value that is owned by the company. The value of an asset (as it appears on the balance sheet) is cost plus installation minus accumulated depreciation. This definition and valuation convention can, however, result in a misleading picture of a company. Importantly, assets, as shown on a balance sheet, represent neither their **value,** if sold, nor their **replacement cost.** (Since March 23, 1976, the Securities and Exchange Commission's Rule 3–17, Regulation SX, has required firms with over $100 million in sales to provide supplementary unaudited estimates of the value of their assets at replacement cost.) Replacement cost refers to what a new asset of the same type would cost if purchased in the current market.

Another way in which balance sheets can be misleading stems from the **convention of omitting "assets"** that are of value to a company but are not "owned" (hence cannot be called "assets"). Obviously, management and employees are not "owned." In an accounting sense, people are resources that are leased or rented. Since leased resources are not "owned," they do not appear on the balance sheet. Thus, for example, the value of IBM's highly trained technical and sales personnel is not reflected on the company's balance sheet.

The final thing to remember about a balance sheet is that it is a **static** picture of an enterprise "as of the close of business on a particular day." Clearly, if you know that you are going to have your picture taken on December 31, you will do whatever you can to look your best on that day.

COMPARATIVE ANALYSIS.   In spite of the definitional problems, the balance sheet can be useful in the **comparative analysis of companies.** A technique that will facilitate this comparison is to represent the two sides of the balance sheet as two equally tall columns. Graphically, these can be thought of as two tall buildings, such as New York's World Trade Towers. This columnar representation is shown in Exhibit 1.

Few people can comprehend the magnitude of the numbers that are reported on financial statements. Consider, for example, the assets of the following, well-known, companies (shown to the nearest $ million) at the close of 1979.

American Telephone and Telegraph Co.	$113,769
International Business Machines, Inc.	24,530
Johnson and Johnson	2,874
Xerox	6,554

Given the size of these numbers, it is useful to think of balance sheet items in terms of **percentages**—not the typically incomprehensible absolute numbers that appear on the balance sheets of large companies. Using percentages, the major categories of a balance sheet can be depicted within the two towers—where each tower represents 100%. That is, beginning on the asset (left) half of the page, the percentage of **current assets** (those most likely to be converted into cash during an operating cycle) is compared to the percentage of fixed assets. **Fixed assets** are items of long-term usefulness to the firm that are not likely to be converted to cash, or consumed, within the next operating cycle. In the illustration (Exhibit 1), the company has half current and half fixed assets.

Within each of the broad categories of current and fixed, assets are listed **in order of decreasing liquidity.** Current assets usually include cash, marketable securities, accounts receivable, and inventories. The inventory category, also listed in order of decreasing liquidity, is typically broken down into finished goods, work-in-process, and raw materials.

EXHIBIT 1   WORLD TRADE TOWERS REPRESENTATION OF A BALANCE SHEET

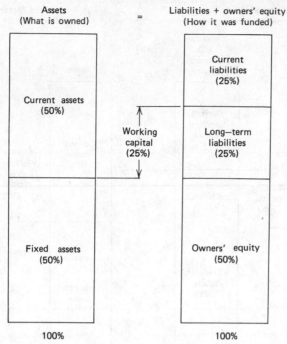

The fixed assets, also listed in order of decreasing liquidity, include items such as equipment, plant, and land. These subcategories of fixed and current assets can also be displayed as percentages in the World Trade Tower representation of a balance sheet.

The right-hand half of the balance sheet shows how the purchases of the assets appearing on the left-hand side of the balance sheets were funded. Basically, there are three funding alternatives. Assets can be purchased with borrowed money (representing **liabilities** of the company), capital invested by stockholders **(owners' equity),** or retained earnings (which are profits added to owners' equity). In Exhibit 1, half the right-hand side of the balance sheet consists of liabilities and half is owners' equity.

Following much the same convention used on the left-hand side of the balance sheet, liabilities are listed in order of "term" or nearness of the obligation. Thus, short-term debt obligations (those that will be retired in one operating cycle) appear first, with owners' equity coming last. In Exhibit 1, half the liabilities of the firm are current and half are long-term.

The graphic representation of a balance sheet can also be used to depict **working capi-tal**—the amount by which the current (most liquid) assets exceed the current (most pressing) liabilities. Other data, such as the percentage of owners' equity—what is owned (assets) minus what is owed (liabilities)—can also readily be derived from this kind of graphic presentation.

Exhibit 2 uses the World Trade Tower approach to contrast the December 31, 1979, balance sheets of General Motors (GM) and Ford Motor Co. While General Motors ($32.2 billion in assets) is larger than Ford ($23.5 billion in assets), the step-by-step comparison

EXHIBIT 2   COMPARATIVE BALANCE SHEETS

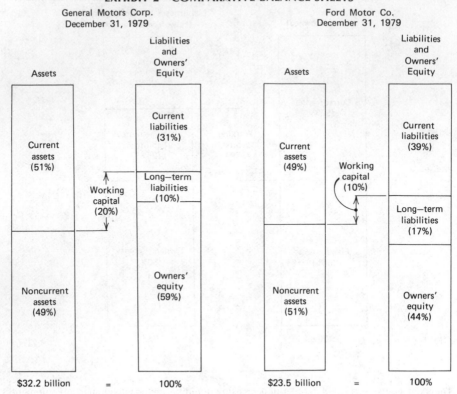

General Motors Corp.
December 31, 1979

Ford Motor Co.
December 31, 1979

$32.2 billion   =   100% $23.5 billion   =   100%

of each balance sheet category is now very easy. The tower comparison reveals, for example, that the assets of General Motors were slightly more liquid. GM had 51% of its assets in the current category compared to 49% for Ford. The fact that GM's working capital accounts for 20% of its assets, versus Ford's 10% shows that money is tighter at Ford.

The comparison also shows that current and long-term liabilities represent 41% of GM's liabilities and equity, against 56% for Ford. Thus, in terms of **three comparisons**—asset liquidity, working capital, and the debt-equity ratio—General Motors has the stronger balance sheet. Thus, assuming a reasonably **efficient market,** one would be surprised to find both General Motors and Ford priced in the stock market equally. In fact, if they were, it might reasonably be concluded that General Motors was undervalued or Ford was overvalued, or both. But, alas, there are few such surprises in the market—just as one would expect, GM's **price-earnings ratio** on December 31, 1979, was roughly 1.5 times that of Ford.

TREND ANALYSIS.   Besides comparing the balance sheets of two (or more) different companies, it is also useful to analyze a single company's balance sheet over time (trend analysis). Using percentages, Exhibit 3 is a percentage balance sheet for General Motors for fiscal years 1970 through 1979. This shows, for example, that 1979 total current assets as a percentage of total assets (51.4%) was at its lowest point since 1970. Trend analysis of financial statements is an effective means to evaluate the progress or deterioration of a firm.

INCOME STATEMENT

TERMS AND STRUCTURE.   The **income statement** (as it is most commonly known) is used to report managerial performance over time. It is a **dynamic** statement reflecting the progress (or lack of progress) of the firm over some period of time. By comparison, the balance sheet is a **static,** or snapshot, picture of the firm's financial condition at a single point in time. Terms used interchangeably here are income statement, profit and loss statement (P & L), and operating statement.

The basic equation for the income statement is

$$\text{income} = \text{revenue} - \text{expenses}$$

No one can disagree with a definition for income as simple as the following: everything brought in (revenue) less everything spent (expenses). Yet, there are many subleties regarding when revenue is recognized as such and which expenses should, at that time, be matched against it. To compound matters, income statements are also replete with many different terms that mean the same thing. There is no difference, for example, among the following: revenues, sales, turnover (in Europe), gross income, and "the top line." Similarly, there is no difference among income, profit, earnings, net income, and "the bottom line."

COMPARATIVE ANALYSIS.   The income statements of different companies can also be compared using the World Trade Tower approach. It merely requires the algebraic rearrangement of the basic equation from

$$\text{income} = \text{revenue} - \text{expenses}$$

to

$$\text{revenue} = \text{expenses} + \text{income}$$

In this format, both sides of the equation are equal so that they represent each side of the equation as easily comparable "towers," as shown in Exhibit 4.

Under the **accounting rules** now in effect (for audited companies), whenever 10% or more of a company's revenues are from a given line of business (e.g., a sales division or a rental segment), the revenues from that segment must be reported separately. Thus the revenue (left-hand) column is merely a graphic representation of the percentages of the company's revenue that are derived from each major segment of its business. Similarly, the expenses and income (right-hand) column, breaks out the percentages of the company's expenses by various categories. And the "bottom line" of the right-hand column shows the amount that is left after expenses have been subtracted from revenues—net aftertax profit, or income.

TREND ANALYSIS.   As with balance sheets, besides comparing the income statements of two (or more) companies, it is also useful to analyze a single company's income statement over time. Two useful techniques can be used to facilitate the interpretation of this information: percentage and base 100 income statement.

EXHIBIT 3 PERCENTAGE BALANCE SHEET FOR GENERAL MOTORS CORP. (ITEMS AS % OF TOTAL ASSETS)

	Year Ending December 31									
	1970	1971	1972	1973	1974	1975	1976	1977	1978	1979
Current Assets										
Cash and equivalents	2.8	18.2	16.1	15.0	6.5	15.6	18.9	12.2	13.3	9.3
Net accounts receivable	12.2	14.9	15.4	15.2	14.7	15.4	16.2	17.6	18.4	15.6
Inventory										
Materials and work-in-process	18.1	13.4	13.8	16.3	21.1	16.7	16.8	17.9	16.5	16.3
Finished goods inventory	10.9	8.5	9.2	9.2	10.2	9.6	9.1	9.0	8.3	8.8
Other current assets	0.0	2.6	3.2	4.2	4.4	2.0	2.3	3.2	2.4	1.4
Total current assets	44.0	57.6	57.7	59.9	56.9	59.3	63.3	59.9	58.9	51.4
Noncurrent Assets										
Net fixed assets	45.1	34.0	33.9	30.8	34.4	32.7	28.5	30.8	31.4	36.1
Intangibles	.4	.3	.2	.2	.2	.1	.1	.1	.0	.0
Investments in subsidiaries and others	7.7	7.5	6.8	7.2	7.6	7.5	7.7	8.0	8.1	9.8
Other assets	2.8	.6	1.4	1.9	1.0	.4	.5	1.3	1.6	2.7
Total noncurrent assets	56.0	42.4	42.3	40.1	43.1	40.7	36.7	40.1	41.1	48.6
Total Assets	100.0	100.0	100.0	100.0	100.0	100.0	100.0	100.0	100.0	100.0

Current Liabilities

Current long-term debt	.3	.1	.1	.5	.3	1.2	.5	.4	.5	.1
Notes payable, other	2.5	2.0	1.4	1.7	3.6	2.6	2.0	2.6	3.2	2.7
Accounts payable	9.0	10.0	12.0	14.0	13.7	11.0	10.0	11.0	11.4	10.5
Accrued taxes	1.4	9.5	4.2	3.0	1.7	3.9	6.8	3.3	3.1	1.5
Other current liabilities	9.6	11.2	9.5	10.3	10.5	11.2	13.1	14.0	14.7	15.8
Total current liabilities	22.7	32.8	27.2	29.4	29.8	29.8	32.4	31.2	32.8	30.6
Long-Term Liabilities										
Total long-term debt	2.0	3.4	4.3	3.7	4.3	5.6	4.4	4.0	3.2	2.7
Deferred taxes	1.1	.8	.9	.9	.9	1.1	1.6	1.4	1.7	2.0
Other liabilities	4.7	3.8	3.6	4.1	3.8	3.1	2.8	4.2	4.8	5.1
Total liabilities	30.5	40.8	36.0	38.1	38.8	39.7	41.1	40.9	42.6	40.5
Stockholders' Equity										
Preferred stock	2.0	1.5	1.6	1.4	1.4	1.3	1.2	1.1	.9	.9
Common stock	3.4	2.6	2.6	2.4	2.3	2.2	2.0	1.8	1.6	1.5
Paid-in surplus	5.4	4.2	4.2	3.8	3.7	3.5	3.2	2.9	2.6	3.2
Retained earnings	58.7	50.9	55.6	54.4	53.7	53.3	52.6	53.4	52.3	53.9
Total Equity	69.5	59.2	64.0	61.9	61.2	60.3	58.9	59.1	57.4	59.5
Total Liabilities and Stockholders' Equity	100.0	100.0	100.0	100.0	100.0	100.0	100.0	100.0	100.0	100.0

EXHIBIT 4   WORLD TRADE TOWERS REPRESENTATION OF A "TYPICAL" INCOME STATEMENT

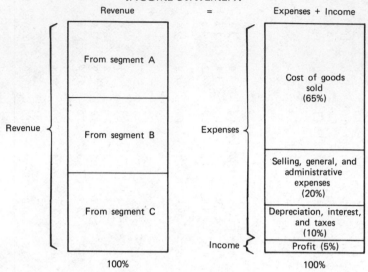

Percentage Income Statement. Exhibit 5 shows a percentage income statement for General Motors for fiscal years 1970–1979. Here all items are expressed as a percentage of net sales (or revenues). This exhibit reveals that the cost of goods sold associated with $100 of sales in 1979 was $84.40. Since 1970 this amount was exceeded only in 1974. The 1979 operating expenses, which include such items as advertising, research and development, and rental expenses, appear to be "in line" with other years (1970 and 1974 appear to be "out of line").

The line showing **depreciation expense** reveals a downward trend over time—from 8.0% in 1970 to 4.8% in 1979. Finally, the net income line reveals that net income, as a percentage of sales is 4.4%—roughly average for recent years.

Base 100 Income Statement. The percentage income statement makes it easier to "see" relationships between items, but it does not show the all-important **amount** of sales and net income. It is a useful way to display the data from **"base 100"** and to calculate **descriptive statistics**—the year-to-year **percentage changes,** the average least squares growth rate, and the standard error.

The base 100 format is shown, for General Motors, in Exhibit 6. First notice the difficulty in interpreting the trends in sales. Now notice the additional information that is provided by the "percent change" line. Unfortunately, a series of year-to-year percentage changes can be misleading. Take, for example, the hypothetical 4-year investment record of up 20%, up 40%, up 20%, down 50%. At a glance, this looks like four up years and one bad year. Using the **"base 100" approach,** however, reveals that this is not the case. Starting with $100, the hypothetical investor ends the first year with $120. In the second year, the investor earns 40% on the $120 and ends the year with $168. In the third year, this amount increases by 20% to $201.60. In the fourth year, however, the return is minus 50%. Thus, the investor finishes the final period with $100.80. Exhibit 6 shows that, in the case of General Motors,

EXHIBIT 5 PERCENTAGE INCOME STATEMENT FOR GENERAL MOTORS CORP. (ITEMS AS % OF SALES)

	Year Ending December 31									
	1970	1971	1972	1973	1974	1975	1976	1977	1978	1979
Net sales	100.0	100.0	100.0	100.0	100.0	100.0	100.0	100.0	100.0	100.0
− Cost of goods sold	83.1	76.8	77.0	78.8	85.3	83.7	80.9	81.1	81.4	84.4
Gross profit	16.9	23.2	23.0	21.2	14.7	16.3	19.1	18.9	18.6	15.6
− Total operating expenses	5.4	3.9	3.8	3.7	4.3	3.7	3.7	3.6	3.6	3.7
Operating income	11.5	19.3	19.2	17.5	10.4	12.6	15.4	15.3	15.0	11.9
+ Net other income	1.0	0.4	0.8	1.0	0.9	0.8	1.6	1.0	0.7	1.2
− Total interest expense	0.3	0.2	0.2	0.3	0.5	0.8	0.6	0.5	0.6	0.6
− Depreciation expense	8.0	6.4	5.9	5.6	5.4	5.9	4.8	4.3	4.8	4.8
Pretax income	4.2	13.1	13.9	12.6	5.4	6.7	11.6	11.5	10.3	7.7
− Total taxes	.9	6.3	6.8	5.9	2.3	3.1	5.4	5.3	4.9	3.3
Net income	3.3	6.8	7.1	6.7	3.1	3.6	6.2	6.2	5.4	4.4

EXHIBIT 6 BASE 100 INCOME STATEMENTS FOR GENERAL MOTORS CORP.

	Year Ending December 31										Growth Rate (%)	Standard Error (%)
	1970	1971	1972	1973	1974	1975	1976	1977	1978	1979		
Sales ($ thousands)	18,752,402	28,263,906	30,435,207	35,798,308	31,549,507	35,724,910	47,181,011	54,961,316	63,221,117	66,311,187		
Percent change	—	50.7	7.7	17.6	−11.9	13.2	32.1	16.5	15.0	4.9		
Sales (base 100)	100.00	150.70	162.30	190.86	168.15	190.35	251.45	292.94	336.88	353.39	13.50	0.25
Net income ($ thousands)	609,087	1,935,709	2,162,807	2,398,103	950,069	1,253,092	2,902,801	3,337,501	3,508,000	2,892,701		
Percent change	—	217.8	11.7	10.9	−60.4	31.9	131.7	15.0	5.1	−17.5		
Net income (base 100)	100.00	317.80	354.98	393.67	155.89	205.62	476.42	547.88	575.82	475.05	13.71	0.90

sales in 1970 base 100 grew to 353.39 at the end of 1979. Similarly, net income in 1970 base 100 grew to 475.05 at the end of 1979. The growth rate column shows the annualized least squares growth rate for both sales and earnings. The **least squares approach** is a statistical method to calculate growth rates based on a straight line drawn through time series points where the **slope** of the line measures the **constant growth rate.** This provides an important perspective on the ability of the company to generate both sales and earnings. The standard error is the standard deviation around the regression line that is used to calculate the least squares growth rate. On average, the variable in question will be within the range of plus or minus 1 standard error roughly 2 out of 3 years (i.e., two-thirds of the time).

FINANCIAL ANALYSIS

OBJECTIVE OF FINANCIAL ANALYSIS.   The facets to analyzing a company include its ability to generate sales from its products and services and its ability to translate these sales into stockholder return. This distinction between **sales** and **translation of sales into stockholder return** is important. Clearly, increases in sales of a company's products will not necessarily translate into stockholder return. Growth of sales is simply not—in and of itself—sufficient to provide future growth of dividends. For a manufacturing company to sell twice as many units, it must first produce these units. Such a doubling of production might mean that the company would have to double its asset base and its manufacturing and distribution costs.

Viewed from this perspective, analysts must consider (1) the expected growth of sales and (2) the managerial and financial resources necessary to transform sales growth into stockholder income. A forecasting technique that does not weigh both these factors provides an incomplete picture of the enterprise. See the section in this *Handbook* entitled "Financial Forecasting."

Thus projections of future growth require two different kinds of information. On the sales side, an analyst must forecast future demand for the firm's products. To do so, a long-term macroeconomic scenario and projected buying patterns must be translated into, first, industry demand, and then, company demand. On the company side, the analyst must analyze a company's ability to finance growth and translate the projected growth into income for the stockholder—the role of financial analysis.

Hence, the objective of financial analysis is to capsulize how efficiently a company employs its assets and how it has chosen to finance the acquisition and carrying costs of those assets. This is accomplished by analyzing the relationships between an enterprise's operating results (income statement) and its financial structure (balance sheet).

KEY FINANCIAL RATIOS.   The sources, data, and relationships for the ratios that summarize these relationships are shown in Exhibit 7. **Asset turnover** compares a key balance sheet item (assets) with a key income statement item (sales) to provide a measure of capacity utilization. **Return on sales** compares two income statement items (sales and income) to provide a measure of a firm's markup, or profit margin. **Return on assets** compares a balance sheet item (assets) with an income statement item (income) to provide a measure of producitivity—the ability of the assets to produce income.

Financial leverage compares two balance sheet items (assets and equity) in analyzing a firm's capital structure. Finally, **return on equity** compares a balance sheet item (equity) with an income statement item (income) to provide a measure of return.

EXHIBIT 7   FINANCIAL RATIOS: SOURCES, DATA, AND RELATIONSHIPS

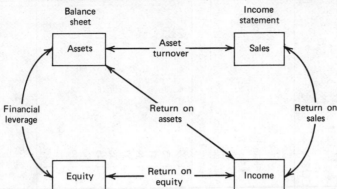

An immediate problem associated with this kind of analysis is that a balance sheet is a **static,** or snapshot, picture of an enterprise—as of the close of business on a particular day. Conversely, an income statement is a **dynamic** statement—reflecting the progress (or lack of progress) of the company throughout an entire period. To reconcile these differences, balance sheet items are generally averaged for the period. Thus, when comparing fiscal year sales (an income statement item) with assets (a balance sheet item), the asset figure that most closely corresponds to the sales figure is the average of the fiscal year's beginning and ending assets.

ANALYSIS OF RETURN ON EQUITY.   The key financial ratios determining return on equity are asset turnover, return on sales, and financial leverage.

Asset Turnover.   Also called operating leverage, this is the ratio of sales per dollar of assets employed during the year. It is calculated by dividing net sales, or revenues, by the average assets. In fiscal 1979 (ended December 31), for example, International Business Machines Corp. had an asset turnover ratio of 1.01 (Exhibit 8). This means that during fiscal 1979 IBM generated $1.01 in sales for each (average) dollar's worth of assets that it owned.

Return on Sales.   Sometimes abbreviated ROS and sometimes called the operating margin or net profit margin, this is the percentage of profit earned on sales. It is calculated by dividing net income, or earnings, by net sales. If we continue with Exhibit 8, in fiscal 1979 IBM had a return on sales of 13.2%. This means that the company earned 13.2¢ in net (aftertax) profit for each dollar of sales.

Return on Assets.   Sometimes abbreviated ROA, this is the percentage of net profit earned on total assets. It is the product of asset turnover and return on sales (sometimes referred to as the **du Pont formula).**

$$\text{asset turnover} \times \text{return on sales} = \text{return on assets}$$

$$\frac{\text{sales}}{\text{assets}} \times \frac{\text{income}}{\text{sales}} = \frac{\text{income}}{\text{assets}}$$

EXHIBIT 8 COMPONENTS OF RETURN ON EQUITY FOR IBM CORP.

	Asset Turnover (Operating Leverage)		Return on Sales (Net Margin)		Return on Assets		Financial Leverage		Return on Equity
	Sales / Average Assets	×	Net Income / Sales	=	Net Income / Average Assets	×	Average Assets / Average Equity	=	Net Income / Average Equity
1971	0.91	×	13.1	=	11.9	×	1.99	=	17.1
1972	0.94	×	13.4	=	12.6	×	1.43	=	18.0
1973	0.95	×	14.4	=	13.7	×	1.41	=	19.2
1974	0.96	×	14.5	=	14.0	×	1.39	=	19.4
1975	0.98	×	13.8	×	13.5	×	1.37	=	18.5
1976	0.98	×	14.7	=	14.4	×	1.38	=	19.8
1977	0.99	×	15.0	=	14.8	×	1.45	=	21.4
1978	1.06	×	14.8	=	15.7	×	1.52	=	23.8
1979	1.01	×	13.2	=	13.3	×	1.59	=	21.2
Least squares growth rate	1.5%		0.72%		2.2%		1.1%		3.3%

Note that when the fraction representing "asset turnover" is multiplied by the fraction representing "return on sales," the "sales" terms in the two fractions cancel each other. Thus, return on assets can be calculated either by multiplying asset turnover times return on sales or merely by dividing income by assets. IBM had a return on assets of 13.3% in fiscal 1979—13.3¢ for each dollar of assets.

Financial Leverage. This is the measure of how many dollars of assets are held in relation to each dollar of stockholders' equity—in other words, how much of a company's asset base is financed with stockholders' equity and how much with borrowed funds. It is calculated by dividing average assets by average stockholders' equity. During fiscal 1979 the leverage ratio for IBM was 1.59, indicating that the company employed $1.59 of assets for each dollar of stockholders' equity.

Return on Equity. Sometimes abbreviated ROE, this is a key measure of the profitability of an equity investment—is the net income earned by a company expressed as a percentage return on the stockholders' investment. Its relationship to return on assets and financial leverage is:

$$\text{return on assets} \times \text{financial leverage} = \text{return on equity}$$
$$\frac{\text{income}}{\text{assets}} \times \frac{\text{assets}}{\text{equity}} = \frac{\text{income}}{\text{equity}}$$

Note that when the fraction representing "return on assets" is multiplied by the fraction representing "financial leverage," the "asset" items in each fraction are canceled out. Thus, return on equity can be calculated either by multiplying the return on assets times financial leverage or merely by dividing income by equity. This is sometimes referred to as the **"modified" du Pont formula.** For fiscal 1979, IBM had an aftertax return on equity of 21.2%.

We can gain much insight into IBM by arraying the ratios that produce return on equity in the format shown in Exhibit 8. We can see that asset turnover, for example, has generally increased since 1971—with a least squares annual growth rate of 1.5%. (The advantage of calculating a "least squares" growth rate is that the procedure minimizes the effect of abnormal years.) We also can see return on sales has tended to increase—with a least squares annual growth rate of 0.7%. Next, we can see that return on assets—reflecting the increases in both asset turnover and return on sales—has risen at an average annual rate of 2.2%. (It should be emphasized that because of the averaging process, the product of the averages will not equal the average of the component ratios.) The fourth column shows that financial leverage has also increased—averaging a 1.1% annual increase. Finally, the net return on equity—reflecting the improvements in asset turnover, return on sales, and leverage—increased at an average annual rate of 3.3%.

COMPONENTS OF RETURN ON SALES. Exhibit 8 showed the components that produce return on equity. Specifically, asset turnover times return on sales equals return on assets; return on assets times financial leverage equals return on equity. A shortcoming of these ratios is that they do not isolate **interest and tax effects** on "net income." Thus one is unable to gauge operating efficiency separately from a company's ability to borrow at low rates or to minimize its tax burden. This shortcoming can be corrected by breaking down return on sales into three components: return on sales before interest and taxes, income retention rate after net interest expenses, and income retention rate after taxes.

Return on Sales Before Interest and Taxes.   This is the percentage of profit earned on sales before the payment of either net interest expenses or taxes. It is calculated by dividing sales into income before net interest expenses and taxes. In fiscal 1979 IBM had a return on sales before interest and taxes of 24.9%. This means that IBM earned 24.9¢ of profit before net interest expenses and taxes on each dollar of sales.

Income Retention Rate After Net Interest Expenses.   This is the proportion of before-tax and before-interest income that is retained after the payment of net interest expenses (interest income less interest expenses). It is calculated by dividing income before interest and taxes into income before taxes. Notice that the difference between the numerator and the denominator of the fraction equals net interest expenses. In fiscal 1979, IBM's income retention rate after net interest expenses was 0.975. This means that IBM retained 97.5% of its before-interest and before-tax income after the payment of net interest expenses.

Income Retention Rate After Taxes.   The income retention rate (after taxes) is the proportion of before-tax income that is retained after the payment of taxes. It is calculated by dividing income after interest but before taxes into net income. Here, the difference between the numerator and denominator of the fraction is the amount of taxes. Thus, if the company pays any taxes, this fraction will be less than 1.0. In fiscal 1979, IBM's income retention rate after taxes was 0.542. This means that IBM retained 54.2% of its income after the payment of taxes.

The relationship among return on sales before interest and taxes, income retention rate after net interest expenses, and income retention rate after taxes is shown in Exhibit 9. Note that when the fraction representing "return on sales before interest and taxes" is multiplied by the fraction representing "income retention rate after net interest expenses," the "income before interest and taxes" terms in each fraction are canceled out. Furthermore, note that when the fraction representing "income retention rate after net interest expenses" is multiplied by the fraction representing "income retention rate after taxes," the "income before taxes" terms in each fraction are canceled out. Thus, the product of the three fractions, after canceling, reduces to "net income" divided by "sales."

The decomposition of return on sales in Exhibit 9 reveals information on IBM that is "masked" by the aggregate return on sales. Notice, for example, that while IBM's return on sales (in column 4) grew at an average annual rate of 0.7%, return on sales before interest and taxes (in column 1) grew by only 0.2% a year. Thus, the majority of the improvement in return in return on sales during the period did not stem from improved profit margins but, instead, from the fact that IBM paid out a smaller proportion of each sales dollar as net interest expenses and taxes.

THREE AVENUES BEYOND RETURN ON EQUITY

Without the decomposition of return on sales, return on equity is defined as:

$$\text{asset turnover} \times \text{return on sales} \times \text{financial leverage} = \text{return on equity}$$

Thus, there are three basic sources of stockholder return: asset turnover, return on sales, and financial leverage. Asset turnover stems from a company's ability to make efficient use of its capacity to manufacture and/or sell its products and/or services. Excess capacity, that is,

EXHIBIT 9 COMPONENTS OF RETURN ON SALES FOR IBM CORP.

	Return on Sales Before Interest and Taxes $\dfrac{\text{Income (BIT)}}{\text{Sales}}$	×	Income Retention Rate After Net Interest Expense $\dfrac{\text{Income (BT)}}{\text{Income (BIT)}}$	×	Income Retention Rate After Taxes $\dfrac{\text{Net Income}}{\text{Income (BT)}}$	=	Return on Sales (Net Margin) $\dfrac{\text{Net Income}}{\text{Sales}}$
1971	25.7		96.7		52.5		13.1
1972	26.3		96.9		52.7		13.4
1973	27.7		96.3		53.5		14.4
1974	27.6		98.0		53.5		14.5
1975	26.2		98.3		53.5		13.8
1976	28.0		99.0		53.1		14.7
1977	28.3		99.2		53.4		15.0
1978	27.8		99.1		53.7		14.8
1979	24.9		97.5		54.2		13.2
Least squares growth rate	0.2%		0.3%		0.3%		0.7%

assets possessed by the firm that are not being used to generate revenues, translates into poor asset turnover. Return on sales stems from the markup that a company places on its products and/or services.

Profitability results from the combination of the first two sources: asset turnover and return on sales (or profit margin). Generally speaking, companies with large investments in fixed assets have low asset turnover and high profit margins. Conversely, companies whose profit margins are typically low, such as supermarkets, must depend on high turnover to achieve a competitive rate of return. Low asset turnover (relative to competing companies) implies excess capacity and/or operating inefficiency. **Excess capacity** generally results from excessive expansion and/or declining demand. Declining sales, in turn, can result from a decline in market share as a result of aggressive competition or can be industrywide and the effect of an economic slowdown.

Profit margins are also influenced by demand and competition. Profit margins typically fall in response to shrinking demand and/or increasing competition. However, even if profit margins are maintained in the face of declining demand, the excess capacity that is likely to result means that fixed costs must be spread over fewer units of output, with a detrimental effect on the company's return on sales.

Conversely, excessively high asset utilization can weaken profitability as production bottlenecks develop and labor becomes less efficient. Thus, to develop or evaluate growth estimates, an analyst must be aware of the factors that have led to changes in the past and, from this perspective, forecast future changes in the underlying components of growth.

Clearly, this analysis and forecasting process must go beyond "return on equity." One must be concerned with the sources of earnings and dividends per share, the financing of growth, and comparative measures of market value. Each of these analyses can be performed by extending the foregoing system of ratios beyond "return on equity" to determine (1) the sources of a company's growth of earnings and dividends per share, (2) a company's sustainable growth, and (3) a company's equity valuation index.

EARNINGS AND DIVIDENDS PER SHARE.   The foregoing system of ratios (which ended with return on equity) can be extended to cover **earnings and dividends per share** by including the following items.

Book Value per Share.   Book value per share is the ratio of the common stockholders' equity to the number of shares used to calculate earnings per share. Thus,

$$\text{book value per share} = \frac{\text{equity}}{\text{shares}}$$

In 1979 IBM's book value per share was $24.39.

Earnings per Share.   Earnings per share is equal to income after taxes divided by the number of shares. The relationship of earnings per share to return on equity and book value per share is:

$$\text{return on equity} \times \text{book value per share} = \text{earnings per share}$$
$$\frac{\text{income}}{\text{equity}} \times \frac{\text{equity}}{\text{shares}} = \frac{\text{income}}{\text{shares}}$$

Note that when the fraction representing ''return on equity'' is multiplied by the fraction representing ''book value per share,'' the ''equity'' terms in the two fractions cancel each other. Thus, earnings per share can be calculated either by multiplying return on equity times book value per share or merely by dividing the number of shares into income.

Dividend Payout Ratio.   The dividend payout ratio is equal to the amount paid out in dividends divided by income. Thus,

$$\text{dividend payout ratio} = \frac{\text{dividends}}{\text{income}}$$

In 1979 IBM's dividend payout ratio was 0.667, which means that the company paid out 66.7% of its aftertax income in dividends.

Dividends per Share.   Dividends per share are equal to dividends divided by number of shares. The relationship to earnings per share and dividend payout is:

$$\text{earnings per share} \times \text{dividend payout} = \text{dividends per share}$$
$$\frac{\text{income}}{\text{shares}} \times \frac{\text{dividends}}{\text{income}} = \frac{\text{dividends}}{\text{shares}}$$

If we use IBM as an example, the system of ratios that produce dividends per share from return on equity is shown in Exhibit 10. Arrayed in this fashion, IBM's earnings per share from 1971 through 1979 can be seen to have enjoyed an annual growth rate of 14.2%. More important, we can readily see that over the same period the two ratios that produce earnings per share—return on equity and book value per share—grew at average annual rates of 3.3 and 10.7%, respectively.

Going beyond earnings per share, Exhibit 10 reveals that from 1971 through 1979 IBM's dividends per share grew at an annual rate of 17.5%. In this case the two ratios that produce dividends per share—earnings per share and dividend payout—grew at average annual rates of 14.2 and 2.9%, respectively.

Exhibit 11 shows the complete system of ratios that produces dividends per share. The ''basic'' ratios are designated by the numbers 1 through 8. The ''resultant'' ratios that are produced by the basic ratios are designated by the letters A through F. Because the resultant ratios A through D serve only to provide interim information, any or all of them can be eliminated from the analysis. Each of the basic ratios, on the other hand, must be included in the determination of dividends per share.

Moving from left to right, Exhibit 11 shows that asset turnover (column 1) times return on sales before interest and taxes (column 2) results in return on assets before interest and taxes (column A). Next, return on assets before interest and taxes (column A) times the income retention rate after net interest expenses (column 3) results in return on assets before taxes (column B). Note, however, that the elimination of the interim ratio ''return on assets before interest and taxes'' in column A would not change the result.

Income Retention Rate after Preferred Dividends.   The series of ratios in Exhibit 11 is self-explanatory except for column 6, ''income retention rate after preferred dividends,'' which is presented here for the first time. **Preferred dividends** are an aftertax expense. The

EXHIBIT 10 RELATIONSHIP AMONG RETURN ON EQUITY, EARNINGS, AND DIVIDENDS PER SHARE FOR IBM CORP.

	Return on Equity $=\dfrac{\text{Income}}{\text{Equity}}$	×	Book Value per Share $=\dfrac{\text{Equity}}{\text{Shares}}$	=	EPS $=\dfrac{\text{Income}}{\text{Shares}}$	×	Dividend Payout Ratio $=\dfrac{\text{Dividends}}{\text{Income}}$	=	Dividends per Share $=\dfrac{\text{Dividends}}{\text{Shares}}$
1971	17.1		10.94		1.88		55.5		1.04
1972	17.1		12.25		2.21		48.9		1.08
1973	19.2		14.02		2.70		41.5		1.12
1974	19.4		16.05		3.12		44.6		1.39
1975	18.5		18.05		3.34		48.8		1.63
1976	19.8		20.08		3.99		50.2		2.00
1977	21.4		21.34		4.58		54.6		2.50
1978	23.8		22.34		5.32		54.1		2.88
1979	21.2		24.39		5.16		66.6		3.44
Least squares growth rate	3.3%		10.7%		14.2%		2.9%		17.5%

ratio introduced here is the proportion of aftertax income that is retained after the payment of preferred dividends. It is calculated by dividing income after the payment of preferred dividends by income after taxes. Thus,

$$\text{income retention rate after preferred dividends} = \frac{\text{income after preferred}}{\text{income after taxes}}$$

Here, the difference between the numerator and the denominator of the fraction is the amount of the preferred dividend. If the company does not pay a preferred dividend, as in the case of IBM, the fraction will be 1.0.

To facilitate algebraic representation, each of the basic ratios and the resultant dividends per share have been abbreviated, so that T = asset turnover; M = return on sales, or profit margin, before interest and taxes; I = the income retention rate after net interest expenses; R = the income retention rate after taxes; L = financial leverage; A = the income retention rate after preferred dividends; B = book value per share; P = dividend payout; and D = dividends per share. Thus we have:

$$T \times M \times I \times R \times L \times A \times B \times P = D$$

It follows that if dividends in any period are derived from these eight sources, **period-to-period changes in dividends** must be derived from period-to-period changes in the same eight sources. This is shown algebraically in Exhibit 11, where T_0 represents asset turnover in one period and T_1 represents asset turnover in the following period. Thus, if $T_0 = T_1$ (i.e., there is no period-to-period change in asset turnover), the ratio T_1/T_0 is 1.0, which does not affect the period-to-period change in dividends per share. The value of T_1 will be greater than that of T_0 when there has been a period-to-period increase in asset turnover. When this happens, the ratio T_1/T_0 will be greater than 1.0, and the ratio will exert a positive influence on the period-to-period change in dividends per share. Moving across Exhibit 11, it is clear that the same period-to-period relationship holds for each of the eight basic ratios that produce changes in dividends per share.

SUSTAINABLE DIVIDEND GROWTH.   We have seen that dividends per share for any company may be expressed as the product of:

asset turnover × return on sales × financial leverage ×
book value per share × dividend payout = dividends per share

Therefore, other things being unchanged, growth in dividends can be derived from increases in any or all of these items. Of all these factors, only increases in **book value per share** can be relied on to sustain dividend growth over a long period of time. Sustainable improvements in **asset turnover**—the ratio of sales to average assets—are limited by such factors as plant size and productive capacity. Clearly, there is a finite limit on the dollar volume of sales that can be generated from a dollar's worth of assets. Similarly, even though year-to-year changes in **profit margins** will doubtless occur, sustainable improvements in a company's **return on sales** are inevitably limited by competition. Nor can reductions in interest expenses and taxes improve return on sales indefinitely. **Financial leverage** is also limited, both by the willingness of creditors to lend and the willingness of management to increase debt. Likewise, it is not possible to have sustainable growth by progressively increasing the dividend payout.

EXHIBIT 11   SYSTEM OF RATIOS THAT

(1)		(2)		(A)		(3)		(B)		(4)		(C)
Asset Turnover (Operating Leverage)	×	Return on Sales (Profit Margin) Before Interest and Taxes	=	Return on Assets Before Interest and Taxes	×	Income Retention Rate After Net Interest Expenses	=	Return on Assets Before Taxes	×	Income Retention Rate After Taxes (Pull-through)	=	Net Return on Assets
$\dfrac{\text{Sales}}{\text{Assets}}$	×	$\dfrac{\text{IBIT}}{\text{Sales}}$	=	$\dfrac{\text{IBIT}}{\text{Assets}}$	×	$\dfrac{\text{IBT}}{\text{IBIT}}$	=	$\dfrac{\text{IBT}}{\text{Assets}}$	×	$\dfrac{\text{IAT}}{\text{IBT}}$	=	$\dfrac{\text{IAT}}{\text{Assets}}$

Each of these ratios can be abbreviated:

$$T \quad × \quad M \quad × \quad I \quad × \quad R$$

Thus, changes in dividends result from changes in:

$$\frac{T_1}{T_0} \quad × \quad \frac{M_1}{M_0} \quad × \quad \frac{I_1}{I_0} \quad × \quad \frac{R_1}{R_0}$$

Perpetual increases in T, M, I, and R are not possible.

Thus, there can be no sustainable improvement in a company's asset turnover, return on sales, financial leverage, or dividend payout rate. Even though each of these factors will doubtless vary, period-to-period changes typically fluctuate about some "normal" value that is dictated by the competitive forces of each company's industry.

Income Reinvestment Rate.   In contrast, **book value per share**—the ratio of equity to shares—can grow through retained earnings at an indefinite and **sustainable rate.** Thus, even if there is no equity financing to change the book value per share (if all other components remain unchanged), growth in dividends per share will result from the return on equity and the proportion of earnings that is retained (i.e., added to equity). Moreover, increases in book value per share **through retained earnings** are the only "sustainable" source of growth!

Sustainable Growth Rate.   A company's sustainable growth rate (see Babcock "The Concept of Sustainable Growth," *Financial Analysts Journal,* May–June 1970) can be defined as the **return on equity** times the **income reinvestment rate.** The income reinvestment rate is equal to 1.0 minus the dividend payout rate. The relationship between return on equity and the income reinvestment rate is:

$$\text{return on equity} × \text{income reinvestment rate} = \text{sustainable growth rate}$$

The sustainable growth rate **(if all else remains unchanged)** can be calculated either by multiplying return on equity times the income reinvestment rate or merely by dividing retained

RESULTS IN DIVIDENDS PER SHARE

(5)		(6)		(D)		(7)		(E)		(8)		(F)
		Income Retention Rate After		Return		Book Value		Earnings		Dividend		Dividends
$\times$ Financial Leverage	$\times$	Preferred Dividends	$=$	on Equity	$\times$	per Share	$=$	per Share	$\times$	Payout Rate	$=$	per Share
$\times$ $\dfrac{\text{Assets}}{\text{Equity}}$	$\times$	$\dfrac{\text{IAP}}{\text{IAT}}$	$=$	$\dfrac{\text{IAP}}{\text{Equity}}$	$\times$	$\dfrac{\text{Equity}}{\text{Shares}}$	$=$	$\dfrac{\text{IAP}}{\text{Shares}}$	$\times$	$\dfrac{\text{Dividend}}{\text{IAP}}$	$=$	$\dfrac{\text{Dividends}}{\text{Share}}$
$\times$ L	$\times$	A			$\times$	B			$\times$	P	$=$	D
$\times$ $\dfrac{L_1}{L_0}$	$\times$	$\dfrac{A_1}{A_0}$			$\times$	$\dfrac{B_1}{B_0}$			$\times$	$\dfrac{P_1}{P_0}$	$=$	$\dfrac{D_1}{D_0}$

Perpetual increases in L, A, and P are not possible. Similarly, perpetual increases in B by (1) selling additional shares above book value, (2) buying existing shares below book value, or (3) using shares as an acquisition currency are not possible. However, B can increase perpetually if the company earns a profit and retains a portion (i.e. increases the equity portion of the book value per share).

income by equity. Using average equity, IBM's sustainable growth rate in fiscal 1979 was 7.1%. This means that if all the factors that contributed to IBM's earnings and dividends in 1979 were to remain unchanged in the future, IBM's future earnings would grow at 7.1% per year.

Exhibit 12 shows the calculation of the sustainable growth rate for IBM from 1971 through 1979. Obviously, since the factors that contribute to earnings do not remain constant, the sustainable growth rate varies from year to year. Nonetheless, Exhibit 12 provides much insight into IBM's internally financed growth, which has averaged 9.5% since 1971. [See Kidder, Peabody and Co., Inc. *Modern Portfolio Theory: Topics and Applications* (No. 5), November 1980, for a technical explanation of why beginning—not average—equity should be used in this calculation.]

By extending this analysis, **dividend growth rates** can be broken down into sustainable and unsustainable parts. The sustainable component is derived from "normal" asset turnover, return, leverage, and dividend payout. The **unsustainable component** is derived from fluctuations above or below the sustainable rate. Therefore, knowledge of the "normal" levels of these components for a particular company, and industry, can be important in analyzing and forecasting growth.

EQUITY VALUATION INDEX.   One way to compare companies is on the basis of management's ability to produce earnings in relation to the total capital that is used to operate the enterprise. As seen earlier, this is the net return on assets (income after taxes divided by average assets). Another comparative measure can be derived from the public's assessment

EXHIBIT 12   COMPONENTS OF SUSTAINABLE GROWTH FOR IBM CORP.

	Return on Equity $\times$	Income Reinvestment Rate $=$	Sustainable Growth Rate
	$\dfrac{\text{Income}}{\text{Equity}}$ $\times$	$\dfrac{\text{Retained Income}}{\text{Income}}$ $=$	$\dfrac{\text{Retained Income}}{\text{Equity}}$
1971	17.1	44.5	7.6
1972	18.0	51.1	9.2
1973	19.2	58.5	11.2
1974	19.4	55.4	10.8
1975	18.5	51.2	9.5
1976	19.8	49.8	9.9
1977	21.4	45.4	9.7
1978	23.8	45.9	10.9
1979	21.2	33.4	7.1
Average	19.8	48.4	9.5
Least squares growth rate	3.3%	− 3.4%	− 0.2%

of management's performance as reflected by the **price** that stockholders are currently paying for an equity share in the enterprise.

In a purely financial sense, management is employed by stockholders to manage the stockholders' equity. Specifically, management is responsible for employing both financial and human resources so that the return to investors will be both large and secure. Moreover, the ability of the management of publicly held companies to use stockholders' equity to produce such returns is scrutinized by millions of investors each day. The resultant "score-card" appears on the daily financial pages—as the price of the stock.

Thus, the price of a stock at any instant reflects investors' expectations about management's ability to convert the company's equity (stockholders' equity and accumulated retained earnings) into a tangible return for the stockholder. This relationship between equity and price can be expressed as:

$$\text{return on equity} \times \text{P/E ratio} = \text{equity valuation index}$$
$$\frac{\text{income after taxes}}{\text{equity}} \times \frac{\text{price}}{\text{income after taxes}} = \frac{\text{price}}{\text{equity}}$$

Note that when the fraction representing "return on equity" is multiplied by the fraction representing the "P/E ratio," the "income after taxes" terms in each fraction are canceled out. Thus, the **equity valuation index** can be calculated either by multiplying return on equity times the price-earnings ratio or by merely dividing equity into price. The resultant figure is the price that investors are currently paying for a dollar's worth of equity that has been entrusted to management through stockholders' equity and retained earnings. The equity valuation index is sometimes referred to as the ratio of **market price to book value of equity** or merely the ratio of price to book.

Exhibit 13, which shows the calculation of the equity valuation index for IBM from 1971 through 1979, reveals, for example, that when the stock was purchased at the end of 1971,

EXHIBIT 13   COMPONENTS OF EQUITY VALUATION INDEX FOR IBM CORP.

	Return on Equity	×	Price-Earnings Ratio	=	Equity Valuation Index
	$\dfrac{\text{Income}}{\text{Equity}}$	×	$\dfrac{\text{Price}}{\text{Income}}$	=	$\dfrac{\text{Price}}{\text{Equity}}$
1971	17.1		35.9		6.15
1972	18.0		36.4		6.56
1973	19.2		22.9		4.40
1974	19.4		13.5		2.62
1975	18.5		16.8		3.11
1976	19.8		17.5		3.47
1977	21.4		14.9		3.20
1978	23.8		14.0		3.34
1979	21.2		12.5		2.64
Average	19.8		20.5		3.94
Least squares growth rate	3.3%		−12.0%		−9.2%

an investor in IBM was paying $6.15 for a dollar's worth of equity. At the end of 1979 an investor was paying $2.64 for a dollar's worth of equity. Thus, equity in IBM was much less expensive in 1979 than in 1971.

TRADITIONAL RATIO ANALYSIS

Traditional ratios, which are based on combining financial statement information and market-related data, can be categorized into at least five groups: liquidity ratios, financial leverage ratios, profitability ratios, turnover or asset management ratios, and market value ratios. Some of the most frequently used ones in each category are described in this section.

LIQUIDITY RATIOS. One of the first concerns of the financial analyst is liquidity: will the firm be able to meet its maturing obligations? Although a full liquidity analysis requires the use of **cash budgets,** ratios, which relate the amount of cash and other current assets to the current obligations, provide quick and easy-to-use measures of liquidity. Two commonly used liquidity ratios are presented below.

Current Ratio. The current ratio is computed by dividing current assets by current liabilities. Current assets normally include cash, marketable securities, accounts receivable, and inventories; current liabilities consist of accounts payable, short-term notes payable, current maturities of long-term debt, accrued income taxes, and other accrued expenses (principally wages). The **current ratio** is the most commonly used measure of **short-term solvency,** since it provides a single indicator of the extent to which the claims of short-term creditors are covered by assets that are expected to be converted to cash in a period roughly corresponding to the maturity of the claims.

An **industry average** is not a magic number that all firms should strive to maintain. In fact, some very well-managed firms will be above it, and other good firms will be below it. However, if a firm's ratios are very far removed from the average for its industry, the analyst must be concerned about why this variance occurs. Thus, a deviation from the industry average should signal the analyst to check further.

Quick Ratio or Acid Test.   The quick ratio is calculated by **deducting inventories from current assets** and dividing the remainder by current liabilities. Inventories are typically the least liquid of a firm's current assets; hence they are the assets on which losses are most likely to occur in the event of liquidation. Therefore, this measure of the firm's ability to pay off short-term obligations without relying on the sale of inventories is important.

$$\text{quick, or acid test ratio} = \frac{\text{current assets} - \text{inventories}}{\text{current liabilities}}$$

FINANCIAL LEVERAGE RATIOS.   The extent to which a firm uses debt financing, or **financial leverage,** has a number of implications. First, creditors look to the equity, or owner-supplied funds, to provide a margin of safety: if owners have provided only a small proportion of total financing, the risks of the enterprise are borne mainly by the creditors. Second, by raising funds through debt, the owners gain the benefits of maintaining control of the firm with a limited investment. Third, if the firm earns more on the borrowed funds than it pays in interest, the return to owners is **magnified.** For example, if assets earn 12% and debt costs only 8%, there is a 4% differential accruing to the stockholders. Financial leverage cuts both ways, however; if the return on assets falls to 5%, the differential between that return and the cost of debt must be made up from equity's share of total profits. In the first instance, where assets earn more than the cost of debt, leverage is favorable; in the second, it is unfavorable.

Firms with low amounts of debt have less risk of loss when the economy is in recession, but they also have lower expected returns when the economy booms. Conversely, firms with high leverage ratios run the risk of large losses but also have a chance of gaining high profits. The prospects of high returns are desirable, but investors are usually averse to risk.

In practice, leverage is approached in two ways. One approach examines balance sheet ratios and determines the extent to which borrowed funds have been used to finance the firm. The other approach measures the risk of default by income statement ratios designed to determine the number of times fixed charges are covered by operating profits. These ratios are complementary, and most analysts examine both types of leverage ratio.

Balance Sheet Ratios.   The ratio of **total debt to total assets,** generally called the **debt ratio,** measures the percentage of total funds provided by creditors.

$$\text{debt ratio} = \frac{\text{total debt}}{\text{total assets}}$$

Debt includes current and long-term liabilities. Creditors prefer low debt ratios, since the lower the ratio, the greater the cushion against creditors' losses in the event of liquidation. In contrast to the creditors' preference for a low debt ratio, the owners may seek high leverage either (1) to **magnify earnings** or (2) because selling new stock means giving up some degree of **control.**

The ratio of **debt to equity** is also used in financial analysis.

$$\text{debt-to-equity ratio} = \frac{\text{total debt}}{\text{total equity}}$$

The debt-to-assets (D/A) and debt-to-equity (D/E) ratios are simply transformations, one of the other. Both ratios increase as a firm of a given size (total assets) uses a greater proportion of debt, but D/A rises linearly and approaches a limit of 100%, while D/E rises exponentially and approaches infinity.

Income Statement Ratios.   The **times-interest-earned ratio** is determined by dividing earnings before interest and taxes by the interest charges.

$$\text{times-interest-earned ratio} = \frac{\text{earnings before interest and taxes}}{\text{interest charges}}$$

The times-interest-earned ratio measures the extent to which earnings can decline without resultant financial embarrassment to the firm because of an inability to meet annual interest costs. Failure to meet this obligation can bring legal action by the creditors, possibly resulting in bankruptcy. Note that the before-tax profit figure is used in the numerator. Because income taxes are computed after interest expense has been deducted, the ability to pay current interest is not affected by income taxes.

$$\text{times interest earned} = \frac{\text{profit before interest and taxes}}{\text{interest charges}}$$

PROFITABILITY RATIOS.   Profitability is the net result of a large number of policies and decisions. The ratios examined thus far reveal some interesting things about the way the firm is operating, but the profitability ratios show the combined effects of liquidity, asset management, and debt management on operating results.

Profit Margin on Sales.   The profit margin on sales, computed by dividing net income after taxes by sales, gives the profit per dollar of sales.

$$\text{profit margin} = \frac{\text{net profit after taxes}}{\text{sales}}$$

Return on Total Assets.   The ratio of net profit to total assets measures the return on total assets.

$$\text{return on total assets} = \frac{\text{net profit after taxes}}{\text{total assets}}$$

Return on Common Equity.   The ratio of net profit after taxes to common equity measures the rate of return on the stockholders' investment.

$$\text{return on common equity} = \frac{\text{net profit after taxes}}{\text{common equity}}$$

TURNOVER OR ASSET MANAGEMENT RATIOS. This group of ratios is designed to measure how effectively the firm is managing its assets. In particular, the asset management ratios answer this question: Does the total amount of each type of asset as reported on the balance sheet seem "reasonable," too high, or too low in view of current and projected operating sales levels?

Inventory Utilization. The inventory utilization ratio, sometimes called the **inventory turnover ratio,** is defined as sales divided by inventories.

$$\text{inventory utilization, or turnover ratio} = \frac{\text{sales}}{\text{inventories}}$$

Two problems arise in calculating and analyzing the inventory utilization ratio. First, sales are at market prices; if inventories are carried at cost, as they generally are, it would be more appropriate to use **cost of goods sold** in place of sales in the numerator of the formula. Established compilers of financial ratio statistics such as **Dun & Bradstreet,** however, use the ratio of sales to inventories carried at cost. To develop a figure that can be compared with those developed by **Dun & Bradstreet,** it is therefore necessary to measure inventory utilization with sales in the numerator, as we do here.

The second problem lies in the fact that sales occur over the entire year, whereas the inventory figure is for one point in time. This makes it better to use an **average inventory.** Preferably, the average inventory is calculated by summing the monthly figures during the year and dividing by 12. If monthly data are not available, one can add the beginning and ending figures and divide by 2. This will adjust for secular trends but not for seasonal fluctuations. If it is determined that the firm's business is highly seasonal, or if there has been a strong upward or downward sales trend during the year, it becomes essential to make some such adjustment.

Average Collection Period. The average collection period, which is used to appraise the accounts receivable, is computed in two steps: (1) annual sales are divided by 360 to get the average day's sales; (2) daily sales are divided into accounts receivable to find the number of days' sales "tied up" in receivables. This is defined as the average collection period, because it represents the average length of time that the firm must wait after making a sale before receiving cash.

$$\text{sales per day} = \frac{\text{sales}}{360}$$

$$\text{average collection period} = \frac{\text{receivables}}{\text{sales per day}}$$

This ratio can also be evaluated by comparison with the terms on which the firm sells its goods. For example, if a firm's credit terms call for payment within 30 days, and the collection period is 40 days, it indicates that customers, on the average, are not paying their bills on time. If the trend in the collection period over the past few years has been rising while the credit policy has not changed, this would be even stronger evidence that steps should be taken to expedite the collection of accounts receivable.

Asset Utilization.

Fixed Assets Utilization.   The ratio of sales to fixed assets, often called the fixed asset turnover ratio, measures the utilization of plant and equipment.

$$\text{fixed assets utilization} = \frac{\text{sales}}{\text{net fixed assets}}$$

Total Assets Utilization.   This ratio measures the utilization or turnover of all the firm's assets. It is calculated by dividing sales by total assets.

$$\text{total assets utilization} = \frac{\text{sales}}{\text{total assets}}$$

We discussed this ratio earlier as one of the key ingredients of return on assets.

MARKET VALUE RATIOS.   Another group of ratios relates the firm's stock price to its earnings and book value per share. These ratios give management an indication of what investors think of the company's past performance and future prospects. If the firm's liquidity debt management, asset management, and profitability ratios are all good, then its market value ratios will probably be high.

Price-Earnings.   The P/E ratio, which was discussed earlier, shows how much investors are willing to pay per dollar of reported profits.

$$\text{P/E ratio} = \frac{\text{price per share}}{\text{earnings per share}}$$

P/E ratios are higher for firms with high growth prospects but lower for firms for which there is a higher risk of achieving the expected returns.

Price-Book.   The ratio of a **stock's market price** to its **book value** gives another indication of how investors regard the company. Companies with high rates of return on equity generally sell at higher multiples of book value than those with low returns.

$$\text{PB ratio} = \frac{\text{price per share}}{\text{book value per share}}$$

DISCRIMINANT ANALYSIS AND FINANCIAL RATIOS

Financial statements quantify the financial position of a firm and the results of its operations. The foregoing ratios capsulize the interrelations between the items that appear on these statements. Nonetheless, two important questions remain unanswered:

When are deviations of a particular ratio significant?
How do ratios offset one another?

Take, for example, the **current ratio** (current assets divided by current liabilities). All other things held constant, high current ratios are desirable. Similarly, all other things held constant, a low debt-to-asset ratio is desirable. But, for example, suppose a company's current ratio is strong and its debt ratio is weak. How do these two ratios offset one another?

Although ratio analysis, as described earlier in this section, provides many insights into firm performance, it still basically is a **subjective,** one-ratio-at-a-time type of analysis. The analyst must eventually draw a conclusion from his calculations, and this decision is made more difficult when the various ratio indicators are giving different signals. A technique that can improve the **information content of financial ratios** is **discriminant analysis.**

Discriminant analysis has been applied to qualitative problems in finance (e.g., bankrupt or nonbankrupt, accept or reject a loan applicant). **Edward Altman's** work in this field has pioneered the approach of combining traditional ratio analysis with the multivariate technique known as discriminant analysis. For an in-depth discussion, see his article "Financial Ratios, Discriminant Analysis and the Prediction of Corporate Bankruptcy" (*Journal of Finance,* September 1968) and his books *Corporate Bankruptcy in America* (Heath, 1971) and *The Analysis and Prediction of Bankruptcy* (Wiley, in press). Altman discusses these works in the section entitled "Bankruptcy and Reorganization" in this *Handbook.* Also E. Brigham, *Financial Management: Theory and Practice* (2nd ed. Dryden Press, 1979, Appendix 6A) provides an excellent summary of discriminant analysis and financial ratios as applied to bankruptcy classification.

CREDIT SCORING. In general, discriminant analysis can use any **quantifiable factor** to help classify observations (e.g., firms) into specific populations (e.g., bankrupt vs. non-bankrupt). In the area of **consumer credit,** applicants may be accepted as high repayment potential or low repayment potential based on personal variables such as employment, income, and owner or renter. This is known as **credit scoring** where each attribute (or ratio) is assigned an **objectively determined weight** and the sum of these attributes times their weights gives a credit score. **Commercial credit scoring** does the same thing but deals with firms rather than individuals. Altman's original (1968) bankruptcy **Z-Score model,** which is still quite accurate despite its "age," is of the form,

$$Z = 1.4X_1 + 1.2X_2 + 3.3X_3 + 0.6X_4 + 1.0X_5$$

where

X_1 = working capital/total assets (%; e.g. .20 for 20 percent)
X_2 = retained earnings/total assets (%)
X_3 = earnings before interest and taxes/total assets (%)
X_4 = market value of equity/total liabilities (%)
X_5 = sales/total assets (number of times, e.g., 2.0 times)

Scores below 1.81 signify a serious problem situation whereas scores above 3.0 indicate a healthy entity. The five ratios used are indicative of liquidity, cumulative profitability, current profitability, leverage, and turnover, respectively. Discriminant analysis can **analyze these ratios simultaneously,** and the overall score or profile is the essence rather than any one ratio or group of ratios.

Altman, Haldeman, and Narayanan, in "Zeta Analysis: A New Model for Identifying Bankruptcy Risk" (*Journal of Banking and Finance,* June 1977) have updated and improved on the 1968 model by explicitly considering such factors as **lease capitalization** (see the section entitled "Leasing" in this *Handbook*), **consolidated financial statements,** and other accounting reporting changes. In addition, they applied income smoothing techniques to level out random fluctuations and trend deviations in the data. The new model was able to classify bankrupt firms very accurately for 2 years prior to failure and was still approximately 70% accurate for about 5 years prior. A more recent study by Dambolana and Khoury, "Ratio Stability and Corporate Failure" (*Journal of Finance,* September 1980) claims to improve on the 1968 Z-Score model by adding variables that capture the time-series dispersion (e.g., standard deviation) of financial ratios.

APPLICATIONS.   Models that combine ratios with rigorous statistical analysis are used with greater frequency by practitioners in the credit, investments, auditing, internal control, and legal areas. As such, academic studies have been adapted to the practical requirements of firms and individuals.

REFERENCES AND BIBLIOGRAPHY

Altman, Edward I., "Financial Ratios, Discriminant Analysis and the Prediction of Corporate Bankruptcy," *Journal of Finance,* Vol. 23, September 1968, pp. 589–609.

————, Haldeman, R. G., and Narayanan, P., "Zeta Analysis: A New Model to Identify Bankruptcy Risk of Corporations," *Journal of Banking and Finance,* Vol. 1, June 1977, pp. 29–54.

Babcock, Guilford C., "The Concept of Sustainable Growth," *Financial Analysts Journal,* Vol. 26, No. 3, May–June 1970, pp. 108–114.

Beaver, William H., "Financial Ratios as Predictors of Failure," in *Empirical Research in Accounting: Selected Studies,* University of Chicago Press, Chicago, 1966 pp. 71–127.

Brigham, Eugene E., *Financial Management: Theory and Practice,* 2nd ed., Dryden Press, Hinsdale, IL, 1979.

Foster, George, *Financial Statement Analysis,* Prentice-Hall, Englewood Cliffs, NJ, 1978.

Foster, Louis O., *Understanding Financial Statements and Corporate Annual Reports,* rev. ed., Chilton, New York, 1968.

Hong, Hai, "Inflationary Tax Effects on the Assets of Business Corporations," *Financial Management,* Fall 1977, pp. 51–59.

Horrigan, James C., "A Short History of Financial Ratio Analysis," *Accounting Review,* Vol. 43, April 1968, pp. 284–294.

Kisor, Manown, Jr., "The Financial Aspects of Growth," *Financial Analysts Journal,* Vol. 20, No. 2, March–April 1964, pp. 46–51.

Larsen, Robert A., and Murphy, Joseph E., Jr., "New Insights into Changes in Earnings per Share," *Financial Analysts Journal,* Vol. 31, No. 2, March–April 1975, pp. 77–83.

Lev, Baruch, *Financial Statement Analysis: A New Approach,* Prentice-Hall, Englewood Cliffs, NJ, 1974.

Smith, Ralph E., and Reilly, Frank K., "Price-Level Accounting and Financial Analysis," *Financial Management,* Vol. 4, Summer 1975, pp. 21–26.

Stanga, Keith G., "Disclosure in Published Annual Reports," *Financial Management,* Winter 1976, pp. 42–52.

Theil, Henri, "On the Use of Information Theory Concepts in the Analysis of Financial Statements," *Management Science,* Vol. 15, May 1969, pp. 459–480.

Viscione, Jerry A., *Financial Analysis: Principles and Procedures,* Houghton Mifflin, Boston, 1977.

Von Furstenberg, George M., and Malkiel, Burton G., "Financial Analysis in an Inflationary Environment," *Journal of Finance,* Vol. 32, May 1977, pp. 575–588.

SECTION **25**

PLANNING AND
CONTROL TECHNIQUES

CONTENTS

FINANCIAL PLANNING 3

Financial Planning Defined 3
Benefits of Planning 3
Steps in Financial Planning 4
  Scenario generation 4
  Translating scenarios into concrete
  numbers 4
  Generating financial statements 4
  Interpreting output and formulating
  plans 6
Planning Horizon 6
Frequency of Revising Financial Plans 6
Strategic and Tactical Planning 6
Responsibility for Financial Planning 6
Generating Pro Forma Statements by
Hand 7
  Sensitivity analysis 9
  Limitations of percent of sales method 9

COMPUTER-ASSISTED FINANCIAL
PLANNING 10

Role of Computers in Planning 10
Growing Use of Computers in Planning 10
Financial Statement Generation 10
  Sources of financial statement
  generators 10
    In-house computer systems 10
    Time-shared computer services 11
    Consulting firms 11
    Banks 11
  Characteristics of financial statement
  generators 11
    Mode of use: Batch versus time-
    sharing 11
    Interface with planner 12
    Ease of data entry 12
    Language level 12
    Degree of realism 12

Flexibility 12
Reporting options 12
Financial planning subsystems 12
  Tax planning 13
  Short-term borrowing needs 13
  Accounts receivable projection 13

PROFIT PLANNING AND BREAK-
EVEN ANALYSIS 13

Cost-Volume-Profit Relationships 13
Types of Cost 13
Determining Cost Types 13
  Department-based classification 13
  Statistical methods 14
  Engineered standards 14
Break-even Analysis 14
  Purposes of break-even analysis 15
  Limitations of break-even analysis 15

BUDGETING AND CONTROL 15

Control Defined 15
Budgets: Definition and Purposes 16
  Planning 16
  Evaluating performance 16
  Motivating actions 16
  Coordinating activities 16
  Authorizing actions 16
Need for Budgeting 16
Types of Budget 17
  Capital budgets 17
  Operational budgets 17
  Financial budgets 18
Budget Preparation 18
Budget Time Horizon 18
Problems of Budgeting 19
  Overbudgeting 19
  Budget inflexibility 19
  Budget masking 19
  Budget pressure 19

FINANCIAL CONTROL SYSTEMS   **19**

Responsibility Centers   **19**
Cost centers   20
Revenue centers   20
Profit centers   20
   Contribution margin   21
   Direct divisional profit   21
   Income before taxes   21
   Net income   21

Investment centers   21
   Return on investment (ROI)   22
   Shortcomings of ROI   23
   Residual income (RI)   23
      Shortcomings of RI   24
      Examples of ROI and RI
      computations   24

PLANNING AND CONTROL TECHNIQUES

Ned C. Hill

FINANCIAL PLANNING

FINANCIAL PLANNING DEFINED. The planning process in general concerns an assessment of possible future states of the world and their impact on the firm. It is intended to enable the planner to formulate courses of action to meet those various states successfully. The description of a specific future state is called a **scenario** and may include brief or extensive assumptions about economic, social, and political events and conditions. It may also include assumptions about the firm's operations. A simple example of a scenario would be: "Assume that next year inflation is 11%, short-term interest rates 13%, and the competition has introduced a new product that will take 10% of our current market share." A more complex scenario could provide many more details of the economic, social, and political world.

Financial planning concerns the financial impact of these scenarios and leads to the development of financial plans. A **financial plan** consists of a set of intended financial actions designed to respond to possible future requirements over the **planning horizon.** Since new information about the future is continually becoming available, no financial plan can ever be considered final. It is always subject to revision.

BENEFITS OF PLANNING. Among the benefits of financial planning are:

1. *Anticipation of future decisions*. Planning requires managers to think about future financial consequences of decision alternatives. The process identifies potential problems as well as opportunities.

2. *Coordination of activities*. The planning process requires communication between the separate activity units of the firm and thereby fosters conflict resolution and efforts to achieve common goals.

3. *Goal clarification*. Planning often brings out the need to set priorities when it is seen that some goals conflict under various scenarios. For example, planning may show that the goal of 15% growth per year is incompatible with a goal of no debt financing, in which case management would have to decide which is more important.

4. *Educational benefits*. Undertaking the planning process is an excellent way to learn about the firm and its workings. Some firms train new managers by having them experiment with financial planning models.

5. *Aid in control.* As discussed later under "Budgeting," planning forms the basis for the budgeting and control process of the firm. Specific plans are translated into budgets, which are used to communicate goals and evaluate performance.

STEPS IN FINANCIAL PLANNING.   Modern financial planning techniques are based on generating possible scenarios, assessing the implications of those scenarios for the firm, generating **pro forma** or future **financial statements,** and deciding from the statements how to respond with financial plans. It is a repetitive process in which the conclusions from a scenario often prompt **sensitivity analysis** or an exploration of how the conclusions would change if the scenario changed slightly. The steps illustrated in Exhibit 1 are discussed in detail below.

Scenario Generation.   Planners first generate a set of scenarios that could possibly be realized in the future. Some scenarios may have a high probability of occurrence, others a low probability. Scenarios often begin with forecasts such as economic forecasts of interest rates, prices, and consumer spending, market forecasts of sales levels, and an assessment of competitive factors. The section of this *Handbook* entitled "Financial Forecasting" deals in detail with these techniques. Scenarios may also include internal factors such as credit policy alternatives or capital investment projects.

"Most likely case" forecasts usually form the basis for one scenario. Though some planners use only the most likely scenario, this neglects the real benefits of planning. Since forecasts are more or less subject to error, most planners develop several scenarios by assuming deviations from forecasts in the "most likely case."

Translating Scenarios into Concrete Numbers.   Scenarios often contain vague, nonspecific terms such as "recession," "inflation," and "high level of sales." These vague notions must be translated into concrete numbers. Consumer spending levels and actions of competitors, for example, are used to generate numerical sales levels; and interest rate estimates are translated into interest costs and customer credit payment patterns. For this step, planners usually solicit guidance from many managers in the firm: marketing, production, tax, operations, and so on. Here, as in all other steps in the process, planning cannot be successful if done in a vacuum.

Generating Financial Statements.   Once specific numbers have been generated, the impact of the scenarios on the firm is quantitatively measured and reported in a format readily understood: financial statements. **Pro forma** or future financial statements such as balance sheets, income statements, cash flow reports, and funds statements are generated. **Pro forma statements** provide the basis for measuring profitability, determining cash needs or surpluses, establishing potential dividend policies, and computing key financial ratios.

The generation of financial statements is often performed by a computer. The computer has made possible the examination of many more scenarios and policy variations than was possible when planning was done largely by hand. An example of a firm that uses the computer in this way was reported in a major planning article in *Business Week* (April 28, 1975, p. 49):

The Hewlett-Packard Company using its own H-P 2000 computer, runs as many as 50 different scenarios on four different models—economic statement, intermediate range plan, econometric, and aggregate sales. One major issue last year—whether to sell $100 million of long-term

EXHIBIT 1   FLOW DIAGRAM FOR FINANCIAL PLANNING PROCESS

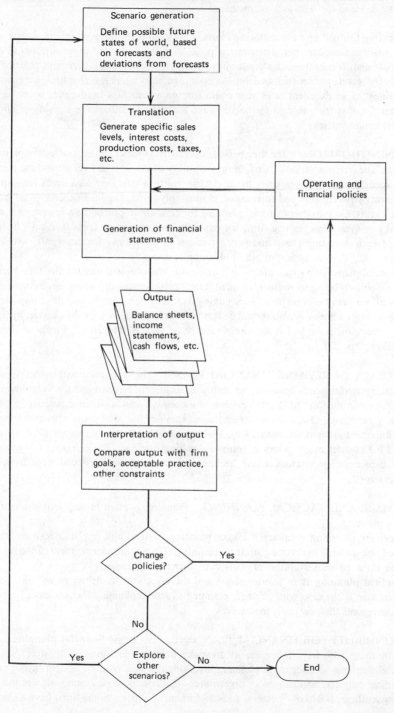

Scenario generation

Define possible future states of world, based on forecasts and deviations from forecasts

Translation

Generate specific sales levels, interest costs, production costs, taxes, etc.

Operating and financial policies

Generation of financial statements

Output

Balance sheets, income statements, cash flows, etc.

Interpretation of output

Compare output with firm goals, acceptable practice, other constraints

Change policies?

Yes

No

Explore other scenarios?

Yes

No

End

debt—involved some 100 different scenarios on the computer. The models helped the company finally decide to stay with in-house financing.

Interpreting Output and Formulating Plans.   By examining the pro forma financial statements, management can then determine if policies in the firm need to be adjusted to meet firm goals and to operate under constraints imposed by prudent management practice and possibly by outside parties such as debtholders or regulatory agencies. One firm, for example, in the midst of an excellent sales year could foresee a reduction in revenues over the next few years. It was then able to formulate plans for orderly cutbacks in operations and for financial contingencies.

PLANNING HORIZON.   The time period covered by a financial plan is called the **planning horizon.** The horizon varies depending on the ability of the firm to forecast and the purpose of the specific plan. For example, in an electric utility where long lead times are required to construct power plants and forecasting is relatively good, capital financing plans extend 10 or 15 years. On the other extreme, planning for cash inflow and outflow requires a horizon of weeks or even days. In one firm, for example, the **corporate treasurer** calls financial heads of each operating group and gets a forecast of cash flows for the coming week and for the coming 4-week period to aid in planning cash needs.

Financial plans for a given planning horizon are often broken into smaller time periods, with near periods being more finely divided. One executive stated: "Many large corporations work with a 5-year business plan. To accommodate short-term needs, and most importantly, to keep current, a business plan should be further broken down by year, by quarter, by month and by week, and reworked at appropriate intervals" (D. N. Judelson, "Financial Controls That Work," p. 22).

FREQUENCY OF REVISING FINANCIAL PLANS.   The frequency with which financial plans are revised depends again on the ability to accurately forecast and the volatility of the economic environment. **Quarterly revision** of the annual plan is common practice, but there are many variations. One firm, for example, reexamines financial plans whenever the price of an important commodity changes by 1% or more. Another firm extends financial plans 2 years but updates every month to achieve a **rolling horizon.** The computer has made the planning process less onerous a task because revisions may be produced more frequently with less cost.

STRATEGIC AND TACTICAL PLANNING.   Planning is often broken into strategic and tactical planning.

Strategic planning connotes a longer planning horizon and implies decisions that, if effected, are difficult to reverse. Strategic planning affects a broader segment of the firm and is more involved with overall firm goals than is tactical planning.

Tactical planning is of shorter range and the effects of its decisions are more easily reversed than is the case with strategic planning. Tactical planning focuses more on means to achieve goals than on goals themselves.

RESPONSIBILITY FOR FINANCIAL PLANNING.   **Strategic financial planning** is best done by those who have the authority to make financial decisions in the firm. Strategic financial planning—longer range planning involving issuance of stock or debt, major capital investment projects, acquisitions or divestitures—is done by some combination of the chief executive officer, board of directors, and chief financial officer. Some firms have a planning committee and planning staff to do the background work such as setting up the scenarios, producing the forecasts, and distilling details down to essential elements. Generally, however, the more decision makers are directly involved in the process, the more effective the planning will be.

Tactical financial planning—involving cash flow projections, credit line or commercial paper usage, and short-term investments—generally comes under the direction of the **treasurer** and, in the multidivision firms, the division financial officer. The treasurer may have a cash management staff to assist in this level of planning.

GENERATING PRO FORMA STATEMENTS BY HAND.   Generating pro forma financial statements is a key element of financial planning. A simple example using a "quick and dirty" approach will serve to illustrate the general procedure. A common method used is the **percent of sales method.** This method assumes that several balance sheet and income statement accounts vary directly with sales. For example, inventory might always be 30% of sales. When sales increase, inventory will increase by a corresponding amount to maintain the same percentage. To determine this percentage, past financial statements serve as a guide. In the example, we use only the previous year for our projections. Exhibit 2 gives the balance sheet and income statement for the year ending 19X1. The task at hand is to project financial statements for 19X2 and determine whether additional financing will be needed to support additional sales and planned plant expansion.

Step 1.   Using the percent of sales method, accounts are identified that are likely to vary with sales, and percentages are computed based on past data. Such accounts are cost of goods sold in the income statement and accounts receivable, inventory, and accounts payable in the balance sheet. The percentages are given next to the appropriate accounts in Exhibit 2. Note that if more years of data had been available, percentages from those years would have been averaged with consideration given to trends.

Step 2.   Based on marketing projections under the "most likely" scenario, a sales increase to $15 million is forecast. Other information provided by the firm is given as follows.

1.   General selling and administrative expenses will remain constant.
2.   A new facility will be constructed at a cost of $3 million partly financed by a $2 million term loan. The new plant will not affect total depreciation during the coming year.
3.   No existing long-term debt will be retired.
4.   Dividends will not be paid.
5.   Cash and marketable securities will be maintained at $5 million.

Step 3.   The income statement is computed from the information given above. As shown in Exhibit 2, net income after taxes is $2.7 million.

Step 4.   The balance sheet is next computed given the information above. Cash and marketable securities is set at $5 million by assumption 5. Accounts receivable, accounts payable, and inventory go up 25% along with the increase in sales. Net property, plant, and equipment is computed by adding the $28 million from last year to the $3 million in new investment minus $1 million for depreciation. Long-term debt goes to $7 million, since $2 million more

EXHIBIT 2   CITY CHEMICAL CO. INCOME STATEMENT AND BALANCE SHEET ($ MILLION)

	19×1	% of Sales	Pro Forma 19×2
INCOME STATEMENT			
Sales	$12.0	—	$15.0
Cost of goods sold	6.0	50%	7.5
Depreciation	1.0	—	1.0
General selling and administration	2.0	—	2.0
Operating profit	3.0	—	4.5
Taxes (40%)	1.2	—	1.8
Net income	$ 1.8	—	$ 2.7
BALANCE SHEET			
Assets			
Cash and marketable securities	$ 4.0	—	$ 5.0
Accounts receivable	6.0	50	7.5
Inventory	12.0	100	15.0
Net property plant and equipment	28.0	—	30.0
Total assets	50.0		57.5
Liabilities and Equity			
Accounts payable	4.0	33	5.0
Long-term debt	5.0	—	7.0
Common equity	30.0		30.0
Retained earnings	11.0		13.7
Total assets	$50.0		$55.7
Additional financing			1.8

was added and none retired. Retained earnings go up by the amount of aftertax net income, since no dividends are distributed.

Step 5.   The total assets are $57.5 million, while total liability and equity are $55.7 million. Since the two sides of the balance sheet must balance, a **balancing account** is created on the liability side for $1.8 million. This represents the additional financing required.

Step 6 (Optional).   To see the need for the extra $1.8 million in financing from a different perspective, it is helpful to produce a cash flow statement. Exhibit 3 shows cash inflows and outflows. A net cash outflow shows the need for additional funds. Note that some balance sheet changes have the effect of a cash flow. For example, an increase in accounts receivable

EXHIBIT 3   CITY CHEMICAL CO.
CASH FLOW STATEMENT, 19X2
($ MILLIONS)

CASH INFLOWS AND ADJUSTMENTS

Sales	$15.0
New debt	2.0
Increase in accounts payable	1.0
Cash inflows	18.0

CASH OUTFLOWS AND ADJUSTMENTS

Cost of goods sold	$7.5
General selling and administration	2.0
Taxes	1.8
Increase in inventory	3.0
Increase in accounts receivable	1.5
New construction	3.0
Increase in cash	1.0
Cash outflows	19.8

Net cash flow = 18.0 − 19.8 − −1.8

---

has the effect of a cash outflow, since added receivables correct for the overstatement of cash inflows from sales. Combining the inflows with the outflows shows a net outflow of $1.8 million. Hence, to balance cash flows, an additional inflow of $1.8 million is needed. This is (and must be, if correct procedures have been followed) the same number as that computed in generating the pro forma balance sheet.

Sensitivity Analysis.   Using this kind of procedure, future financing needs may be determined. The planner will also want to see how financing needs depend on assumptions made at the outset. For example, what if sales increased 40% instead of 25%? What would happen if sales dropped 5%? Exploring how results change as input varies is called **sensitivity analysis.** Appropriate steps in the planning process are repeated and new statements generated.

Limitations of Percent of Sales Method.   The method illustrated is widely used because it is simple and easy to do. Drawbacks are that most accounts do not vary directly with sales. For example, cost of goods sold generally includes costs that are fixed, or fixed over a certain range of sales, as well as variable costs. Accounts receivable also do not depend on current sales levels alone, but on past sales and customer payment patterns, as well. Correcting these approximations introduces complexities that would make hand computations tedious. Sensitivity analysis would also be quite difficult if performed by hand. A computer is therefore almost mandatory for the generation of realistically complex pro forma statements and the performance of sensitivity analysis.

COMPUTER-ASSISTED FINANCIAL PLANNING

ROLE OF COMPUTERS IN PLANNING.   Financial planning is based on the development of various future scenarios and the evaluation of their effects on the firm under different financial policies. The ability to efficiently express the results of those policies in financial statements is key to the planning process. Many firms use computers to handle the complex and tedious task of generating financial statements.

GROWING USE OF COMPUTERS IN PLANNING.   The use of computers for corporate planning has become widespread as the cost of computing power has decreased and the perceived value to management increased. A 1969 survey found only 20% of firms questioned using computers in planning (G. W. Gershefski, "Corporate Models—The State of the Art," *Management Science,* Vol. 16, No. 6, February 1970, pp. B-303–B-312). However a more recent survey by Naylor and Schauland ("A Survey of Users of Corporate Planning Models," *Management Science,* Vol. 22, No. 9, May 1976, pp. 927–937) reported 88% usage for a similar sample. Their survey showed that cash flow analysis, financial forecasting, and pro forma statement generation topped the list of uses for corporate planning models. Other uses of such models were profit planning, sales forecasting, budgeting, and investment analysis. Reasons most often cited for using computer models were the ability to explore more alternatives, better quality decision making, more effective planning, and better understanding of the business.

FINANCIAL STATEMENT GENERATION.   The computer's role in financial planning is to provide a **financial statement generator** (FSG). An FSG reads in data in the form of sales forecasts, projected costs, current inventory levels, depreciation schedules, tax expenses, and so on, and combines these according to company policies (such as setting the inventory level as a specified fraction of sales) and accounting practices. The output may be in the form of standard financial statements or specialized reports such as a schedule of required borrowing.

Sources of Financial Statement Generators.   There are several alternatives available today for obtaining financial planning assistance in the form of financial statement generators.

In-House Computer System.   The survey by Naylor and Schauland showed that the most common access to a financial statement generator is the firm's in-house computer. Of the firms using in-house computers, the majority have had the model designed and programmed by internal staff. Others either have used outside consultants to customize a model to the firm or have bought packaged computer software available from computer companies. Today it is possible to purchase or lease elementary financial planning software that will run on small business computers.
   Among the advantages of an in-house system are:

1. Lower usage costs once the system is developed.
2. The ability to design a model customized to interface with the firm's current data bases.
3. The ability to design custom reports desired by management.

The main disadvantages are the higher initial costs for purchase or development, system maintenance expense, and possible time delays (if the system is developed in-house).

Time-Shared Computer Services. In time-sharing, the services of a large computer, usually with extensive software support, are made available to customers through a computer terminal. This arrangement provides the computing power of a large system and spreads the costs among many users. The expenses in using a time-shared service include charges for software packages used, connect time, data storage, and hardware rental.
Advantages of time-sharing are:

1. A more powerful system at lower initial cost.
2. Avoidance of delays in developing an in-house system.
3. Often, a wider variety of software (programming packages or models).

Disadvantages include relatively high usage charges and inability to customize the model to the firm's data bases and reporting requirements.

Consulting Firms. Various financial consulting firms and public accounting partnerships offer financial planning services. This service differs from the first two in that the consultants are provided data from the firm. The financial statement generation is done generally outside the firm and planning reports are prepared for management. This approach reduces the planning efforts required of busy managers and obviates the need for an in-house computer system. A drawback is that management participates in the planning process less directly. This may limit a manager's understanding of the plans and lessen the perceived responsibility for implementing plans generated.

Banks. As an outgrowth of credit analysis software, many banks have developed financial planning packages to offer their clients. While some banks offer their models by time-sharing, most require that data be submitted in batches with a planning report being returned at a later time. Some banks have small business groups that offer financial planning assistance at nominal cost.

Characteristics of Financial Statement Generators. There is a wide array of financial statement generators. To help the prospective user compare and contrast essential features of the various types of generator, some of the principal characteristics are listed below.

Mode of Use: Batch Versus Time-Sharing. Most computers operate in one of two modes. **Batch mode** refers to the submission of data and program instructions (usually in the form of data cards) in a batch. After a time delay, the data are processed and output reports are produced. The user does not have an opportunity to alter the course of the program during processing. This mode is less expensive and can run on a simpler computer and elementary operating system.
The other mode is **time-sharing.** Communication with the computer is via a terminal, and many terminals may be connected to the central computer at once. While the program runs, the operator may receive requests from the terminal for data or further instructions. Reports may be printed at the terminal. The value of time-sharing to the financial planner lies in the much greater convenience of posing "what if" questions. By observing reports for a given scenario at the terminal, time-shared programs make it easy to alter some

assumptions and rerun the program. Time-sharing, however, requires a more complex and expensive computer.

Interface with Planner.   Some planning models, especially those operating in batch mode, are run by a staff rather than by the actual planner. The data are entered by staff members and reports are brought to the planner in the form of computer output. This kind of planning is less successful than models allowing the planning executive to interface directly with the model. In models of the latter type, the planning staff is responsible for preparing the background historical data and attending to technical details. The manager then does the actual planning and conducts the "what if" experiments. On the other hand, **executive interface** models are generally more expensive to operate and require a time-sharing computer. They also demand more involvement from the executive.

Ease of Data Entry.   Some models designed for small computers require that all data be entered for each run. This makes sensitivity analysis difficult because of the time required to reenter data over and over. Some models, at the other extreme, store the data from previous runs and allow rerun with slight user-specified changes. Some models interface with the firm's existing accounting system and take data directly from it.

Language Level.   While some models require knowledge of a programming language, many time-shared models are "high level" and require only English. Communicating with the program in English reduces the chance of misunderstanding and eliminates the objections of some people to using computers. The nearer to English a model is, generally the more expensive it is to run.

Degree of Realism.   Most models, while giving reports similar in appearance to the firm's accounting system, make simplifications. They buy understandability at the possible cost of realism. For example, many models assume accounts receivable to be a constant fraction of sales. While this assumption may be more or less correct for many firms, it may be drastically wrong if sales are seasonal or are changing rapidly. The model user should be aware of the tradeoff between the value of realism and the benefits of simplicity in understanding the model.

Flexibility.   Some simple models, for example, allow sales to be specified by a starting value and a constant growth rate. Other models allow sales or other variables to be specified through any number of user-selected options. Again, there is the tradeoff between the complexities of flexibility and the ease of use.

Reporting Options.   While some models produce a standard set of reports, others allow the users to prespecify reports and their organizational content. For performing **sensitivity analysis**, it is helpful to have the option of calling for comparison reports contrasting key financial statement variables side by side.

Financial Planning Subsystems.   Sophisticated financial statement generators offer specialized subsystems or programs that can be invoked to aid in specific areas of financial planning. While an exhaustive listing is inappropriate here, some of the more widely used subsystems are mentioned below.

Tax Planning. This subsystem allows the user to determine the tax effects of such policies as depreciation alternatives, inventory valuation options, equipment leasing, and project abandonment.

Short-Term Borrowing Needs. Many firms draw on bank credit lines or issue commercial paper to meet short-term borrowing needs. This subsystem assists in planning cash requirements on a monthly or shorter basis and takes information from longer range plans of the main system. Credit lines can be determined and commercial paper levels anticipated using this subsystem.

Accounts Receivable Projection. The typical financial statement generator computes accounts receivable in only an approximate way such as a given percentage of sales. An accounts receivable subsystem looks in greater detail at credit terms, past sales, and customer payment patterns. This subsystem is particularly useful when credit terms change or when credit sales show high volatility or seasonality. It is also useful when financial planning output is to be used to monitor actual accounts receivable.

PROFIT PLANNING AND BREAK-EVEN ANALYSIS

COST-VOLUME-PROFIT RELATIONSHIPS. Planning that focuses on the relationship between **costs, sales volume,** and **profits** (C-V-P) has often been called "profit planning." While something of a misnomer—since planning is generally done with an eye to the profitability of the firm—the label is still frequently used in finance and accounting texts. C-V-P relationships are important because they get to the heart of issues such as selling price, policies that may effect volume, different types of cost, and the profitability of the firm. C-V-P analyses are sometimes performed to determine the probable success or failure of a proposed project.

TYPES OF COST. Costs may be roughly divided into three types.

Fixed costs remain constant regardless of the sales volume. Examples of fixed costs are executive salaries, interest expenses, depreciation, long-term leases, and insurance expense. While no costs are truly fixed for all levels of sales, many costs may be considered to be fixed for an appropriate planning range.

Variable costs change as sales volume varies. Examples of variable costs are direct labor and material costs.

Semivariable costs vary, but not in direct proportions to sales. Some costs remain fixed over some range of sales but increase when sales enter a higher range. As an example, expense for a milk delivery truck is fixed up to some level of sales, but another truck must be purchased if sales rise above that level.

DETERMINING COST TYPES. It is not easy to sort out which costs are fixed and which are variable or semivariable. There are three general ways to approximate these distinctions, however.

Department-Based Classification. Departments of a firm or division may themselves be classified as incurring fixed or variable costs. The research and development, accounting, and legal departments, for example, are generally considered to be "fixed" because the

EXHIBIT 4   BREAK-EVEN ANALYSIS

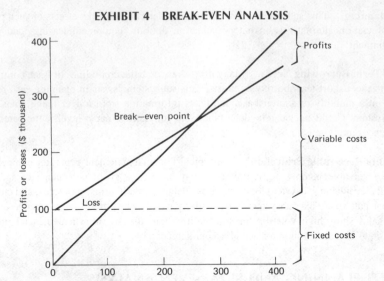

expenses they incur are less sensitive to volume changes, at least over the short run. Expenses for manufacturing and to some extent marketing departments tend more to vary with sales. Hence, classifying each department in this way will give some idea of the variable-fixed expense mix.

Statistical Methods.   By regressing total costs against sales volume using past data, one can approximate fixed costs as the intercept term and variable costs per dollar as the slope of the regression line. This method is generally reliable only when the currently employed technology and operating policies are similar to those employed in the past. Care must also be taken in assuming that the same C-V-P relationships hold over volume levels outside the ranges observed in the past.

Engineered Standards.   Production engineering departments often develop standard unit costs for manufactured products and overhead costs for various levels of activity. These costs from the firm's cost accounting systems may be used for classifying manufacturing costs.

BREAK-EVEN ANALYSIS.   Once fixed and variable costs have been determined (semivariable costs are neglected for the moment), break-even analysis is used to determine what volume of sales will just cover total costs. The break-even graph shown in Exhibit 4 is based on fixed costs of $100,000 and variable costs of 60¢ per dollar of sales. The total costs increase at a slower rate than revenue. At a sales volume of $250,000, revenues just cover total variable plus fixed costs. This is the **break-even point.** Sales above the break-even point generate profits, while sales below that point generate losses. The break-even point may also be found by using the equation:

$$\text{break-even sales level} = \frac{\text{fixed costs}}{1 - \text{variable costs per sales dollar}}$$

Purposes of Break-even Analysis.   Break-even analysis is useful in the following kinds
of decision.

1. *Changing production methods*. Planners need to know how break-even levels change
    to be able to assess the likelihood that sales will be sufficient to cover costs when
    the firm is contemplating a switch to technology involving higher fixed costs and
    lower variable costs (or the reverse).
2. *New product introduction*. Firms often request a break-even analysis for a proposed
    new product. Combining this information with marketing data on potential sales, an
    assessment of likely success can be made.
3. *Expansion of operations*. When general plant expansions are considered, break-even
    analysis helps determine whether added fixed costs can be justified.

Limitations of Break-Even Analysis.   While break-even analysis is relatively simple and
can yield some useful insights into relationships between cost, volume, and profitability, it
is limited as a planning tool when contrasted with planning based on financial statement
generation.

1. Costs are complex: they are not only fixed and variable. While some allowances can
    be made in more sophisticated versions of break-even analysis, most financial state-
    ment generators are flexible enough to handle any kind of cost-volume relationship.
2. Defining "sales volume" is difficult. The same dollar sales may be generated by
    unlimited possible combinations of product mix. Each product mix can be associated
    with different fixed and variable costs.
3. **Break-even analysis** ignores many other financial considerations such as credit and
    borrowing needs, nonexpense-related cash flows, and capital investment. Thus break-
    even analysis focuses only on profitability and cannot handle issues involving overall
    cash flow. Financial statement generators, on the other hand, consider cash flows
    as well as profits.
4. Because cash flows are ignored, break-even analysis cannot reflect the **time value
    of money.** It is therefore an incomplete tool for capital investment decisions. Financial
    statement generators often have subsystems that can perform time-value **capital
    budgeting analysis.**

"Profit planning" or break-even analysis of cost-volume-profit relationships serves a
useful function in identifying important relationships in the firm. The methodology is incomplete, however, as a financial planning or decision-making tool. The methodology was
developed before the widespread availability of computer-based financial planning systems
and is gradually being replaced by that more complete and versatile tool.

BUDGETING AND CONTROL

CONTROL DEFINED.   While planning involves the design of a desirable future state and
the effective means to achieve it, **managerial control** seeks to ensure adherence to those
means or plans. Mockler (*The Management Control Process,* Appleton-Century-Crofts, New
York, 1972, p. 111) defines **management control** as "a systematic effort by business
management to compare performance to predetermined standards, plans, or objectives in

order to determine whether performance is in line with these standards and presumably in order to take any remedial action required to see that human and other resources are being used in the most effective and efficient way possible in achieving corporate objectives.'' Perhaps the most widely used technique for exerting managerial control is **budgeting.**

BUDGETS: DEFINITION AND PURPOSES.   The planning process generates **pro forma financial statements** under a variety of scenarios or assumptions about business policies and economic conditions. A **budget** may be considered to be a set of financial statements resulting from a particular scenario—generally the most likely or hoped for scenario. A budget therefore reflects management opinions regarding future financial circumstances.

Budgets can be applied to the firm's entire operations as in a master budget or broken down into much smaller segments as in a sales representative's expense budget. Budgets serve many functions, among which are the following.

Planning.   By definition, a budget is the outcome of a more or less structured planning process. Hence, to encourage planning activities, some organizations require budgets. Such planning leads management to consider relationships between their areas of responsibility, the economy, and other activities of the firm. The planning process leads to better decision making.

Evaluating Performance.   Budgets are frequently used as a yardstick against which actual performance is measured. To effectively evaluate management performance, it is desirable to consider uncontrollable events during the budget period, recalling that a budget is the expression of only one future scenario.

> Evaluating present performance in terms of past performance assumes that the company's present condition and operating environment are the same as in the past. This is rarely the case. If the purpose of the evaluation is to measure managers' operating abilities as opposed to their forecasting skills, it might also be desirable to remove the effects of uncontrollable or unforeseeable environmental changes that have occurred during the budget period. Examples of uncontrollable environmental variables might be changes in government regulations, labor unrest, and either shortages or unexpected increases in the costs of raw materials. (Barrett and Fraser, ''Conflicting Roles in Budgeting for Operations,'' *Harvard Business Review,* July–August 1977, p. 138).

Motivating Actions.   A budget formalizes and quantifies a plan of action. When appropriately designed, a budget encourages adherence to the plan. It can motivate different units in the firm toward the same goals.

Coordinating Activities.   As budgets from lower levels flow to higher levels within the organization, incompatibilities between various units can be resolved. In an operating unit, budgets from marketing departments, for example, must be coordinated with budgets from the manufacturing department to efficiently utilize resources.

Authorizing Actions.   Especially in government and not-for-profit organizations, budget appropriations provide authorization and spending ceilings on management.

NEED FOR BUDGETING.   Budgeting is found in virtually all industries and in firms of all sizes. The computer has made budgeting a less tedious task to perform. While the volatility of the economy has given management the incentive to look ahead more, it has made forecasting the future extremely difficult. To those who despairingly give up on budgeting, Horngren admonishes (*Cost Accounting: A Managerial Emphasis*, p. 124):

> Many managers claim that the uncertainties peculiar to their business make budgets impractical for them. Yet one can nearly always find at least some companies in the same industry that use budgets. Such companies are usually among the industry leaders, and they regard budgets as indispensable aids. The point is that managers must grapple with uncertainties, either with a budget or without one. The advocates of budgeting maintain that the benefits from budgeting nearly always exceed the costs. Some budget program, at least, will be helpful in almost every organization.

TYPES OF BUDGET.   There are many kinds of budget, but most can be placed into one of three classifications (Exhibit 5).

Capital Budgets.   These express planned and approved expenditures for capital investment projects one or many years into the future. The capital budget is more strategic and points out the need for long-term fund-raising activities. The main role of capital budgets is to plan and coordinate.

Operational Budgets.   These express information about revenues, production costs, and general selling and administration expenses. Pro forma income statements are a type of operational budget and are often prepared for the firm, a division, a product line, and a plant.

EXHIBIT 5   TYPES OF BUDGET

Capital Budgets

Operational Budgets

Budgeted income statement
Production budget
   Materials
   Direct labor
   Factory overhead
   Inventory levels
Cost-of-goods-sold budget
Selling-expense budget
Administrative-expense budget

Financial Budgets

Cash budgets
   Receipts
   Disbursements
Budgeted balance sheet
Budgeted sources and application of funds

Source: Adapted from C. T. Horngren, *Cost Accounting: A Managerial Emphasis*, Prentice-Hall, Englewood Cliffs, NJ, 1977, p. 126.

Operational budgets focus on the tactical plans and have a horizon of a year, a quarter, or a month. They are frequently used in motivating and evaluating management, sales, and production personnel. Operational budgets also serve to coordinate various segments in the firm.

Financial Budgets.   While all budgets relate to financial decisions, the term **financial budget** traditionally refers to budgets of three interrelated types: balance sheet, cash flow budget, and sources and applications of funds budget.

The **budgeted balance sheet** is derived from the budgeted income statement and is useful in controlling trends in key financial ratios.

In contrast to other types of budget, which often contain noncash items (depreciation, credit sales, etc.) that are necessary in accounting profitability measures, the **cash flow budget** focuses directly on cash generated or needed on a monthly, weekly, or daily basis. Cash flow budgets are crucial in planning credit line usage, the issuance of commercial paper, investment in short-term securities, and the establishment of credit and purchasing policies. The **sources and applications of funds budget** is useful in identifying key changes in balance sheet accounts over time.

BUDGET PREPARATION.   There are two extreme approaches in budgeting. In **top-down budgeting,** the highest level of management determines the overall goals of the firm and translates these into sales and production budgets for each division. The division heads then generate sales and production budgets for each operating unit in the division, and the process continues down the organization. The advantages are easy coordination of various units, conformity of unit budgets to overall corporate goals, and speed. The main disadvantages are both motivational and operational. Lower managers who feel that the budget is imposed by others may be less motivated to implement it. In addition, since top management may lack important knowledge possessed by lower management concerning feasible operating and marketing characteristics, there is a potential for serious mistakes in the budgets. For example, unrealistic goals may be established that either are ignored or produce frustration.

At the opposite extreme, **bottom-up budgeting** begins with sales estimates from each sales district or even each sales representative. **Production budgets** are generated from each plant operation. These budgets are consolidated at higher and higher levels until the firm's master budget is produced. The process is slower and costlier and does not guarantee that unit budgets will be coordinated with each other or that they will conform to overall corporate goals. More effort is required to coordinate all the budgets at each level. There may also be a greater tendency for budget "padding." On the other hand, bottom-up budgeting allows greater decentralization and more localized decision making. It places budgeting into the hands of those more familiar with product costs and marketing potential.

In practice, most firms combine the two methods. Overall guidelines are given by top management as a framework for developing unit budgets. Once developed, unit budgets are reviewed and, if needed, revisions are suggested by top management. The process allows all levels of management to participate, each level giving feedback to other levels. The final budget may be the result of several cycles up, down, and across the management structure.

BUDGET TIME HORIZON.   **Capital budgets** often span a period of 10 years or more. Operational and financial budgets generally cover 1 year, broken down into shorter periods for the near future. An annual budget is frequently segmented into months for the first quarter and presented quarterly thereafter. Cash budgeting is sometimes done on a weekly or even daily basis. The horizon of the useful budget period depends to a large degree on the firm's ability to forecast and plan future sales levels, costs, and so on. A freight firm with long-term contracts can budget for a longer period than a ski resort, which must rely on the uncertainties of the weather to forecast sales.

Because more information comes forth as the year evolves, many firms update budgets at frequent intervals. At the end of the first quarter, for example, new data will cause a revision in the budget for the next three quarters.

Continuous or **rolling horizon budgets** are also popular. In such budgets at the end of one quarter, another quarter is added to the end of the budget period. That way management is forced to plan a full year ahead at all times of the year. The time and expense required to update the budget so frequently can be drawbacks.

PROBLEMS OF BUDGETING.   While budgeting provides an important tool to exert financial control in an organization, there are four major problems in the effective use of budgets.

Overbudgeting.   Budgets can become so complex and detailed that the time and expense of preparing them become excessive. Overly complex budgets also tend to be ignored.

Budget Inflexibility.   Because budgets are prepared in advance based on an assumed future, changing circumstances invalidate the underlying assumptions that generated the budget. It is unrealistic to measure current performance against an outdated plan. To overcome this problem, firms sometimes use flexible budgets that take into account the changed environment.

Budget Masking.   Budgets based on past budgets can tend to mask inefficient operations. To overcome this problem, some firms use a **zero-base budgeting review.**

> According to a regular schedule, each ongoing activity is studied intensively, perhaps once every five years. In contrast with the usual budget review, which takes the current level of spending as the starting point, this more intensive review starts from scratch and attempts to build up, *de novo*, the resources that actually are needed by the activity. It may even challenge the need for having the activity at all. These studies are especially important when costs are of the discretionary cost type. Basic questions are raised, such as: (1) Should the function be performed at all? (2) What should the quality level be? Are we doing too much? (3) Should it be performed in this way? (4) How much should it cost? (Anthony and Dearden, *Management Control Systems*, Irwin, Homewood, IL, 1976, p. 408.)

Budget Pressure.   Budgets can sometimes be used as tools to exert pressure on subordinates. When budgets cause resentment and frustration, they have lost their purpose. To reduce this problem, firms often use **participative budgeting,** which gives subordinates an important voice in establishing the budget.

FINANCIAL CONTROL SYSTEMS

RESPONSIBILITY CENTERS.   Budgeting is the chief tool for exerting **financial control** in the organization. This subsection discusses how a **financial control system** is designed. There are four basic types of financial control system, each associated with a **responsiblity**

center. The management of a responsibility center is charged with carrying out the financial plans associated with the budget for that center and is held accountable for performance in relation to the budget. The four types of responsibility center differ in the scope of financial activities they are accountable for. The four types are:

Cost centers, responsible for only the costs incurred by the unit.

Revenue centers, responsible only for the revenues generated by the unit.

Profit centers, responsible for both revenues and costs.

Investment centers, responsible for revenues, costs, and the capital investment base.

Cost Centers.   Dermer has provided the following definition:

> A cost center is the smallest organizational segment for which costs are traced and accumulated and over which an individual has responsibility. Although every unit classified as a cost center produces some useful output, it is usually neither feasible nor desirable to measure these outputs in monetary terms. (Dermer, *Management Planning and Control Systems*, Irwin, Homewood, IL, 1977, p. 15.)

There are two types of cost center: **engineered cost centers** and **discretionary cost centers.** Engineered costs are generally associated with a manufacturing or production facility. Each unit of output has associated with it an **engineered or standard cost.** This is the "acceptable" cost that should be incurred. Engineered cost centers are responsible then for maintaining costs at or below the standard cost per unit.

The discretionary cost center produces output for which there is no readily measurable monetary value. An example of a discretionary cost center is a training staff. The output, training, is likely to be of worth to the firm, but its value and quantity cannot be easily measured in monetary terms. While the efficiency of an engineered cost center can be determined by the extent to which costs are below budgeted costs per unit, the efficiency of a discretionary cost center cannot be so measured. The discretionary cost center manager is generally held responsible for holding to a budget, while efficiency is left to other more qualitative judgments.

The **disadvantage of cost centers** is their emphasis on cost minimization per se, which is not the main goal of the firm. Revenues generated by the firm are obviously important, too.

Revenue Centers.   Marketing units are typically the only revenue centers in most firms. Control is exerted through budgeted sales levels, with incentives for meeting or exceeding budget.

Revenue centers pose some problems when managers have discretion over pricing and/ or credit terms. Revenues can often be increased by lowering price or by liberalizing credit terms. Steps need to be taken to ensure that profitability is maintained by restricting pricing and credit control of the center.

Profit Centers.   When both costs and revenues of a unit can be measured in quantitative terms, the responsibility unit is a profit center. Since profitability is an important goal for the firm, making various units of the firm responsible for pieces of the profit is generally viewed as a desirable organizational objective. In creating an effective profit center, the management of that center is given authority to make decisions regarding operating policies, supply souces, prices, credit terms, and so on. Revenues and expenses must be clearly identifiable and controllable, or a profit center has little meaning.

Measuring the profitability of a profit center is sometimes a difficult task because of three problems:

1. The center may buy from another unit within the firm at an artificially low or high **transfer price.**
2. Revenues may be jointly generated by two or more profit centers within the firm. An allocation must be made on some reasonable basis.
3. Sometimes several profit centers consume joint services from another unit within the firm. Again, the costs have to be fairly allocated.

Anthony and Dearden (*Management Control Systems*, p. 249) describe four profitability measures, discussed briefly below.

Contribution Margin.   Revenues minus the cost of goods sold. Only variable costs are considered, based on the assumption that the profit center may have little control over fixed expenses or allocated corporate expenses.

Direct Divisional Profit.   Although similar to the contribution margin, this measure also contains such costs as fixed expenses and direct charges from other divisions, even though these may be considered uncontrollable.

Income Before Taxes.   Subtracting allocated corporate costs from direct profit gives income before taxes. General corporate expenses are allocated because it is held that the profit center benefits, if only indirectly, from expenses incurred from sources such as general corporate administration, image advertising, and annual report preparation. A profit center, it is argued, has not made a profit until all expenses have been covered.

Net Income.   This measure includes all the expenses above and also subtracts out taxes. This combination serves to keep managers aware of the tax consequences of their decisions. Exhibit 6 illustrates the computation of the various profitability measures.

Investment Centers.   Investment centers are responsible for revenues, costs, and also the **investment base** or the assets generating the revenues and costs. Profits themselves, it is argued, are not really an adequate basis for control unless the assets employed are considered. The profits of two divisions may be identical, but one may employ more assets to generate the profits than the other.

Investment centers imply that management has the responsibility for increasing the investment base or decreasing it. The manager's aims are to generate adequate profits from existing assets and to expand the asset base if an adequate return is likely.

There are two basic methods for **measuring the performance of an investment center:** return on investment and residual income.

EXHIBIT 6   PROFITABILITY MEASURES USED IN PROFIT CENTERS

Revenues	$10,000
Cost of goods sold	− 5,000
Variable costs	− 1,000
Contribution margin[a]	4,000
Fixed division expense	− 1,000
Direct charges from other divisions	− 500
Direct division profit[a]	2,500
Allocation of corporate costs	− 500
Income before taxes[a]	2,000
Taxes	− 1,000
Net income[a]	$ 1,000

[a]A performance measure.

Return on Investment (ROI).   While ROI has long been used to evaluate investments, only in the early 1960s was the measure applied to a division or investment center. Advantages of ROI over other performance measures discussed above are:

1. It incorporates essentially all ingredients of profitability, including the asset base.
2. It can be used to compare the performance of investment centers in the firm with outside firms.
3. It encourages management to think in terms of a broader measure of profitability.

ROI is measured as follows:

$$ROI = \frac{net\ income}{invested\ capital}$$

While the formula is simple, many difficulties arise in measuring both net income and invested capital. Among the issues that must be faced are:

1. How should total assets be measured? The alternatives are total assets and total assets minus liabilities. Some assets may not be under management control. An example is cash, which even in a **divisionalized firm** may be under highly centralized control. Most firms use total assets, even though some may be uncontrollable.
2. When should assets be measured? The options are book value at time of purchase, net book value after subtracting depreciation, and replacement value. Using depreciated value tends to overstate the performance of divisions with older equipment and may discourage beneficial upgrading of assets. **Replacement costs** may be difficult to determine and could be somewhat arbitrary. Hence the preferred method for many firms is to use the undepreciated book value.
3. How should **jointly held assets** be allocated? Accounts receivable, cash, and marketable securities, for example, may be maintained at corporate headquarters. An

allocation to investment centers is generally made on some basis; for example, accounts receivable is often allocated in proportion to sales.

4. How should inventory be valued? While LIFO methods may be desirable for tax purposes, LIFO tends to understate inventory value when prices rise. Hence most firms use FIFO for computing ROI.

Similar problems are encountered in measuring the net income for the ROI computation.

1. Should expenses charged from other divisions within the firm be adjusted if these expenses are different from those that would have been incurred in the open market? Generally **transfer prices** are set so that such adjustments will not have to be made.

2. How should general corporate expenses be allocated to investment centers? Usually some allocation base is used such as sales or fixed assets.

3. How should general corporate revenues be allocated? The marketable securities portfolio, for example, generates a return. If an investment center's asset base includes an allocation of these assets, the proportional revenues are generally also allocated.

4. How does the firm treat research and development costs (or any other cost that will be beneficial in the future)? If the costs are customarily expensed, management may be reluctant to invest in such projects.

While these are only a few of the problems encountered in measuring ROI, they serve to illustrate the kinds of difficulty faced and the caution that must therefore be used in computing and using ROI.

Shortcomings of ROI. Besides the measurement difficulties mentioned above, ROI suffers from several deficiencies. First, accounting measures of return are not cash flows and may not capture the **true economic picture of the investment center.** Second, ROI may encourage a short-term decision horizon that would be bad for the firm in the long run. For example, by selling off assets and leasing them back, the manager might immediately increase ROI; yet such a decision could be harmful over the longer run. Third, the pressure to maintain the current ROI may lead to the rejection of projects that would be beneficial. For example, if a division currently had an ROI of 20%, it would reject investments yielding 16% even if the firm's target were 14%. Fourth, focusing only on keeping ROI high may lead to projects of high risk. Modern managers recognize that ROI and risk are usually directly related.

Residual Income (RI). This performance measure also measures revenues, expenses, and assets but in a different way from ROI. RI is designed to overcome some of the problems encountered by ROI, though RI is also based on accounting measures of assets and profits. RI is defined as the dollar amount left over after subtracting from net income a capital charge for the assets employed:

$$RI = \text{revenues} - \text{operating expenses} - I \times \text{asset base}$$

where I **is the interest rate measuring the cost of providing capital** to the investment center.

The advantage of RI over ROI is that RI encourages the investment center to undertake investments as long as the return is greater than the firm's required return I. Thus a 16%

investment should be pursued when the required return is 14% even if the division currently has an ROI of 20%. Another advantage is that the interest rate can be different for various classes of assets. For risky assets, a higher rate can be applied.

Shortcomings of RI.   Besides similar problems of accounting measures of assets and income also encountered in ROI, RI suffers from other deficiencies. RI is a dollar measure, not a return. Hence it is **difficult to compare divisions**—especially when they are of different sizes. Futhermore, RI does not really overcome two problems associated with ROI: namely, those involving the incentives to reduce assets in the short run and to undertake risky projects with higher returns. So, while RI may be superior for investment decisions, it still has drawbacks that must be considered before it is used to evaluate management performance.

Examples of ROI and RI Computations.   To illustrate the difference in ROI and RI performance measures, consider a very simple example. Assume an investment base of 100 and current net income of 20. Thus ROI for the investment center is 20%. If the rate on invested capital is required to be 14%, the residual income is:

$$RI = 20 - 0.14(100) = 6$$

Now assume that a project is under consideration that would require an investment of 50 and give an annual income of 8, with the same risk as the firm's current projects. The division's return on investment would become

$$ROI = \frac{20 + 8}{100 + 50} = 18.7\%$$

Since this is less than the current ROI of 20%, a manager seeking to maintain a high ROI would not accept the investment. On the other hand, $RI = 28 - 0.14 (150) = 7$. The residual income of the division of the firm increases, so a manager seeking to increase RI would accept the investment project. From the viewpoint of the firm, the investment should be accepted, since it returns 16% and the required return is only 14%.

REFERENCES

Ackoff, Russell L., *A Concept of Corporate Planning,* Wiley-Interscience, New York, 1970.

Anthony, Robert N., and Dearden, John, *Management Control Systems,* 3rd ed., Irwin, Homewood, IL, 1976.

"Corporate Planning: Piercing the Future Fog in the Executive Suite," *Business Week,* April 28, 1975, pp. 46ff.

Dermer, Jerry, *Management Planning and Control Systems,* Irwin, Homewood, IL, 1977.

Horngren, Charles T., *Cost Accounting: A Managerial Emphasis,* 4th ed., Prentice-Hall, Englewood Cliffs, NJ, 1977.

Judelson, David N., "Financial Controls That Work," *Financial Executive,* January 1977, pp. 22–25.

Lorange, Peter, and Vancil, Richard F., "How to Design a Strategic Planning System," *Harvard Business Review,* September–October 1976, pp. 75–81.

Naylor, Thomas H., and Schauland, Horst, "A Survey of Users of Corporate Planning Models," *Management Science,* Vol. 22, No. 9, (May 1976), pp. 927–937.

O'Connor, Rochelle, *Planning Under Uncertainty: Multiple Scenarios and Contingency Planning,* Conference Board, New York, 1978.

Stone, Bernell K., Downes, David H., and Magee, Robert P., "Computer-Assisted Financial Planning: The Planner-Model Interface," *Journal of Business Research,* Vol. 5, (September 1977), pp. 215–233.

Weston, J. Fred, and Brigham, Eugene F., *Managerial Finance,* 6th ed., Dryden Press, Hinsdale, IL, 1978.

Wheelwright, Steven C., and Clarke, Darral G., "Corporate Forecasting: Promise and Reality," *Harvard Business Review,* November–December 1976, pp. 39ff.

SECTION **26**

FINANCIAL FORECASTING

CONTENTS

USES OF FINANCIAL FORECASTS	3
Avoiding Day-to-Day Crises	3
Costs of Forecasting Versus Costs of "Emergencies"	4
Tax Planning	4
"Forecasting" Versus "Budgeting"	4
Uncertainty	5
FORECASTING SALES	5
Importance of Sales Forecasts to Financial Plan	5
Ways to Forecast Sales	5
Subjective method	5
Trend forecasts	6
Causal models of estimation	6
Technique of Regression Analysis	6
Formulating the equation	7
Amount of data required	7
Testing other models	7
Most common factors	7
Interpreting results	8
Coefficient of determination (R^2)	8
"t-Values"	8
Standard error of estimate	8
Other Methods of Sales Forecasting	8
Selecting Appropriate Interval	9
FORECASTING THE CASH POSITION	9
Information for a Cash Budget	9
Example of Cash Budget	9
Cash budget data	10
Interpreting cash budget results	13

Variations in plan and computer-based systems	13
"What if" analysis	13
Most likely	19
Worst case	19
Best case	19
Uses of the Cash Budget	19
FORECASTING BALANCE SHEETS AND INCOME STATEMENTS	20
Uses of Pro Forma Statements	20
Interrelationship of Projected Statements	20
Preparing Pro Forma Income Statements	20
Projected Income Statement Data	21
Preparing Pro Forma Balance Sheets	21
Information required	21
Specific use of pro forma balance sheet	25
Common-Size Balance Sheet	31
A FEASIBLE FINANCIAL PLAN	31
Assessing Overall Financial Forecast	31
Basic Variables	31
Sustainable Growth Model	36
Addition of New Equity	36
Inconsistent Plan	37
Alternative Strategies	37
Increase in leverage	37
Increase in asset turnover	38
Improved profit margin	38
Dividend reduction	38
Inflation and Sustainable Growth	38

FINANCIAL FORECASTING

George G. C. Parker

Financial forecasting in recent years has taken on increasing importance in the overall planning process. This has occurred primarily because of the **larger role that capital has in the conduct of business and the general increase in the cost of that capital.** Many firms have found that both the **cost** and **availability** of funds are as important in determining growth rates as are the traditional factors of market opportunities, supply of labor, or supply of materials. Indeed, many firms are in a position to grow as fast as their financial resources will permit. Thus, good financial forecasting is often a prerequisite to the conduct of a successful business.

Inadequate attention to financial forecasting can lead to unanticipated financial emergencies that could be avoided— partially or entirely—by having **contingency plans** in place. Much as in other business decisions, the formulation of a proper plan is based on a well-formulated forecast. Without good financial forecasts, otherwise successful companies can encounter serious financial trouble in spite of record sales and profits. A good financial forecast goes hand in hand with every other part of the business plan.

This section is organized into five parts, which illustrate the financial forecasting process through the use of both description and example. Every attempt is made throughout to use general business illustrations that can be applied to a broad cross section of companies.

USES OF FINANCIAL FORECASTS

AVOIDING DAY-TO-DAY CRISES. Implicit in the need for careful financial planning is the reality that many financial opportunities in the form of loans, new equity, or investments are not available on short notice, or are not available unless **advance** arrangements have been made. Bank loans require prior approval, a process that is not without delay and occasionally entails uncertainty. New equity financing can require 90 days to 6 months or more to arrange. When cash accumulates, the time-consuming process of deciding how and where to invest excess funds can be significantly enhanced by advance planning. Understanding **when** and **in what amounts** financial resources will be required or become available is essential in the optimal securing or allocation of those resources.

The author acknowledges the helpful cooperation of James Starr, consultant to the Graduate School of Business, Stanford University, in the preparation of the Taft Manufacturing Co. example used in this section. The financial programming used in the example was provided to Stanford University by ADR Services, Inc., of Princeton, New Jersey, through their EMPIRE financial forecasting program.

Accurate estimates of the **timing** and **amount** of funds required are essential in arranging bank financing. Most bankers require that borrowers organize their financial planning before they enter into agreements. These agreements can be tailored to individual requirements if the financial plan is convincingly made and presented. An accurate balance sheet, income statement, and cash flow data for the future should be made available to the banker or other lender. Few tools of financial management are as critical to the orderly operation of the firm as the well-prepared financial forecast.

COSTS OF FORECASTING VERSUS COSTS OF "EMERGENCIES."   An important part of the financial forecasting process is the balancing of the cost of forecasting with the benefits derived from it. These costs must be related to the value of the information generated. Thus in an era of low interest rates (long since past in U.S. history) and ready availability of financing, the time and expense that management devotes to forecasting should be relatively low. When funds are cheap and plentiful the real or **opportunity cost** of holding excess cash (or other liquid assets) is not high. Thus idle resources may be held instead of establishing a tight financial plan. Indeed, financial forecasts are far more important as we enter the 1980s than they were in the 1960s and for a good part of the 1970s. This was true because it was less expensive to protect against uncertainty through holding large cash balances or maintaining large amounts of unused borrowing capacity. Partial evidence of this is that previous editions of the *Financial Handbook* did not include a section on financial forecasting.

TAX PLANNING.   A further major use of financial forecasts concerns planning for an optimal tax strategy. The importance of such planning has increased as the government has expanded the use of tax incentives to stimulate certain sectors of the economy. Capital investment is encouraged through the use of investment tax credits and accelerated depreciation. Employment subsidies may take the form of added tax deductions or tax credits.

While tax subsidies can be an important part of the profit or loss of a business, they require careful financial forecasting to take advantage of available tax savings. Thus in a year when the firm is not scheduled to be profitable, it is not wise to undertake large capital projects and possibly forfeit the investment tax credit or benefits of accelerated depreciation. Furthermore, in a year when profits are scheduled to be high, it may be advantageous to move expenses, to the extent they are discretionary, into the high-profit year. This not only has the effect of "smoothing" earnings from a reporting point of view, but it assures that tax benefits will be realized.

Finally, where capital expenditures or investments are affected by tax considerations, it is important to coordinate tax planning with cash on hand or cash available from external sources. Investment subsidies are not valuable without the resources to make the investment.

"FORECASTING" VERSUS "BUDGETING."   While the terms "budgeting" and "financial forecasting" are sometimes used interchangeably, forecasting is distinct from budgeting in the sense that a **forecast is more passive** in its approach to what will happen. A budget, on the other hand, frequently emphasizes what **ought** to happen if management functions efficiently. Thus a budget is a more active document, and may include a financial forecast as one of the ingredients in its preparation. Budgets may involve a motivational dimension by defining what could happen if everything went well and everyone pulled together. These are sometimes called **"stretch budgets,"** and they are analogous to the rabbit in front of a racing greyhound—it is not expected that the budget will be achieved as much as it is expected that everyone will pursue those figures as a **goal**. Such budgets may involve an element of wishful thinking, but it is injected knowingly.

Forecasts, by contrast, are more objective than budgets in that they attempt to identify what will happen if normal forces are at work. Budgets and forecasts may go hand in hand in a well-managed organization, but they are quite different in their preparation and use.

A further, and final, distinction between budgets and forecasts is that budgets are usually prepared in the accounting office or controller's department, while financial forecasts are more often prepared by the treasurer's department. Of course, in many firms these two functions merge at the level of the financial vice-president. Nonetheless, the distinction remains that **budgets are usually prepared by those responsible for results,** while **financial forecasts are the responsibility of those responsible for planning.**

UNCERTAINTY.   The basis of the need for financial forecasts is uncertainty about the future. Without such uncertainty, the planning process would be much simpler. In many respects financial forecasting could be renamed "coping with uncertainty."

Because uncertainty about the future is involved, and because complete resolution of this uncertainty is impossible, the end result of forecasting is never a perfectly reliable estimate. As noted above, the value of forecast financial information has increased in recent years as financial resources have become more costly. Nonetheless, managers must decide at what point they will stop analyzing data in search of a more perfect model and proceed with the model that is available at a reasonable cost. The examples used in this section are well within the bounds of reasonable cost. More complex systems of forecasting are described in several of the references.

FORECASTING SALES

IMPORTANCE OF SALES FORECASTS TO FINANCIAL PLAN.   Nearly every financial forecast begins with an **estimate of sales.** Since this is the **starting point,** the accuracy or inaccuracy of this estimate will affect the dependability of all other parts of the financial forecast. Pan, Nichols, and Joy emphasized this point in a recent article on sales forecasting: "Sales forecasting is a crucial part of many financial planning activities including . . . profit planning, cash budgeting and merger analysis." They concluded: "Large industrial firms recognize the importance of sales forecasting and commit resources to these efforts on a planned, regular basis." (See Pan, Nichols, and Joy, "Sales Forecasting Practices of Large U.S. Industrial Firms.")

Often the financial executive responsible for preparing the financial plan is not required to produce the sales forecast from which projected financial results are derived. Instead, the sales forecast is generated in the marketing department or in other planning groups within the company. Thus much of the treatment of the process of financial forecasting that follows presumes that a reasonably accurate sales forecast **is available** to the financial manager. Nonetheless, some general discussion of sales forecasting techniques is useful either to assess the **reliability** of the sales estimate or, occasionally, to generate a sales estimate when one is not otherwise provided.

WAYS TO FORECAST SALES.   There are three basic ways to forecast sales: the subjective method, trend forecasts, and causal models of estimation.

Subjective Method.   This essentially is the forecaster's own estimate of what sales will be, based on knowledge of the economy, industry, and generalized past experience. Subjective forecasts may be **individual** or a **consensus of group opinion.** As is true of most subjective techniques, such forecasts are "nonscientific." They are, instead, more visionary and rely on guesswork, imagination, insight, and specialized knowledge about the product and the market. While such forecasts are difficult to "prove" and equally difficult to "defend," there are numerous examples of high degrees of reliability for subjective forecasts of a forecaster whose track record has been good in the past. In most instances, subjective forecasts are enhanced by a group process, with the forecast being a **weighted average** of a **cross section** of **individual judgments.** However, the numerous examples of successful forecasts prepared by particularly gifted individual analysts cannot be ignored.

Trend Forecasts.   This form of sales forecasting, also called time series analysis, is slightly more scientific and is a simple **extrapolation of past trends** to come up with a projection. Trend forecasts generally rely on the premise that "the best estimate for tomorrow is a continuation of yesterday's trend." Refinements of the simple extrapolation technique can include **adjustments for seasonal or cyclical variability** in the historical data. Similarly, data from the past may be weighted more heavily toward the immediate past than toward the distant past.

The most frequently used method of extrapolation is to assemble sales data for the past 4 or 5 years, plot them on a graph, and try to "read a trend." Depending on how well the data **fit** along a simple trend, the reading may be easy or difficult. The obvious disadvantage of the simple extrapolation technique is that it is less than optimal in predicting **turning points** in sales. The prediction of turning points may be better accomplished using the subjective method noted above or the causal method that follows.

Causal Models of Estimation.   Causal models of sales forecasting attempt to identify the **underlying determinants** of sales in a **formal statistical model.** In some sense, causal models are a statistical version of subjective forecasting techniques that assess determinants of sales less "scientifically." In the subjective method, the forecaster uses personal experience of the factors that affect sales to make the forecast. In the causal statistical model, the forecaster examines a variety of numerical relationships from the past to formulate a causal model. **Causal models** are better at predicting **turning points** in sales when the direction or rate of sales may change significantly in response to the external environment.

TECHNIQUE OF REGRESSION ANALYSIS.   Virtually all statistically based predictive models for sales rely on the use of the statistical technique called **regression analysis.** Regression is a mathematical procedure that relates one variable, such as sales, to one or more other variables, such as gross national product (GNP), housing starts, or automobile sales. Regression analysis is a powerful tool that permits the forecaster to **measure** the **statistical impact** (and, by inference, the actual impact) of each **independent** variable on the **dependent variable, sales.** If there appears to be a significant **correlation** between the dependent variable **sales** and the other variables, the regression model is useful in describing the size of the relationship and its predictive value. The hypothetical example of regression that follows was extracted from Parker and Segura, "How to Get a Better Forecast."

In a **hypothetical company** in the **home furnishing industry,** sales might be expected to correlate with such factors as:

- New marriages.
- New housing starts.
- Disposable personal income.
- General time trend.

Formulating the Equation.   It is safe to say that most experienced observers, both within and outside the home furnishings field, will have certain preconceived notions about the effects of the variables listed above on sales of home furnishings. Through the regression technique, however, one can measure precisely **how large** and **how significant** each variable is in its historical relationship with sales. The overall relationship can be described by means of an **industry sales regression equation:**

$$S = B + B_m(M) + B_h(H) + B_i(I) + B_t(T)$$

where S = gross sales for year
$\quad B$ = base sales, or starting point from which other factors have influence
$\quad M$ = marriages during year
$\quad H$ = housing starts during year
$\quad I$ = annual disposable personal income
$\quad T$ = time trend (first year = 1, second year = 2,
$\quad\quad$ third year = 3, etc.)

B_m, B_h, B_i, and B_t represent the amount of influence on sales of the factors M, H, I, and T, respectively. These "B" terms, called **regression coefficients,** indicate the **extent** of the relationship between the dependent variable, sales, and each independent variable on the right-hand side of the equation.

Amount of Data Required.   The estimation of the relationships suggested by the equation generally require the use of several years' data because a meaningful correlation can hardly be judged when trends are measured only for a short time. Furthermore, when more than one variable is being correlated with sales, as in the equation above, the number of years of observations should be increased to make sure the results have reasonable statistical significance.

While there is no definitive cutoff point for the minimum number of years of data that are required, a period of **5 years** is a general rule of thumb when only one variable is being analyzed, and 8 years is a minimum with two. A longer time span is necessary with three or more variables, as is the case in our example.

Testing Other Models.   Regression analysis has the advantage that the basic sales equation can be augmented by the addition of other variables if the forecaster feels they would add to the predictive value of the model. It is the ability of the computer to process large quantities of statistical information that makes regression analyses feasible, since calculations that previously would have taken many, many hours to perform can be done in a matter of a few minutes. In fact, several companies now produce hand-held calculators that will test certain regression equations for those without access to large computer facilities.

Most Common Factors.   The most common macroeconomic factors incorporated into regression equations for sales forecasting are:

1. *Gross national product*. This variable correlates macroeconomic activity with company sales.
2. *Basic demographic data*. Correlations of these factors (e.g., new households, unemployment, housing starts, and age distribution of population) may differ.
3. *Level interest rates*. This factor often has a major impact on sales of higher-priced consumer and capital goods.

Numerous other variables may be selected as long as they can be expected to have a **causal** effect on sales.

Interpreting Results.   Hewlett-Packard, Texas Instruments, and several other manufacturers of calculators provide user information for the application of regression analysis to sales forecasting. This section does not deal in detail with regression analysis as a tool, but readers are referred to the article by Parker and Segura cited in the References or to any of a number of the introductory statistics textbooks with chapters on "regression analysis" (see, e.g., Norman Draper and Harry Smith, *Applied Regression Analysis,* Wiley, New York, 1966).

The major statistics to emerge from a regression equation are discussed next.

Coefficient of Determination (R²).   This statistic indicates the proportion of variation in observed sales in prior years that is explained by the regression equation (model). Theoretically it can range from .00 to 1.00, although, in reality, regression equations seldom demonstrate an R^2 greater than .95 or less than .50. Even the most naive models succeed in capturing some of the variation in sales on a historical basis. Systematic experimentation can improve the R^2.

"t-Values."   These statistics measure the reliability of relationships of the individual variables with the dependent variable (sales). Usually, a *t*-value of at least ±2.0 (assuming adequate sample size) will indicate that the variable is meaningful as a predictor. This does not mean, however, that there is not a better variable available. Only trial and error can establish that.

Standard Error of Estimate.   This indicates the degree to which the estimate is a good predictor. Sales can be expected to fall within ±2.0 standard errors of the estimate of predicted sales. Thus the smaller the standard error of the estimate, the more useful the model is as a predictor.

OTHER METHODS OF SALES FORECASTING.   There are numerous other methods of forecasting sales that are variations and combinations of the subjective and statistical techniques described. It is to be stressed, however, that the financial forecaster is usually somewhat peripheral to the sales forecasting process. The output from the sales forecasting system is the "starting point" for the financial forecaster's task. The partial summary of sales forecasting techniques that follows is from John C. Chambers, Satinder K. Mullick, and Donald D. Smith, "How to Choose the Right Forecasting Technique."

All these methods have pitfalls and may differ vastly in cost and administration. Sales forecasting is a specialty unto itself and requires considerable expertise.

1. Subjective methods
    a. Historical judgment based on similar circumstances.
    b. Market research.
    c. Panel consensus.
    d. Delphi method (a more formal panel consensus relying on sequential questionnaires; results of each questionnaire are used to prepare the subsequent survey).
    e. Individual "guess work."
2. Time series
    a. Moving average—simple and exponentially smoothed.
    b. Box–Jenkins (a highly complex trend forecast).

      c. X-11 (designed to isolate subtrends such as seasonality).
      d. Mechanical trend line.
  3. Causal methods
      a. Regression (as above).
      b. Econometric models (simultaneous regression equations).
      c. Survey of intentions to buy.
      d. Life cycle analysis.

SELECTING APPROPRIATE INTERVAL. Implicit in the sales forecasting process is selection of the appropriate time period to be forecast. Forecasts may be made **monthly** and aggregated for a **yearly forecast.** Some financial planning, however, requires **weekly** and even **daily** forecasting to be maximally useful for the financial planner. **Short-term sales forecasts of the weekly and daily variety are of particular relevance in cash management,** whereas forecasts for planning longer-term needs may more appropriately be done **monthly, quarterly,** or **yearly.** This section emphasizes monthly sales forecasts aggregated to produce an annual sales forecast.

FORECASTING THE CASH POSITION

Often the first report prepared by the financial forecaster is the **cash budget.** This report attempts to estimate the **cash position** of the company, and, indirectly, the **financing requirements** over the forecast period (usually 1 year) presented on a monthly basis. Cash budgets, however, can be prepared on a weekly or even daily basis.

INFORMATION FOR A CASH BUDGET. Supplementing the sales forecast in preparing the cash budget are various **discretionary items** that affect the financial position of the firm and its cash balances. These items include:

1. Scheduled purchases or sales of assets, especially fixed assets such as buildings or equipment.
2. Scheduled new financing such as long-term debt or a new stock issue.
3. Scheduled debt repayments and interest charges.
4. Dividends.
5. Other contractual or planned receipts or disbursements that fall outside the normal operating cycle of the business such as lease payments.

    The sales forecast, in combination with the other known cash inflow and outflow as noted above, is used to produce a schedule of cash receipts and disbursements. A diagram of the relationship of the key financial accounts as they affect cash is shown in Exhibit 1.

EXAMPLE OF CASH BUDGET. To illustrate the preparation of a **monthly cash budget** (forecast for 1980), a hypothetical example, the Taft Manufacturing Co., is presented. The example is a model for the type of data needed to prepare a cash budget in other companies.

1. *Company history.* The hypothetical Taft Co., a distributor of foreign auto parts, has experienced dramatic sales growth over the period 1977–1979, as shown in the historical income statements of Exhibit 2*a.* While sales have been increasing, profits have decreased slightly as shown in the exhibit.

EXHIBIT 1   THE CASH CYCLE[a,b]

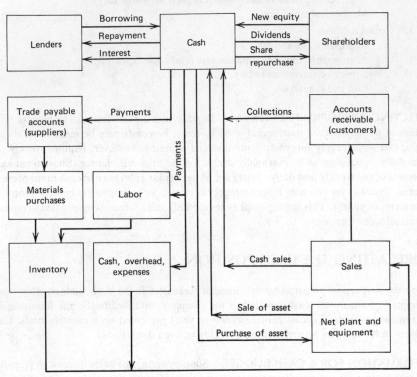

[a]Cash is normally generated by cash sales, collection of accounts receivable, borrowing, new equity, and sale of an asset.

[b]Cash is utilized by cash expenses, payment of accounts payable, debt repayments and interest repayments, dividends or share repurchase, and purchase of an asset.

2. *Year-end balance sheets for 1977–1979.* The year-end financial position of Taft (Exhibit 2*b*) shows a growth in assets from $247,907,000 to $382,659,000, with long-term debt increasing significantly to $96,000,000.

Cash Budget Data.

1. Monthly and annual sales of Taft were estimated by the marketing staff using a **trend forecast** with subjective estimates providing for some seasonal fluctuations. The actual estimates are as follows:

1980 Estimated Monthly Sales
(000 Omitted)

January	$ 58,000
February	59,000
March	61,000
April	62,000

EXHIBIT 2a   TAFT MANUFACTURING CO. ANNUAL INCOME STATEMENTS (000 OMITTED)

	1977	1978	1979
Sales	432,042	504,104	653,242
Cost of goods sold	− 302,436	− 343,829	− 468,850
Gross profit	129,606	160,275	184,392
Operating expense	− 89,056	− 107,068	− 139,179
Operating profit	40,550	53,207	45,213
Interest	− 3,738	− 8,354	− 10,547
Profit before taxes	36,812	44,853	34,666
Income taxes	− 15,980	− 21,171	− 16,016
Net income	20,832	23,682	18,650
Dividends	− 800	− 800	− 800
Change in net worth	20,032	22,882	17,850

EXHIBIT 2b   TAFT MANUFACTURING CO. YEAR-END BALANCE SHEETS (000 OMITTED)

	1977	1978	1979
Assets			
Cash and securities	15,399	39,372	15,940
Accounts receivable	64,487	76,804	101,764
Inventories	117,994	154,485	177,038
Other current assets	4,871	9,724	10,801
Total current assets	202,751	280,385	305,543
Net plant and equipment	39,579	49,998	68,010
Other long-term assets	5,577	6,678	9,106
Total Assets	247,907	337,061	382,659
Liabilities and Net Worth			
Accounts payable	20,729	23,617	33,233
Notes payable	13,096	1,861	22,955
Other current liabilities	19,718	29,525	26,563
Total current liabilities	53,543	55,003	82,751
Long-term debt	31,188	96,000	96,000
Total liabilities	84,731	151,003	178,751
Common stock	48,960	48,960	48,960
Capital surplus	43,563	43,563	43,563
Retained earnings	70,653	93,535	111,385
Net worth	163,176	186,058	203,908
Total capitalization	247,907	337,061	382,659

1980 Estimated Monthly Sales (Continued)	
May	64,000
June	69,000
July	70,000
August	72,000
September	72,000
October	75,000
November	76,000
December	77,000
Total for 1980	$815,000

2. Cash sales accounted for 10% of total sales.

3. Credit terms were net 60 days, thus collections were usually made 2 months after the sale (i.e., January credit sales were collected in March, February credit sales collected in April, etc.). Bad debt losses were expected to be insignificant.

4. The company produced at such a level that year-end inventories were approximately 27.6% of sales. For 1980, this policy required a net increase in inventory of $48 million. Monthly factory schedules were set so that production would be equal to cost of goods sold for the month plus $4 million per month of incremental additions to inventory.

5. Taft followed a policy of "direct" costing; that is, all overhead costs, including depreciation, were charged to period expense. Overhead, exclusive of depreciation, was projected at 19% of sales and was paid in the current month.

6. Cost of goods sold was budgeted at 70% of sales. Since 80% of Taft's production costs were for materials purchased on terms of net 30 days, the company paid for materials 1 month after they were used in production. The remaining production costs were for labor, paid in the current month. All labor expenses were paid currently.

7. Depreciation expense for 1980 was scheduled to be $1.2 million per month, while new capital expenditures were planned as follows:

March	$4,500,000
June	4,600,000
September	4,800,000
December	4,900,000

8. Income taxes for each calendar year were paid in the following year, with 25% due in the first month of each calendar quarter (i.e., 25% on January 15, April 15, July 15, and October 15). Thus for 1980 the 1979 taxes of $16,016,000 were paid in equal installments. Taxes due for 1980 were accrued. For forecasting purposes, Taft assumed a tax rate of 50% of profits.

9. Taft's board of directors declared a quarterly dividend of $200,000 in 1979, paid in the second month of the quarter. Plans for 1980 included a significant increase in the dividend to $2 million quarterly, to be paid in February, May, August, and November.

10. Taft kept at least 18.8% of current monthly sales volume in cash and marketable securities at all times. This was considered a minimum acceptable level of **cash** for contingencies and was useful in maintaining good bank relations.

11. Interest on Taft's $96 million in long-term debt was computed at 8.5% per year. Interest rates on the company's short-term debt (notes payable) varied, but for 1980 it was projected at 13%. Interest was paid at the beginning of each quarter for the 3 preceding months.

12. No amortization of the long-term debt was required before 1985.

13. Taft had other current assets estimated at 1.5% of sales and other long-term assets projected at 1.3% of sales. These were long-run averages based on annual and monthly sales figures. Thus a regular cash receipt or disbursement to bring other asset accounts into line was scheduled.

14. Interest and tax expenses accrued, but not yet paid, were entered as other current liabilities.

Interpreting Cash Budget Results.   Exhibit 3 indicates the **monthly cash flows** as well as the monthly financing needed by Taft based on the sales forecast and other information in items 1–14 presented above. Exhibit 3a indicates a **systematic** increase in short-term notes payable, over the year from $34,662,000 to $82,504,000. The feasibility of such financing can be negotiated with Taft's lender (probably a bank) on the basis of this systematic plan.

The reason for this borrowing can be analyzed on a monthly basis in the January–December period. Here it is seen that there are **wide savings** in monthly cash requirements, which vary from August (the low month), with a net financing need of $832,000, to July (the high month), with a net need of $9,053,000. It is noted further that the discretionary items of "capital expenditures" and "dividends" account for only $28,800,000 million of the incremental financing need of $47,879,000. Thus, if Taft is to permit sales to grow by 25% from 1979 to 1980 as shown in the forecast, the financing requirements will be substantial.

Variations in Plan and Computer-Based Systems.   While the process of preparing a cash budget can be done manually, the forecast can also be prepared using a computer-based system. Many such systems are available in the form of programs or software packages from computer manufacturers and independent computer service bureaus. Many medium-size and large companies also develop forecasting models using their own computer staffs.

The decision to use a prepackaged financial forecasting model instead of an in-house **custom-made model** frequently depends on such considerations as whether the company is operating under unusual loan covenants or experiences unusual seasonal relationships in expenses and sales. With in-house systems, individual company characteristics can be incorporated into the model in specific and highly ingenious ways.

"What If" Analysis.   The key advantage most computer-based systems have over their manual counterparts is the ease with which **sensitivity analysis** can be performed. Sensitivity analysis is often referred to as the process of asking **"what if"** with regard to the impact of certain changes in the planning assumptions or in external market conditions. For example, a computer-based cash budget can forecast the effect on funds requirements for "what if" questions such as:

1. *What if the collection period were to slow down to 75 days from 60 days?* This might be expected to increase the cash requirements significantly. As Exhibit 3b shows, the incremental cash requirement increases each month and, for the year, from

EXHIBIT 3a TAFT MANUFACTURING CO. 1980 CASH BUDGET: BASE PLAN
(000 OMITTED)[a]

	JAN	FEB	MAR	APR	MAY	JUN	JUL	AUG	SEP	OCT	NOV	DEC	1980
CASH RECEIPTS													
Cash Sales	$ 5,800	$ 5,900	$ 6,100	$ 6,200	$ 6,400	$ 6,900	$ 7,000	$ 7,200	$ 7,200	$ 7,500	$ 7,600	$ 7,700	$ 81,500
Collections	50,562	51,202	52,200	53,100	54,900	55,800	57,600	62,100	63,000	64,800	64,800	67,500	697,564
Decrease in Assets	419	0	0	0	0	0	0	0	0	0	0	0	419
Total Receipts	56,781	57,102	58,300	59,300	61,300	62,700	64,600	69,300	70,200	72,300	72,400	75,200	779,483
CASH EXPENDITURES													
Direct Labor	8,920	9,060	9,340	9,480	9,760	10,460	10,600	10,880	10,880	11,300	11,440	11,580	123,700
Direct Materials	35,560	35,680	36,240	37,360	37,920	39,040	41,840	42,400	43,520	43,520	45,200	45,760	484,040
Operating Expenses	11,020	11,210	11,590	11,780	12,160	13,110	13,300	13,680	13,680	14,250	14,440	14,630	154,850
Interest	2,786	0	0	3,117	0	0	3,573	0	0	4,096	0	0	13,572
Taxes	4,004	0	0	4,004	0	0	4,004	0	0	4,004	0	0	16,016
Dividends	0	2,500	0	0	2,500	0	0	2,500	0	0	2,500	0	10,000
Capital Expenditures	0	0	4,500	0	0	4,600	0	0	4,800	0	0	4,900	18,800
Purchase of Assets	0	336	672	336	672	1,680	336	672	0	1,008	336	336	6,384
Total Expenditures	62,290	58,786	62,342	66,077	63,012	68,890	73,653	70,132	72,880	78,178	73,916	77,206	827,362
Net Cash Flow	-5,509	-1,684	-4,042	-6,777	-1,712	-6,190	-9,053	-832	-2,680	-5,878	-1,516	-2,006	-47,879
Initial Cash w/o Loans	-12,449	-17,958	-19,642	-23,684	-30,461	-32,173	-38,363	-47,416	-48,248	-50,928	-56,806	-58,322	-58,322
Cumulative Cash	-17,958	-19,642	-23,684	-30,461	-32,173	-38,363	-47,416	-48,248	-50,928	-56,806	-58,322	-60,328	-60,328
Desired Cash Balance	16,704	16,992	17,568	17,856	18,432	19,872	20,160	20,736	20,736	21,600	21,888	22,176	22,176
Notes Payable	34,662	36,634	41,252	48,317	50,605	58,235	67,576	68,984	71,664	78,406	80,210	82,504	82,504

[a]Explanation for each receipt and expenditure appears under "Cash Budget Data." Notes payable on the bottom line indicates the required level of outside financing at the projected level of receipts and expenditures. It is significant that the Taft financial plan will require an increase in notes payable over the course of the year of nearly $50,000,000 (from $34,662,000 to $82,504,000). Planning for this increased borrowing is a primary use of the cash budget. So, also, is the detail on the *timing* of the requirements.

EXHIBIT 3b TAFT MANUFACTURING CO. 1980 CASH BUDGET: COLLECTION PERIOD 75 DAYS (000 OMITTED)

	JAN	FEB	MAR	APR	MAY	JUN	JUL	AUG	SEP	OCT	NOV	DEC	1980
CASH RECEIPTS													
Cash Sales	$ 5,800	$ 5,900	$ 6,100	$ 6,200	$ 6,400	$ 6,900	$ 7,000	$ 7,200	$ 7,200	$ 7,500	$ 7,600	$ 7,700	$ 81,500
Collections	50,246	50,882	51,701	52,650	54,000	55,350	56,700	59,850	62,550	63,900	64,800	66,150	688,779
Decrease in Assets	419	0	0	0	0	0	0	0	0	0	0	0	419
Total Receipts	56,465	56,782	57,801	58,850	60,400	62,250	63,700	67,050	69,750	71,400	72,400	73,850	770,698
CASH EXPENDITURES													
Direct Labor	8,920	9,060	9,340	9,480	9,760	10,460	10,600	10,880	10,880	11,300	11,440	11,580	123,700
Direct Materials	35,560	35,680	36,240	37,360	37,920	39,040	41,840	42,400	43,520	43,520	45,200	45,760	484,040
Operating Expenses	11,020	11,210	11,590	11,780	12,160	13,110	13,300	13,680	13,680	14,250	14,440	14,630	154,850
Interest	2,786	0	0	3,138	0	0	3,646	0	0	4,267	0	0	13,837
Taxes	4,004	0	0	4,004	0	0	4,004	0	0	4,004	0	0	16,016
Dividends	0	2,500	0	0	2,500	0	0	2,500	0	0	2,500	0	10,000
Capital Expenditures	0	0	4,500	0	0	4,600	0	0	4,800	0	0	4,900	18,800
Purchase of Assets	0	336	672	336	672	1,680	336	672	0	1,008	336	336	6,384
Total Expenditures	62,290	58,786	62,342	66,098	63,012	68,890	73,726	70,132	72,880	78,349	73,916	77,206	827,627
Net Cash Flow	-5,825	-2,004	-4,541	-7,248	-2,612	-6,640	-10,026	-3,082	-3,130	-6,949	-1,516	-3,356	-56,929
Initial Cash w/o Loans	-12,449	-18,274	-20,278	-24,819	-32,067	-34,679	-41,319	-51,345	-54,427	-57,557	-64,506	-66,022	
Cumulative Cash	-18,274	-20,278	-24,819	-32,067	-34,679	-41,319	-51,345	-54,427	-57,557	-64,506	-66,022	-69,378	-66,022
Desired Cash Balance	16,704	16,992	17,568	17,856	18,432	19,872	20,160	20,736	20,736	21,600	21,888	22,176	22,176
Notes Payable	34,978	37,270	42,387	49,923	53,111	61,191	71,505	75,163	78,293	86,106	87,910	91,554	91,554

EXHIBIT 3c TAFT MANUFACTURING CO. 1980 CASH BUDGET: COLLECTION PERIOD 45 DAYS (000 OMITTED)

	JAN	FEB	MAR	APR	MAY	JUN	JUL	AUG	SEP	OCT	NOV	DEC	1980
CASH RECEIPTS													
Cash Sales	$ 5,800	$ 5,900	$ 6,100	$ 6,200	$ 6,400	$ 6,900	$ 7,000	$ 7,200	$ 7,200	$ 7,500	$ 7,600	$ 7,700	$ 81,500
Collections	50,882	51,701	52,650	54,000	55,350	56,700	59,850	62,550	63,900	64,800	66,150	67,950	706,483
Decrease in Assets	419	0	0	0	0	0	0	0	0	0	0	0	419
Total Receipts	57,101	57,601	58,750	60,200	61,750	63,600	66,850	69,750	71,100	72,300	73,750	75,650	788,402
CASH EXPENDITURES													
Direct Labor	8,920	9,060	9,340	9,480	9,760	10,460	10,600	10,880	10,880	11,300	11,440	11,580	123,700
Direct Materials	35,560	35,680	36,240	37,360	37,920	39,040	41,840	42,400	43,520	43,520	45,200	45,760	484,040
Operating Expenses	11,020	11,210	11,590	11,780	12,160	13,110	13,300	13,680	13,680	14,250	14,440	14,630	154,850
Interest	2,786	0	0	3,092	0	0	3,488	0	0	3,897	0	0	13,263
Taxes	4,004	0	0	4,004	0	0	4,004	0	0	4,004	0	0	16,016
Dividends	0	2,500	0	0	2,500	0	0	2,500	0	0	2,500	0	10,000
Capital Expenditures	0	0	4,500	0	0	4,600	0	0	4,800	0	0	4,900	18,800
Purchase of Assets	0	336	672	336	672	1,680	336	672	0	1,008	336	336	6,384
Total Expenditures	62,290	58,786	62,342	66,052	63,012	68,890	73,568	70,132	72,880	77,979	73,916	77,206	827,053
Net Cash Flow	-5,189	-1,185	-3,592	-5,852	-1,262	-5,290	-6,718	-382	-1,780	-5,679	-166	-1,556	-38,651
Initial Cash w/o Loans	-12,449	-17,638	-18,823	-22,415	-28,267	-29,529	-34,819	-41,537	-41,919	-43,699	-49,378	-49,544	-49,544
Cumulative Cash	-17,638	-18,823	-22,415	-28,267	-29,529	-34,819	-41,537	-41,919	-43,699	-49,378	-49,544	-51,100	-51,100
Desired Cash Balance	16,704	16,992	17,568	17,856	18,432	19,872	20,160	20,736	21,600	21,888	22,176	22,176	
Notes Payable	34,342	35,815	39,983	46,123	47,961	54,691	61,697	62,655	64,435	70,978	71,432	73,276	73,276

EXHIBIT 3d TAFT MANUFACTURING CO. 1980 CASH BUDGET: SALES 20% ABOVE FORECAST (000 OMITTED)

	JAN	FEB	MAR	APR	MAY	JUN	JUL	AUG	SEP	OCT	NOV	DEC	1980
CASH RECEIPTS													
Cash Sales	$ 6,960	$ 7,080	$ 7,320	$ 7,440	$ 7,680	$ 8,280	$ 8,400	$ 8,640	$ 8,640	$ 9,000	$ 9,120	$ 9,240	$ 97,800
Collections	50,562	51,202	62,640	63,720	65,880	66,960	69,120	74,520	75,600	77,760	77,760	81,000	816,724
Total Receipts	57,522	58,282	69,960	71,160	73,560	75,240	77,520	83,160	84,240	86,760	86,880	90,240	914,524
CASH EXPENDITURES													
Direct Labor	10,544	10,712	11,043	11,216	11,552	12,392	12,560	12,896	12,896	13,400	13,558	13,736	146,520
Direct Materials	35,560	42,176	42,843	44,192	44,864	46,208	49,568	50,240	51,584	51,584	53,600	54,272	566,696
Operating Expenses	13,224	13,452	13,903	14,136	14,592	15,732	15,960	16,416	16,416	17,100	17,328	17,556	185,820
Interest	2,786	0	0	3,604	0	0	4,111	0	0	4,591	0	0	15,092
Taxes	4,004	0	0	4,004	0	0	4,004	0	0	4,004	0	0	16,016
Dividends	0	2,500	0	0	2,500	0	0	2,500	0	0	2,500	0	10,000
Capital Expenditures	0	0	4,500	0	0	4,600	0	0	4,300	0	0	4,900	18,800
Purchase of Assets	3,479	403	806	403	805	2,015	403	806	0	1,210	403	403	11,139
Total Expenditures	69,597	69,243	73,110	77,555	74,314	80,948	86,606	82,858	85,696	91,888	87,399	90,867	970,084
Net Cash Flow	-12,075	-10,961	-3,150	-6,395	-754	-5,708	-9,086	302	-1,456	-5,128	-519	-627	-55,560
Initial Cash w/o Loans	-12,449	-24,524	-35,485	-38,635	-45,031	-45,785	-51,493	-60,579	-60,278	-61,734	-66,862	-67,381	-67,381
Cumulative Cash	-24,524	-35,485	-38,635	-45,031	-45,785	-51,493	-60,579	-60,278	-61,734	-66,862	-67,381	-68,009	-68,009
Desired Cash Balance	20,045	20,390	21,082	21,427	22,118	23,846	24,192	24,883	24,883	25,920	26,266	26,611	26,611
Notes Payable	44,568	55,875	59,717	66,458	67,903	75,339	84,771	85,161	86,617	92,782	93,647	94,620	94,620

EXHIBIT 3e   TAFT MANUFACTURING CO. 1980 CASH BUDGET: SALES 10% BELOW FORECAST (000 OMITTED)

	JAN	FEB	MAR	APR	MAY	JUN	JUL	AUG	SEP	OCT	NOV	DEC	1980
CASH RECEIPTS													
Cash Sales	$ 5,220	$ 5,310	$ 5,490	$ 5,580	$ 5,760	$ 6,210	$ 6,300	$ 6,480	$ 6,480	$ 6,750	$ 6,840	$ 6,930	$ 73,350
Collections	50,562	51,202	46,980	47,790	49,410	50,220	51,840	55,890	56,700	58,320	58,320	60,750	637,984
Decrease in Assets	2,368	0	0	0	0	0	0	0	0	0	0	0	2,368
Total Receipts	58,150	56,512	52,470	53,370	55,170	56,430	58,140	62,370	63,180	65,070	65,160	67,680	713,702
CASH EXPENDITURES													
Direct Labor	8,108	8,234	8,486	8,612	8,864	9,494	9,620	9,872	9,872	10,250	10,376	10,502	112,290
Direct Materials	35,560	32,432	32,936	33,944	34,448	35,456	37,976	38,480	39,488	39,488	41,000	41,504	442,712
Operating Expenses	9,918	10,089	10,431	10,602	10,944	11,799	11,970	12,312	12,312	12,825	12,996	13,167	139,365
Interest	2,786	0	0	2,873	0	0	3,304	0	0	3,849	0	0	12,812
Taxes	4,004	0	0	4,004	0	0	4,004	0	0	4,004	0	0	16,016
Dividends	0	2,500	0	0	2,500	0	0	2,500	0	0	2,500	0	10,000
Capital Expenditures	0	0	4,500	0	0	4,600	0	0	4,800	0	0	4,900	18,800
Purchase of Assets	0	302	605	302	605	1,512	302	605	0	907	302	302	5,746
Total Expenditures	60,376	53,557	56,958	60,337	57,361	62,861	67,177	63,769	66,472	71,323	67,174	70,375	757,741
Net Cash Flow	-2,226	2,955	-4,488	-6,967	-2,191	-6,431	-9,037	-1,399	-3,292	-6,253	-2,014	-2,695	-44,039
Initial Cash w/o Loans	-12,449	-14,675	-11,721	-16,208	-23,176	-25,367	-31,798	-40,834	-42,233	-45,525	-51,778	-53,793	
Cumulative Cash	-14,675	-11,721	-16,208	-23,176	-25,367	-31,798	-40,834	-42,233	-45,525	-51,778	-53,793	-56,488	-53,793
Desired Cash Balance	15,034	15,293	15,811	16,070	16,589	17,885	18,144	18,662	19,440	19,699	19,958	19,958	19,958
Notes Payable	29,709	27,013	32,020	39,246	41,955	49,682	58,978	60,896	64,188	71,218	73,492	76,446	76,446

$47,879,000 to $56,929,000 (Exhibit 3*a*). The acceptability of this increase can be the basis for deciding whether a relaxation of credit terms can be tolerated.

2. *What if the collection period were reduced to 45 days?* Here the forecast would be that financing requirements will be reduced, as in fact they are by nearly $20,000,000 to $73,276,000, as shown in Exhibit 3*c*.

3. *What if sales were to exceed forecast by an additional 20%?* Under this assumption, financing requirements would be expected to increase. The increase is shown in Exhibit 3*d*, where financing requirements stand at $94,620,000.

4. *What if sales were to fall short of forecast by 10%?* Here, as shown in Exhibit 3*e*, the financing requirement is only $76,446,000, still significantly up from the requirement of $22,955,000 in notes payable at the end of 1979.

Of course numerous other possibilities might be investigated, such as an increase in sales of 40% **combined** with an increase in the collection period to 75 days. This would clearly increase financing requirements significantly.

Similarly, if assumptions about the fixed nature of overhead were examined, overhead might be programmed to be a fixed expense instead of a variable expense, as in the model presented. The number of combinations of possibilities is nearly infinite, so many forecasters arrange their forecasts into three categories: most likely, worst case, and best cases.

Most Likely.　This forecast, often called the "base case," is the forecast of Exhibit 3*a*. It is the forecast we would expect to be most accurate.

Worst Case.　This is the forecast with "everything going wrong." No "worst-case" forecast is made in the Taft example, but it would include a combination of Exhibits 3*b* (75-day collection period) and 3*d* (20% over forecast in sales). Note: **a sales increase might be considered to be a "best case" in terms of profit, but in terms of cash requirements it might be a "worst-case" event.**

Best Case.　This would involve a shortened collection period and modest increases in sales. If "best-case" assumptions are carried to the extreme, the financing requirements may actually drop over the period.

USES OF THE CASH BUDGET.　The primary use of the cash budget is to **estimate funds requirements and cash balances** under a variety of circumstances. Such budgets may also be valuable in formulating **financial strategy.** Examples include:

1. Timing in the declaration and payment of dividends. In some cases the cash budget may even dictate the nonpayment of dividends.

2. Negotiating loan repayment terms and selecting between short-term and long-term debt. This is particularly important where short-term loans are required to be "off the books" during part of the year.

3. Evaluating the cash effects of various accounts receivable policies, including offering discounts for early payment.

4. Planning and modifying capital expenditure policy.

5. Timing short-term investments, particularly marketable securities investments.

Each of these planning decisions is made easier by the basic cash budgets in Exhibits 3, including the variations that may occur.

FORECASTING BALANCE SHEETS AND INCOME STATEMENTS

USES OF PRO FORMA STATEMENTS.   Upon completion of the cash budget, the **projected financial statements** are prepared: the **pro forma balance sheet** and the **pro forma income statement.** These statements are used to:

1. Estimate profit (or loss) for the period (day, week, month, year).
2. Test alternate strategies and their financial effect on **reported** results.
3. Make estimates of asset requirements.
4. Make estimates of financing requirements, both short-term and long-term, for debt and equity.
5. Predict financial "bottlenecks" so that plans may be formulated.

INTERRELATIONSHIP OF PROJECTED STATEMENTS.   Before illustrating the preparation of projected financial statements, it is important to point out that since forecasted balance sheets and income statements are **mutually dependent,** the process may be somewhat circular. This circularity results because it is not possible to know the amount of borrowed funds that will be needed until an estimate of profit for the period is made. On the other hand, the profit estimate will be affected by the amount of funds borrowed, and the interest paid.

Usually the circularity problem is resolved by simply ignoring the interest cost of incremental financing during the forecast period on the assumption that this amount will not materially affect the result—at least not to an extent greater than the forecast error in general.

Because **changes** in interest cost over the planning period are usually small, the preparation of the income statement may be a logical starting point. If the incremental interest changes are significant, usually judged by inspection, the income statement can be reformulated after the balance sheet has been partially estimated; then a closer approximation of actual interest can be incorporated into the income statement. Increased interest will increase borrowing somewhat (by the amount of the added interest), and a slightly more accurate balance sheet and income statement will result.

For the perfectionist, a set of simultaneous equations may bring the balance sheet and income statement into alignment, but this refinement is seldom worth the effort in view of other forecast errors present. Most forecasters resolve the circularity problem by accepting the small amount of imprecision that is implicit in ignoring incremental interest charges.

PREPARING PRO FORMA INCOME STATEMENTS.   There are two methods commonly used to prepare projected income statements. They are:

Percent of Sales Method.   The percent of sales method is a simple method for forecasting the income statement where **historical** expense ratios are applied to the sales forecast. These historical ratios may either be based on the most recent year (or shorter period), or they may be a historical average of the most recent 5 years or 3 years. Deciding on the appropriate historical ratios to apply to the future is a subjective judgment that militates against the otherwise "objective" nature of this technique.

Budgeted Expense Method.   The budgeted expense method is most appropriate when future expenses are expected to deviate substantially from historical expenses. This may be the case when depreciation is expected to increase because of new capital expenditures or the price of labor and raw materials is expected to go up more (or less) than sales prices.

Observers differ on the merits of the two methods. Both have essentially the same results. The percent of sales method tends to be more historical in its orientation, while the budgeted revenue and expense method attempts to capture future performance where it might differ from past history. Depending on the method selected, either **historical** or **target** data may be used.

It is also possible to combine the **percent of sales method** with the **budgeted expense method.** For example, the "cost of goods sold" figure may correlate well with sales, while portions of overhead may be more discretionary, as in the amount of depreciation charged. Thus the pro forma income statement can be purely a percent of sales forecast or a modified percent of sales forecast.

PROJECTED INCOME STATEMENT DATA.   The projected income statement should contain the following items, in the order given:

1. *Sales.* This forecast is taken from marketing department forecasts as in the foregoing cash budget subsection.
2. *Cost of goods sold (COGS).* Projected to be 70% of sales [for the Taft Manufacturing Co. example].
3. *Operating expenses.* Projected at 19% of monthly sales plus $1.2 million depreciation expense per month.
4. *Interest.* Based on 8.5% of long-term debt and 13% of notes payable. For monthly forecasts, one-twelfth of the annual amount is used.
5. *Income taxes.* Estimated at 50% of profit before taxes.
6. *Dividends.* Expected to increase dramatically from 1979 to $10,000,000 over the year paid quarterly.

Exhibit 4*a* shows the pro forma income statement for Taft by month for 1980, with explanations for each line item. The resulting profit figures demonstrate good and consistent profit growth for 1980.

Exhibits 4*b* and 4*c* show the monthly profit figures with a 20% increase in sales over forecast and a 10% decrease in sales from forecast, respectively. Note that profits vary from $26,015,000 to $38,016,000 with the assumptions built into the forecast model. If more of the overhead were fixed, instead of variable, this variation would, of course, increase.

PREPARING PRO FORMA BALANCE SHEETS.   When the cash budget and pro forma income statements are complete, the pro forma balance sheet must be prepared. This statement incorporates the effect of the projected income statement on equity and the effect of the cash budget on the cash position. The pro forma balance sheet presents the **financial condition** of the firm as a result of the financial performance anticipated.

Information Required.   The information for the pro forma balance sheets is primarily derived from the operating data provided for the cash budget and from certain other information as noted in the list below.

Sample pro forma balance sheets are presented in Exhibits 5. Exhibit 5*a* demonstrates the financial position under the **base plan** and corresponds to Exhibits 3*a* in the cash budget and 4*a* in the pro forma income statement.

EXHIBIT 4a TAFT MANUFACTURING CO. 1980 INCOME STATEMENT: BASE PLAN (000 OMITTED)

	JAN	FEB	MAR	APR	MAY	JUN	JUL	AUG	SEP	OCT	NOV	DEC	1980
Sales	58,000	59,000	61,000	62,000	64,000	69,000	70,000	72,000	72,000	75,000	76,000	77,000	815,000
COGS	40,600	41,300	42,700	43,400	44,800	48,300	49,000	50,400	50,400	52,500	53,200	53,900	570,500
Gross Profit	17,400	17,700	18,300	18,600	19,200	20,700	21,000	21,600	21,600	22,500	22,800	23,100	244,500
Operating Expense	12,220	12,410	12,790	12,980	13,360	14,310	14,500	14,880	14,880	15,450	15,640	15,830	169,250
Operating Profit	5,180	5,290	5,510	5,620	5,840	6,390	6,500	6,720	6,720	7,050	7,160	7,270	75,250
Interest	1,010	1,030	1,077	1,149	1,173	1,251	1,347	1,361	1,388	1,457	1,476	1,499	15,219
Profit Before Taxes	4,170	4,260	4,433	4,471	4,667	5,139	5,153	5,359	5,332	5,593	5,684	5,771	60,031
Income Taxes	2,085	2,130	2,216	2,235	2,334	2,569	2,577	2,679	2,666	2,796	2,842	2,885	30,015
Net Income	2,085	2,130	2,216	2,235	2,334	2,569	2,577	2,679	2,666	2,796	2,842	2,885	30,015
Dividends	0	2,500	0	0	2,500	0	0	2,500	0	0	2,500	0	10,000
Change to Net Worth	2,085	-370	2,216	2,235	-166	2,569	2,577	179	2,666	2,796	342	2,885	20,015

EXHIBIT 4b TAFT MANUFACTURING CO. 1980 INCOME STATEMENT: SALES 20% ABOVE FORECAST (000 OMITTED)

	JAN	FEB	MAR	APR	MAY	JUN	JUL	AUG	SEP	OCT	NOV	DEC	1980
Sales	69,600	70,800	73,200	74,400	76,800	92,800	84,000	86,400	86,400	90,000	91,200	92,400	978,000
COGS	48,720	49,560	51,240	52,080	53,760	57,960	58,800	60,480	60,480	63,000	63,840	64,680	684,600
Gross Profit	20,880	21,240	21,960	22,320	23,040	24,840	25,200	25,920	25,920	27,000	27,360	27,720	293,400
Operating Expense	14,424	14,652	15,108	15,336	15,792	16,932	17,160	17,616	17,616	18,300	18,528	18,756	200,220
Operating Profit	6,456	6,588	6,852	6,984	7,248	7,908	8,040	8,304	8,304	8,700	8,832	8,964	93,180
Interest	1,111	1,227	1,266	1,335	1,350	1,426	1,523	1,527	1,542	1,605	1,614	1,623	17,148
Profit Before Taxes	5,345	5,361	5,586	5,649	5,898	6,482	6,517	6,777	6,762	7,095	7,218	7,341	76,032
Income Taxes	2,672	2,681	2,793	2,824	2,949	3,241	3,259	3,389	3,381	3,548	3,609	3,670	38,016
Net Income	2,672	2,681	2,793	2,824	2,949	3,241	3,259	3,389	3,381	3,548	3,609	3,670	38,016
Dividends	0	2,500	0	0	2,500	0	0	2,500	0	0	2,500	0	10,000
Change to Net Worth	2,672	181	2,793	2,824	449	3,241	3,259	889	3,381	3,548	1,109	3,670	28,016

EXHIBIT 4c TAFT MANUFACTURING CO. 1980 INCOME STATEMENT: SALES 10% BELOW FORECAST (000 OMITTED)

	JAN	FEB	MAR	APR	MAY	JUN	JUL	AUG	SEP	OCT	NOV	DEC	1980
Sales	52,200	53,100	54,900	55,800	57,600	62,100	63,000	64,800	64,800	67,500	68,400	69,300	733,500
COGS	36,540	37,170	38,430	39,060	40,320	43,470	44,100	45,360	45,360	47,250	47,880	48,510	513,450
Gross Profit	15,660	15,930	16,470	16,740	17,280	18,630	18,900	19,440	19,440	20,250	20,520	20,790	220,050
Operating Expense	11,118	11,289	11,631	11,802	12,144	12,999	13,170	13,512	13,512	14,025	14,196	14,367	153,765
Operating Profit	4,542	4,641	4,839	4,938	5,136	5,631	5,730	5,928	5,928	6,225	6,324	6,423	66,285
Interest	959	931	983	1,057	1,084	1,163	1,259	1,278	1,312	1,384	1,407	1,437	14,255
Profit Before Taxes	3,583	3,710	3,856	3,881	4,052	4,468	4,471	4,650	4,616	4,841	4,917	4,986	52,030
Income Taxes	1,792	1,855	1,928	1,941	2,026	2,234	2,236	2,325	2,308	2,421	2,458	2,493	26,015
Net Income	1,792	1,855	1,928	1,941	2,026	2,234	2,236	2,325	2,308	2,421	2,458	2,493	26,015
Dividends	0	2,500	0	0	2,500	0	0	2,500	0	0	2,500	0	10,000
Change to Net Worth	1,792	-645	1,928	1,941	-474	2,234	2,236	-175	2,308	2,421	-42	2,493	16,015

It is important to note that the notes payable account in the pro forma balance sheet should correspond to the notes payable line on the cash budget for the corresponding case of assumptions, for example, collection period and sales. If this does not occur, an error has been made in the financial forecast. The three statements, the cash budget, income statement, and balance sheet, should be consistent and should reconcile to each other. If this is not the case, an error has been made.

The items below explain the calculation of each account in the pro forma balance sheet of our example.

1. *Cash/securities*. This represents cash and short-term marketable securities and is maintained at 28.8% of current monthly sales (a historical number).

2. *Accounts receivable*. Calculated to be equal to the amount of credit sales for the current month and the previous month.

3. *Inventories*. Calculated to increase by $4 million per month throughout the year.

4. *Other current assets*. Calculated at 18% of monthly sales, 1.5% (historical number).

5. *Net plant and equipment*. Calculated after deducting the effect of $4 million depreciation expense per month, plus scheduled capital expenditures.

6. *Other long-term assets*. Kept at 15.6% of monthly sales, 1.3% of annual sales.

7. *Accounts payable*. Equal to the direct materials cost for the current month.

8. *Notes payable*. A "plug figure" that equals amount required to maintain the desired level of cash and marketable securities. Calculated after all other accounts have been computed, "notes payable" is the amount required to make the balance sheet balance.

9. *Other current liabilities*. Increases by the amount of accrued interest and taxes for the current month, and decreases by the amount of any payments that take place.

10. *Long-term debt*. The principal amount of $96 million, which is not scheduled to change in 1980.

11. *Common stock and capital surplus*. Not expected to change for 1980 because no new equity issue or share repurchase is scheduled.

12. *Retained earnings*. Increases each month by the amount of profit after taxes, less any dividends paid.

Specific Use of Pro Forma Balance Sheet.   The primary use of the pro forma balance sheet is to assess the financial feasibility of the plan. Judgments may be made about the **liquidity** and **debt ratios** that result to determine whether the financial strength of the company will be compromised in the coming year. In the case of Taft, the pro forma balance sheet indicates that total liabilities will grow over the course of the year to over 50% of assets as shown in Exhibit 5a. Should such growth in liabilities be considered imprudent, a modified plan might include:

1. New equity financing.
2. Postponed capital expenditures.
3. Reduced dividend.
4. Increased prices to improve profits and increase retained earnings.

EXHIBIT 5a TAFT MANUFACTURING CO. 1980 BALANCE SHEET: BASE PLAN
(000 OMITTED)

	JAN	FEB	MAR	APR	MAY	JUN	JUL	AUG	SEP	OCT	NOV	DEC	1980
ASSETS													
Cash/Securities	16,704	16,992	17,568	17,856	18,432	19,872	20,160	20,736	20,736	21,600	21,888	22,176	22,176
Accounts Receivable	103,402	105,300	108,000	110,700	113,400	119,700	125,100	127,800	129,600	132,300	135,900	137,700	137,700
Inventories	181,038	185,038	189,038	193,038	197,038	201,038	205,038	209,038	213,038	217,038	221,038	225,038	225,038
Other Curr Assets	10,440	10,620	10,980	11,160	11,520	12,420	12,600	12,960	12,960	13,500	13,680	13,860	13,860
Total Curr Assets	311,584	317,950	325,586	332,754	340,390	353,030	362,898	370,534	376,334	384,438	392,506	398,774	398,774
Net Plant and Equipment	66,810	65,610	68,910	67,710	66,510	69,910	68,710	67,510	71,110	69,910	68,710	72,410	72,410
Other Long-Term Assets	9,048	9,204	9,516	9,672	9,984	10,784	10,920	11,232	11,232	11,700	11,856	12,012	12,012
Total Assets	387,442	392,764	404,012	410,136	416,884	433,704	442,528	449,276	458,676	466,048	473,072	483,196	483,196
LIABILITIES AND NET WORTH													
Accounts Payable	35,680	36,240	37,360	37,920	39,040	41,840	42,400	43,520	43,520	45,200	45,760	46,320	46,320
Notes Payable	34,662	36,634	41,252	48,317	50,605	58,235	67,576	68,984	71,664	78,406	80,210	82,504	82,504
Other Curr Liabilities	15,107	18,267	21,560	17,824	21,331	25,151	21,497	25,538	29,592	25,746	30,064	34,448	34,448
Total Curr Liabilitie	85,449	91,141	100,172	104,061	110,976	125,226	131,473	138,042	144,776	149,352	156,034	163,273	163,273
Long-Term Debt	96,000	96,000	96,000	96,000	96,000	96,000	96,000	96,000	96,000	96,000	96,000	96,000	96,000
Total Liabilities	181,449	187,141	196,172	200,061	206,976	221,226	227,473	234,042	240,776	245,352	252,034	259,273	259,273
Common Stock	48,960	48,960	48,960	48,960	48,960	48,960	48,960	48,960	48,960	48,960	48,960	48,960	48,960
Capital Surplus	43,563	43,563	43,563	43,563	43,563	43,563	43,563	43,563	43,563	43,563	43,563	43,563	43,563
Retained Earnings	113,470	113,100	115,317	117,552	117,385	119,955	122,532	122,711	125,377	128,173	128,515	131,400	131,400
Net Worth	205,993	205,623	207,840	210,075	209,908	212,478	215,055	215,234	217,900	220,696	221,038	223,923	223,923
Total Capitalization	387,442	392,764	404,012	410,136	416,884	433,704	442,528	449,276	458,676	466,048	473,072	483,196	483,196

EXHIBIT 5b TAFT MANUFACTURING CO. 1980 BALANCE SHEET: COLLECTION PERIOD 75 DAYS (000 OMITTED)

	JAN	FEB	MAR	APR	MAY	JUN	JUL	AUG	SEP	OCT	NOV	DEC	1980
ASSETS													
Cash/Securities	16,704	16,992	17,568	17,856	18,432	19,872	20,160	20,736	20,736	21,600	21,888	22,176	22,176
Accounts Receivable	103,718	105,936	109,135	112,285	115,885	122,635	128,935	133,885	136,135	139,735	143,335	146,485	146,485
Inventories	181,038	185,038	189,038	193,038	197,038	201,038	205,038	209,038	213,038	217,038	221,038	225,038	225,038
Other Curr Assets	10,440	10,620	10,980	11,160	11,520	12,420	12,600	12,960	12,960	13,500	13,680	13,860	13,860
Total Curr Assets	311,900	318,586	326,721	334,339	342,875	355,965	366,733	376,619	382,869	391,873	399,941	407,559	407,559
Net Plant and Equipment	66,810	65,610	68,910	67,710	66,510	69,910	68,710	67,510	71,110	69,910	68,710	72,410	72,410
Other Long-Term Assets	9,048	9,204	9,516	9,672	9,984	10,764	10,920	11,232	11,232	11,700	11,856	12,012	12,012
Total Assets	387,758	393,400	405,147	411,721	419,369	436,639	446,363	455,361	465,211	473,483	480,507	491,981	491,981
LIABILITIES AND NET WORTH													
Accounts Payable	35,680	36,240	37,360	37,920	39,040	41,840	42,400	43,520	43,520	45,200	45,760	46,320	46,320
Notes Payable	34,978	37,270	42,387	49,923	53,111	61,191	71,505	75,163	78,293	86,106	87,910	91,554	91,554
Other Curr Liabilities	15,108	18,272	21,571	17,822	21,341	25,177	21,471	25,543	29,631	25,653	30,010	34,441	34,441
Total Curr Liabilitie	85,766	91,782	101,318	105,665	113,492	128,208	135,375	144,225	151,444	156,959	163,680	172,315	172,315
Long-Term Debt	96,000	96,000	96,000	96,000	96,000	96,000	96,000	96,000	96,000	96,000	96,000	96,000	96,000
Total Liabilities	181,766	187,782	197,318	201,665	209,492	224,208	231,375	240,225	247,444	252,959	259,680	268,315	268,315
Common Stock	48,960	48,960	48,960	48,960	48,960	48,960	48,960	48,960	48,960	48,960	48,960	48,960	48,960
Capital Surplus	43,563	43,563	43,563	43,563	43,563	43,563	43,563	43,563	43,563	43,563	43,563	43,563	43,563
Retained Earnings	113,469	113,095	115,306	117,533	117,354	119,908	122,465	122,613	125,244	128,001	128,304	131,143	131,143
Net Worth	205,992	205,618	207,829	210,056	209,877	212,431	214,988	215,136	217,767	220,524	220,827	223,666	223,666
Total Capitalization	387,758	393,400	405,147	411,721	419,369	436,639	446,363	455,361	465,211	473,483	480,507	491,981	491,981

EXHIBIT 5c   TAFT MANUFACTURING CO. 1980 BALANCE SHEET: COLLECTION
PERIOD 45 DAYS (000 OMITTED)

	JAN	FEB	MAR	APR	MAY	JUN	JUL	AUG	SEP	OCT	NOV	DEC	1980
ASSETS													
Cash/Securities	16,704	16,992	17,568	17,856	18,432	19,872	20,160	20,736	20,736	21,600	21,888	22,176	22,176
Accounts Receivable	103,082	104,481	106,731	108,531	110,781	116,181	119,331	121,581	122,481	125,181	127,431	128,781	128,781
Inventories	181,038	185,038	189,038	193,038	197,038	201,038	205,038	209,038	213,038	217,038	221,038	225,038	225,038
Other Curr Assets	10,440	10,620	10,980	11,160	11,520	12,420	12,600	12,960	12,960	13,500	13,680	13,860	13,860
Total Curr Assets	311,264	317,131	324,317	330,585	337,771	349,511	357,129	364,315	369,215	377,319	384,037	389,855	389,855
Net Plant and Equipment	66,810	65,610	68,910	67,710	66,510	69,910	68,710	67,510	71,110	69,910	68,710	72,410	72,410
Other Long-Term Assets	9,048	9,204	9,516	9,672	9,984	10,764	10,920	11,232	11,232	11,700	11,856	12,012	12,012
Total Assets	387,122	391,945	402,743	407,967	414,265	430,185	436,759	443,057	451,557	458,929	464,603	474,277	474,277
LIABILITIES AND NET WORTH													
Accounts Payable	35,680	36,240	37,360	37,920	39,040	41,840	42,400	43,520	43,520	45,200	45,760	46,320	46,320
Notes Payable	34,342	35,815	39,983	46,123	47,961	54,691	61,697	62,655	64,435	70,978	71,432	73,276	73,276
Other Curr Liabilities	15,105	18,261	21,548	17,825	21,318	25,121	21,522	25,531	29,548	25,862	30,135	34,473	34,473
Total Curr Liabilitie	85,127	90,316	98,891	101,869	108,319	121,652	125,619	131,705	137,502	142,040	147,327	154,069	154,069
Long-Term Debt	96,000	96,000	96,000	96,000	96,000	96,000	96,000	96,000	96,000	96,000	96,000	96,000	96,000
Total Liabilities	181,127	186,316	194,891	197,869	204,319	217,652	221,619	227,705	233,502	238,040	243,327	250,069	250,069
Common Stock	48,960	48,960	48,960	48,960	48,960	48,960	48,960	48,960	48,960	48,960	48,960	48,960	48,960
Capital Surplus	43,563	43,563	43,563	43,563	43,563	43,563	43,563	43,563	43,563	43,563	43,563	43,563	43,563
Retained Earnings	113,472	113,106	115,329	117,575	117,423	120,010	122,617	122,829	125,532	128,366	128,753	131,685	131,685
Net Worth	205,995	205,629	207,852	210,098	209,946	212,533	215,140	215,352	218,055	220,889	221,276	224,208	224,208
Total Capitalization	387,122	391,945	402,743	407,967	414,265	430,185	436,759	443,057	451,557	458,929	464,603	474,277	474,277

EXHIBIT 5d TAFT MANUFACTURING CO. 1980 BALANCE SHEET: SALES 20% ABOVE FORECAST (000 OMITTED)

	JAN	FEB	MAR	APR	MAY	JUN	JUL	AUG	SEP	OCT	NOV	DEC	1980
ASSETS													
Cash/Securities	20,045	20,390	21,082	21,427	22,118	23,846	24,192	24,883	24,883	25,920	26,266	26,611	26,611
Accounts Receivable	113,842	126,360	129,600	132,840	136,080	143,640	150,120	153,360	155,520	158,760	163,080	165,240	165,240
Inventories	181,038	185,038	189,038	193,038	197,038	201,038	205,038	209,038	213,038	217,038	221,038	225,038	225,038
Other Curr Assets	12,528	12,744	13,176	13,392	13,824	14,904	15,120	15,552	15,552	16,200	16,416	16,632	16,632
Total Curr Assets	327,453	344,532	352,896	360,697	369,060	383,428	394,470	402,833	408,993	417,918	426,800	433,521	433,521
Net Plant and Equipment	66,810	65,610	68,910	67,710	66,510	69,910	68,710	67,510	71,110	69,910	68,710	72,410	72,410
Other Long-Term Assets	10,858	11,045	11,419	11,606	11,981	12,917	13,104	13,478	13,478	14,040	14,227	14,414	14,414
Total Assets	405,120	421,187	433,225	440,014	447,551	466,255	476,284	483,822	493,582	501,868	509,737	520,346	520,346
LIABILITIES AND NET WORTH													
Accounts Payable	42,176	42,848	44,192	44,864	46,208	49,568	50,240	51,584	51,584	53,600	54,272	54,944	54,944
Notes Payable	44,568	55,875	59,717	66,458	67,903	75,339	84,771	85,161	86,617	92,782	93,647	94,620	94,620
Other Curr Liabilities	15,796	19,703	23,762	20,314	24,613	29,280	25,946	30,861	35,784	32,341	37,564	42,858	42,858
Total Curr Liabilitie	102,540	118,426	127,671	131,635	138,724	154,187	160,957	167,606	173,985	178,723	185,483	192,422	192,422
Long-Term Debt	96,000	96,000	96,000	96,000	96,000	96,000	96,000	96,000	96,000	96,000	96,000	96,000	96,000
Total Liabilities	198,540	214,426	223,671	227,635	234,724	250,187	256,957	263,606	269,985	274,723	281,483	288,422	288,422
Common Stock	48,960	48,960	48,960	48,960	48,960	48,960	48,960	48,960	48,960	48,960	48,960	48,960	48,960
Capital Surplus	43,563	43,563	43,563	43,563	43,563	43,563	43,563	43,563	43,563	43,563	43,563	43,563	43,563
Retained Earnings	114,057	114,238	117,031	119,855	120,304	123,545	126,804	127,693	131,074	134,622	135,731	139,401	139,401
Net Worth	206,580	206,761	209,554	212,378	212,827	216,068	219,327	220,216	223,597	227,145	228,254	231,924	231,924
Total Capitalization	405,120	421,187	433,225	440,014	447,551	466,255	476,284	483,822	493,582	501,868	509,737	520,346	520,346

EXHIBIT 5e TAFT MANUFACTURING CO. 1980 BALANCE SHEET AS PERCENT OF SALES: SALES 10% BELOW FORECAST

	JAN	FEB	MAR	APR	MAY	JUN	JUL	AUG	SEP	OCT	NOV	DEC	1980
ASSETS													
Cash/Securities	2.4%	2.4%	2.4%	2.4%	2.4%	2.4%	2.4%	2.4%	2.4%	2.4%	2.4%	2.4%	2.7%
Accounts Receivable	15.7	14.9	14.8	14.9	14.8	14.5	14.9	14.8	15.0	14.7	14.9	14.9	16.9
Inventories	28.9	29.0	28.7	28.8	28.5	27.0	27.1	26.9	27.4	26.8	26.9	27.1	30.7
Other Curr Assets	1.5	1.5	1.5	1.5	1.5	1.5	1.5	1.5	1.5	1.5	1.5	1.5	1.7
Total Curr Assets	48.5	47.8	47.3	47.6	47.2	45.3	45.9	45.6	46.3	45.4	45.7	45.9	52.0
Net Plant and Equipment	10.7	10.3	10.5	10.1	9.6	9.4	9.1	8.7	9.1	8.6	8.4	8.7	9.9
Other Long-Term Assets	1.3	1.3	1.3	1.3	1.3	1.3	1.3	1.3	1.3	1.3	1.3	1.3	1.5
Total Assets	60.4	59.4	59.1	59.0	58.1	56.0	56.3	55.6	56.7	55.3	55.4	55.9	63.3
LIABILITIES AND NET WORTH													
Accounts Payable	5.2	5.2	5.2	5.1	5.1	5.1	5.1	5.1	5.1	5.1	5.1	5.1	5.7
Notes Payable	4.7	4.2	4.9	5.9	6.1	6.7	7.8	7.8	8.3	8.8	9.0	9.2	10.4
Other Curr Liabilities	2.4	2.8	3.1	2.5	2.8	3.1	2.5	2.9	3.4	2.8	3.2	3.6	4.1
Total Curr Liabilitie	12.3	12.2	13.1	13.5	14.0	14.9	15.4	15.9	16.7	16.6	17.2	17.9	20.3
Long-Term Debt	15.3	15.1	14.6	14.3	13.9	12.9	12.7	12.3	12.3	11.9	11.7	11.5	13.1
Total Liabilities	27.6	27.2	27.7	27.8	27.9	27.7	28.1	28.2	29.1	28.5	28.9	29.4	33.4
Common Stock	7.8	7.7	7.4	7.3	7.1	6.6	6.5	6.3	6.3	6.0	6.0	5.9	6.7
Capital Surplus	7.0	6.8	6.6	6.5	6.3	5.8	5.8	5.6	5.6	5.4	5.3	5.2	5.9
Retained Earnings	18.1	17.7	17.4	17.4	16.8	15.9	15.9	15.5	15.8	15.4	15.2	15.3	17.4
Net Worth	32.8	32.2	31.4	31.2	30.2	28.3	28.2	27.4	27.7	26.8	26.5	26.4	30.0
Total Capitalization	60.4	59.4	59.1	59.0	58.1	56.0	56.3	55.6	56.7	55.3	55.4	55.9	63.3

Throughout the process of formulating the plan, it is apparent that many interrelationships exist requiring repeated reworking of the plan according to varying assumptions and constraints, such as a debt-assets limit. Fortunately, Taft appears to be able to sustain the growth projected unless the 50% limit on total liabilities proves to be limiting.

COMMON-SIZE BALANCE SHEET. The "common-size" balance sheet is a financial forecasting tool that serves to identify some of the **trends** that will take place under the proposed plan. Through the common-size balance sheet, the financial forecaster can assess the **acceptability** of the plan to the company and to the outside world. The level of debt, assets and equity is portrayed in percentage terms over the forecast period.

Exhibits 6*a-c* show the forecast balance sheets in percentage terms for the base case, for a 75-day collection period, and for sales at 20% over forecast. It is apparent in each of these statements that **equity is not keeping pace with sales growth** as it declines from 53.2% of assets at the beginning of the year to 46.3% of assets in December 1980. Concurrently total debt has increased to fill the gap from 46.8% of assets to 53.7% in December. Thus Taft faces the prospect of new equity financing or the need to reduce future sales, if debt is not to rise above reasonable levels.

It is also apparent from the common-size balance sheet that the liquidity of Taft during 1980 is not in serious **short-term** jeopardy. Only the trend of declining liquidity is alarming, meaning that some increase in long-term financing may be required in the 2–5 year period if sales continue to expand at a rate of 25% per year.

A FEASIBLE FINANCIAL PLAN

ASSESSING OVERALL FINANCIAL FORECAST. One of the most frequent uses of a financial forecast is the assessment of the **feasibility of plans for growth.** The notion of feasibility stems from the fact that most firms do not have unlimited access to external sources of funds; thus many of the funds they require for growth must be generated internally. Therefore, a consistent and logical financial forecast is essential. **Some levels of growth are simply not sustainable without massive infusions of outside capital or significant changes in historical financial ratios.** In the example that follows, the concept of "sustainable" or feasible growth is developed as a financial forecasting tool. This tool supplements the cash budget and pro forma statements in an overall financial plan.

BASIC VARIABLES. To assess the components of a financial plan, it is useful to view financial performance in terms of the **basic variables** that govern the financial process. Thus, beneath the apparent complexity of many financial statements a few **basic financial ratios** serve as the key components of overall financial results. Each of these **prime** variables (Exhibit 7) encompasses several subsidiary strategy variables as noted in Exhibit 8.

Examining these prime variables allows for improved focus on the most sensitive parts of the financial plan to changes in the feasible growth rate. In some sense, each of these variables is a **control lever** in the guidance system of the firm. Although it is often easier to identify relationships than it is to modify them, it is useful to know where attention must be focused.

EXHIBIT 6a   TAFT MANUFACTURING CO. COMMON-SIZE BALANCE SHEET: BASE PLAN

	JAN	FEB	MAR	APR	MAY	JUN	JUL	AUG	SEP	OCT	NOV	DEC	1980
ASSETS													
Cash/Securities	4.3%	4.3%	4.3%	4.4%	4.4%	4.6%	4.6%	4.6%	4.5%	4.6%	4.6%	4.6%	4.6%
Accounts Receivable	26.7	26.8	26.8	27.0	27.2	27.6	28.3	28.4	28.3	28.4	28.4	28.5	28.5
Inventories	46.7	47.1	46.8	47.1	47.3	46.4	46.3	46.5	46.4	46.6	46.7	46.6	46.6
Other Curr Assets	2.7	2.7	2.7	2.7	2.8	2.9	2.8	2.9	2.8	2.9	2.9	2.9	2.9
Total Curr Assets	80.4	81.0	80.6	81.1	81.7	81.4	82.0	82.5	82.0	82.5	83.0	82.5	82.5
Net Plant and Equipment	17.2	16.7	17.1	16.5	16.0	16.1	15.5	15.0	15.5	15.0	14.5	15.0	15.0
Other Long-Term Assets	2.3	2.3	2.4	2.4	2.4	2.5	2.5	2.5	2.4	2.5	2.5	2.5	2.5
Total Assets	100.0	100.0	100.0	100.0	100.0	100.0	100.0	100.0	100.0	100.0	100.0	100.0	100.0
LIABILITIES AND NET WORTH													
Accounts Payable	9.2	9.2	9.2	9.2	9.4	9.6	9.6	9.7	9.5	9.7	9.7	9.6	9.6
Notes Payable	8.9	9.3	10.2	11.8	12.1	13.4	15.3	15.4	15.6	16.8	17.0	17.1	17.1
Other Curr Liabilities	3.9	4.7	5.3	4.3	5.1	5.8	4.9	5.7	6.5	5.5	6.4	7.1	7.1
Total Curr Liabilitie	22.1	23.2	24.8	25.4	26.6	28.9	29.7	30.7	31.6	32.0	33.0	33.8	33.8
Long-Term Debt	24.8	24.4	23.8	23.4	23.0	22.1	21.7	21.4	20.9	20.6	20.3	19.9	19.9
Total Liabilities	46.8	47.6	48.6	48.8	49.6	51.0	51.4	52.1	52.5	52.6	53.3	53.7	53.7
Common Stock	12.6	12.5	12.1	11.9	11.7	11.3	11.1	10.9	10.7	10.5	10.3	10.1	10.1
Capital Surplus	11.2	11.1	10.8	10.6	10.4	10.0	9.8	9.7	9.5	9.3	9.2	9.0	9.0
Retained Earnings	29.3	28.8	28.5	28.2	28.2	27.7	27.7	27.3	27.3	27.5	27.2	27.2	27.2
Net Worth	53.2	52.4	51.4	51.2	50.4	49.0	48.6	47.9	47.5	47.4	46.7	46.3	46.3
Total Capitalization	100.0	100.0	100.0	100.0	100.0	100.0	100.0	100.0	100.0	100.0	100.0	100.0	100.0

EXHIBIT 6b TAFT MANUFACTURING CO. COMMON-SIZE BALANCE SHEET: COLLECTION PERIOD 75 DAYS

	JAN	FEB	MAR	APR	MAY	JUN	JUL	AUG	SEP	OCT	NOV	DEC	1980
ASSETS													
Cash/Securities	4.3%	4.3%	4.3%	4.3%	4.4%	4.6%	4.5%	4.6%	4.5%	4.6%	4.6%	4.5%	4.5%
Accounts Receivable	26.7	26.9	26.9	27.3	27.6	28.1	28.9	29.4	29.3	29.5	29.8	29.8	29.8
Inventories	46.7	47.0	46.7	46.9	47.0	46.0	45.9	45.9	45.8	45.8	46.0	45.7	45.7
Other Curr Assets	2.7	2.7	2.7	2.7	2.7	2.8	2.8	2.8	2.8	2.9	2.8	2.8	2.8
Total Curr Assets	80.4	81.0	80.6	81.2	81.8	81.5	82.2	82.7	82.3	82.8	83.2	82.8	82.8
Net Plant and Equipment	17.2	16.7	17.0	16.4	15.9	16.0	15.4	14.8	15.3	14.8	14.3	14.7	14.7
Other Long-Term Assets	2.3	2.3	2.3	2.3	2.4	2.5	2.4	2.5	2.4	2.5	2.5	2.4	2.4
Total Assets	100.0	100.0	100.0	100.0	100.0	100.0	100.0	100.0	100.0	100.0	100.0	100.0	100.0
LIABILITIES AND NET WORTH													
Accounts Payable	9.2	9.2	9.2	9.2	9.3	9.6	9.5	9.6	9.4	9.5	9.5	9.4	9.4
Notes Payable	9.0	9.5	10.5	12.1	12.7	14.0	16.0	16.5	16.8	18.2	18.3	18.6	18.6
Other Curr Liabilities	3.9	4.6	5.3	4.3	5.1	5.8	4.8	5.6	6.4	5.4	6.2	7.0	7.0
Total Curr Liabilitie	22.1	23.3	25.0	25.7	27.1	29.4	30.3	31.7	32.6	33.1	34.1	35.0	35.0
Long-Term Debt	24.8	24.4	23.7	23.3	22.9	22.0	21.5	21.1	20.6	20.3	20.0	19.5	19.5
Total Liabilities	46.9	47.7	48.7	49.0	50.0	51.3	51.8	52.8	53.2	53.4	54.0	54.5	54.5
Common Stock	12.6	12.4	12.1	11.9	11.7	11.2	11.0	10.8	10.5	10.3	10.2	10.0	10.0
Capital Surplus	11.2	11.1	10.8	10.8	10.4	10.0	9.8	9.6	9.4	9.2	9.1	8.9	8.9
Retained Earnings	29.3	28.7	28.5	28.5	28.0	27.5	27.4	26.9	26.9	27.0	26.7	26.7	26.7
Net Worth	53.1	52.3	51.3	51.0	50.0	48.7	48.2	47.2	46.8	46.6	46.0	45.5	45.5
Total Capitalization	100.0	100.0	100.0	100.0	100.0	100.0	100.0	100.0	100.0	100.0	100.0	100.0	100.0

EXHIBIT 6c TAFT MANUFACTURING CO. COMMON-SIZE BALANCE SHEET: SALES 20% ABOVE FORECAST

	JAN	FEB	MAR	APR	MAY	JUN	JUL	AUG	SEP	OCT	NOV	DEC	1980
ASSETS													
Cash/Securities	4.9%	4.8%	4.9%	4.9%	4.9%	5.1%	5.1%	5.1%	5.0%	5.2%	5.2%	5.1%	5.1%
Accounts Receivable	28.1	30.0	29.9	30.2	30.4	30.8	31.5	31.7	31.1	31.6	32.0	31.8	31.8
Inventories	44.7	43.9	43.6	43.9	44.0	43.1	43.0	43.2	43.2	43.2	43.4	43.2	43.2
Other Curr Assets	3.1	3.0	3.0	3.0	3.1	3.2	3.2	3.2	3.2	3.2	3.2	3.2	3.2
Total Curr Assets	80.8	81.8	81.5	82.0	82.5	82.2	82.8	83.3	82.9	83.3	83.7	83.3	83.3
Net Plant and Equipment	16.5	15.6	15.9	15.4	14.9	15.0	14.4	14.0	14.4	13.9	13.5	13.9	13.9
Other Long-Term Assets	2.7	2.6	2.6	2.6	2.7	2.8	2.8	2.8	2.7	2.8	2.8	2.8	2.8
Total Assets	100.0	100.0	100.0	100.0	100.0	100.0	100.0	100.0	100.0	100.0	100.0	100.0	100.0
LIABILITIES AND NET WORTH													
Accounts Payable	10.4	10.2	10.2	10.2	10.3	10.6	10.5	10.7	10.5	10.7	10.6	10.6	10.6
Notes Payable	11.0	13.3	13.8	15.1	15.2	16.2	17.8	17.6	17.5	18.5	18.4	18.2	18.2
Other Curr Liabilities	3.9	4.7	5.5	4.6	5.5	6.3	5.4	6.4	7.2	6.4	7.4	8.2	8.2
Total Curr Liabilitie	25.3	28.1	29.5	29.9	31.0	33.1	33.8	34.6	35.2	35.6	36.4	37.0	37.0
Long-Term Debt	23.7	22.8	22.2	21.8	21.5	20.6	20.2	19.8	19.4	19.1	18.8	18.4	18.4
Total Liabilities	49.0	50.9	51.6	51.7	52.4	53.7	54.0	54.5	54.7	54.7	55.2	55.4	55.4
Common Stock	12.1	11.6	11.3	11.1	10.9	10.5	10.3	10.1	9.9	9.8	9.6	9.4	9.4
Capital Surplus	10.8	10.3	10.1	9.9	9.7	9.3	9.1	9.0	8.8	8.7	8.5	8.4	8.4
Retained Earnings	28.2	27.1	27.0	27.2	26.9	26.5	26.6	26.4	26.6	26.8	26.6	26.8	26.8
Net Worth	51.0	49.1	48.4	48.3	47.6	46.3	46.0	45.5	45.3	45.3	44.8	44.6	44.6
Total Capitalization	100.0	100.0	100.0	100.0	100.0	100.0	100.0	100.0	100.0	100.0	100.0	100.0	100.0

**EXHIBIT 7   SUSTAINABLE GROWTH MODEL WITHOUT EXTERNAL PRIME
VARIABLE**[a]

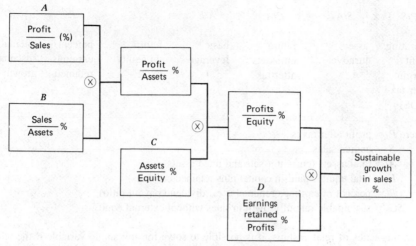

[a]The prime variables A–D may be affected by the strategy variables listed in Exhibit 8.

**EXHIBIT 8   SUSTAINABLE GROWTH MODEL
WITHOUT EXTERNAL FINANCING**

Prime Variables	Strategy Variables
A. Profits/sales	Pricing strategy
	Labor expenses
	Materials costs
	Interest expense
	General overhead
	Depreciation
	Taxes
B. Sales/assets	Cash level
	Accounts receivable level
	Inventory level:
	raw materials
	work in process
	finished goods
	Fixed assets
	Other assets
C. Assets/equity	Short-term borrowing
	Long-term borrowing
D. Earnings retained/profits	Dividend policy

SUSTAINABLE GROWTH MODEL. An internal sustainable growth model can be represented symbolically as follows:

$$P/S \quad \times \quad S/A \quad = \quad P/A \quad \times \quad A/E \quad = \quad P/E \quad \times \quad R \quad = \quad SG$$

operating profit margin after tax (ROS)	asset turnover	return on assets after tax	basic leverage	return on equity (ROE)	percent earnings retained	internally sustainable growth

where P = profit after taxes
   S = annual sales
   A = total assets (current assets and fixed assets)
   E = total equity (paid-in capital plus retained earnings)
   R = percent of earnings retained (i.e., dividend payout ratio)
   SG = sustainable rate of growth in sales without external equity

   In this series of relationships, it is possible to solve for any single variable if the others are known. For example, using the approximate projected relationships of the base plan, Taft may find its sustainable growth based on 1980 data as follows:

$$P/S \times S/A = P/A \times A/E = P/E \times b = SG$$
$$0.037 \times 1.69 = 0.062 \times 2.16 = 0.133 \times 0.68 = 0.090$$

where b is the retention rate.

   The data above indicate that **exclusive of outside equity financing,** the sustainable rate of growth is approximately 9%. The **sensitivity** of Taft's sustainable growth to each of these prime variables is apparent from some further calculations.

1. **If the profit margin increases to 6%,** the revised sustainable growth rate is:
$$P/S \times S/A = P/A \times A/E = P/E \times b = SG$$
$$0.06 \times 1.69 = 0.10 \times 2.16 = 0.22 \times 0.68 = 0.15$$

2. **If the utilization of assets improves to 2.5,** along with an increase in profit margin to 6, the sustainable rate of growth is dramatically improved to 22%.

3. If leverage is increased to 2.5 along with the previous changes, the result is a sustainable growth rate of:
$$P/S \times S/A = P/A \times A/E = P/E \times b = SG$$
$$0.06 \times 2.5 = 0.15 \times 2.5 = 0.375 \times 0.68 = 0.26$$

4. Finally, if the retention rate b were increased to 0.80 (i.e. a reduction in the dividend payout ratio from 0.40 to 0.20), the sustainable growth of all the changes above would be increased to 0.30.

   In inflationary times it is important to recognize that if the level of internal sustainable growth does not at least equal the inflation rate, the firm is shrinking in size in "real" terms.

ADDITION OF NEW EQUITY. It is implicit in the sustainable growth model that a one-time increase in growth is possible with the sale of new equity. Given constancy in the assets to equity ratio (leverage) and the sales to assets ratio (asset turnover) at Taft, the increase in sales possible from a new equity issue would be as follows:

increase in equity (outside funding)		assets to equity		sales to assets		possible growth in sales
$20,000,000	×	1.5	×	2.0	=	$60,000,000

INCONSISTENT PLAN. The calculations above do not imply that it is easy or even feasible to increase profit margins or asset turnover or earnings retention in a short period of time—or even that it is desirable to do so. Rather, the relationships show that there is such a thing as an **inconsistent plan** or forecast, that is, a plan that is simply **not feasible in terms of the basic governing financial relationships.** For example, it is financially inconsistent for Taft to expect sales to go up 35% in 1980 while operating with the ratios shown in the examples in the preceding paragraphs. If, nevertheless, sales were to increase 35% in 1980 and other historical relationships were to hold, it would be possible to illustrate the infeasibility of the plan as follows:

1. Sales = $815,000,000 × 1.35   = $1,100,250,000
2. Profits at 3.7% of sales   = $ 40,709,250
3. Earnings retained = 68% of profits   = $ 27,682,290
4. New total equity = old equity + earnings retained   = $ 251,605,290
5. Total assets at historical
    assets to equity of 2.16   = $ 543,467,420
6. Sales possible at historical
    sales to assets of 1.69   = $ 918,499,930
7. Sales **deficit** due to leverage
    and dividend constraints   = $ 181,750,070

The amount in line 7 represents the infeasibility of a 35% sales revenue increase given historical ratios.

ALTERNATIVE STRATEGIES. If sales growth is to be feasible at a rate above that indicated by the initial sustainable growth model, there are only four financial alternatives.

Increase in Leverage. This is a delicate variable to manipulate for four reasons:

1. When debt levels begin to exceed industry norms, lenders begin to withdraw or charge higher interest.
2. The increased interest may adversely affect the profit margin.
3. Prior covenants or existing debt may prevent the expansion of debt beyond previously agreed levels.
4. A high debt load may affect the stock price in a negative manner.

Thus, while many firms would wish to increase debt financing, the reality is that growth through ever-increasing leverage is often not a feasible solution to the financing problem.

Increase in Asset Turnover.   This option has the effect of improving the productivity of capital. Means of implementing it include operating the plant on a second shift, reducing the ratio of inventory to sales, reducing the ratio of receivables to sales, carrying fewer spare parts, and introducing numerous other strategies to make assets "work harder." While financial planners may wish to incorporate improved asset turnover into plans, it is not always feasible to do so in an operating sense. Often the guideline used is that of comparison with competitors, to determine where asset inefficiencies may be prevalent.

Improved Profit Margin.   This option depends essentially on two variables: the ability to increase price, and the ability to cut operating costs. The latter ability brings up the subject of "labor productivity," about which there is much concern in the United States today. Nonetheless, emphasis on stringent cost control and optimal pricing must be maintained if profit margins are to improve or remain high enough to permit the realization of the overall financial plan.

Dividend Reduction.   Few decisions are as full of complexity as the decision about the optimal dividend. Without entering the broad realm of the effect of dividends on share price, it is clear that reducing the dividend payout ratio is not popular with shareholders. Nonetheless, the concept of the feasible financial plan may indicate that unless one or more of the other basic relationships is modified, such a measure is the only way scheduled growth rates can be achieved.

INFLATION AND SUSTAINABLE GROWTH.   The concept of "sustainable growth" or a "feasible financial plan" has received more attention from financial forecasters in recent years as inflation has had the effect of increasing nominal growth rates rather dramatically, creating the illusion of growth when no real growth has occurred, that is, when growth less inflation is a negative number. The need to improve profit margins to allow real growth to stay even with inflation, or ahead of it, is made clear by the sustainable growth model. Thus the sustainable growth model is of considerable value to the financial planner after the basic cash budget, income statement and balance sheet are complete. (For a more detailed description of the sustainable growth model see Higgins, "How Much Growth Can a Firm Afford?"

REFERENCES AND BIBLIOGRAPHY

Brigham, Eugene F., *Financial Management, Theory and Practice*, 2nd ed., Dryden Press, Hinsdale, IL, 1979, Chapter 7.

Chambers, John C., Mullick, S. K., and Smith, D. D., "How to Choose the Right Forecasting Technique," *Harvard Business Review*, Vol. 49, July–August 1971, pp. 45–74.

Donaldson, G., *Strategy for Financial Mobility*, Irwin, Homewood, IL, 1969.

Francis, Jack C., and Rowell, D. R., "A Simultaneous Equation Model of the Firm for Financial Analysis and Planning," *Financial Management*, Spring 1978, pp. 29–44.

Gentry, James A., and Phyrr, S. A., "Simulating an EPS Growth Model," *Financial Management*, Vol. 2, Summer 1973, pp. 68–75.

Gershefski, George W., "Building a Corporate Financial Model," *Harvard Business Review*, Vol. 47, July–August, 1969, pp. 61–72.

Higgins, Robert C., "How Much Growth Can a Firm Afford?" *Financial Management*, Fall 1977, pp. 7–16.

Helfert, E. A., *Techniques of Financial Analysis,* 3rd ed., Irwin, Homewood, IL, 1977, Chapter 3.

Hunt, P., Williams, C. M., and Donaldson, G., *Basic Business Finance,* Irwin, Homewood, IL, 1974, Chapter 7.

Lyneis, James M., "Designing Financial Policies to Deal with Limited Financial Resources," *Financial Management,* Vol. 4, Spring 1975, pp. 13–24.

Merville, Larry J., and Tavis, L. A., "Long-Range Financial Planning," *Financial Management*, Vol. 3, Summer 1974, pp. 56–63.

Pan, J., Nichols, D. R., and Joy, O. M., "Sales Forecasting Practices of Large U.S. Industrial Firms," *Financial Management,* Fall 1977, pp. 72–76.

Pappas, James L., and Huber, G. P., "Probabilistic Short-Term Financial Planning," *Financial Management,* Vol. 2, Autumn 1973, pp. 36–44.

Parker, George G. C., and Segura E. L., "How to Get a Better Forecast," *Harvard Business Review,* Vol. 49, March–April, 1971, pp. 99–109.

Schall, Lawrence D., and Haley, Charles W., *Introduction to Financial Management,* 2nd ed., McGraw-Hill, New York, 1980, Chapter 13.

Solomon, Ezra, and Pringle, J. J., *An Introduction to Financial Management,* Goodyear Publishing, Santa Monica, CA, 1977, Chapter 3.

Spiro, Herbert T., *Finance for the Non-Financial Manager,* Wiley, New York, 1977, Chapters 7 and 10.

Stone, B., and Wood, R. A., "Daily Cash Forecasting: A Simple Method for Implementing the Distribution Approach," *Financial Management,* Fall 1977, pp. 40–50.

Van Horne, James C., *Financial Management and Policy,* 5th ed., Prentice-Hall, Englewood Cliffs, NJ, 1980, Chapter 26.

CASH MANAGEMENT

CONTENTS

CASH MANAGEMENT PROBLEMS   3

Definition and Concerns   3
Concentration Banking   3
Primary Subproblems   3
Multiple Concentration Banks   5
   Divisional concentration   5
   Regional gathering   5
Direct Collections and Payments   6

THE PAYMENT SYSTEM   6

Definition   6
Alternatives   6
   Checks and drafts   6
   Wires   6
   Automated Clearing House transfers   6

**BANK SERVICES TO SUPPORT CASH
MANAGEMENT**   6

Noncredit Services   6
Lockbox Collections   7
   Invoice match   7
   Photocopy   7
   Data transmission   7
Balance Reporting   7
   Daily balance information   7
   Average balance information   7
   Target balance report   8
   Transfer detail   8
   Transaction detail   8
   Other terminal information   8
   Money transfers   8
Zero-Balance Accounts   8
   Zero-balance disbursement accounts   8
   Controlled disbursing   8
   Zero-balance lockbox concentration   9
   Zero-balance field concentration   9
   Collecting and disbursing   9
   Zero-balance benefits   9

THE COLLECTION SYSTEM   **9**

Definition and Subproblems   **9**
Collection Systems for Noncredit Sales   **9**
   Selecting field banks   9
   Other design issues   10
     Multiple units at one bank   10
     Branch banks   10
     Compensation for field banks   10
     Control   10
     Deposit information gathering   10
     Deposit information gathering:
     Report timing   10
     Coin and currency   10
     Armored car pickup   10
The Collection System for Credit Sales:
Overview   **11**
   Company processing   11
   Lockbox processing   11
Lockbox Processing: Benefits and Costs   **11**
   Mail time improvement   11
   Processing time improvement   11
   Availability time improvement   11
   Costs: Variable and fixed   11
Lockbox Economics   **12**
Collection System Design for Check-
Based Receivables   **12**
   Lockbox design   12
   The design problem   12
   Solution methods   12
   Using a design solution   13
   Data issues   14
     Mail time   14
     Availability time   14
Broader Design Issues   **15**
   Payment alternatives   15
   Changes in collection environment   15
   Future focus   16

THE DISBURSEMENT SYSTEM   **16**

Problem Definition   **16**
Disbursement Bank Location   **16**

Disbursement Float Components 16
  Components of check clearing time 16
  Views on clearing time components 17
  Treating components in disbursement
  system design 17
Recent Developments 17
  Fed collection improvements 17
  Remote disbursing 17
  Controlled disbursing 18
  The 1980 Banking Act 18
  Changing payment terms 18
Design Strategy 19
The Broader Problem 19
Disbursement Design: Synthesis 19

CASH CONCENTRATION 20

Definition 20
Subproblems 20
Types of System 20
Transfer Alternatives 20
  Generic transfer approaches 20
  Wire alternatives 21
  DTC alternatives 21
  ACH-based alternatives 21
Deposit Control 22
Transfer Method Evaluation 22
  The break-even framework 22
  Limitations of break-even framework 22
  Cost comparison framework 24
Cash Transfer Scheduling 24
  The daily transfer solution 24
  Scheduling techniques 24
    Adjusted target anticipation 24
    Time-varying anticipation 24
    Availability anticipation 25
    Weekend timing 25
    Nondaily transfers 25

The scheduling dilemma 25
  Optimal cash transfer scheduling 25
Cash Concentration Design 26
Concentration Banks: Evaluation and
Selection 26
  Past selection criteria 26
  Concentration services 26
  Fast availability as a selection criterion 26
  Limitations of dollar-weighted
  availability 26
  Total cost criterion 27
Multiple Concentration Banks 27
Systematic Design 27
Future Considerations 27

AGGREGATE CASH POSITION
MANAGEMENT 27

Definition 27
Decisions 28
Objectives and Constraints 28
Decision Frameworks 28
  The daily target framework 28
  The control-limit framework 28
  The optimal scheduling framework 28
Framework Evaluation 28
The Daily Target Framework 29
  Management procedure 29
  Evaluation 29
Control-Limit Frameworks 29
  Control limits without forecasts 30
  Control limits with forecasts and
  smoothing 30
  Managing about a target balance 30
Daily Cash Forecasting 31
Month-to-Month Balance Targets and
Annual Smoothing 31

CASH MANAGEMENT

Bernell K. Stone

CASH MANAGEMENT PROBLEMS

DEFINITION AND CONCERNS. **Cash management** is the management of the day-to-day cash flow and the performance of related support activities such as cash forecasting, cash budgeting, and banking relations. The primary focus here is **day-to-day cash flow management.**

There are two primary concerns—management and design. **Design** pertains to structuring the system, for example, selecting banks and transfer methods and setting policies and procedures. **Management** is running the system, as designed, on a day-to-day basis.

CONCENTRATION BANKING. Concentration banking is a technique for managing the movement of cash between a company's banks. The essence of the technique is to select one bank, the primary concentration bank, as the central **cash pool.** Adjustments to balances at all other banks are made by transferring the appropriate amount into or out of the concentration bank.

Exhibit 1 portrays the essential idea of concentration banking. It shows (1) cash moving from customers to deposit banks and then into the concentration bank and (2) cash moving out of the concentration bank to disbursement banks and then to the payees. Classifying most banks as either deposit banks or disbursement banks reflects the typical situation, namely, that most banks serve either for deposits or disbursements but generally not both. Exhibit 1, however, does show one bank used for both deposits and disbursements.

Moving money out of deposit banks is called **cash concentration.** Moving money into disbursement banks is called **disbursement funding.**

PRIMARY SUBPROBLEMS. Within the framework of concentration banking, the task of designing and managing the day-to-day cash flow system involves seven major subproblems—collection, disbursement, cash concentration, disbursement funding, aggregate cash position management, short-term security portfolio management, and short-term debt position management.

The **collection system** is the means by which payments from customers are entered into a company's banking system. A major concern is the selection of lockbox banks for receipt of receivable payments. The selection of field deposit banks is also part of the collection system design task. In addition, there are various direct collect techniques such as preauthorized checks, drafts, and electronic debits.

EXHIBIT 1   CASH CONCENTRATION AND DISBURSEMENT FUNDING: FLOW OF MONEY FROM CUSTOMERS TO DEPOSIT BANKS TO CONCENTRATION BANK AND OUT TO DISBURSEMENT BANKS

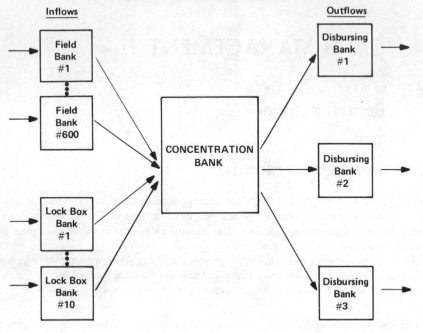

The **disbursing system** is the means by which a company pays its obligations. A major design task is the selection of disbursing banks. With emerging concern for electronic payments, another design task is identification of payment alternatives to checks and the design of systems for electronic payment.

Cash allocation is the task of moving money into and out of the primary concentration bank. **Cash concentration** is the task of moving funds from depository banks into the concentration bank. **Disbursement funding** is the task of moving funds from the concentration bank to accounts at disbursing banks. The major design problems associated with cash concentration and disbursement funding are (1) the selection of the concentration bank or banks and (2) specification of appropriate transfer methods between banks. The primary decision problem of day-to-day management is **cash transfer scheduling,** deciding on the timing and amount of transfers.

Aggregate cash position management (ACPM) is the task of managing the balance at the concentration bank. Once all transfers have been made to a company's other banks, managing the concentration bank balance is tantamount to managing the overall balance. The concentration bank serves as a buffer to handle imbalances in inflows and outflows. If the balance at the concentration bank is too high or too low, adjustments to the overall cash balance are made by borrowing or repaying and/or by short-term security sales or investments. Thus, aggregate cash position management is closely related to the management of both the loan position and the short-term security portfolio, subjects treated in other sections of this *Handbook*. Exhibit 2 shows links to banks and the money market at the concentration bank.

MULTIPLE CONCENTRATION BANKS.   Exhibit 2 shows only a single concentration bank. Actual systems may be more complex, with several **intermediate concentration banks** (intermediate cash pools) and a **primary concentration bank.**

Divisional Concentration.   With divisional concentration, divisions (or other logical sub-units, e.g., group, subsidiary, geographical territory) concentrate deposits and fund disbursements from a **divisional concentration bank.** The divisional cash manager then adjusts the balance at the divisional concentration bank by transfers between the primary concentration bank.

Often, headquarters serves as an "internal bank for the divisions." Cash is borrowed from and repaid to the central cash pool. Hence, divisions are not directly involved in bank borrowing and repayment.

Regional Gathering.   Sometimes deposits made by field units are moved first to a lockbox bank and then to the primary concentration bank. The lockbox bank serves as an intermediate concentration bank. In this context, it is often called a **gathering bank.** It is also called a **regional concentration bank.**

EXHIBIT 2   DAILY CASH FLOW MANAGEMENT: CASH ALLOCATION AND AGGREGATE CASH POSITION ADJUSTMENTS

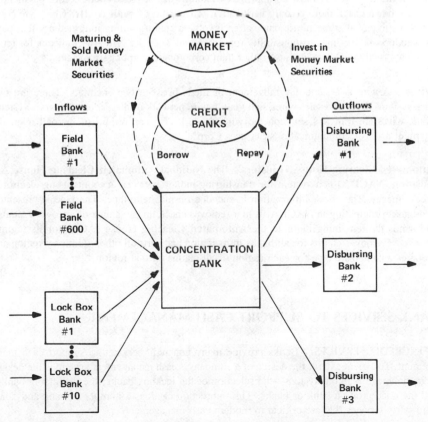

DIRECT COLLECTIONS AND PAYMENTS.   Besides the conventional collection and payment frameworks depicted in Exhibits 1 and 2, there may be collections going directly into the concentration bank from customers (e.g., from preauthorized checks, drafts, or electronic debits). Likewise, a company may make electronic payments directly to its payees' bank accounts.

THE PAYMENT SYSTEM

DEFINITION.   The payment system refers to the variety of means by which funds are transferred from payor to payee.

ALTERNATIVES.   Besides the direct exchange of cash, primary payment means are checks, payable-through drafts, credit drafts (credit card payments), wires, and electronic transfers via check images.

Checks and Drafts.   A **check** is a written authorization to transfer money out of a bank account. A **payable-through draft** is a claim on money in a bank account. A payable-through draft, however, must be approved by the owner of the account before payment is made, while a check requires only verification of signature. **Credit drafts,** which are commitments to pay at some future date, often involve a credit-granting intermediary that pays the vendors and assumes responsibility for collection. They are primarily a means for retail payments (individual to company) rather than corporate-to-corporate payments.

Wires.   A wire is a same-day movement of funds between two accounts. There are two wire systems. **Fed wires** are wires sent via the wire network of the Federal Reserve System. **Bank wires** are transfers sent via the wire network of a consortium of major banks, the Payment and Telecommunications Services Corp.

Automated Clearing House Transfers.   The **National Automated Clearing House Association (NACHA)** is a system for transferring money between accounts using electronic check images. The check information is encoded on magnetic tape. The tape is presented to a bank participating in NACHA. It first removes check image claims on its own accounts and sends the remaining items to the **Automated Clearing House** (ACH) for its region. This ACH removes claims for all banks in its region and sorts all other claims by region and prepares a composite tape for each region of all claims on that region.

BANK SERVICES TO SUPPORT CASH MANAGEMENT

NONCREDIT SERVICES.   Banks provide many noncredit services to support cash management. To a great extent, the design of a company's cash management system is the design of its noncredit banking system—the selection of the lockbox banks, the disbursing banks, and the concentration bank or banks. This subsection catalogs a number of bank and other third-party services that are critical to modern cash management.

LOCKBOX COLLECTIONS. **Lockbox collection service** is offered by many banks. The bank maintains a post office box in the company's name, and bank employees are authorized to pick up mail and process receivable payments. The essence of the service is periodic mail pickup and rapid processing. The benefit of a lockbox service is faster collections because of the reduction of mail time, processing time, and/or check availability time. Mail time is reduced because the services offer more favorable locations (than company processing centers) and frequent, well-timed pickups, with no delivery delay. Processing speedup is attributable to specialized and expeditious attention to checks. Availability is faster because the lockbox is located nearer to the drawee banks, although remote disbursing by the payor can undo this benefit.

There are a wide variety of lockbox services. Most can be placed in three main classes.

Invoice Match. Check amount is compared with invoice amount. Unless the comparison indicates a problem, the check is promptly entered into the clearing process while the invoice and envelope are stored for later transmittal to the company. The bank keeps a microfilm copy of the check and possibly the invoice.

Photocopy. A photocopy of the check is made. The check is entered into the clearing process. The check photocopy, invoice, and envelope are sent on to the company.

Data Transmission. Check, invoice, and possibly envelope postmark data are encoded on magnetic tape or some other computer-readable data storage device. Generally a magnetic tape is sent to the company, although computer-to-computer teleprocessing via high-speed lines is also available. The data preparation involves extra charges and generally requires that the company use a standardized invoice format and machine-readable invoice (e.g., MICR encoding, OCR type, or punch cards).

BALANCE REPORTING. Balance reporting is the generic term that describes the function of a communication system and a variety of reports designed to convey balance and related transaction detail for a company's bank accounts. Cash managers have long obtained current balances and related detail by telephoning their banks and/or arranging to have the banks call them. Since the mid-1970s, major banks have put balance information on **time-shared computers** and provided terminal access with greatly expanded capabilities for reporting both detail and types of report.

The essence of all systems is the provision of account detail available in the usual monthly reconciliation statement on a daily basis via terminal access to a time-sharing system. Differences in the various systems pertain primarily to (1) the amount of detail and the time period for which past data are available, (2) the variety of reports, and (3) the flexibility of the system in terms of user-defined reports.

A **single-bank system** will provide balance reports only for the accounts at the bank offering the service. A **multibank system** allows reports for as many banks as a company can get to transmit the balance data to the time-shared computer. The multibank systems today generally allow only summary information and require use of fairly standard reports.

Daily Balance Information. For every account, standard information is the current available balance, ledger balance, and 1-day and 2 day available additions.

Average Balance Information. Reports typically indicate the average available balance for the month and possibly for longer time periods (e.g., year-to-date average).

Target Balance Report.   Given specification of a target balance, reports indicate deviation between actual average available balance and the target balance and indicate the average balance that must be maintained to meet the target (e.g., the average for the rest of the month, the rest of the year, and possibly other user-specified time periods).

Transfer Detail.   Reports summarize wires received (amount, time, originating bank, originating account identification), wires out (amount, time, receiving bank, receiving account identification), depository transfer check (DTC) deposits, and possibly ACH-based deposits.

Transaction Detail.   The ultimate in detail is an audit trail on checks processed by day (check number, amount, and possibly other detail) and deposits received, wih item detail including return items.

Other Terminal Information.   Besides reports on account status and related detail, the balance reporting systems are often used to convey other pertinent cash management information (e.g., recent quotes for a variety of money market instruments, possibly for a number of dealers).

Money Transfers.   Some of the balance reporting systems allow initiation of wire transfers, wire drawdowns, and possibly DTC transfers from the terminal in accord with a protocol for verification of the transfer amount, the identity of the initiator, and the detail on accounts to be debited and credited. Here it is important to avoid transfer initiation by unauthorized personnel and to prevent errors, especially to make sure that the bank is acting in accord with user instructions for an authorized user.

ZERO-BALANCE ACCOUNTS.   "Zero-balance account" is a generic term for a set of procedures to maintain a zero balance in one or more accounts at a given bank. In the most common version, there is a set of **subaccounts** and a single **master account.** The company and its bank enter into an agreement that instructs the bank to move funds between each subaccount and the master account to achieve a zero balance in each subaccount. The company's residual balance at the bank then resides in the **master account.** Hence, the company can manage the balance at that bank as if there were only a single account. Therefore, a company need make at most one transfer into or out of that bank, namely, an appropriate transfer to the master account.

Zero-Balance Disbursement Accounts.   When a company has several disbursing accounts at a bank, a zero-balance disbursing system has the bank fund each zero-balance subaccount from the master account each day. The company funds the master account. One funding procedure is to receive a balance report via phone or terminal indicating the master account balance and thus the funding requirement. Another funding arrangement is to have the disbursement bank initiate a wire drawdown in an amount that will maintain a target balance. A **wire drawdown** is the initiation of a wire request by the bank to receive the funds.

A special case of zero-balance disbursing is a single account at the disbursing bank. The essence of the zero-balance arrangement is a report early in the day indicating total check presentments and funding requirements. The company then transfers the necessary funds to the disbursing bank.

Controlled Disbursing.   A disbursement funding system driven by a report of each day's funding requirements is called **controlled disbursing.** When a zero-balance is maintained at the disbursing bank, it is controlled disbursing with a zero-balance target. A variant is controlled disbursing with a nonzero target, where the report of each day's funding requirement then tells how much to transfer to maintain the given target.

Zero-Balance Lockbox Concentration.   A company may have several lockbox accounts at a given bank. In a zero-balance system, the funds in each lockbox account are transferred to the company's master account at that bank. The master account balance provides any balance-based compensation to the bank, and other balances are available for transfer. The zero-balance arrangement saves by requiring at most one concentrating transfer rather than one for each lockbox. In addition, it simplifies day-to-day cash management by enabling the cash manager to treat the bank as if all funds reside in a single account.

Zero-Balance Field Concentration.   A company may have several operating units making deposits into their own accounts at a given bank, including different branches of the same bank. With a zero-balance system, each unit's subaccounts are set at zero with the deposits of all units consolidated into the company's master account. Thus, concentrating deposits requires at most a single transfer from the master account. As with lockbox concentration, the zero-balance system saves transfers and simplifies cash management by enabling the cash manager to treat the bank and its branches as a single account for cash concentration purposes.

Collecting and Disbursing.   Zero-balance systems may be set up at banks that are used for both collecting and disbursing. The single master account then serves to net out inflows and outflows.

Zero-Balance Benefits.   Zero-balance systems reduce transfers and simplify cash management. Yet the use of subaccounts provides the company with separate activity detail for logical operating units and/or logical components of the cash flow. Therefore, the company is saved the cost of sorting account detail in its administrative processing. In effect, zero-balance arrangements provide the cash management benefits of a single account and the administrative benefits of multiple accounts. The administrative benefits include forecasting and control, where unit and component detail is the logical focus.

THE COLLECTION SYSTEM

DEFINITION AND SUBPROBLEMS.   The **collection system** refers to the means by which payments from customers are moved into the banking system. The collection system can be logically divided into two subproblems based on the type of payment—credit sales and noncredit sales. Most systematic design attention has been devoted to collection systems for credit sales, especially the design of a lockbox system to accelerate the collection of receivable payments.

COLLECTION SYSTEMS FOR NONCREDIT SALES.   Noncredit sales leave money (cash, checks, credit drafts) at company field units. Here **"field unit"** is used as a generic term for any company entity for distributing goods (e.g., store, catalog showroom, service station, warehouse).

Selecting Field Banks.   The primary design task for the noncredit collection system is selection of the bank for receiving the deposits of the field units, the **field deposit banks.**

The usual selection criterion is geographical proximity to the field unit or convenience for the field unit manager. Hence, selecting field deposit banks is generally viewed as a passive design decision. It is generally not given serious attention in many companies. There are no published papers on the subject.

Other Design Issues.   There are many tactical design issues; however, many of these are company specific or at least industry specific.

Multiple Units at One Bank.   When more than one unit uses the same bank, should a company have separate accounts and transfers for each field unit, or should there be a single master account with zero-balance subaccounts?

Branch Banks.   In states with branch banking (e.g., California), should a company make an effort to use the branches of major banks? The tradeoffs are fewer accounts for transferring but possibly a less convenient depository location.

Compensation for Field Banks.   How should field banks be compensated—fees, compensating balances, a combination? **Compensating balances** are the standard form, primarily because balances are hard to remove and are often needed anyway. All-fee compensation is almost always more costly for field banks.

Control.   Should the branch bank play a role in a company's deposit reporting and deposit control? For instance, should the field bank call corporate headquarters if a deposit is not made by each unit with an account?

Deposit Information Gathering.   How should deposit information be reported—phone calls or point-of-sale (POS) terminal transmission? If phone calls are used, should calls go to a central company location, or should a third-party deposit information gathering service be used? When POS transmission is available, it is generally preferable to phone calls. Deciding whether phone call information should be gathered by the company or by an outside service is a make-or-buy decision. There is generally a higher variable cost with third-party services and a smaller fixed cost. In addition, the company avoids the burden of managing the gathering system.

Deposit Information Gathering: Report Timing.   Most companies report after the deposit is made, frequently late in the day. Alternatives include more than one report per day or a midday report giving deposits (net receipts) for afternoon and evening of previous day and morning. The benefit is more information reported prior to transfer cutoff times, thus faster movement of funds out of deposit banks.

Coin and Currency.   Arrangements must be made to provide coin and currency in some units. Frequency of replenishment and amount involve tradeoffs in management costs and effort versus higher cash balances.

Armored Car Pickup.   If armored car pickup or delivery of cash is pertinent, the frequency and the time of day for both pickup and deposit are decisions that affect cost of services and the amount of cash tied up.

THE COLLECTION SYSTEM FOR CREDIT SALES: OVERVIEW.   The conventional way to pay for a purchase on credit is to send a check by mail. Hence, the standard assumption in designing a receivable collection system for credit sales is to assume that check payments will be mailed in. The essence of a design problem is to "accelerate collections," that is, to reduce the time for a check to become an available balance somewhere in the company's banking system by reducing one or more of the three components of collection time: mail time, processing time, or availability time.

There are two standard ways to process receivable payments: company processing and lockbox processing.

Company Processing.   Payments go first to a company processing center. Envelopes are opened, checks are removed, administrative processing is initiated, and later the checks processed over some time period are taken to a nearby bank and deposited.

Lockbox Processing.   The checks are mailed directly to a company post office box maintained by a bank offering a lockbox collection service. The bank periodically checks the lockbox and takes envelopes to the bank's collection processing center. Alternatively, many banks now have a separate zip code for their customers' lockboxes; this enables them to receive all their lockbox mail directly from the post office and do their own sorting.

Envelopes are opened, checks are removed and entered immediately into the clearing process, and then check information and other remittance data are transmitted to the company for administrative processing.

LOCKBOX PROCESSING: BENEFITS AND COSTS.   The primary benefit of a lockbox collection service is reduced collection time (more rapid collection). The improvement in collection time arises from reducing one or more of the three components of collection time (mailing time, processing time, and availability time).

Mail Time Improvement.   Lockboxes reduce mail time because they are nearer (in mail time terms) to the customer than the company's receivable processing center. Improvements may also be achieved by avoiding the delay of moving mail from a central post office and/ or route delivery. Finally, mail is delivered to lockboxes more often than to the corporate address.

Processing Time Improvement.   A bank specializing in lockbox collections can generally process checks faster than a company. First, the check is removed and deposited, with other processing done subsequently. Second, there may be benefits to specialization, including the use of special equipment for optical character recognition and reading MICR encoding.

Availability Time Improvement.   Improvements in the availability time granted a deposit are achieved in two ways. First, the lockbox bank might be closer to the drawee bank than the company's processing center. Second, the availability cutoff for lockbox deposits is often later than the availability granted over-the-counter deposits, especially those made at bank branches.

Costs: Variable and Fixed.   There are two costs associated with lockbox processing. First, there is a variable cost (per item cost) charged for each check processed in addition to the usual deposit charge. Second, there are certain fixed costs that reflect the lockbox rental, transfer costs (arising from the need to move money into the concentration bank), and possibly additional account charges simply for having a lockbox.

LOCKBOX ECONOMICS.   The essence of lockbox design is trading off the benefits of faster collection time and the incremental processing costs. Insight into this tradeoff is provided by considering a single receivable payment of amount A processed via a lockbox rather than through a company processing center. Let i denote the interest value of funds tied up in the collection process and ΔT the acceleration in collection time at incremental cost Δh. For a receivable of $\$A$, the net value (interest value of faster collection less incremental cost) is given by $iA\Delta T - \Delta h$. Exhibit 3 sketches the net value as a function of receivable size. For small items, the cost exceeds the benefit. Then there is a **break-even size** (given by $A^* = \Delta h/i\Delta T$). Above this size, it pays to use the lockbox in that the interest value of faster collections exceeds the incremental cost. Of course, there must also be sufficient savings to cover the fixed cost of the lockbox.

To illustrate typical magnitudes of the break-even receivable size, consider the special case of 1-day faster processing at 10¢ incremental processing cost and 0.04% interest per day (15.2% per year). In this particular case, the breakeven size is $A^* = \$0.10/(0.0004) = \$250$.

COLLECTION SYSTEM DESIGN FOR CHECK-BASED RECEIVABLES.   There are two broad issues in designing a system for collecting receivables paid by check. One is deciding whether receivables should be collected by the company or by lockbox. The other is selecting lockbox locations and assigning receivables to these locations and/or company processing centers.

Lockbox Design.   The focus of most collection systems studies is the selection of lockbox locations and the assignment of receivables to these locations. The receivables that should be processed by lockboxes are generally decided on in advance, usually on the basis of some kind of break-even analysis for determining whether the receivables are large enough to justify the cost of lockbox processing.

Rather than dealing with the assignment of individual receivables, it is customary to group receivable payments into classes and to deal with the assignment of the receivable classes. The usual criterion for defining a receivable class is a zip code–based **collection zone.** The collection zones are generally defined on the basis of the first two digits of the zip code. The company observes a total number of receivables in each class. The company generally samples its receivable payments to obtain the average check size for each class and possibly other parameters such as the current average collection time for the current mode of processing.

The Design Problem.   The design task is to select **lockboxes** (or lockbox locations) and assign the receivable classes to lockbox locations to minimize the overall cost of processing receivables (the interest value of funds in process of collection less the processing cost). Frequently, a surrogate objective is used, generally minimizing collection time with possibly an average lockbox processing cost used to ensure an appropriate tradeoff between collection time improvement and the cost to attain it. In this case, there is no explicit distinction between lockbox processing costs at different banks.

Solution Methods.   The optimization problem involved in selecting lockboxes and assigning receivables is a standard fixed-cost, assignment-location problem similar to the task of

EXHIBIT 3   BREAK-EVEN RECEIVABLE SIZE: PLOT SHOWING HOW VALUE OF ACCELERATED COLLECTIONS DEPENDS ON RECEIVABLE SIZE

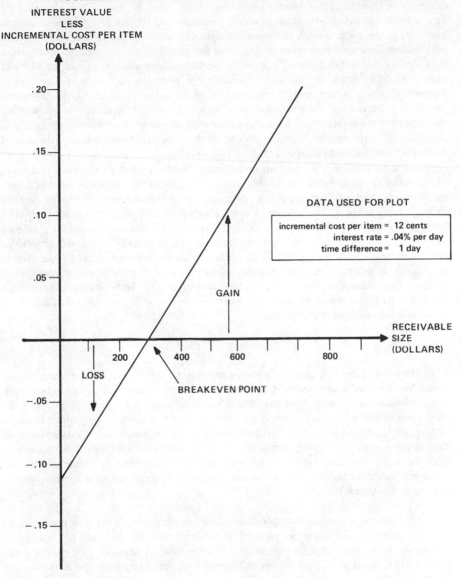

designing a warehousing system. It has been formulated in a number of articles. There are a variety of approaches to solving the problem—heuristic solution, optimal solution, and simulation. Some bank models use a combination of these techniques.

Using a Design Solution.   The essence of arriving at an appropriate **lockbox system design** is deciding whether a company's current lockbox system should be changed to one of the solutions recommended by a design study. Hence, it is necessary to compare one or more alternative systems with the current system and the cost of the change. There are three factors that must be considered in a **change evaluation.** First, since the data used in obtaining the new solution are based on a given sampling procedure and subject to sampling error, it is necessary to recognize that the measured improvements attributed to the alternative systems may include **measurement error** arising from the sampling process used to obtain input data. Second, since the company's accounts receivable compositions, as well as mail and bank availability times, are subject to change, it is necessary to recognize that there is **instability,** which in turn requires consideration of the extent to which measured benefits are likely to be realized for a sustained time period. Third, it is necessary to ask whether the benefits that a company can expect to realize after allowance for measurement error and instability are large enough to justify the cost of changing the system, namely, **the cost of adding or deleting lockboxes** and reassigning receivables.

Because the solution of the lockbox design study is really input to a judgmental evaluation of alternative systems, the accepted industry standard in consulting studies on lockbox design involves organization of the output in a systematic way so that the reports assist the exercise of intelligent judgment. The essence of most reports is to give the best, second best, third best, etc., solutions for different size lockbox systems; here **size** refers to the total number of lockbox locations. Benefits for each solution are generally given as estimated improvement over the company's current system. Exhibit 4 shows how this information can be summarized graphically. In this particular case, one can tell by inspection that the minimum cost system involves five lockboxes. The increase in total cost beyond the fifth lockbox indicates that the collection time savings for additional lockboxes do not justify the additional fixed cost associated with additional lockboxes.

Data Issues

Mail Time.   In a lockbox study, one deals with measurement of mail times and availability times. The standard source for the mail times used by most banks in doing a lockbox study is the **Phoenix-Hecht mail time data base,** which measures average mail time from the downtown central post offices serving a collection zone to downtown post office boxes in lockbox cities. Actual receivable mail time will typically be longer than the data base mail time because most payors do not mail receivable payments from a downtown post office. The justification for using such a sample of mail times is that there is a common bias for all lockboxes, hence no distortion in the selection of the optimal system if appropriate care is used in the design models.

Availability Time.   Another issue pertains to the availability time. In many lockbox studies, Federal Reserve availability times are used. However, many lockbox banks process checks via **direct sends,** which bypass their Federal Reserve bank by depositing the checks at the drawee bank, the drawee bank's Federal Reserve bank, or a clearinghouse in the drawee bank area. Hence, there is an argument for use of actual availability rather than Federal Reserve availability. A study by Ferguson and Maier, "A New Industry Standard for Designing Corporate Collection Systems," shows that there are significant biases in using **Federal Reserve availabilities** rather than actual availabilities including a bias toward too many lockboxes.

The difference between availability times and Phoenix-Hecht mail times is that the sample error in Federal Reserve availabilities is not the same for every location and thus is pertinent to the choice of lockboxes.

EXHIBIT 4   TOTAL COST VERSUS NUMBER OF LOCKBOXES: PLOT SHOWING TOTAL COST FOR FIVE BEST SYSTEMS OF EACH SIZE[a,b]

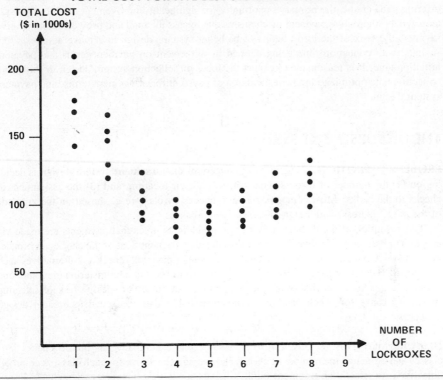

[a]The rapid initial improvement with size and then rather flat curve is typical of most actual situations.
[b]Having many alternatives near the optimum total cost is also typical of most actual situations.

BROADER DESIGN ISSUES.   The conventional design of a receivable collection system assumes check payment via mail. A broader design perspective involves consideration of the means of payment.

Payment Alternatives.   Preauthorized checks (PACs), **preauthorized drafts** (PADs), **preauthorized ACH debits,** and **wires** are alternatives to mail-based check payment. Neither the PAC nor the PAD involves mailing and they ensure timely payment. ACH debits and wires avoid not only mailing but also paper processing and thus provide even further administrative savings.

Changes in Collection Environment.   Prior to 1980, **Fed float** and **free Fed processing** were a disincentive to moving away from check-based payments. With the passage of the **1980 Banking Act,** the pricing of both float and Fed services provides an incentive to convert to **electronic payment.** In effect, there are incentives for payor and payee to negotiate payment form, payment timing, and payment procedures as alternatives to check-based mail payments. The essence of the negotiation is agreeing on means to realize administrative savings and the joint sharing of these savings.

Future Focus.   While check payment sent via the mail (with its associated problem of accelerating collections) will almost always be part of the collection system of most companies offering trade credit, the primary opportunity for significant improvement in collection systems will be alternative payment mechanisms that bypass the mail and provide administrative savings. The crux of the effort here will be better systems design to achieve administrative savings, with collection time being defined by agreement on payment terms and payment initiation time. It is reasonable to expect the focus of collection system design to shift from collection time optimization to consideration of payment form, payment terms, and payment system design.

THE DISBURSEMENT SYSTEM

PROBLEM DEFINITION.   The primary concern of **disbursement system design** is deciding on (1) the number of disbursement banks, (2) their location, and (3) the assignment of checks to the banks. Most companies assign checks by class (e.g., based on the zip code of the payee address) and assign check classes to banks.

This definition of the disbursement design problem assumes that payments are made via check. The assumed objective is to maximize the disbursement float of the checks. A broader perspective of disbursement design includes the form of payment (check vs. alternatives such as wire, ACH debit, or preauthorized draft) and the overall cost of administering the disbursing system. This subsection first treats the conventional disbursement design task of selecting disbursing banks for check payments. The treatment is then expanded to broader design concerns.

DISBURSEMENT BANK LOCATION.   Assume that a company has placed checks into classes and estimated the number of checks and average check size for each class. A common objective is to select **disbursement banks** (disbursement locations) and assign check classes to some disbursing bank. A more appropriate objective is to maximize the value of **disbursement float** less the incremental cost of disbursing from several banks.

DISBURSEMENT FLOAT COMPONENTS.   Fully understanding the issues involved in disbursement float location requires consideration of the three components of disbursement float time—mail time, payee processing time, and check clearing time. Most firms do not engage in "remote mailing" [mailing from one or more sites that are different from the one(s) at which the checks are prepared and written]. Therefore mail time and payee processing time typically are taken as given and independent of the drawee bank location. Hence, the selection of drawee banks to maximize disbursement float is usually tantamount to maximizing the check clearing time.

Components of Check Clearing Time.   Check clearing time can be further resolved into components—**availability time** plus **clearing slippage. Availability time** is the granted availability at the depository bank. It is the time from deposit until the payee (depositor) receives good funds. **Clearing slippage** is any additional time for the check to clear. For example, if the availability time were 2 business days and the actual clearing time were 3 business days, the clearing slippage would be 1 business day.

The clearing slippage benefits the payor but does not cost the payee. It is that part of the disbursement float that is not a **zero-sum game** between payor and payee; that is, it is not a process where the benefit from one party is totally offset by a cost to the other party. This benefit accrues at the cost of the banking system. It is borne by the depository bank, the Fed, and/or the drawee bank. For instance, the depository bank may grant faster availability than its actual collection time. Or, the Fed may not clear checks as fast as the availability it grants the collecting bank. Or, the drawee bank might have delays in its own processing.

Views on Clearing Time Components. While most companies focus on total clearing time, there are reasons to be concerned about its source. One view is that clearing slippage is "risky float" in the sense of being more likely to be eliminated than availability time. Hence, advocates of this view argue for assigning greater value to the availability time component than to the clearing time component. A contrasting view is that the availability extension is achieved at the cost of the customer, is tantamount to "disguised stretching," and should be given lighter weight than clearing slippage, since it involves a cost in customer relations.

Treating Components in Disbursement System Design. Whether a company gives the conventional equal weight to availability and clearing slippage or gives one or the other greater weight clearly will vary from company to company because it is a matter of company policy. All cases can be handled within the framework of current disbursement design models simply by replacing total disbursement float by a weighted float measure that assigns weights to the two components (availability time and slippage). Moreover, the standard algorithms used for maximizing total float time can be used without any change other than modifying the input.

The important points here are recognition that (1) the two components of check clearing time are not necessarily of equal value, and (2) variation in relative importance can be incorporated within the framework of current design methodology.

RECENT DEVELOPMENTS. The environment in which disbursing is conducted has changed significantly in recent years. Major factors include (1) Fed efforts at accelerated check processing to reduce clearing slippage, (2) Fed efforts to discourage remote disbursing, (3) the 1980 Banking Act, (4) evolution in payment terms, and (5) the emergence of a variety of electronic payments mechanisms.

Fed Collection Improvements. In recent years, the Fed has made efforts to eliminate slippage by revising its clearing schedule, insisting on timely presentment by banks, arranging better logistical transmission of checks, and generally improving the rate of check processing.

Remote Disbursing. When the only business reason for writing checks on a given bank is to secure extended float, such practice is called "remote disbursing." In the late 1970s, both Congress and the Fed devoted considerable attention to remote disbursing. In particular, **Fed float** exploitation involves two major issues. First, the cost of increased Fed float is indirectly a cost to taxpayers, since the Fed remits its operating surplus to the U.S. Treasury. Second, companies not exploiting Fed float incur relatively higher net payment costs and are thus subject to a competitive disadvantage relative to companies that do exploit Fed float.

Since most companies set up their disbursing system with the cooperation of their banks, the Fed discouraged remote disbursing by exerting pressure on major banks not to facilitate remote disbursing, especially via correspondent or other cooperative relationships with other banks.

Controlled Disbursing. Controlled disbursing (discussed further in connection with disbursement funding) is the practice of disbursing from banks that receive all check presentments from the Fed early in the day and are able to report the dollar volume of a company's presentments so that there is knowledge of check funding obligations early in the day. This knowledge enables a company to fund its disbursing account on a same-day basis including provision of funds by borrowing, the issuance of commercial paper, and/or the sale of short-term marketable securities. Moreover, in the case of a net surplus, it makes possible timely investment of any excess balances.

The 1980 Banking Act. The 1980 Banking Act mandates changes in the banking system that have drastic implications for disbursing economics. First, the 1980 Banking Act requires that the Fed "price" float. Hence, the Fed's contribution to clearing slippage is no longer free. In 1980 the Fed announced tentative plans to use actual availability based on clearings over the previous 3 months to reduce to zero the expected value of the Fed's net contribution to clearing slippage. While this procedure will eliminate any significant contribution by the Fed to clearing slippage, it does not mean that there will be no slippage in the system. There will be some longer than average clearing times and others that are shorter than average. Hence, there is an opportunity for some companies to gain and some to lose. In particular there is an opportunity now for the more sophisticated companies and banks to gain at the cost of the less sophisticated.

The second important feature of the **1980 Banking Act** is that the **Fed is required to price its services** such as **check clearing** and **money transfers.** Thus, services that the Fed has hitherto given to banks will now be explicitly priced. It is reasonable to expect banks to pass these charges on to their customers. Thus deposits cleared via the Fed should become more expensive. Therefore, remote disbursing on banks using the Fed to clear checks will mean greater costs with no significant float benefit. Hence, the pricing of both services and Fed float jointly means not only no incentive for remote disbursing but a disincentive. Moreover, economic pricing of services means checks and other paper-based payments will be more expensive than electronic payments.

The net effect is that the float disincentive to **electronic transfers** is removed. There is, moreover, also a new economic incentive to shift from paper to electronic transfers. Thus, the underlying assumption of conventional disbursement system design—namely, that payment should occur via checks, with the primary problem being the selection of the banks on which disbursement checks should be written to maximize disbursement float—requires reexamination in preparing for the environment of the 1980s. In particular, one of the major design decisions must be consideration of the form of payment, especially paper versus electronic payments.

Changing Payment Terms. The focus on extending disbursement float arises in part because of the traditional practice of regarding an item as paid when mailed. In recent years the combination of remote disbursing and other stretching practices have led to restatement of credit terms by some companies on the basis of when payment is received or when good funds (collected balances) are received, especially in the case of trade discounts. Moreover, some companies seeking to provide incentive for electronic payment might now state terms conditional on the method of payment; for example, the alternatives might be a 2% discount for check payment if mailed by the seventh day or a 2% discount for electronic payment or preauthorized draft if good funds are "received by the fourteenth day." The extended time is designed to encourage electronic payment and effectively to share savings with the payor. Such changes in credit terms mitigate the benefits of extending disbursement float. Like the Fed pricing of its clearing services and slippage, restatement of payment terms and/or incentives for electronic payment remove, or at least reduce, economic incentives for maximizing disbursement float.

DESIGN STRATEGY.   Pricing Fed float, the economic advantages of an electronic payment over paper-based payment, and changing payment terms are all forcing companies to view the **design of their disbursement systems** in a broader perspective than simply trying to maximize disbursement float. In particular it means than an alternative to checks such as ACH payments, wires, or preauthorized drafts should be given explicit consideration. With electronic payments (either ACH payments or wires), there is no difference in clearing time between banks and there is no mail time at all. In effect, the issue of which bank gives the most disbursement float vanishes simply because there is no difference between disbursing banks in terms of disbursement float time, although there may be significant differences in terms of quality, reliability, or cost of service. Thus, there is no float-based incentive to use multiple disbursing banks when there is no variation across drawee banks with electronic payment.

THE BROADER PROBLEM.   The new focus on disbursing systems requires that to realize administrative savings, companies negotiate terms and procedures for the timing and execution of electronic payments. Such negotiation shifts the emphasis in disbursement system design away from the selection of disbursing banks to **payor and payee negotiation** with respect to the sharing of benefits. Thus, in the future it is reasonable to expect disbursement system design to focus on structuring systems for payments that are administratively efficient rather than concentrating on float optimization. The pioneers in **direct payment systems** today are companies that have set up **electronic payment systems** with payees with whom they have a close and regular relationship (e.g., dealers and franchisees).

DISBURSEMENT DESIGN: SYNTHESIS.   In the 1970s disbursement design focused on extending **disbursement float.** The primary reasons for this emphasis were payment terms based on the mail initiation date and Fed float.

The decision focus in float extension is the selection of disbursing banks. The essence of disbursement bank selection procedures is the identification of candidate disbursing banks, the measurement of disbursement time for various classes of checks, and the solution of a mathematical programming problem to select banks and assign checks (check classes).

Three factors are now forcing a broader look at disbursement system design: (1) an emerging trend toward changing payment terms and defining payment time on the basis of payment receipt and/or good funds receipt, (2) discouragement of remote disbursing by the Fed through the pricing of Fed float and clearing services, and (3) the economies of electronic payment relative to paper, including the economies of ordering and billing as well as paying.

The short-run reaction has been concerned with **controlled disbursing** as an alternative for **remote disbursing** in that it preserves the structure of the current information system. The long-run impact, however, will be a shift away from both remote and controlled disbursing to center disbursement design on broader issues, namely: (1) the method of payment, (2) systems designed to achieve savings from efficient payment, and (3) negotiation between payor and payee on payment terms and timing.

CASH CONCENTRATION

DEFINITION.   **Cash concentration** pertains to the movement of money from deposit banks into the central cash pool at the concentration bank.

SUBPROBLEMS.   Cash concentration can be broken into two major subproblems—design and management. **Cash concentration design** pertains to the selection of the concentration bank (or banks), transfer methods, and transfer initiation time, information system, and a variety of policies and procedures. **Cash concentration management** involves cash transfer scheduling, deciding on the time and amount of transfers, and the day-to-day operation of a deposit information gathering system and an administrative control system.

TYPES OF SYSTEM.   Besides the distinction between design and management, it is useful to identify two primary types of concentration systems—lockbox concentration and field concentration. **Lockbox concentration** is moving money from lockbox banks to the concentration bank. **Field concentration** is moving money from field deposit banks. In general, lockbox concentration is easier to deal with for several reasons. First, there are generally fewer lockbox banks than field banks. Second, lockbox deposits are almost always checks and drafts, not cash. Finally, most lockbox banks are tied into balance reporting systems and/or are able to telephone their reports to the company so that deposit information gathering is fairly straightforward. Finally, lockbox deposits do not involve the fraud-theft control problems that often arise in field deposits.

TRANSFER ALTERNATIVES.   In a cash concentrating transfer the payor and the payee are the same company. Therefore, cash can be concentrated via any payment mechanism available for moving funds between accounts at different banks, namely wires, checks, or ACH transfers. In the case of check-based transfers, the standard method involves a specific type of check known as a **depository transfer check (DTC).** This check has the words "depository transfer check" written on it. With the appropriate legal agreements between a company and its banks, a DTC can be used without a signature as long as it is deposited into specified company accounts. Moreover, it can be used only for deposit into a company account. Thus, the device of the depository transfer check simplifies both problems of check control and administrative procedures.

Banks seeking concentration business provide an **automated DTC service,** namely, the automatic preparation of DTCs from deposit information. Likewise, many major banks are now providing an **automated ACH-based transfer service** in which the preparation of the ACH tape is triggered by deposit information.

The ACH-based transfer is sometimes called a "paperless DTC" or "electronic DTC." It serves the same function as a DTC but without the use of a paper check.

Generic Transfer Approaches.   While each transfer mechanism can be used in a variety of ways, there are two generic approaches—**field initiation** and **central initiation.** With field initiation, the field unit manager or the field bank (or the lockbox bank in the case of lockbox concentration) initiates the transfer and is responsible for deciding on the amount of transfers. With central initiation, transfers are initiated at the concentration bank. Central initiation requires a deposit information gathering system to provide the necessary deposit data at a central location. In contrast, field initiation takes place where the deposit data exist.

Until the early 1970s, most field and even many lockbox concentration systems were field initiated with a few companies running their own centralized deposit information gathering by directing phone calls to a central company location. Since the early 1970s, a number of third-party deposit information gathering services have been created by time-sharing firms and/or major banks. Moreover, most major banks have further facilitated central initiation by developing services to prepare and initiate transfers automatically from deposit information.

Wire Alternatives.   Wire transfers have traditionally been initiated at the depository bank. They might be initiated by a request from a field unit manager. Or more often, a company leaves standing wire instructions especially in the case of lockbox concentration. Typical instructions at the depository bank might be, "wire out each day's deposits" or "wire all funds in excess of $5,000 whenever the balance exceeds $25,000." Such instructions are designed to maintain a target compensating balance while moving funds to the central cash pool.

It is also possible to initiate wires at the concentration bank. In this procedure the concentration bank contacts the depository bank with wire instructions. The initiation of a wire at the request of the receiving bank is called a **drawdown.**

DTC Alternatives.   In the past, the standard method for using a DTC was **mail-based field initiation.** The manager of a field unit would make the deposit and then mail a DTC and deposit slip to a lockbox gathering bank (a regional concentration bank). These funds were then transferred to the primary concentration bank as part of the company's lockbox concentration.

An alternative to mail-based field initiation is **central initiation** at the concentration bank. These are two primary forms of central initiation—company managed and third-party assisted. In **company-managed central initiation,** deposit information is transmitted to a central company location, where it is accumulated. Then the data are used to create a tape of transfer data (e.g., DTC tape images), and the tape is sent to the concentration bank (or possibly teleprocessed). The concentration bank prepares and initiates the transfers.

In **third-party-assisted central initiation,** a third-party information gathering service such as National Data Corp. receives deposit information on behalf of the company and acts first as the information storage manager and then as information forwarder to the company-designated concentration bank. There are now a half-dozen time-sharing firms with deposit information gathering services. Moreover, a number of major banks also provide their own deposit information gathering services, often in partnership with a time-sharing service.

The difference between company-managed and third-party assisted is simply the means by which deposit information is centralized. In the latter, deposit information gathering is performed by a third-party agent rather than by the company itself. In exchange for a charge per call, the company avoids the cost of creating, managing, and maintaining its own deposit information gathering system.

ACH-Based Alternatives.   Field-based initiation of ACH transfers is not viable. Central initiation could be with either company-managed or third-party-assigned deposit information gathering. The only difference is in how the deposit data are gathered for transmission to the concentration bank. Once the data have been received, the process at the concentration bank is the same, namely, the creation of the ACH tape for presentation to the appropriate regional Automated Clearing House.

DEPOSIT CONTROL.   Deposit control is primarily a problem for field concentration. Deposit control involves (1) ensuring timely deposit execution and reporting and (2) preventing fraud and theft. Reporting controls are built into most deposit information gathering systems (e.g., an exception report listing units that have not reported).

The conventional approach to theft prevention involves the rapid removal of deposits from the field bank. An **overdraft** indicates a possible failure to make reported deposits and indicates a need for quick investigation. However, the reporting process, transfer preparation, and transfer clearing involve time delays during which theft losses can occur. Moreover, the process is relatively ineffective for the prevention of "skimming," the taking of only a portion of the day's receipts. The future should see **forecast-based control,** in which actual deposits are compared with pro forma predictions of deposits and exception reports are generated whenever there are significant deviations.

TRANSFER METHOD EVALUATION.   The issue of which transfer method should be used at a particular deposit bank has been traditionally viewed as an issue of cost versus transfer speed. For instance, a wire is faster but more expensive than a DTC, and an EDTC (electronic depository transfer check) offers both 1-day service and relatively low cost. Exhibit 5 summarizes typical cost ranges and availability times for existing ways of using various transfer alternatives.

The Break-Even Framework.   The conventional framework for evaluating transfer methods is a break-even analysis comparing differences in transfer costs with the value of interest that could be earned over the difference in availability times. For instance, if the cost difference and the availability difference between a wire and DTC are $6 and 1 day, respectively, the break-even transfer size at an interest rate of 0.03% per day is $20,000, since it requires $20,000 to earn $6 interest in 1 day at 0.03% per day.

The break-even framework is responsible for the conventional rules of thumb that dictate using DTCs for small transfers and wires for large transfers, say DTCs for transfers of less than $20,000 and wires for amounts greater than $20,000.

Limitations of Break-Even Framework.   While the break-even framework and its implied rules of thumb are in wide use today, the framework is inappropriate for a variety of reasons. First, the difference in availability times for alternative transfer methods is not necessarily the effective delay, as the break-even framework assumes. For instance, a company using DTCs that knows it has $10,000 of transfers in process at a particular depository bank might remove the money tied up in the transfer process by a one-time adjusting transfer and thereby eliminate the transfer delay effect. Or, in the case of check deposits, there is typically a day or more availability delay at the deposit bank. Hence the choice is between a DTC initiated on the day of deposit or a wire on the next business day. In this situation, since the checks deposited are removed the next day with either a DTC or wire, the effective delay difference is zero, not the 1-day difference in availabilities. The key is knowing when each instrument converts deposits into available balances at the concentration bank.

A **second defect of the break-even framework** pertains to differences in granted availability for the transfer at the concentration bank and the actual clearing time involved in removing the funds from the depository bank. For a wire, these are equal. For a DTC, the availability time may be less than, equal to, or greater than the actual clearing time. If the availability time were less by 1 business day, the DTC transfer would mean that the company had credit for available balances in two banks for 1 business day. In this case, the DTC

EXHIBIT 5   DATA ON TRANSFER DELAYS AND COSTS

TRANSFER METHODS	DELAY (DAYS)	TYPICAL COST RANGE [a]	COST COMPONENTS
Wire	0	$6.00–$12.00	1. Outgoing Wire 2. Wire Receipt
EDTC: Third—Party Assisted	1–2	$ .60–$ 1.00	1. Third—Party Charge 2. Deposit Charge 3. DTC Preparation Charge 4. Check Charge
DTC: Centralized Company Initiation	1–2	$ .05–$ .40 plus the cost of bank and/or company preparation of either the DTCs and/or the DTC tape image and any communication costs.	1. Deposit Charge 2. Check Charge 3. Bank Process-ing Charge 4. Company Pro-cessing Cost 5. Communication Cost
DTC: Mail—Based	2–7	$ .30–$ .55	1. Deposit Charge, Lockbox 2. Check Charge 3. Postage/ Envelope
DTC: Third—Party Assisted	1	$ .24–$ .36 plus any bank pre-paration charge	1. Third—Party Charge 2. Electronic Transfer Charge 3. Bank Pre-paration Charge
EDTC: Centralized Company Initiation	1	$ .03–$ .06 plus any bank pre-paration charges and/or the cost of company pre-paration of the EDTC tape and any communication costs.	1. Electronic Trans-fer Charge 2. Bank Prepara-tion Charge 3. Company Pro-cessing Cost 4. Communication Cost

[a]Cost ranges reflect variation in charges across banks and third-party information gathering services.
Source: Bernell K. Stone and Ned C. Hill, "Alternative Transfer Mechanisms and Methods: Evaluation Frameworks," *Journal of Bank Research* (forthcoming).

provides the greater opportunity for interest value for any size transfer, the exact opposite to the conclusion of the break-even framework.

A third defect of the break-even framework is failure to reflect the value of balances in compensating banks for services. A fourth is an implicit assumption of either a one-time transfer or ongoing daily transfers, whereas good cash transfer scheduling (discussed shortly) means the actual situation is almost always more complicated.

Cost Comparison Framework.   An alternative to the incomplete break even framework is a cost comparison framework set forth by Stone and Hill, "Alternative Cash Transfer Mechanisms and Methods: Evaluation Frameworks" (*Journal of Bank Research*, forthcoming, 1981). The Stone-Hill framework is based on comparison of the total scheduling cost associated with each transfer method and the selection of the least-cost alternative. The costs consist of the direct transfer cost, the interest value of any excess balances at the deposit bank, and a measure of the value of any usable dual balances arising from differences in availability times and clearing times. Here, care is necessary to make sure that only dual balances that can be removed and/or used as compensating balances are counted. Finding the minimum value of this cost requires finding the optimal cash transfer schedule for each transfer alternative.

CASH TRANSFER SCHEDULING.   **Cash transfer scheduling** is deciding on the timing and amount of cash transfers.

The Daily Transfer Solution.   Until the mid-1970s, the conventional solution to the cash transfer scheduling problem was a daily transfer of each day's reported deposits. Stress is placed on "reported deposits" because delays in reporting and information gathering and processing could mean that transfers initiated pertained to deposits a day or so earlier.

Daily transfers as soon as deposit information becomes available seem like the fastest possible mobilization of deposits. In fact, it seems that the only way to mobilize money faster would be to reduce reporting and information processing delays. This still widespread view is incorrect. Money can be moved out faster than daily transfers of each day's reported deposits. Moreover, daily transfers can be unnecessarily expensive and can mean forgoing opportunities for cost reductions in cash concentration.

Scheduling Techniques.   Beginning in the mid-1970s, a number of sophisticated cash managers recognized several ways to improve cash transfer procedures by abandoning the automatic transfer of each day's reported deposits. Several rule-of-thumb scheduling techniques were used. While there are many variants, most can be put into one of three classes: anticipation, weekend timing, and nondaily transfers.

Adjusted Target Anticipation.   **Anticipation** is a generic term for a variety of **transfer acceleration methods** that use forecasts of some type to enable initiation of transfers before the company is informed of an available balance addition at the deposit bank. The most common form of anticipation is the so-called **adjusted target framework** in which a company makes a one-time removal of deposits in process. For instance, management might observe from past bank statements that it averages $8,000 deposits in the process of transfer and is overcompensating its banks by $8,000. Hence, the cash manager removes the $8,000 and operates on company books with a target balance that is $8,000 less than the actual target balance.

Time-Varying Anticipation.   A limitation on the adjusted target technique arises from time-varying deposits, especially the strong weekly cycle that is typical of field deposits. Not incurring overdrafts can mean that only part of the average deposits in process can be removed. To remove more, companies may use time-varying anticipation by using deposit forecasts to determine the amount that can be anticipated at any time. In such a system, deposit reports provide a control on the forecast.

Availability Anticipation. For check and credit draft deposits, there is a delay before the company receives credit for an available balance. Knowledge of the ledger balance and the availability delay means that a transfer can be timed to remove deposits as they become available. For instance, a DTC with 1-day clearing time might be initiated to remove tomorrow's available additions as soon as the balance report giving the ledger balance and the schedule of available additions is received. This method is also called **ledger anticipation,** since it involves predictions of the conversion of a ledger balance into an available balance. It is a special case of time-varying anticipation in which a company can forecast available additions over a 1-day horizon with virtually perfect accuracy on a day-to-day basis aside from return items.

Weekend Timing. When the availability time is less than the clearing time, dual balances are created. Timing transfers to increase the amount of the dual balances over the weekend can significantly increase the amount of dual balances. For instance, with a 1–business day availability time and 2–business day clear time, Thursday transfers provide dual balances on Friday, Saturday, and Sunday—3 days rather than 1. Thus any transfer amounts shifted to Thursday can triple the dual balance creation. Hence, transferring the Wednesday deposit, the Thursday deposit, and part of the deposits expected on Friday and the weekend can significantly increase the total dollars, getting the dual balance benefit.

When the availability time received is greater than the clearing time, there is a time period for which the company receives credit for an available balance in neither bank. This situation arises frequently when the deposit bank or its correspondent has an aggressive direct send program. In this case, weekend timing means avoiding weekend transfers. For instance, with 1-day availability and same day clears, Friday transfers should be avoided.

Nondaily Transfers. Moving from daily to less-frequent transfers is a way to reduce direct transfer costs. There are several popular frameworks for managing nondaily transfers. A **trigger point rule** is a type of economic order quantity that initiates a transfer down to a return point whenever the balance exceeds a trigger level. A **periodic frequency rule** is a procedure involving a transfer down to a return point at periodic intervals, say every other business day, every third business day, or once a week.

The Scheduling Dilemma. The transfer schedule influences three cost factors—the direct transfer cost, the value of excess balances at the deposit bank, and the value of usable dual balances. Each of the three generic scheduling techniques focuses on different cost components. Anticipation focuses primarily on reducing excess balances. Weekend timing deals with dual balances. Nondaily transfer rules focus primarily on lowering the direct transfer cost. A good schedule should properly trade off these three cost factors, thus the relative emphasis placed on these techniques. Even more difficult than ensuring a good tradeoff can be resolving conflicts between some of the rule-of-thumb scheduling procedures. For instance, conventional trigger point and periodic frequency rules preclude weekend timing and can complicate the sophisticated use of anticipation.

Optimal Cash Transfer Scheduling. Stone and Hill, in "Cash Transfer Scheduling for Efficient Cash Concentration," formulated a cost measure that properly trades off direct transfer costs, the interest value of excess balances, and the value of usable dual balances, and showed that the least cost schedule can be obtained by solving an integer scheduling problem that optimally incorporates each of the rule-of-thumb scheduling procedures in its most general form. Like the algorithms for lockbox design and disbursement design, at least some cash management banks are now providing algorithms for the optimal solution of this scheduling problem.

CASH CONCENTRATION DESIGN.   Cash concentration design pertains to specification of the structure of the cash concentration system. There are four primary design decisions: (1) the selection of the concentration bank or banks, (2) the assignment of concentration banks to deposit banks whenever there is more than one concentration bank, (3) the selection of the set of transfer methods that a company will support, and (4) the assignment of the transfer method to a deposit bank.

The primary focus of past concentration design has been transfer method assignment, generally in an improperly chosen break-even framework. The systematic evaluation and selection of concentration banks and the merits of several concentration banks tend to be neglected design decisions.

CONCENTRATION BANKS: EVALUATION AND SELECTION.

Past Selection Criteria.   A company's current concentration bank or banks were selected in the past for reasons that have little to do with concentration efficiency today. In the past selection was often based on location: namely, the headquarters city and/or New York City, the latter providing close proximity to major money markets. Another criterion used in the past was selection of the lead credit bank, or at least a major credit bank, since adjustments to the balance at the concentration bank were made by borrowing or lending.

Good communication and same-day **money transfers** mitigate the importance of location. Credit lines can be arranged at most major banks so that logic dictates first selecting the concentration bank, then the credit line.

Concentration Services.   A concentration bank must have reliable, error-free money transfer, communication, and balance reporting services. Automatic preparation of DTC transfers, ACH transfers, and possibly wire drawdowns are essential. Interface to third-party information gathering services is critical for any company using such services and is characteristic of all the banks specializing in concentration. Likewise, ability to accept company tapes or teleprocessing is critical for companies managing their own deposit information gathering.

Some of the concentration banks are now offering their own deposit information gathering. Terminal-based transfer initiation may be pertinent, although most companies use terminal initiation only for occasional transfers (e.g., error correction and other exceptional needs not covered by the standard system).

Banks not providing such services and not committed to staying at the frontiers of cash concentration services are not serious candidates for concentration banks. Probably no more than 100 money center banks are committed to cash concentration.

Fast Availability as a Selection Criterion.   The most common criterion used for systematic evaluation of alternative concentration banks is fast availability. Fastness is often measured by **dollar-weighted availability,** the availability time for a given region weighted by the relative dollars deposited in that region. Presumably the best concentration bank for a particular company is the one with the fastest dollar-weighted availability.

Limitations of Dollar-Weighted Availability.   Dollar-weighted availability as a selection criterion has several defects, although it provides useful information. First, focusing on check availability implicitly assumes the use of DTCs for concentrating transfers. Second, **granted**

availability is not the same as **effective availability** when a company uses anticipation. Third, availability (even a measure of effective availability) is only part of the overall **concentration cost.** There are also direct transfer charges, fixed costs, and, in the case of DTCs, dual balance effects. For instance, a bank might grant uniform 1-day availability but aggressively use direct sends, so that some DTCs clear in less than a day and the company has negative dual balances. Finally, dollar-weighted availability implicitly assumes only a single concentration bank.

Total Cost Criterion.   Superior to availability-only measures are comparisons based on total concentration costs. Of course, cost comparison assumes reliable, quality services that are otherwise comparable. **Measures of concentration costs** should include the impact of concentration bank transfer costs, excess field balances, dual balances, and administrative costs including a variety of fixed costs. Incorporating factors besides availability can make measurement difficult; however, recognizing these factors is clearly superior to ignoring them.

MULTIPLE CONCENTRATION BANKS.   The most common reason today for multiple concentration banks is **divisional concentration.** Another but now less common reason is **regional gathering.** There has been a trend in recent years to move toward fewer concentration banks and often a single bank.

The primary benefit is administrative simplicity. However, the simplicity may be incurred at some cost, especially for DTC-based concentration. Multiple banks provide ability to obtain the best of each bank's granted availability and/or extended clearing (dual balance effect) for check-based transfers.

SYSTEMATIC DESIGN.   The simultaneous consideration of concentration bank selection and assignment and transfer method selection and assignment is a complex problem. Stone and Hill, in "Cash Concentration Design" (Working Paper No. MS-79-7, Georgia Institute of Technology) show that it can be structured as a **fixed-cost assignment-location problem** designed to minimize the overall cost of cash concentration. Once the appropriate **transfer scheduling cost** has been obtained, this design problem is again an assignment location problem similar to the assignment problem arising in lockbox design. Hence, analogous design algorithms can be used for systematically approaching cash concentration design.

FUTURE CONSIDERATIONS.   The **pricing of Fed float** required by the **1980 Banking Act** will reduce the value of dual balances. Rising costs for DTCs and reduced float plus improvements in the system of ACHs will tend to make ACH-based transfers a viable substitute for DTCs. During the transition period, however, companies probably will want to use both DTCs and ACH-based transfers. Besides cost-effective mobilization of cash from deposit banks, future systems should focus on administrative efficiency and good control. Given the changes in the concentration environment, there is a clear value to flexible systems that can support multiple transfer methods and/or multiple concentration banks.

AGGREGATE CASH POSITION MANAGEMENT

DEFINITION.   **Aggregate cash position management (ACPM)** is the task of managing the level of the overall cash balance. After all allocation transfers have been made, managing the aggregate balance is equivalent to managing the balance at the concentration bank relative to its target.

DECISIONS. Day-to-day aggregate cash position management can be structured by identifying three major decisions—the adjustment, the adjustment amount, and the adjustment means. **Adjustment** refers to deciding whether to make any change in the aggregate balance at all. If the answer is yes, the **adjustment amount** must be determined—that is, the amount that should be added to or removed from the current balance. **Adjustment means** are instruments for changing the overall balance, primarily borrowing (including commercial paper issuance) and/or selling securities to increase the cash balance and investing and/or repaying debt (including commercial paper refunding) to decrease the cash balance.

OBJECTIVES AND CONSTRAINTS. The objective of aggregate cash position management is to manage the overall cash balance efficiently while compensating the bank and not incurring overdrafts. Defining "efficiency" precisely usually puts most practicing cash managers in a quandary. The term is generally used to describe maximizing yield on investable cash and/or minimizing the cost of borrowing while providing adequate liquidity and at the same time recognizing that a good yield should not involve significant exposure to default risk. The difficulty is defining "adequate liquidity" or quantifying profitability-liquidity tradeoffs.

DECISION FRAMEWORKS. There are several conceptual frameworks for approaching the problem of aggregate cash position management: the daily target or daily adjustment framework, the control-limit framework, and the balance scheduling framework.

The Daily Target Framework. A target balance is set based on levels of tangible activity, credit lines, borrowing, and compensation agreements with a firm's banks. The cash manager adjusts the balance each day to meet this target balance, or at least to meet the balance to within an efficient money market transaction quantity, say $0.5 million to $1 million for a large company.

The Control-Limit Framework. The cash balance is allowed to fluctuate above and below the target as long as it stays within specified limits or is at least expected to return within the limits in a few days. Adjustments are made only if the balance falls outside the control limits rather than whenever there is a departure from the target.

The Optimal Scheduling Framework. The optimal balance scheduling framework uses mathematical programming to plan all cash adjustments, including purchases of short-term securities and borrowing-repayment timing. Such models have been set forth in works such as Orgler, *Cash Management: Methods and Models,* and Maier and Vander Weide, "A Practical Approach to Short-Run Financial Planning." However, few firms are using this framework. One problem is the assumption that cash flows are known with certainty over a fairly long horizon, say at least 60–90 days. A second is the assumption that interest rates are known with certainty. Third, simplified assumptions are made in many of the articles setting forth this framework such that, for example, sales of short-term securities before maturity may be precluded. Also to be considered are the computational complexity and the information management burden involved in solving the mathematical program required to determine the best adjustment schedule.

FRAMEWORK EVALUATION. The two frameworks meriting serious practitioner consideration are the two in use today—the daily target and the control-limit frameworks, which are similar in many ways. Both allow for uncertainty in day-to-day flows. Both separate the adjustment and adjustment amount decisions from adjustment means. Hence, both separate managing the level of the overall balance from managing both borrowing-repayment scheduling and the short-term security portfolio. In contrast, the failure of the optimal scheduling framework is combining the decisions on adjustment and adjustment amount with the very difficult and complex problems of managing both borrowing-repayment scheduling and the short-term security portfolio. This mixing is the reason for most of the limitations of the optimal scheduling framework noted above.

While the **optimal scheduling approach** may be made into an operationally useful framework in the future, practical means to overcome its many problems must be set forth. At present, the primary value of this framework is pedagogical; that is, it offers a systematic treatment of the problem that shows interdependencies between the cash balance adjustment and management tasks related to the adjustment means.

THE DAILY TARGET FRAMEWORK.

Management Procedure. The daily target framework is very simple. There is always an adjustment unless the balance happens to be within an efficient transaction unit of the target. The adjustment amount is just the difference between the actual balance and the target, possibly rounded up or down for the sake of achieving efficient transaction sizes.

Typical management procedure in the daily target framework is focused on **balance reporting** information. First, the cash manager uses balance reports to ascertain the company's balance position after allowance for transfers in and out of the concentration bank. Then the appropriate adjustment is made. If there is a deficiency, the cash manager makes borrowing arrangements (including the issuance of commercial paper) and/or sells short-term marketable securities. If there is a surplus, the cash manager repays debt and/or contacts a dealer to arrange investment in money market instruments.

The target balance is modified from time to time to reflect changes in bank activity that affect required compensating balances, as well as any past departure from the target. Some balance reporting systems even include target tracking reports to facilitate this modification.

Evaluation. The merit of the daily target framework is its **simplicity.** However, this simplicity may incur costs relative to the control-limit framework, namely, a higher volume of money market trading with its associated transaction costs, greater administrative effort, and lower yield on the money market portfolio and/or higher effective borrowing costs. The lower yield arises from the tendency to invest in very short maturities, especially overnight investments, which generally have a lower yield. The higher effective borrowing costs reflect borrowing at one time and investing at another at a lower rate, when averaging out the borrowing and investment would mean no borrowing or investing and a saving of the spread between the borrowing and investing rate, typically about 150 basis points for a prime borrower. The averaging out can be accomplished in a control-limit framework.

CONTROL-LIMIT FRAMEWORKS. The control-limit framework is based on the control-limit approach to inventories with two-way flows. Thus, the essence of this approach is to view cash as an inventory able to fluctuate within limits. No action is taken as long as the balance remains within the control limits.

The control-limit framework is not a single model but rather a generic approach for which there are many variations. Two key considerations are whether cash forecast information is used and how the forecast information is used.

Control Limits Without Forecasts.   The use of the control-limit framework for cash management without forecasts was first set forth in Miller and Orr, "An Application of Control-Limit Models to the Management of Corporate Cash Balances," and developed in depth by Homonoff and Mullins, *Cash Management: An Inventory Control Limit Approach.*

Without forecasts, the decision to adjust is based on whether the cash balance has moved outside the control limits on a given day. If outside, the balance is restored to a return point within the control limits, generally the target balance. Otherwise, no action is taken.

The primary task is deciding on the control limits and possibly the return point if it is to be different from the target. The benefit of the simple control-limit framework without forecasts is a reduction in the number and volume of transactions. There may also be some smoothing value in avoiding **wash transactions** (i.e., investing at one time with offsetting borrowing at another time, and vice versa). However, the failure to use forecasts means that most of the potential benefits of the control-limit framework go unrealized.

Control Limits with Forecasts and Smoothing.   Most cash managers using a **control-limit framework** would object to the exclusion of forecast data as "too simple." The primary objection would be the failure to use forecast information (including known trends and patterns) in determining the adjustment amount. In fact, most cash managers operating the control-limit framework view it as a way to use forecast information to smooth out peaks and valleys in day-to-day cash flows.

Stone, in "The Use of Forecasts and Smoothing in Control-Limit Models for Cash Management," formalized a common smoothing procedure used judgmentally by cash managers to benefit from cash forecasts. The smoothing procedure is summarized by the rules for the adjustment decision and adjustment amount.

> **Adjustment Decision.**   Do nothing if the balance is within the control limits.
>
> **Adjustment Amount.**   If outside the control limits, consider the position in K days, where K is the look-ahead period, typically 5 business days (1 week) to 10 business days (2 weeks). If the expected balance is still outside the control limit at the end of the look-ahead period, the adjustment amount should return the expected balance to the target at the end of the look-ahead period. However, if the cash balance returns within the control limits by the end of the look-ahead period, then make no adjustment.

Not only does the smoothing average out day-to-day flows, as done in the simple model without forecasts, but the look-ahead also smooths over anticipated future flows. Thus, if a company were at the upper limit, no action would be taken if the company anticipated significant outflows. Likewise, a company at the lower limit would take no action if it anticipated significant inflows. Because of strong weekly cycles in the cash flows of most companies, the look-ahead procedure can dramatically increase smoothing relative to no use of forecasts. Hence, it reduces **wash transactions.** Moreover, because it also averages out daily forecast errors, the procedure is fairly sensitive to forecast errors.

Managing About a Target Balance.   While the look-ahead smoothing rule set forth in Stone, "The Use of Forecasts and Smoothing in Control-Limit Models of Cash Management," incorporates the essence of common smoothing techniques in use today, the framework still has limitations. The crux of the problem is flat control limits relative to a fixed target.

An alternative way to use forecast information in a control-limit framework is to determine a balance plan in which any monthly and weekly patterns are incorporated. The net result is a time-varying target balance, the average value being the target. The key to developing the plan is a measure of the **minimum possible adjustment amount.** It is the difference between the target balance and the average balance that would occur from a starting balance and forecasted flows without any adjustments. If positive, it indicates the average cash addition needed. If negative, it indicates the minimum average investment. Unless exposed to overdrafts, it is the minimum amount that need be transacted as long as there are not significant cumulative forecast errors.

Once a plan for transacting this amount has been determined, control limits can be set about the forecasted balance pattern. Futher adjustments are necessary only if there are significant, persistent forecast errors or large changes in the target balance itself. This approach represents an improvement insofar as it minimizes the expected total change in the cash balance on the basis of a cash forecast and uses the control limits on the forecast error, which is tantamount to time-varying limits on the planned balance.

The benefits are reduction in amount transacted and maximum possible reduction in **wash transactions,** plus insensitivity to forecast error, since day-to-day errors are averaged out.

DAILY CASH FORECASTING.   Many of the benefits to the control-limit framework are smoothing opportunities afforded by forecasting. A framework for structuring daily cash forecasting was set forth in Stone and Miller, in "A Framework for Daily Cash Forecasting." An example of daily cash forecasting within this framework was presented by Stone and Wood, in "Daily Cash Forecasting: A Simple Method for Implementing the Distribution Approach." Forecast techniques are treated further in the Section of this *Handbook* entitled "Financial Forecasting."

MONTH-TO-MONTH BALANCE TARGETS AND ANNUAL SMOOTHING.   Up to this point, it has been assumed that a company knows its target balance at any time in managing the aggregate balance.

There is an opportunity to use **annual smoothing** by appropriately setting month-to-month target balances. The crux of the idea is to provide necessary compensating balances at the time of surplus cash to cover the balance requirement in the period of cash deficiency. The overall effects are to reduce the amount invested in periods of cash surplus and to reduce the amount borrowed in periods of cash deficiency. Hence, the net effect is to reduce the cost of short-term funding by reducing wash transactions across months.

The key idea is to set time-varying targets across months in the annual cash plan. Such targets can be developed by trial and error. Or, variants of a linear programming approach for borrowing-repayment scheduling set forth by Stone, "Models for Allocating Credit, Planned Borrowing, and Tangible Services Over a Company's Banking System," can be used to find the most efficient schedule of target balances for the concentration bank and each credit line bank and major operating bank as a by-product of period-to-period borrowing-repayment scheduling.

REFERENCES

Ferguson, Daniel M., and Maier, Stephen F., "A New Industry Standard for Designing Corporate Collection Systems," Research Publication No. 80-07, Consulting Services Group, First National Bank of Chicago, Chicago, 1980.

Homonoff, Richard, and Mullins, David Wiley, Jr., *Cash Management: An Inventory Control-Limit Approach,* Heath, Lexington, MA, 1975.

Maier, Steven F., and Vander Weide, James H., "A Practical Approach to Short-Run Financial Planning," *Financial Management*, Vol. 7, No. 4, Winter 1978, pp. 10–16.

Miller, Merton, and Orr, Daniel, "An Application of Control-Limit Models to the Management of Corporate Cash Balances," in *Financial Research and Management Decisions*, Alexander A. Robichek (Ed.), Wiley, New York, 1967, pp. 133–151.

Orgler, Yair E., *Cash Management: Methods and Models*, Wadsworth, Belmont, CA, 1970.

Stone, Bernell K., "The Use of Forecasts and Smoothing in Control-Limit Models for Cash Management," *Financial Management*, Vol. 1, No. 1, Spring 1972, pp. 72–84.

———, "Models for Allocating Credit, Borrowing, and Tangible Services Over a Company's Banking System," *Financial Management*, Vol. 4, No. 2, Summer 1975, pp. 65–83.

———, and Hill, Ned C., "Cash Transfer Scheduling for Efficient Cash Management," *Financial Management*, Vol. 9, No. 3, Fall 1980, pp. 35–43.

———, "The Design of a Cash Concentration System," Working Paper No. MS-79-7, Georgia Institute of Technology, Atlanta, 1979.

———, and Miller, Tom W., "A Framework for Daily Cash Forecasting," *Journal of Cash Management*, Vol. 1, No. 1, Spring 1981.

———, and Wood, Robert A., "Daily Cash Forecasting: A Simple Method for Implementing the Distribution Approach," *Financial Management*, Vol. 6, No. 3, Fall 1977, pp. 40–50.

BIBLIOGRAPHY

Arthur D. Little, Inc., *The Consequences of Electronic Funds Transfer*, Arthur D. Little, Inc., Cambridge, MA, 1975.

Beehler, Paul J., *Contemporary Cash Management*, Wiley, New York, 1978.

Business Week, "Making Millions by Stretching Float," November 23, 1974, pp. 88, 90.

Calman, Robert F., *Linear Programming and Cash Management/Cash ALPHA*, M.I.T. Press, Cambridge, MA, 1968.

Commission on Electronic Funds Transfer, *EFT in the United States*, Final Report of the Commission on Electronic Funds Transfer, Washington, D.C., 1977.

Corneugols, Gerard, Fisher, Marshall L., and Nemhauser, George L., "Location of Bank Accounts to Optimize Float: An Analytic Study of Exact and Approximate Algorithms," *Management Science*, Vol. 23, No. 8, April 1977, pp. 789–810.

Donohue, William E., *The Cash Management Manual* P & S Publications, Holliston, MA, 1977.

Fielitz, Bruce D., and White, Daniel L., "A Two-Stage Solution Procedure for the Lock Box Location Problem," *Management Science* (forthcoming).

Fisher, David I., *Cash Management*, Conference Board Report No. 580, Conference Board, Inc., New York, 1973.

Ferguson, Daniel M., Maier, Stephen F., and Vander Weide, James H., "Corporate Disbursement Practice: A Conflict Between Business and the Federal Reserve System," Research Paper No. 80-02, Consulting Services Group, First National Bank of Chicago, Chicago, 1980.

Gitman, Lawrence J., Forrester, D. Keith, and Forrester, John R., Jr., "Maximizing Cash Disbursement Float," *Financial Management*, Vol. 5., No. 2, Summer 1976, pp. 15–24.

Gitman, Lawrence J., Moses, Edward A., and White, I. Thomas, "An Assessment of Corporate Cash Management Practices," *Financial Management*, Vol. 8, No. 1, Spring 1979, pp. 32–41.

Haag, Leonard H., *Cash Management and Short-Term Investments for Colleges and Universities*, National Association of College and University Business Officers, Washington, D.C., 1977.

Hausman, Warren H., and Sanchez-Bell, A., "The Stochastic Cash Balance Problem with Average Compensating Balance Requirements," *Management Science*, Vol. 21, No. 8, April 1976, pp. 849–857.

Hauss, Robert M., and Markland, Robert E., "Solving Lock Box Location Problems," *Financial Management,* Vol. 8, No. 1, Spring 1978, pp. 21–31.

Hill, Ned C., and Riener, Kenneth D., "Determining the Cash Discount in the Firm's Credit Policy," *Financial Management* Vol. 8, No. 1, Spring 1979, pp. 68–73.

Johnson, Theodore O., *Trade Credit Terms and Corporate Cash Management Practices in a Changing Payments Environment,* thesis, Stonier Graduate School of Banking, Rutgers University, New Brunswick, NJ, 1978.

Kraus, A., Janssen, C., and McAdams, A., "The Lock-Box Location Problem," *Journal of Bank Research,* Vol. 1, No. 3, Autumn 1970, pp. 50–58.

Levy, Ferdinand K., "An Application of Heuristic Problem Solving to Accounts Receivable Management," *Management Science,* Vol. 12, No. 6, February 1966, pp. 236–244.

Maier, Steven F., and Vander Weide, James H., "The Lock-Box Location Problem: A Practical Reformulation," *Journal of Bank Research,* Vol. 5, No. 2, Summer 1974, pp. 92–95.

———, "A Unified Location Model for Cash Disbursements and Lock-Box Collections," *Journal of Bank Research* Vol. 7, No. 2, Summer 1976, pp. 166–172.

Metha, Dileep R., *Working Capital Management,* Prentice-Hall, Englewood Cliffs, NJ, 1974.

Payment and Telecommunications Services Corp., *Bank Wire II Functional Description,* Payment and Telecommunications Services Corp., New York, 1977.

Pogue, Gerald A., Faucett, Russell B., and Bussard, Ralph N., "Cash Management: A Systems Approach," *Industrial Management Review,* Vol. 11, No. 2, Winter 1970, pp. 54–74.

Reed, Ward L., Jr., "Profits From Better Cash Management," *Financial Executive,* Vol. 40, No. 5, May 1972, pp. 40–56.

Richardson, Dennis W., *Electronic Money: Evolution of an Electronic Funds Transfer System,* M.I.T. Press, Cambridge, MA, 1970.

Searby, Frederick W., "Use Your Hidden Cash Resources," *Harvard Business Review,* Vol. 46, No. 2, March–April 1968, pp. 71–80.

Shanker, Roy J., and Zoltners, Andris A., "The Corporate Payment Problem," *Journal of Bank Research,* Vol. 3, No. 1, Spring 1972, pp. 47–53.

Stancil, James McNeil, Jr., "A Lock-Box Model," *Management Science,* Vol. 15, No. 2, October 1968, pp. B-84 to B-87.

Stone, Bernell K., "Lock-Box Selection and Collection System Design: Objective Function Validity," *Journal of Bank Research,* Vol. 10, No. 4, Winter 1980, pp. 251–254.

———, *Corporate Cash Management,* Dow Jones–Irwin, New York, 1982.

———, Ferguson, Daniel M., and Hill, Ned C., "Cash Transfer Scheduling: Overview," *Cash Manager,* Vol. 3, No. 3, March 1980, pp. 3–8.

MANAGEMENT OF ACCOUNTS RECEIVABLE AND PAYABLE

CONTENTS

MANAGEMENT OF ACCOUNTS RECEIVABLE	**3**
Determinants of Level of Receivables	3
Credit terms	4
Cash before delivery	5
Cash on delivery	5
Sight draft—bill of lading attached	6
Cash terms	6
Ordinary terms	6
Monthly billing	6
Seasonal dating	6
Consignment	6
Credit analysis and selection	7
Sources of credit information	8
Credit grantor's records	9
Direct investigation	9
Credit reporting agencies	9
Analysis of information	10
Judgmental credit decisions	10
Statistically based credit decisions	10
Collection policies and procedures	12
Statement of account or duplicate of invoice	13
Form letters	13
Telephone calls	13
Adjustments	13
Third-party collection	14

Credit insurance	14
Changing credit policies	15
Evaluation of Management of Accounts Receivable	**18**
Traditional measures of receivable status	19
Days' sales outstanding	19
Aging of receivables	20
Effective measures of receivable status	21
Receivable balance pattern	21
Collection pattern	22
Financing of Accounts Receivable	23
Asset financing	23
Factoring	24

MANAGEMENT OF ACCOUNTS PAYABLE	**25**
Cost of Financing with Trade Credit	**25**
No cash discount	25
Cash discount	26
Evaluation of Management of Accounts Payable	**26**
Traditional measures of payables status	26
Effective measures of payables status	26
Accounting for missed purchase discounts	27

MANAGEMENT OF ACCOUNTS RECEIVABLE AND PAYABLE

Robert W. Johnson

MANAGEMENT OF ACCOUNTS RECEIVABLE

Accounts receivable are customarily classified as current assets on a firm's balance sheet. Like any other asset, accounts receivable represent an investment of funds. Changes in policies that affect the level of the investment in accounts receivable are as much capital budgeting decisions as are investments in plant and equipment. The only difference is that accounts receivable are more liquid than plant and equipment; that is, they may be converted into cash within a few months, whereas it may take years to translate plant and equipment into cash. But the principles of capital budgeting apply. A change in investment in receivables is warranted only if the change maximizes the market value of the firm's common stock. It could also be stated that a change in investment is desirable if the aftertax rate of return resulting from that change exceeds the aftertax cost of capital.

DETERMINANTS OF LEVEL OF RECEIVABLES. The amount of accounts receivable that appears on the firm's balance sheet is a function of the average amount of sales made on credit each day and the average number of days' credit sales outstanding. The higher the average sales made on credit each day and the more days of credit sales outstanding, the larger will be the amount of receivables on the balance sheet. As illustration, if the firm has credit sales of 1,000 units per day at $60 per unit, and if the average time between the sale and collection is 60 days, outstanding accounts receivable will be $3,600,000, as shown in Exhibit 1. The relationship between days' sales and the collection period can be used to estimate receivables for pro forma balance sheets.

The daily amount of credit sales and the collection period are affected by the major credit policies of the firm, as well as by changes in the level of business activity. Since the financial manager has no control over the business cycle, this discussion centers on the credit policies that can be adjusted to affect the level of receivables. The concluding subsection shows how capital budgeting methodology can be used to evaluate proposed changes in these credit policies.

A firm's credit policy has three basic elements: credit terms, credit analysis and selection and collection policies. These features are closely interrelated. Thus if credit terms are stringent, low-risk customers may be the only applicants to receive credit. In that case, credit analysis and collection efforts may be simple and inexpensive. Or, if the firm is effective in its credit analysis and is highly selective in granting credit, its collection costs may be

EXHIBIT 1   ACCOUNTS RECEIVABLE OUTSTANDING

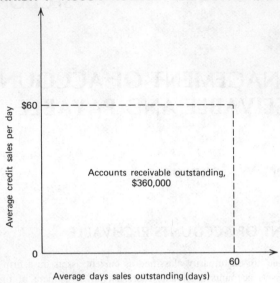

low. Conversely, if credit terms are loose and credit analysis is cursory, collection costs and bad debt expense may be high. An optimal credit policy is one that maximizes the value of the firm as a function of credit sales and the costs of operating the credit function.

Credit Terms.   Credit terms are the agreement between buyer and seller concerning the payment for goods or services. Typically, credit terms are stated on invoices or in the more formal credit agreements found in international trade. This subsection covers the features of credit or payment terms, the factors that influence credit terms, and the major types of credit term.

Credit terms have four basic features. The credit period and the form of the credit arrangement are present in all credit transactions, while a cash discount and a cash discount period are found in most instances.

The **credit period,** or net credit period, is generally the length of time from the date of the invoice to the date on which the payment is due. (Sometimes the credit period is computed from the date on which goods are received by the customer.) For example, if a creditor offers a 2% cash discount for payment within 10 days from the date of invoice, but requires payment in full within 30 days, the credit terms are stated as 2/10, net 30 (or n/30). In this case the credit period is 30 days.

The second feature of credit terms is form of account. In the United States most credit sales are on **open-book account.** The seller merely invoices the buyer and records the obligation on his accounts receivable ledger.

In international trade and in some lines of business more formal credit arrangements, such as trade acceptances, are found. A **trade acceptance** is a draft drawn by the seller on the buyer. Typically, the seller sends the draft with shipping documents to a bank, which delivers the shipping documents to the buyer upon his signing or "accepting" the draft. The bank returns the trade acceptance to the seller, who may hold it or sell it to a third party. On its due date, the trade acceptance is presented through a bank to the buyer for payment. In some instances, especially in foreign trade, the draft is accepted by the bank on behalf of the buyer, in which case it is called a **banker's acceptance.** In essence, the bank has guaranteed payment of the draft at maturity.

Trade debt may be evidenced by a **promissory note:** an unconditional written promise to pay at some specified date. Promissory notes occur in trade credit in two main instances. They are found in lieu of open accounts in certain lines of business, such as wholesale jewelers. In other lines of business that commonly use open-book accounts, a seller may require a customer who is seriously overdue to acknowledge the debt formally with a promissory note specifying a payment date or dates. On the seller's books "notes receivable" replaces "accounts receivable."

The **cash discount** is the deduction from the face amount of the invoice that the buyer is permitted to take for payment within a specified period of time that is shorter than the credit period. In the illustration above, if the amount of the invoice were $5,000, the buyer could deduct 2% if payment were made within 10 days of the date of the invoice; thus the cash discount would be $100.

The **credit discount period** is that time period within which payment must be made to earn the cash discount. In the illustration, the credit discount period is 10 days.

A number of factors influence credit terms, but the dominant factor is competition. Industry standards tend to set "norms" for credit periods, forms of accounts, and terms of cash discounts according to the type of product or service sold and whether the buyer is a retailer or user of the product sold. A seller who varies credit terms among buyers in the same class may be found guilty of price discrimination under the **Robinson-Patman Act.**

Several basic economic factors play a role in setting **industry standard** for credit terms. Attributes of buyers are important. Typically, a seller does not wish to finance a buyer's entire inventory, certainly not inventory plus other assets. Thus terms of sale are related to buyers' rates of stock turnover or marketing periods. The credit period offered by a seller will usually not exceed the time it takes the buyer to convert his inventory into cash. At one extreme are the terms offered to retail grocers on meats and dairy products. Because of the rapid turnover of such goods, the credit period allowed by wholesalers in these lines is usually a week to 10 days. At the other extreme are the terms offered on seasonal products, such as toys and textbooks. Since several months may elapse between shipment and the retailer's conversion of inventory into cash, sellers of seasonal items often extend the credit period from the invoice date to some date near or after the period of peak sales.

The risk characteristics of buyers will also affect credit terms. If individual customers of a firm are especially risky, they may be required to pay at the time of or before delivery. If an entire class of customers is risky, the credit period typically offered by the industry is likely to be short, and high cash discounts may be allowed to encourage prompt payment.

The financial strength of the seller may also affect credit terms. Thus a newly formed business may not have sufficient capital to offer extended credit terms, or even to offer credit. For example, in the early days of the automobile industry, manufacturers sold to dealers on a cash basis.

The major credit terms and their respective uses are listed below in increasing order of liberality of the period of time given to make payment.

Cash Before Delivery (CBD).   Goods must be paid for before the supplier will ship them. A certified check or cashier's draft may be required. These terms are required when the customer represents such a high risk that the supplier is unwilling to extend any credit.

Cash on Delivery (COD).   The goods are shipped to the customer, who must pay in cash, or by certified check or other assured means of payment before taking possession. These terms involve some risk to the seller, since the customer may reject the goods at the time of delivery. In this case, the seller must either absorb the round-trip shipping costs, accept a credit arrangement with a high-risk customer, or find another buyer in the same area.

Sight Draft—Bill of Lading Attached (SDBL).   A bill of lading (shipping document) and a sight draft drawn on the buyer are sent by the seller to the customer's bank or a banking connection in the city. The customer may inspect the goods, but he obtains the bill of lading to release the goods from the carrier only by paying the amount demanded by the draft. The seller faces the same risks and unpleasant alternatives as in the case of COD shipments. SDBL terms are used by automobile manufacturers, meat packers, and canners, and in foreign trade.

Cash Terms.   In spite of the name, "cash terms" involve the extension of credit for a short period of time. Other expressions are net cash, net 10 days, and bill-to-bill. Generally, all these terms mean that the buyer has a week to 10 days to make payment. Bill-to-bill requires that the bill for the previous delivery be paid at the time of a new delivery. Cash terms are found in the sale to retailers of cigars, cigarettes, and tobacco, fresh fruits and produce, meat and poultry, and dairy products.

Ordinary Terms.   These most common credit terms apply to each order individually. The terms usually allow a cash discount if an invoice is paid within a specified discount period and for payment of the bill in full at the end of the credit period. Thus, ordinary terms of 2/10, n/30 require that the buyer either pay for the goods within 10 days of the invoice date, to receive a 2% discount from the invoice price, or pay the full price within 30 days. When the buyer is some distance away or the method of shipment is slow, terms may be 2/10, n/30 AOG (arrival of goods). This arrangement means that the credit period does not start until the buyer has received the goods.

Monthly Billing.   Usually, under this arrangement all purchases made through the 25th of one month are paid for in a single payment in the following month. For example, wholesalers of drugs and drug sundries may sell on terms of 2%-EOM 30. Rather than require separate payments on each individual invoice, the wholesaler accumulates invoices for all shipments from the 26th of the preceding month through the 25th of the current month and sends the druggist a monthly bill for the total. If the druggist wishes to earn the 2% discount, he must pay the total (less discount) by the tenth day of the following month, that is, within 10 days from the end of the month (EOM). The full amount is due by the end of the following month. An alternative means of expressing the credit term is 2/10, prox. net 30, where "prox." stands for "proximo," meaning "the next."

Seasonal Dating.   These credit terms permit the buyer to pay for goods at the end of the selling season. For example, some textbook publishers encourage university bookstores to send in their orders for fall in the early part of the summer by allowing terms of n/30 October 1. This credit arrangement allows publishers to judge their market and level out their producing and shipping activities, as well as to transfer the inventory to bookstores before the peak selling season. In return, the publisher assumes the carrying cost of the investment in the inventory through October 30, when the bookstores are to pay for the books purchased. Seasonal dating is characteristic of businesses with distinct seasons: toys, agricultural and garden supplies, and Christmas cards.

Consignment.   When a sale is made on consignment, title to the goods remains with the seller, while the recipient serves as agent for the seller. The recipient is required to segregate the goods and the proceeds from their sale. Periodically, the proceeds from the sale are sent to the seller, along with reports on the remaining inventory.

Consignments are used when the buyer does not have sufficient funds to pay for goods on delivery or a credit standing high enough to warrant a credit sale. The arrangement may also be made to introduce a new product into distribution, when retailers are unwilling to assume the risk of stocking it. Consignment is common in the magazine publishing business. Retail stores grant display areas to distributors who stock the magazine racks and collect the cost of magazines sold and restock the racks weekly. Consignment terms are also characteristic of rack jobbers serving grocery stores and in the sale of photographic supplies.

Credit Analysis and Selection. Here it is assumed that credit standards have been established by the process of analysis described in the concluding section on changing credit policies. Given those credit standards, the issue here is whether credit applicants meet the standards and can be sold goods or services under the firm's customary credit terms.

The decision process requires, first, information about the credit applicant. Second, the information must be used to judge the riskiness, or risk class, of the applicant. Finally, if the applicant meets the firm's credit standards, a credit limit may be established on the account.

Two types of errors are made in assigning credit applicants to risk classes. On the one hand, an applicant who would have improved the market value of the firm by being a good customer may be rejected, because he was misclassified as a substandard risk. The cost of rejection is an opportunity cost. The firm forgoes the profits that could have been made from selling to that customer. On the other hand, a "bad" customer may be accepted. The customer is "bad" in the sense that the collection costs or bad debt losses resulting from acceptance of the account reduce the value of the firm. The account is misclassified as a risk acceptable under the firm's credit standards.

Neither of these two types of error can be avoided, nor should the intent of credit policies be to minimize the total costs of these errors. It costs money to gather and to analyze information to assign credit applicants to risk classes. At some point the incremental costs of refining this process exceed the marginal benefit of avoiding misclassification errors.

The decision process is illustrated in Exhibit 2. When a purchase order is received, the credit manager may look up the applicant's credit rating in a manual such as Dun & Bradstreet's *Reference Book*. If the rating is very good or very bad, it may not be worthwhile to proceed to the next step of paying for and analyzing a credit report on the applicant. The credit manager must balance the extra cost of $40 against the expected added benefit of having and analyzing the added information. The benefit will result from correcting a misclassification error that would result from halting the credit analysis at the end of stage 1.

The benefit from further credit investigation and analysis is a product of the likelihood that a misclassification error will be corrected and the probable cost of that error. If experience shows that further investigation hardly ever changes a decision to accept or reject when the credit rating is very good or very bad, the merits of proceeding to stage 2 when these ratings are found are slight. The cost of the error is a function of the amount of credit requested and the incremental margin that will be earned (lost) if the order is accepted (rejected). On the one hand, if there is little to gain from correcting a misclassification error by proceeding to stage 2, the value of going to the next stage is small. On the other hand, if a reversal of the decision would add significantly to the value of the firm, either by gaining incremental revenues or by avoiding a substantial loss, further credit investigation and analysis may be warranted.

In summary, the economic advantages to a firm of incurring the costs of added credit investigation and analysis to determine the risk classification of a credit applicant are:

EXHIBIT 2   SEQUENTIAL CREDIT DECISION-MAKING FLOWCHART

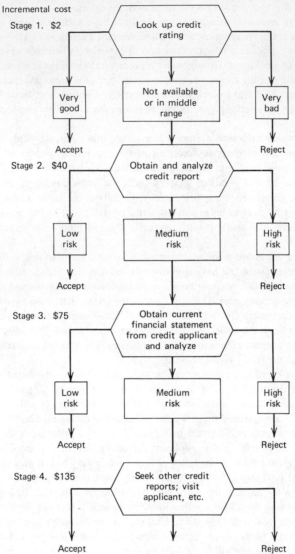

1. Inversely related to the added costs of the credit investigation and analysis.
2. Directly related to the probability that a misclassification error will be corrected.
3. Directly related to the costs of a misclassification error.

Sources of Credit Information.   There are many sources of credit information available to assist in making credit decisions. The extent to which they are used depends on the variables discussed above, as well as the time available to make the credit decision.

Credit Grantor's Records.   If the applicant has previously done business with the firm, the record of payments should be available at fairly low cost. Or the applicant may be a current customer who wishes to exceed his credit limit. Again, the firm's **ledger experience**—record of amounts owed and payment habits—should provide useful data for the credit decision.

Methods of setting **credit limits** vary widely. Cole (*Consumer and Commercial Credit Management,* pp. 616–619) notes that some firms attempt to estimate the limits set by other creditors and match those limits. Sometimes limits are set by observing the "high credit" on credit reports; in other cases the firm's share of sales to the debtor is estimated and the line of credit needed to support this level of sales is then determined. Some firms initially grant only small lines to new customers and increase lines to those who pay promptly. Other firms use "pseudoscientific" methods of setting credit limits, but these are not always based on tested historical experience, as in the case of credit scoring systems.

Modern computer techniques permit instant access to accounts receivable records. As illustration, credit analysts at Rohm and Haas can, in a matter of seconds, bring onto a cathode ray tube (CRT) for any customer "the credit line, agency rating, risk class, date of first sale, purchases this year and last year, high credit this year and last, lockbox assignment, a variety of payment statistics, the collection status, up-to-date aged balance, and a detailed listing of open items" (Stoll, "The Credit Department Goes On-Line," p. 39).

Direct Investigation.   Financial statements may be obtained directly from credit applicants for analysis. In addition, personal interviews by salesmen or persons from the credit office may provide valuable information. Other creditors who have dealt with the applicant may be contacted and will customarily provide their ledger experience with the applicant, including the largest amount owed, any amount past due, and payment habits. This information is especially valuable because it can be obtained quickly and is up to date.

The applicant's commercial bank may also supply information concerning its experience with the applicant or depositor. A bank ordinarily is willing to supply such information as the length of time it has dealt with the applicant, a rough estimate of the average balance carried (e.g., "low five-figure balance"), the bank's experience with the applicant as a borrower, and a general appraisal of the firm's financial condition and reputation.

Credit Reporting Agencies.   Dun & Bradstreet, Inc. (D & B) has had more than a century of experience in the field of credit reporting. Through the use of reporters, D & B gathers credit information directly from business firms, then combines these data with responses to trade inquiries sent to each firm's creditors.

Information gathered by D & B is supplied in a number of forms. The *Reference Book* is published every 2 months and contains ratings of the business firms on which D & B has written credit reports. Each firm is classified by a standard industrial classification (SIC) code number. Following the name of the firm is a three-character D & B rating, such as "BB2." The letters indicate the firm's estimated financial strength (measured by net worth), and the number indicates the composite credit appraisal.

If additional information is required, subscribers may request a credit report. The typical D & B business report contains credit payment records and financial statements. The payments section shows suppliers' ledger experience with the firm: the highest amount of credit extended during the previous year, the amount currently owed and past due, the credit terms, the manner of payment, and the length of time the firm has been a customer. Information is included on the firm's banking relationship and the nature of its operation, as well as a brief history of the firm.

Beginning in 1976, a competitive service was initiated by TRW Business Credit Services and the **National Association of Credit Management** (NACM). The **National Credit Information Service** (NACIS) maintains a central file of credit information drawn from members of the NACM and from Standard & Poor's Corp. Access to the file via teleprinter terminals is available to NACM members within minutes. In conjunction with this program, TRW and NACM are in process of automating the regional credit files that have been used to provide an interchange of credit information among NACM members. The system promises to provide both accurate and timely credit information to members of the NACM.

There are a number of specialized credit reporting agencies that restrict their reports to a single or limited line of trade, to a particular region, or to certain types of information. For example, the **National Credit Office** provides credit rating books in such fields as textiles, leather products, mobile home and travel trailers, and chemical coatings. The **Lyons Furniture Mercantile Agency** provides credit reports on firms in furniture, interior decorating, home appliances, and related fields. Similar mercantile credit agencies operate in other specialized fields.

Analysis of Information.   The next step in the credit granting process is to analyze the information gathered to determine whether the credit applicant falls within the acceptable credit standards of the firm. The credit decision may be based on the judgment of the credit analyst or on mathematical decision models that approximate—or may even improve on—the analyst's judgment.

Judgmental Credit Decisions.   These usually rely on the "five C's of credit": character, capacity, capital, collateral, and conditions. Credit managers view character as the most important. **Character** reflects the customer's willingness or intent to pay obligations; it is an expression of honesty and integrity. It is probably best measured by reviewing the credit reports of the applicant to determine how promptly other creditors have been paid.

Capacity is a measure of the ability of the customer to pay promptly. Trade credit repayments typically are derived from the cash flow cycle from inventory to receivables to cash. (Thus, an applicant's ability to meet current obligations can best be determined by projecting future cash flows and by analyzing such measures of the applicant's current position as the current ratio and turnover of inventory and receivables.)

Capital represents the long-term financial soundness of the customer that may be relied on if cash flows are inadequate. Capital may be measured with such ratios as debt to net worth and times-interest-earned. A fuller explanation of the financial analysis necessary to judge capacity and capital may be found in the section entitled "Financial Statement Analysis."

Conditions refers to the trends in the economy or in the particular industry represented by the credit applicant. In a period of recession, credit managers are in a dilemma. On the one hand, because of slack sales, orders from new customers are desirable to fill idle capacity. On the other hand, the risks of providing credit are increased because of probable delays in collections and potential bad debt losses. Furthermore, particular industries may be depressed, even though the economy as a whole may be prosperous. For example, periodic oil crises threaten the credit standing of manufacturers of snowmobiles and recreational vehicles, even though the rest of the economy may be economically sound.

Statistically Based Credit Decisions.   Past credit experience can be used to develop a mathematical model to predict the probability that credit applicants will pay their debts in the future. While these credit scoring systems are widely used in consumer credit (see section entitled ''Consumer Finance''), they are also used in commercial credit, both to evaluate new applicants and to review purchase orders from existing customers.

To develop a **credit scoring** or point scoring system for trade credit, the credit grantor must first define a ''good'' account and a ''bad'' account. Perhaps a bad account could be defined as any account that has caused undue collection costs, has been more than 90 days delinquent, or has defaulted. For each good and bad account, the creditor compiles all information that might distinguish between the two classes of accounts. Since adequate liquidity is essential to prompt payment of trade receivables, it would be reasonable to compute such variables as the current ratio, the quick ratio, and turnover of inventory and accounts receivable. These data are then examined by a process known as **multiple discriminant analysis** (MDA). This computer analysis makes it possible to identify which, if any, of the characteristics distinguish significantly between good and bad accounts. Then MDA assigns weights or scores to those key characteristics in the one way that best discriminates between the two groups of accounts.

Since a credit scoring system must be based on a creditor's historical experience with a particular group of customers, it is not possible to set forth a generally useful scoring model for trade credit. Purely as illustration of the appearance of a credit scoring model, the final discriminant function might resemble the following. The weights assigned each variable are the coefficients of $X_1, \ldots, X_4$.

$$S = 0.035X_1 + 0.112X_2 + 0.003X_3 + 0.019X_4$$

where X_1 = ratio of working capital to total assets
X_2 = current ratio
X_3 = turnover of inventory
X_4 = turnover of accounts receivable
S = credit score for firms in specified line of business

Finally, the credit grantor must set a **cutoff score.** Applicants having a credit score below that level will be rejected. From this model it appears that the higher the S-score, the greater the probability that the account will be a good account. However, the model will not be a perfect predictor, since some accounts with high scores will become bad accounts, and some with low scores would have been good accounts if they had been accepted. Recognizing the two types of error present in granting credit, the credit grantor sets the cutoff score at the point where the lost profits (or opportunity costs) from rejecting applicants who would have been ''good'' balance the losses from the bad accounts that will be accepted by chance. Some creditors establish two cutoff scores. Applicants scoring less than the bottom cutoff score are rejected, while those with scores above the upper cutoff score are accepted. Those having scores in the middle ''gray area'' are sent to a credit analyst for further review. (See section entitled ''Bankruptcy and Reorganization'' for a further exploration of credit scoring as a predictor of business bankruptcy.)

Simplified versions of credit scoring systems may be used to process initial orders from new customers or orders from established customers. For example, analysis of experience with initial orders may show that they may be accepted without detailed analysis if they are below a specified amount and have a certain credit rating from Dun & Bradstreet. Orders not falling within this blanket authorization will require further analysis, either with a judgmental or credit-scoring system.

Large firms are turning more frequently to **automated credit checking** of orders from established customers. Under this process each customer's order is screened by the computer against predetermined credit tests; the firm then accepts orders that pass the test and refers others to a credit analyst. Ideally, such a system should be based on the firm's experience with repeat orders. Variables used to screen accounts should be those that have been effective in segregating accounts that become bad from those that remain good. The guidelines might include such factors as date of last activity, type of account, date of last financial statement, an order that exceeds a "per order" limit or the credit limit, and type of account. Since a trade creditor would not wish to reject an order from a firm that is past due on only one or two small invoices, tests can be developed to permit certain levels of past due accounts. As an example, the following "automated credit checking report" is reproduced from C. D. Whiteside (*Credit and Financial Management,* Vol. 81, November 1979, p. 25):

Line of Credit	Allowable Past Due
All accounts under $5,000	$ 500
$5,000–$10,000 line of credit	1,000
$10,000–$25,000	3,000
Excess of $25,000	5,000

Obviously, each firm must establish its own tests from its own experience for automated credit checking. Whiteside notes that after a few months of operating such a system, about three-quarters of the orders are approved by the computer.

A final step in the process of credit analysis and selection may be to set credit lines or **credit limits.** Generally, these terms refer to the total outstanding balance permitted a debtor, although a line may also be defined as the total amount of orders from a customer within a given period. If an order is received that would exceed the credit limit, the account is reviewed. The order may be denied or approved as an exception, or the credit limit may be raised. The credit limit is not ordinarily a fixed barrier calling for refusal of any order that would violate the limit.

Although not all companies establish credit limits, the purpose is usually to minimize the number of orders referred to analysts. Taken in conjunction with other tests, credit limits permit a high proportion of orders to be approved automatically. Credit limits are reviewed annually or more frequently for substandard accounts. Credit lines may be set by judgment or through the use of mathematical models designed to provide automated credit checking of orders.

Collection Policies and Procedures.   Once credit has been granted, the next step is to collect the amounts owed. It is worth recalling that collection policy cannot be viewed in isolation from other credit policies. A tradeoff along the following lines is frequently involved:

Restrictive credit terms and tight credit standards   Loose collection policies
Lenient credit terms and loose credit standards   Tight collection policies

The pricing of the goods or service sold on credit may also be relevant to establishing collection policies. Thus selling prices that are low relative to competitors' prices may be accompanied by generally restrictive credit policies (or cash only sales), and vice versa.

Cash outlays on collection efforts are essentially a capital investment with the objective of increasing the present value of cash inflows from collections. The present value of collections is raised either by moving them forward in time or by increasing the expected value of the amount collected. In essence, collection policies should be based on the principle of not throwing good money after bad.

As illustration, consider that a creditor is owed $1,000 by XYZ Furniture Co. Assume that without any collection effort, the probability of collecting the amount owed at the end of 6 months is 0.05, but that with collection effort, the probability of collection shifts to 0.10 at the end of 4 months. (No collections are expected on the account in other months.) Assume that the firm's cost of capital is 12%, or 1% per month. The present value of the collection effort may be calculated as follows:

$$\text{present value with collection effort} = \frac{(0.10)(1,000)}{(1.01)^4} = \$96.10$$

$$\text{present value without collection effort} = \frac{(0.05)(1,000)}{(1.01)^6} = \underline{-47.10}$$

$$\text{incremental present value of collection effort} = \qquad\qquad \$49.00$$

Given these data, it is apparent that the creditor should not spend more than $49 on efforts to increase the present value of expected cash collections from this customer. Estimates of collection results may be based on discriminant analysis of historical collection experience. A critical variable is the length of time that the overdue debt has been outstanding. The longer an overdue debt has been outstanding, the less likely it is for collection activity to be fruitful (Mitchner and Peterson, *Operations Research,* Vol. 5, August 1957, pp. 522–545).

For most accounts, collection procedures follow a fairly set routine. In the great majority of cases it is not necessary to proceed beyond the first few steps listed below.

Statement of Account or Duplicate of Invoice. Initially, delinquent debtors are sent a simple reminder when their account is past due a certain number of days.

Form Letters. If no response is received to the first, polite reminder, creditors may continue collection efforts with a series of form letters. Important accounts may be sent specially written letters. The later in the cycle of collection effort, the more insistent and less polite the letter.

Telephone Calls. This is often an effective collection method, especially as a means of learning the debtor's problems and obtaining a specific commitment for payments. These promises must be monitored closely, so that failure to comply will generate a quick response from the creditor.

Adjustments. If a debtor who is in serious difficulty is an important customer, there are various methods of adjusting the account. Some of these adjustments may still permit the creditor to continue to sell to the customer. In some cases shipments may be continued, provided they are paid for CBD or COD, perhaps with an additional payment to apply to the past due account. In other instances, a creditor may accept a series of promissory notes for the past due balances and continue additional shipments on a cash basis.

An **extension arrangement** should typically be agreed to by all creditors of a firm, or at least by the major creditors. Such arrangements involve a formal extension of the due date of the distressed debtors' obligations. It is binding only on the creditors who sign the agreement and may involve payment of interest for the period of extension.

Under a **composition settlement,** creditors agree to accept a partial payment in final settlement of the amounts owed. For example, creditors may agree to accept 70¢ for each dollar of debt. As in the case of the extension arrangement, the agreement applies only to the creditors who sign the contract. Both forms of settlement should be carefully handled to avoid preferential treatment of some creditors. Often these agreements may be entrusted to the adjustment bureau of the NACM.

If these voluntary settlements cannot be arranged, bankruptcy may be the only alternative (see the section entitled "Bankruptcy and Reorganization").

Third-Party Collection.   If collection letters have failed and a voluntary settlement is not warranted, a creditor may turn the account over to a third party for collection. Usually this action is preceded by a final letter of warning to the delinquent customer. The NACM, Dun & Bradstreet, and many attorneys provide collection services. Collection agencies and attorneys may retain one-fourth to one-third of any amounts collected.

Credit Insurance.   An adjunct to collection activities is the use of credit insurance. Just as in the case of fire insurance, credit insurance is a means of shifting the risk of extraordinary losses to a third party. Banks extending loans secured by accounts receivable may require the use of credit insurance.

Credit insurance is not designed to protect creditors against normal or primary losses. If the experience indicates that normal credit losses amount to 0.7% of credit sales, that percentage of credit sales is established by the credit insurance company as the creditor's primary loss, and that amount is not insurable.

The transfer to the insurance company of abnormal credit losses over and above the primary loss is subject to two limiting features. First, the insurance company will require the creditor to participate in 10–20% of the net loss suffered, depending on the risk involved. This **coinsurance** feature is obviously designed to prevent the careless granting of credit. Second, the insurance company will also limit coverage on individual accounts to an amount that is related to the credit rating of the customer at the time of shipment. For example, the credit insurance company may limit its coverage to $8,000 on each account receivable with a D & B rating of "EE2" at the time of shipment. Unless additional coverage is obtained by special endorsement to the insurance policy, the creditor is liable for all losses over that amount, in addition to the coinsurance share of the amount covered by the policy.

As illustration of the combined effects of the primary loss and coinsurance features, assume that the policyholder's credit sales volume was $600,000, and that the total credit loss was $7,600. The primary loss percentage is 0.7% of credit sales, and the coinsurance is 10%. Under these assumptions the net amount recoverable from the insurance company would be calculated as follows:

Total credit losses	$7,600
Amount of coinsurance (10%)	760
Net covered losses	6,840
Amount of primary loss (0.7% of covered sales)	4,200
Net recoverable from insurance company	$2,640

Delinquent accounts are filed with the insurance company within a specified time period, usually no more than 12 months from the date of shipment. The insurance company then attempts to collect the account, charging the policyholder a fee for this activity. To the extent that collection efforts are successful, the creditor receives a share equal to the coinsurance percentage.

Whether **credit insurance** is desirable depends on the premium and management's attitude toward the changed distribution of risk. The premium is evidently in the range of 0.2% of credit sales and relates directly to the risk level of accounts insured. Clearly, if credit insurance companies are to remain in business, their aggregate premiums must exceed their payments on credit losses, just as in the case of fire insurance companies. However, a creditor may wish to use credit insurance if the risk of nonpayment of the receivables is skewed to such an extent that failure of a few important accounts could jeopardize the financial stability of the firm.

Credit insurance might be used if the creditor has a concentration of sales to a few accounts, in one line of business, or in one geographical area. If adverse business, climatic, or other conditions could jeopardize repayment of a large portion of the dollar amounts of outstanding receivables, credit insurance may be desired to transfer the excess risk to the more diversified insurance company. Similarly, credit insurance may be useful if a firm is engaged in custom manufacturing or in providing services. In these situations, failure of a customer may leave the creditor with a product that is not readily salable, or with no compensation for a service provided.

Changing Credit Policies.   It was observed above that the average amount of receivables outstanding is a function of the average daily credit sales and the average number of days' sales outstanding. Shifts in credit policies that affect either the level of credit sales or the average length of time between the credit sale and collection will be reflected in changes in the level of accounts receivable reported on a firm's balance sheet.

Evaluation of the desirability of a change in credit policies is a capital budgeting problem. At issue is whether a change in the firm's **investment in receivables** will maximize the market value of the owners' equity in the firm. For capital budgeting purposes it is important to distinguish between the amount of receivables as shown on the balance sheet and the **investment** in receivables. Assume that a wholesaler buys a product at $45 per unit and incurs direct, out-of-pocket selling and delivery costs of $5 per unit on the credit sale of each unit at $60. If credit sales average 1,000 units per day, the average day's credit sales is $60,000. If the average time between a sale and collection is 60 days, outstanding accounts receivable will average $3.6 million, as shown in Exhibit 1. However, the wholesaler's cash outlay in the sale of each unit is only $50—the purchase price of $45 plus the direct selling cost of $5. Hence the wholesaler's average investment in receivables is not $3.6 million but $3 million ($50,000 × 60 days). In summary, the firm's investment in receivables is equal to the variable costs, that is, the cash outlays that are incurred if the credit sale is made but would not be present were the credit sale not made.

The key assumption that justifies the use of variable costs to determine the firm's investment in receivables is that the changes in credit sales are **incremental.** To put it another way, it is assumed that without the change in policy, the existing level of credit sales would continue. For example, consider a proposed lowering of credit standards that would leave payment habits of current customers unchanged but would permit credit sales to a more risky group of customers. The added sales do not replace other credit sales that might have been made; they are entirely incremental. In this case the incremental cash investment of the firm is the variable cost of the added receivables that are outstanding as a result of the lowered credit standards. The incremental revenues are the difference between the amounts collected on the marginal accounts and the variable costs of the items sold. As a simple illustration consider that a changed credit policy results in the sale of ten more units on credit at $60 in period 1. A customer buying one unit defaults, with the result that in period 2 a cash inflow of $540 is received (9 units × $60). In summary:

Period 1. Added cash outlay = 10 units × $50 = $500

Period 2. Cash inflow before taxes = 9 units × $60 = $540.

The incremental rate of return for the one period is 8% ($40/$500).

Oh (*Financial Management,* Vol. 5, Summer 1976, pp. 32–36), argues that investment in receivables should be measured by the selling price of the items sold, not by the incremental cash outlays incurred as a direct result of the added credit sales (variable costs). Oh contends that the receivables at selling price represent an opportunity cost that could be realized if the funds were applied to alternative uses. In the example above, Oh would argue that the investment in receivables is $600 (10 units × $60), rather than $500. However, Dyl (*Financial Management,* Vol. 6, Winter 1977, p. 69) correctly points out that the difference ($100 in this case) "is simply uncollected profit and, more important, these 'funds' would be nonexistent without the change in credit standards." Put another way, were it not for the investment to gain the added credit sales of 10 units, only $500 would have been available for other investments.

In the article just cited, Dyl concluded that the opportunity cost does apply if credit policies were changed to lengthen the collection period "on existing sales." But this conclusion overlooks the basic implicit assumption in the capital budgeting approach to investment in receivables. Presumably, a **wealth-maximizing firm** would not change its credit policies to lengthen the collection period on existing accounts out of charity. A change in credit terms on existing accounts must be intended to retain accounts that would otherwise turn to competitors with more lenient credit terms. These credit sales are as incremental as the credit sales added as a result of relaxed credit standards. The same financial analysis must hold in both cases. Thus the investment in those accounts equals the variable cost incurred to **maintain** credit sales to those accounts (in this example, $500), not the receivables at their selling price ($600).

The process of evaluating a change in credit policy will now be illustrated. Assume that the firm is operating under credit policy A, but is considering becoming more lenient in granting credit. The shift toward accepting increasingly risky customers is represented by credit policies B and C. While more lenient credit policies will result in greater sales as shown in column 1 in Exhibit 3, they will also require higher accounts receivable, both because of the larger sales volume and because the more risky accounts can be expected to have a slower turnover. Estimates of the **book value** of receivables are shown in column 2. Additional sales will also require the ordering and stocking of more inventory. The **marginal costs** of selling the added volume of ordering and carrying the added inventory, and of collecting delinquent accounts are shown in column 4. Finally, as the firm accepts more risky classes of customers, bad debts will rise (column 5). The annual cash inflows before taxes are then equal to the revenues from sales, less the cost of goods sold (at 75% of sales), less the marginal costs, and less bad debt losses. If the tax rate is assumed to be 40% (for simplicity), the annual aftertax cash inflows are those shown in column 7.

As noted earlier, the actual cash outflow invested in accounts receivable is not equal to their book value. The data shown in column 1 of Exhibit 4 are based on the assumption that the actual cash investment in accounts receivable is equal to 80% of their book value, composed of investment in cost of goods sold (75% of sales), plus an added 5% for direct selling, handling, and collection costs. The incremental investment in inventory under the three credit policies is shown in column 2, with the total outlay under the three credit policies in column 3. It is assumed that the credit policies will produce incremental cash flows for perpetuity. This is not a drastic assumption, since the cash flows in years beyond the tenth

EXHIBIT 3   EFFECTS OF ALTERNATIVE CREDIT POLICIES ON REVENUES AND EXPENSES ($ THOUSANDS)

Credit Policy	Annual Revenues (1)	Accounts Receivables (2)	Cost of Goods (3)	Marginal Costs (4)	Bad Debts (5)	Cash Inflows Before Tax (6)	Cash Inflows After Tax (7)
A	$ 80	12	60	13	0.3	6.7	4.0
B	140	27	105	21	2.0	12.0	7.2
C	'60	38	120	23	3.7	13.3	8.0

Assumptions
(3) Cost of goods sold = 75% of sales.
(4) Marginal cost = direct selling costs; added collection costs; added costs of ordering and carrying inventory.
(6) = (1) − (3) − (4) − (5).
(7) Tax rate = 40%.

year or so have little effect on the present value of the flows. Thus, assuming a cost of capital of 10%, if credit policy B is adopted, the present value of its incremental cash flows will be $72,000; that is, $7,200/0.10. The **net** present value of credit policy B is simply the present value of aftertax cash flows ($72,000) less the initial cash outlay necessary to implement the policy ($36,300). Since credit policy B has the highest net present value, it is the optimal policy (assuming that the firm is not under capital rationing).

An alternative formulation of Exhibit 4 would be to assess the 10% cost of capital against the incremental investment and then calculate the annual net cash flow after deducting the annual change for funds invested in accounts receivable and inventory. With this approach, the analysis would conclude as shown below:

Amounts ($ Thousands)

Credit Policy	Aftertax Cash Inflows	Capital Cost	Cash Inflows After Taxes and Capital Cost
A	4.0	1.8	2.2
B	7.2	3.6[a]	3.6
C	8.0	4.7	3.3

[a]0.10 × 36.3 (column 3 in Exhibit 4).

Policy B provides the greatest annual cash flows, net after taxes, and the cost of funds invested in accounts receivable and inventory. Thus it is the optimal policy.

It is assumed in this analysis that granting credit to customers in the higher risk class acquired under credit policy B will not change the risk status of the firm. This might occur if only a few accounts were acquired or if they did not otherwise represent a diversified risk. Under such conditions, the firm might wish to insure its receivables.

Furthermore, it is assumed in this illustration that the selling price of the product or service is fixed by competition. Kim and Atkins (*Journal of Finance*, Vol. 33, May 1978,

EXHIBIT 4   NET PRESENT VALUES OF ALTERNATIVE CREDIT POLICIES ($ THOUSANDS)

Credit Policy	Cash Investment in Account Receivable (1)	Inventory (2)	Total (1) + (2) (3)	Present Value Aftertax Cash Flows (4)	Net Present Value (5)
A	9.6	8.4	18.	40	22
B	21.6	14.7	36.3	72	35.7
C	30.4	16.8	47.2	80	32.8

Assumptions
(1)   Cost of goods + direct selling costs = 80% of accounts receivable.
(4)   Column (7), Exhibit 3, discounted in perpetuity at 10% (e.g., 4/0.10 = 40).
(5)   Net present value = (4) − (3).

pp. 403–412,) noted that a change in credit terms is, in effect, a change in the price of the goods sold. However, in a competitive market all components of price—invoice price plus credit terms—are set in the market, and additional risk classes of customers will be served only if they can be charged higher prices. In an imperfectly competitive market, changes in credit policies may increase the market value of the firm, but it is worthwhile in that case to consider the interdependence of pricing and credit policies.

EVALUATION OF MANAGEMENT OF ACCOUNTS RECEIVABLE.   Once credit policies and procedures have been established, a credit manager must design a system to monitor the results. The system should avoid two types of error: (1) signaling that the accounts receivable are out of control, when in fact they are in control; and (2) failing to give a warning signal when the receivables are out of control. A system that is subject to these errors will also be deficient in predicting future levels of accounts receivable outstanding.

To compare the traditional and the more effective methods of assessing the status of receivables, we use a uniform set of data. Based on Lewellen and Johnson (*Harvard Business Review,* Vol. 50, May–June 1972, pp. 101–109), the data assume that the accounts receivable are ''in control''; that is, the pattern of collections and bad debt write-offs is constant, even though credit sales vary from month to month. Specifically, it is assumed that of the credit sales in any given month, 10% are collected (or written off) during the month of sales, 30% the following month, 40% the next month, and the remaining 20% in the final month. Thus if sales of $100,000 are made in month t, collections and receivables outstanding at the end of each month (EOM) will appear as follows:

Month	Amount ($ Thousands) Collections During Month	Receivables Outstanding EOM
t	$10	$90
$t + 1$	30	60
$t + 2$	40	20
$t + 3$	20	0

Traditional Measures of Receivable Status.   The two principal measures of receivable status that are commonly recommended in textbooks and used in business practice are days' sales outstanding (DSO) and aging of the accounts receivable. In a survey of 150 companies, Stone (*Financial Management*, Vol. 5, Autumn 1976, pp. 65–82) found that the great majority used DSO to predict receivables, while the majority used aging schedules as their primary measure of the status of receivables. The analysis that follows concentrates on these two widely used measures.

Days' Sales Outstanding.   Days' sales outstanding is defined as the dollar amount of accounts receivable outstanding at a point in time, divided by the average credit sales per day over some preceding period of time. The reciprocal of this index is the **turnover of accounts receivable.**

The two basic problems with DSO are revealed by examination of Exhibit 5. Credit sales are assumed to be level for the first quarter, rising for the second quarter, and falling for the third. (In the following discussion, all dollar amounts are in thousands.) The first problem is that the sales per day depends on the period of time on which the calculation is based. Consider the calculation at the end of June. If a 30-day peiod is considered, sales per day (column 5) are $3 ($90/30 days), whereas if a 90-day period is used, sales per day (column 6) are $2 ($180/90 days). With the first measure DSO equal 41 days; with the second, 62 days (columns 7 and 8, respectively).

The variation in DSO because of the base period used might not be a problem if one time interval were used consistently. However, DSO is also sensitive to the sales pattern. For example, if DSO is based on 30 days' sales, the index falls during a period of rising sales (April–June) from 51 to 41 days, then rises during a period of declining sales from 41 to

EXHIBIT 5   DAYS' SALES OUTSTANDING (DSO) WITH VARYING SALES PATTERNS AND VARYING AVERAGING PERIODS ($ THOUSANDS)

	Sales (1)	Receivables Outstanding at End of Quarter			Sales per Day for Period of		DSO Based on Period of	
		% of Sales (2)	Dollar Amount (3)	% of Total (4)	30 days (%)	90 days (6)	30 days (7)	90 days (8)
January	$60	20%	$ 12	12%				
February	60	60	36	35				
March	60	90	54	53				
			102	100%	$2	$2	51	51
April	30	20	6	5%				
May	60	60	36	29				
June	90	90	81	66				
			123	100%	$3	$2	41	62
July	90	20	18	22%				
August	60	60	36	45				
September	30	90	27	33				
			81	100%	$1	$2	81	41

81 days. But this is a misleading signal of the status of receivables. In fact, the collection pattern is unchanged. Misleading signals in the opposite direction are provided if DSO is based on 90 days' sales.

While it might be argued that valid comparisons can be made from DSO in June of one year with June of other years, this approach would be justified only if the seasonal pattern of sales were the same in each year. This is seldom true. Nor can valid cross-industry comparisons be made, unless the seasonal movements in credit sales are the same.

Because the DSO is distorted by seasonal movements in sales, projections of receivable balances will also be subject to error. For example, if it is assumed that sales for the fourth quarter will total $200, the estimate of receivables at the end of December, using a DSO based on a period of 90 days, will range from $91.1 to $137.8:

$$\frac{41}{90} \times \$200 = \$\ 91.1$$

$$\frac{62}{90} \times \$200 = \$137.8$$

Aging of Receivables.   An aging schedule lists the percentages of outstanding receivables at points in time that are in different age classes. As shown in column 4, Exhibit 5, as of the end of March, 12% of the amount outstanding ($102) was 60–90 days old. The receivables originated from sales made in January. The percentages necessarily total 100%.

The aging schedule suffers from two deficiencies. First, it is difficult to interpret any series of percentages that is constrained to add to 100%. Compare the aging schedules for June and September in Exhibit 5. Did the proportion of accounts in the 60-to-90-day rise from 5 to 22% because of slothful collection policies, or because of unusually rapid collections from the current month's sales? There is no way to answer this question by examining the aging schedule.

The second deficiency of the aging schedule arises because seasonal sales also cause the system to generate false signals. As may be seen in Exhibit 5, the aging schedule suggests an improvement in the management of receivables from March to June and a worsening by September. In fact, by design, there has been no change in payment behavior. The signals are spurious.

Since the **aging schedule** is deficient for monitoring receivables, it is also lacking as a means of projecting receivables outstanding. To illustrate the point, assume that credit sales of $200 for the fourth quarter are projected on the monthly basis shown below. The aging schedules derived from June and September would produce notably different projections for receivables outstanding at the end of December:

	Projected Sales		Aging Schedule, March (%)		Projected Balance, December 31	Aging Schedule, September (%)	Projected Balance, December 31
October	$ 20	×	5	=	$ 1.0	22	$ 4.4
November	60	×	29	=	17.4	45	27.0
December	120	×	66	=	79.2	33	39.6
	$200		100%		$97.6	100%	$71.0

While there are numerous variations of DSO and aging schedules, the criticisms set forth here apply to the variations as well. Most users of these methods recognize their deficiencies, but it is difficult to make adjustments in their use that will assure that false signals and inaccurate estimates of future levels of receivables are not generated.

Effective Measures of Receivable Status. The basic demand placed on a measure of accounts receivable status is that it not be distorted by seasonal movements in credit sales. Two measures meet that test: the receivable balance pattern and the collection pattern. One is the mirror image of the other, and there do not appear to be convincing arguments that favor one over the other, especially since such computations can readily be handled by computer.

Receivable Balance Pattern. This is the proportion of any month's sales that remains outstanding at the end of each subsequent month. The anticipated decay in outstanding receivables under the assumptions in this section is illustrated in Exhibit 6. This monitoring system is readily usable even by a small business that does not have a computer. Assume a file folder in which are placed invoices amounting to $90 for June credit sales. Invoices are removed when paid or written off as bad debts. At the end of June, one would expect about 90% of the dollar amount of invoices to still be in the folder, or about $81. When the folder is examined at the end of July, there should be about $54 of invoices left (60% × $90). At the end of August, about $18 would remain (20% × $90), and none should be left at the end of September.

EXHIBIT 6   UNCOLLECTED BALANCES AS PERCENTAGE OF CREDIT SALES

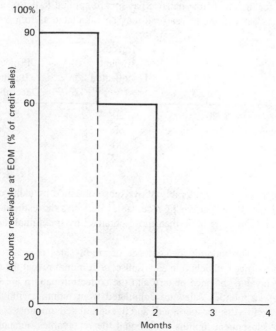

EXHIBIT 7   STATUS REPORT OF ACCOUNTS RECEIVABLE BALANCES

From Sales of:	Accounts Receivable Outstanding (%) at End of:				
	July	August	September	October	November
Same month	92	89	91	88	92
1 month before	58	61	60	58	62
2 months before	19	21	19	18	20
3 months before	0	1	2	1	0

The normal decay pattern can be identified by examining the firm's past experience. Obviously, there will be random variations around the norm, and the norm itself may have a seasonal pattern. A control report might appear as shown in Exhibit 7. At the end of July, 92% of July's sales are still outstanding, 58% of June's sales, and so on. To track the decay pattern of receivables originating in July, the credit manager follows the percentages diagonally across the table as indicated by the arrows. Thus at the end of August, 61% of July's sales are still outstanding, at the end of September, 19%, and at the end of October, 1%. Significant variations from this decay pattern should call for investigation. If the decline in balances is more rapid than usual, credit standards may have become too high, or collections overly vigorous, with a consequent loss in sales. If the decline is less rapid than the norm established by experience, credit standards may have been lowered, or collections may have become lax.

The balance of accounts receivable at the end of some month in the future can readily be predicted, given a forecast of credit sales. Consider the projected sales for the last quarter. If the percentages for the receivable balance pattern are applied to these sales estimates, the expected receivables outstanding at year-end may be calculated as follows:

	Projected Sales		Projected Amount Uncollected (%)		Projected Balance, December 31
October	$ 20	×	20	=	$ 4
November	60	×	60	=	36
December	120	×	90	=	108
					$148

Note that this estimate is considerably above those obtained by using either DSO or the aging schedule. If the decay pattern of receivables persists, the estimate of the year-end balance is significantly more reliable than those obtained by traditional methods.

Collection Pattern.   The monthly percentages of credit sales of a given month that are collected (or written off as bad debts) in each subsequent month reveal the collection pattern. Obviously, the receivables balance pattern and the collection pattern are closely related. If collections of a given month's sales are cumulated from month to month, the difference between the total credit sales for the month and the cumulated amounts collected (or written off) at the end of subsequent months must equal the receivables outstanding, EOM. The relationship between the two methods is illustrated in Exhibit 8. At the end of the first month,

EXHIBIT 8   COLLECTIONS AS PERCENTAGE OF CREDIT SALES

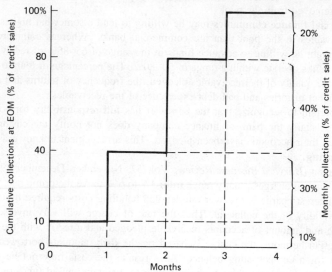

collections amount to 10% of the month's sales, and receivables equal 90% of the month's sales. At the end of the second month, 40% of the initial balances has been collected and 60% remains uncollected.

In the reference cited earlier, B. K. Stone favored use of the monthly collection proportions as a control mechanism for accounts receivable management. Estimates can be made of normal variation around monthly collection percentages, but this is more difficult when dealing with declining percentages of unpaid balances. Each month's unpaid balance is dependent on the balance unpaid in the previous month. Stone also argued that treatment of bad debts is facilitated by use of the monthly collection proportions.

Firms that have adopted either of these systems of monitoring receivables have found that control is most effective if maintained by lines of business, since credit terms and payment patterns vary accordingly. If receivables are aggregated for control purposes, it is not readily apparent whether collection patterns have actually changed or whether the mixture of business has changed. Diners Club has used the receivable balance pattern with excellent results, but has found that payment habits vary by region. Hence it has different control systems according to the region in which cardholders are located.

FINANCING OF ACCOUNTS RECEIVABLE.   As in the case of most other assets, funds may be raised by using accounts receivable, either as a form of collateral or by outright sale.

Asset Financing.   The term "asset financing" is replacing "commercial financing" as a description of the use of assets as collateral for loans from commercial finance companies or commercial banks. In this type of financing a lender is given a security interest in all or a randomly selected portion of the borrower's accounts receivable. In return, the lender agrees to supply funds equal to a percentage of the "pool" of receivables, less a reserve for returns and allowances. Additions to the pool come from new accounts receivable, and deletions occur as daily collections are charged against the pool. Also, past due accounts are usually removed from the pool.

Commercial finance companies may be willing to lend a somewhat higher percentage of the receivables in the pool than are commercial banks. Whereas commercial finance companies might be willing to advance funds in the range of 65–85% of receivables, most commercial banks operate within a range of 50–80%. The percentage of loan to receivables depends on the quality of the receivables pledged, the frequency of returns and allowances, and the payment histories and bad debt experience of the receivables.

It is important to recognize that the borrower has full responsibility for collecting the receivables. Usually the bank or finance company does not notify the customers of the borrower that their accounts have been pledged. This arrangement is known as **nonnotification financing.**

R. Goldman (*Harvard Business Review,* Vol. 57, November–December 1979, p. 210) states that "interest charges usually range from 3% to 6% above the prime rate." However, part of the interest charge is to cover the detailed handling costs required by the lender to assure the validity of the collateral. Thus the rate of charge will vary inversely with the average size and amount of accounts receivable pledged and directly with the turnover of receivables. Furthermore, the charge is based on the daily amounts borrowed, without a requirement for a compensating balance. As a result, the costs may not be significantly greater than bank loans that obligate the borrower to maintain unused funds on deposit.

A variation of asset financing is the use of **finance subsidiaries.** Many firms selling consumer goods and industrial equipment have established captive finance companies that either hold the firm's accounts receivable or lend against the receivables held by the parent. Examples of such finance subsidiaries are General Motors Acceptance Corp., J. C. Penney Financial Corp., and International Harvester Credit Corp. Although the finance subsidiaries seldom pledge their receivables, they comprise most of the subsidiaries' assets. Because of the quality and liquidity of these assets, finance subsidiaries are able to borrow large amounts in relation to their assets on an unsecured basis, especially in the form of commercial paper. Proponents of finance subsidiaries argue that the consolidated firm is able to borrow more than if the accounts receivable were not segregated in a wholly owned subsidiary. In contrast, W. G. Lewellen (*Financial Management,* Vol. 1, Spring 1972, p. 30) has argued that ". . . the best circumstance is one in which parent and subsidiary have the **same** aggregate debt capacity as a combined enterprise. In many instances, a full mutual guarantee of each other's loans would be needed to accomplish even this result. Consequently, finance captives should, if anything, have a negative effect on credit standing." Empirical studies are not available to support or to refute either position.

Factoring.   Factoring involves the selling or transfer of title of accounts receivable to a factoring firm, which acquires the accounts as principal, not as an agent. The receivables are sold without recourse; that is, the factor cannot turn to the seller if it is unable to collect balances owed. If a firm has borrowed against its receivables, the receivables still appear on its balance sheet. If the receivables have been sold to a factor, they disappear from the seller's balance sheet. Most factoring is **notification factoring,** whereby the seller sends invoices to the factor, who then takes over all responsibilities for collection. In nonnotification factoring, the seller collects the payments and remits them to the factor.

Factoring involves two distinct services by the factor, each with a separate fee schedule. First the factor provides credit evaluation and collection services and assumes the total credit risk and bad debt losses on accounts purchased. The factor maintains an extensive credit staff and has a diversified risk exposure that may permit it to buy accounts that the seller might not be willing to extend credit to at its own risk. A factor may, however, reject accounts offered for sale at any time. If a firm uses only the credit and collection services of the factor, the arrangement is called **maturity factoring.** The firm receives payment for the receivables sold each month on the average due date of the factored receivables.

The factor's commission for maturity factoring ranges from about 0.75 to 2%. The greater the expectancy of bad debts and the greater the amount of the handling costs involved, the higher the commission rates.

A second service provided by factors is **discount factoring.** Under this arrangement the firm selling its receivables may draw funds from the factor prior to the average maturity date. Funds available are equal to the net amount of the invoice, after cash discounts, less an allowance to cover estimated claims, returns, and other allowances. In the reference cited above, Goldman quoted the interest rates for this service as ranging from 2 to 3% above the prime rate. The interest charge is based on daily balances, and no compensating balances are required.

In addition to these two basic services, factors may provide other financing arrangements. **Daily cash balance accounts** enable firms selling to retailers "to draw against a receivable from the day it's assigned to the factor" (T. V. Pizzo, *Credit and Financial Management,* Vol. 81, December 1979, p. 18). Interest is charged from that date to the day when the receivable is collected and the advance canceled.

Overadvances permit a firm to borrow from a factor in anticipation of receivables that are yet to be generated. This type of financing permits firms to build inventories in anticipation of their peak selling season.

Factoring is particularly common in the apparel and textile industries, although it is used in a number of other fields. In the reference cited above, Pizzo noted that to use factoring, a firm should have "annual sales of $1 million and up, with outstanding accounts receivable of $300 per invoice or more and a turnover cycle of 30 to 90 days."

MANAGEMENT OF ACCOUNTS PAYABLE

Trade credit is short-term business credit extended by a supplier to a buyer in conjunction with the purchase of goods and services. While accounts receivable are a current asset of the seller of goods and services, accounts payable are the corresponding current liability of the buyer. Thus the forms and credit terms are the same as those discussed in connection with accounts receivable.

Trade credit is an important source of funds to businesses, especially to small firms. Of the $180.7 billion increase in liabilities of nonfinancial corporate business (excluding farms) in 1979, 34% was provided by trade credit (Board of Governors of the Federal Reserve System, Flow of Funds Accounts, May 1980, p. 10). Whereas manufacturing corporations with assets of at least $1 billion financed 8.0% of their assets with trade credit in the second quarter of 1979, manufacturing firms with assets under $5 million financed 17.4% of their assets with trade credit.

COST OF FINANCING WITH TRADE CREDIT.   The cost of trade credit depends on the credit terms offered. There are two classes of credit terms for analysis: those providing no cash discount and those that do include cash discounts.

No Cash Discount.   When cash discounts are not offered, there is no explicit cost associated with the use of trade credit. Obviously, there is an implicit cost. The seller must cover the costs of providing "free" credit services in the selling price of the goods and services. If credit terms are "net 30," the credit should ordinarily be used for the full 30 days. To pay earlier means obtaining and paying for other sources of funds or forgoing the returns from investing idle funds in liquid assets.

Cash Discount.   When cash discounts are available, failure to pay within the discount period bears an explicit cost. Assume that credit terms are 2/10, net 30; if the invoice is for $100, the cost of the goods purchased is really $98, and $2 will be **added** to the cost as a finance charge if the buyer fails to pay $98 by the tenth day. Assume that the buyer would pay by the thirtieth day in any case. The annual percentage rate charged for the use of the supplier's funds for the extra 20 days (from the tenth to the thirtieth day) is as follows:

$$\text{annual percentage rate} = \text{rate per period} \times \text{number of periods per year}$$

$$= \frac{\text{discount percent}}{100\% - \text{discount percent}} \times \frac{365 \text{ days}}{\text{payment period} - \text{discount period}}$$

$$= \frac{2\%}{100\% - 2\%} \times \frac{365 \text{ days}}{30 \text{ days} - 10 \text{ days}}$$

$$= 0.0204 \times 18.25$$

$$= 0.3724 \text{ or } 37.24\%$$

If it were trade practice to stretch out payment to 60 days when the cash discount was missed, the annual percentage rate would be 14.9%. While it may appear that delaying final payment has the effect of lowering the annual percentage cost of missing trade discounts, this may not be the case. The cost of slow payment may be a lowered credit rating and lessened availability of trade credit from desirable suppliers.

EVALUATION OF MANAGEMENT OF ACCOUNTS PAYABLE.   The evaluation of the management of accounts payable is the converse of the management of accounts receivable. Ultimately, failure to manage payables properly will be reflected in a firm's credit report. Since an adverse report levies costs on the firm that are implicit and difficult to measure, management of payables is an important function of financial management.

Traditional Measures of Payables Status.   Just as the status of receivables is commonly measured by the use of days' sales outstanding and aging schedules, the status of accounts payable is measured by **days' purchases outstanding** (DPO) and aging schedules. The former index is calculated by dividing the dollar amount of accounts payable owed at a point in time by the average purchases per day over some preceding period of time. The reciprocal of this index is the **turnover of accounts payable.** An **aging schedule of payables** lists the percentages of outstanding payables at a point in time that are in different age classes: current, 0–30 days past due, 30–60 days past due, and so on.

When purchases vary significantly from month to month, both these measures suffer from the same deficiencies discussed with respect to DSO and aging schedules for accounts receivable. More effective monitoring procedures are available that are easy to employ.

Effective Measures of Payables Status.   Either of two indexes that are not distorted by seasonal variations in purchases may be used to measure the status of accounts payable. Since both are mirror images of the effective procedures used to monitor receivables, they need not be discussed in detail. The **payable balance pattern** is calculated by determining the percentage of each month's purchases that remains outstanding at the end of each subsequent month. The **payment pattern** is shown by the monthly percentages of credit purchases in a given month that are paid in each subsequent month. Given predicted monthly purchases, either procedure can be used to predict levels of accounts payable outstanding.

Accounting for Missed Purchase Discounts.   A final method of evaluating the management of accounts payable is provided by accounting procedures to isolate the cost of missed cash discounts. The cost of purchase discounts missed may be incorporated in "purchases" and carried through to "cost of goods sold." Under this procedure missed purchase discounts merely serve to lower the gross margin. A preferable procedure is to account for purchase discounts missed as a separate expense. For example, if a 2% cash discount were missed on a $100 invoice, $98 would be charged to "purchases" and carried to "cost of goods sold," and $2 would be charged to "purchase discounts missed." This account procedure highlights the cost of the failure of the financial manager to pay bills promptly.

REFERENCES

Cole, R. H., *Consumer and Commercial Credit Management*, 5th ed., Irwin, Homewood, IL, 1976, pp. 391–382.

Credit Management Handbook, Irwin, Homewood, IL, 1965. (New edition planned for 1981.)

Dyl, E. A., "Another Look at the Evaluation of Investment in Accounts Receivable," *Financial Management*, Vol. 6, Winter 1977, pp. 67–70.

Goldman, R. L., "Look to Receivables and Other Assets to Obtain Working Capital," *Harvard Business Review*, Vol. 57, November–December 1979, pp. 206–216.

Kim, Y. H., and Atkins, J. C., "Evaluating Investments in Accounts Receivable: A Wealth Maximizing Framework," *Journal of Finance*, Vol. 33, May 1978, pp. 403–412.

Lewellen, W. G., "Finance Subsidiaries and Corporate Borrowing Capacity," *Financial Management*, Vol. 1, Spring 1972, pp. 21–32.

Lewellen, W. G., and Johnson, R. W., "Better Way to Monitor Accounts Receivable," *Harvard Business Review*, Vol. 50, May–June 1972, pp. 101–109.

Mitchner, M. S. and Peterson, R. P., "An Operations-Research Study of the Collection of Defaulted Loans," *Operations Research*, Vol. 5, August 1957, pp. 522–545.

Oh, J. S., "Opportunity Cost in the Evaluation of Investment in Accounts Receivable," *Financial Management*, Vol. 5, Summer 1976, pp. 32–36.

Pizzo, T. V., "Factoring as a Management Tool," *Credit and Financial Management*, Vol. 81, December 1979, pp. 16–18.

Stoll, D. R., "The Credit Department Goes On-Line," *Credit and Financial Management*, Vol. 81, May 1979, pp. 12–13, 39.

Stone, B. K., "The Payments-Pattern Approach to the Forecasting and Control of Accounts Receivable," *Financial Management*, Vol. 5, Autumn 1976, pp. 65–82.

Whiteside, C. D., "Automated Credit Checking," *Credit and Financial Management*, Vol. 81, November 1979, pp. 23–25.

BIBLIOGRAPHY

Credit Limits Established by Formula and Computer, Credit Research Foundation, Lake Success, NY, 1970.

Hill, N. C., and Reiner, K. D., "Determining the Cash Discount in the Firm's Credit Policy," *Financial Management*, Vol. 8, Spring 1979, pp. 68–73.

Lewellen, W. G., and Edmister, R. W., "A General Model for Accounts-Receivable Analysis and Control," *Journal of Financial and Quantitative Analysis*, Vol. 11, March 1973, pp. 195–206.

Mehta, D. R., "The Formulation of Credit Policy Models," *Management Science*, Vol. 15, October 1968, pp. B30–50.

Mehta, R., *Working Capital Management*, Prentice Hall, Englewood Cliffs, NJ, 1979, pp. 9–67.

Myers, J. H., and Forgy, E. W., "The Development of Numerical Credit Evaluation Systems," *Journal of the American Statistical Association*, Vol. 58, September 1963, pp. 799–806.

Present Value of Debt Settlements, Credit Research Foundation, Lake Success, NY, 1979.

Probability Failure Factors, Credit Research Foundation, Lake Success, NY, 1979.

Schiff, M., and Lieber, Z., "A Model for the Integration of Credit and Inventory Management," *Journal of Finance*, Vol. 24, March 1974, pp. 133–140.

Smith, K. V., *Guide to Working Capital Management*, McGraw-Hill, New York, 1979, pp. 115–140.

Walia, T., "Explicit and Implicit Cost of Changes in the Level of Accounts Receivable and the Credit Policies of the Firm," *Financial Management*, Vol. 6, Winter 1977, pp. 75–78.

Wrightsman, D., "Optimal Credit Terms for Accounts Receivable," *Quarterly Review of Economics and Business*, Vol. 9, Summer 1972, pp. 59–66.

CAPITAL BUDGETING

CONTENTS

**CAPITAL EXPENDITURES AND
FINANCIAL PLANNING** 3

TYPES OF INVESTMENT 4

Independent Projects 4
Mutually Exclusive Investments 5
Types of Decision 5

**RANKING AND CAPITAL
RATIONING** 6

THE CAPITAL BUDGET 6

Coverage 6
Advantages of Capital Budgets 7
Preparation 7
   Status list 7
   Appropriation request 7
   The project summary 8
   Short-cut 8
   Other forms 11

CAPITAL BUDGETING PROCEDURES 11

Objectives of the Firm 11
Use of Cash Flows 12
   Discounted cash flow methods 13
   Time value calculations 13
Methods of Capital Budgeting 14
   Payback method 14
   Return on investment 14
   Discounted cash flow measures 15
     Present value method 15
     Internal rate of return method 16
     Reinvestment rate assumption 17

Net present value profile 18
Mutually exclusive investments 19
What Firms Do: Two Surveys 20

**METHODS OF CALCULATING
DEPRECIATION FOR TAXES** 21

Straight-Line Method 21
Declining-Balance Method 21
Sum-of-the-Years-Digits Method 22
Sensitivity Analysis 24

**CAPITAL BUDGETING UNDER
UNCERTAINTY** 25

Risk-Adjusted Discount Rates 26
Present Value of Paths 26
Certainty Equivalents 27
States of Nature 28
   Conventional present value 28
   Risk-adjusted present value factors
   (RAPVFs) 28
     One-period risk analysis 28
     Dropping the capital asset pricing
     model assumptions 30
Limitation of Risk-Adjusted Present
Values 31

**CAPITAL BUDGETING AND
INFLATION** 32

The Problem 32
An Example 32
Use of Constant Dollars 34

CAPITAL BUDGETING

Harold Bierman, Jr.

Business organizations are continually faced with the problem of deciding whether the commitments of resources—time and money—are worthwhile in terms of the expected benefits. If benefits are likely to accrue reasonably soon after an expenditure is made, and if both expenditure and benefits can be measured in dollars, the solution to such a problem is relatively simple. If the expected benefits are likely to accrue over several years, the solution is more complex. A decision that involves outlays and benefits stretched out through time is called a **capital budgeting decision.** Capital budgeting is a many-sided activity that includes searching for new and more profitable investment proposals, investigating engineering and marketing considerations to predict the consequences of accepting a given investment, and making economic analyses to determine the profit potential of each investment proposal. The objective of this section is to suggest a basic approach to the evaluation of capital budgeting decisions.

CAPITAL EXPENDITURES AND FINANCIAL PLANNING

Capital expenditures should not be analyzed from a narrow or short-term point of view, but should be **integrated into the strategic programs** of a company. The economic justification for a capital expenditures program must be based on a long-term estimate of cash flows, which in turn requires projection of sales and costs of operation for a period of years. **Financial control** over capital expenditures is basic to the proper administration of a business. The effects of decisions involving capital expenditures are permanent and far-reaching; frequently, they determine the success or failure of an enterprise. Once acquired, **capital assets** cannot be disposed of except at a substantial loss. If increased earnings do not result from the purchase of the additional capital assets, the ability of the company to discharge its financial obligations may be impaired. The basic principles involved in evaluating investments apply to every business, regardless of size or industry.

The acquisition of capital assets and the determination of their characteristics will have an important effect on future operating costs. For example, geographical location of plants with relation to markets and sources of raw materials may result in a large difference in operating costs. A general purpose factory building rather than a specialized plant may be more adaptable to new uses in the future, and the structure may have a higher **resale value** if disposal of the plant becomes necessary later. On the other hand, a special purpose plant that costs considerably more initially and is less salable may result in substantial operating economies. Not only must initial expenditures be balanced against estimated savings in future operating costs and estimated **residual value,** but close monitoring of construction in progress is necessary to avoid higher operating costs, delays caused by facility "bottlenecks," or the commitment of capital in idle equipment and plant and partially completed inventories.

Joel Dean (*Capital Budgeting,* 1951) prepared an extremely useful **classification of investments** that may be summarized as follows:

1. Replacement investments:
   - **a.** Like-for-like replacements.
   - **b.** Obsolescence replacements.
2. Expansion investments.
3. Product-line investments:
   - **a.** On new products.
   - **b.** On improving old products.
4. Strategic investments.

Replacement investments substituted for current investments will either reduce cost or increase capacity or quality. **Expansion investments** are directed toward **increasing capacity** rather than toward changing the operating process. Some investments combine elements of replacement and expansion. With respect to **product-line investments,** expenditures may be for purposes of developing new items or for improving those already being produced. Proposals for **strategic investment** are likely to involve basic policy such as a shift to new product lines or new geographic locations.

TYPES OF INVESTMENT

INDEPENDENT PROJECTS.   Another method of **classifying investments** is based on the way the benefits from a given investment are affected by other possible investments. A given investment proposal may be **economically independent** of, or **dependent** on, another investment proposal. The first investment proposal is said to be economically independent of the second if the **cash flows** (or more generally the costs and benefits) expected from the first investment would be the same regardless of whether the second investment were accepted or rejected. If the cash flows associated with the first investment are affected by the decision to accept or reject the second investment, the first investment is said to be economically dependent on the second. It should be clear that when one investment is dependent on another, some attention must be given to the question of whether decisions about the first investment can or should be made separately from decisions about the second.

For investment A to be **economically independent** of investment B, two conditions must be satisfied. First, it must be technically possible to undertake investment A regardless of whether investment B is accepted. For example, since it is not possible to build a school and a shopping center on the same site, the proposal to build one is not independent of a proposal to build the other. Second, the net benefits to be expected from the first investment must not be affected by the acceptance or rejection of the second. If the estimates of the cash outlays and the cash inflows for investment A are not the same when B is either accepted or rejected, the two investments are not independent. Thus it is technically possible to build a toll bridge and operate a ferry across adjacent points on a river, but the two investments are not independent because the proceeds from one will be affected by the existence of the other. The two investments would not be economically independent, in the sense in which the term is used here, even if the traffic across the river at this point were sufficient to support the profitable operation of both the bridge and the ferry.

Sometimes two investments cannot both be accepted because the firm does not have enough cash to finance both. This situation could occur if the amount of cash available for investments were strictly **limited by management** rather than by the capital market, or if increments of funds obtained from the capital market cost more than previous increments. In such a situation the acceptance of one investment may cause the rejection of the other. But we shall not then say that the two investments are economically dependent. To do so would make all investments for such a firm dependent, and this is not a useful definition for our purposes. The cash flows of one independent investment do not directly affect the cash flows of a second independent investment. Thus, leaving out **financial constraints,** the undertaking of one investment does not affect the decision to undertake any of the other independent investments of the firm.

There is a temptation to say two investments with independent cash flows might still compete for funds, thus they are not strictly independent. While conceding that such a competition for funds can exist (in fact, we give this situation a name; it is called **capital rationing**), we still find it useful to use the more restrictive definition of independent investments, given above. Two investments may be economically independent but their sets of cash flows may not be **statistically independent.** If knowing something about the actual level of cash flow of the one investment helps in predicting the cash flow of the second investment, there is **statistical dependency.** The level of dependency will affect a firm's willingness to undertake an investment.

MUTUALLY EXCLUSIVE INVESTMENTS.   When the potential benefits to be derived from the first investment will completely disappear if the second investment is accepted, or when it would be technically impossible to undertake the first if the second were accepted, the two investments are said to be **mutually exclusive.** Frequently, a company will be considering two or more investments, any one of which would be acceptable, but because the investments are mutually exclusive, only one can be accepted. For example, assume that a company is trying to decide where to build a new plant. It may be that either of two locations would be profitable, but because only one new plant is needed, the company must decide which one is likely to be the more profitable. An oil company may need additional transport facilities for its products. Should it build a pipeline or acquire additional tankers and ship by water? Either of these alternatives may result in a net profit to the firm, but the company will wish to choose the one that is more profitable. In these situations, the choice is between mutually exclusive investments.

Mutually exclusive investment alternatives are common. The situation frequently occurs in connection with the engineering design of a new installation. In the process of designing such an installation, the engineers are typically faced with alternatives that are mutually exclusive. Thus a measure of investment worth that does not lead to correct mutually exclusive choices will be seriously deficient. In this light, the fact that the two discounted cash flow measures of investment worth may give different rankings to the same set of mutually exclusive investment proposals becomes of considerable importance.

TYPES OF DECISION.   The primary investment decisions are (1) to **accept or reject decisions** involving independent investments (all the proposals can be undertaken if they are desirable) and (2) to choose the "best of the set" decisions involving mutually exclusive investment. Some managers think it necessary to rank independent investments; however, ranking is not defensible in an exact mathematical sense because it is done in a **subjective manner.**

RANKING AND CAPITAL RATIONING

The **ranking of independent investments** implies that the interest rate being used to discount the future cash flows is not the correct measure of the **opportunity cost of capital** because some of the acceptable (ranked) investments will be rejected. With mutually exclusive investments, this assumption is not implicit in the calculations, since the rejected projects cannot logically be accepted given the nature of the set of mutually exclusive investments. Thus, the choice of the discount rate is not being called into question.

The ranking of independent investments implies that a form of **capital rationing** is taking place. With capital rationing there are more dollars needed for investments than there are investible funds. For one reason or another, the firm chooses not to go to the capital market to raise new capital. This assumption of not being able to raise capital is the **major weakness of capital rationing,** since it is not clear why the firm **cannot** raise more capital at its available cost of funds. The raising of capital would be the logical move, given that the firm has more investment opportunities yielding a higher rate of return than its cost of capital (adjusted for risk) than it has available capital. Despite this apparent logical inconsistency, managers do perceive that capital rationing situations exist and want to rank investments to deal with such situations by eliminating from consideration the lower ranked investments. In fact, what managers are implying is that the costs of raising new capital are prohibitively high relative to expected returns.

While there are no easy calculations that would lead to useful exact rankings, there are several possible solutions. The most popular **academic solution** is a **linear programming model** that will evaluate all investments over the firm's **planning horizon.** However, this solution requires an enormous amount of information. One needs information not only about the current period's investments but also about all the investments of the future periods within the planning horizon. These information requirements tend to discourage firms from using this solution.

A second type of solution is to admit that the rankings are not exactly correct but to use the **internal rate of return** (sometimes adjusted for reinvestment assumptions) or the **present value index** (present value of benefits divided by present value of costs). These techniques are defined shortly. While counterexamples can be prepared to show why the resulting rankings are inexact, the rankings that are derived using these techniques probably do not introduce as much error as is introduced by **faulty estimation of the cash flows.**

In some very well defined situations investments can be unambiguously ranked, but these situations are not likely to occur frequently in the real world with complex cash flow patterns. Investments can be ranked in an **approximate manner.** Ranking cannot be done with exactness in a complex situation entailing a series of investments through time.

THE CAPITAL BUDGET

COVERAGE.   The capital budget covers all proposed outlays for a specified period for the following types of investment:

1. Replacement of units (the salvage value of old items being deducted from the cost).
2. Additions and extensions to plant and equipment.
3. New plant and equipment.
4. Cost of land on which a plant is to be constructed.

5. Furniture, fixtures, and office equipment.
6. Merger decisions.
7. Make-or-buy analyses.
8. Increases in net working capital arising from the items above.

The **capital budget** is known variously as the **construction budget,** the **facilities budget,** the **capital outlay budget,** and the **budget of capital expenditures.**

ADVANTAGES OF CAPITAL BUDGETS. The **administration of capital outlays** is difficult without a capital budget administered by a specific manager (who may have a title such as budget director or vice-president of planning). The treasurer needs to know the capital budget to be able to plan the cash needs of the coming periods. Also, preparing a capital budget facilitates the comparison of the benefits of different projects that are competing for scarce resources.

While having a formal **annual capital budget** does result in a loss of flexibility of action, few companies fail to prepare formal budgets. The annual budget may be supplemented by reviews of individual requests for capital expenditures after the annual budget has been approved. The justification of a project should include an economic analysis, as well.

PREPARATION.

Status List. It is useful to have a list that summarizes the status of all current or planned capital projects. Exhibit 1 shows a sample form that division managers or department heads would use to itemize their projects. This form lists all **projects now underway,** acquisitions for which **commitments have been made,** and the anticipated dates of completion. Items are grouped by fiscal year periods for the next 5 years. The final status list should be approved by the **chief financial officer** and then by the **chief executive officer** before being submitted to the **board of directors** (or one of its committees). Supporting documents for each investment itemized should be readily available for these executives.

Appropriation Request. The **capital budgeting process** starts with the preparation of appropriation requests for each item of capital expenditure. Individual appropriation requests are approved after review by the plant managers and then the division manager, if the size of the expenditure justifies both of these levels. These managers are required to specify the reason for the expenditure if additional authorization is called for. Typical reasons for planned expenditures are:

1. New business activity.
2. Increase in capacity of present business.
3. Replacement of present equipment (nondiscretionary).
4. Replacement of present equipment (discretionary, for increased efficiency, quality, or capacity).
5. New product.
6. Cost reduction.
7. Nonrevenue-producing expenditures.
8. Mandated (by government) expenditures.

EXHIBIT 1   SAMPLE STATUS OF PROJECTS FORM

Capital Projecting Listing

Date

| Division | Capital Projects | | | Expenditures | Estimated Date of Completion | Comments |
	Item Number	Description	Budgeted Total: Amount To Be Expended	Actual to Date		

It is standard for companies to require that the following information be included in the appropriation request:

1. **Purpose of expenditure** (see list above for some general purposes).
2. **Estimated expenditures** involved in acquisition or construction.
3. **Cash flows** resulting from capital expenditure.
4. **Accounting effects** resulting from new capital assets including the loss from the write-off of any present assets.

A sample appropriation request form is shown in Exhibit 2. Forms used vary widely in detail.

Approved appropriations remain valid until the project has been either completed or canceled. Upon completion of the project, if any expended balance remains, the appropriation for it should be canceled and not be made available for other purposes. If the amount of the original appropriation does not prove adequate to cover the full cost of the project, a supplemental appropriation will be needed. A **supplemental appropriation** should be considered as a new investment. Normally, projects once started are eventually completed, but this should not be automatically assumed.

It is common practice to require **approval of appropriation requests** for each project at several managerial levels. The authority required for such approval ordinarily is governed by the **size of both the request and the company.** In instances involving large amounts, the project request for funds requires the approval of the **chief executive officer** and the **board of directors** (or one of its committees).

The Project Summary.   An important tool to use in evaluating an investment is the **project summary sheet** (Exhibit 3), prepared at the **site of the capital budgeting proposal.** This document summarizes the primary relevant economic evaluation measures. We discuss these different methods of capital budgeting.

The **listing of cash flows** gives the person evaluating the investment a feel for the economics of the investment. The major assumption section is used to make explicit the assumptions that go into the cash flow calculations: those regarding the estimated life of the project, the residual value, changes in prices, the rate of inflation, and other important changes in economic or technological variables.

Short-Cut.   The project summary sheet illustrated in Exhibit 3 includes the cash flows of each year. A possible short-cut is to compute the cash flows (after tax) before considering

EXHIBIT 2 SAMPLE APPROPRIATION REQUEST FOR CAPITAL EXPENDITURE

Appropriation for Capital Expenditure

Appropriation No. _____

_____   _____   Date _____
Plant   Division

This appropriation is to cover a capital expenditure made necessary by:

New business ☐   Replacement ☐

Expansion ☐   Change in production method ☐

Other (explain):

Description of Proposed Capital Expenditure

Estimated cost: _____
(prior to implementation)

Estimated useful life of asset: _____

Timing of expenditures (specify years and amounts):

Estimated completion date: . _____

Record of Preparation and Action on This Appropriation			
Plant Record	Date	**Division Record**	Date
Prepared by _____		Received by Division Manager _____	
Approved by _____		Approved by Division Manager _____	

depreciation expense for taxes. The **present value of the tax savings** from depreciation expense is then computed separately.

When the assumptions about the future allow it, one might be able to bypass the year-by-year cash flow calculation completely. For example, if the cash flows before tax considerations are constant for each time period, it is not necessary to show the cash flows of each period.

EXHIBIT 3   SAMPLE PROJECT SUMMARY SHEET

_____   _____   Date:

Project title   Project no.   _____

_____   _____   Purpose of project

Division   Plant

Project Description

Summary of Investment

Maximum outlays (sum)   _____

Net present values   At 0%   _____

                         5%   _____

                        10%   _____

                        20%   _____

Internal rate of return   _____

Payback Information

Cumulative cash flow   After 5 years   _____

                              10 years   _____

Payback period   _____

Discounted payback period   _____

Timing

        Start of expenditures   _____

        Time of first positive flows   _____

Cash Flows

        Time 0 (date___)   _____

              1   _____

              2   _____

              3   _____

              4 (list for all relevant years)

Major Assumptions

Other Forms. Detailed forms can be prepared showing how to compute the cash flows of each period. There are many equally acceptable variations. As suggested above, one useful technique is to compute the basic cash flows without including a **depreciation deduction,** and then treat the depreciation tax savings separately. This type of calculation is illustrated in Exhibits 4 and 5.

Many executives want to know the effect of an investment project on **accounting income.** Conceptually this is simple enough, since it merely entails doing the income statement preparation based on **pro forma information.** Accounting conventions are such that a desirable investment can depress earnings and lower return on investment for one or more of the early time periods. This result occurs because of the **expensing of startup expenses** that theoretically should be **capitalized** and because of large **rapid depreciation expense write-offs.** Such a situation is the result of accounting convention and does not in any way reflect on the economic measures of desirability. If the economic measures indicate that the investment is acceptable, the **accounting measure** (pro forma) should be consistent with the **economic measures. In evaluating investments,** management should either ignore the accounting measures or adjust the accounting to be consistent with the economic measures. Unfortunately this latter path is not always feasible.

CAPITAL BUDGETING PROCEDURES

OBJECTIVES OF THE FIRM. In making **capital budgeting decisions** there is implied some known and agreed on objectives for the business firm. The primary goal of the firm is to **maximize the net present value of the stockholders'** position. The investment decisions are made from the point of view of the stockholders, and it is assumed that their interests are best served by a procedure that systematically assigns a **cost to the capital** that is utilized in the production process.

To be consistent with the best interests of investors, a company must take into consid-

EXHIBIT 4   CASH FLOW WORKSHEET: FORM

	Period 1	Period 2	Period 3
Revenues or savings (cash and receivables)			
Out-of-pocket expenses	——	——	——
Income before taxes			
Taxes (0.48)	$——	——	——
Income after taxes	$——	——	——
Plus: Net working capital decrease			
Less: Net working capital increase	——	——	——
Cash flow	$——	——	——
Present value factors			
Present values	══	══	══
Total present value of savings	$——		
Cost of investment	$——		
Less: Investment tax credit	——		
Present value of			
depreciation times tax rate	——		
Net cost	——		
Net present value	══		

EXHIBIT 5   CASH FLOW WORKSHEET: EXAMPLE

	Period 1	Period 2	Period 3
Revenues or savings (cash and receivables)	10,000	9,000	7,000
Out-of-pocket expenses	5,500	5,500	5,500
Income before taxes	4,500	3,500	2,500
Taxes (0.48)	2,160	1,680	1,200
Income after taxes	2,340	1,820	1,300
Plus: Net working capital decrease			
Less: Net working capital increase	1,000	600	1,600
Cash flow	$1,340	1,220	2,900
Present value factors	0.9091	0.8264	0.7513
Present values	1,218	1,008	1,179

Total present value of savings		$4,405
Cost of investment	$6,000	
Less: Investment tax credit	300	
Present value of depreciation		
times tax rate	2,464	
Tax rate		
Net cost		3,236
Net present value		1,169

Example

An investment costs $6,000 and has a life of 3 years. There is an investment tax credit of 5%. The tax rate is 0.48. The asset will earn $10,000 the first year, $9,000 the second, and $7,000 the third, and there are $5,500 of out-of-pocket expenses per year.

Working capital will be $1,000, then $1,600, then zero. The time discount rate is 10%. Using the sum-of-the-years-digits, the present value of the depreciation per dollar of asset is 0.855427, and with a cost of $6,000 it is $5,133.

---

eration a cost on the capital that is being utilized or, more generally, the **time value of money.** As a second step, the process must **adjust for the risk of the project** being considered. The investors have to be compensated both for time value of money and for risk. Since capital budgeting decisions involve immediate outlays and uncertain benefits that spread out through time, the primary decision problem facing management is to incorporate time value and risk considerations in such a manner that the well-being of the stockholders is maximized.

USE OF CASH FLOWS.   Why use **cash flows** rather than **accounting income measures** for the capital budgeting decisions? The objective is to evaluate the investment over its entire life, and there is no need to determine the year-by-year profitability (as required for accounting) to decide whether the investment is acceptable from an economic point of view. The accountant measures yearly earnings based on complex "accrual" concepts. The cash flow calculations of capital budgeting decisions are much simpler. One needs to find the net amount of cash receipts and expenditures for each time period (an implicit cash outlay will be included when there is a relevant **opportunity cost**).

The analysis of cash flows should use the aftertax cash flows of each period as the inputs into the calculations. The results are consistent with the use of theoretically correct income measures and easier to compute, since they do not require measures of annual depreciation expense and other accounting accruals and assumptions. The primary justifications for the **use of cash flows are simplicity and theoretical correctness.**

Debt flows (i.e., interest expense) are generally excluded from the measure of cash flows. Thus, profitability measures are obtained that are independent of the method of financing. For some purposes the decision maker may want to include all debt flows (principal and interest) to obtain **stockholder equity profitability measures.** These measures of stockholder equity cash flows must be used with care, since they are not comparable to measures that exclude the debt flows. It is a major error to include some of the effects of debt, but not all, or to include all the debt effects but not to recognize that the resulting measures pertain to the stockholders' equity, not to the entire firm.

Discounted Cash Flow Methods.   The **discounted cash flow (DCF) methods** of evaluating investments are now used by almost all the largest industrial firms, and their use is spreading to the smaller firms. Twenty years ago very few firms were using DCF techniques. Users included a few chemical and oil companies and many public utilities, but otherwise DCF was considered to be too theoretical. The **payback period approach** and the **accounting return on investment** were the standard calculations.

All firms face capital budgeting decisions for which the timing of the cash flows of an investment is a relevant factor. For many years business managers did not know how to take time value into consideration in a theoretically correct manner. Now two basic methods are widely used and they are both DCF methods. One method is to find the average return on investment earned through the life of the investment, where the average is a very special type of average. The second method is to apply a rate of discount (interest rate) to future cash flows to bring them back to the present (finding **present value equivalents**). The first method described is the **"internal rate of return"** method and the second calculation is the **"net present value."** A wide range of titles is used for these methods, and there are also variations of calculations, but these two methods are the most common and the most useful.

Time Value Calculations.   A dollar in hand today is worth more than a dollar to be received a year from today. For example, if money can be invested in real assets or lent at 10% per year, $100 held today will be worth $110 a year from today. In like manner, $100 to be received a year from today has a present value now of $90.01 ($90.91 invested to earn 0.10 will earn $9.09 interest and will be worth $100 after one year).

Assuming that we can lend and borrow at an interest of r, the following formula enables us to move cash flows back and forth through time:

$$A = (1 + r)^{-n}C$$

where r = interest rate
   C = future sum to be received in the nth period from now
   A = present value or present equivalent of C

If r, n, and C are properly specified, one is indifferent between C dollars at time n and A dollars now.

For example, assume that a firm is to receive $1 million 2 years from now and r is 0.10. Then

$$A = (1.10)^{-2} \times \$1,000,000 = \$826,446$$

The firm is indifferent between an investment offering $826,444 now or an investment offering $1,000,000 in 2 years if money is worth 0.10. The $826,446 will grow to $909,091 after 1 year and the $909,091 will grow to $1,000,000 at the end of 2 years.

If $r = 0.10$, the present value of $1 million due in 2 years is $826,446. The present value of $1 due in 2 years is $0.826446. Tables can be prepared to give the **present value factors** for different values of r and n. To find the present value equivalent of a future value C, multiply the appropriate present value factor by C. Most **handheld calculators** can be used to determine the value of $(1 + r)^{-n}$. If the calculator has a y^x function, this is equivalent to $(1 + r)^n$, where $y = 1 + r$.

METHODS OF CAPITAL BUDGETING.   Many methods of capital budgeting are used by business firms, but we focus on the four that are most widely used. We consider in sequence the payback, return on investment (ROI), present value, and internal rate of return methods. Only the latter two methods are recommended for general use.

Payback Method.   Over the past 50 years the most widely used method of determining the desirability of an investment has been the "payback" method. The length of time required to recover (earn back) the initial investment is computed, and this measure is compared to maximum payback periods tolerable to the firm for this type of investment. For example, an investment costing $1 million and recovering $250,000 per year would have a payback period of 4 years. Well-informed managers will state that they understand the limitations of payback (not considering either the **time value of money** or the **life of the investment after the payback period**), but they use the payback measure as an indication of the amount of the investment's relative risk—that is, a payback of one year would indicate less risk than a payback of 4 years. **Payback, however, is not a reliable risk measure.**

The **payback period calculation** should not be used as the primary method of evaluating investments. It is, however, an effective safeguard against "game playing" in the preparation of capital budgets. A payback calculation on an investment will expose attempts to load the cash flows of the later years, making the investment appear more desirable than it actually is.

A **discounted variation of payback** is sometimes used. Assume an investment costs $379,000 and will earn a $100,000 cash flow per year. The interest rate is 10%. The **undiscounted payback period** is 3.79 years, but the **discounted payback period** is 5 years (the present values of $100,000 a year for 5 years are equal to the initial outlay of $379,000). This information can also be interpreted to mean that if the forecasted cash flows occur for 5 years, the investment will just break even economically (the investors will receive back their capital and the required return, 10%, on that capital).

Return on Investment.   Another popular method of measuring profitability of an investment, though it is rapidly losing ground as the primary measure, is return on investment (ROI). The ROI of an investment is the **average income divided by the average investment.** Since the income and investment measures used are conventional accounting measures, the ROI measure fails to take into consideration the **time value of money.** While the conventional ROI measure is an unreliable way of evaluating investments, the error is made even worse by incorrect application of the technique. A common practice in industry is to compute the ROI of the first complete year of use. The first year's ROI, as conventionally computed, tends to be smaller than the average return. Thus its use creates a bias against accepting investments that should be accepted.

A distinction should be made between the use of ROI to measure performance of assets being used and the use of ROI to evaluate the acceptability of investments. One cannot judge the effectiveness of a manager by observing the income of a period. The amount of resources used by the manager in earning income on investments is an important variable in measuring performance. The normal procedure is to divide income by beginning of the period investment (or average investment) to obtain a return on investment for the period. If income and investment are reasonably measured, this is an extremely useful calculation. One way or another, it is necessary to measure both income and the resources used and to relate the two measures.

The use of an average ROI to evaluate investments presents problems, since ROI as conventionally computed does not consider the time value of money. A dollar of benefits added to period 10 will affect the ROI as much as a dollar of benefits added to period 1. This is neither theoretically correct nor useful in practice.

Since ROI is widely used to measure performance, **pro forma financial statements** are prepared and pro forma ROI calculations made even where ROI is not used to evaluate investments formally. This implies that in the interest of having consistency between the investment decision criteria and the performance measure calculations, considerable care and thought must be expended to make sure that the **performance measures** are theoretically sound and consistent with the DCF investment criteria being used.

Discounted Cash Flow Measures.   These techniques are more reliable measures of value than the payback and ROI methods described above. The discussion is limited to the internal rate of return and the present value methods. These two measures are recommended because they are widely used and also because they will do everything that alternative methods will do and in some cases will avoid errors in application introduced by these other measures.

Present Value Method.   The present value method of evaluating investments has been increasing in use for the past 20 years. It is hard to find a large industrial firm that does not employ the present value method (generally in conjunction with other measures) somewhere in its organization.

The net present value of an investment is the amount the firm could afford to pay in excess of the cost of the investment and still break even on the investment. It is also the present value of all future profits, where the profits are after the capital costs (interest on the capital) of the investments. If the net present value is positive, the **investment is acceptable.**

The first step in the **computation of the net present value** of an investment is to choose a rate of discount (this may be a required return or **"hurdle rate"**). The second step is to compute on an after tax basis the present value equivalents of all cash flows associated with the investment and sum these present value equivalents to obtain the net present value of the investment.

Example.   Consider an investment costing $864,000 that promises cash flows of $1 million one period from now and $100,000 two periods from now. Using the present value factors for $r = 0.10$ we have:

Time Period	Cash Flows	Present Value Factors (0.10)	Present Value Equivalents
0	$ − 864,000	1.0000	$ − 864,000
1	1,000,000	0.9091	909,000
2	100,000	0.8264	83,000
Net present value			$128,000

The firm could pay $128,000 more than the $864,000 cost and break even; that is, it would just earn the 0.10 capital cost. Thus the $128,000 is in a sense the "excess" incentive to invest and is a measure of the safety margin that exists.

Let us assume the following arbitrary depreciation schedule (any other schedule would give the same present value of income):

Year	Depreciation
1	432,000
2	432,000

The following incomes then result:

Year	Revenues	Depreciation	Income Before Interest	Interest on Book Value	Income	Present Value Factors	Present Value
1	$1,000,000	$432,000	$568,000	$86,400	$481,600	0.9091	$438,000
2	100,000	432,000	− 332,000	43,200	− 375,000	0.8264	− 310,000
	Present value of incomes						$128,000

The present value of the after interest income is $128,000, which is the amount of net present value of cash flows obtained above. This value is **independent of the method of depreciation.**

The argument is sometimes offered that the **present value method** is difficult to use and to understand. Actually it is the simplest of the procedures to use. If the net present value is positive, the investment is acceptable. Also, the interpretation of the measure is easy and useful. The net present value is the amount the firm could pay in excess of the cost and still break even, and it is the sum of the present value of the incomes after capital costs (note the interest on the book value in the table above).

Instead of computing present value, some managers prefer **terminal value.** Following this method, the value as of the end of a project's life is computed. The terminal value at time n is equal to the present value times $(1 + r)^n$. The choice of method is based on preference rather than on a substantive distinction.

The terminal value of the investment being considered is $128,000 \times 1.10^2 = \$155,000$. The terminal value will always be a **larger absolute value** than the present value. If the net present value is greater than zero, the terminal value will also be greater than zero. If investment A has a larger net present value than investment B, investment A will also have a larger terminal value, assuming that both investments are carried out to a common terminal date.

Internal Rate of Return Method. The **present value method** gives a **dollar measure.** Some managers prefer a **percentage measure** that is most frequently called an investment's internal rate of return. Other terms applied to the same measure are the yield, IRR or IROR, return on investment, and time-adjusted rate of return.

The internal rate of return of an investment is the rate of discount that causes the sum of the present values of the cash flows of the investment to be equal to zero. The internal rate of return is found by a **trial-and-error procedure** (when the net present value is equal to zero, the rate of discount being used is the rate of return).

Continuing the example above, we find by trial and error that the net present value is zero using a 0.25 rate of discount. For discount rates larger than 0.25, the net present value would be negative.

		Present Value		
Time	0.00		0.10	0.25
0	−864,000	1.0000	−864,000	1.0000	−864,000
1	1,000,000	0.9091	909,000	0.8000	800,000
2	100,000	0.8264	83,000	0.6400	64,000
Net present value	+236,000		+128,000		0

The **internal rate of return** of an investment has several interesting and relevant economic interpretations. For example, it is the highest rate at which the firm can borrow using the funds generated by the investment to repay the loan. If funds were borrowed at a cost of 0.25, the following repayment schedule would apply:

Initial amount owed	$ 864,000
Year-1 interest (0.25)	+ 216,000
	1,080,000
Repayment using cash flows	−1,000,000
	80,000
Year-2 interest (0.25)	+ 20,000
	$ 100,000
Repayment using cash flows	− 100,000
Amount owed	0

The cash flows generated by the investment are just sufficient to pay the loan costing 0.25.

All **independent investments** with an internal rate of return greater than the **required return** should be accepted. This assumes that cash flows are those of a normal investment, that is, one or more periods of cash outlays followed by cash inflows.

Reinvestment Rate Assumption.   It is frequently said the **present value method** assumes that funds are **reinvested at the cost of money** and that **rate of return method** assumes that funds are **reinvested at the investment's internal rate of return.** This position is not necessarily correct.

Let us consider the example above. The net present value is $128,000 if 0.10 is used as the discount rate and the investment's internal rate of return is 0.25. Both these calculations are independent of the use of the $1 million of cash flows at time 1. For example, the $1 million might be consumed at time 1 and the net present value and the internal rate of return measures remain unchanged.

Let us assume that we know that at time 1 the $1 million could be reinvested in period 2 to earn 0.30. One solution would be to assume the use of a 0.10 discount rate for period 1 and 0.30 for period 2. The net present value *NPV* of the investment is now

$$NPV = -864,000 + \frac{1,000,000}{1.10} + \frac{100,000}{(1.10)(1.30)} = \$115,000$$

The net present value is reduced from \$128,000 to \$115,000, since the time value factor of period 2 has been increased from 0.10 to 0.30.

Previously we computed an internal rate of 0.25 and compared this percentage with the time value factor of 0.10. But now there is not a single time value factor, but rather one for each time period and we cannot use the internal rate of return without an adjustment.

If the rate of return method is used, one solution is to compute an adjusted rate of return based on the reinvestment of the \$1 million at time 1.

Time	Cash Flow	Reinvestment	Sum: Revised Investment
0	−864,000	—	−864,000
1	+1,000,000	−1,000,000	0
2	+ 100,000	+1,300,000	1,400,000

The rate of return of the basic investment is 0.25. The rate of return of the revised investment that assumes reinvestment at time 1 at 0.30 is 0.273. The 0.25 rate of return of the basic investment makes no assumption about reinvestment rates, **though it is consistent with reinvestment and earning 0.25.**

Net Present Value Profile.   A net present value profile can be drawn for any investment. Exhibit 6 shows the **net present value profile** for the example given above. On the *x*-axis are measured the different rates of discount, and on the *y*-axis the net present values that result from the use of the different rates of discount. The **intersection of the net present value profile and the *x*-axis** defines the internal rate of return of the investment (the net present value is equal to zero).

EXHIBIT 6   PROFILE OF NET PRESENT VALUE FOR AN INVESTMENT

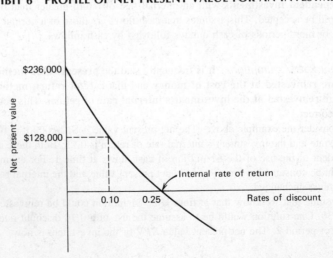

Inspection of Exhibit 6 shows that for a **normal investment** (negative cash flows followed by positive flow) the present value profile slopes downward to the right. Thus, for an investment with an internal rate of return greater than the required return, the net present value will also be positive. With conventional independent investments, the present value method (a dollar measure) and the internal rate of return method (a percentage) will give identical accept and reject decisions.

Mutually Exclusive Investments.   With mutually exclusive investments, the **internal rate of return** cannot be used to choose the best of the set without considering the rate at which the funds can be reinvested. While the basic computation of rate of return does not require a reinvestment assumption, the use of rate of return to **choose the best of a set of mutually exclusive investments** does require that an assumption be made.

Consider the two mutually exclusive investments A and B shown below, having internal rates of return of 0.25 and 0.30, respectively. Which of the investments should be chosen if the appropriate rate of discount is 0.10?

	Period		Internal	Present Value
Investment	0	1	Rate of Return	(0.10)
A	− 80,000	100,000	0.25	$10,910
B	− 20,000	26,000	0.30	$ 2,364

Investment B has a larger internal rate of return than A, but if the appropriate rate of discount is 0.10, investment A has a higher present value. At a 0.233 rate of interest the investor would be indifferent.

Exhibit 7 shows the net present value profiles of the two investments. The curve *AA* represents the net present value profile of investment *A* with a rate of return of r_a. The intersection of the curve with the *X* axis is defined to be the internal rate of return. Investment *B* has an internal rate of return of r_b. The present value of the investments is measured on

EXHIBIT 7   TWO MUTUALLY EXCLUSIVE INVESTMENTS

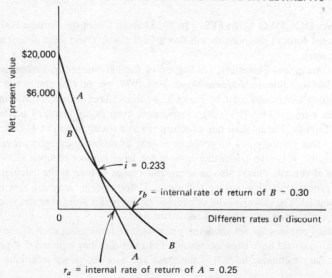

the y-axis for a given rate of discount. Investment B has a larger internal rate of return than A. However, for all rates of discount less than i, investment A has a higher net present value than investment B. Thus if A and B are two mutually exclusive investments (only one can be undertaken), the internal rate of return criterion **incorrectly** indicates that B is to be preferred. The present value method correctly indicates that A is preferred if the appropriate rate of discount is less than i, and B is preferred if the appropriate rate of discount is greater than i.

If the investments are independent and if the firm's required return is less than r_a, both investments are acceptable. In an analysis of **independent investments** with **conventional cash flows,** the internal rate of return and the present value procedures both **give consistent results.** If an investment's internal rate of return is larger than the firm's required return, the investment's present value will also be positive. If the required return is greater than the internal rate of return the investment is not acceptable and the present value is negative. Again the two methods lead to consistent decisions.

Below are two other mutually exclusive investments:

		Period		Internal Rate
Investment	0	1	2	of Return
x	− 100,000	20,000	120,000	0.20
y	− 100,000	—	144,000	0.20

Using internal rates of return, the decision maker is indifferent as to which of the two investments is accepted. The present values of the two investments are equal if and only if .20 is used as the rate of discount. Thus if 0.20 is the appropriate time value factor, the investor is indifferent; otherwise one or the other of the two investments is preferred.

Assume that funds can be reinvested to earn some rate less than 0.20 (say, 0.10), then if the $20,000 is reinvested to earn $22,000, investment X leads to $142,000 at time 2, which is less than the $144,000 of investment Y, and Y would be preferred. However, if the reinvestment rate were greater than 0.20 (say, 0.30), with reinvestment, X leads to $146,000 at time 2, which is greater than the $144,000 of investment Y, and X is preferred.

WHAT FIRMS DO: TWO SURVEYS.   In 1955, about 4% of the Fortune 500 companies were using some form of discounted cash flow calculations. These were almost all chemical and oil companies.

In 1976 Gitman and Forrester (''A Survey of Capital Budgeting Techniques Used by Major U.S. Firms,'' *Financial Management,* Fall 1977, pp. 66–71) conducted a survey of capital budgeting techniques used by major U.S. firms. They found that **discounted cash flow methods** were used by 79% of the respondent firms as the **primary method of evaluating investments.** The internal rate of return is more widely used (54%) than net present value (28%). This choice poses no problem as long as mutually exclusive investments are handled carefully. It is also interesting to note the large number of firms (25%) using the **average rate of return.** This is also an acceptable choice as long as the calculations are not used as the primary decision-making technique. Unfortunately, anything that is computed is likely to be used. The extensive use of average rate of return is unfortunate, since it ignores the time value of money and does not adjust for risk.

Gitman and Forrester did not show the percentage of firms using each of the techniques. This information would have been interesting. For example, they reported that **payback** was used as a primary technique by 9% of the firms and as a secondary technique by 44%. It is possible, however, that some firms used payback as a "backup" procedure (a third calculation) but did not list it. The same is true with the other methods.

Gitman and Forrester also asked for the **hurdle rates** used by firms. They found that 7% of the firms used rates higher than 20%. This probably reflects either a reluctance to go to the markets for capital or a misconception of the purpose of time discounting. It is unlikely that the aftertax cost of obtaining capital in 1976 for a typical large corporation was in excess of 20%. This was no longer the case, however, in 1980, with **risk-free interest rates** exceeding 15%.

Gitman and Forrester also found that 43% of the firms responding adjusted for risk by increasing the minimum rate of return or cost of capital. Adjusting the discount rate or the required return is **not a reliable method** of adjusting for risk. The primary problem is that discount rate increases adjust for **risk and timing** in one compound interest calculation applied to the cash flow of **all** periods, when that may not be the case.

A second survey of large firms, conducted in the early 1970s, avoided some of the omissions of Gitman and Forrester (see Schall, Sundem, and Geijsbeek, "Survey and Analysis of Capital Budgeting Methods," *Journal of Finance,* March 1978, pp. 281–287). The investigators found that 86% of the firms used some form of discounted cash flow method (65% used IRR and 56% used NPV). While payback (74%) and accounting ROI (58%) were also widely used, they were usually used in conjunction with the more theoretically correct methods. For firms using a **weighted average cost of capital** as a hurdle rate (46% of the firms), 11% used a discount rate less than 10% and only 1% used a discount rate greater than 17%. Some firms (17%) used the cost of debt and a measure based on past experience (20%). It would seem that a wide range of numbers is being used at a given moment in time to accomplish **time discounting** and the **adjustment for risk.**

There is still room for improvement in capital budgeting decisionmaking, but the surveys indicate vast improvement in the past 20 years. Both the surveys were conducted using large firms. It can be expected that **smaller firms** are using less sophisticated techniques. There is also reason to conclude that a number of the larger corporations in the United States should be concerned that the techniques they are using are not the best methods of evaluating investments.

METHODS OF CALCULATING DEPRECIATION FOR TAXES

Changes in fixed asset values can be charged off as a depreciation expense to current cost of operations by various methods. The choice of method for calculating the periodic depreciation allowance has important financial consequences, since the amount deducted directly affects the amount of taxes paid in a period.

STRAIGHT-LINE METHOD. The **straight-line method** is by far the easiest to compute. The basic assumption is that depreciation expense is a function of time, and that its amount is uniform with the passage of time. Thus a fixed asset with an estimated life of 10 years would be depreciated 1/10 yearly or 1/120 each month. This is usually expressed as an annual rate (e.g., 10% per annum). The expression "a 10% rate of depreciation" means that the service life of the asset is assumed to be 10 years.

DECLINING-BALANCE METHOD. The 1954 **Internal Revenue Code** marked a significant change from previous law in permitting **liberalized depreciation methods** that increased deductions in the early years of service. Its purpose was to encourage investment in plant and equipment, thereby assisting modernization and expansion of the nation's industrial capacity. In addition to the straight-line method, the 1954 Code specifically mentions the declining-balance method, with a rate not exceeding twice the rate that would have been used if the annual allowance had been computed under the straight-line procedure. Also, the sum-of-the-years-digits (SYD) method was mentioned.

In the **declining-balance method,** the annual depreciation charge represents a fixed percentage of the depreciated book value of an asset or group of assets. This method provides for heavier depreciation deductions in the early years of the life of the asset. For example, with an asset life of 4 years, the straight-line rate is 0.25 and the double declining depreciation rate is 0.50, which is then applied to the **decreasing asset balance.** With an investment of $100,000, the depreciation expense would be $50,000 for year 1, then the 0.50 depreciation rate would be applied to a remaining tax basis of $50,000 and the depreciation expense of year 2 would be $25,000. The firm could then switch to straight-line depreciation and the expenses of both the last two years would be $12,500. One advantage of the declining-balance method is that **salvage value can be omitted** in computing the tax basis that will be multiplied by the rate of depreciation.

A complexity in calculating depreciation expense is that many firms use a **half-year convention** for the first year's depreciation rather than using the exact date the asset is placed into the production stream.

SUM-OF-THE-YEARS-DIGITS METHOD.   In this method, as in the declining-balance method, a larger amount is written off during the early years and a smaller amount in the later years of an asset's life. It is based on the sum of the digits that correspond to the **asset's estimated life.** Thus the numbers representing the periods of life are added and constitute the denominator of a fraction. The numerator is the same numbers in reverse order. For an 8-year asset, $1 + 2 + 3 + 4 + 5 + 6 + 7 + 8 = 36$. For the first year, the fraction would be 8/36; for the second 7/36, and so forth.

A short-cut to adding a series of numbers from 1 to n is to use the formula:

$$\Sigma = n\left(\frac{1 + n}{2}\right)$$

With $n = 8$, we have

$$\Sigma = 8\left(\frac{1 + 8}{2}\right) = 36$$

The logic of the formulation is that the average number $(1 + n)/2$ is multiplied by the number of terms n.

If the asset life is reasonably long (say, in excess of 6 years), and if there are no further complexities, the sum-of-the-years-digits is likely to be the most desirable method; that is, the **present value of the tax savings** from the depreciation deductions will be larger than with any other allowable method of expensing a depreciation asset.

A short-cut in computing the present value of the depreciation deductions is to use tables. For example, *The Capital Budgeting Decision* (Bierman and Smidt) has a set of tables that enables one to determine the present value of depreciation for different interest rates and different lives. Exhibit 8 is extracted from that source. For example, using a 0.10 discount rate and the **sum-of-the-years-digits** method of depreciation, an asset with a depreciable life of 40 years that costs $30 million has a present value of depreciation of:

$$\$30,000,000 \ (0.368548) = \$11,056,000$$

EXHIBIT 8 PRESENT VALUE OF DEPRECIATION CHARGES FROM $1 OF ASSETS DEPRECIATED OVER n YEARS, USING THE SUM-OF-THE-YEARS'-DIGITS DEPRECIATION METHOD, DISCOUNTING AT 6% PER YEAR, ASSUMING NO SALVAGE VALUE[a]

n	6%	7%	8%	9%	10%
3	0.908300	0.894486	0.881048	0.867973	0.855247
4	0.891491	0.875412	0.859841	0.844756	0.830135
5	0.875151	0.856955	0.839408	0.822481	0.806142
6	0.859266	0.839089	0.819715	0.801101	0.783209
7	0.843821	0.821791	0.800728	0.780574	0.761279
8	0.828799	0.805040	0.782417	0.760858	0.740298
9	0.814188	0.788815	0.764753	0.741914	0.720217
10	0.799974	0.773096	0.747709	0.723706	0.700988
11	0.786143	0.757863	0.731257	0.706197	0.682566
12	0.772683	0.743098	0.715372	0.689355	0.664911
13	0.759582	0.728783	0.700031	0.673150	0.647983
14	0.746828	0.714902	0.685210	0.657550	0.631744
15	0.734410	0.701439	0.670888	0.642529	0.616160
16	0.722317	0.688377	0.657043	0.628059	0.601198
17	0.710538	0.675703	0.643657	0.614115	0.586827
18	0.699064	0.663401	0.630710	0.600674	0.573017
19	0.687885	0.651459	0.618184	0.587713	0.559741
20	0.676799	0.639863	0.606063	0.575209	0.546973
21	0.666373	0.628601	0.594329	0.563144	0.534688
22	0.656022	0.617660	0.582967	0.551496	0.522864
23	0.645931	0.607030	0.571963	0.540249	0.511478
24	0.636091	0.596698	0.561302	0.529385	0.500508
25	0.626495	0.586656	0.550970	0.518886	0.489937
26	0.617134	0.576891	0.540955	0.508738	0.479745
27	0.608001	0.567396	0.531244	0.498925	0.469915
28	0.599090	0.558159	0.521826	0.489433	0.460429
29	0.590394	0.549173	0.512689	0.480248	0.451273
30	0.581906	0.540429	0.503823	0.471358	0.442432
31	0.573619	0.531918	0.495217	0.462751	0.433891
32	0.565529	0.523632	0.486861	0.454414	0.425637
33	0.557628	0.515564	0.478746	0.446337	0.417657
34	0.549912	0.507707	0.470863	0.438509	0.409940
35	0.542374	0.500053	0.463203	0.430920	0.402474
36	0.535010	0.492595	0.455758	0.423561	0.395247
37	0.527815	0.485328	0.448521	0.416422	0.388251
38	0.520782	0.478244	0.441483	0.409494	0.381476
39	0.513909	0.471338	0.434638	0.402770	0.374911
40	0.507189	0.464604	0.427978	0.396242	0.368548

[a]Values tabled are:

$$C(n,r) = \sum_{i=1}^{n} \frac{2(n - i + 1)}{n(n + 1)(1 + r)^i}$$

Source: H Bierman, Jr., and S. Smidt, *The Capital Budgeting Decision*, 5th ed., Macmillan, New York, 1980, p. 518.

The 0.368548 represents the present value of the depreciation deductions per dollar of tax basis for the asset acquired. With a tax rate of 0.46, the **depreciation tax shelter** has a value of **$5,086,000:**

$$11,056,000 \ (0.46) = \$5,086,000$$

Inspection of the tables would indicate that SYD is better than the double declining balance method (it has a higher present value). For a firm that is eligible to use double declining balance with a switch to sum-of-the-years-digits, this alternative will be preferable to the others.

The use of the **present value tables** for depreciation greatly simplifies the computation of the net present value of an investment. For example, assume that the investment described above will lead to benefits each year of its 40-year life of $8 million before tax and the firm's time value factor is 0.10. The first step in the analysis is to estimate the **annual benefits after tax:** $8,000,000 (1 − 0.46) = **$4,320,000,** and then compute the present value (PV) of the aftertax benefits: $4,320,000 (P.V. at 0.10) = $4,320,000 (9.7791) = $42,246,000. Assume that the investment tax credit is 0.10 on a $30 million investment: $3 million for the entire investment. The net cost of the asset (net of tax savings) is: $30,000,000 − $3,000,000 − $5,086,000 = **$21,914,000.**

The net present value of the investment is therefore:

$$NPV = \$42,246,000 - \$21,914,000 = \mathbf{\$20,332,000}$$

The net present value is positive and the investment should be undertaken. To test the sensitivity of the investment to different discount rates, repeat the computational process with other rates.

The results of this calculation should be compared to a procedure whereby the cash flows of each period are computed and a present value of cash flows is obtained by multiplying each cash flow by a present value factor and summing. Even though computers can easily do the arithmetic of capital budgeting, there are moments when facility in computing a net present value using the depreciation tables can be extremely valuable.

SENSITIVITY ANALYSIS.   The objective of **sensitivity analysis** is to determine how the profitability of an investment is affected by a change in one or more of the assumptions. Consider the following investment.

Time	Cash Flows
0	$ − 8,000
1	10,000
2	10,000

This investment has a 0.25 internal rate of return and at a discount rate of 10%, the net present value is equal to $9,355 (point A in Exhibit 9). But now assume that we are not sure that the cost of the investment is $8,000. We can test the sensitivity of the net present value to changes in the cost of the investment. We can also plot the different rates of return against the changes in cost. For example, if the initial outlay is $17,355, the rate of return is 0.10, and the present value is zero (point B).

A second possible step in the **risk-sensitivity analysis** would be to allow the benefits to vary as well as the cost of investment. It would be easiest to assume that the percentage

EXHIBIT 9   CHANGE IN NPV GIVEN CHANGES IN COST

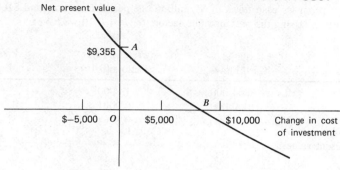

error was the same both for the outlay and for the cash flows after the investment is made. The objective of the analysis is to allow the evaluator to adjust and hopefully eliminate suspected biases in the estimates of the cash flows. In addition, sensitivity analysis enables the analyst to change many of the different key variables in the analysis (e.g., sales, cost of sales, discount rates, cost of the investment) and to observe the effect on the internal rate of return or net present value. In an important article, D. Hertz ("Risk Analysis In Capital Investment," *Harvard Business Review,* Vol. 42, January–February 1964, pp. 96–108) has shown how simulation techniques can provide information on **rate of return sensitivities.**

CAPITAL BUDGETING UNDER UNCERTAINTY

Up to this point (except for the part on sensitivity analysis) it has been assumed that the cash flows were known with certainty. Now we will assume **conditions of uncertainty,** that is, there may be more than one outcome to the situation. The uncertainty may be in the present, as when the costs of construction are not known, or in the future when the costs of production, the selling price, or the number of units that will be sold are not known.

Four basic methods of incorporating uncertainty in the analysis are illustrated. Each of the methods has its uses and also its weaknesses. There is currently **no one "correct" way** of incorporating **uncertainty in a capital budgeting decision.** The four basic methods used are:

1. The use of **risk adjusted discount rates** applied to the expected monetary values of the cash flows.
2. The computation of the present value of the cash flows of different paths using a default-free discount rate or the borrowing rate and then **applying a risk adjustment.**
3. The computation of the **certainty equivalents** of the cash flows of a period, followed by discounting for time.
4. Valuing the cash flows (outcomes) for each **state of nature.**

Implicit in these procedures is the assumption that uncertainty gives rise to **risk aversion** on the part of the investor. That is, if there are two equally likely possible outcomes, a gain of $1 million or a zero cash flow, with an expected value of $500,000 occurring immediately, the average person would not pay $500,000, for this investment. There would necessarily be a discount for risk.

RISK-ADJUSTED DISCOUNT RATES. Let us again consider an investment costing $864,000 that promises cash flows of $1 million one period from now and $100,000 two periods from now. Using the present value factors for $r = 0.10$ we have:

Time Period	Cash Flows	Present Value Factors (0.10)	Present Value Equivalents
0	− 864,000	1.0000	− 864,000
1	1,000,000	0.9091	909,000
2	100,000	0.8264	83,000
Net present value			$128,000

This investment has an internal rate of return of 0.25.

Now we add the information that the cash flows of period 1 can either be $2 million or $0, with both events being equally likely (each event has a .5 probability). We will assume the $100,000 of period 2 is a certain cash flow. The **expected cash flow** of period 1 is $1 million. If it is decided that 0.10 is the appropriate risk-adjusted discount rate to be applied to the **expected values,** the net present value is $128,000 and the investment is acceptable. In fact, as long as the risk-adjusted rate is less than 0.25, the investment will have a positive net present value.

In the past, firms have used a **weighted average cost of capital** (see the section entitled "Long-Term Sources of Funds and the Cost of Capital") as the risk-adjusted discount rate. The same rate is used for all investments. Recent practice of some firms is to use different rates in different operating divisions. The higher the risks of the division the higher the discount rate used.

The difficulty with the application of risk-adjusted discount rates is that two factors, time value and risk, must be taken into consideration with the one calculation. The basic calculation used is to apply $(1 + r)^{-n}$ to the expected cash flow of the period, when r is the risk-adjusted discount rate and n is the number of periods in the future when the cash flows occur. Unfortunately, it is not generally true that risk compounds evenly through time; thus there is no reason to believe that $(1 + r)^{-n}$ can be applied to the cash flows of all future time periods. While 1.10^{-2} may be correct for the cash flows of period 2, the use of 1.10^{-10} for the cash flows of period 10 may not be correct.

PRESENT VALUE OF PATHS. A second procedure is to prepare a **tree diagram** showing all the possible outcomes and compute the present value of each path using a **discount rate that does not reflect risk** and then applying a dollar risk adjustment. Exhibit 10 shows the tree diagram for the investment being considered.

Assume that the default-free rate of interest is 0.05 (or alternatively, the cost of debt capital is 0.05). The present value of path 1 is:

$$PV = \frac{100,000}{1.05^2} + \frac{2,000,000}{1.05} - 864,000 = \$1,131,000$$

The present value of path 2 is:

$$PV = \frac{100,000}{1.05^2} - 864,000 = -773,000$$

EXHIBIT 10   PRESENT VALUE FOR TWO PATHS OF INVESTMENT

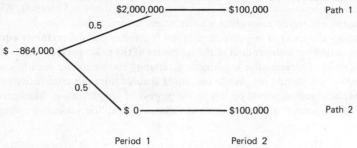

Path	Outcome	Probability	Expectation
1	1,131,000	.5	565,500
2	− 773,000	.5	− 386,500
Expected present value			179,000

The **expected present value** of the two paths is $179,000. But we still have to adjust for the amount of risk. Assume that arbitrary estimate of the adjustment is $51,000. This amount is to be subtracted from the expected present value, that is, an **adjusted present value** of $128,000. If the dollar risk adjustment were $51,000, this procedure would give exactly the same result as the use of the **risk-adjusted discount rate.** While the net value of an investment should be independent of the method of calculation, there is no reason to think that repetitive application of the two procedures to a wide range of investments will always lead to identical value measures.

The primary difficulty with the second procedure is the **determination of the dollar risk adjustments.** There are no exact formulas for the determination of those risk adjustments. They are highly subjective, thus not completely satisfactory inputs into the decision process.

CERTAINTY EQUIVALENTS.   The use of **certainty equivalents** is intuitively appealing. The objective is to make the decision maker indifferent to accepting either the uncertain cash flow or the "certain" one. One can estimate or compute the single cash amount (the certainty equivalent) that represents the value of the uncertain cash flows of the period and then discount the "certainty cash flows" back to the present. Since we are dealing with certainty cash flows, we use a **risk-free discount rate.**

Assume the certainty equivalent (CE) of the cash flow of period 1 is $946,000 (there is .5 probability of $2,000,000 and .5 probability of $0). The certainty equivalent cash flows and their present values are:

Year	CE	Risk-Free Discount Rate	Present Value
0	− 864,000	$(1.05)^{-0}$	− 864,000
1	946,000	$(1.05)^{-1}$	901,000
2	100,000	$(1.05)^{-2}$	91,000
Net present value			128,000

The net present value is again $128,000. Of course, this result was dependent on the fact that the certainty equivalent of period one's uncertain cash flows is $946,000. A different certainty equivalent would have given a different net present value.

The primary weakness of this procedure is that it assumes that the **certainty equivalents** of each time period are **independent of the outcomes of the prior periods.** This assumption may not be valid. Theoretically, to compute a certainty equivalent we need to know what the prior period's outcomes are. While one might abstract from this complexity to simplify the analysis, information would be lost in the process of simplification. Managers are not likely to find the process attractive, given the amount of explicit subjective estimates necessary.

STATES OF NATURE.   Initially it will be assumed that the **capital asset pricing model** (see the section entitled "Modern Portfolio Theory and Management") applies. This assumption implies that only the mean and the variance of an investment portfolio of securities are needed for the investor (holder of the securities) to make a decision, that the securities are well diversified, and that nonsystematic, or firm specific, risk of securities may be ignored. It is assumed that the preferences of investors in securities should determine the investment decision for real assets of the firm. The assumptions of the capital asset pricing model will later be dropped, making the capital budgeting model more general.

Conventional Present Value.   The **conventional present value method** uses present value factors to transform future cash flows into present value equivalents. Each of these present value factors implicitly defines a "price" today for a future dollar. Thus, with a time discount factor of 10%, a dollar one period from now has a price of $0.9091 and a dollar two time periods from now has a price today of $0.8264—that is, 1.10^{-2}. With the use of the present value factors derived from the formulation $(1 + r)^{-n}$, the present value of any future cash flows can be determined. The objective is to search for indifference (i.e., equal preference) amounts between certain sums today and certain future cash flows. With a 10% time discount factor, the investor is indifferent between $82.64 received today or $100 received 2 years from today.

Risk-Adjusted Present Value Factors (RAPVFs).   In a **world of uncertainty** the counterparts of the present value factors are the RAPVFs. These factors are used to transform future dollars back to the present taking into consideration three separate items:

1. Time value.
2. The probability of the event.
3. The risk-return preferences of the market or of the firm and the risk characteristics of the investment.

Each time period is considered as an individual investment and the value of each set of paths for a given time period is computed. It is then necessary to combine the different time periods. The recommended procedure is a **rollback technique** that treats the **future as a series of one-period trials.** Each period is evaluated individually; then periods are combined to obtain the present value equivalents for the entire planning period. For purposes of illustration we shall consider a one-period case.

One-Period Risk Analysis.   Assume a **decision tree** of one period duration with n nodes (cash flows given some event). Each node has a probability. Exhibit 11 shows the situation.

EXHIBIT 11   A ONE-PERIOD DECISION TREE

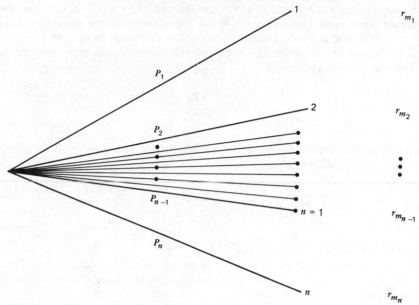

We will define r_m to be the return earned by investing in a well-diversified **"market basket" of securities.** These securities are available to all investors and are vulnerable only to overall market risk. This is referred to as the **market return.**

For each node there is defined a return r_{m_i} to be earned from investing in the market if node i occurs. The market return depends on the state of the world (e.g., overall economic growth) and is a **random event.** If we define the investment's dollar outcome to be equal to 1 for path 1 and zero otherwise, and if we define $s(1)$ to be the RAPVF for path 1, it can be shown that the RAPVF is:

$$\text{RAPVF} = \text{time value} \times \text{probability} \times \text{risk preference adjustment}$$

If a dollar at time 1 and node 1 is worth $1.06 (dollars are valuable, since they are in short supply), and there is 0.15 probability of reaching node 1, and the time discount factor is 0.05, then the RAPVF for node 1 is:

$$\text{RAPVF} = 1.05^{-1}\,(0.15)(1.06) = 0.1514$$

If the outcome at node 1 is $12,000, we multiply $12,000 by 0.1514 to obtain the **risk-adjusted present value** of $1,817. Note that the 1.06 factor incorporates the market's valuation of a dollar at node 1, not the risk preferences of the specific investor.

Returning to the **capital asset pricing model,** we use mathematical notation. If we define $s(1)$ to be the RAPVF for path 1, it can be shown that

$$s(1) = \frac{p_1}{1 + r_f}\,[1 - \lambda\,(r_{m_1} - \bar{r}_m)]$$

where p_1 is the probability of path 1, r_f is the default-free or riskless discount rate, r_m is the market return and $\lambda = (\bar{r}_m - r_f)/\mathrm{var}(r_m)$. The term $[1 - \lambda (r_{m_1} - \bar{r}_m)]$ *is the* **risk preference adjustment.** Thus we have p_1 to take into consideration the probability of path 1, $(1 + r_f)^{-1}$ to take into consideration the one-period time value factor, and $1 - \lambda (r_{m_1} - \bar{r}_m)$ for the **risk return preferences of the market.** We will use R, to represent the risk preference adjustment. Then:

$$s(1) = \frac{p_1 R_1}{1 + r_f}$$

Because an additional dollar has value, we define each $s(i)$ to be positive. If we sum the $s(i)$'s over all paths, we obtain:

$$\sum_{i=1}^{m} s(i) = \frac{1}{1 + r_f}$$

Alternatively, it can be shown that $\Sigma\, p_i R_i = 1$.

Thus the sum of the RAPVFs is equal to the present value factor with no risk. This is intuitively appealing, since it means that if the outcomes of all paths were $1 (thus the outcome is certain) the RAPVF would be $1/(1 + r_f)$, as it should be.

If we define $p_i/(1 + r_f) [\lambda (r_{m_i} - \bar{r}_m)]$ to be the dollar adjustment for risk to be applied to expected present value, the sum of these dollar risk adjustment terms goes to zero if the outcomes of all the nodes are equal. There is zero risk adjustment in total if there is no uncertainty.

The risk adjusted present value may be expressed as:

risk adjusted present value = expected present value − risk adjustment

While it can be shown that this expression is equivalent to the use of RAPVF, and in some respects is easier to understand, the RAPVFs are easier to apply in practice. The RAPVFs are determined for all possible relevant events and they apply to all investments. Once determined, they can be used for any investment being evaluated.

It is necessary to define the events that are uncertain and then estimate the cash flows on those events (or nodes). This is different from defining the cash flows of the investment and then approaching the uncertainty problem.

Dropping the Capital Asset Pricing Model Assumptions.   The **capital asset pricing model** (CAPM) assumptions make the application of the RAPVFs somewhat restrictive, because they are based on either an assumption of normality of outcomes or an assumption that investors have special utility functions. One can drop the assumptions of the CAPM, but retain the requirements that the RAPVF = time value × probability × risk adjustment, that is $s(i) = p_i R_i/(1 + r_f)$. This formulation assumes R_i is not a function of the amount of dollars received, but only of the time period and state of the world. A different formulation would be needed if the **dollar amount of the outcomes** affects their intrinsic value to the investor (i.e., a size effect).

The values of $p_i R_i$ are again constrained so that $\Sigma\, p_i R_i = 1$, where R_i equals the risk preference adjustment of the ith node and we are summing over all nodes of one time period. Constraining the $p_i R_i$ so that they add to 1 ensures that an investment with certain outcomes (giving \$1 no matter what event occurs) will be worth $(1 + r_f)^{-1}$, that is, present value of \$1 discounted at the risk-free rate.

It is important to note that a person or firm evaluating an investment can depart from the CAPM and supply **subjective weights for risk adjustment.** We already know that the probabilities must add to 1. Now we find the $\sum\limits_{i-1} p_i R_i$ must also equal 1. Since $\sum P_i R_i$ equals 1, then

$$\sum s(i) = \sum \frac{p_i R_i}{1 + r_f} = \frac{1}{1 + r_f}.$$

With equal outcomes for all possible events, the cash flows are certain and it is reasonable to use a default-free discount rate. Again, the risk adjustments are constrained so that the product of the risk preference adjustments times their probabilities equals 1, and the sum of the RAPVFs over all nodes is $(1 + r_f)^{-1}$.

LIMITATION OF RISK-ADJUSTED PRESENT VALUES. The limitation of the procedure above is the determination of the values of $s(n)$. If there were markets for investments paying off in only one state of the world (say node 5), the RAPVFs for each node would be determined by market forces. In the absence of such securities and such markets, however, the implementation of the procedure is handicapped. In the **certainty capital budgeting model,** cash flows of each period are multiplied by present value factors. With **uncertainty,** the cash flows of each node are multiplied by multiperiod risk-adjusted present value factors that take into consideration three factors, the time value of money, the probability of the event, and the risk return preferences of the market (or the firm).

While the mathematical derivation tends to be complex, the basic calculations are relatively easy to apply. Most important, the sum of the RAPVFs for each node adds up to the present value factor for that time period using a default-free rate of interest. This restraint on the RAPVF tends to act as a brake preventing one's imagination (or poor intuition) from selecting factors that would give results that are not defensible. Also, the **dollar risk adjustment** is zero if the outcomes are certain.

The **uncertainty model** using the **capital asset pricing model** is built on several assumptions. First, it is a one-period model that assumes the investments to be well diversified. Second, the basic capital asset pricing model assumes that the mean and variance of a portfolio are the only two relevant parameters and that the outcomes are normally distributed. Third, it is assumed that an investment decision of a firm is made from the point of view of the investors in the firm. If these assumptions are not valid, the model cannot be applied to **long-lived real investments of a corporation.**

The approaches involving the use of weighted average cost of capital, risk-adjusted discount rates, or payback period to adjust for risk all have known weaknesses. The procedures suggested in this section are also imperfect, and we can expect improvement in our understanding of the uncertainty problem in the future. By using more complex mathematical formulations, the academic world seems to be leaving behind the **real needs of industry** for feasible capital budgeting techniques. We need to build on the complex theoretical literature and well-known relationships to produce some intuitively appealing and theoretically correct ways of approaching the **capital budgeting decision** under conditions of uncertainty. Patience is needed as we proceed to develop more reliable methods of evaluation.

CAPITAL BUDGETING AND INFLATION

Inflation is frustrating to managers because it is beyond their immediate control. But a wide range of decisions that permit adjustment for inflation is within their control. We now consider to what extent the investment decision process of a corporation (using **present value** or the **internal rate of return method**) should be affected by **forecasts of inflation.** Corporations should be careful that the method being used to adjust for inflation does not introduce new errors into the analysis.

THE PROBLEM.   Because inflation will produce price changes (sometimes dramatic) in the future, adjustments must be made in the capital budget. Four terms figure in the discussion of inflation adjustments:

   Nominal Dollars.   Revenue and costs are measured as they will be measured when the cash is received and disbursed.

   Constant Dollars.   Revenue and costs in current dollars are adjusted to reflect changes in purchasing power.

   Nominal Interest Rates.   The actual, out-of-pocket cost of money.

   Real Interest Rate.   The cost of money if there were market equilibrium and no inflation, an inflation adjustment.

Combining the wrong amount of dollars with the wrong interest rate gives rise to major errors in capital budgeting under inflationary conditions.

AN EXAMPLE.   Assume that the following facts apply for an investment being considered by a firm:

Period	Nominal Dollars: Cash Flows	Price Index
0	− 18,017	100
1	10,000	112
2	10,800	125

The firm can borrow funds at a cost of 9%, and for simplicity we assume that all the capital being used is debt. Using a 9% discount rate, the investment has a net present value of $247 and the investment seems to be acceptable. The conclusion is consistent with the fact that the internal rate of return is 0.10, which is greater than the **cost of capital.**

Many firms do not use such an analysis. They prefer to express the analysis in terms of constant dollars. The initial cash flows were expressed in terms of nominal dollars. To eliminate the change in purchasing power, we convert the flows to constant dollars, which results in the following cash flows:

Period	Nominal Dollars: Cash Flows	Price Level Adjustment	Constant Dollars	Present Value Factor	Present Value
0	− 18,017	1.	− 18,017	1.000	18,017
1	10,000	100/112	8,929	0.917	8,188
2	10,800	100/125	8,640	0.842	7,275
					($ 2,554)

Now the net present value using 9% is a negative ($2,554). When cash flows are analyzed in terms of constant dollars, the investment is not acceptable. However, it is also an error to convert to constant dollars and use the nominal interest rate of 9%.

One can use the nominal dollar cash flows and the nominal interest rates and make a decision that is consistent with **maximizing the well-being of the stockholders.** For example, if $18,017 is borrowed at a cost of 9%, we would have:

Time	Amount Owed	Cash Flow and Amount Paid
0	$18,017	($18,017)
1	19,639	10,000
2	10,506	10,506

After using the $10,800 cash flows of period 2 to pay the debt, there is $294 left over for the residual investors.

The **nominal dollar cash flows** do reflect the forecast of a 8% increase in the benefits of period 2 compared to the benefits of period 1. This might reflect price changes as well as other considerations.

We reach the following conclusion:

The use of **nominal dollars** and **nominal interest rates** is a correct procedure.

The use of constant dollars and **nominal interest rates** is an erroneous procedure in the sense that it can indicate that investment should be rejected even though stockholders benefit from undertaking the investment (see the example above).

It can be argued that the investment should be rejected because the investors will be worse off at the end of the period than at the beginning of the period. We now assume that the investors start with $18,017 of capital at time 0 and can lend to the firm and earn 9%. The 9% is accepted as a reasonable measure of the **opportunity cost of funds.** If the investment is undertaken after two periods, the investor will have:

$$\text{terminal value} = 10,000 \, (1.09) + 10,800 = \$21,700$$

But adjusted for inflation, this amount will only be worth:

$$\frac{21,700}{1.2544} = \$17,299$$

The investors started with $18,017 of purchasing power and ended with $17,299. The position of the investor at time 2 is worse than it was at time 0. However, **this is the wrong comparison.** Let us consider how the investor would have done without the investment. The amount of dollars at time 2 resulting from earning 9% would be:

$$18,017 \times 1.09^2 = \$21,406$$

and price-level adjusted this is:

$$\frac{21,406}{1.2544} = \$17,065$$

The investor is better off with the investment than without it. The fact that the **financial position** of the **investor has deteriorated** is not relevant in that 9% truly represents the return from the best alternative.

USE OF CONSTANT DOLLARS.   Let us define the real interest that an investor earns, in equilibrium conditions, in real terms. If $100 is invested and returns $104 in dollars of the same purchasing power one period later, this is a real interest rate of 4%. In some situations, the investor prefers not to forecast the cash flows in nominal dollars but is willing to forecast the constant dollar cash flows. This approach bypasses the necessity of forecasting the inflation rate (it can be argued that the bypassing is only approximate). If the cash flows are in **constant dollars** the **real interest rate should be used.** Unfortunately, while the nominal borrowing rate can be observed in the capital markets, the **real interest rate** cannot be so observed. Its value must be a rough estimate.

It is difficult to state a given number for the real rate and defend that estimate. All the observed rates are affected jointly by government action and the forces of economics. Isolating out the **real interest rate** for a given year is difficult. A number of the magnitude of 4% can be used, but it should not be thought that we know the real rate is 4%. In equilibrium, we can hypothesize that:

$$\text{nominal rate} = \text{real rate} + \text{inflation rate plus the product of the two}$$

Thus, if the real rate were 0.04 and the inflation rate were 0.12, we would expect the nominal rate to be:

$$\text{nominal rate} = 0.04 + 0.12 + (0.04)(0.12) = 0.1648$$

Assume that $100 is invested to earn $16.48. After 1 year, the investor will have $116.48. But $116.48 converted to constant dollars with an inflation rate of 0.12 is $116.48/1.12 = $104. Thus the investor earned a real return of 0.04 on the initial investment of $100.

If **markets are not in equilibrium,** the expression above must be redefined. One can observe the nominal rate and the inflation rate and compute the real return that is actually earned.

Illustrated above are a correct and an incorrect method for evaluating investments under conditions of inflation. All the possible combinations of incorrect calculations have not been illustrated. The discounted cash flow calculations are powerful tools of analysis, but if the inputs do not have a sound theoretical foundation, the output is often not useful. It is reasonable to want to **adjust for inflation.** The calculation of cash flows using nominal dollars does adjust for inflation in the sense that the nominal dollar forecast reflects expected price changes. While the adjustment to constant dollars is useful in evaluating whether the investor is in a better or a worse position at the end of the period than at the beginning, it is difficult to use constant dollars to make accept or reject investment decisions. The combination of constant dollars and nominal interest rates is a major error.

Further discussion on the impact of inflation on financial management is covered in the section entitled "Financial Management in an Inflationary Environment."

REFERENCES

Bierman, H., Jr., and Smidt, S., *The Capital Budgeting Decision,* 5th ed., Macmillan, New York, 1980.

Clark, J. J., Hindelang, T. J., and Pritchard, R. E., *Capital Budgeting,* Prentice-Hall, Englewood Cliffs, NJ, 1979.

Dean, Joel, *Capital Budgeting,* Columbia University Press, New York, 1951.

Gitman, L. J., and Forrester, J. K., Jr., "A Survey of Capital Budgeting Techniques Used by Major U.S. Firms," *Financial Management,* Fall 1977, pp. 66–71.

Grant, Eugene L., and Ireson, W. Grant, *Principles of Engineering Economy* , 5th ed., Ronald Press, New York, 1970.

Hirshleifer, J. H., "On the Theory of Optimal Investment Decision," *Journal of Political Economy,* August 1958.

Levy, H., and Sarnat, M., *Capital Investment and Financial Decision,* Prentice-Hall International, Englewood Cliffs, NJ, 1978.

Lutz, F., and Lutz, V., *The Theory of Investment of the Firm,* Princeton University Press, Princeton, NJ, 1951.

Schall, L. D., Sundem, G. L., and Geijsheek, W. R., Jr., "Survey and Analysis of Capital Budgeting Methods," *Journal of Finance,* March 1978, pp, 281–287.

Solomon, E., *The Theory of Financial Management* Columbia University Press, New York, 1963.

———, *The Management of Corporate Capital,* Free Press, New York, 1959.

Van Horne, J. C., *Financial Management and Policy,* Prentice-Hall, Englewood Cliffs, NJ, 1977.

Wilkes, F. M., *Capital Budgeting Techniques,* Wiley, London, 1977.

LEASING

CONTENTS

INTRODUCTION 3

Importance of Lease Financing 3
Types of Lease Arrangement 3
  Financial leases 3
  Sale and leaseback arrangements 3
  Leveraged leases 4
  Operating leases 4
Leasing Problems for Financial Analysts 4

ECONOMIC RATIONALE FOR
FINANCIAL LEASING: WHY LEASE? 4

The Lessor as Financial Intermediary 4
Potential Benefits of Leasing 4
Synthesis of Traditional "Advantages"
of Lease Financing 5
  Flexibility and convenience 5
  Lack of restrictions 6
  Avoiding risk of obsolescence 6
  Conservation of working capital 7
  Tax savings 7
  Ease of obtaining credit 7
  Summary 7
Why Lessees Lease: Empirical Evidence 7

LEASE VERSUS PURCHASE 10

Historical Overview 10
  Lease-purchase as a financing decision 11
  Lease-purchase as an investment
  decision 12

Lease-purchase as a financing and
  investment decision 12
Analyzing a Lease versus Purchase
Problem 12
  Step 1: Computing *NPV* 16
  Step 2: Computing *NAL* 17
Empirical Assessment of Industry
Practice: Analysis of Leasing Versus
Purchasing 20
Leasing from the Lessor's Perspective:
Analyzing a Leveraged Lease
Arrangement 22
  Leveraged lease arrangements 22
  Setting lease terms 23
  Setting lease terms: An example 24

ACCOUNTING FOR LEASES 27

Historical Perspective 27
  Accounting Research Bulletin No. 38 27
  Accounting Research Study No. 4 28
  Accounting Principles Board Opinion
  No. 5 28
  Accounting Principles Board Opinion
  No. 31 and Accounting Series Release
  No. 147 28
Lease Capitalization 28
Stock Prices and Lease Capitalization 29
Lease Capitalization and Financial Ratios 31
Lease Capitalization and Bankruptcy
Prediction 31
Security Position in Bankruptcy 32

LEASING

John Martin

INTRODUCTION

IMPORTANCE OF LEASE FINANCING. Leasing has become an increasingly important source of financing during the post-World War II era. It is estimated that the original cost of industrial equipment on lease in 1976 was $100 billion. (R. L. Gallop, *Equipment Leasing and Rental Industries: Trends and Prospects,* U. S. Department of Commerce, Washington D.C., 1976.) New leases accounted for approximately 15% of corporate capital expenditures in that year. S. L. Eichenfield, President of the American Association of Equipment Lessors (Eichenfield, *Fortune,* August 27, 1979, p. 72) estimated total leases for 1979 at $150 billion and projected a worldwide level of over $200 billion by 1985.

TYPES OF LEASE ARRANGEMENT. There are two broad categories of lease arrangement: financial leases and operating leases. Within each category there are various subcategories, and in addition there are hybrid types of lease arrangement that do not fall into either category.

Financial Leases. There are long-term or intermediate-term, noncancelable agreements. The sum of the lease payments over the term of such a lease equals or exceeds the original purchase price of the asset being leased. A purchase option is often included in a financial lease agreement. The option includes a price at which the lessee can purchase the asset from the lessor at termination of the lease. The IRS "true" lease requirements dictate that great care be exercised in writing a purchase option. Violation of the true lease requirements results in loss of the tax deductibility of the lease payments to the lessee as well as loss of the tax deductibility of owner-related expenses (depreciation and interest) to the lessor. Financial leases are written by financial lease companies and commercial banks, as well as equipment dealers and manufacturers.

Sale and Leaseback Arrangements. In this special type of financial lease the lessee firm sells an asset it presently owns to a lessor and enters a financial lease agreement to "reobtain" the asset's services. For example, if a firm owns a building valued at $1 million that is fully paid for and unmortgaged, the firm might sell the building to a lessor for its full value (receiving $1 million in cash) and agree to make lease payments that fully amortize the $1 million over the next 10 years. The firm has exchanged owner financing for lease financing. In the sale and leaseback process the firm has obtained $1 million in cash, incurred a financial lease liability valued at $1 million with the lease payments reflecting the lessor's required rate of return, and in addition, maintained use of the building. Note, however, that the firm might also have borrowed the $1 million, using the building as collateral.

Leveraged Leases.   Another special form of financial lease is the leveraged lease, a financial lease agreement in which the lessor borrows some portion (usually greater than 50%) of the purchase price of the leased asset. The lessor secures the loan by pledging both the asset and the stream of lease payments. The lessee is interested in determining the cost of leasing so that it can be compared with alternative sources of financing, while the lessor wants to determine a set of lease payments that will provide an acceptable return on invested funds.

Operating Leases.   These differ from financial leases in two primary respects. First, an operating lease is cancelable and generally is written for a shorter period of time than is a financial lease. Second, with an operating lease the lessor assumes responsibility for virtually all the expenses of ownership. This type of lease is used when an asset is needed for a short period of time. The lessor captures and passes along to the lessee economies of scale in owning the asset. Operating leases are generally written by firms specializing in this type of agreement or by manufacturers.

Operating leases are an important method of providing temporary financing for the firm. Because financial leases provide a means for financing a firm's asset needs over long periods of time and also present the analyst with a unique set of problems, the balance of this section deals exclusively with financial lease arrangements.

LEASING PROBLEMS FOR FINANCIAL ANALYSTS.   Leasing poses two types of problems for financial analysts: "lease or purchase" (the merits of leasing versus other forms of financing) and **"lease accounting"** (the impact of leasing on the firm's financial statements).

ECONOMIC RATIONALE FOR FINANCIAL LEASING: WHY LEASE?

THE LESSOR AS FINANCIAL INTERMEDIARY.   The lessor serves as a financial intermediary in the sense that he obtains funds externally from the capital markets or internally from undistributed profits and exchanges those funds for a financial lease contract. Exhibit 1 depicts the financial lease process. In the purchase process (left), funds provided by the capital markets are obtained by the purchaser through issuing stock and/or bonds. These funds are then used to obtain title to the assets whose services are being acquired.

In the leasing process (right), the lessor obtains funds from the capital market and acquires title to the asset. The lessor then provides the lessee with the "use value" of the asset while keeping the asset's salvage value in exchange for a series of lease payments as prescribed by the financial lease agreement.

There are two fundamental differences in the lease and purchase alternatives described in Exhibit 1. First, the leasing arrangement includes an additional middleman or financial intermediary (the lessor). Second, the purchase option provides the owner with both the **use value** of the asset and its **salvage value,** whereas the lessee obtains only the use value of the asset. On the surface it appears that the lease arrangement would necessarily be more expensive than the purchase alternative, since leasing includes another financial intermediary who must be rewarded for his services. Thus, to be cost effective, the lessor must offer some saving to the lessee that he cannot obtain for himself.

POTENTIAL BENEFITS OF LEASING.   To understand the potential sources of any benefits from leasing, note the following transactions involved in the purchase scenario described in Exhibit 1. First, the funds needed to acquire the asset must be raised. Second, the asset must

EXHIBIT 1   A COMPARISON OF PURCHASING WITH LEASING

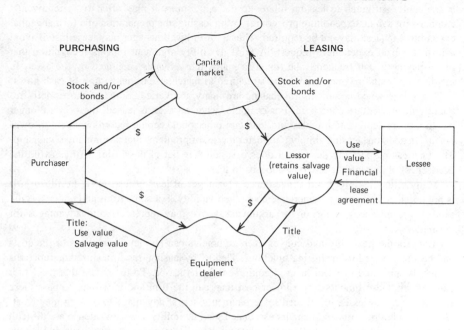

be purchased. Third, the asset must be disposed of at the end of its useful life. These three phases of the purchase process represent the potential sources of economic benefits from leasing. That is, if the lessor can acquire funds from the capital markets on more favorable terms than can the lessee, or purchase the asset at a lower price or achieve a higher salvage value for the asset than can the lessee, then leasing offers the basis for real cost savings to the lessee. For the lessee to realize any cost saving through leasing, however, these cost savings must exceed the required profit of the lessor and they must be passed through to the lessee in the form of reduced lease payments. Thus, although the **financial lease** may prove to be a cheaper form of financing than purchasing, there must be some underlying economic reason for those cost savings to exist.

SYNTHESIS OF TRADITIONAL "ADVANTAGES" OF LEASE FINANCING.   The use of financial leases to finance the acquisition of an asset's services has several purported advantages over purchasing the asset using debt and equity sources of funds. The term "purported" is deliberately used, since many of the advantages attributed to leasing are purely illusory and others are present only some of the time and in varying degrees. This discussion, which places the alleged advantages of lease financing into perspective so that the informed analyst can evaluate them rationally, relies heavily on the work of Martin et al. (*Basic Financial Management*).

Flexibility and Convenience.   It is often claimed that financial leases offer the user a more flexible and convenient source of financing than alternative forms of financing. For example, leasing is said to provide lessees with flexibility because it allows a firm to finance relatively small asset acquisitions in piecemeal fashion without having to sell a bond or stock issue, which is a time-consuming and expensive endeavor. Yet another flexibility advantage that is frequently attributed to leasing relates to the opportunity it may offer to "circumvent" cumbersome capital expenditure procedures. With leasing, the preparation of a formal capital expenditure request may not be required. Thus a lower level manager may lease just to avoid a formal capital expenditure request. A third flexibility argument reflects recognition that rental payments can frequently be timed to match the revenues generated by the asset. In this instance rental payments might be structured to match a seasonal pattern of cash flows.

The convenience arguments for leasing are many and varied. Some of those more frequently mentioned are cited here. For example, when an asset is leased, the firm no longer has to prepare depreciation tables and maintain other bookkeeping records incident to ownership. In addition, leasing simply eliminates the set of problems that accompany ownership. The firm can purportedly do what it does best and stay out of the business (thus avoid the headaches) of owning the assets it chooses to lease.

Many of the flexibility and convenience advantages of leasing just stated are illusory. It is not possible, however, to generalize about their validity. For some firms and under specific sets of circumstances, some of the arguments above may represent valid advantages for leasing.

Many of the flexibility and convenience arguments can be viewed in terms of the costs and benefits derived from shifting functions. That is, by leasing, the firm shifts the functions of bookkeeping and disposal of used equipment to the lessor. To the extent that the lessor can perform these functions at a lower cost than can the firm and is willing to pass these savings on to the lessee in reduced lease payments, a real advantage to leasing may exist. Unfortunately, the costs and benefits associated with flexibility and convenience are difficult to estimate. A subjective approach to evaluating the relative merits of lease financing is thus unavoidable.

Lack of Restrictions. It is often suggested that financial lease agreements do not include the same kinds of restrictive covenant common to bond indentures. In addition, bond indentures may not contain provisions restricting the use of financial leases, even though additional debt may be specifically prohibited or at least restricted. Kim et al. (E.H. Kim, W.G. Lewellen, and J.J. McConnell, "Sale and Leaseback Arrangements and Enterprise Valuation," *Journal of Financial and Quantitative Analysis,* Vol. 13, December 1978, pp. 871–883) demonstrate that the firm's management can exploit the absence of restrictions on its use of financial leases to the benefit of the firm's owners. For such opportunities to exist, however, the firm's creditors would have to be quite naive regarding the impact of financial leases on the firm's debt-carrying capacity.

The extent to which a firm will benefit from the lack of restrictions associated with leasing will depend on the price it must pay for lease financing. The freedom accorded the lessee translates directly into the risk underwritten by the lessor. This is not to say that a favorable set of lease terms cannot be arranged. However, lessor recognition of the lack of restrictions in the lease might result in a prohibitively expensive set of lease terms.

Avoiding Risk of Obsolescence. Leasing is often said to offer the lessee firm a means of avoiding the **risk of obsolescence.** Although cancelable operating leases **may** offer this advantage, a financial lease probably does not. If the lessor is aware of the risk of obsolescence, he is sure to pass the associated costs on to the lessee in the form of higher lease payments. Only when the lessor foresees lower costs associated with obsolescence than the lessee and is willing to pass these on to the lessee in lower lease payments is the risk of obsolescence even partially avoided with a financial lease.

At this point it should be noted that some lessors who specialize in certain types of assets **may** hold an advantage over the lessee in terms of maintaining the asset in good working condition and in selling it upon the lease's termination. These economies of specialization may allow the lessor to offer lease terms that the lessee will find to be cost effective. That is, the lessor provides maintenance services and resale services at a cost the lessee cannot duplicate. Once again, for savings to be realized by the lessee, the lessor **must** pass his savings along as lower lease payments.

Conservation of Working Capital.   Perhaps the most commonly cited advantage of lease financing is that it requires little or no cash down payment. That is, the **lease provides 100% financing.** Although this is true, it is misleading to say that leasing should be favored over other forms of financing for this reason. For example, if bank loan financing is the alternative source of financing being compared with leasing, the down payment itself might be borrowed. Furthermore, the fact that leasing provides 100% nonowner financing means that it uses more of the firm's debt capacity than does a less than 100% loan. Finally, the lease provides the firm with the use value of the asset and **does not** include its **salvage value.** If a substantial salvage value exists, its forfeiture with the lease agreement might be considered a de facto down payment. Thus the lease provides 100% financing of the use value of the asset only.

Tax Savings.   Lease payments are fully tax deductible, whereas only interest and depreciation expense can be deducted from taxable income when an asset is purchased. A full assessment of the relative tax savings associated with leasing and owning can best be accomplished using a lease versus purchase model like the one discussed later.

Ease of Obtaining Credit.   It is sometimes suggested that firms with poor **credit ratings** can obtain lease financing more easily than they can obtain a loan. Since the lessor suffers the risk of default just like any other creditor, the lessee should expect his credit status to be reflected in the level of the lease payments. To the extent that the security position of the lessor is superior to that of a creditor, this might be a valid advantage of leasing.

Summary.   There are a number of advantages frequently attributed to lease financing. The final decision of whether a real advantage exists depends on the particular set of lease terms being evaluated. In every instance the advantages discussed could be converted into dollar savings capable of quantitative analysis via a **lease versus purchase model.** Although estimates of the associated costs and benefits may prove difficult in many cases, the very act of attempting to evaluate the various advantages of leasing in this way should lead to better leasing decisions.

WHY LESSEES LEASE: EMPIRICAL EVIDENCE.   A number of attempts have been made to survey lessees to determine their motives for leasing. Some of the recent studies include H. G. Hamel and G. C. Thompson (in *Theory of Business Finance,* J. F. Weston and D. H. Woods, Eds., Wadsworth, Belmont, CA, pp. 203–213), G. L. Marrah *(Financial Executive,* Vol. 36, 1968, pp. 91–104), R. A. Fawthrop and B. Terry *(Journal of Business Finance and Accounting,* Vol. 2, 1975, pp. 295–314), and P. F. Anderson and J. D. Martin (paper presented at the Ninth Annual Meeting of the Financial Management Association, Boston, October 11–13, 1979).

The discussion presented here is based on the study by Anderson and Martin, since it is the most recent and offers several methodological improvements over earlier work. Specifically, this most recent investigation reports information regarding both the lessee respondent's beliefs about the various "advantages" of leasing **and** the importance the respondent attaches to each advantage in terms of its effect on the respondent's decisions to use lease financing.

The survey produced 191 respondents from lessee firms with sales ranging from $10 million to $300 million annually. The 1976 lease payments of the sample firms ranged from over $50 million to under $10,000. Approximately 76% of the respondents were engaged in manufacturing, 6% were mining companies, 5% were involved in transportation, communications, or public utility service, and the remainder were distributed across a wide variety of industries.

A major problem plaguing previous research efforts was the tendency to focus on the "importance" of leasing's purported advantages without eliciting the respondents' assessment of whether the various advantages were real or illusory. In the survey by Anderson and Martin, respondents were asked to rate each of 40 purported advantages of leasing from 1 to 5, with "1" corresponding to "strongly agree" and "5" corresponding to "strongly disagree." A second scale was used to determine the importance the respondent attached to a particular "advantage" in making leasing decisions. This scale ranged from 1 to 6 with "1" corresponding to "very important" and "6" corresponding to "not at all important."

Of the 40 potential advantages of leasing, the one with the **lowest average agreement score** was: **"All things considered, leasing is less expensive than debt as a means of acquiring equipment."** The agreement score indicates whether the respondent agreed or disagreed that the statement reflects an advangtage of leasing. A low score indicates that the respondent disagreed with the statement. When the "overall" importance of the foregoing advantage was calculated, it was ranked third. The overall importance measure reflects the results obtained from the "importance" scale discussed above. Thus, in this particular instance, the respondents agreed that it is important that the cost of leasing be lower than the cost of debt financing, but they disagreed with the statement that leasing is less costly than debt financing.

The inputs from the agreement scale and importance scale were combined to form an overall measure of the significance of each of the 40 alleged advantages of leasing. The various "advantages" were then arrayed from most significant to least significant, based on this overall measure.

The 10 most significant reasons for leasing appear in Exhibit 2. Note that because of the way the agreement and importance scales were formulated, a low numerical score indicates a high level of importance.

The first point to note in Exhibit 2 is the prominence of tax-related factors. Attributes ranked 1, 8, and 9 relate to the potential tax benefits of leasing. This gives some credence to the view that tax considerations are indeed significant in the leasing decisions of corporations. However, Exhibit 2 also illustrates that other factors are important to the respondents. Moreover, many of these factors, as well as the tax-related factors, would be subsumed by the standard lease versus purchase models existing in the literature.

For example, attributes 1, 3, 7, 8, and 9 would all be accounted for via the discounting mechanism of a lease versus purchase model. Finally, if the "problems" associated with the disposal of secondhand equipment can be quantified, attribute 4 could also be included in any standard analytical model.

Since many of the most significant reasons for leasing are also reflected in the cash flows of lease-purchase models, one might expect the respondents to view leasing as a favorable alternative to debt from a cost perspective. This is suggested by evidence that corporate analysts often use models that compare leasing directly with debt financing. However, as noted previously, the statement "All things considered, leasing is less expensive than debt

EXHIBIT 2   RANK ORDER OF THE 10 MOST SIGNIFICANT REASONS FOR LEASING

Rank	Advantage of Leasing	Mean Significance Score[a]
1.	Leasing provides for 100% deductibility of costs.	6.805
2.	Leasing provides the firm with long-term financing without diluting ownership or control.	8.099
3.	Leasing frees the firm's working capital for other uses.	8.508
4.	Leasing permits the firm to avoid the problems associated with the disposal of secondhand equipment.	8.626
5.	Leasing allows for piecemeal financing of relatively small equipment acquisitions for which debt financing would be impractical.	8.855
6.	Leasing protects the company from the risks of equipment obsolescence.	8.934
7.	The aftertax cost of leasing is less than the aftertax cost of equity financing.	8.994
8.	Leasing is advantageous for firms with low or heavily sheltered earnings because the lessor will be able to pass on the savings from the investment tax credit in a lower lease rate.	9.040
9.	The tax deductibility of lease payments provides a larger and more immediate cash flow than that provided by depreciation and interest deductions.	9.418
10.	Leasing leaves normal lines of credit undisturbed.	9.726

[a]The significance score was calculated as follows:

$$S_i = \sum_{j=1}^{m} B_j I_j$$

where S_i = "significance score" for ith advantage of leasing

B_j = respondent j's belief (agreement score) that leasing possesses attribute i

I_j = respondent j's importance rating for attribute i

Source: P. F. Anderson and J. D. Martin, "Financial Leases: The Corporate Viewpoint," paper presented at the Ninth Annual Meeting of the Financial Management Association, Boston, October 1979.

as a means of acquiring equipment," was rated twentieth in significance and fortieth in overall agreement. This somewhat paradoxical result suggests that perhaps other noncash-flow factors are truly determinant in the leasing decisions of the respondents. This view is reinforced by the growing evidence that some firms and institutions enter into lease arrangements despite rates that are far in excess of debt alternatives. See, for example, the paper by I. W. Sorensen and R. E. Johnson ("Equipment Financial Leasing Practices and Costs: An Empirical Study," *Financial Management,* Vol. 6, 1977, pp. 33–40).

Some suggestion of what these other factors might be can be seen in Exhibit 2. The respondents indicated that the problem of dilution of ownership or control (number 2), piecemeal financing (number 5), obsolescence of equipment (number 6), and maintenance of credit lines (number 10) are all significant motivations for leasing. While these "advantages" are all inconsistent with the assumption of perfect markets, it is clear that the respondents see them as real benefits of leasing. Thus many lessees apparently view themselves as operating in imperfect markets in which non tax and even non cash-flow factors play a role in leasing decisions. "Perfect markets" refers to a set of economic conditions surrounding the writing of lease agreements. A number of authors have demonstrated the irrelevance of the advantages of financial leases under conditions of perfectly competitive capital markets.

The crucial assumptions of these arguments that are violated in reality relate to their reliance on homogeneous expectations and complete and costless information to all market participants. See H. Miller and C. W. Upton, "Leasing, Buying and the Cost of Capital Services" (*Journal of Finance*, Vol. 31, June 1976, pp. 761–786) and W. G. Lewellen, M. S. Long, and J. J. McConnell, "Asset Leasing in Competitive Capital Markets" (*Journal of Finance*, Vol. 31, June 1976, pp. 787–798).

The results of the survey summarized here suggest that lessees consider more than explicit cost advantages in making leasing decisions. Indeed, the evidence indicates that a variety of cash flow and non cash-flow factors may enter into the decision process. Moreover, the respondents generally agree that leasing is more expensive than debt as a source of financing. Thus, it may be argued that "non cost" (i.e., non cash-flow) factors are important in the leasing decisions of the respondents. The lease versus purchase subsection below demonstrates that a judicious analysis of the decision to use lease financing requires quantification of many of these "non cash-flow" items.

LEASE VERSUS PURCHASE

HISTORICAL OVERVIEW.   This section draws heavily on J. D. Martin and P. F. Anderson, "A Practical Approach to the Lease vs. Purchase Problem" (*International Journal of Physical Distribution and Materials Management*, Vol. 9, No. 4, 1979, pp. 150–157).

The **lease versus purchase decision** has intrigued and perplexed both the academician and the practitioner for many years. The enigmatic nature of the problem can be traced to the fact that it is a hybrid containing both financing and investment components. Unlike the related capital investment decision (where analysts and theorists have conveniently separated the financing and investment aspects of the decision through the use of a "weighted average cost of capital" concept—see the section entitled "Capital Budgeting" for a discussion of the capital budgeting decision), the lease versus purchase problem **forces** the analyst to consider both the feasibility of asset acquisition **and** whether lease financing is preferable to normal debt-equity financing.

Traditional capital budgeting procedures incorporate financing considerations into a minimum required rate of return (weighted average cost of debt and equity financing) and proceed to analyze the answer to the first of the questions above. However, when leasing is considered the firm commits itself to what is, in effect, 100% non equity financing of an asset's acquisition. Thus traditional project analyses that relegate financial considerations to a weighted average cost of capital are not immediately amenable to the analysis. One immediate issue in lease-purchase analyses is financial risk differences between lease financing and normal purchase financing. This issue, among others, has provided the basis for a vast academic literature on the lease versus purchase questions. This subsection identifies the troublesome issues arising in lease-purchase analyses and suggests practical solutions.

At least three conflicting viewpoints on the nature of the lease-purchase decision have been expressed in the academic literature. The traditional view is that lease versus purchase analysis is appropriately considered to be a financing decision. A second, but somewhat smaller group of theorists have attempted to deal with the lease versus purchase decision in a strict investment context, devoid of financing implications. More recent theorists have approached the lease-purchase decision as a hybrid financing-investment problem.

Lease-Purchase as a Financing Decision.   Those who take this approach generally view the analysis as a **lease-or-borrow** problem in which the purchase is assumed to be financed with 100% debt. Models have taken one of two basic forms. The most popular format (in terms of the sheer volume of published research) is the **net present value model.** Here the theorist evaluates the lease-purchase problem in terms of the **difference** in the net present value of an asset acquired by a financial lease and its net present value counterpart, where purchase financing is used. When the net present value of purchasing is subtracted from the net present value of leasing, this difference is the **net present value advantage of leasing over purchasing.** If this difference is positive, leasing is favored over purchasing, if it is negative, purchasing is to be preferred.

The second type of lease-or-borrow model involves use of a **rate of return** or **internal rate of return** format. These models consist of finding a rate of interest that makes the net present value advantage of leasing equal to zero. If the internal rate of return exceeds the borrowing rate, the lease is favored; if not, purchasing is favored.

Some of the better known net present value models include A. H. Cohen, *Long Term Leases—Problems of Taxation, Finance and Accounting,* University of Michigan Press, Ann Arbor, 1954; J. F. Weston and E. F. Brigham, *Managerial Finance,* 6th ed., Dryden Press, Hinsdale, IL, 1978; R. F. Vancil, "Lease or Borrow—New Method of Analysis," *Harvard Business Review,* Vol. 39, September–October 1961; R. S. Bower, F. C. Herringer, and J. P. Williamson, "Lease Evaluation," *Accounting Review,* Vol. 41, April 1966, pp. 257–265; and H. Bierman, Jr. and S. Smidt, *The Capital Budgeting Decision,* 5th ed., Macmillan New York, 1980.

In addition, all the prominent internal rate of return models are, by definition, pure financing models (T. H. Beechy, "Quasi-Debt Analysis of Financial Leases," *Accounting Review,* Vol. 44, April 1969, pp. 375–381; T. H. Beechy, "The Cost of Leasing: Comment and Correction," *Accounting Review,* Vol. 45, October 1970, pp. 769 773; M. C. Findlay, III, "Financial Lease Evaluation: Survey and Synthesis," *Financial Review,* 1974, pp. 1–15; G. D. Quirin, *The Capital Expenditure Decision,* Irwin, Homewood, IL, 1967; and R. L. Roenfeldt and J. S. Osteryoung, "Analysis of Financial Leases," *Financial Management,* Vol. 2, Spring 1973.)

There are two practical problems associated with many of these models. First, a majority of these approaches do not properly adjust for the differential risk element in the lease-purchase cash flows. This occurs in many **net present value** (*NPV*) models because the firm's aftertax cost of capital is used to discount nearly riskless contractual tax shield and operating expense flows.

On the other hand, many internal rate of return (*IRR*) models fail to adjust for risky flows such as salvage value. It has been demonstrated elsewhere that because of their failure to adjust for differential risk, the *NPV* and *IRR* approaches tend to be biased against the lease alternative (P. F. Anderson and J. D. Martin, "Lease vs. Purchase Decisions: A Survey of Current Practice and Theory," Working Paper, Virginia Polytechnic Institute and State University, July 1976).

The second problem with pure financing approaches is that many require a justification of the acquisition on a purchase basis before consideration is given to leasing. Thus the investment decision is separated from the financing decision.

The fallacy inherent in this approach has been recognized by a number of writers. As Johnson and Lewellen note, such an ex ante investment analysis can never allow a bargain lease opportunity to reverse an original negative purchase decision (R. W. Johnson and W. G. Lewellen, "Reply," *Journal of Finance,* Vol. 28, September 1973, pp. 1024–1028). Once again, a bias against the lease alternative is introduced.

A final problem associated with pure financing approaches is the basic assumption of these models that 100% debt financing is the appropriate alternative to leasing. It is demonstrated later that this may not be the case, since the optimal debt level for a purchase will depend on the impact of the asset's acquisition on the financial risk of the firm.

Lease-Purchase as an Investment Decision.   At the other extreme from the pure **financing approach** is the pure **investment approach** of Johnson and Lewellen (J & L), "Analysis of the Lease-or-Buy Decision," *Journal of Finance,* Vol. 27, September 1972, pp. 815–823; and "Reply," *Journal of Finance,* Vol. 28, September 1973, pp. 1024–1028. J & L view the lease as a long-term acquisition of services contract that differs in timing but not in financing impact from a purchase. This view of a lease acquisition as something to be financed rather than as a source of financing led J & L to apply the traditional capital budgeting framework to both the lease and purchase options. This, in turn, generated a model that excludes all consideration of interest expense and employs the cost of capital to discount two highly certain flows: the **depreciation tax shield** and the **after tax operating expenses** covered by the lessor.

The **pure investment approach** has attracted few adherents among financial theorists. The academic community does not appear willing to acccept J & L's acquisition-of-services view of leasing. The consensus view appears to be that a lease does provide the firm with an alternative source of financing and that lease-purchase analyses must take this fact into account. Moreover, few writers appear willing to accept their argument that the cost of capital should be applied to flows that are nearly risk-free.

J & L did make an important contribution to the development of **normative lease-purchase theory** by challenging the pure financing approach and demonstrating the importance of the investment element. This has led to a wider recognition of the **lease as a hybrid,** containing elements of both investment and finance.

Lease-Purchase as a Financing and Investment Decision.   The hybrid approach is best illustrated in the work of L. D. Schall ("The Lease-or-Buy and Asset Acquisition Decisions," *Journal of Finance,* Vol. 29, September 1974, 1203–1214). Schall recognizes that a lease is, at one and the same time, an investment in a revenue-generating asset and a source of debt-like financing. Moreover, he is well aware that the financing and investment elements are inextricably linked and cannot be separated if a meaningful choice is to be made between the lease and purchase alternatives. Thus, Schall's model considers the financing and investment decisions simultaneously. In addition, his algorithm overcomes many of the problems associated with earlier approaches.

Although Schall's model gives consideration to all the basic elements of the lease-purchase problem, it offers little guidance with regard to solving the "risk of illiquidity" differences in the alternatives. Theorists have attempted to deal with this issue, notably A. Ofer, "The Evaluation of Lease Versus Purchase Alternatives," *Financial Management,* Vol. 5, Summer 1976, pp. 67–74; L. Allen, J. D. Martin, and P. F. Anderson, "Debt Capacity and the Lease Versus Purchase Problem: A Sensitivity Analysis," *Engineering Economist,* Vol. 24, Winter 1979, pp. 87–108. These contributions are discussed next.

ANALYZING A LEASE VERSUS PURCHASE PROBLEM.   The model presented here builds on the work of Schall ("The Lease-or-Buy and Asset Acquisition Decisions," *Journal of Finance,* Vol. 29, September 1974, pp. 1203–1214). Specifically. a pragmatic **lease-purchase model** is presented that will guide the analyst in three key areas:

1. The adjustment for risk differences in the cash flows.
2. The consideration of "bargain" lease terms that may reverse an unfavorable purchase decision.
3. The necessity for dealing with financial risk differences between leasing and purchase financing.

The model is designed to be practical. That is, it can be implemented using estimates that are both readily available and easily understood.

Schall has proposed that lease-purchase analyses be made using two net present value equations: one to measure the net present value on a project where purchase financing (composed of the firm's optimal debt-equity mix) is used, and the other reflecting the use of lease financing. The analyst, after having calculated both net present values, selects that method of financing which produces the largest positive net present value.

In the procedure discussed here a slightly different form of analysis is used. Specifically, the following two-stage procedure is used.

Stage 1. The **net present value** of the project is calculated for the purchase alternative (designate this quantity *NPV*). This calculation is completely analogous to that which is discussed in standard treatments of the capital budgeting problem.

Stage 2. Regardless of whether *NPV* is found to be positive (signaling a favorable purchase decision) or negative (indicating the asset should **not** be **purchased**), the net present value advantage of leasing over purchasing (*NAL*) is calculated.

The decisions involved in the lease versus purchase analysis can best be described through the use of the flowchart presented in Exhibit 3. To perform the lease-purchase analysis outlined in Exhibit 3, one first calculates project *NPV*. If that *NPV* is positive, the asset offers a positive contribution to the wealth of the firm's shareholders and its purchase is justified. However, even if *NPV* is positive, lease financing may be preferable to purchasing. This possibility is checked using the left-hand side of Exhibit 3. Here *NAL* is calculated and signals "lease" if positive and "purchase" if negative.

Returning to the top of Exhibit 3 where *NPV* is calculated, assume now that the calculated *NPV* is negative (e.g. − $20). Again *NAL* is calculated. However, this time the asset should not be purchased, since *NPV* is negative. Thus the only hope for the project lies in the existence of exceptionally favorable lease terms. In fact, for the asset to be worthy of acquisition (via lease) *NAL* must be not only positive but larger in **absolute value** than *NPV*. For example, if *NPV* is calculated to be − $20 and *NAL* is $10, the asset should **not** be leased, since the positive net present value of leasing is not large enough to offset the negative *NPV* associated with purchase financing.

The right-hand side of Exhibit 3 provides the basis for assessing whether the firm has been offered a "bargain lease." As noted earlier, a number of lease-purchase models assume that the asset has passed an *NPV* hurdle before leasing is considered, an analysis represented by the left-hand side of Exhibit 3. This type of analysis fails to consider the possible availability of bargain lease terms. Such is the objective of performing the analysis on the right-hand side of the flowchart.

To demonstrate the use of the lease-purchase algorithm in Exhibit 3, an example problem is analyzed. Exhibit 4 contains both the *NPV* and *NAL* models, along with the definition of the symbols used by each. Note that *NPV* is calculated in the usual way. That is, the analyst

EXHIBIT 3   THE LEASE VERSUS PURCHASE DECISION

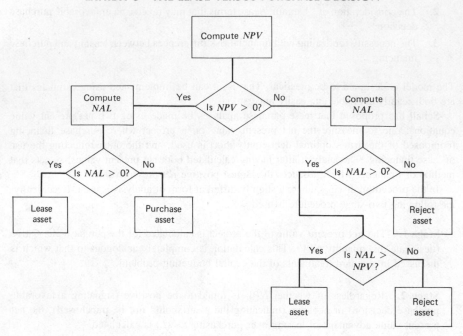

first estimates the project's expected future cash flows (i.e., the ACF_t). These cash flow estimates are then discounted back to the present, using the cost of capital or required rate of return relevant to the project. If the present value of the project's cash flows exceed the initial outlay needed to purchase the asset, purchase of the asset is justified.

Looking at the individual terms contained in NAL, we see that by leasing the asset the firm avoids certain expenses, $O_t (1 - t)$, but incurs the aftertax rentals $R_t (1 - T)$. Furthermore, by leasing, the firm loses the tax shelters on interest TI_t, depreciation TD_t, and the interest on repaid debt or lost debt capacity $T\Delta I_t$. Finally, the firm does not receive the salvage value from the asset V_n, but does not have to make the initial cash outlay to purchase the asset A_o. Thus we see that NAL reflects the cost savings associated with leasing net of the opportunity costs of not purchasing.

The **aftertax debt rate** is employed to discount the contractual, **tax-shield,** and operating expense flows because of their relative certainty. The contractual lease payments are relatively riskless, since they represent legal obligations the firm will have to fulfill. Similarly, the various tax-shield flows are fixed by law and are relatively certain as long as the firm has sufficient other income and tax rates are reasonably stable. Finally, it is assumed that the operating expenses covered by the lessor consist of such highly predictable flows as insurance and maintenance. The predictability of these cash streams is such that they can be discounted at a relatively low rate such as the cost of borrowing (r). Salvage value, on the other hand, represents a highly uncertain cash flow and must be discounted at a higher rate. The firm's aftertax weighted average cost of capital is not an unreasonable approximation of this discount rate. This is particularly true if the value of V_n is based on a stream of expected earnings similar in riskiness to those of the firm as a whole. Alternatively, where V_n is simply scrap

EXHIBIT 4   THE LEASE-PURCHASE MODEL

NET PRESENT VALUE OF ASSET IF PURCHASED

Model

$$NPV = \sum_{t=1}^{n} \frac{ACF_t}{(1 + K)^t} - A_o$$

Definitions

NPV	=	project net present value or expected contribution of project to wealth of firm's common shareholders
ACF_t	=	expected annual cash flow after taxes (but before depreciation) provided by project in year t; interest expense is **not** deducted in arriving at ACF_t.
K	=	firm's minimum acceptable rate of return on projects of riskiness of one being analyzed and reflecting mixture of sources of funds (debt and equity) used to finance project; analysts recommend use of firm's weighted average cost of capital to represent this variable
A_o	=	initial cash outlay required to purchase asset in period zero (now)
n	=	productive life of asset

Note that ACF_n contains any salvage or residual value of the asset plus the return of any working capital invested in the project during its life.

NET PRESENT VALUE ADVANTAGE OF LEASING

Model

$$NAL = \sum_{t=1}^{n} \frac{O_t(1 - T) - R_t(1 - T) - TI_t - T\Delta I_t - TD_t}{(1 + r_T)^t} - \frac{V_n}{(1 + K_s)^n} + A_o$$

Definitions

O_t	=	any operating expense flows in period t that are incurred only where asset is purchased; most often this consists of maintenance expenses and insurance that would be paid by lessor
R_t	=	annual rental for period t
T	=	marginal tax rate on corporate income
I_t	=	tax-deductible interest expense forgone in period t if asset is leased rather than purchased; I_t is interest expenses in period t on funds that would be borrowed **if** asset were purchased
ΔI_t	=	interest on debt that must be repaid if asset is leased, to maintain firm's desired capital structure; recall that leasing entails 100% nonowner financing
D_t	=	depreciation expense in period t for asset
V_n	=	aftertax salvage value of asset expected in year n
K_s	=	discount rate used to find present value of V_n; this rate should reflect risk inherent in estimated V. For simplicity, and to be consistent with computation of NPV, aftertax cost of capital is often used as a proxy for this rate.
A_o	=	purchase price of asset, which is not paid by firm if asset is leased.
r	=	rate of interest on borrowed funds; this rate is used to discount relatively certain contractual, tax-shield, and operating expense cash flows

value, a certainty-equivalent approach may be employed. See M. C. Finlay, III, "Financial Lease Evaluation: Survey and Synthesis" (*Financial Review*, 1974, pp. 1–15).

The two interest tax-shield terms in the *NAL* equation deserve particular mention. The first term, TI_t, represents the interest shield forgone if a lease rather than a loan is used to acquire the asset. On the other hand, the $T\Delta I_t$ term represents an adjustment for financial risk differences between the alternatives. Since **leasing effectively involves 100% leverage financing,** it "uses up" more of the firm's debt capacity than a purchase that involves a mix of debt and equity financing. For example, if the firm seeks to maintain a target debt-equity ratio by financing 60% of all acquisitions with owner's funds, it would have to repay outstanding debt equal to 60% of the asset's cost if it decided to lease. For simplicity, assume that a dollar of lease is equivalent to a dollar of loan. This is only one of several assumptions that might be used. Thus $T\Delta I_t$ represents the lost interest shelter on the repaid debt. Of course, debt may not actually be repaid immediately. However, by leasing the asset, the firm will use more levered financing than the asset will support. Thus to maintain its target debt-equity ratio, the firm must use less levered financing on future projects. In other words, $T\Delta I_t$ represents the tax shield on the debt "displaced" by the lease.

The lease-purchase analysis can be summarized as follows:

1. If *NPV* is positive, the asset **should be** acquired through the preferred financing method as indicated by *NAL*.

2. If *NPV* is negative the asset's services should be acquired via the lease alternative only if *NAL* is positive and greater in absolute value than *NPV*. That is, the asset should be leased only if the cost advantage of lease financing (*NAL*) is great enough to offset the negative purchase *NPV*.

Thus to evaluate a lease-purchase problem the analyst must first calculate *NPV*. If *NPV* is positive, *NAL* is computed, and the appropriate method of financing for the project can be chosen. However, If *NPV* is negative, the only hope for the project's acceptance is an exceptionally favorable set of lease terms, in which case the project would be leased only if *NAL* were positive and greater in absolute value than the negative *NPV*.

Example. This example is modified from the "now standard" problem posed by R. W. Johnson and W. G. Lewellen ("Analysis of the Lease-or-Buy Decision," *Journal of Finance*, September 1972, pp. 815–823). The B. Hilgen Manufacturing Co. (BHM) is presently involved in making a decision regarding the purchase of a new automatic casting machine. The machine will cost $15,000 and has an expected life of 5 years, at which time its aftertax salvage will be $1,050. Note that the $1,050 is an aftertax salvage value, where the asset is depreciated toward a zero expected salvage for tax purposes. The firm's marginal tax rate is 50% and it uses sum-of-the-years'-digits depreciation.

The project is expected to generate annual cash revenues of $5,000 per year over the next 5 years after cash operating expenses but before depreciation and taxes. BHM has a target debt ratio of 40% for projects of this type and estimates its aftertax cost of capital at 12%.

Step 1: Computing *NPV*. The first step in analyzing the lease-purchase problem involves computing the net present value under the purchase alternative. The relevant cash flow computations are presented in Exhibit 5.

The *NPV* then is found by discounting the ACF_t in Exhibit 5 back to the present at the firm's aftertax cost of capital of 12%, adding this sum to the present value of the salvage value, and subtracting the initial cash outlay. These calculations are contained in Exhibit 6.

EXHIBIT 5 COMPUTING ANNUAL AFTERTAX CASH FLOWS, ACF_t

	Year, t				
	1	2	3	4	5
Annual cash revenues	$5,000	$5,000	$5,000	$5,000	$5,000
Less: Depreciation	(5,000)	(4,000)	(3,000)	(2,000)	(1,000)
Earnings before taxes	0	1,000	2,000	3,000	4,000
Less: Income taxes (50%)	(0)	(500)	(1,000)	(1,500)	(2,000)
Net income	0	500	1,000	1,500	2,000
Plus: Depreciation	5,000	4,000	3,000	2,000	1,000
Annual aftertax cash flow ACF	$5,000	$4,500	$4,000	$3,500	$3,000

The project's *NPV* is a positive $421.85, indicating that the asset should be acquired. The next step is to determine how the acquisition should be financed. This can be determined by computing the net advantage to leasing (*NAL*).

Step 2: Computing NAL. To compute *NAL* one must first estimate the operating expenses associated with the asset that will be paid by the lessor, (i.e., the O_t). As discussed earlier, these cash expenses generally consist of certain maintenance expenses and insurance. BHM estimates these expenses at $1,000 per year over the life of the project. The annual rental payments Rt are $4,200.

Next, the interest tax shelters lost as a result of leasing the asset must be estimated. These tax shelters are lost because the firm's normal financing mix is not used and because the firm uses more than its target debt ratio allotment when it finances the asset with a lease. Determining these lost tax shelters involves the calculation of the principal and interest components of two different loans.

Exhibit 7 contains the computations for the $6,000 (0.40 × $15,000) loan used to finance the project under the purchase alternative. (The pretax debt rate is assumed to be 8%.) Note that the interest column supplies the needed information for the interest tax shelter that is lost if the asset is leased. Similarly, to compute ΔI_t the interest on that amount of debt that must be repaid to maintain the firm's target debt ratio must be determined. Since the target debt ratio is 40%, 60% of the purchase price of the asset (0.60 × $15,000 = $9,000) must

EXHIBIT 6 CALCULATING NPV (P)

Year, (t)	Annual Cash Flow (ACF_t)	×	Discount Factor for 12%	=	Present Value
1	$5,000		.893		$ 4,465.00
2	4,500		.797		3,586.50
3	4,000		.712		2,848.00
4	3,500		.636		2,226.00
5	3,000		.567		1,701.00
5	1,050 (Salvage)		.567		595.35
Present value of ACF's and V_n					$15,421.85
$NPV(P) = \$15,421.85 - 15,000$					$421.85

EXHIBIT 7   TERM LOAN AMORTIZATION SCHEDULE ($6,000 LOAN AT 8%)

End of Year, t	Installment Payment, L	Interest, I_t	Principal Repayment, P_t	Remaining Balance, RB_t
1	$1,502.63	$480.00	$1,022.63	$4,977.37
2	1,502.63	398.19	1,104.44	3,872.93
3	1,502.63	309.83	1,192.80	2,680.13
4	1,502.63	214.41	1,288.22	1,391.91
5	1,502.63	111.35	1,391.28[a]	—

[a]This amount does not equal the remaining balance because of rounding errors.

be repaid. Thus, ΔI_t is found just as I_t was, except that the calculations are based on a $9,000 loan rather than a $6,000 loan. The relevant values for ΔI_t are given below:

Year t	Interest, ΔI_t
1	$720.00
2	596.81
3	464.17
4	321.59
5	168.65

Note that both I_t and ΔI_t constitute lost tax shelters where the asset is leased. Also, I_t and ΔI_t correspond to loans equal to 40 and 60% of the purchase price of the asset, respectively. Thus the sum of I_t and ΔI_t is the interest expense on a loan equal to 100% of the asset's purchase price A_o. A more direct and less tedious way to estimate the interest tax shelters lost through leasing would be to compute the annual interest expense on a loan equal to the full purchase price of the asset ($16,000 in the present example). Once all the necessary cash flows have been determined, they are substituted into the *NAL* equation. Exhibit 8 shows these computations.

To summarize the steps in the BHM Co. lease-purchase analysis, first the project's net present value was computed. This analysis produced a positive *NPV* of $421.85, which indicated that the asset should be acquired. However, upon computing the net advantage to leasing it was found that the financial lease is the preferred method of financing the acquisition of the asset's services. As shown in Exhibit 8, the net present value advantage to leasing is a positive $139. Thus the firm should lease the asset rather than purchase it with its target debt-equity ratio (i.e., 40% debt and 60% equity).

This lease versus purchase model attempts to bridge the gap between financial theory and practice. It provides the practitioner with guidance on three specific issues: adjustment for risk differences in the cash flows, consideration of "bargain" lease terms, and correction for financial risk differences between the alternatives. The technique builds on the theoretical model of Lawrence Schall and employs a simple debt-to-assets ratio to control for financial risk differences between leasing and purchase of financing. The reader interested in a more rigorous method for dealing with financial risk is directed to a similar model (C. L. Allen, J. D. Martin, and P. F. Anderson, "Debt Capacity and the Lease-Purchase Problem: A Sensitivity Analysis," *Engineering Economist*, Vol. 24, Winter 1979, pp. 87–108). This

EXHIBIT 8 COMPUTING NET ADVANTAGE TO LEASING, NAL

Step 1

Solving for $\displaystyle\sum_{t=1}^{n}\frac{O_t(1-T) - R_t(1-T) - TI_t - T\Delta I_t - TD_2}{(1+r)^t}$

Year t	Aftertax Operating Expenses Paid by Lessor, $O_t(1-T)$	Aftertax Rental Expense, $R_t(1-T)$	Tax Shelter on Loan Interest,[a] $(TI_t + T\Delta I'_t)$	Tax Shelter on Depreciation, D_tT	= Total	× Discount Factor[b] at 8%, DF	= Present, Value, PV
1	$500	$2,100	$600	$2,500	4,700	.926	$ 4,352
2	500	2,100	498	2,000	4,098	.857	3,512
3	500	2,100	387	1,500	3,487	.794	2,769
4	500	2,100	268	1,000	2,868	.735	2,108
5	500	2,100	140	500	2,240	.681	1,525
							$ -14,266

Step 2

Solving for $-\dfrac{V_n}{(1+K_s)^n} = -\dfrac{\$1,050}{(1+0.12)^5} = -\$1,050 \times .567^c = \$\ -595$

Step 3

Adding purchase price of asset $(A_o) =$ $+\$15,000$

Step 4

Net advantage of leasing, NAL = sum of (1), (2) and (3) = $\$-14,266 - 595 + 15,000 = \underline{\$139}$

[a] This includes interest on the loan that is not used if the lease is undertaken plus interest on the amount of debt that must be repaid to maintain the target debt ratio. Thus for year 1 $(I_t + \Delta I_t)T = (\$480 + 720)0.5 = \$600$.
[b] The debt rate r equals 8%.
[c] The value of K_s was estimated to be the same as the firm's aftertax cost of capital, 12%.

approach employs a **risk of insolvency** criterion to determine the amount of debt "displaced" by a lease.

EMPIRICAL ASSESSMENT OF INDUSTRY PRACTICE: ANALYSIS OF LEASING VERSUS PURCHASING.   A survey of the "state of the art" in industry lease-purchase analysis was conducted in 1976 by Anderson and Martin (P. F. Anderson and J. D. Martin, "Lease vs. Purchase Decisions: A Survey of Current Practice," *Financial Management,* Spring 1977), using some of the 200 largest industrial firms in the United States listed by *Fortune* magazine. Each firm was given a lease versus purchase case problem and a short questionnaire. The case problem was a modified version of the example used in the well-known paper by Johnson and Lewellen, cited earlier.

A total of 48 usable responses were obtained. A distribution of respondent lease payments for 1974 is found in Exhibit 9. The majority of the responding firms were among the largest in the Fortune 200. Of the usable responses, 27 were from firms in the top 100 and 21 were from the top 150. Thus, the sample should indicate which methodologies are used by some of the most sophisticated segments of industry.

Exhibit 10 contains a distribution of the methodologies employed by the respondents. The most used was the traditional internal rate of return model. For a description of the use of internal rate of return models, see, among others, T. H. Beechy, "Quasi-Debt Analysis of Financial Leases" (*Accounting Review,* Vol. 44, April 1969, pp. 375–381), R. C. Doenges, "The Cost of Leasing" (*Engineering Economist,* Vol. 17, Fall 1971, pp. 31–44), G. B. Mitchell, "After- Tax Cost of Leasing" (*Accounting Review,* Vol. 45, April 1970, pp. 308–314, G. D. Quirin, *The Capital Expenditure Decision* (Irwin, Homewood, IL, 1967).

The next most widely used model was the conventional net present value technique. For a discussion of the conventional net present value methodology, see Albert H. Cohen, *Long Term Leases—Problems of Taxation, Finance and Accounting* (University of Michigan Press, Ann Arbor, 1954), James C. Van Horne, *Financial Management and Policy,* 3rd ed., (Prentice-Hall, Englewood Cliffs, NJ, 1974). More than 70% percent of the respondents to

EXHIBIT 9   DISTRIBUTION OF RESPONDENTS BY DOLLAR VALUE OF 1974 LEASE PAYMENTS

Dollar Value	Number of Firms	% of Firms
$100 million or over	2	4.3
$50–$100 million	8	17.4
$25–$50 million	12	26.1
$10–$25 million	13	28.3
Less than $10 million	11	23.9
	46[a]	100.0

[a]Note that two firms returned dual responses such that 48 lease-purchase analyses were available.
Source: Paul F. Anderson and John D. Martin, "Lease vs. Purchase Decisions: A Survey of Current Practice," *Financial Management* (Spring 1977), pp. 41–47.

EXHIBIT 10   CLASSIFICATION OF RESPONDENTS' LEASE VERSUS PURCHASE ANALYSIS MODELS

Model	Frequency of Methodology
Traditional internal rate of return model	24
Conventional net present value model	11
Bierman and Smidt model (1966)	5
Basic interest rate model	4
Weston and Brigham model (1972)	2
Bower, Herringer, and Williamson model	2
	48

Source: Paul F. Anderson and John D. Martin, "Lease vs. Purchase Decisions: A Survey of Current Practice," *Financial Management* (Spring 1977), pp. 41–47.

the study by Anderson and Martin utilized one of these basic approaches to the analysis of the lease-purchase problem. The popularity of the internal rate of return method may well be attributable to a preference by practitioners for the use of rate of return methodology when evaluating financing cost. The relatively widespread use of the traditional net present value model might be due to its similarity to accepted capital budgeting procedures and the fact that this is one of the earliest models developed.

The third most widely used model was proposed in the second edition of *The Capital Budgeting Decision* (H. Bierman, Jr. and S. Smidt, Macmillan, New York, 1966). This model has been shown to be formally equivalent to the 1969 and 1972 Weston and Brigham models. Two of the respondents did indeed use the 1972 version of the Weston and Brigham model. The remaining respondents used either the basic interest rate method (Richard F. Vancil, "Lease or Borrow—New Method of Analysis," *Harvard Business Review*, Vol. 39, September–October 1961) or the BHW model (Richard S. Bower, Frank C. Herringer, and J. Peter Williamson, "Lease Evaluation," *Accounting Review*, Vol. 41, April 1966, pp. 257–275). The differences in these methods are slight, as noted by Findlay (M. Chapman Findlay, III, "Financial Lease Evaluation: Survey and Synthesis," *Financial Review*, 1974, pp. 1–15).

The survey findings indicate that many large industrial firms make use of lease-purchase models that produce results that are **potentially biased in favor of purchasing.** There are two potential sources of bias in the models used: First, a majority of the models do not properly adjust for risk differences in the cash flows attendant to the lease-purchase analysis. Second, many of the models require a justification of the investment on a purchase basis before leasing is considered.

Failure to adjust cash flows for risk differences will tend to overstate the costs of leasing in both net present value and internal rate of return types of models. The conventional net present value model, the basic interest rate model, and the Bower, Herringer, and Williamson models are all subject to this criticism. The source of bias against leasing is related to the use of a relatively high rate of interest, in the form of the weighted average cost of capital, to discount relatively certain contractual and tax-shield cash flows. The bias against leasing results because the cash flow benefits of a lease tend to outweigh its cash flow costs in the latter years of a project's life. Thus the use of an inordinately high rate of interest to discount these cash flows will have the effect of underemphasizing these benefits. There is no consensus among theorists on the proper discount rates; however, most agree that the cost of capital is too high a rate for discounting near riskless cash flows. For supporting arguments see R. S. Bower, "Issues in Lease Financing" (*Financial Management,* Vol. 2, Winter 1973, pp. 25–34), M. Chapman Findlay, III, "Financial Lease Evaluation: Survey and Synthesis" (*Financial Review,* 1974, pp. 1–15), Myron J. Gordon, "A General Solution to the Buy or Lease Decision: A Pedagogical Note" (*Journal of Finance,* Vol. 29, March 1974, pp. 245–250).

In the case of the traditional internal rate of return model, the discount rate bias is related to the failure of the model to consider the uncertainty of the asset's salvage value. This model enters salvage value into the internal rate of return calculation unadjusted for risk differences between the salvage value and the relatively certain tax shield and contractual cash flows. R. L. Roenfeldt and J. S. Osteryoung ("Analysis of Financial Leases," *Financial Management,* Vol. 2, Spring 1973, pp. 74–87) offer a modified internal rate of return methodology that utilizes a **certainty equivalent adjustment to salvage value.** However, none of the respondents cited uses this model.

The second type of bias inherent in many of the lease versus purchase models is related to the requirement that the project be adjudged worthy of purchase by the firm's capital budgeting procedure before lease financing is considered. This ex ante investment analysis fallacy has been recognized by a number of authors. See, for example, Harold Bierman, Jr., and Seymour Smidt, *The Capital Budgeting Decision,* 2nd ed. (Macmillan, New York, 1966), C. Robert Carlson and Donald H. Wort, "A New Look at the Lease-vs.-Purchase Decision" (*Journal of Economics and Business,* Vol. 26, Spring 1974, pp. 199–202). A problem arises, however, because the acquisition of some projects may not be justified on a purchase bias but may be desirable when favorable lease terms are available. The Bierman and Smidt model is the only one of those used by the respondents that does not suffer from this bias.

LEASING FROM THE LESSOR'S PERSPECTIVE: ANALYZING A LEVERAGED LEASE ARRANGEMENT.

Leveraged Lease Arrangements.   A leveraged lease arrangement can be complex; an excellent overview of the details involved in establishing a leveraged lease is found in N. B. Stiles and M. A. Walker, "Leveraged Lease Financing of Capital Equipment" (*Journal of Commercial Bank Lending,* July 1973, pp. 19–39). The essence of the arrangement need not be so complex. This discussion draws on P. R. Smith, "A Straight Forward Approach to Leveraged Leasing" (*Journal of Commercial Bank Lending,* July 1973, pp. 40–47). There are three principal participants in the typical leveraged lease arrangement:

1. The **lessee** or company that will use the leased asset.
2. The **lessor** or owner of the asset (sometimes referred to as the equity participant). The lessor is frequently a financial institution.
3. The **debt participant or lender,** which is a second financial institution.

The basic steps involved in arranging a leveraged lease are as follows:

1. The **lessee** selects the specific asset he desires and usually suggests the term over which he would like to lease it.
2. The **lessor** (owner participant) arranges for a loan of 60–80% of the asset's purchase price and supplies the balance of the funds needed to acquire the asset.
3. The **debt participant** (lender) will generally obtain a *chattel mortgage* on the full

value of the leased equipment as well as an assignment of the lease payments. Note that the lender must look to the mortgaged asset's value and the assigned lease payments as the security for his loan.

In preparing a leveraged lease agreement, the lessor must be very careful to follow the guidelines of the **Internal Revenue Service** regarding a "true lease." That is, if the IRS disallows a leveraged lease on the grounds that it is in fact a **conditional sales contract,** the lessor cannot claim the tax benefits associated with ownership of the leased asset (i.e., depreciation, investment tax credit, and interest expense).The IRS has stated, "In ascertaining such intent no single test, or special combination of tests, is absolutely determinative. No general rule applicable to all cases can be laid down. Each case must be decided in light of its particular facts." (Rev. Rul. 55–540, Section 4.01.) Briefly, the IRS tests of a true lease are as follows:

1. As owner, the lessor must bear the risk of ownership, which includes the possible decline in economic value of the equipment.

2. The lessee cannot build up equity interest in the leased equipment with lease payments, nor can the lessee assume title after making a specified number of lease payments. If the equipment is sold or released at the end of the lease term, it must be at a value not less than an "arm's-length" fair market value.

3. Rental payments that materially exceed the fair market rental over the lease term may be construed to be building up an equity interest in the property.

4. The lease term must be less than the economic life of the equipment so that the equipment has a residual value of at least 15% of its original value and an economic life of at least 2 years or 10% (whichever is greater) of the lease term.

These tests are not ironclad, and previous IRS rulings give evidence of room for flexibility. For this reason, lessors generally seek an opinion from the IRS on any new leases before consummating agreements.

Setting Lease Terms. The lessor is faced with the problem of determining lease terms (payments) every time a new lease is written. The problem is similar to that of the banker who must determine a set of installment payments that will provide the desired rate of return on a loan. The major differences in the positions of the lessor and the lender are that the lessor owns an asset that can be depreciated, whose acquisition may produce an **investment tax credit,** and the lessor will receive any **salvage value** resulting from the disposal of the asset at the termination of the lease. An interesting discussion of the risks inherent in leasing can be found in E. R. Packham, "An Analysis of the Risks of Leveraged Leasing" (*Journal of Commercial Bank Lending,* March 1975, pp. 2–29). This author notes that the greatest risks associated with lessor tax savings relate to the possibility that the IRS will rule that the lease is not a "true lease" (see previous discussion of the true lease requirements), in which case the lessor could not claim the tax shelters associated with ownership (e.g., depreciation expense).

In general terms, the **lessor pricing model** can be defined as follows:

$$A_o = PV[L] + PV[DTS] + ITC + PV[ITS] + PV[S]$$

where A_o represents the purchase price of the leased equipment; $PV[L]$ is the present value of the aftertax lease payments L discounted at a rate commensurate with their riskiness (it is generally recommended that the cost of borrowing be used); $PV[DTS]$ is the present value of the tax savings accruing to the lessor as a result of depreciation charges (again, the cost of borrowed funds is frequently used to discount these tax savings); ITC is the investment tax credit accruing to the lessor in the year in which the asset is acquired; $PV[ITS]$ is the present value of the interest tax savings realized by the lessor due to the tax deductibility of interest expense (the cost of debt is traditionally used to discount these tax savings); and $PV[S]$ is the present value of the estimated aftertax salvage value of the asset upon termination of the lease.

The discount rate used to evaluate the asset's salvage value is one that is commensurate with the risks associated with that salvage value. The determination of such a rate is difficult, and no easy solution to the problem of its estimation exists. The estimation of residual or salvage values remains one of the most difficult issues encountered in evaluating lease terms. In many instances the lessor simply assumes a zero salvage value for the sake of conservatism. This results in the setting of higher lease terms, which may make the lessor noncompetitive. In another approach that has been suggested to deal with this problem the lessor evaluates the residual value in an option pricing framework (see W. Y. Lee, A. J. Ssenchack, and J.D. Martin, "An Option Valuation Approach to Setting Leveraged Lease Terms," Working Paper, University of Texas, Austin, 1980). The proposed methodology involves the potential use of an **option straddle** on the **residual value** where the range of values the asset's terminal value can take on is restrained. The straddle involves the **simultaneous sale of a call option and purchase of a put option** on **the residual value of the leased asset.** The effective use of the strategy depends, of course, on the availability of a market for the needed options. A related discussion of the salvage value problem involved in setting lease terms can be found in J. K. Malernee and R. C. Witt, "Equipment Price Insurance: An Emerging Market" (*Bests Review*, Vol. 79, June 1978, pp. 22, 26, 96, 97).

The lessor's pricing problem involves the determination of a stream of aftertax lease payments L whose present value when combined with that of the other elements on the right-hand side of the lessor pricing model will add up to A_o. This set of lease payments then represents the minimum the lessor can charge the lessee and earn his required rate of return.

There are two fundamental methods that can be used to evaluate a leveraged lease: the **net present value method** and the **internal rate of return method.** The latter has led to a great deal of discussion in the literature (see, for example, W. J. Regan, "The Dual Aspect of Leveraged Leasing," *Banker's Magazine*, Autumn 1976, pp. 75–77).

The problem of **multiple internal rates of return,** which is sometimes encountered in using this method, is related to the fact that the net cash flows to the lessor from a leveraged lease are positive during the early years, then negative in the latter years of the lease. The result is that there can be as many internal rates of return as there are changes in the sign of the project's future cash flows. Hence, for the leveraged lease with two such sign changes, there are two possible internal rates of return.

Internal rate of return methodologies are not further discussed here since the present value method is recognized as providing a correct solution to the problem. Interestingly, Regan recognized the superiority of the present value approach but presented another rate of return criterion based on the perception that **practitioners** are wedded to the use of rates of return in the evaluation of new projects. No such assumption is made in the exposition presented here.

Setting Lease Terms: An Example.   In this simple example a lessor uses the lessor pricing model to set terms on a leveraged lease. The details of the proposed lease are set out in Exhibit 11. Solving for the lease terms (lease payments) involves two steps:

Step 1. Rearrange the terms in the lessor pricing model as follows:

$$PV(L) = A_o - PV[DTS] - ITC - PV[ITS] - PV[S]$$

and solve for $PV[L]$.

Step 2. Having solved for the present value of the aftertax future lease payments $PV(L)$, solve for the annual lease payment annuity cash flow L, which has a present value (when discounted at the lessor's required rate of return on the lease payments) equal to the $PV[L]$ found in step 1. If these aftertax lease payments are charged, the lessor will expect to realize a rate of return equal to its required rate of return. The actual lease payments equal L solved for above divided by 1 minus the lessor's marginal tax rate.

Exhibit 12 contains the cash flow information required to analyze $PV[L]$ in step 1. Having solved for $PV[L]$, the analyst can now proceed to solve for an annuity payment L with a 15-year term (N), which has a present value of $27,800, when discounted at the lessor's required rate of return on the lease payments. For this example, the lessor's required return is set equal to its own borrowing rate of 10%. Parenthetically, it can be argued that the risks inherent in the lessor's receipt of the lease payments are the same as those involved in the lender's receipt of principal and interest on the loan that underlies 80% of the purchase price of the asset. In this case, the required rate of return of the lender on the loan $(r = 10\%$ in this instance) should be the appropriate required rate of return on the lease payments. The

EXHIBIT 11   LEVERAGED LEASE PROBLEM

Leased Asset

Railroad car

Cash Flow Information

Acquisition price (A_0) = $100,000
Lease term (N) = 15 years

Depreciation
Method = Sum-of-the-years' digits
Depreciable life = 11 years
Salvage value = $0.05\, A_0$ = $5,000

Loan Information
Loan amount = $0.75\, A_0$ = $75,000
Interest rate, r = 0.10 or 10%
Term = 15 years
Type of loan = interest only with full principal due at end of year 15

Solution
Investment tax credit = $0.10\, A_o$
Lessor's required rate of return on leased asset's salvage value = 0.20 or 20%
Lessor's marginal tax rate = 0.46 or 46%

EXHIBIT 12   ESTIMATING PRESENT VALUE OF LEASE PAYMENTS IN THE LESSOR PRICING MODEL ($ THOUSANDS)

Solving for $PV[L] = A_o - PV[DTS] - ITC - PV[ITS] - PV[S]$

Year	Depreciation Tax Savings, $(DTS)^a$	+	Interest Tax Savings, $(ITS)^b$	= DTS + ITS	×	Discount Factor^c	=	Present Value of $(DTS + ITS)$
1	$5.46		$3.45	$8.91		.9091		$8.10
2	5.10		3.45	8.55		.8264		7.07
3	4.73		3.45	8.18		.7513		6.16
4	4.37		3.45	7.82		.6830		5.34
5	4.01		3.45	7.46		.6209		4.63
6	3.64		3.45	7.09		.5645		4.00
7	3.28		3.45	6.73		.5132		3.45
8	2.91		3.45	6.36		.4665		2.97
9	2.55		3.45	6.00		.4241		2.59
10	2.19		3.45	5.54		.3855		2.14
11	1.82		3.45	5.27		.3505		1.85
12	1.46		3.45	4.91		.3186		1.56
13	1.09		3.45	4.54		.2897		1.32
14	0.73		3.45	4.18		.2633		1.10
15	0.36		3.45	3.81		.2394		0.91

$$PV(DTS + ITS) = 43.14$$
$$ITC = 0.10 \times \$100 = \$10$$
$$PV[S]^4 = \$5 \times 0.0649 = \$0.32$$
$$A_o = \$100$$

Therefore $PV[L] = \$100 - 53.14 - 10 - 0.32$
$$= \$36.54 \text{ or } \$36,540$$

$^a DTS$ = depreciation expense for the year × marginal tax rate.
$^b ITS$ = interest expense for the year × marginal tax rate. Since the interest component of the assumed loan is constant at $10,000 per year, these annual tax savings equal $10,000 × 0.46 = $4,600.
^{c}Based on the cost of borrowing to the lessor ($r = 10\%$).
^{d}The present value of the asset's salvage or terminal value is calculated here by using the lessor firm's cost of capital of 20%. It is not clear that this rate is appropriate, however, since S is almost certainly more risky than the other cash flows being discounted, a rate higher than the lessor's cost of borrowing justifies.

lessor, of course, is free to set whatever required rate he feels is commensurate with the risks associated with the lease agreement. However, setting too high a required return will produce a set of lease payments so high that the lease will be unattractive to the lessee. The basic point is that the **lessor sets the rate of return on the lease** payments at a level that he would be happy to receive if the lease agreement were consummated. Solving for the lease payments in this example involves the following expression:

$$PV[L] = \$36,540$$

or

$$L \sum_{t=1}^{15} \frac{1}{(1 + 0.10)^t} = \$36,540$$

where

$$\sum_{t=1}^{15} \frac{1}{(1 + 0.10)t} = \text{an annuity discount factor for 10\% and 15}$$
years (obtained from a table
of discount factors)

Therefore

$$L (7.6061) = \$36,540.00$$
$$L = \$ \ 4,804.04$$

The pretax lease payments are $L/(1 - T)$ or $\$4,804.04/(1 - 0.46) = \$8,896.30$.

The lessor can now set the terms of the lease at $8,896.30 per year. Given these lease payments and the remaining estimated cash flows associated with the lease agreement, the lessor will expect to earn his required rate of return on the lease agreement.

ACCOUNTING FOR LEASES

HISTORICAL PERSPECTIVE. This section relies heavily on J. D. Martin, P. F. Anderson, and A. J. Keown, "Lease Capitalization and Stock Price Stability: Implications for Accounting" (*Journal of Accounting, Auditing and Finance,* Vol. 2, Winter 1979, pp. 151–163). The debate over whether leases should be capitalized and included in the lessee's balance sheet spanned almost three decades (see, e.g., A. J. Cannon, "Danger Signal to Accountants in 'Net Lease' Financing," *Journal of Accountancy,* Vol. 85, April 1948, pp. 312–319). Throughout the debate the official accounting literature consistently supported the notion of fuller disclosure of lessee lease commitments; however, until recently, that literature did not support capitalization of most types of lease.

Accounting Research Bulletin (ARB) No. 38. "Disclosure of Long-Term Leases in Financial Statements of Lessees," issued by the American Institute of [Certified Public] Accountants (AICPA) in 1949, provided the first official pronouncement concerning the reporting of leases by lessees. This bulletin recommended disclosure of "material" commitments under long-term leases. In addition, leases that were in effect "installment purchases" were to be capitalized. However, only general guidelines were provided for the determination of the types of leases which should be considered installment purchases.

ARB No. 38 was also noteworthy in that it provided the basis for the **"legal" argument for noncapitalization of leases.** It was argued that only leases that give rise to debt in a strict legal sense should be capitalized. The legal argument is founded on the premise that leases are "executory" contracts as opposed to "executed" contracts. In an executory contract both parties to the contract have continuing agreements that are not fulfilled until the contract is terminated. If leases are indeed executory, it is argued, they cannot give rise to assets and liabilities as generally defined by the accounting profession and should not be capitalized. Indeed, a number of authors have argued that a lease is primarily executory.

(See Donald C. Cook, "The Case Against Capitalizing Leases," *Harvard Business Review*, Vol. 41, January–February 1963, D. M. Hawkins and M. M. Wehle, *Accounting for Leases*, Financial Executives Research Foundation, New York, 1973; and Alvin Zises, "Long-Term Leases: Case Against Capitalization for Full Disclosures," *Financial Analysts Journal*, Vol. 18, May–June 1962, pp. 13–20).

Accounting Research Study No. 4. This report (John H. Myers, "Reporting of Leases in Financial Statements," AICPA, New York, 1962) concluded that certain types of financial leases give rise to "property rights" and should be capitalized. The report became one of the early pronouncements of the "economic" argument for lease capitalization, namely, that "the substance of the transaction should take precedence over its legal form" (D. M. Hawkins and M. M. Wehle, *Accounting for Leases*, Financial Executives Research Foundation, New York, 1973, p. 23). Thus, it was argued that a lease has the same basic economic consequences as debt and therefore should be treated similarly.

Specifically, Accounting Research Study No. 4 recommended lease capitalization for those leases meeting the following provisions:

1. The lease covers substantially the entire useful life of the leased property.

2. The lessee can purchase the property at the termination of the lease for a nominal price.

3. The contract is noncancelable.

4. The lessee pays fixed amounts sufficient to return to the lessor his investment in the property under lease plus a fair return.

5. The lessee pays the taxes, insurance, maintenance, and other ancillary costs associated with the leased property.

The Accounting Principles Board did not, however, adopt the recommendations of Accounting Research Study No. 4. Instead, it took the more moderate position of Accounting Research Bulletin No. 38.

Accounting Principles Board Opinion No. 5. In 1964 the AICPA issued APB Opinion No. 5, "Reporting of Leases in Financial Statements of Lessee," stating that a lease should be capitalized "only in the case in which it is in substance a purchase." In addition, this opinion further clarified the criteria to be used in determining when a lease is essentially a purchase. The opinion also added footnote disclosure requirements for lessee balance sheets.

Accounting Principles Board Opinion No. 31 and Accounting Series Release No. 147. APB Opinion No. 31 ("Disclosure of Lease Commitments by Lessees," AICPA, New York, June 1973) further strengthened the footnote disclosure requirements of APB Opinion No. 5. Meanwhile the **Securities and Exchange Commission** issued Accounting Series Release No. 147 ("Notice of Adoption of Amendments to Regulation S-X Requiring Improved Disclosure of Leases," SEC, Washington, D.C., October 5, 1973). This document included even more stringent footnote disclosure requirements for lessees than did APB Opinion No. 31.

LEASE CAPITALIZATION. Finally, in November 1976 the accounting profession relented and for the first time called for the capitalization of most financial lease agreements. The FASB adopted the basic periods of the "economic argument for capitalization." That is, the economic effect of the transaction should govern its accounting treatment (Financial Accounting Standards Board, Statement of Financial Accounting Standards (SFAS) No. 13, "Accounting for Leases," p. 49). The Board took the point of view that "a lease that transfers substantially all the benefits and risks incident to the ownership of property should be accounted for as the acquisition of an asset and the incurrence of an obligation by the lessee" (SFAS No. 13, p. 49). The Statement further says that capitalized leases need not be "in substance purchases," as was the case in Accounting Principles Board Opinion No. 5.

SFAS No. 13 specifically requires capitalization of all lessee lease agreements that satisfy one or more of the following criteria (pp. 9–10):

1. The lease transfers ownership of the property to the lessee by the end of the lease term.
2. The lease contains a bargain purchase option.
3. The lease term is equal to 75% or more of the estimated economic life of the leased property.
4. The present value of the minimum lease payments equals or exceeds 90% of the excess of the fair value of the leased property over any related investment tax credit retained by the lessor.

The last two requirements are the operational elements in the Board's statement. The first two have not been applicable to most leases for many years because of the Internal Revenue Service's "true lease" requirements (Rev. Rul. 55–540, 1955 CB 41). However, criteria 3 and 4 apply to the majority of the financial leases written in the United States. As a result, most financial leases entered into during 1977 appear in the body of the lessee's balance sheet. Moreover, the Board encouraged immediate retroactive application of the standards, and it requires such application after December 31, 1980.

SFAS No. 13 provides a landmark in terms of the accounting treatment of leases. Since the appearance of this statement, numerous refinements have been made and more are sure to come. Exhibit 13 contains a brief summary of some of these refinements.

STOCK PRICES AND LEASE CAPITALIZATION. The price impact on a lessee firm's common stock of required disclosure of capitalized leases was extensively tested by Ro (Byung T. Ro, "The Disclosure of Capitalized Lease Information and Stock Prices," *Journal of Accounting Research,* Vol. 16, Autumn 1978, pp. 315–340). The specific capitalization requirement tested was SEC Accounting Series Release No. 147 ("Notice of Adoption of Amendments to Regulation S-X Requiring Improved Disclosure of Leases," SEC, Washington, D.C., October 5, 1973, in SEC Docket October 23, 1973). ASR No. 147, which became effective as of November 30, 1973, required the disclosure of lease information that had not previously been called for by the SEC or other accounting regulatory bodies. The release required disclosure of the following items related to noncapitalized financing leases: (1) the present value (PV) of the minimum future lease commitments, (2) the interest rate(s) implicit in computing the PV, and (3) the impact on net income (the income effect, IE) if such leases were capitalized. Detailed disclosure requirements are not presented here because they are not crucial to the interpretation of the Ro test findings.

Two basic groups of tests were made to determine the stock price impact of the lease disclosure requirements of ASR No. 147. Actually, a battery of tests was made but they could be dichotomized in the way described here. One test involved the group of firms that

EXHIBIT 13   ACCOUNTING PRINCIPLES RELATED TO LEASES

STATEMENTS OF FINANCIAL ACCOUNTING STANDARDS[a]

SFAS 13	Accounting for Leases
SFAS 17	Accounting for Leases—Initial Direct Costs
SFAS 22	Changes in the Provisions of Lease Agreements Resulting from Refundings of Tax-Exempt Debt
SFAS 23	Inception of the Lease
SFAS 26	Profit Recognition on Sales-Type Leases of Real Estate
SFAS 27	Classification of Renewals or Extensions of Existing Sales-Type or Direct Financing Leases
SFAS 28	Accounting for Sales with Leasebacks
SFAS 29	Determining Contingent Rentals

FASB INTERPRETATIONS[b]

No. 19	Lessee Guarantee of the Residual Value of Leased Property
No. 21	Accounting for Leases in a Business Combination
No. 23	Leases of Certain Property Owned by a Governmental Unit or Authority
No. 24	Leases Involving Only Part of a Building
No. 26	Accounting for Purchase of Leased Asset by the Lessee During the Term of the Lease
No. 27	Accounting for a Loss on a Sublease

[a]The Financial Accounting Standards Board (FASB) was established in 1973 and had issued 34 Statements of Financial Accounting Standards (SFAS) by October 1979. SFASs are similar in scope to both the Accounting Research Bulletins and Accounting Principles Board Opinions that preceded them. The SFASs amend and supersede these existing pronouncements and establish generally accepted accounting principles in new areas.
[b]These statements represent FASB interpretations of existing pronouncements.

were **PV disclosure firms.** The second consisted of firms that were **both PV and IE disclosure firms.** For each of these groups a total of six different tests were made relating to six sample periods contained within the overall period January 1973–September 1974. Key dates in this period were the announcement of the proposal (June 1973), adoption of the proposal (October 1973), the effective date of the release (November 1973), and the first disclosure (March 1974). Note that all test firms had a December 31 fiscal year-end; thus the first disclosure of lease information was March 1974 for all.

Results of the PV test group are summarized below (Byung T. Ro, "The Disclosure of Capitalized Lease Information and Stock Prices," *Journal of Accounting Research,* Vol. 16, Autumn 1978, p. 331):

> To summarize, evidence from the test results for the PV disclosure firms suggests that the disclosure of capitalized lease information as required by the SEC had no significant effect upon the pricing of securities. This implies that the PV numbers of noncapitalized financing leases, as disclosed under ASR No. 147, did not carry new information to investors for assessing the risk-return attributes of firms with such leases.

The test results for the PV and IE disclosure group were markedly different from those of the PV group. The findings suggested that the lease information disclosure did affect stock prices for five of the six subperiods tested. These results are summarized by Ro as follows (pp. 335–336):

> To summarize, the test results for the PV-IE firms suggest that the information effects of the various events of the SEC lease decision were present when the effects were measured by the changes in the expected values of return distributions. The results also reveal that the market reaction began as early as March 1973, indicating that the effects of the capitalized lease disclosure (as required by the SEC) were anticipated by the investment community prior to the disclosure of the capitalized lease numbers through accounting sources.
>
> The results also show that the capitalized lease disclosure did, overall, have an adverse effect on the valuation of the firms, although a slight upward readjustment of the security prices upon the disclosure of the capitalized lease data was observed for the low-risk firms. This upward readjustment may indicate that the negative effects of the PV and IE numbers (especially the latter) on various financial ratios were not as bad as investors had originally anticipated.

LEASE CAPITALIZATION AND FINANCIAL RATIOS. The capitalization of financial lease obligations can have a significant impact on computed financial ratios that involve either total liabilities or total assets. For example, the debt ratio (total liabilities divided by total assets) is increased by the inclusion of capitalized leases. Likewise the return on total asset ratio (net after tax profits divided by total assets) is reduced when capitalized leases are considered.

Altman et al. (E. I Altman, R. G. Haldeman, and P. Narayanan, "ZETA® Analysis: A New Model to Identify Bankruptcy Risk of Corporations," *Journal of Banking and Finance*, Vol. 1, 1977, pp. 29–54) report that in the sample of firms analyzed, capitalized leases were 17–18% of total assets (including capitalized leases, or 20.5–22% of total assets before lease capitalization). In addition, for bankrupt firms, capitalized leases averaged 23% of total assets (or 30% of total assets before lease capitalization).

To illustrate the **impact of lease capitalization on financial ratios,** consider the following. Using 17.5% as the level of capitalized leases to total assets, a firm with a debt ratio of 50% before capitalization will have a postcapitalization ratio of 59%. Similarly, if the firm's precapitalization return on assets were 20%, the return after capitalization would drop to 16.5%.

The Ro study, discussed above, found virtually no impact of lease capitalization on equity value. This result would suggest that the impact of lease capitalization on financial ratios was known to investors prior to capitalization. Before the issuance of FASB Statement of Financial Accounting Standards No. 13, which required lease capitalization of most types of financial leases, generally accepted accounting practice (APB Opinion No. 31) required substantial footnote disclosure of financial lease obligations. Lease capitalization, however, may have a detrimental effect on a firm's ability to obtain financing on favorable terms when a relatively unsophisticated lender is involved. Furthermore, some equity investors may be so naive as to be unable to properly evaluate uncapitalized leases. However, any fears that a firm may have about the unfavorable impact of capitalization of its lease obligations are based on the presumed naiveté of its financial statement users.

LEASE CAPITALIZATION AND BANKRUPTCY PREDICTION. The prediction of firm failure provides a dramatic and important testing ground for the "usefulness" of reported accounting information. R. Elam ("The Effect of Lease Data on the Predictive Ability of Financial Ratios," *Accounting Review*, January 1975, pp. 25–43) concluded that there is no evidence of improved predictability of bankruptcy that results from the use of lease data in the predictor set of financial ratios. Altman (E. I. Altman, "Capitalization of Leases and the Predictability of Financial Ratios: A Comment," Vol. 1, *Accounting Review,* April 1976, pp. 408–412) questioned Elam's findings on both conceptual and empirical grounds. In an extensive analysis of the bankruptcy prediction problem (E. I. Altman, R. G. Haldeman, and P. Narayanan, "ZETA® Analysis: A New Model to Identify Bankruptcy Risk of Corporations") provide evidence that lease data disclosed in lessee financial statements is indeed useful. The ZETA model was successful in identifying firms that would eventually become bankrupt up to 5 years before their actual failure. Specifically, over 90% of the firms were accurately classified as bankrupt or nonbankrupt one year before the date of failure, and 70% were correctly classified as bankrupt or nonbankrupt up to 5 years before the failure of the bankrupt group.

A number of adjustments were made to reported accounting data before the ZETA model was developed. Altman et al. (1977, p. 33) made the following statement about lease capitalization: "Without doubt, the most important and pervasive adjustment made was to capitalize all non-cancellable operating and finance leases." The resulting ZETA model was more accurate than the original Altman Z-Score model (E. I. Altman, "Financial Ratios, Discriminant Analysis and the Prediction of Corporate Bankruptcy," *Journal of Finance,* Vol. 23, September 1968, pp. 589–609) for predictions made 2–5 years before bankruptcy and provided roughly equivalent predictive accuracy 1 year before failure.

SECURITY POSITION IN BANKRUPTCY.   The security position of the lessor in bankruptcy is generally considered to be superior to that of the firm's general creditors and even the mortgage lenders. If the lessee defaults on the lease payments of a realty lease, the lessor can promptly obtain a court order and taken possession of his property. In the event the lessee firm becomes bankrupt and is liquidated, the lessor's claim to damages is limited to a formula that was recently revised under the **Bankruptcy Reform Act of 1978.**

REFERENCES AND BIBLIOGRAPHY

Anderson, Paul F., and Martin, John D., "Lease vs. Purchase Decisions: A Survey of Current Practice," *Financial Management,* Vol. 6, Spring 1977, pp. 41–47.

Beechy, Thomas H., "Quasi-Debt Analysis of Financial Leases," *Accounting Review,* Vol. 44, April 1969, pp. 375–381.

————"The Cost of Leasing: Comment and Correction," *Accounting Review,* Vol. 45, October 1970, pp. 769–773.

Bierman, Harold, Jr., "Analysis of the Lease-or-Buy Decision: Comment," *Journal of Finance,* Vol. 28, September 1973, pp. 1019–1021.

————, and Hass, Jerome E., "Capital Budgeting Under Uncertainty: A Reformulation," *Journal of Finance,* Vol. 28, March 1977, pp. 119–129.

————, and Smidt, Seymour, *The Capital Budgeting Decision,* 4th ed., Macmillan, New York, 1980.

Bower, Richard S., "Issues in Lease Financing," *Financial Management,* Vol. 2, Winter 1973, pp. 25–34.

Bower, Richard S., Herringer, Frank C., and Williamson, J. Peter, "Lease Evaluation," *Accounting Review,* Vol. 41, April 1966, pp. 257–265.

Carlson, C. Robert, and Wort, Donald H., "A New Look at the Lease-Vs.-Purchase Decision," *Journal of Economics and Business,* Vol. 26, Spring 1974, pp. 199–202.

Clark, Robert A., Jantorni, Joan M., and Gann, Robert R., "Analysis of the Lease-or-Buy Decision: Comment," *Journal of Finance,* Vol. 28, September 1973, pp. 1015–1016.

Cohen, Albert H., *Long Term Leases—Problems of Taxation, Finance and Accounting,* University of Michigan Press, Ann Arbor, 1954.

Cooper, Kerry, and Strawser, Robert H., "Evaluation of Capital Investments Projects Involving Asset Leases," *Financial Management,* Vol. 4, Spring 1975, pp. 44–49.

Doenges, R. Conrad, "The Cost of Leasing," *Engineering Economist,* Vol. 17, Fall 1971, pp. 31–44.

Findlay, M. Chapman, III, "Financial Lease Evaluation: Survey and Synthesis," *Financial Review,* 1974, pp. 1–15.

Johnson, Robert W., and Lewellen, Wilbur G., "Analysis of the Lease-or-Buy Decision," *Journal of Finance,* Vol. 27, September 1972, pp. 815–823.

———, "Reply," *Journal of Finance,* Vol. 28, September 1973, pp. 1024–1028.

Lev, Baruch, and Orgler, Yair E., "Analysis of the Lease-or-Buy Decision: Comment," *Journal of Finance,* Vol. 28, September 1973, pp. 1022–1023.

Lewellen, Wilbur G., Long, Michael S., and McConnell, John J., "Asset Leasing in Competitive Capital Markets," *Journal of Finance,* Vol. 31, June 1976, pp. 787–798.

Lusztig, Peter, "Analysis of the Lease-or-Buy Decision: Comment," *Journal of Finance,* Vol. 28, September 1973, pp. 1017–1018.

Martin, John D., Petty, J. William, Keown, Arthur J., and Scott, David F., Jr., *Basic Financial Management,* Prentice-Hall, Englewood Cliffs, NJ, 1979.

Mitchell, G. B., "After-Tax Cost of Leasing," *Accounting Review,* Vol. 45, April 1970, pp. 308–314.

Myers, Stewart C., "Interactions of Corporate Financing and Investment Decisions—Implications for Capital Budgeting," *Journal of Finance,* Vol. 29, March 1974, pp. 1–25.

———, Dill, David A., and Bautista, Alberto J. "Valuation of Financial Lease Contracts," *Journal of Finance,* Vol. 31, June 1976, pp. 799–819.

———, and Pogue, Gerald A., "A Programming Approach to Corporate Financial Management," *Journal of Finance,* Vol. 29, May 1974, pp. 579–600.

Quirin, G. David, *The Capital Expenditure Decision,* Irwin, Homewood, Il, 1967.

Roenfeldt, Rodney L., and Osteryoung, Jerome S., "Analysis of Financial Leases," *Financial Management,* Vol. 2, Spring 1973, pp. 74–87.

Sartoris, William L., and Paul, Ronda S., "Lease Evaluation—Another Capital Budgeting Decision," *Financial Management,* Vol. 2, Summer 1973, pp. 46–52.

Schall, Lawrence D., "Asset Valuation, Firm Investment, and Firm Diversification," *Journal of Business,* Vol. 45, January 1972, pp. 11–28.

———, "The Lease-or-Buy and Asset Acquisition Decisions," *Journal of Finance,* Vol. 29, September 1974, pp. 1203–1214.

Stapleton, Richard C., "Portfolio Analysis, Stock Valuation and Capital Budgeting Rules for Risky Projects," *Journal of Finance,* Vol. 26, March 1971, pp. 95–117.

Vancil, Richard F., "Lease or Borrow—New Method of Analysis," *Harvard Business Review,* Vol. 39, September–October 1961, reprinted in *Leasing Series,* Harvard Business Review, Cambridge, MA, n.d., pp. 79–93.

Van Horne, James C., *Financial Management and Policy,* 5th ed., Prentice-Hall, Englewood Cliffs, NJ, 1980.

Weston, J. Fred, and Brigham, Eugene F., *Managerial Finance,* 6th ed., Dryden Press, Hinsdale, IL, 1978.

LONG-TERM SOURCES OF FUNDS AND THE COST OF CAPITAL

CONTENTS

DEFINING LONG-TERM FUNDS   3

Liabilities   3
Sources of Funds   3
   Long-term debt   3
   Lease financing   4
   Preferred stock   4
   Common stock   4

DEFINING THE COST OF CAPITAL   5

ESTIMATING THE COST OF CAPITAL: DEFINITIONS   5

Risk-Adjusted Rate of Return   5
Operating Cash Flows After Taxes   6
Cost of Capital for an Unlevered Firm; Its Value   7
Value of the Levered Firm   8
   Market value of debt   8
   Market value versus book value   9
Weighted Average Cost of Capital   9
Cost of Equity for a Levered Firm   10

ESTIMATING THE COST OF SHORT-TERM LIABILITIES   11

Accounts Payable   11
   Trade credit   11
   Credit terms   11
Notes Payable   12
   Line of credit   12
   Compensating balances   12
   Regular term loans   13
   Discount loans   13
   Installment loans   13
   Current portion of long-term debt   14
   Commercial paper   14
Accruals   14

ESTIMATING THE COST OF LEASE FINANCING   14

Accounting for Leasing   14

Direct Cost of Leasing   15
Factors Indirectly Affecting Leasing Costs   16

ESTIMATING THE COST OF LONG-TERM DEBT   16

Yield to Maturity: Definition   16
Coupon Rate   16
Current Yield   17
Yield to Maturity: Calculations   17
   On a consol   17
   On a finite-lived bond   17
Risk-Adjusted Rate of Return   18
Marginal Yield to Maturity   19
Riding the Yield Curve   19
Estimating the Riskiness of Long-Term Debt   20
Effects of Collateral and Indenture Restrictions   21
   Bond covenants that restrict subsequent financing   22
   Bond covenants that restrict dividend payments   22
   Bond covenants that restrict merger activity   23
   Bond covenants that restrict production or investment policies   23
Effects of Term Structure of Interest Rates   24
   Expectations theory   24
   Liquidity preference theory   25

ESTIMATING THE COST OF PREFERRED STOCK   26

Cost of Straight Preferred   26
Cost of Convertible Preferred   27

ESTIMATING THE COST OF EQUITY   27

Dividend Yield   27

Earnings–Price Ratio — 28
Gordon Growth Model — 29
Capital Asset Pricing Model — 29
  Risks in CAPM — 29
  CAPM equation — 30
  Beta defined — 31
  Security market line — 31
  Cost of equity — 32
Cost of Retained Earnings: Flotation Costs — 32
Cost of Depreciation Funds — 33
Cost of Convertible Securities — 33
  Call option — 34
  Convertible debt — 34

COMPUTING WEIGHTED AVERAGE COST OF CAPITAL: AN EXAMPLE — 35

General Algebraic Expression — 35
Cost of Short-Term Liabilities — 35
Costs of Long-Term Debt and Equity — 36
Market Value Weights — 36
Marginal Tax Rate — 37

OPTIMAL CAPITAL STRUCTURE — 37

Debt, Taxes, and Bankruptcy Costs — 37
  Alternate definition of *WACC* — 37
  Cost of equity — 39
  Sample cost of capital problem — 40
  Effect of personal taxes — 42
  Tax advantage tradeoff: Debtfinancing versus bankruptcy costs — 42
Agency Costs — 42
  Agency costs of debt — 43
  Agency costs of external equity — 43

VARIOUS FINANCING SOURCES — 44

Short-Term Instruments — 44
  Commercial paper — 44
  Bankers' acceptances — 44

Leases — 44
  Sale and leaseback — 44
  Service leases — 44
  Financial leases — 45
  Leveraged leasing — 45
Bonds — 45
  Mortgage bonds — 45
  Collateral trust bonds — 45
  Equipment trust certificates — 45
  Debenture bonds — 45
  Subordinated debentures — 45
  Adjustment bonds — 45
  Guaranteed bonds — 45
  Participating bonds — 45
  Joint bonds — 46
  Voting bonds — 46
  Serial bonds — 46
  Convertible bonds — 46
Retirement of Bonds — 46
  Call provisions — 46
  Sinking funds — 47
  The refunding decision — 47
Private Versus Public Placement of Bonds — 47
Preferred Stock — 47
  Par value — 48
  Cumulative dividend feature — 48
  Voting rights — 48
  Participating preferred — 48
Common Stock — 48
  Cumulative voting — 48
  Par value — 49
  Classified common stock — 49
  Founders' shares — 49
  Preemptive right — 49
  Ex rights procedures — 50
  Underwritten issues — 51
  Firm commitment — 51
  Best efforts — 51
Stock Splits and Stock Dividends — 51

LONG-TERM SOURCES OF FUNDS AND THE COST OF CAPITAL

Thomas E. Copeland

DEFINING LONG-TERM FUNDS

LIABILITIES. The liabilities side of a firm's balance sheet can be broken down into the following broad categories:

1. Short-term liabilities:
   a. Accounts payable.
   b. Accruals.
   c. Notes payable.
   d. Current portion of long-term debt.
2. Long-term liabilities:
   a. Leasing.
   b. Long-term debt.
   c. Preferred stock.
   d. Equity.
      1. Common at par.
      2. Common in excess of par.
      3. Retained earnings.
      4. Less treasury stock.

SOURCES OF FUNDS. Long-term sources of funds are recorded as long-term liabilities in item **2** above. Long-term funds are provided from both **external** and **internal sources.** The main internal source is **retained earnings,** which represents the savings of the corporation, namely, earnings not paid out to shareholders as dividends. Historically, about 35% of aggregate savings in the U.S. economy has been provided by retained earnings. The remaining 65% is the personal savings of households. The external sources of capital are debt, leasing, preferred stock, and equity.

Long-Term Debt. This is usually defined as any debt obligation outstanding that comes due more than 1 year hence. The main sources of long-term debt are **commercial banks** (although they seldom lend for maturities longer than 5 years), **insurance companies,** and

investment banking firms that underwrite new issues of bonds to the public and other financial intermediaries (e.g. pension funds). Although the terms of repayment can vary widely, long-term debt is usually characterized by fixed coupon payments, predetermined schedules for the repayment of principal amount of the debt, and indenture clauses that govern the performance of the debt contract. The firm usually considers debt capital to be a favorable source of funds because interest paid on debt is tax deductible, while preferred and common dividends are not. However, this is a complex issue that is discussed in detail later on. Investors view debt capital as less risky than preferred or common stock because debt payments have higher priority. In fact, when debt payments are not made as required by the debt contract, the provisions of the contract usually require that debt holders be given partial or full control of the firm.

Lease Financing. Lease financing provides for the use of buildings and equipment without ownership. In a number of respects leasing is similar to borrowing. It requires contractual fixed payments to the lessor and if the payments are not met, the lessor has the right to take back the leased asset. However, failure to keep up lease payments does not bankrupt the leasing firm. Lease payments, like interest on debt, are tax deductible. A description of various types of lease and a discussion of the cost of lease financing is given later.

Preferred Stock. Although more risky than debt, preferred stock is less risky than common stock. Straight preferred stock has no maturity date and promises to pay a fixed coupon rate. Almost always there is a **cumulative preferred** feature, which stipulates that whenever the firm fails to meet its promised preferred dividend payments, the firm may not make dividend payments to common shareholders until all back payments on preferred have been made. Preferred dividends are usually not tax deductible, and preferred shareholders do not have the right to force the firm into reorganization or bankruptcy if their dividends are not paid. However, if the firm does fail, preferred shareholders take precedence over common shareholders in their claim on the liquidated assets of the firm. In the event of liquidation, preferred shareholders must receive all cumulative dividends before any claim by common shareholders is settled. The main sources of capital from preferred stock are private issues with insurance companies and public issues underwritten by investment banking firms.

Common Stock. The fourth source of external capital is common stock. Shareholders of common stock are the residual claimants on the cash flows of the firm. They own whatever is left after the firm has met production costs, required payments on debt, taxes, and preferred dividends. Residual cash flows are divided into **dividends and retained earnings.** Retained earnings are reinvested in the firm and appear as equity on the long-term liabilities side of the balance sheet. Dividends, on the other hand, are paid out to shareholders as a return on their investment. Needless to say, common stock is the riskiest of the three major sources of long-term capital because it is a residual claim. Common stock has the lowest priority of payment in the event of bankruptcy. Dividends on common stock may be paid only after debtholders and preferred shareholders have received their payments.

Common stock has many different legal forms. For example, there are **voting and nonvoting common stock,** which are usually called **class A and class B.** The New York Stock Exchange has limited this practice, however, by refusing to list stocks of companies that do not give full voting power to all common stock. **Treasury stock** refers to common stock that has been repurchased from shareholders and is held as a contraliability on the balance sheet. In other words, the dollar amount of repurchased treasury stock is subtracted from the equity account on the liabilities side of the balance sheet. Common stock may be issued to the public via investment banking firms or it may be privately held. Newly issued common stock is recorded on the balance sheet as the sum of its **par value** and **common in excess of par.** It is common practice to state a par value that is well below the market value of the common stock. However, if stock is issued for cash at less than its par value, the shareholders will be liable for the difference between the cash and par values if the firm is liquidated.

More complete descriptions of the various types of long-term source of capital are provided at the end of this section.

DEFINING THE COST OF CAPITAL

The cost of capital is the rate of return that could be earned by investors in alternative investments of equal risk. To give greater meaning to this definition, one must consider the relationship between investment decisions and the cost of supplying the funds necessary to undertake them. For the time being it is convenient to assume that we are looking at the investment decisions made by the shareholders of an all equity firm. Suppose that the firm has $1 million of cash flow available for investment. Furthermore, suppose that it has three projects. Each costs $600,000, and the rates of return are 25, 12, and 8%, respectively. Which project should the firm undertake? It is not possible to answer this question without knowing the relative riskiness of each project; and therefore its implicit cost of capital.

Suppose that shareholders are told that the first project is very risky. In fact, if the shareholders were to invest their money elsewhere in projects of equal risk they would require at least 30% return on their investment. This is the rate of return required on alternative projects of equivalent risk. It is the **opportunity cost** of the funds employed and is the correct cost of capital for the project. Given that the cost of capital is 30% and that the project earns 25%, the investment decision is obvious. This first of the three projects should be rejected. Shareholders would be better off if they invested their money elsewhere at 30% than in this equally risky project at a 25% rate of return.

Having eliminated the first project from consideration, suppose that shareholders are told that the opportunity costs of the remaining two projects are 10 and 6%, respectively. With returns of 12 and 8%, both earn more than their cost of capital. To undertake them both, however, the firm would need $1.2 million in funds. Unfortunately, only $1 million is available. What should the shareholders do? They could undertake only one project and pay out the remaining $400,000 as dividends, but this would mean forgoing an opportunity to increase their wealth by undertaking both projects. Instead, they could invest all the firm's available cash flows as well as the additional $200,000. The extra funds could be supplied by issuing new equity.

The example above highlights the relationship between the firm's investment decision and its cost of capital. The cost of capital is the same as the **opportunity cost of funds** that can be invested elsewhere in projects of equivalent risk. The firm cannot make appropriate investment decisions unless it has a good estimate of the relevant cost of capital.

ESTIMATING THE COST OF CAPITAL: DEFINITIONS

RISK-ADJUSTED RATE OF RETURN. Any project that is undertaken must earn enough cash flow to meet the requirements of the two main sources of capital. First, creditors (debtholders) require that the project make enough to cover their required interest payments

EXHIBIT 1   INCOME STATEMENTS FOR REPRESENTATIVE FIRMS

Symbol	Definition	Unlevered Firm	Levered Firm
R	Revenues	1,000	1,000
$-VC$	Variable costs	-600	-600
$-FCC$	Fixed cash costs	-100	-100
$-Dep$	Noncash charges (depreciation)	-100	-100
$EBIT$	Earnings before interest and taxes	200	200
$-rD$	Interest on debt	0	-50
EBT	Earnings before taxes	200	150
$-T$	Taxes at 40% (tax rate $= t_c$)	-80	-60
NI	Net income	120	90

and to pay off the debt principal when it comes due. Second, shareholders require an expected rate of return on their investment that compensates them for the risk they are undertaking. If the **risk-adjusted rate of return** is high enough to meet both types of payment, the project earns its cost of capital. Any return above the cost of capital increases shareholders' wealth.

The income statement shown in Exhibit 1 summarizes the cash flows of two representative corporations. They are alike in every way except that the first carries no debt—that is, it is unlevered; the second has a reasonable amount of financial leverage. Exhibit 2 provides the current balance sheets for the representative firms. Note that the firms are of equal size, but the levered firm has less equity than its unlevered counterpart.

OPERATING CASH FLOWS AFTER TAXES.   As mentioned earlier, the cost of capital is the rate of return that could be earned by investors in alternative investments of equal risk. For simplicity, suppose that the cash flows earned by the representative firms continue, without growth, forever. To maintain these perpetual cash streams, the firms must invest an amount each year equal to their depreciation. This is necessary to maintain the same level of property, plant, and equipment. Investors in the marketplace are willing to pay a price to buy claim to the cash flows of the firm. The rate at which they capitalize the perpetual cash flows is their **opportunity cost, the cost of capital.** For example, take the **case of the**

EXHIBIT 2   BALANCE SHEETS FOR REPRESENTATIVE FIRMS

Unlevered Firm				Levered Firm			
Assets		Liabilities		Assets		Liabilities	
		Debt (D)	0			Debt (D)	500
		Equity (E)	1,000			Equity (E)	500
Total assets	1,000	Total liabilities	1,000	Total assets	1,000	Total liabilities	1,000

unlevered firm. An investor in the unlevered firm will receive the following aftertax cash flows: earnings before interest and taxes *EBIT;* less taxes *t*; plus depreciation (which is a noncash charge against revenues); minus the amount of investment *I*, necessary to maintain the firm at its current level of operations. Algebraically, this cash flow is equal to **operating cash flows after taxes,** *OCFAT*.

$$OCFAT = EBIT - t_c(EBIT) + \text{dep} - I \tag{1}$$

COST OF CAPITAL FOR AN UNLEVERED FIRM; ITS VALUE. It is assumed that investment equals depreciation ($I = \text{dep}$), therefore,

$$OCFAT = EBIT\,(\,1 - t_c)$$
$$OCFAT = 200\,(1 - 0.4) = 120$$

The theoretical value of the unlevered firm V^u is equal to these perpetual cash flows capitalized at the cost of capital appropriate for the riskiness of the firm. Call this the **cost of capital for an unlevered firm,** K_u. We can write the **value of the unlevered** firm as follows:

$$V^u = \frac{OCFAT}{K_u} = \frac{EBIT\,(\,1 - t_c)}{K_u} \tag{2}$$

Suppose that the capital market determines the market value of the unlevered firm to be $1,200. Then, by rearranging equation 2, the cost of capital for the unlevered firm can be computed as 10%.

$$K_u = \frac{OCFAT}{V^u} = \frac{EBIT\,(1 - t_c)}{V^u}$$

$$K_u = \frac{120}{1,200} = 10\%$$

This example illustrates the relationship between the cash flows provided to investors in a firm, the value they are willing to pay for said cash flows, and the cost of capital. If they were willing to pay more for the same cash flows, the implied cost of capital would be lower, and vice versa. Also, note that cash flow received by investors is very different from net income *NI*. This is partly because not all the reported net income is available to be paid out. Some of the firm's cash flows must be reinvested to preserve the productive assets that support future cash flows.

So far the example has been fairly simple because it pertains to an all-equity firm. How does the definition of the cost of capital change when cash flows are paid out to bondholders as well as shareholders? A levered corporation makes payments to two main suppliers of capital: debtholders and shareholders. When the firm is making interest payments, the cash flow received by shareholders is equal to net income *NI*, plus depreciation (which was deducted from revenues as a noncash charge), minus dollars spent on investment *I*. Payment to bondholders is the interest on debt *rD*. Adding these together, total cash flows *CF*, paid to sources of capital in the private sector of the economy, are:

$$CF = NI + \text{dep} - I + rD$$

As before, we assume that investment equals depreciation. Therefore,

$$CF = NI + rD$$

Net income is equal to earnings before interest and taxes $EBIT$, less interest, less taxes. Using this, we can rewrite the cash flow equation as follows:

$$CF = EBIT - rD - t_c(EBIT - rD) + rD \qquad (3)$$
$$CF = EBIT(1 - t_c) + t_c rD$$

Recalling that $EBIT(1 - t_c)$ is also equal to operating cash flows after taxes $OCFAT$, equation 3 may also be written as:

$$CF = OCFAT + t_c rD$$

VALUE OF THE LEVERED FIRM.   In the preceding algebraic manipulation, the cash flows of the firm have been partitioned into two parts with different risks. The first part, operating cash flows after taxes ($OCFAT$), is exactly the same as the cash flows of the unlevered firm. It has exactly the same risk and can, therefore, be capitalized at exactly the same risk-adjusted rate, namely, the cost of equity for an all-equity firm K_u. The second part of the cash flow definition is the corporate tax rate t_c times the interest payments on debt. If the interest payments are risky, this stream of cash flows can be capitalized at a risk-adjusted rate appropriate for risky debt K_d. Capitalizing each cash flow at its risk-adjusted rate provides an expression for the **value of the levered firm**.

$$V^L = \frac{EBIT\,(1 - t_c)}{K_u} + t_c \frac{rD}{K_d} \qquad (4)$$

Market Value of Debt.   Note that the first term in equation 4 is exactly equal to the value of the unlevered firm, V^u, as given in equation 2. The second term is equal to the corporate tax rate t_c, times the **market value of debt** B. The market value of the perpetual debt is the annual interest payment rD, discounted at the cost of risky debt K_d.

$$B = \frac{rD}{K_d} \qquad (5)$$

The analysis above suggests that the value of the levered firm can be written as follows:

$$V^L = V^u + t_c B \qquad (6)$$

If we assume that the market-determined opportunity cost of risky debt K_d is 8%, then by using the numerical example in Exhibit 1, the value of the levered firm is found to be:

$$V^L = \frac{200\,(1 - 0.4)}{0.10} + 0.4\frac{0.10(500)}{0.08}$$
$$V^L = 1,200 + 0.4(526)$$
$$V^L = 1,450$$

Market Value Versus Book Value.   This analysis brings out at least two important points. First, the **market values** of debt and equity are different from the **book values** as stated on the balance sheet. For example, the book value of debt is $500. However, it pays a coupon rate r of 10%, while the market required rate of return is only 8%. Consequently the bond sells for a premium of $125 because it pays a higher nominal rate of interest r than can be obtained from new bonds issued to sell for their face value. The **market value of the firm's common stock** S can be obtained by subtracting the market value of debt B from the market value of the firm V^L.

$$
\begin{aligned}
V^L &= S + B \\
S &= V^L - B \\
S &= 1,450 - 625 \\
S &= 825
\end{aligned}
$$

The book value of equity is $500, while the market value is $825. One would never expect the market and book value of equity to be equal except by chance. The book value of equity is a historical number that reflects the dollars of new equity and retained earnings put into the firm by shareholders in years gone by. It has nothing to do with current market value, which is based on shareholder's expectations of the future cash flows they will receive from the firm.

WEIGHTED AVERAGE COST OF CAPITAL.   A second major point is that the value of the levered firm, $V^L = 1,450$, is greater than the value of the same firm without any debt, $V^u = 1,200$. This gain from leverage arises because interest payments are deductible from earnings before taxes. Hence **interest on debt is a tax shield,** and the value of the firm is higher with the tax shield than without.

Up to this point we have discussed the **cost of equity capital** for the unlevered cash flows of the firm and the cost of debt capital. The final task is to define a single risk-adjusted cost of capital for the levered cash flows of the firm; that is, the rate of return that capitalizes the levered firm's operating cash flows after taxes so that the present value of the cash flows is equal to the market value of the firm. This capitalization rate is called the **weighted average cost of capital** $WACC$. The value of the levered firm is:

$$
V^L = \frac{EBIT(1 - t_c)}{WACC} \tag{8}
$$

and the weighted average cost of capital is:

$$
WACC = \frac{EBIT(1 - t_c)}{V^L} \tag{9}
$$

Using this definition, the weighted average cost of capital is 10% for the unlevered firm and 8.28% for the levered firm. As before, there is an inverse relationship between the value of the firm and the capitalization rate. Holding cash flows constant, if the weighted average cost of capital decreases, the value of the levered firm goes up.

The **traditional definition of the weighted average cost of capital** is that it is equal to the aftertax cost of debt $K_d(1 - t_c)$, multiplied by the percentage of debt in the capital structure of the firm $B/(B + S)$, plus the cost of levered equity capital K_e, multiplied by the percentage of equity in the firm's capital structure, $S/(B + S)$:

$$WACC = K_d(1 - t_c)\frac{B}{B + S} + K_e\frac{S}{B + S} \tag{10}$$

Note that the percentages of debt and equity are computed using market value weights, not book values.

COST OF EQUITY FOR A LEVERED FIRM.   To double check the consistency of this definition of the weighted average cost of capital with that given in equation 9, we need an independent estimate of K_e, the cost of equity for the levered firm. It will be the market-determined capitalization rate for cash flows to shareholders of the levered firm. These cash flows are identified as net income NI, plus depreciation (a noncash charge against earnings), minus the amount of investment needed to replace depreciating assets. Because depreciation and investment cancel each other, we are left with net income. Thus the market value of equity S is

$$S = \frac{NI}{K_e} \tag{11}$$

and the **cost of equity for the levered firm** (which has no growth) is

$$K_e = \frac{NI}{S} \tag{12}$$

$$K_e = \frac{90}{825} = 10.91\%$$

Recall that the cost of equity for the unlevered cash flows K_u was 10%. As the firm takes on debt capital, the riskiness of the shareholders' claim increases. Shareholders require a higher rate of return as compensation for the risk; consequently, the cost of equity for a levered firm increases with leverage. The results above bear this out. The cost of equity has gone from 10% for the firm without any leverage to 10.91% for the firm with leverage of 43.1% of total market value.

If the cost of equity, as calculated from equation 12, is substituted into the formula for the weighted average cost of capital (equation 10), we should obtain the same answer computed earlier from equation 9, namely, that the weighted average cost of capital is 8.28%. This is worked out as follows:

$$WACC = K_d(1 - t_c)\frac{B}{B + S} + K_e\frac{S}{B + S}$$

$$WACC = 0.08(1 - 0.4)\frac{625}{1,450} + 0.1091\frac{825}{1,450}$$

$$WACC = 8.28\%$$

This confirms the consistency of the two definitions of the weighted average cost of capital. Calculated as the market-value weighted average of the market-determined costs of debt (after taxes) and levered equity, it is the discount rate that converts the operating cash flows after taxes (*OCFAT*) into the current market value of the firm.

The next subsection goes into greater detail on the procedure for estimating the market-required rates of return for risky debt and equity for a variety of different debt and equity instruments. Before moving on, a few caveats are necessary. First, it has been assumed that cash flows to debt and equity are perpetuities **without growth**. This assumption must be modified, especially in the case of equity capital, to handle the more realistic situation of future cash flows that are expected to grow. Second, there has been no mention of the effect of bankruptcy costs on the market interest rate on debt. Later, it is argued that this effect, combined with the tax shield provided by interest on debt, is one possible explanation for an **optimal capital structure**.

ESTIMATING THE COST OF SHORT-TERM LIABILITIES

Most textbooks ignore **short-term liabilities** when estimating the cost of capital. Doing so considerably simplifies the exposition. It is argued that short-term liabilities can be ignored either because they are not part of the permanent long-term financing of the firm or because they require no explicit cash payments. For example, accounts payable and accrued taxes have no interest payments. Both the arguments against including short-term liabilities in the cost of capital of the firm are incorrect. First, while it is true that short-term liabilities are not part of the permanent financing of the firm, they still represent the utilization of scarce resources. One need only estimate the average usage of a short-term liability during the year and its economic cost, then include it as part of the weighted average cost of capital. Second, even though there are no direct interest payments, the cost of using trade credit or even deferred taxes as a short-term source of funds is not to be disregarded.

The material that follows describes various short-term liabilities and provides techniques for computing their cost to the firm.

ACCOUNTS PAYABLE.

Trade Credit. Accounts payable represent the trade credit being used by the firm. For example, suppose a firm purchases an average of $1,000 a day and pays its bills after 30 days. Then its accounts payable will be $30,000. If it doubles its purchases to $2,000 a day, it will automatically increase its accounts payable to $60,000, thereby creating an additional $30,000 of financing.

Credit Terms. Trade credit is usually extended with specific credit terms. As an illustration, suppose a firm has just received trade credit where the terms are 2/10 net 30. That is, if the invoice is paid within 10 days of delivery, there is a 2% discount. The cost of not taking cash discounts can be expensive. If the firm pays the bill on the eleventh day, the annualized interest cost is 730%. In general, if n is the number of days **after** the discount period and x is the percentage discount, annual cost is:

$$\text{annual cost} = \frac{365}{n}x \tag{13}$$

The more usual case if the firm forgoes the discount is to pay on the net-day, for example, the thirtieth. The annualized cost is then 36.5%.

Trade credit is a customary part of doing business in most industries. It is convenient and informal. However, as shown above, it is not costless. Even if a firm pays all its bills within the discount period, there is an implicit cost of using trade credit. Usually, the pricing policy of the lending firm is established so that prices are high enough to compensate for the discounts extended.

For an explicit calculation of the cost of trade credit, see the Bethlehem Steel example below (pp. 31·35–37).

NOTES PAYABLE.   Notes payable usually take the form of **short-term loans** from commercial banks. For many firms, particularly small businesses, short-term debt may represent the single largest source of external financing. The costs of using various types of short-term credit are given below.

Line of Credit.   This is an informal understanding between the bank and the borrower: the bank agrees to provide, upon demand, a short-term loan up to a specified amount. If the commitment on the bank's part is formalized, the arrangement is known as a **revolving credit**. Although the terms of a line of credit or revolving credit differ, it is not unusual to pay interest on the amount outstanding plus a commitment fee (e.g., 0.25%) on the unused balance. Also, the borrower is frequently required to "clean up" (reduce the balance to zero) sometime during the year.

The cost of a line of credit is the interest cost per day divided by the balance of the loan outstanding that day plus the commitment fee. Suppose, for example, a firm borrows a line of credit of $100,000 for 6 months at an interest rate of 12% per annum and with an annual commitment fee of 0.5%. Exhibit 3 shows how the credit arrangement would work on a month-to-month basis.

Notice that the total interest charges are $1,200 and the total commitment fees are $200. The firm used an average of $20,000 per month, and the average monthly charge (interest plus commitment fee) was $233. The effective monthly interest was approximately 1.17% (an annual rate of 14.9%). The commitment fee has the effect of raising the true interest rate on the amount borrowed. In Exhibit 3, the firm could have saved commitment fees by having requested a $70,000 line of credit rather than $100,000. The greater the unused credit line, the greater the effective interest will be.

Compensating Balances.   These represent a requirement by the bank that the borrower maintain an average checking account balance of usually 15–20% of the outstanding loan. For example, suppose a firm needs to use $40,000 in debt capital and the bank makes the

EXHIBIT 3   LINE-OF-CREDIT EXAMPLE

	Month					
	1	2	3	4	5	6
Amount used	20,000	70,000	20,000	0	0	10,000
Interest	200	700	200	0	0	100
Unused balance	80,000	30,000	80,000	100,000	100,000	90,000
Commitment fee	33	12	33	42	42	38

loan at an interest rate of 10% with a 20% compensating balance. The firm must borrow $50,000 at 10%, but it gets to use only $40,000 because the remainder is kept in a compensating balance earning no interest. If the firm has no other use for the compensating balance (e.g., using it to meet payrolls), the true cost of the loan is $5,000 ÷ 40,000 or 12.5%. In this way, compensating balances may raise the effective interest on the loan.

Regular Term Loans.   When both principal and interest must be paid back on the maturity date or due date of the loan, the arrangement is called a **regular term loan**. In such cases the effective rate of interest on a 1-year loan is exactly the same as the stated rate. For example, if the firm borrows $100,000 at 12% for 1 year, it will have to pay back $12,000 at year-end. The effective rate of interest is computed as

$$\frac{\text{interest paid}}{\text{principal amount}} = \frac{12,000}{100,000} = 12\%$$

Discount Loans.   Another commonly used device, discount loans require that the interest be paid immediately upon the issue of the loan and that the principal be paid on maturity. Using the above example, the firm would have to pay $12,000 in advance. It would be able to use $100,000 − $12,000 = $88,000 during the year. Although the interest paid is the same as the term loan, the actual amount of funds that the firm can use is less. Hence the **effective rate of interest** is 13.64%:

$$\frac{\text{interest paid}}{\text{amount used}} = \frac{12,000}{88,000} = 13.64\%$$

The example of discount loans emphasizes the critical dependence of the effective rate of interest on the timing of cash flows as well as the amount paid.

Installment Loans.   Here the loan principal must be repaid in equal installments over the life of the loan. Continuing with the example, suppose that the firm borrows $100,000 at a stated interest rate of 12%, but must repay the loan in monthly installments. Furthermore, assume that the annual interest is calculated on the **original** $100,000 (this is not always the way it is done). The borrower has use of the full $100,000 only during the first month. In the second month he can use only $100,000 − (100,000 ÷ 12) = $91,667, in the third month only $83,333, and so on. After using the correct discounting procedures, we would compute that the effective rate of interest on the installment loan is not 12% as stated, but rather close to 23.75%.

For the reader who is familiar with the mathematics of discounting, the nominal rate of interest j is computed from the definition of a monthly annuity. The annuity amount b is assumed to be $1,000 in interest plus $100,000 ÷ 12 = $8,333.33 in principal. The period of payment m is monthly. The formula for present value PV is:

$$PV = 100,000 = (1,000 + 8,333.33)\left[\frac{1 - (1 + j/m)^{-m}}{j/m}\right]$$

$$j \approx 21.5\%$$

The nominal rate j, when compounded annually, equals 23.75%.

Current Portion of Long-Term Debt. This short-term liability is self-explanatory. It is recorded on the short-term portion of the balance sheet to highlight the requirement that the firm repay the stated amount of principal on long-term debt during the upcoming fiscal year. Separating it in this way provides information to financial analysts about the short-term viability of the firm. If short-term liquid assets are insufficient to pay off the current portion of long-term debt, the firm can be forced into **reorganization or bankruptcy**.

Insofar as computing the cost of capital is concerned, the current portion of long-term debt is no different from the remainder of long-term debt. Therefore, further discussion of its cost is deferred until we cover the cost of long-term debt.

Commercial Paper. This consists primarily of **unsecured promissory notes** of large firms sold chiefly to other business firms. In recent years, however, mutual funds have been formed to allow individuals to hold commercial paper. Maturities of commercial paper usually vary from 2 to 6 months, and rates are typically 0.5% below the **prime rate**. Because commercial paper is sold in very large amounts, it is viable only for companies having short-term fund needs large enough to result in **economies of scale**. And because of the economies of scale, commercial paper is a ''cheaper'' source of funds than borrowing at the prime rate.

ACCRUALS. Accruals usually refer to accrued wages and salaries due and to accrued taxes. These are short-term obligations due in the next fiscal year. Although they have no explicit interest cost, they are not free. One might easily argue that when workers agree to receive their paychecks at an interval after the work has been performed, they will compensate for the cost of waiting by asking for a higher wage rate. In effect they are making short-term loans to the firm. Similarly, the government provides services to the economy and finances them with taxes and government debt. One can think of accrued taxes as a short-term loan to the firm by the government. If so, the opportunity cost of accrued taxes due should be taken into account in the cost of capital calculation. On the other hand, it might be argued that the cost to the firm of using accrued taxes as a source of funds is zero because government transfer payments (such as the unearned interest on accrued taxes) are a positive benefit to the private sector.

ESTIMATING THE COST OF LEASE FINANCING

Leasing is a form of **intermediate financing.** Many lease contracts last for the life of the equipment being leased. Until November 1976, there was no uniform code for accounting for lease financing, and many long-term lease commitments did not appear as liabilities on firms' balance sheets. Leasing was referred to as **off-balance-sheet financing.** However, since 1976, the accounting rules have changed.

ACCOUNTING FOR LEASING. From the point of view of the lessee, accounting for leasing is now controlled by Statement No. 13 of the Financial Accounting Standards Board (FASB). Leases are divided into two broad categories: **operating leases** and **capital leases.** A lease is defined as a **capital lease** if it meets one or more of the following four criteria: (1) ownership of the leased asset is transferred to the lessee at the end of the lease, (2) the lease contract gives the lessee an option to purchase the property at a price sufficiently below market value to make exercise of the option likely, (3) the lease term is greater than or equal to 75% of the estimated economic life of the property, or (4) the present value of the lease payments is greater than or equal to 90% of the value of the property at the beginning of the lease. **Capital leases** must be capitalized and shown on the balance sheet both as a fixed asset and a noncurrent liability. **Operating leases** meet none of the aforementioned criteria and are not capitalized on the balance sheet. The lease fees are charged as an expense on the income statement, and disclosure of the lease obligation is made in the footnotes of the firm's annual report.

DIRECT COST OF LEASING. The cost of lease financing is discussed here from the points of view of both the lessor and the lessee. For a complete discussion of the lease-buy decision, the reader is referred to Weston and Brigham (*Managerial Finance,* 6th ed., 1978) and to the section entitled "Leasing" in this *Handbook*.

There has been considerable disagreement about the appropriate cost of capital that should be used in lease financing (see, e.g., Myers, Dill, and Bautista, *Journal of Finance,* June 1976; Schall, *Journal of Finance,* September 1974; and Miller and Upton, *Journal of Finance,* June 1976). Much of the confusion arises from the difficulty of separating the investment decision from the method of financing. The lessee's investment decision should be made by discounting the aftertax cash flows of the project under consideration at the appropriate **risk-adjusted weighted average cost of capital.** However, the project decision is not the main concern of this discussion. Rather, we are interested in the **financing decision,** namely, a comparison between the aftertax cost of lease financing and its close substitute, the aftertax cost of debt financing. Leasing and debt financing both have contractual payments that are deductible for tax purposes, both usually involve contracts of similar length, and **both require an equity base.** Furthermore, they have approximately the same risk.

How, then, shall we compute the aftertax cost of lease financing? First, look at the problem from the point of view of the **lessor.** The lessor receives lease payments L_t, writes off depreciation dep_t as a tax shield, and pays taxes on the net amount. In return, the lessor provides the use of an asset with current market value M. If K is the aftertax rate of return required by the lessor, we have the following relationship:

$$M = \sum_{t=0}^{T} \frac{L_t - dep_t - t_c (L_t - dep_t)}{(1 + K)^t}$$

$$M = \sum_{t=0}^{T} \frac{L_t (1 - t_c) + t_c dep_t}{(1 + K)^t}$$

Given the aftertax required rate of return, the depreciation schedule, and the value of the asset, the lessor can establish his required lease fee L_t. (To keep the analysis simple, it is assumed that there is **no salvage value** for the asset.) The lessor's required rate of return K will be the interest rate on lending operations that have the same risk as leasing. The required rate is also the **lessor's weighted average cost of capital.**

From the lessee's point of view, the cost of the lease K should be compared with the aftertax cost of debt capital, which is a nearly perfect substitute. If the firm decides to take a lease, its debt capacity is reduced by the amount of the lease. Alternatively, if the lessee is already at its **optimal capital structure** prior to the lease, the lease will displace debt. The opportunity cost of the forgone debt is a cost of leasing (see Myers, Dill, and Bautista, *Journal of Finance,* June 1976).

FACTORS INDIRECTLY AFFECTING LEASING COSTS.   These include (1) the riskiness of the **residual value** of the leased property, (2) the **risk of obsolescence,** (3) differences in **maintenance costs,** and (4) **economies of scale** in the leasing operation. From the point of view of the lessor, a lease contract is probably somewhat riskier than a debt contract of equal size and maturity, mainly because of the risk of having the lease terminated before its contract life. This makes leasing more expensive than borrowing. On the other hand, if there are economies of scale in maintenance or financing, or if the lessor has a higher tax rate than the lessee, leasing may be cheaper than borrowing.

ESTIMATING THE COST OF LONG-TERM DEBT

The cost of long-term debt depends on the riskiness of the debt issue, its term to maturity, its indenture restrictions, and special features such as whether it is convertible into common stock or whether it has warrants attached to it. Each of these factors is discussed in turn, beginning with the simple problem of estimating the cost of debt capital from observed market data.

YIELD TO MATURITY: DEFINITION.   Consider the example presented in Exhibit 4, showing the composition of long-term debt of Bethlehem Steel in December 1976.

When trying to estimate the cost of debt capital K_d to employ in equation 10, the **appropriate opportunity cost** must be computed as it is determined by investors in the marketplace. This is called the **yield to maturity** (see below). First, it is useful to discuss two rates that have little to do with the opportunity cost of debt. Nonetheless, because they are often used, it is appropriate to warn the reader against them. The first is the coupon rate, or the historical cost of debt, and the second is the simple yield, shown in column 6 of Exhibit 4.

COUPON RATE.   This is the ratio of the coupon to the **face value** of the bond. For example, in 1955 Bethlehem Steel issued 25-year bonds with a coupon rate of $3\frac{1}{4}$%, due in 1980. This bond issue can be seen on line 2 of Exhibit 4. The $3\frac{1}{4}$% coupon rate is the

EXHIBIT 4   BETHLEHEM STEEL COMPOSITION OF LONG-TERM DEBT, DECEMBER 31, 1976

Issue	Rating (Moody's)	Amount	Call Price	Recent Price	Yield	Year of Issue
Consolidated, Mortgages S.F.3s, K, 1979	Aa	21,800	$100\frac{1}{8}$	NA	NA	1949
Debenture, $3\frac{1}{4}$s, 1980	Aa	3,100	100	$89\frac{1}{2}$	3.6	1955
Debenture, 5.40s, 1992	Aa	109,200	$102\frac{1}{2}$	$84\frac{3}{8}$	6.4	1967
Debenture, $6\frac{7}{8}$s, 1999	Aa	85,800	$104\frac{1}{4}$	$94\frac{1}{4}$	6.6	1969
Debenture, 9s, 2000	Aa	144,000	$105\frac{1}{2}$	$106\frac{1}{2}$	8.5	1970
Debenture, 8.45s, 2005	Aa	250,000	107.45	$103\frac{1}{2}$	8.2	1975
Debenture, $8\frac{3}{8}$s, 2001	Aa	200,000	106.63	$105\frac{1}{2}$	7.9	1976
Subordinated Debenture, $4\frac{1}{2}$s, 1990	A	94,500	102.40	$76\frac{1}{4}$	5.9	1965
Notes payable	—	30,000	—	NA	NA	NA
Subsidiary debt	—	3,200	—	NA	NA	NA
Revenue bonds, $5\frac{1}{4}$s-6s, 2002	—	100,000	—	NA	NA	NA

Source: Moody's Industrial Manual and Bank & Quotation Record, January 1977.

historical cost of the bond, and it reflects the cost of long-term debt for Bethlehem Steel in 1955. This has nothing whatsoever to do with the market cost of debt for Bethlehem Steel as of December 31, 1976.

CURRENT YIELD.   The **current yield** or simple yield is defined as the ratio of the coupon payment to the current **market value** of the bond. The current yield for the Bethlehem Steel $3\frac{1}{4}\%$ debentures due in 1980 is computed as follows

$$\text{current yield} = \frac{\text{coupon rate} \times \text{face value}}{\text{market value}} \tag{14}$$
$$= \frac{0.0325 \times \$1,000}{\$895} = 3.63\%$$

The current yield is the statistic published daily in the *Wall Street Journal*. It has nothing whatsoever to do with the market-determined opportunity cost of the bond that has a **finite life,** which is called the yield to maturity.

YIELD TO MATURITY: CALCULATIONS.   The yield to maturity is the best measure of the correct opportunity cost of a bond. It is the rate of return an investor expects to earn if he **purchases the bond today and holds it to maturity.** In return for the purchase price, he receives the expected coupon payments plus the expected repayment of the principal amount (the face value) at maturity. Readers who are familiar with **capital budgeting techniques** will recognize that the **yield to maturity** is the same as the **internal rate of return** on the bond investment.

On a Consol.   The yield to maturity on a **consol bond** is the easiest to compute. A consol bond is a bond that promises to pay a **constant coupon** at the end of each year, **forever.** It never repays its principal because it never matures. For this special type of bond, the yield to maturity is computed as follows:

$$\text{yield to maturity on a consol} = \frac{\text{coupon rate} \times \text{face value}}{\text{market value}} \tag{15}$$

Note that the yield to maturity on a consol is exactly the same as the current yield described above in equation 14. The implication is that when a bond has a long time to maturity, the current yield may be a reasonable approximation for the yield to maturity. However, more often than not, a bond does not have much time left before it comes due. Therefore, one needs a more accurate way to compute a yield to maturity.

On a Finite-Lived Bond.   Take the example of the **Bethlehem Steel** $3\frac{1}{4}\%$ debentures due in 1980. The coupon payments of $16.25 per $1,000 face value are made on the first day of every May and every November. The issue matures on May 1, 1980. We want to know the yield to maturity as of December 31, 1976, if an investor has to pay $895 for the bond and if he assumes that he will receive all payments with certainty. Exhibit 5 shows the payments and their timing.

   The yield to maturity is the interest rate that equates the discounted present value of the

**EXHIBIT 5   PAYMENTS ON BETHLEHEM STEEL 3¼%
DEBENTURES DUE 1980**

Type of Cash Flow	Expected Amount	Date
Purchase price	− 895.00	December 31, 1976
First coupon	16.50	May 1, 1977
Second coupon	16.50	November 1, 1977
Third coupon	16.50	May 1, 1978
Fourth coupon	16.50	November 1, 1978
Fifth coupon	16.50	May 1, 1979
Sixth coupon	16.50	November 1, 1979
Seventh coupon	16.50	May 1, 1980
Face value	1,000.00	May 1, 1980

Source: Maturities from *Annual Report,* 1976, Bethlehem Steel Corp.

cash inflows (the coupons and the face value) with the current cash price of the bond. Mathematically, this can be expressed as

$$B_O = \sum_{t=0}^{T} \frac{E(\text{coupon}_t)}{(1 + K_d)^t} + \frac{E(\text{repayment of principal})}{(1 + K_d)^T} \tag{16}$$

where B_0 = current price of bond

T = maturity date of bond

$E(\text{coupon}_t)$ = **expected** coupon payment at time t

$E(\text{repayment of principal})$ = **expected** repayment of principal when bond matures

K_d = annual yield to maturity on bond (assumed to be constant across life of bond)

For the Bethlehem Steel example, the yield to maturity is approximately 8%. For an exact solution refer to Copeland and Weston (*Financial Theory and Corporate Policy*, p. 320). During December 1976 all bonds with the same risk, the same maturity, and the same payment dates had approximately the same yield to maturity, because they were nearly perfect substitutes for each other.

RISK-ADJUSTED RATE OF RETURN.   One of the most important things to remember about the definition of the yield to maturity is that it is a **risk-adjusted rate of return.** Bonds of lower quality will require higher yields. Suppose, for example, that instead of being an Aa-rated bond, the Bethlehem Steel debenture had been riskier. Suppose it had a rating of Ba. Bonds of lower quality have a greater probability of delayed payment or default. This must be taken into account when estimating the yield to maturity. One way to do this is to reduce the expected coupon payments or expected repayment of principal in equation 16 to something less than the face values promised in the bond issue. To be specific, assume that the investor is willing to pay only $845 for the lower quality bond and that he expects all the coupons to be paid in full and according to schedule, but he also expects a 30% chance that the bond will repay only $600 in principal and a 70% chance that it will pay the face value of $1,000. This implies that he expects the repayment of principal to be only $880:

0.7(1,000) + 0.3(600) = 880. Under these conditions, the payments in Exhibit 5 would change. The purchase price would become $845 instead of $895, and the **expected** repayment of principal would become $880 instead of $1,000. The recomputed yield to maturity for the Ba-rated bond is approximately 9%. The higher yield is necessary to compensate the investor for the higher risk undertaken. A common error made when estimating the yield to maturity on a risky bond is to use the promised coupon payments and face value rather than the **expected** values as required in equation 16.

MARGINAL YIELD TO MATURITY.   This is the cost of debt capital, were the firm to **issue new debt in the capital market.** In the previous examples we calculated the yield to maturity on a bond that had $3\frac{1}{2}$ years to maturity. Yet by referring to Exhibit 4 it is apparent that when Bethlehem Steel issues new debt, the maturity is typically 25 or 30 years. Therefore, the appropriate marginal cost of new debt capital for Bethlehem is the market-determined yield to maturity on new 25 (or 30) year bonds. The yield to maturity on the 8.45% debentures maturing in 2005 is approximately 8.3%. The 8.375s maturing in 2001 have a similar yield to maturity. Therefore, 8.3% should be used as the marginal cost of new long-term debt in computing the weighted average cost of capital for Bethlehem.

RIDING THE YIELD CURVE.   This anachronistic concept implies that investors can earn abnormal rates of return by purchasing bonds that sell at market prices lower than their face value. For example, suppose that a bond is currently selling for $787.39, that it matures in 4 years, that it has a face value of $1,000, and that it pays an annual coupon of $50. The yield to maturity is 12%. A casual examination of the facts might lead a naive investor to believe that he can make an abnormal profit. After all, he can obtain the coupon payments, and as long as he holds the bond to maturity, he will also earn the difference between the face value, $1,000, and the purchase price, $787.39. Ignoring any possible tax implications, the return on investment appears to be $200 worth of coupons plus $212.61 in capital gains on an investment of $787.39. This is a 52.4% return on investment. However, this logic fails to discount the cash flows. The yield to maturity handles this problem correctly. The actual rate of return is only 12%. Assuming (for convenience) that the yield to maturity does not change over the life of the bond. The price of the bond over its life is graphed in Exhibit 6. Notice that the market price of the bond increases as it gets closer to maturity, reflecting the fact that the bond becomes more valuable as the date of the payoff of the face value draws near.

The usual convention for the payment of interest on bonds is to record interest continuously. For example, suppose that there are only 6 months left before the bond matures and that individual A sells to individual B. Although the final coupon is not paid until the year's end, nevertheless individual A must be compensated for the interest accrued between the last coupon date and the date when the bond is sold. Therefore, with only 6 months to maturity, individual B can expect to receive $25 in interest plus the $1,000 face value. On July 1 this is worth $966.98:

$$\text{bond value on July 1} = \frac{\$25}{1 + 0.12/2} + \frac{\$1,000}{1 + 0.12/2} = \$966.98$$

Thus, at any time to maturity, the yield to maturity will be the same, namely, 12%, even though the price rises in a predetermined fashion as shown in Exhibit 6. If the return is always 12%, no abnormal return can be earned.

EXHIBIT 6   HYPOTHETICAL PRICE OF A BOND OVER ITS LIFE

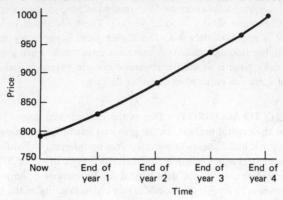

ESTIMATING THE RISKINESS OF LONG-TERM DEBT. The usual method for determining the default risk of corporate long-term debt is to refer to the **bond ratings** supplied by various agencies. Major bond rating agencies are Moody's Investors Service Inc., Standard & Poor's Corp., and Fitch Investor Service. Moody's bond rating has seven classifications ranging from Aaa, which is the highest quality bond, down to Caa, the lowest quality. Weinstein (*Journal of Financial Economics,* December 1977) collected data on 179 new bond issues between 1962 and 1964. Exhibit 7 shows the distribution by risk class. About 40% of the new bonds qualified for the two highest quality ratings. Exhibit 8 shows the yields on bonds of different risk. Just as expected, the high-quality, low-risk bonds have lower yields than do the low-quality, high-risk bonds. A common-sense way of estimating the **marginal cost of new debt** for a firm (assuming that the new debt will not change the firm's bond rating) is to compute the yield to maturity on other bonds with maturities and bond ratings similar to the new issue.

Of the roughly 2,000 major corporations that **are evaluated by the agencies,** approximately 500 are rerated quarterly because they issue commercial paper, another 500 are rerated

EXHIBIT 7   SAMPLE OF NEW ISSUES BY MOODY'S RATING OF ISSUE

Rating	Industrials	% of Total	Utilities	% of Total
Aaa	29	26.1	14	20.6
Aa	18	16.2	14	20.6
A	38	34.3	18	26.5
Baa	20	18.0	20	29.4
Ba	1	0.9	2	2.9
B	5	4.5	0	0
	111	100.0	68	100.0

Source: Adopted from Weinstein, Mark, "The Effect of a Rating Change Announcement on Bond Price," *Journal of Financial Economics,* December 1977.

EXHIBIT 8   COMPARISON OF BOND YIELDS FOR BONDS OF DIFFERENT RISKS

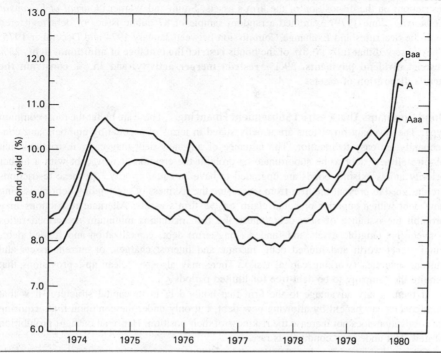

Source: Federal Reserve Bulletins, Board of Governors of the Federal Reserve System, various issues.

annually (most of the utilities), and the remaining 1,000 have no established review date **but are usually reviewed annually.**

From an investor's point of view, one might ask the following question: Do the agencies determine the prices and interest rates paid for bonds or do investors in the capital markets? The evidence collected by Wakeman (University of Rochester, 1978) and Weinstein (*Journal of Finance,* December 1978) shows that changes in bond ratings are not treated as new information by capital markets. In fact, changes in ratings usually occur several months after the capital markets have already reacted to the fundamental change in the bond's quality. Changes in agency ratings do not cause changes in required yields to maturity. It is the other way around. However, this does not imply that bond ratings are without value. On average, the ratings provide unbiased estimates of bond risk and are therefore a useful source of information.

EFFECTS OF COLLATERAL AND INDENTURE RESTRICTIONS.   The riskiness of bonds, and therefore their required yield, is substantively affected by the bond covenants that are written into the bond contract. A good description of the multitude of specific provisions in debt contracts can be found in the American Bar Association compendium called *Commentaries on Model Debenture Indenture Provisions, 1971.* Bond covenants can be divided into four broad categories: (1) those restricting the issuance of new debt, (2) those with restrictions on dividend payments, (3) those with restrictions on merger activity, and (4) those with restrictions on the disposition of the firm's assets. Smith and Warner (*Journal of Financial Economics*, June 1979) examined a random sample of 87 public issues of debt registered with the Securities and Exchange Commission between January 1974 and December 1975. They observed that fully 90.8% of the bonds **restrict the issuance of additional debt,** 23% **restrict dividend payments,** 39.1% **restrict merger activity,** and 35.6% **constrain the firm's disposition of assets.**

Bond Covenants That Restrict Subsequent Financing.   These are by far the most common type. The covenant provisions are usually stated in terms of accounting numbers and consequently are easy to monitor. The issuance of any new debt may carry restrictions that require all new debt to be subordinate or prohibit the creation of new debt with a higher priority unless existing bonds are upgraded to have an equal priority. All these restrictions are designed to prevent the firm from increasing the riskiness of outstanding debt by issuing new debt with a superior or equal claim on the firm's assets. Alternate restrictions may prohibit the issuance of new debt unless the firm maintains minimum prescribed ratios between net tangible assets and funded (long-term) debt, capitalization and funded debt, tangible net worth and funded debt, income and interest charges, or current assets and current liabilities (working capital tests). There may also be "clean-up" provisions that require the company to be debt-free for limited periods.

If there is any advantage to the firm that holds debt in its capital structure, it is that bondholders can benefit by allowing new debt, but only under the condition that acquiring this obligation does not increase the riskiness of their position. Hence an outright prohibition of new debt under any condition is rare.

Other techniques that are used to protect bondholders against subsequent financing include restrictions on rentals, leases, and sale-leaseback agreements; sinking fund requirements (which roughly match the depreciation of the firm's tangible assets); required purchase of insurance; required financial reports and specification of accounting techniques; and required certifications of compliance by the officers of the firm.

Bond Covenants That Restrict Dividend Payments.   These are necessary if for no other reason than to prohibit the extreme case of shareholders voting to pay themselves a liquidating dividend that would leave the bondholders holding an empty corporate shell. Kalay (unpublished Ph.D. thesis, University of Rochester, 1979) reported that in a random sample of 150 firms, every firm had a dividend restriction in at least one of its debt instruments. Restrictions on dividend policy are relatively easy to monitor, and they protect debtholders against the unwarranted payout of the assets that serve as collateral. Appropriately, most indentures refer not only to cash dividends, but to all distributions in respect to capital stock, whether they be dividends, redemptions, purchases, retirements, partial liquidations, or capital reductions and whether in cash, in kind, or in the form of debt obligations to the company. Without such general provisions the firm could, for example, use cash to repurchase its own shares. From the bondholders' point of view, the effect would be the same as payment of cash dividends. No matter what the procedure is called, once cash is paid out to shareholders, it is no longer available for collateral in the event of **reorganization or bankruptcy.**

Most restrictions on the payout of the firm's assets require that dividends increase only if the firm's earnings are positive, if the firm issues new equity capital, or if dividends paid out since the bonds were issued have been kept below a predefined minimum level. Mathematically, the "inventory" of funds allowable for dividend payment D_T^* in quarter T, can be expressed as

$$D_T^* = K \sum_{t=0}^{T} E_t + \sum_{t=0}^{T} S_t + F - \sum_{t=0}^{T-1} D_t \tag{17}$$

where E_t = net earnings in quarter t
    K = predetermined constant, $0 \le K \le 1$
    S_t = net proceeds from issue of new equity
    F = number fixed over life of bonds, known as "dip"
    D_t = dividends paid out in quarter t

Thus the dividend covenant does not restrict dividends per se, rather, it restricts the financing of the payment of dividends with new debt or by sale of the firm's existing assets. This arrangement is in the interest of stockholders because it does not restrict the payment of earned income. It is also in the interest of bondholders because it prevents any dilution of their claim on the firm's assets.

Bond Covenants That Restrict Merger Activity. These may prohibit many mergers but more often will allow mergers, provided certain conditions are met. The effect of a merger on bondholders can be beneficial if the cash flows of the merged firms are not perfectly correlated. Offsetting cash flow patterns can reduce the risk of default, thereby bettering the positions of the bondholders of both firms. Merger can also be detrimental to bondholders. For example, if firm A has much more debt in its capital structure than firm B, the bondholders of B will suffer increased risk after the merger. Or if the maturity of debt in firm A is shorter than for firm B, the bondholders of B will (for all practical purposes) become subordinate to those of firm A after the merger.

To protect against the undesirable effects that can result from a merger, it is possible to require bond covenants that allow merger only if the net tangible assets of the firm, calculated on a postmerger basis, meet a certain dollar minimum or are at least a certain fraction of long-term debt. The merger can also be made contingent on the absence of default of any indenture provision after the transaction is completed.

Bond Covenants That Restrict Production or Investment Policies. These agreements are numerous but are frequently difficult to enforce, given the impossibility of monitoring effectively the investment decisions that the managers of the firm decide not to undertake. Myers (*Journal of Financial Economics*, November 1977) suggests that a substantial portion of the value of a firm is composed of intangible assets in the form of future investment opportunities. A firm with outstanding debt may have the incentive to reject projects that have a positive **net present value** if the benefit from accepting the project accrues to the bondholders.

Direct restrictions on **investment-disinvestment policy** take the following forms: (1) restrictions on common stock investments, loans, extensions of credit, and advances that cause the firm to become a claimholder in another business enterprise, (2) restrictions on the disposition of assets, and (3) covenants requiring the maintenance of assets. Secured debt is an indirect restriction on investment policy. Assets that provide sureity cannot be disposed of under the provisions of the indenture agreement. Collateralization also reduces foreclosure expenses because the lender already has established title via the bond covenant.

EFFECTS OF TERM STRUCTURE OF INTEREST RATES.   Firms always want to issue new debt, at the lowest possible cost. Frequently long-term interest rates are observed to be different from short-term rates. Usually long-term rates are higher [although at the time of writing (early 1980), the opposite was true]. The question then arises, Why not take on shorter-term debt because it has lower interest cost? Another aspect of the same problem is whether to issue debt currently or to wait several months until interest rates (for a given maturity) fall. The answers to these questions lie in an understanding of the term structure of interest rates.

Exhibit 9 gives an example of the term structure of interest rates on U.S. Treasury obligations on January 24, 1979. The simple yield is plotted as a function of the years to maturity. Note that in general, longer term bonds pay lower yields. This reflects the belief, current in the marketplace at that time, that short-run inflation would be worse than long-run inflation. Although the term structure is generally measured by using U.S. government obligations, other debt instruments show similar patterns.

Two major theories have been advanced to explain the term structure: the **expectations theory** and the **liquidity preference theory.**

Expectations Theory.   The expectations theory predicts that any long-run rate of interest is a geometric average of today's observed short-run rate and expected short-term rates in the future. Mathematically, this is expressed as:

$$1 + {}_tR_N = [(1 + {}_tr_1)(1 + {}_{t+1}\bar{r}_1) \cdots (1 + {}_{t+N-1}\bar{r}_1)]^{1/N} \tag{18}$$

where ${}_tR_N$ = average long-term rate on an N-year bond computed in year t

${}_tr_1$ = rate of return on a 1-year bond as observed in year t

${}_{t+1}\bar{r}_1$ = expected rate of return on a 1-year bond issued in year $t + 1$

${}_{t+N-1}\bar{r}_1$ = expected rate of return on a 1-year bond issued in year $t + N - 1$

For concreteness, consider the following example. The 1-year interest rate on a 1-year bond issued on January 1, 1979, is 15%. In addition, the expected interest rate on a 1-year bond issued on January 1, 1980, is 12%, and the expected rate on a 1-year bond issued on January 1, 1981, is 10%. What is the rate of return on a 3-year bond issued on January 1, 1979?

EXHIBIT 9   TERM STRUCTURE OF INTEREST RATES, JANUARY 24, 1979

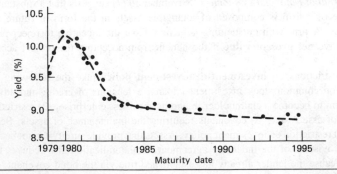

Source: Wall Street Journal, January 24, 1979.

By substituting into equation 18, we have

$$1 + _{1979}R_3 = [(1 + _{1979}0.15_1)(1 + _{1980}0.12_1)(1 + _{1981}0.10_1)]^{1/3}$$
$$1 + _{1979}R_3 = [(1.15)(1.12)(1.10)]^{1/3}$$
$$1 + _{1979}R_3 = (1.4168)^{1/3}$$
$$1 + _{1979}R_3 = 1.123146$$

Thus the rate of return on the 3-year bond is 12.3146%. A similar computation would show the rate of return on a 2-year bond to 13.49%. For this simple example, the term structure of interest rates would be downward sloping as shown in Exhibit 10.

The example shows that if the expectations hypothesis is true, and if people expect future one-period interest rates to be low relative to the current one-period interest rate, the term structure will be falling. Of course if interest rates are expected to be higher in the future, the term structure will rise. Also note that it makes no difference whether the firm issues debt with a 1-year maturity, in which case it rolls the debt over for 2 more years, or whether it issues 3-year debt in the first place. The total interest payment will be the same in either case. Given the term structure of interest rates (and ignoring transactions costs), a policy of issuing short-term debt and rolling it over will have exactly the same cost as the issuance of longer term debt.

Liquidity Preference Theory.   It is sometimes argued that short-term debt is more liquid than long-term debt. Consequently, long-term debt must provide investors with a higher yield than short-term debt. One explanation for the extra liquidity premium required on long-term debt is that investors are exposed to a greater danger of capital losses when interest rates change unexpectedly. The liquidity hypothesis implies (Exhibit 11) that a liquidity premium must be added to the rates of long-term bonds. Exhibit 11 assumes that all future one-period rates are expected to equal today's one-period rate; hence the expectations theory would predict a flat term structure. However, if the liquidity premium theory is correct, a premium must be added to longer term bonds to induce investors to hold them.

The expectations and liquidity theories are not mutually exclusive. In fact, empirical evidence (Roll, *The Behavior of Interest Rates,* Basic Books, 1970; Cargill, 1975; Dobson, Sutch, and Vanderford, *Journal of Finance,* September 1976) suggests that the best explanation of the term structure is unbiased expectations of future rates with liquidity premiums on longer-maturity bonds.

EXHIBIT 10   TERM STRUCTURE FOR 3-YEAR EXAMPLE

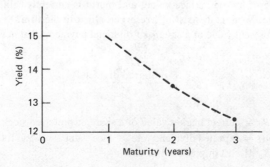

EXHIBIT 11   LIQUIDITY PREMIUM IN THE TERM STRUCTURE

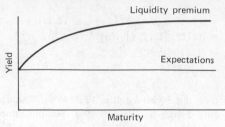

If the term structure reflects unbiased expectations of future rates, the implication is that it rarely pays to follow a **timing strategy for new debt issues,** or for new equity issues either. The reason is simple. Hundreds of thousands of investors and thousands of firms are constantly searching for information that would lead them to find a better forecast of future changes in interest rates. Anyone who can consistently provide a better forecast can earn large capital gains from doing so, and nearly everyone tries. The result is that market interest rates as embedded in the term structure reflect a consensus of thousands of informed forecasts. Empirical evidence has shown these forecasts to be unbiased on average. Therefore, to successfully time a new issue of debt (or equity) one's forecast has to be better than everyone else's. Attempts to "time" new issues usually fail as often as they succeed.

ESTIMATING THE COST OF PREFERRED STOCK

Preferred stock is a hybrid security. It is riskier than debt because preferred dividends are paid only after interest payments on debt have been made and because preferred has lower priority in bankruptcy than debt. On the other hand, preferred is less risky than common stock because it has higher priority in bankruptcy and because no common dividends may be paid until all **cumulative preferred dividends** have been issued. Preferred dividends are like interest payments on debt because they are contractual. Preferred shareholders may not force the firm into reorganization or bankruptcy for failure to pay preferred dividends. Finally, preferred dividends may not be deducted as an expense by the firm.

COST OF STRAIGHT PREFERRED.   Usually, preferred stock is issued as a **perpetuity.** It can be retired only if the firm buys back all outstanding preferred shares in the open market. Suppose that a preferred stock was issued at a par value of $100 per share, that it pays a dividend rate of 8% on its face value, and that it is currently selling (at a discount) for $83.50 per share. What is the **cost of preferred stock** to the firm?

The discounted present value of a stream of dividend payments that never grows is given below.

$$P_0 = \frac{E(\text{preferred dividend})}{K_p}$$

where P_0 = current market value of a share of preferred stock ($83.50)
$E(\text{preferred dividend})$ = expected dividend rate × face value = 8% ($100) = $8
K_p = cost of preferred stock

By rearranging the formula, we can solve for the cost of **straight preferred, K_p**.

$$K_p = \frac{\text{preferred dividend}}{P_0}$$ (19)

$$K_p = \frac{\$8.00}{\$83.50} = 9.58\%$$

This is a reasonable estimate of the cost of nonconvertible preferred stock.

COST OF CONVERTIBLE PREFERRED. Approximately 40% of the preferred stock issued in recent years is convertible into common stock. For example, one share of preferred may be convertible into four shares of the firm's common stock at the option of the preferred shareholder. In this case the investor who purchases one share of convertible preferred pays a market price, P_c, in return for a stream of dividends plus the value of an option to convert, C. Mathematically, this is

$$P_c = \frac{E(\text{preferred dividends})}{K_{cp}} + C$$

If two preferred issues are alike in all respects except that one is convertible and the other is not, investors will pay more for the convertible preferred. The reader who is interested in evaluating the value of the call option, so that the cost of convertible preferred may be estimated, is referred to the section entitled "Options Markets and Instruments."

ESTIMATING THE COST OF EQUITY

The cost of equity is even more difficult to estimate than the cost of debt, mainly because future payments to shareholders are not contractual and are difficult to predict. The principle, however, is the same. **The cost of equity capital is the opportunity cost forgone by not investing in an alternative investment of equal risk.**

We begin by showing some of the difficulties involved in anachronistic measures of the cost of equity such as the dividend yield, the earnings-price ratio, and the **Gordon growth model.** The capital asset pricing model and the **Modigliani-Miller approach** are suggested as "state of the art" approaches. Focus then shifts to problems such as how to handle flotation costs; the cost of retained earnings, the cost of depreciation funds, the effect of financial and operating leverage, trading on the equity, and convertible issues as a source of equity.

DIVIDEND YIELD. Why not use dividend yield or the earnings-price ratio to estimate the cost of equity capital? The **dividend yield** is defined as the ratio of current dividends, d_0 to the current price per share of common stock, S_0.

$$\text{dividend yield} = \frac{d_0}{S_0}$$ (20)

It will be equivalent to the cost of equity capital only under a special set of assumptions, namely, that the current dividend per share d_0 must be paid out at the end of each year forever and that the amount of the dividend must never change (i.e., never grow). This is an extremely unrealistic set of assumptions. Also, if the dividend yield is to be employed as a measure of the cost of equity, the firm must pay a dividend. Equation 20 is useless if current dividend payout is zero. In addition **low dividend yields** imply a cost of equity capital that is less than the cost of debt—which is absurd.

EARNINGS–PRICE RATIO.   Another incorrect definition frequently used to compute the cost of equity is the **earnings-price ratio.** This is the ratio of current annual accounting earnings per share e_0 to the current common stock price per share S_0. Sometimes called the **earnings yield,** it is computed as follows:

$$\text{earnings yield} = \frac{e_0}{S_0} \tag{21}$$

It has the advantage of being "usable" even though the firm has no dividend payout. However, it leads to a number of difficulties. Not the least among them is that it implies a negative cost of equity capital when earnings are negative. Also, it may lead one to conclude that for high price-earnings ratio firms (usually these are high-growth firms) the cost of equity is lower than the cost of debt. Equity in a levered firm, of course, being a residual claimant, is always more risky than debt. A related issue is that some firms have thought that their objective should be to maximize the price-earnings ratio because of the mistaken belief that such a policy would lower the "cost of equity" as measured by the earnings-price ratio. Exhibit 12, which demonstrates the **fallacy** of trying to maximize the firm's price-earnings ratio, shows the relationship between the rate of return on capital and the dollar amount of investment as a declining function of the amount invested. This reflects the fact that as more and more capital is invested in a given year, the list of good projects becomes exhausted and the rate of return on the marginal project falls. The highest price-earnings projects will be those that reflect a high **future** rate of return. The stock price is high relative to current earnings because future earnings are expected to be high. If the firm sticks to high price-earnings projects, it will fail to undertake many projects that earn more than their opportunity cost of capital. Shareholder wealth is maximized at a lower price earnings ratio. This is accomplished at I^*, where the marginal rate of return on the last investment dollar is equal to the opportunity cost of funds. Therefore, as Exhibit 12 illustrates, firms that maximize price-earnings ratios usually are not maximizing shareholder wealth.

EXHIBIT 12   PRICE–EARNINGS RATIO MAXIMIZATION FALLACY

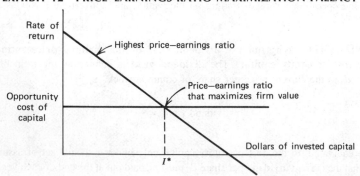

GORDON GROWTH MODEL.   The Gordon growth model expresses the **cost of equity capital** derived under the assumptions that the dividend per share grows at a constant rate g forever and that the risk of the firm will remain unchanged. If we designate K_e as the cost of equity, the model is:

$$K_e = \frac{d_0 (1 + g)}{S_0} + g \qquad (22)$$

This definition of the cost of equity is frequently employed. However, it must be used with care. First, the growth rate g is a long-run growth rate over an infinite horizon, and as such is a difficult parameter to conceptualize. Second, the long-run growth rate must, by definition, be strictly less than the cost of equity, K_e. This can be demonstrated by rearranging terms to solve for the present value of equity:

$$S_0 = \frac{d_0 (1 + g)}{K_e - g} \qquad (23)$$

If the long-run growth rate is equal to the cost of equity, the implied value of the firm is infinite. If $g < K_e$, the implied value is negative. Both results are impossible. Third, the parameters of the Gordon growth model (as given in equation 22) are interdependent. It would seem that a higher growth rate implies a higher cost of equity. However, this is not true because the higher rate of growth will imply a higher current value of the common stock S_0. The net effect will reduce the cost of equity. But if one estimates a higher growth rate, how much greater should S_0 become? The answer is unclear. Finally, the Gordon growth model provides no obvious answer to the question, What cost of equity should be applied when the firm is considering **projects of different risk** than the current operations of the firm? Because of these difficulties, it is recommended that the cost of equity be estimated by using the **capital asset pricing model** (CAPM).

CAPITAL ASSET PRICING MODEL.   Modern finance theory provides an equilibrium model that can be used to estimate the cost of equity. The capital asset pricing model (CAPM) was derived by Sharpe *(Journal of Finance*, September 1964), Lintner *(Review of Economics and Statistics,* February 1965), and Mossin *(Econometrica,* October 1966).

Risks in CAPM.   The **CAPM is a theoretical tradeoff** between the expected return on assets and their expected risk. However, the definition of **risk is not the total volatility of the asset return.** Rather, it is that portion of the variability of an asset's return which cannot be diversified away at virtually no cost. Hence the CAPM argues the **systematic risk,** often called **beta,** is the only relevant measure of risk because it cannot be avoided through **diversification.**

To provide a better intuitive explanation of why only undiversifiable risk is relevant, consider the following train of logic. First, investors can diversify their portfolios at very low cost. For example, one can invest in **no-load mutual funds,** which are composed of hundreds of different assets. In addition, many investors have a good portion of their wealth in pension funds, which are usually well diversified. Second, assuming that diversification costs virtually nothing, one can reduce the total variability of return on his portfolio by holding more and more assets. The portfolio with the greatest possible diversification is the economy as a whole. This portfolio would be composed of every asset (stocks, bonds, real estate, human capital, and personal property) held according to the ratio of its market value to the market value of all assets. In other words, the portfolio would be a **market portfolio,** where each asset is held according to its market value weight. Third, since one cannot escape the risk of the market portfolio, the relevant measure of the risk of an individual asset is its contribution to the risk of the market portfolio. Risk-averse investors will pay a premium to avoid that portion of an asset's **total volatility** which covaries with the market portfolio. They will pay nothing to avoid that portion of an asset's volatility which can be diversified away at no cost (i.e., that portion which is independent of the market return). Consequently, the capital asset pricing model follows from the fact that the total variance of return for every asset can be partitioned into two parts, **undiversifiable** or **systematic risk,** and **diversifiable** or **unsystematic risk:**

$$\text{total return variance} = \text{diversifiable risk} + \text{undiversifiable risk} \qquad (24)$$
$$\text{total return variance} = \text{unsystematic risk} + \text{systematic risk}$$

When estimating the required rate of return on risky assets, the CAPM argues that only the systematic risk is relevant because the unsystematic risk is independent of the market portfolio and can be avoided at no cost through diversification.

For a more detailed explanation of the CAPM, the reader is referred to Modigliani and Pogue (*Financial Analysts Journal,* March–April 1974, May–June 1974) or to Copeland and Weston (*Financial Theory and Corporate Policy,* Chapters 6 and 7). An example taken from Modigliani and Pogue will serve to illustrate the difference between the total variance of return and systematic risk. The actual realized rates of return, their volatility, and their systematic risk for Bayuck Cigar Co. (a NYSE-listed firm) and a randomly selected portfolio of 100 NYSE listed firms are given below. Calculations were made from monthly data between January 1945 and June 1970.

Risk and Return for Bayuck Cigar and Well-Diversified Portfolio

	Annual Return (%)	Total Volatility	Systematic Risk
100-Stock portfolio	10.9	4.45	1.11
Bayuck Cigar	5.4	7.25	0.71

Naturally one would expect the riskier asset to have a higher rate of return over the long run. Note that if total volatility is employed as a measure of risk, the "riskier" asset, Bayuck Cigar, has a lower rate of return. Part of the paradox is that we are comparing the volatility of an individual stock with the volatility of a well-diversified portfolio. Of course the portfolio has lower volatility. A better comparison, one that uses the appropriate measure of risk, is one that does not consider the diversifiable risk, and therefore compares the two alternatives on an equal basis. If one compares the systematic (nondiversifiable) risk of the alternatives, the apparent paradox is resolved. Bayuck Cigar Co. is seen to have lower systematic risk and lower return. It makes sense that the low-risk asset should also have lower return in the long run.

CAPM Equation.   The capital asset pricing model says that there should be a linear tradeoff between the expected rate of return on an asset and its systematic risk. This is shown in Exhibit 13 and equation 25.

$$E(R_j) = R_f + [E(R_m) - R_f]\beta_j$$

where $E(R_j)$ = expected (or required) rate of return on jth asset
R_f = risk-free rate (Treasury bill rate)   (25)
$E(R_m)$ = expected rate of return on market portfolio
β_j = cov $(R_j, R_m)/\text{var}(R_m)$; systematic risk

Beta Defined.   The statistical measure of systematic risk is β (beta). It is computed as the **covariance** between the returns of the asset with the market portfolio, standardized by the variance of the market portfolio. Mathematically, this is

$$\beta = \frac{\text{cov }(R_j, R_m)}{\text{var }(R_m)} = \frac{\sum p_t (R_{jt} - \bar{R}_{jt}) (R_{mt} - \bar{R}_{mt})}{\sum p_t (R_{mt} - \bar{R}_{mt})^2} \tag{26}$$

where p_t = probability of observing R_j in state of nature t
$\bar{R}_{jt}$ = mean (or average) return on asset j
R_{mt} = return on market portfolio in state t
$\bar{R}_{mt}$ = mean (average) return on market portfolio

By definition, the covariance of the market portfolio with itself is equal to the variance of the market portfolio. Therefore, the beta of the market portfolio β_m is always 1.0 (see Exhibit 13).

Security Market Line.   According to the theory, every risky asset traded in secondary markets will have an equilibrium required rate of return that falls exactly on the upward sloping line in Exhibit 13. This line is called the **security market line.** Many empirical studies have verified that the security market line (and its variants) is a reasonably good description of reality. Without going into a long and detailed description of possible extensions and modifications of the theory, we shall proceed by assuming that the model described above is the "state of the art."

EXHIBIT 13   THE CAPITAL ASSET PRICING MODEL

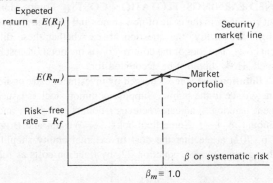

How then, can the CAPM and the security market line be used to conceptualize the cost of equity capital? According to the model (equation 25), it is necessary to estimate the **risk-free rate of return** R_f, the expected rate of return on the **market portfolio** $E(R_m)$, and the **beta** β_j of the risky asset. The rates of return R_f and $E(R_m)$ are nominal rates (they include inflationary expectations) and they are gross rates of return before taxes. Usually, the risk-free rate is interpreted to be the rate on 90-day U. S. Treasury bills.

If we return to the example of the cost of capital for Bethlehem Steel as of December 31, 1976, the 90-day Treasury bill rate was 4.6%. Next, what about the expected rate of return on the market portfolio $E(R_m)$? The expected future rate of return on the market cannot be measured. However, a good way of guessing what it might be is to add three components: (1) the long-run real rate of growth in the economy, 3–4%, (2) an adjustment for inflation next year (in December 1976 a good guess might have been 6–7%), and (3) a risk premium (above the risk-free rate) for the riskiness of the market portfolio of equity (say 4–5%). Using the mean of each of these components, we estimate the expected rate of return on the market as 14.5%. Finally, we need an estimate of the **beta of Bethlehem steel.** Many companies are in the business of estimating financial statistics. It is hard to say who provides better betas. Without revealing the source, we use an estimate of $\beta = 0.9$ for Bethlehem Steel.

Cost of Equity.   Finally, using these estimates we can guess at the **cost of equity of Bethlehem Steel** K_e, because the required rate of return should obey the CAPM. Rewriting equation 25, we have

$$K_e = E(R_j) = R_f + [E(R_m) - R_f]\beta_j \tag{27}$$

and substituting the correct estimates gives

$$K_e = E(R_j) = 0.0467 + [0.145 - 0.0467]0.9$$
$$K_e = 13.52\%$$

This is a "state of the art" ballpark estimate for the cost of equity of Bethlehem Steel as of December 31, 1976. Note that the cost of equity will change with our estimate of expected inflation. It will also change with the systematic risk of Bethlehem. If the basic business risk of Bethlehem changes or if its long-run target capital structure changes, its systematic risk will change correspondingly.

COST OF RETAINED EARNINGS: FLOTATION COSTS.   Equity capital is provided by external sources if it comes from the issue of new shares and from internal sources if provided via retained earnings. Frequently, the question arises whether these different sources of equity have different costs. The root of the controversy is the flotation cost incurred whenever new shares are issued. How should it be accounted for?

An example of a **flotation cost** is fees charged by investment banking firms for the service of underwriting a new issue to the public. Suppose common stock is issued at S_o dollars per share, the investment banking syndicate recieves f dollars per share, and the issuing firm receives the net amount, $S_o - f$. Some textbooks (see Weston and Brigham, *Managerial Finance*, 6th ed., p. 702) argue that the cost of external equity should be computed by adjusting the Gordon growth model, equation 22, by flotation costs as follows:

$$K_e = \frac{d_0(1 + g)}{S_0 - f} + g \tag{28}$$

This technique implies (1) that external equity is more costly than internal equity (retained earnings), (2) that the firm should use up its retained earnings for investment before issuing new equity, and (3) that for a given risk, the marginal cost of capital is upward sloping as shown in Exhibit 14.

Adjusting the cost of equity by flotation costs presents several problems. First, flotation costs are paid when the equity is issued, but the adjusted rate of return method spreads them out over time. Such a procedure violates discounting procedures, which require that cash outflows be recorded as they occur. Second, the cost of equity capital is an **opportunity cost** determined by the rates of return that can be earned elsewhere on projects of equivalent risk. Since flotation costs are irrelevant in determining where else to invest, they are irrelevant in determining the cost of equity.

An alternative to handling flotation costs, as suggested in equation 28, is **not to adjust the cost of equity at all.** Rather, flotation costs can be recognized as a cash outflow to be borne by current shareholders whenever the firm needs to go to the capital markets for external capital (debt as well as equity). This cash outflow can then be combined with the other cash flows of the firm and the net cash flows should be discounted at the weighted average cost of capital determined without flotation costs. Under this recommended procedure the marginal cost of capital does not turn up, as shown by the solid line in Exhibit 14. Rather, for given risk, it stays constant and follows the dotted and dashed line. This approach implies that the cost of retained earnings and external equity are identical.

COST OF DEPRECIATION FUNDS.   In their statements of sources and uses of funds, firms usually list **depreciation charges** as one of the most important sources of funds, if not the most important. Should depreciation be considered "free" capital, should it be ignored completely, or should a charge be assessed against it? The answer is that depreciation funds should be charged at their **opportunity cost,** which is the weighted average cost of capital for the firm as a whole.

Depreciation funds are part of the cash flows generated from operations (defined earlier as *OCFAT*). As such, they represent part of the total funds of the firm that are available to make payments to debtholders and shareholders. The combined opportunity cost for the total funds of the firm is the weighted average cost of capital. Finally, since the cost of depreciation-generated funds is equal to the weighted average cost of capital, depreciation does not enter separately into the calculation of the average cost of capital.

COST OF CONVERTIBLE SECURITIES.   When a firm issues convertible debt (or preferred), it is really issuing a **bond plus a call option on the equity of the firm.** Convertibles

EXHIBIT 14   HYPOTHETICAL MARGINAL COST OF CAPITAL (MCC)

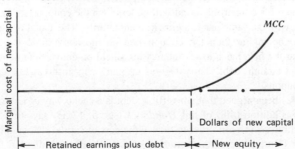

are securities that are exchangeable into common stock at the option of the holder and under specified terms and conditions. The key feature is the **conversion ratio,** which determines the number of shares the holder of the convertible will receive when he surrenders his security on conversion. The **conversion price** is the **exercise price** implied by the conversion ratio. For example, suppose that the XYZ Co. issues a 20-year bond at a par value of $1,000 with a conversion feature that allows the holder to convert into 20 shares of common stock any time before the maturity of the bond. Then the conversion price X_c is

$$X_c = \text{conversion price} = \frac{\text{par value of bond}}{\text{shares received}} = \frac{\$1,000}{20} = \$50 \qquad (29)$$

Sometimes the conversion ratio is stepped up over the life of the bond. For example, the ratio might be 20 shares for the first 5 years, 17.5 shares for the next 5 years, and so on. Still another factor that might affect the conversion ratio is a clause in most bonds that protects against dilution stock splits, stock dividends, and rights offerings.

Call Option.   On the date of offering, the conversion price is always higher than the current stock price so that the bonds are not immediately convertible. If the conversion price is $50 as in the example above, the stock price might be $40. The coupon rate on convertibles is lower than on straight debt of equal risk and maturity because investors receive not only a bond but also a call option (the convertible feature), which allows them to gain if the stock price rises above the conversion price. The rate of return K_c received by an investor who purchases a convertible bond on the date of issue is determined by equating the price he pays for the convertible bond B_0 to the discounted value of the cash payments from the bond (coupons plus face value) plus the present value C of the **call option,** implicit in the right to convert. Mathematically the problem is to solve for K_c in the following formula:

$$B_0 = \sum_{t=0}^{T} \frac{E \,(\text{coupon})_t}{(1 + K_c)^t} + \frac{E(\text{face value})_T}{(1 + K_c)^T} + C \qquad (30)$$

Convertible Debt.   The value of the right to convert C can be determined by using the procedure suggested by Brennan and Schwartz (*Journal of Finance,* December 1977). It may be approximated by using the **European call option** pricing formula (Black and Scholes, *Journal of Political Economy,* May—June 1973), which is discussed in the section entitled "Options Markets and Instruments" of this *Handbook.* The value of the right to convert will increase with the market value of the stock S, the variability of the rate of return on the stock, the time remaining before the conversion privilege runs out, and the risk-free rate of return. It will decrease with a higher conversion price X_c.

The coupon rate on a convertible bond will be less than the coupon rate on an equivalent straight debt issue with the same par value, risk, and maturity. The actual **cost of convertible debt** K_c will also be higher than the coupon rate on the convertible issue. One of the implications is that the firm has a lower interest tax shield on convertible debt than it would have on equivalent straight debt. Thus it gives up part of its **interest tax shield** in return for lower cash coupons.

It has sometimes been argued that convertible debt is a cheap way of issuing new equity. In fact the previous edition (4th) of this *Handbook* (see p. 17.58) says that "management may use a convertible security in order to reduce the cost of capital, taking advantage of the anticipated higher future price of the common stock." We have **indicated** in equation 30 that the actual cost of convertible is higher than the coupon yield and not all the true cost is tax deductible. Therefore, if anything, **convertible debt increases the cost of capital,** not vice versa.

COMPUTING WEIGHTED AVERAGE COST OF CAPITAL: AN EXAMPLE

Cost of capital calculations are as much an art as they are a science. As seen above, this is particularly true when it comes to the problem of estimating the cost of equity. Nevertheless, we can use available methodology to reach a ballpark estimate. The example below estimates the **cost of capital for Bethlehem Steel** as of December 31, 1976. Recall that the weighted average cost of capital is defined as the cost of each type of capital multiplied by its percentage of the total capital employed by the firm.

GENERAL ALGEBRAIC EXPRESSION.   The weighted average cost of capital is computed as follows:

$$WACC = K_{STD}\,(1 - t_c)\,\frac{STD}{TL} + K_{LTD}\,(1 - t_c)\,\frac{LTD}{TL} + K_p\,\frac{P}{TL} + K_c\,\frac{CONV}{TL}$$
$$+ K_e\,\frac{S}{TL} \tag{31}$$

where $WACC$ = weighted average cost of capital
  K_{STD} = market value of short-term liabilities
  TL = market value of total liabilities
  t_c = marginal corporate tax rate
  K_{LTD} = cost of long-term debt
  LTD = market value of long-term debt
  K_p = cost of preferred stock
  P = market value of preferred stock
  K_c = cost of convertible deft or preferred
  $CONV$ = market value of convertible debt and preferred
  K_e = cost of equity
  S = market value of equity

The task of estimating the $WACC$ for Bethlehem Steel is simplified because it has no convertible debt or preferred stock outstanding. Therefore the third and fourth terms in equation (31) are irrelevant.

  We shall assume that Bethlehem contemplates no major changes in its capital structure over time. Consequently, the current percentages of short-term debt, long-term debt, and equity in the capital structure can be taken as the long-term weights for each capital source. Exhibit 15 gives the balance sheet for Bethlehem Steel in 1976.

COST OF SHORT-TERM LIABILITIES.   This component of $WACC$ was discussed earlier. For the sake of convenience, we shall assume that the opportunity cost of short-term liabilities is the same as the interest rate on other short-term obligations of equal risk. A good approximation for Bethlehem Steel is the commercial paper rate, which in December 1976 was 4.91%.

EXHIBIT 15   BALANCE SHEET, BETHLEHEM STEEL, DECEMBER 1976

Assets		Liabilities	
Cash	45,600	Accounts payable	274,800
Marketable securities	355,600	Notes payable	—
Receivables	421,500	Accruals	948,600
Inventories	834,100	Long-term debt[a]	1,023,100
Long-term assets (net)	3,007,600	Common at par[b]	576,000
Total assets	4,939,100	Less Treasury stock	69,300
		Retained earnings	2,185,900
		Total liabilities	4,939,100

[a]Long-term debt is detailed in Exhibit 11.
[b]43,665,578 shares outstanding with a market price of $40.625 per share as of December 31, 1976.
Source: Moody's Industrial Manual.

COSTS OF LONG-TERM DEBT AND EQUITY.   The **cost of long-term debt** for Bethlehem is the rate it would pay if it issued new 25–30 year Aa-rated bonds. This rate was estimated earlier to be approximately 8.3%. Finally, we used the capital asset pricing model to estimate the **cost of equity** to be 13.52% (see earlier discussion).

MARKET VALUE WEIGHTS.   All that remains is to estimate the **market value weights** of each source of capital. For short-term debt we used the book value weights. This is a reasonable approximation for short-term liabilities because there is not much chance for capital gains or losses on assets with short lives. The only exception is the current portion of long-term debt, which may have a market value very different from book. However, since this information was not available, we were forced to use book value. Where possible, we used the market values of long-term debt as given in Exhibit 5, and when market value was unavailable we used book. The easiest source of capital to find market values was equity.

Exhibit 16 gives the market value weights of the three capital sources used by Bethlehem Steel. Note that the market values of long-term debt and equity are much lower than book values. Nevertheless, the market value weights are appropriate because they reflect the current economic value of the firm. Book value weights are irrelevant for current decision making.

EXHIBIT 16   MARKET VALUE WEIGHTS FOR CAPITAL SOURCES

	Market Value ($ Thousands)	% of Total	Cost
Short-term liabilities	1,223,400	32.1	4.9%
Long-term debt	815,945	21.4	8.3%
Equity	1,773,914	46.5	13.5%
	3,813,259	100.0	

Source: Moody's Industrial Manual and Bank & Quotation Record, January 1979.

MARGINAL TAX RATE. Finally, by using equation 31 and the data given in Exhibit 16, we can estimate the weighted average cost of capital for Bethlehem Steel. The **marginal tax rate** is assumed to be 48%.

$$WACC = K_{STD} (1 - t_c) \frac{STD}{TL} + K_{LTD} (1 - t_c) \frac{LTD}{TL} + K_e \frac{S}{TL}$$

$$WACC = 0.049(1 - 0.48) (0.321) + 0.083 (1 - 0.48) (0.214) + 0.135 (0.465)$$

$$WACC = 8.02\%$$

As mentioned earlier, the weighted average cost of capital for a corporation changes from day to day as conditions in capital markets change. In recent years, one of the important causes of change has been the inflation rate. Almost every day, news arrives that changes the term structure of interest rates to reflect inflationary expectations. These changes must be taken into account when estimating the cost of capital.

OPTIMAL CAPITAL STRUCTURE

Until now we have assumed that the ratio of debt to total liabilities employed by the firm remains unchanged. It is time to turn to the question of whether the value of the firm and the weighted average cost of capital can be affected by the mixture of debt and equity financing chosen by the firm. If financing can affect the value of the firm, there is probably an optimal capital structure. Throughout the years there seem to have been empirical regularities in the capital structures employed by various industries. For example, electric utilities use a large percentage of debt, while **computer firms** do not. Why?

Several alternative theories have been put forward. One is that optimal capital structure results from a tradeoff between gains in value from the tax shield provided by utilizing debt capital and losses in value from potential **bankruptcy costs.** Another theory suggests that capital structure can be explained by agency costs that arise as bondholders and stockholders negotiate contracts. In the process of discussing these ideas, we shall also emphasize the relationship between the cost of equity capital K_e and the amount of debt in the capital structure of the firm.

DEBT, TAXES, AND BANKRUPTCY COSTS.

Alternate Definition of WACC. This can be provided if we assume that the only form of taxes is corporate (no personal taxes), that there are no bankruptcy costs, that all cash flows are perpetuities, and that the firm takes on only projects that do not change its risk class. As shown in equation 4, the value of a levered firm may be written as

$$V^L = \frac{EBIT (1 - t_c)}{K_u} + t_c \frac{rD}{K_d} = V^u + t_c B$$

where V^L = market value of levered firm

V^u = market value of unlevered firm

$EBIT$ = earnings before interest and taxes

r = coupon rate on debt

D = face value of debt

K_u = cost of equity for unlevered firm

K_d = cost of debt

B = market value of debt, $B = rD/K_d$

The cost of capital can be defined as the rate of return required on new investment ΔI, which is necessary to guarantee that the anticipated change in shareholders' wealth ΔS^0 will be positive. To discover a cost of capital that fits this definition, we need to examine the way in which the value of the levered firm will change as new investment is undertaken. Any change in the market value of the levered firm must come from one of four sources: the change in the value of original shareholders' wealth ΔS^0, the change in the value of new shareholders' wealth ΔS^n, the change in the value of original bondholders' wealth ΔB^0, or the change in the value of new bondholders' wealth ΔB^n. Mathematically, this can be expressed as:

$$\Delta V^L = \Delta S^0 + \Delta S^n + \Delta B^0 + \Delta B^n \tag{32}$$

Dividing through by the amount of new investment, we have the change in the value of the firm with respect to new investment, ΔI:

$$\frac{\Delta V^L}{\Delta I} = \frac{\Delta S^0}{\Delta I} + \frac{\Delta S^n}{\Delta I} + \frac{\Delta B^0}{\Delta I} + \frac{\Delta B^n}{\Delta I} \tag{33}$$

We further assume that all new debt is subordinate to original debt and that the new project does not increase the risk of the original bondholders' claim on the firm. Therefore, $\Delta B^0/\Delta I = 0$. Also, note that the new project will be financed with new debt and new equity, therefore,

$$\Delta I = \Delta S^n + \Delta B^n \tag{34}$$

Using this fact in equation 33, we have:

$$\frac{\Delta V^L}{\Delta I} = \frac{\Delta S^0}{\Delta I} + \frac{\Delta S^n + \Delta B^n}{\Delta I} = \frac{\Delta S^0}{\Delta I} + 1 \tag{35}$$

Because shareholders are making the investment decision, we assume that they require their wealth to increase. This requirement may be stated by rearranging equation 35:

$$\frac{\Delta S^0}{\Delta I} = \frac{\Delta V^L}{\Delta I} - 1 > 0 \tag{36}$$

Equation 36 requires the value of shareholders' wealth to increase as a result of new investment ΔI. We can expand on this definition by noting that the change in the value of the firm when new investment is undertaken can be derived from equation 4:

$$\frac{\Delta V^L}{\Delta I} = \frac{\Delta EBIT (1 - t_c)}{K_u \Delta I} + t_c \frac{\Delta B^n}{\Delta I} \tag{37}$$

Note that the new investment is expected to change the earnings before interest and taxes ($\Delta EBIT$). This cash flow provides the necessary return on investment. As stated before, the cost of capital is the minimum return on investment that increases shareholders' wealth. We can obtain this definition by substituting 37 into equation 36:

$$\frac{dS^0}{dI} = \frac{\Delta EBIT\,(1 - t_c)}{K_u \Delta I} + \frac{\Delta B^n}{\Delta I} - 1 > 0$$

Solving for the required change in aftertax cash flows with respect to new investment, we have:

$$\frac{\Delta EBIT\,(1 - t_c)}{\Delta I} > K_u \left(1 - t_c \frac{\Delta B^n}{\Delta I} \right) \tag{38}$$

Equation 39 is an **alternate definition of the weighted average cost of capital.**

$$WACC = K_u \left(1 - t_c \frac{\Delta B^n}{\Delta I} \right) \tag{39}$$

Originally derived by Modigliani and Miller (*American Economic Review,* 1963), equation 39 shows the relationship between the weighted average cost of capital and the financial leverage employed in new investment. If we assume that new projects use the average amount of debt and equity, equation 39 becomes:

$$WACC = K_u \left(1 - t_c \frac{B}{B + S} \right) \tag{40}$$

where $B + S$ is the sum of the market values of debt and equity. Of course, their value is identical to the value of the firm

$$V^l = B + S \tag{41}$$

Notice that in equation 40 the cost of capital declines as the percentage of debt in the capital structure of the firm, $B/(B + S)$, increases. This reflects the fact that in a world with only corporate taxes, debt capital provides a tax shield.

Cost of Equity. Modigliani and Miller also derived an expression for the **cost of equity capital** K_e, which shows that the cost of equity rises as more and more debt is used in the firm's capital structure. Their formula is:

$$K_e = K_u + (K_u - K_d)\,(1 - t_c)\,\frac{B}{S} \tag{42}$$

Exhibit 17 shows the relationship between the weighted average cost of capital, the cost of debt, and the cost of equity as the firm increases its debt to equity ratio B/S. The cost of debt is assumed to be invariant to increases in the debt-equity ratio because new debt capital is assumed to be subordinate to old. Hence the riskiness of original debt is assumed to remain unchanged. Equity capital, on the other hand, becomes more risky as the debt-equity ratio increases. This follows because equity is the residual claimant in the cash flows of the firm. As more and more debt is undertaken, the variability of the equity position becomes greater. Shareholders will naturally require higher rates of return on equity to compensate them for

EXHIBIT 17   RELATIONSHIP BETWEEN CAPITAL COSTS AND LEVERAGE

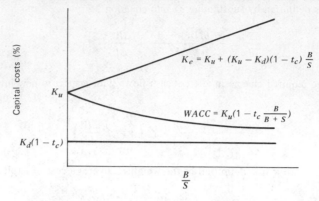

their risk. Finally, the weighted average cost of capital decreases with higher financial leverage because of the tax shield provided by debt.

Sample Cost of Capital Problem.   The usefulness of the theoretical results can be demonstrated by considering the following problem. The United Southern Construction Co. currently has a market value capital structure of 20% debt to total assets. The company's treasurer believes that more debt can be taken on, up to a limit of 35% debt, without losing the firm's ability to borrow at 7%, the prime rate (also assumed to be the risk-free rate). The firm has a marginal tax rate of 50%. The 7% prime rate is used for instructive purposes and does not reflect 1980 rates. The expected return on the market portfolio next year is estimated to be 17% and the systematic risk of the company's equity β_L is estimated to be 0.5.

- What is the company's current weighted average cost of capital, and its current cost of equity?
- What will the new weighted average cost of capital be if the "target" capital structure is changed to 35% debt?
- Should a project with a 9.25% expected rate of return be accepted if its systematic risk is the same as that of the firm?

The data for this problem are all reasonably realistic. For example, the firm's systematic risk can be estimated for its current leverage of 20% by using the definition given in equation 26. Since the systematic risk is $\beta_L = 0.5$, we can use the CAPM, equation 27, to calculate the company's current cost of equity capital:

$$K_e = R_f + [E(R_m) - R_f]\beta$$
$$K_e = 0.07 + [0.17 - 0.07]\,0.5 = 12\%$$

Equation 10, the definition of the weighted average cost of capital, can now be used to compute the firm's current cost of capital, given 20% debt in the capital structure.

$$WACC = K_d\,(1 - t_c)\,\frac{B}{B + S} + K_e\,\frac{S}{B + S} \tag{10}$$

The facts of the problem tell us that the cost of debt is 7% and we have computed the cost of equity as 12%. Substituting these values into the equation, we have:

$$WACC = 0.07(1 - 0.5)(0.2) + 0.12(0.8) = 10.3\%$$

The second question is even more interesting. What will the cost of capital be if the firm increases its usage of debt up to 35% of its capital structure? We cannot directly use the traditional definition of the **weighted average cost of capital** (equation 10) because the cost of equity capital will increase with higher leverage. Only the **Modigliani–Miller approach** to the cost of capital is useful for estimating the new cost of equity and the new weighted average cost of capital.

To compute the new cost of equity we can employ equation 42.

$$K_e = K_u + (K_u - K_d)(1 - t_c)\frac{B}{S}$$

All the necessary parameters are available. For example, we know that the cost of debt (up to a leverage level of 35%) K_d is 7%, the tax rate t_c is 50%, and the ratio of debt to equity will be 53.85%. With 35% debt in the capital structure, we have $B/(B + S) = 0.35$. Solving for B/S we have $B/S = 0.35/(1 - 0.35) = 53.85\%$. The only missing element is the cost of equity for the unlevered cash flow of the firm K_u. This can be estimated by using equation 40:

$$WACC = K_u\left(1 - t_c\frac{B}{B + S}\right)$$
$$K_u = \frac{WACC}{\left(1 - t_c\frac{B}{B + S}\right)} \qquad (40)$$

Substituting in the $WACC$ for 20% debt in the firm's capital structure yields:

$$K_u = \frac{0.103}{(1 - 0.5(0.2))} = 11.44\%$$

Finally, substituting all this into equation 42 gives:

$$K_e = 0.1144 + (0.1144 - 0.07)(1 - 0.5)0.5385 = 12.64\%$$

Thus we see that the cost of equity increases from 12% when leverage is 20% up to 12.64% when leverage increases to 35%. Equity holders require a higher rate of return to compensate them for the greater risk resulting from higher financial leverage.

Having computed the new cost of equity, we can estimate the weighted average cost of capital if the firm increases its debt to 35% of its capital structure.

$$WACC = K_d(1 - t_c)\frac{B}{B + S} + K_e\frac{S}{B + S}$$
$$WACC = 0.07(1 - 0.5)(0.35) + 0.1264(0.65) = 9.44\%$$

Note that the weighted average cost of capital has decreased, even though the cost of equity has increased. This happens because the firm is using a greater percentage of cheaper debt capital, which more than offsets the increased cost of equity.

One might also ask whether equity holders are better off with the new capital structure. The answer is yes—because they are able to keep the gain in the value of the firm that results from the lower cost of capital.

Finally, we are asked to decide whether a project with a 9.25% rate of return is acceptable if its systematic risk (β) is the same as the firm's. The answer is no, because the weighted average cost of capital is 9.44%, that is, higher than the expected return on the project. A common error made in this type of problem is forgetting that the cost of equity capital increases with higher leverage. Had we estimated the weighted average cost of capital using 12% for the old cost of equity and 35% debt as the target capital structure, we would have obtained 9.03% as the cost of capital and we would have (incorrectly) accepted the project.

Effect of Personal Taxes.   The results of the analysis can be considerably altered by the introduction of personal taxes. Miller (*Journal of Finance*, May 1977) has shown that under certain conditions the weighted average cost of capital may remain unchanged as the percentage of debt in the capital structure is increased. It is argued that the before-tax rate of return on corporate debt has to be "grossed up" to compensate bondholders for the personal taxes they must pay on interest received. This effect offsets the advantage of the interest tax shield the firm receives. The net result is that greater use of debt capital will have little or no effect on the firm's weighted average cost of capital.

Tax Advantage Tradeoff: Debt Financing Versus Bankruptcy Costs.   This tradeoff can be used to explain the existence of an optimal capital structure for the firm. Suppose we assume that there is at least some tax benefit from carrying debt. If this were the only effect, firms would try to carry 100% debt in their capital structures. But suppose that the tax benefit from debt is offset by a greater likelihood of incurring bankruptcy costs (defined explicitly in the section on "Bankruptcy and Reorganization") as the firm carries more and more debt. Bondholders bear most of the direct bankruptcy costs such as lawyers' fees, other fees, court costs, and wasted managerial time. Therefore, they require higher and higher interest rates as the firm uses greater amounts of debt in its capital structure. Exhibit 18 shows how the cost of capital changes when we consider a tradeoff between the tax benefit from using debt against the increased cost of bankruptcy. The optimal capital structure is attained at [B/(B + S)]*, where the weighted average cost of capital is lowest. In practice, the choice of an optimal capital structure for a given firm is a subjective decision. Some treasurers make the decision by deciding on the lowest tolerable bond rating, say Aa; then they take on as much debt as possible without falling to the next lowest rating.

AGENCY COSTS.   We have just seen that if there is a gain from financial leverage because of the tax deductibility of interest expenses, and if **bankruptcy costs** are significant, it is possible to construct a theory of optimal capital structure. One troublesome aspect of this approach is that even before income taxes existed in the United States, firms used debt in their capital structure. Furthermore, the same cross-sectional regularities in financial leverage that exist today can also be observed in data from periods before the introduction of corporate taxes. This suggests that optimal leverage (if it exists) may be explained by causes other than debt tax shields and bankruptcy costs. One possibility is a theory of agency costs as postulated by Jensen and Meckling (*Journal of Financial Economics*, October 1976).

EXHIBIT 18   OPTIMAL CAPITAL STRUCTURE AS TRADEOFF BETWEEN BANK-RUPTCY COSTS AND TAX BENEFITS OF DEBT CAPITAL

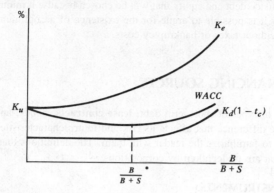

Jensen and Meckling use the notion of **agency costs** to argue that the probability distribution of cash flows provided by the firm is not independent of ownership structure and that this relationship may be used to **explain optimal leverage.** First, there is an incentive problem associated with the issuance of new debt. Suppose that unbeknownst to lenders, the firm has two different investment projects, both having the same systematic risk but different variances. The following are relevant probabilities and end-of-period cash flows:

Probability	Project 1	Project 2
.5	9,000	2,000
.5	11,000	18,000

Both projects cost $8,000 and both have the same expected return. Suppose the firm shows only project 1 to lenders and asks to borrow $7,000. From the lender's point of view, this request seems reasonable because project 1 will always earn enough to pay off the loan. Of course, if creditors lend $7,000 and if the owners of the firm have the ability to switch to project 2, they will do so. The result is a transfer of wealth from bondholders to shareholders.

Agency Costs of Debt.   To prevent such machinations, bondholders insist on protective covenants and monitoring devices of various types, to protect their wealth from expropriation. However, the costs of writing and enforcing such covenants may be considerable. Furthermore, these costs may increase with the percent of financing supplied by bondholders. These costs are the **agency costs of debt.**

Agency Costs of External Equity.   Suppose, on the other hand, that a firm is owned exclusively by a single individual, the owner-manager. He will obviously take every action possible to increase his own wealth. However, if he sells a portion of the ownership rights by selling external equity to new shareholders, conflicts of interest will arise. He then becomes a co-owner with the new shareholders. If, at their expense, he can maximize his wealth by purchasing an executive jet and taking long vacations, he will do so. Co-ownership of equity implies agency problems. The new shareholders will have to incur **monitoring costs** of one form or another to ensure that the original owner-manager acts in their interest.

Jensen and Meckling suggest that given increasing agency costs with higher proportions of equity on one hand and higher proportion of debt on the other, there is an optimum combination of outside debt and equity that will be chosen because it minimizes total agency costs. In this way it is possible to argue for the existence of an optimum capital structure even in a world without taxes or bankruptcy costs.

VARIOUS FINANCING SOURCES

There are dozens of types of short-term debt, **lease contracts,** bonds, and preferred stock, each with a subtle difference that affects its risk and return characteristics. The purpose of this subsection is to familiarize the reader with them. The definitions that follow consist of only **contracts** that are **undertaken** by corporations.

SHORT-TERM INSTRUMENTS.

Commercial Paper.   This consists of any unsecured short-term promissory note issued by a corporation, a finance company, or a bank. Usually issued in denominations of $100,000 or more with maturities of 270 days or less, commercial paper is usually considered to have relatively low risk. Hence interest rates on commercial paper are only 1 or 2% higher than U.S. Treasury obligations of equal duration.

Bankers' Acceptances.   These instruments are created as a means of financing goods in transit. The firm to which the goods are being delivered agrees to pay a given sum within a short period of time, usually 180 days or less. The bank then "accepts" this promise, obligating itself to pay the amount of the note if requested and receiving a claim on the goods as collateral. The note representing the loan becomes a liability of both the bank and the buyer of the goods and is therefore not very risky. Interest rates on bankers acceptances are usually only 1 to 2% above U.S. Treasury obligations of equal maturity.

LEASES.

Sale and Leaseback.   Such an arrangement is created when a firm owning land, buildings, or equipment sells the property to a financial institution and simultaneously enters into a contract to lease back the asset. Land leases are usually arranged with life insurance companies. The sale and leaseback of equipment could be arranged with an insurance company, a commercial bank, or a specialized leasing company. Note that the selling firm receives the value of the asset as an immediate source of cash. The lease payments are sufficient to return the purchase price plus a fair return on investment to the lessor.

Service Leases.   This category includes both financing and maintenance services. The equipment involved is usually computers, automobiles, or trucks. It is the lessor's responsibility to maintain the equipment and the maintenance costs are built into the lease fee. Service leases are usually not fully amortized; that is, the payments do not recover the full cost of the equipment and the lessor maintains property rights to the residual value of the equipment when the lease period ends. Finally, many service leases have a cancellation clause that allows the lessee to stop payment and return the equipment before the lease contract ends.

Financial Leases. These are similar to sale and leaseback except that the equipment is purchased by the lessor from the manufacturer or distributor then leased out. A strict financial lease does not provide for maintenance services, is not cancelable, and is fully amortized.

Leveraged Leasing. Use of this term implies that the lessor does not have full equity interest in the leased asset. Instead, the lessor borrows a portion of the funds needed to acquire the asset for the purpose of leasing it out.

BONDS.

Mortgage Bonds. These are long-term obligations that are secured by specific property. In addition, mortgage bonds are unsecured claims on the general assets of the firm. In the event of default, holders of mortgage bonds receive ownership of the mortgaged property.

Collateral Trust Bonds. Backed by other securities, usually held by a trustee, collateral trust bonds are frequently used by a parent firm when it pledges the securities of a wholly owned subsidiary as collateral.

Equipment Trust Certificates. These are backed by specific pieces of equipment or machinery. Frequently used by airlines, railroads, and shipping companies, these certificates may be issued by a trustee who holds the equipment, issues obligations, and leases the equipment to the corporation that uses it. Cash paid by the corporation is used to pay the interest and principal on the equipment trust certificates. Eventually the firm will take title to the equipment.

Debenture Bonds. Debenture bonds are general obligations of the issuing firm and are unsecured credit. They are claims on the general assets of the corporation only and are protected by their indenture restrictions. As mentioned earlier, the four most common types of indenture provision are provisions against the issuance of more debt, restrictions that limit dividend payments, provisions restricting merger activity, and restrictions on the disposition of the firm's assets.

Subordinated Debentures. Subordinated debentures are junior debt. In the event of bankruptcy, these claims against the firm will not be met unless and until the claims of senior debtholders have been fully satisfied.

Adjustment Bonds. Income bonds pay interest only when the corporation's net income is above a specified level. Occasionally they are called **adjustment bonds** because they may be issued by corporations undergoing reorganization to readjust fixed interest debt. Unfortunately, if the issue bears too many of the characteristics of equity, the Internal Revenue Service may view the interest payments as "essentially equivalent to a dividend" and taxable as such. In this event the interest payments are no longer deductible as an expense before taxes.

Guaranteed Bonds. These are bonds that are guaranteed by the assets of a corporation other than the issuing firm. Usually the guaranteeing corporation is a parent firm.

Participating Bonds. These provide fixed interest payments and, in addition, a portion of surplus earnings accruing over the life of the bond if earnings are above the fixed interest.

Joint Bonds.   Obligations jointly issued by two or more corporations (usually railroads), sometimes called pooled bonds, provide joint collateral.

Voting Bonds.   Usually issued in connection with reorganizations, voting bonds give holders the right to vote for directors if interest payments are not paid for a certain length of time.

Serial Bonds.   Different portions of an issue of serial bonds mature at different (sometimes random) dates. A default on any portion coming due constitutes default on the entire issue.

Convertible Bonds.   At the holder's option, these may be exchanged for other securities, usually common stock. The cost of capital in issuing such bonds was discussed in detail earlier.

RETIREMENT OF BONDS.   One of the important features of bonds is the method of principal repayment. The various types of refunding are discussed below, followed by an economic analysis of the refunding decision.

Call Provisions.   Call provisions give the firm the right to pay off a bond at any time before maturity. This provides an increased degree of flexibility, since debt can be reduced, its maturity altered via refunding, and most important, expensive debt with high interest rates may be replaced with cheaper debt if rates decline. Frequently the call price is established above par value. Nevertheless, from the investor's point of view the call provision establishes an upper limit on the amount of capital gain that can be obtained if interest rates fall. For this reason, the investor will require a higher yield to maturity on callable bonds than on straight debt of equal risk and maturity.

In effect, a callable bond is equal to an ordinary bond with an option contract. On the date of issue the bondholder equates the market price of the callable bond B_0 with the present value of the cash payments from the bond (coupons plus face value) less the present value of the call option C_0, which gives the firm the right to call in the debt early at some predetermined price. Mathematically, this may be expressed as follows:

$$B_0 = \sum \frac{E(\text{coupon})_t}{(1 + K_{ca})^t} + \frac{E(\text{face value})}{(1 + K_{ca})^T} - C_0$$

where B_0 = present value of callable bond
$E(\text{coupon})_t$ = expected coupon payment in year t
$E(\text{face value})$ = expected face value if bond is
refunded at maturity   (43)
K_{ca} = true cost of issuing a callable bond
C_0 = present value of call feature

The expression above is similar to the earlier analysis of convertible debt except that instead of giving the bondholders something of value, namely, the right to convert, with callable bonds the firm is withholding something of value because the call provision limits the amount of capital gain the bondholder can earn.

Investors are usually given some call protection. During the first few years an issue may not be callable. In addition, a premium may be paid when a bond is called. Often this amount becomes smaller, the closer the bond is to its scheduled maturity date. Sometimes an entire issue may be called and other times only specific bonds, drawn by lot by a trustee, are called. In either case, a notice of redemption will appear in advance in the financial press.

Sinking Funds.   Certain bond indenture provisions require the firm to make annual payments into a sinking fund. In this way a portion of the debt outstanding is repaid each year instead of having the entire amount come due at maturity. The corporation may pay cash to the bond trustee, who can then purchase bonds in the open market. Alternately, the firm itself may purchase the bonds, then deposit them with the trustee.

Serial bonds also allow for a portion of a debt issue to be repaid each year. The only difference is that the refunding is done at face value on a prescheduled basis.

The Refunding Decision.   A careful economic analysis, which is fundamentally no different from that entailed by a project selection or capital budgeting decision, must precede the decision to refund. Usually, a firm will consider refunding if a bond has a call provision and if market interest rates have fallen below the coupon rate on the outstanding bonds. The differences of four cost components have to be contrasted against the value of the interest savings. These costs are: (1) the **call premium,** which is tax deductible, (2) the **flotation costs** on the issue of new debt, which can be deducted for tax purposes as an expense amortized over the life of the new bond, (3) the **unamortized portion of the flotation cost** on the outstanding issue; this may be recognized immediately as a tax-deductible expense, however, this must be netted out against the present value of the flotation costs that would have been amortized, and (4) **additional interest** paid because the old bond issue will be outstanding for a short period of time while the new bond has been issued. The present value of these costs can be subtracted from the present value of the interest savings to determine the net present value of the refunding decision. See Weston and Brigham (*Managerial Finance,* 6th ed., pp. 526–530) for a detailed example of a **bond refunding analysis.**

PRIVATE VERSUS PUBLIC PLACEMENT OF BONDS.   Nearly half of all corporate bond sales are issued through private placements sold to insurance companies, pension funds, and other private holders. **Private placement** is the major alternative to underwritten issues of bonds to the public. The principal advantages of private placements are: (1) transactions costs are lower, especially for smaller issues where flotation costs on public issues would be prohibitively high, (2) indenture provisions and the timing of repayment can easily be tailored to meet the needs of both lender and borrower, (3) privately placed issues need not be registered with the **Securities and Exchange Commission,** (4) if the borrowing corporation runs into financial difficulties, the terms of the loan may be more easily renegotiated, and (5) the borrowing firm can schedule to take in funds as needed rather than all at once, as is necessary with a public issue.

The disadvantages of private placements are: (1) they lack marketability because a market has not been established through a public offering, (2) the issuing firm loses the opportunity to repurchase the bonds through open market operations if interest rates fall, and (3) because institutional lenders are sophisticated and frequently much larger than the borrowing corporation, they can exact **indenture restrictions** that are often more restrictive than those on equivalent public offerings.

PREFERRED STOCK.   Preferred stock is given preference over common stock in respect to dividends. Also, in the event of reorganization or bankruptcy, preferred stock has precedence. On the other hand, preferred stock dividends can be paid only after all interest payments on debt have been made, and in bankruptcy, preferred claims are strictly subordinate to all debt claims. Hence preferred stock is a hybrid security, riskier than debt but less risky than common stock.

Par Value.   Unlike the par value of common stock, the par value of preferred stock is a meaningful quantity. First, it establishes the amount of the claim that preferred shareholders have on the assets of the firm in the event of bankruptcy; second, preferred dividends are usually paid as a percentage of par value.

Cumulative Dividend Feature.   Most preferred stock has a cumulative dividend feature. It is a protective device for preferred shareholders because it requires that all past preferred dividends must be paid before any common dividends may be paid.

As mentioned earlier, about 40% of preferred issues are convertible. For example, a share of preferred might be convertible into four shares of common at the discretion of the preferred stockholder. The conversion feature is valuable to preferred shareholders, and they are more willing to accept a lower preferred dividend rate on convertible preferred than on straight preferred. Of course, the lower coupon rate means that the firm has to pay out less cash flow.

Voting Rights.   Sometimes preferred stock is given voting rights, which allow preferred shareholders to elect a minority of the company's board of directors, say two out of ten. Generally the voting privilege takes effect only when preferred dividends have not been paid for a while.

Participating Preferred.   This rare type of security provides for preferred shareholders to receive a predetermined dividend, say $1 per share, for common shareholders to receive dividends up to some fixed amount, say an extra $1 per share, and then for preferred and common shareholders to share in any earnings beyond the first $2 per share.

Although preferred stock usually has no maturity date, sometimes an effective date is established by arranging a **sinking fund** requirement whereby a fixed portion of the out- standing preferred issue must be repurchased in the open market each year.

Another way of retiring preferred is to have a **call provision.** For example, the firm may be able to call in preferred stock with a par value of $100 if a **call premium** of $8 per share is paid. That is, preferred shareholders would be paid $108 per share.

COMMON STOCK.   Whether publicly or privately held, common stock is the riskiest of the major forms of financing. Common shareholders are the residual claimants on the assets of the firm in the event of bankruptcy and receive dividends only after all payments on debt and preferred stock have been completed. However, common stockholders have certain **collective rights.** They elect the corporate board of directors; they may amend the charter of incorporation; they can adopt and amend the firm's bylaws; and they can authorize the sale of fixed assets, enter into mergers, change the amount of authorized common stock, and issue preferred stock, debentures, bonds, and other securities. As individual shareholders they have specific rights, which include voting for directors, selling their stock certificates, and inspecting the corporate books (within certain limits).

Cumulative Voting.   The most common technique for selecting a **board of directors,** cumulative voting permits a shareholder to cast multiple votes for a single director. For example, suppose the firm has 10 directors and Mr. Jones owns 800 shares of stock. Then

Mr. Jones will be given 8,000 votes, all of which may be cast for a single director instead of requiring that 800 votes be given to each of 10 nominees on the slate of directors. The significance of cumulative voting is that minority groups of shareholders can be assured of electing some directors to the board. For a more complete description of cumulative voting, see Weston and Brigham (*Managerial Finance,* 6th ed., pp. 486–488).

Par Value. For common stock, this is an arbitrary accounting designation. For example, if 1 million new shares are issued at $50 each with a $1 par value, $49 million would be recorded in the equity portion of the balance sheet as **common-in-excess-of-par** and $1 million would be recorded as **common-at-par.** However, the selection of a par value is arbitrary. The stock could as easily have a $5 par value or no par value at all. In fact, many corporations issue no par value common stock.

Classified Common Stock. There are voting and nonvoting classes of common stock usually called class A and class B. These designations are sometimes used by new companies seeking to acquire external equity. Class A common will be sold to the public with full voting rights and paying dividends. Class B stock will be retained by the original owners of the firm, will have voting rights, but will not pay individuals until the earnings power of the firm has been established.

Founders' Shares. These are like the class B shares except that they have sole voting rights and do not pay dividends for a predetermined number of years.

Preemptive Right. The preemptive right gives holders of common the first option to purchase additional shares of common stock. Its primary purpose is to protect shareholders against dilution of value when new shares are issued. Shareholders of record may use their preemptive right to purchase new shares, or they can sell the right to someone else who will use it to purchase shares. A second purpose of the preemptive right is to maintain control of the firm in the hands of current shareholders. Without preemptive rights, management could theoretically issue a large number of new shares at a low price, then buy the new shares and gain control of the company.

To illustrate the use of preemptive rights, suppose that the XYZ Corp. currently has earnings of $1 million; 100,000 shares are outstanding, and the market price of a share is currently $100. Earnings per share is $10, the price-earnings ratio is 10, and the market value of the firm's equity is $10 million. Furthermore, assume that the firm wants to raise an additional $5 million in equity via a rights offering. The following questions come to mind:

- What should the terms of the right be?
- How many rights will be required to purchase a share of the newly issued stock?
- What is the value of each right?
- What effect will the rights have on the price of the existing stock?

Let us begin by assuming that the value of the firm's equity will rise $15 million. It might be higher if shareholders believe that the need to issue new equity is a signal that the company's earnings will increase as it undertakes new projects. It might be less if the firm is departing from an optimal long-run capital structure.

Furthermore, suppose that the new shares are to be sold for $62.50 each. This is a considerable discount from the current price of $100, but it ensures that the rights will have a value high enough to permit shareholders to exercise the rights and cover the transactions costs involved. If the price per share were higher, the value of rights would fall and fewer shareholders might exercise their rights.

Ex Rights Procedures.   The number of new shares is determined by dividing the dollar amount of the issue by the price per share as shown below.

$$\text{number of new shares} = \frac{\text{funds to be raised}}{\text{price per share}}$$

$$\text{number of new shares} = \frac{\$5,000,000}{\$62.50} = 80,000 \text{ shares}$$

Currently, there are 100,000 shares outstanding. If we divide the number of old shares by the number of new shares, we obtain the number of rights needed to purchase one new share. Each shareholder receives one right per share but needs 1.25 rights to purchase one new share. Therefore, a stockholder will have to turn in 1.25 rights and $80 to acquire a new share. We now know the number of rights per share. The terms of the rights issue will include the foregoing information and will allow a predetermined amount of time for share-holders of record to exercise their rights. Usually an **ex-rights date** represents the start of the formal rights offering. All shareholders of record as of that date will be given rights. Even though rights are valuable and should be sold or exercised, some stockholders will nevertheless neglect to do so. Therefore, rights offerings usually have an **oversubscription privilege** that allows subscribing stockholders the right to purchase all unsubscribed rights on a pro rata basis.

Next, what is the value of a right and what effect will the rights offering have on the current value of the stock? If we continue to assume that the value of equity after the offering will be $15 million, the price per share will be the total market value of equity divided by the number of shares outstanding.

$$\text{new price per share} = \frac{\text{assumed market value of equity}}{\text{total number of shares}}$$

$$\text{new price per share} = \frac{\$15,000,000}{180,000 \text{ shares}} = \$83.33$$

Therefore, after the financing is completed the price per share will have fallen from $100 to $83.33. Usually the price before the ex-rights date (i.e., $100) is referred to as the price **rights on.** After the ex-rights date the stock price will fall to $83.33 and is called the **ex-rights price.**

For an explicit mathematical derivation of the value of a right, the reader is referred to Smith (*Journal of Financial Economics,* December 1977, pp. 302–304). However, a much simpler approximation is given below. The value of one right, **ex-rights,** is equal to

$$\text{value of one right} = \frac{\text{ex-rights value of stock} - \text{subscription price}}{\text{number of rights per share}}$$

$$\text{value of one right} = \frac{\$83.33 - \$62.50}{1.25} = \$16.67$$

What is the effect of a rights offering on the wealth of a shareholder? Suppose John Doe owned 100 shares of the XYZ Corp. before the rights offering. At $100 per share, his wealth was $10,000. After the rights offering the price per share falls to $83.33, but Doe receives 100 rights, each worth $16.67 in cash. Therefore, the total value of his shares, $8,333, plus the value of his rights, $1,667, is just equal to his original wealth, $10,000. From an arithmetic viewpoint, the shareholder neither gains nor loses from the rights offering.

Underwritten Issues.   There is one main alternative to rights offerings as a means of providing new equity capital to the firm: underwritten issues of stock. In fact, 90% of new equity issues are made via underwritings (see Smith, *Journal of Financial Economics,* December 1977). **Underwriting services** are provided by **investment banking firms,** which write up the required SEC registration statement, guarantee a negotiated price per share to the firm, and form a syndicate to stabilize the price of the new issue and market it.

Firm Commitment.   In this type of underwriting agreement, the underwriting syndicate buys the security issue from the firm and resells it to the public. The firm is therefore guaranteed a net amount from the issue. The underwriting syndicate takes the risk of a decline in the market price between the time the investment banker transmits the money to the firm and the time the securities are placed in the hands of their ultimate buyers. In return for accepting this risk, the underwriter receives a fee that is the difference between the price at which the securities are offered to the public and net amount received by the firm. Sometimes, part of the fee is paid by giving warrants to the investment banker.

Best Efforts.   A type of underwriting less frequently used is called a **best efforts** commitment. In this case the underwriter acts only as the marketing agent for the firm. The underwriter does not agree to purchase the issue at a predetermined price, but sells the security for whatever price it will bring. The underwriter takes a predetermined spread and the firm takes the residual.

There has been a considerable amount of academic research on public issues of new equity. Two recent studies are of particular interest. Ibbotson (*Journal of Financial Economics,* September 1975) investigates the rates of return on newly issued equity and Smith compares the **costs of underwritten issues** with the **costs of rights offerings.**

The study by Ibbotson selected a random sample of 120 new issues between 1960 and 1969 (one issue each month) from among the 2,650 new issues during that time period. Using a procedure to adjust the rate of return for the riskiness of the new issue, he measured the abnormal rate of return on new issues. An **abnormal rate of return** is the rate above (or below) that which is required for investments in securities of equal risk. Ibbotson found that there was an abnormal rate of return during the month of issue but not thereafter. He concluded that the offering price, which is the price at which the underwriting syndicate sells to the public, is set below the equilibrium market price at the time of the issue. This abnormal rate of return does not go to the investment bankers. Rather it is "earned" by investors who buy new issues.

Smith has studied the costs of underwriting versus rights offerings. Exhibit 19 shows a cost comparison of firm commitment underwritings, rights offerings with standby underwriting, and simple rights offerings. The paradox is that although rights offerings appear to have the lowest cost as a percentage of proceeds, almost 90% of new issues are underwritten.

STOCK SPLITS AND STOCK DIVIDENDS.   **Stock splits** and **stock dividends** do not provide any additional capital for the firm, but they do change the number of shares out-

EXHIBIT 19 COSTS OF FLOTATION AS A PERCENTAGE OF PROCEEDS FOR 578 COMMON STOCK ISSUES REGISTERED UNDER THE SECURITIES ACT OF 1933 DURING 1971–1975[a]

Size of Issues ($ Millions)	Underwriting				Rights with Standby Underwriting				Rights	
	Number	Compensation (% of Proceeds)	Other Expenses (% of Proceeds)	Total Cost (% of Proceeds)	Number	Compensation (% of Proceeds)	Other Expenses (% of Proceeds)	Total Cost (% of Proceeds)	Number	Total Cost (% of Proceeds)
Under 0.50	0	—	—	—	0	—	—	—	3	8.99
0.50–0.99	6	6.96	6.78	13.74	2	3.43	4.80	8.24	2	4.59
1.00–1.99	18	10.40	4.89	15.29	5	6.36	4.15	10.51	5	4.90
2.00–4.99	61	6.59	2.87	9.47	9	5.20	2.85	8.06	7	2.85
5.00–9.99	66	5.50	1.53	7.03	4	3.92	2.18	6.10	6	1.39
10.00–19.99	91	4.84	0.71	5.55	10	4.14	1.21	5.35	3	0.72
20.00–49.99	156	4.30	0.37	4.67	12	3.84	0.90	4.74	1	0.52
50.00–99.99	70	3.97	0.21	4.18	9	3.96	0.74	4.70	2	0.21
100.00–500.00	16	3.81	0.14	3.95	5	3.50	0.50	4.00	9	0.13
Total/average	484	5.02	1.15	6.17	56	4.32	1.73	6.05	38	2.45

[a]Issues are included only if the company's stock was listed on the NYSE, AMEX, or regional exchanges prior to the offering, any associated secondary distribution represents less than 15% of the total proceeds of the issue, and the offering contains no other types of securities. The costs reported are (1) compensation received by investment bankers for underwriting services rendered, (2) legal fees, (3) accounting fees, (4) engineering fees, (5) trustees' fees, (6) listing fees, (7) printing and engraving expenses, (8) Securities and Exchange Commission registration fees, (9) Federal Revenue Stamps, and (10) state taxes.

Source: C. W. Smith, Jr., "Alternative Methods For Raising Capital, Rights vs. Underwritten Offerings," *Journal of Financial Economics,* December 1977.

standing, hence the price per share. One often hears that the motivation for stock splits is either to increase the wealth of shareholders (because, e.g., a $100 stock that splits 2 for 1 will be worth more than $50 per share after the split) or to secure the advantage that accrues because the split moves the price per share into an ideal price range where it becomes more "affordable," and therefore more liquid. Empirical studies have shown both the aforementioned ideas to be incorrect. Fama, Fisher, Jensen, and Roll (*International Economic Review*, February 1969) investigated the rates of return for stock for 940 stock splits between January 1927 and December 1959. They found that companies that had been doing well were the ones that underwent stock splits, but there was no abnormal performance either on the split date or during the following time interval. Stock splits do not offer any abnormal rates of return for shareholders.

Copeland (*Journal of Finance*, March 1979) studied the **liquidity of stocks following their splits.** He found that average trading volume declines relative to what it had been before the split, transactions costs increase as a percentage of value traded following stock splits, and bid-ask spreads as a percentage of the value traded increase following splits. Therefore, he concluded that the relative liquidity of stocks declines following splits. This is the opposite of the liquidity motive mentioned above. In sum, no one has yet discovered a good rationale for stock splits or stock dividends.

REFERENCES

American Bar Association, *Commentaries on Model Debenture Indenture Provisions*, Chicago, 1971.

Baranek, W., "The WACC Criterion and Shareholder Wealth Maximization," *Journal of Financial and Quantitative Analysis*, March 1977, pp. 17–32.

Baxter, N. D., "Leverage, Risk of Ruin and the Cost of Capital," *Journal of Finance*, September 1967, pp. 395–403.

Black, F., and Scholes, M. S., "The Pricing of Options and Corporate Liabilities," *Journal of Political Economy*, May–June 1973.

Brennan, M. J., and Schwartz, E. S., "Convertible Bonds: Valuation and Optimal Strategies for Call and Conversion," *Journal of Finance*, December 1977, pp. 1699–1715.

Cargill, Thomas F., "The Term Structure of Interest Rates: A Test of the Expectations Hypothesis," *Journal of Finance*, June 1975, pp. 761–771.

Copeland, T. E., "Liquidity Changes Following Stock Splits," *Journal of Finance*, March 1979.

———, and Weston, J. Fred, *Financial Theory and Corporate Policy*, Addison-Wesley, Reading, MA, 1979.

Dobson, Steven; Sutch, Richard; and Vanderford, David, "An Evaluation of Alternative Empirical Models of the Term Structure of Interest Rates," *Journal of Finance*, September 1976, pp. 1035–1065.

Fama, E., Fisher, L., Jensen, M., and Roll, R., "The Adjustment of Stock Prices to New Information," *International Economic Review*, February 1969, pp. 1–21.

Farrar, D. E., and Selwyn, L., "Taxes, Corporate Financial Policies and Returns to Investors," *National Tax Journal*, December 1967, pp. 444–454.

Galai, D., and Masulis, R., "The Option Pricing Model and the Risk Factor of Stock," *Journal of Financial Economics*, January–March 1976, pp. 53–81.

Hamada, R. S., "The Effect of the Firm's Capital Structure on the Systematic Risk of Common Stocks," *Journal of Finance*, May 1972, pp. 435–452.

Ibbotson, R., "Price Performance of Common Stock New Issues," *Journal of Financial Economics*, September 1975, pp. 235–272.

Jensen, M., and Meckling, W., "Theory of the Firm: Managerial Behavior, Agency Costs, and Ownership Structure," *Journal of Financial Economics,* October 1976, pp. 305–360.

Kalay, A., "Toward a Theory of Corporate Dividend Policy," unpublished Ph.D. thesis, University of Rochester, Rochester, NY, 1979.

Kim, E. H., "A Mean-Variance Theory of Optimal Capital Structure and Corporate Debt Capacity," *Journal of Finance,* March 1978, pp. 45–64.

Lewellen, W., Long, M., and McConnell, J., "Asset Leasing in Competitive Capital Markets," *Journal of Finance,* June 1976, pp. 787–798.

Lintner, J., "The Valuation of Risk Assets and the Selection of Risky Investments in Stock Portfolios and Capital Budgets," *Review of Economics and Statistics,* February 1965, pp. 13–37.

Miller, M., and Upton, C., "Leasing, Buying and the Cost of Capital Services," *Journal of Finance,* June 1976, pp. 761–786.

Miller, M. H., "Debt and Taxes," *Journal of Finance,* May 1977, pp. 261–275.

Modigliani, F., and Miller, M. H., "The Cost of Capital, Corporation Finance, and the Theory of Investment," *American Economic Review,* June 1958, pp. 261–297.

———, "Corporate Income Taxes and the Cost of Capital," *American Economic Review,* June 1963, pp. 433–443.

———, "Some Estimates of the Cost of Capital to the Electric Utility Industry, 1954–57," *American Economic Review,* June 1966, pp. 333–348.

Modigliani, F., and Pogue, G., "An Introduction to Risk and Return," *Financial Analysts Journal,* March–April 1974, May–June 1974, pp. 68–80, 69–85.

Mossin, J. "Equilibrium in a Capital Asset Market," *Econometrica,* October 1966, pp. 768–783.

Myers, S., Dill, D., and Bautista, S., "Valuation of Financial Lease Contract," *Journal of Finance,* June 1976, pp. 799–819.

Myers, S. C. "Determinants of Corporate Borrowing," *Journal of Financial Economics,* November 1977, pp. 147–175.

Roll, Richard, *The Behavior of Interest Rates,* Basic Books, New York, 1970.

Rubinstein, M. E., "A Mean-Variance Synthesis of Corporate Financial Theory," *Journal of Finance,* March 1973, pp. 167–181.

Schall, L., "The Lease-or-Buy and Asset Acquisition Decisions," *Journal of Finance,* September 1974, pp. 1203–1214.

Sharpe, W. F., "Capital Asset Prices: A Theory of Market Equilibrium Under Conditions of Risk," *Journal of Finance,* September 1964, pp. 425–442.

Smith, C. W., Jr., "Alternative Methods for Raising Capital: Rights vs. Underwritten Offerings," *Journal of Financial Economics, December 1977, pp. 273–308.*

———, and Warner, J. B., "On Financial Contracting: An Analysis of Bond Covenants," *Journal of Financial Economics,* June 1979, pp. 117–161.

Stiglitz, J. E., "A Re-Examination of the Modigliani-Miller Theorem," *American Economic Review,* December 1969, pp. 784–793.

———, "On the Irrelevance of Corporate Financial Policy," *American Economic Review,* December 1974, pp. 851–866.

Wakeman, Lee M., "Bond Rating Agencies and the Capital Markets," Working Paper, Graduate School of Management, University of Rochester, Rochester, NY, 1978.

Weinstein, Mark I., "The Effect of a Rating Change Announcement on Bond Price," *Journal of Financial Economics,* December 1977, pp. 329–350.

———, "The Seasoning Process of New Corporate Bond Issues," *Journal of Finance,* December 1978, pp. 1343–1354.

Weston, J. F., and Brigham, E. F., *Managerial Finance,* 6th ed., Dryden Press, Hinsdale, IL, 1978.

DIVIDEND POLICY

CONTENTS

TYPES OF DIVIDEND	**5**
Preferred Stock Dividends	5
Common Stock Dividends	6
Stock dividends and stock splits	6
Other forms of dividend	6
MECHANICS OF DIVIDEND DECLARATION AND PAYMENT	**7**
BOARD OF DIRECTORS AND DIVIDEND DECLARATIONS	**8**
POSTDIVIDEND DECLARATION ACTIVITIES	**11**
Ex-Dividend Date	11
Transfer Agents and Cash Management	11
Dividend Changes or Cancellations	12
WHAT IS A DIVIDEND POLICY?	**12**
Announcement Considerations	13
Dividend Clientele	13
WHEN SHOULD A CORPORATION ADOPT A FORMAL DIVIDEND POLICY?	**13**
Composition of Board of Directors	14
Policy Maintenance and Review	14

DETERMINANTS OF DIVIDEND POLICY	**14**
Cyclicality	14
Stages of Growth	18
Profitability	19
Cash Generation	19
TIMING OF DIVIDEND POLICY	**20**
INVESTOR EXPECTATIONS AND NEEDS	**20**
Owner Versus Manager Control	20
Tax Considerations	21
Dividend Reinvestment Plans	21
CAPITAL STRUCTURE AND DIVIDEND POLICY	**21**
INSOLVENCY TESTS AND CORPORATE DISTRIBUTIONS	**22**
THEORY AND EMPIRICAL EVIDENCE	**22**
Theoretical Controversy	22
Conceptual Models and Empirical Evidence	23
Behavioral models	23
Clientele effect models	24
Information and announcement effects	25

DIVIDEND POLICY

John T. Hackett

In addressing the issue of dividend policy, management and the **board of directors** must make decisions regarding the allocation of its **shareholders' returns** in terms of immediate and/or future benefits. From the shareholders' standpoint, the decision as to how profits are to be divided between dividends and reinvestment is paramount. Management must be sensitive to their shareholders' concerns and aware that dividend decisions are complex.

Over the past 10 years, industrial corporations in the United States have paid out approximately 40% of their total aftertax profits as cash dividends, as shown in Exhibit 1. The remainder of industrial company earnings has been retained for investment in additional fixed assets, working capital, or acquisition of existing businesses.

This section describes the role of dividend policy in corporate financial management. **Corporate dividend policy** is not understood by a large segment of the financial community. There is a misconception that dividend policy is a straightforward and simple aspect of finance as compared with the more technical areas such as taxation, liquidity management, and cost accounting. Some observers of corporate behavior assume that dividend policy is determined easily because dividends represent only the unused portion of corporate profits available to equity investors.

Dividends represent payment to the shareholders for use of **risk capital,** as does the increase in share prices. In a sense, dividends are similar to the payments to suppliers of labor and materials and to the interest payments paid to suppliers of credit. The primary difference is that common stock dividends are not paid as a matter of contractual requirement.

Tax policies, both federal and state, discriminate between those who receive their return on investment as dividends and those who receive interest as creditors. **Interest,** of course, **is a tax-deductible item** to the corporation, whereas dividend payments to shareholders are paid from **profits earned after the payment of taxes.** Legislation to remedy tax treatment differentiation between dividends and interest income have been proposed, but not as a means of eliminating the difference in status between capital sources. The justification for the proposed tax reform is based on a need to **increase capital formation** and **productivity** in the United States.

There are many other interested and affected parties involved in dividend policy determination, including creditors, suppliers, and representatives of labor who seek to influence the determination of the share of current corporate earnings that will go to equity investors rather than being retained by the corporation for other purposes.

The author acknowledges, with appreciation, the sections on "Theory and Empirical Evidence" written by the editor, Edward I. Altman.

EXHIBIT 1   DIVIDEND PAYOUT

	1970	1971	1972	1973	1974	1975	1976	1977	1978	1979
VALUE LINE INDUSTRIAL COMPOSITE										
Earnings per share	$1.32	1.47	1.66	2.23	2.52	2.17	2.76	3.03	3.46	4.87
Dividends per share	$0.74	0.73	0.74	0.80	0.88	0.89	1.01	1.18	1.30	1.50
Net dividend payout (%)	56	50	45	36	35	41	37	39	38	31
STANDARD & POOR'S INDUSTRIALS										
Earnings per share	$5.41	5.97	6.83	8.89	9.61	8.58	10.68	11.56	13.12	16.23
Dividends per share	$3.20	3.16	3.22	3.46	3.71	3.72	4.25	4.96	5.35	6.04
Net dividend payout (%)	59	53	47	39	39	43	40	43	41	37

10-YEAR AVERAGE NET PAYOUTS

Value Line	41%
Standard & Poor's 400	44%

Sources: Value Line Investment Survey, New York, 1980; Standard & Poor's Corp. *Statistics*, S & P, New York, 1980.

TYPES OF DIVIDEND

In describing dividends, a major distinction exists between dividends paid to **preferred shareholders** and to **common shareholders.** Although both classes represent equity investors, there are significant distinctions in terms of payment of dividends and the right of each class of shareholder with respect to claims on corporate earnings.

PREFERRED STOCK DIVIDENDS.   Preferred shareholders are just that. They hold a preferred position with respect to dividend payments. In addition, there may be distinctions among preferred shareholders regarding rights to dividends. Preferred shareholders are usually entitled to a stated dividend before common shareholders receive any dividend. Unlike common stock, both the terms of dividend payment and the rate for preferred are set down in a contractual agreement between the corporation and the shareholder. Agreement regarding the amount of dividends to be received by preferred shareholders is set at the time of the issuance of preferred shares. Unlike common shares, preferred shares receive a **fixed dividend rate,** stated as a percentage of the face value or dollar amount of the preferred shares.

Failure to pay a preferred share dividend usually results in an obligation to pay at a later time, which is referred to as a **cumulative dividend** privilege. A cumulative clause in a preferred shareholders' agreement requires that if a corporation fails to pay a preferred share dividend, or series of dividends, the corporation incurs a liability to pay the dividend at a later time and no common share dividends may be paid as long as such cumulative dividend liabilities on preferred shares remain outstanding. If preferred share dividends are not paid for a prolonged period, preferred shareholders may assume other rights such as the right to select a number of the members of the corporate **board of directors,** approve the issuance of additional preferred shares to existing shareholders, or financial obligation rights senior to those of existing preferred shareholders in the event of corporate liquidation.

Preferred shares may also be classified on the basis of seniority with respect to receipt of dividends. **Straight preferred shares** usually enjoy a senior claim on dividend payments over **convertible preferred shares,** which carry a **subordinated position** both in terms of dividend payments and claim on assets in the event of liquidation. In most instances, straight preferred shares carry a higher dividend rate than convertible preferred shares. However, convertible preferred shares can be converted into a fixed number of common shares of the issuing corporation. The **conversion ratio** is part of the contract between the preferred shareholders and the corporation. In addition, there may be several classes of straight preferred shares with differing rates of dividends and claims on dividends and assets. Agreements between issuing corporations and preferred shareholders sometimes prevent the issuance of additional preferred shares with preferential or even equal dividend rights. In such instances, the corporation may have created a **subordinated straight preferred issue.** The differentiation of the rights of preferred shareholders are sometimes complex.

Most preferred share issues are purchased by institutional investors. The shares are frequently acquired by a **direct (private) placement** with a contract between the issuing corporation and the institutional investor. In arranging the direct placement, elaborate contracts are created to protect the investors. In isolated instances, preferred shareholders may be entitled to dividends other than cash.

The only common differentiation between the values placed on straight preferred shares and on convertible preferred shares is an increase or decrease in the value of common shares that the convertible preferred may have rights to under a convertible preferred issuance agreement. Fluctuations in common share price are normally reflected in the market price of a convertible preferred share.

COMMON STOCK DIVIDENDS.   Nearly all **common stock dividends** fall into two groups: cash and shares. The most familiar form of common stock dividend is a cash payment declared by the **board of directors** and paid **quarterly.** However, it is not uncommon for a corporation to declare additional shares of stock as a dividend. In those instances, the dividend is referred to as a stock dividend. **Stock dividends** and **stock splits** are quite different, although they are frequently assumed to be the same.

Stock Dividends and Stock Splits.   When a **stock dividend** is paid, the **retained earnings or capital surplus** of the corporation is debited and the capital shares account is credited. In addition, the company must have sufficient authorized and unissued shares available; otherwise, an amendment to the charter increasing the authorized shares will have to occur first. Such an amendment normally requires a shareholder meeting. A stock dividend requires no change in **par value.** Stock dividends are declared less frequently than cash dividends and do not follow a uniform pattern, as contrasted with cash dividends.

Unlike a stock dividend, a **stock split** does not affect the retained earnings or the capital surplus account. The capital shares account is also unaffected when a stock split is declared. A stock split does require a change in par value, but the surplus accounts remain unaffected. A corporation may also employ a **reverse stock split** to reduce the number of shares outstanding and increase the par value and market value of the remaining shares. A reverse split, for example, of 1 for 4, will reduce the number of shares outstanding by three-quarters and increase the price fourfold.

There are several reasons a management and board of directors may prefer to pay a stock dividend. For example, a very high price on existing shares, an effort to increase the number of shares outstanding, a desire to increase the number of shareholders, or a desire to retain a larger share of the earnings of the corporation are common reasons a corporation may elect to pay a stock dividend. There is widespread disagreement regarding the benefits that accrue to a shareholder as a result of stock dividends. It appears that when a shareholder receives a stock dividend, he only holds additional pieces of paper rather than receiving an actual increase in wealth. However, proponents of stock dividends contend that there is a benefit from a well-timed and well-designed stock dividend. It may **signal** to the investment community that the corporation is about to enter a new growth phase and, therefore, may result in an increased demand for the shares and improvement in share price. This so-called **dividend announcement effect** is discussed in a later subsection.

Common stock may also be categorized in terms of dividend payments. Some corporations issue different classes of common stock, for example, a **class A and class B common stock.** That is, one class of stock is given a preference with respect to dividend payments and certain liquidation rights; the remaining class may be subordinated with respect to initial dividend payments but the shareholders are entitled to voting rights and profit-sharing privileges not granted to the holders of other shares of common stock outstanding. The **dividend payment** declared may also differ between classes of common stock.

Other Forms of Dividend.   Corporations may issue other forms of dividend, but it is uncommon. Issuance of **warrants** to existing shareholders may represent a type of dividend. Warrants give shareholders the right to purchase additional shares of stock at predetermined prices for a predetermined period of time. If a warrant permits the shareholder to buy additional shares at a price below the current market price and the warrants themselves are traded with a positive value, the shareholder can realize benefits without actually exercising the warrants and purchasing shares.

Preferred shares or debt securities may be issued by corporations as a form of dividend. These instruments are referred to as **bond or scrip dividends.** When a debt security is issued, the corporation is issuing a promise to pay rather than disbursing actual cash.

A corporation may elect to issue warrants, preferred shares, or debt at a time when it is experiencing a shortage of cash or rapid growth when earnings and cash are required to finance the growth or stability of the corporation. The shareholder may be afforded an opportunity to share in future profits by receiving **warrants** or **preferred shares as dividends.** If a corporation elects to employ these techniques for dividend policy, a careful examination of the tax impact on both the corporation and the shareholder should be determined before the actual declaration of the dividend.

Although it is uncommon, in some instances corporations distribute **property dividends.** For example, corporations might distribute products to shareholders as a dividend. Small manufacturers of consumer goods may elect to employ this technique, but it is rarely used. Again, it is important that the tax impact on both the corporation and the shareholders be carefully examined.

Corporations have declared property dividends in which shares of another corporation were distributed to shareholders. A large corporation may choose to dispose of a subsidiary by issuing the shares of the subsidiary directly to its existing shareholders. A large holding in another independent corporation may also be disposed of in this fashion; for example, **General Electric Co.** disposed of **RCA** shares in this fashion. There may be advantages to the shareholders, but the tax implications are complex.

MECHANICS OF DIVIDEND DECLARATION AND PAYMENT

The declaration of a dividend to holders of either preferred or common shares requires a **resolution of the board of directors** of the corporation. In addition, there may be **legal requirements** that must be met before a dividend is declared. The laws of the state that chartered the corporation may impose restrictions on the nature and size of dividends. Corporate laws as well as the tax laws of the state of incorporation should be considered before a dividend resolution is acted on by the board of directors. The **bylaws** of the corporation must be examined and understood by corporate management. A corporation may have adopted bylaws that place restrictions on the declaration of dividends, or it may have entered into agreements with creditors, preferred shareholders, or certain classes of common shareholders that restrict its ability to pay dividends.

Large corporations with outstanding issues of debt securities often have **covenants** within loan agreements that restrict the declaration of dividends. The most common restriction, or negative covenant, prohibits declaration of a dividend that would result in reducing the net worth of the corporation below an absolute figure or a multiple of the total debt outstanding. Other negative covenants may restrict the payment of dividends if earnings of the corporation do not equal a percentage or multiple of the corporation's past earnings. All restrictions on dividend payments are designed to protect the creditor's senior claim in the event of **liquidation or dissolution.**

The declaration of dividends on common shares are undertaken after preferred share dividend requirements are satisfied. A **board of directors** is usually unable to declare or pay a common share dividend in the event any past or present preferred share dividends remain outstanding.

Such restrictions differ according to the type of debt instrument or preference share outstanding. However, institutional lenders have attempted to adopt **uniform negative cov-**

enants. The trend toward uniformity also reflects the influence of **investment banking firms** that act as intermediaries between institutional lenders and the corporations issuing the debt securities.

Foreign corporations are frequently subject to restrictions on dividend payments to shareholders who are not citizens or residents of the country in which the business is incorporated or the assets located. Such restrictions are usually a part of foreign exchange control legislation that is administered by a central bank or a ministry of finance. Restrictions may be placed on the actual declaration and payment of the dividend, or they may prohibit the shareholder from converting the dividend to another currency and withdrawing it from the country in which the dividend was declared. These restrictions are usually complex and are common among developing countries that experience deficits in their balance of payments or difficulty in accumulating sufficient capital to finance economic growth. For an in-depth discussion on this and other related topics, see the section "Financial Decisions for Multinational Enterprises" in this *Handbook*.

The most complex predividend declaration requirements involve the tax implications for both the corporation and the shareholders. Federal, state, and local governments may tax cash dividends as well as other dividend payments. The complexity and diversity of the tax legislation surrounding dividends is a subject that cannot be adequately treated in this section. It is sufficient to caution the reader that an understanding of the tax requirements and implications of a dividend declaration should be thoroughly understood before the actual resolution or declaration by the board of directors. Once a dividend is declared, it is a **legal liability of the corporation.**

Subsidiaries of corporations, both foreign and domestic, may declare dividends payable to the parent corporation as a means of transferring profits. Such dividends may be complex in terms of regulations. When a foreign corporation declares a dividend to a U.S. parent company, there must be an understanding of tax policy and the finance and foreign trade policy of the country in which the subsidiary is located. These issues play a significant role in determining the form and timing of dividends.

Before presenting a recommendation to the **board of directors** regarding dividends, corporate management should be thoroughly familiar with all the limitations placed on dividends by creditors, preference shareholders, and tax and economic policies of local, state, federal, and foreign governments.

Planning for dividend payments requires that in the event of the declaration of either a cash or a stock dividend, the corporation have sufficient cash or unissued shares available for payment of the dividend on the date that the board of directors selects for actual payment. A large dividend payment may require careful cash planning. Corporate management must be assured that all the laws of the state of incorporation have been satisfied regarding authorized but unissued shares in the event that a stock dividend is declared. For example, some states may prohibit issuance of **treasury shares** for a **stock dividend.** States may also require the payment of a tax on newly authorized shares before their actual issuance.

BOARD OF DIRECTORS AND DIVIDEND DECLARATIONS

State laws require a resolution of the **board of directors of a corporation** to declare the payment of any form of dividend to shareholders. Since the board of directors is elected by the shareholders, it is appropriate that they represent the shareholder's interest in determining what portion of a corporation's past and present earnings should be distributed to the shareholders, or if the shareholders' interests are better served by reinvesting the profits. Therefore,

. in addition to declaring dividend payments at regular meetings, boards of directors period-ically review dividend policy. Most corporations declare dividends **quarterly.** Corporations may schedule board of directors meetings around dividend action dates and establish regular meetings once every three months. One of the principal purposes of such a meeting may be the declaration of a dividend.

The **format for dividend declaration** differs among corporations and is determined in part by the technique employed by management in proposing dividend action to the board of directors. The most commonly used technique is to provide the board of directors with a draft of a formal resolution that will be voted on following discussion. The proposed resolution may be approved, amended or rejected; however, total rejection of a management recommendation is uncommon. Corporations differ widely regarding their **approach to determination of dividend rate.** Some corporations consider a change in dividend payments only once a year and routinely declare a quarterly dividend based on the annual determination of the dividend rate. Others prefer to evaluate the dividend rate each quarter and adjust the rate in accordance with the quarterly profit performance of the corporation, expectations of shareholders, trends in the market price of the shares of the corporation, and other matters that the board of directors believe to be appropriate.

Dividend payments are commonly categorized as **regular, interim, extra, final, special,** and **liquidating. Regular dividends** are the cash dividends declared at regular intervals according to a published dividend rate. **Interim dividends** are usually the quarterly dividend payments based on a stated rate. **Final and extra dividends,** the amounts paid at the close of the fiscal year, represent the regular dividend plus an extra amount. **Special dividends** are sometimes called extra dividends, but usually refer to an isolated or special event, for example, profits that result from a nonrecurring event such as the sale of an asset. **Liquidating dividends** usually refer to a return of capital to shareholders as a result of sale of all or a portion of the assets and are treated differently for tax purposes.

Despite the differences in format, a formal written resolution of the board of directors is usually required to fulfill the legal requirements, and the **majority of the board** must approve the action. Approval by more than a majority may be required depending on the corporate charter, corporate bylaws, or restrictions resulting from loan and preferred share agreements.

The **timing of the dividend declaration** is in part dictated by the size of the corporation, the number of shareholders, the number of shares outstanding, the type of dividend declared, and the legal requirements of the state of incorporation. In addition, management usually prefers that dividends be declared well in advance of actual payment to provide appropriate time for postdeclaration requirements and other administrative duties associated with dividend declarations.

Exhibit 2 is a sample resolution that a board of directors might adopt in the declaration of a quarterly cash dividend. Exhibits 3 and 4 are examples of materials that management might provide the board of directors before the actual passage of the resolution to assure that such action does not violate negative covenants in a loan agreement or a dividend policy adopted previously by the board of directors.

EXHIBIT 2   BOARD OF DIRECTORS RESOLUTION: CASH DIVIDEND, COMMON STOCK

RESOLVED, a quarterly cash dividend of $0.50 per share on the outstanding common stock of the Company be and is declared payable on June 16, 1980, to shareholders of record on June 2, 1980.

EXHIBIT 3 LOAN COVENANT LIMITATIONS ON CASH DIVIDENDS

Maximum current liability that may be created at this time for cash dividends **declared** but not yet paid	$ 50,000,000
Maximum retained earnings available to date that may be **paid** over time in cash dividends	$150,000,000
Total cash requirement to pay the recommended quarterly cash dividend on	$ 5,000,000

EXHIBIT 4 RECOMMENDATION FOR DIVIDEND ACTION

Management recommends that the Board of Directors, at its April 20 meeting, declare a $0.50 per share dividend, payable June 16 to holders of record June 2. This action will maintain the dividend at the $2 per share annual rate paid since December 15, 1979. The total quarterly dividend payment will be $5 million.

CURRENT DIVIDEND POLICY

Since reviewing dividend policy at the June 1978 meeting, the Board of Directors has followed the "conservative" dividend policy guidelines:

Basic Policy Guideline	Constraints to Maintain Dividend Stability
30% of previous year's earnings per share	Maximum increase of 20% in 1 year, no decreases

The conservative guideline reflects these objectives:

Retain two-thirds of earnings to capitalize on outstanding investment opportunities over the next 5 years.

Maintain a conservative payment ratio so that the dividend rate can be maintained, and perhaps even increased, during recession periods when earnings growth is restricted.

Attempt to maintain a pattern of consistent and uninterrupted growth of dividends.

REVIEW OF RECENT ACTIONS

Since the September 1979 meeting, the Board of Directors has closely adhered to the conservative dividend policy by maintaining the $0.50 per share dividend rate for three quarters. This policy was confirmed at the December 1979 meeting when the traditional practice of increasing the dividend in the fourth quarter was not followed. In 1979 dividends per share paid were $1.80, which represents a payout of 29% of 1978 earnings.

RECOMMENDATION

It would be an unusual departure from our past practices to increase the dividend rate at this time. Considering that 1980 earnings may be only equal to 1979 earnings, it would be inappropriate to declare a dividend increase. On the other hand, a reduction in the dividend rate would depart from the policy of no decreases and might suggest a poorer financial performance than expected.

We recommend maintaining the current dividend rate.

POSTDIVIDEND DECLARATION ACTIVITIES

Among publicly held corporations, the SEC requires that the declaration of a dividend be made known by a public announcement immediately following the action by the **board of directors.** Exhibit 5 is a sample public announcement to inform shareholders and other interested parties of the action taken by the board of directors regarding dividend payments. Some corporations follow a practice of having the board of directors review the press release at the time the dividend is declared, to assure that the public statement reflects the intent of the board. It is important that both the resolution and the press release state clearly the date on which the dividend is to be paid, as well as the **record date,** the date on which the shareholders of record are to be the recipients of the dividend.

EX-DIVIDEND DATE.   If the shares of the corporation are traded on an organized securities exchange such as the **New York Stock Exchange** or the **American Stock Exchange,** notification of a dividend declaration must be given immediately to officials of the exchange stating the nature and amount of the dividend, the date on which the dividend is to be paid, and the record date. Following notification, an **ex-dividend date** will be established. The ex-dividend date is the trading day prior to the record date on which the price of the shares will be reduced by the amount of the dividend to be paid. Shareholders who purchase shares on or after the ex-dividend date will not receive the current declared dividend because there will not be sufficient time to record the change of ownership before the record date. The seller will be the recipient because his name will still appear on the corporate books on the record date. Therefore, the buyer deducts the value of the dividend from the purchase price. The adjustment is normally at the opening of the **ex-dividend trading day.** The ex-dividend price adjustment is necessary because of the time involved in recording a change in share ownership. In determining the price of the shares, the value of the dividend is deducted, assuring that the new buyer receives the dividend in the form of a reduced price. The seller, who will receive the dividend, has the value of the dividend deducted from the proceeds of the sale of shares. Of course, there are usually tax differentials for most investors on the receipt of dividends compared with capital gains. This might affect the movement of the share price **after the opening on the ex-dividend date.**

TRANSFER AGENTS AND CASH MANAGEMENT.   In addition to notifying the securities exchanges of the declaration of dividend, management must also maintain constant communication with the trust departments of commercial banks that act as the **shareholder registration** and **transfer agents** for the corporation. Maintenance of records of current

EXHIBIT 5   SAMPLE PUBLIC ANNOUNCEMENT OF QUARTERLY DIVIDEND

For Immediate Release
April 20, 1980

COMPANY DECLARES QUARTERLY DIVIDEND

The Board of Directors of the Company, a major manufacturer of components, today declared a quarterly dividend of 50 cents per share, payable June 16, 1980, to shareholders of record on June 2, 1980.

shareholders is a difficult process, particularly among large corporations whose shares are actively traded. The dividend payment process is made more difficult by active trading of shares, as well as by the brokerage house practice of registering shares in **"street names"** (i.e., custodian names) rather than in the names of the primary owners. The trust departments of commercial banks that issue dividend checks, or additional shares in the event a stock dividend is declared, work closely with the management of the paying corporation to assure that sufficient cash is maintained as dividend checks are presented. Large corporations usually maintain records regarding the time lag between issuance and presentation of dividend checks. The **cash management aspect of dividend payments** is an important part of overall cash management procedures.

DIVIDEND CHANGES OR CANCELLATIONS.   Occasionally a question arises regarding failure to pay a dividend following declaration or resolution by the board of directors. Corporate management normally has no authorization to take any action other than that prescribed in the dividend resolution. **A declared dividend** is a short-term debt of the corporation. If alternative actions are deemed necessary, the board of directors must amend the original resolution authorizing the payment of a dividend. Directors may also be held liable for declaring an **illegal dividend.**

When a foreign corporation or a foreign subsidiary of a U.S. corporation declares a dividend, the resolution of the board of directors may have to be approved by the central bank or the ministry of finance of the country in which the dividend-paying corporation is located or chartered before payment can be made. The foreign country authority may insist on approving the dividend action as well as the acquisition of foreign exchange associated with dividend payments to foreign shareholders. In developing countries, governmental authority may require an amendment to the dividend resolution or may even disapprove the entire action. Dividend payments and corporate dividend policy is an integral part of government economic policy among some developing nations.

WHAT IS A DIVIDEND POLICY?

Throughout most of the 1960s equity investors enjoyed a strong stock market and excellent returns in the form of capital appreciation. During this euphoric period it was popular to query whether dividend policy really mattered. During the 1970s the answer became clearer as the stock market faltered and once again dividends became more important to the investor. During the 1960s greater emphasis was placed on reinvestment of earnings on the assumption that the shareholder was better served by realizing capital appreciation on the expected increased market value of shares than by receiving increased cash dividends. However, as the market for equity issues began to deteriorate in the 1970s, dividend policy began to receive increased attention.

A **dividend policy** is a decision by a corporate board of directors and the management to follow a predetermined series of actions regarding the payment of dividends to shareholders. In the case of preferred shareholders, the dividend policy is established by the legal agreement between the shareholders and the corporation. In the case of common shareholders, the board of directors has considerable discretion.

A dividend policy of a corporation may range from a mere decision regarding quarterly dividend action without attempting to define any policy beyond a quarter-to-quarter evaluation, to rather complex formal statements approved by the board of directors and reviewed on a regular basis. The review normally occurs when actions regarding dividend payments are taken by a board of directors. In addition, dividend policy may be reviewed at the **annual shareholders' meeting** or may be published in the **annual report.** Security analysts who follow a particular corporation and evaluate its performance have a strong interest in dividend policies and may ask that management discuss such policies publicly.

ANNOUNCEMENT CONSIDERATIONS.   The dividend policy may also be an explicit statement that serves as a **signal to the shareholders and investment community** of what may be expected in the future. Such statements attempt to establish a relationship between the earnings potential of the corporation and dividend payments. Some policies state explicitly what proportion of the corporation's earnings will be paid out as dividends to the shareholders and under what conditions the shareholders might expect either a reduction or an increase in dividends. In addition, the policy statements may cover stock dividends.

DIVIDEND CLIENTELE.   Dividend policies may serve as a means of attracting and holding the type of buyer that will result in a stable shareholder base and share price. Corporations that want to attract small individual investors, as contrasted with large institutional investors, may prepare a dividend policy that places greater emphasis on a high **payout ratio,** that is, paying out a larger proportion of a corporation's aftertax earnings and dividends. In contrast, large institutional investors may be more interested in realizing appreciation in the value of their shareholdings and may concentrate their investments in corporations that reinvest a substantial proportion of earnings. Thus, corporations interested in attracting institutional investors may design a dividend policy that results in a smaller payout ratio and a higher proportion of total earnings reinvested in additional earning assets. A primary consideration, therefore, is the **tax bracket of shareholders.**

It is difficult to generalize regarding formulation of dividend policies. Efforts to develop a dividend policy must reflect consideration of a variety of issues. The future capital requirements of the corporation, the expected stream of earnings and cash flows and variability of these flows, shareholder expectations and attitudes, changes in corporate tax policy, the future cost and availability of capital, the strategy of the corporation with respect to investment and new product development, and the cash requirements and tax position of the corporation's shareholders all play a role in determining a dividend policy. For an excellent discussion of these determinants, see Weston and Brigham, *Managerial Finance*, Chapter 20.

WHEN SHOULD A CORPORATION ADOPT A FORMAL DIVIDEND POLICY?

Not all corporations require a formal dividend policy. Closely held businesses in which the equity participants hold a position on the board of directors or maintain a working knowledge of the business probably do not require a formal policy. **Formal dividend policies** are normally associated with corporations that have achieved significant size in revenue and number and variety of shareholders. The complexity of financial management and planning play an important part in determining when a formal dividend policy is required. Industrial organizations that are capital intensive and must engage in long-range planning to assure adequate supplies of capital in the future may require a specific dividend policy to assure that sufficient amounts of funds are available when asset acquisition is undertaken. At the same time, it is important to achieve a balance between retained earnings and dividends to assure a market for new equity shares in the event additional equity capital is required.

COMPOSITION OF BOARD OF DIRECTORS.   The composition of the board of directors may influence the need for a formal dividend policy. If a majority of the board of directors are not involved in the management of the company, there may be constrasting views of an appropriate dividend policy for the corporation. Rather than have a debate each time a quarterly dividend declaration is required, it is more effective to devote a significant amount of time to preparing a careful and formal statement of dividend policy on which a majority of the directors agree. Thereafter, each dividend declaration can be measured for compliance with the dividend policy. This assures **continuity in dividend policy,** which has become increasingly important in maintaining a strong market for equity securities.

In the past 10 years, the **outside or independent members of boards of directors** have emerged as a much stronger force in the direction of large corporations. It is assumed, in many cases incorrectly, that management would prefer to pay out smaller proportions of corporate earnings and retain a larger proportion for reinvestment in the corporation to finance growth and diversity. Since outside directors represent the interest of the shareholders of the corporation (although they are usually selected by management), they may require management to justify retention of earnings that otherwise would be available for the payment of dividends to shareholders.

POLICY MAINTENANCE AND REVIEW.   Maintenance of a formal dividend policy is also important to institutional lenders. An erratic dividend policy may endanger the creditors' position if management or the board of directors fails to foresee substantial cash requirements associated with periods of business decline or large investments during times of rapid growth.

As with any policy of a corporation, dividend policies should be subject to **periodic review** by management and the board of directors to assure that dividend actions are in compliance with the policy and that the established dividend policy continues to be relevant to the needs of the corporation and the shareholders. A dividend policy adopted during a period when cash requirements are high to finance rapid growth may not be appropriate as new markets begin to mature and earnings grow significantly. Therefore, it is recommended that the dividend policy of the corporation be reviewed formally once a year with the board of directors to assure both compliance and relevance. Exhibit 6 is an example of a dividend policy review prepared for a board of directors.

Consideration should also be given to a review of dividend policy in the annual report to shareholders and at the annual meeting. At meetings with security analysts and institutional investors management should provide an explanation of dividend policy. These reviews play an important part in maintaining a good information and communication system.

DETERMINANTS OF DIVIDEND POLICY

Formulation of a dividend policy requires consideration of the major **determinants of profitability and cash flow** of a corporation as well as external factors that influence investors' decisions to either acquire or dispose of their investments in the company. A dividend policy refers to the percentage of a firm's earnings paid out to shareholders, although it might be expressed in absolute terms as well.

CYCLICALITY.   One of the most important considerations in determining dividend policy is the **impact of business cycles** on the profitability and cash flow of the corporation. Businesses that experience little cyclicality or fluctuation in demand for their products or services are able to pursue a relatively stable dividend policy, as contrasted with businesses that experience wide fluctuations over the course of a business cycle.

EXHIBIT 6   A REVIEW OF COMPANY DIVIDEND POLICY

The Board of Directors has approved the following dividend policy:

> The Company should continue to increase dividends gradually while directing the bulk of its retained earnings toward maintaining and increasing planned growth as a most effective means of maximizing the stock price. Each dividend recommendation should:
>
> > Be viewed in terms of what is most desirable for Company shareholders.
> >
> > Consider the amount of funds required for planned expansion.
> >
> > Reflect the Company's view of the future.
> >
> > Incorporate the use of strategic increases in critical years.
>
> Inherent in the goals above is the direction to:
>
> > Strive to increase our effective cash dividend rate by 15% annually as a means of demonstrating management's commitment to a 15% average annual growth rate.
> >
> > Retain an average of 70% of our aftertax earnings for reinvestment (i.e., a payout ratio of 30%).

At the last meeting of the Board of Directors the Directors requested a study outlining all relevant factors to be considered in dividend policy formulation. This study identified three factors of paramount importance in determining our dividend policy:

> The market premium that may or may not exist for different payout percentages for firms with similar circumstances to the Company.
>
> The preference of the Company's shareholders for capital gains versus dividend income.
>
> The requirement for funds to fulfill the investment opportunities available to the Company.

The study also concluded that the Company's payout ratio was well below its industry and national averages and that a higher payout would likely produce a higher P/E ratio. However, a higher payout could not be achieved without a reduction in capital expenditures and future growth and additional equity financing.

At the last meeting, the Board reaffirmed its policy of gradually increasing dividends on an annual basis while retaining the bulk of the Company's earnings to carry out planned growth. The Board expressed its acceptance of the following goals:

> Cash dividends should be increased in line with earnings growth, approximately 15% per annum.
>
> An average of 70% of aftertax profits should be retained for reinvestment in internal projects.

The Board further expressed its intent to be guided by three additional factors in deciding appropriate dividend action.

> Near- and longer-term capital requirements to fund the Company's growth,
>
> Near- and longer-term expectations of the Company's profitability,
>
> The possible importance of strategic increases in dividends during years when shareholder expectations require reinforcement.

WHAT FACTORS SHOULD WE CONSIDER IN EVALUATING COMPANY DIVIDEND POLICY?

1. What is an appropriate dividend policy at this stage in the Company's growth?
2. How have investors' attitudes toward dividends changed?
3. Should stability of dividend rate be emphasized?
4. What dividend policy is in the interest of the Company's various stakeholders?
5. What can the Company afford to pay?

EXHIBIT 6 CONTINUED

HAVE INVESTOR ATTITUDES CHANGED?

Investors are focusing more on dividends than in the past. Why?

> They are in a more conservative, defensive mood.
>
> Higher absolute dividend yields are available.
>
> Value placed on $1 paid out has increased more than value on $1 retained.

What does this increased interest in dividends say about the Company policy?

> The individual shareholders' interest will still be best served by a low payout if the Company can invest retained funds at a higher return than a shareholder can receive through reinvesting dividends.
>
> However, if this issue is in doubt, the Company should now lean more toward dividends than retention.

STABILITY OF DIVIDEND RATE

Dividends are meaningful to investors in two ways.

1. Dividends are part of the return on their investment. They prefer to have this cash flow grow steadily and never decline, except in extreme circumstances.
2. Dividends are one of the best indicators of the Board of Directors' outlook for the Company's power to generate earnings and cash flows over the long term. This insight into the Board's outlook is particularly informative to investors when the following factors are all markedly cyclical:

> The economies in which the Company operates.
>
> The industries to which it sells.
>
> Its sales.
>
> Its earnings.
>
> Its financial condition.

Given the Company's cyclicality and its historical pattern of steady dividend growth, it is reasonable to assume that investors are relying heavily on the dividend rate as a proxy for the Board's long-term outlook for the Company.

Management recommends continuation of a steady dividend growth pattern reflective of the Company's earning power.

OTHER STAKEHOLDERS

In addition to common stockholders, the interests of other stakeholders should be considered:

> Lenders.
>
> Employees.
>
> Suppliers.
>
> Customers.
>
> Communities in which the Company operates.

Their interest is in having the Company remain strong financially. A key element of a strong financial position is an equity base adequate to support the current level of operations.

It matters little to these stakeholders how an adequate equity base is maintained. Since dividend policy is only one of several influences on the corporation's equity base, dividend policy in and of itself is of little concern to these stakeholders as long as the combined effect of dividend policy and other influences is maintenance of an adequate equity base.

EXHIBIT 6 CONTINUED

WHAT FACTORS SHOULD WE CONSIDER?

1. What is an appropriate dividend policy at this stage in the Company's corporate life?

   As long as the Company remains in the "established growth" phase, a payout below 40% with steady growth of dividend rate is appropriate.

2. How did investors' attitudes toward dividends change in the 1970s?

   Investors became more interested in dividends; if the decision is not clear, we should lean toward higher payout.

3. Should stability of dividend rate be emphasized?

   Yes, as it has been in the past.

4. What dividend policy is in the interest of the Company's various stakeholder groups?

   They are indifferent as long as an adequate equity base is maintained.

WHAT CAN THE COMPANY AFFORD TO PAY?

There are three alternative policy guidelines.

	Basic Policy Guidelines	Constraints to Maintain Dividend Rate Stability
Conservative	30% of previous year's primary EPS	Maximum increase of 20% in 1 year; no decreases
Moderate	35% of previous year's primary EPS	Maximum increase of 35% in 1 year; no decreases
Aggressive	50% of previous year's primary EPS	Maximum increase of 100% in 1 year; no decreases

AN EXAMPLE

This example applies the conservative policy guideline to the present situation:

	Annual Dividend Per Share
Basic Policy Guideline	$3.00–$4.50
30% of estimated primary EPS of $10–$15	
Constraints	$1.50
Maximum increase of 20% of present $1.50 dividend	
No decrease from present $1.50 dividend	$1.50
Rate Prescribed by Guideline	$1.80

EXHIBIT 6 CONTINUED

RECOMMENDED POLICY GUIDELINE

Until the Board of Directors has approved the long-term operating, capital, and financing plan, a cautious dividend policy is appropriate.

Consequently, we recommend that the conservative dividend policy guideline be adopted, to be reviewed, and affirmed or revised, after a long-term financing plan has been adopted.

Since this guideline is mechanistic, it should be viewed as a guideline only.

RECOMMENDED COMMON DIVIDEND ACTION

In keeping with the cautious approach recommended pending completion of our financing plan, we suggest that the dividend be raised from 37.5¢ quarterly to 45¢ (from $1.50 annually to $1.80).

Corporations that are significantly affected by business cycles often elect to pay out a lower proportion of their total profits during the recovery portion of a business cycle, but strive to maintain the dividend rate during business recessions to provide the shareholder with stability of income. Corporations that experience little change in revenue patterns during the entire course of a business cycle usually require less retention of earnings and are able to pay out a higher proportion of total earnings during recovery and recession periods. **Highly cyclical businesses may be capital intensive,** requiring a larger proportion of their earnings for reinvestment purposes. Therefore, they may be doubly affected by (1) a reduction in cash and profitability during a recession and (2) an increased demand for cash to establish additional manufacturing capacity and working capital requirements in preparation for the forthcoming recovery phase of the business cycle.

STAGES OF GROWTH.   Business operations, like other institutions, experience different **stages** of growth during an entire **life cycle.** The number of growth stages in the life of a business has been the subject of several academic studies. Some scholars attribute a three-phase life cycle to the growth of a business corporation, while others believe that there are five phases. Assuming a three-phase life cycle of **formation, gestation, and maturity,** each of these phases of a business life cycle creates a set of circumstances that may have a major influence on the formulation of a dividend policy.

During the **formation stage,** the typical business enterprise is least profitable and requires its limited profits for reinvestment purposes. Therefore, ability to pay dividends is limited and the emphasis is focused on providing support and growth opportunities to assure survival and protect the shareholders' initial investment. Such a strategy is of far greater value to the shareholders than any limited dividends that might be received during the first phase of the **business life cycle.**

The second phase of growth occurs when a business is succeeding and growing rapidly. This phase may also represent a period of high risk in the growth of a business in that the opportunities for major errors or strategic mistakes are greatest. The phrase **"growing to death"** refers to businesses that experience growth rates so rapid that the internally or externally generated capital or cash flow is insufficient to finance them. As a consequence, management may lose control of its operation and the business may falter or even fail. During the period of gestation it may be difficult for a corporation to pay significant dividends to its shareholders, particularly if shareholders require cash dividends. If the business is experiencing substantial success but requires large additions of capital, it may be appropriate to issue stock dividends rather than cash dividends without denying the corporation the cash required to finance required additions to fixed assets and working capital.

In addition, during the gestation period the business may utilize borrowed capital to a greater extent. Therefore, creditors may prefer a conservative dividend policy to assure that the corporation reinvests a large proportion of earnings, thus assuring continued growth and profitability for the protection of the creditors.

During the next stage of business growth, the **maturity stage,** profitability may increase and needs for cash decrease sufficiently to permit the corporation to pursue a more generous dividend policy and reward the shareholders for forgoing their dividend returns during the earlier stages of growth. In this stage management may discover that **opportunities are diminished** because of a high penetration of the markets in which they compete and fewer opportunities to serve new markets and develop new products.

It is at this stage in the life cycle of a business that its management and board of directors may face a **critical decision,** one that will have a major effect on **dividend policy.** Management and the board of directors may elect to accept the maturation of the business and pay out a large proportion of total earnings to the shareholders, in which case the stock may become a valuable income investment, attractive to those investors who seek immediate income opportunities. On the other hand, management may not be satisfied with such a conservative strategy and may seek new growth opportunities. The latter strategy may lead to **diversification, acquisition, or merger** with other companies, to realize a faster growth rate. Many shareholders may approve of a reconstituted growth strategy because they prefer to realize their returns in the form of ever-increasing appreciation in the market value of the stock as opposed to dividend income. Regardless of which strategy is selected, the impact on dividend policy will be significant, and the policy should be carefully reviewed to be sure that it complements the business strategy.

PROFITABILITY.   Profitability is uneven among different businesses and over the life cycle of an individual business enterprise. Some businesses are characterized by narrow profit margins resulting from strong competition and little value added to the products they distribute (e.g., food merchandising). However, many businesses with narrow profit margins are the most stable. Public utilities are characterized by narrow profit margins; however, they are usually quasi-monopolies, and state and local governments limit their profitability and return on investment by means of rate regulation. Public utilities, like food merchandising firms, experience only small fluctuations in demand for their services over the course of a business cycle.

Predictability and the level of profits play important parts in determining the dividend policy of a corporation. Although food merchandising enterprises and public utilities are similar with respect to cyclicality of profitability, they are dissimilar in terms of the amount and type of capital required to generate profits. In food merchandising a relatively large share of total capital is devoted to inventory or working capital, whereas public utilities require significant investments in fixed assets to generate energy or communication services. Thus the profitability pattern of the corporation and the industry in which it competes must be taken into consideration in determining a dividend policy.

CASH GENERATION.   A dividend policy must also recognize differences that may exist between reported profits and actual **cash generation.** Given the complexity of modern

accounting principles, many corporations show wide variations between profitability and cash flow. High profitability is no assurance of adequate cash from which dividends may be paid. On the other hand, a low level of reported accounting profits is not always indicative of insufficient cash to pay dividends.

Numerous factors that influence reported profits may not affect the cash generation of the corporation. For example, **increased market penetration** resulting from an **extension of credit terms** to customers and maintenance of larger inventories may result in higher reported profits but may deplete the cash reserves of the corporation so greatly that the dividend rate cannot be maintained. In such instances, a corporation may experience cash deficits as it attempts to finance its increasing **accounts receivable and inventory levels.** On the other hand, a corporation suffering a declining profit level may actually be experiencing surpluses of cash as inventories and receivables are reduced and depreciation of fixed assets exceeds the amount invested in new or replacement assets. Accounting for foreign exchange is a more recent phenomenon that has resulted in major changes in corporate profits that may have no impact on cash flow.

In determining the impact of profitability and cash flow on dividend policy, management and the board of directors must evaluate whether the corporation is experiencing a period of temporary or permanent profit growth or decline as well as the ability to maintain or improve the current level of cash flow. Brittain (*Corporate Dividend Policy*) found that post-World War II **accelerated depreciation standards** and added cash flow accounted for a substantial increase in cash dividends paid by U.S. corporations.

TIMING OF DIVIDEND POLICY

All the foregoing determinants of dividend policy must be evaluated in terms of the **length of time these conditions are expected to prevail.** Management and the board of directors should attempt to forecast as far as is reasonably possible the impacts of cyclicality, growth, profitability, and cash generation in evaluating dividend policy and to provide shareholders and the investment community with an evaluation of these issues and a statement of how they are expected to influence dividend policy.

INVESTOR EXPECTATIONS AND NEEDS

OWNER VERSUS MANAGER CONTROL.   Thus far the discussion of dividend policy has centered on the characteristics and requirements of the business enterprise as opposed to the needs and expectations of the shareholders. Various factors influence investors' needs and expectations regarding dividends. If a corporation is owned by a relatively small number of shareholders, the dividend policy may be quite different from that of a publicly held corporation whose shareholders are more dependent on dividends as a means of realizing a return on their investment. If the shareholders of a corporation are restricted to a few individuals, all of whom participate in the operation of the business, the policy may be to avoid the payment of dividends and to emphasize reinvestment of earnings to realize faster growth and greater capital appreciation.

The **Internal Revenue Service** may evaluate the performance of privately held corporations to determine whether the restriction of dividend payments is being used by the shareholders as a means of avoiding federal income tax. If the Internal Revenue Service believes that abuses have occurred, the corporation may be required to pay taxes as if dividends had been paid by the corporation to the shareholders. This is referred to as an **accumulated earnings tax.**

Investor expectations and needs are difficult for corporate management and the board of directors to evaluate, particularly for a large corporation with a wide spectrum of shareholders with differing investment objectives. The dividend policy of a large corporation should be determined by the needs of the corporation. Once dividend policy is determined, management may undertake programs to attract equity investors with investment objectives that coincide with the firm's dividend policy. This requires that management communicate its dividend policy to existing and potential shareholders and the financial community to establish a broad and stable market for equity capital.

TAX CONSIDERATIONS. **Investor expectations** and needs are determined largely by income requirements and federal income tax policy. Investors who do not need immediate income and who have high tax exposure prefer equity investments with high potential for rapid growth, outstanding opportunities for reinvestment of earnings, and promise of continued **capital appreciation.**

Investors who require immediate income are less attracted to growth stocks and may elect to invest in companies with less potential for future capital appreciation that offer more generous immediate cash dividends. In many instances investors are represented by institutions such as insurance companies and pension funds that must satisfy demands for immediate income as well as future capital appreciation. Investors who place greater emphasis on capital appreciation may favor corporations that periodically provide stock dividends, particularly if the corporation continues to demonstrate growth potential and superior profit margins.

DIVIDEND REINVESTMENT PLANS. The use of dividend reinvestment plans is a technique employed by many large corporations that pay a relatively generous dividend, but seek to reinvest a larger share of profits. Dividend reinvestment programs have had limited success. On average, they have been able to attract less than 15% of dividend payments as reinvestments, and they are expensive to administer. They offer the shareholder an opportunity to acquire additional shares without paying brokerage fees. However, the inability to select the purchase price is an unattractive aspect of dividend reinvestment plans. In addition, there is the risk that the Internal Revenue Service will adopt the view that brokerage fees avoided constitute a transfer of value to shareholders, and will levy a tax on the estimated value.

CAPITAL STRUCTURE AND DIVIDEND POLICY

One of the most important decisions in financial management involves the determination of the appropriate capital structure for the corporation, i.e., the mix between debt and equity. Corporations that have relatively large and stable cash flows may undertake the risks of using larger proportions of debt, while corporations that tend to be more significantly affected by the business cycle and interruptions in cash flow usually pursue a more conservative capital structure and rely more heavily on equity.

The more extensively a corporation uses debt or fixed cost capital, the greater the opportunity for equity investors to realize an increasing share of the profits. However, leverage may work against the common shareholder as profits decline. Therefore, equity investors may be less attracted to highly leveraged companies if they surmise the possibility of a cyclical downturn.

A discussion of the appropriate capital structure for a corporation is too extensive to pursue in this section and can be found in the section entitled "Long-Term Sources of Funds and the Cost of Capital." However, it must be realized that dividend policy is an important outgrowth of the decisions regarding capital structure. If a corporation decides to establish a capital structure that emphasizes equity over debt, the dividend policy may be more conservative, to assure that a large proportion of the aftertax profits is retained to build a sufficient equity base. If management elects to pursue a liberal dividend policy and to increase equity simultaneously, new equity issues may be required periodically to replace what otherwise would have been achieved by a greater retention of earnings.

Similar decisions are required with respect to the composition of equity investment (i.e., mix of preferred and common shares). Preferred shares, like debt issues, carry a fixed dividend rate. Thus the use of preferred equity in the capital structure may also offer common shareholders the opportunity to acquire a greater share of the corporation's profits as preferred dividends claim a smaller proportion of increases in aftertax profits.

When management selects the policy regarding capital structure, the mix of debt and equity becomes a principal determinant of the corporate dividend policy. As with dividend policy, it is important that corporate management and the board of directors enunciate clearly the policy regarding capital structure. Information of this kind provided to the shareholders and the financial community is beneficial insofar as it helps attract a stable and supportive group of permanent shareholders who provide continuing markets for additional equity issues.

INSOLVENCY TESTS AND CORPORATE DISTRIBUTIONS

Corporate distributions to shareholders involve (1) the transfer of money or other property (except a corporation's own shares) or (2) the incurrence of indebtedness, whether by **cash dividend** or **share repurchase.** The revised **Model Business Corporation Act (1979)** specifies that the **board of directors** may authorize the corporation to make distributions except when (*a*) the corporation would be unable to pay its debts as they became due in the usual course of business, or (*b*) the corporation's total assets would be less than its total liabilities. The former test describes **equity insolvency** and the latter describes **bankruptcy insolvency.** No longer are the terms **par value, stated value,** and **capital surplus** relevant to a firm's payment of dividends or share repurchase.

Determination of whether a firm would be insolvent as a result of a proposed distribution is to be rendered by the board of directors based on its collective business judgment. This stipulation forces the firm to analyze the future course of its business, including its ability to generate sufficient funds from operations or from the orderly disposition of its assets, and to satisfy its existing and anticipated obligations as they come due.

Discussion of these and other provisions can be found in "Changes in the Model Business Corporation Act—Amendments to Financial Provisions" (*Business Lawyer,* Vol. 34, July 1979). The question of **corporate solvency** may be important in determining shareholder return on investment.

THEORY AND EMPIRICAL EVIDENCE

THEORETICAL CONTROVERSY.   A major issue concerning dividend policy is whether decisions by corporate management as to the amount of dividends paid actually affect the **wealth of the shareholders.** Several determinants of dividend policy have been discussed, but the question of the decision's effect on share prices is difficult to answer.

Conventional corporate finance wisdom specifies that the dividend decision does matter and that the time and effort spent by management and the board of directors on this decision is justified. Such variables as income stability, investment opportunities, cost of alternative financing, and tax bracket of stockholders help to guide management in this important decision. The fact that dividends paid today have more value than those received tomorrow must be considered in the payout decision. In other words, traditional financial theorists and most practitioners feel that **dividends do matter.** Arbitrary changes in dividends, especially dividend cuts, must be carefully considered.

The opposite point of view is advocated by the **"irrelevance school"** led by Miller and Modigliani. In their article "Dividend Policy, Growth, and the Valuation of Shares" (*Journal of Business,* October 1961), they argued that the sole determinant of share price is the **rate of return earned on investment opportunities** and that how these returns are eventually passed through to the owners is irrelevant. Firms that prefer to pay out a greater percentage of earnings to stockholders can finance the investments that are expected to earn a return greater than the firm's **cost of capital** by other means, such as external equity or debt securities. Firms that finance investments all or in part from current earnings, in other words those that pay out small dividends or no dividends, will save the financing "costs" of interest payments on debt or **common stock equity dilution.**

After many years of controversy, the academic world continues to debate **dividend relevancy.** The great majority of practitioners presume that the dividend decision is relevant and important and pay little attention to the academic studies. Whenever a theory is uncertain, the empirical evidence must be examined to help answer the remaining questions. Such evidence and related theoretical constructs are discussed below.

CONCEPTUAL MODELS AND EMPIRICAL EVIDENCE. Researchers have frequently attempted to categorize, explain, and measure the different types of observed corporate dividend behavior. Even before the most recent theoretical controversy was articulated in the early 1960s, models to explain corporate behavior were attempted, some with considerable success. **Behavioral models** were developed that attempted to measure and explain several of the subjects discussed earlier in this section, namely, clientele effects and information and announcement effects of dividend declarations on share values. Only a few of the well-known models are reviewed here. For an excellent discussion entitled "Dividend Policy: Empirical Evidence and Applications," see Copeland and Weston, *Financial Theory and Corporate Policy*, Chapter 14.

Behavioral Models. A classic attempt to explain corporate dividend behavior was made in the article by Lintner entitled "Distribution of Incomes of Corporations Among Dividends, Retained Earnings and Taxes" (*American Economic Review,* May 1956). After conducting interviews with the personnel of numerous large, well-established firms, Lintner concluded (1) that the primary determinants of changes in dividends paid out were the most **recent earnings** and the **past dividends** paid, (2) that management focused on the change in dividends rather than the amount, (3) that changes were made only when management felt secure that the new level of dividends could be maintained, and firms very reluctantly cut or eliminated dividends, (4) that there was a propensity to move toward some **target payout ratio** for most firms, but the **speed of adjustment** toward that level differed greatly among companies, and (5) that investment requirements generally had little effect on dividend behavior. The last point implies that dividend policy and changes in policy constitute an active policy variable of the firm—at least in the opinion of management in the 1950s.

Fama and Babiak, in "Dividend Policy: An Empirical Analysis" (*Journal of the American Statistical Association,* December 1968), found that Lintner's model continued to explain dividend behavior quite well and that a slightly different model with **lagged earnings** (last period's) as well as **lagged dividends** did a slightly better job in that it had higher explanatory power.

Brittain (*Corporate Dividend Policy*) found that accelerated depreciation, increased cash flows, and external cost of financing, among other factors, explained quite well the dividend payout behavior of corporations in the post-World War II period up to the mid-1960s. His study postulated that the key determinant is **cash flows, rather than earnings.** After all, dividends must be paid from cash.

While these studies all had impressive statistical results, the question of why firms pay out the amount of dividends they do was not addressed directly. The following are some empirical attempts to explain this.

Clientele Effect Models.   Do corporations attract a specific type or types of stockholder, and can this phenomenon be measured? Most theoreticians would probably agree that the **payout ratio** and **the dividend yield** of companies do attract individuals, although the tradeoff between dividend income versus capital gains is a complex one. The **clientele effect** is probably one of the reasons for the reluctance of management to make extreme changes in dividend policy, especially when this entails cutting the dividend. Disgruntled shareholders could always sell their shares, although this could possibly lead to unfortunate share price movement and certainly would result in **transaction costs** for those who sold their shares.

Probably the most important clientele effect variable is the **tax bracket** of investors. As mentioned earlier, investors in higher tax brackets should prefer returns in the form of capital gains, not cash dividends. Do stockholders act rationally in this respect? One of the difficulties in translating this conceptual generalization into policy-related action is the problem of determining the tax bracket of a large mass of stockholders of the corporation being managed. Even knowledge of the average tax bracket would be helpful in this respect.

A number of researchers have attempted to "observe" the average tax bracket of stockholders without actually asking them—which would be costly and probably subject to a great deal of bias. Estimates of **average tax brackets** of all U.S. corporation shareholders, usually weighted by proportional stock ownership of individuals, have ranged from 36 to 54%. Most of these estimates were made in the 1960s and early 1970s, and with the increase in state and local taxes in many locations, one would guess that the average is higher in 1980.

A study by Elton and Gruber, "Marginal Stockholders' Tax Rates and the Clientele Effect" (*Review of Economics and Statistics,* February 1970) approached the marginal tax bracket question by examining the **ex-dividend behavior of common stocks.** The authors found that the average price decline of common stocks at the close on the ex-dividend date was lower than the **amount of the dividend** and postulated that this could be explained by the tax bracket or clientele effect. They did find evidence that firms that suffered the greatest decline on the ex-dividend date were those with higher dividend yields, which implied a lower tax bracket. The average tax bracket of all stockholders implied by this ex-dividend price behavior was 36.4%. Copeland and Weston (*Financial Theory and Corporate Policy*) argued, however, that this anomaly in the market (i.e., differential expected movement in share prices dependent on stockholder tax brackets) could not exist. If it did **arbitrageurs** would be able to trade on this information. None of these studies or counterarguments, however, took **transaction costs** into consideration.

Pettit ("Taxes, Transaction Costs, and Clientele Effect of Dividends," *Journal of Financial Economics,* December 1977) examined portfolios of a large number of individuals and found that stocks with **low dividend yields** tended to be held by investors with **high**

income, by **younger investors** (higher risk tolerance), by individuals whose normal versus capital gains tax rates differed greatly, and by those whose portfolios had relatively high **systematic risk,** or **market-related (high-beta) risk.**

Information and Announcement Effects.   One of the more difficult complexities of empirical research is to be confident that when the association between one variable (dividends) and another (share price change) is being measured, significant results indicate direct association between the two. In fact, most theorists and empiricists now believe that it is not the added current cash flow to investors that explains share price increase when dividends increase, but that the **dividend declaration** conveys information about future cash flows.

It is also possible that information about **future investment opportunities** and cash flows could be provided from other sources, although there is a strong intuitive feeling that dividend declarations are clear and not likely to be "window dressing." Unfortunately, **the evidence to date is not conclusive.**

Pettit, in "Dividend Announcements, Security Performance and Capital Market Efficiency" (*Journal of Finance*, December 1972), found evidence that the market does in fact use dividend announcements as important information for assessing security values. He reported that most of the significant **price adjustment** takes place very quickly, either on the dividend announcement date or on the following day. Unfortunately, since no trading rules were tested inclusive of transaction costs it is not clear whether consistent profits could be made by insiders, that is, those who had information not available to the public about dividend announcements.

Watts, in "The Information Content of Dividends" (*Journal of Business*, April 1973), on the other hand, noted a positive dividend announcement effect but concluded that the price movements of shares were not sufficient to earn **abnormal returns,** that is, returns **adjusted for the overall market movement** and the individual stock's **systematic risk,** that are significantly greater than zero.

REFERENCES

Black, F., and Scholes, M., "The Effects of Dividend Yield and Dividend Policy on Common Stock Prices and Returns," *Journal of Financial Economics,* May 1974, pp. 1–22.

Brigham, E., *Financial Management Theory and Practice,* 2nd ed., Dryden Press, Hinsdale, Il, 1979, Chapter 17.

Brittain, J. A., *Corporate Dividend Policy,* Brookings Institution, Washington, D. C., 1966.

Copeland, T., and Weston, J. F., *Financial Theory and Corporate Policy,* Addison-Wesley, Reading, MA, 1979.

Elton, E. J., and Gruber, M. J., "Marginal Stockholders' Tax Rates and the Clientele Effect," *Review of Economics and Statistics,* February 1970, pp. 68–74.

Fama, E., "The Empirical Relationships Between the Dividend and Investment Decisions of Firms," *American Economic Review,* June 1974, pp. 304–318.

———, and Babiak, H., "Dividend Policy: An Empirical Analysis," *Journal of the American Statistical Association,* December 1968, pp. 1132–1161.

Kalay, A., *Essays in Dividend Policy,* Ph. D. thesis, University of Rochester, Rochester, N.Y., 1977.

Khoury, N., and Smith, K., "Dividend Policy and the Capital Gains Tax in Canada," *Journal of Business Administration,* Spring 1977.

Lintner, J., "Distribution of Incomes of Corporations Among Dividends, Retained Earnings and Taxes," *American Economic Review,* May 1956, pp. 97–113.

Miller, M., and Modigliani, F., "Dividend Policy, Growth, and the Valuation of Shares," *Journal of Business,* October 1961, pp. 411–433.

Pettit, R. R., "Dividend Announcements, Security Performance, and Capital Market Efficiency," *Journal of Finance,* December 1972, pp. 993–1007.

———, "The Impact of Dividend and Earnings Announcement: A Reconciliation," *Journal of Business,* January 1976, pp. 86–96.

———, Taxes, Transactions Costs, and Clientele Effect of Dividends," *Journal of Financial Economics,* December 1977, pp. 419–436.

Sorter, D., "The Dividend Controversy—What It Means for Corporate Policy," *Financial Executive,* May 1979, pp. 38–43.

Van Horne, J., and McDonald, J. G., "Dividend Policy and New Equity Financing," *Journal of Finance,* May 1971, pp. 507–520.

Walter, J. E., *Dividend Policy and Enterprise Valuation,* Wadsworth, Belmont, CA. 1967.

Watts, R., "The Information Content of Dividends," *Journal of Business,* April 1973, pp. 191–211.

———, "Comments on the Informational Content of Dividends," *Journal of Business,* January 1976, pp. 81–85.

Weston, J. F., and Brigham, E., *Managerial Finance,* 6th ed., Dryden, Hinsdale, Il, 1978, Chapter 24.

MERGERS AND ACQUISITIONS

CONTENTS

TRENDS IN ACQUISITIONS   3

Merger Movement in the 1970s   3
Reasons for Takeovers   3

FINANCIAL ANALYSIS OF TARGET
COMPANIES   4

Steps in the Analysis   4
  Planning   4
  Search and screen   4
  Financial evaluation   5
Corporate Self-Evaluation   5
  Vulnerability to takeover   5
  Exchange of shares analysis   5
Valuation of Acquisitions   6
  Discounted cash flow (DCF) technique   6
  Forecasting target's cash flows   6
  Assessing acquisition candidate's risk   7

CASE OF ALCAR CORP.   7

Acquisition for Cash   8
  Step 1. Cash flow projections   9
  Step 2. Estimate minimum acceptable
  rate of return for acquisition   11
  Step 3. Compute maximum acceptable
  cash prices   13
  Step 4. Compute rate of return for
  various offering prices and scenarios   13

Step 5. Analyze feasibility of cash
purchase   15
Step 6. Evaluate impact of acquisition
on Alcar's EPS and capital structure   16
Acquisition for Stock   **17**
  Step 1. Estimate value of Alcar shares   17
  Step 2. Compute maximum number of
  shares Alcar can exchange   18
  Step 3. Evaluate impact of acquisition
  on Alcar's EPS and capital structure   19

CONCLUDING NOTE   **20**

DEFINITION OF BUSINESS
COMBINATION TERMS   **20**

Legal   **20**
Tax   **20**
Accounting   **21**
  Pooling of interests   21
    Positive conditions for pooling of
    interests   22
    Negative conditions for pooling of
    interests   22
  Purchase   22
    Conditions for purchase accounting 23
    Guides to cost allocation or
    assigning fair value   23
Economic   **23**

MERGERS AND ACQUISITIONS

Alfred Rappaport

TRENDS IN ACQUISITIONS

MERGER MOVEMENT IN THE 1970s.   Less than a decade after the frantic merger activity of the late 1960s, the late 1970s saw another major wave of corporate acquisitions. In contrast to the 1960s, when acquirers were mainly freewheeling **conglomerates,** the merger movement in the 1970s included such long-established giants of U.S. industry as General Electric, Gulf Oil, and Kennecott Copper. Because of the decline in the value of the dollar and the greater political stability of the United States, foreign companies have become increasingly active buyers of U.S. companies.

Most acquisitions are accomplished with cash today, rather than with packages of securities as was common in the 1960s. Finally, the merger movement involves the frequent use of **tender offers** that often lead to contested bids and to the payment of substantial premiums above the premerger market value of the target company. In 1978 and 1979, cash **tender offer premiums** averaged more than 70% above premerger market values.

REASONS FOR TAKEOVERS.   The popular explanation for the recent merger rage is that the market is "undervaluing" many solid companies, thus making it substantially cheaper to buy rather than to build. Couple this belief with the fact that many corporations are enjoying relatively strong cash positions and the widely held view that government regulation and increased uncertainty about the economy make internal growth strategies relatively unattractive, and we see why mergers and acquisitions have become an increasingly important part of corporate growth strategy.

Despite all the foregoing rationale, more than a few of the recent acquisitions will fail to create value for the acquirer's shareholders. After all, **shareholder value** depends not on premerger market valuation of the target company but on the actual acquisition price the acquiring company pays compared with the selling company's cash flow contribution to the combined company.

Only a limited supply of acquisition candidates is available at the price that enables the acquirer to earn an acceptable return on investment. A well-conceived financial evaluation program that minimizes the risk of buying an economically unattractive company or paying too much for an attractive one is particularly important in today's seller's market. The dramatic increase in **premiums** that must be paid by a company bidding successfully calls for more careful analysis by buyers than ever before.

Because of the competitive nature of the acquisition market, companies not only need to respond wisely but often must respond quickly as well. The growing independence of corporate boards and their demand for better information to support strategic decisions such as acquisitions have raised the general standard for acquisition analysis. Finally, sound analysis convincingly communicated can yield substantial benefits in negotiating with the target company's management or, in the case of tender offers, its stockholders.

FINANCIAL ANALYSIS OF TARGET COMPANIES

Whether companies are seeking acquisitions or are acquisition targets, it is increasingly clear that they must provide better information to enable top management and boards to make well-conceived, timely decisions. The approach presented below is a comprehensive **framework for acquisition analysis based on contemporary financial theory.** Various companies have used this approach for evaluation of serious candidates as well as for initial screening of potential candidates. In the latter case, initial input estimates are quickly generated to establish whether the range of maximum acceptable prices is greater than the current market price of the target companies. With the aid of a computer model, this can be accomplished quickly and at relatively low cost.

Use of the approach outlined here should improve the prospects of creating value for shareholders by acquisitions. By using the analysis, management can estimate how much value a prospective acquisition will in fact create. It provides both management and the **board of directors** of the acquiring company with information to make a decision on the candidate and to formulate an effective negotiating strategy for the acquisition.

STEPS IN THE ANALYSIS.   The process of analyzing acquisitions falls broadly into three stages: **planning, search and screen,** and **financial evaluation.**

Planning.   The **acquisition planning process** begins with a review of **corporate objectives** and product-market strategies for various strategic business units. The acquiring company should define its potential directions for corporate growth and diversification in terms of corporate strengths and weaknesses and an assessment of the company's social, economic, political, and technological environment. This analysis produces a set of acquisition objectives and criteria.

Specified criteria often include statements about industry parameters, such as projected market growth rate, degree of regulation, ease of entry, and capital versus labor intensity. Company criteria for quality of management, share of market, profitability, size, and capital structure also commonly appear in acquisition criteria lists.

Search and Screen.   The search and screen process is a systematic approach to compiling a list of good acquisition prospects. The search focuses on how and where to look for candidates, and the screening process selects a few of the best candidates from literally thousands of possibilities according to objectives and criteria developed in the planning phase.

Financial Evaluation. Finally comes the financial evaluation process, which is the focus of this section. A good analysis should enable management to answer such questions as:

- What is the **maximum price** that should be paid for the target company?
- What are the principal areas of **risk?**
- What are the **earnings, cash flow,** and **balance sheet** implications of the acquisition?
- What is the **best way of financing** the acquisition?

CORPORATE SELF-EVALUATION. The financial evaluation process involves both a **self-evaluation** by the acquiring company and the **evaluation of the candidate** for acquisition. While it is possible to conduct an evaluation of the target company without an in-depth self-evaluation first, in general this is the most advantageous approach. The scope and detail of corporate self-evaluation will necessarily vary according to the needs of each company.

Two fundamental questions are posed by a self-evaluation. (1) How much is my company worth? (2) How would its value be affected by each of several scenarios? The first question involves generating a "most likely" estimate of the company's value based on management's detailed assessment of its objectives, strategies, and plans. The second question calls for an assessment of value based on the range of plausible scenarios that enable management to test the joint effect of hypothesized combinations of product-market strategies and environmental forces.

Corporate self-evaluation viewed as an economic assessment of the value created for shareholders by various strategic planning options promises potential benefits for all companies. In the context of the acquisition market, self-evaluation takes on special significance.

Vulnerability to Takeover. First, while a company might view itself as an acquirer, few companies are totally exempt from a possible takeover. During 1979 alone, 83 acquisitions exceeding $100 million were announced. The recent roster of acquired companies includes Anaconda, Utah International, Babcock & Wilcox, Reliance Electric, Studebaker-Worthington, Seven Up, Pet, Carborundum, and Del Monte. Self-evaluation provides management and the board with a continuing basis for responding to tender offers or acquisition inquiries responsibly and quickly. Second, the self-evaluation process might well call attention to strategic divestment opportunities. Finally, self-evaluation provides acquisition-minded companies a basis for assessing the comparative advantages of a cash versus an exchange of shares offer.

Exchange of Shares Analysis. Acquiring companies commonly value the purchase price for an acquisition at the market value of the shares exchanged. This practice is not economically sound and could be misleading and costly to the acquiring company. A well-conceived analysis for an **exchange-of-shares acquisition** requires sound valuations of **both** buying and selling companies. If the acquirer's management believes the market is undervaluing its shares, then valuing the purchase price at market might well induce the company to overpay for the acquisition or to earn less than the minimum acceptable rate of return. Conversely, if management believes the market is overvaluing its shares, valuing the purchase price at market obscures the opportunity of offering the seller's shareholders additional shares while still achieving the minimum acceptable return.

VALUATION OF ACQUISITIONS.

Discounted Cash Flow (DCF) Technique.   On December 18, 1978 *Business Week* ("The Cash Flow Takeover Formula") reported that as many as half the major acquisition-minded companies were relying extensively on the **discounted cash flow (DCF) technique** to analyze acquisitions. While mergers and acquisitions involve a set of managerial problems considerably more complex than the purchase of an ordinary asset such as a machine or a plant, the economic substance of these transactions is the same. In each case, there is a current outlay made in anticipation of a stream of future cash flows.

Thus the DCF criterion applies not only to internal growth investments, such as additions to existing capacity, but equally to external growth investments, such as acquisitions. An essential feature of the DCF technique is that it explicitly takes into account that a dollar of cash received today is worth more than a dollar received a year from now, because today's dollar can be invested to earn a return during the intervening time.

To establish the maximum acceptable acquisition price under the DCF approach, estimates are needed for (1) the **incremental cash flows** expected to be generated because of the acquisition and (2) the **cost of capital**—that is, the minimum acceptable rate of return required by the market for new investments by the company.

In projecting the cash flow stream of a prospective acquisition, the cash flow contribution the candidate is expected to make to the acquiring company should be taken into account. The results of this projection may well differ from a projection of the candidate's cash flow as an independent company. This is so because the acquirer may be able to achieve operating economies not available to the selling company alone. Furthermore, acquisitions generally provide new postacquisition investment opportunities whose initial outlays and subsequent benefits also need to incorporated in the cash flow schedule. **Cash flow** is defined as:

(earnings before interest and taxes [EBIT]) × (1 − income tax rate) + depreciation and other noncash charges − capital expenditures − cash required for increase in net working capital.

In developing the cash flow schedule, two additional issues need to be considered. (1) What is the basis for setting the **horizon date**—that is, the date beyond which the cash flows associated with the acquisition are not specifically projected? (2) How is the **residual value** of the acquisition established at the horizon date?

Forecasting Target's Cash Flows.   A common practice is to forecast cash flows period by period until the level of uncertainty makes management too "uncomfortable" to go any farther. While practice varies with industry setting, management policy, and the special circumstances of the acquisition, 5 or 10 years appears to be an arbitrarily set forecasting duration used in many situations. A better approach suggests that **the forecast duration for cash flows** should continue only as long as the expected rate of return on incremental investment required to support forecasted sales growth exceeds the cost of capital rate.

If for subsequent periods one assumes that the company's return on incremental investment equals the cost of capital rate, the market would be indifferent to whether management invests earnings in expansion projects or pays cash dividends that shareholders can in turn invest in identically risky opportunities yielding an identical rate of return. In other words, the value of the company is unaffected by growth when the company is investing in projects earning at the cost of capital or at the minimum acceptable risk-ajusted rate of return required by the market.

Thus, for purposes of simplification, we can assume a 100% payout of earnings after the horizon date or, equivalently, a zero growth rate without affecting the valuation of the company. (An implied assumption of this model is that the **depreciation tax shield** can be invested to maintain the company's productive capacity.) The residual value is then the present value of the resulting cash flow perpetuity beginning one year after the horizon date. Of course, if after the horizon date the return on investment is expected to decline below the cost-of-capital rate, this factor can be incorporated in the calculation.

Assessing Acquisition Candidate's Risk. When the acquisition candidate's risk is judged to be the same as the acquirer's overall risk, the appropriate rate for discounting the candidate's cash flow stream is the acquirer's cost of capital. **The cost of capital** or the minimum acceptable rate of return on new investments is based on the rate investors can expect to earn by investing in alternative, identically risky securities.

The cost of capital is calculated as the **weighted average** of the costs of debt and equity capital. For example, suppose a company's aftertax cost of debt is 5% and it estimates its cost of equity to be 15%. Further, it plans to raise future capital in the following proportions—20% by way of debt and 80% by equity. Exhibit 1 shows how to compute the company's average cost.

It is important to emphasize that the acquiring company's use of its own cost of capital to discount the target's projected cash flows is appropriate only when it can be safely assumed that the acquisition will not affect the riskiness of the acquirer. The **specific riskiness of each prospective candidate** should be taken into account in setting the discount rate, with higher rates used for more risky investments.

If a single discount rate is used for all acquisitions, those with the highest risk will seem most attractive. Because the weighted average risk of its component segments determines the company's cost of capital, these high-risk acquisitions will increase a company's cost of capital and thereby decrease the value of its stock.

CASE OF ALCAR CORP.

As an illustration of the recommended approach to acquisition analysis, consider the case of Alcar Corp.'s interest in acquiring Rano Products. Alcar is a leading manufacturer and distributor in the industrial packaging and materials handling market. Sales in 1978 totaled $600 million. Alcar's acquisition strategy is geared toward buying companies with either similar marketing and distribution characteristics, similar production technologies, or a similar research and development orientation. Rano Products, a $50 million sales organization with an impressive new-product development record in industrial packaging, fits Alcar's general acquisition criteria particularly well. Premerger financial statements for Alcar and Rano are shown in Exhibit 2.

EXHIBIT 1 ONE COMPANY'S AVERAGE COST OF CAPITAL

	Weight	Cost	Weighted Cost
Debt	0.20	0.05	0.01
Equity	0.80	0.15	0.12
Average cost of capital			0.13

EXHIBIT 2   PREMERGER FINANCIAL STATEMENTS FOR ALCAR AND RANO ($ MILLIONS)

	Alcar	Rano
STATEMENT OF INCOME, YEAR ENDED DECEMBER 31		
Sales	$600.00	$50.00
Operating expenses	522.00	42.50
EBIT	78.00	7.50
Interest on debt	4.50	0.40
Earnings before taxes	73.50	7.10
Income taxes	36.00	3.55
Net income	$ 37.50	$ 3.55
Number of common shares outstanding (millions)	10.00	1.11
Earnings per share	$ 3.75	$ 3.20
Dividends per share	1.30	0.64
STATEMENT OF FINANCIAL POSITION (AT YEAR-END)		
Net working capital	$180.00	$ 7.50
Temporary investments	25.00	1.00
Other assets	2.00	1.60
Fixed assets	216.00	20.00
Less accumulated depreciation	(95.00)	(8.00)
	$328.00	$22.10
Interest-bearing debt	$ 56.00	$ 5.10
Shareholders' equity	272.00	17.00
	$328.00	$22.10

ACQUISITION FOR CASH. The **interactive computer model for corporate planning and acquisition analysis** used in the Alcar evaluation generates a comprehensive analysis for acquisitions financed by cash or stock, or any combination of cash, debt, preferred stock, and common stock. This analysis concerns only the cash and exchange of shares cases. In the cash acquisition case, the analysis follows six essential steps:

- Develop estimates needed to project Rano's cash flow contribution for various growth and profitability scenarios.
- Estimate the minimum acceptable rate of return for acquisition of Rano.
- Compute the maximum acceptable cash price to be paid for Rano under various scenarios and minimum acceptable rates of return.
- Compute the **rate of return** that Alcar will earn for a range of price offers and for various growth and profitability scenarios.
- Analyze the feasibility of a cash purchase in light of Alcar's current liquidity and target debt-to-equity ratio.
- Evaluate the impact of the acquisition on the earnings per share and capital structure of Alcar.

Step 1. Cash Flow Projections.   The cash flow formula presented earlier may be restated in equivalent form as follows:

$$CF_t = S_{t-1}(1+g_t)(p_t)(1-T_t) - (S_t - S_{t-1})(f_t + w_t)$$

where CF = cash flow
       S = sales
       g = annual growth rate in sales
       p = EBIT as a percentage of sales
       T = income tax rate
       f = capital investment required (i.e., total capital investment net of replacement of existing capacity estimated by depreciation) per dollar of sales increase
       w = cash required for net working capital per dollar of sales increase

When estimates have been provided for five variables, g, p, T, f, and w, it is possible to project cash flow.

Exhibit 3 shows Alcar management's "most likely" estimates for Rano's operations, assuming Alcar control; Exhibit 4 shows a complete projected 10-year cash flow statement for Rano.

Before developing additional scenarios for Rano, some brief comments on how to estimate some of the cash flow variables are in order. The income tax rate is the cash rate rather than a rate based on the accountant's income tax expense, which often includes a portion that is deferred. For some companies, a direct projection of capital investment requirements per dollar of sales increase will prove a difficult task.

To gain an estimate of the recent value of this coefficient, simply take the sum of all capital investments less depreciation over the past 5 or 10 years and divide this total by the sales increase from the beginning to the end of the period. With this approach, the resulting coefficient not only represents the **capital investment historically required per dollar of sales increase** but also impounds any cost increases for replacement of existing capacity.

One should estimate changes in **net working capital requirements** with care. Actual year-to-year balance sheet changes in net working capital may not provide a good measure of the rise or decline in funds required. There are two main reasons for this: (1) the year-end balance sheet figures may not reflect the average or normal needs of the business during the year, and (2) the inventory accounts may overstate the magnitude of the funds committed by the company.

EXHIBIT 3   MOST LIKELY ESTIMATES FOR RANO'S OPERATIONS UNDER ALCAR CONTROL

	Years		
	1–5	6–7	8–10
Sales growth rate, g	0.15	0.12	0.12
EBIT as a percentage of sale, p	0.18	0.15	0.12
Income tax rate, T	0.46	0.46	0.46
Capital investment per dollar of sales increase, f	0.20	0.20	0.20
Working capital per dollar of sales increase, w	0.15	0.15	0.15

Employing the cash flow formula for year 1:
$$CF_1 = 50(1 + 0.15)(0.18)(1 - 0.46) - (57.5 - 50)(0.20 + 0.15) = 2.96$$

EXHIBIT 4   PROJECTED 10-YEAR CASH FLOW STATEMENT FOR RANO ($ MILLIONS)

	Years									
	1	2	3	4	5	6	7	8	9	10
Sales	$57.50	$66.12	$76.04	$87.45	$100.57	$112.64	$126.15	$141.29	$158.25	$177.23
Operating expenses	47.15	54.22	62.36	71.71	82.47	95.74	107.23	124.34	139.26	155.97
EBIT	$10.35	$11.90	$13.69	$15.74	$ 18.10	$ 16.90	$ 18.92	$ 16.95	$ 18.99	$ 21.27
Income taxes on EBIT	4.76	5.48	6.30	7.24	8.33	7.77	8.70	7.80	8.74	9.78
Operating earnings after taxes	$ 5.59	$ 6.43	$ 7.39	$ 8.50	$ 9.78	$ 9.12	$ 10.22	$ 9.16	$ 10.25	$ 11.48
Depreciation	1.60	1.85	2.13	2.46	2.84	3.28	3.74	4.25	4.83	5.49
Less capital expenditures	(3.10)	(3.57)	(4.12)	(4.74)	(5.47)	(5.69)	(6.44)	(7.28)	(8.22)	(9.29)
Less increase in working capital	(1.13)	(1.29)	(1.49)	(1.71)	(1.97)	(1.81)	(2.03)	(2.27)	(2.54)	(2.85)
Cash flow	$ 2.96	$ 3.41	$ 3.92	$ 4.51	$ 5.18	$ 4.90	$ 5.49	$ 3.86	$ 4.32	$ 4.84

To estimate the additional cash requirements, the increased inventory investment should be measured by the variable costs for any additional units of inventory required rather than the absolute dollar amount of the receivable.

In addition to its most likely estimate for Rano, Alcar's management developed two additional (conservative and optimistic) scenarios for sales growth and EBIT-sales ratio. Exhibit 5 gives a summary of all three scenarios. Alcar's management may also wish to examine additional cases to test the effect of alternative assumptions about the income tax rate and capital investment and working capital requirements per dollar of sales increase.

Recall that cash flows should be forecast only for the period when the expected rate of return on incremental investment exceeds the minimum acceptable rate of return for the acquisition. It is possible to determine this in a simple yet analytical, nonarbitrary, fashion. To do so, we compute the **minimum pretax return on sales** P_{min} **needed to earn the minimum acceptable rate of return on the acquisition** (k) given the investment requirements for working capital (w) and fixed assets (f) for each additional dollar of sales and given a projected tax rate (T). The formula for P_{min} is:

$$P_{min} = \frac{f+w)\,k}{(1-T)\,(1+k)}$$

Alcar's management believes that when Rano's growth begins to slow down, its working capital requirements per dollar of additional sales will increase from 0.15 to about 0.20 and its effective tax rate will increase from 0.46 to 0.50. As shown later, the minimum acceptable rate of return on the Rano acquisition is 13%. Thus:

$$P_{min} = \frac{(0.20 + 0.20)\,(0.13)}{(1 - 0.50)\,(1 + .13)}$$
$$= 0.092$$

Alcar's management has enough confidence to forecast pretax sales returns above 9.2% for only the next 10 years, and thus the forecast duration for the Rano acquisition is limited to that period.

Step 2: Estimate Minimum Acceptable Rate of Return for Acquisition.   In developing a company's average cost of capital, measuring the **aftertax cost of debt** is relatively straightforward. The cost of equity capital, however, is more difficult to estimate.

Rational, risk-averse investors expect to earn a rate of return that will compensate them for accepting greater investment risk. Thus, in assessing the company's **cost of equity capital** or the minimum expected return that will induce investors to buy the company's shares, it

EXHIBIT 5   ADDITIONAL SCENARIOS FOR SALES GROWTH AND EBIT/SALES

	Sales Growth			EBIT/Sales		
Years:	1–5	6–7	8–10	1–5	6–7	8–10
Scenario:						
1. Conservative	0.14	0.12	0.10	0.17	0.14	0.11
2. Most likely	0.15	0.12	0.12	0.18	0.15	0.12
3. Optimistic	0.18	0.15	0.12	0.20	0.16	0.12

is reasonable to assume that they will demand the **risk-free rate** as reflected in the current yields available in government bonds, **plus a premium for accepting equity risk.**

In the late 1970s, the risk-free rate on government bonds was in the neighborhood of 8.8%. By investing in a portfolio broadly representative of the overall equity market, it was then possible to diversify away substantially all the unsystematic risk—that is, risk specific to individual companies. Therefore, securities were likely to be priced at levels that reward investors only for the **nondiversifiable market risk**—that is, the **systematic risk** in movements in the overall market.

The **risk premium** for the overall market is the excess of the expected return on a representative market index such as the Standard & Poor's 500 stock index over the risk-free return. Empirical studies have estimated this market risk premium (representative market index minus risk-free rate) to average historically about 5 to 5.5%. I use a 5.2% premium in subsequent calculations.

Investing in an individual security generally involves more or less risk than investing in a broad market portfolio; thus one must adjust the market risk premium appropriately in estimating the cost of equity for an individual security. The risk premium for a security is the product of the market risk premium times the individual security's systematic risk, as measured by its beta coefficient. An in-depth discussion of the cost of equity capital measurement using this CAPM methodology is presented in the section "Long-Term Sources of Funds and Cost of Capital."

The rate of return from dividends and capital appreciation on a market portfolio will, by definition, fluctuate identically with the market, and therefore its beta is equal to 1.0. A **beta** for an individual security is an index of its risk expressed as its volatility of return in relation to that of a market portfolio. Securities with betas greater than 1.0 are more volatile than the market and thus would be expected to have a risk premium greater than the overall market risk premium or the average-risk stock with a beta of 1.0. For a detailed description of beta and its characteristics, see the section entitled "Modern Portfolio Theory and Management."

For example, if a stock moves 1.5% when the market moves 1%, the stock would have a beta of 1.5. Securities with betas less than 1.0 are less volatile than the market and would thus command risk premiums less than the market risk premium. In summary, the cost of equity capital may be calculated by the following equation:

$$k_E = R_F + \beta_j (R_M - R_F)$$

where k_E = cost of equity capital
   R_F = risk-free rate
   β_j = beta coefficient
   R_M = representative market index

The acquiring company, Alcar, with a beta of 1.0, estimated its cost of equity as 14% with the foregoing equation:

$$k_E = 0.088 + 1.0(.052)$$
$$= 0.140$$

Since interest on debt is tax deductible, the rate of return that must be earned on the debt portion of the company's capital structure to maintain the earnings available to common shareholders is the aftertax cost of debt. The aftertax cost of borrowed capital is Alcar's current before-tax interest rate (9.5%) times 1 minus its effective tax rate of 46%, which is 5.1%. Alcar's target debt-to-equity ratio is 0.30, or, equivalently, debt is targeted at 23% and equity at 77% of its overall capitalization as Exhibit 6 shows Alcar's weighted average cost of capital. The appropriate rate for discounting Alcar cash flows to establish its estimated value is then 12%.

For new capital projects, including acquisitions, that are deemed to have about the same risk as the overall company, Alcar can use its 12% cost of capital rate as the appropriate discount rate. Because the company's cost of capital is determined by the weighted average risk of its component segments, the specific risk of each prospective acquisition should be estimated in order to arrive at the discount rate to apply to the candidate's cash flows.

Rano, with a beta coefficient of 1.25, is more risky than Alcar, with a beta of 1.0. Employing the formula for cost of equity capital for Rano:

$$k_E = 0.088 + (0.052)$$
$$= 0.153$$

On this basis, the risk-adjusted cost of capital for the Rano acquisition is as shown in Exhibit 7.

Step 3: Compute Maximum Acceptable Cash Prices. This step involves taking the cash flow projections developed in step 1 and discounting them at the rate developed in step 2. Exhibit 8 shows the computation of the maximum acceptable cash price for the most likely scenario. The maximum price of $44.51 million, or $40.10 per share, for Rano compares with a $25 current market price for Rano shares. Thus, for the most likely case, Alcar can pay up to $15 per share, or a 60% premium over current market, and still achieve its minimum acceptable 13% return on the acquisition.

Exhibit 9 shows the maximum acceptable cash price for each of the three scenarios for a range of discount rates. To earn a 13% rate of return, Alcar can pay at maximum $38 million ($34.25 per share), assuming the conservative scenario, and up to $53 million ($47.80 per share), assuming the optimistic scenario. Note that as Alcar demands a greater return on its investment, the maximum price it can pay decreases. The reverse is, of course, true as well. For example, for the most likely scenario, the maximum price decreases from $44.51 million to $39.67 million as the return requirement goes from 13% to 14%.

Step 4: Compute Rate of Return for Various Offering Prices and Scenarios. Alcar management believes that the absolute minimum successful bid for Rano would be $35 million, or $31.50 per share. Alcar's investment bankers estimated that it may take a bid of as high as $45 million, or $40.50 per share, to gain control of Rano shares. Exhibit 10

EXHIBIT 6 ALCAR'S WEIGHTED AVERAGE COST OF CAPITAL

	Weight	Cost	Weighted Cost
Debt	0.23	0.051	0.012
Equity	0.77	0.140	0.108
Average cost of capital			0.120

EXHIBIT 7   RISK-ADJUSTED COST OF CAPITAL FOR RANO ACQUISITION

	Weight	Cost	Weighted Cost
Debt	0.23	0.054[a]	0.012
Equity	0.77	0.153	0.118
Average risk-adjusted cost of capital			0.130

[a]Before tax debt rate of 10% times 1 minus the estimated tax rate of 46%.

presents the rates of return that will be earned for four different offering prices, ranging from $35 million to $45 million for each of the three scenarios.

Under the optimistic scenario, Alcar could expect a return of 14.4% if it were to pay $45 million. For the most likely case, an offer of $45 million would yield a 12.9% return, or just under the minimum acceptable rate of 13%. This is as expected, since the maximum acceptable cash price as calculated in Exhibit 8 is $44.51 million, or just under the $45 million offer. If Alcar attaches a relatively high probability to the conservative scenario, the risk associated with offers exceeding $38 million becomes apparent.

EXHIBIT 8   MAXIMUM ACCEPTABLE CASH PRICE FOR RANO—MOST LIKELY SCENARIO, WITH A DISCOUNT RATE OF 0.130 ($ MILLIONS)

Year	Cash Flow	Present Value	Cumulative Present Value
1	$ 2.96	$ 2.62	$ 2.62
2	3.41	2.67	5.29
3	3.92	2.72	8.01
4	4.51	2.76	10.77
5	5.13	2.81	13.59
6	4.90	2.35	15.94
7	5.49	2.33	18.27
8	3.86	1.45	19.72
9	4.32	1.44	21.16
10	4.84	1.43	22.59
Residual value	11.48	26.02[a]	48.61
Plus temporary investments not required for current operations			1.00
Less debt assumed			5.10
Maximum acceptable cash price			$44.51
Maximum acceptable cash price per share			$40.10

[a]
$$\frac{\text{year 10 operating earnings after taxes}}{\text{discount rate}} \times \text{year 10} = \frac{\text{discount}}{\text{factor}}$$

$$\frac{11.48}{0.13} \times 0.2946 = 26.02$$

EXHIBIT 9   MAXIMUM ACCEPTABLE CASH PRICE FOR THREE SCENARIOS AND A RANGE OF DISCOUNT RATES

	Discount Rates				
Scenarios	0.11	0.12	0.13	0.14	0.15
1. Conservative					
Total price ($ millions)	$48.84	$42.91	$38.02	$33.93	$30.47
Per share price	44.00	38.66	34.25	30.57	27.45
2. Most Likely					
Total price ($ millions)	57.35	50.31	44.51	39.67	35.58
Per share price	51.67	45.33	40.10	35.74	32.05
3. Optimistic					
Total price ($ millions)	68.37	59.97	53.05	47.28	42.41
Per share price	61.59	54.03	47.80	42.59	38.21

Step 5: Analyze Feasibility of Cash Purchase.   While Alcar management views the relevant purchase price range for Rano as somewhere between $35 million and $45 million, it must also establish whether an all-cash deal is feasible in light of Alcar's current liquidity and target debt-to-equity ratio. The maximum funds available for the purchase of Rano equal the postmerger debt capacity of the combined company less the combined premerger debt of the two companies plus the combined premerger temporary investments of the two companies. (Net working capital not required for everyday operations of the business is classified as "temporary investment.")

In an all-cash transaction governed by purchase accounting, the acquirer's shareholders' equity is unchanged. The postmerger debt capacity is then Alcar's shareholders' equity of $272 million times the targeted debt-to-equity ratio of 0.30, or $81.6 million. Alcar and Rano have premerger debt balances of $56 million and $5.1 million, respectively, for a total of $61.1 million.

EXHIBIT 10   RATE OF RETURN FOR VARIOUS OFFERING PRICES AND SCENARIOS

	Offering Price			
Total ($ millions):	$35.00	$38.00	$40.00	$45.00
Per share:	$31.53	$34.23	$36.04	$40.54
Scenarios				
1. Conservative	0.137	0.130	0.126	0.116
2. Most likely	0.152	0.144	0.139	0.129
3. Optimistic	0.169	0.161	0.156	0.144

The unused debt capacity is thus $81.6 million minus $61.1 million, or $20.5 million. Add to this the combined temporary investments of Alcar and Rano of $26 million, and the maximum funds available for the cash purchase of Rano will be $46.5 million. A cash purchase is therefore feasible within the tentative price range of $35 million to $45 million.

Step 6: Evaluate Impact of Acquisition on Alcar's EPS and Capital Structure.   Because reported earnings per share (EPS) continue to be of great interest to the financial community, a complete acquisition analysis should include a comparison of projected EPS both with and without the acquisition. Exhibit 11 contains this comparative projection. The EPS stream with the acquisition of Rano is systematically greater than the stream without acquisition. The EPS standard, and particularly a short-term EPS standard, is not, however, a reliable basis for assessing whether the acquisition will in fact create value for shareholders.

Several problems arise when EPS is used as a standard for evaluating acquisitions. First, because of accounting measurement problems, the EPS figure can be determined by alternative, equally acceptable methods—for example, LIFO and FIFO. Second, the EPS standard ignores the time value of money. Third, it does not take into account the risk of the EPS stream. Risk is conditioned not only by the nature of the investment projects a company undertakes but also by the relative proportions of debt and equity used to finance those investments.

A company can increase EPS by increasing leverage as long as the marginal return on investment is greater than the interest rate on the new debt. However, if the marginal return on investment is less than the risk-adjusted cost of capital or if the increased leverage leads to an increased cost of capital, then the value of the company could decline despite rising EPS.

Primarily because the acquisition of Rano requires that Alcar partially finance the purchase price with bank borrowing, the debt-to-equity ratios with the acquisition are greater than those without the acquisition (see Exhibit 11). Note that even without the Rano acquisition, Alcar is in danger of violating its target debt-to-equity ratio of 0.30 by the ninth year. The

EXHIBIT 11   ALCAR'S PROJECTED EPS, DEBT-TO-EQUITY RATIO, AND UNUSED DEBT CAPACITY, WITHOUT AND WITH RANO ACQUISITION[a]

	EPS		Debt/Equity		Unused Debt Capacity ($ millions)	
Year	Without	With	Without	With	Without	With
0	$ 3.75	$ 4.10	0.21	0.26	$25.60	$20.50
1	4.53	4.89	0.19	0.27	34.44	9.42
2	5.09	5.51	0.17	0.28	44.22	7.00
3	5.71	6.20	0.19	0.29	40.26	4.20
4	6.38	6.99	0.21	0.30	35.45	0.98
5	7.14	7.87	0.24	0.31	29.67	−2.71
6	7.62	8.29	0.26	0.31	22.69	−7.77
7	8.49	9.27	0.27	0.32	14.49	−13.64
8	9.46	10.14	0.29	0.33	4.91	−22.34
9	10.55	11.33	0.31	0.34	−6.23	−32.36
10	11.76	12.66	0.32	0.35	−19.16	−43.88

[a]Assumed cash purchase price for Rano is $35 million.

acquisition of Rano accelerates the problem to the fifth year. Regardless of whether Alcar purchases Rano, management must now be alert to the financing problem, which may force it to issue additional shares or reevaluate its present capital structure policy.

ACQUISITION FOR STOCK.   The first two steps in the acquisition for stock analysis, projecting Rano cash flows and setting the discount rate, have already been completed in connection with the acquisition for cash analysis developed previously. The remaining steps of the acquisition for stock analysis are:

- Estimate the value of Alcar shares. Compute the maximum number of shares that Alcar can exchange to acquire Rano under various scenarios and minimum acceptable rates of return.
- Evaluate the impact of the acquisition on the earnings per share and capital structure of Alcar.

Step 1: Estimate Value of Alcar Shares.   Alcar conducted a comprehensive corporate self-evaluation that included an assessment of its estimated present value based on a range of scenarios. In the interest of brevity, I consider here only its most likely scenario.

Management made most likely projections for its operations, as shown in Exhibit 12. Again using the equation for the cost of equity capital, the minimum EBIT as a percentage of sales needed to earn at Alcar's 12% cost of capital is 10.9%. Since management can confidently forecast pretax return on sales returns above 10.9% for only the next 10 years, the cash flow projections will be limited to that period.

Exhibit 13 presents the computation of the value of Alcar's equity. Its estimated value of $36.80 per share contrasts with its currently depressed market value of $22 per share. Because Alcar management believes its shares to be substantially undervalued by the market, in the absence of other compelling factors it will be reluctant to acquire Rano by means of an exchange of shares.

To illustrate, suppose that Alcar were to offer $35 million in cash for Rano. Assume the most likely case, that the maximum acceptable cash price is $44.51 million (see Exhibit 8); thus the acquisition would create about $9.5 million in value for Alcar shareholders. Now assume that instead Alcar agrees to exchange $35 million in market value of its shares to acquire Rano. In contrast with the cash case, in the exchange of shares case Alcar shareholders can expect to be worse off by $12.1 million.

With Alcar shares selling at $22, the company must exchange 1.59 million shares to meet the $35 million offer for Rano. There are currently 10 million Alcar shares outstanding.

EXHIBIT 12   MOST LIKELY ESTIMATES FOR ALCAR OPERATIONS WITHOUT ACQUISITION

	Years		
	1–5	6–7	8–10
Sales growth rate	0.125	0.120	0.120
EBIT as a percentage of sales	0.130	0.125	0.125
Income tax rate	0.460	0.460	0.460
Capital investment per dollar of sales increase	0.250	0.250	0.250
Working capital per dollar of sales increase	0.300	0.300	0.300

EXHIBIT 13   ESTIMATED PRESENT VALUE OF ALCAR EQUITY—MOST LIKELY SCENARIO, WITH A DISCOUNT RATE OF 0.120 ($ MILLIONS)

Year	Cash Flow	Present Value	Cumulative Present Value
1	$ 6.13	$ 5.48	$ 5.48
2	6.90	5.50	10.98
3	7.76	5.53	16.51
4	8.74	5.55	22.06
5	9.83	5.58	27.63
6	10.38	5.26	32.89
7	11.63	5.26	38.15
8	13.02	5.26	43.41
9	14.58	5.26	48.67
10	16.33	5.26	53.93
Residual value	128.61	345.10[a]	399.03
Plus temporary investments not required for current operations			25.00
Less debt outstanding			56.00
Present value of Alcar equity			$368.03
Present value per share of Alcar equity			$ 36.80

[a] $\dfrac{\text{year 10 operating earnings after taxes}}{\text{discount rate}} \times \text{year 10 discount factor} =$

$$\frac{128.62}{0.12} \quad \times \quad 0.32197 \quad = \quad 345.10$$

After the merger, the combined company will be owned 86.27%—that is, 10.00/(10.00 + 1.59)—by current Alcar shareholders and 13.73% by Rano shareholders. The $12.1 million loss by Alcar shareholders can then be calculated as shown in Exhibit 14.

Step 2: Compute Maximum Number of Shares Alcar Can Exchange. The maximum acceptable number of shares to exchange for each of the three scenarios and for a range of discount rates appears in Exhibit 15. To earn a 13% rate of return, Alcar can exchange no more than 1.033, 1.210, and 1.442 million shares, assuming the conservative, most likely, and optimistic scenarios, respectively. Consider, for a moment, the most likely case. At a market value per share of $22, the 1.21 million Alcar shares exchanged would have a total

EXHIBIT 14   CALCULATION OF LOSS BY ALCAR SHAREHOLDERS ($ MILLIONS)

Alcar receives 86.27% of Rano's present value of $44.51 million (see Exhibit 8)	$38.4
Alcar gives up 13.73% of its present value of $368.03 million (See Exhibit 13)	(50.5)
Dilution of Alcar shareholders' value	$12.1

EXHIBIT 15   MAXIMUM ACCEPTABLE SHARES (MILLIONS) TO EXCHANGE FOR THREE SCENARIOS AND A RANGE OF DISCOUNT RATES

	Discount Rates				
Scenarios	0.11	0.12	0.13	0.14	0.15
1. Conservative	1.327	1.166	1.033	0.922	0.828
2. Most likely	1.558	1.367	1.210	1.078	0.967
3. Optimistic	1.858	1.630	1.442	1.285	1.152

value of $26.62 million, which is less than Rano's current market value of $27.75 million—that is, 1.11 million shares at $25 per share. Because of the market's apparent undervaluation of Alcar's shares, an exchange ratio likely to be acceptable to Rano will clearly be unattractive to Alcar.

Step 3: Evaluate Impact of Acquisition on Alcar's EPS and Capital Structure.   The $35 million purchase price is just under 10 times Rano's most recent year's earnings of $3.55 million. At its current market price per share of $22, Alcar is selling at about six times its most recent earnings. The acquiring company will always suffer immediate EPS dilution whenever the price-earnings ratio paid for the selling company is greater than its own. Alcar would suffer immediate dilution from $3.75 to $3.54 in the current year. A comparison of EPS for cash versus an exchange-of-shares transaction appears as part of Exhibit 16. As expected, the EPS projections for a cash deal are consistently higher than those for an exchange of shares.

However, the acquisition of Rano for shares rather than cash would remove, at least for now, Alcar's projected financing problem. In contrast with a cash acquisition, an exchange of shares enables Alcar to have unused debt capacity at its disposal throughout the 10 year

EXHIBIT 16   ALCAR'S PROJECTED EPS, DEBT-TO-EQUITY RATIO, AND UNUSED DEBT CAPACITY—CASH VERSUS EXCHANGE OF SHARES[a]

	EPS		Debt/Equity		Unused Debt Capacity (millions)	
Year	Cash	Stock	Cash	Stock	Cash	Stock
0	$ 4.10	$ 3.54	0.26	0.21	$20.50	$25.60
1	4.89	4.37	0.27	0.19	9.42	35.46
2	5.51	4.93	0.28	0.17	7.00	46.62
3	6.20	5.55	0.29	0.18	4.20	48.04
4	6.99	6.23	0.30	0.20	0.98	46.37
5	7.87	7.00	0.31	0.21	−2.71	44.29
6	8.29	7.37	0.31	0.23	−7.77	40.90
7	9.27	8.22	0.32	0.24	−13.64	36.78
8	10.14	8.98	0.33	0.26	−22.34	29.90
9	11.33	10.01	0.34	0.27	−32.36	21.79
10	12.66	11.17	0.35	0.29	−43.88	12.29

[a]Assumed purchase price for Rano is $35 million.

forecast period. Despite the relative attractiveness of this financing flexibility, Alcar management recognized that it could not expect a reasonable rate of return by offering an exchange of shares to Rano.

CONCLUDING NOTE

The experience of companies that have implemented the approach to acquisition analysis described here indicates not only that it is an effective way of evaluating a prospective acquisition candidate, but also that it serves as a catalyst for reevaluating a company's overall strategic plans. The results also enable management to justify acquisition recommendations to the board of directors in an economically sound, convincing fashion.

DEFINITION OF BUSINESS COMBINATION TERMS

LEGAL.

Statutory Merger.   A combination of two or more firms in which one company survives under its own name while the others cease to exist as legal entities (Exhibit 17).

Statutory Consolidation.   All the companies involved in the combination cease to exist as legal entities and a new corporation is created (Exhibit 18).

Parent-Subsidiary Relationship.   One company acquires a controlling interest of another corporation's voting stock but does not assume legal title to its assets or responsibility for its liabilities. The acquired company continues to exist as a separate legal entity (Exhibit 19).

Purchase of Assets.   The acquiring corporation purchases the other corporation's assets, leaving the selling corporation's legal existence intact. The selling company may choose to use the proceeds to retire its outstanding debt and distribute any remainder to its shareholders (Exhibit 20).

TAX.   **Taxable combinations** include taxable acquisition of stock and taxable acquisition of assets.

EXHIBIT 17   STATUTORY MERGER OF COMPANY T INTO COMPANY A

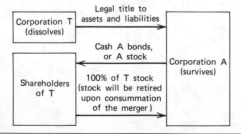

Source: Reinhardt, *Mergers and Acquisitions: A Corporate Finance Approach*, General Learning Corp., 1972.

EXHIBIT 18   STATUTORY CONSOLIDATION OF COMPANY A AND COMPANY T

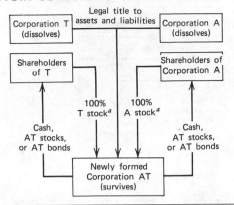

[a]Stock will be retired upon consummation of the consolidation.
Source: Reinhardt, *Mergers and Acquisitions: A Corporate Finance Approach*, General Learning Corp., 1972.

Tax-free "reorganizations" may take one of three forms:

Type A.   Statutory merger or consolidation.

Type B.   Exchange of stock for stock.

Type C.   Exchange of stock for assets.

ACCOUNTING.

Pooling of Interests.   Accounting treatment is prescribed by the AICPA's Accounting Principles Board Opinion No. 16 when combination meets a specified set of criteria (e.g., voting common stock be given in exchange for at least 90% of voting common stock of one of the combining companies).

EXHIBIT 19   AFFILIATION BETWEEN COMPANY A AND COMPANY T

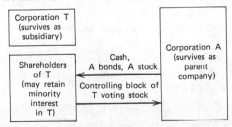

Source: Reinhardt, *Mergers and Acquisitions: A Corporate Finance Approach*, General Learning Corp., 1972.

EXHIBIT 20   A "PURCHASE OF ASSETS" COMBINATION

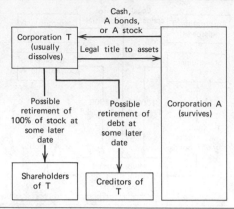

Source: Reinhardt, *Mergers and Acquisitions: A Corporate Finance Approach*, General Learning Corp., 1972.

Positive Conditions for Pooling of Interests.   Each company in a pooling must have been an active independent company for at least 2 years before the plan of combination is initiated. This means that companies that were subsidiaries or divisions of another corporation within that period cannot be pooled. Note the implications for **divestitures**.

  The exchange must be common stock for common stock in a single transaction or under a plan accomplished within a year. Common stock in exchange for outstanding preferred stock is permitted.

  The "common stock" requirement is met if the corporation issuing its common stock to complete the business combination is deemed to have obtained in exchange at least 90% of the common stock of its "pooling partner."

  Shareholders' relative interests must be maintained; that is, the same exchange offer must be made to all stockholders except, of course, the **dissident stockholders** whose interests are acquired for cash (subject to the 90% rule above).

  Generally, the existence of arrangements for contingent issuances of stock or other consideration will prohibit the use of pooling.

Negative Conditions for Pooling of Interests.   To account for a business combination as a pooling, there must be an **absence of any plan to:**

  Retire or reacquire any of the common stock issued to effect the combination.

  Make arrangements for the benefit of a former stockholder of the combining company, such as the guarantee of debt.

  Dispose of any significant part of the assets of the combining companies within 2 years after the combination (except to eliminate duplicate facilities, excess capacity, etc.).

Purchase.   Accounting treatment is prescribed by Accounting Principles Board Opinion No. 16 when combination does not meet pooling of interests criteria.

Conditions for Purchase Accounting.

If a transaction does not meet pooling criteria, it is treated as a purchase.

Assets of the purchased company are written up to fair values, and resulting difference from purchase price is deemed to be **goodwill,** which must be written off over a period not to exceed 40 years.

Guides to Cost Allocation or Assigning Fair Value.

Accounts Receivable.   Present value of amounts deemed to be collectible.

Work in Process.   Estimated selling price as finished goods less cost to complete, sell, dispose, and reasonable profit.

Raw Material.   Current replacement cost.

ECONOMIC.

Horizontal Merger.   One company acquires the stock or assets of another company that is a direct competitor in the same product line and in the same market.

Vertical Merger.   One company acquires the stock or assets of another company that is a customer (forward vertical integration) or supplier (backward vertical integration) of the acquired company.

Market Extension Merger.   One company acquires the stock or assets of another company that sells the same products as the acquiring company but in different markets.

Product Extension Merger.   One company acquires the stock or assets of another company operating in a common market but selling products related to those of the acquirer.

Conglomerate Merger.   One company acquires the stock or assets of another company that is not in a competitive relation and does not have a customer-supplier relationship with the acquiring company.

REFERENCES

Alberts, William W., and McTaggart, James M., "The Short-Term Earnings per Share Standard for Evaluating Prospective Acquisitions," *Mergers and Acquisitions,* Winter 1978.

Bradley, James W., and Korn, Donald H., "Bargains in Valuation Disparities: Corporate Acquirer Versus Passive Investor," *Sloan Management Review,* Winter 1979, pp. 51–64.

Brigham, Eugene F., *Financial Management: Theory and Practice,* Dryden Press, Hinsdale, IL, 1977.

Business Week, "The Cash-Flow Takeover Formula," December 18, 1978.

Ibbotson, Roger G., and Sinquefield, Rex A., *Stock, Bonds, Bills and Inflation: The Past and the Future,* Financial Analysts Research Foundation, New York, 1977.

Mueller, Dennis C., "Effect of Conglomerate Mergers—Survey of the Evidence," *Journal of Banking and Finance,* December 1977, pp. 315–347.

Rappaport, Alfred, "Measuring Company Growth Capacity During Inflation," *Harvard Business Review,* January–February 1979, pp. 91–95.

———, "Strategic Analysis for More Profitable Acquisitions," *Harvard Business Review,* July–August 1979, pp. 99–110.

Rappaport, Alfred, "Do You Know the Value of Your Company?" *Mergers and Acquisitions,* Spring 1979, pp. 12–17.

Reinhardt, Uwe E., *Mergers & Acquisitions: A Corporate Finance Approach,* General Learning Corp., 1972.

Salter, Malcolm S., and Weinhold, Wolf A., "Diversification via Acquisition: Creating Value," *Harvard Business Review,* July–August 1978, pp. 166–176.

Steiner, Peter O., *Mergers: Motives, Effects and Policies,* University of Michigan Press, Ann Arbor, 1975.

Stern, Joel M., "Earnings per Share Don't Count," *Financial Analysts Journal,* July–August 1974, pp. 39–43, 67–75.

Troubh, Raymond S., "Purchased Affection: A Primer on Cash Tender Offers," *Harvard Business Review,* July–August, 1976, pp. 79–91.

PENSION AND PROFIT-SHARING PLANS

CONTENTS

NATURE OF THE COMMITMENT 3

EVOLUTION OF PENSION PLAN
REPORTING AND ISSUES 3

Definitions and Pension Plan Reporting 3
Vested, Past, and Prior Service Cost
Benefits 5
Insured Pension Benefits 6
Potential Unpaid Pension Liabilities: An
Example 6
Recognizing Costs and Liabilities 6
Deferred Profit-Sharing Plans 8
Tax Benefits 8

PLAN OBJECTIVES 9

Financial Versus Nonfinancial Factors 9
    Early retirement costs 9
    Postretirement benefit adjustments 9
    Vesting standards 9
Alternatives to Defined Benefits 10

ROLE OF THE ACTUARY 11

Plan Design 11
Estimating Costs 11

DEFINING INVESTMENT OBJECTIVES 12

Purpose 12
Nature of the Investment Problem 13
Corporate Factors 14
The Asset Mix Decision 15

SELECTING INVESTMENT MANAGERS 17

The Active Management Decision 17
Single-Manager Case 18
Multiple-Manager Structure 18
    Guaranteed investment contract 18
    Immunization 19
    Real estate pools 19
    Managing the managers 19
Manager Selection 20

PERFORMANCE MEASUREMENT 20

LESS CONVENTIONAL INVESTMENTS 22

The Prudence Constraint 22
International Diversification 22
Real Estate 23
Option and Futures Contracts 23
Tangible Assets 24

PENSION AND PROFIT-SHARING PLANS

Roger F. Murray

NATURE OF THE COMMITMENT

The provision of retirement income supplemental to **Social Security benefits** is an aspect of corporate policy, personnel and salary administration, and employee relations that extends far beyond the **corporate finance function.** Related to **overall corporate objectives** are effective recruiting, good employee motivation and morale, systematic retirement rules to facilitate orderly advancement of career employees, and recognition of employees' contributions to the company. These objectives can be met by different means, and the choices among alternatives have distinct financial implications. In collectively bargained pension plans, the negotiating of benefits or contributions involves a wide range of financial considerations.

The nature of the **retirement income commitment** affects the firm's financial position and cost structure. For example, a **profit-sharing retirement plan** involves a cost contingent on profitability; but avoiding a "fixed charge" may turn out to be an expensive method of providing benefits perceived to be of less value by the employee because of contingency. **A defined contribution plan,** common among multiemployer union pension programs, appears to limit liability to the negotiated pension benefits. The problems of such plans in **declining industries** may result, however, in obstacles to withdrawal, or in the assumption of liabilities of other participants who do fail. The **defined benefit plan** involves a specific commitment and the **Employee Retirement Income Security Act of 1974 ("ERISA")** requires systematic funding and corporate backing of the plan. Defined benefits are desirable to employees because of the financial security provided.

The other financial dimension associated with retirement income benefits is, of course, the investment of funds set aside for providing them. This is entirely the financial officer's responsibility. Accordingly, **investment management** is the major topic of this section. Before discussing corporate policies with respect to pension plans, some definitions are supplied and the evolution of pension plan reporting is covered briefly.

EVOLUTION OF PENSION PLAN REPORTING AND ISSUES

DEFINITIONS AND PENSION PLAN REPORTING. Pension plans were first defined, in an official reporting context, in Accounting Report Bulletin No. 47, 1956, and reprinted in *Financial Accounting Standards, Original Pronouncements as of July 1978* (Commerce Clearing House, 1978, p. 77) as follows:

> A formal arrangement for employee retirement benefits, whether established unilaterally or through negotiation, by which commitments, specific or implied, have been made which can be used as the basis for estimating costs. It does not include profit sharing plans or deferred-compensation contracts with individuals. It does not apply to informal arrangements by which voluntary payments are made to retired employees.

ARB No. 47 only indicated guides that are acceptable for dealing with costs of pension plans in the accounts of companies that already have plans. It was not concerned with how these plans should be funded. It was the opinion of the committee that past service benefit costs, that is, costs related to services rendered by employees prior to adoption of a plan, "should be charged to operations during the current and future periods benefited, and should not be charged to earned surplus at the inception of the plan." If the plan already exists, it is appropriate to charge to earned surplus the amount that should have been accumulated by past charges to income since the inception of the plan. The bulletin also states that for accounting purposes it is reasonable to assume that the plan, though modified or renewed, will continue for an indefinite period. The costs based on current and future services should be systematically accrued during the expected period of active service of the covered employees. Costs based on past services should be charged off over some reasonable period, provided the allocation is made on a "systematic and rational" basis and does not cause distortion of the operating results in any one year. The 1956 bulletin concluded that since the general opinion of accounting for pension costs had not been "crystallized sufficiently," differences in methods and procedures would be expected to continue.

Because of the lack of any standardized accounting method, lack of a definition of "vested," and an increased significance of pension costs in relation to the financial position of many companies, pension costs were reviewed again in 1966 in an Accounting Principles Board document, **APB Opinion No. 8.** This opinion was mainly concerned with the determination of pension costs for accounting purposes. It pointed out that the actual pension cost to be charged to expense is not necessarily the same as the amount to be funded for the year. The Board recognized that companies limit their "legal obligation by specifying that pensions shall be payable only to the extent of the assets in the pension fund . . . that plans continue indefinitely and that termination and other limitations of liability are not invoked while the company continues in business" (p. 152). The Board states that the costs of the plan will ultimately be charged to income and should not be charged directly to retained earnings at any time. The amortization of the costs will be a yearly provision between the minimum and maximum limits.

In September 1974 the **Employee Retirement Income Security Act (ERISA)** became law. It was concerned with the **funding of pension plans,** the conditions for **employee participation** and for **vesting of benefits,** and the protection of employees' pension rights. All pension plans adopted after January 1, 1974, are subject to the requirements of the Act. To protect employees' benefits, ERISA imposes an obligation on employers to make **annual contributions,** as determined by a recognized actuarial method, in amounts that will be sufficient over time to pay all pension benefits. ERISA also established the **Pension Benefit Guaranty Corp. (PBGC),** a federal corporation, to administer terminated plans and to guarantee the basic benefits of all participants who have vested rights under a pension plan. If a plan is terminated, the PBGC can obtain a lien against the employer's assets for the

excess of any present value of guaranteed benefits over plan assets, which is limited to 30% of the **fair value of corporate net worth.** This lien has the same status as a federal tax lien in the event of bankruptcy; it has priority over the claims of all but those of secured creditors. We will return to this point shortly.

In December 1974 the **Financial Accounting Standards Board (FASB)** issued **Interpretation No. 3,** "Accounting for the Cost of Pension Plans Subject to the Employee Retirement Income Security Act of 1974." Although it stated that no change was necessary in the minimum and maximum limits for the annual provision for pension costs, the Board did not believe that the Act created a legal obligation for unfunded pension costs that warrant accounting recognition as a liability. There are two exceptions:

1. A company must fund the minimum requirement yearly unless it receives a waiver from the Treasury. The amount not funded shall then be a liability.

2. In the event of termination, or when there is convincing evidence of possible termination, the Act imposes a liability of the excess of prior accruals over funded assets, that is, the **unfunded vested benefits.**

Reviewing this evolution one can easily see that much confusion exists over how unfunded pension costs should be treated, not to mention confusion over the terminology. All agree that if the plan terminates, the unfunded vested benefits should be paid. They are earned; thus they are legal. **Unfunded past or prior service costs** should be amortized, but they are not a legal obligation. It is argued that since they apply only to current employees as a result of new benefits or actuarial changes, they are unearned, thus not legal. Because there is confusion over the legal obligation of unfunded vested benefits for companies that have continuing plans and are amortizing the amount required annually, companies do not report on their balance sheets the unfunded vested benefits. This off-balance sheet "liability" can be a threat to the financial health of a company (see Blissert, *Unfunded Pension Liabilities).*

VESTED, PAST, AND PRIOR SERVICE COST BENEFITS.   The liabilities incurred in the establishment or revisions of defined benefit plans can be measured in two ways: the present value of **vested benefits** and the present value of accumulated or **past service plan benefits. Vested benefits** are the benefits that have been accrued to date and are not contingent on the employee's continuing in the service of the employer or on the plan's termination. They may be insured or uninsured. In either case they are a **legal obligation of the firm. Nonvested benefits** have been earned but are not a legal liability. When the pension benefits are increased, without a corresponding increase in assets, unfunded vested and unvested benefits of course reflect this increase. The significant item to be reported is the **unfunded vested benefits.** The new, earned yet unfunded benefits, payable to former and some current employees, are amortized over 30–40 years.

When a plan is improved, the overall value of the plan increases in proportion to the increase in benefit levels. Since the **assets** (the **funded section**) do not usually increase instantaneously when the plan is improved, the unfunded area will grow. The unfunded future portions are the **unfunded prior service costs** or **past service costs.** Past service costs are those assigned to years **prior to the inception of a new plan,** while prior service costs are those assigned to years prior to the date of a **particular actuarial valuation.** Thus, past service costs are new, yet unearned, benefits **under a new plan,** and prior service costs are those unearned arising through adjustments to the **existing plan** for changes in the actuarial assumptions, such as interest rates and turnover. In both cases the costs apply only to current employees (contingent upon employment) and are amortized over 30–40 years.

Vesting liabilities can be triggered if a firm's plant or division is closed, resulting in the reduction in its labor force, even if the firm itself continues. The **unfunded present value of vested benefits** need not be carried over to the plan sponsor's balance sheet as a liability. Nevertheless, the value of the company—for example in a merger or acquisition—will obviously be affected by the size of this item, since it is essentially a liability of the firm.

INSURED PENSION BENEFITS.   In the event of a pension plan's discontinuance, employees' vested benefits are insured through the **Pension Benefit Guaranty Corp. (PBGC).** The company itself is liable to the PBGC for pension claims paid by the latter with a **maximum liability of 30% of its net worth.** "Net worth" is not defined clearly in the legislation except that it refers to the "fair value" of stockholders' equity. "Fair value" appears to refer to economic value, not to the firm's book value or market value; therefore it is not directly measurable. In addition, the amount and status of the PBGC claim is not clear. In any event, creditors and potential lenders take account of such contingent liabilities in their appraisal of firm creditworthiness.

POTENTIAL UNPAID PENSION LIABILITIES: AN EXAMPLE.   It was only too clear that **Chrysler Corp.** would have gone bankrupt in 1979 or 1980, had the government's loan guarantee bailout not been instituted. In early 1980, Chrysler had 11 separate **defined benefit pension plans** that were covered by ERISA. According to PBGC, assets of 7 of the 11 plans were insufficient to pay vested claims of workers and therefore would have resulted in a PBGC payout and subsequent claim (see Bear Stearns, *Accounting Issues Update,* April 2, 1980). The estimated **plan asset insufficiency** was slightly over $1 billion with an unknown amount collectible from Chrysler. Therefore, PBGC's possible liability also exceeded $1 billion.

If Chrysler's plans had been terminated, but the firm itself did not go bankrupt, the PBGC claim would have been equivalent to any government claim and presumably would have preceded those of the other unsecured creditors. If Chrysler had gone **bankrupt** and had attempted to reorganize under the **new Bankruptcy Code,** the situation would have been less clear because the Code does not specifically mention PBGC. It is not clear, however, that the pension plans will be terminated even in a bankruptcy. Bankruptcy does not always result in a **plan termination,** assuming the firm attempts rehabilitation. Plans could be **assumed,** as well, by purchasers of the relevant assets.

The impact of a **Chrysler bankruptcy** and plan termination on PBGC could have been disastrous. In early 1980, PBGC only had $250 million in assets, against liabilities already totaling $380 million (Bear Stearns, *Accounting Issues Update,* p. 2). Since payments are usually spread out among the pensioners and the Chrysler pension fund assets would also have been available, the total impact would not have hit PBGC immediately. The insurance entity would probably have had no choice, however, but to go to Congress to obtain an increase in its own premium rate, which in 1980 was **$2.60 per covered employee** per year. The result of the Chrysler plan's discontinuance would have resulted, therefore, in an increased cost to all companies with pension plans. That is, the costs of the **Chrysler** problem—or the more definite **White Motor Co. bankruptcy (1980)**—could be spread to other firms.

RECOGNIZING COSTS AND LIABILITIES.   Retirement income expectations should not, according to public policy, be created without steps taken to assure their realization. Govcrnment-approved plans must provide for **systematic funding of prospective benefits** and must keep the funds independent of the plan sponsor's financial position. The **Pension Benefit Guaranty Corp.** ensures a minimum level of benefit payments to participants in **defined benefit plans.**

Determining the cost of a plan is a primary objective of financial management. At the time of adopting a plan, only estimates are available. No one really knows what the plan costs until the last employee has retired, perhaps 40 years later. Even then, **postretirement pension adjustments** may add to costs.

Company policies dictate some of the assumptions about the future. For example, pension planners and **actuaries** rely on projections of the numbers, types, age, sex distribution, and turnover characteristics of the work force to help estimate future costs. Other decisions relate to early retirement incentives, death and disability benefits, vesting provisions, and benefit formulas.

A plan that is successful in providing a standard of living in retirement commensurate with that achieved in a person's active years is almost inevitably a **final pay plan.** For example, a formula that provides 1.5% of the highest 5 of the last 10 years' compensation for each year of service up to 30 years, less half the Social Security benefit (less for shorter service), would be expected to produce the following fractions of the final year's compensation in the case of an employee with 30 years' service:

Final Year's Compensation	Fraction Replaced by Benefits (%)
$ 9,000	61
15,000	53
25,000	48
50,000	45

Because of the reduced expenses and taxes applicable to retired persons, 10–15 percentage points can be added to the fractions above to arrive at the level of **replacement in terms of disposable income.**

The cost of the plan will depend on salary levels and other factors that will prevail far into the future. Actuaries can estimate with some reliability such factors as mortality, turnover, early retirements, disability cases, and other characteristics of the work force. But the major cost elements will turn out to be **changes in Social Security,** the effects of **price level fluctuations on wages and salaries,** and the rates of return that financial pension assets will earn.

Estimating the cost of a pension plan given such uncertainties is an elusive goal. The best that the financial manager can do is to insist on realistic assumptions and regular revisions in light of unfolding developments. A series of successive approximations will then result, rather than a single cost projection. Reasonable stability in the percentage of payroll attributable to pension costs is the primary goal for this aspect of financial management. Since the past has an appealing certainty, the inclination is strong to use the present work force distribution, past turnover rates, and historical investment returns as the basis for calculating future costs. The assumption that the future will mirror the past, however, is seldom if ever valid. The financial manager, therefore, must insist that **cost estimates be forward-looking,** not simply retrospective views of a retirement program that will never again be in operation.

Generally accepted accounting principles as defined by **Accounting Principles Board Opinion No. 8** and the **Securities and Exchange Commission** are under review and prospective revision. The **thrust** of the rules for **financial reporting and disclosure of pension plans,** however, is well established. The minimum level of cost recognition (regardless of the rate of funding) for a defined benefit plan is the normal cost for the period plus interest on any unfunded prior service cost and amortization of such costs over 40 years (30 years for newly created plans or new past service liabilities). This is also the **minimum funding standard** under **ERISA.**

The familiar emphasis on consistency in reporting requires **footnote explanations** of any changes in actuarial methods and assumptions. In the past, companies used **variable cost recognition methods** to ''manage'' or smooth reported earnings. Present and prospective reporting and disclosure rules are designed to make clear what methods of cost recognition and changes in them the firm has adopted.

To avoid transitory variations in cost pension managers should spread actuarial gains and losses over a relatively long period of time (e.g., 15 years).

DEFERRED PROFIT-SHARING PLANS.   The financial reporting and disclosure necessary to comply with the standards of the accounting profession, the SEC, and ERISA have undoubtedly discouraged some firms, especially those that have not yet established stable earning power, from establishing **defined benefit pension plans. Proft-sharing plans** in which the amounts credited to each individual's account are deferred until retirement have more appeal because they create no past service liability. From the standpoint of the employee, however, there are serious deficiencies in such plans. Length of service is not fully recognized until many years after adoption of a plan, and there is no firm expectation of retirement benefits on which the employee may rely.

Profit-sharing plans have become more advantageous since the provision of ERISA under which the employee has the option of deferring the capital gains tax on a lump-sum distribution by placing the proceeds in an **Individual Retirement Account (IRA)** for accumulation until retirement. In essence, this is a type of forced saving-investment plan with tax benefits.

Whatever the plan formula, whether fixed or contingent on profits, the extent to which provision has **already been made** for employees' retirement income is a measure of **financial position.** If future periods will be burdened with greater cost contributions than in the case of competitors, for funding a comparable level of benefits, the firm will be at a **cost disadvantage.** The higher percentage of payroll represented by contributions will be one measure. Another indicator is the size of the unfunded (pension benefits not specifically set aside by the firm) commitment. As **financial reporting and disclosure practices** become more complete, it will be possible for the financial officer to **compare his firm's situation** with that of competitors in terms of the adequacy, cost, and funding status of benefits.

TAX BENEFITS.   To qualify for special **tax treatment** under the Internal Revenue Code, a plan must not discriminate in favor of higher paid employees, must include the total work force, and must accumulate funds for the sole benefit of the pensioners and their beneficiaries. If the plan qualifies, the employer contributions are not recognized as income to covered employees until received as pension benefits. In addition, the funds accumulate without taxes on income or capital gains. The **employer contribution,** like any other expense, is **deductible for income tax purposes.** The funding requirements of ERISA are consistent with the **favorable tax treatment afforded a qualified plan.**

For the self-employed individual, the **Keogh plans,** established in 1962 and amended in 1974, permit taxpayers to **deduct** from taxable income the **lesser** of 15% of earned, non-salaried, income or $7,500 **in any year** if contributions are segregated in an insurance contract or trust account. If employees are not covered under any qualified Keogh plan, they can set aside up to 15% of compensation but not more than $1,500 ($1,750 in certain cases) in an **Individual Retirement Account** (IRA). The tax benefit is the reduction of taxes on the contributions and the deferral of taxes as investment earnings until retirement.

The **tax treatment** of **pension fund investments** makes them an attractive alternative to direct investment in the business (i.e., retained earnings), where profits are subject to the corporate income tax. The lower the marginal aftertax rate of return on new direct investment, the greater the overall advantage of **fully funded pension benefit commitments.**

PLAN OBJECTIVES

FINANCIAL VERSUS NONFINANCIAL FACTORS.   Recruiting key personnel, particularly at later ages, is facilitated by a wide range of personal incentives, of which pension benefits are only one. However, it is desirable to have retirement plans equal to or better than those of others in the industry and/or in the community. The financial management objective of incurring only costs that are moderate and stable relative to payrolls may have to be compromised in the interest of competing effectively for talent and commitment to the firm.

Early Retirement Costs.   From a financial cost standpoint, the **actuarial reduction for early retirement** is usually one-fifteenth per year; for example, at age 62, the employee would be entitled to 80% of what the benefit would be at age 65 (3 years $\times \frac{1}{15} = \frac{3}{15}$ reduction from retirement age benefits). To encourage early retirement, many plans provide for no reduction or one of 3 or 4% for each year prior to age 65, provided the employee has 10 or 15 years of service. Our 62-year-old employee would receive 91% of retirement benefits under a 3% reduction plan. The questions to be raised are: How many employees will elect early retirement? Which kinds of employees will they be? What will be the advantages to the company? Can these advantages be quantified and compared with the additional expense? Disability benefits are a similar analytical problem, although generally not as expensive to a plan.

Postretirement Benefit Adjustments.   Postretirement adjustments are included in benefits to take some **account of inflation** and higher living costs. They can easily add one-third to one-half to costs even if a limit is placed on the extent of indexing. Companies have made periodic ad hoc adjustments since the increase in the rate of inflation, thereby incurring only known costs and not committing in advance for an escalation in benefits of unknown size and duration. Such adjustments have been well received by employees and their unions and are requested with increasing frequency at the bargaining table.

Death benefits may be included in the pension plan or dealt with separately through group life insurance plans. The latter are simpler, more readily communicable, and therefore more effective, especially during service prior to retirement. Small death benefits for retirees are sometimes included at modest cost to take care of funeral and final illness expenses. The important benefit, required under ERISA, is the **joint and survivor annuity option.** Typically, this is 50% of the deceased employee's accrued or projected pension.

Vesting Standards.   The minimum **vesting standards** for individuals established by **ERISA** is **one** of the following:

1. 100% vesting after 10 years of service after age 22.
2. Graduated vesting beginning with 25% after 5 years of service after age 22, increasing 5% a year for the next 5, and 10% a year for each year after 10, to 100% after 15 years.
3. 50% vesting after the earlier of 10 years of service or when the combination of years of service (at least 5) and the employee's age total 45, increasing 10% a year for the next 5 years to 100%. Years of service before age 22 count.

In a typical case, the cost element in choosing among these three standards is not substantial; but **patterns of turnover,** both timing and extent, should be examined thoroughly. There is little advantage and some unnecessary expense in creating small vested benefits for relatively young groups of employees to whom more immediate forms of compensation would be more appreciated.

ALTERNATIVES TO DEFINED BENEFITS.   Given the uncertainties as to the costs of a **defined benefit final pay plan** and the liabilities it creates for the plan sponsor, alternative approaches have been developed. A **money purchase plan,** for example, produces whatever pension benefit the sum in each employee's individual account will buy on retirement. The **defined contribution,** usually a fixed percentage of payroll, produces an accumulation that reflects capital market returns and the quality of investment management applied to it. The employer has fulfilled all obligations in making the defined contribution. All subsequent gains and losses affect only the participating employee.

There are several deficiencies in this approach, especially in a sustained period of rising wages and prices. The contributions invested for the longest periods are those based on the earliest, lower salaries, while those related to the highest years' earnings just prior to retirement are invested only for short periods. A rate of contribution that will produce a satisfactory level of benefits for young entrants will not yield adequate benefits for older entrants.

A special form of **money purchase pension plan** is provided by a **variable annuity.** The pioneer plan was that of the **College Retirement Equities Fund (CREF),** launched in 1952 as a companion to the fixed-dollar annuity benefits provided by **Teachers Insurance & Annuity Association (TIAA)** for the faculties and staffs of colleges, universities, independent schools, and their related associations. During the period of accumulation, the employer and employee contributions are invested in a portfolio of common stocks. At retirement, the accumulation units are used to acquire annuity units in the dollar equivalent of which benefits are paid. The level of retirement income is adjusted to reflect changes in the market value of the stock portfolio each year.

The **variable annuity concept** is essentially that the total return on equities across extended periods of time will, as in the past, equal a basic rate, such as 4%, plus the rate of inflation and possibly plus the rate of improvement in the general standard of living. There is the potential, then, for maintaining the real **purchasing power of pension benefits.** Variable annuities using assets other than common stocks are possible. The major problem with variable annuities during the 1970s was the long lag of security returns in reflecting price-level changes.

Some of the same disadvantages relate to **deferred profit-sharing plans** designed to provide retirement income. If the plan provides that forfeitures (i.e., the interests of employees who leave before full vesting) accrue to the benefit of those who stay, the result may be to produce a good salary replacement level for career employees.

Profit-sharing plans serve two purposes, which may be partially in conflict. One is to provide **long-term financial security** without burdening the firm with a fixed commitment. This argues for a conservative investment program, to ensure that a sufficient level of benefits is generated from profitable operations. The other purpose is to strengthen the employees' **interest in the growth and profitability of the enterprise.** This may be magnified by investing the fund, or a major portion of it, in company stock. The result is not a diversified portfolio, well designed to assure the payment of benefits. In fact, the employment risk has been compounded by the equity risk. The **combination** of a **profit-sharing plan** with a **fixed benefit pension plan,** however, has the incentive advantages without the exposure to serious shortfall in retirement income.

An **incentive savings plan** under which the employer matches, say, 50% of the employees' savings with shares of company stock is another approach to creating an interest in the enterprise among shareholders and employees.

Finally, there is the least acceptable course of providing benefits, namely, on a **pay-as-you-go basis.** There is no liability for prior service to be amortized when each pension is voted on an ad hoc basis. (Any systematic treatment would be a defined benefit plan.) The employee lacks financial security and the employer lacks expense control, since this cost rises each year with a maturing work force. This is the classic case of failure to match costs and revenues, which is rapidly disappearing from the scene in the corporate world, although still characteristic of some public programs and the Armed Services Retirement System.

None of the alternatives has, in effect, the simplicity, clarity, and assurance to the employee of a defined benefit plan. Such a pension program is relatively easy to communicate and has high value as an employee benefit. For this reason, companies seek to establish such plans as soon as their earning power warrants assuming such long-term obligations. Smaller and newer firms may substitute deferred **profit-sharing plans,** until they feel secure enough to provide a defined benefit plan.

ROLE OF THE ACTUARY

PLAN DESIGN. Deciding on the terms of a pension plan is important because once provisions have been established, it is virtually impossible to revise them downward. To be sure, a new plan can be adopted for new employees and for the future service of existing plan participants, but prospective changes take decades to become fully effective. The permanence of a plan, then, justifies obtaining at the outset **professional counsel** from pension planning experts and consulting actuaries. Based on complete information (age, sex, length of service, compensation, etc.) about the work force, **actuaries** can provide crucial insights on the relative costs of different provisions. They can also describe prevailing and competitive plans.

Actuaries, with legal assistance at certain points, are the principal resource for assuring the qualification of plans under the **Internal Revenue Code** and the requirements of **ERISA.** The corporate financial officer may find himself the named fiduciary under the Act, which means that he must take all necessary steps to avoid both corporate and personal liability.

ESTIMATING COSTS. As observed earlier, the **total cost of a pension plan,** especially in the case of a defined benefit final pay plan, cannot be determined for 30 or 40 years after its adoption. But cost estimates are required year by year to satisfy the rules on funding in accordance with acceptable standards.

Within limits it is possible to change the timing of the incidence of costs. **Front-end loading** tends to anticipate that wage rates will continue to rise and that plan provisions will increase the level of benefits. **Back-loading** assumes that such events will occur gradually, that employees will elect later retirement (especially if **Social Security payments** are changed in that direction), that growth in the employee group will long delay the maturing of the plan, and that the current period's costs should not be burdened with costly provisions adopted in future periods. A neutral stance is to seek a **level percentage of payroll** for the present and the future based on reasonable actuarial assumptions and projections.

Complete actuarial valuations every 3 years at a minimum, supplemented by annual reviews, provide the necessary support for the deduction of contributions for tax purposes, for ascertaining the current level of contributions for satisfying ERISA standards, making expense projections for financial planning, for an analysis of gains and losses, and the reporting of funding status. The certification that normal costs are being met and that prior service liabilities are being amortized is an essential statement for all purposes.

The key variables for discussion with the actuary are (1) the maturing of the work force, (2) the trend toward or away from early retirement, (3) priorities in collective bargaining demands, (4) competitors' plans and cost recognition, and (5) any other factors peculiar to the firm that might differentiate its position from the typical case in the actuary's experience. On the basis of these specifics and corporate expectations about the future economic environment (stability, inflation levels, industry developments, tax policy, etc.), **actuarial assumptions** have to be made. None of these questions about the future is easy to answer with confidence, but each is as germane to the elements of **cost recognition** and pace of funding as to the corporate capital budgeting decision on a major investment in plant and equipment or a new product development. Integration of the actuarial considerations with all other elements of financial planning is both logical and essential. The financial executive must fight against treating the pension decisions as a mysterious world apart from the firm's basic long-term strategic plans.

Apart from the assumptions as to **salary progression** and **investment return,** which are discussed below, the specific cost factors the actuary provides are mortality rates, employee turnover, incidence of disability, and retirement ages. These reflect general trends as modified by company experience. Also, the actuary must make an assumption about the future of the Social Security wage base and benefits. The financial officer has little reason to challenge these estimates when they are carefully made. He should save his principal questions for, and apply his experience to, the assumptions regarding investment returns and salary progression. These, in turn, should be derived from the investment objectives carefully defined as a matter of corporate policy.

DEFINING INVESTMENT OBJECTIVES

PURPOSE. In the past, corporate managements have given an investment manager such a vague statement of **objectives** as "seek the maximum return consistent with an acceptable level of risk." Since such a statement provides no measurable standard of performance expectations, the appraisal of results becomes a matter of hindsight and subjective judgment rather than objective appraisal. In addition, the term "risk" has so many meanings that its precise definition in this context is essential.

Beyond the question of holding an investment manager accountable for results is the major question of determining corporate policy thoughtfully and analytically. Some consistency with other policies is desirable, and stability of attitudes and expectations is essential. Absent this kind of measured consideration, decisions will be reached on the spur of the moment under the overwhelming influence of the euphoric or doomsday atmospheres that periodically invade the boardroom. Evidence of the reality of such distortions of expectations in reflection of events of the most recent past is found in the dismal record of corporate pension funds over an extended period. After a long period of excellent equity returns in the 1950s and 1960s, when stock prices were peaking in the early 1970s, corporate pension funds sold bonds to put more than 100% of new money in common stocks. By the middle and late 1970s, when stocks had been revalued downward some 50% in relation to earning power, new money was directed predominantly into bonds on the eve of the worst bond market experience in history. After the 5-year favorable experience of common stocks (1975–1979), stocks regained favor once again.

Human and peer pressures are so powerful in the direction of sharing the expectations for the future derived from yesterday's events that only a clearly thought out and understood **definition of objectives** can keep the investment program on a course consistent with maximizing its productivity over a 30-year funding span. Business executives who commit resources to the launching of new products, the building of new plants, and the opening of new markets with full recognition of the risks involved sometimes shrink from investing in a **well-diversified portfolio of seasoned companies.** This paradoxical behavior was illustrated in the 1970s when companies that were increasing the bond component of their pension funds at the same time were bidding 30, 40, and 50% premiums over market prices to make major acquisitions.

A clear and explicit statement of **objectives,** constantly reviewed and reaffirmed, is the best available antidote to the loss of perspective and the emotional reactions to transitory events that periodically influence the investment decision-making process. A measured framing of objectives and expectations that can be adhered to across time will do more to enhance the productivity of pension fund assets than any other single step.

NATURE OF THE INVESTMENT PROBLEM.   The investment management of a pension fund has certain important characteristics that are favorable to the achievement of excellent results:

1. *Absence of tax considerations.* None of the usual differentiations among capital gains and ordinary income, short-term and long-term gains, or forms of holding period returns has any significance.

2. *Absence of distinctions between principal (capital) and income.* The total return or productivity of the invested assets is what matters; that is, the interest and dividend flow plus or minus changes in capital values, whether realized or not.

3. *Absence of liquidity needs.* With rare exceptions, the fund is not subject to unanticipated withdrawals that require emphasis on stability of market values or substantial assets readily convertible into cash on short notice without material risk of loss. (An exception would be a profit-sharing plan covering few members.)

4. *A long time horizon.* Results over a 20- or 30-year period are what really matter. Short-term aberrations from good long-term rates of return are not important. The long view of investment strategy can be taken.

These favorable dimensions of the investment problem must be exploited to the fullest because the achievement of the desired solution is so difficult. The provision of a standard of living that is comparable to today's standard in real terms at some far distant date implies that reasonably constant purchasing power can be delivered by earning a real rate of interest plus an inflation premium. There is substantial evidence that a continuous investment in U.S.

Treasury bills will earn the inflation rate over long periods of time. By giving up the price stability and liquidity of a Treasury bill, positive real returns have been earned historically. The long **record of real returns** (i.e., nominal returns minus changes in the Consumer Price Index) has been tabulated as follows by Ibbotson and Sinquefield, in *Stocks, Bonds, Bills, and Inflation: Historical Returns (1926–1978)*:

Geometric Mean Total Return, 1926–1978

	Nominal Return (%)	−	Inflation Rate (%)	=	Real Return (%)
U.S. Treasury bills	2.5		2.5		0
Long-term government bonds	3.2		2.5		0.7
Long-term corporate bonds	4.0		2.5		1.5
Common stocks	8.9		2.5		6.4

Each of these asset categories, except Treasury bills, provided an **incremental return over inflation rates** as a form of reward for accepting price variability and illiquidity. For the same period, Ibbotson and Sinquefield calculated the **standard deviation of nominal returns** (a widely accepted measure of variability) for Treasury bills at 2.2%, while long-term corporate bond returns showed a standard deviation of 5.6% and common stocks one of 22.2%. Although stocks provided a significantly higher average return, it was highly erratic, fluctuating between −13.3 and +31.1% [about two-thirds of the time (standard deviation) during this 53-year period].

The logic and economic underpinnings of a **positive relationship between rate of return and the variability of that return** support the expectation that the historical risk, variability, and illiquidity premiums will persist in the future, even though their size may vary with capital market conditions. A pension plan sponsor is in a good position to accept such generally undesirable attributes of investment experience and to earn those premiums. Indeed, it would be poor judgment to give up a return increment to secure the price stability and liquidity that a pension fund does not require.

CORPORATE FACTORS.   Capital market expectations are not the only factors to be considered in **defining investment objectives**. The characteristics of the pension plan, as we have seen, affect the timing of cash flows and the nature of the employer's commitments and liabilities. Even more relevant are the **characteristics of the firm**. A young firm in a period of strong growth can accept a level of variability in pension fund returns that would be undesirable for a mature company in a cyclically sensitive industry. **The pension fund should be looked on as a major capital investment** to be compared with corporate direct investments in production facilities for particular lines of business. If those areas of activity are profitable and stable, there are fewer reasons to emphasize stability in the returns sought from the pension fund portfolio.

A major asset on a **defined pension plan's balance sheet** is the **present value of future contributions**. The stronger the plan sponsor (i.e., the higher the credit rating for that long-term ''receivable''), the greater the proportion of variable, risky assets the plan can hold to earn a higher return. At the other extreme, if the viability of the company is open to question, the assets on hand should logically be exposed to less variability and possible loss.

Financial leverage is another useful measure for setting objectives consistent both with **corporate financial policy** and protection of the interests of present and future pensioners. If the plan sponsor, as a matter of policy, creates a highly leveraged capital structure that results in variability of earnings, the funding of pension benefits with variable assets might be restricted. There are, indeed, some who advocate borrowing by corporations to repurchase equity while concentrating the pension plan investments in fixed return assets, like high-quality bonds. The validity of this approach depends on a series of assumptions about which serious questions can be raised; but there can be no challenge to the logic of taking an integrated view of the combined financial position of the pension fund and the plan sponsor.

The previously described characteristics of pension funds, especially the absence of liquidity needs and the long time horizon, suggest that the pension fund is a better holder of variable, illiquid assets like common stocks than is the sponsoring corporation. If such assets are described as "risky" because of the uncertainty of the timing of the realization of returns, it is clear that a typical defined benefit pension plan of a growing enterprise is an almost ideal holder of "risky" assets. This type of risk must be clearly distinguished from what can be thought of as the risk of permanent or nonrecoverable losses of the kind that are sustained when a company goes bankrupt, scales down its obligations, and retains little if any of its equity. This **default risk** can result in losses that are subtractions from the total returns realized across time, not just temporary fluctuations.

While stable costs are a normal corporate objective, stability is not necessarily to be valued more highly than lower average costs. In the case of regulated industries and defense contractors, however, the stable return that produces a stable percentage of payroll in the cost structure may have advantages in the setting of rates and the determination of allowable expenses. Whatever the tradeoff between **return** and **variability**, the actuarial methods applied can dampen short-run variations significantly by the use of average rather than single-point market values and by spreading investment gains and losses over future periods.

THE ASSET MIX DECISION. The decision as to the **allocation of pension fund assets among different classes of securities** is the most important single choice to be made by the financial officer and his board. Even the selection of a **single manager** to whom complete discretion is granted does not provide escape from responsibility for this decision. The selection of that single manager must be made with full knowledge of how he will diversify the portfolio, so that the act of selecting the manager is the act of determining the **asset mix**. The situation is even clearer when two or more managers are employed because then each allocation of cash flow to a manager is a choice of that person's style and an asset mix decision.

Portfolio theory commends as one type of **"efficient" portfolio** that which produces the best expected return for a given level of variability. If the best estimate is that the variability of an equity portfolio is equal to the market's (a **beta** of 1.00, in the popular jargon), one might well accept the lower return commensurate with 10% less variability (a beta of 0.90). The economic theorist would describe this whole process as determining the **corporate utility function**. This is a useful formal concept: a way to think about the question. For example, at what point will corporate management value increments of stability and predictability more highly than units of additional expected return? In most instances, such risk-return tradeoffs **cannot** be derived by observation and discussion with money managers but an **asset allocation model** will help.

Investment simulations that answer the question "what if?" are widely available from pension consultants and investment managers. These exercises are designed to estimate the probability of a pension portfolio failing to earn an assumed rate of total return over a 10-year period with various **bond-stock ratios** and with various expected returns from each type of security. These models permit the decision maker to insert his own judgments as to future trends in inflation, bond yields, and stock returns. Relating these factors to the estimated rate of increase in wages and salaries will indicate whether expected returns will be at least equal to, preferably greater than, the progression in pay scales and vested pension benefits.

The use of **asset allocation models** for determining the specific investment objectives at a single point in time may lead to bad decisions. The asset allocation model's application assumes an equilibrium relationship between, say, bond and stock expected returns. If, on the contrary, either class of asset is materially over- or undervalued relative to the other, the results will be disappointing. In other words, asset allocation models are no substitute for an informed, careful judgment of prospective returns from the different asset types. This difficulty of making infallible judgments about future capital market trends is another reason for diversifying the portfolio among different types of assets.

However reached, the decision regarding **asset mix** is the most important one for the plan sponsor in addressing the question of acceptable levels of return and variability. For example, the decision might be to define investment objectives in terms of the following asset mix:

	Normal Proportion (%)	Authorized Range (%)
Long-term bonds	25	10–30
Common stocks	65	50–75
Real estate	5	0–10
Cash equivalents	5	5–40

Such an asset mix expresses the following conclusions about the future:

1. Variable returns are not a cause of concern and the plan sponsor will accept them to earn a higher return across time. **Liquidity and price stability** are portfolio characteristics of little value relative to their cost in the form of total return forgone.

2. While skeptical about the ability of investment managers to make consistently successful market timing decisions, the plan sponsor provides scope for significant shifts to **cash equivalents** when managers consider prices for any asset class excessive and vulnerable to correction.

3. A relatively high positive correlation between bond and stock returns is expected in the future. As a result, aggregate returns cannot be materially stabilized by shifts between long-term bonds and common stocks. The assumption is that only cash equivalents (money market instruments) will serve that purpose.

The **asset mix decision** can be translated into a **total return expectation** by another set of assumptions regarding inflation (nominal and real rates). An example might be:

	Proportion (%)	Expected Real Return (%)	Expected Inflation Rate (%)	Expected Nominal Return (%)	Expected Portfolio Return (%)
Long-term bonds	25	2.5	8	10.5	2.63
Common stocks	65	7.5	8	15.5	10.08
Real estate	5	8.5	8	16.5	0.83
Cash equivalents	5	0.5	8	8.5	0.42
					13.96

Return expectations, therefore, can be expressed to investment managers in either real or nominal terms (e.g., approximately 14% nominal or 6% real). Ideally, the portfolio manager will add enough to the fund's asset value to pay for his management fee and other portfolio expenses. Measures of variability like the **standard deviation of returns** can be specified to make expectations more precisely framed.

The resulting statement of expectations as to asset mix, returns, and variability comprises the statement of **investment objectives**. Some additional specifications can be provided to control the rate of permanent losses from investments in companies that prove to have marginal creditworthiness. Illustrations would be the setting of quality standards in terms of **Moody's** or **Standard & Poor's ratings**, and specifying limits on the concentration of investments and measures of **diversification**, **yield targets for common stocks**, and a **range of beta coefficients** as a measure of sensitivity to broad market fluctuations. Other guidelines might include the extent of **international diversification** or the authorization of **option activity**.

However defined, investment objectives must be reviewed regularly and revised to take account of changes in plan or corporate factors, changes in attitudes toward different types of risk, and fundamental changes in the capital markets that materially affect expected returns and differentials among them. Frequent review and reexamination also serve to keep stable the plan sponsor's commitment to basic policy.

SELECTING INVESTMENT MANAGERS

THE ACTIVE MANAGEMENT DECISION.   Since security markets are highly efficient in pricing individual issues, some argue that a market fund will perform as well as a fund that is actively managed. **Market or index funds** seek to replicate a market index, like Standard & Poor's 500 Stock Index, by owning a very broadly diversified portfolio of stocks in the index in proportion to the market values of their capitalizations. Such a **passive portfolio** will presumably exceed the average performance of all actively managed portfolios by the **saving in transaction costs**. Engaging in **active management** to secure superior returns (after adjustment for relative variability) is often referred to as a **zero sum game**; that is, the winners' gains are equaled by the losses of unsuccessful managers.

The plan sponsor's decision to employ **active management** for part or all of the pension fund's assets presumes that he can identify managers who will produce superior returns across a market cycle. These returns must be sufficiently better than the market returns available from a passive market portfolio to pay the cost of transactions and a return warranted by the level of specific risk.

Some plan sponsors select a compromise by having a **"core" market portfolio** that is passively managed while having **specialist managers** who seek to add return by their skills in selecting stocks from such market sectors as emerging companies, growth stocks, basic value issues, and yield stocks.

The financial officer, in identifying active managers likely to add value by **active management**, must satisfy himself that the prospective manager has a style, a discipline, and a quality control system to support the marketing presentation. The term "style" refers to the general approach or strategy of an investment manager. It may be the development of expertise in selecting growth or basic value stocks, in rotating from one market sector to another, in timing bond and stock market changes, or in identifying small-capitalization stocks with strong growth potential.

But a portfolio manager's style is not meaningful unless it is reinforced by a well-defined discipline that assures a systematic and consistently applied **analytical valuation approach** to security selection. This must be a valid and tested decision-making process or there can be no assurance that past results will be achieved in the future.

Finally, the investment management function must be able to track performance, identify aberrations from expected results, and determine on a current basis whether the product being delivered in the form of a portfolio has uniformly defined characteristics. Active management without these safeguards may turn out to be unreliable and unpredictable.

SINGLE-MANAGER CASE.   **For passive management**, only a single qualified manager is required. **For active management**, the plan sponsor has a choice. The simplicity, convenience, and lower cost of working with a single manager are appealing but not persuasive reasons for selecting a single manager. Most organizations have special strengths, and the best results will always be achieved by hiring managers to do what they do best. A good bond manager may not be good at equities, and vice versa. Placing a balanced portfolio with a single manager requires separate analyses of capabilities in each area.

The commingled fund run by banks, **life insurance company separate accounts**, and **mutual funds** managed by investment advisers permit having **multiple portfolio managers** with specialized skills for funds of even modest size. Small size is, then, no longer a reason for using a single manager.

The principal arguments against the employment of a single manager are the need to obtain **specialized skills** and the reduction in **manager selection risk**. Since organizations change, professionals leave, ownership shifts, leadership becomes complacent, and past performance is a thoroughly unreliable guide to future results, even the most careful process of selecting managers can fail. Thus if the plan sponsor has a perception of a manager that proves to be inaccurate, too long a time may elapse before the situation is fully recognized and a change made. That period is likely to be one of underperformance. **Diversifying the manager risk** is, therefore, worth considering.

MULTIPLE-MANAGER STRUCTURE.   If the goal is not merely to diversify, but more affirmatively to obtain the benefit of superior skills in different market sectors, the plan sponsor can consider a **multiple-manager structure** for active management. If the managers add value by actively managing portfolios in their several styles, they will produce aggregate results superior, after adjustment for variability, to a **market fund**.

Active bond portfolio managers also differ in their styles. Some rely almost exclusively on the anticipation of **interest rate changes**. Others give emphasis to "**sector swaps**"; that is, seeking additional returns by shifting from a relatively fully valued market sector to a relatively undervalued one on the basis of yield spreads between them. Another approach is to use **credit analysis** to select issues that are about to be upgraded and avoid those whose credit rating is about to be downgraded. There are also substantial differences in the aggressiveness with which a manager will back his interest rate forecasts.

Guaranteed Investment Contract.   Another form of fixed income management is the **guaranteed investment contract (GIC)** issued by life insurance companies. Some minimum rate of return is guaranteed by the issuer for a specified period in the future. The GIC, for accounting and actuarial purposes at least, is presumed to have a **fixed value**. Typically the funds are invested in a broadly diversified portfolio of corporate direct placements.

Immunization. Investment managers have designed and offer a **bond "immunization" program** (see the sections entitled "Bond Management Issues" and "Specialized Fixed Income Security Strategies"). The bond portfolio is invested so that for a specific period (e.g., 7 years) the return will not vary significantly from what was initially projected. This **immunity from interest rate changes** is accomplished by resetting the portfolio periodically to meet the calculated objective. Funding benefits promised to retired employees through a GIC or an immunization program are designed to fix the cost of those benefits by reducing the interest rate risk. Buying **immediate annuity contracts** from insurers would shift the mortality risk in addition.

Contracts that are designed to shift the uncertainties of future interest levels and fluctuations to an insurer must, of necessity, have limited lives. In relation to a 30-year funding period for long deferred benefits, a 5- or 10-year period of protection is helpful but still leaves the plan sponsor carrying the bulk of the risk.

Real Estate Pools. Life insurance companies also offer participations in **pools of real estate equity investments,** providing a degree of diversification not otherwise available to any but the largest funds. Since inflows and outflows of funds occur at appraised values, as distinguished from prices set in an active trading market, participation in **real estate separate accounts** may be more or less advantageous depending on the extent to which the valuation smoothing of appraisals brings unit values into line with the effects of interest rate and other capital market factors.

With such a wide range of alternatives (and so-called unconventional assets have not even been mentioned), it is evident that the plan sponsor has choices to make in selecting the combination of investment management styles and skills that is most likely to achieve the firm's defined objectives for the pension fund. Internal resources for making these decisions can be usefully supplemented by counsel from consultants. Their role is to provide information about the styles and disciplines of individual managers and to assist in the analysis of the suitability of any combination of them for matching the defined investment objectives. Whether a particular manager should be hired is, of course, the decision of the plan sponsor. If the "chemistry" of the relationship is not good, no style or discipline, however appropriate for the task, should dictate the selection.

Managing the Managers. Once the **multiple-manager structure** has been established, the plan sponsor has the task of managing it. **Managing the managers,** obviously, is not managing the portfolios. The principal tasks of the sponsor are now (1) the review and revision of investment objectives in light of changes in the external environment, plan factors, and corporate factors, (2) the allocation of new money among managers in accordance with a plan consistent with defined objectives, (3) the analysis of and rationalization for the performance of managers across a market cycle (typically 3 or 4 years), and (4) effective communication with corporate executives and investment managers of progress in and prospects for realizing the defined objectives.

The worst hazards to successful management of managers are (1) lack of effective communication and understanding, (2) impatience and hasty reactions to capital market developments, and (3) turnover in personnel without adequate transitional guidance. There is a strong tendency to increase attention to this investment pool when it is performing poorly, perhaps because of temporary capital market factors. Vastly superior rates of returns may, in fact, be a better reason for more careful analysis because they may be due to an unsustainable aberration in the relationships among asset values.

Finally, the corporate sponsor must fight the managers' tendency to hold diversified portfolios. Each manager needs to be prodded in the direction of **concentrating in the market sector of his expertise,** avoiding broad diversification and overlap with other managers. Only the plan sponsor should look at the total result and test the adequacy of its diversification, to prevent either seriously disappointing results or exposure to large permanent losses of capital. Related questions are, of course, whether a different mix of styles is more likely to serve the objectives better in the future and whether more specific guidelines should be furnished to individual managers to assure the uniform character of their output. **The plan sponsor** must be sure that what he is asking of a manager is drawing on that manager's deepest reservoir of experience, conviction, and skill.

MANAGER SELECTION.   Regardless of whether outside consultants are employed to assist in the **manager selection process,** the corporate financial officer and the **board of directors** must arrive at independent judgments and make informed decisions. Screening the very large number of capable investment managers to identify those who have the potential of performing a particular function in the manager mix is the most useful function of the consultant. His role is also helpful in preparing the questionnaire, if one is used, or the interview materials needed to ensure that time is productively employed. The consultant should also help in interpreting the **interview results, sample portfolios** and **performance records,** and to assess the effects on **total portfolio characteristics of different manager mixes.**

Those involved from the corporate side and the portfolio manager who is being considered for the account must meet and discover the "chemistry," good or bad, of the relationship. Before any final choice is made, a **visit to the working quarters of the manager** is essential, to observe this element of the firm's style. Proprietary information involving financial position, ownership, compensation, management of growth, turnover in employees and accounts, and so on, is relevant and suitable for discussion. The extensive survey of alternatives and the intensive study of individual candidates is very cost effective because of the **high costs of changing managers:** both the loss of continuity and the high transaction costs of extensive portfolio shifts.

PERFORMANCE MEASUREMENT

The appropriate measurement for **investment management performance** is the **time-weighted total rate of return** with or without adjustment for variability. The measure is of the **productivity of capital** for the periods of time under management. The manager has no control over the timing of contributions and should be neither benefited nor penalized for decisions beyond his control. The method essentially involves calculating total returns for each period in which there is no fund inflow or outflow. A simple example follows:

A fund has $1 million market value of assets on January 1.

It earns interest and dividends of $40,000 during the first 6 months.

Assets increase in value $60,000 during the period.

On July 1, $500,000 is added to the fund.

During the second half of the year, the fund earns $60,000 but has a decrease in market value of $100,000, with the result that the fund's December 31 value is $1,560,000.

What was the time-weighted rate of return?

The total return for the first half of the year was

$$\frac{\$40,000 + \$60,000}{\$1,000,000} = 10\%$$

For the second half of the year, the total return was

$$\frac{\$60,000 - \$100,000}{\$1,600,000} = -2.5\%$$

At the end of June, each dollar at the start of the year had a value of $1.10.

Each July 1 dollar was worth only $0.975 at the end of the year. For the year as a whole, therefore, a dollar grew to $1.0725, making the **time-weighted total return** 7.25%, compounded semiannually.

When inflows and outflows do not neatly coincide with valuation dates as in the example, approximations can be made without serious distortions of results. (The authoritative and widely accepted study on this subject is the **Bank Administration Institute's** "Measuring the Investment Performance of Pension Funds," 1968.)

The more conventional **dollar-weighted rate of return** would be lower in the example because more dollars were invested during the period of inferior returns. However, for the evaluation of progress toward funding a liability, this **internal rate of return** is the correct measure and will be used in actuarial valuations to determine investment gains and losses, that is, realized and unrealized returns across time compared with the assumed interest rate.

The **adjustment of time-weighted returns** to reflect their **variability** is a logical step, especially if (1) the data are used to make comparisons with other funds or (2) the variability is greater or less than contemplated in the definition of investment objectives. Frequently, the **beta coefficient** (the historical sensitivity of the portfolio's returns to those of market indexes) is used for such adjustments. Ratios of return to variability are also useful to determine whether the investment manager is realizing adequate rewards for risk assumed in the form of the variability of returns.

When a manager's performance lags, he may be tempted to "play catch-up ball"—to buy lower quality, volatile securities in the hope that a positive market environment will produce returns far above average. The plan sponsor's task is to make sure that such a strategy is not placing fund assets at a higher than contemplated level of risk. Conversely, a manager may seek an unnecessarily **defensive position** in terms of price stability and liquidity at material sacrifice in return to avoid exposure to possible client disappointments resulting in the loss of investment management business.

Refinements in the measurement of portfolio characteristics have made it possible to describe a risk-return profile with a fair degree of precision. The use of **fundamental betas** (those that take account of earnings, size, growth, and financial leverage factors in addition to historical price variability relative to the market) has increased the visibility of investment styles and the sources of superior or inferior returns. **Measures of portfolio diversification** like the R^2 (percent of the variance of return explained), and measures of **variability** like the **standard deviation** also guide the corporate financial officer in determining whether a **multiple-manager structure** can be expected to produce superior returns.

Such data on the **sources of performance results** permit **diagnostic analysis:** the analysis of performance for the purpose of identifying the strategies and tactics that added to or subtracted from realized returns. This should not be just an exercise in hindsight. Diagnostic analysis extends to the review of defined objectives and the corporate factors in their influence on investment management policies. The effective use of this analytical step is not as grounds for recriminations but as an early warning of any misperceptions of the basic asset management plan.

For an in-depth discussion on portfolio evaluation see the section entitled "Performance Measurement."

LESS CONVENTIONAL INVESTMENTS

THE PRUDENCE CONSTRAINT.   In addressing the question of whether less conventional or even **unconventional investments** are eligible for pension funds, the corporate financial officer must recognize that Section 404.(a)(1) of ERISA has not been definitively interpreted by the courts. Nevertheless, the language is fairly explicit:

> . . . a fiduciary shall discharge his duties with respect to a plan solely in the interest of the participants and beneficiaries and (A) for the exclusive purpose of: (i) providing benefits to participants and their beneficiaries; and (ii) defraying reasonable expenses of administering the plan; (B) with the care, skill, prudence, and diligence under the circumstances then prevailing that a prudent man acting in a like capacity and familiar with such matters would use in the conduct of an enterprise of a like character and with like aims; (C) by diversifying the investments of the plan so as to minimize the risk of large losses, unless under the circumstances it is clearly prudent not to do so. . . .

Undivided **loyalty, prudence,** and **diligence** are not new requirements for a fiduciary; but the standard of **"a prudent man acting in a like capacity and familiar with such matters"** appears to call for specific expertise in managing pension funds. Being informed about the terms of the plan, the investment alternatives, and risks of loss implies some specialized knowledge of the field.

The traditional **personal trust standard of prudence,** which treats each investment as an individual case, does not recognize a gain on one as an offset to a loss on another. The **emerging definition of prudence** in pension fund asset management appears to recognize the effects of diversification and to apply the standard to a portfolio rather than to single securities. As is well known in portfolio theory, a well-diversified portfolio of risky securities may have very little exposure to large losses. Individual securities might not be clearly prudent—shares of new and unseasoned companies, for example—but a well-diversified portfolio of them could be quite acceptable.

In short, the prudent expert constraint appears to be more analytically grounded by relating investment decisions to the characteristics of a growing pool of assets with a long time horizon. The range of investment alternatives appears to have been broadened, provided the decision maker systematically studies their place in and effects on the characteristics of a total asset mix.

The other reassuring phrase is "under the circumstances then prevailing." This says that decisions will be judged not based on hindsight but on the basis of the reasonableness of judgments reached in the environment in which the investments were made.

INTERNATIONAL DIVERSIFICATION.   Diversifying bond and stock portfolios across the world's capital markets is both logical and consistent with the objective of creating the most efficient portfolio, that is, securing the best return at a given level of variability. Since securities returns in different markets, including the effects of currency fluctuations, are not likely to show high positive correlations, distributing investments among the half-dozen largest markets has typically resulted in a higher return and less variability than a portfolio invested in domestic markets.

International diversification has, therefore, become widely adopted by corporate pension funds but on a modest scale. Some funds invest in a portfolio that mirrors an **international market index** while others opt for active management. **Commingled funds** are available from banks and investment advisory organizations. For a discussion on this and other related factors, see the section entitled ''International Portfolio Diversification and Foreign Capital Markets.''

REAL ESTATE. Investing in **real estate equities** has become almost conventional. The major life insurance company **real estate open-end separate accounts** provide broad diversification and experienced management for very large aggregations of capital. Other organizations assemble **closed-end packages of investments for pension funds** with the expectation that the investments will be liquidated in a decade or so. Valuation of properties becomes important in the case of open-end pools.

Comprehensive data on returns from real estate equity investments in the hands of tax-free investors are not available. Experience suggests, however, that **real estate is a good diversifying asset,** providing ample returns as the reward for accepting its illiquidity. Investments need to be well diversified because of the uniqueness of each property and the factors that may affect its holding period return. Except for the largest pension funds, therefore, participation in a **pool of real estate investments** is the prudent course.

OPTION AND FUTURES CONTRACTS. The purchase and sale of **option contracts** by themselves raise questions as to prudence because options have no claim on assets or earning power, provide no current return, and have a very short life. It is generally thought that the purchase of such a contract is pure **speculation** on an unpredictable price change or a device to provide high leverage without borrowing.

When combined with other assets, however, options can become **risk-reducing instruments. Writing (selling) calls** on stocks in the portfolio, for example, is recognized as a prudent step in **reducing volatility.** The premium received for writing the call is a cushion (hedge) against the loss from a decline in the stock price. A portfolio of stocks on which calls are regularly written will typically have the variability of its return reduced by 30–40% at a modest sacrifice of total return. The simultaneous purchase of stocks and writing of calls may produce an asset with no more variability than a portfolio of long-term bonds but with a higher total return.

Less widely recognized is an essentially similar strategy of buying **"protective puts"** covering some or all of a portfolio of stock positions. Prospective returns are reduced by adding the **cost of the protective puts** to the cost of the shares, but the exposure to loss is absolutely limited to the difference between the combined cost and the exercise value of the put contract.

Some fund managers have purchased what are sometimes called **"fiduciary calls."** The amount of the **exercise price is earmarked in cash equivalents tied to the purchased call.** The combination of the calls and the money market instruments provides the upside potential of owning the shares but with possible loss limited to the value of the calls. It is a **fiduciary call** because the exercise price is fully funded in riskless investments that earn interest and are highly liquid. The combination of calls and cash equivalents is also an attractive substitute for convertible securities of the same companies.

Still in the experimental stage is **writing puts against assured future cash flows on stocks** the manager plans to buy as soon as the funds are available. The premium received for writing the put in effect reduces the cost of acquiring the selected stocks. Earmarking cash reserves or expected cash flows to the extent of the exercise prices of the puts makes them **"fiduciary puts."**

In contrast to option contracts that may or may not be exercised, **financial futures contracts** are firm commitments to pay for or deliver Treasury bills, Treasury bonds, GNMAs, or other financial instruments at a fixed price on a specified date. Entering into such contracts without the securities to make delivery or the funds to accept delivery cannot be considered prudent. However, the use of financial futures to hedge positions or in arbitrage transactions is entirely appropriate.

Timing risks in the bond market are among the major exposures to loss of earnings. Futures contracts can be used to reduce such risks and to compensate for arbitrary fluctuations in the flow of contributions to the pension fund. If investment managers use financial futures as a tool of portfolio management, the plan sponsor should establish some specific guidelines for the extent of use and for the provision of coverage for contracts with liquid or maturing assets. Such guidelines will prevent exposure to losses from forward commitments.

These rapidly developing markets in options and futures afford investment managers new tools for modifying the risk-return characteristics of a portfolio in ways not achievable by converting a proportion of it into cash. The markets in such contracts are, however, highly sophisticated. The authorization for using these tools should be given only after the corporate financial officer has satisfied himself that the manager is fully qualified. Complete discussions on "Options Markets and Instruments" and "Futures and Commodities Markets" can be found in earlier sections of this *Handbook*.

TANGIBLE ASSETS.   The **ownership of gold, silver, and other precious metals** is no longer "unthinkable" for a pension fund. But the time-tested measures of **prudence** imply or perhaps even demand that the asset have some form of earning power or contractual return. Is an expected appreciation in value sufficient? The same question applies to paintings, rare coins and stamps, and the vast array of articles that have come to be known as **collectibles.**

A security has value because it promises to pay a contractual rate of interest or represents a share in the earning power of an enterprise. It has an intrinsic value derived from these qualities. Precious metals and collectibles, on the other hand, depend for their return entirely on the owner's ability to sell them to someone else at a higher price. Ownership is not productive of return but only of expense for storage and insurance. When time is a source of expense instead of revenue, the question arises as to whether these classes of assets fit the basic characteristics of a pension fund. Perhaps only a period of persistent inflationary pressures could bring them to serious consideration.

REFERENCES AND BIBLIOGRAPHY

Accounting Issues Update, "Chrysler Pension Liabilities: What Will Happen to Creditors, Workers, and PBGC in Bankruptcy?" Bear Stearns, New York, April 2, 1980.

Bagehot, Walter, "Risk and Reward in Corporate Pension Funds," *Financial Analysts Journal,* January–February 1972, pp. 80–83.

Bank Administration Institute, *Measuring the Investment Performance of Pension Funds,* Park Ridge, IL, 1968.

Blissert, Joan, *Unfunded Pension Liabilities,* New York University Working Paper, New York, May 1979.

Burianek, Frank G., "An Actuary's Views in Pension Plan Accounting and Reporting," *Management Accounting,* January 1979, pp. 46–49.

Cottle, Sidney, et al., *Pension Asset Management: The Corporate Decisions,* Financial Executives Research Foundation, New York, 1980.

Ehrbar, A. F., "Those Pension Plans Are Even Weaker than You Think," *Fortune,* November 1977, pp. 104–114.

Financial Analysts Research Foundation, *Evolving Concepts of Prudence: The Changing Responsibilites of the Investment Fiduciary in the Age of ERISA,* FARF, Charlottesville, VA, 1976.

Fratar, Tom, and Gilbert, Barry, "Pension Cost Accounting and the Implications of the Unfunded Vested Liabilities for Financial Statement Analysis," *Journal of Commercial Bank Lending,* July 1977, pp. 32–44.

Gewirtz, Paul A., and Phillips, Robert C., "Unfunded Pension Liabilities: The New Myth," *Financial Executive,* August 1978, pp. 32–42.

Gravitz, David H., "Plan Mergers, Spinoffs and Transfers Under ERISA," *Financial Executive,* May 1978, pp. 38–42.

Ibbotson, Roger G., and Sinquefield, Rex A., *Stocks, Bonds, Bills, and Inflation: Historical Returns, 1926–1978,* Financial Analysts Research Foundation, Charlottesville, Va, 1979.

Leo, Mario, Bassett, Preston, C., and Kachline, Ernest S., *Financial Aspects of Private Pension Plans,* Financial Executives Research Foundation, New York, 1975.

McGill, Dan M., *Fundamentals of Private Pensions,* 4th ed., Richard D. Irwin, for Pension Research Council, Homewood, IL, 1979.

Paul, Robert D., "Impact of Pension Reform on American Business," *Sloan Management Review,* Fall 1976, pp. 59–71.

Pension Benefit Guaranty Corp., *Annual Reports,* Washington, D.C., 1977–1980.

———, *Guidelines on Voluntary Termination.* Washington, D.C., Publication No. 503, PBGC, 1978.

Phillips, Susan, and Fletcher, Linda, "The Cost of Funding Benefits Under the ERISA: A Statistical Survey," *Journal of Risk and Insurance,* December 1976.

Regan, Patrick J., "Potential Corporate Liabilities Under ERISA," *Financial Analysts Journal,* March–April, 1976, pp. 26–32.

———, "Interpreting the Pension Data in 1977 Annual Reports," *Financial Analysts Journal,* March–April, 1978, pp. 14–15.

Treynor, Jack L., "Principles of Corporate Pension Finance," *Journal of Finance,* May 1977, pp. 627–638.

———, Regan, Patrick J., and Priest, William W., Jr., *The Financial Reality of Pension Funding under ERISA,* Dow Jones-Irwin, Homewood, IL, 1976.

———, "Pension Claims and Corporate Assets," *Financial Analysts Journal,* May–June 1978, pp. 84–88.

Williams, Arthur, III, *Managing Your Investment Manager,* Dow Jones-Irwin, Homewood, IL, 1980.

BANKRUPTCY AND REORGANIZATION

CONTENTS

BANKRUPTCY AND
REORGANIZATION THEORY   3

COSTS OF BANKRUPTCY   5

DEFINING CORPORATE PROBLEMS   5

INSOLVENCY TESTS AND
CORPORATE DISTRIBUTIONS   6

EVOLUTION OF THE BANKRUPTCY
PROCESS IN THE UNITED STATES   7

Equity Receiverships   7
The Chandler Act of 1938   8
   Chapter XI   8
   Chapter X   8
Liquidation   10

THE BANKRUPTCY REFORM ACT OF
1978   11

Rationale for the New Act   11
Bankruptcy Filings   12
Claims and Protections   12
Lessor Claims   13
Priorities   13
Bank Setoffs   13
Chapter 11 Reorganizations   14
   Creditors' committee   14
   Reorganization plan filing   14
   Role of the SEC   14
   Reorganization valuation   15
   Absolute priority of claims   15
   Execution of the plan   16
   Confirmation of the plan   16
   Reorganization time in bankruptcy   17
   Changes in the judiciary and procedure   17
   U.S. Trustee program   20

BANKRUPTCY TAX ISSUES   20

Discharge of Indebtedness   20
Recapture Rule   21
Exchange of Equity for Debt   21
Tax Loss Carry-Forwards   22
   Importance   22
   The old tax laws   22
   The new tax bill and reorganization   22
Triangular Reorganization   23
Modification of the Absolute Priority
Rule   23

BUSINESS FAILURE   23

Bankruptcy Statistics and Business
Failure   23
   Sources of data   23
   Bankruptcy filings by chapter and
      occupation   25
   Statistics since October 1979   29
Aggregate Influences on Business Failure   29
New Business Formation and Age of
Business Failures   31
Causes of Business Failure   32

PREDICTING CORPORATE
BANKRUPTCY   32

Predicting Bankruptcy: Why?   32
   Credit analysis   33
   Investment analysis   33
   Audit risk analysis   33
   Legal issues of bankruptcy prediction   33
   Diverse applications   35
Predicting Bankruptcy: How?   35
   The Z-score model   35
   Failure prediction services   37

**INVESTING IN BANKRUPT
SECURITIES**   37

Valuation and Investing   37
Investing in Recent Bankrupts   37
A Caveat on Successful Reorganizations   38

PERSONAL BANKRUPTCY   38

The New Personal Bankruptcy Rules   38

Exempt Property   39
Chapter 13 Repayment Plans   39
Codebtor Clause and Refiling Restrictions   44
Chapter 7: Straight Bankruptcy
Liquidation   44
Filing Costs and Lawyer Fees   44

BANKRUPTCY AND REORGANIZATION

Edward I. Altman

Business failure, including the legal procedures of **corporate bankruptcy liquidation and reorganization,** is a sobering economic reality reflecting the uniqueness of the American way of corporate death. The business failure phenomenon has received a great deal of exposure during the decade of the 1970s and this attention is heightened as the nation moves into the 1980s. Between 1975 and 1979, 29,500 to 35,200 firms a year petitioned the courts to liquidate or to reorganize under the protection of the nation's bankruptcy laws. In fiscal 1980 the number increased 55% over that posted in 1979 to a record 45,841, of which 36,433 were individual businesses. Although business failure is a worldwide phenomenon, this section concentrates on events, data, and commentary on bankruptcy in the United States.

Corporate failure is no longer the exclusive province of the small, undercapitalized entity but is increasingly found among the large industrial and financial corporations. The 1970s decade was a watershed in this respect, from the $5 billion **Penn Central bankruptcy** (in 1970), heralding the new wave of larger firm failures, to the $12 billion all-but-bankrupt **Chrysler Corporation** problem and subsequent government bailout beginning in 1979. Exhibit 1 lists the largest U.S. bankruptcies—all of which have taken place during or since 1970. The list does not include financial organizations such as commercial banks and savings and loan associations but does include real estate investment trusts (REITs). Certainly, inflation accounts for the increase in size of all firms, including those that go bankrupt, but the astounding increase in the average liability of business failures (next subsection) goes beyond inflationary influences.

Among the 26 largest bankruptcies, in terms of assets and liabilities, are six retailers, six REITs, and four railroads. A noticeable dearth of large manufacturers is evident, but even this sector appears increasingly vulnerable with the near failure of Chrysler (as of March 1981) and the recent *Penn Dixie Co.* and *White Motor Co.* cases—the latter is the largest bankruptcy filed thus far (March 1981) under the **Bankruptcy Reform Act of 1978** which went into effect in October 1979.

BANKRUPTCY AND REORGANIZATION THEORY

In any economic system, the continuous entrances and exits of productive entities are natural components. Since there are costs to society inherent in the failure of these entities, laws and procedures have been established (1) to protect the contractual rights of interested parties,

EXHIBIT 1   THE LARGEST U.S. BANKRUPTCIES[a] (IN TERMS OF DOLLAR LIABILITIES) AS OF OCTOBER 1980[e]

	Total Liabilities ($ Millions)	Bankruptcy Petition Date	Filed Under[b]
1. Penn Central Transportation Co.	3,300	June 1970	Chapter VIII, Section 77
2. W. T. Grant Co.	1,000	October 1975	Chapter XI
3. Continental Mortgage Investors	607	March 1976	Chapter XI–X[c]
4. United Merchants & Manufacturing	552	July 1977	Chapter XI
5. Commonwealth Oil Refining Co.	421	March 1978	Chapter XI
6. W. Judd Kassuba	420	December 1973	Chapter XI
7. Erie Lackawanna Railroad	404	June 1972	Chapter VIII, Section 77
8. White Motor Corp.	399	September 1980	Chapter 11[d]
9. Investors Funding Corp.	379	October 1974	Chapter X
10. Food Fair Corp.	347	October 1978	Chapter XI
11. Great American Mortgage & Trust	326	March 1977	Chapter XI[c]
12. U.S. Financial Services	300	July 1973	Chapter XI
13. Chase Manhattan Mortgage & Realty Trust	290	February 1979	Chapter XI[c]
14. Daylin, Inc.	250	February 1975	Chapter XI
15. Guardian Mortgage Investors	247	March 1978	Chapter XI[c]
16. Chicago, Rock Island & Pacific	221	March 1975	Chapter VIII, Section 77
17. Equity Funding Corp. of America	200	April 1973	Chapter X
18. Interstate Stores, Inc.	190	May 1974	Chapter XI
19. Fidelity Mortgage Investors	187	January 1975	Chapter XI[c]
20. Omega, Alpha Corp.	175	September 1974	Chapter X
21. Reading Railroad	158	November 1971	Chapter VIII, Section 77
22. Boston & Maine Railroad	148	December 1975	Chapter VIII, Section 77
23. Westgate–California	144	February 1974	Chapter X
24. Colwell Mortgage & Trust	142	February 1978	Chapter XI[c]
25. Pacific Far East Lines	132	January 1978	Chapter XI
26. Allied Supermarkets	124	June 1977	Chapter XI
27. Penn Dixie Co.	122	April 1980	Chapter 11[d]

[a]Does not include commercial banking entities.
[b]Old Bankruptcy Act (Chandler Act; see below) prior October 1979 as noted.
[c]Real estate investment trust.
[d]Filed under Bankruptcy Reform Act of 1978 (new Act).
[e]Seatrain Corporation filed under Chapter 11 in February, 1981.
Source: Author compilation.

(2) to provide for the orderly liquidation of unproductive assets, and (3) when deemed desirable, to provide for a temporary moratorium on certain claims, to give the debtor time to become rehabilitated and to emerge from the process as a continuing entity. Both liquidation and reorganization are available courses of action in most countries of the world and are based on the following premise. If an entity's **intrinsic or economic value** is greater than its current **liquidation value,** then from both the public policy and entity ownership viewpoints, the firm should attempt to reorganize and continue. If, however, the firm's assets are worth more dead than alive—that is, if liquidation value exceeds economic value—liquidation is the preferable alternative.

The **theory of reorganization in bankruptcy** is basically sound and has potential economic and social benefits. The process is designed to enable the financially troubled firm to continue in existence and maintain whatever goodwill it still possesses, rather than liquidate its assets for the benefit of its creditors. Justification of this attempt is found in the belief that continued existence will result in a healthy going-concern operation worth more than the value of its assets sold in the marketplace. Since this rehabilitation process often requires several years, the **time value of money** should be considered explicitly through a **discounted cash flow procedure.** If, in fact, economically productive assets continue to contribute to society's supply of goods and services above and beyond their **opportunity costs,** the process of reorganization has been of benefit, to say nothing of the continued employment of the firm's employees. These benefits should be weighed against the **costs of bankruptcy** to the firm and to society.

The primary groups of interested parties are the firm's creditors and owners. The experience of these parties is of paramount importance in the evaluation of the bankruptcy-reorganization process, although the laws governing reorganization reflect the legislators' concern for overall **societal welfare.** The primary immediate responsibility of the reorganization process is to relieve the burden of the debtor's liabilities and realign the capital structure so that financial problems will not recur in the foreseeable future.

COSTS OF BANKRUPTCY

From the firm's standpoint, bankruptcy includes direct and indirect costs. **Direct bankruptcy costs** are the tangible, out-of-pocket expenses of either liquidating or attempting a reorganization of the ailing enterprise. These include bankruptcy filing fees and legal, accountant, and other professional service costs. Some analysts, such as J. Warner ("Bankruptcy Costs: Some Empirical Evidence," *Journal of Finance,* May 1977), include in the direct cost category the costs involved with **lost managerial time,** a difficult "expense" to measure empirically. I prefer to include lost managerial time with other **intangible opportunity costs or indirect costs.** The primary **indirect cost** is the lost sales and profits of the firm due to the perceived potential bankruptcy—primarily from customer reluctance to buy from a firm that may fail. This cost was dramatically illustrated when sales of Chrysler products dropped during the 1978–1980 financial crisis.

Continuing research in this area centers on trying to quantify the **magnitude** of these direct and indirect costs to permit their comparison with the **tax benefit** that a firm receives from additional leverage. Many theorists believe that the increasing bankruptcy possibility, due to increased leverage, and the attendant costs of bankruptcy, help explain why firms seek some **optimal capital structure;** in other words, an optimal mix of debt and equity capital.

DEFINING CORPORATE PROBLEMS

The unsuccessful business enterprise has been defined in numerous ways in attempts to depict the formal process confronting the firm and/or to categorize the economic problems involved. Three generic terms that are commonly found in the literature are **failure, insolvency,** and **bankruptcy.** Although these terms are sometimes used interchangeably, they have distinctly different meanings.

Failure, by economic criteria, means that the realized rate of return on invested capital, with allowances for risk considerations, is significantly and continually lower than prevailing rates on similar investments. Somewhat different economic criteria have also been utilized, including insufficient revenues to cover costs and cases of the **average return on investment** being below the firm's **cost of capital.** These economic situations make no positive statements about the existence or discontinuance of the entity. Normative decisions to discontinue operations are based on expected returns and the ability of the firm to cover its variable costs. It should be noted that a company may be an **economic failure** for many years, yet never fail to meet its current obligations because of the absence or near absence of legally enforceable debt. When the company can no longer meet the legally enforceable demands of its creditors, it is sometimes called a **legal failure.** The term "legal" is somewhat misleading because the condition, as just described, may exist without formal court involvement.

The term "business failure" has also been adopted by Dun & Bradstreet (D&B)—a leading supplier of relevant statistics on unsuccessful enterprises—to describe various unsatisfactory business conditions. **Business failures** include businesses that cease operation following assignment or bankruptcy; those that cease with loss to creditors after such actions as execution, foreclosure, or attachment; those that voluntarily withdraw leaving unpaid obligations, or have been involved in court actions such as **receivership, reorganization,** or **arrangement;** and those that voluntarily **compromise with creditors.** In actuality, business failures as defined by D&B are a fraction, although a significant one, of the enterprises that are discontinued each year.

Insolvency is another term depicting negative firm performance and is generally used in a more technical fashion. The state of **technical insolvency** exists when a firm cannot meet its current obligations, signifying a **lack of liquidity.** Another term used to describe the same situation is **insolvency in an equity sense.** Walter ("Determination of Technical Insolvency," *Journal of Business,* January 1957, pp. 30–43) discussed the measurement of technical insolvency and advanced the theory that net cash flows relative to current liabilities should be the primary criterion used to describe technical insolvency, not traditional working capital measurement. **Technical insolvency** may be a temporary condition, although it often is the immediate cause of formal bankruptcy declaration.

Insolvency in a bankruptcy sense is more critical and indicates a chronic rather than temporary condition. A firm finds itself in this situation when its total liabilities exceed a fair valuation of its total assets. The **real net worth** of the firm is, therefore, **negative.** Technical insolvency is easily detectable, whereas the more serious bankruptcy insolvency condition requires a comprehensive valuation analysis, which is usually not undertaken until **asset liquidation** is contemplated. Insolvency, as it relates to the **formal bankruptcy process,** is defined explicitly in Section 101, clause 26, of the **Bankruptcy Reform Act of 1978.**

Finally, we come to **bankruptcy** itself. One type of bankruptcy is described above and refers to the net worth position of an enterprise. A second, more observable type, is a firm's formal declaration of bankruptcy in a federal district court, accompanied by a petition to either liquidate its assets or attempt a recovery program. The latter procedure is legally referred to as a **bankruptcy-reorganization** and is discussed later. The judicial reorganization is a formal procedure that is usually the last measure in a series of attempted remedies.

INSOLVENCY TESTS AND CORPORATE DISTRIBUTIONS

Corporate distributions to shareholders involve the transfer of money or other property (except its own shares) or the incurrence of indebtedness, whether by **cash dividend** or **share repurchase.** The revised **Model Business Corporation Act** specifies that the **board of directors** may authorize and the corporation may make distributions except where (*a*) the corporation would be unable to pay its debts as they become due in the usual course of its business, or (b) the corporation's total assets would be less than its total liabilities, sometimes known as the **balance sheet test.** The former test describes **equity insolvency** and the latter describes **bankruptcy insolvency.** No longer are the terms **par value, stated value,** or **capital surplus** of any relevance to a firm's payment of dividends or share repurchase.

Whether a firm would be insolvent as a result of a proposed distribution is to be determined by the board of directors based on its collective business judgment. This is stipulated to involve judgments as to the future course of the corporation's business, including an analysis of the firm's ability to generate sufficient funds from operations or from the orderly disposition of its assets, to satisfy its existing and reasonably anticipated obligations as they come due.

Discussion of these and other provisions can be found in "Changes in the Model Business Corporation Act—Amendments to Financial Provisions" (*Business Lawyer,* Vol. 34, July 1979). The question of **corporate solvency** is now explicit and fundamental to the concept of shareholder return on investment.

EVOLUTION OF THE BANKRUPTCY PROCESS IN THE UNITED STATES

The Constitution empowers the U.S. Congress to establish uniform laws regulating bankruptcy. By virtue of this authority, various acts and amendments have been passed, starting with the **Bankruptcy Act of 1898.** Several bankruptcy acts have been passed in this century, and in 1978 Congress enacted the **Bankruptcy Reform Act of 1978,** which is the current standard. To appreciate the bankruptcy process, it is necessary to review the previous statutes and codes that have helped to form the present system.

EQUITY RECEIVERSHIPS. The **Bankruptcy Act of 1898** provided only for a company's liquidation and contained no provisions allowing corporations to reorganize and thereby remain in existence. Reorganization could be effected, however, through **equity receiverships.** Although the basic theory of corporate reorganization is sound, the equity receivership procedure proved to be ineffective. It was developed to prevent disruptive seizures of property by dissatisfied creditors who were able to obtain liens on specific properties of the financially troubled concern. Receivers were appointed by the courts to manage the corporate property during financial reorganization. This procedure presented serious problems, however, and essentially was replaced by provisions of the **Bankruptcy Acts of 1933 and 1934. Receivership in equity** is not the same as **receivership in bankruptcy.** In the latter case, a **receiver** is a court agency that administers the bankrupt's assets until a trustee is appointed. While receivership is still available to companies, it has been almost entirely replaced by reorganization under the new Bankruptcy Act.

Equity receivership was extremely time-consuming and costly, as well as susceptible to severe injustices. The courts had little control over the reorganization plan, and the committees set up to protect security holders were usually made up of powerful corporate insiders who used the process to further their own interests. The initiative for equity receivership was usually taken by the company in conjunction with some friendly creditor. There was no provision made for independent, objective review of the plans that were invariably drawn up by a biased committee or friendly receiver. Since ratification required majority creditor support, it usually meant that companies offered cash payoffs to powerful dissenters to gain their support. This led to long delays and charges of unfairness. Because of these disadvantages, the procedure was ineffective, especially when the number of receiverships skyrocketed during the Depression years.

THE CHANDLER ACT OF 1938.   In 1933 a new Bankruptcy Act with a special Section 77 (for railroad reorganizations) was hastily drawn up and enacted. The following year Section 77B was enacted, to provide for general corporate reorganizations. The Act was short-lived: in 1938 it underwent a comprehensive revision and was thereafter known as the **Chandler Act.** This legislation was the result of the joint efforts of the National Bankruptcy Conference, the **Securities and Exchange Commission** (SEC), which had embarked on its own study of reorganization practices, and various other interested committees and associations.

Chapter XI.   For our purposes, the two most relevant chapters of the Chandler Act were those related to corporate bankruptcy and to subsequent attempts at reorganization. **Chapter XI arrangements** applied only to the unsecured creditors of corporations and removed the necessity to get all creditor types to agree on a plan of action. A Chapter XI arrangement was a **voluntary proceeding** that could be initiated by corporate or noncorporate entities or persons. The court had the power to appoint an **independent trustee or receiver** to manage the corporate property or, in many instances, to permit the old management team to continue its control during the proceedings. The bankrupt's petition for reorganization usually contained a preliminary plan for financial relief. The prospect of continued management control and reduced financial obligations made **Chapter XI** particularly attractive to present management. During the proceedings, a referee called the creditors together to go over the proposed plan and any new amendments that had been proposed. If a majority in number and amount of each class of unsecured creditors consented to the plan, the court could confirm the arrangement and make it binding on all creditors. Usually, the plan provided for a scaled-down creditor claim, **composition of claims,** and/or **extension of payment over time.** New financial instruments could be issued to creditors in lieu of their old claims.

In addition to the advantages noted above, **Chapter XI** placed the bankrupt's assets strictly in the custody of the court and made them free from any prior pending court proceeding. Also, the debtor could borrow new funds that had preference over all unsecured indebtedness. Although the interest rate on such new credit was expectedly high, it still enabled the embarrassed firm to secure an important new source of financing. As in all corporate reorganizations, the assets were protected by the court during these proceedings. Also the Chapter XI arrangements, if successful, were of relatively short duration compared to the more complex Chapter X cases, since administrative expenses were a function of time. Chapter XI was usually less costly than proceedings that involved all security holders. Successful **out-of-court settlements,** however, were usually even less costly. Finally, the arrangement was binding in all states of the country.

Chapter X.   The least common but most important type of corporate bankruptcy-reorganization was the **Chapter X proceeding.** The importance of this bankruptcy form is clearly illustrated by the dollar amount of liabilities involved, the size and importance of the petitioning companies, and the fact that most of the empirical data utilized in bankruptcy analysis involved Chapter X bankrupts.

Chapter X proceedings applied to **publicly held corporations** except railroads, and to those that had **secured creditors.** This bankruptcy process could be initiated **voluntarily by the debtor or involuntarily by three or more creditors** with total claims of $5,000 or more. It was generally felt that Section 77B of the 1934 Act was too liberal to the small creditors, since only $1,000 in claims was required. The bankruptcy petition had to contain a statement of why adequate relief could not be obtained under Chapter XI. The aim of this requirement was to make Chapter X proceedings unavailable to corporations having simple debt and capital structures. On the other hand, the court had the right (and exercised it on several occasions) to refuse to allow a Chapter XI proceeding and to require that a reorganization be processed under Chapter X. This usually happened when a substantial **public interest was deemed present** by the court or by the SEC, and the firm had originally filed a Chapter XI voluntary petition. The SEC on particular occasions filed motions in Chapter XI proceedings to force companies into Chapter X because Chapter XI could not adequately handle the case when a substantial public interest was involved.

In most cases, a Chapter XI was preferred by the debtor because Chapter X automatically provided for the **appointment of an independent, disinterested trustee or trustees** to assume control of the company for the duration of the bankruptcy proceeding. Actually the Act provided for the appointment of the independent trustee in every case in which indebtedness amounted to $250,000 or more. Where the indebtedness was less than $250,000, the judge could either continue the **debtor in possession** or appoint a disinterested trustee. The only prescribed qualification of the trustee, in addition to disinterestedness, was competence to perform the duties.

The **independent trustee** was charged with the development and submission of a reorganization plan that was "fair and feasible" to all the parties involved. The **Interstate Commerce Commission** (ICC) was charged with this task in the case of railroad bankruptcies. Invariably, this plan involved all the creditors as well as the preferred and common stockholders. This important task was in addition to the day-to-day management responsibilities, although the trustee usually delegated the latter authority to the old management or to a new management team. New management was often installed, since management incompetence, in one form or another, was by far the most common cause of corporate failure. In most contemporary Chapter X bankruptcies, the trustee was aided by various experts in the development and presentation of **reorganization plans,** as well as by committees representing the various creditors and stockholders. This practice will no doubt continue under the new Act. At the outset, the creditors, indenture trustees, and stockholders were permitted to file answers controverting the allegations of a voluntary or involuntary petition. While bankruptcy initiation action was curtailed by the 1938 Act, the ability to answer was enhanced.

Another extremely important participant in **Chapter X** proceedings was the **SEC.** This is clearly not the case under the current code, which all but eliminates the role of the SEC. Although the Commission did not possess any decision-making authority, its involvement, via the **SEC Adivsory Reports,** was in my opinion a powerful **objective force in the entire process.** The SEC was charged with rendering its Advisory Report if the debtor's **liabilities exceeded $3 million,** but the court could ask for SEC assistance regardless of liability size.

The advisory reports usually took the form of a critical evaluation of the reorganization plan submitted by the trustee and an opinion on the **fairness and feasibility of the plan.** This involved a comprehensive valuation of the debtor's existing assets in comparison with the various claims against the assets. In the event of a discrepancy between the SEC evaluation and that of the trustee, the former usually suggested alternative guidelines. Ultimately, the decisions on (1) whether the firm was permitted to reorganize, and (2) the submission of the plan for final acceptance, rested with the federal judge (and with the new bankruptcy judge under the 1978 Bankruptcy Act).

The Chandler Act provided that the reorganization plan, after approval by the court, be submitted to each class of creditor and stockholder for final approval. **Final ratification required approval of two-thirds of each class of stockholder.** Of course if the plan, as accepted by the court, completely eliminated a particular class, such as the common stockholders, this excluded group had no vote in the final ratification, although it could always file suits on its own behalf. **Common stockholders were eliminated** when the firm was deemed **insolvent in a bankruptcy sense,** that is, when the liabilities exceeded a fair valuation of the assets. Regardless of whether the old stockholders were permitted to participate in the reorganized enterprise, the plan invariably entailed a restructuring of the old capital accounts as well as plans for improving the productivity of the debtor. This will no doubt be the case in the future, as well.

The entire bankruptcy reorganization process, including those relevant features and conditions of the Bankruptcy Code of 1978, is summarized in Exhibit 2, which follows the discussion of liquidation and the new Code.

LIQUIDATION.   When, either through a court petition or a trustee decision, it is deemed that there is no hope for rehabilitation or if prospects are so poor as to make it unreasonable to invest further efforts, costs, and time, the only alternative remaining is liquidation. **Economically, liquidation** is justified when the value of the assets sold individually **exceeds the capitalized value of the assets in the marketplace.** Usually, the key variables are **time and risk.** For instance, it may be estimated that the absolute economic value of the firm will exceed the liquidation value but the realization of the economic benefits is subject to uncertainty, because of time and subjective probability estimates, resulting in a lower discounted value. In this case, final liquidation may take the form of an assignment or a formal bankruptcy liquidation.

An assignment is a private method whereby assets are assigned to a trustee, usually selected by the creditors, to be liquidated by him. The **net liquidation value** realized is equal to the funds received less the creditor claims against the company. Rarely are the funds sufficient to pay off all creditors in full. All creditors must agree to the settlement. Since the assignment is generally handled in good faith, it is customary for the creditors to release the debtor from further liability. This process is usually faster and less costly than the more rigid bankruptcy procedure, but it is not feasible when the debtor has a complicated liability and capital structure.

The expanded Act (1938) continued to provide for the orderly liquidation of an insolvent debtor under court supervision. Regardless of who filed the petition, liquidations were handled by referees who oversaw the operation until a trustee was appointed. The latter liquidated the assets, made a final accounting, and paid the liquidating dividends—all subject to referee approval. **Payments of** receipts usually entailed the so-called **absolute priority doctrine,** under which claims with priority must be paid in full before less prior, or subordinated claims, can receive any funds at all.

The **liquidation fate is primarily observed in the small firm.** The large bankrupt firm is more likely to attempt a reorganization and/or a merger with another entity. Sometimes, however, the basis for merger terms while a corporation is in bankruptcy is based on the **net liquidating value** of the company, not its capitalized income value. This was precisely the basis for negotiation in the ICC hearings on the **Penn Central–New York New Haven & Hartford Railroad merger in 1968.**

Although larger firms usually attempt to reorganize or merge in bankruptcy, the result is often not successful, and liquidation eventually occurs. In an earlier study (Altman, *Corporate Bankruptcy in America,* Chapter 6) I showed that a large percentage of firms are not successfully reorganized and as much as 56% of the cases resulted in a total loss to common stockholders. A glaring example of a recent failure to reorganize successfully was the billion dollar **W.T. Grant** case. The firm filed under Chapter XI in 1975 and attempted to reorganize, but was forced to liquidate several months later in 1976. This is in contrast to several more recent, large successful reorganizations, including the billion dollar (in assets) **United Merchants & Manufacturing** Chapter XI proceeding in July 1977. The firm was reorganized and emerged as a going concern in less than one year.

The delays caused by court action to determine whether a firm should file under Chapter X or Chapter XI were often costly and took time to settle because of the ambiguity in the Chandler Act. One could argue that in both the W.T. Grant and United Merchants cases, a large **public interest** was involved and parties other than unsecured creditors were affected. Still, persuasive pressures were brought to bear by the debtors and their legal counsels, and the courts ruled that these cases could be handled more efficiently, without adverse effects to other interested parties, under Chapter XI. **Under the new Bankruptcy Code,** the old Chapters X and XI are combined under a new reorganization title, **Chapter 11,** and this no longer is an issue.

THE BANKRUPTCY REFORM ACT OF 1978

RATIONALE FOR THE NEW ACT.   Forty years after the passage of the Chandler Act, Congress enacted the **Bankruptcy Reform Act of 1978,** which revised the administrative and, to some extent, the procedural, legal, and economic aspects of corporate and personal bankruptcy filings in the United States. The complete text of the new Act can be found in **Bankruptcy Law Reports,** No. 389, October 26, 1978, Part II, published by the **Commerce Clearing House, Chicago, Illinois.**

The following reasons were presented **in 1970** in a joint Congressional resolution to create a commission to look into the nation's bankruptcy laws (S.J.R. 88, 91st Congress, 1st Session, July 24, 1970). An accompanying report from the Committee on the Judiciary, Report No. 91–230, strongly endorsed the proposal. I served as an advisor to the Commission on the Bankruptcy Laws of the United States. Charles Seligson, a member of the Commission, enumerated some current problems in "Major Problems for Consideration By the Commission on the Bankruptcy Laws of the United States" (*American Bankruptcy Law Journal,* Winter 1977, pp. 73–112).

1. In the 30 years since the last major revision, there has probably been even greater change in the social and economic conditions of the country than in the 40 years prior to the enactment of the 1938 Act.

2. Population has increased by 70 million people, while installment credit has skyrocketed from about $4 billion to $80 billion. The number of total bankruptcies has risen to an annual rate of more than 200,000 from a rate of 110,000 in 1960. By far, the major increase has been in personal bankruptcies.

3. More than one-quarter of the referees in bankruptcy have problems in the administration of their duties and have made suggestions for substantial improvement in the Act.

4. There is little understanding by the federal government and the commercial community in evaluating the need to update the technical aspects in the Act.

In 1979 the problems under the old Act were even more acute. The long-term **worldwide problems of inflation and recession** had further increased the number of bankruptcy filings in the U.S. court system. Transitions in credit policies—for example, greater reticence to **delay default proceedings in large corporations,** and other not so definable changes—have contributed to making the old bankruptcy laws awkward and the 1978 Code desirable. Whether the structure of the new Code will alleviate pressures and make the system more efficient will be determined empirically as the new Code is implemented. One thing is certain, the new Code is being tested immediately as the number of filings increase in the face of the 1979–1980 recession and credit restraints.

The new Act, which went into effect on October 1, 1979, is divided into four titles, with Title I containing the substantive and much of the procedural law of bankruptcy. This part, known as ''the Code,'' is divided into eight chapters: 1, 3, 5, 7, 9, 11, 13, 15. Chapter 1 (General Provisions), Chapter 3 (Case Administration), and Chapter 5 (Creditors, the Debtor and the Estate), apply generally to all cases, and Chapter 7 (Liquidation), Chapter 9 (Adjustment of Municipality Debt), Chapter 11 (Reorganization), Chapter 13 (Adjustment of Debts of Individuals with Regular Income), and Chapter 15 (U.S. Trustee Program). For an informative review of the new code, see Duberstein, ''A Broad View of the New Bankruptcy Code'' (*Brooklyn Barrister*, April 1979). The major provisions of the new Act are discussed in the subsections that follow.

BANKRUPTCY FILINGS.   The debtor must reside or have a domicile or place of business or property in the United States. Liquidation cases of banks and insurance companies engaged in business in this country are excluded. A foreign bank or foreign insurance company that is not engaged in business in the United States but does have assets here may become a debtor under the Code, but an involuntary petition cannot be filed against a foreign bank even if it has property here. The debtor may file a **petition for liquidation or reorganization.** The filing of the petition constitutes what is known as ''an order for relief.'' An involuntary case may be commenced only under Chapter 7, dealing with liquidation, or Chapter 11, dealing with reorganization. This route is not permitted for municipalities under Chapter 9, nor in Chapter 13 cases. An involuntary petition is prohibited against farmers, ranchers, and charitable institutions.

CLAIMS AND PROTECTIONS.   The provision for an **involuntary Chapter 11** case is a change from the old law: involuntary cases were permitted under Chapter X, dealing with corporate reorganization, and Chapter XII, dealing with real property arrangements, but not under a Chapter XI arrangement. **Acts of bankruptcy** are no longer the criteria for the commencement of an involuntary case. Instead, it will be necessary to show that the debtor is generally not paying its debts as such debts become due, or that within 120 days before the filing of the petition, a custodian (e.g., an assignee for the benefit of creditors) was appointed and took possession of the debtor's assets. If the debtor has more than 12 creditors, three creditors must join in the **involuntary petition** whose claims must aggregate at least $5,000. If there are fewer than 12 creditors, two creditors or a single creditor holding claims of at least $5,000 may file. An indenture trustee representing the holder of a claim against the debtor may be a petitioning creditor.

Section 10, paragraph (4) of the Code defines **''claim.''** The effect of the definition is a significant departure from the old Act, which never defined ''claim'' in straight bankruptcy. The term was simply used, along with the concept of provability, to limit the kinds of obligations that were payable in a bankruptcy case. The new definition adopts a broader meaning: **a claim is any right to payment,** whether or not reduced to judgment, liquidation, unliquidated, fixed, contingent, matured, unmatured, disputed, undisputed, legal, equitable, secured, or unsecured. The definition also includes as a **claim an equitable right to performance** that does not give rise to payment. The use of the term throughout the Act seems to imply that all legal obligations of the debtor, no matter how remote or contingent, will be dealt with in a bankruptcy case.

One of the most important parts of the Code deals with **stays of secured and unsecured creditor action** and the right of the debtor to continue to use the creditor's collateral in his business. The **automatic stay** is one of the fundamental **debtor protections provided by the bankruptcy laws.** It gives the debtor a breathing spell from creditors. It stops all collection efforts, all harassment, and all foreclosure actions. It permits the debtor to attempt a repayment or reorganization plan, or simply to be relieved of the financial pressures that drove the firm into bankruptcy.

Section 361–64 removes some of the uncertainty concerning the **rights of secured creditors.** The basic requirement that secured creditors be afforded **"adequate protection"** is not formally defined, but some guidelines are offered in Section 361, which suggests that such protection might include cash payments, additional collateral, or replacement collateral, but would not include the simple giving of any **priority.**

LESSOR CLAIMS.   Under the old Bankruptcy Act, a lessor was entitled to a claim on unpaid rents of a maximum of 1 year of lease or rental payments in a **straight bankruptcy liquidation** and a maximum of 3 years in a **reorganization.** Under the new Code's Section 502 b(7), a formula replaces the 1–3 year rule for both liquidations and reorganizations. In essence the claim for damages resulting from the termination of a lease of real property is now **the greater** of 1 year of payments, or 15%, not to exceed 3 years, of the remaining term of the lease, plus any unpaid rent due under such lease. Such terms start the earlier of (1) the petition date or (2) the date on which the lessor repossessed the leased property, or the lessee surrendered it.

Section 365 of the Code deals with **executory contracts** and **unexpired leases** and specifies under what provisions a trustee, or the court, can assume continuance of a lease while in reorganization. Essentially, the Code specifies that lessors must be **cured** or **compensated** for their claims or that **adequate assurance** of prompt compensation be given. The trustee must assume a lease or executory contract within 60 days of the petition date.

PRIORITIES.   The concept of **provability of claims,** apparently troublesome under the previous Act, has been discarded in favor of simple sections (501–503), dealing with the allowance of claims; among other things, these sections require that contingent or unliquidated claims be estimated. Many of the familiar priorities for claims remain, but significant changes have been made to protect employees. The new Act expands and increases the **wage priority.** The amount entitled to priority is raised from $600 to $2,000. The priority is expanded to cover fringe benefits, which is new (Section 507). A **new priority** has been established for **consumer creditors who have deposited money** in connection with the purchase, lease, or rental of property, or the purchase of services, for their personal, family, or household use, when such properties or services **are not delivered or provided.**

BANK SETOFFS.   Banks may specify that, in the event of bankruptcy, all existing balances of the debtor will be **set off** against the outstanding claim of the bank and the balance of the loan will be included among general creditor claims. One can argue that this is unfair to the debtor, since once a loan is made, the proceeds can be used in any manner that the borrower chooses. The banks can argue, on the other hand, that the balances are a type of "security" against repayment of the loan. In any event, the new Act provides for the continuation of setoffs, but the court must ratify them in a manner that is more formal than in the past.

As in the old law, the **right of setoff** is unaffected **except** when the creditor's claim is disallowed by the court or the creditor has acquired the claim, other than from the debtor, during a 90-day period preceding the case at a time when the debtor was insolvent. **An exception to the right of setoff** is the **automatic stay** provided for in Section 362 of the Code. The automatic stay refers to an injunction against the creditor and prohibits any action to further set off the loan **after the petition is filed.**

The Code does contain an additional limitation on the rights of creditors who have offset a mutual debt on or within 90 days before the filing of a petition when the creditor receives a **preferential payment.** For example, assume that a debtor owes a bank $150,000 and has $50,000 on deposit 90 days prior to the filing. If the bank exercises its right of setoff 30 days before filing, when the debtor owes $75,000, the bank will recover all but $75,000 of the amount owed to it by the debtor; if the bank had set off the amount 90 days before bankruptcy, on the other hand, it would have received $50,000. Thus by waiting 60 days before exercising its right of setoff, the bank recovered an additional $25,000 and therefore **improved its position** by that amount. This $25,000 is **the amount that the trustee may recover** for the debtor under Section 553 (b).

The setoff section operates only in the case of **prefiling setoffs,** thus encouraging creditors to work with the debtor rather than attempting to recover as much as appears possible at the time. In any case, a **default** must exist before there is a setoff right. It appears that the **right of setoff** is somewhat constrained under the new Code compared to the old law. Still, we can expect that financial institutions and others will continue the practice and it will be up to the trustee to recover the funds.

CHAPTER 11 REORGANIZATIONS.   An extremely important change in the new act appears in Chapter 11, which is a consolidated chapter for business rehabilitations. It adopts much of the old **Chapter XI arrangement** and incorporates a good portion of the public protection of the old **Chapter X** and also a major part of **Chapter XII real property arrangements.**

Under Chapter 11, the debtor continues to operate the business unless the court orders a **disinterested trustee** for cause shown, or if it would be in the best interests of the creditors and/or the owners. "Cause" includes fraud, dishonesty, incompetence, or gross mismanagement, either before or after commencement of the case.

Creditors' Committee.   After the petition for a Chapter 11 rehabilitation has been filed, the court, or a U.S. Trustee, where available, appoints a **committee of unsecured creditors.** Chapter 11 is permitted to affect secured debts and equity security holders and, upon request of a party in interest, the court may order the appointment of additional committees of creditors or of equity security holders. Ordinarily, committees consist of the holders of the **seven largest claims** or interests to be represented, if they are willing to serve. The Code permits continuation of a committee selected before the case is filed if the committee is fairly chosen and is representative of the different kinds of claims to be represented. A designated committee of equity security holders ordinarily consists of the persons willing to serve who hold the **seven largest amounts of shares** of the debtor. On the request of a party in interest, the court is authorized to change the size of membership of the creditors of the equity security holders' committee if the membership is not representative of the different claims or interests.

Reorganization Plan Filing.   The essence of the reorganization process is the **plan of reorganization for financial and operating rehabilitation.** The new Code gives the debtor, or its trustee if appointed, the exclusive right for 120 days to file a plan. The debtor has up to **180 days after the reorganization petition is filed** to receive the requisite consents from the various creditors and owners (if relevant). The court, however, is given the power to increase or reduce the 120- and 180-day periods. If the debtor fails to meet either of these deadlines or others established by the court, creditors and other interested parties may file a plan for approval.

Role of the Securities and Exchange Commission.   The SEC may raise and be heard on any issue but **may not appeal** from any judgment order or decree. Greater expediency for completing reorganization and alleged uneven performance of the SEC in past cases are reasons that have been given for the exclusion of the SEC. Although any interested party can still petition the courts and appeal any perceived inequities, the role of the SEC as the public's representative has been greatly diminished. For example, the SEC had often petitioned to change a Chapter XI arrangement to a Chapter X reorganization. There is no need for such a petition under the new Code. Despite the SEC's performance in Chapter X cases, it has issued some rather excellent commentary and suggestions in its reorganization reports, particularly in the valuation process.

Reorganization Valuation.   The reorganization plan has as its centerpiece the valuation of the debtor as a continuing entity. Traditionally, valuation is based on the capitalization of future earnings flows, which involves **a forecast of expected after tax earnings** and the attachment of an appropriate **capitalization rate** (discount rate). The capitalized value can then be adjusted for excess working capital and tax and other considerations. If the resulting value is **greater** than the liquidation value of the assets, reorganization is justified. If the value is **less** than the allowed claims, the firm is **insolvent in a bankruptcy sense** and the old shareholders are usually eliminated. Typically, the creditors become the new shareholders along with any new shareholders that might purchase shares.

Absolute Priority of Claims.   Since the inception of the bankruptcy laws, most reorganization plans have been guided by the so-called **absolute priority doctrine.** This "doctrine" stipulates that creditors should be compensated for their claims in a certain hierarchical order and that the more senior claims must be paid in full before a less senior claim can receive anything. In fact, however, plans are often based on a combination of **absolute** and **relative priorities** whereby lesser claimants receive partial payment even though a claim that is more senior is "not made whole" (not paid off completely). This arrangement is often expedient, and it permits compromise with creditors who are likely to vote against the plan unless some satisfactory payment to them is forthcoming.

Creditors are frequently compensated for their claims with a combination of cash and securities different from the original securities. It is quite common for the old debtholders to become the new stockholders. For example, the old debtholders of the **Penn Central Transportation Co.** received a combination of new series debt securities, new preferred stock, and shares of the common stock, while the old stockholders received but a fraction of their old shares, 1 for each 25 shares owned.

The objective of the reorganization plan is to provide for a **fair and feasible rehabilitation.** The term "fair" refers to the priority of claims, and "feasible" implies that the recapitalized company will be structured so that the new fixed cost burden will realistically be met without a recurrence of default. The reorganization plan must therefore provide the cash flow analysis necessary to make that assessment. The costs involved with negotiations for restructuring—both in bankruptcy or what takes place out of reorganization, that is, **a quasi-reorganization,** are referred to as **agency costs** and represent a **deadweight loss** to the firm, a loss that is not someone else's gain in society.

Priorities are spelled out in Section 507 of the Code. Expenses and claims have priority in the following order:

1. Administration expenses of the bankruptcy, such as legal and accounting fees and trustee fees.

2. **Unsecured claims** arising in the ordinary course of the debtor's business or financial affairs **after the commencement of the case,** for example, supplier claims on goods delivered and accepted, with some exceptions as spelled out in Section 502(f).

3. Unsecured claims for wages, salaries, or commissions, including vacation, severance, and sick leave pay (*a*) earned by an individual within 90 days before the filing of

the petition or the date of the cessation of the debtor's business but only (*b*) to the extent of $2,000 per individual.

4. Unsecured claims for contributions to employee benefit plans, with the same limitations noted in item 3.

5. Unsecured claims to individuals up to $900 arising from the deposit, before bankruptcy, of money in connection with the future use of goods or services from the debtor.

6. Unsecured claims of governmental units, that is, taxes on income, property, and employment, and excise and tax penalties.

Secured debts, that is, debt that has specific assets as collateral, has priority over the funds received in the liquidation of that asset. To the extent that the funds received are insufficient to cover the entire allowed claim, the balance is owed by the debtor and is considered part of the remaining unsecured claims. **Senior debt** has priority over all debt that is specified as **subordinated** to that debt but has equal priority with all other unsecured debt. The terms of most loan agreements spell out these priorities.

After the unsecured claims are satisfied, the remaining "claimants" are the equity holders of the firm—preferred and common stockholders, in that order. As noted earlier, these individuals should not receive any payment or securities in the new firm if the value of the firm's assets is less than the allowed claims.

Execution of the Plan. A plan must provide adequate means for its execution. It may provide for the satisfaction or modification of any lien, the waiver of any default, and the merger or consolidation of the debtor with one or more entities. The issuance of **nonvoting equity securities** is prohibited, and the plan must provide for distribution of voting powers among the various classes of equity securities. It may impair, or leave unimpaired, a class of claims, secured or unsecured; provide for the assumption or rejection of executory contracts or unexpired leases not previously rejected; and propose the sale of all or substantially all of the estate property and the distribution of the proceeds among creditors and equity security holders, making it a **liquidating plan.**

Confirmation of the Plan. A **plan may place a claim** in a particular class if such claim is substantially similar to other claims of the class. **Confirmation of a plan** requires that every claimant or holder of an interest accept the plan or if it is not accepted by all classes, the creditors must receive or retain under the plan an amount that is not less than the amount that they would receive or retain if the debtor were liquidated on the date of the plan. At least one class of creditors must accept the plan. Thus, for example, if the only class affected by the plan is comprised of a mortgagee, the **plan cannot be confirmed without the mortgagee's consent.** A plan is deemed **accepted by a class of creditors** if at least two-thirds in amount and more than one-half in number of the allowed claims of the class that are voted are cast in favor of the plan. Shareholders are deemed to have accepted the plan if at least two-thirds in amount of the outstanding shares actually voted are cast for the plan. These terms are reviewed in Exhibit 2.

The Code deals with the **impairment of claims,** which is a new concept. A plan may be confirmed over the dissent of a class of creditors. If all the requirements for confirmation of the plan are satisfied, except that a class of impaired claimants or shareholders has not accepted it, the court may nevertheless confirm the plan if the plan does not discriminate unfairly and is "fair and equitable" with respect to each class of claims or interests impaired.

This is the new Code's version of the **"cram-down"** clause, which appeared in Chapters X and XII. The test for what is **"fair and equitable"** with regard to a class of secured claimants impaired under a plan is met, in general, if the plan provides (1) that said class will retain its lien on the property whether the property is retained by the debtor or transferred, (2) that the property will be sold and the lien transferred and the secured creditor will receive deferred cash payments of a least the allowed amount of the claims of the value on the date of confirmation, and (3) that the secured class will realize the "indubitable equivalent" of its claims under the plan. If a class of unsecured claims that are impaired under the plan will receive property or payment equal to the allowed amount of the claims, or if the holders of the claims junior to such class will receive nothing under the plan, the plan has met the **"fair and equitable" test of the Code.**

Reorganization Time in Bankruptcy.   One of the important goals of the new Act is to reduce the time it takes for a firm to go through the reorganization process and devise a plan for restructuring its capital financing and rehabilitating its operations. The new Act, in and of itself, will certainly **not provide any novel solutions to the typical problems** that cause firms to fail. But the requirement that the debtor submit a reorganization plan within 120 days is likely to speed up the initial process. One wonders whether large, complicated cases are amenable to the 4-month time frame; only time will tell.

The attempt to reduce reorganization time is important, since there is a positive correlation between the time spent in reorganization and the **direct costs of bankruptcy.** The latter include legal and accounting fees, trustee and filing fees, and any other tangible costs involved with the bankruptcy process. In a study of almost 90 reorganizations, I found that the average industrial reorganization took 27 months, with the median period being 20 months (Altman, *Corporate Bankruptcy in America,* Chapter 6). Another study concentrating on more complex **railroad bankruptcies** (Chapter 7 of the same source) concluded that the average and median **Section 77 reorganization** took slightly more than 7 years. A more recent study (Warner, "Bankruptcy Costs: Some Empirical Evidence," *Journal of Finance,* May 1977), found that railroad reorganizations took even longer. Clearly, it would be desirable to reduce the time needed to reorganize entities.

Changes in the Judiciary and Procedure.   The Code creates a U.S. Bankruptcy Court in each of the present districts where there is a U.S. District Court. **The new court will be established April 1, 1984.** The **bankruptcy judges** will be appointed by the President, with the advice and consent of the the Senate, for a term of 14 years. The established bankruptcy courts are to continue from October 1, 1979, to March 31, 1984.

The Code eliminates the present jurisdictional dichotomy between summary and plenary jurisdiction; the bankruptcy court is given exclusive jurisdiction of the property of the debtor wherever it is located. All cases under the Code and all civil actions and proceedings arising from its enforcement will be held before the bankruptcy judge unless he decides to abstain from hearing a particular proceeding that is already pending in the state court or in another court that he believes to be more appropriate.

Appeals from the bankruptcy judge will go to the **district judge,** except that if the **circuit counsel of the circuit court** so orders, the chief judge of the circuit shall designate panels of three bankruptcy judges to hear appeals in the bankruptcy court. The panel may not hear an appeal from an order entered by a panel member. An appeal from the panel will go directly to the U.S. Court of Appeals. An appeal can go directly from the bankruptcy court to the court of appeals if the parties so agree.

EXHIBIT 2 SUMMARY OF FINANCIAL REHABILITATION PROCEDURES

Function	Chapter X	Chapter XI	Section 77 (1933 Act)	Chapter 11 (New Code)
1. Initiation of proceedings	1. a. Voluntary by the debtor b. Involuntary—three or more creditors with claims totaling $5,000 or more	1. a. Voluntary only b. Noncorporate and corporate c. Affects only unsecured creditors	1. a. Railroad only b. Voluntary c. Involuntary by creditors representing 5% or more of total indebtedness	1. a. Voluntary by debtor b. Involuntary—by three creditors with claims of at least $5,000 (where more than 12 creditors exist); fewer than three creditors with $5,000 or more in claims where less than 12 creditors exist
2. Custody of property	2. Court appoints disinterested trustee (mandatory if debts exceed $250,000) a. Cannot be officer or employee b. Cotrustee from previous management to aid in operation	2. Court may or may not appoint receiver or trustee	2. Trustees appointed who act as operating managers	2. Court may or may not appoint a trustee; trustee may or may not act as operating manager
3. Creditor protection	3. Committees representing each class of creditors and stockholders are formed	3. Court conducts meetings; may use advisory creditors' committee	3. Committee for each class of creditor	3. Creditors' committee comprised of seven largest creditors plus any others sanctioned by the court
4. Reorganization plan	4. a. Trustee creditors, or creditors' committee prepares plan; confers with committees b. Court hearings on plan c. SEC renders advisory report (mandatory if debts over $3 million)	4. Debtor proposes arrangement	4. Presented by one of the following: a. Trustee b. Debtor c. Holders of 10% or more of each security	4. Debtor proposes plan within 120 days; adequate approval required within 180 days of petition; if deadline not met, any interested party may submit a plan

5. Court review	5. Court approves plan if it is: a. Fair b. Feasible	5. Court holds hearings	5. a. Hearings before Interstate Commerce Commission b. ICC submits plan to court c. Court approval	5. Court holds hearings on the plan and will approve if fair and feasible
6. Reorganization plan	6. Provides for: a. Provision for exchange of securities b. Provision for selection of new management c. Adequate means for execution of plan	6. Composition—claims of unsecured creditors scaled down, or extension in time of payment, or both	6. Same as Chapter X	6. Provides for any or all aspects of old Chapters X, XI, and XII
7. Approval	7. Two-thirds of each class of creditors by value; majority of stockholders (unless total liabilities exceed total assets)	7. Majority in number and amount of each class	7. Same as Chapter X	7. Two-thirds in amount and one-half in number of the allowed claims. Where an equity exists, two-thirds in amount of outstanding shares actually voted; "Cram-down" provision possible (i.e. court may approve plan despite dissatisfied creditors). In all cases, creditors must receive an amount that is greater than if the firm was liquidated
8. Execution of plan	8. Court confirms plan	8. Receiver, trustee, or disbursing agent to carry out arrangement	8. Plan executed by ICC	8. Plan is confirmed by the court and executed by U.S. Trustee or by the court

U.S. Trustee Program.   To aid bankruptcy judges in avoiding involvement in many administrative functions, and to allow them to devote more time to the area of judicial determination, the Code establishes a **5-year trial pilot program** of U.S. Trustees that will be operative in only 10 geographical areas of the country, covering 18 present judicial districts. It will include the Southern District of New York (but not the Eastern District), the District of New Jersey, the Central District of California (which includes Los Angeles), and the Northern District of Illinois (which includes Chicago). The program will run to April 1, 1984, at which time Congress will decide whether to fully implement the U.S. Trustee system. The U.S. Trustees will not be serving the bankruptcy courts either as assistants to the bankruptcy judges or as arms of the court, but will be **under the supervision of the Attorney General,** who will appoint them.

BANKRUPTCY TAX ISSUES

The Bankruptcy Reform Act of 1978 completely rewrote the laws that govern bankruptcy procedures and principles but was essentially silent with respect to tax considerations. In bankruptcy proceedings the government acts both as a creditor and as a force to aid in the rehabilitation of an entity. The two roles are not easy to reconcile, and the tax laws that are relevant present considerable problems and are the subject of much debate. A proposed tax bill contemporaneous with the new Bankruptcy Code was so controversial, for solvent as well as nonsolvent firms, that it never was voted on by Congress; instead, the **Bankruptcy Tax Bill of 1980** (H.R. 5043) was evaluated by the House Ways and Means Committee and passed by the House of Representatives on March 24, 1980. As a consequence, the nation was governed for a period of time by a Bankruptcy Code that had **no relevant tax law.** The Tax Bill of 1980 was finally passed and went into effect in early 1981. Copies of the bill are available from the **Commerce Clearing House,** Chicago, Illinois, 60646.

The new bill deals with all aspects of bankruptcy and reorganization and, indeed, affects solvent firms as well, especially on the **repurchase of outstanding debt.** Three issues of the reorganization process will be discussed: (1) **the discharge or reduction in outstanding debt,** (2) **exchange of equity for debt,** and (3) **tax loss carry-forwards.** All are common to almost every bankruptcy reorganization and are often important elements in the estimation of the value of an emerging company—on an aftertax basis.

DISCHARGE OF INDEBTEDNESS.   In Public Law 95–598, Congress repealed provisions of the old Bankruptcy Act governing income tax treatment of a **discharge of indebtedness** in bankruptcy for cases filed on or after October 1, 1979. The Bankruptcy Tax Bill of 1980 fills this vacuum by providing that no amount of debt discharge is to be **included in income** for federal income tax purposes if the debtor is insolvent. Instead, the **amount of debt reduction** can be applied at the debtor's election first to **reduce the debtor's depreciable asset basis.** This policy can, however, affect reported income in the future, and the government will eventually be rewarded for its "generosity" if the firm becomes a profitable, going concern. In essence, the government is helping to provide a "fresh start" but is not totally forgiving the benefits for all time.

If the debtor does not choose to apply the reduction to depreciable assets, the amount is applied to reduce the taxpayer's tax attributes in the following order:

1. Net **operating losses and carryovers.**
2. Carryovers of **investment tax credits** and other tax credits.

3. **Capital losses** and carryovers.
4. The basis of the **taxpayer's assets.**

The reduction in each category of carryovers is made in the order of taxable years in which the items would be used, with the order based on the year of discharge and the taxes that would have been paid. After reduction of the specified carryover, any remaining debt discharge is applied to reduce the debtor's asset basis, but not below the amount of the taxpayer's remaining **undischarged liabilities.** Finally, any remaining debt discharge is disregarded; see page 10 of the Bankruptcy Tax Bill of 1980, as reported in *Bankruptcy Law Reports.*

For example, assume that a debtor borrows $1 million on a short-term note and later issues $600,000 worth of stock in cancellation of the note. Under the **old bankruptcy law,** the creditor recognized a $400,000 loss, but the debtor neither recognized income nor reduced tax attributes. Under the new bill, **the creditor can still recognize the loss,** but the debtor corporation must account for a **debt discharge** of $400,000. This ruling, which applies to all corporations, was the subject of heated debate because it was viewed as an attempt by the Treasury Department to eliminate an alleged tax loophole and recover an estimated $500 million a year in taxes (B. Greene, "What Big Teeth You Have, Grandma," *Forbes,* February 4, 1980). Therefore, **solvent companies** will have to pay income taxes on profits made when they buy back their own bonds at a discount. For companies being reorganized in bankruptcy, the "gain" on an exchange of the type noted above will be treated as a **debt discharge** and will be subject to the tax rules as specified above.

RECAPTURE RULE.   To ensure that the **debt discharged** amount eventually will result in ordinary income, the bill provides that any gain on a subsequent **sale of an asset** that had been reduced in value, by virtue of the provisions of the bill, will be subject to "recapture" under rules similar to standard **recapture tax law.**

EXCHANGE OF EQUITY FOR DEBT.   One of the most common provisions of a recapitalization plan in a bankruptcy reorganization is a **compensation arrangement** involving the exchange of stock in the reorganized firm for all or part of the outstanding indebtedness of the debtor-bankrupt. In essence, the old creditors become the new owners. If a debtor issues stock to its creditor for an outstanding security, such as a bond, there is no debt discharge amount. Thus there are no consequences of the type discussed above. There will be no recognition of a gain or loss for the creditors. If stock is issued for other debts, such as a supplier claim or short-term note, the debtor is treated as having satisfied the claim with an amount of money equal to the stock's value. A value can be placed on the stock either by the bankruptcy court in a proceeding in which the **IRS had the right to intervene** or in an **out-of-court agreement** in which the debtor and creditor had adverse interests in the tax consequences of the valuation. The new tax bill provides that the special limitations on **net operating loss carryovers** generally **will not apply** to the extent that creditors receive stock in exchange for their claims. See Section 382 of the Internal Revenue Code for more details.

If both stock and other property are issued to satisfy a debt, the stock is treated as issued for a proportion of the debt equal to its proportion of the total value exchanged. For example, if $20 million of cash and $30 million in stock are issued for a claim of $100 million, the cash is to be treated as satisfying $40 million of the debt and the stock for the other $60 million, with no income resulting nor attribute reduction required.

Some recent stock for debt exchanges in large firm reorganization plans involved Equity Funding of America (1976), Interstate Stores (1978), King Resources (1978), and Daylin Corp. (1979). Debt is not always replaced by equity, however, as witnessed by the reorganization plans of **Penn Central Co.** [combination of debt and equity but mostly debt (1978)] and **United Merchants and Manufacturing** (1978). For a discussion and evaluation of the postbankruptcy performance of reorganization plan securities, see "A Caveat on Successful Reorganizations," below, especially Exhibit 8.

TAX LOSS CARRY-FORWARDS.

Importance.   **Tax loss carry-forwards** are an extremely important element in any reorganization, especially if the value of the new firm is relevant, as it almost always is. Tax loss questions are irrelevant, of course, in a straight liquidation. Theoretically, the **value of a firm** is equal to the discounted present value of its future **earnings after taxes.** Since tax loss carrybacks or carry-forwards will affect taxes paid, they have a potentially powerful impact on the earnings to be discounted. The most appropriate procedure is to discount the expected aftertax earnings projection and then add the **present value of tax loss carry-forwards** to arrive at the net overall value.

The Old Tax Laws.   Under the Chapter X, **tax-free transfers** of corporate assets to a successor corporation were generally provided for. But **no reference** was made to the carryover of tax losses, and this caused considerable confusion. Certain cases established the **clean-slate rule,** which held that a firm emerging from bankruptcy that had discharged its old debts was **precluded** from using losses from the "old" business.

Other cases ruled on the so-called **continuity of business doctrine,** and allowed carryovers of losses when there was a **continuity of interest and of the business.** When the principal purpose of a merger (in or out of bankruptcy) was **tax avoidance,** carryovers were disallowed (see Section 269 of the Internal Revenue Code). In practice, this has come to mean that the tax loss carryover is not allowed when a greater than 50% change in ownership or a change in business occurs after the transfer of assets. This highly subjective test probably has not been very effective in curbing takeovers for tax purposes. In addition, the debtor or creditor could petition for a favorable IRS ruling in a bankruptcy-merger reorganization plan that was the only feasible alternative to liquidation.

The New Tax Bill and Reorganization.   The bill introduces a new category of **tax-free reorganization,** known as a **"G" reorganization,** which is more flexible than other types and is, in the belief of the Congress, a means to facilitate the rehabilitation of a problem firm. For instance, a "G" does not require a **statutory merger** (type A), nor does it require that the financially distressed corporation receive solely stock of the acquiring corporation in exchange for its assets (type C), and former shareholders do not have to be in control of a "split-off" company (type D). This new type of reorganization is intended to facilitate the reorganization of bankrupt companies. In light of the debt discharge rules of the bill, which adjust tax attributes of a reorganized corporation to reflect changes in debt structure, the statutory rule regarding **loss carryovers** will apply in "G" reorganizations.

Since "G" reorganizations are subject to the same rules on security exchanges for shareholders and other security holders that apply generally to reorganizations, any party receiving new securities whose principal value is greater than that of the securities surrendered is taxed on the excess, and vice versa. Money or other property received in a "G" will be subject to the dividend equivalency tests (as to whether the property is a **return on capital),** which apply to reorganizations generally. Likewise, securities transferred to creditors based on claims **attributable to accrued or unpaid interest** on securities surrendered, will be subject to tax as if interest income were received.

TRIANGULAR REORGANIZATION.   The new bill permits a firm to purchase a company in bankruptcy in exchange for stock of the parent company of the acquiring firm rather than its own stock. This is known as a **triangular reorganization.** In addition, the creditors of the insolvent company are permitted to exchange their claims for voting stock of the **surviving company** when the stock received equals at least 80% of the value of the debts of the insolvent firm.

MODIFICATION OF THE ABSOLUTE PRIORITY RULE.   The House Ways and Means Committee Report made it clear that the continuity of interest rule would be clarified with regard to creditors. The report also advised that the **absolute prioirty rule** should be modified to permit junior creditors and shareholders to retain an interest in the reorganized business even when senior creditors do not receive full settlement; that is, it favored **relative priority rules.** Junior and senior claims should be considered as **proprietary interests** for purposes of the continuity of interest test.

BUSINESS FAILURE

BANKRUPTCY STATISTICS AND BUSINESS FAILURE.

Sources of Data.   The two primary sources of aggregate business failure and bankruptcy statistics in the United States are **Dun & Bradstreet Corp.** and the **Administrative Office of the U.S. Courts,** Division of Bankruptcy. Dun & Bradstreet has been compiling failure statistics since 1857 and presents annual data in the *Business Failure Record* publication and monthly data in *News from D&B, Monthly Failures.* The Bankruptcy Division source assembles summary reports from the 96 U.S. district courts and breaks down bankruptcy filings by chapter filed, whether business or personal, and by sector of the economy.

Exhibit 3 combines information from the two sources just named, presenting data for 1950–1980. Column 2 indicates that the number of business bankruptcy filings has increased dramatically since 1950, with the major increases registered in 1975 and 1976 and most dramatically in 1980. The aftermath of the 1974–1975 recession saw bankruptcy filings rise to a record, over 35,000. This record was recently surpassed with a great increase in 1980 to over 36,000 individual company filings, and in 1980 a continuation into 1981 appeared likely (see my forecast in "The Economic Case Against Government Bailouts," *Business Week,* March 24, 1980). The current rise reflects both recessionary activity and a relatively tight money and credit market in response to inflationary pressures.

The most continuous time series bankruptcy statistic is D&B's **business failure rate.** This index, which records the **number of failures** recorded **per 10,000 firms** that D&B covers, is an excellent barometer of relative changes in business "exiting" in the United States and Canada. Column 4 of Exhibit 3 shows that the failure rate has been relatively low in recent years, with less than 0.5% of the firms followed actually ceasing operations in a given year, following assignment or bankruptcy, loss to creditors, receivership, reorganization or arrangement. D&B data do not include certain industries, including railroads, most financial enterprises, real estate companies, and many small service firms. The data are also less than comprehensive, since far fewer business failures (column 3) are recorded than business bankruptcy filings (column 2).

The three final columns of Exhibit 3 show that although there has not been a noticeable trend in business failures or failure rates, the **average liability per failure** has been moving steadily upward since 1950, with a peak of over $400,000 in 1978. This can be explained

EXHIBIT 3 NUMBER OF BANKRUPTCY CASES FILED AND NUMBER OF BUSINESS FAILURES AND FAILURE RATES REPORTED SINCE 1950

Year	Number of Business Bankruptcies[a]	Number of Business Failures[b]	Business Failure Rate per 10,000 Firms[b]	Average Liability per failure [b]
1950	8,352	9,162	34	$ 27,099
1951	7,387	8,058	31	32,210
1952	6,542	7,611	29	37,224
1953	6,772	8,862	33	44,477
1954	8,888	11,086	43	41,731
1955	9,185	10,969	42	40,968
1956	9,748	12,686	48	44,356
1957	10,144	13,739	52	44,784
1958	11,403	14,964	56	48,667
1959	11,729	14,053	52	49,300
1960	12,284	15,445	57	60,772
1961	15,241	17,075	64	63,843
1962	15,644	15,782	61	76,898
1963	16,303	14,274	56	94,100
1964	16,510	13,501	53	98,454
1965	16,910	13,514	53	97,800
1966	16,430	13,061	52	106,091
1967	16,600	12,364	49	102,332
1968	16,545	9,636	39	97,654
1969	15,430	9,154	37	124,767
1970	16,197	10,748	44	175,638
1971	19,103	10,326	42	185,641
1972	18,132	9,566	38	209,099
1973	17,490	9,345	36	245,972
1974	20,747	9,915	38	307,931
1975	30,130	11,432	43	383,150
1976	35,201	9,628	35	312,762
1977	32,189	7,919	28	390,872
1978	30,528	6,619	24	401,270
1979	29,500	7,564	28	353,000
1980	45,841[c]	11,742	42	394,744

[a]From the U.S. Administrative Bankruptcy Courts, Washington, D.C., 1980. Statistical year ends June 30.

[b]From Dun & Bradstreet, *Failure Record, 1979*. Failures include businesses that ceased operations following assignment or bankruptcy ceased with loss to creditors; and voluntarily withdrew, leaving unpaid obligations, or were involved in court actions such as receivership, reorganization, or arrangement. Certain industries such as financial enterprises, railroads, insurance, real estate companies, and many small services are not represented. Figures for 1979 are based on the first 10 months of data. Failure liabilities do not include publicly held debt, nor most long-term liabilities and as such underestimate average liabilities.

[c]Includes 9,308 joint husband and wife filings; individual bankruptcies were 36,433.

only partially by inflation, since the average size of U.S. firms, and the consequent liabilities, have grown with price level increases. As noted earlier, however, I feel that the major change in the profile of business failures in the United States is the **susceptibility of the larger firm** to total demise. The last column of Exhibit 3 does not include any long-term publicly held debt and primarily reflects short-term claims. As such, it understates failure claims—in some years, for example, 1975 and 1977—significantly.

Bankruptcy Filings by Chapter and Occupation.   Exhibits 4 and 5 list the nation's bankruptcy filings by chapter of the Bankruptcy Act (prior to 1980) and by type of business. "Straight bankruptcy," whether voluntary or involuntary, means that the firm had to liquidate its assets and repay its creditors in some manner reflecting their priorities. This filing, now

EXHIBIT 4   FILINGS BY CHAPTER OF THE (OLD) BANKRUPTCY ACT SINCE 1950

Fiscal Year	Total	Voluntary Straight Bankruptcy	Involuntary Straight Bankruptcy	Chapter IX	X	XI	XII	XIII	Section 77 (1933 Act)
1950	33,392	25,263	1,369	4	134	583	31	6,007	0
1951	35,193	26,594	1,099	3	88	459	22	6,924	0
1952	34,873	25,890	1,059	15	74	413	21	7,397	0
1953	40,087	29,815	1,064	0	86	437	15	8,670	0
1954	53,136	41,335	1,398	2	104	649	12	9,634	0
1955	59,404	47,650	1,249	1	73	547	19	9,864	0
1956	62,086	50,655	1,240	1	40	597	15	9,535	0
1957	73,761	60,335	1,189	0	65	599	24	11,549	0
1958	91,668	76,048	1,417	2	67	720	23	13,391	0
1959	100,672	85,502	1,288	3	78	787	21	12,993	0
1960	110,034	94,414	1,296	0	90	622	12	13,599	0
1961	146,643	124,386	1,444	0	112	947	31	19,723	0
1962	147,780	122,499	1,382	1	77	903	37	22,880	0
1963	155,493	128,405	1,409	0	128	1,188	33	24,329	0
1964	171,719	141,828	1,339	0	125	1,088	47	27,292	0
1965	180,323	149,820	1,317	0	88	1,022	49	28,027	0
1966	192,354	161,840	1,173	2	93	909	75	28,261	1
1967	208,329	173,884	1,241	1	138	1,033	68	31,963	1
1968	197,811	164,592	1,001	3	128	953	69	31,065	0
1969	184,930	154,054	946	0	87	867	66	28,910	0
1970	194,399	161,366	1,085	0	115	1,262	58	30,510	3
1971	201,352	167,149	1,215	2	179	1,782	120	30,904	1
1972	182,869	152,839	1,094	1	105	1,361	92	27,374	3
1973	173,197	144,929	985	0	101	1,458	92	25,632	0
1974	189,513	156,962	1,009	1	163	2,172	172	29,019	15
1975	254,484	208,064	1,266	0	189	3,506	280	41,178	1
1976	246,549	207,926	1,141	2	141	3,235	525	33,579	0
1977	214,399	180,062	1,132	1	96	3,046	640	29,422	0
1978	202,951	167,776	995	2	75	3,266	650	30,185	2
1979	226,476	182,344	915	1	63	3,042	669	39,442	0
1980	360,960	—	—	a	a	a	—	—	—

[a] 4,664 Chapter 11 filings under New Code—9 months (1980).

Source: U.S. Bankruptcy Courts, Administrative Office of the President, Table of Bankruptcy Statistics, 1980.

EXHIBIT 5 NUMBER OF BANKRUPTCY CASES FILED BY OCCUPATIONS IN THE BUSINESS AND NONBUSINESS GROUPS FOR FISCAL YEARS 1950–1980

| Fiscal Year | Non-Business | | | Business | | | | | | Grand Total | National Population |
	Employee	Others Not in Business	Total	Merchants	Manufacturers	Farmers	Professionals	Others in Business	Total		
1950	22,933	2,107	25,040	2,565	803	290	126	4,568	8,352	33,392	151,677,000
% of total	68.7	6.3	75.0	7.7	2.4	.8	0.4	13.7	25.0	100.0	
1951	25,984	1,822	27,806	2,360	522	205	127	4,173	7,387	35,193	154,360,000
% of total	73.8	5.2	79.0	6.7	1.5	0.6	0.4	11.8	21.0	100.0	
1952	26,527	1,804	28,331	2,319	532	196	137	3,358	6,542	34,873	156,981,000
% of total	76.1	5.2	81.3	6.6	1.5	0.6	0.4	9.6	18.7	100.0	
1953	31,253	2,062	33,315	2,402	518	214	140	3,498	6,772	40,087	159,696,000
% of total	78.0	5.1	83.1	6.0	1.3	0.5	0.4	8.7	16.9	100.0	
1954	40,889	3,359	44,248	3,191	745	322	154	4,476	8,888	53,136	162,409,000
% of total	77.0	6.3	83.3	6.0	1.4	0.6	0.3	8.4	16.7	100.0	
1955	46,163	4,056	50,219	3,317	750	386	217	4,515	9,185	59,404	165,248,000
% of total	77.7	6.8	84.5	5.6	1.3	0.6	0.4	7.6	15.5	100.0	
1956	48,784	3,824	52,608	3,155	730	400	212	4,981	9,478	62,086	168,091,000
% of total	78.6	6.2	84.8	5.1	1.2	0.6	0.3	8.0	15.2	100.0	
1957	59,053	4,564	63,617	3,160	665	405	204	5,710	10,144	73,761	171,191,000
% of total	80.1	6.2	86.3	4.3	0.9	0.5	0.3	7.7	13.7	100.0	
1958	73,379	6,886	80,265	3,504	758	332	284	6,525	11,403	91,668	174,000,000
% of total	80.1	7.5	87.6	3.8	0.8	0.4	0.3	7.1	12.4	100.0	
1959	81,516	7,427	88,943	3,400	634	408	430	6,857	11,729	100,672	177,128,000
% of total	81.0	7.4	88.4	3.4	0.6	0.4	0.4	6.8	11.6	100.0	
1960	89,639	8,111	97,750	3,157	624	453	495	7,555	12,284	110,034	180,670,000
% of total	81.4	7.4	88.8	2.9	0.6	0.4	0.4	6.9	11.2	100.0	

Year											Total
1961	119,117	12,285	131,402	4,244	790	546	623	9,038	15,241	146,643	182,868,000
% of total	81.2	8.4	89.6	2.9	0.5	0.4	0.4	6.2	10.4	100.0	
1962	120,742	11,383	132,125	4,295	735	548	771	9,306	15,655	147,780	186,482,000
% of total	81.8	7.7	89.5	3.0	0.4	0.4	0.5	6.2	10.5	100.0	
1963	127,156	12,034	139,190	4,271	859	554	753	9,866	16,303	155,493	189,278,000
% of total	81.8	7.7	89.5	2.7	0.6	0.4	0.5	6.3	10.5	100.0	
1964	141,550	13,659	155,209	5,064	819	565	785	9,277	16,510	171,719	191,851,000
% of total	82.4	8.0	90.4	2.9	0.5	0.3	0.5	5.4	9.6	100.0	
1965	148,965	14,448	163,413	4,856	852	589	780	9,833	16,910	180,323	193,818,000
% of total	82.6	8.0	90.6	2.7	0.5	0.3	0.4	5.5	9.4	100.0	
1966	160,299	15,625	175,924	4,683	747	551	632	9,817	16,430	192,354	196,843,000
% of total	83.3	8.2	91.5	2.4	0.4	0.3	0.3	5.1	8.5	100.0	
1967	174,205	17,524	191,729	4,929	729	443	704	9,732	16,600	208,329	199,118,000
% of total	83.6	8.4	92.0	2.4	0.4	0.2	0.3	4.7	8.0	100.0	
1968	162,879	18,387	181,266	4,567	749	567	1,087	9,575	16,545	197,811	200,996,000
% of total	82.3	9.3	91.6	2.3	0.4	0.3	0.5	4.9	8.4	100.0	
1969	150,235	19,265	169,500	3,969	680	606	1,301	8,874	15,430	184,930	203,216,000
% of total	81.3	10.4	91.7	2.1	0.4	0.3	0.7	4.8	8.3	100.0	
1970	156,397	21,805	178,202	4,413	858	658	1,304	8,964	16,197	194,399	205,395,000
% of total	80.5	11.2	91.7	2.3	0.4	0.3	0.7	4.6	8.3	100.0	
1971	156,143	26,106	182,249	5,113	1,160	788	1,474	10,568	19,103	201,352	207,006,000
% of total	77.5	13.0	90.5	2.5	0.6	0.4	0.7	5.3	9.5	100.0	
1972	139,466	25,271	164,737	4,757	801	631	1,562	10,381	18,132	182,869	208,837,000
% of total	76.2	13.8	90.1	2.6	0.4	0.3	0.9	5.7	9.9	100.0	
1973	131,153	24,554	155,707	4,851	746	431	1,452	10,010	17,490	173,197	209,724,000
% of total	75.7	14.3	90.0	2.8	0.4	0.2	0.9	5.7	10.0	100.0	
1974	141,930	26,836	168,766	5,634	309	308	1,587	12,409	20,747	189,513	211,909,000
% of total	74.9	14.2	89.1	3.0	0.4	0.2	0.8	6.5	10.9	100.0	

EXHIBIT 5 CONTINUED

Fiscal Year	Non-Business			Business						Grand Total	National Population
	Employee	Others Not in Business	Total	Merchants	Manufacturers	Farmers	Professionals	Others in Business	Total		
1975	184,178	40,176	224,354	6,345	938	550	2,547	19,750	30,130	254,484	213,466,000
% of total	72.4	15.8	88.2	2.4	0.4	0.2	1.0	7.8	11.8	100.0	
1976	166,499	44,849	211,348	6,417	740	672	2,813	24,559	35,201	246,549	214,988,000
% of total	67.5	18.2	85.7	2.6	0.3	0.3	1.1	10.0	14.3	100.0	
1977	144,840	37,370	182,210	6,881	849	736	2,685	21,038	32,189	214,399	216,168,000
% of total	67.6	17.4	85.0	3.2	0.4	0.3	1.3	9.8	15.0	100.0	
1978	139,910	32,513	172,423	5,759	907	751	2,353	20,758	30,528	202,951	217,916,000
% of total	68.9	16.0	85.0	2.8	0.4	0.4	1.2	10.2	15.0	100.0	
1979	164,150	32,826	196,967	4,306	653	592	2,249	21,700	29,500	226,476	219,759,000
% of total	72.5	14.5	87.0	1.9	0.3	0.3	0.9	9.6	13.0	100.0	
1980	n.a.	n.a.	314,875	n.a.	n.a.	n.a.	n.a.	n.a.	45,841	360,716	n.a.
% of total			87.2						12.8	100.0	

n.a. not available.
Source: U.S. Bankruptcy Courts, Administrative Office of the President, Table of Bankruptcy Statistics, 1980.

known as **Chapter 7 straight bankruptcies,** encompasses individuals as well as companies. **Personal bankruptcies** are discussed at the end of this section in the context of the new Bankruptcy Code.

If we compare the number of Chapter X and XI filings with the total number of business bankruptcies, it appears that the combined total is a small percentage (slightly over 10%) of all business filings and is relatively insignificant. Nothing could be further from the truth, however: the size, complexity, and public policy issues involved far outweigh the relatively small number that represents the remaining bankruptcies. To my knowledge, no accurate combined or separate compilation of **Chapter X and XI liabilities** exists.

The breakdown of filings by sector indicates that merchants and professional service firms account for a large proportion, but the total is dominated by "Others in Business." Certain financial and real estate firms make up the bulk of the "other" category. This explains why the **number of bankruptcy filings exceeds** D&B's **number of business failures,** since the latter source does not include them. A more complete breakdown of failures by sector can be found in Dun & Bradstreet's *Failure Record,* published annually.

Statistics Since October 1979.   As we discuss at the end of this section, the new Code will have its major impact in terms of numbers of filings on personal bankruptcies. After just 9 months under the new Code (June 1980), the number of all filings was up more than 60% from the comparable period in 1979, and the total number of filings in the statistical year 1980 had increased 55% over 1979. The two main reasons are the recession of late 1979 and 1980 and the **liberal changes in the new Act,** particularly those affecting Chapters 7 and 13, determining how much individuals can retain after bankruptcy and who is eligible to file.

The **number of Chapter 11 reorganizations** also rose dramatically in 1980, with 4,684 filings in the first 9 months since the new Code went into effect, compared to 3,774 for Chapters X, XI, and XII in all of 1979. The effects of the recession are probably the primary reason for this increase. Next we discuss the **macroeconomic influences on business failures,** indicating that the state of the overall economy is a direct influence on firm performance.

AGGREGATE INFLUENCES ON BUSINESS FAILURE.   Most analysts of business failures and bankruptcies concentrate their efforts on microeconomic causes and indicators. The relatively large number of studies that have attempted to classify and predict bankruptcy (see References, and the discussion on predicting bankruptcies) have obscured the relevance and influence of **macroeconomic influences on the failure phenomenon.** It can be shown, however, that in addition to individual firm inefficiencies, certain aggregate conditions are closely associated with the causes of business failures and contribute to the explanation of why marginally continuing enterprises are forced to declare bankruptcy or to simply close down.

In a recent study (in Altman, *The Analysis and Prediction of Corporate Bankruptcy,* Chapter 2), I explored several macroeconomic influences on the **business failure rate** from 1950 to 1978. Utilizing a first-difference, distributive lag regression model, I concluded that the following time series helps to **explain cyclical movements in business failures:**

1.   Percentage change in real growth in the gross national product (GNP).
2.   Percentage change in the money supply (M-1B).
3.   Percentage change in the Standard & Poor's 500 stock market index.
4.   Percentage change in new business incorporations.

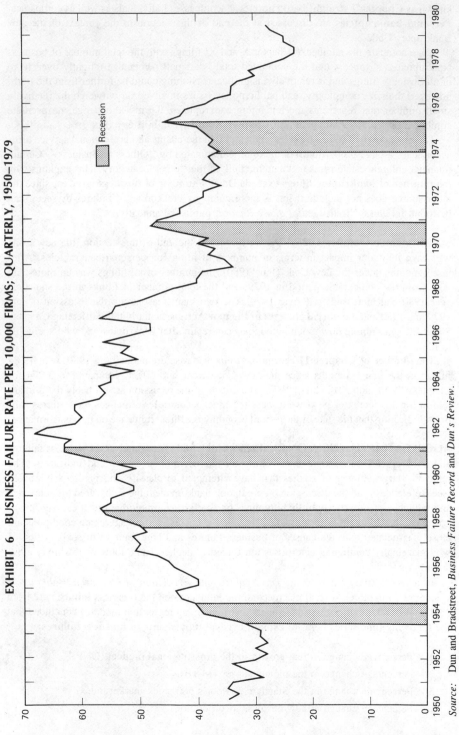

EXHIBIT 6   BUSINESS FAILURE RATE PER 10,000 FIRMS; QUARTERLY, 1950–1979

Source: Dun and Bradstreet, *Business Failure Record* and *Dun's Review.*

I found that the cumulative **change in real GNP growth** over the four quarters preceding and including the quarter in which specific **business failure rate changes** take place helps to explain the changes. The **inverse or negative association** between **aggregate GNP activity and business failures** is shown in Exhibit 6, where the shaded areas depict the recession periods since 1950. One can observe the upsurge in business failures surrounding these recessions. It is intuitively clear why overall economic activity changes and failure rates are negatively correlated, since the aggregate performance of individual firms comprises the overall GNP index.

It can also be seen that changes in the **availability of credit** (money supply) and in **capital market expectations** (stock market index) are inversely associated with the **business failure rate.** A firm will continue to exist as long as it can pay its bills, either through internal generation of funds or from external sources. When the money and capital markets are increasingly stringent or when credit is essentially unavailable to the marginal firm, pressures can be expected to build and failures to start increasing among all firms, particularly the most vulnerable entities. One type of vulnerable firm is the young company.

NEW BUSINESS FORMATION AND AGE OF BUSINESS FAILURES.   The rate of business formation can affect the failure rate in subsequent periods, since it is well documented that there is a **greater propensity for younger firms to fail** than for more mature companies. Exhibit 7 shows this propensity and breaks down failures by age for different sectors and for all concerns. Note that more than 53% of all firms that failed did so in the first five years of their life. This percentage has been remarkably stable over the years, with the rate between 53 and 60% since 1952. Before 1952 an even higher percentage of younger firms failed.

Although almost 28% of the firms that failed did so in their first three years, only about 1% failed in the first year. This is not surprising: **it takes time to fail!** Even when a firm

EXHIBIT 7   AGE OF FAILED BUSINESSES BY FUNCTION, 1978

Age (Years)	Business Type (%)					
	Manufacturing	Wholesale	Retail	Construction	Service	All Concerns
1 or less	0.9	0.6	1.4	0.5	0.9	1.0
2	10.6	7.2	13.6	6.4	7.8	10.5
3	13.6	14.7	19.1	13.6	16.0	16.4
Total 3 years or less	25.1	22.5	34.1	20.5	24.7	27.9
4	13.0	16.3	15.8	14.0	14.6	14.9
5	9.2	10.0	10.3	11.2	11.8	10.4
Total 5 years or less	47.3	48.8	60.2	45.7	51.1	53.2
6	6.6	8.9	7.7	10.0	9.5	8.3
7	6.4	5.2	6.5	9.3	7.5	7.0
8	5.6	4.0	5.0	5.8	3.9	5.0
9	3.3	4.2	3.6	4.9	3.5	3.8
10	4.3	3.5	2.6	3.4	4.5	3.3
Total 6–10 years	26.2	25.8	25.4	33.4	28.9	27.4
Over 10	26.5	25.4	14.4	20.9	20.0	19.4
Total	100.0	100.0	100.0	100.0	100.0	100.0
Number of failures	1,013	740	2,889	1,204	773	6,619

Source: Dun & Bradstreet, *Business Failure Record, 1978*, p. 10.

is in its worst competitive situation (i.e., when it starts out), there is usually sufficient capital to keep it going for a period of time, and default on loans is usually not immediate. Because of this phenomenon, any model observing the association between **new business formation** and changes in **failure rates** must attempt to exploit this sequence.

In fact, there is a very definite positive relationship between new business formation change in some quarter *t* and the change in failures in the subsequent 4–14 quarters. That is, a **lagged relationship** is observed, and when the various lagged quarterly rates have differential influences, the **distributed lagged** relationship (differential importance of the same phenomena over time, e.g., new business formation) helps to explain and predict subsequent failures. For example, with new business formation declining in the first two quarters of 1980, we can probably expect a reduction in the business failure rate starting some time in 1981 or 1982—everything else held equal. Unfortunately, everything else rarely stays the same, and the negative economic performance of the overall economy, if it continues into 1981, will have a countervailing **adverse effect on failure rates.**

As noted earlier, the recent trend in the aggregate economic influences, discussed above—namely, negative real economic growth, a restrictive credit policy due to inflationary pressures, poor stock market performance in 1979, and accelerated business formation in 1978—implied that **business failures and bankruptcy filings would be way up in 1980.** In fact, total filings in 1980 increased by over 16,000 cases, an increase of 55%!

CAUSES OF BUSINESS FAILURE. The overwhelming cause of individual firm failures is **managerial incompetence.** In 1979 over 92% of all failures were identified with the **lack of experience or unbalanced experience** (45%), or just plain incompetence (47%). The remaining causes are categorized as neglect (0.9%), fraud (0.5%), and reasons unknown (5.8%). These statistics represent the opinions of informed creditors and information from D&B reports for over 6,000 business failures. Of course, if **debtors' management** were asked why businesses fail, the category of inexperience and incompetence would receive much lower significance.

PREDICTING CORPORATE BANKRUPTCY

PREDICTING BANKRUPTCY: WHY?   The corporate bankruptcy phenomenon has intrigued researchers and practitioners for several decades because it presents an event that is clearly defined and promises significant rewards to the forecaster who supplies accurate, timely predictions. Ever since the late 1960s, the established methodology has been to classify and predict bankruptcy by combining traditional financial analysis techniques with rigorous statistical procedures. Essentially, analysts have attempted to build **early warning systems** for this negative, but extremely important event. The reference list of this section contains a fairly complete bibliography of these early warning technique studies, and this discussion highlights some of the attempts and comments on their effectiveness.

The reasons for constructing and implementing bankruptcy prediction models are fairly obvious. They involve:

1.   Credit analysis for financial institutions and firms.
2.   Investment analysis for capital market participants.
3.   Audit risk analysis for accounting firms.
4.   Failing company analysis and prudent man considerations for legal and antitrust issues.

5. Various diverse applications such as loan guarantees, government subsidy programs, and merger analysis.

Credit Analysis.   The **objective of credit analysis** is to determine the repayment probability of a potential or existing customer, to assist in the **accept-reject decision** and the pricing policy, as well as the **loan review evaluation.** Most of these applications are primarily related to the operations of financial institutions which have a large number of loan requests and portfolio clients that need to be evaluated quickly and effectively. A related application is in the **accounts receivable management function** of a firm providing goods and services.

In all cases, the **optimal decision criterion** should be to extend credit up to the point at which the marginal expected return from the lowest credit risk is equal to the marginal expected loss from taking on the account. Marginal returns and losses are a function of pricing (interest rates on loans) and costs of **default** or **delinquency** on outstanding credits. For an analysis of these costs for commercial banks, see Altman ("Commercial Bank Lending: Process, Credit Scoring and the Costs of Lending Errors," *Journal of Financial and Quantitative Analysis,* November 1980). The expected return variable is derived from the probability of failure or nonrepayment and its inverse, the probability of successful repayment, hence the significant importance of techniques that seek to quantify failure probabilities.

Investment Analysis.   Later we discuss the **investment performance of securities of bankrupt firms** that went through the reorganization process. An obvious extension of that investigation is to analyze the investment implications of models for predicting bankruptcy. The sale of securities of firms that have a high propensity to fail is one implication. More aggressive strategies might include **short sale** or **option trades,** where precipitous drops in price always accompany a firm's path toward failure.

Audit Risk Analysis.   One of the more controversial issues in the accounting profession is the auditor's responsibilities toward **going-concern qualifications.** If there is a substantial likelihood that a firm will no longer be operating as a continuing entity, the auditor is obliged to state this **contingency** in the **opinion** attached to the audited financial statements. Several firms view their responsibility as mainly expressing their expert opinion on their **ability to realize asset values** and determine whether these values are sufficient to cover outstanding liabilities. Most accountants do not believe that they should be responsible for assessing the **probability of failure.** At the same time, however, most would agree that it is important to counsel clients when the outlook is grim and failure is not an insignificant possibility.

A recent exposure draft of the American Institute of Certified Public Accountants (Accounting Standards Board, Exposure Draft, "The Auditor's Considerations When a Question Arises About an Entity's Continued Existence," March 24, 1980), attempts to specify **auditor responsibilities in high-risk situations.** The draft identifies several pieces of "information that may indicate solvency problems," including **"negative trends** and **adverse key financial ratios, recurring operating losses, working capital deficiencies,** and **negative cash flows."** The AICPA is expected to issue a final report in early 1981.

Regardless of the position accountants take toward the future viability of their clients, both existing and potential ones, the value of an **early warning financial system** is obvious. For a specialized reading list on this subject, see the references.

Legal Issues of Bankruptcy Prediction.   Legal applications of models that attempt to classify firms as having financial profiles similar to bankrupt companies involve two con troversial issues. The **failing company doctrine** is an **antitrust defense** whereby an **otherwise illegal merger** could be allowed because one of the partners is a **failing entity** and no other **good-faith purchaser** exists. This "doctrine" was first applied in the *International Shoe Co.* v. *FTC* [280 U.S. 291 (1930)], but has been infrequently and inconsistently applied ever since. In a recent paper it is argued that such mergers should be sanctioned only if the costs of bankruptcy to society exceed the costs to society from the anticompetitive effects of the merger (Altman and Goodman, "An Economic and Financial Analysis of the Failing Company Doctrine," Salomon Brothers Center Working Paper No. 196, New York University, 1980).

The application of bankruptcy prediction models in failing company cases could provide an objective test for whether the so-called failing company is indeed on the verge of serious financial problems (Blum, "Failing Company Discriminant Analysis," *Journal of Accounting Research,* Vol. 12, No. 1, Spring 1974). For example, the merger in 1978 between two large companies, whose principal subsidiaries were **Youngstown Sheet & Tube** and **Jones & Laughlin Steel** (of Lykes Corp. and LTV Corp.), was sanctioned by the U.S. Attorney General over the objection of his own staff. The degree of seriousness of the steel companies' problems was questioned, as well as the economic justification of permitting the nation's seventh and eighth largest steel manufacturers to merge. We believe that such models, as will be described, can be helpful in understanding the situation. The steel merger was consummated and, indeed, one of the failure classification models (Z-Score) did show that Lykes was a definite candidate for insolvency. Incidentally, the **going-concern qualification** that Youngstown Sheet & Tube received from its auditor in 1977 was removed in the year following the merger.

A **second area of legal application** concerns the investment manager's **fiduciary responsibility** to examine each individual security in his portfolio for its expected return and risk. Portfolio theorists and some legal commentators have argued (see Langbein and Posner, "Market Funds and Trust Investment Law," *American Bar Foundation Research Journal,* December 1975) that the primary responsibility of the **portfolio manager** is to maximize the overall return of the portfolio; individual firm performance is of no relevance. (These authors do concede, however, that an inexpensive screen for assessing security risk would probably be worthwhile to **minimize legal risk.**) One can argue that on the contrary, the manager can and should assess insolvency risk of the securities combined into a portfolio and that companies that possess significant failure potential should not be purchased or, if owned, should be sold (see Altman, "Bankruptcy Identification: Virtue or Necessity," *Journal of Portfolio Management,* Spring 1977).

The application of an **early warning screen** to investment securities is particularly applicable to index fund management. **Index funds** are portfolios of securities theoretically comprised of the entire list of some established stock market index such as the **Standard & Poor's 500** or S & P's **Industrial 400.** The theory is that portfolio managers have rarely, if ever, consistently outperformed the indexes, so why try, and in the process incur substantial personnel and transaction costs. In fact, however, index funds rarely invest in the entire index; rather, they **select a subgroup of the index** in which to concentrate funds. For example, a fund might hold the highest 200 stocks in terms of market capitalization instead of the entire 500.

This situation is ideal for application of failure prediction models. Instead of investing in the top 200 or 300, why not, for example, screen out of that group of 200 the stocks whose companies possess significant failure risk, substituting other stocks that are part of the overall index. Indeed, several **index funds** are utilizing bankruptcy prediction screens in their analysis today. Portfolio management companies are concerned that the stockholders of index and other **mutual funds** will sue management for negligence and mismanagement. This is not likely to occur very often, but one investment manager estimated that a single lost lawsuit could wipe out 5–6 years of profits on a $25 million fund (see McWilliams, "Failure Models and Investment Management," in *Financial Crises: Institutions and Markets in a Fragile Environment,* Altman and Sametz, Eds.)

Diverse Applications.   Other applications for failure models include (1) criteria for **loan guarantees** or other **subsidy programs,** (2) **merger target** analysis, and (3) **bond rating analysis.** In all cases, the aim is to assess creditworthiness and insolvency risk in such a manner as to objectively analyze opportunities and risks.

PREDICTING BANKRUPTCY: HOW?   Since the late 1960s there has been considerable interest among researchers in the development and testing of models for classifying and predicting business failures. Probably the two most important works were by Beaver (1967) and Altman (1968) (references to this topic are listed together at the end of this section), who presented a methodology that has been replicated and improved on for many different types of firms. **Beaver** segregated for analysis a sample of bankrupt firms and a matched sample of nonbankrupt firms and studied the two samples' financial performance indicators for up to 5 years before failure. Beaver's work was a type of **univariate analysis** whereby each measure, or ratio, was analyzed separately and the **optimal cutoff point** was selected so that the number of accurate classifications was maximized for that particular sample. When his analysis is evaluated based on the original samples, the technique is known as **classification analysis.** When a model is tested on a sample of firms other than the original one, preferably from a period after the original model's data source, the analysis takes on a **predictive** flavor.

Beaver tested 14 ratios and found that the **cash flow to total debt ratio** was the best classifier of corporate bankruptcy. Other important financial measures found by Beaver were the debt to total assets and net income to total assets ratios, and the "no credit interval" (for precise definitions, see Beaver, 1967).

The Z-Score Model.   Altman (1968), was the first to apply the technique known as **discriminant analysis** to failure classification problem. The analysis is **multivariate** in that a number of variables are combined simultaneously to analyze a firm for its failure potential. That particular technique, known as the **Z-Score model, applied to manufacturing entities,** has been applied by many practitioners to problems of **credit analysis, investment analysis,** and **going-concern evaluation,** among others. The Z-Score model is expressed as follows:

$$Z = 1.2x_1 + 1.4x_2 + 3.3x_3 + 0.6x_4 + 0.99x_5$$

where: x_1 = (current assets − current liabilities)/total assets
  x_2 = retained earnings/total assets
  x_3 = earnings before interest and taxes/total assets
  x_4 = market value of preferred and common equity (number of shares × price of stock/total debt)
  x_5 = sales/total assets

x_1, **Working Capital/Total Assets.**   The ratio of working capital to total assets, frequently found in studies of corporate problems, is a measure of the **net liquid assets** of the firm relative to the total capitalization. **Working capital** is defined as the difference between current assets and current liabilities. Liquidity and size characteristics are explicitly considered. Ordinarily, a firm experiencing consistent operating deficits will have shrinking current assets in relation to total assets.

x_2, **Retained Earnings/Total Assets. (RE/TA).**   This is a measure of **cumulative profitability** over time. The **age of a firm** is implicitly considered in this ratio. For example, a relatively young firm will probably show a low RE/TA ratio because it has not had time to build up its cumulative profits. Therefore, it may be argued that the young firm is somewhat discriminated against in this analysis, and its chance of being classified as bankrupt is relatively higher than that of another, older firm. But this is precisely the situation in the real world. As we have shown, the incidence of failure is much higher in a firm's earlier years.

x_3, **Earnings Before Interest and Taxes/Total Assets.**   This ratio is calculated by dividing the earnings before interest and tax reductions into the total assets of a firm. In essence, it is a measure of the **true productivity of the firm's assets,** abstracting from any tax or leverage factors. Since a firm's ultimate existence is based on the earning power of its assets, this ratio appears to be particularly appropriate for studies dealing with corporate failure. Furthermore, insolvency in a bankruptcy sense occurs when the total liabilities exceed a fair valuation of the firm's assets, with the value determined by the **earning power of the assets.** This is the most important measure of the five ratios, based on **univariate tests.**

x_4, **Market Value of Equity/Book Value of Total Debt.**   Equity is measured by the combined market value of all shares of stock, preferred and common, whereas debt includes both current and long-term obligations. The measure shows how much the firm's assets can decline in value (measured by market value of equity plus debt) before the liabilities exceed the assets and the firm becomes insolvent. For example, a company with a market value of its equity of $1,000 and debt of $500 could experience a two-thirds drop in asset value before insolvency. However, the same firm with $250 in equity will be insolvent if its drop is only one-third in value. The ratio adds a **market value dimension.** It appears to be a more effective predictor of bankruptcy than a similar, more commonly used ratio, the net worth to total debt (book values).

x_5, **Sales/Total Assets.**   This capital turnover ratio is a standard financial ratio illustrating the sales-generating ability of the firm's assets. It is one measure of management's capability in dealing with competitive conditions. This final ratio is interesting because it is the least significant ratio on an individual basis. Because of its unique relationship to other variables in the model, however, the **sales/total assets ratio** ranks second in its contribution to the overall discriminating ability of the model.

Any firm with a **Z-Score below 1.8** is considered to be a prime candidate for bankruptcy, and the lower the score, the higher the failure probability. This model has been over 90% accurate in classifying bankrupt firms correctly one statement prior to failure and over 80% accurate in subsequent prediction tests, see Altman (1975) and Altman et al. (1977).

With the many important changes in reporting standards since the late 1960s, the **Z-Score model** is somewhat out of date in the 1980s. A second-generation model known as **Zeta Analysis** (Altman et al., 1977) adjusts for these changes, primarily the **capitalization of financial leases.** The resulting linear Zeta discriminant model is extremely accurate for up to 5 years before failure. Since this analysis is a proprietary one, the exact weights for the model's seven variables cannot be specified here (see source below).

Failure Prediction Services. There are at least four statistical "services" that seek to assess the **insolvency risk of industrial companies:**

1. The **Z-Score model.** This model is in the public domain, and it is not necessary to subscribe to a statistical service, although some firms, such as **Merrill Lynch,** will provide Z-Scores.

2. The **Zeta Model.** Available from Zeta Services, Inc., Mountainside, New Jersey.

3. The **Gambler's Ruin Model.** Developed by J. Wilcox (1971, 1976). Available from Advantage Financial Systems, Boston.

4. The **QES Score.** Available from the Trust Division of the First Union Bank, Charlotte, North Carolina.

INVESTING IN BANKRUPT SECURITIES

VALUATION AND INVESTING.   Not only is the reorganization valuation process critical to the debtor, it is also an important determinant of the potential investment opportunities for those interested in **bankrupt securities.** Although a majority of bankrupt firms end in total liquidation or are evaluated as insolvent in bankruptcy (i.e., liabilities are greater than an assessed value of the assets), the firms that are reorganized successfully present potentially excellent investment returns, especially on debt securities. A study performed in 1969 (Altman, "Corporate Bankruptcy Potential, Stockholder Returns and Share Valuation," *Journal of Finance,* December 1969) showed that equity investors of bankrupt firms tended to do as well as all other equity investors if the reorganized firm **lasted at least 5 years** after its initial bankruptcy petition. Admittedly, the percentage (33%) of the firms studied that did last 5 years was relatively small.

The trick is to determine which firms are likely candidates for a successful reorganization and then to **wait at least one month** after the petition date to purchase the securities. It was found that the price of bankrupt firm equities **falls on average 25%** from one month before failure to one month after. This drop in price, sometimes referred to as the **bankruptcy information effect,** implies that the market was not totally anticipating the bankruptcy, or else the price would have been fully discounted.

INVESTING IN RECENT BANKRUPTS.   The postbankruptcy price movement of both the equity shares and debt claims for a number of recent, sizable business failures have been observed. Exhibit 8 lists 11 recent failures, the terms of the reorganization (if any), the price of the debt and equity one month prior to bankruptcy, and the value of these securities as of June 30, 1980. The June 30 value has not been discounted back to the bankruptcy date to adjust for opportunity costs over the period, nor have intermediate values for these securities between the bankruptcy date and the most current date been noted. One who is interested in these adjustments and additions can pursue the matter in as detailed a fashion as is desired. Our purpose for showing these values is to highlight the overall investment potential.

Some of the **investment returns on debt securities** have been enormous and would be even more impressive if the investor had waited until after the bankruptcy to purchase the bonds. For example, **United Merchants & Manufacturing's** $9\frac{1}{2}\%$, 1995 debentures dropped to $420 per bond in the wake of the July 1977 bankruptcy, and subsequently the price rose to almost par value. As interest rates skyrocketed in 1979, the price of all debt fell and the most current value was $890. Several other debt securities received common stock in the reorganization and the subsequent price rise in the common shares helped make the "investment" look very good indeed. For example, **Interstate Stores'** successful transition to **Toys "R" Us** showed a $220 value, before failure, increase to over $4,168 on the 1992 convertibles and over $3,500 compared to a prebankrupt $450 value on the 1981 convertible debt. **King Resources** also showed a large increase.

With the notable exceptions of **Miller-Wohl** and Interstate Stores, the **common stockholders** have not done exceptionally well in their postbankruptcy experience, but in most cases the performance has been acceptable, especially since the stock market in general has not done well in the past decade.

A CAVEAT ON SUCCESSFUL REORGANIZATIONS.   This exercise should not be construed as an endorsement of **investment strategies** that concentrate on bankrupt securities. Bankruptcy does not automatically mean a loss of one's total investment. The key, again, is the **successful reorganization potential** of the debtor, which is usually a function of sound valuation analysis during bankruptcy and favorable economic performance after reorganization. Most bankrupt entities attempt to recover by liquidating, or selling to another firm, the parts of the business that caused most of the problems in the past and by concentrating on the parts that have the greatest earnings potential. Of course, management should have been following this strategy while solvent, but usually the **"crisis principle"** is the motivating force for change. Unfortunately, drastic changes are usually attempted too late to keep a bankrupt from liquidating. For firms that emerge successfully, however, the **reorganization process** is critical to all interested parties, including past and future investors.

PERSONAL BANKRUPTCY

THE NEW PERSONAL BANKRUPTCY RULES.   The **Bankruptcy Reform Act of 1978** made sweeping changes in the rules that govern the personal bankruptcy filings in the United States. In fact, the changes were so dramatic that the number of filings jumped considerably after the Act went into effect on October 1, 1979. For the first 6 months of 1980, the number of personal bankruptcies increased more than 75% over the comparable period in 1979. **Total bankruptcy filings** in 1980 exceeded 360,000, with 314,875 filings in the personal sector. Exhibit 9 shows the trend in personal filings since 1950 (see also Exhibit 5).

Note that, as expected, the number of personal filings increases during recessionary periods and, in all but the 1974–1975 recession, the increase tends to continue for a short time after the recession has ended. Also, with the exception of 1968–1969, 1972–1973, and 1976–1978, the number of filings has been consistently increasing, and we can expect the trend to continue in the 1980s.

There are two reasons for the great increase in personal filings under the new Code (1980 and beyond): (1) the recession and the attendant credit restraints, which had harsh effects on the individual, and (2) the increased liberality of the new Code, particularly in the **exemptions** that are available. See "The New Rules About Bankruptcy," *Changing Times,* May 1979 for details of the new Code related to personal filings.

Personal bankruptcy rationale is based on the premise that individuals should have the opportunity to work out a liquidation or repayment schedule that is feasible and be able to get a **fresh start** on a "new life." The new Code creates a broad set of federal **exemptions** that normally apply to debtors in all states. In states that provide more liberal allowances, a debtor can opt for them. Also, states can pass laws prohibiting the use of federal exemptions, and many of them have done so since the new act went into effect.

EXEMPT PROPERTY.   The following property is **exempted by the federal code:**

1. Up to $7,500 in equity in a **home or burial plot.** Some states (e.g., New York) permit up to $10,000.

2. An individual's interest up to $1,200 in a **motor vehicle.**

3. An individual's interest up to $200 for **any single item** in household goods, furnishings, clothes, appliances, books, animals, crops, and musical instruments.

4. Up to $500 in **jewelry.**

5. Any **property** worth up to $400 plus any unused part of the household exemption (item 1 above).

6. Up to $750 worth of implements, books, or **tools of trade.**

7. Any professionally prescribed **health aids.**

8. Protection includes **social security and veterans' benefits, unemployment compensation, alimony** and **child support,** and **pension and profit-sharing payments.**

If husband and wife file for bankruptcy jointly, the dollar limit doubles. The new Code is far more liberal in its exemptions. For example, under the old act the **federal homestead exclusion** was only $2,000.

Just because property falls into an exempt category, however, a bankrupt cannot necessarily keep it. If a person owns the property completely, he can keep it. Property that is **security for a purchase or a loan** can be repossessed, regardless of whether it is exempted. Once repossessed, the property is sold to satisfy the debt; if there is something left over, in the case of exempt property, the debtor can then list the asset's value under the exclusion categories noted above (e.g., $7,500 for a home). The court might, however, invalidate certain repossessable property **in favor of the debtor** for such items as furniture, tools of trade, and other necessities. In addition, the law limits a **creditor's claim** against certain property **to the value of the property,** regardless of how much is still owed. So if a washing machine that cost $500 on credit has $300 still outstanding but the repossessed value was only $200, the debtor could pay the store the $200 and the remaining $100 of the debt would be eliminated.

CHAPTER 13 REPAYMENT PLANS.   **Chapter 13 of the new Bankruptcy Code** deals with the small business debtor and the individual. Whereas previously the law was limited to "**wage earners,**" now it is possible for any individual with **regular income** to file a Chapter 13 if he has unsecured debts of less than $100,000 and secured debts of less than $350,000.

The debtor has the right to propose a **repayment plan** that may provide for payments over a period of up to 3 years, with the court having the power to extend a repayment period up to 5 years. The debtor may make his payments from future income only or from a combination of future income and a liquidation of his assets. A repayment plan may modify the rights of secured creditors, but not claimants who hold a security interest in real property that is the debtor's principal residence. A plan may not be confirmed unless each **secured creditor** accepts the plan, or the plan provides that the creditor retain the lien securing his claim and that he receive property valued at no less than the allowed amount of his claim. There is no requirement that unsecured creditors vote on or accept a plan.

The key aspect of a Chapter 13 repayment plan is the **monthly budget,** listing expected revenues and expenses for the debtor. Any surplus then becomes the basis for the repayment schedule over the 3–5 year repayment period. It is not uncommon for the debtors to petition

EXHIBIT 8 INVESTMENT PERFORMANCE OF DEBTHOLDERS AND STOCKHOLDERS OF BANKRUPT FIRMS

Original Company and (Reorganization Filing Date)	Total Liabilities (Millions)	Security of Bankrupt Company	Prebankruptcy Market Value of 1 Bond or 100 Shares	New Company and (Date Reorganization Completed)	Securities in New Company or Cash Received in Reorganization or Liquidation for 1 Bond or 100 Shares	Value Based on Recent Market (June 30, 1980)
Penn Central Transportation Co., (June 1970)	$3,600	New York Central 6% bonds due 1980	$ 720	Penn Central Corp., (October 1978)	0.275 Series A and 0.164 Series B mortgage bonds + 21.98 shares B preferred + 9.91 shares common + $147	$ 837.25
Penn Central Co. (100% Owner of P.C.T.C.) (July 1976)	$ 125	Common	$ 150		4 Shares common	$ 80
W.T. Grant Co. (October 1975)	$1,031	4¾% Sinking fund debentures due 1978	$ 360	Company is in liquidation.	$1,000	$ 1,000
		4% Convertible subordinated debentures due 1990	$ 317.50		14% of Face value (judge's approval February 1980 pending 90% agreement of recipients)	$ 140
		4¾% Convertible subordinated debentures due 1966	$ 235		14% of face value (judge's approval February 1980 pending 90% agreement of recipients)	$ 140
		Common stock	$ 338		Probably none	—
Equity Funding Corp. of America, (April 1973)	$ 594	9½% Debentures due 1990	$1,098	Orion Capital Corp., (March 1976)	71.2 Shares common	$ 961.20
		5½% Convertible subordinated debentures due 1991	$ 800		25.5 Shares common	$ 344.25
		Common stock	$2,538		28.7 Shares common	$ 387.45

Company		Security		Successor (date)	Terms	
Interstate Stores, Inc. (May 1974)	$ 208	4% Convertible subordinated debentures 1992	$ 220	Toys ''R'' Us, Inc. (April, 1978)	117 Shares common	$ 4,168.13
		4⅝% Convertible subordinated debentures due 1981	$ 450		1 Share per $10 claim; total claims unavailable	At least $ 4,562
	$ 117	Common Stock	$ 163		66.7 Shares common	$ 2,376.18
King Resources Co., (August 1971)		5½% Convertible subordinated debentures due 1988	$ 90	Phoenix Resources Co., (January 1978)	55.5 Shares B common + $2.83	$ 2,070.20
		Common Stock	$ 181		1 Share B common + $2.13	$ 39.38
Bowmar Instrument Corp., (February 1975)	$ 51	No public debt		Bowmar Instrument, (April, 1977)	—	—
		Common stock	$ 438		66.7 Share common	$ 268
Miller-Wohl Co., Inc., (September 1972)	$ 32	No public debt		Miller-Wohl Co., Inc., (November 1973)		
		Common stock	$ 675		100 Shares common	$18,800
United Merchants & Manufacturing, Inc., (July 1977)	$ 380	9½% Sinking fund debentures due 1995	$ 890	United Merchants & Manufacturers, Inc., (June 1978)	50% of Principal + accrued interest. 9½% interest on remainder to be retired 1989	$ 760
		4½% Convertible subordinated debentures due 1990	$ 502.50		All interest and principal pursuant to original indenture	$ 350
	$ 112	Common stock	$ 538		100 Shares common	$ 675
Unishops, Inc., (November 1973)		No public debt		Unishops, Inc., (April 1975)		
		Common stock	$ 163		66.7 Shares common	$ 217.75

EXHIBIT 8 CONTINUED

Original Company and (Reorganization Filing Date)	Total Liabilities (Millions)	Security of Bankrupt Company	Prebankruptcy Market Value of 1 Bond or 100 Shares	New Company and (Date Reorganization Completed)	Securities in New Company or Cash Received in Reorganization or Liquidation for 1 Bond or 100 Shares	Value Based on Recent Market (June 30, 1980)
Neisner Bros., Inc., (December 1977)	$ 46	No public debt		Merged with Ames Department Stores, Inc., (October 1978)		
		Common stock	$ 325		25 Shares Ames convertible preferred (convertible to 1.25 shares common)	$ 437.50
Daylin, Inc., (February 1975)	$ 250	8.35% Debentures due 1997	$ 700	Daylin, Inc., (November 1976), merged with W. R. Grace, (March 1979)	$158 + 0.121 "A" notes + 0.558 "A" debentures + 54 shares common	$ 1,053
		5% Subordinated debentures due 1989	$ 220		0.085 Class "B" notes + 0.032 class "B" debentures + 290 shares common	$ 1,327.63
		Common stock	$ 150		100 Shares common—Received $4.0625 a share in Grace merger	$ 406.25

EXHIBIT 9 PERSONAL BANKRUPTCY FILINGS IN THE UNITED STATES, 1950–1980

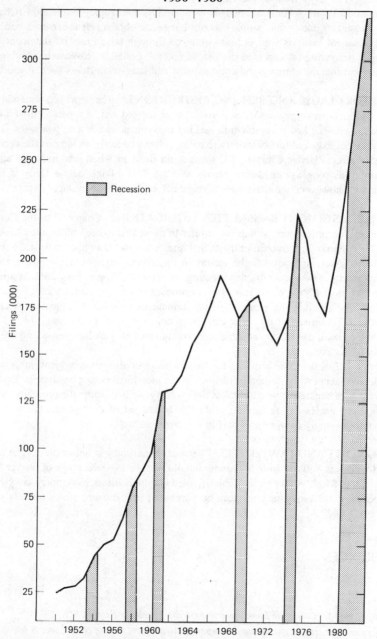

Source: Administrative Office of the U.S. District Courts, Bankruptcy Divisions, *Table of Statistics,* Washington, D.C., 1980.

for and receive confirmation on very low repayment schedules including the so-called 1% (of liabilities) or **$5 (a month) plans.**

Chapter 13 offers several advantages over straight bankruptcy liquidation (Chapter 7) filings. The major one is that people can **discharge,** or **obtain release from** a wider range of debts. Student loans as well as loans obtained through false financial statements can be discharged depending on expected disposable income available. **Nondischargeable debts,** however, still include alimony and child support and **long-term debts** such as mortgages.

CODEBTOR CLAUSE AND REFILING RESTRICTIONS.   The court now extends its protection to codebtors or guarantors of a loan. Under the old Act, if a person filed a Chapter XIII plan, a creditor had no problem in seeking repayment from a loan guarantor. The new Code stipulates that creditors cannot try to collect from a codebtor **as long as the repayment plan is in effect.** Under **Chapter 13,** there is **no limit to when one may file again for bankruptcy** as long as the debtor repays at least 70% of the debts. Under Chapter 7 (liquidation), however, one must **wait 6 years** before filing for bankruptcy again.

CHAPTER 7: STRAIGHT BANKRUPTCY LIQUIDATION.   Chapter 7 of the Code deals with liquidation procedures, which are similar to those that existed under the old Act. The new Code provides for the court, or the U.S. Trustee, to appoint an interim trustee to liquidate the debtor's assets and pay off the claims in their order of priority (see the material on absolute priority, above). At the first meeting, creditors holding at least **20% in amount of claims** may elect a trustee. At least 20% in amount of claims must actually vote, and the candidate who receives the majority of the amount of the claims is elected. A creditors' committee is comprised of no fewer than three nor more than 11 creditors for the purpose of consulting with the trustee and making recommendations to him respecting the administration of the estate.

Section 727 of the Code provides for the discharge of all remaining debts after the estate is liquidated except when certain infractions of the individual debtor preclude it. Essentially, when one goes bankrupt, the court takes the property, sells it, splits the proceeds among the creditors, and erases any remaining debt. The **broad set of exemptions** discussed earlier for Chapter 13 apply for the most part to Chapter 7 as well.

FILING COSTS AND LAWYER FEES.   Personal bankruptcy is not costless. The filing fee for individuals is $60, up from $50 under the old Act. In 1980 the range of lawyer fees was usually $150–$400. Although the majority of individuals hire a bankruptcy lawyer, this is not necessary: the requisite forms can be purchased in stationery stores for less than $10 (in 1980).

REFERENCES

Books

Altman, Edward I., *Corporate Bankruptcy in America,* Heath, Lexington, MA, 1971.

———, *The Analysis and Prediction of Corporate Bankruptcy,* Wiley, New York, in press (1982).

———, and Sametz, A.W., *Financial Crises, Institutions and Markets in a Fragile Environment,* Wiley-Interscience, New York, 1977.

Argenti, John, *Corporate Collapse: The Causes and Symptoms,* McGraw-Hill, London, 1976.

Sinkey, Joseph, *Problems and Failed Institutions in the Commercial Banking Industry,* JAI Press, Greenwich, CT, 1979.

Stanley, David, and Girth, Marjorie, *Bankruptcy: Problem, Process of Reform,* Brookings Institution, Washington, D.C., 1971.

Periodicals and Occasional Papers

Administrative Office of the U.S. Courts, Bankruptcy Division, *Annual Reports,* Washington, D.C.

American Institute of Certified Public Accountants, Exposure Draft, "The Auditor's Considerations When a Question Arises About an Entity's Continued Existence," AICPA Accounting Standards Board, New York, March 24, 1980.

Bankruptcy Reform Act of 1978, *Bankruptcy Law Reports,* No. 389, October 26, 1978, Part II, *Commerce Clearing House,* Chicago.

Bankruptcy Tax Bill of 1980 (H.R. 5043), Commerce Clearing House, Chicago.

Business Week, "The Economic Case Against Government Bailouts," March 24, 1980, pp. 104–107.

Collier on Bankruptcy, 15th ed., 1980, Bender, New York.

Dun & Bradstreet, *The Failure Record,* D&B, New York, annual.

————, *News From D&B, Monthly Business Failure Record,* D&B, New York, monthly.

Green, B., "What Big Teeth You Have, Grandma," *Forbes,* February 4, 1980.

Herzog, Asa, and King, Lawrence, P., *Bankruptcy Code: With Legislative History and Explanatory Comment on Bankruptcy Reform Act, 1978,* 1979 Collier pamphlet ed., Bender, New York, 1979.

"New Rules About Bankruptcy," *Changing Times,* May 1979.

Security and Exchange Commission, *Corporate Reorganizations Releases,* Chapter X cases, periodic, SEC, Washington, D.C.

Journal Articles: Failure Prediction Studies

Altman, Edward I., "Financial Ratios, Discriminant Analysis and the Prediction of Corporate Bankruptcy," *Journal of Finance,* September 1968, pp. 589–609.

————, "Corporate Bankruptcy Prediction and Its Implications for Commercial Loan Evaluation," *Journal of Commercial Bank Lending,* December 1970, pp. 8–22.

————, "Predicting Railroad Bankruptcies in America," *Bell Journal of Economics and Management Science,* Vol. 4, No. 1, Spring 1973, pp. 184–211.

————, "The Z-Score Bankruptcy Model: Past, Present, and Future," in *Financial Crises* (E. I. Altman and A. W. Sametz, Eds.), Wiley-Interscience, New York, 1977, pp. 89–139.

————, "Predicting Performance in the Savings and Loan Association Industry," *Journal of Monetary Economics,* October 1977, pp. 443–466.

————, Haldeman, R. G., and Narayanan, P., "Zeta Analysis: A New Model to Identify Bankruptcy Risk of Corporations," *Journal of Banking and Finance,* June 1977, pp. 29–54.

————, Margaine, M., Schlosser, M., and Vernimmen, P., "Financial and Statistical Analysis for Commercial Loan Evaluation: A French Experience," *Journal of Financial and Quantitative Analysis,* March 1974, pp. 195–214.

Beaver, W. H., "Financial Ratios as Predictors of Failure," *Empirical Research in Accounting: Selected Studies 1966,* January 1967, pp. 71–111.

————, "Alternative Accounting Measures as Predictors of Failure," *Accounting Review,* January 1968, pp. 113–122.

————, "Market Prices, Financial Ratios, and the Prediction of Failure," *Journal of Accounting Research,* Autumn 1968, pp. 179–192.

Blum, M., "Discussion: The Z-Score Bankruptcy Model," in *Financial Crises* (E. I. Altman and A. W. Sametz, Eds.) Wiley–Interscience, New York, 1977, pp. 120–129.

Deakin, E. B., "A Discriminant Analysis of Predictors of Business Failure," *Journal of Accounting Research,* Spring 1972, pp. 167–179.

———, "Business Failure Prediction: An Empirical Analysis," in *Financial Crises* (E. I. Altman and A. W. Sametz, eds.), Wiley-Interscience, New York, 1977, pp. 62–88.

Edmister, R. O., "An Empirical Test of Financial Ratio Analysis for Small Business Failure Prediction," *Journal of Financial and Quantitative Analysis,* March 1972, pp. 1477–1493.

Elam, R., "The Effect of Lease Data on the Predictive Ability of Financial Ratios," *Accounting Review,* January 1975, pp. 25–43.

"How to Figure Who's Going Bankrupt," *Dun's Review,* October 1975, pp. 63, 64, 107, 108.

Korobow, L., and Stuhr, D. P., and Martin, D., "A Probabilistic Approach to Early Warning of Changes in Bank Financial Condition," *Monthly Review,* Federal Reserve Bank of New York, July 1976, pp. 187–194.

Martin, D., "Early Warning of Bank Failure: A Logit Regression Approach," *Journal of Banking and Finance,* November, 1979, pp. 249–276.

Meyer, P. A., and Pifer, H. W., "Prediction of Bank Failures," *Journal of Finance,* September 1970, pp. 853–868.

Mullin, R. A., "The National Bank Surveillance System," in *Financial Crises* (E. I. Altman and A. W. Sametz, Eds.), Wiley-Interscience, New York, 1977, pp. 49–55.

Sinkey, Joseph, "Problem and Failed Banks, Bank Examinations, and Warning Systems: A Summary," in *Financial Crises* (E. I. Altman and A. W. Sametz, Eds.), Wiley-Interscience, New York, 1977, pp. 24–47.

———, "The Collapse of Franklin National Bank of New York," *Journal of Bank Research,* Summer 1977, pp. 113–122.

———, "A Multivariate Statistical Analysis of the Characteristics of Problem Banks," *Journal of Finance,* March 1975, pp. 21–36.

Stuhr, D. P., and Van Wicklen, R., "Rating the Financial Condition of Banks: A Statistical Approach to Bank Supervision," *Monthly Review,* Federal Reserve Bank of New York, September 1974, pp. 233–238.

Wilcox, J. W., "A Gambler's Ruin Prediction of Business Failure Using Accounting Data," *Sloan Management Review,* Spring 1971, pp. 1–10.

———, "A Prediction of Business Failure Using Accounting Data," *Journal of Accounting Research* (Supplement), October 1973, pp. 163–171.

———, "The Gambler's Ruin Approach to Business Risk," *Sloan Management Review,* Fall 1976, pp. 33–46.

Journal Articles: Other

Altman, Edward I., "Corporate Bankruptcy Potential, Stockholder Returns and Share Valuation," *Journal of Finance,* December 1969, pp. 886–900.

———, "Bankruptcy Identification: Virtue or Necessity?" *Journal of Portfolio Management,* Spring 1977, pp. 63–67.

———, and McGough, T., "Evaluation of a Firm as a Going Concern," *Journal of Accountancy,* December 1974, 50–57.

———, and Goodman, L., "An Economic and Statistical Analysis of the Failing Company Doctrine," Salomon Brothers Center, Working Paper No. 196, New York University, 1980.

Blum, Marc, "Failing Company Discriminant Analysis," *Journal of Accounting Research,* Spring 1974, pp. 1–25.

Committee on Corporate Laws, "Changes in the Model Business Corporation Act—Amendments to Financial Provisions," *Business Lawyer*, Vol. 34, July 1979, pp. 1867–1881.

Duberstein, Conrad, "A Broad View of the New Bankruptcy Code," Reprint from *Brooklyn Barrister*, April 1979, pp. 1–19.

Langbein, J., and Posner, R., "Market Funds and Trust Investment Law," *American Bar Foundation Research Journal*, December 1975.

Seligson, Charles, "Major Problems for Considerations by the Commission on Bankruptcy Laws of the United States," *American Bankruptcy Law Journal*, Winter 1977, pp. 73–112.

Walter, James, "Determination of Technical Insolvency," *Journal of Business*, January 1957, pp. 30–43.

Warner, Jerold, "Bankruptcy Costs, Some Empirical Evidence," *Journal of Finance*, May 1977, pp. 337–348.

PUBLIC UTILITY FINANCE

CONTENTS

BACKGROUND 3

THE REGULATORY ENVIRONMENT 3

A Simplified View of Regulation 4
Inflation and Regulatory Lag 6
Changes in Cost of Capital 6
Mandatory Investment 9
Accounting Policies Under Regulation 9
  Tax accounting 10
  Construction accounting 10

CAPITAL BUDGETING 12

Traditional Utility Capital Budgeting 12
Capital Budgeting in the 1980s 13
  Demand forecasting 13
  Cost forecasting 13
  Cost of capital considerations 14
    Current environment of capital
budgeting decision making 14
Regulatory approval 14

Commission Participation in the Decision
  Process 15
Joint Facilities Planning 16

COST OF CAPITAL 17

Cost of Capital in Rate Cases 17
  Comparable earnings method 17
  DCF method 17
  Risk premium methods 20
  Capital asset pricing model (CAPM) 20
Adjustment for Flotation Costs 21
Cost of Capital for Capital Budgeting 22

CAPITAL STRUCTURE 23

Capital Structure Theory 23
Capital Structure in Rate Cases 24
Parent–Subsidiary Issues 26
  Differences among subsidiaries 26
  Double leverage 27

DIVIDEND POLICY 29

PUBLIC UTILITY FINANCE

Eugene F. Brigham

BACKGROUND

Other sections of this *Handbook* deal with such topics as cash management, dividend policy, and capital budgeting techniques. However, the application of these techniques must vary somewhat from firm to firm and from industry to industry, depending on each entity's characteristics and operating environment. This is especially true of the public utilities, defined here to include electric, gas, telephone, and water companies, and, in certain respects, some of the transportation companies.

The utilities' prices are controlled by regulatory agencies, and the companies are required to provide a specified level of service as a condition for maintaining their operating franchises. This combination of controlled prices and required new investment has had a profound effect on the **financial policies of utilities** vis-à-vis the policies of industrial corporations. For example, the decision of an industrial company to invest or not to invest in a new plant would depend on whether the present value of the expected cash flows from the plant exceeded the cost of building it. Utilities, on the other hand, have traditionally proceeded by (1) deciding that a new plant would be needed 10 or 12 years down the road, (2) building the plant, and (3) **then** trying to persuade the regulatory authorities to permit the company to set prices (on the whole system's output) sufficient to cover costs and to provide a **fair and reasonable return on invested capital.** Similarly, if an industrial company's profits were "too low" and its cash flows "inadequate," it would raise prices or, if competition did not permit price increases, cut back on its investment or even close down the operation, redeploying capital into more profitable areas. A utility, on the other hand, must go before its regulatory commission and seek permission to raise prices to correct financial problems.

Because of the critical—indeed, dominant—importance of regulation, this section begins with a discussion of regulatory practices and their effects on the financial posture of the utility industries. Then, building on this background, we consider the following aspects of financial policy: capital budgeting, cost of capital determination, capital structure decisions, and dividend policy. For the other aspects of financial management, which are less influenced by regulation, see the appropriate sections of this *Handbook*.

THE REGULATORY ENVIRONMENT

Utility companies are, to a large extent, **natural monopolies**—one firm can provide service to a particular territory more efficiently than could two or more companies. Thus, to minimize total operating costs, **utilities** are granted **franchises,** which give them exclusive rights within a given region. Because each firm is a monopoly, and because the service supplied is a necessity, utilities have the potential for earning excessive profits. As a result, utilities are subject to **price regulations** designed to limit them to a "fair" rate of return on invested capital.

A SIMPLIFIED VIEW OF REGULATION.   In theory, regulatory procedures call for first estimating demand and cost schedules under "normal" conditions, then using these schedules to produce estimates of profits at various prices. These relationships are illustrated in Exhibit 1, where for simplicity we assume that the utility provides but one type of service. At a price P, Q units are demanded. The cost per unit at Q units of output is C. The profit per unit is $P - C$, and this unit profit, multiplied by Q units, gives total profits, the shaded area in the graph. If the company operated without regulation, it would set marginal revenue *(MR)* equal to marginal cost *(MC)*, set a **monopoly price** higher than P, sell fewer units of output, and earn larger operating profits in spite of its lower level of operations. Clearly, some type of regulation is desirable to prevent this result.

In a simple world, regulators would (1) determine the **assets** necessary to supply a given level of service (the **rate base**), (2) recognize that money capital of the same amount is required to acquire the **rate base assets,** and (3) authorize a price for the utility's service such that the company's operating profits were just sufficient to cover its **cost of capital.** For example, if the required level of assets and capital were $100 million, and if the cost of capital were 12%, the **target operating profit level** would be $12 million. Service rates would have to be set at a level that would provide sufficient revenues to cover fuel, operating and maintenance (O & M) costs, and taxes, and **still leave $12 million to compensate the investors** who supplied capital to the utility enterprise.

Obviously, the real world is much more complex than this. First, it is impossible to determine the cost and demand schedules exactly. Second, utilities serve several classes of customers, which means that a number of different cost and demand schedules, with varying elasticities, are involved, so that any number of different rate schedules could be used to produce the desired level of profits. Third, the actual size of the rate base is subject to dispute, and it is not necessarily equal to the capital supplied by investors. In particular, as discussed in detail later, part of the capital supplied by investors is invested in operating assets, on which a cash return is earned, and part is invested in **"construction work in progress,"** which is generally not in the rate base and consequently does not provide a current cash return.

Furthermore, utility regulation is not and should not be nearly as rigid as the example in Exhibit 1 suggests. For one thing, such rigidity, even if it were possible, would leave little or no room for managerial incentive: the profit motive for efficiency would be totally removed if the companies were simply guaranteed a specified profit. Consequently, it is often argued that rates should be set sufficiently low so that companies must strive to keep costs down and demand up to attain the profit goal. Furthermore, rates are changed with a lag, so if a particular company were especially efficient and were thus able to keep its costs lower than those that had been estimated when the rate schedule was set, it would be able to earn a higher than prescribed rate of return—at least until the regulatory agency ordered a rate reduction. Conversely, if costs rose and profits fell, there would be a lag before a rate increase could be obtained. These lags provide a powerful stimulus for utilities to operate efficiently.

To summarize, regulators in theory are supposed to do the following: (1) **determine the amount** of investment the company has made in facilities to serve the public, which in general is close to the amount of capital investors have supplied, (2) **determine a "fair rate**

EXHIBIT 1   HYPOTHETICAL DEMAND-COST RELATIONSHIPS FOR A UTILITY COMPANY

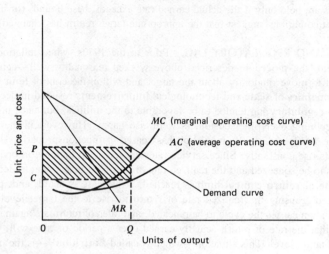

of return," which is based on the cost of capital, and (3) **set prices** that result in profits just high enough to actually provide that "fair return."

As they typically operate, commissions establish a **"target rate of return"** equal to the **weighted average cost of capital** and then, implicitly or explicitly, establish upper and lower bounds around this target. Exhibit 2a illustrates this concept. Even under reasonably stable economic conditions, actual earned rates of return could be expected to vary somewhat from year to year depending on weather conditions and other random factors. Furthermore,

EXHIBIT 2   TYPICAL RATE OF RETURN PATTERNS UNDER INFLATIONARY CONDITIONS: (a) WITHOUT REGULATORY LAG, (b) WITH REGULATORY LAG

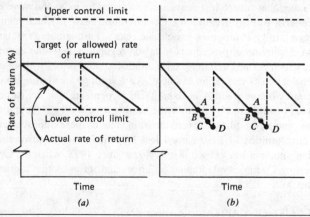

Source: Brigham and Pettway, "Capital Budgeting by Utilities, *Financial Management*, Autumn 1973, p. 13.

it would not be feasible to hold a rate case every time the actual rate of return varied even slightly from the target. Thus, **upper and lower control limits** (implicit or explicit) are set, and rate cases are held only if the actual earned rate exceeds these bounds (or if changes in capital market conditions suggest that the appropriate target return has changed).

INFLATION AND REGULATORY LAG.   Prior to the 1970s, when inflation became a major problem, the procedure described above worked reasonably well—actual rates of return tended to move randomly about the target and within the control limit boundaries.

Indeed, **economies of scale** and **technological improvements** resulted in declining costs over time, so **regulatory lag** tended to be favorable to the utilities, but since utility service rates were declining over time, customers were also happy. However, in the inflationary climate of the 1970s and 1980s, regulation has ceased to function properly. Under strong inflation, costs rise constantly. Since service rates are fixed, an increase in operating costs causes profits to be squeezed and the realized rate of return on investment to decline. When the **lower rate of return control limit** is reached, a rate case is heard, and, presumably, rates are raised, causing the realized rate of return to rise to the target level. However, continued inflation causes the cycle to be repeated, and rates of return are again eroded. The net result is that the rate of return actually earned over a period of time will, on average, be below the target level. This situation—which is called **"attrition"**—is the one depicted in Exhibit 2.

Exhibit 2*b* shows how **administrative lags** exacerbate the problem. At point *A* the actual rate of return penetrates the lower control limit, prompting the company to seek a rate hearing, which occurs at point *B*. At point *C* an order is issued permitting the company to raise rates, and the rate increase takes effect at point *D*. As shown here, the actual rate of return at point *D* does not return to the target level. The cost figures generally used in the point *B* rate cases are those of the **most recent past year.** If inflation continues, the cost figures will be outdated (i.e., too low) by the time new rates take effect. Hence, the calculated utility rates are too low to boost the rate of return on investment up to the target level. It would, of course, be possible for regulatory authorities to anticipate price increases—in utility parlance, this is called **"using a future test year"**—and this would lessen the impact of **regulatory lag.** However, a **historic test year** is used in most jurisdictions, and this has a **negative impact** on utility profits under **inflationary conditions.**

It should be noted that **future test years** are being used by more and more commissions, including the **Federal Energy Regulatory Commission** (FERC), which regulates the sale of power **between utility companies** (wholesale rates). Furthermore, regulatory agencies are beginning to employ other procedures to lessen regulatory lag—the automatic fuel adjustment clause, which permits certain electric utilities to raise prices without going through a rate case when fuel costs rise, is an example. Also, utilities are starting to project trends and to file rate cases before point *A* in Exhibit 2*b*, recognizing that the earned return will be below the lower control limit by the time the hearing is held even if the limit has not been penetrated at the time of the filing. Nevertheless, in spite of these improvements, 93 of the 100 largest electric utilities in 1980 earned **less** than their authorized or **target rates of return.** A similar situation has existed in every year since 1973, when the Organization of Petroleum Exporting Countries quadrupled oil prices and set in motion a dramatic spurt in the inflation rate.

CHANGES IN COST OF CAPITAL.   Another problem faced by utility companies is the rapidly rising cost of capital they have experienced during the past few years. Controversy exists over the exact measurement of the cost of capital, but because of the general **increase**

EXHIBIT 3   ILLUSTRATION OF RISING COST OF CAPITAL COMBINED WITH LAGGED CHANGES IN ALLOWED RATE OF RETURN

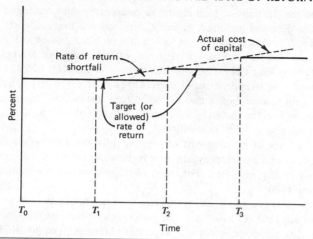

Source: Brigham and Pettway, "Capital Budgeting by Utilities," *Financial Management,* Autumn 1973, p. 14.

in interest rates, no one seriously questions the contention that the cost of capital has been rising. However, because of regulatory lags, the target rate of return has generally been set below the actual cost of capital. Exhibit 3 illustrates this situation. From T_0 to T_1, the cost of capital is both stable and equal to the allowed rate of return. At T_1 the cost of capital begins to rise, and during the interval from T_1 to T_2 the **rate of return shortfall** widens. At T_2 a rate case is held, and the allowed rate of return is adjusted upward. However, the continuing increase in the cost of capital causes the cycle to be repeated, and over the entire period the actual rate of return averages less than the cost of capital.

The following data are from *Standard & Poor's Statistical Services, Federal Reserve Bulletin,* and *The Wall Street Journal;* estimated equity costs are from Brigham and Shome, "Estimating the Market Risk Premium," Public Utility Research Center Working Paper, July 1979. This tabulation presents dramatic evidence of the **rise in the cost of capital** that occurred from the mid-1960s to the early 1980s.

	1965	1970	1977	1978	1979	November 1980
1-Year Treasury notes	4.00%	6.50%	6.09%	8.34%	10.67%	15.75%
20-Year Treasury bonds	4.21	6.58	7.67	8.48	9.33	12.85
Aaa utility bonds	4.52	8.11	8.14	8.83	9.64	14.81
Baa utility bonds	4.77	9.11	8.86	9.48	10.69	16.04
Utility common stock dividend yields	3.24	5.83	7.39	8.33	9.19	13.50
Estimated cost of common equity	8.00	10.92	13.19	14.17	15.65	N.A.

One might think that if the **rate of inflation** stabilized, the cost of capital for a utility would also stabilize, and the "cost of capital" line in Exhibit 3 would level out. However, this is not correct. A utility's cost of capital for rate-making purposes is a weighted average (k_a) of the cost of debt (k_d), preferred stock (k_p), and common stock equity (k_s),

$$k_a = w_d k_d + w_p k_p + w_s k_s, \qquad (1)$$

where the w's are the fractions of total capital represented by debt, preferred stock, and common stock. For debt and preferred, k_d and k_p represent the **average costs of all out-standing securities.** The typical utility issues 30- or 40-year bonds, so some of the currently outstanding debt was issued years ago at very low interest rates. For example, the Bell System has outstanding long-term debt with interest rates as low as 2.625%, even though more recently issued long-term debt carries interest rates of up to 14.25%. Thus, since the **marginal cost of debt** is much higher than k_d, the average cost of debt, the issuance of new debt for expansion or to retire maturing old issues will keep utilities' cost of capital rising for years, even if the rate of inflation stabilizes.

The combined effects of a **rising cost of capital, inflation,** and **regulatory lags** are shown in Exhibit 4, in which a company's average realized rate of return is depicted as being substantially below its cost of capital. For most utility companies, this situation existed in the 1970s and early 1980.

Whenever a company is earning, and is expected to earn, a return on common equity less than its **cost of equity,** the stock will sell at a market price below its book value. Exhibit 5 shows cost of equity capital estimates (k_s), actual earned returns on equity (ROE), the ratio of ROE to k_s, and market price/book value ratios (M/B) for the electric utility industry from 1966 to 1979. It is apparent from the exhibit that before 1973, the electrics typically earned more than their cost of capital, hence sold at prices above book, while after 1973 the industry on average has earned less than the cost of capital and consequently has sold below book. Other utility industries—for example, the **telephone companies**—have faced a generally similar situation.

EXHIBIT 4   COMBINED EFFECT OF RISING COSTS, RISING COST OF CAPITAL, AND REGULATORY LAG

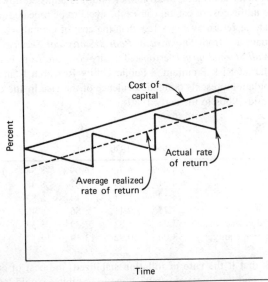

Source: Brigham and Pettway, "Capital Budgeting by Utilities," *Financial Management*, Autumn 1973, p. 15.

EXHIBIT 5 ESTIMATED COST OF EQUITY, EARNED ROE, AND MARKET/BOOK RATIOS FOR THE ELECTRIC UTILITY INDUSTRY, 1966–1979[a]

Year	(1) Estimated Cost of Equity Capital, k_s	(2) Rate of Return on Average Common Equity, ROE	(3) Ratio of ROE to k_s	(4) Market/Book Ratio
1966	8.56%	12.84%	1.50	2.17 times
1967	9.34	12.84	1.37	1.93
1968	9.51	12.29	1.29	1.93
1969	10.19	12.25	1.20	1.68
1970	10.92	11.82	1.08	1.54
1971	10.67	11.55	1.08	1.41
1972	10.95	11.78	1.08	1.33
1973	12.61	11.34	0.90	0.95
1974	15.24	10.40	0.68	0.64
1975	15.30	11.26	0.74	0.88
1976	13.46	11.53	0.86	0.99
1977	13.19	11.49	0.87	0.97
1978	14.17	11.22	0.79	0.83
1979	15.66	11.15	0.71	0.75

[a]The theoretical relationship between the market/book ratio M/B and the ROE is given by:

$$M/B = \frac{\text{expected ROE} - b(\text{expected ROE})}{k_s - b(\text{expected ROE})}$$

where b is the fraction of earnings the company is expected to retain in the future. Column 2 shows actual ROEs, which are not necessarily the expected future ROEs. Still, the correlation between ROE/k_s and M/B is 0.9886.

Source: Column 1: Brigham and Shome, "Estimating the Market Risk Premium," Public Utility Research Center Working Paper, July 1979. Column 2: ROE and M/B ratios calculated from Standard & Poor's Compustat Industrial and Utility tapes.

MANDATORY INVESTMENT.   Whereas industrial companies typically undertake capital projects only if the expected rates of return on the projects exceed their costs of capital, **regulation causes utilities to operate differently.** Utilities are required to provide service on demand, so they must anticipate future demand and then build the facilities necessary to meet this demand. Thus, most of their **investment is mandatory** in the sense that it is necessary to provide service as demanded by new or existing customers. Even though the cost of capital may exceed the projected rate of return from certain projects, utility managements have operated on the premise that mandatory investments simply must be undertaken and that eventually regulators will allow the company to recover the cost of the project, including its cost of capital. More and more, as we shall discuss in connection with capital budgeting, this premise is being questioned.

ACCOUNTING POLICIES UNDER REGULATION.   Utility **financial managers** must be concerned with both **profits** and **cash flows**—profits are nice and are necessary for a viable operation, but profits are not synonymous with cash, and cash is necessary for the payment of interest and dividends, as well as for making purchases of all types. Furthermore, the accounting policies used by regulators to determine costs have a significant effect on cash flows—two accounting policies can produce the same reported profits but vastly different cash flows. The two major areas where utility accounting practices differ from those of unregulated firms are (1) with respect to the **reporting of tax liabilities** and (2) with respect to the **capitalizing of financing costs during construction periods.**

Tax Accounting.   Most corporations, utility and nonutility alike, use **accelerated depreciation** for tax purposes but charge depreciation to cost of goods sold on a **straight-line basis.** The result, for a company whose net assets are growing (as most are, because of inflation if not as a result of **real growth**), is a relatively low current tax bill combined with the certain knowledge that taxes will rise, assuming stable tax rates, at some future time when accelerated tax depreciation is less than straight-line book depreciation (Brigham and Nantell, ''Normalization Versus Flow Through for Utilities,'' *Accounting Review,* July 1974, pp. 436–477). Industrial companies are required, as a condition for an **unqualified audit report,** to report as a charge against income the difference between taxes currently paid and the taxes that would have been paid if the company had used straight-line depreciation for both tax and book purposes—this charge is the item **''deferred taxes,''** which is shown on the income statements and balance sheets of most industrial firms.

The theory of deferred taxes is straightforward and logical—accelerated tax depreciation postpones, or defers, federal income taxes, but these deferred taxes will someday have to be paid; hence they should be shown as a cost. This is called **normalizing** the effects of accelerated depreciation. Not to normalize understates costs, overstates profits, and can be construed as providing misleading information to investors. This is why the accounting profession (and the SEC implicitly) requires corporations to show deferred taxes as a cost, that is, to normalize.

Although many utilities do follow the standard practice of reporting profits after deferred taxes, in about half the states **regulators forbid** this practice. The result is a (relative) understatement of costs and a corresponding overstatement of current profit. The benefits of accelerated depreciation are, in effect, ''flowed through'' to current ratepayers, hence this practice is called **flow through.**

Advocates of flow-through accounting argue that a **growing company** will never have to ''pay off the deferred taxes.'' Opponents point out (1) that under all conceivable conditions, the use of flow through shifts the tax burden associated with current operations from current customers to future customers, hence creates an intergenerational inequity, (2) that flow-through utilities are forced to request rate increases more often, and that if these increases are delayed because of regulatory lag, the problem of rate of return attrition is compounded, (3) that the **cash flows** of **flow-through companies** are lower than those of normalizing utilities, forcing the flow-through firms to raise more money in the capital markets, and (4) that flow-through companies' cash coverages of interest and dividends are lower than those of similar normalizing utilities. The net effect of all this is to raise the cost of debt and equity to flow-through companies vis-à-vis normalizing ones.

If there are so many conceptual problems with the use of flow through, why do almost half the utilities use it? The reason seems to be **political:** the use of flow through postpones a cost—income taxes—to some future date; hence it **shifts the cost of utility service from today's customers to future ones.** Apparently, a number of politicians involved in regulation are more concerned with today's customers than with those of future years.

Construction Accounting.   The other major aspect of public utility accounting that distinguishes it from the accounting practices of unregulated firms relates to construction projects. Visualize a situation in which an electric utility has net assets of $4 billion, represented primarily by generating plant and transmission facilities. The company has a capacity of 10 million kilowatts (kW) at a book cost of $400 per kilowatt of capacity. The company now decides that it must expand generating capacity by 20%, or by 2 million kW. Under current federal regulations, **any new capacity** must be either **coal or nuclear.** A new coal plant started in 1981 would probably have a cost of close to $1,000 per kilowatt of capacity; nuclear would cost about $2,000. Thus, a 20% capacity expansion would call for the expenditure of about $2 billion (50% of existing assets) for a coal plant or $4 billion (100% of existing assets) for a nuclear one.

The **construction time for a new coal plant** is 8–10 years, and it takes at least 12 years to build a **nuclear plant.** The funds invested in the new plant will accumulate over the construction period, and, of course, any increase on the asset side of the balance sheet must be matched by an increase on the liability-capital side. Thus, to pay for the cost of constructing the plant, securities (stock and bonds) will have to be sold years ahead of the time the facility will be put into service.

The investors who supply the new capital must be compensated for the use of their money, both during the construction period and after the plant goes into service. The compensation for capital used during construction—interest on debt plus dividends and retained earnings on equity—has long been recognized as a legitimate cost that should be borne by the utility's customers. However, it is traditional to handle this element as follows: (1) **construction work in progress** (CWIP) is segregated from plant-in-service, (2) only plant-in-service is included in the rate base on which customer bills are based, (3) an **allowance for funds used during construction** (AFUDC) is calculated by **multiplying CWIP by a figure** approximately **equal to the weighted average cost of capital,** (4) AFUDC is reported as income, (5) AFUDC is added to beginning-of-period CWIP (this is called **capitalizing AFUDC**), and (6) customers end up paying, and the company earning, a cash return on capitalized AFUDC when the new plant is completed and added to the rate base. This procedure is logical because it requires current customers to pay only for plant that is currently "used and useful," while future customers, who will receive the output of the new plant, will pay its full cost, including the financing costs incurred during its construction phase.

Although **capitalizing AFUDC** does have the significant merit of requiring those who receive the services of a plant to pay all costs associated with the plant, it also has some severe **financial drawbacks.** First, as in our example, under inflationary conditions a utility can have a very large fraction of its assets invested in CWIP, hence be earning a great deal of AFUDC relative to cash income. For example, Florida Power & Light had 26% of its assets in CWIP in 1979, and AFUDC represented 34% of the company's net income to common. The AFUDC–net income percentage was much higher for many companies—for the 12 months ended June 30, 1980, it averaged 49% for the electric industry, and 8 of the 100 largest companies obtained more than 100% of their reported profits from AFUDC (Salomon Brothers, *Electric Utility Quality Measures,* November 14, 1980). In the 1960s, before new plants became so expensive, the AFUDC–net income ratio generally ran about 5% for the average electric utility, so AFUDC income was not significant.

AFUDC is not cash, but interest and dividends must be paid in cash. Therefore, if a utility obtains a large fraction of its income as AFUDC, it has a **cash flow problem.** Such a company can be forced to sell new bonds and stock to raise the cash necessary to pay interest and dividends on its old bonds and stock. Some security analysts have likened this to a **Ponzi, or Pyramid, scheme,** and research has shown very clearly (1) that **AFUDC income** is regarded as being of **low "quality"** and (2) that utilities that have significant amounts of AFUDC tend to have **lower rated bonds,** hence higher costs of both debt and equity capital (see Brigham, "The Treatment of CWIP," University of Florida, Public Utility

Research Center, 1980). Perhaps even more important, since most utility bond indentures have minimum **coverage requirements** for the sale of new bonds, and since the amount of AFUDC income that can be included to compute coverages is limited, a number of utilities have at times literally been unable to sell new bonds—Georgia Power, Alabama Power, and Portland General Electric are three examples. Being unable to obtain conventional financing, such companies are forced either to stop their construction programs or to undertake expensive, unconventional financing programs.

It should also be noted that industrial firms were not permitted to **capitalize construction financing costs** before 1980, but Statement of Financial Accounting Standards No. 34, "Capitalization of Interest Costs," issued in October 1979 by the Financial Accounting Standards Board (FASB), permits industrials to capitalize the **interest component** (only). However, since industrial firms typically use less debt than utilities, since their construction periods are generally shorter, and since their fixed assets are a smaller fraction of total assets, the industrials' AFUDC–net income ratios are far lower than those of the utilities.

CAPITAL BUDGETING

Conceptually, the correct method of **capital budgeting by unregulated firms** calls for (1) estimating the investment cost associated with a project, (2) estimating the net cash flows each year over a project's life, (3) determining the cost of capital required to complete the project, (4) using these data to calculate the project's net present value (NPV), and (5) accepting the project if its NPV is positive or rejecting it if NPV is negative. It is not a simple matter to obtain accurate estimates of the input data, but from a conceptual standpoint this procedure is correct because it is market oriented and because it optimizes the welfare of both customers and investors within the constraints of a market economy.

TRADITIONAL UTILITY CAPITAL BUDGETING. The utilities have traditionally operated in a different manner. Before the mid-1970s, their capital budgeting process was as follows: (1) demand for service (electricity, gas, telephone service, etc.) was estimated, largely by extrapolating past trends, (2) the plant capacity needed to meet this projected demand was determined, (3) alternative plant designs (e.g., coal- vs. oil-powered plants, or electric vs. manual switching for telephone service) were considered, and (4) the plant design that would provide the needed service at the lowest present value of expected future costs was chosen. The **discount rate** used to find the present values was generally taken to be the **authorized rate of return.**

The whole process was **dominated by engineers,** who forecasted demand, designed the plants, estimated capital requirements, and generally ran the companies. The role of the **financial officer** was mainly to raise the capital the engineers indicated they needed. Regulatory involvement was minimal: because of technological improvements and economies of scale, new plants, when they went on line, generally lowered costs, so rate increases were not required. Indeed, **periodic rate reductions** to keep the rate of return within reasonable bounds were common in the electric, telephone, and gas distribution industries.

Although this procedure worked well for decades, it contained four fatal flaws, which surfaced during the 1970s:

1. The (electric) utilities' demand forecasts did not take adequate account of the relationship between the prices charged and the amount of service demanded (price elasticity).

2. It was assumed that customers wanted the highest quality service (essentially, close to zero probability of power failures, power shortages, filled telephone lines, etc.) and were willing to pay the costs for such systems, regardless of the level of costs.

3. The relationships between the amount of capital raised and the cost of this capital, between the riskiness of cash flows associated with a project and the project's cost of capital, and between the marginal and average costs of capital were not adequately recognized and dealt with.

4. The companies assumed that **public utility commissions** would authorize rate increases to cover the cost increases that would necessarily occur when new plants, whose costs under inflation were far higher than the costs of existing plants, were put on line.

With 20–20 hindsight, it is easy to see that the assumptions embodied in the utilities' capital budgeting procedures were incorrect. Experience during the 1970s taught us that **price elasticity** does indeed exist for utility services—higher prices result in reduced demand, and this demand reduction increases over time as customers adapt to higher prices by insulating houses better, buying more energy-efficient appliances, and the like. Similarly, it is now clear that while customers may have been willing to pay the cost of carrying a 30% reserve margin to assure uninterrupted electric service when capacity cost only $200/kW and when the cost of carrying this spare capacity was based on 5% interest rates, they prefer lower reserve margins when capacity costs $1,000/kW and carrying costs are based on 15% interest rates. Finally, every utility in the country has learned that commissions will not automatically pass the costs of new, high-cost plants on to customers without an argument and without delays.

CAPITAL BUDGETING IN THE 1980s. Even though 20–20 hindsight suggests that the traditional method of capital budgeting by utilities, and especially by electric utilities, had major shortcomings, it is not at all clear that this methodology produced incorrect decisions during the 1960s and early 1970s. In retrospect, it appears that many utility companies started plants that probably should have been deferred for several years; but most of these decisions would have been made under any capital budgeting procedure, given the information available at the time the decisions were actually made. Nevertheless, the methodology employed earlier should not be used during the 1980s. The essential **elements of a viable capital expenditure decision system for the 1980s** are outlined next.

Demand Forecasting. The most important element in the system is a good demand forecasting process. The **demand forecast** must recognize **price elasticity.** This means that a utility must forecast all the elements of cost that will go into service rates, hence influence demand. Furthermore, for telecommunications companies and other utilities that are subject to competition, the company must forecast both total market demand and its own share of the market.

Cost Forecasting. The utility must forecast the cost of building facilities as well as the fuel, operating, maintenance, and capital costs after the plant goes into service. Since plants of alternative types can be built (e.g., coal vs. nuclear power plants, or satellite vs. microwave telecommunication transmission systems), it is necessary to forecast the construction, fuel, and O & M costs of alternative systems to be able to build the least-cost (lowest present value of future cost) system to meet a given forecasted demand. If these cost forecasts are incorrect, the result will be a relatively high-cost, inefficient system, and if these high costs are passed on to consumers in the form of higher service rates, demand may be reduced, further compounding the problem.

Cost of Capital Considerations.   Although many utilities apparently use their **authorized rates of return as the discount rate** for capital budgeting, **this procedure is incorrect** and can lead to substantial errors. The first major problem is that authorized rates of return are based on the **historic average cost** of debt and preferred stock, not on **marginal costs;** hence the authorized rate of return understates the cost of the capital used today to finance capital projects. Second, the authorized rate of return on equity may not correctly reflect the current cost of equity. Third, the cost of capital raised during a period depends (1) on the amount of capital raised and (2) on the perceived riskiness of the investment being made, whereas the authorized rate of return, to the extent that it reflects actual conditions at all, reflects average conditions in the past, not marginal conditions at the present time. Thus electric utilities have at times used the same cost of capital to evaluate nuclear and coal plants, even though far more capital must be raised to construct a nuclear plant, and nuclear plants are generally regarded as being riskier than coal plants from an investment standpoint. The use of the same cost of capital for these two types of plant would tend to **bias the decision toward nuclear** and, possibly, lead to costly mistakes.

Current Environment of Capital Budgeting Decision Making.   No forecasting methodology is or can possibly be perfect. Therefore, a utility may, on the basis of the best available data, forecast its future demand at a given level, build a plant to meet forecasted demand, and find, 10 years or so later when the plant is completed, that the plant is not needed because demand has grown more slowly than had been anticipated. Or, fuel and other cost elements may have changed, or a new design may not have worked out as anticipated, making the newly completed plant's costs higher than they would have been if some other type of plant had been built. Of course, such ex-post mistakes may be identified before a plant is completed—during the latter half of the 1970s, many utilities recognized that conditions were changing, and they slowed down or canceled plant construction, or converted partially completed plants from one fuel to another, often at substantial costs. And, of course, the costs of all new plants have tended to exceed original expectations because of inflated construction costs. The opposite situation existed in the 1960s, when actual demand often exceeded forecasted demand, and electric utilities were forced to generate power with high-cost peaking units because they could build these units and get them on line quickly.

Regulatory Approval.   Since it is clear that not all capital budgeting decisions will turn out to be good ones, it is important that major **investment decisions** be made with the best information available. Furthermore, if consumers are expected to pay for plants, inputs from the public should enter the decision process. This leads to the conclusions, discussed in more detail below, (1) that **commission approval should be obtained** for all major projects as an integral part of the capital budgeting process, and (2) that **commissions should be kept apprised** of new developments during the construction of a major facility and should participate in decisions to slow down, speed up, cancel, or modify projects. Utility companies may resist what they consider to be "commission interference," and commissions may resist being asked to give prior approval to major investment decisions, but commission involvement appears to be an essential ingredient in a viable capital budgeting system.

COMMISSION PARTICIPATION IN THE DECISION PROCESS. In some states, commissions have long had the authority to approve or reject major capital expenditure programs, and in most other states commissions have the right to approve or deny security issues, which gives them de facto authority to block projects. However, **utility managements** have traditionally regarded the **level and composition of the construction program** as a management prerogative, hence have not actively solicited commission inputs into the process, and commissions have not sought active involvement. Utilities have, for the most part, simply designed and built facilities (but obviously with the full knowledge of their commissions) and then, when the plants were completed, asked their commissions to put them into **rate base.**

As noted above, in the pre-1970s era, this procedure worked well because costs were generally declining and demand increased at a steady, predictable rate. During the 1970s, however, costs rose dramatically, and demand has generally fallen short of the projections that were made at the time construction was begun. As a result, many electric utilities began plants expecting their output to have a given cost and to be demanded in full, only to complete the project and find the cost per kilowatt-hour much higher than was originally forecasted and the plant not really needed because of lower than expected demand. In such instances consumer advocates have argued, sometimes successfully, that the plants should not go into rate base, or that the company should be "punished" in some other way for having made a mistake. Even if plants are not excluded from rate base, questions of **excess capacity** or **higher than required costs** may delay rate case decisions, result in low authorized returns, or hurt the company and its investors in other ways.

In view of the very long construction periods for electric utility plants, and the volatile nature of both construction and fuel costs, planning is obviously difficult, and mistakes will occasionally be made. In other words, risks are high. If the utilities were unregulated, then (1) the cost of ex-post errors would be borne by investors in the form of lower profits for some companies in some years, but (2) these risks would be priced into the cost of capital and would be reflected in both service rates and earned returns on investment. Manufacturing companies, for example, sometimes build excess capacity, or the wrong type of capacity, and suffer losses (or low rates of return) as a result; but over time these risks are compensated in the form of high (but variable) average returns. The customers of these firms pay for the inherent **business risks** through product prices.

Since utility plant is built for the **benefit of customers,** the customers must pay the costs associated with these plants, including the costs associated with "mistakes." These costs can be assessed in two different ways: (1) by permitting all plant to go immediately into rate base and to earn the cost of capital, or (2) by excluding certain plant, but recognizing the risk this throws on investors by allowing a higher rate of return on investment. Under the first procedure, the risks associated with a construction program would be **borne directly by the utility's customers;** under the second procedure, these risks would be **borne directly by investors,** who would be compensated for bearing them by a higher allowed and earned (on average) rate of return on invested capital.

It is debatable whether it would be better for construction risks to be borne directly by investors or by customers. However, three things are clear:

1. Authorized and earned rates of return during the past decade were set by commissions, and accepted by investors, on the premise that **customers** would bear **construction risks.** The data in Exhibit 6, which show that the utilities have on average earned significantly lower returns than the industrials, demonstrate this point.

EXHIBIT 6   RETURNS ON EQUITY AND MARKET/BOOK RATIOS FOR ELECTRIC, TELEPHONE (AT&T), AND INDUSTRIAL COMPANIES, 1970–1979

Year	Standard & Poor's 399 Industrials[a]		Compustat Electric Utilities		AT&T[b]	
	ROE	M/B	ROE	M/B	ROE	M/B
1970	11.33%	2.11	11.82%	1.54	9.16%	1.11
1971	12.09	2.28	11.55	1.41	8.88	0.98
1972	12.90	2.54	11.78	1.33	9.32	1.12
1973	15.70	1.90	11.34	0.95	10.30	1.01
1974	15.88	1.19	10.40	0.64	10.46	0.87
1975	13.27	1.50	11.26	0.88	9.79	0.96
1976	15.37	1.62	11.53	0.99	11.22	1.15
1977	15.07	1.30	11.49	0.97	12.39	1.05
1978	15.56	1.23	11.22	0.83	13.09	1.00
1979	17.83	1.26	11.15	0.75	12.90	0.93
Average	14.50%	1.69	11.35%	1.03	10.75%	1.02

[a]The Standard & Poor's 400 Index companies minus AT&T. These data and all others in the exhibit are weighted averages.
[b]AT&T represents 80% of the regulated sector of the telephone industry.
Source: Standard & Poor's Compustat Industrial and Utility Tapes.

2.   If it is decided that construction risks are to be allocated differently in the future, this decision must be reflected in **authorized "normal times" returns.** If failure is to be penalized, then success must be rewarded, and average returns over time must reflect the risk exposure of investors.

3.   To the extent that the choice has not been explicitly made, a utility company's management is taking a tremendous chance if it goes forward with a major construction program, particularly one that involves new and unproved technology of any type. If the plant is built on time and at or under the projected cost, and if it operates at or better than expected efficiency, the company's customers will benefit. If things do not work out well, the company's investors may be the ones who suffer. In other words, the company is taking a chance that the commission will end up playing "heads I win, tails you lose."

JOINT FACILITIES PLANNING.   Some of the uncertainties inherent in **construction planning** could be reduced by cooperative planning and **joint ownership of facilities,** especially among the **smaller utilities.** For example, an electric company and/or its customers are exposed to increased risks if the utility relies on only one type of fuel. However, **economies of scale** are such that it would be inefficient for smaller utilities to have a good mix of plants that utilized different types of fuel. For example, many utilities could not utilize all the output from several large coal and nuclear units, and unless they had several units of each type, they would be exposed to the risk of power shortages in the event of unscheduled plant outages. Similarly, to guard against plant failures, a smaller utility would have to have larger reserve margins than would a larger company with more units. Both types of problem can be reduced by cooperative planning, joint construction and ownership of plants, and intertie arrangements whereby utilities can **buy or borrow power** from neighboring companies. **Cooperative arrangements** of all types increased dramatically during the 1970s, and it can be anticipated that this trend will continue during the 1980s and beyond.

COST OF CAPITAL

A utility must estimate its cost of capital for two major purposes: (1) as the requested rate of return in rate cases, and (2) as the discount rate for use in capital budgeting decisions.

COST OF CAPITAL IN RATE CASES.   The **weighted average cost of capital,** set forth earlier in Equation 1, is generally used as the basis for setting service rates in a rate case; to repeat:

$$k_a = w_d k_d + w_p k_p + w_s k_s$$

The **weights** are generally based on the **book value** fractions of investor-supplied, long-term capital, although sometimes total debt rather than long-term debt is used. The costs of debt and preferred stock are the **weighted averages of the historic** costs of the outstanding debt and preferred, and they can be estimated precisely, and generally without much controversy. However, it is more difficult to estimate the **cost of equity**, and this is often a controversial issue in rate cases.

A landmark case decided by the U.S. Supreme Court in 1944 [*FPC* v. *Hope Natural Gas Co.,* 320 U.S. 591, 603 (1944)] established the general criteria for setting the rate of return on equity:

> . . . The return to the equity owner should be commensurate with returns on investments in other enterprises having corresponding risks. That return, moreover, should be sufficient to assure confidence in the financial integrity of the enterprise, so as to maintain its credit and to attract capital.

The following procedures can be used to implement the Hope case requirements.

Comparable Earnings Method.   The Hope decision **did not specify how the return on equity should be measured.** However, the method used at the time the case was tried was the **comparable earnings method,** whereby one calculates the **average rate of return on book equity** for a sample of companies that have risks comparable to those of the utility in question, and allows the utility to earn a return equal to that average. The comparable earnings approach has two major problems:

1. **Other utilities** are most comparable, but their actual earned returns may be quite different from the rate of return that is required by investors; see Exhibit 5 above for an example.
2. If **nonutilities** are used for the comparison, it is virtually impossible to establish comparability with regard to risk.

DCF Method.   To avoid the very difficult problems associated with the comparable earnings approach, analysts in the mid-1960s began to use the **constant growth discounted cash flow (DCF) method:**

$$k_s = \frac{D_1}{P_0} + g \tag{2}$$

where D_1 is the dividend expected during the coming 12 months, P_0 is the current stock price, and g is the expected (constant) future growth rate in earnings, dividends, and the stock price. (See Brigham, *Financial Management: Theory and Practice*, 2nd ed., Chapter 4, for an extended discussion of the **constant growth model.**)

The constant growth DCF model is, of course, appropriate only if the expected **future growth rate is a constant.** If growth is not expected to remain constant in the future, a **nonconstant model** should be used. One such model that has been used in rate cases and is widely applied by **security analysts** in the investments business is the following:

$$P_0 = \sum_{t=1}^{n} \frac{D_t}{(1 + k_s)^t} + \left(\frac{D_n (1 + g_n)}{k_s - g_n}\right) \left(\frac{1}{1 + k_s}\right)^n \qquad (3)$$

Here n is a period during which growth is not expected to be constant and g_n is the normal (and constant) growth rate expected to exist beyond year n.

To illustrate both the constant and the nonconstant DCF models, we can use data on The Southern Co. Southern's stock has traded recently in the range of $11–11\frac{1}{2}$ (down from a 1965 high of over \$36); its expected dividend during the next 12 months is \$1.62, and its past compound growth rates have been as follows:

	Dividends	Earnings	Stock Price
1965–1980	3.6%	2.5%	−6.6%
1970–1980	2.2	0.3	−6.5
1975–1980	2.2	−2.4	+0.4
1978–1980	0.0	17.4	−11.1

Southern's **current dividend yield**, using $11\frac{1}{4}$ as P_0, is 14.4%:

$$\frac{D_1}{P_0} = \frac{\$1.62}{\$11.25} = 14.4\%$$

The proper value for Southern's expected future growth rate is not obvious from the data shown above. Indeed, the only conclusions we can reach from examining the historic growth rates are (1) that they certainly are not constant, and (2) that by selecting data series and time periods, many different growth rates can be calculated. Thus, most objective analysts have come to follow the lead of Myron Gordon, the man who pioneered the DCF model (often called the **"Gordon model"**) in a rate case involving AT&T heard before the Federal Communications Commission. That is, they estimate the expected future growth rate as $g = b(\text{ROE})$, where b is the fraction of earnings the utility will probably retain in the future and ROE is the **expected future return on equity.** If Southern earns in the range of 12–14% on equity and retains 20–30% of its earnings (these values are good ballpark figures and are consistent with most analysts' expectations), its future growth rate will be in the 4.2–2.4% range:

High. $g = b(\text{ROE}) = 0.3(14\%) = 4.2\%$
Low. $g = b(\text{ROE}) = 0.2(12\%) = 2.4\%$

Combining the **dividend yield** with the **expected growth rate** gives an **indicated DCF cost of capital** in the range of 18.6–16.8%:

High. $k_s = \dfrac{D_1}{P_0} + g = 14.4\% + 4.2\% = 18.6\%$

Low. $k_s = \dfrac{D_1}{P_0} + g = 14.4\% + 2.4\% = 16.8\%$

The **nonconstant growth model** is a bit more complicated to utilize. It requires estimates of dividends on an individual year basis during the period of nonconstant growth, as well as the expected constant growth rate beyond the nonconstant period, and it requires that one solve an equation to obtain the value of k. The best and most objective sources of data for the nonconstant model are reports published by **security analysts.** Using data from the October 3, 1980, report of **Value Line,** a major investment advisory service, we can illustrate Equation 3:

Projected retention rate in 1984: $b = 0.22$

Projected ROE in 1984 (and assumed constant beyond 1984): $\text{ROE} = 12.80\%$

Derived long-run growth rate: $g = b(\text{ROE}) = 2.82\%$

Dividend projections (shown in equation below):

$\$11.25 =$

$$\frac{\$1.60}{(1 + k_s)^1} + \frac{\$1.67}{(1 + k_s)^2} + \frac{\$1.73}{(1 + k_s)^3} + \frac{\$1.80}{(1 + k_s)^4} + \left(\frac{\$1.80(1.0282)}{k_s - 0.0282}\right)\left(\frac{1}{1 + k_s}\right)^4$$
$$(1984)$$

This equation has but one unknown, k_s, so it can be solved to determine the value of k_s. The solution value, obtained by using the **internal rate of return function** on a hand-held financial calculator, is 17.45%. This is an estimate of Southern's DCF **cost of equity** based on the nonconstant growth model.

The 17.4% estimate is based on the assumption that the **Value Line** projections represent a good proxy for the expectations of investors in general. A study done by the University of Illinois Survey Research Center (Linke, "Estimating Growth Expectations for AT&T: A Survey Approach," August 1980) demonstrates convincingly that institutional investors, who have dominated the securities markets in recent years, rely on analysts' projections when making investment decisions. Furthermore, several studies (e.g., Brigham and Vinson, "Value Line Forecasts versus Other Analysts' Forecasts," and Brown and Rozeff, "The Superiority of Analyst Forecasts as Measures of Expectations,") suggest that analysts make similar forecasts (regarding future earnings and dividends, but not regarding future stock prices) for large companies such as Southern. It would be preferable to obtain the published forecasts of a number of different organizations, use each of them with Equation 3 to obtain nonconstant model estimates of the cost of equity, and then average these results. (This procedure was used by the author to estimate AT&T's cost of equity in 1980 rate cases filed in Texas, Arkansas, Missouri, and Pennsylvania.) However, it is often difficult to obtain up-to-date analysts' forecasts, making it necessary to rely on only one or perhaps two such forecasts.

Before leaving this subject, a few words on **incorrect DCF procedures** are appropriate. First, the DCF method requires **future growth expectations,** not past realized growth. Unless the future is expected to be very similar to the past—and this is certainly not the case for utilities today—past growth rates cannot be used as estimates of future growth rates. (The

Linke study referenced above demonstrated that when making buy-sell decisions on stocks, investors follow logic and give very little weight to past growth rates, but much weight to expected future growth.) Second, the **dividend yield** component of the DCF cost of capital should be the projected 12-month dividend divided by the **current stock price.** Some analysts use the average dividend yield over some past period. This results in an estimate of the **past cost of equity,** not in the best estimate of the future cost of equity.

Risk Premium Methods.   Equity is riskier than debt, and investors must be compensated for bearing the additional risks of holding stock rather than bonds. Recognizing this fact, analysts frequently estimate the **cost of equity** by adding to a bond rate an estimated **risk premium:**

$$k_s = \text{riskless (or low-risk) rate } + \text{ risk premium}$$
$$= R_F + RP \tag{4}$$

The company's own bond rate, or else the yield on long-term U.S. Treasury bonds, can be used for R_F. The risk premium term (RP) is more difficult to estimate. (See Brigham and Shome, "The Risk Premium Approach to Estimating the Cost of Common Equity Capital," for a discussion.) Research suggests that the risk premium over Treasury bonds is in the range of 5–6 percentage points for most electric and telephone companies, and 4–5 percentage points over their own current bond yields. Thus, when the Treasury bond rate is 12% and its subsidiaries' bonds are yielding about 14%, The Southern Co.'s cost of equity would be estimated to be about 18%.

Capital Asset Pricing Model (CAPM).   The CAPM is a special, rigorous version of the risk premium method. To use the **CAPM,** this formula is applied:

$$k_s = R_F + b(k_M - R_F) \tag{5}$$

Here R_F is a **risk-free rate,** k_M is the expected **rate of return on an average stock (the market),** and b is a stock's **beta coefficient.** Beta measures the relative volatility of stocks, with an average stock having $b = 1.0$, less volatile stocks having betas less than 1.0, and more volatile stocks having betas greater than 1.0. The concept of the CAPM is discussed at length in Chapter 5 of *Financial Management* by Brigham and in the section entitled "Modern Portfolio Theory" in this *Handbook.*

The **CAPM** is a great favorite among many academicians, and it has been applied fairly often in rate cases. Two state commissions (Oregon and South Carolina) explicitly relied on it in 1980 decisions. However, most authorities who have actually tried to apply the CAPM in rate cases have concluded that while it appears to be quite precise, objective, and free of biases and judgments, it is actually highly judgmental, though the judgments are well hidden.

The vast amount of literature available on the CAPM (see References and Bibliography at the end of the section) makes clear the dangers lurking in the CAPM for use in rate cases, but one example can be used to illustrate the point. A witness, who shall remain nameless, testified against some 15 to 20 utilities, including The Southern Co.'s subsidiary Georgia Power, in the period 1976–1978. His recommendations were adopted, or at least given heavy weight, by a number of commissions, including that of the State of Georgia. He used the 30-day Treasury bill rate for R_F, a beta that was generally very close to 0.7 for electrics and telephone companies, and a market risk premium $(k_M - R_F)$ equal to about 7.8% based on data going back to 1926. In the 1976–1978 period, Treasury bills generally had yields in the 4.5–6.5% range, so his CAPM cost of capital estimates for companies such as Georgia Power generally fell into the range of 10–12%:

$$k_s = 4.5\% + 0.7(7.8\%) = 4.5\% + 5.5\% = 10\%$$
$$k_s = 6.5\% + 0.7(7.8\%) = 6.5\% + 5.5\% = 12\%$$

These numbers were quite satisfactory to many consumer groups, and the witness was in great demand to testify in rate cases. However, the application of his methodology in the fall of 1980, when Treasury bill rates were quite high, produced cost of equity estimates of over 23%:

$$k_s = 17.95\% + 0.7(7.8\%) = 17.95\% + 5.46\% = 23.41\%$$

Other methods put Georgia Power's cost of equity in the 17–18% range, and, to most observers, demonstrate a basic problem in the CAPM approach when applied to public utilities.

ADJUSTMENT FOR FLOTATION COSTS. The **DCF** or **risk premium cost of equity** (called the **"market value"** or **"bare bones"** cost) is appropriate for equity raised as retained earnings, but not for equity raised by selling **new common stock.** The bare bones cost of equity must be increased somewhat to recognize the **flotation expenses** and market pressure associated with new stock offerings. **Underwriting costs and expenses** average about 4% of gross proceeds for utility stock offerings (see Brigham, *Financial Management,* Chapter 13), while market pressure (the temporary decline in a stock's price when the company adds to the supply of shares through a new offering) amounts to about 1% (see Brigham, *Financial Management,* Chapter 14, as well as Bowyer and Yawitz, "The Effect of New Equity Issues on Utility Stock Prices," *Public Utilities Fortnightly,* May 22, 1980). Thus, **total issuance costs** amount to about 5% of gross proceeds.

The most appropriate method of **accounting for issuance costs** in a rate case is as follows:

1. Estimate the market value or bare bones cost of equity. For illustrative purposes, assume that this value is

$$k_s = \frac{D_1}{P_0} + g = \frac{\$1.62}{\$11.25} + 3.0\% = 14.4\% + 3.0\% = 17.4\%$$

2. Use this formula (developed in Brigham, *Financial Management,* Chapter 16) to estimate the **cost of new external common equity** from sale of stock, where F = percentage flotation costs:

$$k_e = \frac{\text{expected dividend yield}}{(1 - F)} + g$$
$$= \frac{14.4\%}{1.0 - 0.05} + 3.0\%$$
$$= 15.2\% + 3.0\% = 18.2\%.$$

3. Determine the percentage of equity that has been raised since the company's inception by **retained earnings versus sale of stock.** These figures can be approximated from the balance sheet as follows, using Southern Co. as an example:

Common stock plus paid-in capital	$1,871,304,000	74.9%
Retained earnings	628,118,000	25.1
Total common equity	$2,499,422,000	100.0%

4. Calculate a weighted average of the bare bones and flotation-adjusted cost of equity and use this figure as the **allowed rate of return on equity** for **rate-making purposes:**

$$k_s(\text{revenue requirements}) = 0.251(17.4\%) + 0.749(18.2\%)$$
$$= 18.0\%$$

There has been a great deal of confusion in rate cases on the matter of a proper flotation adjustment. **Company witnesses** have often overstated the adjustment by assessing a flotation cost, in effect, against retained earnings, while **opposition witnesses** have underestimated the adjustment by applying the adjustment only to the fraction of total equity raised (or expected to be raised) during the current period. However, the method set forth above is, in my opinion, the proper one.

COST OF CAPITAL FOR CAPITAL BUDGETING.   The **discount rate used to evaluate capital expenditure proposals** is different from the cost of capital for rate-making purposes, and it is estimated as follows:

1. The proper debt component is the **after-tax cost of new debt,** not the weighted average **(or "embedded") interest rate** on outstanding debt. Thus, for a company whose embedded cost of debt is 8%, which has an effective tax rate of $t = 40\%$ and must pay 15% for new debt, the cost of debt for capital budgeting purposes is $k_d (1 - t) = 15\%(0.6) = 9\%$.

2. The preferred stock component is the flotation-adjusted **yield on new preferred,** not the embedded cost of preferred. Thus, for a company whose embedded cost of preferred is 10% but whose preferred currently has a yield of 14%, and assuming that flotation costs of new preferred would be 3%, the cost of preferred for capital budgeting purposes is $k_p = 14\%/(1 - 0.03) = 14.43\%$.

3. Since capital coming in the form of **deferred taxes** represents an **interest-free loan from the federal government,** it should be entered as having a zero cost.

4. The proper cost of equity is a weighted average of the bare bones cost of equity and the flotation-adjusted cost of equity, using as weights the fraction of equity that the company actually expects to obtain **in the future** from retaining earnings and from the sale of new common stock. For example, if the company expects to obtain 50% of its new equity as retained earnings at a cost of 17.4% and 50% by selling new common at a cost of 18.2%, the average cost of new equity would be

$$k_s = 0.5(17.4\%) + 0.5(18.2\%) = 17.8\%$$

5. A **weighted average cost of capital** should then be developed, using as weights the actual percentages of each type of capital, including deferred taxes, that the company expects to raise in the future, not the balance sheet capital structure. For example the balance sheet might show 50% debt, 10% preferred, 28% common equity, and 12% deferred taxes, but the company might have a **target capital structure** of 45%

debt, 8% preferred, 36% common, and 11% deferred taxes, and it might be planning to raise capital in the future in these proportions. Then, with the numbers shown above, its basic cost of capital for capital budgeting purposes would be

$$k_a = 0.45(k_d) + 0.08(k_p) + 0.36(k_s) + 0.11(0)$$
$$= 0.45(9\%) + 0.08(14.3\%) + 0.36(17.8\%) + 0.11(0)$$
$$= 11.6\%$$

Several other points should be noted in connection with the cost of capital for capital budgeting purposes. First, since actual market costs are used, they can be expected to vary substantially over time, causing significant changes in the estimated average cost of capital, k_a. This may mean, for example, that a decision to build a nuclear plant made when the cost of capital was low, may not look as good as the alternative of building a coal plant looks later, when capital costs are high. Awareness of this potential problem may tempt managements to use some type of average cost of capital that is forced to be stable over time. Such a procedure may make managers feel better, but it is **incorrect** and it is likely to lead to incorrect decisions.

Second, **depreciation** is a major source of funds for capital budgeting, yet no mention was made of it above. The reason is that the **cost of depreciation,** for a nonliquidating company, is approximately equal to the **weighted average cost of capital** as calculated above (see Brigham, *Financial Management,* Appendix 16A).

Third, in general, the cost of capital is an increasing function of the amount of capital raised during a given period of time. This means that if a company has an exceptionally large construction program (relative to its "normal" situation), its cost of capital will be higher than normal, other things held constant. From this it follows that when comparing two major **mutually exclusive projects** with radically different capital costs (e.g., a nuclear plant and a coal-fired plant), it may be appropriate to evaluate the larger project using a higher cost of capital.

Fourth, different types of project often differ in risk, and it is appropriate to evaluate riskier projects using a somewhat higher cost of capital. Unfortunately, there is no precise method of measuring **relative project risk,** nor is there a precise way of estimating just how project risk affects the cost of capital. Still, if management judges one project to be riskier than another, the riskier project should be evaluated with a somewhat higher cost of capital.

CAPITAL STRUCTURE

Establishing the **target capital structure** for a utility is a major task, and a highly controversial one. The academic and professional literature offers quite a bit of advice on the subject, but, unfortunately, different advisers frequently offer conflicting advice, and no one can prove his position. To complicate the matter still further, most of the theoretical academic work on capital structure has been implicitly addressed to unregulated industrial concerns, and major changes are required to apply the **theory to utilities.**

CAPITAL STRUCTURE THEORY. The theory of capital structure is based on **valuation—** the relationship between the value of a firm and its capital structure is set forth, and then, based on this value/capital structure relationship, the relationship between capital structure and the cost of capital is established. For an **unregulated firm,** value increases with debt because interest on debt is tax deductible: hence the greater the use of debt, the larger the proportion of operating income that goes to investors, hence the greater the value of the firm. However, there are offsets to the tax advantage of debt:

1. The **probability of bankruptcy,** with its attendant costs, increases with leverage.
2. Firms that have high levels of debt are cut off from the capital markets during credit crunches, thus impairing operations.
3. Managements of firms with an excessive amount of leverage are often more preoccupied with raising capital, or even survival, than with operations, and efficiency suffers.
4. Both the monetary and the nonmonetary costs associated with debt and preferred stocks rise sharply if the use of leverage is excessive.

These considerations give rise to value/capital structure and cost of capital–capital structure relationships like those shown in Exhibit 7. Note particularly that the capital structure that maximizes the firm's value also **minimizes its weighted average cost of capital;** this particular capital structure is defined as the **optimal capital structure.**

The situation is conceptually different for a public utility. Theoretically, a utility should be allowed to earn its cost of capital, no more and no less. Furthermore, if it does earn its cost of capital, its stock will sell at book value. Therefore, a utility's stock price should remain constant regardless of its capital structure. There are, of course, tax benefits from the use of leverage, but these benefits accrue to **ratepayers,** not to stockholders. Therefore, for a utility, the "net addition of leverage to value" in Exhibit 7 should be relabeled "net value of leverage to ratepayers," and the value of a utility should remain constant at the level V_0. The "cost of capital" section of the exhibit remains unchanged.

Under any reasonable set of circumstances, a utility's management would have no reason to establish any capital structure other than the one that minimizes its weighted average cost of capital and thereby minimizes customers' charges. Stockholders would not be helped or hindered by the selection of one capital structure or another.

CAPITAL STRUCTURE IN RATE CASES.   In rate cases, utilities' opponents occasionally argue that the capital structure employed by the company is nonoptimal. They then state an opinion as to the **optimal capital structure,** calculate an average cost of capital based on this hypothetical capital structure, and recommend that the company be allowed to earn this hypothetical return rather than a return based on its actual capital structure. Invariably, the hypothetical capital structure calls for the use of more debt than the company actually uses, and the resulting average cost of capital is relatively low.

In looking at the application of these hypothetical capital structures, observers could be struck with several thoughts:

1. The utility's opponent has little or no basis for asserting that the company's capital structure has too little debt.
2. The adjustments (increases) in the cost of both debt and equity that would be necessary if the capital structure were changed either are not made or are arrived at in some unsupported and essentially arbitrary manner.
3. The whole exercise seems designed more to obtain a low cost of capital, hence to scale back the company's rate increase, than to determine what the cost of capital really is.

EXHIBIT 7   RELATIONSHIP AMONG STOCK PRICE, COST OF CAPITAL, AND LEVERAGE

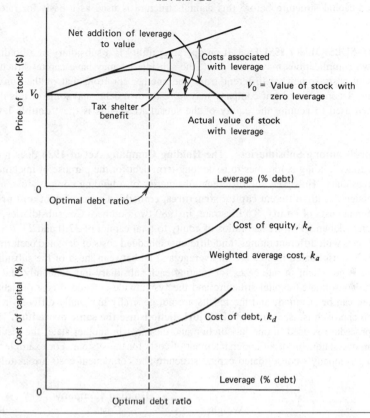

Source: Brigham, *Financial Management: Theory & Practice*, 3rd ed. Dryden Press, Hinsdale. IL, 1981.

4. However, the utility's position is equally tenuous, and management is generally unable to defend its choice of capital structure in a convincing manner.

In truth, it is impossible to identify and to prove the existence of an optimal capital structure. Academicians can offer advice about the factors in the determination of the optimal structure, and **investment bankers** and other professionals can give their opinions on what type of financing a company should employ, but nobody can truly prove his position. This being the case, how should a company and its commission approach the capital structure issue? Probably the best solution would be for a company and its commission to meet (outside of the pressures of a rate case), discuss the company's long-term financial plans, and decide jointly what the company will do and how the commission will treat the capital structure in future rate cases. Obviously, as conditions change, plans will need to be modified; so periodic meetings would be necessary.

Commissions and managements may resist the preceding suggestion on the grounds that financing decisions are a management prerogative, and also that regulatory commissions have little expertise in these matters. This may be true, but if a commission is going to get into the business of making de facto capital structure decisions, this ought to be done outside the framework of a rate case, and the regulated company ought to have time to adjust to the mandated capital structure before this capital structure is used as a basis for rate-making decisions.

PARENT–SUBSIDIARY ISSUES. If an operating utility is a subsidiary of a holding company, two complications may arise. First, the subsidiaries may have capital structures and component costs somewhat different from one another, or from that of the consolidated company. Second, the parent company may have its own debt, and some of this debt may have been used to acquire the equity of the subsidiaries—this is the **"double leverage"** issue.

Differences among Subsidiaries. The **Holding Company Act of 1934** does not permit electric utility holding companies to issue long-term debt for the purpose of injecting equity into a subsidiary. However, the different subsidiaries of a holding company can and often do have significantly different **capital structures, embedded costs of debt and preferred**, and different **costs of equity**. To illustrate, in 1980 two Southern Co. subsidiaries, Georgia Power and Alabama Power, had ratios of equity to total capital of 32.0 and 27.7%, respectively, bonds with different ratings, and different embedded costs of debt and preferred stock. Southern's consolidated figures are an average and lie between those of the subsidiaries.

There is precedent in rate cases for treating each subsidiary independently and also for using the consolidated capital structure and the systemwide embedded cost of debt. Either procedure can be justified, and the results are not generally materially different regardless of which approach is used, **provided all jurisdictions use the same procedure.** However, if one procedure is used in one jurisdiction and the other in another state, the result can be either an overstatement or an understatement of costs for the system. For example, suppose a holding company's consolidated capital structure and component costs are as follows:

		Weight	×	**Holding Company** Cost	=	Product
Debt	$100	50%		9%		4.5%
Preferred	20	10		10		1.0
Common	80	40		15		6.0
	$200	100%				11.5% $= k_a$

Its two subsidiaries each have the same capital structure and both are assigned the parent's cost of equity. But, because its recent growth has been quite rapid, Subsidiary B has sold most of its debt and preferred in the recent high rate market, so its embedded costs of debt and preferred are relatively high:

		Weight	×	**Subsidiary A** Cost	=	Product
Debt	$ 50	50%		8%		4.0%
Preferred	10	10		9		0.9
Common	40	40		15		6.0
	$100	100%				10.9% $= k_a$

		Weight	×	Subsidiary B Cost	=	Product
Debt	$ 50	50%		10%		5.0%
Preferred	10	10		11		1.1
Common	40	40		15		6.0
	$100	100%				12.1% = k_a

If Subsidiary A is allowed to earn 10.9% and B 12.1%, the parent company will earn its 11.5% cost of capital. The parent would also earn its required return if both subsidiaries earned 11.5%. However, if the commission in Subsidiary A's state used the individual company method and authorized 10.9%, while B's commission adopted the consolidated method and authorized 11.5%, the parent company would earn only 0.5 (10.9%) + 0.5 (11.5%) = 11.2%, which is below its cost of capital.

Similar, but more complex, problems can arise if the different subsidiaries have different capital structures, and if different equity capital costs are assigned to the various subsidiaries. These problems can become quite severe if a large number of subsidiaries are involved, as is the case in the **telephone industry**. The only rational solution to this situation is through some type of agreement among commissions on how the **multistate holding companies** are to be regulated, but at present no such agreement exists, and this has contributed to the telephone companies' financial problems.

Double Leverage. Double leverage exists whenever a holding company has outstanding, at the parent company levels, debt that has been used to buy the equity of the subsidiaries. The double leverage situation is trivial in the electric industry because of the Holding Company Act's prohibition of parent company debt, but it does exist in the **telephone industry**. To illustrate, consider the following tabulation of assets versus liabilities/capital for a parent company with two subsidiaries.

PARENT COMPANY

Assets		Liabilities/Capital	
Investment in operating companies	$200	Debt (10%)	$100
		Equity (15%)	100
	$200		$200

$$k_a = 0.5(10\%) + 0.5(15\%) = 12.5\%$$

Subsidiary A (Wholly Owned)

Operating assets	$200	Debt (10%)	$100
		Equity (all from parent)	100
	$200		$200

Subsidiary B (Wholly Owned)

Operating assets	$200	Debt (10%)	$100
		Equity (all from parent)	100
	$200		$200

Assets		Liabilities/Capital	
	Consolidated		
Operating assets	$400	Debt (parent)	$100
		Debt (subs)	200
		Equity	100
	$400		$400

Now assume that all debt has a cost of 10%, and that the parent's cost of equity is 15%. The **cost of capital to the subsidiaries** for ratemaking purposes could be calculated in several ways:

1. Based on **consolidated data**:

$$k_a = 0.75(10\%) + 0.25(15\%) = 11.25\%$$

2. **"Double leverage."** Use parent's average cost of capital as the cost of equity for the subsidiary:

$$k_{a(\text{parent})} = 0.5(10\%) + 0.5(15\%) = 12.5\%$$
$$k_{a(\text{sub})} = 0.5(10\%) + 0.5(12.5\%) = 11.25\%$$

3. **Wrong.** Use parent's cost of equity and subsidiary's own capital structure:

$$k_a = 0.5(10\%) + 0.5(15\%) = 12.5\%$$

which is too high.

This is all simple enough **as long as the two subsidiaries have identical capital structures, and as long as the parent company has no assets except its investment in subsidiaries.** However, subsidiaries generally do not have identical structures, and most of the major telephone companies, where double leverage concepts are especially important, do have substantial amounts of other assets, and much of the parent company's debt is used to support the investment in these other assets rather than to buy the equity of the subsidiaries. Because the subsidiaries do have different capital structures, the utilities' opponents can attempt to "whipsaw" the companies by using whatever combination of capital structure and embedded costs produces the lowest calculated return for the jurisdiction in question, regardless of practices in other jurisdictions, and regardless of whether, in total, the parent can earn its overall cost of capital. Similarly, but more important, utility opponents can make the implicit assumptions (1) that all assets owned by the parent company are equally risky and (2) that parent company debt is used to acquire stock in subsidiaries rather than in other types of assets, and, based on these assumptions, they can develop a weighted average cost of capital and then use it as the cost of equity for the subsidiaries as was done in method 2, "double leverage," above. Although much has been written about double leverage in the literature, these issues are far from resolved.

DIVIDEND POLICY

Exhibit 8 shows the dividend payout ratios for the **Standard & Poor's industrials,** the **electrics,** and **AT&T** (whose payout ratios were similar to those of other telephone companies) during the 1970s. Clearly, the electric and telephone companies pay out a larger percentage of their earnings than do the industrials.

The utilities' high **payout ratios** are something of an anomaly with respect to financial theory, which suggests that companies that need large amounts of new equity capital should have low payout ratios. (See Brigham, *Financial Management*, Chapter 17, and the section entitled "Dividend Policy" of this *Handbook* for a discussion.) This difference between what academic theory says the companies ought to be doing and what they actually are doing could have one of two causes: (1) there is something wrong with the theory as applied to utilities, or (2) utility company managements are grossly misguided.

It is impossible to prove which position is correct, and a case can be made for each of them. The academic position, set forth in all the basic textbooks, in essence goes like this:

1. There are reasons that would lead some investors to prefer **dividends** to **reinvestment and capital gains** (a need for current cash income, possibly less risk in cash-in-hand dividends versus hoped-for-capital gains). On the other hand, there are reasons for some investors to prefer reinvestment and capital gains (primarily the lower tax rate on capital gains income). It is impossible to decide on a theoretical basis how these two opposing forces offset each other, and empirical investigations of the issue have been inconclusive.

2. However, it does seem clear that because of **flotation costs** involved with the **issuance of new stock,** the greater the need of a company for new equity capital, the lower its **dividend payout ratio** should be. Therefore, since utilities need large amounts of new equity, they should have **low** payout ratios. Since their actual payouts are high, management is acting contrary to the principles found in finance theory.

EXHIBIT 8   DIVIDEND PAYOUT RATIOS, 1970–1979

Year	Standard & Poor's 399 Industrials	Electric Utilities	AT&T
1970	51.11%	67.85%	65.16%
1971	47.77	67.53	65.16
1972	41.18	63.31	62.21
1973	33.43	65.71	57.63
1974	30.93	69.70	61.48
1975	34.35	64.59	66.28
1976	31.88	64.21	62.81
1977	35.24	67.72	60.26
1978	34.34	67.53	59.43
1979	30.83	70.13	62.19
Average	37.11%	66.83%	62.26%

Source: Standard & Poor's Compustat Industrial and Utility Tapes.

The academic argument has an implicit assumption that **capital markets are efficient** in the sense that investors can move among companies to find one with a dividend policy that suits the particular investor, and also that investors are reasonably sophisticated. Knowledgeable **investment bankers** argue that market efficiency simply does not hold in the case of the utilities, making the high payout ratios logical. Their argument goes like this:

1. Traditionally, the utilities were regarded as being safe, "widow and orphan" stocks that were well suited for retirees and others who needed safe, assured income. Because of their "clientele" of stockholders who wanted high current income, the utilities paid out a high percentage of their earnings as dividends.

2. In the 1970s, because of **regulatory lag** and other problems, the utilities' **perceived risk** vis-à-vis the industrials rose, yet their ROEs did not rise to keep pace with their increasing costs of capital. This caused the price of their stocks to decline, and most of them have sold below book value during most of the 1970s. (See Exhibit 6.)

3. The more sophisticated investors (especially **institutional investors**) have largely abandoned the utility stocks. (Approximately 95% of the utilities' stocks are owned by individuals and only 5% by institutions, in comparison to 60% of the industrials' stocks owned by individuals and 40% by institutions.) The present **owners of utility stocks** are (1) very much income oriented, (2) generally retirees or others on relatively low fixed incomes, hence in low tax brackets, and (3) not very sophisticated.

4. To an unusually large degree, utility stocks are "sold" rather than "bought"; that is, stockbrokers solicit purchasers of utility stocks rather than having potential buyers come in with their buy orders.

5. The major competition for utility investors' capital includes bonds, bank certificates, and other securities that are oriented toward yield (as opposed to growth).

6. Therefore, if a utility needs to raise new equity capital, the investment bankers find it easier to interest purchasers if the stocks pay a high dividend, and thus compete well with bonds in terms of current income, than if the stocks paid lower dividends but promised higher future growth rates. In other words, to sell to the people who buy utility stocks, brokers find it easier to base their pitch on dividend yield than on total return.

There is probably some truth in both the academic and the investment banking positions—the academic position is logical, but it does not quite hold because the sophisticated investors who are needed to make markets efficient have deserted the utility stocks. This desertion has occurred because of the decade-long experience of the utilities with regulatory lag, returns less than the cost of capital, declining stock prices (both absolute and relative to the industrials), and other unresolved problems. Thus, one may conclude that the **utilities' dividend policy** is probably not the one they should be following, nor the one they would be following if they were earning their costs of capital; rather, it is the only policy they can follow under their present operating conditions.

REFERENCES AND BIBLIOGRAPHY

BankAmeriLease Group, *On-the-Spot Leasing for Utilities*, BankAmeriLease Group; San Francisco, 1978.

Bowyer, J. W., and Yawitz, J. B., "The Effect of New Equity Issues on Utility Stock Prices," *Public Utilities Fortnightly*, May 22, 1980.

Brigham, Eugene F., *Financial Management: Theory and Practice*, Dryden Press, Hinsdale, IL, 2nd ed., 1979, 3rd ed., 1981.

———, "The Treatment of CWIP," University of Florida, Public Utility Research Center, 1980.

———, and Crum, Roy L., "On the Use of the CAPM in Public Utility Rate Cases," *Financial Management*, Summer, 1977, pp. 7–15.

———, and Nantell, T. J., "Normalization versus Flow Through for Utilities," *Accounting Review*, July 1974, pp. 436–477.

———, and Pappas, James L., *Liberalized Depreciation and the Cost of Capital*, Michigan State University, Institute of Public Utilities, 1970.

———, and Pettway, Richard H., "Capital Budgeting by Utilities," *Financial Management*, Autumn, 1973, pp. 11–22.

———, and Shome, Dilip K., "International Harvester Lecture: Effects of Inflation on Capital Structure and the Cost of Capital in the 1980s," *Journal of the Midwest Finance Association*, Vol. 9, May 1980, pp. 1–21.

———, and ———, "The Risk Premium Approach to Estimating the Cost of Common Equity Capital," Proceedings of the Iowa State Regulatory Conference, May 1980.

———, and Vinson, S. R., "Value Line Forecasts versus Other Analysts' Forecasts," University of Florida, Public Utility Research Center, 1980.

Brown, L. D. and M. S. Rozeff, "The Superiority of Analyst Forecasts as Measures of Expectations," *Journal of Finance*, March 1980.

Deloitte, Haskins, and Sells, *Public Utilities Manual*, Public Document No. 8003, Government Printing Office, Washington, D.C., 1980.

Evans, Robert E., "On the Existence, Measurement, and Economic Significance of Market Pressure in the Pricing of New Equity Shares," Ph.D. thesis, Department of Economics, University of Wisconsin, 1978.

Gordon, Myron J., *The Cost of Capital to a Public Utility*, Michigan State University, Institute of Public Utilities, 1974.

Harrington, Diana R., "The Capital Asset Pricing Model and Regulated Utility Cost of Equity Estimation," D.B.A. dissertation, University of Virginia, 1978.

Ibbotson, R. G., and Sinquefield, R. A., *Stocks, Bonds, Bills, and Inflation: The Past (1926–1976) and the Future (1977–2000)*, Financial Analysts Research Foundation, Charlottesville, VA, 1977.

Kahn, Alfred E., *The Economics of Regulation: Principles and Institutions*, Vols. I and II, Wiley, New York, 1970.

Linke, C. M., "Estimating Growth Expectations for AT&T: A Survey Approach," University of Illinois, Survey Research Center, August 1980.

Myers, Stewart C., "The Application of Finance Theory to Public Utility Rate Cases," *Bell Journal of Economics and Management Science*, Spring 1972, pp. 58–97.

Peseau, Dennis E., et al., "Utility Regulation and the CAPM: A Discussion," *Financial Management*, Autumn 1978, pp. 52–76.

Pomerantz, Lawrence S., and Suelflow, James E., *Allowance for Funds Used during Construction: Theory and Application*, Michigan State University, Institute of Public Utilities, 1975.

Reeser, Marvin P., *Introduction to Public Utility Accounting*, American Gas Association, Washington, D.C. 1976.

Salomon Brothers, *Electric Utility Quality Measures*, Salomon, New York, November 14, 1980.

FINANCIAL MANAGEMENT IN AN INFLATIONARY ENVIRONMENT

CONTENTS

INFLATION EXPERIENCE AND TAX
LAW ADJUSTMENTS: AN
INTERNATIONAL COMPARISON   3

INFLATION AND THE FIRM'S
FINANCIAL POSITION   4

Inventory   5
Depreciation   7
Treatment of Inventory and Depreciation
and Its Effect on Earnings and Taxes   7
Inflationary Holding Gains on Assets   8
  Unlevered firm   8
  Levered firm   8
  Numerical illustration   10
Liquidity   12

CREDIT TERMS AND INFLATION   12

Changing the Discount Percentage   14
Changing the Credit Period   14

INFLATION, DEPRECIATION,
INCOME TAX, AND CAPITAL
BUDGETING

Effect of Inflation on a Project's Net
Present Value   17

Neutral inflation   17
Nonneutral inflation   21
Riskless interest rate   21
Ranking Mutually Exclusive Investment
Projects: Incentives Not Considered   21
Effectiveness of Investment Incentives 24
  Accelerated depreciation   24
  Investment tax credit   28
Ranking of Mutually Exclusive
Investment Projects: Incentives
Considered   28
Can Overcompensation or
Undercompensation for Inflation Be
Avoided?   31

INFLATION AND COMMON STOCK
RETURNS   31

Classical Theory and Cost of Capital
Under Inflation   33
Stock Prices and Inflation in the Classical
Framework   34
Empirical Evidence   35
Explaining the Empirical Evidence   39

IS INDEXATION THE ANSWER TO
ALL INFLATION PROBLEMS?   40

FINANCIAL MANAGEMENT IN AN INFLATIONARY ENVIRONMENT

Moshe Ben-Horim
Haim Levy

INFLATION EXPERIENCE AND TAX LAW ADJUSTMENTS: AN INTERNATIONAL COMPARISON

One marked consequence of the **energy crisis** for Western economies in recent years has been the high and often accelerating inflation rates. In the United States, the **Consumer Price Index** (CPI) rose by 13.3% in 1979, the highest increase in almost four decades. Furthermore, contrary to the traditional view, the rapid inflation was not accompanied by low unemployment, and the period was characterized by simultaneous high inflation and high unemployment, a condition termed **stagflation.** Exhibit 1 presents the annual inflation rates in a number of countries for 1961–1979. In the United States the average annual inflation rate was 3.1% in 1961–1972, rising to 8.5% in 1972–1979. The average inflation rate was also higher in 1972–1979 in all other countries except Brazil, which experienced its highest rates in the 1960s.

Inflation normally reduces investment profitability and often slows down investment, which is what happened in the 1970s. In an attempt to reactivate the economy and offset inflation losses to firms, some governments have introduced **investment incentives.** For example, in the United States, firms may elect to use the LIFO method of inventory accounting, which relieves them of some of the tax on inflationary profits. Other incentives are **accelerated depreciation,** introduced by the Eisenhower administration, and the **reduced asset lives system** for tax purposes, introduced by the Kennedy and Nixon administrations. The **investment tax credit,** which first appeared in 1962, is another important incentive. With the high inflation rates experienced in the past few years, however, all these devices combined do not always compensate the firm for inflation loss.

In the United Kingdom, a 100% first-year depreciation of plant and equipment has been permitted since 1972 (see Hale, "Inflation Accounting and Public Policy Around the World," *Financial Analysts Journal,* November–December 1978, pp. 28–40). In another incentive introduced in 1975, the difference in the inventory value between the first and last days of the fiscal year became a deductible expense. Canada grants a relatively small tax relief. Firms are **not permitted** to adopt LIFO recording, but 3% of the opening value of their inventory is a deductible expense. The LIFO method is also **not permitted** in Australia, but the depreciation code offers other significant investment incentives. The **trading stock**

EXHIBIT 1   INFLATION RATES IN SELECTED COUNTRIES, 1961–1979

Year	United States	Canada	United Kingdom	Australia	Brazil	Netherlands
1961	1.0	0.0	3.9	1.0	43.3	2.9
1962	1.0	1.9	2.8	0.0	60.8	0.0
1963	1.9	1.0	1.8	1.0	82.0	4.7
1964	0.9	1.8	4.5	3.7	84.4	5.4
1965	1.8	3.7	5.1	4.9	41.0	6.0
1966	3.6	3.5	4.1	2.6	46.0	4.0
1967	3.8	3.5	2.4	5.0	32.8	3.4
1968	4.1	4.1	4.6	2.6	22.0	3.8
1969	5.3	4.4	5.4	2.8	22.5	7.4
1970	5.9	3.4	6.3	3.9	22.0	3.6
1971	4.3	2.7	9.4	6.1	20.0	7.5
1972	3.2	4.7	7.1	5.8	16.1	7.8
1973	6.3	7.5	9.2	9.4	12.8	7.9
1974	10.8	10.9	16.0	14.5	27.0	9.8
1975	9.1	10.7	24.2	24.2	28.8	10.5
1976	5.8	7.5	16.5	16.5	41.9	8.8
1977	6.5	8.0	15.8	15.8	43.7	6.4
1978	7.8	9.0	8.3	7.9	38.7	4.1
1979	13.3	12.5	21.3	12.3	61.0	5.2
Average						
1961–1972	3.1	2.9	4.8	3.2	41.1	4.7
1972–1979	7.9	9.4	15.9	14.4	36.3	7.5
1961–1979	5.1	5.3	8.9	7.2	39.3	5.8

valuation adjustment (TSVA) allows as a deductible expense an amount equal to 50% of the difference between the opening value of the inventory and that value multiplied by the goods component of the consumer price index. Brazil experienced an average inflation rate of 39.3% in 1961–1979. Following the 1964 revolution, the government introduced indexation, which applies to companies' accounts, government bonds, bank deposits, rents, loans, and so on. That is, firms' assets and depreciation are revalued each year to reflect the upward trend in the **wholesale price index.**

Although most countries have amended their tax laws to compensate firms for inflation loss, the incentives included in tax laws are generally insufficient when price levels change as rapidly as they have in the past few years in some Western countries.

INFLATION AND THE FIRM'S FINANCIAL POSITION

In view of high and persistent inflation rates in recent years in the United States and elsewhere, it has become increasingly important to understand the implications of the changes in price levels for the relationships between the financial position of a firm, as reflected in its financial statements, and the firm's real financial position.

Perhaps a reasonable point of departure for making this distinction is the measurement of income. A firm's **economic income** is defined as the income that it can distribute during the period, so that at the end of the period it is left with sufficient physical assets to carry on the same level of activity as at the beginning of the period.

Corporate income as reported under **generally accepted accounting practices (GAAP)** usually deviates from economic income. In the absence of inflation, however, the two measures of income are quite closely related, and income reported under GAAP gives a fair idea of both the trend of a firm's economic income and the way it compares with the economic income of other firms in the industry. The same holds for related measures such as earnings per share and the price-earnings ratio. Under inflation, however, the relationships between reported and economic incomes are substantially distorted. In addition, because assets are recorded at historical cost, while revenues and expenses are recorded in current dollars, some of the financial ratios traditionally used to analyze a firm's financial position are affected by inflation and must consequently be carefully analyzed at periods of rapid price increase.

Inflation accounting has been debated for a number of years now, and, in its Statement of Financial Accounting Practices No. 33, the **Financial Accounting Standards Board** (FASB) has recently taken action to compel large public companies (specifically, those with $1 billion of assets or $125 million of inventories and gross property) to report the effects of inflation on their financial statements.

The Board has decided to retain historical cost recording in the primary financial statements, but Statement No. 33 specifies requirements for supplementary information in annual reports to reveal the effects of the changing price level. The new requirements are effective for accounting years ending after December 24, 1979, but companies may postpone disclosure of the current cost information for 1979 until their 1980 annual report. The Board requires companies to report the effect of inflation in two different ways: (*a*) using **constant dollar accounting,** and (*b*) on a **current cost basis,** a method that employs specific price changes for each asset.

Inflation accounting is at an experimental stage. The bulk of financial reporting is still on a **historical cost basis.** Let us then examine the main problems and some consequences of the GAAP rules during times of inflation.

INVENTORY.   The accounting treatment of inventories can affect the firm's reported earnings, tax bill, and cash position. The magnitude of the effect depends particularly on whether the firm uses the **first-in first-out** (FIFO) or the **last-in first-out** (LIFO) formula. To demonstrate this point in detail, consider a firm that has revenues of $200 million and for simplicity assume that there are no costs or expenses except the cost of goods sold. Additional information about the firm is:

	Units (Millions)	Cost per Unit
Inventory at the beginning of the year	100	$ 1.0
Inventory bought during the year	100	$ 1.5
Sales during the year	100	
Inventory at the end of the year	100	

The cost of goods sold is equal to:

inventory at beginning of year + new purchases during year − inventory at end of year

It is therefore clear that the method by which we evaluate the end-of-year inventory affects the cost of goods sold. The tax and profit will be affected as follows:

	Amount ($ Millions)	
	FIFO	LIFO
Revenue	200	200
Cost of goods sold	100	150
Net profit before tax	100	50
Tax (50%)	50	25
Net profit after tax	50	25

(The tax rate of 50% is used for purposes of illustration. In practice it would be different.)

Under FIFO, the units sold during the year are the ones bought by the firm at $1 each. Thus the end-of-year inventory is $150 million (i.e., 100 million units at $1.5 each). Under LIFO, the units sold are those bought during the year at $1.5 so that the end of year inventory is $100 million (i.e., 100 million units at $1.0).

What are the implications for a firm of switching from FIFO to LIFO? As illustrated, the FIFO method allows the firm to show a higher profit than that shown by using LIFO ($50 million vs. $25 million in the example). Thus switching will reduce reported earnings. Nonetheless, economic analysis reveals that switching from FIFO to LIFO is advantageous to the firm. Recall that the cash outlay for the materials purchased during the year was $150 million; thus the total cash flow under the two alternative methods is:

	Firm's Cash Flow ($ Millions)	
	FIFO	LIFO
Revenue	+200	+200
New purchases	−150	−150
Tax	− 50	− 25
Net cash flow	0	+ 25

Switching from FIFO to LIFO increases the net cash flow of the firm by $25 million because of the lower tax burden. Since the replacement cost of the 100 million inventory units sold during the year is $150 million, the firm's true pretax profit is $50 million, no matter how the firm records the inventory. LIFO reveals the true economic profit **when inflation is neutral.** However, with nonneutral inflation, neither LIFO nor FIFO measures precisely the true economic profit.

The LIFO procedure results in a tax bill of $25 million, or a 50% tax on real earnings, but, in this illustration, FIFO results in a tax bill of $50 million, or an **effective tax rate** of 100% i.e., as a percentage of economic income. Despite the advantage of LIFO over FIFO in terms of its effect on economic profit, only about one-third of the companies in the United States use LIFO. The main reason for this is probably that firms must use the same method both for tax purposes and for financial reporting. Along with a lower tax rate and a higher real profit, switching from FIFO to LIFO would reduce reported profit. Many financial managers hold the view that the performance of a firm is evaluated and judged largely on the basis of reported earnings per share, even if they are partly illusory, which accounts for the willingness to pay more tax than called for under LIFO, merely to keep the level of reported profit high. In particular, financial managers hesitate to switch to LIFO because the firm might report a lower profit than other firms in the same industry.

DEPRECIATION. If a firm invests $100 million in depreciable assets with a 10 year lifetime, **straight-line depreciation** comes to $10 million per annum. If the inflation rate is 20%, the first year's depreciation (i.e., 1 year after purchasing the assets) should be $12 million on the basis of purchasing power. However, the federal income tax code admits only historical cost depreciation; it does not permit replacement cost depreciation, nor does it permit adjustment for the price level. Thus although the $12 million represents the first year's depreciation in current dollars, the tax code recognizes only $10 million of this for tax purposes. Clearly, if inflation persists, depreciation adjusted for purchasing power will continue to increase while the amount recognized for tax purposes will remain constant. In the tenth year adjusted depreciation will come to $61.9 million $[= 10(1.2)^{10}]$, but it will still only be $10 million at historical cost. It is in this way that historical cost depreciation creates illusory profits and the consequently high effective tax rates and low cash flow. A number of investment incentives have been introduced over the years to rectify this situation, among them **accelerated depreciation** and **investment tax credit.** These incentives, discussed below, are often insufficient to fully compensate firms for their inflation losses.

TREATMENT OF INVENTORY AND DEPRECIATION AND ITS EFFECT ON EARNINGS AND TAXES. In 1978 U.S. business earned a total of $202 billion before taxes and $118 billion after taxes, the pretax earnings being 16% above those of 1977 and 68% over the 1975 figure. One should not, however, interpret this as an increase in real profit. About one-third of the 1978 earnings reflects the nominal effect of inflation, and if the earnings are adjusted by extracting inflationary inventory gains and valuing depreciation at replacement cost, the 1978 aftertax income is found to be lower by $42 billion.

If inventory and depreciation are adjusted for inflation, the tax bill would be $17 billion less. This would reduce the tax rate considerably below the figure computed on the basis of reported earnings. In 1978 cash dividends amounted to $49 billion, or 42% of reported net income. However, on the basis of adjusted net income, the cash dividends come to as much as 65%. Exhibit 2 summarizes relevant data for nonfinancial corporations in the United States for the years 1973–1977; the inflation-adjusted aftertax income was obtained after adjusting the inventory and depreciation to reflect changes in the price level. Exhibit 2 shows

EXHIBIT 2   INCOME, TAXES, AND DIVIDENDS OF NONFINANCIAL CORPORATIONS IN THE UNITED STATES, 1973–1977 ($ BILLIONS)

	1973	1974	1975	1976	1977
Income before tax	92.7	102.9	102.3	130.6	141.8
Tax	39.6	42.7	40.8	53.7	57.0
Income after tax	53.1	60.2	61.5	76.9	84.8
Inflation-adjusted income after tax	36.3	16.8	37.5	48.3	53.2
Dividends	23.9	25.4	28.8	32.2	37.9
Payout ratio (%) based on					
Reported income	45.0	42.2	46.8	41.9	44.7
Adjusted income	65.8	151.2	76.8	66.7	71.2

Source: David Hale, "Inflation Accounting and Public Policy Around the World," *Financial Analysts Journal,* November–December 1978, pp. 28–40.

a considerable gap between reported and inflation-adjusted aftertax income throughout the period.

The **dividend payout ratio** is fairly stable when based on reported net income, but on the basis of inflation-adjusted net income, it is much higher and fluctuates more. The greatest difference between reported and inflation-adjusted net income occurred in 1974, when the effective payout ratio reached a high of 151.2%. Firms apparently found it hard to cut back on cash dividends, because of the increasing stream of reported profits.

INFLATIONARY HOLDING GAINS ON ASSETS.

Unlevered Firm.   An increase in the price level creates **holding gains** on assets by increasing the nominal value of the assets. Consider the effect of such holding gains on the **earnings per share** (EPS) of a no-growth and unlevered firm. Suppose the price level is stable up to time 0, when a **fully anticipated neutral inflation** starts at a rate h. For simplicity, assume that the price level becomes stable again a year later, at time 1. Since the inflation is neutral, it increases revenues, costs, expenses, asset values, and so on, in the same proportion. Denote before-tax income at time 0 by X, the corporate tax rate by T, and the number of common shares outstanding by n; then the EPS at time 0, EPS_0, is:

$$EPS_0 = \frac{(1 - T)X}{n}$$

One period later, at time 1, the nominal EPS is

$$EPS_1 = \frac{(1 - T)X(1 + h)}{n} = EPS_0(1 + h)$$

The value of EPS in constant dollars at time 1, EPS_1^c, is obtained by discounting EPS_1 at rate h.

$$EPS_1^c = \frac{EPS_1}{1 + h} = \frac{EPS_0(1 + h)}{1 + h} = EPS_0$$

Denote the value of the firm's assets at time 0 by V; the firm gets an amount hV of holding gains on these assets, and it is assumed that these gains are spread over all the firm's assets in equal proportions. This assumption is made for simplicity, but it does not impair the generality of the discussion. The holding gains hV, however, do not represent real gain, since to keep the profitability in real terms unchanged, the value of assets at time 1 must be $V(1 + h)$. As Hicks put it (*Value and Capital*, 2nd ed., Clarendon Press, Oxford, 1957, p. 174), "income . . . must be defined as the maximum amount of money which the individual can spend this week, and still expect to be able to spend the same amount **in real terms** in each ensuing week." Thus holding gains should not be added to income for the EPS calculations.

Levered Firm.   Consider now a levered firm. With no inflation, the situation is quite simple. Denote the market value of the debt by D and the interest rate paid on the firm's debt by r; the EPS is then

$$\text{EPS}_0 = \frac{(1 - T)(X - rD)}{n}$$

For the case of inflation, it is assumed that the market value of the debt is not affected by it, but the interest rate rises from r to $(1 + r)(1 + h) - 1 = r + h(1 + r)$. In other words, we assume that bondholders are compensated for inflation by the increase in their interest to a level equal to the sum of the no-inflation interest (rD) **plus** compensation for the decrease in the value of the principal (hD) **plus** compensation for the decrease in the value of the no-inflation interest (hrD). Interest on long-term bonds does not actually adjust fully to current inflation rates, since it is largely a function of bondholders' long-term inflation expectations. Also note that personal tax is ignored in this analysis. All the interest is assumed to be tax deductible for the firm. Nominal EPS at time 1 excluding holding gains is

$$\begin{aligned}
\text{EPS}_1 &= \frac{(1 - T)[X(1 + h) - rD - hD(1 + r)]}{n} \\
&= \frac{(1 - T)[(X - rD)(1 + h) - hD]}{n} = \text{EPS}_0(1 + h) - \frac{(1 - T)hD}{n}
\end{aligned}$$

and EPS at time 1 in constant dollars is

$$\text{EPS}_1^C = \frac{\text{EPS}_1}{1 + h} = \text{EPS}_0 - \frac{(1 - T)hD}{n(1 + h)}$$

In this case, inflation appears to have reduced the value of EPS. However, this is not so, since the holding gains on the levered firm's assets have thus far been ignored. Unlike the pure equity firm, a part of the holding gain for a levered firm is real income for the stockholders.

When calculating EPS_1^C, holding gains were not considered, although just as with the unlevered firm, there is a gain of hV. Since the holding gain "belongs" only to the equity, it is in excess of what is needed to create future income for stockholders that is equal in real terms to their past income. To see this, start with the identity $V = E + D$ (where E denotes equity), which implies that $hV = hE + hD$. As long as D is positive, the (nominal) holding gains exceed hE, that is, there are **excess holding gains** in the amount hD.

Suppose that the excess holding gains are distributed (the firm liquidates some of the fixed assets) and are subject to the tax rate T. In this case, the aftertax income (including the excess holding gains) available to stockholders is

$$(1 - T)[(X - rD)(1 + h) - hD + hD]$$

so that

$$\text{EPS}_1 = \frac{(1 - T)[(X - rD)(1 + h)]}{n} = \text{EPS}_0(1 + h)$$

This implies that EPS should be adjusted for the excess holding gains and for inflation to obtain the **real** value of EPS at time 1, EPS_1^R:

$$\text{EPS}_1^R = \frac{\text{EPS}_0(1 + h)}{1 + h} = \text{EPS}_0$$

Note the distinction between constant and real EPS: EPS^C is the deflated value of the unadjusted nominal EPS, whereas EPS^R is the deflated EPS, adjusted for excess holding gains.

It has so far been assumed that the excess holding gains on the equity are distributed to stockholders. If this amount hD is distributed by liquidating assets worth hD, the firm's debt-equity ratio will change and EPS in the year after the inflation year will not be the same (in real terms) as in the year before inflation. However, this would happen whatever the reason for the alteration in the capital structure, since in general, EPS varies with it. Denoting the preinflation debt-equity ratio by D/E, the postinflation ratio is $D/[E(1 + h) + hD]$ before the distribution of holding gains and $D/[E(1 + h)] < D/E$ after it. Since the debt-equity ratio has declined, we expect a lower EPS.

It is now shown that if the debt-equity ratio in the postinflation year at time 2 is restored to its original level by issuing additional debt hD, the EPS in real terms will revert to its original level.

The nominal value of the assets is $V(1 + h) = (E + D)(1 + h)$ and earnings before interest and tax (EBIT) is $X(1 + h)$. The interest rate is back at r, since it is assumed that there is no inflation in the postinflation years; after additional debt of hD has been issued, total outstanding debt is $D(1 + h)$, and total interest is then $rD(1 + h)$. Therefore nominal EPS is given by:

$$EPS_2 = \frac{(1 - T)X(1 + h) - rD(1 + h)}{n} = EPS_0(1 + h)$$

However, the earnings per share in constant preinflation dollars is given by:

$$EPS^C = \frac{EPS_2}{1 + h} = \frac{EPS_0(1 + h)}{1 + h} = EPS_0$$

That is, the distribution of excess holding gains at the end of the inflation year leaves the real EPS in the following year the same as before inflation.

The discussion has assumed a 1-year period of inflation followed by a period of stable prices. However, the same result holds if prices continue to rise. Note also that if the excess holding gains are not realized, they are not taxed, and the real EPS of a levered firm will rise with inflation.

Numerical Illustration.   To begin, assume the absence of leverage. Suppose that the total value of the firm's assets is $100 at the beginning of the period, EBIT is $20, the tax rate is 50%, and there are 10 shares outstanding. Exhibit 3 presents the data for the current and the next year, assuming a 10% (neutral) inflation.

Disregarding depreciation, there is a holding gain of $10, since the value of assets has risen to $110 by the beginning of the second year from $100 at the beginning of the first year. However, the gain is only nominal. The real value of the assets at the beginning of the second year is $110/1.1 = $100. If the firm did not have $110 worth of assets at the beginning of the second year, it could not end up with EBIT of $22. Thus there is **no real holding gain,** and the result is that real EPS has not changed. Looking at it in another way, suppose that the real discount rate is 10%. Then, before inflation, $V = 10/1.1 + 10/(1.1)^2 + \cdots + 10/(1.1)\infty = 100; after the 10% inflation (which occurs only in the first year), the nominal value is $11/1.1 + 11/(1.1)^2 + \cdots + 11/(1.1)\infty = 110, and its **real** value is $100.

EXHIBIT 3   EXAMPLE SHOWING EFFECT OF 10% NEUTRAL INFLATION ON EPS OF UNLEVERED FIRM ($)

	First	Second Year
Assets	100	110
EBIT	20	22
Tax	10	11
Net income	10	11
Number of shares	10	10
EPS	1	1.1
EPS^R	1	1

Consider now a levered firm. Assume that the leverage is 50% at the beginning of the first year, and the firm pays 10% interest on its debt. Assume also that the inflation rate is 10% and the interest rate in the second year is 21%, to compensate bondholders for the inflation. Earnings per share calculations that do not consider holding gains are EPS expressed in constant dollars EPS^C, as shown in Exhibit 4. Thus EPS^C has declined when the stockholders' excess holding gains are not considered. However, the equity value in the example has risen beyond what is needed to keep up with inflation: with 10% inflation, the $50 of equity has to rise to $55 to keep up with inflation; but in the example it has risen to $60; hence there is an excess holding gain hD of $5 ($= 0.10 \times 50$), and stockholders have had a **real** gain.

From the debt side, it is seen that the value of the debt remains unchanged at $50, and there is a decrease in the real value of the debt that generates $5 of excess holding gain on the equity. If the $5 holding gain is subject to 50% tax, the net profit available for stockholders is $8.25 ($= 5.75 + 0.5 \times 5$), and EPS_1 is $1.65 ($= 8.25/5$) or in real terms, EPS_1^R is $1.5 ($= 1.65/1.1$). Thus $EPS_1^R = EPS_0 = \$1.5$, since a neutral inflation should not affect the EPS^R as long as the appropriate adjustments are carried out. No such correction should be made for unlevered firms, since for them $hD = 0$.

If the $5 excess holding gain is subject to a lower tax rate, the real EPS is even higher. Suppose, for example, that the holding gain is not realized. In this case, $EPS_1 = \$2.15$ $[= (5.75 + 5.00)/5 = 10.75/5]$, and $EPS_1^R = \$1.955 ($= 2.15/1.1$).

EXHIBIT 4   EXAMPLE SHOWING IMPACT OF 10% NEUTRAL INFLATION ON EPS^C OF LEVERED FIRM ($)

	First	Second Year
Assets	100	110
Debt	50	50
Equity	50	60
EBIT	20	22
Interest	5	10.5
Taxable income	15	11.5
Tax	7.5	5.75
Net income	7.5	5.75
Number of shares	5	5
EPS	1.5	1.150
EPS^C	1.5	1.045

While the standard EPS calculation, which ignores holding gains, shows a decline in EPS^C as a result of inflation, the correction for holding gains shows that EPS^R increases as a result of inflation. This, of course, has implications for the way EPS growth and the firm's cost of capital are to be measured. Modigliani and Cohn ("Inflation, Rational Valuation and the Market," *Financial Analysts Journal*, March–April 1979, pp. 24–44) have also described the effect of inflation on earnings. However, in their model the stockholders' gain originates in the decline in the market value of the debt.

LIQUIDITY.   It has been demonstrated that the EPS of an unlevered firm will not be affected by inflation, whereas the EPS of a levered firm will increase. However, the negative effect of the treatment of inventory and depreciation on the firm's net income was ignored in arriving at these conclusions. When it is taken into consideration, the unlevered firm may experience reduced profitability in times of rising prices. While the levered firm would incur inflationary losses on its inventory and depreciation, it would benefit from excess holding gains on its debt. Thus the net effect of inflation on a levered firm is unclear. Both unlevered and levered firms are bound to find themselves in a **liquidity crunch** if the inflation is severe enough.

The reduced economic earnings of the unlevered firm will not necessarily be reflected in reported earnings. Consequently, **dividend payout ratios** computed on the basis of economic earnings will tend to rise. Coupled with the high effective tax rate, the firm is likely to find that its cash flow is insufficient for new investments.

Levered firms will find themselves in a similar situation. Although the levered firm's excess holding gains improve its profitability, they must be realized if they are to provide liquidity relief. The liquidity problem is illustrated in Exhibit 4 above, where a 10% anticipated inflation reduces net income from $7.5 in the first year to $5.75 in the second. The levered firm gets a $5 excess holding gain, but since it is not realized, it does not affect the firm's cash flow or its liquidity. To overcome the liquidity problem, the firm can either liquidate some of its assets or raise additional debt. The latter choice is more likely. Note that the illustration of the unlevered firm under inflation (Exhibit 3) shows no decrease in the firm's net income.

Most firms cope with the liquidity problem by issuing more debt. For example, in 1975 Du Pont tripled its outstanding debt to $793 million, and in late 1979 IBM issued $1 billion of notes and debentures for financing investments and growth, the largest single debt issue by an industrial company in the United States. Kepcke ("Current Accounting Practices and Proposals for Reform," *New England Economic Review*, Federal Reserve Bank of Boston, September–October 1976, p. 23), shows that the debt-equity ratio of U.S. nonfinancial corporations rose from 0.97 to 1.34 in the period 1965–1975. However, on the basis of current value (rather than conventional) reporting, the ratio hardly changed during the period: it was 0.91 in 1965 and 0.92 in 1975.

CREDIT TERMS AND INFLATION

Sales terms specify the period for which credit is extended and the discount, if any, given for early payment. If for example, the terms are "2/10 net 30," a 2% discount is granted if payment is made within 10 days, and the full sales price is due within 30 days from the invoice date if the discount is not taken. To get the percentage **opportunity cost** if the discount not taken is easily calculated, the textbook calculation is:

annual percentage cost (APC)

$$= \frac{\text{discount \%}}{100 - \text{discount \%}} \times \frac{360}{\text{days credit outstanding} - \text{discount period}}$$

See, for example, Brigham (*Financial Management,* Dryden Press, 1977, p. 387). The effective annual rate is in fact even higher, since the formula given here disregards compound interest during the year. Considering the compound interest we set $\lambda = 360/($days credit outstanding $-$ discount period). The rate that takes this effect into account is APC $= [1 + ($discount \%$)/(100 - $discount \%$)]^\lambda - 1$, and for "2/10 net 30" this comes to 0.438 $= (1 + 0.0204)^{18} - 1$, or 43.8\%.

Ignoring the compound interest we find that for "2/10 net 30" the APC is:

$$\text{APC} = \frac{2}{100 - 2} \times \frac{360}{30 - 10} = 0.367$$

or 36.7\%. This is an **opportunity cost.** It can also be derived as follows. Suppose that XYZ Corp. has annual purchases of \$367.2 million. If the 2\% discount is taken, the daily purchases are $367.3 \times (0.98)(1/360) = \$1$ million. Since each bill will be paid on the tenth day, accounts payable will be \$10 million. Most accountants record payables net of discount, then report the higher payments that result from not taking discounts as an additional expense. If the discount is not taken, the bills will be paid on the thirtieth day and payables will amount to \$30 million, an increase of \$20 million. A 2\% discount on the annual sales then amounts to \$7.346 million, which is 36.7\% of the \$20 million.

Under inflation, the discount becomes less advantageous, since the real difference between the discounted price and the full price paid at the end of the period is reduced by the decline in the purchasing power of the dollar during the credit period.

To see how the gain from the discount changes with inflation, consider a firm that purchases P dollars worth of materials per day. Consider now the credit policy "α/t_1 net t," and assume a daily inflation rate h. If the discount is taken, the purchases are paid for after t_1 days and the purchase price in real terms is $(1 - \alpha)P/(1 + h)^{t_1}$; if the discount is not taken, the bill will be paid after t days, the real purchase price is $P/(1 + h)^t$, and the real benefit from the discount is:

$$\text{real benefit} = \frac{P}{(1 + h)^t} - \frac{(1 - \alpha)P}{(1 + h)^{t_1}}$$

Expressing the benefit as a proportion γ of the real purchase price if the discount is taken, we obtain:

$$\gamma = \frac{\dfrac{P}{(1 + h)^t} - \dfrac{(1 - \alpha)P}{(1 + h)^{t_1}}}{\dfrac{(1 - \alpha)P}{(1 + h)^{t_1}}} = \frac{1}{(1 - \alpha)(1 + h)^{t_2}} - 1$$

where $t_2 = t - t_1$. The benefit γ is obtained over t_2 days. On an annual basis, it is

$$(1 + \gamma)^\lambda - 1 = \frac{1}{[(1 - \alpha)(1 + h)^{t_2}]^\lambda} - 1$$

where $\gamma = 360/t_2$.

It can be shown that the derivative of γ with respect to h is negative, which means that the percentage benefit decreases as inflation increases. Moreover, if h is sufficiently large, the expression $(1 - \alpha)(1 + h)^{t_2}$ could be greater than 1, in which case γ would be negative, and it certainly would be advantageous for the purchasing firm to forgo the discount.

CHANGING THE DISCOUNT PERCENTAGE.   The financial manager who wants to get the greatest cash flow possible from the firm's sales and to exploit the firm's credit to the utmost should take the effect of inflation on γ into account and should consider an increase in the nominal rate of discount to maintain a desired level of γ, the **real** percentage benefit resulting from the discount. It is thus of interest to determine the discount rates that will yield the same real benefit as a given discount in the absence of inflation. To do so, note first that in the absence of inflation ($h = 0$), $\gamma_0 = 1/(1 - \alpha) - 1$. Given an inflation rate $h = 0$, put

$$\frac{1}{(1 - X)(1 + h)^{t_2}} - 1 = \frac{1}{1 - \alpha} - 1 = \gamma_0$$

and solve for X, the rate of discount that makes the real percentage benefit equal the no-inflation rate γ_0:

$$X = 1 - \frac{1 - \alpha}{(1 + h)^{t_2}}$$

A numerical example will illustrate this. Suppose the credit policy is "2/10 net 30" and the inflation rate is zero. Then $\alpha = 0.02$ and $\gamma_0 = 1/(1 - 0.02) = 0.0204$, which translates into 0.438 on an annual basis. Now with a 12% per annum inflation rate, $(1 + h)^{t_2} = 1.0063$ ($= 1.12^{1/18}$); that is, over 20 days the inflation comes to 0.63%. Substituting $(1 + h)^{t_2} = 1.0063$ in the expression for X, we obtain $X = 0.0262$; that is, a 2.62% discount at 12% per annum inflation will yield the same real percentage benefit as a 2% discount in the absence of inflation. In other words, the discount rate must be raised significantly if it is to provide the same real percentage benefit. If this is not done, the selling firm can expect the number of cash-paying purchasers to decline, with adverse effects on the seller's liquidity.

Exhibit 5 shows the values for X for different credit terms and for a variety of annual inflation rates. Exhibit 6 portrays the ratio X/α for selected inflation rates and credit periods.

CHANGING THE CREDIT PERIOD.   Instead of changing the percentage discount and keeping the credit period unchanged, the selling firm may adjust its credit terms to inflation by shortening the credit period, keeping the discount percent unchanged. The opportunity cost of forgoing the discount is given by

$$APC = \frac{1}{[(1 - \alpha)(1 + h)^{t_2}]^{\lambda}} - 1$$

If $h = 0$, this reduces to $1/(1 - \alpha)^{360/t_2} - 1$. When $h > 0$, t_2 may be shortened to some value t_2^* such that

$$\frac{1}{[(1 - \alpha)(1 + h)^{t_2^*}]^{360/t_2^*}} - 1 = \frac{1}{(1 - \alpha)^{360/t_2}} - 1$$

EXHIBIT 5   INFLATION-ADJUSTED DISCOUNT PERCENTAGE FOR SELECTED
CREDIT TERMS AND INFLATION RATES

EQUIVALENT DISCOUNT ADJUSTED FOR INFLATION

ANNUAL INFL. RATE	NET 30 DAYS					NET 60 DAYS					NET 90 DAYS				
	1/10	2/10	3/10	4/10	5/10	1/10	2/10	3/10	4/10	5/10	1/10	2/10	3/10	4/10	5/10
5.	1.27	2.27	3.26	4.26	5.26	1.67	2.66	3.66	4.65	5.64	2.07	3.06	4.05	5.04	6.03
6.	1.32	2.32	3.31	4.31	5.31	1.80	2.79	3.79	4.78	5.77	2.28	3.27	4.26	5.24	6.23
7.	1.37	2.37	3.36	4.36	5.36	1.93	2.92	3.91	4.90	5.89	2.49	3.47	4.46	5.44	6.43
8.	1.42	2.42	3.41	4.41	5.41	2.06	3.05	4.04	5.03	6.02	2.69	3.68	4.66	5.64	6.62
9.	1.47	2.47	3.46	4.46	5.45	2.18	3.17	4.16	5.15	6.14	2.90	3.88	4.86	5.84	6.82
10.	1.52	2.52	3.51	4.51	5.50	2.31	3.30	4.28	5.27	6.26	3.10	4.08	5.05	6.03	7.01
11.	1.57	2.57	3.56	4.56	5.55	2.43	3.42	4.41	5.39	6.38	3.30	4.27	5.25	6.23	7.20
12.	1.62	2.62	3.61	4.60	5.60	2.56	3.54	4.53	5.51	6.50	3.49	4.47	5.44	6.42	7.39
13.	1.67	2.67	3.66	4.65	5.65	2.63	3.66	4.65	5.63	6.61	3.69	4.66	5.63	6.61	7.58
14.	1.72	2.71	3.71	4.70	5.69	2.80	3.78	4.77	5.75	6.73	3.88	4.85	5.82	6.79	7.77
15.	1.77	2.76	3.75	4.75	5.74	2.92	3.90	4.88	5.86	6.84	4.07	5.04	6.01	6.98	7.95
20.	2.00	2.99	3.98	4.97	5.96	3.51	4.48	5.46	6.43	7.41	5.01	5.97	6.93	7.89	8.85
25.	2.23	3.21	4.20	5.19	6.18	4.07	5.04	6.01	6.97	7.94	5.91	6.86	7.81	8.76	9.71
30.	2.44	3.43	4.41	5.40	6.38	4.61	5.57	6.53	7.50	8.46	6.77	7.71	8.65	9.59	10.54
35.	2.65	3.63	4.62	5.60	6.58	5.13	6.08	7.04	8.00	8.96	7.60	8.53	9.46	10.40	11.33
40.	2.85	3.83	4.81	5.79	6.78	5.62	6.58	7.53	8.48	9.44	8.40	9.32	10.25	11.17	12.10
45.	3.04	4.02	5.00	5.98	6.96	6.11	7.06	8.00	8.95	9.90	9.16	10.08	11.00	11.92	12.84
50.	3.23	4.21	5.13	6.16	7.14	6.57	7.52	8.46	9.40	10.35	9.91	10.82	11.73	12.64	13.55
60.	3.58	4.56	5.53	6.51	7.43	7.46	8.39	9.33	10.26	11.20	11.32	12.22	13.11	14.01	14.90
70.	3.92	4.89	5.86	6.83	7.80	8.29	9.22	10.14	11.07	11.99	12.65	13.53	14.41	15.29	16.18
80.	4.23	5.20	6.17	7.13	8.10	9.07	9.99	10.91	11.83	12.75	13.89	14.76	15.63	16.50	17.37
90.	4.53	5.49	6.46	7.42	8.39	9.81	10.72	11.64	12.55	13.46	15.07	15.93	16.79	17.64	18.50
100.	4.81	5.77	6.73	7.70	8.66	10.52	11.42	12.32	13.23	14.13	16.19	17.03	17.88	18.73	19.57

**EXHIBIT 6   RATIO BETWEEN INFLATION-ADJUSTED DISCOUNT PERCENTAGE *X*
AND NO-INFLATION PERCENTAGE**

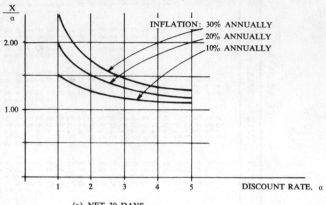

(a) NET 30 DAYS

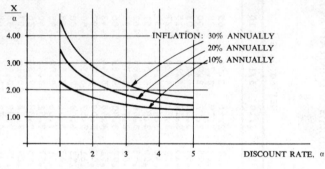

(b) NET 60 DAYS

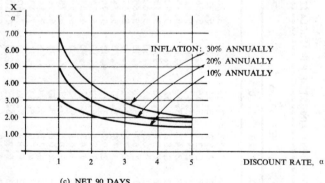

(c) NET 90 DAYS

Solve for t_2^* to get

$$t_2^* = \frac{t_2^*[\log(1 - \alpha)]}{\log(1 - \alpha) - t_2[\log(1 + h)]}$$

Values of t_2^* can be derived from this expression for various combinations of t_2, α, and h. Note that the derivative of t_2^* with respect to h is negative, which means that other things being equal, the higher the inflation rate, the shorter should be the credit period for a constant real opportunity cost. Note that $t_2^* = t_2$ when $h = 0$, and when h approaches infinity, t_2^* approaches zero. Exhibit 7 gives the values of $t^* = t_1 + t_2^*$ (to the nearest whole day) for a variety of combinations of t, α, and h. For example, a credit policy "2/10 net 30" in the absence of inflation gives the same real percentage benefit as "2/10 net 24" with annual inflation of 15%. Exhibit 8 presents the ratios t^*/t for selected combinations of t, α, and h.

INFLATION, DEPRECIATION, INCOME TAX, AND CAPITAL BUDGETING

A characteristic of investment in a fixed asset is that the cash flow derived from it is obtained long after it was acquired. For both financial reporting and income tax calculations, an asset's cost is spread over its lifetime so that the depreciation expense can be matched with the revenues. Depreciation, however, is based on the historical cost of the asset, which during periods of inflation is less than current replacement cost. Over the years, various tax incentives have been introduced that in part aim to provide real or close to real depreciation in periods of inflation, the most important being accelerated depreciation and the investment tax credit. The class life **asset depreciation range system** (ADR) is another such incentive. The system provides upper and lower limits for recommended lifetimes of broad classes of assets, so that a firm may not need to work with more than one lifetime. However, the ADR system is not as important an incentive as the two mentioned here and therefore is not discussed.

EFFECT OF INFLATION ON A PROJECT'S NET PRESENT VALUE.   The net present value (NPV) of an investment project is a widely accepted measure of investment profitability. As with other measures of profit and profitability, special care is required in applying the NPV criterion to a cash flow in conditions of inflation—a project that would be accepted in the absence of inflation could very well be rejected when inflation is present, and inflation increases a project's riskiness. Investment incentives are ignored for the time being.

Neutral Inflation.   The analysis begins by assuming neutral inflation, in which all prices increase at the same rate h.

Suppose that the **cost of capital** in real terms is k, say 10% per annum, so that an investment of $100 will be attractive only if the cash flow at the end of the year is at least $110 in real terms. If the cash flow is exactly $110, the net present value (NPV) of the investment is 0 ($= -100 + 110/1.1$). If the real cash flow exceeds $110, the project's NPV is positive and it will be accepted.

With a 20% neutral inflation, the minimum nominal cash flow required is $132, since its real value is only $110. The project's net present value is then

$$NPV = -100 + \frac{\$132/1.2}{1.1} = -100 + \frac{\$132}{1.32} = 0$$

EXHIBIT 7 INFLATION-ADJUSTED CREDIT PERIOD BY SELECTED CREDIT TERMS AND INFLATION RATES

EQUIVALENT NET DAYS ADJUSTED FOR INFLATION

ANNUAL INFL. RATE	NET 30 DAYS					NET 60 DAYS					NET 90 DAYS				
	1/10	2/10	3/10	4/10	5/10	1/10	2/10	3/10	4/10	5/10	1/10	2/10	3/10	4/10	5/10
5.	26.	28.	28.	29.	29.	40.	47.	51.	53.	54.	48.	62.	69.	73.	76.
6.	25.	27.	28.	29.	29.	38.	46.	49.	52.	53.	45.	59.	66.	71.	74.
7.	25.	27.	28.	28.	29.	36.	44.	48.	51.	52.	42.	56.	63.	68.	72.
8.	24.	27.	28.	28.	28.	34.	43.	47.	50.	51.	39.	53.	61.	66.	70.
9.	24.	26.	27.	28.	28.	33.	41.	46.	49.	50.	37.	51.	59.	64.	68.
10.	23.	26.	27.	28.	28.	31.	40.	45.	48.	50.	36.	49.	57.	62.	66.
11.	23.	26.	27.	28.	28.	30.	39.	44.	47.	49.	34.	47.	55.	61.	65.
12.	22.	25.	26.	27.	28.	29.	38.	43.	46.	48.	33.	45.	54.	59.	63.
13.	22.	25.	26.	27.	28.	28.	37.	42.	45.	47.	31.	44.	52.	58.	62.
14.	22.	25.	26.	27.	27.	28.	36.	41.	44.	47.	30.	42.	51.	56.	61.
15.	21.	24.	25.	26.	27.	27.	35.	40.	44.	46.	29.	41.	49.	55.	60.
20.	20.	23.	24.	25.	26.	24.	32.	37.	41.	43.	26.	36.	44.	50.	54.
25.	19.	22.	23.	25.	26.	22.	30.	35.	38.	41.	23.	33.	40.	46.	50.
30.	18.	22.	23.	24.	25.	21.	28.	33.	36.	39.	21.	30.	37.	42.	47.
35.	17.	21.	23.	24.	25.	20.	26.	31.	34.	37.	20.	28.	35.	40.	44.
40.	17.	20.	22.	23.	24.	19.	25.	29.	33.	36.	19.	27.	33.	38.	42.
45.	16.	19.	21.	23.	24.	18.	24.	28.	32.	35.	18.	25.	31.	36.	40.
50.	16.	19.	21.	22.	23.	17.	23.	27.	31.	33.	17.	24.	30.	34.	38.
60.	15.	18.	20.	21.	23.	16.	22.	26.	29.	32.	16.	22.	27.	32.	35.
70.	15.	18.	20.	21.	23.	16.	20.	24.	27.	30.	15.	21.	26.	30.	33.
80.	15.	18.	20.	21.	22.	16.	20.	23.	26.	29.	15.	20.	24.	28.	32.
90.	14.	17.	19.	20.	22.	15.	19.	22.	25.	28.	15.	19.	23.	27.	30.
100.	14.	17.	19.	20.	21.	15.	18.	22.	24.	27.	15.	19.	22.	26.	29.

EXHIBIT 8   RATIO BETWEEN THE INFLATION-ADJUSTED NET (t^*) AND THE NO-INFLATION NET PERIOD (t) FOR SELECTED NET PERIODS AND DISCOUNT PERCENTAGES

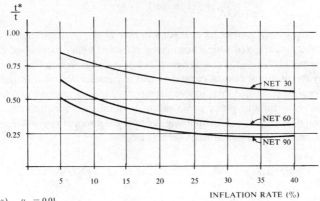

(a) $\alpha = 0.01$

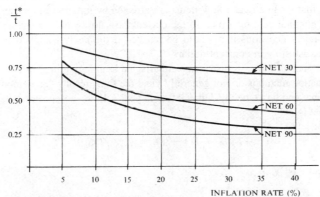

(b) $\alpha = 0.02$

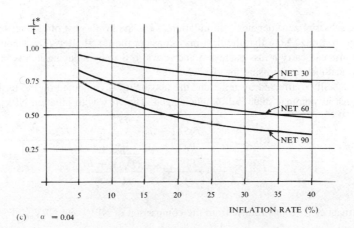

(c) $\alpha = 0.04$

The proper cost of capital adjusted for inflation deduced from this example is 32%. More generally, if k is the **real cost of capital**, the **nominal rate** k_N is

$$k_N = (1 + k)(1 + h) - 1$$

Should an investment project be evaluated in current or constant dollars? Since all cash flow components are affected proportionally by inflation, either method of evaluation will lead to the same investment decision, provided that in current dollars the cash flow is discounted by the **nominal cost of capital** k_N and in constant dollars it is discounted by the **real cost of capital** k. To see this, ignore depreciation for the moment and assume that the real annual net cash flow in year t is S_t, and with an inflation (neutral) rate h, the current annual net cash flow is $S_t(1 + h)^t$. Applying the nominal discount rate to the nominal annual net cash flow, the NPV computed from current amounts is

$$\text{NPV} = -I + \sum_{t=1}^{n} \frac{S_t(1 + h)^t}{[(1 + k)(1 + h)]^t} = -I + \sum_{t=1}^{n} \frac{S_t}{(1 + k)^t}$$

where I is the initial investment outlay and $(1 + k)(1 + h) = 1 + k_N$. The real cost of capital can also be applied to the real cash flow to obtain the second summation directly.

It is clear that when all cash flow items are affected by inflation in the same proportion, applying the nominal cost of capital to the current cash flow yields the same NPV and the same accept-reject decisions that would be reached if the analyst applied the real cost of capital to the cash flow in constant dollars.

In practice, not all the cash flow items are affected by inflation in the same way; and thus the two evaluation methods do not generally yield the same results. To demonstrate this, let T be the tax rate and let D_t be the depreciation in year t. In the absence of inflation, the cash flow for year t is

$$(1 - T)(S_t - D_t) + D_t = (1 - T)S_t + TD_t$$

and the project's NPV is

$$\text{NPV}_0 = -I + \sum_{t=1}^{n} \frac{(1 - T)S_t}{(1 + k)^t} + \sum_{t=1}^{n} \frac{TD_t}{(1 + r)^t}$$

where the subscript zero denotes "no inflation," k is the firm's cost of capital, and r is the riskless interest rate. Note that the firm may consider the **tax shelter** TD_t, a nonrisky cash flow (the firm can carry a loss backward and forward, thereby reducing its tax bill in years of profit), and discount it using the riskless rate r.

While S_t will be affected by inflation, the tax shelter is computed on the basis of book value so that its nominal value will be unchanged. The NPV with inflation NPV_{inf} is

$$\text{NPV}_{\text{inf}} = -I + \sum_{t=1}^{n} \frac{(1 - T)S_t(1 + h)^t}{[(1 + k)(1 + h)]^t} + \sum_{t=1}^{n} \frac{TD_t}{[(1 + r)(1 + h)]^t}$$

$$= -I + \sum_{t=1}^{n} \frac{(1 - T)S_t}{(1 + k)^t} + \sum_{t=1}^{n} \frac{TD_t/(1 + h)^t}{(1 + r)^t}$$

Three main conclusions follow from the comparison of NPV_0 and NPV_{inf}.

1. Since NPV_{inf} is the correct net present value under inflation, the firm can separate its cash flow into two components. The part of the cash flow whose nominal value changes proportionally to the price level will not be affected by inflation. The depreciation tax shelter, however, will be reduced in value. For both components, though, it is true that **one can apply either the real rate of discount to the constant dollar cash flow or the nominal rate of discount to the nominal value of the cash flow.**

2. It can be seen that $NPV_0 > NPV_{inf}$, which means that other things being equal, investment projects become less attractive under inflation. The higher the inflation rate, the greater the gap between NPV_0 and NPV_{inf}. Moreover, it is quite possible that $NPV_0 > 0$ while $NPV_{inf} < 0$, so that a project that would be accepted in the absence of inflation may be rejected when there is inflation.

3. Firms having fixed obligations (such as lease contracts) may gain from inflation, since the NPV of their fixed commitments decreases in real terms.

Nonneutral Inflation.   In reality, inflation is rarely neutral. The price of oil, for example, has risen in recent years much faster than the price of larger cars, the prices of food products do not change at the same rate as the prices of durable goods, and so on. If stockholders consume a well-mixed basket of goods and services, it is only reasonable to assume that their required rate of return on investment will change proportionally to the average price change. Thus the firm's cost of capital changes from k to $(1 + k)(1 + h) - 1$ with inflation. The firm that produces only a limited number of products may increase its prices by a rate h^*, which generally differs from h. Thus under inflation, a project's NPV will be

$$NPV_{inf} = I + \sum_{t=1}^{n} \frac{(1 - T)S_t(1 + h^*)^t}{[(1 + k)(1 + h)]^t} + \sum_{t=1}^{n} \frac{TD_t}{[(1 + r)(1 + h)]^t}$$

Under neutral inflation, the real cost of capital k can be considered constant. Since h^* differs from h, however, inflation introduces a new dimension of risk to the firm. The differential inflation rates increase the business risk of all firms, and this may increase the real cost of capital, thus reducing NPV.

Riskless Interest Rate.   In the absence of inflation the tax shelter TD_t is assumed to be riskless, and the riskless discount rate r applies to it. In the presence of inflation that includes unexpected elements, the depreciation tax shelter is no longer riskless, and a rate $r^* > r$ should be applied to it. The difference between the two, $r^* - r$, is simply the risk premium for the uncertainties of inflation. Both neutral and nonneutral inflation increase the riskiness of the cash flow. The result is higher discount rates and lower NPV.

RANKING MUTUALLY EXCLUSIVE INVESTMENT PROJECTS: INCENTIVES NOT CONSIDERED.   To simplify the discussion of the ranking of mutually exclusive investment projects, without any loss of generality, the same cost of capital k is used to discount the uncertain component of the cash flow and the certain depreciation tax benefit.

Nelson ("Inflation and Capital Budgeting," *Journal of Finance*, Vol. 31, No. 3, June 1976, pp. 923–931) has examined some of the implications of inflation for the ranking of investment projects. Among other things he demonstrated that the NPV ranking of **mutually exclusive investment projects** depends, in general, on the rate of inflation. He showed that at higher rates of inflation, ranking will usually change in favor of projects with shorter duration. Nelson also showed that inflation generally affects replacement policy: the higher the rate of inflation, the greater the likelihood of replacement being deferred.

When projects with unequal lifetimes are compared, their net present values are not adequate as a measure of relative profitability, since the length of time over which a given amount of profit is generated must be taken into account. For example, if projects A and B have $NPV_A = \$100$ and $NPV_B = \$200$, respectively, project B should not automatically be preferred to A without regard to the project's lifetime. If, for example, the lifetimes are 2 and 10 years for A and B, respectively, project A might very well be preferred. In particular, it will be preferred if it can be assumed that other equally profitable investments will become available in years 3–10. If so (such an assumption is common in replacement chain analyses), the profitability of investments can be compared on the basis of their **uniform annuity series** (UAS), which is defined as the annuity whose present value equals the NPV:

$$NPV = \frac{UAS}{(1 + k)} + \frac{UAS}{(1 + k)^2} + \cdots + \frac{UAS}{(1 + k)^n}$$

Thus if a project's net present value is $200 and its lifetime 10 years, its UAS, assuming a 9% cost of capital, is $31.16, since

$$200 = \frac{31.16}{1.09} + \frac{31.16}{(1.09)^2} + \cdots + \frac{31.16}{(1.09)^{10}}$$

Similarly, if the NPV is $100 and the lifetime is 2 years, the UAS is $56.85. The UAS criterion leads to selection of the second project, and this is justified if it can be assumed that an equally profitable investment will appear in two years' time.

Exhibit 9 compares five investment projects; the UAS is the basis for capital budgeting of projects with unequal lifetimes, and the cost of capital is taken as 9%. The five projects have two things in common: they all require the same initial outlay, and in all five the UAS is $100.

Assume now an inflation of 20% per annum. The cost of capital is $(1.09)(1.2) - 1 = 0.308$, the (book value) depreciation is unchanged, and S_t rises by 20% per annum starting in the first year. Exhibit 10 illustrates the cash flow of project B with and without inflation.

The real NPV of project B in the presence of 20% per annum inflation is

EXHIBIT 9   PROJECTS A–E CASH FLOWS AND NPV AND UAS

	Project				
	A	B	C	D	E
n	1	2	5	10	∞
I	1,000	1,000	1,000	1,000	1,000
S_t	1,380	837	514	412	380
D_t	1,000	500	200	100	0
$(1 - T)S_t + TD_t$	1,190	668	357	256	190
NPV	92	176	390	642	1,111
UAS	100	100	100	100	100

EXHIBIT 10   PROJECT B's CASH FLOW, WITH AND WITHOUT INFLATION

	Year		
	0	1	2

NO INFLATION

I_0	$-1,000$	—	—
S_t	—	836.95	836.95
D_t	—	500.00	500.00
$(1 - T)S_t + TD_t$	—	668.48	668.48

WITH INFLATION

I_0	$-1,000$	—	—
S_t	—	1,004.34	1,205.21
D_t	—	500.00	500.00
$(1 - T)S_t + TD_t$ ·		752.17	852.61

$$NPV_B = -1,000 + \frac{752.17}{1.308} + \frac{852.61}{1.308^2} = 73.4$$

The UAS_B is then derived by solving $73.39 = UAS_B/1.09 + UAS_B/1.09^2$, where $1.09 = 1.308/1.2$; this UAS_B, which equals \$41.72, is thus a real value, its nominal value being $(41.72)(1.2) = \$50.06$ in the first year, and $(41.72)(1.2^2) = \$60.08$ in the second. The real NPV and UAS of the five projects, A–E is as follows:

	A	B	C	D	E
n	1	2	5	10	∞
NPV	15.28	73.39	239.87	472.15	1,111.11
UAS	16.65	41.72	61.67	73.57	100.00

With no inflation, the UAS of all five projects is \$100; thus the table shows that a project's UAS is reduced by inflation (unless, as with project E, it is infinite); moreover, the shorter the lifetime, the greater the decrease. It is clear from the example that when mutually exclusive investment projects differing in lifetimes are ranked by NPV or UAS, inflation could change the ranking because it affects the real value of the tax shelter differently in each case.

The effect of inflation on the **internal rate of return** (IRR) can now be examined. Exhibit 11 lists the **no-inflation cash flow** of five investments as well as their nominal IRR (IRR_N) and real IRR (IRR_R) in the face of a 20% inflation rate. In the absence of inflation, the IRR of all five projects (IRR_O) is 10%. The project's real IRR, given an inflation rate h, is

$$IRR_R = \frac{1 + IRR_N}{1 + h} - 1$$

EXHIBIT 11   PROJECTS F–J CASH FLOWS AND IRR$_N$ AND IRR$_R$

	Project				
	F	G	H	I	J
n	1	2	5	10	∞
I_0	1,000	1,000	1,000	1,000	1,000
S_t	1,200.00	652.38	327.59	225.49	200.00
D_t	1,000.00	500.00	200.00	100.00	0.00
$(1 - T)S_t + TD_t$	1,100.00	576.19	263.80	162.75	100.00
IRR$_N$	22.00	22.76	24.77	27.12	32.00
IRR$_R$	1.70	2.30	3.98	5.93	10.00

where IRR$_N$ is the nominal value of IRR; the last two lines of Exhibit 11 IRR$_N$ and IRR$_R$. To show their derivation, consider project G, in Exhibit 12. The project's IRR$_N$ is 22.76%, since

$$-1,000 + \frac{641.43}{1.2276} + \frac{719.72}{1.2276^2} = 0$$

and

$$IRR_R = \frac{1.2276}{1.20} - 1 = 2.3\%$$

Comparison of the IRR$_R$ of the five projects shows that the profitability of short-lived projects is more adversely affected by inflation, and project J, with infinite lifetime, is not affected at all. Thus inflation may alter the IRR ranking of projects.

EFFECTIVENESS OF INVESTMENT INCENTIVES.

Accelerated Depreciation. Let us reexamine capital budgeting, considering the main investment incentives and their effectiveness at times of inflation. Landskroner and Levy ("Inflation, Depreciation and Optimal Production," *European Economic Review*, Vol. 12, 1979, pp. 353–367) have examined the effectiveness of two accelerated depreciation methods, the double declining balance (DDB) and the sum-of-the-years-digits (SYD) **as investment incentives.**

To determine effectiveness, they compared the **present value of the depreciation tax shelter** TD_t for assets of various lifetimes and under alternative inflation rates. In the absence of inflation, the present value of the tax shelter is given by

$$PV(TD) = \sum_{t=1}^{n} \frac{TD_t}{(1 + r)^t}$$

whatever the method. Once inflation at an annual rate h is taken into account, the tax saving is:

$$PV(TD, h) = \sum_{t=1}^{n} \frac{TD_t/(1 + h)^t}{(1 + r)^t} = \sum_{t=1}^{n} \frac{TD_t}{[(1 + r)(1 + h)]^t}$$

EXHIBIT 12   CASH FLOW DATA FOR PROJECT G

	Year 0	Years 1, 2, No Inflation	20% Inflation	
			Year 1	Year 2
I_0	$-1,000$			
S_t		652.38	782.86	939.43
D_t		500.00	500.00	500.00
$(1 - T)S_t + TD_t$		576.19	641.43	719.72

Accelerated depreciation is generally a more effective investment incentive than straight-line depreciation (SL) because with the accelerated methods the bulk of the asset is depreciated in the early periods. But the relative effectiveness of DDB and SYD is not necessarily clear.

Exhibit 13 presents the present value of the depreciation using the three methods and assuming that the real discount rate is $r = 0.05$, for different lifetimes and inflation rates. Exhibit 13 disregards the tax rate T, which is assumed to be constant; in other words, it has no bearing on effectiveness. A number of conclusions concerning the relation between the parameters and the methods of depreciation may be drawn from Exhibit 13. First, as the inflation rate increases, the accelerated methods have an increasing advantage over SL. This is because higher inflation rates mean higher nominal discount rates, which in turn increase the relative weight of the charges in the early years. Second, it can be observed that short service life and high inflation rate, separately or together, favor DDB over the SYD. At the high end of the inflation range, the greater the rate of inflation, the later the point at which DDB becomes preferable. However, this delaying effect is fairly small: assuming the 5% real discount rate used in Exhibit 13, the point at which DDB and SYD change places is 5–6 years for annual inflation rates of up to 20%, 6–7 years for inflation rates of 20–35%, and 7–8 years for 40% inflation. This stability of the relative effectiveness of the depreciation methods is the most important result of Exhibit 13. In the relevant range of inflation for the United States ($h \leq 20\%$), if $n \leq 5$, DDB is the more effective, and SYD is more effective still if $n > 5$.

Exhibits 14 and 15 illustrate the present value of the tax depreciation charge as a function of the asset's service life for selected inflation rates, with an assumed real discount rate of 5%. The curves in Exhibit 15 are closer to the horizontal axis than those of Exhibit 14; this implies that the tax saving declines as the inflation rate increases under all these methods. Also, the SYD and DDB curves cross each other, which illustrates that the relative effectiveness of the accelerated method is a function of inflation rate and service life.

Inflation reduces the firm's real net cash inflows because depreciation is based on historical cost and is not adjusted to change with inflation, while revenues and cash expenses usually increase with inflation. Comparing the present value of straight-line depreciation in the absence of inflation with the present value under an inflation rate of $h\%$, it is obvious that $PV(TD) > PV(TD, h)$: **inflation reduces the firm's real tax savings.** The DDB and SYD accelerated depreciation methods will reduce this inflation loss. However, it is interesting to question the extent to which these procedures protect the firm against inflation loss, or how much compensation they provide for it. Exhibit 16 shows the ratio of the present value of depreciation of the two accelerated methods under inflation to the present value of the straight-line method in the absence of inflation.

An entry greater than unity means that the accelerated method overcompensates for inflation, less than unity means undercompensation, and unity exact compensation. For example, if an asset has a service life of 8 years, both accelerated methods will overcom-

EXHIBIT 13 PRESENT VALUE OF DEPRECIATION BY SELECTED SERVICE LIVES AND INFLATION RATES: SL, DDB, SYD, FOR $r = 0.05$

Inflation Rate, h	Service Life of Asset, n (years)								
	3	4	5	6	7	8	12	16	20
0.00									
SL	0.908	0.886	0.866	0.846	0.827	0.808	0.739	0.677	0.623
DDB	0.923	0.914	0.896	0.878	0.861	0.845	0.784	0.730	0.682
SYD	0.923	0.908	0.894	0.880	0.867	0.854	0.804	0.759	0.718
0.02									
SL	0.873	0.845	0.818	0.792	0.767	0.744	0.658	0.587	0.526
DDB	0.907	0.882	0.858	0.835	0.813	0.792	0.716	0.652	0.598
SYD	0.893	0.874	0.855	0.837	0.820	0.803	0.740	0.685	0.636
0.05									
SL	0.825	0.788	0.753	0.721	0.690	0.661	0.561	0.482	0.419
DDB	0.870	0.837	0.806	0.776	0.749	0.723	0.632	0.561	0.503
SYD	0.852	0.827	0.802	0.779	0.757	0.735	0.659	0.595	0.540
0.10									
SL	0.755	0.707	0.663	0.622	0.586	0.552	0.442	0.363	0.305
DDB	0.816	0.772	0.731	0.694	0.661	0.629	0.528	0.453	0.396
SYD	0.791	0.757	0.726	0.696	0.668	0.643	0.544	0.483	0.427
0.15									
SL	0.694	0.638	0.588	0.544	0.505	0.469	0.360	0.286	0.235
DDB	0.768	0.715	0.669	0.627	0.590	0.556	0.452	0.380	0.327
SYD	0.737	0.698	0.661	0.628	0.597	0.569	0.475	0.405	0.351
0.20									
SL	0.641	0.580	0.527	0.481	0.440	0.405	0.300	0.234	0.190
DDB	0.725	0.666	0.616	0.571	0.533	0.498	0.395	0.327	0.279
SYD	0.690	0.646	0.606	0.571	0.538	0.508	0.414	0.346	0.297
0.40									
SL	0.486	0.418	0.381	0.319	0.283	0.254	0.176	0.133	0.106
DDB	0.591	0.522	0.466	0.420	0.382	0.350	0.263	0.210	0.175
SYD	0.547	0.495	0.451	0.414	0.381	0.353	0.270	0.217	0.181

EXHIBIT 14   PRESENT VALUE OF DEPRECIATION STREAM OF SL, DDB, AND SYD

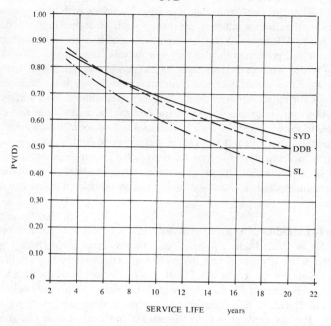

EXHIBIT 15   PRESENT VALUE OF DEPRECIATION STREAM OF SL, DDB AND SYD

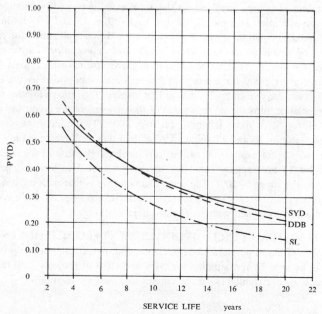

pensate for inflation at a rate of 1% per annum: the real present value of depreciation is increased by 1% under DDB and by 2% under SYD, as compared with SL in the **absence** of inflation. Taking the same asset but assuming 5% inflation, both accelerated methods undercompensate the firm for inflation: the present value of depreciation is reduced by 11% under DDB and by 9% under SYD. The main finding of Exhibit 16 is that the accelerated methods provide full protection only at very low inflation rates, up to 1% of inflation with DDB and up to 2% with SYD. This result is independent of the asset's service life. It is interesting to note that within the range of inflation rates in which the accelerated methods overcompensate for inflation, overcompensation increases with the asset's lifetime. The rate of increase, however, is greater for SYD: for example, at an inflation rate of 1%, using SYD, the ratio increases from 1.00 for a 3-year asset to 1.08 for a 20-year asset; using DDB, the increase is only from 1.01 to 1.02. That is, during periods of low inflation the accelerated methods will induce investment in long-lived projects. The opposite occurs when inflation exceeds 2%. At this level, the degree of undercompensation increases with the asset's life; the accelerated methods thus encourage investment in short-lived assets that minimize inflation losses.

Investment Tax Credit.   The investment tax credit was first incorporated into the federal income tax law in 1962. Under its provisions, business firms could claim a specified percentage of the dollar amount of new investment in certain assets as a credit against their income tax. Originally, the credit was 7% of new investment in assets with a lifetime of 8 or more years: two-thirds of 7% for assets with 6 or 7 years of life, and one-third of 7% for assets with 4 or 5 years of life; no credit could be claimed for assets with a lifetime of less than 4 years. The tax credit was twice suspended and reinstated as Congress used it to encourage investment when economic conditions required it. In 1975, the basic credit rate was raised from 7 to 10%.

The investment tax credit supplements the accelerated depreciation methods in encouraging capital investments. In view of the data of Exhibits 13 and 16, the investment tax credit clearly makes economic sense. It provides an additional incentive for capital investments in years of undercompensation under accelerated depreciation. Furthermore, as seen in Exhibit 16, the degree of undercompensation increases with the asset's life, and this justifies the higher tax credit for assets with longer lifetimes provided by the law.

Exhibit 17 is similar to Exhibit 16, except that it shows the ratio of present value of DDB and SYD depreciation **plus** the present value of the investment tax credit (assuming a 10% rate) to (as before) SL without inflation, for $r = 0.05$. Two conclusions emerge from a comparison of Exhibits 16 and 17. First, it is evident that the investment tax credit adds a significant tax saving for assets with various service lives. Because of the tax structure, the ratios of Exhibit 17 are roughly equal for service lives of 3 to 8 years, particularly for inflation rates in the range 5–10%. The second conclusion is that with inflation rates of 5% or more, the tax credit is not a strong enough incentive and does not fully compensate for inflation even when combined with accelerated depreciation.

RANKING OF MUTUALLY EXCLUSIVE INVESTMENT PROJECTS: INCENTIVES CONSIDERED.   The effect of accelerated depreciation and investment tax credit on the ranking of projects can be seen by reexamining the NPV and UAS of projects A–E (Exhibit 9) and the IRR projects F–J (Exhibit 11).The incentives assumed are as follows:

Project A, F   No incentives
Project B, C   Double declining balance depreciation (DDB)

EXHIBIT 16 RATIO OF PRESENT VALUE OF DDB AND SYD DEPRECIATION UNDER INFLATION TO SL WITHOUT INFLATION, FOR $r = 0.05$

Inflation Rate, h	Service Life of Asset, n (years)									
	3	4	5	6	7	8	12	16	18	20
0.00										
DDB	1.03	1.03	1.03	1.04	1.04	1.05	1.06	1.08	1.09	1.09
SYD	1.02	1.02	1.03	1.04	1.05	1.06	1.09	1.12	1.14	1.15
0.01										
DDB	1.01	1.01	1.01	1.01	1.01	1.01	1.01	1.02	1.02	1.02
SYD	1.00	1.00	1.01	1.01	1.02	1.02	1.04	1.06	1.07	1.08
0.02										
DDB	1.00	0.99	0.99	0.99	0.98	0.98	0.97	0.96	0.96	0.96
SYD	0.98	0.99	0.99	0.99	0.99	0.99	1.00	1.01	1.02	1.02
0.03										
DDB	0.99	0.98	0.97	0.96	0.96	0.95	0.93	0.91	0.91	0.90
SYD	0.97	0.97	0.97	0.97	0.96	0.96	0.96	0.96	0.96	0.96
0.05										
DDB	0.96	0.94	0.93	0.92	0.91	0.89	0.86	0.83	0.82	0.81
SYD	0.94	0.93	0.93	0.92	0.92	0.91	0.89	0.88	0.87	0.87
0.10										
DDB	0.90	0.87	0.84	0.82	0.80	0.78	0.71	0.67	0.65	0.64
SYD	0.87	0.85	0.84	0.82	0.87	0.80	0.75	0.71	0.70	0.69
0.15										
DDB	0.85	0.81	0.77	0.74	0.71	0.69	0.61	0.56	0.54	0.52
SYD	0.81	0.79	0.76	0.74	0.72	0.70	0.64	0.60	0.58	0.56
0.20										
DDB	0.80	0.75	0.71	0.68	0.64	0.62	0.53	0.48	0.46	0.45
SYD	0.76	0.73	0.70	0.67	0.65	0.63	0.56	0.51	0.49	0.48
0.40										
DDB	0.65	0.59	0.54	0.50	0.46	0.43	0.36	0.31	0.29	0.28
SYD	0.60	0.56	0.52	0.49	0.46	0.44	0.37	0.32	0.30	0.29

EXHIBIT 17   RATIO OF PRESENT OF DEPRECIATION OF DDB AND SYD PLUS VALUE OF INVESTMENT TAX CREDIT (ASSUMING 10%) TO SL WITH ZERO INFLATION, $r = 0.05$

Inflation Rate, h	Service Life of Asset, n (years)								
	3	4	5	6	7	8	12	16	20
0.00									
DDB	1.03	1.06	1.06	1.09	1.10	1.13	1.16	1.18	1.21
SYD	1.02	1.05	1.06	1.09	1.10	1.14	1.18	1.22	1.26
0.01									
DDB	1.01	1.04	1.04	1.07	1.07	1.10	1.11	1.12	1.13
SYD	1.00	1.03	1.04	1.07	1.08	1.11	1.14	1.17	1.20
0.02									
DDB	1.00	1.02	1.02	1.04	1.04	1.07	1.06	1.07	1.07
SYD	0.98	1.01	1.01	1.04	1.05	1.08	1.10	1.12	1.13
0.03									
DDB	0.99	1.00	1.00	1.02	1.01	1.04	1.02	1.02	1.01
SYD	0.97	0.99	0.99	1.02	1.02	1.05	1.06	1.07	1.08
0.05									
DDB	0.96	0.97	0.96	0.97	0.96	0.98	0.95	0.93	0.92
SYD	0.94	0.96	0.95	0.98	0.97	1.00	0.99	0.98	0.98
0.10									
DDB	0.90	0.90	0.87	0.88	0.86	0.87	0.81	0.77	0.75
SYD	0.87	0.88	0.86	0.88	0.88	0.88	0.84	0.82	0.80
0.15									
DDB	0.85	0.83	0.80	0.80	0.77	0.77	0.71	0.66	0.64
SYD	0.81	0.81	0.79	0.80	0.78	0.79	0.74	0.60	0.68
0.20									
DDB	0.80	0.78	0.74	0.73	0.70	0.70	0.63	0.59	0.56
SYD	0.76	0.75	0.73	0.73	0.71	0.72	0.65	0.61	0.59
0.40									
DDB	0.65	0.61	0.56	0.55	0.52	0.52	0.45	0.41	0.39
SYD	0.60	0.59	0.55	0.54	0.52	0.52	0.46	0.42	0.40

Project C, H	DDB with a switchover to straight line (SL) plus 3.33% investment tax credit
Project D, I	DDB with a switchover to SL, plus 10% investment tax credit
Project E, J	10% investment tax credit

Each of the projects requires an initial investment of $1,000, all of it depreciable and eligible for investment tax credit.

The results under the assumption of 20% inflation are summarized in Exhibit 18 and presented graphically in Exhibit 19.

Several valid points emerge in spite of any reservation one might have about generalizing from numerical examples. First, the profitability of short-lived assets is more adversely affected by inflation than that of long-lived assets (other things being equal). This applies to both UAS and IRR. Second, the tax incentives currently in force are inadequate as inflation compensation for assets with lives of 10 years or less. Calculations, not presented above, show that such investments do not receive full compensation if the inflation exceeds 10% per annum. Third, the combination of inflation and investment incentives could change the ranking of investment projects by both UAS and IRR. It should also be borne in mind that unexpected inflation adds risk that was not considered in the analysis.

CAN OVERCOMPENSATION OR UNDERCOMPENSATION FOR INFLATION BE AVOIDED? Is there a simple procedure for adjusting the depreciation tax benefit so that its real value is the same under any inflation rate as it is under no inflation? One way to achieve this is by adjusting depreciation to the general price level, at least for tax purposes. However, this method has its drawbacks. It can also be argued that a replacement cost method should be used.

There is, however, a method by which exact compensation can be given to the firm without requiring price level adjustment or replacement cost determination. Recall that under- or overcompensation is measured relative to $PV(TD)$; **a possible solution is to allow a tax credit of $PV(TD)$ at the time the asset is purchased.** This has a few notable advantages. First, exact compensation is given regardless of the rate of inflation and the asset's service life. Second, the procedure removes the **uncertainty** of inexact compensation, since the firm knows the real value of the tax benefit in advance. Removing such uncertainty is in itself an incentive, assuming that firms are risk averse. Third, because the method is insensitive to the inflation rate, it avoids the need for frequent legislation in response to changing inflation rates and changing expectations concerning them.

Finally, Congress might also want to use the tax credit as a fiscal policy tool. This would be easy to implement. For example, if Congress wished to stimulate investment, a credit of $1.10PV(TD)$ would be allowed, whereas if a slowdown were sought the credit would be reduced to $0.90PV(TD)$.

INFLATION AND COMMON STOCK RETURNS

The determinants of stock prices and returns have long been a target of theoretical and empirical research by students of finance and capital markets. The **capital asset pricing model** (CAPM) developed by Sharpe, Lintner, and Mossin, which is an extension of the portfolio selection framework suggested by Markowitz, has opened the way to a better

EXHIBIT 18   NPV, UAS, AND IRR OF PROJECTS UNDER DIFFERENT INCENTIVE ASSUMPTIONS

	n (years)				
	1	2	5	10	∞
Project:	A	B	C	D	E

NPV

	A	B	C	D	E
No incentives, no inflation	91.7	175.9	389.0	641.8	1,111.1
Incentives, no inflation	91.7	194.9	446.8	774.9	1,211.1
Incentives and 20% inflation	15.3	118.0	321.2	621.5	1,211.1

UAS

	A	B	C	D	E
No incentives, no inflation	100.0	100.0	100.0	100.0	100.0
Incentives, no inflation	100.0	110.87	114.85	120.7	109.0
Incentives and 20% inflation	16.7	67.3	82.6	96.8	109.0

	n (years)				
	1	2	5	10	∞
Project:	F	G	H	I	J

IRR

	F	G	H	I	J
No incentives, no inflation	10.0	10.0	10.0	10.0	10.0
Incentives, no inflation	10.0	11.8	12.6	13.7	11.1
Incentives and 20% inflation	1.7	5.2	7.1	9.7	11.1

understanding of capital assets. This model distinguishes between diversifiable and nondiversifiable risk, and shows that as the number of securities in a portfolio increases, the relative importance of the nondiversifiable risk increases while the importance of each security's own risk diminishes. The model was developed on a set of restrictive assumptions but, as Lintner ("Inflation and Security Returns," *Journal of Finance,* Vol. 30, No. 2, May 1975) asserts, "subsequent work has shown that the essential structure of the model is remarkably robust to generalizations" (p. 263).

Nevertheless, most of the studies to date have been concerned with nominal rather than

**EXHIBIT 19 EFFECT OF INVESTMENT INCENTIVES ON UAS AND IRR UNDER
20% ANNUAL INFLATION AS A FUNCTION OF A PROJECT'S LIFETIME**

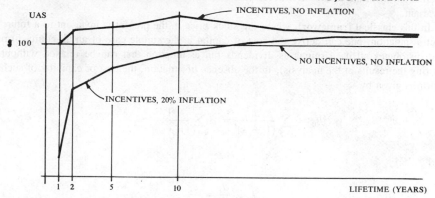

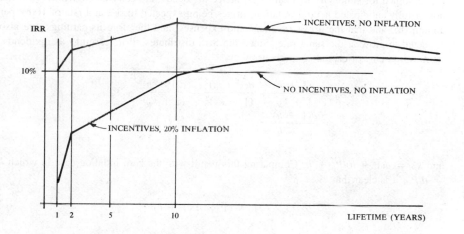

real returns on capital assets. With the persistent inflation of recent years, it must be asked
how stock returns and price react to inflation. Here, classical as well as recent findings must
be considered.

CLASSICAL THEORY AND COST OF CAPITAL UNDER INFLATION. The **classical
model** of the effect of inflation on the cost of capital and stock prices advanced by Irving
Fisher (*The Purchasing Power of Money*, Macmillan, New York, 1920) and John Burr
Williams (*Theory of Investment Value*, Harvard University Press, Cambridge, MA, 1938)
reaches three major conclusions. First, the real return on capital assets is invariant to the
price level, since the returns depend on production functions that are not affected by the
general price level. Second, the real rate of interest is also invariant to the price level. Third,
the real market value of claims against capital assets is equal to the real return on capital

goods capitalized at the real rate of interest. Since the real return as well as the real rate of interest are invariant to the price level per se, it is clear that the real market value is also invariant.

In this **classical framework** where the stock price in the present is invariant to a future neutral inflation, one can derive the cost of capital in the simple case of an all-equity firm that distributes all its earnings as dividends (an assumption that can be relaxed without altering the results of the analysis). In the absence of inflation, the cost of capital k of such a firm is given by

$$P_0 = \sum_{t=1}^{\infty} \frac{d_t}{(1 + k)^t} = d \sum_{t=1}^{\infty} \frac{1}{(1 + k)^t} = \frac{d}{k}$$

and

$$k = \frac{d}{P_0} = \frac{e}{P_0}$$

where P_0 denotes the present market price of the stock, and d_t is the dividend per share in year t, which by assumption is equal to e_t, the earnings per share in year t. Note also that it is assumed for simplicity that earnings, hence dividends, are constant over time. Assume now a fully anticipated neutral inflation, prices being expected to rise at a rate of 100% per annum (h), and that the firm's revenues and expenses, and therefore its earnings, are also expected to grow at the same rate. Since the firm distributes all its earnings as dividends, its **nominal** cost of capital k_N is given by

$$\begin{aligned} P_0 &= \frac{d(1 + h)}{1 + k_N} + \frac{d(1 + h)^2}{(1 + k_N)^2} + \frac{d(1 + h)^3}{(1 + k_N)^3} + \cdots \\ &= \frac{d(1 + h)}{k_N - h} \end{aligned}$$

and $k_N = d(1 + h)/P_0 + h$. Comparing this result with the zero inflation case in which $k = d/P_0$, it is clear that

$$k_N + 1 = (1 + h)(1 + k)$$

or

$$k_N = k(1 + h) + h = k + h + kh$$

where k is the **real** cost of capital and k_N is the nominal cost of capital.

This approach can be clarified by considering a simplified numerical example. Suppose that in the absence of inflation, the minimum required real rate of return on investment is 10%; that is, the firm requires a minimum return of $110 on a $100 investment with a duration of 1 year. What will be the effect of an expected rate of inflation of, say, 10% on the nominal cost of capital k_N? Using $k_N = h(1 + k) + h$, the result is $k_N = 0.10(1.10) + 0.10 = 21\%$.

STOCK PRICES AND INFLATION IN THE CLASSICAL FRAMEWORK. The relationship between stock prices and inflation has been the source of some confusion. Consider a simple case of **no growth,** that is, a firm with constant earnings per share, e, which distributes all these earnings as dividends so that $e = d$, the price of the stock in period t is given by

$$P_t = \frac{d}{1 + k} + \frac{d}{(1 + k)^2} + \cdots = \frac{d}{k}$$

The price of the stock 1 year later, in period $t + 1$, is the same, $P_{t+1} = P_t$.

Now assume a fully anticipated neutral inflation. Today's stock price is given by the capitalization of the new stream of dividends (= earnings) which, by the definition of neutral inflation, will rise at the inflation rate (k_N denotes the new nominal cost of capital):

$$P_t = \frac{d(1 + h)}{1 + k_N} + \frac{d(1 + h)^2}{(1 + k_N)^2} + \cdots = \frac{d(1 + h)}{k_N - h} = \frac{d(1 + h)}{k(1 + h)} = \frac{d}{k}$$

There is no immediate impact on the stock price, since $k_N - h = k(1 + h)$. However, the price of the share one year later is given by:

$$P_{t+1} = \frac{d(1 + h)^2}{1 + k_N} + \frac{d(1 + h)^3}{(1 + k_N)^2} + \cdots = \frac{d(1 + h)^2}{k_N - h}$$

or, $P_{t+1} = P_t(1 + h)$, so that the end-of-period share price rises at the inflation rate. Thus, under the assumptions made, common stocks do provide a **hedge against inflation.**

In the classical framework, the return to the stock of a levered firm increases when the inflation rate over the remaining life of the outstanding debt increases above its expected value. Since the total real value of the firm is invariant to the price level, the loss of real market value of such debt is accompanied by a gain in the real market value of the stock.

Lintner ("Inflation and Common Stock Prices in a Cyclical Context," in National Bureau of Economic Research, 53rd Annual Report, September 1973) points out that subsequent works in the classical framework have replaced leverage by the concept of **net debtor position** (financial liabilities in excess of financial assets). Firms in a net debtor position will enjoy real capital gains when inflation rates rise above the expected rates over the remaining life of their debt.

Since the consolidated balance sheet of U.S. nonfinancial corporations has consistently been in the net-debtor position since 1945 (see Lintner, 1973, op. cit.), the classical theory would predict that the current market value of their stocks should show a more than proportionate capital gain in current money terms to the rates of inflation.

EMPIRICAL EVIDENCE.   The **accumulated empirical evidence** on the relationship between inflation and stock prices does not confirm the classical view. While the classical theory concludes that common stocks provide a hedge against inflation, the empirical evidence is that they fail to do so.

Lintner has examined the relationship between annual stock price changes and annual changes in the general price level. His main findings are as follows:

1. A simple regression between the annual percentage change in stock prices and the annual percentage change in the wholesale price index over a 70-year period showed **no correlation** between these two variables. This result is obtained largely because high inflation rates and serious deflation tend to reduce stock returns. Lintner found that a 10% deflation would reduce stock prices by 15% and a 10% inflation would reduce them by 4.1%.

2. When percentage changes in earnings and interest rates were added to the equation, the explained variance of stock price changes (i.e., the dependent variable) rose to about 33%. Deflation was the most powerful explanatory variable in the equation. A 10% price fall was estimated to **reduce** prices by 33%. A 10% inflation, on the other hand, was estimated to **reduce** stock prices by about 6.7%. Since these are estimates in a multiple regression analysis where percentage changes in earnings and interest rates are included as explanatory variables, these effects on stock prices are **net** of the effect of earnings and interest rates.

Lintner concluded that the classical theory of the relationship between changes in the price level and stock prices is not valid. He noted that the classical theory will hold if (*a*) the **real** returns to ownership of capital goods and (*b*) the real interest rate are invariant to inflation; but there is a good reason to believe that neither premise holds.

Additional evidence contradicting the classical theory is provided in the work of Zvi Bodie ("Common Stocks as a Hedge Against Inflation," *Journal of Finance*, Vol. 31, No. 2, May 1976, pp. 459–470). Bodie's approach to the question of common stock returns and inflation is essentially a portfolio approach. He focuses on the variance of a bond free of default. The risk of such a bond originates solely from the **inflation uncertainty.** Bodie tried to find out to what extent an investor can reduce the uncertainty of the real return on such a nominal bond by combining it with a well diversified portfolio of common stocks.

Consider Exhibit 20 which shows the expected return and standard deviation of a **default-free bond** and (*B*) a **well-diversified portfolio** of common stocks (*S*). Elementary portfolio theory shows that *B* and *S* can be combined into a portfolio whose expected return and standard deviation lie along the curve *BS*. The precise location of the portfolio depends on the proportion of investment allocated to *B* and *S*, and Bodie was concerned with the proportions that bring the portfolio's variance (or standard deviation) to a minimum. If a combination of *B* and *S* can result in a portfolio such as *H* in Exhibit 20, where the standard deviation of *H* (σ_H) is smaller than the standard deviation of *B* (σ_B), equities do provide (at least some) hedge against inflation. Common stocks provide a perfect hedge against

EXHIBIT 20   EFFICIENT FRONTIER BETWEEN *S* AND *B*: STOCK PORTFOLIO *S* IS HELD LONG AT MINIMUM VARIANCE PORTFOLIO *H*

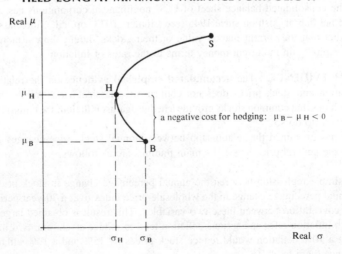

EXHIBIT 21   EFFICIENT FRONTIER BETWEEN S AND B: STOCK PORTFOLIO S IS HELD SHORT AT MINIMUM VARIANCE PORTFOLIO H

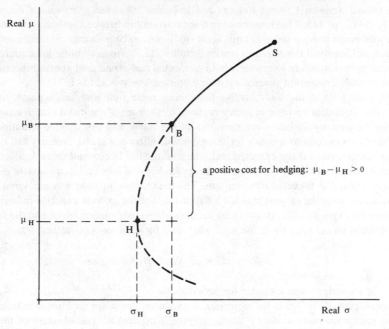

inflation when $\sigma_H = 0$ and a partial hedge when $\sigma_H > 0$. The **cost of hedging** is defined as the difference between the mean real return on the nominal bond (μ_B) and the mean real return on the minimum variance portfolio (μ_H). In Exhibit 20, $\mu_B - \mu_H < 0$. The cost is negative because combining a well-diversified portfolio of common stocks with B not only decreases the risk from σ_B to σ_H, it also increases the return from μ_B to μ_H.

The situation described by Exhibit 20 is not the only possible one, however. In Exhibit 21 the minimum variance portfolio H is not located between the points B and S, but on the extension of the curve SB beyond B. **Portfolio theory** advises that to attain portfolio H, B must be **held** long and S **short.** If empirical findings indicate that the minimum variance portfolio includes the well-diversified stock portfolio S with a negative proportion, that is, S is held short, the situation corresponds to Exhibit 21, and the conclusion is that stocks do not provide a hedge against inflation (when held in long position). The cost of hedging in Exhibit 21 is positive; $\mu_B - \mu_H > 0$, so that one can reduce the variance below σ_B, but only at the cost of reducing the expected value below μ_B.

Using data for 1953–1972, Bodie found that the minimum variance portfolio could indeed be attained only when the common stock portfolio was held short (!), not long. To attain the **minimum variance portfolio,** the investor must sell short about $0.03 worth of equity for every $1.03 invested in nominal bonds. By doing so, the hedger can eliminate roughly 18% of the variance of the real return on the bonds. The cost of such a hedge is a reduction in expected return of 0.34.

Furthermore, Bodie found not only that the real return on equity is negatively correlated with unanticipated inflation, it is also inversely related to anticipated inflation. The estimate he obtained was that an increase of 1 percentage point in the expected rate of inflation is associated with a decline of 4 percentage points in the real return on equity.

Fama and Schwert ("Asset Returns and Inflation," *Journal of Financial Economics,* Vol. 5, 1977, pp. 115–146) have examined the relationship between realized rates of return on various assets and the inflation rate. Their study concerned both expected and unexpected inflation and involved the return to stock portfolios, U.S. Treasury bills, longer term U.S. government bonds, return to privately held residential real estate, and nominal income from human capital. The period covered by their empirical study is 1953–1971.

The main tests in the study involve time series regression analyses, separate for each asset. The dependent variable in such a regression is the asset's nominal rate of return, and the two explanatory variables are measures of **expected and unexpected inflation.** The variable that was used as a proxy for the expected inflation was the Treasury bill nominal rate of interest, since if the expected real return on the bill is constant through time, and if the bill market is efficient, the nominal rate on the bill will be equal to a constant expected real return plus the expected inflation rate. The unexpected inflation was measured by the difference between the **ex post** realized inflation rate and the **ex ante** expected inflation rate. Denoting the expected inflation proxy by x_1, the unexpected inflation by x_2, and the nominal rate of return on an asset by R, the regression used for each asset of interest was

$$R_t = \beta_0 + \beta_1 X_{1t} + \beta_2 X_{2t}$$

where the subscript t denotes value for period t.

A coefficient $B_1 = 1.0$ in the regression would mean that when anticipated inflation rises by one percentage point so does ("on the average") the nominal rate of return on the asset, indicating that the asset is a **hedge against anticipated inflation.** Similarly, a coefficient $\beta_2 = 1.0$ means that when unanticipated inflation rises by 1 percentage point so does ("on the average") the nominal rate of return on the asset, and the asset is a hedge against unanticipated inflation.

Fama and Schwert reached the following main conclusions:

1. Of all assets, only **private residential real estate** was a complete hedge against both expected and unexpected inflation during 1953–1971.

2. Government debt instruments (i.e., bonds and bills) are a complete hedge against **expected** inflation, but not against unanticipated inflation.

3. Common stock returns are negatively related to expected and unexpected inflation. They are also negatively related to changes in expected inflation.

Irwin Friend and Joel Hasbrouck ("Effect of Inflation on the Profitability and Valuation of U.S. Corporations," unpublished paper, Wharton School) have examined the relationship between **rates of return on equity** and the rates of inflation. They found that the negative correlation between these two variables is attributable to two main factors: a decline in **real dividends and earnings of the firms,** and an increase in the **real required rates of return** on stocks. They found that 1 percentage point increase in steady-state inflation is accompanied by 5% decline in dividends and about 10% in real economic earnings per share. Thus inflation tends to decrease economic earnings per share more sharply than cash dividends, implying that the payout ratio increases under inflation. The decrease in dividends and the increase in risk depress stock prices and cause the negative relationship between rates of return on stocks and inflation.

EXPLAINING THE EMPIRICAL EVIDENCE. Lintner ("Inflation and Security Returns," *Journal of Finance*, Vol. 30, No. 2, May 1975, pp. 259–280) advanced a new theory to explain the negative relationship between inflation and stock prices. He assumes **neutral inflation** so that the firm's input and output prices all rise proportionally. He further assumes that capital stock and current rates of real investment are proportional to physical output, depreciation is taken at replacement cost for tax purposes, corporate profits are taxed at a fixed rate, and dividends are a fixed fraction of aftertax profits. With these assumptions, the excess of current dollar outlays for fixed investment over gross funds retained from operations (retained earnings plus depreciation) is a fixed fraction of current dollar sales. These excess outlays are denoted by bS_t, where b is a constant fraction of sales S_t.

Because sources of funds must equal their application, Lintner believes that additional external financing is needed to cover increases in **cash and accounts receivable.** Assuming that cash balances are a fixed ratio of current dollar sales, that a fixed proportion of sales is made on credit, and that the collection period of receivables is not affected by inflation, Lintner argues that the additional demands for external funds is a fixed fraction a of the increase in current dollar sales. The total demand for external funds is therefore $F_t = bS_t + aS_t$.

Exhibit 22 presents a numerical example to demonstrate that in these circumstances the ratio of external funds to sales F_t/S_t increases with inflation rates. The assumptions are: 10% inflation from year 1 to year 2, 30% inflation from year 2 to year 3, $a = 0.6$, and $b = 0.1$. As can be seen, the ratio of external financing to sales increases from 15.4% in year 2 to 23.8% in year 3. Since by assumption profits before and after taxes rise proportionally to sales, and since dividends are a fixed proportion of net profit, it follows that the **ratio of external to internal financing** (retained earnings plus depreciation) **also increases with inflation.** It is important to note that the dependence on external financing increases when inflation **rates** increase, that is, when the price level rises at an increasing rate. If the price level rises at a constant rate, external funds will be proportional to sales and internal funds; if inflation rates decline, the dependence on external funds will decrease. The case of constant inflation rates is illustrated in the last column of Exhibit 22, in which the inflation rate is assumed to be 10% from year 3 as well as from year 1 to year 2. As can be seen, $F_t/S_t = 15.4\%$, as in the year 1 column.

This analysis led Lintner to conclude ("Inflation and Security Returns," *Journal of Finance*, Vol. 30, May 1975, pp. 273–274) that under the assumptions made, the real value of the firm's profits will not change with inflation, but more external financing will be

EXHIBIT 22   NEED FOR EXTERNAL FUNDS UNDER CONSTANT INFLATION RATE AND UNDER INCREASING INFLATION RATE

	Year 1	Year 2	Year 3 Case 1	Year 3 Case 2
Inflation rate per annum	—	10%	30%	10%
S_t	1,000	1,100	1,430	1,210
ΔS_t	—	100	330	110
$bS_t = 0.1S_t$	100	110	143	121
$a\Delta S_t = 0.6\Delta S_t$	—	60	198	66
$F_t = (3) + (4)$	—	170	341	187
F_t/S_t (%)	—	15.4	23.8	15.4

required with rising inflation. Consequently, the share of the **outstanding stock** in the firm's profits (whose real value is unchanged) is reduced. This in turn reduces the **outstanding equity value.**

IS INDEXATION THE ANSWER TO ALL INFLATION PROBLEMS?

In a number of countries, among them some Latin American countries and Israel, indexation has been tried as a way of coping with inflation. The procedure involves price level adjustment of such items as depreciation, inventory, and wages. Theoretically, applying complete indexation would allow firms to avoid the negative effects of inflation. In practice, complete indexation is virtually impossible to achieve. One difficulty is that inflation is not neutral. It affects various revenue and cost items differently. For example, suppose that wages and other cost items fluctuate proportionally to the Consumer Price Index. The firm's product price may rise more slowly, significantly reducing the firm's profit. Indexation theoretically reduces the uncertainty about future prices, thus encouraging investment and lowering the real cost of capital. In some cases, however, indexation may create uncertainty. For example, an exporting firm may suffer losses if exchange rates do not fully adjust to changes in the price level. Indexation (say, of wages) would only reduce the firm's flexibility. The history of indexation shows that in fact it does not provide an effective means of fighting inflation. Its mere existence, moreover, often creates the illusion that a way has been found, and this illusion prevents the search for a really effective solution.

REFERENCES

Bodie, Zvi, "Common Stocks as a Hedge Against Inflation," *Journal of Finance*, Vol. 31, No. 2, May 1976, pp. 459–470.

Brigham, Eugene F., *Financial Management*, Dryden Press, Hinsdale, IL, 1977.

Fama, Eugene F., and Schwert, William G., "Asset Returns and Inflation," *Journal of Financial Economics*, Vol. 5, 1977, pp. 115–146.

Fisher, Irving, *The Purchasing Power of Money*, Macmillan, New York, 1920.

Friend, Irwin, and Hasbrouck, Joel, "Effect of Inflation on the Profitability and Valuation of U.S. Corporations" (unpublished working paper, Wharton School, University of Pennsylvania, 1979).

Hale, David, "Inflation Accounting and Public Policy Around the World," *Financial Analysts Journal*, November–December 1978, pp. 28–40.

Hicks, John R., *Value and Capital*, 2nd ed., Clarendon Press, Oxford, 1957.

Kepcke, R. W., "Current Accounting Practices and Proposals for Reform," *New England Economic Review*, Federal Reserve Bank of Boston, September–October 1976.

Landskroner, Yoram, and Levy, Haim, "Inflation, Depreciation and Optimal Production," *European Economic Review*, Vol. 12, 1978, pp. 353–367.

Lintner, John, "Inflation and Security Returns," *Journal of Finance*, Vol. 30, No. 2, May 1975, pp. 259–280.

———, "Inflation and Common Stock Prices in a Cyclical Context," in National Bureau of Economic Research, 53rd Annual Report, September 1973.

Modigliani, Franco, and Cohn, Richard A., "Inflation, Rational Valuation and the Market," *Financial Analysts Journal*, March–April 1979, pp. 24–44.

Nelson, Charles R., "Inflation and Capital Budgeting," *Journal of Finance*, Vol. 31, No. 3, June 1976, pp. 923–931.

Williams, John Burr, *Theory of Investment Values*, Harvard University Press, Cambridge, MA, 1938.

SECTION **38**

FINANCIAL DECISIONS FOR MULTINATIONAL ENTERPRISES

CONTENTS

WORKING CAPITAL MANAGEMENT 3

International Cash Management 3
    Organization 4
    Cash planning and budgeting 4
    Collection and disbursement of funds 5
    Optimal worldwide cash levels 8
    Management of the short-term
        investment portfolio 9
Accounts Receivable Management 10
    Credit management 10
    Credit extension 10
Inventory Management 12
    Advance inventory purchases 12
    Inventory stockpiling 12

MANAGING INTRACORPORATE
FUND FLOWS 13

The Multinational Financial System 13
    Mode of transfer 13
    Timing flexibility 13
    Value 14
Intracorporate Fund Flow Mechanisms 15
    Transfer pricing 16
    Fees and royalties 17
    Leading and lagging 18
    Intracorporate loans 19
    Dividends 19

FOREIGN INVESTMENT ANALYSIS 21

Capital Budgeting for Multinational
Corporations 21
    Parent versus project cash flows 21
    Financial incentives 22
    Political and economic risk analysis 22
    Currency controls 24
    Exchange rate changes and inflation 25
Cost of Capital for Foreign Investments 27
    Discount rates for foreign projects 27

Empirical evidence on MNC risk 28
Restrictions on international portfolio
    diversification 29
Portfolio diversification versus foreign
    direct investment 29
Management implications of MNC
    investment 30
Political Risk Analysis and Management 30
    Measuring political risk 31
    Avoiding political risk 31
    Political risk insurance 32
    Modifying the environment 33
    Structuring foreign investment 33
    Planned divestment 34
    Short-term profit maximization 34
    Changing the ratio of cost to benefit 34
    Developing local stakeholders 35
    Adaptation 35

FINANCING FOREIGN OPERATIONS 36

Multinational Financial Strategy 36
Foreign Finance Subsidiaries 36
Financing Foreign Subsidiaries 37
    Debt versus equity financing 37
    Government credit and capital controls 37
    Government subsidies 37
    Import financing strategy 38
    Diversification of fund sources 38
    Worldwide financial structure 38
    Subsidiary financial structure 38
    Parent company guarantees and
        consolidation 40
Sources of Funds for MNC Affiliates 41
    Short-term financing 41
    Medium-term financing 41
    Long-term financing 42
    Development banks 42
Evaluating Foreign Currency Borrowing 44

Methodology   44

Short-term financing cost calculations   45

Long-term financing cost calculations   47

Exposure management considerations   49

Borrowing cost comparisons and
market efficiency   49

FINANCIAL DECISIONS FOR MULTINATIONAL ENTERPRISES

Alan C. Shapiro
Richard Karl Goeltz

WORKING CAPITAL MANAGEMENT

INTERNATIONAL CASH MANAGEMENT. International money managers attempt to attain worldwide the traditional domestic objectives of cash management: (1) bringing the company's cash resources within control as quickly and efficiently as possible and (2) achieving the optimum conservation and utilization of these funds. Accomplishing the first goal requires establishing accurate, timely forecasting and reporting systems, improving cash collections and disbursements, and decreasing the cost of moving funds among affiliates. The second objective is achieved by minimizing the required level of cash balances, making money available when and where it is needed, and increasing the risk-adjusted return on the funds that can be invested.

The **principles of domestic and international cash management** are identical, except that international cash management is a more complicated exercise because of its wider scope and the need to recognize the customs and practices of other countries. When considering the movement of funds across national borders, a number of external factors inhibit adjustment and constrain the money manager.

The most obvious is a set of restrictions that impede the free flow of money into or out of a country. Numerous examples exist, such as former U. S. **Overseas Foreign Direct Investment** (OFDI) restrictions, Germany's **Bardepot,** and the requirements of many countries that their exporters repatriate the proceeds of foreign sales within a specific period. Many observers have argued that floating exchange rates would permit the global dismantling of capital controls. Although these regulations have become somewhat less prevalent and more relaxed, they continue to impede the free flow of capital and thereby hinder an **international cash management** program.

There is really only one generalization that can be made about this type of regulation: controls become more stringent during periods of crisis, precisely when financial managers want to act. Thus a large premium is placed on foresight, planning, and anticipation. Aside from a broad statement that borders on being a truism, the basic rule is that government restrictions must be scrutinized on a country-by-country basis to determine realistic options and limits of action.

This section is divided into five key areas of international cash management: organization, **cash planning and budgeting, collecting and disbursing of funds,** setting an optimal level of **worldwide corporate cash balances,** and **investing excess funds.** Currency risk management and netting are covered in the section of this *Handbook* entitled "Exchange Rates and Currency Exposure"; see also "Cash Management."

Organization. Compared with a system of autonomous operating units, a fully centralized international cash management program offers a number of advantages.

- The corporation is able to operate with a smaller amount of cash; pools of excess liquidity are absorbed and eliminated. Each operation maintains transactions balances only and does not hold speculative or precautionary ones.
- By reducing total assets, profitability is enhanced and financing costs reduced.
- The headquarters staff, with its purview of all corporate activity, can recognize problems and opportunities that an individual unit might not perceive.
- All decisions can be made using the overall corporate benefit as the criterion.
- Greater expertise in cash and portfolio management exists if one group is responsible for these activities.
- The corporation's total assets at risk in a foreign country can be reduced. Less will be lost in the event of an expropriation or the promulgation of regulations restricting the transfer of funds.

The foregoing and other benefits have long been understood by many experienced multinational firms. Today, the combination of volatile currency and interest rate fluctuations, questions of capital availability, increasingly complex organizations and operating arrangements, and a growing emphasis on profitability virtually mandates a highly centralized international cash management system. There is also a trend to place much greater responsibility in corporate headquarters. This trend applies to European as well as American firms; see *New Techniques in International Exposure and Cash Management* (Business International Corporation) and *Foreign Exchange Markets Under Floating Rates* (The Group of Thirty).

It should be recognized that centralization does not necessarily imply control by headquarters of all facets of cash management. Instead, it requires a concentration of decision making at a sufficiently high level within the corporation so that all pertinent information is readily available and can be used to maximize the firm's position.

Cash Planning and Budgeting. Cash receipts and disbursements must be reported and forecast in a comprehensive, accurate, and timely manner. If the headquarters staff is to utilize fully and economically the company's worldwide cash resources, they must know the financial positions of affiliates, the forecast cash needs or surpluses, the anticipated cash inflows and outflows, local and international money market conditions, and likely movements in currency values. The form of these reports will vary, depending on the characteristics of the individual firm. Exhibit 1 (pp. **38** · 6–7) shows the reporting format of one multinational firm.

As a result of rapid and pronounced changes in the international monetary arena, the need for more frequent reports has become acute. Firms that had been content to receive information quarterly are now requiring monthly, weekly, or even daily data. Key figures are often transmitted by telex or telecopier instead of by mail.

Collection and Disbursement of Funds.   Accelerating collections both within a foreign country and across borders is a key element of international cash management. Potential benefits exist because long delays often are encountered in collecting receivables, particularly on export sales, and in transferring funds among affiliates and corporate headquarters. Allowing for mail time and bank processing, delays of 8–10 business days are common from the moment an importer pays an invoice to the time when the exporter is credited with funds available for use. Given high interest rates, wide fluctuations in the foreign exchange markets, and the periodic imposition of **credit restrictions** that have characterized financial markets in recent years, cash in transit has become more expensive and more exposed to risk.

With increasing frequency, corporate management is participating in the establishment of an affiliate's **credit policy** and monitoring of **collection performance.** The principal goals of this intervention are to minimize **float** (the transit time of payments), to reduce the investment in **accounts receivable,** and to lower banking fees and other transaction costs. By converting receivables into cash as rapidly as possible, a company can increase its portfolio or reduce its borrowing, earning a higher investment return or saving interest expense.

Considering either national or international collections, accelerating the receipt of funds usually involves: (1) defining and analyzing the different available payment channels, (2) selecting the most efficient method (which can vary by country and customer), and (3) giving specific instructions regarding procedures to the firm's customers and banks.

In addressing the first point, the full costs of using the various methods must be determined and the inherent delay of each calculated. There are **two main sources of delay in the collections process:** the time between the dates of payment and of receipt and the time for the payment to clear through the banking system. Inasmuch as banks will be as "inefficient" as possible to increase **their float,** understanding the subtleties of **domestic and international money transfers** is requisite if a firm is to reduce the time funds are held and extract the maximum value from its banking relationships. A number of multinational banks, particularly U.S. ones, now offer to corporations consulting services that focus on accelerating collections and utilizing funds within a country, the transnational movement and employment of money, or both. Even sophisticated industrial firms are likely to find these services valuable, particularly when they are applied to collections within a country.

Turning to international cash movements, having all affiliates transfer funds by telex enables the corporation to plan better because the vagaries of mail time are eliminated. Third parties, too, are asked to use wire transfers.

To cope with the transmittal delays associated with checks or drafts, customers are instructed in some cases to remit to **"mobilization" points,** which are centrally located in important regions with large sales volumes. The funds are managed centrally or transmitted to the selling subsidiary. For example, all European customers may be told to make all payments to Switzerland, where the corporation maintains a staff specializing in cash and portfolio management and collections. A variation is to intercept all collections within a country and forward them to a central corporate point. **Intracountry collection methods** vary, but they are usually constrained by prevailing trade customs.

Sometimes customers are asked to pay directly into a designated account at a branch of the bank that is mobilizing the funds of the multinational corporation internationally. This is particularly useful when banks have large branch networks. Another technique that is used both domestically and internationally is to have customers remit funds to a designated **lock box,** which is a postal box in the company's name. A local bank or branch of a multinational bank takes and opens the mail received at the lock box one or more times daily. Any deposit or transfer made is immediately reported to the national or regional mobilization office.

EXHIBIT 1 FORM OF CASH FLOW STATEMENT FOR A MULTINATIONAL FIRM

	1st Month		2nd Month		3rd Month			12th Month	
	Plan	Actual	Plan	Actual	Plan	Actual	. . . . .	Plan	Actual
Receipts									
Collections									
Domestic									
Export to nonaffiliates									
Export to affiliates									
Discounted trade bills									
Other Receipts									
Total cash receipts									
Disbursements									
Wages, salaries, and benefits									
Capital expenditures									
Maturing inventories									
Other inventories									
Payments to affiliates									
Advertising and marketing expenses									
Import duties and excise taxes									
Circulation tax (sales tax)									
Income and capital taxes									

Interest
External
Intracompany
Other expenses
 Total disbursements
Net receipts/(disbursements)
Cash, beginning of period
Plus:
 External borrowing
 Intracompany borrowing
Less: Repayments
 External borrowing
 Intracompany borrowing
Cash, end of period

Memo: Short-term borrowing, end of period

Credit for the funds is then given to the company, usually on the same day. The period spent in transit can thereby be reduced from up to a week to 1 or 2 days.

To reduce clearing time, some companies set up accounts in their customers' banks, a useful device if there are only a few large customers or the check clearing time is quite lengthy. Some firms have gone one step further and directly debit their customers. In **direct debiting**, or preauthorized payment, the customer allows its account to be charged periodically by the supplier or the supplier's bank up to a maximum amount. With this method, there is no customer payment delay, intentional or inadvertent, and mail delay is eliminated. Clearing time can also be reduced by initiating debiting the correct number of days before the due date.

Regarding disbursements, most European banks operate on a **debit transfer** basis, whereby the customer's account is charged immediately, giving the bank, as opposed to the payer, the advantage of the float. By contrast, U.S. banks operate on a **credit transfer** basis, granting the payer the benefit of the float until the check clears. Furthermore, on international transactions, European banks will debit a company's account 2 days before foreign funds are made available. American banks, though, usually provide a firm with **value compensation;** that is, the firm does not give up domestic funds until the foreign funds are provided.

Optimal Worldwide Cash Levels.   Centralized cash management typically involves the transfer of an affiliate's cash in excess of minimal operating requirements into a central account (pool) where all corporate funds are managed by corporate staff. Some firms have established a special corporate entity that collects and disburses funds through a single bank account.

With **cash pooling,** each affiliate need hold **locally** only the minimum cash balance required for transaction purposes. All **precautionary balances** are held by the parent or in the pool. As long as the demands for cash by the various units are reasonably independent of each other, centralized cash management can provide an equivalent degree of protection with a lower level of cash reserves. For example, assume that each of a multinational's three foreign affiliates has the following probability distribution of cash demands during the next month: a 70% chance of needing \$100,000, a 25% chance of needing \$250,000, and a 5% chance of needing \$500,000. If cash management is decentralized, each of the three units must hold \$250,000 (or a total of \$750,000) to achieve a safety level of 95%, that is, to ensure that the probability that a given affiliate will run short of cash is no greater than 5%. However, on a worldwide bases, the likelihood that all three affiliates will require at least \$250,000 simultaneously is only $.30^3 = .027$, provided these cash demands are independent of each other. Unless funds can be shifted, the probability that at least one unit will run short of cash is $1 - .95^3 = .1426$, even though \$750,000 is being held overall (i.e., the overall safety level is only 85.74%). With centralization, only \$600,000 need be held to achieve a safety level of 84.16% for the corporation as a whole because funds are no longer restricted as to use. Cash reserves of \$750,000 will increase the overall safety level to 93.09%, while \$850,000 will reduce the probability of a cash shortage anywhere in the firm to less than 2%.

The derivation of these probabilities is shown in Exhibit 2. Events A, B, and C denote cash requirements, of \$100,000, \$250,000, and \$500,000, respectively. The various possible event sets, their probabilities, and the funds required to satisfy the demand associated with each event are listed in order of ascending cash requirements. For instance, the event AAB refers to any two affiliates facing cash demands of \$100,000 and one unit needing \$250,000, for a total funds requirement of \$450,000 with probability $3(.7)^2(.25) = .3675$.

EXHIBIT 2   CASH FLOW POOLING PROBABILITIES: A FORECASTING EXAMPLE

Event	Probability	Cumulative Probability	Cash Requirement
AAA	$.7^3 = .343$	.343	$ 300,000
AAB	$3(.7)^2(.25) = .3675$	.7105	450,000
ABB	$3(.7)(.25)^2 = .13125$	.84175	600,000
AAC	$3(.7)^2(.05) = .0735$	.91525	700,000
BBB	$.25^3 = .015625$	.930875	750,000
ABC	$6(.7)(.25)(.05) = .0525$	.983375	850,000
BBC	$3(.25)^2(.05) = .009375$	.99275	1,000,000
ACC	$3(.7)(.05)^2 = .00525$	.998	1,100,000
BCC	$3(.25)(.05)^2 = .001875$	.999875	1,250,000
CCC	$.05^3 = .000125$	1.0	1,500,000
Event A	cash requirement of $100,000		
Event B	cash requirement of $250,000		
Event C	cash requirement of $500,000		

Management of the Short-Term Investment Portfolio. A major task of international cash management is to determine the levels and currency denominations of the multinational group's investment in cash balances and money market instruments. Firms with seasonal or cyclical cash flows have special problems such as arranging investment maturities to coincide with projected needs.

To manage this investment properly requires a forecast of future cash needs based on the company's current budget and past experience as well as an estimate of a minimum cash position for the coming period. These projections should take into account the effects of inflation and anticipated currency changes on future cash flows.

Common-sense **guidelines for managing the marketable securities portfolio globally** include:

1. The instruments in the portfolio should be diversified to minimize the risk for a given level of return or to maximize the yield for a given level of risk. Government securities should not be used exclusively. Eurodollar and other instruments may be nearly as safe.

2. The portfolio must be reviewed daily to decide which securities are to be liquidated and what new investments made.

3. In revising the portfolio, care should be taken to ensure that the incremental interest earned more than compensates for added costs such as clerical work, the income lost between investments, fixed charges, such as the foreign exchange spread, and commissions on the sale and purchase of securities.

4. If conversion to cash rapidly is an important consideration, the marketability (liquidity) of the instrument should be carefully evaluated. Ready markets exist for some securities but not others.

5. The maturity of the investment should be tailored to the firm's projected cash needs or a secondary market with high liquidity should exist.

6. Opportunities for **covered** or **uncovered interest arbitrage** should be carefully considered.

Some observers have attributed a major portion of the turbulence in foreign exchange markets to multinational corporations and their aggressive (or defensive) international cash management programs. Corporations do exercise control over massive amounts of liquidity and clearly possess the power to disrupt markets. Their activities, particularly in **leading and lagging payments,** have contributed on occasion to a sharp appreciation or depreciation of individual currencies, but whether they are primarily responsible for the tumult of recent years is a more difficult question to answer. In May 1971 the U.S. Department of Commerce stated, "major multinational corporations . . . played only a limited role in recent massive movements of dollars into foreign central banks." More recently, an article in the Federal Reserve Bank of Boston's *New England Economic Review* (March–April 1979) examined the role of corporations and banks as foreign exchange speculators. Admitting that only a tentative conclusion was possible, the author said, "the foreign exchange market activity reported by U.S. firms is not demonstrably destabilizing."

ACCOUNTS RECEIVABLE MANAGEMENT.   Multinational corporations (MNCs) and domestic firms face the same decisions regarding the appropriate level of accounts receivable. In the multinational firm, though, this exercise is complicated by the existence of different rates of inflation, **foreign exchange fluctuations,** and restrictions within a market or on currency transfers.

Credit Management.   Firms grant trade credit to customers, both domestically and internationally, because they expect the investment in receivables to be profitable, either by expanding sales volume or by retaining sales that otherwise would be lost to competitors. Some companies also earn a profit on the financing charges they levy on credit sales.

The need to scrutinize credit terms is particularly important in countries experiencing rapid rates of **inflation.** The incentive for customers to defer payment, liquidating their debts with less valuable money in the future, is great. Furthermore, **credit standards** abroad are often more relaxed than in the home market, especially in countries lacking alternative sources of credit for small customers. To remain competitive, MNCs may feel compelled to loosen their own credit standards. Finally, the compensation system in many companies tends to reward higher sales more than it penalizes an increased investment in accounts receivable. Local managers frequently have an incentive to expand sales even if the corporation overall does not benefit.

Credit Extension.   The easier credit terms are, the more sales are likely to be made. Generosity is not always the best policy. The risk of default, increased interest expense on the larger investment in receivables, and the deterioration through **currency devaluation** of the dollar value of accounts receivable denominated in the buyer's currency must be balanced against higher revenues. These additional costs may be partly offset if liberalized **credit terms** enhance a firm's ability to raise its prices.

Another factor that tends to increase accounts receivable in foreign countries is an uneconomic expansion of local sales, which may occur if managers are credited with dollar sales when accounts receivable are denominated in the local currency (LC). Sales managers should be charged for the expected depreciation in the value of local currency accounts receivable. For instance, if the current exchange rate is LC_1 = $0.10 but the expected exchange rate 90 days hence (or the 3-month forward rate) is $0.09, managers providing 3-month credit terms should be credited with only $0.90 for each dollar in sales booked at the current spot rate.

Whether judging the implications of inflation, devaluation, or both, it must be remembered that when a unit of inventory is sold on credit, a **real asset** has been transformed into a **monetary asset.** The opportunity to raise the local currency selling price of the item to maintain its dollar value is lost. This point is obvious but frequently disregarded.

Assuming that both buyer and seller have access to credit at the same cost and reflect in their decisions anticipated currency changes and inflation, it should normally make no difference to a potential customer whether he receives additional credit or an equivalent cash discount. The MNC may benefit by revising its credit terms, however, in three circumstances:

1. The buyer and seller hold different opinions concerning the future course of inflation or currency changes, leading one of the two to prefer term-price discount tradeoffs (i.e., a lower cost if paid within a specified period).

2. Because of market imperfections, the MNC has a lower risk-adjusted cost of credit than does its customer. In other words, the buyer's higher financing cost must not be a result of its greater riskiness.

3. During periods of credit restraint in a country, the affiliate of an MNC may, because of its parent, gain a marketing advantage over its competitors through having access to funds that are not available to local companies. Absolute availability of money, rather than its cost, may be critical.

The following analytical approach enables a firm to compare the expected benefits and costs associated with **extending credit internationally.** The same analysis can also be used in domestic credit extension decisions, with inflation rather than currency fluctuations being the complicating factor. Let ΔS and ΔC be the incremental sales and costs, respectively, associated with an easing of credit terms. If the expected credit cost per unit of sales revenues R is expected to increase to $R + \Delta R$ because of a more lenient credit policy, terms should be eased if, and only if, incremental profits are greater than incremental credit costs or

$$\Delta S - \Delta C \geqq S\Delta R + \Delta S(R + \Delta R)$$

It should be noted that ΔR reflects forecast changes in currency values as well as the cost of funds over the longer collection period. This analysis can be used to ascertain whether it would be worthwhile to tighten credit, accepting lower sales but at the same time reducing credit costs.

To illustrate the use of this approach, suppose that a subsidiary in France currently has annual sales of $1 million with 90-day credit terms. It is believed that sales will increase by 6% ($60,000) if terms are extended to 120 days. Of these additional sales, the cost of goods sold is $35,000. Monthly (30-day) credit expenses are 1% in financing charges. In addition, a 1.5% depreciation of the franc is expected over the next 90 days.

Ignoring currency changes for the moment but considering financing costs, the value today of $1 of receivables to be collected at the end of 90 days is approximately $0.97. Taking into account the 1.5% expected franc devaluation, this value declines to $0.97(1 - 0.015)$ or $0.955. Similarly, $1 of receivables collected 120 days from now is worth $[1 - (0.01)4]$ $[1 - (0.015 + d_4)]$ today or $0.945 - 0.96d_4$, where d_4 (unknown) is the amount of currency change during the fourth month. Then, the cost of carrying French franc receivables for 3 months is 4.5%, while the incremental cost for the fourth month equals $0.955 - (0.945 - 0.96d_4)$ dollar or $1\% + 96d_4\%$.

Using the formula previously presented, $\Delta S - \Delta C = \$25,000$, $S\Delta R = \$1,000,000$ $(0.01 + 0.96d_4) = \$10,000 + \$960,000d_4$, and $\Delta S(R + \Delta R) = \$60,000 (0.045 + 0.01 + 0.96d_4) = \$3,300 + \$57,600d_4$. Then, credit extension is worthwhile only if the incremental profit, \$25,000, is greater than the incremental cost, $\$13,300 + \$1,017,600d_4$ or

$$d_4 < \frac{11,700}{1,017,600} = 1.15\%$$

One potential problem when evaluating the desirability of extending credit to obtain greater sales is the **reaction of competition.** It is likely that in an oligopoly, if one firm cuts its effective price by granting longer payment terms, its competitors will be forced to follow to maintain their market positions. The result could well be no incremental sales and profits for any firm, but only greater accounts receivable for all.

INVENTORY MANAGEMENT.   Although conceptually the **inventory management problems** faced by multinational firms are not unique, they may be exaggerated in the case of foreign operations. For instance, MNCs typically have greater difficulty in controlling their overseas inventory and realizing inventory turnover objectives for a variety of reasons, including long and variable transit times if ocean transportation is used, lengthy customs proceedings and possibilities of dock strikes, import controls, supply disruption, anticipated changes in currency values, and higher customs duties.

Advance Inventory Purchases.   In many developing countries, forward contracts for foreign currency are limited in availability or nonexistent. In addition, restrictions often preclude free remittances, making it difficult if not impossible to convert excess funds into a hard currency. One means of **hedging** is anticipatory purchases of goods, especially imported items. The tradeoff involves owning goods for which local currency prices may be increased, thereby maintaining the dollar value of the asset even though inflation and devaluation are virulent, versus forgoing the return on local portfolio investments or not being able to take advantage of potentially favorable fluctuations in the specific prices of these materials. (The attractiveness of holding investments in **local currency money market instruments** is frequently overlooked; the aftertax dollar yield, adjusted fully for devaluation, may be positive, sometimes spectacularly so.)

Inventory Stockpiling.   The problem of supply failure is of particular importance for any firm dependent on foreign sources because of long delivery lead times, the often limited availability of transport for economically sized shipments, and currency restrictions. These conditions may make the knowledge and execution of an optimal stocking policy under a threat of a disruption to supply more critical in the MNC than in the firm that purchases domestically.

The traditional response to such risks has been advance purchases. According to Business International (*Decision-Making in International Operations*): "If sourcing from a risky area for international corporations, stockpile goods outside the country and plan for and cultivate alternative supply sources." Holding large quantities of inventory can be quite expensive, though. In fact, the high cost of stockpiling inventory, including financing, insurance, storage, and obsolescence, has led many companies to identify low inventories with effective management. In contrast, production and sales managers typically desire a relatively large inventory, particularly when a cutoff in supply is anticipated.

It is obvious that as the probability of disruption increases or as holding costs go down, more inventory should be ordered. Similarly, if the cost of a stockout rises or if future supplies are expected to be more expensive, it will pay to stockpile additional inventory. Conversely, if these parameters move in the opposite direction, less inventory should be stockpiled.

MANAGING INTRACORPORATE FUND FLOWS

THE MULTINATIONAL FINANCIAL SYSTEM.   The ability to adjust intracorporate fund flows and accounting profits on a global basis is potentially of great advantage to the multinational corporation. However, inasmuch as most of the gains derive from the MNC's proficiency at taking advantage of openings in tax laws or regulatory barriers, conflicts between a government and the firm are quite likely.

Financial transactions within the MNC result from the internal transfer of goods, services, technology, and capital. These product and factor flows range from intermediate and finished goods to less tangible items such as management skills, trademarks, and patents. The transactions not liquidated immediately give rise to some type of financial claim such as royalties for the use of a patent or accounts receivable for goods sold on credit. In addition, capital investments lead to future flows of dividends and/or interest and principal repayments. Some of the myriad financial linkages possible in the MNC are depicted in Exhibit 3.

Although all the links portrayed in Exhibit 3 can and do exist among independent firms, as pointed out by Lessard ("Transfer Prices, Taxes, and Financial Markets," in Robert G. Hawkins, Ed., *The Economic Effects of Multinational Corporations*, JAI Press, Greenwich, CT, 1979), the MNC has greater control over the mode and timing of these financial transfers.

Mode of Transfer.   The MNC has considerable freedom in selecting the **financial channels** through which to move funds, allocate profits, or both. For example, patents and trademarks can be sold outright or transferred in return for a contractual stream of royalty payments. By varying the prices at which transactions occur, profits and cash can be shifted within the worldwide organization. Similarly, funds can be moved from one unit to another by adjusting **transfer prices** on intracorporate sales and purchases of goods and services. With regard to **investment flows,** capital can be sent overseas as debt with at least some choice of interest rate, currency of denomination, and repayment schedule, or as equity with returns in the form of dividends. The multinational firm can use these various channels, singly or in combination, to transfer funds internationally, depending on the specific circumstances encountered. Furthermore, within the limits of various national laws and with regard to the relations between a foreign affiliate and its host government, these flows may be more advantageous than those that would result from dealings with independent firms.

Timing Flexibility.   Some of the internally generated financial claims require a fixed payment schedule; others can be accelerated or delayed. This leading and lagging is most often applied to **interaffiliate trade credit** where a change in open account terms from, say, 90 to 180 days, can involve massive shifts in liquidity. (Some nations, both developed and less developed, have regulations concerning the repatriation of the proceeds of export sales. Thus, typically, there is not complete freedom to move funds by **leading and lagging.**) In addition, the timing of fee and royalty payments may be modified when all parties to the agreement

EXHIBIT 3   FINANCIAL LINKAGES FOR THE MNC[a]

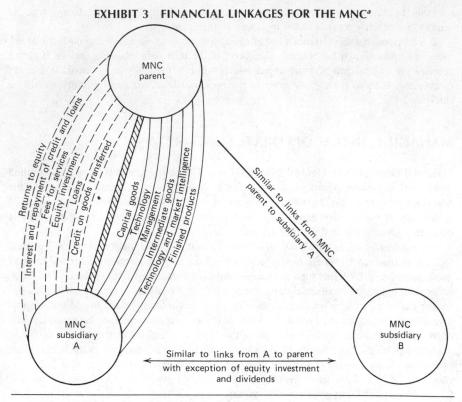

[a]Solid lines, real flows; dotted lines, financial flows.
Source: Reprinted with permission from Donald R. Lessard, "Transfer Prices, Taxes, and Financial Markets," in Robert G. Hawkins, Ed., *The Economic Effects of Multinational Corporations,* JAI Press, Greenwich, CT, 1979.

are related. Even if the contract cannot be altered once agreed upon, the MNC generally has latitude when the terms are established initially.

In the absence of **exchange controls,** firms have the greatest amount of flexibility in the timing of equity claims. The earnings of a foreign affiliate can be retained or used to pay dividends which, in turn, can be deferred or paid in advance.

Value.   Lessard also points out that the ability to transfer funds and to reallocate profits internally presents multinationals with three different types of arbitrage opportunity:

1. *Tax arbitrage.* By shifting profits from units located in high-tax nations to those in lower tax nations or from those in a taxpaying position to those with tax losses, MNCs can reduce their burden.

2. *Financial market arbitrage.* By transferring funds among units, MNCs may be able to circumvent exchange controls, earn higher risk-adjusted yields on excess funds, reduce their risk-adjusted cost of borrowed funds, and tap previously unavailable capital sources.

3. *Regulatory system arbitrage*. Where **subsidiary profits** are a function of government regulations (e.g., where a government agency sets allowable prices on the firm's goods) or union pressure, rather than the marketplace, the ability to disguise true profitability by reallocating profits among units may provide the multinational firm with a negotiating advantage.

There is also a fourth arbitrage opportunity—the ability to permit an affiliate to negate the effect of credit restraint or controls in its country of operation. If a government limits access to additional borrowing locally, the firm with the ability to draw on external sources of funds not only can achieve greater short-term profits, but it may also be able to attain a more powerful market position over the long term.

INTRACORPORATE FUND FLOW MECHANISMS.   The MNC can be visualized as **unbundling** the total **flow of funds** between each pair of affiliates into separate components, which are associated with resources transferred in the form of products, capital, services, and technology. For example, dividends, interest, and loan repayments can be matched against capital invested as equity or debt, while fees, royalties, or corporate overhead can be charged for various corporate services, trademarks, or licenses.

As part of the analysis of these transfer techniques of multinationals, it is useful to look first at the historical remittance patterns of U.S. firms. Exhibit 4 contains a breakdown of earnings repatriated as either **fees and royalties** or **dividends** and **interest** during the years 1966 through 1976. It also shows the percentage of overseas earnings actually remitted.

The most noticeable point is the stable relative contribution of each component. On average, dividend and interest payments account for approximately 75% of these flows with fees and royalties making up the remaining 25%. The data suggest a slight growth in the relative importance of fees and royalties. One can also conclude that the earnings payout rate (the ratio of remitted to total earnings) has been declining somewhat over time, from 85.5% in 1966 to 77.6% in 1976.

These data present only a partial description, however, in that MNCs have a large degree of flexibility in shifting funds by means other than the traditional dividend or fee remittance

EXHIBIT 4   AGGREGATE REMITTANCE PRACTICES OF U.S. MULTINATIONALS, 1966–1976 ($ MILLIONS)

Year	Total Earnings	Total Remittances	% of Total Earnings	Dividends and Interest	% of Total Remittances	Fees and Royalties	% of Total Remittances
1966	5,259	4,497	85.5	3,467	77.1	1,030	22.9
1967	5,605	4,983	88.9	3,847	77.2	1,136	22.8
1968	6,592	5,431	82.4	4,152	76.4	1,279	23.6
1969	7,449	6,501	87.3	4,819	74.1	1,682	25.9
1970	8,169	6,911	84.6	4,992	72.2	1,919	27.8
1971	9,159	8,143	88.9	5,983	73.5	2,160	26.5
1972	10,949	8,845	80.8	6,416	72.5	2,429	27.5
1973	16,542	11,222	67.8	8,384	74.7	2,838	25.3
1974	19,156	14,449	75.4	11,379	78.8	3,070	21.2
1975	16,615	12,110	72.9	8,567	70.7	3,543	29.3
1976	18,841	14,648	77.6	11,126	76.0	3,522	24.0

Source: U.S. Department of Commerce, *Survey of Current Business,* various issues.

routes. The most important additional channels include transfer price adjustments, leading and lagging, and intracorporate loans.

Transfer Pricing. The pricing of goods and services traded internally is one of the most sensitive of all management subjects, and executives are typically reluctant to discuss it. Each government normally presumes that multinationals use transfer pricing to the detriment of the host country. For this reason, a number of home and host governments have set up policing mechanisms to review the **transfer pricing policies of MNCs.**

The most important uses of transfer pricing include:

1. Diminishing taxes.
2. Reducing tariffs.
3. Avoiding exchange controls.

To illustrate the **tax effects** associated with a change in transfer price, suppose that subsidiary A is selling 100,000 circuit boards annually to subsidiary B at a unit price of $10. A change in price to $10.50 would simultaneously increase A's income by $50,000 and reduce B's income by the same amount. Assuming that the marginal tax rates on income for A and B, respectively, are 0.35 and 0.50, this transfer price change will increase A's taxes by $17,500 (0.35 × $50,000) and lower B's taxes by $25,000 (0.5 × $50,000) for a net corporate tax saving of $7,500 annually. In effect, profits are being shifted from a higher to a lower tax jurisdiction. In the extreme case, an affiliate may be in a loss position because of high startup costs, heavy depreciation changes, or substantial investments that are expensed. The MNC would forecast when that affiliate would pay taxes and determine the net present value tax rate, which by definition must be less than the statutory one.

With respect to tariffs, companies will usually set a relatively low price on goods exported to countries with high ad valorem duties. This practice will enable the purchasing affiliate to price the goods competitively with no loss of revenue to the corporation overall.

Most countries have specific regulations governing transfer prices. For instance, **Section 482 of the U.S. Revenue Code** grants the Secretary of the Treasury the following powers:

> In any case of two or more organizations, trades, or businesses (whether or not incorporated, whether or not organized in the United States, and whether or not affiliated) owned or controlled directly or indirectly by the same interests, the Secretary or his delegate may distribute, apportion, or allocate gross income, deductions, credits, or allowances between or among such organizations, trades, or businesses, if he determines that such distribution, apportionment, or allocation is necessary in order to prevent evasion of taxes or clearly to reflect the income of any of such organizations, trades, or businesses.

The regulations specify three methods of pricing, which are to be applied in the following order: (1) comparable uncontrolled price, (2) resale price, (3) cost plus (Fuller, "Section 482 Revisited," *Tax Law Review,* Vol. 31, 1976). The government's strong and stated preference is for **arm's-length prices,** those that a willing buyer and a willing, unrelated seller would freely accept.

In light of Section 482, the U.S. government's willingness to use it, and similar authority in most other nations, the current practice by MNCs appears to be set standard prices for standardized products. However, the innovative nature of the typical multinational ensures a continual stream of new products for which no market equivalent exists. Some flexibility is possible in setting transfer prices. Furthermore, many of the items sold internally are components and subassemblies for which no external market exists. Firms also have a great deal of latitude in setting prices on rejects, scrap, and returned goods.

Based on their detailed interviews with 39 U.S.-based MNCs, Robbins and Stobaugh (*Money in the Multinational Enterprise*), concluded that although tax minimization is a principal goal of transfer pricing, reducing the effect of **exchange controls** is also quite important. For example, the MNC may raise the intracompany price for sales to an affiliate with blocked funds, accepting a larger global tax liability but reducing the affiliate's funds exposed to devaluation and other types of loss. To determine the attractiveness of this step, the effective income tax rates of the selling and purchasing subsidiaries, the probable duration of the blocking, and alternative investment opportunities for the affiliate with the excess funds must be known or estimated.

Fees and Royalties.   Management services such as headquarters advice, allocated overhead, patents, and trademarks are often unique and, therefore, without a reference market price. The consequent difficulty in pricing these corporate resources makes them suitable for use as additional routes for international fund flows by varying the fees or royalties charged for the use of these intangible factors of production.

Transfer prices for services have the same tax and **exchange control** effects as transfer prices on goods do, but they are often subject to even greater scrutiny. However, host governments often look with more favor on payments for industrial know-how than for **profit remittances.** Restrictions that do exist are more likely to be modified to permit a fee for technical knowledge rather than dividends.

Leading and Lagging.   A highly favored means of shifting liquidity between affiliates is an acceleration or delay (leading and lagging) in the payment of interaffiliate accounts by modifying the credit terms extended by one unit to another. For example, suppose affiliate A sells goods worth $1 million monthly to affiliate B on 90-day credit terms. On average, A has $3 million of accounts receivable from B and is, in effect, financing $3 million of working capital for B. If the terms are changed to 180 days, there will be a one-time shift of an additional $3 million to B. Conversely, a reduction in credit terms to 30 days will involve a flow of $2 million from B to A. This is shown in Exhibit 5.

Inasmuch as incremental accounts receivable are financed typically by short-term debt, the costs of leading and lagging are evaluated in the same way as any other use of different sources of borrowing, that is, by considering relevant interest and tax rates and the likelihood of changes in currency value.

A 1977 survey by Business International (*New Techniques in International Exposure and Cash Management*) indicates how prevalent leading and lagging is. According to that survey, over 65% of all European and U.S.-based multinationals engage in this direct form of intracompany lending. Some firms prefer not to use this technique because they feel it compromises discipline. The attitude that invoices should be paid on time, not before or after, seems to be more prevalent among European companies. To the extent that greater control is concentrated in corporate headquarters, this technique can be used more readily and effectively.

Intracorporate Loans.   A principal means of financing foreign operations and moving funds internationally is intracorporate lending activities. Although a variety of types of intracorporate loan exist, the most important methods currently are **direct loans, back-to-back financing, parallel loans,** and **currency swaps.** The first is a straight extension of

EXHIBIT 5   FUND TRANSFER EFFECTS OF LEADING AND LAGGING: SUBSIDIARY A SELLS $1 MILLION IN GOODS MONTHLY TO SUBSIDIARY B

Balance Sheet Accounts	Credit Terms		
	Normal (90 days)	Leading (30 days)	Lagging (180 days)
Subsidiary A Accounts receivable from B	$3,000,000	$1,000,000	$6,000,000
Subsidiary B Accounts payable to A	3,000,000	1,000,000	6,000,000
Net Cash Transfers From B to A	—	$2,000,000	—
From A to B	—	—	$3,000,000

credit from the parent to an affiliate or from one affiliate to another. The others typically involve an intermediary.

Back-to-back loans (also called **fronting loans** or **link financing**) are often employed to finance affiliates located in nations with high interest rates or restricted capital markets, especially when there is a danger of **currency controls,** or when different rates of withholding tax are applied to loans from a financial institution. In the typical arrangement, the parent company deposits funds with a bank in country A, which in turn lends the money to a subsidiary in country B. In effect, a back-to-back loan is an **intracorporate loan** channeled through a bank. From the bank's point of view, the loan is risk-free because the parent's deposit fully collateralizes it. The bank just acts as an intermediary or a "front"; compensation is provided by the margin between the interest received from the borrowing unit and the rate paid on the parent's deposit.

A back-to-back loan may offer several potential advantages compared with a direct intracorporate loan. Two of the more important are:

1. Certain countries apply different withholding tax rates to interest paid to a foreign parent and to a financial institution. A cost saving in the form of lower taxes may be available with a back-to-back loan.

2. If currency controls are imposed, the government will usually permit the local subsidiary to honor the amortization schedule of a loan from a major multinational bank; to stop payment would hurt the nation's credit rating. Conversely, local monetary authorities would have far fewer reservations about not authorizing the repayment of an intracompany loan. In general, back-to-back financing provides better protection against expropriation and/or exchange controls than does an intracompany loan.

Some authors argue that a back-to-back loan conveys another benefit. The subsidiary seems to have obtained credit from a major bank on its own, possibly enhancing its reputation. This appearance is unlikely to be significant in the highly informed international financial community.

A **parallel loan** is a method of effectively repatriating **blocked funds** (at least for the term of the arrangement), circumventing exchange control restrictions, avoiding a premium exchange rate for investments abroad, or obtaining foreign currency financing at attractive rates. It consists of two related but separate, or parallel, borrowings and usually involves four parties in two different countries. The parent A will extend a loan in its home country and currency to a subsidiary of B, whose foreign parent will lend the local currency equivalent in its country to the subsidiary of A. Drawdowns, repayments of principal, and payments of interest are made simultaneously. The differential between the rates of interest on the two loans is determined in theory by the cost of money in each country and anticipated changes in currency values.

A **currency swap** achieves an economic purpose similar to a **parallel loan** but generally is simpler, involving only two parties and one agreement. Two companies sell currencies to each other and undertake to reverse the exchange after a fixed term. Unlike parallel loans, interest is not paid by both parties; in a currency swap, a fee or commission is paid by one to the other. This commission in effect is equivalent to the **forward foreign exchange premium or discount,** which in turn should reflect interest rate differentials. The **spread** is fixed for a number of years and consequently does not fluctuate as a forward discount or premium will.

Depending on the tax positions of the parent and its affiliate, the commission in a currency swap may offer some benefits to the corporation overall compared with the alternative of interest income and expense involved in a parallel loan arrangement. In addition, the **right of offset** may be more firmly established in a currency swap.

For both transactions, an exchange adjustment, or **"topping-up,"** clause may be sought. If one currency were to depreciate sharply, the borrower of it would be required to advance additional funds to the other party so that both amounts would remain roughly equivalent in value at the spot rates prevailing throughout the term of the agreement. This convenant provides protection against credit risk; see Suhar and Lyons, "Choosing Between a Parallel Loan and a Swap" (*Euromoney*, March 1979).

Since the **currency swap** is not a loan, it is not reflected as a liability on the parties' balance sheets. Whether a parallel loan appears in a corporation's consolidated financial statements depends on whether a **right of offset** exists. If one does, the net of the asset and liability need be shown; this will, of course, be zero when the loans receivable and payable in U.S. dollars are identical, as they will be if currency values do not change or a topping-up provision exists. If a right of offset is not one of the provisions in the agreement, the asset and liability are shown gross (SEC Staff Accounting Bulletin Topic 10-E, paragraph 7805).

Dividends.   This is by far the **most important means of transferring funds from foreign affiliates to the parent company,** accounting for over 50% of all remittances to U.S. firms in 1977. Among the various factors that MNCs consider when deciding on dividend payments by their affiliates are taxes, financial statement effect, exchange risk, currency controls, financing requirements, availability and cost of funds, and the parent's dividend payout (dividends-earnings) ratio. Firms differ, though, in the relative importance they place on these variables, as well as on how systematically they are incorporated in an overall remittance policy.

A major consideration in the dividend decision is the effective tax rate on payments from different affiliates. By varying payout ratios among its foreign subsidiaries, the corporation can reduce its total tax burden. Total tax payments are dependent on the regulations of both the foreign and home nations. The foreign country ordinarily has two types of tax that directly affect tax costs: **corporate income taxes** and **withholding taxes on dividend remittances.** In addition, several countries, such as Germany and Austria, **tax retained earnings** at a higher rate than earnings paid out as dividends. Many nations, such as the United States, tax dividend income received from abroad at the regular corporate tax rate. When this rate is higher than the combined foreign income and withholding taxes, the receipt of dividend income will normally entail an incremental tax cost. A number of countries, including Canada, Holland, and France, do not impose any additional taxes on dividend income from subsidiaries in which the parent holds more than a certain percentage ownership. The United States also taxes certain unremitted profits known as **Subpart F income,** including dividends paid to holding companies located in tax havens. Canada has similar tax regulations known as **FAPI** (foreign accrual property income).

As an offset to these additional taxes, most countries, including the United States, provide tax credits for taxes already paid by affiliates in countries of operation. For example, if a foreign subsidiary has $100 in pretax income, pays $40 in local income taxes, and a $6 dividend withholding tax and then remits the remaining $54 to its U.S. parent in the form of a dividend, the IRS will impose a $46 tax (0.46 × $100) but will provide a dollar-for-dollar tax credit for the $46 already paid in foreign taxes, leaving the parent with no U.S. income tax bill. **Foreign tax credits** from other remittances may be used in certain cases to offset these additional taxes. There are also a number of tax treaties between countries, established to avoid the double taxation of the same income and to provide for reduced dividend withholding taxes.

Some caution is in order. The determination of the full corporate tax cost of dividends is not as straightforward as the preceding paragraph may imply. U.S. income tax law (Regulation 1.861-8 of the Internal Revenue Code) limits the amount of foreign tax credits that can be used each year.

Putting aside qualitative considerations (which nevertheless may be quite important), the policy regarding dividends from affiliates to the parent is essentially a pure financial decision. The funds employed to make the remittance must be replaced to leave the affiliate whole. The economic effects of this substitution must be evaluated carefully. Unless constrained, once the firm has determined the amount of dividends to be received from its foreign operations, it will withdraw funds from the locations with the lowest comprehensive transfer costs.

Currency controls are another major factor in the dividend decision. Nations with balance of payments problems are likely to restrict the payment of dividends to foreign companies. These controls vary by country, but, generally, they limit the size of **dividend remittances** either in absolute terms or as a percentage of earnings, equity, or registered capital.

A number of firms attempt to reduce the danger of such interference by maintaining a record of consistent dividends that is designed to show that these payments are part of an established financial program rather than an act of speculation against the host country's currency. Dividends are paid every year, regardless of whether justified by financial and tax considerations, just to demonstrate a continuing policy to the local government and central bank. Even when they cannot be remitted, dividends are sometimes declared for the same reason, namely, to establish grounds for making future payments when these controls are lifted or modified.

Some companies even set a uniform **dividend payout ratio** throughout the corporate system to set a global pattern and maintain the principle that affiliates have an obligation to pay dividends to their stockholders. If challenged, the firm can then prove that its French or Brazilian or Italian subsidiaries must pay an equivalent percentage dividend. MNCs are often willing to accept higher tax costs to maintain the principle that dividends are a necessary and legitimate business expense. According to many executives, a record of consistently paying dividends (or at least declaring them) is a contributing factor in getting approval for further dividend disbursements.

FOREIGN INVESTMENT ANALYSIS

CAPITAL BUDGETING FOR MULTINATIONAL CORPORATIONS. The standard capital budgeting analysis involves calculating the expected aftertax values of all cash flows associated with a prospective investment, then discounting those cash flows back to the present using the firm's weighted average cost of capital. If the net present value of those cash flows is positive, the investment should be undertaken; if negative, it should be rejected. Formally, this net present value equals

$$NPV = -I_0 + \sum_{i=1}^{n} \frac{X_i}{(1 + k^*)^i}$$

where NPV = net present value of project
I_0 = net present value cost of investment
X_i = aftertax project cash flow in year i (no financial costs included)
n = anticipated life of project
k^* = required rate of return

The **analysis of a foreign project** raises three issues in addition to those encountered in domestic project analysis:

1. Should cash flows be measured from the viewpoint of the project or the parent?
2. How should the availability of subsidized loans be reflected in the project analysis?
3. Should the additional economic and political risks that are uniquely foreign be reflected in cash flow or discount rate adjustments?

Parent Versus Project Cash Flows. A substantial difference can exist between the cash flow of a project and the amount that is remitted to the parent because of tax regulations and exchange controls. Furthermore, many project expenses, such as management fees and royalties, are returns to the parent company. In addition, the incremental revenue contributed to the parent MNC by a project can differ from total project revenues if, for example, the project involves substituting local production for parent company exports or if transfer price adjustments shift profits elsewhere in the system. Given the differences that are likely to exist, the relevant cash flows to use in project evaluation must be determined.

One position suggested by Rodriguez and Carter (*International Financial Management*, p. 409) is that "to the extent that the corporation views itself as a true multinational, the effect of restrictions on repatriation may not be severe." Shapiro (*Financial Management*, Spring 1978, pp. 7–16), however, claims that according to economic theory, the value of a project is determined by the net present value of future cash flows back to the investor. Thus the parent MNC should value only the cash flows that are or can be repatriated, less any transfer costs (such as taxes), because only accessible funds can be used to pay dividends and interest, to amortize the firm's debt, and for reinvestment. (This principle also holds, of course, for a domestic firm. For example, only 15% of dividends received by a U.S. firm from a domestic subsidiary that is not consolidated for tax purposes are taxed; hence this earning stream has a value of 91.9% of the original dividend paid.)

To simplify **project evaluation,** a three-stage analysis is recommended. In the first stage, project cash flows are computed from the subsidiary's standpoint, exactly as if it were a separate, national corporation. The perspective then shifts to the parent company. The second stage of analysis requires specific forecasts concerning the amounts, timing, and form of transfers to headquarters. It reflects the taxes and other expenses that will be incurred by the remittances. Finally, the firm must take into account the indirect benefits and costs that this investment confers on the rest of the system, such as an increase or decrease in export sales by another affiliate. In general, incremental cash flows to the parent can be found only by subtracting worldwide parent company cash flows (without the investment) from postinvestment parent company cash flows.

Financial Incentives.   As a means of attracting foreign investment into a country to a region or for a specific purpose, many governments offer low-cost or subsidized loans. This type of incentive may be available in the United States as well, but it is much more likely to be encountered in less developed countries. If such a loan is granted, how should the benefit be incorporated in the project analysis? Some suggest that the amount of the subsidized loan be subtracted from the total investment and the anticipated cash flows compared with the net commitment. This approach does not seem valid; the corporation's total **debt capacity** is consumed as much by a low-cost loan as by one at the market rate of interest. (This is true in accounting terms; in an economic sense, the principal amount of the debt would be reduced to reflect recognition that the terms of the subsidized borrowing lower the true value of the liability compared with value at market rates.) Rather, a credit should be taken in the cash flow for the differential between the rates of interest on the incentive financing and that available on a commercial basis.

Another inducement often provided to attract foreign investment is tariff protection. Many multinational firms have learned to their dismay that an investment predicated wholly or even partially on trade barriers that promise insulation against external competition is extremely risky. This protection may be withdrawn or diminished substantially once the investment is in place; the anticipated returns vanish. Furthermore, when this type of incentive is necessary, the underlying economic attractiveness of the project is suspect. Extreme caution and skepticism are generally warranted.

Political and Economic Risk Analysis.   All else being equal, firms prefer to invest in countries with stable currencies, healthy economies, and minimal political risks such as expropriation. But since all else is usually not equal, firms must devote resources to evaluating the consequences of various political and economic risks for the viability of potential investments.

Four principal methods exist for incorporating the additional political and economic risks, such as currency fluctuations and expropriation, that are encountered overseas.

1. Shortening the minimum payback period.
2. Raising the investment's required rate of return.
3. Adjusting cash flows for the costs of risk reduction, for example, charging a premium for political risk insurance.
4. Adjusting cash flows to reflect the specific impact of a given risk.

The two most prevalent approaches among multinationals are to use a higher discount rate for foreign operations and to require a shorter **payback period** (Wickes, "A Comparative Analysis of the Foreign Investment Evaluation Practices of U.S.-Based Multinational Companies"). For instance, if exchange restrictions are anticipated, a normal required return of 15% might be raised to 20% or a 5-year payback period may be shortened to 3 years.

Neither approach, however, lends itself to a careful evaluation of the potential impact of a particular risk on investment returns, although the use of payback may be appropriate if the political environment is so uncertain that the possibility of a total loss is high. Thorough analysis requires an assessment of the magnitude and timing of risks and their implications for the projected cash flows. For example, an **expropriation** 5 years hence is likely to be much less threatening than one expected next year, even though the probability that the event will occur later may be higher. Thus using a uniformly higher discount rate just distorts the meaning of a project's present value by penalizing future cash flows relatively more heavily than current ones without allowing for a careful risk evaluation. Furthermore, the choice of a **risk premium** (or premiums, if the discount rate is allowed to vary over time) is an arbitrary one, whether it is 2 or 10%. Instead, adjusting cash flows makes it possible to incorporate fully all available information about the impact of a specific risk on the future returns from an investment.

In the sophisticated cash flow adjustment technique known as **uncertainty absorption,** each year's flows are charged a premium for **political and economic risk insurance.** Political risks such as currency inconvertibility or expropriation could be covered by insurance bought through the **Overseas Private Investment Corporation,** a U.S. government agency. The premiums that would be charged are a notational expense for the project. (If insurance is actually purchased, the premium is a cost, and uncertainty absorption is not really used.) This solution, however, does not really measure the effect of a given political risk on a project's present value. In the case of expropriation, political risk insurance normally covers only the book value, not the economic value of expropriated assets. The relationship between the book value of a project's assets and the project's economic value as measured by its future cash flows is tenuous at best. It is worthwhile, of course, to compare the cost of political risk insurance with its expected benefits. Insurance is the third step, however, in a sequential process of, first, identifying and quantifying risks, and second, taking any steps that can be cost justified to reduce them. It is not a substitute for a careful evaluation of the political risk for a given project.

Economic risk, such as currency fluctuations, could be hedged in the **forward exchange market.** In this case, the uncertainty absorption approach would involve adjusting each period's dollar cash flow X_i by the cost of an exchange risk management program. Thus if D_i is the expected forward discount in period i, the value of period i's cash flow is $X_i(1 - D_i)$. The uncertainty absorption technique is particularly useful if local currency cash flows are fixed, as in the case of interest on a bond denominated in a foreign currency. Where income is generated by an ongoing business operation, local currency cash flows will vary with the exchange rate. As indicated in section 11 of the *Handbook* entitled "Exchange Rates and Currency Exposure," there is a set of equilibrium conditions tending to hold in efficient financial markets that generally cause exchange rate changes and inflation to have only a minimal impact on real cash flows. The recommended approach is to adjust a project's cash flows to reflect the specific impact of a given risk, primarily because there is normally more and better information on the specific impact of a given risk on a project's cash flows than on its required return.

Although the suggestion that cash flows from politically risky areas should be discounted at a rate that ignores those risks is contrary to current practice, the difference is more apparent than real. As Lessard ("Evaluating Foreign Projects," in Donald R. Lessard, Ed., *International Financial Management*), points out, most firms evaluating foreign investments discount most likely (modal) rather than expected (mean) cash flows at a **risk-adjusted rate.** If an **expropriation** or **currency blockage** is anticipated, the mean value of the probability distribution of future cash flows will be significantly below its mode. From a theoretical standpoint, of course, cash flows should always be adjusted to reflect the change in expected values caused by a particular risk, but only if the risk is systematic should these cash flows be further discounted. This **adjusted cash flow approach** is illustrated for the case of currency controls.

Currency Controls.   Cash flow adjustments must take into account the likelihood that the effect of currency controls will vary over the life of the investment. Often the impact is initially advantageous and only gradually becomes unfavorable when the venture turns into a net generator of cash. In the early phase of an investment, a corporation may be able to import capital goods at a favorable exchange rate if the equipment is assigned a high priority by the host nation. (By using **multiple exchange rates,** many governments effectively subsidize the import of products deemed essential.) Moreover, the company's foreign affiliate may be able to arrange local currency financing at attractive rates by borrowing **blocked funds** held by other foreign-owned companies. It is only when a project is generating a substantial amount of cash that **restrictions on profit repatriation** are likely to be onerous; until then, controls may be advantageous.

When faced with the possibility of exchange controls, the parent company may find that probability **break-even analysis** is necessary to ascertain under what risks the project would be worth undertaking. By applying break-even analysis, the firm will not have to pinpoint the exact likelihood of risk but merely to determine whether it is smaller or larger than the benchmark figure. Probability analysis may indicate that a project generating large sums of blocked cash is still acceptable, particularly if the funds are likely to be blocked only temporarily and can be invested in local money market instruments and have their dollar value preserved.

Consider, for example, a project that requires an initial outlay of $1 million, with expected annual cash flows to the parent of $375,000, all to be remitted in equal installments over 5 years. The net present value of the investment, discounted at 20%, is $121,250—a positive sum that means that the project is acceptable. But what if exchange controls are imposed before the second remittance, and full repatriation occurs at the end of the fifth year? Assuming either that the blocked funds cannot be reinvested locally or that they can be invested only at a rate of interest that maintains and does not augment their dollar value, the investment's net present value becomes −$84,625 (Exhibit 6A).

If p is the probability that controls will be imposed in the second year or not at all, the project's expected net present value equals −$84,625p + $121,250(1 − p)$. As long as −$84,625p + $121,250(1 − p) > 0$, or $p < .59$, the expected net present value is positive. Hence, from the standpoint of its expected value, the project is worth undertaking only if the probability is less than 59% that exchange curbs will be imposed during the second year and not lifted until the end of the fifth year.

If the funds can be reinvested to yield an annual dollar rate of return of 5%, the net present value rises to −$37,893, and to $12,006 if the rate is 10%. The respective break-even probabilities are .76 and 1. Thus, with a dollar reinvestment rate of 5%, the expected net present value will be positive if the probability of controls in the second year is no greater than 76%; with a dollar reinvestment rate of 10%, net present value will be positive even if it is certain that currency controls will be imposed during the second year. (The computations for a 5% reinvestment rate are presented in Exhibit 6B.)

Probability break-even analysis is useful, since normally fewer data are required to ascertain whether p is smaller or larger than the benchmark needed to determine the absolute value of p. For instance, if the break-even level is 76%, it is unnecessary to spend time determining whether the chance of currency curbs is 30 or 40%, because the project's net present value will be positive in either case.

If exchange restrictions are not anticipated until just before the third remittance, the net present value with no reinvestment equals $24,875 (see Exhibit 6C). That means that regardless of either the likelihood of currency controls after the second year or the magnitude of the rate of return on blocked funds, the investment can be undertaken, provided all funds can be repatriated at the end of the fifth year.

Exchange Rate Changes and Inflation.   Projected cash flows can be stated in nominal (current) or real (constant) domestic or foreign currency terms. Ultimately, to ensure comparability between the various cash inflows and home currency outlays today, all cash flows must be expressed in real terms (i.e., units of constant purchasing power). Nominal cash flows can be converted to real cash flows by adjusting either the cash flows or the discount rate. Both methods yield the same results.

Let C_t be the nominal expected foreign currency cash flow in year t, e_t the nominal spot exchange rate in t, and i_h the home currency inflation rate. Then $C_t e_t$ is the nominal home currency value of this cash flow in year t and $C_t e_t / (1 + i_h)^t$ is its real value in current units of home currency.

Discounting at the real required rate of return k, which equals the real interest rate plus a risk premium, the present home currency value of this cash flow is:

$$\frac{C_t e_t}{(1 + k)^t (1 + i_h)^t}$$

Usually, however, the nominal cash flow in home currency terms, $C_t e_t$, is discounted at the nominal required rate of return k^*, which equals the nominal interest rate plus a premium for risk. But according to the **Fisher effect,** the nominal interest rate incorporates a premium for anticipated inflation or $1 + k^* = (1 + k)(1 + i_h)$. Therefore,

$$\frac{C_t e_t}{(1 + k^*)^t} = \frac{C_t e_t}{(1 + k)^t (1 + i_h)^t}$$

or discounting nominal cash flows using a nominal discount rate is identical in equilibrium to discounting real cash flows using a real rate of return. These possibilities are summarized in Exhibit 7.

If **purchasing power parity** holds

$$e_t = \frac{e_0 (1 + i_h)^t}{(1 + i_f)^t}$$

where e_0 is the current spot rate and i_f is the foreign currency inflation rate. Then:

$$\frac{C_t e_t}{(1 + k)^t (1 + i_h)^t} = \frac{\bar{C}_t e_o}{(1 + k)^t}$$

EXHIBIT 6   PRESENT VALUE CALCULATIONS UNDER DIFFERENT CONDITIONS OF REINVESTMENT AND EXCHANGE CONTROLS

				Present Value	
Year	Project Cash Flow	Cash Flow to Parent	20% Present Value Factor	Without Exchange Controls	With Exchange Controls

A.   NO REINVESTMENT : (EXCHANGE CONTROLS IMPOSED DURING YEAR 2)

Year	Project Cash Flow	Cash Flow to Parent	20% Present Value Factor	Without Exchange Controls	With Exchange Controls
0	−$1,000,000	−$1,000,000	1.0	−$1,000,000	−$1,000,000
1	375,000	375,000	0.833	312,375	312,375
2	375,000	0	0.694	260,250	0
3	375,000	0	0.579	217,125	0
4	375,000	0	0.482	180,750	0
5	375,000	375,000 × 4	0.402	150,750	603,000
Net present value				$121,250	−$ 84,625

Year	Project Cash Flow	Cash Flow to Parent	20% Present Value Factor	Present Value With Controls

B.   WITH 5% REINVESTMENT RATE : (EXCHANGE CONTROLS IMPOSED DURING YEAR 2)

Year	Project Cash Flow	Cash Flow to Parent	20% Present Value Factor	Present Value With Controls
0	−$1,000,000	−$1,000,000	1.0	−$1,000,000
1	375,000	375,000	0.833	312,375
2	375,000	0	0.694	0
3	375,000	0	0.579	0
4	375,000	0	0.482	0
5	375,000	375,000 × $(1 + 1.05 + 1.05^2 + 1.05^3)$	0.402	649,732
Net present value				−$ 37,893

Break-even probability calculation

$$-37,893p + 121,250 (1 - p) > 0$$

or

$$p < \frac{121,250}{37,893 + 121,250} = 0.76$$

Year	Project Cash Flow	Cash Flow to Parent	20% Present Value Factor	Present Value With Controls

C.   NO REINVESTMENT : (EXCHANGE CONTROLS IMPOSED DURING YEAR 3)

Year	Project Cash Flow	Cash Flow to Parent	20% Present Value Factor	Present Value With Controls
0	−$1,000,000	−$1,000,000	1.0	−$1,000,000
1	375,000	375,000	0.833	312,375
2	375,000	375,000	0.694	260,250
3	375,000	0	0.579	0
4	375,000	0	0.482	0
5	375,000	375,000 × 3	0.402	452,250
Net present value				$ 24,875

EXHIBIT 7   EVALUATING FOREIGN CURRENCY CASH FLOWS

	Real	Nominal
Cash flow	$\dfrac{\bar{C}_t e_t}{(1 + i_h)^t}$	$C_t e_t$
Discount rate	k	$k^* = k + i_h + k i_h$
Present value	$\dfrac{\bar{C}_t e_t}{(1 + k)^t (1 + i_h)^t}$	$\dfrac{C_t e_t}{(1 + k^*)^t} = \dfrac{C_t e_t}{(1 + k)^t (1 + i_h)^t}$

where $\bar{C}_t = C_t/(1 + i_f)^t$ is the expected foreign currency cash flow expressed in real terms.

This demonstrates again that to evaluate foreign cash flows, it is necessary to abstract from offsetting inflation and exchange rate changes. It is worthwhile, however, to analyze each effect separately because there is often a lag between a given rate of inflation and the implied exchange rate change to maintain international equilibrium. This is particularly true when government intervention occurs, such as in a **fixed rate system** or a **managed float.** Furthermore, local **price controls** may not permit or may even retard the effect of internal price adjustments. The possibility of relative price changes within the foreign economy can be incorporated easily by altering nominal project cash flows (the C_t's). Thus the present value of future cash flows can be calculated by converting nominal foreign currency cash flows into nominal home currency terms, then discounting them at the nominal domestic required rate of return. This is identical to converting nominal foreign currency cash flows into real home currency terms and discounting them at the real domestic required rate of return.

COST OF CAPITAL FOR FOREIGN INVESTMENTS. The cost of capital for a given investment is the minimum risk-adjusted return required by shareholders of the firm undertaking that investment. As such, it is the basic measure of financial performance. Unless the investment generates sufficient funds to compensate the suppliers of capital adequately, the firm's value will suffer. This return requirement is met only if the net present value of future project cash flows, using the corporation's cost of capital as the discount rate, is positive.

Discount Rates for Foreign Projects. A key issue for the MNC is whether a higher rate of return should be required of foreign projects than of domestic ones with comparable commercial risks. Many firms believe that the additional **risks associated with foreign investments**—currency controls, exchange risk, expropriation, and other forms of government intervention—mean that the greater a firm's international involvement, the riskier its stock should be, hence the greater its cost of equity capital.

In fact, there is good reason to believe that being international may actually reduce the riskiness of a firm. To understand this assertion, it is necessary to realize that risk is generally measured by the total variability of returns. The less variable a security's returns, the lower the risk of that security. **The capital asset pricing model** (see the section entitled ''Modern Portfolio Theory and Management'') assumes that the total variability of an asset's returns can be attributed to two sources: (1) marketwide influences such as the state of the economy that affect all assets to some extent, and (2) developments or aspects that are specific to a given firm. The former is usually termed a **systematic, or nondiversifiable risk,** and the latter an **unsystematic,** or diversifiable risk.

By holding a portfolio of stocks whose returns are not all subject to the same risks, an investor can eliminate some of this return variability. The risk of a portfolio of stocks will be less than the average riskiness of its component securities. Thus unsystematic risk is largely irrelevant to the holder of a highly diversified share portfolio; the effects of disturbances can be expected to be **offset on average** in the portfolio. On the other hand, no matter how well diversified a stock portfolio is, systematic risk, by definition, cannot be eliminated; the investor must be compensated for bearing that risk.

The importance of this theory for the international company is that the relevant component of risk in pricing a firm's stock is its systematic risk, in other words, that portion of return variability that cannot be eliminated by diversification. Most of the systematic, or general, market risk is related to the cyclical nature of the national economies in which the firm operates. The **diversification effect** that comes from dealing in a number of countries whose economic cycles are not perfectly synchronous should reduce the variability of an MNC's earnings.

In fact, less developed countries (LDCs), where **political risks** are greatest, may provide the maximum diversification benefits. They are less likely to be closely linked to the U.S. or other major economies, whereas the business cycles of developed countries tend to be closely correlated with each other. Thus investments in LDCs could be regarded as a plus, rather than a minus, for a company.

Of course, the systematic risk of projects even in relatively isolated LDCs is unlikely to be too far below the average for all projects; these countries are still tied into the world economy. The important point is that the ratio of systematic risk to total risk may be quite small in those countries, not necessarily that the systematic risk itself is small.

Even if a nation's economy is not closely linked to the world economy, the systematic risk of a project located in that country might still be rather large. For example, a mining venture in a foreign nation, whether in Canada, Chile, or Zaire, will probably have systematic risk that is very similar to that of an identical investment in the United States. The major element of systematic risk in any extractive project is related to variations in the price of the mineral being mined, which is set in a world market. The global price in turn is a function of worldwide demand, which itself is systematically related to the state of the world economy.

By contrast, a market-oriented project in an LDC, whose risk depends largely on the evolution of the domestic demand in that country, is likely to have a systematic risk that is small both in relative and absolute terms.

Empirical Evidence on MNC Risk.   An analysis of the available evidence on the impact of foreign operations on firm riskiness suggests that if there is an effect, it is generally to reduce both actual and perceived riskiness. Both Cohen (*Multinational Firms and Asian Exports,* Yale University Press, New Haven, CT, 1975) and Rugman (*Journal of International Business Studies,* Fall 1976, pp. 75–80) have shown that there is little correlation between the earnings of the various national components of MNCs. To the extent that foreign cash flows are not perfectly correlated with those of domestic investments, the overall risk associated with variations in total corporate returns might be reduced. Thus the greater riskiness of individual projects overseas could well be offset by beneficial portfolio effects. Furthermore, it is generally assumed that most of the economic and political risks specific to the multinational corporation are nonsystematic and can, therefore, be eliminated through diversification.

The **benefits of international diversification** should reduce the cost of equity for an MNC. However, if international portfolio diversification can be accomplished as easily and cheaply by individual investors, the required rates of return on an MNC's securities should reflect only their contribution to the systematic risk of a fully diversified world portfolio. In fact, though, very little foreign portfolio investment is actually undertaken by U.S. investors.

Restrictions on International Portfolio Diversification. The limited amount of **investment in foreign securities** is normally explained by a lack of information and the various legal and economic barriers that serve to segment national capital markets. Currency controls, specific tax regulations, relatively less efficient and less developed capital markets abroad, exchange risk, and the paucity of adequate, readily accessible, and comparable information on potential investments in foreign securities increase the perceived riskiness of foreign securities and deter investors. Furthermore, no other country in the world has the breadth or depth of industry that the United States has. Hence, to diversify adequately in a foreign economy, it will usually be necessary to acquire shares of multinational firms in industries operating in nations where indigenous firms do not exist. Diversifying into the computer industry in Venezuela, for example, means buying the shares of IBM or some other multinational computer manufacturer with operations there. Thus U.S. investors may be able to achieve low-cost international diversification by acquiring the shares of the U.S.-based MNCs. Moreover, when countries impose restictions on overseas portfolio investment, investors may be able to achieve international portfolio diversification only by purchasing shares in the multinational corporations domiciled in their own nations.

The value of international diversification appears to be significant. Lessard (*Financial Analysts Journal,* January–February 1976, pp. 32–38) and Solnik (*Financial Analysts Journal,* July–August 1974, pp. 48–54) have presented evidence that national factors have a strong impact on security returns relative to that of any common world factor. In addition, they find that returns from the different national equity markets have relatively low correlations with each other. These results imply that international diversification may be able to reduce significantly the risk of portfolios. In fact, the **variance of an internationally diversified portfolio** appears to be as little as 30% of that of individual securities. Moreover, as Solnik's data indicate (Exhibit 8), the benefits from international diversification are significantly greater than those that can be achieved solely by adding more domestic stocks to a portfolio.

Portfolio Diversification Versus Foreign Direct Investment. The ability of MNCs to provide an indirect means of international diversification may be an important advantage to investors. However, for foreign activities to affect an MNC's cost of equity capital, the market must be able to distinguish between the international and domestic operations of firms.

In an important study, Agmon and Lessard (*Journal of Finance,* September 1977, pp. 1049–1055) examined the price behavior of U.S.-based multinational corporations listed on the New York Stock Exchange. They asserted that if MNCs do indeed supply global diversification for U.S. investors, price movements of the securities of multinational firms should reflect their degree of international involvement; that is, the greater the extent of foreign activity, the more closely the movements in the price of an MNC share will be related to a world market factor than to a U.S. market factor. Their regression analysis supports the hypothesis that investors recognize and reward **international diversification.** (In technical terms, beta was found to be a decreasing function of the percentage of foreign to overall sales.) However, their results are just barely statistically significant.

In a related work, Jacquillat and Solnik (*Journal of Portfolio Management,* Winter 1978, pp. 8–12) concluded that although multinational firms do provide some diversification for investors, they are poor substitutes for **international portfolio diversification.** Their results indicate that an internationally diversified portfolio leads to a much greater reduction in variance than does a portfolio comprising firms with widespread international activities. For

EXHIBIT 8   BENEFITS OF INTERNATIONAL PORTFOLIO DIVERSIFICATION

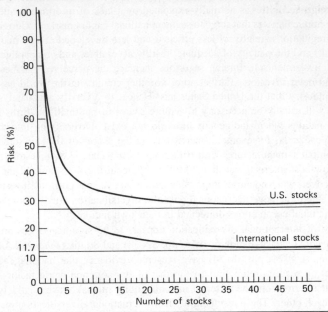

Source: Reprinted from Bruno H. Solnik, "Why Not Diversify Internationally Rather Than Domesti-cally?" *Financial Analysts Journal,* July–August 1974, p. 51, by permission of the publisher.

a detailed discussion of international portfolio diversification, see the section entitled "International Portfolio Diversification and Foreign Capital Markets."

Management Implications of MNC Investment.   Corporations should continue investing abroad as long as profitable opportunities exist. Retrenching based on a belief that investors desire less extensive or smaller international operations will lead to forgoing both profitable foreign investments and valuable diversification; the firm's shareholders would be penalized, not rewarded. At the very least, executives of multinational firms should seriously question whether a premium rate of return should be employed to account for the added political and economic risks of overseas operations when evaluating prospective foreign investments. The use of any such premium ignores the fact that the risk of an individual overseas investment within the context of the firm's other investments, domestic as well as foreign, will be less than that project's total risk. How much less depends on how highly correlated the outcomes of the firm's different investments are. Thus the automatic inclusion of a premium when evaluating a foreign project is not necessarily an element of conservatism. Before additional conclusions can be reached, more empirical testing of investor perceptions of the riskiness of MNCs is required. These perceptions are likely to be affected by the location as well as the percentage of foreign source earnings (e.g., developed versus less developed countries).

POLITICAL RISK ANALYSIS AND MANAGEMENT.   Rising nationalism both in developing and developed countries and in economic blocks has increased the political risks to which MNCs have been exposed historically. These take many forms, from currency controls to expropriation, from a change in tax laws to requirements for additional local production or expensive pollution control equipment. Their common denominator is government action that adversely affects the value of the firm. Despite the potentially severe consequences of political risk, surveys of how firms view and respond to this exposure reveal a pattern of few attempts at systematic analysis. The findings of these surveys, which are remarkably consistent, are summarized by Kobrin (*Journal of International Business Studies*, Spring–Summer 1979, p. 75) as follows:

> First, it is clear that managers consider political instability or political risk, typically quite loosely defined, to be an important factor in the foreign investment decision. Second, it is just as clear that rigorous and systematic assessment and evaluation of the political environment is exceptional. Most political analysis is superficial and subjective, not integrated formally into the decision-making process and assumes that instability and risk are one and the same. The response frequently is avoidance; firms simply do not get involved in countries, or even regions, that they perceive to be risky. Last, managers appear to rely for environmental information primarily on sources internal to the firm. When they look for outside data, they are most likely to go to their banks or the general and business media.

Measuring Political Risk. The characteristics of each company will, to a large extent, determine the susceptibility to political risk and the effects on the present value of its foreign investment. Governments, even revolutionary ones, rarely **expropriate foreign investments** indiscriminately. This assertion is supported by studies by Truitt (*Journal of International Business Studies*, Fall 1970, pp. 21–34) and Hawkins, Mintz, and Provissiero (*Journal of International Business Studies*, Spring 1976, pp. 3–15) on the post-World War II experiences of U.S. and British MNCs. The data clearly show that except for the countries in which Communist governments gained control, companies differ in their susceptibilities to political risk, depending on the industry, size, composition of ownership, level of technology, and degree of vertical integration with other affiliates. For example, expropriation, overt or creeping, is more likely to occur in the extractive, utility, and financial service sectors of an economy than in manufacturing. Moreover, some firms may be benefited by the same event that harms other firms. A company that relies on imports will be hurt by trade restrictions, whereas an import-competing firm may well be helped.

In general, the greater the perceived benefits provided by a subsidiary to the host economy and the more expensive its replacement by a purely local operation, the smaller the degree of risk to the MNC. The implication is that governments select their expropriation targets according to nonpolitical criteria. This degree of selectivity suggests that companies can take actions to control their exposure to political risk.

Avoiding Political Risk. The easiest way to **manage political risk** is to avoid it, which many firms do by screening out investments in politically uncertain nations. However, inasmuch as all governments make decisions that influence the profitability of business, all investments, including those made in the United States, face some degree of political risk. For example, American steel companies have had to cope with stricter environmental regulations requiring the expenditure of billions of dollars for new pollution control devices, and American oil companies are beleaguered by so-called windfall profit taxes, price controls, and mandatory allocations. Risk avoidance is impossible.

The real issue is the degree of political risk a company is willing to tolerate and the return required to bear it. A policy of avoiding countries considered to be politically unstable ignores the potentially high returns available and the extent to which a firm can·control the risks. After all, companies are in business to take risks, if these are recognized, intelligently managed, and provide compensation.

Political Risk Insurance.   Most developed countries sell political risk insurance to cover the foreign assets of domestic companies. The coverage provided by the U.S. government through the **Overseas Private Investment Corporation** (OPIC) is typical. By insuring assets in unstable areas, firms can concentrate on managing their businesses and forget about this risk—or so it appears.

The OPIC program provides U.S. investors with insurance against loss due to the specific political risks of expropriation, currency inconvertibility, war, revolution, or insurrection. To qualify, the investment must be a new one or a substantial expansion of an existing facility and must be approved by the host government. Coverage is restricted to 90% of equity participation. For very large investments or for projects deemed especially risky, OPIC coverage may be limited to less than 90%. The only exception is institutional project loans to unrelated third parties, which may be insured for the full amount of principal and interest. The cost of the coverage varies by industry and risk insured (Exhibit 9). It is apparent that the costs are not based solely on objective criteria but also reflect certain political aims, such as fostering development of additional energy supplies.

There are two fundamental problems associated with relying on insurance as a protection against political risk. First, as previously mentioned, the economic value of an investment is the present value of its future cash flows, but only the investment in assets is covered by insurance. Thus, although insurance can provide some insulation against political risk, it falls far short of being a comprehensive solution. Second, there is an asymmetry involved. If an investment proves unprofitable, it is unlikely to be expropriated. Since business risk is not covered, any losses must be borne by the firm itself. On the other hand, if the

EXHIBIT 9   OPIC INSURANCE FEES (%) (AS OF 1980)

Coverage	Manufacturing and Services Projects	Natural Resource Projects (Other Than Oil and Gas)	Oil and Gas Projects Exploration	Oil and Gas Projects Production	Institutional Loans
Inconvertibility	0.30	0.30	0.10	0.30	0.25
Expropriation	0.60	0.90	0.40	1.50	0.30
War, revolution, insurrection (WRI)	0.60	0.60	0.60	0.60	0.60
Interference with operations	—	—	0.40	0.40	—
Inconvertibility, expropriation (combined)	—	—	—	—	0.50
Inconvertibility, expropriation, WRI (combined)	—	—	—	—	0.90

Source: Overseas Private Investment Corporation, *Investment Insurance Handbook.*

investment is successful and then is expropriated, the firm is compensated only for the value of its assets, not for the lost future earnings.

Modifying the Environment. As an alternative to insurance, therefore, some firms try to reach an understanding with the host government before undertaking the investment, defining the rights and responsibilities of both parties. Such a concession agreement, in effect, specifies the rules under which the firm can operate locally.

Concession agreements were quite popular among firms investing in less developed countries, especially in colonies of the home country. They often were negotiated with weak governments. In time, many of these countries became independent or their governments were overthrown. Invariably, the new rulers repudiated the old concession agreements, arguing that they were a form of exploitation.

Concession agreements are still being negotiated today, but they seem to carry little weight among the LDCs and are observed usually only in developed countries. Their high rate of obsolescence has led many firms to pursue a more active policy of political risk management.

Structuring Foreign Investment. Once a firm has decided to invest in a country, it can try to minimize its exposure to political risk by adjusting its operating policies in the areas of production, logistics, exporting, and technology transfer, and its financial policies.

One key element of such a strategy is to keep the local affiliate dependent on sister companies for markets and/or supplies. Similarly, by concentrating research and development facilities and proprietary technology, or at least key components thereof, in the home country, a firm can raise the cost of nationalization. To be effective, other multinationals with licensing agreements must be unable to service an affiliate if nationalized, or must be forbidden to do so. Another element of this strategy is to establish single, global trademarks that cannot be legally duplicated by a government. In this way, the incentive for a government to expropriate a local subsidiary of a consumer products company would be reduced significantly because the use of the recognized brand name would be precluded.

Control of transportation, including shipping, pipelines, and railroads, has also been used at one time or another by the **United Fruit Co.** and other MNCs to gain leverage over governments. Similarly, diversifying production among multiple plants changes the balance of power between government and firm by reducing the government's ability to hurt the worldwide firm by seizing a single facility.

Involving external **financial stakeholders** in the venture is another defensive measure that may be particularly useful in extractive industries. **Capital for a venture** is raised from the host and other governments, international financial institutions, and customers (with payment to be provided out of production) rather than employing funds supplied or guaranteed by the parent company. In addition to spreading risks, an international response will be elicited by any expropriation move or other adverse action by a host government. This protection is not necessarily free, and it may be obtained only by accepting expensive capital. As an example, **project financing** to develop mineral and hydrocarbon resources has been used extensively by multinational firms. By placing international banks between the company and the host government, a degree of insulation is obtained.

A last approach, particularly for extractive projects, is to obtain unconditional **host government guarantees** for the amount of the investment, which enable creditors to threaten or to institute legal action in foreign or international courts against harmful (to the MNC) commercial transactions between the host country and third parties if a subsequent government repudiates the nation's obligations. Such guarantees provide investors with potential sanctions against a foreign government without having to rely on the uncertain support of their home government. In reality, these guarantees are difficult to enforce.

Planned Divestment.   Once the multinational has invested in a project, its ability to influence the susceptibility to political risk is greatly diminished but not ended. Planned divestment involves the orderly sale by a multinational firm of all or a majority of its ownership of a foreign investment to local investors. Such an arrangement, however, may be difficult to conclude to the satisfaction of all parties involved. If a *buyout price* has been set in advance on an investment that turns out to be unprofitable, the host government probably will not honor the purchase commitment or permit local investors to honor it. Moreover, with the constant threat of expropriation present during the bargaining, it is unlikely that a fair price can be negotiated. This disadvantageous position for the multinational firm is not restricted to cases of danger of full expropriation. Legislation in a number of countries requires certain percentages of local ownership. Often these laws were enacted after the investments had been made, and grandfather clauses may not be available. For example, the **Andean Pact** nations agreed to limit foreign ownership in commercial (i.e., wholesaling and retailing) companies to 20%.

Short-Term Profit Maximization.   Confronted with the need to divest itself wholly or partially of an equity position, the multinational corporation may respond by attempting to withdraw the maximum from the local operation. By deferring maintenance expenditures, cutting investment to the minimum necessary to sustain the desired level of production, curtailing marketing expenditures, producing lower quality merchandise, setting higher prices, and eliminating training programs, cash generation will be maximized for the short term, regardless of the effects of such actions on longer run profitability and viability. This policy, which almost guarantees that the company will not be in business locally for long, is a response of desperation. Of course, the behavior is likely to accelerate expropriation if such is the government's intention (and perhaps even if it was not originally).

The firm must select its time horizon for augmenting cash outflow and consider how this behavior will affect government relations and actions. The secondary implications of the short-term profit maximization strategy must be evaluated as well. The unfriendly government could be replaced by a new government more receptive to foreign investment, or the multinational firm may want to supply the local market from affiliates in other countries. In either case, an aggressive tactic of withdrawing as much as possible from the threatened affiliate probably will be considered a hostile act and will vitiate all future dealings between the multinational firm and the country.

One alternative to this indirect form of divestment is to do nothing, hoping that even though the local regime could, at a minor cost, take an affiliate over, it will choose not to do so. This is not necessarily a vain wish, since it rests on the premise that the country needs foreign direct investment and will be unlikely to receive it if potential investors fear that existing operations may be expropriated without fair and full compensation. Whether this passive approach will succeed is a function of the host country's dependence on foreign investment to realize its own development plans and the degree to which economic growth will be sacrificed for philosophical, religious, or political reasons.

Changing the Ratio of Cost to Benefit.   If the government's objectives in an **expropriation** are rational (i.e., based on the belief that economic benefits will more than compensate for the costs), the multinational firm can initiate a number of programs to reduce the perceived advantages of local ownership and thereby diminish the incentive to expel foreigners. These steps include establishing local research and development facilities, developing export markets for the affiliate's output, training local workers and managers, expanding production facilities, and manufacturing a wider range of products locally as substitutes for imports. It should be recognized that many of the foregoing actions simultaneously lower the cost of expropriation and, consequently, reduce the penalty for the government. A delicate balance must be considered.

Realistically, however, it appears that the countries most prone to expropriate view the benefits (real, imagined, or both) of local ownership as more important than the cost of replacing the foreign investor. Although the value of a subsidiary to the local economy can be important, its worth may not be sufficient to protect against political risk. Thus one aspect of a protective strategy must be to raise the cost of expropriation by increasing the negative sanctions that would be exerted. This includes achieving and maintaining control over export markets, transportation, technology, trademarks and brand names, and components manufactured in other nations. Some of these tactics may not be available once the investment has been made, but others may still be implemented.

Developing Local Stakeholders.   A more positive strategy is to cultivate local individuals and groups who have a stake in the affiliate's continued existence as a unit of the parent multinational. Potential stakeholders include consumers, suppliers, the subsidiary's local employees, local bankers, and joint venture partners.

Consumers worried about a change in product quality or suppliers concerned about a disruption in their production schedules (or even a switch to other suppliers) brought about by a government takeover may have an incentive to protest. Similarly, well-treated local employees may lobby against expropriation. Local borrowing could help give local bankers a stake in the health of the MNC's operations if any government action threatened the affiliate's cash flows and jeopardized loan repayments.

Having local private investors as partners would appear to provide protection. In fact, this shield is likely to be of limited value because the local investors will be deemed to be tainted by association with the multinational. A government probably would not be deterred by the existence of local shareholders from expropriation or enacting discriminatory laws. Moreover, the action could be directed solely against the foreign investor. The local partners even could be the genesis of a move to expropriate, to enable them to acquire the whole of a business at little or no cost.

Adaptation.   A more radical approach to political risk management is being tried by some firms today. Rather than resisting potential expropriation, this policy entails adapting to the inevitability of it and trying to earn profits on the firm's resources by entering into **licensing and management agreements.** Oil companies whose properties were nationalized by the Venezuelan government received management contracts to continue their exploration, refining, and marketing operations. These firms have recognized that it is not necessary to own or control an asset such as an oil well to earn profits. This form of arrangement is likely to be more common in the future as countries develop greater management abilities and decide to purchase from foreign firms only the skills that remain in short supply at home. Firms unable to surrender control of their foreign operations because of the integration of these operations in a worldwide production planning system or some other form of global strategy are also those least likely to be troubled by the threat of property seizure. An expropriated automobile assembly plant is of little value in the absence of facilities for producing engines, transmissions, and body stampings.

FINANCING FOREIGN OPERATIONS

MULTINATIONAL FINANCIAL STRATEGY. In selecting an appropriate **strategy for financing** its **worldwide operations,** the availability of different sources of funds and their relative costs and effects on the multinational firm's operating risks must be considered. Some of the key variables in the evaluation are rates of interest and taxes, exchange risk, diversification of fund sources, the freedom to move funds across borders, and a variety of **government credit and capital controls and subsidies.** The eventual funding strategy selected must reconcile a variety of potentially conflicting objectives such as minimizing expected financing costs, reducing economic exposure to foreign exchange fluctuations, providing protection against **currency controls** and other forms of **political risk,** and assuring availability of funds in times of tight credit.

A general framework by Lessard and Shapiro ("Designing a Global Financing Strategy ") separates the financing of international operations into three facets and offers the following directions.

1. Seek to profit from market distortions. This includes:
   a. Taking advantage of deviations from equilibrium exchange or interest rates that may exist because of government controls and subsidies.
   b. Speculating based on forecasts divergent from those held by the market in general.
   c. Exploiting the company's unique position vis-à-vis taxes, exchange controls and other restrictions, based on its ability to adjust **intracompany fund flows.**
2. Arrange financing to reduce the riskiness of the operating cash flows. This includes:
   a. Offsetting the firm's projected economic exposure by borrowing, if cost justified, in appropriate currencies.
   b. Reducing various political risks, either by giving lenders a vested interest in the continuing viability of the firm's operations or by decreasing the firm's assets that are exposed.
   c. Selling the output from the plant or project in advance to customers to decrease sales uncertainty and then using the sales contracts to obtain funds.
   d. Securing a continuing supply of financing for corporate activities worldwide by diversifying sources of funds and, possibly, borrowing in anticipation of needs.
3. Meet the financial structure goals of the multinational corporation overall. This includes:
   a. Establishing a worldwide capital structure that balances the aftertax costs and benefits of leverage.
   b. Selecting the appropriate affiliate capital structures.

FOREIGN FINANCE SUBSIDIARIES. The United States imposes on dividend and interest payments to foreigners a withholding tax at rates up to 30%, depending on the double tax treaty between this country and that of the investor. Inasmuch as investors are concerned with the net yield on a debt instrument, U.S. firms issuing bonds directly in international markets are at a disadvantage: either they will not be able to market the debt, or they will be required to pay a higher gross rate of interest so that the return to the holder net of the withholding tax is equivalent to that offered on instruments of similar quality foreign firms. To avoid this tax penalty and to be competitive in the **Eurodollar market,** a number of American companies established foreign finance subsidiaries that are incorporated domestically (an **80–20 corporation**) or abroad (an **offshore finance company**). Although the former arrangement technically worked and was employed to some extent to borrow internationally to finance foreign operations, great care had to be exercised to ensure that U.S. legal requirements were satisfied. Thus offshore finance companies, particularly those incorporated in the **Netherlands Antilles,** which has an especially attractive tax treaty with the United States, have been used more extensively. In virtually all cases, a parent guarantee of the subsidiary's obligations is required.

The need for U.S. corporations to rely on a circuitous and artificial mechanism to raise money in international capital markets may disappear. Congress currently is debating whether to eliminate the withholding tax on interest paid to foreigners.

FINANCING FOREIGN SUBSIDIARIES. The following factors should be considered when selecting the method of financing affiliates abroad.

Debt Versus Equity Financing. Interest payments on debt, extended by either the parent or a financial institution, generally are deductible by an affiliate for its local tax purposes, but dividends are not. In addition, the repayment of borrowing usually does not attract taxes. Thus an incentive exists to employ leverage.

Government Credit and Capital Controls. Governments intervene in their financial markets for a number of reasons: to restrain the growth of lendable funds, to make certain types of borrowing more or less expensive, and to direct funds to certain favored economic activities. When access to local funds markets is restricted, interest rates in them are usually below the risk-adjusted equilibrium level. There is often an incentive to borrow as much as possible where nonprice credit rationing is used.

Restraints on overseas borrowing, or incentives to promote it, are often employed as well. There are numerous examples of this. Certain countries have limited the amount of local financing obtainable by the subsidiary of a multinational firm to that required for working capital purposes; any additional needs must be satisfied from abroad. A precondition for obtaining official approval for a new investment or acquisition often is a commitment to inject external funds. Conversely, when a nation is concerned about excess capital inflows, a portion of any new foreign borrowing might have to be placed on deposit with the government, thereby raising the effective cost of external debt.

The multinational firm with access to a variety of sources and types of funds and the ability to shift capital with its **internal transfer system** has more opportunities to secure the lowest risk-adjusted cost of money and to circumvent credit restraints. These attributes should give it a substantial advantage over a purely domestic company.

Government Subsidies. Despite the often hostile rhetoric directed against the multinational firm, many governments offer a growing list of incentives to MNCs to influence their production and export sourcing decisions. Direct investment incentives include interest rate subsidies, loans with long maturities, guarantees of repatriation, grants related to project size, favorable prices for land, corporate income tax holidays, accelerated depreciation, and a reduction in or elimination of the payment of other business taxes and import duties on capital equipment and raw materials. Governments sometimes make the infrastructure investments as well, thereby providing the base to support a new industrial project.

In addition, all governments of developed nations have some form of export financing agency whose purpose is to boost exports by providing loans with long repayment periods at rates of interest below the market level and low-cost political and economic risk insurance.

These **export credit programs** can often be employed advantageously by multinationals. The use depends on whether the firm is seeking export or import goods or services, but the basic strategy remains the same—examining the various incentives for the best possible financing arrangement.

Import Financing Strategy.   If sizable imports are part of an investment, it may be possible to finance these purchases on attractive terms. A number of countries, including the United States, make credit available to foreign purchasers at low (below market) interest rates and with long repayment periods. These loans are tied to procurement in the agency's country; thus the firm must compile a list of goods and services required for the project and relate them to potential sources, country by country. Where there is overlap among the potential suppliers, the purchasing firm may have leverage to extract more favorable financing terms from the various export credit agencies involved.

Diversification of Fund Sources.   A key element of any MNC's global financial strategy should be to gain access to a broad range of fund sources to lessen its dependence on any one financial market. An ancillary benefit is that the firm broadens its sources of economic and financial information, providing a useful supplement to its domestic resources and aiding in its financial decision-making process.

Worldwide Financial Structure.   The multinational firm, like a purely domestic one, has as one of its key objectives a capital structure which minimizes the overall aftertax cost of capital. This determination is complicated when a firm is operating in more than one country because the laws and regulations of other nations must be considered. The worldwide capital structure, however, need not be just a residual of the decisions made for individual subsidiaries. The parent does have the ability to offset a highly leveraged overseas financial structure with a more conservative one elsewhere to maintain a target **debt-equity mix** for the firm as a whole. The focus is on the consolidated financial structure because suppliers of capital to a multinational firm associate the risk of default with the MNC's worldwide debt ratio. Shareholders look to the entire corporation for their dividends and the **cost of equity capital** is a function of the enterprise's overall profitability.

Subsidiary Financial Structure.   Once a decision has been made regarding the appropriate mix of debt and equity for the entire corporation, questions about individual operations can be raised. What factors are relevant in establishing foreign affiliates' capital structures? Should they:

Conform to that of the parent company?
Reflect the capitalization norms in each foreign country?
Vary to take advantage of opportunities to minimize the MNC's cost of capital?

Disregarding public and government relations and legal requirements for the moment, the parent company could decide to raise funds in its own country and inject sufficient amounts of equity to satisfy fully all subsidiaries' financial requirements. The overseas operations would then have a zero debt ratio. Alternatively, the parent could avoid the direct financial burden on itself. It would hold only one dollar of share capital in each affiliate and require all to borrow locally or internationally, with or without guarantees. In this instance, the debt ratios approach 100%. Or, the parent could itself borrow from external markets and relend the moneys as **intracompany advances.** Here again, the affiliates' debt ratios would be close to 100%. In all these cases, the total amount of borrowing and the **debt-equity mix** of the consolidated corporation are identical. Thus the question of an optimal capital structure for a foreign affiliate is completely distinct from the corporation's overall debt-equity ratio. Assets in a foreign country are to be financed; how is it to be done?

Adler (*Journal of Finance*, March 1974, pp. 119–132), moreover, has argued that any accounting rendition of a separate capital structure for the subsidiary is wholly illusory **unless** the parent is willing to allow its affiliate to default on its debt. As long as the rest of the MNC group has a legal or moral obligation or sound business reasons for preventing the affiliate from defaulting, the individual unit has no independent capital structure. Rather, its true debt-equity ratio is equal to that of the consolidated group.

The **irrelevance of subsidiary financial structures** when considering the entire corporation seems to be recognized by multinationals. A survey of eight U.S.-based MNCs by Business International (*Business International Money Report*, September 21, 1979, pp. 319–320) reported that most of the firms expressed little concern with the debt-equity mixes of their foreign affiliates; the primary focus was on the worldwide, rather than individual, capital structure. (Admittedly, for most of the firms interviewed, the debt ratios of affiliates had not significantly raised the MNC's consolidated indebtedness.) The third option of manipulating affiliate financial structures to take advantage of local financing opportunities appears to be the preferred choice. Thus, within the constraints set by **foreign** statutory or **minimum equity rules,** the need to appear to be a responsible and a good guest, and the requirements of a worldwide financial structure, a multinational corporation should finance its affiliates to minimize its total **weighted average cost of capital.**

A subsidiary with a capital structure similar to its parent may forgo profitable opportunities to lower its cost of funds. For example, rigid adherence to a **fixed debt-equity ratio** may not allow a subsidiary to take advantage of government subsidized debt or low-cost loans from international agencies. Furthermore, it may be worthwhile to raise funds locally if the country is politically risky. If the affiliate were expropriated, for instance, it would default on all loans from local financial institutions. Similarly, borrowing funds in the country will decrease the company's vulnerability to exchange controls. On the other hand, forcing a subsidiary to raise funds locally to meet parent norms may be quite expensive in a country with a high-cost capital market.

The cost-minimizing approach would be to direct subsidiaries in low-cost countries to exceed the parent company capitalization norm, while affiliates in high-cost nations would have lower target debt-equity ratios. This assumes that capital markets are at least partially segmented. Although there are no definite conclusions on this issue at present, the variety and degree of governmental restrictions on capital market access lend credence to the segmentation hypothesis. In addition, the behavior of MNCs in lobbying against regulations such as the OFDI restrictions indicates that they believe that capital costs vary substantially among countries.

A counterargument by Stonehill and Stitzel (*California Management Review*, Fall 1969, pp. 91–96) is that a **subsidiary's financial structure** should conform to local norms. Then, because German and Japanese firms are more highly leveraged than, say, companies in the United States and France, the Japanese and German subsidiaries of an American firm should have much higher debt-equity ratios than the U.S. parent or a French subsidiary. There are two problems with this argument. First, according to Naumann-Etienne (*Journal of Financial and Quantitative Analysis*, November 1974, pp. 859–870), it ignores the strong linkage between U.S.-based multinationals and the U.S. capital market. Since most of their stock is owned and traded in the United States, it follows that the firms' **target debt-equity ratios** are dependent on U.S. shareholders' risk perceptions. Similar argments hold for multinationals that are not based in the United States. Furthermore, the level of **foreign debt-equity**

ratios is usually determined by institutional factors that have no bearing on foreign-based multinationals. For example, **Japanese and German banks** own much of the equity as well as the debt issues of local corporations. Combining the functions of stockholder and lender may reduce the perceived risk of default on loans to captive corporations and increase the desirability of substantial leverage. This would not apply to a wholly owned subsidiary. However, a **joint venture** with a corporation tied to the local banking system may enable an MNC to lower its local cost of capital by leveraging itself, without a proportional increase in risk, to a degree that would be impossible otherwise.

Second, for purposes of capital budgeting and intercorporate comparisons, **delevered cash flows** must be used. To prescribe a financial structure as Stonehill and Stitzel suggest seems close to violating this tenet.

Parent Company Guarantees and Consolidation.   Multinational firms are sometimes reluctant to guarantee explicitly the debt of their subsidiaries, even when a more advantageous interest rate can be negotiated. First, they argue, affiliates should be able to stand alone. In the case of a joint venture when the other partner is unable or unwilling to provide a valuable counterguarantee, a penalty rate of interest may be accepted to avoid overfinancing other shareholders. A cost is incurred to maintain a principle and avoid a dangerous precedent. Second, the protection against **expropriation** provided by an affiliate's borrowing may be lost if the parent guarantees those debts. Third, many corporations believe lenders should be reasonable, requesting a guarantee when the affiliate is operating at a loss or with a debt-heavy capital structure and lending without one when the borrower itself is creditworthy. Fourth, providing explicit support for one operation could lead to lenders' demands in other cases.

The issue of whether to issue guarantees may be more important in theory than in fact. It is likely that a parent company would "keep lenders whole" if a subsidiary defaulted even if it had no legal obligation to do so. A survey by Stobaugh (*Journal of International Business Studies,* Summer 1970, pp. 43–64) showed that not one of a sample of 20 medium and large multinationals (average foreign sales of $200 million and $1 billion annually, respectively) would allow their subsidiaries to default on debt that did not have a parent company guarantee. (There have been, however, two instances involving major multinational firms in which the parent refused to honor its subsidiaries' defaulted obligations.) Of the small multinationals interviewed (average annual sales of $50 million), only one out of 17 indicated that it would allow a subsidiary to default on its obligations under some circumstances. The previously cited study by Business International (*Business International Money Report,* September 21, 1979, pp. 319–320) had similar findings. The majority of firms interviewed said they would make good the nonguaranteed debt of a subsidiary in the event of a default. This attitude is not the result of benevolence nor, possibly, even a sense of morality. A multinational firm relies on financial institutions in many countries. In a real sense, it could rarely, if ever, function without them. Any action that jeopardizes these relations, such as allowing an affiliate to become bankrupt, has an extremely high cost. Multinational firms also may distinguish between international and local banks. The former could be kept whole and the latter directed to their own government for repayment if an affiliate were expropriated and unable to pay its debts.

If an explicit guarantee will reduce a subsidiary's borrowing costs, it is usually in the parent's best interest to give this support, provided there is an actual commitment to satisfy the subsidiary's obligations. An overseas creditor may not be as certain regarding the firm's intentions, and its ties to the multinational may be less substantial. The fact that the parent does not guarantee its subsidiaries' debt may then convey some information, namely, that the commitment to subsidiary debt is not strong.

The Internal Revenue Service recently argued that by guaranteeing foreign affiliates' debts, a U.S. corporation is providing a valuable service for which it should be compensated. The IRS, therefore, has begun imputing income to the guarantor and levying a tax. This additional tax cost should be incorporated in the determination of whether parent support should be given to an overseas subsidiary's borrowing.

SOURCES OF FUNDS FOR MNC AFFILIATES.   A distinctive feature of the financial strategy of multinational firms is the wide range of internal and external sources of funds available to them. Those external sources include commercial banks, export financing agencies, public (government) financial institutions, development banks, insurance companies, pension plans, private and public bond placements, and lease financing.

Short-Term Financing.   Like most domestic firms, affiliates of multinational corporations generally attempt to finance their **working capital requirements** locally both for convenience and for exposure management purposes. Commercial banks are the prime source of short-term financing. This usually takes the form of overdrafts and discounting facilities, but may be a straight loan for a set period such as 90 days or longer. Nonbank sources of funds include export financing and factoring and commercial paper.

In countries other than the United States, banks tend to lend through **overdrafts.** An overdraft is simply a line of credit against which drafts (checks) can be drawn (written), up to a specified maximum amount. These overdraft lines are often extended and expanded year after year, thus providing, in effect, a form of medium-term financing. The borrower pays interest on the debit balance only. **Commitment fees** on the unused portion of the credit line may be required, but unlike the practice in the United States, **compensating balances** (required minimum balances) are rarely requested.

The **discounting of trade bills** is the preferred short-term financing technique in many developed and less developed countries. It is popular because these bills often can be rediscounted with the central bank at a rate that does not fully reflect all the commercial risks involved (i.e., at a subsidized rate). Discounting usually results from the following set of transactions. A manufacturer selling goods to a retailer on credit draws a bill on the buyer, payable in, say, 30 days. The buyer endorses (accepts) the bill, or his bank accepts it on his behalf (at which point it becomes a **banker's acceptance**). The manufacturer gives the bill to his bank, which accepts it for a fee if the buyer's bank has not done so already. The bill is then sold at a discount to the manufacturer's bank or to a money market dealer. The rate of interest varies with the term of the bill and the general level of local money market interest rates.

Medium-Term Financing.   Loans with maturities between 1 and 7 years constitute medium-term financing. Customarily, these take the form of **renewable overdrafts** or discounting facilities (revolving acceptance credits) with the rate of interest fluctuating. They are used as a continuing source of funds or as **bridge financing** while the borrower obtains medium- or long-term fixed rate financing, usually from a financial institution other than a commercial bank. Banks that extend bridging loans also may act as agents in syndicating the substitute financing that is used to repay the bank debt. Such arrangements are common in Germany and Italy.

Medium-term loans typically are made on the basis of cash flows expected to be generated by the borrower's investments. Thus the repayment schedule is geared to the borrower's estimated operating cash flows. A formal agreement is involved, which often contains collateral requirements as well as **restrictive covenants,** such as limits on working capital, debt-equity ratios, and dividends. Medium-term credits are available in Australia and a number of European countries including the United Kingdom, Belgium, France, Germany, the Netherlands, and Switzerland. Elsewhere, they are difficult to arrange; bankers in Japan, for example, generally prefer to provide medium-term credits by rolling over short-term loans.

Long-Term Financing.   Long-term debt is normally used to purchase fixed assets, leading lenders to focus on the firm's ability to generate cash flows to service these liabilities rather than on its liquidity position. Security is often required, but the lender's principal concern remains the borrower's earnings prospects and the various technological, managerial, and market resources that affect these prospects. The major forms of long-term debt financing include loans from banks and other financial institutions (e.g., pension funds), bonds, and leasing.

In contrast to U.S. banks, commercial banks or their affiliates in many other countries, including Germany, Japan, the United Kingdom, France, Italy, Belgium, the Netherlands, and Australia, supply long-term credits to industry. The type of collateral required varies with the borrower's credit rating but often takes the form of a mortgage or a bank or parent company guarantee.

Funds from pensions and insurance plans are an important source of long-term financing in the United States, the United Kingdom, Germany, the Netherlands, and a number of other countries; such funding is growing in importance in Japan. In France and Italy, however, where private pension plans virtually do not exist, no separate pool of investable funds is available.

Compared with the United States, **leasing** is in the embryonic stage in most countries. The implicit cost tends to be quite high. Its value and use depends on the tax regulations relating to **depreciation write-offs** in a particular country and the importance of these tax shields to companies contemplating fixed asset acquisitions.

Bond placements are closely controlled in most countries, either directly by the government or by the major commercial and merchant banks. Public offerings are relatively rare in countries such as France and Italy where government agencies dominate the capital markets with their own issues or high rates of local inflation make lenders unwilling to commit their funds for extended periods. The weakness of Japan's capital market seems to stem both from investor preferences for bank deposits, which may be related to the lack of a strong secondary market and to the strength of banking institutions, and from strict government regulations. **New bond issues in Japan** are sold mainly to financial institutions, although there is currently a large demand for yen-denominated bonds from non-Japanese sources.

Unrestricted by a local counterpart of the **Glass-Steagall Act,** commercial banks outside the United States play a major role in the underwriting and placement, both public and private, of long-term debt issues. They usually form syndicates to market the securities, filling the role that only investment banks are allowed to perform in this country.

Development Banks.   To help provide the huge financial resources required to promote growth in less developed areas, the United States and other countries have established a variety of development banks whose lending is directed to investments that would not otherwise be funded by private capital. The projects include dams, communication systems, roads, and other infrastructure items whose economic benefits could not be completely captured by private investors, as well as investments such as steel mills and chemical plants whose value lies in perceived political or social advantages to the host nation (or at least to its leaders). The loans generally are medium to long term and carry concessionary rates.

Even though most lending is done directly to a government, this type of financing has two implications for the private sector. First, the projects require goods and services that corporations can provide. Second, once an infrastructure has been established, new investment opportunities become available for multinational corporations.

There are three different types of development bank: the **World Bank Group,** regional development banks, and national development banks.

The **World Bank Group,** a multinational financial institution, was established after World War II to facilitate provision of long-term capital for the reconstruction and development of member countries. It comprises three related financial organizations: the **International Bank for Reconstruction and Development (IBRD),** also known as the **World Bank,** the **International Finance Corporation (IFC),** and the **International Development Association (IDA).**

The **World Bank** makes loans at nearly conventional terms to countries for projects of high economic priority. To qualify for financing, a project must have costs and revenues that can be estimated with reasonable accuracy. A **government guarantee** is a necessity for World Bank funding. The bank's main emphasis has been on large infrastructure projects such as roads, dams, and power plants, and educational and agricultural activities. Besides its members' subscriptions, the World Bank raises funds by issuing bonds.

The **IFC** finances various projects in the private sector through loans and equity participations. In contrast to the World Bank, the IFC does not require government guarantees and emphasizes providing risk capital for firms in the manufacturing field that (a) have a reasonable chance of earning the investors' required rate of return and (b) will provide economic benefits to the nation.

The World Bank concentrates on projects that have a high probability of being profitable; consequently, many of the poorest of the less developed countries are unable to gain access to its funds. **IDA** was founded in 1960 to remedy this shortcoming. As distinguished from the World Bank, IDA is authorized to make "soft" (highly concessionary) loans with maturities to 50 years and no interest. It does require a government guarantee, however. The establishment of IDA illustrates a major unresolved issue for the **World Bank Group:** should its emphasis be on making sound loans to developing countries, or should it concentrate on investing in projects most likely to be of benefit to the host country? It is not clear, of course, that these goals are in conflict.

The past two decades have seen a proliferation of **national and regional development banks,** with the Middle East being a recent spawning ground for many new ones. The functions of a development bank are to offer debt and equity financing to aid in the economic growth of underdeveloped areas. This includes extending intermediate- to long-term capital directly, strengthening local capital markets, and supplying management consulting services to new companies. The professional guidance helps to safeguard, and thereby encourage, investments in a firm.

National and regional **development banks** have the same basic function: to provide funds for the financing of manufacturing, mining, agricultural, and infrastructure projects considered important for growth. The characteristics for success are the same for both types of organization. They must attract capable, investment-oriented management and they must propose enough economically viable projects to enable management to select a reasonable portfolio of investments.

As the names imply, a difference does exist in the orientation of these institutions. National development banks may focus on particular industries or geographical areas in a country. Regional banks tend to support projects that promote regional cooperation and economic integration. The loans typically have a 5–15 year term and carry a favorable rate of interest.

The list that follows includes some of the leading regional development banks:

1. *European Investment Bank (EIB).* Founded in 1958, if offers funds for certain public and private projects in European and other nations associated with or linked to the Common Market by cooperative agreements for financial aid. Loans to less developed areas are emphasized.

2. *Inter-American Development Bank (IADB).* The IADB is one of the key sources of long-term capital in Latin America. Founded in 1959 by the United States and 19 Latin American countries, the IADB had granted a net total of 1,022 loans with a total value of $11.9 billion through 1977. It lends to joint ventures, both minority and majority foreign owned.

3. *Atlantic Development Group for Latin America (ADELA).* Formed in 1964, this international private investment company, incorporated in Luxembourg, is dedicated to the socioeconomic development of Latin America. Its objective is to strengthen private enterprise by providing capital and entrepreneurial and technical services. The 230-odd shareholders are many of the leading industrial and financial companies of Europe, South America, Japan, and Latin America.

4. *Asian Development Bank (ADB).* Its 42 members include the countries of the UN Commission for Asia and the Far East, Canada, the United Kingdom, and the United States, and Germany, and several other West European countries. It guarantees or makes direct loans to private ventures in Asia-Pacific countries and helps develop local capital markets by underwriting securities issued by private enterprises.

5. *African Development Bank (ADB).* Founded in 1964 by member states of the Organization of African Unity, the bank's primary purpose is to promote the economic and social development of its member states. It makes or guarantees loans and provides technical assistance in the preparation, financing, and implementation of development projects. Beneficiaries of ADB loans and activities are normally governments or government-related agencies.

6. *Arab Fund for Economic and Social Development (AFESD).* Oldest of the multilateral Arab funds (established in 1968), the AFESD has $1.4 billion (1979) in capital paid in by its members, which are all Arab League states. It actively seeks projects in Arab League countries and assumes responsibility for project implementation by conducting feasibility studies, contracting, controlling quality, and supervising the work schedule.

EVALUATING FOREIGN CURRENCY BORROWING.   Firms continually face the choice of financing their overseas affiliates with dollars or with foreign currencies. Even if markets are efficient in the sense of equating pretax expected dollar financing costs, the impact of taxation of foreign exchange gains or losses on loans will generally cause aftertax costs to diverge. Thus tax effects can be a significant determinant of the financing decision when firms have the option of raising funds in several different currencies. Other important factors involved in the borrowing decision include relative interest rates, anticipated currency changes, and exposure management considerations.

Methodology.   Folks and Advani ("Alternative Methods for Analyzing the Currency of Denomination Decisions for Long-Term Bonds," University of South Carolina Working Paper, April 1977) give the following steps for evaluating the appropriate currency for a loan or a bond issue:

1. Determine the effective cost (yield) of dollar (or other base currency) financing.
2. For each currency under consideration, estimate the future exchange rates, period by period.
3. Use these forecasts to convert into dollars the projected foreign currency cash outflows needed to service and repay the foreign currency debt.
4. Calculate that discount rate (the internal rate of return) that equates the present dollar value of these outflows with the dollar value of the proceeds from the financing.
5. Select that financing source with the lowest dollar cost.

Several variations on this basic methodology are possible. One is to determine the interest rate on a foreign currency borrowing that after adjustments for taxes and currency changes, provides the same yield as on dollar debt. If the projected **foreign currency interest rate** is above this break-even level, dollar debt would be preferred; the foreign currency should be borrowed when its anticipated dollar cost is below the break-even rate.

Another approach is to compute the annualized rate of currency appreciation or depreciation that would just equate the aftertax borrowing costs of dollar and foreign currency debt. The forecast devaluation or revaluation is then compared with the break-even rate and the less expensive option selected.

Short-Term Financing Cost Calculations.   The aftertax U.S. dollar cost of a local currency loan at an interest rate of r_L by a foreign affiliate when the expected local currency (LC) **exchange rate depreciation** versus the dollar is d equals the aftertax interest expense less the exchange gain on principal payment:

$$\text{interest cost } - \text{ exchange gain}$$
$$r_L (1 - d)(1 - t_i) - d$$

where t_i is the affiliate's marginal tax rate on interest expense. The first term is the aftertax dollar interest cost paid at year-end after an LC devaluation of d; the second is the exchange gain in dollars of repaying the local currency loan worth $1 - d$ dollars at the end of the year. The gain has no local tax effect for the affiliate because the same amount of local currency was borrowed and repaid. In the case of a forecast revaluation, a loss is entailed by local currency borrowing, and $1 + d$ is substituted for $1 - d$ and $+d$ for $-d$.

The aftertax cost of a dollar loan is the difference between the aftertax interest expense and the tax deduction (expense) arising from the effect of the currency change on the principal repayment:

$$\text{interest cost } - \text{ tax gain (loss) due to change in local currency value of principal amount}$$
$$r_{U.S.} (1 - t_i) - dt_x$$

where t_x is the affiliate's marginal tax rate on exchange gains and losses. The first term is the aftertax interest expense of borrowing dollars. The second reflects the fact that if the exchange rate fluctuates, the local currency units required to repay a dollar loan will increase (with a devaluation) or decrease (with a revaluation). Depending on the country involved and whether exchange losses or gains on a capital transaction are a taxable event, the affiliate's local tax burden may be smaller or greater.

One approach to determining whether local currency or dollar financing is less expensive is to equate the costs of each and calculate the break-even rate of LC depreciation or appreciation, that is, the value for d at which the firm is indifferent to borrowing in one currency or the other. This is given by:

$$d = \frac{(1 - t_i)(r_L - r_{U.S.})}{(1 - t_i)\,r_L + (1 - t_x)}$$

There are two special cases that are frequently of interest:

- When $t_i = t_x$ (which is true for many countries).

$$d = \frac{r_L - r_{U.S.}}{r_L + 1}$$

- When $t_x = 0$ (which is true, e.g., in the United Kingdom).

$$d = \frac{(1 - t_i)(r_L - r_{U.S.})}{(1 - t_i),\,r_L + 1}$$

The foregoing analysis can be applied when the dollars are provided by an intracompany advance from the United States rather than obtained directly by the affiliate from a financial institution. In this case:

$$d = \frac{(1 - t_p)(r_{U.S.} - I_c) + (1 - t_i)(r_L - I_c)}{(1 - t_i)\,r_L + (1 - t_x)}$$

where t_p is the parent company's marginal tax rate(s) on interest income and expense, and I_c is the parent company's interest charge to the affiliate. (It should be noted that $r_{U.S.}$ here is the parent's, not the affiliate's, cost of dollar debt.)

With this **break-even analysis,** the treasurer can readily see the amount of foreign currency fluctuation necessary to make one type of borrowing cheaper than the other. He will then compare the firm's actual forecast, determined objectively or subjectively, of currency change with this benchmark.

For example, a Brazilian subsidiary requires funds to finance working capital for one year. It can borrow cruzeiros at a cost of 45% or dollars from a bank at 12%. The tax rates for calculating the effective cost of interest expense and a devaluation loss are identical. Then, the break-even value of d is $(0.45 - 0.12)/1.45 = 22.76\%$. If the cruzeiro is expected to devalue by less than this amount over the course of the next year, dollar debt will be less expensive. Conversely, a more rapid rate of devaluation renders cruzeiro debt preferable.

It is imperative to recognize that the devaluation is measured by the decline in the value of the local currency versus the dollar, **not** by the increased number of local currency units required to purchase the dollar. To illustrate, if the exchange rate at the beginning of the year was NCr 20/U.S.\$ and NCr 30/U.S.\$ at the end, the devaluation is 33.3%, that is, (NCr 30 − NCr 20)/NCr 30. Initially, one cruzeiro was worth \$0.0500 and declined in value over 12 months to \$0.0333. Its devaluation in dollar terms was \$0.0167; this is the reduction in worth that is to be compared with the initial value.

The error of determining the rate of devaluation by dividing the change in local currency units to one dollar by the initial exchange rate is readily apparent if one remembers that a 100% devaluation is virtually impossible. When Uruguay devalued its peso some years ago from pesos 100/U.S.\$ to pesos 200/U.S.\$, many newspapers and business magazines referred to the event as a 100% devaluation. If in fact the devaluation had been of that magnitude, the Uruguayan peso would have been worthless by definition. Yet, it retained a value. The amount of the devaluation in the case was 50% because the currency had lost one-half its value in U.S. dollar terms.

The logic of the foregoing break-even analysis can be extended to **financing options** other than those cited here, for example, having the parent extend interest-free financing through adjustments in the intracompany merchandise account. In all situations, the cost of each source of funds must be calculated in terms of the relevant variables (interest rates, tax rates, and future exchange rates) and the expense compared with that of all other possibilities.

Long-Term Financing Cost Calculations. Assume that a firm can borrow dollars abroad or the local (foreign) currency for n years at fixed interest rates of $r_{U.S.}$ and r_f, respectively. Interest is to be paid at the end of each year and the principal in a lump sum at the end of year n. Suppose that the foreign currency undergoes a cumulative devaluation (revaluation) of d_i between now and the end of year i, with $d_i = (e_0 - e_i)/e_0$ (d_i is negative for a revaluation), where e_0 is the current exchange rate ($\$e_0 = LC1$), e_i is the exchange rate at the end of period i, and t is the foreign tax rate. Then it can be shown that the **aftertax yield on a foreign currency–denominated bond** issued by a local affiliate can be found as the solution r to:

$$-1 + F_1(1 - t) + \sum_{i=1}^{n} \frac{r_f(1 - d_i)(1 - t)}{(1 + r)^i} + \frac{1 - d_n}{(1 + r)^n} = 0$$

Similarly, the effective aftertax cost of dollar debt is the solution k to:

$$-1 + F_2(1 - t) + \sum_{i=1}^{n} \frac{r_{U.S.}(1 - t)}{(1 + k)^i} + \frac{1 - d_n t}{(1 + k)^n} = 0$$

The terms F_1 and F_2 are the flotation costs for issuing the foreign currency and dollar bonds, respectively. It is assumed that these costs are tax deductible as soon as they are incurred.

To illustrate the application of these formulas, suppose that Global Industries, Inc., is planning to float a 7-year $30 million bond issue. It has the choice of having its Swiss subsidiary borrow U.S. dollars at a coupon rate of 9.625% or Swiss francs at 3.5%. Both bond issues are sold at par. The flotation costs are 3% for the Swiss franc and 1.2% for the dollar issue, leading to effective pre-tax rates of 4% for the Swiss franc debt and 9.87% for the dollar debt. Repayment is in a lump sum at the end of year 7.

The current exchange rate is SFr 1.75 to the dollar. Thus Global Industries' subsidiary can either borrow $30 million or SFr 52.5 million. Assume that the Swiss tax rate is 45%. Exhibits 10 and 11 contain the year-by-year Swiss franc cash flows and dollar cash flows associated with both issues. The projected exchange rates for the coming 7 years are listed in Exhibit 11. On the basis of these data, the effective aftertax yield on the Swiss franc issue is 8.40% and on the dollar debt issue 8.02%.

Such detailed currency projections are generally not made, given the uncertainties involved. Instead, it is simpler to project an average rate of currency change over the life of the debt and to calculate effective aftertax dollar costs on that basis. For example, if a steady appreciation of the foreign currency at a rate of g per annum is anticipated, the **effective aftertax dollar yield on the foreign currency bond** issued by a local affiliate can be found by solving the following equation for r:

EXHIBIT 10 AFTERTAX CASH FLOWS ASSOCIATED WITH SWISS FRANC DEBT

Year	Cash Flow Category	Swiss Franc Cash Flows (1)	÷	Rate of Exchange (2)	×	Aftertax Factor (3)	=	Aftertax Dollar Cash Flows (4)
0	Bond sale	− 52,500,000		1.75		1		− $30,000,000
	Flotation charge	1,575,000		1.75		0.55		495,000
1	Interest	1,837,500		1.665		0.55		606,981.98
2	Interest	1,837,500		1.580		0.55		639,636.09
3	Interest	1,837,500		1.495		0.55		676,003.35
4	Interest	1,837,500		1.410		0.55		716,755.33
5	Interest	1,837,500		1.325		0.55		762,735.88
6	Interest	1,837,500		1.240		0.55		815,020.14
7	Interest	1,837,500		1.155		0.55		875,000.01
	Principal repayment	52,500,000		1.555		1		$43,454,545.45

$$-1 + \sum_{i=1}^{n} \frac{r_f(1 + g)^i (1 - t)}{(1 + r)^i} + \frac{(1 + g)^n}{(1 + r)^n} = 0$$

The solution r equals $r_f(1 + g)(1 - t) + g$, the same as in the one-period case.

Assuming a nominal yield r_f equal to 6%, $t = 45\%$, and $g = 3\%$, the effective cost of foreign currency borrowing is $0.06 \times 1.03 \times 0.55 + 0.03$ or 6.4%. In the absence of taxes, this cost would be 9.18% ($0.06 \times 1.03 + 0.03$).

EXHIBIT 11 AFTERTAX CASH FLOWS ASSOCIATED WITH DOLLAR DEBT

Year	Cash Flow Category	Dollar Cash Flow (1)	×	Aftertax Factor (2)	=	Aftertax Dollar Cash Flows (3)
0	Bond sale	− $30,000,000		1		− $30,000,000
	Flotation charge	360,000		0.55		198,000
1	Interest	2,887,500		0.55		1,588,125
2	Interest	2,887,500		0.55		1,588,125
3	Interest	2,887,500		0.55		1,588,125
4	Interest	2,887,500		0.55		1,588,125
5	Interest	2,887,500		0.55		1,588,125
6	Interest	2,887,500		0.55		1,588,125
7	Interest	2,887,500		0.55		1,588,125
	Principal repayment	$30,000,000		1		$30,000,000
	Capital gain recognized by Swiss tax authorities	$15,454,545[a]		0.45		$6,954,545.30

[a]At $0.87, 17,850,000 Swiss francs.

Exposure Management Considerations. These approaches all assume that firms are interested only in minimizing expected costs. However, foreign currency borrowing can be used to reduce the variance of total corporate cash flows and as a hedge against economic exposure. This aspect of long-term financing is important to most managers, who usually are concerned with total as opposed to systematic risk, regardless of shareholder perceptions and academic advice.

It is necessary to recognize, however, that if firms have the option of neutralizing in the **forward foreign exchange market** any exposure resulting from financial decisions, the **currency of denomination of corporate debt** may not be as important in exposure management as the role sometimes assigned to it. If a sufficiently broad and deep forward market does exist, the hedging possibilities provided by debt that is denominated in foreign currency can be replicated by forward exchange contracts. (In the absence of capital controls and other impediments to the free functioning of the forward market, arbitrage will operate to ensure that spot and future exchange rates reflect perfectly the home and foreign interest rate structures.)

At times, however, forward contracts in a particular currency are either nonexistent or unavailable in the quantity required. From the standpoint of exchange risk management, therefore, a firm may wish to borrow another currency even if it is not the theoretically least expensive form of financing on an expected value basis. The formulas above can be used to estimate the expected cost of deviating from the cost-minimizing alternative. This penalty is the benchmark for gauging foreign exchange risk management benefits.

Borrowing Cost Comparisons and Market Efficiency. Implicit in the various approaches used to compare borrowing costs is an assumption that interest differentials among currencies do not efficiently incorporate all available information concerning future exchange rates. These interest differentials can, however, be used in an efficient market to provide relatively unbiased forecasts of currency changes. Thus substituting one's own judgment about the future course of exchange rates is questionable, unless there is reason to believe that one of the following conditions holds:

1. Certain barriers (e.g., controls on capital flows), distortions (e.g., credit rationing with interest ceilings), or interventions in the marketplace (e.g., massive government sales or purchases of securities) are likely to push the interest differential out of line with generally held exchange rate expectations.
2. The individual's forecasts are superior to the market's because of inside information or the more effective use of publicly available information.

The probability of the first condition holding is undoubtedly much greater than the probability of the second one.

REFERENCES

Adler, Michael, "The Cost of Capital and Valuation of a Two-Country Firm," *Journal of Finance,* March 1974, pp. 119–132.

Agmon, Tamir, and Lessard, Donald R., "Investor Recognition of Corporate International Diversification," *Journal of Finance,* September 1977, pp. 1049–1056.

Business International, *Decision-Making in International Operations,* Business International Corp., New York, 1970.

————, *New Techniques in International Exposure and Cash Management, Vol. I, The State of the Art,* Business International Corp., New York, 1977.

Cohen, Benjamin I., *Multinational Firms and Asian Exports,* Yale University Press, New Haven, CT, 1975.

Fieleke, Norman S., "Foreign Exchange Speculation by U.S. Firms: Some New Evidence," *New England Economic Review,* March–April 1979, pp. 5–17.

Folks, William R., Jr., and Advani, Ramesh, "Alternative Methods for Analyzing the Currency of Denomination Decision for Long-Term Bonds," University of South Carolina Working Paper, presented at the Eastern Finance Association meeting, Boston, April 1977.

Group of Thirty, *Foreign Exchange Markets Under Floating Rates,* Group of Thirty, New York, 1980.

Hawkins, Robert G., Mintz, Norman, and Provissiero, Michael, "Government Takeovers of U.S. Foreign Affiliates," *Journal of International Business Studies,* Spring 1976, pp. 3–15.

Jacquillat, Bertrand, and Solnik, Bruno H., "Multinationals Are Poor Tools for Diversification," *Journal of Portfolio Management,* Winter 1978, pp. 8–12.

Kobrin, Stephen J., "Political Risk: A Review and Reconsideration," *Journal of International Business Studies,* Spring-Summer 1979, pp. 67–80.

Lessard, Donald R., "World, Country, and Industry Relationships in Equity Returns: Implications for Risk Reduction Through International Diversification," *Financial Analysts Journal,* January–February 1976, pp. 32–38.

————, "Evaluating Foreign Projects—An Adjusted Present Value Approach," in Donald R. Lessard, Ed., *International Financial Management,* Warren, Gorham & Lamont, Boston, 1979.

————, "Transfer Prices, Taxes, and Financial Markets: Implications of Internal Financial Transfers within the Multinational Firm," in Robert G. Hawkins, Ed., *The Economic Effects of Multinational Corporations,* JAI Press, Greenwich, CT, 1979.

————, and Shapiro, Alan C., "Designing a Global Financing Strategy," University of Southern California Working Paper, February 1980.

Naumann-Etienne, Ruediger, "A Framework for Financial Decisions in MNCs," *Journal of Financial and Quantitative Analysis,* November 1974, pp. 859–874.

"Policies of MNCs on Debt/Equity Mix," *Business International Money Report,* September 21, 1979, pp. 319–320.

Robbins, Sidney M., and Stobaugh, Robert B., *Money in the Multinational Enterprise,* Basic Books, New York, 1973.

Rodriguez, Rita M., and Carter, E. Eugene, *International Financial Management,* 2nd ed., Prentice-Hall, Englewood Cliffs, NJ, 1979, Chapter 10.

Rugman, Alan M., "Risk Reduction by International Diversification," *Journal of International Business Studies,* Fall–Winter 1976, pp. 75–80.

Shapiro, Alan C., "Evaluating Financing Costs for Multinational Subsidiaries," *Journal of International Business Studies,* Fall 1975, pp. 25–32.

————, "Capital Budgeting for the Multinational Corporation," *Financial Management,* Spring 1978, pp. 7–16.

————, "The Impact of Taxation on Currency-of-Denomination Decision for Long-Term Foreign Borrowing," University of Southern California Working Paper, December 1978.

Solnik, Bruno H., "Why Not Diversify Internationally Rather than Domestically?" *Financial Analysts Journal,* July–August 1974, pp. 48–54.

Stobaugh, Robert B., "Financing Foreign Subsidiaries of U.S.-Controlled Multinational Enterprises," *Journal of International Business Studies,* Summer 1970, pp. 43–64.

Stonehill, Arthur I., and Stitzel, Thomas, "Financial Structure and Multinational Corporations," *California Management Review,* Fall 1969, pp. 91–96.

Suhar, V. Victor, and Lyons, Douglas D., "Choosing Between a Parallel Loan and a Swap," *Euromoney*, March 1979, pp. 114–119.

Truitt, J. Frederick, "Expropriation of Foreign Investment: Summary of the Post-World War II Experience of American and British Investors in the Less Developed Countries," *Journal of International Business Studies*, Fall 1970, pp. 21–24.

Wickes, M. E. "A Comparative Analysis of the Foreign Investment Evaluation Practices of U.S.-Based Multinational Companies," unpublished doctoral dissertation, Pennsylvania State University, March 1980.

BIBLIOGRAPHY

Aharoni, Yair, *The Foreign Investment Decision Process*, Harvard Graduate School of Business Administration, Division of Research, Cambridge, MA, 1966.

Arpan, Jeffrey S., *International Intracorporate Pricing*, Praeger, New York, 1972.

Bavishi, Vinod, "Capital Budgeting for U.S.-Based Multinational Corporations: An Assessment of Theory and Practice," University of Connecticut Working Paper, Storrs, CT, 1979.

Bradley, David, "Managing Against Expropriation," *Harvard Business Review*, July–August 1977, pp. 75–83.

Business International, *Financing Foreign Operations*, Business International Corp, New York, various issues.

Choi, Frederick D. S., and Mueller, Gerhard G., *An Introduction to Multinational Accounting*, Prentice-Hall, Englewood Cliffs, NJ, 1978.

Eiteman, David K., and Stonehill, Arthur I., *Multinational Business Finance*, 2nd ed., Addison-Wesley, Reading, MA, 1979.

Folks, William R., Jr., "Analysis of Short-Term, Cross-Border Financing Decisions," *Financial Management*, Autumn 1976, pp. 19–27.

Giddy, Ian H., "The Demise of the Product Cycle Model in International Business Theory," *Columbia Journal of World Business*, Spring 1978, pp. 90–97.

Goeltz, Richard K., "The Composition of Parent Financial Assistance to Foreign Subsidiaries," unpublished Esso Memorandum, 1968.

———, "Managing Liquid Funds Internationally," *Columbia Journal of World Business*, July–August 1972, pp. 59–65.

Kobrin, Stephen J., "When Does Political Instability Result in Increased Investment Risk?" *Columbia Journal of World Business*, Fall 1978, pp. 113–122.

Levy, Haim, and Sarnat, Marshall, "International Diversification of Investment Portfolios," *American Economic Review*, September 1970, pp. 668–675.

Rutenberg, Davis P., "Maneuvering Liquid Assets in a Multi-National Company," *Management Science*, June 1970, pp. B-671–684.

Shapiro, Alan C., "Optimal Inventory and Credit-Granting Strategies Under Inflation and Devaluation," *Journal of Financial and Quantitative Analysis*, January 1973, pp. 37–46.

———, "International Cash Management—The Determination of Multicurrency Cash Balances," *Journal of Financial and Quantitative Analysis*, December 1976, pp. 893–900.

———, "Financial Structure and Cost of Capital in the Multinational Corporation," *Journal of Financial and Quantitative Analysis*, June 1978, pp. 211–226.

Stobaugh, Robert B., "How to Analyze Foreign Investment Climates," *Harvard Business Review*, September–October 1969, pp. 100–108.

Stonehill, Arthur, and Nathanson, Leonard, "Capital Budgeting and the Multinational Corporation," *California Management Review*, Summer 1968, pp. 39–54.

Wasserman, Max J., Prindle, Andreas R., and Townsend, Charles C., Jr., *International Money Management*, American Management Association, New York, 1973.

Weston, J. Fred, and Sorge, Bart W., *Guide to International Financial Management*, McGraw-Hill, New York, 1977.

Zenoff, David B., "Remitting Funds from Foreign Affiliates," *Financial Executive*, March 1968, pp. 46–63.

———, "International Cash Management: Why It Is Important and How to Make It Work," *Worldwide Projects and Installations Planning*, July–August 1973.

———, and Zwick, Jack, *International Financial Management*, Prentice-Hall, Englewood Cliffs, NJ, 1969.

The Internal Revenue Service recently argued that by guaranteeing foreign affiliates' debts, a U.S. corporation is providing a valuable service for which it should be compensated. The IRS, therefore, has begun imputing income to the guarantor and levying a tax. This additional tax cost should be incorporated in the determination of whether parent support should be given to an overseas subsidiary's borrowing.

SOURCES OF FUNDS FOR MNC AFFILIATES. A distinctive feature of the financial strategy of multinational firms is the wide range of internal and external sources of funds available to them. Those external sources include commercial banks, export financing agencies, public (government) financial institutions, development banks, insurance companies, pension plans, private and public bond placements, and lease financing.

Short-Term Financing. Like most domestic firms, affiliates of multinational corporations generally attempt to finance their **working capital requirements** locally both for convenience and for exposure management purposes. Commercial banks are the prime source of short-term financing. This usually takes the form of overdrafts and discounting facilities, but may be a straight loan for a set period such as 90 days or longer. Nonbank sources of funds include export financing and factoring and commercial paper.

In countries other than the United States, banks tend to lend through **overdrafts**. An overdraft is simply a line of credit against which drafts (checks) can be drawn (written), up to a specified maximum amount. These overdraft lines are often extended and expanded year after year, thus providing, in effect, a form of medium-term financing. The borrower pays interest on the debit balance only. **Commitment fees** on the unused portion of the credit line may be required, but unlike the practice in the United States, **compensating balances** (required minimum balances) are rarely requested.

The **discounting of trade bills** is the preferred short-term financing technique in many developed and less developed countries. It is popular because these bills often can be rediscounted with the central bank at a rate that does not fully reflect all the commercial risks involved (i.e., at a subsidized rate). Discounting usually results from the following set of transactions. A manufacturer selling goods to a retailer on credit draws a bill on the buyer, payable in, say, 30 days. The buyer endorses (accepts) the bill, or his bank accepts it on his behalf (at which point it becomes a **banker's acceptance**). The manufacturer gives the bill to his bank, which accepts it for a fee if the buyer's bank has not done so already. The bill is then sold at a discount to the manufacturer's bank or to a money market dealer. The rate of interest varies with the term of the bill and the general level of local money market interest rates.

Medium-Term Financing. Loans with maturities between 1 and 7 years constitute medium-term financing. Customarily, these take the form of **renewable overdrafts** or discounting facilities (revolving acceptance credits) with the rate of interest fluctuating. They are used as a continuing source of funds or as **bridge financing** while the borrower obtains medium- or long-term fixed rate financing, usually from a financial institution other than a commercial bank. Banks that extend bridging loans also may act as agents in syndicating the substitute financing that is used to repay the bank debt. Such arrangements are common in Germany and Italy.

Medium-term loans typically are made on the basis of cash flows expected to be generated by the borrower's investments. Thus the repayment schedule is geared to the borrower's estimated operating cash flows. A formal agreement is involved, which often contains collateral requirements as well as **restrictive covenants,** such as limits on working capital, debt-equity ratios, and dividends. Medium-term credits are available in Australia and a number of European countries including the United Kingdom, Belgium, France, Germany, the Netherlands, and Switzerland. Elsewhere, they are difficult to arrange; bankers in Japan, for example, generally prefer to provide medium-term credits by rolling over short-term loans.

Long-Term Financing.   Long-term debt is normally used to purchase fixed assets, leading lenders to focus on the firm's ability to generate cash flows to service these liabilities rather than on its liquidity position. Security is often required, but the lender's principal concern remains the borrower's earnings prospects and the various technological, managerial, and market resources that affect these prospects. The major forms of long-term debt financing include loans from banks and other financial institutions (e.g., pension funds), bonds, and leasing.

In contrast to U.S. banks, commercial banks or their affiliates in many other countries, including Germany, Japan, the United Kingdom, France, Italy, Belgium, the Netherlands, and Australia, supply long-term credits to industry. The type of collateral required varies with the borrower's credit rating but often takes the form of a mortgage or a bank or parent company guarantee.

Funds from pensions and insurance plans are an important source of long-term financing in the United States, the United Kingdom, Germany, the Netherlands, and a number of other countries; such funding is growing in importance in Japan. In France and Italy, however, where private pension plans virtually do not exist, no separate pool of investable funds is available.

Compared with the United States, **leasing** is in the embryonic stage in most countries. The implicit cost tends to be quite high. Its value and use depends on the tax regulations relating to **depreciation write-offs** in a particular country and the importance of these tax shields to companies contemplating fixed asset acquisitions.

Bond placements are closely controlled in most countries, either directly by the government or by the major commercial and merchant banks. Public offerings are relatively rare in countries such as France and Italy where government agencies dominate the capital markets with their own issues or high rates of local inflation make lenders unwilling to commit their funds for extended periods. The weakness of Japan's capital market seems to stem both from investor preferences for bank deposits, which may be related to the lack of a strong secondary market and to the strength of banking institutions, and from strict government regulations. **New bond issues in Japan** are sold mainly to financial institutions, although there is currently a large demand for yen-denominated bonds from non-Japanese sources.

Unrestricted by a local counterpart of the **Glass-Steagall Act,** commercial banks outside the United States play a major role in the underwriting and placement, both public and private, of long-term debt issues. They usually form syndicates to market the securities, filling the role that only investment banks are allowed to perform in this country.

Development Banks.   To help provide the huge financial resources required to promote growth in less developed areas, the United States and other countries have established a variety of development banks whose lending is directed to investments that would not otherwise be funded by private capital. The projects include dams, communication systems, roads, and other infrastructure items whose economic benefits could not be completely captured by private investors, as well as investments such as steel mills and chemical plants whose value lies in perceived political or social advantages to the host nation (or at least to its leaders). The loans generally are medium to long term and carry concessionary rates.

APPENDIX **A**

MATHEMATICS OF FINANCE

CONTENTS

INTEREST RATE MATHEMATICS	**3**
Definitions	**3**
Basic Types of Interest	**3**
Ordinary interest	4
Exact interest	4
Nature of exact interest	4
Interest on U.S. government securities	5
Anticipation	5
Bank Discount	**6**
Loans and discounts	6
Types of note	7
Basis for calculating proceeds	7
Due date of notes	7
Computing proceeds and discount on noninterest-bearing paper	8
Discounting interest-bearing paper	8
Finding principal to yield given proceeds	9
Computation of interest under partial payment plans	9
Merchant's rule	9
United States rule	10
Bank discount versus true discount	10
Relation of bank discount rate to true discount rate	11
Chain Discounts	**12**
Definition	12
Finding equivalent single discount	13
Compound Interest	**13**
Definitions	13
Finding the compound amount	14
Computing compound value using tables	15
Computing compound value using a financial calculator	17
Present Value	**17**
Computing present value using tables	18
Computing present value using a financial calculator	18
Other Converse Cases	**18**

Finding value of n	18
Computing n using tables	20
Computing n using a financial calculator	20
Finding value of i	20
Computing i using tables	20
Computing i using a financial calculator	21
Annuities	**21**
Definitions	21
Final value of ordinary annuity	22
Formula for compound value of an annuity	23
Computing compound value of annuity using tables	23
Computing compound value of annuity using a financial calculator	23
Sinking Fund Calculations	**24**
Finding amount of sinking fund installments	24
Computing value of annuity using tables	24
Schedule of sinking fund installments	24
Computing value of annuity using a financial calculator	26
Finding number of payments in a sinking fund	26
Computing number of years n using tables	27
Computing number of years n using a financial calculator	27
Final value of annuity due	27
Computing final value of annuity due using tables	28
Computing final value of annuity due using a financial calculator	28
Present value of ordinary annuity	28
Computing present value of annuity using tables	29
Computing present value of	

annuity using a financial calculator   29
Annuity that $1 will buy   31
  Computing an annuity amount using
  tables   31
  Computing an annuity amount using
  a financial calculator   31
Finding number of payments to
amortize a loan   33
  Computing period n using tables   33
  Computing period n using a
  financial calculator   33
Present value of annuity due   34
  Computing present value of annuity
  due using tables   34
  Computing present value of annuity
  due using a financial calculator   34
Bond Valuation: Definitions and
Calculations   **35**
  Bond definitions   35
  Premium and discount on bonds   35
  Nominal and effective interest rates   35
  Determining basis price of bonds   35

Computing the price using tables   36
  Short method for finding basis price   36
  Computing the price using a
  financial calculator   36
Amortization schedule   37
Short-cut method for discount bonds   38
Schedule of accumulation   38
Bond valuation tables   39
Basis price for bonds bought between
interest dates   39
  Computing bond prices using tables   39
  Computing bond prices using a
  financial calculator   41
Accruing bond interest between
interest dates   42
Determining profit or loss on sale of
bonds   43
Finding yield between interest dates   43

OPTION PRICING MATHEMATICS   **44**

The Black-Scholes Formula   **44**
Nomograms for Option Valuation   **46**

MATHEMATICS OF FINANCE

Marti G. Subrahmanyam

This appendix introduces the reader to concepts and computational methods in **interest rate mathematics** and **option pricing mathematics.**

The first part is oriented toward elucidating the basic concepts in interest rate calculations, with the assistance of examples of computation using tables. Since the pocket financial calculator has largely eliminated the tedium of detailed calculations using tables, the latter are used to illustrate the concepts rather than for computation per se. Every sub section also includes the computational method using a **financial calculator.**

There is a vast array of pocket **financial calculators** on the market today beginning with simple calculators that have financial function keys in addition to the basic function keys. Besides these, there are general purpose **programmable calculators** that are sufficiently powerful to handle a wide range of financial calculations. To provide a feel for the use of the pocket calculator in financial calculations, rather than an exhaustive listing of programs for a wide variety of calculators, the programs here are restricted to those suitable for a common type of machine, specifically, the Hewlett-Packard HP37E/HP 38E. Readers interested in a more detailed exposition are referred to Greynolds, Aronofsky, and Frame (1980), in addition to the handbooks published by the manufacturers of calculators.

INTEREST RATE MATHEMATICS

DEFINITIONS.   Interest is ordinarily defined as consideration paid for the use of money. To the borrower it represents the cost of the loan, to the lender it is a source of income. The amount of interest depends on three factors: principal, rate, time.

Principal.   The principal is any sum of money on which interest is to be computed. It may represent invested capital, as in the instance of partnership equities, or a loan in the form of notes or more formal bond indentures.

Rate.   The interest rate is usually expressed as a percentage of the principal per unit of time; for example, 14% per annum, 7% semiannually.

Time.   The time refers to the period for which interest is to be calculated. Unless otherwise stated, interest formulas use the year as a unit.

BASIC TYPES OF INTEREST.   There are two basic types of interest, simple and compound. These may be represented as follows:

1. Simple interest.
   a. Ordinary.
   b. Exact—commercial practice.
   c. Exact—government securities.
2. Compound.

Simple interest refers to interest that is always computed on the original principal. If the interest is not paid when due, it is not added to the principal. Thus the amount of interest is always proportional to the time.

Ordinary interest represents a type of simple interest computed on a 360-day year, commonly referred to as the **commercial year.** Under this method the year is divided into 12 months of 30 days each. Although the method is used in many commercial transactions, modifications are often introduced. For example, in discounting commercial paper, ordinary interest is calculated, but it is based on the exact number of days in the discount period.

Exact interest is interest based on a 365-day year, or 366 days in leap years. It is generally employed by banks in allowing interest on daily balances, and also in governmental calculations other than interest on government securities. In the latter instance special tables are available from which the accrued interest may be read.

Compound interest is discussed below.

Ordinary Interest.   Ordinary interest is the product of the principal, the rate, and the time:

$$I = Pit$$

where
I = amount of interest
P = principal
i = rate
t = time (years)

For example, to find the ordinary interest on \$12,148.72 for 153 days at 14% (per year), the formula yields:

$$12,148.72 \times \frac{14}{100} \times \frac{153}{360} = \$722.85$$

Exact Interest.

Nature of Exact Interest.   A given amount of principal earns in 365 days as much exact interest as the same principal earns in 360 days at ordinary interest. For 360 days therefore the exact interest is only 360/365 of the amount of ordinary interest. For practical purposes it is easier to compute ordinary interest first and then to adjust the result to get exact interest. Since 360/365 = 72/73, it is evident that exact interest is 72/73 of ordinary interest; therefore to calculate exact interest, figure ordinary interest and subtract 1/73.

Example.   Municipal taxes in the town of X are due November 1 and may be paid without penalty up to and including November 30. Thereafter an interest penalty is charged at 7%

per annum from the first due date. (November 1). For a tax bill of $4,850, find the total paid to the town, if payment is made on December 11 of the same year.

Solution.   Elapsed time November 1–December 11, 40 days.

7% ordinary interest	$ 37.722
Less $\frac{1}{73}$	0.517
Exact interest, 7%	$ 37.21
Amount of bill	4,850.00
Total paid	$4,887.21

Interest on U.S. Government Securities.   Interest on bonds or notes issued by the U.S. government is computed on the basis of exact interest for the exact number of days falling within the interest period. Exhibit 1 shows that the length of an interest period may vary from 181 days to 184 days. The daily accrual of interest may be computed as follows. First, determine the number of days in the interest period. Then, compute the accrual after adjusting for the number of days and the principal amount.

Anticipation.   This is a customary term used in connection with purchase invoices that have extra dating where interest is allowed if payment is made before the expiration of the final due date of the invoice. The effect of the extra dating is to extend the time within which a proffered **cash discount** may be taken. Thus, if merchandise is purchased at 2%, 10 days, 90 days extra, with anticipation at 6%, a discount of 2% is allowed for payment any time within 100 days. In addition, the purchaser may deduct interest for the number of days before the final due date. The exact procedure is first to find the amount payable on the last day of the discount period. From this amount is deducted **exact interest** at the stipulated anticipation rate for the number of days anticipated.

Example.   An invoice is dated April 12, 1980, for $5,653.75, terms 2%, 10 days, 60 days extra, f.o.b. destination, anticipation at 6%. The purchaser paid $45.60 freight. What was the amount due if payment was made on May 22, 1980?

EXHIBIT 1   EXACT NUMBER OF DAYS IN 6-MONTH INTEREST PERIOD

Ending Dates	Ordinary Year	Leap Year
January 1 or 15	184	184
February 1 or 15	184	184
March 1 or 15	181	182
April 1 or 15	182	183
May 1 or 15	181	182
June 1 or 15	182	183
July 1 or 15	181	182
August 1 or 15	181	182
September 1 or 15	184	184
October 1 or 15	183	183
November 1 or 15	184	184
December 1 or 15	183	183

The number of days from April 12 to May 22 is 40. Hence payment is anticipated 30 days. The calculation appears as follows:

Invoice	$5,653,75
Less: Freight paid	45.60
Net invoice	$5,608.15
Less: 2% discount	112.16
Balance subject to anticipation	$5,495.99
Anticipation for 30 days at 6% per annum (exact)	27.10
Amount payable on May 22, 1966	$5,468.89

It is the custom of some stores to compute the discount on the face of the invoice and the anticipation on the net amount after deducting the discount, finally deducting the freight charges. This plan, which favors the purchaser, is illustrated below:

Invoice	$5,653.75
Less: 2% discount	113.08
Balance	$5,540.67
Anticipation for 30 days at 6% per annum	27.33
Balance	$5,513.34
Less: Freight paid	45.60
Amount of check	$5,467.74

Extra dating is sometimes secured by stores as a result of certain trade customs. Invoices are frequently dated, say, 2%, 10 days, e.o.m. (end of month). This means that if an invoice is dated June 17, it is due 10 days after the end of June (i.e., July 10). Both discount and anticipation would then be allowed if payment is made before July 10.

Again, purchase orders sometimes contain conditional clauses in which "the seller agrees that merchandise shipped on or after the twenty-fifth of a month, will be billed as of the first of the following month." Thus, merchandise shipped on April 26, terms 2%, 10 days, is billed as of May 1, with discount and anticipation available until May 10. Ordinarily the anticipation may not amount to much because of the short time. However, if the above-quoted clause is coupled with e.o.m. dating, the effect is to secure an extra month's dating. In short, if goods are shipped on April 26, terms 2%, 10 days, e.o.m., and the purchase order contains the billing clause above, the invoice becomes due on June 10, that is, 10 days after the first of the month in which the invoice would otherwise fall due.

BANK DISCOUNT.

Loans and Discounts.   One of the important functions of a commercial bank is the making of loans, which produce a source of income for the bank and fulfill a necessary function in the economic life of the community served by the bank. Technically **loans** are distinguished from **discounts** chiefly by the fact that in the case of loans, interest is paid periodically, during the existence of the loan or at its maturity, whereas in the case of discounts the interest or "discount" is deducted at the time the advance is made. Thus, in the case of a $1,000 loan at 16% for 6 months, the borrower receives $1,000 and pays back $1,080 at the end of 6 months. On the other hand, if he discounts a $1,000 note at 6%, he receives $920 and pays back $1,000 at the end of the 6-month term. In short, bank discount is the consideration deducted by the bank from the face of a note or draft prior to its maturity date.

Since the 1930s, finance companies and banks have been making **long-term loans,** especially in the field of **home financing**. These loans are usually amortized, principal and interest, through equal monthly payments. They are dealt with later in this Section in connection with annuities.

Types of Note.   Notes may be variously classified, but for computation purposes it is necessary only to know whether a note is **interest bearing** (see, e.g., Exhibit 2) or **noninterest bearing** (Exhibit 3).

In discounting a note, the bank pays only what the note is worth at the time of discount. Thus, a **noninterest-bearing note** is worth its face value at maturity and not before. Any time before maturity the note is valued at less than face value by the amount of interest the bank charges. An **interest-bearing note,** however, provided the interest and discount rates are the same, is worth approximately its face value on the date of issue and thereafter increases in value each day by the amount of interest earned until maturity.

The amount that a bank pays for a note or that it credits to a borrower's account is called the **proceeds** of the note.

Basis for Calculating Proceeds.   Ordinarily, banks use the actual number of days in figuring the discount period on short-term notes, but interest or discount is computed on the basis of a 360-day year (ordinary interest). In the case of the Federal Reserve System, **exact interest** is used.

Due Date of Notes.   Promissory notes are payable at a stated number of days or months after date. **Drafts** may be payable so many days **after date** or **after sight.** If days are specified, the exact number of days is counted. Thus, if the note states "60 days after date . . ." and is dated May 14, it is due July 13. However, when months are specified, the note falls due in the month of maturity on the same date as is specified in the date of the note. For example, a note dated May 14 due in 2 months is due on July 14.

If a note is dated on the last day of a 31-day month, and falls due in a 30-day month, the due date would be the last of the 30-day month. To illustrate, a note dated May 31, due

EXHIBIT 2   INTEREST-BEARING PROMISSORY NOTE

$ 3,400 ⁰⁰/100	*New York April 2* 19—

$ 3,400 ^{00}/100   *New York   April 2* 19—

_____ *Two (2) months* _____ AFTER DATE ___*I*___ PROMISE TO PAY TO

THE ORDER OF _____ *Barrows & Co.*

_____ *Thirty—four hundred and* ^{00}/100 ～～～～～ DOLLARS

AT _____ *Irving Trust Co. with interest @ 15%*

VALUE RECEIVED

No.   *1*   DUE *June 2* 19—   *J. Doe*

EXHIBIT 3   NONINTEREST-BEARING PROMISSORY NOTE

$ 500 00/100	New York May 15 19—
Twenty (20) days AFTER DATE _I_ PROMISE TO PAY TO	
THE ORDER OF _J. Doe_	
Five hundred and 00/100 ~~~~~~~~~~~ DOLLARS	
AT _Irving Trust Co._	
VALUE RECEIVED	
No. 273 _R. Roe_	

in four months, matures on September 30. But a note dated May 31, due in 120 days, is payable September 28.

Computing Proceeds and Discount on Noninterest-Bearing Paper. Three steps are neccessary to calculate the proceeds or deposit credit:

1. Calculate the time from the discount date to maturity.
2. Compute the interest to maturity for the time computed in step 1. This is the discount.
3. Deduct the discount from the face value.

Example 1. Find the proceeds or deposit credit on a note for $1,875, dated July 5, for 30 days, discounted at 14% per annum on the date of issue. The note is due August 4, that is, 30 days from July 5.

Face value of note	$1,875.00
Discount, 30 days, 14% on $1,875	− 21.87
Proceeds	$1,853.13

Example 2. Find the proceeds on a note for $2,863.79 dated February 8, 1981, due in 60 days, discounted on March 2 at $14\frac{1}{2}\%$ per annum. The maturity date is April 9, 1981, and the time to maturity (March 2 to April 9) 38 days.

Face value	$2,863.79
Discount on above for 38 days at $14\frac{1}{2}\%$	− 43.83
Proceeds	$2,819.96

Discounting Interest-Bearing Paper. The general rule in discounting interest-bearing paper is to compute and then discount the maturity value. In calculating the maturity value, the interest from the date of the note to maturity is added to the face value. Next the discount is computed for the discount period and deducted from the maturity value.

Example. A merchant arranges to pay for a shipment by borrowing the exact amount required to pay the invoice. The net amount of the invoice is $5,960.34 and the bank agrees to discount the merchant's note at 4% for 120 days.

Maturity value

Face value	$5,350.00
Interest August 12 to November 12	205.08

(92 days on $5,350 at 15%)

Maturity value	$5,555.08
Discount from September 27 to	
November 12 (46 days, 14%)	− 99.37
Proceeds	$5,455.71

Finding Principal to Yield Given Proceeds.   Occasionally it becomes necessary to reverse the process above; that is, a debtor wishes to borrow enough so that the proceeds will exactly cover the net amount of an invoice that is to be paid. Thus the face value of the note is unknown. If the note is **noninterest bearing,** the face value to yield the given proceeds is found by dividing the given proceeds by the proceeds of $1. The expression "proceeds of one dollar" means one dollar minus the interest or discount on $1.

Example.   A merchant arranges to pay for a shipment by borrowing the exact amount required to pay the invoice. The net amount of the invoice is $5,960.34 and the bank agrees to discount the merchant's note at 4% for 120 days.

$$\text{proceeds of } \$1 \text{ for 120 days at } 4\% = \$1 - \$0.01\tfrac{1}{3} = \$0.98\tfrac{2}{3}$$

$$\frac{\text{given proceeds}}{\text{proceeds of } \$1} = \frac{\$5,960.34}{.98\tfrac{2}{3}} = \frac{\$17,881.02}{2.96} = \underline{\$6,040,89}$$

Face value	$6,040.89
Interest for 120 days at 4%	80.55
Proceeds	$5,960.34

Computation of Interest Under Partial Payment Plans.   When a short-term indebtedness is reduced through periodic payments, the interest is computed upon either one of two bases. The basis used commonly in business is known as the **"merchant's rule."** This method gives the results more quickly but not as accurately as the computation under the other, the **"United States rule."**

Merchant's Rule.   In following the merchant's rule, the interest is computed on the total indebtedness from the date of inception to the date of maturity, and from this total is deducted the interest earned from the date that each partial payment is made to the date of maturity of the debt.

Example.   The following payments were made on a $16,500, 6% note, dated June 22, 1981, due in 6 months:

October 20, 1981	$ 300
November 15, 1981	3,500

What is the amount due at maturity?

Solution

June 22	Face value		$16,500.00
December 22	Interest at 6% on above, June 22 to		503.25
	December 22 = 183 days		
	Maturity value of note		$17,003.25
October 20	First payment	$ 300.00	
	Interest on above October 20 to		
	December 22 = 63 days	3.15	
November 15	Second payment	3,500.00	
	Interest on above November 15 to		
	December 22 = 37 days	21.58	
	Total credits		3,824.73
December 22	Maturity: balance due		$13,178.52

United States Rule.   Under the United States rule, each installment is first applied against the interest due at the date the partial payment is made, and the balance of the installment is then applied to reduce the principal. Interest is always computed on the reduced principal. In the event that a partial payment is insufficient to cover the accrued interest, it is held in suspense. There is no reduction of principal until the suspended payment together with subsequent payments exceeds the accrued interest. Using the same figures as in the example for the merchant's rule, the solution appears as follows:

June 22	Face value		$16,500.00
October 20	First payment	$ 300.00	
	Interest on $16,500 for 120 days		
	(June 22 to October 20)	330.00	
	Reduction of principal		—0—
November 15	Second payment	$3,500.00	
	Add first payment	300.00	
	Total	$3,800.00	
	Interest on $16,500 for 146 days		
	(June 22 toNovember 15)	401.50	
	Reduction of principal		3,398.50
	Balance due		$13,101.50
December 22	Maturity		
	Interest on $13,101.50 for 37 days		
	(November 15 to		
	December 22)		80.79
	Balance due		$13,182.29

Bank Discount Versus True Discount.   In a discounting operation, the interest charge, as in the case of noninterest-bearing notes, is taken out in advance. Thus the borrower receives the maturity value minus the discount. He is paying interest calculated on the maturity value for the use of a smaller sum, the proceeds. A 60-day note for $1,000, discounted at 18%, yields $970 proceeds. The borrower pays $30 for the use of $970, which is therefore more than 18%. The discount calculated as above is called **bank discount.** So-called true discount is an interest charge based on the **present value** of the note, that is, on a sum that at the discount rate would produce the face value of the note. To find the present value of a note, it is necessary merely to divide the maturity value by the amount of $1 (at the given rate and for the given time). The "amount of $1" means one dollar plus the interest on $1.

Example.   Find the proceeds and present value of a note for $5,632.50, dated June 22, 1980, due in 90 days, and discounted at 18% per annum on July 27, 1980. The note is due September 20, 1980.

Proceeds

Maturity value (since this is a noninterest-bearing note)	$5,632.50
Discount at 18% for 55 days; (i.e., from July 27–September 20)	154.89
Proceeds	$5,477.61

Present Value

Maturity value	$5,632.50
Amount of $1 at 18% per annum	
for each of 55 days	1.0275
Present value	$5,632.50 ÷ 1.0275 = $5,481.75

In this example, the **bank discount** is $154.89 but the **true discount** is $150.75 ($5,632.50 − $5,481.75).

Relation of Bank Discount Rate to True Discount Rate.   Since the bank discount is based on a larger sum than the borrower receives, he evidently pays more than the indicated rate of interest. To discover the true interest rate, it is necessary to express the bank discount as a percentage of the proceeds, assuming the loan ran for 1 year. Actually, the amount is immaterial, since the calculation can be put on a unit dollar basis.

Example.   A note for $10,000, due in 12 months, is discounted at 16% per annum. What is the equivalent annual interest charge?

Solution a   Here it is necessary to compute the annual discount:

Maturity value	$10,000.00
Discount 16%, one year	1,600.00
Proceeds	$ 8,400.00

The borrower, in effect, pays $1,600 for the use of $8,400 for a year. Hence the interest rate is

$$\frac{1,600}{8,400} = 0.1905 = \underline{\underline{19.05\%}}$$

Solution b   By putting the calculation on a unit dollar basis a general formula may be derived as follows:

Maturity value	$1.00
Discount	0.16
Proceeds	$0.84

$$\text{Interest rate} = \frac{0.16}{0.4} = 0.1905 = 19.05\%.$$

Let d = discount rate. Then

$$1 - d = \text{proceeds of \$1 due in 1 year}$$
$$r = \text{interest rate}$$

Hence

$$r = \frac{d}{1 - d} \times 100$$

In the problem above substitution in the formula yields;

$$\frac{0.16}{0.84} \times 100 = 19.05\%$$

Thus a discount rate of 16% per annum is equal to an annual interest charge of 19.05% approximately.

CHAIN DISCOUNTS.

Definition.   Chain discounts are two or more discounts that are applied in succession to a quote price. The latter is usually referred to as the **list price,** that is, the price at which the item is listed in the manufacturer's or jobber's catalog. Each discount is applied to the net amount remaining after the previous discount has been taken. For example, an article quoted at $25 less 30 and 10 means $25 less 30%, and then less 10% on the diminished amount.

List price	$25.00
Less: First discount—30%	7.50
Balance	$17.50
Less: Second discount—10%	1.75
Net price	$15.75

If many chain discounts are involved in connection with a given list price, this method may be cumbersome. An alternative method is to multiply the list price by the net cost factors, that is, the percentage remaining after deducting the chain discount from 100%. Thus, in the example above, the purchaser pays

$$\$25 \times 70\% \times 90\% = 25 \times 0.63 = \$15.75$$

Finding Equivalent Single Discount.   It is often convenient to convert chain discounts into equivalent single discounts. To find an equivalent single discount rate equal to two chain discounts, add the discounts and subtract their product.

Examples.   Find single discounts equal to chain discount of:

1. 40 and 30.
2. 20 and 20.
3. 15 and 10.
4. 10 and 5.
5. 10 and 5.

1	2	3	4	5
0.40	0.20	0.15	0.20	0.10
+0.30	+0.20	+0.10	+0.05	+0.05
0.70	0.40	0.25	0.25	0.15
−0.12	−0.04	−0.015	−0.01	−0.005
0.58	0.36	0.235	0.24	0.145
58%	36%	23.5%	24%	14.5%

In practice, the decimal points are omitted to speed up the work. Thus problem 5 would be solved: $10 + 5 = 15$, minus $0.5 = 14.5\%$. In fact, these problems can and should be done mentally.

The same rule may be applied to three or more chain discounts, provided only two discounts are taken at a time. The order in which the discounts are taken is immaterial.

COMPOUND INTEREST.

Definitions.   In compound interest calculations, the interest is computed at the end of each fiscal period and added to the principal at the beginning, the total representing the new principal on the basis of which a new interest calculation is made. Compound interest may therefore be defined as that form of interest in which the interest for each period is added to the principal. Because interest is added to the principal, and interest for the next period is calculated on the new total, interest sometimes is said to be **converted** into principal.

The time for which interest is calculated and converted is known as the **conversion period.** It represents the elapsed time between two successive interest dates. The time—that is, the conversion period—may be a month, or a quarterly, semiannual, or annual period, or any other convenient time period.

The conversion period is sometimes referred to as an **accumulation period** because the principal accumulates—that is, it increases by the amount of interest added to the principal. No such term was necessary in the instance of simple interest, because the interest was not converted but always computed on the original principal. But in compound interest, the interest is computed on an ever-increasing amount, because of the repeated addition to the existing principal.

Finding the Compound Amount.   The principle behind the method of compound interest calculations can be illustrated by reference to an example.

Example.   Find the compound amount on $1,500 for 3 years at 6% per annum, compounded semiannually (or at 3% per 6 months).

Investment	$1,500.00
Interest 6 months, $1,500 at 3%	45.00
Amount at end of first 6 months	$1,545.00
Interest 6 months, $1,545 at 3%	46.35
Amount at end of second 6 months	$1,591.35
Interest 6 months, $1,591.35 at 3%	47.74
Amount at end of third 6 months	$1,639.09
Interest 6 months, $1,639.09 at 3%	49.17
Amount at end of fourth 6 months	$1,688.26
Interest 6 months, $1,688.26 at 3%	50.65
Amount at end of fifth 6 months	$1,738.91
Interest 6 months, $1,738.91 at 3%	52.17
Compound amount at end of 3 years	$1,791.08

If the principal amount is reduced to say $1, the tabulation above can be restated as follows:

Investment	$1.00
Interest 6 months, $1 at 3% or	0.03
Amount at end of first 6 months	$1.03
Interest 6 months, $1.03 at 3%	0.0309
Amount at end of second 6 months	$1.0609
Interest 6 months, $1,0609 at 3%	0.031827
Amount at end of third 6 months	$1.092727
Interest 6 months, $1.092727 at 3%	0.032782
Amount at end of fourth 6 months	$1.125509
Interest 6 months, $1.125509 at 3%	0.033765
Amount at end of fifth 6 months	$1.159274
Interest 6 months, $1.159274 at 3%	0.034778
Compound amount at end of 3 years	$1.194052

It is obvious therefore that if the rate of interest per period is represented by i, the statement immediately above may be recast as follows:

Compound amount at end of first 6 months	$1.03	$= (1 + i)$
Compound amount at end of second 6 months	1.0609	$= (1 + i)^2$
Compound amount at end of third 6 months	1.092727	$= (1 + i)^3$
Compound amount at end of fourth 6 months	1.125509	$= (1 + i)^4$

Compound amount at end of fifth 6 months $1.159274 = (1 + i)^5$
Compound amount at end of sixth 6 months $1.194052 = (1 + i)^6$

Thus the compound amount of $1,500 for 3 years at 6%, converted semiannually, is

$$\$1,500 \times 1.194052 = \underline{\$1,791.08}$$

The difference between the compound amount and the original principal is the compound interest.

Compound amount, end of 3 years	$1,791.08
Principal at beginning	1,500.00
Compound interest	$ 291.08

Similarly for n periods the compound amount for $1 is $FVIF_{i,n} = (1 + i)^n$. In this formula

$$FVIF_{i,n} = \text{compound amount of \$1}$$
$$i = \text{interest rate}$$
$$n = \text{number of periods}$$

The compound amount of any given number of dollars can then be found easily by multiplying the principal by the value of $(1 + i)^n$. In general terms,

$$A = P(1 + i)^n = P \times FVIF_{i,n}$$

where A = compound amount
      P = principal (i.e., initial investment)

Computing Compound Value Using Tables. The arithmetical method for finding the compound amount is obviously too cumbersome. The formula may be solved either through the use of prepared tables or by use of a calculator. Exhibit 4 gives the compound amount of $1 for periods from 1 to 60 for various interest rates. The use of the table is illustrated below.

Example. Find the compound amount of $2,634.56 for 12 years at 5% annually.

$$A = \quad P \quad \times (1 + i)^n$$
$$= \$2,634.56 \times 1.05^{12}$$

Locate the 5% column in Exhibit 4, run down the column to the twelfth period. The figure on that line represents the compound amount of $1 for 12 years at 5%; in short, 1.05^{12}. Hence,

$$A = \$2,634.56 \times 1.7959$$
$$= \underline{\$4,731.29}$$

EXHIBIT 4 FUTURE VALUE OF $1 AT THE END OF n PERIODS

$$FVIF_{i,n} = (1 + i)^n$$

Period	1%	2%	3%	4%	5%	6%	7%	8%	9%	10%	12%	14%	15%	16%	18%	20%	24%	28%	32%	36%
1	1.0100	1.0200	1.0300	1.0400	1.0500	1.0600	1.0700	1.0800	1.0900	1.1000	1.1200	1.1400	1.1500	1.1600	1.1800	1.2000	1.2400	1.2800	1.3200	1.3600
2	1.0201	1.0404	1.0609	1.0816	1.1025	1.1236	1.1449	1.1664	1.1881	1.2100	1.2544	1.2996	1.3225	1.3456	1.3924	1.4400	1.5376	1.6384	1.7424	1.8496
3	1.0303	1.0612	1.0927	1.1249	1.1576	1.1910	1.2250	1.2597	1.2950	1.3310	1.4049	1.4815	1.5209	1.5609	1.6430	1.7280	1.9066	2.0972	2.3000	2.5155
4	1.0406	1.0824	1.1255	1.1699	1.2155	1.2625	1.3108	1.3605	1.4116	1.4641	1.5735	1.6890	1.7490	1.8106	1.9388	2.0736	2.3642	2.6844	3.0360	3.4210
5	1.0510	1.1041	1.1593	1.2167	1.2763	1.3382	1.4026	1.4693	1.5386	1.6105	1.7623	1.9254	2.0114	2.1003	2.2878	2.4883	2.9316	3.4360	4.0075	4.6526
6	1.0615	1.1262	1.1941	1.2653	1.3401	1.4185	1.5007	1.5869	1.6771	1.7716	1.9738	2.1950	2.3131	2.4364	2.6996	2.9860	3.6352	4.3980	5.2899	6.3275
7	1.0721	1.1487	1.2299	1.3159	1.4071	1.5036	1.6058	1.7138	1.8280	1.9487	2.2107	2.5023	2.6600	2.8262	3.1855	3.5832	4.5077	5.6295	6.9826	8.6054
8	1.0829	1.1717	1.2668	1.3686	1.4775	1.5938	1.7182	1.8509	1.9926	2.1436	2.4760	2.8526	3.0590	3.2784	3.7589	4.2998	5.5895	7.2058	9.2170	11.703
9	1.0937	1.1951	1.3048	1.4233	1.5513	1.6895	1.8385	1.9990	2.1719	2.3579	2.7731	3.2519	3.5179	3.8030	4.4355	5.1598	6.9310	9.2234	12.166	15.916
10	1.1046	1.2190	1.3439	1.4802	1.6289	1.7903	1.9672	2.1589	2.3674	2.5937	3.1058	3.7072	4.0456	4.4114	5.2338	6.1917	8.5944	11.805	16.059	21.646
11	1.1157	1.2434	1.3842	1.5395	1.7103	1.8983	2.1049	2.3316	2.5804	2.8531	3.4785	4.2262	4.6524	5.1173	6.1759	7.4301	10.657	15.111	21.198	29.439
12	1.1268	1.2682	1.4258	1.6010	1.7959	2.0122	2.2522	2.5182	2.8127	3.1384	3.8960	4.8179	5.3502	5.9360	7.2876	8.9161	13.214	19.342	27.982	40.037
13	1.1381	1.2936	1.4685	1.6651	1.8856	2.1329	2.4098	2.7196	3.0658	3.4523	4.3635	5.4924	6.1528	6.8858	8.5994	10.699	16.386	24.758	36.937	54.451
14	1.1495	1.3195	1.5126	1.7317	1.9799	2.2609	2.5785	2.9372	3.3417	3.7975	4.8871	6.2613	7.0757	7.9875	10.147	12.839	20.319	31.691	48.756	74.053
15	1.1610	1.3459	1.5580	1.8009	2.0789	2.3966	2.7590	3.1722	3.6425	4.1772	5.4736	7.1379	8.1371	9.2655	11.973	15.407	25.195	40.564	64.358	100.71
16	1.1726	1.3728	1.6047	1.8730	2.1829	2.5404	2.9522	3.4259	3.9703	4.5950	6.1304	8.1372	9.3576	10.748	14.129	18.488	31.242	51.923	84.953	136.96
17	1.1843	1.4002	1.6528	1.9479	2.2920	2.6928	3.1588	3.7000	4.3276	5.0545	6.8660	9.2765	10.761	12.467	16.672	22.186	38.740	66.461	112.13	186.27
18	1.1961	1.4282	1.7024	2.0258	2.4066	2.8543	3.3799	3.9960	4.7171	5.5599	7.6900	10.575	12.375	14.462	19.673	26.623	48.038	85.070	148.02	253.33
19	1.2081	1.4568	1.7535	2.1068	2.5270	3.0256	3.6165	4.3157	5.1417	6.1159	8.6128	12.055	14.231	16.776	23.214	31.948	59.567	108.89	195.39	344.53
20	1.2202	1.4859	1.8061	2.1911	2.6533	3.2071	3.8697	4.6610	5.6044	6.7275	9.6463	13.743	16.366	19.460	27.393	38.337	73.864	139.37	257.91	468.57
21	1.2324	1.5157	1.8603	2.2788	2.7860	3.3996	4.1406	5.0338	6.1088	7.4002	10.803	15.667	18.821	22.574	32.323	46.005	91.591	178.40	340.44	637.26
22	1.2447	1.5460	1.9161	2.3699	2.9253	3.6035	4.4304	5.4365	6.6586	8.1403	12.100	17.861	21.644	26.186	38.142	55.206	113.57	228.35	449.39	866.67
23	1.2572	1.5769	1.9736	2.4647	3.0715	3.8197	4.7405	5.8715	7.2579	8.9543	13.552	20.361	24.891	30.376	45.007	66.247	140.83	292.30	593.19	1178.6
24	1.2697	1.6084	2.0328	2.5633	3.2251	4.0489	5.0724	6.3412	7.9111	9.8497	15.178	23.212	28.625	35.236	53.108	79.496	174.63	374.14	783.02	1802.9
25	1.2824	1.6406	2.0938	2.6658	3.3864	4.2919	5.4274	6.8485	8.6231	10.834	17.000	26.461	32.918	40.874	62.668	95.396	216.54	478.90	1033.5	2180.0
26	1.2953	1.6734	2.1566	2.7725	3.5557	4.5494	5.8074	7.3964	9.3992	11.918	19.040	30.166	37.856	47.414	73.948	114.47	268.51	612.99	1364.3	2964.9
27	1.3082	1.7069	2.2213	2.8834	3.7335	4.8223	6.2139	7.9881	10.245	13.110	21.324	34.389	43.535	55.000	87.259	137.37	332.95	784.63	1800.9	4032.2
28	1.3213	1.7410	2.2879	2.9987	3.9201	5.1117	6.6488	8.6271	11.167	14.421	23.883	39.204	50.065	63.800	102.96	164.84	412.86	1004.3	2377.2	5488.8
29	1.3345	1.7758	2.3566	3.1187	4.1161	5.4184	7.1143	9.3173	12.172	15.863	26.749	44.693	57.575	74.008	121.50	197.81	511.95	1285.5	3137.9	7458.0
30	1.3478	1.8114	2.4273	3.2434	4.3219	5.7435	7.6123	10.062	13.267	17.449	29.959	50.950	66.211	85.849	143.37	237.37	634.81	1645.5	4142.0	10143.
40	1.4889	2.2080	3.2620	4.8010	7.0400	10.285	14.974	21.724	31.409	45.259	93.050	188.88	267.86	378.72	750.37	1469.7	5455.9	19426.	66520.	—a
50	1.6446	2.6916	4.3839	7.1067	11.467	18.420	29.457	46.901	74.357	117.39	289.00	700.23	1083.6	1670.7	3927.3	9100.4	46890.	—a	—a	—a
60	1.8167	3.2810	5.8916	10.519	18.679	32.987	57.946	101.25	176.03	304.48	897.59	2595.9	4383.9	7370.1	20555.	56347.	—a	—a	—a	—a

a FVIF > 99999.

A · 16

Computing Compound Value Using a Financial Calculator.   The calculator can be used to obtain both greater accuracy as well as a much larger variety of both interest rates and number of time periods. For the example above, the keystrokes would be:

Keystroke	Display	Comment
ALL	0.00	Clear
END	0.00	Set payment switch
2634.56	2,634.56	Principal
PV	2,634.56	—
5	5	—
i	5.00	Interest rate
12	12	—
n	12.00	Number of periods
FV	−4,731.29	—
CHS	4,731.29	Compound amount

PRESENT VALUE.   The general formula $A = P(1 + i)^n$ may be used to find any of the variables contained in it. The most common converse case is finding the present value [P]. This is the value at the present moment of money due at a future time. It is the reciprocal of the compound amount, and may also be defined as that sum of money that, when placed at compound interest for the full number of periods involved, will amount to the given sum.

Example. $1,500 at compound interest for six periods at 3% per period will amount to $1,791.08. Hence the present worth of $1,791.08 due six periods hence at 3% per period compounded is $1,500.

The formula for the present value of $1 is:

$$PVIF_{i,n} = \frac{1}{(1 + i)^n}$$

where $PVIF_{i,n}$ = present value of $1
        i = interest rate
        n = number of periods

The formula for the present value of any number of dollars is:

$$P = A \frac{1}{(1 + i)^n}$$

that is,

$$A \times PVIF_{i,n}$$

This formula is used whenever prepared present value tables are available. When, because of table limitations, direct calculation must be used, the formula is more convenient for computation when written in the form

$$P = \frac{A}{(1 + i)^n}$$

where A = given sum (i.e., the compound amount, the end value after n conversion periods)
    P = present value (the initial investment)

Computing Present Value Using Tables.   Exhibit 5 shows the present value of $1 for a number of interest rates from 1 to 60 periods. The use of the table is illustrated below.

Example.   Find the present value of $6,975 received 5 years from now at 10% per annum. Locate the 10% column in Exhibit 5 and run down the column to the sixth period: the present value of $1 for 6 periods is seen to be $0.5645:

$$P = A \times \frac{1}{(1 + i)^n}$$
$$P = 6,975 \times 0.5645 = \underline{\$3,937.21}$$

The difference between the present value and the given compound amount is sometimes called the **compound discount**. In the illustration above, the compound discount is

$$\$6,975 - \$3,937.21 = \underline{\$3,037.79}$$

The compound discount represents the amount of interest that $3,937.21 would earn in 6 years at 10% per annum.

Computing Present Value Using a Financial Calculator.   The keystrokes for the calculator to compute the present value in the example above would be:

Keystroke	Display	Comment
ALL	0.00	Clear
END	0.00	Set payment switch
6975	6,975	—
FV	6,975.00	Future value
10	10	—
i	10.00	Interest rate
6	6	—
n	6.00	Number of periods
PV	−3,937.21	—
CHS	3,937.21	Present value

OTHER CONVERSE CASES.   Occasionally it becomes necessary to find how long it will take for a given sum to amount to another sum at some future time; or what interest rate is being realized on a given principal. In short, the problem is to find n or i in the general formula. These may be found either by interpolation in a table or by using a calculator.

Finding Value of *n*.   There are two methods for finding n. These are illustrated to solve the following problem: how long will it take for $765 to amount to $1,350 if money is worth 8% per annum?

EXHIBIT 5 PRESENT VALUE OF $1

$$PVIF = 1/(1 + i)^n$$

Period	1%	2%	3%	4%	5%	6%	7%	8%	9%	10%	12%	14%	15%	16%	18%	20%	24%	28%	32%	36%
1	.9901	.9804	.9709	.9615	.9524	.9434	.9346	.9259	.9174	.9091	.8929	.8772	.8696	.8621	.8475	.8333	.8065	.7813	.7576	.7353
2	.9803	.9612	.9426	.9246	.9070	.8900	.8734	.8573	.8417	.8264	.7972	.7695	.7561	.7432	.7182	.6944	.6504	.6104	.5739	.5407
3	.9706	.9423	.9151	.8890	.8638	.8396	.8163	.7938	.7722	.7513	.7118	.6750	.6575	.6407	.6086	.5787	.5245	.4768	.4348	.3975
4	.9610	.9238	.8885	.8548	.8227	.7921	.7629	.7350	.7084	.6830	.6355	.5921	.5718	.5523	.5158	.4823	.4230	.3725	.3294	.2923
5	.9515	.9057	.8626	.8219	.7835	.7473	.7130	.6806	.6499	.6209	.5674	.5194	.4972	.4761	.4371	.4019	.3411	.2910	.2495	.2149
6	.9420	.8880	.8375	.7903	.7462	.7050	.6663	.6302	.5963	.5645	.5066	.4556	.4323	.4104	.3704	.3349	.2751	.2274	.1890	.1580
7	.9327	.8706	.8131	.7599	.7107	.6651	.6227	.5835	.5470	.5132	.4523	.3996	.3759	.3538	.3139	.2791	.2218	.1776	.1432	.1162
8	.9235	.8535	.7894	.7307	.6768	.6274	.5820	.5403	.5019	.4665	.4039	.3506	.3269	.3050	.2660	.2326	.1789	.1388	.1085	.0854
9	.9143	.8368	.7664	.7026	.6446	.5919	.5439	.5002	.4604	.4241	.3606	.3075	.2843	.2630	.2255	.1938	.1443	.1084	.0822	.0628
10	.9053	.8203	.7441	.6756	.6139	.5584	.5083	.4632	.4224	.3855	.3220	.2697	.2472	.2267	.1911	.1615	.1164	.0847	.0623	.0462
11	.8963	.8043	.7224	.6496	.5847	.5268	.4751	.4289	.3875	.3505	.2875	.2366	.2149	.1954	.1619	.1346	.0938	.0662	.0472	.0340
12	.8874	.7885	.7014	.6246	.5568	.4970	.4440	.3971	.3555	.3186	.2567	.2076	.1869	.1685	.1372	.1122	.0757	.0517	.0357	.0250
13	.8787	.7730	.6810	.6006	.5303	.4688	.4150	.3677	.3262	.2897	.2292	.1821	.1625	.1452	.1163	.0935	.0610	.0404	.0271	.0184
14	.8700	.7579	.6611	.5775	.5051	.4423	.3878	.3405	.2992	.2633	.2046	.1597	.1413	.1252	.0985	.0779	.0492	.0316	.0205	.0135
15	.8613	.7430	.6419	.5553	.4810	.4173	.3624	.3152	.2745	.2394	.1827	.1401	.1229	.1079	.0835	.0649	.0397	.0247	.0155	.0099
16	.8528	.7284	.6232	.5339	.4581	.3936	.3387	.2919	.2519	.2176	.1631	.1229	.1069	.0930	.0708	.0541	.0320	.0193	.0118	.0073
17	.8444	.7142	.6050	.5134	.4363	.3714	.3166	.2703	.2311	.1978	.1456	.1078	.0929	.0802	.0600	.0451	.0258	.0150	.0089	.0054
18	.8360	.7002	.5874	.4936	.4155	.3503	.2959	.2502	.2120	.1799	.1300	.0946	.0808	.0691	.0508	.0376	.0208	.0118	.0068	.0039
19	.8277	.6864	.5703	.4746	.3957	.3305	.2765	.2317	.1945	.1635	.1161	.0829	.0703	.0596	.0431	.0313	.0168	.0092	.0051	.0029
20	.8195	.6730	.5537	.4564	.3769	.3118	.2584	.2145	.1784	.1486	.1037	.0728	.0611	.0514	.0365	.0261	.0135	.0072	.0039	.0021
25	.7798	.6095	.4776	.3751	.2953	.2330	.1842	.1460	.1160	.0923	.0588	.0378	.0304	.0245	.0160	.0105	.0046	.0021	.0010	.0005
30	.7419	.5521	.4120	.3083	.2314	.1741	.1314	.0994	.0754	.0573	.0334	.0196	.0151	.0116	.0070	.0042	.0016	.0006	.0002	.0001
40	.6717	.4529	.3066	.2083	.1420	.0972	.0668	.0460	.0318	.0221	.0107	.0053	.0037	.0026	.0013	.0007	.0002	.0001	—[a]	—[a]
50	.6080	.3715	.2281	.1407	.0872	.0543	.0339	.0213	.0134	.0085	.0035	.0014	.0009	.0006	.0003	.0001	—[a]	—[a]	—[a]	—[a]
60	.5504	.3048	.1697	.0951	.0535	.0303	.0173	.0099	.0057	.0033	.0011	.0004	.0002	.0001	—[a]	—[c]	—[a]	—[a]	—[a]	—[a]

[a] The factor is zero to four decimal places.

A · 19

Computing n Using Tables. In Exhibit 4, in the 8% column, locate the number of periods for which $FVIF_{i,n}$ is closest to $1,350/765 = 1.7647$. It is between 7 and 8 years. By **linear interpolation,** the period n can be computed as follows:

Year	$FVIF_{i,n}$
7	1.7138
8	1.8509
?	1.7647

$$n = 7 + \frac{1.7647 - 1.7138}{1.8509 - 1.7138}$$
$$= 7.37 \text{ years}$$

This calculation is only approximate, since the true relationship between $FVIF_{i,n}$ and n is nonlinear, not linear as assumed here.

Computing n Using a Financial Calculator. The number n can be determined exactly (without rounding errors) using the financial calculator without resorting to the linear interpolation approximation method, above. The keystrokes for this example would be:

Keystroke	Display	Comment
ALL	0.00	Clear
END	0.00	Set payment switch
1350	1,350	—
FV	1,350.00	Future value
765	765	—
CHS	− 765.00	—
PV	− 765.00	Present value
8	8	—
i	8.00	Interest rate
n	7.38	Number of periods

Finding Value of i. The methods of the solution by interpolation and using a calculator are illustrated below.

Example. Find the yield on U.S. government bonds sold at $18.75 redeemable in 10 years for $25.

Computing i Using Tables. Proceed as in the previous solution.

$$(1 + i)^{10} = \frac{25}{18.75} = 1.3333$$

Now look in Exhibit 4 on the tenth period line and find values on that line just above and below 1.3333. The value is evidently between 2% and 3%. The computation is as follows:

Interest Rate	$FVIF_{i,n}$
2	1.2190
3	1.3439
?	1.3333

$$i = 2 + \frac{1.3333 - 1.2190}{1.3439 - 1.2190}$$
$$= 2.92\%$$

Again, the foregoing calculation is only approximate because a linear relationship has been assumed, rather than a nonlinear relationship, between $FVIF_{i,n}$ and i.

Computing i Using a Financial Calculator.   The keystrokes for the calculation are:

Keystroke	Display	Comment
ALL	0.00	Clear
END	0.00	Set payment switch
18.75	18.75	—
PV	18.75	Present value
25	25	—
CHS	− 25	—
FV	− 25.00	Compound value
10	10	—
r	10.00	Number of years
i	2.92	Interest rate

ANNUITIES.

Definitions.   An annuity is the payment of a fixed sum of money at uniform intervals of time. An example of an annuity is rent on the use of property. Payments of annuities are commonly called **rents.**

Ordinary Annuity.   An ordinary annuity is a series of equal payments each of which is made at the end of a period of time.

Annuity Due.   An annuity due is one in which the payments are due at the beginning of each payment period. A life insurance premium is an example of an annuity due, since such premiums are always payable in advance.

Deferred Annuity.   A deferred annuity is one in which payments are due after a number of periods have elapsed.

Amount or Final Value of Annuity.   The total of all annuity payments made, together with the interest earned by these payments, is the amount of annuity. It is technically referred to as the final value of an annuity.

Perpetuity.   An annuity in which the payments continue without end is a perpetuity. An example of this type is to be found in the payments made from endowment funds.

Life Annuity.   An annuity whose duration depends on the life expectancy of one or more persons is called a contingent or life annuity.

Annuity Certain.   This is an annuity that has a definite number of periods to run.

Example.   A mortgage on a piece of property is to be paid off through 20 equal quarterly payments beginning 4 years from the present time. This is an ordinary annuity deferred 4 years; it is certain because it runs for 5 years, once it becomes effective.

Final Value of Ordinary Annuity.   The total accumulation of an annuity may be illustrated by reference to the following example:

Example.   What is the **accumulated value** of an annuity of $200 per year for 5 years if the annual interest rate is 14% and the annuity is paid **at the end** of each year?

Payment end of first year	$ 200.00
Interest second year (14%)	28.00
Payment end of second year	200.00
Total end of second year	$ 428.00
Interest third year	59.92
Payment end of third year	200.00
Total end of third year	$ 687.92
Interest fourth year	96.31
Payment end of fourth year	200.00
Total end of fourth year	$ 984.23
Interest fifth year	137.79
Payment end of fifth year	200.00
Total accumulation (final value)	$1,322.02

In effect, the final value of an annuity is the sum of the compound amounts of the individual payments. Thus as shown below, the first payment made at the end of the year bears interest for 4 years, the second for 3 years.

	1	2	3	4	5
Payments (end of each year)	$1	$1	$1	$1	$1
Compound amount (end of fifth year)	1.14^4	1.14^3	1.14^2	1.14	1
Total value (Exhibit 5)	1.6890 +	1.4815 +	1.2990 +	1.140	+ 1 = $6.6101

Assuming money is worth 14%, the compound amount of each $1 payment is shown underneath the payments. When the values are totaled, it is found that an ordinary annuity of $1 per year annually for 5 years at 14% amounts to $6.6101. For an annuity of $200 under these conditions, the final amount is

$$200 \times 6.6101 = \underline{\$1,322.02}$$

Instead of laboriously calculating the compound amount of each payment, recourse may be had to prepared annuity tables (Exhibit 6). Thus in the illustration above, the answer may be found directly in the 14% column of line 5 of Exhibit 6.

Formula for Compound Value of an Annuity. The symbol for the final value of an ordinary annuity of $1 per annum is $FVIFA_{i,n}$.

$$FVIFA_{i,n} = (1 + i)^{n-1} + (1 + i)^{n-2} + \cdots + (1 + i) + 1$$

$$= \sum_{t=1}^{n} (1 + i)^{n-t}$$

$$= \frac{(1 + i)^n - 1}{i}$$

where i = interest rate

      n = number of periods

The numerator of the fraction is evidently the compound interest for n periods.

$$FVIFA_{i,n} = \frac{\text{compound interest}}{\text{interest rate}}$$

The final value for any number of dollars is expressed by the following formula:

$$A = R \times FVIFA_{i,n}$$

where A = final value of annuity

      R = amount of each payment

Example. Find the final value of an annuity of $2,000 received quarterly for 5 years when invested at 8% per annum.

Computing Compound Value of Annuity Using Tables.   Proceed as follows:

$$A = R \times FVIFA_{i,n}$$
$$A = 2,000 \times FVIFA_{2,20}$$

Note that interest is at 2% per period for 20 periods; hence look for the value in the 2% column, line 20 of Exhibit 6. Therefore,

$$A = \$2,000 \times 24.297 = \underline{\$48,594}$$

Computing Compound Value of Annuity Using a Financial Calculator.   The keystrokes are as follows:

Keystroke	Display	Comment
ALL	0.00	Clear
END	0.00	Set payment switch
2000	2,000	—

Keystroke	Display	Comment
CHS	−2,000	—
PMT	−2,000	Annuity amount
2	2	—
i	2.00	Interest rate
20	20	—
n	20.00	Number of periods
FV	48,594.74	Compound amount

SINKING FUND CALCULATIONS.   Sinking funds are commonly used to accumulate, by periodic contributions, sufficient amounts for the extinction of a debt or the replacement of an asset. In the latter event, the fund is more generally referred to as a **replacement fund.** In either instance the periodic payments are annuity rentals. Many bond issues of both private and municipal corporations are of the sinking fund type. The payments are usually turned over to a trustee or municipal sinking fund commission that invests these amounts and accumulates them to maturity or uses them to retire some of the bonds each year. In some issues, no part of the debt is extinguished until maturity even if the trustee invests his receipts in the bonds to be redeemed. In the latter case, he merely collects the coupons and adds the interest to the sinking fund just as in the case of investment in any other bonds.

There are two mathematical problems involved in the **flotation** of sinking fund bond issues. The first is one of determining what sum shall be set aside periodically to provide the required amount at maturity. The other problem is concerned with determining the life span of the bond issues once the size of the periodic sinking fund payment the corporation can afford to make is known. These are presented below.

Finding Amount of Sinking Fund Installments.   Determination of the installment or rent necessary to be set aside periodically is equivalent to finding R in the annuity formula.

$$R = \frac{A}{FVIFA_{i,n}}$$

The value of $FVIFA_{i,n}$ can be obtained from Exhibit 6. Its reciprocal represents the periodic payment of an annuity that will amount to $1 in n periods.

Example.   A corporation on June 1, 1980, issued bonds due June 1, 1986 to the amount of $200,000. Provision was made to set up a sinking fund to retire the entire issue by means of semiannual payments. If the fund earns 6% semiannually, what is the size of each installment? There are 12 payments compounded at 6% every 6 months.

Computing Value of Annuity Using Tables.   From Exhibit 6, in the 6% column, line 12, the value of $FVIFA_{i,n}$ can be obtained.

$$R = \frac{200,000}{16.869} = \underline{\underline{\$11,856.07}}$$

Schedule of Sinking Fund Installments.   The schedule below shows the periodic amounts set up and the interest earned on the accumulated balances in the sinking fund. The total semiannual installments plus the accumulated interest earned by the sinking fund equal

EXHIBIT 6 SUM OF AN ANNUITY OF $1 PER PERIOD FOR *n* PERIODS

$$FVIFA_{i,n} = \sum_{t=1}^{n} (1 + i)^{n-t} = \frac{(1 + i)^n - 1}{i}$$

Number of Periods	1%	2%	3%	4%	5%	6%	7%	8%	9%	10%	12%	14%	15%	16%	18%	20%	24%	28%	32%	36%
1	1.0000	1.0000	1.0000	1.0000	1.0000	1.0000	1.0000	1.0000	1.0000	1.0000	1.0000	1.0000	1.0000	1.0000	1.0000	1.0000	1.0000	1.0000	1.0000	1.0000
2	2.0100	2.0200	2.0300	2.0400	2.0500	2.0600	2.0700	2.0800	2.0900	2.1000	2.1200	2.1400	2.1500	2.1600	2.1800	2.2000	2.2400	2.2800	2.3200	2.3600
3	3.0301	3.0604	3.0909	3.1216	3.1525	3.1836	3.2149	3.2464	3.2781	3.3100	3.3744	3.4396	3.4725	3.5056	3.5724	3.6400	3.7776	3.9184	4.0624	4.2296
4	4.0604	4.1216	4.1836	4.2465	4.3101	4.3746	4.4399	4.5061	4.5731	4.6410	4.7793	4.9211	4.9934	5.0665	5.2154	5.3680	5.6842	6.0156	6.3624	6.7251
5	5.1010	5.2040	5.3091	5.4163	5.5256	5.6371	5.7507	5.8666	5.9847	6.1051	6.3528	6.6101	6.7424	6.8771	7.1542	7.4416	8.0484	8.6999	9.3983	10.146
6	6.1520	6.3081	6.4684	6.6330	6.8019	6.9753	7.1553	7.3359	7.5233	7.7156	8.1152	8.5355	8.7537	8.9775	9.4420	9.9299	10.980	12.135	13.405	14.798
7	7.2135	7.4343	7.6625	7.8983	8.1420	8.3938	8.6540	8.9228	9.2004	9.4872	10.089	10.730	11.066	11.413	12.141	12.915	14.615	16.533	18.695	21.126
8	8.2857	8.5830	8.8923	9.2142	9.5491	9.8975	10.259	10.636	11.028	11.435	12.299	13.232	13.726	14.240	15.327	16.499	19.122	22.163	25.698	29.731
9	9.3685	9.7546	10.159	10.582	11.026	11.491	11.978	12.487	13.021	13.579	14.775	16.085	16.785	17.518	19.085	20.798	24.712	29.369	34.895	41.435
10	10.462	10.949	11.463	12.006	12.577	13.180	13.816	14.486	15.192	15.937	17.548	19.337	20.303	21.321	23.521	25.958	31.643	38.592	47.061	57.351
11	11.566	12.168	12.807	13.486	14.206	14.971	15.783	16.645	17.560	18.531	20.654	23.044	24.349	25.732	28.755	32.150	40.237	50.398	63.121	78.998
12	12.682	13.412	14.192	15.025	15.917	16.869	17.838	18.977	20.140	21.384	24.133	27.270	29.001	30.850	34.931	39.580	50.894	65.510	84.320	108.43
13	13.809	14.680	15.617	16.626	17.713	18.882	20.140	21.495	22.953	24.522	28.029	32.088	34.351	36.786	42.218	48.496	64.109	84.852	112.30	148.47
14	14.947	15.973	17.086	18.291	19.598	21.015	22.550	24.214	26.019	27.975	32.392	37.581	40.504	43.672	50.818	59.195	80.496	109.61	149.23	202.92
15	16.096	17.293	18.598	20.023	21.578	23.276	25.129	27.152	29.360	31.772	37.279	43.842	47.580	51.659	60.965	72.035	100.81	141.30	197.99	276.97
16	17.257	18.639	20.156	21.824	23.657	25.672	27.888	30.324	33.003	35.949	42.753	50.980	55.717	60.925	72.939	87.442	126.01	181.86	262.35	357.69
17	18.430	20.012	21.761	23.697	25.840	28.212	30.840	33.750	36.973	40.544	48.883	59.117	65.075	71.673	87.068	105.93	157.25	233.79	347.30	514.66
18	19.614	21.412	23.414	25.645	28.132	30.905	33.999	37.450	41.301	45.599	55.749	68.394	75.836	84.140	103.74	128.11	195.99	300.25	459.44	700.93
19	20.810	22.840	25.116	27.671	30.539	33.760	37.379	41.446	46.018	51.159	63.439	78.969	88.211	98.603	123.41	154.74	244.03	385.32	607.47	954.27
20	22.019	24.297	26.870	29.778	33.066	36.785	40.995	45.762	51.160	57.275	72.052	91.024	102.44	115.37	146.62	180.68	303.60	494.21	802.86	1298.8
21	23.239	25.783	28.676	31.969	35.719	39.992	44.865	50.422	55.764	64.002	81.698	104.76	118.81	134.84	174.02	225.02	377.46	633.59	1060.7	1767.3
22	24.471	27.299	30.536	34.248	38.505	43.392	49.005	55.456	62.873	71.402	92.502	120.43	137.63	157.41	206.34	271.03	469.05	811.99	1401.2	2404.6
23	25.716	28.845	32.452	36.617	41.430	46.995	53.436	60.893	69.531	79.543	104.60	138.29	159.27	183.60	244.48	326.23	582.62	1040.3	1850.6	3271.3
24	26.973	30.421	34.426	39.082	44.502	50.315	58.176	66.764	76.789	88.497	118.15	158.65	184.16	213.97	289.49	392.48	723.46	1332.6	2443.8	4449.9
25	28.243	32.030	36.459	41.645	47.727	54.864	63.249	73.105	84.700	98.347	133.38	181.87	212.79	249.21	342.60	471.98	898.09	1706.8	3226.8	6052.9
26	29.525	33.670	38.553	44.311	51.113	59.156	68.676	79.954	93.323	109.18	150.33	208.33	245.71	290.08	405.27	567.37	1114.6	2185.7	4260.4	8233.0
27	30.820	35.344	40.709	47.084	54.669	63.705	74.483	87.350	102.72	121.09	169.37	238.49	283.56	337.50	479.22	681.85	1388.1	2798.7	5624.7	11197.9
28	32.129	37.051	42.930	49.967	58.402	68.528	80.697	95.338	112.96	134.20	190.69	272.88	327.10	392.50	566.48	819.22	1716.0	3583.3	7425.6	15230.2
29	33.450	38.792	45.218	52.966	62.322	73.639	87.346	103.96	124.13	148.63	214.58	312.09	377.16	456.30	669.44	984.06	2128.9	4587.6	9802.9	20714.1
30	34.784	40.568	47.575	56.084	66.438	79.058	94.460	113.28	136.30	164.49	241.33	356.78	434.74	530.31	790.94	1181.8	2640.9	5873.2	12940.	28172.2
40	48.886	60.402	75.401	95.025	120.79	154.76	199.63	259.05	337.88	442.59	767.09	1342.0	1779.0	2360.7	4163.2	7343.8	22728.	69377.	—[a]	—[a]
50	64.463	84.579	112.79	152.66	209.34	290.33	406.52	573.76	815.08	1163.9	2400.0	4994.5	7217.7	10435.	21813.	45497.	—[a]	—[a]	—[a]	—[a]
60	81.669	114.05	163.05	237.99	353.58	533.12	813.52	1253.2	1944.7	3034.8	7471.6	18535.	29219.	46057.	—[a]	—[a]	—[a]	—[a]	—[a]	—[a]

[a] FVIFA > 99999.

$200,000, the accumulated amount in the sinking fund on June 1, 1986, the date of maturity of the bonds. Note that the last figure in the last column contains a rounding error.

Date	Semiannual Installment	Interest at 6% on Accumulated Sinking Fund	Total Additions to Sinking Fund	Accumulated Amounts in Sinking Fund
June 1, 1980	—	—	—	—
December 1, 1980	11,856.07	—	11,856.07	11,856.07
June 1, 1981	11,856.07	711.36	12,567.43	24,423.50
December 1, 1981	11,856.07	1,465.37	13,320.73	37,742.85
June 1, 1982	11,856.07	2,264.57	14,119.97	51,862.82
December 1, 1982	11,856.07	3,111.77	14,967.17	66,829.99
June 1, 1983	11,856.07	4,009.80	15,865.20	82,695.19
December 1, 1983	11,856.07	4,961.71	16,817.11	99,512.30
June 1, 1984	11,856.07	5,970.74	17,826.13	117,338.44
December 1, 1984	11,856.07	7,040.31	18,895.71	136,234.15
June 1, 1985	11,856.07	8,174.05	20,029.45	156,263.60
December 1, 1985	11,856.07	9,375.82	21,231.22	177,494.81
June 1, 1986	11,856.07	10,649.69	22,505.09	199,999.90

Computing Value of Annuity Using a Financial Calculator. The keystrokes are as follows:

Keystroke	Display	Comment
ALL	0.00	Clear
END	0.00	Set payment switch
200000	200,000	—
CHS	− 200,000	—
FV	− 200,000.00	Compound value
12	12	—
n	12.00	Number of years
6	6	—
i	6.00	Interest rate
PMT	11,855.41	Annuity amount

Finding Number of Payments in a Sinking Fund.   A corporation floating a sinking fund bond issue needs to prepare a long-range budget to determine what it can spare for sinking fund payments. Once that is known, the time to build up the proper size sinking fund can easily be calculated. This involves finding the number of payments (n in the formula) from which the maturity of the bonds may be determined. The simplest solution is through interpolation using Exhibit 6.

Example.   A corporation wishes to raise $300,000 through the issuance of sinking fund bonds paying 5% semiannually. It can spare $50,000 a year for sinking fund purposes and interest on the bonds. If the fund earns 4% semiannually, when should the bonds be made to mature?

Computing Number of Years n Using Tables.   This task is straightforward:

Total annual payment	$50,000.00
Annual interest charge (300,000 × 0.05)	15,000.00
Sinking fund contribution	$35,000.000

$$FVIFA_{i,n} = 300,000 \div 35,000$$
$$FVIFA_{i,n} = \underline{\underline{8.5714}}$$

Now look in Exhibit 6 in the 4% column for the amounts directly above and below the given figure. The time is evidently between 7 and 8 periods. Since the results are approximations in any event, only four decimals are used.

Years	$FVIFAi_,n$
7	7.893
8	9.2142
?	8.5714

$$n = 7 + \frac{8.5714 - 7.8983}{9.2142 - 7.8983}$$
$$= 7.52 \text{ periods}$$

Since bond maturities such as this are practically unknown, the borrower must decide whether the bonds are to mature in 3 or 4 years. If $50,000 represents the limit of what the borrower can spare, the maturity must be extended to 4 years and the exact amount of R (sinking fund contribution) recalculated. If a maturity of 3 years is more desirable, the total annual burden will be greater that $50,000 and can easily be found by the formula for R.

Computing Number of Years n Using a Financial Calculator.   The keystrokes on the calculator are as follows:

Keystroke	Display	Comment
ALL	0.00	Clear
END	0.00	Set payment switch
300000	300,000	—
CHS	−300,000	—
FV	−300,000.00	Compound value
35000	35,000	—
PMT	35,000.00	—
4	4	—
i	4.00	Interest rate
n	7.52	Number of years

Final Value of Annuity Due.   In the case of an annuity due, the payments are made at the end of the period, i.e., the last payment earns interest for the last period. The symbol for final value of an annuity due of $1 is $FVIFAB_{i,n}$. The simplest formula for it is:

$$FVIFAB_{i,n} = (1 + i)^n + (1 + i)^{n-1} + \ldots$$
$$+ (1 + i)^2 + (1 + i)$$
$$= \sum_{t=1}^{n} (1 + i)$$
$$= \sum_{t=1}^{n+1} (1 + i)^{n+1-t} - 1$$
$$= FVIFA_{i,n+1} - 1$$

Example.   Find the final value of an annuity due to $6,500 for 10 years at 12%.

Computing Final Value of Annuity Due Using Tables.   Start with the following formula:

$$\text{annuity due} = R \times FVIFAB_{i,n}$$
$$= \$6,500 \times (FVIFA_{i,n+1} - 1)$$
$$= \$6,500 \times 19.654$$
$$= \$127,751$$

In looking up $FVIFAB_{i,n}$ start in the 12% column in Exhibit 6, read the figure on the eleventh line, and subtract $1: that is, look up $FVIFA_{i,n+1}$ and decrease this value by $1, to get 19.654.

Computing Final Value of Annuity Due Using a Financial Calculator.   The keystrokes are as follows:

Keystroke	Display	Comment
ALL	0.00	Clear
BEGIN	0.00	Set payment switch
6500	6,500	—
CHS	−6,500	—
PMT	−6,500.00	Annuity amount due
12	12	—
i	12.00	Interest rate
10	10	—
n	10.00	Number of periods
FV	12,7754.79	Compound amount

Present Value of Ordinary Annuity.   The present value of an annuity is an amount that represents the sum of the discounted or present values of a series of equal payments made at uniform time intervals. Note that the future payments are equal, but are discounted. Hence, each payment represents in part principal and in part interest on the remaining debt. This is a contrast to final value problems, where payments are accumulated to wipe out a future debt at maturity. Hence, wherever the annuity payments represent principal and interest, the problem is one of present value.

The symbol to represent the present value of a single dollar per annum payable at the end of each year (i.e., an ordinary annuity of $1) is $PVIFA_{i,n}$. The formula is as follows:

$$PVIFA_{i,n} = \frac{1 - 1/(1 + i)^n}{i}$$

$$= \frac{1 - PVIF_{i,n}}{\text{interest rate}}$$

Exhibit 7 shows the present values represented by the formula above and may therefore be used to solve present value problems. The present value of any number of dollars is representd by the following formula:

$$A = R \times PVIFA_{i,n}$$

where A = present value of R dollars
 R = amount of each annuity payment

Example.   A lumber company signs a contract with a syndicate that owns a large tract of timber land. The company agrees to cut 20,000,000 feet of timber a year for 3 years and to pay $360,000 every 6 months for the cut timber. The syndicate, desiring to anticipate the payments under its contract, applies to its bankers for the cash value of the contract, offering as security the contract itself and a mortgage on the timber land. What is the present worth of the contract if the interest rate is 8% per annum, compounded semiannually?

Computing Present Value of Annuity Using Tables.   The number of periods is 6 and the interest rate is 4% per period. The present value annuity factor $PVIFA_{i,n}$ can be determined from Exhibit 7.

$$A = 360,000 \times PVIFA_{i,n}$$
$$= \$360,000 \times 5.2421$$
$$= \underline{\underline{\$1,887,160}}$$

Computing Present Value of Annuity Using a Financial Calculator.   The keystrokes are:

Keystroke	Display	Comment
ALL	0.00	Clear
END	0.00	Set payment switch
360000	360,000	—
CHS	− 360,000	—
PMT	− 360,000.00	Annuity amount
6	6	—
n	6.00	Number of periods
4	4	—
i	4.00	Interest rate
PV	1,887,169.27	Present value

This answer represents the amount the syndicate can borrow on its contract. This means

EXHIBIT 7 PRESENT VALUE OF AN ANNUITY OF $1 PER PERIOD FOR n PERIODS

$$PVIFA_{i,n} = \sum_{i=1}^{n} \frac{1}{(1+i)^n} = \frac{1 - \dfrac{1}{(1+i)^n}}{i}$$

Number of Payments	1%	2%	3%	4%	5%	6%	7%	8%	9%	10%	12%	14%	15%	16%	18%	20%	24%	28%	32%
1	0.9901	0.9804	0.9709	0.9615	0.9524	0.9434	0.9346	0.9259	0.9174	0.9091	0.8929	0.8772	0.8696	0.8621	0.8475	0.8333	0.8065	0.7813	0.7576
2	1.9704	1.9416	1.9135	1.8861	1.8594	1.8334	1.8080	1.7833	1.7591	1.7355	1.6901	1.6467	1.6257	1.6052	1.5656	1.5278	1.4568	1.3916	1.3315
3	2.9410	2.8839	2.8286	2.7751	2.7232	2.6730	2.6243	2.5771	2.5313	2.4869	2.4018	2.3216	2.2832	2.2459	2.1743	2.1065	1.9813	1.8684	1.7663
4	3.9020	3.8077	3.7171	3.6299	3.5460	3.4651	3.3872	3.3121	3.2397	3.1699	3.0373	2.9137	2.8550	2.7982	2.6901	2.5887	2.4043	2.2410	2.0957
5	4.8534	4.7135	4.5797	4.4518	4.3295	4.2124	4.1002	3.9927	3.8897	3.7908	3.6048	3.4331	3.3522	3.2743	3.1272	2.9906	2.7454	2.5320	2.3452
6	5.7955	5.6014	5.4172	5.2421	5.0757	4.9173	4.7665	4.6229	4.4859	4.3553	4.1114	3.8887	3.7845	3.6847	3.4976	3.3255	3.0205	2.7594	2.5342
7	6.7282	6.4720	6.2303	6.0021	5.7864	5.5824	5.3893	5.2064	5.0330	4.8684	4.5638	4.2883	4.1604	4.0386	3.8115	3.6046	3.2423	2.9370	2.6775
8	7.6517	7.3255	7.0197	6.7327	6.4632	6.2098	5.9713	5.7466	5.5348	5.3349	4.9676	4.6389	4.4873	4.3436	4.0776	3.8372	3.4212	3.0758	2.7860
9	8.5660	8.1622	7.7861	7.4353	7.1078	6.8017	6.5152	6.2469	5.9952	5.7590	5.3282	4.9464	4.7716	4.6065	4.3030	4.0310	3.5655	3.1842	2.8681
10	9.4713	8.9826	8.5302	8.1109	7.7217	7.3601	7.0236	6.7101	6.4177	6.1446	5.6502	5.2161	5.0188	4.8332	4.4941	4.1925	3.6819	3.2689	2.9304
11	10.3676	9.7868	9.2526	8.7605	8.3064	7.8869	7.4987	7.1390	6.8052	6.4951	5.9377	5.4527	5.2337	5.0286	4.6560	4.3271	3.7757	3.3351	2.9776
12	11.2551	10.5753	9.9540	9.3851	8.8633	8.3838	7.9427	7.5361	7.1607	6.8137	6.1944	5.6603	5.4206	5.1971	4.7932	4.4392	3.8514	3.3868	3.0133
13	12.1337	11.3484	10.6350	9.9856	9.3936	8.8527	8.3577	7.9038	7.4869	7.1034	6.4235	5.8424	5.5831	5.3423	4.9095	4.5327	3.9124	3.4272	3.0404
14	13.0037	12.1062	11.2961	10.5631	9.8986	9.2950	8.7455	8.2442	7.7862	7.3667	6.6282	6.0021	5.7245	5.4675	5.0081	4.6106	3.9616	3.4587	3.0609
15	13.8651	12.8493	11.9379	11.1184	10.3797	9.7122	9.1079	8.5595	8.0607	7.6061	6.8109	6.1422	5.8474	5.5755	5.0916	4.6755	4.0013	3.4834	3.0764
16	14.7179	13.5777	12.5611	11.6523	10.8378	10.1059	9.4466	8.8514	8.3126	7.8237	6.9740	6.2651	5.9542	5.6685	5.1624	4.7296	4.0333	3.5026	3.0882
17	15.5623	14.2919	13.1661	12.1657	11.2741	10.4773	9.7632	9.1216	8.5436	8.0216	7.1196	6.3729	6.0472	5.7487	5.2223	4.7746	4.0591	3.5177	3.0971
18	16.3983	14.9920	13.7535	12.6593	11.6896	10.8276	10.0591	9.3719	8.7556	8.2014	7.2497	6.4674	6.1280	5.8178	5.2732	4.8122	4.0799	3.5294	3.1039
19	17.2260	15.6785	14.3238	13.1339	12.0853	11.1581	10.3356	9.6036	8.9501	8.3649	7.3658	6.5504	6.1982	5.8775	5.3162	4.8435	4.0967	3.5386	3.1090
20	18.0456	16.3514	14.8775	13.5903	12.4622	11.4699	10.5940	9.8181	9.1285	8.5136	7.4694	6.6231	6.2593	5.9288	5.3527	4.8696	4.1103	3.5458	3.1129
25	22.0232	19.5235	17.4131	15.6221	14.0939	12.7834	11.6536	10.6748	9.8226	9.0770	7.8431	6.8729	6.4641	6.0971	5.4669	4.9476	4.1474	3.5640	3.1220
30	25.8077	22.3965	19.6004	17.2920	15.3725	13.7648	12.4090	11.2578	10.2737	9.4269	8.0552	7.0027	6.5660	6.1772	5.5168	4.9789	4.1601	3.5693	3.1242
40	32.8347	27.3555	23.1148	19.7928	17.1591	15.0463	13.3317	11.9246	10.7574	9.7791	8.2438	7.1050	6.6418	6.2335	5.5482	4.9966	4.1659	3.5712	3.1250
50	39.1961	31.4236	25.7298	21.4822	18.2559	15.7619	13.8007	12.2335	10.9617	9.9148	8.3045	7.1327	6.6605	6.2463	5.5541	4.9995	4.1666	3.5714	3.1250
60	44.9550	34.7609	27.6756	22.6235	18.9293	16.1614	14.0392	12.3766	11.0480	9.9672	8.3240	7.1401	6.6651	6.2402	5.5553	4.9999	4.1667	3.5714	3.1250

that six annual payments of $360,000 will pay off the loan and the interest on the outstanding balances. The amortization of the loan is illustrated below:

Year	Amount Outstanding at Beginning of Period	Interest at 4% on Outstanding Balance	Annuity Payment	Principal Repaid
1	$1,887,169.28	$ 75,486.77	$ 360,000.00	$ 284,513.23
2	1,602,656.05	64,106.24	360,000.00	295,893.76
3	1,306,762.29	52,270.49	360,000.00	307,729.51
4	999,032.78	39,961.31	360,000.00	320,038.69
5	678,994.09	27,159.76	360,000.00	332,840.24
6	346,153.85	13,846.15	360,000.00	346,153.85
		$272,830.72	$2,160,000.00	$1,887,169.28

Annuity That $1 Will Buy.   The annuity that $1 will buy is equivalent to a series of annuity payments the sum of whose present values is $1. This type of problem is found where the size of the annuity rent (R) is to be determined. The formula is as follows:

$$R = A_n \times \frac{1}{PVIFA_{i,n}}$$

The fraction is the reciprocal of the present value of $1 and represents the annuity that $1 will purchase. The annuity factors can be obtained by taking the reciprocals of the numbers in Exhibit 7, as illustrated below.

Example 1.   Mr. X buys a property for $150,000 agreeing to pay $50,000 down and the balance in 25 equal annual installments that include interest at 14% What is the size of each installment?

The debt amounts to $100,000 after deduction of the down payment.

Computing an Annuity Amount Using Tables.   From Exhibit 7, $PVIF_{i,n}$ is found to be 6.8729 for $i = 14\%$ and $n = 25$.

$$R = A \times \frac{1}{PVIF_{i,n}}$$
$$= \$100,000 \times \frac{1}{6.8729}$$
$$= \underline{\$14,549.90}$$

Computing an Annuity Amount Using a Financial Calculator.   The keystrokes for the problem are:

Keystroke	Display	Comment
All	0.00	Clear
END	0.00	Set payment switch

Keystroke	Display	Comment
100000	100,000	—
CHS	− 100,000	—
PV	+ 100,000.00	Present value
25	25	—
n	25.00	Number of periods
14	14	—
i	14.00	Interest rate
PMT	14,549.90	Annuity amount

Example 2.   The Steel Wire Co. floated a $300,000, 12% bond issue on May 1, 1980, due May 1, 1984. Interest is payable quarterly; the bonds are in denominations of $1,000, and callable at par and accrued interest. What is the standard rent that will wipe out the debt and interest?

$$R = A \times \frac{1}{PVIFA_{i,n}}$$

$$= \$300,000 \times \frac{1}{12.5611}$$

$$= \underline{\$23,883.26}$$

Exhibit 8 is a table of bond retirements. Since the bonds are issued in fixed denominations, the total semiannual charge cannot be exactly as stated above, but should be kept as near that figure as possible. Thus on August 1, 1980, $9,000 of the $23,883.27 is due as interest and the balance of $14,883.27 can be applied against principal outstanding. But the bonds must be retired in even amounts; in this case 15 bonds are retired. As a result, the first quarter

EXHIBIT 8   SCHEDULE OF INTEREST PAYMENTS AND BOND RETIREMENTS FOR SERIAL BOND ISSUE

Date	Outstanding	Interest at 3%	Amount Retired	Amount To Pay Interest and Retire Bonds	Number of Bonds Retired	Over (+) and Short (−) Current	Over (+) and Short (−) Cumulative
May 1, 1980	$300,000	—	—	—	—	—	—
August 1, 1980	300,000	$ 9,000	$ 15,000	$ 24,000	15	+ 117	+ 117
November 1, 1980	285,000	8,550	15,000	23,550	15	− 333	− 216
February 1, 1980	270,000	8,100	16,000	24,100	16	+ 217	+ 1
May 1, 1981	254,000	7,620	16,000	23,620	16	− 263	− 262
August 1, 1981	238,000	7,140	17,000	24,140	17	+ 257	− 5
November 1, 1981	221,000	6,630	17,000	23,630	17	− 253	− 258
February 1, 1982	204,000	6,120	18,000	24,120	18	+ 237	− 21
May 1, 1982	186,000	5,580	18,000	23,580	18	− 303	− 324
August 1, 1982	168,000	5,040	19,000	24,040	19	+ 157	− 167
November 1, 1982	149,000	4,470	20,000	24,470	20	+ 587	+ 420
February 1, 1983	129,000	3,870	20,000	23,870	20	− 13	+ 407
May 1, 1983	109,000	3,270	20,000	23,270	20	− 613	− 206
August 1, 1983	89,000	2,670	21,000	23,670	21	− 213	− 419
November 1, 1983	68,000	2,040	22,000	24,040	22	+ 157	− 262
February 1, 1984	46,000	1,380	23,000	24,380	23	+ 497	+ 235
May 1, 1984	23,000	690	23,000	23,690	23	− 193	+ 42
		$82,170	$300,000	$382,170	300		

involves an expenditure of $24,000 instead of $23,883. The excess payment is reflected in the column showing the excess or deficiency of any one period. A cumulative column is also provided; the purpose is to keep the cumulative error as low as possible. In the case of a $1,000 bond the maximum deviation from the standard charge should not exceed ±$500, that is half the value of the bond. In case the cumulative error threatens to become more than $500, it is best to redeem one bond more or less, so as to keep the error within the stated limits.

Finding Number of Payments to Amortize a Loan.   If the amount that can be spared for principal and interest is known, the borrower must also know how long it will take to amortize the debt. This involves finding n, that is, the number of payments to be made.

Example.   The Brass Fixture Co. on July 1, 1981 issued $300,000, 12% bonds, interest payable semiannually. The bonds are in denominations of $1,000 and are to be redeemed at par and accrued interest. How long will it take to pay them off if the corporation has budgeted $30,000 each period for interest and bond redemption?

Computing Period n Using Tables.   First do the following calculations:

$$r = 6\%, \text{ semiannually}$$

$$R = A \times \frac{1}{PVIFA_{i,n}}$$

$$PVIFA_{i,n} = \frac{A}{R} = \frac{300,000}{30,000} = 10$$

Now look for the values in the 6% column of Exhibit 7 and interpolate. Evidently, n lies between 15 and 16 periods.

Years	$PVIFA_{i,n}$
15	9.7122
16	10.1059
?	10.0

$$n = 15 + \frac{10.0 - 9.7122}{10.1059 - 9.7122}$$
$$= \underline{15.73 \text{ periods} \simeq 8 \text{ years}}$$

Computing Period n Using a Financial Calculator.   The keystrokes are as follows:

Keystrokes	Display	Comment
ALL	0.00	Clear
END	0.00	Set payment switch
300000	300,000	—
PV	300,000.00	Present value
30,000	30,000	—
CHS	−30,000	—

Keystrokes	Display	Comment
PMT	− 30,000.00	Annuity
6	6	—
i	6.00	Interest rate
n	15.73	Number of periods

Present Value of Annuity Due.   The symbol for the present value of an annuity due of $1 per period is $PVIFA_{i,n}$. The formula is as follows:

$$PVIFAB_{i,n} = 1 + \frac{1}{1 + i} \cdots + \frac{1}{(1 + i)^{n-2}} + \frac{1}{(1 + i)^{n-1}}$$
$$= 1 + PVIFA_{i,n-1}$$

This means that the present value tables for ordinary annuities (Exhibit 7) may be used in computing the present value of an annuity due. For instance, if $PVIAB_{12,10}$ is wanted, it can be found by looking in the 12% column of Exhibit 7 on line 9 and adding $1. In this case the answer is 6.3282.

Example.   What is the cash value of a lease that has 5 years to run and that calls for rentals of $1,365 quarterly, payable in advance? Assume money is worth 16% per annum, compounded quarterly.

The lease has 20 periods to run and is discounted at 4% per period. Since payments are made in advance, it is an annuity due.

Computing Present Value of Annuity Due Using Tables.   The value of $PVIFAB_{4,20}$ can be obtained from Exhibit 7:

$$AD = R \times PVIFAB_{i,n}$$
$$= R \times (1 + PVIFA_{i,n-1})$$
$$= \$1,365 \times 14.1339$$
$$= \underline{\underline{\$19,292.77}}$$

Computing Present Value of Annuity Due Using a Financial Calculator.   The keystrokes are as follows:

Keystroke	Display	Comment
ALL	0.00	Clear
BEGIN	0.00	Set payment switch
1365	1,365	—
CHS	− 1,365	—
PMT	− 1,365.00	Annuity amount due
4	4	—
i	4.00	Interest Rate
20	20	—
n	20.00	Number of periods
PV	19,292.83	Present value

BOND VALUATION: DEFINITIONS AND CALCULATIONS.

Bond Definitions.   A bond may be defined as a long-time **promissory note** under "seal." It promises to pay to the owner of the bond a specified principal sum called the face value on a definite date in the future, called the maturity date. It also promises to pay the interest based on the face value on the interest dates as called for in the bond indenture.

The **par value** of a bond is the amount stated on its face. The **redemption value** is the price at which the bond will be redeemed. In many issues this is the same as the par value; in others, premiums are paid when bonds are redeemed before maturity.

Premium and Discount on Bonds.   When bonds sell at a price greater than par, they are said to sell at a **premium,** and when at a price less than par they are said to sell at a **discount.**

Nominal and Effective Interest Rates.   The **nominal rate,** also known as the **coupon rate** or the cash rate, is the rate, based on the par value, stipulated in the bond.

The **effective rate,** also called the **yield** or **market rate,** is the return that the bonds earn on the price at which they are purchased if they are held to maturity. Note that the yield is based on the price paid for the bond, not on its par value. When the nominal rate is in excess of the yield rate, that is, in excess of what in the opinion of the market is considered a fair rate of return for that type of security, the bond sells at a **premium.** When the bond rate is less than the yield rate, the bond sells at a **discount.** The amount of the premium or discount can be mathematically determined and is based on principles of compound interest and annuities.

Determining Basis Price of Bonds.   The price at which a bond will sell on the open market depends on a number of factors:

1. The security for the payment of the principal and interest.
2. The bond rate.
3. The rate realized by like investments, or to be realized by the investor.
4. The time to the maturity of the bond.
5. The price at which the bond will be redeemed.
6. The tax status of the principal and interest.

From a purely mathematical point of view, once the desired yield is known, the basis price, that is, the purchase price, of a bond depends on two factors:

1. The present value of the principal.
2. The present value of the interest payments.

The sum of these two present values represents the basis price of the bond. The first factor represents the present value of a lump sum, the second the present value of an annuity.

Example.   What is the price paid by Mr. X on November 1, 1980, for 100 bonds, par value $100,000, paying 16% nominal to yield 14%? The bonds pay interest May 1 and November 1, through coupons, and mature November 1, 1983.

The nominal rate per period is 8%, the effective rate 7%.

Computing the Price Using Tables.   The present value of the principal six periods from now is

$$
\begin{aligned}
P &= A \times PVIF_{i,n} \\
&= A \times PVIF_{7,6} \\
&= \$100,000 \times 0.6663 \text{ (Exhibit 5)} \\
&= \underline{\underline{\$66,630}}
\end{aligned}
$$

The present value of the coupons is calculated by means of the annuity formula. The size of each coupon is determined from the nominal rate. In this example, the semi-annual coupons have a face value of $8,000 (i.e., $100,000 × 8%). Their present value is then found:

$$
\begin{aligned}
A &= R \times PVIFA_{i,n} \\
&= R \times PVIF_{7,6} \\
&= \$8,000 \times 4.7665 \text{ (Exhibit 7)} \\
&= \underline{\underline{\$38,132}}
\end{aligned}
$$

Basis price of bonds:

$$
\$66,630 + 38,132 = \underline{\underline{\$104,762}}
$$

Note that the yield rate is always used except for calculating the amount of cash coupon.

Short Method for Finding Basis Price.   Since the difference between the coupon and yield rates gives rise to premium or discount on bonds, it is possible to compute the premium, and hence the basis price, directly from such difference. This method is illustrated below, using the same example as above.

	Rate (%)	Amount
Nominal interest	8	$8,000
Effective interest	7	7,000
Excess interest		$1,000

The bond pays $8,000 interest per period. It should pay $7,000 to sell at par. There is, therefore, $1,000 excess interest per period. The excess interest constitutes an annuity for the life of the bond. The present value of this annuity represents the premium to be paid.

$$
\begin{aligned}
A &= R \times PVIFA_{7,6} \\
&= \$1,000 \times 4.7665 \text{ (Exhibit 7)} \\
&= 4,766.50
\end{aligned}
$$

$$
\begin{aligned}
\text{Par value} &= \$100,000 \\
\text{Basis price} &= \$104,766.50
\end{aligned}
$$

Computing the Price Using a Financial Calculator.   The keystrokes are as follows:

Keystroke	Display	Comment
ALL	0.00	Clear
END	0.00	Set payment switch
8	8	—
ENTER	8.00	Nominal interest
7	7	Effective interest
—	1.00	—
100000	100,000.00	Par value
STO	100,000.00	—
1	100,000.00	—
×	100,000.00	—
100	100.00	—
÷	1,000.00	Excess interest
CHS	−1,000.00	—
PMT	−1,000.00	—
7	7.00	—
i	7.00	Interest rate
6	6.00	—
n	6.00	Number of periods
PV	4,766.54	—
RCL	4,766.54	—
1	100,000.00	—
+	104,766.54	Basis price

Amortization Schedule. Although an investor may have paid a premium for the bond, generally speaking, he collects only the par value at maturity. This shrinkage in value takes place gradually during the life of the bond. It means that each coupon collection represents two things:

1. Return on the investment at the yields rate.
2. Partial return of the premium paid.

That this is the case can be shown by a so-called amortization table. Exhibit 9 is based on the premium bond illustrated in the last example.

EXHIBIT 9 AMORTIZATION SCHEDULE

Date	Coupon Income 8%	Effective Income 7%	Amortization	Remaining Book Value
November 1, 1980	—	—	—	$104,766.54
May 1, 1981	$8,000	$7,333.66	666.34	104,100.20
November 1, 1981	8,000	7,287.01	712.99	103,387.21
May 1, 1982	8,000	7,237.10	762.90	102,624.32
November 1, 1982	8,000	7,183.70	816.30	101,808.02
May 1, 1983	8,000	7,126.56	873.44	100,934.58
November 1, 1983	8,000	7,065.42	934.58	100,000.00

The coupon income is 8% a period based on the par value of the bonds. The effective income or yield is 7% based on the remaining investment. Thus, on May 1, 1981, 7% is earned on $104,766.54 or $7,333.66. This is the true income for the period. The balance of the $8,000 coupon interest collected on that day represents a partial liquidation of the investment. Hence, the book value is reduced on May 1, 1981, by $666.34. Six months later, the effective income is 7% of the new book value of $104,100.20, and so on.

Short-Cut Method for Discount Bonds.   The short-cut method just illustrated works equally well for bonds selling at a discount, as shown in the example below.

Example.   Find the basis price of $10,000 bond paying 10% nominal interest on February 1 and August 1, to yield 12%. The bond was purchased February 1, 1980, and matures August 1, 1982.

	Rate (%)	Amount
Nominal interest	5	$500
Effective interest	6	$600
Deficiency of interest		$100

$$A = R \times PVIFA_{i,n}$$
$$= \$100 \times PVIFA_{6,5}$$
$$= \$100 \times 4.2124 \text{ (Exhibit 7)}$$
$$= \$421.24$$
$$\text{par value} = \$10,000.00$$
$$\text{basis price} = \$ \ 9,578.76$$

Schedule of Accumulation.   A bond purchased at a discount approaches par or other redemption value gradually. The increase in value is spread over the life of the bond. Hence, the **true income** each period consists of:

1.   Coupon interest.
2.   Increase in book value, known as the accumulation.

Exhibit 10 is an accumulation table for the last illustration, under the short-cut method for discount bonds.

EXHIBIT 10   ACCUMULATION TABLE FOR $10,000 BOND

Date	Coupon Interest 5%	Effective Interest 6%	Accumulation	New Book Value
February 1, 1980	—	—	—	$ 9,578.76
August 1, 1980	$500	$574.73	$74.73	9,653.49
February 1, 1981	500	579.21	79.21	9,732.69
August 1, 1981	500	583.96	83.96	9,816.66
February 1, 1982	500	589.00	89.00	9,905.66
August 1, 1982	500	594.34	94.34	10,000.00

The figures in the effective interest column are obtained by taking 6% of the last book value. Thus on August 1, 1980, 6% of $9,578.76 yields $574.73. Six months later 6% of $9,653.49 amounts to $579.21, and so on. In each instance, the difference between coupon and yield interest is **added** to the previous book value.

Bond Valuation Tables.   Bond tables have been devised to simplify the labor involved in determining:

1. The price to be paid when the yield is known.
2. The yield when the cost is known.

Thus it is possible to read the basis price of a bond directly from the table. The **standard bond tables** usually give the value of a million dollar bond correct to the nearest cent for a great variety of nominal and effective interest rates and for periods ranging from 6 months to 50 years at 6-month intervals, and at longer intervals thereafter. However, with the easy availability of pocket calculators, these tables are virtually obsolete.

Basis Price for Bonds Bought Between Interest Dates.   The basis price of a bond changes from day to day. Hence, if a bond is bought between interest dates, its basis price must be computed by interpolation between the basis prices of the last preceding and next succeeding interest dates. In addition, the purchaser will have to pay **accrued interest** on the bonds to the seller for the time since the last interest date.

Bonds may be quoted either "and interest" or "flat." The **"and-interest" price** is the quoted price plus the accrued interest. The **"flat" price** includes the accrued interest in the quotation. To find the value of a bond between interest dates, proceed as follows:

1. Find the basis price on the preceding interest day and on the succeeding interest day, and thus determine the decrease or increase in book value for the entire period.
2. Find the fractional part of the period that has elapsed to the day of purchase. Find this fractional part of the period's change in book value.
3. Add to the book value of the preceding interest day the increase found in step 2 or subtract from it the decrease found in step 2 for the part of the period that has elapsed. The result is the "and-interest" price or "ex-interest" price.
4. Add to the ex-interest price in either instance the accrued interest, or seller's share of the current period's bond interest. The result is the **total price** or flat price.

Example.   Find the "and-interest" and "flat" prices for a $1,000 bond, due February 1, 1991, bearing interest at 14% per annum, payable February 1 and August 1, if purchased April 1, 1981, to yield 12%.

The life of the bond on the last interest date (February 1, 1981) was 10 years; at the next interest date it has $9\frac{1}{2}$ years to run. The basis prices on these two dates can be found by the methods presented earlier (determining the basis prices of bonds) by using tables or a financial calculator.

Computing Bond Prices Using Tables.   The values of the bond to yield 12% are as follows:

Step 1	10 years (February 1, 1981)	$1,114.70
	$9\frac{1}{2}$ years (August 1, 1981)	$1,111.58
	Amortization for 6 months	$ 3.12

Step 2   From February 1 to April 1 is one-third of a period. Therefore the basis price decreased

$$\tfrac{1}{3} \times \$3.12 = \$1.04$$

Step 3   "And-interest" price April 1, 1981 = \$1,114.70 − \$1.04 = \$1,113.66
Step 4   Accrued interest

14% per annum on \$1,000 for 2 months	23.33
Flat price	\$1,136.99

It is possible also to determine the flat price directly. The seller is entitled to the book value on the preceding interest day, plus interest on this válue at the yield rate, for the time elapsed since that day. The procedure is as follows:

1. Find the basis price on the preceding interest day.
2. Find the time elapsed since the last interest day, and add to the basis price on the preceding interest day interest on it at the yield rate for the elapsed time on a 360-day year basis. The result is the **total price.**
3. From the total price **subtract** the accrued interest. The result is the and-interest price or the ex-interest price.

Using the same illustration as above, the method works out as follows:

Step 1	February 1, 1981, basis price	\$1,114.70
Step 2	Interest at 12% per annum for 2 months on above	22.29
Step 3	April 1, 1981, flat price	\$1,136.99

If only the total price to be paid by the purchaser or to be received by the seller is wanted, this method offers a short-cut. For the purpose of setting up a schedule of amortization or accumulation, the and-interest price must be used. The first four lines of the amortization table for the bond above appear as follows:

Date	Bond Interest 14%	Effective Interest 12%	Amortization	Book Value
April 1, 1981	—	—	—	\$1,113.66
August 1, 1981	\$46.67	\$44.59	\$2.08	1,111.58
February 1, 1982	70.00	66.69	3.31	1,108.28
August 1, 1982	70.00	66.50	3.50	1,104.77

The figures for August 1, 1981, are obtained as follows:

1. Bond interest. The total coupon interest for a period is \$70, one-third of which (\$23.33) was paid over to the vendor on April 1. Hence, the net interest collected on August 1 is \$46.67.
2. Effective interest. This must be calculated on the basis price as of the last interest date (February 1, 1981) for 4 months. In this case \$1,114.70 at 12% for 4 months is \$44.59.

3. Amortization. Difference between the two preceding columns. $46.67 − $44.54 = $2.08. It could also be found by taking the amortization for the full 6-month period ($3.12) and subtracting the amortization from February 1 to April 1 ($1.04).

4. Book value. Book value April 1, 1981, less current amortization. $1,114.70 − $2.08 = $1,112.62.

Computing Bond Prices Using a Financial Calculator.   The keystrokes are as follows:

Keystroke	Display	Comment
ALL	0.00	Clear
END	0.00	Set payment switch
0.07	0.07	—
ENTER	0.07	—
1000	1,000.00	—
×	70.00	Coupon interest
STO	70.00	—
1	70.00	—
CHS	− 70.00	—
PMT	− 70.00	—
6	6.00	—
i	6.00	Yield
20	20.00	—
n	20.00	Number of periods
PV	802.89	—
0	0.00	—
PMT	0.00	—
1000	1,000	—
CHS	− 1,000	—
FV	− 1,000.00	—
PV	311.80	—
+	1,114.70	Bond base price, $n = 20$
STO	1,114.70	—
2	1,114.70	—
19	19.00	—
n	19.00	—
PV	330.51	—
RCL	330.51	—
1	70.00	—
CHS	− 70.00	—
PMT	− 70.00	—
0	0.00	—
FV	0.00	—
PV	781.07	—
+	1,111.58	Bond base price, $n = 19$
RCL	1,111.58	—
2	1,114.70	—
$x \gtrless y$	1,111.58	—
−	3.12	—

Keystroke	Display	Comment
2	2.00	—
×	6.24	—
6	6.00	—
÷	1.04	Decrease in base price
CHS	− 1.04	—
RCL	− 1.04	—
2	1,114.70	—
+	1,113.66	"And-interest" price
STO	1,113.66	—
3	1,113.66	—
RCL	1,113.66	—
1	70.00	—
3	3.00	—
÷	23.33	Accrued interest
RCL	23.33	—
3	1,113.66	—
+	1,136.99	Flat price

Accruing Bond Interest Between Interest Dates.   The interest accrued at time of purchase or sale depends on whether the bond is a corporate or a government bond. For corporate bonds delivery must be made on the fourth working day after the sale and interest is accrued on the basis of a 360-day year up to and including the day before delivery. In the case of government bonds, delivery is on the next working day, and the seller receives interest up to and including the day of the sale.

The rules are further clarified by the Committee on Securities of the New York Stock Exchange as follows:

Interest at the rate specified on a bond dealt in "and-interest" shall be computed on a basis of a 360-day year, i.e., each calendar month shall be considered to be 1/12 of 360 days, and each period from a date in one month to the same date in the following month shall be considered to be 30 days.

Note: The number of elapsed days shall be computed in accordance with the examples given in the following table:

From	To
30th to 31st	1st of the following month to be figured as 1 day
30th or 31st	30th of the following month to be figured as 30 days
30th or 31st	31st of the following month to be figured as 30 days
30th or 31st	1st of the second following month to be figured as one month one day

Thus if a January and July 15 bond were bought on March 15, 2 months are said to have elapsed since January 15. If a June and December 1 bond were bought on January 16, following the above rule there are:

From December 1 to January 1	30 days
From January 1 to January 16	15 days
Elapsed time	45 days

Determining Profit or Loss on Sale of Bonds.   When bonds that have been purchased as an investment are subsequently sold, the profit or loss on the transaction is determined by comparison of the book value (i.e., the and-interest price) on the date of sale with the selling price.

The profit or loss figure represents the capital gain or loss for tax purposes and is of course exclusive of the coupon interest less amortization regularly reported as income.

Finding Yield Between Interest Dates.   The calculation by tables of yield between interest dates is complex, since it requires a double interpolation, once for the basis price of the bond and then for the yield. Hence, only the method using the financial calculator is given below.

Example.   A price of $102 is quoted for a bond with 26 semiannual coupon payments remaining. The coupon rate is 12.75%. The current coupon period contains 183 days, and the settlement date is 60 days into the period. Assuming that the bond is redeemable at par, what is the yield?

The steps in the calculation are as follows:

1. Compute the yield ignoring the adjustment in the basis price of the bond.
2. Compute the adjusted basis price of the bond to take into account the time away from the settlement date.
3. Repeat steps 1 and 2 iteratively, till the change in yield between iterations is negligible.

The keystrokes for the financial calculator are as follows.

Keystroke	Display	Comment
ALL	0.00	Clear
END	0.00	Set payment switch
59	59	Days to settlement
ENTER	59.00	—
183	183	Days in coupon period
÷	0.32	—
STO	0.32	—
5	0.32	—
6.375	6.375	Coupon
×	2.06	—
STO	2.06	—
6	2.06	—
6.375	6.375	—
CHS	−6.375	—
PMT	−6.38	—
100	100	Future value
CHS	−100	—
FV	−100.00	—
STO	−100.00	—
4	−100.00	—
102	102.00	—
PV	102.00	Present value
STO	102.00	—

Keystroke	Display	Comment
1	102.00	—
124.	124.00	Days from previous settlement
÷	0.82	—
25	25.00	Coupon payments remaining other than present
+	25.82	—
n	25.82	—
STO	25.82	—
2	25.82	Coupon payments remaining including fraction of present
i	6.22	Iteration 1
0	0.00	—
PV	0.00	—
RCL	0.00	—
5	0.32	—
n	0.32	—
FV	2.01	—
CHS	−2.01	—
RCL	−2.01	—
6	2.06	—
+	0.04	—
PV	0.04	—
RCL	0.04	—
1	102.00	—
+	108.22	—
PV	108.22	—
RCL	108.22	—
4	−100.00	—
FV	−100.00	—
RCL	−100.00	—
2	25.82	—
n	25.82	—
i	5.76	Iteration 2
0	0.00	Continue to iteration 3
PV	0.00	—
.	.	
.	.	
.	.	
i	5.79	Iteration 5

OPTION PRICING MATHEMATICS

THE BLACK–SCHOLES FORMULA.   The most commonly used formula for pricing call options is one developed by **Black and Scholes** in "The Pricing of Options and Corporate Liabilities" (*Journal of Political Economy*, May–June 1973). It is often used, with minor variations, to determine the gap between the market price of a **call option** and its **intrinsic value.**

The key assumptions of the **Black-Scholes model** are:

1. The short-term interest rate is known and is constant through time.

2. The stock price follows a random walk in continuous time with a variance rate proportional to the square of the stock price.

3. The distribution of possible stock prices at the end of any finite interval is log normal.

4. The variance rate of return on the stock is constant.

5. The stock pays no dividends and makes no other distributions.

6. The option can be exercised only at maturity.

7. There are no commissions or other transaction costs in buying or selling the stock or the option.

8. It is possible to borrow any fraction of the price of a security to buy it or to hold it, at the short-term interest rate.

9. A seller who does not own a security (a short seller) will simply accept the price of the security from the buyer and will agree to settle with the buyer on some future date by paying him an amount equal to the price of the security on that date. While this short sale is outstanding, the short seller will have the use of, or interest on, the proceeds of the sale.

10. The tax rate, if any, is identical for all transactions and all market participants.

The assumption that the distribution of the stock price at the end of any finite time interval be log normal is equivalent to saying that the distribution of the stock's returns in each instant will be normal with a constant variance. Under these assumptions and using the hedging arguments outlined in the section entitled "Option Markets and Instruments," the price of a call option is determined by:

$$P_o = P_s N(d_1) - \frac{E}{e^{rt}} N(d_2)$$

where $d_1 = \dfrac{\ln (P_s/E) + (r + \frac{1}{2}\sigma^2)t}{\sigma\sqrt{t}}$

$d_2 = \dfrac{\ln (P_s/E) + (r - \frac{1}{2}\sigma^2)t}{\sigma\sqrt{t}}$

where P_o = current value of option

P_s = current price of stock

E = exercise price of option

e = 2.71828

t = time remaining before expiration (years)

r = continuously compounded riskless rate of interest

σ = standard deviation of continuously compounded annual rate of return on the stock

$\ln (P_s/E)$ = natural logarithm of (P_s/E)

$N(d)$ = probability that a deviation less than d will occur in a normal distribution with a mean of 0 and a standard deviation of 1

Example.   Suppose the price of a share of XYZ Corp. is $50 and the exercise price of the call option is $40. The option has 3 months to maturity (i.e., 0.25 of a year). If the riskless rate of interest is 5% per year, and the standard deviation of the continuously compounded annual return is 50%, determine the price of the option, using the following data:

P_s = $36
E = $40
t = 0.25 (i.e., one-fourth of a year, or 3 months)
r = 0.05 (i.e, 5% per year, continuously compounded)
· σ = 0.50 (i.e., the standard deviation of the continuously compounded annual return is 50%)

Using the formula, we write:

$$d_1 = \frac{\ln (36/40) + [0.05 + \frac{1}{2}(0.50^2)]\, 0.25}{0.50\sqrt{0.25}} \approx -0.25$$

$$d_2 = \frac{\ln (36/40) + [0.05 - \frac{1}{2}(0.50^2)]\, 0.50}{0.50\sqrt{0.25}} \approx -0.50$$

From Exhibit 11, which furnishes values of the $N(d)$, the standard normal-variate for various values of d, we see that

$$N(d_1) = N(-0.25) = 0.4013$$
$$N(d_2) = N(-0.50) = 0.3085$$

Thus:

$$P_o = (36 \times 0.4013) - \left(\frac{40}{e^{0.05 \times 0.25}} \times 0.3085\right) \approx \$2.26$$

Only a hand calculator is needed to estimate the value of an option using the Black-Scholes formula. In fact, a pocket calculator can be programmed to make the calculations directly. The details of such a program are furnished in Rubinstein (1977) or Rubinstein and Cox (1981).

NOMOGRAMS FOR OPTION VALUATION.   An alternative method using a **nomogram** is illustrated in Exhibit 12. To value an option, it is necessary to construct a box. The position on the left-hand side is determined by the maturity of the option. The top of the left-hand side is determined by the standard deviation of the stock's annual return and the bottom by the annual interest rate. The position of the right-hand side of the box is determined by the ratio of the current stock price to the exercise price (here, based on the location of the upper right-hand corner). In this case, the nomogram indicates that the option value is somewhat more than 5% of the exercise price, or $2(0.05 × $40); see Exhibit 13.

Exhibit 12 shows that, other things equal, an option is generally more valuable:

The **higher** the current stock price relative to the exercise price.

The **longer** the time remaining before expiration.

The **higher** the riskless rate of interest.

The **greater** the risk of the underlying stock.

EXHIBIT 11   VALUES OF N(d) FOR SELECTED VALUES OF d

d	N(d)	d	N(d)	d	N(d)
		−1.00	.1587	1.00	.8413
−2.95	.0016	−0.95	.1711	1.05	.8531
−2.90	.0019	−0.90	.1841	1.10	.8643
−2.85	.0022	−0.85	.1977	1.15	.8749
−2.80	.0026	−0.80	.2119	1.20	.8849
−2.75	.0030	0.75	.2266	1.25	.8944
−2.70	.0035	−0.70	.2420	1.30	.9032
−2.65	.0040	−0.65	.2578	1.35	.9115
−2.60	.0047	−0.60	.2743	1.40	.9192
−2.55	.0054	−0.55	.2912	1.45	.9265
−2.50	.0062	−0.50	.3085	1.50	.9332
−2.45	.0071	−0.45	.3264	1.55	.9394
−2.40	.0082	−0.40	.3446	1.60	.9452
−2.35	.0094	−0.35	.3632	1.65	.9505
−2.30	.0107	−0.30	.3821	1.70	.9554
−2.25	.0122	−0.25	.4013	1.75	.9599
−2.20	.0139	−0.20	.4207	1.80	.9641
−2.15	.0158	−0.15	.4404	1.85	.9678
−2.10	.0179	−0.10	.4602	1.90	.9713
−2.05	.0202	−0.05	.4801	1.95	.9744
−2.00	.0228	0.00	.5000	2.00	.9773
−1.95	.0256	0.05	.5199	2.05	.9798
−1.90	.0287	0.10	.5398	2.10	.9821
−1.85	.0322	0.15	.5596	2.15	.9842
−1.80	.0359	0.20	.5793	2.20	.9861
−1.75	.0401	0.25	.5987	2.25	.9878
−1.70	.0446	0.30	.6179	2.30	.9893
−1.65	.0495	0.35	.6368	2.35	.9906
−1.60	.0548	0.40	.6554	2.40	.9918
−1.55	.0606	0.45	.6736	2.45	.9929
−1.50	.0668	0.50	.6915	2.50	.9938
−1.45	.0735	0.55	.7088	2.55	.9946
−1.40	.0808	0.60	.7257	2.60	.9953
−1.35	.0885	0.65	.7422	2.65	.9960
−1.30	.0968	0.70	.7580	2.70	.9965
−1.25	.1057	0.75	.7734	2.75	.9970
−1.20	.1151	0.80	.7881	2.80	.9974
−1.15	.1251	0.85	.8023	2.85	.9978
−1.10	.1357	0.90	.8159	2.90	.9981
−1.05	.1469	0.95	.8289	2.95	.9984

EXHIBIT 12   THE CALL OPTION VALUATION NOMOGRAM

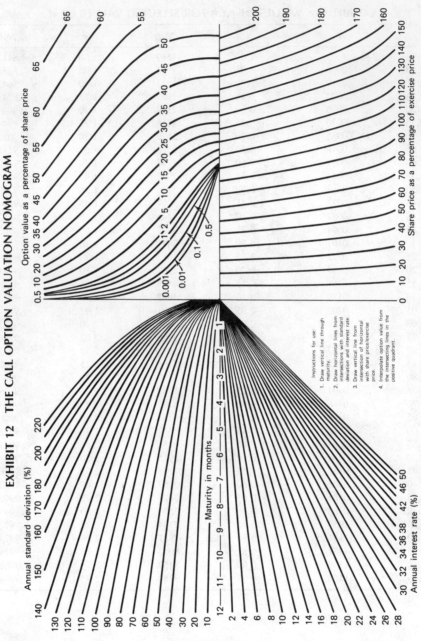

Source: E. Dimson, "Instant Option Valuation," *Financial Analysts Journal,* May–June 1977.

EXHIBIT 13 · EXAMPLE OF THE USE OF CALL OPTION VALUATION NOMOGRAM

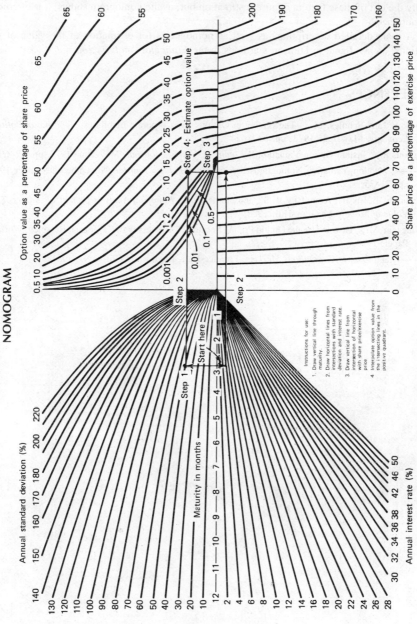

Source: E. Dimson, "Instant Option Valuation," *Financial Analysts Journal,* May–June 1977.

Only the last of these factors requires estimation but, as the nomogram shows, it is of crucial importance.

A more detailed description, as well as nomograms for estimation of the value of put options, are available in Dimson's articles in the *Financial Analysts Journal*.

REFERENCES

Black, F., and Scholes, M., "The Pricing of Options and Corporate Liabilities," *Journal of Political Economy*, May–June 1973, pp. 637–654.

Dimson, E., "Instant Option Valuation," *Financial Analysts Journal*, May–June 1977, pp. 62–69.

———, "Option Valuation Nomograms," *Financial Analysts Journal*, November–December 1977, pp. 71–75.

Greynolds, E. B., Jr., Aronofsky, J. S., and Frame, R. J., *Financial Analysis Using Calculators: Time Value of Money*, McGraw-Hill, 1980.

Rubinstein, M., "How to Use the Option Pricing Formula," University of California, Berkeley, Working Paper, 1977.

———, and Cox, J. C., *Options Markets*, Prentice-Hall, Englewood Cliffs, NJ, 1981.

SOURCES OF INVESTMENT INFORMATION

This suggested list of materials covers basic sources of information that the serious student and practitioner of investment strategies will want to consult. Several bibliographies are compiled regularly to provide up-to-date evaluations of what is being published in the field. As a general guide the *Investment Bibliography* published by the New York Stock Exchange is recommended. The Baker Library of the Harvard University Graduate School of Business Administration prepares a *Mini-List on Investment Sources* each year, which lists major reference works and investment services. "Recommended Business Books of the Year" is a list published annually by *Library Journal* that includes books on investment techniques and current business conditions. The quarterly issues of *Wall Street Review of Books* contain lengthy reviews of books on investment strategy. To keep abreast of new computerized databases, the serious investor should consult issues of *Information and Data Base Publishing Report,* a biweekly newsletter published by Knowledge Industry Publications, Inc., and issues of *Online* and *Database* magazines, published by Online, Inc. For a detailed discussion of investment information sources, see section 16 of this *Handbook.*

BOOKS

On Learning to Invest

Darst, David M., *The Handbook of the Bond and Money Markets,* McGraw-Hill, New York, 1981.

Gastineau, Gary L., *The Stock Options Manual,* 2nd ed., McGraw-Hill, New York, 1979.

Sokoloff, Kiril, *The Paine Webber Handbook of Stock and Bond Analysis,* McGraw-Hill, New York, 1979.

Touhey, John, *Stock Market Forecasting for Alert Investors,* AMACOM, New York, 1980.

Tracy, John, *How to Read a Financial Report,* John Wiley & Sons, New York, 1980.

For Experienced Investors

Bernstein, Jacob, *The Investor's Quotient: The Psychology of Successful Investing in Commodities and Stocks,* John Wiley & Sons, New York, 1980.

Hardy, C. Colburn, *The Investor's Guide to Technical Analysis,* McGraw-Hill, New York, 1978.

"Sources of Investment Information" was prepared by Madeline Cohen, Manager of Library Services at ABC News and Chairman of the Business and Finance Group of the New York Chapter of the Special Libraries Association. An experienced consultant on information delivery and database development, she was formerly with Research Institute of America, McGraw-Hill, Inc., and the American Bankers Association.

Jastram, Roy, *Silver: The Restless Metal,* John Wiley & Sons, New York, 1981.

Kaufman, P.J., Ed., *Technical Analysis in Commodities,* John Wiley & Sons, New York, 1980.

Noddings, Thomas, *Advanced Investment Strategies,* Dow Jones-Irwin, Homewood, Ill., 1978.

Powers, Mark and Vogel, David, *Inside the Financial Futures Market,* John Wiley & Sons, New York, 1981.

Stewart, Joseph T., Jr., *Dynamic Stock Option Trading,* John Wiley & Sons, New York, 1981.

Textbooks

Bellmore, Douglas, *Investment Analysis and Portfolio Selection: An Integrated Approach,* South-Western Publishing Company, Cincinnati, Ohio, 1979.

Christy, George A. and Clendenin, John C., *Introduction to Investments,* 7th ed., McGraw-Hill, New York, 1978.

Cohen, Jerome B., *Investment Analysis and Portfolio Management,* 3rd ed. Dow Jones-Irwin, Homewood, Ill., 1977.

Curley, Anthony J. and Bear, Robert M., *Investment Analysis and Management,* Harper and Row, New York, 1979.

Fischer, Donald E. and Jordan, Ronald J., *Security Analysis and Portfolio Management,* 2nd ed., Prentice-Hall, Englewood Cliffs, N.J., 1979.

Francis, Jack Clark, *Portfolio Analysis,* 2nd ed., Prentice-Hall, Englewood Cliffs, N.J., 1979.

Hagin, Robert, *The Dow Jones-Irwin Guide to Modern Portfolio Theory,* Dow Jones-Irwin, Homewood, Ill., 1979.

Loll, Leo M. and Buckley, Julian G., *The Over-the-Counter Securities Market,* 4th ed., Prentice-Hall, Englewood Cliffs, N.J., 1981.

Reilly, Frank K., *Investment Analysis and Portfolio Management,* Dryden Press, Hinsdale, Ill., 1979.

BANK LETTERS

Monthly Economic Letter, Citibank, monthly.

The Morgan Guaranty Survey, Morgan Guaranty Trust Co. of New York, monthly.

General Business Indicators, The Bank of New York, monthly.

Business in Brief, Chase Manhattan Bank, bimonthly.

Federal Reserve Bank Monthly Bulletins, published by each of the 12 Federal Reserve Banks.

SOURCES OF ECONOMIC AND FINANCIAL STATISTICS

Federal Reserve Bulletin, Board of Governors of the Federal Reserve System, monthly.

Chart Book on Business, Economic and Financial Statistics (monthly) and *Historical Chart Book* (annual), Board of Governors of the Federal Reserve System.

Survey of Current Business, U.S. Department of Commerce, monthly. Annual compilation: *Business Statistics.*

Economic Indicators, President's Council of Economic Advisors, monthly. Also publishes *Annual Economic Review.*

Business Conditions Digest, U.S. Department of Commerce, monthly.

Quarterly Financial Report for Manufacturing Corporations, U.S. Federal Trade Commission and the U.S. Securities and Exchange Commission, quarterly.

Standard and Poor's Statistical Service, Standard and Poor's Corporation, updated monthly.

NEWSPAPERS

American Banker, daily
Barron's, weekly.
Commercial and Financial Chronicle, weekly.
Financial Times (London), daily.
Journal of Commerce, daily.
M/G Financial Weekly Market Digest, weekly.
Money Manager, weekly.
Wall Street Journal, daily.
Wall Street Transcript, weekly.

PERIODICALS

Bank and Quotation Record, monthly.
Business Week, weekly.
Euromoney, monthly.
Financial Planner, monthly.
Financial Analysts Journal, bimonthly.
Financial Executive, monthly.
Financial World, semi-monthly.
Forbes, biweekly.
Fortune, biweekly.
Insider's Chronicle, weekly.
Institutional Investor, monthly.
Investment Dealer's Digest, weekly.
Journal of Finance, five times a year.
Journal of Financial and Quantitative Analysis, five times a year.
Journal of Portfolio Management, quarterly.
Official Summary of Security Transactions and Holdings (magazine of the SEC), monthly.
SEC Monthly Statistical Review, monthly.
Securities Week, weekly.
Stock Market Magazine, monthly.
Technical Trends, weekly.
Venture Capital, monthly.
Wright Investment Analyses, weekly.

PERIODICALS INDEX

F & S United States and *F & S International*. Predicasts, Inc., Cleveland. Updated weekly. Loose-leaf
services. Comprehensive business periodicals indexes covering all industries and companies in the
U.S. and worldwide. Access is by SIC code and by company name.

INVESTMENT AND FINANCIAL SERVICES

Arnold Bernhard & Co., Inc., New York.

Value Line Investment Survey. Weekly. Covers over 1,700 stocks and situations.

Value Line Options & Convertibles. 48 times per year. Data on options, convertibles and warrants.

Commerce Clearing House, Inc., Chicago.

American Stock Exchange Guide

Capital Changes Reporter

Commodity Futures Law Reporter

Federal Securities Law Reporter

Mutual Funds Guide

NASD Manual

New York Stock Exchange Guide

Loose-leaf services containing the latest information in each field of investment.

Dunn & Hargitt, Inc., Lafayette, Indiana.

The Dunn & Hargitt Commodity Service. Weekly. Contains charts and trading advice based on technical analysis of commodity futures prices. Includes commentary on supplies and demand for selected commodities.

Moody's Investors Service, Inc., New York.

Moody's Handbook of Common Stocks. Quarterly. Financial and business information on over 900 stocks.

Moody's Manuals of Investment. Annual, updated semiweekly. Individual volumes: Bank and Finance, Industrials, Municipals and Government, OTC Industrial, Public Utilities, Transportation.

National Quotation Bureau, Inc., New York.

National Monthly Bond Summary

National Monthly Stock Summary

Monthly, with semiannual bound volumes. Contains quotations on OTC and inactive listed securities that have appeared in *National Daily Services*.

R.H.M. Associates, Inc., Great Neck, N.Y.

The R.H.M. Survey of Warrants, Options & Low-Price Stocks. Weekly. Advisory service on investments.

Standard & Poor's Corporation, New York.

Analysts Handbook. Updated monthly. Composite corporate per share data from 1946 for nearly 100 industries and the S&P 400 Industrial Index.

Daily Stock Price Record. Quarterly. Individual volumes covering NYSE, ASE, and OTC.

Dividend Record. Five times per week. Contains complete information on dividends.

Earnings Forecaster. Weekly. Provides new and revised earnings estimates on over 1,600 companies.

Fixed Income Investor. Weekly. Comments on new corporate and municipal issues and includes the S&P rating plus a "rating rationale."

Industry Surveys. Annual. Basic Survey and three Current Surveys in the course of the year on each of 65 leading industries in the United States and Canada.

The Outlook. Weekly. Reports S&P's stock market investment policy and comments on the investment merits of a wide range of securities.

Security Owner's Stock Guide. Monthly. Summary of investment data on over 5,100 common and preferred stocks.

Bond Guide. Monthly. Contains descriptive and statistical data on over 5,700 corporate bonds.

Standard Corporation Descriptions. Updated daily. Basic financial information on over 5,900 corporations.

Stock Reports. Periodically revised. Two-page reports on nearly 3,600 companies listed on the NYSE, ASE, and OTC.

Trendline's Current Market Perspectives. Monthly. Provides price action charts and basic financial data for 972 listed stocks.

United Business Service, Boston.

United Business & Investment Report. Weekly. Investment advisory service with commentary and evaluation of economic conditions.

Vickers Associates, Inc., Huntington, N.Y.

Vickers Guide to Bank Trust Portfolios.

Vickers Guide to College Endowment Portfolios.

Vickers Guide to Investment Company Portfolios.

Loose-leaf services. Cover stock purchases, sales and portfolio holdings.

Wiesenberger Investment Companies Service, New York.

Investment Companies. Annual. Gives background data, management policy, income, dividends and price ranges for each listing.

SELECTED REFERENCE WORKS

Fact Books

AMEX Data Book. American Stock Exchange.
Mutual Fund Fact Book. Investment Company Institute.
NASDAQ/OTC Market Fact Book. National Association of Security Dealers.
Fact Book. New York Stock Exchange.
Yearbook. Securities Industry Association.
Commodity Year Book. Commodity Research Bureau.

Directories, Handbooks and Encyclopedias

Feng, Paul, *The Dividend Reinvestment Handbook*, PMF Research Co., Kenilworth, Ill, 1981.

Grant, Mary McNierney and Cote, Norma, eds., *Directory of Business and Financial Services*, 7th ed., Special Libraries Association, 1976.

The New Encyclopedia of Stock Market Techniques, Investors Intelligence, New York, 1977.

Security Dealers of North America, Standard and Poor's Corporation, New York, twice a year with periodic supplements.

Stock Market Encyclopedia of the S&P "500", Standard and Poor's Corporation, New York, semiannual.

COMPUTERIZED DATABASES

Compustat

S&P Compustat Services, New York. Contains income statement, balance sheet, sources and application of funds information, line of business and market information for publicly held U.S. and some non-U.S. corporations. Annual data are included for about 6,000 industrial and nonindustrial companies. Quarterly data are available for 2,800 companies.

Disclosure Online

Disclosure, Inc., Washington, D.C. Contains information from the more than 11,000 publicly owned
companies that file reports with the Securities and Exchange Commission (SEC). Information in
each listing includes name, principal office address, state of incorporation, fiscal year end, exchange
on which its common stock is traded, Standard Industrial Classification (SIC) codes, description
of business, and a list of all SEC reports filed by the company. Extracts of Form 10K or 20K
include shareholder information, number of employees, subsidiaries, directors and officers, legal
proceedings, balance sheet and income statement information, and auditor. Extracts of 10Q, 8K,
prospectuses, registration statements, and proxies are also included.

Dow Jones News/Retrieval Service

Dow Jones and Co., Princeton, N.J. Contains full-text, edited news stories and articles from *The Wall
Street Journal, Barron's,* and *Dow Jones News Service.* Retrieval is by corporate stock symbol,
industry, and government codes.

Dow Jones Stock Quote Reporter. Contains price quotations on approximately 6000 companies. Includes
all companies listed on the New York, American, Midwest, and Pacific Stock Exchanges and the
NASDAQ Over-The-Counter market. Covers preferred stocks and warrants, bonds, options, mutual
funds, and selected U.S. Treasury issues.

DRI-SEC (Securities Data Bank)

Data Resources, Inc., Washington, D.C. Contains current and historical trading, financial, and descriptive information for thousands of security issues of all different types. Data are obtained primarily
from Telstat Systems, Inc. Price and yield data on about 18,000 bonds are obtained from Merrill
Lynch Economics, Inc.

Moody's Electronic Fact Sheets

Moody's Investors Service, Inc., New York. Updated daily. Information is similar to that contained in
published volumes of *Moody's Investors Fact Sheet* on 4,000 companies. Includes all NYSE and
AMEX companies and 1,500 OTC firms. Provides complete dividend information on more than
8,000 companies comprising 12,000 issues.

Security Market Data

Interactive Data Corporation (IDC), Waltham, Mass. Contains the following files of stock market data:
Security Master (security description and status information on over 45,000 securities in the United
States and Canada), *Prices* (daily high, low, close or bid and asked prices and volume data for
over 12,000 North American equity and fixed income securities from 1968), *Masterprice* (weekly
bid prices for over 15,000 unlisted corporate bonds and 7000 OTC stocks from January 1975),
Municipal Bonds (descriptive information and daily evaluations for more than 1.7 million municipal
issues from 1976), *Split & Dividend* (daily stock splits and stock and cash dividends for more than
12,000 North American securities and dividends for over 100 Dow Jones and S&P indexes, from
1971), *Monthly/Quarterly* (quarterly earnings per share and monthly shares outstanding for 8000
companies and over 100 indexes for companies listed on the NYSE and AMEX and monthly
holding period returns for NYSE, AMEX and NASDAQ-listed issues).

Value Line

Value Line Data Services, Arnold Bernhard and Co., New York. Contains financial histories, projections, earnings estimates, target price forecasts, quarterly results, industry composites, accounting practices, risk measures, earnings predictability measures, stock price histories, restated sales and earnings, and trading volume figures for over 1600 major industrial, transportation, utility, retail, bank, insurance, and savings and loan companies. Covers major companies on the NYSE and selected companies on AMEX and OTC.

INDEX

Abnormal Rate of Return, 31·51
Absolute Priority Doctrine
  Bankruptcy and, 35·2, 35·15–16, 35·23
Absolute Purchasing Power Parity, 12·19–20
Accelerated Depreciation, 16·23, 32·17, 37·3
  Inflation accounting and, 37·38
Acceleration upon Default
  As creditor remedy, 9·19
Accepting Bank, 1·21
Accounting Return on Investment, 29·13
Accounting
  Acquisitions and mergers, 33·21–23
  Bankruptcy prediction and, 35·33
  Futures and, 21·15–18
  Inflation, see Inflation
  Missed purchase discounts, 28·27
  Public utilities and, 36·9–12
  see also Leasing
Accounting Income
  Investment project and, 29·11, 29·12
Accounts Payable, see Short-Term Liabilities
Accounts Receivable
  Determinants of level of, 28·3–4
    Collection policies and procedures,
      28·12–18
    Credit analysis and selection, 28·7–12
    Credit policy change, 28·15–18
    Credit Terms, 28·4–7
  Evaluation of management of, 28·18
    Effective measures of receivable status,
      28·21–23
    Traditional measures of receivable status,
      28·19–21
  Financial statement and, 25·13
  Financing of, 28·23–25
  See also Multinational Corporations
Accruals, 31·14
Accumulated Earnings Tax, 32·21
ACH-Based Transfer Service, 27·20, 27·21
Acid Test (Quick Rates), 24·26
Acquisitions, see Mergers and Acquisitions
Active Management Decision
  Pension and profit-sharing plans, 34·17–18
Actuarial Method
  Consumer credit prepayment, 9·20–21
Actuary
  Pension and profit-sharing plans, 34·11–12
Add-On Rate
  Consumer credit and, 9·15
Adela Investment Company, 13·32
Adjustable Rate Bands, 4·5–6
Adjusted Balance Method
  Revolving credit account and, 9·16

Adjusted Cash Flow Approach, 38·23–24
Adjusted Target Framework, 27·24
Adjusters
  Insurance claims and, 8·33–34
Adjustment, 27·28, 27·30, 27·31
Adjustment Bands, 4·5, 31·45
Administrative Office of the U. S. Courts
  Statistics and, 35·23, 35·24
Advance Deposit
  Permitted imports and, 11·17
Advance on Drafts, 14·19
Advanced Refunding Bonds
  Municipalities and, 2·6
Adversary Theory
  Transaction costs and, 12·12
Advertising Age, 16·8
Affiliated Banks, 14·13
Affiliation, Mergers and Acquisition of, 33·20,
    33·21
African Development Bank (ADB), 13·32, 38·44
Aftertax Yield on a Foreign Currency
  Denominated bond, 38·47
Agencies, see Federal Agencies
Agent
  Insurance, 8·6, 8·31–32
  Liability for acts, 8·22
Agent Banks, 9·11
Aggregate Approach
  Future earnings, 16·24–25
Aggregate Cash Position Management (ACPM),
    see Cash Management
Aging of Receivables, 28·20
Aging Schedule of Payables, 28·26
Agricultural Loans
  Commercial banks and, 6·6, 6·11
Allowance for Funds Used during Construction
    (AFUDC), 36·11–12
American Express Co.
  Credit cards, 6·4
American Lloyd's, 8·13
American Stock Exchange (AMEX), 5·14
  Commodities Exchange, 5·14
  Dividend declaration and, 32·11
Amortization
  Bonds, 18·8–10
  Loans, A·33–34
  Mortgage, 23·12–14
  Schedule, A·37–38
Amsterdam
  As world financial center, 13·8
Analysts Handbook, 16·9
Andean Development Corporation, 13·32
Andean Pact, 38·34

1

Annual Economic Review, 16·7
Annual Percentage Rate (APR)
  Consumer credit and, 9·15, 9·16
Annual Smoothing, 27·31
Annuities
  Amount or final value of, A·21
  Compound value of, A·23–24
  Definitions, A·21–22
  Due, A·21
  Ordinary annuity, A·22–23
  Pension plan and, 8·31
  Variable, 1·10, 34·10
  See also Sinking Fund
Annuity Certain, A·22
Anticipation, 27·24–25, A·5–6
Apartments
  Investment characteristics, 23·32–33
Appreciation, 22·8
Appropriation Request
  Capital budgeting process, 29·7–8, 29·9
Approximation
  Average rate of return and, 22·13–14
Arab Fund for Economic and Social Development (AFESD), 38·44
  In Africa, 13·32
Arbitrage
  Cash and Futures, 2·13
  Commodity market, 12·19
  Covered interest, 12·9, 12·26, 14·30–31
  Foreign Exchange, 12·5, 12·7, 12·8–9
  International financial market, 13·20
  Multinational corporation, 38·14–15
  Risk-free, 12·7, 12·26
  Spatial, 12·8
  Term repurchase transactions and, 10·12–13
  Triangular, 12·8–9, 12·13
Arbitrage Pricing Theory, 17·7
ARB Opinion No. 8 and 47
  Pension and profit-sharing plans, 34·4
Arithmetic Average, 22·9–10
Armored Car Pickup of Cash, 27·10
Arm's Length Prices, 38·16
Asian Development Bank, 13·32, 38·44
Ask Price, 5·20
Asset Accounts, *see* Commercial Bank
Asset Allocation Model
  Pension plan investments, 34·15, 34·16
Asset Depreciation Range System (ADR), 37·17
Asset Financing
  Accounts receivables, 28·23–24
Asset Management Ratios (Turnover Ratios), *see* Financial Statement Analysis
Asset Mix Decision
  Pension fund investments and, 34·15–17
Asset Pairs
  Interest rate parity theory, 13·22
Assets
  Balance sheet and, 24·4–5
  Commerical banks, 7·4–5
  Current, 24·4–5
  Fixed, 24·4–5
  Inflationaly holding gains on, 37·8–12
  Insurer, 8·34
  Purchase of Combination, 33·20, 33·22
  Return on, 24·12, 24·13, 24·15, 24·16
  Return on total, 24·27
  Savings institutions, 7·4–5

Assets (*Continued*)
  Tangible, 34·24
  Utilization, 24·29
Asset Turnover, 24·12, 24·13, 24·16, 24·18
  Dividends per share, 24·22
  Sales growth feasibility, 26·38
  Sustainable dividend growth, 24·21
Asset Value
  Bank stock and, 16·28
Assignable Letter of Credit, 14·24
Assignment, 35·10
Atlantic American Group for Latin America (ADELA), 38·44
Attorney's Fee Charges
  As creditor remedy, 9·18
Auction Market, 5·6
Audit Risk Analysis
  Bankruptcy predictions and, 35·33
Authority to Purchase, 14·24
Automated Clearing House (ACH), 6·28, 27·6
  Charge for, 6·23
Automated Teller Machines (ATMs), 6·27
Automatic Reinsurance, 8·15
Automatic Transfer Service (ATS), 6·15–16, 6·31
Automation, *see* Computers
Automobile Credit
  Commercial banks, 2·10, 9·11
  Consumer credit industry, 9·10
  Credit unions, 9·11
Automobile Insurance Contracts, 8·22
Automobile Paper, 9·5–6, 9·7, 9·8
Automobile Stocks, 16·27
Availability, 27·26–27
Availability Time, 27·14
Average Collection period, 24·28
Average Rate of Return, *see* Performance Measurement
Averaging
  Average rate of return and, 22·9–10
Awarding Bonds, 3·9

Back Loading
  Pension and profit-sharing plans, 34·12
Bahamas
  World financial center, 13·8
Bailees
  Liability of, 8·22, 8·23
Balance of Payments, 11·18
  Capital account, 11·19
  As current account, 11·18–19
  See also International Financial Markets
  Trade account, 11·18
Balance Reporting
  Daily target framework, 27·29
Balance Sheet, *see* Financial Statement Analysis
Balance Sheet Ratios, 24·26–27
"Ballon payment," 23·12, 23·13
Bancor, 11·6
Bank
  Certificate of deposit, 2·9
  Consumer credit, 9·7–8
  Corporate loans, 1·24, 1·25–26
  Financial planning packages and, 25·11
  Indexed loans, 1·7
  Internationalization of, 6·3
  Leasing financing and, 1·8
  Money market certificates and, 1·10

Bank (*Continued*)
Negotiable certificates of deposits, *see* Money Market
Repurchase agreements, 2·8–9
Setoffs and, 35·13–14
Subsidiaries, 14·14
Term deposits, *see* Money Market
See also Cash Management; International Banking *specific banks*
Bankamerica's *Finance America*, 6·21
Bank Burglary and Robbery Policy, 8·28
Bank Credit Cash, *see* Credit Cards
Bank for Corporatives, 10·9
Bank Debentures
Japanese, 15·18
Bank Discount
Definition, A·6–7
Rates, A·7–8
Calculating proceeds, A·7
Due date, A·7–8
Face value determination, A·9
Interest bearing paper discounting, A·7, A·8–9
Noninterest-bearing paper proceeds and discounts, A·7–8
Trade debt, 28·5
Vs. true discount, A·10–12
Bank Drafts, *see* Drafts
Bank of England
Account with, 15·21
Gold standard and, 11·4
Banker's Acceptance (BA), 1·21, 1·24, 1·26, 10·4, 10·5–6, 14·20, 14·23, 28·5
Definition, 31·44
Market, 1·19
Multinational affiliates and, 38·41
Bankers' Blanket Bonds, 8·28
Bank Guaranty, 14·20
Bankhaus Herstatt
Failure of, 12·10
Bank Holding Companies, 6·3
Bank Holding Company Act of 1970, 6·20–22
Federal Reserve and, 6·5
Commercial banks and, 1·9
Holding company device, 6·21
See also Commercial Bank
Banking Act of 1980, 27·15
Disbursement system, 27·18
Fed float and, 27·27
Banking Act of 1933 ("Glass-Steagall Act"), 3·6
Bank-Related Commercial Paper, 1·21
Bank Reserves
Federal Reserve and, 1·18
Bankruptcy Act of 1848, 35·7
Bankruptcy Act of 1978, 35·7
Bankruptcy Act of 1934, 35·7
Bankruptcy Acts of 1933, 35·7
Bankruptcy Reform Act of 1978, *see* Bankruptcy and Reorganization
Bankruptcy and Reorganization, 35·3, 35·4
Bankruptcies, 35·4
Bankruptcy process evaluation, 35·7–11
Chandler Act of 1938, 35·8–10
Chapter XI, 35·8, 35·18–19
Equity receiverships, 35·7
Personal bankruptcy and, 35·38, 35·39, 35·44

Bankruptcy Reforme Act of 1978, 30·32, 35·3, 35·6, 35·7, 35·11–19
Bankruptcy Filings, 35·12
Bank Setoffs, 35·13–14
Chapter 11 Reorganizations, 35·12–20, 35·29
Lessor Claims, 35·13
Priorities, 35·13, 35·15–16
Rationale for, 35·11–12
Bond Covenants, 31·22
Business Failure, 35·3, 35·5–6, 35·23–32
Causes of, 35·32
Filings by chapter and occupation, 35·25–29
Influences on, 35·29, 35·30, 35·31
New Business Formation and, 35·31–32
Sources of data, 35·23–25
Chrysler, 34·6
Consumer credit and, 9·25–26
Costs of, 35·5, 35·17, 35·44
Current position of long-term debts and, 31·14
Debt Financing *vs.*, 31·42, 31·43
Definition, 35·6
Information, 35·37
Insolvency, 35·6, 32·22, 35·7
Investing in Bankrupt Securities, 35·37–38
Judges, 35·17
Lease capitalization and, 30·31–32
Pensions and profit-sharing plans and, 34·6
Personal Bankruptcy, 35·38–39, 35·43–44
Predicting, 35·32–37
Credit analysis, 35·33
Credit risk analysis, 35·33
Failure predictions services, 35·37
Investment analysis, 35·33
Legal issues, 35·33–35
Z-score model, 24·30, 35·35–37
Priority, 30·32
Restricting dividend payments and, 31·22
Tax Issues, 35·20–23
Absolute Priority Rule, 35·23
Discharge of Indebtedness, 35·20–22
Exchange of Equity for Debt, 35·21–22
Recapture Rule, 35·21
Tax-free, 33·21
Tax Loss Carry-Forwards, 35·22–23
Triangular Reorganization, 35·23
Theory, 35·3–5
White Motor Company, 34·6
Bankruptcy Tax Act of 1980, 4·7
Bankruptcy Tax Bill of 1980, 35·20
Bank Stocks, 16·27–28
Bank Wires, 27·6, 27·8
BANs, *see* Bond Anticipation Notes
Barbell Strategy, 18·24
Bardeport, 38·3
Barron's, 16·8
Base Case Forecast, 26·14, 26·19
Base 100 Income Statement, 24·10, 24·11, 24·12
Base Rate, 13·13
Basic Analysis, 16·8
Basic Earning Power, 16·22
Basic Interest Rate Method
Leasing and, 30·21
Basis, 21·19–20
Price of bonds, A·35–37
Basket Currencies, 11·10
Euromarket and, 15·12

Batch Mode
  Computers and, **25**·11
Bearer Bonds
  Municipal bonds as, **3**·6
"Beginning Balance" Method
  Revolving credit account and, **9**·16
Best Efforts Commitment, 31·51
Best's Fire and Casualty Aggregates and
    Averages, 8·36
Best's Insurance Reports, 8·36
Best's Key Rating Guide Property and Liability,
    8·36
  Performance measurement and, **34**·21
Beta Coefficient, 17·16, **22**·16–18
  Risk-adjusted rate of return, **22**·19–20
Bid and Ask Quotes, 22·5, **22**·6
Bid-ask Spread, 12·12, **12**·13
Bid Price, 5·20
Bilateral Exchange Rate, 12·14, **12**·16
Black
  Option theory of corporate securities
    evaluation, **20**·40
Black-Scholes Formula, A·44–46, **A**·47
  Option evaluation and, **20**·31–34
Blanket Bonds, 8·23–29
Blanket Contract, 8·16
Blanket Crime Policy, 8·28
Blanket Mortgage, 23·19
Blanket Security
  As creditor remedy, **9**·18
Blue Cross, 8·13
Blue List of Current Municipal Offerings,
    3·10–11
Blue Shield, 8·13
Board of Governors, *see* Federal Reserve System
Boiler and Machinery Contracts, 8·26–27
Bond Anticipation Notes (BANs), 3·12
Bond Index Funds, 18·21–24
Bonds, A·35
  Accumulation schedule, **A**·38–39
  Amortization schedule, **A**·37–38
  Bases price, **A**·35–37
    Bought between interest dates, **A**·39–41
  Bearer, **3**·6
  Bond life, **18**·15–16
  Call Provision, **16**·11
  Contractual provisions (indenture), **16**·11
  Currency option, **13**·17
  Discount, **3**·9, **A**·35
    Short-cut method, **A**·38
    Dividends, **32**·7
  Duration, **19**·6–7
    Duration-based rebalancing, **19**·20–25
    GNMAs and, **18**·30
    Limitations, **19**·14
    Macaulay, **19**·6–8, **19**·17, **19**·36
    Price volatility and, **19**·3, **19**·11–14
    Rebalancing using, **19**·18–20
    Yield curve and, **19**·16
    Zero-coupon bonds, **19**·8–9
  Fire and casualty insurance companies, **1**·8,
    1·11
  Foreign, **13**·7, **13**·19–20
  General obligation, **3**·13, **3**·14, **3**·15, **3**·29
  Guaranteed, **3**·22–23
  Immunization, **18**·24, **19**·3–11, **34**·19

Bonds (*Continued*)
  Duration-based rebalancing, **19**·20–25
  Investment management, **34**·19
  Multiple rate changes, **19**·17–18
  Over time, **19**·9–11
  Rebalancing and, **19**·18–20
  Reinvestment risk and, **19**·4–6
  Vulnerability, **19**·37
  Yield curve, **19**·28, **19**·29, **19**·30, **19**·31,
    19·34–36
  Yield-to-maturity, **19**·32–33
Income measurement, **22**·7
Industrial aid, **3**·17–18
Information on, **16**·9–10
Insured, **3**·23
Interest-on-Interest, **19**·4–5, **19**·9
Interest rates
  accruing between interest dates, **A**·35–37
Market
  Inflation and, **I**·4
  Japanese, **15**·15, **15**·16, **15**·17–18
Multinational affiliates and, **38**·42
Mutual savings banks, **7**·24
Options and, **20**·41
Par value, **A**·35
Portfolio performance evaluation, **22**·25–26
Price, **A**·39–41
  Volatility, **19**·3, **19**·11–14
Private placement market and, **4**·22
Profit or loss on sale of, **A**·43
Ratings
  Corporate, **4**·15, **4**·17–21
  Municipals, **3**·18–22, **3**·28
Redemption value, **A**·35
Rebalancing
  Intricacies of, **19**·36–37
  Proxy for zero-coupon bond over time,
    19·20–25
  Using duration, **19**·18–20
  Using horizon volatility, **19**·25–26, **19**·27,
    19·28, **19**·30, **19**·36
  Along yield curve, **19**·26–27
Revenue, **3**·13–14, **3**·15, **3**·29
Savings institutions, **1**·6, **1**·8
Sinking funds and, **4**·7–11, **16**·11–12
Special assessment, **3**·13
Valuation, **22**·6
  Tables, **A**·39
  Yield concepts, **16**·12
    Between interest dates, **A**·43–44
Yield curve case, **19**·14, **19**·15, **19**·16,
    19·26–27
  Changing shapes, **19**·33–34
  Nonparallel shifts, **19**·33–36
  Parallel shifts of, **19**·30–33
  Portfolio rebalancing along, **19**·26–27
  Reinvestment and, **19**·5–6
  Rolling yield, **19**·27–36
  Sequences, **19**·34–36
  Simulation of, **19**·34–36
Yield-to-maturity, **19**·5, **19**·11, **19**·32–33
Yield tradeoffs, **16**·12–13
See also Corporate Bonds; Eurobonds;
  Government Obligations; Securities
  Industry; State and Local Government
  Obligations

Book Value per Share, 24·18, 24·22
  Dividends per share, 24·23
  Market value *vs.*, 22·5, 31·9
  Receivables, 28·16
  Sustainable dividend growth, 24·23
Bordereau, 8·14
Boston Stock Exchange, 5·14
Bottom-Up Budgeting, 25·18
Bowmar Instrument Corp., 35·41
Branch Banking, 6·3, 6·23–25
  Foreign branches, 14·12
  Insurance and, 8·32
  International banking and, 14·45
  Noncredit sales collection system, 27·10
  See also Commercial Bank
Breach of Warranty, 8·22
Break-Even Analysis
  Foreign currency borrowing, 38·45–46
  Multinational corporations, 38·24–25
  Transfer methods evaluation, 27·22–23
Break-Even Marginal Tax
  Tax-exempt securities and, 3·26–27
Break-Even Point, 25·14
Break-Even Receivable, 27·12, 27·13
Bretton Woods Agreement, 11·6–7, 11·19, 12·9
  IMF quotas and, 11·25
Bridge Financing
  Multinational affiliates, 38·41
Broad-Form Storekeepers' Policy, 8·28
Broad Market, 16·4
Brokerage Firm
  Types of, 5·12
Brokers
  Commercial bank loans to, 6·10–11
  Foreign exchange market and, 12·7, 14·27
  Futures trading and, 21·13, 21·18, 21·27
  Insurance, 8·6, 8·31–32
Brussels
  World financial center, 13·8
Budget
  Cash, *see* Forecasting
  Definition, 25·16
  Forecasting and, 26·4–5
  Need for, 25·16–17
  Preparation, 25·18
  Problems of, 25·19
  Rolling horizon, 25·19
  Stretch, 26·4
  Time horizon, 25·18–19
  Types of, 25·17–18, 25·19
  Zero-based, 25·19
  See also Capital Budgets
Budget of Capital Expenditures, *see* Capital
  Budgeting
Budgeted Balance Sheet, 25·18
Budgeted Expense Method
  Pro forma income statement, 26·20–21
Business in Brief, 16·7
Business Conditions Digest, 16·7
Business Failure, 25·3, 25·5–6
  See also Bankruptcy and Reorganization
Business Liability, 8·9
Business Life Cycle, Dividend Policy, 32·14, 32·18–19
Business Periodicals Index, 16·8
Business Review, 16·7

Business Risk, 16·4
  Inflation and, 1·5
Business Week, 16·7, 16·8
Buy Hedge, 21·25–26
Buy-and-Sell Agreements, 8·29

Callable Bonds, 18·13
  Eurobonds, 14·42
Call Option, *see* Options
Call Premium
  Bond refunds, 31·47
Call Refunding
  Risk of, 18·12–14
Canadian Rollover Mortgage (CRM), 1·7, 23·14–15
Capacity
  Credit decisions and, 28·10
Capital
  Credit decisions and, 28·10
  Risk of loss, 1·12
  See also Cost of Capital
Capital Accounts, *see* Commercial Bank
Capital Appreciation
  Dividends and, 32·21
Capital Asset Pricing Model (CAPM), 17·7, 17·15–16, 29·29–31
  Cost of equity, 31·29–32
  Inflation and common stock returns, 37·31–32
  Public utilities and, 36·20–21
Capital Budgeting, 30·10
  Capital budget
    Advantages, 29·7
    Coverage, 29·6
    Definition, 25·17
    Preparation, 29·7–11
    Time horizon, 25·18
  Capital expenditures, 29·3–4
  Cash flow use, 29·8–11, 29·12–14
    Discounted cash flow methods, 29·13, 29·15–20
    Time value calculations, 29·13–14
  Depreciation calculated for taxes, 29·9, 29·21–25
    Declining-balance method, 29·21
    Depreciation deduction, 29·11
    Sensitivity analysis, 29·24–25
    Straight-line method, 29·21
    Sum-of-the-years-digits method, 29·22–24
  Inflation and, 29·32–34
  Internal rate of return method, 29·16–17, 29·19–20
  Investment classification, *see* Investments
  Mutually exclusive investments, 29·19–20
  Net present value profile, 29·18–19
  Objectives of firm and, 29·1–12
  Payback method, 29·14
  Present value method, 29·15–16, 29·17, 29·19–20
  Ranking and capital Rationing and, 29·5, 29·6
  Reinvestment rate assumption, 29·17–18
  Return on investment, 29·14–15
  Under uncertainty, 29·25–32
    Conventional present value, 29·28–31
    Risk-adjusted discount rates, 29·26
    Risk-adjusted present value factors

Capital Budgeting (*Continued*)
(RAPVEs), 29·29–31
See also Multinational Corporations; Public
Utilities
Capital controls
Sovereign risk and, 13·28
Capital Expenditures, 29·3–4
See also Capital Budgeting
Capital Flow Approach
Financial market integration, 13·21
Capital gain
Bonds and, 19·5, 19·9, 19·10
Convertible preferred stocks, 4·28
Options and, 20·28
Capitalization
Of leases, 30·27–29
Utility and, 16·31
Capitalizing AFUOC, 36·11–12
Capital Leases, *see* Lease Financing
Capital Loss Carry-Forwards
Option investment, 20·28
Capital Market
Overseas, 1·6
See also Internationalization
Capital Market Risk, 17·15
Capital Market Theory, 17·2, 17·3, 17·7, 17·15
Capital Asset Pricing Model, 17·16, 17·17
Capital Movements
Exchange controls and, 11·17
Capital Outlay Budget, *see* Capital Budgeting
Capital Rationing, 29·5, 29·6
Capital Stock Associations, 7·6
Capital Structure
Dividend Policy, 32·21–22
See also Optimal Capital Structure; Public
Utilities
Cap Loans, 1·26
Caribbean Development Bank, 13·32
Carrying Charge Market, 21·20
"Carry" Spread, 10·12
Carte Blanche
Credit cards, 6·4
"Carter Bonds," 2·8
Cash Account
Commercial banks, 6·6–8
Cash Acquisition, 33·7–17
Cash Balance
Aggregate cash position management and, *see*
Cash Management
Cash before Delivery (CBD), 28·5
Cash Budgets, 25·18–19
See also Forecasting
Cash Concentration, *see* Cash Management
Cash Discount, 28·5
Trade credit, 28·26
Cash Flow, 22·10–13
Acquisition analysis, 33·6, 33·9–11
Bonds, 19·6
Macaulay duration and, 19·6–8
Day-to day, *see* Cash Management
Real estate, 23·29–30
Multinational corporation, 38·5–6, 38·21
Adjusted approach, 38·23, 38·24
Cash policy and, 38·8–9
Delivered, 38·40
Foreign exchange controls and, 38·24–25
Inflation and, 38·25–27

Cash Flow (*Continued*)
Risk and, 38·36
See also Capital Budgeting
Cash Flow Yield
GNMAs and, 18·30
Cash Foreign Exchange, 12·4
Cash Generation
Dividend policy, 32·19–20
Cash Items in Process of Collection, 6·6
Cash Management
Aggregate cash position management (ACPM),
27·27–31
Control-limit frameworks, 27·28, 27·29–31
Daily cash forecasting, 27·31
Daily target framework, 27·28, 27·29
Decision frameworks, 27·28
Definition, 27·4, 27·27
Objectives, 27·28
Smoothing, 27·30, 27·31
Bank services to supporting, 27·6–9
Balance reporting, 27·7–8
Lockbox collections, 27·3, 27·5
Noncredit services, 27·6
Zero-balance accounts, 27·8–9
Cash concentration, 27·20–27
ACH-based alternatives, 27·20–21
Cash transfer scheduling, 27·24–26
Definition, 27·3, 27·4, 27·20
Deposit control, 27·22
Design, 27·26
DTC alternatives, 27·20, 27·21
Generic transfer approaches, 27·20–21
Lockbox concentration and, 27·20
Scheduling techniques, 27·24–25
Transfer alternatives, 27·20–21
Transfer method evaluation, 27·22–24
Wire alternatives, 27·21
Collection system, 27·9–16
Availability time, 27·14
Check-based receivables, 27·12–16
Credit sales, 27·11
Definition, 27·3, 27·6
Deposit information gathering, 27·9
Field banks compensation, 27·10
Field banks selection, 27·3, 27·9
Lockbox processing, 27·11–12, 27·13
Mail time, 27·14
Noncredit sales, 27·9–10
Zero-balance systems, 27·9
Concentration banking, 27·3–4, 27·5,
27·26–27
Costs, 27·29
Design, 27·29
Divisional, 27·5, 27·27
Multiple, 27·5–6, 27·27
Regional, 27·5, 27·27
Selection, 27·26–27
Services, 27·26
Definition, 27·3
Disbursement system, 27·16–19
Bank location, 27·16
Check clearing time, 27·16–17
Controlled disbursing, 27·18, 27·19
Definition, 27·3, 27·4, 27·16
Design, 27·19
Fed collection and, 27·17
Float components, 27·16–17

Cash Management (*Continued*)
Improvements, 27·17–19
1980 Banking Act, 27·18
Payment terms, changing, 27·18–19
Remote disbursing, 27·17, 27·19
Zero-balance system and, 27·9
Lockbox, 6·15, 38·7
Check-based receivables, 27·12, 27·13, 27·14
Collections, 27·3, 27·5, 27·7
Concentration, 27·9, 27·20
Economics, 27·12, 27·13, 27·15
Processing, 27·11–12
Payment system, 27·6
Cash Management Systems
Demand deposits and, 6·6, 6·14–15
Cash Market, 21·3
Cash on Delivery (COD), 28·5–6
Cash Pool, 27·3, 38·8
Cash Terms
Credit terms and, 28·6
Catastrophe, 8·7
Catastrophe excess, 8·15
Causal Models of Estimation
Sales forecasting, 25·6, 25·9
Cedel, 15·14
Central American Bank for Economic Integration, 13·32
Central Bank, 2·8
See also Federal Reserve Banks
Central Initiation, 27·21
Central Limit Order Book, 5·24
Centralization
Hedging and, 12·36–37
Certainty Capital Budgeting Model, 29·31
Certainty Equivalents, 29·27–28
Certificates of Deposit (CDs), 2·9, 10·3, 10·4, 10·5, 13·12, 13·14
Citibank and, I·9
Commercial banks, 6·16–17, 6·18
Euromarket innovation, 14·34, 14·35
Floating rate, 14·41, 14·42
Future trading, 21·8
Negotiable, *see* Money Market
Savings and loan associations, 7·8
See also Eurodollar Certificates of Deposit
Cession, 8·14
Chain Discount, A·12–13
Chandler Act of 1938, 35·8–10
Chapter II, 35·12–20, 35·29
Chapter XI, 35·8
Chapter VII
Seasonal bankruptcy and, 35·44
Chapter X, 35·8–10, 35·22
Chapter XIII, 35·39, 35·44
Character
Credit decisions and, 28·10
Chart Book on Business, Economic, and Financial Statistics, 16·7
Check, 27·6
Balance reporting and, 27·8
Clearing charge for, 6·23
Commercial banks, 6·6–7, 6·23
Time components, 27·16–17
Collecting receivables paid by, 27·12–16
Depository transfer (DTC), 27·20
Federal Reserve banks and, 1·17

Check (*Continued*)
Lockbox services and, 27·7
Preauthorized, 27·15
Check Credit Plans
Commercial banks and, 9·11
Checking Account
As demand deposit, *see* Commercial Bank
Check Truncation, 6·29
Chemical Stock, 16·27
Chemical Week, 16·8
Chicago Board Options Exchange (CBOE), 5·14
Option changes initiated by, 20·6–7, 20·9
Chicago Board of Trade, 2·12, 21·3, 21·14
See also Futures Trading
Chicago Mercantile Exchange, 21·4
Chrysler Corporation
Bankruptcy problem, 34·6, 35·3
Cincinnati Stock Exchange, 5·14
"Cincinnati experiment," 5·24
Citibank
Certificate of deposit, I·9
Information sources from, 16·7
Citicorp's *Person to Person Finance,* 6·21
Classified Common Stock, 31·49
Clean Draft, 14·16
Clearing Account, 6·8, 14·31
Clearinghouse
Funds, 10·5
Futures trading and, 21·3, 21·15–18
Clearing Services
Correspondent banks and, 6·7
Euromarket and, 15·13–14
Clearing Slippage, 27·16
Cleveland City
Bond anticipation note, 3·13
Closed End Contracts, 9·6–7
Close Market, 16·5
Closing Costs of Mortgage, 23·15–17
Codebtor Clause
Personal bankruptcies and, 35·44
Coefficient of Determination
Regression analysis, 26·8
Coinsurance
Clause, 8·17–18
Credit insurance, 28·14
Plan, 8·15
Collateral
Corporate bonds and, 16·15
Collateral Risk
International banking and, 14·16
Collateral Trust Agreement, 16·14
Collateral Trust Bonds, 4·4, 31·45
Collectibles
Pension and profit-sharing plan, 34·24
Collection Drafts
Exporter financing, 14·16–17
Collection Practices, 28·22–23
Consumer credit contract, 9·19
See also Cash Management
College Retirement Equities Fund (CREF), 34·10
Combination Option, 20·3
Combination Safe Depository Policy, 8·28
Combinations, *see* Mergers and Acquisitions
Commercial Bank
Asset accounts, 6·6–12
Cash account, 6·6–8, 6·23
Commercial loans, 6·6, 6·10–12

Commerical Bank (*Continued*)
   Investment securities, 6·6, 6·8–10
  Assets, 1·6, 1·8
   Financing and, 28·23–24
  Branch banking, 6·3, 6·23–25
  Changes in, 6·3
  Check credit, 9·11
  Consumer credit and, 9·7, 9·10–11, 9·12
  Definition, 6·4–5
  Demand deposits, 6·4, 6·12–16
  Dividend declaration and, 32·11–12
  Federal reserve credit control, 6·25–29
   Bank credit cards, 6·4, 6·26–27
   Electronic funds transfer system (EFT),
    6·27–29
  Floating term loans, 1·7
  Foreign exchange trading and, 12·13–14
  Funds supplied by, 1·5, 1·7
  Government securities, 2·8
  Liability and capital accounts of, 6·12–20
   Demand deposits, 6·4, 6·12–16
   Deposit rate ceilings, 6·18–20
   Time and savings deposit, 6·13–17, 6·18
  Mortgages, 23·4, 23·7, 23·8
  One-day repurchase agreement and, 10·12
  Regulation, 6·3, 6·5, 6·20
   Bank Holding Company Act of 1970,
    6·20–22
   Depository Institutions Deregulation and
    Monetary Control Act of 1980, 6·5, 6·22–23
   International Banking Act of 1978, 6·22
  Repo transactions and, 2·9
  Share drafts, 6·4
  As shareholder and transfer agents, 32·11
  Small bank and, 6·29–30
  Tax-exempt securities and, 3·23–25
  Treasury bills and, 10·7–8
  Treasury debt and, 2·6, 2·7
  See also International Banking
Commercial Credit Scoring
  Discriminant analysis, 24·30
Commercial and Financial Chronicle, 16·8
Commercial Finance Companies
  Asset financing and, 28·23–24
Commercial Insurance, 8·10, 8·11
  See also Insurance
Commercial Letter of Credit, 14·20–21
Commercial Loans
  Commercial bank, 6·6, 6·10–12
  Floating rate, 6·26
Commercial Paper, 1·21, 1·22–23, 1·24, 1·26
  Cost of, 31·14
  Definition, 31·44
  Futures market and, 21·7, 21·11
  Liquidity and, 16·5
  Market, 6·4
   Business firms and, 6·11
   Commercial bank and, 6·14, 6·17
  Parent holding company, 6·21
  Savings and loan associations, 7·20
  Tax-exempt, 10·10–11
  See also Corporate Obligations
Commercial Property Coverage, 8·24–25
Commercial Year, A·4
Commingled Fund, 34·18
Commission Rates
  Securities and, 5·20

Commitment Fees
  Eurocurrency rate, 14·37
  Multinational affiliates and, 38·41
Commodities, *see* Futures Trading
Commodities Exchange Act, 21·27
Commodity Futures Trading Commission (CFTC),
  5·12, 5·15, 21·18, 21·27–29
Commodity-Linked Bonds, 14·35
Commodity Market Arbitrage
  Purchasing power parity and, 12·19
Commodity Pool Operators, 21·27
Commodity Trading Advisers, 21·27
Common-Size Balance Sheet, 16·21, 26·31,
  26·32–34
Common-Size Income Statement, 16·20
Common Stock, 4·30–33, 16·19–32
  Bankruptcy, 35·38
  Bank stocks, 16·27–28
  Best efforts, 31·51
  Characteristics, 4·31–32, 16·14, 16·19
  Cumulative voting, 31·48–49
  Dividends, 32·6–7
  Exrights procedures, 39·50–51
  Financial securities, 16·27–28
  Firm commitment, 31·51, 31·52
  Flounders' shares, 31·49
  Indexation, 37·40
  Industrial securities, 16·26–27
  Inflation and, 37·31–33
   Classical framework and, 37·34–35
   Classical theory and cost of capital,
    37·33–34
   Empirical evidence and, 37·35–40, 37·40
  Insurance stocks, 16·28
  Issuing, 4·32–33
  Par value, 31·5, 31·49
  Pooling of interests, 33·22
  Preemptive right, 31·49–50
  Preferreds convertible into, 4·28
  Private placement, 4·22, 4·23, 4·24
  Projecting earnings, 16·24–26
   Aggregate approach, 16·24–25
   Historical growth rate, 16·24
   Industrial life cycle, 16·25–26
   Information on, 16·9–10
   Return on investment, 16·25
  Public utility securities, 16·29–32
  Record of real returns, 34·14
  Risk, 4·32
  Risk-return tradeoff and, 16·20, 20·14
  Secondary market, 4·33
  Securities and Exchange Commission,
   4·32–33
  Split, 32·6
  Stockholders' rights, 4·30–31
  Underwritten issues, 31·51
  Valuation concepts, 16·19–20
  Warrants, 32·6
  See also Dividends, Policy; Financial
   Statement Analysis
Communications systems
  Securities industry, 5·22
Comparative Analysis
  Balance sheets and, 24·4–6
  Income statement and, 24·7
Compensating Balance, 1·26, 14·35, 31·12–13
  Multinational affiliates and, 38·41

Competitive Bidding
Tax-exempt securities and, 3·6
Component Depreciation, 23·29
Composition Settlement
Credit adjustment, 28·13–14
Compound Average, 22·9–10
Compound Average Total Return, 22·11, **22**·12
Compound Interest, *see* Interest
Compound Option Approach, 20·35
**Comprehensive Dishonesty, Disappearance, and
Destruction (3-D), 8**·28
Comptroller of the Currency
Commercial bank regulation, 6·5
Compustat, 16·10
Computers
ACH-based transfer service, 27·20
Acquisitions and mergers, 33·8–17
Automated DTC services, 27·20, 27·21
Balance reporting and, 27·7–8
Cash budget and, 26·13
Credit decision and, 28·9, 28·11
Investment information and, 16·10–11
Option evaluation and, 20·16
Securities industry and, 5·21–24
Stock exchanges and, 16·10
See also Financial Planning
Concealment, 8·20
Concentration Banking, *see* Cash Management
Concentration Ratios, Branch Banking and, 6·25
Concession Agreements, 38·33
Conditionality
IMF loans and, 11·25, 13·27
Conditional Sales Contract, 30·23
Conditions
Credit decisions and, 28·10
Confirmation Slip, 5·21
Confirmed Letter of Credit, 14·23
Confiscation
Sovereign risk and, 13·29
Conglomerate Merger, 33·23
Conglomerates, 6·21, **33**·3
See also Mergers and Acquisitions
Consequential Loss Contracts, 8·27
Consignment, 28·6–7
Exporter financing and, 14·16
Consol Bond
Yield to maturity, 31·17
Consortium Banks
International banking and, 14·13–14
Constant Dollars
Inflation and, 29·32–34
**Constant Growth Discounted Cash Flow (DCF)
Method**
Public utilities and, 36·17–19
Construction Accounting
Public utilities and, 36·10–12
Construction Budget, *see* Capital Budgeting
Construction Loans, 23·18, **23**·19
Construction Risks
Public utilities and, 36·15–16
Construction Work in Progress (CWIP), 36·11
Consulting Firms
Financial planning services, 25·11
Consumer Credit
Commercial bank and, 1·6, 1·8
Consumer credit outstanding, 9·3–6
Consumer uses of, 9·23–26

Consumer Credit (*Continued*)
Controls, 6·25–29
Definition of, 9·3
Discriminant analysis and, 24·30–31
Federal Reserve and, 6·5, 6·25–29
Finance charges, 9·13
Specifying, 9·14–16
Funds demanded by, 1·5, 1·7
Holders, 9·7–8, 9·9
Industry development and, 9·8–12
Commercial banks, 9·10–11, 9·12
Consumer finance companies, 9·10
Credit unions, 9·4, 9·12
Retailers, 9·11
Inflation and, 1·5
Installment credit, 9·7
Use of, 9·23–25
Other contract terms, 9·17–21
Collection practices, 9·19
Credit insurance, 9·21
Creditors' remedies, 9·17–19
Delinquency, 9·25–26
Equal Credit Opportunity Act (1975), 9·23
Fair Credit Billing Act (1969), 9·22
Fair Credit Reporting Act (1971), 9·22
Fair Debt Collection Practices Act (1977),
9·23
Laws regulating, 9·21–23
Prepayment provisions, 9·19, 9·21
State laws, 9·23
Truth-in-Lending Act (1969), 9·14, 9·15,
9·22
Rate determination, 9·13, 9·14
Revenues from, 9·13–14
Revolving credit, 9·6, 9·7, 9·8, 9·9
Commercial banks and, 9·10, 9·11
Nominal rate *vs.* yields on, 9·16
Risk evaluation, 9·16–17
Savings institutions and, 1·6, 1·8
Consumer Credit Protection Act, 9·22
Consumer Finance Companies
Consumer credit industry and, 9·10
Consumer Loans, 9·10
Commercial banks, 6·6, 6·12, 6·26,
9·10–11
Credit unions and, 7·3, 7·29
Floating rate, 6·26
Savings and loan associations and, 7·20
Consumer Price Index (CPI), 37·3
Inflation and, 1·4
Contacting Third Parties
Creditor remedy, 9·19
Contingent Orders, 21·18
Contracts
Foreign exchange and, 12·4–7
Contractual Liability, 8·23
Contribution Margin, 25·21, **25**·22
Control, 25·15–16
See also Budget; Financial Control Systems
Controlled Disbursing, 27·8, **27**·18, **27**·19
Control-Limit Frameworks, 27·28, **27**·29–31
Conventional GPM, 23·14
**Conventional Mortgage Pass-Through Certificates,
18**·29–30
**Conventional Mortgages Savings and Loan
Associations, 7**·12
Conventional Present Value, 29·28

Conversion
Puts and, 20·19–20
Convertibility Risk, 14·15
Convertible Bonds, 4·4, **18·**5, **31·**46
Convertible Debt
Cost of, 31·34–35
Exchange offers for, 4·4–5
Convertible Preferreds, 4·28
Cost of, 31·27, 33–35
Core Portfolio, 18·20
Corporate Bonds, 1·27, **1·**28, **16·**12–13
Adjustable rate, 4·5–6
Bond portfolios management, 18·17
Active management strategies, 18·18–21
Guaranteed investment contracts, 18·25
Immunization, 18·24
Index funds, 18·21–24
Constant maturity strategies, 18·24
Passive fixed income management,
18·21–25
Private placements, 18·24–25
Turnover, 18·20–21
Call and refunding features, 4·6, 18·5
Collateral trust, 4·4
Commercial Bank and, 1·6, 1·8
Commercial paper, 10·4, 10·6–7
Convertible bonds, 4·4–5, 18·5
Covenants, 31·21–23
Coupon rate, 18·5, 31·16–17
Credit of issuer, 16·13–14
Current portion of, 31·14
Debenture bonds, 4·4, 18·4
Definition, 31·3
Equipment trust certificates, 4·4, 18·4–5
Fire and casualty insurance company and, 1·8,
1·11
Floating rate securities, 18·28–29
Funds demanded by, 1·8, 1·5, 1·7
Guaranteed, 4·5
Horizon, 18·7
Income, 4·5
Index for, 22·22–23
Inflation and, 1·6
Intermediate term, 1·7
Investing in bankruptcies and, 35·37–38,
35·40–42
Joint, 4·5
Life insurance company, 1·6, 1·11
Maintenance and replacement fund, 18·6
Master notes, 10·7
Maturity date, 18·5
Mortgage bonds, 4·3, 18·4
Mutual savings banks and, 7·24
Participating, 4·5
Pension funds and, 1·12
Price amortization, 18·8–10
Principal amount, 18·5
Privately placed, 1·7, 31·47
Protective provisions, 16·14–15
Put and call provisions and, 20·40
Quantitative techniques
Performance measurement, 18·26–27
Portfolio simulations, 18·25–26
Valuation models, 18·27–28
Ratings, 16·15–16, 31·20–21
Services, 1·27, 1·28
Realized compound yield, 18·7–8

Corporate Bonds (*Continued*)
Retirement of, 4·6–7, 31·46–47
Returns on, 18·3–4
Risk management, 31·20–21
Call and sinking funds, 18·12–14
Duration, 18·15–16
Horizon, 18·12, 18·16
Mean absolute charge, 18·16–17
Measurement, 18·12
Price volatility risk, 18·15
Quality risk, 18·14–15
See also Bonds, Rating
Reinvestment risk, 18·15
Term to maturity, 18·15
Risk-return tradeoff, 20·14
Serial, 4·5
Sinking fund provisions, 18·5–6
Sources, 31·3–4
State and local government retirement assets,
1·8, 1·11
Subordinate debenture bonds, 4·4, 18·4
Term structure of interest rates, 18·11–12,
31·24
Expectation theory, 31·24–25
Liquidity preference theory, 31·25–26
Voting, 4·5
Weighted average cost of capital, 31·36
Yield curves, 18·10, 18·11
Riding the, 31·19
Yield to maturity, 18·6–7, 18·8, 18·9–10,
31·16, 31·17
Consol bond, 31·17
Finite-lived bond, 31·17–18
Risk adjusted rate of return, 31·18–19
Marginal, 31·19
Corporate Capital, 4·3
Bank loans, 1·24, 1·25–26
Bankers' acceptances, 1·24, 1·26
Bonds, *see* Corporate Bonds
Commercial paper, 1·24, 1·26
Common stock, 4·27–30
See also Common Stock
Finance company loans, 1·24, 1·26
Long-term debt securities, *see* Corporate
Bonds
Mortgage, 1·27, 1·28
Preferred stock, 4·27–30
See also Preferred Stock
Profit tax payable, 1·24, 1·26
Ratings, 4·15, 4·17–21
Securities industry and, 5·6
Sinking funds
Bonds, 4·7–11
Nominal *vs.* realized, 4·11–15, 4·16–17
Preferred stock with, 4·27–28
Pricing considerations, 4·7–11
Purchase, 4·7–8
Trade credit, 1·24, 1·25
See also Common Stock; Corporate Bonds;
Preferred Stock; Private Placement
Corporate Treasurer
Commercial paper and, 6·17
Electronic reporting and movement of funds,
6·28
Options and, 20·40–41
Quotation of rate exchange, 14·28–29
Corporate Utility Function, 34·15

Corporations
Edge Act, 6·22
Electronic reporting and movement of funds, 6·28
Information on, 16·8–10
Leveraged leasing and, 1·6
Options and, 20·40–41
Preferred stock purchasers, 4·30
Correspondent Balance
International banking, 14·5
Correspondent Banks
Clearing services and, 6·7
Confirmed letter of credit, 14·23
D/A draft and, 14·17
Federal Reserve Bank as, 6·8
International banking and, 14·12
Cosigner Agreement
Creditor remedy, 9·19
Cost of Capital
Acquisition analysis and, 33·7
Defining, 31·5
Estimating
Of levered firm, 31·8–9
Operating cash flows after taxes, 31·6–7
Risk-adjusted rate of return, 31·5–6
Unlevered term, 31·7–8
Inflation and, 37·33–34
Multinational corporations, 38·27–30
Optional capital structure, 31·37–44
Agency costs and, 31·42–44
Cost of capital problem and, 31·40–42
Cost of equity, 31·39–40
Debt financing *vs.* bankruptcy costs, 31·42, 31·43
Personal taxes, 31·42
Weighted average cost of capital and, 31·37–39
See also Public Utilities
Risk adjusted and acquisition analysis, 33·13, 33·14
Weighted average, 31·9–10
Computing, 31·35–37
Leasing and, 31·15
Optimal capital structure, 31·37–39
Risk-adjusted, 31·15
Cost Centers, 25·20
Cost Comparison Framework
Cash transfer evaluation, 27·24
Cost Forecasting
Public utility capital budget, 36·13–14
Cost-Volume-Profit Relationships, 25·13–14
Country Risk, 12·13
Eurobanks and, 14·40
Coupon Bond
Durations, 19·17, 19·18
Japanese, 15·18
Coupon Equivalent Yield
Treasury bills, 2·10
Coupon Rate, 18·5, 31·16–17
Covenant of Prior or Equal Coverage, 16·14
Covered Call Writing, 20·10, 20·12–13, 20·19
Covered Interest Arbitrage, 12·9, 12·26, 13·22, 13·23, 14·30–31
Multinational corporations, 38·9
Cox
Option evaluation, 20·35
"Crom-Down", Chapter 11 and, 35·17

Credit
Analysis and selection, 28·7–12
Bankruptcy prediction, 35·33
Branch banking, 6·25
Collection system for, 27·11
Commercial bank and, 1·6, 1·8
Federal Home Loan Bank Board and, 7·17–18
Federal Reserve Board control of, 6·25–29
Insurance, 9·21, 28·14–15
Fees, 9·14
Leasing and, 30·7
Limits, 28·9
Line of, 31·12
Business firms and, 6·12
Eurobanks, 14·41, 14·42
Multinational corporations, 28·7, 38·10–12
Government, 38·38
Period, 29·4
Restrictions, 38·3
Terms, 28·4–7
See also Accounts Receivable; Consumer Credit; Inflation
Credit Assistance Programs
Tax-exempt securities, 3·22–23
Credit Cards, 6·4
Bank, 6·4, 6·12, 6·26–27, 9·11
Credit unions and, 7·31
Retail charge account plans and, 6·12
See also Consumer Credit; Credit
Credit Assistance Programs
Tax-exempt securities, 3·22–23
Credit Discount Period, 28·5
Credit Draft, 27·6
Credit and Finance Companies
Private placement market, 4·24
Creditors' Remedies
Consumer credit contracts, 9·17–19
Credit Reporting Agencies, 28·9
Consumer credit, 9·17
Credit Risk, 12·13
Eurobanks and, 14·40
International banking and, 14·15
Credit Scoring System
Consumer credit, 9·17
Discriminant analysis, 24·30–31
Trade credit and, 28·11
Credit SWAR, 14·39
Credit Union National Association, 7·28
Credit Unions, 7·3, 7·27–31
Administration
Asset distribution, 7·4–5, 7·28
Consumer credit, 7·3, 7·29, 9·7–8, 9·11–12
Funds supplied by, 1·5, 1·7
Income and expense, 7·30–31
Regulation, 7·27, 7·28
Savings deposits, 7·4, 7·29
Share draft, 6·4, 6·15, 6·31, 7·30–31
Sources and uses of funds, 7·29–30
Structure of, 7·27–38
Taxation, 7·31
Crime Insurance Contracts, 8·28
Cross-Default Clause
Eurocurrency loan agreements, 14·38
Cross-Hedge, 21·24
Cross-Rate
Triangular arbitrage, 12·8

Currency Basket Bond
Euromarket innovation, **14**·34
Currency and Coin Account, 6·7–8, **6**·23
Charge for, **6**·23
Currency Controls
Sovereign risk, **13**·23
Currency Futures, 14·35
Currency Option Bonds, 13·17
Euromarket innovation, **14**·34
Currency Option Clause
Eurocurrency loan and, **14**·38
Currency Risk, 12·31–32, **13**·25–26
Eurobanks and, **14**·40
Foreign investments and, **15**·10
International banking and, **14**·15–16
Currency SWAP, 14·39, **38**·19
Current Account
Balance of payments, **11**·18–19
Current Assets, 24·4–5
Balance sheet, **16**·21
Current Liabilities
Balance sheet, **16**·21
Current-Noncurrent Approach
Foreign exchange exposure, **12**·33, **12**·34
Current Rate Approach
Foreign exchange exposure, **12**·34
Current Ratio, 16·22, **24**·25–26, **24**·30
Current Yield, 31·17
Cutoff Score
Credit decision, **28**·11
Cyclicality
Dividend policy, **32**·14, **32**·18–19

D/A Drafts, 14·16–17
Daily Cash Balance Accounts, 28·25
Daily Cash Forecasting, 27·31
Daily Target Framework, 27·28, **27**·29
Daylin, Inc., 35·42
Days' Purchase Outstanding (DPO)
Accounts payable status and, **28**·26
Days' Sales Outstanding (DSD), 28·19–20
Day Traders, 21·18–19
"Dealer Banks"
Government securities and, **2**·8
Dealer Placed Commercial Paper, 1·21, **1**·22
Dealers
Commercial bank loans to, **6**·10–11
Death Benefits, 34·9
Debenture Bonds, 4·4, **18**·14, **31**·45
Debenture Issues, 4·4
Debit Transfer, 38·8
Debt
Market value of, **31**·8
Mortgage, **23**·3, **23**·4–6
See also National Debt; Treasury Debt
Debt-Equity Mix
Foreign affiliates, **38**·39–40
Debt-Equity Ratios
Inflation and, **I**·5
Debt Flows, 29·13
Debt-to-Assets Ratio, 24·27
Debt Equity Financing
Financing foreign subsidiaries and, **38**·37–38
Debt-to-Equity Ratio, 24·27
Debt Funds
Mutual fund industry and, **I**·8
Debt Ratios, 24·26
Business sector, **I**·6

Decision Tree
One-period risk analysis and, **29**·28–29
Declarations, 8·17
Declared Dividend, 32·12
Declining-Balance Method
Depreciation, **29**·21–22
"Default-Free" Yield Curve, 18·10
Default Risk, I·7, **18**·14
Consumer credit and, **9**·13, **9**·16–17
International/financial markets, **13**·26
Pension plan investments, **34**·15
Deferred Annuity, A·21
Deferred Compensation, 8·30
Deferred Profit-Sharing Plans, 34·8, **34**·10
"Deferred Taxes"
Public utilities, **36**·10
Deficiency Judgment
Creditor remedy, **9**·18
Defined Benefit Plan, 8·31
Defined Benefits, 34·3, **34**·7
Alternatives to, **34**·10–11
See also Pensions and Profit-Sharing Plans
Defined Contribution Plan, 8·31, **34**·3
See also Pension and Profit-Sharing Plans
Deflation
Financial institutions, **I**·9
Delayed Delivery
Government securities, **2**·10
Delivered Cash Flows, 38·40
Demand Deposit, *see* Commercial Bank
Demand Forecasting
Public utility capital budget, **36**·13
Demonetize Gold, 11·24
Department of Housing and Urban Development
Projected notes, **10**·10
Department of Treasury, *see* Treasury Department
Deposit Collateral Mortgages, 23·20
Depository Institutions Deregulation Committee (DIDC), 7·19
Depository Institutions Deregulations and Monetary Decontrol Act of 1980, 6·5, **6**·22, **23**·7
Electronic fund transfer system, **6**·27
Savings and loan industry, **7**·19–21
Depository Transfer Check (DTC), 27·20, **27**·21
Transfer method, **27**·22, **27**·23
Depository Trust Co., 5·14
Depreciation
Accelerated Method of, **16**·23, **37**·7–8, **37**·17, **37**·24–28
Component, **23**·29
Foreign exchange rate, **38**·45–46
Inflation accounting, **37**·7–8
Public utilities, **36**·23
Real estate, **23**·29
Straight-line method, **16**·23
Depreciation Funds Costs
Cost of equity capital and, **31**·33
Depreciation Tax Shield
Acquisition's analysis, **33**·7
Depreciation Write-Offs
Multinational affiliates, **38**·42
Deregulation, Financial
Inflation and, **I**·3
Designated Order Turnaround (DOT), 5·24
Detroit Stock Exchange, 5·14
Development Banks, 13·32, **13**·33
Multinational affiliates, **38**·42–44

Development Banks (*Continued*)
See also *specific banks*
Diagonal Model, see Single-Index Model
Diners Club
Credit cards, 6·4
Direct Dealing
Foreign exchange market, 12·7
Direct Debiting, 38·8
Direct Divisional Profit, 25·21, 25·22
Direct Loans, 38·17–18
Direct Placement, see Private Placement
Direct Rates
Triangular arbitrage, 12·8
Direct Writing, 8·32
Directors' Liability, 8·23
Disbursement Float, 27·19
Disbursement Funding, see Cash Management
Discount
Credit terms and inflation, 37·12–14,
  37·15–16
Treasury bills and, 2·10
Discount Bonds, 3·9, 16·12
Discount of Drafts, 14·19
Discounted Acceptance, 14·16
Discounted Cash Flow (DCF)
Acquisitions analysis, 33·6
Bankruptcy and reorganization, 35·5
Investment profitability, 29·13, 29·15–20
Methods, 29·13
Discount Factoring, 28·25
Discount Notes
Federal agencies, see Money Market
Discount Payback Period, 29·14
Discount Rate, 1·16
Consumer credit and, 9·15–16
Federal Reserve and, 1·18
Risk-adjusted, 29·27
Risk-free, 29·27
Yield to maturity and, 18·6
Discretionary Cost Centers, 25·20
Discriminant Analysis
Failure classification problem, 35·35
Financial ratios and, 24·29–31
Disintermediation, 1·4, 23·24
Mutual savings banks, 23·8
Distribution
Underwriters and, 3·6, 3·8
Utility loss, 8·4–5
Divergence Indicator
European monetary system, 11·11
Diversible Risk
Pricing model, 31·30
Diversification
Corporate bonds, 18·4
Multinational corporations, 38·27–30, 38·38
R-squared, 17·18
See also *International Portfolios*
Divestment
Multinational corporations, 38·34
Pooling of interests, 33·22
Dividend Discount Models, 17·22–23
Dividend Growth Rate, 24·23
Dividend Payout Rate
Dividends per share, 24·23
Dividend Payout Ratio, 24·19
Inflation, 37·12
Inflation-adjusted net income and, 37·8
Dividend Reinvestment Plans, 5·27, 32·21

Dividends, 31·51, 31·53, 32·3–4
Bankruptcy, 35·6–7
Behavioral models of corporate dividend
  behavior, 32·23–24
Bond Covenants Restricting, 31·22–23
Corporate distributions, 32·22
Declaration
  Board of Directors and, 32·8–10, 32·11
  Ex-dividend date, 32·11
  Mechanics of, 32·7–8
  Postdividend Declaration Activities,
    32·11–12
  Role of, 32·25
Income retention rate after preferred, 24·21
Insolvency tests, 32·22
Investor expectations and needs, 32·20–21
Life insurance, 8·17
Modern portfolio theory, 17·19–22, 17·23
Multinational corporations, 38·15, 38·19–21
Payment
  Categories, 32·9
  Mechanisms, 32·7–8
Period-to-period changes in, 24·21
Policy, 32·12–13
  Capital structure and, 32·21–22
  Clientele effect and, 32·24–25
  Determinants of, 32·14–20
  Formal, 32·13–14
  Maintenance and review, 32·15–18
  Timing of, 32·20
Public utilities, 36·29–30
Relevancy of, 32·22–23
  Sales growth feasibility, 26·38
Stock, 31·51, 31·53, 32·5, 32·7
  Common, 32·6–7
  Per share, 24·19, 24·20, 24·22–23
  Preferred, see Preferred Stock
Sustainable growth, 24·21–23, 24·24
Dividend Yield
Cost of equity capital, 31·27–28
Divisional Concentration Bank, 27·5, 27·27
Documentary Draft, 14·16
Dollar
Main currency for international trade, 13·8,
  14·29
Vehicle currency, 12·8–9, 12·12
Dollar Premium
Multiple exchange rates and, 11·18
Dollar Price Repurchase Agreement, 10·13
Dollar Risk Adjustment, 29·31
Dollar-Weighted Availability, 27·26
Dollar-Weighted Rate of Return, 22·10–11
Domestic (U.S.) Certificates of Deposit, see
  Certificates of Deposit
Double-Barreled Obligation, 3·14
Double Indemnity, 8·17
Double Leverage
Public utilities, 36·26, 36·27–28
Double Taxation Agreements, 15·18
Douglas Amendment, 6·20, 6·23, 6·25
Dow Jones Industrial Average (DJIA), 17·5
D/P Draft, 14·16
Drafts
Advance on, 14·19
Bankers' acceptances as, 10·4, 10·5–6
Collection, 14·16–17
Documents and, 14·19, 14·24–25
Due date, A·7

Drafts (*Continued*)
Foreign exchange, 12·4
Payable-through credit, 27·6
Preauthorized, 27·15, 27·19
Trade acceptance as, 28·4–5
Draw Down, 27·21
Credit line, 6·12
Drawings
International Monetary Fund and, 11·7
Drug Stock, 16·27
Dual-Currency Convertible Bonds
Euromarket innovation, 14·34
"Duality"
Credit card companies, 6·26
Due-From Accounts, 6·6, 6·7
"Due To" Accounts, 6·16
Dun and Bradstreet, Inc. (D & B)
Credit reporting and, 28·9
Statistics and, 35·23, 35·24
Du Pont Formula, 24·13
Modified, 24·15
Duration, *see* Bonds

Earnings Before Interest and Taxes/Total Assets Ratio
Z-score model, 35·36
Earnings Coverage Ratios
Inflation and, I·5
Earnings and Dividends Per Share, *see* Financial Analysis
Earnings Forecaster, 16·9
Earnings-Price Ratio
Cost of equity, 31·28
Econometric Forecasts
Exchange rate forecasting, 12·29
Economic Exposure, 12·33
Economic Income
Firm, 37·4–5
Economic Indicators, 16·7
Economics of Scale, 31·16
Public utilities, 36·16
Economist, 16·8
Edge Act Corporations, 6·22
Edge Act Subsidiaries, 14·8, 14·14
Education Student Loan Marketing Association, 2·11
Effective Aftertax Dollar Yield on the Foreign Currency Bond, 38·47–48
Effective Availability, 27·27
Effective Exchange Rates, 12·15
Record of, 12·17–18
Effective Yield, *see* Yield to Maturity
Efficient Market Hypothesis, 16·6
Modern portfolio theory, 17·7
Efficient Portfolios, 15·4
Efficient Sets
Modern portfolio theory, 17·11–13
Electronic Depository Transfer Check, 27·22, 27·24
Electronic Funds Transfer System (EFT), 6·27–29
Credit unions, 7·31
Electronic Payment
Collections and, 27·15
Disbursements and, 27·18, 27·19
Electronic Terminals Across State Lines
Branch banking, 6·25
Emergency Home Finance Act of 1970, 7·25, 18·29, 23·9

Employee Retirement Income
Security Act (1974) (ERISA), 5·11–12, 8·31, 20·40, 34·3, 34·4–5
Ending Balance Method
Revolving credit account, 9·16
Engineered Cost Centers, 25·20
Entrepôt Financial Centers, 13·7, 13·30
Entry Restrictions
Foreign banks and, 14·51
Equal Credit Opportunity Act (1975) 9·17, 9·23
Equal Principal Payment Approach, 23·13–14
Equilibrium Model
International capital market, 15·8
Equipment Trust Certificates, 4·4, 18·4–5, 31·45
Equity
Cost of, 31·27
Acquisitions analysis and, 33·11–13
Capital asset pricing model (CAPM), 31·29–32
Earnings price ratio, 31·28
Convertible securities cost, 31·33–35
Depreciation Funds cost, 31·33
Dividend yield, 31·27–28
Earnings-price ratio, 31·28
Flotation costs and, 31·32–33
Gordon Growth Model, 31·29
For levered firm, 31·10–11
Optimal capital structure and, 31·39–40
Public utilities and, 36·8, 36·26
Retained Earnings, 31·32–33
Security Market Line, 31·31–32
Weighted average cost of capital and, 30–36
Return on, 24·12, 24·14, 24·15, 24·16, 24·18, 24·22, 24·23
See also Return on Equity
Equity Funding Corp. of America, 35·40
Equity Insolvency, 32·22, 35·7
Equity Interest in Foreign Bank, 14·13
Equity Investments, *see* Common Stocks; Real Estate Finance
Equity Market
Japanese equity, 15·14, 15·15
Equity Receiverships, 35·7
Equity Valuation Index, 24·23–25
Escrows
Real estate, 23·23–24
Estoppel, 8·20
Eurobank, 14·32
Liability management, 14·41, 14·42
Eurobonds, 11·9, 13·7, 13·14, 13·16–19, 15·12, 15·13
Eurobanks and, 14·41
Euromarket innovation, 14·34
First issue, 15·12
Yields, 15·13
Euroclear, 15·14
Eurocommercial paper, 14·35
Eurocredit Market, 13·14–16, 14·33
Eurocurrency, 11·8–9, 14·5
Availability, 14·38
Deposits, 11·9
Foreign exchange, 14·26, 14·27
Loan participation certificates, 14·35
Syndication, 14·35–37
See also International Banking; International Financial Markets
Eurodollar Certificates of Deposit, 1·24, 10·4, 10·5, 14·41, 14·42

Eurodollar Certificates of Deposit (*Continued*)
  Futures trading and, 21·8
  Negotiable, 14·43
Eurodollar Deposits, I·8, 10·5
Eurodollar Interest Rate Futures, 14·35
Eurodollar Placement Market, 10·5
Eurodollars, 11·8, 13·10, 14·33
  Euromarket innovation, 14·34
Euroequity, 14·35
Euroloans Syndicated, 14·35–37
Euromarket
  Characteristics, 15·10, 15·12
  Clearing procedures, 15·13–14
  History of, 15·12
  Innovations, 14·34
  Investing in, 15·9, 15·10, 15·12–14
  Trading, 15·13
European Call Option Pricing Formula, 31·34
European Coal and Steel Community, 13·32
European Composite Unit (EURCO), 13·9
European Currency Unit (ECU), 13·10
  European monetary system, 11·11, 11·14,
    11·16
European Development Fund, 13·32
European Economic Community, 14·33
European Investment Bank (EIB), 13·32, 38·44
European Monetary Cooperation Fund, 11·17
European Monetary System, 11·11, 11·14–17
European Unit of Account (EUA), 13·10
Exact Interest, A·4, A·6, A·7
Excess of Loss Ratio, 8·15
Excess Return, 17·17
Exchange Clearinghouse, Futures Contracts,
    12·4
  Foreign currency and, 12·4
Exchange controls, *see* International Monetary
    System
Exchange-of-Shares Acquisition, 33·5
Exchange Offers
  Convertible debt, 4·4–5
Exchange Rate Change Hedge, 21·25–26
Exchange Rate Overshooting, 12·23
Exchange Rate Risk
  Foreign exchange trading and, 12·13
Exchange Rates
  Determination, 12·19–21
  Dynamics
    Overshooting, 12·23–25
    Volatility, 12·21–23
  Fluctuations and foreign investments, 15·10
  Forecasting, 12·27–29
    Attitudes of companies toward, 12·38
    Commercial services for, 12·29
    Evaluating, 12·30–32
    Forward rate and, 12·29–30
  Forward, 13·23–24
  Movements
    Currency value, 12·14–16
    Recent exchange rate behavior, 12·16–19
  See also Foreign Exchange; International
    Monetary System
Exchange Risk, 14·39, 38·49
Exchanges, 5·13–15
  Continuous auction process and, 5·19
  History of, 5·8–10
  See also Exchanges; Futures Trading; *Specific
    exchanges*
Exclusions, 8·17

Ex-Dividend Date, 32·11
Exercise Price, 20·3
  See also Options
Eximbank, 14·25
Expansion Investments, 29·4
Expectations Theory, 18·12
  Term structure of interest rates, 31·24–25
Expected Inflation, 37·38
Expected Return
  Modern portfolio theory, 17·19–22, 17·23
Expiration Date, 20·4, 20·7
  See also Options
Export Credit Programs, 38·38
Export Financing, 14·8, 14·9
  See also International Banking
Export Letters of Credit, 14·22
Exposure
  Currency, *see* Foreign Exchange
  Economic, 12·33
  Forward rates, 12·4
  Transaction, 12·32
  Translation, 12·32
Expropriation, 38·31, 38·32, 38·33, 38·34–35,
    38·40
  See also Political Risk
Ex Rights Procedures
  Common stock, 31·50–51
Extension Arrangement, Credit Adjustment,
    28·13–14
External Currency Accounts, *see* Eurodollars
Extra Dating, A·6
Extra Dividends, 32·9
Extramarket Risk, 17·15

Face Value of Note
  Determining, A·9
Facilities Budget, *see* Capital Budgeting
Factoring
  Accounts receivable financing, 28·24–25
Facultative Reinsurance, 8·15
Failing Company Doctrine, 35·34
Fair Credit Billing Act (1969), 9·23
Fair Credit Reporting Act (1971), 9·22
Fair Debt Collection Practices Act (1977), 9·23
False Invoicing
  Multiple exchange rates and, 11·18
Fama
  Option evaluation, 20·34
"Fannie Mae," *see* Federal National Mortgage
    Association
FAPI, 38·20
Farm Credit Act of 1971, 10·9
Farm Credit Administration, 2·11
Farmers Home Administration, 23·5, 23·9
Federal Advisory Council, 1·14
Federal Agencies, 2·10–12, 2·14–15
  Costs, 31·42–44
  Fund Demanded by, 1·5, 1·7
  Issues
    Commercial bank and, 1·6, 1·8, 6·6, 6·9
    Credit unions, 7·30
    Fire and casualty insurance company, 1·8,
      1·11
    Life insurance company and, 1·6, 1·11
    Mutual savings banks and, 7·24
  Mortgage holdings of, 23·5, 23·9
  Pension funds and, 1·12

Federal Agencies (*Continued*)
Savings institutions, 1·6, 1·8
State and local government retirement assets,
1·8, 1·11
See also specific agencies
Federal Credit Union Act of 1934, 7·27, 9·11
Federal Crop Insurance Program, 8·13
Federal Debt, *see* National Debt
Federal Deposit Insurance Corporation (FDIC),
6·5, 8·13
International banking regulation and, 14·45
Mutual savings banks and, 7·22
Federal Fair Debt Collection Practices Act, 9·19
Federal Farm Credit System
Discount notes, 10·4, 10·9
Federal Funds, 1·19, 6·6, 6·10
Federal Reserve and, 1·18
Government securities and, 2·10
Interest rate, 1·23, 1·30
Market, 6·7
See also Money Market
Federal Home Loan Bank, 18·29
Discount notes, 10·4, 10·8
Issues, 2·10, 10·4, 10·8
Mortgages, 23·7
Federal Home Loan Bank Board (FHLBB), 2·11,
7·6, 7·10, 7·17–18, 7·28, 23·3, 23·7
Mutual associations, 7·6
Federal Home Loan Mortgage Corporation
(FHLMC), 7·8, 7·9, 7·12, 7·13, 7·18, 23·5,
23·9
"Freddie Mac" pass-through securities, 2·10,
2·11, 18·29
Federal Housing Administration (FHA), 6·10,
23·9, 23·11, 23·18
Mortgage, 7·25, 7·26
Federal Housing and Veterans Administration,
23·5, 23·9
Federal Intermediate Credit Bank, 7·28, 10·9
Federal Land Bank, 10·9, 23·5
Federal National Mortgage Association ("Fannie
Mae"), 2·10, 2·11, 10·4, 10·8–9, 23·5, 23·9,
23·25
Discount notes, 10·4, 10·8–9
Federal Open Market Committee (FOMC), 1·14,
1·16, 1·17
Federal Reserve Act of 1913, 1·13, 1·14
Federal Reserve Banks, 1·14, 1·15, 1·16–17
Charge for services, 6·23
Disbursements systems, 27·17–18
Banking Act of 1980 and, 27·18
Federal funds, 6·6, 6·10
Treasury debt and, 2·8
Federal Reserve Board
Consumer credit and, 9·3, 9·7
Credit controls, 6·25–29
Edge Act subsidiaries, 14·14
International banking regulations, 14·45, 14·46
Regulation M, 14·43
Regulation Z, 23·17
Securities industry regulation and, 5·15
Federal Reserve Bulletin, 1·16, 16·7
Federal Reserve Open Market Committee, 10·11
Federal Reserve System, 1·13–14
Availabilities, 27·14
Bank regulation and, 6·5, 6·8
See also Regulation M; Regulation Q

Federal Reserve System (*Continued*)
Board of Governors, 1·14, 1·16
Bank holding companies and, 6·21
Reserve requirements, 6·8, 6·22
See also Regulation Q
Check clearing, 6·7
Currency and coin account, 6·7–8, 6·23
Federal Advisory Council, 1·14
Federal Open Market Committee, 1·14, 1·16,
1·17
Member banks, 1·14
Money supply and, 6·13
Operation, 1·14–19
Policy directives, 1·17–18
Services, 1·17
Tools, 1·18–19
See also Money Market
Federal Savings and Loan Insurance Corporation
(FSLIC),
Savings and loan associations and, 7·5, 7·6,
7·10, 7·18–19, 7·20
"Federal Securities Code," 5·12
Federal Truth-in-Lending Act, 9·14, 9·15
Federally Chartered Savings and Loan
Associations, 7·6
Fed Float, 27·15, 27·17, 27·18, 27·19, 27·27
Fed Wires, 27·6, 27·8
Fidelity Bonds, 8·28–29
"Fiduciary Calls"
Pension and profit-sharing plans, 34·23
Field Banks, 27·3, 27·9
Compensation for, 27·10
Filter Rule
Foreign exchange market efficiency, 12·26
Final Dividends, 32·9
Final Value of Annuity Due, A·27–28
Finance Charges, *see* Consumer Credit
Finance Companies
Commercial bank loans to, 6·10–11
Federal Reserve Board and, 6·21
Funds demanded by, 1·5, 1·7
Loans, 1·24, 1·26
Stocks of, 16·28
Finance Subsidiaries, 28·24
Financial Accounting Standards Board (FASB)
Foreign Exchange Exposure, 12·34
Inflation accounting and, *see* Inflation
Pension and profit-sharing plans and, 34·5
Financial Analysis, 24·12–13
Asset turnover, 24·12, 24·13, 24·16, 24·18,
24·21, 24·22
Bank stocks, 16·28
Earnings and dividends per share, 24·2
Book value per share, 24·18, 24·21, 24·22,
24·23
Dividends payment ratio, 24·19, 24·23
Dividends per share, 24·19, 24·20, 24·22–23
Earnings per share (EPS), 24·18–19, 24·23,
33·16–17, 33·19–20, 37·8–12
Income retention rate after preferred
dividends, 24·19, 24·21, 24·23
Equity valuation index, 24·23–25
Financial leverage, 24·12, 24·15, 24·16,
24·21, 24·23
Objective of, 24·12
Return on Assets, 24·12, 24·13, 24·15, 24·16,
24·22

Financial Analysis (*Continued*)
  Return on equity, 24·12, 24·14, 24·15, 24·16,
    24·18, 24·22, 24·23
  Return on sales, 24·12, 24·13, 24·15–16,
    24·17, 24·18, 24·22
    Income retention rate after net interest
      expenses, 24·16, 24·22
    Income retention rate after taxes, 24·16,
      24·22
    Return on sales before interest and taxes,
      24·16, 24·22
    Sustainable dividend growth and, 24·21
  Sustainable dividend growth, 24·21, 24·23,
    24·24
    Income reinvestment rate, 24·22
    Sustainable growth rate, 24·22–23, 24·24
  See also Financial Statement Analysis
Financial Budgets, 25·17, 25·18
Financial Companies
  Commercial paper, 1·22
Financial Control Systems, 25·19–24
  Cost centers, 25·20
  Investment centers, 25·20, 25·21–24
  Profit centers, 25·20–21
  Revenue centers, 25·20
Financial Environment, 1·3
  Responses
    Financial institutions and, 1·8–10
    Financial instruments and, 1·8
    Financial intermediation, 1·7
    Financial markets and, 1·8
    Real sector, 1·6–7
  Shifts
    Business and financial risk, 1·5
    Inflation and, 1·3–5
      Internationalization and, 1·6
      Regulatory policy and, 1·5
Financial Institutions
  Changes in, 1·8–10
  Commercial bank loans to, 6·6, 6·10–11
  Crime insurance contracts, 8·28
  Deregulation of, 1·5
  Restructure of, 1·3
  6-month treasury, 2·17
  See also Nonbank Finance Companies
Financial Intermediary
  Risk aversion, 1·4
Financial Leases, 30·5
  See also Leasing
Financial Leverage, 24·12, 24·15, 24·16
  Dividends per share, 24·23
  Pension plan investment and, 34·14–15
  Ratios, *see* Financial Statement Analysis
  Sustainable dividend growth and, 24·21
Financial Markets
  Inflation and, 1·5, 1·8
  Integration, 13·21
Financial Planning
  Benefits of, 25·3–4
  Break-even analysis, 24·14–15
  Computer-assisted, 25·10–13
  Cost-volume-profit relationships, 25·13–14
  Definition, 25·3
  Planning horizon, 25·6
  Profit plannings and, 25·13–14
  Pro forma statements, 25·4
    Per cent of sales methods, 25·7–9

Financial Planning (*Continued*)
  Sensitivity analysis, 25·4, 25·9, 25·12
  Revising, 25·6
  Steps in, 25·4–6
  Strategic and tactical, 25·6–7
  Subsystems, 25·3
Financial Ratios, *see* Financial Analysis;
    Financial Statement Analysis
Financial Risk, 16·4
  Inflation and, 1·5
Financial Statement Analysis, 16·20, 24·3
  Balance Sheet, 16·21–22, 26·20
    Comparative analysis, 24·4–6
    Description, 24·3, 24·13
    Pro forma, *see* Forecasting
    Ratios, 24·26–27
    Risk and, 8·4
    Shortcomings, 24·4
    Test, 35·7
    Trend analysis, 24·6, 24·8–9
  Deficiencies, 16·23–24
  Definition, 24·3
  Discrimination analysis and financial ratios,
    24·29–31
  Financial leverage ratios, 24·26–27
    Balance sheet ratios, 24·26–27
    Income statement ratios, 24·27
  Generating statements, 25·4–5
    Computers and, 25·4, 25·6, 25·10–13
  Income statement, 16·20–21
    Base 100 income statement, 24·10, 24·11,
      24·12
    Comparative analysis, 24·7
    Description, 24·7, 24·13
    Percentage income statement, 24·10, 24·11
    Pro forma, *see* Forecasting
    Ratios, 16·21, 24·7
    Risk analysis, 8·4
    Trend analysis, 24·7, 24·10–12
  Liquidity ratios, 24·25–26
    Current ratio, 24·25–26, 24·30
    Quick ratio (acid test), 24·26
  Market value ratios, 24·29
    Price book, 24·29
    Price-earnings, 24·29
  Profitability ratios, 24·27–28
    Profit margin on sales, 24·27
    Return on common equity, 24·27–28
    Return on total assets, 24·27
  Sources and uses of funds statement,
    16·22–23
  Turnover on asset management ratios,
    24·28–29
    Asset utilization, 24·29
    Average collection period, 24·28
    Bond portfolios, 18·20–21
    Inventory utilization, 24·28
  See also Forecasting
Financial Statement Generator (FSG), 25·10
Financial Times, 16·8
Financial World, 16·8
Finite-Lived Bond
  Yield to maturity, 31·17–18
Fire and Casualty Insurance Companies, *see*
  Insurance
Firm Commitment, 31·51, 31·52
First-In First-Out (FIFO), 16·23, 37·5–7

Fisher Open Effect, 38·25
 Foreign exchange exposure, 12·33
Fitch Publishing Co.
 Commercial paper and, 10·6
Fixed Assets, 24·4–5
 Utilization, 24·29
Fixed Benefit Pension Plan, 34·11
Fixed Charge Coverage
 Corporate bonds, 16·13
Fixed Costs, 25·13
Fixed-Income Securities, see Bonds; Preferred
 Stock
Fixed Price Offering System, 13·18
Flitcraft Compend, 8·36
Float
 Multinational corporations, 38·7, 38·8
Floater Contract, 8·16, 8·26
Floating Rate System, 11·8
 CD's, 14·35, 14·43
  Eurobanks and, 14·41
 Eurocredit market, 13·26
 Loans, 1·7, 6·26
 Interest rates, 6·11
  Eurocredit, 13·15
 Notes, 12·16, 14·35, 14·43
  Eurobanks and, 14·41
  International banking and, 14·5
 Pricing, 6·3
 Securities, 18·28–29
Floor Brokers, 21·13, 21·18, 21·27
Floor Traders, 21·13
Flotation Costs
 Bond refunds and, 31·47
 Common stock and, 4·33
 Cost of equity capital, 31·32–33
 Public utilities, 36·21–22, 36·29
Flow of Funds, 1·4–12
Flow through Accounting, 36·10
Forbes, 16·8
Forecasting, 25·4, 26·3
 Acquisition analysis, 33·6–7
 Budgets and, 26·4–5
 Cash budget, 26·9–19
  Base case, 26·14, 26·19
  Example of, 26·9–19
  Information for, 26·9, 26·10, 26·12–13
  Interpreting, 26·13, 26·14–18
  Sensitivity analysis, 26·13, 26·19
  Uses of, 26·19
 Classical security analysis, 17·3–5
 Control-limit framework and, 27·28, 27·29–31
 Corporate earnings, 16·24–26
 Daily cash, 27·31
 Dividend discount model, 17·22–23
 Feasible financial plan (sustainable growth),
  26·31, 26·35–38
 Inflation and, 26·36, 26·38
 Information sources and, 16·7–8
 Interest rate, 18·25–26
 Pro forma balance sheets, 26·20
  Common size, 26·31, 26·32–34
  Data, 26·21, 26·25, 26·26–30
  Preparing, 26·21
  Uses, 26·25
 Pro forma financial statements, 25·4, 25·16
 Pro forma income statement, 25·17, 26·20
  Data, 26·21, 26·22–24

Forecasting (Continued)
  Preparing, 26·20–21
 Public utilities, 36·13–14
 Sales forecasts, 26·5–9
  Importance of, 26·5
  Methods, 26·5–6, 26·8
  Regression analysis, 26·6–8
 Security analysis, 16·6
 Uses of, 26·3–5
 See also Exchange Rates; Financial Planning;
  Modern Portfolio Theory
Foreclosure
 Creditor remedy, 9·19
Foreign Bonds, 13·7, 13·19–20
Funds Demanded by, 1·5, 1·7
 Savings institutions, 1·6, 1·8
 See also Eurobonds
Foreign Corporations, see Multinational
 Corporations
Foreign Credit Insurance Associations, 14·25
Foreign Eurodollar CDs, 10·5
Foreign Exchange
 Actors, 12·17
 Arbitrage, 12·8–9
 Balance of payment settlement, 11·19, 11·24
 Borrowing, 38·44–49
 Commercial banks and, 12·13–14
 Contracts, 12·4–7
 Controls
  Cash flow and, 38·24–25
  Dividends and, 38·20
  Equity claims, 38·14
  Transfer prices for services, 38·17
 Currency exposure
  Accounting approaches to measuring,
   12·33–34
  Defining, 12·32–35
  Hedging techniques, 12·35–37
  Economic approaches to measuring,
   12·34–35
  Impact of, 12·37–39
  Management strategies toward, 12·35–39
  Sources of exposure to exchange rate
   changes, 12·32–33
 Evaluating, 38·44–49
 Fluctuations
  Accounts receivable, 38·10
  Inflation and, 38·25, 38·27
  Multinational corporations, 38·10
 Forward market, 38·49
 Future market and, 21·7, 21·8, 21·11, 21·12,
  21·20, 21·23
 Intervention
  Bretton Woods Agreement, 11·6
 Market, 11·3, 12·3–4
  Dimensions, 12·10–13
  Efficiency, 12·25–27
 Money market instruments denominated in,
  10·9–10
 National debt and, 2·8
 Options, 14·35
 Risk, 38·49
 Speculation, 12·9
 Trading, 12·9–10
 See also Exchange Rates; International
  Banking; International Monetary System
Foreign Exchange Rate Depreciation, 38·45–46

Foreign Exchange Trader, 12·3
Foreign Markets, 15·14
  See also International Portfolios
Foreigners
  National debt and, 2·3–4
Forfeiting
  Euromarket innovation, 14·34
Forgery Bonds, 8·28
Fortune, 16·8
Forward Contracts, 21·3
  See also Futures Trading
Forward Currency Contract, 11·8
Forward Currency Markets, 13·21, 13·22
Forward Eurodollar CD, 14·43
Forward Foreign Exchange
  Contract, 10·9, 14·27–28
  Market, 12·4, 38·49
    Economic risk, 38·23
  Rates, 14·29
"Forward-Forward," 14·28, 14·43
Forward-forward CDs
  Euromarket innovation, 14·34
Forward Markets
  Efficiency, 12·26–27
  Floating rate system and, 11·8
  Foreign exchange, 12·4, 38·23, 38·49
  Mortgages and, 23·25–26
  See also International Monetary System
Forward Option Contracts, 14·28
Forward Rate
  Exchange rate forecasting, 12·29–30
  Formula for, 12·17
Founders' Shares, 31·49
Four-Year Certificates
  Maturity of, 7·21
Four-Year Floating Interest Rate Ceiling
  Certificate, 7·10, 7·12
FPC v. *Hope Natural Gas Co.,* 36·17
France
  Investing in capital markets of, 15·11,
  15·24–26
Franchises
  Public utility, 16·29
Frankfurt
  World financial center, 13·8
Franklin National Bank, 12·10
Frank Russell and Co.
  Fixed income performance measurement
  technique, 18·26–27
"Freddy Mac," 2·10, 2·11, 23·9
Free Fed Processing, 27·15
Frequency Compounding
  Mortgages and, 23·11, 23·12
Front-End Loading
  Pension and profit-sharing plans, 34·12
Front-End Management Fees
  Eurocurrency loan and, 14·37
Full Faith and Credit Bonds, 3·13
Fully Accumulated Issue
  Price of, 4·8
Fully Amortized Loan, 23·12
Fundamental Betas
  Performance measurement, 34·21
Fundamental Disequilibrium
  Bretton Woods Agreement, 11·6
Funding Risk
  Eurobanks and, 14·40

Fungibility
  Options and, 20·7
Futures Trading, 2·12
  Chicago Board of Trade Characteristics, 21·14
  Clearinghouse, 21·13
  Commission merchants, 21·8, 21·13, 21·15,
    21·27
  Commodities traded, 21·6
  Contracts
    Attributes, 21·3–4
    Conditions necessary for viable, 21·8, 21·10
    Forward contracts, 21·3
    Features, 21·4–5, 21·12
    Foreign currency and, 12·4–5
    Grade, 21·4
    Innovations, 1·8
    Largest, 21·11
    Liquidation, 21·15
    Months, 21·4
    Offset provision, 21·15
    Pension and profit-sharing plans and, 34·24
    Portfolio futures, 21·5
    Proposed and pending, 21·8
    Sellers' options and, 21·4
  Development, 21·3–10
    Growth in, 21·3, 21·4, 21·23
    Origins of, 21·3
  Exchanges
    Functions, 21·13
    Operations, 21·13–14
  Financial
    Basis and, 21·19, 21·20, 21·22
    Contract Features, 21·4–5, 21·11, 21·12
    Currencies traded, 21·7, 21·8, 21·11, 21·12,
      21·20, 21·23
    Instruments traded, 21·7, 21·8, 21·11,
      21·12, 21·18, 21·22, 21·23
  Foreign futures exchange, 21·9–10
  Functions, 21·12–13
    As hedge, 1·6
    Buy, 21·25–26
    Definition, 21·10, 21·11–12, 21·21
    Exchange rate change hedge, 21·25–26
    Interest rate change hedge, 21·24–25, 21·26
    Long hedge, 21·25–26
    Partial, 21·21, 21·23
    Price change hedge, 21·23–24
    Short hedge, 21·21, 21·23–25
    Spread, 21·26
    Straddle, 21·26
    Total hedge, 21·21, 21·23
    Using portfolio futures, 21·5
  Mechanics, 21·5–21
    Accounting, 21·15–18
    Basis, 21·19–20, 21·21, 21·23
    Carrying charge market, 21·20
    Contract liquidation, 21·15
    Inverted market, 21·20–21, 21·23
    Margin, 21·15
    Order flow, 21·18
    Order types, 21·18
    Trading types, 21·18–19
  Mortgages and, 23·25–26
  Personnel, 21·27
  Regulation, 5·12, 21·27–29
    Commodity Futures Trading Commission,
      21·18

Futures Trading (*Continued*)
Required reporting, 21·28–29
Speculation and, 21·12, 21·18–19
See also Interest Rate Futures

Gambler's Ruin Model, 35·37
Gambling, 16·3
Garnishment
Creditor remedy, 9·18
Gas and Oil Companies
Consumer credit, 9·7–8
Gastineua-Madansky Model, 20·35–37
Option profitability and, 20·37–38
Gathering Bank, 27·5
General Business Indicators, 16·7
General Electric Co.
Property dividends, 32·7
"General Obligation Bond," 3·13, 3·14, 3·15,
3·29, **16**·16
See also State and Local Governments
Obligations
Generally Accepted Accounting Practices (GAAP)
Inflation accounting, *see* Inflation
Pension and profit-sharing plans and, 34·7–8
Genoa Conference of 1922, 11·4
Germany, *see* West Germany
Geske
Option evaluation and, 20·34
Gilt Market, 15·19, 15·20–21
Ginnie Maes, *see* Government National Mortgage
Association
Gladstein
Option profitability and, 20·37–38
Glass-Steagall Banking Act of 1933, I·9, 3·6,
5·26
Multinational affiliates and, 38·42
GNP
Business failure, 35·30, 35·31
Deflator and inflation, I·4
Gold
Balance of payments and, 11·3–4, 11·24
Bloc, 11·5
Demonetizing, 11·24
Exchange standard, 11·4
Pool, 11·24
Standard, *see* International Monetary System
Tranche, 11·24–25
Goodwill
Acquisitions and mergers and, 33·23
Gordon Growth Model, 36·17–21
Cost of equity capital, 31·27, 31·29
Government Agencies, *see* Federal Agencies;
specific agencies
Government National Mortgage Association
(GNMA), 2·12, **10**·13, **23**·5, **23**·9, **23**·25
Cash flow patterns, 18·30
Futures contracts (Ginnie Maes), 2·12, 2·16,
2·17, 21·7, 21·11, 23·9
Mutual savings banks, 7·24, 7·25
Pass-through index, 18·21
Pass-through securities, 18·29
Government Obligations
Credit Unions, 7·30
Federal Reserve and, 1·18
As hedge, 37·38
Interest on, A·5
Liquidity and, 16·5

Government Obligations Inflation (*Continued*)
Mutual savings banks, 7·24
Repo (RP) transactions, 2·8–9
Yields on, 1·31
See also Federal Agencies; Interest Rate
Futures; State and Local Government
Obligations: *under* Treasury
Grace Period, 14·36
Graduated Payment Mortgage (GPM), 23·14
Grain Futures Act, 21·27
"G" Reorganization, 35·22
Gross Leases, 23·22
Group Health Insurance, 8·30
Group Life Insurance, 8·30
Growth
Feasibility of plans for, 26·31, 26·35–38
Inflation and, I·3
Sustainable dividend, 24·21–23, 24·24
Growth Rate
Common stock analysis and, 16·24
Least squares approach to, 24·12
Growth Stock, 4·31–32
Guarantee Clause
Eurocurrency loan and, 14·38
Guaranteed Bonds, 4·5, **31**·45
Guaranteed Insurability, 8·17
Guaranteed Investment Contracts (GICs), 18·25,
19·4, **34**·18–19
Guaranteed Par Value Date (GPVD), 4·8, 4·9

Half-Year Convention
Depreciation and, 29·22
Hazard, 8·3
Health Insurance, *see* Insurance
Health Maintenance Organization Act of 1973,
8·30
Hedging, 8·5, **38**·23
Adjustable rate securities and, 4·6
Asset as, 37·38
Common stocks, 37·35, 37·36–37
Cost of, 37·37
Currency exposure and, 12·35–37
Currency risk and, 14·15–16
Default risk and, I·7
Financial institutions and, I·7
Foreign currency and, 12·4
Government obligations debt instruments,
37·38
Households and, I·6
Money market certificate and, 2·17
Multinational corporations and inventory,
38·12
Options and, 20·32–33
Real estate, 37·38
Reinvestment of interest income, 18·4
Selling in forward markets, 11·8
Stocks, I·4
Transaction costs, 12·12
See also Futures Trading
Hidden Reserves
Bank stock and, 16·28
High Tax Bracket Individuals
Options and, 20·28
High Yield Bonds, 16·15
Historical Chart Book, 16·7
Historical Growth Rate
Forecasting future earnings, 16·24

Holding Company
Operating utility as, **36**·26–28
Holding Company Act of 1934, 36·26
Holding Company Device
Bank holding companies, **6**·21
Holding Gains on Assets
Inflationary, **37**·8–12
Homogeneity, 8·6
Hope Natural Gas Case, 16·30
Horizon, 18·8
Bonds and, **18**·12
Date and acquisition analysis, **33**·6
Horizontal Merger, 33·23
Horizon Volatility, 18·12, **18**·16, **19**·25–26,
19·27, **19**·28, **19**·30, **19**·36
Household
Direct investment, **1**·4
Inflation, **I**·6
Tax-exempt securities and, **3**·23–25
Treasury debt, **2**·7
House Resolution 133, 1·14
Housing Expenditures
Inflation and, **I**·5
Housing and Urban Development (HUD)
Local housing authority notes, **3**·11, **3**·12
See also Federal National Mortgage
Association
Housing and Urban Development Act of 1968,
23·9
Hunt Commission, 6·22
Hurdle Rates, 29·15
Use of, **29**·21

Illegal Dividend, 32·12
Immediate Annuity, 8·31
Immunization, *see* Bonds
Import
Exchange controls and, **11**·17
See also International Banking
Import Financing
International banking and, **14**·8
Strategy, **38**·38
Import Letters of Credit, 14·22
Incentive Savings Plan, 34·11
Income
Risk of loss, **1**·12
Income Before Taxes, 25·21, **25**·22
Income Bonds, 4·5
Income Growth
Evaluating, **22**·21
Income Reinvestment Rate, 24·22
Sustainable growth rate, **24**·22
Income Retention Rate
After Net Interest Expenses, **24**·16
Dividends per share, **24**·22
After preferred dividends, **24**·19, **24**·21,
24·23
After taxes, **24**·16
Dividends per share and, **24**·22
Income Statement, *see* Financial Statement
Analysis; Forecasting
Income Tax, see Taxation
Income Yield, 22·7–8
Indebtedness
Discharge of, **35**·20–21
Indemnity, 8·19
Indenture, **16**·11

Index
Investment performance comparison,
22·22–23
Indexation
Inflation and, **37**·40
Index Funds
Bankruptcy and, **35**·34
Bonds and, **18**·21–24
Index-Linked Bonds, 14·35
Indifference Curves
Modern portfolio theory, **17**·9–10
Individual Bonds, 8·28
Individual Loans, *see* Consumer Loans
Individual Retirement Account (IRA), 34·8, **34**·9
Industrial Aid Bonds, 3·17–18
Industrial Banks
Consumer credit and, **9**·11–12
Japanese, **15**·18
Industrial Companies
Private placement market, **4**·24
Industrial Life Cycle, 16·25–26
Industrial Securities, 16·26–27
Industries
Information on, **16**·8–10
Industry Sales Regression Equation, 26·7
Industry Standard
Credit terms and, **28**·5
Industry Surveys, 16·8
Inefficient Sets
Modern portfolio theory, **17**·10, **17**·11, **17**·12
Inflation
Accounting practices, **37**·4–5
Depreciation, **37**·78
Holding gains on assets (inflationary), **37**·8–12
Inventory, **37**·5–8
Liquidity, **37**·12
Anticipated rate of, **1**·4
Bond returns and, **18**·3–4
Business risk and, **I**·5
Capital budgeting and, **29**·32–34, **37**·21–24
Consumer credit and, **9**·24
Credit terms and, **37**·12–14
Changing credit period, **37**·14, **37**·17, **37**·18,
37·19
Changing discount percentage, **37**·14,
37·15–16
Expected, **37**·38
Financial environment and, **I**·3–5
Financial risk and, **I**·5
Financial sector and, **I**·7–10
Floating rate securities and, **18**·28
Housing expenditures and, **I**·5
Interest rates and, **I**·5, **1**·31, **1**·32
Internal rate of return, **37**·23–24
International comparison, **37**·3–4
Investment incentives and, **37**·3
Accelerated depreciation, **37**·24–28
Investment tax credit, **37**·28, **37**·29, **37**·30,
37·31
Multinational corporations credit and, **38**·10
Exchange rate changes, **38**·25, **38**·27
Net present value and, **37**·17
Neutral inflation, **37**·17, **37**·20–21, **37**·34
Nonneutral inflation and, **37**·21
Riskless interest rates and, **37**·21
Overcompensation or undercompensation for,
37·31

Inflation (*Continued*)
Public utilities and, **36**·6
Cost of capital and, **36**·7–8
Ranking of mutually exclusive investment
projects, **37**·21–22
Incentives considered, **37**·21–24, **37**·28,
37·31, **37**·32, **37**·33
Real Sector and, **I**·6–7
Reborrowing and, **2**·8
Sinking fund preferreds, **4**·27–28
Sustainable growth and, **26**·36, **26**·38
Unanticipated range of, **I**·4
Unexpected, **37**·38
See also Common Stock; Hedging
Ingersoll
Option theory of corporate securities, **20**·40
In-House Computer System
Financial statement generator, **25**·10–11
Inland Marine Contracts, **8**·26
Insolvency, **35**·6
See also Bankruptcy and Reorganization
Insolvency Tests
Dividends and, **32**·22
Installment Credit, **9**·8, **9**·9
Installment Loan, **31**·13
"Instinct," **5**·21
Institutional Investors
Euromarket investor group, **15**·13
German fixed income, **15**·24
Investment portfolio of, **5**·4, **5**·17
New York Stock Exchange trading, **5**·21
United Kingdom Markets, **15**·21
Institutional Mortgages, **23**·17
Instrument Intermediation, *see* Hedging
Insurance
Agent, **8**·31–32
Associations, **8**·14–36
Bank, **6**·5
Bonds, **3**·23
Broker and, **8**·31–32
Commercial liability, **8**·9, **8**·11
Contracts, **8**·16, **8**·17–19, **8**·23
Contractual liability, **8**·23
Insurers, **8**·13, **8**·14
Investments, **8**·34
Liabilities, **8**·34
Liability for acts of agents, **8**·22
Liability of bailees, **8**·22–23
Liability of landlords and tenants, **8**·21–22
Liability of owners and operators of
vehicles, **8**·22
Negligence, **8**·20, **8**·22
Officers' and directors' liability, **8**·23
Product liability, **8**·22
Professional liability, **8**·9, **8**·23–24
Premiums, **8**·11–12
Rate, **8**·33
Reinsurance in, **8**·14
Underwriting, **8**·32–33
Workers' compensation and employers'
liability, **8**·9, **8**·16, **8**·20–21
Commercial property insurance, **8**·7–9, **8**·11
Boiler and machinery contracts, **8**·26–27
Consequential loss contracts, **8**·27
Contracts, **8**·16, **8**·17–19
Coverage, **8**·24–25
Crime insurance contracts, **8**·28

Insurance (*Continued*)
Fire and allied lines, **8**·14, **8**·16, **8**·19, **8**·24,
8·27
Inland marine contracts, **8**·14, **8**·26–27
Insurers, **8**·13, **8**·14
Investments, **8**·34
Jewelers' block contract, **8**·24
Liabilities, **8**·34
Manufacturers' output conract, **8**·25
Mercantile block contract, **8**·24–25
Ocean marine contracts, **8**·14, **8**·25–26
Physical damage contracts, **8**·27
Premiums, **8**·11–12
Rate, **8**·33
Reinsurance in, **8**·15
Special multiperil contract, **8**·25
Suretyship, **8**·28–29
Underwriting, **8**·32–33
Contracts, **8**·16–20, **8**·27, **9**·21
Concealment, **8**·20
Consumer credit, **9**·14, **9**·21
Estoppel, **8**·20
Indemnity, **8**·19
Insurable interest, **8**·19
Representations, **8**·19
Structure, **8**·16–17
Types of, **8**·16
Waiver, **8**·20
Warranties, **8**·19–20
Credit, **28**·14–15
Finance, **8**·34–35
Policyholders' surplus, **8**·35
Ratios, **8**·34–35
Underwriting profit or loss, **8**·35
Fire and casualty, **1**·7
Funds supplied by, **1**·5, **1**·7
Fire insurance, **8**·14, **8**·16, **8**·19, **8**·24
Health insurance, **8**·9
Group, **8**·30
Insurers, **8**·13, **8**·14
Premiums, **8**·11
Insurers selection, **8**·36–37
Interest, **8**·19
Life insurance, **8**·9
Buy-and-sell agreements, **8**·29
Contracts, **8**·17
Deferred compensation, **8**·30
Group, **8**·30
Insurers, **8**·14
Investments, **8**·34
Key man insurance, **8**·29
Premiums, **8**·11
Rates, **8**·33
Real estate pools and, **34**·19
Reinsurance in, **8**·15–16
Retirement income plans, **8**·30–31
See also Pension Profit Sharing Plans
Split-dollar, **8**·30
Underwriting, **8**·33
Marketing, **8**·31–32
Meeting risk and, **8**·6–11
Commercial, **8**·10, **8**·11
Insurable risks, **8**·6–7
Insurance characteristics, **8**·6
Limitations on, **8**·7
Mechanism characteristics, **8**·6
Self-insurance, **8**·10–11

Insurance (*Continued*)
Mortgage, 23·18
Political and economic risk, 38·23, 38·32–33
Premiums and bill futures and, 2·17–18
Rate computations, 8·33
Rating, 8·33
Regulation of, 8·36
Reinsurance, 8·6, 8·14–16
Settlement of loss, 8·33–34
Stocks, 16·28
Fire and casualty insurance companies, 16·28
Life insurance companies, 16·28
Structural characteristics of institution, 8·11–14
Insurer, 8·12–13
Insurer, organized, 8·14
Insurer types, 8·12–14
Number and size of, 8·11–12
Premiums, 8·11–12
Underwriting, 8·32–33
Profit and loss, 8·35
Variable annuities, I·10
See also Risk
Insurance Companies
Assets, I·6–8, 1·9–11
Corporate bonds, 4·7
Expanding functions of, 2·9
Funds supplied by, 1·5, 1·7
Mortgages, 23·4, 23·8–9
Preferred stock purchases, 4·30
Private placement market and, 4·24
Reinsurance contracts, I·7
Risk and, I·7
Separate accounts, 34·18
Sources of long-term debt, 31·3
Tax-exempt securities, 3·23–25
Treasury debt and, 2·7
Insurance Services Office, 8·14
Insuring Agreement, 8·17
Interactive Data Corporation (IDC), 16·10
Inter-America Development Bank (IADB), 13·32, 38·44
Interbank Bid Rate, 13·12
Interbank Lines of Credit
Eurobanks, 14·41–42
Interbank Market
Foreign exchange trading, 12·9
Interchange
Consumer credit and, 9·14
Interest Adjusted Index, 8·36
Interest-Bearing Note, A·7
Interest-Bearing Paper Discounting, A·7, A·8–9
Interest Equalization Tax, 13·17, 13·28–29
Interest-on-Interest
Bonds and, 19·4–5, 19·9, 19·10
Interest Rate Adjustment Act, 7·10
Interest Rate Effect
Bond performance measurement techniques, 8·26
Interest Rate Futures, 2·12–13
Bill futures, 2·17–19
Cash pushes futures, 2·13
Futures push cash, 2·13
Government National Mortgage Association and, 2·12–13, 2·16

Interest Rate Futures (*Continued*)
Intermarket trades, 2·17
Money market certificate costs and, 2·17
6-month treasury bills, 2·17
Spread trades, 2·13, 2·16
Trading yield curve, 2·16
Interest Rate Parity, 13·26
Foreign exchange and, 14·30
Theorem (IRPT), 12·5
Theory, 13·21–22
Interest Rate Risk, 12·13, 14·16, 14·37, 16·4
Eurobanks and, 14·40
International borrowers and, 13·25
Interest Rates
Bond management, 18·18–19
Capital certainty *vs.* income certainty, 1·12
Ceilings, 6·18–20
Adjusting, 7·21
Certificate of deposit, 1·21, 1·24
Certificate of deposit and, 6·31
Change as hedge, 21·24
Compound
Computing, A·14–17
Definitions, A·13
Computation, *see also* Bank Discount
Merchant's rule, A·9–10
United States rule, A·10
Cost of capital, 36·7
Cyclical pattern of, 1·28–32
Inflation and, 1·31, 1·32
Quality considerations, 1·30, 1·32
Yield curve, 1·28–30, 1·31
Definition, A·3
Depository Institutions Deregulation and Monetary Control Act of 1980 and, 6·23, 7·19
Equilibrating process, 1·13
Eurocurrency loans and, 14·43–44
Exact, A·4–6
Expectations, 1·13
Floating rate pricing, 6·3, 6·11
Forecast and bond portfolio management, 18·25–26
Gold standard and, 11·4
Immunization and, *see* Bonds
Inflation and, I·4, 8·5
Money market instruments in foreign countries, 10·10
Mortgages, 23·10–11, 23·24–25
National debt and, 2·3, 2·4
Ordinary, A·4
Risk, 14·16
Savings and loans associations, 7·10, 7·11
Simple, A·4
Tax-exempt securities, 3·25–27
Term risk and, I·7
Term structure of, 18·11–12
See also Corporate bonds
U.S. Government Securities, A·5
Treasury bonds, 2·10
See also International Financial Markets; Regulation Q
Interim Dividends, 32·9
Interinsurers, 8·13
Intermarket Trading System (ITS), 5·24
Intermediate Concentration Banks, 27·5
Intermountain Stock Exchange, 5·14

Internal Rate of Return, 22·10, **29**·13
  Consumer credit and, **9**·15
  Inflation and, **37**·23–29
  Lease and purchase problem and, **30**·11
  Leasing, **30**·20, **30**·21, **30**·22
    Leveraged lease, **30**·24
  Method, **29**·16–17, **29**·19–20
  Yield to maturity and, **18**·6
  See also Bonds
Internal Revenue Service
  Dividend payments, **32**·20–21
  Dividend reinvestment plans and, **32**·21
  Leveraged lease agreement and, **30**·23
Internal Trade
  Bankers' acceptances, **1**·26
  Exchange markets and, **12**·
  See also International Banking; International
    Financial Markets
International Bank Act of 1978 (IBA), 14·45
  Edge Act subsidiaries, **14**·14
**International Bank for Reconstruction and
Development (IBRD), 13**·33, **38**·43
International Banking
  Activities, **14**·3–9
    Environmental changes, **14**·5
    Expansion strategies, **14**·5, **14**·8–9
  Foreign exchange, **14**·26–31
    Covered interest arbitrage, **14**·30–31
    Forward exchange rates, **14**·29
    Forward transactions, **14**·27–28
    Market, **14**·26–27
    Quotation of rates, **14**·28–29
    Spot transactions, **14**·27
    Sway transactions, **14**·28, **14**·29, **14**·39,
      14·41
  Funding in, **14**·40–44
    Eurocurrency market, **14**·40–41
    Instruments, **14**·42–43
    Interbank lines of credit, **14**·41–42
    Liability management, **14**·41, **14**·42
    Onshore *vs.* offshore funding, **14**·41,
      14·43–44
  International lending, **14**·32–40
    Borrowers from international banks, **14**·33
    Credit swaps, **14**·39
    Eurocurrency lending practices **14**·33–37
    Eurocurrency loan pricing, **14**·37–38
    Loan agreement provisions, **14**·31–39
    Parallel loans, **14**·39
    Risk protection, **14**·40
    Swaps, **14**·39
  International payments, **14**·31–32
  International trade finances, **14**·14–25
    By exporter, **14**·16–17, **14**·18
    By exporter's bank, **14**·19
    By importer, **14**·17, **14**·19
    By importer's bank, **14**·19–25
    Letters of credit, **14**·20–24
    Problems and risks of, **14**·15–16
    Public sources of export, **14**·25
    U.S. export-import bank (Eximbank), **14**·25
  Organizing for, **14**·9–14
    Correspondent banking, **14**·12
    Edge Act subsidiaries, **14**·14
    Export financing department, **14**·9
    Foreign affiliates, **14**·13
    Foreign branches, **14**·12
    Global customer organization, **14**·11

International Banking (*Continued*)
    International and regional department,
      14·9–10
    Joint banking ventures and consortia,
      14·13–14
    Legal *vs.* managerial organization, **14**·9
    Majority-owned banking subsidiaries, **14**·14
    Representative offices, **14**·12–13
    Service or functional organization, **14**·10–11
  Problems in, **14**·5, **14**·6–7
  Regulations, **14**·44–51
    Other countries' regulation of foreign banks,
      14·46–51
    Risk and, **14**·40
    U.S. regulation of American banks, **14**·45
    U.S. regulation of foreign banks, **14**·45
  See also International Financial Markets
International Banking Act of 1978 (IBA), 6·22
International Borrowers
  Interest rate risk, **13**·25
International Development Agency (IDA), 13·33,
  38·48
International Finance Corporation (IFC), 13·33,
  38·43
International Financial Decisions, *see*
  Multinational Corporations
International Financial Markets
  Current account, **13**·3–4
    Asset pairs, sovereign risk, **13**·22
    Balances, **13**·4, **13**·5
    Currency risk and, **13**·25–26, **14**·15–16,
      14·40
    Eurocredit and, **12**·15–16
    Financial market integration, **13**·20–24
    Forward exchange rates, **13**·23–24
    Interest rate parity theory, **13**·21–22,
      13·23–24
    Sources for financing, **13**·4–5
    Term structure of, **13**·24–25, **13**·26
    Transaction costs, **13**·23
  Eurocurrency system
    Deposits, **13**·14
    Eurobonds, **13**·7, **13**·14, **13**·16–19
    Eurocredits, **13**·14–16
    Eurocurrencies, **13**·8, **13**·10–12
    Eurodollar, **13**·10, **13**·12, **13**·13
    Foreign bonds, **13**·7, **13**·19–20
    Interest rates, **13**·12–14
  Function, **13**·3–4
  Interest rates
    Eurocurrency system and, **13**·12–14, **13**·16
    Levels, **13**·20
  Investing and borrowing, **13**·6
    Currencies for, **13**·7–9
    Multicurrency financing, **13**·9–10
  Petrodollar recycling, **13**·6
  Risk in, **13**·25–29, **14**·15–16
    Collateral risk, **14**·16
    Convertibility risk, **14**·15
    Credit risk, **14**·15
    Currency risk, **13**·25, **14**·16, **14**·37, **14**·40
    Default risk, **13**·26
    Effects, **13**·26–27
    Eurobanks and, **14**·40
    Foreign exchange rate, **14**·28, **14**·39
    Interest rate risk, **13**·25, **14**·16, **14**·37,
      14·40
    Sovereign risk, **13**·28–29, **14**·40

International Financial Markets (*Continued*)
World financial centers, 13·6–7, 13·8, 13·29–33
Emerging centers, 13·32
Germany, 13·8, 13·31
Japan, 13·8, 13·32
London, 13·7, 13·8, 13·31
Luxembourg, 13·7, 13·8, 13·31
Major international capital markets, 13·30–32
New York, 13·7, 13·8, 13·30–31
Official international financial institutions, 13·32, 13·33
Switzerland, 13·8, 13·31–32
See also International Banking
Internationalization
Banking and, 6·3
International Banking Act of 1978 and, 6·22
Eurodollar and, i·8
Increase in, I·6
Private placements and, 4·26
Securities industry and, 5·15
Securities markets, 5·24–25
International Monetary Fund (IMF), 13·4, 13·5, 13·27
Bretton Woods Agreement and, 11·7
Freely floating exchange rates and, 11·19
Proposed substitution account, 11·26–28
Quotas and, 11·25
Reserve positions in, 11·24–25
International Monetary Market, 12·5
International Monetary System, 11·3
Bretton Woods system, 11·6–7, 11·19, 11·25, 12·9
Eurocurrencies, 11·8–9
Eurodollars, 11·8
Exchange controls, 11·17–18
International diversification, 11·5, 11·8
Tripartite agreement, 11·5–6
Floating rate system, 11·8, 12·16
Transaction costs and, 12·12
Gold standard
Britain's return to gold, 11·5
Gold bloc, 11·5
Gold exchange standard, 11·4
History of, 11·3–4
Managed floating (intervention), 11·9–10, 12·13, 12·16
European monetary system, 11·11, 11·14–17
Minidevaluation systems, 11·10–11
Tied exchange rates, 11·10
Settlements
Foreign exchange, 11·19, 11·24
Gold, 11·3–4, 11·24
IMF reserve positions, 11·24–26
Proposed substitution account, 11·24–26
Smithsonian agreement, 11·7–8, 11·24
Special Drawing Right of, 11·10, 13·9
Tripartite agreement, 11·5–6
United States, 11·20–23
See also Balance of Payments; Exchange Rate; Foreign Exchange
International Payments, 14·31–32
See also International Banking
International Portfolios, 15·3
Empirical studies on, 15·5–7
Costs of, 15·8–9

International Portfolios (*Continued*)
International funds performance, 15·8
Models of, 15·8
Structure of returns, 15·7–8
Investment efficiency, 15·3–5
Major capital markets, 15·9–10, 15·14
Euromarket, 15·9, 15·10, 15·12–14
France, 15·11, 15·24–26
Japan, 15·11, 15·14–19
Performance, 15·8
United Kingdom, 15·8–9, 15·11, 15·19–22
West Germany, 15·11, 15·22–24
Multinational corporations and, 15·9
Pension and profit-sharing plans, 34·22–23
Risk and, 15·6, 15·7, 38·27–30
International Reserve Currency
Dollar as, 13·8
International Shoe Co. v. *FTC*, 35·34
Interstate Commerce Commission
Railroad bankruptcies, 35·9
Interstate Stores, Inc., 35·38, 35·41
Intervention Process (Managed Floating), *see* International Monetary System
Intracorporate Loans, 38·17–19
Intramarket Spread Trades 2·13, 2·16
Inventories
Coinsurance and, 8·16
Inflation accounting and, 37·3, 37·5–8
Methods for valuing, 16·23
Multinational firms and, 38·12–13
Inventory Risk
Underwriters and, 3·8
Inventory Turnover
Corporate liquidity and, 16·14
Ratio, 24·28
Inverted Market, 21·20–21, 21·23
Investment, 29·18–19
Classical security analysis and, 17·3–5
Classification of, 16·3, 29·4
Expansion, 29·4
Independent project, 29·4–5
Mutually exclusive investments, 29·5
Product-line, 29·4
Replacement, 29·4
Strategic, 29·4
Definition, 16·3
Diversification, 16·4
Equity, *see* Common Stock; Real Estate Finance
Fixed income, *see* Bonds; Preferred Stock
Incentives, 37·3
Accelerated depreciation, 37·24–28
Inflation and, 37·17
Marketability, 16·4–5
Public utilities and, 36·9
Receivables, 28·15–18
Risk, 16·4
Risk-return tradeoff and, 16·4, 20·13–14, 20·15
Security analysis, 16·5–6
Sources of information, 16·7–11
Computer-based information, 16·10–11
Economic conditions and business outlook, 16·7–8
Industries and companies, 16·8–10
Tax status, 16·5
Uncertainty in, 1·12
See also Capital Budgeting; Modern Portfolio

Investment (*Continued*)
Theory; Pension and Profit-Sharing Plans;
Performance Measurement; Return on
Investment
Investment Advisors Act (1940), 5·11
Investment Banker
Issuing common stock and, 4·32, 4·33
Investment Banking Firms
Sources of long term debt, 31·4
Underwriting services, 31·51
Investment Capital Management, 5·8
Investment Company Act (1940), 5·10–11
Investment Disinvestment Policy
Bond covenants restricting, 31·23
Investment Managers, *see* Pension and Profit-
Sharing Plans
Investment Securities
Commercial banks, 6·6, 6·8–10
Investment Services, 16·8–9
Investment Tax Credit, 37·3, 37·17, 37·28,
37·29, 37·30, 37·31
Inflation accounting, 37·7–8
Leasing and, 30·23
Investors Management Sciences, Inc. (IMS),
16·10
Invoice Currency
Foreign exchange, 12·37
Irrevocable Letters of Credit, 14·22–23

Jamaica Agreement, 11·24
Japan
Investing in capital market of, 15·11,
15·14–19
World financial center, 13·8, 13·32
Jewelers' Block Contract, 8·24
Joint Bonds, 4·5, 31·46
Joint Float (European Monetary System), 11·11,
11·14–17
Joint and Survivor Annuity Option, 34·9
Joint Ventures
International banking, 14·13
Jones and Laughlin Steel, 35·34
Judge, Bankruptcy, 35·17, 35·20
Judgmental Approach
Exchange rate forecasting, 12·29
Judgmental Risk Evaluation System
Consumer credit and, 9·17
Judgment Currency
Eurocurrency loan, 14·38
Junior Issues, 4·4
"Junk Bonds," 16·15
Jurisdiction
Eurocurrency loan and, 14·38

Kassouf
Option profitability and, 20·37–38
Keogh Plans, 34·8–9
Key Currency
Gold exchanges standard, 11·4
Key Man Insurance, 8·29
Keynes, John Maynard, 11·6
Keynes's Bancors
SDRs and, 11·26
Key Rates, 13·13
Kidder, Peabody Security Valuation System
(SALUS), 17·24–25
King Resources, 35·38, 35·41

Laddered Maturity, 18·24
Land Development Financing, 23·18–19
Landlords
Liability, 8·21
Land Trusts, 23·24
Large Block Trades, 5·21
Last-In First-out (LIFO), 37·3, 37·5–7
Late Charges
Mortage and, 23·17
Late Payment Charges
Creditor remedy, 9·18
Law of Large Numbers, 8·6
Law of One Price
Purchasing power parity and, 12·19
Lead Bank, 6·15, 13·14–15
Syndicate and, 14·35, 14·36
Leading, 38·15, 38·17, 38·18
"Lead Underwriter," 5·25
Leasco Data Processing Equipment Co. (Leasco),
6·21
Lease Capitalization, *see* Lease Financing
Lease Financing
Accounting for, 30·4, 30·28–32, 31·14–15
Historical perspective, 30·27–28
Lease capitalization, 30·27–29
Bankruptcy prediction and, 30·31–32
Financial ratios and, 30·31
Stock prices and, 30·29–31
Advantages, 30·4–7
Banks and, i·8
Bankruptcy claims, 35·13
Capital lease, 31·14–15
Estimating cash, 31·14–16
Federal Reserve Board, 6·21
Financial leases, 30·3, 30·5, 31·45
Gross lease, 23·22
Importance of, 30·3
Lease *vs.* purchase, 30·4, 30·5, 30·7,
30·10–27
Financing decision, 30·11–12
Industry analysis of, 30·20–22
Investment decision, 30·12
Lease-purchase model, 30·12–20
Net present value, 30·13–17, 30·18,
30·20–21
Net present value advantage of leasing over
purchasing, 30·13, 30·14, 30·15,
30·17–18, 30·19
Lessor as financial intermediary, 30·4–5
Leveraged leasing, 30·4, 30·22–23, 31·15
Corporations and, i·6
Evaluating, 30·29
Terms, 30·23, 30·24–27
Long-term, 16·24, 23·20–22
Net leases, 23·21
Operating leases, 30·4, 31·14–15
Provisions, 23·22
Reasons for, 30·7–10
Sale-leaseback financing, 23·21, 23·22–23,
30·3, 31·44
Service leases, 31·44
Tax savings, 30·7, 30·9, 30·12, 30·14, 30·16
Variable rent leases, 23·22
See also Real Estate Finance
Leasehold Mortgages, 23·19–20
Lease Rental Obligations
Corporate bonds and, 16·13

Least Squares Approach
Growth rates and, 24·12
Ledger Experience
Credit decision and, 28·9
Lehman Brothers Kuhn Loeb Index, 18·21, 18·23
Lessor Pricing Model, 30·23–24
Letter of Credit Agreement, 1·21
Assignable, 14·24
Commercial, 14·20–21
Confirmed and unconfirmed, 14·23
Import and export, 14·22
International banking and, 14·8
Revocable and irrevocable, 14·22–23
Revolving, 14·23–24
Letter of Guaranty, 14·24
Letter of Hypothecation
General assurance, 14·25
Letter of Intent
International Monetary Fund and, 11·7
Level Payment Mortgage Loan, 23·12, 23·13
Level Percentage of Payroll
Pension and profit-sharing plans, 34·12
Leverage
Sales growth feasibility, 26·37
Leveraged Leases, see Lease Financing
Levered Firm
Cost of equity, 31·10–11
Inflationary holding gains or assets, 37·8–11,
37·12
Value of, 31·8–9
Liabilities
Balance sheet and, 24·5
Insurer, 8·34
Long term, 31·3
See also Bonds; Common Stock; Equity;
Lease Financing; Preferred Stock
Pension and profit-sharing plans, 34·6–8
Savings and loan, 7·8, 7·9
See also Short-Term Liabilities
Liability Accounts, see Commercial Bank
Liability Insurance, see Insurance
Liability Management
Banks and, 6·16
Eurobank, 14·41
Liability Products, 6·3
See also Commercial Bank
Licensee, 8·21
Liens
Mortgage and, 23·17–18
Life Annuity, A·22
Life Insurance, see Insurance
LIFO, 16·23
Limited-Liability Special Tax Bond, 3·14
Limit Orders, 5·17–18, 21·18
Liquid Assets
Savings and loan associations, 7·7–8
Liquidating Dividends, 32·9
Liquidating Lease, 23·21, 23·22–23
Liquidation, 35·4, 35·6, 35·10–11, 35·12
Value of portfolio, 22·6
See also Bankruptcy and Reorganization
Liquidity
Corporate bonds, 16·14
Financial intermediaries, 1·4
Inflation, 37·12
Investment, 16·5
Working capital position, 16·22

Liquidity Preference
Term structure of interest rates, 13·25,
31·25–26
Liquidity ratios, see Financial Statement
Analysis
Liquidity Risk
Foreign exchange, 12·8
Transaction costs, 12·12
Liquidity Theory
Transaction costs, 12·12, 12·13
Listed Options, see Options
Lloyd's of London, 8·13
Load Factor
Utility and, 16·31
Loans
Commercial bank, 1·6, 1·8
Definition, A·6
Discount, 31·13
Finance company, 1·24, 1·26
Installment, 31·13
International, see International Banking
Multinational corporations and intracorporate,
38·17–19
Payments amortizing, A·33
Regular Term, 31·13
See also Consumer Credit; Credit; Mortgages
Loan Section, 8·17
Loan-to-Home Price Ratio, 23·9
Loan-to-Value Ratio, 23·28
Local Clearinghouse
Check clearing and, 6·7
Local Governments, see State and Local
Government Obligations
Local Housing Authority Notes, 3·11–12
Locals, 21·13
Lockbox, see Cash Management
Logging, 38·13, 38·17, 38·18
London
World financial center, 13·7, 13·8, 13·31
London Dollar CDs, 14·43
Euromarket innovation, 14·34
London Interbank Offer Rate (LIBOR), 13·12,
13·13, 13·26, 14·37
Long Hedge, 21·25–26
Long-Term Debt, see Bonds
Long-Term Leases, 23·20–22
Long-Term Net Lease, 23·21
Loss Distributions, 8·4–5
Luxembourg
World financial center, 13·7, 13·8, 13·31
Luxembourg Stock Exchange
Euromarket trades, 15·13
Lyons Furniture Mercantile Agency, 28·10

Macaulay Duration, 19·6–8, 19·17, 19·36
McCullach v. *Maryland* 3·3
McFadden Act, 6·23
Madansky, 20·35–37
Option profitability and, 20·37–38
Maintenance Costs
Leasing costs, 31·16
Maintenance Margin, 21·15
Maintenance and Replacement Fund, 18·6
Manage Floating, see International Monetary
System
Managerial Control, 25·15–16
See also Budget; Financial Control Systems

Managing Banks
  Syndicate and, 14·36
Mandelbrot
  Option evaluation and, 20·34
Manufacturers' Output Contract, 8·25
Margin, 5·18–19
  Futures trading, 21·15
Marginal Costs, 28·16
Market, efficiency of, 12·25
Marketability of Investments, 16·4–5
Market Extension Merger, 33·23
Market on Close (MOC), 21·18
Market Extension Merger, 33·23
Market Model, 17·16
Market Orders, 5·17, 21·18
Market Price to Book Value of Equity, 24·23–25
Market Return, 29·29
Market Segmentation Theory, 18·12
Market Timing Strategy
  Bond management, 18·18–19
Market Value
  Book values vs, 22·5, 31·9
  of Debt, 31·8
  Z-score model of Equity/Book value of total
    debt rates, 35·36
Market Value Ratios, see Financial Statement
    Analysis
Market Value Weights
  Weighted average cost of capital, 31·36
Markowitz Model 17·7, 17·8, 17·14
Maryland Automobile Insurance Fund, 8·13
Master Account
  Zero-balance account, 27·8
Master Notes, 10·7
Maturity
  Mortgage, 23·11–12
  Municipal bonds, 16·17
  Price risk measure, 18·15
Maturity Date, 16·11, 18·5
Maturity Factoring, 28·25
Maturity Mismatching, 14·16
Maxidevaluation, 11·11
Mean Absolute Change in Price (MACP), 18·17
Mercantile Block Contract, 8·24–25
Mercantile Interior Robbery Policy, 8·28
Mercantile Messenger Robbery Policy, 8·28
Mercantile Open Stock Theft Policy, 8·28
Mercantile Paymaster Robbery Policy, 8·28
Merchant Banking Activities, 14·4
Merchant Discount
  Consumer credit, 9·14
"Merchant's Rule," A·9–10
Mergers and Acquisitions
  Acquisition analysis
    Acquisition for cash, 33·7–17
    Acquisition for stock, 33·17–20
    Corporate self-evaluation, 35·5–6
    Financial evaluation, 33·5
    Planning, 33·4
    Search and screen, 33·4
    Valuation of acquisitions, 33·6–7
  Bond covenants, 31·23
  Business combination terms
    Accounting, 33·21–23
    Economic, 33·23
  Legal, 33·20, 33·21, 33·22
  Tax, 33·20–21

Mergers and Acquisitions (Continued)
  Preferred stock and, 16·18
    Convertible, 4·28
  Private placements and, 4·26
  Reasons for, 33·3–4
  Restricting, 31·23
  Securities industry and, 5·28
  Trends in, 33·3–4
Merrill Lynch Cash Management Account, 6·4
Merton
  Option evaluation and, 20·31
  Option profitability and, 20·37–38
Midwest Stock Exchange, 5·14
Milan
  World financial center, 13·8
Miller-Wahl Co., Inc., 35·38, 35·41
Minidevaluation Systems, 11·10–11
Mint Parity
  Gold standard and, 11·3
Mobile Home Credit, 9·8
  Commercial banks and, 9·10–11
  Consumer credit industry and, 9·10
Mobile Home Paper, 9·6, 9·7
Model Business Corporation Act (1979), 32·22,
    35·6
Modern Capital Market Theory
  Black-Scholes evaluation of options, 20·33
Modern Portfolio Theory (MPT)
  Classical security analysis, 17·3–5
  Decision process, 17·5–6
  Definition, 17·3
  Dividend discount models, 17·22–23
  Futures on stock indices and, 21·5
  Judgment in, 17·6–7
  Options and, 20·10
    Covered calls and, 20·14–15
  Relationships among securities, 17·8–13
    Concept of utility, 17·8–9
    Efficient sets, 17·11–13
    Indifference curves, 17·9–10
    Inefficient sets, 17·11–13
  Research results, 17·23–25
  Return, 17·13–15
    Capital market theory, 17·3, 17·7, 17·15,
      17·16, 17·17
    Market model, 17·16–17
    Markowitz model, 17·7, 17·8, 17·14
    Portfolio theory, 17·7, 17·15
  Risk, 17·13–14, 17·15–18
    Capital asset pricing model, 17·15–16,
      17·17
    Capital market theory and, 17·15
    Market model, 17·16–17
    R-squared, 17·18
    Security characteristic lines, 17·17–18
  Theoretical foundation for, 17·7–8
  Valuation theory, 17·18–19, 17·23
    Kidder, Peabody Security Valuation System
      (SALUS), 17·24–25
    Use of, 17·19–22
  Volatility and, 19·3
Modified Coinsurance Plan, 8·15
Modigliani-Muller Approach
  Cost of equity and, 30·37, 30·39
Momentum Services
  Exchange rate forecasting, 12·29
Monetary Control Act of 1980, 6·7

Monetary-Nonmonetary Approach
Foreign exchange exposure and, **12**·33
Monetary Policy
Inflation and, **1**·5
Monetary Theory
Exchange rate determination, **12**·20–21
Money Brokers
Eurodollar deposits, **10**·5
Federal funds market, **10**·11
Money Market, 10·3
Certificates (MMCs), **6**·31, **7**·10
Commercial banks and, **6**·19
Competition for, **1**·8
Costs, **2**·17
Inflation and, **1**·7.
Interest on, **7**·21
Mortgages and, **23**·24–25
Mutual savings banks, **7**·22
Savings and loan associations, **7**·10, **7**·16, **7**·17
Corporate obligations, **10**·6–7
Commercial paper, **10**·4, **10**·6–7
Master notes, **10**·7
Federal agency discount notes, *see* Federal Farm Credit System; Federal Home Loan Bank; Federal National Mortgage Association
Federal funds market, **10**·3, **10**·11–13
Dollar price repurchase agreement, **10**·13
Domestic certificates of deposit and, **10**·3
Eurodollar certificates of deposit and, **10**·5
Repurchase agreements, **10**·11–12
Reverse repurchase agreements, **10**·11–12
"Rollover" market, **10**·11
"Spot" market, **10**·11
Term, **10**·5
Term repurchase transactions arbitrage instrument, **10**·12–13
"Yankee" certificates of deposit, **10**·5
Federal Reserve control of, **1**·19, **1**·20
Bankers' acceptances **1**·21
Commercial paper, **1**·21, **1**·22–23
Federal funds, **1**·19
Negotiable certificates of deposit, **1**·21, **1**·24
Rates, **1**·18
Repurchase agreements, **1**·19
Treasury bills, **1**·19
Foreign currency, **10**·9–10, **14**·26, **14**·27
Instruments
Commercial banks **6**·16, **6**·18–19
Multinational corporations, **38**·12
Savings institutions, **1**·6, **1**·8
Mutual fund, **1**·6, **6**·31
Performance evaluation, **22**·26
Negotiable certificates of deposit (CDs), **1**·8, **1**·21, **1**·24, **10**·3, **10**·4, **10**·5
Domestic (U.S.) certificates of deposit, **10**·3, **10**·4, **10**·5
Eurodollar certificates of deposit, **10**·4, **10**·5
Futures trading and, **21**·8
"Yankee" certificates of deposit, **10**·5
Tax exempt, **10**·10–11
Banker's acceptances, **10**·4, **10**·5–6
Eurodollar deposits, **10**·5
Term Federal Funds, **10**·5
Treasury bills, **10**·4, **10**·7–8

Money Market Hedge
Currency exposure, **12**·35–36
Money Purchase Pension Plan, 34·10
Money and Securities Broad-Form Policy, 8·28
Money Supply
Demand deposits and, **6**·13
Monopolies
Utility companies as, **36**·34
Monthly Billing, 28·6
Monthly Economic Letter, 16·7
Monthly Review, 16·7
Moody's Handbook of Common Stocks, 16·9
Moody's Investors Service, 1·27, **3**·19, **3**·20–21, **16**·9
Bond ratings and, **16**·15
Commercial paper and, **10**·6
Corporate bond ratings and, **4**·17–18, **4**·21
Preferred stock ratings, **4**·29
"Moral Obligation"
State credit assistance and, **3**·23
Morgan Guaranty Survey, The, 16·7
Mortgage-Backed Securities
Bonds, **23**·9
Insurance companies and, **23**·8
Revenue bonds, **3**·14
Mortgage Banker (Company), 23·7, **23**·8–9, **23**·25
Mortgage Banking
Federal Reserve Board and, **6**·21
Savings and loans associations and, **7**·13
Mortgage Bonds, 18·4, **31**·45
Corporations and, **4**·3
Mortgage Clause, 8·18–19
Morgage Companies
Commercial bank loans to, **6**·10–11
Mortgage Debt
Households and, **1**·6
Mortgage Participation Interests, 23·9
Mortgage Pools, 23·3, **23**·5
Funds demanded by securities, **1**·5, **1**·7
Mortgages
Amortization and repayment plans, **23**·12–14
Blanket, **23**·19
"Canadian" 5-year rollover, **1**·7, **23**·14–15
Closing costs and origination fees, **23**·15–17, **23**·18, **23**·19
Commercial bank, **1**·6, **1**·8
Construction loans, **23**·18, **23**·19
Corporate bonds and, **16**·14
Corporation and, **1**·27, **1**·28
Credit unions, **7**·30
Debt, **23**·3, **23**·4–6
Deposit collateral, **23**·20
Federal Housing Association—Veterans Administration Loans, **7**·25, **7**·26
Federal National Mortgage Association and, **10**·4, **10**·8–9
Found markets, **23**·25–26
Frequency compounding, **23**·11, **23**·12
Fully amortized, **23**·12
Funds demanded by, **1**·5, **1**·7
Futures, **23**·25–26
Graduated payment mortgage (GPM), **23**·14
Growth, **9**·3–5
Inflation and, **1**·7
Institutional, **23**·17
Insurance, **23**·18

Mortgages (*Continued*)
Interest rates on mortgages, 23·10–11, 23·14, 23·24–25
Ceilings, 1·5
Investment performance and, 22·6
Land development financing, 23·18–19
Late charges, 23·17
Leasehold, 23·19–20
Level payment, 23·12, 23·13
Liens, 23·17–18
Life insurance company, 1·6, 1·11
Maturity, 23·11–12
Mortgage-backed securities, 23·9
Mutual savings banks, 7·3, 7·23–25
Open-end, 23·20
Package, 23·20
Pension funds and, 1·12
Pools, 23·3
Prepayment charges, 23·15, 23·16
Purchase money, 23·17–18
Residential, 7·3
Savings and loans associations and, 7·5, 7·12
Reverse annuity, 23·14, 23·15
Savings institutions, 1·6, 1·8
Savings and loan associations, 7·3, 7·5, 7·7, 7·9, 7·12, 7·13–14, 7·15, 7·17, 7·20
Secondary market, 7·13, 7·15
Secondary, 7·13, 7·15, 7·25–26, 23·9, 23·17, 23·25–26
State and local government retirement assets, 1·8, 1·11
Straight-term, 23·12, 23·13
Thrift institutions and, 1·9
Variable rate, 23·14, 23·15
Variable rate rollover rate, 7·17
Wraparound, 23·19
See also Real Estate Finance
Moving Average Approach, 16·24
Multibank System
Balance reports, 27·7
Multicurrency Financing, 13·9–10
Multicurrency Option Loan, 14·35
Eurocurrency loan, 14·38
Multinational Banks, 14·3
See also International Banking
Multinational Corporations (MNCs), 14·5
Accounts receivable management, 38·7, 38·10–12
Credit extension, 38·10–12
Credit management, 38·10
Capital budgeting for, 38·21–27
Currency controls, 38·24–25
Exchange rate changes and inflation, 38·25–27
Financial incentives, 38·22
Parent versus project cash flows, 38·15–16
Political and economic risk analysis, 38·22–24
Capital controls and, 13·28
Cost of capital, 38·27–30
Discount rates, 38·27–28
Diversification, 38·27–30, 38·38
Management, 38·9–10
Edge Act subsidiaries, 14·14
Exchange rate forecasts and, 12·28–29
Financial system, 38·13, 38·14
Arbitance opportinity and, 38·14–15

Multinational Corporations (MNCs) (*Continued*)
Mode of transfer, 38·13
Timing flexibility, 38·13–14
Financing, 38·36–49
Foreign subsidiaries, 38·36–41
Sources of funds for, 38·41–44
Strategy, 38·36
Foreign currency borrowing
Evaluation, 38·44–49
Fund flow mechanisms, 38·15–21
Dividends, 38·15, 38·19–21
Fees and royalties, 38·17
Intracorporate loans, 38·17–19
Leading and lagging, 38·13, 38·17, 38·18
Transfer pricing, 38·16–17
International banking organization for, 14·11
International cash management
Cash planning and budgeting, 38·4–6
Collection and disbursement of funds, 38·7–8
Optimal worldwide cash levels, 38·8–9
Organization, 38·4
International lending and, 14·33
Inventory management, 38·12–13
Investing in, 15·9
Dividend declaration, 32·12
Dividend payments, 32·8
Political risk, 38·22–24, 38·28, 38·30–35, 38·36
See also International Banking
Multiple Concentration Banks, 27·5–6, 27·27
Multiple Discriminant Analysis (MDA)
Credit decision, 28·11
Multiple Exchange Rates
Exchange control and, 11·17–18
Multiple Internal Rates of Return, 30·24
Multiple-Location Contract, 8·16
Multiple-Manager Structure
Pension and profit-sharing plans, 34·18–20
Performance measurement, 34·21
Multiplier Process
Eurodollar market and, 11·9
Municipal Bonds *see* State and Local Government Obligations
Municipal Securities Rulemaking Board, 3·11
Mutual Associations, 7·6, 7·20
Mutual Capital Certificates (MCCs)
Savings and loan associations, 7·20
Mutual Funds
Bankruptcy prediction, 35·35
Debt funds and, 1·8
German equity markets, 15·24
Japanese, 15·15
Money market investments and, 1·6
Multiple portfolio managers for, 34·18
See also Money Market
Mutually Exclusive Investments, 29·5
Mutuals
As insurer, 8·12, 8·13
Mutual Savings Banks, 7·3, 7·21–22
Assets, 7·4–5
Consumer credit, 9·7–8
Funds supplied by, 1·5, 1·7
Uses of, 7·23, 7·24
Sources of, 7·22–23
Mortgages, 23·4, 23·8
Negotiable order of withdrawal accounts, 6·15, 6·31

Mutual Savings Bonds (*Continued*)
Nonmortgage assets, 7·24, 7·25
Profitability, 7·26–27
Savings deposits, 7·4
Secondary market, 7·25–26
Mutual Savings Central Fund, Inc., 7·22

Name Schedule Bonds, 8·28
**National Association of Credit Management
(NACM),** 28·10
National Association of Insurance Commissioners,
8·36
Sinking fund preferreds, 4·27–28
National Association of Securities Dealers (NASD),
5·14, 5·15
**National Automated Clearing House Association
(NACHA),** 27·6
National Banks
Comptroller of currency and, 6·5
National Credit Information Service (NACIS),
28·10
National Credit Office, 28·10
National Credit Union Administration (NCUA),
7·27, 7·28
**National Credit Union Share Insurance Fund
(NCUSIF),** 7·29
National Debt
Borrowing cycle, 2·6, 2·7
Certainty of payment, 2·6, 2·7
Dealers in, 2·8
Evolution of, 2·3, 2·4
Foreign currencies, 2·8
Interest on, 2·3, 2·4
Length of debt maturity, 2·4, 2·5, 2·6
Ownership of, 2·6, 2·7
Types of obligations, 2·3–4, 2·5
See also Government Obligations; *under*
Treasury
National Development Banks, 38·43–44
National Exchange Market System (NSTS), 5·12,
5·23, 5·24
**National Exchange Market System (NEMS) Act
(1975),** 5·11
See also Securities Act Amendments
Nationalization
France and, 15·24
National Treatment Principle
Foreign banks and, 14·45
Navy Federal Credit Union, 7·28
Negative Pledge, 13·15
Negligence, 8·20, 8·22
Negotiable Certificates of Deposit, *see* Money
Market
Negotiable Order of Withdrawal (NOW) Account,
6·4, 6·15, 6·19–20, 6·23, 7·22
Savings and loan associations and, 7·20
Thrift institutions and, 1·9
Negotiated Underwritings
Tax-exempt securities and, 3·6
Neisner Bros. Inc., 35·42
Net Debt
Bond ratings and, 3·22
Net Income, 25·21, 25·22
Small banks, 6·29 30
Net Income to Average Assets
Savings and loan associations and, 7·16
Net Income to Equity (ROE)
Small banks and, 6·30

Net Interest Cost (NIC)
Awarding bonds, 3·9
Net Leases, 23·21
Net Present Value, 29·13, 29·18
Lease-purchase problem, 30·11
Leasing and, 30·13–17, 30·18, 30·20–21
Leveraged lease and, 30·24
Uniform annuity series, 37·22
See also Inflation
Net Rates of Return
Consumer credit and, 9·13, 9·14
Neutral Hedge Ratio, 20·20
Neutral Inflation, 37·39
Net present value, 37·17, 37·20–21
Neutral Option Hedge, 20·32, 20·33
New Convertible Bonds, 4·4
New issues
Public utilities, 36·21–22, 36·29
Sale of, 5·26–28
Securities Act (1933), 5·11
Newsweek, 16·8
New York
Bond anticipation note and, 3·12–13
World financial center, 13·7, 13·8, 13·30–31
New York Clearing House Association, 14·31
New York Fed, 1·19
New York Futures Exchange, 12·5
New York Insurance Exchange, 8·13
New York State Urban Development Corporation
State authority BAN and, 3·12
New York Stock Exchange (NYSE), 5·6, 5·14
Depository Trust Co., 5·14
Designated Order Turnaround system, 5·24
Dividend declaration and, 32·11
History of, 5·9–10
Institutional trading and, 5·21
Intermarket Trading System (ITS), 5·24
Large block trades, 5·21
Margins and, 5·19
Member brokerage firms, 5·12
Odd-lot orders, 5·19
Securities Clearing Corp. (NSCC), 5·14–15
Securities firms and, 1·9
Securities Industry Automation Corp. (SIAC),
5·14–15
Transactions and, 5·19–21
New York Times, 16·8
Ninety-Nine-Year Leases, 23·21
Nominal Dollars
Bilateral exchange and, 12·14
Inflation and, 29·32–34
Nominal Exchange Rates, 12·16
Nominal Interest Rates
Inflation and, 29·32–34
Nomograms
Option valuation, A·46, A·48–50
Nonbank Commercial Paper, 1·21
Nonbank Finance Companies, 2·6–7
Funds supplied by, 1·6, 1·7
Nonbank Subsidiaries
Loan, 6·21
Nonconstant Growth Model, 36·18, 36·19
Nonfinancial Assets
Inflation and, 1·5
Nonfinancial Companies
Commercial paper and, 1·22
Funds supplied by, 1·6, 1·7
Tax-exempt securities and, 3·23–25

Nonfinancial Companies (*Continued*)
  Treasury debt, 2·7
Nonforfeiture Section, 8·17
Noninstallment Credit, 9·7
Noninterest-Bearing Note, A·7, A·8
Nonmarketable Assets
  Investment performance and, 22·6
Nonmarket Risk, 17·15
Nonneutral Inflation
  Net present value and, 37·21
Nonnotification Financing, 28·24
Nonresident Aliens
  Option investment, 20·28
Nonrevolving Charge Accounts, 9·7
Nonvested Benefits, 34·5
Normative Lease-Purchase Theory, 30·12
Nostro Account, 14·31
Note, *see* Bank Discount; Treasury Notes
Notes Payable, *see* Short-Term Liabilities
Notification Factoring, 28·24
NOW Accounts, *see* Negotiable Order of
  Withdrawal Accounts

Obsolescence, 30·6–7
  Leasing costs, 31·16
  See also Lease Financing
Ocean Marine Contracts, 8·24, 8·25–26
Occupation
  Bankruptcies filed by, 35·25–29
Odd Lots, 5·19
Offering Price
  Common stock and, 4·33
Office Buildings
  Investment characteristics, 23·32
Officers' Liability, 8·23
Offset Provision
  Futures contract, 21·15
Offshore Finance Company, 38·37
Oil Stock, 16·27
**Old Age, Survivors, and Disability Insurance
  Program, 8·13**
One-Factor Model, *see* Single-Index Model
One-Period Risk Analysis, 29·28–30
OPEC, 13·6
Open-Book Account
  Credit sales, 28·4
  Shipment on, 14·16
Open-End Contracts
  Revolving credit, *see* Consumer Credit
Open-End Mortgages, 23·20
Open Interest, 21·18
Open Market Commercial Paper (CPs)
  Negotiable nature of, 1·8
Open Market Operations
  Federal Reserve and, 1·18, 1·19, 2·8
Open Market Paper
  Commercial bank and, 1·6, 1·8
  Funds demanded by, 1·5, 1·7
  Life insurance company and, 1·6, 1·11
Operating Cash Flows After Taxes, 31·6–7
Operating Leases, *see* Lease Financing
Operating Statement (Income Statement), *see*
  Financial Statement Analysis
Operational Budgets, 25·17–18
Opportunity Cost, 26·4, 29·12
  Bankruptcy and reorganization, 35·5
  Cost of capital, 31·5, 31·6

Opportunity Cost (*Continued*)
  Currency exposure and, 12·35
  Depreciation funds, 31·33
  Discount not taken, 37·12–14
  Funds, 29·33
  Transaction costs and, 12·12
Optimal Capital Structure, 36·24
  See also Cost of Capital; Public Utilities
Options, I·8
  Advisory services, 20·42–44
  Bankruptcy prediction and, 35·33
  Buyer, 20·4
    Option fair value and, 20·28–29
    Taxation and, 20·22, 20·23–26
  Call option, 16·11, 18·5
    Convertible securities cost and, 31·34
    Corporate securities and, 20·40
    Covered, 20·10, 20·12, 20·13, 20·14–15,
      20·19
    Definition, 20·3
    Risk-reward characteristics of, 20·4–6,
      20·15
    Value of, 20·30–31
    Writing, 34·23
  Combination option, 20·3
  Conversion, 20·19–21
  Corporate securities, 20·9
    Definition, 20·3
    Early exercise of, 20·21–22
    Fiduciary, 34·23
  Definition, 20·3
  Expiration date, 20·4, 20·7
  Evaluation of, 20·16–17, 20·28–37
    Black-Scholes model, 20·31–34
    Cox, 20·35
    Fair values of, 20·29–31
    Gastineau-Madansky model, 20·35–37
  Hedge, 8·6
  Listed, 20·6–10, 20·41
    Chicago Board Options Exchange changes,
      20·6–7, 20·9
    Conventional options *vs.*, 20·8–9
    Transaction costs, 20·7, 20·9–10
  Pension and profit-sharing plans, 32·23–24
  Premium, 20·4, 20·5, 20·12, 20·13
    Variations, 20·15–16
  Pricing theory, 17·7
    Black-Scholes Formula, A·44–46, A·47
    Nomograms for, A·46, A·48–50
  Probability distribution problem and, 20·35–37
  Profitability of, 20·37–39
  Protective, 34·22
    Risk-reward characteristics, 20·4–6,
      20·18–19
  Put options, 20·18
  Real estate, 23·23
  Risk and, 20·4–6, 20·17–18, 20·20–21
  Risk-adjusted returns, 20·15, 20·16
  Risk modification and, 20·4
  Risk-return trade-off, 20·13–14, 20·15
  Risk-reward characteristics of, 20·4–6, 20·10,
    20·12
  Ross, 20·35
  Rubinstein, 20·35
  Samuelson-Merton model, 20·31
  Significance of, 20·28–31
  Specialists, I·9

Options (*Continued*)
  Spread, 20·4
  Sprenkle model, 20·31
  Straddle, 20·3, 30·24
  Striking price (exercise), 20·3
  Taxation and, 20·22–28
    Capital loss carry-forwards and, 20·28
    High tax bracket individuals and, 20·28
    Nonresident aliens and, 20·28
    Option buyer and, 20·22, 20·23–26
    Option writer and, 20·22, 20·27
    Treasurer and, 20·40–41
    Writer, 20·4
      Taxation and, 20·22–27
Options Clearing Corp., 20·7, 20·9
Ordinary Annuity, A·21, A·22–23
Ordinary Interest, A·4
Ordinary Terms
  Credit terms and, 28·6
**Organization of Petroleum Exporting Countries
  (OPEC),** 13·6
Origination Fees
  Construction loans and, 23·18
  Consumer credit and, 9·14
  Mortgage, 23·15–17
Origination Services
  Underwriters and, 3·6–8
Overadvances, 28·25
Overall Debt
  Bond rating and, 3·22
Overdraft
  Multinational affiliates, 38·41
Overseas Money and Capital Markets, *see*
  International Banking; International Financial
  Markets
Overseas Private Investment Corporation (OPIC),
  38·32, 38·23
Overshooting
  Exchange rate, 12·23–25
Over-the-Counter Market, 5·21

Pacific Stock Exchange, 5·14, 5·23–24
Package Contract, 8·16
Package Mortgages, 23·20
Panama
  World financial center, 13·8
Parallel Loan, 14·39, 38·19
  Euromarket innovation, 14·34
Parent-Subsidiary Relationship, 33·20, 33·21
Paris
  World financial center, 13·8
Parity Grid System
  European monetary system and, 11·11
Partial Hedge, 21·23
Partially Amortized Loan, 23·13
Partial Payment in Advance
  Importer financing and, 14·17, 14·19
Participating Banks
  Syndicate and, 14·36
Participating Bonds, 4·5, 31·45
Participating Preferreds, 4·28, 31·48
Participation Fee, 13·15
Participative Budgeting, 25·19
Par Value
  Bond, A·35
  Bretton Woods system and, 11·6
  Commercial banks and, 6·17

Par Value (*Continued*)
  Common stock, 31·49
  Inflation and, 1·7
  Mutual savings banks and, 7·23
  Preferred stock, 31·48
  Savings and loan associations and, 7·8, 7·10,
    7·12
Passive Fixed Income Management, 18·21–25
Passive Management
  Pension and profit plans, 34·18
Pass-Through Packaging
  Nonnegotiable instruments, 1·8
Pass-Through Securities, 23·9, 23·25
Past Service Costs, 34·5
Past Service Plan Benefits, 34·5
Payable Balance Pattern, 28·26–27
Payable-Through Draft, 27·6
Pay-As-You-Go Basis
  Providing benefits, 34·11
Payback Method, 29·14
  Use of, 29·20–21
Payback Period, 29·13
  Multinational corporations, 38·23
Payment on Documents
  Importer financing and, 14·19
Payment with Order
  Importer financing and, 14·17
Payout Ratio, 16·21
Pegged Rate System
  Floating exchange rate system *vs.*, 12·12
**Penn Central-New York New Haven and Hartford
  Railroad merger,** 35·10
Penn Central Railroad
  Bankruptcy, 1·21, 35·3, 35·40
  Commercial paper obligations, 6·17
Penn Central Transportation Co., 35·15, 35·40
Pension Benefit Guaranty Corp. (PBGC), 34·4–5,
  34·6, 34·7
Pension and Profit-Sharing Plans, 8·31
  Accounting, 34·7–8
  Actuary role, 34·11–12
  Alternatives to defined benefits, 34·10–11
  Conventional investments, 34·22–24
    Approximation for total return, 22·13
    Assets, 1·12
    Cash flows and, 22·10–12
    Corporate bonds, 4·7
    Current service liability, 16·23
    International Diversification, 34·22–23
    Option and Futures Contracts, 20·40,
      34·23–24
    Options and, 20·40
    Past service liability, 16·23–24
    Private placement market, 4·24
    Prudence constraint, 34·22
    Real estate, 34·23
    State and local government, 1·11
    Tangible assets, 34·24
    Treasury funds, 2·7
    Variable annuities and, 1·10
  Costs and Liabilities, 34·6–8, 34·11–12
  Deferred Profit-Sharing Plans, 34·8
  Definitions, 34·3–5
  Employee Retirement Income Security Act
    (ERISA), 5·12, 34·4–5, 34·8, 34·9, 34·11,
    34·22
  Financial *vs.* Nonfinancial Objectives, 34·9–10

Pension and Profit-Sharing Plans (*Continued*)
Early retirement costs, 34·9
Postretirement benefit adjustments, 34·7,
34·9
Vesting standards, 34·9–10
Insured pension benefits, 34·6
Potential unpaid pension liabilities, 34·6
Investment Managers Selection, 34·17–20
Active Manager Decision, 34·17–18
Guaranteed investment contract, 34·18–19
Immunization, 34·19
Managing the Managers, 34·19–20
Multiple-Manager Structure, 34·18–20,
34·21
Real estate pools, 34·19, 34·23
Single Manager Case, 34·18
Investment Objectives
Asset Mix Decision, 34·15–17
Corporate Factors, 34·14–15
Nature of Investment Problem, 34·13–14
Purpose, 34·12–13
Nature of Commitment, 34·3
Performance Measurement, 22·4, 34·20–22
Reporting, 33·3–5
Tax Benefits, 34·8–9
Vested, Past, and Prior Service Cost Benefits,
34·5–6
Percentage Income Statement, 24·10, 24·11
Percentage-of-Parity Basis
Government securities, 2·9–10
Percent of Sales Method
Pro forma income statements and, 25·7–9,
26·20, 26·21
Performance Bonds, 21·15
Performance Measurement
Average rate of return over several time
periods, 22·9–14
Averaging, 22·9–10
Approximations, 22·13–14
Cash flows, 22·10–13
Dollar-weighted rate of return, 22·10–11
Time-weighted rate of return, 22·11, 22·12
Unit values, 22·11, 22·13
Bond portfolio, 22·25–26
Comparing performances, 22·21–25
Rate of return comparisons, 22·22–23
Risk-adjusted comparisons, 22·23–24
Special services, 22·24
Usefulness of, 22·24–25
Evaluating performance, 22·20–21
Evolution of, 22·3–4
Rate of return for single period, 22·4–9
Appreciation, 22·8
Calculation, 22·8–9
Income measurement, 22·7
Income yield, 22·7–8
Total return, 22·4–5, 22·7
Valuation, 22·5–6
Real estate portfolio, 22·26
Risk measurement, 22·14–18
Beta-Coefficients, 22·16–18
Market risk, 22·16
Standard deviation, 22·15–16
Uncertainty, 22·14–15
Risk and return measures combined, 22·18–20
Risk-adjusted rate of return, 22·18–20,
22·23–24
Short-term securities portfolios, 22·26

Performance Measurement (*Continued*)
See also Capital Budgeting; Pension and
Profit-Sharing Plans
Peril, 8·3
Periodic Frequency Rule, 27·25
Perpetual Annuity, 16·19
Perpetual Bond Volatility, 19·11
Perpetual Obligations
Treasury and, 2·8
Perpetuity, A·21
Personal Bankruptcy, *see* Bankruptcy and
Reorganization
Personal Liability, 8·9
Petrodollar Recycling, 13·6
Petroleum Companies
Stock in, 16·27
Phoenix-Hecht Mail Time
Data base, 27·14
**Pittsburgh, Baltimore, Washington Stock
Exchange, (PBW), 5·14**
Placement Memorandum, 14·36
Planning, *see* Financial Planning
Planning Horizon
Financial plan and, 25·6
Pledged Savings Account
Mortgages and, 23·14
Point-of-Sale (POS)
Electronic movement of funds, 6·27–28
Policyholders' surplus, 8·35
Policy Loans
Life insurance company and, 1·6, 1·11
Political Risk, 13·22, 13·28
Interest rate parity theory and, 13·22
Multinational corporations, 38·22–24, 38·28,
38·30–36
Pollution Control Revenue Bonds, 1·27, 1·28
Ponzi Scheme, 36·11
Pooling of Interests
Acquisitions and mergers, 33·21–22
Portfolio
Efficient, 15·4
Minimum variance, 37·37
See also International Portfolios; Modern
Portfolio Theory
Portfolio Balance Theory
Exchange rate determination and, 12·21
Overshooting and, 12·24
Portfolio of Currencies, 13·9
Portfolio Futures Contract, 21·5
Portfolio Manager
Bankruptcy prediction, 35·34–35
Portfolio Theory, 5·17, 7·7, 7·15
Hedging, 37·37
Portfolio Yields, 7·16–17
Position Schedule Bonds, 8·28
Postretirement Benefit Adjustments, 34·9
Postretirement Pension Adjustments, 34·7
Preauthorized ACH Debits, 27·15
Preauthorized Checks (PACs), 27·15
Preauthorized Drafts (PADs), 27·15, 27·19
Precious Metals
Pension profit-sharing plans, 34·24
Preemptive Right
Common stock, 31·49–50
Preference Stocks, 4·28–29
Preferred Dividends, 24·19
Preferred Habitat
Term structure of interest rates and, 13·25

Preferred Stock, 4·27–30, **31**·4,
  31·47–48
  Analysis, **16**·18–19
  Convertible, 4·28, **16**·18, **31**·27, **32**·5
  Dividends, 32·5
    Cumulative dividend feature, **31**·4,
    31·48
  Estimating cost of, 31·26–27
  Issues, 4·29–30
  Par and liquidation values, 4·29, **31**·48
  Participating preferreds, 4·28, **31**·48
  Preference stocks, 4·28–29
  Private placement, 4·22
  Purchasers, 4·30
  Ratings, 4·29
  Sinking fund preferreds, 4·27–28, **16**·11
  Straight, **31**·26–27, **32**·5
  Voting rights, **31**·48
  See also Dividends; Policy
Preliminary prospectus, 5·27
Premium
  Bond and, **16**·12
  Floating rate system and, **11**·8
  Mergers and Acquisition, **33**·4
  Options and, **20**·4, **20**·5, **20**·12, **20**·13
  See also Insurance
Prepayment Provisions
  Consumer credit contract and, **9**·19–21
  Eurocurrency loan and, **14**·38
  Mortgage and, **23**·15, **23**·16
Presale Marketing
  Underwriters and, 3·8
Present Value, **29**·15–16, **29**·17,
  29·19–20
  Annuity due, A·34
  Computing, 2·17–18, A·19
  Conventional, **29**·28
  Depreciation, **29**·23, **29**·24
  Equivalents, **29**·13
  Interest rate, A·20–21
  Number of payments, A·18, A·20
  Ordinary Annuity, A·28–31
  Paths, **29**·26–27
  Pension plan and investments, **34**·14
  Risk-adjusted factors, **29**·28–31
  Stocks, **17**·20–22
Press
  Option evaluation and, **20**·34
Pretax Sales Returns
  Acquisition analysis, **33**·11
Previous Balance Method
  Revolving credit account and, **9**·16
Price-Book Ratio, 24·29
Price Change Hedge, **21**·23–24
Price Discovery
  Futures markets and, **21**·13
Price-Earnings Ratios (P/E), 24·6, 24·29
  Classical security earnings and, **17**·3–5
  Inflation and, **I**·4
Price Elasticity
  Utility service, **36**·13
Price Issue
  Fully accumulated, 4·8
Price Risk
  Transaction costs and, **12**·12
Price Volatility, **19**·3, **19**·11–14
  Risk, **18**·15
Primary Concentration Bank, **27**·5

Prime Formula, 1·26
Prime Rate, 1·26
Principal
  Definition, A·3
Principal Amount, **18**·5
Principal Banks, **9**·11
Private Debt
  Inflation and, **I**·7
Private Export Funding Corp. (PEFCO), **14**·25
Private Pension Funds
  Funds supplied by, 1·5, 1·7
Private Placement, 4·21–23
  Adjustable rate securities and, 4·6
  Bond portfolio management, **18**·24–25, **31**·47
  Commercial banks and, **I**·9
  Commercial paper, 1·21, 1·22
  Evaluation, 4·23–24
  Japanese, **15**·18
  Market participants, 4·24
  New issues, 5·27
  Outlook, 4·26–27
  Preferred share and, **32**·5
  Project financing, 4·27
  Public markets and, 4·25–26
  Resale of, 4·26
  Sinking funds, 4·8, 4·11, 4·15
Proceeds and Discounts, A·7, A·8
Product Extension Merger, **33**·23
Production Budgets, **25**·18
Productivity, Economic
  Inflation and, **I**·3
Product Liability, **8**·22
Product-Line Investments, **29**·4
Professional Liability, **8**·9, **8**·23–24
Profitability, 24·18
  Dividend policy, **32**·19
  Measures, **25**·21, **25**·22
  Ratio, *see* Financial Statement Analysis
Profit Centers, **25**·20–21
Profit and Loss Statement (Income Statement), *see*
  Financial Statement Analysis
Profit Margins, 24·18
  On sales, 24·27
  Sales growth feasibility and, **26**·38
  Sustainable dividend growth and, 24·21
Profit Planning, **25**·13–14
Profit-Sharing Plans, *see* Profit and Pension-
  Sharing Plans
Profit Tax Payable, 1·24, 1·26
Pro Forma Statements, *see* Forecasting
Programmable Calculators
  Yield tables, **18**·6
Project Financing, 4·27
Project Notes, **10**·10
Project Summary Sheet, **29**·8, **29**·10
Promissory Note, *see* Bank Discount
Property
  Personal bankruptcy, **35**·39
Property and Casualty Insurance Companies, *see*
  Insurance Companies
Property Dividends, **32**·7
Pro Rata Distribution Clause, **8**·18
Pro Rata Liability Clause, **8**·18
"Protective Puts"
  Pension and Profit-sharing plans, **34**·23
Proxmire-Reuss Depository Institutions
  Deregulation and Monetary Control Act of
  1980, **7**·19

Prudence Constraint
  Pension and profit-sharing plans, 34·22
Public Debt, see National Debt; Treasury Debt
Public Placement
  Of bonds, 31·47
Public Securities Association, 5·16
Public Utilities
  Background, 36·3
  Capital Budgeting
    Commission participation in decision
      process, 36·15–16
    Cost of capital, 36·14
    Cost forecasting, 36·13–14
    Current, 36·13–17
    Current environment of, 36·14
    Demand forecasting, 36·13
    Joint facilities planning, 36·16–17
    Regulatory approval, 36·14
    Traditional, 36·12–13
  Capital structure, 36·23
    Capital structure theory, 36·23–24, 36·25
    Double leverage, 36·26, 36·27–28
    Parent-subsidiary issues, 36·26, 36·27–28
    In rate cases, 36·24–26
  Cost of capital
    Capital asset pricing model (CAPM),
      36·20–21
    Capital budgeting and, 36·14, 36·22–23
    Changes in, 36·6–9
    Discounted cash flow method (DCF),
      36·17–21
    Floatation costs adjustment, 36·21–22, 36·29
    Nonconstant growth model, 36·19
    In rate cases, 36·17
    Risk premium methods, 36·20
    to Subsidiaries, 36·28
  Dividend policy, 36·29–30
  Modern portfolio theory and, 17·8–9
  Preferred stock and, 4·29–30, 16·18
  Regulatory environment, 36·3–4
    Accounting policies, 36·9–12, 36·21–22
    Cost of capital charges, 36·6–9
    Inflation and regulatory log, 36·6, 36·8
    Mandatory investment, 36·9
    Simplified view of, 36·4–6
  Securities, 16·29–32
Purchase
  Acquisitions and mergers, 33·22–23
"Purchase of Assets" Combination, 33·20, 33·22
Purchase and Leaseback, 23·21, 23·22–23
Purchase Money Mortgage, 23·17–18
Purchasing Power Parity Theory (PPP)
  Exchange rate determination, 12·19–21
Purchasing Power Risk, 16·4
Put Option, see Options
Pyramid, Scheme, 36·11

QES Score, 35·37
Quality Risk, 18·14–15
Quantitative Restrictions, Imports and, 11·17
*Quarterly Financial Report for Manufacturing
  Corporations,* 16·8
Quick Ratio (Acid Test), 16·22, 24·26
Quota-Share Arrangement, 8·15

Random Event
  Market return as, 29·29

Random Walk Hypothesis, 12·26
Ranking of Independent Investment, 29·5, 29·6
RANS, see Revenue Anticipation Notes
Rate
  Definition, A·3
Rate of Return
  Abnormal, 31·51
  Acquisition analysis, 33·11–13, 33·13–14,
    33·15
  Dollar-weighted
    Performance measurement, 34·21
  Lease and purchase problem, 30·11
  Public utilities, 36·45
  Risk-adjusted and, 22·14, 22·18–19, 31·5–6
    Bonds and, 31·18–19
    Comparison, 22·23–24
    Options and, 20·15, 20·16
  Time-weighted total and investment
    management performance, 34·20–22
  See also Performance Measurement
Ratings
  Bond, see Bonds; Corporate Bonds; State and
    Local Government Obligations
  Commercial paper, 10·6–7
  Real estate investment and, 23·27
Ratio Analysis, see Financial Analysis; Financial
    Statement Analysis
Ratio of External to Internal Financing Inflation,
    37·39
Reaffirmation of Debts After Bankruptcy
  Creditor remedy, 9·19
Real Effective Exchange Rate, 12·15–16,
    12·18–19
Real Estate Finance
  Escrows, 23·23–24
  Hedge, 37·38
  Investment features
    Apartments, 23·32–33
    Office buildings, 23·32
    Ratings, 23·27
    Risk characteristics, 23·26–31
    Shopping centers, 23·32
    Single-family houses, 23·33
    Taxes, 23·29–30
    Valuation, 23·31–32
  Investment performance and, 22·6, 22·26
  Land trusts, 23·24
  Lending sources, 23·3, 23·4–6
    Commercial banks, 6·6, 6·10, 23·4, 23·7,
      23·8
    Credit agencies, 23·5, 23·9 See also specific
      agencies
    Federal and quasi-federal mortgage,
      23·9–10
    Life insurance companies, 23·4, 23·8–9
    Mortgage companies, 23·7, 23·8–9, 23·25
    Mutual savings bank, 23·4, 23·8
    Options, 23·23
  Pension and profit-sharing funds, 34·23
  Pools, 34·23
  Real Estate Investment Trusts (REITs), 23·8,
    23·10
  Risk, 23·26–31
  Savings and loan associations, 23·3, 23·4,
    23·7
  See also Lease Financing; Mortgages
Real Estate Investment Trust Act of 1960, 23·10

Real Estate Investment Trusts (REITS), 23·8, 23·10
  Commercial bank loans to, 6·10–11
Real Exchange Rate, 12·14–15
Real Interest Rate
  Inflation and, 29·32–34
Realized Compound Yield, 18·7–8
Real Return on Investments
  Inflation and, I·4
  Nonfinancial assets and, I·5
  Short-term debt market and, I·4
Rebalancing, see Bonds
Reborrowing
  Treasury debt and, 2·8
Recapture Rule, 35·21
Receivable Balance Pattern, 28·21–22
Receivables, see Accounts Receivable
Reciprocals, 8·13
Reciprocal Tax Exemption, 3·3
Reciprocity
  Foreign banks and, 14·45
Reconciliation
  Working capital, 16·23
Record of Real Return, 34·14
Redemption Provisions
  Municipal bonds and, 16·17
Redemption Value of Bond, A·35
Reduced Asset-Lives System, 37·3
Refiling Restrictions
  Personal bankruptcy, 35·44
Refinancing Bill, 14·19
Refunding, 18·5, 18·6
  Bonds and, 31·47
  Risk, 18·12–14
Regional Concentration Bank, 27·5
Regional Development Banks, 38·43–44
Regional Gathering, 27·27
Registered Commodity Representative (RCR), 21·18
Registration Statement, 5·27
Regression Analysis
  Aggregate approach, 16·24–25
  Sales forecasting and, 26·6–8
"Regular Delivery"
  Government securities and, 2·10
Regular Dividends, 32·9
Regular Term Loan, 31·13
Regulation M, 14·44
Regulation Q, 14·43, 6·16–17
  Depository Institutions Deregulation and
    Monetary Control Act of 1980 and, 6·23
  Eurocurrency deposits and, 11·9
  Expires, 7·19
  Interest, 1·21
  Money market fund and, 6·19
  Passbook savings account and, 6·17
  Time deposits
    Interest ceilings, I·5
Regulatory Lag
  Utilities and, 36·6
Regulatory Risk
  Eurobanks and, 14·40
Reinsurance
  Contracts, I·7
  Specialists, I·9
Reinvestment
  Dividends, 32·21

Reinvestment (Continued)
  Risk, 18·15
    Immunization and, 19·4–6
    Yield-to-maturity and, 18·7
Relative Purchasing Power Parity, 12·20
Remonetization of Gold, 11·24
Remote Disbursing, 27·19
Remote Service Units (RSUs)
  Savings and loan associations and, 7·20
Renewable Overdrafts
  Multinational affiliates, 38·41
Reorganization, see Bankruptcy and
    Reorganization
Repayment Plans
  Personal bankruptcy, 35·39, 35·44
Replacement Cost, 25·22
Replacement Cost New, 8·18
Replacement Fund, A·24
Replacement Investments, 29·4
Reported Book
  Bank stock and, 16·28
Reported Earnings
  Utility, 16·31
Repossession
  Creditor remedy, 9·18
Representations, 8·19
Representative Offices, 14·45
Repurchase Agreements (repos), 1·19, 2·8–9,
    2·13, 6·15, 10·11–13
  Commercial banks and, 6·6, 6·9–10
  Treasury bills and, 2·13
Research and Development
  Investment in, 16·23
Resell Agreement, see Reverse Repurchase
    Agreement
Reserve Currencies
  Settlements of, 11·24
Reserve Currency Country
  United States as, 11·19
Reserve Requirements
  Depository Institution Deregulation and
    Monetary Control Act (DIDMCA), 6·22
  Eurobanks and, 14·41
  Eurocurrency loan and, 14·38
  Eurodollars, 11·9, 14·44
  Federal Reserve and, 1·18, 6·8, 7·21
    See also Regulation Q
  Foreign banks and, 14·51
  Savings and loan associations and, 7·20
Reserve Tranche, 11·25
Residential Mortgage, see Mortgages
Residual Effect
  Bond performance measurement techniques
    and, 18·26, 18·27
Residual Income (RI)
  Investment evaluation and, 25·23–24
Residual Risk, 17·15
Residual Value
  Acquisition analysis, 33·6
Respondent Banks
  Due-from accounts and, 6·7
Restrictive Covenants
  Multinational affiliates, 38·41
Retail Charge Account Plans, 6·12
Retailers
  Consumer credit, 9·7–8, 9·11
Retail Stocks, 16·27

Retained Earnings Cost
  Cost of equity capital, 31·32–33
Retained Earnings/Total Assets (RE/TA) ratio
  Z-score model, 35·36
Retirement, *see* Pension and Profit-Sharing Plans
Retirement of Bonds, *see* Corporate Bonds
Retirement Income Commitment, 33·3
  See also Pension and Profit-Sharing Plans
Retirement Income Plans, 8·30–31
  See also Pension and Profit-Sharing Plans
Retrocession, 8·14
Return
  Excess, 17·17
  See also Expected Return
Return on Assets (ROA), 24·12, 24·13, 24·15,
  24·16
  Dividends per share and, 24·22
  Small banks and, 6·29–30
Return on Common Equity, 24·22–28
Return on Equity (ROE), 24·12, 24·13, 24·14,
  24·15, 24·16
  Dividends per share, 24·23
  Public utilities, 36·17
  Sustainable growth rate and, 24·22
Return on Investment (ROI), 16·34
  Forecasting earnings and, 16·25
  Investment center evaluation and, 25·22–23,
  25·24
  Investment profitability and, 29·14–15
Return on Sales, 24·12, 24·13, 24·15–16, 24·17,
  24·18
  Dividends per share and, 24·22
  Before interest and taxes, 24·16
  Sustainable dividend growth and, 24·21
Return on Total Assets, 24·27
Revenue Anticipation Notes, 3·12, 10·10
Revenue Bonds, 3·13–14, 3·15, 3·29, 16·16–18
Revenue Centers, 25·20
Reverse Annuity, 23·14, 23·15
Reverse Repurchase Agreements, 2·9, 10·11–12
Reverse Stock Split, 32·6
Revocable Letter of Credit, 14·22–23
Revolving Credit, *see* Consumer credit
Revolving Letter of Credit, 14·23
Reward-Risk Tradeoff, 19·14
  Yield curve and, *see* Bonds
Right of Offset
  Currency swap, 38·19
Risk, 8·3
  Acquisition analysis, 33·7
  Adjusting, 29·21
  Capital asset pricing model, 31·29–36
  Capital budgeting under uncertainty and, *see*
    Capital Budgeting
  Capital loss and, 1·12
  Classification, 8·4
  Currency choice and international finances,
    13·7–8
  Definition, 8·3
  Extramarket, 17·15
  Identification and analysis, 8·3–4
  Income loss and, 1·12
  Leveraged leasing, 30·23
  Management, 8·5
  Measurement, 8·4–5
    See also Performance Measurement
  Meeting, 8·5

Risk (*Continued*)
  Obsolescence, 30·6–7
    See also Lease financing
  Selection, 17·15
  Specific, 17·15
  Transfer of, 8·5
  Zero selection, 17·18
    See also Modern Portfolio Theory;
      Performance Measurement; *specific
      aspects of risk*
Risk-Adjusted Discount Rate, 29·27
Risk-Adjusted Present Value Factors (RAPVFs),
  29·28–31
Risk Adjustment
  Subjective weights for dollar, 29·31
Risk Analysis Questionnaire
  Risk analysis and, 8·4
Risk Bearing
  Underwriters and, 3·6, 3·8
Risk Capital
  Dividends, 32·3
Risk-Free Arbitrage
  Foreign exchange and, 12·7, 12·26
Risk-Free Rate
  Credit contracts pricing and, 9·13
Risk and Insurance Management Society (RIMS),
  8·5
Risk Preference Adjustment, 29·30
Risk Premium Methods, 17·16
  Public utilities and, 36·20
Risk Return Preferences of Market, 29·30
Risk-Return Tradeoff
  Common stock and, 16·20
  Investment, 20·13–14, 20·15
Risk-Reward Characteristics
  Call contracts and, 20·4–6, 20·15
  Option, 20·4–6, 20·10, 20·12
  Option evaluation, 20·28–29
  Put contracts, 20·4–6, 20·18–19
Risk-Sensitivity Analysis, 29·24–25
Robinson-Patman Act
  Price discrimination and, 28·5
Rolling Horizon
  Budgets, 25·19
  Financial plans and, 25·6
Rolling Yield, *see* Bonds
Rollover, 14·28
  Credit
    Eurocredit and, 13·15
    Euromarket innovation, 14·34, 14·37
  Foreign currency and, 12·5
  Market, 10·11
**Rollover (Or Renegotiable) Rate Mortgages
  (RRMs),** 7·17
Ross
  Option evaluation and, 20·35
R-Squared, 17·18
Rubinstein
  Option evaluation and, 20·35
Rule of 78, 9·20–21

Sale-Leaseback Lease, 23·21, 23·22–23
Sales
  Profit margin on, 24·27
Sales Forecasts, *see* Forecasting
Sales/Total Assets Ratio
  Z-score model, 35·36

Salomon Brothers Bond Indexes, 18·21, 18·22
Salomon Brothers Long Term, High Grade
    Corporate Bond Index, 22·23
Salvage Value, 30·4, 30·7, 30·22, 30·23
    Declining-balance method, 29·22
Samuelson-Merton Model
    Option evaluation and, 20·31
Samurai bond, 15·17, 15·18
Savings Deficit Sectors, 1·3
Savings Deposits, 7·10
    Commercial banks and, 7·4
    Credit unions, 7·29
    Mutual savings banks, 7·24
    Savings and loan associations, 7·4, 7·8,
        7·9, 7·10–12
    See also Time Deposit
Savings Institutions, 7·3–5
    Assets, 1·6, 1·8
    See also Credit Unions; Mutual Savings
    Banks; Savings and Loan Associations
Savings and Loan Associations, 1·7, 7·3, 7·5
    Asset and liability structure, 7·7–10
    Asset size distribution, 7·4–5, 7·8
    Consumer credit, 9·7–8, 9·11–12
    Depository Institutions Deregulation and
        Monetary Control Act of 1980, 7·19–20
    Federal Home Loan Bank Board (FHLBB),
        7·6, 7·10, 7·17–18
    Federal Home Loan Mortgage Corporation,
        7·8, 7·9, 7·12, 7·13, 7·18
    Federal Savings and Loan Insurance
        Corporation, 7·5, 7·6, 7·10, 7·18–19, 7·20
    Funds supplied by, 1·5, 1·7
    Insurance, 7·19, 7·20
    Interest rates, 7·21
    Mortgage lending, 7·3, 7·5, 7·7, 7·9, 7·12,
        7·13–14, 7·15, 7·17, 7·20, 23·3, 23·4, 23·7
    Number of, 7·6
    Organization, 7·6
    Profitability, 7·14, 7·16, 7·17
        Variability in, 7·16–17, 7·18
    Revenues and expenses, 7·13–14, 7·16
    Savings deposits, 7·4, 7·8, 7·9, 7·10–12
    Secondary mortgage market, 7·13, 7·15
    Transaction account of bill payment service,
        6·15
Savings and Loan Holding Companies
    Stocks of, 16·28
Savings Surplus Sectors, 1·3
Scalpers, 21·18–19
Schedule Contract, 8·16
Scholes
    Option evaluation model and, 20·31–34
    Option profitability and, 20·37–38
    Option theory of corporate securities
        evaluation, 20·40
Scrip Dividends, 32·7
Search and Screen
    Acquisition prospects, 33·4
Sears Roebuck and Co.
    Credit cards and, 6·4
Seasonal Cycles
    Short-term loans and, 6·11
Seasonal Dating, 28·6
SEC Disclosure Act of 1933, 18·24
Secondary Market
    Agency securities and, 6·9

Secondary Market (Continued)
    Bankers' acceptances, 10·6
    Common stock and, 4·33
    Eurodollar CDs, 10·5
    Federal Farm Credit System discount notes,
        10·9
    Federal Home Loan Bank discount notes and,
        10·8
    Federal National Mortgage Association
        discount notes, 10·9
    Mortgages and, 7·13, 7·15, 23·9, 23·25–26
    Negotiable certificates of deposit and, 10·3–4
    Nonnegotiable instruments, 1·8
    Options and, 20·7
    Private placement and, 4·26
    Tax-free anticipation notes, 10·10
    "Yankee" certificates of deposit, 10·5
Second Mortgages, 23·17
    Specialists, 1·9–10
Sector-Quality Effect
    Bond performance measurement technique
        and, 18·26, 18·27
Secured Debts
    Bankruptcy priorities, 35·16
Securities Act of 1933, 5·10, 5·11
    Private placement market and, 4·21
Securities Acts Amendments (1975), 5·12
    Municipal Securities Rulemaking Board, 3·11
Securities Clearing Corp. (NSCC), 5·14
Securities Exchange Act (1934), 5·10, 5·11
    Short selling and, 5·18
Securities and Exchange Commission, 5·15, 5·16
    Chandler Act and, 35·8
    Chapter 11 and, 35·14–15
    Chapter X, 35·9
    Commission schedules, 1·8
    Common stock registration, 4·32–33
    Dividend declaration, 32·11
    Establishment of, 5·11
    Eurobonds and, 13·19
    Financial reports to, 5·7
    Foreign and domestic issues requirements of,
        13·31
    Municipal Securities Rulemaking Board, 3·11
    New security issues, 5·11
    Private placement market and, 4·21, 31·47
        Resale and, 4·26
    Registration statement, 5·27
Securities Exchanges
    Leading world, 13·29, 13·30
    See also specific exchanges
Securities Firms, 1·9–10
    Changing functions of, 1·9–10
Securities Industry
    Description, 5·3–5
    Functions of, 5·5–8
    Investment banking, 5·25–28
        Competition, 5·26
        Nature of, 5·25
        New capital raised by, 5·6–7
        New issues, 5·26–28
        Types of, 5·25–26
    Securities trading, 5·16–25
        Computers and, 5·21–24
        Customer classes, 5·16–17
        Exchange execution, 5·19–21
        Internationalization, 5·24–25

Securities Industry (*Continued*)
  Order types, 5·17–19
  Structures of, 5·8–16
    Brokerage firm, 5·12–13
    Government regulatory, 5·15–16
    History, 5·8–10
    Instability of, 5·16
    Legal environment, 5·10–12
    See also specific laws
  Trends, 5·28
  See also Bonds; Corporate Capital;
    Government Obligations; Stocks
Securities Industry Association, 5·16
Securities Industry Automation Corp. (SIAC),
  5·14–15
Securities Investor Protection Corporation Act
  (SIPC) (1970), 5·11, 5·15
Securities Price Data Base, 16·10
Securities Rand
  Multiple exchange rates, 11·18
Security Analysis, 16·5–6
Security Characteristic Lines, 17·17–18
Security Market Line
  Cost of equity capital, 31·31–32
Selection Risk, 17·15
Self-Insurance, 8·10–11
Self-Regulating Organizations, *see* Exchanges
Semivariable Costs, 25·13
Senior Debt
  Bankruptcy priorities, 35·16
Sensitivity Analysis
  Cash budgets and, 26·13, 26·19
  Computer and, 25·12
  Investment profitability and, 29·24–25
  Pro forma statement and, 25·4, 25·9
Serial Bonds, 4·5, 31·46
Serial Maturities
  Tax-exempt security and, 3·6, 3·7
Service Credit, 9·7
Setoffs
  Bankruptcies and, 35·13–14
Settlement Date, 5·21
Share Drafts, 6·4, 6·15
  Commercial banking and, 6·4
  Credit union industry and, 6·4, 6·31, 7·30, 7·31
Shares
  Credit unions and, 7·29
"Shelf Registrations," 5·27
Shopping Centers, 23·26
  Investment characteristics, 23·32
Short Selling, 5·18
Short-Term Business Loans
  Funds demanded by, 1·5, 1·7
Short-Term Debt Instruments, *see* Money Market
Short-Term Debt (Deposit) Market
  Inflation and, 1·4
Short-Term Instruments, *see* Banker's
  Acceptances; Commercial Paper
Short-Term Liabilities
  Accounts payable
    Credit terms, 31·11–12
    Management of, 38·25–27
    Trade credit, 31·11–12
  Accruals, 31·14
  Categories, 31·3
  Estimating weighted average cost of capital,
    31·35

Short Term Liabilities (*Continued*)
  Notes payable, 31·12
    Commercial paper, 31·14
    Compensating balances, 31·12–13
    Current portion of long-term debt, 31·14
    Discount loans, 31·13
    Installment loans, 31·13
    Line of credit, 31·12
    Regular term loans, 31·13
Short-Term Tax-exempt Securities, *see* State and
  Local Government Obligations
Shrinkage
  Duration values and, 19·7
Sight Draft, 14·16, 28·6
Simple Interest, A·4
Single-Bank System
  Balance reports, 27·7
Single-Index Model, 17·14, 17·16
Single-Payment Loans, 9·7
Sinking Fund, 16·11–12
  Active management strategies, 18·20
  Annuity that $1 will buy, A·31–33
  Bond retirement, 31·47
  Final value of annuity due, A·27–28
  Installments, A·24
    Annuity using value computing, A·24, A·25,
      A·26
    Schedule of, A·24, A·26
  Payment, 16·11, A·26–27
  Preferred stock and, 31·48
  Present value of ordinary annuity, A·28–31,
    A·34
  Provisions, 18·5–6
  Risk, 18·13
  See also Annuities; Corporate Capital
Small Loan Laws, 9·23
Smithsonian Agreement, 11·7–8, 11·24
Smoothing Techniques, 27·30
"Snake," (European Monetary System), 11·11,
  11·14–17
Social Security Administration, 8·13
Social Security Payments, 33·4
  Automated Clearing House and, 6·28
  See also Pension and Profit-Sharing Plans
Southeastern Underwriters Association, 8·36
Sovereign Risk, *see* Political Risk
Spatial Arbitrage
  Foreign exchange market and, 12·8
Special Assessment Bonds, 3·13
Special Dividends, 32·9
Special Drawing Right (SDR), 13·9
  Currencies, 11·10
  Euromarket and, 15·12
  International Monetary Fund and, 11·25,
    11·26
Specialists, 5·19–20
Special Multiperil Contract, 8·25
Specific Contract, 8·16
Specific Risk, 17·15
Speculation
  Definition, 16·3
  Foreign exchange market and, 12·9
  Futures and, 21·12, 21·18–19
  Modern portfolio theory and, 17·12–13
Speculators, 5·17
Split-Dollar Life Insurance, 8·30
Split Ratings, 4·21

Spokane Stock Exchange, 5·14
Spot Contract, 12·4
Spot Foreign Exchange Market, 12·4
Spot Market, 10·11, 21·3, 21·10
  Efficiency, 12·26
Spot Rate Term Structure of Interest Rates, 18·12
Spot Transaction, 14·27
Spread
  Carry, 10·12
  Currency swap, 38·19
  Eurobonds and, 13·18
  Future trading and, 21·20, 21·26
  Government securities and, 6·9
  New issues and, 5·28
  Options and, 20·4
  Underwriters, 3·8–9
  Yield, see Yield Spreads
Spreader, 21·19
Spread-Loss Cover, 8·15
Spread Trades, 2·13, 2·16
Sprenkle Model
  Option evaluation and, 20·31
Stabilization Accounts
  Exchange rates and, 11·5
Stable Market, 16·5
Stagflation, 37·3
Standard Deviation of Nominal Returns, 34·14
  Risk measurement and, 8·5
  Total risk in investment, 22·15–16
Standard Error of Estimate, 26·8
Standard N.Y.S.E. Stock Reports, 16·9
Standard & Poor's, 1·27, 16·8
  Bond rating, 4·19–20, 4·21, 16·5
  Commercial paper and, 10·6
  Preferred stock ratings, 4·29
Standard & Poor's 400 Industrial Index, 16·9,
  35·34
Standard & Poor's 500 Stock Index, 22·22, 22·23,
  35·34
Standard & Poor's Standard Corporation Records
  16·9
Standard & Poor's Stock Guide, 16·9
Standby Line of Credit, 1·26
State Banking Departments, 6·5
State-Chartered Savings and Loan Associations,
  7·6
State and Local Government Obligations, 3·3,
  3·23–25, 7·24, 16·12, 16·16
  Commercial bank and, 1·6, 1·8, 6·6, 6·9
  Commercial paper, 10·10–11
  Contractual position and remedies, 16·7
  Credit risk evaluation, 3·18–22, 3·28,
    16·17–18
  Demand for, 3·23–25
  Fire and casualty insurance company and, 1·8,
    1·11
  General obligations, 16·16
  Guaranteed, 3·22–23, 3·25–27
  Inflation and, 1·6
  Insured, 3·2
  Interest rates on, 1·28, 1·30, 3·25–27
  Legality, 16·7
  Life insurance company, 1·6, 1·11
  Marketing, 3·5–10
  Maturity structure of, 3·27–28, 16·7
  Municipal securities rulemaking board, 3·11
  New issues, 5·26

State and Local Government Obligations (Continued)
  Pollution control revenue bonds and, 1·27,
    1·28
  Project notes, 10·10
  Purposes for, 3·16–18
  Quality evaluation, 3·18–22, 3·28
  Redemption provisions, 16·7
  Retirement assets, 1·8, 1·11
  Revenue bonds, 16·16–18
  Risk and, 3·18–22
  Savings institutions and, 1·6, 1·8
  Secondary market, 3·10–11
  Security features of long-term
    General obligations, 3·13, 3·15, 3·29
    Revenue bonds, 3·13–14, 3·15, 3·29
    Special assessment bonds, 3·13
    Volume, 3·3–4
  Security features of short-term
    Bond anticipation notes (BANs), 3·12–13
    Local housing authority notes, 3·11–12
    Marketing, 3·6
    Revenue anticipation notes (RANs), 3·12
    Tax anticipation notes (TANs), 3·12
    Urban renewal project notes, 3·11, 3·12
    Volume, 3·3–4
  Tax-free anticipation notes, 10·10
  Treasury debt, 2·6–7
  Trends in, 3·14–16
    Volume, 3·3–5
  Yields, 3·28–29
States of Nature, 29·28–31
State Usury Ceilings, 9·23
  Mortgage loans and, 7·20
Status List
  Capital budgeting and, 29·7, 29·8
Statutory Consolidation, 33·20, 33·21
Statutory Merger, 33·20
Sterling Depreciation, 11·5
Stock Broker
  Commission schedules, 1·8
Stock exchanges, see Exchanges; specific
  exchanges
Stockholder Equity Profitability Measures, 29·13
Stock Insurers, 8·12, 8·13
Stock Options, see Options
Stocks
  Acquisition for, 33·17–20
  Bankruptcy prediction, 35·33
  Earnings and dividends per share, see
    Financial Analysis
  Expected return, 17·19–22, 17·23
  Fire and casualty insurance companies, 1·8,
    1·11
  Futures on, 21·5
  Income measurement, 22·7
  Inflation hedge, 1·4
  Investing in bankruptcies, 35·37–38, 35·40–42
  Lease capitalization and, 30·29–31
  Mutual savings banks, 7·24
  Pension funds and, 1·12
  Savings institutions and, 1·6, 1·8
  Splits, 31·51, 31·53, 32·6
  State and local government retirement assets,
    1·8, 1·11
  See Also Common Stock; Dividends; Modern
    Portfolio Theory; Preferred Stock; Securities
    Industry

Stop Limit Order, 21·18
Stop-Loss Cover, 8·15
Stop-Loss Orders, 5·18
Store of Value
  Domestic currency, 12·4
Straddle, 20·3
  Futures trading and, 21·26
  See also Options
Straight Bankruptcies, 35·25, 35·29
Straight Bankruptcy, liquidation
  Personal bankruptcy, 35·44
Straight-Line Depreciation, 29·21
  Inflation accounting and, 37·7–8
Straight Preferred Stock
  Cost of, 31·26–27
Straight-Term Loans, 23·12–13
Strategic Investment, 29·4
Strategic Planning, 25·6–7
Striking Price, 20·3
  See also Options
Subaccounts
  Zero-balance account and, 27·8
Subjective Method
  Sales forecasting and, 26·5–6, 26·8
Subordinated Debentures, 4·4, 7·22, 18·4
Subpart F Income, 38·20
Subrogation Clause, 8·19
Subsidiaries
  Banking, 14·14
  Finance, 28·24
    Foreign, 38·36–41
  International banking and, 14·45
Sum-of-the-Years-Digits Method
  Depreciation, 29·22–24
Sunk Cost
  Currency exposure, 12·35
Surety Bonds, 8·28, 8·29
Suretyship, 8·28–29
Surplus Treaty, 8·15
Survey of Current Business, 16·7
Sustainable Dividend Growth, 24·21–23, 24·24
Sustainable Growth Model (Feasible Financial
  Plan), 26·31, 26·35–38
Sustainable Growth Rate, 24·22–23, 24·24
Swap, 14·28, 14·29, 14·41
  Currency credit, 14·39
  Euromarket innovations, 14·34
  Foreign exchange, 12·5–7
    Exposure and, 12·36, 12·37
SWIFT, 14·31
Switzerland
  World financial center, 13·8, 13·31–32
Syndicated Credits, 14·36
Syndicated Loans
  Charges on, 14·37–38
Syndicates
  New issues and, 5·26
Systematic Risk, 16·4, 16·20
  Pricing Model, 31·30

Tactical Planning, 25·6–7
TANs, *see* Tax Anticipation Notes
"Tap" Certificate of Deposit, 13·14, 14·43
Target Balance Report, 27·8
Tariffs, 11·17
Taxable Combinations, 33·20–21

Tax Accounting
  Public utilities, 36·10
Tax Anticipation Notes (TANs), 312
Taxation, 10·10–11
  Credit union, 7·31
  Deferred compensation, 8·30
  Depreciation and, *see* Capital Budgeting
  Dividends, 32·3, 32·21
    Accumulated earnings tax, 32·21
  Euromarket investments and, 15·12
  Financial forecasts and, 26·4
  French capital market and, 15·25–26
  German capital market, 15·24
  Income retention rate after, 24·16, 24·22
  Interest equalization tax, 13·17, 13·28–29
  Investments and, 16·5
  Japanese capital market investments and,
    15·18–19
  Leasing and, 30·7, 30·8, 30·9, 30·12, 30·14,
    30·16, 30·23
  Multinational corporations
    Dividends, 38·19–20
    Transfer pricing, 38·16
  Mutual savings banks, 7·27
  Pension and profit-sharing plans, 34·8–9
  Personal
    Optimal capital structure and, 31·42
  Planning, 25·13
  Profit tax payable, 1·24, 1·26
  Real estate and, 23·29–30
  Return on assets before interest and, 24·22
  Return on sales before interest and, 24·16,
    24·22
  Savings and loans associations and, 7·14
  Sovereign risk and, 13·28–29
  United Kingdom market and, 15·22
  See also Bankruptcy and Reorganization;
    Options; State and Local Government
    Obligations
Tax Bracket
  Dividend policy and, 32·24
Tax-Exempt Commercial Paper, 10·10–11
Tax-Exempt Securities, *see* State and Local
  Government obligations
Tax-Free Anticipation Notes, 10·10
Tax-Loss Carry Forwards
  Reorganization, 35·22
Tax Operating Expenses
  Leasing and, 30·12
Tax Reform Act of 1969, 7·27
Tax Reform Act of 1976, 20·22, 20·40
Tax Shield
  Convertible debt, 31·34
  Interest on debt as, 31·9
  Leasing and, 30·14, 30·16
  Real estate and, 23·29
Teachers Insurance and Annuity Association
  (TIAA), 34·10
Technical Services
  Exchange rate forecasting, 12·29
Telephone Bill Payment Service, 6·15
Telestate Pricing Tapes, 18·26, 18·27
Temporal Approach
  Foreign exchange exposure, 12·34
Tenants
  Liability of, 8·21

Tender Offer, 33·3
  Leasco and, 6·21
10K Reports, 16·9
Term Deposits, *see* Money Market
Term Funds, 1·19
  Federal, 10·5
Terminal Value, 29·16
Term Intermediation
  Inflation and, i·7
Term to Maturity, 18·15
Term Repurchase Transactions, 1·19
  Arbitrage instrument, 10·12–13
Term Risk, i·7
Terms Loans, 14·36
  Commercial banking and, 6·11
  Eurocredit and, 13·15
Term Structure of Interest Rates, 13·12
  Bonds and, 18·11–12
  International interest, 13·24–25, 13·26
Thin Market, 16·5
Third-Party Collection
  Credit collection and, 28·14
Thrift Institution
  Asset portfolio powers of, 6·23
  Deposit rate ceilings, 6·18
  Expanding functions of, I·9
  Mortgage servicing, I·9
  Passbook savings account and, 6·17
  See also Savings Institutions
Tied Exchange Rates, 11·10
Time, 16·8
Time
  Definition, A·3
Time Deposit
  Commercial banks and, 6·13–17, 6·18
  Eurocurrency banks and, 13·14
  Interest ceilings on, I·5
  Mutual savings banks, 7·24
Time Draft, 14·16
Time Element Losses, 8·27
Time Horizon
  Budget, 25·18–19
Time Series Analysis
  Sales forecasting and, 26·6
Time-Shared Computer Services, 25·11–12
Times-Interest-Earned Ratio, 24·27
Time Value of Money
  Bankruptcy and reorganization calculations,
    29·12, 29·13–14, 33·5
  Return on investment, 29·14, 29·15
  Yield-to-maturity and, 18·6
Time-Varying Anticipation, 27·24, 27·25
Time-Weighted Rate of Return, 22·11, 22·12
  Adjustment and performance measurment,
    34·21
  Investment management performance,
    34·20–22
Tobacco Stock, 16·27
Tokyo
  World financial center, 13·8
  See also Japan
"Tombstone Advertisements," 5·26
"Tomorrow-Next" Swap, 14·28
  Foreign currency and, 12·5
Top-Down Budgeting, 25·18
"Topping-Up," 38·19

Toronto
  World financial center, 13·8
Tort, 8·20
Total Assets utilization, 24·29
Total Hedge, 21·21, 21·23
Total Return, 22·4–5, 22·7
Total Return Expectation
  Asset mix decision, 34·16–17
Toys "R" Us, 35·38
Trade Acceptance, 14·17, 28·4–5
Trade Account
  Balance of payments, 11·18
Trade Bills
  Discounting and multinational affiliates, 38·41
Trade Credit, 1·24, 1·25, 28·25, 31·11–12
  Cost of financing, 28·25–26
  Fire and casualty insurance companies and,
    1·8, 1·11
  Funds supplied by, 1·6, 1·7
Trader
  Foreign exchange market and, 12·7
Trading Pit, 21·18
Trading Stock Valuation Adjustment (TSVA),
    32·34
Traditional Ratio Analysis, *see* Financial
    Statement Analysis
"Tranche" Certificate of Deposit, 13·14, 14·43
Transaction Account
  Savings and loan associations, 6·15
Transaction Costs
  Foreign exchange trading and, 12·12–13
  Forward exchange market, 12·4
Transaction Date, 5·21
Transaction Exposure, 12·32
Transfer
  Evaluation of methods, 27·22–24
Transfer Acceleration Methods, 27·24
Transfer Agents
  Commercial bank as, 32·11
Transfer Prices
  Multinational Corporations, 38·13, 38·16
  Return of investment, 25·23
Translation Exposure, 12·32
Transportation Contracts, 8·26
Treasury Bills, 1·19,2·5, 2·7, 6·8, 10·4, 10·7–8
  Certificates of, 6·16
  Competition for, I·8
  Delivery and payment, 2·10
  Deposit and, 6·16
  Eurocurrency interest rates, 13·12–13
  Futures, 2·13, 2·17–19
  Inflation and, I·7
  Interest rate, 1·28, 1·30
  Money market certificates, 6·19, 7·10
  Pricing, 2·10
  Record of real returns, 34·14
  Risk return tradeoff and, 20·14
  6-month, 2·17
  United Kingdom, 15·20
Treasury Bonds, 2·5,2·7,6·8,16·12,21·4–5,
    21·7,21·8,21·11,21·12,21·18,21·22,21·23
  Debt extension and, 2·6
  Delivery and payment, 2·10
  Futures, 2·13, 2·17
  Interest, 2·10
  Intramarket spread trades, 2·13, 2·16

Treasury Bonds (*Continued*)
Pricing, 2·9–10
Record of real returns, 34·14
Treasury Bulletin Monthly Statements of the
Public Debt of the United States, 2·4
Treasury Debt
Foreign currencies and, 2·8
Lengthening maturity of, 2·6
Ownership, 2·6–7
Reborrowing, 2·8
Regularization, 2·6, 2·7
Rise in, 2·6
See also National Debt
Treasury Department
Foreign countries' treatment of U.S. banks,
14·46–51
Proposed substitution account, 11·27–28
Securities industry regulation, 5·15
Treasury Issues, 31·4
Commercial banks, 1·6, 1·8, 6·6, 6·8–9
Fire and casualty insurance company and, 1·8,
1·11
Futures trading bills, 21·7, 21·8, 21·11
Life insurance company and, 1·6, 1·11
Notes, 21·7, 21·8
Pension funds and, 1·12
Savings institutions and, 1·6, 1·8
State and local government retirement assets,
1·8, 1·11
See also Treasury Bills; Treasury Bonds;
Treasury Notes
Treasury Notes, 6·8
Delivery and payment, 2·10
Interest, 2·5, 2·7, 2·10
Maturity, 2·6
Pricing, 2·9–10
Treasury Yield Curve, 2·16, 18·10
Treaty Reinsurance, 8·15
Tree Diagram
Present value of paths, 29·26, 29·27
Trend Analysis
Balance sheets, 24·6, 24·8–9
Income statement and, 24·7, 24·10–12
Trend Forecasts, 26·10
Sales forecasting and, 26·6
Trespassers, 8·21–22
Triangular Arbitrage
Foreign exchange market and, 12·8, 12·13
Triangular Reorganization, 35·23
Triffin Dilemma, 11·7
Trigger Point Rule, 27·25
Tripartite Agreement, 11·5–6
Trust
Land, 23·24
Trust Fund
Income yield, 22·7–8
Trust Indenture Act (1939), 5·10, 5·11
Truth-in-Lending Act (1969), 9·22
"Truth-in-Lending" Mortgage, 23·17
Turnover (Asset Management Ratios), *see*
Financial Statement Analysis
Turnover of Accounts Payable, 28·26
Turnover of Accounts Receivable, 28·19
t-Values
Regression analysis and, 26·8
21-Year Lease, 23·21
Two-Tier Agreements, 11·24

Two-Way Quotation
Direct dealing and, 12·7

Uncertainty
Capital budgeting and, *see* Capital Budgeting
Measures of, 22·14–15
See also Risk
Uncertainty Absorption, 38·23, 38·24
Unconfirmed letter of credit, 14·23
Uncovered Interest Arbitrage
Multinational corporations, 38·9
Underwriting
Best efforts, 31·51
Compensation (spread), 3·8–9
Firm Commitment, 31·51, 31·52
Insurance and, 8·32–33
Underwriting Syndicates
Eurobonds and, 13·18
Euromarket, 15·13
Tax-exempt securities and, 3·6–10
Underwritten Issues
Investment banking firms, 31·51
Undiscounted Payback Period, 29·14
Undiversible Risk
Capital asset, 31·30
Unemployment Insurance, 8·13
Unexpected Inflation, 37·38
Unfunded Present Value
Vested benefits, 34·6
Unfunded Prior Service Costs, 34·5
Unfunded Vested Benefits, 34·5
Uniform Annuity Series (UAS), 37·22, 37·23
Uniform Management of Institutional Funds Act,
22·8
Uniform Negative Covenants
Dividend policy and, 32·8
Uniform Small Loan Law, 9·8, 9·9
Unishaps, Inc., 35·41
United Kingdom
Investing in capital market, 15·8, 15·9, 15·11,
15·19–22
United Merchants and Manufacturing, Inc.,
35·37, 35·41
Chapter XI and, 35·10, 35·11
United States
Balance of payments, 11·20–23
Foreign exchange market transactions, 12·11,
12·12
Reserve currency country, 11·19
See also Government Obligations; Treasury
United States Bankruptcy Court, 35·17
United States Certificates of Deposit, *see*
Certificates of Deposit
United States Export-Import Bank (Eximbank),
14·25
United States Government Obligations, *see*
Government Obligations; *under* Treasury
United States Overseas Foreign Direct Investment
(OFDI), 38·3
United States Rule, A·10
United States Trustee Program
Chapter 11 and, 35·20
Unit Values
Use of, 22·11, 22·13
Unlevered Firm
Cost of capital, 31·7–8
Inflationary holding gains or assets and,

Unlevered Firm (*Continued*)
37·8–11, 37·12
Unlimited-Tax General Obligations Bonds, 3·13
Unsystematic Risk, 16·4, 17·15
Capital asset, 31·30
Urban Renewal Project Notes, 3·11, 3·12
U.S. News and World Report, 16·8
Usury Ceilings
Mortgages, 1·5
State, 6·23
Utilities, *see* Public Utilities
Utility Distribution, 8·4
Utility Revenue Bonds, 3·14

Valuation, 22·5–6
Bonds, 18·27–28
Tables, A·39
Real estate, 23·31–33
Reorganization, 35·15
See also Modern Portfolio Theory
Value of Call, 20·30–31
Value Compensation, 38·8
Value Line Data Services, 16·11
Value Line Industrial Composite Dividend Payout, 32·4
Value Line Investment Survey, 16·9, 22·17
Variability
Term structure of interest rates, 13·25
Variable Annuities, 1·10, 8·31, 34·10
Variable Ceiling Accounts
Savings and loan associations, 7·11
Variable Costs, 25·13
Variable Interest Obligations
Inflation and, 1·7
Variable Rate Mortgages (VRMs), 7·17, 23·14, 23·15
Inflation and, 1·7
Variable Rent Leases, 23·22
Variable Reserve Requirements
Savings and loan associations and, 7·20
Variance, 17·13–14
Variation Margin, 21·15
Vehicle Currency
Dollars as, 12·8–9, 12·12
Venture Capital
Risk-return tradeoff, 20·14
Vertical Merger, 33·23
Vested Benefits, 34·5, 34·6
Vesting Liabilities
Unfunded present value of, 34·6
Vesting Standards
ERISA and, 34·9–10
Veterans Administration (VA), 6·10, 23·9, 23·18
Mortgages, 7·25, 7·26
Volatile Market, 16·5
Volatility Risk, 19·11–14
Voting Bonds, 4·5, 31·46

Wage Assignment
Creditor remedy, 9·18–19
Waiver, 8·20
Waiver of Premium in Event of Disability, 8·17
Waiver of Statutory Exemption
Creditor remedy, 9·18
Wall Street Journal, 16·8
Warranties, 8·5, 8·19–20
Breach of, 8·22

Warrant Pricing, 20·31
Warrants, 32·6, 32·7
Washington Post, 16·8
Wash Transactions, 27·31
Weighted Average Cost of Capital, *see* Cost of Capital
West Germany
Investments in capital market of, 15·11, 15·22–24
World financial center, 13·8, 13·31
White, Henry Dexter, 11·6
Wholesale Price Index
Inflation and, 37·4
Wholesalers, 5·25–26
Wires, 27·15, 27·19
Balance reporting and, 27·8
Bank, 27·6, 27·8
Drawdown, 27·8
Fed, 27·6, 27·8
Wire Systems
Demand accounts and, 6·14, 6·23
Wire Transfers, 6·15, 6·23, 27·21
Charge for, 6·23
Electronic reporting and movement of funds, 6·28
Multinational corporations and, 38·7
Withdrawal Penalty Formula, 7·21
Withholding Tax
Nonresident aliens, 20·28
Workers' Compensation and Employers' Liability, 8·9, 8·16, 8·20–21
Working Capital
Balance sheet and, 24·5
Leasing and, 30·7
Position, 16·21–22
Reconciliation, 16·23
Working Capital/Total Assets
Z-score model and, 35·35–36
World Bank, 13·33, 14·33, 38·43
World Bank Group, 38·43
World Economic Conference of 1933, 11·5
World Financial Centers, 13·8
See also International Financial Markets
Wraparound Mortgages, 23·19
Writing (selling) Calls
Pension and profit sharing plans, 34·23
W. T. Grant, 35·40
Chapter XI and, 35·10, 35·11

"Yankee" Certificates of Deposit, 10·5
Yearly Renewable Term Plan, 8·15
Yield
Gilt issues and, 15·21
Repurchase agreement, 10·12
Yield to Call
Call and, 18·13
Yield Curve, 1·28–30, 1·31, 18·10, 18·11
Tax-exempt securities, 3·27–28
See also Bonds
Yield to Maturity, 16·12, 18·6–7, 18·8, 18·9–10
Bond performance measurement techniques, 18·26–27
Call and, 18·13
Formula, 18·7
Realized compound, 18·7–8
Reinvestment rate and, 18·15
Treasury bills, 2·10

Yield Spreads
  Preferreds with sinking funds, 4·28
  Private placement market, 4·26
  Savings and loan associations and, 7·16, 7·17,
    7·18
Yield Tables, 18·6, 18·8, 18·9
Yield Tradeoffs, 16·12–13
Youngstown Sheet and Tube, 35·34

"Z" Account, 15·21
Zero-Balance Accounts, 27·8–9
Zero-Balance Disbursement Accounts, 27·8–9
Zero-Balance Field Concentration, 27·9

Zero-Balance Lockbox Concentration, 27·9
Zero-Base Budgeting Review, 25·19
Zero-Coupon Bonds
  Duration equivalents, 19·8
  Rebalancing and, 19·20–25
Zero Selection Risk, 17·18
Zero-Sum Game, 27·16
Zeta Analysis, 35·36, 35·37
Z-Score Model, 35·35–37
  Discriminant analysis and, 24·30–31
Zurich
  World financial center, 13·8